DEVELOPMENTAL
PSYCHOPATHOLOGY

DEVELOPMENTAL PSYCHOPATHOLOGY

Volume 1: Theory and Methods

Editors

DANTE CICCHETTI

AND

DONALD J. COHEN

A Wiley-Interscience Publication

John Wiley & Sons, Inc.

New York • Chichester • Brisbane • Toronto • Singapore

This text is printed on acid-free paper.

Library of Congress Cataloging-in-Publication Data:

Developmental psychopathology / Dante Cicchetti and Donald J. Cohen,
editors.
v. <1- > cm. — (Wiley series on personality processes)
Includes index.
Contents: v. 1. Theory and methods — v. 2. Risk, disorder, and
adaptation.
ISBN 0-471-53257-6 (set). — ISBN 0-471-53243-6 (v. 1). — ISBN
0-471-53244-4 (v. 2)
1. Mental illness—Etiology. 2. Developmental psychology.
3. Mental illness—Risk factors. 4. Adjustment (Psychology)
I. Cicchetti, Dante. II. Cohen, Donald J. III. Series.
RC454.4.D483 1995
616.89′071–dc20 94-36391

Printed in the United States of America

10 9 8 7 6 5 4 3 2 1

To Alex Siegel and Phyllis Cohen

Contributors

Thomas M. Achenbach, Ph.D.
Professor of Psychiatry and Psychology and,
Director, Center for Children, Youth and Families
University of Vermont
Burlington, Vermont

Junko Aimi, Ph.D.
Postdoctoral Fellow
Nancy Pritzker Laboratory
Department of Psychiatry and Behavioral Sciences
Stanford University School of Medicine
Stanford, California

Adrian Angold, MRCPsych.
Assistant Professor
Department of Psychiatry, Developmental Epidemiology Program
Duke University
Durham, North Carolina

Simon Baron-Cohen, Ph.D.
Lecturer in Psychopathology
Departments of Experimental Psychology and Psychiatry
University of Cambridge
Cambridge, United Kingdom

Francine M. Benes, M.D., Ph.D.
Director, Laboratory for Structural Neuroscience
McLean Hospital
Belmont, Massachusetts

Elizabeth A. Carlson, Ph.D.
Institute of Child Development
University of Minnesota
Minneapolis, Minnesota

Alice S. Carter, Ph.D.
Assistant Professor
Department of Psychology and Yale Child Study Center
Yale University
New Haven, Connecticut

Michael Chandler, Ph.D.
Department of Psychology
University of British Columbia
Vancouver, British Columbia
Canada

Christopher Chase, Ph.D.
Associate Professor
School of Communications and Cognitive Science
Hampshire College
Amherst, Massachusetts

Roland D. Ciaranello, M.D.
Professor
Nancy Pritzker Laboratory
Department of Psychiatry and Behavioral Sciences
Stanford University School of Medicine
Stanford, California

Dante Cicchetti, Ph.D.
Professor of Psychology, Psychiatry, and Pediatrics and,
Director, Mt. Hope Family Center
University of Rochester
Rochester, New York

Donald J. Cohen, M.D.
Director, Yale Child Study Center and,
Irving B. Harris Professor of Child Psychiatry, Pediatrics, and Psychology
Yale University
New Haven, Connecticut

Elizabeth J. Costello, Ph.D.
Associate Professor of Medical Psychology
Department of Psychiatry
Duke University
Durham, North Carolina

Eric Courchesne, Ph.D.
Professor
Neurosciences Department
University of California at San Diego
La Jolla, California

Robin R. Dean, Ph.D.
Research Associate
Nancy Pritzker Laboratory
Department of Psychiatry and Behavioral Sciences
Stanford University School of Medicine
Stanford, California

Edward L. Deci, Ph.D.
Professor
Department of Psychology
University of Rochester
Rochester, New York

Peter Fonagy, Ph.D.
Freud Memorial Professor
Psychoanalysis Unit, Department of Psychology
University College London and,
Research Director, Anna Freud Centre
London, United Kingdom

Uta Frith, Ph.D.
Professor
Medical Research Council Cognitive Development Unit
University College London
London, United Kingdom

Darren R. Fuerst, Ph.D.
Neuropsychologist
Department of Psychology
Harper Hospital
Detroit, Michigan

Andrew Gerber, M.Sc.
Research Associate
Psychoanalysis Unit, Department of Psychology
University College London
London, United Kingdom

Wendy S. Grolnick, Ph.D.
Associate Professor
Department of Psychology
Clark University
Worchester, Massachusetts

Paul Harris, D. Phil.
Department of Experimental Psychology
University of Oxford
Oxford, United Kingdom

Stuart T. Hauser, M.D., Ph.D.
Professor of Psychiatry
Harvard Medical School and,
Director, Judge Baker Children's Center
Boston, Massachusetts

Karen L. Hershey, Ph.D.
Department of Psychology
University of Oregon
Eugene, Oregon

Carroll E. Izard, Ph.D.
Unidel Professor
Department of Psychology
University of Delaware
Newark, New Jersey

Chris LaLonde, Ph.D. Candidate
Research Associate
University of British Columbia
Vancouver, British Columbia
Canada

David A. Morilak, Ph.D.
Research Associate
Nancy Pritzker Laboratory
Department of Psychiatry and Behavioral Sciences
Stanford University School of Medicine
Stanford, California

Robin Morris, Ph.D.
Associate Professor
Department of Psychology
Georgia State University
Atlanta, Georgia

John Morton, Ph.D.
Professor
Medical Research Council Cognitive Development Unit
University College London
London, United Kingdom

Gil G. Noam, Ed.D., Dipl. Psych.
Associate Professor of Psychology/Psychiatry and Education
Harvard University and,
Director, Hall-Mercer Laboratory of Developmental Psychology and Developmental Psychopathology
McLean Hospital and Harvard Medical School
Cambridge, Massachusetts

Bruce F. Pennington, Ph.D.
Professor
Department of Psychology
University of Denver
Denver, Colorado

Robert Plomin, Ph.D.
Professor
College of Health and Human Development and,
Director, Center for Developmental and Health Genetics
Pennsylvania State University
University Park, Pennsylvania

Matthew H. Porteus, M.D., Ph.D.
Intern
Nancy Pritzker Laboratory
Department of Psychiatry and Behavioral Sciences
Stanford University School of Medicine
Stanford, California

Michael I. Posner, Ph.D.
Professor
Department of Psychology
University of Oregon
Eugene, Oregon

Gary Racusin, Ph.D.
Associate Research Scientist
Department of Psychiatry and Yale Child Study Center
Yale University
New Haven, Connecticut

David Reiss, M.D.
Professor of Psychiatry, Psychology, and Medicine
Department of Psychiatry and Behavioral Science
The George Washington University Medical Center
Washington, DC

Richard Rende, Ph.D.
Assistant Professor of Clinical Psychology in Psychiatry
Department of Psychiatry
Columbia University College of Physicians and Surgeons
New York, New York

Paola Giovanardi Rossi, L.D.
Professore di Neuropsichiatria Infantile
Institute di Clinica Neurologica
Dell Universita di Bologna
Bologna, Italy

Mary K. Rothbart, Ph.D.
Professor
Department of Psychology
University of Oregon
Eugene, Oregon

Byron P. Rourke, Ph.D.
Professor
Department of Psychology
University of Windsor
Windsor, Ontario and,
Yale Child Study Center
Yale University
New Haven, Connecticut

Richard M. Ryan, Ph.D.
Professor
Department of Psychology
University of Rochester
Rochester, New York

Andrew W. Safyer, Ph.D.
Assistant Professor
School of Social Work
Boston University
Boston, Massachusetts

Arnold J. Sameroff, Ph.D.
Professor of Psychology
Center for Human Growth and Development
University of Michigan
Ann Arbor, Michigan

Sara S. Sparrow, Ph.D.
Professor of Psychology
Department of Psychology and Yale Child Study Center
Yale University
New Haven, Connecticut

L. Alan Sroufe, Ph.D.
William Harris Professor of Child Psychology
Institute of Child Development
University of Minnesota
Minneapolis, Minnesota

Miriam Steele, Ph.D.
Lecturer in Psychology
Psychoanalysis Unit, Department of Psychology
University College London and,
Senior Research Fellow, Anna Freud Centre
London, United Kingdom

Barbara Swarzenski, M.D.
Instructor
Department of Psychiatry (Child)
Washington University School of Medicine
St. Louis, Missouri

Mary Target, Ph.D.
Lecturer in Psychology
Psychoanalysis Unit, Department of Psychology
University College London and,
Senior Research Fellow, Anna Freud Centre
London, United Kingdom

Richard D. Todd, M.D., Ph.D.
Professor of Psychiatry and Genetics
Washington University School of Medicine
St. Louis, Missouri

Jeanne Townsend, Ph.D.
Research Neuroscientist
Neuropsychology Research Laboratory
University of California at San Diego
La Jolla, California

Paola Visconti, L.D.
Reparto di Neuropsichiatria Infantile
Institute di Clinica Neurologica
Dell Universita di Bologna
Bologna, Italy

Barry M. Wagner, Ph.D.
Assistant Professor
Department of Psychology
The Catholic University of America
Washington, DC

Marilyn Welsh, Ph.D.
Associate Professor
University of Northern Colorado
Greeley, Colorado

Series Preface

This series of books is addressed to behavioral scientists interested in the nature of human personality. Its scope should prove pertinent to personality theorists and researchers as well as to clinicians concerned with applying an understanding of personality processes to the amelioration of emotional difficulties in living. To this end, the series provides a scholarly integration of theoretical formulations, empirical data, and practical recommendations.

Six major aspects of studying and learning about human personality can be designated: personality theory, personality structure and dynamics, personality development, personality assessment, personality change, and personality adjustment. In exploring these aspects of personality, the books in the series discuss a number of distinct but related subject areas: the nature and implications of various theories of personality; personality characteristics that account for consistencies and variations in human behavior; the emergence of personality processes in children and adolescents; the use of interviewing and testing procedures to evaluate individual differences in personality; efforts to modify personality styles through psychotherapy, counseling, behavior therapy, and other methods of influence; and patterns of abnormal personality functioning that impair individual competence.

IRVING B. WEINER

Tampa, Florida

Preface

If the value of a scientific course of inquiry can be measured, then, at least in part, its contribution can be judged by the role it exerts on generating new questions and discovering new truths, and through its impact and visibility in the literature. By these criteria, the importance of the field of developmental psychopathology to the basic research and applied aspects of developmental and clinical psychology, psychiatry, the neurosciences, and related disciplines cannot be denied. In the past two decades, the presence of the developmental psychopathology perspective has been manifested in a number of arenas: through the growing number of theoretical, review, and empirical papers that reflect this orientation; through its enhanced influence on work in the fields of prevention and intervention; and through its increased application to the areas of advocacy and social policy. In addition, there has been a proliferation of journal special sections devoted to the topic, as well as the publication of a number of journal special issues, beginning with the landmark volume in *Child Development* (Cicchetti, 1984).

The scientific importance of developmental psychopathology also was formally acknowledged through its inclusion as a topic in the fourth edition of the *Handbook of Child Psychology* (Mussen, 1983; see the chapter by Rutter and Garmezy). In 1989, *Development and Psychopathology,* a journal devoted exclusively to the discipline of developmental psychopathology, was initiated. Moreover, there have been numerous scientific meetings focused on the theoretical and empirical advances that have been fostered by the developmental psychopathology framework.

Despite the relatively recent ascendance of developmental psychopathology, its roots can be traced to a variety of areas and disciplines (Cicchetti, 1990; Cohen, 1974). Although a more comprehensive historical perspective on the discipline of developmental psychopathology has been presented elsewhere (Cicchetti, 1990), some highlights of contributions to the formation of developmental psychopathology will be helpful in embedding this area of inquiry within a broader context. Specifically, the origins of developmental psychopathology can be seen in a number of developmental theories, including organismic-developmental theory (Werner, 1948), psychoanalytic theory (Freud, 1940/1955), and structural-developmental theory (Piaget, 1971), all of which stress the dynamic relationship between the individual and the environment.

For scientists working within each of these developmental traditions, the study of pathological populations resulted in the confirmation, expansion, or modification of the developmental principles on which their theories were based. As stated by Werner (1948), "[P]sychopathology will shed light on the genetic data of other developmental fields . . . the results of psychopathology . . . become valuable in many ways for the general picture of mental development, just as psychopathology is itself enriched and its methods facilitated by the adoption of the genetic approach" (pp. 33–34). In their recognition of the importance of understanding the abnormal in order to inform the normal, and vice versa, theoreticians and researchers such as Werner were promulgating a well-established tradition that can be traced to Goethe, who believed that psychopathology resulted from "regressive metamorphoses" and stressed the close connection between abnormal and normal functioning. In essence, for Goethe, the study of pathology allowed one to see, magnified, the normal processes of development and functioning. William James (1902), too, emphasized the role that abnormal mental functioning could play in enhancing the understanding of human nature. Much of psychoanalytic theory also has been grounded in the belief that a knowledge of normal development is a prerequisite to understanding abnormality (Marans & Cohen, 1991). Working within this tradition, Sigmund Freud (1940/1955) drew no sharp distinction between normal and abnormal functioning. Likewise, Anna Freud (1965) argued against adopting a symptomatological diagnostic system for psychopathology, advocating instead the evaluation of disturbances in children based on their ability to perform age-appropriate developmental tasks. Examples such as these serve to elucidate the historical origins of one of the central tenets of developmental psychopathology: that the studies of normal and abnormal development are mutually enriching.

In addition to the important contributions of the early developmental theorists to the emergence of developmental psychopathology, this young field owes much to the influences derived from a variety of disciplines, including cultural anthropology, epidemiology, embryology, genetics, the neurosciences, experimental psychology, and psychiatry (see Cicchetti, 1990). Many of the eminent theorists and great systematizers in these fields conceived of psychopathology as a magnification or distortion of the normal condition and believed that the examination of psychopathology could sharpen our understanding of normal biological and psychological processes.

The reason for the relatively recent crystallization of a number of subdisciplines into a line of inquiry subsumed under developmental psychopathology can be attributed to the maturation of related disciplines. Only after a sufficient corpus of research knowledge on normal biological and psychological development across the life span had been accumulated could researchers interpret the findings of their investigations of psychopathological processes and atypical development. The current work in developmental psychopathology, much of which is contained in these volumes, attests to the rich history that has contributed to this discipline, as well as to the promising future that remains to be discovered.

This two-volume set utilizes a developmental approach to elucidate processes and mechanisms associated with risk, disorder, and adaptation across the life course. As suggested by the title, *Developmental Psychopathology* applies a developmental perspective to the ever-fluctuating relationship between adaptive and maladaptive outcomes, between pathology and normality, and between intrinsic and extrinsic influences on ontogenesis. Because developmental psychopathologists are as invested in understanding those individuals who evidence adaptation despite risk as they are in examining manifestations of psychopathology, we have chosen not to organize these volumes exclusively around thematic psychiatric disorders. Rather, we have opted to explore developmentally relevant theories, methods of assessment, and domains of functioning. Although many chapters address specific disorders, processes that eventuate in psychopathology rather than the psychiatric disturbances per se are emphasized.

In Volume 1, *Theory and Methods,* various approaches to understanding developmental influences are presented. The volume begins with an explication of the discipline of developmental psychopathology. After issues of epidemiology, taxonomy, and assessment are examined, biological and genetic processes are addressed. The volume concludes with analyses of cognitive and social-cognitive processes, socioemotional processes, and systems theory approaches.

Volume 2, *Risk, Disorder, and Adaptation,* begins with a series of chapters that examine the impact of ecological and relational risk factors on development, ranging from societal to more micro-level processes. The volume then examines the emergence of disorder in a variety of populations. To conclude, in their discussions of adaptation and protective processes, a number of authors address the occurrence of resilient outcomes despite the presence of stressors often associated with maladaptation.

In a work of this breadth and scope, it is important that readers understand the goals of these volumes. *Developmental Psychopathology* was not intended to serve as a "how to" manual or as a compendium of research knowledge on the extensive array of psychiatric disorders across the life course. Rather, we invited premier scholars to conceptualize their work within a developmental psychopathology framework and to discuss the implications of their theory and research for enhancing knowledge of normal and atypical development. Toward this end, the utilization of dimensional approaches affecting development, as well as more categorical approaches, was considered to be necessary. We also chose to focus these volumes on theory and research. Although generalizations to implications for treatment of various disorders can be made by the knowledgeable reader, these volumes were not conceived to provide information on various psychotherapeutic approaches. Because we felt that a chapter or two on psychotherapy could not possibly provide the necessary depth to address the topic adequately, intervention techniques are not presented other than when an author chooses to incorporate therapeutic considerations into a chapter. These volumes are concerned with methods of approaching and understanding normal and atypical development, not with providing guidelines for intervention.

As the editors of *Developmental Psychopathology,* we are honored to contribute yet another link to the chain that has been forged from this exciting area of inquiry. The contributors to these volumes have many suggestions and recommendations for furthering the growth that has occurred, and we believe that developmental psychopathology will be enriched and will continue to exert a growing influence on theory and research in normal and abnormal development as a result of their insights.

Collectively, we wish to acknowledge the generations of developmentalists and the several decades of personal contributions of the individuals whose ideas flow throughout these volumes and whose foresight, vision, courage, and passion helped to create the field of developmental psychopathology.

Dante Cicchetti has had the privilege and good fortune of working closely with a number of scholars who have influenced his thinking and supported his work in this field, as well as provided inestimable sources of support, love, and friendship. Without the belief and guidance, as well as the ongoing love and "fatherly concern" of Alex Siegel, Dante would not have embarked on the "developmental psychopathology journey" that began in his undergraduate years and has continued through to the present. In following Alex's footsteps to the University of Minnesota, Dante studied with and was deeply influenced by three incredible intellects and persons: Norman Garmezy, Paul Meehl, and Alan Sroufe. Words cannot express Dante's indebtedness to these individuals for believing in him, providing a supportive environment, encouraging him to pursue his dreams to the fullest, and having the wisdom to look beneath the surface. When he left the University of Minnesota for Harvard University, a number of scholars and friends contributed to Dante's breadth and depth as a scientist, theorist, and clinician. In particular, his colleagues, Jules Bemporad, Phil Holzman, Jerome Kagan, Steve Kosslyn, Duncan Luce, Brendan Maher, and Shep White; his closest friends, David Buss, Heidi Mitke, Ross Rizley, and James Stellar; and his students, especially Larry Aber, Marjorie Beeghly, Vicki Carlson, Wendy Coster, Petra Hesse, and Karen Schneider-Rosen—all enhanced Dante's personal and professional growth. In his current environment at the Mt. Hope Family Center at the University of Rochester, Dante has been fortunate to be surrounded by a group of first-rate intellects and high-integrity individuals. First and foremost among these is Sheree

Toth, a phenomenal example of a scientist-clinician who has already made numerous contributions to this field. In addition, his colleagues and friends, Douglas Barnett, Kathleen Holt, Michael Lynch, Jody Todd Manly, and Fred Rogosch have greatly contributed to the exciting and productive environment that exists at Mt. Hope. Knowing that these talented individuals have chosen to become developmental psychopathologists bodes well for the continued growth of the field. Finally, Dante acknowledges the support, influence, and inspiration of Thomas Achenbach, William Charlesworth, Byron Egeland, Irving Gottesman, Larry Kohlberg, Ping Serafica, Michael Rutter, and Edward Zigler.

Donald Cohen acknowledges the influential role that his colleagues at the Yale Child Study Center have had in contributing to his thinking in the area of developmental psychopathology. Although the team is too large for everyone to be recognized by name, Donald extends special recognition to Albert Solnit and Edward Zigler.

REFERENCES

Cicchetti, D. (Ed.). (1984). Developmental psychopathology [Special issue]. *Child Development, 55,* 1–314.

Cicchetti, D. (1990). A historical perspective on the discipline of developmental psychopathology. In J. Rolf, A. Masten, D. Cicchetti, K. Nuechterlein, & S. Weintraub (Eds.), *Risk and protective factors in the development of psychopathology* (pp. 2–28). New York: Cambridge University Press.

Cohen, D. J. (1974). Competence and biology: Methodology in studies of infants, twins, psychosomatic disease and psychosis. In E. J. Anthony & C. Koupernik (Eds.), *The child in his family: Children at psychiatric risk* (pp. 361–394). New York: Wiley.

Freud, A. (1965). *Normality and pathology in childhood.* New York: International Universities Press.

Freud, S. (1955). An outline of psycho-analysis. In J. Strachey (Ed. and Trans.), *The standard edition of the complete works of Sigmund Freud* (Vol. 23, pp. 139–207). London: Hogarth Press. (Original work published 1940)

James, W. (1902). *The varieties of religious experience.* London: Longmans, Green.

Marans, S., & Cohen, D. J. (1991). Child psychoanalytic theories of development. In M. Lewis (Ed.), *Child and adolescent psychiatry: A comprehensive textbook* (pp. 613–621). Baltimore: Williams & Wilkins.

Mussen, P. (Ed.). (1983). *Handbook of child psychology* (4th ed.). New York: Wiley.

Piaget, J. (1971). *Biology and knowledge.* Chicago: University of Chicago Press.

Werner, H. (1948). *Comparative psychology of mental development.* New York: International Universities Press.

DANTE CICCHETTI
DONALD J. COHEN

Rochester, New York
New Haven, Connecticut
January 1995

Contents

Volume 1
Theory and Methods

PART FOUR COGNITIVE AND SOCIAL-COGNITIVE PROCESSES

Volume 2
Risk, Disorder, and Adaptation

PART ONE ECOLOGICAL AND RELATIONAL RISK FACTORS

PART TWO DISORDERS

PART ONE

Introduction

CHAPTER 1

Perspectives on Developmental Psychopathology

DANTE CICCHETTI and DONALD J. COHEN

In this chapter, we discuss those aspects of developmental psychopathology that we consider to be central to its uniqueness. We want to emphasize that, if taken in isolation, many components of a developmental psychopathology perspective are equally applicable to other disciplines. However, the incorporation and integration of previously discrete concepts serve to set developmental psychopathology apart. Specifically, a focus on the interplay between normal and atypical development, an interest in diverse domains of functioning, and an emphasis on the utilization of a developmental framework for understanding adaptation across the life course are among those elements that are integral to a developmental psychopathology approach. To begin, we examine the historical origins of developmental psychopathology. We then explicate the definitional parameters of the discipline and discuss issues that are central to research conducted within a developmental psychopathology framework. We conclude by describing implications for intervention and perspectives on the future of developmental psychopathology.

HISTORICAL ROOTS OF DEVELOPMENTAL PSYCHOPATHOLOGY

Despite its ascendance as a discipline that holds great promise for promoting research and theory on risk conditions and disorders, developmental psychopathology continues to be somewhat elusive. If one were to poll leading developmentalists for a definition of developmental psychopathology, it is likely that descriptive divergences would outweigh convergences. In truth, developmental psychopathology is broad enough to be able to comfortably mirror differences in emphasis, thereby contributing to some apparent definitional disparities. However, despite assertions that its breadth may, in fact, exclude it from status as a unique discipline, we believe that developmental psychopathology possesses a core set of assumptions that serve to distinguish it as a distinct discipline. It owes the emergence and coalescence of its framework to many historically based endeavors. Therefore, we begin our explication of developmental psychopathology by placing it within a historical context.

During the course of the past several decades, developmental psychopathology has emerged as a new science that is the product of an integration of various disciplines, the efforts of which had been previously distinct and separate (Achenbach, 1990; Cicchetti, 1984b, 1990). The publication of Achenbach's textbook (Achenbach, 1974/1982), the chapter by Rutter and Garmezy in the *Handbook of Child Psychology* (Mussen, 1983), the Special Issue of *Child Development* (Cicchetti, 1984a), the Rochester Symposium on Developmental Psychopathology (see, e.g., Cicchetti, 1989), and a journal devoted exclusively to the discipline, entitled *Development and Psychopathology,* are among its landmark works, but the field of developmental psychopathology has historical roots within a variety of areas and disciplines (Cicchetti, 1990; Cohen, 1974).

Many of the great theorists in embryology, the neurosciences, ethology, psychoanalytic theory, clinical, developmental, and experimental psychology, and psychiatry have reasoned that we can learn more about the normal functioning of an organism by studying its pathology and, likewise, more about its pathology by investigating its normal condition. A number of these integrative thinkers conceived of psychopathology as a magnifying mirror in which normal biological and psychological processes could better be observed. Because these systematizers conceptualized psychopathology as a distortion or exaggeration of the normal condition, the study of pathological phenomena was thought to throw into sharper relief the understanding of normal processes.

A basic theme appears in the writings of these earlier thinkers: because all psychopathology can be conceived as a distortion, disturbance, or degeneration of normal functioning, it follows that, if one wishes to understand pathology more fully, then one must understand the normal functioning against which psychopathology is compared (Cicchetti, 1984b). Not only is knowledge of normal biological, psychological, and social processes very helpful for understanding, preventing, and treating psychopathology (Benes, Turtle, Khan, & Farol, 1994; Cohen, 1992; Cohen & Donnellan, 1987; Cohen & Leckman, 1993; Institute of Medicine, 1989, 1994), but also the deviations from and distortions of normal development that are seen in pathological processes indicate in exciting ways how normal ontogenesis may be better investigated and understood (see, e.g., Baron-Cohen, Tager-Flusberg, & Cohen, 1993; Broman & Grafman, 1994; Cicchetti, 1993; Freud, 1965; Koretz, 1991; Leslie & Thaiss, 1992; Milner, Corkin, & Teuber, 1968; Omenn, 1976; Rutter, 1986; Rutter & Garmezy, 1983; Sroufe, 1990; Tager-Flusberg, 1994; Weddell, 1994). Indeed, for many thinkers, the very essence and uniqueness of a developmental psychopathology approach lies in its focus on both normal and abnormal, adaptive and maladaptive, ontogenetic processes (Cicchetti, 1984b; Rutter, 1986; Sroufe, 1989, 1990).

Although not considered to be empiricists in the traditional model, the great pioneers of child psychoanalysis, such as Anna Freud, Melanie Klein, Ernst and Marianne Kris, Erik Erikson, Donald Winnicott, and John Bowlby contributed significantly to the emergence of developmental psychopathology through their detailed observations of children in naturalistic settings. The work of these visionaries exerted a profound impact on developmental psychopathology in relation to our understanding of stages of normal development. Concepts such as attachment theory and evolving representational models, personal identity, the constructive use of imagination, and the role of defensive mechanisms in the reduction of anxiety all emerged from the observations of analytic thinkers and subsequently contributed to the formulation of investigations of normal and atypical development (Marans & Cohen, 1991).

An example of one such area that has been examined extensively by both analytic theorists and empiricists pertains to the many uses of play in the course of development (Cohen, 1992; Slade & Wolf, 1994; Solnit, Neubauer, & Cohen, 1993). Play not only reflects what is of current import in a child's life, but also operates as a psychological process that moves development forward. Play allows a child to explore diverse roles, to reenact prior experiences, and to explore hypotheses, all in a safe, contained fashion. Although the overt manifestation of play becomes altered over the course of development, the psychological process of playing continues. The emergence and uses of play and imagination, and the manner in which various factors distort this process, could serve as an important measure of development in relation to psychopathology (Solnit et al., 1993).

Writing in the late 1970s, Eisenberg (1977) urged his psychiatric brethren to adopt a developmental framework, presenting it as a helpful unifying perspective that would enable clinical investigators to frame the difficulties they encounter in investigating and treating psychopathology. Eisenberg believed that the concept of development could serve as "the crucial link between genetic determinants and environmental variables, between . . . psychology and sociology, [and between] . . . 'physiogenic and psychogenic' causes . . . " (p. 225). Moreover, he proposed that the term *development* be used in a broad sense, and felt that it should include "not only the roots of behavior in prior maturation as well as the residual of earlier stimulation, both internal and external, but also the modulation of that behavior by the social fields of the experienced present" (p. 225).

Because developmental psychology exerted a major influence on the emergence of developmental psychopathology, its course is relevant to our discussion. Moreover, the influences of psychiatry, clinical psychology, and developmental psychopathology can be seen increasingly in the research endeavors of developmental psychologists. Most historians of the field of developmental psychology date its onset as a scientific area of investigation to the late 19th century (Cairns, 1983; Kuhn & Meacham, 1983; Parke, Ornstein, Reiser, & Zahn-Waxler, 1992; Siegel & White, 1982; White, 1990). Despite the relatively recent ascendance of developmental psychology as a discipline of scientific inquiry, philosophical and biological thinkers were concerned with many of the influential ideas and themes of development for at least the prior century (Cairns, 1983; Kaplan, 1967).

One of the most dominant ideas that contributed to the blossoming of this perspective was Spencer's (1862/1900) "Developmental Hypothesis," in which ontogenesis was depicted as a uniform process that was governed by universal laws and principles (see also Glick, 1992; Kaplan, 1967). Throughout the ensuing century, the maturation of developmental psychology as a discipline has exerted a profound effect on the field of developmental psychopathology. Additionally, important contributions have been made by individuals such as Gesell (1925) and Buhler (e.g., Buhler & Hertzer, 1935), whose observations of early childhood development provided a framework for developmental psychopathology by elucidating the expectable pathways of development to which deviations from normality could be compared. The advances made in our knowledge of basic psychobiological, perceptual, cognitive, linguistic, representational, social, social-cognitive, emotional, and motivational ontogenetic processes have provided a firm empirical basis against which developmental psychopathologists could discover new truths about the processes underlying adaptation and maladaptation, as well as the best means of preventing and treating psychopathology.

Despite its impact on the field of developmental psychopathology, developmental psychology had been, until the past several decades, largely concerned with basic theoretical and empirical issues (Reese, 1993). In fact, during one of its major growth eras, in the 1960s and 1970s, developmental psychology focused more and more on theoretical issues and less and less on applied problems (Reese, 1993). Among the exceptions to this practice, during this period groups of developmentalists increasingly became interested in social policy issues. Aging and the efficacy of early intervention on the functioning of disadvantaged children were two of developmental psychology's major applied foci. Undoubtedly, these particular phenomena rose into prominence because of the influence of the life-span development movement (Baltes, Reese, & Lipsitt, 1980) and the war on poverty in our country (Zigler & Valentine, 1979), respectively.

As developmental psychology has evolved toward becoming an ever more applied area of specialization, field placements, research opportunities in diverse settings, and exposure to a range of cultural, racial, and ethnic groups are becoming more commonplace in doctoral training programs. Moreover, the growing recognition for the need to integrate developmental psychology with other scientific fields has contributed to the influx of training opportunities in settings as diverse as day care centers, family court, detention centers, mental health clinics, early intervention programs, and the schools.

This expanded focus has contributed to the emergence of a new subdiscipline, applied developmental psychology. The theoretical formulations of Bronfenbrenner (1979) have played a catalytic role in moving developmental psychology beyond the confines of the laboratory. Since being described as "the science of the strange behavior of children in strange situations with strange adults for the briefest periods of time" (Bronfenbrenner, 1977, p. 513), developmental psychology has increasingly extended its vision to applied issues and has expanded the horizons of its research efforts into an accumulating number of populations and contexts (Bronfenbrenner, Kessel, Kessen, & White, 1986; Cahan, 1992; Reese, 1993).

In parallel to the enhanced concern for applied and policy-relevant issues, applied developmental psychologists have brought their expertise in research methodology and theory to bear on social problems. Included in these research endeavors has been work on a variety of pressing societal issues such as the impact of poverty on the process of development (Duncan, Brooks-Gunn, & Klebanov, 1994; Huston, 1991; Huston, McLoyd, & Garcia-Coll, 1994), the effects of divorce on children's functioning (Hetherington, 1989), the sequelae of child abuse and neglect (Cicchetti & Carlson, 1989), the consquences of being reared by an adolescent parent (Furstenberg, Brooks-Gunn, & Morgan, 1987), and the effects of day care attendance on socioemotional development (Belsky, 1988). One consquence of this evolution has been increased attention to investigations of person–context relations (Hinde, 1992; Lerner & Kauffman, 1985; Valsiner, 1987; Wertsch, 1979). Rather than focusing predominantly on individual ontogenetic change, developmental scientists have undertaken enhanced investigation of the actual contexts within which individuals reside. An outgrowth of this developmental–contextual perspective that has obvious connections with a developmental psychopathology approach is that scholars have developed an increasing appreciation for the diversity of patterns of individual and family development that exist across cultures and settings (Cicchetti & Garmezy, 1993; Lerner, 1991). Topics such as ethnic, gender, racial, cultural, handicap, and psychopathology-based diversity were for too long ignored by researchers in mainstream academic developmental psychology. Now that we are accruing more knowledge about diversity in development, we are learning that the same rules of normal ontogenesis do not necessarily exist for, or apply to, all children and families (see, e.g., Baldwin, Baldwin, & Cole, 1990). Without a sophisticated understanding of the range of diversity in normal development, we would be severely hampered in our attempts to elucidate the pathways to adaptation and maladaptation in high-risk and disordered individuals of varying backgrounds. Thus, developmental psychology was integral to fostering the emergence of developmental psychopathology.

In their seminal article, Sroufe and Rutter (1984) proposed that developmental psychopathology could be defined as "*the study of the origins and course of individual patterns of behavioral maladaptation,* whatever the transformations in behavioral manifestation, and however complex the developmental pattern may be" (p. 18; italics theirs). More recently, we served as members of the Steering Committee for the Institute of Medicine's "Study of Research on Child and Adolescent Mental Disorders." The Institute of Medicine (1989) report, written from the integrative perspective of developmental psychopathology, and highly influential in the development and implementation of the National Plan for Research on Child and Adolescent Mental Disorders (National Advisory Mental Health Council, 1990; see also Jensen et al., 1993), stated that the developmental psychopathology perspective should take into account ". . . the emerging behavioral repertoire, cognitive and language functions, social and emotional processes, and changes occurring in anatomical structures and physiological processes of the brain" (p. 14) *throughout the life course.* Although some definitional divergence exists, it is generally agreed that developmental psychopathologists should investigate functioning through the assessment of ontogenetic, biochemical, genetic, biological, physiological, cognitive, social–cognitive, representational, socioemotional, environmental, cultural, and societal influences on behavior (Achenbach, 1990; Cicchetti, 1993; Cohen, 1990; Cohen & Leckman, 1993; Plomin & McLearn, 1993; Rutter & Garmezy, 1983).

In view of the intimate link between the study of normal and abnormal ontogenesis, it is not surprising that theoreticians and researchers who predominantly focus on normal processes espouse similar perspectives about the nature of development. For example, Cairns (1990) conceptualized the study of normal development as necessitating a holistic, synthetic science. As Cairns articulated: "Maturational, experiential, and cultural contributions are inseparably coalesced in ontogeny. Hence developmental studies should be multi-level, concerned with ontogenetic integration, and employ person-oriented as well as variable-oriented analyses" (p. 42).

In a related vein, Gottlieb (1991) depicted individual normal development as characterized by "an increase of complexity of organization (i.e., the emergence of new structural and functional properties and competencies) at all levels of analysis (e.g., molecular, subcellular, cellular, organismic) as a consequence of horizontal and vertical coactions among the organisms' parts, including organism–environment coactions" (p. 7). For Gottlieb (1992), horizontal coactions take place at the same level of analysis (e.g., gene–gene, cell–cell, person–person, environment–environment), whereas vertical coactions occur at a different level of analysis (e.g., cell–tissue, organism–environment, behavioral activity–nervous system) and are reciprocal. As such, vertical coactions are capable of influencing developmental organization from either lower-to-higher or higher-to-lower levels of the developing system (Gottlieb, 1992). Thus, epigenesis is viewed as probabilistic rather than predetermined, with the bidirectional nature of genetic, neural, behavioral, and environmental influence over the course of individual development capturing the essence of Gottlieb's conception of probabilistic epigenesis. From the influential psychiatrist Adolf Meyer came a psychobiological orientation that bore striking similarity to Gottlieb's position. For Meyer, the psychobiological approach depicted humans as integrated organisms such that their thoughts and emotions could affect their functioning all the way down to the cellular and biochemical level, and, conversely, that occurrences at these lower biological levels could influence thinking and feeling (Lidz, 1993; Meyer, 1950–1952; Rutter, 1988).

THE ORGANIZATIONAL PERSPECTIVE

Although developmental psychopathology is not characterized by the acceptance of any unitary theoretical approach, the organizational perspective on development (Cicchetti, 1993; Sroufe & Rutter, 1984) offers a powerful theoretical framework for conceptualizing the intricacies of the life-span perspective on risk and psychopathology, as well as on normal ontogenesis. Similar to Gottlieb's viewpoint (1991, 1992), the organizational perspective focuses on the quality of integration both within and among the behavioral and biological systems of the individual. This focus on variations in the quality of integration provides the building blocks on which the developmental psychopathologist characterizes developmental status. Further, the organizational perspective specifies how development proceeds. Development occurs as a progression of qualitative reorganizations within and among the biological, social, emotional, cognitive, representational, and linguistic systems proceeding through differentiation and subsequent hierarchical integration and organization. The orthogenetic principle (Werner, 1984) specifies that the developing individual moves from a state of relatively diffuse, undifferentiated organization to states of greater articulation and complexity by differentiation and consolidation of the separate systems, followed by hierarchic integration within and between systems. Initially, separate systems within the infant are relatively undifferentiated; however, through development, the various systems increasingly become more distinct or differentiated, and repeated hierarchical integrations among these systems lead to increasingly complex levels of organization.

At each juncture of reorganization in development, the concept of hierarchic motility specifies that prior developmental structures are incorporated into later ones by means of hierarchic integration. In this way, early experience and its effects on the organization of the individual are carried forward within the individual's organization of systems rather than having reorganizations override previous organizations. As a result, hierarchic motility suggests that previous areas of vulnerability or strength within the organizational structure may remain present although not prominent in the current organizational structure. Nevertheless, the presence of prior structures within the current organization allows for possible future access by way of regressive activation of those previous structures in times of stress or crisis. Thus, for example, a behavioral or symptomatic presentation of a depressed individual may appear discrepant with recently evidenced adaptations, but in effect indicates the activation of prior maladaptive structures that were retained in the organizational structure through hierarchical integration.

Organizational theorists believe that each stage of development confronts individuals with new challenges to which they must adapt. At each period of reorganization, successful adaptation or competence is signified by an adaptive integration within and among the emotional, cognitive, social, representational, and biological domains, as the individual masters current biological and psychological developmental challenges. Because earlier structures of the individual's organization are incorporated into later structures in the successive process of hierarchical integration, early competence tends to promote later competence. An individual who has adaptively met the developmental challenges of the particular stage will be better equipped to meet successive new challenges in development. This is not to say that early adaptation ensures successful later adaptation; major changes or stresses in the internal and external environment may tax subsequent adaptational capacities. However, early competence does provide a more optimal organization of behavioral and biological systems, thus offering, in a probabilistic manner, a greater likelihood that adaptive resources are available to encounter and cope with new developmental demands (see, e.g., Cicchetti, 1993; Erikson, 1950; Sroufe, 1989; Sroufe, Egeland, & Kreutzer, 1990).

In contrast, incompetence in development is fostered by difficulties or maladaptive efforts to resolve the challenges of a developmental period. Inadequate resolution of developmental challenges may result in a developmental lag or delay in, for example, one of the biological or behavioral systems. As a result, less than adequate integration within that domain will occur, and that poor within-domain integration will compromise adaptive integration among domains as hierarchical integration proceeds. Thus, incompetence in development may be viewed as a problematic integration of pathological structures. Over time, as hierarchical integration between the separate systems occurs, difficulty in the organization of one biological or behavioral system may tend to promote difficulty in the way in which other systems are organized (cf. Hinde, 1992). The organization of the individual may then appear to consist of an integration of poorly integrated component systems.

Early incompetence—the converse of the effects of early competence—tends to promote later incompetence because the individual arrives at successive developmental stages with less than optimal resources available for responding to the challenges of that period. Again, however, this progression is probabilistic, not inevitable. Changes in the internal and external environment may lead to improvements in the ability to grapple with developmental challenges, resulting in a redirection in the developmental course (Sroufe & Rutter, 1984).

To understand adaptive versus maladaptive development over time, it is important to consider the dialectic nature of two epistemologies employed to classify problems and disorders: (a) categorical approaches (e.g., DSM IV; ICD-10) and (b) dimensional or more "developmentally heuristic" models. These two models reflect mutually enriching perspectives, but each has limitations as well as benefits. From a developmental psychopathology perspective, we tend to be interested in continuities and discontinuities, both over time and with regard to normal and deviant development. Developmental psychopathologists also are invested in understanding the whole continuum of functioning, from normal to abnormal, and the associated pathways. However, categorical approaches that delimit specific disorders also are useful. It is sometimes difficult to draw a clear delineation between, for example, issues such as a few tics and Tourette's syndrome (Cohen, Bruun, & Leckman, 1988), but it cannot be assumed that categorical diagnoses are therefore without merit. Rather, developmental psychopathologists are committed to understanding the origins of categorically definable conditions as well as to providing alternative ways of considering and describing psychopathology.

DEFINITIONAL PARAMETERS OF DEVELOPMENTAL PSYCHOPATHOLOGY

With the organizational perspective on development in mind, it is possible to examine some of the definitional parameters of developmental psychopathology. Developmental psychopathologists focus their interests predominantly on the investigation of high-risk and disordered populations. Inherent to this approach is a commitment to the importance of applying our knowledge of normal development to the study of atypical populations. Thus, even before the emergence of a psychopathological disorder, certain pathways signify adaptational failures in normal development that probabilistically forebode subsequent pathology. Similarly, developmental psychopathologists recognize the value in examining abnormality in order to enhance our understanding of normal processes. Accordingly, developmental psychopathologists are equally interested in individuals who are at risk for the development of pathology but do not manifest it and individuals who develop an actual disorder (Masten, Best, & Garmezy, 1990; Sroufe & Rutter, 1984). Developmental psychopathologists also are committed to understanding pathways to competent adaptation despite exposure to conditions of adversity (Masten, 1989; Rutter, 1990; Rutter & Garmezy, 1983).

A related aspect of the developmental psychopathology perspective involves an interest in the mechanisms and processes that moderate the ultimate outcome of risk factors (Cicchetti & Lynch, 1993; Rutter, 1988). The approach suggested by a developmental psychopathology framework requires a comprehensive assessment of functioning, including multidisciplinary, multidomain, and multicontextual measurement strategies.

Finally, although many active theoreticians and researchers in developmental psychopathology have focused their efforts on childhood disorders, we believe that a life-span perspective is necessary because it is only by examining a range of conditions and populations from infancy through adulthood and into old age that developmental continuities and discontinuities can be elucidated fully. Moreover, because all periods of the life course usher in new biological and psychological challenges, strengths, and vulnerabilities (Erikson, 1950; Noam & Valiant, 1994), the process of development may embark on an unfortunate turn at any point in the life span (Bell, 1986). Where as change in functioning remains possible at each transitional turning point in development, prior adaptation does place constraints on subsequent adaptation. In particular, the longer an individual continues along a maladaptive ontogenic pathway, the more difficult it is to reclaim a normal developmental trajectory (Sroufe, 1990). Furthermore, recovery of function to an adaptive level of developmental organization is more likely to occur following a period of pathology if the level of organization prior to the breakdown was a competent and adaptive one (Sroufe et al., 1990). Additionally, the examination of the relations between the risk condition or disorder of interest and other emergent difficulties throughout the life span, including comorbidity (Caron & Rutter, 1991) and pleiotropy (Gottesman & Goldsmith, 1994), presents opportunities for investigating fundamental developmental processes such as the changing manifestation of an underlying diathesis with maturation (Cohen, 1992).

In addition to emphasizing the study of developmental processes throughout the life span, developmental psychopathology is committed to a multigenerational perspective that highlights an essential point: parents transmit their genes *and* provide a context for development. Development must be understood within this framework. For a number of specific disorders, such as Tourette's syndrome, there is a clear multigenerational pattern (Cohen & Leckman, 1993); for others, such as depression, there are clear influences (Gershon, Bunney, Leckman, Van Eerdewegh, & DeBauche, 1976; Kendler, Neale, Kessler, Heath, & Eaves, 1992). By studying gene–environment interactions over the course of development, the reciprocal interactions between constitutional and psychosocial factors can be better understood. The study of discordance among monozygotic twins provides a useful approach for examining gene–environment interaction from infancy through adulthood (Gottesman & Bertelsen, 1989; Rutter et al., 1990). Although genetic factors are not all expressed at birth, they play a prominent role at each phase of development. The age of onset of disorders is most likely affected by timed biological events (e.g., pruning of the CNS, endocrine surges, etc.) as well as by the emergence of stage-salient issues of development.

Developmental psychopathologists view disorders of childhood and adulthood from within the broader context of knowledge that has been accrued about normal biological, psychological, and sociological processes (Cohen, 1980, 1990, 1992). Moreover, from the integrative perspective of developmental psychopathology, it is critical to engage in a comprehensive evaluation of these factors and how they may influence the nature of individual differences, the continuity of adaptive or maladaptive behavioral patterns, and the different pathways by which the same developmental outcomes may be achieved.

In practice, this requires an understanding of and appreciation for the biological and psychological developmental transformations and reorganizations that occur over time (Cohen, 1992; Sroufe, 1989); an analysis and appropriate weighing of the risk and protective factors and mechanisms operating in the individual and his or her environment throughout the life course (Cicchetti & Lynch, 1993; Rutter, 1990); the investigation of how emergent functions, competencies, and developmental tasks modify the expression of risk conditions or disorder or lead to new symptoms and difficulties (Angold & Costello, 1991; Rutter, 1987, 1988; Rutter & Garmezy, 1983; Sroufe & Rutter, 1984); and the recognition that a specific stress or underlying mechanism may, at different times in the developmental process and in varied contexts, lead to different behavioral difficulties. Consequently, individuals may experience similar events differently, depending on their level of functioning across all domains of psychological and biological development. Accordingly, various occurrences will have different meanings for an individual because of both the nature and the timing of their experience. The interpretation of the experience, in turn, will affect the adaptation or maladaptation that ensues.

Because of the interrelations involved in investigation of normal and abnormal ontogenesis, developmental psychopathologists need to be aware of normal pathways of development, uncover deviations from these pathways, articulate the developmental transformations that occur as individuals progress through these deviant ontogenetic courses, and identify the factors and mechanisms that may divert an individual from a particular pathway and onto a more or less adaptive course (cf. Kopp & Recchia, 1990; Sroufe, 1989). According to Zigler and Glick (1986), a central tenet of developmental psychopathology is that persons may move between pathological and nonpathological forms of functioning. Additionally, developmental psychopathology underscores that, even in the midst of pathology, patients may display adaptive coping mechanisms. Moreover, depending on contextual constraints, the definition of normality may vary. For example, affective inhibition may be adaptive for a child with maltreating parents, but it may result in victimization by peers. This life-span perspective on psychopathology enables developmental considerations to be brought into harmony with clinical concepts used to define the natural history of disorder, such as prodrome, onset, course, offset, remission, and residual states (Cohen, 1992).

We believe that the field of developmental psychopathology provides a framework for integrating knowledge within and across disciplines, contexts, and domains of inquiry. In this regard, developmental psychopathology as a field will be enriched by increased interactions with biologists, anthropologists, sociologists, and epidemiologists. Research conducted within a developmental psychopathology framework may challenge assumptions about what constitutes health or pathology and may redefine the manner in which the mental health community operationalizes, assesses, classifies, communicates about, and treats the adjustment problems and functioning impairments of infants, children, adolescents, and adults (see, e.g., Richters & Cicchetti, 1993; Sameroff & Emde, 1989; Toth & Cicchetti, 1993; Zeanah, 1993). Through its principles and tenets, developmental psychopathology transcends disciplinary boundaries and provides fertile ground for moving beyond mere symptom description to a process level understanding of normal and atypical developmental trajectories. Rather than competing with existing theories and facts, the developmental psychopathology perspective provides a broad, integrative framework within which the contributions of separate disciplines can be fully realized in the broader context of understanding individual functioning and development.

CONCEPTUAL ISSUES

To elucidate the breadth and integrative potential of developmental psychopathology, we next discuss some core concepts. We believe that research conceived through a consideration of these issues will continue to further our understanding of the course of psychopathology across the life span.

Developmental Pathways

Diversity in process and outcome are hallmarks of the developmental psychopathology framework. It is expected that: (a) there are multiple contributors to disordered outcomes in any individual, (b) the contributors vary among individuals who have the disorder, (c) among individuals with a specific disorder, there is heterogeneity in the features of their disturbance, and (d) there are numerous pathways to any particular manifestation of disordered behavior. In this vein, the principles of equifinality and multifinality derived from general systems theory (von Bertalanffy, 1968) are germane.

Equifinality refers to the observation that a diversity of paths, including chance events or what biologists refer to as nonlinear epigenesis, may lead to the same outcome. Consequently, a variety of developmental progressions may eventuate in a given disorder, rather than expecting a singular primary pathway to the disorder. Achenbach (1993), for example, argued cogently for the existence of two different yet overlapping syndromes of antisocial behavior, one with and one without significant levels of overt aggression. Even among those with similar patterns of aggressive behavior, however, there may be multiple, alternative causal pathways influencing aggression. Similarly, Sroufe (1989) suggested that there were multiple pathways to attention deficit/hyperactivity disorder (ADHD), one predominantly biological, the other largely attributable to insensitive caregiving. Likewise, Newman and Wallace (1993) proposed that there were diverse etiological pathways to disinhibitory psychopathology (i.e., conduct disorder, ADHD, and their comorbid syndromes) in children. Finally, Cicchetti, Rogosch, Lynch, and Holt (1993) discovered that there were different developmental pathways for resilient maltreated and resilient nonmaltreated children. Notably, ego overcontrol appeared to operate differentially among maltreated and nonmaltreated resilient children. Ego overcontrol, or a more reserved, guarded approach, appeared to be better suited for maltreated children in adapting to their particular environments. Restraining from emotional reactivity in volatile family circumstances may serve a protective function. Conversely, this style may be problematic for nonmaltreated children.

In contrast, multifinality suggests that any one component may function differently, depending on the organization of the system in which it operates. Thus, for example, having an insecure attachment relationship with one's primary caregiver in childhood may eventuate in any number of outcomes for children, depending on the context of their environments and their individual competencies and coping capacities (Cummings & Cicchetti, 1990; Greenberg, Speltz, & DeKlyen, 1993). Conduct disorder may be one such outcome, for example, in a child who has the biological diathesis, who has an insecure representational model of the self, and who faces extremes of additional stress in the form of a violent home and/or community environment in conjunction with minimal support or nurturance from caregivers (Gottesman & Goldsmith, 1994; Richters & Cicchetti, 1993).

Risk Factors

The investigation of risk factors as they relate to the development of maladaptation and/or psychopathology has been an active area of inquiry in recent decades (Rolf, Masten, Cicchetti, Nuechterlein, & Weintraub, 1990). Many of the internal and external processes implicated in the causes and consequences of maladaptive and/or disordered outcomes tend not to occur in isolation (Walker, Downey, & Nightingale, 1989). This co-occurrence of risk factors often renders difficult the critical task of disentangling mediating and moderating influences on outcome. In some instances, suspected causal processes may be genuinely the products of other converging systems and only spuriously related to the risk or disordered condition being studied. In other instances, a process may indeed influence a risk condition or a psychopathological disorder, but the nature and extent of its causal influence may be masked or clouded by the influences of other interacting systems. One strategy for disentangling causal influence among multiple, interacting systems is to identify and study the functioning of individuals who possess specific functioning deficits and not others. Multiple processes, when studied individually in this way, may yield significant insights into their roles in normal adaptation, and into how those roles might change and require reconceptualization within a broader matrix of functioning deficits.

In concert with our developmental formulation, it is likely that a multitude of rather general factors across the broad domains of biology, psychology, and sociology will be at least indirectly related to the etiology, course, and sequelae of risk conditions and psychopathology. A comprehensive articulation of the processes and mechanisms that have promoted or inhibited the development of competent adaptation over the course of ontogenesis may be more important than specific predictors of the immediate or proximal onset of a psychopathological disorder (Sroufe, 1989; Sroufe & Rutter, 1984).

Toward this end, an examination of factors that may contribute to adaptive or maladaptive functioning is necessary. Vulnerability factors are typically regarded as enduring or longstanding life circumstances or conditions that promote maladaptation (Zubin & Spring, 1977). Major domains of influence on the child, including those external (intrafamilial, social–environmental) and internal (biological, psychological) to the individual, may become sources of vulnerability because they detract from the achievement of successful adaptation and competence. Throughout ontogenesis, these vulnerability factors transact with the evolving organization of the biological and psychological behavioral systems of the individual child to detract from the attainment of competence, and they may promote a pathological organization across the emotional, social, cognitive, representational, linguistic, and biological domains of development.

In contrast, there also are enduring protective factors that promote competent adaptation in the child. These features are likely to enhance rather than hinder development. Protective factors may operate in a compensatory manner, counterbalancing the effects of known risks. Alternatively, protective factors may operate interactively, influencing outcomes more potently under conditions of high risk and providing minimal influence under conditions of low risk; the protective factor moderates or reduces the strength of the effect of high levels of risk (Rutter, 1990).

In addition to these enduring competence-detracting and competence-promoting factors, transient influences exist which, although temporary in duration, may have a critical positive or negative impact, depending on the timing of such events or transitions in circumstances and the pertinent developmental issues for the child at the time. Further, the potency of specific risk and protective factors in influencing development will vary as a result of the developmental period during which they occur (Bell, 1986); a specific factor may be more influential in one developmental period as compared to another. Additionally, the same factor may function differently, depending on the context in which it occurs. For example, the loss of a job by a parent may have varying degrees of impact on children, depending on the socioeconomic conditions of the family. Thus, it is important to evaluate the effect of risk and protective processes based on both the developmental and the social–environmental context in which they occur.

For any individual child, the specific enduring factors encountered—both vulnerability factors and protective factors—will vary and exist within a dynamic balance. A greater likelihood for the development of incompetence and pathological organization will occur for those children for whom vulnerability and risk factors outweigh the protective and buffering influences. Psychopathological disorders have the potential to emerge in those individuals for whom a pathological organization has evolved transactionally through development and whose coping capacities and protective resources are no longer effective in counteracting longstanding vulnerabilities and current stressors or acute risk factors.

Rutter (1990) cautioned that risk, vulnerability, and protective factors are not variables causing pathological outcomes per se; rather, they are indicators of more complex processes and mechanisms that impact on individual adaptation. Specification of the process or mechanism involved is therefore essential. In our conceptualization, these factors are expected to operate primarily through the significance they have in promoting or detracting from the development of competence at progressive stages of development and the consequent likelihood of an emerging pathological organization. For example, parental death per se does not cause depressive disorder, but in some children it may contribute to a sequence of negative transformations in the psychological and biological systems over the course of development. These changes, in turn, may result in the emergence of a prototypic depressive organization and a strong potential for depressive outcomes.

Perspectives on the Interface between Normal and Atypical Development

Throughout history, prominent theoreticians, researchers, and clinicians have adopted the premise that knowledge about normal and atypical development is reciprocally informative (Cicchetti, 1990). Embryologists, geneticists, ethologists, neuroscientists, psychiatrists, and psychologists have underscored that research on the normal and atypical must proceed hand-in-hand, in order for an integrative theory of development that can account for normal as well as deviant forms of ontogenesis to emerge.

In a prescient plea, the embryologist Weiss (1961) stated: "Pathology and developmental biology must be reintegrated so that our understanding of the 'abnormal' will become but an extension of our insight into the 'normal,' while . . . the study of the 'abnormal' will contribute to the deepening of that very insight. Their common problems should provide foci for common orientation so that, as they advance in joint directions, their efforts may supplement and reinforce each other to mutual benefit" (p. 150). More recently, the anthropologist Gould (1980) articulated the central role that the discovery of anomalies could play in elucidating the history of evolution. Gould noted that while "good fits" between organisms and their ecological niches generate so great an array of interpretations as to be uninformative, the identification of anomalies greatly decreases the amount of explanations possible. As Gould (1986) stated: "We must look for imperfections and oddities, because any perfection in organic design or ecology obliterates the paths of history and might have been created as we find it" (p. 63).

Research conducted in embryology has made significant contributions to development theory (Fishbein, 1976; Gottlieb, 1976, 1983; Waddington, 1957). From their empirical efforts to unravel the mysteries of normal embryological functioning through isolation, defect, and recombination experiments, and their investigation of surgically altered and transplanted embryos, early embryologists derived the principles of differentiation, of a dynamically active organism, and of a hierarchically integrated system (Waddington, 1966; Weiss, 1969). These three principles form the cornerstone beliefs of most contemporary developmental theories (Cairns, 1983; Gottlieb, 1983).

Moreover, throughout time, experiments conducted on genetic mutations have enhanced our understanding of normal functioning by magnifying the processes involved in normal ontogenesis (see Lawrence, 1992; Plomin, Rende, & Rutter, 1991; Pritchard, 1986; Sarnat, 1992). For example, investigations of inborn errors of metabolism eventuated in the "one gene, one enzyme" hypothesis that is viewed as the major mechanism underlying normal gene action (Beadle & Tatum, 1941). Mutagenesis has evolved into one of the primary strategies in the geneticists' research armamentarium. Investigators initially relied on spontaneously occurring mutations; now, genetically engineered mutations are being initiated. These mutagenesis experiments are designed to produce specific effects, including causing lesions in a particular gene and impacting on genes in a biochemical pathway (Lawrence, 1992). Through the examination of aberrant genetic makeup, the normal functioning of genes can be elucidated (Cohen & Leckman, 1993).

As Weiss (1961) stated, it is important to emphasize that "even the grossest deformity is produced by the same rigorously lawful molecular and cellular interactions that govern normal development. All that has happened is that the proportions among the component processes, whose harmony is predicated on proper closing and timing, have become grossly distorted during the course of development because of either some major initial flaws in the . . . endowment or some disruptive variations in the environment . . ." (p. 150).

Unfortunately, despite the adherence of developmental psychopathologists to the belief that normal and abnormal ontogenetic processes must be examined concurrently, most contemporary theory and research in developmental psychopathology have focused on the contributions that normal development can make to advancing our knowledge of psychopathology. As Weiss (1961) articulated this state of affairs: "[T]here is . . . no doubt that understanding of development has been furthered by the study of abnormalities . . . the preoccupation with the grossly abnormal has also had the unfortunate side effect of grooving the mental habit of separating the 'normal' as a distinct and disparate phenomenon, as if the processes themselves were less sound in one case than in the other . . ." (p. 150).

In a historically important chapter, Shakow (1968) reflected, with great surprise, on the lack of general acceptance of the proposition that knowledge of the psychopathological could be useful for understanding normal functioning. After addressing some of the reasons for the neglect of this viewpoint in the literature, Shakow stated that he felt encouraged that the "broadening trends" in the field would help break down existing barriers between disciplines and bring about progress in accepting the position that the normal and abnormal were closely interrelated. Unfortunately, Shakow's optimistic prediction took quite a long time to be borne out.

In view of the contributions that the study of psychopathological phenomena and extreme risk conditions have made to theory development and refinement in other disciplines, it is curious that, until recently, there has been less recognition and acceptance that the examination of high-risk and pathological conditions can affirm, expand, and challenge extant development theories. As Chess (1974) eloquently described, ". . . not infrequently highly abnormal sets of circumstances create varying stresses and adaptive necessities which elucidate normal mechanisms and capacities" (p. 255). This reluctance to apply knowledge derived from atypical populations to normal developmental theory is even more surprising in view of the historical interest in children who developed in unusual circumstances.

Dating to the turn of the 19th century, case studies of the Wild Boy of Aveyron, a child who was deprived of all contact with his own species, caused scholars to question the unfolding of the developmental process in conditions severely discrepant from more normative childhood experiences (Humphrey & Humphrey, 1932). Examinations of aberrant circumstances such as those endured by the Wild Boy shed light on theories of the interrelation among biological, cognitive, linguistic, and social development.

More recently, case studies have been utilized to examine Lenneberg's (1967) claims that there is a "sensitive period" for the acquisition of language (see also Newport, 1990). Because investigations of the determinants of human behavior are greatly hampered by the ethical impossibility of conducting experiments that will compromise the integrity of biological and psychological ontogenetic processes, so-called "experiments of nature" can be examined in order to elucidate our understanding of the processes and mechanisms underlying the course of development (cf. Leslie & Thaiss, 1992; Milner et al., 1968). Along these lines, Curtiss (1977, 1988) investigated the acquisition of a first-draft language by examining two women who were not exposed to linguistic input until they entered adulthood. One of them, Genie (Curtiss, 1977), was deprived of exposure to language by her abusive father until after puberty. In the interim, she resided in isolation in a back room in her home. When she was discovered, Genie was removed from her home and provided with intensive tutoring in the English language. Genie's linguistic development proved to be extremely atypical. Specifically, Curtiss (1977) reported that Genie acquired only limited syntactic and morphological development.

In 1988, Curtiss discussed the language development of a deaf woman, Chelsea, who had been deprived of linguistic experience, both to auditory amplification and to gestural input, for the first 32 years of her life. Despite the fact that Chelsea was successfully exposed to spoken language via auditory amplification, she, as was the case with Genie, also manifested profoundly abnormal linguistic functioning.

The findings of these detailed case investigations provide support for Lenneberg's (1967) assertion regarding the presence of a critical period for the acquisition of language. Moreover, as Skuse (1984) summarized in his review of the literature on individuals who had experienced extreme deprivation, a number of important insights can be gained from case studies more generally. Specifically, Skuse noted that case investigations provide information concerning which experiences must minimally occur if development is to proceed along a normal trajectory. Moreover, case studies offer a perspective on whether there are sensitive periods in development during which inadequate exposure to critical experiences results in enduring or permanent deleterious consequences. In addition, Skuse described how case studies might shed light on the compensatory factors or protective mechanisms that could mollify the psychological problems that ensue from adverse early rearing experiences.

Research on groups of institutionally reared infants likewise has revealed serious behavioral and socioemotional problems (Dennis, 1973; Freud & Burlingham, 1973; Provence & Lipton, 1962; Spitz, 1945). Furthermore, a recent investigation of the social and cognitive development of toddlers and preschoolers residing in Romanian orphanages revealed that children who showed problems in one developmental domain tended to demonstrate difficulties in the other, thereby underscoring the interdependence of these ontogenetic systems (Kaler & Freeman, 1994). Additionally, congruent with the theoretical beliefs that cognition and language are multifaceted in nature (Bellugi, Bihrle, Neville, Doherty, & Jernigan, 1993; Gardner, 1983), empirical investigations of the relation between syntactic and functional aspects of language in autistic (Tager-Flusberg, 1994) and maltreated (Beeghly & Cicchetti, 1994) children, representational and linguistic aspects of self-development in children with Down syndrome (Beeghly, Weiss-Perry, & Cicchetti, 1990), cognitive and affective development in infants with Down syndrome (Cicchetti & Sroufe, 1978) and in maltreated toddlers (Schneider-Rosen & Cicchetti, 1984), and affective and linguistic development in adolescents with Williams syndrome (Reilly, Klima, & Bellugi, 1990), all uncovered dissociations between the developmental systems examined.

A compelling example of the mutually enriching nature of studies of psychopathology and normal development stems from recent work on theory of mind. Studies of the difficulties with respect to the emergence of theory of mind among children with autism elucidate how research on psychopathological conditions can highlight normal processes. Specifically, the problems experienced by children with autism on joint attention between parent and child, and understanding of intentions, narrations, and implicit social messages help to illustrate relations among normal developmental systems (Baron-Cohen et al., 1993).

Despite these important contributions, caveats and limitations must be noted, and competing explanations must be explored in future work before findings obtained on atypical populations can be used to formulate theories of normal development. We agree with Rutter's (1989) assertion: "[T]here can be no presupposition that normal and abnormal development do, or do not, share the same qualities; rather, there must be a concern empirically to test for similarities and dissimilarities" (p. 26).

Often, the investigation of a system in its smoothly operating normal or healthy state does not afford us the opportunity to comprehend the interrelations among its component subsystems. Chomsky (1968) reflected on this state of affairs when he asserted: "One difficulty in the psychological sciences lies in the familiarity of the phenomena with which they deal. . . . One is inclined to take them for granted as necessary or somehow 'natural.'" Because pathological conditions such as brain damage, mental disorders, and growing up in malignant environments enable us to isolate the components of the integrated system, their investigation sheds light on the normal structure of the system and prevents us from falling prey to the problem identified by Chomsky. Hence, examinations of psychopathological populations and developmental extremes must be conducted. If we choose simply to ignore or bypass the study of these atypical phenomena, then the eventual result is likely to be the construction of theories that are contradicted by the revelation of critical facts in psychopathology (cf. Lenneberg, 1967).

When extrapolating from abnormal populations with the goal of informing developmental theory, however, it is important that a range of populations and conditions be considered. The study of a single psychopathological or risk process may result in spurious conclusions if generalizations are made based solely on that condition or disorder. As Rutter (1982) aptly articulated: "The causal processes for abnormality may not always be identical with those that underlie variations within the normal range" (p. 106). However, if we view a given behavioral pattern in the light of an entire spectrum of diseased and disordered modifications, then we may be able to attain significant insight into the processes of development not generally achieved through sole reliance on studies of relatively more homogeneous nondisordered populations.

Resilience

Examinations of risk and psychopathology across the life course all too often portray the developmental process as somewhat deterministic, resulting in maladaptive and adverse outcomes. Investigations ranging from genetic and biological contributions to pathology, to assaults on development associated with inadequate caregiving and acute and chronic stressors, graphically convey the multiplicity of risks that eventuate in maladaptation and/or psychopathology (Aber, 1994; Anthony & Cohler, 1987; Elder, 1974; Rutter & Garmezy, 1983; Jensen & Shaw, 1993; Leavitt & Fox, 1993; Murphy & Moriarty, 1976; Werner & Smith, 1992). As the developmental perspective has assumed a more prominent role in psychopathology research, there has been a growing interest in the study of resilience (Garmezy & Masten, 1994; Masten, Best, & Garmezy, 1990). What individual, familial, or environmental/societal factors stem the trajectory from risk to psychopathology, thereby resulting in adaptive outcomes even in the presence of adversity? The current efforts to understand the mechanisms and processes contributing to resilient functioning have been facilitated by researchers conducting work within the area of developmental psychopathology (Cicchetti & Garmezy, 1993; Cohen, 1992; Rutter, 1987, 1990).

For example, the recognition of the diversity of developmental pathways has led to a growing interest regarding the presence of successful adaptation despite adversity. In their exposition of the domain and boundaries of developmental psychopathology, Sroufe and Rutter (1984) also stressed the need to understand "patterns normally predictive of disorder but which *for reasons to be discovered, do not do so with a particular subgroup of subjects*" (pp. 18–19, italics ours). By uncovering the mechanisms and processes that lead to competent adaptation despite the presence of adversity, our understanding of both normal development and psychopathology is enhanced.

The incorporation of a developmental perspective into work in the area of resilience also underscores the need to examine functioning across domains of development. For example, even though a child may appear to be adapting positively within the school arena if outcome measures focus solely on cognitive abilities, the same child may manifest impaired social relationships. Unless multiple domains of development are assessed, only a partial picture of adaptation can be formulated. This is especially problematic if significant maladaptation subsequently emerges: it would appear to be an unexplained divergence when, in reality, the earlier portrayal of adaptive functioning was incorrect. As illustrated in the seminal work of Luthar and her colleagues, disadvantaged adolescents who are manifesting resilient functioning in some areas are often at risk for difficulties in other realms of functioning (Luthar, 1991; Luthar, Doernberger, & Zigler, 1993). We believe—and there is growing evidence to support our belief (see, e.g., Baltes, Smith, & Staudinger, 1992; Staudinger, Marsiske, & Baltes, 1993)—that this state of affairs is characteristic of the nature of resilience throughout the life course.

An organizational perspective on development highlights the importance of assessing multiple developmental systems concurrently. Although various domains may be studied independently, organizational theorists seek an integrated understanding of the organization of various psychological and biological developmental systems. Psychopathologists who adhere to an organizational view of the developmental process must increasingly incorporate age-appropriate assessments of the effects of biological, psychological, and sociocultural factors on the same individuals, in their strivings to uncover the roots of resilient adaptation.

Along these lines, the investigation of multiple aspects of the developmental process concurrently can shed light on the nature of the interrelation among various ontogenetic domains. For example, how do cognition, affect, and neurobiological growth relate with one another at various points during ontogeny? When an advance or a lag occurs in one system, what are the consequences for other systems? Pursuing answers to questions such as these will not only enable researchers to formulate more precise definitions of resilience, but will help to ensure that individuals who are labeled resilient are persons who genuinely have been exposed to the biological, psychological, and sociocultural stressors under investigation (cf. Richters & Weintraub, 1990). The issue of magnitude of risk cannot be minimized, and risk should not be assumed merely in response to the presumed presence of a stressor. Adherence to an organizational perspective underscores the importance of obtaining more comprehensive information on the nature of risk in all samples. The simultaneous assessment of a diverse array of intra- and interindividual factors called for by organizational theorists holds promise for elucidating our knowledge of resilient adaptation throughout the life course.

Investigations of how some individuals can "bounce back" from traumatic experiences while others apparently have grave difficulty doing so shed further light on the understanding of the construct of resilience. A number of researchers studying resilience have emphasized how examinations of the processes underlying recovery of function from traumatic experiences or other vicissitudes of life can enhance our knowledge of the mechanisms of developmental change (Garmezy, 1990; Murphy & Moriarty, 1976; Werner, 1993), as well as provide an important opportunity for testing the propositions of a probabilistic conceptualization of epigenetic change. Thus, for example, if individuals who manifest adaptive functioning on prior developmental tasks are more likely to rebound from maladaptive periods than those individuals who display prior poor quality adaptation on those tasks, then support would be found for claims that development is hierarchically integrated, with past and current factors playing central roles in determining the quality of outcome (cf. Sroufe et al., 1990).

As is true for all developmental phenomena, resilience is a dynamic process, not a static phenomenon (Egeland, Carlson, & Sroufe, 1993). We believe that the concept of resilience as "invulnerability" must be avoided. Resilient individuals, although giving the impression of being somewhat herculean in their resistance to stress, must also undergo struggles associated with this process (cf. Jamison, 1993). These resilient persons may also need support to deal with the emotional difficulties that are often associated with coping with the adverse experiences they have had to address and surmount.

Another vital aspect of the scientific study of resilience is that it affords another avenue for examining biological and social constraints that may operate on aspects of the developmental process throughout the life course (Masten et al., 1990; Skuse, 1984). Moreover, through investigating the determinants of resilient adaptation, we are in a position to discover the range and variability in individuals' attempts to respond adaptively to challenge and ill fortune (Masten, 1989).

Developmental psychopathologists not only take into account the interrelations among dynamic systems and the processes characterizing system breakdown, but also are committed to explaining the mechanisms by which compensatory, self-righting tendencies are initiated whenever higher-level monitors detect deviances in a subsystem (Sameroff & Chandler, 1975; Waddington, 1957). From his earliest writings on the topic, Garmezy (1971, 1974) emphasized that most children maintain the ability to show some resilience strivings in the presence of serious and chronic adversity. A recent investigation of the processes leading to adaptive outcomes in high-risk maltreated children provided confirmation of Garmezy's thesis (Cicchetti et al., 1993). The results of this study revealed that, in contrast to the largely pessimistic depictions of maltreated children in the extant literature, the preponderant number of maltreated and nonmaltreated children displayed at least one index of adaptive functioning in the face of chronic adversity to which they had been exposed. Thus, it appears that most of these children continue to have resilient strivings as they actively cope with the vicissitudes of their stressful lives.

Despite these encouraging findings, not all children were as fortunate. In a number of maltreated and nonmaltreated children, there was a total absence of resilient strivings. Although this outcome was more characteristic of the maltreated children, the absence of such strivings seems especially aberrant because self-righting tendencies are important characteristics of living organisms (Waddington, 1957). By continuing to investigate the factors that either contribute to or conspire against the ability of individuals to persist in their self-strivings against the backdrop of extreme difficulties, insights into the nature of positive life-sustaining motivational processes may be gleaned.

Finally, the ability to function resiliently in the presence of biological and/or environmental disadvantage may be achieved through the use of developmental pathways that are less typical than those negotiated in the course of usual circumstances. Thus, an important question for researchers to pursue is whether the use of alternative pathways to attaining competence renders individuals more vulnerable to manifesting subsequent delays or deviations in development. Only longitudinal investigations can fully address this issue, but it will be critical to ascertain whether these individuals are more prone to developing pathology later in life.

A DEVELOPMENTAL PSYCHOPATHOLOGY PERSPECTIVE ON INTERVENTION

Despite the logical links that exist between the provision of interventions to children, adolescents, and adults and developmental theory and research, far too few bridges have been forged between these realms of knowledge (Cicchetti & Toth, 1992; Cohen, 1992; Cohen & Donnellan, 1987; Fonagy & Moran, 1991). During the past several decades, there has been increased dialogue between basic researchers and those invested in providing developmentally guided prevention and intervention (see, e.g., Guidano & Liotti, 1983; Lieberman, 1991; Selman, Schultz, & Yeates, 1991; Shirk, 1988; Zeanah, 1993). Specifically, as the investigation of the relation between normal and abnormal development has burgeoned, so, too, has the application of findings conceptualized within this genre to prevention and intervention efforts. The upsurgence of developmentally guided work on treatment is reflected in a recently published Institute of Medicine (1994) report that employs several concepts from the field of developmental psychopathology. The authors of the report used the developmental perspective as an organizing conceptual framework for reviewing what is known about interventions throughout the life span, from infancy to senescence.

Now that psychopathologists have begun to acknowledge that ontogenesis is an integrated and multiply determined process, there is a growing realization that interventions developed for disordered individuals must attend to the developmental dimension. Thus, for example, psychotherapists have become increasingly sensitive to the fact that no particular treatment will be efficacious throughout the life course. In essence, in order to integrate potential compensatory factors and protective mechanisms into an intervention successfully, an in-depth understanding of an individual's level of developmental organization is necessary.

Because the discipline of developmental psychopathology is concerned with the detection of developmental deviation before an actual psychiatric disturbance crystallizes, as well as with the course of disorders once exhibited (Sroufe, 1989), knowledge derived from research in this field possesses considerable relevance for application to the prevention and treatment of high-risk and psychopathological conditions. The value of applying a developmental psychopathology perspective to prevention and intervention efforts was captured by Sroufe and Rutter (1984), who stated: "[B]y thoroughly understanding factors that pull subjects toward or away from increased risk at various age periods, one not only acquires a deeper understanding of development but one also gains valuable information for primary prevention" (p. 19). Additionally, once a disorder has become manifested, knowledge of the mechanisms that contributed to the maladaptive outcome can be applied to its remediation.

Specifically, considerations such as when (i.e., the timing) and why a disorder occurs, how long it persists, and what precursors to the disordered functioning can be identified, all require a developmental approach to ensure that prevention and intervention strategies are timed and guided. The life-span perspective that characterizes a developmental psychopathology approach underscores that even adults and elderly persons continue to be confronted with challenges that present opportunities for new strengths or usher in new vulnerabilities (Erikson, 1950; Noam & Valiant, 1994: Staudinger et al., 1993). Thus, the developmental timing of a preventive intervention may be even more critical than its particular content. Minimally, we contend that the effect of an intervention will be enhanced or decreased in relation to its sensitivity to the temporal dimension of the developmental process.

Because periods of developmental transition and "sensitive periods" offer opportunities for reorganization and change, it might be especially important to target prevention and intervention efforts at these periods of intersystemic reorganization. For example, depending on when a pathology-inducing insult occurred or a deviant process was initiated, interventions might be more efficiently targeted. By developing more specific and circumscribed approaches, intervention effectiveness could increase and the need for more prolonged treatment might decrease. The knowledge of early developmental deviations and their link with subsequent psychopathology also could be used to prevent the emergence of full-blown psychopathology, thereby decreasing both time and money expended in the treatment of more entrenched and often severe clinical conditions (Carnegie Corporation, 1994; Hamburg, 1992; Institute of Medicine, 1989, 1994).

In addition, we believe that developmentally based preventive interventions may serve as a vehicle for testing the claims of existing developmental theories (Koretz, 1991). Akin to research in clinical neurology and developmental psychobiology, where recovery of a given function has been demonstrated to follow its natural sequential appearance during ontogeny (i.e., from the simple to the complex; from lower to higher brain centers; see Denny-Brown, Twitchell, & Saenz-Arroyo, 1949;

Sherrington, 1906; Teitelbaum, 1971, 1977), it will be important to ascertain whether the achievement of competent functioning on stage-salient developmental issues that had been previously unsuccessfully resolved will follow the same emergence as observed during normal ontogenesis (e.g., if rehabilitation of attachment must occur before gains can be made in the development of the self-system and of effective peer relations).

Conversely, strategies of prevention and intervention can be based on normal developmental principles. For example, the notion that development is a hierarchically integrated and organized process and that epigenesis is probabilistically determined, in concert with our extant knowledge of the link between the successful resolution of stage-salient developmental issues and future adaptation, suggests that programs to prevent the emergence of psychopathology can benefit from our knowledge of the progression through these stage-salient issues in nondisordered children.

Resilience, discussed earlier, also holds promise as an avenue for facilitating the development of prevention and intervention programs, as well as for contributing to developmental theory. By examining the distal and proximal processes and mechanisms that contribute to positive adaptation in situations that more typically result in maladaptation, researchers will be better equipped to devise ways of promoting positive outcome in high-risk populations.

Likewise, the concepts of equifinality and multifinality that are inherent to a developmental psychopathology perspective should alert all clinicians to the importance of utilizing multiple strategies of treatment predicated on issues such as individuals' stage in the life cycle, their current level of functioning and developmental organization on the stage-salient issue of their developmental period and across psychological and biological domains, and any special characteristics to the group of individuals being treated. As a corollary, it is essential that interventions be directed at a range of developmental domains. Moreover, because multiple risk factors, both intra- and extraorganismic, drawn from psychological, biological, and environmental forces, characterize the various pathways to maladaptive and disordered outcomes, interventions must address the broader causal matrix or be destined to produce ineffective and short-lived results. Additionally, because the presence of many risk factors at multiple levels of the ecology and the individual is associated with more chronic, enduring, and maladaptive outcomes than those characterized by fewer and more circumscribed risk factors, interventions with more serious pathological conditions (e.g., bipolar illness; schizophrenia) must incorporate a longitudinal perspective and employ a series of interventions over time, in an effort to reduce the risk factors to a manageable minimum.

As this discussion begins to elucidate, the application of a developmental psychopathology perspective to the prevention and remediation of clinical disorders also possesses important implications for formulating social policy (Institute of Medicine, 1989, 1994). The existence of a conservative fiscal climate has resulted in mental health advocates' being increasingly expected to justify expenditures on behalf of the research and treatment of psychopathology. A theory-based approach such as that espoused by developmental psychopathologists can be utilized to devise treatment strategies and evaluate outcomes, thereby warranting the provision of resources so vital for this area (Institute of Medicine, 1989, 1994).

CONCLUSION AND FUTURE DIRECTIONS

Investigations conceived within a developmental psychopathology framework have enhanced our knowledge of the sundry pathways by which adaptive and maladaptive outcomes may eventuate, underscored the variegated ways in which individuals can respond after being exposed to the same risk factors and traumatic experiences, and elucidated links between the study of normal and abnormal development. A great deal of progress has occurred and a considerable amount of excitement has been generated for this approach. However, in order to sustain enthusiasm and advance beyond our current state of knowledge, continued growth must take place as developmental psychopathology moves to join the ranks of mature scientific disciplines.

Thus, for example, future investigations must strive to attain enhanced fidelity between the elegance and complexity of our theoretical models and the measurement and data-analytic strategies employed in our studies. To provide one example, transactional models require commensurately complex measurement and statistical strategies. We are now fully cognizant that analysis of variance and covariance, as well as multiple regression techniques, engender deceptive conclusions when utilized to sort multiple interacting risk factors and interdependent influences on pathological outcomes.

Moreover, it is imperative that we examine individual subject pathways and not overlook or obscure important aspects of our findings by focusing only on group means. Hinde (1992) chastised developmental psychology for being predominantly concerned "with age and . . . group averages," stating that it also needed "*to understand individuals, the primary concern of much clinical and personality psychology*" (p. 109, italics ours). Likewise, developmental psychopathologists, with their emphasis on tracking individual patterns of adaptation across developmental transformations and reorganizations, must increasingly endeavor to comprehend the unique lives of individuals. Because major variability exists within and across all psychological and biological developmental domains, it is crucial, for both scientific and sociopolitical reasons, that we investigate the processes that underlie these individual differences.

An approach to addressing the issue of individual differences was advocated by Hinde (1992), who conjectured that developing group profiles might be a fruitful strategy for eventually elucidating a fuller understanding of the unique aspects of persons. Hinde felt that the investigation of those individuals who prove to be exceptions to their initial placement was especially important because it could generate new information for a more refined categorization of the groups. A continued iteration of this process through successive classifications of persons over time could conceivably move toward a comprehension of individuals.

Cicchetti and Rogosch (1994) have embarked on a procedure similar to the one advocated by Hinde. In an ongoing longitudinal study of the adaptation of maltreated and nonmaltreated children from early school age through the adolescent years, participants are classified as globally evidencing adequate adaptation or incompetent adaptation during childhood and during adolescence. Individuals are then grouped according to four patterns: adaptation over time, prior poor adaptation but competent adaptation in adolescence (recovery), prior adequate adaptation but emergence of difficulty in adolescence ("sleeper effects"), and continuous incompetent adaptation over time. In this continuing longitudinal study of these children, these four patterns of adaptation will be explored in efforts to ascertain the ways in which the risk and protective factors of individuals so characterized might differentially contribute to further diverging developmental pathways.

There also is a need for unbroken dialogue between developmental psychopathologists and developmentalists of all persuasions, so that a premature compartmentalization does not occur. As Hinde (1992) noted, the field of "developmental psychology has . . . become a field in its own right but, as a result, has become partially cut off from clinical, personality, physiological and social psychology and from biology" (p. 108). Ongoing progress in developmental psychology will contribute to generating a more sophisticated developmental psychopathology. Likewise, more growth will occur in the field of developmental psychology if it is receptive to the incorporation of research from the investigation of risk and psychopathology.

Historically, a number of developmentalists have called for cross-fertilization of developmental psychology with other disciplines (see, e.g., Cicchetti, 1990; Fishbein, 1976; Gottesman, 1974; Hinde, 1992; Kagan, 1984; Piaget, 1970). Recent national conferences on graduate training in applied developmental science have advocated an integration of perspectives from pertinent biological, social, and behavioral sciences (Fisher et al., 1993). Discussions of training in the area of developmental psychopathology similarly have called for a broad-based, multi- and interdisciplinary approach (Cicchetti & Toth, 1991; Institute of Medicine, 1989). In addition, scientists and clinicians are increasingly in agreement over the importance of incorporating diversity in graduate training programs (Cantor, Spiker, & Lipsitt, 1991; Cicchetti & Toth, 1991; Fisher et al., 1993), including calls for cultural pluralism and racial/ethnic diversity (Highlen, 1994).

As the field of developmental psychopathology ushers in its next era of scientific and clinical challenges, opportunities for fascinating collaborations on pressing theoretical and social issues should abound as a consequence of enhanced sensitivity to the urgent sociopolitical issues of our times. A major stumbling block could be the relatively large amounts of funding needed to initiate and carry out large, multidomain, interdisciplinary research projects of basic and applied import with high-risk and psychopathological populations. Educating legislators to the benefits of research in developmental psychopathology, and stressing the costs associated with failure to learn more about psychopathology and its effective prevention and treatment, will be critical avenues worth pursuing. Thus far, we have not succeeded in educating society about the importance of research in the area of mental health. It is imperative that we become more effective at conveying the benefits that will be derived from developmentally informed research conducted on high-risk and disordered populations.

In a related vein, it is important that researchers and clinicians maintain open lines of communication. To ensure that their research findings are disseminated most effectively, researchers must convey their results not only to their scientific brethren, but also to a wide array of persons, including social policy advocates, clinicians, and individual consumers. Receptivity to input from these same persons will enhance the research pursuits of developmental psychopathologists and augment the probability that their results will be assimilated into practical applications.

Finally, we cannot lose track of the importance of linking research with good-quality patient care (Cohen, 1992; Cohen & Donnellan, 1987). Because a goal of the developmental psychopathology perspective is to break down the schisms that typically occur between basic and applied research, and between clinical practice and academic pursuits, we believe that researchers in this field should have exposure to a range of normal, high-risk, and psychopathological populations. This does not mean that developmental psychopathologists must engage in the provision of therapy, but we think it is critical for them to have firsthand experience with atypical populations (Cicchetti, 1993; Cohen, 1992; Institute of Medicine, 1989). We should not forget that many of the progenitors of our field, including the great psychiatrists Bleuler and Kraepelin, not only saw patients but also actually took up residence at the facilities where their patients resided. It is not at all surprising that these systematizers' rich clinical experiences in the field enabled them to discover so many exciting phenomena.

In a relatively brief period of time, developmental psychopathology has contributed significantly to enhancing our understanding of risk, disorder, and adaptation across the life span. Its contributions to theory development and enhancements in research design and methodology also have been noteworthy. Much of the momentum of developmental psychopathology has stemmed from an openness to preexisting knowledge in combination with a willingness to question established theory, thereby continuing to promote growth. Moreover, the integration of methods and concepts derived from areas of endeavor that are too often isolated from each other has resulted in knowledge gains that might have been missed in the absence of cross-disciplinary dialogue. If its illustrious beginning presages future advances, developmental psychopathology will continue to engender much enthusiasm and to foster significant advances in our knowledge of normal and atypical development.

REFERENCES

Aber, J. L. (1994). Poverty, violence and child development: Untangling family and community level effects. In C. A. Nelson (Ed.), *Minnesota Symposia on Child Psychology: Volume 27. Threats to optimal development: Integrating biological, psychological and social risk factors* (pp. 229–272). Hillsdale, NJ: Erlbaum.

Achenbach, T. (1982). *Developmental psychopathology* (Vol. 1). New York: Wiley. (Original work published 1974)

Achenbach, T. (1990). What is "developmental" about developmental psychopathology? In J. Rolf, A. Masten, D. Cicchetti, K. Nuechterlein, & S. Weintraub (Eds.), *Risk and protective factors in the development of psychopathology* (pp. 29–48). New York: Cambridge University Press.

Achenbach, T. M. (1993). Taxonomy and comorbidity of conduct problems: Evidence from empirically based offenders. *Development and Psychopathology, 5,* 51–64.

Angold, A., & Costello, E. J. (1991). Developing a developmental epidemiology. In D. Cicchetti & S. L. Toth (Eds.), *Rochester Symposium on Developmental Psychopathology: Volume 3. Models and integrations* (pp. 75–96). Rochester, NY: University of Rochester Press.

Anthony, E. J., & Cohler, B. (Eds.). (1987). *The invulnerable child.* New York: Guilford.

Baldwin, A., Baldwin, C., & Cole, R. (1990). Stress-resistant families and stress-resistant children. In J. Rolf, A. Masten, D. Cicchetti, K. Nuechterlein, & S. Weintraub (Eds.), *Risk and protective factors in the development of psychopathology* (pp. 257–280). New York: Cambridge University Press.

Baltes, P., Reese, H., & Lipsitt, L. (1980). Life-span developmental psychology. *Annual Review of Psychology, 32,* 65–110.

Baltes, P., Smith, J., & Staudinger, U. (1992). Wisdom and successful aging. In T. Sonderegger (Ed.), *Nebraska Symposium on Motivation* (Vol. 39; pp. 123–167). Lincoln, NE: University of Nebraska Press.

Baron-Cohen, S., Tager-Flusberg, H., & Cohen, D. J. (Eds.). (1993). *Understanding other minds: Perspectives from autism.* New York: Oxford University Press.

Beadle, G. W., & Tatum, E. L. (1941). Experimental control of developmental reaction. *American Naturalist, 75,* 107–116.

Beeghly, M., & Cicchetti, D. (1994). Child maltreatment, attachment, and the self system: Emergence of an internal state lexicon in toddlers at high social risk. *Development and Psychopathology, 6,* 5–30.

Beeghly, M., Weiss-Perry, B., & Cicchetti, D. (1990). Beyond sensorimotor functioning: Early communicative and play development of children with Down syndrome. In D. Cicchetti & M. Beeghly (Eds.), *Children with Down syndrome: A developmental perspective* (pp. 329–368). New York: Cambridge University Press.

Bell, R. Q. (1986). Age-specific manifestations in changing psychosocial risk. In *Risk in intellectual and psychosocial development* (pp. 169–185). New York: Academic Press.

Bellugi, U., Bihrle, A., Neville, H., Doherty, S., & Jernigan, T. (1993). Language, cognition, and brain organization in a neurodevelopmental disorder. In M. Gunnar & C. Nelson (Eds.), *Minnesota Symposia on Child Psychology: Developmental behavioral science* (pp. 201–232). Hillsdale, NJ: Erlbaum.

Belsky, J. (1988). The "effects" of infant day care reconsidered. *Early Childhood Research Quarterly, 3,* 235–272.

Benes, F., Turtle, M., Khan, Y., & Farol, P. (1994). Myelination of a key relay zone in the hippocampal formation occurs in the human brain during childhood, adolescence, and adulthood. *Archives of General Psychiatry, 51,* 477–484.

Broman, S., & Grafman, J. (Eds.). (1994). *Atypical cognitive deficits in developmental disorders: Implications for brain function.* Hillsdale, NJ: Erlbaum.

Bronfenbrenner, U. (1977). Toward an experimental ecology of human development. *American Psychologist, 32,* 513–531.

Bronfenbrenner, U. (1979). *The ecology of human development: Experiments by nature and design.* Cambridge, MA: Harvard University Press.

Bronfenbrenner, U., Kessel, F., Kessen, W., & White, S. (1986). Toward a critical social history of developmental psychology: A propaedeutic discussion. *American Psychologist, 41,* 1218–1230.

Buhler, C., & Hertzer, H. (1935). *Testing children's development from birth to school age.* New York: Farrar & Rinehart.

Cahan, E. (1992). John Dewey and human development. *Developmental Psychology, 28,* 205–214.

Cairns, R. (1983). The emergence of developmental psychology. In P. Mussen (Ed.), *Handbook of child psychology* (Vol. 1; pp. 41–102). New York: Wiley.

Cairns, R. (1990). Toward a developmental science. *Psychological Science, 1,* 42–44.

Cantor, D., Spiker, C., & Lipsitt, L. (Eds.). (1991). *Child behavior and development: Training for diversity.* Norwood, NJ: Ablex.

Carnegie Corporation of New York. (1994, April). *Starting point: Meeting the needs of our young children.* New York: Author.

Caron, C., & Rutter, M. (1991). Comorbidity in child psychopathology: Concepts, issues, and research strategies. *Journal of Child Psychology and Psychiatry, 32,* 1063–1080.

Chess, S. (1974). The influence of defect on development in children with congenital rubella. *Merrill-Palmer Quarterly, 29,* 255-274.

Chomsky, N. (1968). *Language and mind.* New York: Harcourt Brace Jovanovich.

Cicchetti, D. (Ed.). (1984a). *Developmental psychopathology.* Chicago: University of Chicago Press. [Special issue of *Child Development, 55,* pp. 1–318.]

Cicchetti, D. (1984b). The emergence of developmental psychopathology. *Child Development, 55,* 1–7.

Cicchetti, D. (Ed.). (1989). *Rochester Symposium on Developmental Psychopathology: Vol. 1. The emergence of a discipline.* Hillsdale, NJ: Erlbaum.

Cicchetti, D. (1990). A historical perspective on the discipline of developmental psychopathology. In J. Rolf, A. Masten, D. Cicchetti, K. Nuechterlein, & S. Weintraub (Eds.), *Risk and protective factors in the development of psychopathology* (pp. 2–28). New York: Cambridge University Press.

Cicchetti, D. (1993). Developmental psychopathology: Reactions, reflections, and projections. *Developmental Review, 13,* 471–502.

Cicchetti, D., & Carlson, V. (Eds.). (1989). *Child maltreatment: Theory and research on the causes and consequences of child abuse and neglect.* New York: Cambridge University Press.

Cicchetti, D., & Garmezy, N. (Eds.). (1993). Milestones in the development of resilience [Special issue]. *Development and Psychopathology, 5*(4), 497–774.

Cicchetti, D., & Lynch, M. (1993). Toward an ecological/transactional model of community violence and child maltreatment: Consequences for children's development. *Psychiatry, 56,* 96–118.

Cicchetti, D., & Rogosch, F. (1994). *Childhood maltreatment and developmental psychopathology.* Grant proposal, William T. Grant Foundation, New York.

Cicchetti, D., Rogosch, F., Lynch, M., & Holt, K. (1993). Resilience in maltreated children: Processes leading to adaptive outcome. *Development and Psychopathology, 5,* 629–647.

Cicchetti, D., & Sroufe, L. A. (1978). An organizational view of affect: Illustration from the study of Down's syndrome infants. In M. Lewis & L. Rosenblum (Eds.), *The development of affect* (pp. 309–350). New York: Plenum.

Cicchetti, D., & Toth, S. L. (1991). The making of a developmental psychopathologist. In J. Cantor, C. Spiker, & L. Lipsitt (Eds.), *Child behavior and development: Training for diversity* (pp. 34–72). Norwood, NJ: Ablex.

Cicchetti, D., & Toth, S. L. (1992). The role of developmental theory in prevention and intervention. *Development and Psychopathology, 4,* 489–493.

Cohen, D. J. (1974). Competence and biology: Methodology in studies of infants, twins, psychosomatic disease and psychosis. In E. J. Anthony & C. Koupernik (Eds.), *The child in his family: Children at psychiatric risk* (pp. 361–394). New York: Wiley.

Cohen, D. J. (1980). The pathology of the self in primary childhood autism and Gilles de la Tourette syndrome. *Psychiatric Clinics of North America, 3,* 383–402.

Cohen, D. J. (1990). Tourette's syndrome: Developmental psychopathology of a model neuropsychiatric disorder of childhood. *University of Pennsylvania Hospital Strecker Monograph Series, XXVII,* 11–64.

Cohen, D. J. (1992, November). *Applying developmental concepts and methods to the study of child and adolescent psychopathology.* Paper presented at the NIMH conference on Developmental Approaches to the Assessment of Psychopathology, Washington, DC.

Cohen, D. J., Bruun, R. D., & Leckman, J. F. (Eds.). (1988). *Tourette syndrome and tic disorders: Clinical understanding and treatment.* New York: Wiley.

Cohen, D. J., & Donnellan, A. (Eds.). (1987). *Handbook of autism and pervasive developmental disorders.* New York: Wiley.

Cohen, D. J., & Leckman, J. (1993). Developmental psychopathology and neurobiology of Tourette's syndrome. *Journal of the American Academy of Child and Adolescent Psychiatry, 33,* 2–15.

Cummings, E. M., & Cicchetti, D. (1990). Attachment, depression, and the transmission of depression. In M. T. Greenberg, D. Cicchetti, & E. M. Cummings (Eds.), *Attachment during the preschool years* (pp. 339–372). Chicago: University of Chicago Press.

Curtiss, S. (1977). *Genie: A psycholinguistic study of a modern-day "wild child."* New York: Academic Press.

Curtiss, S. (1988). *The case of Chelsea: A new test case of the critical period for language acquisition.* Unpublished manuscript, University of California, Los Angeles.

Dennis, W. (1973). *Children of the creche.* New York: Appleton-Century-Crofts.

Denny-Brown, D., Twitchell, T. E., & Saenz-Arroyo, I. (1949). The nature of spasticity resulting from cerebral lesions. *Transactions of the American Neurological Association, 74,* 108–113.

Duncan, G., Brooks-Gunn, J., & Klebanov, P. (1994). Economic deprivation and early childhood development. *Child Development, 65,* 296–318.

Egeland, B., Carlson, E., & Sroufe, L. A. (1993). Resilience as process. *Development and Psychopathology, 5,* 517–528.

Eisenberg, L. (1977). Development as a unifying concept in psychiatry. *British Journal of Psychiatry, 131,* 225–237.

Elder, G. (1974). *Children of the Great Depression.* Chicago: University of Chicago Press.

Erikson, E. H. (1950). *Childhood and society.* New York: Norton.

Fishbein, H. (1976). *Evolution, development, and children's learning.* Pacific Palisades, CA: Goodyear Publishing.

Fisher, C., Murray, J., Dill, J., Hagen, J., Hogan, M., Lerner, R., Rebok, G., Sigel I., Sostek, A., Smyer, M., Spencer, M., & Wilcox, B. (1993). The National Conference on Graduate Education in the Applications of Developmental Science. *Journal of Applied Developmental Psychology, 14,* 1–10.

Fonagy, P., & Moran, G. (1991). Understanding psychic change in child analysis. *International Journal of Psycho-Analysis, 72,* 15–22.

Freud, A. (1965). *Normality and pathology in childhood: Assessments of development.* New York: International Universities Press.

Freud, A., & Burlingham, D. (1973). *Infants without families: Reports on the Hamstead Nurseries 1939–1945.* New York: International Universities Press.

Furstenberg, F. F., Brooks-Gunn, J., & Morgan, S. P. (1987). *Adolescent mothers in later life.* New York: Cambridge University Press.

Gardner, H. (1983). *Frames of mind: The theory of multiple intelligences.* New York: Wiley.

Garmezy, N. (1971). Vulnerability research and the issue of primary prevention. *American Journal of Orthopsychiatry, 41,* 101–116.

Garmezy, N. (1974). The study of competence in children at risk for severe psychopathology. In E. J. Anthony & C. Koupernik (Eds.), *The child in his family* (pp. 77–98). New York: Wiley.

Garmezy, N. (1990). A closing note: Reflections on the future. In J. Rolf, A. Masten, D. Cicchetti, K. Nuechterlein, & S. Weintraub (Eds.), *Risk and protective factors in the development of psychopathology* (pp. 527–534). New York: Cambridge University Press.

Garmezy, N., & Masten, A. (1994). Chronic adversities. In M. Rutter, E. Taylor, & L. Hersov (Eds.), *Child and adolescent psychiatry: Modern approaches* (3rd ed.; pp. 191–208). London: Blackwell.

Gershon, E., Bunney, W., Leckman, J., Van Eerdewegh, M., & DeBauche, B. (1976). The inheritance of affective disorders: A review of data and of hypotheses. *Behavior Genetics, 6,* 227–261.

Gesell, A. (1925). *Mental growth in the preschool child.* New York: Macmillan.

Glick, J. (1992). Werner's relevance for contemporary developmental psychology. *Developmental Psychology, 28,* 558–565.

Gottesman, I. I. (1974). Developmental genetics and ontogenetic psychology: Overdue detente and propositions from a matchmaker. In A. Pick (Ed.), *Minnesota Symposia on Child Psychology* (pp. 55–80). Minneapolis: University of Minnesota Press.

Gottesman, I. I., & Bertelsen, A. (1989). Confirming unexpressed genotypes for schizophrenia. *Archives of General Psychiatry, 46,* 867–872.

Gottesman, I. I., & Goldsmith, H. (1994). Developmental psychopathology of antisocial behavior: Inserting genes into its genesis and epigenesis. In C. A. Nelson (Ed.), *Minnesota Symposia on Child Psychology: Vol. 27. Threats to optimal development: Integrating biological, psychological, and social risk factors.* (pp. 69–104). Hillsdale, NJ: Erlbaum.

Gottlieb, G. (1976). Conceptions of prenatal development: Behavioral embryology. *Psychological Review, 83,* 215–234.

Gottlieb, G. (1983). The psychobiological approach to developmental issues. In P. Mussen (Ed.), *Handbook of Child Psychology* (Vol. 2; pp. 1–26). New York: Wiley.

Gottlieb, G. (1991). Experiential canalization of behavioral development: Theory. *Developmental Psychology, 27*(1), 4–13.

Gottlieb, G. (1992). *Individual development and evolution: The genesis of novel behavior.* New York: Oxford University Press.

Gould, S. (1980). *The panda's thumb.* New York: Norton.

Gould, S. (1986). Evolution and the triumph of homology, or why history matters. *American Scientist, 74,* 60–69.

Greenberg, M. T., Speltz, M. L., & DeKlyen, M. (1993). The role of attachment in the early development of disruptive behavior problems. *Development and Psychopathology, 5,* 191–213.

Guidano, V. F., & Liotti, G. (1983). *Cognitive processes and emotional disorders: A structural approach to psychotherapy.* New York: Guilford.

Hamburg, D. A. (1992). *Today's children: Creating a future for a generation in crisis.* New York: Times Books.

Hetherington, E. M. (1989). Coping with family transitions: Winners, losers, and survivors. *Child Development, 60,* 1–14.

Highlen, P. (1994). Racial/ethnic diversity in doctoral programs of psychology: Challenges for the twenty-first century. *Applied & Preventive Psychology, 3,* 91–108.

Hinde, R. (1992). Developmental psychology in the context of other behavioral sciences. *Developmental Psychology, 28,* 1018–1029.

Humphrey, G., & Humphrey, M. (1932). *The Wild Boy of Averyron.* New York: Appleton-Century-Crofts.

Huston, A. (Ed.). (1991). *Children in poverty: Child development and public policy.* New York: Cambridge University Press.

Huston, A., McLoyd, V., & Garcia-Coll, C. (1994). Children and poverty: Issues in contemporary research. *Child Development, 65,* 275–282.

Institute of Medicine. (1989). *Research on children and adolescents with mental, behavioral, and developmental disorders.* Washington, DC: National Academy Press.

Institute of Medicine. (1994). *Reducing risks for mental disorders: Frontiers for preventive intervention research.* Washington, DC: National Academy Press.

Jamison, K. (1993). *Touched with fire: Manic-depressive illness and the artistic temperament.* New York: Free Press.

Jensen, P., Koretz, D., Locke, B., Schneider, S., Radke-Yarrow, M., Richters, J., & Rumsey, J. (1993). Child and adolescent psychopathology research: Problems and prospects for the 1990s. *Journal of Abnormal Child Psychology, 21,* 551–580.

Jensen, P., & Shaw, J. (1993). Children as victims of war. *Journal of the American Academy of Child and Adolescent Psychiatry, 32,* 697–708.

Kagan, J. (1984). *The nature of the child.* New York: Basic Books.

Kaler, S., & Freeman, B. J. (1994). Analysis of environmental deprivation: Cognitive and social development in Romanian orphans. *Journal of Child Psychology and Psychiatry, 35,* 769–781.

Kaplan, B. (1967). Meditations on genesis. *Human Development, 10,* 65–87.

Kendler, K., Neale, M., Kessler, R., Heath, A., & Eaves, L. (1992). A population-based twin study of major depression in women: The impact of varying definitions of illness. *Archives of General Psychiatry, 49,* 257–266.

Kopp, C., & Recchia, S. (1990). The issues of multiple pathways in the development of handicapped children. In R. Hodapp, J. Burack, & E. Zigler (Eds.), *Issues in the developmental approach to mental retardation* (pp. 272–293). New York: Cambridge University Press.

Koretz, D. (1991). Prevention-centered science in mental health. *American Journal of Community Psychology, 19,* 453–458.

Kuhn, D., & Meacham, J. (Eds.). (1983). *Contributions to human development: Vol. 8. On the development of developmental psychology.* Basel, Switzerland: Karger.

Lawrence, P. A. (1992). *The making of a fly: The genetics of animal design.* Oxford, England: Blackwell.

Leavitt, L., & Fox, N. (Eds.). (1993). *Psychological effects of war and violence on children.* Hillsdale, NJ: Erlbaum.

Lenneberg, E. (1967). *Biological foundations of language.* New York: Wiley.

Lerner, R. (1991). Changing organism–context relations as the basic process of development: A developmental contextual perspective. *Developmental Psychology, 27,* 27–32.

Lerner, R., & Kauffman, M. (1985). The concept of development in contextualism. *Developmental Review, 5,* 309–333.

Leslie, A., & Thaiss, L. (1992). Domain specificity in conceptual development: Neuropsychological evidence from autism. *Cognition, 43,* 225–251.

Lidz, T. (1993). Images in psychiatry: Adolf Meyer. *American Journal of Psychiatry, 150*(7), 1098.

Lieberman, A. (1991). Attachment theory and infant–parent psychotherapy: Some conceptual, clinical and research considerations. In D. Cicchetti & S. L. Toth (Eds.), *Rochester Symposium on Developmental Psychopathology: Vol. 3. Models and integrations* (pp. 261–288). Rochester, NY: University of Rochester Press.

Luthar, S. (1991). Vulnerability and resilience: A study of high-risk adolescents. *Child Development, 62,* 600–616.

Luthar, S., Doernberger, C., & Zigler, E. (1993). Resilience is not a unidimensional construct: Insights from a prospective study of inner-city adolescents. *Development and Psychopathology, 5,* 703–717.

Marans, S., & Cohen, D. J. (1991). Child psychoanalytic theories of development. In M. Lewis (Ed.), *Child and adolescent psychiatry: A comprehensive textbook* (pp. 613–621). Baltimore: Williams & Wilkins.

Masten, A. (1989). Resilience in development: Implications of the study of successful adaptation for developmental psychopathology. In D. Cicchetti (Ed.), *Rochester Symposium on Developmental Psychopathology: Vol. 1. The emergence of a discipline* (pp. 261–294). Hillsdale, NJ: Erlbaum.

Masten, A., Best, K., & Garmezy, N. (1990). Resilience and development: Contributions from the study of children who overcome adversity. *Development and Psychopathology, 2,* 425–444.

Meyer, A. (1950–1952). *The collected papers of Adolf Meyer* (4 Vols.). Baltimore: Johns Hopkins University Press.

Milner, B., Corkin, S., & Teuber, H. (1968). Further analysis of the hippocampal amnesic syndrome: 14-year follow-up study of H.M. *Neuropsychologia, 6,* 215–234.

Murphy, L., & Moriarty, A. (1976). *Vulnerability, coping, and growth: From infancy to adolescence.* New Haven: Yale University Press.

Mussen, P. (Ed.). (1983). *Handbook of child psychology* (Vol. 1). New York: Wiley.

National Advisory Mental Health Council. (1990). *National plan for research on child and adolescent mental disorders.* Rockville, MD: National Institute of Mental Health.

Newman, J., & Wallace, J. (1993). Diverse pathways to deficient self-regulation: Implications for disinhibitory psychopathology in children. *Clinical Psychology Review, 13,* 699–720.

Newport, E. L. (1990). Maturational constraints on language learning. *Cognitive Science, 14,* 11–28.

Noam, G., & Valiant, G. (1994). Clinical–Developmental psychology in developmental psychopathology: Theory and research of an emerging perspective (pp. 229–331). In D. Cicchetti & S. L. Toth (Eds.), *Rochester Symposium on Developmental Psychopathology: Vol. 5. Disorders and dysfunctions of the self.* Rochester, NY: University of Rochester Press.

Omenn, G. (1976). Inborn errors of metabolism: Clues to understanding human behavioral disorders. *Behavior Genetics, 6,* 263–284.

Parke, R., Ornstein, P., Reiser, J., & Zahn-Waxler, C. (1992). Editors' introduction to the APA Centennial Series. *Developmental Psychology, 28,* 3–4.

Piaget, J. (1970). Piaget's theory. In P. Mussen (Ed.), *Carmichael's manual of child psychology* (3rd ed.; pp. 703–732). New York: Wiley.

Plomin, R., & McLearn, G. (Eds.). (1993). *Nature, nurture, and psychology.* Washington, DC: American Psychological Association.

Plomin, R., Rende, R., & Rutter, M. (1991). Quantitative genetics and developmental psychopathology. In D. Cicchetti & S. L. Toth (Eds.), *Rochester Symposium on Developmental Psychopathology: Vol. 2. Internalizing and externalizing expressions of dysfunction* (pp. 155–202). Rochester, NY: University of Rochester Press.

Pritchard, D. (1986). *Foundations of developmental genetics.* London: Taylor & Francis.

Provence, S., & Lipton, R. (1962). *Infants in institutions.* New York: International Universities Press.

Reese, H. (1993). Developments in child psychology from the 1960s to the 1990s. *Developmental Review, 13,* 503–524.

Reilly, J., Klima, E. S., & Bellugi, U. (1990). Once more with feeling: Affect and language in atypical populations. *Development and Psychopathology, 2,* 367–392.

Richters, J., & Cicchetti, D. (1993). Mark Twain meets DSM-III-R: Conduct Disorder, development and the concept of harmful dysfunction. *Development and Psychopathology, 5,* 5–29.

Richters, J. E., & Weintraub, S. (1990). Beyond diathesis: Toward an understanding of high-risk environments. In J. Rolf, A. S. Masten, D. Cicchetti, K. G. Nuechterlein, & S. Weintraub (Eds.), *Risk and protective factors in the development of psychopathology* (pp. 67–96). New York: Cambridge University Press.

Rolf, J., Masten, A., Cicchetti, D., Nuechterlein, K., & Weintraub, S. (Eds.). (1990). *Risk and protective factors in the development of psychopathology.* New York: Cambridge University Press.

Rutter, M. (1982). Epidemiological–longitudinal approaches to the study of development. In W. A. Collins (Ed.), *Minnesota Symposia on Child Psychology: Vol. 15. The concept of development* (pp. 105–142). Hillsdale, NJ: Erlbaum.

Rutter, M. (1986). Child psychiatry: The interface between clinical and developmental research. *Psychological Medicine, 16,* 151–169.

Rutter, M. (1987). Psychosocial resilience and protective mechanisms. *American Journal of Orthopsychiatry, 57,* 316–331.

Rutter, M. (1988). Epidemiological approaches to developmental psychopathology. *Archives of General Psychiatry, 45,* 486–495.

Rutter, M. (1989). Age as an ambiguous variable in developmental research: Some epidemiological considerations from developmental psychopathology. *International Journal of Behavioral Development, 12,* 1–34.

Rutter, M. (1990). Psychosocial resilience and protective mechanisms. In J. Rolf, A. S. Masten, D. Cicchetti, K. H. Nuechterlein, & S. Weintraub (Eds.), *Risk and protective factors in the development of psychopathology* (pp. 181–214). New York: Cambridge University Press.

Rutter, M., & Garmezy, N. (1983). Developmental psychopathology. In P. Mussen (Ed.), *Handbook of child psychology* (Vol. 4; pp. 775–911). New York: Wiley.

Rutter, M., Macdonald, H., LeCouteur, A., Harrington, R., Bolton, P., & Bailey A. (1990). Genetic factors in child psychiatric disorders: II. Empirical findings. *Journal of Child Psychology and Psychiatry, 31,* 39–83.

Sameroff, A. J., & Chandler, M. J. (1975). Reproductive risk and the continuum of caretaking casualty. In F. D. Horowitz (Ed.), *Review of child development research* (Vol. 4; pp. 187–244). Chicago: University of Chicago Press.

Sameroff, A., & Emde, R. (Eds.). (1989). *Relationship disturbances in early childhood: A developmental approach.* New York: Basic Books.

Sarnat, H. (1992). *Cerebral dysgenesis: Embryology and clinical expression.* New York: Oxford University Press.

Schneider-Rosen, K., & Cicchetti, D. (1984). The relationship between affect and cognition in maltreated infants: Quality of attachment and the development of visual self-recognition. *Child Development, 55,* 648–658.

Selman, R., Schultz, L. H., & Yeates, K. O. (1991). Interpersonal understanding and action: A development and psychopathology perspective on research and prevention. In D. Cicchetti & S. L. Toth (Eds.), *Rochester Symposium on Developmental Psychopathology: Vol. 3. Models and integrations* (pp. 289–329). Rochester, NY: University of Rochester Press.

Shakow, D. (1968). Contributions from schizophrenia to the understanding of normal psychological function. In M. Simmel (Ed.), *The reach of mind: Essays in memory of Kurt Goldstein* (pp. 173–199). New York: Springer.

Sherrington, C. (1906). *The integrative action of the nervous system.* New York: Scribner's.

Shirk, S. (1988). *Cognitive development and child psychotherapy.* New York: Plenum.

Siegel, A., & White, S. H. (1982). The child study movement: Early growth and the development of the symbolized child. *Advances in Child Development and Behavior, 17,* 233–285.

Skuse, D. (1984). Extreme deprivation in early childhood—II. Theoretical issues and a comparative review. *Journal of Child Psychology and Psychiatry, 31,* 893–903.

Slade, A., & Wolf, D. (Eds.). (1994). *Children at play.* New York: Oxford University Press.

Solnit, A. J., Neubauer, P., & Cohen, D. J. (1993). *The many meanings of play: A psychoanalytic perspective.* New Haven: Yale University Press.

Spencer, H. (1900). *First principles* (6th ed.). New York: Appleton. (Original work published in 1862)

Spitz, R. A. (1945). Hospitalism: An inquiry into the genesis of psychiatric conditions in early childhood. *Psychoanalytic Study of the Child, 1,* 53–74.

Sroufe, L. A. (1989). Pathways to adaptation and maladaptation: Psychopathology as developmental deviation. In D. Cicchetti (Ed.), *Rochester Symposium on Developmental Psychopathology: Vol. 1. The emergence of a discipline* (pp. 13–40). Hillsdale, NJ: Erlbaum.

Sroufe, L. A. (1990). Considering normal and abnormal together: The essence of developmental psychopathology. *Development and Psychopathology, 2,* 335–347.

Sroufe, L. A., Egeland, B., & Kreutzer, T. (1990). The fate of early experience following developmental change: Longitudinal approaches to individual adaptation in childhood. *Child Development, 61,* 1363–1373.

Sroufe, L. A., & Rutter, M. (1984). The domain of developmental psychopathology. *Child Development, 55,* 17–29.

Staudinger, U., Marsiske, M., & Baltes, P. (1993). Resilience and levels of reserve capacity in later adulthood: Perspectives from life-span theory. *Development and Psychopathology, 5,* 541–566.

Tager-Flusberg, H. (Ed.). (1994). *Constraints on language acquisition: Studies of atypical children.* Hillsdale, NJ: Erlbaum.

Teitelbaum, P. (1971). The encephalization of hunger. In E. Stellar & J. Sprague (Eds.), *Progress in physiological psychology* (Vol. 4). New York: Academic Press.

Teitelbaum, P. (1977). Levels of integration of the operant. In W. K. Honig & J. Staddon (Eds.), *Handbook of operant behavior.* Englewood Cliffs, NJ: Prentice-Hall.

Toth, S. L., & Cicchetti, D. (1993). Child maltreatment: Where do we go from here in our treatment of victims? In D. Cicchetti & S. L. Toth (Eds.), *Child abuse, child development, and social policy* (pp. 399–438). Norwood, NJ: Ablex.

Valsiner, J. (Ed.). (1987). *Culture and the development of children's action.* New York: Academic Press.

von Bertalanffy, L. (1968). *General system theory.* New York: Braziller.

Waddington, C. H. (1957). *The strategy of genes.* London: Allen & Unwin.

Waddington, C. H. (1966). *Principles of development and differentiation.* New York: Macmillan.

Walker, E., Downey, G., & Nightingale, N. (1989). The nonorthogonal nature of risk factors: Implications for research on the causes of maladjustment. *Journal of Primary Prevention, 9,* 143–163.

Weddell, R. (1994). Effects of subcortical lesion site on human emotional behavior. *Brain and Cognition, 25,* 161–193.

Weiss, P. (1961). Deformities as cues to understanding development of form. *Perspectives in Biology and Medicine, 4,* 133–151.

Weiss, P. (1969). The living system: Determinism stratified. In A. Koestler & J. Smythies (Eds.), *Beyond reductionism* (pp. 3–55). Boston: Beacon Press.

Werner, E. (1993). Risk, resilience, and recovery: Perspectives from the Kauai Longitudinal Study. *Development and Psychopathology, 5,* 503–515.

Werner, E., & Smith, R. (1992). *Overcoming the odds: High-risk children from birth to adulthood.* Ithaca, NY: Cornell University Press.

Werner, H. (1984). *Comparative psychology of mental development.* New York: International Universities Press.

Wertsch, J. (1979). From social interaction to higher psychological processes: A clarification and application of Vygotsky's theory. *Human Development, 22,* 1–22.

White, S. H. (1990). Child study at Clark University: 1894–1904. *Journal of the History of the Behavioral Sciences, 26,* 131–150.

Zeanah, C. (Ed.). (1993). *Handbook of infant mental health.* New York: Guilford.

Zigler, E., & Glick, M. (1986). *A developmental approach to adult psychopathology.* New York: Wiley.

Zigler, E., & Valentine, J. (Eds.). (1979). *Project Head Start: A legacy of the war on poverty.* New York: Free Press.

Zubin, J., & Spring, B. (1977). Vulnerability: A new view of schizophrenia. *Journal of Abnormal Psychology, 56,* 103–126.

PART TWO

Epidemiology, Taxonomy, and Assessment

CHAPTER 2

Developmental Epidemiology

ELIZABETH J. COSTELLO and ADRIAN ANGOLD

In this chapter, we discuss developmental psychopathology from the viewpoint of epidemiology, "the study of health and illness in human populations" (Kleinbaum, Kupper, & Morgenstern, 1982, p. 2). After a brief introduction to some of the basic concepts of the epidemiological method, we present a short history of child psychiatric epidemiology, illustrating how it has changed in the past century as society's concerns about the mental health of children have changed. We then review recent epidemiological studies of children and adolescents, from the perspective of what they can tell us about the interaction between developmental processes as they occur in children and in the psychiatric illnesses to which they are vulnerable. Next, we discuss what modern epidemiology is and does, what questions it addresses, some of the key methods it uses, and how these methods can be applied to the special problems of psychiatric epidemiology. In the final section of the chapter, we discuss what we mean by developmental epidemiology, and set out some ideas for a program of research that could inform both psychiatric epidemiology and developmental science.

By the end of the chapter, we hope to have made the case that: (a) the goal of epidemiological research is disease prevention; (b) understanding the development of a disease and intervening to prevent it are equally important aspects of epidemiological research; (c) understanding the development of a disease may point to different kinds of intervention at different stages in the developmental process; and (d) understanding individual development is a critical part of understanding and intervening in the disease process, because both risk for, and expression of, disorder change over the life course.

This chapter was written in part with the support of William T. Grant Foundation Faculty Scholar awards to both authors, and of the Leon Lowenstein Foundation.

Modified versions of parts of this chapter have appeared in D. Cicchetti and S. Toth (Eds.), *Rochester Symposium on Developmental Psychopathology,* Volume 3 (Hillsdale, NJ: Lawrence Erlbaum and Associates, 1991), and are included here with the permission of the publisher.

WHAT IS EPIDEMIOLOGY?

Epidemiology is the study of patterns of disease in human populations (Kleinbaum et al., 1982). Patterns, or nonrandom distributions, of disease occur in both time and space; the task of epidemiology is to understand observed patterns of pathology along these two dimensions, and to use this understanding as a basis for prevention and treatment. For example, a pattern has been observed linking exposure to environmental lead in infancy with the development of behavioral and learning problems in later years (Needleman & Bellinger, 1991). The causal relationship appears to be sufficiently strong to justify primary preventive measures to remove lead from gas and domestic paint, in order to protect those children who might otherwise be vulnerable to such exposures.

Epidemiology, "an exact and basic science of social medicine and public health" (Earls, 1979, p. 256), emerged as an influential branch of medicine in the 19th century. Like the rest of medicine, it is an action-oriented discipline, whose purpose is intervention to control disease. Epidemiology has both similarities to and differences from clinical medicine. Scientific knowledge about the cause and course of disease is one of the tools that both share. Epidemiology reflects clinical medicine also in using two methods of attack: (a) a tactical method, concerned with the practical and administrative problems of disease control at the day-to-day level, and (b) a strategic method, concerned with finding out what causes disease so that new weapons of control and cure can be engineered (Earls, 1980; Susser, 1973). Thus, epidemiologists can be found, in their tactical or public health role, reporting on the prevalence of AIDS and advising on how to control its spread, while, at the same time, others working under the label "clinical epidemiology" carry out multicenter clinical research trials of new vaccines and treatments.

Epidemiology is also like clinical medicine in its understanding of the concept of "disease" in broad terms. In this chapter, we adopt the definition of diseases as *pathological processes,* which may have biological, psychological, and social dimensions (Kleinbaum et al., 1982; Susser, 1973). Disease in this sense includes, but is not limited to, identified syndromes of known etiology. It may equally apply to a single phenomenon, such as blood pressure or anxiety, at the point at which the level becomes pathological. The unifying theme is that, at some point, a decision is made that a pathological process is present in an individual, who then becomes a case. The thorny problems of case identification in child and adolescent psychopathology are discussed later in this chapter.

Epidemiology diverges from clinical medicine to the extent that it concentrates on understanding and controlling disease processes in the context of the *population at risk,* whereas the primary focus of clinical medicine is the *individual patient.* This does not mean that epidemiology is not concerned with the individual; on the contrary, it is very much concerned with understanding the individual's illness and the causes of that illness. The difference lies in the frame of reference. Put crudely, clinical medicine asks: "What is wrong with this person *and how should I treat him or her?*" Epidemiology asks: "What is wrong with this person *and what is it about him or her that has resulted in this illness?*" Why is this child depressed, but not her brother? If her mother is also depressed, is the child's depression a cause, a consequence, or an unrelated, chance co-occurrence? Such questions immediately set the individual child within a frame of reference of other children, or other family members, or other people of the same sex or race or social class. As we shall discuss later, this approach to understanding pathology has important effects on the way information is collected, the kind of information collected, the methods used to analyze it, and the conclusions that can be drawn.

As the study of patterns of disease distribution in time and space, epidemiology thus encompasses a great deal more than simply counting how many people have smallpox or AIDS. "Epidemiology counts" (Freedman, 1984, p. 931), but it does far more than that. The methods developed to count cases are useful for many purposes—for example, to estimate the need for and probable cost of mental health services, or to monitor the effect of a new treatment. However, these methods provide only one part of the information needed to understand the course, causes, and prevention of disease. Figure 2.1 (adapted from Kleinbaum et al., 1982) shows how the study of disease patterns in time and space informs both public health and scientific epidemiology (Susser, 1973).

Scientific Epidemiology

From the strategic or scientific point of view, the issues at each level have to do with identifying the stages by which a disease progresses through its natural course, generating and testing hypotheses about causal pathways, and inventing and testing methods for prevention to be implemented by the tactical, public health arm of the health care professions. The success or failure of attempts to prevent a disorder can then provide important information about the causes of the problem. The course of disease can be divided into three stages (see Figure 2.1): (a) exposure, dealing with causes; (b) disorder, dealing with the manifestation of a disease in clinical signs and symptoms; and (c) outcome, examining what leads to different outcomes for different patients. These three stages invite different kinds of preventive intervention: (a) primary prevention attacks the exposure phase; (2) secondary prevention is directed at preventing those exposed to causal factors from developing the disease; and (c) tertiary prevention focuses on reducing the damage caused in those who actually become ill. Although this developmental approach to disease prevention was first articulated at a time when acute, infectious diseases such as cholera and smallpox were the chief preoccupation of epidemiology, it applies with minor modifications to chronic or episodic diseases, such as heart disease and cancer, which are the main causes of mortality in industrialized countries today. Applied to psychopathology, it provides a model for exploring the development of the psychiatric disorders (Rutter, 1990).

Public Health Epidemiology

At the tactical level, public health and primary care workers are often involved in what has been called "shoe-leather epidemiology" (Kleinbaum et al., 1982, p. 25). This might take the form of tracing the pathways by which a cluster of suicides spreads through a high school, or isolating the source of a neurotoxic element in the water supply, or advocating life-style changes to reduce the risk of stress-related disease. The aim is to identify key points in the development and transmission of a disease at which intervention can act to reduce the prevalence of the disease or the harm caused by it. Such interventions may be directed at preventing exposure to the causes of the disorder, at preventing the onset of the disorder in those who are vulnerable to it, or at minimizing death rates or residual impairment in those who survive. Taking substance abuse as an example of a public health problem,

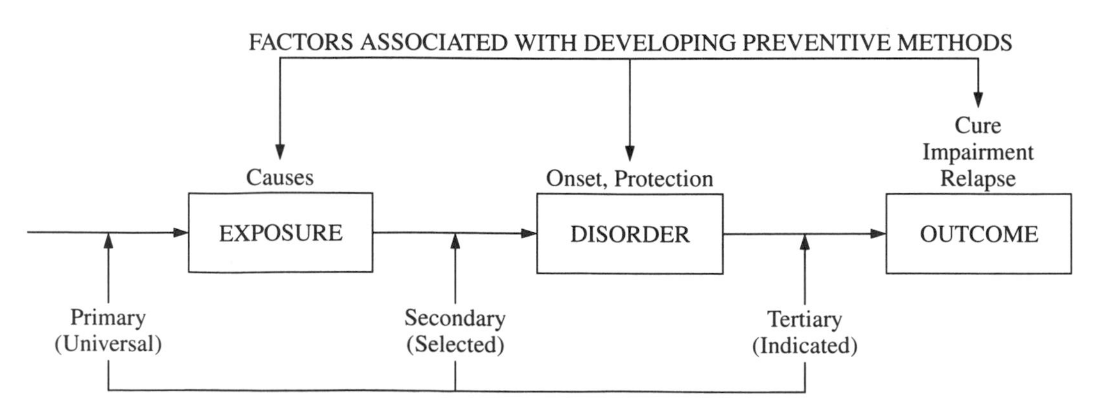

Figure 2.1 Uses of epidemiology: Understanding factors associated with developing preventive methods.

primary prevention might involve school programs of the "Just Say No" variety, directed at all children; secondary prevention could include helping to organize community support programs and extra policing in areas where street drugs are widely sold, or support groups for the children of addicts; tertiary prevention includes treatment and rehabilitation programs for adolescent substance abusers, behavioral training for families, and so on.

There is a great deal of interchange between the public health aspects and the scientific aspects of epidemiology, and also between different levels of investigative and preventive effort. At each of these levels, both strategic and tactical efforts are needed. Indeed, the "real world" nature of epidemiology means that the answers to many scientific questions, such as the paths of disease transmission, have at some stage to be tested by regarding a preventive intervention as a scientific experiment. The classic example is the story of how John Snow, by removing the handle from the Broad Street water pump during the 1853 cholera epidemic in London, tested his hypothesis that (a) cholera was caused by an invisible, self-reproducing agent living in water; (b) the agent flourished in water heavily contaminated with sewage; and (c) therefore, if a community drawing its water from a contaminated supply was forced (by his action in disabling the pump) to use water from a different water company, drawn from a purer source, the rate of disease would fall (Snow, 1855).

A BRIEF HISTORY OF CHILD PSYCHIATRIC EPIDEMIOLOGY

In this section, we trace the historical background of developmental epidemiology. Work on the psychiatric disorders of children and adolescents was first undertaken within an epidemiological framework in the late 19th century, to answer the most pressing question that faced the emerging discipline of child psychiatry: how to classify and care for children with severe disabilities, many of whom were likely to be a public expense for much of their lives. In this context, the main concerns were to identify the nature of the deficits shown by severely impaired children, and to find out how many of such children there were. By the mid-20th century, in the context of a growing concern with the role of social factors in mental illness (Earls, 1979), epidemiologists focused on the other end of the spectrum of severity, examining the borderline between normality and abnormality. In the past two decades, influenced by psychiatry's move back to a more phenomenological taxonomy of psychiatric disorder, a major concern has been to develop ways of "counting" the number of children in the community who have psychiatric disorders that meet the criteria of the *Diagnostic and Statistical Manual* (DSM) of the American Psychiatric Association (American Psychiatric Association, 1952, 1968, 1980, 1987, 1994). Despite these changes of emphasis, the basic tasks of epidemiology outlined earlier—to identify causal links between risk factors and cases of disorder, with the goal of prediction and control—can be seen to have guided the research process throughout the century. What has been missing until the past couple of decades has been any drive to incorporate developmental issues into the knowledge base or developmental methods into the technology of epidemiological research.

The Origins of Psychiatric Epidemiology

In the 19th century, the disease concept of psychiatric illness came to dominate the earlier view of psychiatric illness as "moral insanity" (Prichard, 1837). "Mental disease was regarded as a 'thing' residing within the affected individual; cases could therefore be counted in the same way as in the epidemiology of physical disease. At the same time, reforms in the administration of psychiatric services (e.g., the assumption by the state of responsibility for mental hospitals) increased the need for statistics and paved the way for epidemiological studies" (Jablensky, 1986, p. 274). There appear to have been few children in mental hospitals or asylums in the 19th century (von Gontard, 1988), but an analogous problem arose here, too: how to identify children who could never be expected to become self-sufficient adults, and for whom long-term care, probably at public expense, would be needed. As Grob (1985) pointed out, the fact that local government has had to take more financial responsibility for those with severe and persistent mental illness than for almost any other group of the sick has had a profound effect on the course of psychiatric epidemiology as a branch of research. Right from the start, the focus was on prevalence rates, or numbers of people using mental health services, and, in particular, hospital beds. To the extent that psychiatric epidemiology paid attention to prevention, it concentrated on tertiary prevention of relapse and rehospitalization of the severely mentally ill, rather than on primary or secondary prevention of exposure or onset.

Distinguishing Psychiatric Disorder from Severe Mental Retardation

An important and basic distinction was made in the 19th century between "imbeciles" and "lunatics." As universal education spread across Europe and America in the second half of the century, children who could not handle the demands of the educational system became a visible and troubling group. In their historical overview of child psychiatry, Chess and Habibi (1986) pointed out that the distinction between, and division of responsibility for, "idiots" and "lunatics" was far from clear throughout the 19th century; in 1876, all the charter members of the American Association on Mental Deficiency were psychiatrists, and the child guidance movement in America began at the University of Pennsylvania in a clinic set up by Witmer in 1894 primarily to care for the feebleminded. The distinction between the psychiatrically ill child and the severely mentally retarded child emerged slowly over the second half of the 19th century. It was not a distinction made in the aims and methods of England's first institutions for severely handicapped children. The school set up in Bath in 1846 by the Misses White, and the asylum for idiots founded in 1848 by a distinguished psychiatrist, John Conolly, were both inspired by the French and German educational traditions for the mentally retarded, but were equally concerned with "Moral culture . . . control of temper, obedience, order, kindness to each other" (von Gontard, 1988, p. 576). Gradually, specific groups of children were described, and causes for their disabilities were identified. John Langdon Down, a psychiatrist and superintendent of a large asylum for idiots, described Down syndrome (Down,

1867), and William Ireland, superintendent of the Scottish National Institution for Imbecile Children, developed a classification into such categories as epileptic, microcephalic, and inflammatory idiocy, demonstrating that the same phenomenon of idiocy could result from many different causes (Ireland, 1877). Mental retardation slowly became recognized as a problem to be treated separately from behavioral and emotional problems. Children with severe developmental deficits began to be seen as lying on a continuum of disability with children who were struggling to survive the new compulsory education system, rather than as simply part of the general class of severely dysfunctional children (although, of course, some children might have both intellectual and psychiatric problems). For example, special classes for the "feeble minded" were mandated in England by the Elementary Education Act (Defective and Epileptic Children) of 1899. Throughout the industrialized world, as the right of all children to education was acknowledged, the care of the mentally retarded largely moved out of the sphere of psychiatry, unless emotional or behavioral problems were also severe. Causal theories focused on genetics, perinatal insults, and early environmental adversity; treatment centered on pinpointing precise deficits and maximizing children's potential, rather than "curing" them, as the pioneers in the treatment of idiocy had hoped to do.

Distinguishing among Psychiatric Disorders

From the same period, descriptions can be found of children whose cognitive development was normal but who showed serious emotional or behavioral problems. James Prichard (1786–1848), a physician, was clear that the distinction was real. In 1835, he wrote that "idiotism and imbecility are observed in childhood, but insanity, properly so termed, is rare before the age of puberty" (Prichard, 1837, p. 127). He defined as *moral insanity* "madness consisting in a morbid perversion of the natural feelings, affections, inclinations, temper, habits, moral dispositions, and natural impulses, without any remarkable disorder or defect of the intellect or knowing and reasoning faculties, and particularly without any insane illusion or hallucination" (p. 16). Following Pinel, the French psychiatrist who had first described "madness without delirium," Prichard distinguished moral insanity from, on the one hand, "mania, or raving madness . . . in which the mind is totally deranged" (p. 16), and which he attributed to physical causes such as convulsions, and, on the other hand, imbecility or mental retardation. He thus used "moral" in its 18th-century sense of pertaining to personality or character. Henry Maudsley (1879), writing 30 years later, used the term in its 19th-century sense, referring to ethics and norms. He distinguished between *instinctive insanity,* which was "an aberration and exaggeration of instincts and passions," and *moral insanity,* which was a defect of the moral qualities along a dimension of "viciousness to those extreme manifestations which pass far beyond what anyone would call wickedness" (p. 289). In the process, he broadened the realm of child psychiatry to include problems of conduct previously seen to be the responsibility of religion and the law. Maudsley preferred to use the term *affective* (where Prichard used *moral*) ". . . as being a more general term and expressing more truly the fundamental condition of nerve-element, which shows itself in affections of the mode of feeling generally, not of the special mode of moral feeling only" (Maudsley, 1879, p. 280).

When writing about etiology rather than classification, however, Prichard and Maudsley followed the French tradition in distinguishing between *moral* and *physical* causes of mental disorder, using moral in the sense of what came to be called exogenous causes. Prichard (1837), quoting Georget, listed among moral causes of insanity domestic grief, disappointment in love, political events, fanaticism, jealousy, poverty or reversal of fortune, reading romances, and excessive study. Mental retardation was seen as stemming exclusively from physical causes: either convulsions of some type in the early years, or some defect transmitted from the parent. This defect might itself be inherited, or it might be "traceable to parental intemperance and excess" (Maudsley, 1879, p. 44). The dominant causal theory of psychopathology in the second half of the 19th century was genetic: heredity and degeneration caused disease, which started with scarcely perceptible signs in early childhood, but took a progressive and irreversible course and would probably be transmitted to future generations if the affected individual were permitted to breed. Even when the proximal cause of insanity was a moral one, ". . . the different forms of insanity that occur in young children . . . are almost always traceable to nervous disease in the preceding generation" (p. 68).

Psychiatrists in the 19th century thus had a developmental causal theory about psychopathology, but it was a narrow form of developmental theory: the development of the disease was progressive and irreversible, tied to the development of the child only in that it manifested itself differently as the child grew, but impervious to other influences, such as treatment or learning. "All one could do was to prevent the most extreme manifestations by strict punishment and to protect those not affected" (von Gontard, 1988, p. 579). The most effective defense for society was to prevent the procreation of the insane, and eugenics and lifelong segregation in asylums were seen as more effective intervention strategies than attempting treatment or cure. Although a continuum of severity was documented in child psychiatric disorders, as it was in mental retardation, the continuum was interpreted quite differently. It took the form of a continuum of degeneration caused by the disease within the individual across time, rather than a distribution of severity that would remain fairly constant across individuals over time, as was the case for mental retardation. Thus, the prognosis, even for children who presented with mild symptoms, was believed to be gloomy.

Psychoanalytic Theory and Developmental Psychopathology

One of the strengths of the psychoanalytic approach to psychopathology, as its theory and treatment methods developed around the turn of the 20th century, was that it rejected the therapeutic pessimism of much contemporary child psychiatry. Although Sigmund Freud himself accepted that individuals had innate or constitutional characteristics, he developed what his daughter, Anna Freud, described as an "etiological formula of a sliding scale of internal and external influences: that there are people whose 'sexual constitution would not have led them into a neurosis if they had not had . . . [certain] experiences, and these experiences would not have had a traumatic effect on them if their libido had been otherwise disposed' (S. Freud, 1916–17, p. 347)" (A. Freud, 1965, p. 520). "Hereditary factors depend for their pathogenic impact on the accidental influences with which they interact" (A. Freud, 1965, p. 138). Children whose libido "disposed" them to pathology could be saved by the right environment, or therapy, or both. Thus, although even mild symptoms could be ominous, the course was not inevitable. Psychoanalytic theory was fundamentally developmental at a time when the term had no place in mainline child psychiatry; as an example, the entries under the heading "Development" in the index of Anna Freud's *Normality and Pathology in Childhood* (1965) take up two columns, whereas there is not a single entry under that heading in two of the classics of mid-20th-century American child psychiatry (Chess & Habibi, 1978, 1986; Kanner, 1945, 1972). Psychoanalytic theory was also developmental in the multiple senses discussed later in this chapter and throughout this volume (see Cicchetti, 1990a); that is, it emphasized multiple determination of outcomes, the transformation and hierarchical integration of behavior, and the emergence of novelty. In the words of Anna Freud:

> According to our psychoanalytic conceptions, the final achievement of social adaptation is the result of a number and variety of developmental advances. To enumerate these in detail is useful, because in this way we create the prerequisites for predicting future massive disturbance at a time when only the merest indications of disharmony, unevenness in growth, or faulty response to the environment are present. This endeavor also disposes effectively of the conception of dissociality as a nosological entity which is based on one specific cause, whether this is thought to be internal (such as "mental deficiency" or "moral insanity") or external (such as broken homes, parental discord, parental neglect, separations, etc.). As we abandon thinking in terms of specific causes of dissociality, we become able to think increasingly in terms of successful or unsuccessful transformations of the self-indulgent and asocial trends and attitudes which normally are part of the original nature of the child. This helps to construct developmental lines which lead to pathological results, although these are more complex, less well defined, and contain a wider range of possibilities than the lines of normal development." (A. Freud, 1965, pp. 166–167)

In the past two decades, the influence of Freudian developmental psychopathology on clinical teaching and practice has declined as a more phenomenological approach to describing psychopathology has gained popularity, particularly in the United States. The nosologies currently in use for describing psychiatric problems, such as the International Classification of Diseases (ICD) (World Health Organization, 1992) and the *Diagnostic and Statistical Manual* (American Psychiatric Association, 1994), are essentially nondevelopmental in their approaches, searching for common denominators that describe the manifestations of a disorder at every age, rather than attempting, as the Freudian approach does, to describe the development of the disease in the context of the development of the individual. In this, they follow the example of medicine, which looks for diseases that have a standard etiology and set of manifestations, and of some branches of psychology, which seek to pin down concepts like intelligence in forms that are deliberately designed to transcend differences that are a function of developmental factors (Cairns & Cairns, 1991). Although the *content* of psychodynamic theories as an explanation of severe child psychopathology has not stood up to empirical research, the *form,* with its emphasis on how the development of the child and of the disease are intertwined, retains considerable attraction as a model for developmental psychopathology.

Distinguishing Normal from Abnormal

In contrast to the earlier concentration on severe disorder, work began in the 1940s to differentiate between what Lapouse and Monk (1958) called "deviations from the usual pattern" and behavior that could be seen (at least in hindsight) to be part of the picture of normal development:

> One of the great psychiatric dilemmas of our time is the decision as to what is normal and what is abnormal in human behavior. Lacking specific tests to make the distinction, the diagnostician has recourse mainly to his clinical judgment which rests on his training, experience, perceptiveness, and theoretical persuasion. . . . In child psychiatry, Leo Kanner points out that recorded symptoms "are of necessity those of selected groups and not of the total population of children"; and, he continues, "This selectiveness, in the absence of 'normal controls' has often resulted in a tendency to attribute to single behavior items an exaggerated 'seriousness' with regard to their intrinsic psychopathologic significance. The seriousness becomes attached to the signal regardless of what it announces and who announces it. The high annoyance threshold of many fond and fondly resourceful parents keeps away from clinics and out of reach of statistics a multitude of early breath holders, nail biters, nose pickers and casual masturbators who, largely because of this kind of parental attitude, develop into reasonably happy and well-adjusted adults" (Kanner, 1945). (Lapouse & Monk, 1958, p. 1136)

One of the achievements of the early child psychiatric epidemiologists, such as Lapouse and Monk (1958) in the United States, and Shepherd, Oppenheim, and Mitchell (1971) in England, was to document just how common *individual* "abnormal" behaviors are in the general population of children. For example, in their survey of a random sample of 6- to 12-year-olds in Buffalo, New York, Lapouse and Monk found that 43% of children were reported by their mothers to have seven or more fears or worries, 49% to be overactive, and 48% to lose their tempers twice a week or more (Lapouse & Monk, 1958). Similarly, Shepherd et al. (1971) found that, on their scale of 25 "deviant" behaviors, only 40% of a population sample of elementary school children in Buckinghamshire were *not* deviant. However, only 2.6% of the children were deviant in seven or more areas.

Measuring Child and Adolescent Psychopathology

The problem with the "questionnaire" approach to child psychiatric epidemiology used in these two studies was illuminated by a review of prevalence studies commissioned for President Carter's Commission on Mental Illness (Gould, Wunsch-Hitzig, & Dohrenwend, 1980). Prevalence estimates of childhood psychopathology varied widely, depending on whether parents or teachers were surveyed (at that time, children were rarely asked about their own problems). Estimates of the prevalence of "maladjustment" varied widely even when they were based on data from the same informant group: from 6.6% to 22% according to teachers, and from 10.9% to 37% according to mothers. It is difficult either to plan service delivery systems or to examine causal factors if the rate of the disorder itself is so imprecise. The questionnaires used in the 1950s and 1960s had two other disadvantages for epidemiological research: (a) they were not designed to distinguish clearly among different syndromes or diagnostic clusters of symptoms, and (b) they did not, as a rule, differentiate symptoms of a disorder from any impairment in functioning that might accompany those symptoms but not be a part of the syndrome itself. For example, failing to perform at age-appropriate levels in school could be a symptom of general mental retardation, a specific learning difficulty, attentional problems associated with attention deficit hyperactivity disorder (ADHD) or depression; or, it could result from repeated absence from school because of acute separation anxiety or a chronic physical illness. General "maladjustment" scales did not make it easy to study the relationship between symptoms and impaired functioning in a way that might illuminate causal relationships.

The problem of syndrome identification was tackled in the 1970s, most effectively by Achenbach and his colleagues (see Achenbach, Chapter 3 of this volume). They set out to develop a set of interrelated symptom questionnaires whose items derived from real evidence about the patterns of symptoms as they were found to be distributed in the population. The original set of behavioral and emotional problems was compiled from clinical sources, but the process of reducing the list to the 113 finally selected was based on studies using general population samples. The first of the questionnaires, the Child Behavior Checklist (Achenbach & Edelbrock, 1983), was designed for use by parents whose children were ages 4 through 16. Items endorsed by fewer than 5% or more than 95% of parents were rejected, and language was simplified so as to be understandable by anyone with a fourth-grade education. Achenbach and Edelbrock carried out extensive studies of how items clustered together in children of different age groups and genders. For four groups of children—boys and girls, ages 4 through 11 and 12 through 16—they identified two "broad-band" and eight or nine "narrow-band" syndromic clusters that could be reliably identified in each group and had many similarities across groups. These syndromes also proved to have considerable similarity to many of the clusters of symptoms identified by other empirically based symptoms checklists (Achenbach, Conners, Quay, Verhulst, & Howell, 1989), and many syndromes showed clear links to the standard diagnostic labels used in psychiatry. The two broad-band syndromes, labeled "internalizing" and "externalizing," proved to be the most consistently identified and reliable dimensions for classifying children's emotional and behavioral problems, and reflected the distinction between disorders of conduct and disorders of emotion made in the International Classification of Diseases (World Health Organization, 1978). Within each broad-band syndrome, the narrow-band factors varied by age and sex; different symptoms of anxiety and depression, for example, were grouped together in the depression factor, and, in the case of boys ages 12 through 16, no depression factor was identified. A recent revision of the Child Behavior Checklist identifies the same factors for each age and sex group. Not all the items among the 113 behavior problems listed fall into the factors; some, like bed-wetting, address isolated problems.

The work of Achenbach and his colleagues has provided some powerful tools for developmental epidemiology, both practically and conceptually. First, the extensive data collection and careful standardization on large samples set high standards for instrument development, and rooted the identified syndromes in the real world of evidence about the ways that thousands of parents actually saw their children and their problems. Second, the team has developed a closely integrated set of scales associated with the original Child Behavior Checklist—a version for parents of children ages 2 through 4, self-report versions for those 12 through 16 years old and for young adults, and a Teacher Report Form. Thus, it is possible to link repeated assessments across a wide age range. For example, Verhulst and van der Ende (1992) used the Checklist to trace patterns of continuity and change in emotional and behavioral problems in a large community sample of children in Holland. Third, the list of emotional and behavioral problems is set in the context of questions about the child's social competencies and school performance; basic sociodemographic information also is collected. Fourth, a lot of work has gone into language and layout, and the 4-page questionnaires collect a great deal of information in a brief time (around 20 minutes). As a result of these virtues, these instruments are very widely used for both clinical and epidemiological purposes. They have been translated into many languages, so that cross-cultural studies of the generalizability of the identified symptoms and syndromes and their correlates become possible (see, for example, Verhulst, Achenbach, Althaus, & Akkerhuis, 1988; Weisz, 1989).

The many virtues of the approach adopted by Achenbach and colleagues make it all the more important to recognize its dangers and limitations (Achenbach, 1985). First, the strategy of omitting rarely endorsed symptoms means that this method cannot be used to describe some of the most severe and disabling problems, such as those seen in autistic children, for example. Thus, it has limitations as a general tool for assessing psychopathology. Second, it is important to note that the questionnaire method is predicated on the assumption that the respondent knows the child well enough to be able to make ratings on items like "Feels too guilty" or "Lying or cheating." The Checklist is thus a very well-designed form for *recording* information about a child that the respondent already possesses, and can also serve as a guide for finding out more about important areas of symptomatology. Unfortunately, its very simplicity can beguile people into thinking that it can be validly completed on the basis of only limited knowledge of the child; for example, by a caseworker or pediatrician who rarely sees the child in his or her normal environment. The data that the Checklist provides can only be as good as the respondent's knowledge of the child in question. Third, this method produces a series of scale scores for each child, standardized relative to a population sample matched for age, sex, and social class. These scores cannot be used to answer such public health questions as "How many children need treatment?", unless certain decision rules are applied to them. A "clinical cutpoint" has been identified for the global behavioral problem score of the Checklist, based on a comparison of the scores of children who had been referred for mental health services during the previous year with the scores of nonreferred children (Achenbach & Edelbrock, 1981). However, as we shall discuss later, there is reliable evidence from national data and community surveys that fewer than 2% of children are receiving mental health treatment at any time, despite similarly strong evidence that one child in five has a psychiatric problem that entails significantly impaired functioning (see Table 2.1). Receipt of services is a poor criterion for defining need for services

TABLE 2.1 Summary of Longitudinal Surveys of the Prevalence and Continuity of Child Psychiatric Disorders

Key References and Setting	Population Base for Prevalence Estimates (Approximate)	Sample Size at Wave 1, Stage 1 (Stage 2)	Sample Size at Both Wave 1 and Wave 2 (Percent of Wave 1)	Age at Each Wave (Years between Waves)	Informant (Method)	Diagnostic Instrument (Diagnostic System)	Prevalence	Continuity: Proportion with W1 Diagnosis Who Have W2 Diagnosis
Rutter et al., 1970; Graham & Rutter, 1973: United Kingdom (Isle of Wight and London)	2,193	1,900 (284)	NA	W1 10–11 W2 14–15 (4)	W1 PC(I) W2 C(I) PT(Q)	Clinical Interview (ICD)	W1 6.8% W2 21.0%	60%
Anderson et al., 1987; McGee et al., 1992: New Zealand (Dunedin)	1,661	792	750 (95%)	W1 11 W2 15 (4)	W1 C(I) PT(Q) W2 C(I) P(Q)	DISC (DSM)	W1 17.6% (8.8%)[4] W2 19.6%	42%
Velez et al., 1989; Cohen et al., 1993: USA (New York State)	NA	776	734 (95%)	W1 9–18 W2 11–20 (2)	W1 PC(I) W2 PC(I)	DISC (DSM)	W1 17.6% W2 15.8%	23%–56%[1]
Verhulst & van der Ende, 1992: Netherlands (Zuid-Holland)	NA	2,076 (1,497 = 4–11)	(4 waves) 936 (63%)	W1 4–16 W2 8–16[2] (4)	W1 P(Q) W2 P(Q)	CBCL (DSM)	W1 NA W2 NA	r = .39[5]
Offord et al., 1987; Offord et al., 1992: Canada (Ontario)	NA	2,679 (1,617 = 4–11)	1,172 (54%)	W1 4–16 W2 8–16[2] (4)	W1 PCT(Q)[3] W2 PCT(Q)	CBCL-based Q (DSM)	W1 18.1% (15.8%)[4] W2 15.6%	30%–46%[4]
Laucht & Schmidt, 1987; Esser et al., 1990: Germany (Mannheim)	1,444	399	356 (89%)	W1 8 W2 13 (5)	W1 C(I) W2 C(I) P(I)	Clinical Interview (ICD)	W1 16.2% W2 16.2%	51%
Richman et al., 1982: United Kingdom (London)	4,000	705 (212)	185 (87%)	W1 3 W2 8 (5)	W1 P(I) (Q) W2 P(I) PT(Q)	Clinical Interview (ICD)	W1 Any: 22.3% Mod/Severe 7.7% (16.3%)[4] W2 25.5%	56%
McConaughy et al., 1992: USA (National sample)	National	2,734	2,479 (91%)	W1 4–16 W2 7–19 (3)	W1 P(Q) W2 PCT(Q)[3]	ACQ (NA) CBCL (NA)	W1 NA W2 NA	r = .585
Costello et al., 1988; Costello, 1992: USA (Pennsylvania)	2,800	789 (300)	278 (93%)	W1 7–11 W2 12–18 (5–7)	W1 PC(I) W2 PC(I)	DISC (DSM)	W1 22% W2 26.6%	61%

[1]Data presented by diagnosis: 23% = overanxious disorder, 56% = oppositional disorder.
[2]Only those ages 4–12 at Wave 1 were reassessed.
[3]Between ages 4 and 11, parent and teacher completed questionnaire. Between ages 12 and 16, parent and child completed it.
[4]Prevalence in members of Wave 1 who were also in Wave 2.
[5]Pearson correlation coefficient.
[6]Data presented by diagnosis at Wave 1: 30% = emotional disorder, 46% = conduct disorder.
Abbreviations: ACQ = Achenbach, Conners, Quay Questionnaire; C = Child; CBCL = Child Behavior Checklist; DISC = Diagnostic Interview Schedule for Children; DSM = Diagnostic and Statistical Manual; I = Interview; ICD = International Classification of Diseases; NA = Not Applicable; P = Parent; Q = Questionnaire; T = Teacher; W1 = Wave 1; W2 = Wave 2.

(Costello, Burns, Angold, & Leaf, 1993). Because the scale scores were standardized so as to identify *a priori* a certain percentage of the population as being in the clinical range, they cannot be used to make prevalence estimates.

The Checklist approach has proved valuable for identifying which children are seen by themselves, their parents, or their teachers as having a high rate of emotional and behavioral problems, relative to the distribution of these problems in the general population. It could not, however, provide the detailed information about symptom severity, duration, age at onset, and associated impairment that is needed, together with symptom reports, to make a diagnosis or devise a treatment plan. A method was needed that was more closely related to the process of clinical decision making.

Prevalence of Child and Adolescent Psychiatric Disorders

Beginning with Rutter and his colleagues in the late 1960s, several groups have carried out studies of representative community samples of children and adolescents, using methods designed to mirror clinical diagnostic processes, with the aim of establishing the prevalence of the major clinically defined psychiatric disorders in child and adolescent populations. Such studies require samples representative of the population to which they seek to generalize, and a standardized method of data collection. Decisions have to be made about who should collect diagnostic information and make diagnoses, who should provide the information, and how often. Thus, in the first systematic, diagnostic survey based on a clearly defined population (Rutter, Tizard, & Whitmore, 1970), child psychiatrists and other clinicians interviewed parents and children, using an approach based on a standard clinical interview. A similar method, employing clinicians as interviewers, was used by Vikan in Norway (Vikan, 1985), by Schmidt and colleagues in Germany (Esser, Schmidt, & Woerner, 1990; Laucht & Schmidt, 1987), and by Connell and colleagues in Australia (Connell, Irvine, & Rodney, 1982). Other researchers have relied on identifying cases of disorders reported in children's medical records or hospital admission records (Magnusson & Bergman, 1990). In the United States, psychiatrists have generally been too expensive to use as interviewers, at least for large-scale surveys. Interviews were developed that could be used by trained "lay" interviewers. This method has been used in studies in New York State and Pennsylvania. In Missouri, Puerto Rico, and New Zealand, a hybrid process was used: psychiatrists or psychologists were the interviewers, employing one of the standardized interview formats developed in the previous decade for research purposes. Finally, a series of studies carried out in Canada, Holland, and the United States has used questionnaires completed by parents, children, and teachers. The diagnosis-like syndromes derived from them have generally reflected the symptom structure of the major DSM categories, but have omitted any criteria based on date of onset or duration of symptoms.

Table 2.1 summarizes the major prevalence surveys of the past 25 years that provide information relevant to developmental epidemiology. Because developmental epidemiology is concerned with how individuals change over time (see below), all studies cited involved at least two waves of data collection. Details of the individual studies, and of others that involved only a single wave of data collection, can be found in the references given and in recent review papers (Brandenburg, Friedman, & Silver, 1990; Costello, 1989). In this section, we summarize the methods and findings of three of these research efforts (all of which are still in progress), with an emphasis on their contribution to developmental epidemiology. We make no claim that this section is exhaustive; the aim is rather to give a sense of the issues that have preoccupied child psychiatric epidemiologists over the past quarter century, and how they have been tackled in three of the most important ongoing research endeavors.

The Isle of Wight Studies

The series of studies carried out by Rutter and his colleagues (generally referred to as the "Isle of Wight studies," although some components of the research program were carried out in London) provided the first large-scale survey data that could be used as a basis for estimates of the prevalence of child psychiatric disorders in the general population. To make psychiatric diagnoses on children, a two-stage design was used. First, parents and teachers of all 10- and 11-year-olds living on the Isle of Wight (a small, rural island off the south coast of England) completed brief questionnaires about the children's emotional and behavioral problems. A previously determined cutpoint was used as a basis for selecting children at high risk for psychiatric disorder for more detailed assessment, and a small number of other children were also assessed in detail. By weighting the rates of disorder in the high-risk group by their sampling fraction, and combining the rates from the two groups, it was possible to estimate prevalence rates for the entire population of around 2,000 children in the age group. Psychiatrists and other clinicians were employed as interviewers for the detailed assessments, and made diagnoses based on the classification system of the International Classification of Diseases (World Health Organization, 1978). They used a semistructured interview based on the standard procedures for diagnostic interviewing at the Maudsley Hospital in London, the psychiatric hospital where Rutter and many of the research team worked. The ". . . parents were interviewed about their social circumstances and the behavior of their children; the teachers were asked to provide further information; and the children themselves had a psychiatric interview. . . . The data relating to the emotional state and behavior of the children were collated and a judgment was made about the presence and type of psychiatric disorder" (Graham & Rutter, 1973, p. 1226). This procedure led to the conclusion that between 6% and 7% of 10- and 11-year-olds on the island had a psychiatric disorder comparable in severity to those seen by the research team in their clinical work, and "for whom it was felt psychiatric services could usefully be employed" (Rutter & Graham, 1966, p. 385). One third had a neurotic or emotional disorder (roughly comparable with anxiety or depression, using current DSM terminology), two thirds had "antisocial or mixed conduct-emotional disorders" (Yule, 1981, p. 32). Only 13 children had diagnoses that fell outside these two broad categories: 8 with enuresis only, and 5 others with assorted problems. Although close to 7% of children were diagnosed as in need of treatment, the actual treatment rate at the time was less than 1%.

After 4 to 5 years, when the children were 14 to 15, the same population was surveyed again, using a similar methodology, including in the interviewed sample all the children identified as high-risk in the first wave of the study (Rutter, Graham, Chadwick, & Yule, 1976). This time, the weighted prevalence estimate was 21% (Graham & Rutter, 1973): 58% of those selected by the screening process, and 15% of the rest. Emotional disorders were the most common, affecting an estimated 12.9% of the total population, followed by mixed conduct and emotional disorders (5.8%) and conduct disorder (2.1%).

In the early 1970s, a second survey compared rates of psychiatric disorder among children on the Isle of Wight with rates found in a poor, inner-city area of London. Ten-year-olds were surveyed in both settings, providing a partial replication of the first Isle of Wight study. However, some aspects of the methodology differed (only a teacher questionnaire was used for screening; only 10-year-olds were surveyed; the parent but not the child was interviewed). Combining information from parent and teacher, the prevalence rate of psychiatric disorder was 12% on the Isle of Wight and 25.4% in inner London. On the Isle of Wight, 2% of adolescents (16% of those with a disorder) were attending a mental health clinic at the time of the survey.

The Dunedin Study

A longitudinal study begun in New Zealand in 1973 is providing some of the most valuable information yet collected about the development of psychiatric disorders in childhood. Between April 1, 1972, and March 31, 1973, 1,661 babies were born in the local maternity hospital to mothers from the Dunedin metropolitan area. These children were fairly representative of the population of New Zealand, except for being slightly less likely to be poor, Maori, or Polynesian. Aspects of the health, mental health, and academic attainment of the children who have remained in the Dunedin area have been studied at ages 3, 5, 7, 9, 11, 13 and 15, and the study is still going on. At age 9, depressive disorders were studied using a standard diagnostic interview (the Kiddie Schedule for Affective Disorders and Schizophrenia, Epidemiologic Version (K-SADS-E)) (Kashani et al., 1983); and at ages 11 and 15, the Diagnostic Interview Schedule for Children (DISC) (Costello, Edelbrock, Kalas, Kessler, & Klaric, 1982) was used to assess children for a broad range of DSM-III disorders. A psychiatrist interviewed the children, and information from questionnaires to parents and teachers was incorporated into the decision about the presence or absence of disorder. To get over the problem of multiple informants, an ordinal scale of diagnostic rigor was developed (Anderson, Williams, McGee, & Silva, 1987):

> Level 1 indicates diagnostic criteria met by more than one source, independently (strong, pervasive). Level 2 indicates diagnostic criteria met by one source and symptoms confirmed by one or both of the other sources (strong, pervasive). Level 3 indicates diagnostic criteria met by one source without confirming symptoms from either of the other sources (situational). Level 4 indicates diagnostic criteria met only by combining symptoms from all three sources, with the same symptoms reported by several sources counted only once (weak, pervasive). (p. 72)

This important survey has much in common with the Isle of Wight studies (psychiatrist-administered, standard interview of the child, combined with questionnaires for parent and teacher). It differs in using the DSM rather than the ICD taxonomy, and having a single-stage design. However, the overall prevalence rate is within the same range as all but the first Isle of Wight study: at age 11, 17.6% of children received one or more diagnoses based on the combined information of child, parent, and teacher. Twice as many boys as girls had "externalizing" disorders (attention deficit, conduct, or oppositional disorders). On the whole, anxiety disorders and phobias were seen more frequently in girls, but of the 14 cases of depression and dysthymia, 12 occurred in boys. At age 15, no teacher data were collected, but 22% of the adolescents were judged to have one or more diagnoses (McGee et al., 1990). At this stage, all internalizing disorders except for social phobia were more common in girls. Attention deficit disorders and aggressive conduct disorder were more frequently seen in boys; however, in this sample, more girls than boys showed nonaggressive conduct disorder and oppositional disorder.

The New York Study

The third example of a longitudinal, epidemiological study of children comes from the United States. In 1976, 976 mothers in northern New York State were interviewed about their children, then aged between 1 and 10 (Velez, Johnson, & Cohen, 1989). The sample was followed up in 1983 and 1985, and a fourth wave of interviews is currently in progress. At waves 2 and 3, mothers and children were interviewed using the DISC, and we concentrate on these two data waves here. Rates of disorder were in the same range as most other DISC-based community studies, ranging from 15.6% for 11- to 14-year-olds in wave 3 to 19.4% for 9- to 12-year-olds in wave 2. As in almost all community studies, adolescents reported more disorders than did children. The risk factors studied included demographic characteristics, family structure, ethnicity, parental mental health problems, and earlier characteristics of the child. In general, all types of risk predicted externalizing disorders (conduct, oppositional, and attention deficit disorders) better than they did anxiety or depression. But the best predictors of depression and overanxious disorder at ages 11 through 20 were parental emotional problems 2 years earlier (see Table 2.2). School failure and stressful life events also predicted internalizing disorders. Interestingly, separation anxiety was associated with the indicators of low socioeconomic status that also predicted externalizing disorders, but not with the child stress and parental emotional problems that predicted other types of anxiety.

As Table 2.1 shows, several other community surveys around the world in the past two decades have given us some glimpses of the development of child psychopathology and the key risk factors. In general, the series of population surveys that have followed (and usually copied) the Isle of Wight studies have replicated its findings to an extraordinary extent. The one deviant finding is the low

TABLE 2.2 Relative Risk of Factors Measured at Ages 9 to 18 on DSM-III-R Diagnoses Measured at Ages 11 to 20[1]

	Time 3 Diagnoses					
	Externalizing			Internalizing		
Time 2 Factors	CD	ADD	OPP	OVA	SEP	MDD
Sociostructural						
Demographics						
Age/Sex	0.98	0.89	0.93		0.77	
Sex/Age	1.39			0.70		0.50
Low SES	2.26	3.79	1.99	1.91	5.41	
Low income	2.90	3.15	2.24		3.59	
Low education—mother		2.78	1.92		4.12	
Low education—father	1.78[2]		2.53		3.90	
Income/mo. ed/fa. ed	Inc.	Inc.	Inc.		Inc., mo. ed	
Residential stability						
Frequent moves						
Recent moves	1.85					
Family structure						
Mother only/SES	2.03		1.74			
Stepfather/SES		2.02				
Race						
Nonwhite/SES	2.69					
Parental Characteristics						
Sociopathy	1.54	1.47			1.52	
Father emotional problems/SES				2.33		
Mother emotional problems/SES				2.32		3.56
Both parents with emotional problems				5.35		6.61
Child Characteristics						
Ever repeated grade	2.40	3.84	1.72	1.93		2.62
Mental health treatment by Time 2	2.29	2.75	2.46	2.29		
Stressful life events (7 or more) since Time 2 vs. 2 or less	3.65	2.39	2.14	1.67		1.91

[1]Always controlling for age and sex, and SES when indicated, estimated by adjusted odds.
[2]Significant in simultaneous estimation.
Abbreviations: ADD = Attention Deficit Disorder; CD = Conduct Disorder; OPP Oppositional Disorder; OVA Overanxious Disorder; SEP Separation Anxiety Disorder; MDD Major Depressive Disorder; SES Socioeconomic Status; mo. ed. = mother's educational level; fa. ed. = father's educational level; Inc. = income
From "A Longitudinal Analysis of Selected Risk Factors of Childhood Psychopathology" by C. N. Velez, J. Johnson, and P. Cohen, 1989, *Journal of the American Academy of Child and Adolescent Psychiatry, 28,* p. 863. Adapted by permission.

(7%) prevalence rate reported in the first wave of Isle of Wight interviews. Thereafter, the studies consistently find that information from any single informant—parent, child, or teacher—yields a prevalence rate in the 10% to 12% range, with an overall rate, combining information from different sources, in the region of 20%. The rate of treatment in a mental health setting is still, 25 years later, close to 1%.

CONTINUITY AND CHANGE IN CHILD PSYCHIATRIC DISORDERS

Public health epidemiology has an interest in tracking changes in prevalence rates of various disorders over time, so that services can be tailored to the needs of the population. But epidemiology as a scientific activity is concerned with causes, and, as a developmental science, with continuity and change in individuals. Some epidemiological studies have begun to take what Magnusson (1988) called a *person-based approach* to understanding the relationship among exposure to risk, onset of disorder, course, and outcome. In this section, we examine how the longitudinal studies described earlier, and some others, have used person-based analytic methods to explore continuity and change at the level of the individual. The last column of Table 2.1 summarizes the level of continuity of psychopathology found when the same children were assessed over time; that is, the proportion of children receiving a diagnosis at the first assessment who also received one (though not necessarily the same diagnosis) at a second evaluation.

Evidence for Continuity and Change

The Isle of Wight studies address two kinds of developmental questions: continuity and change in the expression of psychiatric disorder, and risk factors for onset and continuity of disorder.

Graham and Rutter (1973) reported that a diagnosis in childhood considerably increased the likelihood of a psychiatric diagnosis in adolescence: compared with a prevalence rate of 21% in those with no childhood disorder, the rates of adolescent disorder were 46% in those with childhood emotional disorders, 58% in those with childhood mixed disorders, and 75% in those with childhood conduct disorders. There was also persistence in the type of disorder: over half of those with conduct disorders in childhood had conduct or mixed disorders in adolescence, and one third of children with emotional disorders reported similar problems in adolescence. This persistence cannot be taken to imply continuity of the same illness episode; a child may have recovered and relapsed, possibly more than once. But it does imply a continuity in vulnerability.

Graham and Rutter (1973) reported that 70% of those with persistent disorders (using the term loosely, as discussed in the last paragraph) were boys, compared with only 56% of those with new disorders. Although there was no difference in IQ, there were considerable differences in reading ability at the time of the first interview: 14% of children with persistent disorder, compared with 3% of those with only adolescent disorder, had shown reading retardation at the age of 10–11. Rutter et al. (1976) presented evidence that several other factors, including having been in residential care, not living with both biological parents, marital discord, and maternal psychiatric disorder, occurred more commonly in the persistent group.

To look at continuity and change from ages 11 through 15 in the New Zealand children, McGee, Freehan, Williams, and Anderson (1992) recalculated the data from the 11-year-old wave, using only the sources of data (essentially, self-report interview and parental questionnaire) available at both times. This procedure reduced the proportion of children with one or more diagnoses to 8.8% at age 11, and 19.6% at age 15. Different patterns of continuity and change were found for boys and girls (Figure 2.2). For girls, internalizing disorders showed considerable persistence (in the broad sense discussed earlier); a girl with anxiety or depression at age 11 was 6.2 times more likely to have anxiety or depression at age 15 than a girl with no internalizing disorder in childhood. Girls showed no comparable pattern of persistence of externalizing disorders. Boys, by contrast, were 4.2 times more likely to have an adolescent externalizing disorder if they reported conduct or oppositional disorder or attention deficit disorder (ADD) as children. However, they were also 5.8 times more likely to have an adolescent externalizing disorder if they reported anxiety or depression as children. There was no persistence for internalizing disorders, as there was for the girls. Thus, the persistence of ICD conduct disorder reported by Graham and Rutter (1973) was found in the New Zealand sample only in the boys (the same may well have been true of the Isle of Wight sample; most of those with conduct disorders were boys, and the results were not reported separately by sex), and the persistence of emotional disorders was found in New Zealand only in girls.

One of the strengths of the Dunedin survey is the amount of work that has been done on developmental aspects of childhood psychopathology—too much work to be reviewed in detail here. One or two examples will give a flavor of how the researchers have capitalized on their longitudinal data and of the range of

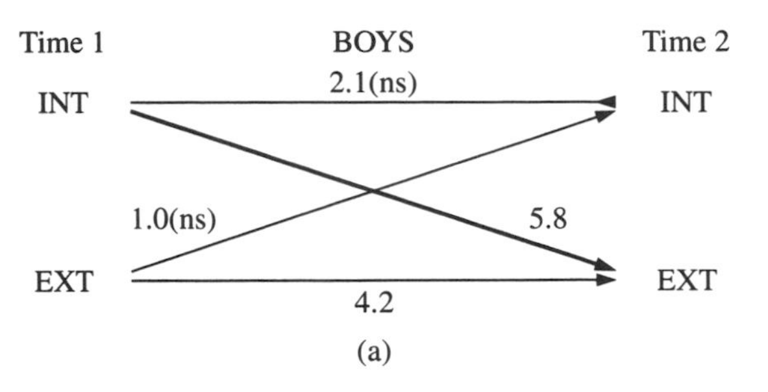

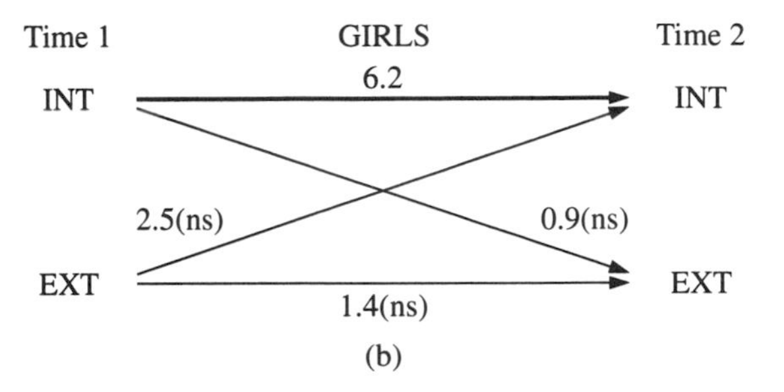

Figure 2.2 Odds ratios of diagnosis of boys and girls at age 15 given the presence/absence of diagnosis at age 11.

areas studied, to test some important hypotheses about causes and consequences of psychopathology. At the age of 3, 2% of the sample (21 children) were identified as "pervasively hyperactive" (McGee, Partridge, Williams, & Silva, 1991). The developmental progress of this group was compared 12 years later with that of 31 children who, like the hyperactive group, were described by their mothers as "very difficult to manage," but who were not hyperactive; and with a "developmental control group" of 21 children matched to the hyperactive group on sex, IQ, and family adversity at age 3, and verbal comprehension at age 5, but who were not hyperactive or difficult to manage.

By age 11, one third of the hyperactive group met criteria for a diagnosis of ADD, but by age 15 the rate had fallen to 10%—still higher than the 2% rate found in the rest of the sample, but only 1 in 10 of the original group (see Table 2.3). However, 50% of the hyperactive group had one or more DSM-III diagnoses, compared with 24% or less in the other groups. No one diagnosis predominated. Furthermore, when the research team looked at "recovery" by identifying children with no significant problems or mental health service use, only 25% of the hyperactive group were problem-free at age 15, compared with 75% of the "developmental controls." Thus, early hyperactivity in this group seems to have been a precursor of adolescent psychiatric disorder in general, rather than just of hyperactivity.

In another set of analyses, Anderson, Williams, McGee, and Silva (1989) looked at factors predicting which children would be diagnosed with multiple DSM-III disorders at age 11. Most of this group, which made up 2% of the sample, had ADD and conduct disorder, and many also reported anxiety and/or depression. Ninety percent were boys, and the study shows that risk factors for this constellation of problems could be seen as early as age 5. Verbal and performance IQ scores were significantly lower at

TABLE 2.3 DSM-III Disorders in Four Groups at Age 11

	Group			
Type of Disorder	Hyperactive (N=18)	Difficult to Manage (N=21)	Developmental Control (N=20)	Remainder of Sample (N=724)
Attention deficit disorder (ADD)	6	2	3	42
Other DSM-III disorder	3	2	0	80
No disorder	9	17	17	602
Percent of disorder	50%	19%	18%	17%

From "A Twelve-Year Follow-Up of Preschool Hyperactive Children" by R. McGee, F. Partridge, S. Williams, and P. A. Silva, 1991, *Journal of the American Academy of Child and Adolescent Psychiatry, 30,* p. 224–232. Adapted by permission.

every age for this group (and for the "pure ADD" group) than for children with other diagnoses or no disorder. Reading and spelling skills were lower too, and, not surprisingly, self-esteem was poor. A measure of peer relationships showed that the group with multiple diagnoses started out school life no less popular than other children, but, over time, they became increasingly disliked and solitary (see Figure 2.3). This was noticeably less true of the children with pure ADD, although their academic performance mirrored that of the multiply disordered group. The authors pointed out that family disadvantage and poor school performance appeared to contribute separately to the likelihood of multiple psychiatric disorders in middle childhood, which implies that prevention focusing on either domain could be expected to have an impact on the number of children developing multiple disorders.

The value of the Dunedin study has grown and continues to grow. Because of the low dropout rate and the wide range of data collected, it is possible to look at the interaction of risk factors from many domains: education, health, economics, and family psychopathology. It is interesting that these data from the other side of the world show such a high degree of concordance with British and North American studies on the overall rates of disorder, the major risk factors, and the low rate of service use. They also concur in demonstrating that although psychopathology in general shows considerable continuity, the continuity of specific disorders is much lower. Such information is critical to improving the taxonomy of psychiatric disorders, and only longitudinal studies like this provide the necessary information about continuity and change in symptomatology.

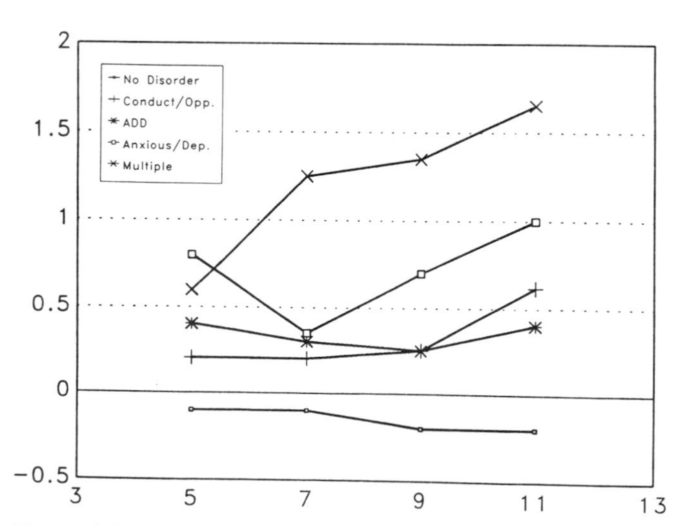

Figure 2.3 Peer sociability and acceptance for disorder groups, by age.

Stability of Specific Disorders

Within the global pattern of continuity and change in psychopathology, a certain amount of stability can be found for broad diagnostic groupings. McGee et al. (1991) found that externalizing disorders in 11-year-old boys predicted externalizing disorders at age 15, and internalizing disorders in 11-year-old girls predicted internalizing disorders at age 15. Cohen, Cohen, and Brook (1993), in the New York study, calculated the odds of receiving a specific diagnosis for adolescents who had the same diagnosis 2.5 years earlier, relative to adolescents without that diagnosis. The odds ratios were significantly above the chance level for ADHD, conduct disorders, oppositional disorder, overanxious disorder, and alcohol abuse. Furthermore, with the exception of alcohol abuse, the more severe the Time 1 diagnosis, the greater the odds ratio (i.e., the gap between children with and without the Time 1 diagnosis in the likelihood of having the disorder at Time 2). In Canada, Offord et al. (1992) found that the strongest predictor of a conduct disorder in their community sample was a conduct disorder diagnosis 4 years earlier (44% of those with the earlier diagnosis received the same diagnosis at follow-up). Of children with hyperactivity, 34% had received the same diagnosis at Time 1, while one quarter of children with a diagnosis of emotional disorder (anxiety or depression) had received the same diagnosis 4 years earlier. In a study of 300 children in Pittsburgh, Pennsylvania, who were reinterviewed 5 years later, in adolescence, Costello, Stouthamer-Loeber, and DeRosier (1993) found that internalizing disorders in childhood predicted internalizing disorders in adolescence, and externalizing disorders predicted externalizing disorders, for both boys and girls.

All these studies show a level of continuity across time that greatly exceeds what would be expected by chance alone. It is not safe to assume that these children had the same disorders continuously over the period of time covered by the studies, because there was an interval of 2.5 to 5 years during which no data were collected, and retrospective data were not sought. But it is safe to conclude from these studies that a psychiatric disorder in childhood greatly increases the risk of having a similar disorder in adolescence. Furthermore, Cohen et al.'s analysis by severity level suggests that the more severe the childhood disorder, the greater the risk of a later diagnosis at the same or a higher level of severity (Cohen et al., 1992). The accumulated information from several thousands of children thus gives the lie to the comfortable assumption that "It's only a phase" and "He'll grow out of it." It is equally disturbing to link these results with the information about onset of adult disorders collected for the adult Epidemiological Catchment Area (ECA) studies (Burke, Burke, Regier, & Rae, 1990). These surveys of over 20,000 people aged 18 years and older in the United States asked about age at onset for symptoms that contributed to the diagnosis of each disorder. Figure 2.4 shows the hazard rate for age of onset of three disorders. Many adults reported (retrospectively) the onset of symptoms in childhood or adolescence. The median ages of onset for 3 out of 7 disorders examined were in the teens (bipolar illness, 19; phobias, 13; drug abuse or dependence, 18). Retrospective data from people whose ages ranged from 18 to 94 may not be very reliable, but taken in conjunction with the prospective evidence of considerable continuity from childhood to adolescence, they have to make us wonder about the long-term prospects for the children interviewed in the studies in Table 2.1. Some of these studies are still going on, and they include subjects now in their late teens and early 20s (the New Zealand and New York State studies) or even in their 30s (Isle of Wight study), so information will soon be available that does not rely on retrospective recall of childhood problems. A further follow-up of the Isle of Wight study is being planned, to assess the consequences for adult functioning of child and adolescent psychopathology, and to trace patterns of continuity and change into the next generation.

Reasons for Continuity and Change in the Development of Pathology

It is easier to define this as the key question for developmental epidemiology than to point to good examples of relevant research. An example of the kind of work that needs to be done will serve to illustrate (a) that it can be done and (b) how much more similar work is needed in other diagnostic areas. Loeber and his colleagues (Loeber, Keenan, & Zhang, 1994) have made important progress in providing empirical support for a series of *developmental pathways* in the area of the disruptive behavior disorders, in which different constellations of risk factors lead to different outcomes (see Figure 2.5). Furthermore, they have begun to link these developmental pathways to constellations of risk factors, some of which operate to increase the likelihood that a child will *start* on a particular pathway, while others operate to *maintain* a behavioral pattern once it has started. For example, Loeber, Stouthamer-Loeber, Van Kammen, and Farrington (1991) reported that in their

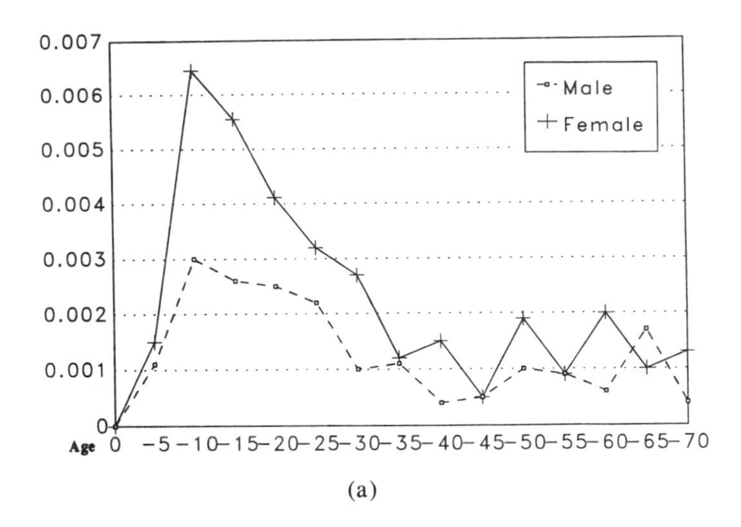

(a)

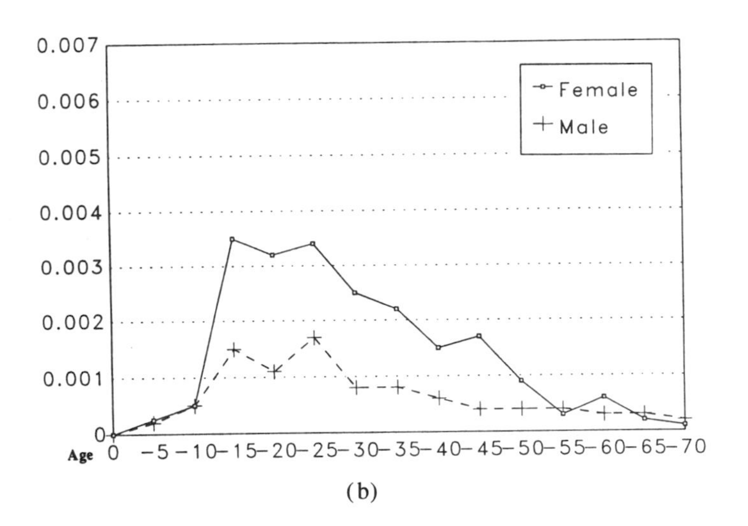

(b)

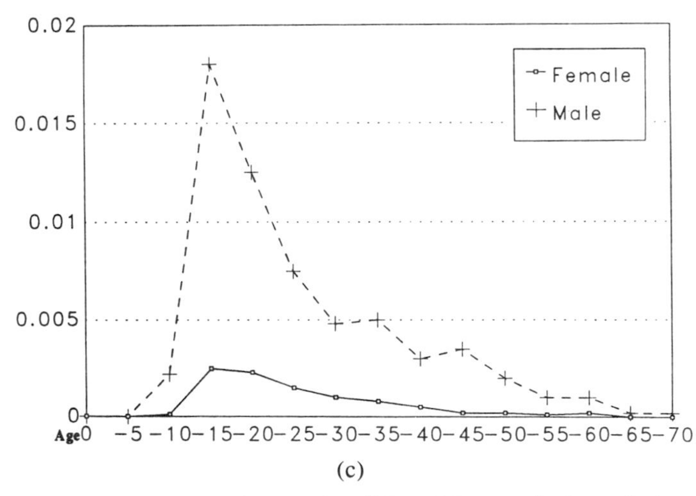

(c)

Figure 2.4 Hazard rate by life table survival analysis, DIS/DSM-III: (a) phobias; (b) affective disorders; (c) alcohol abuse/dependence.

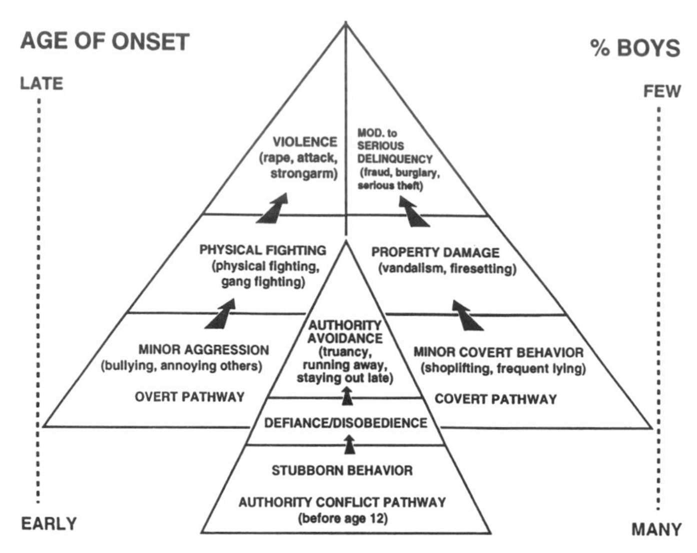

Figure 2.5 Three pathways to boys' problem behavior and delinquency.

longitudinal study of 1,500 inner-city boys ages 7, 10, and 13 at intake, initiation into antisocial behavior was predicted by some factors (e.g., poor relations with parents, physical aggression) that were common across the three age groups, and others (e.g., shyness at age 7, depression at age 10) that were age-specific. Furthermore, the environments of children who remained antisocial differed from those of children whose antisocial behavior dropped or disappeared; for example, good supervision seems to have been particularly important in helping the older children (13 at intake) to reduce their antisocial behavior, but less important for younger children than their attitude to school.

The studies discussed in this section lead to two general conclusions of importance for developmental epidemiology. The first is that the rate of psychiatric disorder, however it is measured and whoever provides the information, appears to show a consistent pattern that could be summarized in the rule of thumb: "Ten percent agreement between informants; ten percent prevalence per informant; ten percent treated." The second conclusion is that we are still at the very start of the search for specific causes of specific child psychiatric disorders. There is little to link one risk factor or group of risk factors to one disorder. Even when children are identified on the basis of the presence of that disorder in themselves (McGee et al., 1991) or their parents (Weissman et al., 1987), this increases their vulnerability to psychiatric disorder *in general,* as well as to that same disorder. One of the problems with risk research is that we can only look for the effects of factors that we have thought to include in the study to begin with. Furthermore, we have to face the possibility that, for example, the risk factors for parent-reported depression are different from the risk factors for child-reported or teacher-reported depression. Some causal pathways may begin to reveal themselves only when we have solved the many methodological problems inherent in this kind of research. The major problems are described later, when we discuss the future of developmental epidemiology.

CHARACTERISTICS OF EPIDEMIOLOGICAL RESEARCH

This brief introduction to what child psychiatric epidemiology has dealt with substantively during the past century brings us back to the question of what distinguishes epidemiological research from other research paradigms, and how these methodological or epidemiological characteristics influence, and are influenced by, taking child psychopathology as their topic. The introductory section discussed epidemiology less as a body of substantive knowledge than as a way of looking at problems. The great historical victories over infectious diseases, and the recent achievements in helping to reduce mortality and morbidity from chronic illnesses such as cardiovascular disease (Dawber, 1980), came as a result of looking at clinical problems in a different way. Here we introduce the basic requirements for studying the epidemiology of any disorder (Kleinbaum et al., 1982, chapter 1), and discuss their implications for the study of developmental psychopathology. They are: (a) the ability to measure disease frequency (i.e., the rates of cases); (b) the ability to make valid generalizations from sample to population (i.e., to avoid sampling or ascertainment bias); and (c) the ability to control bias in estimates of risk factors (i.e., to distinguish between confounding factors and effect modifiers).

Measuring the Frequency of Disease

The question of how many people exposed to a risk factor for a disease actually become sick, and how many die or recover, is central to epidemiological research. The most frequently used measures involve the concept of a *rate,* "an instantaneous potential for change in one quantity per unit change in another quantity" (Kleinbaum et al., 1982, p. 3). Typically, the second quantity is time. Epidemiology deals most often with *incidence rates,* which measure the extent to which new cases of a disorder appear in the previously healthy population over a specified period of time, and *prevalence rates,* which measure all the cases, whether new or previously existing, observed during a specified period. Usually, the epidemiologist is concerned with *relative rates* of disease onset in two or more groups of people who differ on exposure to a risk or preventive factor; for example, in a Swedish study, the prevalence of drunkenness in adolescence among girls who reached menarche earlier than the norm for the population was found to be high, relative to the rate found in girls of the same age whose menarche occurred within the normal age range (Stattin & Magnusson, 1990). Relative rates thus become the metric for answering questions about a possible causal role played by putative risk factors in the onset of disorder. In this example, Stattin and Magnusson found that, at age 14, 75% of girls who had reached menarche before age 11 had been drunk at least once, compared with only 29% of girls who reached menarche after age 13. Furthermore, the rate of frequent drunkenness remained higher across adolescence for early than for later maturing girls.

Defining a "Case"

A corollary of epidemiology's concern with measuring the frequency of disease is the importance attached to diagnosis. Making a diagnosis means putting an individual into a category: "Has Disorder X" or "Does not have Disorder X." In any context where decisions have to be made leading to action to prevent or treat illness, categories have to be created. Even if the goal is to eliminate a risk factor that potentially affects everyone in the community (such as environmental pollutants or unsafe automobiles), it is still necessary to define categories of affected and nonaffected individuals in order to measure the outcome of a primary prevention or to calculate costs and benefits (e.g., how many cases of learning disability were prevented by reducing environmental lead? How much does it cost to prevent one case of learning disability, and how much is saved by doing so?). The relationship among symptoms, diagnosis, and the concept of disease has exercised many brains (Meehl, 1992). A diagnosis encapsulates a mixed bag of information: the number and severity of symptoms, the duration of symptomatology, the date of onset, and the level of functional impairment. All of these have implications for a decision about whether intervention is indicated. For some forms of pathology, there is little ambiguity about how the diagnosis should be made; either it is fairly self-evident, like a broken bone, or the rules have been sanctified by use, like the stages of cervical cancer, or there is a clearly identifiable pathogen that acts as a marker for the disease, as in tuberculosis. Few types of psychopathology can invoke any one of these methods for decision making. There are no reliable pathognomic markers; the boundaries between one disorder and another, or between normality and disorder, are generally ill-defined, as Kendell (1976) demonstrated in his exploration of the boundaries of depression. Every generation sees a new classification system, usually based on a new set of ideas about where to look for the causes of illness. Thus, as outlined in the previous section, the past 100 years of child psychopathology have seen a move from a classification based on genetic causes, with biological degeneration as the manifestation, through the psychodynamic era in which disorders were defined by their etiology, to the current effort to define disorders by their observable characteristics, as far as possible avoiding etiological inferences that are not empirically testable, at least in theory (American Psychiatric Association, 1987). Meanwhile, older classifications may still retain some of their sway, and, to confuse matters further, psychiatry often makes use of familiar language in its diagnostic terminology (for example, "depression," "separation anxiety"), not necessarily in the vernacular meaning of the term. In his review of childhood depression, for example, Angold (1988) identified eight different ways in which the term "depression" is used in the description of psychopathology:

1. As the low end of normal mood fluctuations;
2. As a description of psychic pain felt in response to some unpleasant situation;
3. As a trait;
4. As an individual symptom;
5. As a syndrome;
6. As a disorder;
7. As a disease; or
8. As a cause of handicap or disability.

The implications for treatment are likely to differ, depending on which definition is being used.

As a result of the current emphasis on operationally definable criteria for psychiatric disorders, *taxonomy,* the study of how phenomena cluster together, has become a central concern to psychiatry. Evidence of this is the enormous effort put into successive editions of the American Psychiatric Association's *Diagnostic and Statistical Manual* (DSM) (American Psychiatric Association, 1952, 1968, 1980, 1987, 1994), which have been published over the past 30 years at ever shorter intervals and greater length. The 1994 *Diagnostic and Statistical Manual* (DSM-IV) states: "The purpose of DSM-IV is to provide clear descriptions of diagnostic categories in order to enable clinicians and investigators to diagnose, communicate about, study, and treat the various mental disorders" (American Psychiatric Association, 1994, p. xxvii). Thus, the issue of "what is a case?" (Wing, Bebbington, & Robins, 1981) has become as critical for clinical psychiatry as it is for psychiatric epidemiology. An industry has grown up around the successive DSMs, dedicated to developing instruments to identify "cases" of each diagnosis accurately and consistently in both clinical and community settings. In some ways, the task facing epidemiology is even more difficult than that facing clinical psychiatry. The clinician can assume a certain level of suffering in a patient who has come seeking help, so that the problem is to figure out what exactly is the nature of the problem. Epidemiologists, working most frequently in the community, have to identify cases among people most of whom are not seeking treatment. They have to convince themselves and others that the criteria they use are valid: that a clinician would identify this person as a "case" of a given disorder, whether or not the individual came seeking treatment.

For child psychiatry, this problem of case definition is even more complex. Children rarely refer themselves for treatment even when severely symptomatic. Thus, the rule of thumb that equates illness with seeking treatment is even less accurate for children than it is for adults. Referral for treatment may have more to do with characteristics of a child's mother, teacher, or pediatrician than with the child's behavior or feelings (Costello & Janiszewski, 1990; Dulcan et al., 1990; Shepherd et al., 1971). Because the criteria for caseness have to be applicable in the community as a whole, not only in a clinical setting, the criteria defining the level of both symptom severity and functional impairment necessary to distinguish a "case" have to be specified very clearly. Epidemiology has historically been involved in community studies; it has had to confront these problems before. Psychiatric epidemiologists have been active collaborators with clinicians in the work carried out around the world in the past 25 years to improve psychiatric taxonomies as the basis for research and intervention (Robins, 1985, 1989). There are two aspects to this process: (a) developing a taxonomy to classify psychiatric disorders, which involves specifying the criteria to be used to define each disorder, and (b) translating the taxonomic criteria into practical tools for case identification: interviews, checklists, and the like.

Cases in the Clinic and the Community

The problem of equating cases found in community studies with referred cases has been addressed in several ways in child psychiatric epidemiology. First, diagnostic instruments have been developed that meticulously translate clinical diagnostic criteria into methods for identifying the same symptoms in nonreferred cases (e.g., Angold, Cox, Prendergast, Rutter, & Simonoff, 1992; Chambers et al., 1985; Costello et al., 1982; Herjanic & Campbell, 1977; Hodges, Klein, Fitch, McKnew, & Cytryn, 1981; Shaffer, Fisher, Schwab-Stone, Piacentini, & Wicks, 1989).

Second, most measures for community use now include, or are used with, measures of functional impairment, so that the relationship between symptoms and a child's ability to carry out the normal tasks of daily life can become the subject of empirical review. At the same time, current attempts to classify psychiatric disorders into a coherent taxonomy have adopted a "multiaxial" system by which a clinician is encouraged to describe the patient from several points of view, of which psychiatric diagnosis is only one (American Psychiatric Association, 1994; Rutter et al., 1969; Rutter, Shaffer, & Sturge, 1979). Several current epidemiological assessment instruments adopt the same multiaxial approach (Angold et al., 1992; Shaffer et al., 1989). In addition, the psychometric studies that are carried out as part of the process of instrument development include studies of referred and nonreferred samples, and interviews using both clinicians and trained "lay" interviewers. Instruments can then be revised so that "caseness" has the same meaning wherever a child is recruited or assessed.

Epidemiology and Case Identification

It is important to distinguish between the problems that can be solved by a well-designed instrument and those that have to be solved at the level of the taxonomic system (Meehl, 1992). For example, Robins (1989) presented evidence that some DSM disorders are consistently diagnosed more validly (using several criteria of validity) than others, using both clinical and epidemiological methods. This, Robins believes, suggests that "part of the source of invalidity lies in the diagnostic grammar of the systems whose criteria standardized interviews evaluate" (1989, p. 57). She uses the phrase "diagnostic grammar" because, she argues, "[D]iagnosis is much like a language. The criteria include elements that have special relations to each other like parts of speech—symptoms (nouns?); severity (adjectives?); clustering (verbs?); age of onset, frequency, and duration (adverbs?)" (p. 61). If the grammar is wrong, the sentence will not make sense, however clearly it is articulated. Much of the process of developing a good diagnostic grammar is carried out through careful clinical work; epidemiology, however, can contribute in several ways. It provides feedback about the relationship between symptom patterns seen in clinical and community samples, which can throw light on possible referral biases (see below). It can also provide information about the prevalence of different disorders in the community, and their patterns of distribution by age, sex, and so on. This information can then influence clinicians' expectations about the relative likelihood that a given patient has one disorder rather than another. In practice, it is well known that physicians make diagnostic judgments on the basis of very few items of information (Cantwell, 1988; Meehl, 1954). Good prevalence information can be a very important part of the clinician's database.

Given a taxonomy that accurately reflects the phenomenology of illness, another important role of epidemiology in case identification is to develop accurate tests for the disease in question. Testing for the AIDS virus has brought the technical problems associated with case identification painfully to public attention in recent years. Newspaper articles have educated us about such esoteric points as: if the base rate of a disease in the population is very low, then even if a test for that disease rarely identifies a healthy person as diseased (i.e., has a very low false-positive rate), most people identified as diseased by the test will not actually have the disease. Many psychiatric disorders are extremely rare, and testing for the presence of a disorder is hampered by the lack of pathognomic tests such as those available to identify HIV. Psychiatry is still largely dependent on question-and-answer methods for case identification. Epidemiologists have been closely involved in the development and testing of numerous questionnaires and interviews designed to translate the current taxonomy into accurate "tests" for caseness in both clinical and community settings. They have also wrestled with the problems of how to quantify the accuracy of tests. The basic rules and statistical tests were developed in the context of psychological testing (Anastasi, 1986) and clinical pathology (Galen & Gambino, 1975). There has been much debate about the applicability to psychopathology of some of these standard methods, such as the kappa statistic for quantifying agreement between observers about the presence of a disorder (Cohen, 1960, 1990), especially when dealing with rare disorders (Cicchetti, Sparrow, Volkmar, Cohen, & Rourke, 1991; Shrout, Spitzer, & Fleiss, 1987; Spitznagel & Helzer, 1985). Psychiatry confronts two problems that make it particularly difficult to develop reliable and accurate measures of symptoms and diagnoses. One is that there are no "gold standard" measures that can be used to evaluate the accuracy of a test: a postmortem or a PET scan will not tell us whether a child really had separation anxiety disorder. The second problem is with the standard procedure for assessing the reliability of a measure: the test–retest reliability procedure, which uses two interviewers to interview the same subject on two different occasions about the same period of time. Whereas one can take someone's temperature repeatedly without appreciably altering body temperature, interviewing someone at length about emotionally sensitive topics can hardly be done without affecting how the individual thinks or feels about these issues. The first interview is thus likely to affect how the subject responds to the second interview. For example, Angold and Costello (1993) found that boys who, at the first of two parallel interviews, admitted that they told a lot of lies, were much more likely than other boys to deny, at the second interview, other kinds of deviant behavior to which they had previously admitted. It is a tribute to the efforts of a generation of researchers that interview methods for psychiatric disorders are as reliable as they currently are.

Developmental Epidemiology and Case Identification

One reason why establishing rates of disorder is a serious problem for child psychiatric epidemiology is that there is a need to reconcile a nondevelopmental psychiatric taxonomy, such as the DSM system, with the realities of child development. The DSM system sticks closely to an implicit medical model according to which a disease, although it has a developmental course along the lines sketched earlier, is defined as a disease by virtue of the fact that every case has roughly the same etiology, pathogenesis, risk factors, presentation, course, and treatment response. Measles is measles is measles. For example, the diagnostic criteria for DSM-IV major depressive episode are described as being similar in their essential features in children, adolescents, and adults (American Psychiatric Association, 1994). In the list of diagnostic criteria, the only differences specified are additions to two of the symptoms: "(1) depressed mood. In children and adolescents, can be irritable mood" and "(3) significant weight loss or weight gain. . . . In children, consider failure to make expected weight gains" (p. 327). A section on age-specific features of depression (p. 220) discusses symptoms or forms of comorbidity with other disorders that may occur with different frequency at different ages, but no reference is made to any aspect of children's cognitive, social, and bodily development that might influence a child's ability to experience, or respond to, different symptoms. Neither the similarities nor the differences specified by the DSM have a firm basis in developmental data about the manifestation of depression at different stages of life (Angold & Worthman, 1993; Cicchetti & Schneider-Rosen, 1984, 1986; Digdon & Gotlib, 1985). We shall return to this issue in more detail later. The point to be made here is that current views about the best way to identify cases of psychiatric disorders, for research and treatment, have emphasized the value of a single, development-free set of criteria, and that this creates considerable problems for child psychopathology and for epidemiologists involved in the task of operationalizing the DSM criteria for case identification.

In summary, epidemiology shares with clinical psychiatry a concern for, and involvement in, the problems of case identification. These problems occur at two levels: (a) the level of defining the characteristics of a disorder, and (b) the level of developing methods for identifying those who have the disorder so defined. Arguments about the "reliability" and "validity" of psychiatric assessment have frequently confused these two levels, as Robins has so clearly demonstrated (Robins, 1985, 1989). Only when we can clearly describe the causal pathway for each disorder, from exposure through onset to outcome, as in Figure 2.1, shall we be in a position to be satisfied with the validity of our taxonomy and the reliability of our diagnostic tools.

Controlling Bias in the Identification of Cases and Risk Factors

It is the nature of epidemiological research that questions of causality can rarely be answered by laboratory studies in which all but the key variable are carefully controlled or randomly varied. It is not feasible to test the causal role of poverty, for example, by randomly assigning newborns to be raised in high- and low-income households, or the role of maternal temperament by the sort of cross-fostering studies that are considered ethical with other primates (e.g., Suomi, 1991). One way to compensate is to pay very careful attention to the characteristics of the population from which the study samples are drawn; that is, not only to the *numerator* of a rate of disease (the number of cases within a given period) but also to the *denominator* of the rate (the population at risk). Only when we know that the sample selected for study accurately mirrors the population from which it is drawn (or when we know exactly what the biases are and how to control for them) can we specify exactly to whom our causal analyses apply. This necessity usually rules out samples of convenience and mandates very careful thought about the choice of population for a study. For example, if the question has to do with the causal role played by the peer group in adolescent delinquency, and the sample consists of young people recruited from 10th-grade classrooms, neither the denominator nor the numerator can, by definition, include persons who have dropped out of school. Thus, the conclusions about causal processes that can be drawn from such a study are limited to those relevant to 10th graders who attend school, not to the age-group in general. Because dropping out of school and delinquency are known to be associated, the selection of a school-based population may result, not just in a randomly unrepresentative sample, but in a sample that is biased in important ways.

Bias is a distortion in an estimate of the frequency of a disease that threatens the validity of an observed link between a putative causal factor and a disorder. A causal association can only be accepted as valid after a whole series of tests to eliminate possible causes of bias. One of the most dangerous forms of bias to which clinical studies of pathology are liable is ascertainment bias, often called "Berkson's bias" after the physician who first quantified it (Berkson, 1946). Berkson was concerned that physicians assumed "that cholecystic [gall bladder] disease is a provocative agent in the causation or aggravation of diabetes. In certain medical circles, the gall bladder was being removed as a treatment for diabetes" (Berkson, 1946, p. 48). A study of records at the Mayo Clinic, where Berkson worked, showed that cholecystitis was indeed more common in patients with diabetes than in the general population or in some other patient groups: for example, in patients who came to the clinic to get their eyes checked for glasses. But he went on to demonstrate that when the proportion of the population hospitalized with a disease is small, the ratio of multiple diagnoses to single diagnoses in the hospital will always be higher than in the population; and:

> [If] a patient is suffering from two diseases, each disease is itself aggravated in its symptoms and more likely to be noted by the patient . . . [the] . . . effect would be to increase relatively the representation of multiple diagnoses in the hospital, and in general to increase the discrepancy between hospital and parent population, even more than if the probabilities were independent. . . . This applies also to other similar problems, as for instance whether the incidence of say, heart disease, is different for laborers and farmers, if it is known that laborers and farmers are not represented in the hospital in the proportion that they occur in the community. . . . there does not appear to be any ready way of correcting the spurious correlation existing in the hospital population by any device that does not involve the acquisition of data which would themselves answer the primary question [i.e., by carrying out another study on a properly selected community sample]. (p. 50)

Berkson thus argued that it is more cost-efficient to carry out properly representative community studies earlier rather than later in the process of studying comorbidity and etiology, because bias-free studies have to be done at some point in any case. Meehl

(1992) is another writer who has pointed out that "Millions of dollars of tax money have been wasted" performing studies in clinical settings where the biases inherent in case selection mean that the studies cannot answer the questions about causal association that they are designed to address (p. 124).

The danger of ascertainment bias is one reason why many epidemiological studies use samples that are carefully selected to be representative of the general population. The disease of interest may be quite rare in the community, which often means that the case-identification stage of such studies is expensive; large numbers of people must be surveyed in order to identify a relatively small number of cases. With child psychiatric disorders, the issue is compounded because reports from different informants—parents, children, teachers, peers—identify very different children as "cases" (Achenbach, McConaughy, & Howell, 1987; Rutter et al., 1970). Depending on the question being studied, it may be necessary to interview three or more people in order to establish whether a child is or is not a case according to the study criteria. The risk factors for a disorder identified by one informant may also be quite different from the risk factors for the disorder as identified by another informant. For example, in a study of children with symptoms of hyperactivity, inattention, and impulsivity (Costello, Loeber, & Stouthamer-Loeber, 1991), 61% of children identified as hyperactive by both parents and teachers were boys; however, boys made up 77% of children identified as hyperactive by teachers alone, but only 38% of children identified by mothers alone. The utmost care is needed at every level of the process of case ascertainment, if the resulting sample is to be a valid reflection of the population from which it was drawn. If it is not, then the study findings relating causal factors to disease and outcome run the risk of being a poor reflection of the world outside that particular sample, and are therefore useless as a basis for public health policy. In the example cited, use of mothers' reports alone as the basis for case identification would have led to the conclusion that girls are more likely to be hyperactive than boys, and a study based on teachers' reports alone would have led to the opposite conclusion. For the researcher interested in developmental influences on the expression of psychopathology, the situation becomes even more complex. For example, Figure 2.6 shows the rate of separation anxiety symptoms reported by children between the ages of 7 and 11, and by parents about their children. The parents' report data showed low rates of symptoms, and no effect of the child's age on the rate of symptoms. The rate of symptoms reported by the children, in contrast, fell sharply as the age of the child increased. If the purpose of the study had been to select a sample of "cases" of separation anxiety disorder, the bias caused by relying exclusively on one informant or the other would have varied, depending on the age of the children surveyed.

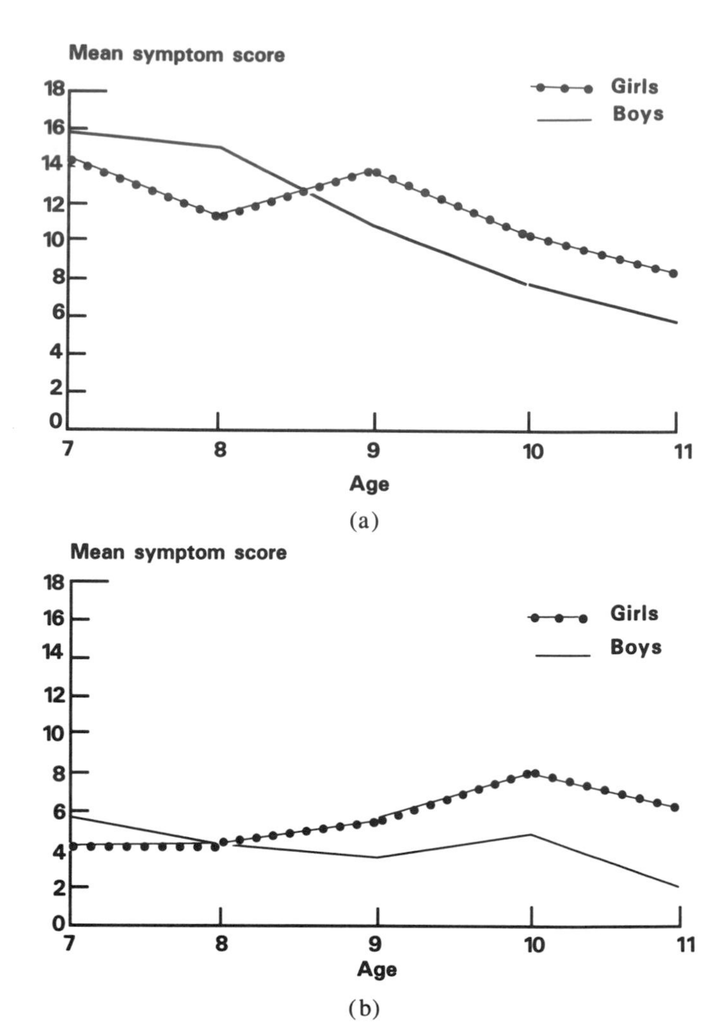

Figure 2.6 Separation anxiety symptoms in children ages 7 through 11: (a) children's reports; (b) parents' reports.

Controlling Bias in Estimating the Influence of Risk Factors

Apart from selection bias, the other major types of bias that threaten the validity of a causal link go under the general heading of *confounding*. In most etiological studies, more than one risk factor is involved. The problem is to figure out the relative importance of various risk factors, so that decisions about intervention can be focused where they will be most effective. It is useful to distinguish between two distinct characteristics of factors that influence the probability of disease: confounding and effect modification (Miettinen, 1974). *Confounding* distorts the impact of a risk factor on the risk of disease, because of the presence of some extraneous variable. A factor may act as a confounder in one study but not in another; for example, if race and poverty were strongly associated in one community and not in another, and one race but not the other carried a genetic risk factor for a particular disease, a "real" relationship between poverty and disease might be obscured in the first community, but not in the second. Almost everyone in the first community who was poor would also be from the affected race, so it would not be possible to say which factor was causing the disorder. In the second community, where not all the poor were of the affected race and not all the affected race were poor, it would be possible to look separately at the rates of disorder in four groups (poor nonaffected, rich nonaffected, poor affected, rich affected), and figure out which variable, race or poverty, carried the risk.

Effect modification or *synergy* refers to the different impact of a risk factor at different levels of another variable (Rothman, 1976). This relationship is not specific to any particular study; it is a "real" relationship among two or more risk factors. For example, if both the gene for phenylketonuria and a diet high in phenylalanine are necessary for PKU to occur, rates of the disorder will vary in different communities, depending on how many people inherit the gene and how many eat a high phenylalanine diet. The relationship between gene and diet remains constant across sites, but diet will act as an effect modifier, controlling the expression of the gene. Another example is the relationship among peak height velocity (PHV: the "growth spurt" of early adolescence), change of school, and depressive symptoms. The period of PHV may be a time when youngsters are particularly vulnerable to symptoms of depression (Simmons & Blyth, 1987), particularly when they have to deal with stressful events. It happens that, in the American school system, most children move from middle school to high school between eighth and ninth grades. This coincides with the time when many girls, but few boys, are at PHV. School change could thus be acting as an effect modifier, increasing the risk of depression in girls but not in boys.

Although a primary goal of epidemiology is to identify the causes of disease, most researchers prefer to use the term *risk factor* rather than *cause.* In practice, causal investigation rarely yields the pure, unique, perfectly predictable connection between two phenomena that etiologic research aims for. The term risk factor was coined by cardiovascular epidemiologists in the 1960s, when longitudinal community studies showed that their initial hypothesis of a single cause for cardiovascular disease was untenable (Kannel, 1990). Risk factors are associated with an increased probability of disease, but may not be causally related. Most diseases appear to have more than one cause—and most risk factors, more than one pathological effect. For example, many pathogens, such as the polio virus and the cholera vibrio, can exist in the human body without causing disease; they appear to be necessary for a specific disease to become manifest, but are not sufficient in themselves to cause disease (Rothman, 1976). Conversely, a causal agent can increase the probability of several diseases, and can do so via several different mechanisms; for example, smoking is a risk factor, by different causal pathways, for lung cancer, emphysema, and coronary heart disease.

In his discussion of causation from an epidemiological point of view, Rothman (1976) pointed out that a specific disorder may result from one or more "constellations of component causes," which may or may not have a common element. The idea is illustrated in Figure 2.7. The disorder in question has three "causal complexes"; each, in itself, is sufficient to cause the onset of illness. Each complex has five component causes. Component A is a necessary cause; it is present in each sufficient causal complex. Components B, C, and F appear in two, but not in all three sufficient causal complexes. They are not necessary causes: the disorder can occur without any one of them. Figure 2.7 demonstrates that the rate of occurrence of a disorder with multiple component causes will depend on many factors, among which the rate of occurrence of the least common component will act as a limit. This has important implications for prevention; if it is possible to identify a sufficient causal complex with reasonable confidence (Angold & Hay, 1993), it may make more sense to target the least frequently occurring component, or the component easiest to eradicate, rather than a necessary component. Thus, it is likely that there is a necessary genetic component to some psychiatric disorders. However, prevention of actual cases of such a disorder might be possible by eradicating other components of the causal complex that are more amenable to intervention than is DNA.

Another corollary of this model of causation pointed out by Rothman is that the same causal factor can interact in different ways with other causal factors. Two or more factors that are part of the same causal complex are synergistic; that is, neither can have any effect (within that causal complex) without the other's presence. However, one, another, or all may also be components of a different causal complex. This phenomenon would account for the observation that causal factors rarely appear to have complete synergy. In Figure 2.7, D and E are completely synergistic; they co-occur in causal complex I and nowhere else. Factors B and C are partially synergistic: they co-occur in one sufficient cause, but also appear independently (B in causal complex II and C in causal complex III). A and B would appear to be completely synergistic (and necessary) in environments where J was absent,

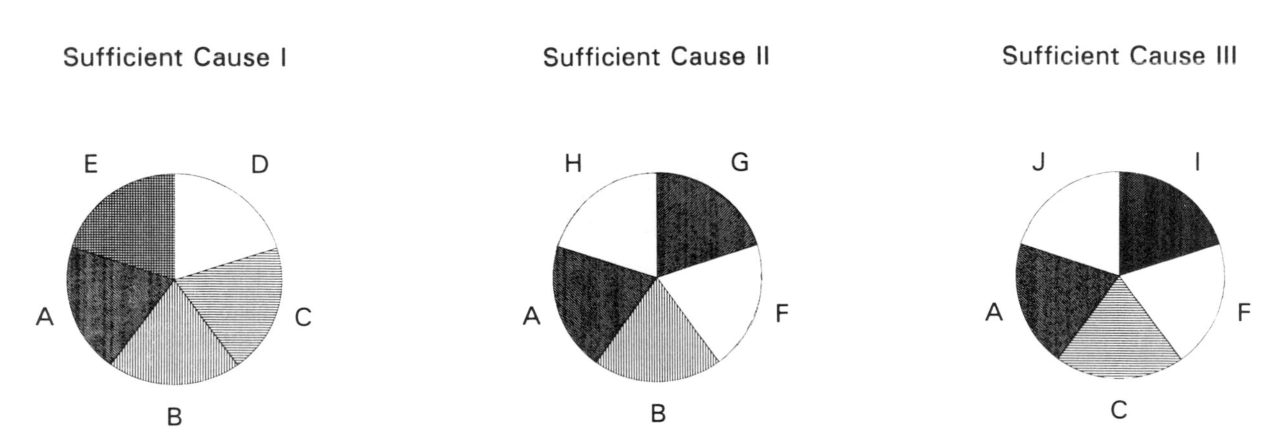

Figure 2.7 Conceptual scheme for the causes of a hypothetical disease.

because sufficient cause III would never occur. Where J was present, however, A and B would be only partially synergistic because within one causal complex the disorder could occur when A was present but B was not.

This approach to the search for causes has obvious developmental implications. It is easy to imagine, for example, a causal complex of genetic and environmental factors that could only give rise to overt disorder when the child was developmentally capable of certain cognitive or physical acts. For example, some of the behaviors included in the diagnostic criteria for conduct disorder, such as forced sex or armed robbery, require a level of physical strength or sexual development that rule them out until a certain age. But once that developmental stage is reached, the other component causes may already be in place.

Rothman's approach is appealing, if only because it shows how risk factors can operate independently, or additively, in some contexts, and synergistically, or multiplicatively, in others (Bebbington, Tennant, Sturt, & Hurry, 1984; Harris & Brown, 1985), but it is not an easy model to apply in the real world. How does one go about determining how many causal complexes there are for a single disorder (always assuming that the boundaries of the disorder in question have been clearly defined)? Despite these difficulties, the implications for prevention make this approach worth taking seriously. For example, the intensive Infant Health and Development Program, an intervention program for almost 1,000 low-birth weight, premature infants, sponsored in eight states by the Robert Wood Johnson Foundation, was shown to have a marked effect on the behavioral problems of these high-risk children *only if the mother was of low educational level.* In the rest of the group, the children's behavioral problems at age 3 were not affected by the intensive day-care program (Infant Health and Development Program, 1990). Birthweight by itself, among this sample of children weighing 2,500 grams or less at birth, did not predict behavioral problems at age 3. Low maternal educational level, however, did predict behavioral problems in the child. Because the causal complex leading from low birthweight to behavioral problems required low maternal education as part of the complex, it follows that the intervention only affected behavioral problems in children with both risk factors. Birthweight did affect the impact of the intervention program on the children's intelligence scores at age 3, whereas maternal educational level did not. Thus, by extension, an intervention study aimed at preventing behavioral problems in low-birthweight babies would need to be different from an intervention whose goal was raising intelligence; the first, perhaps, focusing on mothers' child-rearing skills, and the second directly on the children.

Adolescent depression provides another example of how normal developmental processes may be incorporated into a multistage causal model of disease onset. The problem is to explain the marked increase in depressive disorders observed in girls, but not in boys, once they reach adolescence (Angold & Rutter, 1992; Rutter, 1986a). In this case, one would postulate different causal clusters for boys and girls. Both may include many of the same risk factors—genetic predisposition, maternal depression, lack of an adult confidante, for example—but one of the clusters for girls would include physical maturation. It is not clear yet whether the crucial factor is hormonal, morphological, or social/maturational, or some combination of the three (Worthman, Stallings, & Gubernick, 1991). None of the causal clusters for depression in boys would include puberty as a component risk factor; in fact, recent evidence (Angold et al., 1994) suggests that it acts as a protective factor. For conduct disorders, by contrast, puberty may contribute in very different ways. Maturing earlier than the majority of girls, rather than puberty itself, seems to be part of one risk cluster for girls; puberty itself may possibly be a risk factor for boys (Angold & Worthman, 1993).

An example of a disorder with at least two identified causal clusters is alcohol abuse, according to Bohman, Sigvardsson, and Cloninger (1981). They studied a cohort of 862 illegitimate children adopted in infancy, of whom 151 had some record of alcohol abuse as adults. They identified a "Type I" causal cluster involving both genetic predisposition and adverse environmental factors (e.g., adoptive parents who abused alcohol), and a "Type II" cluster that was found only in males and was nine times as likely in the sons of biological fathers with a serious criminal record, independent of postadoption factors. Type I alcoholism had onset in adulthood and a milder course than Type II alcoholism, which had onset in adolescence. Others, however, have questioned the reality of the distinction between the two causal clusters, seeing a difference of degree of genetic liability rather than two distinct causal patterns (Hodgkinson, Mullan, & Murray, 1991).

Promotion and Detection Factors

Risk factors associated with a higher probability of the actual onset of disease are called *promoters;* those that are associated only with a higher probability of detection, but appear to have no etiologic importance, are called *detection factors* (Kleinbaum et al., 1982, p. 30). So far, little has been done in child psychiatric epidemiology to distinguish promotion from detection factors, or to trace their interrelationship developmentally. The idea that certain environmental phenomena could conversely be identified as *protective factors* has been widely discussed recently, in the context of developmental psychopathology (Garmezy, 1988). As Rutter (1985) has pointed out, there are logical problems in identifying something as a protective factor except in the presence of a risk or vulnerability; the concept of protection implies the presence of risk. However, in terms of Figure 2.1, it is reasonable to talk about protection from risk factors for a disease, as well as protection from risk of disease, given exposure. For example, decent sewage systems protect the whole community from exposure to the cholera vibrio, while good nutrition might help to protect an individual exposed to the infection from actually developing the disease.

One implication of the view of causality described here is that it is possible to rank risk factors in terms of their relative importance to the rate of observed disorder, and thus to make decisions about the most cost-efficient preventive strategies. There are several ways to calculate the importance of a risk factor in contributing to the prevalence of a disease. We shall refer to two of these: (a) risk ratio or *relative risk,* and (b) excess or *attributable risk.* Relative risk is a ratio comparing two risks of disease—often, the risk of a disease in a group exposed to a risk factor compared with the risk in a nonexposed group (e.g., the risk of depression in children of divorced parents compared with the risk to children in intact families). Attributable risk is an estimate of the extra cases of disease (above the rate in the nonexposed population) attributable to exposure to the risk factor. Attributable risk is a function of two factors: (a) the relative risk in groups exposed and not exposed to the risk factor, and (b) the frequency of the risk factor in the population. Thus, even if the relative risk associated with a risk factor is high, the attributable risk, and thus the decrease in incidence of the disease if that risk factor were removed, may be low if the proportion of people in the population exposed to that risk factor is low. For example, there might be a high relative risk for lung cancer associated with exposure to a chemical used only in one particular industry, but the excess risk would be low if only a few people worked in that industry and so were exposed to that chemical. In absolute terms, a greater reduction in the number of cases of lung cancer might be achieved by removing a risk factor with a lower relative risk but to which more people are exposed, for example, asbestos or cigarette smoke (Lilienfeld & Lilienfeld, 1980; Rothman, 1976). Another aspect of risk that has practical implications is the relationship between the prevalence of the disease and the prevalence of the risk factor. Even if the relative risk of the disease is high in the presence of the risk factor, if the disease is rare and the risk factor common, the effort required to prevent the disease by eliminating the risk factor may be disproportionately high.

Measures of relative risk are particularly important for the scientific aspect of epidemiology, because they are a way of estimating the causal impact of risk factors. Measures of attributable risk are of particular interest from the practical point of view, because they can generate an estimate of the impact of a risk or protective factor in real or proportional terms. For example, the risk attributable to smoking, based on 1976 data, was 79% for lung cancer and 26.7% for coronary heart disease (CHD). But because CHD was much commoner than lung cancer, the absolute number of CHD deaths that would have been prevented if no one had smoked was over twice the number of lung cancer deaths prevented (Kleinbaum et al., 1982, p. 170).

This discussion of causality begs an underlying question of whether it makes sense to think about human behavioral development at all in terms of continuity and causes. Some developmental psychologists have argued that prediction is not only difficult but also not a necessary concept for the study of psychopathology (Lewis, 1990). Epidemiology has not adopted this approach; on the contrary, it has put its money on its ability to control disease through the prediction of causal pathways, and historically this has been an immensely successful bet. The interesting question is whether it is an approach that will prove to be as effective in the area of developmental psychopathology as it has been for infectious diseases.

WHAT IS DEVELOPMENTAL EPIDEMIOLOGY?

The epidemiological model of the development of a disease is of particular interest in the context of child psychopathology because it has to be set alongside the other, implicit, developmental model: the model that describes the development of the individual. From this point of view, developmental epidemiology can be seen as concerned with the interaction between the developmental processes of the organism (the child) and of the disease. The importance of understanding this interaction was pointed out by Anna Freud (Cicchetti, 1990a; Freud, 1965; Rutter, 1988), but her view of what develops was somewhat different from the view of both developmental psychology and developmental psychopathology today. In this chapter, our use of the concept of development, which follows that of developmental psychology and biology, will be familiar to developmentalists, but carries different implications from those invoked for most child psychiatrists in the United States, who use the term "development" either in the context of psychodynamic theories of personality (Dare, 1985), or to refer to specific, largely cognitive abilities (American Psychiatric Association, 1994). For clarification, we preface the next section with a brief review of what we understand by development.

The Concept of Development

Earlier in this chapter, we discussed epidemiology as a scientific method of understanding the development of disease (see Figure 2.1). This approach shows marked similarities with the way the word *development* is applied to biological organisms (Hay & Angold, 1993). As Nagel (1957) defined it:

> [T]he concept of development involves two essential components: the notion of a system possessing a definite structure and a definite set of pre-existing capacities; and the notion of a sequential set of changes in the system, yielding relatively permanent but novel increments not only in its structure but in its modes of operation. (p. 15)

The process of disease progression has much in common with development: it is "programmed" by the nature of the transformation of the organism that begins the process, and in general it follows a reasonably regular course, although with wide variations in its rate. Furthermore, there is hierarchical integration as diseases develop. Each stage in the progress of a given disease builds on the previous stages, and many of the manifestations of earlier stages are "integrated" into later symptomatology. This has much in common with the idea of *epigenesis,* as developed by Gottlieb (1991), which is central to our thinking about development:

> Individual development is characterized by an increase of complexity of organization (i.e., the emergence of new structural and functional properties and competencies) at all levels of analysis (molecular, subcellular, cellular, organismic) as a consequence of horizontal and vertical coactions among the organisms' parts, including organism--environment coactions. Horizontal coactions are those that occur at the same level (gene–gene . . ., organism–organism), whereas vertical coactions occur at different levels (. . . cell–tissue, . . . behavioral activity–nervous system) and are reciprocal, meaning that they can influence each other in either direction, from lower to higher or from higher to lower levels of the developing system. (p. 7)

For example, the genome controls cell structure, but environmentally induced cytoplasmic changes are capable of switching genes on and off (e.g., Ho, 1984; Jollos, 1934); neural differentiation in the mammalian visual cortex is dramatically affected by sensory experience (e.g., Black & Greenough, 1986); neuroendocrine mechanisms are powerfully affected by sociocultural factors (e.g., Mineka, Gunnar, & Champoux, 1986; Worthman, 1987, 1990; Worthman & Konner, 1987). This concept of development (a) presupposes change and novelty, (b) underscores the importance of timing in behavioral establishment and organization, (c) emphasizes multiple determination, and (d) leads us *not* to expect invariant relationships between causes and outcomes across the span of development (Caccioppo & Tassinary, 1991; Cairns, 1991). (See Caspi and Moffitt (1991) and Magnusson (1988) for empirical examples of these points.)

Behavior is seen as resulting from the dynamic interaction of multiple interdependent systems in both the individual and the environment. As summarized by Eisenberg (1977), ". . . the process of development is the crucial link between genetic determinants and environmental variables, between individual psychology and sociology . . ." (p. 225). It is characteristic of such systems that they consist of feed-back and feed-forward loops of varying complexity. Organism and environment are mutually constraining, however, with the result that developmental pathways show relatively high levels of canalization (Angoff, 1988; Cairns, Gariépy, & Hood, 1990; Gottlieb, 1991; Greenough, 1991; McGue, 1989; Plomin, DeFries, & Loehlin, 1977; Scarr & McCartney, 1983). For example, consider the well-established path to substance abuse (Kandel & Davies, 1982):

Beer or wine → Cigarettes or hard liquor →
Marijuana → Other illicit drugs

It is characteristic of this pathway that the number of individuals at each level becomes smaller, but that those at the higher levels continue to show behaviors characteristic of the earlier stages. Having described such a pathway, the task is to understand the process by which it is established and invent preventive strategies appropriate to the various stages of the developmental pathway. Such strategies must be appropriate to the developmental stage of both the individual at risk and the disorder.

Research based on this view of development has been going on for several decades, as these volumes attest, but only recently has there been an effort to rethink child psychiatric epidemiology in terms of current views of development (Angold & Costello, 1991; Costello & Angold, 1993; Rutter, 1988). Conversely, until recently, developmental psychopathology has paid less attention to some of the key concerns of epidemiology—in particular, the importance of representative samples.

Implications of a Developmental Approach for Child Psychiatric Epidemiology

Child psychiatry, in its current manifestation in the United States, has modeled its nosology and its concepts of health and disease on adult psychiatry, using the same nomenclature and assumptions about causality, risk factors, course, and outcome. But children are not scaled-down adults, and this approach causes serious problems for the epidemiologist concerned with explaining patterns of disease distribution in the community. Why, for example, do rates of depressive disorders, which are low in prepubertal children of both sexes, continue low in postpubertal boys but rise very sharply in postpubertal girls (Angold & Rutter, 1992)? Is the increase causally associated with age, or with pubertal status, or with something else entirely? To understand these phenomena, it seems reasonable to postulate the need to take into account the reality that children are organisms developing at a different rate from adults; organisms in whom developmental changes dramatically alter both the ways in which they can manifest their genetic endowment and the nature of their interactions with their surroundings. Here we consider the implications of some basic principles of developmental theory for the epidemiology of child psychiatric disorders.

Development Implies Change

This may seem to be an obvious statement, but child psychiatric epidemiology has not always taken the idea of change very seriously. This is partly the result of the current systems for the classification of diseases, which are essentially nondevelopmental. Most disorders have definitions that take no account of age or developmental level, sometimes in spite of overwhelming evidence that age-dependent changes are a central feature of the phenomenology of the disorders involved. Conduct disorder is a good example. Figure 2.5 (from Loeber et al., 1994) summarizes three different developmental pathways involving antisocial behavior. If a cross-sectional, "snapshot" view is taken of their behavior, children who pursue any of these three pathways share many characteristics. Longitudinal studies, however, reveal different patterns. Children who follow the authority conflict path tend to show conduct problems early in life, to have trouble at school because of hyperactivity and learning difficulties as well as conduct problems, to explore a wide range of different deviant behaviors, and to remain deviant well into adulthood. Some of the same behaviors can be found in other children at any given time, but a group of these will follow a different, covert pathway, with a higher remission rate. These children tend to have started showing deviant behavior later in childhood than the first group, and to have had fewer problems at school or with peers. Longitudinal studies also suggest the existence of a third group who, like the first, are aggressively deviant in adolescence, but who showed little or no early conduct disorder. The evidence for these different developmental patterns has been pieced together from a multitude of different studies, using both clinical and population samples, and is much stronger for boys than for girls (Loeber & Baicker-McKee, 1990). As discussed earlier, child psychiatric epidemiology has followed the guidance of the American Psychiatric Association's *Diagnostic and Statistical Manual* (DSM-IV) (American Psychiatric Association, 1994) in largely ignoring changes in the expression of conduct disorder with age. Indeed, despite the strong evidence that conduct disorders, at least in the context of the aggressive/versatile pathway, are precursors of antisocial personality disorder in adults (Robins & Price, 1991; Robins & Wish, 1977), the DSM codes conduct disorders on Axis I (Clinical Disorders), and antisocial personality disorder in adults on Axis II (Personality Disorders and Mental Retardation).

Development Is Goal-Directed

If we accept what Mayr (1982) called the biological "metaphor" or "heuristic" of development, then we accept a teleonomic, goal-directed explanation as part of that metaphor. In Mayr's (1982) words:

> A physiological process or a behavior that owes its goal-directedness to the operation of a program can be designated as teleonomic . . . . All the processes of individual development (ontogeny) as well as all seemingly goal-directed behaviors of individuals fall in this category, and are characterized by two components: they are guided by a program, and they depend on the existence of some endpoint or goal which is foreseen in the program regulating the behavior. . . . Each particular program is the result of natural selection and is constantly adjusted by the selective value of the achieved endpoint. (p. 48)

Teleonomic activities are distinguished by Mayr from other types of teleological processes—most importantly, for our purposes, from those performed by *adapted systems* (e.g., the cardiovascular or respiratory systems) that "owe their adaptedness to a past selectionist process" (Mayr, 1982, p. 49; see also Hay & Angold, 1993).

A teleonomic, or orthogenetic, approach has particular advantages for developmental epidemiology, given its concern with disease elimination and service provision. It enables us to conceive of disease states in terms of inability to achieve one or more of the goals of development, and it points preventive efforts in the direction of those situations in which a particular process or task seems to be particularly salient at a certain phase of life. For example, Sroufe and Rutter (1984) have outlined "a series of developmental issues . . . based on the collective experience of numerous developmentalists . . . cutting across affective, cognitive, and social domains" (p. 22, reproduced in Table 2.4).

Table 2.4 has two major implications for epidemiology. First, it implies that if we want to prevent, for example, conduct disorders, we need to define the goal of orderly conduct and the various "systems" (affect, cognition, muscular control) that are most involved with regulating conduct at different developmental stages. For example, do children who have achieved the goal of forming secure attachments around one year of age find behavioral control easier than insecurely attached children? Although the links between emotional security and impulse control or socially responsible behavior are not simple ones, it is possible to use interventions to test a hierarchical, causal relationship among the various stages. (See Cicchetti (1990b) and Cicchetti and Toth (1992) for a more detailed discussion of this point.)

TABLE 2.4 Salient Development Issues

Age (Years)	Issues
0–1	Biological regulation; harmonious didactic interaction; formation of an effective attachment relationship
1–2.5	Exploration, experimentation, and mastery of the object world (care-giver as secure base); individualization and autonomy; responding to external control of impulses
3–5	Flexible self-control; self-reliance; initiative; identification and gender concept; establishing effective peer contacts (empathy)
6–12	Social understanding (equity, fairness); gender constancy; same-sex chumships; sense of "industry" (competence); school adjustment
13 +	"Formal operations" (flexible perspective taking; "as if" thinking); loyal friendships (same sex); beginning heterosexual relationships; emancipation; identity

From "The Domain of Developmental Psychopathology," by L. A. Sroufe and M. Rutter, 1984, *Child Development, 55*, p. 22.

A second, linked implication is that pathology that looks very different at different stages may be causally linked; for example, the "anxious attachment" of a 1-year-old may be causally linked to the emotional lability and superficial friendliness of the same child at age 5, and to an inability to form lasting intimate relationships as an adult. If this were the case, then, from a public health point of view, efforts to support secure attachments in infants would be justified, not just by the manifest anxiety of some 1-year-olds, which probably is not in itself a major public health issue, but by the chance of preventing the social disruption caused by those same children as adolescents and adults. However, there is very little empirical evidence so far for direct, causal links between failure to achieve a goal at one stage and specific pathologies at a later stage. Demonstrating such links as the basis for thoughtful interventions is, we believe, part of the task of developmental epidemiology.

The Goal of Development Is Normality

Normality is *a state not requiring intervention:* We would argue the value for developmental epidemiological research of taking the position that the goal of development is "normality." That is, among the multiple outcomes of any developmental process there exists a wide range that is not likely to cause a child any problems in moving to the next developmental phase or task; any of these outcomes should be defined as normal. Normality and pathology in an epidemiological context can thus be defined in terms of decision making: Is some sort of intervention indicated? In this respect, epidemiology moves along a different track from much of developmental psychopathology, which has tended to adopt the viewpoint of developmental psychology, that many phenomena of interest are best measured on some sort of continuous scale, representing a hypothesized underlying distribution of symptoms or capacities in the population. This makes sense for disciplines whose aim is to map out the pathways by which children's thoughts, feelings, and actions change over time under different internal and external controls. The specific concern of epidemiology, however, functioning as it does at the interface between scientific understanding and public health, is with those patterns of thought, feeling, and action about which "something must be done" at a given stage, for the sake of the child's present or future well-being, or in response to pressures from families, schools, or society in general. Thus, we define a developmental abnormality from an epidemiological point of view as "a state in which intervention is indicated," and normality as "a state in which intervention is not indicated." These definitions do not necessarily require that an effective intervention be available, only that pathology has a social meaning as well as a medical and a developmental one, and that a corollary of defining a syndrome as pathological is that one would intervene if it were feasible. In this, public health and clinical medicine are alike.

This view of normality and abnormality requires us to take into account not only the symptom or behavior, but also the developmental stage at which it occurs, in deciding whether to devote major efforts to prevention. Taking an example from externalizing behaviors, Loeber and Le Blanc (1990) pulled together evidence from many studies to argue that behavior that is not highly predictive of later conduct disorder in most children at a certain stage may be highly predictive in a specific child if (a) it first occurs earlier than in "normal" children; (b) it occurs with greater frequency than in "normal" children; and (c) it forms part of a "larger-than-normal" or more diversified symptom cluster. These developmental abnormalities frequently go together (Cohen, 1986; Farrington, 1983; Tolan, 1987). This implies that, for example, boys younger than 12 who commit minor acts of theft, vandalism, and substance abuse should be treated as showing a serious problem for which intervention is needed, whereas boys who first commit such acts after age 12 should not be treated so seriously. This is based on evidence that children who begin such acts early are likely to show a much higher rate of delinquency in their late teens than those who begin later (Fréchette & Le Blanc, 1987; Tolan, 1987), and to continue showing delinquent behavior for a longer period of time (Le Blanc & Fréchette, 1989).

These characteristics of development—goal-directed change toward developmentally appropriate, "normal" behavior—provide a framework within which to study patterns of pathology in time and space, and link the study of human development to the study of disease under the heading of developmental epidemiology.

EPIDEMIOLOGY AS A DEVELOPMENTAL METHOD

In this section, we consider ways in which epidemiology has tackled some of the problems of identifying and measuring causal processes leading to chronic disease, and we review their applicability to psychopathology. Much of this section is inspired by Breslow and Day's two volumes on *Statistical Methods in Cancer Research* (Breslow & Day, 1980, 1987). As those authors pointed out: "Most chronic diseases are the results of a process extending over decades, and many of the events occurring in this period play a substantial role. . . . In the study of physical growth, of mental and hormonal development, and in the process of aging, the essential feature . . . is that changes over time are followed at the individual level. Longitudinal surveillance and recording of these events is therefore a natural mode of study to obtain a complete picture of disease causation" (Breslow & Day, 1987, p. 2). Many psychiatric disorders fall into the category of chronic diseases, and the methods developed by cancer and cardiovascular epidemiologists to explore causal relationships in such diseases can, we believe, provide at least a useful starting place for thinking about psychiatric disorders. Chronic disease epidemiologists view the diseases they study as having inherent developmental processes of their own—processes that obey certain laws and follow certain stages even as they destroy the individual in whom they develop (Hay & Angold, 1993). In adopting this model of pathogenesis, developmental epidemiology takes a somewhat different viewpoint from that of developmental psychopathology in general (e.g., Cicchetti, 1984, 1990a; Cicchetti & Toth, 1992; Rutter, 1986b; Sroufe & Rutter, 1984). The focus of the latter has generally been on failures, delays, and distortions in "normal" development. Developmental epidemiology takes from medicine the model of a disease process with its own developmental processes and patterns, and asks what happens when the two developmental processes collide.

Risk, Exposure, and Time

Many questions can only be answered by methods that take into account temporal characteristics of risk factors, including their onset, and the "dose," or level of exposure, over time. Age at first exposure, time since first exposure, duration of exposure, and intensity of exposure are all interrelated aspects of timing that may have different implications for causality and thus for prevention. The kinds of questions we are thinking of include the following:

1. Does physical abuse by parental figures cause psychiatric disorders in children? Is a single blow a sufficient cause, or does abuse have to go on for a period of time, are at a certain level of severity, before it constitutes a risk factor? Are children of different ages or developmental stages differentially vulnerable to physical abuse as a risk factor? What risks are associated with removing children from home because of physical abuse? Is there a net reduction in risk attributable to the child protection policies currently in force?
2. Are children whose mothers are depressed at greater risk for psychopathology? Is the apparent excess of behavioral problems in these children an artefact of maternal overreporting? Is there a period during which maternal depression poses more of a risk than it does at other periods of development? Is there a genetic vulnerability expressed as depression in mothers and behavior problems in children?
3. Why are depressive disorders rare in both prepubertal girls and boys, but much more common in postpubertal girls? What causes the observed sex difference to develop? Is it associated with hormonal, morphological, or social changes occurring around puberty? Why is earlier-than-average maturation apparently a positive event for boys but a negative one, associated with increased risk of behavioral and school problems, for girls?

In this section, we examine methods that epidemiologists have used to examine risk factors for several chronic diseases, in terms of timing, duration, and dose or intensity of exposure. We then consider some examples that illustrate the applicability of this approach to developmental psychopathology.

Timing, Duration, and Dose

A risk factor may have a different impact on the risk of disease, depending on when it first occurs, how long it is present, and the level of intensity at which it occurs. For example, insulation workers exposed to asbestos had a cumulative risk of dying of mesothelioma over a 20-year period (controlling for other causes of death) that was the same irrespective of age at first exposure (Peto, Seidman, & Selikoff, 1982) (see Figure 2.8). In contrast,

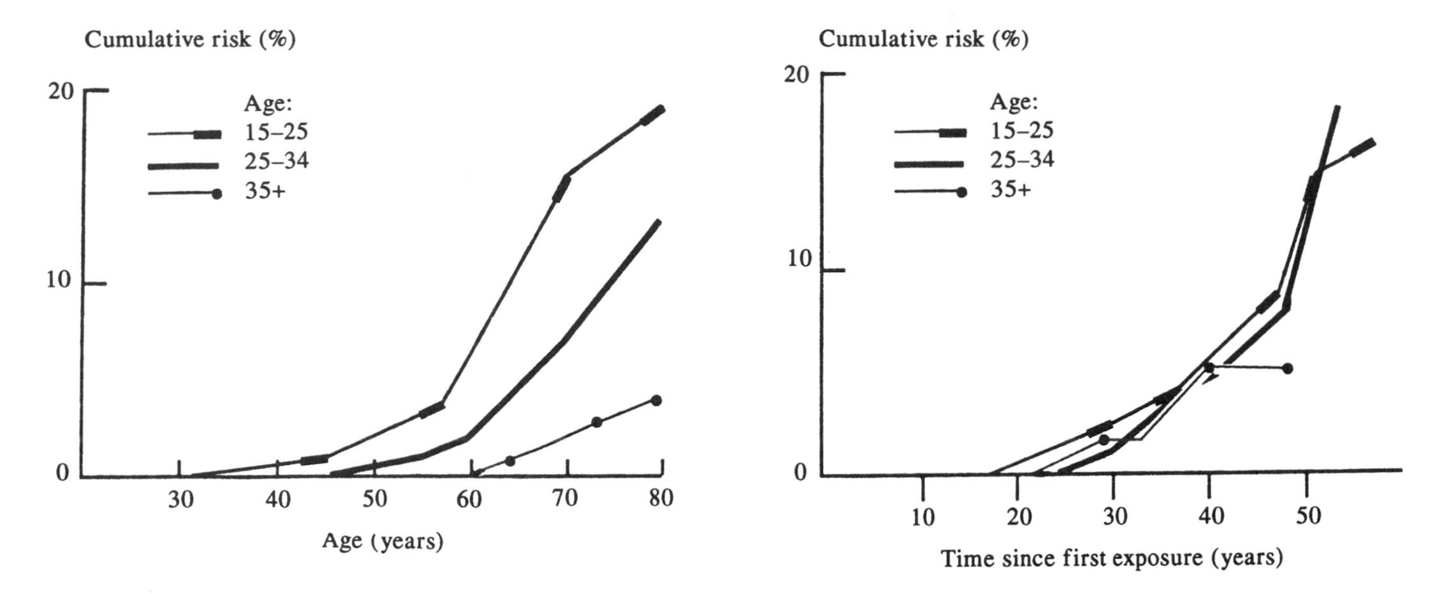

Figure 2.8 (a) Age at exposure and (b) years since exposure to disease.

the risk of breast cancer following irradiation appears to be highest in girls exposed at ages 0 through 9, falling with age until there is little excess risk for breast cancer associated with exposure to radiation after age 40. Cases of breast cancer attributable to irradiation begin to occur some 10 years after exposure, and continue thereafter at a roughly constant level, suggesting that the absolute excess risk increases with time since exposure (Howe, 1982). However, different sorts of radiation can have different durations as risk factors for cancer; for example, bone sarcomas occurring after exposure to the radioisotope ^{224}Ra, which has a half life of 3.6 days, cluster in a period of 5 to 10 years following first exposure, whereas bone sarcomas following exposure to ^{226}Ra, which has a half life of 1,600 years, occur at a constant rate beginning 5 years after first exposure (Mays & Spiess, 1984). In the latter case, exposure to the decay products of the radioisotope continue at virtually constant levels after absorption of the radium. A longitudinal study of British male doctors' smoking provides an example of dose-related risk: the annual death rate per 100,000 men, between 1951 and 1971, standardized for age, was 1,317 for nonsmokers, 1,518 for those currently smoking 1 to 14 cigarettes a day, 1,829 for those currently smoking 15 to 24 a day, and 2,452 for those smoking over 24 a day (Doll & Peto, 1976). For lung cancer deaths, the dose--response relationship was even more marked: 10 per 100,000 men for nonsmokers, 52 for those smoking 1 to 14 cigarettes a day, 106 for those smoking 15 to 24 a day, and 224 for those smoking over 24 a day.

These examples illustrate the importance, for causal research, of thinking separately about age at first exposure, time since first exposure, duration of exposure, and intensity of exposure. Thus, in the case of cigarette smoking and lung cancer, it appears that it is not the time since beginning to smoke, the age at beginning to smoke, or the duration of exposure (number of years of smoking) that matters so much as the absolute amount of the dose (total number of cigarettes smoked). However, time since the end of exposure (giving up smoking) proved to be important also: after 10 years without smoking, age-adjusted mortality rates among smokers fell to the level of those found in people who had never smoked (Breslow & Day, 1987).

Examples from Developmental Psychopathology

In child psychopathology, the importance of *age at first exposure* has been studied most intensively of all the aspects of risk over time, because of the theoretical importance attached to early experiences in the Freudian and other psychodynamic models of development. For example, researchers investigating the role of attachment in children's development have concentrated on the very early months and years of life as the crucial period during which the inability to form one or more such relationships may have damaging effects that last into childhood and perhaps even into adulthood (Sroufe, 1988). The critical date of onset of risk appears to occur after 6 months, but the duration of the risk period is not yet clear. Hay has presented evidence that maternal depression, which presumably interferes with mothers' ability to form normal relationships with their infants, affects motor development if it occurs during the first year of life, and language development but not motor development if it occurs during the second year of life (Hay, Kumar, & Everitt, 1992; Hay, Kumar, Sharp, Pawlby, & Schmücker, 1992). This is a case where age at first exposure appears to interact with the developmental processes most salient at a particular age.

Time since first exposure has rarely been treated separately in studies of child psychopathology. Brown and colleagues, in their work on the social origins of depression, argued that women who lost their mothers in the first decade of life were more vulnerable as adults to depressive episodes in the face of severe life events (Brown & Harris, 1978). However, theirs was a retrospective study that did not address the question of whether these women were also at greater risk of depressive episodes during later childhood and adolescence. It is not clear whether the crucial factor was the length of time since exposure to the risk factor of mother's death, or the age of the child at the time of exposure, or some combination of the two. In another example of the importance of timing of exposure to a risk factor, Rutter has pointed out that once children have achieved urinary continence at around age 2, there is a period of risk for relapse into incontinence that appears to coincide with starting school (Rutter, 1985). Once this period of risk is over, the chance of developing enuresis is very slight. In this case, age at exposure is clearly the critical developmental risk factor, because no parallel increase in functional enuresis occurs at later times of stress, such as moving to middle or high school, and there is no delay between the stress and the symptoms.

Duration of exposure to poverty was examined by Offord et al. (1992). In their repeated surveys of a representative sample of children in Ontario, they showed that children whose families were living below the poverty level at two measurement points were at increased risk of behavioral disorders, compared with children whose families were below the poverty level on one occasion only, or never. In the longitudinal study from New Zealand described earlier, Moffitt (1990) found that children identified at age 13 as both delinquent and hyperactive had experienced significantly more family adversity (poverty, poor maternal education and mental health), consistently from the age of 7, than children who were only delinquent or only hyperactive at age 13.

An example of work examining the combined effect of *timing and duration of exposure* is the research on the hospitalization of young children that was carried out in England in the 1950s and 1960s. The Robertsons' studies of children's distress and behavioral problems during and after going to a hospital (Robertson & Robertson, 1971) were probably overinterpreted at first, but subsequent studies (e.g., Douglas, 1975) led to a more refined model that more precisely defined the timing that was most likely to result in symptoms, the role played by duration of hospitalization, and the precise characteristics of the experience (separation from mother/pain/lack of predictability) that were most distressing, as a way of explaining the causal pathway from the experience to the symptoms. These exercises in description and explanation led to predictions about situations that minimize the dangers of hospitalization for young children, and to preventive interventions (mothers rooming in, preadmission preparation sessions) that are now standard practice in most hospitals.

Intensity of exposure to lead (Needleman & Bellinger, 1991), provides an example of a definite dose–response relationship. Another aspect of intensity is the number of different risk factors to which a child is exposed. Sameroff, Rutter, and others have pointed out that children exposed to one risk factor are at increased risk of exposure to others (e.g., poverty and no father in the home), and that the dose–response relationship to an increasing number of different risk factors is not a simple linear one. Most children appear to be able to cope with a single adverse circumstance, but rates of psychopathology rise sharply in children exposed to several adverse circumstances or events (Seifer, Sameroff, Baldwin, & Baldwin, 1989).

These examples show that it is possible to design studies that at least begin to allow us to tease out the respective roles played by time since first exposure, age at first exposure, duration of exposure, and intensity of exposure. The challenge is to incorporate all these aspects of risk into a single model, because all are clearly aspects of the risk–disease relationship for each disorder. Multistage models of risk, which have been developed to address the complexities of causality in chronic disease, are one way of putting the pieces together. Several such models have been proposed, particularly in the context of carcinogenesis (Peto, 1984), and have been reviewed in terms of developmental psychopathology by Pickles (1993).

Implications of Multistage Models for Understanding Causality

In cancer epidemiology, it has been possible to use observations about the onset of different cancers to develop and test theories about the characteristics of a hypothesized cause, and there is no reason why similar models should not be applied to psychopathology (see Pickles, 1993). For example, a useful distinction can be made between factors that act at an early phase in the process of carcinogenesis and factors that act at a late stage (Peto, 1984). Figure 2.9 illustrates the impact on rates of new cases across time of an exposure that operates continuously once it begins to operate, as a function of whether it operates on an early or a late stage of the process leading to overt disease. Relative to the "background" incidence rate in the population not exposed to the risk factor, the incidence rate if the risk factor affected an early stage in the development of the disease would rise sharply, because time since first exposure is of prime importance. However, if a late stage in the development of the disease is affected

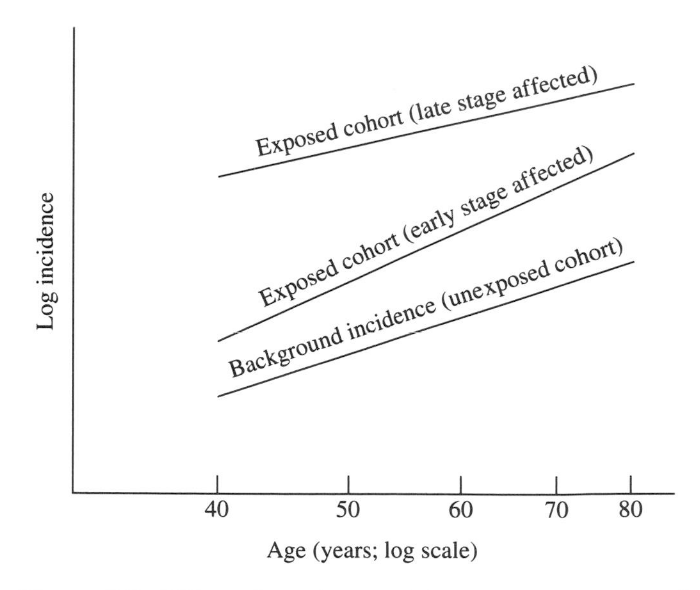

Figure 2.9 Effect of continuous risk exposure on onset of disease.

by the risk factor, age rather than time since first exposure is of primary importance, and relative risk is nearly independent of age at first exposure, for a given duration of exposure. Thus, the distribution of mesotheliomas in asbestos workers has been shown to fit the distribution that would be predicted from early-stage effects—that is, it can be described simply in terms of time since first exposure (Peto et al., 1982). In the case of lung cancer, however, asbestos appears to operate as a late-stage agent. In cancers of hormonally dependent organs such as the breast, models that fit the epidemiological data best are those that include age-related (or development-related) variations in the susceptibility of the target organ (Pike, Krailo, Henderson, Casagrande, & Hoel, 1983). Such variations include the decrease in susceptibility to breast cancer that comes with increasing parity, and endogenous late-stage agents related to ovarian activity that decrease after menopause (Breslow & Day, 1987). From these models come predictions about the relationships among risk, dose, and time that can be empirically tested.

Child psychiatry is still a long way from being able to make full use of the kinds of sophisticated developmental models of disease that characterize cancer or cardiovascular epidemiology. The problem is not so much inability to measure the component variables—as discussed elsewhere, measurement of both risk factors and disorders has improved markedly in recent years—as lack of good data tied to clear questions. Doll and his colleagues collected data for 20 years, from more than 43,000 male British doctors and 6,000 female doctors, to develop their multistage model of lung cancer. The follow-up of survivors of the Hiroshima and Nagasaki nuclear attacks involved some 30,000 people over 30 years. In both instances, the researchers were clear at the outset about the risk factor of interest, and had some ideas, however imprecise, about the causal chain linking exposure and outcome. Also, there was a national commitment to understanding the disease process, and a concomitant investment in the research.

Although there have been several fairly large, prospective studies of children in the past half-century (see Table 2.1), most have measured a wide variety of possible risk factors and outcomes in a fairly atheoretical fashion. One example of how data currently being collected can be used to look at developmental risk is the work of Moffitt on antecedents of ADD and delinquency in 13-year-olds (Moffitt, 1990). Using the longitudinal data from the Dunedin study (see above), Moffitt showed, for example:

> The most striking increase in the antisocial behavior of ADD+delinquent boys [diagnosed at age 13] occurred between the ages of 5 and 7, when they attained a mean antisocial rating that was not reached by other delinquent boys until 6 years later. School entry and reading failure coincided temporally with this exacerbation of antisocial behavior. These data suggest that the problem behavior of this group, despite being generally persistent, *is* responsive to experience. The data also reveal a key point of vulnerability that could be a target for intervention: reading readiness. (p. 906; see Figure 2.10)

In other analyses (see Figure 2.11), Moffitt showed that, on an index of family adversity constructed from measures of poverty, parental education and occupation, single parenting, family size, and maternal mental health, the ADD+delinquent children suffered greater adversity than all other groups at every age from 3 onward. The delinquent-only group reported greater adversity only at ages 11 and 13, not before that; nor could they be distinguished from the nondisordered and ADD-only groups earlier on measures of antisocial behavior. This suggests that (a) family adversity was not a sufficient cause of delinquency, in the absence of ADD, and (b) some of the markers of family adversity could have been family responses to the teenage boys' increasing delinquency rather than causes of it (again, in the absence of ADD).

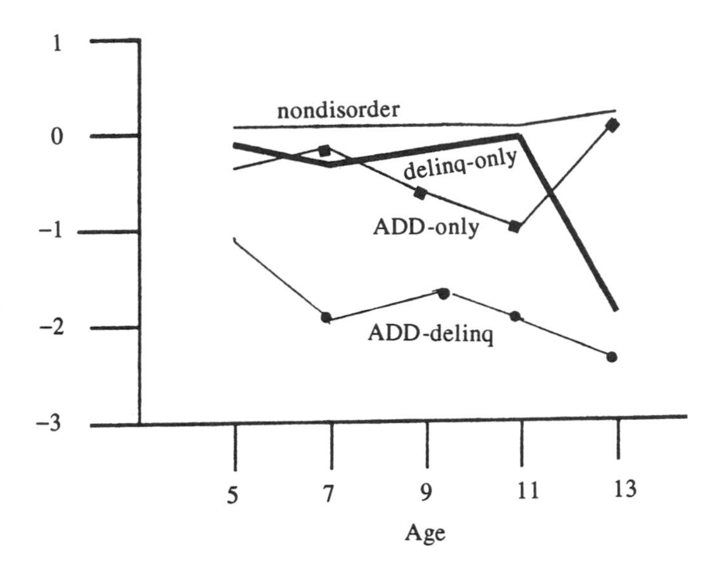

Figure 2.10 Effect of school entry on the antisocial behavior of boys with ADD + delinquency at age 13.

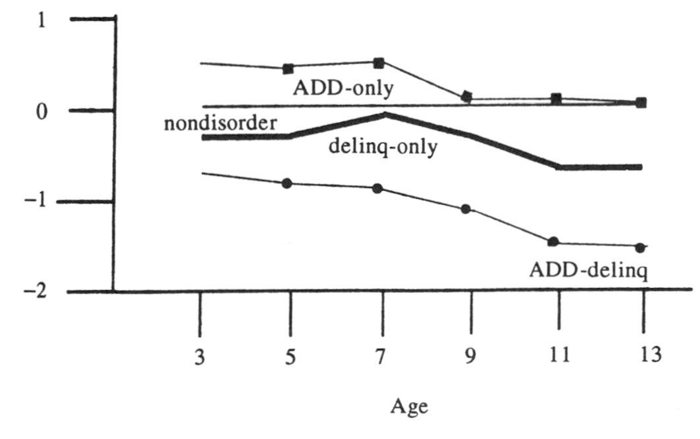

Figure 2.11 Family adversity and ADD + delinquency in adolescence.

As another example of a multistage model applied to a psychiatric outcome, consider the analysis by Kendler, Neale, Heath, Kessler, and Eaves (1991) of their data on current depressive symptoms and life events during the previous year, collected from 461 pairs of monozygotic twins and 363 pairs of dizygotic twins. First, they replicated the finding of McGuffin, Katz, and Bebbington (1988) that life events were familial, even when events that would clearly affect both twins, such as deaths of family members, were excluded. Second, they went on to show that if they divided life events into those that were clearly dependent on the subject's own behavior and those that were probably or clearly independent, heritable influences accounted for around 20% of the variation in "dependent" events, and familial/environmental factors around 10%, whereas for independent events the amount of variation attributable to heritable factors was negligible, compared with individual and familial/environmental factors, which together accounted for around 35% of the variance. Third, current depressive symptoms were modestly correlated; some 15% of the variance in scores could be attributed to genetic and familial/environmental factors, and the rest were the result of aspects of the individual environment, and measurement error. Fourth, the analyses carried out (structural equation modeling) gave the authors no reason to reject the hypothesis that the same genetic and familial/environmental factors influenced depressive symptoms in both low-stress and high-stress environments: "[T]hese findings are not consistent with the hypothesis that exposure to high levels of stress 'turns on' new genetic or familial environmental factors that are 'dormant' in low-stress environments" (Kendler et al., 1991, p. 161). However, genetic and/or familial environmental factors played a greater role in influencing depression in high-stress than low-stress environments. Finally, age at the time of the assessment, which varied from 18 to 50 years, did not affect the proportion of the variance in life events explained by familial environment. Data from this study could be used to test a multistage model in which the most vulnerable group throughout life would be individuals genetically at risk both for depression and for the kinds of life events that are dependent on one's own behavior. If such an individual lived in an environment that gave rise to life events that were independent of the individual's own behavior, the risk of depression would rise just as it would for anyone else. Thus, genetic risk for depression would contribute to at least two casual clusters, while genetic risk for dependent life events would contribute to one of those, as well as to a third cluster.

One of the problems with causal research in child psychopathology has been that the same set of risk factors—low socioeconomic status, parental mental or physical illness, inconsistent parenting—seems to recur in association with every disorder. Even specific psychiatric disorders in parents appear to increase the likelihood of childhood psychopathology in general, rather than simply the disorder from which the parent suffers (Weissman et al., 1987). However, these examples show that it is possible to develop causal models that begin to put risk factors into the kind of "causal complexes" that Rothman postulates, and to look for differences among age at exposure, duration of exposure, intensity of exposure, and multiplicity of exposures, as predictors of the onset of psychiatric disorders.

THE DEVELOPMENT OF DEVELOPMENTAL EPIDEMIOLOGY

The term *developmental epidemiology,* coined in the 1970s (Kellam, Brown, Rubin, & Ensminger, 1983), has recently come back into use as a focus for psychiatric epidemiological research that goes beyond "nose counting," to try to understand and control the onset of childhood disorders. Very few studies yet completed combine epidemiological standards of sampling and bias control with a developmental approach to questions of causality, although some are now in progress or planned (Costello, Angold, Burns, & Tweed, 1990; Earls, 1993; Jensen, 1992; Rutter, 1988). This final section summarizes the main themes that have been developed in this chapter, and points to where, we believe, research needs to be focused in the next decade if it is to make the best use of current developmental epidemiological methods to improve the mental health of children and adolescents.

This chapter has expanded on the theme that developmental epidemiology is about continuity and change in psychopathology; *describing* how disorders develop, *explaining* the observed patterns in terms of what is known about both human development and the development of the disease, *predicting* the distribution of disorders in the population, and using this knowledge for *controlling* the development of disorders (cf. Kleinbaum et al., 1982, p. 21). Describing continuity and change involves us in asking questions about rates of disorder across development; for example, what is the age of onset of various disorders? What is the time lag between onset and identification or diagnosis? Does the prevalence of different disorders change as children develop? What is the pattern of continuity from childhood into adolescence and adulthood? To explain what we observe, we have to understand the changing impact of risk factors for disorders over time. The questions about prediction and control of the development of disorders deal with whether, and how, treatment and prevention need to take developmental issues into account.

Continuity and Change in the Prevalence of Disorders

The evidence from recent studies using DSM categories, summarized in Table 2.1, suggests that, although the rates of specific psychiatric disorders change considerably across childhood and adolescence, there is also a certain amount of continuity over time; children who have a psychiatric disorder at one assessment are more likely to have one at a second assessment than are children originally without disorder.

Reasons for Change in Rates of Disorder

Prevalence studies, even longitudinal ones, provide only one piece of the information needed to understand the development of psychiatric disorders in terms of the model shown in Figure 2.1. Unfortunately, research in the areas of risk factor and outcome research has even further to go than research on the basic issues of continuity and change. For the most part, we lack both adequate measures and even an adequate understanding of the questions that have to be asked. Studies like that of Loeber and colleagues (Loeber et al., 1991), described earlier, begin to provide some of the information needed to fill in Figure 2.1 for conduct problems, and also to show us how the necessary studies can be designed and carried out. However, even within the single area of conduct disorders, there are still many questions to be answered. One of the most important is the nature of the developmental pathways for girls (there are no girls in Loeber et al.'s study). Another critical area is the temporal sequencing of symptoms in children with more than one disorder. For example, across a range of community studies, conduct disorders are between four times and ten times as common in children and adolescents with a depressive disorder as in other children (Angold & Costello, 1993, in press). Does this mean that depression is a risk factor for conduct disorder, or vice versa; or does some other causal complex underlie both? At present, we lack even reliable information about the sequence in which depressive and conduct symptoms develop in comorbid children.

Treatment and Prevention as Developmental Epidemiological Tools

This chapter has reiterated that the goal of epidemiology is to control illness, and treatment and prevention are the ways to do this. On the road toward that goal, it is important to make use of prevention and treatment trials as opportunities to test hypotheses about how psychopathology develops. Every clinical trial is implicitly a test of a causal theory. Unfortunately, referral biases or failures to control for potential confounders often reduce the value of such studies for epidemiological purposes. In particular, clinical and prevention studies that take developmental issues seriously are very rare (exceptions are: Kellam, Rebok, Ialongo, & Mayer, 1992; Kovacs, Feinberg, Crouse-Novak, Paulauskas, & Finkelstein, 1984a; Kovacs et al., 1984b; Kovacs, Gatsonis, Paulauskas, & Richards, 1989).

The Research Program for Developmental Epidemiology

The outlook is good for some useful work to be done in the next few years. The key descriptive and explanatory tasks are clearer than they ever have been, and trail-blazing studies like that of Loeber et al. (1991) provide guidance on how the work can be done. Methodologically, some good instruments for assessing psychopathology across the age range in the community have been developed, although there is a great deal still to be done, particularly in linking early childhood problems with later pathology. New instruments are also available in related areas, such as service seeking and barriers to treatment (Farmer, Angold, Burns, & Costello, in press; Goodman, Alegria, Hoven, Leaf, & Narrow, 1992). The assessment of risk factors is still patchy, but the need is recognized and progress is being made, both to adapt measures from developmental psychology (e.g., measures of peer relationships (Coie, Underwood, & Lochman, 1991) and early temperament and cognitive development (Earls & Reiss, 1991), and to develop new measures where none is available (e.g., traumatic life events (Angold et al., 1992)). Major advances have been made in the statistical analysis of large, complex data sets that include categorical variables, repeated waves of data collection, nested variables (e.g., children within families), and missing data, all of which are likely to occur in developmental epidemiological research.

Most importantly, there is now a growing group of researchers who see that development, as it is understood in contemporary biological thought, is a crucial concept for modern psychiatric epidemiology. Hay and Angold (1993) have shown that "the medical model" is inherently developmental; in this chapter, we have widened the argument to include one of medicine's basic sciences: epidemiology. We have found basic developmental principles, such as differentiation and hierarchical integration, to be helpful in identifying and formulating the key questions for epidemiological research. Of equal importance is the perception that epidemiology offers insights and methods that can be valuable for developmental psychopathology. The next decade will be an interesting one.

REFERENCES

Achenbach, T. M. (1985). *Assessment and taxonomy of child and adolescent psychopathology.* Beverly Hills, CA: Sage.

Achenbach, T. M., Conners, C. K., Quay, H. C., Verhulst, F. C., & Howell, C. T. (1989). Replication of empirically derived syndromes as a basis for taxonomy of child/adolescent psychopathology. *Journal of Abnormal Child Psychology, 17,* 299–323.

Achenbach, T. M., & Edelbrock, C. S. (1981). Behavioral problems and competencies reported by parents of normal and disturbed children aged four through sixteen. *Monographs of the Society for Research in Child Development, 46*(1, Serial No. 188).

Achenbach, T. M., & Edelbrock, C. S. (1983). Manual for the Child Behavior Checklist and Revised Child Behavior Profile. Burlington: University of Vermont, Department of Psychiatry.

Achenbach, T. M., McConaughy, S. H., & Howell, C. T. (1987). Child/adolescent behavioral and emotional problems: Implications of cross-informant correlations for situational specificity. *Psychological Bulletin, 101,* 213–232.

American Psychiatric Association. (1952, 1968, 1980, 1987, 1994). *Diagnostic and statistical manual of mental disorders* (1st ed., 2nd ed., 3rd ed., 3rd ed. rev., 4th ed.). Washington, DC: Author.

Anastasi, A. (1986). Evolving concepts of test validation. *Annals of Developmental Psychology, 37,* 1–15.

Anderson, J. C., Williams, S., McGee, R., & Silva, P. A. (1987). DSM-III disorders in preadolescent children: Prevalence in a large sample from the general population. *Archives of General Psychiatry, 44,* 69–77.

Anderson, J. C., Williams, S., McGee, R., & Silva, P. A. (1989). Cognitive and social correlates of DSM-III disorders in preadolescent children. *Journal of the American Academy of Child and Adolescent Psychiatry, 28,* 842–846.

Angoff, W. H. (1988). The nature–nurture debate, aptitudes, and group differences. *American Psychologist, 43,* 713–720.

Angold, A. (1988). Childhood and adolescent depression II: Research in clinical populations. *British Journal of Psychiatry, 153,* 476–492.

Angold, A., & Costello, E. J. (1991). Developing a developmental epidemiology. In D. Cicchetti & S. Toth (Eds.), *Rochester Symposium on Developmental Psychology* (Vol. 3, pp. 75–96). Rochester, NY: University of Rochester Press.

Angold, A., & Costello, E. J. (1993). Depressive comorbidity in children and adolescents: Empirical, theoretical, and methodological issues. *American Journal of Psychiatry, 150,* 1779–1791.

Angold, A., & Costello, E. J. (in press). A test–retest reliability of child-reported psychiatric symptoms and diagnoses using the Child and Adolescent Psychiatric Assessment (CAPA-C). *Psychological Medicine.*

Angold, A., Cox, A., Prendergast, M., Rutter, M., & Simonoff, E. (1992). *The Child and Adolescent Psychiatric Assessment (CAPA).* Unpublished document. Developmental Epidemiology Program, Duke University, Durham, NC.

Angold, A., & Hay, D. F. (1993). Precursors and causes in development and psychopathology: An afterword. In D. F. Hay & A. Angold (Eds.), *Precursors and causes in development and psychopathology* (pp. 293–312). Chichester, England: Wiley.

Angold, A., & Rutter, M. (1992). The effects of age and pubertal status on depression in a large clinical sample. *Development and Psychopathology, 4,* 5–28.

Angold, A., & Worthman, C. M. (1993). Puberty onset of gender differences in rates of depression: A developmental, epidemiologic and neuroendocrine perspective. *Journal of Affective Disorders, 29,* 145–158.

Bebbington, P. E., Tennant, C., Sturt, E., & Hurry, J. (1984). The domain of life events: A comparison of two techniques of description. *Psychological Medicine, 14,* 219–222.

Berkson, J. (1946). Limitations of the application of fourfold table analysis to hospital data. *Biometrics Bulletin, 2,* 47–52.

Black, J. E., & Greenough, W. T. (1986). Induction of pattern in neural structure by experience: Implications for cognitive development. In M. E. Lamb, A. Brown, & B. Rogoff (Eds.), *Advances in developmental psychology* (Vol. 4, pp. 1–50). Hillsdale, NJ: Erlbaum.

Bohman, M., Sigvardsson, S., & Cloninger, C. R. (1981). Maternal inheritance of alcohol abuse: Cross-fostering analysis of adopted women. *Archives of General Psychiatry, 38,* 965–969.

Brandenburg, N. A., Friedman, R. M., & Silver, S. E. (1990). The epidemiology of childhood psychiatric disorders. *Journal of the American Academy of Child and Adolescent Psychiatry, 29,* 76–83.

Breslow, N. E., & Day, N. E. (1980). *Statistical methods in cancer research: Vol. I. The analysis of case control studies.* Lyons, France: WHO International Agency for Research on Cancer.

Breslow, N. E., & Day, N. E. (1987). *Statistical methods in cancer research: Vol. II. The design and analysis of cohort studies.* Lyons, France: WHO International Agency for Research on Cancer.

Brown, G. W., & Harris, T. (1978). *Social origins of depression: A study of psychiatric disorder in women.* Cambridge, England: Tavistock Publications.

Burke, K. C., Burke, J. D., Jr., Regier, D. A., & Rae, D. S. (1990). Age at onset of selected mental disorders in five community populations. *Archives of General Psychiatry, 47,* 511–518.

Caccioppo, J. T., & Tassinary, L. G. (1991). Inferring psychological significance from physiological signals. *American Psychologist, 45,* 16–26.

Cairns, R. B. (1991). Multiple metaphors for a singular idea. *Developmental Psychology, 27,* 23–26.

Cairns, R. B., & Cairns, B. D. (1991). Social cognition and social networks: A developmental perspective. In D. J. Pepler & K. H. Rubin (Eds.), *The development and treatment of childhood aggression* (pp. 249–278). Hillsdale, NJ: Erlbaum.

Cairns, R. B., Gariépy, J. L., & Hood, K. E. (1990). Development, microevolution, and social behavior. *Psychological Review, 97,* 49–65.

Cantwell, D. P. (1988). DSM-III studies. In M. Rutter, A. H. Tuma, & I. S. Lann (Eds.), *Assessment and diagnosis in child psychopathology* (pp. 3–36). New York: Guilford.

Caspi, A., & Moffitt, T. E. (1991). Individual differences are accentuated during periods of social change: The sample case of girls at puberty. *Journal of Personality and Social Psychology, 61,* 157–168.

Chambers, W. J., Puig-Antich, J., Hirsch, M., Paez, P., Ambrosini, P. J., Tabrizi, M. A., & Davies, M. (1985). The assessment of affective disorders in children and adolescents by semistructured interview; test–retest reliability of the Schedule for Affective Disorders and Schizophrenia for School-age Children, Present Episode Version. *Archives of General Psychiatry, 42,* 696–702.

Chess, S., & Habibi, M. (1978). *Principles and practice of child psychiatry.* New York: Plenum.

Chess, S., & Habibi, M. (1986). *Principles and practice of child psychiatry* (2nd ed.). New York: Plenum.

Cicchetti, D. (1984). The emergence of developmental psychopathology. *Child Development, 55,* 1–7.

Cicchetti, D. (1990a). An historical perspective on the discipline of developmental psychopathology. In J. Rolf, A. Masten, D. Cicchetti, K. Neuchterlein, & S. Weintraub (Eds.), *Risk and protective factors in the development of psychopathology* (pp. 1–28). New York: Cambridge University Press.

Cicchetti, D. (1990b). Perspectives on the interface between normal and atypical development. *Developmental Psychopathology, 2,* 329–333.

Cicchetti, D., & Schneider-Rosen, K. (1984). Toward a developmental model of the depressive disorders. *New Directions for Child Development, 26,* 5–27.

Cicchetti, D., & Schneider-Rosen, K. (1986). An organizational approach to childhood depression. In M. Rutter, C. E. Izard, & P. B. Read (Eds.), *Depression in young people: Developmental and clinical perspectives* (pp. 71–134). New York: Guilford.

Cicchetti, D. V., Sparrow, S. S., Volkmar, F., Cohen, D., & Rourke, B. P. (1991). Establishing the reliability and validity of neuropsychological disorders with low base rates: Some recommended guidelines. *Journal of Clinical and Experimental Neuropsychology, 13,* 328–338.

Cicchetti, D., & Toth, S. L. (1992). The role of developmental theory in prevention and intervention. *Development and Psychopathology, 4,* 489–493.

Cohen, J. (1960). A coefficient of agreement for nominal scales. *Educational Psychology Measurement, 20,* 37–46.

Cohen, J. (1986). Research on criminal careers: Individual frequency rates and offense seriousness. In A. Blumstein, J. Cohen, J. A. Roth, & C. A. Vishar (Eds.), *Criminal careers and career criminals* (Vol. I, pp. 292–418). Washington, DC: National Academy Press.

Cohen, J. (1990). Things I have learned (so far). *American Psychologist, 45,* 1304–1312.

Cohen, P., Cohen, J., & Brook, J. (1993). An epidemiological study of disorders in late childhood and adolescence: 2. Persistence of disorders. *Journal of Child Psychology and Psychiatry, 34,* 869–877.

Coie, J. D., Underwood, M., & Lochman, J. E. (1991). Programmatic intervention with aggressive children in the school setting. In D. J. Pepler & K. H. Rubin (Eds.), *The development and treatment of childhood aggression* (pp. 389–410). Hillsdale, NJ: Erlbaum.

Connell, H. M., Irvine, L., & Rodney, J. (1982). Psychiatric disorder in Queensland primary schoolchildren. *Australian Pediatrics Journal, 18,* 177–180.

Costello, A. J., Edelbrock, C. S., Kalas, R., Kessler, M. D., & Klaric, S. H. (1982). *The National Institute of Mental Health Diagnostic Interview Schedule for Children (DISC).* Rockville, MD: National Institute of Mental Health.

Costello, E. J. (1989). Developments in child psychiatric epidemiology. *Journal of the American Academy of Child and Adolescent Psychiatry, 28,* 836–841.

Costello, E. J., & Angold, A. (1993). Toward a developmental epidemiology of the disruptive behavior disorders. *Development and Psychopathology, 5,* 91–101.

Costello, E. J., Angold, A., Burns, B. J., & Tweed, D. (1990). *Service use for alcohol, drug, and mental disorder comorbidity in rural adolescents* (NIMH RO1 MH48085). Rockville, MD: National Institute of Mental Health.

Costello, E. J., Burns, B. J., Angold, A., & Leaf, P. J. (1993). How can epidemiology improve mental health services for children and adolescents? *Journal of the Academy of Child and Adolescent Psychiatry, 32,* 1106–1113.

Costello, E. J., Costello, A. J., Edelbrock, C., Burns, B. J., Dulcan, M. K., Brent, D., & Janiszewski, S. (1988). Psychiatric disorders in pediatric primary care: Prevalence and risk factors. *Archives of General Psychiatry, 65,* 1107–1116.

Costello, E. J., & Janiszewski, S. (1990). Who gets treated? Factors associated with referral in children with psychiatric disorders. *Acta Psychiatrica Scandinavica, 81,* 523–529.

Costello, E. J., Loeber, R., & Stouthamer-Loeber, M. (1991). Pervasive and situational hyperactivity—confounding effect of informant: A research note. *Journal of Child Psychology and Psychiatry, 32,* 367–376.

Costello, E. J., Stouthamer-Loeber, M., & DeRosier, M. (1993, February). *Continuity and change in psychopathology from childhood to adolescence.* Paper presented at the annual meeting of the Society for Research in Child and Adolescent Psychopathology, Santa Fe, NM.

Dare, C. (1985). Psychoanalytic theories of development. In M. Rutter & L. Hersov (Eds.), *Child and adolescent psychiatry: Modern approaches* (2nd ed., pp. 204–215). Oxford, England: Blackwell.

Dawber, T. R. (1980). *The Framingham Study: The epidemiology of coronary heart disease.* Cambridge, MA: Harvard University Press.

Digdon, N., & Gotlib, I. H. (1985). Developmental considerations in the study of childhood depression. *Developmental Review, 5,* 162–199.

Doll, R., & Peto, R. (1976). Mortality in relation to smoking: 20 years' observations on male British doctors. *British Medical Journal, ii,* 1525–1536.

Douglas, J. W. B. (1975). Early hospital admission and later disturbance of behavior and learning. *Developmental Medicine and Child Neurology, 17,* 456–480.

Down, J. (1867). Observations on an ethnic classification of idiots. *Journal of Mental Science, 13,* 121–123.

Dulcan, M. K., Costello, E. J., Costello, A. J., Edelbrock, C., Brent, D., & Janiszewski, S. (1990). The pediatrician as gatekeeper to mental health care for children: Do parents' concerns open the gate? *Journal of the American Academy of Child and Adolescent Psychiatry, 29,* 453–458.

Earls, F. (1979). Epidemiology and child psychiatry: Historical and conceptual development. *Comprehensive Psychiatry, 20,* 256–269.

Earls, F. (1980). Prevalence of behavior problems in 3-year-old children: A cross-national replication. *Archives of General Psychiatry, 37,* 1153–1157.

Earls, F. (1993). *Third annual report of the developmental epidemiology unit of the program on human development and criminal behavior.* Cambridge, MA: Harvard School of Public Health.

Earls, F., & Reiss, A. J. (1991). *Annual report of the program on human development and criminal behavior.* Cambridge, MA: Harvard School of Public Health.

Eisenberg, L. (1977). Development as a unifying concept in psychiatry. *British Journal of Psychiatry, 131,* 225–237.

Esser, G., Schmidt, M. H., & Woerner, W. (1990). Epidemiology and course of psychiatric disorders in school-age children—results of a longitudinal study. *Journal of Child Psychology and Psychiatry, 31,* 243–263.

Farmer, E. M. Z., Angold, A., Burns, B. J., & Costello, E. J. (in press). Reliability of self-reported service use: Test–retest consistency of children's responses to the Child and Adolescent Services Assessment (CASA). *Journal of Child and Family Studies.*

Farrington, D. P. (1983). Offending from 10 to 25 years of age. In K. T. VanDusen & S. A. Mednick (Eds.), *Prospective studies of crime and delinquency* (pp. 17–38). Boston: Kluwer-Nijhoff.

Fréchette, M., & Le Blanc, M. (1987). *Délinquences et délinquants.* Chicoutimi, Québec: Gaetan Morin.

Freedman, D. X. (1984). Psychiatric epidemiology counts. *Archives of General Psychiatry, 41,* 931–933.

Freud, A. (1965). *Normality and pathology in childhood.* New York: International Universities Press.

Galen, R. S., & Gambino, R. (1975). *Beyond normality: The predictive value and efficiency of medical diagnosis.* New York: Wiley.

Garmezy, N. (1988). Longitudinal strategies, causal reasoning and risk research: A commentary. In M. Rutter (Ed.), *Studies of psychosocial risk* (pp. 29–44). Cambridge, England: Cambridge University Press.

Goodman, S., Alegria, M., Hoven, C., Leaf, P., & Narrow, W. (1992). *Core service utilization and risk factor (SURF) modules.* Unpublished document.

Gottlieb, G. (1991). Experiential canalization of behavioral development: Theory. *Developmental Psychology, 27,* 4–13.

Gould, M. S., Wunsch-Hitzig, R., & Dohrenwend, B. P. (1980). Formulation of hypotheses about the prevalence, treatment and prognostic significance of psychiatric disorders in children in the United States. In B. P. Dohrenwend (Ed.), *Mental illness in the United States: Epidemiological estimates* (pp. 9–44). New York: Praeger.

Graham, P., & Rutter, M. (1973). Psychiatric disorders in the young adolescent: A follow-up study. *Proceedings of the Royal Society of Medicine, 66,* 1226–1229.

Greenough, W. T. (1991). Experience as a component of normal development: Evolutionary considerations. *Developmental Psychology, 27,* 14–17.

Grob, G. (1985). The origins of American psychiatric epidemiology. *American Journal of Public Health, 75,* 229–236.

Harris, T., & Brown, G. W. (1985). Interpreting data in aetiological studies of affective disorder: Some pitfalls and ambiguities. *British Journal of Psychiatry, 147,* 5–15.

Hay, D. F., & Angold, A. (1993). Introduction: Precursors and causes of development and pathogenesis. In D. F. Hay & A. Angold (Eds.), *Precursors and causes in development and psychopathology* (pp. 1–21). Chichester, England: Wiley.

Hay, D. F., Kumar, R., & Everitt, B. (1992). Material presented at the British Psychological Society Developmental Section Conference, Edinburgh, Scotland.

Hay, D. F., Kumar, R., Sharp, D., Pawlby, S., & Schmücker, G. (1992). Material presented at the British Psychological Society Developmental Section Conference, Edinburgh, Scotland.

Herjanic, B., & Campbell, W. (1977). Differentiating psychiatrically disturbed children on the basis of a structured interview. *Journal of Abnormal Child Psychology, 5,* 127–134.

Ho, M. W. (1984). Environment and heredity in evolution. In M. W. Ho & P. T. Saunders (Eds.), *Beyond neo-Darwinism: An introduction to the new evolutionary paradigm* (pp. 267–289). San Diego, CA: Academic Press.

Hodges, K., Klein, J., Fitch, P., McKnew, D., & Cytryn, L. (1981). The Child Assessment Schedule. *Catalog Selected Documents Psychology, 11,* 56.

Hodgkinson, S., Mullan, M., & Murray, R. (1991). The genetics of vulnerability to alcoholism. In P. McGuffin & R. Murray (Eds.), *The new genetics of mental illness* (pp. 183–197). Oxford, England: Butterworth-Heinemann.

Howe, G. R. (1982). Epidemiology of radiogenic breast cancer. In J. D. Boice, Jr. & J. R. Fraumeni, Jr. (Eds.), *Radiation carcinogenesis: Epidemiology and biological significance* (pp. 119–129). New York: Raven Press.

Infant Health and Development Program, The. (1990). Enhancing the outcomes of low-birth-weight, premature infants: A multi-site, randomized trial. *Journal of the American Medical Association, 263,* 3035–3042.

Ireland, W. W. (1877). *On idiocy and imbecility.* London: Churchill.

Jablensky, A. (1986). Epidemiological surveys of mental health of geographically defined populations in Europe. In M. M. Weissman, J. K. Myers, & C. E. Ross (Eds.), *Community surveys of psychiatric disorders* (pp. 257–313). New Brunswick, NJ: Rutgers University Press.

Jensen, P. (1992, December). *National Institute of Mental Health: Conference on Developmental Approaches to the Assessment of Psychopathology.* Rockville, MD: National Institute of Mental Health.

Jollos, V. (1934). Inherited changes produced by heat treatment in Drosophila melanogaster. *Genetics, 16,* 476–494.

Kandel, D. B., & Davies, M. (1982). Epidemiology of depressive mood in adolescents: An empirical study. *Archives of General Psychiatry, 39,* 1205–1212.

Kannel, W. B. (1990). Contribution of the Framingham Study to preventive cardiology. *Journal of the American College of Cardiology, 15,* 206–211.

Kanner, L. (1945). *Child psychiatry.* Springfield, IL: Thomas.

Kanner, L. (1972). *Child psychiatry* (4th ed.). Springfield, IL: Thomas.

Kashani, J. H., McGee, R. O., Clarkson, S. E., Anderson, J. C., Walton, L. A., Williams, S., Silva, P. A., Robins, A. J., Cytryn, L., & McKnew, D. H. (1983). Depression in a sample of 9-year-old children: Prevalence and associated characteristics. *Archives of General Psychiatry, 40,* 1217–1223.

Kellam, S. G., Brown, C. H., Rubin, B. R., & Ensminger, M. E. (1983). Paths leading to teenage psychiatric symptoms and substance use: Developmental epidemiological studies in Woodlawn. In S. B. Guzé, F. J. Earls, & J. E. Barrett (Eds.), *Childhood psychopathology and development* (pp. 17–51). New York: Raven Press.

Kellam, S. G., Rebok, G. W., Ialongo, N., & Mayer, L. S. (1992). The course and malleability of aggressive behavior from early first grade into middle school: Results of a developmental epidemiologically based preventive trial. *Journal of Child Psychology and Psychiatry, 35,* 281–295.

Kendell, R. E. (1976). The classification of depressions: A review of contemporary confusion. *British Journal of Psychiatry, 129,* 15–28.

Kendler, K. S., Neale, M. C., Heath, A. C., Kessler, R. C., & Eaves, L. J. (1991). Life events and depressive symptoms: A twin study perspective. In P. McGuffin & R. Murray (Eds.), *The new genetics of mental illness* (pp. 146–164). Oxford, England: Butterworth-Heinemann.

Kleinbaum, D. G., Kupper, L. L., & Morgenstern, H. (1982). *Epidemiologic research: Principles and quantitative methods.* New York: Van Nostrand-Reinhold.

Kovacs, M., Feinberg, T. L., Crouse-Novak, M. A., Paulauskas, S. L., & Finkelstein, R. (1984a). Depressive disorders in childhood: I. A longitudinal prospective study of characteristics and recovery. *Archives of General Psychiatry, 41,* 229–237.

Kovacs, M., Feinberg, T. L., Crouse-Novak, M., Paulauskas, S. L., Pollock, M., & Finkelstein, R. (1984b). Depressive disorders in childhood: II. A longitudinal study of the risk for a subsequent major depression. *Archives of General Psychiatry, 41,* 643–649.

Kovacs, M., Gatsonis, C., Paulauskas, S. L., & Richards, C. (1989). Depressive disorders in childhood: IV. A longitudinal study of comorbidity with and risk for anxiety disorders. *Archives of General Psychiatry, 46,* 776–782.

Lapouse, R. L., & Monk, M. A. (1958). An epidemiologic study of behavior characteristics in children. *American Journal of Public Health, 48,* 1134–1144.

Laucht, M., & Schmidt, M. H. (1987). Psychiatric disorders at the age of 13: Results and problems of a long-term study. In B. Cooper (Ed.), *Psychiatric epidemiology: Progress and prospects* (pp. 212–224). London: Croom Helm.

Le Blanc, M., & Fréchette, M. (1989). *Male criminal activity from childhood through youth: Multilevel and developmental perspectives.* New York: Springer-Verlag.

Lewis, M. (1990). Challenges to the study of developmental psychopathology. In M. Lewis & S. M. Miller (Eds.), *Handbook of developmental psychopathology* (pp. 29–40). New York: Plenum.

Lilienfeld, A. M., & Lilienfeld, D. E. (1980). *Foundations of epidemiology* (2nd ed.). New York: Oxford University Press.

Loeber, R. (1991). Questions and advances in the study of developmental pathways. In D. Cicchetti & S. Toth (Eds.), *Rochester Symposium on Developmental Psychopathology, Volume 3: Models and Integrations* (pp. 97–116). Rochester: University of Rochester Press.

Loeber, R., & Baicker-McKee, C. (1990). *The changing manifestations of disruptive antisocial behavior from childhood to early adulthood: Evolution or tautology.* Unpublished.

Loeber, R., Keenan, K., & Zhang, Q. (1994). Boys' experimentation and persistence in developmental pathways toward serious delinquency. Unpublished.

Loeber, R., & Le Blanc, M. (1990). Toward a developmental criminology. In M. Tonry & N. Morris (Eds.), *Crime and justice: An annual review* (12th ed., pp. 375–473). Chicago: University of Chicago Press.

Loeber, R., Stouthamer-Loeber, M., Van Kammen, W., & Farrington, D. P. (1991). Initiation, escalation and desistance in juvenile offending and their correlates. *The Journal of Criminal Law and Criminology, 82,* 36–82.

Magnusson, D. (1988). *Individual development from an interactional perspective: A longitudinal study.* Hillsdale, NJ: Erlbaum.

Magnusson, D., & Bergman, L. R. (1990). A pattern approach to the study of pathways from childhood to adulthood. In L. Robins &

M. Rutter (Eds.), *Straight and devious pathways from childhood to adulthood* (pp. 101–115). Cambridge, England: Cambridge University Press.

Maudsley, H. (1879). *The pathology of mind* (3rd ed.). London: Macmillan.

Mayr, R. (1982). *The growth of biological thought: Diversity, evolution and intelligence.* Cambridge, MA: Harvard University Press.

Mays, C. W., & Spiess, H. (1984). Bone sarcomas in patients given radium-224. In J. D. Boice, Jr. & J. F. Fraumeni, Jr. (Eds.), *Radiation carcinogenesis: Epidemiology and biological significance* (pp. 241–252). New York: Raven Press.

McConanghy, S. H., Stanger, C., & Achenbach, T. M. (1992). Three-year course of behavioral/emotional problems in a national sample of 4- to 16-year-olds: I. Agreement among informants. *Journal of the American Academy of Child and Adolescent Psychiatry, 31,* 932–940.

McGee, R., Feehan, M., Williams, S., & Anderson, J. C. (1992). DSM-III disorders from age 11 to age 15 years. *Journal of the American Academy of Child and Adolescent Psychiatry, 31,* 50–59.

McGee, R., Freehan, M., Williams, S., Partridge, F., Silva, P. A., & Kelly, J. (1990). DSM-III disorders in a large sample of adolescents. *Journal of the American Academy of Child and Adolescent Psychiatry, 29,* 611–614.

McGee, R., Partridge, F., Williams, S., & Silva, P. A. (1991). A twelve-year follow-up of preschool hyperactive children. *Journal of the American Academy of Child and Adolescent Psychiatry, 30,* 224–232.

McGue, M. (1989). Nature–nurture and intelligence. *Nature, 340,* 507–508.

McGuffin, P., Katz, R., & Bebbington, P. (1988). The Camberwell collaborative depression study: III. Depression and adversity in the relatives of depressed problems. *British Journal of Psychiatry, 152,* 755–782.

Meehl, P. E. (1954). *Clinical versus statistical prediction: A theoretical analysis and review of the evidence.* Minneapolis: University of Minnesota Press.

Meehl, P. E. (1992). Factors and taxa, traits and types, differences of degree and differences in kind. *Journal of Personality, 60,* 117–174.

Miettinen, O. S. (1974). Confounding and effect modification. *American Journal of Epidemiology, 100,* 350–353.

Mineka, S., Gunnar, M., & Champoux, M. (1986). Control and early socioemotional development: Infant rhesus monkeys reared in controllable versus uncontrollable environments. *Child Development, 57,* 1241–1256.

Moffitt, T. E. (1990). Juvenile delinquency and attention deficit disorder: Boys' developmental trajectories from age 3 to age 15. *Child Development, 61,* 893–910.

Nagel, E. (1957). Determinism and development. In D. B. Harris (Ed.), *The concept of development* (pp. 15–26). Minneapolis: University of Minnesota Press.

Needleman, H. L., & Bellinger, D. (1991). The health effects of low-level exposure to lead. *Annual Review of Public Health, 12,* 111–140.

Offord, D. R., Boyle, M. H., Racine, Y. A., Fleming, J. E., Cadman, D. T., Blum, H. M., Byrne, C., Links, P. S., Lipman, E. L., MacMillan, H. L., Grant, N. I. R., Sanford, M. N., Szatmari, P., Thomas, H., & Woodward, C. A. (1992). Outcome, prognosis, and risk in a longitudinal follow-up study. *Journal of the American Academy of Child and Adolescent Psychiatry, 31,* 916–923.

Offord, D. R., Boyle, M. H., Szatmari, P., Rae-Grant, N. I., Links, P. S., Cadman, D. T., Byles, J. A., Crawford, J. W., Munroe-Blum, H., Byrne, C., Thomas, H., & Woodward, C. A. (1987). Ontario child health study. II. Six month prevalence of disorder and rates of service utilization. *Archives of General Psychiatry, 44,* 832–836.

Peto, J. (1984). Early- and late-stage carcinogenesis in mouse skin and in man. In M. Börzsönyi, N. E. Day, K. Lapis, & H. Yamasaki (Eds.), *Models, mechanisms and etiology of tumour promotion (IARC Scientific Publications No. 56)* (pp. 359–371). Lyons, France: International Agency for Research on Cancer.

Peto, J., Seidman, H., & Selikoff, I. J. (1982). Mesothelioma mortality in asbestos workers: Implications for models of carcinogenesis and risk assessment. *British Journal of Cancer, 45,* 124–135.

Pickles, A. (1993). Stages, precursors and causes in development. In D. F. Hay & A. Angold (Eds.), *Precursors and causes in development and psychopathology* (pp. 23–49). Chichester, England: Wiley.

Pike, M. C., Krailo, M. D., Henderson, B. E., Casagrande, J. T., & Hoel, D. G. (1983). "Hormonal" risk factors, "breast tissue age" and the age-incidence of breast cancer. *Nature, 303,* 767–770.

Plomin, R., DeFries, J. C., & Loehlin, J. C. (1977). Genotype–environment interaction and correlation in the analysis of human behavior. *Psychological Bulletin, 84,* 309–322.

Prichard, J. C. (1837). *A treatise on insanity and other disorders affecting the mind.* Philadelphia: Haswell, Barrington & Haswell.

Richman, N., Stevenson, J., & Graham, P. (1982). *Preschool to school: A behavioral study.* London: Academic Press.

Robertson, J., & Robertson, J. (1971). Young children in brief separations: A fresh look. *Psychoanalytic Study of the Child, 26,* 262–315.

Robins, L. N. (1985). Epidemiology: Reflections on testing the validity of psychiatric interviews. *Archives of General Psychiatry, 42,* 918–924.

Robins, L. N. (1989). Diagnostic grammar and assessment: Translating criteria into questions. *Psychological Medicine, 19,* 57–68.

Robins, L. N., & Price, R. K. (1991). Adult disorders predicted by childhood conduct problems: results from the NIMH epidemiologic catchment area project. *Psychiatry, 54,* 113–132.

Robins, L. N., & Wish, E. (1977). Childhood deviance as a developmental process: A study of 223 urban Black men from birth to 18. *Social Forces, 56,* 448–473.

Rothman, K. J. (1976). Review and commentary: Causes. *American Journal of Epidemiology, 104,* 587–592.

Rutter, M. (1985). Resilience in the face of adversity: Protective factors and resistance to psychiatric disorder. *British Journal of Psychiatry, 147,* 598–611.

Rutter, M. (1986a). The developmental psychopathology of depression: Issues and perspectives. In M. Rutter, C. Izard, & P. Read (Eds.), *Depression in young people: Issues and perspectives* (pp. 3–30). New York: Guilford.

Rutter, M. (1986b). Child psychiatry: The interface between clinical and developmental research. *Psychological Medicine, 16,* 151–169.

Rutter, M. (1988). Epidemiological approaches to developmental psychopathology. *Archives of General Psychiatry, 45,* 486–495.

Rutter, M. (1990). Changing patterns of psychiatric disorders during adolescence. In J. Bancroft & J. M. Reinisch (Eds.), *Adolescence and puberty* (pp. 124–145). New York: Oxford University Press.

Rutter, M., & Graham, P. (1966). Psychiatric disorder in 10- and 11-year-old children. *Proceedings of the Royal Society of Medicine, 59,* 382–387.

Rutter, M., Graham, P., Chadwick, O. F. D., & Yule, W. (1976). Adolescent turmoil: Fact or fiction? *Journal of Child Psychology and Psychiatry, 17,* 35–56.

Rutter, M., Lebovici, S., Eisenberg, L., Sneznevskij, A. V., Sadoun, R., Brooke, E., & Tsung-Yi, L. (1969). A tri-axial classification of mental disorders in childhood: An international study. *Journal of Child Psychology and Psychiatry, 10,* 41–61.

Rutter, M. L., Shaffer, D., & Sturge, C. (1979). *A guide to a multi-axial classification scheme for psychiatric disorders in childhood and adolescence.* London: Frowde & Co.

Rutter, M., Tizard, J., & Whitmore, K. (1970). *Education, health, and behaviour.* London: Longman.

Scarr, S., & McCartney, K. (1983). How people make their own environments: A theory of genotype–environment effects. *Child Development, 54,* 424–435.

Seifer, R., Sameroff, A. J., Baldwin, C. P., & Baldwin, A. (1989, April). *Risk and protective factors between 4 and 13 years of age.* Paper presented at the annual meeting of the Society for Research in Child Development, San Francisco, CA.

Shaffer, D., Fisher, P., Schwab-Stone, M., Piacentini, J., & Wicks, J. (1989). *The Diagnostic Interview Schedule for Children (DISC 2.1).* Rockville, MD: National Institute of Mental Health.

Shaffer, D., Schwab-Stone, M., Fisher, P., Davies, M., Piacentini, J., & Gioia, P. (1987). *Revised Diagnostic Interview Schedule for Children (DISC-R).* Rockville, MD: National Institute of Mental Health.

Shepherd, M., Oppenheim, B., & Mitchell, S. (1971). *Childhood behavior and mental health.* London: University of London Press.

Shrout, P. E., Spitzer, R. L., & Fleiss, J. L. (1987). Quantification of agreement in psychiatric diagnosis revisited. *Archives of General Psychiatry, 44,* 172–394.

Simmons, R. G., & Blyth, D. A. (1987). *Moving into adolescence: The impact of pubertal change and school context.* Hawthorne, NY: Aldine de Gruyter.

Snow, J. (1855). *On the mode of communication of cholera* (2nd ed.). London: Churchill.

Spitznagel, E. L., & Helzer, J. E. (1985). A proposed solution to the base rate problem in the kappa statistic. *Archives of General Psychiatry, 42,* 725–728.

Sroufe, L. A. (1988). The role of infant–caregiver attachment in development. In J. Belsky & T. Nezworski (Eds.), *Clinical implications of attachment* (pp. 18–38). Hillsdale, NJ: Erlbaum.

Sroufe, L. A., & Rutter, M. (1984). The domain of developmental psychopathology. *Child Development, 55,* 17–29.

Stattin, H., & Magnusson, D. (1990). *Paths through life—Volume 2: Pubertal maturation in female development.* Hillsdale, NJ: Erlbaum.

Suomi, S. J. (1991). Adolescent depression and depressive symptoms: Insights from longitudinal studies with rhesus monkeys. *Journal of Youth and Adolescence, 20,* 273–287.

Susser, M. (1973). *Causal thinking in the health sciences: Concepts and strategies in epidemiology.* New York: Oxford University Press.

Tolan, P. H. (1987). Implications of age of onset for delinquency risk. *Journal of Abnormal Child Psychology, 15,* 47–65.

Velez, C. N., Johnson, J., & Cohen, P. (1989). A longitudinal analysis of selected risk factors of childhood psychopathology. *Journal of the American Academy of Child and Adolescent Psychiatry, 28,* 861–864.

Verhulst, F. C., Achenbach, T. M., Althaus, M., & Akkerhuis, G. W. (1988). A comparison of syndromes derived from the Child Behavior Checklist for American and Dutch girls aged 6–11 and 12–16. *Journal of Child Psychology and Psychiatry, 29,* 879–895.

Verhulst, F. C., & van der Ende, M. S. (1992). Six-year developmental course of internalizing and externalizing problem behaviors. *Journal of the American Academy of Child and Adolescent Psychiatry, 31,* 924–931.

Vikan, A. (1985). Psychiatric epidemiology in a sample of 1,510 ten-year-old children: I. Prevalence. *Journal of Child Psychology and Psychiatry, 26,* 55–75.

von Gontard, A. (1988). The development of child psychiatry in 19th century Britain. *Journal of Child Psychology and Psychiatry, 29,* 569–588.

Weissman, M. M., Gammon, G. D., John, K., Merikangas, K. R., Warner, V., Prusoff, B. A., & Sholomskas, D. (1987). Children of depressed parents: Increased psychopathology and early onset of major depression. *Archives of General Psychiatry, 44,* 847–853.

Weisz, J. R. (1989). Culture and the development of child psychopathology: Lessons from Thailand. In D. Cicchetti (Ed.), *Rochester Symposium on Developmental Psychopathology, Volume I: The emergence of a discipline* (pp. 89–117). Hillsdale, NJ: Erlbaum.

Wing, J. K., Bebbington, P., & Robins, L. N. (1981). *What is a case?* London: Grant McIntyre.

World Health Organization. (1978). *Manual of the International Classification of Diseases, Injuries, and Causes of Death* (9th ed.). Geneva, Switzerland: Author.

World Health Organization. (1992). *Mental disorders: Glossary and guide to their classification in accordance with the International Classification of Diseases* (10th ed.). Geneva: Author.

Worthman, C. M. (1987). Interactions of physical maturation and cultural practice in ontogeny: Kikuyu adolescents. *Cultural Anthropology, 2,* 29–38.

Worthman, C. M. (1990). Socioendocrinology, key to a fundamental synergy. In T. E. Ziegler & F. B. Bercovitch (Eds.), *The socioendocrinology of primate reproduction* (pp. 187–212). New York: Liss-Wiley.

Worthman, C. M., & Konner, M. (1987). Testosterone levels change with subsistence hunting effort in !Kung San men. *Psychoneuroendocrinology, 12,* 449–458.

Worthman, C. M., Stallings, J. F., & Gubernick, D. (1991). Measurement of hormones in blood spots: A non-isotopic assay for prolactin. *American Journal of Physical Anthropology, 85,* 186–187.

Yule, W. (1981). The epidemiology of child psychopathology. In B. B. Lahey & A. E. Kazdin (Eds.), *Advances in clinical child psychology* (Vol. 4, pp. 1–51). New York: Plenum.

CHAPTER 3

Developmental Issues in Assessment, Taxonomy, and Diagnosis of Child and Adolescent Psychopathology

THOMAS M. ACHENBACH

The linkage of *developmental* with *psychopathology* in the title of a weighty volume implies a fait accompli. The linkage between studies of development and studies of psychopathology remains, however, more of a goal than an accomplished fact. It is not a goal to be achieved through any single type of research or theory. Instead, it involves advancing our understanding of psychopathology by taking account of developmental considerations whenever possible. This is not merely an admonition to append yet another counsel of perfection to the long list of desiderata for doing proper research. Rather, it involves imbuing our thinking with developmental perspectives that shape the research questions we ask, as well as the studies done to answer them.

In this chapter, I focus on developmental issues in the assessment, taxonomy, and diagnosis of childhood disorders. (For brevity, I use the term *childhood* to include adolescence.) Assessment, taxonomy, and diagnosis are especially fundamental in research on child psychopathology, because these enterprises aim to distinguish the normal from the pathological and one kind of pathology from another. If we are to imbue the study of psychopathology with developmental perspectives, there is no more crucial place to start than in the assessment, taxonomy, and diagnosis of the problems to be studied.

As a preface to developmental issues in relation to assessment, taxonomy, and diagnosis, it is helpful to introduce what I mean by *developmental* and *psychopathology.* I use both of these concepts broadly, with a minimum of theoretical assumptions. Although particular theories of development and of psychopathology may help us understand particular phenomena, the value of these concepts would be reduced by limiting them to the meanings prescribed by particular theories.

Much of the work reported here was supported by NIMH Grant 40305, the W. T. Grant Foundation, and University Associates in Psychiatry, a nonprofit health service and research corporation of the University of Vermont Department of Psychiatry.

THE DEVELOPMENTAL COMPONENT

Rather than limiting its meaning, I use developmental to encompass processes, changes, sequences, and characteristics that are typically associated with age. Chronological age (CA) is the most obvious developmental yardstick, but it may serve as a proxy for many other developmental parameters. For some purposes, it may be preferable to use other developmental parameters that do not necessarily correlate highly with CA. Mental age (MA) and other indexes of cognitive developmental level, for example, would not correlate highly with CA in samples that included retarded children, whose cognitive levels would be below their CAs, or very bright children, whose cognitive levels would be above their CAs. Nevertheless, even when a parameter other than CA provides a more precise index of developmental variables, CA remains an important common denominator because of CA-related differences in biological maturity and social status. My use of developmental is intended to stimulate new ideas rather than to restrict thinking to the dictates of any single developmental theory.

In addition to identifying characteristics that are associated with particular developmental parameters, a developmental perspective focuses on adaptational processes. By identifying adaptive and maladaptive processes, we can shed light on the origins of favorable versus unfavorable outcomes. This, in turn, provides a basis for inferring causal factors in psychopathology and for interventions to prevent or treat psychopathology by influencing the causal factors.

Developmental Concepts

Some of the most influential views of human psychological functioning have been developmental. Psychoanalytic theory, for example, interprets adult psychopathology in terms of childhood precursors involving psychosexual stages, fixations, and regressions (Freud, 1940). Piaget's (1983) theory portrays adult cognitive functioning as an outgrowth of stagelike advances and reorganizations. Learning theories attribute deviant behavior to the environmental contingencies experienced throughout the individual's lifetime (Bandura, 1977). Genetic hypotheses about psychopathology focus on sequences of organic determinants starting at conception and continuing through the eventual emergence of child or adult disorders (Rutter, 1991).

It may seem obvious that an organism's behavior at a particular point is in some respect an outgrowth of its previous history. It is much less obvious how and to what extent the organism's previous history determines successful adaptation versus pathological maladaptation at particular points. The diverse theories attest to the range of possible ways to view development and to the multiplicity of variables that may be associated with differences in developmental periods and levels. Although it may not be feasible to take account of all variables posited by all the different views of development, these views provide a rich array of clues and concepts for guiding the developmental study of psychopathology.

Depending on the developmental level of the subjects and the kinds of disorders to be studied, particular bodies of developmental research and theory can guide our understanding of psychopathology. For example, knowledge of cognitive development would argue against using interviews that require children to judge their own behavioral and emotional problems before they are cognitively capable of making and communicating such judgments. Knowledge of development can thus be helpful in tailoring assessment methods to the specific capabilities of the subjects. Even in areas where knowledge of development is meager, assessment should be designed to detect possible developmental differences.

In designing assessment procedures to take account of developmental differences, it is important to be sensitive to developmental variation in the *content* and *patterning* of the relevant phenomena, as well as to parameters that can be measured in a uniform fashion across broad age spans. For example, height, weight, and IQ are expressed in similar numerical ways for individuals of different ages. Yet, the physical and cognitive configurations underlying these parameters change markedly across the life span. Thus, children who weigh 40 pounds at age 5 and 120 pounds at age 15 have not merely grown three times as large. Their body proportions have changed, pubertal development has occurred, and their adolescent appearance causes them to be treated differently by other people.

Analogously, the cognitive processes and specific responses that yield an IQ of 100 at age 5 are very different from those that yield an IQ of 100 at age 15. By the same token, psychopathological conditions that bear the same diagnostic label at different ages, such as Attention Deficit/Hyperactivity Disorder at ages 5 and 15, may be phenotypically quite different at the different ages, may involve different underlying processes, and may have different consequences for the individual's adaptation. We should therefore avoid reifying diagnostic constructs as if they represented encapsulated disease entities that retain the same form regardless of the child's developmental level and other characteristics.

Developmental Methodology

Developmental approaches contribute essential methodology for studying variations in functioning at different ages and for linking variables assessed at one age with those assessed at other ages. Longitudinal research is a hallmark of developmental methodology and is essential for determining relations between variables assessed at different ages. Certain classic longitudinal studies have had major impacts on views of relations between childhood factors and later functioning (e.g., Bayley, 1968; Kagan & Moss, 1962).

Despite their importance, "real-time" longitudinal studies are costly, can seldom use broadly representative samples, and take a long time to produce results. Easier methods for obtaining longitudinal data have therefore been sought. These include "follow-up" (or "catch-up") studies, in which a sample assessed at one age is sought for reassessment at a later point in time, and "follow-back" studies, which seek to obtain records of the earlier history of subjects for whom outcomes are known. Follow-up and follow-back studies are usually quicker and more economical than real-time longitudinal studies. Follow-up and follow-back designs may also be used to select subjects who have particular risk or outcome characteristics that would be difficult to study with real-time longitudinal designs because of obstacles to repeatedly assessing large enough samples of such subjects.

Examples of influential follow-up studies of childhood disorders include Robins's (1966) study of adults who had been assessed at a child guidance clinic many years earlier and a long-term follow-up of autistic children by Kanner, Rodrigues, and Ashenden (1972). Follow-back studies that started with known adult outcomes include comparisons of the early school records of people who differed in adult psychiatric diagnoses (Lewine, Watt, Prentky, & Fryer, 1980).

Longitudinal research is essential for linking early characteristics with later outcomes. However, the ability of traditional longitudinal designs to shed light on psychopathology has been limited by the difficulty of maintaining subject samples, research teams, and funding over long periods. In addition, most longitudinal studies have been handicapped by their inability to detect differences among cohorts and by their reliance on different assessment procedures at different ages. These handicaps are found in real-time, follow-up, and follow-back studies alike.

Life-span developmental psychologists have emphasized the need to take account of differences related to birth cohorts and times of measurement, as well as differences related to age (e.g., Baltes, 1987). Unfortunately, cohort and time-of-measurement comparisons make longitudinal research on psychopathology still more difficult.

Cohort-Sequential Designs

One way to improve longitudinal research on psychopathology is to assess multiple birth cohorts by the same methods over several uniform intervals. Such designs have been variously called "convergence" (Bell, 1953, 1954), "longitudinal-sequential" (Schaie, 1965), "mixed-longitudinal" (van't Hoff, Roede, & Kowalski, 1991), and "cohort-sequential" (Baltes, Cornelius, & Nesselroade, 1979). Because several birth cohorts are assessed in the same way over the same period, the longitudinal findings for each cohort can be compared with the findings for each other cohort. We can thus determine whether changes with age are similar in all cohorts or whether the changes differ among cohorts or times of measurement.

An additional strength of cohort-sequential designs is that they can potentially reveal developmental sequences over a longer period of time than the real time spanned by the study. How can we perform this magic of accelerating longitudinal research? The logic is as follows:

1. At Time 1, children from several adjoining birth cohorts are assessed in a uniform fashion. For example, in June 1996, a test is administered to cohorts of children who are 6, 7, 8, or 9 years old (designated as Cohorts 6, 7, 8, and 9).

2. At Times 2, 3, and 4, the same test is readministered to the same children. In the example given above, the test is readministered in 1997, 1998, and 1999 to Cohorts 6, 7, 8, and 9, who will be 9 to 12 years old at the final administration in 1999.

3. Individual subjects from one cohort are matched to subjects in another cohort. For example, subjects from Cohort 6 are matched to subjects in Cohort 7 with respect to demographic variables and test scores obtained at ages 7 and 8. That is, a particular Cohort 6 middle-income-family boy named Chris is matched to a particular Cohort 7 middle-income-family boy named Scott whose test scores at ages 7 and 8 were similar to the scores obtained by Chris at ages 7 and 8.

4. The accuracy of predicting scores obtained by subjects in one cohort from earlier scores obtained by matched subjects in another cohort is then tested. For example, we compute the correlation between scores obtained at age 6 by Cohort 6 subjects and scores obtained at age 9 by their matched counterparts from Cohort 7. For purposes of comparison, we then compute the correlation between the scores obtained at age 6 by the Cohort 6 subjects and the scores obtained at age 9 by these same subjects. Suppose the correlation between age 6 and 9 scores within Cohort 6 is significant. Suppose also that the between-cohort correlation from scores obtained at age 6 by Cohort 6 subjects to the age 9 scores obtained by their matched Cohort 7 counterparts is of the same magnitude as the correlation from age 6 to age 9 within Cohort 6. These findings would indicate that the score obtained at age 6 by a Cohort 6 subject such as Chris can be used to predict the score obtained at age 9 by a Cohort 7 subject such as Scott with as much accuracy as prediction of Scott's age 9 score from his own age 6 score.

5. If the findings outlined in step 4 above are replicated for the other combinations of cohorts in the study, it may become possible to create matched sets of subjects across the four cohorts to predict scores obtained by Cohort 9 at age 12 from scores obtained by Cohort 6 at age 6. A cross-sequential study that requires 3 years of real time (1996–1999) could thus yield results spanning 6 years of development (ages 6 to 12).

Although developmental psychologists have long discussed the cohort-sequential concept, it has had little application to accelerating longitudinal research on psychopathology by matching subjects from different birth cohorts. Instead, the applications have been limited mainly to identifying cohort and time-of-measurement effects in personality and cognitive tests (e.g., Nesselroade & Baltes, 1974; Schaie, Labouvie, & Buech, 1973).

The need for uniform assessment of multiple birth cohorts over several years might seem to make accelerated longitudinal studies of psychopathology prohibitive. On the other hand, accelerated longitudinal studies could be far more cost-effective than traditional longitudinal studies that require as many years to collect data as the developmental period spanned. But would the magic of predicting from early assessments of psychopathology in one cohort to later assessments in another cohort actually work? The answer depends on the specific assessment procedures, subject samples, and developmental periods spanned. The magic has, in fact, worked tolerably well in at least one accelerated longitudinal study of psychopathology, as outlined in the following section.

Application of the Accelerated Longitudinal Strategy

Stanger, Achenbach, and Verhulst (1994) applied accelerated longitudinal analyses to a general population sample of Dutch children who were assessed 5 times at 2-year intervals from 1983 to 1991. The children were selected randomly from population registers of 13 birth cohorts that were 4 through 16 years old in 1983 (Verhulst, Akkerhuis, & Althaus, 1985). The accelerated longitudinal analyses were applied to the 7 birth cohorts (cohorts initially aged 4 to 10) for which the same assessment procedure was employed at Time 1 through Time 5. The primary assessment procedure was a standardized form, the Child Behavior Checklist (CBCL; Achenbach, 1991c), on which parents rated problem items on 3-point scales.

To perform accelerated longitudinal analyses, Stanger et al. (1994) matched subjects from each birth cohort to subjects in the cohort that was 2 years older. (Cohorts differing by 2 years were matched to take account of the 2-year intervals between assessments.) Subjects of the same sex and similar socioeconomic status (SES) were matched for total problem scores at two assessment points. For example, Cohort 4 boys, who were 4 years old at Time 1 in 1983, were matched to Cohort 6 boys, who were 6 years old at Time 1 and who were similar to their Cohort 4 matches in SES and in the total problem scores they had obtained at ages 6 and 8 (Times 1 and 2 for the Cohort 6 boys, Times 2 and 3 for the Cohort 4 boys).

To test the between-cohort predictive relations, correlations were computed from early scores obtained by children in one cohort to later scores obtained by their counterparts in an older cohort. For example, correlations were computed (separately for each sex) between the age 4 scores from Cohort 4 and the age 10 scores for the matched subjects in Cohort 6. Analogous correlations were computed between the age 4 scores for the Cohort 4 subjects and their own age 10 scores. The between-cohort correlations were then compared to the within-cohort correlations. Surprisingly, it was found that the between-cohort correlations were of about the same magnitude as the analogous within-cohort correlations. This was true in all comparisons where the between-cohort correlations spanned developmental periods that included at least one age when the cohorts had been matched. As Figure 3.1 shows, even over a 6-year period when cohorts had been matched at only one age, the mean between-cohort correlation was only .01 less than the mean within-cohort correlation (.51 vs. .52). Similarly, over 2- and 4-year periods, the mean between-cohort correlation was also only .01 less than the mean within-cohort correlation (.67 vs. .68 for the 2-year interval; .59 vs. .60 for the

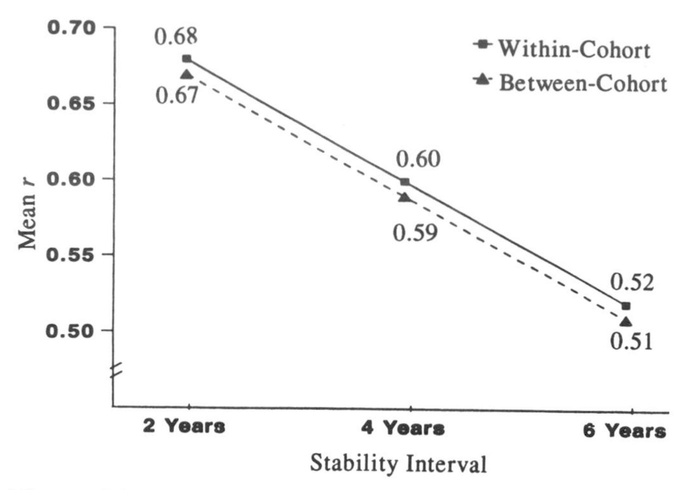

Figure 3.1 Mean Pearson correlations between CBCL total problem scores within cohorts (same children at two ages) and between cohorts (matched cohorts of children at two ages) obtained in accelerated longitudinal analyses (data from Stanger, Achenbach, & Verhulst, 1994).

4-year interval). With a loss of only .01 from the size of the correlation obtained between the subjects' own scores, the magic of between-cohort prediction thus actually worked over developmental periods of 2, 4, and 6 years.

Based on the evidence for predictive relations across pairs of cohorts, between-cohort predictions could potentially be made from Time 1 scores obtained by one cohort to Time 4 scores obtained by its matched cohort when 8 years older. For example, Time 1 scores obtained at age 4 by the Cohort 4 subjects could be used to predict Time 4 scores obtained at age 12 by their matched counterparts in Cohort 6. A study spanning 6 years of real time could thus be used to test predictive relations over 8 years of development. Furthermore, the availability of so many cohorts offers the possibility of expanding the predictive period to 12 years by matching subjects from successive cohorts to provide predictive correlations between age 4 scores obtained by Cohort 4 subjects at Time 1 with age 16 scores obtained by Cohort 10 subjects at Time 4. The success of the accelerated longitudinal strategy greatly increases the attractiveness of short-term longitudinal studies, which are usually far more feasible and economical than long-term studies.

The accelerated longitudinal strategy is just one of many potential methodological contributions of developmental approaches to psychopathology. It illustrates both the complexity and the promise of developmental perspectives for advancing the study of psychopathology. Cohort and time-of-measurement effects, as well as intraindividual developmental sequences, highlight the need for complex multivariate conceptualizations. The complexity should not deter efforts to cope with the challenges of interrelations between development and psychopathology, however, because powerful research tools are available for coping with such challenges. In the next section, we turn to the psychopathology component of our topic.

THE PSYCHOPATHOLOGY COMPONENT

I use the term *psychopathology* broadly to encompass persistent behavior, thoughts, and emotions that are likely to impede the accomplishment of developmental tasks necessary for long-term adaptation. For children in Western societies, the important developmental tasks include at least the following: regulation of biological functions relevant to eating, sleeping, elimination, and energy expenditure; maintenance of close relationships with family and peers; acquisition of academic and social skills; preparation for adult occupational and social roles; and formation of a stable sense of personal identity.

A key aim of this chapter is to advance our ways of thinking about psychopathology. Because psychopathology can be conceptualized in different ways for different purposes, it is important to consider the relative utility of various approaches.

Nosological Approaches

Nosological approaches to psychopathology originated in the 19th century with efforts to bring psychopathology out of the realm of demonology and into the realm of organic medicine. An important thrust of these efforts was to model the classification of mental disorders on classifications of diseases, called *nosologies.*

Contemporary psychiatric nosologies stem largely from Emil Kraepelin's (1883) efforts to construct descriptive categories of major adult disorders that might ultimately be found to have different organic causes. Diagnostic categories such as schizophrenia (originally called *dementia praecox,* i.e., premature or early dementia) and manic-depressive (bipolar) disorder were featured in Kraepelin's nosology and have remained hallmarks of psychiatric nosologies ever since. These diagnostic categories, in turn, have continued to mold clinical practice, training, and funding mechanisms.

In the United States, psychiatric nosology has been embodied in successive editions of the American Psychiatric Association's (1952, 1968, 1980, 1987, 1994) *Diagnostic and Statistical Manual* (hereinafter, DSM-I, DSM-II, DSM-III, DSM-III-R, DSM-IV). Elsewhere, the International Classification of Diseases (World Health Organization, 1978, 1992; hereinafter, ICD-9, ICD-10) has provided the official psychiatric nosology.

Despite their influence on the way psychopathology is viewed, the official nosologies have had limited utility for advancing knowledge of the behavioral/emotional problems of childhood. Unlike the differentiation among numerous categories of adult disorders in the 19th century, official nosologies offered little differentiation among childhood disorders until late in the 20th century. Until 1968, for example, the DSM provided only two categories specifically for childhood disorders: (a) Adjustment Reaction of Childhood and (b) Schizophrenic Reaction, Childhood Type. Even after the introduction of more differentiated categories of childhood disorders in DSM-II and DSM-III, Adjustment Reaction remained a common diagnosis (American Academy of Child Psychiatry, 1983; Cerreto & Tuma, 1977). Furthermore, current versions of this diagnostic category are often used to avoid the stigma that might be associated with other disorders (Setterberg et al., 1991).

As successive editions of the DSM have become more differentiated with respect to childhood disorders, the categories and criteria have changed markedly. However, these changes have not been derived from data on actual samples of children, nor have they been calibrated from one edition of DSM to the next. The changes have markedly altered the distributions of diagnoses even in the same samples of children (Lahey et al., 1990). Furthermore, the changes in DSM have not been well-coordinated with ICD.

Although nosological categories are intended to mark boundaries between disorders that might have different etiologies, different etiologies have not in fact been found for most categories of child psychopathology specified by the DSM and ICD. Progress in understanding etiologies is likely to require flexibility in conceptualizing disorders and their boundaries on the basis of empirically identified relations between causal factors and outcomes. To advance our understanding, we must therefore experiment with various conceptualizations that can be tested and compared with respect to reliability, validity, and utility.

Theoretically Based Approaches

There has been abundant theorizing about the nature of particular disorders and also about the nature of psychopathology in general. Nineteenth-century nosological efforts were initially based on the theory that all mental disorders are caused by brain diseases (Griesinger, 1845). Kraepelin's (1883) initial aim was to describe differences among disorders for which different physical causes could then be found. However, by the 1915 version of his nosology, Kraepelin included disorders thought to be of psychological origin. He also included personality disorders viewed as bordering between illness and eccentricity. Although subsequent psychiatric nosologies have continued to be modeled on physical diseases, they have not been dictated by any single etiological theory.

Historically, the most influential general theory of psychopathology has been psychoanalysis. Sigmund Freud (1917/1963) proposed theoretical explanations for the development of particular disorders, such as obsessive-compulsive versus hysterical neurosis. With respect to childhood disorders, Anna Freud (1965) proposed a Developmental Profile for assessing individual children in terms of developmental sequences hypothesized by analytic theory. The Developmental Profile includes diagnostic categories specified in terms such as the following: "There is permanent drive regression to fixation points which leads to conflicts of a neurotic type" (A. Freud, 1965, p. 147). Little has been published on how children are to be distinguished with respect to the assessment criteria or diagnostic categories of the Developmental Profile; instead, most publications illustrate how it might look for a particular child (e.g., Yorke, 1980).

Another theoretically based classification for childhood disorders was proposed by the Group for the Advancement of Psychiatry (GAP; 1966). The GAP classification was intended to operationally define disorders with a minimum of inference. Although the GAP classification provided far more categories than Anna Freud's Developmental Profile, many of its categories required extensive psychodynamic inferences, and no assessment operations were actually specified for determining whether a child met the criteria for particular categories. As an example, the GAP category of Psychoneurotic Disorders was defined as:

> . . . disorders based on unconscious conflicts over the handling of sexual and aggressive impulses which, though removed from awareness by the mechanism of repression, remain active and unresolved. . . . The anxiety, acting as a danger signal to the ego, ordinarily sets into operation certain defense mechanisms, in addition to repression, and leads to the formation of psychological symptoms which symbolically deal with the conflict, thus achieving a partial though unhealthy solution. (GAP, 1966, pp. 229–230)

Empirically Based Approaches

Kraepelin (1883) designated his nosology as "descriptive." That is, the nosology was intended to describe the characteristics of different disorders in the hope that a specific etiology would ultimately be found for each type of disorder. Kraepelin's descriptions were based on his own observations of symptoms that tended to co-occur, characteristics observed in people having particular kinds of symptoms, and the course of what he judged to be a particular type of disorder. For example, Kraepelin described dementia praecox in terms of psychological symptoms of thought disorder, onset in early adulthood, and differentiation from manic-depressive psychosis by a chronic and deteriorating course.

Kraepelinian nosology was intended to be "empirical" in the sense of being based on experts' observations of patients in clinical settings such as mental hospitals. For adult disorders involving extreme forms of behavioral, emotional, and cognitive deviance, such as dementia praecox and manic-depressive disorders, this approach succeeded in establishing categories that remain cornerstones of psychiatric nosology. In addition, some disorders that were early recognized as involving both mental and physical abnormalities were eventually found to have specific organic causes. An example is *general paresis,* which involves mental and physical deterioration that in the late 19th century was found to result from syphilitic infection. Another example is *Down syndrome,* which was described by Langdon Down in 1866, although it was not until 1959 that the cause was found to be a chromosomal abnormality (Lejeune, Gautier, & Turpin, 1959/1963).

Efforts to describe disorders clinically and then to find organic etiologies have thus yielded some notable successes. The 19th-century success in discovering the etiology of paresis helped to establish the organic disease model for psychiatric nosology. Success in pinpointing the etiology of Down syndrome, on the other hand, had to wait for nearly a century of advances in genetic research.

Organic hypotheses abound for some childhood behavioral/emotional problems, such as attention deficits. Organic factors may ultimately be implicated in others as well. However, physical abnormalities have not been firmly established for most of the common behavioral/emotional problems for which child mental health services are sought. For those problems lacking recognized physical abnormalities, it is important to avoid prematurely imposing nosological boundaries that may incorrectly distinguish among disorders. Instead, we need to optimize the use of data that will facilitate understanding of the similarities and differences among particular problems, their causes, prognoses, and optimal treatments.

Multivariate statistical methods can be used to identify groupings of problems far more systematically and rigorously than the clinical observations on which descriptive nosology has been based. These methods make it easy to take account of large numbers of potentially useful variables assessed in much larger samples of children than individual clinicians can evaluate. Using multivariate methods, we can thus derive syndromes from large samples chosen to be representative of populations of children rather than being limited to particular clinical caseloads. To take account of the potential variations in problems related to children's age and other important characteristics, we can do separate multivariate analyses for children grouped according to these characteristics. Results for the different groups of children can then be compared in order to identify similarities and differences in problem patterns related to characteristics of the children.

Nosologies such as the DSM and ICD must serve many masters. These masters include mental health professionals seeing different kinds of clients in different types of settings; different factions within the organizations that promulgate the nosologies; third-party payers; government agencies; and record librarians. It should therefore not be surprising that nosologies of poorly understood disorders are subject to vicissitudes other than those of empirically based science. It is to be hoped that scientific criteria and knowledge will be applied to the improvement of nosologies. However, efforts to advance knowledge of childhood disorders should not be subservient to official nosologies in which children's problems are subordinated to conceptual models for adult disorders. Instead, to advance knowledge of childhood behavioral/emotional problems, research needs to be closely geared to both the developmental aspects of children's functioning and to the actual problems manifested by children in various contexts, rather than being dictated by nosological categories of theories about the childhood precursors of adult disorders. The next section outlines a conceptual framework for the developmental study of psychopathology.

A FRAMEWORK FOR THE DEVELOPMENTAL STUDY OF PSYCHOPATHOLOGY

To advance the developmental study of psychopathology, it is helpful to outline a framework of issues that research must contend with. No single study can contend simultaneously with all the issues, but programmatic efforts to improve the assessment, taxonomy, and diagnosis of child psychopathology are needed to resolve these issues.

Developmental Differences

We previously stressed the importance of developmental parameters in all research on child psychopathology. To obtain an accurate picture of psychopathology, it is essential to gear assessment procedures to the developmental level of the subjects, to determine what features are associated with clinical deviance at each level, and to construct taxonomies that reflect features characterizing each developmental level. The features that discriminate between forms of deviance are apt to change with development. It is therefore important for assessment and taxonomy to take account of developmental changes occurring in individual children, so that the same children can be studied longitudinally. Both the differences and links between developmental levels must be rigorously tested.

Multiple Sources of Data

The study of adult psychopathology focuses largely on data obtained from the patient in the clinical setting via interviews, observations, and tests. Most adults being assessed for psychopathology accept the role of patient and contribute to the assessment process by reporting on their history and symptoms. The dominant approaches to assessment of psychopathology are based on adult patients who are the main sources of data about themselves.

The adult model of assessment has been extended to children by means of structured psychiatric interviews, such as the Diagnostic Interview Schedule for Children (DISC; Shaffer, 1992) and the Diagnostic Interview for Children and Adolescents (DICA; Reich, Shayka, & Taibleson, 1992). These interviews aim to assign diagnoses by questioning children about the presence of the criterial features specified by DSM categories. One edition of the DISC, for example, has questions such as "Have you held someone up or mugged someone?" (Shaffer, Fisher, Piacentini, Schwab-Stone, & Wicks, 1989, p. 169). Answers of "yes" to these questions count toward a diagnosis of Conduct Disorder. A child who acknowledges enough criterial features of the DSM diagnostic category of Conduct Disorder is diagnosed as having a conduct disorder. On the other hand, a child who acknowledges one less feature is diagnosed as not having a conduct disorder.

Although adult psychiatric patients are appropriate sources of data about their own condition, children are much less adequate sources, for several reasons. First, before adolescence, children are not apt to be cognitively capable of judging whether they have the types of problems that define diagnostic categories. As a consequence, their yes-or-no answers to questions about these problems may be much less accurate than answers by adult interviewees. Research on the test–retest reliability of children's responses to structured interviews shows that they affirm far more problems in an initial interview than in a repeat interview. As an example of this *attenuation effect,* 6- to 9-year-old children were found to report 33% more symptoms in an initial DISC interview than in a repeat DISC several days later (Edelbrock, Costello, Dulcan, Kalas, & Conover, 1985). Even at ages 10 to 13, there was a 24% test–retest decline, and at ages 14 to 18, a 16% decline. Although adult informants also tend to report fewer problems on a retest interview (Robins, 1985), the attenuation effect is generally much smaller than is found with child interviewees.

The marked decline found by Edelbrock et al. (1985) evidently stemmed from an initial "yea-saying" response set, whereby children responded "yes" rather indiscriminately. The yea-saying set at the first interview was then replaced by a "nay-saying" set at the second interview, when the children responded "no" to many of the same items they had previously affirmed. In neither the initial nor the retest interview were the children's responses likely to provide an adequate assessment of disorders, because little agreement was found between diagnoses made from the child interviews and those made either from DISC interviews with the children's parents ("DISC-P") or from complete clinical work-ups (Costello, Edelbrock, Dulcan, Kalas, & Klaric, 1984). Similar problems continue to afflict newer versions of these interviews (Costello, Burns, Angold, & Leaf, 1993).

Although child interviews will no doubt remain key components of clinical assessment, it seems clear that they are not likely to provide an adequate basis for diagnosis. Even when the interviewers' observations are added to children's self-reports, the behavior seen in the clinical setting may be quite unrepresentative of the child's behavior elsewhere. Physical aggression, stealing, suicide attempts, and disruptiveness in school are problems for which professional help is often sought but which are unlikely to be directly observed by clinicians or reported by children in clinical interviews. Instead, reports of such problems by others, such as parents, teachers, and observers, are needed for comprehensive assessment of children.

Children's behavior varies from one context and interaction partner to another, and informants may differ in their sensitivity to particular behaviors. As a result, correlations between reports of children's problems by different informants tend to be modest. Meta-analyses of many studies have yielded a mean Pearson correlation of .60 between ratings by informants who play generally similar roles with respect to children (e.g., parent × parent, teacher × teacher); a mean correlation of .28 between informants who play different roles with respect to children (e.g., parent × teacher, teacher × mental health worker); and a mean correlation of .22 between children's self-ratings and ratings by others, such as parents and teachers (Achenbach, McConaughy, & Howell, 1987). Different sources can provide useful data on different aspects of children's functioning, but no one source can substitute for all others. It is therefore necessary to make explicit use of multiple sources of data, as detailed in subsequent sections of this chapter.

Epidemiological Aspects

Research on both development and psychopathology often employs samples chosen for convenience. This is understandable in light of the need to find children, parents, and other collaterals, such as teachers, who are willing and able to participate in a particular study. Many selective factors affect the composition of the convenience samples that are used for research. As a result, the distributions of variables and the findings in such samples cannot necessarily be generalized to larger, more typical populations.

If our knowledge of psychopathology is derived mainly from subjects who are conveniently available, we may become overfocused on problems that are of low frequency, do not actually distinguish normal from deviant individuals, or might have different meanings in other contexts.

As an example, both the early psychoanalytic and behavioral literature used children's fears of animals to model theories of the etiology and treatment of psychopathology. Sigmund Freud (1909/1953) devoted a 145-page paper to the hypothesized psychodynamic determinants of Little Hans's horse phobia. Freud (1926/1959) then used the same case to illustrate his revised theory of neurosis 17 years later. In the behavioral tradition, Watson and Rayner (1920) experimentally conditioned Little Albert to fear a white rat, and Jones (1924) applied Watson's principles to the treatment of 2-year-old Peter's fear of a white rabbit.

Both the psychodynamic and behavioral traditions made children's fears paradigmatic for the subsequent literature on psychopathology. Yet, epidemiological studies have shown that fears of specific animals, situations, or places (other than school) are not actually much more common among children considered to be clinically deviant than among representative samples of nonreferred children (Achenbach & Edelbrock, 1981; Achenbach, Howell, Quay, & Conners, 1991). Furthermore, epidemiological research has shown that some problems employed as criteria for nosological categories do not actually discriminate between clinically referred children. "Always on the go," for example, was a criterial feature for the DSM-III category of Attention Deficit Disorder and is also a criterial feature of the DSM-IV category of Attention Deficit/Hyperactivity Disorder (American Psychiatric Association, 1980, 1994). Yet, this item was reported more often for a nationally representative sample of *nonreferred* children than for demographically matched *referred* children (Achenbach et al., 1991). Most other nosological criteria for childhood disorders have likewise been chosen without epidemiological evidence that they actually discriminate between deviant and normative populations.

Few childhood disorders are decisively distinguished by a specific abnormality whose presence serves as a litmus test for the disorder. Instead, most childhood disorders involve problems that many children manifest in some degree at some time in their lives. To identify children as being clinically deviant, we therefore need to know the distribution of particular problems among children considered to be relatively normal, as well as among those who are considered deviant enough to need professional help. Because many selective factors affect referral to particular services, we also need data on children who are seen in different settings. And we need to know the outcomes of particular problems in both referred and nonreferred populations. This requires that epidemiological samples be reassessed longitudinally to determine which problems have relatively good versus poor outcomes when treated versus untreated and what other child and family variables predict outcomes. Such research is important not only to determine what problems distinguish children who need help from those who do not, but also to identify risk and protective factors on which preventive and therapeutic efforts can be based.

Multivariate Aspects

Because so many different kinds and degrees of problems may evoke concern, it is important to standardize the recording and analysis of problems. The difficulty of assessing and aggregating multiple problems in large samples argues for using multivariate approaches to the aggregation and analysis of data. Each score on an individual problem obtained from informants, observations, or tests is subject to many kinds of sampling and measurement error. However, by using multivariate methods, we can aggregate scores on numerous problems from multiple sources to identify patterns that characterize groups of children. This is analogous to computed tomography (CT scanning), where numerous low-grade x-ray pictures are integrated by computer to produce high-grade images. Once we identify patterns of scores, we can use them to group children for research on the etiology, course, prognosis, and effectiveness of treatment for each pattern. Those multivariate patterns that are found to be reliable and to validly discriminate between children who differ in other important ways can then serve a taxonomic function, as detailed in later sections.

Operational Definitions

A key tool of science is the operational definition of variables. Although scientific thought and theory employ numerous abstractions that are not operationalized, empirical tests of scientific ideas require that the variables to which they refer be specifiable in terms of assessment operations. The results of the assessment operations should yield reliable values for variables, which, in turn, provide the empirical content of the science.

Discussions of child psychopathology are replete with terms that are used as if their meaning were self-evident. Terms (and their abbreviations) such as Attention Deficit/Hyperactivity Disorder (ADHD), Conduct Disorder (CD), and Oppositional Defiant Disorder (ODD) are common examples from the DSM nosology. Terms such as Seriously Emotionally Disturbed (SED) and Learning Disabled (LD) are used with similar aplomb in special education circles, reflecting the influence of Public Law 94-142 (P.L. 94-142), the Education of the Handicapped Act (*Federal Register,* 1977, 1981), which specifies eligibility for special education services (reauthorized as P. L. 101-476, Individuals with Disabilities Act, 1990).

The need for operational definitions has been acknowledged in efforts to improve nosologies. The diagnostic classification of childhood disorders proposed by the Group for the Advancement of Psychiatry (GAP; 1966), for example, "attempted to set forth operational definitions of clinical categories" (p. 209). DSM-III (American Psychiatric Association, 1980) was also heralded as an effort to provide operational definitions. However, neither the GAP classification nor the DSM has defined behavioral/emotional disorders according to specific assessment operations. What about the DSM's lists of explicit criteria that are required for particular diagnoses? These criteria do not constitute operational definitions, because no operations are specified for determining whether a child manifests each criterial feature. Nor are operations specified for combining the assessment data from multiple sources. This lack of truly operational definitions for nosological categories of childhood disorders may be one reason for the mediocre reliability found for these categories (Achenbach, 1992, provides a review of reliability data).

In the absence of more complete knowledge about childhood disorders, categories such as those specified by the DSM and P. L. 101-476 will continue to serve administrative functions, such as providing guidelines for reimbursement of services. However, these categories were not derived from empirical findings on distinctions among disorders in actual samples of troubled children. The categories should therefore not be mistaken for "types" of children. Although children may indeed have the kinds of problems highlighted by administrative categories, children do not necessarily come packaged according to these categories. That is, we should not assume that children are intrinsically ADHD, CD, ODD, SED, or LD. Unless we empirically test (a) the associations among features that are used to define the categories and (b) the power of the features to discriminate between normal and troubled children, we cannot know how best to distinguish among kinds of disorders. To improve our ability to distinguish between normal and clinically deviant children, as well as among patterns of clinical deviance, we need long-term programmatic research that is more robust than most administrative categories have proven to be. Such research is needed to advance our overall understanding of child psychopathology, as addressed in the following sections.

THE ROLES OF ASSESSMENT AND TAXONOMY IN THE DEVELOPMENTAL STUDY OF PSYCHOPATHOLOGY

To improve our ways of distinguishing the normal from the deviant and one kind of deviance from another, it is helpful to distinguish between two related tasks. One task is to *assess individual cases* in order to identify their distinguishing features. The second task is to *construct a taxonomy* for grouping cases according to their distinguishing features. These tasks are essential steps in identifying the target disorders to be studied in each developmental period. They also form the basis for diagnostic decisions about individual cases. To improve diagnostic decision making, we need reliable and valid procedures for identifying the distinguishing features of individual cases, for grouping cases according to their distinguishing features, and for effectively integrating all the relevant data into optimal decisions. To clarify the different tasks, I first address assessment and taxonomy as scientific endeavors that can be better understood if we avoid the complex connotations associated with the term diagnosis.

Assessment

Assessment refers to gathering data with which to identify the distinguishing features of individual cases. Every case can be distinguished from other cases in many ways. Effective assessment requires selecting optimal features for the kinds of decisions that we must make. To know what features are likely to be optimal, we need data from representative samples of cases in which the distributions, reliability, validity, and utility of various features have been tested.

Psychometric principles provide guidance for determining the methodological adequacy of assessment data. As applied to the assessment of children's behavioral/emotional problems, these principles can be summarized as follows:

1. Assessment should employ standardized procedures.
2. Multiple items should be used to sample each aspect of functioning.

3. Items should be aggregated to provide quantitative scores for each aspect of functioning.
4. Scores should be normed to indicate how an individual compares with relevant reference groups.
5. For variables potentially related to development, the normative reference groups should be formed according to age levels or other indexes of development.
6. To be considered psychometrically sound, assessment procedures must be reliable and valid, although the types of reliability and validity vary with the type of procedure.

In addition to these principles, psychometric theory prescribes specific standards for constructing sound assessment procedures. Psychometric theory does not, however, tell us *which* of the many features of individual cases should be assessed. Instead, we should select features that are found to discriminate between children whose behavioral/emotional problems differ with respect to etiology, course, prognosis, and/or the most appropriate intervention. Because we do not yet know which features specifically discriminate between children according to these variables, research is needed to test the discriminative power of various features. Rather than attempting to test every possible feature one-by-one, it is preferable to identify sets of features that tend to co-occur. Because assessment of each feature is subject to unique sources of variance, scores for sets of covarying features are likely to be more reliable than scores for individual features. Furthermore, sets of covarying features are likely to be more useful than individual features for generating and testing hypotheses, as well as for managing individual cases. The task of aggregating covarying features into sets with which to identify similar cases is the task of taxonomy, to which we now turn.

Taxonomy

It is helpful to distinguish between *classification* in general and *taxonomy* in particular. Classification refers to any systematic ordering of phenomena into classes, groups, or types. Many classifications are constructed merely for the convenience of users. Administrative classifications, for example, are often developed to meet particular organizational needs. The people who develop such classifications may start with knowledge of the organization's needs and the ways in which prospective users of a classification customarily view the phenomena to be classified. They then attempt to mesh the users' classificatory behavior with the organizational functions that the classification is to serve.

As an example, health insurers take medical nosologies as representative of how providers distinguish among disorders. The insurers then construct their own schemes for classifying disorders and services in order to specify reimbursements. A key question is whether a classification scheme enables the insurer's actuaries to compute costs accurately enough for the insurer to charge rates that are competitive but high enough to be profitable after covering the costs. For third-party payers that are not funded by premiums based on costs, such as Medicaid, the problem is complicated by unpredictable changes in the size and nature of the covered population, variations in the services obtained, providers' techniques for coping with low reimbursement rates, and the vicissitudes of government funding. Considering the variety of factors that affect insurers' classification schemes, it should be no wonder that the thousands of insurers in the United States have thousands of classifications for determining reimbursability.

In contrast to the broad concept of classification, *taxonomy* refers to a subset of classifications that are intended to reflect intrinsic differences between cases assigned to different classes. Taxonomies of plants and animals, for example, are based on features that are intended to capture important differences among species. Various features can be chosen to distinguish among groups of plants and animals, such as physical characteristics, interbreeding, and hypothesized evolutionary relations. Although the concept of species is so familiar as to seem self-evident, species is not an intrinsic property of living things. Instead, species is a taxonomic construct that is imposed on subsets of features selected from all the features that might be used to distinguish among individual plants and animals (Levin, 1979). Taxonomic constructs such as species involve systematic efforts to distinguish among individuals on the basis of scientifically identified characteristics of those individuals, rather than being imposed without regard to intrinsic differences among the individuals.

In constructing taxonomies of behavioral/emotional problems, we should remember that many different features can be aggregated according to many different criteria. Certain features and ways of aggregating them may be useful at one stage of knowledge and for one developmental stage but not at other stages of knowledge or development. Furthermore, different taxonomic principles may be useful for different kinds of disorders or for different purposes at the same stage of knowledge or for the same developmental stage. Cognitive measures, for example, may be useful for grouping children according to ability levels, whereas behavior problems may be useful for grouping the same children for management purposes.

It should also be remembered that the features chosen to characterize cases represent abstractions with which to link cases that are expected to have other important characteristics in common with each other. When we abstract a subset of features from the many features that could be identified, we form a hypothetical construct of the case—a conceptual abstraction intended to capture the important aspects of the case. If our notion of the individual case and our grouping of cases according to features they share both involve hypothetical constructs, how should we match our construct of the individual case to the constructs of a taxonomy? Answers to this question must take account of both the methodological possibilities for assessing individual cases and the mental processes involved in matching the features of the individual case to the features used to define taxonomic groupings of cases.

Prototypes as Taxonomic Models

Classification systems have traditionally defined categories in terms of criteria that are "singly necessary and jointly sufficient" for classifying individual cases (Cantor, Smith, French, & Mezzich, 1980, p. 182). That is, a case was assigned to a particular category if, and only if, it met all the criteria for that category. Conversely, all cases that met the criteria for a particular category were ipso facto assigned to that category.

Cognitive research indicates that people's mental use of categories does not conform to the classical model whereby cases are categorized according to features that are both necessary and sufficient. As illustrated by familiar categories such as furniture, for example, the objects that people categorize together do not all share the same defining features (Rosch & Mervis, 1975). Instead, certain objects classified as furniture, such as tables and chairs, have little similarity to other objects that are also classified as furniture, such as lamps and rugs.

Objects that have the most features of a category are considered to be the most typical of the category and are more quickly and reliably categorized than are objects that have fewer of the category's features (Smith, 1978). Objects that have features of multiple categories are difficult to categorize reliably. As an example, tomatoes are difficult to categorize as fruits or vegetables, because they have features of both categories.

Instead of being rigidly defined by criterial features that must all be present in all members of a category, people's mental representations of categories consist of sets of imperfectly correlated features known as *prototypes* (Rosch, 1978). Category membership can thus be judged according to the degree of overlap between the features of a case and the set of prototypical features that define a category. Cases having many features of a prototype are considered to be very typical of the category represented by that prototype. Cases that have few features of a prototype are less typical of that category. Cases that manifest features of more than one prototype may be viewed as being on the border between the categories represented by those prototypes.

According to the prototype view, there is a quantitative basis for judging the resemblance between particular cases and particular categories. That is, the degree of resemblance between a case and a category is judged according to the number of prototypical features they have in common. Furthermore, if each prototypical feature can be scored in terms of the intensity or certainty with which it is manifested, quantification can be extended beyond the number of prototypical features to include a total score comprising the sum or other aggregation of scores on all the prototypical features.

If the human minds that must use taxonomies conceptualize categories in terms of quantifiable prototypes, why not design taxonomies to mesh these facets of human information processing with the phenomena to be embodied in the taxonomies? The possibilities for doing this will be presented after we consider conventional diagnostic thinking.

DIAGNOSIS

The term *diagnosis* conveys an aura of clinical authority, implying that it reveals an essential truth about what is really wrong with a patient. Yet, the term has multiple meanings that sow confusion when we move from the research tasks conceptualized in terms of assessment and taxonomy to clinical practice conceptualized in terms of diagnosis. To clarify relations between the research tasks and diagnostic practice, it is helpful to distinguish among the different meanings of diagnosis discussed next.

Diagnostic Process

The diagnostic process is the gathering of data on which to base decisions about individuals. It is analogous to what we earlier defined as assessment. However, because it implies gathering data in order to determine which disease a person has, diagnostic process connotes a narrower range of possibilities than the more neutral term, assessment.

Formal Diagnosis

Formal diagnosis is the assignment of cases to the categories of a diagnostic classification. Accordingly, a leading psychiatric diagnostician, Samuel Guze (1978), has defined diagnosis as "the medical term for classification" (p. 53). This is the sense in which the categories of the DSM, GAP, and ICD nosologies are "diagnoses." When a clinician states that a child meets the DSM criteria for Conduct Disorder, for example, the clinician is making a formal diagnosis.

Diagnostic Formulation

Whereas formal diagnosis has quite a narrow meaning, diagnostic formulation has a much broader meaning that encompasses efforts to elucidate multiple aspects of an individual's condition. When a clinician interprets a child's problems in terms of organic vulnerabilities, developmental history, family dynamics, academic stress, and rejection by peers, for example, the clinician makes a diagnostic formulation. A diagnostic formulation should weave all the findings of the diagnostic process into a comprehensive picture of the case. The diagnostic formulation thus provides a broader basis for developing a treatment plan than does a formal diagnosis. Yet, it is by means of the formal diagnosis that the individual case is linked to others like it.

The formal diagnosis helps the clinician apply knowledge gained from similar cases to constructing a diagnostic formulation for the current case. To do this, the diagnosis of individual cases must be reliable with respect to the gathering of data, the integration of data into a diagnosis, and the selection of the appropriate formal diagnosis. Furthermore, the system from which the formal diagnosis is selected must be reliable, must be valid with respect to important correlates of its diagnostic categories, and must encompass cases like the one being diagnosed. In short, the credibility of diagnosis depends on the same methodological standards as assessment and taxonomy. Shorn of its connotations, diagnosis involves gathering data to identify the distinguishing features of individual cases and grouping cases according to their distinguishing features, just as do assessment and taxonomy. Whichever terminology is used, the value and credibility of such procedures rest on their contributions to knowledge about how to help the people to whom they are applied.

The Issue of Comorbidity

Since the introduction of explicit diagnostic criteria by DSM-III (American Psychiatric Association, 1980), many children have been found to meet the criteria for more than one disorder (e.g., Costello et al., 1984; Livingston, Dykman, & Ackerman, 1990; Weinstein, Noam, Grimes, Stone, & Schwab-Stone, 1990). Termed *comorbidity,* the tendency for a particular disorder to be diagnosed in individuals who also have another disorder has a variety of implications. The apparent co-occurrence of two disorders could mean, for example, that one disorder results from the other; or that the same risk factors lead to both disorders; or that the two disorders are not really separate but are manifestations of the same underlying condition.

The DSM and ICD categories for childhood disorders are not based on evidence for the independent existence of a separate disorder for every category. Nor do the DSM and ICD specify assessment operations for identifying each disorder independently of others. Where procedures have been developed to operationally assess DSM criteria for childhood disorders, high base rates and overlapping criteria for certain disorders have made comorbidity almost inevitable. For example, two studies have shown that 96% of boys who met DSM criteria for Conduct Disorder also met criteria for Oppositional Defiant Disorder (Faraone, Biederman, Keenan, & Tsuang, 1991; Walker et al., 1991). In addition, the DSM-III-R field trials found that 84% of clinic-referred children who met criteria for Conduct Disorder also met criteria for Oppositional Defiant Disorder (Spitzer, Davies, & Barkley, 1990). Because the DSM criteria for these disorders have not been proven to distinguish between separate entities, the very high rates of overlap between diagnoses suggest that the diagnostic criteria are interdependent.

The specific rates of comorbidity reported in many studies may be misleading, because they reflect computation of the overlap between diagnoses in only one direction. That is, they reflect the percentage of children having Diagnosis A who also have Diagnosis B. If the two diagnoses have different base rates, this "unidirectional" computation yields a different rate of comorbidity than would be obtained by computing the percentage of children having Disorder B who also have Disorder A. By recomputing published comorbidity rates "bidirectionally" (i.e., as the mean of the comorbidities of A to B and B to A), McConaughy and Achenbach (1994a) obtained quite different rates from those based on the unidirectional comorbidities.

Apparent comorbidity among disorders may also be misleading in other ways, as detailed elsewhere (Achenbach, 1991a; Caron & Rutter, 1991). Suppose, for example, that individuals manifesting a particular disorder have X probability of referral. Suppose, too, that individuals manifesting another disorder have Y probability of referral. Even if the disorders do not tend to co-occur in the population as a whole, people who have both disorders have $X + Y - XY$ probability of referral. This is obviously higher than individuals who have only X or Y probability of referral. If we study only referred people, we may conclude that the two disorders tend to occur together. Yet, if we study the entire population (including nonreferred people), we might find that the two disorders have no more than chance co-occurrence, because individuals having only one disorder without the other are common in the nonreferred portion of the population. Known as *Berkson's bias* (Berkson, 1946), this effect of referral biases on apparent comorbidity is one of many artifactual ways in which findings of co-occurrence between even independently verifiable disorders can arise. The different effects of the referral bias on different problems has been demonstrated by comparing comorbidities obtained among empirically based syndromes in demographically similar referred and nonreferred samples (McConaughy & Achenbach, 1994a).

If two disorders are operationally defined according to mutually independent assessment procedures, and if the two disorders are demonstrated to occur together with greater than chance frequency in unbiased samples of the general population, then the comorbidity of these particular disorders may be quite informative. However, if diagnoses are not based on operational definitions of empirically separable disorders, findings of comorbidity may merely reflect a lack of appropriate boundaries between diagnostic categories or an inability of diagnosticians to validly distinguish between disorders that do not actually co-occur at any more than chance rates.

Thus, rather than taking findings of comorbidity at face value as reflecting the co-occurrence of two distinct disorders, it is important to examine the diagnostic system itself for possible artifactual sources of apparent comorbidity. The high rate of overlap found between DSM-III diagnoses of Oppositional Disorder and Conduct Disorder (Faraone et al., 1991; Spitzer et al., 1990; Walker et al., 1991) for example, invites scrutiny of the diagnostic system to determine whether they should really be viewed as separate disorders. The arbitrariness of these diagnostic categories is highlighted by the major changes they underwent from DSM-III to DSM-III-R, with further changes in DSM-IV. DSM-III (American Psychiatric Association, 1980) listed five criteria for Oppositional Disorder, of which only two criteria were required for the diagnosis. DSM-III-R (American Psychiatric Association, 1987), by contrast, listed nine criteria, of which five were required for the diagnosis. DSM-IV lists eight criteria, of which four are required for the diagnosis. Furthermore, the DSM criteria for diagnoses of Conduct Disorder also underwent major changes from DSM-III to DSM-III-R, with further changes in DSM-IV. DSM-III provided four distinct categories, plus a residual category of Atypical Conduct Disorder. DSM-III-R, by contrast, provided only one set of explicit criteria for Conduct Disorder, although once the prescribed number of criteria were met, the disorder could be categorized as "group type," "solitary aggressive type," or "undifferentiated type," according to the diagnostician's judgment. DSM-IV has dispensed with these types in favor of "childhood onset type" versus "adolescent onset type."

Any classification system should be subject to change as knowledge advances. However, the DSM-III-R and DSM-IV revisions were not derived from empirical tests of the co-occurrence of particular features or of whether the criteria for Oppositional Disorder and Conduct Disorder actually discriminated between distinctly different disorders in representative samples of children. Furthermore, no provision was made for correlating or calibrating diagnoses made from one edition of the DSM with those made from previous editions. It should not be surprising, therefore, that very different distributions of oppositional and conduct disorders were obtained when applying DSM-III versus DSM-III-R to the same children, and that many children met criteria for both diagnoses (Lahey et al., 1990). DSM-IV diagnostic criteria are likely to yield still different distributions of diagnoses.

DSM-III-R and DSM-IV specify that the diagnosis of Oppositional Defiant Disorder is not to be made if the criteria for Conduct Disorder are met. Does this mean that Oppositional Defiant Disorder is a mild version of Conduct Disorder, a developmentally early version, or a by-product, or that the two disorders are intrinsically related in some other way? Similar questions arise from overlaps among other diagnostic categories that are not derived from actual data on relations among children's problems. As an alternative to a priori diagnostic categories, the following section addresses possibilities for a more empirical approach.

AN EMPIRICAL BASIS FOR ASSESSMENT, TAXONOMY, AND DIAGNOSIS

The lack of well-defined childhood disorders in psychiatric nosologies has prompted efforts to identify disorders empirically by analyzing associations among problems reported for children. In the earliest efforts, combinations of bivariate statistical analyses and clinical judgments were applied to problems scored as present versus absent in the case histories of children referred to guidance clinics (Hewitt & Jenkins, 1946; Jenkins & Glickman, 1946). This approach yielded three broad sets of problems designated as the Overinhibited Child, the Unsocialized Aggressive Child, and the Socialized Delinquent Child.

In the 1960s and 1970s, the advent of computers made it easy to use multivariate analyses, such as factor analysis and principal components analysis, to identify groups of problems that tend to occur together. Multivariate analyses were applied to numerous rating forms completed by a variety of raters using different kinds of information on diverse samples of children. The variations in methodology and data sets made it risky to generalize from the findings of one study to the findings of each other study. Nevertheless, despite all the variations among different studies, reviews of the multivariate findings identified certain syndromes that appeared to be fairly consistent in multiple studies (Achenbach, 1985; Achenbach & Edelbrock, 1978; Quay, 1986).

A Second Generation Effort to Derive Syndromes

The first generation multivariate studies were exploratory. That is, they started with a potpourri of items that were analyzed to see what syndromes would emerge. However, the convergence of exploratory findings on certain syndromes prompted a "second generation" effort to test syndromes hypothesized on the basis of the first generation findings. After reviewing the syndromes found in the first generation studies, Achenbach, Conners, and Quay (1983) constructed the ACQ Behavior Checklist ("ACQ") to tap 12 syndromes for which evidence had been found in at least some of the previous studies. The items selected to tap the 12 syndromes were drawn from the existing Achenbach (1981) Child Behavior Checklist (CBCL), Conners (1978) Parent Questionnaire (PQ), and Quay and Peterson (1982) Revised Behavior Problem Checklist (RBPC). Additional items were written as needed to tap the 12 hypothesized syndromes. The ACQ was then completed by parents of 5,364 children referred to 18 mental health services distributed throughout the United States. The item scores were subjected to principal components analysis with varimax rotations. The results were compared with similar analyses of the CBCL (which has 115 problem items in common with the ACQ), analyses of the subset of 115 ACQ items that are counterparts of CBCL items, and analyses of the Dutch translation of the CBCL, all scored for children referred to a variety of mental health services in the United States and the Netherlands (Achenbach, Conners, Quay, Verhulst, & Howell, 1989).

Syndromes were identified that repeatedly occurred in multiple varimax rotations of principal components derived separately for each sex at ages 6 to 11 and 12 to 16. For most syndromes, the versions obtained from the different data sets correlated highly with one another when scored for a particular sample of children. This indicated good consistency in the composition of syndromes, despite differences in the instruments and samples from which they were derived.

The items that were found in the versions of a syndrome for a particular sex/age group in three or more of the four data sets were selected to represent a *core* version of the syndrome for children of that sex and age. Ten core syndromes were constructed in this fashion. Most of these syndromes had counterparts in all four sex/age groups, but some were restricted to one sex or a particular age range.

To assess the degree of consistency among the core syndromes identified for the four sex/age groups, correlations were computed among the core versions of a particular syndrome scored for groups of children of both sexes and different ages. (A child's score for a particular syndrome was the sum of the scores obtained by that child on the items comprising the syndrome.) Most of the core versions of a particular syndrome correlated highly with each other, indicating consistency for particular groupings of problems among children of both sexes and different ages. To represent the common elements of syndromes across the four data sets for both sexes and the two age ranges, *central core syndromes* were constructed from the items that were present in each core syndrome for a majority of the sex/age groups. All the central core syndromes were found to discriminate very well between demographically matched referred and nonreferred children. Thus, despite variations in the prevalence rates and patterning of problem items for boys and girls of different ages assessed with different instruments in different settings, this second generation effort yielded syndromes that, in turn, discriminated well between referred and nonreferred children.

A Third Generation Effort to Derive Cross-Informant Syndrome Constructs

The second generation effort moved beyond the first generation research in rigorously identifying a common set of syndromes in multiple data sets derived from parents' ratings. However, the modest correlations between reports of children's problems by different informants (Achenbach et al., 1987) indicate that parents' reports cannot substitute for reports by other informants. The need to obtain data from multiple informants makes it essential to determine whether data from different informants should focus on similar syndromes or on syndromes differing according to the type of informant.

To test the similarities and differences among syndromes derived from different informants, we have undertaken a third generation effort that builds on the methodology and findings of the first and second generation efforts. We have done this by obtaining ratings of clinically referred children from the informants who are usually most relevant to assessment of children's problems—their parents, their teachers, and the children themselves. The parents' ratings were obtained with the CBCL, the teachers' ratings were obtained with the Teacher's Report Form (TRF; Achenbach, 1991d), and self-ratings were obtained from 11- to 18-year-olds with the Youth Self-Report (YSR; Achenbach, 1991e). Although these forms have fewer problem items than the ACQ, the analyses of the ACQ did not yield any syndromes that were not also found in the CBCL. The CBCL, TRF, and YSR have 89 problem items in common, plus additional items that are specific to one or two of the informants.

To identify syndromes that might be similarly assessable by the different informants, we performed principal components analyses of the 89 common items scored on 8,542 CBCLs, TRFs, and YSRs for clinically referred children, separately for each sex in different age ranges. As in the second generation effort, the subjects were drawn from a large variety of clinical settings. Varimax rotations were performed on the largest principal components obtained for each sex/age group on each instrument. Sets of items that were found together in multiple rotations were considered to reflect syndromes that were robust for a particular sex/age group, as scored by a particular kind of informant (Achenbach, 1991b).

After syndromes were derived for each sex/age group on a particular instrument, the syndromes were compared across all the sex/age groups for that instrument. For those syndromes that had counterparts in multiple sex/age groups on a particular instrument, we constructed a *core syndrome* consisting of the problems that occurred together in a majority of the sex/age groups for which the syndrome was found. For example, versions of a Somatic Complaints syndrome were found on the CBCL in separate analyses of each sex at ages 4 to 5, 6 to 11, and 12 to 18. The items that obtained rotated factor loadings of at least .30 on the version of the syndrome derived from each sex/age group were printed in a list beside the items from the other five sex/age groups. Items that loaded ≥.30 on at least four of the six versions were retained for the core CBCL Somatic Complaints syndrome.

After identifying core syndromes from the CBCL, TRF, and YSR, we listed the items of the corresponding syndromes from the three instruments side-by-side. We then identified items that were present in the corresponding core syndromes for at least two of the three instruments. For example, we listed the items of the core Somatic Complaints syndromes from the CBCL, TRF, and YSR side-by-side. The items that were present in at least two of the three core syndromes were used to define a *cross-informant syndrome construct* for the Somatic Complaints syndrome. The term *construct* is used to signify that the items common to the core syndromes from multiple instruments represent a hypothetical variable that may not be completely measured by any of the three instruments alone. The Somatic Complaints construct represents the common elements of the different versions of the Somatic Complaints syndrome that were derived empirically from ratings of clinically referred boys and girls of different ages on the CBCL, TRF, and YSR.

In terms of categorical concepts, each cross-informant syndrome construct serves as a *prototype* (Rosch, 1978) consisting of correlated items that define a particular category of problems. In statistical terms, each cross-informant syndrome construct can be viewed as a "latent" (inferred) variable that is represented by a syndrome scale scored from the CBCL, TRF, and YSR. A syndrome scale scored from one instrument may differ somewhat from the scale for the same syndrome scored from the other instruments, in that the specific wording of items and some of the items included in a scale vary from one instrument to another. Ratings by one type of informant on a syndrome scale of one of the three instruments provide one operational definition for a syndrome construct. Ratings by the other types of informants on their respective instruments provide other operational definitions for the same construct. Ratings by the different informants can all be used to assess the same construct, but the ratings are not necessarily expected to correlate highly with one another.

Table 3.1 lists the problem items defining the eight cross-informant syndrome constructs that were derived from analyses of the CBCL, TRF, and YSR. These are the items that comprised the core versions of the corresponding syndromes derived from at least two of the three instruments.

The cross-cultural construct validity of the eight syndromes was supported by a separate factor analysis of CBCLs from 2,339 clinically referred Dutch children (De Groot, Koot, & Verhulst, 1994). Even though the factor analytic methodology differed from that used to derive the American syndrome constructs, the Dutch syndromes correlated .82 to .99 with the American syndromes. Furthermore, confirmatory factor analysis (CFA) showed that the American and Dutch factor models were virtually identical. According to three goodness-of-fit measures, the CFA findings on a second cross-validation sample of 2,335 clinically referred Dutch children were just as similar to the American factor model as to the model derived separately on the initial Dutch sample of 2,339 children. The syndrome constructs were thus taxonomically very robust despite methodological differences in deriving them and the differences in language, culture, and mental health systems. Similar findings have been obtained with Dutch translations of the TRF and YSR (De Groot, Koot, & Verhulst, submitted).

Besides the eight cross-informant syndromes, an additional syndrome designated as Sex Problems was found in parents' CBCL ratings of younger boys and girls, and a syndrome designated as Destructive was found in parents' CBCL ratings of girls (Achenbach, 1991c). A syndrome designed as Self-Destructive/Identity Problems was also found in boys' self-ratings on the YSR (Achenbach, 1991e). These syndromes reflect problems that co-occurred in ratings by one type of informant but were not found to co-occur in ratings by the other types of informants. They are apt to be quite important in the assessment of children according to ratings by the relevant type of informant. However,

TABLE 3.1 Items Defining the Cross-Informant Syndrome Constructs Derived from the Child Behavior Checklist (CBCL), Youth Self-Report (YSR), and Teacher's Report Form (TRF)[1]

Internalizing Scales		Neither Internalizing nor Externalizing		Externalizing Scales	
Withdrawn	*Anxious/Depressed*	*Social Problems*	*Attention Problems*	*Delinquent Behavior*	*Aggressive Behavior*
42. Would rather be alone	12. Lonely	1. Acts too young	1. Acts too young	26. Lacks guilt	3. Argues
65. Refuses to talk	14. Cries a lot	11. Too dependent	8. Can't concentrate	39. Bad companions	7. Brags
69. Secretive	31. Fears impulses	25. Doesn't get along with peers	10. Can't sit still	43. Lies	16. Mean to others
75. Shy, timid	32. Needs to be perfect	38. Gets teased	13. Confused	63. Prefers older kids	19. Demands attention
80. Stares blankly[2]	33. Feels unloved	48. Not liked by peers	17. Daydreams	67. Runs away from home[3]	20. Destroys own things
88. Sulks[2]	34. Feels persecuted	62. Clumsy	41. Impulsive	72. Sets fires[3]	21. Destroys others' things
102. Underactive	35. Feels worthless	64. Prefers younger kids	45. Nervous, tense	81. Steals at home	23. Disobedient at school
103. Unhappy, sad, depressed	45. Nervous, tense		61. Poor school work	82. Steals outside home	27. Jealous
111. Withdrawn	50. Fearful, anxious	*Thought Problems*	62. Clumsy	90. Swearing, obscenity	37. Fights
	52. Feels too guilty	9. Can't get mind off thoughts	80. Stares blankly[2]	101. Truancy	57. Attacks people
Somatic Complaints	71. Self-conscious	40. Hears things		105. Alcohol, drugs	68. Screams
51. Feels dizzy	89. Suspicious	66. Repeats acts			74. Shows off
54. Overtired	103. Unhappy, sad, depressed	70. Sees things			86. Stubborn, irritable
56a. Aches, pains	112. Worries	84. Strange behavior			87. Sudden mood changes
56b. Headaches		85. Strange ideas			93. Talks too much
56c. Nausea					94. Teases
56d. Eye problems					95. Temper tantrums
56e. Rashes, skin problems					97. Threatens
56f. Stomachaches					104. Loud
56g. Vomiting					

[1]Items are designated by the numbers they bear on the CBCL, YSR, and TRF and by summaries of their content.
[2]Not on YSR.
[3]Not on TRF.
From Achenbach, 1991b, pp. 48–50.

because they did not meet our criteria for cross-informant syndromes, we will not deal with them in the following sections.

Profiles for Scoring Cross-Informant Syndromes

To aid in assessing children according to the eight syndromes, separate profiles have been constructed for scoring the CBCL, TRF, and YSR. The CBCL profile, for example, displays scales comprising the items used to score the CBCL versions of the eight cross-informant syndromes. Each item is scored 0 = Not True (of the child), 1 = Somewhat or Sometimes True, and 2 = Very True or Often True. The scores for the items of a syndrome scale are summed to provide a raw scale score for that syndrome as reported by a particular informant. To provide a normative basis for comparison, the raw scale scores are converted to *T* scores derived from national normative samples. To take account of sex and age differences in the distributions of scores, a child's *T* score is based on a normative sample of the child's sex and age. The profile displays a child's score on each syndrome scale in relation to the distribution of scores for the appropriate normative sample. The profile also indicates a normal, borderline, and clinical range for each scale. Figure 3.2 summarizes relations among the derivation of syndromes, formulation of cross-informant syndrome constructs, and construction of scales for scoring the syndromes on the CBCL, TRF, and YSR profiles.

Internalizing and Externalizing Groupings

Previous research on children's problems has distinguished between broad groupings variously designated as Personality Problem versus Conduct Problem (Peterson, 1961), Internalizing versus Externalizing (Achenbach, 1966), Inhibition versus Aggression (Miller, 1967), and Overcontrolled versus Undercontrolled (Achenbach & Edelbrock, 1978). To test this distinction in the cross-informant syndromes, we performed second-order principal factor/varimax analyses of scores obtained on the eight syndrome scales. We did this separately for clinically referred children of each sex in each age range, as scored from the CBCL, TRF, and YSR. The two largest factors in each solution were rotated to the varimax criterion for simple structure.

Averaged across all sex/age groups on all three instruments, the loadings of the syndrome scales showed that the Withdrawn, Somatic Complaints, and Anxious/Depressed syndromes formed one distinct grouping. The Aggressive Behavior and Delinquent Behavior syndromes formed another distinct grouping. The Attention Problems syndrome had a moderately high mean loading

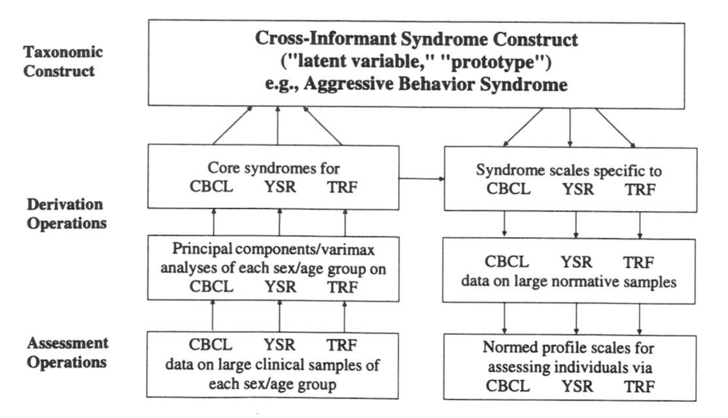

Figure 3.2 Relations among derivation of syndromes, formulation of cross-informant syndrome constructs, and construction of profile scales (from Achenbach, 1991b).

of .618 on the second-order factor that included the Aggressive and Delinquent syndromes. However, because the mean loading of .618 obtained by the Attention Problems syndrome was substantially below the mean loadings of .791 and .778 obtained by the Aggressive and Delinquent syndromes, respectively, the Attention Problems syndrome was not assigned to the Externalizing grouping. The Social Problems and Thought Problems syndromes did not have consistently high loadings on either of the second-order factors.

The CBCL, TRF, and YSR profiles are arranged in a uniform format to reflect the Internalizing grouping of the Withdrawn, Somatic Complaints, and Anxious/Depressed scales on the left, followed by the Social Problems, Thought Problems, and Attention Problems syndromes in the middle, and the Delinquent and Aggressive syndromes on the right. To assess children in terms of the Internalizing–Externalizing distinction, raw scores and *T* scores are computed for the sum of Internalizing items and the sum of Externalizing items, respectively. Normal, borderline, and clinical ranges have been derived from comparisons between the Internalizing and Externalizing scores of nonreferred versus referred children (Achenbach, 1991c, 1991d, 1991e).

Cross-Informant Comparisons

To facilitate comparisons among multiple informants on the cross-informant syndromes, a cross-informant computer program is available (described by Achenbach, 1991b, 1993). Data from up to five informants, such as the CBCLs completed by parents, TRFs completed by teachers, and the YSR can be entered into the program. The program then scores a separate profile from each informant's data. In addition, the program displays side-by-side the raw scores for each of the 89 problem items common to all three types of informant and the *T* scores for the eight syndrome scales, Internalizing, Externalizing, and total problems, as scored by each type of informant. The program also indicates whether each scale score is in the normal, borderline, or clinical range, enabling the user to identify agreements and disagreements among the levels of the scale scores obtained from the different informants. In addition, the program displays intraclass correlations between the child's profile pattern that is scored from each informant and profile types that were derived from cluster analyses (Achenbach, 1993).

To provide quantitative indexes of the degree of agreement between informants, the program computes *Q* correlations between each combination of informants for the 89 item scores and also for the eight syndrome scale scores. (A *Q* correlation is a correlation between two sets of scores where all the scores in one set are derived from one source, such as the father's 89 item scores, and all scores in the other set are derived from another source, such as the mother's 89 item scores. The more familiar *R* correlation, by contrast, is computed between scores on two variables, where the two variables are scored for multiple subjects.)

To give users a basis for judging the *Q* correlations between pairs of informants rating a particular child, the cross-informant program also prints out the 25th percentile, the mean, and the 75th percentile correlations obtained in large reference samples. Thus, if the correlation between the CBCLs obtained from a particular father and mother is below the 25th percentile for a large reference sample of mothers and fathers, their agreement is considered to be relatively low. If the correlation between the CBCLs from the father and mother is above the 75th percentile, on the other hand, their agreement is relatively high. The cross-informant program provides precise information on specific agreements and disagreements among informants for parallel problem items, syndromes, Internalizing, Externalizing, total problem scores, and profile patterns. A child can thus be simultaneously viewed from the perspectives of different informants. Interventions with the informants as well as with the child can then be tailored to these different perspectives.

Applications of Cross-Informant Syndromes

As described in the foregoing sections, the cross-informant syndromes have been empirically derived from multivariate analyses of large clinical samples scored by parents, teachers, and the subjects themselves. Standard scores for the syndromes have been normed on national samples of nonreferred children rated by each type of informant. The scoring profiles are designed to coordinate and compare data on multiple syndromes as seen by multiple informants. The rating forms and scoring profiles can be used in clinical practice, as well as in research and theoretical work.

Profiles of quantitatively scored syndromes avoid the problems of comorbidity arising from categorical definitions of disorders whose boundaries have not been empirically established. Because each child obtains a score on all syndromes, there is no need for forced choices between different diagnostic categories. Furthermore, because any pattern of scores is possible, a child may obtain high scores on several syndromes without necessarily being diagnosed as having several coexisting disorders. Instead, a profile pattern characterized by peaks on multiple syndromes may reveal a disorder that is more multifaceted than separate diagnostic categories can reveal. Or, the relative elevation of multiple syndrome scales may reflect responses to conditions that differ across the situations in which a child functions or that change with time. By preserving quantitative variations in scores across multiple syndromes and multiple informants, we can avoid premature closure on categories that may short-circuit the detailed assessment process needed for effective diagnostic thinking.

A Taxonomic Decision Tree

Where decisions need to be made about the predominant areas of deviance, data from multiple sources can be integrated according to the decision-making strategy illustrated in Figure 3.3. Called a *taxonomic decision tree,* this strategy starts with data from several sources that yield scores for similar sets of syndromes, which are normed for particular developmental periods. The eight cross-informant syndromes scorable from the CBCL, TRF, and YSR are examples. Other sources of data might include clinical interviews and direct observations. As an example of a clinical interview, the Semistructured Clinical Interview for Children and Adolescents (SCICA; McConaughy & Achenbach, 1994b) has been developed to derive syndromes from interview responses and observations, using methods like those employed with the CBCL, TRF, and YSR. To provide observational data, the Direct Observation Form (DOF; see Achenbach, 1991c) is designed to score behavior observed in group settings, such as classrooms, in terms of empirically derived syndromes.

As shown in Figure 3.3, the decision maker starts at the top of the decision tree with data from any combination of sources, such as father, mother, teachers, structured self-reports, interviews, and observations. After the syndrome scales are scored from each source, the initial screening question is whether any scales are in the clinical range. A global screen for deviance would include total problem, Internalizing, and Externalizing scores, as well as syndrome scales from each source. If no scores are in the clinical range, this would indicate that the child is not clinically deviant. Nevertheless, individual items should be examined for evidence of problems that are important in their own right, such as suicidal behavior and fire setting, whether or not any scales are in the clinical range.

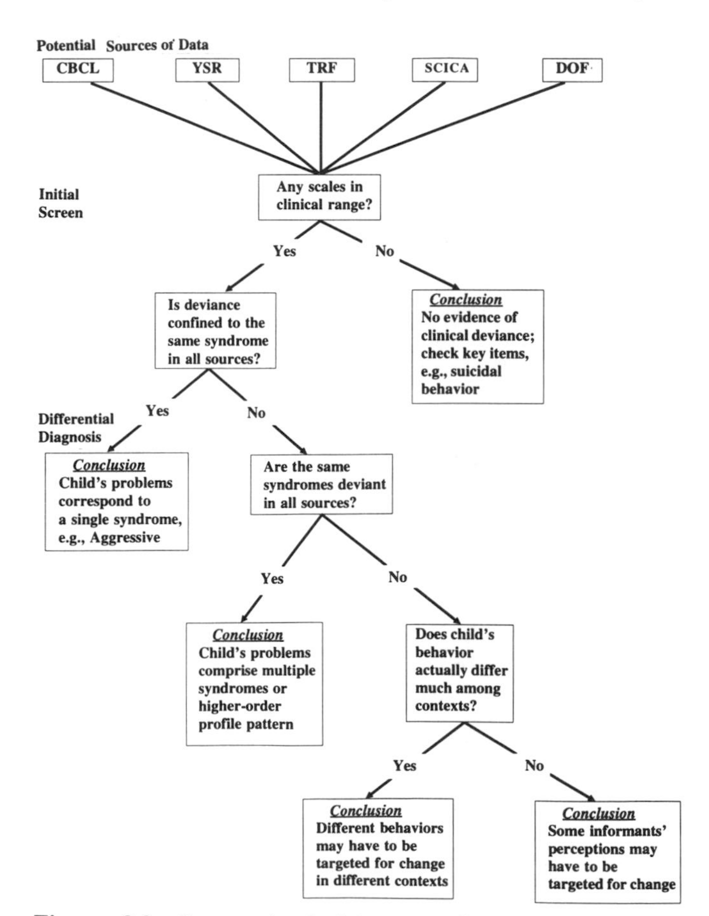

Figure 3.3 Taxonomic decision tree for using empirically based assessment procedures (from Achenbach, 1991b).

If any scales are in the clinical range, the next question is whether deviant scores occur on the same syndromes in all sources of data that show any deviance. This is a question of differential diagnosis. If deviance is confined to the same syndromes in all data, this indicates focalized problems in the area of that syndrome.

If deviant scores are not confined to a single syndrome, we then ask whether the same combination of syndromes is deviant in all data. If the answer is yes, this indicates that the child's problems comprise multiple syndromes or a complex profile pattern that might correspond to profile types identifiable through cluster analysis.

On the other hand, if different syndromes are deviant according to different sources, we need to determine whether the child's behavior actually differs much among contexts. If the answer is yes, we can conclude that different behaviors may have to be targeted for change in different contexts. If the answer is no, however, this suggests that some of the informants' perceptions of the child may need changing.

Additional choices besides those represented in the decision tree are possible, as are additional sources of data, such as medical examinations, interviews with parents and teachers, family assessment, and psychological tests. However, the taxonomic decision tree and cross-informant program are especially valuable for focusing research, training, and diagnostic decision making on taxonomic distinctions that can be made from multiple sources relevant to the assessment of most children.

Research on the Developmental Course of Psychopathology

In addition to clinical applications, the cross-informant syndromes can facilitate research on the development of psychopathology. The low cost, standardization, and wide applicability of the assessment procedures make them practical for use in large general population samples as well as in clinical samples. The use of representative general population samples avoids biases that are associated with referral to particular clinical facilities. The parallel forms enable users to obtain data from multiple sources that are relevant to functioning in different contexts and different developmental periods. Furthermore, because the norms span extensive age ranges, relations between syndromes and other variables can be tested over numerous developmentally significant periods.

As an example of developmental research on psychopathology using the cross-informant syndromes, Stanger, McConaughy, and Achenbach (1992) tested predictive relations among family variables, stressful experiences, and syndrome scores over a 3-year period for children who were 4 to 16 years old at Time 1. In a home interview survey, parents of a nationally representative sample of 2,734 children initially completed the ACQ Behavior Checklist and provided data on socioeconomic status (SES), family constellation, marital status of the parents, child care arrangements for the subjects, and mental health services received by family members. Three years later, the parents completed the CBCL, again provided data on family variables, and reported on stresses experienced by the child since the Time 1 assessment. In addition, teachers of children who were attending school completed the TRF. Those of the subjects who were 11 to 19 years old completed the YSR and provided self-reports of their own stressful experiences.

Path analyses were done for subjects of each sex at initial ages 4 to 11 and 12 to 16, to identify significant predictors of the eight cross-informant syndromes, as scored by parents, teachers, and the subjects themselves. Some significant predictors varied with the age and sex of the subjects. However, to identify predictors that were especially robust despite sex and age variations, beta weights that were significant in at least 3 of the 4 sex/age groups were selected. Figure 3.4 illustrates the path relations found for prediction of Time 2 parents' ratings on the Delinquent syndrome when the standardized beta weights significant in 3 or more sex/age groups were averaged across all 4 groups. As Figure 3.4 shows, not only Time 1 Delinquent Behavior scores but also Time 1 Attention Problems and Aggressive Behavior syndrome scores made significant independent contributions to the prediction of Time 2 Delinquent Behavior scores 3 years later. Furthermore, parents' marital status (married or widowed versus other) made an indirect contribution through its significant prediction of Time 1 Delinquent Behavior. And the number of family members (besides the subject) receiving mental health services made an indirect contribution through its significant prediction of Time 1 Aggressive Behavior.

Path analyses of the national sample over 6 years have revealed important sex differences in predictive pathways (Achenbach, Howell, McConaughy, & Stanger, in press a, b). For example, even though the literature on ADHD focuses mainly on boys, we found that the empirically based Attention Problems syndrome predicted a greater variety of later problems among girls than boys. Conversely, even though the literature on affective disorders tends to focus on girls, the empirically based Anxious/Depressed syndrome predicted more diverse problems among boys than girls.

IMPLICATIONS FOR UNDERSTANDING, PREVENTING, AND TREATING PSYCHOPATHOLOGY

Neither researchers nor practitioners can be expected to master all aspects of both development and psychopathology. Instead, conceptual paradigms are needed to selectively organize thinking and activities around subsets of variables and to provide tools for dealing with those variables. Because so many variables may be associated with both development and psychopathology, no single paradigm can encompass all of them. Furthermore, paradigms should engender research that yields new knowledge which, in turn, will require the paradigms to be revised or replaced.

The 20th century has produced a remarkable range of paradigms concerning development and psychopathology. Global theories for explaining vast domains of human functioning have generally given way to much more specialized foci. In the study of development, for example, the specialized foci tend to be on specific phenomena, such as attachment behavior (e.g., Fox, Kimmerly, & Schafer, 1991), and specific functions, such as memory (e.g., Friedman, 1991). In the study of psychopathology, the specialized foci tend to be on specific categories of disorders, which have proliferated since the DSM-III added numerous new categories of childhood disorders. Many books on child

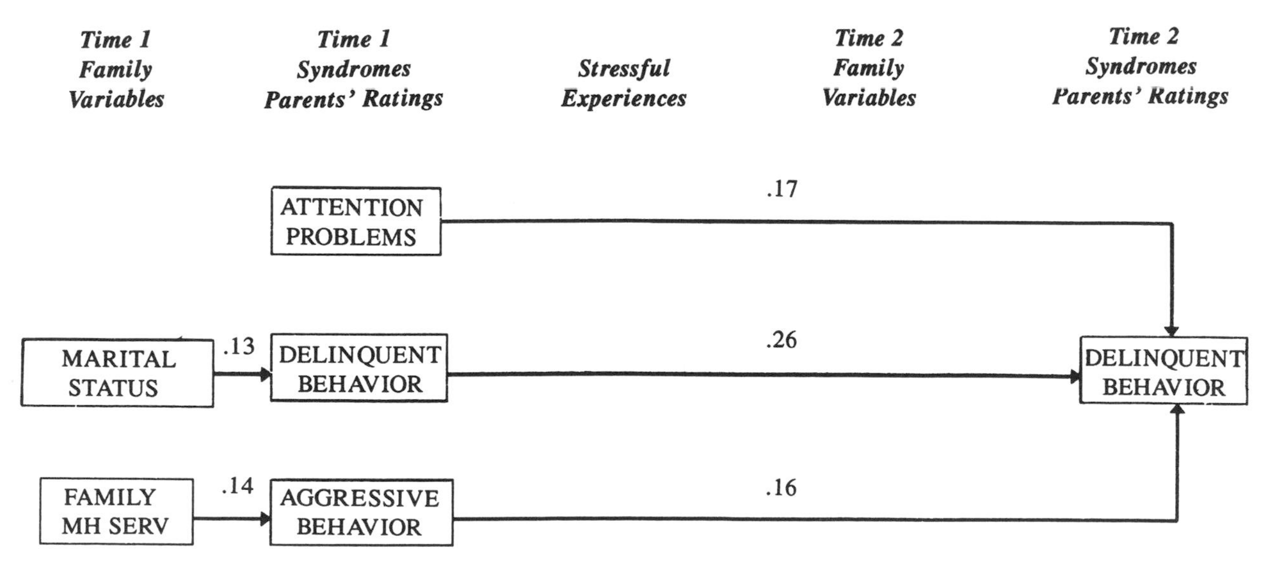

Figure 3.4 Path analysis of 3-year predictors of parents' ratings of the Delinquent Behavior syndrome in a national sample of children and youth (from Stanger, McConaughy, & Achenbach, 1992).

psychopathology are now organized mainly around lists of disorders, although there is little evidence that each disorder is really a separate entity that exists independently of all the others.

As a field grows, it inevitably becomes more differentiated and specialized. However, advances in the level of understanding and in the effectiveness with which a field's knowledge is applied also require progressive *integration* of data, methods, and ideas. Like the process of individual development described by Heinz Werner (1957), the development of a field involves both "differentiation and hierarchic integration." At this particular stage in the development of developmental psychopathology, an empirically based approach to assessment and taxonomy offers a way of integrating many aspects of the study, prevention, and treatment of childhood problems. Rather than classifying childhood problems in terms of categorical disorders that are judged to be either present or absent, the empirically based approach provides standardized procedures for quantitatively assessing the problems of individual children from multiple perspectives. To reflect developmental variations in the composition of syndromes, as well as variations in relation to other subject characteristics such as sex, and differences among informants, syndromes are derived separately for different groups of subjects and different sources of data. Those syndromes that are similar across different developmental periods, both sexes, and/or different informants are normed to reflect developmental, sex, and informant variations.

Because all children obtain quantitative scores on each empirically derived syndrome, diagnosticians are not forced to choose between diagnostic categories. Nor do high scores on multiple syndromes necessarily imply comorbidity among separate disorders. Instead, any combination of syndrome scores may be informative about the pattern of a particular child's problems. Furthermore, the empirically based approach can identify groups of children who have similar profiles of syndrome scores as a basis for a taxonomy that may be more comprehensive and powerful than taxonomies based on individual syndromes. Children who are deviant on a particular syndrome may share certain etiological factors in common. However, those who manifest similar patterns across multiple syndromes may be similar in a greater variety of ways, including how they respond to pathogenic factors, as well as similarities in the pathogenic factors themselves. The empirically based approach is closely tied to research data, provides a source of research hypotheses, and is open to revision as knowledge advances.

Improving Diagnostic Decision Making

Diagnostic decisions about children typically involve a variety of data, such as reports from parents and teachers, developmental histories, interviews with the children, observations, medical data, and cognitive, achievement, and personality tests. The practitioner must elicit, process, remember, and integrate these diverse kinds of data in order to determine what the problems are and how best to help. For some forms of persistent, pervasive, and extreme deviance, such as infantile autism and Down syndrome, the practitioner can match salient patterns to relatively clear diagnostic categories. These particular categories have well-established prognostic correlates. By contrast, most behavioral/emotional problems of childhood present much less salient patterns and greater disparities among different sources of data. It is for problems of this sort, which characterize the majority of children referred for mental health services, that the empirically based approach can be especially helpful in diagnostic thinking.

Research has demonstrated numerous sources of bias in people's judgments of clinical data (reviewed by Achenbach, 1985). Many of the biases arise from information processing strategies that are appropriate for the regularities of everyday life but are inadequate for clinical assessment. As an example, the unaided human mind is not very good at detecting systematic covariation among attributes observed across large numbers of cases. Cognitive research has shown that, even when attributes are specified in a concrete present-versus-absent fashion, people tend to infer *illusory correlations* among them where no correlations exist (Arkes, Harkness, & Biber, 1988). Under certain conditions, people also fail to detect associations between attributes that are perfectly correlated in a series of cases (Chapman & Chapman, 1971). Training people to beware of illusory correlations does not prevent the trainees from inferring them (Kurtz & Garfield, 1978). Covariation is especially difficult to detect among attributes that do not occur in concrete present-versus-absent form but that need to be judged over a variety of situations and gradations. Most behavioral/emotional problems of childhood present difficulties of this sort.

Another bias in processing complex clinical data is the *confirmatory bias*. This is the tendency for people to weight data that confirm their beliefs more heavily than disconfirming data (Arkes & Harkness, 1983). In clinical information processing, it has been found that initial judgments are retained despite disconfirming data. Worse yet, confidence in the initial judgments increases greatly as the amount of data increases, even though the judgments do not become more accurate (Nisbett, Zukier, & Lemley, 1981). Furthermore, experienced clinicians seem to be more susceptible to the biasing effects of their initial judgments than nonclinicians, who have less confidence in their own judgments (Friedlander & Phillips, 1984).

Empirically based assessment can avoid information processing biases in the collection of clinical data by providing standardized quantitative data on each of a large number of problems, as scored by multiple informants from their own perspectives. The initial clinical database is thus free of the practitioner's biases in deciding what data to obtain in what way, from which informants, and how to process it. Similarly, empirically based taxonomy can avoid information processing biases in combining data, because the data are combined by means of quantitative procedures (Achenbach, 1993).

Decisions about the degree to which a child is reported to manifest each syndrome are protected from information processing biases when the child's scores are computed in a standardized fashion for comparison with norms for the child's sex and age, as scored by the relevant type of informants. Furthermore, the process of comparing and integrating clinical data from multiple informants can be protected from biases by using the cross-informant computer program (Achenbach, 1993) to explicitly compare data from each pair of informants and to quantify the level of agreement between informants.

These procedures do not obviate the need for clinical judgment, which is ultimately required to make decisions about what to do in each case and how to deal with all the relevant people. However, by providing standardized means for obtaining, aggregating, and comparing data, empirically based assessment and taxonomy can free clinical thinking for the tasks that require creative solutions, rather than overburdening it with tasks that can be better handled by other means. By employing developmentally appropriate procedures and norms, empirically based assessment and taxonomy also avoid reifying diagnostic constructs as if they represented entities that retain the same form across the course of development.

Prevention and Treatment

To improve our ways of preventing and treating psychopathology, we need economical procedures that can be used to assess large samples of children who are candidates for preventive or therapeutic efforts. The same procedures need to be applicable at developmentally later periods to assess outcomes. Furthermore, the assessment procedures should be able to differentiate among various kinds of problems in order to test interactions between the type of problems and type of interventions.

Preventive research typically requires identification of large numbers of individuals who are at risk for later problems but who have not yet been referred for clinical services. Whether the risk factors are external to the child subjects, such as parental divorce, or are characteristics of the subjects, such as aggressive behavior, it is far more feasible to recruit representative samples for pre- and postpreventive assessments if the assessments are not intrusive, do not require much time or highly skilled personnel to administer, and can be done in the subjects' everyday environments. Similarly, for rigorous pre–post comparisons of children receiving experimental therapeutic interventions, it is more feasible to obtain representative samples of referred children if the assessment procedures can be readily included in routine clinical intakes, without being burdensome to the subjects or their families. Their low cost, self-administration format, and broad applicability make empirically based assessment and taxonomic procedures easy to use in pre–post assessments of preventive and therapeutic efforts in conjunction with whatever other assessment procedures are chosen for a particular study.

FUTURE DIRECTIONS

Applications of developmental perspectives to the study of psychopathology are still in their infancy. Many important tasks lie ahead. This chapter has laid groundwork on which to build new structures. We will now consider some forms that future work may take.

Extensions to Adult Psychopathology

Findings and theories regarding adult psychopathology have long influenced views of child psychopathology. A key task of developmental psychopathology has been to replace unsupported assumptions based on adult psychopathology with empirical findings on relations between development and psychopathology. For a variety of reasons, the downward extrapolation from adult to child psychopathology now shows signs of being reversed.

Adult Attention Deficit Disorders

One reason for extending developmental approaches from the study of children upward to the study of adults is the wide publicity being given adult attention deficit disorders, even by popular media such as television talk shows and *Newsweek* magazine (Cowley & Ramo, 1993). Until recently, attention deficit disorders were assumed to be outgrown in adolescence. However, follow-up studies of children diagnosed as having attention deficit disorders have shown that many continue to have significant behavioral problems in young adulthood (Mannuzza, Klein, Bessler, Malloy, & LaPadula, 1993; Weiss & Hechtman, 1993). The problems often extend well beyond the DSM criteria for childhood attention deficit disorders. Are such problems adult continuations of childhood attention deficit disorders? Or do they reflect maladaptive developmental consequences of earlier attention deficits? Or are they continuations of conduct or other disorders that are often reported to accompany attention deficits? We do not yet have answers to these questions.

The DSM and ICD do not provide specific criteria for adult attention deficit disorders. Furthermore, influential epidemiological surveys that include adolescents as well as adults have not employed criteria for attention deficit disorders (e.g., Kessler et al., 1994). To determine whether attention deficit disorders indeed continue into adulthood, whether their form changes, what their consequences are, and how they should be treated, we must adapt methodology and criteria developed on children to the study of adults.

Longitudinal Research Extending into Adulthood

A second reason for applying developmental approaches to the study of adults is that several longitudinal studies of psychopathology that began when their subjects were children are now reassessing their subjects in early adulthood (e.g., Achenbach, Howell, McConaughy, & Stanger, in press c; Ferdinand & Verhulst, 1994; Ferdinand, Wiznitzer, & Verhulst, in press; Reinherz, 1994). To provide methodological continuity between assessment of child and adult psychopathology, upward extensions of the CBCL and YSR are being used to assess subjects at ages 19 to 28. Called the Young Adult Behavior Checklist (YABCL) and Young Adult Self-Report (YASR), these instruments are similar in format to the CBCL and YSR and have many adult counterparts of the same items. In addition, however, the YABCL and YASR have items geared to the different developmental pathways that young adults may follow, including higher education, work, military service, and conjugal partnerships.

Principal components/varimax analyses of these instruments have yielded several syndromes that are similar to the cross-informant syndromes derived from the CBCL, YSR, and TRF, plus other syndromes that do not have clear counterparts at younger ages. Syndrome scores obtained on the CBCL and YSR have been found to predict scores on the adult syndromes 3 years later with as much accuracy as prediction of CBCL and YSR scores from the same instruments over 3 years of adolescence (Achenbach et al., in press c). In addition, scores on the adult instruments predict subsequent DSM diagnoses and discriminate more accurately between young adults seen for mental health services and normative samples of young adults than do the General Health Questionnaire and Symptom Checklist-90, which are widely used to assess adult psychopathology (Achenbach et al., in press c; Wiznitzer et al., 1992).

Long-Term Outcomes of Childhood Disorders

A third reason for extending developmental approaches is to compare long-term outcomes for different kinds of psychopathology, as well as for different preventive and therapeutic efforts. Because there is a paucity of hard data on relations between specific childhood problems and specific adult disorders, it is important to determine the typical adult outcomes for different types of childhood problems. It is also important to determine whether these outcomes are affected by preventive and therapeutic interventions. Rather than using child-oriented assessment procedures initially and then very different adult-oriented outcome measures later, it is preferable to use a series of similar procedures that are calibrated to successive developmental periods. This is especially true for the transitional period between adolescence and adulthood, from roughly about age 17 to age 25. Even though major adult disorders such as schizophrenia and bipolar conditions begin to emerge during this period, it is often unclear whether early adult behavioral/emotional problems are forerunners of major disorders, are developmentally specific phenomena, or are continuations of earlier problems. To sort out the various possibilities, it is necessary to use assessment procedures that are tailored more closely to the various developmental pathways of this period than are instruments focused on either child nosology or adult nosology. Neither the traditional child instruments nor adult instruments may adequately tap problems characteristic of the transitional period.

Bridging the Gap between Research and Practice

The research literature on child psychopathology is steadily growing, as is the number of practitioners who deal with troubled children. However, the research is spread over diverse publications, while the practitioners have diverse orientations. They see children in contexts ranging from private psychiatric, psychological, and social work practices, to mental health clinics, pediatric settings, schools, courts, hospitals, and residential treatment centers. Few practitioners have the time to distill large quantities of research literature for applications to their practice. As a result, there is a wide gap between most research on child psychopathology and the services that children actually receive. Certain assessment concepts and procedures may be idiosyncratic to particular practitioners, may be unsupported by research or may even be discredited by research.

Although the DSM provides an administrative classification system for purposes of record keeping and third-party payment, it does not provide assessment operations. The means for making DSM diagnoses therefore vary widely, and DSM diagnoses of children are of questionable utility for guiding treatment. Furthermore, settings that provide a large proportion of the services for troubled children, such as schools, have their own administrative classifications, such as those based on P. L. 101-476 (Individuals with Disabilities Act, 1990). Even classifications based on P. L. 101-476 vary widely, however, because states and localities differ in their interpretations and terminology for the P. L. 101-476 categories.

Empirically based assessment and taxonomy provide procedures that can be readily employed in most settings in conjunction with procedures that are specific to particular settings. Because the results of empirically based assessment and taxonomy directly reflect reports by relevant informants for a particular child, they are directly applicable to decisions about the child. They also provide a baseline against which to evaluate change over the course of interventions by readministering the same procedures. The derivation of empirically based assessment and taxonomy from extensive research that supports its reliability and validity (Achenbach, 1991c, 1991d, 1991e, 1993), plus over 1,500 studies establishing numerous correlates in many populations (Brown & Achenbach, 1995), provide practitioners with the fruits of research. Conversely, the continual input of practitioners to the development of these procedures contributes to their user friendliness for practitioners as well as for researchers. Both practice and research can benefit from progressively increasing the degree to which they share the same assessment, taxonomic, and information systems, despite the necessary differences between their day-to-day agendas.

Reforming Health Care Financing

The system for financing health care in the United States is under great stress for a variety of reasons. One reason is the soaring cost of medical technology that prolongs the lives of severely impaired people who would previously have died. A second reason is increased usage of health services owing to the aging of the population. A third reason is the readiness to seek costly specialized care for ailments that would not have received specialized care previously. A fourth reason for stress is the increasing number of uninsured people who are at high risk for serious illness due to poverty, homelessness, drug addiction, failure to obtain treatment in a timely fashion, and neglect. A fifth reason is the inability of employers and government to pay for steep rises in costs for those whom they insure. And a sixth reason is the pervasive effort to shift costs by reducing government reimbursements below the actual costs of care, transferring the costs of nonpaying patients to paying patients, limiting insurance coverage, and juggling coverage among insurance companies, health maintenance organizations, and managed care plans.

The financing of mental health services raises additional problems. These services are not uniformly accepted as health care costs, they are harder to define in terms of specific health care needs, and some people may be heavy users without having verifiable needs for service. Furthermore, people who are least likely to be covered by insurance often need the greatest care, at a time when government facilities, such as mental hospitals, have been drastically curtailed.

Changes are certainly needed in the way health care is financed in the United States. Whatever changes are made, however, financing of mental health care for children will continue to present unique problems. Because children cannot arrange for their own mental health care, services are typically sought when adults, such as parents, teachers, or pediatricians, decide that help is needed. Because of a lack of clarity about which behavioral/emotional problems of childhood warrant mental health services, and because there is seldom a specific treatment of proven efficacy, the type of service sought and obtained varies widely. When mental health services are sought on a fee-for-service basis, the adequacy and source of payment often affect the diagnostic process as well as access to particular practitioners and types of service. If a family has insurance or Medicaid, for example, the diagnosis is apt to hinge on what is reimbursable by that third-party payer. As a consequence, official diagnoses cannot necessarily be taken at face value as reflecting children's needs in the same way as if third-party payment were not a factor. If special education services are sought, ambiguities arise in the application of local, state, and federal regulations to children's eligibility for services. Like diagnoses, administrative classifications of children for special education are often affected by efforts to shift or avoid the costs.

Despite the unpredictable flux of health care financing, it is important to protect diagnostic practices from being distorted by financial exigencies. Although economic and political factors will continue to shape administrative classifications, mental health professionals should apply state-of-the-art knowledge to the diagnostic process. Because empirically based assessment and taxonomy are derived from multiple sources of data on children's problems rather than being shaped by economic and political exigencies, they can guide decision making about how to help children regardless of the vicissitudes of administrative classifications. A major challenge will be to advance the empirical basis for choosing and rendering services to troubled children within managed care systems dominated by cost-cutting. In the long run, a better empirical basis for services will enhance both cost-effectiveness and the overall quality of care.

CONCLUSION

Assessment, taxonomy, and diagnosis are especially fundamental in the developmental study of psychopathology, because these endeavors distinguish the normal from the pathological and one kind of pathology from another. In this chapter, the term *developmental* was used broadly to encompass processes, changes, sequences, and characteristics that are typically associated with chronological age or with other developmental parameters, such as mental age. The term *psychopathology* was used to encompass persistent behavior, thoughts, and emotions that impede the accomplishment of developmental tasks necessary for long-term adaptation. Diverse theoretical perspectives can contribute to our developmental understanding of psychopathology, but no single theory is currently adequate for explaining all the relevant phenomena.

Rather than limiting ourselves to a particular theoretical approach at this stage, it is useful to draw on methods and concepts from diverse approaches in order to build a better empirical basis for assessment, taxonomy, and diagnosis. As an example, cohort-sequential research designs offer a means for carrying out accelerated longitudinal studies of the development of psychopathology in less time than is required for the developmental periods to be spanned. To take advantage of such designs, it is necessary to have standardized assessment procedures that can be repeatedly readministered across a wide age range at low cost.

Nosological approaches to classifying psychopathology have shaped concepts of adult psychopathology since the 19th century. However, these approaches provided little differentiation among childhood disorders until late in the 20th century. When official nosologies, such as the DSM, began to differentiate among childhood disorders, adult diagnostic formats were applied to children and adolescents. The categories for child/adolescent psychopathology have undergone rapid changes in each edition of the DSM, with neither a firm empirical basis for the changes nor calibration of criteria from one edition to the next. Theoretical approaches to the classification of child/adolescent psychopathology, such as those based on psychoanalytic theory, have also lacked firm empirical support.

As an alternative to *a priori* classification of psychopathology in terms of either nosological categories or theoretical inferences, multivariate statistical methods have been used to identify syndromes of problems that tend to occur together in large samples of clinically referred children. To take account of variations in problems related to children's age, sex, and other characteristics, separate multivariate analyses have been performed for children grouped according to these characteristics. Furthermore, empirically based norms and clinical cutpoints have been established according to the distributions of scores obtained by representative normative and clinical samples.

The following tasks face the developmental study of psychopathology: to gear assessment and taxonomy to the developmental level of the subjects; to take account of developmental changes occurring in individual subjects studied longitudinally; to integrate multiple sources of assessment data; to provide an epidemiological basis for the selection of diagnostic criteria and cutpoints; to rigorously aggregate large numbers of data points; and to provide operational definitions for disorders.

To improve research and diagnostic decision making, we need reliable and valid procedures for identifying the distinguishing features of cases (*assessment*), for grouping cases according to their distinguishing features (*taxonomy*), and for integrating relevant data into optimal diagnostic decisions. Conceptual *prototypes* provide taxonomic models that mesh the quantitative and correlational aspects of cognitive processing with the quantitative and correlational aspects of syndromes.

The term *diagnosis* has multiple meanings that obscure relations among the tasks of assessment, taxonomy, and decision making about individual cases. Diagnostic decisions based on the DSM often raise problems of *comorbidity* when children meet criteria for multiple disorders. If diagnoses are not based on operational definitions of empirically separable disorders, apparent comorbidity may reflect a lack of clear boundaries between categories or diagnosticians' inability to validly distinguish between disorders that do not actually co-occur.

An empirical basis for assessment, taxonomy, and diagnosis was outlined in terms of three generations of efforts to move from the empirical identification of syndromes, to the testing of syndromes hypothesized from the first generation of findings, and thence to the derivation of cross-informant syndrome constructs from reports by multiple informants. The cross-informant constructs serve as prototypes for taxonomic categories of problems that tend to co-occur in reports by different informants. Profiles have been developed for scoring and coordinating multisource data in terms of the cross-informant constructs. Applications of the cross-informant constructs to decisions about individual children and to longitudinal–epidemiological research on national samples were illustrated.

Implications of the empirically based approach were discussed for diagnostic decision making, prevention, and treatment. Future directions were outlined in terms of applications to adult psychopathology, bridging gaps between research and practice, and reform of health care financing.

REFERENCES

Achenbach, T. M. (1966). The classification of children's psychiatric symptoms: A factor-analytic study. *Psychological Monographs, 80* (No. 615).

Achenbach, T. M. (1981). Child Behavior Checklist. Burlington, VT: University of Vermont Department of Psychiatry.

Achenbach, T. M. (1985). *Assessment and taxonomy of child and adolescent psychopathology.* Newbury Park, CA: Sage.

Achenbach, T. M. (1991a). "Comorbidity" in child and adolescent psychiatry: Categorical and quantitative perspectives. *Journal of Child and Adolescent Psychopharmacology, 1,* 271–278.

Achenbach, T. M. (1991b). *Integrative guide for the 1991 CBCL/4–18, YSR, and TRF profiles.* Burlington: University of Vermont Department of Psychiatry.

Achenbach, T. M. (1991c). *Manual for the Child Behavior Checklist/4–18 and 1991 Profile.* Burlington: University of Vermont Department of Psychiatry.

Achenbach, T. M. (1991d). *Manual for the Teacher's Report Form and 1991 Profile.* Burlington: University of Vermont Department of Psychiatry.

Achenbach, T. M. (1991e). *Manual for the Youth Self-Report and 1991 Profile.* Burlington: University of Vermont Department of Psychiatry.

Achenbach, T. M. (1992). Developmental psychopathology. In M. H. Bornstein & M. E. Lamb (Eds.), *Developmental psychology: An advanced textbook* (3rd ed.). Hillsdale, NJ: Erlbaum.

Achenbach, T. M. (1993). *Empirically based taxonomy: How to use syndromes and profile types derived from the CBCL/4–18, TRF, and YSR.* Burlington: University of Vermont Department of Psychiatry.

Achenbach, T. M., Conners, C. K., & Quay, H. C. (1983). *The ACQ Behavior Checklist.* Burlington: University of Vermont Department of Psychiatry.

Achenbach, T. M., Conners, C. K., Quay, H. C., Verhulst, F. C., & Howell, C. T. (1989). Replication of empirically derived syndromes as a basis for taxonomy of child/adolescent psychopathology. *Journal of Abnormal Child Psychology, 17,* 299–323.

Achenbach, T. M., & Edelbrock, C. (1978). The classification of child psychopathology: A review and analysis of empirical efforts. *Psychological Bulletin, 85,* 1275–1301.

Achenbach, T. M., & Edelbrock, C. (1981). Behavioral problems and competencies reported by parents of normal and disturbed children aged four to sixteen. *Monographs of the Society for Research in Child Development, 46* (1, Serial No. 188).

Achenbach, T. M., Howell, C. T., McConaughy, S. H., & Stanger, C., (in press a). Six-year predictors of problems in a national sample of children and youth: 1. Cross-informant syndromes. *Journal of the American Academy of Child and Adolescent Psychiatry.*

Achenbach, T. M., Howell, C. T., McConaughy, S. H., & Stanger, C., (in press b). Six-year predictors of problems in a national sample of children and youth: 2. Signs of disturbance. *Journal of the American Academy of Child and Adolescent Psychiatry.*

Achenbach, T. M., Howell, C. T., McConaughy, S. H., & Stanger, C., (in press c). Six-year predictors of problems in a national sample: 3. Transitions to young adult syndromes. *Journal of the American Academy of Child and Adolescent Psychiatry.*

Achenbach, T. M., Howell, C. T., Quay, H. C., & Conners, C. K. (1991). National survey of competencies and problems among 4- to 16-year-olds: Parents' reports for normative and clinical samples. *Monographs of the Society for Research in Child Development, 56* (3, Serial No. 225).

Achenbach, T. M., McConaughy, S. H., & Howell, C. T. (1987). Child/adolescent behavioral and emotional problems: Implications of cross-informant correlations for situational specificity. *Psychological Bulletin, 101,* 213–232.

American Academy of Child Psychiatry. (1983). *Child psychiatry: A plan for the coming decades.* Washington, DC: Author.

American Psychiatric Association. (1952, 1968, 1980, 1987, 1994). *Diagnostic and statistical manual of mental disorders* (1st ed., 2nd ed., 3rd ed., 3rd ed. rev., 4th ed.). Washington, DC: Author.

Arkes, H. R., & Harkness, A. R. (1983). Estimates of contingency between two dichotomous variables. *Journal of Experimental Psychology: General, 112,* 117–135.

Arkes, H. R., Harkness, A. R., & Biber, D. (1988). *Salience and the judgment of contingency.* Paper presented at the Midwestern Psychological Association meeting, St. Louis, MO.

Baltes, P. B. (1987). Theoretical propositions of life-span developmental psychology: On the dynamics between growth and decline. *Developmental Psychology, 23,* 611–626.

Baltes, P. B., Cornelius, S. W., & Nesselroade, J. R. (1979). Cohort effects in developmental psychology. In J. R. Nesselroade & P. B. Baltes (Eds.), *Longitudinal research in the study of behavior and development* (pp. 61–87). New York: Academic Press.

Bandura, A. (1977). *Social learning theory.* Englewood Cliffs, NJ: Prentice-Hall.

Bayley, N. (1968). Correlates of mental growth: Birth to thirty-six years. *American Psychologist, 23,* 1–17.

Bell, R. Q. (1953). Convergence: An accelerated longitudinal approach. *Child Development, 24,* 145–152.

Bell, R. Q. (1954). An experimental test of the accelerated longitudinal approach. *Child Development, 25,* 281–286.

Berkson, J. (1946). Limitations of the application of fourfold table analysis to hospital data. *Biometrics Bulletin, 2,* 47–53.

Brown, J. S., & Achenbach, T. M. (1995). *Bibliography of published studies using the Child Behavior Checklist and related materials: 1995 edition.* Burlington: University of Vermont Department of Psychiatry.

Cantor, N., Smith, E. E., French, R. de S., & Mezzich, J. (1980). Psychiatric diagnosis as prototype categorization. *Journal of Abnormal Psychology, 89,* 181–193.

Caron, C., & Rutter, M. (1991). Comorbidity in child psychopathology: Concepts, issues and research strategies. *Journal of Child Psychology and Psychiatry, 32,* 1063–1080.

Cerreto, M. C., & Tuma, J. M. (1977). Distribution of DSM-II diagnoses in a child setting. *Journal of Abnormal Child Psychology, 5,* 147–155.

Chapman, L. J., & Chapman, J. P. (1971). Associatively based illusory correlation as a source of psychodiagnostic folklore. In L. D. Goodstein & R. I. Lanyon (Eds.), *Readings in personality assessment.* New York: Wiley.

Conners, C. K. (1978). *Parent questionnaire.* Washington, DC: Children's Hospital National Medical Center.

Costello, E. J., Burns, B. J., Angold, A., & Leaf, P. J. (1993). How can epidemiology improve mental health services for children and adolescents? *Journal of the American Academy of Child and Adolescent Psychiatry, 32,* 1106–1113.

Costello, A. J., Edelbrock, C., Dulcan, M. K., Kalas, R., & Klaric, S. H. (1984). *Report on the Diagnostic Interview Schedule for Children (DISC).* Pittsburgh, PA: University of Pittsburgh Department of Psychiatry.

Cowley, G., & Ramo, J. C. (1993, July 26). The not-young and the restless. *Newsweek,* pp. 48–49.

De Groot, A., Koot, H. M. & Verhulst, F. C. (1994). Cross-cultural generalizability of the Child Behavior Checklist cross-informant syndromes. *Psychological Assessment, 6,* 225–230.

De Groot, A., Koot, H. M. & Verhulst, F. C. Cross-cultural generalizability of the Youth Self-Report and Teacher's Report Form cross-informant syndromes. Submitted for publication.

Edelbrock, C., Costello, A. J., Dulcan, M. K., Kalas, R., & Conover, N. C. (1985). Age differences in the reliability of the psychiatric interview of the child. *Child Development, 56,* 265–275.

Education of the Handicapped Act (P.L. 94-142). (1977). *Federal Register, 42,* p. 42,478. Amended in *Federal Register* (1981), *46,* p. 3,866.

Faraone, S. V., Biederman, J., Keenan, K., & Tsuang, M. T. (1991). Separation of DSM-III attention deficit disorder and conduct disorder: Evidence from a family-genetic study of American child psychiatric patients. *Psychological Medicine, 21,* 109–121.

Ferdinand, R. F., & Verhulst, F. C. (1994). The prediction of poor outcomes in young adults: Comparison of the Young Adult Self-Report, The General Health Questionnaire, and the Symptom Checklist. *Acta Psychiatricia Scandinavica, 89,* 405–410.

Ferdinand, R. F., Wiznitzer, M., & Verhulst, F. C. (in press). Continuity and changes of self-reported problem behaviors from adolescence into young adulthood. *Journal of the American Academy of Child and Adolescent Psychiatry.*

Fox, N. A., Kimmerly, N. L., & Schafer, W. D. (1991). Attachment to mother/attachment to father: A meta-analysis. *Child Development, 62,* 210–225.

Freud, A. (1965). *Normality and pathology in childhood.* New York: International Universities Press.

Freud, S. (1940). *An outline of psychoanalysis.* New York: Norton.

Freud, S. (1953). Analysis of a phobia in a five-year-old boy. In J. Strachey (Ed. and Trans.). *The standard edition of the complete works of Sigmund Freud* (Vol. 7). London: Hogarth Press. (Original work published 1909)

Freud, S. (1959). Inhibition, symptoms, and anxiety. In J. Strachey (Ed. and Trans.). *The standard edition of the complete psychological works of Sigmund Freud* (Vol. 20). London: Hogarth Press. (Original work published 1926)

Freud, S. (1963). Introductory lectures on psychoanalysis. Part III. General theory of neuroses. In J. Strachey (Ed. and Trans.). *The standard edition of the complete psychological works of Sigmund Freud* (Vol. 16). London: Hogarth Press. (Original work published 1917)

Friedlander, S., & Phillips, S. D. (1984). Preventing errors in clinical judgment. *Journal of Consulting and Clinical Psychology, 52,* 123–133.

Friedman, W. J. (1991). The development of children's memory for the time of past events. *Child Development, 62,* 139–155.

Griesinger, W. (1845). *Die Pathologie und Therapie der psychischen Krankheiten (Mental pathology and therapeutics).* C. L. Robertson & J. Rutherford (Trans.). London: New Sydenham Society, 1867.

Group for the Advancement of Psychiatry. (1966). *Psychopathological disorders in childhood: Theoretical considerations and a proposed classification.* GAP Report No. 62. New York: Author.

Guze, S. (1978). Validating criteria for psychiatric diagnosis: The Washington University Approach. In M. S. Akiskal & W. L. Webb (Eds.), *Psychiatric diagnosis: Exploration of biological predictors.* New York: Spectrum.

Hewitt, L. E., & Jenkins, R. L. (1946). *Fundamental patterns of maladjustment: The dynamics of their origin.* Springfield, IL: State of Illinois.

Individuals with Disabilities Act (P.L. 101-476). (1990). 104 Stat. 1103–1151.

Jenkins, R. L., & Glickman, S. (1946). Common syndromes in child psychiatry: I. Deviant behavior traits. II. The schizoid child. *American Journal of Orthopsychiatry, 16,* 244–261.

Jones, M. C. (1924). A laboratory study of fear: The case of Peter. *Pedagogical Seminary, 31,* 308–315.

Kagan, J., & Moss, H. A. (1962). *Birth to maturity.* New York: Wiley.

Kanner, L., Rodrigues, A., & Ashenden, B. (1972). How far can autistic children go in matters of social adaptation? *Journal of Autism and Childhood Schizophrenia, 2,* 9–33.

Kessler, R. C., McGonagle, K. A., Zhao, S., Nelson, C. B., Hughes, M., Eshleman, S., Wittchen, H.-U., & Kendler, K. S. (1994). Lifetime and 12-month prevalence of DSM-III-R psychiatric disorders among persons aged 15–54 in the United States: Results from the National Comorbidity Study. *Archives of General Psychiatry, 51,* 8–19.

Kraepelin, E. (1883, 1915). *Compendium der Psychiatrie* (1st ed., 8th ed.). Leipzig: Abel; Barth.

Kurtz, R. M., & Garfield, S. L. (1978). Illusory correlation: A further exploration of Chapman's paradigm. *Journal of Consulting and Clinical Psychology, 46,* 1009–1015.

Lahey, B. B., Loeber, R., Stouthamer-Loeber, M., Christ, M. A. G., Green, S., Russo, M. F., Frick, P. J., & Dulcan, M. (1990). Comparison of DSM-III and DSM-III-R diagnoses for prepubertal children: Changes in prevalence and validity. *Journal of the American Academy of Child and Adolescent Psychiatry, 29,* 620–626.

Lejeune, J., Gautier, M., & Turpin, R. (1963). Study of the somatic chromosomes of nine mongoloid idiot children. In S. H. Boyer (Ed.), *Papers on human genetics.* Englewood Cliffs, NJ: Prentice-Hall.

Levin, D. A. (1979). The nature of plant species. *Science, 204,* 381–384.

Lewine, R. R. J., Watt, N. F., Prentky, R. A., & Fryer, J. H. (1980). Childhood social competence in functionally disordered psychiatric patients and in normals. *Journal of Abnormal Psychology, 89,* 132–138.

Livingston, R. L., Dykman, R. A., & Ackerman, P. T. (1990). The frequency and significance of additional self-reported psychiatric diagnoses in children with attention deficit disorder. *Journal of Abnormal Child Psychology, 18,* 465–478.

Mannuzza, S., Klein, R. G., Bessler, A., Malloy, P., & LaPadula, M. (1993). Adult outcome of hyperactive boys: Educational achievement, occupational rank, and psychiatric status. *Archives of General Psychiatry, 50,* 565–576.

McConaughy, S. H., & Achenbach, T. M. (1994a). Comorbidity of empirically based syndromes in matched general population and clinical samples. *Journal of Child Psychology and Psychiatry, 35,* 1141–1157.

McConaughy, S. H., & Achenbach, T. M. (1994b). *Manual for the Semistructured Clinical Interview for Children and Adolescents.* Burlington: University of Vermont Department of Psychiatry.

Miller, L. C. (1967). Louisville Behavior Checklist for males, 6–12 years of age. *Psychological Reports, 21,* 885–896.

Nesselroade, J. R., & Baltes, P. B. (1974). Adolescent personality development and historical change: 1970–1972. *Monographs of the Society for Research in Child Development, 39* (Serial No. 154).

Nisbett, R. E., Zukier, H., & Lemley, R. E. (1981). The dilution effect: Nondiagnostic information weakens the implications of diagnostic information. *Cognitive Psychology, 13,* 248–277.

Peterson, D. R. (1961). Behavior problems of middle childhood. *Journal of Consulting Psychology, 25,* 205–209.

Piaget, J. (1983). Piaget's theory. In P. H. Mussen (Ed.), *Handbook of child psychology* (4th ed.). W. Kessen (Vol. Ed.), *Vol. 1. History, theory, and methods.* New York: Wiley.

Quay, H. C. (1986). Classification. In H. C. Quay & J. S. Werry (Eds.), *Psychopathological disorders of childhood* (3rd ed., pp. 1–42). New York: Wiley.

Quay, H. C., & Peterson, D. R. (1982). *Revised Behavior Problem Checklist.* Coral Gables, FL: University of Miami Department of Psychology.

Reich, W., Shayka, J. J., & Taibleson, C. (1992). *Diagnostic Interview for Children and Adolescents.* St. Louis: Washington University Department of Psychiatry.

Reinherz, H. Z. (1994). *Early Adulthood Research Project.* Boston: Simmons College School of Social Work.

Robins, L. N. (1966). *Deviant children grown up.* Baltimore: Williams & Wilkens.

Robins, L. N. (1985). Epidemiology: Reflections on testing the validity of psychiatric interviews. *Archives of General Psychiatry, 42,* 918–924.

Rosch, E. (1978). Principles of categorization. In E. Rosch & B. B. Lloyd (Eds.), *Cognition and categorization.* Hillsdale, NJ: Erlbaum.

Rosch, E., & Mervis, C. B. (1975). Family resemblances: Studies in the internal structure of categories. *Cognitive Psychology, 7,* 573–605.

Rutter, M. (1991). Nature, nurture, and psychopathology: A new look at an old topic. *Development and Psychopathology, 3,* 125–136.

Schaie, K. W. (1965). A general model for the study of developmental problems. *Psychological Bulletin, 64,* 92–107.

Schaie, K. W., Labouvie, G. V., & Buech, B. V. (1973). Generational and cohort-specific differences in adult cognitive functioning: A fourteen-year study of independent samples. *Developmental Psychology, 9,* 151–166.

Setterberg, S. R., Ernst, M., Rao, U., Campbell, M., Carlson, G. A., Shaffer, D., & Staghezza, B. M. (1991). Child psychiatrists' views of DSM-III-R: A survey of usage and opinions. *Journal of the American Academy of Child and Adolescent Psychiatry, 30,* 652–658.

Shaffer, D. (1992). *Diagnostic Interview Schedule for Children, Version 2.3.* New York: Columbia University Division of Child Psychiatry.

Shaffer, D., Fisher, P., Piacentini, J., Schwab-Stone, M., & Wicks, J. (1989). *Diagnostic Interview Schedule for Children—2.* New York: Columbia University Division of Child Psychiatry.

Smith, E. E. (1978). Theories of semantic memory. In W. K. Estes (Ed.), *Handbook of learning and cognitive processes* (Vol. 5). Hillsdale, NJ: Erlbaum.

Spitzer, R. L., Davies, M., & Barkley, R. A. (1990). The DSM-III-R field trial of disruptive behavior disorders. *Journal of the American Academy of Child and Adolescent Psychiatry, 29,* 690–697.

Stanger, C., Achenbach, T. M., & Verhulst, F. C. (1994). Accelerating longitudinal research on child psychopathology: A practical example. *Psychological Assessment, 6,* 102–107.

Stanger, C., McConaughy, S. H., & Achenbach, T. M. (1992). Three-year course of behavioral/emotional problems in a national sample of 4- to 16-year-olds: II. Predictors of syndromes. *Journal of the American Academy of Child and Adolescent Psychiatry, 31,* 941–950.

van't Hoff, M. A., Roede, M. J., & Kowalski, C. (1991). A mixed longitudinal data analysis model. *Human Biology, 49,* 165–179.

Verhulst, F. C., Akkerhuis, G. W., & Althaus, M. (1985). Mental health in Dutch children: (I) A cross-cultural comparison. *Acta Psychiatrica Scandinavica, 72* (Suppl. 323).

Walker, J. L., Lahey, B. B., Russo, M. F., Christ, M. A. G., McBurnett, K., Loeber, R., Stouthamer-Loeber, M., & Green, S. M. (1991). Anxiety, inhibition, and conduct disorder in children: I. Relations to social impairment. *Journal of the American Academy of Child and Adolescent Psychiatry, 30,* 187–191.

Watson, J. B., & Rayner, R. (1920). Conditioned emotional reactions. *Journal of Experimental Psychology, 3,* 1–14.

Weinstein, S. R., Noam, G. G., Grimes, K., Stone, K., & Schwab-Stone, M. (1990). Convergence of DSM-III diagnoses and self-reported symptoms in child and adolescent inpatients. *Journal of the American Academy of Child and Adolescent Psychiatry, 29,* 627–634.

Weiss, G., & Hechtman, L. T. (1993). *Hyperactive children grown up: Empirical findings and theoretical considerations* (2nd ed.). New York: Guilford.

Werner, H. (1957). The concept of development from a comparative and organismic point of view. In D. B. Harris (Ed.), *The concept of development.* Minneapolis: University of Minnesota Press.

Wiznitzer, M., Verhulst, F. C., van den Brink, W., Koeter, M., van der Ende, J., Giel, R., & Koot, H. M. (1992). Detecting psychopathology in young adults. A comparison of the Young Adult Self-Report, the General Health Questionnaire, and the Symptom Checklist-90 as screening instruments. *Acta Psychiatrica Scandinavica, 86,* 32–37.

World Health Organization. (1977). *Manual of the International Classification of Diseases, Injuries, and Causes of Death* (9th ed.). Geneva, Switzerland: Author.

World Health Organization. (1978, 1992). *Mental disorders: Glossary and guide to their classification in accordance with the International Classification of Diseases* (9th ed., 10th ed.). Geneva: Author.

Yorke, C. (1980). The contributions of the Diagnostic Profile and the assessment of developmental lines to child psychiatry. *Psychiatric Clinics of North America, 3,* 593–603.

CHAPTER 4

Comprehensive Psychological Assessment Through the Life Span: A Developmental Approach

SARA S. SPARROW, ALICE S. CARTER, GARY RACUSIN, and ROBIN MORRIS

In this chapter, we present a developmental model of comprehensive psychological assessment appropriate for conceptualizing both clinical and research questions. In doing so, we do not intend to review the large library of currently available assessment instruments or to instruct the reader in the administration of these instruments. Rather, our aim is to advance the reader's understanding of critical conceptual and theoretical issues regarding comprehensive psychological assessment through the life span. We advocate employing a comprehensive, developmentally sensitive conceptual framework even when pragmatic considerations dictate limited assessments.

The chapter begins with a historical overview and presentation of our model of comprehensive assessment, including the developmental systems levels in which individual assessment occurs (e.g., community, institutional, and family settings) and the relevant assessment domains within the individual (e.g., biologic, cognitive, language, social/emotional, achievement/vocational, and adaptive behavior). In contrast to traditional models of assessment that focus primarily on the individual, we emphasize the family context of the developmental systems level as an example of the significance of context in individual assessment. Next, issues related to test construction and scaling and to methods of assessment are discussed, highlighting developmental and psychometric issues and dimensions of assessment that are salient at specific life stages. Subsequently, we discuss contextual issues to be considered in implementing the model. We conclude with recommendations for future research and clinical directions.

DEVELOPMENTAL COMPREHENSIVE ASSESSMENT

Our use of the term *comprehensive* refers to a multidimensional investigation of an individual's functioning within the context of developmental influences and multilevel systems. Multidimensional evaluation is necessary because it is impossible to understand the individual through a single score in one domain, or a global summary score that averages across domains. Adequate appreciation of individual complexity requires information from multiple functional domains generating a profile of strengths and weaknesses. In part, this approach is required because all available assessment instruments, even when designed to be unidimensional, probe multiple dimensions of functioning. Although various domains of functioning have been discussed historically as if they are independent, interdependence across domains is in fact the norm. Further, skill acquisition and/or deficit in one domain will influence functioning in other domains. Similarly, one gains a richer understanding of the individual from longitudinal rather than from single cross-sectional or "snapshot" assessment. Multilevel refers to the importance of viewing individuals within the contexts in which they are currently and have previously been nested. These include the individual's culture, community, institutional environments, and family.

HISTORICAL PERSPECTIVES

The model presented in this chapter, which appreciates individual development across the life span, is rooted in earlier work in the study of individual differences in both Europe and the United States. In particular, the assessment field owes much to 19th-century scientists who sought to understand mental retardation through the measurement of individuals (Bellack & Hersen, 1980). Galton's publication of *Classification of Men According to their Natural Gifts* in 1892 provided the foundation for the modern study of individual psychology. Some 35 years later, Alfred Binet developed the first widely accepted test of intelligence used for screening schoolchildren (Binet & Simon, 1905). Binet undertook this task at the request of the French government in order to provide information for program planning and placement of children who were mentally retarded. Shortly thereafter, in 1910, Goddard, director of the Psychology Laboratory at Vineland Training School in New Jersey, translated Binet's scale into English, a development that launched the large-scale use of individual intelligence testing in the United States.

Major controversies in the assessment movement have involved the diagnosis and labeling of mental retardation, the relative contributions of nature and nurture to intelligence, the definition and factor structure of intelligence, and issues of racial and cultural bias. Each of these areas continues to witness debate, but the most intense controversy in the past three decades has involved the appropriateness of using test findings for purposes that have political or social ramifications. A well-known example of this controversy was the California case of *Larry P. v. Wilson Riles,* where the court ruled that tests used for placement of African American children in special classes for the mentally retarded were culturally biased (*Larry P. v. Wilson Riles,* 1979). As a result of this ruling, some school districts have chosen to prohibit the use of intelligence tests for placement in special education classes.

Other educators and researches have argued that, rather than abandon the use of individual tests for these purposes, the lessons learned from these controversies should be the basis for producing more socially sensitive tests. Substantial effort has been devoted to constructing tests that minimize bias through sophisticated standardization procedures, development of normative groups for special populations, and careful delineation of the limits on inference imposed by inherent test biases.

MODEL OF COMPREHENSIVE ASSESSMENT

Multilevel Interactive Systems

Within the assessment model to which we now turn, we emphasize the importance of understanding systemic processes in relation to the individual being evaluated. This emphasis is consistent with the general acknowledgment that individuals must be viewed within the contexts of their families and the broader social institutions within which they live (Bronfenbrenner, 1986). A diagram of the individual within the transaction of developmental systems levels is presented in Figure 4.1. The transaction of the individual and context through development is highlighted in recent research on family functioning. Shared family environment appears to exert some influence on children's development; however, a child's unique experience within the family appears to have a much greater impact on that individual child's development (Plomin, 1986). Several factors are most likely to influence unique experience both within and outside of the family: (a) the transaction of the child's genetic endowment within ongoing systemic processes (i.e., two children who experience the same family phenomena differently as a function of different emotional reactivity); (b) the cognitive and emotional understanding associated with prior experience (i.e., children of different ages will experience the same phenomena differently as a function of individual cognition and affect); and (c) the unique responses a particular child may evoke in the system (e.g., parents may employ different parenting strategies in response to two children's differing temperamental or physical presentation). Therefore, although it is essential to evaluate general aspects of systemic functioning, new strategies for assessment must attempt to evaluate the way in which the individual perceives or experiences the family, the community, and relevant institutions. In addition, the availability of potentially positive influences (e.g., church groups) within the broader community is typically not taken into consideration. Finally, assessment strategies should acknowledge the potential influence of personal history and "sleeper effects" (i.e., delayed sequelae of previous experiences) on development (Bornstein, 1987; Gurman & Kniskern, 1981). Although space precludes a complete discussion of each of these contexts, we will highlight the role of

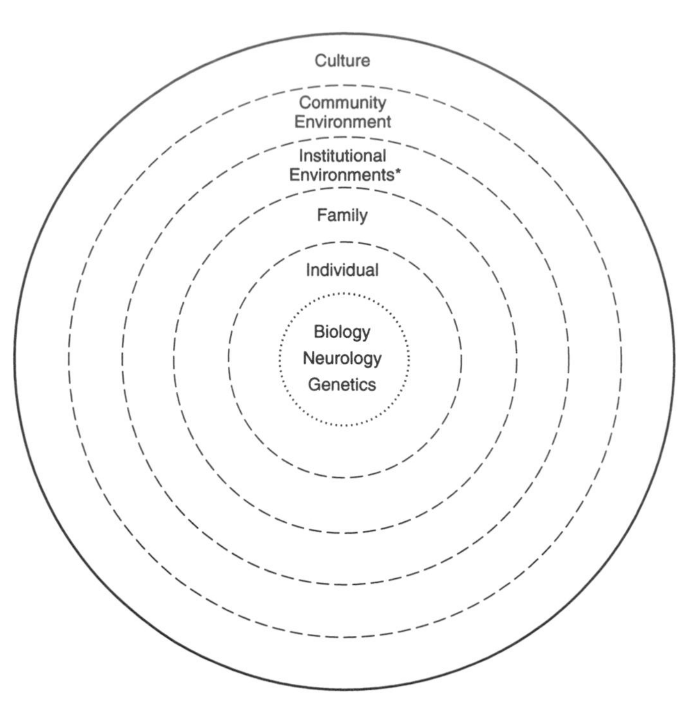

Figure 4.1 The contextual nexus of comprehensive developmental assessment.

the family system as an example of the influence of contextual systems on comprehensive assessment of an individual.

The Family Context: An Example of Developmental Systems Levels

In the past 10 to 15 years, significant advances in family assessment have clarified and identified central dimensions of family functioning that warrant assessment, and have improved the psychometric properties of existing scales (Bloom, 1985; Schumm, 1990). At the same time, our sophistication regarding developmental processes has increased dramatically (Cicchetti, 1990). Despite these advances, little work has bridged these two lines of research by addressing the assessment of transitions in family functioning through the life span. To date, researchers involved in family assessment have created instruments that can detect how "given interactions are related to prior interactions in the family and . . . [have] implications for future interactions and outcomes" (Bradbury & Fincham, 1990, p. 37). What the field still lacks, however, are the methods to evaluate the family within a developmental context. We advocate a developmental approach that recognizes the importance and complexity of evaluating the life stage of each family member, intrafamilial dyadic relationships, and the family as a unit. In doing so, we distinguish between assessing the impact of time and the influence of developmental processes. Consistent with the application of developmental psychopathology to individual functioning, this approach to family assessment acknowledges that the tasks of family life shift and that different psychological issues come to the fore, depending on the constellation of life stages within the family.

Critical Dimensions for Assessing Family Functioning

We will highlight several critical dimensions of family functioning that appear throughout various theoretical perspectives and are presumed to serve a contributory role in the expression of multiple categories of psychopathology. Many authors have generated lists of critical dimensions of family functioning. Some specified as many as 15 dimensions (e.g., Bloom, 1985), others as few as 3 (e.g., Olson, Russell, & Sprenkle, 1989; Olson, Sprenkle, & Russell, 1979). Based on our review of the literature and our clinical experience, we will generate a moderate list of central dimensions. These dimensions are not orthogonal; each, however, adds explanatory power to our ability to capture the complexities inherent in family functioning. Further, these dimensions are central to overall family functioning. Dimensions relevant to subsystem functioning (e.g., marital satisfaction, parenting) will not be addressed. Further, a review of family assessment instruments is beyond the scope of this paper. However, currently available instruments have been reviewed recently (McCubbin & Thompson, 1987; Touliatos, Perlmutter, & Straus, 1990).

Careful consideration of individual instruments is critical. Although there are several psychometrically sophisticated paper-and-pencil family assessment instruments (e.g., Family Adaptability and Cohesion Scale (FACES)—Olson et al., 1979; Olson, Portner, & Bell, 1982; Family Environment Scale (FES)—Moos, 1974; Moos & Moos, 1981), and there is some overlap across instruments, each highlights different aspects of perceived family functioning. This reflects the fact that family functioning is not a unitary construct. Choice of appropriate instruments, therefore, must selectively highlight those dimensions of family functioning on which the instrument is theoretically or empirically based.

Cohesion

Cohesion, which ranges between the polarities of enmeshment and disengagement, refers to the extent to which family members perceive themselves and behave in an emotionally bonded manner. When cohesion is high (i.e., at the enmeshed pole), family members are overidentified, such that loyalty to and agreement within the family prevent individuation. When cohesion is low (i.e., at the disengaged pole), high levels of autonomy are encouraged, with family members displaying limited connection or commitment to the family. In the midrange between these poles, family members experience and balance the competing demands of individuation and connectedness (Olson, Russell, & Sprenkle, 1983).

Adaptability

Adaptability is defined as the capacity of the system to change in response to developmental and situational stress. As employed by Olson and colleagues (1983), this dimension focuses on change in power structure, role relationships, and relationship rules. When adaptability is unusually high (i.e., chaotic at one extreme), the family is characterized by rapidly oscillating rules, boundaries, and structures, making it difficult for family members to have a sense of continuity and predictability in family life. When adaptability is unusually low (i.e., rigid at the extreme), the family demonstrates an inability to change rules, boundaries, and structures, which leads to a constricted capacity to adapt to developmental challenges.

Expression and Modulation of Emotion

Expression and modulation of emotion is defined in terms of (a) experiencing and expressing a wide range of affects; (b) shifting flexibly between affective states; (c) regulating the intensity with which these affects are experienced and expressed; and (d) employing contextually appropriate social display rules. This construct is primarily assessed utilizing observational methods. The extent to which positive and negative affects are expressed within the family provides an index of the emotional climate within the family. For example, parental expressions of positivity and negativity have been repeatedly associated with a range of social-emotional outcomes in children (Lewis, Dlugokinski, Caputo, & Griffin, 1988). Similarly, a considerable body of research on expressed emotion has demonstrated that the type, manner, and intensity of feelings that are displayed in verbal and/or nonverbal communication are related to severity of psychopathology and to recovery and maintenance following psychotherapeutic interventions (Doane, Goldstein, Miklowitz, & Falloon, 1986; Doane, West, Goldstein, Rodnick, & Jones, 1981). Further, the sequence of affective displays may reveal important aspects of family functioning. For example, the expression of depressive affect, which appears to inhibit aggressive displays in other family members, has been labeled the suppression effect (Hops et al., 1987; Nelson & Beach, 1990).

Communication

An emphasis on communication has a long history in the field of family therapy and has been incorporated in a variety of questionnaire and observational assessment methods. Concepts associated with this school of thought include the "double bind," "family homeostasis," and "family rules." Dimensions of communication that have been operationalized include clarity, consistency, and blaming (Napier & Whitaker, 1978). More recently, communication has been emphasized within the cognitive behavioral marital and family models associated with Oregon.

Structure

A structural analysis of family functioning places an emphasis on the articulation and wielding of executive authority and the delineation of family subsystems (Minuchin, 1974). Specifically, focus is placed on the extent to which the family has established clear boundaries between subsystems (e.g., parental, marital, sibling) and the permeability of these boundaries. In addition, an assessment is made of the locus of authority and power and whether it is held by the developmentally appropriate family members or subsystems. This assessment must take place in the context of a developmentally sensitive evaluation of adaptability, cohesion, and communication patterns.

Dynamic Issues

Dynamic issues in family assessment and therapy are most clearly conceptualized by the object relational school of family therapy (e.g., Scharff, 1989). Object relational family theorists believe that a fundamental motive in life is the need for satisfying interpersonal relationships. At the same time, the individual strives to acquire and maintain a sense of autonomy and independence. The extent to which family members achieve an adaptive balance of these drives is the primary focus of analysis. In addition to a focus on current interactional processes, an object relational family evaluation includes an emphasis on understanding how individual and dyadic historical events impact or distort current interactional processes. For example, strong affects associated with prior traumatic events in a parent's childhood may be evoked in the current parent-child relationship. Further, these personalized affects may distort the parent's perception of the child's behavior and interfere with the parent's ability to employ adaptive parenting behaviors. As a consequence, the parent's sense of efficacy and autonomy in the parenting role and the establishment of intimacy are compromised. It would be difficult to understand the intensity of the parent's affective response relying solely on an assessment of the immediate behavioral antecedents in the observed interactional process. Evaluation of family dynamic issues relies on close observations of family interaction patterns, as well as a clinician's own subjective experiences of the family. Because the interactional expression of these dynamic issues often involves a recreation or enactment of experiences in the family of origin, the inclusion of intergenerational assessment strategies may be useful. A potentially fruitful area of research might develop a combined assessment approach that would include a reliable observational coding scheme along with reliable clinical ratings of these dimensions of family function. Humphrey and Benjamin (1986) have developed one application in this direction. Benjamin's Structured Analysis of Social Behavior (SASB) coding system (Benjamin, 1974) is based on a circumplex model of interpersonal relations and their intrapsychic representations. For example, this coding system operationalizes two core dynamic constructs—affiliation and interdependence—by coding aspects of interpersonal and intrapsychic functioning.

Achievement Orientation

The assessment of a family's achievement orientation, or the extent to which it values and strives for academic and occupational advancement, as well as the extent to which it provides intellectually stimulating or enriching experiences for the children, is incorporated in many family assessment instruments (e.g., FES). Assessment in this domain is often useful for understanding family conflict and "underachievement." For example, when there are discrepancies in the extent to which family members adhere to a shared achievement orientation and there is a high degree of cohesion, there is usually family conflict. Similarly, when a child evidences a high IQ but low academic achievement, an examination of the family's achievement orientation may reveal a lack of investment in the child's academic success as opposed to an information processing deficit within the child.

Family Satisfaction

Family satisfaction is a dimension that can be assessed along with these other aspects of family functioning to determine family members' degree of pleasure with family functioning. Both global and specific areas of satisfaction can be assessed in order to evaluate the extent of unanimity and distress among family members regarding family functioning. Evaluating family satisfaction provides information regarding motivation for change and alliances within the family.

As stated above, it is our belief that these dimensions of family functioning must be evaluated within the context of the family's overall developmental circumstances. We recognize the complexity of this endeavor, but our hope is to inspire greater collaboration between researchers and clinicians to create developmentally oriented family assessment instruments. Salient family transitions present developmental challenges that individual family members and subsystems must negotiate (e.g., transition to parenthood, entry of sibling, death of a parent, children leaving home). It is important to keep in mind that, in many families, these events co-occur, thus presenting multiple developmental challenges. Although it is true that many facets of family life can undergo dramatic change while overall family functioning remains relatively stable, typically it is only in the context of the family transition that a shift in family functioning can be understood fully.

As stated previously, the field of family assessment has made dramatic strides in the past decade. A critical task deserving focus and effort is to develop assessment instruments that integrate relevant dimensions of family functioning into the developmental contexts created by individual and systemic life-stage transitions. Inferences drawn regarding two families presenting with identical scores on important dimensions of family functioning (e.g., cohesion, communication, achievement orientation) will be quite different, depending on where each family lies in its family life cycle. One could envision the need for a different set of norms for families adjusting to developmental demands at different phases of life. A second task for family assessment researchers involves developing improved methods for integrating information across multiple informants and across methods of assessment (e.g., interviews, observations, and questionnaires). Finally, our sophistication regarding the assessment of family functioning has not yet been incorporated into such formal diagnostic nosologies as DSM-IV (American Psychiatric Association, 1994). Limited attention is paid to family functioning with the assignment of "conditions not attributable to a mental disorder but worthy of treatment" (V codes on Axis I of the DSM-IV), but the current level of knowledge is not reflected in such gross characterizations of families. It is likely that a multidimensional nominal approach may be more feasible than a unidimensional discrete approach to diagnosis.

Comprehensive Assessment of the Individual

Having provided an example of developmental assessment of one contextual system in which an individual is embedded, we will now narrow our focus to assessment of the individual. To do so, we first discuss the biological substrate of the individual. As seen in Figure 4.1, the different pictorial representation circumscribing biology/neurology/genetics reflects the fact that this substrate is always present and inextricably intertwined with observed functioning. Next, we discuss several domains of functioning that we believe to be critical to comprehensive developmental assessment.

Biology

In recent years, the nature-nurture pendulum has swung back to a keen interest in biological aspects of human functioning. Technological advances in such fields as human genetics, brain imaging, and molecular biology account, in part, for this trend. We appreciate the importance of knowing about specific genetic configurations and/or compromises in neurological integrity as a necessary but insufficient portion of an assessment strategy designed to fully understand an individual's functioning across developmental domains. Variability in the range of functioning across developmental domains has been demonstrated in multiple studies of individuals with documented or suspected genetic and neurologic abnormalities (e.g., Down Syndrome, meningitis, closed head injury). These conditions may set some limits on the range of possible outcomes these individuals may achieve, but learning or other nonbiologic influences may be more crucial to the individual's current and future functioning. At the same time, it behooves the evaluator to be familiar with the research and clinical literature describing individuals with known genetic or neurologic abnormalities. Many of these disorders are associated with specific patterns of functioning. Thus, areas of functioning known to be associated with the disorder might receive more attention in the evaluation (e.g., expressive language delay in children with Down syndrome). Similarly, evaluators must be aware of changes in areas of functioning associated with development in terms of both acquisition of new skills and changes associated with the aging process.

DEVELOPMENTAL RESOURCE PARAMETERS AND THEIR FUNCTIONAL MANIFESTATIONS

Our model of primary domains of assessment (see Figure 4.2) is an attempt to capture aspects of an individual's development across six domains that are integral to a synthetic description of current resources and functioning: (a) Cognition, (b) Language, (c) Sensorimotor, (d) Social-Emotional, (e) Academic/Occupational Performance, and (f) Adaptive Behavior. Because of the complexity of human beings, there are innumerable ways to partition aspects of functioning. The selection of the specific domains included in the model was guided by findings from relevant research and clinical experience and from our conceptualization of interrelationships among relevant domains of functioning. In these areas, the available instruments have attained the greatest scientific rigor and are most likely to provide reliable and valid results. In choosing relevant domains of assessment, there is a tension between selecting a larger number of more discrete categories and at the same time reducing the number for the sake of

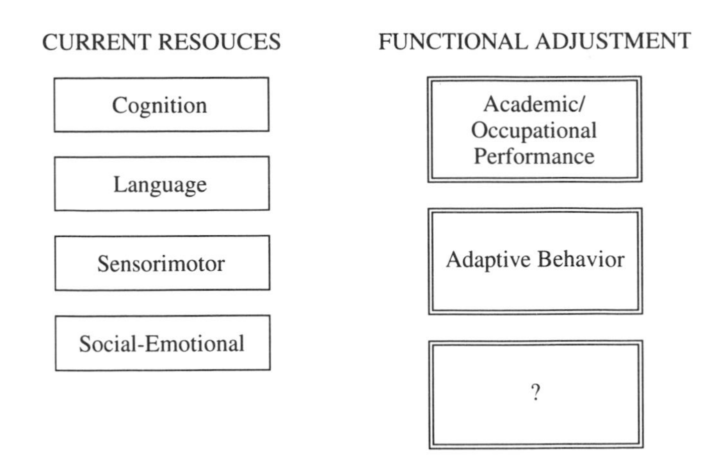

Figure 4.2 Comprehensive assessment of the individual: Developmental resource parameters and their functional manifestations.

parsimony. Parsimony facilitates efficiency in evaluation, which is often critical for making timely recommendations. Efficiency in the process of assessment also contributes to preserving the boundary of an evaluatory relationship as contrasted to a therapeutic relationship. The six spheres shown in Figure 4.2 are discrete enough to capture fundamental aspects of individual functioning but broad enough to characterize the whole person, thus comprising a comprehensive assessment strategy.

By functional domains, we mean categorical areas of behavior or abilities that emerge and are transformed in a developmental sequence throughout the life span and that can be operationally defined for psychometric purposes. From a developmental perspective, it is understood that the boundaries between these domains are frequently permeable; that is, developments within domains may reciprocally influence or drive developments within other domains. From a psychometric or test construction perspective, however, the placement of specific behaviors within domains may result in boundaries that are arbitrary, because the demands of test construction may require the assignment of specific behaviors to one (as opposed to another) domain. For example, although the Wechsler Intelligence Scale for Children—Third Edition (WISC-III; Wechsler, 1991) is a measure of a child's cognitive functioning, the Comprehension subtest carries a high social loading and thus could be understood as a measure of a child's social functioning. Although the goal of this model of comprehensive assessment is to derive an integrated view of an individual's functioning, this integrated view is derived from a preliminary understanding of functioning within each specific domain.

These functional domains can be operationally defined for psychometric purposes. An integrated view of an individual's functioning is facilitated by organizing the data into the abilities assessed by each subtest, the relation of the abilities to functional domains, and interrelations between functional domains and the manifestations of the assessed abilities in terms of functional adjustment (see Figure 4.3). This is an example of the first step employed in interpretation of test data. As multiple subtests are examined in this manner, the evaluator can begin to explore patterns of shared and unique abilities across subtests and domains,

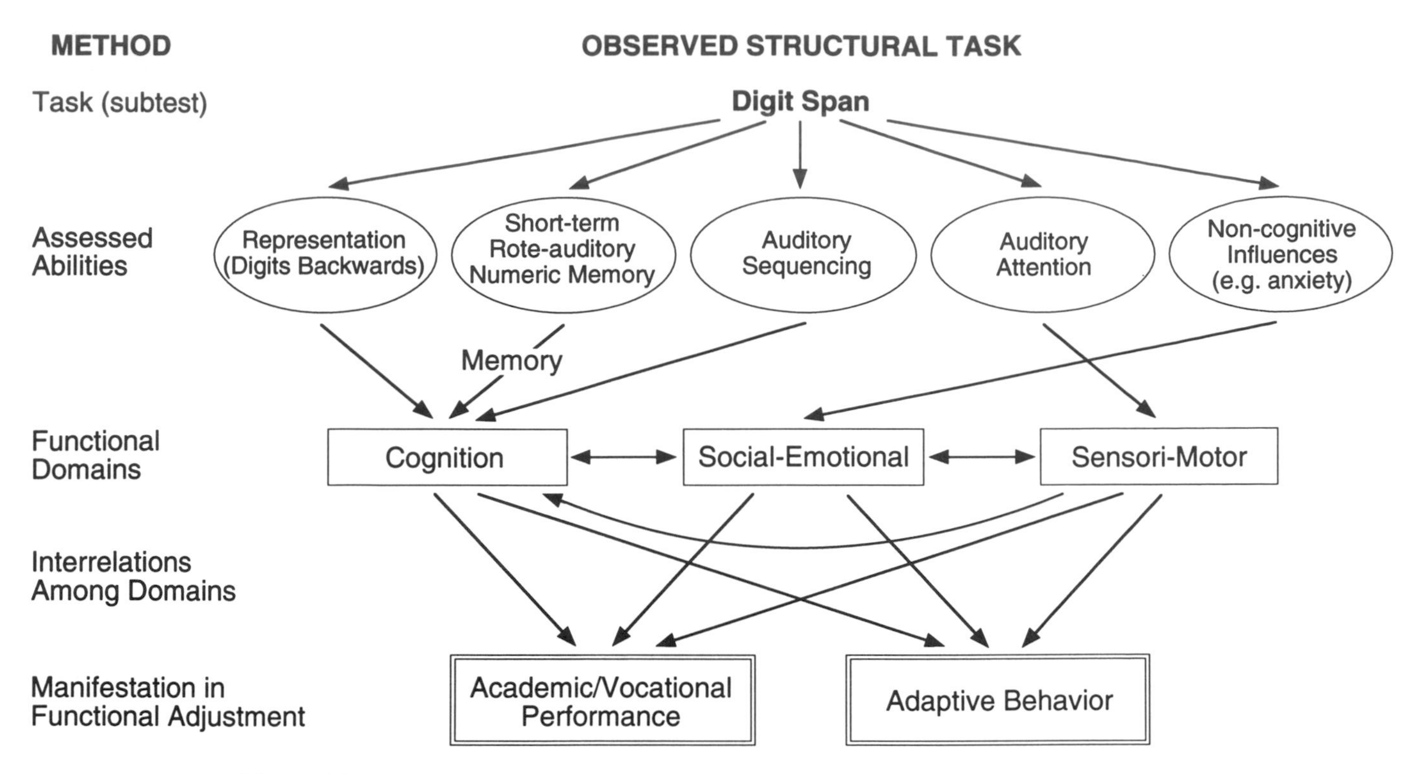

Figure 4.3 Examples of lines of inference from assessment task to functional adjustment.

to better understand the processes influencing functional adjustment. In the example presented in Figure 4.3, if convergent evidence across subtests suggests a problem in visual representation and minimal anxiety, the evaluator will place greater emphasis on the contribution of the cognitive domain when interpreting an individual's functional adjustment in the domains of academic/occupational achievement and adaptive behavior. In addition to overlap of the abilities assessed in the domains of functioning, one must attend to inconsistencies in abilities that may be a function of employing different sources of information (e.g., parent report versus child report, structured versus unstructured instruments) as well as situational factors that may have influenced performance on a given subtest.

We are especially concerned with identifying (a) the individual's current resources, in terms of developmentally emerging competencies, skills, and endowments, as well as cognitive, social-emotional, and behavioral styles; and (b) the adaptive integration of these resources into a functioning whole, which we will term *functional adjustment.* Although it is not possible to evaluate resources and adjustment independently, different assessment approaches place relatively greater emphasis on either individual capacities or integrative functioning. For example, this distinction is evident when the capacity for visual acuity on a structured test of perception is compared to the capacity to read and understand an assignment that is written on a classroom blackboard. A comprehensive assessment approach includes evaluating individual capacities as well as appreciating how these capacities are embedded within the broader context of other developmentally emerging skills and interactions with the environment. The particular approach taken should be informed by knowledge of normative developmental processes relevant to the domain of study as well as knowledge of impaired processes within different psychopathological groups. For example, if asked to evaluate a preschool child described as phobic of vacuum cleaners, the evaluator would need to appreciate developmentally normative fears characterizing this age group. Even if the behavior is quite normative, the evaluator should draw on knowledge of other psychopathological conditions to determine whether the form and intensity of the behavior are normal or pathological, and whether concomitant behaviors exist that would provide evidence of psychopathology (e.g., extreme withdrawal, ritualistic behaviors, necessity for sameness, or problems in peer relations). Although the referral question may be quite narrow (e.g., Does this individual have a learning disability?), a comprehensive assessment strategy addresses multiple aspects of the individual's current development and the manner in which the answer to the narrow question may be influencing broader aspects of functioning (e.g., Is the learning disability influencing self-esteem and/or peer relationships?).

Our emphasis on functional adjustment outcomes as a means of capturing integrative functioning through psychological assessment differs from other psychological assessment models. One means of measuring functional adjustment is to assess adaptive behavior, which refers to the daily performance of personal and social sufficiency. A second way to assess functional adjustment is to evaluate performance in the individual's school or workplace. Functional adjustment has not typically been included as an independent domain of assessment, or, if included, it is listed as one of many domains. Too often, emphasis is on the assessment of capacities or resources without due attention to how these capacities influence behavior in the contexts that comprise an individual's "real world."

In any assessment, the inherent goal is to determine how the domains of development affect the individual's everyday life (e.g., school performance, peer relationships); however, information concerning the individual's performance of age-appropriate tasks is often neglected. One exception is the routine assessment of academic achievement, which represents an aspect of evaluating academic performance. In combination with the use of behavioral assessment in the classroom, this strategy provides information regarding academic performance. A second strategy is the assessment of adaptive behavior. Traditionally, and even today, adaptive behavior is primarily considered an important domain for the classification of mental retardation (Sattler, 1988a, 1988b). However, in our clinical and empirical work with individuals who vary widely in terms of cognitive level and psychopathology, we have become convinced that adaptive behavior contributes to comprehensive assessment, especially in terms of quantifying functional adjustment.

By assessing the performance of age-appropriate behaviors in the adaptive behavior domains of communication, daily living, socialization, and motor skills, we can evaluate how the individual is implementing currently available resources. Furthermore, we can address the role of context in facilitating or inhibiting the implementation of such available resources. For example, using traditional psychological assessment instruments, we can characterize carefully the motor functioning of an individual with cerebral palsy and can document his or her levels of cognitive, social-emotional, and language functioning. However, the picture that emerges will be incomplete unless we know how the combination of functioning in these domains interfaces to impinge on behavior in the world outside of the testing room. In our empirical studies, the assessment of adaptive behavior permits an understanding of the heterogeneity of preschool precocious readers by providing a context within which to appreciate this unique achievement. Similarly, the assessment of adaptive behavior is extremely valuable in discriminating children who are experiencing psychological difficulties and require inpatient versus outpatient treatment (Cicchetti, Sparrow, & Carter, 1991).

Current Resources

When we conduct a psychological assessment, we are taking a snapshot of the individual's functioning. Current functioning reflects the past integration of endowment and experience and has predictive value for the future.

Sensorimotor

Sensorimotor abilities are those behaviors that might be best thought to link all mental and cognitive processes with the external world. Sensory systems embody those operations that allow external stimulus information into the brain for processing. These systems are among the earliest to fully develop, and deficits in their functioning have numerous implications for a person's further development and ultimate functional adjustment. Although the primary sensory systems of vision and hearing are typically the focus of assessments, deficits in tactile/kinesthetic abilities can have lasting impact on early development in infants, most notably in the motor domain. Taste and olfactory senses are rarely assessed, and developmental deficits in their functioning have not been a primary area of concern; yet, they may impact early eating behaviors, which, in turn, may have additional consequences for development.

Motor functions represent the only mode that humans have for the output of their behavioral choices, if one considers the vocal/speech system to be primarily a motor system. Fine motor and vocal skills continue to develop during childhood. It is also important to note that, without adequate development of these latter skills, writing/graphomotor and spoken language are not possible. An individual who has compromised motor development and is without speech, however, can still develop language abilities by utilizing alternative motor modes for expression (e.g., sign language).

A special relationship between sensory and motor systems appears to provide for their integration and development. For example, eye movements are critical for tracking visual information and for ensuring that the visual information is centrally focused on the retina. At the same time, basic sensory information provides for almost reflexive orienting responses that trigger motor movements toward the stimulus. The sensorimotor systems develop jointly and are the foundation on which all other behavior is constructed.

Cognition

Cognition refers to the highest levels of mental processes such as perception, memory, and the more integrative and control processes related to executive functions. Although there are many different theoretical models of such cognitive processes, almost all are based on some form of modularity. Modularity represents the functional subsystems of cognition, and although these subsystems may differ in their degree of independence, it is suggested that each unit operates differently and through unique underlying principles. This orientation regarding modularity as a basic property of the cognitive system has also resulted in strong arguments that such functional modules are based on neuroanatomically discrete systems. In recent years, these neurobehavioral or neuropsychological models of cognition have become pervasive in most assessment models of cognitive functions. Most of these neuropsychological assessment models require the independent evaluation of attention; auditory, visual, and tactile perceptual functions; verbal/language and spatial/constructional processing abilities; memory and learning; and executive functions (conceptual, reasoning, problem-solving, planning, set-switching, and control abilities).

The development of the various component processes underlying cognition does not occur at the same rate. During infancy and early childhood, the more basic attentional and perceptual elements undergo the fastest development; in later childhood and adolescence, the development of higher-order linguistic, spatial, and executive elements is primary. Because of this developmental pattern of differential emerging abilities, deficits or delays in the development of any of these various subcomponents can lead to diverse configurations of the cognitive system. Such outcomes may have adaptive or nonadaptive significance for a person's functional adjustment.

We do not consider the term *cognition* to be a synonym of IQ or intelligence. IQ represents the summary score on standardized "intelligence" tests, which may include measures of cognition but also assess sensorimotor and related abilities that are not typically included under cognition. For example, individuals with motor dyscontrol (e.g., cerebral palsy) may score poorly on IQ measures reflecting timed tasks with motor components, despite the fact that they possess high levels of cognitive abilities. In addition, infants have been shown to have a wide variety of cognitive abilities, but standardized IQ measures are not able to adequately assess them because of heavy reliance on sensorimotor skill assessment at early ages. Finally, there is significant contention that IQ tests measure only what persons have learned in the past, which is partly dependent on their opportunity, and not what their innate cognitive abilities or future potential actually represents. In many ways, from a comprehensive developmental assessment perspective, the concept of IQ as a global index of cognitive functioning is considered to be obsolete—not the tests themselves, but their traditional use and theoretical interpretations. Because such measures are so multifactorial and complex, additional independent measures of cognitive functions are typically required for adequate interpretation and integration into current assessment models.

At a minimum, the adequate assessment of cognition requires the measurement of each of the major modules within one's model of cognition. Because we consider the assessment of language functions to be a unique and critical component of this process in humans, they are described in more detail below. The assessment of the spatial processing abilities, including (but not limited to) those related to visual discrimination, closure, angulation, integration, and figure-ground processes, are also major areas of interest. Such assessments must include careful evaluation not only of the attentional and perceptual subcomponents involved in the initial processing of spatial information, but also of the ability of the cognitive system to store such information into its memory elements and to retrieve it later, when needed.

Attention is the process that focuses on the relevant information in a stimulus array while also inhibiting nonrelevant information from further processing. Attention, considered to be a limiting front-end feature of the perceptual process, controls the amount and quality of the information available for higher-order cognitive processes. Perception, the next step in the processing of sensory/attentional information, transforms the information into higher-order codes for use by the various higher-order cognitive subsystems. Memory is the set of processes that temporarily holds new information while it is being utilized or processed for other purposes, or more permanently holds learned information for future reference and use.

The final component of the cognitive assessment is the evaluation of executive functioning. This term has not been typically well defined, but includes those control and regulatory processes that integrate the processed stimulus information from the external world, compare the information to what is stored in memory from the past, and blend it with information about the person's internal physiological state and biological drives. This system makes decisions regarding the appropriate behavioral response to a given situation, decides what are appropriate goals and then develops plans to meet them, and provides the required behavioral programs to carry them out. It also is considered to be the primary subsystem involved in conceptual problem-solving and reasoning abilities not directly performed by the language and spatial subsystems.

Language

The capacity for spoken language is a unique human attribute, although other primates may possess the basic subcomponents of language systems. Language is the system that receives, comprehends, formulates, and uses symbols to communicate. Although communicative competence may take many forms, spoken and written language are the most common avenues for this unique cognitive system.

Assessment of the language system is one of the most fundamental aspects of any complete evaluation. Often, the initial assessment of language functioning is subsumed within broader aspects of cognitive functioning (e.g., Verbal Scale on the WISC-III tests; Wechsler, 1991). A more detailed assessment of language functioning must evaluate both receptive and expressive language capacities for the processing of the phonological, morphological, syntactic, and semantic aspects of the language system. This process is complicated by the need to evaluate the language system via different input and output modalities (e.g., auditory, visual, oral, gestural). The input of symbolic/language information may be made via most modalities, although the most common are the auditory and visual channels; the output system typically utilizes either the oral or gestural/written mode. In addition, evaluation of a person's pragmatic linguistic skills is required in order to understand his or her ability to utilize these complex abilities in a social context.

Because of these considerations, the basic capacities of each of these input/output channels must be clearly evaluated. For example, evaluation of the auditory system is critical in understanding factors that may affect language development. Although children who are congenitally deaf have difficulty learning oral language skills, they are able to develop and learn a language system via manual symbols. The pace of developmental change is most dramatic in the first 6 to 7 years of life. In this brief period of time, children undergo drastic changes in their observable language functioning, from being nonverbal to developing a complex expressive and receptive gestural and verbal repertoire, as well as acquiring the skills of reading and writing.

Although there is a great deal of information regarding normal language system development, there are still many questions regarding the factors that influence its emergence. Many of these factors appear to be related to the basic neurological substrates of the language system, but many are also related to the environmental characteristics (family or cultural) in which a person develops. These developmental changes, and their underlying neurological and environmental influences, also have effects during later aging, when these input and output channels undergo further changes that affect the language system's functioning and ability to be assessed.

Because language functioning represents one of the most complex but socially important behaviors, its evaluation must be made a priority in any assessment, and it should be assessed in the cultural context within which it developed or is used. In addition, knowledge regarding normal language development must be integrated within any evaluation process, in order to adequately understand the natural changes the language system undergoes with increasing age.

Social-Emotional

Social-emotional functioning refers to intra- and interpersonal regulation of emotion, cognition, and behavior. Emotional regulation involves: modulating the expression and experience of a wide range of emotions; developing skills to label emotions; decoding and empathizing with others' emotions; and integrating emotional information from the self and others by using appropriate contextual cues to inform adaptive responses to the environment. Personality organization refers to the individual's characteristic styles of behaving and relating; they provide a coherent sense of self while allowing others to make predictions about behavior. These aspects of personality are influenced by innate characteristics of temperament in their transaction with the interpersonal environment.

It is not possible to conduct a psychological assessment without appreciating the central role of social and emotional factors. There is a strong tradition of viewing emotion as an adaptive organizer of cognitive processing and behavior (Easterbrook, 1959; Leeper, 1948; Mandler, 1975). Recent theoretical and empirical advances in the study of emotion and social processes in social, clinical, and developmental psychology and psychiatry must be incorporated into developmentally informed models of assessment. Thus, concepts such as emotional intelligence (Salovey & Mayer, 1990), emotional competence (Saarni, 1989), and relational disturbances in early childhood (Emde, 1989; Sameroff, 1989) provide organizing templates for data typically collected in the social-emotional domain of functioning. In addition, it behooves clinical researchers to evaluate the utility of instruments developed to examine basic psychological processes in work with clinical populations.

To evaluate an individual's performance on any task, whether motoric, cognitive, or achievement-related, a variety of social-emotional and personality factors must be taken into consideration. These include the individual's motivation to perform the task (e.g., achievement orientation, attempts to convey a positive or negative impression), anxiety or depression that compromises attention regulation (e.g., selective attention, distractibility), and relation to authority, which may influence compliance and fearfulness or wariness. Some of these factors are readily apparent in the pattern of the individual's responses. For example, when there is dramatic improvement in performance as the tester establishes rapport, it is likely that wariness or social anxiety was interfering. If an examiner believes initial wariness or social anxiety may be the most parsimonious explanation for a relative weakness, administering additional tasks that assess the domain of relative weakness helps to determine whether the poorer performance was an artifact of the individual's emotional state. A similar profile may be seen when individuals (e.g., adolescents) do not recognize that the evaluator is a potential advocate for them.

It is important to determine the individual's understanding of the purpose of the evaluation and how the information that is obtained will be used. Significant social-emotional difficulty increases the likelihood of distortions regarding each of these issues. In addition, when individuals feel coerced into an assessment and/or do not believe the assessment will be used to advocate for their best interest, they are less likely to provide information that accurately reflects their true capacities.

Although most psychologists can agree that intelligence tests measure intelligence, there is not a similar general consensus regarding the assessment of personality and social-emotional functioning (Goldstein & Hersen, 1984). Traditionally, the kinds of instruments that have been employed to assess social-emotional functioning include play assessments for younger children, problem behavior checklists (e.g., Child Behavior Checklist (CBCL)—Achenbach & Edelbrock, 1986; Symptom Checklist-90 (SCL-90)), projective assessments such as the Rorschach inkblot task (Rorschach, 1948), story-telling tasks with ambiguous pictorial stimuli (e.g., Thematic Apperception Test (TAT)—Bellak, 1916), sentence completion tasks, figure drawings, personality inventories (e.g., Minnesota Multiphasic Personality Inventory-Adolescent (MMPI-A), Millon Clinical Multiaxial Inventory-II (MCMI-II)), and clinical profile interpretation of cognitive instruments (e.g., see Sattler, 1988a, 1988b, regarding interpretation of the Wechsler instruments). In terms of the assessment of psychopathology, self- and other-report inventories or rating scales that address specific symptoms for particular disorders are available (e.g., the Conners rating scale to assess Attention Deficit Disorder—Conners, 1985; the Beck Depression Inventory—Beck, 1967; Beck, Steer, & Garbin, 1988) as well as structured and semistructured interviews that yield diagnoses tied to research or clinical criteria. Because the social-emotional domain of the assessment often relies on instruments that have lower reliability and validity estimates than other components of the assessment, the use of multiple sources and methods of assessment is recommended. In this manner, greater confidence can be placed in hypotheses generated about social-emotional functioning and psychopathology.

Academic Achievement

Almost all achievement assessment is focused on evaluating an individual's current factual knowledge and skill, and probably represents an area in which change in abilities is expected with additional training and development. Most achievement assessment focuses on basic reading, decoding, and comprehension, and on spelling, writing, and arithmetic skills; in-depth evaluations will also assess more specific areas of knowledge (science, social studies, history, and so on). We are limiting the assessment of academic achievement resources to the individual's learned capacities, as contrasted to the academic skills the individual employs in everyday life. Thus, if an individual "can" read on a tenth-grade level but never reads, he or she has resources that do not contribute to functional adjustment.

Functional Adjustment

Achievement and Occupational Functioning

Achievement and occupational functioning represent the outcome of very specific areas of formal learning. Typically, achievement assessment is focused on academic-related abilities gained in formal learning environments such as school. These assessments almost always represent the implementation of what a child or adult has acquired from educational opportunities, and rarely suggest future potential or ability in other domains. The assessment of such abilities is highly affected by cultural, environmental, and curriculum factors.

Vocational assessment traditionally has had two different foci. The first has tried to evaluate a person's career interests and how they match those of others from various vocational groups and contribute to personality assessment. The second type of assessment, which is more clearly linked to achievement measurement, has as its goal the measurement of a person's basic abilities as they relate to specific job requirements and demands. These abilities have been learned, typically through formal educational or vocational training, and can be modified with additional experience. In many cases, basic achievement skills (i.e., reading, writing, and problem-solving skills) are considered to be the foundation or minimal requirements of any vocational assessment. In this model, vocational assessment is the developmental extension of achievement assessment as a person enters adulthood. Vocational assessment is typically even more specialized than achievement assessment, because of the specific needs of a particular job.

Adaptive Behaviors

Although adaptive behaviors are typically thought of as sets of concrete behaviors that connote personal sufficiency in day-to-day life, acquiring information concerning an individual's adaptive behavior skills provides a window into the individual's ability to integrate competencies across developmental domains. As can be seen in our discussion of adaptive behavior at various developmental phases, mastery of stage-specific tasks will be manifest in the practical negotiation of the everyday integration of the domains illustrated in Figure 4.2. Sroufe and Rutter (1984), Greenspan (1990), Sander (1962), and others described salient tasks at various developmental stages. For example, in the preschool years, a critical developmental task is negotiation of peer relations. When using a multidomain developmental measure of adaptive behavior (e.g., the Vineland Adaptive Behavior Scales—Sparrow, Balla, & Cicchetti, 1984), peer relations will be assessed within the socialization domain in terms of the child's ability to have friends, to have a best friend, and to have the related capacity to engage in fantasy play. In addition, a complex psychological construct such as individuation is concretely operationalized in the daily living skills domain, in terms of the child's habitual performance of self-help skills such as dressing, toileting, and bathing. When preschoolers are having difficulty negotiating the task of separating from their parents and developing age-appropriate peer attachments, difficulties are also likely to appear in the domain of daily living skills, which becomes the battleground for working through these psychological struggles. Deficiencies in socialization and daily living skills may appear whether the source of the difficulty is a cognitive delay or an emotional disturbance. At the same time, the child may appear age-appropriate in motor skills and communication skills. Knowledge of salient tasks of development, coupled with an adaptive behavior profile, provides a vehicle for evaluating the individual's practical integration of competencies across developmental domains.

Although development in cognition, language, social-emotional, and motor domains drives the acquisition of adaptive behaviors, adaptive behavior in this model is largely thought of as an outcome measure. However, it is essential to recognize that adaptive behavior is modifiable, and that teaching an individual how to behave in an age-adequate manner is likely to exert reciprocal influences, especially in the domain of social-emotional development.

Currently Unknown Domains

The domains reviewed so far represent one approach for understanding the complexity of human behavior. As our knowledge of human development increases, other currently unaddressed domains will likely be incorporated into standard assessment strategies. Just as the evaluation of IQ is currently a core concept for a broad spectrum of outcomes, concepts such as reaction time, which were once prominent but are currently receiving less attention, and concepts such as intersubjectivity, empathy, and habituation, which are receiving intensive study by a small number of researchers, may move into the mainstream practice of psychological assessment.

CURRENT RESOURCES AND FUNCTIONAL ADJUSTMENT THROUGHOUT THE LIFE SPAN

To highlight the importance of a developmentally informed approach, we discuss here the issues that emerge in different life stages for the functional domain illustrated in Figure 4.2. Because of the rate of change in the sensorimotor domain during infancy, the preschool years, and the geriatric phase of life, assessment of this domain is of particular relevance during each of these phases. Assessment of sensorimotor functioning is common in infancy, but, at later points in development, sensorimotor functioning is typically the focus of attention only when conducting specialized (e.g., neuropsychological) evaluations. In contrast, tasks designed to assess motor functioning are commonly employed with preschool and geriatric populations.

Infancy

Infancy is a time of rapid change and development marked by both quantitative and qualitative shifts, as evidenced across domains of functioning. The rate and degree of change in infancy make assessment of individual differences an inherently complex task. In addition, there is less homology across domains, which does not necessarily reflect any future delays or difficulties. For example, some 12-month-olds appear preoccupied with achieving increased motor competence; other 12-month-olds appear preoccupied with achieving increased linguistic competence. By 18 months of age, the focus of developmental attention may be reversed, resulting in equal competence across these two learning paths. Because of the rapid and spiraling quality of development in this phase, infants are especially vulnerable to environmental deprivation or insult.

Cognition. The fundamental aspect of Piaget's theory—that intelligence is not something that a child has or knows, but something that a child does—is critical to understanding cognition in infancy (0 to 2 years). According to Piagetian theory, human development can be understood in terms of functions and structures. Functions are innate biological mechanisms that facilitate the construction of internal cognitive structures. Structures, also referred to as schemas, reflect organized underlying knowledge that guides the child's interactions with the world as the child adapts to his or her environment. Further, the child's interactions with the world can modify existing schema as the child assimilates consistent information and accommodates new information. Through the process of unfolding biology and increased environmental experience, children construct knowledge about the world. Piaget, a stage theorist, described infant cognition in the first two years of life as falling within the sensorimotor stage of development. This refers to initial schemes based on simple reflexes that are gradually elaborated into larger, more flexible units of action. Because symbolic functions are not yet established, knowledge about the world is limited to physical interactions.

A majority of infant developmental assessment tools evaluate a variety of sensorimotor capacities (Bayley, 1969; Uzgiris & Hunt, 1975). These include attainment of various levels of: object permanence; use of objects as means; learning and foresight, or demonstrating expectancies; understanding causality; conception of objects in space; and imitation. With the exception of infants evidencing extreme delays in these areas, sensorimotor capacities are not predictive of performance on intelligence tests at later ages. Problems inherent in infant assessment include the highly variable rate of development, the profound influence of state changes on infant performance, and difficulties in discriminating problems in attention and concentration from problems in specific areas of development.

In addition to understanding sensorimotor development, assessment in infancy must be informed by knowledge of infants' capacity to be conditioned and to learn. Infants can be conditioned through both operant and classical paradigms from birth. The simplest form of learning involves habituation, which describes the decrease or disappearance of a reflex response by the repeated presentation of the same stimulus. For example, after multiple presentations of an interesting visual image, the infant will decrease the amount of time spent gazing at the image. The recovery of a habituated response is called dishabituation. Knowledge of this process has led to a host of discoveries about infant capacities, especially capacities involving sensation, perception, and memory. Indeed, Fagan, Singer, Montie, and Shepard (1986) have demonstrated that individual variability in rates of infant habituation is related to IQ in the preschool years.

Language. In the first two years of life, infants shift from reflexive communication (e.g., cries, movements, and facial expressions) to a vocabulary of more than 200 words, a complex gestural communication system, and comprehension. Intermediate stages include a range of meaningful noises (2 months); elaboration of sounds, including vowel sounds (3 to 6 months); babbling, including both consonant and vowel sounds and repeated syllables (6 to 10 months); comprehension of simple words and intonation, and use of simple gestures (10 months); first words (12 months); and slow growth of vocabulary, up to approximately 50 words (12 to 18 months). These phenomena are followed by an accelerated increase in vocabulary and the use of two-word phrases (16 to 20 months), and, finally, a vocabulary of approximately 200 words accompanied by the use of simple grammatical constructions (24 months).

Assessment of language functioning can be difficult in the second year of life because many infants are inhibited when they meet a strange examiner, and this results in reduced vocalizations. With increased understanding of the range of communication skills infants are acquiring (i.e., both gestural and verbal modalities), assessment of language functioning is shifting from a focus on expressive and receptive vocabulary to an emphasis on communicative competence (Bates, 1976).

Sensorimotor. In the first two years of life, infants develop increasing control over their bodies. Born with extremely limited capacities and control over movement, normally developing infants will eventually run, kick a ball, and scribble with a pencil or crayon. Motor assessments will include evaluations of the infant's ability to lift and gain control over the head and upper torso (2 months); roll over (3 to 4 months); sit up unsupported, grab an object (6 months); pull up to a standing position, release an object (7 to 8 months); stand alone (11 to 12 months); coordinate grabbing with thumb and forefinger (pincer grasp, 9 to 14 months); walk well unsupported (12 to 14 months); walk up steps (17 months); and kick a ball (20 to 24 months). Because parents are less aware of the subtleties of early language acquisition, delayed motor development is often the initial presenting problem for evaluation of infants who evidence more general cognitive delays. On the other hand, many infants who evidence delays in language and social-emotional functioning appear extremely competent in motor functioning, and this competence may prolong an appropriate referral for evaluation or services.

Social-Emotional. It is critical to consider infants' social-emotional development within the context of their primary caregiving relationships. Recent infancy research has highlighted the range of capacities and competencies that infants are born with (Haith & Campos, 1983; Osofsky, 1987), but the infant cannot organize these capacities independently. Innate and early emerging capacities develop and are shaped within the caregiving relationship, resulting in a wide range of adaptive and maladaptive patterns (Tronick & Giannino, 1986). As described by Emde (1989), the functional aspects of the caregiving relationship involve attachment, vigilance, physiological regulation, affect regulation and sharing, learning, play, and self-control. At the same time, parental functions include emotional availability and commitment, protection, provision of organized structure, responsiveness to needs, empathic responsiveness, teaching, play, and discipline.

Social-emotional development in infancy evolves through a series of salient developmental transformations. At approximately 2 months of age, the infant begins to evidence social smiling and vocalizations and increased eye-to-eye contact. By 7 to 9 months, along with locomotion in the motor domain and the beginning of object permanence in the cognitive domain, the infant begins to evidence affective reactions such as pleasure and fear, in anticipation of events that will evoke such responses. Stranger anxiety also emerges at this time. With the transition to toddlerhood, early in the second year of life, we see infants begin to use affective expressions in an instrumental or intentional manner. Further, infants will use social referencing to gain information from the caregiver when faced with an ambiguous or unknown situation. Parents typically begin to socialize their infants more actively, for example, using the word "no" to inhibit behavior. Between 18 and 22 months, the infant is once again transformed, and begins to focus on issues related to autonomy and dependency (Mahler, Pine, & Bergman, 1975). This is the beginning of the phase of development that is often referred to as "terrible 2." At this time, infants begin to become involved in the use of symbols, both in language and play. Toddlers develop new levels of competence in social play, and the role of peer relations becomes increasingly important. Several measures and coding schemes have been developed for research that addresses infants' social-emotional functioning. However, there is a paucity of standardized instruments that can be employed in clinical settings to determine an infant's status in this domain.

Academic Achievement. Major tools leading to academic achievement are the development of language and fine motor skills as well as feelings of self-efficacy and agency in the world. In addition, infants as young as 18 months of age are beginning to acquire familiarity with books and the notion of storytelling and reading. Experience with spoken language (including following simple commands), reading, and freedom to explore a range of objects will facilitate the child's readiness for later preacademic pursuits.

Adaptive Behavior. Many of the language, social-emotional, and motor competencies just described (e.g., babbling, social smiling, vocalizing pleasure, waving, using people's names) are integral to the infant's ability to attain personal and social sufficiency on a day-to-day basis. Generally, adaptive behavior is only moderately correlated with IQ; in infancy, however, the child's adaptive level is more closely linked to developmental or mental level. Competencies in the areas of language, motor, and social-emotional functioning enable the infant to make its needs known to family members and to begin independent activities (e.g., self-feeding). In addition, adaptive behavior reflects the infant's developing understanding of basic social conventions (e.g., clocks are important; you can talk on a telephone, to someone who is not present; the stove is hot and dangerous; people have names). Because the infancy period is typically viewed as a time of dependence, parents sometimes have difficulty understanding the value of promoting the acquisition of adaptive behavior skills at this early age. Indeed, the assessment of adaptive behavior will sometimes reveal a pattern of overprotection, which will lead to difficulties later in childhood in an infant who appears competent on more traditional measures of infant developmental assessment.

Early Childhood

Cognition. Piaget's description of preschoolers' cognitive development has been challenged and revised, but it continues to be a major influence on the study of cognition in this phase of development. According to Piaget (1928/1962), the most significant gain in cognition occurs in the area of symbolic thought. Beginning in rudimentary form in the second half of the second year of life, toddlers and preschoolers (ages 2 to 7) solve problems mentally, using symbolic representations as they develop the capacity to have thoughts stand for objects or actions. Although children's capacity to relate symbols to each other increases dramatically, it is considered "preoperational" in Piaget's stage theory because children tend to center on one idea and have difficulty applying more than one logical principle at a time. Because they also think in terms of absolutes rather than continuous dimensions, they also have difficulty with transitions and transformations. The emergence of symbolic thought, although primarily considered a cognitive advance, has far-reaching implications across multiple developmental domains and is especially significant in the areas of language and social-emotional development.

Language. Increases in vocabulary continue during the preschool years. The most notable gains in language are in complexity, as preschoolers begin to master a number of complex semantic relations and learn more about the pragmatics of everyday usage. Children tend to learn the rules prior to learning the exceptions to the rules, and their language is therefore characterized by overregularization (e.g., "I brushed my tooths"). Gains in cognitive and linguistic capacities permit utilization of a broad range of formalized assessment strategies that cannot be employed with younger children or with children who have not reached this developmental level (e.g., children who are mentally retarded or who have specific language delays).

Sensorimotor. When thought and action are no longer so intimately intertwined, preschool children continue to make dramatic gains in the area of motor development (e.g., running, hopping, skipping, writing). In fact, by the end of this phase of development, they will have acquired the basic skills necessary for adult motoric activities. Refinement or coordination of these skills continues to be modified throughout the life span and is strongly influenced by practice.

Social-Emotional. A concomitant development to the emergence of symbolic thought is pretend or "as if" play. The quality of children's pretend play appears to be a critical variable to include in a comprehensive assessment strategy because research has demonstrated that such play correlates with the quality of parental attachment and the development of subsequent age-appropriate peer relationships (Main, Kaplan, & Cassidy, 1985; Matas, Arend, & Sroufe, 1978). Within this line of research, rating scales have been developed to assess the developmental quality (Belsky & Most, 1981) of the use of symbols in play, as well as the coherence and elaboration of thematic content in both unstructured and semistructured play situations (Cicchetti & Wagner, 1990). Similarly, in this developmental stage, children make dramatic advances in their capacities to identify and label their own and others' feelings, and to modulate the expression and experience of feelings (Harris, 1989). These gains in emotional development are paralleled by dramatic shifts in the social realm. Sroufe & Rutter (1984) and Cicchetti & Schneider-Rosen (1986) have argued that the most salient developmental task in the preschool years is the negotiation of peer relationships. Observational research tools are available to assess peer relations at this stage of development, but there are few instruments that can be used in clinical settings. Given the centrality of these aspects of functioning and their power to predict subsequent adaptation, development of normative assessment instruments should be given high priority.

Academic Achievement. In this domain, preschoolers are acquiring the skills that will prepare them for formal instruction in reading, mathematics, and other academic subjects. Among these skills are: beginning awareness of visual or written symbols (e.g., company logos, first letter of name), and one-to-one correspondence. School readiness requires sufficient progress across developmental domains.

Adaptive Behavior. After infancy, the preschool years represent the second most rapid phase of child development. Consistent with the complexity of development at this time, children typically make dramatic advances in performance across many areas of adaptive functioning. Acquisition of adaptive communicative skills at this phase of development centers around more social aspects of communication. Consistent with the emphasis on pragmatic speech, noted earlier, preschoolers become more effective in letting their needs and wants be known to caregivers. In the realm of daily living skills, there is a significant move toward more independence in eating, toileting, dressing, and other self-help skills, preparatory to upcoming activities located away from the home (e.g., school). Age-appropriate adaptive socialization entails entry into more sophisticated interpersonal functioning, including rudimentary concerns for the feelings of others, development of group and individual friendships, and increasing mastery of community standards of acceptable social functioning (e.g., manners, sharing of possessions). Motorically, development of most fundamental gross and fine motor skills permits application to participation in more age-appropriate social activities, such as sports and a wide variety of school-related activities (e.g., using scissors, riding tricycles).

Middle Childhood (Ages 6 to 12)

Cognition. Building on preschoolers' preoperational cognitive processes, children in this age group move into the Piagetian cognitive stage of concrete operations. Children's thought at this phase of development becomes more logical, rule-bound, and integrated. Employing their preliminary acquisition of symbolic thinking, these older children increasingly focus on the rules and defining properties of objects and events in the world, a process that permits them to engage in more sophisticated problem solving by entertaining alternative hypotheses. For example, school-age children often appear more invested in negotiating the rules of a game than in the game's outcome. At this stage of cognitive development, however, this type of reasoning can still be applied only to tangible objects. The development of cognitive abilities enables children to "decenter," that is, to apply more than one logical principle at a time. Additionally, increased capacity to think in terms of symbols rather than images allows the children to grasp specific symbol systems, such as reading and mathematics.

School-age children's broadened and more complex thinking renders their cognitive processes more accessible to measurement and assessment. Further, their increased capacities to concentrate and attend to relevant stimuli contribute to a marked increase in the reliability of measurement and the accuracy of prediction of future intellectual development and academic achievement.

Language. As in the preschool years, in middle childhood there is continued increase in vocabulary acquisition and continued refinement of syntactic and semantic usage. Additionally, children in this phase of development exhibit an increased grasp of the pragmatic aspects of language, such as joke telling and polite speech. A further important development in this domain is metalinguistic awareness, or the ability to think about language. For instance, an interest in writing poems reflects a developing awareness of a variety of components of words, such as sounds and syllables, subparts, and connotations. This ability has been shown to be important in the acquisition of age-appropriate reading skills.

Social-Emotional. School-age children are involved in the initial stages of the complex task of achieving a coherent sense of self and a sense of self-identity. The school is a major arena for developing this sense of self. The process involves a self-evaluation of competencies in relation to peers. During this stage, the importance of peer relationships is in ascendance and the definition of family relationships takes on increasing complexity. Paralleling these developments, school-age children develop increasingly sophisticated abilities to label a spectrum of affects, and must achieve greater mastery of their capacity to regulate the form and intensity of their affective expression.

Academic Achievement. As defined by Erikson (1963), a sense of industry versus inferiority is the core developmental outcome of this developmental period. Given this task, academic achievement assumes crucial developmental significance. School-age children struggle to win approval for task mastery and to develop greater knowledge of personal strengths and weaknesses. The "tools" (e.g., reading, writing, mathematics) to succeed in a literate society must be acquired during this time.

Adaptive Behavior. Building on adaptive behavior acquired from earlier phases of development, school-age children continue to make strides in the realm of adaptive functioning. Communication skills are more focused around school skills, such as improvement in reading and writing abilities. In daily living skills, more independence is exhibited in dressing and personal hygiene. Advances are observed in capacities to tell time, to utilize a telephone, and to understand basic monetary concepts, and household chores assume more importance. In the socialization domain, the development of skills required to negotiate individual and group friendships is accelerated, as is knowledge and mastery of organized games and sports. School-age adaptive behavior in this domain also requires increased sensitivity to others' feelings and interests.

Adolescence

Cognition. In the cognitive domain, the most basic change in adolescence is the emergence of the Piagetian cognitive developmental stage of formal operations, which is accompanied by a dramatic increase in metacognitive processes. This stage is characterized by the developmentally acquired capacity to engage in abstract thinking, to utilize abstractions in problem solving (Flavell, 1985), and to reflect on the success of one's own abstract problem-solving strategies. Adolescents are increasingly able to abstract rules or principles that greatly enhance their ability to generalize learning across situations and contexts. Although there is some controversy about whether a stage theory most adequately captures the developmental process, there is consensus that this cognitive developmental stage represents a qualitative shift in reasoning ability and is not simply an extension of the cognitive abilities of younger children.

Language. The major task in the language domain during adolescence is the continued development and refinement of pragmatic skills. For the purposes of this model of assessment, pragmatic skills are the skills required to vary verbal communications according to the social level of the speaker's audience as well as the context within which communication occurs. At the same time, adolescents begin to refine their understanding of and become competent in the sophisticated use of nonliteral, figurative language as it occurs in the social context (e.g., "drop dead"). Adolescents must learn the nuances that influence how one speaks to one's social and developmental peers and how one must communicate with individuals in positions of authority. In terms of test development, this area of pragmatic language skills represents one of the greatest challenges for future design.

Social-Emotional. Adolescent development in the realm of personality and social-emotional functioning is characterized by more salient struggles regarding separation and individuation from primary caregivers, usually the family. This struggle also entails emerging questions regarding self-definition, interpersonal intimacy, and sexual object choice outside the family. Research findings (Offer & Offer, 1975; Rutter, 1980) contest the generally held assumption that these developmental struggles are typically tempestuous or rebellious in nature.

Adaptive Behavior. The most salient tasks of adolescence in the adaptive behavior domain involve acquisition of the skills required for developmentally appropriate interpersonal relationships and preparation for career or long-term academic goals. These skills entail, for instance, mastery of the interpersonal skills involved in dating, and social activities in and away from school. Occupationally, the adolescent must acquire abilities that will facilitate accomplishment of career goals, such as negotiating authority relationships, being on time for appointments, and frustration tolerance.

Academic Achievement. The primary academic requirement of adolescence is to utilize previously acquired learning skills (e.g., reading, writing, and mathematics) in order to increase a progressively more complex and specialized knowledge base.

Adulthood

Cognition. To understand the developmental processes central to the cognitive domain in adulthood, we must pay attention to distinctions between fluid and crystallized intelligence. Throughout adulthood, crystallized intelligence becomes increasingly preeminent and fluid intelligence declines (Kaufman, 1994). The largest decline in fluid intelligence occurs between the ages of 30 and 60 (Horn, 1982, 1985; Kaufman, 1994, p. 227), although this finding is mediated by educational and family life experiences (Kaufman, 1994, p. 230; Willis, 1985).

Language. Recent research (e.g., McLean, Kaufman, & Reynolds, 1988) indicates that this is the principal domain in which functional capacity actually increases with age, a clear example of the differential effects of development on crystallized as opposed to fluid abilities. Increase in language functioning with age appears to be facilitated in those adults whose activities include practice of language skills (e.g., lecturing, going to union meetings, writing, teaching, and so on) (Kaufman, 1994, chap. 7).

Social-Emotional. The area in which developmental processes in adulthood has received the most attention has been social-emotional and personality development. Erikson (1963), who was strongly influenced by Freud's drive-reduction theory, was one of the first to extend the notion of life stages into adulthood and lay the groundwork for a proliferation of further studies (e.g., Levinson, 1978, 1986; Loevinger, 1976; Vaillant, 1977). More recent theorists have shifted from stages of internally driven conflict resolution to a model more influenced by social psychology. For example, Levinson (1986), among others, has articulated a stage model with intervening transitional periods. The model is impelled by the challenges and demands of moving forward with one's life in the world. This involves articulating a "life dream" and establishing a "life structure" that permits the realization of the life dream.

Adaptive Behavior. For developmentally appropriate functioning in this domain, adults should have acquired the behaviors of routinely doing that which is necessary to sustain intimate family functioning, work within or outside of the home, and appropriate interpersonal relationships outside the family. In addition to these aspects of adaptive behavior functioning, adults face new developmental challenges to carve out leisure time from the multiplicity of their responsibilities, and to acquire capacities to engage in gratifying leisure activities.

Academic Achievement. Many adults will pursue traditional educational opportunities (e.g., high school, college and/or graduate degrees, additional vocational training, or adult education courses), but work performance in adulthood may be viewed as the upward extension of school performance in childhood and adolescence. A major task of adulthood is to address three related dimensions of work adjustment: (a) determining the relative personal significance of work achievement, in or out of the home, in the "life dream"; (b) determining the contributions of intrinsic and extrinsic rewards to motivation for work success; and (c) determining whether work is viewed as a static performance of previously mastered activities or a process of acquiring new skills and competencies that will lead to new developmental attainments. At the same time, certain responsibilities in any work situation—arriving on time, phoning that one will be late or absent, and filling out job applications—may be better understood within the domain of adaptive behavior.

Geriatrics

Cognition. During the developmental period of the geriatric years, the most basic function in the cognitive domain is adjustment to the changing capacity to engage in new problem-solving activities, abstract thinking, and flexible processing of novel stimuli. There are minimal declines in these functions before 50 or 60 years of age, but they may become more limited with progressing age. In addition, speed of processing, typically assessed via reaction time measures, may show a gradual decline with age, as changes occur in the sensory, motor, and nervous systems. Although complaints regarding memory abilities may be very common during this period, actual deficits in memory functions are rare except in disease states (i.e., dementia). There is some suggestion that new learning occurs at slower rates, and there may be an increasing problem with the retrieval of information from memory. A primary characteristic of this developmental level is an increased variability across most areas of cognitive functioning, with illness and disease states increasing the severity of related deficits. This relationship is best observed in what has been described as the "terminal drop," which marks impending death via acutely observed deficits in cognitive functioning.

Language. Language domain functioning is one of the most stable areas of abilities during the geriatric years (a) because this system has its foundation in what persons have previously learned rather than in what can be learned in a new situation, and (b) because central nervous system changes appear to have only limited effects on functional language capacity. The exception to this pattern is seen in individuals who suffer strokes or other nervous system insults that affect the underlying biological substrate of the language system. A more common problem is hearing loss, which can result in increased communicative and social isolation, even in the face of adequate language skills. This language system represents a major component of what has been described as "crystallized intelligence" as compared to "fluid intelligence." With increased age and decreasing perceptual-motor skills, communication skills become increasingly important.

Sensorimotor. As in other functional domains during this developmental period, there is great variability in the motor functioning of individuals. No clear pattern of decrements for all persons can be identified. There is a suggestion, however, that changes in life styles, in muscle mass and tone, in sensory system functioning, and in speed of central nervous system processes, all can interact to affect the functional motor abilities of persons within this period. Because of these effects on fine and gross motor functions, individuals may become more limited in doing job or leisure activities at the same level of performance or rate of speed.

Social-Emotional. Personality changes during the geriatric period are generally considered to be limited. When there are changes, they have been described as representing a change from an active style to a passive or introverted style in relating to the world. In addition, there appears to be a decrease in the number of social interactions in which older persons participate, and this may affect their emotional states. The principal challenges of this developmental period involve addressing the limitations placed on the individual by society (i.e., forced retirement) or by his or her own biological systems (i.e., changes in sensory functioning or in mental or motor capacity). These challenges are also related to the primary emotional issues that face elderly persons: loneliness, social isolation, and dealing with losses. As might be expected from this listing of challenges, the geriatric period carries increased risk for depression and feelings of decreased independence. Regardless of the changes observed, most authors consider personality functioning to be a key mediating factor in predicting how a person will deal with the challenges of this final developmental period. One of the primary tasks of this time in life has been described as an "identity review" in which a person evaluates the past and adjusts to a final identity.

Adaptive Behavior. The most salient task during the geriatric period of development in adaptive behavior involves the evaluation, adjustment, and performance of the skills required for basic living and self-help skills, in the face of changing sensory/cognitive abilities and societal expectations. In addition, these years require an ability to adapt to vocational retirement, to the increased challenges of nonstructured leisure time, and to changing roles in the family and community.

Academic Achievement. The geriatric period typically involves a major change in vocational functioning, often because of societal limitations. With such a change can come related revisions in income, marital, or social roles or activities, which might impact an individual in both positive and negative ways. There is little evidence that this change in vocational functioning must have an adverse effect; many persons substitute volunteer or part-time working roles. The active pursuit of specific leisure activities (i.e., gardening, traveling) then becomes their new "vocation."

TEST CONSTRUCTION AND SCALING ISSUES

A developmentally informed comprehensive perspective on psychological assessment can only be achieved with a basic understanding of psychometric and methodological issues. We begin our discussion of these issues with a focus on standardization, reliability, and validity. Although these concepts are frequently given only passing attention in clinical practice or research, conceptual issues such as item scaling and a test's factor structure are critical considerations for assessing the development of an individual or group. The following section briefly reviews some of the influences of psychometric issues on measures that try to describe developmental processes.

Item Selection

One psychometric issue in test construction that will influence a test's sensitivity to developmental change is item selection. The seemingly simple act of developing or choosing a specific item (or a specific behavior, if using a behavioral approach to assessment) for a specific measure depends on our understanding of the normal progression and unfolding of abilities. Items are typically chosen based on their content, structure, and statistical characteristics. An item's content represents a sample of the measured domain or function; its structure represents the item's format. For example, if one were developing a vocabulary measure, content could be varied by changing the words included in the item, and structure, by changing the response required by the individual (e.g., asking the individual to provide a definition, to point to a picture that best represents the word, or to use the word in a sentence).

Critical developmental considerations are involved in decisions regarding content. For instance, the population of words that can be used across development changes significantly, from few if any during early infancy, to thousands, if not hundreds of thousands, during adulthood. To best represent and assess an individual's vocabulary, an understanding of the normal developmental progression of language abilities is necessary. In addition, developmental considerations are inherent in choosing the structure for an item. Younger children have been shown to have a more extensive receptive vocabulary than an expressive or written vocabulary. Therefore, an item requiring a young child to point to the best pictorial representation of the word would yield a very different view of "vocabulary" than an item requiring a verbal definition or use in a sentence. Although this example has obvious developmental considerations, there are few measurement domains in which this is not the case. One of the problems in some measurement areas, such as social-emotional functioning, is our relatively limited knowledge about normal development (Cicchetti, 1990). Once an item pool is selected that varies in both content and structure, sophisticated statistical item-scaling methods can be employed to determine the difficulty level of items and to assign developmentally appropriate ordering of scale items (e.g., Rasch scaling method; Woodcock & Dahl, 1971).

Some theoretical statistical models are conceptually useful for guiding the construction of developmentally appropriate items and measures. For example, based on its underlying assumptions, (i.e., item parameter invariance across groups), item response or latent trait theory suggests that a general measure can be developed with scaling that can be compared across subjects of greatly differing abilities. In addition, this model suggests that one can use completely different groups of items for different groups of subjects and still compare their results. Given these assumptions, one could choose different sets of developmentally appropriate items for groups of subjects who are at very different developmental stages, develop measures from each set of items, and still be able to compare the actual scores obtained across the groups or within a group across time. Although this item development model is considered to be very strong in theory, there are few actual examples of its use outside of the achievement or adaptive behavior domains. Even within the achievement area, the use of sets of anchor or calibration items has been required to help this model work.

The statistical properties of each item within a particular measure also have to be considered within the developmental context. One of the most difficult measurement problems in assessing developmental functions occurs when a distribution of scores is nonnormal, especially when there is a positive or negative skew. Most often, nonnormal distribution of scores occurs with those items that fall at either end of the continuum of difficulty. When a large portion of the chosen items is either too easy or too difficult for a specific developmental level, there will be little variability in performance on those items. Items that are too easy will result in many individuals' obtaining the highest scores possible on the measure (ceiling effect), and items that are too difficult will result in a majority of individuals' obtaining very low scores (floor effect). This problem is easily illustrated if one considers what would happen if a majority of the items on a reading test were at the 5th-grade reading level and it was given either to a group of 1st graders (floor effect) or 12th graders (ceiling effect). In either situation, it is not possible to accurately scale or measure an individual's true abilities because they fall within the tail end of either distribution. It is also extremely difficult to examine change, over time, in individuals who are already scoring at the ceiling of a measure, or who may be limited to scoring at the floor end of a measure. Such developmentally insensitive measures also severely limit one's ability to compare relations between constructs. In part, this is due to the statistical restrictions in variance that ceiling and floor effects cause. Restriction in variance (i.e., all respondents obtaining approximately the same score) will always limit the amount of covariance possible between measures (i.e., the ability of scores on one measure to predict scores on another measure, or on the same measure at a future point in time).

Normatization

Traditional assessment as practiced is inherently developmental because of its use of standardization samples and norms. In many ways, the concept of "norms" is central to a developmental perspective for assessment. Although traditionally a norm is considered to represent the average test performance of a standardization sample, it is very easy to consider a norm as representing the average, median, or modal performance of a particular developmental level or stage. There is always a difficulty in operationally defining a group of individuals at a particular developmental level, because development occurs on a continuum (regardless of one's orientation regarding steps, stages, linear or nonlinear models of development). In a majority of the tests available, the most typical way to operationalize development has been based on chronological age, partly because of ease of use. A developmental level or stage, though, may be defined based on an individual's ability to perform a particular cognitive task (i.e., object permanency) or even on his or her marital status, depending on the developmental area of interest. Regardless of the dimension chosen as an index of developmental level, and in order to obtain a "norm" for reference purposes, a decision on where to partition the dimension has to be made. A true developmental assessment model is therefore not actually possible, because any "norms" represent an arbitrary piece of a lifelong process.

Normative data also have to be considered within the cultural, historical, and societal frameworks in which they are developed. There has been considerable discussion regarding the concept of cohort in developmental research. In some domains, the historical events of the nation (i.e., the Great Depression, World War II) or of a local community (i.e., a flood, a special business development) may have very strong effects on an individual's developmental progression in a number of domains. Norms developed in such situations may not be adequate representations of a different cohort that has not had similar environmental/historical experiences.

The reliability of a measure is also a critical consideration when one is concerned with developmental assessments. First, there are some conceptual difficulties in the use of some reliability coefficients. For example, the test-retest reliability measure is in some ways directly related to change during the course of development. Typically, one would test a group of subjects at one point in time and then again at a later point in time. One issue involved in this simple method is the length of time between measurements. Traditionally, this period of time is between 2 weeks and 2 months. But within a developmental framework, even 2 weeks does not necessarily represent a constant period of change. For example, a 2-week period in a 1-month-old infant represents a large portion of the infant's life and a period of rapid change in abilities. In contrast, a 2-week period in the life of a 50-year-old constitutes a very small percentage of development and may represent a period in which little change is occurring. This issue is very similar to the changing interval problems involved in using age- or grade-equivalent scores. Given that a test-retest reliability coefficient is designed to assess the consistency of a measure and is dependent on the stability of the assessed behavior, one has to consider that it may also include some variance caused by true individual changes that occur during certain periods of development.

Reliability

The role that measurement reliability plays in the comparison between and among different measures underlies most developmental assessments. When comparing the scores from two different measures, a statistically significant difference is based on the standard error of the difference scores, which is calculated using the reliability coefficients of each measure. The lower the reliability, the greater the score difference required before one is secure in deciding that there is a significant discrepancy. As has been shown in previous research, individuals at different developmental levels may require larger or smaller score differences because of differences in the reliability of the measures used at different levels. A simple example is found in the Stanford-Binet Intelligence Scale, 4th Edition (Thorndike, Hagen, & Sattler, 1986), which shows that a 3-year-old child requires almost a 14-point standard age score difference between Verbal Comprehension and Nonverbal Reasoning/Visualization factor scores, but a 17-year-old requires only a 10-point factor score difference to achieve statistical significance (at the .01 probability level). Given that younger children may also have a more limited range of scores on such a scale, especially when one considers their limited raw score performances, it may be psychometrically rare for them to ever exhibit such a magnitude of differences between the measures. These points are also of concern if there are floor or ceiling effects on the measures involved. In such situations, the reliabilities are artificially inflated, the standard error of the differences is therefore artificially decreased, and interpretations are wrongly made that there are true differences between measures when this might not be the case.

Validity

The construct validity of a measure also may be affected by developmental processes. Although many measures are analyzed by using factor analytic methods to confirm their underlying traits or constructs, very few are analyzed within a developmental framework. Such an analytic plan is required in order to describe the changing patterns of the traits or constructs over development. An assumption that a particular measure has the same structure, or even measures the same traits/constructs over development, is generally unwarranted unless there is adequate assessment of its validity using an appropriate developmental analytic framework. In addition to a measure's construct validity, there are developmental considerations regarding its predictive validity. Most measures are more predictive over shorter time periods than over longer periods, but there may be exceptions when individuals enter a new stage of development. Again, the measure's reliability and developmental appropriateness will affect its predictiveness.

As has been described, all of these test construction issues are bound by developmental considerations but are also critically important in assessing an individual's or a group's developmental change. The key purpose of all assessment measures within a developmental framework is to accurately describe the change that is continually occurring, regardless of the dimensions of interest. Measures that are not developed to meet strict psychometric criteria will artificially limit our understanding of both the underlying dimensions and the processes of change that are occurring. Therefore, such basic psychometric considerations are central to any strong developmental model for assessment.

Sensitivity-Specificity

Although a test or measure may be a very reliable and valid measure of an underlying construct or behavior, there is still an issue of how useful it might be for a given diagnostic purpose. Of most concern within this realm is the problem of misclassification and its impact on the person being classified. The measures of sensitivity (proportion of a sample found to fall within a diagnostic category) and specificity (proportion of a sample not falling within a diagnostic category) help to determine how well any test can be used for a specific diagnostic purpose. In addition, the measures of predictive value of a positive result (pvP) and predictive value of a negative result (pvN) provide information regarding how useful a particular test is for a specific population being classified. These latter concepts have significant applicability in evaluating a specific test for use with various populations during different developmental periods. One should not expect any one test to have stable sensitivity and specificity for a particular diagnostic decision across the developmental spectrum. For example, there are many specific diagnostic conditions (e.g., dementia, depression, speech disorders) that might have different base rates at different ages. If we have a test that has very good sensitivity and specificity (e.g., 80% to 90%) at one developmental level, and try to use it with another developmental group that has a different base rate of the disorder, then the sensitivity and specificity could change significantly and the test may not be adequate for the purpose at hand, even though its reliability and psychometric properties remain strong and stable.

METHODS

In approaching specific assessment strategies, whether for clinical or research applications, a common starting point is to review available tests or instruments. We advocate an alternative approach: begin by determining the constructs most relevant to the questions being asked. Once these constructs are determined, it is important to select the methods that one will use to assess the constructs. The methods may include standardized tests, which represent the most structured of available procedures, but other available methods should also be considered. In isolation, standardized tests are rarely sufficient to answer the questions that researchers and clinicians attempt to answer. For example, even when evaluating intelligence, the obtained scores on a particular IQ test can only be interpreted in the context of observational and situational data (e.g., compliance, attention, motivation). To the extent that a multitrait, multimethod matrix can be developed to address the questions of interest, multiple sources of method error variance can be examined and a clearer understanding of the constructs under consideration will emerge (Campbell & Fiske, 1959).

For heuristic purposes, we have chosen to discuss the sources of method variance that are particularly relevant to a comprehensive developmental assessment approach and that demonstrate how the use of multiple methods enriches the validity and generalizability of the outcome. The sources are: (a) reporting sources, (b) interviews, rating scales, and questionnaires; (c) observational methods; and (d) projective methods.

Reporting Sources

The routine evaluation of individuals in isolation is artificial and provides only a partial picture of current functioning. There are numerous sources for obtaining relevant information for multiple domains of functioning. For children and adolescents, examples include contacting teachers and caregivers to obtain additional information in the domains of academic, cognitive, social-emotional, and adaptive functioning; and reviewing school records for academic achievement. For adults, examples include interviewing spouses and family members to obtain relevant information in the domains of personal, social, and adaptive functioning; and reviewing medical charts as an adjunct to a neuropsychological evaluation. Because multiple informants often provide conflicting information, their inclusion often complicates data integration. However, conflicting data are often informative and contribute an added dimension to the assessment, especially in terms of understanding the systems in which the individual functions. Because informants may have access to different samples of behavior in multiple settings, conflicting information may reflect true variability in current functioning. On the other hand, conflicting information may be a function of observer or interviewer biases. When the informant will be involved in implementing recommendations, having some knowledge of these biases may be extremely useful. It should also be acknowledged that, in some situations, the use of other informants is the only way to obtain information about a relevant domain, either because the behaviors of interest have such a low base rate of occurrence and are unlikely to occur in the testing situation or because the individual is unable to provide the information (e.g., because of coma, psychosis, dementia, severe retardation, infancy). When considering the inclusion of multiple informants, care must be taken to protect the individual's confidentiality. Informed consent must be secured from the individual or his or her legal guardian prior to obtaining information from outside sources.

Interviews, Rating Scales, and Questionnaires

Although interviews are more commonly employed in clinical assessments, and rating scales or questionnaires are used more in research applications, each form of data collection is applicable to both situations. Indeed, as more questionnaires and rating scales become available with appropriate normative information, and as clinical interview methods are standardized, the versatility of these methods increases. For each method, the adequacy of the sample on which normative data are based should be evaluated carefully along a number of dimensions, including: sample size; representativeness of age, sex, and socioeconomic status; ethnicity; and size of community. A well-normed instrument must be representative of the group with whom the individual being tested is compared. For example, when evaluating an individual to rule out a diagnosis of mental retardation, both intelligence and adaptive behavior must be assessed with instruments that have been normed on a large sample that is representative of the total population. However, it may also be important to determine how a mentally retarded individual is functioning relative to other individuals who are diagnosed as mentally retarded. Therefore, the existence of additional norms, including a representative sample of individuals who are mentally retarded, might influence the selection of a specific instrument for this purpose.

A central concern when employing interviews, rating scales, and/or questionnaires is the bias of the informant, typically discussed in terms of response styles. For example, an informant may attempt to present in a negative light in order to gain access to treatment or services. Some scales have incorporated social desirability indexes or veracity scales that can detect such response biases and provide correction formulas (e.g., MMPI-2—Graham, 1991). A second concern is the reliability of the instrument. For both rating scales and interviews, the more structured the format, the easier it is to obtain adequate test-retest and interrater reliability coefficients. Similarly, the lower the inference level required to make ratings (either for the informant or the interviewer), the greater the probability that adequate reliability can be obtained. There is a tradition of giving greater credibility to observational or standardized test data, but, in many cases, the best approach is to ask the individual. Such inquiry can be accomplished with a rating scale, a questionnaire, or an interview. For example, when assessing suicidality, a valid method is to ask whether an individual has considered killing himself or herself, whether an attempt has been made in the past, and whether a feasible plan is in place.

Observational Methods

Consistent with data from interviews, rating scales, and questionnaires, observational methods vary along a continuum of structure and of the level of inference required to evaluate the constructs of interest. In addition, observational data add the dimension of time: decisions must be made regarding the time frame of the analysis (e.g., continuous versus time or event sampling). The unit of analysis must also be considered in terms of a microanalytic or macroanalytic focus. Such decisions will be driven by the constructs under study. When conducting evaluations, we continually make observations that guide our subsequent behavior and decision-making processes. To this extent, the use of observational methods is not new. Research employing observational methods (e.g., interpersonal processes and play) has made significant contributions to our knowledge base. However, few structured observational methods have been developed and standardized sufficiently to permit their use in clinical applications. One exception is Katherine Barnard's Nursing Child Assessment Satellite Training (NCAST) teaching scale (Barnard, 1979), which has been employed with large numbers of socially high- and low-risk mother-infant dyads, as well as with infants with disabilities (Barnard & Kelly, 1990).

Projective Methods

Freud introduced the term *projection* in 1894 and explained it as a strategy for assigning attributions (see Exner, 1991). Since the introduction of projective techniques in the United States in the 1930s, their use has been highly controversial. Their basic underlying assumption is that individuals' responses to an ambiguous stimulus or set of stimuli reveal something about the way in which the individuals perceive, interpret, and organize the information presented (Maloney & Ward, 1976). A further assumption is that these perceptions, interpretations, and organizational strategies inform the examiner about personality, unconscious processes, psychopathology, and reality testing. A primary feature of all projective techniques is that they involve a relatively unstructured demand or task. Typically, the examinee is not aware of how the test will be interpreted. Controversy has centered around issues of reliability and validity and has led to attempts to standardize administration, scoring, and interpretation by developing methods of quantifying ratings of responses. Over the years, many systems have been proposed for one of the most widely used projective techniques, the Rorschach Inkblot task. For example, early systems were developed by Beck (1944), Klopfer and Donaldson (1962), and Rappaport, Gill, and Schaffer (1968). More recently, Exner (1991) built on previous methods to develop for the Rorschach Inkblot task a comprehensive system that includes normative data. Other currently employed projective methods include sentence completion tasks, figure drawings, and storytelling tasks. Despite the controversy, projective techniques continue to be employed as a primary means of assessing and understanding personality and emotional development in school-age children and adults. Play interview techniques are also employed with preschool-age children, making use of the same set of projective assumptions to assess social-emotional functioning. At present, a paucity of tools is available to evaluate young children's social-emotional functioning in clinical and research settings. A task currently employed by the MacArthur Network collaborative study of children's use of narratives, directed by Robert Emde, builds on sentence completion tasks and play interviews (Robinson, Mantze-Simmons, & Macfie, 1993). This task involves the presentation of structured story stems that are organized around relevant themes (e.g., attachment, separation, misbehavior) and are accompanied by toy props. This kind of methodology presents an opportunity for developing a quantifiable, normed projective instrument for use with preschoolers.

IMPLEMENTING THE MODEL: HYPOTHESIS-DRIVEN ASSESSMENT

The terms *comprehensive* and *developmental,* emphasized throughout this chapter, must remain salient at each phase of implementation. To recapitulate, by comprehensive, we refer to obtaining data about the individual's functioning across a broad range of domains (i.e., cognition, language, social-emotional and personality, adaptive behavior, and academic/occupational achievement). The assessment should address not only functioning within domains, but also reciprocal influences between domains. By developmental, we refer to the notion that an individual's functioning in these domains can only be understood within the context of normative expectations for performance during a given developmental period (Cicchetti, 1984).

Goals of the Assessment

Assessment is aimed at painting a comprehensive picture of an individual's functioning within and across domains as they relate to the level of development. This model of comprehensive developmental assessment is applicable to the evaluation of individuals and groups for research or for clinical purposes. In each case, one must establish (a) the goals of the assessment; (b) the relevant domains of assessment; (c) appropriate instruments; (d) the relations among selected instruments; (e) contextual factors that influence performance on these instruments; (f) a synthesis and interpretation of the obtained information, which provides a parsimonious understanding of the individual's current functioning; and (g) communication of this understanding of the individual's functioning to relevant levels of the developmental system, along with recommendations for any indicated interventions. When the model is actually implemented, these component parts are not necessarily discrete or sequential. Rather, the examiner engages in an ongoing interactive feedback loop among all of these component parts at each phase of the evaluation.

Because of the multifactorial characteristics of any single measure, it is critical to use multiple measures and to have a good understanding of unique and shared abilities (i.e., latent constructs) that will contribute to the score obtained on a specific instrument. At the individual level, the use of multiple measures permits an analysis of patterns of convergence and divergence across instruments. Once measurement error is minimized, it is possible to determine patterns of relative strengths and weaknesses across multiple domains of development. Thus, the use of multiple instruments heightens one's confidence in a given finding because the error contribution from a single measurement source is minimized. At the nomothetic level, cluster and factor analytic approaches have been employed to identify patterns of functioning across relevant developmental domains that can lead to the successful classification of discrete subtypes or groups of individuals. An example of employment of this approach can be seen in clinical research that seeks to identify specific subtypes of learning disabilities (Fletcher, 1985; Morris, Blashfield, & Satz, 1986; Rourke, 1985).

Hypothesis-Driven Assessment Approach

In clinical situations, we endorse utilizing a strategy of hypothesis-driven assessment. Hypothesis-driven assessment refers to a process in which each step in the evaluation is guided by hypotheses generated from currently available information. A dynamic process is involved: the available information changes throughout the course of the assessment. A comparison between this approach and a standard comprehensive battery is analogous to the distinction between theory-driven research and shotgun research. The hypothesis-driven approach has a higher probability of hitting the relevant target in terms of obtaining information that is truly explanatory in the individual case. Kaufman (1979, 1983, 1994) has written widely about this approach to assessment. His major focus has been on intelligence and the most widely used tests of intelligence. In this model, we advocate the application of this approach across the spectrum of assessed domains. At points in the life span when developmental changes may play a larger role (i.e., in childhood and old age), it is critical to apply a developmentally informed perspective to hypothesis generation, instrument selection, and inferences derived from observational and quantitative data.

When presented with the task of selecting the initial goals of the assessment and choosing the domains that will be emphasized, the first piece of information that is available is typically the referral question. Based on the referral question, initial hypotheses are generated. These initial hypotheses guide the identification of relevant domains to assess, which in turn guide the selection of available instruments. Ideally, each domain of assessment relevant to the referral question will be addressed in a preliminary way in the first session with the individual. Based on the preliminary data, the next step of the assessment is designed. The preliminary data may support or disconfirm the initial hypotheses or may suggest additional hypotheses meriting further exploration. This approach is in marked contrast to administering a standard, lengthy battery to all individuals. A practical implication of this approach is that multiple assessment sessions over time are preferred to one or two extended sessions.

The use of multiple sessions provides an opportunity to score and evaluate information, refine hypotheses, and customize selection of instruments to elucidate strengths and weaknesses of the individual being evaluated. In addition, intersession variability has often been considered a component of unexplained or error variance from a test-and-measurement perspective. When dealing with an individual case, however, this variability may be quite informative. One can weigh the relative impact of such variables as initial performance anxiety and the development of rapport by observing improvements or decrements in performance over time. Thus, the use of multiple sessions often provides a more reliable and accurate estimate of the individual's behavior. This is especially important when evaluating children, whose behavior is likely to change and be more variable over time.

Appropriate and Inappropriate Referral and Research Questions

To implement this approach to assessment successfully, referral questions should be specific and should be based on information about the individual in multiple settings of the developmental system. Specific questions facilitate the generation of preliminary hypotheses to be pursued during the assessment. This is true for research studies that investigate groups of individuals and make clinical evaluations of individuals. For example, a global request regarding an individual's IQ score when there is a nonstated concern about language functioning may interfere with the selection of the most appropriate instruments for evaluating intelligence and language in this individual, because different IQ tests vary in their emphasis on verbal functioning in the determination of global intelligence. Similarly, when conducting research, it is important to determine the specific construct being measured and the interaction of the construct with the dependent variables under study. For example, if the interest is in evaluating children diagnosed with Attention Deficit/Hyperactivity Disorder (ADHD) and non-ADHD children on listening vocabulary, the selection of a cognitive test must take into consideration how much the instrument is influenced by the attentional behavior associated with the diagnosis of ADHD. Thus, if an instrument is selected and used in isolation (e.g., a test of listening vocabulary such as the Peabody Picture Vocabulary Test, Revised—Dunn & Dunn, 1981), it is critical to recognize all the known influences that may contribute to the obtained scores. Attentional difficulties may well compromise performance on this task, such that presumed group differences in listening vocabulary are more parsimoniously explained in terms of differences in attentional ability.

Steps to Interpretation from a Developmental and Conceptual Perspective

The steps to interpretation we will describe assume that multiple measures have been employed to evaluate multiple domains of functioning. The initial phase of interpretation involves a systematic analysis of each of the individual measures administered. Because many of the measures are comprised of multiple subtests, this process involves identifying the unique and shared abilities assessed within the subtests that comprise each of the individual tests administered. Consistent with the approach described by Kaufman (1979, 1990) for the Wechsler scales and by Sparrow et al. (1984) for the Vineland Adaptive Behavior Scales, we advocate beginning the analysis of individual tests by analyzing the most global and psychometrically robust level (e.g., Full Scale IQ (FSIQ) or Adaptive Behavior Composite). In this first step, it is essential to recognize the contribution of the variability in the subtests or subdomains underlying the global scores (e.g., statistically and/or clinically significant Verbal IQ (VIQ) and Performance IQ (PIQ) discrepancies, or communication, socialization, daily living skills, and/or motor discrepancies). Often, a global score may misrepresent an individual's functioning because of the variability of the component scores. Subsequently, we proceed from the most molar (i.e., global score) to the next most robust level of analysis, proceeding systematically to the most molecular level of analysis (i.e., an individual item within a particular subtest). To guide this exploration and prevent interpretations of differences that may be a function of chance, it is critical to use available psychometric data. For example, prior to interpreting a profile of strengths and weaknesses based on a pattern of subtest scores, one must account for the fact that there are differences in the reliabilities of each of the subtests that comprise various scales. This is accomplished by determining whether observed subtest scatter is meaningful. Both in research and clinical settings, the evaluator must address both statistical and clinical significance. The latter case involves the clinician's examining the normative data to determine whether a particular degree of variability is markedly unusual. A common fallacy in test interpretation is that statistical significance is viewed as clinically meaningful, even when 40% of the population may evidence a statistically significant level of variability.

A further caution at the level of individual test analysis is to employ developmental knowledge to inform the interpretation of particular patterns of subtest variability. Specifically, one must be sensitive to the fact that individual subtests on a given instrument may reflect different underlying abilities at different developmental levels. For example, this developmental shift in latent variables is seen on the Kaufman Assessment Battery for Children (K-ABC) Photo Series subtest, which reflects different processing styles at different developmental levels (Kaufman & Kaufman, 1983), and on the Arithmetic subtest on the WISC-III (Wechsler, 1991), in which the task demand makes a qualitative shift as item difficulty increases.

Employing a comprehensive developmental assessment approach increases the level of interpretive complexity, in part because of a lack of empirical guidelines for synthesizing information across different tests. Thus, when there is variability in the information obtained across two or more tests, there are no empirical data to guide the determination of whether the variability is statistically or clinically meaningful. The interpreter must rely on his or her knowledge of the specific task demands of and latent abilities assessed by the different tests. This knowledge must be complemented by a grasp of the contextual influences present when each of the tasks was administered. To help clarify discrepant information about a specific ability, it is often valuable to administer additional measures that illuminate the specific ability with greater precision. The recent increase in journals dedicated to research on measurement and assessment should provide an additional source of guidance on interpreting test information. For example, studies employing comprehensive assessment approaches with large numbers of subjects provide important information about patterns of functioning evidenced by individuals with specific disorders such as learning disabilities or neurological dysfunction (see Kaufman, 1994).

Contextual factors to be considered in evaluating performance on multiple measures include not only influences evident in the testing situation, but also available background information and a profile of the individual's functioning within the developmental systems levels. For example, when evaluating an individual with suspected depression, it is critical to consider the salient developmental challenges in which the individual is engaged (e.g., peer relations and individuation, in adolescence; loss, in the geriatric phase of life), developmentally appropriate modes of expression (e.g., capacities for affective expression, attention, behavioral control), and domains of functioning known to influence the onset and maintenance of depression (e.g., social support, life events).

Once a parsimonious understanding of the individual's functioning across the relevant domains is achieved and appropriate recommendations are determined, it is critical to communicate this information to the pertinent individuals in the applicable levels of the individual's developmental system. Often, an exquisite evaluation is conducted, resulting in interpretations and recommendations that offer great potential for assistance to the individual, but the results are communicated inadequately or in a manner that interferes with the implementation of the recommendations. Even when the individual receiving the recommendation agrees with the evaluator, failure to implement recommendations may occur because the recipient fails to understand the findings on which the recommendations are based. When an understanding of the relation of the findings to the recommendations is achieved, the intervenors can generalize the bases of the recommendations to new situations. A second difficulty emerges when the individual receiving the recommendations understands the findings and agrees with the recommendations, but does not have the skills or knowledge to communicate the findings to the appropriate agents within the developmental systems levels in which the individual assessed will require intervention. Thus, it is incumbent on the evaluator to take the time to make certain that the pertinent individuals in the developmental systems level understand the findings and the relation of the findings to the recommendations. In addition, more often than not, recipients of the information will require guidelines and support, to ensure implementation of the recommendations they accept.

DIRECTIONS FOR FUTURE RESEARCH

Although significant gains are being made in the field of assessment, a number of issues continue to pose problems for any attempts to implement the comprehensive developmental model. Our goals in highlighting these issues are: to promote research, including the development of new assessment instruments that will improve our ability to describe functioning, and to recommend appropriate interventions for all levels of functioning across the life span.

First, the most critical problems in assessment are seen at the high and low ends of the chronologic age and developmental functioning distributions. In terms of chronologic age, infancy and the geriatric phases of life remain less understood, and fewer instruments are available to address multidimensional domains of functioning in an integrated manner. Similarly, within a given age span, assessment of individuals whose developmental functioning is well above or well below normative levels is complicated by psychometric issues such as item density, and floor and ceiling effects that will compromise the reliability of assessments within a given domain. Thus, the lower reliability and specificity of scores across domains interferes with the ability to document a profile of existing strengths and weaknesses. For example, it is not possible to discuss cognitive strengths and weaknesses when a 50-year-old individual obtains raw scores of 1 on ten of the eleven Weschler subtests and a raw score of 2 on the eleventh. This individual would obtain a VIQ of 56, a PIQ of 62, and an FSIQ of 54. It is interesting to note that an individual who obtained raw scores of 0 across each subtest would achieve a VIQ of 52, a PIQ of 57, and an FSIQ of 48. Thus, it is not only at young ages that item restriction precludes a rich description of functioning.

At the gifted end of the cognitive spectrum, ceiling effects often limit the range of scores obtained. For example, when the Weschler Adult Intelligence Scale—Revised (WAIS-R) is given to a 16-year-old, sums of scale scores ranging from 164 to 209 (a perfect score) all result in an FSIQ of 150. At the same time, it is difficult to discern patterns of strengths and weaknesses between domains. Widely variable scaled scores may not be significantly different from one another because of the unreliability of the scales at the upper end of the distribution.

Second, many tests now in use do not meet currently acceptable standards of psychometric or technical competence. Thus, more attention must be paid to issues of standardization, instrument reliability, and generalizability. For example, many informal tests are very useful in clinical settings and have been shown to discriminate between very impaired and nonimpaired populations. Unfortunately, lack of technical competence renders the results of such instruments difficult to interpret and limits the power of these instruments to inform decision making. Many measures are currently being standardized and revised to meet technical standards, but more work is needed in this area.

A third issue that requires further research is emphasis on the validity of various constructs across development. Factor analytic studies at a given age or level of developmental functioning may not hold across other ages or levels of functioning. As mentioned earlier, the same subtest may reflect different latent conceptual abilities at different points in development (e.g., Photo Series on the K-ABC).

A fourth issue is the need for more empirical work on methods to make use of multiple data points. In research and clinical settings, information is obtained across multiple informants, methods, and functional developmental domains. Although methods have been developed to analyze patterns of strengths and weaknesses within a given test (e.g., WISC-III), guidelines for integrating information across tests and informants are in a much more preliminary stage. To develop these guidelines, data from the most widely used or informative tests must be collected on the same population of individuals. Ideally, such a study would include both a comprehensive assessment of multiple domains of functioning and assessments of developmental system level functioning. Such a study would also permit a better understanding of the associations between functional adjustment and current resources.

A fifth issue involves the need for better assessments of cognitive strategies, learning abilities, problem-solving skills, motivation, and self-concept. These mediators of the relation between current resources and functional adjustment require greater study, to enhance our knowledge of how a particular deficit may or may not impact multiple domains of functioning. For example, a learning disabled child who develops good compensatory learning strategies and maintains a positive and motivated stance toward learning will likely achieve a more satisfying functional adjustment than a learning disabled child who has the same initial resources but adopts an avoidant learning style and a negative stance toward learning. In this manner, we will move away from simplistic formulas that identify a diagnostic category (e.g., Learning Disabled) and toward comprehensive descriptions that allow for more appropriate interventions.

Finally, more work is needed to understand the role of family functioning and other developmental systems levels. For example, tools that can be used in school settings are needed to assess dimensions of the classroom environment and the match among classroom, family, and community environments.

CONCLUSION

In the past 10 to 15 years, there has been a resurgence of interest in the field of assessment, as evidenced by the proliferation of new tests, revisions of old tests, and emergence of journals devoted exclusively to the topic. Considerable progress has been made in the assessment of many domains of development, and the goal of this chapter has been to provide an explicit framework for integrating these advances in research and clinical practice. Most researchers and clinicians have an implicit model that guides their work, but there are few contexts in which one is compelled to make such a model explicit. We have found that the process of articulating a working model or conceptual framework for developmental comprehensive assessment facilitates a more systematic approach to data collection and interpretation in both clinical and research settings.

Our model of comprehensive developmental assessment, although based on the theoretical and empirical literature, is primarily derived from our clinical and teaching experiences. The specific domains we have chosen to include in this chapter are less important than the process of employing a comprehensive developmental approach. Indeed, our inclusion of a subsection entitled "Currently Unknown Domains" was intended to reflect our expectation that new empirical findings will inform the organization, classification, and number of domains that span individual resources and functional adjustment. Thus, in addition to the future directions we discussed, research addressing the utility and validity of competing comprehensive developmental models is required. Efforts to validate these models should be conducted from the perspective of knowledge of both normative and psychopathological populations.

We hope we have conveyed our position that the better one understands development, the better one can design a test. The better the available tests, the more likely it is that one will obtain a profile of results that accurately reflects the individual's developmental competencies and environmental resources. Similarly, the richer the information about the population in which the individual or family is nested, the more successful the interpretation is likely to be. Understanding individual functioning within relevant developmental systems levels should result in increased knowledge about development in normative and psychopathological populations. When this process succeeds, the outcome is improved identification of the needs and strengths of the individual being assessed and the resources within the developmental systems that are available to provide a means of remediation or intervention.

REFERENCES

Achenbach, T. M., & Edelbrock, C. S. (1986). *Child Behavior Checklist—and Young Self Report.* Burlington, VT: University of Vermont, Department of Psychology.

American Psychiatric Association. (1994). *Diagnostic and statistical manual of mental disorders* (4th ed.). Washington, DC: Author.

Barnard, K. (1979). *Instructor's learning resource manual.* Seattle: NCAST Publications, University of Washington.

Barnard, K., & Kelly, J. F. (1990). Assessment of parent-child interaction. In S. J. Meisels & J. P. Shonkoff (Eds.), *Handbook of early childhood intervention* (pp. 278–302). New York: Cambridge University Press.

Bates, E. (1976). *Language and context: The acquisition of pragmatics.* New York: Academic Press.

Bayley, N. (1969). *Bayley Scales of Infant Development: Birth to Two Years.* San Antonio, TX: Psychological Corp.

Beck, A. (1967). *Depression: Causes and treatment.* Philadelphia: University of Pennsylvania Press.

Beck, A., Steer, R., & Garbin, M. (1988). Psychometric properties of the BDI: 25 years of evaluation. *Clinical Psychology Review, 8,* 77–100.

Beck, S. J. (1944). *Rorschach's test I—basic processes.* New York: Grune & Stratton.

Bellack, A. S., & Hersen, M. (1980). *Introduction to clinical psychology.* New York: Oxford University Press.

Bellak, L. (1916). *Thematic Apperception Test (TAT).* Cambridge, MA: Harvard University Press.

Belsky, J., & Most, R. (1981). From exploration to play: A cross-sectional study of infant free play behavior. *Developmental Psychology, 17,* 630–639.

Benjamin, L. S. (1974). Structural analysis of social behavior. *Psychological Review, 81,* 392–425.

Binet, A., & Simon, J. (1905). Méthodes nouvelles pour le diagnostic du niveau-intellectuel des anormaux. *L'Annec' Psychologique, 11,* 191–244.

Bloom, B. J. (1985, June 24). A factor analysis of self-report measures of family functioning. *Family Process, 2,* 225–239.

Bornstein, M. H. (1987). *Sensitive periods in development.* Hillsdale, NJ: Erlbaum.

Bradbury, T. N., & Fincham, F. D. (1990). Dimensions of marital and family interaction. In J. Touliatos, B. F. Permutter, & M. A. Straus (Eds.), *Handbook of family measurement techniques* (pp. 37–60). Newbury Park, CA: Sage.

Bronfenbrenner, U. (1986). Ecology of the family as a context for human development research perspectives. *Developmental Psychology, 22,* 723–742.

Butcher, J. N., Williams, C. L., Graham, J. R., Archer, R. P., Tellegen, A., Ben-Porath, Y. S., & Kaemmer, B. (1992). *Manual for administration, scoring, and interpretation; Minnesota Multiphasic Personality Inventory-Adolescent.* Minneapolis: University of Minnesota.

Campbell, D. T., & Fiske, D. W. (1959). Converted and discriminant validations by the multitrait-multimethod matrix. *Psychological Bulletin, 56,* 81–105.

Cicchetti, D. (1984). The emergence of developmental psychopathology. *Child Development, 55,* 1–7.

Cicchetti, D. (1990). A historical perspective on the discipline of developmental psychology. In J. Rold, A. Mastter, D. Cicchetti, K. Neuchterlein, & S. Weintraub (Eds.), Risk and protective factors in the development of psychopathology (pp. 2–28). New York: Cambridge University Press.

Cicchetti, D., & Schneider-Rosen, K. (1986). An organizational approach to childhood depression. In M. Rutter, C. Izard, & P. Read (Eds.), *Depression in young people: Clinical and developmental perspectives* (pp. 71–134). New York: Guilford.

Cicchetti, D. V., Sparrow, S. S., & Carter, A. S. (1991, August 16). *Development and validation of two Vineland Adaptive Behavior Screening Instruments.* Paper presented at the annual meeting of the American Psychological Association, San Francisco.

Cicchetti, D., & Wagner, S. (1990). Alternative assessment strategies for the evaluation of infants and toddlers: An organizational perspective. In S. J. Meisels & J. P. Shonkoff (Eds.), *Handbook of early childhood intervention* (pp. 246–277). New York: Cambridge University Press.

Conners, C. K. (1985). *The Conners Rating Scales: Instruments for assessment of childhood psychopathology.* Unpublished manuscript, Children's Hospital National Medical Center, Washington, DC.

Derogatis, L. (1977). SCL-90 Administration, scoring, and procedures manual-I. Baltimore: Johns Hopkins University Press.

Doane, J. A., Goldstein, M. J., Miklowitz, D. H., & Falloon, I. R. H. (1986). The impact of individual and family therapy on the affective climate of families of schizophrenics. *British Journal of Psychiatry, 148,* 279–287.

Doane, J. A., West, K. L., Goldstein, M. J., Rodnick, E. H., & Jones, J. E. (1981). Parental communication and affective style predictions of subsequent schizophrenic-spectrum disorders in vulnerable adolescents. *Archives of General Psychiatry, 38,* 679–681.

Dunn, L. M., & Dunn, L. M. (1981). *Peabody Picture Vocabulary Test—Revised.* Circle Pines, MN: American Guidance Service.

Easterbrook, J. A. (1959). The effects of emotion on cue utilization and the organization of behavior. *Psychological Review, 66,* 183–200.

Emde, R. N. (1989). The infant's relationship experience: Developmental and affective aspects. In A. J. Sameroff & R. N. Emde (Eds.), *Relationship disturbances in early childhood: A developmental approach* (pp. 33–51). New York: Basic Books.

Erikson, E. H. (1963). *Childhood and society* (2nd ed.). New York: Norton.

Exner, J. E. (1991). *The Rorschach: A comprehensive system: Vol. 2. Interpretation* (2nd ed.). New York: Wiley.

Fagan, J. F., III, Singer, L. T., Montie, J. E., & Shepard, P. A. (1986). Selective screening device for the early detection of normal or delayed cognitive development in infants at risk for mental retardation. *Pediatrics, 78,* 1021–1026.

Flavell, J. H. (1985). *Cognitive development* (2nd ed.). Englewood Cliffs, NJ: Prentice-Hall.

Fletcher, J. M. (1985). External validation of learning disability typologies. In B. P. Rourke (Ed.), *Neuropsychology of learning disabilities* (pp. 147–166). New York: Guilford.

Galton, F. (1892). Classification of men according to their natural gifts. In *Hereditary genius: An inquiry into its laws and consequences* (pp. 12–32). New York: Macmillan.

Goddard, H. H. (1910). A measuring scale of intelligence. *Training School, 6,* 146–155.

Goldstein, G., & Hersen, M. (1984). *Handbook of psychological assessment.* New York: Pergamon.

Graham, J. R. (1991). *MMPI-2: Assessing Personality and Psychopathology.* Minneapolis: University of Minnesota Press.

Greenspan, S. I. (1990). Comprehensive clinical approaches to infants and their families: Psychodynamic and developmental perspectives. In S. J. Meisels & J. P. Shonkoff (Eds.), *Handbook of early intervention* (pp. 150–172). New York: Cambridge University Press.

Gurman, A., & Kniskern, D. P. (1981). Family therapy outcome research: Knowns and unknowns. In A. Gurman & D. Kniskern (Eds.), *Handbook of family therapy* (pp. 742–745). New York: Brunner/Mazel.

Haith, M. M., & Campos, J. J. (Eds.). (1983). *Handbook of child psychology: Vol. 2. Infancy and developmental psychobiology.* New York: Wiley.

Harris, P. L. (1989). *Children and emotion: The development of psychological understanding.* New York: Blackwell.

Hops, H., Biglan, A., Sherman, O., Arthur, J., Friedman, L., & Osteen, V. (1987). Home observation of family interactions of depressed women. *Journal of Consulting and Clinical Psychology, 55,* 341–346.

Horn, J. L. (1982). The theory of fluid and crystallized intelligence in relation to concepts of cognitive psychology and aging in adulthood. In F. I. M. Craik & S. Trehub (Eds.), *Advances in the study of communication and affect: Vol. 8. Aging and cognitive processes* (pp. 237–278). New York: Plenum.

Horn, J. L. (1985). Remodeling of models of intelligence. In B. Wolman (Ed.), *Handbook of intelligence* (pp. 267–300). New York: Wiley.

Humphrey, L., & Benjamin, L. (1986). Using structural analysis of social behavior to assess critical but elusive family processes: A new solution to an old problem. *American Psychologist, 41,* 979–989.

Kaufman, A. S. (1979). Role of speed on WISC-R performance across the age range. *Journal of Counseling and Clinical Psychology, 47,* 595–597.

Kaufman, A. S. (1983). Intelligence: Old concepts—new perspective. In G. W. Hynd (Ed.), *The school psychologist: An introduction* (pp. 95–117). Syracuse, NY: Syracuse University Press.

Kaufman, A. S. (1994). *Intelligent testing with the WISC-III.* New York: Wiley.

Kaufman, A. S., & Kaufman, N. L. (1983). *Kaufman Assessment Battery for Children—K-ABC.* Circles Pines, MN: American Guidance Service.

Klopfer, B., & Donaldson, H. H. (1962). *The Rorschach technique: An introductory manual.* New York: Harcourt.

Larry P. v. Wilson Riles. (1979). U. S. District Court, Northern District of California, Case No. C-71-2270 RFP, 1974–1979.

Leeper, R. W. (1948). A motivational theory of emotions to replace "Emotions as disorganized response." *Psychological Review, 55,* 5–21.

Levinson, D. (1978). *The seasons of the man's life.* New York: Ballantine Books.

Levinson, D. (1986). A conception of adult development. *American Psychologist, 41,* 3–13.

Lewis, R. J., Dlugokinski, E. L., Caputo, L. M., & Griffin, R. B. (1988). Children at risk for emotional disorders: Risk and resource dimensions. *Clinical Psychology Review, 8,* 417–440.

Loevinger, J. (1976). *Ego development: Conception and theories.* San Francisco: Jossey-Bass.

Mahler, M. S., Pine, F., & Bergman, A. (1975). *The psychological birth of the infant: Symbiosis and individuation.* New York: Basic Books.

Main, M., Kaplan, N., & Cassidy, J. (1985). Security in infancy, childhood, and adulthood: A move to the level of representation. *Monographs for the Society of Research in Child Development, 50,* 66–104.

Maloney, M. P., & Ward, M. P. (1976). *Psychological assessment: A conceptual approach.* New York: Oxford University Press.

Mandler, G. (1975). *Mind and emotion.* New York: Wiley.

Matas, L., Arend, R., & Sroufe, L. A. (1978). Continuity in adaptation in the second year: The relationship between quality of attachment and later competence. *Child Development, 49,* 547–556.

McCubbin, H. I., & Thompson, A. I. (1987). *Family assessment inventories for research and practice.* Madison: Family Stress Coping and Health Project, University of Wisconsin.

McLean, J. E., Kaufman, A. S., & Reynolds, C. R. (1988, November). What role does formal education play in the IQ-age relationships across the adult life-span? *Mid-South Educational Researcher, 17*(1), 6–8, 13–18.

Millon, T. (1987). *Manual for the MCMI-II* (2nd ed.). Minneapolis: National Computer Systems, Inc.

Minuchin, S. (1974). *Families and family therapy.* Cambridge, MA: Harvard University Press.

Moos, R. H. (1974). *Family Environment Scale.* Palo Alto, CA: Consulting Psychologist Press.

Moos, R. & Moos, B. S. (1981). *Family Environment Scale.* Palo Alto, CA: Consulting Psychologist Press.

Morris, R., Blashfield, R., & Satz, P. (1986). Developmental classification of reading-disabled children. *Journal of Clinical and Experimental Neuropsychology, 8*(4), 371–392.

Napier, A. Y., & Whitaker, C. A. (1978). *The family crucible.* New York: Harper & Row.

Nelson, G. M., & Beach, S. R. H. (1990, Spring). Sequential interaction in depression: Effects of depressive behavior on spousal aggression. *Behavior Therapy, 21*(2), 167–182.

Offer, D., & Offer, J. (1975). *From teenage to young manhood.* New York: Basic Books.

Olson, D. H., Portner, J., & Bell, R. (1982). *FACES II: Family Adaptability and Cohesion Evaluation Scales.* St. Paul: Social Science Department, University of Minnesota.

Olson, D. H., Russell, C. S., & Sprenkle, D. H. (1983, March 22). Circumplex model of family process: VI. Theoretical update: *Family Process, 1,* 69–83.

Olson, D. H., Russell, C. S., & Sprenkle, D. H. (1989). *Circumplex model: Systemic assessment and intervention.* New York: Haworth.

Olson, D. H., Sprenkle, D. H., & Russell, C. (1979). Circumplex model of marital and family systems: I. Cohesion and adaptability dimension, family types, and clinical applications. *Family Process, 18,* 3–28.

Osofsky, J. D. (Ed.). (1987). *Handbook of infant development* (2nd ed.). New York: Wiley.

Piaget, J. (1962). *Judgment and reasoning in the child.* Marjorie Warden (Trans). London: Routledge & Kegan Paul. (Original work published 1928)

Plomin, R. (1986). *Development, genetics and psychology.* Hillside, NJ: Erlbaum.

Rappaport, D., Gill, M. M., & Schaffer, R. (1968). *Diagnostic psychological testing* (rev. ed.). New York: International Universities Press.

Robinson, J., Mantze-Simmons, L., Macfie, J., & The MacArthur Narrative Working Group. (1993). Narrative Coding Manual. Boulder, CO.

Rorschach, H. (1948). *Rorschach psychodiagnostic plates.* New York: Grune & Stratton.

Rourke, B. P. (1985). Overview of learning disability subtypes. In B. P. Rourke (Ed.), *Neuropsychology of learning disabilities* (pp. 3–14). New York: Guilford.

Rutter, M. (1980). *Changing youth in a changing society: Patterns of development and disorder.* Cambridge, MA: Harvard University Press.

Saarni, C. (1989). Children's understanding of strategic control of emotional expressions in social transitions. In C. Saarni & P. L. Harris (Eds.), *Children's understanding of emotion.* Cambridge, England: Cambridge University Press.

Salovey, P., & Mayer, J. D. (1990). Emotional intelligence. *Imagination, Cognition and Personality, 9*(3), 185–211.

Sameroff, A. J. (1989). Principles of development in psychopathology. In A. J. Sameroff & R. N. Emde (Eds.), *Relationship disturbances in early childhood: A developmental approach* (pp. 17–32). New York: Basic Books.

Sander, L. (1962). Issues in early mother-child interacion. *Journal of the American Academy of Child Psychiatry, 1,* 141–166.

Sattler, J. M. (1988a). *Assessment of children.* San Diego: Author.

Sattler, J. M. (1988b). Issues related to the measurement and change of intelligence. In S. Lifland & J. Ostock (Eds.), *Assessment of Children* (p. 71). San Diego: Author.

Scharff, J. S. (1989). *Foundations of object relations family therapy.* Northvale, NJ: Aronson.

Schumm, W. R. (1990). Evolution of the family field: Measurement principles and techniques. In J. Touliatos, B. F. Perlmutter, & M. A. Straus (Eds.), *Handbook of family measurement techniques* (pp. 23–36). Newbury Park, CA: Sage.

Sparrow, S. S., Balla, D. A., & Cicchetti, D. V. (1984). *The Vineland Adaptive Behavior Scales: Survey Form.* Circle Pines, MN: American Guidance Service.

Sroufe, L. A., & Rutter, M. (1984). The domain of developmental psychopathology. *Child Development, 55*(1), 17–29.

Thorndike, R. L., Hagen, E. P., & Sattler, J. M. (1986). *Stanford-Binet Intelligence Scale: Fourth Edition.* Chicago: Riverside.

Touliatos, J., Perlmutter, B. F., & Straus, M. A. (Eds.). (1990). *Handbook of family measurement techniques.* Newbury Park, CA: Sage.

Tronick, E. Z., & Giannino, A. F. (1986). The transmission of maternal disturbance to the infant. In E. Z. Tronick & T. Field (Eds.), *Maternal depression and infant disturbance* (pp. 5–11). New York: Wiley.

Uzgiris, I. C., & Hunt, J. McV. (1975). *Assessment in infancy: Ordinal scales of psychological development.* Urbana: University of Illinois Press.

Vaillant, G. E. (1977). *Adaptation to life.* Boston: Little Brown.

Wechsler, D. (1991). *Wechsler Intelligence Scale for Children—Third Edition.* San Antonio, TX: Psychological Corp.

Willis, S. L. (1985). Towards an educational psychology of the older adult learner: Intellectual and cognitive bases. In J. E. Birren & K. W. Schaie (Eds.), *Handbook of the psychology of aging* (2nd ed., pp. 818–847). New York: Van Nostrand-Reinhold.

Woodcock, R. W., & Dahl, M. N. (1971). *A common scale for the measurement of person ability and test item (AGS Paper No. 10).* Circle Pines, MN: American Guidance Service.

PART THREE

Biological and Genetic Processes

CHAPTER 5

Fundamentals of Molecular Neurobiology

ROLAND D. CIARANELLO, JUNKO AIMI, ROBIN R. DEAN, DAVID A. MORILAK, MATTHEW H. PORTEUS, and DANTE CICCHETTI

Researchers and clinicians concerned with developmental psychopathology are focusing increasing attention on brain development (Benes, 1991; Cicchetti, 1993; Collins & Depue, 1992; Davidson, 1991; Feinberg, 1982; Huttenlocher, 1979; Weinberger, 1987). There are several reasons for this: an increasing recognition that developmental disorders, particularly the severe disturbances such as infantile autism, arise from exogenous or endogenous disruptions in brain development; a veritable explosion in our knowledge of developmental neurobiology, that area of neuroscience that focuses on factors regulating the development of neurons, neural circuitry, and complex neuronal organization systems, including the brain; and the exciting contributions of molecular genetics to neurologic disease, which for the first time enable us to understand the genetic basis of certain diseases without requiring foreknowledge of the underlying biochemical abnormalities.

It is difficult, if not impossible, to overstate the importance of this last point. We know virtually nothing about the biologic substrates of the severe developmental disorders, despite years of intensive study. The same statement can be made about psychiatric diseases in adults, where an even greater, more prolonged research endeavor has failed to disclose even a single consistent biologic deficit that can guide the diagnosis or treatment of any psychiatric disorder. Until recently, this lack of knowledge was a major obstacle to progress in psychiatric research. Although it remains a formidable impediment today, the ability to identify defective genes without *a priori* knowledge of their protein products or the underlying pathophysiology now exists and has contributed to breathtaking advances in medicine just within the past few years. There is every reason to believe as well that such advances hold great hope for breakthroughs in psychiatric diseases (Plomin, Rende, & Rutter, 1991) and, in particular, the developmental disorders. Genetic disorders of behavior that are characterized by a variable age of onset and/or remissions and exacerbations should offer the most exciting possibilities for integrating psychopathology, biology, and development (cf. Gottesman, 1974).

In this chapter, we guide the reader through the basic principles of molecular neurobiology, the branch of neuroscience that is concerned with regulation of nervous system function at the molecular and cellular level. As one might expect, this relatively new discipline draws from many other disciplines, including neuroanatomy, neurophysiology, neuropharmacology, endocrinology, and genetics, as well as molecular biology, and it derives its clinical sustenance from pediatrics, neurology, and psychiatry. This chapter is organized to provide the reader with a basic understanding of the genetic, metabolic, and cellular processes underlying brain development before considering how disruptions in these processes might lead to disturbances in brain maturation and, ultimately, behavior and social functioning.

ANATOMY AND PHYSIOLOGY OF CELL TYPES PRESENT IN THE BRAIN

Neuroglia

Rudolph Virchow, a 19th-century German anatomist, was perhaps the first to identify the two distinct cell types found in the brain: neurons and neuroglia. Neuroglia means "nerve glue"; the name is apt because these cells fill in the spaces between and around neurons. Neuroglia are identified by their characteristic microscopic appearance: astrocytes possess numerous processes that radiate out from the cell body, giving the cell a starlike appearance; oligodendrocytes (oligo = few, dendro = branches) possess fewer, thinner processes than astrocytes; microglia are small, with very fine processes. Astrocytes are ubiquitous throughout the central nervous system. Microglia migrate to injury sites, proliferate, and consume cellular debris; their role in the nervous system is analogous to macrophages in the cellular immune response. Oligodendrocytes are responsible for the formation of the myelin sheath that surrounds many axons and determines the rate at which action potentials propagate down the axon. Neuroglia make up approximately 90% of the cells in the brain. It was initially thought that glia were analogous to connective tissue in some other organs,

Work from the authors' laboratory described in this chapter was supported by a program-project grant from the National Institute of Mental Health (MH 39437), by a Research Scientist Award (RDC) from the NIMH (MH 00219), by the endowment fund of the Nancy Pritzker Laboratory, and by the Spunk Fund, Inc. (JA), the Meyer Fund, the John Merck Fund, the Rebecca and Solomon Baker Fund, and the Edward and Marjorie Gray Endowment Fund (DAM). MHP is an M.D., Ph.D. student in the Medical Scientist Training Program. In addition, support from the Spunk Fund, Inc. was provided to DC.

predominantly playing a support role to neurons. Little is yet known about the functions of the neuroglia, but it is clear that they do more than support, segregate, and insulate neurons. More recently, it has been suggested that neuroglia may have trophic effects on neurons, providing metabolic elements, growth factors, and other compounds essential for neuronal function. Specific neurotransmitter uptake systems and receptors have been described on neuroglia, but the extent of their function is not yet well understood. No role in information processing or memory storage has yet been established for neuroglia.

Neurons

The structure of nerve cells, or neurons, is uniquely poised to enable them to carry out their function. Nerves carry information in the form of electrochemical impulses throughout the body, over distances as long as a few meters or as short as the space between adjacent cells. Nerves may be very simple in structure, or exceedingly complex, but regardless of their superficial appearance, all neurons have four main components (Figure 5.1): (a) the *soma,* (b) a network of *dendrites,* (c) the *axon,* and (d) the *nerve terminal,* with its specialized axonal ending, the *synapse.*

The soma, or cell body, is the metabolic center of the neuron. Within the cell body reside a number of important subcellular organelles whose function is the regulation of critical cellular events and chemical reactions. These organelles consist of the nucleus, which contains the nucleic acids (DNA and RNA) and proteins necessary for transforming the information in the cellular genome into protein molecules the cell can use for all its functions; the endoplasmic reticulum (ER), whose membrane surface is studded with polyribosome bodies (rough ER that carry out the synthesis of all cellular proteins); the Golgi apparatus, which receives proteins and lipids from the endoplasmic reticulum and dispatches them to other compartments within the cell; mitochondria, which generate the energy-rich phosphate compounds (e.g., adenosine triphosphate, ATP) that drive many metabolic reactions; lysosomes, which contain the digestive enzymes involved in degrading senescent intracellular structures and proteins; and peroxisomes, which contain enzymes involved in oxidative biochemical reactions.

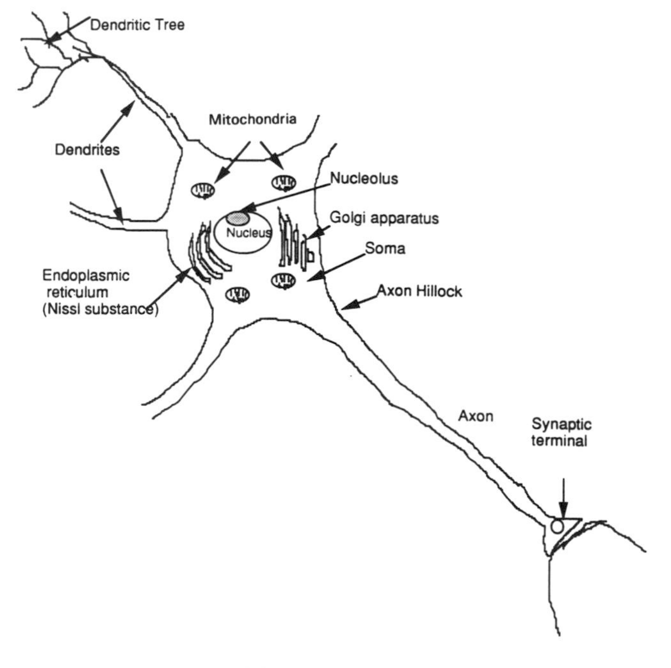

Figure 5.1 Neuronal ultrastructure.

A neuron's dendritic arborization is probably its most unique structural feature. The dendrites of a nerve cell receive input from other neurons in the form of chemical stimuli. The dendritic tree may be exceedingly complex or quite simple, but, in either case, it transmits information from the membrane surface of the dendrite to the soma. An individual neuron may receive hundreds or even thousands of stimuli from other neurons through its dendrites, yet it makes a single response. This requires the existence of a fairly elaborate mechanism to resolve all this information into one appropriate output.

Regardless of their dendritic complexity, nerve cells contain a single axon, down which electrical impulses flow. As the dendrites represent the signal input apparatus of the neuron, so does the axon represent its response output apparatus. The axons of some neurons traverse meters in length; others may travel only a few hundred microns (one-millionth of a meter). Conduction of electrical impulses down the length of an axon occurs by the flow of sodium (Na^+) and potassium (K^+) ions across the axonal membrane, resulting in a progressive reversal of the membrane's electrical potential, and propagation of the electrical impulse. This process occurs more rapidly in neurons surrounded by a fatty (myelin) sheath that is interrupted only at regular intervals along the axon length (nodes of Ranvier). In these rapidly conducting myelinated neurons, the electrical impulse jumps from node to node rather than from point to point. Conduction velocity in these neurons is very fast compared to nerves that lack the myelin sheath altogether.

The nerve terminal represents the specialized end of the axon, the synapse. The synapse is (a) the site where the nerve cell physically ends and (b) the structural element that makes chemical neurotransmission possible. An electrical impulse propagated down the axon to the nerve terminal does not jump across the space between the axon and its target as a spark or an electrical arc. Instead, neurotransmitters (chemicals stored in synaptic vesicles) are released from the nerve terminal, diffuse across the small gap between the terminal and its target (the synaptic cleft), and chemically activate the target cell, causing it to respond (see Figure 5.2). Depending on the target cell, its response may be to initiate a new electrical impulse (e.g., if the target cell is another neuron), secrete a hormone if it is a glandular cell, or contract and do physical work if it is a muscle cell.

In many respects, neurons (as well as neuroglia) resemble any other cell in the body. The genomic DNA in the nucleus of any neuron is identical to that in all other cells of the same organism. The diameter of the neuronal soma can vary from 5 mm to about 70 mm (McGeer, Eccles, & McGeer, 1987). The size of the nucleus also varies widely in different neurons and in different locations within the brain. Finally, like all other cells, the

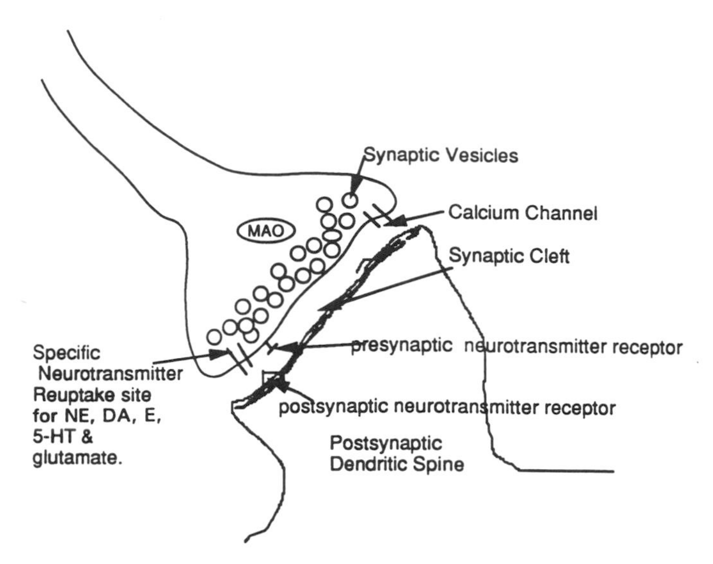

Figure 5.2 Ultrastructure of synapse.

neuron is enclosed by a lipid bilayer plasma membrane. Signaling between neurons requires precise control of the movements of ions across this plasma membrane. Specialized proteins integrated into the membrane selectively move or pump ions across the membrane, some in the direction of concentration gradients, others against concentration gradients. Because maintaining ionic gradients requires energy, neurons typically possess large numbers of mitochondria, and generate substantial amounts of adenosine triphosphate (ATP), which they use as an energy source to drive ion pumps.

Like other cells, neurons carry out extensive synthesis of proteins. The ribosomes present synthesize the many proteins needed by the cell. They are found in the endoplasmic reticulum (ER) and the rough ER, which is typically quite dense in the vicinity of the nucleus. Staining of this accumulation of ER near the nucleus gives rise to the "Nissl substance," a characteristic feature of neurons. The Golgi apparatus, frequently associated with the smooth ER, packages proteins and lipids from the ER and transports them to their final destination within the cell. The Golgi apparatus was originally discovered in neurons, which are richly endowed with Golgi bodies. Posttranslational modifications of proteins, such as disulphide bond formation and glycosylation, occur in the ER and Golgi apparatus. Lysosomes and peroxisomes, containing degradative and oxidative enzymes respectively, are also present in nerve cells. Unlike most other cells of the body, neurons are nondividing cells.

Physiology of Neurons

Excitable Membranes. The neuron is a specialized excitable cell. The processing of information in the brain is electrochemical in nature. The unique cellular specializations of the neuron underlie this process. Intercellular communication is chemically mediated by release of neurotransmitter from the axon terminal and its subsequent diffusion to regions of the target cell specialized to respond to the specific signal. The intracellular conductance of information to distal portions of the cablelike axon is electrochemical (ionic) in nature. This process is dependent on numerous specialized integral membrane proteins, which are responsible for the regenerative flow of ions between the interior and exterior of the cell membrane, and gives rise to the one-way propagation of the signal down the axon. The components of the specialized nerve cells that carry out these complex phenomena are briefly described below.

A potential difference exists across the plasma membrane of a neuron, as it does in most other cells. Unlike other cells, rapid changes in this membrane potential, in the form of action potentials, can be propagated unidirectionally down the axon. The lipid bilayer membrane surrounding nerve cells contains a unique complement of ion channels, which play a crucial role in this process. When a cell receives a depolarizing stimulus that exceeds the threshold for that cell, it responds with a very large change in membrane potential that lasts several milliseconds. This is followed by a slightly slower return of the membrane potential to its resting prestimulus level (see Figure 5.3(a)). Stimuli that exceed the membrane threshold will elicit an action potential, giving rise to the all-or-none character of neuronal transmission. This action potential is responsible for information transmission in the nervous system. The threshold feature effectively filters out noise, allowing the generation of an action potential only when a stimulus of sufficient intensity is received, or when multiple temporally convergent signals simultaneously excite a cell. Small subthreshold perturbations in the membrane potential do not produce action potentials. Another consequence of the all-or-nothing

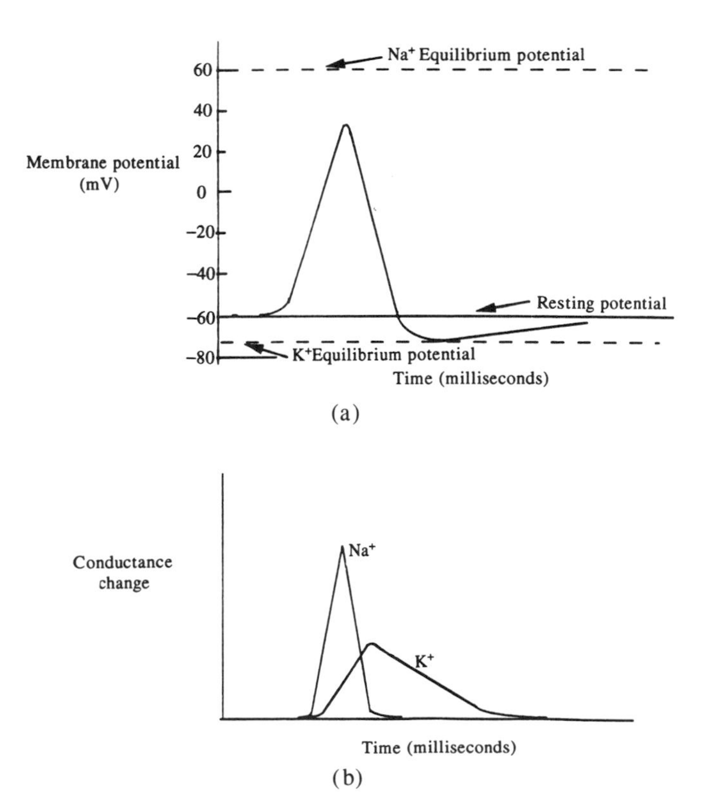

Figure 5.3 (a) Time course of action potential and (b) Na^+ and K^+ conductances.

character of the action potential is that any stimulus that exceeds the threshold will result in an action potential of the same size (amplitude) regardless of the initial stimulus intensity. The time between the stimulus onset and the peak of the resulting action potential, known as the latency, can be influenced by the stimulus intensity: the stronger the signal, the shorter the latency. The frequency of firing is also influenced by stimulus intensity.

The ionic basis for the action potential is now reasonably well understood, and the actual molecular mechanisms are being intensely studied. The action potential is characterized by a rapid inward flow of positive ions, predominantly Na^+, which increases, then decreases until it reverses, and subsequently there is a net outward flow of positive ions (predominantly K^+) until the membrane potential returns to the resting potential (see Figure 5.3(a) and 5.3(b)). The initial inward current is a voltage-dependent sodium current conducted by a channel that selectively passes sodium ions. Depolarization beyond the threshold level leads to the opening of additional Na^+ channels and then to more rapid depolarization. At approximately the peak of the action potential, an inactivation process induces the sodium channels to spontaneously close. The return of the membrane potential toward the resting level is initiated by the delayed outward potassium current, which appears to account for most of the membrane repolarization and is mediated by a voltage-dependent K^+ channel (see Figure 3(b)). The initial distribution of ions (sodium predominantly outside the cell and potassium with a greater intracellular concentration) is restored and maintained by ATP-driven ion pumps.

Ion replacement experiments and the use of naturally occurring toxins, such as tetrodotoxin and apamin, aided in establishing the ionic currents underlying the different phases of the action potential. In most neurons, a voltage-dependent calcium current contributes to the inward current phase of the action potential. The ionic mechanisms underlying the action potential and its propagation were originally worked out by Hodgkin and Huxley (1952a, 1952b) in the giant squid axon. Although some differences have been found in some vertebrates studied, the principles appear to apply to the function of neurons in higher animals as well as invertebrates.

Ion Channels

Sodium Channels. Classical biochemical techniques have revealed little about the structural features and underlying mechanisms of ion channels. Gene cloning and recombinant DNA techniques have revealed a wealth of structural information about ion channel proteins. Primary sequence comparisons have shown that the ligand-gated anion channels (glycine receptor, GABA receptor) and the voltage-gated cation channels (Na^+, K^+, and Ca^{++}) appear to be members of a molecular family or subfamilies. Ligand-gated channels are composed of several protein subunits, a particular combination of which is required for full activity. Voltage-gated channels all appear to contain four repeated elements with high sequence homology; each contains six hydrophobic (alphahelical) domains. Fully functional voltage-gated sodium channels appear to require only the presence of the larger alpha subunit. The putative Drosophila potassium channel appears to differ from the sodium and potassium channels described to date in that it consists of several relatively short subunits but still exhibits the same characteristic pattern of repeating domains observed in the larger channel protein subunits. This characteristic structure will be described in more detail for the voltage-dependent sodium channel. (For reviews of voltage-sensitive ion channels, see Eisenman & Dani, 1987; Guy & Conti, 1990; Jan & Jan, 1989; Stuhmer, 1991.)

Three sodium channels from rat brain have been cloned and characterized (Noda et al., 1986). The rat brain channels consist of three subunits, one larger (260 kd) and two smaller (33 kd and 36 kd). The larger alpha subunit sequence was similar to the previously cloned electroplax sodium channel (sequences obtained from cDNA prepared from whole rat brain poly(A) + mRNA) (Noda et al., 1984) possessing four internal repeats of a homologous sequence (I-IV). Each of these repeats contains six transmembrane helices, S1-S6. Both the amino-terminal and the carboxy-terminal ends are exposed on the cytosolic surface of the membrane (see Figure 5.4). The S4 domain contains positively charged residues that line up along one side of the transmembrane helix. Site-directed mutagenesis studies (Stuhmer et al., 1989), altering the amino acid sequence in this region, support the hypothesis that the S4 domain is "the voltage sensor" and is responsible for the voltage-dependent activation of the channel. Further site-directed mutagenesis experiments by the same group revealed that the cytosolic loop between repeats III and IV is important in inactivation of the sodium channel. Tryptic digest of this linker or treatment with an antibody directed against this region (Vassilev, Scheuer, & Catterall, 1988) significantly slowed inactivation and provided further evidence for the involvement of this region in channel inactivation.

A conformational change associated with a net movement of charge through the lipid bilayer is thought to result in channel activation and opening. Inactivation is voltage-independent and is thought to be regulated by a different domain than that regulating activation (for models of activation, gating, and inactivation see, e.g., Guy & Conti, 1990; Noda et al., 1984). The timer of the cycle is thought to be the inactivation domain, because it appears to control the duration of ion flow. Inactivation is virtually independent of voltage. Return of the channel to the closed but ready-for-activation state requires repolarization and is thus voltage-dependent. Several conformations of the sodium channel may exist, and cycling through these conformations with each

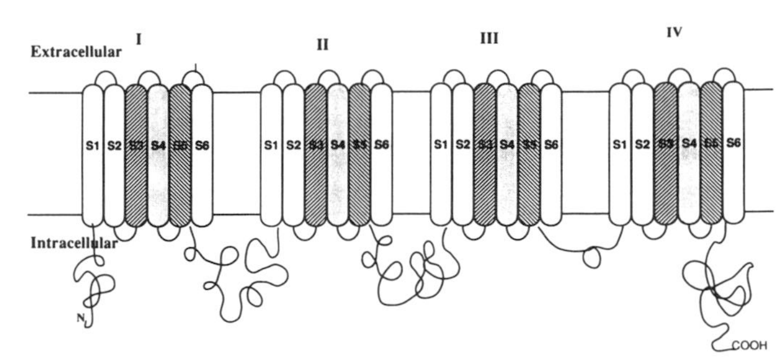

Figure 5.4 Proposed structure of the sodium channel.

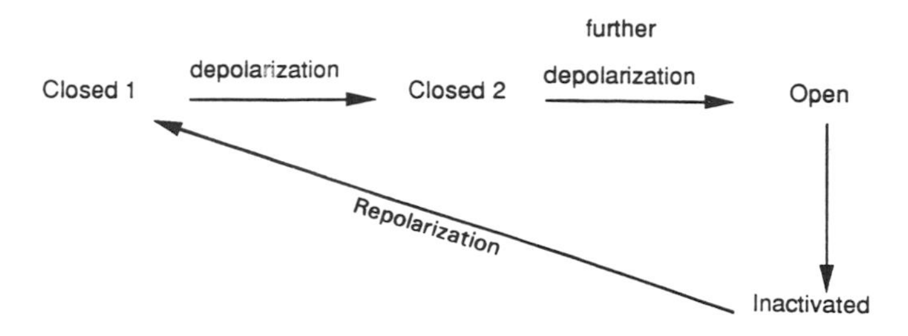

Figure 5.5 Model of Na^+ channel activation-inactivation cycle.

opening, as shown in Figure 5.5, effectively permits only one opening of the sodium channel per action potential. After an action potential has been propagated, the cell undergoes a transient refractory period during which it is unresponsive to further stimulation.

The sodium channel shows an elevenfold selectivity for sodium over potassium ions. This channel is well conserved across evolution, being highly homologous in mammals, flies, and eels. These observations indicate that the sodium channel evolved prior to the divergence of vertebrates and invertebrates. At least three distinct sodium channels, each encoded by a different gene, are thought to be present in the nervous system. It remains to be determined whether different types of sodium channels are preferentially expressed in particular neurons or subcellular locations within a neuron.

Potassium Channels. The potassium channels represent the largest, most diverse family of ion channels described to date. The various potassium channels can be differentiated on the basis of kinetics, voltage sensitivity, and modulation by calcium or different neurotransmitters. The family of potassium channels includes:

1. "K" channels, or outward delayed rectifying channels, like those first described by Hodgkin and Huxley in the giant squid axon, which were responsible for repolarization of the membrane. These channels remain open as long as the membrane is depolarized, and therefore, inactivation is voltage-dependent. K channels are found in axons.

2. "A" channels, or fast transient channels, which are present in action potential-generating membranes such as dendrites and, to a lesser extent, cell bodies. The potassium current through this channel begins immediately upon depolarization and turns off after about 10 to 100 ms, independent of the membrane repolarization. This channel is capable of opening when the membrane is in a more hyperpolarized state than the K potassium channel. These channels enable the membrane to fire repetitively at a slow rate and are thought to play a role in spacing successive action potentials in neurons that fire rhythmically.

3. "C" channels, or calcium-dependent potassium channels, are found in association with voltage-sensitive calcium channels. Calcium entering the cell through the calcium channel activates and opens the C channel, allowing the efflux of potassium, which in turn inactivates the calcium channel, thus providing a negative feedback loop.

4. "M" channels, also called anomalous channels because they close in response to depolarization. They are frequently neurotransmitter-gated channels activated by second messengers.

5. "S" channels, or serotonin-sensitive potassium channels, found in sensory neurons of the sea snail *Aplysia californica.* Serotonin closes these channels rather than opens them, thus leading to a longer duration action potential and enhanced cellular excitability. This is thought to be the mechanism responsible for behavioral sensitivity, a simple model of learning in *Aplysia* (Smith, 1989). For a review of potassium channels see Miller (1991), Smith (1989), and Yellen (1987).

The discovery that the *Shaker* locus in Drosophila was a member of the potassium A channel family (Papazian, Schwarz, Tempel, Jan, & Jan, 1987; Pongs et al., 1988) yielded new insight into mechanisms responsible for potassium channel diversity. Alternate splicing of the mRNA was found to give rise to at least five different A channels with unique characteristics (Pongs et al., 1988). The Shaker channel was found to be multimeric. Tandem dimers formed functional channels, suggesting that the native configuration probably contained four subunits. A diverse array of channel types and characteristics is possible by combining alternate splicing and heteromultimer formation. An obvious question arises as to why there are so many potassium channels. One possible answer is that the wide range of different potassium channels with different kinetics, latencies, and inactivation times endows the neurons containing them with a wide range of potential firing patterns.

The potassium channel was found to contain only one domain analogous to the four found in sodium and calcium channels, but does possess the six membrane-spanning domains within this region. Furthermore, the S4 segment is highly conserved in the potassium channel and in all voltage-dependent ion channels and is thought to play a role in voltage sensing. Site-directed mutagenesis studies of the potassium channel S4 segment confirms this hypothesis (Papazian et al., 1987). In contrast to the sodium channel, fast inactivation of the potassium current appears to involve the amino terminal region instead of the region linking domains III and IV (Timpe et al., 1988). The ion pore-forming region is thought to be located in two unusual membrane-spanning domains between S5 and S6 (Miller, 1991). The potassium channel is thought by some to be the oldest of the voltage-dependent ion channels because there are related channels even in fungi and plants (Stuhmer, 1991).

Calcium Channels. Voltage-dependent calcium channels have been found in almost all cell types studied to date. Calcium channels in the terminal regions play a crucial role in the release of neurotransmitters from presynaptic elements. They are also found in the membrane of the initial segment, where, in conjunction with calcium-dependent potassium channels, they are thought to influence the adaptation of neurons (Smith, 1989). Smaller numbers of calcium channels are found in dendritic and cell body membranes.

Calcium channels are very selective; the voltage-dependent calcium current is a hundredfold more selective for calcium than for sodium (in the heart). This is essential because the physiological extracellular concentration of Ca^{++} is about 3 mM; that of Na^{+} is 145 mM. Studies of calcium channel ion selectivity, kinetics, and molecular domains important in activation and inactivation have been hampered by the fact that X. laevis oocytes, used successfully in the study of the sodium and potassium channels, have proven inadequate for the study of calcium channels. Similar to many other voltage-gated ion channels studied to date, the activation-inactivation cycle appears to be more complex than a simple two-stage, open-shut cycle. The molecular basis for the ion selectivity and kinetics is not yet understood.

The calcium channels cloned so far resemble the classic voltage-dependent ion channel: the alpha subunit is composed of four homologous domains (I to IV); about 300 amino acids are present, each containing six transmembrane regions (S1 to S6); and both the C-terminal and amino-terminal ends are cytoplasmic. S1, S2, S3, S5, and S6 contain some hydrophobic regions, S4 is a positively charged segment. The highly conserved S4 domain is probably involved in voltage sensing because it is in the other voltage-gated ion channels.

At least two and probably three distinct classes of calcium channels are thought to exist on central and peripheral neurons, which can be differentiated from one another on the basis of their kinetics, voltage dependence for inactivation and activation, single-channel conductance, and pharmacology. The low-voltage activation (LVA) type calcium channel has a low threshold of activation (< -50 mV) and inactivates quickly (10–40 ms) by a voltage-dependent mechanism. In contrast, the high-voltage activation (HVA) type calcium channel exhibits a high activation threshold (-20 mV) and inactivates at a slower rate (>50 ms), which appears to depend on the internal calcium concentration. The LVA channel is also called the T-type (transient,) and the HVA channel is also called the L-type (long-lasting). An additional HVA calcium channel has been suggested, the N channel (neither L nor T). These N-type calcium currents, with intermediate characteristics, are frequently observed in neurons. Inactivation of N channels is variable, depending on the neuronal preparation from which it was recorded, suggesting that inactivation is complex and probably is both voltage- and calcium-ion-dependent (Swandulla, Carbone, & Lux, 1991). N channels are clustered in nerve terminals and are coupled to neurotransmitter release (Speddings, Kilpatrick, & Alps, 1989).

The HVA and LVA calcium currents have different time courses of inactivation; the HVA channels are approximately an order of magnitude faster. The two basic types of calcium channels can also be differentiated pharmacologically. Cadmium ions (Cd^{2+}) at concentrations below 20 μM attenuate HVA currents; LVA currents are unaffected (Fox, Nowycky, & Tsien, 1987a). Similarly, omega-conotoxin GVIA in micromolar concentrations blocks neuronal HVA (N and L) calcium channels without affecting LVA (T) channels (effect is more pronounced in peripheral neurons) (Feldman, Olivera, & Yoshikami, 1987; McClesky, Fox, Feldman, Cruz, & Olivera, 1987; Swandulla et al., 1991). Nickel (μM concentrations) or amiloride selectively blocks LVA channels in some but not all neurons (Swandulla et al., 1991). Pharmacological methods have as yet been unsuccessful at clearly differentiating the N-type calcium channel. (For a discussion of calcium channel types, see Fox et al., 1987a, 1987b; Miller, 1987; Swandulla et al., 1991).

Calcium channels can be modulated by a number of neurotransmitters and drugs, most often acting through G protein-linked receptors. This can result in an enhancement or inhibition of calcium channel activity, depending on the particular receptors activated. Neurotransmitters that have an inhibitory effect on calcium channel activity include: GABA, some adenosine analogs, norepinephrine, serotonin, enkephalins, and somatostatin. This effect may play a role in some autoreceptor mechanisms. For example, the negative coupling of alpha-2 adrenergic receptors to calcium channels may decrease the activity of synaptic terminal calcium channels, thereby decreasing the calcium-dependent release of norepinephrine from a noradrenergic neuron.

The early investigation of action potential and nerve conduction mechanisms by Hodgkin and Huxley was conducted using the giant squid axon. More recently, studies of many neurons from different animals have shown that the depolarizing inward current has kinetics quite different from those described by Hodgkin and Huxley in the squid axon. In most neurons, a voltage-dependent calcium current contributes to the inward current phase of the action potential. Pharmacological and ion replacement experiments have shown that the sodium current can be blocked or even eliminated without significantly impairing the cells' ability to generate action potentials. In some cases, the calcium current accounts for most (or occasionally all) of the depolarizing inward phase, with the rising phase of the action potential appearing normally in the complete absence of sodium ions (Levitan & Kaczmarel, 1991). (For a review of calcium channels in neurons see Carbone & Swandulla, 1989; Hess, 1990; Miller, 1987; Swandulla et al., 1991).

Gating and the movement of charges through voltage-gated ion channels are difficult to study in native excitable tissue because they generally occur in association with other voltage-gated channels. Thus, currents arising from the different types of channels are virtually impossible to separate. By using alternate expression systems, such as the X. laevis oocyte system, in which high densities of a particular channel can be expressed and the resulting currents accurately and temporally measured, much has been learned about the movement of charges, gating, and the domains that play roles in the different phases of channel activity. Site-directed mutagenesis and site-directed antibody studies can reveal domains of the protein that are important in different aspects of channel operation. Further studies are bound to yield new insight into voltage-gated channel mechanisms.

Intracellular calcium is much more than just an ion contributing to the net charge flow across the membrane. It has the unique distinction of being a "transducer," converting the electrical signal of the action potential into a chemical signal in the synapse and making interneuronal communication possible. Clusters of calcium channels are seen in nerve terminals in close proximity to neurotransmitter vesicles and sites of neurotransmitter release. Transmitter release requires external calcium entry through the calcium channel. Depolarization of the presynaptic membrane activates the voltage-dependent calcium channel, resulting in calcium influx. The elevated calcium is thought to activate kinases that phosphorylate certain synaptic vesicle proteins, leading to fusion of the synaptic vesicle with the plasma membrane, and expulsion of the neurotransmitter into the synaptic cleft (Hess, 1990). Transmitter release is very rapid, despite evidence suggesting that the binding of several calcium ions is required. In addition to this important function of calcium, it plays a variety of other roles by binding to different calcium-binding proteins that regulate or modulate cellular enzymes. Calcium channels are also regulated or modulated by a number of neurotransmitters and peptides.

Action potentials cannot continue to fire indefinitely without restoring the ion concentrations across the membrane. When currents flow, they follow their concentration gradients. If action potentials were to continue to fire in the absence of a restoring mechanism, eventually the sodium and potassium concentrations on either side of the membrane would be equal and the membrane potential would be zero. Thus, continued operation requires restoration of those ionic gradients. The sodium-potassium ATPase pump is an enzyme that uses energy from the hydrolysis of ATP to move three sodium ions into the cell and pump two potassium ions out of the cell. This is an important ion pump in neurons, particularly in axons.

Some neuronal cell bodies lack the rapid voltage-dependent sodium channels described above. Furthermore, cell bodies may possess a variety of ion currents in addition to or instead of those typically found in axons associated with action potential propagation. These ion currents are conducted by specific ion channels, which may be regulated by neurotransmitters binding to the extracellular side of the channel, intracellular metabolites, or calcium-binding proteins. Typically, the ionic current in cell bodies and dendrites is more varied than that found in the axons. One such ion channel is the chloride channel associated with the GABA receptor complex. GABA represents the primary inhibitory neurotransmitter in the nervous system. A number of psychoactive drugs, including barbiturates and benzodiazepines, modulate the chloride channel through action on this receptor complex.

Dendrite Structure

Dendrites are neuronal processes that are specialized for the receipt of information. In general, they are much shorter and more highly branched than axons. The extensive network of branching observed in many dendrites gives rise to what has been called the dendritic tree because of its microscopic appearance. The electron microscope reveals that the dendrites of many cells are studded with numerous stubby, fingerlike projections, called dendritic spines. The spines are sites where synaptic contact is made by axon terminals of other neurons. Until recently, it was believed that dendrites were only capable of receiving information, but now evidence is accumulating that in some circumstances a two-way flow of information can occur, apparently through the same set of dendritelike processes, thus making dendritic release of neurotransmitter possible. Typically, the external surface of the soma and dendrites is densely covered by synaptic knobs of various sizes and shapes.

Axon Structure

Axons are neuronal processes that are specialized for the transfer of information from one brain region to another over short to very long distances. Axons can vary in length from a few micrometers to a few meters. They originate at a thickened portion of the soma called the axon hillock. This region of the soma has fewer organelles and ribosomes. The neurofilaments and microtubules are grouped into fascicles in the axon hillock. The axon's diameter remains constant throughout its length. An extensive cytoskeletal system (microfilaments, neurofilaments, and microtubules) is thought to maintain the structure of both axons and dendrites, as well as play an essential role in the transport of proteins and metabolites in both directions, via axoplasmic flow. No protein synthesis occurs in axons, so they are dependent on axoplasmic transport for their supply of proteins. The importance of a functional cytoskeletal system is suggested in Alzheimer's disease, which is associated with highly disorganized neurofilaments, the characteristic neurofilamentous tangles. At this time, it is unclear whether these tangles have any pathological consequences or are simply a result of the pathology.

In myelinated axons, the portion of the axon between the hillock and where myelination begins is called the initial segment. The initial segment of some types of neurons (motorneurons and some spinal neurons) has a lower depolarization threshold. Large axons are most frequently myelinated and, in general, the larger the axon, the thicker the myelin sheath. Myelin is produced by oligodendrocytes in the central nervous system (CNS) and by Schwann cells in the peripheral nervous system (PNS). These cells wrap the axon with a lipid coating many layers thick. Myelin is no longer thought to be exclusively associated with axons and has been described in some instances (e.g., in the olfactory bulb) around soma and dendrites. There is a gap, called the node of Ranvier, about 1 m long between the myelin produced by neighboring oligodendrocytes/Schwann cells. Sodium channels are clustered in high densities (3,000 per mM^2) at the node, where they play an important role in action potential propagation. Potassium channels are found in much lower abundance at the node (about $1/mM^2$). The repolarizing potassium current may be absent or nonessential at the node of Ranvier of many myelinated axons, because sodium channel inactivation alone appears to account for repolarization. Conduction along myelinated axons is sped up by the signal's traveling from node to node along the axon rather than traversing the entire length of the axon. The smaller axons, which are more prevalent in the CNS, are generally unmyelinated. Neurons with short axons are also more numerous in the CNS. There is only one axon per neuron, but it may be branched, giving rise to collateral axons.

The Synapse

The synapse provides the structural basis of neurochemical transmission: it is the highly specialized neuronal structure that mediates the interneuronal transfer of information. The term *synapse* was first used by Sherrington in 1906 to describe the specialized nerve terminal endings that he hypothesized must exist. However, it was not until the mid-1950s that E. G. Gray, using electron microscopy, confirmed the existence of synapses. The presynaptic axon is expanded at its end, forming a terminal bulb. Vesicles localized in this presynaptic terminal bulb are concentrated close to the synaptic cleft, a very narrow space that completely separates the external surfaces of the synaptic bulb/knob from that of the dendrite/soma with which it is communicating. The vesicular packing of neurotransmitter prevents degradation of the neurotransmitter by metabolizing enzymes present in the cytoplasm. The synaptic cleft is relatively uniform in width (about 20 nm) across synapses. Stains used to localize sugars have revealed large amounts of carbohydrates in the synaptic cleft; their function is as yet unknown. All synapses made by a given neuron onto other neurons are of the same type and release the same neurotransmitter(s) and peptide(s).

Electrical synapses, in which transmission appears to be by the flow of electrical current directly from the presynaptic to the postsynaptic element, have a much narrower synaptic cleft (2–4 nm) and have been called gap junctions. Gap junctions are found predominantly in invertebrates and lower vertebrates, and are not thought to be important in the mammalian CNS. Chemical synapses are more commonly found in the mammalian CNS and will be the focus of discussion.

The soma, dendrites, and axon terminal regions, but not the axon proper, are capable of synthesizing neurotransmitters. Some of the neurotransmitters, neuropeptides, and many other proteins required for synaptic activity are synthesized only in the soma and therefore must be transported to the terminal region. Axoplasmic transport mechanisms carry vesicles, enzymes, and other material from the perikaryon toward the synaptic terminal (antegrade flow), and damaged membranes and other salvaged materials from the terminal toward the perikaryon (retrograde flow). Thus, a diversity of intracellular traffic must be carefully choreographed to ensure proper nerve functioning.

Three major classes of cytoskeletal elements are involved in transport processes: (a) microfilaments, composed of actin subunits; (b) intermediate filaments; and (c) microtubules, composed of polymerized tubulin subunits. Microtubules are generally found in association with microtubule accessory proteins (MAPs) and tau proteins, which appear to be required for polymerization and stabilization of tubulin subunits. The marked differential subcellular localization of MAPs and tau proteins contributes to the neuronal asymmetry and may have important functional consequences. Tau proteins are more abundant in axons; a high molecular weight MAP^2 is predominantly localized to dendrites (Goedert, Crowther, & Garner, 1991). These proteins, in conjunction with microtubules, have been implicated in cell migration, axonal outgrowth, and axonal transport.

Neurotransmitter Release

Invasion of the axon terminal by a wave of depolarization conducted down the axon leads to the Ca^{++}-dependent fusion of the neurotransmitter-containing vesicle with the presynaptic plasma membrane and to the release of the neurotransmitter into the synaptic cleft. The neurotransmitter then diffuses across the synaptic cleft and binds to a specific integral-membrane postsynaptic receptor on the target neuron. Different neurotransmitters bind to a variety of receptors that are selective for the particular transmitter. The various receptor types have distinct distributions within the CNS. Methods borrowed from molecular biology have revealed a greater diversity of receptor types than was previously predicted by binding methods. Some receptors are directly coupled to ion channels; others are coupled indirectly to ion channels through G proteins and second messenger systems. Receptors and second messengers are discussed in detail in a later section.

In addition to postsynaptic receptors, there are usually, in the terminal region, presynaptic autoreceptors that are capable of binding the released neurotransmitters when stimulated autoreceptors signal a decrease in neurotransmitter release. Presynaptic autoreceptors have been described in virtually all the neurotransmitter systems. This anatomical arrangement provides a negative feedback mechanism where the concentration of released neurotransmitter modulates subsequent transmitter release in response to further depolarization. The neuron is thus able to monitor the level of neurotransmitter present in the synapse and to make homeostatic adjustments by increasing or decreasing the release of the transmitter.

Efficient transfer of information between cells requires the rapid termination of the signal and a return to the baseline condition. Synaptic specializations have evolved that aid in this function. The cellular mechanism(s) utilized are dependent on the specific neurotransmitter system involved. There are selective reuptake sites, which are integral membrane proteins, for norepinephrine, glutamate, dopamine, and serotonin. In addition, there are enzymes that metabolize/degrade the transmitters: monoamine oxidase A and B, with slightly different substrate specificities for serotonin and the monoamines; and acetylcholinesterase for breaking down acetylcholine. Most peptide neurotransmitters have specific degredative enzymes.

A new dimension in neuronal communication has been added with the localization immunohistochemically of nitric oxide (NO) synthetase in neuronal cells of specific brain areas. In adult rat brain, high expression was found in the cerebellum, olfactory bulb neurons, and neural innervation of the posterior pituitary (Bredt, Hwang, & Snyder, 1990). At least two isoforms of NO synthetase may show tissue-specific expression. The synthetic enzyme is activated by calcium/calmodulin. Released NO reaches neighboring cells by simple diffusion, and can affect a number of neighboring cells. Its action is most likely limited by the short half-life of this highly reactive compound. NO stimulates guanylyl cyclase activity and decreases cytosolic calcium by a cGMP-independent mechanism. By modulating cGMP and cytosolic calcium levels, NO may play an important role in regulating the level of excitability of neurons as well as the release of neurotransmitters.

One last distinction between neurons and other cells of the body is worth noting. Unlike most other cells, mature CNS neurons do not undergo further division (they are said to be terminally mitotic) and hence cannot be replaced when damaged. Because of this, it is likely that the nervous system has evolved some novel strategies to prevent or minimize neuronal loss. Recently, one such strategy was reported by Joly, Muche, and Oldstone (1991). Most cells are "marked" with unique antigens as self. These recognition molecules, the major histocompatibility class I molecules, play a role in detecting foreign antigens and aiding in their destruction by the immune system (typically, by cytotoxic T cells). It has been observed that neurons infected by multiple viruses do not appear to be targeted by the immune system. Neurons appear to avoid cytotoxic lymphocyte detection and lysis by failing to express MHC class I antigens on their cell surface, and thereby fail to present viral peptides complexed with MHC class I antigens on their cell surface. This represents a unique survival mechanism that allows viral-infected neurons to survive, but also leaves them vulnerable to infection by neurotropic viruses.

FUNDAMENTALS OF MAMMALIAN BRAIN DEVELOPMENT

In this section, we summarize what is known about mammalian brain development at a molecular level. We accomplish this in a four-part way. (a) We give a broad overview of the basic embryology of the developing brain. This overview is intended as a review and to establish a common ground from which further discussion will emanate. (b) We outline certain developmental events and concepts that are particularly relevant to molecular research in brain development. Much of this section focuses on interesting cell biological experiments. (c) We address at a molecular level the developmental problems outlined in the preceding part of the chapter. (d) We speculate about where we perceive the focus of molecular brain research will be in the future. Our intent in this section is not to provide a comprehensive list of all the known molecular events. Instead, our goal is to highlight examples of what is probably happening throughout the brain. What is striking about this summary is that, although bits and pieces are known for different aspects, there is no comprehensive picture of mammalian brain development. Many hypotheses about brain development are derived from experiments in other developmental systems that remain to be confirmed or repudiated in the mammalian brain.

Elements of Neuroembryology

The beginning of neurogenesis, and differentiation from the rest of the embryo, starts with the formation of the neural plate (Nowakowski, 1987). The neural plate is a thickening of ectodermal cells on the dorsal aspect of the developing embryo that runs the entire length of the embryo. The ectodermal plate is induced to form neural tissue by the underlying notochord, a mesodermal structure (Schoenwolf & Smith, 1990). At the lateral edges of the plate, ridges form. Eventually, the ridges extend to meet at the dorsal midline to form the neural tube. The cavity created by the tube is called a ventricle. The closure of the neural tube does not occur simultaneously along the rostral-caudal axis of the embryo. Instead, closure first occurs in the middle and then "zippers" its way rostrally and caudally. The last parts of the neural tube to close are those at the tail of the embryo and those at its head.

Initially, the neural plate looks uniform along its entire axis. The differential closure of the neural tube begins to morphologically differentiate one part of the neural tube from another. Moreover, even as closure is occurring, the neural tube is morphologically regionalizing by differential cell division and migration. In this way, the neural tube can initially be split into the spinal cord, the rhombencephalon, the mesencephalon, and the prosencephalon. The rhombencephalon, mesencephalon, and prosencephalon all develop into structures in the brain. The rhombencephalon gives rise to the hindbrain, the mesencephalon to the midbrain, and the prosencephalon to the forebrain. These are what are known as the three cardinal subdivisions of the brain and are based on three ventricular swellings of the neural tube (Sadler, 1985).

Among the three subdivisions, there is further division. The rhombencephalon divides into the mylencephalon and metencephalon. The mesencephalon stays undivided. The prosencephalon divides into the diencephalon and telencephalon. This further division helps to establish where structures in the mature brain originate:

1. The medulla oblongata comes from the mylencephalon;
2. The pons and cerebellum come from the metencephalon;
3. The midbrain comes from the mesencephalon;
4. The hypothalamus, thalamus, epithalamus, and subthalamus come from the diencephalon;
5. The cerebral cortex, hippocampus, olfactory bulb, amygdala, and basal ganglia come from the telencephalon. (Sadler, 1985)

These five subdivisions have been in the textbooks for some time. Recently, interest has been revived in transient structures known as rhombomeres. First described in the 19th century (Keynes & Lumsden, 1990), the rhombomeres are nine bulges in the rhombencephalon that appear early and then disappear. Analysis of the boundaries of the rhombomeres shows that cells do not seem to cross these borders (Keynes & Lumsden, 1990). Moreover, each cranial nerve that comes from the hindbrain has a unique origin in a particular set of rhombomeres (Keynes & Lumsden, 1990). Thus, a transient morphological structure early in development has a distinct relationship to structures in the mature brain. We believe that such phenomena are going to be the rule rather than the exception in brain development. The rediscovery and appreciation of rhombomeres as important segmental units in the developing brain have led scientists to look closely at more rostral parts of the developing brain for analogous structures.

At this point, we should introduce some cellular terms and concepts. Lining the cavity of the neural tube and forming the wall is a layer of ectodermal pseudostratified neuroepithelial cells. These cells are called ventricular zone cells because they lie in the ventricular zone, the region next to the ventricle. The ventricular zone cells are small, round, actively mitotic cells that eventually give rise to all of the mature cell types, both neurons and glia, in the fully developed brain. These cells might be thought of as stem cells of the nervous system; for this reason, the ventricular zone is also known as the germinal zone.

A common feature of brain development is that a ventricular zone cell will stop dividing, become terminally postmitotic, and migrate to a destination away from the ventricular zone. The postmitotic cells that become neurons become organized in two different ways: (a) into layers, giving a "laminar" organization to the structure (the cerebral cortex and lateral geniculate nucleus are two examples of structures that show laminar organization), or (b) into clumps, giving a "nuclear" organization to the structure. The striatum and most parts of the hindbrain are examples of structures that have a nuclear organization.

In addition to the laminar organization, the cerebral cortex is also organized into columns. The columns run perpendicular to the laminar plane and are a group of cells that are functionally related. The mature mammalian cerebral cortex consists of millions of these columns (Rakic, 1988).

In sum, the development of the brain is a process of progressive regional specialization. An inherent key to the function of the brain is its structural organization. A useful way to understand the structural organization is to try to understand how different parts of the brain become regionally specialized and how cell types within a given region become determined.

Basic Problems in Brain Development

In the previous section, we provided an overview of the embryology of brain development. In this section, we describe some cell biological experiments that relate to five important developmental questions:

1. What is the cell lineage of neurons in the brain?
2. How do cells migrate to their appropriate destinations?
3. How do cells and regions differentiate?
4. How do neurons make the correct axonal connections?
5. How plastic is the developmental process?

These questions are based on the problems that an undifferentiated ventricular zone cell must solve in order to become a functional neuron. There are no complete answers to any of these questions; however, in this section, we strive to provide a sense for what some of the answers might be.

Cell Lineage

To summarize what is known about cell lineage of neurons in the brain, we focus on three types of experiments: (a) birthdating studies, (b) transplantation studies, and (c) retroviral tracing experiments. Birthdating studies of neurons are studies designed to determine whether there is a temporal determinant to the final destination of the cell; that is, does the dating of when a ventricular zone cell becomes postmitotic determine where it is going to migrate to? These studies are done by giving a pulse of tritiated labeled thymidine to an embryonic animal. When a cell replicates its DNA, it will incorporate tritiated thymidine and become labeled. If a cell continues to divide, however, the label will dilute among its daughter cells and become undetectable by autoradiography. Thus, the most intensely labeled cells are those that divide once and then stop dividing. A certain amount of time after giving the pulse—usually, when the animal becomes an adult—the brain is sectioned and the location of the labeled cells is determined. In this way, it can be determined when neurons of a particular location become terminally postmitotic.

Birthdating studies have shown that the cerebral cortex develops like an "inside-out sandwich" (Rakic, 1988). The first group of postmitotic cells migrates to form a layer below the pial surface. The second wave of cells splits the first group into the marginal zone at the pial surface, which will become layer 1 of the mature cerebral cortex and the subplate, which is a transient structure that is not present in the mature cerebral cortex. The second wave of cells is destined to become the deepest layer of the cerebral cortex, layer 6 cells. The cells in the third wave, which are destined to be layer 5 cells, migrate through the subplate cells and layer 6 progenitors to form a new layer below the marginal zone. Thus, in the mature cerebral cortex, layer 1 is formed first but then deeper layers are formed before more superficial layers.

The corpus striatum, unlike the cerebral cortex, has a nuclear organization of patch and matrix cells, not a laminar organization. Birthdating studies in the striatum have shown that, compared to matrix cells, patch cells have a distinctly earlier time at which they become postmitotic (Van der Kooy & Fishell, 1987). Thus, the cerebral cortex and striatum are two examples of a temporal determinant to final cell location during normal development.

Birthdating studies show that the cerebral cortex develops in a well characterized sequential manner. Such studies do not show whether the cells migrate "dumbly" or "smartly": do they migrate according to specific instructions from the surrounding environment, or do they already "know" where they are supposed to go? Transplantation studies have shed some light on this question. Experiments were done by transplanting labeled ventricular zone cells that normally migrate to layer 6 to a ventricular zone that was making layer 2/3 cells (McConnell & Kaznowski, 1991). The studies showed that if the cells incorporated labeled thymidine while in the layer 6 environment, they migrated to layer 6 even when placed in the new environment; if they incorporated labeled thymidine in culture, they migrated to layer 2/3. Thus, there is a complicated relationship involving the time at which the cell becomes postmitotic, the environment in which it undergoes its final DNA synthesis, and the layer to which it will migrate. A not altogether surprising conclusion is that cells may be both "dumb" and "smart."

Retroviral lineage studies are designed to determine whether a given ventricular zone cell gives rise to different cell types or to cells of a single cell type. These studies are carried out by infecting ventricular zone cells with a small number of disabled retroviruses bearing a genetic marker. The retrovirus will insert itself into the host cell genome during DNA replication and give the cell a novel genetic marker. Once in the genome, that marker will be passed on to all of the infected cell's progeny. The retrovirus has been designed, however, so that it is incapable of replicating itself and infecting other cells. Theoretically, all the cells that show the marker are clonally related to the single original cell that was infected. These studies can address whether cells within a clonal population are restricted in their final destination and whether cells within a clonal population are restricted in their mature phenotype.

Retroviral lineage studies in the cerebral cortex have shown that, early in brain development, a given ventricular zone cell can give rise to every cell type in the brain. This suggests that each ventricular zone cell is a stem cell for the nervous system in a way that is analogous to how bone marrow stem cells can give rise to the different cell types of the hematopoietic system. However, at later stages of development, a given cell becomes restricted in its range of potential offspring. For instance, an early split in lineage is between the astrocytes of the grey matter and other cells of the brain (Price & Thurlow, 1988). Some studies suggest that eventually a given cell becomes restricted to only generating neurons (Luskin, Pearlman, & Sanes, 1988). Thus, at some stage, the multipotency of ventricular zone cells becomes restricted. In all retroviral lineage studies done so far, a given germinal zone cell is able to give rise to cells of all cortical layers within a vertical column, and some ventricular zone cells give rise to cells separated widely in the horizontal plane as well (Price & Thurlow, 1988; Walsh & Cepko, 1988). These studies point out that we only are beginning to understand the factors that determine the offspring of a given ventricular zone cell.

Cell Migration

Once a cell becomes postmitotic, how does it get to its final destination? The prevailing hypothesis is that cells reach their final destination by migrating along radial glia cells (Hatten, 1990; Rakic, 1988). Radial glia cells have processes that are anchored at both the pial surface and the ventricular surface in the cerebral cortex. They seem to form a scaffold throughout the developing brain. There are three basic lines of evidence that neurons migrate along radial glia cells. As mentioned earlier, it is known that the cerebral cortex is organized into vertical columns, with each column being functionally related. It has been hypothesized that each column is developmentally related as well. The vertical organization of the radial glia cells suggests that they would provide an excellent framework in establishing the columnar organization of the cerebral cortex. Thus, this line of evidence is mainly theoretical. A second line of evidence is that, using the electron microscope, which can only record a snapshot of an ongoing process, putative migrating cells are seen closely apposed to the radial glial fibers. They "look" as if they are creeping up the fiber. Real time video microscopy shows that cerebellar neurons *in vitro* move along Bergmann glial cells and that the migrating cells resemble the migrating cells seen in the electron microscope (Hatten, 1990). Finally, there are mouse mutants that show neuronal migration defects. In *weaver,* migrating granule cells are unable to attach to the Bergman radial glia in the cerebellum and do not migrate correctly (Caviness & Rakic, 1978; Hatten, 1990). The incorrect migration leads to the death of the granule cell. In *reeler,* the cerebral cortex develops "outside-in" rather than "inside-out," but there is no cell death (Caviness & Rakic, 1978; Hatten, 1990). In this mutation, it seems that the migrating cells are unable to detach from the radial glia cell and thus form a roadblock; later migrating cells cannot get by. Thus, the cumulative evidence seems quite strong that neurons migrate to their final destinations at least in part along radial glial cells.

Cell Differentiation

Once a ventricular zone cell becomes terminally postmitotic, it must not only migrate to its correct destination but also differentiate into its mature phenotype. The broad process of differentiation encompasses all the topics of this section: cell lineage, cell migration, axonal outgrowth, and plasticity. Here, we will focus primarily, though not exclusively, on how particular regions of the brain become specified rather than on individual cells. This question of regional specification is one of the most actively studied and debated areas in developmental neurobiology. There are two fundamental views of regional specification: (a) it is an intrinsic, genetically controlled process, or (b) it is an extrinsic, environmentally controlled process. We believe that this split is an artificial distinction, because the genome and the environment are inextricably intertwined. In the following section, we describe some experiments that address how cortical regions become specified.

A major experimental approach has been cell transplantation. The principle is to transplant cells from one environment to another and then to examine whether the transplanted cells adopt the phenotype of the donor environment or of the acceptor environment.

The most interesting of these experiments has been to transplant part of the developing occipital cortex to the developing sensory cortex. These experiments showed that the transplanted tissue adopted the phenotype of the acceptor environment. In one set of experiments, the occipital donor tissue was found to maintain a projection through the pyramidal tract, which it normally does not maintain, when it was transplanted to the rostral neocortex, an area that normally does maintain that projection (O'Leary & Stanfield, 1989). In a second set of experiments, the occipital cortex was found to make "barrels," a functionally unique architecture to the host somatosensory cortex, when transplanted to somatosensory cortex (Schlagger & O'Leary, 1991). Retroviral tracing and transplantation studies described earlier point to the importance of a temporal analysis of these studies. It may be that if the transplantations were done later, the donor tissue would not have taken on host tissue characteristics. A related concern is whether the only tissue that could survive was the tissue that took on host characteristics. Thus, the experiment would only be selecting for tissue that could adapt and not for whether the donor tissue was already determined. Nonetheless, it seems likely, based on these experiments, that the local environment does play an important role in specifying the local phenotype, although what exactly the local environment contributes is not known.

Another approach has been to alter the input into a particular region of the cerebral cortex. A basic way of altering the input to the visual cortex is to study an anophthalmic animal. Rakic (1988) showed that the visual cortex of an anophthalmic mouse maintained its correct topography and connections. This suggests that the visual cortex does not need environmental cues to develop correctly. A second approach to altering the input to the visual cortex is to enucleate the eyes of an embryonic cat. Such a procedure causes cell death in the lateral geniculate nucleus, the thalamic relay center for the visual system, and a corresponding decrease in the number of thalamic inputs into the visual cortex. The visual cortex of such an animal appeared biochemically and cytologically normal (Rakic, 1988). A decrease in the size of the visual cortex was attributable to a decrease in the number of columns in the visual cortex. But each column seemed functionally normal, despite the lack of normal input. A third type of experiment was to reroute retinal ganglionic afferents to the medial geniculate nucleus, the thalamic auditory relay center (Rakic, 1988). After such an alteration, what would have normally been the auditory cortex became capable of processing visual information. Thus, the functional specificity of a cortical region was altered by changing its functional input.

No discussion of regional specialization would be complete without mentioning the concept of a protomap. The protomap is proposed to be an underlying genetic determination to the different regions of the cortex (Rakic, 1988). That is, the seemingly homogeneous ventricular zone is actually obscuring a complex genetic code that leads to the specification of different parts of the brain. The experimental evidence concerning a protomap is slim, mostly because study of brain development at a genetic level has just begun, although there are examples of the equivalent of a protomap in other developmental systems. For instance, in the Drosophila embryo, there is a well defined pattern of gene expression in a field of apparently homogeneous cells (Akam, 1987; Ingham, 1988).

Axonal Outgrowth

Given that a neuron has embarked on its correct pathway of differentiation, it faces a major developmental obstacle in making appropriate connections. There is no evidence that a cell has to connect with one particular cell in one particular way, but the degree of organization of axonal connections, in the face of long distances traversed and a myriad of potential connections shunned, is striking. For example, in every sensory system studied, there is a map on the cortex such that neighboring neurons process information from neighboring parts of the environment (Kandel & Schwartz, 1985).

The most well-studied system of axonal pathfinding is the developing visual system. The simple, mature mammalian visual pathways consists of a retinal ganglion cell forming a synapse with a neuron in the lateral geniculate nucleus. The lateral geniculate nucleus neuron then sends projections to layer 4 neurons of the visual cortex. The striking aspect of this pathway is the organization and maintenance in both the LGN and visual cortex of a retinotopic map. That is, the visual world can be mapped precisely onto both the LGN and the visual cortex.

One of the ways this organization develops is believed to involve making pioneer neurons that serve as a scaffold on which the mature pathway is made. The concept of pioneer neurons was first proposed in the developing grasshopper (Bentley & Keshishian, 1982). Recently, it has been proposed that cells in the subplate act as pioneer neurons in the cerebral cortex (MConnell, Ghosh, & Shatz, 1989). Subplate cells are present only in development and are some of the first cells to become postmitotic in the developing cerebral cortex. Thus, they have characteristics that suggest they might serve a pioneer function. To test whether subplate neurons pioneered mature pathways, a lipophilic dye was injected into the subplate of a fixed section of developing cat brain. This dye migrates along the membrane of all the processes that arise from the area injected. In this way, the dye highlights how the subplate neurons make connections with the LGN before layer 4 cells are even born. Moreover, these studies seemed to show that the LGN sent axons that docked on the subplate cells of the visual cortex. Before growing into layer 4 and synapsing there, the LGN axons waited at the subplate until layer 4 cells, the mature destination of LGN axons, had been born and migrated into place (Ghosh, Antonini, McConnell, & Shatz, 1990). If the subplate cells beneath the developing visual cortex were removed, the LGN axons grew past the visual cortex and never found a place to dock. These studies highlight the idea that a cellular scaffold may be important in guiding axonal outgrowth. They do not address, however, how the LGN axons got to the subplate neurons and how the subplate axons got to the LGN in the first place.

A chemoaffinity hypothesis to explain how axons find their correct location was proposed by Sperry in the 1940s. The chemoaffinity hypothesis proposes that axons follow a chemical gradient in order to find their correct destination (Purves & Lichtman, 1985). Experiments in which a target tissue is cocultured with the tissue of origin for an axon show that the axon preferentially grows toward the natural target tissue and not toward other tissues (Heffner, Lumsden, & O'Leary, 1990). Moreover, the floor plate of the developing neural tube, which is induced by the underlying notochord, releases a substance that attracts axons to the midline (Dodd & Jessell, 1988). When the floor plate is removed or prevented from forming by removal of the notochord, the axons fail to migrate to the midline. These types of experiments suggest that there probably are chemoattractants to guide axonal outgrowth.

Plasticity

The final developmental phenomenon we wish to discuss is the plasticity of the developing brain. The developing brain shows an amazing ability to adapt to changes in its environment and to fine-tune its connections during development. It is this process of adaptation and fine-tuning that we refer to as plasticity. Again, the visual system provides the best backdrop to explain plasticity. The mature visual system consists of a series of alternating columns, called ocular dominance columns, that respond preferentially to one eye or the other. When radioactive tracer is injected into one eye or the other, it is retrogradely transported back to the visual cortex. Autoradiography of the labeled visual cortex shows a series of alternating stripes of labeling corresponding to the ocular dominance columns (Hubel & Wiesel, 1963). This organization is created by the axonal arborization of a particular LGN neuron, which is driven by one eye or the other. The arborization of a given LGN neuron is limited to a single column. During development, however, the axonal arborization of LGN neurons driven by opposite eyes overlaps. Only by pruning of the arborization are the ocular dominance columns formed. If activity from one eye is blocked, either pharmacologically or physically, during a particular time called the critical period, the normal ocular dominance columns do not form (Shatz, 1990). Instead, the stripes corresponding to the blocked eye become narrower and the stripes corresponding to the unblocked eye get wider. The unblocked eye seems to take over the columns normally controlled by the blocked eye. It has been proposed that the organization into ocular dominance columns, therefore, is the result of some sort of activity-dependent competition between neurons. In the next section, we discuss what might be a molecular mechanism to this competition.

This activity-dependent competition has a temporal profile (Shatz, 1990). If activity is blocked after the critical period, there is no effect; if the block is removed before the critical period, there is also no effect. The block has to span a specific period of time during development in order to effect the organization of ocular dominance columns.

The developing brain is much more plastic than the mature brain, but the mature brain is capable of learning and memory, which are analogous to developmental plasticity, although probably at a subtler level. Moreover, a recent experiment showed that the mature brain is capable of profound changes and significant plasticity if it is given enough time. When the brains of monkeys that had had their brachial plexuses severed 10 years earlier were examined, it was found that the area of the brain that normally processed information from the brachial plexuses was processing information from the face (Pons et al., 1991). Thus, critical periods should probably be viewed more as "sensitive" periods than as absolute critical periods (Aslin, 1981; Bornstein, 1989; Gottlieb, 1983).

We have discussed here some of the obstacles that cells in the developing brain have to overcome. We have been able to use examples from the developing cerebral cortex, although we expect the concepts to be more general. In the next part of the chapter, we focus on potential molecular mechanisms that may explain the developmental phenomena discussed here. Unfortunately, most of the examples in the next discussion are not from the developing cerebral cortex. We expect and hope that the examples we do use, however, will prove to have similar mechanisms in the developing cerebral cortex.

A Molecular Viewpoint of Brain Development

The techniques of molecular biology allow scientists to study individual genes and gene products in a unique and powerful way. Molecular biology has, therefore, been critical in understanding the molecular mechanisms in many biological systems. Only recently, however, have those techniques been applied to the study of mammalian brain development. Thus, our knowledge of possible molecular mechanisms underlying the developmental phenomena described in the preceding section is only a beginning.

Cell Lineage

An important "decision" for a ventricular zone cell is when to divide and when to stop dividing. Dividing cells progress through a series of steps called the cell cycle. As a dividing cell progresses through the cell cycle, it must pass certain checkpoints. Studies in yeast have shown that the product of the cdc2 gene must be phosphorylated in order for the cell to pass from G1 into S phase (Lee & Nurse, 1988). If the cdc2 gene product is unphosphorylated, the cell remains arrested in G1. Further, it has been shown that the mammalian homologue of the cdc2 gene product serves as an identical functional checkpoint in mammalian cells (Lee & Nurse, 1988). The gene product of the cdc2 gene is known as p34cdc2 because it is 34 kd protein. Biochemically, the phosphorylated form of p34cdc2 has protein kinase activity *in vitro;* the dephosphorylated form shows no protein kinase activity *in vitro.* Thus, progression through the cell cycle seems to require phosphorylated p34cdc2, which is itself an active protein kinase. Moreover, a number of genes have been isolated that regulate the state of phosphorylation of p34cdc2 in both yeast and vertebrates (Lee & Nurse, 1988). There is a complex relationship of phosphorylation and dephosphorylation among the gene products that control passage through the cell cycle, but this process has been found to be quite general to all dividing cells. It is likely, therefore, that dividing germinal zone cells are also regulated through the p34cdc2 pathway, but there is little data on what gene products present in ventricular zone cells may uniquely regulate its cell cycle. More importantly, there are presently no molecular data on what triggers a neuron to keep its p34cdc2 gene product unphosphorylated or perhaps even unexpressed and thus become terminally postmitotic.

As retroviral lineage studies show, for a dividing ventricular zone cell to give rise to different cell types, there must be some mechanism of generating asymmetry among its daughter cells. Either the dividing cell must partition its cellular contents asymmetrically, or there must be local environmental asymmetries to differentiate one daughter cell from another. At present, there are no data to determine how these potential asymmetries are created in the ventricular zone.

Cell Migration

As discussed previously, cells are thought to migrate to their final destination along radial glia cells. Understanding neuronal migration will require knowledge about the molecular relationship between the radial glia cell and the migrating neuron. Cloning of the genes involved in the mouse mutants—for instance, *reeler* and *weaver*—that show migration defects might be a first step in understanding that relationship. One molecule that is missing or defective in *weaver* mouse granule cells, the cells that require the gene product from the *weaver* gene, is astrotactin. Antibodies against astrotactin, but not antibodies against L1 or NCAM (two cell adhesion molecules), were able to block the adherence of granule cells to radial glia in culture (Hatten, 1990). Thus, astrotactin is probably a molecule that is involved in neuron-glia interactions.

Cell Differentiation

Cell differentiation is the process by which a cell changes from one phenotype to another—usually, the phenotype it is "destined" to achieve. The term implies that a cell moves from a more pluripotent phenotype to a more specialized one. This transition can roughly be assigned to cell autonomous or cell nonautonomous factors. We consider transcription factors as examples of factors causing cell autonomous shifts, and cell signaling and morphogens as examples of factors causing cell nonautonomous shifts.

In Drosophila melanogaster, the fruit fly, there are mutants that cause a transformation of one body segment into another (Gehring, 1987; Lewis, 1978). Two examples are the mutation *antennepedia,* which causes antennae to be transformed into legs, and *ultrabithorax,* which causes the fly to have two sets of wings instead of one. These mutations are called "homeotic" transformations because they transform one body part "into the likeness of something else" (Bateson, 1894). When the genes underlying these and similar mutations were cloned, many were found to share a common 180 necleotide structure called a homeobox, which encodes a 60 amino acid homeodomain (Gehring, 1987). Biochemical analysis of homeodomain-containing proteins showed that they mediate their effects by regulating the transcription of genes (Hayashi & Scott, 1990). Thus, by changing the expression of a subset of genes, homeotic genes have a critical function in fly development. In Drosophila, a set of homeotic genes is arranged in two clusters in the genome. It is likely that these two clusters were once joined in a particular orientation in an evolutionary precursor. These genes are expressed in a fashion corresponding to their location within the cluster such that genes more 3′ in the cluster have a more anterior boundary of expression (Akam, 1989).

Over 30 mammalian homologues of homeobox genes have been cloned (Kessel & Gruss, 1990). There is evidence that these mammalian homeobox genes play developmental roles similar to those of their counterparts in flies. A subset of mammalian homeobox genes, called Hox genes, is organized into 4 clusters. Each cluster looks like a duplication of a common ancestral cluster that was present before flies and mammals diverged; that is, genes most homologous to each other have the same relative position within the cluster. Moreover, as in Drosophila, the genes most 3′ in the cluster have a more anterior boundary of expression (Kessel & Gruss, 1990). Interestingly, the anterior boundaries of expression for the Hox genes correspond to the boundaries of the rhombomeres (Keynes & Lumsden, 1990). Thus, the Hox genes and rhombomeres provide a nice molecular-morphological correspondence. Overexpression of the mammalian genes in flies recreates in part the phenotype of overexpression of the homologous fly gene in flies (Malicki, Schughart, & McGinnis, 1990; McGinnis, Kuziora, & McGinnis, 1990). This demonstrates that the genes can functionally complement each other. Misexpression of the Hox 1.1 gene causes a homeotic transformation in the vertebral column, suggesting that the mammalian homeobox genes may also control the identity of particular segments (Kessel, Balling, & Gruss, 1990) Finally, creating homozygous null mutations in the Hox 1.5 or Hox 1.6 genes causes embryonic lethality consistent with these genes' playing important developmental roles (Chisaka & Capecchi, 1991; Lufkin, Dierich, LeMeur, Mark, & Chambon, 1991). Importantly, the Hox 1.6 mutation caused disruption of rhombomere development.

The rostral boundary or expression of the Hox genes is the rhombencephalon. Some homeobox genes discovered outside of the clusters have more rostral limits of expression but are also expressed in the caudal nervous system (Holland & Hogan, 1988). In fact, some even show layer-specific expression in the cerebral cortex (He et al., 1989). Only recently have homeobox genes been cloned that are exclusively expressed in the forebrain of the nervous system (Porteus, Bulfone, Ciaranello, & Rubenstein, 1991; Price, Lemaistre, Pischetola, DiLauro, & Duboule, 1991). The homeobox gene Tes-1, for example, is expressed only in the ventral forebrain, and not in the dorsal forebrain, during certain stages of development. It may contribute, therefore, to the differentiation of ventral tissues of the forebrain. Tes-1 and Dlx, another mouse homeobox gene, show discontinuous patterns of expression in the diencephalon. These two genes help to define molecular boundaries in the diencephalon of the developing brain.

In Drosophila nervous system development, a cluster of genes, called proneural genes, when mutated causes an alteration in the number of sensory neurons in the periphery (Ghysen & Dambly-Chaudiere, 1988; Jimenez & Campos-Ortega, 1990). When these genes were cloned, they were found to code for a domain called the "basic-helix-loop-helix" (bHLH). bHLH proteins also act as transcriptional regulators. Studies of these and other bHLH proteins have shown that they are intimately involved in specifying particular cell fates (Weintraub et al., 1991). For example, when MyoD, a mammalian muscle determination gene, is induced in myoblasts, the myoblasts mature into multinucleate muscle cells. Roughly, the homeobox genes seem to establish the pattern of the embryo, and the bHLH genes seem to control particular cell identities. This is just a generality, but it is a useful way to think about the different classes of transcriptional factors. Two mammalian homologues of the Drosophila genes have been cloned and have been found to be expressed in many parts of the nervous system during development (Johnson, Birren, & Anderson, 1990; Lo, Johnson, Wuenschell, Saito, & Anderson, 1991). They are likely to control the specification of cell fate in the mammalian nervous system during development.

Cells can also differentiate based on cell nonautonomous factors. These factors can either be proteins or chemicals. In Drosophila, mutations in the gene *wingless* cause abnormal development. The wingless gene has been cloned, and biochemical analysis of its gene product suggests that it is a secreted protein and it mediates its effects through signaling to cells immediately around it (Rijsewijk et al., 1987; Van den Heuvel, Nusse, Johnston, & Lawrence, 1989). Many mammalian homologues of the wingless gene have been cloned; these are called the Wnt genes. Different Wnt genes are expressed in different parts of the developing nervous system and show sharp boundaries of expression (Roelink & Nusse, 1991). When a homozygous null mutant was created in the Wnt-1 gene, the mouse showed abnormal hindbrain development, a region where the gene is normally expressed (McMahon & Bradley, 1990; Thomas & Capecchi, 1990). It is likely, therefore, that these gene products are important in cell determination via their cell signaling properties in the developing brain.

During development, the notochord, a mesodermal derivative, induces the overlying neural plate, an ectodermal derivative, to form nervous tissue. Careful analysis of transplantation studies shows that the notochord induces the floor plate to release a diffusable factor, which then causes the overlying spinal cord to form cells of the appropriate types, such as motoneurons, and morphology (Placzek, Tessier-Lavigne, Yamada, Jessell, & Dodd, 1990; Yamada, Placzek, Tanaka, Dodd, & Jessell, 1991). The diffusible factor has not been isolated, but it is clear that induction is a molecular mechanism by which cell differentiation can be caused.

A morphogen is a substance that causes differentiation to occur along different pathways, depending on its concentration. It is often thought of as originating at a single location, where it will have a high concentration, and then diffusing away, creating gradually lower concentrations. The concept of a morphogen is an important one in developmental biology. A good example of a graded morphogen is the gene product of a bicoid gene in Drosophila (Nusslein-Volhard, Frohnhofer, & Lehman, 1987). Very early in normal Drosophila embryogenesis, the bicoid protein is distributed in a gradient with very high concentrations at the anterior pole and gradually lower concentrations posteriorly. In this way, bicoid protein establishes the anterior pole of the embryo. Bicoid has been shown to act as a morphogen by experimentally manipulating its concentration through the embryo. Thus, if anterior pole cytoplasm, which contains high concentrations of bicoid protein, is injected into the posterior pole, which contains no bicoid protein, the posterior pole takes on anterior characteristics. Moreover, if bicoid protein is found in higher concentrations than normal posteriorly, it induces those regions to take on more anterior characteristics. Conversely, if the bicoid protein is reduced in areas in which it normally is present, those regions take on more posterior characteristics. Thus, bicoid is a classic morphogen in that its level directly determines the identity of a particular region.

Retinoic acid (RA), or its metabolites, is thought to act as a morphogen in vertebrate development. The evidence that retinoic acid can act as a morphogen is fivefold. First, it is known that retinoic acid acts as a teratogen during development (Summerbell & Maden, 1990). Thus, it can impinge on the developmental process. Second, the receptor for RA belongs to the steroid receptor superfamily of genes (Giguere, Ong, Segui, & Evans, 1987). This family is able to directly alter the transcription of genes after binding of their appropriate ligand. Thus, by regulating the transcription of other genes, RA can conceivably act as a morphogen. Third, in the chick wing bud, during development, RA can cause a mirror duplication of wing structures (Smith et al., 1989). It causes this duplication in a concentration-dependent manner and thus can act as a morphogen in another developmental system. Fourth, studies of RA in cell culture show that the concentration of RA can have differential effects on gene expression. That is, the genes at the 3′ end of the Hox-2 cluster were induced to express at lower concentrations of RA than the genes at the 5′ end in teratocarcinoma cells (Simeone et al., 1990). This effect is intriguing because, as discussed previously, the genes at the 3′ end of the Hox-2 cluster have a more anterior border of expression, and the gene products of the Hox cluster are likely to play important regulatory roles during development. Finally, RA was shown to cause an anteroposterior transformation in the frog nervous system and anteroposterior transformations in the mouse vertebral column (Durston et al., 1989; Kessel & Gruss, 1991). In the mouse experiment, RA had altered the normal expression pattern of Hox genes. Although retinoic acid is a likely, but not proven, candidate to act as a morphogen in cell determination during development, there are few, if any, other candidates. Thus, morphogens remain undiscovered and elusive in brain development.

Axonal Pathfinding

A number of genes that play important roles in axonal outgrowth have been cloned. In Drosophila, certain mutants show axonal pathfinding defects. That is, particular axons normally have well-characterized tracts (called fascicles) that they follow. In certain mutants, axons would either choose the wrong tract or stop growing entirely (Harrelson & Goodman, 1988). The genes fasciclin-1,2,3 and neuroglian were cloned and proven to be the genes underlying a few of the various mutations (Bieber et al., 1989; Harrelson & Goodman, 1988; Snow, Bieber, & Goodman, 1989; Zinn, McAllister, & Goodman, 1988). Structural analysis of the protein products showed that two belong to the immunoglobulin superfamily because they contain domains that are homologous to conserved domains in immunoglobulin proteins. Biochemical analysis of the gene products shows that each works by binding to itself, a homophilic adhesion. Homophilic adhesion was shown by transfecting the gene into a cell line that normally is dispersed and does not express any of the cell adhesion molecules. After transfection, the cells clump, indicating that the product of the transfected gene binds itself to the surface of another cell. It is proposed that axons find the correct tract by matching the homophilic adhesion molecule on its surface with the tract that expresses the same homophilic adhesion molecule.

In the vertebrate spinal cord, certain axons must cross the midline. As mentioned previously, the floor plate is thought to release a substance that causes the axons to grow toward the midline. These axons have been examined at a molecular level with antibodies (Dodd & Jessell, 1988). Antibody staining showed that the axon expresses Tag-1, another member of the immunoglobulin superfamily, on its surface while it is on the same side of the spinal cord as its cell body and as it passes through the midline. But after passing the midline, the axon no longer expresses Tag-1. Instead, it expresses another cell adhesion molecule called L1. This expression pattern and the ability of Tag-1 and L1 to promote neurite outgrowth (Dodd & Jessell, 1988) suggest that these molecules are acting as guides for axonal outgrowth.

Axons probably find their correct targets both by reading the signs on other axons, such as in the insect fasciclin molecules, and by reading signals along the extracellular matrix. The importance of cell-substrate interactions in axonal outgrowth has been shown by growing developing retinal ganglion explants on various substrates in culture (Walter, Allsopp, & Bonhoeffer, 1990). These studies showed that certain substances promoted axonal outgrowth more robustly than did other substrates. Moreover, when given a choice, the explant would choose tissue homogenates from its normal target, rather than from a closely related abnormal target, to grow axons on. The factor(s) that mediate this preferential outgrowth have not been cloned, but these experiments show that there is an important molecular determinant to pathfinding by growing axons.

Plasticity

Plasticity of neurons and neuronal connections has been studied in many systems. The molecular studies of desensitization and sensitization in the invertebrate sea slug Aplysia are likely to have important ramifications in our understanding of brain development. But we will focus on the role of correlated activity as an important determinant during brain development. Tetrodotoxin (TTX), a toxin from puffer fish, blocks the sodium channel in axons and thereby blocks action potentials. When TTX is injected into the pathway of the developing visual system, the normal segregation of the LGN into eye-specific layers, and the visual cortex into ocular dominance columns, is blocked (Shatz, 1990). At a cellular level, it is found that TTX prevents the normal pruning of the extensive axonal arborization that is present during development.

The N-methyl-d-aspartate (NMDA) receptor is a glutamate neurotransmitter receptor. When opened, it allows Na^+, K^+, and Ca^{++} to flow through its channel. It is the only known glutamate-gated channel that allows Ca^{++} to pass. But the NMDA-gated channel only opens if it binds glutamate, or agonistlike NMDA, and the cell is depolarized. Thus, Ca^{++} only enters the cell if the receptor is activated in a correlated manner with another input. A Hebbian synapse is one whose ability to influence the postsynaptic cell depends on the synchronous convergence of two inputs.

Thus, the properties of the NMDA channel suggest that it may be involved in strengthening inputs that are cotemporal in a Hebbian fashion. If NMDA receptor antagonists are used to treat developing or regenerating visual system pathways, the normally precise retinotopic maps are disrupted (Shatz, 1990). This disruption may be the result of the cell's being unable to correlate normally synchronous inputs because the NMDA receptor has been disabled. The recent cloning of the NMDA receptor will help to unravel the role it plays in the developing brain (Moriyoshi et al., 1991).

In conclusion, we have sketched the characteristics of various transcription factors, cell signaling molecules, morphogens, cells adhesion molecules, and neurotransmitter receptors, in order to show that brain development is beginning to be understood at a molecular level. In the next section, we speculate about the future directions of brain research at the molecular level.

Future Directions

In the immediate future, there will be a better understanding of genes that have already been cloned. Molecular biology allows genes to be expressed at high levels in bacteria and thus much more easily purified. The purified proteins can then be analyzed biochemically and structurally, in order to understand how they function. In addition, there are now techniques to study mammalian genes genetically. Transgenic mouse technology gives the ability to put an altered copy of the gene randomly back into the genome. In the past few years, gene targeting by homologous recombination has allowed the generation of mice that have null mutations in specific genes (Mansour, Thomas, & Capecchi, 1988). In this section, we have discussed how creating null mutations in two Hox genes and one Wnt gene has helped underscore their importance in development. In the future, many mouse mutants will be created by the gene-targeting technology in a multitude of different genes. Thus, brain development can be understood and manipulated at a genetic level in mammals for the first time.

We have focused primarily on two organisms, the mouse and the fly, to understand the molecular nature of brain development while minimizing the fragmentation of our discussion. But active and fruitful study of other organisms, such as the frog, chicken, and zebrafish, has and will likely continue to have an important part in our understanding of brain development.

We believe that two general fields of study will be the focus of future research in brain development: (a) the relationship between the genome and the brain and (b) the possibility of somatic cell recombination during brain development. The classic genetic code is the one that translates nucleotide sequence into amino acid sequence. We believe this code is merely embedded in a much larger code that is involved in translating the genome, with all of its associated structure, into an organism. This code includes but is not limited to: characterizing regulatory elements of specific genes, characterizing the signals for alternative splicing of a gene, characterizing how chromatin is folded and bent in order to make regions transcriptionally active or unactive, and characterizing the role of DNA modification, such as methylation, in gene expression. Because brain development is probably the most complicated task facing an organism, it is likely that study of the genomic code in the sense we have just outlined will have direct relevance to the study of brain development.

The immune system is known to rearrange its genomic content, by a process called somatic cell gene rearrangement, to create a diversity of response. Recently, experiments showed that the brain might also rearrange its genomic content. In these experiments, a transgenic mouse was made with marker gene that could only be expressed if the marker gene was rearranged by somatic cell recombination (Matsuoka et al., 1991). As expected, the marker gene was found to be expressed in the cells of the immune system that are known to undergo somatic cell recombination. Surprisingly, however, the marker gene was found to be expressed in many parts of the brain in a differential fashion, suggesting that somatic cell recombination also occurs in the brain. If these experiments are confirmed, it will revolutionize the molecular study of brain development.

Researchers estimate that there are about 100,000 different genes in higher mammals, perhaps 30% to 60% of which are uniquely expressed in the brain. At present, only about 5% have been cloned. The nature of cloning suggests that this 5% is skewed toward the most abundantly expressed genes. Thus, 95,000 genes still remain to be cloned, and these genes are likely to control the subtle aspects of brain development. The use of subtractive hybridization (Porteus, Ciaranello, & Rubenstein, in press), which isolates genes based on their preferential expression in one tissue over another, and enhancer/promoter traps (Friedrich & Soriano, 1991), which identify genes by trapping the regulatory elements of a gene using a marker transgene, are promising methods to isolate genes involved in brain development. But, in general, many more genes need to be cloned, by whatever method. It is highly probable that, as more genes are cloned, there will be many interesting surprises. In 20 years, we are likely to look back at our present molecular studies of brain development and conclude that we did not yet know the right questions to ask, much less the answers to those questions.

FUNDAMENTALS OF CHEMICAL NEUROTRANSMISSION

Overview

The transmission of neural impulses between neurons and their target cells takes place by the liberation of chemicals, called neurotransmitters, from the nerve terminal. Neurotransmitters are synthesized primarily in the nerve terminal by enzymes specialized for this task. The process of neurotransmitter synthesis is tightly regulated so as to maintain the usual concentration of neurotransmitters in the cell's basal state, and to ensure the rapid availability of neurotransmitters when conditions of high metabolic demand, such as stress, arise. The process of neurotransmitter release is regulated by the concentration of calcium ions in the cytoplasm of the nerve terminal. The released neurotransmitter diffuses across a short synaptic gap between the nerve terminal and its target cell, where it interacts with a membrane-bound receptor protein to stimulate a response in the target cell. In all cells, mechanisms exist to terminate neurotransmitter action, so that the cell can return to its resting state. All these processes are described in detail in the sections that follow.

The brain utilizes a bewildering array of neurotransmitters to carry out its function. These belong to a number of chemical families and, depending on the family from which they arise, the regulation of their metabolism differs. To prevent this review from becoming impossibly complicated, we first describe some of the properties of neurotransmitter metabolism that are common to all transmitters, regardless of their chemical origins. These processes are precursor uptake (processing for neuropeptides), transmitter synthesis, transmitter storage, release, interaction with receptors, and termination of transmitter action. We then describe the control of these processes for individual neurotransmitters.

Precursor Uptake

Most neurotransmitters are derived from parent (precursor) compounds through one or more enzyme-catalyzed conversions. For example, the catecholamine neurotransmitters—dopamine, norepinephrine, and epinephrine—are all derived from the amino acid tyrosine. Neurons possess specific transport systems that recognize and bind these precursor molecules and transport them into the cell for conversion into active neurotransmitter. The transport systems consist of protein molecules whose transport function is driven by metabolic energy from ATP; these are capable of transporting transmitter precursors into the cell against large concentration gradients.

An interesting exception to the transport of precursors into cells is seen in the neuropeptide family of compounds. Peptides are small polymers of amino acids (<100) that play an important role in metabolism as hormones (e.g., insulin), growth factors, and modulators of cell activity. Neuropeptides are peptides that are synthesized and stored within neurons, often colocalized with specific neurotransmitters, and are released upon neural stimulation. They interact with specific receptors and often play a neuromodulatory role, rather than acting as neurotransmitters. That is, they are coreleased with a transmitter, and, in interacting with their receptor, they modulate the action of the neurotransmitter with which they are released.

Neuropeptides arise from precursor compounds, but these are synthesized within the neuron, rather than taken up from the external environments. The propeptide precursors are usually large peptides or proteins (>100 amino acids). After synthesis in the endoplasmic reticulum, they undergo proteolytic cleavage into the shorter, biologically active peptide molecule.

Transmitter Synthesis

The conversion of a precursor into a neurotransmitter requires one or more metabolic reactions. Specific enzymes carry out these steps, which are usually subject to complex modes of regulation whose result is the acceleration or attenuation of the rate of neurotransmitter production, depending on specific demand conditions.

Transmitter Release

Once its synthesis is complete, the transmitter then enters a storage compartment, usually a membranous vesicle, where it resides until it is to be released. Transmitter release occurs when action potentials coursing down the axon cause a shift in the concentration of intracellular K^+ and Na^+ ions. This shift in ion concentration causes changes in intracellular voltage, which promotes the opening of voltage-gated calcium channels, allowing entry of calcium into the neuron. Calcium regulates the release of several neurotransmitters. The transmitter, and often the other chemical constitutents of the storage vesicle, is released into the synaptic space, where the transmitter interacts with specific receptor proteins.

Receptor Interaction

Receptors are protein molecules that interact with neurotransmitters in a highly specific manner; this interaction leads to a series of cellular events. Neurotransmitter receptors may be located on the presynaptic nerve terminal or on postsynaptic target cells. Presynaptic receptors are neurotransmitter receptors located on the nerve terminal; they act as sensors, monitoring the concentration of neurotransmitter released into the synaptic cleft. The interaction between a transmitter and a presynaptic receptor constitutes a form of negative feedback, in that stimulation of the presynaptic receptor leads to an attenuation of transmitter release.

Postsynaptic receptors also interact with neurotransmitters; here, their action may be either stimulatory (the target cell is activated) or inhibitory (target cell activity is attenuated). Most neurotransmitters can be either stimulatory or inhibitory, depending on the type of receptor they act on, where in the brain the interaction occurs, and what other neuronal circuits are impinging on the same target. Thus, with only a few exceptions, it is usually not possible to specify a particular neurotransmitter as being wholly stimulatory or wholly inhibitory.

The interaction between a receptor and a neurotransmitter follows certain basic rules. First, the interaction is specific for a particular neurotransmitter molecule and receptor. Thus, dopamine, a catecholamine neurotransmitter, binds with high affinity to dopamine receptors, but poorly to norepinephrine receptors, despite the close structural similarity between dopamine and norepinephrine, and not at all to serotonin receptors. Second, the interaction of a receptor and its ligand (any small molecule binding to a larger one, such as a protein) is stereospecific. Most biologic compounds, because they are organic molecules, contain an asymmetric center, usually a nitrogen atom, which allows them to exist in two mirror-image forms. These mirror images are termed isomers. In solution, they bend the plane of polarized light in different directions; thus, they are often termed optical isomers. One isomer will bend the plane of polarized light to the left (levo-isomer); the other will deflect it to the right (dextro-isomer). The levo-isomer is the active form of many biologic compounds (although not, interestingly enough, in the case of some hallucinogens, where the dextro-isomer is the biologically active form). Neurotransmitter receptors, and indeed any binding protein, can easily distinguish between the stereoisomers of a biologic compound, and can exhibit a preference of a millionfold or more between them. Third, the binding of a ligand to its receptor is saturable. At any given receptor concentration, only a certain fraction of the free ligand will be bound to it; increasing the ligand concentration further will not increase the amount of ligand bound.

Receptor-ligand interactions adhere to the basic rules of equilibrium kinetics for bimolecular reactions. Thus, the binding of a transmitter and receptor reaches an equilibrium after time, resulting in the formation of a receptor-ligand complex. At equilibrium, the concentration of each reactant and the receptor-ligand complex can be described by equation (1):

$$[R] + [L] \underset{k_{-1}}{\overset{k_1}{\rightleftarrows}} [RL] \qquad (1)$$

where [R] is the concentration of receptor, [L] is the concentration of ligand, and k_1 and k_{-1} are the reaction rate constants for the forward and reverse reactions, respectively. The relation between reactants and product is given by the equilibrium association constant, K_a, as:

$$K_a = \frac{[RL]}{[R][L]} = \frac{k_1}{k_{-1}}$$

Reference to equation (1) gives some useful insights into receptor-ligand interactions. At any given concentration of R or L, there will be a certain amount of RL formed (governed by k_1); at the same time, a certain amount of RL will dissociate back to free R and free L (governed by k_{-1}). The position of the equilibrium (whether favoring RL formation or dissociation) is given by the ratio of k and k_{-1}, which also defines the equilibrium constant. As this equation is written, the equilibrium constant K represents an association constant, because it specifies the amount of RL that is formed. Thus, if K is very small, most of the R and L will be free reactants, and the amount of RL will be small (equilibrium lies to the left). Conversely, if K is large, most R and L will be tied up in RL, and the equilibrium will lie to the right.

The position of the equilibrium is a measure of the affinity of the ligand for its receptor, and is an important way in which researchers compare different drugs or neurotransmitters for their affinity at receptor sites. By convention, receptor ligand interactions are described by the equilibrium *dissociation* constant, rather than the *association* constant. The equilibrium dissociation constant, K_d, is the inverse of the equilibrium association constant. Thus:

$$K_d = \frac{1}{K_a} = \frac{k_{-1}}{k_1} = \frac{[R][L]}{[RL]}$$

In receptor terminology, when K_d is low, most of R and L exist as RL; thus, the ligand has high affinity for the receptor, stays bound to it for prolonged periods, and dissociates slowly from it (k_{-1} low relative to k_1). K_d is always expressed in units of concentration (M or molar). Drugs or transmitters with high affinity for receptors usually have low K_ds, in the range of 10^{-10} to 10^{-8} M (0.1 nM to 10 nM).

Neurotransmitter receptors exist in myriad forms; however, they can be subdivided into two large families, based on their structural similarities and their probable origin from common ancestral genes. One family is the group of G-protein coupled receptors, the second family is the ligand-gated ion channel receptors. Both families exist in the brain and throughout the body, and both are used by the same neurotransmitters.

G-Protein Coupled Receptors

G-protein linked receptors are so named because they initiate cellular responses by coupling to an effector enzyme through an intermediary protein (guanyl nucleotide binding protein) known as a G-protein. This family includes receptors for nearly all of the known neurotransmitters. The common features that unite this family are: (a) G-protein linked receptors transduce signals by interacting with a G-protein, which connects them to an effector enzyme; activation of the receptor by the binding of neurotransmitter results in a modulation of the activity of the effector enzyme, leading to amplification or attenuation of cellular reactions; (b) G-protein linked receptors are monomeric proteins, that is, they consist of a single protein molecule; in contrast, ligand-gated channels and hormone receptors are made up of multiple protein subunits. All G-protein receptors so far characterized by molecular cloning techniques contain seven segments of 20 to 28 hydrophobic amino acids arranged in an α-helical configuration; these are thought to be membrane-spanning domains.

Much of our knowledge of the structure of G-protein receptors comes from molecular cloning. To date, the structures of more than two dozen G-protein linked receptors have been deduced from cloned cDNAs.

The interaction among the receptor, G-protein, and effector enzyme is complicated. A receptor acting through a G-protein modulates activity of the effector enzyme, causing a change in the rate of formation of the enzyme product, or "second messenger." This change may be either an increase or a decrease in second messenger formation, depending on whether receptor activation is stimulatory or inhibitory on the effector enzyme. Second messengers directly or indirectly activate a class of enzymes known as protein kinases, which in turn phosphorylate other intracellular target molecules, usually proteins. The process of phosphorylation can be associated with an increase or a decrease in the target molecule's biological activity.

Each element in the signal transduction cascade is represented by multiple subtypes, so that a great diversity in cellular responses is available. For example, each neurotransmitter interacts with at least 2 (and usually several more) transmitter-specific receptor subtypes. For example, dopamine acts on at least 4 discrete dopamine receptors; serotonin may act on as many as 10. These differ in their affinity for the transmitter and in the G-proteins to which they couple.

G-Proteins. There are several different G-proteins; each acts to activate or inhibit the activity of a particular effector enzyme. One form of G-protein, Gs, stimulates the enzyme adenylyl cyclase; another, Gi, inhibits the enzyme. A third G-protein, Gp, activates a completely different effector enzyme, phospholipase C. Other G-proteins probably inhibit this enzyme, and still others act on different effector enzymes.

Effector Enzymes. To date, three principal effector enzymes have been identified: (a) adenylyl cyclase, (b) phospholipase C, and (c) phospholipase A2. Adenylyl cyclase is the oldest and best studied of this group. Its activity can be stimulated or inhibited, depending on whether it is interacting with Gs or Gi. Adenylyl cyclase catalyzes the conversion of cyclic AMP from ATP. Phospholipase C catalyzes the conversion of the phospholipid phosphatidylinositol bis-phosphate (PIP2) into inisitol 1,4, 5-tris-phosphate (IP3) and diacyglycerol (DAG). Phospholipase A2 catalyzes the formation of arachodonic acid from a variety of phospholipid substrates.

Second Messengers. Cyclic AMP activates a protein kinase (protein kinase A), which in turn phosphorylates a variety of substrates, including proteins and sugars. Cyclic AMP also can bind to a protein (cyclic AMP binding protein), which acts as an initiator of gene transcription. Among the more important protein substrates for protein kinase A are neurotransmitter receptors, whose activity is modulated by phosphorylation, enzymes in the biosynthetic pathways for neurotransmitters, and ion channel proteins, whose patency is regulated by the addition or removal of a phosphate group.

IP3 and DAG are second messengers that act in different ways. IP3 directly activates a protein kinase, protein kinase C, which, like protein kinase A, phosphorylates a variety of substrates. DAG activates a different protein kinase, but does it indirectly. DAG causes a shift in intracellular calcium flux, leading to the efflux of calcium from stored intragranular pools into the cytoplasm. This results in the mobilization of calmodulin, a calcium binding protein, which in turn leads to activation of yet another protein kinase, CAM (calcium/calmodulin) kinase. Among the more interesting substrates for CAM kinase are proteins that when phosphorylated, act as initiators of gene transcription.

As this discussion illustrates, the final common pathway of receptor activation is the modulation of the activity of one or more protein kinases, all of which phosphorylate a wide variety of protein as well as nonprotein substrates. The subject of protein phosphorylation as a critical regulator of receptor activity, enzyme activity, membrane protein function, ion channel activity, membrane protein function, ion channel patency, and gene transcription, to name just a few events, has received enormous scientific attention over the past decade. The other side of this regulatory coin, the enzymatic removal of phosphate from proteins by phosphatases, is just now beginning to receive significant attention. This field is likely to be a very active area of investigation in the next few years.

Ligand-Gated Ion Channels

Some important brain neurotransmitters interact with receptors belonging to the ligand-gated family. In contrast to G-protein receptors, which act through effector enzymes and second messengers, ligand-gated receptors are ionic channels whose opening is triggered by binding to a neurotransmitter. Ligand-gated channels are large, structurally complex macromolecules through which flow sodium, potassium, chloride, or calcium ions.

All ligand-gated channels whose structures have been so far identified are made up of at least 3, and usually 4, distinct protein subunits. Thus, their molecular weights are quite large compared to the G-protein receptors (>200,000 daltons). The individual subunits of the ligand-gated receptors are encoded by distinct genes, whereas each G-protein receptor is encoded by a single gene. Moreover, several different forms of each ligand-gated channel subunit gene are likely to exist, based on what is known for existing channels. Thus, the potential for diversity among the ligand-gated channels is even greater than for the G-protein linked receptors. Consider the hypothetical possibility of a ligand-gated channel consisting of four protein subunits, a, b, g, and d. Each subunit is encoded by a distinct gene. However, at least 5 different forms of the α-subunit of this receptor have been identified, each the product of a different gene. If there are 5 α-subunit genes, and as few as 3 for each of the other subunits, then as many as $5 \times 3 \times 3 \times 3 = 135$ different combinations of this one neurotransmitter receptor could potentially exist. Based on what is already known for this family of receptors, 5 discrete forms of a particular subunit is not an unrealistic estimate, so the possibility of an astonishing variety of ligand-gated receptors for each neurotransmitter exists. The features that distinguish the subunit variants identified so far are subtle but definite differences in binding affinity for the neurotransmitter. This lends even further credence to the idea that the diversity of receptor subtypes for a given transmitter leads to important differences in the cell's potential for response to that transmitter.

Hormone Receptors

Hormones such as insulin, insulinlike growth factors, and others exert their cellular action via specific membrane-bound receptors. The hormone receptors belong to yet another receptor family, distinct from the G-protein and ligand-gated receptor families. The hormone receptors, of which the insulin receptor is a good model, consist of multimeric proteins made up of two subunits, a and b, with the structural formula a2b2.

ANATOMY AND DEVELOPMENT OF NEUROTRANSMITTER SYSTEMS IN THE BRAIN

Communication between nerve cells, and hence the conveying of neural information between functional regions of the brain, is a chemical process, and the specialized chemicals that mediate this process are called neurotransmitters. In neurobiological research, a number of criteria are used to determine that a chemical serves as a neurotransmitter in the brain (adapted from Cooper, Bloom, & Roth, 1982). The first is demonstration that a putative neurotransmitter is present in presynaptic terminals of select neural pathways. This has been accomplished using various chemical-anatomical techniques, such as uptake of radio-labeled transmitter agents, aldehyde-induced histofluorescence, enzyme histochemistry, and immunohistochemistry.

The second criterion is a demonstration that the transmitter candidate is released from nerve terminals in an appropriate activity-dependent or depolarization-dependent fashion. This has most easily been accomplished with *in vitro* preparations, where access to neural pathways is more direct and the extracellular chemical environment is easily monitored. However, with the development of such techniques as *in vivo* voltammetry and *in vivo* microdialysis, transmitter release can now be monitored in intact living animals, and even in conscious behaving animals, thus giving a truer indication of the behavioral and physiological correlates of neurotransmitter release.

The third criterion requires a similarity between the effects obtained with exogenous, pharmacological application of the presumed transmitter and those obtained by activating the endogenous pathway in which it exists. These studies have been conducted using physiological bioassays in isolated tissue (e.g., contraction of the isolated vas deferens), using systemic or local application of chemicals, or monitoring the electrophysiological activity of identified cells while applying drugs by pressure injection or microiontophoresis.

Similar preparations have been used in studies fulfilling the fourth criterion, which requires that pharmacological agents that block, or facilitate, or otherwise influence the action of the administered transmitter candidate also must exert identical effects on the neurally released substance. With a few notable exceptions, it has been difficult to fulfill all of the criteria described above for any putative neurotransmitter substances. However, by combining neuroanatomical, neurochemical, and neuropharmacological observations, and by relying on convergent indirect evidence (such as the direct demonstration that the synthetic enzymes for a presumed neurotransmitter exist in nerve terminals, and that the substance itself can be measured biochemically in the region), neuroscientists have now identified a number of chemical substances that are believed to serve as neurotransmitters in the brain.

Presumed neurotransmitters have traditionally been grouped together into a number of subclasses based on a variety of chemical and/or functional characteristics. The most straightforward classification of brain neurotransmitters has been on the basis of their chemical composition. The major chemical classes of transmitter include the monoamines (e.g., serotonin, dopamine, norepinephrine, epinephrine, and histamine), the amino acids (e.g., glutamate, aspartate, GABA, and glycine), acetylcholine, and the neuropeptides.

Further classifications are based on either functional or historical characteristics (see Bloom, 1984, 1986). One functional classification has become very useful in understanding the interactions between transmitters; it has to do with the nature of the postsynaptic response induced by the substance. On the one hand are the "classical" neurotransmitters, those that act postsynaptically to induce a direct excitation or inhibition in their target cells, most often through selective opening or closing of ion channels. On the other hand is a more recently defined class of "neuromodulators." The postsynaptic response induced by neuromodulators is subtler and more indirect; neuromodulators act to facilitate or attenuate the effects of other neurotransmitter inputs to the same target cell, often without exerting any direct effects of their own. To further complicate matters, the same substance can act both as a classical transmitter and as a neuromodulator in different, or even in the same brain regions, depending on the postsynaptic receptors present on the target cell, and the effectors to which they are coupled. Moreover, the influence of a neuromodulator on the response to a primary neurotransmitter may itself be dependent on the local context. A case in point is the interaction of the glutamatergic NMDA receptor with the more classical excitatory glutamatergic receptors (see below); the modulatory influence of glutamate acting at the NMDA receptor is itself dependent on the state of depolarization and recent activational history of the cell.

Another important issue for understanding neurotransmitter function and organization is that of colocalization of transmitters. Almost all conceivable combinations of transmitter classes have now been demonstrated to coexist within the same neurons (Lundberg & Hokfelt, 1983). Indeed, numerous peptides often coexist in a single cell, along with other neurotransmitters. Thus, although we can deal with each transmitter class and with the specific transmitter substances individually and independently for the purposes of discussion and review, it must be emphasized that the ultimate effect of transmitter release is always in a context that includes corelease of other substances from the same terminals, and convergence with other transmitters from other pathways released onto the same postsynaptic target. In fact, important functional subclassifications of neural cell types are emerging, based not only on the identity of a primary transmitter used by a group of cells, but also on the full complement of colocalized transmitters exhibited by subpopulations of cells within a group.

In this review, we present the major transmitter systems in the brain, grouped according to neurochemical classification. We first describe the primary neural systems that are known or believed to utilize these transmitters. We then discuss what is known about the development of these neurotransmitter systems. Finally, we examine a sampling of clinical disorders in which these identified neurotransmitter systems are thought to play a role.

Monoamines

First isolated in peripheral tissue, the monoamines are so named because they are synthesized from an amino acid or an amine precursor through a sequential process of enzymatic modification. The catecholamines (dopamine, norepinephrine, and epinephrine) are all synthesized from the amino acid tyrosine. Serotonin arises from tryptophan, and histamine is derived from histidine. Acetylcholine is derived from an amine, choline, rather than an amino acid. The monoamines, being not as ubiquitous nor as concentrated as the amino acids, tend to exist in regionally enriched brain tissue in nanomolar extracellular concentrations (Bloom, 1984; Krieger, 1986). The monoamines are also similar to each other in many functional characteristics; they are contained within a relatively small number of brain cells, which tend to be clustered in a limited number of nuclear regions within portions of the brain stem. However, these very defined and delimited clusters of monoaminergic cells tend to have widespread and divergent projections throughout all levels of the neuraxis. Thus, the monoaminergic systems represent key points through which specific external or internal stimuli can exert widespread effects through the entire brain via a well-localized system of neurochemical afferents. The functional roles attributed to monoaminergic systems, including regulation of sleep, stress, emotion, and selective attention, reflect this divergence in that they represent overriding modulatory influences on the functioning of the brain as a whole, rather than mediating any specific and defined response.

The monoaminergic systems as a whole develop very early in the course of neuronal ontogeny. The cells are among the first to be born and to differentiate. They also express the appropriate synthetic enzymes and neurotransmitters soon after they are born, and begin to send processes out shortly after reaching their final destinations. Moreover, monoaminergic nerve terminals reach their targets early in development. Because of the precocity of these systems, it has been suggested that they may play a role in the development of their target regions (Lauder, 1983, 1990). However, because of the observations that the monoaminergic neurons express their transmitters well before the maturation of their targets, and before they can make any synaptic connections (in fact, even while they are migrating to their respective brain stem locations), it has been suggested that any developmental role they play may be hormonal or paracrine rather than as a neurotransmitter, though very little data exist directly addressing this issue.

Catecholamines

The catecholamines are derived from the amino acid tyrosine. The first step in this biosynthetic pathway is conversion of tyrosine into L-dopa (L-dihydroxyphenyalanine) by tyrosine hydroxylase, the rate-limiting enzyme in all catecholamine biosynthesis. L-dopa is transformed by the action of dopa-decarboxylase into dopamine, which is the first catecholaminergic neurotransmitter in the series. In a number of cells, synthesis stops there and dopamine is the presumed neurotransmitter. However, in a subset of catecholaminergic cells containing the enzyme dopamine-B-hydroxylase, the transmitter norepinephrine (or noradrenaline) is synthesized from dopamine. Likewise, in a smaller subpopulation of cells, norepinephrine is further processed by phenylethanolamine-N-methyl transferase (PNMT) into epinephrine (adrenaline). Each of the catecholaminergic neurotransmitters is represented in a defined set of nerve cells, and each has a characteristic projection pattern and acts at a specific set of receptor subtypes. Each system has been implicated in a unique variety of physiological, behavioral, and neuropsychiatric processes.

The catecholaminergic cells in the brain were originally described by Dahlstrom and Fuxe (Dahlstrom & Fuxe, 1964b) and their colleagues, using the technique of aldehyde-induced catechol histofluorescence (Falck, Hillarp, Thieme, & Torp, 1962). They identified the major subgroups of catecholaminergic cells in the brain stem, and subsequently catalogued them (Dahlstrom & Fuxe, 1964a), along with the serotonergic brain stem neurons. They described the monoaminergic organization into series of cell clusters to which they applied a classification nomenclature in which catecholamine cell groups were numbered A1 to A13 (A14 and A15 were added later), and the serontonergic groups were designated B1 to B9. Catecholaminergic cell groups with the designation A1 to A7 contain norepinephrine, while groups A8 to A15 contain dopamine. Using histofluorescence, it was impossible at the time to distinguish epinephrine from norepinephrine; however, with the development of immunohistochemical techniques using antibodies to the synthetic enzyme PNMT, it was shown that epinephrine also exists in a group of cells distributed similarly to the medullary noradrenergic cell groups (A1 to A3). These adrenergic cell clusters were designated C1 to C3.

Dopamine

Localization and Function. Aside from a few minor dopaminergic cell groups located in the nucleus tractus solitarius and dorsal motor nucleus of the medulla oblongata, the dopamine-containing cells of the brain have been localized to a series of cell clusters occupying a region of the ventral brain stem from the rostral mesencephalon through the olfactory bulb (Dahlstrom & Fuxe, 1964a; Lindvall & Bjorklund, 1978, 1983; Ungerstedt, 1971).

The most rostral dopaminergic cell group is the A15 group of periglomerular cells in the olfactory bulb. These represent interneuronal components of local circuits in the olfactory bulb. The hypothalamus and surrounding regions contain several clusters of dopaminergic cells, A11 to A14, extending from the zona incerta and posterior hypothalamus (A11) through the dorsal and periventricular hypothalamic nuclei (A12 to A14). The hypothalamic cell groups provide the dopaminergic innervation of the spinal cord, thalamus, and hypothalamus, as well as interconnecting with other brain stem nuclei. A specialized component of the hypothalamic dopamine system, the tuberoinfundibular pathway, consists of the A12 cells of the arcuate and periventricular hypothalamic nuclei. Projecting primarily to the median eminence of the hypothalamus and to the intermediate lobe of the pituitary, the pathway acts to regulate the neuroendocrine release of prolactin.

The A9 dopaminergic cell group, located in the substantia nigra pars compacta is perhaps the most extensively studied of the catecholaminergic systems, because of its postulated role in the etiology of Parkinson's disease. These cells make up the nigrostriatal pathway, providing dopaminergic innervation of the neostriatum (the caudate nucleus and the putamen). The nigral dopaminergic neurons engage in a reciprocally interconnected feedback loop with a subset of the GABAergic projection neurons in the striasomal patch compartment of the neostriatum (Graybiel, 1990).

The other major projection system utilizing dopamine as a neurotransmitter is the mesotelencephalic system, originating in the A8 and A10 dopaminergic cells of the ventral tegmental area just medial to the substantia nigra. These cells project forward to areas of limbic cortex and related structures, including the prefrontal, cingulate, pyriform, and entorhinal cortices, the nucleus accumbens, olfactory tubercle, and septal nuclei. Because of their relative locations and the pattern of their projection systems, the A8, A9, and A10 dopamine groups have been postulated to form a somewhat topographic continuum rather than distinct systems, although there are important differences in the pattern of activity of cells within these regions, and different functional attributes ascribed to their target areas. The A9 nigrostriatal system has been primarily associated with extrapyramidal motor integration, but it has been suggested that the mesolimbic and mesocortical projection systems are important in reward and motivational processes.

Clinical Relevance. Among the most studied of roles for a putative neurotransmitter is the hypothesized involvement of dopamine in extrapyramidal motor control in the basal ganglia (substantia nigra, caudate, putamen, globus pallidus), and the role of dopamine in the pathological degeneration of this control system seen in Parkinson's syndrome. The most effective agent in alleviating the symptoms of Parkinson's disease, especially in its early stages, is the administration of L-dopa or carbidopa. The definitive histopathological feature of Parkinson's disease is a very selective and extensive loss of the dopaminergic striatonigral projection neurons (Hornykiewicz, 1982). The mesotelencephalic neurons do not seem to be affected to the same extent. Numerous laboratory studies have shown the importance of dopamine in the striatum in maintaining a coordinated extrapyramidal motor control, although the precise nature of this role has remained elusive. Perhaps the most dramatic clinical demonstration of the importance of the dopamine pathway in this system, and the effect of selectively lesioning it, was provided by the tragic case of MPTP (N-methyl-4-phenyl-1,2,5,6-tetrahydropyridine). This highly toxic synthetic drug was the unintentional byproduct of sloppy attempts to illicitly manufacture meperidine analogs for self-administration. Meperidine and related opiate derivatives had gained popularity as substitutes for heroin, and certain street supplies of home-synthesized meperidine congeners contained varying percentages of MPTP. When administered systemically (usually intravenously), a metabolite of MPTP ultimately proved to act as a potent and selective neurotoxin for dopamine-containing cells of the substantia nigra, and produced a debilitating condition that was neurologically and histologically identifiable with Parkinson's disease (Davis et al., 1979; Langston, Ballard, Tetrud, & Irwin, 1983). Subsequent animal studies have confirmed the toxic nature and mechanism of action of this compound, and have led to the development of an animal model that most closely approximates the human syndrome of Parkinson's in nonhuman primates (Phillips & Burns, 1984).

Conversely, hyperactivity of the striatonigral and the mesolimbic dopamine systems have also been implicated in important clinical situations. In contrast to Parkinson's, increased dopamine release in the limbic forebrain and prefrontal cortex has been implicated in the etiology of schizophrenia (Losonczy, Davidson, & Davis, 1987), and the most commonly used antipsychotic agents share in common the ability to block the action of dopamine. An important consideration in the pharmacological treatment of either of these syndromes is that anti-Parkinsonian agents (e.g., L-dopa) and antipsychotic drugs both interact with dopaminergic transmission, but in opposite directions and perhaps in different systems (nigrostriatal vs. mesotelencephalic). Thus, a careful titration of dose must be maintained to avoid undesirable side effects; overdosage in the first instance can produce psychotomimetic effects, and in the second case can produce a Parkinson's-like motor symptomatology. Likewise, the development of postsynaptic supersensitivity and rebound increases in dopaminergic transmission following the reduction or cessation of neuroleptic therapy can cause an exacerbation of psychotic symptoms, related to a rebound supersensitivity in the mesolimbic dopamine system, or to the motor syndrome of tardive dyskinesia, related to rebound supersensitivity in the nigrostriatal dopaminergic system (Diamond & Borison, 1986).

Another clinical syndrome related to dopaminergic activity, and especially important to child psychiatrists and pediatricians, is Attention Deficit/Hyperactivity Disorder (ADHD) (Shaywitz, Yager, & Klopper, 1986). This syndrome, and especially the hyperkinesis and attentional disorders with which it is associated, has been attributed at least in part to dysfunctions in the mesocortical and mesolimbic projection pathways from the ventral tegmental region. Although the mechanism is not well understood, the apparently paradoxical ability of stimulants such as amphetamine or methylphenidate to alleviate many of the behavioral disorders associated with ADHD are perhaps related to imbalances in the normal regulation of dopaminergic synaptic activity and feedback.

Also important clinically is the role that catecholaminergic neurotransmitters play in the process of drug abuse and addiction. Amphetamine and related compounds act primarily to release and prevent reuptake of catecholamines, and different components of the behavioral and physiological effects of amphetamines, especially hyperactivity, euphoria, and psychoticlike mentation, can be attributed to different catecholamine systems. Dopamine in particular has been implicated in the mechanism of action of cocaine, particularly its very powerful reinforcing and addictive properties. Cocaine acts mainly to prevent the reuptake of synaptically released dopamine, and increases in extracellular dopamine have been shown to occur in regions of the brain involved in reward and motivation following cocaine administration (Damsma, Day, & Fibiger, 1989; Fibiger & Phillips, 1987). The precise mechanisms are not well understood yet, but it seems likely that the ability of cocaine to directly activate the mesolimbic reward system is directly related to its potential for abuse, and this system represents a possible target for pharmacologic therapies intended to alleviate drug craving and dependence.

Norepinephrine

Localization and Function. The noradrenergic cell groups of the brain are all located within the caudal brain stem, from the rostral pons back to the caudal medulla, and are loosely organized into two discontinuous columns. One column, situated in the ventral and lateral aspects of the brain stem, comprises, from caudal to rostral, the A1, A3, A5, and A7 cell groups. The second column, situated in the dorsal and medial portions of the pons and medulla, includes the A2, A4, and A6 groups (Dahlstrom & Fuxe, 1964a; Lindvall & Bjorklund, 1978, 1983; Ungerstedt, 1971).

The medullary noradrenergic cell groups include the A1 cluster in the caudal ventrolateral medulla and the A2 neurons in the caudal nucleus tractus solitarius. The A3 cells are a poorly defined group found rostral to the A1 cluster, in the region just dorsal to the inferior olive. These medullary cell groups, which are heavily interconnected with each other as well as with other catecholaminergic cell regions in the rostral medulla and pons, have been primarily implicated in control of the cardiovascular system and fluid homeostasis. Activation of the noradrenergic groups of cells in the medulla appears to exert an inhibitory influence on other regions that act to maintain normal blood pressure, although there has been some dispute as to whether these effects are in fact related to noradrenergic activity. Both the A1 and A2 cell groups also innervate the paraventricular and supraoptic nuclei of the hypothalamus. The noradrenergic input to these neuroendocrine regions has been most strongly connected to a regulation of vasopressin release, with activation of the ascending noradrenergic pathways enhancing the release of vasopressin (Blessing & Willoughby, 1985; Day, Ferguson, & Renaud, 1984).

In the caudal pons, along the ventrolateral edge of the brain stem, is found the A5 cell group. This small cluster of cells projects to the spinal cord, where it may influence sympathetic outflow via a connection with the autonomic intermediolateral cell column (Loewy, 1982), and may also be involved in modulation of spinal and lower brain stem motor activity. Within the brain stem, the A5 cells are interconnected with other catecholaminergic nuclei, as well as with cranial nerve motor nuclei (Grzanna, Chee, & Akeyson, 1987; Lyons & Grzanna, 1988).

Proceeding forward, the next group of noradrenergic cells in the ventrolateral column is the A7 collection of neurons. The A7 group actually is composed of several small clusters of noradrenergic cells in the rostral pons, including the parabrachial region, the Kolliker-Fuse nucleus, and portions of the lateral reticular formation. The A7 cells also are heavily interconnected with the other catecholamine cell groups in the brain stem. They innervate several brain stem cranial nerve motor nuclei, both autonomic (e.g., dorsal motor nucleus of the vagus) and somatic (e.g., facial and trigeminal motor nuclei) (Fulwiler & Saper, 1984; Grzanna et al., 1987; Lyons & Grzanna, 1988). The A7 neurons, like most of the other noradrenergic cell groups, project to the spinal cord, innervating the ventral motor regions, and also forward to the hypothalamus and the amygdala. It has been suggested that the A7/parabrachial region is a junction in an important, reciprocally interconnected circuit linking areas of the limbic forebrain, such as the amygdala and septal nuclei, to primary autonomic regulatory regions of the medulla (e.g., NTS, dorsal motor nucleus), and that this circuit serves to translate emotional or perceptual information into physiological autonomic responses (Block & Hoffman, 1987; Cechetto, Ciriello, & Calaresu, 1983).

Also in the pons is the A6 noradrenergic cell group of the locus coeruleus (LC). The LC, located along the lateral edges of the fourth ventricle in the central gray, contains the majority of noradrenergic cells in the brain. The A6 neurons in the LC are highly responsive to sensory stimuli of several modalities, and their activity is most highly correlated with the level of behavioral arousal. This cell group has been implicated in several higher-order processes such as sleep, arousal and attention, the integration of emotional stimuli with autonomic responses, anxiety and the stress response, and the mechanisms of selective attention (for reviews, see Amaral & Sinnamon, 1977; Foote, Bloom, & Aston-Jones, 1983; Mason & Fibiger, 1979; Redmond & Huang, 1979). The LC is heavily interconnected with other catecholaminergic and monoaminergic nuclei, but also has numerous projections throughout the entire neuraxis, being the sole source of noradrenergic innervation to the cerebral cortex, hippocampus, and cerebellum, and also projecting to a variety of limbic and sensory nuclei in the amygdala, basal forebrain, thalamus, and hypothalamus. The A6 neurons innervate sensory nuclei in the mesencephalon, pons, and medulla, including the superior and inferior colliculi. The LC provides noradrenergic input to the dorsal horn of the spinal cord, and it has even been suggested that the LC provides the noradrenergic innervation of pial blood vessels in the brain. In this regard, given the extent of its CNS innervation pattern, the nature of the multimodal stimuli to which it responds, its relation to stress and arousal, and the close correlation between LC and the activity of the peripheral sympathetic nervous system, it has been postulated that the LC represents a central branch of the sympathetic nervous system with the brain as its target. This widespread influence and the dynamic response to a number of complex stimuli are even more remarkable, given that this very compact nucleus receives input from a very limited number of regions in the brain, with the major afferents being in the rostral ventrolateral medulla and the nucleus prepositus hypoglossi, both in the medulla. These two regions contain, among other cell clusters, the C1 and C3 adrenergic cell groups. Thus, the LC represents an important means by which peripheral input, via a limited number of medullary relays, is disseminated throughout the brain and spinal cord, and influences the operation of a vast number of neural structures. This divergent characteristic is reflected in the higher-order, complex behavioral and integrative functions with which it has been connected.

Associated with the A6 neurons in the LC is a small cluster of noradrenergic cells—the A4 cell group—extending up into the roof of the fourth ventricle. There are also a number of noradrenergic cells extending ventrally and laterally into the reticular formation of the brain stem below the LC, and these comprise the subcoeruleus region. These cells are distinct from the nearby A7 neurons of the lateral pontine reticular formation. The demarcation between the A7 neurons and those of the subcoerulear complex is not entirely clear, especially in species in which the LC itself is not a compact, homogenous structure. Nonetheless, both the A4 and the subcoerulear region are typically considered together with the A6/LC complex.

A great deal of research has been generated to investigate the presumed neuromodulatory role of norepinephrine—specifically, the A6 noradrenergic system—in the CNS. Several electrophysiological results have suggested that the primary effects of norepinephrine on target cell activity are in modulating the excitatory or inhibitory effects of other neurotransmitters (Segal, 1985; Woodward, Moises, Waterhouse, Hoffer, & Freedman, 1979). Extrapolating from neurophysiology to behavior is often difficult, especially in circuits as complex as those in the cerebral cortex, but it has been suggested that these neuromodulatory cellular effects are related to such behavioral and physiological processes as attention, arousal, stress response, or vigilance (Aston-Jones, 1985; Foote et al., 1983).

Clinical Significance. It has been suggested, mostly from animal work, that the A6 noradrenergic cell group in the LC is involved in the processes mediating stress and arousal. An extension of this has been to suggest that this group may be an important component of the neuropathology arising from the stress response (Stone, 1983). The LC may be an important integrator of emotional or perceptual processes and the autonomic responses to stressful stimuli. Experimental work in both animals and humans has shown that increases in noradrenergic neurotransmission can induce anxiety, and that stress-induced behaviors in animals as well as humans' perception of anxiety are both associated with increased noradrenergic synaptic activity. This has been extended clinically to the etiology of panic disorders (Charney et al., 1990). Hyperactivity or, more importantly, hyperreactivity in the LC noradrenergic system may be the basis of the clinical syndrome involving panic attacks. In a related context, the physiological and emotional/behavioral symptoms of distress that occur during withdrawal from opioid drugs such as heroin have been associated with hyperactivity in central noradrenergic neurons, particularly in the LC. Clonidine, an alpha-2 noradrenergic agonist, inhibits noradrenergic neuronal activity through an autoreceptor mechanism, and is effective in reducing the symptoms of opioid withdrawal. Moreover, it appears that clonidine and opioid agents acting at the mu receptor subtype induce similar effects on noradrenergic neurons, and may in fact share an overlapping effector substrate within these cells.

A good case has also been made for an involvement of the ascending noradrenergic system in the etiology of ADHD (Zametkin & Rapoport, 1987). Biochemical measurements indicate a disorder in the metabolism of catecholamines and the current therapeutic agent of choice, methylphenidate, as well as amphetamine affect neurotransmission at both noradrenergic and dopaminergic synapses. The mechanism of action of the stimulant drugs in alleviating the behavioral and cognitive abnormalities of ADHD is still not clearly understood. The efficacy of stimulants is somewhat paradoxical: hyperactivity and the cognitive symptoms of ADHD would most likely be associated with an increased central catecholaminergic transmission, which is also a common component of stimulant action in the CNS. Thus, it is possible that ADHD represents a disorder in the postsynaptic receptor sensitivity for catecholamines, or that the primary deficit is not an abnormal tonic release of central catecholamines, but an inappropriate reactivity in response to activating stimuli. Given the presumed role of norepinephrine as a global neuromodulator, a disruption of normal catecholaminergic receptor sensitivity or of the coordinated pattern of release in response to activating stimuli could well produce the characteristic behavioral and thought disorders of ADHD. It is possible that the mechanism of action of stimulants could be to restore the normal homeostatic balance in effective noradrenergic neurotransmission. In support of this, other agents that have therapeutic benefit in the treatment of ADHD include a class of tricyclic antidepressants (e.g., desipramine) that have a degree of selectivity for the noradrenergic system, and monoamine oxidase inhibitors, which also increase effective noradrenergic transmission (Zametkin & Rapoport, 1987). These treatments, while affecting many systems, have been shown to normalize noradrenergic metabolism in the periphery to a degree that is indicative of the therapeutic efficacy in alleviating the symptoms of ADHD.

Although such symptoms as anxiety and panic attack have been associated with increased noradrenergic transmission in the A6 system, a vast literature has related decreases in noradrenergic functioning to other affective disorders, particularly depression (Sweeney & Maas, 1979; Weiss, Glazer, Pohorecky, Bailey, & Schneider, 1979). Certain of the tricyclic antidepressants, such as imipramine, while influencing all monoaminergic systems to a certain extent, have particularly potent and somewhat selective effects on the noradrenergic systems. The mode of action of this class of drug is to block the reuptake of synaptically released norepinephrine—hence, in theory, prolonging its synaptic action and facilitating overall noradrenergic transmission. Numerous experiments in animals support the idea that depression is related to a decrease in functional noradrenergic transmission. An animal model for human depression in which decreased noradrenergic activity has been demonstrated is the paradigm of learned helplessness (see Weiss et al., 1979). Following a series of inescapable, unpredictable, and uncontrollable shocks, experimental animals will assume a behavioral condition with characteristics very similar to those of depression. They ultimately will not attempt to escape even when it is possible to do so (Overmeier & Seligman, 1967). Neurochemical data suggest that this behavioral syndrome is associated with a decrease in effective noradrenergic transmission in the A6 system. This model also suggests a mechanism for the association between stress and depression. However, it is very difficult to specify cause and effect in paradigms such as this, and evidence that is at least as compelling implicates other neurotransmitter systems, especially serotonin, in the etiology of depression.

Another set of arousal-related dysfunctions with which the noradrenergic cells of the rostral pons have been associated involves sleep disorders. A long history of research links the noradrenergic cell groups with the mechanisms of sleep. In general, agents that elevate noradrenergic activity (e.g., amphetamine) are arousing; agents that decrease noradrenergic activity are sedating. The locus coeruleus, which provides the main ascending and descending adrenergic output to most of the neural axes, appears to be important in the regulation of sleep (Ramm, 1979; Steariade & Hobson, 1976). This brain region is active during waking and silent during rapid eye movement (REM) sleep (Aston-Jones & Bloom, 1981; Rasmussen, Morilak, & Jacobs, 1986). An elevation of α2-adrenergic receptors in this region has been found in nacoleptic canines (Fruhstoffer et al., 1989). Elevations in alpha 1-adrenergic receptors have also been found in specific brain regions (Mignot et al., 1989), particularly limbic areas, of narcoleptic canines. Prazosin, an alpha-1 adrenergic antagonist, induces severe attacks of cataplexy (loss of muscle tone analogous to that which occurs during REM sleep) in narcoleptic patients as well as canines (Mignot, Guilleninault, & Bowersox, 1988; Mignot, Guilleminault, Bowersox, Kilduff, & Dement, 1987; Mignot, Guilleminault, Bowersox, Rappaport, & Dement, 1988). Thus, it is clear that alterations in brain adrenergic systems can profoundly influence sleep and wakefulness. Because changes in sleep patterns are associated with many psychiatric disorders, insight into the underlying biochemical abnormality or imbalance may be gained.

The noradrenergic cell groups in the rostral part of the brain stem have been implicated in the integration of behavioral and physiological functions; those in the medulla have been linked to more basic autonomic regulatory processes. A variety of experimental models for hypertension have been associated with changes in central noradrenergic neurotransmission (Chalmers, 1978), and pharmacological agents that reduce central noradrenergic activity are effective antihypertensives. Several stimuli, including stress, can induce release of both central and peripheral norepinephrine. This finding, together with the fact that sympathetic vasoconstriction induced by peripheral norepinephrine is the primary mechanism by which phasic increases in arterial blood pressure occur, makes it highly probable that at least a subset of hypertensive syndromes can be attributed to central and/or peripheral dysfunctions in the noradrenergic neurotransmitter systems.

Epinephrine

Localization and Function. The final step in the catecholaminergic synthetic pathway is a conversion of norepinephrine to epinephrine, also called adrenaline. Epinephrine is the major transmitter secreted hormonally into the bloodstream by the chromaffin cells of the adrenal medulla. It plays a powerful role in blood glucose regulation, blood pressure maintenance, and heart rate control, and it participates in the overall responses of the sympathetic nervous system. In the brain, epinephrine is located in a subset of catecholaminergic cells in the medulla oblongata (Hokfelt, Johansson, & Goldstein, 1984; Mefford, 1988). The C1, C2, and C3 adrenergic cell groups show a distribution very similar to the A1, A2, and A3 noradrenergic groups, although the adrenergic cells all lie just rostral to their noradrenergic counterparts.

The C1 group of adrenergic cells, by far the most numerous, reside in the rostral ventrolateral medulla, just below the nucleus ambiguus, and just caudal to the facial motor nucleus. At their most caudal extent, there is considerable overlap with the A1 noradrenergic neurons of the caudal ventrolateral medulla. The C1 cells have been mostly associated with cardiovascular regulatory processes, being located in a part of the medulla that is heavily involved with excitatory drive to the sympathetic nervous system. This area receives input from the nucleus tractus solitarius and the caudal ventrolateral medulla, and the adrenergic cells in this region project primarily to the intermediolateral cell column in the spinal cord and the paraventricular nucleus of the hypothalamus. There are minor projections to other regions, especially to other monoaminergic cell groups such as the A6 group in the LC. It has been very difficult, however, to ascribe specific functions to any particular group of cells in this region because it is a highly heterogenous part of the reticular formation. The ventrolateral medulla contains a number of intermingled cell types utilizing a variety of transmitters and cotransmitters, with different functions and interconnections.

The C2 group of adrenergic cells in the rostral nucleus tractus solitarius also projects to the spinal cord and hypothalamus, as well as to the ventrolateral medulla, and this group has also been implicated primarily in autonomic regulation. The remaining C3 adrenergic group of cells is a very small cluster located in the dorsomedial medulla at its juncture with the caudal pons in the vicinity of the nucleus prepositus hypoglossi extending down near the midline into the reticular formation. Very little is known about this group of cells, although there is indication that they may also project to the spinal cord and hypothalamus.

Clinical Significance. There is little data regarding the role of the adrenergic brain cells in any clinical disorder, other than characteristics that they may have in common with the noradrenergic systems discussed above, including common target sites and similar receptors and postsynaptic receptor mechanisms. It has been suggested, for instance, that the C1 adrenergic cells in the rostral ventrolateral medulla may participate in the development of hypertension, although more recent evidence suggests that excitatory amino acids may be the descending transmitters responsible for activation of the sympathetic nervous system (Guyenet, Haselton, & Sun, 1989). Epinephrine may contribute to the coordination and integration of the stress response via projections to the neuroendocrine portions of the hypothalamus, and interconnections with other brain stem catecholaminergic cell groups, and thus may also contribute to the pathology of stress. However, no firm or convincing data implicate the adrenergic systems as distinct from the noradrenergic cell groups.

Development of Catecholamine Pathways. In the rat (gestation 22 days), final division and differentiation of noradrenergic neurons occur between embryonic days E10 and E13, and the process for dopaminergic neurons occurs between embryonic days E11 and E15 (Lauder & Bloom, 1974). Tyrosine hydroxylase is detectable immunohistochemically by E12.5 (Specht, Pickel, Joh, & Reis, 1981a), after the cells have completed their final mitotic division but while they are still migrating to their final destinations. At this time, there are four identifiable groups of TH-containing neurons, corresponding to the A1–3, A4–7, A8–10, and A11–14 groups of cells. Shortly thereafter (E13 for DA and E14 for NE), catecholamine histofluorescence is first observed, indicating the presence of neurotransmitter (Lauder & Bloom, 1974; Olson & Sieger, 1972). These still-immature catecholaminergic cells begin to send out processes bearing growth cones as the cells continue migration. By E14.5, dopamine-containing terminals first appear in limited portions of the neostriatum. By E18, the catecholaminergic cell distribution and appearance essentially resemble those of the adult, with the exception that the dopaminergic cells in the olfactory bulb emerge later, and a few tyrosine hydroxylase-immunoreactive cells are evident in the cerebral cortex. Whether these transiently expressed cortical catecholaminergic cells are dopaminergic or noradrenergic, they disappear by E21 and are not observed in the adult brain (Specht, Pickel, Joh & Reis, 1981b). In the late prenatal period, E18–E21, the efferent fiber pathways become much more extensive. At this stage, all the major catecholaminergic pathways to the spinal cord and forebrain, and within the brain stem, have become apparent. Terminal fields in the striatum, hypothalamus, basal forebrain, and cortex increase in density, although terminal innervation is still not present in all target areas by this time. In the cortex, the fibers run in two parallel bundles in the superficial molecular layer, and in a region below the cortical plate in the subplate region. Prenatal innervation of the cortex is limited primarily to this transient subplate area (Specht et al., 1981b). The adult pattern of target innervation is not established until 3 to 5 weeks postnatally

(Coyle, 1973). Within the catecholamine cell regions themselves, synapse formation on the somata and dendrites of the neurons begins in the late postnatal period, between E18 and E21, but the majority of afferent connections are established postnatally, with a period of accelerated synapse formation occurring between day 15 and day 30 (Lauder & Bloom, 1975). The monoaminergic systems in the brain are among the earliest to develop. The majority of the prenatally appearing afferents to these monoamine cell groups would themselves also be monoaminergic, with the majority of nonmonoaminergic afferents making synaptic connections in the period of postnatal synaptogenesis. However, electrophysiological studies have shown that, although the majority of noradrenergic cells recorded in fetal E18 rats are not spontaneously active, they can be activated phasically in response to various sensory stimuli, and their responses are similar to those of the adult LC (Sakaguchi & Nakamura, 1987). This suggests that at least a portion of functional afferent inputs, presumably glutamatergic, must be established in the late prenatal period. Also, regarding the functional output of the catecholamine systems, a limited number of behavioral pharmacological studies employing releasers such as amphetamine have suggested that these systems have made functional connection with their targets in the early neonate (Fibiger, Lytle, & Campbell, 1970).

A similar pattern of early catecholaminergic development has been described in the human CNS (Freeman et al., 1991; Verney, Zecevic, Nikolic, Alvarez, & Berger, 1991). In one study, tyrosine hydroxylase immunoreactive cells were reported to appear in the mesencephalic ventricular zone at 6.5 weeks, with a few cells beginning to migrate toward the ventral mesencephalon at that time (Freeman et al., 1991). In another study, both TH- and DBH-positive migrating cells were observed in the ventral mesencephalon, primordial locus coeruleus, and medulla oblongata as early as 5 weeks gestational age (Verney et al., 1991). These cells show extensive process elaboration and extension by 6 weeks, and display axonal tracts representing the ascending ventral and dorsal noradrenergic bundles and the nigrostriatal tract. At 8.5 weeks, a larger number of dopaminergic cells appear in the ventral mesencephalon and extend neuritic processes toward the striatum. The first dopaminergic axons reach the neostriatum by 9 weeks, and dopaminergic neurogenesis is essentially complete by approximately 11 weeks. Thus, in the human, as in the rat and other species studied, the catecholaminergic neurotransmitter systems are among the first to develop, acquiring the capability to synthesize and perhaps release neurotransmitter well before they themselves are innervated by extrinsic afferents, and preceding the establishment of synaptic contact with their still immature target areas.

Serotonin, Histamine, and Acetylcholine

Serotonin

Serotonin, like norepinephrine, exists in a widely divergent projection system originating in a very restricted, well-defined set of cells. Also, like norepinephrine, the serotonergic projection system innervates all levels of the neuraxis, from neocortex through spinal cord. This divergent system is thus in a position to influence several functionally distinct regions of the CNS simultaneously, in response to a common stimulus. The postsynaptic action of serotonin has also been classified as neuromodulatory in several of these target regions, and the proposed functions of serotonin in these systems reflect the divergent and neuromodulatory nature of this neurotransmitter.

Localization and Function. Serotonin is localized to a series of cell groups from the most caudal portion of the brain stem, at the spinomedullary juncture, up through the rostral mesencephalon (Steinbusch, 1984). Numbered B1-B9 in early classification studies, these cell groups tend to be situated on the midline of the brain stem. As a group, they are referred to as the raphe nuclei. The various raphe nuclei can be identified as distinct regions of the brain stem, but varying proportions of cells in each region actually contain serotonin. Also, there is a great deal of overlap between regions in terms of the projection targets and sources of innervation. Thus, in the description that follows, we merely provide an outline of the major projection systems of the raphe nuclei as a whole, bearing in mind that this is something of a generalization.

Starting at the hindmost aspect of the brain stem, the B1 and B2 cell groups are located on the medullary midline, in the nucleus raphe pallidus on the ventral midline and the nucleus raphe obscurus just above it. The third medullary group of serotonergic neurons, B3, is in the nucleus raphe magnus in the rostral medulla, located on the midline at the very bottom of the brain, with two well-defined lateral extensions in the rostral ventrolateral medulla on either side. These medullary serotonergic cells project primarily to the spinal cord, innervating all regions, including the dorsal and ventral horns, as well as the intermediolateral cell column. These spinal projections are thought to be involved in sensorimotor modulation, pain perception and analgesia, and basic autonomic regulation. The lateral B3 cells represent a serotonergic component of the rostral ventrolateral medullary pressor region, involved in primary control of the cardiovascular system. The midline B3 cells are believed to be important in the mediation of pain perception and pain modulation. In addition to their spinal connections, this group of cells is connected with the brain stem central gray. This circuit is thought to underlie serotonin's involvement in analgesia, and is possibly a target for the analgesic effects of opiates such as morphine (Basbaum & Fields, 1984). There are also numerous interconnections between medullary catecholamine cell groups and medullary serotonergic cell groups; their interaction is maintained in the more rostral regions as well.

In the pons are found the B5 serotonergic neurons of the nucleus raphe pontis, situated just dorsal to the most rostral extension of the raphe magnus. The density of serotonin-containing cells in this region is very low. Just above the raphe pontis, underlying the cerebellum, is another sparse group of serotonergic cells, the B4 group. These cells merge rostrally with the caudal extension of the B6 cell group, being the most posterior portion of the dorsal raphe complex.

The rostral pons and caudal mesencephalon contain the sources of most of the ascending serotonergic projections to the forebrain and cortex. The B6 cells caudally and B7 cells rostrally make up the serotonergic components of the dorsal raphe nucleus. The rostral B7 group is a very dense collection of serotonergic cells in the central gray, lying between the fiber pathways of the medial longitudinal fasciculus. An impressive cluster of serotonergic cells extends up and fans outward to form lateral "wings" in the pontine-mesencephalic reticular formation. Just below the dorsal raphe, located in the nucleus raphe medianus, are the B8 serotonergic cells. Included in this rostral serotonergic complex are the B9 cells in the interpeduncular nucleus and the nucleus linearis. The B6 to B9 complex of cells provides serotonergic innervation of the basal forebrain, striatum, hippocampus, neocortex, and amygdala. They also innervate the hypothalamus and limited regions of the thalamus, as well as several brain stem nuclei and the cerebellum. The rostral serotonergic neurons are heavily interconnected with catecholaminergic neuronal groups in the brain stem, including the locus coeruleus and substantia nigra.

As with norepinephrine, the behavioral and physiological functions ascribed to serotonin, as well as the neuropathological conditions with which it has been associated, reflect the divergent and widespread nature of its CNS projection systems. Serotonin has been implicated in sleep and arousal, stress, feeding, anxiety and affect, learning and memory, developmental regulation, circadian rhythmicity, thermoregulation, hormonal regulation, motor control, sexual behavior, hallucinogenesis, cardiovascular regulation, pain modulation, and aggression (Wilkinson & Dourish, 1991). These various processes are perhaps more indicative of the variety of primary target circuits that are innervated by serotonin than of an essential role in the mediation of any of them; serotonin, like norepinephrine, has been postulated to act as a typical neuromodulatory neurotransmitter.

Clinical Significance. Clinically, serotonin has been most strongly associated with affective disorders such as depression. Dysfunctions of serotonergic metabolism and receptors have been noted in patients suffering from depression, and particularly in suicide victims (Mann, Arango, & Underwood, 1990). One class of antidepressants, including chlorimipramine, blocks the reuptake of serotonin and, in the short term at least, increases the effective transmission at serotonergic synapses. The most common and most effective antidepressant currently in clinical application is fluoxetine, a very selective blocker of serotonin uptake. A novel class of drugs that act as agonists at the 5-HT1A receptor has also been shown to be effective in learned helplessness, the animal model for depression (Wilkinson & Dourish, 1991).

However, although all these agents may be effective antidepressants, there is a general problem of time course: a significant "therapeutic delay" of several days to weeks occurs before these pharmacological agents relieve the behavioral, physiological, and cognitive signs of depression; the cellular and biochemical effects are much more rapid. Thus, an alternative explanation has been proposed that evokes a selective action at serotonergic autoreceptors (Blier, de Montigny, & Chaput, 1990; de Montigny, Chaput, & Blier, 1990). Activation of the 5-HT1A receptor, thought to be a somatodendritic autoreceptor, shuts off the activity of serotonergic neurons. Likewise, 5-HT1B autoreceptors are located on serotonergic nerve terminals and inhibit the release of serotonin into the synapse. Persistent tonic activation of the autoinhibitory 5-HT1A and 5-HT1B receptors, through reuptake blockade or direct pharmacological activity, leads to a powerful down-regulation and desensitization of these receptors. As they are themselves thought to homeostatically inhibit serotonergic neurotransmission, the result is a rebound activation, or "escape," resulting in a more stable increase in release of serotonin from the terminals (Blier et al., 1990; de Montigny et al., 1990). Not only does this hypothesis explain the mechanism of action of a diverse array of antidepressant agents, but it also reconciles the time course of action with the "therapeutic lag" of most drug treatments.

Another neuropsychiatric syndrome that has been associated with a decrease in serotonergic function is the spectrum of obsessive-compulsive disorders (Winslow & Insel, 1990). Most of the evidence supporting this hypothesis is derived from clinical observations of the efficacy of (a) serotonergic reuptake blockers in alleviating the symptoms of obsessive-compulsive disorder, and (b) serotonergic antagonists to exacerbate the condition.

Similar inferences have been made about the role of serotonin in certain feeding disorders. Decreased central serotonergic activity has been implicated in bulimia nervosa (Goldbloom & Garfinkel, 1990). This is again related to the alleviating effects of serotonin reuptake blockers, and also to reduced metabolite concentrations in CSF. Moreover, animal experiments have suggested a role for serotonin in feeding behavior and satiety mechanisms. It has been suggested that bulimia may be the result of a disrupted feedback loop in which dieting or abnormal eating patterns could cause disregulation of central serotonin synthesis through effects on tryptophan metabolism. This in turn could cause an impairment in central control of feeding and satiety (Goldbloom & Garfinkel, 1990).

With regard to drugs of abuse, serotonin has a long history in research on the mechanism of action of hallucinogens. The hallucinogenic activity of phenyalkylamines, indolealkylamines, and related chemical agents such as LSD is correlated with the degree to which they act as agonists or partial agonists at serotonergic receptors, particularly of the 5-HT2 subtype (Glennon, 1990; Heym & Jacobs, 1987).

Development of Serotonin Pathways. Serotonergic neuronal systems also develop quite early relative to their target sites (Lauder & Bloom, 1974; Lidov & Molliver, 1982; Wallace & Lauder, 1983). In the rat, serotonin neurons begin differentiating at about E11. Serotonin is first detected by histofluorescence or immunohistochemistry in neurons of the rostral raphe at E13, just after they leave the ventricular zone and are still migrating. The caudal raphe cells develop serotonin immunoreactivity about 1 to 2 days later. The serotonergic neurons extend processes immediately after they appear, and axon terminals first invade the cortex from E17 to E18. The cells of the raphe also achieve their mature position by this time.

A similarly precocious developmental pattern for serotonergic systems has been described in the human brain (Olson, Boreus, & Sieger, 1973; Shen, Luo, Zheng, & Yew, 1989). The same rostral-caudal developmental gradient observed in the rat is also seen in the human brain. The serotonergic cells of the primordial rostral raphe appear as early as 7 weeks of gestational age, and by 10 weeks they have organized into distinct recognizable nuclei representing the B4-B9 groups. Cells in the caudal raphe emerge slightly later, by about 14 weeks. By 27 to 28 weeks of gestation, the serotonergic cells have basically assumed their final configuration.

Histamine

Histamine has long been known to exist in the brain, although most of the CNS histamine content is associated with mast cells, as it is in the periphery. Only recently, advances in anatomical and biochemical techniques to demonstrate localization and neural release of histamine have enabled a conclusive role as a neurotransmitter to be sufficiently confirmed (see Hough, 1988, for review).

Localization and Function. Histamine is derived from histidine by the enzymatic action of histidine decarboxylase. Much of what is known about the localization of histaminergic neurons in the brain was revealed by immunohistochemistry's use of antibodies against this synthetic enzyme (Watanabe et al., 1984) in a manner analogous to the demonstration of catecholaminergic or serotonergic localization by visualizing immunoreactivity to their synthetic enzymes (see above). In addition, recent innovations allowing the generation of antibodies to small neurotransmitter molecules such as the monoamines or amino acids have made it possible to visualize directly the localization of the transmitter itself, and this too has been applied to histamine (Airaksinen & Panula, 1988; Inagaki et al., 1988; Steinbusch & Mulder, 1984).

Histamine-containing neurons, located in a highly restricted region of the brain, nonetheless project fairly extensively. Histaminergic neurons are found almost exclusively within magnocellular nuclei of the posterior hypothalamus, from the ventral premamillary nuclei back through the caudal postmamillary region. Histaminergic projections are most dense in the hypothalamus and thalamus. Most functions ascribed to neurally released histamine have to do with the innervation of they hypothalamus, which is most concentrated in rostral hypothalamic regions and in the median eminence, arcuate nuclei, and infundibulum extending into the neurohypophysis. Such postulated functions include thermoregulation and neuroendocrine regulation, especially modulation of vasopressin and prolactin release. Other histaminergic targets include the posterior hypothalamus, cerebral cortex, amygdala, and basal forebrain; fewer fibers are seen in the hippocampus and striatum. These ascending projections have been postulated to play a role in arousal. In the brain stem, considerably fewer histaminergic fibers are found in fewer areas, such as the superior and inferior colliculi, central gray, locus coeruleus, parabrachial region, raphe nuclei, and several cranial nerve nuclei.

Clinical Significance. There is very little evidence linking histaminergic neurotransmission to any important clinical disorders. Ascending histamine afferents have been linked to arousal mechanisms, and the sedative effects of antihistamine drugs may in part be due to blockade of central histamine receptors. Evidence also exists that histamine participates in the central control of blood pressure. However, very little is known about histaminergic function in the CNS, and even less about its clinical relevance as a neurotransmitter.

Acetylcholine

Acetylcholine was the first neurotransmitter identified. It is the transmitter released in the heart when the vagus nerve is stimulated, inducing a decrease in heart rate. Acetylcholine, synthesized by the enzymatic activity of choline acetyltransferase, is the primary transmitter in the output nerves of the CNS. It is contained in somatic motorneurons in the ventral horn of the spinal cord and in the cranial nerve nuclei of the brain stem, and is the transmitter acting at the neuromuscular junction to induce contraction of striated muscle. Acetylcholine is also the transmitter in all autonomic preganglionic nerves; these are the major outputs of the sympathetic and parasympathetic nervous systems. The cholinergic preganglionic neurons in the intermediolateral cell column of the thoracolumbar spinal cord innervate the noradrenergic neurons making up the sympathetic postganglionic neurons. In cervical and sacral spinal cord, the cholinergic preganglionics send nerve fibers out to the peripheral target organs, where they contact the parasympathetic postganglionic cells that innervate vascular smooth muscle, the heart, glands, and other parasympathetic target tissues. These postganglionic parasympathetic effectors also utilize acetylcholine. Thus, all autonomic preganglionic transmission is cholinergic; all somatic motor transmission is cholinergic; all parasympathetic postganglionic transmission is cholinergic, and sympathetic postganglionic outflow is noradrenergic.

Acetylcholine has been known to be a transmitter in the periphery for a long time; only recently has conclusive evidence of its existence in the CNS, sufficient to classify it as a neurotransmitter, been gathered. Presumed cholinergic neurons have been visualized using an enzyme histochemical technique to demonstrate the presence of acetylcholinesterase, the metabolic enzyme that breaks down acetylcholine (Lewis & Shute, 1967; Shute & Lewis, 1967). It had been assumed that neurons demonstrating a high level of cholinesterase activity were in fact cholinergic. This has now been shown to have been true in many cases, but it is not universally applicable. For example, what was thought to be a cholinergic system originating in the ventral tegmentum has since been shown to contain dopamine and not acetylcholine, but the dopaminergic neurons in this pathway contain a high level of cholinesterase activity. More recently, polyclonal and monoclonal antibodies have been raised to choline acetyltransferase and applied in immunohistochemical studies to provide a more valid indication of the localization of cholinergic neurons in the CNS. These observations have been substantiated by biochemical as well as pharmacological experiments, although only very recently has direct measurement of acetylcholine released *in vivo* from activated neural pathways been possible, using microdialysis (Damsma et al., 1987).

Localization and Function. The cholinergic neurons in the central nervous system are located in 5 major systems, as well as in the spinal motor neurons, autonomic preganglionic neurons, and parasympathetic postganglionic neurons. The primary CNS cholinergic systems have been broken down and classified in various ways by different authors, and, depending on the species, the organizational subdivisions are more or less distinct.

The first central cholinergic subgrouping is directly analogous to the somatic motor aspect of the peripheral cholinergic system. Acetylcholine is the neurotransmitter in the oculomotor and somatic motor cranial nerve nuclei of the brain stem (Armstrong, Saper, Levey, Wainer, & Terry, 1983). Cholinergic oculomotor neurons include the third (oculomotor), fourth (trochlear), and sixth (abducens) nerve motor neurons. Other somatic motor nuclei include the fifth (trigeminal), seventh (facial), and twelfth (hypoglossal) motor nuclei. All of these contain characteristic large multipolar cholinergic motor neurons which extend their axonal processes out to the periphery via the appropriate cranial motor nerve branch, innervating muscles controlling eye movement as well as musculature of the face (especially for mastication) and mouth, including the tongue and pharynx. The second group of cholinergic neurons in the brain is again analogous to peripheral counterparts, this time of the visceromotor category. Visceral (i.e., cranial parasympathetic) motor neurons residing in the Edinger-Westphal nucleus, dorsal motor nucleus of the vagus, and nucleus ambiguous are cholinergic, and innervate postganglionic cells in the head (e.g., salivary glands, pupillary muscles) as well as bodily parasympathetic targets via long axonal projections.

The rest of the cholinergic neuronal groups in the brain are unique to the CNS, and resemble more closely their monoaminergic counterparts, with which they are heavily interconnected in terms of their distribution, projection patterns, and presumed functions. In keeping with the scheme of classification in place for the monoaminergic cell groups, some of the CNS cholinergic groups have also been labeled the Ch1–Ch6 cell groups (Mesulam, Mufson, Wainer, & Levey, 1983). However, this classification is only partially inclusive: it was expressly intended to classify brain stem cholinergic projection neurons, and thus ignores intrinsic cholinergic interneurons such as those in the striatum (Armstrong et al., 1983). The nuclear and cytoarchitectonic demarcation of the Ch1–Ch4 cell groups is dependent on the species. In monkeys and humans, these are closely related but distinct cell clusters (Mesulam & Mufson, 1984; Mesulam, Mufson, Levey, & Wainer, 1983), whereas in the rat they are a continuous column of cells in the basal forebrain, differentiated only by their projection patterns (Fibiger, 1982; Woolf & Butcher, 1986; Woolf, Eckenstein, & Butcher, 1984). Even so, the Ch1–Ch4 cell groups are often considered as parts of a continuum, each with more or less its own projection pattern, but all comprising the basal forebrain cholinergic cell population.

The Ch1–Ch4 groups are related in that they all reside in subregions of the basal forebrain, extending from the medial septal region, olfactory tubercle, and diaganol band nucleus caudally to the substantia innominata underlying the globus pallidus. This broad group of cells provides cholinergic input to the cortex and limbic forebrain, and the individual cell clusters can be differentiated on the basis of their target structures. The Ch1 and Ch2 groups are located in the medial septal region and the vertical limb of the nucleus of the diagonal band, respectively. These neurons provide, via the fornix, the cholinergic innervation of the hippocampus, especially the CA2 and CA3 fields and the hilar region of the dentate gyrus. This septohippocampal cholinergic system has been postulated to be important in the processes of learning and memory (Squire & Davis, 1981). Cholinergic antagonists or lesioning of this pathway can disrupt both the retrieval and acquisition of learned information, and has especially deleterious effects on spatial learning (Miyamoto, Kato, Narumi, & Nagaoka, 1987; Whishaw, O'Conner, & Dunnett, 1985). Activity in the cholinergic septohippocampal pathway has been associated with the generation of the hippocampal EEG, and may be involved in arousal and/or attentional processes (Vanderwolf & Stewart, 1986).

The next forebrain cholinergic group is the Ch3 component, situated in the lateral portion of the horizontal limb of the diagonal band nucleus. These neurons innervate the olfactory bulb and related areas of the ventral forebrain. There is a degree of overlap between the cells of the Ch3 and those of the Ch1 and Ch2 neurons. Especially in the rat, it is easier to think of these as different components of the same cell group than as different subgroups entirely.

The most studied but still not well understood collection of cholinergic neurons in the brain is the Ch4 neurons in the basal nucleus of Meynert, the caudal portions of the nucleus of the diagonal band, and extending caudally into the substantia innominata at the base of the globus pallidus. This cell group provides the major if not the sole cholinergic innervation of the entire cerebral cortex and the amygdala. This component of the cholinergic forebrain system has also been shown to be important in learning and memory processes (Miyamoto et al., 1987; Whishaw et al., 1985). Interestingly, the only areas of the cortex that supply a reciprocal innervation to the basal nucleus are areas of the limbic cortex, including the prepyriform, insular, entorhinal, and orbitofrontal cortex. Other inputs to the Ch4 group include the septal region, the ventral pallidum/nucleus accumbens, and portions of the lateral hypothalamus. Recordings of cellular activity in this region in monkeys have shown some connection with complex behavioral operations, indicating some possible involvement in motivational and arousal processes (Richardson & DeLong, 1988). The relationship of this area to the limbic cortex, amygdala, and other limbic forebrain regions, and the interconnection of these areas in a circuit involving the parabrachial region and the cardiovascular portions of the medulla also suggest some integrative function of emotion and autonomic responses with specific sensorimotor processes, although, again, it is difficult to determine whether these interregional connections involve subsets of cells of a certain neurochemical signature (i.e., cholinergic), because these are highly heterogenous areas of the brain, subserving many and varied functions. The Ch4 group also supplies the cholinergic innervation of the mesencephalic interpeduncular nucleus, the densest cholinergic target in the brain. The pathway by which this innervation is supplied may include inputs to the habenular complex en route via the fasciculus retroflexus to the interpeduncular nucleus. The habenula and IPN together are components of a dorsal brain stem limbic circuit, and thus represent another means by which limbic structures of the forebrain are interconnected.

The Ch5 and Ch6 groups are found in the pedunculopontine nucleus and lateral dorsal tegmental nucleus, respectively, both in the pontine reticular formation. These two areas provide the cholinergic input to the thalamus, including the anterior, medial dorsal, central medial, and reticular nuclei of the thalamus, the lateral geniculate and posterior thalamus, as well as the habenula, pretectal area, superior colliculus, substantia nigra, globus pallidus, lateral hypothalamus, subthalamic area, and regions of the basal forebrain that contain cell groups Ch1–Ch4. These pontomesencephalic cholinergic neurons also are interconnected with noradrenergic neurons as well as nonnoradrenergic neurons in the pons (A6 and A7 regions), and with brain stem serotonergic neurons. These cells are thought to be involved in arousal and sleep mechanisms, specifically in the maintenance of waking arousal, as well as in the activation of the brain during active or REM sleep (Hobson, McCarley, & Wyzinski, 1975; McCarley & Hobson, 1975; Sakai, 1988; Vanderwolf & Stewart, 1986). These pontine cholinergic cells are implicated in the physiology of dreaming and other aspects of REM sleep, including the generation of so-called PGO waves in the pons, lateral geniculate, and occipital cortex, and in the motor paralysis that accompanies REM sleep (Hobson et al., 1975; McCarley & Hobson, 1975; Sakai, 1988).

The final group of cholinergic neurons to be considered is the caudate nucleus of the neostriatum. These cholinergic cells are most likely striatal interneurons that participate in local circuitry involving ascending dopamine terminals, glutamatergic corticostriatal afferents, and striatal GABAergic neurons projecting to the globus pallidus as well as back to the substantia nigra (Graybiel, 1990). The striatal cholinergic interneurons are medium-to-large type II aspiny neurons. Although they represent only about 1% of total neuronal number in the striatum, they seem to be evenly distributed, in contrast to the patch/matrix organization of many other striatal components, including muscarinic receptors (Graybiel, 1990). These cholinergic neurons apparently do not project at all outside the striatum.

Clinical Significance. The cholinergic neurons of the periphery have been associated with a number of important clinical conditions, primarily involving motor nerve function. The one most directly related to cholinergic mechanisms is myasthenia gravis, an autoimmune disorder resulting in a selective loss of cholinergic receptors at the neuromuscular junction. Amyotropic lateral sclerosis, another peripheral motor disorder, also results from a selective disruption of cholinergic motor neuron function.

A clinically important, widespread, and costly affliction involving cholinergic mechanisms is addiction to nicotine and the craving that accompanies it. It had been thought that nicotinic cholinergic receptors were limited to the periphery, and therefore that the signs of nicotine withdrawal were presumably peripheral feedback symptoms. Many of the sensations of cigarette smoking are due to activation of peripheral nicotinic receptors. However, the number of nicotinic receptors in the CNS is limited, especially in the basal forebrain and hippocampus, and these regions have been implicated in motivational and reward processes. Indeed, these are some of the same target regions that have been implicated in the dopaminergic mechanisms of cocaine addiction (see above). The action of nicotine through cholinergic receptors most likely induces a release of forebrain and hippocampal dopamine and norepinephrine (Brazell, Mitchell, & Gray, 1991; Damsma et al., 1989), and this cholinergic/catecholaminergic interaction in the brain reward systems may be the basis of nicotine addiction (Fibiger & Phillips, 1987).

A very strong case has been made for an involvement of septohippocampal cholinergic pathways in learning and memory. Disruption of this circuit induces specific learning and memory deficits, and total or partial destruction of this pathway may contribute to memory deficits seen following injury, or after surgical removal of portions of the hippocampus, amygdala, or temporal lobe to alleviate severe epilepsy. Degeneration of this pathway may also contribute to the memory deficits seen with Alzheimer's disease (see below), although the precise neurochemical mechanisms underlying these very complex functions are not well understood.

The most important clinical connection for the basal forebrain neurons is in relation to the etiology and symptomatology of Alzheimer's disease. In Alzheimer's disease, there is a fairly selective decrease in cortical acetylcholine, and a loss of cholinergic neurons in the basal forebrain, particularly in the region of the Ch4 cells in the basal nucleus of Meynert/substantia innominata (Jacobs & Butcher, 1986; Whitehouse, Price, Clark, Coyle, & DeLong, 1981). Although this selective loss of cells preferentially innervating neocortical areas almost certainly contributes to the debilitating behavioral and cognitive disorders seen with Alzheimer's disease, no cause-and-effect relationship between this cholinergic cell loss and the primary mechanisms underlying the widespread cortical degeneration and histological anomalies seen with Alzheimer's disease has yet been established. It is not currently known whether the selective cell death is a result of a primary degenerative process in the cortex, such as a defect in the processing of amyloid protein, or whether the primary defect is in the cholinergic cells themselves, and the widespread histopathological alterations in the cortex are a secondary reaction to cell death and perhaps ultimate liberation of a locally toxic substance released by the dying cells. Nonetheless, the loss of cholinergic innervation of the cortex could well be a major determinant of the degree of cognitive incapacity, but pharmacological therapies utilizing agents to enhance cholinergic transmission have not been very successful in treating Alzheimer's disease.

There is also a degree of cholinergic cell loss in Parkinson's disease, and this could, in part, account for some of the cognitive deficits seen with this disorder. However, the main dysfunction in Parkinson's disease, resulting primarily in extrapyramidal motor symptoms, at least in the earlier stages of the disease, appears to be an imbalance in the various neurotransmitter components involved in the neostriatal circuitry, caused by the loss of the major dopaminergic input from the striatum. Use of cholinergic antagonists to restore the balance among dopamine, GABA, and acetylcholine has been effective in attenuating the symptoms of Parkinson's disease (Tarsy, 1977).

Development. The development of the cholinergic systems in many ways resembles that of the monoaminergic systems, in that the cells and pathways making up this system are established relatively early in development. However, unlike the monoamines, the emergence of functional neurotransmission may in fact appear quite late in the cholinergic pathways.

Cholinergic neurons of the basal forebrain are born during early prenatal development (E12-E17 in the rat), overlapping with the period of neurogenesis of the monoaminergic cells

(Armstrong, Bruce, Hersh, & Gage, 1987; Henderson, 1991). Acetyl cholinesterase activity is high, from a very early stage, in the nucleus basalis, in cells of the region, and in target terminal processes. However, although this enzyme has been used as a marker for cholinergic neurons, it is only indicative of degradative capability and is not a reliable marker for the cholinergic phenotype, nor does it reflect the capability to synthesize acetylcholine. The synthetic enzyme, choline acetyltransferase, first appears, at low levels, in the late prenatal period. Immunohistochemical labeling for ChAT remains minimal or below detectability in cells of the basal nucleus, as well as in the cortex before and shortly after birth (Henderson, 1991; McDonald, Speciale, & Parnavelas, 1987). Cortical terminal labeling emerges in significant amounts 2 to 3 weeks postnatally in the rat (McDonald et al., 1987), gradually increasing to adult levels during subsequent postnatal development. It appears, however, that fiber projections to the cortex are established long before the expression of ChAT, and hence the ability to synthesize acetylcholine is acquired (Henderson, 1991).

The development of the cholinergic system in humans has also been described (Kostovic, 1986). Acetyl cholinesterase activity emerges and increases in the nucleus basalis between 8 and 35 weeks of gestation. AchE appears in the region of the primordial nucleus basalis even before the cells in the area begin to differentiate. At 9 weeks, AchE reactive neuronal processes start to extend out of the region. From 10 to 11 weeks, the majority of cells in the nucleus basalis become differentiated, and there is a substantial increase in the AchE activity of the neuropil. At 15 weeks, AchE activity is first seen in cell bodies, and the distribution of reactive cells within the forebrain cholinergic complex essentially assumes that of the adult. Between 15 and 22 weeks, fibers reach the most distal regions of the cortex; however, these terminals, which course through the external capsule and the outer white strata of the cortex, do not penetrate the cortical layers, but innervate the transient subplate of the cortex and hippocampus. From 24 to 30 weeks, the nucleus basalis increases in size and cell number, and terminals begin to penetrate the cortical layers, corresponding to a period of some maturation and synaptogenesis in the cortex. It is presumed that the majority of cholinergic synapses are formed from 30 weeks until birth and postnatally, coinciding with the emergence of some cholinergic functions in the fetus and neonate, including the development of behavioral arousal states and the differentiation of REM sleep and quiet sleep (see Kostovic, 1986, for discussion). However, recent studies have shown that the development of AchE activity, the differentiation and maturation of cells in the nucleus basalis, and even the establishment of anatomical connections with the cortex far precede the expression of cholinergic synthetic capability (Henderson, 1991).

Amino Acids

A second chemical class of neurotransmitter is made up simply of a number of amino acids, including glutamate, aspartate, glycine, GABA (gamma-amino butyric acid), and perhaps taurine. The amino acid transmitters are the most ubiquitous and most abundant of all neurotransmitter substances in the brain. They exist in micromolar concentrations and are found throughout the brain. In fact, in terms of distribution and concentration, it may be assumed that amino acid neurotransmitters participate in the vast majority of neural circuits and functions in the CNS. One problem, however, in studying the specific neurotransmitter functions of the amino acids has been the difficulty in separating the amino acids acting as transmitters (i.e., contained in and released from presynaptic terminals in an activity-dependent manner and acting as specific postsynaptic receptors) from those same substances when they fulfill a metabolic and biosynthetic role in nerve cells and glia. Thus, although the amino acid transmitters exist in great abundance and are found in neural components throughout the brain, it is only with recent advances in neuroanatomical, electrophysiological, and neurochemical techniques that a better understanding of their specific neurotransmitter roles has been gained. The amino acids can be divided generally into two categories: (a) the excitatory amino acids, including glutamate and aspartate, which act to depolarize and hence excite their target neurons, and (b) the inhibitory amino acids, GABA, glycine, and taurine, which hyperpolarize and thus inhibit the activity of their targets.

Glutamate and Aspartate

L-glutamate is the most plentiful amino acid in the CNS (McGeer, Eccles, & McGeer, 1978). This very important amino acid accounts for many metabolic and synthetic functions: it is involved in protein and fatty acid synthesis, it participates in brain ionic regulation and maintenance of ammonia levels, and it serves as a component in several steps of the Krebs cycle. In addition, glutamate is the immediate precursor for the inhibitory amino acid GABA. A vast amount of evidence points to a specific excitatory neurotransmitter role for L-glutamate and the closely related amino acid, L-aspartate. However, only with recent advances in neuroanatomical techniques—the development of and subsequent immunohistochemical application of antibodies against the enzymes involved in amino acid synthesis and then against the amino acids themselves (Ottersen & Storm-Mathisen, 1987)—could these substances be localized to appropriate presynaptic neuronal elements, thus fulfilling the first of the essential transmitter criteria. Further developments in the techniques for monitoring the *in vivo* release and subsequent measurement of amino acids have allowed additional verification of their role as neurotransmitters.

It could probably be argued that glutamate represents the quintessential "classical" excitatory neurotransmitter. Postsynaptically, it elicits a direct and rapid excitation of its target cell by opening ion channels. However, it is equally true that glutamate also serves as a typical neuromodulator through its actions at one subclass of glutamatergic receptor, the NMDA receptor (so named because N-methyl-D-aspartate is a selective agonist). These receptors, which presumably underlie the phenomenon of long-term potentiation and perhaps other forms of neural plasticity, are also excitatory ion channel linked receptors. They appear to be operational only when activated in conjunction with another depolarizing stimulus (often glutamatergic as well, acting via the kainate or quisqualate receptor subtypes). Thus, when NMDA receptors are solely activated, no response ensues. When activated in conjunction with a second excitatory stimulus, the effect is a dramatic enhancement and alteration of the overall response, a typical neuromodulatory effect (Cotman & Iversen, 1987; Mayer & Westbrook, 1987).

Localization and Function. A number of important brain regions and circuits utilize excitatory amino acids, which, in the context of local circuitry, serve very specific functions. Glutamate and aspartate play an important excitatory role in the cerebellum. The excitatory parallel fiber inputs to Purkinje cells arising from the cerebellar granule cells utilize glutamate, and a large number of cells in the inferior olivary nucleus, the source of the powerfully excitatory climbing fiber inputs to the Purkinje cells, contain aspartate (Aoki, Semba, Kato, & Kashiwamata, 1987; Madl, 1987). Interestingly, all of the other intrinsic cerebellar connections and cell types are believed to utilize inhibitory amino acids (either GABA or glycine); exogenous afferents from other brain regions, providing modulatory inputs to this primary cerebellar circuitry, utilize a variety of other transmitters, including the monoamines serotonin and norepinephrine.

Many cells in the cerebral cortex contain excitatory amino acids, and many of these constitute the primary excitatory projections from the neocortex to various subcortical regions. Major subcortical projections include the excitatory corticothalamic and corticostriatal pathways, providing a highly topographic connection between the cerebral cortex and corresponding regions of the thalamus and basal ganglia. There also are ascending excitatory amino acid pathways from the thalamus to the cortex (see Graybiel, 1990, for review).

Excitatory amino acids make up several components of hippocampal circuitry, including pyramidal and granule cells as well as both intrinsic and extrinsic fiber pathways (Liu, Grandes, Matute, Cuenod, & Streit, 1989; Ottersen & Storm-Mathisen, 1984). Excitatory amino acids in the hippocampus are thought to play important roles in various forms of associative learning and memory, and one of the best neural models of associative conditioning to date (long-term potentiation, or LTP) is dependent on excitatory amino acid mechanisms in the hippocampus.

A very strong case has been made that glutamate may be the transmitter, or at least a cotransmitter, in a number of visceral and somatic primary sensory afferents from the periphery to the CNS. Glutamate is in high abundance in the dorsal horn of the spinal cord, and has been demonstrated in dorsal root ganglia. High-affinity glutamate uptake is present in primary cardiovascular afferents to the brain stem, and application of glutamate mimics activation of these afferents. Glutamate antagonism blocks the elicitation of cardiovascular reflexes by activation of primary sensory afferents. Second-order neurons in the brain stem, which are involved in cardiovascular or sympathoadrenal regulation, also contain excitatory amino acids, providing both ascending and descending excitatory inputs to other regions of the brain and spinal cord.

As new glutamatergic pathways are identified, it is becoming increasingly clear that excitatory amino acids serve an important and widespread role as the primary excitatory transmitters in the brain. Activation of glutamate/aspartate receptors produces an almost universal excitatory effect, regardless of the location or identity of the target cell or structure. This presents something of a paradox, however: with recent anatomical and neurochemical advances (see above), it has become apparent that these transmitters are in fact localized to discrete and specific pathways within the brain. Thus, there may be a degree of dissociation between the presence of active amino acid receptors on a neural target and an appropriate neurotransmitter-containing substrate innervating that target. This raises the possibility that a certain degree of extrasynaptic neurotransmission may take place; that is, transmitter substances diffusing in sufficient concentration in the extracellular fluid may gain access to these "unattached" receptors and thus evoke cellular responses that are not dependent on presynaptic innervation, and are not, in fact, strictly activity-dependent but are more hormonal or paracrinelike in nature. With respect to the excitatory amino acids, there is a ready supply of potential transmitter in the extracellular fluid related to the metabolic pools and overflow of these substances. However, there also exist very efficient and rapid mechanisms for the reuptake and degradation of amino acids by nerve cells and, especially by glia. Thus, perhaps only in cases of metabolic overload or disruption of the normal homeostatic maintenance of optimal levels of extracellular excitatory amino acid levels may such putative extrasynaptic transmission take place.

Clinical Significance. The most important clinical connection of the excitatory amino acids is related to their apparent neurotoxicity in high concentration. Excessive local release of excitatory amino acids resulting from anoxia, ischemia, stroke, or hypoglycemia, or even in response to certain hormonal states (e.g., excessive steroid levels), has been strongly linked to a degree of tissue damage and cell death associated with these conditions. Many of the behavioral or cognitive deficits that can be associated with these events may in part be attributable to the excitotoxic effects of excitatory amino acids. Glutamate neurotoxicity has been implicated in focal lesions associated with seizures and epilepsy. Indeed, long-lived glutamate analogs such as kainic acid or ibotenic acid have long been used experimentally not only as pharmacological tools to activate nerve cells, but also as selective neural excitotoxins that specifically induce death of the neuronal cell bodies that they excite (Rothman & Olney, 1987).

Glutamatergic neurotoxic effects have also been implicated in the etiology of Huntington's disease (DiFiglia, 1990), a genetic abnormality in which alterations in amino acid metabolism have been observed. The major histopathological disorder seen with Huntington's disease is a very selective degeneration of the projection neurons, presumably GABAergic, in the striatum. It has been suggested that this is the result of glutamate neurotoxicity, and this subpopulation of cells is particularly sensitive to the excitotoxic effects of glutamate (Rothman & Olney, 1987).

Excessive glutamate release from corticostriatal afferents may also be partly responsible for the neurologic symptoms of Parkinson's disease. Glutamate and dopamine exert opposite cellular effects on a common set of target neurons in the striatum, both interneurons and striatal projection neurons. A delicate balance of neurotransmitter activity must be maintained in the striatum, involving the glutamatergic and dopaminergic afferents, the cholinergic interneurons, and the GABAergic projection neurons, to ensure the normal coordinated functioning of the extrapyramidal system. Disruptions of this balance, through selective cell death, leading to a disproportionate hyper- and hypoactivity in one or more of these systems, have devastating consequences and lead to the pathological conditions seen in Parkinson's disease, Huntington's disease, hemiballismus, choreoathetosis, and tardive dyskinesia.

Glutamatergic hypoactivity has been implicated as a mechanism in schizophrenia (Carlsson & Carlsson, 1990). Phencyclidine (PCP, or "angel dust"), a noncompetitive antagonist at the glutamate NMDA receptor, is a psychotomimetic drug of abuse, the effects of which have been reported to most closely mimic chronic undifferentiated schizophrenia. The glutamate hypothesis for schizophrenia would also be consistent with the reported inverse relationship between epilepsy and schizophrenia in patients stricken with both illnesses. During periods of high seizure activity, which would be associated with increased excitatory amino acid transmission, the occurrence of psychotic symptoms is low, and vice versa. Treatment for either condition in these patients can exacerbate the other. Thus, the commonly prescribed dopamine antagonist antipsychotic agents may be acting to restore the normal opposing balance between the dopaminergic and glutamatergic systems.

GABA and Glycine

Gamma-amino butyric acid (GABA) was first identified as the principal inhibitory neurotransmitter in invertebrate preparations. Subsequently, it was found to be a widespread inhibitory neurotransmitter in the mammalian CNS. GABA is synthesized from glutamate by the action of glutamic acid dehydrogenase (GAD). Like glutamate, GABA appears to be widely distributed, and GABA or GABA analogs have a ubiquitous inhibitory influence throughout the CNS. GABA has been localized anatomically by uptake and transport of radiolabeled ligand, and more recently by immunohistochemical means to visualize GAD as well as GABA (Oertel, Schmechel, Mugnaini, Tappaz, & Kopin, 1981; Somogyi, Hodgson, Chubb, Penke, & Erdei, 1985). Even though the local tissue concentration of GABA is, like glutamate, in the micromolar range, it is not found in high extracellular concentration, mostly because of an extremely rapid and efficient reuptake mechanism, both into neurons and into glial cells. With further development of techniques, especially in monitoring and measuring neuronal release of GABA (Tossman, Segovia, & Ungerstedt, 1986), important roles for GABA in normal and pathological processes are becoming more amenable to study.

Localization and Function. GABA is found throughout the brain and spinal cord in inhibitory local interneurons. In the spinal cord, glycine is thought to be the neurotransmitter in inhibitory interneurons, activated by a collateral of excitatory inputs and serving as a negative feedback mechanism in a local circuit. GABA is also located in intraspinal neurons. These are thought to be involved in presynaptic inhibition of release from primary afferents, and also in more complex inhibitory circuits, in some cases producing disinhibition by suppressing inhibitory interneurons. Actually, this mode of double inhibition is a common one in the nervous system, especially for GABAergic neurons.

Other regions in which GABA inhibitory interneurons are prominent are the cerebral cortex and hippocampus. In the cortex, GABA interneurons of many morphological cell types have been observed (Somogyi et al., 1985; Somogyi & Soltesz, 1986). In the hippocampus, they are primarily the basket cells, although other cell types have been seen (Liu et all, 1989; Somogyi et al., 1985). GABAergic interneurons also function in the thalamus, hypothalamus, and amygdala, and in several brain stem nuclei.

GABA neurons play several specialized roles in the cerebellum. GABA is the transmitter in the Purkinje cells, the sole output of the cerebellar cortex. In fact, all cells in the cerebellar cortex, except for the excitatory granule cells, including the basket, stellate, and golgi cells, are GABAergic (Oertel et al., 1981; Somogyi et al., 1985). These form a variety of local inhibitory circuits, again representing a case of double inhibition.

GABA is also a major component in several circuit loops involving the cortex-neostriatum-thalamus-substantia nigra pathways. Separate populations of GABA neurons in the striatum project to the globus pallidus and to the substantia nigra pars reticulata. These in turn send GABAergic projections to the brain stem and thalamus. These double-inhibitory GABAergic side loops act to modulate the excitatory activity of the thalamocortical pathway. The result is that excitatory glutamatergic transmission from the cortex serves to ultimately disinhibit the excitatory thalamocortical afferents, and inhibitory dopaminergic input tends to inhibit thalamocortical activation (Graybiel, 1990). Another set of GABA neurons in the striasomal patches projects back to the dopaminergic neurons of the substantia nigra pars compacta, forming another closed feedback loop.

GABA has also been demonstrated as a neurotransmitter in several cell groups and pathways in the pons and medulla. GABAergic projections from the cardiovascular regions of the nucleus tractus solitarius and caudal ventrolateral medulla inhibit sympathoexcitatory neurons in the rostral ventrolateral medulla. GABA also is colocalized, along with neuropeptides such as TRH and substance P, in serotonergic neurons of the rostral ventrolateral medulla as well as the raphe nuclei, and GABA has been shown to be an inhibitory component of several local circuits and short projection paths in the brain stem.

A conclusive neurotransmitter role for glycine, on the other hand, has been confirmed in only a small number of systems in the CNS. Glycine is located in interneurons in the spinal cord, where it appears to participate as an inhibitory interneuron in local circuits (Basbaum, 1988; van den Pol & Gorca, 1988). Glycine has been implicated as the transmitter involved in producing the paralysis associated with REM sleep, by a direct inhibition of spinal and brain stem motor neurons (Soja, Lopez-Rodriguez, Morales, & Chase, 1991). Glycine also has been localized to a subset of inhibitory neurons in the cerebellum.

Clinical Significance. GABAergic mechanisms have been implicated in the mode of action of several therapeutic drug classes, including anxiolytics, sedatives, antiepileptics, and barbiturate anesthetics. The GABAA receptor complex, the site of action of many clinically useful drugs, taps into the ubiquitous and potent inhibitory influence of GABA in the CNS. The receptor itself is a ligand-gated chloride channel, activation of which results in an increase in chloride conductance and a decrease in target cell excitability. Associated with the GABAA receptor complex are binding sites for the benzodiazepines and barbiturates, and this receptor is thought to be the site at which these agents exert their anxiolytic and anesthetic effects, respectively. A similar mechanism may account for the reduction in seizure activity by antiepileptic agents, and the sedative or narcotic influence of several drugs. It is difficult to say whether the efficacy of these drugs acting via GABAergic mechanisms implies a defect in those mechanisms that underlie the pathology, or whether the ubiquitous inhibitory nature of the GABAergic system is a convenient and effective means of eliciting a variety of therapeutic effects regardless of the underlying mechanism.

Much evidence for a deficit in GABAergic neurotransmission exists in certain extrapyramidal motor dysfunctions, including Parkinson's disease, hemiballismus, choreoathetosis, and Huntington's disease (DeLong, 1990; DiFiglia, 1990; Reiner et al., 1988; Walters & Chase, 1977). In many cases, these may represent imbalances involving several neurotransmitter systems. With the complex arrangement of opposing influences and double inhibitory circuits involving GABAergic projection neurons as well as interneurons in the various loops connecting the thalamus, striatum, brain stem, and cortex, it is easy to understand how relative imbalances can produce such devastating disorders.

In Huntington's disease, it appears that the primary pathology is in the GABAergic system itself. Huntington's disease, a genetic disorder linked to chromosome 4 in humans, is characterized by a massive and selective loss of striatal GABAergic neurons (DiFiglia, 1990; Reiner et al., 1988). Different subpopulations of GABAergic cells in the striatum, defined by their cotransmitters and projection targets, degenerate at different rates, but ultimately almost all striatal projection cells are affected (Reiner et al., 1988). This selective cell death may in fact be a result of glutamate-induced neurotoxicity, to which the GABAergic striatal neurons are particularly sensitive (DiFiglia, 1990).

Another rare motor disorder in which GABAergic dysfunction has only recently been suggested is Stiff-Man syndrome, presumed to be an autoimmune disorder affecting central motor systems. Recently, an antibody against glutamate decarboxylase (GAD), the synthetic enzyme for GABA, has been isolated from patients suffering from this disorder (Solimena & De Camilli, 1991). This antibody selectively labels GABAergic neurons in the CNS, and, surprisingly, also labels pancreatic islet cells, suggesting the possibility of a common autoimmune disorder, affecting GABAergic systems, underlying both Stiff-Man syndrome and certain forms of insulin-dependent diabetes. Indeed, there appears to be a degree of coincidence of insulin-dependent diabetes, as well as epilepsy, with Stiff-Man syndrome (Solimena & De Camilli, 1991).

Development of Amino Acid Neurotransmitters. Considerably less information exists regarding the development of amino acid transmitter systems as compared to the monoamines. This is due, in part, to the very recent development of such tools as specific antibodies for the amino acid transmitters and their synthetic enzymes, and, in part, to the fact that the amino acid transmitters are also important components of more general metabolic processes.

Although many aspects of glutamate biochemical processing in the brain arise quite early, it is difficult to separate metabolic from neurotransmitter-related processing by biochemical measures alone—or even by neuroanatomical measures—because all cells apparently contain glutamate (Ottersen & Storm-Mathisen, 1984). The ontogeny of glutamate receptors has recently been characterized quite extensively, but far less is known about the development of the glutamatergic neuronal systems themselves. Independent of postsynaptic receptors, functional indexes of glutamate neurotransmission, such as glutamate uptake into synaptic vesicles, emergence of synthetic enzymes, and neural synthesis, suggest that most of the development of these systems may occur in the first 2 weeks postnatally in the rat (Kish, Kim, & Ueda, 1989).

As detected immunohistochemically, GABAergic neurons appear to develop very early in the prenatal period (Cobas, Fairen, Alvarez-Bolado, & Sanchez, 1991; Lauder, Han, Henderson, Verdoorn, & Towle, 1986; Van Eden, Mrzljak, Voorn, & Uylings, 1989). Several other indexes of GABAergic activity, such as the appearance of the synthetic enzyme glutamate decarboxylase (GAD), GABAergic receptors, or electrophysiological responses to GABA, suggest, however, that most of the development and maturation of functional GABAergic transmission in the rat occurs in the first 3 weeks postnatally (Seress & Ribak, 1988). This period corresponds to the first few years in humans. GABA-containing fibers first appear in the caudal brain stem in the rat as early as E12. From E13 to E14, GABAergic neurons first appear in the primordial cortex. Within the cortex, the GABA neurons are concentrated in the plexiform region, which splits into the superficial marginal zone and the subplate region to make way for the developing cortical plate. These GABA neurons increase in number, differentiate, and mature over the next few days, and more GABA cells populate the lower intermediate and subventricular region as well as the cortical plate itself. This concentration of GABA neurons in the transient ontogenetic regions of the developing cortex, as well as a dense fiber innervation of several emerging monoaminergic regions of the brain stem, has led researchers to propose a developmental regulatory or guidance role for early prenatal GABAergic systems (Cobas et al., 1991; Lauder et al., 1986; Van Eden et al., 1989). Cells in the cortex and neostriatum begin to differentiate and mature rapidly from E16 to E18. The cortical population of GABAergic neurons continues to increase until birth, at which time the cells in the lower intermediate, subventricular, and subplate regions decrease dramatically; a small number persist into adulthood as the interstitial cells of cortical layers I and VI. The cells in the cortical plate proper will have assumed near-adult distribution and form in the late prenatal period, with only slight development occurring postnatally.

Neuropeptides

The final major class of neurotransmitters to be considered is the neuropeptides. These molecules, like all peptides, are made up of several amino acids linked in a linear chain by peptide bonds between the primary amino and carboxylic acid moieties of the amino acids. The neuropeptides are derived from much larger precursor protein molecules that are synthesized in the endoplasmic reticulum of the cell bodies. These proteins are transcribed directly from mRNA, modified, packaged, and transported to the terminal release sites for final enzymatic processing. Countless neuropeptides are now proposed as neurotransmitter candidates, and the number grows almost continually. These substances are typically localized by immunocytochemical methods, or by local biochemical measurement using radioimmunoassay. However, special difficulties exist in fulfilling all of the criteria for positively identifying the neuropeptides as neurotransmitters. First, they have exceedingly low concentrations in the brain, on the order of 10^{-6} to 10^{-12} moles/mg, orders of magnitude less than the amino acids, acetylcholine, or the monoamines (Bloom, 1984; Krieger, 1986). Second, the neuropeptides, in several instances, coexist with other neurotransmitters, and the effect of the peptide on target cells is often neuromodulatory in nature, being evident only in the presence of cotransmission of the accompanying transmitter. Such effects are often elusive, and this is compounded by the general lack of specific and selective pharmacological agents for studying neuropeptide mechanisms. Finally, neuropeptide precursors can often be processed differentially into any of several products, and the metabolic products of neuropeptide degradation themselves often possess biological activity. This has made it very difficult to establish which, if any, of the substances under study is the effective neurotransmitter. In addition, the existence of related peptides, derived from the same as well as different precursors, has presented the problem of cross-reactivity, making both the anatomical localization and the biochemical measurement of released peptides sometimes equivocal or tentative. Nonetheless, there is very convincing circumstantial if not direct evidence that several neuropeptides and neuropeptide families function as neurotransmitters. In the review that follows, we describe the neuropeptide systems for which the best evidence exists supporting such a role.

Opioid Peptides

The opioid family of peptides is derived from three precursor proteins:

1. Proenkephalin A is the precursor for the family of enkephalins, relatively short peptides that all share the N-terminal amino acid sequence Tyr-Gly-Gly-Phe-X, with X being Met or Leu.
2. Proenkephalin B, or Prodynorphin, is the precursor molecule for the dynorphin and neo-endorphin family of opioid peptides.
3. Proopiomelanocortin (POMC) is the precursor for beta-endorphin and related peptides (as well as adrenocorticotropic hormone and a variety of other important neuroendocrine substances).

These substances are all considered part of the same category of opioid peptides in that they all contain the enkephalin sequence in their biologically active region, and their actions are all antagonized by naloxone (and related substances), which itself was first identified for its ability to antagonize the effects of morphine and related narcotic opiates. Aside from these similarities, the three classes of opioids act with varying degrees of selectivity, at three subtypes of endogenous opioid receptors, and are distributed differentially throughout the brain. The opioid peptides as a whole are among the most studied of neuropeptides, for several reasons: some are related to the importance of the functions with which they have been associated, and some are related to the availability of useful research tools with which they can be studied, such as specific antibodies for anatomical localization and neurochemical measurement, and very specific, selective, and well-characterized agonist and antagonist drugs for the different receptors.

Localization and Function. The several peptides representing the three general classes of opioid peptides are localized differentially in the CNS, although there is a great deal of overlap in their distribution and target innervation, as well as in their proposed functions. In many cases, the different opioids appear to produce similar behavioral or physiological effects, at the same or even different receptors. At other times, the different systems subserve different and sometimes opposing functions, in the same or in different regions of the CNS. The opioids as a whole have been implicated in such diverse but often related functions as analgesia of many forms, the response to stress, affective processes and reward mechanisms, neuronal-immune system interactions, and basic autonomic regulation (Olson, Olson, & Kastin, 1989).

Beta-endorphin, derived from the POMC molecule, which also generates ACTH and related substances, is located primarily in the corticotroph cells of the anterior pituitary and the melanotrophs of the intermediate lobe (Akil et al., 1984), and is often colocalized and coreleased with ACTH. The peripheral release of beta-endorphin has been implicated in the response to stress. Beta-endorphin is also found in hypothalamic neurons in the arcuate nuclei and in neurons of the nucleus tractus solitarius. These neuronal beta-endorphin systems innervate extensive regions of the forebrain, hypothalamus, amygdala, and mesencephalon, as well as periventricular regions and reticular formation of the pons and medulla (Lewis, Khachaturian, Schafer, & Watson, 1986). Beta-endorphin acts primarily at the opioid mu receptor, the same receptor at which morphine and heroin act.

The enkephalins and related peptide derivatives of proenkephalin A are localized to several regions of the CNS (Fallon & Leslie, 1986; Khachaturian, Lewis, & Watson, 1982; Uhl, Goodman, Kuhar, Childers, & Snyder, 1979). They are prominent components of the basal ganglia, amygdala, hypothalamus, periaqueductal gray, brain stem autonomic regions, and spinal cord. Enkephalins have been implicated in a number of processes subserved by the variety of primary circuits of which they are components; in many cases, the enkephalins have been shown to subserve a modulatory function as cotransmitters rather than a primary mediating role. The enkephalins act primarily at the opioid delta receptors, as well as at the mu receptors.

The final class of opioid peptides, the dynorphins and neo-endorphins, are derived from proenkephalin B, also called prodynorphin, and are also found in a number of pathways in the brain (Fallon & Leslie, 1986; Khachaturian, Watson, et al., 1982). The dynorphins are the primary opioid ligands at the kappa receptor subtype, and they too have been implicated in certain forms of analgesia.

Clinical Significance. The endogenous opioids have been most heavily implicated in analgesic mechanisms. Opioid action at several levels of the CNS, from spinal cord through forebrain, have been associated with analgesia of several forms (Akil et al., 1984), including stress-induced analgesia, acupuncture, analgesia associated with childbirth, and analgesia associated with stimulation of several regions of the brain stem. Morphine, the prototypic exogenous opiate drug, has long been used as an analgesic. However, complications with this application of opioid mechanisms derive from another set of processes in which the opioids have been implicated, those of affect, reward mechanisms, and addiction. Morphine and related synthetic opiate alkaloids such as heroin act through the opioid mu receptors to induce the euphoria associated with opiate narcotic intoxication. They also produce the craving of opiate addiction and the negative physiological and psychological effects associated with opiate withdrawal.

At one time, there was a suggestion of dysregulation of endogenous opioids underlying schizophrenia (Koob & Bloom, 1983; Nemeroff, Berger, & Bissette, 1987). However, this theory has subsequently been refuted, and the observed disorders in normal opioid function and metabolism, if indeed they do exist, are no more implicated than dysfunctions in any other system in schizophrenia, and may in fact be secondary to alterations in other transmitter systems. More recent suggestions have arisen regarding the role of opioids in depression. However, inconsistent or conflicting results and a general lack of experimental support have led to a general abandonment of theories suggesting a primary dysfunction in opioid systems as the basis for either schizophrenia or depression (see Nemeroff et al., 1987; Olson et al., 1989).

Development. Beta-endorphin is first detectable in the rat brain at E13, and continues to increase through the first few weeks postnatally (McDowell & Kitchen, 1987). Enkephalin-containing neurons, detected immunohistochemically, first appear in the primordial brain stem reticular formation of the rat embryo at day E16. These cells increase in both number and distribution during the late prenatal period, and through the first 10 days postnatally (Pickel, Sumal, & Miller, 1982; Senba et al., 1982). Forebrain enkephalinergic cells emerge slightly later, in the late prenatal and early postnatal periods (McDowell & Kitchen, 1987). Also, in the late prenatal period, enkephalin-containing nerve terminals are first seen in some target regions, although most major terminal field elaboration occurs postnatally. Prodynorphin-related peptides first appear in the late prenatal period; most dynorphin development occurs postnatally (McDowell & Kitchen, 1987).

The differential development of the three opioid peptide families is also seen with the development of opioid receptor subtypes. Mu receptors are the first to appear, shortly after the first appearance of beta-endorphin. Kappa receptors also appear prenatally, although levels remain very low until birth, after which there is a gradual increase to adult levels. In contrast, there is a disparity between the developmental time course of the enkephalins and their corresponding delta receptors. The enkephalins themselves appear relatively early, but the delta receptors are not apparent until 2 to 3 weeks postnatally (De Vries, Hogenboom, Mulder, & Schoffelmeer, 1990; Rius, Barg, Bem, Coscia, & Loh, 1991; Spain, Roth, & Coscia, 1985). Thus, the connectivity and ability to synthesize transmitter in the enkephalin system far precede the establishment of synaptic contact with target delta receptors, or the majority of enkephalinergic effects are mediated by mu receptors until quite late in development.

Substance P

Localization and Function. Substance P, an 11-amino acid peptide first isolated based on its peripheral effects as a vasodilator, has been most firmly established as a neurotransmitter in primary sensory afferent fibers, and especially in the fine-caliber type C and type Ad fibers that transmit pain information to the dorsal horn of the spinal cord and spinal trigeminal nucleus in the brain stem (Hokfelt, Kellerth, Nilsson, & Pernow, 1975). Evidence exists that substance P may subserve a similar role in primary cardiovascular afferents conveying chemoreceptor and baroreceptor information to autonomic sensory regions of the brain stem (Haeusler & Osterwalder, 1980; Helke, O'Donohue, & Jacobowitz, 1980). The central release of substance P from sensory afferents is believed to excite second-order neurons involved in sensory processing, but the release of substance P from the peripheral sensory endings of these fibers is responsible for t he vasodilation underlying the wheal-and-flare response to local mechanical or chemical irritation (the "axon reflex") (Foreman, Jordan, Oehme, & Renner, 1983).

Substance P also is located in several regions of the spinal cord, brain stem, and forebrain, and substance P pathways innervate widespread regions of the CNS (Cuello & Kanazawa, 1978; Ljungdahl, Hokfelt, & Nilsson, 1978). The influence of substance P in many of these pathways has been investigated, but its role has typically been related to the function of the particular pathway under study (e.g., amygdala, striatum, nucleus tractus solitarius), rather than to any specific function of a central substance P "system" per se.

Clinical Significance. The most widely known drug effect associated with a substance P mechanism is that of capsaicin. Capsaicin is a rather selective releaser of substance P, an effect responsible for the familiar sensation associated with the ingestion of capsaicin-containing foods, such as jalapeno peppers (Dun & Kiraly, 1983). However, capsaicin, when administered to neonatal animals, induces a long-lasting depletion of substance P and a loss of a subclass of primary afferent pathways. This has been associated with sensory and cardiovascular deficits in experimental animals, although the relevance of this model to a human clinical condition is unclear.

Development. Substance P is first detectable in brain stem primordial neurons of the rat at about E15 (Inagaki et al., 1982; Pickel et al., 1982; Sakanaka et al., 1982). Between E15 and E18, an extensive network of substance P-containing fibers develops, with a distribution comparable to that of the adult. This fiber network increases in density until adulthood. However, although numerous fibers are apparent early in development, very few terminal fields (i.e., varicose terminals associated with release sites) are observed at this time (Pickel et al., 1982). Thus, it is possible that substance P cells and fibers themselves may develop relatively early, but functional communication with CNS targets may emerge much later. A steady increase in the number and extent of substance P cells through the first two weeks postnatally is followed by a decrease in number to an adult level. However, this apparent decrease is actually related to the activation of neuronal transport mechanisms that shuttle the newly synthesized peptide out of the cell body and into the terminal region, thus rendering the cell itself nonimmunoreactive in the absence of transport inhibitors such as colchicine. Unlike many other transmitters in the brain stem, like serotonin, substance P shows a caudal to rostral developmental gradient. Cells in the rostral forebrain do not display substance P immunoreactivity until several days after the first appearance of substance P cells in the caudal brain stem.

The course of substance P development in the human brain has also been described (Del Fiacco, Dessi, & Levanti, 1984; Nomura et al., 1982), and is roughly analogous to that in the rat. Substance P first appears perhaps as early as 4 months' gestation; by 18 to 25 weeks, there is extensive development of substance P-containing cells and fiber networks. By 8 months' gestation, the basic pattern of substance P distribution is very similar to that of the adult, although a considerable increase and elaboration in the overall level and extent of substance P immunolabeling occurs postnatally.

FUNDAMENTALS OF MOLECULAR BIOLOGY

In the previous sections, we surveyed the diversity of neuronal phenotypes and the complexity of cellular connections that make up the structural basis for the functions of the nervous system. Here, we consider the regulation of neurobiology at the molecular level.

The essence of molecular biology has been best summarized by Francis Crick's central dogma of molecular biology: "DNA makes RNA and RNA makes protein." With few exceptions, the major flow of information proceeds from nucleic acids to protein. It is, after all, the products encoded by the genes that contribute to the overall phenotypic diversity of the nervous system. Over the past decade, advances in molecular biology have brought a new level of understanding to developmental molecular neurobiology. In addition, the development and applications of recombinant DNA technology have led to the integration of molecular genetics and protein chemistry. These advances have enabled us to focus on the roles played by the genes in the regulation of neuronal development and in the expression of a multitude of phenotypes, and to examine the factors that influence gene expression. Further, these studies have allowed us to gain an insight into some of the genetic etiology of neurological disorders.

In this section, we provide a brief review of the basic principles and techniques of genetics and molecular biology. We outline the key steps involved in the process from gene transcription to protein synthesis. We also include an analysis of the basic tools of molecular biology, the cloning of cDNAs, and the isolation of the corresponding genes. Because it is beyond the scope of this chapter to elaborate in depth on each of these topics, interested readers are encouraged to refer to texts by Lewin (1990) and Watson and colleagues (e.g., Watson, Tooze, & Kurtz, 1983), as well as to other citations throughout this section, for a more comprehensive review.

Mendelian Genetics

The genetic information used by cells to replicate themselves and to carry out their biological functions is contained on the chromosomes. These chromosomes, which reside solely within the cell nucleus, are highly compact structures made up of nucleic acids and proteins known as histones. The total number of chromosomes is unique for each species; however, each has a pair of sex chromosomes (XX or XY) and varying numbers of paired homologous autosomes. The total set of hereditary information of an individual, its genotype, consists of basic units called genes, which are arranged in a specific linear array along the chromosomes. The existence of genes was discovered by the Austrian monk Gregor Mendel during the 1860s. He postulated the existence of "particulate factors" that were passed on from parent to progeny without alteration. Mendel recognized that a gene may exist in alternative forms, which we now call alleles. An organism is said to be homozygous when both alleles are identical. Alternatively, if the alleles are different, then the organism is said to be heterozygous. Results of his breeding experiments with peas are summarized in Mendel's two laws. His first law describes the segregation of alleles. It recognizes that the genotype of a heterozygote includes both alleles, even though only one (dominant) allele may contribute to the phenotype (physical appearance). Mendel's second law predicted that individual genes segregate independently. Therefore, if two traits are determined by distinct genes, the ratio of phenotypes arising from the first mating (F1 generation) and from a subsequent crossing ($F1 \times F1 = F2$) can be predicted by supposing an entirely random association between one of the two alleles for each of the two traits. We now know that this concept of independent gene segregation holds true only for unlinked genes, that is, genes located on separate chromosomes or on separate regions of a chromosome.

DNA Structure

Genes are composed of deoxyribonucleic acid (DNA) which, in turn, consists of two polymeric strands that are intertwined to form a right-handed helical duplex (Figure 5.6). The double-stranded helix model was originally proposed in 1953 by Watson and Crick and was subsequently supported by X-ray crystallographic structure of partially purified DNA (Watson & Crick, 1953). The building blocks of DNA include 4 bases: 2 purines (adenine (A) and guanine (G)) and 2 pyrimidines (cytosine (C) and thymine (T); see Figure 5.7). Each base is linked to a modified sugar, 2-deoxyribose phosphate, to form deoxyribonucleotides (Figure 5.7). The chains are formed by linkages between phosphate groups. Each DNA strand has a defined polarity. One end has a free 5′-phosphate group and the other end has a free 3′-hydroxyl group. The polarity of each strand in a nucleic acid paired duplex runs in opposing directions and is said to be antiparallel, as shown in Figure 5.6. The two strands of DNA are held together in the interior of the helix by hydrogen bonding (H-bonding) between two opposing base pairs. The phosphate and sugar moieties are placed on the outside of the helix and form the backbone of the structure. The base pairing is strictly governed to maintain a uniform and stable

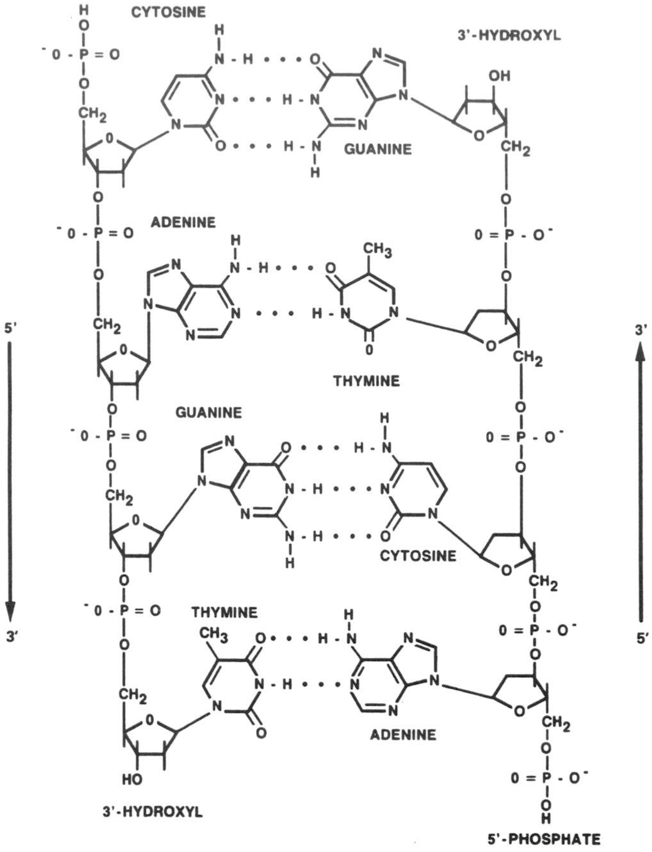

Figure 5.6 Desoxyribonucleic acid (RNA).

structure. The most stable H-bonding occurs between A-T and G-C pairs (Figure 5.6). Each of these base pairs is said to be complementary. The complex order of the nucleotides in the DNA strand establishes a code. Only one strand encodes the genetic information. This strand is termed the sense strand; the second, opposing strand, which harbors the complementary sequence, is called the antisense strand. The principle of precise molecular complementarity is a crucial structural feature of DNA. It explains why single-stranded nucleic acids are able to combine to form stable duplexes. Moreover, the fidelity of complementation is necessary to achieve an accurate replication and transfer of genetic information in dividing cells.

DNA Replication

Cells must replicate themselves by passing on genetic information without copying error. Precise self-replication is an essential property of DNA. During DNA replication, the two strands unwind to allow specific DNA polymerases to bind to and travel along the unwinding double helix. Each strand serves as a template for the synthesis of a complementary "daughter" strand. The daughter strand is synthesized by the addition of the 5′-phosphate of a deoxyribonucleotide to a free 3′-hydroxyl group on the growing strand. Because the chain growth takes place in the 5′ to 3′ direction, the growing strand traverses along the template in the 3′

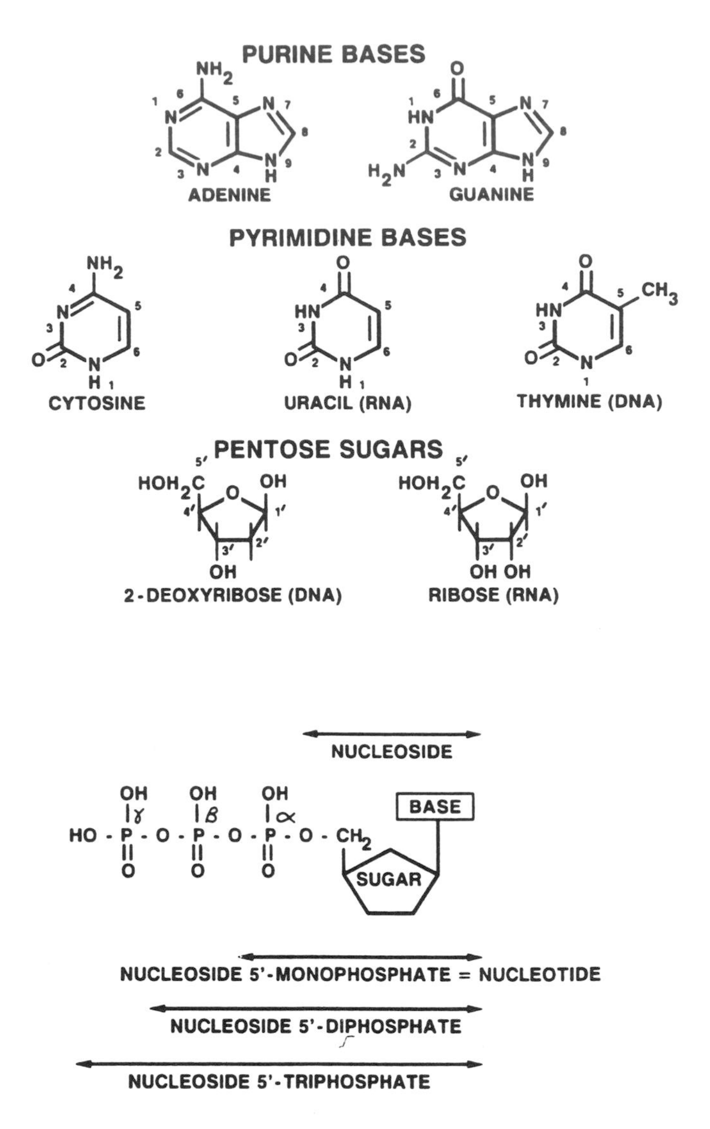

Figure 5.7 The building blocks of DNA.

to 5′ direction such that each parent strand (template) gives rise to a complementary daughter strand with which it immediately forms a new antiparallel duplex structure, which is joined by H-bonding. This is illustrated in Figure 5.6. Two new DNA duplexes are generated at the end of each replication cycle. Because each duplex consists of one original strand and one newly synthesized strand, this process is termed semiconservative replication.

Gene Structure

Although eukaryotic genes are often organized as extremely complex units, they also share common structural features. A schematic diagram of a "generic" gene is illustrated in Figure 5.8. The 5′ end harbors clusters of bases that are termed 5′ regulatory elements or upstream activator sequences (UAS). The elements consist of short consensus sequences of approximately 8 to 12 bp and are located at variable distances from the start of transcription. These elements are involved in the modulation of gene

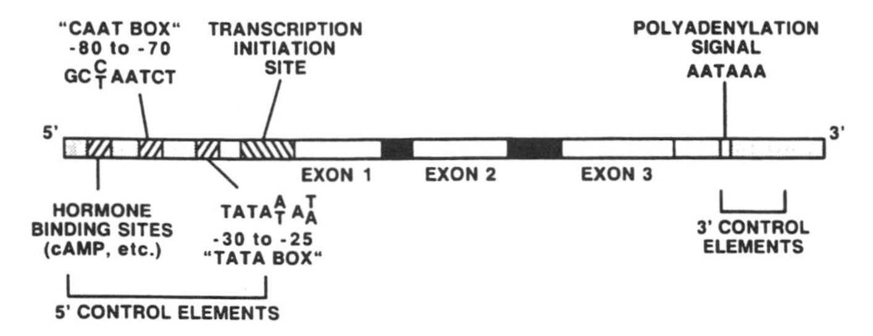

Figure 5.8 Schematic diagram of a "generic" gene.

expression either by activation or inhibition (for reviews, see He & Rosenfeld, 1991; Roeder, 1991). Collectively, this group of elements constitutes the promoter region. The promoter is essential for activation of gene transcription. An absence or mutation may result in severe loss or attenuation of gene transcription.

The most basic and prevalent promoter element is the TATA box. This region is frequently identified by the presence of a short stretch of repeating TA sequences which are located upstream (5′) of the transcription initiation site. The TATA sequence is thought to act as a signal for RNA polymerase to initate gene transcription at a site approximately 30 base pairs downstream.

Another promoter element found in many different genes is the CAAT box. The identity and mechanism of these and other UAS continue to generate interest among molecular biologists as new genes are characterized and new transcription regulatory factors are sought. The precise mechanism by which transcription is modulated is not yet clearly understood. However, regulatory factors are DNA-binding proteins that are believed to interact physically with both the DNA promoter elements and with RNA polymerases through specific binding sites for both. Thus far, the diversity and flexibility in gene expression patterns appear to be accomplished with relatively few transcription factors. The expression of the regulatory factors is dynamic, changing throughout development and in response to extracellular signals. It is evident that the combined action of transcriptional regulatory proteins is essential to generate the complexity of gene expression patterns in multicellular organisms.

The coding portion of the gene includes the region between the transcription initiation and termination sites, which will be transcribed into the primary messenger RNA. The coding regions of eukaryotic cells vary in length from a few hundred bases to as many as a few million. The coding region is usually arranged in a linear fashion. However, most gene segments are split into coding regions, which are expressed (exons) and interrupted by regions not found in the mature mRNA (introns). Consequently, the primary gene transcript, termed hnRNA (heterogeneous nuclear RNA) contains extra RNA sequences representing introns. These introns must be edited or "spliced" out before the mRNA can successfully direct protein synthesis. The length of an intron also ranges from a few hundred to several thousand bases. Moreover, some genes may be interrupted by many introns. The gene encoding dystrophin, the protein involved in muscle membrane integrity, spans 2 million bases and has over 60 introns (Hoffman, Brown, & Kunkel, 1987). The function of these introns is not clearly understood; only a few intronless genes (e.g., neurotransmitter receptors) have been identified (Weinshank et al., 1991).

Evidence for precise excision of introns has been predicted by the presence of short, conserved consensus sequences that define the site at which splicing of primary mRNA transcript is to take place. The dinucleotide sequence –GT– lies on the 5′ end of the intron; –AG– sequences appear at the 3′ end. The sequences are referred to as the splice donor and acceptor sites, respectively, representing the only conserved elements that are present among the ends of the introns.

Regulatory elements are also found downstream of the coding region. The most prominent of these elements is the sequence AATAAA, which functions as a polyadenylation signal. The polyadenylation signal apparently instructs the cleavage by a nuclease of the mRNA chain 10 to 15 bases further downstream. A second enzyme adds a homopolymer of 100 to 200 bases of As to the mRNA chain. The function of the polyA tail is unclear, although many investigators have postulated a role in stabilizing mRNA.

DNA Transcription

DNA is considered the master molecule, because it is replicated and passed on to subsequent generations, but RNA molecules actually direct the chemical synthesis of proteins during their short life span. The process in which DNA makes RNA is called transcription.

RNA is a single-stranded polymer that shares structural properties with DNA. However, RNA does possess some unique features: (a) RNA substitutes uridylic acid (U) for thymidylic acid (T), and (b) ribose (which has a hydroxyl group at the 2′ position of pentose) is substituted for deoxyribose. Two major types of RNA will be discussed here and in the subsequent section. Messenger RNA (mRNA) functions as the information carrier of the genetic information copied from the DNA. Transfer RNA (tRNA) plays an important role in protein synthesis as a carrier for amino acids that are to be incorporated into proteins. Although RNA exists in the cell as a single-stranded molecule, RNA strands are able to form stable hybrid duplexes with single-stranded DNA molecules. In addition, some forms of RNA (e.g., transfer RNA) harbor extensive intramolecular complementary sequences, which allow regions within the strand to self-hybridize and form intrastrand loops.

RNA synthesis is carried out in the cell nucleus by specific RNA polymerases that can faithfully transcribe mRNA from a DNA template. Initiation of transcription begins in the promoter region, where the two DNA strands separate. As was observed in DNA replication, mRNA synthesis also proceeds in a 5′ to 3′ direction with the addition of a 5′-ribonucleotide to the 3′-hydroxyl on the growing chain. In contrast, however, only one DNA strand will be transcribed into the primary transcript. By convention, the DNA strand that is copied will be considered the positive strand and will be an exact copy of the primary mRNA except that U will substitute for T in the mRNA. It follows, then, that the negative strand will always serve as the template for mRNA synthesis.

RNA Processing

The primary RNA transcript, termed heterogeneous nuclear RNA (hnRNA), must undergo further editing. This processing involves a series of highly specific splicing reactions in which exons are connected through the removal of introns. The mature mRNAs, which are now a continuous structure comprising only exons, are exported from the nucleus to the cytoplasm.

A less common mode of transcriptional control occurs at this stage. Alternative splicing of exons results in differential patterns of gene expression. Altered transcripts are generated by switching the coding exons to be utilized and discarding others. The mechanism for this type of control is clearly more complicated and as yet not well understood.

RNA Translation

In the cytoplasm, the mature mRNA is ready for protein synthesis. This process is termed translation because the nucleic acid sequences are "translated" into amino acid sequences. The translation process is even more complex than the mechanism of transcription. The machinery includes ribosomes, tRNAs, mRNAs, amino acids, aminoacyl synthetases, and a number of initiation, elongation, and termination factors. As the mature mRNA moves from the nucleus to the cytoplasm, specific ribosomes are assembled onto mRNA, which will then be used as a template to direct protein synthesis. Translation initiates at a specific AUG site in the 5′ terminus of the RNA. The base sequences of the mRNA corresponding to codons are read as nonoverlapping triplets. The AUG codon, which encodes methionine, dictates a reading frame such that sequential bases will be read as triplets, and directs incorporation of correct amino acids into the final protein product. There are 60 specific codons encoding for the existing 20 amino acids as well as 3 additional codons that signal termination of synthesis. The excess of codons relative to the number of amino acids means that multiple codons can encode the same amino acid. The number of codons employed is related to the frequency of usage of the particular amino acid.

Assembly of the polypeptide chain first requires that the tRNA be activated. Complementary sequence regions of this molecule undergo internal hybridization to form a double-stranded, cloverleaf structure containing looped regions. One of these loops contains a base triplet, an "anticodon," which is complementary to the codon sequence in the mRNA. Every tRNA has an anticodon, and a unique tRNA exists for every functional codon. An amino acid binding site lies on the opposite end of the tRNA molecule. The tRNA is said to be "charged" when an amino acid is chemically linked to this site by a specific aminoacyl synthetase. During protein synthesis, charged tRNA binds to mRNA through codon-anticodon pairing. Proteins also possess a defined polarity. Polypeptide chains grow by stepwise addition of single amino acids, starting with the amino-terminal amino acid and terminating with the carboxy-terminal amino acid. These amino acids are linked to the growing polypeptide chain with a specific enzyme, aminoacyltransferase, along with other cofactors. The ribosomes move along the mRNA template, to facilitate the proper insertion and linkage of amino acid into this protein. It is possible for multiple ribosomes to be assembled along the same mRNA template at any given time; therefore, several polypeptides are usually synthesized simultaneously. When the ribosome complex encounters the termination codon, the complex disassembles and the released polypeptide chain folds itself into its tertiary structure as its amino acid residues interact with each other and with their local chemical environment.

Protein Processing

After translation has been completed, the finished polypeptide often must undergo additional processing to become a mature, biologically active protein. A number of proteins, including receptors and ion channels, are composed of several polypeptide subunits. The finished protein requires assembly of these constituent subunits, which may be identical or different polypeptides. Different subunits may be products encoded by distinct genes or products of alternatively spliced primary transcripts.

Secreted proteins and peptide neurotransmitters are often synthesized with an additional stretch of approximately 20 residues at the amino-terminal end. These sequences are referred to as signal sequences. These extra residues appear to be necessary for attachment of a ribosome to the endoplasmic reticular (ER) membrane and for initial insertion of the protein into the lumen of the ER. Once inside the ER, these residues are immediately cleaved.

Other forms of posttranslation modification commonly observed in higher organisms include glycosylation and phosphorylation—the addition of sugar residues or phosphate groups at specific amino acid residues, respectively—in the polypeptide. Both processes appear to be essential to the activation and modulation of many proteins. Moreover, posttranslation processing by proteolytic cleavage of large precursor proteins at specific residues is often observed to yield small biologically active forms. A prime example is the endogenous enkephalin opioid. The large precursor, pro-opio-melanocortin (POMC; 265 amino acids) undergoes extensive posttranslation processing to yield several pituitary hormones (e.g., ACTH, aMSH, and bMSH) as well as the α- and β-endorphins.

Molecular Biology Tools

Significant advances in molecular biology over the past two decades are due in part to the discovery and development of three powerful technical achievements: (a) nucleic acid sequencing methods; (b) identification of restriction enzymes (RE); and (c) development of small plasmids. In the past few years, an exciting, innovative technique, the polymerase chain reaction (PCR), has also significantly advanced our analysis capabilities.

Nucleic Acid Sequencing

The ability to determine the nucleic acid sequences of DNA segments was based primarily on two methods developed in the 1970s: (a) the chemical modification procedure of Maxam and Gilbert (1977) and (b) the dideoxy chain termination method of Sanger (see, e.g., Sanger & Coulson, 1975). (The details of the chemistry for these methods will not be discussed here.) Over the years, improved modifications of these two techniques have facilitated the determination of sequences several thousands of bases in length, and have afforded a powerful tool for genetic analysis. With the knowledge of DNA sequences at hand, it is possible to deduce the sequence of RNA and, ultimately, the amino acid sequence of the gene product, without laborious purification of the protein itself. Comparison of the sequences found within the mRNA and that of the genomic DNA enables us to determine the intron-exon junctions. Moreover, comparison of DNA sequences and their predicted protein sequences to previously characterized nucleic acid or protein sequences in a computerized database has provided an opportunity to discover homologies and gain an insight into functional features of the encoded molecules. Some of the structural features that emerge from sequence comparison include hydrophobic and hydrophilic domains, and consensus sequences for potential posttranslation modifications of proteins and regulatory promoter elements of genes.

Restriction Endonucleases

In 1970, Hamilton Smith described an enzyme isolated from *Haemophilus influenzae,* which enzymatically degraded *E.coli* DNA (Smith & Wilcox, 1970). This enzyme was purified and shown to cleave the following specific double-stranded DNA sequences:

5′-GTPy ∅ PuAC-3′

3′-CAPu–PyTC-5′

(Py and Pu represent a pyrimidine and purine residue, respectively.)

Numerous restriction endonucleases (RE) have since been purified and characterized to cleave at very specific recognition sites that average 4 to 6 base pairs. The DNA fragments generated are sometimes called restriction-length fragments. Restriction enzymes have proven extremely useful in mapping DNA fragments because of their specificity and have also played a major role in cloning of foreign DNA into plasmids. The use of restriction fragment length polymorphisms (RFLPs), which are restriction sites created or deleted by random nucleotide modifications, has led to the discovery of several disease genes, including the gene involved in cystic fibrosis, Duchenne muscular dystrophy, and neurofibromatosis (Cawthon et al., 1990; Hoffman & Kunkel, 1989; Karem et al., 1989; see also Plomin et al., 1991, for a discussion of the role that RFLPs can play in elucidating the etiology of various forms of child and adult developmental psychopathology).

Plasmids

Also generically known as vectors, this class of mobile genetic elements is composed of a circular duplex of DNA into which foreign DNA may be inserted. Propagation of the bacterial cells that harbor the plasmid will produce multiple copies of the recombinant DNA. This is the process commonly referred to as molecular cloning. The most useful plasmids in recombinant DNA technologies share several basic common features:

1. The bacterial origin of replication is present, allowing for autonomous replication.
2. The plasmid does not integrate into bacterial chromosomes; therefore, it is readily isolated from a bacterial genetic material.
3. The presence of antibiotic resistance genes provides a selectable marker for cells that have taken up plasmid.
4. Several unique restriction sites have been engineered into plasmids so that foreign DNA may be readily inserted into them.

The combination of features provided by these multifunctional plasmid vectors and the ability to sequence DNA can be exploited to isolate, identify, and characterize nucleic acid sequences that represent a small fraction of an organism's genome.

Polymerase Chain Reaction (PCR)

This new tool for molecular biology is a very sensitive technique in which single DNA molecules can be produced without prior purification or cloning and with minimal sequence information. Basically, PCR is an *in vitro* method for DNA synthesis by which a particular segment of DNA can be specifically replicated. Two oligonucleotide primers, which flank the DNA fragment of interest, are amplified by repeated cycles of heat denaturation of DNA, annealing of primers to complementary sequences, and extension of annealed primers with a heat-stable DNA polymerase. This results in an exponential accumulation of specific target fragments. One of the most common applications of this technique is the specific amplification of single copy sequences from complex genomic samples. However, many other applications of this useful method are being successfully carried out (for review, see Erlich, 1989).

DNA Cloning

The information afforded by DNA cloning has been enormous. Not only has it revealed a vast body of protein sequence information, but it has enabled us to generate large quantities of the product of interest in order to examine its functional properties in a controlled environment. Manipulations by genetic engineering have allowed us to gain a better understanding of the consequences of altering DNA molecules. Genomic DNA cloning has enabled us to analyze gene structure and to transfer genes from one host to another, for example, by creating transgenic animals.

Construction of a cDNA

One of the initial steps in studying a gene product at the molecular level is the isolation and characterization of the mRNA encoding the protein. This involves the synthesis and cloning of DNA molecules complementary to the mature mRNA isolated from a specific tissue. The product is commonly termed cDNA. Because the level of mRNAs often reflects the amount of protein produced, it is generally a distinct advantage to generate a cDNA library from a tissue that contains an enriched source of the protein of interest. This limits the number of recombinant plasmids that must be screened in order to obtain the clone of interest. The principles involved in cDNA cloning are relatively straightforward, although the actual process is subject to various optimization steps. Here, we will simply outline the basic steps involved in cDNA cloning into plasmid vectors (see Figure 5.9). The synthesis of cDNA is facilitated by an enzyme, reverse transcriptase, which is isolated from RNA viruses. Its ability to transcribe DNA from an RNA template is the one exception to the central dogma of molecular biology. RNA viruses utilize DNA in the viral replication cycle. The complementary DNA molecule is synthesized from the 3′ to 5′ end of the mRNA to create a DNA-RNA hybrid. Another attractive feature of reverse transcriptase is that it inserts a few additional bases, using the newly synthesized cDNA as a template, after it reaches the 5′ end of the mRNA. This creates a hairpin loop in the cDNA. The mRNA is chemically removed at this stage because it is no longer required for subsequent steps. This first strand of cDNA is complementary to the coding mRNA strand; therefore, the second opposing strand of cDNA, which is synthesized by DNA polymerase, will be a copy of the mRNA sequence. The subsequent double-stranded DNA fragment must undergo several more steps (see Figure 5.9) before it can be inserted in the vector for propagation and further analysis. Numerous customized vectors are now available for cloning, including plasmids, bacteriophages, and cosmids, each of which is designed for efficiency and convenience. Short DNA fragments that harbor a particular RE site are attached to the mixture of double-stranded cDNAs such that they may be enzymatically linked to the vector. The next step will be to amplify this mixture of cDNA, called a

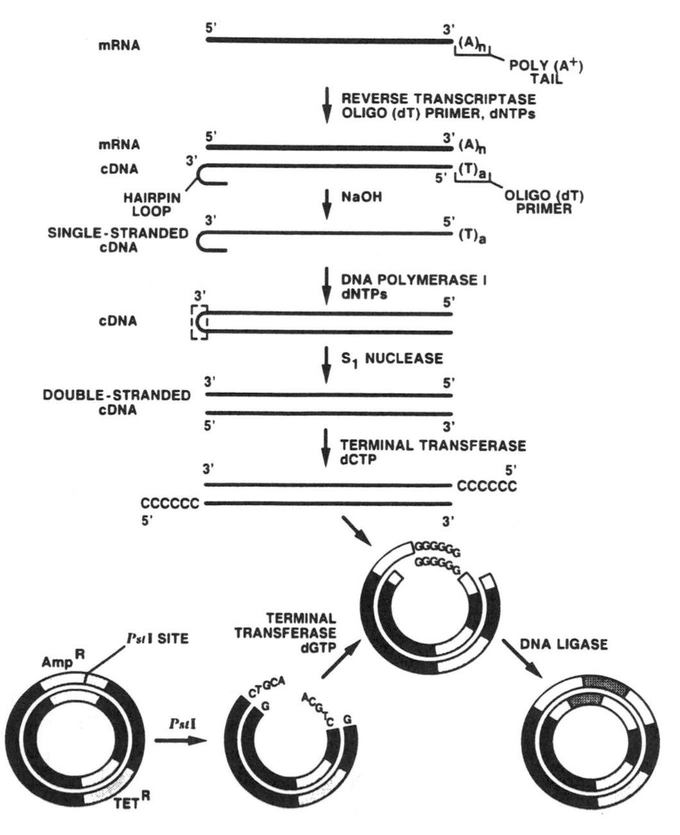

Figure 5.9 The process of cDNA cloning.

cDNA library, because the number of distinct cDNAs corresponds to the abundance of each unique mRNA molecule present in the tissue, and this frequency is presumed to be very low (~1 in 105). Amplification is accomplished by inoculating bacteria with the plasmid vectors, which now contain the cDNAs. This will allow the bacteria to be transformed and replicated. The copy number of the plasmid within each bacterial cell will increase by one or two magnitudes.

Once this library has been constructed and amplified, there are several ways to identify the cDNA of interest, depending on the specific tools available to the investigator. For example, if some amino acid sequence information is known, then it is possible to deduce the potential nucleic acid sequence based on our knowledge of genetic codons. Short nucleotide sequences may be synthesized and tagged radioactively and then used as probes to search for the complementary DNA fragment that will hybridize with probe. Alternatively, if the protein of interest has been purified but not sequenced, then an antibody directed against this protein may be used to identify the cDNA sequence that transcribes and translates the protein of interest. In this case, a bacteriophage vector, such as lgt11, has been developed to suit this purpose. Whatever the method of choice, the particular cDNA clone that has been identified may be further purified from the "library" and grown in larger quantities for further analyses.

Complementary DNA clones now exist for many peptides and peptide precursors. They include the sodium channel protein (Noda et al., 1986), acetylcholine receptor (Noda et al., 1984), serotonin receptor subtypes (Julius, Huang, Livelli, Axel, & Jessel, 1990), dopamine receptors (Weinshank et al., 1991), and enzymes such as tyrosine hydroxylase (O'Malley et al., 1987).

Genomic DNA Cloning

Analyses of gene structure and subsequent characterization of UAS elements involved in transcriptional regulation require the construction of a genomic DNA library. To accomplish this, chromosomal DNA is first digested with a suitable restriction enzyme. The resulting pool of DNA fragments is introduced into a cloning vector, such as the 1 bacteriophage, which supports growth and amplification of a large insert of foreign DNA. Isolation of the gene of interest may be achieved in several ways. The most common approach is to utilize a radiolabeled probe containing sequences complementary to those found in the gene, including cDNA probes. Once identified, the gene can be isolated, purified, and replicated for analyses of its structure. The principal techniques are generally related to those described above for cDNA cloning.

BRAIN DEVELOPMENT AND DEVELOPMENTAL PSYCHOPATHOLOGY

At the outset of this chapter, we expressed our conviction that new developments in developmental and molecular neurobiology could provide important new insights about brain development, which would be useful to researchers and clinicians concerned with developmental psychopathology. Now that the reader is well versed in the fundamental concepts of these disciplines, perhaps we can raise some additional issues for consideration. We believe the following points are pertinent to this discussion: (a) the relative importance of environmental vs. genetic factors in brain development; (b) the need for fresh conceptualizations of developmental disorders; (c) the importance of biologic markers to researchers in this field; and (d) the recognition that investigations of the molecular neurobiology of developmental disorders can enhance our understanding of basic molecular neurobiological processes (Ciaranello, Wong, & Rubenstein, 1990).

First, if we have learned anything from developmental neurobiology research over the past two decades, it is that the normal development of the nervous system unfolds as a series of timed genetic events whose expression depends on properly timed and delivered environmental stimuli (Nowakowski, 1987). We also know that the degree of malleability of the nervous system—the ability of the genetic hard-wiring to be influenced by environmental events—varies greatly across cell types, brain regions, and periods of time (Greenough, Black, & Wallace, 1987). Cellular phenotype is a good example: the maturational course of cells is "genetically determined," by which we usually mean that if cells are undisturbed their developmental outcome is predictable. However, there is abundant evidence that cellular phenotype can be altered if cells are exposed to a different chemical milieu at a critical point in maturation. What, then, does the phrase genetically determined mean? We take it to mean that when a developing cell remains in its normal environment, the properties it assumes will be governed by its genetic programming. But if the environment is altered at a sensitive period in development, then gene expression, too, may be altered, and the cell's development may take a quite different course. Deprived of light, sections of the visual cortex will not develop, even though they have all the genetic information they need to do so. If infant rat pups do not receive the proper tactile stimulation from the mother, important metabolic enzymes are not activated, even though their structural genes are perfectly intact.

And so it goes. There are literally hundreds of examples in developmental neurobiology where gene-environment interactions determine the pattern of normal development (Scarr & McCartney, 1983). Indeed, such interactions should probably be taken as the norm rather than the exception, because we can think of few examples where genetic programming is entirely insensitive to environmental input.

Second, we believe a fresh view of developmental disorders is needed. We really have no understanding of the structural deficits—if indeed there are any—in the brains of autistic or retarded children. These have been some intriguing clues: fewer dendritic spines, loss of specific cell types, persistence of fetal innervation patterns (Coyle, Oster-Granite, & Gearhart, 1986; Huttenlocher, 1979), but no unequivocal neuropathologic lesion that we can point to with certainty. Does this mean there are none, or that we lack the right tools for measurement?

It is possible that, in the nervous system, abnormal function is unrelated to abnormal structure, but such a conclusion would make the brain different from all other organs. It does not seem necessary to postulate that the brain disobeys the basic rules of biology to explain how it functions. In every other biologic system, structure and function are intimately joined, so that changes in one predispose to changes in the other. Until proven otherwise, we should assume that brain neurons follow this principle.

Why then can we not reliably identify changes in brain morphology in even the most severe developmental disorders? We suspect it is because the tools we now use cannot answer the questions we should be asking. Let us use infantile autism as a case in point.

Autism is a devastating clinical disorder characterized by extreme social dysfunction, stereotypic behaviors, failure to develop normal language, and, in most cases, mild to moderate mental retardation. It begins in infancy; both its temporal course and its outcome suggest it is a disorder of central nervous system development. But with few exceptions, no neurologic or neuropathologic deficits have been found in the brains of autistic children, and those that have been found are inconsistent and inadequate to explain the clinical deficits.

What new concepts emerging from research in developmental neurobiology give us some fresh ideas about autism? One is the notion of transient expression, either at the gene or cellular level, which we described earlier. We now know that certain genes are actively expressed only during certain times in development; after that, they are silent. We know most about the class of transiently expressed genes that turns on (or turns off) other genes, but we know that these genes are critical to normal nervous system development. Similarly, we know that certain neurons in the developing subplate live briefly to help migrating neurons find their targets, then disappear. Both examples illustrate an important point about developmental disorders: despite their clinical severity, their underlying neuropathology must be very subtle because we do not see them with existing research methodologies (Ciaranello, VandenBerg, & Anders, 1982). Deficits in synaptic connection, cell migration, axonal pruning, dendritic arborization—all of these could give rise to considerable neurologic impairment but not be prominent either on autopsy or microscopic examination. Defects in transiently expressed events, either at the gene or cellular level, could be even subtler, and thus less likely to be detected with current methodologies, which really are anatomic survey tools. Only if a researcher were expressly searching for them (and thus using the proper research methodologies) would defects in these events be likely to be found.

This reasoning suggests, then, that one approach to the biology of developmental disorders is to address them using models from developmental neurobiology, testing specific hypotheses derived therefrom. At the genetic level, for example, although our knowledge about transiently expressed genes is incomplete, there are already several candidate genes from flies and mice that could be tested for mutations in children with developmental disorders. (It is important for readers unfamiliar with molecular biology to recall that, even though such a gene is no longer expressed, it has not disappeared from the genome, so mutations in it can still be identified.)

This takes us to our third point. This field is still in great need of reliable, consistent markers that can be used to unambiguously classify developmental disorders. Clinically, these represent a frustrating hodgepodge of overlapping entities whose similarities often outweigh the differences among them. Attempts to differentiate among them usually follow lines set out by diagnostic committees whose clinical judgments, however refined and sophisticated, do not substitute for objective markers.

Decades of biologic and psychosocial research have failed to identify a single marker that can be used to diagnose, plan treatment, or predict the outcome of any psychiatric disorder. Working without reliable objective markers greatly handicaps our ability to ask questions and frame testable hypotheses that could lead us to important advances. As new fields emerge and make their contributions, we should not lose sight of their potential to contribute new ideas, concepts, and, especially, markers that could be used to make advances in our own field.

Finally, throughout history, theoreticians, researchers, and clinicians, working within diverse disciplines—embryology, the neurosciences, clinical and experimental psychology and psychiatry—have utilized high-risk, atypical, and psychopathological populations to affirm, challenge, elucidate, and expand the basic underlying principles of normal developmental theory (see Cicchetti, 1990, for a review). In view of the close link between the study of normal and abnormal development, the views of those who study normal development are equally applicable to atypicality: "Individual development is characterized by an increase of complexity of organization (i.e., the emergence of new structural and functional properties and competencies) at all levels of analysis (e.g., molecular, subcellular, cellular, organismic) as a consequence of horizontal and vertical coactions among the organisms' parts, including organism-environment coactions" (Gottlieb, 1991, p. 7). A "developmental analysis" (Cicchetti, 1990), such as that espoused by Gottlieb, assumes change and novelty, emphasizes the importance of timing in the manifestation and organization of behavior, underscores multiple determination, and warns against assuming invariant cause-and-effect relationships over the course of ontogenesis (Cairns, 1991).

One of the basic tenets of a developmental perspective on psychopathology is that we can learn more about the normal functioning of an organism by investigating its pathology, and, likewise, more about its pathology by examining its normal condition (Cicchetti, 1984). In essence, disorders or aberrations are conceived as a kind of magnifying lens in which normal psychological processes can be better observed. Precisely because many developmentalists construe psychopathology as a distortion or exaggeration of the normal, the investigation of pathological conditions is believed to throw into sharper relief one's understanding of normal processes. Although most contemporary research in the field of psychopathology has primarily focused on the contributions that normal development can make to advancing our knowledge of atypical ontogenesis, research in molecular neurobiology has paid more attention to both halves of the normal-abnormal equation. We believe that continued explorations on the molecular neurobiology of disorder will shed important light in the understanding of the processes and mechanisms underlying normal neurobiological development.

REFERENCES

Airaksinen, M. S., & Panula, P. (1988). The histaminergic system in the guinea pig central nervous system: An immunohistochemical mapping study using an antiserum against histamine. *Journal of Comparative Neurology, 273,* 163–186.

Akam, M. (1987). The molecular basis for metameric pattern in the Drosophila embryo. *Development, 101,* 1–22.

Akam, M. (1989). Hox and HOM: Homologous gene clusters in insects and vertebrates. *Cell, 57,* 347–349.

Akil, H., Watson, S. J., Young, E., Lewis, M. E., Khachaturian, H., & Walker, J. M. (1984). Endogenous opioids: Biology and function. *Annual Review of Neuroscience, 7,* 223–255.

Amaral, D. G., & Sinnamon, H. M. (1977). The locus coeruleus: Neurobiology of a central noradrenergic nucleus. *Progress in Neurobiology, 9,* 147–196.

Aoki, E., Semba, R., Kato, K., & Kashiwamata, S. (1987). Purification of specific antibody against aspartate and immunocytochemical localization of aspartergic neurons in the rat brain. *Neuroscience, 21,* 755–765.

Armstrong, D. M., Bruce, G., Hersh, L. B., & Gage, F. H. (1987). Development of cholinergic neurons in the septal/diagonal band complex of the rat. *Developmental Brain Research, 36,* 249–256.

Armstrong, D. M., Saper, C. B., Levey, A. I., Wainer, B. H., & Terry, R. D. (1983). Distribution of cholinergic neurons in rat brain: Demonstration by the immunocytochemical localization of choline acetyltransferase. *Journal of Comparative Neurology, 216,* 53–68.

Aslin, R. N. (1981). Experimental influences and sensitive periods in perceptual development: A unified model. In R. N. Aslin, J. R. Alberts, & M. R. Peterson (Eds.), *Development of perception: Psychobiological perspectives* (Vol. 2, pp. 45–93). New York: Academic Press.

Aston-Jones, G. (1985). Behavioral functions of locus coeruleus derived from cellular attributes. *Physiological Psychology, 13,* 118–126.

Aston-Jones, G., & Bloom, F. (1981). Activity of norepinephrine containing locus coeruleus neurons in behaving rats anticipates fluctuations in the sleep-waking cycle. *Journal of Neuroscience, 1,* 876–886.

Basbaum, A. I. (1988). Distribution of glycine receptor immunoreactivity in the spinal cord of the rat: Cytochemical evidence for a differential glycinergic control of lamina I and V nociceptive neurons. *Journal of Comparative Neurology, 278,* 330–336.

Basbaum, A. I., & Fields, H. L. (1984). Endogenous pain control systems: Brain stem spinal pathways and endorphin circuitry. *Annual Review of Neuroscience, 7,* 309–338.

Bateson, W. (1894). *Materials for the study of variation treated with special regard to discontinuity in the origin of species.* London: Macmillan.

Benes, F. (1991). Toward a neurodevelopmental understanding of schizophrenia and other psychiatric disorders. In D. Cicchetti & S. L. Toth (Eds.), *Rochester Symposium on Developmental Psychopathology: Vol. 3. Models and integrations* (pp. 161–184). Rochester, NY: University of Rochester Press.

Bentley, D., & Keshishian, H. (1982). Pathfinding by peripheral pioneer neurons in grasshoppers. *Science, 218,* 1082–1088.

Bieber, A. J., Snow, P. M., Hortsch, M., Patel, N. H., Jacobs, J. R., Traquina, Z. R., Schilling, J., & Goodman, C. S. (1989). Drosophila neuroglian: A member of the immunoglobulin superfamily with extensive homology to the vertebrate adhesion molecule L1. *Cell, 59,* 447–460.

Blessing, W. W., & Willoughby, J. O. (1985). Inhibiting the rabbit caudal ventrolateral medulla prevents baroreceptor-initiated secretion of vasopressin. *Journal of Physiology, 367,* 253–265.

Blier, P., de Montigny, C., & Chaput, Y. (1990). A role for the serotonin system in the mechanism of action of antidepressant treatments:

Preclinical evidence. *Journal of Clinical Psychiatry, 51*(4, Suppl.), 14–20.

Block, C. H., & Hoffman, G. E. (1987). Neuropeptide and monoamine components of the parabrachial pontine complex. *Peptides, 8,* 267–283.

Bloom, F. E. (1984). The functional significance of neurotransmitter diversity. *American Journal of Physiology, 246,* C184–C194.

Bloom, F. E. (1986). Identifying neuropeptides by gene cloning. *Psychopharmacology Bulletin, 22,* 701–707.

Bornstein, M. H. (1989). Sensitive periods in development: Structural characteristics and causal interpretation. *Psychological Bulletin, 105,* 179–197.

Brazell, M. P., Mitchell, S. N., & Gray, J. A. (1991). Effect of acute administration of nicotine on *in vivo* release of noradrenaline in the hippocampus of freely moving rats: A dose-response and antagonist study. *Neuropharmacology, 30,* 823–833.

Bredt, D. S., Hwang, P., & Snyder, S. H. (1990). Location of nitric oxide synthetase indicating a neural role for nitric oxide. *Nature, 347,* 768.

Cairns, R. B. (1991). Multiple metaphors for a singular idea. *Developmental Psychopathology, 27,* 23–26.

Carbone, E., & Swandulla, D. (1989). Neuronal calcium channels; kinetics, blockade and modulation. *Progress in Biophysics and Molecular Biology, 54,* 31–58.

Carlsson, M., & Carlsson, A. (1990). Interactions between glutamatergic and monoaminergic systems within the basal ganglia: Implications for schizophrenia and Parkinson's disease. *Trends in Neuroscience, 13,* 272–276.

Caviness, V. S. J., & Rakic, P. (1978). Mechanisms of cortical development: A view from mutations in mice. *Annual Review of Neuroscience, 1,* 297–326.

Cawthon, R. M., Weiss, R., Xu, G., Viskochil, D., Culver, M., Stevens, J., Robertson, M., Dunn, D., Gesteland, R., O'Connell, P., & White, R. (1990). A major segment of the neurofibromatosis type 1 gene: cDNA sequence, genomic structure, and point mutations. *Cell, 621,* 193–201.

Cechetto, D. F., Ciriello, J., & Calaresu, F. R. (1983). Afferent connections to cardiovascular sites in the amygdala: A horseradish peroxidase study in the cat. *Journal of the Autonomic Nervous System, 8,* 97–110.

Chalmers, J. P. (1978). Nervous system and hypertension. *Clinical Science and Molecular Medicine, 55,* 45s–56s.

Charney, D. S., Woods, S. W., Nagy, L. M., Southwick, S. M., Krystal, J. H., & Heninger, G. R. (1990). Noradrenergic function in panic disorder. *Journal of Clinical Psychiatry, 51 (Suppl. A),* 5–11.

Chisaka, O., & Capecchi, M. R. (1991). Regionally restricted developmental defects resulting from targeted disruption of the mouse homeobox gene Hox-1.5. *Nature, 350,* 473–479.

Ciaranello, R. D., Vandenberg, S. R., & Anders, T. F. (1982). Intrinsic and extrinsic determinants of neuronal development: Relations to infantile autism. *Journal of Autism and Developmental Disorders, 12*(2), 115–146.

Ciaranello, R., Wong, D., & Rubenstein, J. (1990). Molecular neurobiology and disorders of brain development. In S. Deutsch, A. Weizman, & R. Weizman (Eds.), *Applications of basic neuroscience to child psychiatry* (pp. 9–32). New York: Plenum.

Cicchetti, D. (1984). The emergence of developmental psychopathology. *Child Development, 55,* 1–7.

Cicchetti, D. (1990). A historical perspective on the discipline of developmental psychopathology. In J. Rolf, A. Masten, D. Cicchetti, K. Nuechterlein, & S. Weintraub (Eds.), *Risk and protective factors in the development of psychopathology* (pp. 2–28). New York: Cambridge University Press.

Cicchetti, D. (1993). Developmental psychopathology: Reactions, reflections, projections. *Developmental Review, 13,* 471–502.

Cobas, A., Fairen, A., Alvarez-Bolado, G., & Sanchez, M. P. (1991). Prenatal development of the intrinsic neurons of the rat neocortex: A comparative study of the distribution of GABA-immunoreactive cells and the GABAA receptor. *Neuroscience, 40,* 375–397.

Collins, P., & Depue, R. (1992). A neurobehavioral systems approach to developmental psychopathology: Implications for disorders of affect. In D. Cicchetti & S. L. Toth (Eds.), *Rochester Symposium of Developmental Psychopathology: Vol. 4. Developmental perspectives on depression* (pp. 29–101). Rochester, NY: University of Rochester Press.

Cooper, J. R., Bloom, F. E., & Roth, R. H. (1982). *The biochemical basis of neuropharmacology* (4th ed.). New York: Oxford University Press.

Cotman, C. W., & Iversen, L. L. (1987). Excitatory amino acids in the brain: Focus on NMDA receptors. *Trends in Neuroscience, 10,* 263–265.

Coyle, J. T. (1973). The development of catecholaminergic neurons of the central nervous system. *Neuroscience Research, 5,* 35–52.

Coyle, J. T., Oster-Granite, M., & Gearhart, J. (1986). The neurobiologic consequences of Down syndrome. *Brain Research Bulletin, 16,* 773–787.

Cuello, A. C., & Kanazawa, I. (1978). The distribution of substance P immunoreactive fibers in the rat central nervous system. *Journal of Comparative Neurology, 178,* 129–156.

Dahlstrom, A., & Fuxe, K. (1964a). Evidence for the existence of monoamine-containing neurons in the central nervous system. I. Demonstration of monoamines in the cell bodies of brain stem neurons. *Acta Physiologica Scandinavica, 62*(Supp. 232), 1–55.

Dahlstrom, A., & Fuxe, K. (1964b). A method for the demonstration of monoamine-containing nerve fibres in the central nervous system. *Acta Physiologica Scandinavica, 60,* 293–294.

Damsma, G., Day, J., & Fibiger, H. C. (1989). Lack of tolerance to nicotine-induced dopamine release in the nucleus accumbens. *European Journal of Pharmacology, 168,* 363–368.

Damsma, G., Westerink, B. H. C., Imperato, A., Rollema, H., de Vries, J. B., & Horn, A. S., (1987). Automated brain dialysis of acetylcholine in freely moving rats: Detection of basal acetylcholine. *Life Sciences, 41,* 873–876.

Davidson, R. (1991). Cerebral asymmetry and affective disorders: A developmental perspective. In D. Cicchetti & S. L. Toth (Eds.), *Rochester Symposium on Developmental Psychopathology: Vol. 2. Internalizing and externalizing expressions of dysfunction* (pp. 123–154). Hillsdale, NJ: Erlbaum.

Davis, G. C., Williams, A. C., Markey, S. P., Ebert, M. H., Caine, E. D., Reichert, C. M., & Kopin, I. J. (1979). Chronic Parkinsonism secondary to intravenous injection of meperidine analogs. *Psychiatry Research, 1,* 249–254.

Day, T. A., Ferguson, A. V., & Renaud, L. P. (1984). Facilitatory influence of noradrenergic afferents on the excitability of rat paraventricular nucleus neurosecretory cells. *Journal of Physiology, 355,* 237–249.

de Montigny, C., Chaput, Y., & Blier, P. (1990). Modification of serotonergic neuron properties by long-term treatment with serotonin reuptake blockers. *Journal of Clinical Psychiatry, 51*(12, Suppl. B), 4–8.

De Vries, T. J., Hogenboom, F., Mulder, A. H., & Schoffelmeer, A. N. M. (1990). Ontogeny of m-, d- and k-opioid receptors mediating inhibition of neurotransmitter release and adenylate cyclase activity in rat brain. *Developmental Brain Research, 54,* 63–69.

Del Fiacco, M., Dessi, M. L., & Levanti, M. C. (1984). Topographical localization of substance P in the human post-mortem brain stem: An immunohistochemical study in the newborn and adult tissue. *Neuroscience, 12,* 591–611.

DeLong, M. R. (1990). Primate models of movement disorders of basal ganglia origin. *Trends in Neuroscience, 13,* 281–285.

Diamond, B. I., & Borison, R. L. (1986). Basic and clinical studies of neuroleptic-induced supersensitivity psychosis and dyskinesia. *Psychopharmacology Bulletin, 22,* 900–905.

DiFiglia, M. (1990). Excitotoxic injury of the neostriatum: A model for Huntington's disease. *Trends in Neuroscience, 13,* 286–289.

Dodd, J., & Jessell, T. M. (1988). Axon guidance and the patterning of neuronal projections in vertebrates. *Science, 242,* 692–699.

Dun, N. J., & Kiraly, M. (1983). Capsaicin causes release of a substance P-like peptide in guinea-pig inferior mesenteric ganglia. *Journal of Physiology, 340,* 107–120.

Durston, A. J., Timmermans, J. P. M., Hage, W. J., Hendricks, H. F. J., de Vries, N. J., Heideveld, M., & Nieuwkoop, P. D. (1989). Retinoic acid causes an anteroposterior transformation in the developing central nervous system. *340,* 140–144.

Eisenman, G., & Dani, J. A. (1987). An introduction to molecular architecture and permeability of ion channels. *Annual Review of Biophysics and Biophysical Chemistry, 16,* 205–226.

Erlich, H. A. (1989). *PCR technology.* New York: Stockton Press.

Falck, B., Hillarp, N.-A., Thieme, G., & Torp, A. (1962). Fluorescence of catecholamines and related compounds condensed with formaldehyde. *Journal of Histochemistry and Cytochemistry, 10,* 348–354.

Fallon, J. H., & Leslie, F. M. (1986). Distribution of dynorphin and enkephalin peptides in the rat brain. *Journal of Comparative Neurology, 249,* 293–336.

Feinberg, I. (1982). Schizophrenia: Caused by a fault in programmed synaptic elimination during adolescence? *Journal of Psychiatric Research, 17,* 319–334.

Feldman, D. H., Olivera, B. M., & Yoshikami, D. (1987). Omega conus geographus toxin: A peptide that blocks calcium channels. *FEBS Letters, 214,* 295–300.

Fibiger, H. C. (1982). The organization and some projections of cholinergic neurons of the mammalian forebrain. *Brain Research Reviews, 4,* 288–327.

Fibiger, H. C., Lytle, L. D., & Campbell, B. A. (1970). Cholinergic modulation of adrenergic arousal in the developing rat. *Journal of Comparative and Physiological Psychology, 72,* 384–389.

Fibiger, H. C., & Phillips, A. G. (1987). Role of catecholamine transmitters in brain reward systems: Implications for the neurobiology of affect. In J. Engel & L. Oreland (Eds.), *Brain reward systems and abuse* (pp. 61–74). New York: Raven Press.

Foote, S. L., Bloom, F. E., & Aston-Jones, G. (1983). Nucleus locus coeruleus: New evidence of anatomical and physiological specificity. *Physiological Reviews, 63,* 844–914.

Foreman, J. C., Jordan, C. C., Oehme, P., & Renner, H. (1983). Structure-activity relationships for some substance P-related peptides that cause wheal and flare reactions in human skin. *Journal of Physiology, 335,* 449–465.

Fox, A. P., Nowycky, M. C., & Tsien, R. W. (1987a). Kinetic and pharmacological properties distinguishing three types of calcium currents in chick sensory neurones. *Journal of Physiology (London), 394,* 149–172.

Fox, A. P., Nowycky, M. C., & Tsien, R. W. (1987b). Single-channel recordings of three types of calcium channels in chick sensory neurones. *Journal of Physiology (London), 394,* 173–200.

Freeman, T. B., Spence, M. S., Boss, B. D., Spector, D. H., Strecker, R. E., Olanow, C. W., & Kordower, J. H. (1991). Development of dopaminergic neurons in the human substantia nigra. *Experimental Neurology, 113,* 344–353.

Friedrich, G., & Soriano, P. (1991). Promoter traps in embryonic stem cells: A genetic screen to identify and mutate developmental genes in mice. *Genes and Development, 5,* 1513–1523.

Fruhstoffer, B., Mignot, M., Bowersox, S., Nishino, S., Dement, W. C., & Guilleminault, C. (1989). Canine narcolepsy is associated with an elevated number of alpha 2 receptors in the locus coeruleus. *Brain Research, 500,* 209–214.

Fulwiler, C. E., & Saper, C. B. (1984). Subnuclear organization of the efferent connections of the parabrachial nucleus in the rat. *Brain Research Reviews, 7,* 229–259.

Gehring, W. (1987). Homeo boxes in the study of development. *Science, 236,* 1245–1252.

Ghosh, A., Antonini, A., McConnell, S. K., & Shatz, C. J. (1990). Requirement for subplate neurons in the formation of thalamocortical connections. *Nature, 347,* 179–181.

Ghysen, A. & Dambly-Chaudiere, C. (1988). From DNA to form: The achaete-scute complex. *Genes and Development, 2,* 495–501.

Giguere, V., Ong, E. S., Segui, P., & Evans, R. M. (1987). Identification of a receptor for the morphogen retinoic acid. *Nature, 330,* 624–629.

Glennon, R. A. (1990). Do classical hallucinogens act as 5-HT2 agonists or antagonists? *Neuropsychopharmacology, 3,* 509–517.

Goedert, M., Crowther, R. A., & Garner, C. C. (1991). Molecular characterization of microtubule-associated proteins tau and MAP2. *Trends in Neuroscience, 14,* 193–199.

Goldbloom, D. S., & Garfinkel, P. E. (1990). The serotonin hypothesis of bulimia nervosa: Theory and evidence. *Canadian Journal of Psychiatry, 35,* 741–744.

Gottesman, I. (1974). Developmental genetics and ontogenetic psychology: Overdue detente and propositions from a matchmaker. In A. Pick (Ed.), *Minnesota Symposium on Child Psychology* (pp. 55–80). Minneapolis: University of Minnesota Press.

Gottlieb, G. (1983). The psychobiological approach to developmental issues. In P. Mussen (Ed.), *Handbook of child psychology* (pp. 1–26). New York: Wiley.

Gottlieb, G. (1991). Experimental canalization of behavioral development: Theory. *Developmental Psychology, 27*(1), 4–13.

Graybiel, A. (1990). Neurotransmitters and neuromodulators in the basal ganglia. *Trends in Neuroscience, 13,* 244–254.

Greenough, W., Black, J., & Wallace, C. (1987). Experience and brain development. *Child Development, 58,* 539–559.

Grzanna, R., Chee, W. K., & Akeyson, E. W. (1987). Noradrenergic projections to brain stem nuclei: Evidence for differential projections from noradrenergic subgroups. *Journal of Comparative Neurology, 263,* 76–91.

Guy, H. R., & Conti, F. (1990). Pursuing the structure and function of voltage-gated channels. *Trends in Neuroscience, 13,* 201–206.

Guyenet, P. G., Haselton, J. R., & Sun, M. -K. (1989). Sympathoexcitatory neurons of the rostroventrolateral medulla and the origin of the sympathetic vasomotor tone. *Progress in Brain Research, 81,* 105–116.

Haeusler, G., & Osterwalder, R. (1980). Evidence suggesting a transmitter or neuromodulatory role for substance P at the first synapse of the baroreceptor reflex. *Naunyn-Schmiedeberg's Archives of Pharmacology, 314,* 111–121.

Harrelson, A. L., & Goodman, C. S. (1988). Growth cone guidance in insects: Fasciclin II is a member of the immunoglobulin superfamily. *Science, 242,* 700–708.

Hatten, M. E. (1990). Riding the glial monorail: A common mechanism for glial-guided neuronal migration in different regions of the developing mammalian brain. *Trends in Neurosciences, 13*(5), 179–184.

Hayashi, S., & Scott, M. P. (1990). What determines the specificity of action of Drosophila homeodomain proteins? *Cell, 63,* 883–894.

He, X., & Rosenfeld, M. G. (1991). Mechanisms of complex transcriptional regulation: Implications for brain development. *Neuron, 7*(2), 183–196.

He, X., Treacy, M. N., Simmons, D. M., Ingraham, H. A., Swanson, L. W., & Rosenfeld, M. G. (1989). Expression of a large family of POU-domain regulatory genes in mammalian brain development. *Nature, 340,* 35–42.

Heffner, C. D., Lumsden, A. G. S., & O'Leary, D. D. M. (1990). Target control of collateral extension and directional axon growth in the mammalian brain. *Science, 247,* 217–220.

Helke, C. J., O'Donohue, T. L., & Jacobowitz, D. M. (1980). Substance P as a baro- and chemoreceptor afferent neurotransmitter: Immunocytochemical and neurochemical evidence in the rat. *Peptides, 1,* 1–9.

Henderson, Z. (1991). Early development of the nucleus basalis-cortical projection but late expression of its cholinergic function. *Neuroscience, 44,* 311–324.

Hess, P. (1990). Calcium channels in vertebrate cells. *Annual Review of Neuroscience, 13,* 337–356.

Heym, J., & Jacobs, B. L. (1987). Serotonergic mechanisms of hallucinogenic drug effects. *Monographs in Neural Sciences, 13,* 55–81.

Hobson, J. A., McCarley, R. W., & Wyzinski, P. W. (1975). Sleep cycle oscillation: Reciprocal discharge by two brain stem groups. *Science, 189,* 55–58.

Hodgkin, A. L., & Huxley, A. F. (1952a). The components of membrane conductance in the giant axon of Loligo. *Journal of Physiology (London), 116,* 473–496.

Hodgkin, A. L., & Huxley, A. F. (1952b). Currents carried by sodium and potassium ions through the membrane of the giant axon of Loligo. *Journal of Physiology (London), 116,* 449–472.

Hoffman, E. P., Brown, R. H., & Kunkel, L. M. (1987). Dystrophin: The protein product of the Duchenne muscular dystrophy locus. *Cell, 51,* 919–928.

Hoffman, E. P., & Kunkel, L. M. (1989). Dystrophon abnormalities in Duchenne/Becker muscular dystrophy. *Neuron, 2,* 1019–1029.

Hokfelt, T., Johansson, O., & Goldstein, M. (1984). Central catecholamine neurons as revealed by immunochemistry with special reference to the adrenaline neurons. In A. Bjorklund & T. Hokfelt (Eds.), *Handbook of neuroanatomy* (pp. 157–276). Amsterdam: Elsevier.

Hokfelt, T., Kellerth, J. O., Nilsson, G., & Pernow, B. (1975). Substance P: Localization in the central nervous system and in some primary sensory neurons. *Science, 190,* 889–890.

Holland, P. W. H., & Hogan, B. L. M. (1988). Expression of homeobox genes during mouse development: A review. *Genes & Development, 2,* 773–782.

Hornykiewicz, O. (1982). Brain neurotransmitter changes in Parkinson's disease. In C. D. Marsden & S. Fahn (Eds.), *Movement disorders* (pp. 41–58). London: Butterworth.

Hough, L. B. (1988). Cellular localization and possible functions for brain histamine: Recent progress. *Progress in Neurobiology, 30,* 469–505.

Hubel, D. H., & Wiesel, T. N. (1963). Shape and arrangement of columns in cat's striate cortex. *Journal of Physiology, 165,* 559–568.

Huttenlocher, P. (1979). Synaptic density in human frontal cortex: Developmental changes and effects of aging. *Brain Research, 163,* 195–205.

Inagaki, S., Sakanaka, M., Shiosaka, S., Senba, E., Takatsuki, K., Takagi, H., Kawai, Y., Minigawa, H., & Tohyama, M. (1982). Ontogeny of substance P-containing neuron system of the rat: Immunohistochemical analysis—I. Forebrain and upper brain stem. *Neuroscience, 7,* 251–277.

Inagaki, N., Yamatodani, A., Ando-Yamamoto, M., Tohyama, M., Watanabe, T., & Wada, H. (1988). Organization of histaminergic fibers in the rat brain. *Journal of Comparative Neurology, 273,* 283–300.

Ingham, P. W. (1988). The molecular genetics of embryonic pattern formation in drosophila. *Nature, 335,* 25–34.

Jacobs, R. W., & Butcher, L. L. (1986). Pathology of the basal forebrain in Alzheimer's disease and other dementias. In A. B. Scheibel & A. F. Wechsler (Eds.), *The biological substrates of Alzheimer's disease* (pp. 87–100). New York: Academic Press.

Jan. L. Y., & Jan, Y. N. (1989). Voltage-sensitive ion channels. *Cell, 56,* 13–25.

Jimenez, F., & Campos-Ortega, J. A. (1990). Defective neuroblast commitment in mutants of the achaete-scute complex and adjacent genes of D. melanogaster. *Neuron, 5,* 81–89.

Johnson, J. E., Birren, S. J., & Anderson, D. J. (1990). Two rat homologues of Drosophila achaete-scute specifically expressed in neuronal precursors. *Nature, 346,* 858–861.

Joly, E., Muche, L., & Oldstone, M. B. A. (1991). Viral persistence in neurons explained by lack of MHC class I expression. *Science, 253,* 1283.

Julius, D., Huang, K. N., Livelli, T. J., Axel, R., & Jessel, T. M. (1990). The 5HT2 receptor defines a family of structurally distinct but functionally conserved serotonin receptors. *Proceedings of the National Academy of Sciences, 87,* 928–932.

Kandel, E. R., & Schwartz, J. H. (1985). *Principles of neural science.* New York: Elsevier.

Kerem, B. -S., Rommens, J. M., Buchanan, J. A., Markiewicz, D., Cox, T. K., Chakravarti, A., Buchwald, M., & Tsui, L. -C. (1989). Identification of the cystic fibrosis gene: Genetic analysis. *Science, 245,* 1073–1080.

Kessel, M., Balling, R., & Gruss, P. (1990). Variations of cervical vertebrae after expression of a Hox-1.1 transgene in mice. *Cell, 61,* 301–308.

Kessel, M., & Gruss, P. (1990). Murine developmental control genes. *Science, 249,* 374–379.

Kessel, M., & Gruss, P. (1991). Homeotic transformations of murine vertebrae and concomitant alteration of Hox codes induced by retinoic acid. *Cell, 67,* 89–104.

Keynes, R., & Lumsden, A. (1990). Segmentation and the origin of regional diversity in the vertebrate central nervous system. *Neuron, 2,* 1–9.

Khachaturian, H., Lewis, M. E., & Watson, S. J. (1982). Enkephalin systems in diencephalon and brain stem of the rat. *Journal of Comparative Neurology, 220,* 310–320.

Khachaturian, H., Watson, S. J., Lewis, M. E., Coy, D., Goldstein, A., & Akil, H. (1982). Dynorphin immunocytochemistry in the rat central nervous system. *Peptides, 3,* 941–954.

Kish, P. E., Kim, S. Y., & Ueda, T. (1989). Ontogeny of glutamate accumulating activity in rat brain synaptic vesicles. *Neuroscience Letters, 97,* 185–190.

Koob, G. F., & Bloom, F. E. (1983). Behavioural effects of opioid peptides. *British Medical Bulletin, 39,* 89–94.

Kostovic, I. (1986). Prenatal development of nucleus basalis complex and related fiber systems in man: A histochemical study. *Neuroscience, 17,* 1047–1078.

Krieger, D. T. (1986). An overview of neuropeptides. In J. B. Martin & J. D. Barchas (Eds.), *Neuropeptides in neurologic and psychiatric disease* (pp. 1–32). New York: Raven Press.

Langston, J. W., Ballard, P., Tetrud, J. W., & Irwin, I. (1983). Chronic Parkinsonism in humans due to a product of meperidine-analog synthesis. *Science, 219,* 979–980.

Lauder, J. M. (1983). Hormonal and humoral influences on brain development. *Psychoneuroendocrinology, 8,* 121–155.

Lauder, J. M. (1990). Ontogeny of the serotonergic system in the rat: Serotonin as a developmental signal. In P. M. Whitaker-Azmitia & S. J. Peroutka (Eds.), *The neuropharmacology of serotonin* (pp. 297–314). New York: New York Academy of Sciences.

Lauder, J. M., & Bloom, F. E. (1974). Ontogeny of monoamine neurons in the locus coeruleus, raphe nuclei and substantia nigra of the rat: I. Cell differentiation. *Journal of Comparative Neurology, 155,* 469–481.

Lauder, J. M., & Bloom, F. E. (1975). Ontogeny of monoamine neurons in the locus coeruleus, raphe nuclei and substantia nigra of the rat: II. Synaptogenesis. *Journal of Comparative Neurology, 163,* 251–264.

Lauder, J. M., Han, V. K. M., Henderson, P., Verdoorn, T., & Towle, A. C. (1986). Prenatal ontogeny of the GABAergic system in the rat brain: An immunocytochemical study. *Neuroscience, 19,* 465–493.

Lee, M., & Nurse, P. (1988). Cell cycle control genes in fission yeast and mammalian cells. *Trends in Genetics, 4*(10), 287–290.

Levitan, I. B. (1991). *The neuron cell.* New York: Oxford University Press.

Lewin, B. (1990). *Genes IV.* Oxford, England: Oxford University Press.

Lewis, E. B. (1978). A gene complex controlling segmentation in Drosophila. *Nature, 276,* 565–570.

Lewis, M. E., Khachaturian, H., Schafer, M. K. -H., & Watson, S. J. (1986). Anatomical approaches to the study of neuropeptides and related mRNA in the central nervous system. In J. B. Martin & J. D. Barchas (Eds.), *Neuropeptides in neurologic and psychiatric disease* (pp. 79–109). New York: Raven Press.

Lewis, P. R., & Shute, C. D. (1967). The cholinergic limbic system: Projections to hippocampal formation, medial cortex, nuclei of the ascending cholinergic reticular system, and the subfornical organ and supra-optic crest. *Brain, 90,* 521–540.

Lidov, H. G. W., & Molliver, M. E. (1982). Immunohistochemical study of the development of serotonergic neurons in the rat CNS. *Brain Research Bulletin, 9,* 559–604.

Lindvall, O., & Bjorklund, A. (1978). Organization of catecholamine neurons in the rat central nervous system. In L. L. Iversen, S. D. Iversen, & S. H. Snyder (Eds.), *Handbook of psychopharmacology* (pp. 139–231). New York: Plenum.

Lindvall, O., & Bjorklund, A. (1983). Dopamine- and norepinephrine-containing neuron systems: Their anatomy in the rat brain. In P. C. Emson (Ed.), *Chemical neuroanatomy* (pp. 229–255). New York: Raven Press.

Liu, C. -J., Grandes, P., Matute, C., Cuenod, M., & Streit, P. (1989). Glutamate-like immunoreactivity revealed in rat olfactory bulb, hippocampus and cerebellum by monoclonal antibody and sensitive staining method. *Histochemistry, 90,* 427–445.

Ljungdahl, A., Hokfelt, T., & Nilsson, G. (1978). Distribution of substance P-like immunoreactivity in the central nervous system of the rat: I. Cell bodies and nerve terminals. *Neuroscience, 3,* 861–943.

Lo, L., Johnson, J. E., Wuenschell, C. W., Saito, T., & Anderson, D. J. (1991). Mammalian achaete-scute homolog 1 is transiently expressed by spatially restricted subsets of early neuroepithelial and neural crest cells. *Genes and Development, 5,* 1524–1537.

Loewy, A. D. (1982). Descending pathways to the sympathetic preganglionic neurons. *Progress in Brain Research, 57,* 267–277.

Losonczy, M. F., Davidson, M., & Davis, K. L. (1987). The dopamine hypothesis of schizophrenia. In H. Y. Meltzer (Ed.), *Psychopharmacology: The third generation of progress* (pp. 715–726). New York: Raven Press.

Lufkin, T., Dierich, A., LeMeur, M., Mark, M., & Chambon, P. (1991). Disruption of the Hox-1.6 homeobox gene results in defects in a region corresponding to its rostral domain of expression. *Cell, 66,* 1105–1119.

Lundberg, J. M., & Hokfelt, T. (1983). Coexistence of peptides and classical neurotransmitters. *Trends in Neuroscience, 6,* 325–333.

Luskin, M. B., Pearlman, A. L., & Sanes, J. R. (1988). Cell lineage in the cerebral cortex of the mouse studied *in vivo* and *in vitro* with a recombinant retrovirus. *Neuron, 1,* 635–647.

Lyons, W. E., & Grzanna, R. (1988). Noradrenergic neurons with divergent projections to the motor trigeminal nucleus and the spinal cord: A double retrograde neuronal labeling study. *Neuroscience, 26,* 681–693.

Madl, J. E. (1987). Monoclonal antibodies specific for fixative-modified aspartate: Immunocytochemical localization in the rat CNS. *Journal of Neuroscience, 7,* 2639–2650.

Malicki, J., Schughart, K., & McGinnis, W. (1990). Mouse Hox 2.2. specifies thoracic segmental identity in Drosophila embryos and larvae. *Cell, 63,* 961–967.

Mann, J. J., Arango, V., & Underwood, M. D. (1990). Serotonin and suicidal behavior. In P. M. Whitaker-Azmitia & S. J. Peroutka (Eds.), *The neuropharmacology of serotonin* (pp. 476–485). New York: New York Academy of Sciences.

Mansour, S. L., Thomas, K. R., & Capecchi, M. R. (1988). Disruption of the proto-oncogene int-2 in mouse embryo-derived stem cells: A general strategy for targeting mutations to nonselectable genes. *Nature, 336,* 348–352.

Mason, S. T., & Fibiger, H. C. (1979). Noradrenaline and selective attention. *Life Sciences, 25,* 1949–1956.

Matsuoka, M., Nagawa, F., Okazaki, K., Kingsbury, L., Yoshida, K., Muller, U., Larue, D., Winer, J. A., & Sakano, H. (1991). Detection of somatic DNA recombination in the transgenic mouse brain. *Science, 254,* 81–86.

Maxam, A. M., & Gilbert, W. (1977). A new method of sequencing DNA. *Proceedings of the National Academy of Sciences (USA), 74,* 5463–5467.

Mayer, M. L., & Westbrook, G. L. (1987). The physiology of excitatory amino acids in the vertebrate central nervous system. *Progress in Neurobiology, 28,* 197–276.

McCarley, R. W., & Hobson, J. A. (1975). Neuronal excitability modulation over the sleep cycle: A structural and mathematical model. *Science, 189,* 58–60.

McClesky, E. W., Fox, A. P., Feldman, D. H., Cruz, L. J., & Olivera, B. M. (1987). Omega-conotoxin: Direct and persistent blockade of specific types of calcium channels in neurons but not muscle. *Proceedings of the National Academy of Sciences (USA), 84,* 4327–4331.

McConnell, S. K., Ghosh, A., & Shatz, C. J. (1989). Subplate neurons pioneer the first axon pathway from the cerebral cortex. *Science, 245,* 978–982.

McConnell, S. K., & Kaznowski, C. E. (1991). Cell cycle dependence of laminar determination in developing neocortex. *Science, 254,* 282–285.

McDonald, J. K., Speciale, S. G., & Parnavelas, J. G. (1987). The laminar distribution of glutamate decarboxylase and choline acetyltransferase in the adult and developing visual cortex of the rat. *Neuroscience, 21,* 825–832.

McDowell, J., & Kitchen, I. (1987). Development of opioid systems: Peptides, receptors and pharmacology. *Brain Research Reviews, 12,* 397–421.

McGeer, P. L. (1978, 1987). *Molecular neurobiology of the mammalian brain* (1st ed., 2nd ed.). New York: Plenum.

McGinnis, N., Kuziora, M. A., & McGinnis, W. (1990). Human Hox-4.2 and Drosophila: Deformed encode similar regulatory specificities in Drosophila embryos and larvae. *Cell, 63,* 969–976.

McMahon, A. P., & Bradley, A. (1990). The Wnt-1 (int-1) proto-oncogene is required for development of a large region of the mouse brain. *Cell, 62,* 1073–1085.

Mefford, I. N. (1988). Epinephrine in mammalian brain. *Progress in Neuropsychopharmacology and Biological Psychiatry, 12,* 365–388.

Mesulam, M. -M. & Mufson, E. J. (1984). Neural inputs to the nucleus basalis of the substantia innominata (Ch4) in the rhesus monkey. *Brain, 107,* 253–274.

Mesulam, M. -M., Mufson, E. J., Levey, A. I., & Wainer, B. H. (1983). Cholinergic innervation of cortex by the basal forebrain: Cytochemistry and cortical connections of the septal area, diagonal band nuclei, nucleus basalis (substantia innominata), and hypothalamus in the rhesus monkey. *Journal of Comparative Neurology, 214,* 170–197.

Mesulam, M. -M., Mufson, E. J., Wainer, B. H., & Levey, E. J. (1983). Central cholinergic pathways in the rat: An overview based on an alternative nomenclature (Ch1-Ch6). *Neuroscience, 10,* 1185–1201.

Mignot, E., Guilleminault, C., Aldrich, M., Quera-Sedra, M. A., Tiberge, M., & Partinen, M. (1988). Prazosin contraindicated in patients with narcolepsy. *Lancet, 2,* 511.

Mignot, E., Guilleminault, C., & Bowersox, S. (1988). Effect of 1-adrenergic blockade with prazosin in canine narcolepsy. *Brain Research, 444,* 184–188.

Mignot, E., Guilleminault, C., Bowersox, S. S., Frusthofer, B., Nishino, S., Maddaluno, J., Ciaranello, R. D., & Dement, W. C. (1989). Central a1 adrenoceptor subtypes in narcolepsy-cataplexy: A disorder of REM sleep. *Brain Research, 490,* 186–191.

Mignot, E., Guilleminault, C., Bowersox, S. S., Kilduff, T., & Dement, W. C. (1987). The effects of alpha-1 adrenoceptor agonist and antagonist in canine narcolepsy. *Sleep Research, 16,* 393.

Miller, C. (1991). 1990: Annus Mirabilus of potassium channels. *Science, 252,* 1092–1096.

Miller, R. J. (1987). Multiple calcium channels and neuronal function. *Science, 235,* 46–52.

Miyamoto, M., Kato, J., Narumi, S., & Nagaoka, A. (1987). Characteristics of memory impairment following lesioning of the basal forebrain and medial septal nucleus in rats. *Brain Research, 419,* 19–31.

Moriyoshi, K., Masu, M., Ishii, T., Shigemoto, R., Mizuno, N., & Nakanishi, S. (1991). Molecular cloning and characterization of the rat NMDA receptor. *Nature, 354,* 31–37.

Nemeroff, C. B., Berger, P. A., & Bissette, G. (1987). Peptides in schizophrenia. In H. Y. Meltzer (Ed.), *Psychopharmacology: The third generation of progress* (pp. 727–743). New York: Raven Press.

Noda, M., Ikeda, T., Kayano, T., Suzuki, H., Takeshima, H., Kuraski, M., Takahashi, H., & Numa, S. (1986). Existence of distinct sodium channel messenger RNAs in rat brain. *Nature, 320,* 188–192.

Noda, M., Shimizu, S., Tanabe, T., Takai, T., Kayano, T., Ikeda, T., Takahashi, H., Hirose, T., Inayama, S., Hayashida, M., Miyata, T., & Numa, S. (1984). Primary structure of electroplax electricus sodium channel deduced from cDNA sequence. *Nature, 312,* 121–127.

Nomura, H., Shiosaka, S., Inagaki, S., Ishimoto, I., Senba, E., Sakanaka, M., Takatsuki, K., Matsuzaki, T., Kubota, Y., Saito, H., Takase, S., Kogure, K., & Tohyama, M. (1982). Distribution of substance P-like immunoreactivity in the lower brain stem of the human fetus: An immunohistochemical study. *Brain Research, 252,* 315–325.

Nowakowski, R. S. (1987). Basic concepts of CNS development. *Child Development, 58,* 568–595.

Nusslein-Volhard, C., Frohnhofer, H. G., & Lehman, R. (1987). Determination of anteroposterior polarity in Drosophila. *Science, 238,* 1675–1681.

Oertel, W. H., Schmechel, D. E., Mugnaini, E., Tappaz, M. L., & Kopin, I. J. (1981). Immunocytochemical localization of glutamate decarboxylase in rat cerebellum with a new antiserum. *Neuroscience, 6,* 2715–2735.

O'Leary, D. D. M., & Stanfield, B. B. (1989). Selective elimination of axons extended by developing cortical neurons is dependent on regional locale: Experiments utilizing fetal cortical transplants. *Journal of Neuroscience, 9*(7), 2230–2246.

Olson, L., Boreus, L. O., & Sieger, A. (1973). Histochemical demonstration and mapping of 5-hydroxytryptamine- and catecholamine-containing neuron systems in the human fetal brain. *Zeitschrift fur Anatomie und Entwicklungs-Geschichte, 139,* 259–282.

Olson, G. A., Olson, R. D., & Kastin, A. J. (1989). Endogenous opiates: 1987. *Peptides, 10,* 205–236.

Olson, L., & Sieger, A. (1972). Early prenatal ontogeny of central monoamine neurons in the rat: Fluorescence histochemical observations. *Zeitschrift fur Anatomie und Entwicklungs-Geschichte, 137,* 301–316.

O'Malley, K. L., Anhalt, M. J., Martin, B. M., Kelsoe, J. K., Winfield, S. L., & Ginns, E. I. (1987). Isolation and characterization of the human tyrosine hydroxylase gene: Identification of 5' alternative splice sites responsible for multiple mRNAs. *Biochemistry, 26,* 2910–2914.

Ottersen, O. P., & Storm-Mathisen, J. (1984). Neurons containing or accumulating transmitter amino acids. In A. Bjorklund, T. Hokfelt, & M. J. Kuhar (Eds.), *Handbook of chemical neuroanatomy* (pp. 141–246). Amsterdam: Elsevier.

Ottersen, O. P., & Storm-Mathisen, J. (1987). Localization of amino acid neurotransmitters by immunocytochemistry. *Trends in Neuroscience, 10,* 250–255.

Overmeier, J. B., & Seligman, M. E. P. (1967). Effects of inescapable shock upon subsequent escape and avoidance learning. *Journal of Comparative and Physiological Psychology, 63,* 23–33.

Papazian, D. M., Schwarz, T. L., Tempel, B. L., Jan, Y. N., & Jan, L. Y. (1987). Cloning of genomic and complementary DNA from Shaker, a putative potassium channel gene from Drosophila. *Science, 237,* 749–753.

Phillips, J. M., & Burns, R. S. (1984). The MPTP-treated monkey: An animal model of Parkinson's disease. *ILAR News, 27*(3), 8–11.

Pickel, V. M., Sumal, K. K., & Miller, R. J. (1982). Early prenatal development of substance P and enkephalin-containing neurons in the rat. *Journal of Comparative Neurology, 210,* 411–422.

Placzek, M., Tessier-Lavigne, M., Yamada, T., Jessell, T., & Dodd, J. (1990). Mesodermal control of neural cell identity: Floor plate induction by the notochord. *Science, 250,* 985–988.

Plomin, R., Rende, R., & Rutter, M. (1991). Quantitative genetics and developmental psychopathology. In D. Cicchetti & S. L. Toth (Eds.), *Rochester Symposium on Developmental Psychopathology: Vol. 2. Internalizing and externalizing expressions of dysfunction* (pp. 155–202). Rochester, NY: University of Rochester Press.

Pongs, O., Kecskemethy, N., Muller, R., Krah-Jentgens, I., Baumann, A., Kutz, H. H., Canal, I., Llamazares, S., & Ferrus, A. (1988). Shaker encodes a family of putative potassium channel proteins in the nervous system of Drosophila. *EMBO Journal, 7,* 1087–1096.

Pons, T. P., Garraghty, P. E., Ommaya, A. K., Kaas, J. H., Taub, E., & Mishkin, M. (1991). Massive cortical reorganization after sensory deafferentation in adult macaques. *Science, 252,* 1857–1860.

Porteus, M. H., Bulfone, A., Ciaranello, R. D., & Rubenstein, J. L. L. (1991). Isolation and characterization of a novel cDNA clone encoding a homeodomain that is developmentally regulated in the ventral forebrain. *Neuron, 7,* 221–229.

Porteus, M. H., Brice, A. E., Bulfone, A., Usdin, T. B., Ciaranello, R. D., & Rubenstein, J. L. L. (1992). Isolation and characterization of a library of cDNA clones that are preferentially expressed in the embryonic telencephalon. *Molecular Brain Research, 12,* 7–22.

Price, M., Lemaistre, M., Pischetola, M., DiLauro, R., & Duboule, D. (1991). A mouse gene related to Distal-less shows a restricted expression in the developing forebrain. *Nature, 351,* 748–751.

Price, J., & Thurlow, L. (1988). Cell linage in the rat cerebral cortex: A study using retroviral-mediated gene transfer. *Development, 104,* 473–482.

Purves, D., & Lichtman, J. W. (1985). *Principles of neural development.* Sunderland, MA: Sinauer Associates.

Rakic, P. (1988). Specification of cerebral cortical areas. *Science, 241,* 170–176.

Ramm, P. (1979). The locus coeruleus, catecholamines and REM sleep: A critical review. *Behavior Neural Biology, 26,* 415–448.

Rasmussen, K., Morilak, D. A., & Jacobs, J. L. (1986). Single unit activity of locus coeruleus neurons in the freely moving cat: I. During naturalistic behaviors and in response to simple and complex stimuli. *Brain Research, 371,* 324–334.

Redmond, D. E., & Huang, Y. H. (1979). New evidence for a locus coeruleus-norepinephrine connection with anxiety. *Life Sciences, 25,* 2149–2162.

Reiner, A., Albin, R. L., Anderson, K. D., D'Amato, C. J., Penney, J. B., & Young, A. B. (1988). Differential loss of striatal projection neurons in Huntington's disease. *Proceedings of the National Academy of Sciences, 85,* 5733–5737.

Richardson, R. T., & DeLong, M. R. (1988). A reappraisal of the functions of the nucleus basalis of Meynert. *Trends in Neuroscience, 11,* 264–267.

Rijsewijk, F., Schuermann, M., Wagenaar, E., Parren, P., Weigel, D., & Nusse, R. (1987). The Drosophila homolog of the mouse mammary oncogene int-1 is identical to the segment polarity gene wingless. *Cell, 50,* 649–657.

Rius, R. A., Barg, J., Bem, W. T., Coscia, C. J., & Loh, Y. P. (1991). The prenatal developmental profile of expression of opioid peptides and receptors in the mouse brain. *Developmental Brain Research, 58,* 237–241.

Roeder, R. G. (1991). Complexities of eukaryotic transcription initiation: Regulation of preinitiation complex assembly. *Trends in Biological Sciences, 16,* 402–408.

Roelink, H., & Nusse, R. (1991). Expression of two members of the Wnt family during mouse development: Restricted temporal and spatial patterns in the developing neural tube. *Genes and Development, 5,* 381–388.

Rothman, S. M., & Olney, J. W. (1987). Excitotoxicity and the NMDA receptor. *Trends in Neuroscience, 10,* 299–302.

Sadler, T. W. (1985). *Langman's medical embryology.* Baltimore: Williams & Wilkins.

Sakaguchi, T., & Nakamura, S. (1987). Some *in vivo* electrophysiological properties of locus coeruleus neurones in fetal rats. *Experimental Brain Research, 68,* 122–130.

Sakai, K. (1988). Executive mechanisms of paradoxical sleep. *Archives Italiennes de Biologie, 126,* 239–257.

Sakanaka, M., Inagaki, S., Shiosaka, S., Senba, E., Takagi, H., Takatsuki, K., Kawai, Y., Iida, H., Hara, Y., & Tohyama, M. (1982). Ontogeny of substance P-containing neuron system of the rat: Immunohistochemical analysis—II. Lower brain stem. *Neuroscience, 7,* 1097–1126.

Sanger, F., & Coulson, A. R. (1975). A rapid method for determining sequences in DNA by primed synthesis with DNA polymerase. *Journal of Molecular Biology, 94,* 444–448.

Scarr, S., & McCartney, K. (1983). How people make their own environments: A theory of genotype-environment effects. *Child Development,* 54, 424–435.

Schlagger, B. L., & O'Leary, D. D. M. (1991). Potential of visual cortex to develop an array of functional units unique to somatosensory cortex. *Science, 252,* 1556–1560.

Schoenwolf, G. C., & Smith, J. L. (1990). Mechanisms of neuralation: Traditional viewpoint and recent advances. *Development, 109,* 243–270.

Segal, M. (1985). Mechanisms of action of noradrenaline in the brain. *Physiological Psychology, 13,* 172–178.

Senba, E., Shiosaka, S., Hara, Y., Inagaki, S., Kawai, Y., Takatsuki, K., Sakanaka, M., Iida, H., Takagi, H., Minagawa, H., & Tohyama, M. (1982). Ontogeny of the leucine-enkephalin neuron system of the rat: I. Lower brain stem. *Journal of Comparative Neurology, 205,* 341–359.

Seress, L., & Ribak, C. E. (1988). The development of GABAergic neurons in the rat hippocampal formation: An immunohistochemical study. *Developmental Brain Research, 44,* 197–209.

Shatz, C. J. (1990). Impulse activity and the patterning of connections during CNS development. *Neuron, 5,* 745–756.

Shaywitz, B. A., Yager, R. D., & Klopper, J. H. (1986). Selective brain dopamine depletion in developing rats: An experimental model of minimal brain dysfunction. *Science, 191,* 305–308.

Shen, W. Z., Luo, Z. B., Zheng, D. R., & Yew, D. T. (1989). Immunohistochemical studies on the development of 5-HT (serotonin) neurons in the nuclei of the reticular formation of human fetuses. *Pediatric Neuroscience, 15,* 291–295.

Shute, C. C. D., & Lewis, P. R. (1967). The ascending cholinergic reticular system: Neocortical, olfactory, and subcortical projections. *Brain, 90,* 497–519.

Simeone, A., Acampora, D., Arcioni, L., Andrews, P., Boncinelli, E., & Mavilio, F. (1990). Sequential activation of Hox2 homeobox genes by retinoic acid in human embryonal carcinoma cells. *Nature, 346,* 763–766.

Smith, C. U. M. (1989). *Elements of molecular neurobiology.* New York: Wiley.

Smith, H. O., & Wilcox, K. W. (1970). A restriction enzyme from Haemophilus influenzae: Purification and general properties. *Journal of Molecular Biology, 51,* 379–391.

Smith, S. M., Pang, K., Sundin, O., Wedden, S. E., Thaller, C., & Eichele, G. (1989). Molecular approaches to vertebrate limb morphogenesis. *Development (Suppl.),* 121–131.

Snow, P. M., Bieber, A. J., & Goodman, C. S. (1989). Fasciclin III: A novel homophilic adhesion molecule in Drosophila. *Cell, 59,* 313–323.

Soja, P. J., Lopez-Rodriguez, F., Morales, F. R., & Chase, M. H. (1991). The postsynaptic inhibitory control of lumbar motoneurons during the atonia of active sleep: Effects of strychnine on motoneuron properties. *Journal of Neuroscience, 11,* 2804–2811.

Solimena, M., & De Camilli, P. (1991). Autoimmunity to glutamic acid decarboxylase (GAD) in Stiff-Man syndrome and insulin-dependent diabetes mellitus. *Trends in Neuroscience, 14,* 452–457.

Somogyi, P., Hodgson, A. J., Chubb, I. W., Penke, B., & Erdei, A. (1985). Antisera to g-aminobutyric acid: II. Immunocytochemical application to the central nervous system. *Journal of Histochemistry and Cytochemistry, 33,* 240–248.

Somogyi, P., & Soltesz, I. (1986). Immunogold demonstration of GABA in synaptic terminals of intracellularly recorded horseradish peroxidase-filled basket cells and clutch cells in the cat's visual cortex. *Neuroscience, 19,* 1051–1065.

Spain, J. W., Roth, B. L., & Coscia, C. J. (1985). Differential ontogeny of multiple opioid receptors (mu, delta, kappa). *Journal of Neuroscience, 5,* 584–588.

Specht, L. A., Pickel, V. M., Joh, T. H., & Reis, D. J. (1981a). Light-microscopic immunocytochemical localization of tyrosine hydroxylase in prenatal rat brain: I. Early ontogeny. *Journal of Comparative Neurology, 199,* 233–253.

Specht, L. A., Pickel, V. M., Joh, T. H., & Reis, D. J. (1981b). Light-microscopic immunocytochemical localization of tyrosine hydroxylase in prenatal rat brain: II. Late ontogeny. *Journal of Comparative Neurology, 199,* 255–276.

Speddings, M., Kilpatrick, A. T., & Alps, B. J. (1989). Activators and inhibitors of calcium channels: Effects in the central nervous system. *Fundamentals of Clinical Pharmacology, 3,* 3s–29s.

Squire, L. R., & Davis, H. P. (1981). The pharmacology of memory: A neurobiological perspective. *Annual Review of Pharmacology, 21,* 323–356.

Steariade, M., & Hobson, J. A. (1976). Neuronal activity during the sleep-waking cycle. *Progress in Neurobiology, 6,* 155–376.

Steinbusch, H. W. M. (1984). Serotonin-immunoreactive neurons and their projections in the CNS. In A. Bjorklund, T. Hokfelt, & M. J. Kuhar (Eds.), *Handbook of chemical neuroanatomy* (pp. 68–125). Amsterdam: Elsevier.

Steinbusch, H. W. M., & Mulder, A. H. (1984). Immunohistochemical localization of histamine in neurons and mast cells in the rat brain. In A. Bjorklund, T. Hokfelt, & M. J. Kuhar (Eds.), *Handbook of chemical neuroanatomy* (pp. 126–140). Amsterdam: Elsevier.

Stone, E. A. (1983). Problems with current catecholamine hypotheses of antidepressant agents: Speculations leading to a new hypothesis. *The Behavioral and Brain Sciences, 6,* 535–577.

Stuhmer, W. (1991). Structure-function studies of voltage-gated ion channels. *Annual Review of Biophysics and Biophysical Chemistry, 20,* 65–78.

Stuhmer, W., Conti, F., Suzuki, H., Wang, X., Noda, M., Yahagi, N., Kubo, H., & Numa, S. (1989). Structural parts involved in activation and inactivation of the sodium channel. *Nature, 339,* 597–603.

Summerbell, D., & Maden, M. (1990). Retinoic acid: A developmental signalling molecule. *Trends in Neuroscience, 13,* 142–147.

Swandulla, D., Carbone, E., & Lux, H. D. (1991). Do calcium channel classifications account for neuronal calcium channel diversity? *Trends in Neuroscience, 14,* 46–51.

Sweeney, D. R., & Maas, J. W. (1979). Stress and noradrenergic function in depression. In R. A. DePue (Ed.), *The psychobiology of the depressive disorders: Implications for the effects of stress* (pp. 161–176). New York: Academic Press.

Tarsy, D. (1977). Dopamine-acetylcholine interaction in the basal ganglia. In W. S. Fields (Ed.), *Neurotransmitter function: Basic and clinical aspects* (pp. 213–246). New York: Symposia Specialists; Stratton Intercontinental Medical Book Corp.

Thomas, K. R., & Capecchi, M. R. (1990). Targeted disruption of the murine int-1 proto-oncogene resulting in severe abnormalities in midbrain and cerebellar development. *Nature, 346,* 847–850.

Timpe, L. C., Schwarz, T. L., Tempel, B. L., Papazian, D. M., Jan, Y. N., & Jan, L. Y. (1988). Expression of functional potassium channels from Shaker cDNA in Xenopus oocytes. *Nature, 331,* 143–145.

Tossman, U., Segovia, J., & Ungerstedt, U. (1986). Extracellular levels of amino acids in striatum and globus pallidus of 6-hydroxydopamine-lesioned rats measured with microdialysis. *Acta Physiologica Scandinavica, 127,* 547–551.

Uhl, G. R., Goodman, R. R., Kuhar, M. J., Childers, S. R., & Snyder, S. H. (1979). Immunohistochemical mapping of enkephalin-containing cell bodies, fibers, and nerve terminals in the brain stem of the rat. *Brain Research, 166,* 75–94.

Ungerstedt, U. (1971). Stereotaxic mapping of the monoamine pathways in the rat brain. *Acta Physiologica Scandinavica (Suppl.) 367,* 1–48.

Van den Heuvel, M., Nusse, R., Johnston, P., & Lawrence, P. A. (1989). Distribution of the wingless gene product in Drosophila embryos: A protein involved in cell-cell communication. *Cell, 59,* 847–850.

van den Pol, A. N., & Gorca, T. (1988). Glycine and glycine receptor immunoreactivity in brain and spinal cord. *Journal of Neuroscience, 8,* 472–492.

Van der Kooy, D., & Fishell, G. (1987). Neuronal birthdate underlies the development of striatal compartments. *Brain Research, 401,* 155–161.

Vanderwolf, C. H., & Stewart, D. J. (1986). Joint cholinergic-serotonergic control of neocortical and hippocampal electrical activity in relation to behavior: Effects of scopolamine, ditran, trifluoperazine and amphetamine. *Physiology and Behavior, 38,* 57–65.

Van Eden, C. G., Mrzljak, L., Voorn, P., & Uylings, H. B. M. (1989). Prenatal development of GABA-ergic neurons in the neocortex of the rat. *Journal of Comparative Neurology, 289,* 213–227.

Vassilev, P. M., Scheuer, T., & Catterall, W. A. (1988). Identification of an intracellular peptide segment involved in sodium channel inactivation. *Science, 241,* 1658–1661.

Verney, C., Zecevic, N., Nikolic, B., Alvarez, C., & Berger, B. (1991). Early evidence of catecholaminergic cell groups in 5- and 6-week-old human embryos using tyrosine hydroxylase and dopamine-b-hydroxylase immunocytochemistry. *Neuroscience Letters, 131,* 121–124.

Wallace, J. A., & Lauder, J. M. (1983). Development of the serotonergic system in the rat embryo: An immunohistochemical study. *Brain Research Bulletin, 10,* 459–479.

Walsh, C., & Cepko, C. L. (1988). Clonally related cortical cells show several migration patterns. *Science, 241,* 1342–1345.

Walter, J., Allsopp, T. E., & Bonhoeffer, F. (1990). A common denominator of growth cone guidance and collapse? *Trends in Neuroscience, 13*(11), 447–452.

Walters, J. R., & Chase, T. N. (1977). GABA systems and extrapyramidal function. In W. S. Fields (Ed.), *Neurotransmitter function: Basic and clinical aspects* (pp. 193–211). New York: Symposia Specialists; Stratton Intercontinental Medical Book Corp.

Wantanabe, T., Taguchi, Y., Shiosaka, S., Tanaka, J., Kubota, H., Terano, Y., Tohyama, M., & Wada, H. (1984). Distribution of the histaminergic neuron system in the central nervous system of rats: A fluorescent immunohistochemical analysis with histidine decarboxylase as a marker. *Brain Research, 295,* 13–25.

Watson, J. D., & Crick, F. H. C. (1953). Molecular structure of nucleic acids: A structure for deoxyribose nucleic acid. *Nature, 171,* 737–738.

Watson, J. D., Tooze, J., & Kurtz, D. T. (1983). *Recombinant DNA: A short course.* New York: Freeman.

Weinberger, D. R. (1987). Implications of normal brain development for the pathogenesis of schizophrenia. *Archives of General Psychiatry, 44,* 660–669.

Weinshank, R. L., Adham, N., Macchi, M., Olsen, M. A., Branchek, T. A., & Hartig, P. A. (1991). Molecular cloning and characterization of a high affinity dopamine receptor (D1b) and its pseudogene. *Journal of Biological Chemistry, 266*(33), 22427–22435.

Weintraub, H., Davis, R., Tapscott, S., Thayer, M., Krause, M., Benezra, R., Blackwell, T. K., Turner, D., Rupp, R., Hollenberg, S., Zhuang, Y., & Lassar, A. (1991). The myoD gene family: Nodal point during specification of the muscle cell lineage. *Science, 251,* 761–766.

Weiss, J. M., Glazer, H. I., Pohorecky, L. A., Bailey, W. H., & Schneider, L. H. (1979). Coping behavior and stress-induced behavioral depression: Studies of the role of brain catecholamines. In R. A. DePue (Ed.), *The psychobiology of the depressive disorders: Implications for the effects of stress* (pp. 125–160). New York: Academic Press.

Whishaw, I. Q., O'Conner, W. T., & Dunnett, S. B. (1985). Disruption of central cholinergic systems in the rat by basal forebrain lesions or atropine: Effects on feeding, sensorimotor behavior, locomotor activity and spatial navigation. *Behavioural Brain Research, 17,* 103–115.

Whitehouse, P. J., Price, D. L., Clark, A. W., Coyle, J. T., & DeLong, M. R. (1981). Alzheimer's disease: Evidence for selective loss of cholinergic neurons in the nucleus basalis. *Annals of Neurology, 10,* 122–126.

Wilkinson, L. O., & Dourish, C. T. (1991). Serotonin and animal behavior. In S. J. Peroutka (Ed.), *Serotonin receptor subtypes: Basic and clinical aspects* (pp. 147–210). New York: Wiley.

Winslow, J. T., & Insel, T. R. (1990). Neurobiology of obsessive compulsive disorder: A possible role for serotonin. *Journal of Clinical Psychiatry, 51*(8, Suppl.), 27–31.

Woodward, D. J., Moises, H. C., Waterhouse, B. D., Hoffer, B. J., & Freedman, R. (1979). Modulatory actions of norepinephrine in the central nervous system. *Federation Proceedings, 38,* 2109–2116.

Woolf, N. J., & Butcher, L. L. (1986). Cholinergic systems in the rat brain: III. Projections from the pontomesencephalic tegmentum to the thalamus, tectum, basal ganglia, and basal forebrain. *Brain Research Bulletin, 16,* 603–637.

Woolf, N. J., Eckenstein, F., & Butcher, L. L. (1984). Cholinergic systems in the rat brain: I. Projections to the limbic telencephalon. *Brain Research Bulletin, 13,* 751–784.

Yamada, T., Placzek, M., Tanaka, H., Dodd, J., & Jessell, T. M. (1991). Control of cell pattern in the developing nervous system: Polarizing activity of the floor plate and notochord. *Cell, 64,* 635–647.

Yellen, G. (1987). Permeation in potassium channels: Implications for channel structure. *Annual Review of Biophysics and Biophysical Chemistry, 16,* 227–246.

Zametkin, A. J., & Rapoport, J. L. (1987). Noradrenergic hypothesis of attention deficit disorder with hyperactivity: A critical review. In H. Y. Meltzer (Ed.), *Psychopharmacology: The third generation of progress* (pp. 837–842). New York: Raven Press.

Zinn, K., McAllister, L., & Goodman, C. S. (1988). Sequence analysis and neuronal expression of fasciclin I in grasshoppers and Drosophila. *Cell, 53,* 577–587.

CHAPTER 6

Structural and Functional Development of the Human Brain

RICHARD D. TODD, BARBARA SWARZENSKI,
PAOLA GIOVANARDI ROSSI, and PAOLA VISCONTI

The substrates of personality, cognition, emotion, and other human qualities we consider to be a part of the psyche are found in the central nervous system. In this chapter, we attempt to describe how the development and organization of the human central nervous system are characterized both by important stereotypic features that are common to all individuals and by mechanisms that produce individual differences. Too often, psychological and psychiatric theories take birth as a starting point for considering both the development of psychopathology and the development of individual differences. From an evolutionary or comparative anatomy viewpoint, however, birth is an arbitrary starting point for discussing development and, as will be stressed in this chapter, both pre- and postnatal influences can have important effects on brain structure and function. Too often, biological theories ignore the qualitative differences in environmental and psychological experiences before and after birth. Little discussion is usually given to the interactions of the current biological state of the child and the impact of a given experience; an example is the difference in the biological response and the psychological meaning of spoken language before and after a child develops the ability to understand speech. In an average environment, the ability of an average child to understand spoken language is contingent only on the development of the proper auditory centers, including the appropriate neuronal connections. The psychological and physiological responses to speech, however, change dramatically with the establishment of meaning. Even at the level of brain blood flow, it is easy to demonstrate changes in the activation of different brain structures in response to words versus nonsense syllables.

As a convenient starting point, we will consider brain development to begin with neurulation (the process of neural tube formation). This is a critical event in the life histories of all individuals. Failure of this developmental event leads to catastrophic malformations of the central nervous system. It is less clear, however, what long-lasting impact there is from minor injury or from environmental manipulations during this period. However, before starting a detailed description of the development of the central nervous system, we give an overview of the structural and functional anatomy of the adult brain. Next, we deal more specifically with particular principles of brain development, review what is known about the environmental and genetic control of brain development, and discuss areas of potential modulation of brain development, both pre- and postnatally. We include discussions of sex differences in brain structure and function and the possible neurobiology of psychosocial development.

Our main goal here is to present the fundamentals of neurobiological development of the human brain, synthesizing this complex literature in a fashion that will make relevant, in neurobiological terms, much of the literature on enriched environments, personality, and various developmental states. This chapter should thus provide an understanding of the neurodevelopmental principles that govern both normal and abnormal outcomes. One may speculate that normal and pathological states are part of the same neurodevelopmental continuum. This means that all neuro- or psychopathology can be regarded as deviance from the usual ontogenetic pathways, and that a study of abnormal development of the nervous system can enhance our understanding of normal development. These two concepts underlie the emerging discipline of developmental psychopathology (Cicchetti, 1987; Pepper, 1942), which is presented more thoroughly elsewhere in this volume. In our chapter, we provide several examples of this developmental approach to neuro- or psychopathology—for example, mental retardation. Other chapters in this volume illustrate the application of this model in more detail, using a variety of syndromes and disorders of childhood and adulthood. This approach serves to lessen the mainly artificial gap between the study of child and adult psychopathology.

Various approaches are possible for the presentation of the fundamentals of brain development. Ideally, genetic, molecular, cellular, neural systems, family, and environmental aspects and interrelations would be presented simultaneously, to give a more realistic view of the complicated and interrelated process in which changes in one area have secondary and tertiary effects in other areas. Unfortunately, our level of understanding of most aspects of nervous system development does not currently allow such a cohesive presentation. Hence, many aspects and levels of development will be described individually in a temporal format across the life cycle.

We recognize that development is neither a collection of linear processes nor a simple interactive process in which the endowment of the individual, the past occurrence of both detrimental and advantageous environmental events, and the ongoing environmental milieu contribute to the characteristics of the individual. Both of these models neglect the environment-organizing and modifying capacities of individuals. This latter type of developmental model has been called transactional (e.g., Sameroff & Chandler, 1975) to emphasize that the individual is an active participant in his or her own development and that environments can be self-modified to minimize the untoward effects of earlier developmental events. In fact, the interactive and self-manipulating aspects of development should be of greatest interest to the study of psychopathology and the generation of individual differences. We note that the possibility of genes whose action is to modify the environment may confound attempts to separate the genetic and environmental components of development. When experimentally documented or of particular theoretical relevance, examples of interactions and nonlinear developmental models will be given.

OVERVIEW OF THE STRUCTURAL ANATOMY OF THE ADULT BRAIN

The brain is usually described as the part of the nervous system that is contained within the cranial cavity. It can be conveniently divided into four areas: (a) cerebrum, (b) thalamus and hypothalamus (diencephalon), (c) midbrain (mesencephalon), pons, and medulla, and (d) cerebellum. In addition, there are collections of brain regions that form functional systems of special interest to psychologists and psychiatrists. Two of these are the basal ganglia and the limbic systems. Specific connections among the different major brain areas have led many authors to consider the brain as a single organ. However, it is quite feasible to consider the brain as a collection of individual organs with more or less specialized functions and connections. The actions of these individual brain areas are coordinated through higher-level organizations to form coherent patterns or integrations of neural activity for the input and output of information.

The Major Brain Areas

The Cerebrum

The cerebrum is divided into right and left hemispheres. These hemispheres are subdivided along deep surface folds called sulci, which define the regions of the cortex: the frontal lobe, the parietal lobe, the occipital lobe, and the temporal lobe (Figure 6.1(a) and 6.1(b); Garoutte, 1987). The developing primate brain differs from the brains of other species in its pronounced overgrowth of the forebrain compared to the midbrain and cerebellum. Consequently, the primate cortex has numerous additional foldings that permit a very large amount of cortical tissue to fit into a relatively small cranial cavity. The thin outer layer of the cerebrum is known as the cerebral cortex. The cortex (gray matter) usually consists of four to six layers of cells beneath which lies a thick core of white matter, which receives its coloring from the myelin sheaths surrounding nerve fibers (Lewis & Clarke, 1878). The primary cortical areas and association cortex, which integrate information from one functional system, typically exhibit six well-defined cellular layers (Mesulam, 1985b). According to some investigators, association cortex that integrates the information from more than one functional system may have slightly less differentiation of the cellular layers (Mesulam, 1985a). How such subtle differences in cellular structure arise in primary and associative cortical areas during nervous system development, and the functional significance of these differences, are not well understood. In contrast, it is generally agreed that the much less

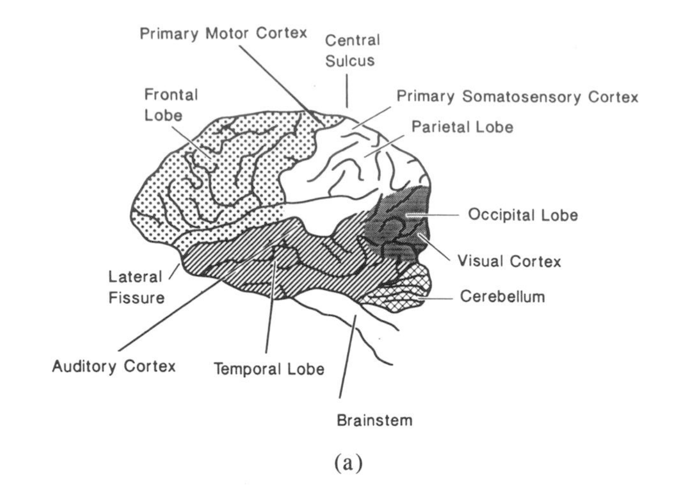

(a)

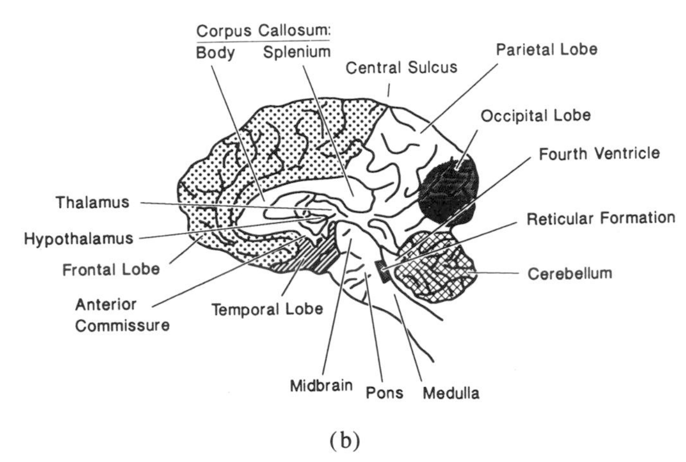

(b)

Figure 6.1 The brain—the locations and major divisions of several structures of the human central nervous system. (a) Side view, showing the boundaries between the cerebral lobes and two major grooves produced by the foldings of the brain: (i) the central sulcus, which courses between the primary motor and sensory areas, and (ii) the lateral fissure, which separates the temporal lobe from the frontal and parietal lobes. (b) Midline view, showing several landmarks, including the thalamus and hypothalamus (diencephalon) and the major neural tracts connecting the two hemispheres: (i) the corpus callosum and (ii) the anterior commissure. Also shown are the components of the brain stem: the midbrain (mesencephalon), pons, and medulla.

structured morphology of parts of the limbic cortex (see below) reflects its phylogenetically earlier origin.

To a large extent, the layer in which a cortical neuron is found (see Figure 6.7, below) defines the pattern of its connections. In general, layer I, the most exterior layer, contains mostly glial cells. Layer IV contains cells that receive input from the thalamus. Cells in layers II and III project to other cortical cells, and cells in layers V and VI provide output that leaves the cortex (Kuffler, Nicholls, & Martin, 1984, pp. 88–91).

The primate brain is further distinguished from the brains of other species in that most of the primate cerebral cortex is association or integration cortex, which is thought to be crucial for the processing of many cognitive functions. Only a relatively small proportion of the human cortex processes primary motor and sensory information. This is in contrast to the rodent brain, which has much less association cortex (Kupferman, 1985a; Thompson, 1975).

The primary areas of the cortex are (a) the primary motor area, in the precentral gyrus of the frontal lobe; (b) the primary visual area, in the occipital lobe; (c) the primary auditory area, in the temporal lobe; and (d) the primary somatosensory area, in the parietal lobe (Figure 6.1(a)). Primary refers to areas that have direct projections from the motor cortex to the periphery or, for the sensory system, receive projections from the periphery. The analogous areas of the two hemispheres frequently serve the same type of function (Witelson & Kigar, 1987). For example, the primary motor area of the left hemisphere serves the right side of the body, and the right motor cortex serves the left side of the body. Within a functional area of the cortex, there is frequently a topological representation of the body. For example, the cortical neurons that control the hand are located near the neurons that control the forearm, which are located next to neurons that control the arm, and so on.

The right and left hemispheres may show significant differences in anatomy and function. The lateralization of behaviors to one hemisphere or the other may be the rule rather than the exception for many behaviors, although this remains a controversial topic. A well-known example is that, in the majority of individuals, the primary speech areas are located only in the left cortex. The analogous areas in the right hemisphere are primarily involved in nonverbal tasks. There is also evidence that the two hemispheres may function independently of each other and use fundamentally different ways of assimilating information. Some researchers feel that right-left differences in function may have been overemphasized.

Two major midline connections or tracts course between the two hemispheres: (a) the corpus callosum and (b) the anterior commissure (Figure 6.1(b)). The corpus callosum is partially organized by modality (i.e., motor, visual, auditory, and somatosensory) (Pandya & Seltzer, 1986). There is controversy about the functional role of the corpus callosum, although most agree that it mediates communication between the two hemispheres.

The Diencephalon

The diencephalon (between-brain) connects the cerebrum with many other brain areas (Figure 6.2). There is no clear distinction in humans between the diencephalon and the cerebrum.

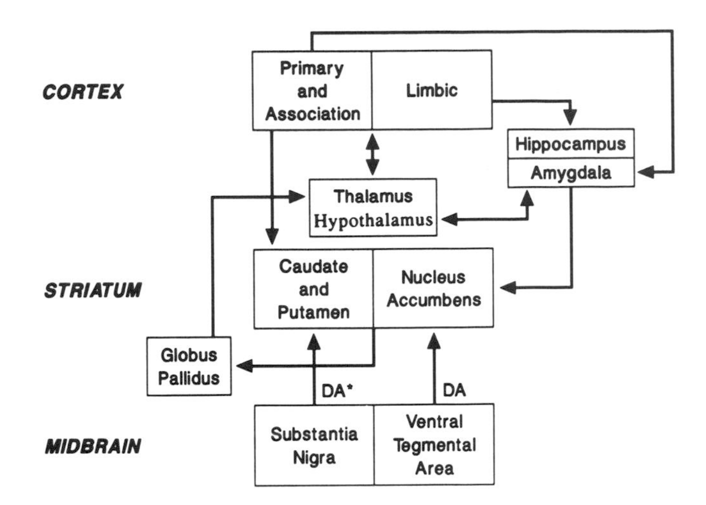

Figure 6.2 Schematic representation of the diencephalon, basal ganglia, and limbic system—the functional units of the human brain that are involved in the expression of most behaviors. The arrows give the direction of major neuronal projections. Emphasized are: the output neural tracts from the striatum through the globus pallidus to the thalamus; the dopaminergic input (DA = dopaminergic pathway) from the brain stem to higher cerebral centers; and the interconnections between the areas of cortex (primary and association; limbic) and other parts of the brain.

Structures in the diencephalon are the thalamus, hypothalamus, and pineal gland. The thalamus is a major relay station for information between the cerebrum and other parts of the brain. It has groups of cell bodies, known as nuclei, that have a key role in the control of sensation and motor activity. The thalamus also has reciprocal connections with the hypothalamus, which is a major center for controlling homeostatic mechanisms (endocrine and autonomic systems). The function of the pineal gland in humans is not well understood.

The Brain Stem

The brain stem is composed of the mesencephalon (midbrain), pons, and medulla (Figure 6.1(b)). All three structures contain numerous nuclei, which have specific functions. The reticular formation, which has a role in maintaining the level of arousal, consists of a collection of cells and their processes and extends through much of the brain stem. The mesencephalon also serves as a connection between the forebrain and the spinal cord. Many of the fibers originating in the cerebrum or diencephalon course through the brain stem. The mesencephalon's primary structures are the cerebral peduncles. In addition to other nuclei, the peduncles contain the substantia nigra, which primarily sends axons to the caudate and putamen and to motor nuclei in the thalamus (Figure 6.2). The pons contains cranial nerve nuclei and a variety of other nuclei. The medulla, the most caudal part of the brain stem, is continuous with the spinal cord. It contains other cranial nerve nuclei and is flanked by two pyramidal motor tracts. These consist principally of axons from primary cortical motor neurons, which synapse on spinal cord neurons.

The Cerebellum

The cerebellum is located posterior to the brain stem; its appearance resembles a fern leaf (Figure 6.1(a) and 6.1(b)). It has two hemispheres, a central part called the vermis, three cortical cell layers, and white matter. In addition, there are nuclei deep in the cerebellum, including the dentate nucleus, which sends fibers controlling motor function to the thalamus. The cerebellum receives input from the motor cortex and also has sensory information mapped onto its surface. It is usually thought of as being involved in modulating and coordinating complex muscular movement. The cerebellum may also process some aspects of motor learning and visceral control.

Selected Systems

Two systems that are of great interest to psychologists and psychiatrists are the basal ganglia and the limbic system. The basal ganglia are large nuclei deep within the brain which are thought to be involved in the feedback control of many motor movements. These structures are also thought to be involved in memory and other cognitive processes. In humans, the basal ganglia consist of the striatum and globus pallidus (Figure 6.2). The striatum has several components, including the caudate, the putamen, and the nucleus accumbens. The striatum receives descending cortical input mainly from the primary and association cortices and ascending dopaminergic input from the substantia nigra (Garoutte, 1987). The nucleus accumbens receives input from the limbic system (Heimer & Wilson, 1975). The globus pallidus may be thought of as a relay station from the striatum to the thalamus and thus also plays a key role in motor control. Many theories of severe psychiatric dysfunction have centered on the involvement of the basal ganglia.

The limbic system consists of a number of cerebral structures adjacent to the hypothalamus. This system is usually thought to be involved in the control of many behavioral and emotional reactions (MacLean, 1955; Papez, 1937). Lesions of the limbic system frequently result in problems with emotional control, affective blunting, or memory. The limbic system consists of the amygdala, the hippocampus, the mammary body, and the limbic cortex. The limbic cortex is usually considered to consist of the cingulate gyrus and the parahippocampal gyrus. The amygdala, which has reciprocal connections with the hypothalamus and also receives input from the cortex, is thought to be involved in the regulation of drive (motivation). Memory disturbances are particularly associated with defects of the hippocampus and amygdala.

The Ventricular System

The brain contains a series of cavities called ventricles, which are filled with cerebrospinal fluid (CSF). The ventricles are connected to each other and to the fluid surrounding the spinal cord and the brain. The ventricular system consists of two lateral ventricles located in the cerebral hemispheres, a third ventricle within the diencephalon, and a fourth ventricle in the caudal part of the brain stem. Cerebrospinal fluid is produced within the entire ventricular system by specialized structures called the choroid plexus. This fluid also circulates around the exterior surfaces of the brain. The CSF is thought to help provide and regulate the appropriate neurochemical environment for the central nervous system. If the circulation or reabsorption of CSF is interfered with, hydrocephalus or increased cranial pressure results.

The Major Neural Pathways

Connections between the Major Brain Areas

These different gross brain areas have numerous interconnections. In general, these can be divided into input connections and output connections. As discussed above, many areas of the brain appear to be organized as a representation of the body. In addition, many sensory modalities appear to project to specific brain regions. This will be described in more detail in the functional anatomy sections to follow. The diencephalon acts as the major connection between the cerebral cortex and the rest of the brain. Most messages are relayed through the thalamus. The hypothalamus exerts at least part of its function through directly influencing the endocrine system. This is achieved through direct release of products into the general circulation and also through direct connections to the pituitary gland.

Methods of Information Transfer along Neural Pathways

Along the course of a neuron, information is transmitted by the passage of electrical action potentials. This process is rapid and is initiated at the neuronal synapse, a specialized connection between cells with a high electrical resistance. Transfer of information between cells is via the diffusion of chemicals called neurotransmitters (Bloom, 1990; Cooper, Bloom, & Roth, 1986b). In general, the arrival of an action potential at a synapse (see Figure 6.4(c), below) results in the release of a neurotransmitter, which diffuses across the synaptic space. The neurotransmitter interacts with specific proteins called neurotransmitter receptors, which interpret the information by causing changes in the electrical potential of the postsynaptic neuron and changes in the intracellular metabolism of the neuron. The information transmitted by the receptor may be stimulatory or inhibitory. The speed of neural transmission is principally limited by the number of synaptic contacts in a pathway. The action potential is generated by the opening of ion channels in the membrane, which allows for the influx and efflux of cations such as K^+ and Na^+ and anions such as Cl^- (Cooper, Bloom, & Roth, 1986a; Mommaerts, 1978).

Discrete Pathways for Neurotransmitters

Specification of which neurotransmitters are used within the brain occurs by the projection of nerve fibers containing different neurotransmitters to different parts of the brain. For the biogenic amines serotonin, dopamine, and norepinephrine, most of the cell bodies that synthesize these neurotransmitters are found in discrete nuclei in the midbrain and the hind brain. The majority of serotonin-producing neurons have their cell bodies in the raphe nuclei (Parent, Descarries, & Beaudet, 1981). The dopamine-producing cell bodies are primarily found in the substantia nigra, the ventral tegmental area near the brain stem, and the hypothalamus (Lindvall & Björklund, 1983). The cell bodies for norepinephrine are principally found in the pons and medulla, with the largest concentration present in the locus ceruleus (Lindvall & Björklund, 1983). The serotonergic and noradrenergic systems project widely in the central nervous system; the dopaminergic systems have very discrete projections to the basal ganglia and the cerebral cortex. In addition to the biogenic amines, there are probably hundreds of other types of neurotransmitters, many of whose projections and locations are only grossly understood (Fagg & Foster, 1983; Krieger, 1983). In the coming years, there will most likely be major revisions of our understanding of the distributions of particular neurotransmitter systems. Neuroanatomical tracing techniques are also improving, and changes in some of the neural connections that have been classically described can be expected.

In general, the majority of cerebral or diencephalic neurons do not directly connect with peripheral organs but synapse with interneurons located in relay nuclei or the spinal cord. From these relay nuclei, further connections are made to the peripheral nervous system and the peripheral organs, to form a communication system that is based on synaptic relays.

OVERVIEW OF THE FUNCTIONAL ANATOMY OF THE ADULT BRAIN

Enough is known about the functional anatomy of many behavioral systems to provide a general understanding of how we perceive and react to ourselves and the environment. The functional systems discussed here are: consciousness and attention, sensory modalities, motor areas, associative areas, language, emotion (affect), memory processes, and cognition (thought). Human behavior may be considered to be the sum of these processes. Most neuroscientists today agree that these functions have anatomic localization to specific areas of the brain. Although the neuronal pathways often are not precisely known for each functional system nor is it always clear how different systems are interconnected, several principles of brain function can be highlighted. First, discrete brain functions have discrete anatomical representations. In adults, specific brain lesions result in predictable functional deficits or syndromes. This appears to be true for simple motor systems as well as for functions such as memory, which are harder to precisely define. Second, many brain areas are organized as topological representations of the body. This has been demonstrated not only for motor systems but for many sensory pathways at each relay level. Third, some brain areas serve only one side of the body. Depending on the pathways of the projecting neurons, this relationship may be ipsilateral (same side of the body) or contralateral (opposite side of the body) to where the neurons are located.

In addition, some types of neural processing function in several areas of the brain. Many neuronal pathways are connected in a hierarchical (serial) manner: one neuron is directly linked to another as part of a linear arrangement. Neural networks are often also constructed in parallel, which means that the same information can reach a given neuron using different routes. One advantage of parallel processing is that breakdown in one area may still leave the overall function intact. Also, efficiency of information transfer may be improved. However, some "parallel" networks can have opposing actions. Columnar organization (described below) is another major method for processing of information in many parts of the cortex.

Consciousness and Attention

There are numerous definitions of consciousness; however, most concepts of consciousness assume or imply an ability to maintain or shift attention. Attentional mechanisms are thought to involve interactions among the brain stem, thalamus, and neocortex (Mesulam, 1985a). As previously mentioned, the brain stem contains cells belonging to the reticular formation. These neurons send projections to the thalamus and neocortex using cholinergic and monoaminergic neurotransmitters (Chu & Bloom, 1973; Spehlmann & Smathers, 1974). The reticular formation may have the role of a pacemaker in setting the level of consciousness. What role the neocortex has in controlling the level of arousal is not well understood.

Sensory Modalities (Brodal, 1981; Kolb & Whishaw, 1990c)

Sensation refers to the perception and neural processing of stimuli that originate from the outside world (vision, audition, sensations of the skin, and so on) or from the interior of the body (temperature, heart rate, and so on), or that provide information about the position of the body in space. By definition, primary sensory areas are the first cortical areas to receive information, via thalamic relay nuclei, from the periphery. Subsequently, sensory information is conveyed to association areas. From there, it is relayed to other cortical areas for further integration (see below). Three sensory modalities will be discussed here: vision, audition, and the somatosensory system.

Vision

Light, interacting with rod and cone cells in the retina, produces nerve impulses that travel in the optic nerve to the thalamus. These impulses are then relayed to the visual cortex (see Figure 6.1(a)). Each visual cortex (located in the occipital portion of each hemisphere) receives information about the opposite (contralateral) side of the world. This means that if the left visual cortex is injured, the brain won't visually perceive the right side of the environment, and vice versa. Each retina collects light from both visual fields. For example, the left side of each retina sees the right visual field. This information is sorted such that the left side of each retina sends nerve projections to the left visual cortex. This is achieved by the merging and branching of the neuronal supply from each retina at the optic chiasm prior to projecting to the lateral geniculate nucleus of the thalamus and the occipital cortex. For sensory systems, a major principle is that nerve cells that deal with related messages are found in proximity to each other. This principle holds true for all levels of the visual system, from the retinal receptor cells to the visual cortex. For the visual system, this means that information arriving from neighboring areas in outside visual fields will be handled in the retina by nerve cells that are close to each other. This may help ensure that information processing will be both faster and more accurate at any given level. Receptive fields, which are defined as the areas that activate a given receptive cell, can be small or large. The smaller the field, the finer the discrimination will be. Information coming from the retina is relayed in topological arrangement to (or is mapped in a point-to-point manner to) the lateral geniculate nucleus and then to the occipital cortex. Not all parts of the retina are represented with equal weight in central areas: areas of the retina with smaller receptive fields (i.e., higher relay neuron density in the retina) have greater representation in the geniculate bodies and the cortex.

The cellular layers of the visual cortex are arranged in a manner analogous to that of other cortical areas. In addition, the visual cortex is arranged in dominance and orientation columns, which have the function of providing, respectively, binocular and depth vision, and information about visual orientation. Columns handle different types of information, coming from small, discrete areas of the retina, in a repetitive and overlapping manner. For example, columns that detect differences in depth, orientation, or color, or similar information for a given retinal area, are located together in the cortex. Columnar organization is also found in the somatosensory, motor, and auditory cortices.

Audition

The primary auditory cortex (Figure 6.1(a)) lies within Heschl's gyrus of the temporal lobe. It receives aural information from both ears, but the contralateral ear predominates. An injury to one cortical side usually will not cause deafness on the other side because of this bilateral input. Auditory information is initially processed in the medial geniculate nucleus of the thalamus and then relayed to the auditory cortex. Different parts of the inner ear respond to different frequencies of aural input, which in turn are represented in different areas centrally. Hence, the topological map for auditory input is based on frequency.

Somatosensory System

This system integrates sensory information from the external world (exteroceptive component) with information about the position of body parts relative to each other and about the position of the body in space (proprioceptive components). The inputs, just as for the other modalities, are processed in several parts of the thalamus; from there, the projections reach the postcentral gyrus of the parietal lobe. Information about pain, surface temperature, fine and crude touch, and stereognosis (ability to perceive three-dimensional space) is processed via different pathways (Figure 6.3). The contralateral body surface is mapped point-to-point to each cerebral hemisphere; in some cases, one pathway can at least partially take over the function of another that is damaged (parallel processing). For example, a tract that usually carries information predominantly about pain may be able to convey information about touch, should the former nerve fibers become damaged.

Motor Areas (Kolb & Whishaw, 1990b)

Many nerve projections involved in the control of motor activity have their origin in the primary motor cortex, which is located in the precentral gyrus of the frontal lobe. These fibers then travel through the internal capsule in each hemisphere and cross over to the contralateral side at the lower boundary of the brain stem, forming the pyramidal tracts (Figure 6.3). These projections, also known as the corticospinal tracts (upper motor neurons), are the predominant regulators of voluntary motor output. Additional cortical projections regulating motor activity stem from other areas of the frontal cortex and also from the parietal cortex. These primary cortical motor neurons synapse on anterior horn cell (lower motor neuron) bodies found in the spinal cord (Figure 6.3) and send out processes that course through the ventral root of the spinal cord and end at a muscle fiber. The body representation of the motor cortex is similar to that of the somatosensory cortex in that a disproportionately large amount of the motor cortex is represented by the hands and face. Additional control and integration mechanisms for motor systems are provided for by the numerous corticocortical inputs both from the same hemisphere and from the opposite side via the corpus callosum. The thalamus also sends fibers to the cortex for control purposes, including integration of sensory information with motor movement.

Various other brain areas also contribute to the control of movement. Injury to the cerebellum typically will not produce motor weakness or sensory deficits, but, instead, causes impaired coordination because of faulty or absent communication with the descending motor (from the cortex) pathways. The basal ganglia are subcortical structures that, as a group, function to

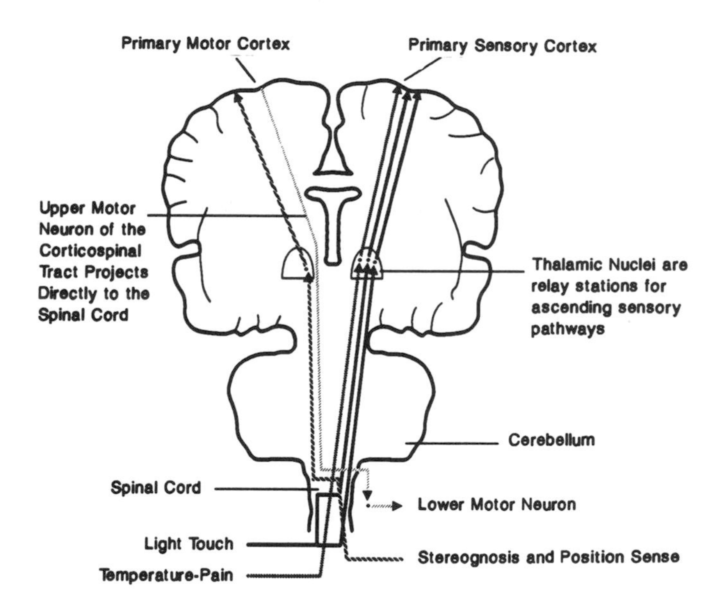

Figure 6.3 The major sensory and motor systems. These systems have different anatomic pathways. In the sensory system, messages from the periphery are processed first in specific nuclei in the thalamus and then are relayed to the sensory cortex. The direct motor system contains cortical neurons that project directly onto motor neurons in the spinal cord. The sensory and motor systems are integrated with each other by a variety of other neural pathways (not shown).

control movement. Injury to the basal ganglia causes emergence of involuntary movements—for example, tremors or slowness of movement. As for the cerebellum, the basal ganglia have reciprocal connections with the thalamus and cortex.

Association Areas (Kupferman, 1985; Mesulam, 1985b; Thompson, 1975)

The primary cortices so far described are thought to be important for first-level information processing. Each of the sensory modalities—vision, audition, somatosensation, and the motor area—has modality-specific association areas, also located in the cortex. These areas connect primary cortical areas with higher-level association areas, which are integrative centers that process information from more than one modality. Many cognitive processes characteristic of humans appear to require associative ability.

Language (Damasio & Geschwind, 1984; Kandel & Mayeux, 1985)

The functional units of language are phonemes. These are the sounds that make up the syllables (and thus, the words) and the grammar that provides the rules for how words are put together into phrases and sentences. Much of the ability to produce language is thought to be innate (genetically coded). For example, children from different cultures start to babble the same sounds, say individual words, and form sentences at similar ages. Very little is known about how language is achieved at the level of physiology (smaller-scale neural units or genes). However, some of the larger-scale anatomical substrates of language have been defined.

Language processing reflects hemispheric specialization. For most individuals, the left (so-called dominant) cerebral hemisphere can control language without any right hemispheric involvement. This has been shown both in stroke patients and through split-brain experiments, in which the two halves of the brain could not communicate with one another. Rudimentary linguistic capabilities have been found in the right hemisphere. In addition, the right hemisphere may be preferentially specialized to modulate the emotional components of language—for example, speech inflection. It is not well understood how such lateralization occurred during development of the central nervous system, nor is any advantage of lateralization completely evident. Nonlanguage lateralities have been observed in species other than humans or primates (see below). Lateralization of function within the brain may facilitate increased specialization of function.

Emotions (Affect)

As in other functional systems, neural units are thought to deal with the experience, expression, and memory of feelings. It is not generally known how this occurs. How emotions are integrated with other components of behavior is even less well understood. Nonetheless, some anatomic and physiologic abnormalities have been associated with specific emotions. For example, major depression is a syndrome involving extreme emotional states that has been correlated to varying degrees with localizable brain abnormalities (e.g., a characteristic syndrome, including depression, following stroke in the left anterior frontal cortex; Robinson & Starkstein, 1989). Epilepsy and other neuropsychiatric disorders have also been associated with characteristic affective states (Gloor, Olivier, Quesney, Andermann, & Horowitz, 1982).

Although some of the findings are ambiguous, several investigators have noted that there may be hemispheric differences in the type of emotion processed. In particular, some believe that the right hemisphere preferentially processes dysphoric emotions, and the left hemisphere handles elevated emotions (Dimond, Farrington, & Johnson, 1976; Reuter-Lorenz & Davidson, 1981; Sackeim et al., 1982). Thus, a patient with a left hemispheric impairment often will appear depressed while a patient with a right hemispheric impairment will present with superficially happy affect. The point here is that possibly both hemispheres are needed for appropriate and rich affective experience.

More certainty exists that the limbic system has a key role in the regulation of emotional tone (MacLean, 1955; Papez, 1937; Stumpf, 1980). Specifically, the parahippocampal area and the cingulate gyrus receive many neural inputs from cortical association areas. Other parts of the limbic system receive extensive neural projections directly from the hypothalamus, which also is involved in affect and drive (motivation) regulation as well as in autonomic function. For this reason, the limbic system is often known as the visceral brain.

Memory Processes (Kolb & Whishaw, 1990a; Kupferman, 1985)

Memory is usually defined as the retention of information. Various aspects of memory are well accepted by investigators and several types of memory are used by the brain. At the risk of oversimplification, they may be divided into memory necessary to handle pieces of information in a manner that requires awareness about the topic (declarative memory), and memory that operates on an automatic (reflexive memory) level. An example of declarative memory is remembering that one has read a specific book—recalling its title, its content, and so on. Automatic memory allows performance of a previously learned activity without conscious thought concerning the activity. Different components of memory use different neural pathways. Evidence for this differentiation comes from the clinical finding that injury to specific areas in the brain may result in one type of memory loss but not another.

Memory may be placed into stores, both short-term and long-term, and retrieved at another time. Placement into stores presumably causes physical changes, either transient or permanent, at the level of the neuron. Placement and retrieval both may be more or less accurate. With repeated stimulation, memory improves; instead of lasting for seconds, it may persist for minutes, hours, or much longer. Events that happened further in the past are remembered more easily by brain-injured patients, presumably because long-term memory involves more permanent structural changes and thus is less susceptible to perturbation.

An additional point concerning memory processes is that, although specific lesions to the brain can result in specific memory deficits, the same memory required for a given task may be stored in different neural pathways (another example of parallel processing). This means that, in some cases at least, there is not just one part of the brain that can carry out the functions of learning or memory for a given situation. This duality has obvious value in case of neural injury (Cohen, 1982).

The parts of the brain that have been defined as being important for memory include the limbic system, especially the hippocampus and amygdala, and the frontal cortex. Long-term potentiation, which has been reported in hippocampal output cells, refers to an increase of the amplitude of postsynaptic electrical signals after being stimulated by high-frequency stimuli of short duration. This effect may last from hours to weeks and may be associated with a substantial increase in the number of synaptic contacts and with changes in phospho-proteins within the neurons exhibiting this phenomenon (Lee, Schottler, Oliver, & Lynch, 1980). These neuroanatomic and physiological changes may serve as bases for permanent memory formation.

THE CELLULAR COMPONENTS OF THE CENTRAL NERVOUS SYSTEM

Neurons (from the Greek word for sinew) (Kuffler, Nicholls, & Martin, 1984; Peters, Palay, & Webster, 1976) are a diverse class of cells that share the common characteristics of transmitting changes in membrane potential unidirectionally (carrying action potentials) and transmitting information between cells synaptically (the release into and diffusion across the synaptic cleft of neurotransmitter molecules). As a result, nerve cells are unique in their ability to transfer information in a highly directable manner over long distances. Neurons possess a cell body (soma), axons, and dendrites (Figure 6.4). The axon is specialized by being wrapped in a myelin sheath to carry action potentials away from the cell body. With its end branches, an axon may contact up to 1,000 other neurons. Axon tips contain the machinery for the production, storage, and release of neurotransmitters. In the human, an axon may reach 1 meter in length but usually is less than 100 microns in length. Presynaptic neurotransmitter receptors are frequently found on axon terminals. They have autoregulatory functions and are sensitive to the neurons' own neurotransmitters.

Dendrites are specialized to receive information. Purkinje cells, inhibitory output neurons of the cerebellum, each have an elaborate dendritic tree that receives about 150,000 terminals of other cells. (Most neurons receive approximately 1,000 contacts.) Dendrites contain high concentrations of both stimulatory and inhibitory neurotransmitter receptors and can give rise to action potentials. In general, dendrites receive synapses from a variety of cell types using different neurotransmitters; an axon usually releases only one or two types of neurotransmitter. If more than one chemical is released from the same synapse, the additional transmitter is usually a peptide.

In the simplest situation, the summed input to the dendrites results in changes in membrane potential, which may or may not be sufficient to generate an action potential. The axon responds to the action potential by releasing a neurotransmitter(s) that interacts with the next dendrite and causes changes in the postsynaptic

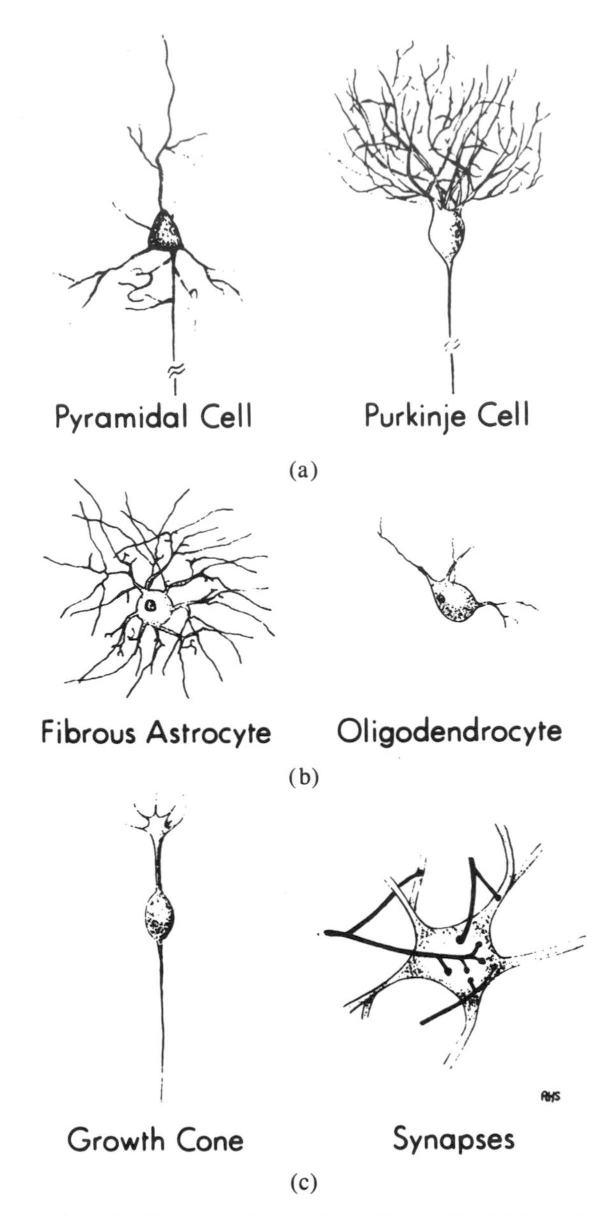

Figure 6.4 (a) Neurons: Pyramidal cells and Purkinje cells are the major output neurons of the cerebral and cerebellar cortices. The central nervous system contains several other classes of neurons that can be morphologically distinguished. Axons are the single processes which carry information away from the cell body. Dendrites form elaborate networks and generally receive input from another neuron. (b) Glial cells: Astrocytes and oligodendrocytes are the two main types of glial cells of the central nervous system. They have a variety of functions (see the text description). (c) (Left) An immature cortical neuron of the type frequently seen in tissue culture. The broadened area of the end of one of the neuronal processes is known as the growth cone, which is involved in the outgrowth of the cell. The genetic and physiological factors that regulate the growth of neuronal extensions (axons and branches) are currently an active area of research in developmental neurobiology. (Right) Synapses making multiple contacts with the cell body and branches of a single neuron.

cell's membrane potential. Factors such as stores of neurotransmitter, activity of intracellular second-messenger systems, functional state of the receptors on the cell surface, and chemical composition of the environment of the synapse often make it difficult to predict the response of a postsynaptic cell.

Glial cells (from the Greek word for glue) (Kuffler, Nicholls, & Martin, 1984; Peters et al., 1976) are nonneuronal cells found in intimate contact with neurons that are thought to play important roles in the maintenance and development of neuronal properties. Glial cells are small supportive elements that give substance and form to the brain; they act as connective tissue does for other body organs. Two principal types of brain glial cells are the astrocyte and the oligodendrocyte (Figure 6.4(b)). The number of glial cells is usually 10 to 50 times that of neurons. Mature oligodendrocytes wrap around axons and produce brain myelin, which acts as an electrical insulator to speed action potential conduction velocities. Astrocytes are thought to provide nutritional support to neurons and to buffer changes in extracellular potassium ion concentrations produced by neuronal firing. Glial cells also help terminate synaptic transmission by removing released neurotransmitters from the extracellular space. Interestingly, many glial cells possess receptors for many neurochemicals, including the classical neurotransmitters (Kimelberg, 1988). The functions of these nonneuronal receptors are presently unclear.

Vasculature, the *blood-brain barrier,* and *cerebrospinal fluid* (Cutler & Spertell, 1982; Purves, 1972) are characteristic of the adult brain, one of the most metabolically active organs in the body. In times of nutritional or metabolic distress, the brain is given preference in receiving nutrients. This priority is especially critical because the brain has limited energy reserves and cannot produce its own glucose. In addition to receiving preferential nutritional support, the brain is relatively isolated from circulating drugs, toxins, and antibodies because of two features of brain vascular cells: (a) tight cellular junctions between the vascular endothelial cells allow only small, uncharged molecules to diffuse from the blood capillaries to the extracellular space, and (b) there is a relative paucity of transport mechanisms for the transfer of large molecules across brain capillary walls.

In many parts of the brain, only a single vessel supplies blood. Occlusion of such a vessel, then, results in death or damage of that brain area. The arrangement of the vasculature is so similar among individuals that the clinical symptoms resulting from a stroke or other vascular accident allow the clinician to say with high probability that a certain branch of a certain vessel is involved. Lack of collateral blood supply in particular parts of the brain has allowed the mapping of many neural functions in humans through comparisons of clinical and neuropathological exams in stroke patients.

Cerebrospinal fluid (CSF) is a clear fluid that is almost devoid of cells and has a low protein content. It is made mainly by epithelial cells in the choroid plexus, within the four ventricles of the brain. The CSF flows from the ventricles into the subarachnoid space, which lies within the meninges. The CSF protects the brain from mechanical shock, provides a pathway for the movement of chemical substances and hormones, and holds the internal environment of the brain chemically more constant than that of the blood. This last achievement seems to be particularly important because the brain may, at any time, need to quickly generate specific neural activity.

Three membranes, collectively called the *meninges,* envelop the entire central nervous system, including the spinal cord. The innermost membrane, the pia mater, lies directly on the surface of the brain and spinal cord, and follows the contours of the nervous tissue. Most of the meninges have their origin in mesoderm. The membranes have a structural function of encapsulation and, both prenatally and postnatally, may influence glial and neuronal migration (O'Rahilly & Muller, 1986; Sievers, Pehlemann, & Berry, 1986).

OVERVIEW OF BRAIN DEVELOPMENT

Cell Birth and Migration

Neurulation and gross brain development (Jacobson, 1978; Lund, 1978; Purves & Lichtman, 1985, p. 332) are first apparent with the establishment of the neural plate during the third embryonic week in human development. This process of neurulation (neural tube formation) is divided into primary and secondary phases. During the primary phase of neurulation, the ectodermal neural plate is transformed, through four stages, into a neural tube. These stages are recognizable but show considerable overlap. They consist of (a) formation of the plate by ectodermal thickening, (b) shaping of the neural plate, (c) bending of the plate, and (d) closure of the neural groove. With closure of the neural tube, there is formation of the neural crest and its overlying surface epithelium. The process of secondary neurulation results in the formation of the most caudal portion of the spinal cord. As in primary neurulation, there are several overlapping stages. In humans, this entire process takes approximately 2 weeks. Subsequently, uneven rates of cell division along the inner surface of the neural tube (the eventual ventricular surface) result in formation of the various brain centers. From week 5 to about week 18 during human gestation, neural precursor cells divide at a rapid rate along the ventricular surface, leading to marked increases in the size of the brain. After about week 18, division of the precursor cells of the neurons ceases in most parts of the brain, and the division of glial precursor cells rapidly increases. This phase of extensive glial cell proliferation and the subsequent formation of myelin, referred to as the brain growth spurt, continues from about week 19 of gestation until 2.5 years of age (Dobbing & Sands, 1973). The steps of neuronal and glial cell division are accompanied by stereotyped gross morphological changes in the external appearance of the brain. As shown in Figure 6.5, the brain increases in size and the surface becomes progressively folded. Primary gyri become well defined at about 28 weeks of gestation. There are gross changes in appearance until at least 4 years of age. The timing of initial development of major human brain structures is given in Table 6.1. The fate of cells that give rise to these structures presumably is set at earlier times during gestation. Nonetheless, the sequential development is interesting to consider in terms of how intrinsic or extrinsic insults to the nervous system at specific gestational times may result in characteristic psychopathological conditions.

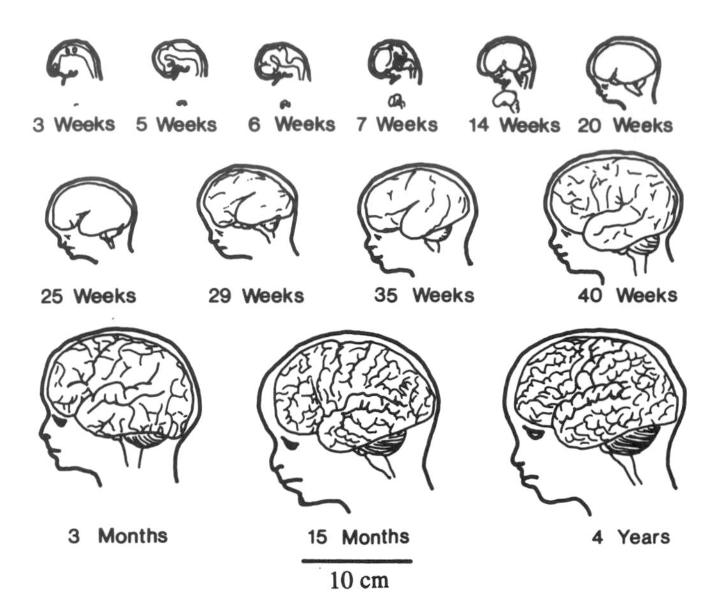

Figure 6.5 Morphological development of the human brain. These schematic drawings depict the external surface of the brain at a succession of embryonic, fetal, and early postnatal ages. The first 5 embryonic stages are represented at both an arbitrary scale (top) to better illustrate structural details and at the same scale (bottom) as the later developmental stages. The bar represents 10 cm. The brain is relatively immature at birth and increases markedly in surface complexity through the first few years of life (Cowan, 1979). After Sikich & Todd, 1988.

A comparison of the development of the brain in different mammalian species is shown in Figure 6.6. We are comparing here the gross brain weight as a function of pre- and postnatal age for rats, rhesus monkeys, and humans. As can be seen on the figure, the time of birth is arbitrary with respect to brain weight development. In the rat, the brain is approximately 12% of its adult size at the time of birth but reaches its full mature characteristics in the course of approximately 40 days. In the rhesus monkey, about 80% of the adult brain size is achieved by the time of birth. Humans are somewhat intermediate between these two, with about 25% of the adult brain weight being achieved at the time of birth. A long progressive period of increases of brain weight extends over the first several years of life in humans (Dobbing & Sands, 1979).

Neuroblast Migration and Brain Topology

Neuronal cell birth is also a temporally regulated process. For each brain region, neuroblast division begins at a characteristic time during development and continues for a specific time. Following their final cell division, most neurons retain simple shapes as they migrate from their region of birth to their final location. Following arrival at their controlled location, the neurons extend elaborate processes. As will be discussed later, these immature neurons are also metabolically active. They can secrete neurotransmitters from growth cones (Hume, Role, & Fischbach, 1983; Young & Poo, 1983) and respond to environmental and neurotransmitter cues from surrounding neurons (Haydon, McCobb, & Kater, 1984; Sikich, Hickok, & Todd, 1990). For cortical structures, the final positions of neurons depend on the time of their birth (Rakic, 1974). As shown in Figure 6.7, for primate visual cortex, the last cells to divide migrate to the most superficial layers of the cortex.

TABLE 6.1 Timing of Earliest Detectable Appearance during Gestation of Major Human Brain Structures

Structure	Time of Appearance (Weeks)	Reference
1. Thalamus	4	(Lemire, Loeser, Leech, & Alvord, 1975)
2. Hypothalamus distinct from thalamus	4	"
3. Anlage of striatum and amygdaloid complex	5	"
4. Hippocampus	5	"
5. Cells in the alar plate (hindbrain) form precursors of cerebellum	5	"
6. Amygdala, caudate, and putamen identifiable	5–6	"
7. Pineal gland	5–6	(Dooling, Chi, & Gilles, 1983a)
8. Substantia nigra	7	(Lemire et al., 1975)
9. Interhemispheric fissure begins to expand rostrally	8	(Dooling, Chi, & Gilles, 1983b)
10. Corpus callosum (primordium)	8	(Gilles, 1983)
11. All layers of hippocampus distinct	9	(Lemire et al., 1975)
12. Fibers of comissural pathways cross midline	10	(Gilles, 1983)
13. Interhemispheric fissure separates the two hemispheres	10	(Dooling et al., 1983b)
14. Hippocampal sulcus in frontal lobe	10	(Dooling et al., 1983b)
15. Optic tracts and lateral geniculate bodies of thalamus seen distinctly	12	(Gilles, 1983)
16. Dentate nucleus of cerebellum	12	(Lemire et al., 1975)
17. Sylvian fissure in frontal, temporal, and parietal lobes	14	(Dooling et al., 1983b)
18. Cortical development of cerebellar vermis fairly advanced (precedes cortical development of the lateral cerebellar hemispheres by 6–8 weeks)	16	(Lemire et al., 1975)
19. Calcarine fissure in occipital lobe	16	(Dooling et al., 1983b)
20. Cingulate gyrus	18	"
21. Parahippocampal gyrus	23	"

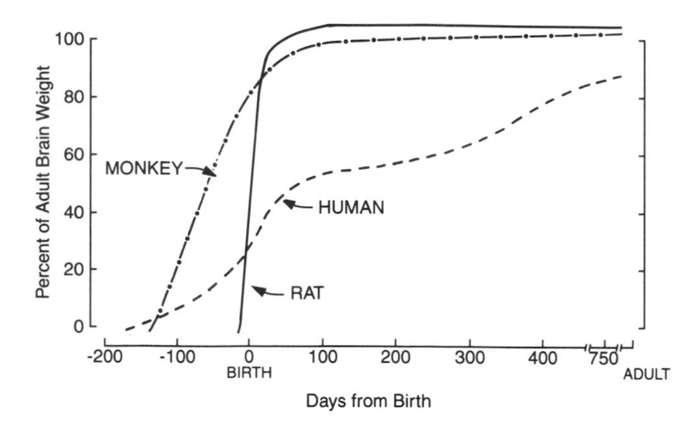

Figure 6.6 Development of the brain in different species. The rates of brain maturation in rats, rhesus monkeys, and humans are dramatically different. At birth, the rat's brain is only 12 percent its adult weight. However, the rat's postnatal development is extremely rapid and it attains its adult weight within 40 days. In contrast, the rhesus monkey's brain growth is nearly complete (76 percent) at birth. The period of human brain growth is markedly prolonged and extends until 2.5 years of age. Thus, we would expect structural neurodevelopmental effects of both intrinsic (for example, hormonal) and extrinsic influences to occur during a circumscribed perinatal period in rats, primarily prenatally in rhesus monkeys, and over a prolonged period encompassing both the latter half of gestation and the first few years of life in humans (Dobbing & Sands, 1979). After Sikich & Todd, 1988.

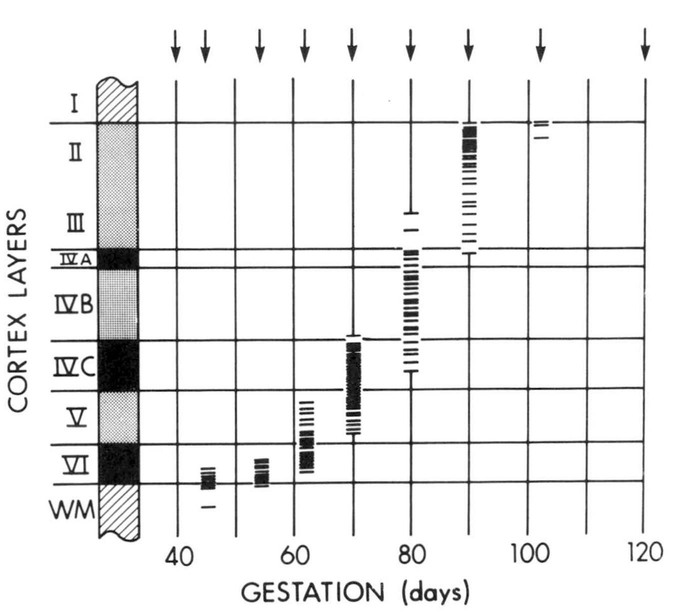

Figure 6.7 Cell birth and cortical layers. The final position of neurons in the monkey visual cortex depends on the time of birth. Cell divisions at a particular time were marked by injection of radioactive thymidine, which is incorporated into DNA shortly before cell division. The visual cortex (area 17) of the monkeys was examined several months after birth. The horizontal lines define the cortical layers, and the vertical lines define the gestational age. Arrows mark the time of ^{3}H-thymidine injections and the hatch marks represent the locations of labeled neurons. The neurons generated late in development have a more superficial location in the cortex. Because all neurons divided in the periventricular zone, the superficial neurons migrated through regions of older cells. This has been called the "inside-out" relationship between cell birth and final location (Carlson, Earls, & Todd, 1988; Purves & Lichtman, 1985, p. 93; Rakic, 1974).

The principles that govern this three-dimensional organization of neuronal destinations are not clear. As will be discussed later in this chapter, their organization probably involves both positive and negative regulators of migration pathway and cell process outgrowth. Most of the brain structures follow the same general outline of development described for the cerebrum. An exception is the cerebellum. The cerebellum is somewhat unusual in its development in that the time of origin and migration of its neurons is over both the pre- and postnatal periods (Sidman & Rakic, 1973). In humans, Purkinje cell neurons complete their migration by the end of the first trimester of pregnancy. But the granule cell neurogenesis and migration starts much later and continues until about 2 years of age. Interestingly, this process may be guided by specific neurotransmitter systems. Some of the first axons to enter the cerebellum and make contact with cerebellar neurons are serotonergic. This serotonergic projection is transient and correlates with the formation of the cortical layers in the cerebellum. The prolonged neurogenesis and cell migration in the cerebellum allows for long periods of vulnerability to environmental and other insults. However, some authors would also view this as a longer period of potential plasticity for recovery of function following injury, as will be described later in this chapter.

Astrocytes and oligodendrocytes arise relatively late in brain development and come from precursor cells distinct from neurons. Most cell birth and migration of glial cells occurs postnatally in humans, and the process of cell death is not known to occur. There is evidence that certain classes of glial cells play a role in neuroblast migration and may be involved in the outgrowth of neurites. In primates, an early, prominent class of glial cells forms networks that extend from the ventricular surface to the cerebral cortex. These so-called radial glia appear to form the surface that cortical neuroblasts adhere to during migration (Varon & Somjen, 1979). Molecules on the surface of other glial cells have also been identified as inhibitors of the movement of growth cones, the part of the neuron that is involved in outgrowth (Caroni & Schwab, 1988). Glial cells then may have important developmental roles in both neuroblast migration and neurite extension.

Angiogenesis in the brain occurs early in embryonic development and, in part, appears to be regulated by various growth factors. Astrocytes, which are closely approximated to brain capillaries, may play a role in blood brain barrier induction early in embryogenesis and in maintenance of the blood brain barrier postnatally (Janzer & Raff, 1987; Risau & Wolburg, 1990).

Functional Development

The development of functional characteristics of the brain follows a somewhat similar course. Synapses are sent out once neurons arrive at their final location to go through competitive and complex processes of cell death and synapse elimination (described below). Very early on in the lives of neurons, however, neurotransmitters are produced, synaptic connections are made, and preliminary functional networks are established (Huttenlocher, 1979; Huttenlocher, de Courten, Garey, & van der Loog, 1982). It appears that this process is more rapid for the sensory systems (Gottlieb, 1972). In the human infant, there is relatively advanced development of sensory systems such as vision, hearing, and touch at the time of birth. The motor systems, however, show considerable delay in their development, partly because of the differences in nerves involved in myelination processes. In part, however, this probably represents differential development of the relay nuclei involved in processing information from the periphery versus sending information back to the peripheral organs.

Neuronal Cell Death

For most brain regions, more neurons are formed than are present in the mature animal. This process of cell elimination or death begins soon after the formation of neurons and is over for most brain regions before birth (Hamburger & Oppenheim, 1982). In mammals, this process appears to be competitive. Immature neurons send out neurites to target cells. More than one cell competes for a given target. The target cell secretes a limited amount of a trophic substance that is essential for neuronal survival (Hamburger, 1980). The cell that successfully competes for the trophic substance survives to make mature synaptic connections with the target cell (Figure 6.8). The neuron that loses the competition for the trophic substance must withdraw its neurite and find another cell to synapse on or die. If the size of the target tissue is experimentally increased or decreased in size, the number of neurons that survive is correspondingly increased or decreased. This process of competitive cell death is different from the process that occurs in invertebrates. For example, in the simple organism *C. elegans,* there are many identified neurons for which, following the last neuroblast cell division, one of the sister cells is programmed to die (Horvitz, Ellis, & Sternberg, 1982). Even if the cell destined to live is experimentally destroyed, the sister cell dies. Such programmed cell death has not been established in vertebrate species. This may in part be due to technical problems in identifying specific sister cells in the more complex vertebrate nervous system. The competitive process of neuronal cell death and survival, however, is well established. The relationship of target size to neuronal survival in vertebrate animals illustrates another important principle of neural development (Katz & Lasek, 1978). Within a given genetic endowment, environmental manipulations can change the architecture of the nervous system. This is one mechanism for creating individual diversity.

The trophic factors that promote neuronal survival appear to be soluble proteins secreted by the postsynaptic target cell. The best studied example is from the peripheral nervous system. The so-called nerve growth factor is a soluble protein produced in

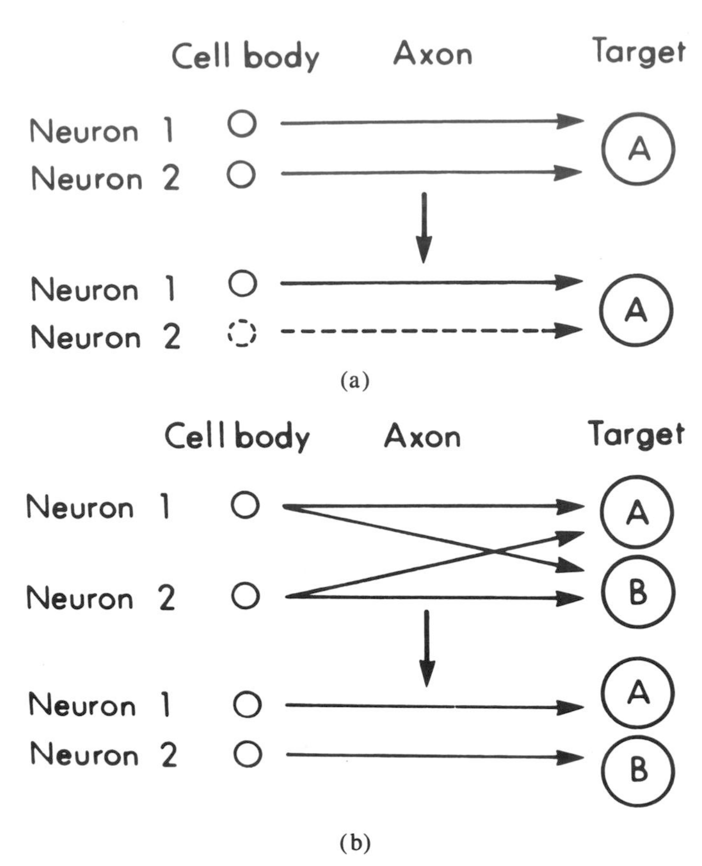

Figure 6.8 Neuronal death and process elimination. (a) During the process of neuronal death, more than one neuron competes for a target (another neuron, a muscle cell, and so on), but only one maintains a successful contact. The unsuccessful neuron dies from lack of a requisite trophic interaction with the target. (b) During process elimination, neurons initially make contacts with more than one target. A neuron successfully competes at one target, but not another. The axon at the unsuccessful target is withdrawn. Neuronal death occurs early in prenatal development; process elimination begins during late prenatal development and extends to at least the early postnatal period (Carlson, Earls, & Todd, 1988).

limited quantities by peripheral target cells (Levi-Montalcini, 1976). Released nerve growth factor interacts with a receptor (analogous to a neurotransmitter receptor) on sympathetic neurons. Nerve growth factor is then taken up by the neuron and retrogradely transported along the neuron's cell body. The interaction of nerve growth factor with its receptor, and its subsequent transport to the cell body, results in a variety of metabolic changes in the presynaptic cell that promotes its survival. Several brain-derived growth factors that appear to act by analogous mechanisms have recently been described.

Synapse Formation and Elimination

The process of synapse formation starts soon after the final cell division forms the immature neuroblast. During cell migration, rudimentary neurites (the eventual axons and dendrites) are formed, but these remain relatively short and ill-defined until neurons reach their final positions. Next follows a phase of rapid extension of axons and dendrites toward their targets. The processes that guide axons and dendrites appear to be both extrinsic and intrinsic. Immature mammalian neurons transplanted from one part of the cerebral cortex to another can still find their targets, suggesting important intrinsic guidance mechanisms for at least these cells (Lund, McLoon, McLoon, Harvey, & Jaeger, 1983). The extracellular matrix also appears to be important in defining allowable pathways for cell process growth. Proteins in the extracellular matrix act as attachment factors for extending processes (Edelman, Cunningham, & Tiery, 1990). Neurites extend by elongation from specialized structures at their tips called growth cones (Figure 6.4(c)) (Kater & Letourneau, 1985). These processes can branch repeatedly, forming complex arborization. Growth cones can respond to extracellular cues such as extracellular matrix composition or neurotransmitters (Kater & Mills, 1989). Calcium seems to be important as an intracellular signal in causing changes in growth rate and growth direction. Recent studies suggest that some of the classical biogenic amine neurotransmitters may have important developmental roles in regulating neurite outgrowth (Haydon, McCobb, & Kater, 1986). For example, stimulation of serotonin type 1a receptors on immature frontal cortical neurons decreases the branching of growing neurites (Sikich et al., 1990). In contrast, stimulation of dopamine D_2–like receptors on the same cells results in increased branching and outgrowth of neurites (Todd, 1992). As described below, these neurotransmitters and their receptors are present early in development and may serve as important neural morphogens.

Initially, more neurites are produced and attempt to form synapses than survive in the mature animal (Hamburger & Oppenheim, 1982). As shown in Figure 6.9, in contrast to the process of cell death, which primarily occurs prenatally in humans, synapse and process elimination continue long after birth. The decrease in the number of synapses is accompanied by increased facilitation of the remaining synapses. These changes correlate with the development of functional abilities and appear to be dependent on synaptic activity. This process is best understood for the visual system, where experimental modulations of optical input have been demonstrated to change synaptic density and cortical organization. In the mature visual cortex, input from both eyes is segregated into alternating columns of neurons that span the cortical layers. These visual columns are not present at birth at all or may be only rudimentarily developed at birth, depending on the species. Initially, axons from both lateral geniculate bodies (relay nuclei for transmitting visual information from the two retina) equally project to all parts of the visual cortex (Hubel, Wiesel, & LeVay, 1977). As visual information starts to be received from both eyes and causes synaptic activity in the visual cortex, axons from one geniculate body recede from each eventual visual column (Figure 6.10). If input from one eye is blocked, then only axons that should have carried input from that eye recede (Rakic, 1981). If input from both eyes is blocked, then regression does not occur and no visual columns develop. The

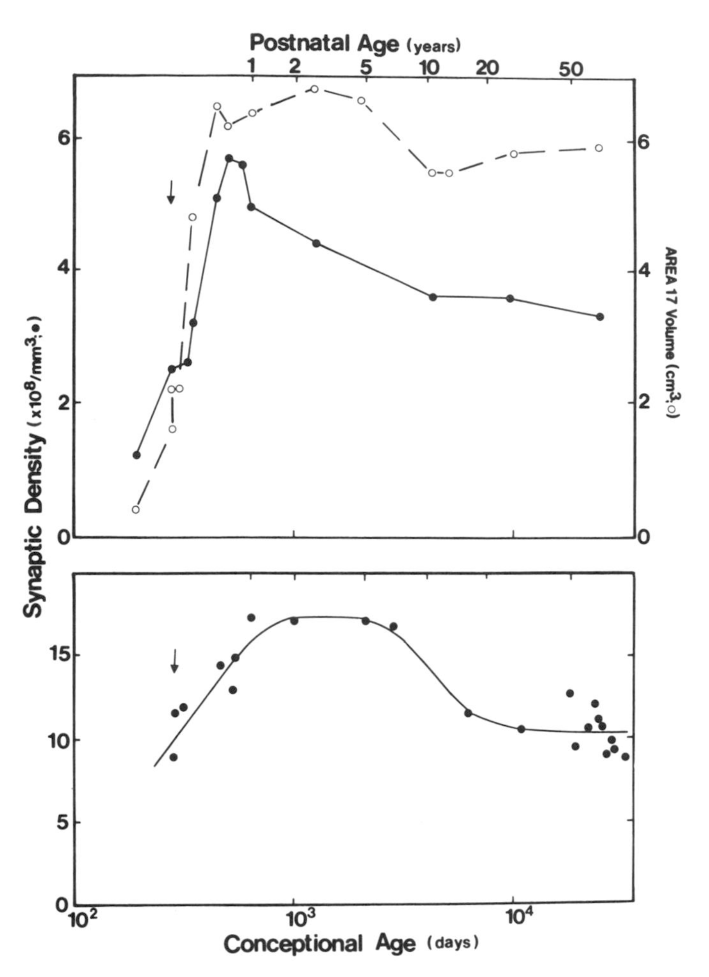

Figure 6.9 Combined Huttenlocner synapse elimination data: synaptic counts as a function of age in human primary visual cortex, also known as area 17 (top graph), and in human frontal cortex (bottom graph). Synaptic density is highest in early life and decreases with age. For the visual cortical area, synaptic density is greatest at 8-12 months, at about 50–60% above the value reached in adulthood (•). Synapse elimination is pronounced until the age of 12 years; subsequently, a more gradual loss occurs. Cortical volume, in contrast, reaches adult values in very early life in this area of the cortex (○). Synapse density in the frontal cortex likewise peaks in the early postnatal period and then declines—at first, rapidly; then more slowly, until age 16 years. These data suggest that regulation of synapse number occurs in the early and late postnatal period as a normal component of human central nervous system development (Huttenlocher, 1979; Huttenlocher, de Courten, Garey, & van der Loog, 1982).

mechanism whereby the activity of one synapse results in the regression of competing synapses is not known. This is particularly puzzling because most neurons make and receive multiple synaptic contacts. There is evidence that the joint activity of a pre- and postsynaptic neuron pair preserves and facilitates the strength of the synaptic connection (Hamburger, 1980). A presynaptic neuron that does not elicit postsynaptic activity

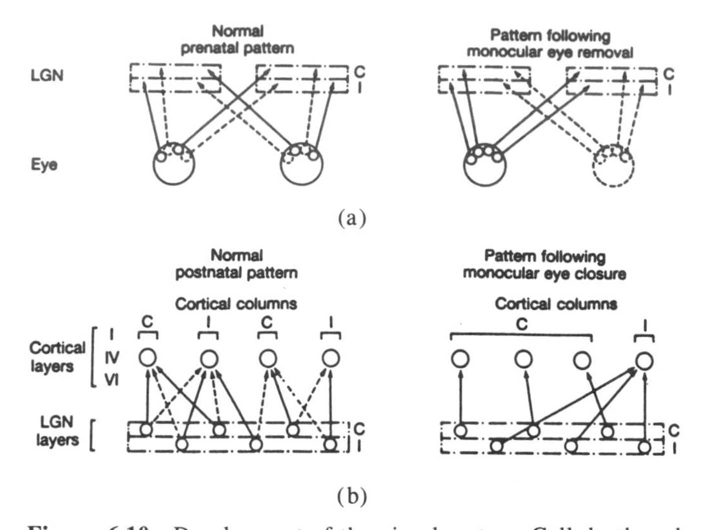

Figure 6.10 Development of the visual system. Cell death and process elimination in the primate visual system depends on competition between the eyes. (a) Retinal-thalamic connections. Between embryonic (E) days 50-90 (of a 165-day gestation period in macaques), the number of axons in the optic nerve rises to more than twice the number found at birth or in the adult. During this period, both eyes project to all layers of the cortex. As axons of retinal ganglion cells begin to form synapses in the lateral geniculate nucleus (LGN) of the thalamus (E90-E120), inputs from the contralateral (C) and ipsilateral (I) eye segregate into eye-specific layers. This segregation is achieved by selective retraction of neurons projecting to inappropriate layers (dashed lines) and stabilization of those projecting to appropriate layers (solid lines). If one eye is removed prior to this segregation, the remaining eye stabilizes projections to both the C and I layers. Approximately 37% more axons than normally exist are found in the remaining optic nerve (Rakic & Riley, 1983; Stryker & Harris, 1986). (b) Thalamic-cortical connections. During the late prenatal period, following segregation of retinal input to the LGN, LGN neurons project in an overlapping pattern to cells in layer IV of the visual cortex. As the result of spontaneous activity in the retina and LGN in the prenatal period, and of visual experience in the early postnatal period, half of the left- and right-eye axons form stabilized synapses (solid lines) and half of the axons retract (dashed lines). If, postnatally, one eye is sutured (the ipsilateral eye in this example), thereby reducing patterned vision, the final cortical projection pattern is altered from that of normal animals. The open eye will stabilize more processes than the deprived eye, resulting in an expanded ocular dominance column for the open eye relative to the closed eye (Carlson, Earls, & Todd, 1988; Carlson, O'Leary, & Burton, 1987).

because of low activity levels or weak synaptic impulses, then, would be withdrawn. As will be discussed in greater detail below, there is a limited time period postnatally during which the activity-dependent regression of synapses and axons can occur or be modulated in the visual system. This appears to be a general theme, in that the biological or genetic program of brain development can only be modulated during certain sensitive time periods (sometimes called critical periods). For different brain regions, different times are involved. For many of the structures of interest to psychologists or psychiatrists, the timing of these sensitive or critical periods is not well documented.

The modulation of synapse number and organization by neuronal activity may represent a major mechanism for generating individual differences. For the sensory systems, differences in environmental experiences will result in differences in synaptic organization. Motor or cognitive responses to different sensory input may secondarily result in differences in synaptic organization in these systems. If these systems have sensitive or critical periods when developmental changes in synaptic organization can occur, then enduring differences will be established between individuals. This would be true even if the individuals have the same genotype.

The modulation of synapse number and organization also offers a potential mechanism for experimentally or clinically altering individual abilities. Because synapse and process elimination continue through at least early childhood in humans, increasing or decreasing different types of activities or stimuli could alter synaptic organization. As will be discussed below in conjunction with studies on the effects of rearing animals in different environments, there is evidence that such environmental manipulations may one day result in clinically meaningful effects in at-risk infants and children. A major empirical question is whether sufficient quantities of a specific type of stimulation can be administered to effect synaptic organization in the desired manner. Present methods of assessing change may not be sufficiently sensitive to document clinically relevant changes.

Myelination of the Central Nervous System

Myelin, a lipid substance found in vertebrates, surrounds many axons in the central and peripheral nervous systems. Myelin electrically insulates nerve fibers and thereby provides a means for rapid nerve conduction along the axon. Generally, larger axons that carry messages over a long distance are myelinated, although more locally active axons with much smaller diameters are also often myelinated, especially in the central nervous system. Although attempts have been made for many years, it has been difficult to use myelination of the brain as a measure of the onset of cerebral function. For example, neurons can conduct impulses without myelin, and early reflex arcs are functional before their fibers are myelinated. As will be discussed subsequently, changes in dendritic and synaptic organization during development have more readily provided clues for understanding behavioral and cognitive maturation. However, interest in the myelination of the nervous system has not waned and even now serves as a useful index of brain growth and integrity. Further study of myelination is warranted, given the closeness of interaction of CNS nerve cells and myelin-producing cells (oligodendrocytes), and the evidence that abnormalities of myelin, whether dysmyelination or demyelination, are often seen in neurological and neurodevelopmental disorders. A well-known example of a demyelinating disorder is multiple sclerosis, in which, typically early in the disease, sensory and motor performance is impaired. Mood and cognitive disturbances may also occur. Usually, young adults are first affected and may continue to show evidence of neurological damage for years. Occasionally, there are long-lasting remissions. The cause of multiple sclerosis remains unknown. Although multiple sclerosis is usually not considered a developmental disorder, it provides an interesting model for the study of possible behavioral correlates to demyelination of the central nervous system over a prolonged time period. Another example of a clinical syndrome that has been regarded in terms of changes in myelination is schizophrenia. In a recent study, it was speculated that the on-schedule myelination during adolescence of key areas in the cortical-limbic circuit, which have been implicated in the pathogenesis of schizophrenia, may be associated with the onset of symptoms (Benes, 1989). Lastly, there is continued interest in studying the myelination of children and infants, especially with the introduction of noninvasive imaging techniques such as magnetic resonance imaging (MRI). Significant differences in myelination between normal children and those with developmental delay have been noted (Dietrich et al., 1987).

An overview of myelination in the human central nervous system is given in Table 6.2. Myelination proceeds at different rates in different neural systems and in different tracts of the same system (Gilles, Shankle, & Dooling, 1983). Early myelination occurs in the brain stem at 20–30 weeks of gestation; myelination in the forebrain follows at 30–40 weeks of gestation. In the human, the time of most rapid myelination is in the first two years of life (Dobbing & Sands, 1973). Primary motor and sensory areas of the brain are relatively completely myelinated by age 6. Associative areas become fully myelinated only in the second decade, and some investigators have documented myelination of the prefrontal cortex up to the fourth decade (Yakolev & Le Cours, 1967). In the human brain, myelination thus proceeds over an extended time period ranging from the fetal stage to adolescence and beyond. As noted elsewhere in this chapter, another structural change that occurs in the human brain over a similar time period, or at least until adolescence, is the elimination of synapses in the cerebral cortex. The mechanisms of myelination and of synapse elimination are not known, but an interplay of intrinsic with environmental factors presumably occurs in both over a large part of the human life span. The prolonged time of development of myelin offers numerous opportunities for the disruption of myelination by toxins, nutrition, and other environmental factors. Such effects on myelination have been well documented (Wiggins, 1986).

TABLE 6.2 Approximate Onset and Completion of Myelination in the Human Nervous System

Structure	Onset	Postnatal Completion
Motor roots	3 months (prenatal)	1 month
Sensory roots	4 months "	6 months
Cerebellar peduncles	5 months "	6 years
Limbic system	7 months "	6 years
Mammilothalamic tract	8 months "	7 months (50% completion)
Optic radiation and tract	Birth	4 months
Acoustic radiation	Birth	6 years
Reticular formation	Birth	2 decades
Cerebral commissures	2 months (postnatal)	1 decade
Intracortical neuropil	3 months "	2–4 decades (associative areas last)

Times of onset and completion of myelination were observed by light microscopy. After "The Myelogenetic Cycles of Regional Maturation of the Brain" by P. I. Yakolev and A. R. Le Cours, 1964. In *Regional Development of the Brain in Early Life* (pp. 3–70), A. Minkowski, Ed. Oxford, England: Blackwell.

Development of Neurotransmitter Production and Function

Both neurotransmitter receptors and neurotransmitters are present early in development. In the developing rat brain, messenger RNA for dopaminergic receptors can be found as early as embryonic day 14 (Mack, O'Malley, & Todd, 1991). The neurotransmitter receptor proteins and their neurotransmitters are present during the same developmental period (Lanier, Dunn, & Van Hartesveldt, 1978). Perhaps more relevant to human development are the elegant studies of Goldman-Rakic and Brown (1982). Using monkeys as a model system, these investigators have mapped regional cortical distributions of classical neurotransmitters (serotonin, dopamine, norepinephrine) and their receptors in cortex throughout postnatal development. There is great variety in the developmental courses for the different neurotransmitters. For example, in postnatal cortex, serotonin has essentially the same concentration and distribution of concentrations in 2-month-old and 36-month-old animals. In contrast, dopamine and norepinephrine show large fluctuations in levels during the same period. In addition to changes in absolute concentration, the distribution is very different for the neurotransmitters. Serotonin is in uniform concentration throughout the cortical areas surveyed; dopamine has a pronounced rostral-caudal gradient, with the highest concentrations being found in prefrontal cortex. Norepinephrine has a varied distribution, with low levels in prefrontal and occipital cortex but higher levels in the postcentral cortical regions.

Many authors, as early as the 1960s or before, have argued that these neurotransmitters may have important developmental roles in establishing specific pathways in brain topology. As discussed earlier, neural activity is an important determinant of which synapses are retained. In addition to synaptic activity effects, however, there is increasing evidence that both serotonin and dopamine can affect neuronal morphology directly. This is highlighted by recent studies of the effect of stimulating serotonin 5-HT_{1A} receptors on cortical neurons in culture. Specific stimulation of 5-HT_{1A} receptors results in dramatic decreases in the branching of neurites (Sikich et al., 1990). As seen in Figure 6.11(a), the overall length of the neurite is unaffected, suggesting that this may be a normal mechanism for the pruning or elimination of synaptic processes. In addition, this may be a quantitatively important mechanism because the majority of cortical neurons, both during development and in adulthood, possess serotonin receptors. In contrast, stimulation of dopamine D_2 receptors appears to enhance both neurite branching and outgrowth in cells that possess dopamine receptors (Figure 6.11(b)) (Todd, 1992; Swarzenski et al., 1994).

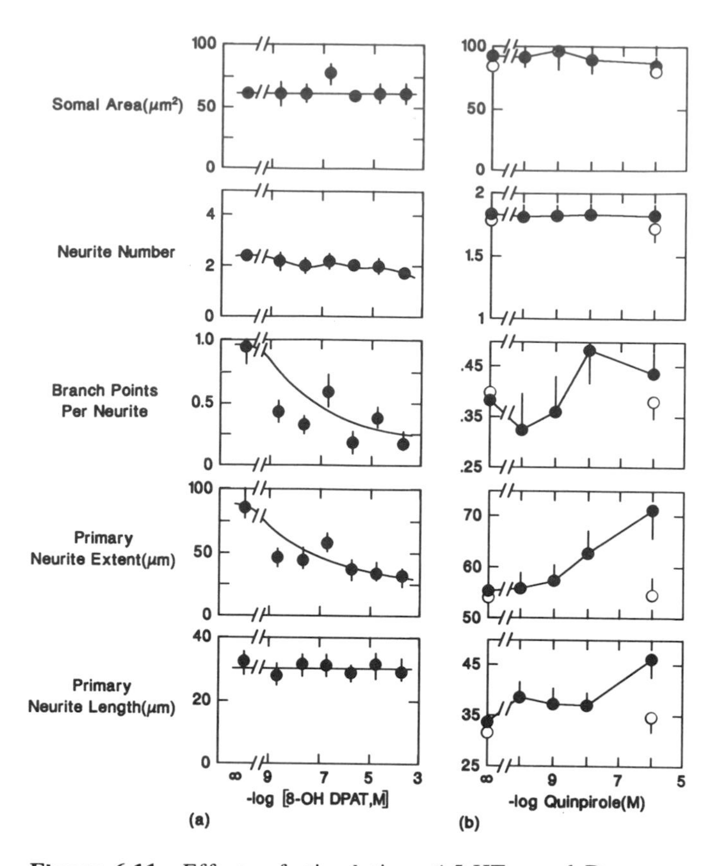

Figure 6.11 Effects of stimulation of 5-HT_{1A} and D_2 receptors. (a) Effects of 8-OH DPAT, a specific 5-HT_{1A} serotonin receptor agonist, on neuronal morphology. Rat frontal cortical neurons of gestational age 19 days (E19) were cultured for 48 hours in the indicated concentrations of 8-OH DPAT. All values are mean ± SEM for 100 cells. There were no significant concentration effects on somal area, neurite number per cell, primary neurite number per cell, or primary neurite length per cell. All concentrations of 8-OH DPAT resulted in significant (Mann-Whitney analyses $p < 0.001$) reductions in the number of branch points per neuron and the total neuritic extent per neuron. Similar results were obtained in a repeat experiment (Sikich, Hickok, & Todd, 1990). (b) Effects of D_2 ligands on neurite outgrowth and branching. E17 cells of rat frontal cortex were cultured for 48 hours in the indicated concentrations of quinpirole (•), a selective D_2 dopamine receptor agonist, and/or 1 μm eticlopride (○), a selective D_2 dopamine receptor antagonist. All values are mean ± SEM for 100 cells. There were no significant effects on somal area, or on neurite number per cell. There were significant increases in branch points per cell, primary neurite length, and total neuritic extent (Todd, 1992).

Both these effects occur at physiologically relevant concentrations and may represent competing processes that help establish a mature neuronal morphology. In this context, the program of development would be specified in part by which neurotransmitter receptors are expressed on particular neurons. There would be a combination or interaction of the genotype and functional phenotype of the cell with local neurochemical and environmental cues that determine the overall developmental process.

As a clinical footnote to this discussion, it should be recognized that many psychoactive pharmacological agents used in the treatment of severe mental and behavioral disorders interact in either inhibitory or stimulatory fashion with these classical neurotransmitter receptors. In the treatment of either pregnant or lactating females, we may be inadvertently affecting developmental processes in either the pre- or early postnatal period. These types of neuronal morphological alterations would be very difficult to define on postmortem or brain imaging techniques. This kind of difficulty would more likely be documented in behavioral or cognitive testing paradigms.

In general, the distribution of neurotransmitter concentrations in the adult individual mimics the pattern of innervation of particular neurotransmitter systems. It must be appreciated, however, that the distribution of neurotransmitters only overlaps in part with the distribution of neurotransmitter receptors. There are regional differences in the expression of different neurotransmitter receptor subtypes. For example, in the dopaminergic system, there are two families of receptors, D_1 and D_2. Both are present in the basal ganglia. In contrast, in the substantia nigra, where a large number of the cell bodies of dopamine-producing cells are found, there is a paucity of D_1-like receptors but an abundance of D_2-like receptors (Cooper, Bloom, & Roth, 1986c; Creese, 1987). It is thought that these D_2-like receptors are so-called autoreceptors, which help in the regulation of dopamine synthesis. This identity has also been found for other neurotransmitter subtypes. For example, there are at least a dozen types of receptors for serotonin (for example $5\text{-HT}_{1A, B, C, D}$, 5-HT_2, and 5-HT_3). 5-HT_{1A} receptors are found predominantly in the hippocampus and lateral septum, and are present in smaller numbers in other parts of the brain (Doyer, 1990; Hamon et al., 1990). The 5-HT_{1C} receptor is found in the highest abundance in the choroid plexus and at a much lower concentration in other brain regions. Because activation of different receptor subtypes by the same neurotransmitter can result in inhibitory or excitatory effects on the postsynaptic cell membrane, the distribution of receptor subtypes is considered by some to be more fundamental than the distribution of neurotransmitters themselves.

As a reflection of the complex physiology of neurotransmission, it may be fairer to state that there are increasing layers of signal amplification and diversity at each step in the information transfer process. The action potential releases, at the synapse, one or a few neurotransmitters, which diffuse across the synaptic cleft to interact with receptors. Depending on what form of neurotransmitter receptor is present on the postsynaptic cell, there may be an inhibitory or excitatory response at the cell membrane. In addition, depending on what second-messenger system the neurotransmitter couples to or interacts with within the cell, there may be various short- and long-term responses to the arrival of information from the presynaptic action potential. The second-messenger interactions, which in part are specified by the presence of particular types of G proteins, can result in a variety of immediate changes in the metabolic machinery of the cell or in more long-term gene activation changes (Watson, Hopkins, Roberts, Steitz, & Weiner, 1987). In the coming decades, it is hoped, there will be substantial increases in our understanding of the important regulatory features of the interactions of the multiplicity of neurotransmitter types with the multiplicity of neurotransmitter receptor subtypes and the multiplicity of post-synaptic coupling events resulting from neurotransmission.

Changes in Brain Organization after Childhood

The brain is not a static structure. It continues to change and to have the potential to change throughout the life of the individual. These changes are not restricted to atrophy or degenerative phenomena; they also include important changes associated with puberty, memory, and experience. With age, neuronal cell loss continues at a lower but measurable rate in cognitively normal individuals. As previously stated, synapse number also appears to decrease significantly. During puberty, there are important changes in many measures of brain function and structure. Although the cellular or subcellular basis for memory is largely unknown, new memories are acquired throughout life, presumably reflecting changes in synaptic organization. As will be discussed later in more detail, there is growing evidence that postnatal environmental experience can affect numbers of synaptic contacts in both developing and mature animals. Much of this work has been done using experimental animals, and the generalizability to humans is debatable. Even so, the important implications of such approaches for realistic treatment interventions argue for careful evaluation of these difficult studies.

SEX DIFFERENCES IN BRAIN STRUCTURE AND FUNCTION

Although our culture is often concerned with the differences between the sexes, men and women share most behavioral characteristics. Some behavioral scientists hypothesize that even in the presence of structural (anatomical) sex differences, each individual organism may have the functional capacity to display many of the stereotypical masculine and feminine behaviors (Södersten, 1984). Different biological and social experiences during development possibly allow significant departure from expected sex differences in both structure and function. However, various sex differences in brain structure and function have been described for several species. A typical example of differences in behavior between males and females about which there is little dispute is the complex mating rituals of many species. These frequently stereotyped rituals are found both in invertebrates and vertebrates. For example, as part of courtship behavior, the male housefly has chasing rituals not demonstrated by the female (Hausen & Strausfeld, 1980; Purves & Lichtman, 1985, p. 344). Chasing behavior of the male housefly has been anatomically localized to a neuronal structure consisting of two columns of neurons and specialized cells in the brain. This neural structure is not present in the female brain. This is a clear example of a sexual dimorphism (different in males versus females) in neuroanatomy and function that serves to govern reproductive behavior.

The human brain also contains several neural structures that have vital roles in sexual behavior and undergo sexual differentiation during development. Sexual differentiation of the brain refers to the process beginning in the fetal period and continuing postnatally, whereby anatomical and behavioral differences (such that exist) between the sexes are established. This process does not appear to be primarily due to genetic differences acting within individual brain cells. The regulatory mechanisms for this developmental process, which involves differences in neuronal organization, are hypothesized to be guided primarily by circulating sex hormones (gonadal hormones; androgens and estrogens) acting directly on neurons. These hormones, and their receptors, are present in the central nervous system at early developmental stages. Although sex differences in brain structure have been clearly documented in humans, considerable controversy exists about their significance for behavior (whether reproductive, cognitive, or social).

One compelling reason for understanding the nature of sex differences in anatomy is the possibility of obtaining more neurobiological insight into the development and maintenance of a healthy organism. Significant sex differences are found in the incidence, clinical course, and severity of many medical diseases. Similarly, significant sex differences are found in many psychopathological diseases (Table 6.3) (Dohrenwend & Dohrenwend, 1976; Earls, 1987). For example, boys are more likely to be afflicted with disorders such as dyslexia and infantile autism. Conversely, girls appear to be more susceptible to some forms of depression. Adult males more commonly are afflicted with antisocial personality disorder, in which severe aggression is often the predominant finding. For a given illness, there may be different degrees of severity between the sexes. For example, girls are more likely than boys to have a more severe form of autism. In contrast, men who have schizophrenia, for which the sex ratio is equal, often have a much poorer clinical course than women. Interestingly, males develop schizophrenia at an earlier age than females. Given the assumption that these and other psychopathological conditions have much of their origin in abnormal neurobiological development, and given the knowledge that there are truly significant sex differences in psychopathology, one may hypothesize that the effects of gonadal hormones during development, both prenatally and postnatally, may have direct consequences on the development of abnormal psychological states.

Initially, structural and functional sex differences for the mammalian brain are discussed in this section. Specific examples are given and discussed in a developmental context. Subsequently, the role of gonadal hormones in the sexual differentiation of

TABLE 6.3 Sex Differences in the Incidence of Neuropsychiatric and Developmental Disorders

Condition	Boy:Girl Ratio	Reference
Hyperactivity	4:1–9:1	(Cantwell, 1977)
Tourette's syndrome	3:1	(Shapiro, Shapiro, Bruun, & Sweet, 1978)
Obsessive-compulsive disorder	2:1	(Rapoport, 1986)
Autism	~ 3:1	(Rutter & Garmezy, 1983)
Reading retardation	3.5:1	(Rutter & Yule, 1977)
Cross-gender behaviors*	7:1	(Bradley, 1990)

*Cross-gender behaviors may not be part of a disorder. Ratio of 7:1 was found in a psychiatric clinic population. After Sikich and Todd, 1988.

the brain and the development of the central nervous system is examined.

Structural Sex Differences in the Central Nervous System

A few gross anatomical differences of brain structure between the sexes have been consistently described. These include differences in speech areas and in total brain weight. A sex difference in brain weight in humans (males heavier than females, when corrected for height) appears during the second year of life. By this time, the brain has reached about 80% of its adult value (Swaab & Hofman, 1984). The weight of the developing male brain increases faster than that of the female brain for about the first 5 years of life. The functional significance of this developmental sex difference in weight is not clearly understood, but may be related to differences in the rates of maturation for cognitive abilities between boys and girls (see below).

One of the first brain areas demonstrated to have left-right differences also differs between the sexes. The planum temporale is a gyrus within the temporal lobe that is contained within the cortical region known as Wernicke's area. This region has a primary role in the perception (understanding) of language. Language abilities seem to differ between men and women. In both sexes, the left planum is usually larger than the right (range in some studies varies from 65% to 82% of cases) (Geschwind & Levitsky, 1968; Wada, Clarke, & Hamm, 1975). This asymmetry is clearly present in infants (Witelson & Pallie, 1973) and has been observed as early as the 28th week of gestation (Dooling, Chi, & Gilles, 1983b). Most females have a leftward biased anatomic asymmetry; however, more females than males have a larger right planum (Wada et al., 1975). Presently, it is unclear what role the planum temporale has in the development of language and what is the functional significance of the observed sex difference.

Several other gross anatomical differences between the sexes have been described. These include differences in the massa intermedia (Landsdell & Davie, 1972) (fibers joining the two thalami) and in both of the commissural pathways (the corpus callosum and the anterior commissure). The functional meaning of the sex differences in the thalamus and anterior commissure is still unclear. A substantial literature exists on structural sex differences in the corpus callosum, much of which appears to be contradictory or of undetermined significance. One recent study on sex differences in the corpus callosum will be reviewed in a subsequent section.

In contrast to the fairly small number of gross anatomical sex differences that have been described in the literature, numerous smaller-scale morphological sex differences have been consistently found in the mammalian central nervous system, both in the brain and spinal cord. Examples that will be described in more detail include differences in the gross volume of certain nuclei, in individual neuronal size, and in cellular organization, including synaptic and dendritic organization. Differences in enzyme activities and in neurotransmitter systems (including receptors) have also been described, although not as consistently. Such differences have been noted in multiple brain areas, including the hypothalamus, parts of the limbic system (amygdala and hippocampus), and cerebral cortex. The hypothalamus and limbic system are connected with each other by an abundance of bidirectional neural tracts. A main task of the hypothalamic/limbic system is the regulation of drive or motivation, which involves the expression of reproductive, aggressive, and other social behaviors, so it may not be surprising that there are sex differences in structure in these areas.

Functional Sex Differences in the Central Nervous System

In this section, evidence for sex differences in behavior will be reviewed. Behavioral sex differences, like structural sex differences, most likely reflect interactions among chromosomal, hormonal, and environmental influences during embryonic and postnatal development and in adulthood. In theory at least, it should be possible to link behavioral sex differences directly to ultrastructural and physiological sex differences. In practice, as previously stated, such direct correlation is not often achieved. Differences in human brain function and behavior and their possible relationships to differences in human brain anatomy and development will be discussed. Finally, effects of gonadal hormones on brain and behavior in rodents, nonhuman primates, and humans will be reviewed.

Sex Differences and Functional Anatomic Lateralization

Cerebral function in both sexes frequently is organized in an asymmetric manner, meaning that the left and right hemispheres can perform different tasks or may be specialized to perform a function particularly well. Hemispheric asymmetry or lateralization of function is found across species, including primates (Wada et al., 1975), rodents (Kolb, Sutherland, Nonneman, & Whishaw, 1982), and birds (Nottebohm, 1977). Sex differences in cerebral function are most consistently found in specific cognitive abilities (some of which appear to be lateralized) and in handedness (which also is thought to reflect specialization of one hemisphere over the other). A simple example of lateralization of function in which there is a sex difference is left-handedness. Although most people of both sexes are right-handed in writing (Annett, 1980), left-handedness is more frequent in men. This example raises two questions: (a) How does cerebral functional asymmetry develop? and (b) Does sex influence the manner in which the cerebral hemispheres develop? The answer to the first question is not clear, but there is sufficient evidence to provide a partial response to the second. Some of the evidence for the presence of asymmetries in function and anatomy at birth and for developmental sex differences in such asymmetries is discussed to provide a framework for a subsequent discussion of sex differences in cognition and handedness.

Functional lateralization probably has already appeared by birth. For example, infants soon after birth respond to different stimuli (e.g., speech vs. musical sounds) using preferentially one hemisphere over the other (left and right hemispheres, respectively) (Molfese, Freeman, & Palermo, 1975). Infants also show functional asymmetry for other nonverbal perceptual skills that are lateralized to the right hemisphere (Witelson & Swallow,

1988). This is the same pattern as in the adult. Boys appear to develop nonverbal perceptual skills (right hemispheric lateralization) significantly earlier than girls, often by many years (Witelson, 1976). Girls in turn exhibit certain verbal skills (left hemispheric lateralization) earlier than boys (Morley, 1957). These findings argue fairly convincingly for differential timing of development of neuroanatomical substrates for some cognitive skills in boys and girls. Different timing of right and left hemispheric development in boys and girls is also suggested by the clinical observation that young girls are more able to transfer linguistic skills to the right hemisphere after left hemispheric injury than boys with a similar injury (Kelly, 1985). This last point is particularly important. Sex-based differences in the timing of developmental events may provide a mechanism for the development of sex differences in the rates of particular neurological or psychiatric disorders.

As described above for the adult, the functional organization of the right and left hemispheres usually differs in both sexes. The left hemisphere appears to process mostly linguistic and analytic functions, and the right hemisphere emphasizes form recognition and integration (Zaidel, Clarke, & Suyenobu, 1990). This dichotomy in function may be an oversimplification, but there clearly is some validity to this model, as evidenced by brain-injured patients and numerous experiments. Perhaps as a consequence of differential development of the right and left hemispheres in males and females, certain cognitive functions are performed more easily by males and others more easily by females. This differential development of the hemispheres in the young does not necessarily imply that in the adult the left hemisphere is developed better in females, or vice versa. In fact, it remains unclear what the implications of differential hemispheric development in the sexes are for many adult cerebral functions.

As described above, the left planum temporale is usually larger than the right in both sexes, but more females than males have a reversed asymmetry. A recent intriguing finding is that dyslexics, who are more frequently males than females, show more symmetry in this area than nondyslexics (Galaburda, Sherman, Rosen, Aboitiz, & Geschwind, 1985). Dyslexia is a reading disorder characterized by abnormalities in both visuospatial and linguistic processes, presumably as a result of abnormal neural organization (Witelson, 1974). The greater likelihood for males to have dyslexia could reflect a greater probability in males for such abnormal cerebral development at the level of neural organization, possibly because of the relatively prolonged period of hemispheric development in males. There is also evidence of more widespread cortical malformations in disorders that predominate in boys, such as dyslexia and autism.

The corpus callosum is an important structure that, according to some, may have roles in interhemispheric communication and control (Cooke, 1986). Sex differences in this collection of nerve fibers might be expected to result in differences in the ways the two cerebral hemispheres function relative to each other. A recent intriguing study suggests that callosal (isthmus) size predicts handedness in adult males but not in females. This may mean that lateralization of handedness develops differently in males and females, again implying a possible functional sex difference (Witelson, 1989).

Sex Differences in Human Cognition

Frequently, the statement is made that women are more proficient than men in verbal skills and that men have greater ability than women in visuospatial skills, for example, mental rotation and map reading (Harris, 1978). This dichotomy may be too simple. For example, women do not excel in verbal reasoning more frequently than males (Hutt, 1972). However, women may solve some types of visuospatial problems as well as men by using different mental processes or by practicing similar mental processes. Nonetheless, it is interesting with respect to developmental differences in the sexes that girls are capable of some more advanced linguistic functions at an earlier age than boys (Horgan, 1976). For example, girls are verbally more fluent and have larger vocabularies at an earlier age than boys. In contrast, boys, according to some data, excel in verbal analogies. Also, boys appear to develop some mathematical skills earlier and more consistently than girls (Benbow & Benbow, 1984). Possibly, these developmental cognitive differences reflect differences in the development of the left and right hemispheres in the sexes.

Sex Differences in Handedness

Most people of both sexes are right-handed. This is thought to represent a usual left hemispheric specialization for this function. Cross-culturally, an incidence of 10% in left-handed writing is usually found. However, there are sex differences in the prevalence of types of handedness. Men have a higher incidence of mixed- or left-handedness (Annett, 1970) and women more often have a stronger right-handed preference than men (Annett, 1980). Unlike the language capabilities for most people, who usually have minimal right hemispheric linguistic abilities, handedness for a variety of tasks is not as clearly confined to one hemisphere (Annett, 1970).

The development of handedness has frequently been discussed in relation to the development of cognitive abilities. So far, no single theory fully explains the development of handedness. Here, only a hormonal model to explain handedness will be presented; the model addresses several aspects of cerebral functional asymmetry and sex differences in brain structure and function. The major tenet of this theory (known as the Geschwind and Galaburda hypothesis) is that the high levels of testosterone normally found in males slow down or prolong the neuronal development of the left hemisphere (Geschwind & Galaburda, 1987). The prolonged development of the left hemisphere lengthens the vulnerable period for environmental or other insults. In the human male, testosterone is elevated during gestation and early postnatal life. Such insults could interfere with the development of the left hemispheric functions or could prompt the transfer of some functions to the other hemisphere. Why the left hemisphere should be preferentially inhibited is not clear. Although this theory does not explain how, in terms of neural mechanisms, testosterone influences handedness, it is consistent with many observations. As previously stated, left-handedness is more common in males, and males have a higher incidence of some developmental disorders associated with left-hemispheric dysfunction. In addition, there is an increased incidence of non-right-handedness among patients with several developmental disorders—for example, mental retardation and dyslexia (Telzrow, Century, Redmond, Whitaker, & Zimmerman, 1983).

Role of Gonadal Hormones in Sex Differences

Sexual Differentiation of the Brain

Over the past few decades, evidence has accumulated suggesting that gonadal hormones have important direct influences on the sexual differentiation of the brain during development and on behavioral sex differences in the adult. These include reproductive, social, and cognitive behaviors. These effects may be divided into long-lasting organizational effects (Phoenix, Goy, Gerall, & Young, 1959) and short-term, reversible, activational effects (Grant & Young, 1952). Specific areas in the mammalian central nervous system are thought to be sensitive to gonadal hormones during critical developmental periods; primarily, these are prenatal and perinatal, but they can also be postnatal. During such critical periods, gonadal hormones have been shown to exert direct effects on nerve cell division, migration, and survival. These influences result in relatively permanent, organizational changes in neural structure that do not require the continued presence of hormones. Other differences are detectable only in the presence of hormones. An example of such an activational effect is the cyclic ability of estrogen in females to induce hypothalamic cells to secrete luteinizing hormone-releasing hormone (LHRH). This hormone causes the release of luteinizing hormone, which, in females, will result in ovulation. If a male is gonadectomized in the perinatal period, then later exposure to estrogen will cause hypothalamic secretion of LHRH (Feder & Whalen, 1964; Gorski, 1988).

Organizational effects during development are thought to underlie the ways the organism can respond to activational hormonal messages during adolescence and adulthood. One example of a developing structure that is clearly sensitive to the organizational effects of gonadal hormones and for which functional significance has been postulated is the sexually dimorphic nucleus of the preoptic area (SDN-POA), located close to the anterior hypothalamus (Gorski, Gordon, Shryne, & Southam, 1978; Jacobsen, Csernus, Shryne, & Gorski, 1981). Although it is not known what the precise functions of the SDN-POA are, or the neurobiological bases for such functions, there is evidence that this area has a role in endocrine activity and regulation of sexual activity. This includes luteinizing hormone regulation and possibly copulatory behavior, both of which differ in males and females (Arendash & Gorski, 1983; Halász & Gorski, 1967). Most work on sexual dimorphisms in the anterior hypothalamic area has been done with rodents.

There are several structural differences in the SDN-POA between males and females. First, the SDN-POA has a much larger volume in males (Gorski et al., 1978; Gorski, Harlan, Jacobsen, Shryne, & Southam, 1980). This difference is observed postnatal day 1 in the rat and is maintained during adulthood. The volume difference is due to a greatly increased number of neurons in the male (Jacobsen & Gorski, 1981). Second, male rats and male monkeys have longer and more highly branched dendrites in the SDN-POA. The orientation of the dendrites is also different (Ayoub, Greenough, & Juraska, 1983; Greenough, Carter, Steerman, & de Voogd, 1977). Third, male SDN-POA neurons in the rat have more dendritic spines. This results in different patterns of synapses between males and females (Raisman & Field, 1973).

It has been shown clearly that the developing SDN-POA responds to gonadal hormones and that there is a perinatal critical period for these effects. A single injection of testosterone in neonatal female rats markedly increases the volume of the SDN-POA when measured in adulthood (Gorski et al., 1978). In contrast, perinatal castration of male rats decreases the volume of the SDN-POA. Gonadectomy of male rats or androgen treatment of female rats has no effect on SDN-POA volume if conducted after the initial sexual differentiation period (Gorski et al., 1978).

Two current studies of human brains show structural sex differences between homosexual and heterosexual males, which may provide useful leads to understanding some components of human sexual behavior. In the first study, the suprachiasmatic nucleus (SCH) was shown to be significantly larger in homosexual compared to heterosexual male brains (Swaab & Hofman, 1990). It is not known whether this center in humans has a role in the governing of reproductive behavior. This area is usually thought to be involved in establishing periodic changes in behavior. In rodent species, the SCH-medial preoptic area has been linked to mating behavior (Södersten, Hansen, & Srebro, 1981) and may be involved in the regulation of gonadotropin-releasing hormone activity (Goodman, 1978). The second study showed the size of a nucleus in the anterior hypothalamus (the INAH-3 nucleus) to be the same size in homosexual men as in heterosexual women (LeVay, 1991). In both studies, other sexually diphorphic nuclei did not differ between homosexual and heterosexual males. Thus, certain areas of the human brain, either close to or within the anterior hypothalamus, show marked structural differences in males with different sexual orientation. Whether a causative relationship exists between nuclear size and sexual orientation is not known. It is also not known what physiologic factors contribute to the development of these structural differences. Differences in sex hormone action on neuronal nuclei during early development hypothetically provide a mechanism for the establishment of such structural differences.

Gonadal Endocrine Function during Development

Genetic sex (genotype) depends on whether an ovum, which has an X chromosome, is fertilized by a Y- or an X-containing sperm. This determines only whether the developing embryo will have testes in males or ovaries in females. After fertilization, the development of the reproductive tract and sexual differentiation of the brain results in the female phenotype (form) unless the androgen testosterone is present in sufficient amounts. Very early in gestation, the embryo may be considered to be bipotential in that both male and female sexual differentiation requires specific hormonal influences to proceed normally (Toran-Allerand, 1976). Males and females are morphologically indistinguishable until the end of the 6th week of in utero development. From then on, testicular development progresses rapidly, and the testes begin to secrete testosterone (Sitteri & Wilson, 1974). In the human male fetus, testosterone secretion is high between 3 and 5 months of gestation and again in the first 6 weeks postnatally (Reyes, Boroditsky, Winter, & Faiman, 1974; Winter, Hughes, Reyes, & Faiman, 1976). Testosterone levels in the male during these periods are several times higher than in the adult male. It is during these critical periods that testosterone is thought to exert pronounced influences on neural organization. The active form of testosterone in the hypothalamus and limbic system is its metabolite estradiol (E2), which is produced by an aromatization reaction (Selmanoff, Brodkin, Weiner, & Siiteri, 1977). As previously mentioned, these two areas exhibit pronounced sex differences in structure and function. A major effect of testosterone, at least in some species (Reinisch & Sanders, 1984), is therefore achieved via an estrogenic hormone that requires an estrogen receptor to function. Testosterone also has androgen metabolites—for example, dihydroxytestosterone (DHT), which interacts with androgen receptors in various parts of the body, including the brain (Hamilton & Ofner, 1982), during male sexual development. Thus, both female and male hormones are important in establishing the male phenotype during development. Presumably, a larger number of modulators (i.e., estrogens and androgens) for sexual development in one sex permits more developmental flexibility.

The developing female brain also contains receptors for both estrogens and androgens. These appear to be in amounts and distributions similar to those in the male brain (McEwen, 1983). Both in utero and postnatally, the female brain is capable of responding to estrogens and androgens.

A well-known example of the sensitivity of the female fetus to testosterone is that female mice that are closer to males than to females in utero have higher amounts of testosterone in their amniotic fluid and blood (Vom Saal & Bronson, 1980). In postnatal life, these female mice have differences in activity levels and in acceptability as mates to males, compared to less masculinized females that were further removed from male fetuses in utero. The placenta and fetal liver produce testosterone in both males and females, so a female fetus is normally exposed to testosterone. However, compared to males, the amount of testosterone is much less in females during development. The role of androgens in normal female development is not well understood, but it is clear that sufficiently high androgen levels in the female will prevent normal female sexual development and result in masculinization of both anatomy and behavior.

There is agreement among several authors that complete female differentiation of the brain may require estrogen (Döhler et al., 1984, pp. 99–103 and 104–109; Shapiro, Goldman, Steinbeck, & Neumann, 1976). In other words, relative absence of androgen may not be sufficient for normal female development. For example, tamoxifen, acting as an estrogen antagonist when given postnatally to rats, results in a significant inhibition of the neuroanatomical development of the preoptic area in both males and females (Döhler et al., 1984, pp. 99–103). In addition, tamoxifen has been reported to result in defeminization of female behavior with no emergence of male behaviors (Hancke & Döhler, 1980).

The sources of estrogen in the human during pregnancy are the fetal adrenals and the placenta, not the ovaries (Döhler et al., 1984, pp. 104–109). The ovaries of the human female begin to develop in the 4th week postconception but do not secrete estrogen during gestation. It is not completely clear what prevents the developing female brain from becoming masculinized by estrogens. Possible ways in which the same gonadal hormones could have different roles in the sexual differentiation of the brain include sex differences in concentration of the hormones and neurotransmitter systems (De Vries, Buijs, & van Leeuwen, 1984; Döhler, 1978; Döhler et al., 1984, pp. 99–103). The brain, for both sexes, continues to show similarity in estrogen and androgen receptor distributions during development.

Possible Mechanisms of Action of Gonadal Hormones

The temporal correlation of periods of high testosterone secretion and major events in neural development, including neural differentiation and synapse formation, suggests neurodevelopmental roles for sex hormones. There is evidence that gonadal hormones participate in the regulation of a variety of stages in neural development, including neurogenesis, neuronal migration, neurite outgrowth, and neuron survival and death (Gorski, 1988, pp. 257–259; Toran-Allerand, Gerlach, & McEwen, 1980). How these effects are achieved is not well understood. Receptors for sex hormones are located within the cytoplasm or possibly within the nucleus itself (O'Malley & Birnbaumer, 1978). After binding to the receptor, gonadal hormones influence transcriptional and posttranscriptional events within the nucleus (Schneider & McCann, 1970). Presumably, the changes in gene expression determine the specific consequences of sex hormone exposure.

Gonadal Hormone Effects on Sociosexual Behavior

The development of certain sociosexual behaviors may be thought to be gonadal hormone-dependent to a degree determined strongly by environmental and individual differences. This model is considered to apply to a variety of species, including rodents, nonhuman primates, and humans. Several effects, on brain and behavior, of early postnatal castration of male rats and testosterone treatment of female rats have been consistently described. These effects, summarized in Table 6.4, represent stereotyped responses to gonadal hormone effects. Possibly similar effects may occur in nonrodents in specific phases of development, which are then subject to modulation by other (e.g., genetic and environmental) factors. Normal (i.e., not subjected to experimental manipulations) adult male and female rats are capable of exhibiting masculine and feminine pseudocopulatory behaviors in nonsexual situations. For example, the adult male rat, when threatened, may assume a position that is similar to the typical lordotic posture taken by the female during sexual intercourse. Similarly, mounting behavior can be seen in the normal female (Christensen & Gorski, 1978).

Gonadal hormone effects may be influenced by social conditions. This has been well documented in numerous nonhuman primate studies. For example, in one study, androgen treatment of gonadectomized male monkeys was only able to increase male sexual activity in socially dominant and not in nondominant males (Dixon & Herbert, 1977). Thus, position in social hierarchy was shown to determine the response to androgen.

Sex differences in gonadal hormones have been implicated by a variety of human behavioral studies in the production of typical male versus female behaviors. For example, it has been noted that

TABLE 6.4 Direct Effects of Perinatal Gonadal Manipulation on Rodent Brain and Behavior

Manipulation	Observed Effect	Reference
Castration of Males (~ PND1-7)	↓ volume of sexually dimorphic nucleus of the preoptic area (SDN-POA)	Gorski, Gordon, Shryne, & Southam, 1978
		Jacobsen, Csernus, Shryne, & Gorski, 1981
	↓ shaft synapses in amygdala	Nishizuka & Arai, 1981
	cyclic gonadotropin release	Raisman & Field, 1973
	↓ mounting and ejaculation	Gorski et al., 1978
	↑ lordosis (female copulatory posture)	Raisman & Field, 1973
	↓ play-fighting	Meaney & Stewart, 1981
	↑ open field activity	Pfaff & Zigmond, 1971
	↑ norepinephrine content in hypothalamus	Wilson & Agrawal, 1979
	↓ serotonin in midbrain	"
Testosterone Treatment		Gorski et al., 1978
of Females (~ PND1-7)	↑ volume of SDN-POA	Jacobsen et al., 1981
	↑ shaft synapses of amygdala	Nishizuka & Arai, 1981
	noncyclic gonadotropin release	Raisman & Field, 1973
	↓ lordosis	"
	↑ mounting	Ward, 1969
	↑ play-fighting	Meaney & Stewart, 1981
	↓ open field activity	Pfaff & Zigmond, 1971
	↓ dopaminergic neurons in anterolateral periventricular nucleus of POA	Simerly, Swanson, Handa, & Gorsgi, 1985
	↑ serotonin in midbrain	Wilson & Agrawal, 1979

Adapted from Sikich & Todd, 1988.

boys engage in more play-fighting (rough-and-tumble play) than girls. This sex difference in play has been observed in rodents and, in these animals, has been associated with the effects of testosterone on the amygdala in males (Meaney, Dodge, & Beatty, 1981; Meaney & Stewart, 1981). Female primates may spend less time on social play but more time on caretaking behavior—for example, nurturing infants (Frodi & Lamb, 1978; Lancaster, 1971).

There are two frequently discussed conditions in which gonadal hormone exposure during early development may provide clues about the roles of sex hormones in the production of sociosexual behaviors. Female patients with congenital adrenal hyperplasia, a condition in which there is an excess of androgens in utero and the early postnatal period, have been reported by some studies to show increased amounts of "male" behavior, for example, play-fighting (Ehrhardt, Epstein, & Money, 1968). Female patients with this disorder have also been reported to demonstrate less interest in infant care (Ehrhardt & Baker, 1974); but again, other studies have found no difference. Studies on prenatal estrogen exposure are often based on the effects of the synthetic estrogen diethylstilbestrol (DES). DES may act as a potent estrogen in a manner analogous to androgens that are converted to estradiol. DES exposure in utero has been correlated with changes in sexual behaviors in mature rodents (Hines, 1982). Exposure to DES during the perinatal period may sex-reverse the SDN-POA volume in female rodents (Döhler et al., 1982). In humans, DES exposure has been associated with an increased incidence of homosexuality and bisexuality in females (Ehrhardt et al., 1985).

The origins of sociosexual behaviors and the extent to which sex hormones contribute to their development remain difficult to determine in many species. In humans, the development of sociosexual behaviors may be both more enriched and more complicated than in other species by the greater degree of developmental flexibility of the human central nervous system. As discussed in other sections, this developmental flexibility is found at both early and late developmental stages.

EFFECTS OF EXPERIENCE ON NEURAL ORGANIZATION AND BEHAVIOR

In higher vertebrates, the complete maturation of some central nervous system structures, such as the sensory systems (visual and others), requires interaction with the environment. These interactions have been shown to result in alterations in neuronal processes at the levels of synapses, dendrites, and axons. Without such environmental input, structural development can become severely hindered or not occur at all. In contrast, some behaviors seem to require little or no input from the environment in order to occur. An example of such a behavior may be the intrinsic ability of motor neurons in the spinal cord to be electrically active and so effect muscle contraction without experiencing any sensory input (Hamburger, Wenger, & Oppenheim, 1966; Purves & Lichtman, 1985, p. 332; Ripley & Provine, 1972). Spontaneous electrical activity has also been reported for retinal ganglion cells in the rat during gestation, prior to their exposure to light (Galli & Maffei, 1988). Whether other cues within the central nervous system activate these neural cells early in development or whether this is true spontaneous activity is unclear. However, this finding supports the contention that neuronal activity for developing systems may have an intrinsic component independent of environmental (outside of the body) influences, which then may act as a template for experiential factors during development.

As previously described, a neuronal activity-dependent process is well documented for the development of the mammalian visual system. Although much of the circuitry necessary for vision is already present at birth (Hubel & Wiesel, 1963), stimulation of the visual system after birth is required for the complete maturation of visual dominance columns in the occipital cortex (Hubel et al., 1977; Shatz & Stryker, 1978). If this stimulation does not occur during the early postnatal period, vision will not develop at all. In the kitten, this critical period begins in the latter part of the 3rd postnatal week and has passed by about 12 weeks of age (Hubel & Wiesel, 1970). Closure of an eye during this time can cause a significant decrease in the number of cortical cells that receive input from that eye. Consequently, the architecture of the dominance columns will be abnormal. For example, a 3-month period of eye closure after birth can result, in the kitten, in an approximately 80% drop in the usual number of cortical nerve cells that can respond to visual stimulation (Hubel & Wiesel, 1970). In contrast, unilateral eye closure for over a year in an adult cat does not lead to gross morphological changes in the cortical ocular dominance columns (LeVay, Wiesel, & Hubel, 1980). Even after this prolonged time of visual deprivation, the cortical cells are driven normally by both eyes.

Experience-driven changes in synapse formation are not limited to the postnatal period or to the visual system. Although, with aging, the magnitude of possible changes seems to diminish, activity-dependent modulation probably continues throughout life. Greenough, who considered this a problem of information storage, argued that different mechanisms may be used during different life stages because the character of the relevant information is fundamentally different (Greenough, 1986). He proposed two categories for considering how experience influences brain development: (a) experience-expectant information storage and (b) experience-dependent information storage.

Experience-Expectant Environmental Effects

The early developmental period of overproduction and elimination of synapses and neuronal processes is referred to as experience-expectant. The overproduction of synapses is considered a mechanism whereby the organism prepares itself for the input from experiences it can reasonably expect to have. The input includes the frequency range of sounds and the orientation of visual stimuli that are assumed to have been reasonably constant or predictable on an evolutionary time scale. The overproduction of synapses allows for the fine-tuning of the experiences received and allows the individual to adapt to the specifics of an otherwise stereotyped environment. This matching of inputs to targets by regression of axons is a relatively efficient and flexible mechanism for large-scale absorption of general environmental characteristics over a short time scale. The disadvantage of this process is that if the experiential input does not arrive, the large excess of synaptic inputs cannot be maintained and the synaptic organization is formed on the available information. Hence, some brain regions have windows or periods of time when experiential input can modulate this process. Critical periods may extend, with varying degrees of susceptibility, over a relatively prolonged time (as described above for the visual system in the kitten). The interval of maximum susceptibility to environmental effects, however, may be relatively short. For example, in the kitten, one-sided eye closure for only 3 days in the period of maximum susceptibility results in as dramatic a decrease in the number of responsive cortical cells as eye closure for weeks or months in other phases of the critical period (Hubel & Wiesel, 1970). Abnormal experience during these critical periods, which are generally early in development, can clearly result in irreversible abnormalities of structural development. Different environmental exposures during critical periods thus can be a source of profound individual differences.

Experience-Dependent Environmental Effects

Experience-dependent effects on the brain include the synaptic changes occurring as a result of environmental differences that are unique to the individual. Thus, they may occur at different times during development, both early and late. New synapse formation is thought to be the major mechanism for incorporating experience-dependent information. One example of new synapse formation in the adult is the increase in hippocampal synapses seen in long-term potentiation, as previously mentioned. Another example of new synapse formation in the adult is seen in the mature rat under specific conditions discussed later in this section. The major behavioral correlate of experience-dependent environmental effects is thought to be the establishment of new memories.

As previously stated, cortical synaptic density reaches a maximum of about twice the adult value during the first few years of human life. A fairly high level of synaptic density continues for a relatively long time, until about age 10, after which there is a gradual decline, until the later teen years, to the lower adult cortical synaptic density (Huttenlocher, 1979; Huttenlocher et al., 1982). This suggests that the early "overproduction" of synapses and slow regression may be an important mechanism for the development of many cortical functions, including the maturation of cognitive abilities and the handling of unique environmental input, for a prolonged part of the life span. Thus, the neural mechanisms for experience-expectant and experience-dependent processes may overlap during a significant part of human life.

Enriched and Impoverished Environmental Effects

Manipulations of the environment can result in morphological and physiological changes in the central nervous system. The studies that have produced the most replicable results in this regard are those in which rats are exposed to environments that differ in complexity. The environments are usually referred to as enriched condition (EC) versus impoverished condition (IC). Generally, enriched condition refers to a group of rats' living in a cage that contains a variety of objects with which the rats can interact—for example, blocks and ladders. Impoverished condition usually means a single rat or a group of rats isolated in a cage that contains no objects. The various conditions may take place before weaning (weaning occurs at age 26 days in rats) or in the older animal. The effects of enrichment and impoverishment are more pronounced in the weaned rat after a certain amount of cortical development has taken place (Diamond, 1990). The studies summarized here refer to postweaned, i.e. maturing and mature, rats living in enriched or impoverished conditions for varying lengths of time, often up to several hundred days or more. Although it has been difficult to quantify environmental complexity, various parameters of behavior, when measured, have indicated differences in performance ability, and neuroanatomical studies on sacrificed animals have yielded much information about morphological changes in the two conditions. Earlier in this chapter, the point was made that it often is not possible to directly link anatomical differences with behavioral differences. This is also the case for environmental complexity studies.

An example of a behavioral difference in EC versus IC rats is that rats raised in seclusion may show an increase in aggressiveness and other socially inappropriate behavior (Baenningen, 1967). Other studies have not shown this finding (Renner & Rosenzweig, 1986). The severely impaired socialization of primates raised in isolation, to the degree of inability to mate, has been noted by Harlow and Harlow (1973), suggesting that, also in this species, appropriate environmental stimuli may be necessary for the development of socialization. Further examples of behavioral differences in EC versus IC rats are that EC rats display significantly superior ability in running mazes and escaping predation (Bennett, Rosenzweig, & Diamond, 1970; Greenough, Madden, & Fleischmann, 1972; Roeder, Chetcuti, & Will, 1980) and in demonstrating exploratory behavior (Renner, 1987).

As noted in the thorough review by Renner and Rosenzweig (1987), the most consistent changes in neurobiological parameters have been described in the neocortex, hippocampus, and cerebellum. The area of the cortex that changes the most in EC rats is part of the occipital cortex. Cortical thickness in this area is about 8–9% greater in EC rats (Diamond, Krech, & Rosenzweig, 1964). The corpus callosum underlying this area of the cortex is also slightly larger in EC rats. The increase in cortical thickness is due to numerous ultrastructural changes. Neuronal density decreases (Diamond et al., 1964), but there is a significant increase in dendritic complexity, including an increase in the number of dendrites (Uylings, Kuypers, Diamond, & Veltman, 1978; Volkmar & Greenough, 1972) and in the number of synaptically active spines on the dendrites (Globus, Rosenzweig, Bennett, & Diamond, 1973). The numbers of both oligodendrocytes and astrocytes increase (Diamond et al., 1966; Szeligo, 1977). Metabolic activity is higher in the occipital cortex of EC rats. This is reflected in part by the presence of larger capillaries in EC rats (Diamond et al., 1964). Differences in RNA production (Ferchmin, Eterovic, & Caputto, 1970) have also been reported. Interestingly, right and left hemispheric differences and sex differences (Juraska, 1984; McShane et al., 1988) are also described for neurobiological changes in EC and IC rats.

Given the information currently available about the effects of the environment on several nonhuman species, it seems reasonable to assume that similar processes can occur in humans. Examples of changes in human neural substrates occurring as the environment changes are not readily available. However, there appears to be support for the validity of the concepts of critical periods and activity-dependent maturation of the central nervous system in humans, for example, in language and cognitive development. Social development in humans may also occur predominantly in younger years. This is supported by recent work that suggests behaviorally disturbed children appear to have the best chance for rehabilitation if treated prior to the onset of adolescence.

APPLICATION OF DEVELOPMENTAL PRINCIPLES TO MENTAL RETARDATION

In this chapter, we have reviewed the basic structural and functional anatomy of the adult human brain and the developmental principles by which it arrives at that structure. In this section, we will describe the application of these principles to understand the forms and varieties of mental retardation syndromes. A comprehensive review of this area is beyond the scope of this chapter. A brief review is indicated, however, in order to illustrate the fundamental importance of some of these developmental principles.

Epidemiological data indicate that the prevalence of mental retardation in the more developed countries is 2–3% of the general population (Lyon & Evrad, 1987). Severe mental retardation occurs in about 0.5% of the general population. A comprehensive analysis of the causes of mental retardation has recently been reported for the Swedish cities of Uppsala, Göterberg, and Västerbotten (Evrad, De Saint-George, Kadhim, & Gadisseux, 1989). Overall evidence could be found for biological origins of 81% of the cases of severe mental retardation and 43% of the cases of moderate mental retardation. Prenatal etiological factors could be associated with 55% of the cases of severe mental retardation and 23% of the cases of moderate retardation. Perinatal factors were present in 15–20% of cases of severe and moderate mental retardation. Overall, it appears that 80–85% of severe mental retardation cases have suffered some form of brain damage prior to birth.

These findings need to be put into the perspective of normal brain development on a population basis. It is estimated that 70% of conceptions are spontaneously aborted (Hagberg, Hagberg, Lewerth, & Lindenberg, 1981). At least 25% of these aborted conceptions are affected by developmental problems of the central nervous system. In addition, 40% of deaths occurring during the first year of life appeared to be related to prenatal malformations. The stereotypic pattern of normal brain development allows a variety of prenatal spontaneous abortions to be timed as to the point of gestation where problems occurred. In addition, anatomical studies of the brains of individuals suffering from mental retardation syndromes suggest that specific developmental times and developmental processes are involved in their genesis. These can be grossly divided into the first and second half of pregnancy. As reviewed above, the first half of pregnancy results in the generation of the cells and structures associated with the mature brain, whereas the second half of pregnancy is associated with growth and differentiation to define the structural detail of the fully developed brain. Abnormalities associated with the first half of pregnancy include early microencephaly (small brain size), macroencephaly, abnormalities of the formation of gyra (microgyria or lissencephaly), and abnormalities of the development of the commissures between the hemispheres. These anomalies can be thought of as problems with the multiplication and migration of neural elements. Anomalies associated with the second half of pregnancy have been more difficult to associate with specific mental retardation syndromes, but include problems with the outgrowth and maturation of axons and dendrites, problems with myelination of axons, and differentiation of individual cell functioning. These abnormalities are thought to give rise to laterdevelopment microencephaly by interrupting the normal processes of neuronal death and synapse elimination. These have been associated in anatomical studies with the presence of too many or too few surviving neurons and too many or too few surviving synapses.

The two most important prenatal processes in the development of mental retardation are ischemia and infarction. However, a variety of factors, including chromosomal aberrations, genetic mutations, and fetal intoxication syndromes (such as from alcohol, or other drugs) can contribute to deficient maternal-fetal circulation (Lou, 1980; Lyon & Evrad, 1987). Chromosomal abnormalities account for up to 30% of cases of severe mental retardation. The most common syndrome is trisomy 21 (Down syndrome). For males, Fragile X syndrome is associated with 6–10% of mental retardation cases. Among alcoholic mothers, 20–25% of infants will be born with fetal alcohol syndrome. There is an increasing incidence of brain abnormalities and behavioral syndromes associated with maternal addiction to other substances such as cocaine. The principal mechanism for many of these disorders has been hypothesized to be the loss of self-regulation of cerebral perfusion (Lou, 1980; Lou, Greisen, & Tweed, 1989). In newborns, it has been demonstrated that cerebral blood flow regulation is very sensitive to prenatal hypoxic conditions. Increased stress in the newborn period, caused by previous exposure to alcohol, drugs, infections, or other etiological factors, increases the likelihood of newborn ischemic problems.

Most of these severe insults result in the death or severe developmental malformation of the surviving fetal brain. However, less dramatic changes in brain structure have been associated with specific cognitive difficulties. Many of these will be addressed more fully in other chapters in this volume. In particular, though, there is now good evidence for difficulties with formation of cortical structures in syndromes with cognitive deficits, such as dyslexia and infantile autism. Most of these structural changes are below the levels of resolution of imaging techniques such as magnetic resonance imaging (MRI) or positron emission tomography (PET). The demonstration of abnormal developmental processes in many of these disorders will have to await the collection of cases for postmortem analysis.

Currently, however, a significant number of minor cerebral developmental anomalies have been reported for cases of mental retardation of known etiology. These include minor anomalies of gyral patterns, and changes in neuronal density and synaptic density. In addition, changes in cerebellar structure have been reported in cases of mental retardation and infantile autism (Courchesne, Yeung-Courchesne, Press, Hesselink, & Jernigan, 1989; Lyon, 1989).

In summary, a variety of mental retardation syndromes can, in many instances, be correlated with specific interruptions in the normal developmental processes of neuronal proliferation and migration and synapse formation. The stereotypic pattern of human brain development allows many of these abnormalities to be placed in specific developmental periods. These studies suggest that the timing of ischemic or other events may result in different effects on brain structure. In addition, population studies of the outcome of conception suggest that lethal anomalies of central nervous system structure are common. As imaging and neuropathological techniques improve, it should be possible to better correlate specific retardation syndromes with abnormalities of specific central nervous system developmental processes.

FUTURE DIRECTIONS

Historically, advancement in understanding brain structure and function has been dependent on exploitation of experiments of nature, the development of new technologies, or the application of ideas from other fields. For example, the current models of cerebral hemispheric localization were built on the combined clinical and pathological analysis of unfortunate individuals who had suffered brain injuries. Recent localization studies of different forms of memory have also relied on the study of brain injury cases. Many recent advancements in cognitive science relied on the application of models of information processing developed for computers (parallel versus series processes, and so on). The study of cognitive models has also relied on the development of computer-based simulations. Now such cognitive models have gone beyond the original analogies with different computing methods. Likewise, functional localization studies can now utilize in vivo imaging techniques and normal individuals. Even so, it is likely that advancements in other areas of brain development, structure, and function will rely on serendipity and intellectual and technological advancement in other fields. Several avenues of investigation are sufficiently developed to allow speculation as to new directions of research and to suggest new potential areas of synthesis. These include studies of both normal and abnormal development of structure and function and, in some cases, make life-span studies more feasible.

In other cases, complications may arise from unexpected sources. For example, classically, brain dopamine was thought to interact with two types of neurotransmitter receptor, D_1 and D_2 (Kebabian & Calne, 1979). There was debate as to whether these same receptors also functioned in the periphery. Gene cloning studies have recently demonstrated the existence of at least three genes coding for distinct D_2-like receptors (called D_2, D_3, and D_4; Bunzow et al., 1988; Sokoloff, Giros, Martres, Bouthenet, & Schwartz, 1990; Van Tol et al., 1991) and at least two genes coding for D_1-like receptors (called D_1 and D_5; see, e.g., Sunahara et al., 1990, 1991). Within each class, receptors have different but related pharmacological characteristics, different patterns of expression within the central nervous system, and, presumably, different functions. In addition, at least in the rat, the D_4 receptor is expressed at higher levels in the cardiovascular system than in the brain (O'Malley, Harmon, Tang, & Todd, 1992). These molecular pharmacology results call into question the interpretation of a large literature of physiological and behavioral studies on the role(s) of dopamine during development and in normal and pathological states. In addition, at least D_2-like receptors have been found to have morphogenic properties which may effect early brain development (Todd, 1992). Whether the other newly described dopamine receptor types also have morphogenic effects is unknown. It is difficult to predict when such field-expanding findings will occur, or when simplifying results, such as the discovery of the double helical structure of DNA, will clarify concepts of function.

In this section, we describe several areas that we think will be important in the next decade, and we suggest some areas that we feel should receive increased attention.

Anatomical and Neurotransmitter Studies

An important advancement in our current understanding of brain functioning was the acceptance of the notion of functional localization. For humans, this initially relied on the correlation of clinical symptoms with pathological results and the confirmation of these findings in animal lesion studies. As more neurochemicals were identified and the neurotransmitter status of some confirmed, links between certain functions and particular neurochemical pathways were established. The number of putative neurotransmitters has grown enormously over the past 20 years, and the functional roles of these transmitters are poorly understood at many levels. The activity of neurotransmitters is, of course, usually dependent on interactions with receptors. As described above for dopamine neurotransmitter receptors, the number of known receptors has grown at least as fast as the number of neurotransmitters. In many ways, this explosion of basic molecular information poses serious problems for interpreting and synthesizing studies of neurotransmitter function beyond the single cell or synapse level. This is particularly true for pharmacological/behavioral studies that depend on the selectivity of challenge compounds. The coding of different but related receptor types by different genes also introduces new genetic potential for the control of receptor expression and hence the effect of stimulating particular neurotransmitter pathways. These are not simply concerns for molecular biologists; they represent potential confounding or illuminating mechanisms for developmentalists at all levels. For example, the mechanisms for environmental modification of individual development or homeostasis or for individual modification of environment may be based on selective gene activation or inhibition of receptor subtypes.

The basic neuroanatomical, pharmacological, and molecular aspects of where transmitters are present, what receptors are expressed, and what cellular processes are affected will continue to be a major area of interest for neuroscientists. The developmental course of expression of both classical and more recently described neurotransmitters and receptors will be important in defining potential roles and interactions of these systems. A major accomplishment in pursuing these goals will be the development of pharmacological compounds or techniques that allow the stimulation of individual components of complex systems. Another approach will be the development of simple model systems in which individual receptors can be studied in isolation. The application of genetic engineering approaches to neuronal cells makes this feasible now; it will allow the development of specific pharmacological probes and the identification of receptor subtype-specific characteristics or functions, which could then be studied in a more focused fashion in more complex systems or in vivo.

Higher Organizational Level Studies of Function

Conceptual and technological advances have allowed the beginnings of new types of studies of higher levels of brain function in humans. In particular, new imaging and electrophysiological techniques have greatly increased the power of concurrent behavioral or psychological measures and anatomical measures. This has been most strikingly shown by positron emission tomography (PET) studies of blood flow during simple tasks such as thinking single words or sustaining attention (Pardo, Fox, & Raichle, 1991; Petersen, Fox, Posner, Mintun, & Raichle, 1988). Such studies define brain areas that respond to particular tasks or stimulations by increasing or decreasing energy consumption (the assumption is that blood flow is directly related to neuronal activity). The goal of many of these studies is to use simple paradigms to build temporal and topographical maps of brain activity in order to define, in a building block fashion, what pathways participate in complex activities such as attention. Similar technological advances are being made in the application of a number of structural and functional approaches that allow the in vivo study of neural systems at increasingly fine levels of resolution. Although individuals with circumscribed brain lesions are still important in the localization of functions, there is now much less reliance on experiments of nature to define normal processes in humans. These combined imaging and physiological approaches are also allowing more refined studies of complex disorders such as schizophrenia, which lack specific gross neuropathological findings.

The application of information theory to detailed neuroanatomical and electrophysiological studies of the visual system has allowed the construction of elegant and integrated maps of visual activity, which demonstrate varied approaches to information processing and association within a single sensory modality (Van Essen, Anderson, & Felleman, 1992). Clear evidence is found for parallel and serial processing of information input and output, duplication of information processing, and filters to information transmission. Similar advances should be possible for other sensory modalities in the adult animal. When such models are available, specific tests can be made in humans using the in vivo imaging and physiological techniques described above. What will take longer, but is of great interest to developmental psychopathologists, is the definition of similarly detailed maps of developmental events for sensory or cognitive systems, including processes that modulate the environment and processes that can be modulated by the environment.

It seems to us that the long-term goal of these and other studies should be similar to the quest of physics to develop a grand unified theory. Any theory of higher-level functioning of the brain or mind must include the principles of self-organization, self-regulation, modulation of the environment, and modulation by the environment. In addition, theories should provide specific predictions for the consequences of different types of modulations or insults. Just as with cosmological tests of competing physics theories, which are in essence developmental tests that look back in time, the most stringent tests of brain or mind theories will be developmental in nature. In part, this is because the greatest changes occur at early developmental times. More generally, though, as is discussed below, the brain is best understood as always being in a developmental state. The forms of change or the regions involved will vary quantitatively with time, but there is little evidence that any brain region is ever static, except after catastrophic incidences.

Modulation of Neural Properties Late in the Life Cycle

Most examples of induced changes in brain organization occur during the pre- and early postnatal developmental periods. As discussed above, however, it has been possible to demonstrate changes in brain structure by rearing adolescent or young adult animals in environments of varying complexity. It has been difficult to relate these types of structural changes with specific functional or physiological changes. The detailed studies of primary sensory systems, and the accompanying technologies, have now allowed the detection of changes in functional organizations in adult animals after specific manipulations. For example, the somatosensory system of the skin has a specific topological representation in the cortex. The area representing the hand is disproportionately large, to accommodate the density of touch receptors in the hand. The cortical representation of specific digits can be determined by electrical recordings. If areas of hand skin and the corresponding nerves are grafted to new locations on the hand, the cortical representation of the hand changes. This demonstrates that changing input for the periphery can induce functional changes in cortical organization. This also suggests that ongoing input is necessary for maintenance of cortical organization, at least with respect to local effects. Similarly, if the bilateral retinal input to particular visual cortex columns is removed, these columns become responsive to input from adjacent visual areas (Gilbert & Wiesel, 1992). Within given functional areas, then, it appears that significant reorganization or transfer of cortical function is possible in mature animals. In contrast, the corresponding area of the lateral geniculate body (the first relay nucleus in the visual pathway) remains silent following removal of input and apparently does not change organization. This suggests that different principles govern the ongoing ability of different brain areas to respond to changes in input and that injury or modulation of input to a particular neural system or network may have different consequences, depending on what component is affected. How widespread these phenomena are and whether similar principles will apply to nonsensory systems is unknown. Most researchers assume some reorganizational principles must apply to the establishment of memories. It may be that the study of reorganization of sensory information may provide clues to the other modulation processes.

Sex Differences in Brain Organization

As described above, it has become easy to demonstrate differences between the sexes in the structure of various brain regions, at least in nonhuman mammals. Except for areas thought to be directly involved in reproductive functions, it has been much harder to relate anatomical differences to functional or psychological differences. Even in the studies of homosexuality by Schwab and colleagues (1990) and LeVay (1991), it is difficult to separate cause from effect. If sex- or sexual orientation-based differences in brain structure exist, it seems important to understand their developmental consequences. As discussed above, there are important differences between females and males in the incidence, course, and outcome of many psychiatric disorders (Sikich & Todd, 1988). Understanding sex differences in either normal or abnormal brain function and development could inform treatment and etiological studies of disease. New studies of sex-based differences in brain structure will take advantage of improved imaging and electrophysiological procedures for humans. This should allow better correlative studies of brain areas and volumes with concurrent behavioral and psychological measures. Many of the newer imaging techniques, such as magnetic resonance imaging (MRI), can be used on children and adolescents and will extend studies to prepubertal periods. Sadly, neuropathological studies of sexual orientation and gender differences will continue to be able to take advantage of victims of acquired immunodeficiency syndrome (AIDS). The increased incidence of HIV infection in heterosexual and adolescent groups should allow studies that better control for age, developmental, and disease effects, in addition to sexual orientation.

Psychopathological and Family Studies

The establishment of imaging and electrophysiological techniques that are safe for children and adolescents will allow the determination of developmental courses for brain maturation in many areas and in any diagnostic group desired. This outcome also potentially allows for the prospective evaluation of individuals based on presumed risk for psychopathology. The in vivo course of changes in many brain features can now be assessed in conjunction with cognitive or other measures. Such studies are beginning for disorders such as dementia and schizophrenia, and will presumably be concurrently done for normal aging as well. It is hoped that investigators will apply similar methods to disorders first manifested in early life, such as Attention Deficit/Hyperactivity Disorder (ADHD).

In combination with newer family designs, such as the use of cousins to control for family-specific environmental factors, the potential exists for utilizing developmental imaging or electrophysiological data with quantitative genetic models. These approaches, whose description is beyond the confines of this chapter, should increase the ability to detect both genetic and nongenetic factors in the development of psychopathology. This is not simply the application of new tests to the old high-risk study designs. Rather than selecting a high-risk and a low-risk group based on a dichotomous variable, such as parental illness, newer (at least to psychiatric studies) family designs incorporate information from all or a subset of relatives and can use quantitative study variables and outcomes. Such approaches have allowed the detection of minor gene effects in disorders such as hypertension. The use of special classes of relatives, such as first cousins, should help control for age effects and cultural factors while maintaining a known degree of genetic relatedness. In fact, in many instances, cousins can provide more genetic information than siblings or parents (see, e.g., Risch, 1990). Family studies also provide a natural prospective, high-risk design where the degree of relatedness to affected family members can be used as a more complex variable than high or low risk per se (Todd, Reich, & Reich, 1994). The joint application of clinical and laboratory measures to family studies should increase both the power and the developmental focus of these studies.

REFERENCES

Annett, M. (1980). Sex differences in laterality: Meaningfulness versus reliability. *Behavioral Brain Science, 3,* 227–228.

Annett, M. A. (1970). A classification of hand preference by association analysis. *British Journal of Psychology, 61,* 303–321.

Arendash, G. W., & Gorski, R. A. (1983). Effects of discrete lesions of the sexually dimorphic nucleus of the preoptic area or other medial preoptic regions on the sexual behavior of male rats. *Brain Research Bulletin, 10,* 147–154.

Ayoub, D. M., Greenough, W. T., & Juraska, J. M. (1983). Sex differences in the dendritic structure of the preoptic area of the juvenile macaque monkey brain. *Science, 221,* 197–198.

Baenningen, L. P. (1967). Comparison of development in socially isolated and grouped rats. *Animal Behavior, 15,* 312–323.

Benbow, C. M., & Benbow, R. M. (1984). Biological correlates of high mathematical reasoning ability. In G. J. De Vries, J. P. C. De Bruin, H. B. M. Uhylings, & M. A. Corner (Eds.), *Progress in brain research* (Vol. 61, pp. 469–490). Amsterdam: Elsevier.

Benes, F. M. (1989). Myelination of cortical-hippocampal relays during late adolescence. *Schizophrenia Bulletin, 15*(4), 585–593.

Bennett, E. L., Rosenzweig, M. R., & Diamond, M. C. (1970). Time courses of effects of differential experience on brain measures and behavior of rats. In W. L. Byrne (Ed.), *Molecular approaches to learning and memory* (pp. 55–89). New York: Academic Press.

Bloom, F. E. (1990). Neurohumoral transmission and the central nervous system. In A. G. Gilman, T. W. Rall, A. S. Nies, P. Taylor (Eds.), *The pharmacological basis of therapeutics* (8th ed.). New York: Pergamon.

Bradley, S. J. (1990). Gender dysphorias of childhood and adolescence. In B. D. Garfinkel, G. A. Carlson, & E. B. Weller (Eds.), *Psychiatric disorders in children and adolescents* (pp. 121–134). Philadelphia: Saunders.

Brodal, A. (1981). *Neurological anatomy in relation to clinical medicine* (3rd ed.). New York: Oxford University Press.

Bunzow, J. R., Van Tol, H. H., Grandy, D. K., Albert, P., Salon, J., Christie, M., Machida, C. A., Neve, K. A., & Civelli, O. (1988). Cloning and expression of a rat D_2 dopamine receptor cDNA. *Nature, 336,* 783–787.

Cantwell, D. (1977). The hyperkinetic syndrome. In M. Rutter & L. Herson (Eds.), *Child psychiatry: Modern approaches.* London: Blackwell.

Carlson, M., Earls, F., & Todd, R. D. (1988). The importance of regressive changes in the development of the nervous system: Towards a neurobiological theory of child development. *Psychiatric Developments, 1,* 1–22.

Carlson, M., O'Leary, D. D. M., & Burton, H. (1987). Potential role of thalamocortical connections in recovery of tactile function following somatic sensory cortex lesions in infant primates. *Society for Neuroscience Abstracts, 13,* 75.

Caroni, P., & Schwab, M. E. (1988). Two membrane protein fractions from rat central myelin with inhibitory properties for neurite growth and fibroblast spreading. *Journal of Cell Biology, 106,* 1281–1288.

Christensen, L. W., & Gorski, R. A. (1978). Independent masculinization of neuroendocrine systems by intracerebral implants of testosterone or estradiol in the neonatal female rat. *Brain Research, 146,* 325–340.

Chu, N., & Bloom, F. E. (1973). Norepinephrine-containing neurons: Changes in spontaneous discharge patterns during sleeping and waking. *Science, 179,* 907–910.

Cicchetti, D. (1987). Developmental psychopathology in infancy: Illustration from the study of maltreated youngsters. *Journal of Consulting and Clinical Psychology, 55,* 837–848.

Cohen, D. H. (1982). Central processing time for a conditioned response in a vertebrate model system. In C. D. Woody (Ed.), *Conditioning: Representation of involved neural functions* (pp. 517–534). New York: Plenum.

Cooke, N. D. (1986). *The brain code: Mechanisms of information transfer and the role of the corpus callosum.* London: Methuen.

Cooper, J. R., Bloom, F. E., & Roth, R. H. (1986a). Bioelectric properties of the nerve cell. In J. House (Ed.), *The biochemical basis of neuropharmacology* (5th ed., pp. 15–33). New York: Oxford University Press.

Cooper, J. R., Bloom, F. E., & Roth, R. H. (1986b). Introduction. In J. House (Ed.), *The biochemical basis of neuropharmacology* (5th ed., pp. 3–6). New York: Oxford University Press.

Cooper, J. R., Bloom, F. E., & Roth, R. H. (1986c). Receptors. In J. House (Ed.), *The biochemical basis of neuropharmacology* (5th ed., pp. 88–89). New York: Oxford University Press.

Courchesne, E., Yeung-Courchesne, R., Press, G., Hesselink, J., & Jernigan, T. (1989). Hypoplasia of cerebellar vermal lobules VI and VII in autism. *New England Journal of Medicine, 318,* 1349–1354.

Cowan, W. M. (1979). The development of the brain. *Scientific American, 241,* 106–117.

Creese, I. (1987). Biochemical properties of CNS dopamine receptors. In H. Y. Meltzer (Ed.), *Psychopharmacology: The third generation of progress* (pp. 257–264). New York: Raven Press.

Cutler, R. W. P., & Spertell, R. B. (1982). Cerebrospinal fluid: A selective review. *Annals of Neurology, 11,* 1–10.

Damasio, A. R., & Geschwind, M. (1984). The neural basis of language. *Annual Review of Neuroscience, 7,* 127–147.

De Vries, G. J., Buijs, R. M., & van Leeuwen, F. W. (1984). Sex differences in vasopressin and other neurotransmitter systems in the brain. In G. J. De Vries, J. P. C. De Bruin, H. B. M. Uhylings, & M. A. - Corner (Eds.), *Progress in brain research: Sex differences in the brain* (Vol. 61, pp. 185–203). Amsterdam: Elsevier.

Diamond, M. C. (1990). Morphological cortical changes as a consequence of learning and experience. In A. B. Scheibel & A. F. Wechsler (Eds.), *Neurobiology of higher cognitive function* (pp. 1–12). New York: Guilford.

Diamond, M. C., Krech, D., & Rosenzweig, M. R. (1964). The effects of an enriched environment on the histology of the rat cerebral cortex. *Journal of Comparative Neurology, 123,* 111–120.

Diamond, M. C., Law, F., Rhodes, H., Lindner, B., Rosenzweig, M. R., Krech, D., & Bennett, E. L. (1966). Increases in cortical depth and glia numbers in rats subjected to enriched environment. *Journal of Comparative Neurology, 187,* 726–727.

Dietrich, R. B., Bradley, W. G., Zaragoza, E. J., IV, Otto, R. J., Taira, R. K., Wilson, G. H., & Kangarloo Hooshang, M. R. (1987). Evaluation of early myelination patterns in normal and developmentally delayed infants. *American Journal of Radiology, 150,* 889–896.

Dimond, S. J., Farrington, L., & Johnson, P. (1976). Differing emotional response from right and left hemisphere. *Nature, 261,* 690–692.

Dixon, A. F., & Herbert, J. (1977). Gonadal hormones and sexual behavior in groups of adult talapoin monkeys (miopithecus talapoin). *Hormone Behavior, 8,* 141–154.

Dobbing, J., & Sands, J. (1973). Quantitative growth and development of the human brain. *Archives of Disease in Childhood, 48,* 757–767.

Dobbing, J., & Sands, J. (1979). Comparative aspects of the brain growth spurt. *Early Human Development, 3,* 79–83.

Döhler, K. D. (1978). Is female sexual differentiation hormone mediated? *Trends in Neuroscience, 1,* 138–140.

Döhler, K. D., Hancke, J. L., Srivastava, S. S., Hofmann, C., Shryne, J. E., & Gorski, R. A. (1984). Participation of estrogen in female sexual differentiation of the brain: Neuroanatomical, neuroendocrine, and behavioral evidence. In G. J. De Vries, J. P. C. De Bruin, H. B. M. Uhylings, & M. A. Corner (Eds.), *Progress in brain research* (Vol. 61). Amsterdam: Elsevier.

Döhler, K. D., Hines, M., Coquelin, A., Davis, F., Shryne, J. E., & Gorski, R. A. (1982). Pre- and postnatal influence of diethylstilbesterol on differentiation of the sexually dimporphic nucleus in the preoptic area of the female rat brain. *Neuroendocrinology Letter, 4*(6), 361–365.

Dohrenwend, B. P., & Dohrenwend, B. S. (1976). Sex differences and psychiatric disorders. *American Journal of Sociology, 81,* 1447–1454.

Dooling, E. C., Chi, J. G., & Gilles, F. H. (1983a). Dorsal mesodiencephalic function: Pineal subcommissural organ, and mesocephalic recess. In J. Wright (Ed.), *The developing human brain: Growth and epidemiologic neuropathology* (pp. 105–116). Littleton, MA: John Wright.

Dooling, E. C., Chi, J. G., & Gilles, F. H. (1983b). Telencephalic development: Changing gyral patterns. In J. Wright (Ed.), *The developing human brain: Growth and epidemiologic neuropathology* (pp. 94–112). Littleton, MA: John Wright.

Doyer, D. (1990). Serotonin 5-HT_3, 5-HT_4, and 5-HT-M receptors. *Neuropsychopharmacology, 3*(5/6), 371–383.

Earls, F. (1987). Sex differences in psychiatric disorders: Origins and developmental influences. *Psychiatric Development, 1,* 1–23.

Edelman, G. M., Cunningham, B. A., & Tiery, J. P. (1990). *Morphoregulatory molecules* (p. 1628). New York: Wiley.

Ehrhardt, A. A., & Baker, S. W. (1974). Fetal androgens, human central nervous system differentiation, and behavioral sex differences. In R. C. Friedman, R. M. Richart, & R. L. van de Wiele (Eds.), *Sex differences in behavior* (pp. 33–51). New York: Wiley.

Ehrhardt, A. A., Epstein, R., & Money, J. (1968). Fetal androgens and female gender identity in the early treated adrenogenital syndrome. *Johns Hopkins Medical Journal, 122,* 160–167.

Ehrhardt, A. A., Meyer-Bahlburg, H. F. L., Rosen, L. R., Feldman, J. F., Veridiano, N. P., Zimmerman, I., & McEwen, B. S. (1985). Sexual orientation after prenatal exposure to exogenous estrogen. *Archives of Sexual Behavior, 14,* 57–77.

Evrad, P., De Saint-George, P., Kadhim, H. J., & Gadisseux, J. F. (1989). Pathology of prenatal encephalopathies. In J. H. French, S. Harel, & P. Casaer (Eds.), *Child neurology and developmental disabilities* (p. 153). Baltimore: Brooks.

Fagg, G. E., & Foster, A. C. (1983). Amino acid neurotransmitters and their pathways in the mammalian central nervous system. *Neuroscience, 9,* 701.

Feder, H. H., & Whalen, R. E. (1964). Feminine behavior in neonatally castrated and estrogen-treated male rats. *Science, 147,* 306–307.

Ferchmin, P. A., Eterovic, V. A., & Caputto, R. (1970). Studies of brain weight and RNA content after short periods of exposure to environmental complexity. *Brain Research, 20,* 49–57.

Frodi, A., & Lamb, M. (1978). Sex differences in responsiveness to infants: A developmental study of psychophysical and behavioral responses. *Child Development, 49,* 1182–1188.

Galaburda, A. M., Sherman, G. F., Rosen, G. D., Aboitiz, F., & Geschwind, N. (1985). Developmental dyslexia: Four consecutive patients with cortical anomalies. *Annals of Neurology, 18,* 222–223.

Galli, L., & Maffei, L. (1988). Spontaneous impulse activity of rat retinal ganglion cells in prenatal life. *Science, 244,* 90–91.

Garoutte, B. (1987). *Survey of functional neuroanatomy* (2nd ed.). Greenbrae, CA: Jones Medical Publications.

Geschwind, N., & Galaburda, A. M. (1987). *Cerebral lateralization: Biological mechanisms, associations, and pathology.* Cambridge, MA: MIT Press.

Geschwind, N., & Levitsky, W. (1968). Human brain: Left-right asymmetries in temporal speech region. *Science, 161,* 186–187.

Gilbert, C. D., & Wiesel, T. N. (1992). Receptive field dynamics in adult primary visual cortex. *Nature, 356,* 150–152.

Gilles, F. H. (1983). Telencephalon medium and the olfactocerebral outpouching. In J. Wright (Ed.), *The developing human brain: Growth and epidemiologic neuropathology.* Littleton, MA: John Wright.

Gilles, F. H., Shankle, W., & Dooling, E. C. (1983). Myelinated tracts: Growth patterns. In J. Wright (Ed.), *The developing human brain: Growth and epidemiologic neuropathology.* Littleton, MA: John Wright.

Globus, A., Rosenzweig, M. R., Bennett, E. L., & Diamond, M. C. (1973). Effects of differential experience on dendritic spine counts in rat cerebral cortex. *Journal of Comparative and Physiological Psychology, 82,* 175–181.

Gloor, P., Olivier, A., Quesney, L. F., Andermann, F., & Horowitz, S. (1982). The role of the limbic system in experiential phenomena of temporal lobe epilepsy. *Annals of Neurology, 12,* 129.

Goldman-Rakic, P. S., & Brown, R. M. (1982). Postnatal development of monoamine content and synthesis in the cerebral cortex of rhesus monkeys. *Developmental Brain Research, 4,* 339–349.

Goodman, R. L. (1978). The site of the positive feedback action of estradiol in the rat. *Endocrinology, 102,* 151–159.

Gorski, R. A. (1988). Sexual differentiation of the brain: Mechanisms and implications for neuroscience. In S. S. Easter, Jr., K. F. Barald, & B. M. Carlson (Eds.), *From message to mind.* Sunderland, MA: Sinauer Associates.

Gorski, R. A., Gordon, J. H., Shryne, J. E., & Southam, A. M. (1978). Evidence for a morphological sex difference within the medial preoptic area of the rat brain. *Brain Research, 148,* 333–346.

Gorski, R. A., Harlan, R. E., Jacobsen, C. D., Shryne, J. E., & Southam, A. M. (1980). Evidence for the existence of a sexually dimorphic nucleus in the preoptic area of the rat. *Journal of Comparative Neurology, 193,* 529–539.

Gottlieb, G. (1972). Ontogenesis of sensory functions in birds and mammals. In E. Tobach, L. A. Ronson, & E. Shaw (Eds.), *The biopsychology of development* (pp. 67–128). New York: Academic Press.

Grant, J. A., & Young, W. C. (1952). Differential reactivity of individuals and the response of male guinea pigs to testosterone propionate. *Endocrinology, 51,* 237–248.

Greenough, W. T. (1986). What's special about development? Though ts on the bases of experience-sensitive synaptic plasticity. In W. T. Greenough & J. M. Juraska (Eds.), *Developmental neuropsychobiology* (pp. 387–407). New York: Academic Press.

Greenough, W. T., Carter, C. S., Steerman, C., & de Voogd, T. J. (1977). Sex differences in dendritic patterns in hamster preoptic area. *Brain Research, 126,* 63–72.

Greenough, W. T., Madden, T. C., & Fleischmann, T. B. (1972). Effects of isolation, daily handling, and enriched rearing on maze learning. *Psychonomic Science, 27,* 279–280.

Hagberg, B., Hagberg, G., Lewerth, A., & Lindenberg, U. (1981). Mild mental retardation in Swedish school children: I. Prevalence. *Acta Paediatrica Scandinavica, 70,* 405–444.

Halász, B., & Gorski, R. A. (1967). Gonadotropic hormone secretion in female rats after partial or total interruption of neural afferents to the medial basal hypothalamus. *Endocrinology, 80,* 608–622.

Hamburger, V. (1980). Trophic interactions in neurogenesis: A personal historical account. *Annual Review of Neuroscience, 3,* 269–278.

Hamburger, V., & Oppenheim, R. W. (1982). Naturally occurring neuronal death in vertebrates. *Neuroscience Commentary, 1,* 35–55.

Hamburger, V., Wenger, E., & Oppenheim, R. (1966). Motility in the chick embryo in the absence of sensory input. *Journal of Experimental Zoology, 162,* 133–160.

Hamilton, D. W., & Ofner, P. (1982). Androgen action and target-organ androgen metabolism. In D. W. Hamilton & F. Naftolin (Eds.), *Basic reproductive medicine: Vol. 2. Reproductive function in man.* Cambridge, MA: MIT Press.

Hamon, M., Lanfumey, L., El Mestikawy, S., Boni, C., Miquel, M.-C., Balaños, Schechter, L., & Gozian, H. (1990). The main features of central 5-HT_1, receptors. *Neuropsychopharmacology, 3*(5/6), 349–360.

Hancke, J. C., & Döhler, K. D. (1980). Postnatal estradiol treatment prevents tamoxifen-induced defeminization of the female rat brain. *Acta Endocrinologie, 94* (Suppl. 234), 102.

Harlow, H. F., & Harlow, M. K. (1973). Social deprivation in monkeys. In W. T. Greenough (Ed.), *Readings from the* Scientific American: *The Nature and nurture of behavior* (pp. 108–116). San Francisco: Freeman.

Harris, L. J. (1978). Sex differences in spatial ability: Possible environmental, genetic and neurological factors. In M. Kinsbourne (Ed.), *Asymmetrical functions of the brain* (pp. 405–522). Cambridge, England: Cambridge University Press.

Hausen, K., & Strausfeld, N. J. (1980). Sexually dimorphic interneuron arrangements in the fly visual system. *Proceedings of the Royal Society of London Series B, 208,* 57–71.

Haydon, P. G., McCobb, D. P., & Kater, S. B. (1984). Serotonin selectively inhibits growth cone motility and synaptogenesis of specific identified neurons. *Science, 226,* 561–564.

Haydon, P., McCobb, D. P., & Kater, S. B. J. (1986). Dopamine and serotonin inhibition of different identified neurons. *Journal of Neurobiology, 18,* 197–215.

Heimer, L., & Wilson, R. D. (1975). The subcortical projections of the allocortex: Similarities in the neural associations of the hippocampus, the piriform cortex and the neocortex. In M. Santini (Ed.), *Golgi Centennial Symposium Proceedings* (pp. 177–193). New York: Raven Press.

Hines, M. (1982). Prenatal gonadal hormones and sex differences in human behavior. *Psychological Bulletin, 92,* 56–80.

Horgan, D. (1976). Sex differences in language development. Cited by Harris, L. J. (1978). Sex differences in spatial ability: Possible environmental, genetic and neurological factors. In M. Kinsbourne (Ed.), *Asymmetrical functions of the brain* (pp. 405–422). Cambridge, England: Cambridge University Press.

Horvitz, H. R., Ellis, H. M., & Sternberg, P. W. (1982). Programmed cell death in nematode development. *Neuroscience Commentary, 1,* 56–65.

Hubel, D. H., & Wiesel, T. N. (1963). Receptive fields of cells in striate cortex of very young, visually inexperienced kittens. *Journal of Neurophysiology, 26,* 994–1002.

Hubel, D. H., & Wiesel, T. N. (1970). The period of susceptibility to the physiological effects of unilateral exposure in kittens. *Journal of Physiology, 206,* 419–436.

Hubel, D. H., Wiesel, T. N., & LeVay, S. (1977). Plasticity of ocular dominance columns in monkey striate cortex. *Philosophical Transactions of the Royal Society of London Series B, 278,* 377–409.

Hume, R. I., Role, L. W., & Fischbach, G. D. (1983). Acetylcholine release from growth cones detected with patches of acetylcholine receptor-rich membrane. *Nature, 305,* 632–634.

Hutt, C. (1972). *Males and females.* Middlesex, England: Penguin.

Huttenlocher, P. R. (1979). Synaptic density in human frontal cortex: Developmental changes and effects of aging. *Brain Research, 163,* 195–205.

Huttenlocher, P. R., de Courten, C., Garey, L. J., & van der Loog, H. (1982). Synaptogenesis in human visual cortex: Evidence for synapse elimination during normal development. *Neuroscience Letter, 33,* 247–252.

Jacobsen, C. D., Csernus, V. J., Shryne, J. E., & Gorski, R. A. (1981). The influence of gonadectomy, androgen exposure, or a gonadal graft in the neonatal rat on the volume of the sexually dimorphic nucleus of the preoptic area. *Journal of Neuroscience, 14,* 1142–1147.

Jacobsen, C. D., & Gorski, R. A. (1981). Neurogenesis of the sexually dimorphic nucleus of the preoptic area of the rat. *Journal of Comparative Neurology, 196,* 512–529.

Jacobson, M. (1978). *Developmental neurobiology* (pp. 5–20). New York: Plenum.

Janzer, R. C., & Raff, M. C. (1987). Astrocytes induce blood-brain barrier properties in endothelial cells. *Nature, 325,* 253–257.

Juraska, J. M. (1984). Sex differences in dendritic response to differential experience in the rat visual cortex. *Brain Research, 295,* 27–34.

Kandel, E. R., & Mayeux, R. (1985). Natural languages, disorders of language and other localizable disorders of cognitive functioning. In E. R. Kandel & J. H. Schwartz (Eds.), *Principles of neural science* (2nd ed., pp. 688–703). New York: Elsevier.

Kater, S. B., & Letourneau, P. (Eds.). (1985). *The biology of the neuronal growth cone.* New York: Liss.

Kater, S. B., & Mills, L. R. (1989). Neurotransmitter activation of second messenger pathways for the control of growth cone behaviors. In J. M. Lauder, A. Privat, E. Giacobini, P. Timiras, & A. Vernadakis (Eds.), *Molecular aspects of development and aging of the nervous system* (pp. 217–225). New York: Plenum.

Katz, M. J., & Lasek, R. J. (1978). Evolution of the nervous system: Role of ontogenetic mechanisms in the evolution of matching populations. *Procedures of the National Academy of Science, 75,* 1349–1352.

Kebabian, J. W., & Calne, D. B. (1979). Multiple receptors for dopamine. *Nature, 277,* 93–96.

Kelly, D. D. (1985). Sexual differentiation of the brain. In E. R. Kandel & J. H. Schwartz (Eds.), *Principles of neural science* (2nd ed., pp. 781–782). New York: Elsevier.

Kimelberg, H. K. (1988). *Glial cell receptors.* New York: Raven Press.

Kolb, B., Sutherland, R. J., Nonneman, A. J., & Whishaw, I. Q. (1982). Asymmetry in the cerebral hemispheres of the rat, mouse, rabbit, and cat: The right hemisphere is larger. *Experimental Neurology, 78,* 348–359.

Kolb, B., & Whishaw, I. Q. (1990a). Memory. In R. C. Atkinson, G. Lindzey, & R. F. Thompson (Eds.), *Fundamentals of human neuropsychology* (3rd ed., pp. 525–567). New York: Freeman.

Kolb, B., & Whishaw, I. Q. (1990b). Organization of the motor systems. In R. C. Atkinson, G. Lindzey, & R. F. Thompson (Eds.), *Fundamentals of human neuropsychology* (3rd ed., pp. 257–282). New York: Freeman.

Kolb, B., & Whishaw, I. Q. (1990c). Organization of the sensory systems. In R. C. Atkinson, G. Lindzey, & R. F. Thompson (Eds.), *Fundamentals of human neuropsychology* (3rd ed., pp. 203–225). New York: Freeman.

Krieger, D. T. (1983). Brain peptides: What, where, and why? *Science, 222,* 975–985.

Kuffler, S. W., Nicholls, J. G., & Martin, A. R. (1984). *From neuron to brain: A cellular approach to the function of the nervous system* (2nd ed., pp. 88–91). Sunderland, MA: Sinauer Associates.

Kupferman, I. (1985a). Hemispheric asymmetries and the cortical localization of hemispheric cortical functions. In E. R. Kandel & J. H. Schwartz (Eds.), *Principles of neural science* (2nd ed., pp. 674–675). New York: Elsevier.

Kupferman, I. (1985b). Learning. In E. R. Kandel & J. H. Schwartz (Eds.), *Principles of neural science* (2nd ed., pp. 811–814). New York: Elsevier.

Lancaster, J. (1971). Play-mothering: The relations between juvenile females and young infants among free-ranging vervet monkeys. *Folis Primatology, 15,* 161–182.

Landsdell, H., & Davie, J. (1972). Massa intermedia: Possible relation to intelligence. *Neuropsychologia, 10,* 207–210.

Lanier, L. P., Dunn, A. J., & Van Hartesveldt, C. (1978). Development of neurotransmitters and their function in brain. In S. Ehrenpreis & I. J. Kopin (Eds.), *Reviews of neuroscience* (Vol. 3, pp. 195–256). New York: Raven Press.

Lee, K. S., Schottler, F., Oliver, M., & Lynch, G. (1980). Brief bursts of high frequency stimulation produce two types of structural changes in rat hippocampus. *Journal of Neurophysiology, 44,* 247–258.

Lemire, R. J., Loeser, J. D., Leech, R. W., & Alvord, E. C. (1975). *Normal and abnormal development of the human nervous system* (pp. 173–181). Hagerstown, MD: Harper & Row.

LeVay, S. (1991). A difference in hypothalamic structure between heterosexual and homosexual men. *Science, 253,* 1034–1037.

LeVay, S., Wiesel, T. N., & Hubel, D. H. (1980). The period of susceptibility to the physiological effects of unilateral eye closure in kittens. *Journal of Comparative Neurology, 191,* 1–51.

Levi-Montalcini, R. (1976). The nerve growth factor: Its role in growth differentiation and function of the sympathetic adrenergic neuron. *Progress in Brain Research, 45,* 235–258.

Lewis, B., & Clarke, H. (1878). The cortical lamination of the motor area of the brain. *Proceedings of the Royal Society of London, 27,* 38–49.

Lindvall, O., & Björklund, A. (1983). Dopamine- and norepinephrine-containing neuron systems: Their anatomy in the rat brain. In P. C. Emson (Ed.), *Chemical neuroanatomy.* New York: Raven Press.

Lou, H. C. (1980). Perinatal hypoxic-ischemic brain damage and intraventricular hemorrhage: A pathogenetic model. *Archives of Neurology, 41,* 825–829.

Lou, H. C., Greisen, G., & Tweed, A. (1989). Vascular flow and metabolic study of the neonatal brain. In J. French, S. Harel, & P. Casaer (Eds.), *Child neurology and developmental disabilities* (p. 191). Baltimore: Brooks.

Lund, R. D. (1978). *Development and plasticity of the brain* (pp. 13–21). New York: Oxford University Press.

Lund, R. D., McLoon, L. K., McLoon, S. C., Harvey, A. R., & Jaeger, C. B. (1983). Transplantation of the developing visual system of the rat. In F. J. Seil (Ed.), *Nerve, organ and tissue regeneration: Research perspectives* (pp. 303–323). New York: Academic Press.

Lyon, G. (1989). Bases neurologiques de la communication [The neurological bases of communication]. In G. Lelord, J. P. Muh, M. Petit, & D. Sauvage (Eds.), Autisme et troubles du développement global de l'enfant [The neurological basis of communication in autism and impairment of global development of the infant] (pp. 22–37). Paris: Expansion Scientifique Française.

Lyon, G. & Evrard, P. (1987). Troubles desfonctions cognitives—Déficience mentale [Disorders of cognitive function—Mental retardation]. In G. Lyon & P. Evrard (Eds.), Neuropédiatrie [*Neuropediatric*] (pp. 385–397). Paris: Masson.

Mack, J. K., O'Malley, K. L., & Todd, R. D. (1991). Differential expression of dopaminergic D_2 receptor messenger RNAs during development. *Developmental Brain Research, 59,* 249–251.

MacLean, P. D. (1955). The limbic system ("visceral brain") and emotional behavior. *Archives of Neurological Psychiatry, 73,* 130–134.

McEwen, B. S. (1983). Gonadal steroid influences on brain development and sexual differentiation. In R. O. Greep (Ed.), *Reproductive physiology IV* (pp. 99–145). Baltimore: University Park Press.

McShane, S., Glaser, L., Grear, E. R., Houtz, J., Tong, M. F., & Diamond, M. C. (1988). Cortical asymmetry—a preliminary study: Neurons–glia, female–male. *Experimental Neurology, 99,* 353–361.

Meaney, M. J., Dodge, A. M., & Beatty, W. W. (1981). Sex dependent effects of amygdaloid lesions on the social play of prepubertal rats. *Physiological Behavior, 26,* 467–472.

Meaney, M. J., & Stewart, J. (1981). Neonatal androgens influence the social play of prepubescent rats. *Hormone Behavior, 15,* 197–213.

Mesulam, M. M. (1985a). Biology of the attentional matrix. In F. Plum (Ed.), *Principles of behavioral neurology* (pp. 134–140). Philadelphia: Davis.

Mesulam, M. M. (1985b). Patterns in behavioral neuroanatomy: Association areas, the limbic system, and hemispheric specialization. In F. Plum (Ed.), *Principles of behavioral neurology* (p. 7). Philadelphia: Davis.

Molfese, D. L., Freeman, R. B., & Palermo, D. S. (1975). The ontogeny of brain lateralization for speech and nonspeech stimuli. *Brain and Language, 2,* 356–368.

Mommaerts, W. F. H. M. (1978). Excitation and conduction. In G. Ross (Ed.), *Essentials of human physiology* (pp. 35–53). Chicago: Year Book Medical Publishers.

Morley, M. E. (1957). *The development and disorder of speech in childhood.* London: Livingston.

Nishizuka, M., & Arai, Y. (1981). Sexual dimorphism in synaptic organization in the amygdala and its dependence on neonatal hormone environment. *Brain Research, 212,* 31–38.

Nottebohm, F. (1977). Asymmetries in neural control of vocalization in the canary. In S. R. Harnard, R. Doty, L. Goldstein, J. James, & G. Krauthamer (Eds.), *Lateralization in the nervous system* (pp. 23–44). New York: Academic Press.

O'Malley, B. W., & Birnbaumer, L. (Eds.). (1978). *Receptor and hormone action II.* New York: Academic Press.

O'Malley, K. L., Harmon, S., Tang, L. & Todd, R. D. (1992). The rat dopamine D_4 receptor. *The New Biologist, 4,* 137–146.

O'Rahilly, R., & Muller, F. (1986). The meninges in human development. *Journal of Neuropathology and Experimental Neurology, 45*(5), 558–608.

Pandya, D. N., & Seltzer, B. (1986). The topography of commissural fibers. In F. Lepore, M. Ptito, & H. H. Jasper (Eds.), *Two hemispheres—one brain: Functions of the corpus callosum* (pp. 47–73). New York: Liss.

Papez, J. W. (1937). A proposed mechanism of emotion. *Archives of Neurological Psychiatry, 38,* 725–743.

Pardo, J. V., Fox, P. T., & Raichle, M. E. (1991). Localization of a human system for sustained attention by positron emission tomography. *Nature, 349,* 61–64.

Parent, A., Descarries, L., & Beaudet, A. (1981). Organization of ascending serotonin systems in the adult rat brain: A radioautographic study after intraventricular administration of ^{3}H5-hydroxy tryptamine. *Neuroscience, 6,* 115.

Pepper, S. (1942). *World hypotheses.* Berkeley: University of California Press.

Peters, A., Palay, S. L., & Webster, H. deF. (1976). *The fine structure of the nervous system: The neurons and supporting cells.* Philadelphia: Saunders.

Petersen, S. E., Fox, P. T., Posner, M. I., Mintun, M., & Raichle, M. E. (1988). Positron emission tomographic studies of the cortical anatomy of single-word processing. *Nature, 331,* 585–589.

Phoenix, C. H., Goy, R. W., Gerall, A. A., & Young, W. C. (1959). Organizing action of prenatally administered testosterone propionate on the tissues mediating mating behavior in the female guinea pig. *Endocrinology, 65,* 369–382.

Purves, D., & Lichtman, J. W. (1985). The development of behavior. In *Principles of neural development.* Sunderland, MA: Sinauer Associates.

Purves, M. J. (1972). *The physiology of the cerebral circulation.* London: Cambridge University Press.

Raisman, G., & Field, P. M. (1973). Sexual dimorphism in the neuropil of the preoptic area of the rat and its dependence on neonatal androgen. *Brain Research, 54,* 1–29.

Rakic, P. (1974). Neurons in rhesus monkey visual cortex: Systematic relation between time of origin and eventual disposition. *Science, 183,* 425–427.

Rakic, P. (1981). Development of visual centers in the primate brain depends on binocular competition before birth. *Science, 214,* 928–931.

Rakic, P., & Riley, K. P. (1983). Overproduction and elimination of retinal axons in the fetal rhesus monkey. *Science, 219,* 1441–1444.

Rapoport, J. L. (1986). Childhood obsessive compulsive disorder. *Journal of Child Psychological Psychiatry, 27,* 289–295.

Reiman, E. M., Raickle, M. E., Butler, F. K., Herscovitch, P., & Robins, E. (1984). A local brain abnormality in panic disorder, a severe form of anxiety. *Nature, 310,* 683–685.

Reinisch, J. M., & Sanders, S. A. (1984). Prenatal gonadal steroidal influences on gender-related behavior. In G. J. De Vries, J. P. C. De Bruin, H. B. M. Uhylings, & M. A. Corner (Eds.), *Progress in brain research* (Vol. 61, p. 408). Amsterdam: Elsevier.

Renner, M. J. (1987). Experience-dependent changes in exploring behavior in the adult rat (Rattus Norvegicus): Overall activity level and interactions with objects. *Journal of Comparative Psychology, 101,* 1.

Renner, M. J., & Rosenzweig, M. R. (1986). Social interactions among rats housed in grouped and enriched conditions. *Developmental Psychobiology, 19*(5), 303–313.

Renner, M. J., & Rosenzweig, M. R. (1987). *Enriched and impoverished environments: Effects on brain and behavior* (pp. 14–15). New York: Springer-Verlag.

Reuter-Lorenz, P., & Davidson, R. J. (1981). Differential contributions of the two cerebral hemispheres to the perception of happy and sad faces. *Neuropsychologia, 19,* 609–613.

Reyes, F. I., Boroditsky, R. S., Winter, J. S. D., & Faiman, C. (1974). Studies on human sexual development: II. Fetal and maternal serum gonadotropin and sex steroid concentrations. *Journal of Clinical Endocrinology and Metabolism, 38,* 612–617.

Ripley, K. L., & Provine, R. P. (1972). Neural correlates of embryonic motility in the chick. *Brain Research, 45,* 127–134.

Risau, W., & Wolburg, H. (1990). Development of the blood-brain barrier. *Trends in Neuroscience, 13*(5), 174–178.

Risch, N. (1990). Linkage strategies for genetically complex traits: II. The power of affected relative pairs. *American Journal of Human Genetics, 46,* 229–241.

Robinson, R. G., & Starkstein, S. E. (1989). Mood disorders following stroke: New findings and future directions. *Journal of Geriatric Psychiatry, 22*(1), 1–15.

Roeder, J.-J., Chetcuti, Y., & Will, B. (1980). Behavior and length of survival of populations of enriched and impoverished rats in the presence of a predator. *Biology of Behavior, 36,* 1139–1145.

Rutter, M., & Garmezy, N. (1983). Developmental psychopathology. In E. M. Hetherington (Ed.), *Socialization, personality, and social development* (4th ed., Vol. 4, pp. 775–911). New York: Wiley.

Rutter, M., & Yule, W. (1977). Reading difficulties. In M. Rutter & L. Herson (Eds.), *Child psychiatry: Modern approaches.* London: Blackwell.

Sackeim, H. A., Greenberg, M. S., Weiman, A. L., Gur, R. C., Hungerbuhler, J. P., & Geschwind, N. (1982). Hemispheric asymmetry in the expression of positive and negative emotions: Neurological evidence. *Archives of Neurology, 39,* 210–218.

Sameroff, A. J., & Chandler, M. J. (1975). Reproductive risk and the continuum of caretaking casuality. *Review of Child Development Research, 4,* 187–244.

Schneider, H. P. G., & McCann, S. M. (1970). Estradiol and the neuroendocrine control of LH release in vitro. *Endocrinology, 87,* 330–338.

Selmanoff, M. K., Brodkin, L. D., Weiner, R. I., & Siiteri, P. K. (1977). Aromatization and 5α-reduction of androgens in discrete hypothalamic and limbic regions of the male and female rat. *Endocrinology, 101,* 841–848.

Shapiro, B. H., Goldman, A. S., Steinbeck, H. F., & Neumann, F. (1976). Is feminine differentiation of the brain hormonally determined? *Experientia, 32,* 650–651.

Shapiro, A. K., Shapiro, E. S., Bruun, R. D., & Sweet, T. R. D. (1978). *Gilles de la Tourette syndrome.* New York: Raven Press.

Shatz, C. J., & Stryker, M. P. (1978). Ocular dominance in layer IV of the cat's visual cortex and the effects of monocular deprivation. *Journal of Physiology, 281,* 267–283.

Sidman, R. L., & Rakic, P. (1973). Neuronal migration, with special reference to developing human brain: A review. *Brain Research, 62,* 1–35.

Sievers, J., Pehlemann, F.-W., & Berry, M. (1986). Influences of meningeal cells on brain development. *Naturwissenschaften, 73,* 188–194.

Sikich, L., Hickok, J. M., & Todd, R. D. (1990). 5-HT_{1A} receptors control neurite branching during development. *Developmental Brain Research, 2,* 269–274.

Sikich, L., & Todd, R. D. (1988). Are the neurodevelopmental effects of gonadal hormones related to sex differences in psychiatric illnesses? *Psychiatric Developments, 4,* 277–309.

Simerly, R. B., Swanson, L. W., Handa, R. J., & Gorsgi, R. A. (1985). The influence of perinatal androgen on the sexually dimorphic distribution of tyrosine hydroxylase immunoreactive cells and fibers in the anteroventral periventricular nucleus of the rat. *Neuroendocrinology, 40,* 501–510.

Sitteri, P., & Wilson, J. D. (1974). Testosterone formation and metabolism during male sexual differentiation in the human embryo. *Journal of Clinical Endocrinological Metabolism, 38,* 113–125.

Södersten, P. (1984). Sexual differentiation: Do males differ from females in behavioral sensitivity to gonadal hormones? In G. J. De Vries, J. P. C. De Bruin, H. B. M. Uhylings, & M. A. Corner (Eds.), *Progress in brain research* (Vol. 61, pp. 257–270). Amsterdam: Elsevier.

Södersten, P., Hansen, S., & Srebro, B. (1981). Suprachiasmatic lesions disrupt the daily rhythmicity in the sexual behavior of normal male rats and treated neonatally with antiestrogen. *Journal of Endocrinology, 88,* 125.

Sokoloff, P., Giros, B., Martres, M. P., Bouthenet, M. L., & Schwartz, J. C. (1990). Molecular cloning and characterization of a novel dopamine receptor (D_3) as a target for neuroleptics. *Nature, 347,* 146–151.

Spehlmann, R., & Smathers, C. C. (1974). The effects of acetylcholine and of synaptic stimulation in the sensorimotor cortex of cats: II. Comparison of the neuronal responses to reticular and other stimuli. *Brain Research, 74,* 243–253.

Stryker, M. P., & Harris, W. A. (1986). Binocular impulse blockade prevents formation of ocular dominance columns in cat visual cortex. *Journal Neuroscience, 6,* 2117–2133.

Stumpf, W. E. (1980). Anatomical distribution of steroid hormone target neurons and circuitry in the brain. In M. Motta (Ed.), *The endocrine functions of the brain* (pp. 43–49). New York: Raven Press.

Sunahara, R. K., Guan, H. C., O'Dowd, B. F., Seeman, P., Laurier, L. G., Ng, G., George, S. R., Torchia, J., Van Tol, H. H., & Niznik, H. B. (1991). Cloning of the gene for a human dopamine D_5 receptor with higher affinity for dopamine than D_1. *Nature, 350,* 614–619.

Sunahara, R. K., Niznik, H. B., Weiner, D. M., Stormann, T. M., Brann, M. R., Kennedy, J. L., Gelernter, J. E., Rozmahel, R., Yang, Y. L., & Israel, Y. (1990). Human dopamine D_1 receptor encoded by an intronless gene on chromosome 5. *Nature, 347,* 80–83.

Swaab, D. F., & Hofman, M. A. (1984). Sexual differentiation of the brain: A historical perspective. In G. J. De Vries, J. P. C. De Bruin, H. B. M. Uhylings, & M. A. Corner (Eds.), *Progress in brain research* (Vol. 61, pp. 361–374). Amsterdam: Elsevier.

Swaab, D. F., & Hofman, M. A. (1990). An enlarged suprachiasmatic nucleus in homosexual men. *Brain Research, 537,* 141–148.

Swarzenski, G. C., Tang, L., Oh, Y. J., O'Malley, K. L., & Todd, R. D. (1994). Morphogenic potentials of D_2, D_3, and D_4 dopamine receptors revealed in transfected neuronal cell lines. *Proc. Nat'l Acad Sci USA, 91,* 649–653.

Szeligo, F. (1977). Quantitative differences in oligodendrocytes and myelinated axons in the brains of rats raised in enriched, controlled and impoverished environments. *Anatomical Record, 187,* 726–727.

Telzrow, C. F., Century, E., Redmond, C., Whitaker, B., & Zimmerman, B. (1983). The Boder test: Neuropsychological and demographic features of dyslexic subtypes. *Psychology in the Schools, 20,* 427–432.

Thompson, R. F. (1975). *Introduction to physiological psychology.* New York: Harper & Row.

Todd, R. D. (1992). Neural development is regulated by classical neurotransmitters: Dopamine D_2 receptor stimulation enhances neurite outgrowth. *Biological Psychiatry, 31,* 794–807.

Todd, R. D., Reich, W., & Reich, T. (1994). Prevalence of affective disorder in the child and adolescent offspring of a single kindred. *Journal of the American Academy of Child and Adolescent Psychiatry, 33,* 198–207.

Toran-Allerand, C. D. (1976). Sex steroids and the development of the newborn mouse hypothalamus and preoptic area in vitro: Implications for sexual differentiation. *Brain Research, 106,* 407–412.

Toran-Allerand, C. D., Gerlach, J. L., & McEwen, B. S. (1980). Autoradiographic localization of ^3H estradiol related to steroid responsiveness in cultures of the hypothalamus and preoptic area. *Brain Research, 184,* 517–522.

Uhylings, H. B. M., Kuypers, K., Diamond, M. C., & Veltman, W. A. M. (1978). The effects of differential environments on plasticity of dendrites of cortical pyramidal neurons in adult rats. *Experimental Neurology, 62,* 658–677.

Van Essen, D. C., Anderson, C. H., & Felleman, D. J. (1992). Information processing in the primate visual system: An integrated systems perspective. *Science, 255,* 419–423.

Van Tol, H. H., Bunzow, J. R., Guan, H. C., Sunahara, R. K., Seeman, P., Niznik, H. B., & Civelli, O. (1991). Cloning of the gene for a human dopamine D_4 receptor with high affinity for the antipsychotic clozapine. *Nature, 350,* 610–614.

Varon, S. S., & Somjen, G. F. (1979). Neuron-glia interactions. *Neurosciences Research Bulletin, 17*(1) 3-239.

Volkmar, F. R., & Greenough, W. T. (1972). Rearing complexity affects branching of dendrites in the visual cortex of the rat. *Science, 176,* 1445–1447.

Vom Saal, F. S., & Bronson, F. H. (1980). Sexual characteristics of adult female mice are correlated with their blood testosterone levels during prenatal development. *Anatomy Record, 157,* 173–180.

Wada, J. A., Clarke, R., & Hamm, A. (1975). Cerebral hemispheric asymmetry in humans. *Archives of Neurology, 32,* 239–246.

Ward, I. L. (1969). Differential effects of pre- and postnatal androgen on the sexual behavior of intact and spayed rats. *Hormone Behavior, 1,* 5–36.

Watson, J. D., Hopkins, N. H., Roberts, J. W., Steitz, J. A., & Weiner, A. M. (1987). The control of cell proliferation. In J. R. Gillen (Ed.), *Molecular biology of the gene* (4th ed., pp. 978–982). Menlo Park, CA: Benjamin/Cummings.

Wiggins, R. C. (1986). Myelinization: A critical stage in development. *Neurotoxicity, 7*(2), 103–120.

Winter, J. S. D., Hughes, I. A., Reyes, F. I., & Faiman, C. (1976). Pituitary-gonadal relations in infancy: II. Patterns of serum gonadal steroid concentrations in man from birth to two years of age. *Journal of Clinical Endocrinology and Metabolism, 42,* 679–686.

Witelson, S. F. (1974). Hemispheric specialization for linguistic and nonlinguistic tactual perception using a dichotomous stimulation technique. *Cortex, 11,* 3–17.

Witelson, S. F. (1976). Sex and the single hemisphere: Specialization of the right hemisphere for spatial processing. *Science, 193,* 425–427.

Witelson, S. F. (1989). Hand and sex differences in the isthmus and genu of the human corpus callosum: A postmortem morphological study. *Brain, 112,* 799–835.

Witelson, S. F., & Kigar, D. L. (1987). Neuroanatomical aspects of hemispheric specialization in humans. In D. Ottoson (Ed.), *Duality and unity of the brain: Unified functioning and specialization of the hemispheres* (pp. 446-495). Hampshire, England: Macmillan.

Witelson, S. F., & Pallie, W. (1973). Left hemisphere specialization for language in the newborn: Neuroanatomical evidence of asymmetry. *Brain, 96,* 641–646.

Witelson, S. F., & Swallow, J. (1988). Neuropsychological study of the development of spatial cognition. In J. Stiles-Davis, J. M. Kritchevsky, & U. Bellugi (Eds.), *Spatial cognition: Brain bases and development* (pp. 373–409). Hillsdale, NJ: Erlbaum.

Yakolev, P. I., & Le Cours, A. R. (1964). The myelogenetic cycles of regional maturation of the brain. In A. Minkowski (Ed.), *Regional development of the brain in early life* (pp. 3–70). Oxford, England: Blackwell.

Young, S. H., & Poo, M. (1983). Spontaneous release of transmitter from growth cones of embryonic neurons. *Nature, 305,* 634–637.

Zaidel, E., Clarke, J. M., & Suyenobu, B. (1990). Hemispheric independence: A paradigm case for cognitive neuroscience. In A. B. Scheibel & A. F. Wechsler (Eds.), *Neurobiology of higher cognitive function* (pp. 299-300). New York: Guilford.

CHAPTER 7

Neurodevelopmental Principles Guide Research on Developmental Psychopathologies

ERIC COURCHESNE, JEANNE TOWNSEND, and CHRISTOPHER CHASE

This chapter discusses why theories and views based on adult lesion effects or on symptoms (behavioral and biological) so frequently fail to account for the brain bases of developmental disorders. The fetal brain differs greatly from the adult brain, and *symptoms, which are end products of development,* can be far removed from beginning causes. Erroneous is the notion that if the most critical or pathognomonic behavioral or biological symptoms of a developmental disorder could be identified, then one should necessarily be able to travel backward from them to root causes. The history of research on developmental disorders (e.g., autism, dyslexia, schizophrenia, and so on) is replete with examples of dead ends resulting from this simplistic approach. Because of the special nature of neurodevelopmental processes, particular problems are encountered when seeking the precipitating perturbations underlying developmental disorders.

THE TRADITIONAL APPROACH IN RESEARCH ON DEVELOPMENTAL PSYCHOPATHOLOGIES

Research on developmental psychopathologies traditionally begins at the end: with symptoms—their appearance, treatment, and speculated neural substrates. In this chapter, neurobehavioral symptoms refer to all behavioral and biological expressions of structure and function, including, for example, positron emission tomography (PET), functional magnetic resonance imaging (fMR), or electrophysiological measures of functional brain activity; MR or autopsy measures of anatomy; biochemical assays; and neuropsychological performance.

The traditional approach begins by asking what behavioral/psychological defects or treatment effects are characteristic of or specific to a disorder. Next, it asks what the neural substrates are for these types of behavioral/psychological functions or treatment effects. To answer this second question, tradition turns to data on the effects of brain lesions and treatments in adult humans and animals. For instance, some theories of dyslexia have revolved around the idea that it is caused by damage to the same cortical regions which, when damaged in adults, lead to reading and language deficits. Similarly, some theories of infantile autism, a disorder that involves deficits in "executive" functions, have revolved around the idea that it is caused by frontal lobe damage, which, in adults, may sometimes lead to impaired executive functions. Yet fetuses and infants with observable focal lesions in these frontal and posterior cortical regions do not become dyslexic or autistic. Likewise, some theories of schizophrenia, a developmental disorder that may be responsive to treatment of the dopamine system, have revolved around the idea that it is caused by abnormal dopaminergic function. Yet evidence of fetal maldevelopment has not been seen in brain stem dopaminergic nuclei (Bogerts, Meertz, & Schonfeldt-Bausch, 1985), but rather in medial temporal lobe structures (Beckmann & Jakob, 1991; Jakob & Beckmann, 1986, 1989).

Looking across decades of research, we can see that symptoms, whether biologic or behavioral, have unfortunately not proven to be the key to finding the root causes or origins of developmental psychopathologies. Instead, symptoms offer quite different information, such as information about pathognomonic features (i.e., a diagnostically defining characteristic defect); treatable features or mechanisms; key debilitating features; and prognostic features. At best, examination of symptoms has sometimes helped add a layer or two of explanation beneath abnormal behavior. For instance, infantile autism is characterized by a profound deficiency in social knowledge, affect, and communication. A possible explanation may emerge from the discovery that autistic patients have a marked deficit in joint social attention (Curcio, 1978; Loveland & Landry, 1986; Mundy, Sigman, Ungerer, & Sherman, 1986), which is a function considered critical for normal social, affective, and language development (Bruner, 1975; Tronick, 1982).[1] Important though this explanation is, it leaves unanswered the question of what is the root cause of joint social attention deficits in

Supported by funds from NIMH (1-RO1-MH-36840) and NINDS (5-RO1-NS-19855) awarded to Eric Courchesne. Thanks to Naomi G. Singer and Heather J. Chisum for helpful advice and insightful comments on this paper.

[1] Joint social attention normally develops by 12 to 15 months (Bakeman & Adamson, 1984). In joint attention, two persons coordinate their focus of attention on each other and an object of mutual interest.

autism. In a parallel fashion, abnormal metabolic activity has been found in the frontal lobes in autistic patients and may help explain the behavioral impression that frontal lobe functions are impaired in autism. Interesting though this association may be, it leaves unanswered the key developmental question of how and where abnormalities first began in the autistic brain.

Despite decades of research, the when, where, and how of the events that trigger abnormal development and the sequence of ensuing maldevelopmental steps that lead to the symptoms we see in the child, have remained largely a mystery for nearly every developmental psychopathology (e.g., autism, dyslexia, dysphasia, schizophrenia, Attention Deficit/Hyperactivity Disorder (ADHD), Rett syndrome, and so on). Why has the traditional approach not yielded key insights into these two crucial questions about each disorder: (a) when, where, and how did it begin, and (b) how did this beginning result in final symptomatology? Perhaps it is because of conceptual miscues inherent in the traditional approach.

These conceptual miscues may be best understood by first considering a simple analogy. Symptoms of a cold are familiar: a runny nose, a slight rise in body temperature, chill sensations, general achiness, and basic indisposition. We now know, of course, what causes colds and that there are different types (e.g., viral colds, June colds, rose colds). We treat a cold by taking decongestants and aspirin, drinking plenty of water, and getting lots of sleep.

Based on treatment effects, does it make sense to conclude that colds are caused by a deficiency in decongestants, aspirin, water, or a dozen hours of sleep? No. But is this not analogous to the logic that drives much research and theory in developmental psychopathologies? Based on symptoms, does it make sense to conclude that colds are caused by too much nasal mucus, poor temperature regulation, weak muscles, an irascible disposition, or irritated skin around the nose? No. But is this not also analogous to the logic that drives much research and theory in developmental psychopathologies? Would we ever find the causes of colds if we conducted experiments measuring how much mucus normal people and affected people produce; or how mucus production is affected by varying doses of aspirin, water, and sleep? Because some people have relatively less mucus production while still having general achiness, but others have the opposite symptomatology, should we conclude that symptom differences necessarily reflect different causes? Should we assume that all people with similar cold symptoms necessarily have similar causes for their colds? Irritated skin around the nose is an undeniable anatomic feature that accompanies many viral colds; does the cold virus directly cause this or is it linked to the viral infection only through indirect mechanisms? The latter, clearly, is correct. Do all people with colds always have the same symptoms? No; the same perturbation in different individuals can produce different end symptoms.

As with colds, behavioral and biological symptoms in developmental psychopathologies orient us to the phenomena. Attention to these phenomena defines the domain of later experiments on the underlying causes and the symptoms that candidate causes must ultimately explain. However, it is instructive and sobering to consider that accurate explanations of the mechanisms underlying cold symptoms were not obtained until after the discovery of the triggering perturbations. In much the same way, accurate explanations of the developmental origins and transformations behind the far more intricate symptomatology of developmental psychopathologies will require discovery of triggering events. We will not get there by limiting ourselves to experimenting on the end products of maldevelopment (e.g., theory of mind deficits; frontal lobe metabolic peculiarities; eye movement abnormalities; arousal deficits; and so on). We have to seek evidence that takes us to beginning events, and then from that foundation, build explanations of how final symptoms come about.

PRINCIPLES GOVERNING NORMAL AND ABNORMAL NEURODEVELOPMENT

Normal Development

Normal development is a self-organizing phenomenon. During developmental differentiation, emergent structures and functions at any given point enable the construction of new structures and functions and the further elaboration of those that had previously emerged. Unlike a mature system, the developing neural network is undergoing continuous, rapid, and profound global change from one of fewer elements, fewer interactions among elements, less stability, and less structural and functional differentiation to one of more elements, more complex interactions, stability, and structural and functional parcellation and specialization.

Initially there is an *overabundance* (see Figure 7.1) of neural elements (i.e., neurons and synapses) and axonal connections (Cowan, Fawcett, O'Leary, & Stanfield, 1984; O'Leary & Koester, 1993). *Regressive events* (see Figures 7.1 and 7.2) follow, during which some neural elements and connections are

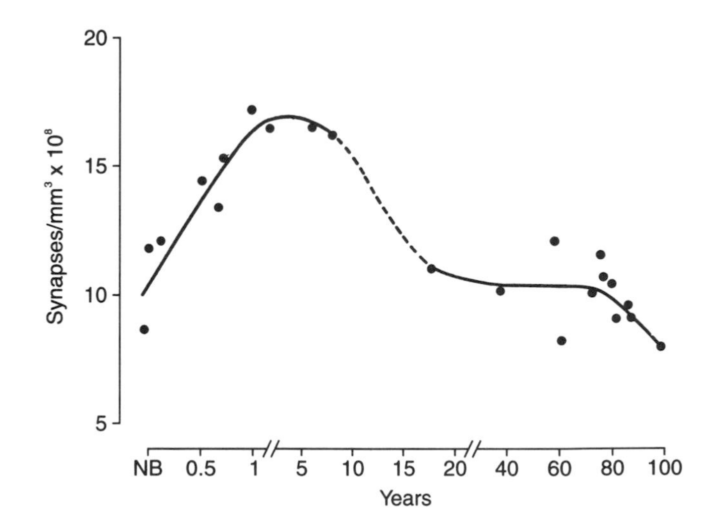

Figure 7.1 Synapse counts in layer 3 of the middle frontal gyrus as a function of age in humans. From "Synaptic Density in Human Frontal Cortex—Developmental Changes and Effects of Aging" by P. R. Huttenlocher, 1979, *Brain Research, 163,* p. 218. Copyright 1979 by Elsevier Science Publishing BV, Amsterdam, The Netherlands. Reprinted by permission.

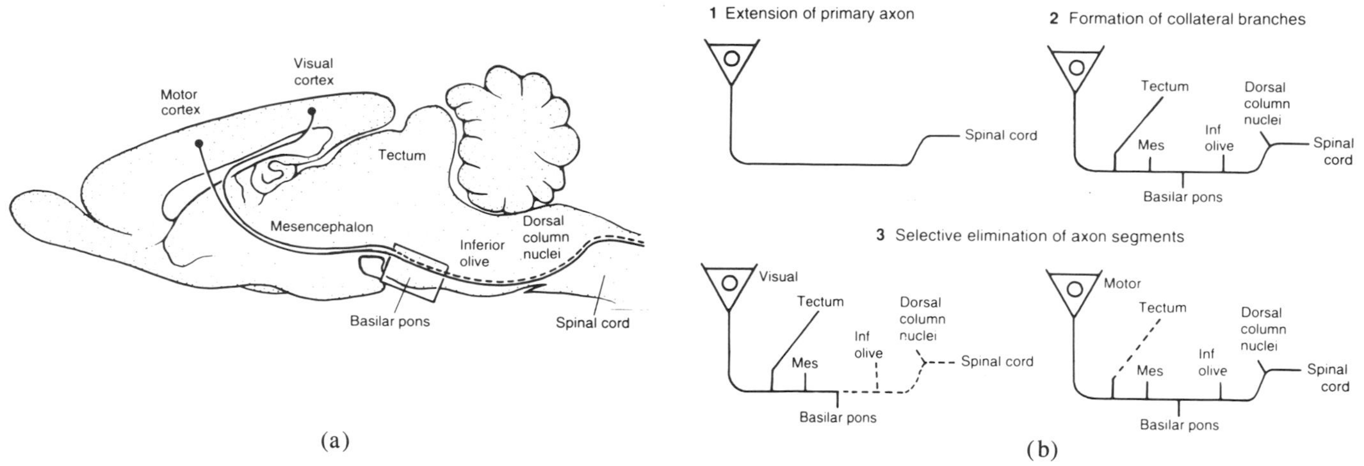

Figure 7.2 Branches of developing axons in the central nervous system are pruned during development. (a) Schematic, parasagittal view of the basic, subcortical trajectory of the parent axons that form the corticospinal and corticopontine projections. The pathway originating in the visual cortex is transient (the dashed part of trajectory) beyond the basilar pons. (b) Phases in the development of projections of layer 5 cortical neurons. 1. The initial projection of the primary axon to the spinal cord is the same for neurons in both motor and visual cortex. 2. The pattern of collateral branches from the primary axons is similar for neurons in motor and visual cortex. 3. Neurons in the motor and visual cortex eliminate different branches, resulting in distinctive projection patterns at maturity. From *Principles of Neural Science,* 3rd ed. (p. 924) by E. R. Kandel, J. H. Schwartz, and T. M. Jessell, 1991, Norwalk, CT: Appleton & Lange. Adapted from O'Leary and Terashima, 1988. Copyright 1988 by Cell Press, Cambridge, MA.

selectively eliminated and others are retained (Chalupa & Killackey, 1989; Cowan et al., 1984; Innocenti, 1981; Killackey, 1990; O'Leary & Koester, 1993; O'Leary, Stanfield, & Cowan, 1981; Stanfield, O'Leary, & Fricks, 1982). *Functional activity* often determines what is retained and what is eliminated (Killackey, 1990; Stryker, 1990; see below). Thus, competition between and correlated activity within neural networks drive the elimination of some connections and the selective stabilization of others (Katz, 1993; Siegler, 1989) (see Figures 7.3–7.5). To paraphrase, "neurons that fire together, wire together." At successive stages of development, new patterns of firing together (either spontaneous or evoked) create new patterns of wiring together (see Figure 7.6). From such dynamic processes shaped through individual-specific experiences, it is possible to see that two individuals with similar beginning states may follow progressively divergent developmental paths (see Figure 7.7);

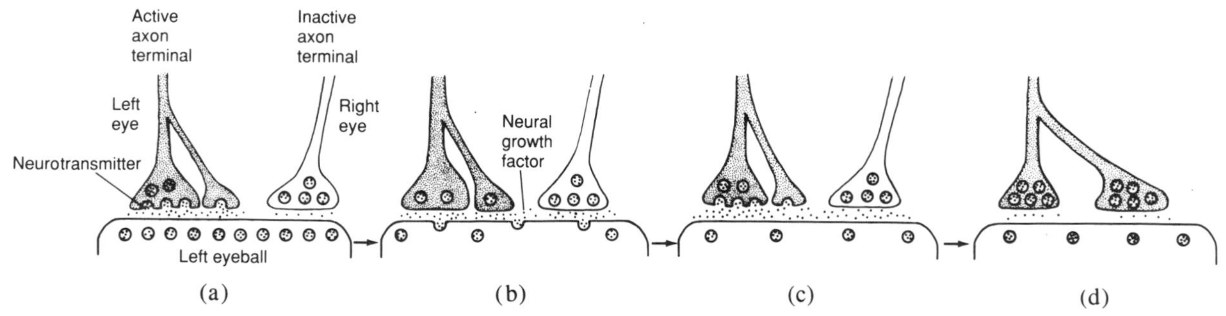

Figure 7.3 A possible mechanism for cooperation and competition. According to this model, stabilization of a synapse depends on factors released from the postsynaptic cell (in this case, a cell responding to the left eye) that act on and stimulate the growth of active presynaptic inputs. Active axon terminals that take up a factor enlarge and grow additional terminals that thereby reinforce the strength of the synapse. The more frequently the postsynaptic cell is stimulated, the more its internal store of the factor is depleted and the lower is the rate of spontaneous release. Thus, inactive axon terminals competing with active ones (a) will fail to obtain adequate amounts of growth factor and consequently will shrink and eventually withdraw (b), (c), and (d). When two axon terminals are active at different times, they will compete with one another for the limited amount of growth factor that the postsynaptic cell contains. A large terminal will take up more growth factor, which in turn will make it larger still. The outcome of such competition may thus depend on slight differences in initial size of the synaptic terminal (a). From *Principles of Neural Science,* 3rd ed. (p. 956) by E. R. Kandel, J. H. Schwartz, and T. M. Jessell, 1991, Norwalk, CT: Appleton & Lange. Modified from Alberts et al., 1989. Copyright 1989 by Garland Publishing, New York.

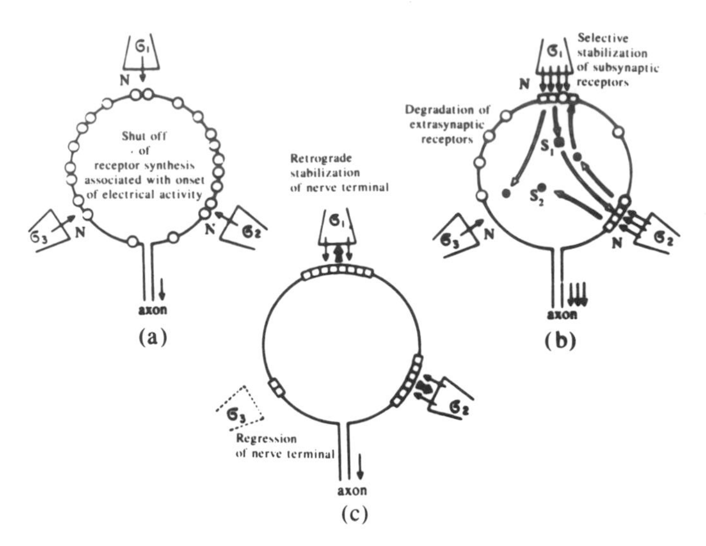

Figure 7.4 The selective localization of the receptor on the surface of a neuron receiving several nerve terminals. The labile and mobile state of the receptor for the neurotransmitter is represented by a circle; the stable and immobilized one, by a square. The different signals postulated are represented by arrows: N = the anterograde factor, for instance, the neurotransmitter: S = the internal coupling factor: a thick arrow indicates the retrograde factor. At the onset of activity, a "shut off" factor stops the synthesis of labile receptor molecules. The model allows for the segregation of different receptor molecules if the nerve terminals secrete different anterograde factors. From "Selective Stabilization of Developing Synapses as a Mechanism for the Specification of Neural Networks" by J. P. Changeux and A. Danchin, 1976, *Nature, 264,* p. 709. Copyright 1976 by Macmillan Magazines Ltd. Reprinted by permission.

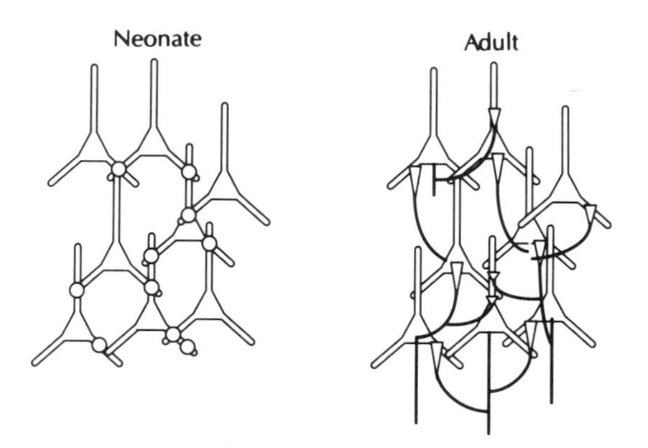

Figure 7.5 Diagram of the hypothetical transition from gap-junction coupled networks to synaptically linked arrays. Correlated activity in the form of Ca^{2+} transients may contribute to the formation of synapses between coupled cortical assemblies that are repeatedly coactivated by early synaptic inputs. From "Coordinate Activity in Retinal and Cortical Development" by L. C. Katz, 1993, *Current Opinion in Neurobiology, 3,* p. 97. Copyright 1993 by Current Science. Reprinted by permission.

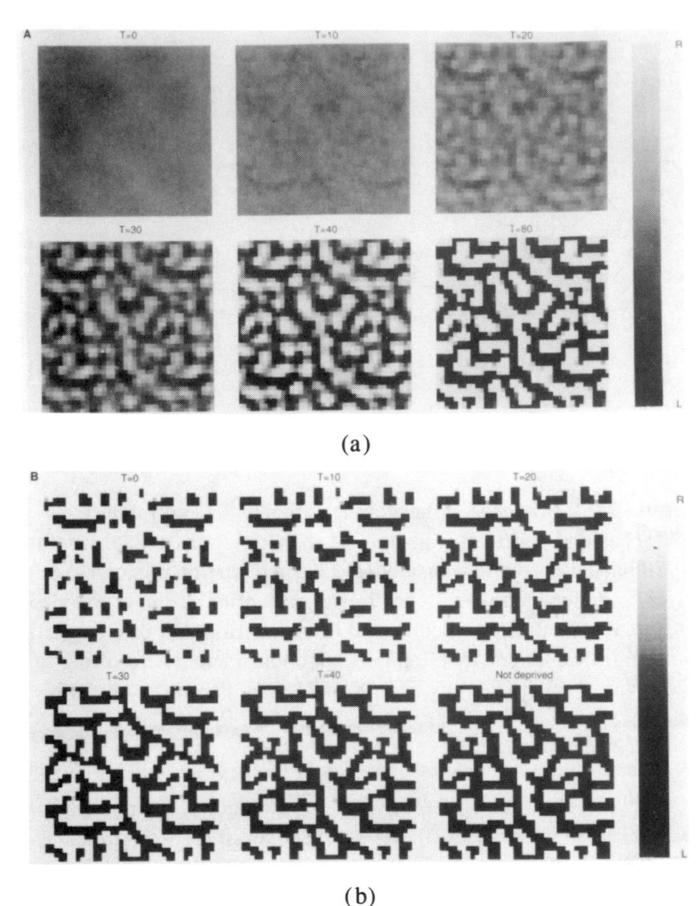

Figure 7.6 A computer-generated simulation of the development of ocular dominance columns. (a) These examples illustrate different stages in the normal development of ocular dominance columns. Each square represents a single cortical cell. White and black signify complete dominance of inputs from one or the other eye. Shades of gray indicate the degree of convergent input from both eyes. With time (T) in arbitrary units roughly comparable to days, this model generates a progressive segregation of inputs from each eye until, at T = 80, there is almost no overlap. The resulting pattern is similar to that observed experimentally. (b) Similar image showing the consequences for segregation of eye inputs when monocular deprivation has been carried out at various starting times (T) (ranging from 0 to 40). When segregation is started early (T = 0), the input of the remaining eye expands significantly during the initial period. As the onset of monocular deprivation is delayed (T = 10, 20, 30, 40), the expansion of the input of the intact eye decreases. In this example, the critical period lasts from T = 0 to T = 20. After T = 30, monocular deprivation has little effect; this can be seen by comparison to the nondeprived "normal" case in (a). From "Ocular Dominance Column Development: Analysis and Simulation" by K. D. Miller, J. B. Keller, and M. P. Stryker, 1989, *Science, 245,* pp. 609, 612. Copyright 1989 by the American Association for the Advancement of Science. Reprinted by permission.

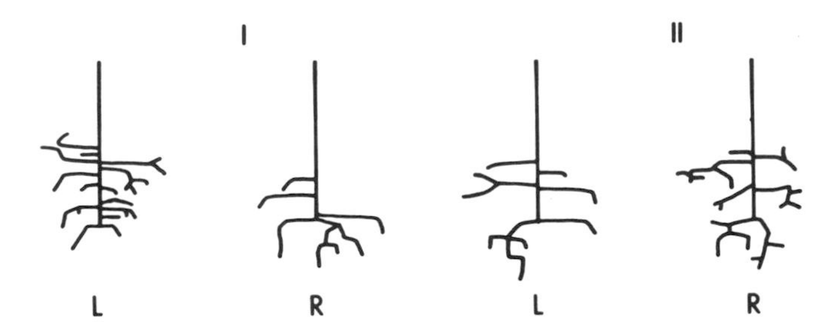

Figure 7.7 Drawing of computer reconstructions of the branching pattern of the same retinal axon on left (L) and right (R) sides of the brain of two Daphnia specimens (I and II), to show the considerable variability experienced. The two specimens are isogeneic members of a single parthenogenetic clone. From *Development and Plasticity of the Brain* (p. 6) by R. D. Lund, 1978, New York: Oxford University Press. Copyright 1978 by Oxford University Press. After Macagno, Lopresti, and Levinthal, 1973. Reprinted by permission.

conversely, two individuals with different beginning states may follow progressively convergent developmental paths.

As a result of this dynamic process of emergence and transformation, there develop successively more complex, specialized, and stable neural network configurations that differ greatly from antecedent ones. All signs of intermediate neural states and operations are often eliminated by this developmental process. For instance, operations or neural configurations that may have been essential for the initial construction of a particular function may not be needed thereafter to maintain, use, or elaborate that function; other operations or configurations may come into play at these later stages.

In the end, what remain clearly detectable are the neurobehavioral end products *of this self-constructive, epigenetic process, rather than the intervening steps.*[2] Numerous pitfalls plague attempts to use backward solutions to derive the intermediate processes, events, and configurations antecedent to any particular neurobehavioral phenotypic profile. By analogy, for instance, the blossoming full-grown fruit tree bears little resemblance to the emergent sapling, and the Hawaiian valley with its richly diverse rain-forest ecosystem bears no resemblance to its fiery volcanic origins. Thus, in biologic systems of all sorts, often no obvious clues remain as to the states or events antecedent to observed end conditions.

Appearances—or, in our case, neurobehavioral end products—can be deceptive. Figure 7.7, for example, shows that the pattern of axonal connections may differ sharply between two genetically identical individuals. In different individuals, dissimilar appearances (i.e., phenotypic features) could have similar biologic bases and vice versa. So, although different individuals may have similar neurodevelopmental starting points, they may experience differences in patterns of genetic-environmental interactions that drive them down *divergent developmental paths.* Despite the divergent developmental outcomes, such divergent symptoms may be thought of as *homologous* to each other because each had a comparable developmental basis. Conversely, similar neurobehavioral end products in different individuals may be thought of as *analogous* to each other if they reflect only superficial similarities in structure or function, but are actually derived from different developmental origins. Such similarity may come about through *convergent developmental paths.*

Ironically and fortuitously, these principles of normal development are derived in large part from the results of experiments in which the nervous system is subjected to abnormal perturbations of one sort or another (e.g., lesions, sensory deprivation, and so on) at different developmental stages. Therefore, the principles of normal development gleaned from these perturbation experiments apply directly and equally to abnormal development.

Abnormal Development

Like normal development, abnormal development is a self-organizing phenomenon, but with one critical twist: the end result includes some significant degree of *misorganization.* Abnormal perturbations at one stage disable the construction of some new structures and functions, distort the form of other later-emerging ones, enable the construction of ones that normally never appear, and/or limit the elaboration and usage of previously emerged ones.

Damaging perturbations that lead to "alterations of the 'ecological balance' of the processing system" in adults (Kosslyn & Intriligator, 1992) could, in the developing system, lead to "ecological chaos." That is, a perturbation to the developing brain can set off a cascade of growth and function changes that lead the system irrevocably down a path that deviates from normal. Eventually, successively more complex, specialized, and stable *abnormal* neural network configurations and operations develop that differ greatly from antecedent ones. Under the most favorable conditions, the final outcome is a successful relocation of structure and function (see below); more typically, the final outcome is a system with impoverished capacity in one or more structural and functional domains (see below).

A number of rules govern the response of the developing brain to abnormal perturbations (e.g., migration errors, lesions, receptor defects, sensory defects, and so on). The remainder of this section discusses these rules.

First, abnormal functional activity may determine what is retained and what is eliminated. For example, elimination of retinal activity (by blocking it with tetrodotoxin or eye removal) during early development causes hypoplasia of primary visual cortex (Dehay, Horsburgh, Berland, Killackey, & Kennedy, 1989) (see Figure 7.8); increases the number of area 18 neurons with callosal projections (Dehay et al., 1989); and eliminates the normal segregation of geniculocortical afferents into eye-specific alternating patches (Antonini & Stryker, 1992) so that ocular-dominance columns do not develop normally (Stryker

[2] "End products" are phenotypic features that are the manifest structural and functional characteristics of a person; they result from both heredity and environment.

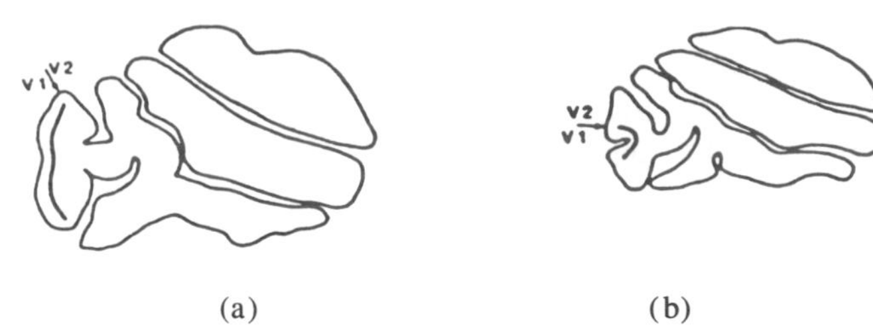

Figure 7.8 Schematic drawing of the area 17/18 border diagramming region of callosally projecting cells in the newborn monkey. (a) Normal. (b) After eye removal at E77. The continuous line in the operculum indicates the extent of area 17. Area 17 occupies most of the operculum of the normal animal, but after eye removal at E77, area 17 seems considerably shrunken. From "Maturation and Connectivity of the Visual Cortex in Monkey Is Altered by Prenatal Removal of Retinal Input" by C. Dehay, G. Horsburgh, M. Berlaud, H. Killackey, and H. Kennedy, 1989, *Nature, 337,* p. 266. Copyright 1989 by Macmillan Magazines Ltd. Adapted by permission.

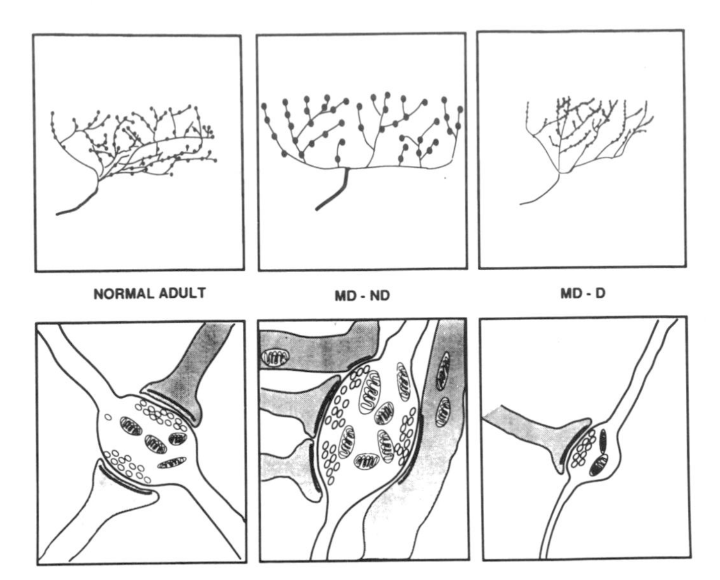

Figure 7.9 Summary diagram illustrating major significant differences in axon aborizations and ultrastructure of individual synapses for Y axon geniculocortical contacts in layer 4 of area 18 in normal and MD (monocular deprived) cats.

MD causes arborizations of individual Y axons to change in their extent and the density of boutons. ND (nondeprived eye) axons in MD cats cover a larger extent (mediolateral × rostrocaudal) and space their boutons more widely. The D (deprived eye) axons' extent of cortical coverage is reduced, and their density of boutons is higher (with the centermost part of their arborizations). They also contain more isolated peripheral branches with sparse bouton coverage. The individual boutons of ND axons are larger than those of D axons. (Boutons of Y axons in area 18 of normal cats are intermediate in size.) The boutons of ND axons vary considerably in the number of targets contacted, but, in many cases, contact multiple targets (4–12). These targets include a greater proportion of dendritic shafts than for axons from normal animals or D boutons in MD animals. The ND boutons contain more mitochondria and innervate zones with larger postsynaptic densities on dendritic shafts. The D boutons are generally smaller, contact fewer targets, prefer spines as do normal axons, have fewer mitochondria, and often do not form any synapses. From "Effects of Monocular Visual Deprivation on Geniculocortical Innervation of Area 18 in Cat" by M. J. Friedlander, K. A. C. Martin, and D. Wassenhove-McCarthy, 1991, *The Journal of Neuroscience, 11,* p. 3285. Copyright 1991 by Society for Neuroscience. Reprinted by permission.

& Harris, 1986) Fig. 7.10. After monocular deprivation during early development, activity-deprived Y-type geniculocortical axons have a a variable reduction in arbor size, an increase in bouton density, smaller bouton size, fewer bouton mitochondria, and synapse on only a single target or on no target at all (Friedlander, Martin, & Wassenhove-McCarthy, 1991) (see Figure 7.9). In the monocular deprived animal, the Y-type geniculocortical axons from the nondeprived eye are also abnormal (see Figure 7.9); they have expanded axonal arbors, form ectopic synapses, and form more synapses per bouton than normal.

Activity-mediated effects have been found in a variety of systems (for a review, see Hockfield & Kalb, 1993; Jensen & Killackey, 1987; Van der Loos & Woolsey, 1973; Voyvodic, 1989) (see Figures 7.8 to 7.11) and demonstrated via computer simulation (see Figure 7.6). Most striking of all are studies showing that, by routing visual information to either auditory or somatosensory cortex, cells in those normally nonvisual areas become responsive to visual information and can display some of the distinctive response features characteristic of normal visual cortical cells (Frost & Metin, 1985; Sur, Garraghty, & Roe, 1988) (see Figure 7.12). Thus, because a host of studies show that extensive mis-organization can occur in sensory systems under the influence of abnormal activity, it is reasonable to predict that future research will also demonstrate that so-called "higher-order" systems are capable of substantial mis-organization as well.

The evidence demonstrates that abnormal activity can trigger the formation of a wide range of structural and functional mis-organizations even in sites distant from the point of the actual abnormal perturbation. These experiments illustrate another very important concept: The existence of structural or functional abnormalities at a particular site does not mean that it is the site of the precipitating defect. Such a site might well have been potentially perfectly normal except for some defect that arose elsewhere. *Thus, structural or functional mis-organizations may be either the end product of abnormal perturbations elsewhere or the originating site of abnormality.* In human developmental psychopathologies, experimental evidence is required to demonstrate which possibility is true. For example, very subtle growth changes have been detected in limbic structures in four cases of infantile autism (Bauman, 1991; Raymond, Bauman, & Kemper, 1989); whether they reflect the end product of abnormality originating elsewhere or the originating site of abnormality is unknown.

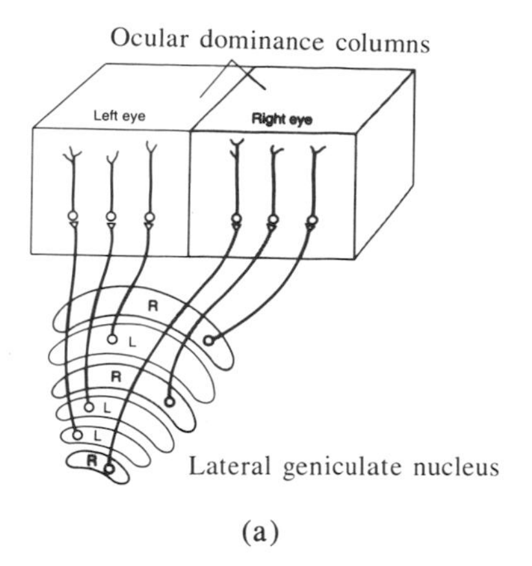

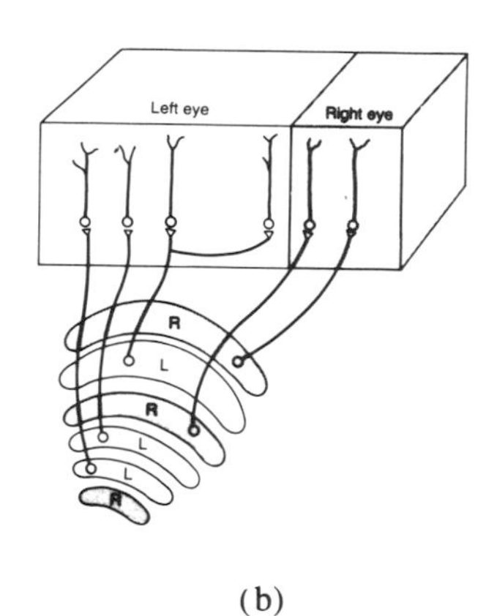

(a) (b)

Figure 7.10 How lack of vision in one eye might affect development of the ocular dominance columns. (a) Normal. Ocular dominance columns are normally equal in size for each eye. (b) Right eye closed. Without vision in the right eye, the columns devoted to the right eye become narrow compared to those of the left eye. According to the hypothesis illustrated here, deprivation of one eye changes the normal balance between eyes. The geniculate cells receiving input from the nonfunctional (right) eye regress and lose some of their connections with cortical cells, whereas the geniculate cells receiving input from the left eye sprout and connect to cortical cells previously occupied by geniculate neurons from the right eye. From *Principles of Neural Science,* 3rd ed. (p. 953) by E. R. Kandel, J. H. Schwartz, and T. M. Jessell, 1991, Norwalk, CT: Appleton & Lange. Copyright 1991 by Appleton & Lange. Reprinted by permission.

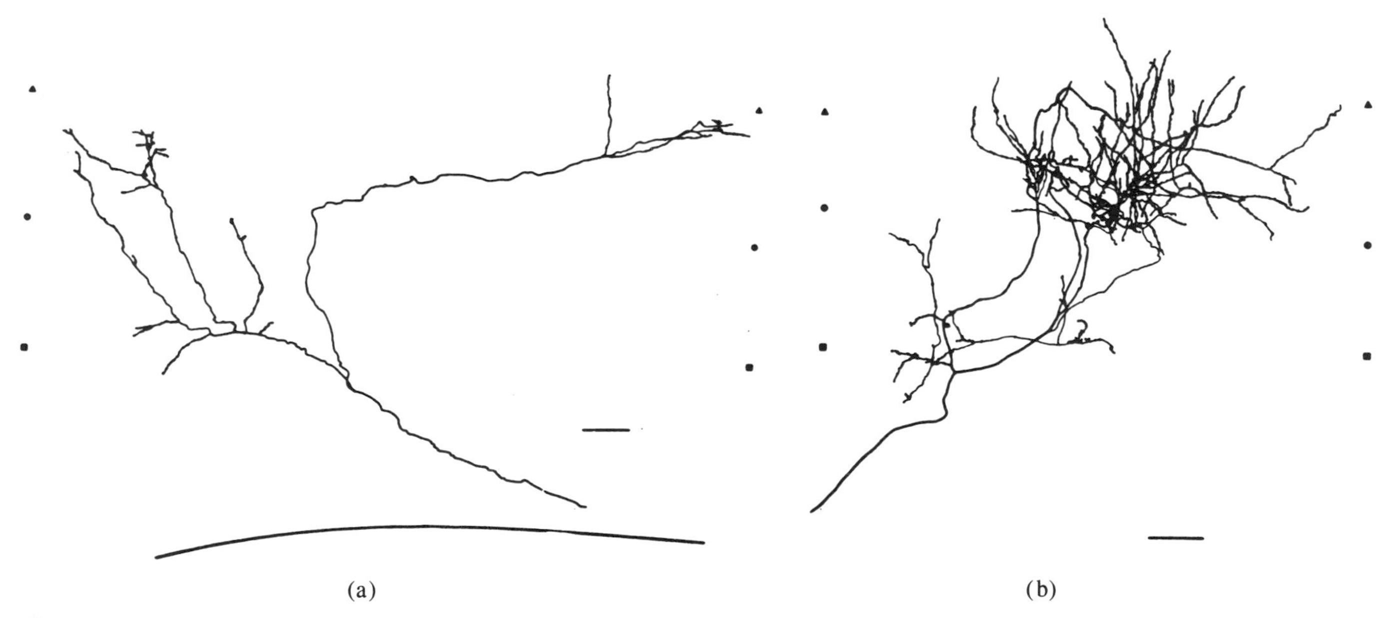

(a) (b)

Figure 7.11 Neuronal activity during early development alters the size and pattern of axonal branching of developing thalamocortical somatosensory fibers. (a) Normal adult animal. Size and pattern of terminal branching from region in somatosensory cortex where the mystacial vibrassae are represented. The medial to lateral extent of the layer IV axonal branching is 1,500 μm. The bottom line represents the white matter of the internal capsule. Triangles indicate the border of layers III and IV. Circles indicate the border of layers IV and V. Squares indicate the border of layers V and VI. Scale line = 100 μm. (b) Neuronal activity-deprived animal. At birth, the infraorbital nerve was cut, depriving the developing animal of sensory neural signals from the face region. In the activity-deprived animal at adulthood, the size and pattern of terminal branching is substantially altered (compare to normal size and pattern in (a)). The medial to lateral extent of the layer IV plexus of this arbor in the activity-deprived animal is 430 μm. Details as in (a). From "Terminal Arbors of Axons Projecting to the Somatosensory Cortex of the Adult Rat . . ." by K. F. Jensen and H. P. Killackey, 1987, *The Journal of Neuroscience, 7,* pp. 3548, 3550. Copyright 1987 by Society for Neuroscience. Reprinted by permission.

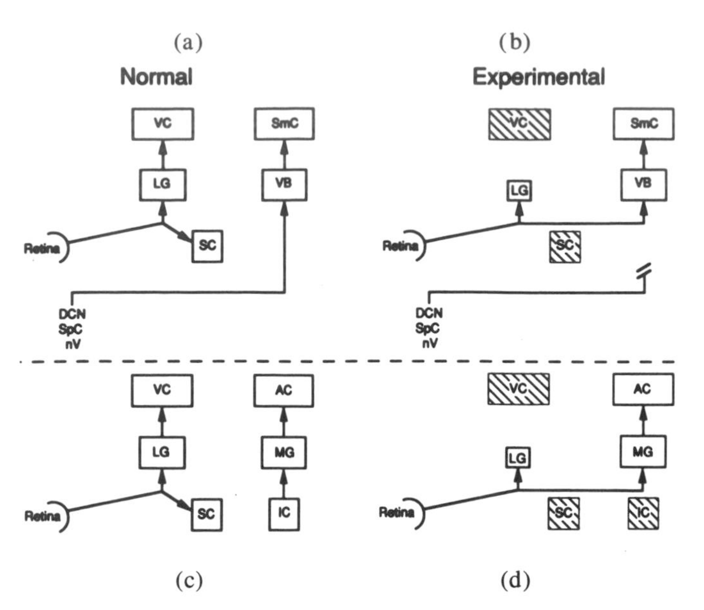

Figure 7.12 Aberrant routing of visual input into somatosensory and auditory cortex. (a) In normal hamsters, the retina projects to the primary visual thalamic nucleus, the lateral geniculate nucleus (LG), and the superior colliculus (SC). The LG relays visual information to the visual cortex (VC). Somatosensory information is sent from the dorsal column nuclei (DCN), spinal cord (SpC), and trigeminal nuclei (nV) to the primary somatosensory thalamic nuclei, termed the ventrobasal complex (VB), which in turn relays it to the somatosensory cortex (SmC).

(b) The retina can be induced to project to VB by reducing its normal targets (by removing at birth the SC and the VC, which results in atrophy of the LG) and making terminal space available in the VB (by removing at birth its normal input). Under these conditions, SmC receives visual input from VB.

(c) In normal ferrets, the retina projects to the LG and the SC. The LG projects to several visual cortical areas. The primary auditory thalamic nucleus, the medial geniculate (MG), receives auditory information from the inferior colliculus (IC) and relays it to the auditory cortex (AC).

(d) The retina can be induced to project to MG by a strategy similar to the one described above; retinal targets are reduced (by removing the SC and visual cortical areas 17 and 18, which results in atrophy of the LG) and terminal space is made available in MG (by removing IC). Under these conditions, AC receives visual input from MG. From "Do Cortical Areas Emerge from a Protocortex?" by D. D. M. O'Leary, 1989, *Trends in Neuroscience, 12,* p. 401. Copyright 1989 by Elsevier Trends Journals. Adapted from Frost and Metin, 1985; Sur, Garraghty, and Roe, 1988. Reprinted by permission.

Thus, abnormal competition between and abnormal correlated activity within undamaged as well as damaged neural networks can drive the abnormal elimination of some connections and neural elements (e.g., remote loss) and the abnormal selective stabilization of others (e.g., aberrant connections retained or created) (Hockfield & Kalb, 1993; O'Leary & Koester, 1993; Stryker, 1990; Wall, 1988). To paraphrase a colloquialism, during abnormal development, "Neurons that abnormally fire together, abnormally wire together," or "Neurons that abnormally fail to fire together, abnormally fail to wire together," and so on.

Second, neural loss in a particular location will trigger loss in additional locations, including those that are remote from the primary location. For instance, Rosenzweig and colleagues (1984) have shown in rats that occipital damage leads to remote loss in many locations, even those as removed as motor cortex (see Figure 7.13). The amount of primary loss affects the amount of remote loss, and remote loss increases with time across development as shown in the figure. Furthermore, remote loss is inevitable even when the lesioned animal is placed in an enriched environment; that is, learning and enrichment do not seem to protect the lesioned developing animal from the debilitating effects of remote loss. Some neural structures, such as motor and somatosensory cortex, appear to be especially vulnerable to remote loss; others, such as the cerebellum, seem to be resistant.

Presumably, such effects operate in developing humans, but there is an absence of research on this phenomenon. One possible example comes from autism. Autopsy evidence indicates that primary damage in infantile autism involves massive loss of Purkinje neurons throughout the posterior cerebellar vermis and hemispheres, probably during fetal development and many MR studies have confirmed hypoplasia in these regions (see Table 7.1). Autopsy studies have found no evidence of primary damage in cerebral cortex, but MR evidence shows what could potentially be

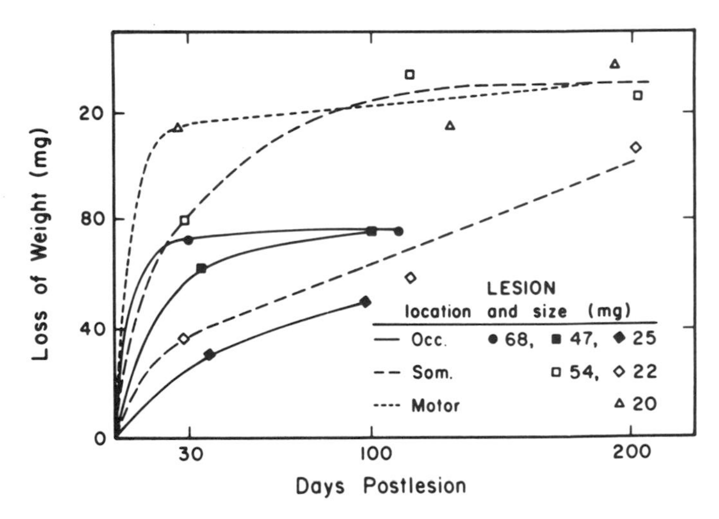

Figure 7.13 Loss of weight in the total brain outside of the region in which a lesion had been made.

Bilateral lesions of various sizes were made in motor (Motor), somatosensory (Som.), or occipital (Occ.) areas of the cerebral cortex. Groups of animals were sacrificed after various postlesion durations, approximately 30, 100, or 200 days. Each point is based on at least nine lesion versus control pairs of rats. From "Multiple Effects of Lesions on Brain Structure in Young Rats" by M. R. Rosenzweig, E. L. Bennett, and M. Alberti, 1984, in S. Finger & C. R. Almli (Eds.), *Early Brain Damage: Vol. 2. Neurology and Behavior* (p. 59), Orlando, FL: Academic Press. Copyright 1984 by Academic Press. Reprinted by permission.

TABLE 7.1 Quantitative MR and Autopsy Studies of the Cerebellum in Infantile Autism

Studies Finding Abnormalities	Studies Finding No Abnormalities
Williams et al., 1989 (autopsy)	Garber et al., 1989 (MR)
Bauman & Kemper, 1985 (autopsy)	Garber et al., 1992 (MR)
Bauman & Kemper, 1986 (autopsy)	Holttum et al., 1992 (MR)
Ritvo et al., 1986 (autopsy)	
Gaffney et al., 1987 (MR)	
Courchesne et al., 1988 (MR)	
Murakami et al., 1989 (MR)	
Bauman & Kemper, 1990 (autopsy)	
Ciesielski et al., 1990 (autopsy)	
Arin et al., 1991 (autopsy)	
Bauman, 1991 (autopsy)	
Piven et al., 1992 (MR)[a]	
Kleinmen et al., 1992 (MR)[a]	
Courchesne, Saitoh, Yeung-Courchesne, Press et al., 1994 (MR)	
Saitoh et al., 1994 (MR)	
Hashimoto et al., in press (MR)	

[a]Evidence based on re-analysis of study data by Courchesne, Townsend, and Saitoh 1994.

a remote loss effect: in 43% of autistic adolescents and young adults, there is atrophy of posterior parietal, somatosensory, and motor cortex (Courchesne, Press, & Yeung-Courchesne, 1993). Behavioral and neurophysiological evidence confirms that those patients with this MR abnormality have associated functional impairment of spatial attention (Townsend, 1992; Townsend & Courchesne, 1994; submitted for publication; Townsend, Courchesne, & Egaas, 1992; see below); PET studies have also reported abnormal metabolic findings in parietal cortex in autistic patients (Horwitz, Rumsey, Grady, & Rapoport, 1988).

Third, neural abnormality in a particular location can alter the normal course of regressive events at other locations.

Normal development in a vertebrate nervous system is marked by an initial phase of overproduction of neural elements followed by a regressive phase wherein excess elements are eliminated (see Figures 7.1 and 7.2) (Cowan et al., 1984; Edelman, 1987; Purves, 1988; Rakic, Bourgeois, Eckenhoff, Zecevic, & Goldman-Rakic, 1986). Prenatally, there is an overproliferation of neurons (roughly double the number seen in the normal adult brain); this phase is followed by the death of excessive neurons and this continues until about age 2. Beginning prenatally, there is an exuberant production of axon collaterals to many more destinations than is normal for the adult brain; this phase is followed by the gradual elimination of excess axon collaterals. There is also an exuberant production of synapses, beginning prenatally; peak numbers are reached in young children, who have nearly double the number seen in adults (Huttenlocher, 1979). The gradual pruning of excessive synapses continues throughout childhood and preadolescence.

Developmental changes in cerebral functioning can be studied more directly with PET, which measures the rate of cerebral glucose metabolism. Consistent with neurobiological and microscopic evidence, the PET data closely correspond, following a similar developmental course. Cortical metabolic values of neonates are 30% lower than those of adults; they then increase to exceed adult values by the age of 2–3, presumably reflecting the increased metabolic activity necessary to support the many additional synaptic contacts. These PET values remain high until about the age of 10, at which time the rate gradually declines to reach adult levels around the age of 16–18 (Chugani, Phelps, & Mazziota, 1987; Chugani & Phelps, 1991) (see Figure 7.14).

Regressive events are thought to be the result of competitive interactions, between neurons or their processes, for some required resource (e.g., trophic factor, electrical stimulation) that is in limited supply (see Figures 7.3 and 7.4). When a neuron or its processes are deprived of this resource, the size of the axonal and dendritic arbors is reduced, processes are withdrawn from the regions of competition, or the cell degenerates (Changeux & Danchin, 1976; Rakic, 1984). Through a process of competitive selective (i.e., not random) elimination, connections are lost, producing functionally segregated cortical areas. For example, Rakic (1981, 1988) has shown that ocular dominance columns in the LGN, which are groups of cells that selectively respond to one eye or the other, are primarily formed by the pruning of axon collaterals from the inappropriate eye.

Virtually every neural target site receives input from two or more sources. When lesions or other kinds of disrupting perturbations reduce or remove one or more sources of neural activity to a target site, remaining inputs experience less competition for trophic resources at the target site. With less competition and more trophic resources available, such remaining functional neural inputs may undergo less regression of connectivity, and may instead retain or develop an abnormally large domain of connectivity at the target site (see Figure 7.9). For example, when neural projections from the retina of one eye are disrupted during embryonic development, the remaining eye continues, after birth, to maintain many retinal projections to inappropriate columns of cells in the LGN that would normally have been filled by axon terminals from the damaged eye (Rakic, 1981). Also, as mentioned above, in kittens deprived of visual input through one eye but not the other, Y-type geniculocortical axons from the non-deprived eye have unusually expanded

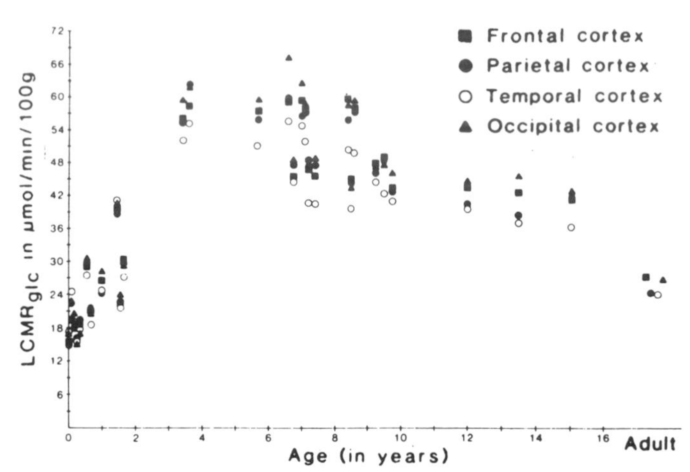

Figure 7.14 Absolute values of local cerebral glucose (ICMR-Glc) for frontal, parietal, temporal, and occipital regions, plotted as a function of age for 29 infants and children and corresponding adult values.

In the infants and children, points indicate individual values; in adults points are mean values of 7 subjects. Adapted from Chugani, Phelps, and Mazziotta, 1987. Reprinted by permission.

axonal arbors and have more synapses per bouton than normal (Friedlander et al., 1991) (see Figure 7.9).

Fourth, early developmental abnormalities lead to aberrant neural circuitry and often to permanent behavioral abnormalities. For example, in rats, lesions of the superior colliculus can prompt incoming axons from the retina to make permanent connections with several subcortical sites they would normally either avoid or with which they would make only temporary connection (Schneider, 1979). Unilateral lesions of the cerebellar dentate nucleus during early development can lead to a variety of abnormal neural connections: those made by cerebral cortical axons that project to brain stem sites as well as those made by axons from the undamaged side of the cerebellum (Gramsbergen & Ijkema-Paassen, 1984) (see Figure 7.15). In both examples, the time of damage determines the final details of the aberrant circuit, and this in turn determines whether visually guided behavior (Schneider, 1979) or motor behavior (Gramsbergen & Ijkema-Paassen, 1984) is permanently abnormal. In rodents that suffer Purkinje neuron loss during early stages of development, basket, stellate, and granule neurons are reduced in number, and their connections with the few remaining Purkinje neurons are abnormal (Altman, 1982). Additionally, climbing fibers that normally follow the *one climbing fiber-one Purkinje neuron* rule, break that rule by making multiple connections (see Figure 7.16). It is likely that, without competing Purkinje input to the deep cerebellar nuclei, the excitatory climbing, mossy, and aminergic fibers will make an abnormally excessive number of connections with the spontaneously excitatory deep cerebellar neurons. Mutant mice (e.g., nervous mice) that undergo early Purkinje neuron loss show permanent deficits in emotional and exploratory behavior (Sidman & Green, 1970).

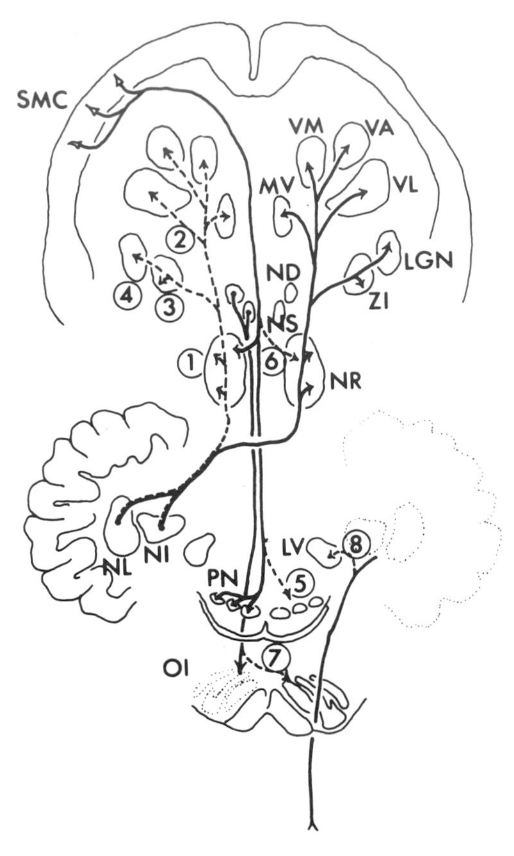

Figure 7.15 Aberrant fiber connections found after cerebellar hemispherectomy up to the 10th day of life in rats.

Dotted lines = removed cerebellar hemisphere (the inferior olivary complex contralateral to the cerebellar lesion degenerates secondarily). *Continuous lines* = normally occurring projections. *Discontinuous lines* = aberrant projections. Numbers mark additional sites of aberrant connections. LGN: n. geniculate lateralis; LV: n. vestibularis lateralis; MV: n. medialis ventralis thalami; ND: n. of Darkschewitsch; NI: n. interpositus cerebelli; NL: n. lateralis cerebelli; NR: n. ruber; NS: n. subparafascicularis; OI: inferior olivary complex; PN: pontine nuclei; VA: n. ventralis anterior thalami; VL: n. ventralis lateris thalami; VM: n. ventralis medialis thalami; ZI: zona incerta. From "Cerebellar Hemispherectomy at Young Ages in Rats" by A. Gramsbergen and J. Ijkema-Paassen, 1984, in J. R. Bloedd, J. Dichgans, and W. Precht (Eds.), *Cerebellar Functions* (p. 165), New York: Springer-Verlag. Copyright 1984 by Springer-Verlag. Reprinted by permission.

Fifth, functional or structural abnormalities should be greatest following abnormal perturbations in systems with the greatest divergent and convergent neural connectivity; the inverse should also be true. This follows from the idea that spontaneous and evoked neural activity selectively stabilizes some neural connections rather than others and leads to the normal parcellation of neural systems (e.g., protocortex) into specific structural and functional units (O'Leary, 1989). Killackey (1990) proposed that labeled line systems—for instance, sensory systems

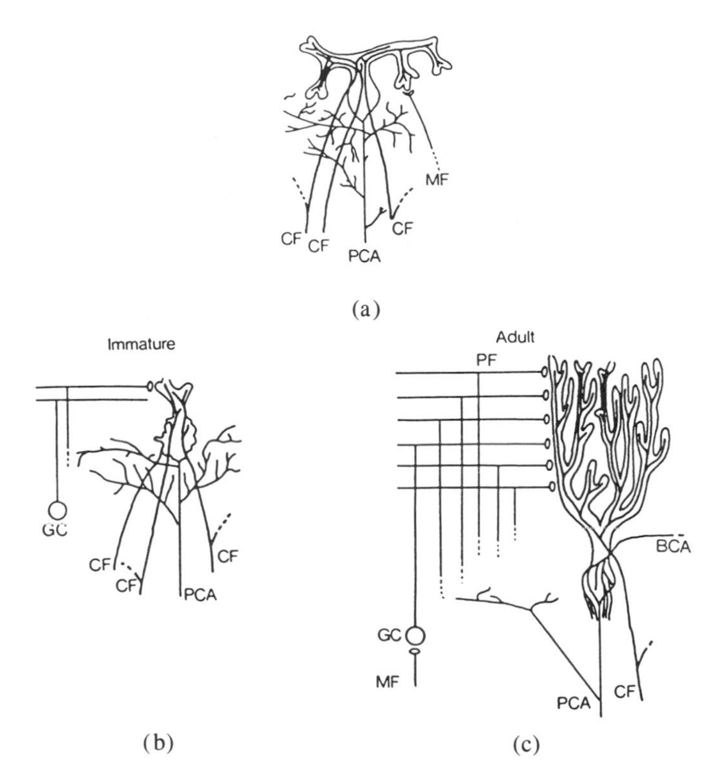

Figure 7.16 In normal immature mice, each Purkinje cell is contacted by many climbing fibers (panel b), but in the normal adult, each Purkinje cell is contacted by only a single climbing fiber (panel c). In mutant or X-irradiated mice, regression of immature neural circuitry does not occur, and aberrant circuitry and cell features are retained into adulthood (panel a). GC: granule cells; CF: climbing fibers; PCA: Purkinje cell axon; MF: Mossy fibers; BCA: basket cell axon. From "Regression of Functional Synapses in the Immature Mammalian Cerebellum" by F. Crepel, 1982, *Trends in Neuroscience, 5,* pp. 267–268. Copyright 1982 by Elsevier Trends Journals. Reprinted by permission.

and the cerebellum—are critical in this selective specification process in cerebral cortex. In dyslexia, neural pathology exists within only a single subset of the labeled line sensory systems—the thalamic relay station for low-frequency visual and auditory information (Galaburda & Eidelberg, 1982; Galaburda, Rosen, & Sherman, 1985; Galaburda, Sherman, Rosen, Aboitiz, & Geschwind, 1985; Livingstone, Rosen, Drislane, & Galaburda, 1991); relatively limited functional abnormality would therefore be predicted. This possibility is discussed in detail below.

In contrast, much more extensive functional abnormality would be predicted in autism because neural pathology exists throughout the entire posterior cerebellum, which is a structure with highly divergent and convergent connectivity. It has input from and output to all major regions of the human central nervous system, including the spinal cord, brain stem, diencephalon, limbic system, and cerebral cortex (Ghez, 1991; Ito, 1984). Specific structures and functional systems or operations affected by or sending input to the posterior cerebellum include arousal and attention systems; hippocampal memory systems; serotonergic, noradrenergic, and dopaminergic systems; opiate system; hypothalamic nuclei; speech systems; semantic association operations; visual, auditory, and somatosensory activity at brain stem, thalamic, and cortical levels; brain stem autonomic systems; vestibular system; classical conditioning operations; and motor planning and execution systems.

How might adverse functional effects come about in autism? Purkinje cells are the principal inhibitory control for the spontaneous excitatory output of the cerebellum. So, rather than the normal temporally precise oscillatory output from the cerebellum, which smoothly modulates neural activity (Llinas, 1988), their loss should result in uncontrolled excitatory output to the wide range of systems to which it projects. [Such hypothesized patches of aberrant excitation may be responsible for the randomly distributed patches of abnormally high levels of cortical metabolic activity that have actually been detected in some PET studies of autism (Horwitz et al., 1988)].

Sixth, under favorable conditions, following damage at one location, functions may be relocated to a neighboring undamaged site. For example, in rat pups, a focal lesion in somatosensory cortex will cause the developing representational maps of the facial vibrissae to be relocated to neighboring nondamaged cortex, but only if the lesion occurs on or before postnatal day 10 (Seo & Ito, 1987) (see Figure 7.17). After this date, similar lesions result in defects within the representational map. These results show that (a) even for primary sensory cortex, organizational patterns are not rigidly prefixed, and (b) early developmental

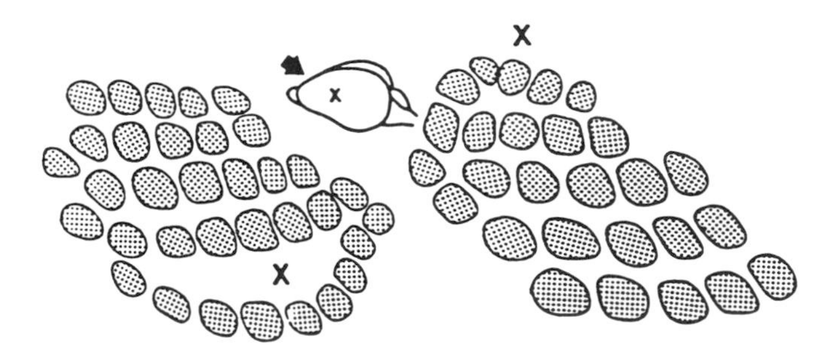

Figure 7.17 Relocation of cortical sensory maps following very early postnatal cortical lesions. In the rat, the pattern of different facial vibrissae is represented in the cortex as a "map" with a highly characteristic pattern of rows and columns of "barrels" (stippled circles), each reflecting a vibrissal location on the face. A focal lesion in the vicinity of the vibrissae cortical sensory map in rat pups (X on brain surface, center) causes developing barrels to avoid the lesioned site. As a result, lesions (X) are subsequently found between rows in the vibrissae map (left), or displaced to the periphery of the vibrissae map (right). These avoidance changes occur if lesions are made before postnatal day 10, but do not occur with later lesions. These findings suggest that the future pattern of cluster locations is not prefixed during the first several postnatal days. From "Reorganization of Rat Vibrissa Barrelfield as Studied by Cortical Lesioning on Different Post-Natal Days" by M. L. Seo and M. Ito, 1987, *Experimental Brain Research, 65,* p. 256. Copyright 1987 by Springer-Verlag GmbH & Co. KG. Reprinted by permission.

perturbations can cause structural and functional respecification of cortex. It is unknown how such relocations affect other representations, particularly those that would otherwise have occurred in the cortical locations taken over by vibrissal maps.

THE NEURODEVELOPMENTAL APPROACH: CONSIDERATIONS

General

Because abnormal development is a self-mis-organizing process, developmental perturbations can act through a variety of mechanisms (remote loss, formation of aberrant connections, and so on) to trigger a complex chain of abnormal structural and/or functional transformations. Potentially, even a single perturbation can reverberate outward to affect multiple neural structures and functions across time. Not surprisingly then, very different perturbations may eventually produce abnormal neural configurations that overlap to some degree in structure or function. Thus, diverse pathogenic processes may lead to convergent, overlapping neurobehavioral end symptoms. The converse is also true: similar pathogenic processes may lead to some degree of divergence and nonoverlapping of end symptoms (see Figure 7.18).

The causal chain of transformations is, therefore, extremely difficult to determine in developmental disorders. In fact, the literature shows that knowledge of structure or function underlying end symptoms has not revealed for any developmental psychopathology the causal chain of events that led to those final features. That is, there is no example of disorder in which the "inverse" solution approach has demonstrated the causal chain of transformations from overt behavioral symptoms to biologic origins. Unfortunately, this approach is traditionally the most common one in research on developmental psychopathologies. The idea that the inverse solution from behavioral symptoms to biologic origins of developmental psychopathologies is possible is the holy grail of neuropsychiatry—it may exist, but no one has ever seen it.

Nonetheless, knowledge of how the end abnormal neural network functions can enhance the chances of early and accurate diagnosis and effective treatment of end symptoms. Also, much fundamental information about the brain basis of behavior may be gleaned in this way.

The literature also demonstrates that, even when there is knowledge of the precise precipitating defect, there remains a very incomplete understanding of how neurobehavioral end symptoms came about. For instance, at the present time, for all cognitive and psychiatric developmental disorders in which a specific genetic defect has been conclusively identified (e.g., Fragile X, Lesch-Nyhan syndrome, PKU, Williams syndrome), the causal chain of transformations linking the gene defect to neurobehavioral end symptoms typically remains incomplete. At best, of the multiple paths that certainly must link the gene defect to the end symptoms in each disorder, only sketchy outlines or guesses are available for a few. This lack of full understanding of these extremely complex human neurogenetic disorders should

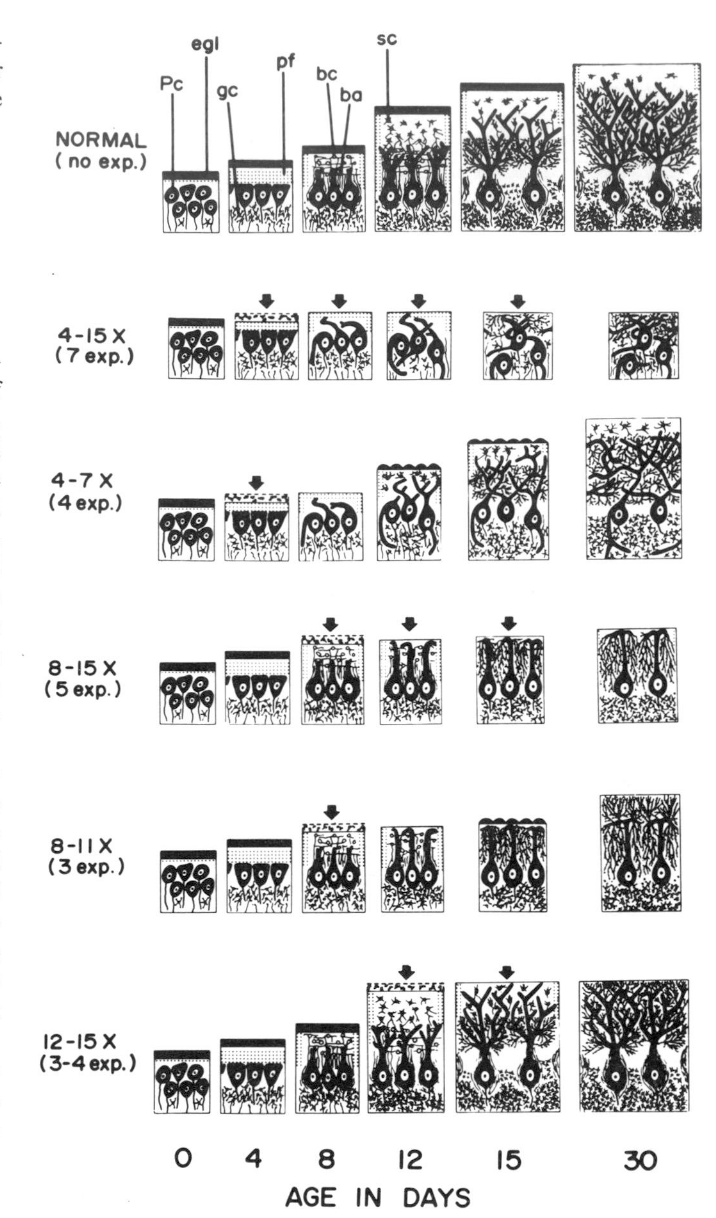

Figure 7.18 Schematic summary of the stages and time course of Purkinje cell dendritic development in normal rats (top row) and in rats X-irradiated between the postnatal days, and the number of X-ray exposures specified in the legend column on the left.

Arrows indicate X-irradiation; fragmented EGL symbolizes its destruction by irradiation; absence of EGL indicates its failure to recover after irradiation or its natural dissolution; corrugated EGL symbolizes its recovery after irradiation. ba: basket cell axons; bc: basket cell bodies; egl: external germinal layer; exp: exposure; gc: granule cells; Pc: Purkinje cells; pf: parallel fibers; sc: stellate cells. From "Morphological Development of the Rat Cerebellum and Some of Its Mechanisms" by J. Altman, 1982, in S. L. Palay and V. Chan-Palay (Eds.), *The Cerebellum—New Vistas* (p. 38), Heidelberg, Germany: Springer-Verlag. Copyright 1982 by Springer-Verlag GmbH & Co. KG. Reprinted by permission.

not be surprising; developmental causal chains for simple neurogenetic disorders in lower mammals (e.g., neurogenetic mechanisms controlling the expression of vibrissal maps in mice; Welker & Van der Loos, 1986) are often incompletely understood.

Specific

Remediation and Treatment

The end product of abnormal neural development in many cases is a relatively fixed system having distinctly abnormal neurocomputational properties. In attempting to provide remedial intervention to correct the behavioral consequences of these abnormalities, one must take into consideration the principles described herein.

First, after abnormal development is complete, treatment always or correction of primary precipitating events or defects may not be possible. In most cases, the damage already has been done to the nervous system during early development and cannot be undone through later intervention. After abnormal neural configurations have developed, it is likely to be beyond current technology to deconstruct and then reconfigure a complex neural network. To illustrate, if the damage suffered by a tree during its early development has produced a malformed trunk, one cannot reverse the process and straighten the trunk. The outcome is the result of changes that occurred during development, and these usually cannot be corrected after growth has occurred.

Second, after abnormal development is complete, even successful treatment of the primary precipitating defect may not be effective in correcting many end symptoms. For example, a rare metabolic disorder called cystinosis is a genetic defect that affects the ability of cells to metabolize cystine. Intracellular accumulation of cystine crystals eventually causes widespread damage to the kidney, thyroid gland, cornea, and CNS, but the addition of a food supplement, cysteamine, which the affected individuals are unable to synthesize in their own bodies, can normalize cystine metabolization. Unfortunately, even children who have received cysteamine diet supplements since birth continue to evidence mental and physical characteristics such as small physical stature and poor visual memory skills, which are commonly associated with the untreated condition (Gahl, Renlund, & Thoene, 1989; Trauner, Chase, Scheller, Katz, & Schneider, 1988). PKU is another vivid example (see below). Dietary restrictions do not restore a PKU child to normal.

Third, when end symptoms can be treated, such successes are usually not the result of changes that correct the primary precipitating defect. In many cases, the end symptoms are associated with behavioral syndromes that represent another level of complexity in CNS functioning. The behavioral problems can often be remediated, but this treatment in no way corrects the underlying developmental pathology. For example, developmental dyslexia can be remediated through intensive individual tutoring. A recent study showed that, compared to a study skills control group, dyslexic children over a 10-week summer period, responded to several different methods of intervention and improved their reading skills (Lovett, Ransby, Hardwick, Johns, & Donaldson, 1989). Many neuropsychologically based remediation procedures, such as perceptual motor training, movement therapies, ocular-motor exercises, antihistamine drugs, or use of colored lenses, have been proposed as interventions that would correct the underlying primary defect. However, most of these ideas are based on poorly substantiated or incorrect theories about the developmental pathology associated with dyslexia, and these treatment programs usually fail to demonstrate any significant reading improvement under well-controlled experimental conditions. A complete understanding of the neurobiological etiology of dyslexia still may provide little concrete guidance about how to best teach reading to dyslexic children, and certainly a successful reading remediation program reveals little about the neurobiology of the disorder.

Fourth, just because treatment has been effective for one end symptom does not mean it will be effective in the remediation of other symptoms as well. If, as is almost always the case, successful treatment of an end symptom does not correct the underlying cause of a disorder, then this treatment will not necessarily be effective in the remediation of other end symptoms.

Fifth, treatment effectiveness principally reveals the malleability of the underlying mechanisms that control end symptoms, but not necessarily the primary precipitating events or defects. Some developmental disorders have end symptoms that are easier to treat than others; for example, teaching dyslexic children to read is much easier than correcting the social and emotional problems associated with autism. Important neurobiological differences between these two disorders include what parts of the nervous system have been affected, what subsequent CNS regions are further disrupted during development as a result of inadequate stimulation from these regions of primary abnormality, and what cognitive functions depend on these regions for normal development. Successful treatment of end symptoms rarely has any impact on these neurological abnormalities, but often depends on the neurological specificity of the end symptom (that is, how many different ways the CNS can accomplish the same behavior using different anatomical regions and functional pathways) and on the plasticity of other cortical areas to adapt and subsume these functions. Do not confuse the cause with the treatment. Taking aspirin, drinking 12 glasses of water a day, and getting 12 hours of sleep may improve the symptoms of a cold, but no one would suggest that colds can be prevented by these treatments.

Behavioral End Symptoms

In the study of behaviorally defined pathology, it is not necessarily the behavioral end symptoms that initially guide the search for neurodevelopmental origins of the disorder. The manner in which behavioral symptoms are used to define groups and subgroups of a disorder will critically affect the ability to discover the underpinnings of that disorder.

First, the idea of a "spectrum" of disorder may be behaviorally descriptive but will not necessarily be biologically correct. Appearances can be deceptive; qualitatively or quantitatively similar neurobehavioral phenotypes may have entirely different biological bases. For example, 40 years ago, senile dementia was characterized by many as a spectrum disorder, but we now know that very different biologic defects can result in very similar behavioral symptoms of dementia. In fact, dementia can be caused by more than 60 disorders (Katzman, 1986) with widely disparate underlying pathologies (Joynt & Shoulson, 1985). Other mental disorders that have been treated as spectrum disorders include autism and schizophrenia. Before Kanner (1943) identified autism as a separate entity, it is likely that some would have been autistic children diagnosed as childhood schizophrenics. In DSM-II (1968), infantile autism was classified as "schizophrenia, childhood type." Subsequent classification systems (DSM-III, 1980; DSM-III-R, 1987; DSM-IV, 1994) delineate autism and schizophrenia as distinct and separate entities, but there are still a few who maintain that there may be at least a subgroup of autism that is actually early onset schizophrenia. Autism and schizophrenia are heterogeneous disorders with heterogeneous etiologies, but there is no evidence of a common underlying biologic base.

Second, inclusion, into a single group, of all individuals who fall within a broad spectrum of a disorder will not likely lead to detection of underlying neurobehavioral abnormalities. If patients representing multiple diagnostic syndromes are combined into a single study group, the true and different biologic abnormalities underlying each will be masked. For example, patients grouped together on the basis of dementia or memory loss, (general symptoms occurring in diverse disorders) would be likely to show functional and structural abnormalities associated with a wide variety of brain sites (e.g., hippocampus, frontal cortex, basal ganglia), and an equally diverse set of etiologies (e.g., head trauma, genetic abnormalities, vascular disease).

Third, to optimize the possibility of uncovering underlying neurobehavioral abnormalities in complex disorders, patients should be grouped carefully on the basis of complex behavioral patterns of pathognomonic and normal features. Homogeneity of diagnostic groups is of crucial importance in the search for neurodevelopmental origins, but that homogeneity must be based on critical defining features that are specific to the disorder in question. If progress is to be made toward uncovering the true origins of a disorder, the patterns of characteristics by which a subject group is formed should serve to set that group apart from other syndromes. When patients are diagnosed and grouped carefully, consistent associations between a disorder and its structural or functional underpinnings may begin to emerge. For example, cerebellar abnormalities involving 240 autistic cases have now been found in 16 autopsy and quantitative MR reports from 9 different laboratories (review Courchesne, Townsend, & Saitoh, 1994 and Table 7.1). Diagnostic groupings of patients with complex disorders like developmental psychopathologies will be altered as knowledge about the disorders and their origins advances. The expectation should always be that further research will uncover additional distinctive features that may be used to refine groupings. For example, data from 4 separate MR studies involving 78 autistic patients were recently reexamined, and mean anatomical measurements of patients and control subjects were found to be quite similar despite small differences in measurement methodology (Courchesne, Townsend, & Saitoh, 1994). Results showed that, in each of the 4 studies, the majority of patients (84–92%) displayed hypoplasia of vermal lobules VI-VII, and the rest comprised a subgroup (8–16%) displaying vermal hyperplasia. The hyperplastic subgroup could prove to have a different etiology and should be further examined for associated behavioral traits that further distinguish them from other autistic patients.

Biological End Symptoms

First, similar neurobehavioral phenotypes do not necessarily imply similar pathogenic events. For example, individuals with dementia do not all have the same pathogenic origins. In the strict sense of the term, there is not a "spectrum" (a *continuous* sequence) of dementias. There are now known to be distinctly different pathogenic mechanisms and neural substrates for "dementia." Even within a "single" type, Alzheimer's dementia, there now is evidence of heterogeneous mechanisms that lead to a final similar phenotype (see above). In developmental psychopathology, the idea of a spectrum of disorder (e.g., "autism spectrum disorder") is popular among some practitioners. However, as with dementia, it seems likely that more accurate, biologically based clusters will eventually emerge from research, and that the utility of the behaviorally based spectrum concept will become obsolete. To optimize prevention or treatment, diagnostic and biologic precision in distinguishing different pathogenic types must be a central goal.

A corollary is that overlapping structural or functional abnormalities may (via the effects of abnormal activity, remote loss, aberrant connections, and so on) result from different types or sites of pathogenic events. A simple example is volume loss in motor cortex, which may follow lesions of either visual or somatosensory cortex.

Second, functional abnormalities do not necessarily mark the type and time of pathogenic perturbations. Therefore, functional abnormalities should be considered phenotypic end products of a cascade of reactions and transformations until proven otherwise. Such abnormalities are nearly always nonspecific. For example, a variety of metabolic (e.g., PET, MR spectroscopy), neurophysiologic (e.g., EEG, ERP), and behavioral abnormalities indicative of frontal lobe dysfunction have been reported in a wide range of developmental and degenerative disorders (ADHD, schizophrenia, autism, Down syndrome, Alzheimer, and so on). No such functional abnormality has yet been proven to be part of the initial pathogenic steps in any disorder; none has revealed any information about the time of onset of pathogenesis; and none has proven to be disorder-specific. A similar absence of pathogenic information holds for a host of other neurobiological and neurobehavioral abnormalities reported in nearly all neuropsychiatric disorders. *The claim that a functional abnormality is at the point from which pathogenic perturbations emanated must be experimentally substantiated; otherwise, the abnormality should be assumed to be an end product (symptom).* When the claim is proven to be true, as in the case of abnormal phenylalanine levels (PKU), it can be key (see below).

Third, structural abnormalities do not necessarily mark the site or time of pathogenic perturbations. Therefore, structural abnormalities should also be considered phenotypic end products of a cascade of reactions and transformations until proven otherwise. As noted above, numerous experiments have amply demonstrated that structural abnormalities ranging from microscopic to macroscopic (e.g., abnormal dendritic arbors; remote loss; reduced neuron size and increased cell packing density; aberrant axon connections; reduced cortical volume) can mark the *end* result of a perturbation. For example, abnormal dendritic arbors and reduced volume in occipital cortex can result from abnormal retinal activity (Friedlander et al., 1991; see above), and, though it becomes abnormal in structure, is obviously not the site from which pathogenic perturbations emanated. The claim that a structural abnormality is at the point from which pathogenic perturbations emanated as opposed to an end product must be experimentally substantiated.

Fourth, abnormality in multiple structures or functions does not necessarily mean multiple points or types of initial pathogenic perturbations. Multiple abnormalities may come about either via a single site or type of defect whose effects reverberate outward to affect multiple structures and functions, or via multiple sites or types of defects.

THE NEURODEVELOPMENTAL APPROACH: CONCLUSIONS AND EXAMPLES

The study of human brain-behavior associations and of the etiological mechanisms underlying human neurobehavioral disorders is in a fledgling state. Little is known about the specific function of particular brain systems or of particular sequences of genetic material. Both must rely heavily on the use of abnormalities to establish knowledge of normal function, much as knowledge and principles of normal development have been largely derived from studies of abnormal systems. The validity of neurodevelopmental findings, therefore, depends critically on the precision and validity of the specification of the abnormal system. Psychopathological abnormalities are particularly challenging because these syndromes are complex and are behaviorally defined; some subjectivity unavoidably enters into the specification of defining abnormal features. The pathogenic mechanisms and subsequent abnormal developmental transformations will most likely be complex. Therefore, to discover the pathogenic bases of developmental psychopathologies, it is particularly important to employ approaches that optimize the opportunity for success.

To discover the origins of developmental psychopathologies, the most fruitful research approach aims to begin at the beginning—that is, with signs that, most likely, directly mark the earliest pathogenic perturbations. To find the basis of a disorder, as opposed to the basis of a particular neurobehavioral end symptom, means to find the *root cause* or *origin*—the etiology—of the disorder. Evidence that points to the when, where, or how of initial *precipitating* events or processes must be sought. Research evidence must be evaluated as to whether it provides such vital information.

How are such likely markers of early perturbations found? We start by describing the history behind the first time that a specific pathogenic defect was found for a developmental disorder involving "social failure."

The Early History of Phenylketonuria

Phenylketonuria (PKU) was discovered in 1934 by a Norwegian biochemist and physician, Dr. Asbjorn Folling, after a concerned and observant Norwegian mother brought her two mentally retarded children, ages 4 and 7, to his attention. At that time, such children were simply considered to be "social failures" and "mentally deficient" and were placed in institutions. Their mother, however, had noticed that both children had a "musty" odor that clung to them constantly and seemed to be associated with their urine. She had brought the children to numerous psychiatrists and other physicians, none of whom was able to provide for her any satisfactory diagnosis, or any explanation for the similarity in both siblings' apparent disorders.

Rather than focusing on an explanation for the psychiatric features of the children, Dr. Folling turned his attention to analyzing the children's urine specimens. He initially noted that a particular compound turned the urine green, rather than other colors usually associated with metabolic disorders. Through careful and creative biochemical assays, he was able to identify the core biochemical marker for this deficiency.

Since this somewhat serendipitous beginning, 50 years' research has led to a detailed understanding of the key genetic mechanisms that constitute the pathogenic bases of the disorder. The classic PKU defect is an absence of phenylalanine hydroxylase activity, the result of which is phenylalaninemia, an abnormal increase in blood phenylalanine concentrations. The result of this single abnormality is a cascade of biochemical, neuroanatomical, and neurobehavioral abnormalities (see Figure 7.19). As Blau (1979) wrote, "The importance of the phenylalanine hydroxylase system in human metabolism was not realized until it became apparent how serious its absence could be."

Because PKU has been characterized in detail at the molecular pathogenic level and at the neurobehavioral end symptom level, it is informative in many ways. First, diverse molecular genetic defects can produce comparable neurobehavioral end symptoms. Yet, knowing the precipitating defects have not resulted in an understanding of the chain of transformations that create the critical neurobehavioral end abnormalities. Second, a single abnormality (hyperphenylalaninemia) produces an enormous diversity of structural and functional defects throughout the brain. In retrospect, even great knowledge of the neurobehavioral features of the PKU child (e.g., PET, MR spectroscopy, ERP, autopsy, neuropsychological, and psychiatric data) might never have led to the determination that all defects were ultimately due to elevated levels of this single amino acid that is normally present and essential to life. That is, the triggering defect normally has no unique or specific role to play in the structural, functional, and developmental bases of the many systems (memory, perception, motor action, language, social, and so on) affected in the PKU child. Were it not for the detection of markers (abnormal urine odor and elevated levels of an amino acid that is essential and normally present) that are completely independent of the neurobiological abnormalities in PKU, the disorder would likely still be of unknown etiology. Third, early dietary treatment begun prior to the onset of the cascade of abnormal neurobiological changes can largely prevent them; but once the cascade of abnormal neural transformations has taken place, no treatment is corrective and detailed knowledge of the molecular cause offers no help.

Each of these lessons offered by PKU could also have been readily derived from any one of a number of other disorders for which much is known about the molecular pathogenic bases on the one hand, and the neurobehavioral end products on the other. For example, it appears that identification of a gene defect involved in Williams syndrome may be near at hand (Ewart et al.,

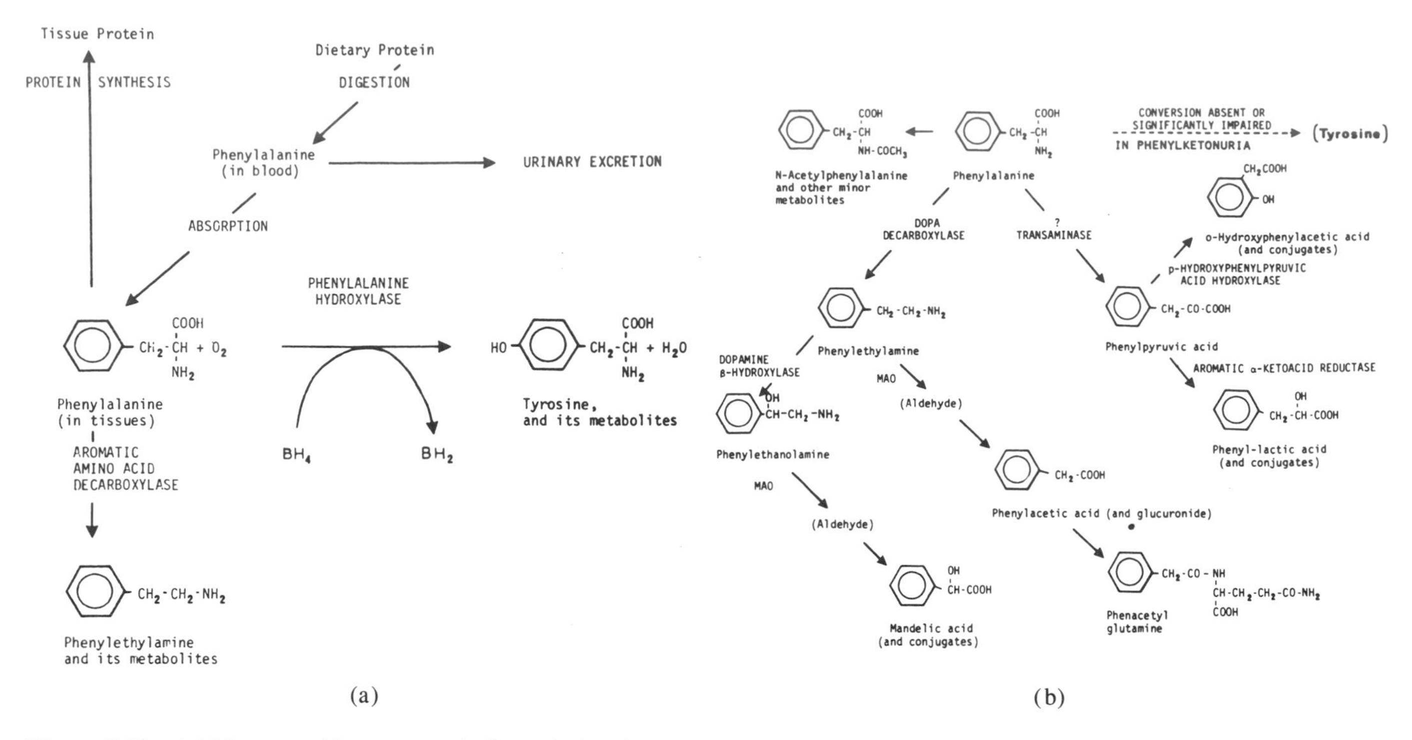

Figure 7.19 (a) The normal human metabolism of phenylalanine. (b) Metabolism of phenylalanine in states of hyperphenylalaninemia. From "Phenylalanine Hydroxylase Deficiency . . . " By K. Blau, 1979, in M. B. H. Youdim (Ed.), *Aromatic Amino Acid Hydroxylase and Mental Disease,* Chichester, England: John Wiley & Sons Ltd. Copyright 1979 by John Wiley & Sons Ltd. Reprinted by permission.

1993). Determination of this potential defect was via knowledge of a defect in a different gene (the elastin gene) that may well have nothing to do with the unique and fascinating social, language, and cognitive abnormalities manifested in Williams syndrome (Bellugi, Wang, & Jernigan, 1994).

As another example, the Lesch-Nyhan syndrome (LNS) (Lesch & Nyhan, 1964) is a disorder resulting from mutation in a single gene, the HPRT gene, that codes for hypoxanthine-guanine phosphoribosyltransferase, an enzyme involved in the recycling of purines (Jinnah, Gage, & Friedmann, 1990). As with PKU and Williams syndrome, behavioral symptomatology did not lead to the discovery of the gene defect. Newborns with LNS appear normal at birth, but by 3 to 6 months neurological features begin to appear and eventually include self-injurious behavior, hypotonia, extensor spasticity, dysarthria, choreoathetosis, opisthotonos, and mental retardation. Anatomical abnormalities have not been detected, in sharp contrast to PKU. However, the principal biochemical features resulting from this defect are known; a number of biochemical and transgenic animal models have been developed, and a number of hypotheses concerning neurobehavioral pathogenesis have been proposed and tested (Jinnah et al., 1990). Despite the seeming simplicity of the genetic and biochemical system involved, the relationship between the HPRT deficiency and the neurobehavioral end symptoms remains unknown. Indeed, mouse models with the identical gene defect show little evidence of the principal neurobehavioral symptoms characteristic of the human with LNS (Jinnah et al., 1990; Jinnah, 1992). In addition, despite detailed knowledge of the LNS genetic defect and consequent biochemical abnormalities, there is neither effective treatment nor corrective intervention.

The Current Status of Autism

Infantile autism was first identified as a disorder in 1943 by Leo Kanner. The characteristic features of the disorder described by Kanner form the core of today's diagnostic criteria. These features include a profound deficiency in social knowledge, affect, and communication, including imitation, turn-taking, representational play, and the ability to exchange experiences and emotions with others about topics of mutual interest (Kanner, 1943). Subsequent work has suggested that joint social attention, the developmental precursor of these complex communication skills, is also profoundly deficient in autism (Curcio, 1978; Landry & Loveland, 1988; Loveland & Landry, 1986; Mundy, Sigman, & Kasari, 1990; Mundy et al., 1986; Wetherby & Prutting, 1984). Although autism is defined as a disorder of social communication, there is increasing evidence that the core dysfunction may actually lie in attentional systems. Numerous behavioral, electrophysiological, and metabolic studies have suggested that autism involves attentional disturbance (Courchesne, 1987; Courchesne, Akshoomoff, & Townsend, 1990; Dawson & Lewy, 1987; Frith, 1989; Sigman, Ungerer, Mundy, & Sherman, 1987; Martineau, Garreau, Roux, & Lelord, 1987; Martineau et al., 1992; Schreibman & Lovaas,

1973). To date, there is little information on the etiology of autism.

Autism, like all other developmental disorders for which no clear biochemical or genetic marker has been identified, presents a formidable challenge. Researchers must attempt to identify patients who typify the disorder and then search for common abnormalities among them that may lead to the source of the disorder. Until there are biologic markers, however, these disorders must be behaviorally defined. One has only to examine the history of the classification process in schizophrenia to understand how the subjectivity inherent in forming homogeneous groups can affect the search for common abnormalities (Cancro, 1985). Diagnostic subjectivity is, of course, not the only obstacle. Because of complex biologic and environmental interactions, not only can a single biologic abnormality result in a variety of behavioral manifestations, but a variety of biologic abnormalities can also result in very similar behavioral patterns. In spite of these somewhat daunting hurdles, some important progress has been made.

Recent research and theorizing on the brain bases of infantile autism serve to illustrate one approach to understanding the mechanisms and the origins of a developmental psychopathology that is largely, and by necessity, driven from the top (specification of functional abnormalities in a well-defined group) with some key information from the bottom (anatomical abnormalities occurring early in development). The resulting model of autism rises not from a single serendipitous finding, as in PKU, but from an accumulation of evidence from a variety of studies conducted over more than two decades.

A Model

Courchesne and colleagues (1985, 1987, 1989; Courchesne, Akshoomoff, Townsend, & Saitoh, 1994; Courchesne, Chisum, & Townsend, 1994; Courchesne, Townsend, Akshoomoff, Saitoh et al., 1994; Courchesne, Townsend, Akshoomoff, Yeung-Courchesne et al., 1994) have suggested that, in autism, there is a cascade of abnormal development in which:

1. The loss of Purkinje cells in the posterior cerebellum causes failure of modulation of cerebellar output, allowing deep cerebellar nuclei to generate uncontrolled and potentially chaotic excitatory output to other parts of the brain.
2. Cerebellar connections to brain areas involved in attentional processes (e.g., reticular-activating system, posterior parietal cortex, dorsolateral prefrontal cortex, superior colliculus, cingulate gyrus, pulvinar) provide the means by which unmodulated cerebellar output produces attentional impairments that are analogous to cerebellar motor impairments (i.e., "attentional asynergia").
3. Unmodulated cerebellar excitatory output may also contribute to functional mis-specification or structural abnormalities in later developing brain regions such as parietal cortex.
4. Attentional processing impairments resulting from cerebellar damage (e.g., slowness to shift or reorient attention) cause an autistic infant to experience temporal and spatial gaps in dynamic information processing.
5. Gaps in spatial and temporal contiguity interfere with the ability to discern causal relationships and the ability to engage in joint social attention, thus creating a fragmented, imprecise, and misleading representation of the environment that interferes with the ability to acquire language as well as with social and affective development.

The following section is a review of evidence from which this model was constructed.

Anatomical Evidence

Cerebellar Abnormalities from MR and Autopsy Studies (Table 7.1). As researchers attempted to peel away the levels at the top of the disorder to uncover core functional deficits (e.g., attentional deficits), some key information from autopsy studies suggested a very early, and therefore possibly primary, site of anatomical brain abnormality—extensive Purkinje cell loss in the cerebellum (Williams, Hauser, Purpura, DeLong, & Swisher, 1980). Subsequently, cerebellar abnormality was also found on MR from autistic patients (Courchesne et al., 1987,

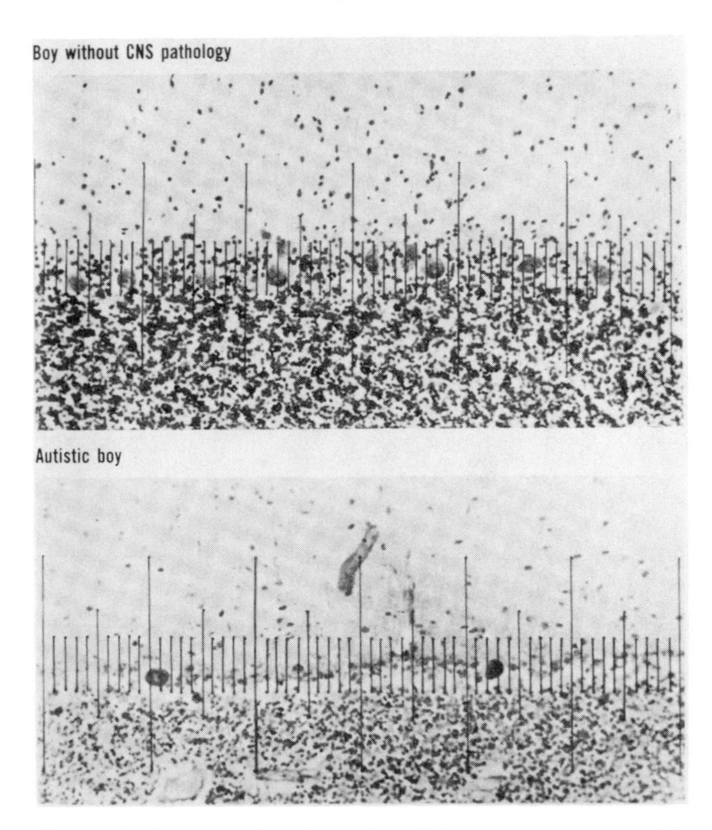

Figure 7.20 Cerebellar Purkinje cell loss has been reported in 12 autopsy cases of infantile autism. Shown here are specimens from the cerebellum of a 13-year-old boy without CNS pathology and a 10-year-old autistic boy. Original magnification = 100X. Interval between vertical elements = 20 μm. From "Lower Purkinje Cell Counts in the Cerebella of Four Autistic Subjects . . ." by E. R. Ritvo et al., 1986, *American Journal of Psychiatry, 143,* p. 864. Copyright 1986 by the American Psychiatric Association. Reprinted by permission.

1988; Gaffney et al., 1987), and additional autopsy studies of autistic cases also found cerebellar Purkinje cell loss (Table 7.1 and Figure 7.20). That the neuron loss is not accompanied by gliosis suggests a prenatal event, perhaps as early as the second trimester (Bauman, 1991; also review Courchesne, 1991). As Figure 7.21 shows, a number of MR studies have now generalized this finding to much larger samples of autistic patients, showing *hypo*plasia in 84% to 92% of the subjects (Table 7.1). Larger samples have also revealed a subgroup of 8% to 16% who show extreme enlargement of the cerebellar vermis or *hyper*plasia (Courchesne, Saitoh, Townsend et al., 1994; Courchesne, Saitoh, Yeung-Courchesne, et al., 1994; for a review, see Courchesne, Townsend, & Saitoh, 1994). The vermian hypoplasia observed in autistic patients might result from either genetic abnormalities or environmental insults, or a combination of both. Hyperplasia, however, is most likely genetic in origin. Animal studies have demonstrated that very specific environmental events can lead to a localized increase in numbers of neurons (Cowan, Fawcett, O'Leary, & Stanfield, 1984), but there is no precedent in human literature for focal neuronal hyperplasia that results from known environmental insults (e.g., radiation, toxins, infections, hypoxia, and so on). However, because normal development is marked by a phase of neural overgrowth followed by selective elimination (Cowan et al., 1984), it is conceivable that genetic defects that interfere with regressive events could result in hyperplasia.

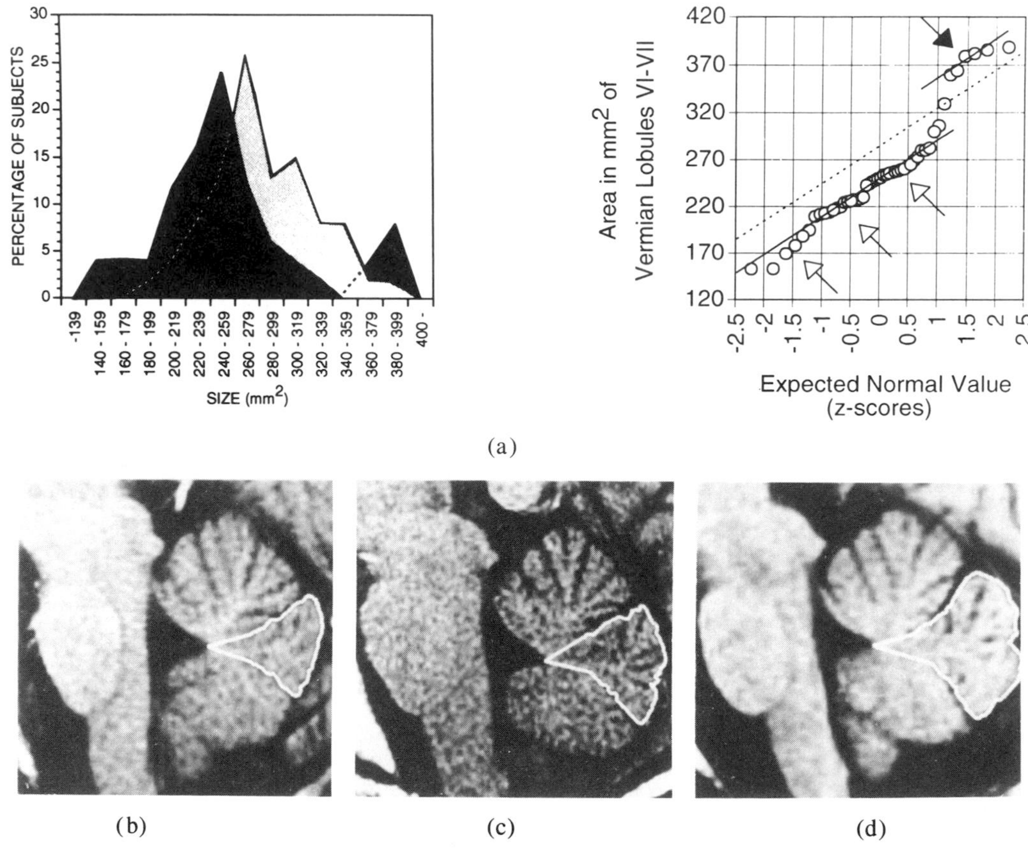

Figure 7.21 In patients with infantile autism, two types of cerebellar abnormality have been identified by quantitative analyses of MR images. (a) (left) Comparison of the midsagittal area of vermian lobules VI and VII in 50 autistic and 53 normal subjects. Shows the graph of the area of vermian lobules VI and VII by the percentage of subjects with that size. For the autistic group, a few subjects apparently have enlargement of lobules VI and VII, while the majority have values smaller than the normal mean size. (a) (right) For the 50 autistic patients, plot of the size of vermian lobules VI-VII against expected values on a Gaussian curve showed a bimodal distribution. There were two separate clusters of autistic patients: one, a *hypo*plasia subtype (open arrows), and another, a *hyper*plasia subtype (closed arrow). The dotted line is based on normal data values. (b–d) Examples of midsagittal T1-weighted (TR = 600ms; TE = 12ms) magnetic resonance images of (b) an autistic patient with small vermian lobules VI and VII (216.5 mm^2), (c) a normal control with lobules of average size (288.5 mm^2), and (d) an autistic patient with enlarged lobules (379.3 mm^2). From "Abnormality of Cerebellar Vermian Lobules VI and VII in Patients with Infantile Autism . . ." by E. Courchesne, O. Saitoh, R. Yeung-Courchesne et al., 1994, *American Journal of Roentgenology, 162,* p. 126. Copyright 1994 by The Lancet Ltd. Reprinted by permission.

Autism and the Role of the Cerebellum in Attention and Other Nonmotor Functions. Although the cerebellum has traditionally been associated most frequently with motor function, there is mounting evidence for involvement of the cerebellum in nonmotor function of the sort that might underlie the behavioral abnormalities in autism. For example, the cerebellum may be important for timing production and perception of time (Ivry & Keele, 1989; Ivry, Keele, & Diener, 1988) and for cognitive functions such as attention, learning, speed of information processing, planning, visual-spatial organization, programming sequences of events, language, and abstract thinking (Akshoomoff & Courchesne, 1992, 1994; Akshoomoff, Courchesne, Press, & Iragui, 1992; Botez, Botez, Elie, & Attig, 1989; Botez, Gravel, Attig, & Vezina, 1985; Bracke-Tolkmitt et al., 1989; Leiner, Leiner, & Dow, 1986, 1989; Townsend, 1992; Wallesch & Horn, 1990).

Both the opportunity and the means by which the cerebellum may influence attention are suggested by current literature. In normal processing, selective attention operations may require coordinated interactions among frontal and parietal systems and the brainstem-thalamic-reticular systems (Crick, 1984; Harter & Aine, 1984; LaBerge, 1990; Mesulam, 1981; Rafal & Posner, 1987). Connections have been documented between the neocerebellum and systems implicated in selective attention, including the reticular activating system, posterior parietal cortex, dorsolateral prefrontal cortex, superior colliculus, cingulate gyrus, and pulvinar (Courchesne, 1987, 1989; Dow, 1988; Itoh & Mizuno, 1979; Nieuwenhuys, Voogd, & van Huijzen, 1988; Sasaki, Jinnai, Gemba, Hashimoto, & Mizuno, 1979; Sasaki, Matsuda, Kawaguichi, & Mizuno, 1972; Schmahmann & Pandya, 1989; Vilensky & Van Hoesen, 1981). Damage to these systems, their interconnections, or their afferent or efferent paths might be expected to interfere with selective processing. The abnormalities seen in the neocerebellar cortex in autism, reflecting greatly reduced numbers of Purkinje cells, could, in fact, result in this sort of interference (Courchesne, 1987; Courchesne, Chisum, & Townsend, 1994). Purkinje cells provide inhibitory modulation for cerebellar output from the deep cerebellar nuclei to neural systems throughout the brain, including the brainstem-thalamic-reticular systems and cerebral cortex, which are thought to be involved in selective attention. Failure of this modulation could interrupt interactions among these systems, affecting attentional mechanisms. Consistent with this possibility are PET data demonstrating that, compared to normal controls, autistic subjects did, in fact, show reduced functional associations among regions thought to subserve selective attention (Horwitz et al., 1988).

Neurophysiologic studies employing single-cell recording in animals further suggest that the neocerebellum may interact with cortical systems to affect attentional operations. Several studies have shown that activation of neocerebellar neurons is associated with modulation of neuronal responses to visual, auditory, and somatosensory stimulation in brain stem, thalamus, hippocampus, and cerebral cortex (Crispino & Bullock, 1984; Newman & Reza, 1979). For example, there is an interval of time during which stimulation of the neocerebellum will lead to a significant amplification of the response in superior colliculus to a visual stimulus (see Figure 7.22).

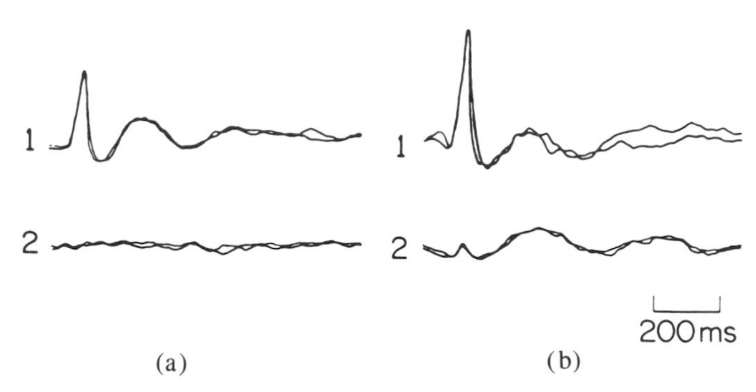

Figure 7.22 The cerebellum modulates neural responses to visual stimulation. (a) No cerebellar stimulation conditions. Flash of light elicits visual evoked responses in the superior colliculus in the absence of cerebellar stimulation. (a1) Control visual evoked response to flash of light. (a2). Abolition of such response by addition of background light. (b) With stimulation of cerebellar vermian lobules VI and VII preceding the flash of light. (b1) Response to the flash. (b2) Response to the flash with background illumination added. Superimposed averages, 64 stimulus presentations. From "Cerebellum Mediates Modality-Specific Modulation of Sensory Responses of the Midbrain and Forebrain in Rat" by L. Crispino and T. H. Bullock, 1984, *Proceedings of the National Academy of Science, 81,* p. 2919. Reprinted by permission.

Because the cerebellar damage to an infant with autism likely occurs between the second prenatal trimester and the first year of postnatal life (Bauman & Kemper, 1985; Hashimoto et al., in press; Courchesne, in press), the resulting functional disabilities (e.g., impaired attentional operations) affect critical developmental stages of learning and behavior. Additionally, there may be a sort of neurodevelopmental domino effect in autism, in which primary abnormalities of the developing cerebellum might lead to further brain abnormalities, which, in turn, produce additional functional deficits (Courchesne, 1985, 1987, 1989; Courchesne, Chisum, & Townsend, 1994; Courchesne, Townsend, Akshoomoff, et al., 1994). As previously discussed, neurobiological data show that there are a number of ways in which early damage in one system can alter organization in other systems with which it is interconnected. Early cerebellar damage in autism could conceivably contribute to abnormal organization and functioning within attention, arousal, memory, limbic, sensory, hypothalamic, serotonergic, dopaminergic, noradrenergic, and motor systems with which it is interconnected (Bava, Manzoni, & Urbano, 1966; Chambers & Sprague, 1955; Crispino & Bullock, 1984; Haines & Dietrichs, 1987; Itoh & Mizuno, 1979; Moruzzi & Magoun, 1949; Nieuwenhuys et al., 1988; Newman & Reza, 1979; Sasaki et al., 1972, Schmahmann & Pandya, 1989; Snider, 1950, 1967; Steriade & Stoupel, 1960; Vilensky & Van Hoesen, 1981; Watson, 1978). An example is the evidence in some autistic patients of abnormalities in posterior parietal cortex that are corollary or additional to those found in the posterior cerebellum (Courchesne et al., 1993).

Parietal Lobe Abnormalities from MR Studies. Neuroradiological examination of MR scans from 21 autistic adolescents and adults found that 43% of this group had abnormalities in appearance of parietal lobes, suggesting reduction in cortical volume (Courchesne et al., 1993). The most frequent positive finding in this subgroup was bilateral increased sulcal width in superior parietal regions (see Figure 7.23). The mesial, lateral,

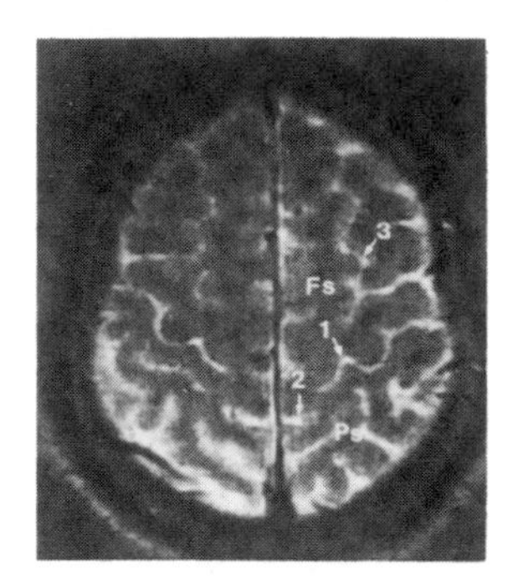

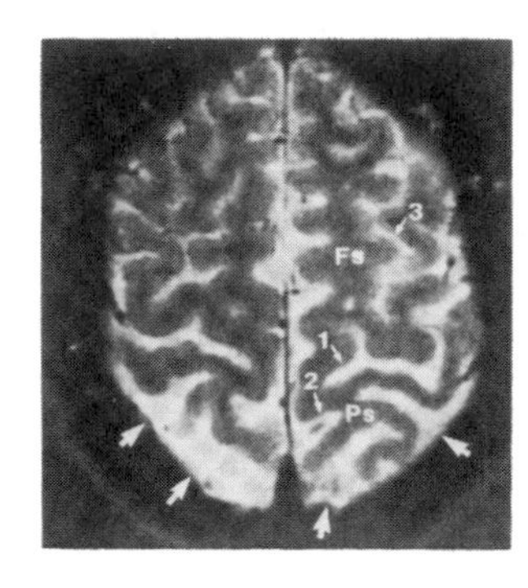

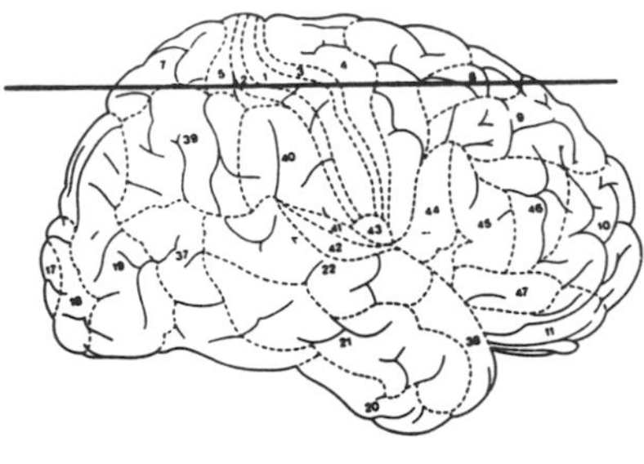

Figure 7.23 Example of abnormalities of parietal cortex in autistic patients, as seen on MR images. Transverse MR images (SE 2000/80, TR ms/RE ms), from a young adult normal control (top left) and an autistic young adult with increased sulcal width in superior parietal lobe (top right). Numbers and letters on images identify the following anatomical landmarks: (1) central sulcus, (2) marginal ramus of cingulate sulcus, (3) superior frontal sulcus, (FS) superior frontal regions, and (PS) superior parietal regions. Arrows at the base of the image of the autistic patient (top right) mark regions of abnormal sulcal width. The line through the tracing at the bottom shows the approximate position for the MR slices, from which quantitative estimates of parietal volume loss in autistic patients were computed. Numbers in brain schematic corresponding to Brodmann's cytoarchitectonic areas. MR images from "Parietal Damage and Narrow 'Spotlight' Spatial Attention" by J. Townsend and E. Courchesne, 1994, *Journal of Cognitive Neuroscience, 6*(3), pp. 389. Copyright 1994 by MIT Press. Adapted from Courchesne, Press, and Yeung-Courchesne, 1993. Reprinted by permission. Brain schematic from *The Human Central Nervous System* by R. Nieuwenhuys, J. Voogd, and C. von Huijzen, 1988, (p. 10), Berlin: Springer-Verlag. Copyright 1988 by Springer-Verlag. Reprinted by permission.

and orbital frontal lobes and temporal lobes were judged normal in appearance in all autistic subjects. Additionally, there is recent evidence of parietal abnormality in autism from a MR study of the corpus callosum. In 51 age and sex matched pairs of autistic patients and normal controls, there was significant size reduction of the corpus callosum in autistic children and adolescents localized to the posterior subregions where parietal fibers are concentrated (Egaas, Courchesne, & Saitoh, in press).

The time of onset of these cortical abnormalities and their relation, if any, to cerebellar abnormalities in autism are unknown, but there are several possibilities to consider (Courchesne, et al., 1993). The increased sulcal width might be part of a larger pattern of abnormal CNS growth and development, possibly related in time or causality to the cerebellar hypoplasia. For example, the proposed window for onset of the cerebellar hypoplasia (Bauman & Kemper, 1985; Courchesne, in press; Hashimoto et al., in press) is during a time frame in normal development in which there is enlargement of subarachnoid spaces that is maximal over the parietal convexity and tapers off over anterior occipital and posterior frontal regions (McArdle et al., 1987). McArdle and colleagues propose that this space is filled by growth of parietal lobes during late prenatal and early postnatal development. Retarded growth during this critical period might fail to fill sulcal space, resulting in the increased sulcal width over superior parietal and adjacent regions that is observed in some autistic subjects.

An alternate possibility is that the same mechanisms (genetic or nongenetic) that underlie Purkinje cell loss in the cerebellum also alter neuronal growth in the cerebrum. Yet another possibility is based on a recent theory by Killackey (1990), who proposed that the cerebellum is part of a "labeled line system" critical to structural development and functional specification of cerebral cortex. Because Purkinje neurons provide the principal inhibitory control for spontaneous excitatory cerebellar output, reduced numbers of Purkinje cells in random patches of cerebellar vermis and hemispheres should result in uncontrolled excitatory output to patches of cerebral cortex (Courchesne, 1985, 1987). Such aberrant signals in a labeled line system should produce aberrant cortical specification and development, and perhaps cell death in neurons receiving excessive unmodulated excitation over time (Choi, 1992). Finally, in the absence of definitive evidence to support these proposals, a progressive atrophy that results in the observed focal parietal volume loss must be considered as well.

Behavioral Evidence

With potential sites of primary and secondary neural pathology identified, studies linking those sites to the behavioral manifestations of the disorder can enable the construction of a model of autism. For example, evidence of time-related deficits in shifting attention between and within modality and between spatial locations in autistic and cerebellar lesion patients comes from a series of behavioral and electrophysiological studies (Akshoomoff, 1992; Akshoomoff & Courchesne, 1992, 1994; Courchesne, Townsend, Akshoomoff, Saitoh et al., 1994; Courchesne, Townsend, Akshoomoff, Young-Courchesne et al., 1994; Townsend, 1992; Townsend et al., 1992; Townsend & Courchesne, 1994; submitted for publication). As Figure 7.24 shows, when their attention was focused on a single

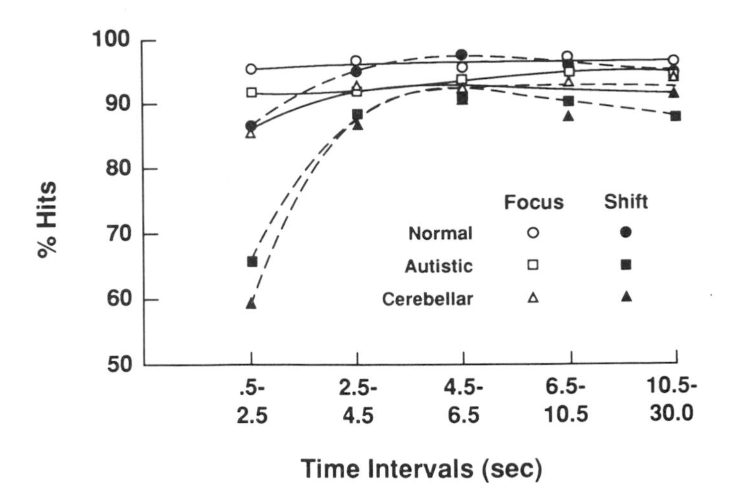

Figure 7.24 Focus vs. Shift Attention: Behavioral evidence that autistic patients are severely impaired in their capacity to rapidly and accurately shift attention back and forth between auditory and visual sensory modalities. Shows the mean percentage hits for normal control (circles), autistic (squares), and cerebellar (triangles) groups in the baseline focused attention tasks (open symbols) and shift attention task (closed symbols). All data were analyzed at five intervals of time (in sec) elapsed since onset of every immediately preceding target that had been correctly detected. There is no statistically significant difference in performance between groups at any time interval in the focused attention tasks. In the shift attention task, autistic and cerebellar groups are significantly less accurate than normal controls, with less than 2.5 seconds between targets. From "A New Finding: Impairment in Shifting Attention in Autistic and Cerebellar Patients" by E. Courchesne, J. Townsend, N. A. Akshoomoff et al., 1994, in S. H. Broman and J. Grafman (Eds.), *Atypical Cognitive Deficits in Developmental Disorders* (p. 122), Hillsdale, NJ: Erlbaum. Copyright 1994 by Lawrence Erlbaum Associates, Inc. Reprinted by permission.

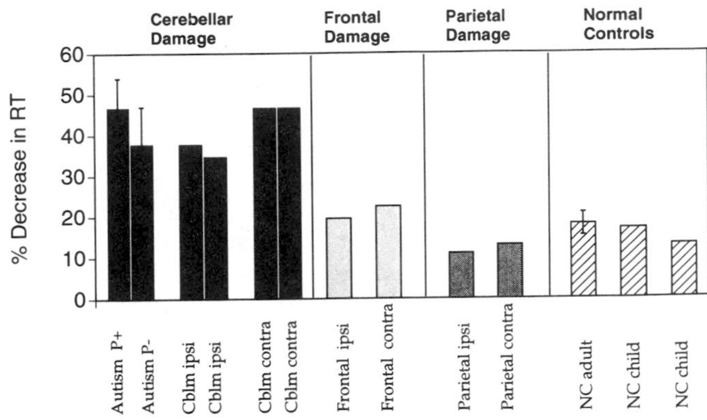

Figure 7.25 On a Posner-type task, autistic patients and patients with acquired cerebellar lesions are slow to orient visual attention. Greater decrease in RT indicates slowed response to target at cued location when there is only 100 ms between cue and target. Orienting effects (percent improvement in RT at 800 ms vs. 100 ms cue-to-target delay) are shown for: autistic patients with (P +) and without (P-) parietal abnormalities; two cerebellar patients on targets ipsilesional and contralesional to their focal lesions; patients with unilateral frontal lobe damage (Petersen et al., 1989) and unilateral parietal damage (Posner et al., 1984) adult normal control subjects; and two groups of normal control children. (Swanson et al., 1991, and pilot data from Sharon Nichols and Beverly Wulfeck, Language Research Center, Children's Hospital, San Diego). From "A New Finding: Impairment in Shifting Attention in Autistic and Cerebellar Patients" by E. Courchesne, J. Townsend, N. A. Akshoomoff et al., 1994, in S. H. Broman and J. Grafman (Eds.), *Atypical Cognitive Deficits in Developmental Disorders* (p. 125), Hillsdale, NJ: Erlbaum. Copyright 1994 by Lawrence Erlbaum Associates, Inc. Reprinted by permission.

modality, autistic and cerebellar patients were as fast and as accurate as normal control subjects, even with short intervals between targets. Following a cue to shift target modalities, however, autistic and cerebellar patients required up to 5 seconds between target stimuli to perform at normal levels of accuracy (Akshoomoff & Courchesne, 1992; Courchesne, Townsend, Akshoomoff, Saitoh et al., 1994; Courchesne, Townsend, Akshoomoff, Yeung-Courchesne et al., 1994). These same subjects were also quite slow to orient attention in a series of tasks derived from those developed by Posner (Posner, Walker, Friedrich, & Rafal, 1984), involving shifts of attention between spatial locations (Townsend, 1992; Townsend et al., 1992; Townsend & Courchesne, 1994; submitted for publication). In these tasks, autistic and neocerebellar patients had significantly delayed responses to targets at a cued location when the target was presented shortly after the cue (see Figure 7.25). With longer cue-to-target delays, the patients' responses were not different from those of control subjects. This time-related delay has not been reported for other patient groups (e.g., those with acquired lesions of frontal, parietal, temporal, thalamic, or midbrain), but it is an abnormality consistent with the time-related delays that these autistic and cerebellar patients displayed in the attention-shifting tasks described above.

Autistic patients having parietal as well as cerebellar abnormalities would be expected to exhibit a different, perhaps more complex, phenotypic profile, including deficits in spatial attention that are commonly associated with parietal damage. Evidence that parietal cortex plays a critical role in spatial attention comes from clinical reports of hemi-inattention in patients with damage to parietal lobes (Heilman, Watson, & Valenstein, 1985), and from studies showing that specific deficits in target detection are characteristic of patients with acquired parietal lesions (Petersen, Robinson, & Currie, 1989; Posner et al., 1984; Posner, Walker, Friedrich, & Rafal, 1987). In spatial cuing tasks, adult patients with acquired parietal damage are extremely slow to respond to simple visual targets in the visual field contralateral to their lesion, after their attention has been directed to the opposite (ipsilesional) side (Petersen et al., 1989; Posner et al., 1984). In spatial cuing paradigms, autistic patients with parietal abnormalities, like previously studied patients with acquired parietal damage, were extremely slow to respond to targets in uncued and therefore unexpected locations (Courchesne, Townsend, Akshoomoff, Saitoh et al., 1994; Townsend et al., 1992; Townsend & Courchesne, submitted for publication). Because their parietal abnormality was bilateral, however, these autistic patients showed this deficit in both visual fields. Importantly, this performance deficit was significantly correlated with quantitative measures of parietal abnormality (see Figure 7.26). There is also electrophysiological data that suggest a possible mechanism underlying these spatial deficits (see Figure 7.27). Autistic patients with parietal abnormalities show evidence of extremely narrowed regions of attention-related sensory enhancement of visual stimulation (Townsend, 1992; Townsend & Courchesne, 1994; submitted for publication).

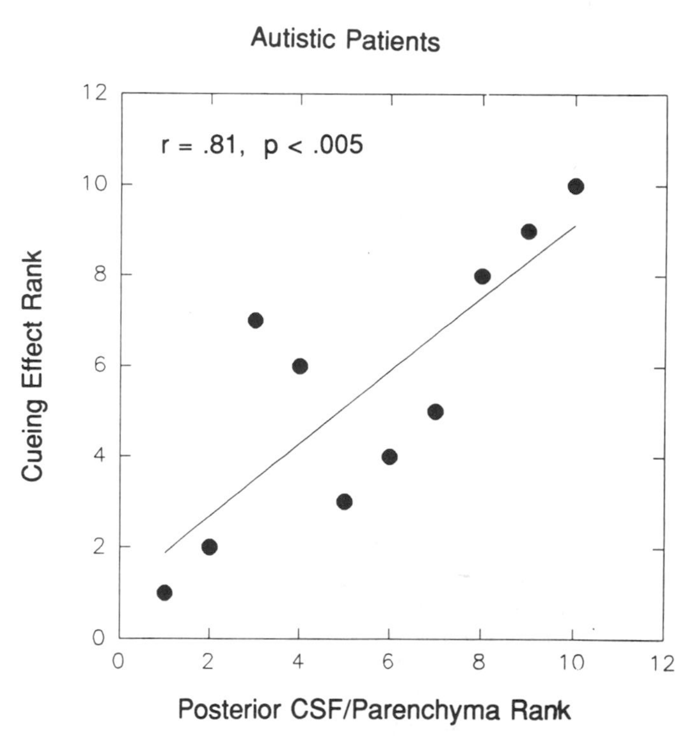

Figure 7.26 Across autistic subjects, those with more parietal abnormality have greater deficits in detecting information at unexpected (uncued) locations. Scattergram with regression line shows the relationship in autistic patients between the rank for a subject of the ratio of intrasulcal cerebral spinal fluid (CSF) to parenchyma and that subject's rank for the overall cuing effect (i.e., differences between response time to correctly and incorrectly cued targets). From "A New Finding: Impairment in Shifting Attention in Autistic and Cerebellar Patients" by E. Courchesne, J. Townsend, N. A. Akshoomoff et al., 1994, in S. H. Broman and J. Grafman (Eds.), *Atypical Cognitive Deficits in Developmental Disorders* (p. 127), Hillsdale, NJ: Erlbaum. Copyright 1994 by Lawrence Erlbaum Associates, Inc. Reprinted by permission.

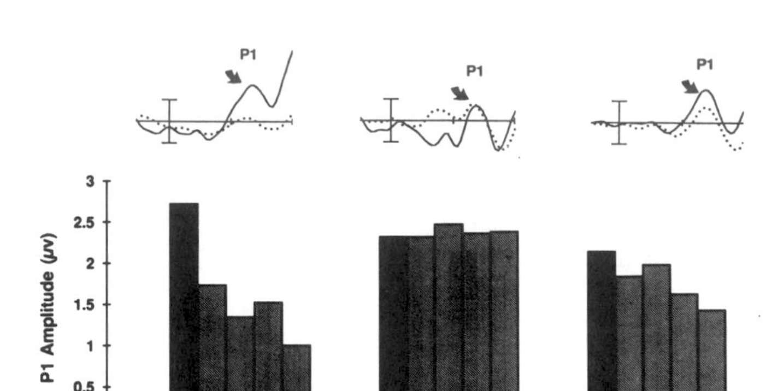

Figure 7.27 Autistic patients with parietal abnormalities show evidence of extremely narrowed regions of attention-related sensory enhancement of visual stimulation. Bar graphs for autistic patients with and without parietal abnormalities, and normal control subjects. Shows P1 peak amplitude responses at occipital scalp sites to stimuli at attended location (dark bar), compared to P1 responses at that location when attention was focused one, two, three, and four locations away (light bars in order, left to right). Locations were separated by 2.7 degrees of visual angle. Waveforms at the top show P1 responses at occipital sites to attended (solid line) compared to unattended (dashed line) locations. From "Parietal Damage and Narrow 'Spotlight' Spatial Attention" by J. Townsend and E. Courchesne, 1994, *Journal of Cognitive Neuroscience, 6*(3). Copyright 1994 by MIT Press. Adapted with permission.

Attentional Dysfunction and Deficits of Social Communication

An examination of the development of social communication skills in normal infants suggests the link by which deficits in attention could produce the deficiencies in social behavior that characterize autism. In his book on affect, cognition, and communication in infancy, Tronick (1982) proposed that, in normal development, social interchanges involve the coordination of frequent and rapid changes in the direction of a mutual focus of attention. A failure to engage in this regulatory process will interfere with an infant's social and affective development. Early developmental failure of this system, such as that observed in autistic subjects who are unable to execute rapid shifts of attention between and within sensory modalities, would disrupt the most fundamental causal associations and so would interfere with normal development of meaning, on which concepts about the world are based.

Related observations have come from Mandler (1992), who proposed that concepts about the world that precede the acquisition of language are formed when an infant attentively analyzes a "perceptual array" to abstract new or recoded information.

Even very young infants who have limited control over their own motor function learn about the world by association. They are, Mandler said, "surrounded by people who interact contingently among themselves and who respond from a distance to the infant's actions and vocalizations" (1992, p. 594). A responsiveness to contingency has, in fact, been demonstrated in neonates as young as 2 months of age (Watson, 1972). Infants for whom there is discontinuity in the sorts of temporal information on which contingencies are based would be unable to form such contingency-based concepts, or might form false concepts. At 4 months of age, normal babies are able to distinguish causal relationships that occur when one ball touches and moves another (Leslie, 1982, 1988). *If, however, there is a spatial or a temporal gap in the movement of two objects, infants do not connect the events.* An autistic infant unable to execute rapid shifts of attention in space—from objects to people or from gesture to voice—would experience spatial and temporal gaps in information, and so would fail to make the crucial associations on which effective social communication depends. Electrophysiological data supporting this view come from studies showing that autistic children have abnormally reduced brain responses reflecting conditioned association of cross-modal stimuli (Lelord, Laffont, Jusseaume, & Stephant, 1973; Martineau et al., 1987, 1992). An infant who is unable to associate component parts that are close in time and space will undoubtedly fail to integrate important concepts and to understand causal relationships, including the consequences of his or her own acts.

Summary and Implications

The evidence reviewed here forms the core for a model in which abnormalities of the cerebellum and parietal cortex underlie primary dysfunction in attention-related information processing, ultimately resulting in the higher-level disorder of social communication that characterizes autism.

Critical to the development of this model has been the careful specification of the behavioral abnormalities that define autism and that have led to diagnosis of more homogeneous groups of autistic patients. Also critical is information from basic science about the action of Purkinje neurons and functional connections of the cerebellum with other brain systems. Finally, numerous studies of many behavioral end symptoms have provided evidence that links the anatomic damage to the final behavioral outcome of the disorder.

There are, of course, many remaining questions, not the least of which is whether the cerebellum is actually a primary site of damage or is preceded by some earlier structural abnormality, and whether there are major subgroups in autism with different patterns of anatomic pathology. In any case, an increased understanding of the underlying mechanisms of the disorder is critical and should allow treatment to become increasingly specified and, therefore, more effective. Additionally, the identification of a potential site of primary structural damage may help to narrow the search for genetic and nongenetic causes. *In the end, however, it must be recognized that a model such as this one provides only a framework from which to continue the search.*

Models based on converging evidence from studies of abnormal function and anatomy are also emerging from other developmental psychopathologies. There is now evidence, for example, implicating what may be primary sites of brain abnormalities that underlie developmental disorder of reading and language, and a model for the way in which these anatomical abnormalities may affect these cognitive processes (Chase & Tallal, 1991; Galaburda et al., 1985, 1989; Galaburda & Eidelberg, 1982; Livingstone et al., 1991). Although language delay and reading problems are the symptomatology that define this disorder, the onset of these symptoms is hypothesized to be preceded by abnormalities of sensory perception and attention (Tallal, 1988; Tallal & Piercy, 1973; Tallal, Stark, & Mellits, 1985). Among the end symptoms that probably provide the best clue to precipitating events in this disorder are abnormalities of the thalamic magnocellular system (Galaburda & Eidelberg, 1982; Livingstone et al., 1991). Cellular abnormalities observed in the lateral and medical geniculate are likely to occur early in prenatal development and may underlie the perceptual processing impairments. For example, the small cell size and disorganization of the magnocellular system are likely to affect the quality of sensory experience by slowing the speed with which information is processed in the magnocellular pathway. Additionally, this abnormal sensory experience may contribute to abnormal symmetry of language areas in the brain, also observed in this disorder, as well as to difficulties with language acquisition and reading (Livingstone et al., 1991). Alternatively, the pathology that underlies the abnormal development of the magnocellular system may also act directly on the development of language areas of the brain. In either case, the magnocellular abnormalities provide an end symptom that is likely to precede other symptoms and so bring us closer to the origins of this disorder.

THE CONTRIBUTION OF STUDIES OF DEVELOPMENTAL PSYCHOPATHOLOGY TO THE UNDERSTANDING OF NORMAL BRAIN FUNCTION AND DEVELOPMENT

The study of abnormal developmental perturbations[3] using animal models is the central foundation on which knowledge and principles of normal neurodevelopment have been built (see above). Many of the types of perturbations studied in animal models are much the same as those that could well underlie developmental psychopathologies (e.g., genetic mutations or exposure to neurodevelopment-altering agents such as viruses,

[3] In animal models, a wide range of abnormal perturbations have been studied, including brain lesions; genetic mutations (naturally occurring as well as artificially created ones); brain tissue transplants; sensory, neural, or behavioral deprivation (e.g., monocular deprivation or tetrodotoxin injection in the retina) or excitation (e.g., via pharmacological agents or behavioral "enrichment"); exposure to neurodevelopment-altering agents (e.g., viruses, alcohol, X-irradiation, lead, neuropharmacological agents); and extraction of brain cells for in vitro growth manipulations.

alcohol, lead, or neuropharmacological agents). Indeed, for this very reason, findings from animal models provide an indispensable basis for understanding human developmental psychopathologies.

By extension, therefore, it seems reasonable to suggest that the study of human developmental psychopathologies could theoretically provide a foundation on which knowledge and principles of normal human development could be built. Unlike studies of abnormal animals, studies of developmental psychopathology hold tremendous *potential* for revealing neurobiologic factors underlying functions of special interest to us all: language, social skills and affect, memory, attention, and intelligence. This potential, however, has seldom been realized.

Among the possible reasons stand two that are particularly compelling. *First, research in developmental psychopathology has traditionally begun at the end—with neurobehavioral end symptoms* (see above discussion). For instance, although there is evidence of neuronal migration errors within the medial temporal lobe in schizophrenia, this unusual developmental clue has not prompted fundamentally new neurodevelopmental models or experimental approaches in the schizophrenia field. Instead, after decades of research and thousands of articles, the theories, experiments, and findings on schizophrenia remain largely at the end symptom level, whether they have to do with the effects of dopamine manipulation, abnormal executive functions, or reduced P3 amplitude. Although hypofrontality in PET studies of schizophrenia garners much interest, this effect is as much a neurobehavioral end symptom as is the presence of hallucinations. As such, neither symptom offers deep insight into neurobiologic factors that underlie the normal development of human attention, memory, affect, or cognition.

Second, studies of developmental psychopathology have disadvantages not present in animal models. For developmental psychopathologies, the precipitating abnormal perturbations are typically unknown. The neural sites and type of defect are typically unknown. Recognition that an individual is abnormal typically comes well after developmental transformations are largely complete; because of this, in vivo examination of the unfolding neurodevelopmental process of self-*mis*-organization is not possible. Systematic manipulation of the type, time, site, and extent of damage is out of the question. Lastly, without knowing all possible sites of pathology within the abnormal brain, it is impossible to ever be certain that one has isolated effects due solely to one site of neural defect.

There are instances, however, where these methodological disadvantages can be removed from research on developmental psychopathology. In such cases, as with animal models, much can be learned from developmental psychopathologies about normal development. A good example comes from autism. There is now abundant evidence (see above) supporting the theory that the cerebellum is one of the key sites of developmental damage in infantile autism (Courchesne, 1985, 1987, 1989, in press). As described above, since the first report of Purkinje neuron loss in the cerebellum of an autistic patient (Williams et al., 1980), every autopsy study on autism has reported the same defect (review Courchesne, Townsend, & Saitoh, 1994 and Table 7.1). Quantitative MR and autopsy studies agree that the defect is greatest in the posterior cerebellum with the maximum Purkinje neuron loss (50–60%) in vermal lobules VI-X. Also, because this neuron loss is unaccompanied by gliosis, it can be inferred to have occurred early in brain development, quite likely before birth. Moreover, a new MR imaging study (Hashimoto et al., in press) of 96 autistic patients provides the first direct evidence that this cerebellar hypoplasia occurs as early as the first year of life, which is prior to the onset of critical social and language developmental milestones.

Therefore, in infantile autism, we know one site of damage (the cerebellum) and the type (Purkinje neuron loss), extent (maximal in vermian and hemisphere lobules VI, VII, VIII, IX, and X) and approximate time (between the second trimester and early postnatal life) of this damage.

What can this tell us about normal development and brain functioning? This sort of specific neurobiologic information makes three contributions: (a) to hypotheses about the development of joint social attention, (b) to hypotheses about the role of labeled lines systems in brain development, and (c) to theories about the functional role of the human cerebellum.

First, a major hypothesis is that, during normal human development, joint social attention is a critical milestone along the road to complex social and language abilities and appears by 12 to 15 months of age (see above). Prominent behaviors marking the presence of joint attention in the infant include orienting attention to gestures, words, or tactile information, and the shifting of attention back and forth between mother's gestures, words, and so on, and some other object or event of interest. It has been observed that in autism there is a failure to develop joint attention and a failure to control attention even in nonsocial situations (see above). These observations, combined with the evidence for early cerebellar maldevelopment, lead to a new cerebellar theory of autism (see above). Studies based on this theory provide the best available neurobiologic information about what cognitive operations and brain structures might be important for the normal developmental expression of joint attention. As discussed above, new evidence indicates that damage to the cerebellum severely impairs the ability to rapidly orient to attention-getting information (e.g., when mother moves a toy train near baby) and the ability to rapidly and accurately shift attention back and forth between two sources of information (e.g., between mother's words or facial expressions and the toy train) (see Figures 7.24 and 7.25). In autism, MR imaging evidence indicates that cerebellar hypoplasia occurs prior to the expected appearance of joint attention Hashimoto et al., in press. The operations of orienting and shifting attention would therefore not be available to the developing autistic baby when they are needed to achieve this critical milestone at 12–15 months of age. The study of autism, then, raises the hypothesis that, during normal development, Purkinje neuron function and orienting and shifting attention operations are among the structures and functions needed for the normal expression of joint attentional behavior. Other sites and functions might be just as important, if not more so. For instance, bilateral parietal abnormality (Figure 7.23) recently discovered in some cases of autism might result in an abnormally narrowed "spotlight" of attention (Figure 7.27) leading to a profound sensory inattention in autistic infants (Townsend & Courchesne, 1994; submitted for publication), not unlike the neglect syndromes that follow focal parietal lesions in adults (Critchley, 1966; Denny-Brown & Banker, 1954; Heilman, Valenstein, & Watson, 1983; Heilman et al., 1985).

Second, another major hypothesis is that, during normal development, correlated neural activity is critical to the development of normal neuronal structure and function (see above; Figures 7.3 to 7.6 and 7.8 to 7.11). Killackey (1990) speculated that correlated neural activity from labeled line systems is crucial to normal cerebral cortical specialization. According to Killackey (1990), labeled line systems include sensory systems and the cerebellum. The idea that the cerebellum is involved has never been experimentally tested; autism may be a unique, naturally occurring test of this hypothesis. Animal experiments show that neural activity deprivation can lead to increased cell packing density and/or reductions in cell size, axon arborizations, and dendritic arborizations (see above). Also, animal experiments show that activation of vermian lobules VI and VII modulates neural activity in brain stem sensory pathways and in limbic structures (see above). Autism involves not only a heavy loss of Purkinje neurons in this region of the vermis, but also heavy loss of vermian output neurons in the fastigial nucleus. Based on Killackey's (1990) concept, this damage in autism would be predicted to lead to activity deprivation of this portion of the labeled line system and therefore to some effects in systems to which it projects. In fact, increased cell packing density, reduced cell size, and reduced dendritic arbors consistent with late developmental growth retardation have been reported in some limbic structures in several cases of autism at autopsy (see above), and reduced size of the brain stem (Hashimoto et al., in press) and unusual auditory brain stem neurophysiology have been reported by others.

An extremely interesting contrast exists in the cerebellar system in autism: Whereas activity reduction should occur down one portion of the cerebellar labeled line projection system because of loss of fastigial output neurons, *excessive* activity should occur down a different portion because dentate and interpositus output neurons are intact. Dentate and interpositus output neurons are spontaneously excitatory, and normally, this excitation is controlled by the inhibitory action of Purkinje neurons. With roughly 50% of their controlling Purkinje neurons gone, patches of dentate and interpositus neurons might be sending uncontrolled, excessive, excitatory activity down their portion of the labeled line system. Scattered patches of abnormal hypermetabolic activity throughout numerous subcortical and cortical structures have been reported in some PET studies of autism (Horwitz et al., 1988). Much is understood about the effects of activity deprivation or uncorrelated activity on normal neural development (Figures 7.6 and 7.8 to 7.11; see above), but the effects of excessive nonseizure-like correlated neural activity on normal neural development and function are not known with certainty. Cerebellar abnormalities in autism suggest that duplication of this pattern of pathology in animals could offer an unparalleled model system for testing activity-dependent and labeled line hypotheses of normal development.

Third, for nearly 200 years, a major hypothesis of normal brain function has been that the human cerebellum is primarily involved in motor coordination. By 1984, although a number of animal studies had identified its potential for modulating sensory activity in brain stem, thalamic, cortical, and hippocampal systems, no one had seen how such operations could be linked to higher-order attentional and cognitive behavior. Moreover, no study using normal infants or children had ever linked the cerebellum to any such behavior. Beginning in 1985, in our laboratory, observations of patients with infantile autism led to theories and experiments that for the first time made such links between the cerebellum and higher-order attentional behavior (Courchesne, Townsend, Akshoomoff, Saitoh et al., 1994; Courchesne, Townsend, Akshoomoff, Yeung-Courchesne et al., 1994; Courchesne, Townsend, & Saitoh, 1994; Townsend & Courchesne, submitted for publication). Many have been described herein. Moreover, at about the same time, other researchers began to make links between the cerebellum and higher-order cognitive functions (Ivry & Keele, 1989; Leiner et al., 1986), some also based on clinical observations (e.g., Botez, Gravel, Attig, & Vezina, 1985; Hamilton, Frick, Takahashi, & Hopping, 1983). More recent studies of normal subjects have confirmed these links; for instance, a recent PET study has confirmed an earlier theory (Leiner et al., 1986) by showing that the lateral cerebellum is activated during semantic tasks (Petersen et al., 1989) and a functional MR study found activation of cerebellar dentate nuclei during cognitive processing in normal subjects (Kim, Ugurbil, & Strick, 1994).

Thus, research on infantile autism illustrates that, with regard to the understanding of normal human brain function and development, the major contribution of developmental psychopathologies is to bring to our attention the startling examples of important function gone wrong. That contributions by clinical cases are possible is attested to by the long history of invaluable contributions made by adult patients. For example, the famous case of Phineas P. Gage made us aware of the importance of frontal lobes for personality, affect and motivation, attention, and high-level cognitive function. Another clinical case made us aware of the importance of "Broca's" area for speech (Broca, 1861), and other cases highlighted the importance of different cortical areas in speech and language (Wernicke, 1874). Similarly, observations of patient HM first made us aware of the importance of medial temporal lobe structures for human memory (Scoville & Milner, 1957), and patients made us aware of the importance of posterior cortical areas for attention (Critchley, 1966; Denny-Brown & Banker, 1954; Heilman et al., 1983; Heilman et al., 1985; Posner et al., 1984). Discussion in this chapter makes clear that progress in forming links between abnormal behavior and underlying brain structure and function will typically be easier with patients with adult onset lesions than with patients with developmental psychopathologies. Both types of patients, however, hold the potential to ultimately reveal brain mechanisms that might otherwise remain hidden.

When development is progressing normally, it is sometimes difficult to identify underlying causal processes. In animals, scientist-made perturbations (see Note 3) allow us to shake up the normal sequence of development and to see underlying causal processes. As the result of naturally occurring perturbations, however, developmental psychopathologies make us aware of major rifts in the normal human developmental landscape.

Like geologic faults that remain invisible to us until forces perturb them sufficiently to perturb us, factors that normally shape the neural landscape remain invisible to us until scientists or naturally occurring events apply forces that perturb them sufficiently to disrupt the normal course of development.

FUTURE DIRECTIONS

At the time of Folling's discovery of the key biochemical marker for one form of "social failure," the biologic tools and concepts necessary to unravel its pathogenic bases were unavailable. Nearly half a century passed before biologic tools and concepts became sophisticated enough to identify the specific genetic mechanisms underlying this simple biochemical marker. The story of PKU, then, puts into perspective the rate of progress that has been made in unraveling the biologic bases of much subtler developmental psychopathologies.

In the past, progress has been slow because of the absence of sufficiently sensitive and powerful biologic and diagnostic tools and sufficiently sophisticated knowledge of neurodevelopmental mechanisms. In the past, therefore, theories of the brain bases of developmental psychopathologies have been unavoidably, yet undeniably, simplistic and inaccurate.

At present, in the neurosciences, we have new tools and concepts that can be used to study etiological mechanisms, the brain bases of aberrant functional development, and treatment. For example, many model disorders (Williams, PKU, Lesch-Nyhan, Alzheimer, Huntington, cystic fibrosis) now exist that can guide the design for studies seeking the genetic etiologies underlying developmental psychopathologies. Studies of Alzheimer's disease show that several distinctly different etiologic paths may lead to nearly the same neuropathology and neurobehavioral disorder. Some paths involve inheritance in an autosomal dominant fashion; others apparently occur spontaneously, without evidence of familial inheritance. Some may be solely dependent on genetic defects; others may involve the co-occurrence of genetic defect and environmental insult (e.g., virus, head injury). Also instructive is the amazing story of Williams syndrome, a fascinating disorder affecting language, social, and cognitive development (e.g., Bellugi et al., 1994), in which the pursuit of a genetic explanation for developmental heart valve defects may soon lead to the discovery of genetic defects that produce the unusual language, social, and cognitive features characteristic of

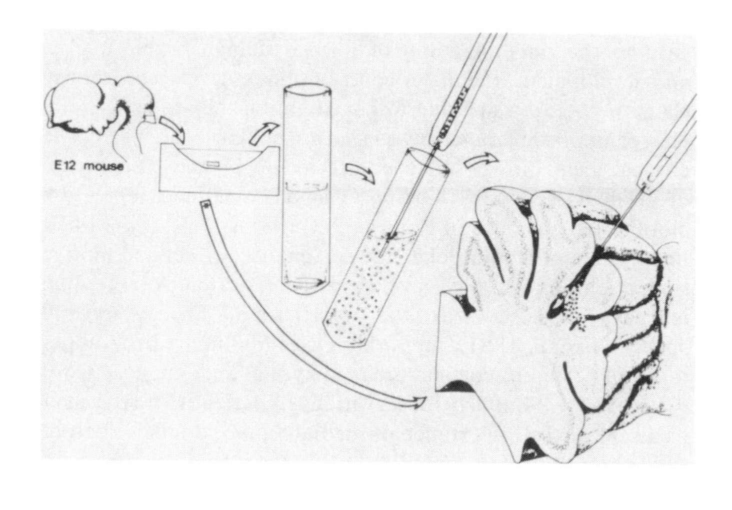

(a)

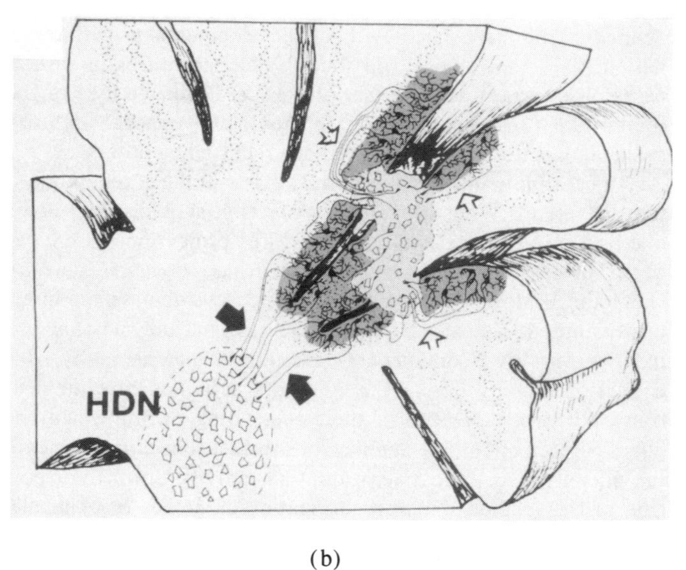

(b)

Figure 7.28 Transplantation of embryonic Purkinje cells into the cerebellum.

(a) In the *"pcd"* mouse, a genetic defect causes cerebellar Purkinje cell death to occur in early postnatal life. The dotted circles along the perimeter of the cerebellar cortex indicate the location of these missing cerebellar neurons. After this Purkinje cell death, healthy embryonic Purkinje cells are transplanted back into the cerebellum. Two transplantation procedures have been used, as indicated by the various arrows: either solid pieces of the cerebellar primordium (long arrow) or cell suspensions (small arrows) have been injected into the host cerebellar cortex.

(b) Schematic representation of one result of Purkinje cell transplantation. When the distance between the grafted embryonic Purkinje cells and the host deep cerebellar nuclei (HDN) is less than 600 μm (but not when greater than 600 μm), some Purkinje cell axons (solid arrows) cross the white matter and make synaptic contact with deep cerebellar neurons, and so partially reconstruct the normal corticonuclear circuit. Although most Purkinje axons do not complete this circuit to HDN (open arrows), the fact that initial experiments have succeeded in partial reconstruction of circuits proves that the reconstruction task is possible. From "The Reconstruction of Cerebellar Circuits" by C. Sotelo and R. M. Alvarado-Mallart, 1991, *Trends in Neuroscience, 14,* pp. 351, 354. Copyright 1991 by Elsevier Trends Journals. Adapted with permission.

this disorder (Ewart et al., 1993). Lastly, the story of the unraveling of the genetic defects behind cystic fibrosis provides a compact model for researchers. [An entire issue of *Science* (November 8, 1989) was devoted to it.]

New in vivo, noninvasive methods for studying in humans the brain bases of aberrant behavioral development have recently appeared. Most are too new to have been used to study changes in structure and function in developmental psychopathologies, but they almost certainly will be used in the future. For instance, it has recently been shown that it is possible to image and map myeloarchitectonic features of cerebral cortex in the living human brain using MR imaging (Clark, Courchesne, & Grafe, 1992). Using this new method, coupled with improved high-resolution, fast MR imaging procedures, it should be possible in the near future to noninvasively map the size of and developmental changes in more than 50 cortical areas in the living human. Another method, functional MR (fMR) imaging, is the first noninvasive method with the potential to image at a specific location within the living brain some physiologic effects that are associated with motor, sensory, attention, memory, and language processes (Belliveau et al., 1991; Kwong et al., 1992; Le Bihan, Turner, Moseley, & Hyde, 1993). Still other methods (Dale, 1994) are being developed for calculating the approximate neuroanatomical locations of sources of event-related brain potentials (ERPs) and magnetoencephalograms (MEGs). This would add a powerful new dimension to functional imaging with ERPs and MEGs; they already offer a temporal resolution for functional activity that is higher than available by any other in vivo method in humans and can be used in babies as well as adults to index a variety of sensory, motor, attention, memory, and language functions (Regan, 1989). In the past two decades, new methods have been invented for analyzing microstructural and histochemical characteristics of autopsy material, but almost none of these methods has been used in autopsy studies of cases with developmental psychopathologies.

In addition to continued advances in existent behavioral or pharmacological treatment modalities, entirely new treatment modalities, such as gene therapy or neural transplants, are on the horizon. For example, in a strain of mice called "pcd," a genetic defect causes cerebellar Purkinje cells to die suddenly in early postnatal life (Mullen, Eicher, & Sidman, 1976). Recent experiments have transplanted embryonic Purkinje cells back into the cerebellum of the pcd mouse (Sotelo & Alvarado-Mallart, 1991) (Figure 7.28). These grafted embryonic Purkinje cells migrate, grow, differentiate, and make many of the connections that are normal for cerebellar circuits. One of several difficulties encountered in the pcd mouse experiments is that, when grafted embryonic Purkinje cell axons attempt to grow out to their normal target site, the deep cerebellar nuclei, they are blocked by gliosis (a kind of brain scar) left behind by the earlier death of the mouse's natural Purkinje cells. In autism, there might not be this particular block to reconstruction of this cerebellar connection because there is no gliosis.

Future progress hinges not only on the use of sophisticated tools and designs, but also on the use of sophisticated neurodevelopmental concepts. Indeed, this latter point rests at the heart of this chapter. Overly simplistic hypotheses that clearly ignore modern neurodevelopmental concepts should be strongly discouraged. Hypotheses to take seriously will be recognized by clear attempts to place results into a realistic neurodevelopmental framework.

REFERENCES

Akshoomoff, N. A. (1992). Neuropsychological studies of attention and the role of the cerebellum (Doctoral dissertation, University of California, San Diego).

Akshoomoff, N. A., & Courchesne, E. (1992). A new role of the cerebellum in cognitive operations. *Behavioral Neuroscience, 106,* 731–738.

Akshoomoff, N. A., & Courchesne, E. (1994). Intramodality shifting attention in children with damage to the cerebellum. *Journal of Cognitive Neuroscience, 6, 388–399.*

Akshoomoff, N. A., Courchesne, E., Press, G., & Iragui, V. (1992). Contribution of the cerebellum to neuropsychological functioning: Evidence from a case of cerebellar degenerative disorder. *Neuropsychologia, 30,* 315–328.

Alberts, B., Bray, D., Lewis, J., Raft, M., Roberts, K., & Watson, J. D. (1989). *Molecular biology of the cell* (2nd ed.). New York: Garland.

Altman, J. (1982). Morphological development of the rat cerebellum and some of its mechanisms. In S. L. Palay & V. Chan-Palay (Eds.), *The cerebellum—New Vistas* (pp. 8–49). New York. Springer-Verlag.

American Psychiatric Association. (1968, 1980, 1987, 1994). *Diagnostic and statistical manual of mental disorders* (2nd ed., 3rd ed., 3rd ed. rev., 4th ed.). Washington, DC: Author.

Antonini, A., & Stryker, M. P. (1992). Morphological changes of single geniculocortical axons in the cat visual cortex during normal development and in the absence of retinal activity. *Investigative Ophthalmology and Visual Science, 33,* 1217.

Arin, D. M., Bauman, M. L., & Kemper, T. L. (1991). The distribution of Purkinje cell loss in the cerebellum in autism. *Neurology, 41* (Suppl. 1), 307.

Bakeman, R., & Adamson, L. B. (1984). Coordinating attention to people and objects in mother-infant and peer-infant interaction. *Child Development, 55,* 1278–1289.

Bauman, M. L. (1991). Microscopic neuroanatomic abnormalities in autism. *Pediatrics, 87,* 791–796.

Bauman, M. L., & Kemper, T. (1985). Histoanatomic observations of the brain in early infantile autism. *Neurology, 35,* 866–874.

Bauman, M. L., & Kemper, T. (1986). Developmental cerebellar abnormalities: A consistent finding in early infantile autism. *Neurology, 36* (Suppl. 1), 190.

Bauman, M. L., & Kemper, T. (1990). Limbic and cerebellar abnormalities are also present in an autistic child of normal intelligence. *Neurology, 40* (Suppl. 1), 359.

Bava, A., Manzoni, T., & Urbano, A. (1966) Cerebellar influences on neuronal elements of thalamic somatosensory relay-nuclei. *Archives of Scientific Biology, 50,* 199.

Beckmann, H., & Jakob, H. (1991). Prenatal disturbances of nerve cell migration in the entorhinal region: A common vulnerability factor in functional psychoses? *Journal of Neural Transmission: General Section, 84* (1-2), 155–164.

Belliveau, J. W., Kennedy, D. N., McKinstry, R. C., Buchbinder, B. R., Weisskoff, R. M., Cohen, M. S., Vevea, J. M., Brady, T. J., & Rosen, B. R. (1991). Functional mapping of the human visual cortex by magnetic resonance imaging. *Science, 254,* 621–768.

Bellugi, U., Wang, P. P., & Jernigan, T. L. (1994). Williams syndrome: An unusual neuropsychological profile. In S. H. Broman & J. Grafman (Eds.), *Atypical cognitive deficits in developmental disorders: Implications for brain function* (pp. 23–56). Hillsdale, NJ: Erlbaum.

Blau, K. (1979). Phenylalanine hydroxylase deficiency: Biochemical, physiological, and clinical aspects of phenylketonuria and related phenylalaninemias. In M. B. H. Youdim (Ed.), *Aromatic amino acid hydroxylases and mental disease* (pp. 77–139). Chichester, England: Wiley.

Bogerts, B., Meertz, E., & Schonfeldt-Bausch, R. (1985). Basal ganglia and limbic system pathology in schizophrenia: A morphometric study of brain volume and shrinkage. *Archives of General Psychiatry, 43,* 36–42.

Botez, M. I., Botez, T., Elie, R., & Attig, E. (1989). Role of the cerebellum in complex human behavior. *The Italian Journal of Neurological Sciences, 10,* 291–300.

Botez, M I., Gravel, J., Attig, E., & Vezina, J. L. (1985). Reversible chronic cerebellar ataxia after Phenytoin intoxication: Possible role of cerebellum in cognitive thought. *Neurology, 35,* 1152–1157.

Bracke-Tolkmitt, R., Linden, A., Canavan, A. G. M., Rockstroh, B., Scholtz, E., Wessel, K., & Diener, H. C. (1989). The cerebellum contributes to mental skills. *Behavioral Neuroscience, 103*(2), 442–446.

Broca, P. (1861). Rémarques sur le siege de la faculté du language articule, suives d'une observation d'aphemie. *Bulletin de la Société Anatomie, 2,* 330–357.

Bruner, J. (1975). The ontogenesis of speech acts. *Journal of Child Language, 2,* 1–19.

Cancro, R. (1985). History and overview of schizophrenia. In H. Kaplan & B. J. Sadock (Eds.), *Comprehensive textbook of psychiatry/IV* (4th ed.). Baltimore: Williams & Wilkins.

Chalupa, L. M., & Killackey, H. P. (1989). Process elimination underlies ontogenetic change in the distribution of callosal projection neurons in the postcentral gyrus of the fetal rhesus monkey. *Proceedings of the National Academy of Sciences, 86,* 1076–1079.

Chambers, W. W., & Sprague, J. M. (1955). Functional localization in the cerebellum: II. Somatotopic organization in cortex and nuclei. *Archives of Neurologic Psychiatry, 74,* 653–680.

Changeux, J. P., & Danchin, A. (1976). Selective stabilisation of developing synapses as a mechanism for the specification of neural networks. *Nature, 264,* 705–712.

Chase, C. H., & Tallal, P. (1991). Cognitive models of developmental reading disorders. In J. E. Obrzut & G. W. Hynd (Eds.), *Neuropsychological foundations of learning disabilities* (pp. 199–240). San Diego: Academic Press.

Choi, D. W. (1992). Bench to bedside: The glutamate connection. *Science, 258,* 241–243.

Chugani, H. T., & Phelps, M. E. (1991). Imaging human brain development with positron emission tomography. *Journal of Nuclear Medicine, 32,* 23–26.

Chugani, H. T., Phelps, M. E., & Mazziota, J. C. (1987). Positron emission tomography study of human brain functional development. *Annals of Neurology, 22,* 487–497.

Ciesielski, K. T., Allen, P. S., Sinclair, B. D., Pabst, H. F., Yanossky, R., & Ludwig, R. (1992). Hypoplasia of cerebellar vermis in autism and childhood leukemia. In *Proceedings of the Fifth International Child Neurology Congress* (p. 650). New York: Karger.

Clark, V. P., Courchesne, E., & Grafe, M. (1992). In vivo myeloarchitectonic analysis of human striate and extrastriate cortex using magnetic resonance imaging. *Cerebral Cortex, 2,* 417–424.

Courchesne, E. (1985, May). *The missing ingredients in autism.* Paper presented at the Conference on Brian and Behavioral Development: Biosocial Dimension, Elridge, MD.

Courchesne, E. (1987). A neurophysiologic view of autism. In E. Schopler & G. Mesibov (Eds.), *Neurobiological issues in autism* (pp. 258–324). New York: Plenum.

Courchesne, E. (1989). Neuroanatomical systems involved in infantile autism: The implications of cerebellar abnormalities. In G. Dawson (Ed.), *Autism: New perspectives on diagnosis, nature, and treatment* (pp. 119–143). New York: Guilford.

Courchesne, E. (1991). Neuroanatomic imaging in autism. *Pediatrics, 87,* 781–790.

Courchesne, E. (in press). New evidence of cerebellar and brainstem hypoplasia in autistic infants, children and adolescents: The Hashimoto et al., study. *Journal of Austism & Developmental Disorders.*

Courchesne, E., Akshoomoff, N. A., & Townsend, J. (1990). Recent advances in autism. *Current Opinion in Pediatrics, 2,* 685–693.

Courchesne, E., Akshoomoff, N. A., Townsend, J., & Saitoh, O. (1994). A model system for the study of attention and the cerebellum: Infantile autism. In G. Karmos, M. Molnar, V. Csepe, L. Czigler & J. E. Desmedt (Eds.), Perspectives of Event-Related Potentials, *Journal of Electroencephalography & Clinical Neurophysiology* (Suppl. 44), 315–325.

Courchesne, E., Chisum, H. J., & Townsend, J. (1994). Neural activity-dependent brain changes in development: Implications for psychopathology. *Development and Psychopathology, 6,* 699–723.

Courchesne, E., Hesselink, J. R., Jernigan, T. L., & Yeung-Courchesne, R. (1987). Abnormal neuroanatomy in a nonretarded person with autism: Unusual findings with magnetic resonance imaging. *Archives of Neurology, 44,* 335–341.

Courchesne, E., Press, G. A., & Yeung-Courchesne, R. (1993). Parietal lobe abnormalities detected on magnetic resonance images of patients with infantile autism. *American Journal of Roentgenology, 160,* 387–393.

Courchesne, E., Saitoh, O., Townsend, J. P., Yeung-Courchesne, R., Press, G. A., Lincoln, A. J., Haas, R. H., & Schreibman, L. (1994). Cerebellar hypoplasia and hyperplasia in infantile autism. *Lancet, 343,* 63–64.

Courchesne, E., Saitoh, O., Yeung-Courchesne, R., Press, G. A., Lincoln, A. J., Haas, R. H., & Schreibman, L. (1994). Abnormality of cerebellar vermian lobules VI and VII in patients with infantile autism: Identification of hypoplastic and hyperplastic subgroups by MR imaging. *American Journal of Roentgenology, 162,* 123–130.

Courchesne, E., Townsend, J., Akshoomoff, N. A., Saitoh, O., Yeung-Courchesne, R., Lincoln, A.J., James, H., Haas, R., Schreibman, L., & Lau, L. (1994). Impairment in shifting attention in autistic and cerebellar patients. *Behaviorial Neurosciences, 108,* 1–18.

Courchesne, E., Townsend, J., Akshoomoff, N. A., Yeung-Courchesne, R., Press, G., Murakami, J., Lincoln, A., James, H., Saitoh, O., Haas, R., & Schreibman, L. (1994). A new finding: Impairment in shifting attention in autistic and cerebellar patients. In S. H. Broman & J. Grafman (Eds.), *Atypical cognitive deficits in developmental disorders: Implications for brain function* (pp. 160–393). Hillsdale, NJ: Erlbaum.

Courchesne, E., Townsend, J., & Saitoh, O. (1994). The brain in infantile autism: Posterior fossa structures are abnormal. *Neurology, 44,* 214–223.

Courchesne, E., Yeung-Courchesne, R., Press, G. A., Hesselink, J. R., & Jernigan, T. L. (1988). Hypoplasia of cerebellar vermal lobules VI and VII in autism. *The New England Journal of Medicine, 318,* 1349–1354.

Cowan, W. M., Fawcett, J. W., O'Leary, D. D. M., & Stanfield, B. B. (1984). Regressive events in neurogenesis. *Science, 225,* 1258–1265.

Crepel, F. (1982). Regression of functional synapses in the immature mammalian cerebellum. *Trends in Neurosciences, 5,* 266–269.

Crick, F. (1984). Function of the thalamic reticular complex: The searchlight hypothesis. *Proceedings of the National Academy of Science, 81,* 4586–4590.

Crispino, L., & Bullock, T. H. (1984). Cerebellum mediates modality-specific modulation of sensory responses of the midbrain and forebrain in rat. *Proceedings of the National Academy of Science, 81,* 2917–2920.

Critchley, M. (1966). *The parietal lobes.* New York: Hafner.

Curcio, F. (1978). Sensorimotor functioning and communication in mute autistic children. *Journal of Autism and Childhood Schizophrenia, 8,* 281–292.

Dale, A. M. (1994). Source localization and spatial discriminant analysis of event-related potentials: Linear approaches. Doctorial dissertation, University of California, San Diego, Special Collection Archives, BF 310.6.D35.

Dawson, G., & Lewy, A. (1989). Arousal, attention and the socioemotional impairments of individuals with autism. In G. Dawson (Ed.), Autism: Nature, diagnosis and treatment (pp. 49–74). New York: Guilford.

Dehay, C., Horsburgh, G., Berland, M., Killackey, H., & Kennedy, H. (1989). Maturation and connectivity of the visual cortex in monkey is altered by prenatal removal of retinal input. *Nature, 337,* 265–267.

Denny-Brown, D., & Banker, B. Q. (1954). Amorphosynthesis from left parietal lesions. *Archives of Neurological Psychiatry,* 71, 302–313.

Dow, R. S. (1988). Contributions of electrophysiological studies to cerebellar physiology. *Journal of Clinical Neurophysiology, 5,* 307–323.

Edelman, G. M. (1987). *Neural Darwinism.* New York: Basic Books.

Egaas, B., Courchesne, E., & Saitoh, O. (in press). Reduced size of corpus callosum in autism. *Archives of Neurology.*

Ewart, A. K., Morris, C. A., Atkinson, D., Jin, W., Sternes, K., Spallone, P., Stock, A. D., Leppert, M., & Keating, M. T. (1993). Hemizygosity at the elastin locus in a developmental disorder, Williams syndrome. *Nature Genetics, 5,* 11–16.

Friedlander, M. J., Martin, K. A. C., & Wassenhove-McCarthy, D. (1991). Effects of monocular visual deprivation on geniculocortical innervation of area 18 in cat. *Journal of Neuroscience,11,* 3268–3288.

Frith, U. (1989). A new look at language and communication in autism. *British Journal of Disorders of Communication, 24,* 123–150.

Frost, D. O., & Metin, C. (1985). Induction of functional retinal projections to the somatosensory system. *Nature, 317,* 162–164.

Gaffney, G. R., Tsai, L. Y., Kuperman, S., & Minchin, S. (1987). Cerebellar structure in autism. *American Journal of Diseases in Children, 141,* 1330–1332.

Gahl, W., Renlund, M., & Thoene, J. (1989). Lysosomal transport disorders: Cystinosis and sialic acid storage disorder. In C. Scriver, A. Beaudet, W. Sly, & D. Valle (Eds.), *The metabolic basis of inherited disease* (6th ed.) (pp. 2619–2647). New York: McGraw-Hill.

Galaburda, A. M., & Eidelberg, D. (1982). Symmetry and asymmetry in the human posterior thalamus: II. Thalamic lesions in a case of development dyslexia. *Archives of Neurology, 39,* 333–336.

Galaburda, A. M., Rosen, G. D., & Sherman, A. F. (1989). The neural origin of developmental dyslexia: Implications for medicine, neurology, and cognition. In A. M. Galaburda (Ed.), *From reading to neurons* (pp. 377–388). Cambridge, MA: MIT Press.

Galaburda, A. M., Sherman, G. F., Rosen, G. D., Aboitiz, F., & Geschwind, N. (1985). Developmental dyslexia: Four consecutive patients with cortical anomalies. *Annals of Neurology, 18,* 222–233.

Garber, H. J., Ritvo, E. R., Chui, L. C., Griswold, V. J., Kashanian, A., & Oldendorf, W. H. (1989). A magnetic resonance imaging study of autism: Normal fourth ventricle size and absence of pathology. *American Journal of Psychiatry, 146,* 532–535.

Garber, H. J., & Ritvo, E. R. (1992). Magnetic resonance imaging of the posterior fossa in autistic adults. *American Journal of Psychiatry, 149,* 245–247.

Ghez, C. (1991). The cerebellum. In E. R. Kandel, J. H. Schwartz, & T. M. Jessell (Eds.), *Principles of neural science* (3rd ed., pp. 626–636). New York: Elsevier.

Gramsbergen, A., & Ijkema-Paassen, J. (1984). Cerebellar hemispherectomy at young ages in rats. In J. R. Bloedel, J. Dichgans, & W. Precht (Eds.), *Cerebellar functions* (pp. 164–167). New York: Springer-Verlag.

Haines, D. E., & Dietrichs, E. (1987). On the organization of interconnections between the cerebellum and hypothalamus. In J. E. King (Ed.), *New concepts in cerebellar neurobiology* (pp. 113–149). New York: Liss.

Hamilton, N. G., Frick, R. B., Takahashi, T., & Hopping, M. W. (1983). Psychiatric symptoms and cerebellar pathology. *American Journal of Psychiatry, 140,* 1322–1326.

Harter, M. R., & Aine, C. J. (1984). Brain mechanisms of visual selective attention. In R. Parasuraman & D. R. Davies (Eds.), *Varieties of attention.* New York: Academic Press.

Hashimoto, T., Tayama, M., Murakawa, K., Yoshimoto, T., Miyazaki, M., Harada, M., & Kuroda, Y. (in press). Development of the brain stem and cerebellum in autistic patients. *Journal of Autism and Development Disorders.*

Heilman, K. M., Valenstein, E., & Watson, R. T. (1983). Localization of neglect. In A. Kertesz (Ed.). *Localization in neuropsychology* (pp. 471–492). New York: Academic Press.

Heilman, K. M., Watson, R. T., & Valenstein, E. (1985). Neglect and related disorders. In K. M. Heilman & E. Valenstein (Eds.), *Clinical neuropsychology* (2nd ed.). New York: Oxford University Press.

Hockfield, S., & Kalb, R. G. (1993). Activity-dependent structural changes during neuronal development. *Current Opinion in Neurobiology, 3,* 87–92.

Holttum, J. R., Minshew, N. J., Sanders, R. S., & Phillips, N. E. (1992). Magnetic resonance imaging of the posterior fossa in autism. *Biological Psychiatry, 32* 1091–1101.

Horwitz, B., Rumsey, J., Grady, C., & Rapoport, S. (1988). The cerebral metabolic landscape in autism. *Archives of Neurology, 45,* 749–755.

Huttenlocher, P. R. (1979). Synaptic density in human frontal cortex—developmental changes and effects of aging. *Brain Research, 163,* 195–205.

Innocenti, G. M. (1981). Growth and reshaping of axons in the establishment of visual callosal connection. *Science, 212,* 824–826.

Ito, M. (1984). *The cerebellum and neural control.* New York: Raven Press.

Itoh, K., & Mizuno, N. (1979). A cerebello-pulvinar projection in the cat as visualized by the use of antero-grade transport of horseradish peroxidase. *Brain Research, 106,* 131–134.

Ivry, R. B., & Keele, S. W. (1989). Timing functions of the cerebellum. *Journal of Cognitive Neuroscience, 1,* 136–152.

Ivry, R. B., Keele, S. W., & Diener, H. C. (1988). Dissociation of the lateral and medial cerebellum in movement timing and movement execution. *Experimental Brain Research, 73,* 167–180.

Jakob, H., & Beckmann, H. (1986). Prenatal developmental disturbances in the limbic allocortex in schizophrenics. *Journal of Neural Transmission, 65,* 303–326.

Jakob, H., & Beckmann, H. (1989). Gross and histological criteria for developmental disorders in brains of schizophrenics. *Journal of the Royal Society of Medicine, 82*(8), 466–469.

Jensen, K. F., & Killackey, H. P. (1987). Terminal arbors of axons projecting to the somatosensory cortex of the adult rat: I. The altered morphology of specific thalamocortical afferents. *Journal of Neuroscience, 7,* 3529–3543.

Jinnah, H. A. (1992). The neurologic consequences of hypoxanthine-guanine phosphoribosyltransferase deficiency in a genetic mouse model of Lesch-Nyhan disease (Doctoral dissertation, University of California, San Diego).

Jinnah, H. A., Gage, F. H., & Friedmann, T. (1990). Animal models of Lesch-Nyhan syndrome. *Brain Research Bulletin, 25,* 467–475.

Joynt, R. J., & Shoulson, I. (1985). Dementia. In K. M. Heilman & E. Valenstein (Eds.), *Clinical neuropsychology* (2nd ed., pp. 453–480). New York: Oxford University Press.

Kandel, K. R., Schwartz, J. H., & Jessell, T. M. (1991). *Principles of neural science* (3rd ed.). Norwalk, CT: Appleton & Lange.

Kanner, L. (1943). Autistic disturbances of affective contact. *Nervous Child, 2,* 217–250.

Katz, L. C. (1993). Coordinate activity in retinal and cortical development. *Current Opinion in Neurobiology, 3,* 93–99.

Katzman, R. (1986). Alzheimer's disease. *The New England Journal of Medicine, 314,* 964–973.

Killackey, H. P. (1990). Neocortical expansion: An attempt toward relating phylogeny and ontogeny. *Journal of Cognitive Neuroscience, 2,* 1–17.

Kim, S.-G., Ugurbil, K., & Strick, P. L. (1994). Activation of a cerebellar output nucleus during cognitive processing. *Science,* 265, 949–951.

Kleiman, M. D., Neff, S., & Rosman, N. P. (1992). The brain in infantile autism: Are posterior fossa structures abnormal? *Neurology, 42,* 753–760.

Kosslyn, S. M., & Intriligator, J. M. (1992). Is cognitive neuropsychology plausible? The perils of sitting on a one-legged stool. *Journal of Cognitive Neuroscience, 4,* 96–106.

Kwong, K. K., Belliveau, J. W., Chesler, D. A., Goldberg, I. E., Weisskoff, R. M., Poncelet, B. P., Kennedy, D. N., Hoppel, B. E., Cohen, M. S., Turner, R., Cheng, H-M., Brady, T. J., & Rosen, B. R. (1992). Dynamic magnetic resonance imaging of human brain activity during primary sensory stimulation. *Neurobiology, 89,* 5675–5679.

LaBerge, D. (1990). Thalamic and cortical mechanisms of attention suggested by recent positron emission tomographic experiments. *Journal of Cognitive Neuroscience, 2,* 358–372.

Landry, S. H., & Loveland, K. A. (1988). Communication behaviors in autism and developmental language delay. *Journal of Child Psychology and Psychiatry and Allied Disciplines, 29,* 621–634.

Le Bihan, D., Turner, R., Moseley, M. E., & Hyde, J. S. (1993, June). Functional MRI of the brain. A report on the SMRM/SMRI workshop. *Magnetic Resonance Medicine, 30,* 405–408.

Leiner, H. C., Leiner, A. L., & Dow, R. S. (1986). Does the cerebellum contribute to mental skills? *Behavioral Neuroscience, 100,* 443–454.

Leiner, H. C., Leiner, A. L., & Dow, R. S. (1989). Reappraising the cerebellum: What does the hindbrain contribute to the forebrain? *Behavioral Neuroscience, 103*(5), 998–1008.

Lelord, G., Laffont, F., Jusseaume, P., & Stephant, J. L. (1973). Comparative study of conditioning of averaged evoked responses by coupling sound and light in normal and autistic children. *Psychophysiology, 10,* 415–427.

Lesch, M., & Nyhan, W. L. (1964). A familial disorder of uric acid metabolism and central nervous system function. *American Journal of Medicine, 36,* 561–570.

Leslie, A. M. (1982). The perception of causality in infants. *Perception, 11,* 173–186.

Leslie, A. M. (1988). The necessity of illusion: Perception and thought in infancy. In L. Weiskrantz (Ed.), *Thought without language* (pp. 185–210). Oxford, England: Clarendon.

Livingstone, M. S., Rosen, G. D., Drislane, F. W., & Galaburda, A. M. (1991). Physiological and anatomical evidence for a magnocellular defect in developmental dyslexia. *Proceedings of the National Academy of Sciences, 88,* 7943–7947.

Llinas, R. R. (1988). The intrinsic electrophysiological properties of mammalian neurons: Insights into central nervous system function. *Science, 242,* 1654–1664.

Loveland, K. A., & Landry, S. H. (1986). Joint attention and language in autism and developmental language delay. *Journal of Autism and Developmental Disorders, 16,* 335–349.

Lovett, M. W., Ransby, M. J., Hardwick, N., Johns, M. S., & Donaldson, S. A. (1989). Can dyslexia be treated? Treatment-specific and generalized treatment effects in dyslexic children's response to remediation. *Brain and Language, 37,* 90–121.

Lund, R. D. (1978). *Development and plasticity of the brain* (pp. 1–15). New York: Oxford University Press.

Macagno, E. R., Lopresti, V., & Levinthal, C. (1973). Structure and development of neuronal connections in isogeneic organisms: Variations and similarities in the optic system of Daphnia magna. *Proceedings of the National Academy of Sciences, 70,* 57–61.

Mandler, J. (1992). How to build a baby: II. Conceptual primitives. *Psychological Review, 99*(4), 587–604.

Martineau, J., Garreau, B., Roux, S., & Lelord, G. (1987). Auditory evoked responses and their modifications during conditioning paradigm in autistic children. *Journal of Autism and Developmental Disorders, 17*(4), 525–539.

Martineau, J., Roux, S., Adrien, J. L., Garreau, B., Barthelemy, C., & Lelord, G. (1992). Electrophysiological evidence of different abilities to form cross-modal associations in children with autistic behavior. *Electroencephalography and Clinical Neurophysiology, 82,* 60–66.

McArdle, C. B., Richardson, C. J., Nicholas, D. A., Mirfakhraee, M., Hayden, C. K., & Amparo, E. G. (1987). Developmental features of the neonatal brain: MR imaging part II. Ventricular size and extracerebral space. *Radiology, 162,* 230–234.

Mesulam, M. (1981). A cortical network for directed attention and unilateral neglect. *Annals of Neurology, 10,* 309–325.

Miller, K. D., Keller, J. B., & Stryker, M. P. (1989). Ocular dominance column development: Analysis and simulation. *Science, 245,* 605–615.

Moruzzi, G., & Magoun, H. W. (1949). Brain stem reticular formation and activation of the EEG. *Electroencephalography and Clinical Neurophysiology, 1,* 455–473.

Mullen, R. J., Eicher, E. M., & Sidman, R. L. (1976). Purkinje cell degeneration: A new neurological mutation in the mouse. *Proceedings of the National Academy of Science, 73,* 208–212.

Mundy, P., Sigman, M., & Kasari, C. (1990). A longitudinal study of joint attention and language development in autistic children. *Journal of Autism and Developmental Disorders, 20,* 115–128.

Mundy, P., Sigman, M., Ungerer, J., & Sherman, T. (1986). Defining the social deficits of autism: The contribution of non-verbal communication measures. *Journal of Child Psychology and Psychiatry and Allied Disciplines, 27,* 657–669.

Murakami, J. W., Courchesne, E., Press, G. A., Yeung-Courchesne, R., & Hesselink, J. R. (1989). Reduced cerebellar hemisphere size and its relationship to vermal hypoplasia in autism. *Neurology, 46,* 689–694.

Newman, P. P., & Reza, H. (1979). Functional relationships between the hippocampus and cerebellum: An electrophysiological study of the cat. *Journal of Physiology, 287,* 405–426.

Nieuwenhuys, R., Voogd, J., & van Huijzen, C. (1988). *The human central nervous system* (pp. 221–226). Berlin: Springer-Verlag.

O'Leary, D. D. M. (1989). Do cortical areas emerge from a protocortex? *Trends in Neuroscience, 12,* 400–406.

O'Leary, D. D. M., & Koester, S. E. (1993). Development of projection neuron types, axon pathways, and patterned connections of the mammalian cortex. *Neuron, 10,* 991–1006.

O'Leary, D. D. M., Stanfield, B. B., & Cowan, W. M. (1981). Evidence that the early postnatal restriction of the cells of origin of the callosal projection is due to the elimination of axon collaterals rather than to the death of neurons. *Developmental Brain Research, 1,* 607–617.

O'Leary, D. D. M., & Terashima, T. (1988). Cortical axons branch to multiple subcortical targets by interstitial axons budding: Implications for target recognition and "waiting periods." *Neuron, 1,* 901–910.

Petersen, S. E., Robinson, D. L., & Currie, J. N. (1989). Influences of lesions of parietal cortex on visual spatial attention in humans. *Experimental Brain Research, 76,* 267–280.

Piven, J., Nehme, E., Simon, J., Barta, P., Pearlson, G., & Folstein, S. E. (1992). Magnetic resonance imaging in autism: Measurement of the cerebellum, pons and fourth ventricle. *Biological Psychiatry, 31,* 491–504.

Posner, M. I., Walker, J. A., Freidrich, F. A., & Rafal, R. D. (1984). Effects of parietal injury on covert orienting of attention. *Journal of Neuroscience, 4*(7), 1863–1874.

Posner, M. I., Walker, J. A., Freidrich, F. A., & Rafal, R. D. (1987). How do the parietal lobes direct covert attention? *Neuropsychologia, 25*(1A), 135–145.

Purves, D. (1988). *Body and brain: A trophic theory of neural connections.* Cambridge, MA: Harvard University Press.

Rafal, R. D., & Posner, M. I. (1987). Deficits in human visual spatial attention following thalamic lesions. *Proceedings of the National Academy of Science, 84,* 7349–7353.

Rakic, P. (1981). Development of visual centers in the primate brain depends on binocular competition before birth. *Science, 214,* 928–931.

Rakic, P. (1984). Defective cell-to-cell interactions as causes of brain malformations. In E. S. Gollin (Ed.), *Malformations of development: Biological and psychological sources and consequences.* New York: Academic Press.

Rakic, P. (1988). Specification of cerebral cortical areas. *Science, 241,* 170–176.

Rakic, P., Bourgeois, J. P., Eckenhoff, M. F., Zecevic, N., & Goldman-Rakic, P. S. (1986). Concurrent overproduction of synapses in diverse regions of the primate cerebral cortex. *Science, 232,* 232–235.

Raymond, G., Bauman, M. L., & Kemper, T. (1989). The hippocampus in autism: Golgi analysis. *Annals of Neurology, 26,* 483–484.

Raz, N., Torres, I. J., Spencer, W. D., White, K., & Acker, J. D. (1992). Age-related regional differences in cerebellar vermis observed in vivo. *Archives of Neurology, 49,* 412–416.

Regan, D. (1989). *Human brain electrophysiology: Evoked potentials and evoked magnetic fields in science and medicine.* New York: Elsevier.

Ritvo, E. R., Freeman, B. J., Scheibel, A. B., Duong, T., Robinson, H., Guthrie, D., & Ritvo, A. (1986). Lower Purkinje cell counts in the cerebella of four autistic subjects: Initial findings of the UCLA-NSAC autopsy research report. *American Journal of Psychiatry, 143,* 862–866.

Rosenzweig, M. R., Bennett, E. L., & Alberti, M. (1984). Multiple effects of lesions on brain structure in young rats. In S. Finger & C. R. Almli (Eds.), *Early brain damage: Vol. 2. Neurobiology and behavior,* Orlando, FL: Academic Press.

Saitoh, O., Courchesne, E., Egaas, B., Lincoln, A. J., & Schreibman, L. (1994). Cross-sectional area of the posterior hippocampus in autistic patients with cerebellar and corpus callosum abnormalities. *Neurology.*

Sasaki, K., Jinnai, K., Gemba, H., Hashimoto, S., & Mizuno, N. (1979). Projection of the cerebellar dentate nucleus onto the frontal association cortex in monkeys. *Experimental Brain Researach, 37,* 193–198.

Sasaki, K., Matsuda, Y., Kawaguichi, S., & Mizuno, N. (1972). On the cerebello-thalamo-cerebral pathway for the parietal cortex. *Experimental Brain Research, 16,* 89–103.

Schmahmann, J., & Pandya, D. N. (1989). Anatomical investigation of projections to the basis pontis from the posterior parietal association cortices in rhesus monkey. *Journal of Comparative Neurology, 289,* 53–73.

Schneider, G. E. (1979). Is it really better to have your brain lesion early? A revision of the "Kennard Principle." *Neuropsychologia, 17,* 557–583.

Schreibman, L., & Lovaas, O. (1973). Overselective response to social stimuli by autistic children. *Journal of Abnormal Child Psychology, 1,* 152–168.

Science. (1989). *245,*1021–1152. (Special issue.)

Scoville, W. B., & Milner, B. (1957). Loss of recent memory after bilateral hippocampal lesions. *Journal of Neurology and Neurosurgery in Psychiatry, 20,* 11–21.

Seo, M. L., & Ito, M. (1987). Reorganization of rat vibrissa barrelfield as studied by cortical lesioning on different postnatal days. *Experimental Brain Research, 65,* 251–260.

Sidman, R. L., & Green, M. C. (1970). "Nervous," a new mutant mouse with cerebellar disease. In M. Sabourdy (Ed.), *Les mutants pathologiques chez l'animal, leur interêt pour la récherche biomedicale* (pp. 69–79). Paris: Editions du Centre National de la Récherche Scientifique.

Siegler, R. S. (1989). Mechanisms of cognitive development. *Annual Review of Psychology, 40,* 353–379.

Sigman, M., Ungerer, J. A., Mundy, P., & Sherman, T. (1987). Cognition in autistic children. In D. Cohen & A. M. Donnellan (Eds.), *Handbook of autism and pervasive developmental disorders* (pp. 103–120). New York: Wiley.

Snider, R. S. (1950). Recent contributions to the anatomy and physiology of the cerebellum. *Archives of Neurological Psychiatry, 64,* 196–219.

Snider, R. S. (1967). Functional alterations of cerebral sensory areas by the cerebellum. In C. A. Fox & R. S. Snider (Eds.), *Progress in brain research: V. The cerebellum, 25* (pp. 322–332). Amsterdam: Elsevier.

Sotelo, C., & Alvarado-Mallart, R. M. (1991). The reconstruction of cerebellar circuits. *Trends in Neuroscience, 14,* 350–355.

Stanfield, B. B., O'Leary, D. D. M., & Fricks, C. (1982). Selective collateral elimination in early postnatal development restricts cortical distribution of rat pyramidal tract neurones. *Nature, 298,* 371–373.

Steriade, M., & Stoupel, N. (1960). Contribution a l'étude des relations entre l'aire auditive du cerebelet et l'ecore cerebrale chez le chat. *Electroencephalography and Clinical Neurophysiology, 12,* 119–136.

Stryker, M. P. (1990). Summary: The brain in 1990. *Cold Spring Harbor Symposia on Quantitative Biology,* 1049–1067.

Stryker, M. P., & Harris, W. A. (1986). Binocular impulse blockade prevents the formation of ocular dominance columns in cat visual cortex. *Journal of Neuroscience, 6,* 2117–2133.

Sur, M., Garraghty, P. E., & Roe, A. W. (1988). Experimentally induced visual projections into auditory thalamus and cortex. *Science, 242,* 1437–1441.

Swanson, J. M., Posner, M. I., Potkin, S., Bonforte, S., Youpa, D., Fiore, C., Cantwell, D., & Crinella F. (1991). Activating tasks for the study of visual-spatial attention in ADHD children: A cognitive anatomic approach. *Journal of Child Neurology, 6,*(Suppl. S) 119–127.

Tallal, P. (1988). Developmental language disorders. In J. F. Kavanagh & T. J. Truss, Jr. (Eds.), *Learning disabilities: Proceedings of the national Conference* (pp. 181–272). Parkton, MD: York Press.

Tallal, P., & Piercy, M. (1973). Defects of nonverbal auditory perception in children with developmental aphasia. *Nature, 241,* 468–469.

Tallal, P., Stark, R., & Mellits, F. (1985). Identification of language-impaired children on the basis of rapid perception and production skills. *Brain and Language, 25,* 314–322.

Townsend, J. (1992). Abnormalities of brain structure and function underlying the distribution of visual attention in autism. Doctoral dissertation, University of California, San Diego.

Townsend, J., & Courchesne, E. (1994). Parietal damage and narrow "spotlight" spatial attention. *Journal of Cognitive Neuroscience, 6,* 218–230.

Townsend, J., & Courchesne, E. (submitted for publication). Slowed orienting of visual-spatial attention in autism: Specific deficits associated with cerebellar and parietal abnormalities.

Townsend, J., Courchesne, E., & Egaas, B. (1992). *Visual attention deficits in autistic adults with cerebellar and parietal abnormalities.* Paper presented at the annual meeting of the Society for Neuroscience, Anaheim, CA. (Abstracts Vol. 18, Part 1. 144.7, 332.)

Trauner, D., Chase, C., Scheller, J., Katz, B., & Schneider, J. (1988). Neurologic and cognitive deficits in cystinosis. *Journal of Pediatrics, 112,* 912–914.

Tronick, E. Z. (1982). Affectivity and sharing. In E. Z. Tronick (Ed.), *Social interchange in infancy: Affect, cognition and communication* (pp. 1–6). Baltimore: University Park Press.

Van der Loos, H., & Woolsey, T. A. (1973). Somatosensory cortex: Structural alterations following early injury to sense organs. *Science, 179,* 395–398.

Vilensky, J. A., & Van Hoesen, G. W. (1981). Corticopontine projections from the cingulate cortex in the rhesus monkey. *Brain Research, 205,* 391–395.

Voyvodic, J. T. (1989). Peripheral target regulation of dendritic geometry in the rat superior cervical ganglion. *Journal of Neuroscience, 9,* 1997–2010.

Wall, J. T. (1988). Variable organization in cortical maps of the skin as an indication of the lifelong adaptive capacities of circuits in the mammalian brain. *Trends in Neurosciences, 11,* 549–557.

Wallesch, C. W., & Horn, A. (1990). Long-term effects of cerebellar pathology on cognitive functions. *Brain and Cognition, 14,* 19–25.

Watson, J. (1972). Smiling, cooing, and "the game." *Merrill-Palmer Quarterly, 18,* 323–340.

Watson, P. J. (1978). Nonmotor functions of the cerebellum. *Psychological Bulletin, 85,* 944–967.

Welker, E., & Van der Loos, H. (1986). Quantitative correlation between barrel-field size and the sensory innervation of the whiskerpad: A comparative study in six strains of mice bred for different patterns of mystacial vibrissae. *Journal of Neuroscience, 6,* 3355–3373.

Wernicke, C. (1874). *Der aphasiche symptomencomplex.* Breslau, Poland: Cohn & Weigart.

Wetherby, A., & Prutting, C. (1984). Profiles of communicative and cognitive-social abilities in autistic children. *Journal of Speech and Hearing Research, 27,* 264–377.

Williams, R. S., Hauser, S. L., Purpura, D. P., DeLong, R., & Swisher, C. N. (1980). Autism and mental retardation: Neuropathologic studies performed in four retarded persons with autistic behavior. *Archives of Neurology, 37,* 749–753.

CHAPTER 8

A Neurodevelopmental Approach to the Understanding of Schizophrenia and Other Mental Disorders

FRANCINE M. BENES

. . . any behavioral condition must be a function both of experience and of the constitution that does the experiencing.

D. O. HEBB, 1949, p. 261

For many decades, the prevailing view concerning disorders of the central nervous system was that they were either neurological or psychiatric in nature. Neurological disorders were considered to be those that altered the substance of the brain; psychiatric disorders were those that involved the emotions and were "functional" in nature. With the advent of pharmacological agents that are effective in the treatment of psychosis, depression, and anxiety, it became clear that a mental illness might entail alterations of brain circuitry and, in this respect, bear some similarity to the neurological disorders. This perspective has provided an impetus for investigations of the pathophysiology and treatment of mental illness that have burgeoned over the past 20 years. Because schizophrenia has been the most extensively studied, the discussion that follows will give a primary focus to psychosis, although affective and, to a lesser extent, anxiety disorders also are addressed.

A popular hypothesis for the etiology of schizophrenia has been that patients with this disorder might have excessive amounts of dopaminergic activity (Carlsson, 1978). With previous family studies revealing a higher incidence of schizophrenia among the relatives of schizophrenics (Kety, Rosenthal, Wender, & Schulsinger, 1968), it was suggested that a genetic factor might be responsible for the proposed increase of dopaminergic activity in schizophrenia (Kety & Matthysse, 1972). Viewing schizophrenia as a genetically transmitted disorder, however, left certain clinical observations unexplained. For example, the concordance rate for schizophrenia among monozygotic twins was found to be only 40–50% (Gottesman & Shields, 1972; Kety, 1983), making it virtually impossible to explain the occurrence of this disorder solely on the basis of an inherited trait. In addition, because many schizophrenics show a characteristic deterioration of functioning during the first several years of illness, it seemed that a neurodegenerative process might be involved in the etiology of this disorder. It is noteworthy that several studies have indicated that schizophrenics as a group have a much higher than expected incidence of obstetrical complications (Jacobsen & Kinney, 1980; Parnas et al., 1982). The most prevalent type of birth complication noted was prolonged labor. Because this is thought to be associated with hypoxemia, many believed that an early brain insult occurring in this setting might be a risk factor for schizophrenia.

It has long been thought that schizophrenia might be a heterogeneous group of disorders, with some patients having a genetically transmitted disease, and others, a neurodegenerative one. This idea is appealing because these two etiologies could potentially explain some of the differences in the clinical appearance of schizophrenic patients. Some patients show a preponderance of so-called positive symptoms (e.g., hallucinations and delusions); others show a preponderance of negative symptoms (e.g., poor motivation, flat affect, anhedonia, and anergia). Consistent with this idea, schizophrenics with prominent negative symptoms were found to be more likely to show volume loss in computerized axial tomography (CT) scans of their brains. This typology, however, failed to account for the fact that most schizophrenic patients show the occurrence of both positive and negative features and cannot be easily segregated into these two categories. In addition, obstetrical complications alone could not explain the occurrence of neurodegeneration in schizophrenia because birth complications are not exclusively found in the past records of schizophrenics. For example, individuals with cerebral palsy have experienced profound brain damage from severe anoxia early in life, but carry no increased risk for schizophrenia. It seemed that a "two-factor" model for schizophrenia might better explain these various observations (Parnas et al., 1982). According to this view, if a subtle brain insult occurs in the setting of a preexisting risk factor for schizophrenia, then perhaps the two together could give rise to the disorder. Accordingly, a model of schizophrenia in which both an early brain insult and a predisposing genetic trait are necessary for the occurrence of schizophrenia (Parnas et al., 1982) seems more plausible. Such a two-factor model of schizophrenia is consistent with the idea of Hebb (1949) that both constitution and environment play central roles in the occurrence of mental illness. Interestingly, a model of this type could help explain some of the heterogeneity of schizophrenia as a result of varying degrees of brain insult and/or genetic loading. Moreover, the precise time during early development when a brain insult occurs could further determine the specific aspects of brain circuitry that are disrupted and this, in turn, might influence the specific behavioral manifestations that are observed clinically.

A key issue for a two-factor model of schizophrenia is to identify the genetically transmitted latent trait for schizophrenia. Although evidence for a primary defect in dopamine transmission has not been forthcoming, some investigators have looked toward identifiable phenotypic markers. For example, alterations of smooth pursuit eye movements found both in schizophrenics and in their first-degree relatives could be related to a fundamental difference in the constitution of an individual who carries a gene for schizophrenia (Holzman et al., 1988). Similarly, the schizotypal personality trait, which is more prevalent among the first-degree relatives of schizophrenics than it is among those of normal individuals (Kety, 1985), could also represent a predisposing constitutional trait (Parnas et al., 1982). Because schizotypes characteristically are withdrawn, suspicious, have magical thinking, and experience some perceptual disturbances (DSM-IV; American Psychiatric Association, 1994), it is not difficult to imagine that an individual with such a personality profile, when exposed to an early brain insult, could develop the more exaggerated symptoms seen in schizophrenia.

The discussion that follows will address the question of how developmental neurobiology can provide a framework for investigating the nature, course, and etiology of psychiatric disorders. The chapter begins with a discussion of how we might conceptualize the interaction of "constitution" with "environment" in determining patterns of human personality and behavior. Next, the basic nature of personality is discussed in relation to several core defects in schizophrenia, to help identify corticolimbic brain regions that might play a role in the mediation of some functional aspects of the "personality" disturbed in schizophrenia. This is followed by a review of basic developmental neurobiology, particularly with regard to the ontogenesis of corticolimbic brain areas and the major neurotransmitter systems found in them. This latter discussion lays the groundwork for a description of some recent postmortem findings in schizophrenic brain and a discussion of how neurodevelopmental disturbances might have theoretically given rise to them. Finally, the chapter concludes with a discussion of the future directions that neurobiologic studies of schizophrenia and other psychiatric disorders might follow so that a neurodevelopmental understanding of mental illness can eventually emerge.

CONSTITUTION AND THE ENVIRONMENT AS DETERMINANTS OF PERSONALITY AND VULNERABILITY

Through the pioneering work of Jerome Kagan, the idea that there is a neurobiologic basis for constitutional differences among human subjects has gained widespread acceptance. This concept has grown out of the observation that a distinct subgroup of children can be identified by their fearful response to novel settings (Kagan, Reznick, Snidman, Gibbons, & Johnson, 1988). These "inhibited" children show distinct changes in heart rate, blood pressure, and glucocorticoid release when presented with unfamiliar settings (Kagan, Reznick, & Snidman, 1988). A similar constitutional subtype in cats is also recognized. This "harm-avoidant" cat type has a reduced ability to interact socially with strangers and tends to hide when presented with novel stimuli (Adamec, 1991). In these fearful felines, there is an increase in the firing of neurons in the basomedial amygdala and the ventromedial hypothalamus (Adamec, 1978), and lesions that interrupt the connections between these latter two structures eliminate fearful responses (Pellis et al., 1988). It is noteworthy that the harm-avoidant temperament in cats appears very early in postnatal life when early experience tends to bring out innate differences in temperament (Adamec, Stark-Adamec, & Livingston, 1980). For example, kittens showing more exploratory tendencies show aggressive responses to rats; those with harm-avoidant tendencies become defensive when exposed to rats early in development. If a defensive cat is exposed to a dead prey, a decrease of defensive behavior is noted. Thus, postnatal experience may modify the basic temperament of cats (Adamec et al., 1980). The inhibited temperament in children also shows a tendency for postnatal modification (Kagan, Reznick, & Gibbons, 1989; Kagan et al., 1988; Kagan & Snidman, 1991a, 1991b). For example, when inhibited children were reevaluated at age 4, the harm-avoidant patterns, in many instances, were less apparent. Experiential factors, such as parental reinforcement of nonavoidant behaviors, might serve to modify basic constitutional tendencies and become integrated as part of a child's temperament.

The idea that aspects of the temperament are environmentally influenced was first suggested by the observations of Spitz (1949) on children reared either in a stimulus-enriched, nurturant environment or in an environment with both social and sensory isolation. The latter group developed an "anaclitic" depression characterized by withdrawal, lack of curiosity, and infection proneness. An animal model for environmental effects on the development of behavioral characteristics was later developed in primates to investigate whether social isolation during critical periods of early postnatal life might result in a permanent tendency toward social isolation (Harlow, 1958; Harlow, Dodsworth, & Harlow, 1965). It was found that isolative behavior can be modified by exposure of young monkeys to other, more gregarious monkeys.

Cloninger (1991) described two additional basic temperaments identifiable in humans. The "novelty-seeking" type includes features such as exploratory excitability, impulsiveness, extravagance, and disorderliness; the "reward-dependent" type shows sentimentality, persistence, attachment, and dependence. As suggested above, the schizotypal personality may be another constitutional variant in humans. It would be difficult to fit every individual into such categories, but aspects of several prototypes may occur in a variety of permutations and account for the diverse array present in the general population.

The above discussion supports the general notion that an innate tendency toward certain behavioral responses occurs in higher mammals, particularly humans, but this can be modified by experience early in life. Each individual may carry a predisposition to certain types of basic behavioral responses, but it is likely that each also has experienced extensive modification of a constitutional framework through environmental experience. It might be operationally useful to define the individual personality as a complex function in which a dynamic equilibrium exists between basic constitution and cumulative experience (environment) (Figure 8.1). According to such a model, constitution and experience would be interacting throughout the lifetime of an individual, and both would have the ability to continually modify the other. The cumulative experience of an individual and its interplay with basic constitutional tendencies would influence not only how that person responds to subsequent experience, but also how normal changes in brain maturation (see below) might alter the overall response set or personality of the individual. The idea that personality is not immutable, but rather fluid, has come from the provocative work of George Vaillant (1983), in which the "alcoholic personality," with its passive, dependent features, was found to be a state-dependent phenomenon. Individuals who have abstained from alcohol for long periods of time do not show this profile.

With regard to the question of how postnatal development may play a role in the occurrence of the mental disorders, the above discussion provides some clues. Each individual who presents with a particular mental disorder may have a preexisting set of constitutional and experiential variables that will contribute to the nature, course, and prognosis of that illness. As noted previously, for a person "at risk" for schizophrenia, a schizotypal constitution may provide a predisposing substrate in which an early brain injury might produce the full schizophrenic syndrome. Moreover, the severity of a brain insult could potentially determine how responsive the individual might be to conventional treatments and how debilitating the illness is. For example, schizophrenics who show evidence of volume loss in their brains also show an impaired performance on neuropsychological tests and only a partial response to antipsychotic medication (Weinberger, 1987). Thus, the specific ways in which constitutional and experiential factors interact for a particular individual may theoretically result in differences in both the degree of vulnerability and the severity of the resulting illness.

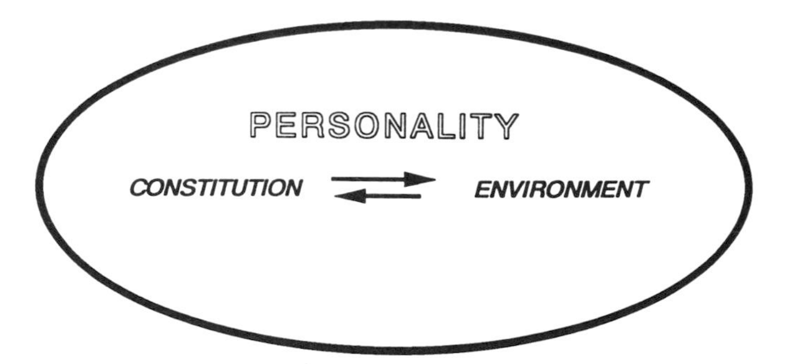

Figure 8.1 Interaction of constitution and environment as determinants of personality. Constitution may be a genetically defined set of behavioral responses that interplay with environmental events. During the life of an individual, these two factors interact in a reciprocal fashion and give rise to what we identify as "personality." In individuals "at risk" for mental illness, constitution may impart selective vulnerability to individuals who have various abnormal genes related to the psychiatric disorders. In such individuals, environmental factors can influence whether and/or the degree to which the selective vulnerability is expressed.

THE CORTICOLIMBIC SYSTEM

Personality and the Symptoms of Schizophrenia

In evolving a developmental psychopathology of the mental disorders, it is necessary to consider how the risk factors for each may alter circuitry. To do this, it is necessary to understand the mechanisms through which various types of human behavior are integrated within the central nervous system.

MacLean (1990) has suggested that a careful analysis of psychiatric disorders can potentially help us to identify such mechanisms. Toward this end, an initial step is to consider what brain regions can be reasonably implicated in the generation of a particular syndrome, an approach that has already been applied to the study of schizophrenia (Benes, 1993). The symptoms of schizophrenia typically involve changes of behaviors—emotion, motivation, attentional responses, sociability, and reasoning. In a broad sense, the behaviors disturbed in schizophrenia are also central features of personality, which is defined by Dorland's Medical Dictionary as "the total reaction of an individual to the surrounding environment." It has been suggested that alterations of temperament can be induced in both monkeys (Ward, 1948) and humans (Tow & Whitty, 1953) following surgical ablations of certain corticolimbic regions, such as the anterior cingulate cortex. In the discussion that follows, several features of personality, known to be abnormal in schizophrenia, will be considered in relation to the anterior cingulate cortex and other corticolimbic areas with which it is extensively connected.

Affectivity

A hallmark feature of schizophrenia, particularly when it takes on a chronic course, is a progressive disappearance of affect (Bleuler, 1952). Schizophrenics characteristically show a facial expression that lacks emotion—a reflection of their inability to generate appropriate affective responses to surrounding events. In some cases, an affective response is noted but is inappropriate; in others, it may be "shallow." In general, schizophrenics are unable to tolerate a high degree of emotion expressed by others around them; such an occurrence seems to predispose them to relapse (Barrelet, Ferrero, Szogethy, Giddey, & Pellizzer, 1990).

Emotional expression is an attribute that first became apparent in mammals. It is probably mediated in part by phylogenetically primitive brain regions such as the brain stem reticular formation, hypothalamus, amygdala, and septal nuclei. This mediation would help to account for the suggestion that fearfulness in cats appears to be modulated by these same limbic structures (Adamec, 1992). Papez (1937) was the first to postulate that the cingulate gyrus may play a central role in the integration of emotional experience with cognition because it not only has extensive connections with the limbic system, but it also has rich reciprocal connectivity with other associative cortical regions involved in higher cognitive functions. These patterns of connectivity lay the groundwork for the simultaneous occurrence of visceral responses with thinking. Consistent with this, autonomic responses have been altered by either stimulation or ablation of the anterior cingulate cortex. With electrical stimulation of this region in primates, visceromotor responses, such as eyelid-opening, pupillary dilatation, respiratory movements, cardiovascular changes, and piloerection (Anand & Dua, 1956; Kaada, Pribam, & Epstein, 1940; Smith, 1945) have been induced. Notably, changes in facial expression (Smith, 1945) and motor arrest (Dunsmore & Lennox, 1950; Smith, 1945) have also been observed. Extensive surgical ablation of the anterior cingulate cortex, on the other hand, has resulted in a decrease of emotional responsiveness (Ward, 1948). Personality changes characterized by either inappropriate purring or growling without provocation have been observed in cats with cingulate lesions (Kennard, 1955); in humans, bilateral infarction of the cingulate gyrus has been associated with increased docility and indifference (Laplane, Degos, Baulac, & Gray, 1981). Interestingly, an inability to either express or experience emotion has been described in patients with bilateral cingulate gyrus infarction (Damasio & Van Hoesen, 1983). The decrease in emotional responsiveness seen in cingulotomized patients bears some resemblance to the flat affect seen in schizophrenics.

Selective Attention

Bleuler (1952) was perhaps the first to emphasize that schizophrenics have great difficulty selectively focusing and shifting their attention. In support of this, studies using the continuous performance task (CPT) have demonstrated that schizophrenics do not score well (Kornetsky & Orzack, 1978). One proposed explanation for the loss of selective attention in schizophrenia is that there may be a defective central filtering mechanism (Detre & Jarecki, 1971) that gives rise to "over-inclusive" thinking (Cameron, 1938; Payne & Friedlander, 1962). These patients frequently cannot distinguish relevant objects in the perceptual field, a defect that seems to arise early in the course of the illness and one that was thought to involve an impairment of inhibitory mechanisms (McGhie & Chapman, 1961; see below). Some believe that the cingulate and parietal cortices may cooperate in the performance of directed attention (Mesulam, 1983). In monkeys, lesions of the anterior cingulate cortex bilaterally have been associated with neglect of surrounding objects and even cage mates (Glees, Cole, Whitty, & Cairns, 1950). A similar syndrome has been observed in cats with cingulate ablations (Kennard, 1955). In humans with bilateral infarction of the cingulate gyrus, a lack of attentiveness to the surrounding environment has been observed (Laplane et al., 1981). A recent cerebral blood flow study reported that human subjects show a marked increase of activity in the anterior cingulate region during performance of a Stroop attentional conflict paradigm (Pardo, Pardo, Janer, & Raichle, 1990). In schizophrenic subjects, there was a slower response to targets in the right, but not the left, visual fields, and attentional deficits similar to those following left hemispheric lesions were also noted (Posner, Early, Reisman, Pardo, & Dhawan, 1988). It is noteworthy that abnormalities of smooth pursuit eye movements also have been found in schizophrenics and in their first-degree relatives, and are believed to reflect the "latent trait" for this disorder (Holzman et al., 1988). The neglect occurring with lesions of the cingulate cortex is thought to involve alterations in the relationship of the cingulate region with frontal eye field 8 (Belaydier & Maugierre, 1980), but this may be an indirect effect mediated through connections of this region with the prefrontal and inferior parietal areas. Nevertheless, the smooth pursuit abnormalities seen in schizophrenic subjects may reflect a role of frontal eye field 8 in the attentional deficits also seen in patients with this disorder. Patients with unilateral neglect syndromes arising from lesions of the frontal or parietal regions also show some emotional disturbances and these defects are consistent with a "parallelism in the integrity of attention and emotion" (Mesulam & Geschwind, 1978, p. 252), a concept that Bleuler first suggested to be pertinent to our understanding of schizophrenia.

Motivation

Lack of motivation is another core feature of schizophrenia. A model for understanding a loss of motivation and interest comes from the description of massive frontal lobe lesions resulting in the apathico-akinetico-abulic syndrome (Luria, 1973). As in schizophrenia, individuals with such lesions are passive, lack desires, and have poor hygiene (Luria, 1973). It is noteworthy that schizophrenics who fail to activate cerebral blood flow in the dorsolateral prefrontal cortex also perform poorly on the Wisconsin Card Sort, a functional marker for this area (Weinberger, Berman, & Zec, 1986), and the differences do not appear to be related to either poor attention (Berman, Zec, & Weinberger, 1986) or global cortical dysfunction (Berman et al., 1986).

Bleuler may have been the first to suspect a link between affect and motivation. He wrote, "The will, a resultant of all the various affective and associative processes, is of course disturbed in a number of ways, but above all by the breakdown of the emotions" (1952, p. 70). The interaction of motivation and affect in humans is illustrated by a distinctive syndrome called "akinetic mutism," seen in patients with bilateral destructive lesions of the anterior cingulate cortex (Barris & Schumann, 1953). Acute infarctions of this type are associated with an inability to move or speak, as well as considerable negativism. This is quite similar to the catatonic state in which muteness, lack of movement, and negativism are also observed. Patients who had akinetic mutism arising from bilateral occlusion of the anterior cerebral arteries and who later recovered have described a sudden loss of the experience of affect and a concomitant absence of the will to move (Damasio & Van Hoesen, 1983). A similar concurrence of defects in motivation and emotional experience, seen in schizophrenia, could arise from a disturbance in communication between the dorsolateral prefrontal area and the anterior cingulate cortex.

Sociability

Schizophrenics have great difficulty engaging in relationships with other people, and this results in marked isolation. It is no surprise that these patients rarely marry and raise families. Female schizophrenics, in general, are unable to nurture their children. The inability of these patients to "relate" to others and share empathetically in their feeling states is probably central to their impaired social skills, both within family units and outside them.

The cingulate gyrus has been implicated in the mediation of interpersonal relations because ablations of this region are associated with a loss of maternal activities, such as nursing, nest building, and retrieval of the young (Slotnick, 1967; Stamm, 1955). It has been suggested that separation calls and play activities, key features associated with the appearance of social interaction, may have emerged in parallel with the development of the cingulate gyrus during the phylogenetic progression of reptiles into mammals (MacLean, 1985). MacLean has suggested that separation calls that also first appeared in mammals may be mediated by the cingulate gyrus. In support of this, vocalizations can be elicited by stimulation of the anterior cingulate region in monkeys (Ploog, 1970; Smith, 1945); more extensive ablations that also include the medial prefrontal cortex and the subcallosal and preseptal cingulate cortices result in a complete loss of spontaneous isolation calls (MacLean, 1985).

If the cingulate gyrus plays a role in social interactions, it is possible that the unrelatedness and poor social skills typically observed in schizophrenia may also be related, at least in part, to associated defects in motivation and attentiveness. It seems likely, however, that lack of interest in and neglect of one's surroundings might also contribute to diminished interactiveness.

Logical Processing

One of the most significant core defects in schizophrenia is a formal thought disorder, in which there are illogical sequences of unrelated concepts. Attempts have been made to characterize the nature of the defective thinking found in schizophrenic patients. Toward this end, methodologies for evaluating the central processing of incoming information have been developed to study thought disorder in schizophrenia. One such study characterized the abnormalities of central integration in schizophrenics as involving serial processing of information, but with a limited channel capacity (Callaway & Naghdi, 1982). It has also been found that, when an informational target stimulus is followed at varying intervals by a noninformational masking stimulus, a temporal delay in a two-choice forced discrimination task is observed in schizophrenics (Saccuzzo & Braff, 1986). This information processing defect appears to be trait-dependent, rather than an epiphenomenon of the psychotic state, because individuals with the schizotypal personality profile also show it (Saccuzzo & Braff, 1986). This latter finding implies that the thought disorder seen in schizophrenia might be a genetically transmitted attribute, perhaps one arising from a specific alteration in neural circuitry. The left inferior parietal lobe has been implicated in the construction of logical-grammatical relationships, and patients with focal left inferior parietal lesions demonstrate a marked impairment in the ability to formulate thoughts that involve the communication of relationships among ideas (Luria, 1973). It is noteworthy that neurons in monkey posterior parietal cortex are activated by hand-eye coordinated movements, particularly when "desirable" objects that can satisfy thirst or hunger are used (Mountcastle, Lynch, Georgopoulos, Sakata, & Acuna, 1975). This motivationally driven response is believed to require not only limbic connections with the parietal region but also an attentional component (Mesulam & Geschwind, 1978). Consistent with this proposal, the inferior parietal region has extensive connections with the anterior cingulate cortex and the presubiculum (Jones & Powell, 1970; Pandya & Kuypers, 1969; Petras, 1971; Seltzer & Pandya, 1978, 1984; Seltzer & Van Hoesen, 1979; Van Hoesen, 1982). Thus, interactions of this type may provide at least part of the limbic component to inferior parietal responses to desirable objects. Luria (1973) emphasized the role of the left (dominant) inferior parietal region in the construction of logical-grammatical relationships; he also described unilateral neglect syndromes in patients with right-sided posterior parietal lesions. These patients do not pay attention to extracorporeal space on the left side, but they also show a peculiar inability to perceive their defects. The failure to perceive one's defects is commonly seen in schizophrenics with illogical thinking who are unable to notice the inability of a listener to comprehend what they are saying. The simultaneous occurrence of illogical thinking and neglect in schizophrenia is consistent with the idea that both the left and right inferior parietal areas might be dysfunctional in this disorder. As noted above, neglect of the surrounding environment occurs with cingulate lesions, and the coincidence of attentional problems and disturbances of thinking could reflect the extensive connections between the anterior cingulate and inferior parietal cortices.

Corticolimbic Involvement in Disorders of Mood and Anxiety

Based on the above discussion of the symptoms of schizophrenia and the functions of several corticolimbic regions, it has been suggested that the anterior cingulate cortex as well as the dorsolateral prefrontal region, inferior parietal lobe, and hippocampal formation with which it connects, may be of central importance to the symptomatology, and possibly even the etiology, of schizophrenia. The functions collectively subsumed by these regions cover a broad range of behaviors, including affect, attention, motivation, social behavior, and cognition. It is relevant to this discussion to consider whether other psychiatric disorders may possibly involve alterations in similar cortical regions. In bipolar mood disorder, as mania alternates with depression, patients may show increases or decreases of emotional expression, motivation, attention, interpersonal relations, and thinking. Manic individuals typically show rapid thinking and a flight of ideas from one concept to another, frequently of a grandiose nature; patients with depression show thinking that is slowed and fixated on only certain ideas, usually of a self-deprecatory type. Opposite disturbances in social behavior also occur, with manic patients being inappropriately interactive or intrusive and depressed patients being very withdrawn or isolative. In considering the brain areas that might play a role in these mood disturbances, it is noteworthy that chronically depressed patients show improvement of their mood following bilateral anterior cingulotomy (Ballantine, Cassidy, Flanagan, & Marino, 1967; Brown & Lighthill, 1968; Tow & Whitty, 1953), a procedure that does not produce deficits in, and may even improve, overall cognitive function (Long, Pueschel, & Hunter, 1978). Other psychiatric syndromes, such as panic disorder and phobias, frequently occur comorbidly with depression. Individuals with phobias have been found to have been prone to separation anxiety as children and many were branded as school phobics during childhood (Klein, Zitrin, & Woerner, 1978). The suggestion by MacLean (1985) that the cingulate area might mediate separation behaviors (see above) could provide a theoretical basis for understanding this syndrome, which also responds well to treatment with antidepressant medication. Another syndrome occurring comorbidly with depression is panic disorder, characterized by episodes of acute anxiety in which an individual experiences shortness of breath, tachycardia, profuse sweating, and pallor in response to an irrational perception of impending doom. Because the cingulate cortex is involved in the cortical regulation of autonomic visceromotor responses (Anand & Dua, 1956; Kaada et al., 1940), it is possible that this region, and/or areas with which it connects, could participate in the generation of panic attacks as well.

"Le Grande Lobe Limbique"

In parallel with the first appearance of mammalian features in vertebrates, Broca (1878) noted that a "limbic lobe," consisting of the septal nuclei, amygdala, hippocampus, parahippocampal (entorhinal) cortex, and cingulate gyrus, appeared along the midsagittal plane of virtually all mammalian forms (Figure 8.2). Interestingly, the elaboration of this limbic lobe coincided with the appearance of audition, vocalization, maternal nurturance, and separation calls by the young, suggesting that the integration of visceral responses with cortically mediated behaviors might have facilitated the protection of young offspring (MacLean, 1985). Accordingly, the evolutionary trend toward developing more elaborate behaviors to nurture the young and presumably perpetuate species probably involved a corresponding increase in both the amount and complexity of cortical ties with limbic structures. Within the spectrum of mammalian forms, there has been a striking increase in the relative proportion of neocortex to Broca's limbic lobe. Figure 8.2 shows a comparison of the limbic lobe in rat, cat, and monkey brain (MacLean, 1954). It is evident from the figure that there has been a progressive increase in the volume of neocortex surrounding the cingulate and parahippocampal gyri. In primates and humans, this has been accompanied by the most extensive elaboration of connectivity between associative cortical regions, such as the cingulate region and the hippocampal formation, with the subcortical limbic system (Figure 8.3). The above discussion illustrates that the brain, not having a specific mechanism for deleting phylogenetically older circuits, has integrated older circuits with newly acquired ones within the corticolimbic system. As a result, there has been a progressive increase in the integration of higher cognitive processes with visceral and instinctual behaviors mediated through subcortical limbic structures. In the human brain, this additive tendency that has occurred during phylogeny has probably been adaptive because it is doubtful that the human species could have survived without limbicly driven emotions and instincts together with cortically driven logical planning and volition.

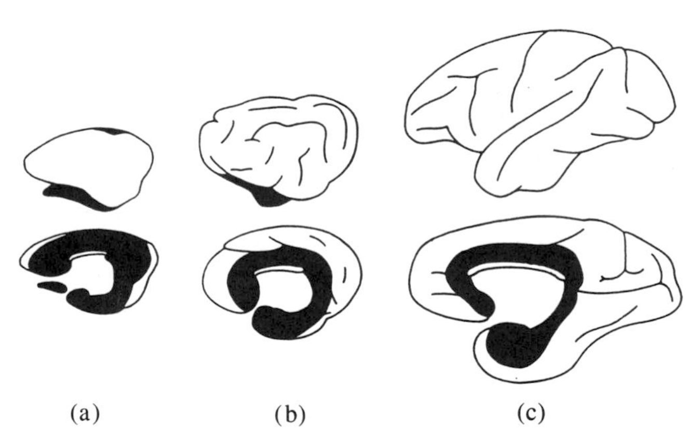

Figure 8.2 The appearance of the brain in the rat (a), cat (b), and monkey (c), shown both in a lateral (above) and a midsagittal (below) view. All three brains show a contiguous loop (black) of limbic structures (including the cingulate gyrus, parahippocampal gyrus, and amygdala) that has remained remarkably similar during phylogenesis. This so-called "limbic lobe" is surrounded, above and laterally, by neocortex that has shown a progressive increase during phylogeny. From "Studies on Limbic System (Visceral Brain) and Their Bearing on Psychosomatic Problems" by P. D. Maclean, 1954, in E. Wittkower and R. Cleghorn, (Eds.), *Recent Developments in Psychosomatic Medicine* (p. 106), Philadelphia: Lippincott.

The Anterior Cingulate Cortex Occupies a Key Location in Corticolimbic Circuitry

The anterior cingulate region has extensive reciprocal connections with several different cortical areas that include the prefrontal region, the presubiculum, and the inferior parietal lobe (Jones & Powell, 1970; Pandya & Kuypers, 1969; Petras, 1971; Seltzer & Pandya, 1978; Seltzer & Van Hoesen, 1979; Van Hoesen, 1982). Very importantly, the anterior cingulate region also has both afferent and efferent connections with nuclear groups that mediate autonomic functions (Figure 8.4), such as the periaqueductal gray (Beckstead, 1979; Domesick, 1969; Hurley, Herbert, Moga, & Saper, 1991; Wyss & Sripanidkulchai, 1984), the nucleus solitarius, the dorsal motor nucleus of the vagus (Hurley et al., 1991; Terreberry & Neafsey, 1983, 1987; Van der Kooy, McGinty, Koda, Gerfen, & Bloom, 1982), and preganglionic sympathetic neurons in the intermediolateral cell column of thoracic spinal cord (Hurley et al., 1991). Accordingly, the anterior cingulate cortex interacts directly with centers that mediate both viscerosensory and visceromotor responses in the periphery—relationships that are believed to be fundamental to its role in integrating emotional responses at the cortical level (Neafsey, Terreberry, Hurley, Ruit, & Frysztak, 1992). Either ablation (Kennard, 1955; Laplane et al., 1981; Ward, 1948) or stimulation (Anand & Dua, 1956; Kaada, 1960; Kaada et al., 1940; Smith, 1945) of the anterior cingulate cortex has resulted in both autonomic and affective changes. In humans with documented seizure activity arising from the cingulate cortex (Devinsky & Luciano, 1992), emotional stimulation is a frequent precipitant of ictal activity (Mazars, 1970). The majority of such patients exhibit limbicly related features such as temper tantrums and fixed

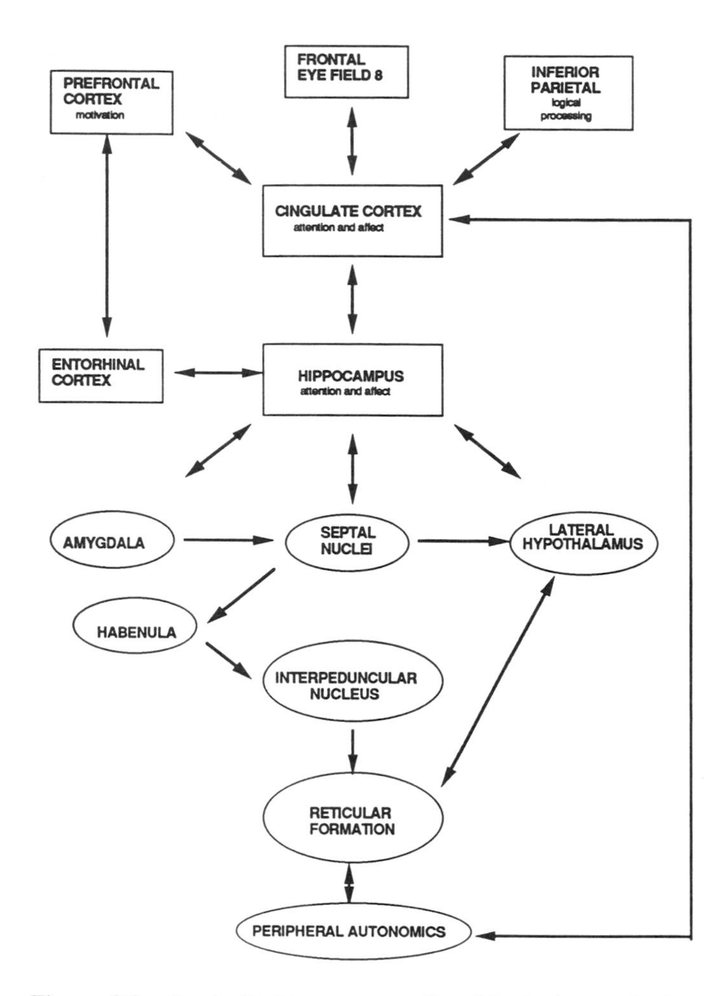

Figure 8.3 Corticolimbic structures found in the human brain. The corticolimbic system is composed of both cortical (rectangles and subcortical (ovals) regions that are extensively interconnected. The hippocampal formation is archicortex that first appeared in reptiles and has extensive connections with subcortical limbic regions, such as the amygdala, septal nuclei, and lateral hypothalamus. The entorhinal and cingulate regions are transitional mesocortex that first appeared in early mammals. The latter two areas form a link between the primitive hippocampal formation and the most recently evolved neocortical regions, which include the prefrontal area, frontal eye field 8, and the inferior parietal lobe. Together, the various cortical components of this network subsume a complex set of motivational, attentional, and affective responses, to which the inferior parietal lobe imparts a logical framework. The cingulate gyrus has extensive connections with centers in the brain stem and spinal cord that regulate visceral sensory and motor functions.

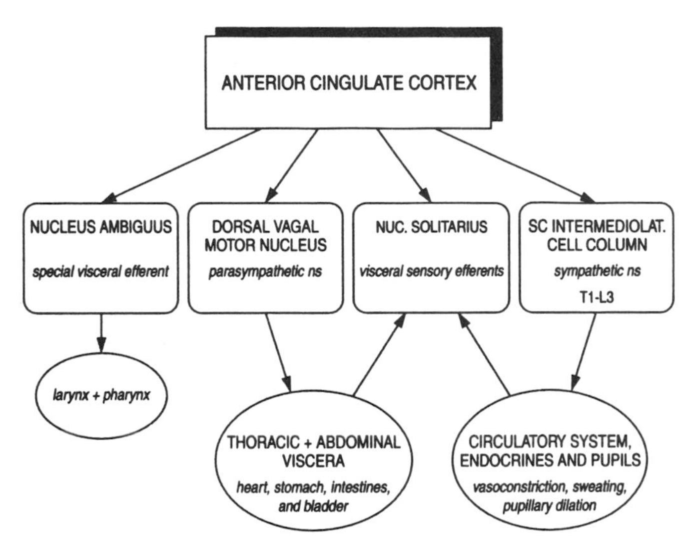

Figure 8.4 The anterior cingulate cortex and its corticobulbar and corticospinal connections, which are involved in the mediation of visceral motor and sensory responses. The anterior cingulate cortex plays a unique role in the integration of affective experience with higher cognitive function via its extensive interactions with both brain stem and spinal centers involved in autonomic processing. Corticobulbar fibers, originating in the anterior cingulate region, project to the nucleus ambiguous and the dorsal vagal motor nucleus and the preganglionic sympathetic fibers of the intermediolateral cell column to influence the outflow of activity to special visceral efferent muscles (e.g., larynx and pharynx), thoracic and abdominal viscera (e.g., the heart, esophagus, stomach, intestines, and bladder), and blood vessels and sweat glands. Extensive connections of the anterior cingulate region with the nucleus solitarius probably influence the inflow of sensory information from all viscera of the body.

psychoses (Mazars, 1970). In one reported case, a child with cingulate seizures was noted to run toward her mother during ictal episodes (Geier et al., 1977), a manifestation consistent with the proposed role of the cingulate cortex in mammalian separation behaviors (MacLean, 1985). Thus, the various corticolimbic connections of anterior cingulate cortex and the behavioral manifestations associated with its lesions support the idea that this region may play a particularly central role in the integration of limbic functions with higher cognitive processing (Papez, 1937).

The cingulate region is a central component in broadly distributed networks of cortical and subcortical regions that subsume functions altered in schizophrenia and other psychiatric disorders. In Figure 8.3, the cingulate cortex is connected with the dorsolateral prefrontal area, frontal eye field 8, the inferior parietal lobe, the hippocampal formation, and frontal eye field 8. The entorhinal region provides a key relay of information from the prefrontal area to the hippocampal formation. The prefrontal, anterior cingulate, and entorhinal cortices receive a rich supply of dopamine afferents from the midbrain ventral tegmental area (Lindvall & Bjorklund, 1984). Some of the areas indicated in Figure 8.3 are phylogenetically newer cortical regions (e.g., the dorsolateral prefrontal and inferior parietal regions) and are most extensively developed in human brain. In contrast, the hippocampal formation is phylogenetically the oldest cortical region that first appeared in a rudimentary form in reptiles (Ulinski, 1990).

The cingulate and entorhinal cortices are transitional limbic cortices that first appeared in early mammals and provide a link between the hippocampal formation and the neocortical regions represented in Figure 8.3 (e.g., the dorsolateral prefrontal and inferior parietal regions) that are particularly well developed in humans.

By examining the corticolimbic regions and their interconnections, represented in Figures 8.3 and 8.4, it can be appreciated that defective integration in one or several of these areas could give rise to abnormalities in the cortical integration of limbicly derived functions, such as emotional experience, with functions integrated primarily at the neocortical level, such as volition and logic. A psychopathological process—schizophrenia, for example—that impacts on one or several corticolimbic regions could potentially give rise to a broad variety of symptoms that encompass the emotional and cognitive spheres.

Three- and Six-Layered Cortex

To understand how defects in the corticolimbic system can influence the processing of activity in subcortical regions, it is useful to examine more closely the cytoarchitectural organization within the cortex of higher mammals. The cortex of reptiles has a simple three-layered organization (Ulinski, 1977); mammalian neocortex has been expanded into six layers, which can be distinguished from one another according to the density and size of neurons, as well as their morphological appearance (see Figure 8.6, p. 000). For example, layer I has sparse numbers of relatively small interneurons; layers II, III, V, and VI contain large numbers of projection cells called pyramidal neurons. These latter cells typically send their axons out of the cortex to other distal sites. In contrast to the pyramidal cell layers, layer IV contains abundant numbers of excitatory interneurons, called granule cells. Relative to layer IV, the deeper layers V and VI are called infragranular layers and the superficial layers I–III, supragranular layers.

Interestingly, there is a basic dichotomy between the superficial and deep layers of mammalian cortex. Pyramidal neurons in layers V and VI project axons primarily to subcortical structures; those in layers II and III send their axons preferentially to other cortical sites (Jones, 1984). Layer IV receives a rich supply of afferents from the thalamus (White, 1986), and layer I has a large number of incoming associative inputs from other cortical regions (Marin-Padilla, 1984). Thus, these latter two receptive layers reflect this subcortical and corticocortical relationship of the other infragranular and supragranular projection layers, respectively. In a very general sense, then, the phylogenetic development of the cortex has involved an expansion from three to six layers, and it is of more than passing interest that the three supragranular layers have a more specific role in processing associative activity and an ever-increasing role in phylogenetically more advanced species, such as primates and humans. The thickness of the supragranular layers is proportional to the amount of associative activity that a particular region mediates. For example, the primary visual cortex has a rudimentary amount of layers I–III; the tertiary visual association area 19 has a well-developed supragranular zone. Supramodal (tertiary) cortical regions such as the cingulate, prefrontal areas, and inferior parietal areas, which are associative in nature, have upper layers that are thicker than the deeper layers. Overall, the marked expansion of associative cortex that has occurred in relation to phylogenesis of the brain has involved a dramatic increase in supragranular laminar processing.

In any study of the corticolimbic system of schizophrenic brain, the six-layered organization of the cortex is relevant to consider because alterations that occur in superficial laminae would be more likely to impact on higher cognitive processes (see below).

NORMAL ONTOGENESIS OF CORTICOLIMBIC BRAIN REGIONS

It is now pertinent to consider the manner in which components of the corticolimbic system undergo ontogenetic development during pre- and postnatal life. The discussion that follows will consider the ontogenesis of the hippocampal formation, followed by the neocortex. The ingrowth of afferents to the cortex and myelination of the cortex are discussed. Finally, the sequential changes that occur for both intrinsic and extrinsic transmitters of the cortex are described.

Ontogenesis of the Hippocampal Formation

The hippocampal formation of human brain is a very complex structure composed of several different subsidiary regions, including the area dentata, the hippocampus proper, the subicular complex, and the entorhinal cortex (Stanfield & Cowan, 1988). The developmental changes that occur in the hippocampal formation as described below have been previously reviewed (Benes, 1993). This process involves a carefully timed sequence of events, although the period during which the sequential changes occur may differ for various mammalian species. For example, in rats, the cells of the regio superior (CA1–CA2) appear during the last half of gestation (Angevine, 1965; Stanfield & Cowan, 1988); in monkeys, they appear during the first half (Rakic & Nowakowski, 1981). There is also a general tendency for neurons of the hippocampus to be generated by mitotic proliferation of precursor elements within a zone closely apposed to the ventricular surface (Angevine, 1965; Rakic & Nowakowski, 1981; Stanfield & Cowan, 1988). When a given cell has completed its mitotic proliferation, it begins to migrate upward and eventually assumes its proper position in an "inside-out" progression. This latter process occurs for the hippocampus proper, the subicular complex, and the entorhinal cortex. For the area dentata, however, the disposition of this subregion within the hippocampal formation is such that the cells migrate in an "outside-in" manner. Thus, the direction of migration occurs relative to where the proliferative epithelial zone has generated the cells. Another developmental gradient occurs along the axis lying between the entorhinal cortex and the area dentata (Stanfield & Cowan, 1988). Neurons along the ends of this so-called rhinodentate axis develop earlier; cells in the center (subicular complex and hippocampus proper) appear later (Rakic & Nowakowski, 1981; Schlessinger, Cowan, & Swanson, 1978).

The development of the area dentata may continue well beyond birth. In rats, for example, the numbers of dentate granule cells seem to increase during both the preadult weanling and adult periods (Bayer, Yackel, & Puri, 1982), and the cells arising postnatally are thought to originate from mitotic neuroblasts (Kaplan & Bell, 1984). These newly generated granule cells of the area dentata are thought to give rise to axons that project into subfields CA3 and CA4 of the hippocampus (Stanfield & Trice, 1988). Evidence for postnatal granule cell increases has not been found in rhesus monkeys (Eckenhoff & Rakic, 1988); however, there have not, as yet, been any studies to determine whether similar postnatal changes may occur in the area dentate of human brain. Thus, it is difficult to know whether postnatal neurogenesis might play a role in human maturation.

Parallels between the ontogenetic development of the hippocampal formation and its phylogeny in vertebrates have been described. At 8 weeks in utero, the human telencephalon is thought to be comparable to that found in mature amphibians (Hoffman, 1963). At 10 weeks, however, it is similar to that of reptiles (Crosby, 1917) and early mammalian species. In the 8-week-old fetus, rostral levels of the forebrain contain the septal nuclei situated immediately ventral to the fornix and medial frontal cortex; at more caudal levels, the fornix is contiguous with the hippocampus (Rakic & Yakovlev, 1968), also having a medial location. The appearance of limbic cortical structures in the medial forebrain of the human fetus early in prenatal development parallels that of phylogenetically earlier forms lacking neocortical structures. Thus, there are some striking similarities in the anatomical relationships of cortical and limbic forebrain structures found in reptiles, early mammals, and the human fetus. This parallelism underscores the notion that these regions are developmental precursors to transitional cortices (such as the cingulate gyrus) that predate neocortical areas such as the prefrontal and inferior parietal regions (see below).

Ontogeny of the Cortex

Cortical regions undergo ontogenesis at varying rates that, to some degree, reflect phylogeny. For example, limbic cortical areas tend to differentiate early in gestation. At 16–19 weeks in humans, the cingulate region can be distinguished as a gyrus; at 20–23 weeks, the parahippocampal gyrus is apparent in the medial temporal area (Gilles, Shankle, & Dooling, 1983). In contrast, the superior and medial frontal gyri (prefrontal regions) do not take on a clear gyral configuration until 24–27 weeks of gestational age, and the angular and supramarginal gyri (inferior parietal area) are not distinguished until 28–31 weeks (Gilles et al., 1983).

Cortical ontogenesis follows a carefully timed sequence of events (Poliakov, 1965; Sidman & Rakic, 1973) that also reflects phylogenesis. In a manner similar to the hippocampal formation, all cortical neurons are generated along the ventricular surface in the "marginal zone." This area appears early and is increasingly displaced toward the surface as cells undergo several mitotic divisions and give rise to an intermediate zone between them. Poliakov (1965) described five stages of cortical development in human brain. In the fetus, Stage I begins at approximately week 7, when postmitotic cells begin to move upward. These cells assume a position between the intermediate and marginal zones and form the *cortical plate.* Stage II occurs at 10–11 weeks, when the cortical plate becomes increasingly thick and compact. During this period, the first afferent fibers, probably derived from the thalamus, appear in the intermediate zone below the cortical plate. Stage III occurs at 11–13 weeks, when the cortical plate has developed an *inner zone,* with more mature cells that have an elongated shape and a diffuse distribution, and an *outer zone,* which has densely packed immature cells. In Stage IV, the ventricular zone becomes less prominent; cells are completing their mitotic divisions and migrating outward toward the cortical plate. Stage V, the longest period, occurs between fetal week 16 and the early postnatal period. During Stage V, postmitotic neuronal cells continue migrating and reach their final destination within the cortical plate. As neurons enter the cortical plate, those destined for more superficial layers arrive later than those that occupy deeper layers. Accordingly, the cortex, like the hippocampus, shows an inside-out progression of development (Rakic, 1974, 1975). Studies in humans have shown that, by 7 months of gestation, layers V and VI have attained a more advanced degree of development than layers II and III (Marin-Padilla, 1970a; Zilles, Busching, & Schleicher, 1986). The morphological differentiation of neurons in the various layers mirrors this migratory process, such that large pyramidal neurons with a well-developed dendritic arborization and basket cells (inhibitory interneurons) can be distinguished in deeper layers sooner than in superficial layers (Marin-Padilla, 1970b). By 7.5 months in utero, pyramidal neurons in deeper portions of layer III are first beginning to show differentiation of an apical dendrite extending into layer I; in layers V and VI, these cells already have elaborate dendritic arborizations. During this same interval, incoming afferent fibers are present in virtually all layers of the cortex. In the months immediately prior to birth, interneurons with a basket cell appearance begin to appear in the deeper portions of layer III; in layer II and the outer portions of layer III, they are first beginning to form. By birth, both the second and third laminae contain pyramidal neurons; however, basket cells in layer II are largely absent (Marin-Padilla, 1970b). By 2.5 months postnatally, pyramidal neurons continue to mature, showing a dramatic increase in overall size, the amount of dendritic branching, and the numbers of dendritic spines (Michel & Garey, 1984). Layers VI and I (the marginal zone) are the first laminae to appear and differentiate; layers II and III are the last to form and the latest to mature (Marin-Padilla, 1970a).

The Development of Afferent Inputs to the Cortex

During normal brain development, the entry of various types of afferent fibers to the cortex follows a carefully timed sequence. Two principal inputs to the cortex, one arising from the thalamus and one from the contralateral cortex, show such a sequential progression. During prenatal stages in rats, fibers from the thalamus extend toward the cortical mantle and either stop immediately beneath or begin to enter layer IV (Wise & Jones, 1978). In rat somatosensory cortex, the ingrowth of thalamocortical fibers toward specific neuronal elements, particularly those in layer IV, continues after parturition and is not complete until approximately the third postnatal day (Wise & Jones, 1978). In contrast, commissural inputs arising from homologous cortex of the opposite hemisphere begin entering the somatosensory cortex at 5 days postnatally and attain a mature degree of connectivity by postnatal day 7 (Wise & Jones, 1978). Thus, pyramidal cell axons grow toward their sites of termination before their dendritic arbors have developed, suggesting that the elaboration of the dendritic tree and the formation of spines on pyramidal neurons may be regulated by extrinsic influences from incoming afferent fibers originating in other cortical areas (Wise, Fleshman, & Jones, 1979).

In primates, the destination toward which commissural afferents travel is determined by the region from which they have originated (Goldman-Rakic, 1981). Commissural afferents arising from cortex surrounding the principal sulcus of the dorsolateral prefrontal area will grow toward the principal sulcus of the opposite hemisphere during the prenatal period (Goldman-Rakic, 1981). If, however, the contralateral cortex to which the fibers would ordinarily project is surgically removed, these commissural afferent fibers will deviate from their intended path and course toward a more dorsal location where they will then enter the cortex to form synaptic connections. Although much of normal brain development is tightly programmed, cortical afferents appear to have considerable flexibility as to where they can terminate. Thus, perturbations of normal developmental sequences can potentially result in the formation of aberrant connections in the cortex of primates and, likely, of humans. Such a process could contribute to the development of psychopathology later in life (Benes, 1991).

Myelination of Key Corticolimbic Pathways

A broadly accepted marker for the functional maturation of the central nervous system is the acquisition of myelin sheaths around axon shafts. Myelin, the insulating sheath surrounding axons, enhances conduction velocity; its appearance during development signals the acquisition of functional capabilities for pathways in which it occurs. It has long been known that various neural pathways myelinate at different stages of development (Flechsig, 1920). There is a general tendency, however, for more cephalad structures to myelinate later than those more caudad, and for subcortical pathways to myelinate before cortical associational paths (Yakovlev & Lecours, 1967). For example, the medial longitudinal fasciculus, a pathway that is found along the entire extent of the spinal cord and brain stem, begins myelinating as early as week 20 of the gestational period. The medial lemniscus, a pathway confined to the brain stem, shows similar changes at week 24 (Gilles et al., 1983). Within the cerebral hemispheres, the posterior limb of the internal capsule begins myelinating at week 32; the anterior limb does not show evidence of myelin until week 38. Interestingly, proximal portions of the cingulum bundle do not show evidence of myelin until gestational weeks 38–39 (Gilles et al., 1983), but probably continue myelinating well into the postnatal period (see below). Some paths that are not associative in nature, such as the fornix and mammilothalamic tract, do not begin to myelinate until weeks 44 and 48, respectively. The fornix provides an efferent flow from the hippocampal formation to the mammillary body of the posterior hypothalamus, and the mammilothalamic tract, in turn, conveys information to the anterior nucleus of the thalamus. Both of these pathways are components of the loop of Papez and, in a larger sense, of the corticolimbic system (see above).

Other cortically based links within this system, however, do not myelinate until well into the postnatal period (Benes, 1989; Benes, Turtle, Kahn, & Farol, 1994). For example, the superior medullary lamina of the parahippocampal gyrus medially contains the perforant pathway (entorhinal cortex to area dentata) and laterally includes distal portions of the cingulum bundle (cingulate cortex to presubiculum). The medial part actively myelinates from birth through the first decade, but lateral portions seem to myelinate through the sixth decade of postnatal life (Figures 8.4 and 8.5). The observation of increasing myelination in the superior medullary lamina is noteworthy for two reasons. First, it has long been believed that late postnatal changes of this type may occur in the human brain. Yakovlev and Lecours (1967), in noting sequential myelination of spinal cord, brain stem, and telencephalic structures, suggested that the intracortical associational pathways might continue myelinating as late as the fourth decade. Although their paper is often cited as if it had presented empiric evidence for such changes, no data were in fact included. The first empirical evidence for such adult developmental changes did not appear until the aforementioned study (Benes, 1989; see Figure 8.5) and a more recent replication and extension (Benes et al., 1994). Second, the observation of late myelination of the superior medullary lamina may present an unexpected paradox regarding human behavior and development. It has been generally held that late postnatal myelination probably occurs last in the phylogenetically most sophisticated associative neocortex because this would reflect the overall tendency for brain development to parallel phylogeny. It is ironic that this latter idea would have been correct if the associative cortical areas showing these late postnatal changes were of the neocortical type. Instead, the areas implicated in this late myelination are mesocortical transitional types (i.e., the cingulate cortex), and the fibers showing the changes, rather than projecting "upward," send fibers "downward" toward the primitive allocortex of the hippocampal formation. It may be inferred from the known connection patterns of this latter cortical region (Figure 8.1) that increased conduction occurring along the distal cingulum bundle would probably enhance the flow of activity toward the limbic system. If the identity of these fibers is correct, it can be concluded that late postnatal maturational changes in the human brain, and presumably in human behavior, would involve a tighter modulation of emotional responses in relation to neocortically driven mechanisms. Thus, it would appear from the discussion of the findings in Figure 8.5 that the advanced phase of adult human development during adulthood might involve a more effective interplay between cognitive processing and emotional reactivity (Benes et al., 1994).

Developmental Changes in Neurotransmitter Systems

The functional maturation of the central nervous system must involve obligatory changes in the various neurotransmitter systems that mediate neural activity. Neurotransmitters participating in cortical integration are of two basic types: (a) those that arise from the cortex itself, which are referred to as *intrinsic,* and (b) those that are derived from noncortical locations, which are considered *extrinsic* in nature. The discussion that follows will consider developmental changes of cortical neurotransmitters

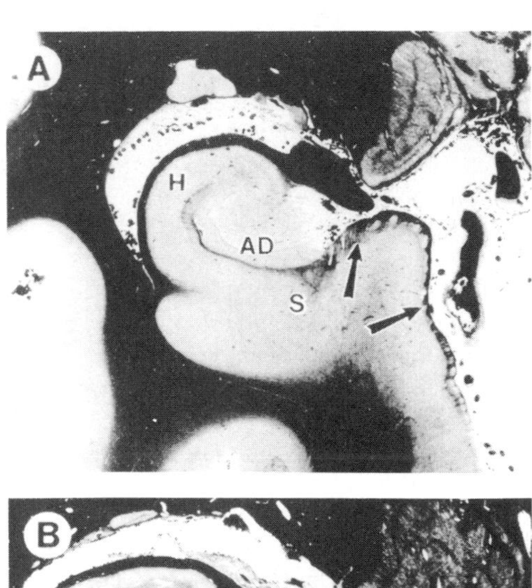

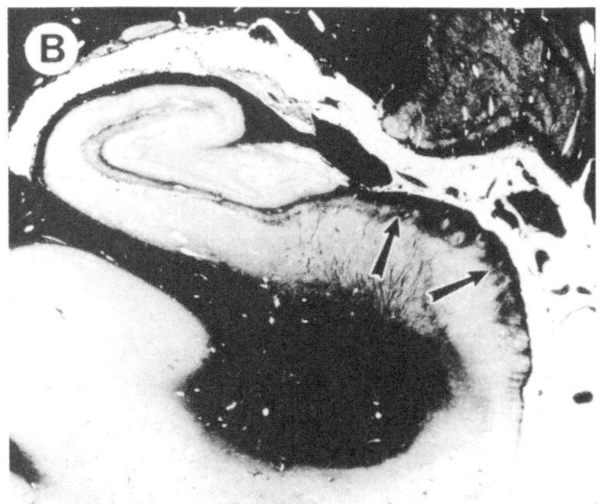

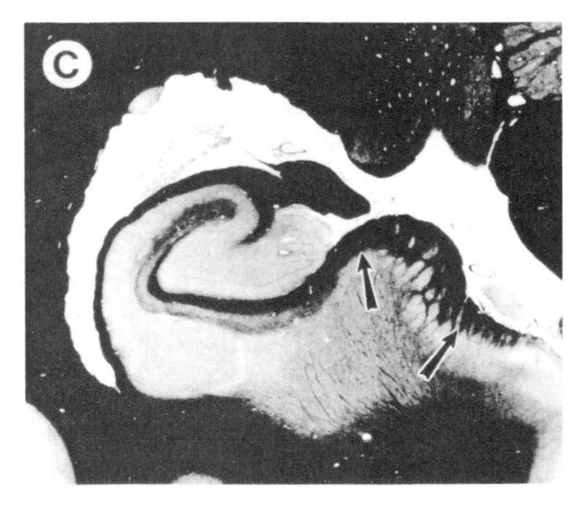

Figure 8.5 Weigert-stained sections of the hippocampal formation from normal human brains of a 6.5-year-old (a), a 17-year-old (b), and a 35-year-old (c). The area dentata (AD), hippocampus proper (H), and subiculum-presubiculum (S) are present in each of the cross-sectional profiles. Along the surface of the subiculum-presubiculum and extending along the parahippocampal gyrus, there is a region showing black staining of myelin sheath material (arrows) that medially contains fiber of the perforant path and laterally distal portions of the cingulum bundle. The amount of Weigert-stained myelin material shows a progressive increase between the first and second decades of life and again later during advanced adulthood.

according to this distinction. It is true that the specific timing of developmental changes in the central nervous system can vary considerably from one species to another, but there are, nevertheless, some general principles that apply for most mammalian forms. For this reason, it is useful to review what has been learned from extensive studies of subhuman species, such as rats, to gain some insight into the possible sequence of changes that may occur in the human brain. As previously discussed, neurotransmitter systems show extensive postnatal maturational changes that continue well beyond the perinatal period and, in some instances, into adulthood (Benes, 1993b). For the purpose of the discussion that follows, it is useful to point out that the equivalent of pubescence for rats occurs between 4–6 weeks of postnatal life; thereafter, rats are considered to be adult. Where available, studies in the developing human brain will also be described.

Intrinsic Neurotransmitters

Intrinsic neurotransmitters can be divided into two basic types, according to whether they exert *excitatory* or *inhibitory* effects on postsynaptic target sites.

Excitatory Cortical Transmitters. Glutamate, an amino acid, and aspartate, a closely related compound, are generally considered to be the transmitters employed by pyramidal axons projecting to both cortical and subcortical locations, as well as to the collateral branches that participate in local cortical circuits (Streit, 1984). Studies suggest that the time at which various glutamatergic pathways mature may be different. For example, the corticocortical glutamate projections of the visual system in rat brain attain mature levels of transmitter before their corticostriate counterparts projecting from cortex to caudate nucleus (Johnston, 1988). Two days after birth, the activity of the glutamate reuptake mechanism is 30% of what it will eventually be at postnatal day 15. In the visual cortex and the lateral geniculate nucleus, this mechanism attains adult levels by postnatal days 15 and 20, respectively (Kvale, Fosse, & Fonnum, 1983). The high-affinity glutamate receptor also continues to change postnatally. Between postnatal days 10 and 15, the amount of glutamate binding increases by 30% and is approximately ten times higher than it will eventually be during adulthood (Schliebs, Kullman, & Bigl, 1986). After day 15, however, it declines substantially through postnatal day 25 (Schliebs et al., 1986). In rats monocularly deprived of visual input, the overall binding of glutamate is reduced in the lateral geniculate nucleus but not in the visual cortex, and these reductions are maintained into adulthood (Schliebs et al., 1986). In the hippocampus, glutamate binding increases up to postnatal day 23 (Baudry, Arst, Oliver, & Lynch, 1981), possibly reflecting the continuing acquisition of long-term potentiation that may be important to both learning and memory (Johnston, 1988).

Inhibitory Cortical Transmitters. Gamma-amino butyric acid (GABA) has long been recognized as the most important inhibitory neurotransmitter in mammalian brain, particularly in humans. Several markers for GABA neurotransmission have been used to trace the development of this system; they include GABA itself, the reuptake mechanism for GABA, the enzyme responsible for the synthesis of GABA (glutamate decarboxylase or GAD), and the receptor that mediates its activity, the GABA-benzodiazepine complex (Bruun-Meyer, 1987). Generally speaking, in rats, the activity of the reuptake mechanism for GABA seems to increase before the activity of GAD (Coyle & Enna, 1976). At birth, the amount of GABA is 50% of adult levels, but these concentrations are not attained until the second postnatal week. In contrast, GAD levels are negligible at birth but reach adult levels by the third postnatal week (Johnston & Coyle, 1980). The amount of GABA and benzodiazepine receptor activity does not begin to increase until the first postnatal week, but then rises sharply through the second week (Candy & Martin, 1979). High-affinity GABA binding continues to increase an additional 15% between the second and seventh postnatal weeks (Candy & Martin, 1979). In contrast, the reuptake mechanism for GABA plateaus by the second postnatal week, but later, in the seventh week, it decreases. In the human brain, unlike that of the rat, the amount of GABA binding demonstrates an overshoot phenomenon (Brooksbank, Atkinson, & Balasz, 1981; Diebler, Farkas-Bargeton, & Wehrle, 1979). The density of GABAergic receptors shows a fivefold increase during the perinatal period and another 100% increase for several weeks thereafter (Brooksbank et al., 1981). GAD activity rises more slowly. It is noteworthy that functional inputs may regulate the ontogenesis of the GABA system. For example, in cat visual cortex, dark-rearing from birth through the sixth postnatal week results in an attenuation of GAD levels (Fosse, Heggelund, & Fonnu, 1989), suggesting that visual activation probably plays some role in regulating the expression of genes for this enzyme.

In the hippocampal formation, GABAergic neurons become postmitotic and begin migrating on embryonic day 14 (Amaral & Kurz, 1985; Lubbers, Wolff, & Frotscher, 1985). As in cortex, GABAergic cells of the hippocampus are generated prenatally; however, unlike the cortex (Marin-Padilla, 1970b), where pyramidal cells differentiate before basket cells, the peak of neurogenesis for GABAergic cells of the hippocampus occurs before that of other non-GABAergic neurons (Soriano, Cobas, & Fairen, 1986). Like cortex, on the other hand, GABA-immunoreactive neuronal cell bodies are detectable in the hippocampus as early as the third postnatal day (Rozenberg, Robain, Jardin, & Ben-Ari, 1989), although cells positive for both GABA and GAD are not close to adult levels until postnatal day 18 (Seress & Ribak, 1988). Terminal boutons positive for GABA first appear at postnatal day 6 and continue to increase in number through the third postnatal week (Rozenberg et al., 1989).

Extrinsic Neurotransmitters

Many different afferent systems project into regions of the neocortex and the hippocampal formation, but most are intrinsic to the cortex and are likely to use either glutamate or aspartate as a neurotransmitter. Afferent projections that are extrinsic to the cortex—those arising from noncortical locations—are of several different types; however, four have been particularly well investigated: (a) projections from the basal forebrain, pons, midbrain, and a diffuse region lying along the brain stem median raphe; they use acetylcholine (basal nucleus of Meynert; Mesulam, Mufson, Levey, & Wainer, 1983), (b) norepinephrine (locus coeruleus; Levitt & Moore, 1978; Lindvall, Bjorklund, & Divac, 1978), (c) serotonin (the raphe nuclei; Descarries, Beaudet, & Watkins, 1975), and (d) dopamine (ventral tegmental nuclei and substantia nigra; Berger, Tassin, Blanc, Moyne, & Thierry, 1974; Thierry, Blanc, Sobel, Stinus, & Glowinski, 1973). The developmental changes in each of these neurotransmitter systems are discussed separately below:

Acetylcholine. Most of the acetylcholine (Ach) found in the cortex is derived from the basal forebrain (Johnston, McKinney, & Coyle, 1979), although a small amount may be synthesized by intrinsic cholinergic neurons (Levey, Wainer, Raye, Mufson, & Mesulam, 1984). The neuronal cell bodies of the cholinergic system are generated early in gestation (Bayer, 1985), but they do not begin to accumulate appreciable amounts of choline acetyltransferase (ChAT) until after the first postnatal week, although this enzyme continues to increase at least until the sixth postnatal week (Johnston & Coyle, 1980). These changes in ChAT parallel the amount of binding activity at the receptor that mediates cholinergic effects in the cortex, the *muscarinic binding site* (Coyle & Yamamura, 1976), except that high-affinity sites for Ach are already fairly abundant at birth, and ChAT is not. The ingrowth of cholinergic fibers into the cortex occurs first in deeper layers and later in the superficial layers, a pattern that mirrors the inside-out progression seen for cortical ontogeny. In humans, cholinergic fibers have been observed to enter the cortex as early as 12–22 weeks of gestation (Candy et al., 1985); however, by birth, the overall levels of ChAT remain low, and adult levels are not attained until approximately age 10 (Diebler et al., 1979). In sharp contrast to rodents, muscarinic receptor activity in human cortex is highest at birth and progressively diminishes during the second through sixth decades (and possibly longer), perhaps as a result of synaptic "pruning" (Ravikumar & Sastary, 1985). In human cortex, acetylcholinesterase, the enzyme that degrades Ach, is found principally in interneurons during the first postnatal week, but later shows a progressive increase in pyramidal cell bodies of layer III, where it reaches peak levels in young adults (Kostovic, Skavic, & Strinovic, 1988). Because upper cortical layers are predominantly involved in associative connections, these latter changes could reflect maturational changes in cognitive activity.

Norepinephrine. Noradrenergic cell bodies of the locus coeruleus undergo their last mitotic division in rat brain at gestational days 12–14 (Lauder & Bloom, 1974) and, in monkeys, at gestational days 27–36 (Levitt & Rakic, 1982). By birth, there is a rather extensive network of noradrenergic fibers in the cortex, and their density is considerably greater than that seen in adults (Coyle & Molliver, 1977). In rats, tyrosine hydroxylase (TH), the enzyme involved in the synthesis of norepinephrine and dopamine, increases steadily between the first and seventh postnatal weeks (Johnston & Coyle, 1980). The beta-adrenergic receptor increases sharply between the first and second postnatal weeks, before plateauing (Harden, Wolfe, Sporn, Perkins, & Molinoff, 1977). Studies of the cat have suggested that norepinephrine may play a key role in the plasticity of synaptic connections (Kasamatsu & Pettigrew, 1976). Following monocular visual deprivation, cats depleted of norepinephrine (Kasamatsu & Pettigrew, 1976) or given clonidine, a drug that inhibits the release of this transmitter (Nelson, Schwartz, & Daniels, 1975), have binocularly-driven neurons that have failed to convert to a monocularly-driven pattern. Parallel information is not available for primate or human brain. Norepinephrine together with other transmitters could play a similar role in the cortex of more advanced mammalian species.

Serotonin. The timing of developmental changes for serotonin (5-hydroxytryptamine or 5-HT) is similar to that observed for the noradrenergic system (Hamon & Bourgoin, 1977; Hedner & Lundberg, 1980). Serotonin-containing neurons are first visualized between gestational days 13 and 17, when some of their axons have already grown toward the primitive pyriform cortex (Wallace & Lauder, 1983). As seen with other transmitter systems, 5-HT levels increase rapidly between birth and the fourth postnatal week (Johnston, 1988). The synthesizing enzyme for 5-HT, tryptophan hydroxylase, is 10% of adult levels by birth, but rises to adult levels by postnatal day 30 (Deguchi & Barchas, 1972). Cortical receptors for 5-HT, on the other hand, are more than a third of adult levels during the perinatal period, but do not attain adult levels until the sixth postnatal week (Uphouse & Bondy, 1981). In primates, 5-HT afferents to the cortex appear to have established an adult pattern by postnatal week 6, and t he levels of 5-HT continue to increase for an additional 2–3 weeks (Goldman-Rakic & Brown, 1982). In the human brain, however, maturational declines in the density of 5-HT_2 binding sites persist throughout life, in the frontal cortex. They show a linear decline between 17 and 100 years of age. A similar but less striking change in this receptor also occurs in the hippocampus (Marcusson, Morgan, Winblad, & Finch, 1984).

It has been suggested that the pattern of ingrowth for serotonergic fibers may vary according to the particular degree of maturity of intrinsic circuits within a given region (Lidov & Molliver, 1982). Around birth, the serotonin projection to sensory cortex is found preferentially within layers IV and VI, the two laminae predominantly involved in receiving thalamic afferents. Because the arrival of serotonin fibers precedes that of the thalamocortical afferents found beneath the cortical mantle, awaiting their time for entry (Wise & Jones, 1978), it has been suggested that the serotonergic innervation to cortex may provide a trophic influence on either incoming fibers from the thalamus and/or their target neurons within the cortical mantle (D'Amato et al., 1987). Such an interaction, if it occurs, might promote the entry of thalamocortical fibers and the formation of synaptic connections with intrinsic neurons of layers IV and VI.

Dopamine. Dopamine cells of rat midbrain begin to differentiate on embryonic day 11, and they continue this process through day 15 (Lauder & Bloom, 1974). Afferent dopamine fibers first arrive near the frontal cortex at approximately embryonic day 16 (Verney, Berger, Vigny, & Gay, 1982); however, at birth, these axons have penetrated into the cortical mantle, where they establish an abundant innervation by postnatal week 2 for the frontal area and postnatal week 3 for the cingulate region (Berger & Verney, 1984). Dopamine afferents to the prefrontal region follow the typical inside-out progression seen for cholinergic inputs (see above), entering the infragranular layers first, and the supragranular layers last (Kalsbeek, Voorn, Buijs, Pool, & Uylings, 1988), and establishing a full distribution by adulthood (Verney et al., 1982). Neonatal rats have dopamine concentrations that are lower than those seen in adults (Johnston, 1988). Before birth, however, the dopamine receptors have already been expressed in the cortex. They continue to increase toward adult levels through postnatal day 31 (Bruinink, Lichtensteiner, & Schlumpf, 1983; Deskin, Seidler, Whitmore, & Slotkin, 1981).

Developmental Similarities among Transmitter Systems

Some general principles concerning the development of neurotransmitter systems can be derived from the above discussion. First, the progenitor cells that give rise to neuronal cell bodies responsible for the elaboration of both intrinsic and extrinsic transmitter activity in the cortex become postmitotic long before they show appreciable differentiation of their respective neurotransmitters. Second, at birth, virtually all neurotransmitter systems are present in the cortex, but they are not yet fully matured. Third, in rats, the postnatal maturation of certain aspects of most transmitter systems continues for up to 4–7 weeks and either overlaps or, in some cases, exceeds the weanling period, during which important pubertal changes are occurring. Although there is a dearth of detailed information concerning the ontogenesis of transmitter systems in the cortex of human brain, evidence from both the cholinergic and serotonergic systems suggests that postnatal changes may continue much longer than in rats and probably persist through most of the life span of the normal individual.

RECENT POSTMORTEM FINDINGS IN CORTICOLIMBIC REGIONS OF SCHIZOPHRENIC BRAIN

Evidence for a Defect in GABA Transmission in the Anterior Cingulate Cortex of Schizophrenics

In a subsequent study that attempted to replicate the first cell-counting analysis of associative cortex in schizophrenic brain (Benes, Davidson, & Bird, 1986), neurons were further differentiated as large pyramidal cells or small cells (interneurons). In so doing, it was unexpectedly found that there were preferential losses of interneurons in layers II–VI of the anterior cingulate cortex of schizophrenic cases, although pyramidal neuron density showed little difference when compared to similar specimens from normal individuals. Because schizophrenic individuals also have lower neuronal densities in other brain areas—such as the primary motor cortex (Benes et al., 1986), pulvinar nucleus of the thalamus (Dom, 1976), hippocampus (Falkai & Bogerts, 1986), and entorhinal cortex (Falkai, Bogerts, & Rozumek, 1988)—it seems plausible that this pattern might have a broad distribution in the brains of chronically psychotic individuals. Such widely distributed changes could arise from a generalized insult at birth (Jacobsen & Kinney, 1980; Parnas et al., 1982). This current study and three previous reports (Benes et al., 1986; Benes, McSparren, Bird, Vincent, & SanGiovanni, 1991; Roberts et al., 1986) failed to show any increase in glial numbers in schizophrenic brain, indicating that an ongoing degenerative process is probably not occurring in these patients. In this regard, it is of interest to note that perinatal hypoxia has been shown to result in neuronal loss but not in gliotic reactions (Windle & Becker, 1944). Thus, the results reported here are consistent with the possibility that a hypoxic event or some other environmental insult might have occurred early in the life of the patients included in this study and may account for these findings (see discussion of acquired insults, below).

Layer II of the cingulate area showed the most robust reductions in the density of interneurons, as did this same lamina in the prefrontal area. Because many different types of interneurons are known to occur in the cortex, it was pertinent to know whether only one or perhaps all categories of interneurons were reduced in the schizophrenics studied. Only a few of these nonpyramidal cases show a diffuse distribution throughout the layers. For example, Cajal-Retzius cells are found in layer I (Marin-Padilla, 1984), Martinotti cells in layers V and VI (Fairen, DeFelipe, & Regidor, 1984), granule cells in layer IV (Lund, 1984), and double bouquet cells in layers II and III (Somogyi & Cowey, 1984). In contrast, basket (Jones & Hendry, 1984) and chandelier cells (Peters, 1984) are found in layers II–VI, a distribution that overlaps with the reduction of interneurons in the anterior cingulate cortex of schizophrenic patients. Because both of these latter cell types are believed to be GABAergic inhibitory neurons (Jones & Hendry, 1984; Peters, 1984), it appeared that strategies aimed at localizing and quantitating this transmitter system might help to identify the missing cells.

Using a high-resolution technique for analyzing receptor binding activity, it was found that GABA-A binding, defined by inhibition of ^{3}H-muscimol binding by bicuculline and enhancement by benzodiazepines, was well preserved in postmortem specimens of human brain tissue (Benes, Vincent, & SanGiovanni, 1989). When this technique was applied to both normal and schizophrenic specimens of the anterior cingulate cortex and blindly analyzed using a semiautomated technique, there was an 84% increase of GABA-A receptor binding on individual neurons in layer II and a 74% increase on neuronal cell bodies in layer III, but no difference was found on neurons in layers V and VI of the schizophrenic cases when compared to normal controls (Benes, Sorensen, Vincent, Bird, & Sathi, 1992). The data for the neuropil showed significant increases of GABA-A receptor binding in layer I only. The findings of increased GABA-A receptor activity in layers I–III of schizophrenics are consistent with the hypothesis that there might be a preferential loss of GABAergic interneurons in layer II and possibly layer III of the cingulate region of schizophrenics. These data were particularly striking because the upper cortical or superficial layers are preferentially involved in associative information processing (Jones, 1984).

It is well known that GABA-mediated inhibition is essential to the normal functioning of the central nervous system (Jones, 1987). For example, in visual cortex, bicuculline-induced disruptions of this transmitter system can produce alterations in directional and orientational selectivity of simple and complex neurons (Sillito, 1984). It is not difficult to conceptualize that a loss of GABAergic inhibitory cells in associative cortex of schizophrenic brain could result in profound disturbances in central information processing and provide a neurobiological basis for understanding some phenomena observed in this disorder, such as the putative loss of the central filtering mechanism (Detre & Jarecki, 1971; see the section on "Selective Attention," above). Roberts (1972) was the first to suggest that schizophrenia might involve a defect in GABA neurotransmission. The findings described above are consistent not only with this latter possibility, but also with other empirical data showing increased ^{3}H-muscimol binding (Hanada, Mita, Nishinok, & Tankaka, 1987), decreased glutamate decarboxylase (Bird, Spokes, & Iversen, 1979), and decreased GABA uptake (Simpson, Slater, Deakin, Royston, & Skan, 1989) in frontal cortex of schizophrenic brain. It is important to note, however, that deficits in the GABA system may not be present in subcortical brain areas of schizophrenics (Cross, Crow, & Owen, 1979; Perry, Buchanan, Kish, & Hansen, 1979).

Evidence for Increased Associative Inputs to the Anterior Cingulate Cortex of Schizophrenics

Two separate studies have demonstrated an increase of vertical fibers in superficial layers of anterior cingulate cortex of schizophrenic subjects (Benes, Majocha, Bird, & Marrotta, 1987; Benes, Vincent, & Molloy, 1993). In the first study, antibodies against axon cytoskeletal proteins were used to visualize fibers in postmortem specimens, and a quantitative analysis revealed that the schizophrenics had significantly more fibers with a vertical, but not horizontal, orientation (Benes et al., 1987). The vertical orientation of these fibers, showing increases in the schizophrenics, was consistent with their possibly being incoming afferents from other regions, possibly cortical ones. If this interpretation were correct, it seemed that such axons might employ glutamate as a neurotransmitter, and strategies aimed at this system might yield more specific clues as to their identity. Using antibodies against glutamate, it was found that abundant numbers of vertical processes could be visualized. When this technique was blindly applied to postmortem specimens of anterior cingulate cortex from normal and schizophrenic cases, it was found that the patient group had a density that was 74% higher than the controls (Benes et al., 1993). No such difference was observed in the prefrontal cortex.

It is important to critically evaluate the possible origin(s) of the small-caliber vertical fibers found to be increased in density in the schizophrenic group. Vertical fibers in the superficial layers represent a heterogeneous population of afferent fibers from both cortical and subcortical regions. Subcortical areas, such as the nucleus basalis of Meynert (Mesulam et al., 1983), raphe nuclei (Descarries et al., 1975; Lindvall & Bjorklund, 1984), locus coeruleus (Levitt & Moore, 1978; Lindvall & Bjorklund, 1984), and the ventral tegmental area (Berger et al., 1974; Lindvall & Bjorklund, 1984; Thierry et al., 1973) send afferent fibers that are typically varicose in appearance and form a dense network of both horizontal and vertical processes in superficial and deep cortical laminae. Inputs arising from these latter regions use acetylcholine, serotonin, norepinephrine, and dopamine, respectively, as transmitters. Because the monoclonal antibodies employed in this study recognized glutamate bound to the carboxy-terminus of alpha-tubulin and exclusively visualized nonvaricose fibers with a vertical orientation, it is unlikely that these fibers originated from these latter subcortical nuclei. This region also receives afferent fibers from the amygdala (Vogt & Pandya, 1987) and thalamus (Vogt, Pandya, & Rosene, 1987; Vogt, Rosene, & Peters, 1981), projections that terminate in superficial layers. The amygdala is reportedly reduced in volume in schizophrenics (Bogerts, Meertz, & Schonfieldt-Bausch, 1985). In the case of the thalamus, no difference in either large or small neurons was noted in anterior nuclei, but posterior nuclei were found to have a substantial decrease in the density of small, nonprojection neurons (Dom, 1976). Although both amygdala and thalamus must be considered as potential sources of the vertical fibers that show an increased density in superficial laminae of anterior cingulate cortex in schizophrenics, more compelling histopathologic evidence would be needed to support this idea. Within the cortex itself, some pyramidal neurons, particularly in layer V (Martin, 1984), as well as in the Martinotti cells found in deeper laminae (Fairen et al., 1984), project axons in a vertical direction toward layer I and could theoretically contribute to the small-caliber fibers that were found in superficial laminae of the schizophrenic group in this study. The transmitter employed by Martinotti cells has not been identified. For pyramidal cells, including those in deeper laminae, the transmitter is probably glutamate or aspartate (Conti, Fabri, & Manzoni, 1988; Monaghan & Cotman, 1985). Pyramidal neurons of layer V in the anterior cingulate cortex, however, probably do not account for the substantial increase in the density of vertical processes observed here, because an earlier study demonstrated a lower neuronal density in layer V in this region of schizophrenics (Benes et al., 1986). In contrast, the density of pyramidal neurons in layer V of the prefrontal cortex is higher in schizophrenic brain (Benes et al., 1991). Because associative afferents that project in a rostral-caudal direction may originate in layer V (Galaburda & Pandya, 1983), it is conceivable that the glutamate-immunoreactive vertical processes showing an increased density in the anterior cingulate region of schizophrenic subjects may be derived from the prefrontal area. Alternatively, the increased numbers of afferent fibers could theoretically have arisen from fiber sprouting (Stevens, 1992) in the outer layers of anterior cingulate cortex. Such a mechanism is conceivable because a reduced density of neurons (Benes et al., 1986; Benes et al., 1991) occurring without volume loss could give rise to an increase in the amount of neuropil relative to cell bodies as a result of an increase in the processes contained therein. Nevertheless, a sprouting of fibers would not produce axon shafts with a straight vertical course.

Functional Implications

An increase of incoming activity to the cingulate region would likely produce important shifts in the relationship of this area with the various regions to which it, in turn, projects. Recent investigations of anterior cingulate cortex from schizophrenic patients have also suggested a model (Figure 8.6) in which there may be a loss of GABAergic neurons, particularly in layer II (Benes, 1991; Benes et al., 1991; Benes, Vincent, Alsterberg, Bird, & SanGiovanni, 1992). In this setting, excessive excitatory activity emanating from increased associative inputs could theoretically be exacerbated by diminished inhibitory activity from GABAergic basket neurons (Benes, Sorensen, Vincent, Bird, & Sathi, 1992). It has been suggested that the effects of increased excitatory inputs and decreased inhibitory activity (Benes, Vincent et al., 1992) could contribute to the overinclusive thinking and loss of a "central filtering" mechanism, respectively, that have been described in this disorder (Detre & Jarecki, 1971). In addition, superabundant glutamatergic inputs could themselves be responsible for GABA neuron loss as a result of an excitotoxic injury (Rothman & Olney, 1986). Such an effect on inhibitory interneurons has been experimentally induced in adult rats using the excitotoxin, kainic acid (Zhang et al., 1990). Because excitotoxic mechanisms have been associated with ischemic injuries to the brain (Rothman & Olney, 1986), it is possible that perinatal complication, such as prolonged labor (Jacobsen & Kinney, 1980), could result in a lower oxygen tension, or high levels of glucocorticoids. Hypoxia does not appear to be a likely source of early neuronal damage in schizophrenic subjects because many different complications have been found in their obstetrical records, but most are *not* associated with a low oxygen tension. Rather, a nonspecific stress response, with unusually high circulating titers of glucocorticoid hormone, would be a more likely setting in which damage to the immature brain might occur (Sapolsky & Meaney, 1986). Reductions in neuronal cell content (Cotterrell, Balazs, & Johnson, 1972) have been observed in rats exposed to high levels of corticosterone early in life, making it plausible that a variety of stressors could induce alterations of brain circuitry by triggering a nonspecific stress response. It is noteworthy that glucocorticoids seem to potentiate the excitotoxic effects of kainic acid (Stein-Behrens et al., 1992), and such a mechanism could influence the proposed role of glutamatergic afferents in the pathophysiologic changes that occur in the anterior cingulate cortex of schizophrenic subjects. Because the cortex develops in an inside-out fashion (Marin-Padilla, 1970a; Rakic, 1974, 1981; Sidman & Rakic, 1973) and basket cells of layer II are particularly immature in human brain at the time of birth (Marin-Padilla, 1970b), it is possible that GABAergic interneurons may be particularly vulnerable to the effects of perinatal complications (Benes, 1991, 1993, 1994; Benes, Sorensen, et al., 1992; Benes, Vincent, et al., 1992). In this regard, it is worth noting that, in immature rat brain, neurons with N-methyl-D-aspartate (NMDA) receptors may have periods in which they exhibit hypervulnerability to even moderate amounts of receptor stimulation (Ikonomidou, Mosinger, Shahid Sallet, Labruyere, & Olney, 1989). Apparently, different populations of neurons show their own periods of peak vulnerability (Olney & Sesma, 1993). Because GABAergic neurons of corpus striatum are particularly sensitive to excitotoxic degeneration in adult rats (Schwarcz & Coyle, 1977), it is possible that basket cells in various layers of immature cortex also show selective hypersensitivity to stimulation of NMDA receptors at particular stages of development. Indeed, excessive numbers of glutamatergic inputs to superficial laminae might be a predisposing factor for a perinatal hypoxic insult to result in a failure of cortical basket neurons to mature.

Although current hypotheses regarding the etiology of schizophrenia favor a model in which an early brain injury plays a key role in this disorder (Benes, 1991; Benes et al., 1986; Jakob &

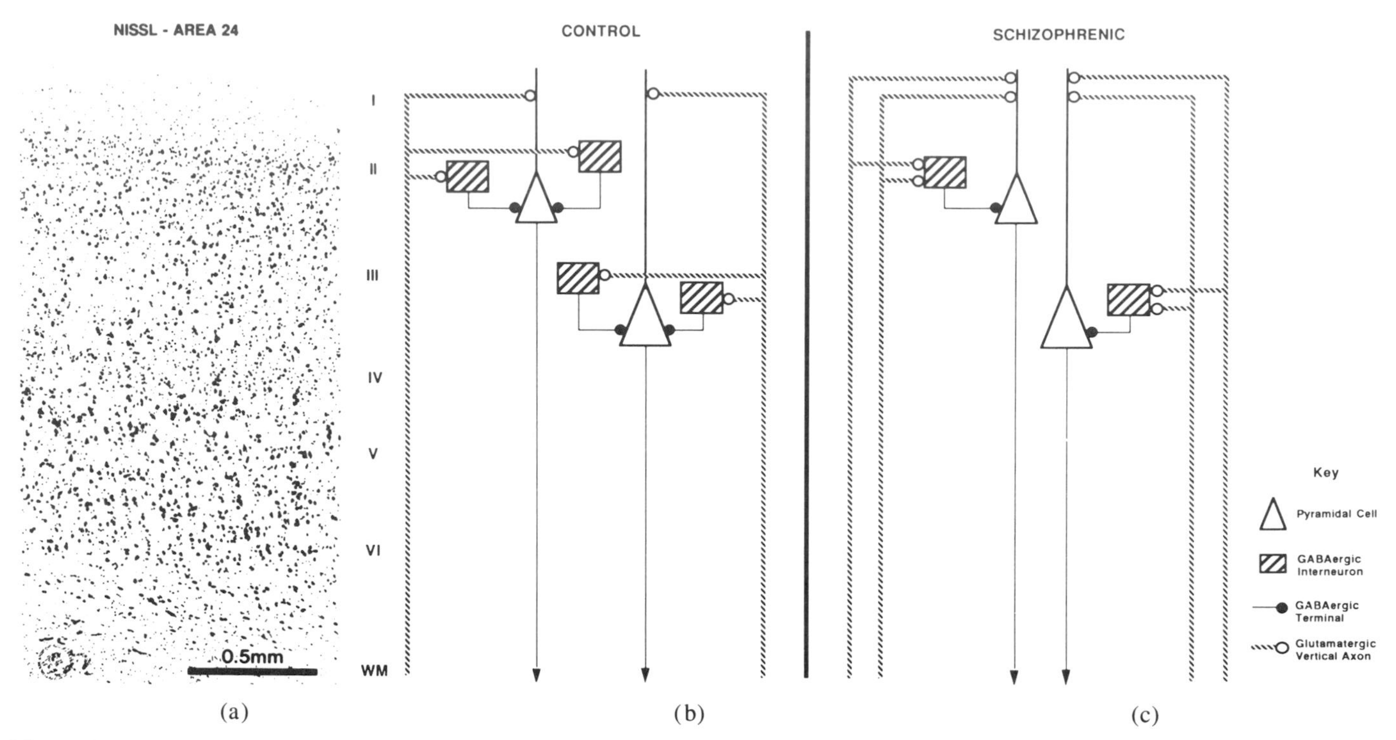

Figure 8.6 Abnormalities thought to occur in the anterior cingulate region of schizophrenic brain: (a) a Nissl-stained section of anterior cingulate cortex, showing its six-layered appearance; (b) schematic depiction of an intrinsic circuit in a normal individual; (c) schematic depiction of an altered circuit in a schizophrenic. In the normal circuit, two pyramidal neurons receive GABAergic inputs from four inhibitory interneurons. Two separate glutamatergic vertical fibers ascend to layer I, where they travel horizontally before forming excitatory connections with the distal portions of pyramidal cell dendrites. Before reaching layer I, collateral branches of these latter fibers form excitatory connections with the inhibitory interneurons. In the schizophrenic circuit, there are four glutamatergic vertical fibers coursing toward layer I, forming excitatory connections with pyramidal cell dendrites, and giving off collateral branches in layers II and III. There are, however, only two GABAergic interneurons. In the schizophrenic circuit, less inhibitory activity would be available to modulate the excessive excitatory activity arising from the vertical associative inputs. A circuit of this type could help account for the loss of filtering and overinclusive thinking seen in schizophrenics.

Beckmann, 1986; Kovelman & Scheibel, 1984; Murray & Lewis, 1987; Weinberger, 1987), it is also possible that an excitotoxic injury might occur later in the life of a schizophrenic individual (Benes, Sorensen et al., 1992). In this regard, it is pertinent that this disorder has a characteristic onset between 16 and 25 years of age (Kraepelin, 1919), a period during which the human brain shows active myelination of a key corticolimbic relay area (Benes, 1989; Benes, Sorensen et al., 1992). Because the occurrence of myelination would be associated with an increased velocity of conduction (Huxley & Stampel, 1949), this developmental change might be expected to enhance associative processing in corticolimbic areas also found to have structural alterations in schizophrenics (Benes et al., 1994; Bogerts et al., 1985; Jakob & Beckmann, 1986; Kovelman & Scheibel, 1984). In the setting of excessive associative inputs to the anterior cingulate cortex, an increased release of glutamate occurring in response to developmental changes in other corticolimbic areas with which it is reciprocally connected could theoretically trigger an excitotoxic response in the anterior cingulate cortex of schizophrenics during the second or third decade of life.

Implications for the Study of Mood Disorders

Based on the idea discussed in the section on evidence for increased associative inputs, a limited number of interconnected cortical regions could be involved in the generation of a wide gamut of psychiatric symptoms and syndromes. This raises some important issues concerning postmortem investigations of other disorders, such as unipolar depression and manic depressive illness. Because of the complexity of cortical circuitry, it is not difficult to imagine that many different types of abnormalities may potentially occur in and among various cortical regions. Accordingly, different types of behavioral manifestations could also arise, depending on the alterations of circuitry that occur. For example, alterations of monoaminergic mechanisms have been hypothesized for disorders of mood and anxiety (Maas, 1985; Praag, 1978; Schildkraut & Kety, 1967), and these could potentially involve abnormalities in the projections of certain brain stem monoaminergic nuclei to the anterior cingulate, prefrontal, inferior parietal, entorhinal, and hippocampal regions. In manic depressive illness, such alterations could include increases and decreases, respectively, in the effect of monoaminergic systems on intrinsic circuits of the cingulate cortex and other regions.

It has been suggested that exposure to environmental stressors may result in a sensitization during subsequent stressful episodes, such that changes become encoded at the level of gene expression (Post, 1992). Thus, abnormal behavioral states, like those seen in psychiatric disorders, could arise either from alterations of the intrinsic circuitry within the corticolimbic system (as might be the case in schizophrenia) or from changes in the extrinsic modulation of the activity of intrinsic circuits in these same regions (as, perhaps, in manic depressive illness). An analogy for manic depressive illness might be a piano whose internal mechanism is wired appropriately, but, depending on how it is played, it may give off sounds that are shrill and chaotic, solemn and melancholic, or harmonious and soothing. Unlike schizophrenics, who show stable defects of emotional and cognitive function suggestive of intrinsic cortical "mis-wiring," individuals in a manic state who are receiving treatment with lithium carbonate and sedatives, or depressed patients who are being treated with antidepressants, typically return to a state of health in which their affect, attention, motivation, interpersonal relations, and thinking are once again normal. The return to normalcy in mood disorder implies that the pattern of connectivity in brain circuitry is not constitutively changed; rather, the setpoint for its activity may be modulated upward or downward, such that the behavioral output becomes *reversibly* abnormal. Because monoaminergic systems interact with intrinsic cortical circuits whether or not they are abnormal, drugs that influence monoaminergic transmission, such as dopamine receptor blockers, could be effective in treating psychopathologic states that arise from alterations of either the dopamine system itself or the intrinsic cortical elements with which it interacts. A theoretical framework of this type could help to explain the fact that the dopamine receptor blockers are effective in treating both mania and schizophrenia.

FUTURE DIRECTIONS

Based on the above discussion, there are several directions that developmental neurobiologic studies of schizophrenia and other psychiatric disorders can follow in the coming years. These directions are discussed here in detail.

Identification of How Circuitry Is Altered

The most essential phase of developmental neurobiologic studies of schizophrenia and other psychiatric disorders is the precise identification of abnormalities in the intrinsic circuits of involved brain regions. Each psychiatric disorder will require appropriate neurobiologic strategies.

Schizophrenia

As noted above, in the discussion of recent postmortem studies of the anterior cingulate cortex of schizophrenics, evidence is suggesting the possibility that two separate abnormalities may be present. On the one hand, there seem to be excessive numbers of incoming fibers that project to layer I; on the other, there appears to be a defect in GABA transmission in layers II and III of the same region. It will be important to establish whether these changes might have appeared before, during, or perhaps even after the onset of illness in the subjects studied. One approach to this problem is to determine whether subjects in the earliest phases of illness show findings that are similar in both degree and kind to those observed in individuals who have been chronically ill for several years. For example, the increased density of vertical glutamate-containing fibers (Benes, Sorensen, et al., 1992) and the increased GABA-A receptor binding (Benes, Vincent, et al., 1992) were both found to an equivalent degree in young and old schizophrenic subjects. Based on these observations, it seems likely that both these changes were present early in the course of the illness; however, it is not yet known whether one or both of these changes appeared at the time the illness began or whether perhaps they were present before symptoms appeared. In the latter case, it is conceivable that one or both of these findings were present from birth. To obtain further information about their time of appearance, it will be useful to relate each to the established risk factors for schizophrenia (see below).

Affective Disorders

With regard to the affective disorders, where much less postmortem work has been performed, little is known about brain circuitry. Because depression improves and mania is worsened by antidepressant compounds that influence the noradrenergic and serotonergic systems, it seems likely that the affective disorders will involve, either directly or indirectly, disturbances in monoaminergic integration. With regard to the corticolimbic system, it will be important to assess whether—and if so, how—these monoaminergic systems are altered in individuals with depression and/or mania. Using immunocytochemical techniques, the distribution of noradrenergic or serotonergic fibers can be analyzed with respect to discrete subregions, layers, or neuronal cell types. This information can, in turn, be used to interpret the results of receptor binding activity associated with each transmitter's system. For example, depressed patients have up-regulated 5-HT_2 serotonin (Meltzer & Lowy, 1987) and $beta_1$-noradrenergic (Siever, 1987) receptor binding activity that becomes down-regulated when they are treated with antidepressant compounds (Charney, Menkes, & Heninger, 1981). It will be important to determine which corticolimbic regions show these latter changes, what types of neurons within these regions mainly account for the differences, and how the intrinsic circuits within each region have been altered as a result of such changes. In this latter regard, several different mechanisms could potentially result in increased receptor binding activity: (a) decreased synthesis or release of norepinephrine and 5HT, (b) an increased rate of transmitter inactivation following release, (c) an increase in the synthesis of receptor molecules ($beta_1$ or 5HT_2, or (d) a decrease in the rate of degradation of the receptor molecule. Each of the aforementioned mechanisms could, in turn, be either primarily or secondarily altered; that is, changes may arise either from an intrinsic dysregulation of the genetic mechanisms involved in their regulation or as a result of effects exerted by pre- or postsynaptic neuronal elements influencing the cell in which they are found. It will be of central importance to determine the *specific* genetic and cellular mechanisms through which the activity of the relevant transmitter system has been modified. It will also be important to assess when these changes may have appeared during the life cycle of an individual with a mood disorder. A neurodevelopmental strategy may then yield information that might eventually lead to preventive, rather than ameliorative, treatment approaches.

Linking Risk Factors to Histopathologic Abnormalities

It will be essential to define what the risk factors for a particular illness are and whether they may be inherited or acquired. As previously discussed with respect to schizophrenia, it is now widely believed that a genetically determined latent trait acting alone or in combination with an early brain insult may play an etiologic role in the occurrence of this disorder. Once the risk factors are specifically identified, it will be necessary to develop strategies that aim to elucidate the neurobiologic consequences for an individual who carries these risk factors—that is, how they might result in specific circuitry alterations within corticolimbic regions.

Genetic Traits

One approach that postmortem investigations can use to relate certain histopathologic abnormalities to a genetic risk factor for schizophrenia is to carefully analyze the data observed in different subtypes of schizophrenia. For example, schizophrenia both with and without superimposed mood disturbances may be variations of the same illness, but with somewhat different patterns of inheritance. Bleuler was the first to suggest that schizophrenia may be a heterogeneous group of illnesses (Bleuler, 1952) and the so-called schizoaffective disorder is probably one of its subtypes. A genetic etiology has been suggested for schizophrenia (Gottesman & Shields, 1972; Kendler, Gruenberg, & Tsuang, 1985; Kety et al., 1968; Kety & Matthysse, 1972), but schizoaffective disorder has not been extensively studied. It is possible that particularly severe affective disorder could give rise to a syndrome that, in many respects, is indistinguishable from schizophrenia (Levitt & Tsuang, 1988). Family studies have shown different findings for the two types of schizophrenia. For example, both affective disorder and schizophrenia tend to occur among the family members of schizoaffective patients (Fowler, 1978; Levitt & Tsuang, 1988), and a prevalence for schizotypal personality and schizophrenia has been found in the first-degree relatives of schizophrenics (Kendler et al., 1985). Thus, although genetic factors for the two disorders are different in some respects, they also seem to overlap. Schizoaffective patients are believed to represent a genetically heterogeneous group of patients (Fowler, 1978; Levitt & Tsuang, 1988), so it might be expected that a microscopic finding emanating from a heritable trait that is common to both disorders would be more striking in the schizophrenic patients without mood disturbances who might be considered genotypically more homogeneous. However, from the data reported for neuronal cell density in the anterior cingulate and prefrontal cortices (Benes et al., 1991), the opposite was true. In the latter study, the small neuron density was even lower in the schizoaffective group when compared to the schizophrenics without superimposed mood disturbances. This latter finding might therefore argue in favor of the lower density of interneurons not having arisen from a primary genetic defect, but rather from birth complications (Jacobsen & Kinney, 1980; Parnas et al., 1982) or some other environmental insult. The fact that reduced numbers of neurons have also been reported in other corticolimbic regions, including the hippocampus (Falkai & Bogerts, 1986) and entorhinal regions (Falkai et al., 1988; Jakob & Beckmann, 1986), provides further support for such a conclusion.

In the future, if microscopic analyses can demonstrate that an abnormality is present in schizophrenics and schizoaffectives but not in manic depressive illness, this could potentially lay the groundwork for identifying the effects of a putative genetic trait. The next step will be to assess what types of genes might be involved in generating such an abnormality and to begin the arduous task of using molecular genetic approaches to determine which products of gene expression are involved. Once the gene is identified, it will be necessary to establish what the gene normally encodes for and how this encoding process could go awry at specific developmental stages, and then produce an alteration of brain circuitry like that seen in the disorder. A general discussion of this goal is straightforward, but the specific details of how to do this are awesome in their implications.

Current approaches to the genetics of schizophrenia deal with familial tendencies for particular characteristics and as such are at the most gross phenomic level. Because our current understanding of human genetics is at a rather rudimentary level, it is difficult to identify the phenomic equivalents for particular genes. There are genes that encode for both structural and functional protein molecules, but there are also loci that regulate the transcription of these genes by either turning them on or shutting them down. Accordingly, an alteration in the phenomic expression of a particular gene in human subjects could arise through changes in its own nucleotide sequence or the sequence for sites that regulate its expression, the so-called "switches." It will also be important to determine whether a genetic variant involved in a psychiatric illness is uniformly expressed throughout the central nervous system. It is theoretically possible that there may be regional variations in the degree to which an abnormal gene is expressed, an issue that derives from the unique neurobiologic properties of the central nervous system. For example, an abnormality related to the GABA system that results in excessive GABA receptor activity could arise from a primary defect in the structure of the receptor molecule and affect its affinity properties or, alternatively, it could be derived from a change in the postsynaptic regulation of gene expression for this locus as the receptor undergoes a compensatory upregulation. There could also be primary alterations in the mechanisms through which GABA-A receptor molecules are packaged and transported to the surface of neuronal cell bodies in anterior cingulate cortex of schizophrenics. Alternatively, there could be a primary defect in the expression of glutamate decarboxylase, the enzyme that synthesizes GABA, and this could give rise to a decrease in the amount of GABA available to interact with the receptor. The latter situation would also result in a compensatory upregulation of GABA-A binding that secondarily, but not primarily, produces a change in the regulation of expression for the receptor gene.

The finding of increased glutamatergic afferents in superficial layers of the anterior cingulate cortex could also be attributable to a primary gene defect. In this instance, however, it will be even more complicated to define the specific mechanisms through which such a change might arise, because there is little general information regarding the genetic regulation of neuronal differentiation and the establishment of connectivity during brain ontogeny. Thus, the elucidation of such mechanisms related to specific types of neurons and specific types of fibers is not likely to be forthcoming for some time. Nevertheless, we can look forward to a time in the foreseeable future when information of this type will begin to emerge and will be available to developmental psychopathologists for the study of mental illness.

Acquired Risk Factors

The strategies required for assessing the role of environment in the occurrence of schizophrenia and other mental disorders will, in some respects, be different from those needed for the genetic factors. In addition to human genetic studies, it will be necessary to use animal models to assess how various types of environmental perturbations may induce alterations of brain structure and function. Animal models of behavior relevant to psychiatry have distinct limitations; nevertheless, they provide carefully controlled paradigms for evaluating the role of certain acquired factors (Henn & McKinney, 1987), and a critical use of such models can provide meaningful information.

Many different types of acquired insult have been traced to the records of schizophrenic subjects, including prolonged labor, viral infections in utero, head trauma, emotional trauma, and others. The heterogeneity of these factors makes it difficult to model for an early insult, unless a common denominator to all can be established. As noted above, stressful conditions of any type result in an elevation of adrenal glucocorticoid levels in the blood as part of a general adaptive responsive of the body (see above). It seems plausible that early traumatic events of any type could potentially produce a generalized insult to the brain. It does not seem likely, however, that such events would be sufficient to explain schizophrenia or other mental illnesses, because individuals exposed to even severe anoxia resulting in cerebral palsy do not show any increased risk for psychosis. Nevertheless, studies of the effects of pre- and postnatal exposure to glucocorticoids on the development of the corticolimbic circuitry will provide important insights into the role of early stress in the etiology of schizophrenia (see below).

With regard to affective disorders, environmental factors are also thought to play an etiologic role, and a variety of animal models have been proposed for the study of this relationship. These have included maternal separation (Jensen & Tolman, 1962), learned helplessness (Overmeier & Seligman, 1967), behavioral despair (Porsolt, Bertin, & Jalfre, 1977) and chronic unpredictable stress (Katz, Roth, & Carroll, 1981). Studies using these various models have attempted to establish construct validity by measuring various neurochemical markers related to monoaminergic transmitter systems to determine whether changes similar to those found in depressed patients can be elicited. For example, with the separation model, low CSF norepinephrine levels are thought to be a trait marker that predicts a greater vulnerability, and reduction of CSF HIAA may be a state marker reflecting the behavioral response to this experimental manipulation (Kraemer, Ebert, Lake, & McKinney, 1984). In contrast, the observation that a tricyclic antidepressant can reverse the potentiated response of such animals to subsequent separation (Kraemer & McKinney, 1979) suggests that this paradigm may also have predictive validity as a model for depression. None of these models is completely satisfactory, but they are powerful research tools for studying the role of environmental conditions in the occurrence of mental illness.

The Interaction of Genetic and Acquired Risk Factors

As suggested by Hebb (1949), the influence of environment on the occurrence of mental illness is probably dependent on the constitution of the individual on whom it is acting. In modeling developmentally for the etiology of mental disorders, it seems appropriate to postulate that an environmental factor will likely interact with constitutional factors to give rise to schizophrenia, mood disturbances, and other psychiatric illnesses. Thus, a nonspecific insult associated with the release of neurotoxic levels of glucocorticoids could result in a diffuse loss of neurons, although the specific loci for such loss may depend on other factors that impart a *selective vulnerability.* For example, with regard to schizophrenia, a preexisting increase of glutamatergic afferents to superficial layers of the anterior cingulate cortex could potentiate an excitotoxic injury to neurons with which they interact (Benes, Vincent et al., 1992). In the setting of a stress response, the increased levels of circulating glucocorticoids could provide a precipitant for the increased release of glutamate at NMDA-mediated synapses (Stein-Behrens et al., 1992). Selectively bred strains of rodents will be a potent research tool to investigate the interaction of environmentally induced stress on genetically determined vulnerability for various psychiatric disorders. For example, operant responses of alcohol-preferring and alcohol-nonpreferring rats are being characterized (Murphy, Gatto, McBride, Lumeng, & Li, 1989) and differential responses of various neurotransmitters in these strains are being identified (McBride, Murphy, Lumeng, & Li, 1990). Selectively bred recombinant strains of mice are also being developed for the study of depression (Swanson, Hingtgen, Simon, & Nurnberger, 1991). This general strategy will undoubtedly provide important insights into the interplay of genetic vulnerability with environmental factors.

Critical Stages for the Development of Psychopathology

It has been recognized for some time that various mental disorders frequently show a characteristic age of onset. Most schizophrenic patients will first present with symptoms at approximately 15–25 years of age (Kraepelin, 1919), and this observation has led to the suggestion that normal ontogenetic changes during adolescence and early adulthood could theoretically play a role in the appearance of schizophrenic symptoms (Benes, 1988, 1989). Empiric support for such a viewpoint comes from studies of monkeys that received unilateral extirpative lesions of the dorsolateral prefrontal cortex soon after birth. There was no difference in the performance of lesioned and unlesioned monkeys on the delayed response task following recovery from the surgical procedure (Goldman-Rakic, 1981). When both sets of monkeys were again tested at approximately 2–3 years of age (their equivalent of pubescence), the unlesioned monkeys showed an age-appropriate performance but the lesioned monkeys now showed a marked impairment of performance on the same task (Goldman-Rakic, 1981). These results were interpreted as indicating that late postnatal changes in the dorsolateral prefrontal region of monkeys might have provided a framework in which the previously latent effects of the lesioning could become manifest. The nature of these putative ontogenetic changes is, however, not understood. Possible alterations that could play a role in the onset of schizophrenia include: (a) a defect of synaptic elimination, which normally occurs in the cortex between 5 and 15 years of age (Feinberg, 1982), or (b) the maturation of the cortical dopamine innervation during adolescence (Weinberger, 1987).

As discussed above, it is also known that changes in the myelination of a key corticolimbic relay zone occur during adolescence (Benes, 1989; Benes, Turtle, Khan, & Farol, 1994) and again during the fifth and sixth decades of life. The fibers showing these postnatal changes probably derive from the cingulate cortex, and possibly also from the entorhinal region and hippocampal formation, and all of these regions have been implicated by recent postmortem investigations in the pathophysiology of schizophrenia (Bogerts et al., 1985; Jakob & Beckmann, 1986; Kovelman & Scheibel, 1984). An increase in the velocity of conduction would occur on these associative fibers as myelin sheaths form (Huxley & Stampel, 1949). An increased release of glutamate at NMDA-mediated synapses would also occur in relation to the overall increase of associative activity within this corticolimbic relay zone. In the setting of increased numbers of glutamatergic fibers into the anterior cingulate cortex, such changes elsewhere in the corticolimbic system could trigger an excitotoxic injury within this latter region. Thus, late postnatal changes in the maturation of the corticolimbic system could conceivably play a role in the appearance of schizophrenic symptoms during adolescence. As discussed above, most neurotransmitter systems, both intrinsic and extrinsic to the cortex, show appreciable postnatal changes, and associated changes in synaptic elimination (Feinberg, 1982) or the dopamine system (Weinberger, 1987) could create an overall environment that is "permissive" for the onset of schizophrenia.

A neurodevelopmental approach to the study of mental illness will require that we obtain a clearer understanding of how various neurotransmitter systems may be undergoing normal ontogenetic changes during the critical stages identified for each illness. For example, with regard to the model of schizophrenia described above, the glutamate and GABA systems both show extensive postnatal maturation up to and, in some cases, including adulthood (see above). The dopamine system also undergoes extensive postnatal development. It will be important to know the extent to which the dopamine system interacts with the GABA (Berger, Febvret, Greengard, & Goldman-Rakic, 1990; Vincent, Molloy, & Benes, 1992) and glutamate (Goldman-Rakic, Leranth, William, Mons, & Geffard, 1989) systems, and the degree to which such interactions could play a role in the etiology and/or treatment response of this disorder at different stages of the illness. Ultimately, abnormal interactions among these various neurotransmitter systems will be understood in relation to postnatal brain ontogeny and the complex symptomatology of the disorder.

With regard to mood disorders, maturational changes in both the noradrenergic and serotonergic systems also proceed well beyond birth and, at least in some cases, even into adulthood (see above). If a genetic factor related to monoaminergic transmission plays a role in the etiology of the affective disorders, then it will be important to define the critical developmental periods during which the expression of a relevant gene is switched "on" or "off." Information of this type can potentially be related to periods of the life cycle when environmental factors might contribute to the actual development of a mood disorder in an individual with genetic vulnerability. The experiences of such a person could be "learned" through neuroplastic changes that give rise to permanently altered networks of associative connections. Because norepinephrine and serotonin have both been implicated in the establishment of cortical connectivity during ontogenesis as well as (see above) the pathophysiology of depression, an abnormal gene related to these transmitter systems could theoretically play a role in the acquisition of maladaptive responses, such as learned helplessness or separation sensitivity, in individuals with a selective vulnerability for affective disorder.

Our understanding of the pathophysiology of psychiatric illness will have to take into account a complex interplay between the various risk factors for these illnesses and normal developmental changes in the brain. On the one hand, it is likely that a genetic factor and/or an acquired insult to the brain can alter normal brain development, perhaps focally or in a generalized way. On the other hand, once the brain of an individual who is "at risk" for a mental illness has been affected by environmental risk factors, then normal ontogenetic changes may trigger their expression during critical periods of postnatal development. The inherited risk factor for affective disorder is probably different from that for schizophrenia, and the types of environmental factors that influence their expression may also be different. In applying a developmental approach to the study of schizophrenia and mood disorders, it will be necessary to define the unique neurobiologic consequences of abnormal genes found in relation to each of these illnesses, and to establish an understanding of how the expression of such genes interplays with normal ontogenetic events during a critical period of life when an individual at risk for such an illness is apt to become symptomatic.

The Challenge for the Future

The progress of a developmental neurobiology of the mental disorders will depend on a clear definition of the neural substrates of constitutional vulnerability for various disorders.

Toward this end, we will need to know:

1. The precise variations of neural circuits associated with various constitutional types;

2. The particular genes that impart selective vulnerability to certain constitutions;
3. The phenotypic expression of these latter genes within these neural circuits;
4. The effect of environmental factors on the *de novo* expression of such genes, or the changes they impart to the involved circuits;
5. The normal ontogenetic changes that influence the activity of these neural circuits at "critical stages."

As discussed above, extensive and complex alterations in many different neurotransmitter systems normally occur well into adulthood. The question is no longer whether such ontogenetic changes normally occur; instead, we need to know what these changes are, the regions in which they are occurring, and how they impact preexisting circuitry. Thus, all normal developmental changes influence, either primarily or secondarily, circuitry that lies both upstream and downstream within the human brain. Our ultimate challenge for the future is to understand how the risk factors for each mental illness alter the normal development of the corticolimbic system early in life, and how, in turn, normal developmental changes during critical stages of postnatal life permit the appearance of particular mental illnesses.

REFERENCES

Adamec, R. E. (1978). Normal and abnormal limbic system mechanism of emotive biasing. In K. E. Livingston & O. Hornykiewicz (Eds.), *Limbic mechanisms* (pp. 405–455). New York: Plenum.

Adamec, R. E. (1991). Individual differences in temporal lobe sensory processing of threatening stimuli in the cat. *Physiology and Behavior, 49,* 445–464.

Adamec, R. E. (1992). Anxious personality in the cat: Its ontogeny and physiology. In B. J. Carroll & J. E. Barrett (Eds.), *Psychopathology and the brain* (pp. 153–168). New York: Raven Press.

Adamec, R. E., Stark-Adamec, C., & Livingston, K. E. (1980). The development of predatory aggression and defense in the domestic cat (Felinus Catus): I. Effects of early experience on adult patterns of aggression and defense. *Behavioral Neurology and Biology, 30,* 389–409.

Amaral, D. G., & Kurz, J. (1985). The time of origin of cells demonstrating glutamic acid decarboxylase-like immunoreactivity in the hippocampal formation of the rat. *Neuroscience Letter, 59,* 33–39.

American Psychiatric Association. (1994). *Diagnostic and statistical manual of mental disorders* (4th ed.). Washington, DC: Author.

Anand, B. K., & Dua, S. (1956). Circulatory and respiratory changes induced by electrical stimulation of the limbic system (visceral brain). *Journal of Neurophysiology, 19,* 393–400.

Angevine, J. B. (1965). Time of neuron origin in the hippocampal region: An autoradiographic study in the mouse. *Experimental Neurology, 13* (Suppl.), 1–70.

Ballantine, H. T., Cassidy, W. L., Flanagan, N. W., & Marino, R. (1967). Stereotaxic anterior cingulotomy for neuropsychiatric illness and intractable pain. *Journal of Neurosurgery, 26,* 488–495.

Barrelet, L., Ferrero, F., Szogethy, L., Giddey, C., & Pellizzer, G. (1990). Expressed emotion and first-admission schizophrenia: Nine-month followup in a French cultural environment. *British Journal of Psychiatry, 156,* 357–362.

Barris, R. W., & Schumann, H. R. (1953). Bilateral anterior cingulate gyrus lesions: Syndrome of the anterior cingulate gyri. *Journal of Neurology, 3,* 44–52.

Baudry, M., Arst, D., Oliver, M., & Lynch, G. (1981). Development of glutamate binding sites and their regulation by calcium in rat hippocampus. *Developmental Brain Research, 1,* 37–38.

Bayer, S. A. (1985). Neurogenesis of the magnocellular basal telencephalic nuclei in the rat. *International Journal of Developmental Neuroscience, 3,* 229–243.

Bayer, S. A., Yackel, J. W., & Puri, P. S. (1982). Neurons in the dentate gyrus granular layer substantially increase during juvenile and adult life. *Science, 216,* 890–892.

Beckstead, R. M. (1979). An autoradiographic examination of corticocortical and subcortical projections of the mediodorsal-projection (prefrontal) cortex in the rat. *Journal of Comparative Neurology, 184,* 43–62.

Belaydier, C., & Maugierre, F. (1980). The duality of the cingulate gyrus in monkey: Neuroanatomical study and functional hypothesis. *Brain, 130,* 525–554.

Benes, F. M. (1988). Post-mortem structural analyses of schizophrenic brain: Study designs and the interpretation of data. *Psychiatric Developments, 6,* 213–226.

Benes, F. M. (1989). Myelination of cortical-hippocampal relays during late adolescence: Anatomical correlates to the onset of schizophrenia. *Schizophrenia Bulletin, 15,* 585–594.

Benes, F. M. (1991). Toward a neurodevelopmental understanding of schizophrenia and other psychiatric disorders. In D. Cicchetti & S. L. Toth (Eds.), *Rochester Symposium on Developmental Psychopathology: Vol. 3. Models and integrations* (pp. 161–184). Rochester, NY: University of Rochester Press.

Benes, F. M. (1993). Relationship of cingulate cortex to schizophrenia and other psychiatric disorders. In B. A. Vogt & M. Gabriel (Eds.), *The neurobiology of cingulate cortex and limbic thalamus* (pp. 581–605). Boston: Birkhauser.

Benes, F. M. (1994). Development of the corticolimbic system. In G. Dawson & K. Fischer (Eds.), *Human behavior and the developing brain* (pp. 176–206). New York: Guilford.

Benes, F. M., Davidson, J., & Bird, E. D. (1986). Quantitative cytoarchitectural studies of cerebral cortex of schizophrenics. *Archives of General Psychiatry, 43,* 31–35.

Benes, F. M., Majocha, R., Bird, E. D., & Marrotta, C. A. (1987). Increased vertical axon numbers in cingulate cortex of schizophrenics. *Archives of General Psychiatry, 44,* 1017–1021.

Benes, F. M., McSparren, J., Bird, E. D., Vincent, S. L., & SanGiovanni, J. P. (1991). Deficits in small interneurons in schizophrenic cortex. *Archives of General Psychiatry, 48,* 996–1001.

Benes, F. M., Sorensen, I., Vincent, S. L., Bird, E. D., & Sathi, M. (1992). Increased density of glutamate-immunoreactive vertical processes in superficial laminae in cingulate cortex of schizophrenic brain. *Cerebral Cortex, 2,* 503–512.

Benes, F. M., Turtle, M., Khan, Y., & Farol, P. (1994). Myelination of a key relay zone in the hippocampal formation occurs in human brian during childhood, adolesence and adulthood. *Archives of General Psyhicatry, 51,* 477–484.

Benes, F. M., Vincent, S. L., Alsterberg, G., Bird, E. D., & SanGiovanni, J.-P. (1992). Increased GABA-A receptor binding in superficial layers of cingulate cortex in schizophrenics. *Journal of Neuroscience, 11,* 925–947.

Benes, F. M., Vincent, S. L., & SanGiovanni, J. P. (1989). High resolution imaging of receptor binding in analyzing neuropsychiatric disease. *Biotechniques, 7,* 970–979.

Berger, B., Febvret, A., Greengard, P., & Goldman-Rakic, P. S. (1990). DARPP-32, a phosphoprotein enriched in dopaminoceptive neurons bearing dopamine D_1 receptors: Distribution in the cerebral cortex of the newborn and adult rhesus monkey. *Journal of Comparative Neurology, 299,* 327–348.

Berger, B., Tassin, J. P., Blanc, G., Moyne, M. A., & Thierry, A. M. (1974). Histochemical confirmation for dopaminergic innervation of rat cerebral cortex after the destruction of noradrenergic ascending pathways. *Brain Research, 81,* 332–337.

Berger, B., & Verney, C. (1984). Development of the catecholamine innervation in rat neocortex: Morphological features. In L. Descarries, T. R. Reader, & H. H. Jasper (Eds.), *Monoamine innervation of cerebral cortex* (pp. 95–121). New York: Liss.

Berman, K. F., Zec, R. F., & Weinberger, D. R. (1986). Physiologic dysfunction of dorsolateral prefrontal cortex in schizophrenia: II. Role of neuroleptic treatment, attention, and mental effort. *Archives of General Psychiatry,* 126–135.

Bird, E. D., Spokes, E. G. S., & Iversen, L. L. (1979). Increased dopamine concentration in limbic areas of brain from patients dying with schizophrenia. *Brain, 102,* 347–360.

Bleuler, E. (1952). Dementia praecox or the group of schizophrenias. New York: International Universities Press.

Bogerts, B., Meertz, E., & Schonfieldt-Bausch, R. (1985). Basal ganglia and limbic system pathology in schizophrenia: A morphometric study of brain volume and shrinkage. *Archives of General Psychiatry, 42,* 784–791.

Broca, P. (1878). Anatomie comparée des circonvolutions cérébrales: Le grand lobe limbique et la scissure limbique dans la serie des manmifères. *Révue d'Anthropologie, 1,* 385–498.

Brooksbank, B. W. L., Atkinson, D. J., & Balasz, R. (1981). Biochemical development of the human brain: II. Some parameters of the GABAergic system. *Developmental Neuroscience, 1,* 267–284.

Brown, M. H., & Lighthill, J. A. (1968). Selective anterior cingulotomy: A psychosurgical evaluation. *Journal of Neurosurgery, 29,* 513–519.

Bruinink, A., Lichtensteiner, W., & Schlumpf, M. (1983). Pre- and postnatal ontogeny and characterization of dopaminergic D_2, serotonergic S_2, and spirodecanone binding sites in rat forebrain. *Journal of Neurochemistry, 40,* 1227–1237.

Bruun-Meyer, S. E. (1987). The GABA/benzodiazepine receptor-chloride ionophore complex: Nature and modulation. *Progress in Neuropsychopharmacology, 11,* 365–387.

Callaway, E., & Naghdi, S. (1982). An information processing model for schizophrenia. *Archives of General Psychiatry, 39,* 339–347.

Cameron, N. (1938). Reasoning, regression and communication in schizophrenics. *Psychology Monograph, 50,* 1–33.

Candy, J. M., Bloxham, C. A., Thompson, J., Johnson, M., Oakley, A. E., & Edwardson, J. A. (1985). Evidence for the early prenatal development of cortical cholinergic afferents from the nucleus of Meynert in the human fetus. *Neuroscience Letters, 61,* 91–95.

Candy, J. M., & Martin, I. L. (1979). The postnatal development of the benzodiazepine receptor in the cerebral cortex and cerebellum of the rat. *Journal of Neurochemistry, 32,* 655–658.

Carlsson, A. (1978). Mechanism of action of neuroleptic drugs. In M. A. Lipton, A. DiMascio, & K. F. Killam (Eds.), *Psychopharmacology: A generation of progress* (pp. 1057–1070). New York: Raven Press.

Charney, D. S., Menkes, D. B., & Heninger, G. R. (1981). Receptor sensitivity and the mechanisms of action of antidepressant treatment. *Archives of General Psychiatry, 38,* 1160–1180.

Cloninger, C. R. (1991). Brain networks underlying personality development. In B. J. Carroll & J. E. Barrett (Eds.), *Psychopathology and the brain* (pp. 183–208). New York: Raven Press.

Conti, F., Fabri, M., & Manzoni, T. (1988). Glutamate-positive corticocortical neurons in the somatic sensory areas I and II of cats. *Journal of Neuroscience, 8,* 2948–2960.

Cotterrell, M., Balazs, R., & Johnson, A. L. (1972). Effects of corticosteroids on the biochemical maturation of rat brain: Postnatal cell formation. *Journal of Neurochemistry, 19,* 2151–2167.

Coyle, J. T., & Enna, S. (1976). Neurochemical aspects of the ontogenesis of GABAergic neurons in the rat brain. *Brain Research, 111,* 119–133.

Coyle, J. T., & Molliver, M. (1977). Major innervation of newborn rat cortex by monoaminergic neurons. *Science, 196,* 444–447.

Coyle, J. T., & Yamamura, H. I. (1976). Neurochemical aspects of the ontogenesis of GABAergic neurons in the rat brain. *Brain Research, 118,* 429–440.

Crosby, E. C. (1917). The forebrain of alligator mississippiensis. *Journal of Comparative Neurology, 27,* 325–402.

Cross, A. J., Crow, T. J., & Owen, F. (1979). Gamma-aminobutyric acid in the brain in schizophrenia. *Lancet, 1,* 560–561.

Damasio, A. R., & Van Hoesen, G. W. (1983). Emotional disturbances associated with focal lesions of the limbic frontal lobe. In K. M. Heilman & P. Satz (Eds.), *Neuropsychology of human emotion* (pp. 85–110). New York: Guilford.

D'Amato, R. J., Blue, M., Largent, B., Lynch, D., Leobetter, D., Molliver, M., & Snyder, S. (1987). Ontogeny of the serotonergic projection of rat neocortex: Transient expression of a dense innervation of primary sensory areas. *Proceedings of the National Academy of Sciences, 84,* 4322–4326.

Deguchi, T., & Barchas, J. (1972). Regional distribution and developmental change in tryptophan hydroxylase in rat brain. *Journal of Neurochemistry, 19,* 927–929.

Descarries, L., Beaudet, A., & Watkins, K. C. (1975). Serotonin nerve terminals in adult rat neocortex. *Brain Research, 100,* 563–588.

Deskin, R., Seidler, F. J., Whitmore, W. L., & Slotkin, T. A. (1981). Development of noradrenergic and dopaminergic receptor systems depends on maturation of their presynaptic nerve terminals in the rat brain. *Journal of Neurochemistry, 36,* 1683–1690.

Detre, T. P., & Jarecki, H. G. (1971). *Modern psychiatric treatment* (pp. 108–116). Philadelphia: Lippincott.

Devinsky, O., & Luciano, D. (1992). The contribution of cingulate cortex to human behavior. In B. A. Vogt & M. Gabriel (Eds.), *The neurobiology of cingulate cortex and limbic thalamus.* Boston: Birkhauser.

Diebler, M. F., Farkas-Bargeton, E., & Wehrle, R. (1979). Developmental changes of enzymes associated with energy metabolism and synthesis of some neurotransmitters in discrete areas of human neocortex. *Journal of Neurochemistry, 32,* 429–435.

Dom, R. (1976). Neostriatal and thalamic interneurons: Their role in the pathophysiology of Huntington's chorea, Parkinson's disease and catatonic schizophrenia. *Acta Psychiatrica Scandinavica, 265* (Suppl.), 103–123.

Domesick, V. B. (1969). Projections from the cingulate cortex in the rat. *Brain Research, 12,* 296–320.

Dunsmore, R. H., & Lennox, M. A. (1950). Stimulation and strychninization of supracallosal anterior cingulate gyrus. *Journal of Neurophysiology, 13,* 207–213.

Eckenhoff, M. F., & Rakic, P. (1988). Nature and fate of proliferative cells in the hippocampal dentate gyrus during the life span of the rhesus monkey. *Journal of Neuroscience, 8,* 2729–2747.

Fairen, A., DeFelipe, J., & Regidor, J. (1984). Nonpyramidal neurons. In A. Peters & E. G. Jones (Eds.), *Cerebral cortex: Vol. 1. Cellular components of the cerebral cortex* (pp. 201–253). New York: Plenum.

Falkai, P., & Bogerts, B. (1986). Cell loss in the hippocampus of schizophrenics. *European Archives of Psychiatry and Neurological Sciences, 236,* 154–161.

Falkai, P., Bogerts, B., & Rozumek, M. (1988). Cell loss and volume reduction in the entorhinal cortex of schizophrenics. *Biological Psychiatry, 24,* 515–521.

Feinberg, I. (1982). Schizophrenia: Caused by a fault in programmed synaptic elimination during adolescence? *Journal of Psychiatric Research, 17*(4), 319–334.

Flechsig, P. (1920). *Anatomie des menschlichen gehirns und ruckenmarks auf myelogenetischer gundlange.* Leipzig: Thieme.

Fosse, V. M., Heggelund, P., & Fonnu, F. (1989). Postnatal development of glutamatergic, GABAergic and cholinergic neurotransmitter phenotypes in the visual cortex, lateral geniculate nucleus pulvinar and superior colliculus in cats. *Journal of Neuroscience, 9,* 426–435.

Fowler, R. C. (1978). Remitting schizophrenia as a variant of affective disorder. *Schizophrenia Bulletin, 4,* 68–77.

Galaburda, A. M., & Pandya, D. N. (1983). The intrinsic architectonic and connectional organization of the superior temporal region of the rhesus monkey. *Journal of Comparative Neurology, 221,* 169–184.

Geier, S., Bancaud, J., Talairach, J., Bonis, A., Szikla, G., & Enjelvin, M. (1977). The seizures of frontal lobe epilepsy: A study of clinical manifestations. *Neurology, 27,* 951–958.

Gilles, F. H., Shankle, W., & Dooling, E. C. (1983). Myelinated tracts: Growth patterns. In F. H. Gilles, A. Leviton, & E. C. Dooling (Eds.), *The developing human brain: Growth and epidemiologic neuropathology* (pp. 117–183). Boston: John Wright.

Glees, P., Cole, J., Whitty, W. M., & Cairns, H. (1950). The effects of lesions in the cingulate gyrus and adjacent areas in monkeys. *Journal of Neurology and Neurosurgery, 13,* 178–190.

Goldman-Rakic, P. (1981). Development and plasticity of primate frontal association cortex. In F. O. Smith (Ed.), *The organization of the cerebral cortex.* Cambridge, MA: MIT Press.

Goldman-Rakic, P. S., & Brown, R. M. (1982). Postnatal development of monoamine content and synthesis in the cerebral cortex of rhesus monkeys. *Developmental Brain Research, 4,* 339–349.

Goldman-Rakic, P. S., Leranth, C., William, S. M., Mons, N., & Geffard, M. (1989). Dopamine synaptic complex with pyramidal neurons in primate cerebral cortex. *Proceedings of the National Academy of Sciences, 86,* 9015–9019.

Gottesman, I. I., & Shields, J. (1972). *Schizophrenia and genetics: A twin study vantage point.* New York: Academic Press.

Hamon, M., & Bourgoin, S. (1977). Biochemical aspects of the maturation of serotonergic neurons in the rat brain. In S. R. Berenger (Ed.), *Brain: Fetal and infant* (pp. 239–261). The Hague: Nijoff.

Hanada, S., Mita, T., Nishinok, N., & Tankaka, C. (1987). ^{3}H-Muscimol binding sites increased in autopsied brains of chronic schizophrenics. *Life Science, 40,* 259–266.

Harden, T. K., Wolfe, B. B., Sporn, J. R., Perkins, J. P., & Molinoff, P. B. (1977). Ontogeny of beta-adrenergic receptors in rat cerebral cortex. *Brain Research, 125,* 99–108.

Harlow, H. F. (1958). The nature of love. *American Psychology, 13,* 673–685.

Harlow, H. F., Dodsworth, R. O., & Harlow, M. K. (1965). Total social isolation in monkeys. *Proceedings of the National Academy of Sciences, 54,* 90–97.

Hebb, D. O. (1949). *Organization of behavior* (p. 261). New York: Wiley.

Hedner, T., & Lundberg, P. (1980). Serotonergic development in the postnatal rat brain. *Journal of Neurological Tranm., 49,* 257–279.

Henn, F. A., & McKinney, W. T. (1987). Animal models in psychiatry. In H. Y. Meltzer (Ed.), *Psychopharmacology: The third generation of progress* (pp. 687–695). New York: Raven Press.

Hoffman, H. H. (1963). The olfactory bulb, accessory olfactory bulb and hemisphere of some anurans. *Journal of Comparative Neurology, 120,* 317–368.

Holzman, P. S., Kinglem, E., Matthysse, S., Flanagan, S., Lipton, R., Cramer, G., Levin, S., Lange, K., & Levy, D. L. (1988). A single dominant gene can account for eye tracking dysfunctions and schizophrenia in offspring of discordant twins. *Archives of General Psychiatry, 45,* 641–647.

Hurley, K. M., Herbert, H., Moga, M. M., & Saper, C. B. (1991). Efferent projections of the infralimbic cortex of the rat. *Journal of Comparative Neurology, 308,* 249–276.

Huxley, A. F., & Stampel, R. (1949). Evidence for saltatory conduction in peripheral myelinated nerve fibres. *Journal of Physiology (London), 108,* 315–339.

Ikonomidou, C., Mosinger, L. L., Shahid Sallet, K., Labruyere, J., & Olney, J. W. (1989). Sensitivity of the developing rat brain to hyperbaric/ischemic damage parallels sensitivity to N-methyl-D-aspartate neurotoxicity. *Journal of Neuroscience, 9,* 2809–2818.

Jacobsen, B., & Kinney, D. K. (1980). Perinatal complications in adopted and non-adopted schizophrenics and their controls: Preliminary results. *Acta Psychiatrica Scandinavica, 238,* 103–123.

Jakob, H., & Beckmann, H. (1986). Prenatal developmental disturbances in the limbic allocortex in schizophrenics. *Journal of Neural Transmission, 65,* 303–326.

Jensen, G. D., & Tolman, C. W. (1962). Mother-infant relationship in the monkey, Macaca nemestrina: The effect of brief separation and mother infant specificity. *Journal of Comparative Physiology and Psychology, 55,* 131–136.

Johnston, M. V. (1988). Biochemistry of neurotransmitters in cortical development. In A. Peters & E. G. Jones (Eds.), *Cerebral cortex: Vol. 7. Development and maturation of cerebral cortex* (pp. 211–236). New York: Plenum.

Johnston, M. V., & Coyle, J. T. (1980). Ontogeny of neurochemical markers for noradrenergic, GABAergic and cholinergic neurons in neocortex lesioned with methylazoxymethanol acetate. *Journal of Neurochemistry, 34,* 1429–1441.

Johnston, M. V., McKinney, M., & Coyle, J. T. (1979). Evidence for a cholinergic projection to neocortex from neurons in basal forebrain. *Proceedings of the National Academy of Sciences, 76,* 5392–5396.

Jones, E. G. (1984). Laminar distribution of cortical efferent cells. In A. Peters & E. G. Jones (Eds.), *Cerebral cortex: Vol. 1. Cellular components of the cerebral cortex* (pp. 521–554). New York: Plenum.

Jones, E. G. (1987). GABA-peptide neurons in primate cerebral cortex. *Journal of Mind and Behavior, 8,* 519–536.

Jones, E. G., & Hendry, S. H. C. (1984). Basket cells. In A. Peters & E. G. Jones (Eds.), *Cerebral cortex: Vol. 1. Cellular components of the cerebral cortext.* New York: Plenum.

Jones, E. G., & Powell, T. P. S. (1970). An anatomical study of converging sensory pathways within the cerebral cortex of the monkey. *Brain, 93,* 793–820.

Kaada, B. R. (1960). Cingulate, posterior orbital, anterior insular and temporal pole cortex. In J. Field (Ed.), *Handbook of physiology* (Vol. 2, pp. 1345–1372). Washington, DC: American Physiological Society.

Kaada, B. R., Pribram, K. H., & Epstein, J. A. (1940). Respiratory and vascular responses in monkeys from temporal pole, insula, orbital surface and cingulate gyrus. *Journal of Neurophysiology, 12,* 347–356.

Kagan, J., Reznick, J., & Gibbons, J. (1989). Inhibited and uninhibited types of children. *Child Development, 60,* 838–845.

Kagan, J., Reznick, J. S., & Snidman, N. (1988). Biological bases of childhood shyness. *Science, 240,* 167–171.

Kagan, J., Reznick, J. S., Snidman, N., Gibbons, J., & Johnson, M. A. (1988). Childhood derivatives of inhibition and lack of inhibition to the unfamiliar. *Child Development, 59,* 1580–1589.

Kagan, J., & Snidman, N. (1991a). Infant predictors of inhibited and uninhibited profiles. *Psychological Science, 2,* 40–44.

Kagan, J., & Snidman, N. (1991b). Temperamental factors in human development. *American Psychologist, 48,* 856–862.

Kalsbeek, A., Voorn, P., Buijs, R. M., Pool, C. W., & Uylings, H. B. (1988). Development of the dopaminergic innervation in the prefrontal cortex of rat. *Journal of Comparative Neurology, 269,* 58–72.

Kaplan, M. S., & Bell, D. H. (1984). Mitotic neuroblasts in the 9-day-old and 11-month-old rodent hippocampus. *Journal of Neuroscience, 4,* 1429–1441.

Kasamatsu, T., & Pettigrew, J. W. (1976). Depletion of brain catecholamines: Failure of monocular dominance shift after monocular conclusion in kittens. *Science, 194,* 206–209.

Katz, R. J., Roth, K. A., & Carroll, B. J. (1981). Acute and chronic stress effects on open field activity in the rat: Implications for a model of depression. *Neuroscience and Biobehavioral Research, 5,* 247–251.

Kendler, K. S., Gruenberg, A., & Tsuang, M. T. (1985). Psychiatric illness in first-degree relatives of schizophrenic and surgical control patients. *Archives of General Psychiatry, 42,* 770–779.

Kennard, M. A. (1955). The cingulate gyrus in relation to consciousness. *Journal of Nervous and Mental Disorders, 121,* 34–39.

Kety, S. (1983). Mental illness in the biological and adoptive relatives of schizophrenic adoptees: Findings relevant to genetic and environmental factors in etiology. *American Journal of Psychiatry, 140,* 720–727.

Kety, S. (1985). Schizotypal personality disorder. An operational definition of Bleuler's latent schizophrenia. *Schizophrenia Bulletin, 11,* 590–594.

Kety, S., & Matthysse, S. (1972). Prospects for research on schizophrenia. An overview. *Neuroscience Research Bulletin, 10,* 456–467.

Kety, S., Rosenthal, D., Wender, P., & Schulsinger, F. (1968). The type and prevalence of mental illness in the biological and adoptive families of adopted schizophrenics. In D. Rosenthal & S. Kety (Eds.), *The transmission of schizophrenia* (pp. 25–37). Oxford, England: Pergamon.

Klein, D. F., Zitrin, C. M., & Woerner, A. (1978). Antidepressant, anxiety, panic and phobia. In M. A. Lipton, A. Dimascio, & K. F. - Killam (Eds.), *Psychopharmacology: A generation of progress* (pp. 1401–1410). New York: Raven Press.

Kornetsky, C., & Orzack, M. H. (1978). Physiological and behavioral correlates of attention dysfunction in schizophrenia patients. *Journal of Psychiatric Research, 14,* 69–79.

Kostovic, I., Skavic, J., & Strinovic, D. (1988). Acetylcholinesterase in the human frontal associative cortex during the period of cognitive development: Early laminar shifts and late innervation of pyramidal neurons. *Neuroscience Letters, 90,* 107–112.

Kovelman, J. A., & Scheibel, A. B. (1984). A neurohistological correlate of schizophrenia. *Biological Psychiatry, 19,* 1601–1621.

Kraemer, G., & McKinney, W. T. (1979). Interactions of pharmacological agents which alter biogenic amino metabolism and depression: An analysis of contributing factors within a primate model of depression. *Journal of Affective Disorders, 1,* 33–54.

Kraemer, G. W., Ebert, J. H., Lake, C. R., & McKinney, W. T. (1984). Cerebrospinal fluid measures of neurotransmitter changes associated with pharmacological alteration of the despair response to social separation in rhesus monkeys. *Psychiatry Research, 11,* 303–315.

Kraepelin, E. (1919). Dementia Praecox and Paraphrenia. Edinburgh, Scotland: Livingston.

Kvale, I., Fosse, V. M., & Fonnum, F. (1983). Development of neurotransmitter parameters in lateral geniculate body, superior colliculus and visual cortex of the albino rat. *Developmental Brain Research, 7,* 137–145.

Laplane, D., Degos, J. D., Baulac, M., & Gray, F. (1981). Bilateral infarction of the anterior cingulate gyri and of the fornices. *Journal of Neurological Science, 51,* 289–300.

Lauder, J. M., & Bloom, F. E. (1974). Ontogeny of monoamine neurons in the locus coeruleus, raphe nuclei and substantia nigra of the rat: I. Cell differentiation. *Journal of Comparative Neurology, 155,* 469–482.

Levey, A. I., Wainer, B. H., Raye, D. B., Mufson, E. J., & Mesulam, M. M. (1984). Choline acetyltransferase immunoreactive neurons intrinsic to rodent cortex and distinction from acetylcholinesterase-positive neurons. *Neuroscience, 13,* 341–353.

Levitt, P., & Moore, R. Y. (1978). Noradrenaline neuron innervation of the neurocortex in the rat. *Brain Research, 139,* 219–231.

Levitt, P., & Rakic, P. (1982). The time of genesis, embryonic origin and differentiation of brainstem monoamine neurons in the rhesus monkey. *Brain Research, 4,* 35–37.

Levitt, J. J., & Tsuang, M. T. (1988). The heterogeneity of schizoaffective disorder: Implications for treatment. *American Journal of Psychiatry, 145,* 926–936.

Lidov, H. G., & Molliver, M. E. (1982). An immunohistochemical study of serotonin neuron development in the rat: Ascending pathways and terminal fields. *Brain Research Bulletin, 8,* 389–430.

Lindvall, O., & Bjorklund, A. (1984). General organization of cortical monoamine system. In L. Descarries, J. R. Reader, & H. H. Jasper (Eds.), *Monoamine innervation of cerebral cortex* (pp. 9–40). New York: Liss.

Lindvall, O., Bjorklund, A., & Divac, I. (1978). Organization of catecholamine neurons projecting to frontal cortex in the rat. *Brain Research, 142,* 1–24.

Long, C. J., Pueschel, K., & Hunter, S. E. (1978). Assessment of the effects of cingulate gyrus lesions by neurophysiological techniques. *Journal of Neurosurgery, 49,* 264–271.

Lubbers, K., Wolff, J. R., & Frotscher, M. (1985). Neurogenesis of GABAergic neurons in the rat dentate gyrus: A combined autoradiographic and immunocytochemical study. *Neuroscience Letters, 62,* 317–322.

Lund, J. S. (1984). Spiny stellate neurons. In A. Peters & E. G. Jones (Eds.), *Cerebral cortex: Vol. 1. Cellular components of the cerebral cortex* (pp. 255–308). New York: Plenum.

Luria, A. R. (1973). *The working brain* (pp. 147–160). New York: Basic Books.

Maas, J. W. (1985). Biogenic amines and depression: Biochemical and pharmacological separation of two types of depression. *Archives of General Psychiatry, 42,* 405–417.

MacLean, P. D. (1954). Studies on limbic system (visceral brain) and their bearing on psychosomatic problems. In E. Wittkower & R. Cleghorn (Eds.), *Recent developments in psychosomatic medicine* (p. 106). London: Pribram; Philadelphia: Lippincott.

MacLean, P. D. (1985). Brain evolution relating to family, play and the separation call. *Archives of General Psychiatry, 42,* 405–417.

MacLean, P. D. (1990). *The triune brain* (pp. 242–243). New York: Plenum.

Marcusson, J. O., Morgan, D. G., Winblad, B., & Finch, C. E. (1984). Serotonin-2 binding sites in human frontal cortex and hippocampus: Selective loss of S-2A sites with age. *Brain Research, 311,* 51–56.

Marin-Padilla, M. (1970a). Prenatal and early post-natal ontogenesis of the human motor cortex: A Golgi study. I. The sequential development of the cortical layers. *Brain Research, 23,* 167–183.

Marin-Padilla, M. (1970b). Prenatal and early post-natal ontogenesis of the human motor cortex: A Golgi study. II. The basket-pyramidal system. *Brain Research, 23,* 185–191.

Marin-Padilla, M. (1984). Neurons of layer I: A developmental analysis. In A. Peters & E. G. Jones (Eds.), *Cerebral cortex: Vol. 1. Cellular components of the cerebral cortex* (pp. 447–478). New York: Plenum.

Martin, K. A. C. (1984). Neuronal circuits in cat striate cortex. In A. Peters & E. G. Jones (Eds.), *Cerebral cortex: Vol. 2. Functional properties of cortical cells* (pp. 241–284). New York: Plenum.

Mazars, G. (1970). Criteria for identifying cingulate epilepsies. *Epilepsia, 11,* 41–47.

McBride, W. J., Murphy, J. M., Lumeng, L., & Li, T. K. (1990). Serotonin, dopamine and GABA involvement in alcohol drinking of selectively bred rats. *Alcohol, 7,* 199–205.

McGhie, A., & Chapman, J. (1961). Disorders of attention and perception in early schizophrenia. *British Journal of Medical Psychology, 34,* 103–116.

Meltzer, H. Y., & Lowy, M. T. (1987). The serotonin hypothesis of depression. In H. Y. Meltzer (Ed.), *Psychopharmacology: The third generation of progress* (pp. 513–222). New York: Raven Press.

Mesulam, M.-M. (1983). The functional anatomy and hemispheric specialization of directed attention. The role of the parietal lobe and its commentary. *Trends in Neuroscience, 6,* 384–387.

Mesulam, M.-M., & Geschwind, N. (1978). On the possible role of neocortex and its limbic connections in the process of attention and schizophrenia: Clinical cases of inattention in man and experimental anatomy in monkey. *Journal of Psychiatric Research, 14,* 249–259.

Mesulam, M.-M., Mufson, E. J., Levey, A. I., & Wainer, B. H. (1983). Cholinergic innervation of cortex by the basal forebrain: Cytochemistry and cortical connections of the septal area, diagonal band nuclei, nucleus basals (Substantia innominata) and hypothalamus in the rhesus monkey. *Journal of Comparative Neurology, 214,* 140–191.

Michel, A. E., & Garey, L. H. (1984). The development of dendritic spines in the human visual cortex. *Human Neurobiology, 3,* 223–227.

Monaghan, D. T., & Cotman, C. W. (1985). Distribution of N-methyl-D-aspartate-sensitive L-^{3}H-glutamate-binding sites in rat brain. *Journal of Neuroscience, 5,* 2905–2919.

Mountcastle, V. B., Lynch, J. C., Georgopoulos, A., Sakata, H., & Acuna, C. (1975). Posterior parietal association cortex of the monkey: Command functions for operations within extrapersonal space. *Journal of Neurophysiology, 38,* 871–908.

Murphy, J. M., Gatto, G. J., McBride, W. J., Lumeng, L., & Li, T. K. (1989). Operant conditioning for oral ethanol in the alcohol-non-preferring NP lines of rats. *Alcohol, 6,* 127–131.

Murray, R. M., & Lewis, S. W. (1987). Is schizophrenia a neurodevelopmental disorder? *British Medical Journal, 95,* 681–682.

Neafsey, E. J., Terreberry, R. R., Hurley, K. M., Ruit, K. G., & Frysztak, R. J. (1992). Anterior cingulate cortex in rodents: Connections, visceral control functions and implications for emotion. In B. A. Vogt & M. Gabriel (Eds.), *The neurobiology of cingulate cortex and limbic thalamus.* Boston: Birkhauser.

Nelson, S. B., Schwartz, M. A., & Daniels, J. D. (1975). Clonidine and cortical plasticity: Possible evidence for noradrenergic involvement. *Developmental Brain Research, 23,* 39–50.

Olney, J. W., & Sesma, M. A. (1993). Glutamatergic, cholinergic and GABAergic systems in posterior cingulate cortex: Interactions and possible mechanisms of limbic system disease. In B. A. Vogt & M. Gabriel (Eds.), *The neurobiology of cingulate cortex and limbic thalamus* (pp. 557–580). Boston: Birkhauser.

Overmeier, J. B., & Seligman, M. E. (1967). Effects of inescapable shock upon subsequent escape and avoidance responding. *Journal of Comparative Physiology and Psychology, 63,* 28–33.

Pandya, D. N., & Kuypers, H. G. (1969). Cortico-cortical connections in the rhesus monkey. *Brain Research, 58,* 13–36.

Papez, J. W. (1937). A proposed mechanism of emotion. *Archives of Neurological Psychiatry, 38,* 725–743.

Pardo, J. V., Pardo, P. J., Janer, K. W., & Raichle, M. E. (1990). The anterior cingulate cortex mediated processing selection in the Stroop attentional conflict paradigm. *Proceedings of the National Academy of Sciences, 87,* 256–259.

Parnas, J., Schulsinger, F., Teasdale, W., Schulsinger, H., Feldman, P. M., & Mednick, S. A. (1982). Perinatal complications and clinical outcome. *British Journal of Psychiatry, 140,* 416–420.

Payne, R. W., & Friedlander, D. (1962). Short battery of simple tests for measuring over-inclusive thinking. *Journal of Mental Science, 108,* 362–367.

Pellis, S. M., O'Brien, D. P., Pellis, V. C., Teitelbaum, P., Wolgin, D. L., & Kennedy, S. (1988). Escalation of feline predation along a gradient from avoidance to "play" to killing. *Behavioral Neuroscience, 102,* 760–777.

Perry, T. L., Buchanan, J., Kish, S. J., & Hansen, S. (1979). Gamma-aminobutyric acid deficiency in brains of schizophrenic patients. *Lancet, 1,* 237.

Peters, A. (1984). Chandelier cells. In A. Peters & E. G. Jones (Eds.), *Cerebral cortex: Vol. 1. Cellular components of the cerebral cortex* (pp. 361–380). New York: Plenum.

Petras, J. M. (1971). Connections of the parietal lobe. *Journal of Psychiatric Research, 8,* 189–201.

Ploog, D. W. (1970). Phonation, emotion, cognition with references to the brain mechanisms involved. In *Brain and Mind Ciba Foundation Series* (pp. 79–98). Amsterdam: Exerpta Medica.

Poliakov, G. I. (1965). Development of the cerebral neocortex during the first half of intrauterine life. In S. A. Sarkisov (Ed.), *Development of the child's brain* (pp. 22–52). Leningrad, USSR: Medicina.

Porsolt, R. D., Bertin, A., & Jalfre, M. (1977). *Archives of International Pharmacodynamics, 229,* 327–336.

Posner, M. K., Early, T. S., Reisman, E., Pardo, P. J., & Dhawan, M. (1988). Asymmetries in hemispheric control of attention in schizophrenia. *Archives of General Psychiatry, 45,* 814–821.

Post, R. M. (1992). Transduction of psychosocial stress into the neurobiology of recurrent affective disorder. *American Journal of Psychiatry, 149,* 999–1010.

Praag, H. M. van (1978). Monoamine hypotheses of affective disorders. In S. D. Iverson & S. H. Snyder (Eds.), *Handbook of psychopharmacology* (Vol. 13, pp. 187–297). New York: Plenum.

Rakic, P. (1974). Neurons in rhesus monkey visual cortex: Systematic relation between time of origin and eventual disposition. *Science, 183,* 425–427.

Rakic, P. (1975). Timing of major ontogenetic events in the visual cortex of the rhesus monkey. In N. A. Buchwald & M. Brazier (Eds.), *Brain mechanisms of mental retardation* (pp. 3–40). New York: Academic Press.

Rakic, P. (1981). Developmental events leading to laminar and area organization of the neocortex. In F. O. Schmitt (Ed.), *The organization of the cerebral cortex* (pp. 7–28). Cambridge, MA: MIT Press.

Rakic, P., & Nowakowski, R. (1981). The time of origin of neurons in the hippocampal region of the rhesus monkey. *Journal of Comparative Neurology, 196,* 99–128.

Rakic, P., & Yakovlev, P. I. (1968). Development of the corpus callosum and septum cavi in man. *Journal of Comparative Neurology, 132,* 45–72.

Ravikumar, B. V., & Sastary, P. S. (1985). Muscarinic cholinergic receptors in human fetal brain: Characterization and ontogeny of [^{3}H]quinuclidinyl benzilate binding sites in frontal cortex. *Journal of Neurochemistry, 44,* 240–246.

Roberts, E. (1972). An hypothesis suggesting that there is a defect in the GABA system in schizophrenia. *Neuroscience Research Bulletin, 10,* 469–482.

Roberts, G. W., Colter, N., Lofthouse, R., Bogerts, B., Zec, M., & Crow, T. J. (1986). Gliosis in schizophrenia: A survey. *Biological Psychiatry, 39,* 1043–1050.

Rothman, S. M., & Olney, J. W. (1986). Glutamate and the pathology of ischaemic/hypoxic brain damage. *Annals of Neurology, 19,* 105–111.

Rozenberg, F., Robain, O., Jardin, L., & Ben-Ari, Y. (1989). Distribution of GABAergic neurons in late fetal and early postnatal rat hippocampus. *Developmental Brain Research, 50,* 177–187.

Saccuzzo, D. P., & Braff, D. L. (1986). Information-processing abnormalities: Trait- and state-dependent component. *Schizophrenia Bulletin, 12,* 447–456.

Sapolsky, R., & Meaney, M. (1986). Maturation of the adrenocortical stress response: Neuroendocrine control mechanisms and the stress hyporesponsive period. *Brain Research Reviews, 11,* 65–76.

Schildkraut, J., & Kety, S. (1967). Biogenic amines and emotion. *Science, 156,* 21–30.

Schlessinger, A. R., Cowan, W. M., & Swanson, L. W. (1978). The time of origin of neurons in Ammon's horn and the associated retrohippocampal fields. *Anatomy and Embryology, 154,* 153–173.

Schliebs, R., Kullman, E., & Bigl, V. (1986). Development of glutamate binding sites in the visual structures of the rat brain: Effect of visual pattern deprivation. *Biomedical and Biophysical Acta, 45,* 4495–4506.

Schwarcz, R., & Coyle, J. T. (1977). Neurochemical sequela of kainate injections in corpus striatum and substantia nigra of the rat. *Life Sciences, 20,* 431–436.

Seltzer, B., & Pandya, D. M. (1978). Afferent cortical connections and architectonics of the superior temporal sulcus and surrounding cortex in the rhesus monkey. *Brain Research, 192,* 1–24.

Seltzer, B., & Van Hoesen, G. W. (1979). A direct inferior parietal lobule projection to the presubiculum in the rhesus monkey. *Brain Research, 179,* 157–161.

Seress, L., & Ribak, C. E. (1988). The development of GABAergic neurons in the rat hippocampal formation. An immunocytochemical study. *Developmental Brain Research, 44,* 197–202.

Sidman, R., & Rakic, P. (1973). Neuronal migration with special reference to developing human brain. *Brain Research, 62,* 1–35.

Siever, L. J. (1987). Role of noradrenergic mechanisms in the etiology of the affective disorders. In H. Y. Meltzer (Ed.), *Psychopharmacology: The third generation of progress* (pp. 493–504). New York: Raven Press.

Sillito, A. M. (1984). Functional considerations of the operation of GABAergic inhibitory processes in the visual cortex. In A. Peters & E. G. Jones (Eds.), *Cerebral cortex: Vol. 2. Functional properties of cortical cells* (pp. 91–118). New York: Plenum.

Simpson, M. D., Slater, P., Deakin, J. F., Royston, M. C., & Skan, W. J. (1989). Reduced GABA uptake sites in the temporal lobe in schizophrenia. *Neuroscience Letters, 107,* 211–215.

Slotnick, B. M. (1967). Disturbances of maternal behavior in the rat following lesions of the cingulate cortex. *Behavior, 24,* 204–236.

Smith, W. D. (1945). The functional significance of the rostral cingulate cortex as revealed by its responses of electrical excitation. *Journal of Neurophysiology,* 241–255.

Somogyi, P., & Cowey, A. (1984). Double bouquet cells. In A. Peters & E. G. Jones (Eds.), *Cerebral cortex: Vol. 1. Cellular components of the cerebral cortex* (pp. 337–360). New York: Plenum.

Soriano, E., Cobas, S. A., & Fairen, A. (1986). Asynchronism in the neurogenesis of GABAergic and non-GABAergic neurons in the mouse hippocampus. *Developmental Brain Research, 30,* 88–92.

Spitz, R. A. (1949). Hospitalism: An inquiry into the genesis of psychiatric conditions in early childhood. *Psychoanalytic Study of the Child, 1,* 53–74.

Stamm, J. S. (1955). The function of the median cerebral cortex in maternal behavior of rats. *Journal of Comparative Physiology and Psychology, 48,* 347–356.

Stanfield, B. B., & Cowan, W. M. (1988). The development of hippocampal region. In A. Peters & E. G. Jones (Eds.), *Cerebral cortex: Vol. 7. Development and maturation of cerebral cortex* (pp. 91–132). New York: Plenum.

Stanfield, B. B., & Trice, J. E. (1988). Evidence that granule cells generated in the dentate gyrus of adult rats extend axonal projections. *Experimental Brain Research, 72,* 399–406.

Stein-Behrens, B., Elliott, E., Miller, C., Schilling, J., Newcombe, R., & Sapolsky, R. (1992). Glucocorticoids exacerbate kainic acid-induced extracellular accumulation of excitatory amino acids in the rat hippocampus. *Journal of Neurochemistry, 58,* 1730–1734.

Stevens, J. R. (1992). Abnormal reinnervation as a basis for schizophrenia: An hypothesis. *Archives of General Psychiatry, 49,* 238–243.

Streit, P. (1984). Glutamate and aspartate as transmitter candidates for systems of the cerebral cortex. In A. Peters & E. G. Jones

(Eds.), *Cerebral cortex: Vol. 2. Functional properties of cortical cells* (pp. 119–144). New York: Plenum.

Swanson, C. L., Hingtgen, J. N., Simon, J. R., & Nurnberger, J. (1991). Cholinergic and serotonergic parameters of behavior in two inbred strains of mice: C57BL/6J and DBA/2J. *Biological Psychiatry, 29,* 78A.

Terreberry, R. R., & Neafsey, E. J. (1983). Rat medial frontal cortex: A visceromotor region with a direct projection to the nucleus solitarius. *Brain Research, 278,* 245–249.

Terreberry, R. R., & Neafsey, E. J. (1987). The rat medial frontal cortex projects directly to autonomic regions of the brainstem. *Brain Research Bulletin, 19,* 639–649.

Thierry, A. M., Blanc, G., Sobel, A., Stinus, L., & Glowinski, J. (1973). Dopaminergic terminals in the rat cortex. *Science, 182,* 499–501.

Tow, P. W., & Whitty, C. W. M. (1953). Personality changes after operations on the cingulate gyrus in man. *Journal of Neurology, Neurosurgery and Psychiatry, 16,* 186–193.

Ulinski, P. S. (1977). Intrinsic organization of snake medial cortex: An electron microscope and Golgi study. *Journal of Morphology, 152,* 247–280.

Ulinski, P. S. (1990). The cerebral cortex of reptiles. In A. Peters & E. G. Jones (Eds.), *Cerebral cortex: Vol. 8A. Comparative structure and evolution of cerebral cortex, Part 1* (pp. 139–215). New York: Plenum.

Uphouse, L. L., & Bondy, S. C. (1981). The maturation of cortical serotonergic binding sites. *Developmental Brain Research, 1,* 415–417.

Vaillant, G. E. (1983). *The natural history of alcoholics* (pp. 1–332). Cambridge, MA: Harvard University Press.

Van der Kooy, D., McGinty, J. F., Koda, L. Y., Gerfen, C. R., & Bloom, F. E. (1982). Visceral cortex: Direct connections from prefrontal cortex to the solitary nucleus in the rat. *Neuroscience Letters, 33,* 123–127.

Van Hoesen, G. W. (1982). The parahippocampal gyrus. *Trends in Neuroscience, 5,* 345–350.

Verney, C., Berger, B. A. J., Vigny, A., & Gay, M. (1982). Development of the dopaminergic innervation of the rat cerebral cortex: A light microscopic immunocytochemical study using anti-tyrosine hydroxylase antibodies. *Developmental Brain Research, 5,* 41–52.

Vincent, S. L., Molloy, R. P., & Benes, F. M. (1992). Interaction of dopaminergic fibers with GABAergic interneurons in rat medial prefrontal cortex. *Society for Neuroscience Abstracts, 18*(1), 465.

Vogt, B. A., & Pandya, D. N. (1987). Cingulate cortex of the rhesus monkey: II. Cortical afferents. *Journal of Comparative Neurology, 262,* 271–289.

Vogt, B. A., Pandya, D. N., & Rosene, D. L. (1987). Cingulate cortex of the rhesus monkey: I. Cytoarchitecture and thalamic afferents. *Journal of Comparative Neurology, 262,* 256–270.

Vogt, B. A., Rosene, D. L., & Peters, A. (1981). Synaptic terminations of thalamic and callosal afferents in cingulate cortex of rat. *Journal of Comparative Neurology, 201,* 265–283.

Wallace, J. A., & Lauder, J. M. (1983). Development of the serotonergic system in the rat embryo: An immunocytochemical study. *Brain Research Bulletin, 10,* 459–479.

Ward, A. A. (1948). The anterior cingulate gyrus and personality. In *The frontal lobes.* Baltimore: Williams & Wilkins.

Weinberger, D. R. (1987). Implications of normal brain development for the pathogenesis of schizophrenia. *Archives of General Psychiatry, 44,* 660–669.

Weinberger, D. R., Berman, K. F., & Zec, R. F. (1986). Physiologic dysfunction of dorsolateral prefrontal cortex in schizophrenia: I. Regional cerebral blood flow evidence. *Archives of General Psychiatry, 43,* 114–124.

White, E. L. (1986). Termination of thalamic afferents in the cerebral cortex. In A. Peters & E. G. Jones (Eds.), *Cerebral cortex: Vol. 5. Sensory-motor areas and aspects of cortical connectivity* (pp. 271–289). New York: Plenum.

Windle, W. F., & Becker, R. F. (1944). Alterations in brain structure after asphyxiation at birth. *Journal of Neuropathology and Experimental Neurology, 3,* 224–238.

Wise, S. P., Fleshman, J. W., & Jones, E. G. (1979). Maturation of pyramidal cell form in relation to developing afferent and efferent connections of the rat somatic sensory cortex. *Journal of Neuroscience, 4,* 1275–1297.

Wise, S. P., & Jones, E. G. (1978). Developmental studies of thalamocortical and commissural connections in the rat somatic sensory cortex. *Journal of Comparative Neurology, 178,* 187–208.

Wyss, J. M., & Sripanidkulchai, K. (1984). The topography of the mesencephalic and pontine projections from the cingulate cortex of the rat. *Brain Research, 293,* 1–15.

Yakovlev, P., & Lecours, A. (1967). The myelinogenetic cycles of regional maturation of the brain. In A. Minkowski (Ed.), *Regional development of the brain early in life* (pp. 3–70). Oxford, England: Blackwell.

Zhang, W. Q., Rogers, B. C., Tandon, P., Hudson, P. M., Sobotka, T. J., Hong, J. S., & Tilson, H. A. (1990). Systemic administration of kainic acid increases GABA levels in perfusate from the hippocampus of rats in vivo. *Neurotoxicology, 11,* 593–600.

Zilles, K. W. R., Busching, U., & Schleicher, A. (1986). Ontogenesis of the laminar structure in areas 17 and 18 of the human visual cortex. A quantitative study. *Anatomy and Embryology, 174,* 339–353.

CHAPTER 9

Neuropsychology and Developmental Psychopathology

BRUCE F. PENNINGTON and MARILYN WELSH

In this chapter, we discuss the utility of a neuropsychological perspective for understanding developmental psychopathologies. We include both a consideration of general conceptual and methodological issues raised by a neuropsychological approach to developmental psychopathology and a review of neuropsychological studies of particular disorders.

These general issues are important because developmental psychopathology has rarely been examined from an explicitly neuroscientific perspective, and mainstream developmental psychopathologists may be wary of such a perspective, for both bad and good reasons. For instance, such an approach could be viewed as reductionistic, exclusively biological, or even antidevelopmental, to name a few of the concerns that may spring to mind. Instead, we would like to show how a neuroscientific perspective offers a broad integrative framework that encompasses (a) different levels of analysis, (b) developmental continuity and discontinuity, and (c) a broad range of etiologies and processes, including genetic, bioenvironmental, and social-environmental factors. Indeed, we believe such a broad framework is needed to prevent premature and misleading closure on core issues; such premature closure has hampered progress in understanding developmental psychopathologies in the past.

This chapter is divided into four main sections, three of which are concerned with general conceptual and methodological issues: the neuroscientific perspective, the neuropsychological level of analysis within neuroscience, and, to close the chapter, implications for future research. The penultimate section contains a review of empirical studies of the neuropsychology of four specific developmental psychopathologies:

1. Schizophrenia;
2. Attention Deficit/Hyperactivity Disorder (ADHD);
3. Autism;
4. Dyslexia.

During preparation of this chapter, author Pennington was supported by an NIMH RSDA (MH00419) and MERIT award (MH38820 and MH45916), as well as by grants from the March of Dimes (12-135) and the Orton Dyslexia Society. He was also supported in part by an NICHD Center Grant (HD 27802).

A NEUROSCIENTIFIC PERSPECTIVE

In taking a neuroscientific perspective on either abnormal or normal behavioral development, several levels of analysis need to be considered. We organize the discussion of specific psychopathologies into four broad levels: (a) etiology, (b) brain mechanisms, (c) neuropsychology, and (d) symptoms or surface levels (Pennington, 1991). These are similar to the four levels proposed by Leslie (1991) in his analysis of autism: (a) biology, (b) neural circuits, (c) cognitive architecture, and (d) behavior. The use of only four levels is, of course, a simplification: within some of these levels, such as brain mechanisms, many finer divisions are possible. For instance, Sejnowski and Churchland (1989) proposed six levels of analysis for understanding relations between brain structure and computation: molecules, synapses, neurons, networks, maps, and systems. They emphasized that it is an empirical matter to determine how many levels of analysis will be needed to understand a complex behavior. Thus, our identification of only four levels is provisional and heuristic.

The important overall point of a neuroscientific perspective is that analyses of normal or abnormal function need to be informed by an understanding of the brain structures and processes that implement the function. In other words, "hardware" matters, and it provides important constraints for developmental theories, whether they are theories of neo-Piagetian cognitive operations or internal working models in attachment theory. Taking a neuroscientific perspective forces us to confront a latent "dualism" in much of developmental psychology: the assumption that analyses of behavioral function can proceed completely independently of analyses of brain. As Patricia Goldman-Rakic (1987) aptly said in discussing the relation between neuroscience and developmental psychology, "The 'empty organism' has long since been filled with intentionality and information-processing skills, but not necessarily with a central nervous system" (p. 601).

To draw out the implications of this point, let us take as an example a hypothetical developmental psychopathology that is *entirely* determined by the social (i.e., interpersonal) environment—no genetic influence, and no traumatic, toxic, or other noninterpersonal environmental alteration of brain development. It is very easy to catch oneself thinking that, in such a case, the pathogenetic social influences are registered somewhere besides the brain—in the attachment system, in object relations, or what have you. The point of a neuroscientific perspective is that *all* pathological influences affect brain development in some way. In other words, the familiar clinical distinction between "functional" and "organic" is misleading and, in a strict sense, fundamentally incorrect. There is no autonomous substrate for functional pathologies, nor does the functional/organic distinction neatly divide disorders either by treatability or mode of treatment. For instance, it is frequently assumed that functional disorders call for behavioral treatments and are more amenable to treatment, whereas organic ones are less treatable and call for biological interventions. However, many counter-examples, such as phenylketonuria (PKU) on the one hand, and posttraumatic stress disorder (PTSD) on the other, can be cited. The former is a genetic disorder that is readily treated by a behavioral intervention—dietary control of phenylalanine intake. The latter disorder is produced by environmental trauma that alters neurologic function and development, sometimes irreversibly. To return to our hypothetical case of a purely socially determined pathology, we would argue that information about the brain mechanisms underlying social learning and responses to social stressors (e.g., limbic memory and arousal modulation mechanisms, and the scope and limits of their plasticity) would have significant implications for understanding and treating this pathology (Sapolsky, 1990).

Having argued for the relevance of brain mechanisms in understanding a pure social pathology, we hasten to point out that this is not an argument for reductionism. Explanatory "bedrock" will be reached at different levels of analysis for different developmental psychopathologies: the molecular level for some, and the network or systems level for others. Most importantly, integration across levels of analysis does not imply elimination of higher levels in favor of lower levels. Thus, to understand a purely interpersonal pathology, the optimum level of explanation may well be at an interpersonal systems level, similar to the one used in family systems theory. However, no level of analysis is entirely autonomous or encapsulated; interpersonal systems do not exist in some "social ether" outside of human organisms. When we learn and use such systems, we are constrained by the real human brain, which evolved for just that function, among others. Moreover, dynamic principles that describe network properties within a brain may well have some utility in describing the dynamics of social networks.

Instead of being reductionistic, our claims about the relevance of neuroscience for purely social pathologies are integrative. The point is that neuroscience potentially provides a paradigm broad enough to encompass *all* of developmental psychopathology. A complete explanation for some pathologies will require more levels of analysis than the explanation of others, but all can fit within the same broad paradigm. A pathology caused in part by genetic influences will require an explanation that begins at the deepest explanatory level, with an altered DNA sequence, and proceeds across many levels of analysis up to the level of observable behavior. In contrast, a pathology that is completely caused by aberrant parenting will require fewer levels of analysis, but these will overlap with those used in the previous example; we should not have to invoke a totally different paradigm.

We return here to the four levels of analysis mentioned above, and will next define each level. The *etiological* level is concerned with genetic and environmental influences that cause the pathology in question. Genetic and environmental influences may act independently, but they may also interact with each other or be correlated with each other. The latter situation has some similarities to what developmental psychopathologists call transactions (Pennington & Ozonoff, 1991). An obvious but frequently overlooked methodological point is that clear answers about environmental etiologies cannot be obtained without controlling for genetic influences (see Reiss, Hetherington, & Plomin, 1994, for a landmark behavior/genetic study of nonshared social environmental influences on adolescent development). Unfortunately, many existing studies of supposed environmental influences on developmental psychopathology include only nontwin, biological families, in which genetic and environmental influence are inherently confounded.

The next level of analysis concerns how these etiological influences act on the development of *brain mechanisms*. One of the important recent discoveries in neuroscience is that early experience plays a very important role in sculpting the connectivity of the developing brain; with about 10^{11} neurons and a total of about 10^{15} connections between them, it is logically impossible for 10^{5} genes to specify neuronal location and connections in a hard-wired fashion (Changeux, 1985). Instead, the developing brain overproduces neurons, dendrites, and synapses and then lets experience "select" which elements are preserved through a kind of "neural darwinism" (Edelman, 1987). Later experience also changes brain structure both by adding or subtracting dendrites and synapses and by tuning existing synapses (Greenough, Black, & Wallace, 1987). A fundamental account of how experience alters brain structure is emerging within neuroscience; this account is of obvious relevance to psychopathologists who ponder why some experiences are so formative and others are so surprisingly neutral in their long-term effects.

On the genetic side, the substantial heritabilities found for many normal and abnormal individual differences in behavior mean that there are genetically caused variations in brain structures within our species. What aspects of brain development are likely targets for genetic influence? Although it has been shown that genetic influences on behavior can "turn on" across the life span (Plomin, 1990), it is likely that many genetic influences on brain structure, especially those important for developmental psychopathologies, act on early brain developmental processes, such as neuronal proliferation, migration, and differentiation. Numerous animal examples exist of specific genetic mutations that affect the development of specific brain structures, such as the mouse mutants with specific cerebellar and hippocampal malformations (Changeux, 1985). There is neuropathological evidence of similar early alterations of brain structures in some human pathologies, such as dyslexia and schizophrenia (Nowakowski, 1987). Such mutations not only affect neuronal migration and lamination in a specific brain structure, but also alter neural connectivity more widely and would presumably alter the computational properties of neural networks. Hence, there is a resolution to the apparent paradox of how a seemingly small early change in brain development can have major effects, despite the sometimes impressive plasticity of the developing brain given a later (and larger) acquired lesion. Other psychopathologies may involve alterations in brain structure at a finer scale, such as changes in the distribution of synapses or neurochemicals; these aspects of brain structure are also partly under genetic control.

The next level of analysis, *neuropsychology,* attempts to bridge the chasm separating brain and behavior, body and mind. Whether it can do so in a way that satisfies philosophers of mind is a contentious issue (Churchland, 1986; Churchland, 1988; Dennett, 1987; Fodor, 1983). What is important for our purposes is that it attempts to do so in a way that has some plausibility for students of psychopathology. Although there are levels of analysis within neuropsychology, by and large neuropsychology has been focused on a level of analysis of behavior that is molar enough so that the domains it studies are not completely outside the view of functional, cognitive psychology. Yet, unlike functional psychology, it constrains these categories by what we know about brain function. Thus, neuropsychology finds spatial cognition an acceptable category, but has rejected categories such as a general-purpose short- or long-term memory, and has generally avoided concepts like the self, will, consciousness, and object relations. (The fact that both folk and real psychologists use these latter concepts—at times, effectively—to predict and explain behavior is a phenomenon that neuropsychology must eventually account for; see Dennett, 1987.) One can think of neuropsychology as a kind of amalgam of concepts and categories from cognitive psychology, developmental psychology, and neuroscience. Sometimes, this amalgam leads to a coherent explanation of the connection between brain and behavior. Or, we could think of neuropsychology as a kind of scaffolding; once we have completed the edifice of neuroscience, neuropsychology in its present form may be nowhere within it. One reason for this possible eventual outcome is that most of current neuropsychology is not computational. The long-term goal of neuroscience is to provide a computational account of molar functions; our current, preliminary notions about the cognitive architecture will eventually be explained in terms of the workings of neural systems (Arbib, 1989). To summarize, current neuropsychology is mostly about molar functions that we can recognize, with the constraint that these molar functions fit with what we currently know about how the real brain works; eventually, current neuropsychology will be replaced by a more precise computational account of how the real brain accomplishes these functions.

For a psychopathologist, what is important about neuropsychology is that it provides an underlying level of behavioral analysis that is closer to and more consistent with brain mechanisms than the phenomenological account of a syndrome given in the language of symptoms. Neuropsychological analyses can help clarify the often confusing array of symptoms found in a complex behavioral disorder.

The *symptom or surface* level is the last level of analysis, the one at which most current developmental psychopathologies are defined. A psychopathology is a syndromal cluster of defining symptoms, a putative cluster or "hump" in the continuum of multivariate behavioral space, for which an explanation is sought. The other lower levels of analysis considered above can (a) provide this explanation; (b) organize symptoms according to which are primary, secondary, correlated, and artifactual (Pennington, 1991; Rapin, 1987); (c) redefine syndrome boundaries; (d) clarify comorbidities; and (e) explain developmental continuities and discontinuities in the symptoms of a disorder (Pennington & Ozonoff, 1991).

When we review each of the specific developmental psychopathologies below, we will consider three of these four levels of analysis: brain mechanisms, neuropsychology, and symptoms; a review of the etiological level is given elsewhere in this volume. We will also demonstrate how deeper levels of analysis can clarify issues at more superficial levels. We now explain the neuropsychological level of analysis in more detail.

THE NEUROPSYCHOLOGICAL LEVEL OF ANALYSIS

In this section, we examine different uses of neuropsychology in developmental psychopathology, the reciprocal relation between studies of normal and abnormal neuropsychological development, and neuropsychological domains that are particularly relevant for developmental psychopathology.

Different Uses of Neuropsychology

There are at least three different uses of neuropsychology in the study of developmental psychopathology. One is *exploratory:* to see whether a particular disorder or risk factor has associated neuropsychological deficits. For instance, one could ask whether depressed or maltreated children, or children with a chronic illness (such as asthma), have neuropsychological deficits. In other words, do these risk factors compromise some basic neuropsychological processes, like memory or executive functions? Are these conditions, somewhat unexpectedly, neurodevelopmental disorders? To answer this question, a broad battery of neuropsychological measures is administered to both the at-risk group and an appropriate control group. Because this is not a hypothesis-driven research strategy, any positive results must be interpreted cautiously. Ascertainment biases in the at-risk group as well as an inappropriate control group can lead to spurious positive results. Often, it is useful to have two control groups, a chronological age (CA) control group without the risk factor in question, and a second control group that is similar to the at-risk group on potentially confounding variables, such as socioeconomic status (SES) in the case of maltreatment, or chronic illness and school disruption in the case of asthma. In any event, positive results need to be followed up with tests of specific hypotheses of how and why the risk factor influences some brain functions and not others. If it is possible to manipulate the hypothesized risk mechanism (e.g., steroid medication in asthma) or if the risk mechanism varies naturally within the at-risk group (e.g., phenylalanine levels in children with early-treated PKU), then more powerful tests of the relation between risk mechanism and brain function are possible.

A second use of neuropsychology is to *further define the underlying neuropsychological deficit* in a disorder that is already known to be a neurodevelopmental disorder. For instance, current research on dyslexia, autism, and Williams syndrome all fall in this category. In each case, the field of possible deficits has been narrowed considerably by previous studies, and the main remaining task is to determine which of the possible deficits are primary and how the primary deficit(s) explain both the other deficits and the symptoms of the disorder.

The defining criteria for a primary deficit include specificity, universality, persistence, and, most importantly, causal precedence (Pennington & Ozonoff, 1991). Different, converging methodologies are needed to address these different criteria. First, there must be a consistent pattern of positive results from cross-sectional studies demonstrating impairment in the candidate primary deficit relative to groups matched on developmental level (e.g., a reading age control group in dyslexia studies; a Down syndrome or other developmentally disabled control group, similar in age and IQ, in the case of autism and Williams syndrome). Such a pattern of results begins to satisfy the requirement for specificity. Universality can be addressed in various ways. One empirical test is a discriminant function analysis that can evaluate whether the proposed primary deficit correctly distinguishes the large majority of individuals with the diagnosis of interest from controls matched on developmental level. Persistence can be addressed by cross-sectional studies across a broad age range and by studies of compensated adults. Because a primary deficit lies at the core of the disorder, it is likely to be among the most persistent features of the disorder; thus, high-functioning adults who previously had the disorder can provide very useful information about core or primary deficits. Similarly, individuals with a subclinical form of the disorder, such as relatives of an affected proband in the case of a genetic disorder, can be informative about primary deficits. So, contrary to the traditional wisdom, the most clearly and most severely affected individuals are not always the most informative about the neuropsychology of a disorder. Studies of persistence need to use developmentally appropriate measures of the construct in question; we are very unlikely to find that individuals with a given developmental psychopathology are impaired on exactly the same task at all stages of development. This consideration is related to the issue of homotypic versus heterotypic continuity, which is a core issue in developmental psychopathology.

The final criterion is the most important: a primary deficit must precede and predict the disorder. The ideal way to address this question is through a longitudinal study of children at high risk for developing the disorder in question. If the disorder is genetically influenced, then risk can be defined by family history. (In the future, genetic risk status may be more precisely defined by genetic markers linked to the disorder.) In rare or early-onset disorders, such as autism, longitudinal studies may not be feasible. Two other, less powerful methods for examining causal precedence are behavior genetic studies of genetic covariance and retrospective archival studies using family movies or videotapes.

Behavior genetic analyses of genetic covariance or correlation address the issue of whether the same genetic influences are acting on two related behavioral phenotypes, such as a diagnostic dimension and a putative primary deficit or precursor. As an example, consider the relation between imitation skill and autism. Imitation skill is one putative primary deficit in autism, based on evidence from the other kinds of studies discussed above (Rogers & Pennington, 1991). Moreover, developmental studies have provided us with evidence that the normal onset of imitation precedes the usual age of onset in autism. Given this information, and the knowledge that autism is genetically influenced in part, behavior genetic analyses of the genetic correlation between autism and imitation skill in twin pairs identified through an autistic proband could be informative about the primacy of an imitation deficit in autism. If present, the genetic correlation could be due to (a) imitation deficits causing autism; (b) a third factor, (c) a reciprocal causal relation between imitation skill and autism; or even (d) autism causing later imitation deficits, in spite of the normal developmental timetable. Heath and Martin (1991) described a method whereby cross-sectional twin data can be modeled to test these competing causal models.

The other method, the retrospective archival technique (Walker, Davis, & Gottlieb, 1991), has the obvious disadvantage that the investigator has no control over what behaviors were sampled and uses real-life films or videos. This technique may be quite informative, especially if the putative primary deficit is in the social domain.

The third use of neuropsychology is to *identify a behavioral or physiological marker for the disorder* or its diathesis. In this case, the neuropsychological phenotype so identified is not considered to be necessarily the primary underlying deficit, or even to explain the disorder at a neuropsychological level. Instead, the marker is a neurological "hard" or "soft" sign whose value consists in its being universal and specific either to individuals with the disorder, or a substantial subset of their relatives—or both. That is, the marker may be a sign for a genetically mediated diathesis for the disorder, and hence may be found in all affecteds and a substantial number of relatives; or, it may be one pleiotropic manifestation of a latent trait, with the disorder itself being the other. In this second, pleiotropic situation, not all individuals with the disorder have the marker, whereas in the diathesis situation, they do. A second important distinction concerns trait versus state markers. If the marker precedes the onset of the disorder, it is considered to be a trait marker. If, on the other hand, it follows the onset of the disorder, or is only present in an acute or active phase of the disorder, then it is considered to be a state marker. For example, disruptions in smooth pursuit eye movement (SPEM) appear to be a trait marker in schizophrenia (Holtzman & Matthysse, 1990), whereas abnormalities in the dexamethasone suppression test (DST) are only a weak state marker in depression. Markers are measurable correlates or consequences of the pathogenetic disruption in brain mechanisms underlying the disorder. The link between the marker and the pathogenetic disruption could be very close, in which case, the marker is straightforwardly informative about the primary neuropsychological deficit; however, this is not required for a marker to be useful.

Parenthetically, markers and the disordered brain mechanisms they point to have the potential for expanding or revising traditional neuropsychological categories, which have been heavily influenced by cortical functions and molar behavioral categories. Some developmental psychopathologies, such as schizophrenia and autism, may involve subcortical pathology and not map directly onto our traditional set of neuropsychological functions.

Finally, trait markers can play a special role in elucidating the genetics of complex disorders, since what may be genetically transmitted is not the disorder *per se,* but, instead, a diathesis or latent trait. Genetic studies of diagnosed individuals may be misleading about genetic mechanisms; the diathesis or latent trait may be transmitted in a major gene fashion, but the disorder itself may look polygenic or multifactorial. Meehl (1989) and others (Holtzman & Matthysse, 1990) have emphasized this possibility for the genetics of schizophrenia.

The Reciprocal Relation between Studies of Normal and Abnormal Development

As indicated above, studies of disorders have the potential to recast our categories of normal behavior (Cicchetti, 1984). Without studies of brain damage, who would have thought of phenomena like blindsight, neglect, or the nondependence of long-term memory on short-term memory? Similarly, without studies of developmental psychopathology, who would have thought that the self could be fragmented, that there may be a specific neurological basis for our theory of other minds, or that mental obsessions and motor tics both spring from the same underlying pathology? Studies of disorders help us to carve the seamless whole of normal behavior at its frequently unexpected joints, and to glimpse the intricate machine that lies under the smooth mask of the self. Conversely, our ability to understand developmental psychopathology is directly dependent on progress in analyzing normal development, especially in the domain where the pathology occurs. This reciprocal relation is beautifully illustrated by recent work on autism and the normal development of theory of mind, where there is intensive interaction between workers in each area, as well as overlapping studies. (This work is discussed below.)

Neuropsychological Domains Important for Developmental Psychopathology

We consider here three broad neuropsychological domains that appear to be important for developmental psychopathology: (a) executive functions, (b) social cognition, and (c) phonological functions. Two other domains that are important in child neuropsychology, but arguably less important for developmental psychopathology, are spatial cognition and long-term memory. (For a review of childhood disorders affecting these domains, see Pennington, 1991.) We will briefly define each of the three domains and consider the limitations of this list. More detail on some of the domains will be added when we consider specific developmental psychopathologies in the next section of the chapter.

Executive Functions

This domain is jointly defined by cognitive accounts of executive processes and by neuropsychological studies of the functions of the prefrontal lobes in humans and animals (Welsh & Pennington, 1988). Luria (1966) proposed that the frontal lobes are important for the programming, regulation, and verification of activity. Note that, on his proposal, preprogrammed activity, such as is simulated in a production system, would not require frontal or executive involvement; in contrast, complex novel tasks would.

Several other theoretical accounts of either frontal function or complex task performance have contributed to the view we are developing here. Principal among these is the work of Goldman-Rakic (1987, 1988), who has emphasized that the prefontal cortices serve working memory rather than associative memory. Working memory holds goal-related representations on-line so that the animal can solve problems that cannot be solved strictly on the basis of previously learned associations.

Shallice (1988) provided a cognitive account in which the prefontal lobes function as a supervisory attentional system (SAS) "involved in the genesis of willed actions and required in situations where the routine selection of actions was unsatisfactory—for instance, in coping with novelty, in decision making, in overcoming temptation, or in dealing with danger" (p. 335).

Carpenter and Just (1989; Carpenter, Just, & Shell, 1990) have used cognitive experiments and simulations to better define the role of a dynamic working memory system in complex and novel problems, whether parsing double center-embedded sentences, solving the Tower of Hanoi problem, or performing the Raven's Progressive Matrices. Although they do not relate their work to brain theory, their work is nonetheless relevant to the characterization of prefrontal and executive functions pursued here. They conceive of working memory as a "computational arena" whose main function is the "transient storage of partial results in the service of computation," and whose "capacity should be construed not just as storage capacity (perhaps measured in chunks), but as operational capacity or throughput" (Carpenter & Just, 1989, p. 34).

Cohen and Servan-Schreiber (1992) postulated that the core function of the prefrontal cortices is to maintain an "internal representation of context" (IRC) in working memory to guide behavior in complex or novel situations. In their connectionist account, this IRC competes with other response tendencies evoked by the task situation; the outcome of this competition determines whether the eventual response selected is adaptive or not. Their theory is an explicitly computational account of how a frontally mediated working memory system may function or malfunction, as in the case of schizophrenia. Moreover, their account is explicitly tied to underlying brain biology (i.e., the effects of variations in dopamine levels on a neural parameter called "gain").

Cohen and Servan-Schreiber (1992) suggested that there are essentially two critical dimensions for evaluating the extent to which a task taps prefrontal function: (a) the strength of the competing prepotent or automatic response and (b) the working memory load required to maintain an internal representation of context. Thus, they predict that tasks that are high on both of these dimensions should be most sensitive to prefrontal functions. Roberts, Hager, & Heron (in press) have used these dimensions to classify various prefrontal tasks. They also conducted experiments in which they manipulated working memory load on the antisaccade task. They found that, with a greater working memory load, normal subjects' performance resembled that of patients with frontal lobe lesions. This approach is exciting because it begins to provide a unified, theoretical account of the diverse and often complex clinical tasks that have been shown to be sensitive to prefrontal damage, and it leads to specific, testable predictions.

Integrating across these various theories, we may say that, when faced with nonroutine tasks, the organism must compute a new response, rather than just activating an established production based on associative memory. The organism must hold several things on-line (e.g., the relevant representations, the partial and final products of computation, and the goals of the computation), in a dynamic, frontally mediated working memory system. Proper functioning of this possibly unitary system undergirds the organism's success at (a) strategic allocation of attention, (b) inhibition of irrelevant responses, (c) appropriate shifting of cognitive set, (d) relating information appropriately over time and space, and (e) adjusting behavior in relation to evolving contexts. (For a theory of how prefrontally mediated working memory relates to individual and developmental cognitive differences, see Pennington, in press.)

Much of social behavior and social development would appear to depend on these capacities. Social behavior is context-dependent, with the context shifting frequently and often unexpectedly. Social behavior requires:

1. The integration of multiple sources of information in the computation of an appropriate response;
2. The on-line simulation of others' mental states, which task can be, potentially, computationally intensive;
3. The inhibition of inappropriate, but possibly prepotent responses;
4. Rapid shifting of attentional resources.

Consequently, we would expect the domain of executive functions to be particularly important for understanding deficits in social behavior, which is the domain of much of developmental psychopathology. Indeed, executive function deficits are being found in a number of developmental psychopathologies, as we will illustrate later.

Social Cognition

As we discussed above, some aspects of social cognition appear to be mediated by the prefrontal lobes and to require executive functions, so this is not a wholly independent category. However, it does appear that other parts of the brain, such as the limbic system and parts of the posterior right hemisphere, are also important for some social and emotional functions; hence, a separate category with separate pathologies is warranted. Our list of specific functions that fall in this domain includes emotion perception (whether of faces or intonation), the pragmatic aspects of language comprehension, and, perhaps, production, attachment, and affect regulation. Not all of these meet usual definitions of social *cognition,* so perhaps we should emphasize that we are talking about *early* social cognition or just particular social skills. The overall point is that some developmental psychopathologies appear to involve disruptions in these early or basic social processes, perhaps without disrupting the development of executive functions. We next turn to a neuropsychological domain that has only indirect or secondary effects on social-emotional development.

Phonological Functions

In the majority of normal adults, phonological processing is subserved by the perisylvian areas of the left hemisphere, including Wernicke's area in the posterior left temporal lobe and Broca's area in the premotor portion of the left frontal lobe. Lateralization of speech processes to the left hemisphere is evident quite early in development (Witelson, 1987). In terms of function, some discrimination of speech sounds may be present in neonates and is clearly present in infants by a few months of age (Eimas, 1974). Although the ability to produce different phonemes is commonly viewed as emerging in the babbling phase of speech development, both the perception and production of discrete phonemic segments appear to be protracted, with preschoolers processing words more at the syllabic than the phonemic level (Menyuk & Menn, 1979; Nittrouer & Studdert-Kennedy, 1987). Similarly, articulatory competence for the full repertoire of phonemes is not completed until about age 8 (Templin, 1957). Moreover, there are steady increases in articulatory speed at least into adolescence (Baddeley, 1986; Case, Kurland, & Goldberg, 1982). Consonant with their late evolution and protracted development, phonological processes are subject to considerable individual variation, and disorders of phonological processes have a high prevalence rate. Developmental articulation disorders have an approximate prevalence rate of 5% (Beitchman, Nair, Clegg, Ferguson, & Patel, 1986). Developmental dyslexia, which we will discuss as a developmental phonology disorder, and which overlaps somewhat with developmental articulation disorders (Catts, 1989; Lewis, Ekelman, & Aram, 1990), has a prevalence rate of 5% to 10%.

There are other developmental language disorders besides these two, just as there are other levels of language processing besides phonology. Developmental language disorders that only affect nonphonological language processes such as syntax, semantics, and/or pragmatics, are rarer. Some of these rarer developmental language disorders overlap with autistic spectrum disorder.

More generally, language processes are very important in understanding developmental psychopathology, both because primary deficits in language processes can disrupt the development of social skills and because primary deficits in social skills can disrupt language development. Given this close reciprocal relation, it is not surprising that there is a considerable overlap between developmental language disorder (DLD) and developmental psychopathology (e.g., autism and attention deficit/hyperactivity disorder). Understanding the causal basis of such overlap (or comorbidity) is one of the challenges for developmental psychopathology.

Differential Vulnerability of Modules

The prevalences of pathologies that affect different modules are not equal; thus, we must ask why some modules are more vulnerable to developmental perturbation than others. One answer would be anatomical: the brain regions subserving some of these domains of function are larger and more complexly interconnected to other brain regions than are others. This answer has clear applicability for the prefrontal areas of the brain, which are both the largest and most complexly connected portions of cortex (Goldman-Rakic, 1988). Various authors have argued that there may be less behavioral plasticity after early frontal versus nonfrontal insults, because no other portion of cortex has quite the same pattern of reciprocal connectivity with much of the rest of the brain (Price, Daffner, Stowe, & Mesulam, 1990). However, the hippocampus also has extensive reciprocal connectivity with the rest of the brain, especially the cortex, but we lack clear examples of developmental perturbations of hippocampal function. (It is true that the trauma associated with closed head injuries most affects these two systems with extensive connectivity, because long fiber tracts are more vulnerable to shearing.)

Another answer would be evolutionary: different modules have different evolutionary histories; some are recently evolved (e.g., those subserving language; see Liberman, 1984) and others are much older (e.g., those subserving spatial cognition). Rapid recent evolution would generally lead to more genetic variation for that trait within a species. On this account, both the phonological and executive domains should be the most vulnerable, which accords fairly well with the differential prevalences of developmental disorders affecting different neuropsychological domains.

Although we do not have definitive answers to these questions, they are important to consider. For instance, it would be useful to ground the concepts of risk and protective factors in an understanding of underlying biological mechanisms.

NEUROPSYCHOLOGY OF SPECIFIC DEVELOPMENTAL PSYCHOPATHOLOGIES

In this main section of the chapter, we review research on the neuropsychology of schizophrenia, attention deficit/hyperactivity disorder (ADHD), autism, and dyslexia. The first two are discussed as executive function (EF) disorders. Autism is discussed as a disorder of social cognition, but the role of EF deficits in autism is reviewed as well. Dyslexia is discussed as a phonological processing disorder. Research on these four disorders is at different stages of development and has captured the attention of different disciplines. Schizophrenia has received by far the most attention from neuroscientists working at more basic levels of analysis, but the cognitive neuropsychology of schizophrenia is much less well developed, and a developmental perspective is frequently absent from schizophrenia research, even though (or, perhaps, because) this disorder poses profound developmental puzzles. At perhaps the other extreme, we now have a fairly mature cognitive and developmental psychology of normal and abnormal reading, and some understanding of which brain structures are relevant, but we know almost nothing about dyslexia at a neurochemical level.

For each of the four disorders considered in this chapter, the research review is organized to discuss *clinical description, brain mechanisms,* and *neuropsychological phenotype.* These topics correspond to three of the four levels of analysis discussed in the introduction.

Disorders of Executive Function

Schizophrenia

Clinical Description. Although several subtypes of schizophrenia are distinguished by unique behavioral features, a group of major characteristics sets it apart from other acute psychoses (Sarason & Sarason, 1989). Both the form and content of thought are disordered in schizophrenia. The structure of thought may be characterized by loose associations or autistic thinking, and its content will often reflect an inappropriate interpretation of reality, as in delusions. Normal perceptual processes also can be severely affected; both auditory and visual hallucinations can occur (Sarason & Sarason, 1989). Emotional responses to daily experiences may be absent, unpredictable, or inappropriate, and there may be a weak sense of self as a separate, unique individual who can control one's own behavior. Motor behavior may be wildly frenetic or catatonic and motionless. Overall motivational level is very depressed, and this often extends to social interactions that are characterized by withdrawal and detachment. Finally, there is a certain degree of intellectual deterioration based on standardized instruments, some of which may be secondary to the thought and perceptual disorders described above. In this chapter, cognitive deficits in attention and executive function will be a particular focus.

Brain Mechanisms. The search for neuroanatomical correlates of the devastating mental disorder of schizophrenia has been pursued for nearly a century, with mixed results. Given the major recent technological advances in anatomical and imaging techniques, such research has clearly grown in precision and sophistication. However, the hope that a single brain structure or system might be identified as relevant to the pathophysiological process has *not* been realized. As is the case with any human research, one's selection of subjects, choice of comparison group, and employment of particular investigative techniques will influence the data generated. The following is a selective review of the most recent evidence regarding neuroanatomical and neurochemical abnormalities observed in the brains of schizophrenics. Such information is meant to serve as a backdrop for the subsequent discussions of a potential behavioral marker of schizophrenia manifested in the brain's electrophysiological response to stimuli, and of characteristic neuropsychological deficits that appear to have more direct relevance to the functional disabilities associated with this mental illness.

The neuroanatomical abnormalities linked with schizophrenia have been isolated primarily through neuropathological studies of the postmortem brains of patients, although more recent *in vivo* imaging studies of schizophrenia have gathered generally convergent evidence (Mesulam, 1990). This research has implicated several brain structures, including, but not restricted to, the limbic system (e.g., hippocampus and amygdala), the frontal cortex and cingulate gyrus, and regions of the left hemisphere. Ventricular enlargement is also a frequent finding; such enlargement implies atrophic changes in adjacent brain tissue. The great variability in findings must be viewed in light of the fact that the composition of schizophrenic samples is inconsistent across studies, in terms of premorbid functioning, history of medication and hospitalization, and precise diagnosis. In addition to these differences, studies vary in the comparison group selected (e.g., normals, "organic" neurological patients, other psychiatric groups). The choice of control group will affect which brain differences are identified in the schizophrenics. In many neuropathological studies, anatomical differences between patients and normal controls are slight, and there is substantial normal variation; thus, groups will overlap to a significant degree (Suddath, Christison, Torrey, Casanova, & Weinberger, 1990).

To reduce the extraneous variation between patients and controls, Suddath et al. (1990) used magnetic resonance imaging

(MRI) to compare the brains of monozygotic twins who were discordant for schizophrenia, yet had a common genome and similar socioeconomic backgrounds. The investigators found bilateral increases in the size of the lateral and third ventricles in most of the affected twins. This result is consistent with previous reports of enlarged lateral and third ventricles in the brains of schizophrenic patients (Kelsoe, Cadet, Pickar, & Weinberger, 1988; Suddath et al., 1989; Weinberger, Torrey, Neophytides, & Wyatt, 1979). However, enlarged ventricles are neither a necessary nor a sufficient condition for schizophrenia; not all schizophrenics exhibit increased ventricular size, nor is it restricted to this diagnosis.

The brains of the schizophrenic twins also exhibited a smaller anterior hippocampus, primarily on the left side. Several postmortem studies have identified abnormalities in anteriomedial limbic structures (Bogerts, Meertz, & Schonfeldt-Bausch, 1985; Conrad & Scheibel, 1987; Falkai, Bogerts, & Rozumek, 1988), suggesting a potential role of this brain system in the pathophysiology of the illness. This part of the brain has also been implicated in neurochemical studies demonstrating abnormalities in the hippocampus and amygdala (Kerwin, Patel, Meldrum, Czudek, & Reynolds, 1988; Reynolds, Czudek, & Andrews, 1990).

The brains of the affected twins also showed a reduction in the total volume of grey matter in the left temporal lobe. Pathology of the temporal lobe has been implicated in postmortem studies (Bruton et al., 1990; Colter et al., 1987) as well as in imaging studies that have demonstrated hypermetabolism in the left temporal lobe (Andreasen, 1988; Gur et al., 1985). The "positive" symptoms characteristic of schizophrenia also have been observed in temporolimbic epilepsy, especially if the focus is in the left hemisphere (Andreasen, 1988; Mesulam, 1988). Furthermore, there is evidence of primarily left-sided differences in the brains of schizophrenics in terms of structure (Largen, Calderon, & Smith, 1983; Reveley, Reveley, & Baldy, 1987), biochemistry (Losonczy et al., 1986; Reynolds, 1983), and electrophysiology (Reite et al., 1988).

Another brain system found to be abnormal in schizophrenia is the frontal cortex and cingulate gyrus. Cytoarchitectural studies by Benes, Davidson, and Bird (1986) reported decreased numbers of neurons in the prefrontal, cingulate, and motor cortices of the brains of schizophrenics. Additionally, hypometabolism in the frontal lobe has been found in cerebral blood flow studies with this patient population (Andreasen, 1988; Gur et al., 1985). Given the higher concentrations of dopamine in the frontal cortex, the well-known dopamine excess hypothesis of schizophrenia and collateral findings suggest a dysfunction in this brain region. This hypothesis derives from the production of schizophrenialike symptoms by amphetamine (a DA agonist) and the ameliorative effects of drugs such as chlorpromazine (a DA antagonist). This central dopaminergic hypothesis has not as yet been conclusively proven; however, dopamine and to a lesser extent its metabolite, homovanillic acid, have been found to be increased in the left amygdala of schizophrenics (Reynolds et al., 1990). These convergent findings regarding a possible dysfunction of the frontal cortex are seen by Mesulam (1990) as consistent with the "negative" symptoms of schizophrenia that bear some resemblance to the behavioral sequelae to frontal lobe damage in adults (e.g., impaired initiation and motivation, flattened affect). Later in this section, we will describe specific neuropsychological findings that also suggest a possible frontal lobe dysfunction in schizophrenia.

Of particular relevance to a chapter on developmental psychopathology is the degree to which we can identify developmental periods during which the presumed CNS insults underlying behavioral dysfunction occur. The disorder of schizophrenia presents a unique and potentially informative case example in this regard, given its interesting developmental course and apparent genetic etiology. The relatively late manifestation of the mental illness (from the teens to the early 30s) would suggest the involvement of some late-acting neuropathological agent in adulthood, such as a slow virus or other neurotoxin. However, the overwhelming evidence for at least a partial genetic contribution to schizophrenia would tend to implicate prenatal and early postnatal deviations in normal neuroanatomical development (although, as mentioned earlier, genetic mutations do not always operate early in development and may involve a phenotypic expression later in life, such as in Huntington's disease). In light of the evidence for the particular anatomical differences observed in the brains of schizophrenics reviewed above, several hypotheses for the developmental timing of the neuropathological process have been offered.

The findings of Suddath et al. (1990) highlight the need to consider extragenetic, postnatal, and environmental contributions to schizophrenia. In their study, monozygotic twins were not only discordant for the psychiatric condition, but were discordant for the brain abnormalities as well. These abnormalities were not correlated with exposure to neuroleptic medication or duration of illness, implying that the neuropathology was not a secondary effect of "psychic suffering" or specific treatment modality (Mesulam, 1990). Such a conclusion is supported by findings of a similar dissociation between ventricular size and the treatment, course, and duration of the illness (Iacono, Smith, Moreau, 1988; Kelsoe et al., 1988; Schlusinger et al., 1984; Shelton & Weinberger, 1986; Suddath et al., 1989; Weinberger et al., 1979; Weinberger, DeLisi, Perman, Targum, & Wyatt, 1982; Williams, Reveley, Kolakowska, Arden, & Madelbrote, 1985).

Suddath and colleagues (1990) proposed that the schizophrenia research to date is not consistent with a progressive degenerative disorder, and, instead, supports a neurological dysfunction that predates the onset of the illness. They suggested that some subtle developmental dysfunction, perhaps in neuronal migration, might account for the abnormalities observed in schizophrenic brains. A smaller hippocampal structure in schizophrenics, found by Suddath et al. (1990) and by others, might imply an early postnatal insult, given that neuronal migration occurs late in this structure and, unlike most of the cortex, continues postnatally. Neuromigration is, however, complete in the whole brain before the end of the first year of life. A postnatal onset of the neuropathological process is also consistent with the discordance seen between monozygotic twins in the size of this brain structure. It would seem that the peri- and early postnatal periods would be the most likely times when some agent could selectively alter the course of one twin's brain development.

According to the authors, the absence of gliosis accompanying a decrease in tissue volume (Roberts et al., 1987) and abnormal cytoarchitecture of the hippocampus (Jakob & Beckmann, 1986) also is convergent with an early postnatal mechanism. Similarly, the findings of Benes et al. (1986), in which the columnar organization of the frontal cortex and cingulate gyrus of schizophrenics is abnormal, are thought to reflect a very early phenomenon, possibly during the prenatal period.

In summary, the bulk of recent empirical evidence of neuropathology in schizophrenia points to the hippocampus, frontal cortex, and selected left hemisphere structures as the potential sites of neurological insult. Moreover, current theorizing regarding the developmental timing of such insults converges on the notion of early onset, that is, during the prenatal and early postnatal periods. However, a single specific pathogenetic brain mechanism, whether structural or neurochemical, has not yet been clearly established. As with many other complex behavioral disorders, the possibility of neurological subtypes must be considered. The following section reviews recent work exploring possible behavioral markers of schizophrenia that may serve as another window on the neurological substrates of the disorder.

Neuropsychological Phenotype: Biological Marker Level. The search for biological markers of schizophrenia and other psychological disorders has as its objective a clarification of both genetic and neurological mechanisms underlying the disorder. Clementz and Sweeney (1990) suggested that the following criteria should be satisfied, for a behavior to be considered as a biological marker: (a) low base rate in the population, (b) temporal stability, (c) genetic transmission, (d) ability to identify individuals at risk for syndromal and subsyndromal manifestations of the illness, (e) specificity to the diagnostic category, (f) presence during symptom remission, and (g) evidence in first-degree relatives of the proband at a higher rate than is observed in the general population.

These criteria can be related to the four criteria for a primary neuropsychological deficit, discussed earlier in this chapter. The specificity criterion is relevant for both biological markers and primary neuropsychological dysfunctions. However, as discussed earlier, a valid marker need not be universal within the clinical population of interest, because the marker could be one of several pleiotropic manifestations of a latent trait. The criterion of persistence is related to several of the above characteristics of biological markers: temporal stability, identification of individuals at risk for the disorder who are currently in a subclinical state, and presence of the behavior during symptom remission. Finally, the criterion of causal precedence is satisfied by evidence for genetic transmission and observation of the marker in first-degree relatives of the schizophrenic proband.

A great deal of recent research has focused on *eye movement dysfunction (EMD)* as a potentially valid biological marker of schizophrenia. Of the many functional classes of eye movement patterns, the smooth pursuit and saccadic systems are the two domains that have captured the most research interest. A critical review of this literature appears elsewhere in this volume. Here, we will focus on another potential biological marker of schizophrenia: a neurophysiological index of sensory processing known as sensory gating.

The *sensory gating* response is presumed to reflect the operation of the inhibitory neuronal pathways in the brain, which are responsible for filtering and regulating the amount of sensory input processed (Freedman et al., 1987). Well-documented deficits in the perceptual and attentional processes of schizophrenia (Braff & Saccuzzo, 1982; Gruzlier, 1975; Landau, Buchsbaum, Carpenter, Strauss, & Sacks, 1975; McGhie & Chapman, 1961; Roemer, Shagass, Straumanis, & Amadeo, 1979; Roth & Cannon, 1972; Saccuzzo & Braff, 1981; Zahn, 1976) are hypothesized by Freedman and colleagues (Baker et al., 1987; Franks, Adler, Waldo, Alpert, & Freedman, 1983; Freedman et al., 1987; Siegel, Waldo, Miznor, Adler, & Freedman, 1984) to be caused by a dysfunction of this sensory gating system. However, the localizing significance of such a dysfunction has not yet been established, given that inhibitory pathways can be found in diverse neurological systems, including the hippocampus, thalamus, and cerebral cortex (Eccles, 1969).

The sensory gating response is measured by inspecting the P50 wave of the auditory evoked potential (AEP). This early wave component was selected because it is easily reproducible and it is relatively unaffected by the subject's level of attention or by stimulus intensity (Hillyard, Pfefferbaum, Hink, Schment, & Pieton, 1973; Pfefferbaum, Horvath, Roth, Tinklenberg, & Kopell, 1980). The sensory gating response is elicited by means of the conditioning-testing (C-T) paradigm, which includes a first (conditioning) stimulus followed by a second (test) stimulus at .5, 1.0 or 2.0 second intervals. Both auditory stimuli should evoke AEPs; however, the second stimulus should be accompanied by a smaller potential because of inhibitory activity of the neuronal pathways (Freedman, Adler, Waldo, Pachtman, & Franks, 1983). That is, the first stimulus activates or "conditions" the inhibitory mechanism, and the second stimulus "tests" the strength of that inhibition (Eccles, 1969; Freedman et al., 1987). A C-T ratio has been developed to quantify the degree of inhibition exhibited by a given individual; it is derived by dividing the test response by the conditioned response and is generally expressed as a percentage. A high ratio or percentage, such as 80%, reflects that the test response is equivalent to 80% of the conditioned response. This high percentage is indicative of very poor suppression or sensory gating. In contrast, a low ratio or percentage, such as 15%, represents a test response that is only 15% of the conditioned response. In this case, very good suppression of the AEP has occurred, and one assumes adequate functioning of the relevant inhibitory neuronal pathways (Baker et al., 1987).

In the original study exploring the adequacy of sensory gating in schizophrenics, Adler et al. (1982) compared unmedicated schizophrenics to normal controls on the C-T paradigm using AEPs. The authors found greater suppression of the test stimulus P50 in controls than in schizophrenics. For example, the mean C-T ratios at the .5 second interval were 10% for controls and 86% for schizophrenics, suggesting a dysfunction of the inhibitory pathway responsible for gating auditory stimulation in the latter group.

Given clear evidence of a sensory gating deficit in schizophrenics compared with normal controls (Adler et al., 1982; Baker et al., 1987; Franks et al., 1983; Freedman et al., 1983; Siegel et al., 1984), one can evaluate the research with regard to the biological marker status of this abnormality. The studies conducted to date address three broad domains that are considered to be criteria for biological marker status (Clementz & Sweeney, 1990): (a) pervasiveness (e.g., presence during symptom remission), (b) specificity, and (c) causal precedence or genetic transmission (e.g., manifestation in first-degree relatives of affected individuals). These three characteristics of biological markers will be discussed in turn, with respect to the relevant studies.

The pervasiveness of the suppression deficit observed in the AEPs of schizophrenics was explored when Freedman et al. (1983) compared medicated and unmedicated schizophrenics on the C-T paradigm. Replicating Adler et al. (1982), they found greater inhibition of P50 in controls than in schizophrenics. Moreover, neuroleptic medication did *not* increase suppression of the P50 response, nor was the C-T ratio correlated with ratings of clinical status. In contrast, neuroleptic treatment *did* enhance the amplitude and latency of the P50 response; such normalization of evoked potentials with medication has been found previously (Shagass, 1977). Thus, although amplitude and latency parameters of the P50 may represent transient phenomena linked to catecholaminergic function, the abnormal C-T ratio may be a relatively stable, pervasive feature related to a pathophysiological mechanism underlying the schizophrenic disorder (Freedman et al., 1983).

Later work has continued to clarify the neurochemical contributions to evoked potential responses in schizophrenics, which may provide a window on the relevant neurological structures. Freedman and colleagues found that normalization of P50 amplitude was related to decreases in the dopamine (DA) metabolite, homovanillic acid (HVA), suggesting that increased DA may be responsible for the smaller waves in unmedicated schizophrenic patients (reported in Freedman et al., 1987). This finding is consistent with animal model research in which amphetamine (DA agonist) and haloperidol (DA antagonist) modulated the size of the P50 wave (Adler, Rose, & Freedman, 1986). Freedman et al. (1987) proposed that there may be two distinct abnormalities in the schizophrenic's neuronal processing of auditory stimulation: (a) a reversible effect on P50 amplitude, dependent on DA, and (b) a fixed deficit in sensory gating, independent of DA. Both dysfunctions may then combine to produce the abnormal sensory perceptions characteristic of schizophrenia. The DA-dependent mechanism may be reflected in the changes observed in symptomatology across the course of the illness; DA-independent mechanisms may be responsible for the more chronic, medication-resistant, negative symptoms of the disorder.

The specificity criterion for biological marker status has been addressed by studies comparing the sensory gating of schizophrenics to that of other psychiatric populations. Franks et al. (1983) measured the C-T ratio in normal controls and in bipolar patients; the latter group was split into subgroups of manic and euthymic. The results demonstrated that the acutely manic subjects exhibited less suppression of the P50 wave than the euthymic and control subjects, who did not differ from each other. Moreover, clinical status, as assessed by the Manic State Rating Scale, correlated with degree of suppression of the test response. Sensory gating was more variable across trials in the manic subjects, as well as across subjects within the manic group, suggesting a high level of sensitivity of the C-T ratio to both transient changes in behavioral state and more stable individual differences in clinical condition. Therefore, the common sensory gating deficit observed in both schizophrenia and mania implies that this abnormality is *not* diagnostically specific, and it may reflect some common features of the two mental illnesses, such as distractability and indiscriminant responding to stimuli (Abrams & Taylor, 1981; Baker et al., 1987; Franks et al., 1983). However, an important difference between the findings for schizophrenia and mania tends to mitigate this lack of specificity. In mania, and *not* in schizophrenia, sensory gating is influenced by clinical state and pharmacological treatment (Freedman et al., 1987). That is, both schizophrenic and manic patients may manifest the abnormality; however, only in the former group is the deficit insensitive to current clinical status, symptom remission, and neurochemical perturbations. Both abnormalities appear to be pervasive, fixed, and perhaps genetically controlled *traits* in schizophrenia, but *state*-dependent features in manic individuals (Freedman et al., 1987).

Evidence for a genetic mode of transmission of the sensory gating dysfunction was provided by one study that explored the phenomenon in first-degree relatives of schizophrenics (Siegel et al., 1984). These family members as a group exhibited poor inhibition of P50 at a rate of more than five times that seen in normal controls. The mean C-T ratio of the relatives (56.1%) fell between that of the normal controls (18.6%) and that of the schizophrenics (86.2%). The relatives of schizophrenics displayed great variability in their C-T ratios: one subgroup resembled controls (good suppression) and one subgroup resembled schizophrenics (poor suppression). Family members showing good gating were more likely to have married into a schizophrenic kindred and to exhibit less elevated MMPI scales. All the relatives had normal amplitude and latency of the P50 wave, consistent with the notion that these parameters are more closely linked with current symptomatology and neurochemical function. These data suggest that sensory gating may have a genetic etiology and may be useful in identifying unaffected individuals who are nevertheless at risk for a subclinical manifestation on the disorder because of this genetic predisposition. Consistent with this, Siegel et al. (1984) found that two-thirds of the schizophrenics and one-third of their relatives showed *both* abnormal C-T ratios and eye movement deficits. Although the discordance of the two abnormalities implies different genetic mechanisms, the high concordance, especially in schizophrenics, is intriguing and warrants further study.

Based on a relatively small set of recent studies, there appears to be good reason to pursue sensory gating as another potential biological marker of schizophrenia. Although there has been much more study of EMD as a marker of schizophrenia, many common findings have emerged from both bodies of research. First, both sensory gating abnormalities and EMD have been found to be relatively pervasive, stable, and fixed deficits in schizophrenia, as opposed to more transient, perhaps secondary, symptoms in mania. Second, both disorders are exhibited by first-degree relatives of probands at a much higher rate than is seen in normal controls. Further study of the sensory gating phenomenon with regard to additional criteria clearly is required before its status as a biological marker can be fully assessed. Finally, there is a pressing need for a broader theoretical framework in which to understand these biological marker results. Understandably, research on these markers has been largely empirically driven, with the goal of establishing the particular phenomenon as a valid marker. Eventually, however, we need to understand how those fragments of behavior fit into several broader contexts, such as the total symptom picture of schizophrenia, an integrated account of brain functions, and an account of normal and abnormal cognitive development. The approaches and perspectives provided by developmental psychopathology could be useful in this regard.

Neuropsychological Phenotype: Functional Level. There is general consensus among researchers in psychopathology that schizophrenics manifest a range of *cognitive deficits* that may directly or indirectly contribute to their dysfunctional behavior. Given sufficient motivation and appropriate structure, schizophrenics perform relatively normally on tasks tapping sensorimotor skills, associative memory, and basic language abilities (Goldman-Rakic, in press; Mesulam, 1990). However, their cognitive deficits emerge in task situations that demand focused and sustained attention (Asarnow & MacCrimmon, 1978; Kornetzky & Orzack, 1978), the creation of anticipatory sets (Rodnick & Shakow, 1940), flexible switching of problem solving strategies (Kolb & Whishaw, 1983), and general information processing speed (Nelson et al., 1990; Yates, 1966). This section discusses executive function, a domain of cognition that is presumed to be mediated by the prefrontal cortical system, and that may serve as a model to integrate the diverse findings regarding cognitive impairments in schizophrenia.

As described earlier in this chapter, *executive function* refers to the skills necessary to generate and execute goal-directed behavior, especially in novel situations. Goal-oriented actions require that information in the form of plans and expectations be computed and held "on-line" in working memory, and flexibly changed in response to feedback. Otherwise, behavior is dominated by prepotent responses. Kraepelin (1919) implied a blatant impairment of executive function when he commented that schizophrenics "are wholly incapable of . . . carrying out a well-considered plan" (pp. 221–222).

A well-established measure of one executive function skill, the ability to shift mental set in response to negative feedback, is the Wisconsin Card Sorting Test (WCST; Grant & Berg, 1948; Heaton, 1981). The WCST includes a deck of 128 stimulus cards varying along the dimensions of color, shape, and number of items, and 4 standard cards that represent a unique combination of these three features (e.g., one red triangle, two green stars). The subject is instructed to sort each of the cards in the deck to one of the standard cards, and the experimenter provides accuracy feedback after each sort. Once the subject has made 10 correct consecutive sorts to the color category, the experimenter, without warning, switches the criterion to shape. The test proceeds until each of the three categories has been completed twice or the deck is exhausted. The most important behavioral measure derived from this test is perseveration, defined as sorting to an incorrect category in the face of negative feedback. There is considerable empirical evidence demonstrating that individuals with frontal lobe damage commit significantly more perseverative responses than comparison groups (Drewe, 1975; Kolb & Whishaw, 1983; Milner, 1966).

The following is a review of studies of schizophrenics' performance on the WCST. These studies have found that, like frontal patients, schizophrenics also show abnormally high levels of perseveration on the WCST. Moreover, some of these studies provide direct evidence that this impairment may indeed reflect prefrontal dysfunction in schizophrenia.

Comparing schizophrenics with normal controls, Fey (1951) found the former group to be impaired on the WCST in terms of the number of categories completed and the amount of perseverative responding. Malmo (1974) found that frontal-damaged patients performed worse on the WCST than four psychiatric patient groups, but among the psychiatric groups, the chronic schizophrenics exhibited the most perseveration. Exploring possible differences among schizophrenic subtypes, Bornstein et al. (1990) discovered that all the schizophrenic groups performed more poorly than controls on a range of tests tapping functions of both hemispheres and both frontal and posterior cortex. However, the nonparanoid group displayed pronounced deficits on the WCST compared with the other clinical subtypes. This finding contrasts with that of Rund (1986), in which the paranoid subjects displayed greater perseveration. This deficit in WCST performance appears to be quite profound; even when schizophrenic subjects were taught how to solve the task with regard to the nature of the categories and set shifts, their performance did not improve (Goldberg, Weinberger, Berman, Pliskin, & Podd, 1987).

Utilizing a regional cerebral blood flow (rCBF) technique, recent studies by Weinberger and colleagues have not only replicated this impairment in WCST performance in schizophrenics, but have also identified possible neurophysiological mechanisms. Reduced metabolism in the dorsolateral prefrontal cortex has been observed in both medicated (Berman, Zec, & Weinberger, 1986) and unmedicated (Weinberger, Berman, & Zec, 1986) chronic schizophrenics during WCST performance. In contrast, abnormally low metabolic levels in this brain region were *not* observed in a number-matching task presumed to elicit posterior cognitive functions. Lowered rCBF in the prefrontal cortex does not merely reflect difficulty with the task and poor performance. Comparing a schizophrenic group with a Huntington's disease group, Goldberg, Berman, Mohr, and Weinberger (1990) found *both* groups to be impaired on the WCST, but only the schizophrenics showed the characteristic hypometabolism in the prefrontal cortex. Similarly, other tasks on which schizophrenics perform poorly, such as the CPT and the Raven's Progressive Matrices, are not necessarily accompanied by low rCBF in the dorsolateral prefrontal cortex (Berman et al., 1986). The finding that impaired performance on the contingent version of the CPT was not related to lower metabolic activity in schizophrenics (Berman et al., 1986) is somewhat surprising, given that the anticipatory set encouraged by the task might be considered a frontal lobe executive function. One possible explanation for this result is that the version of the CPT used did not sufficiently tax working memory. (See Cohen and Servan-Schreiber (1992), for an extensive discussion of this point.)

The finding of hypometabolism in the dorsolateral prefrontal cortex of schizophrenics specifically during WCST performance appears to be replicable and reliable. Weinberger and colleagues have speculated as to the neurophysiological mechanisms underlying this phenomenon, suggesting that at least a subgroup of schizophrenics exhibits executive function impairments because of a reduced ability to increase prefrontal cortex metabolism when the situation demands it (Weinberger et al., 1986). A recent finding that the reduced rCBF in the prefrontal cortex during WCST performance was correlated with lowered CSF dopamine levels has led to the proposal that the cognitive dysfunction may be secondary to a neurochemical perturbation. Specifically, Berman et al. (1988) suggested that there may be reduced presynaptic dopamine activity in the mesocortical system, perhaps as a result of a structural enlargement of the ventricles often observed in schizophrenia.

Goldman-Rakic (in press) has suggested that a key aspect of executive function, working memory, is not only a cardinal feature of frontal lobe functioning, but also contributes to many of the major symptoms of schizophrenia. Working memory can be defined as mental representations of the external world that are transiently held "on-line" in service of some goal-directed behavior. In contrast to semantic memory (Tulving, 1983), which, by definition, refers to stored information that is stable, permanent, and associative, the content of working memory is dynamic, temporary, and context-dependent. Goldman-Rakic (in press) proposes that working memory subserves flexible, spontaneous, and planful behavior by allowing the individual to guide actions by internal representations (e.g., ideas, thoughts), as opposed to immediate external stimulation. She points out that many of the key clinical symptoms of schizophrenia can be interpreted as behavior that appears to lack appropriate internal controls. Goldman-Rakic and Friedman (1991) presented extensive evidence for frontal cortex mediation of working memory.

Goldman-Rakic (in press) highlights the similarities in neuropsychological performance between schizophrenics and individuals with frontal lobe damage, and suggests that this performance pattern may reflect an underlying working memory dysfunction. Both clinical groups perform poorly on spatial delay tasks (Malmo, 1974), the Wisconsin Card Sorting Test (Goldberg et al., 1987), and the Category Test of the Halstead-Reitan Battery (Klonoff, Fibiger, & Hutton, 1970). Each of these tasks could be thought to require the development of symbolic mental representations to drive problem-solving behavior.

Another test of working memory skills is the Tower of Hanoi, one of several variants of disk-transfer tasks. This task demands that the subject keep a variety of dynamic information "on-line" during problem solving: important subgoals, a series of disk moves, and the implications of such moves for achieving the subgoals. The Tower of Hanoi has been found to be sensitive to frontal lobe lesions in adults (Shallice, 1982) and to the cognitive deficits of chronic schizophrenics (Goldberg & Weinberger, 1988).

Related to the notion that working memory represents a particular deficit area for schizophrenics was the suggestion by C. D. Frith and U. Frith (1991) that this psychiatric group is impaired in the generation and use of what they call second-order mental representations. Although first-order representations are relatively veridical pictures of external stimuli, second-order representations reflect "meta-pictures" of the world. That is, they are "once removed" (Frith & Frith, 1991) or decoupled (Leslie, 1987) from reality as it is directly perceived by the senses. Examples of these second-order representations would include metacognition (knowing about knowing), pretend play (acting on an object as if it were something else), and "theory of mind" (awareness of the mental states of others). According to our working memory perspective being developed here, second-order representations are internal, context-specific representations that differ from the more stable, primary representations encoded in associative memory. Frith and Frith (1991) make a strong case for the contribution of an impairment in second-order representation to the symptomatology of schizophrenia. For instance, the overall poverty of communication production and content, as well as abnormalities in cohesion (Rochester & Martin, 1979), discourse planning, inference generation (Allen, 1984), and syntax (Morice & Ingram, 1983), could all be attributed to a failure in the schizophrenic's second-order representations, including theory of mind.

Furthermore, these authors speculate as to the neurophysiological mechanisms underlying a deficit in second-order representations. They propose that the temporal lobes may be the site where permanent, stable, first-order representations are built and stored, and that arbitrary, context-dependent, second-order representations may be generated in the frontal cortex. If, as Leslie (1987) proposed, second-order representations are essentially decoupled first-order representations, then an intact connection between the posterior and frontal cortical systems would be critical for their generation (Frith & Frith, 1991). As discussed earlier, both the frontal and temporal lobes are cortical areas in which morphological abnormalities have been observed in the brains of schizophrenics.

Perhaps the most searching cognitive account of schizophrenia as a frontal disorder has been provided by Cohen and Servan-Schreiber (1992). (Parts of their work have been discussed earlier.) They modeled normal and schizophrenic performance on three widely different working memory tasks (Stroop, CPT-AX, and a lexical disambiguation task) using a connectionist architecture. In each simulation, a particular set of hidden-layer units performed the working memory function of maintaining an internal representation of context; reducing the gain parameter selectively in these units produced a schizophrenic pattern of performance in all three simulations. The choice of the gain parameter was biologically motivated in that other work has demonstrated that reducing dopamine decreases gain. The work of these two authors relates directly to the dopamine hypothesis of schizophrenia, but unexpectedly posits dopamine *depletion* as an explanation for at least part of the schizophrenic symptom picture. As we said earlier, their theoretical analysis of frontal tasks is both elegant and computational, and it begins to provide the integrative framework needed to better understand not only schizophrenia, but also frontal function and dysfunction in general.

In summary, although hardly conclusive, many lines of evidence converge to support the hypothesis of frontal dysfunction and resultant executive function or working memory deficits in schizophrenia. The evidence is contributed from neuroanatomical, neuroimaging, and neuropsychological studies. The frontal hypothesis has been particularly compelling as an account for the so-called negative symptoms in schizophrenia, but more recent accounts have shown how a frontal hypothesis might account for the positive symptoms of hallucinations and delusions as well (e.g., Cohen & Servan-Schreiber, 1992; Frith & Frith, 1991; Goldman-Rakic, in press). As suggested above, it will be important for future work on both neuropsychological markers and deficits in schizophrenia to be less paradigm-driven and more broadly integrative. Coherent cognitive explanations of the wide array of symptomatology and deficits on experimental tasks that are seen in this disorder are needed; the working memory hypothesis is one candidate for such an explanation.

Attention Deficit/Hyperactivity Disorder (ADHD)

Clinical Description. The diagnosis of ADHD can be difficult because of the number of confounding conditions (e.g., chaotic family life) that must be excluded, because of fundamental disagreements in the field on how to define the syndrome, and because objective tests of ADHD are much less well developed than those for the impaired cognitive processes in other learning disorders, such as dyslexia.

Although we also lack similarly objective tests for diagnosing schizophrenia and autism, these are rarer and more severe disorders whose key symptoms do not overlap as much with either those of other disorders or behaviors that are developmentally normal. Identifying attention problems in children is difficult because even normal children are less attentive, more active, and more impulsive than the average adult. Because the diagnosis is based primarily on history and symptoms, much of the research on diagnosis has focused on developing both lists of critical or primary symptoms and (for parents and teachers) behavioral rating scales that incorporate these critical symptoms. The core symptoms that appear to be primary to the disorder fall into three categories: (a) inattention, (b) impulsivity, and (c) hyperactivity. Behavioral problems that may be correlated with ADHD involve sleep disturbances and emotional lability. Other symptoms that demonstrate an association with ADHD, but do not appear to be primary, include aggressive behavior, conduct disorder, learning disabilities, depression, and poor self-esteem.

Another complication for diagnosis is that primary symptoms may differ according to the age of the child. In infancy, symptoms may include a high activity level, less need for sleep, colic, frequent crying, and poor soothability—characteristics that overlap with what is called a "difficult" infant. In toddlerhood, the ADHD child often has a low sense of danger, an unusual amount of energy, and a tendency to move from one activity to another very quickly. ADHD children nearly always come to clinical attention in the early school years, because of the behavior management problems they pose in a classroom setting: frequent talking, getting out of their seat, difficulty keeping their hands to themselves, and problems finishing school work. A diagnosis of ADHD is usually made if the child has a history of these and related problematic behaviors in the early school years, and these problems do not appear to be due to acquired causes, such as a closed head injury.

Brain Mechanisms. In the neuropsychological section that follows this one, we develop the general hypothesis that ADHD is caused by dysfunction in the prefrontal areas of the brain. What direct evidence is there to support this hypothesis or the more global hypothesis that ADHD is due to brain dysfunction?

Early attempts to relate ADHD to brain dysfunction utilized neurological soft signs as the brain measure. The results of these studies were mixed and discouraging in terms of elucidating a brain basis for ADHD (Rutter, Graham, & Yule, 1970; Werry et al., 1972).

There is likewise a weak association between minor physical anomalies (MPAs) and hyperactivity (Burg, Rapoport, Bartley, Quinn, & Timmins, 1980; Rapoport & Quinn, 1975), but the association is not specific to hyperactivity and is not clinically useful in a predictive way. The potential neurological significance of observable MPAs is that they may be correlated with less observable developmental anomalies of the CNS. However, this line of research is more likely to bear fruit if specific genetic syndromes with MPAs (e.g., Fragile X syndrome) are studied instead of the undoubtedly heterogeneous group of all children with MPAs.

In terms of more direct measures of brain structure and function, the best evidence for differences in ADHD comes from measures of brain function, including measures of electrophysiology, regional cerebral blood flow, and catecholamines (dopamine and norepinephrine). With regard to brain structure, earlier work (Harcherik et al., 1985; Shaywitz, Shaywitz, Cohen, & Young, 1983) found no evidence of structural differences in computed tomography (CT) scan studies of ADHD children. Hynd and colleagues (Hynd, Semrud-Clikeman, Lorys, Novey, & Eliopulas, 1991), however, did find absence of the usual right > left frontal asymmetry in ADHD children using MRI scans. When they contrasted ADHD subjects with both dyslexics and controls, the frontal finding was present in both clinical groups, but did not differentiate between them, even though the dyslexic group was selected to be non-ADHD. As we discuss later, there is an association between the right frontal lobe and measures of sustained attention, so this neuroanatomical difference has theoretical relevance to ADHD. More studies are needed to examine the replicability and specificity of this candidate neuroanatomical difference in ADHD.

In terms of brain function, the electrophysiological measures have supported the hypothesis of CNS underarousal in at least a subgroup of hyperactive children (Ferguson & Rapoport, 1983). Lou, Henriksen, and Bruhn (1984) found decreased blood flow to the frontal lobes in ADHD children; the flow increased after the children received Ritalin. Ritalin treatment also decreased blood flow to the motor cortex and primary sensory cortex, "suggesting an inhibition of function of these structures, seen clinically as less distractibility and decreased motor activity during treatment" (p. 829). These investigators recently replicated this result in an expanded sample (Lou, Henriksen, Bruhn, Borner, & Nielson, 1989); in this second report, they emphasized the basal ganglia as the locus of reduced blood flow in ADHD. Zametkin et al. (1990) used the PET scan technique to study the parents of ADHD children; these parents had residual-type ADHD. They found an overall reduction in cerebral glucose utilization, particularly in right frontal areas, but increased utilization in posterior medial orbital areas. Because hyperfrontality of blood flow is characteristic of the normal brain, hypofrontality in ADHD could explain the low central arousal found in the electrophysiological studies.

In terms of brain biochemistry, Shaywitz, Cohen, and Bowers (1977) found lower levels of homovanillic acid—HVA (the main dopamine metabolite)—in the cerebro-spinal fluid of ADHD children compared to controls. Dopamine has a preponderant distribution in the frontal regions of the cortex. Moreover, a well-validated animal model of ADHD involves dopamine depletion (Shaywitz et al., 1983); however, there is also evidence of depletion of norepinephrine (NE) in ADHD (see Shaywitz & Shaywitz, 1988). Posner and Petersen (in press) have recently reviewed evidence supporting the view that NE pathways are involved in maintaining alertness, mainly by acting on the posterior attention systems of the right hemisphere. An alternative view of ADHD is that it involves NE depletion in these posterior right hemisphere systems.

In summary, one plausible theory of brain mechanisms in ADHD is as follows. The executive function deficit of ADHD children is caused by functional hypofrontality, which in turn is caused by either structural and/or biochemical changes in the prefrontal lobes, and is detectable as reduced frontal blood flow. Biochemically, the cause would be low dopamine levels, which Ritalin treatment reverses, at least in part.

Unfortunately, the story is not that simple. One study found that dopamine agonists were not effective in treating hyperactive children (Mattes & Gittelman, 1979); however, certain dopamine antagonists did have unexpected beneficial effects in ADHD children (Zametkin & Rapoport, 1987). Both of these results are opposite to what would be predicted by the dopamine depletion hypothesis. The neurochemical mechanisms may be more complex, although the ubiquitous problem of heterogeneity in ADHD samples is another explanation.

Zametkin and Rapoport (1987) argued that no single neurotransmitter is exclusively involved in the pathogenesis of ADHD, both because stimulant medications always affect more than one neurotransmitter and because of the multiple interrelations among specific catecholamines and their precursors and metabolites. Along with Oades (1987), they argue that the combined action of dopaminergic and noradrenergic systems should be considered in the biology of ADHD.

Much more research is needed, preferably using familial samples that are as phenotypically homogeneous as possible. For instance, as suggested above, one subtype of ADHD children may have hypoarousal of the right posterior hemisphere secondary to NE depletion, whereas others may have the hypofrontal subtype of ADHD discussed here. Although the posterior and anterior attentional systems interact, separate deficits in each system are possible.

Neuropsychological Phenotype. Historically, phenotypic research on ADHD has shifted from a focus on activity per se to research on attentional processes and then to a focus on other cognitive processes that appear to underlie the surface symptoms of restlessness and inattention. Research on activity level in ADHD generally found that it was not the *quantity* but the *quality* of activity that mainly differentiates ADHD children from controls (Cromwell, Baumeister, & Hawkins, 1963), a result that is similar to the research on eye contact in autism. Research on attention clarified that specific aspects of attention were impaired in ADHD children. For instance, Porges, Walter, Korb, and Sprague (1975) used an ingenious experiment to demonstrate that there were no differences between ADHD children on and off Ritalin in reactive or orienting attention, but there were clear differences in focused or selective attention. Other studies have shown that, contrary to the prevailing belief, ADHD children are no more vulnerable to extraneous stimuli, which engage orienting attention, than are normals (Douglas & Peters, 1979). In contrast, on measures of vigilance or sustained attention, ADHD children have a clear deficit, especially when prolonged attention is required and time of presentation is experimenter- (vs. self-) paced (Sykes, Douglas, & Morgenstern, 1973; Sykes, Douglas, Weiss, & Minde, 1971). Recent studies of both adult lesion patients and blood flow studies of adult normals support a right frontal localization for the mechanisms involved in sustained attention (Wilkins, Shallice, & McCarthy, 1987).

As is the case for research exploring attentional abnormalities in schizophrenia, vigilance and reaction time tasks have been invaluable tools for investigating similar deficits in children with ADHD. The common demands across a variety of paradigms include the need to maintain effortful attention over time, inhibit irrelevant and impulsive responding, and generally perform in a systematic and organized fashion. There is now a large body of literature demonstrating that children with ADHD exhibit deficits on vigilance tasks like the CPT (Barkley, 1977; Douglas, 1972; Douglas & Peters, 1979). They make more errors of commission and omission and have slower and more variable reaction times than control children (Douglas, 1984). When presented with reaction time tasks that include a preparatory interval prior to the target, ADHD subjects, like schizophrenics, perform poorly. Douglas (1984) interpreted this impaired performance on a variety of vigilance measures as a reflection of both unsystematic and inconsistent responding to target stimuli and a failure to inhibit maladaptive responding.

During the past two decades, emphasis has shifted from sustained attention to a search for the core cognitive deficits associated with ADHD. Douglas (1988) summarized this work as supporting the hypothesis that ADHD children have a generalized self-regulatory deficit that affects the organization of information processing, the mobilization of attention throughout information processing, and the inhibition of inappropriate responding across visual, auditory, motor, and perceptual-motor modalities. In her formulation, organization of information processing encompasses planning, executive function, metacognition, optimum set maintenance, regulation of arousal and alertness, and self-monitoring. The arousal/alertness component refers especially to the deployment of attentional resources in relation to task demands, including maintenance of attention over time. The inhibition component refers to controlling interference from irrelevant but sometimes prepotent response patterns, stimuli, and reinforcers. Douglas explicitly uses the term *executive functions,* and her list of impaired cognitive processes includes many of the executive functions we have already discussed.

In an early study, Conners (1970), another important contributor to our understanding of the neuropsychological phenotype in ADHD, compared neurotic and hyperkinetic children from the same clinic setting on a variety of measures. The hyperkinetic children had significantly lower verbal IQ (VIQ) and performance IQ (PIQ), performed significantly less well on the Porteus Mazes (which have been validated as a frontal lobe measure), and exhibited deficits in the *voluntary* inhibition of motor responses. The paradigm used to evaluate motor inhibition is worthy of note, because it permitted a distinction between voluntary and involuntary motor responses. With a Luria tremograph attached to both hands, subjects were instructed to make responses to target stimuli with the right hand only; some stimuli were very loud noises (gun shots), which initially produced a startle response in both hands. This startle response habituated over trials. The hyperactive subjects did not differ from controls in left-hand performance, either for errors or rate of habituation of startle responses, indicating similar involuntary motor control. In contrast, hyperactives made more errors and habituated more slowly with their right hands, indicating a deficit in higher cortical mechanisms concerned with the inhibition of voluntary movement. (See Conners & Wells, 1986, for a summary of these studies.) Conners interpreted these results as consistent with frontal lobe dysfunction.

In a later series of studies, Conners used a neuropsychological test battery to define six subtypes within a sample of hyperkinetic children. These subtypes exhibited differential drug responsiveness, among other things, and so appear to possess some external validity. Two groups did not give evidence of academic or cognitive disabilities, and their overactivity appeared to be mainly due to anxiety. One group appeared to have attention deficits in the context of learning disabilities; medication did not help this group. Perhaps this latter group had ADHD as a superficial secondary symptom of dyslexia or other LD, as discussed above. A fourth group had an isolated deficit in motor impulsivity, which also did not respond to drug treatment. A fifth group had mainly a visuospatial pattern of deficits.

Conners labeled the final group "frontal lobe dysfunction" because of distinctively poor performance on the Porteus Mazes. Although these children had the lowest IQ scores of all the groups, they were not depressed on measures of academic achievement or paired associate learning, both results indicating intact language processing and long-term memory skills. Their cognitive profile is reminiscent of the one described by Douglas (1988) in her studies of ADHD children, and best fits the executive function deficit definition of ADHD espoused here. Moreover, their response to drug treatment was different from the responses seen in all the other groups, in that significant change on teacher ratings was in the areas of defiance, hyperactivity, and overall psychopathology. In other words, medication helped these children inhibit socially inappropriate responses, whereas medication in the other groups was either ineffective or mainly seemed to affect anxiety-related behaviors. This and other work by Conners underscores the clinical importance of distinguishing anxious from nonanxious (and LD from non-LD) hyperactive children, with the nonanxious, non-LD subtype best exemplifying the syndrome of ADHD as we are describing it here. Conners (1975) and Klove and Hole (1979) found that nonanxious hyperactives have low autonomic arousal and a significantly greater history of CNS risk events.

Across studies, what are some of the specific cognitive tasks on which ADHD children have been found to be impaired and not impaired? In the impaired list, we find monitoring tasks, such as the Continuous Performance Test; perceptual search tasks, such as the Matching Familiar Figures Test; logical search tasks, such as Raven's Progressive Matrices; and motor control and visuomotor tasks, such as Porteus Mazes, Bender Gestalt, and the Rey-Osterrieth Complex Figure. ADHD children have also been found to be impaired on validated measured of prefrontal function, including the Wisconsin Card Sorting Test (Chelune & Baer, 1986; Parry, 1973), the Tower of Hanoi planning task (Pennington, Groisser, & Welsh, 1993; Welsh, Wall, & Towle, 1989), and conflictual motor responding tasks, such as the "go-no-go" paradigm (Douglas, 1988). In the unimpaired list are various verbal memory tasks, such as Digit Span, paired associates and story recall; and various nonverbal memory tasks, such as recurring figures and recall of spatial positions. We can offer the generalization that performance on working memory tasks is impaired, whereas performance on associative memory tasks is not. Similar tasks can elicit or fail to elicit deficits in ADHD children, depending on task conditions such as reinforcement schedule, number of items and distractors, and processing speed. This dependence of deficits on task conditions reinforces the hypothesis that the underlying deficit is not in a particular information processing domain, like verbal memory, but in executive functions that regulate all of information processing.

Studies targeting specific executive function deficits in ADHD children have been a relatively recent phenomenon. Because executive skills are conceptualized, operationalized, and assessed in different ways across studies, some conflicting findings are to be expected. Research in our laboratory has utilized a relatively consistent battery of executive function measures that tap the efficiency and organization of visual and semantic search, planning ability (Tower of Hanoi), flexibility of strategies (Wisconsin Card Sorting Test), and impulse control (Matching Familiar Figures Test and Continuous Performance Test) (Welsh, Pennington, & Groisser, 1991). In one study, young children (mean age = 7 years) presenting to a child evaluation clinic with attention problems were compared with age- and IQ-matched children presenting with speech and language difficulties (Welsh et al., 1989). The latter group was impaired on a speech and language screening test; the former group was not. The attention problem group exhibited less efficiency in visual search, more perseveration on a verbal fluency task, and poorer planning on the Tower of Hanoi than the language problem group, which did not differ from age-appropriate norms (Welsh et al., 1991). In a later study, well-defined nonoverlapping groups of children (mean age = 9 years) with ADHD only and dyslexia only were compared on a set of executive function tasks, including the Tower of Hanoi, Continuous Performance Test, and Wisconsin Card Sorting Test, as well as on a set of discriminant tasks tapping phonological skills (Pennington, Groisser, & Welsh, 1993). The ADHD group, but not the dyslexic group, was significantly impaired on the executive function tasks, compared with normal controls. In contrast, the dyslexic group, but not the ADHD group, exhibited significant deficits on the phonological tasks. These two studies together suggest that, in their "pure" forms, language-related disorders (e.g., dyslexia) are neuropsychologically independent from executive function disorders (e.g., ADHD) with regard to the core cognitive deficits and the underlying brain mechanisms involved.

In summary, studies of the neuropsychological phenotype in ADHD are consistent with the hypothesis of a primary executive function deficit, but hardly provide conclusive evidence for this hypothesis. Of the various converging empirical criteria needed to establish primacy, only a few have been met. We do not know whether executive function deficits are among the most persistent features of the disorder, although adult outcome studies provide indirect evidence for this view. We do not know whether executive function deficits are clearly distinctive in nonanxious, non-conduct-disordered ADHD children. We do not know whether executive function deficits are coheritable with ADHD. Most importantly, we do not know whether executive function deficits in early life predict later ADHD. Much research still needs to be done on the neuropsychological phenotype in ADHD. Moreover, because there is evidence for executive function deficits in both schizophrenia and autism, such deficits are not specific to ADHD. We return to this important discriminant validity issue in the last section of this chapter. Before concluding this section on executive function disorders, it is important to mention some other developmental psychopathologies in which executive function deficits may play a key role. These are conduct disorder and Tourette's syndrome.

Autism Spectrum Disorder: Disorder of Social Cognition

Both autism and its close cousin, Asperger's syndrome, were first described in the 1940s and consequently have much shorter research histories than dyslexia or schizophrenia. Autism research has undergone the same kind of paradigm shifts that characterized schizophrenia research, being initially considered by Kanner (1943) as a constitutional defect (i.e., a brain disorder), then as a psychogenic disorder, and now again as a brain disorder. As is true for schizophrenia, the nature of the underlying neuropsychological deficit in autism and Asperger's syndrome poses significant challenges for traditional neuropsychological theory, but we will attempt to demonstrate that we are closer to a developmental understanding of autism than we are for schizophrenia. Recent autism research is exemplary developmental psychopathology: the potential reciprocal relation between studies of normal and abnormal development has been fruitfully realized.

Clinical Description

Autism spectrum disorder involves several types of behavioral impairment affecting social interactions and communication and the preferred activities and interests of the child (Sarason & Sarason, 1989). The core symptoms of autism may lie in the domain of social relations. Autistic children exhibit an unusual lack of awareness of the existence and feeling of others, and they will not seek comfort when distressed nor offer empathic responses to others. They avoid being held and making eye contact, lack an understanding of social norms, and prefer to play with objects as opposed to people. Often correlated with autism are deficits in intellectual function and other cognitive and language skills, as well as self-injurious behavior and seizures. Language and communication abnormalities in autistic children are quite profound. Although many are mute, those children who develop language use it in a bizarre manner that fails to show communicative intent. For example, their speech may be characterized by echolalia, inappropriate pronoun use, and a monotonous or sing-song quality. Finally, autistic children's range of activities and interests is particularly limited and unusual (Sarason & Sarason, 1989). These children may spend inordinate amounts of time inspecting a repetitive, moving object or engaging in behavioral sterotypies, such as rocking and hand flapping.

Most researchers regard Asperger's syndrome as part of autism spectrum disorder (Schopler, 1985; Volkmar, Paul, & Cohen, 1985; Wing, 1986), yet the IQ profiles of many reported cases of Asperger's syndrome are unlike those for autism. In autism, verbal IQ is relatively depressed; the opposite is often true in Asperger's syndrome. In this respect, Asperger's syndrome is more like nonverbal learning disorder, discussed elsewhere in this volume. Because early social cognition is itself not a unitary domain, it would not be surprising to find subtypes in its pathology, with each subtype reflecting a primary deficit in a different aspect of early social cognition.

Other disorders considered in this chapter affect social cognition in various ways, as do other disorders covered in other chapters of this volume but not reviewed here. Our purpose here is to focus on autism and Asperger's syndrome, which are overlapping disorders and in which there may be a *primary* neuropsychological deficit in social cognition. Thus, in considering these disorders, we need to address both the question of which portions of the brain seem to be particularly important for social cognition, and the vexing and perhaps misstated issue of whether the primary deficit in autism is social or cognitive. We later consider the relation between executive functions and social cognition as a possible resolution to this issue.

Brain Mechanisms. The neurological basis of autism has been puzzling, partly because we lack good analogies from classic neuropsychological studies of adults with acquired lesions. Analogies with aphasia syndromes have made the search easier for brain mechanisms in dyslexia and other developmental language disorders. Confusion over what is the core behavioral deficit in autism has likewise contributed to confusion in attempts to identify its neurological basis. Different brain regions need to be considered, depending on whether the core deficit is in language, social cognition, attention, arousal level, or executive functions. The search for brain mechanisms in autism has not been mainly driven by theoretical considerations and thus has been less constrained than attempts to understand brain mechanisms in a disorder like dyslexia. Neurological theories of autism have variously focused on the brain stem, the cerebellum, the limbic system, the thalamus, the left hemisphere, and the frontal lobes. We argue in the next section that current evidence best supports the view that the core behavioral deficit is in early social cognition, although there is recent evidence for core deficits in executive function, which may cause the social cognitive deficits. Dysfunction in the frontal lobes or closely related structures, such as the limbic system, might provide an explanation for such functional deficits. There is some research support for anomalies in these brain regions in autism, but there is also evidence for anomalies elsewhere, including the cerebellum. Because there are no group studies of brain mechanisms in Asperger's syndrome, the following review is restricted to autism.

Two reviews of neuroimaging studies have appeared recently (Aitken, 1991; Filipek, Kennedy & Caviness, 1992), and we will include the broad conclusions of those reviews in this summary. Our review of structural findings will be followed by a review of functional findings. CT and MRI studies of autistic subjects are rarely abnormal on clinical interpretation (about 15% of the time) and less than half of these demonstrate focal lesions (Filipek et al., 1992). These lesions have been found in a variety of locations, including the cerebellum, the frontal lobes, other cortical lobes, the basal ganglia, the limbic system, and the corpus callosum. Ventricular enlargement of the lateral or fourth ventricles accounted for the remainder of the clinical anomalies. Lateral ventricular enlargement is one of the more consistent findings. It has been found using pneumoencephalography (Aarkrog, 1968; Hauser, DeLong, & Rosman, 1975); CT scans (Campbell et al., 1982; Damasio, Maurer, Damasio, & Chui, 1980); and MRI scans (Gaffney, Kuperman, Tsai, & Minchin, 1989). These findings of ventricular enlargement suggest developmental atrophy in adjacent limbic and associated frontal structures. However, ventricular enlargement is not found in all studies or all autistic subjects (Creasey, Rumsey, & Schwartz, 1986; Harcherik et al., 1985). Moreover, ventricular enlargement is not specific to autism; it is found in other psychiatric disorders, such as schizophrenia.

Another fairly consistent finding is atrophy of the cerebellum, especially the vermis (Courchesne, Yeung-Courchesne, Press, Hesselink, & Jernigan, 1988; Ritvo et al., 1986).

Although the cerebellar atrophy identified by these researchers could be primary and causal in autism, it could also be a correlate of the primary neurological cause. The neocerebellum and parts of the limbic system, such as the hippocampus, undergo late neurogenesis at the same time. Neuronal migration is still occurring postnatally in both structures, unlike the rest of the brain, and thus both structures would be similarly vulnerable to a late-acting embryonic insult, whether genetic or environmental (or both). In a careful autopsy study of autistic individuals, structural anomalies have been found in both limbic and cerebellar areas (Bauman & Kemper, 1985). Such a correlation could be produced by an earlier insult. Courchesne et al. (1988) have argued that the neocerebellar hypoplasia found in autism is caused by abnormal cell migration occurring between 3 and 5 months' gestation.

Evidence for cortical migrational anomalies in autism has recently been reported (Piven et al., 1990). In this MRI study of 13 high-functioning males, cortical malformations were found in 7 subjects (54%). The authors pointed out that this rate of cortical malformations is much higher than the rate reported in previous large samples of pediatric (about 2%) or retarded populations (about 5%). Most of the subjects had polymacrogyria. Malformations were not consistently found in either a given lobe or hemisphere; however, 3 of the 7 abnormal subjects had malformations in the frontal lobes.

In summary, migrational defects leading to malformations, whether in the cerebellum, limbic system, or cortex, appear to be a somewhat consistent finding in autism. More research with large representative samples is needed to test the extent and consistency of these findings. There may turn out to be several different loci in which early insults can lead to autistic symptoms.

There have been fewer functional than structural neuroimaging studies of autism. Three studies have found brain hypermetabolism in autism (DeVolder, Bol, Michel, Cogneau, & Goffinet, 1987; Minshew, Dombrowski, Panchalingham, & Pettegrew, 1993; Rumsey et al., 1985) and one small study has not (Herold, Frakowiak, LeCouteur, Rutter, & Howlin, 1988). Brain hypermetabolism would be consistent with a hypothesis of less efficient and perhaps less integrated information processing.

In a follow-up analysis of the Rumsey study, Horwitz, Rumsey, Grady, and Rapoport (1988) found significantly lower correlations in autistics vs. controls between frontal and parietal regions, as well as between certain subcortical structures (thalamus, caudate nucleus, and lenticular nucleus) and frontal and parietal regions. Correlated brain activity among brain centers such as these can be thought of as reflecting the integrated function of a distributed processing system; hence, lower correlations would indicate less integrated function, consistent with the hypermetabolism results discussed above. The key question is: Which brain centers are failing in the task of integration? These could be lower centers, such as the neocerebellum, as argued by Courchesne (1991), or they could be higher centers, such as the frontal lobes. Horwitz et al. (1988) interpreted their results as indicating dysfunction in a distributed system that subserves directed attention; however, other neuropsychological interpretations are possible, such as a working memory interpretation.

The recent Minshew et al. (1993) study is of considerable interest because it used a new measure of brain metabolism: *in vivo* ^{31}P nuclear magnetic resonance spectroscopy (MRS), which was recorded from dorsal prefrontal cortex. This technique images various phosphorous-containing compounds such as adenosine triphosphate (ATP), which are critical to neuronal metabolism. The autistic group had decreased levels of several of these phosphorous-containing compounds. Neuropsychological test performance within the autistic group correlated with levels of phosphorous metabolites. Taken together, these results are consistent with a hypothesis of a metabolic disturbance in autism, in the prefrontal cortex and perhaps elsewhere, that exerts a strong effect on cognitive functioning. Because MRS studies have not been done on other parts of the brain in autism, we do not know how widespread this metabolic disturbance is.

In summary, neuroimaging studies of autism have not yet established a consistent morphological or functional correlate of autism. Instead, they have found widespread anomalies, including ventricular enlargement, migrational anomalies, and alterations in brain metabolism. This pattern of results suggests that there is very likely more than one neurological cause for the behavioral phenotype we call autism. It also suggests that a focal lesion hypothesis of autism may be misguided, and that, instead, we perhaps should be thinking of a distributed neural system that plays a key role in the integration of behavior and can be disrupted by a variety of changes in brain development.

Neuropsychological Phenotype. It will be useful in this section to distinguish between developmental and neuropsychological studies of the core deficit in autism, although the two certainly overlap. We will deal first with the developmental research, which has identified an unusual configuration of the impaired and intact early skills that any theory of autism must account for. We will then examine the ability of competing neuropsychological theories to account for this configuration.

As mentioned elsewhere in this chapter, recent research on autism provides an excellent case example of the power of the developmental psychopathology approach. This work is interdisciplinary, involving child clinicians, cognitive developmental psychologists, developmental psycholinguists, and even philosophers and primatologists. Moreover, in this work, the relation between studies of normal and abnormal development is clearly viewed as reciprocal. Not only has autism research drawn on the latest theories and paradigms from studies of normal early development, but also it has become an important stimulus for these studies, as witnessed by the numerous articles on normal children's theory of mind in the recent developmental literature. Autism research has brought the early social and cognitive abilities of normal human infants into sharper relief, making clearer what needs to be explained in early development and which early skills may be useful to examine in both within-species and cross-species comparisons. These research accomplishments have relevance for deep and fundamental questions in psychology and philosophy. For instance, how do we become aware of other minds? What is a person and how do infants form a concept of persons? How does the self develop? What are the cognitive requirements for intersubjectivity and later human relatedness? How are early social and cognitive development intertwined? We touch on the relevance of autism research for these issues in the review that follows.

Theorizing about the nature of the primary behavioral deficit in autism has recently come full circle. Kanner (1943), in the original description of the autistic syndrome, suggested the possibility that autistic children were born "with an innate inability to form the usual, biologically provided affective contact with people" (p. 42). But he also suggested that some of this "disturbance of affective contact" might be due to inadequate social stimulation from parents. A psychogenic hypothesis prevailed during the next two decades in psychoanalytic accounts of autism (e.g., Mahler, 1952). As evidence for an organic etiology of autism accumulated, researchers concerned with the underlying processing deficit shifted their focus to various cognitive possibilities, neglecting Kanner's original insight that the disorder might represent a primary *social* deficit of constitutional origin. Various possible primary cognitive deficits were investigated, including deficits in arousal, language, symbolic thought, memory, and cross-modal processing. However, when autistic children were compared to nonautistic retarded children similar in mental age, few reliable differences were found in these various cognitive processes. Even when reliable differences were found, there were other reasons why the apparent deficit in these areas was unlikely to be primary (Fein, Pennington, Markowitz, Braverman, & Waterhouse, 1986). Specifically, most of these cognitive processes develop after the onset of autistic symptoms, are theoretically inadequate to explain autistic aloofness, cannot be found in all autistic children, and may be the very cognitive abilities that depend most heavily on normal social functioning. Other reasons for regarding the social symptoms as primary in autism include: (a) the dissociability of social and cognitive impairments both within and across developmentally disabled populations; (b) the special difficulty autistic children have with social stimuli; and (c) the rarity of social relatedness deficits, even in severely damaged babies, and its resistance to change in autism.

Research published subsequent to the Fein et al. (1986) review has refined our understanding of which social processes are impaired and intact in autism. We have reviewed this work in later papers (Ozonoff, Pennington, & Rogers, 1990; Rogers & Pennington, 1991) and will summarize it here. Somewhat surprisingly, some early social cognitive processes have proved *not* to be specifically impaired in autism, compared to MA controls. These include attachment behaviors, self-recognition, person recognition, and differential social responsivity. Other early social cognitive processes are specifically impaired: imitation, emotion perception, joint attention, theory of mind, pragmatics, and symbolic play. At a very general level, each of these impaired processes requires representation of another person's underlying mental state (motor intentions, feelings, attentional focus, belief, and knowledge), although the complexity of that mental state obviously varies across these different processes, which also vary in their time of onset in normal development. Following Stern (1985), we can construe each of these early social cognitive processes as an aspect of developing intersubjectivity, and thus recast the primary deficit in autism as an underlying deficit in intersubjectivity, which will manifest itself as a failure on different social tasks at different ages. Thus, autistic children have been described as "behaviorists," whereas normal children are "mentalists," even from a fairly early age (Baron-Cohen, 1989; Bartsch & Wellman, 1989). That is, autistic children's understanding of behavior is based on observable consequences and instrumental contingencies, and we would thus expect social behaviors mediated by such an understanding to be relatively unimpaired in autism. In contrast, social behaviors that require an understanding of mental states are impaired.

The intriguing discovery that autistic children are specifically impaired in theory of mind was made by a group of British researchers (Baron-Cohen, Leslie, & Frith, 1985, 1986). They have since replicated this result with different tasks and different autistic samples (Baron-Cohen, 1989; Perner, Frith, Leslie, & Leekam, 1989). Perhaps the most convincing demonstration of this deficit involves the use of a false belief task. Children were shown a box of a well-known candy, "Smarties" (essentially equivalent to M&Ms), and were asked "What's in here?" All subjects answered "Smarties" or "sweets." They were then shown (and told) that, in fact, the box contained a pencil. After the pencil was put back in the box, they were asked to predict what the next subject would say was in the box, as well as to say what was really in the box. Similar to previous results on other theory of mind tasks, about 80% of the autistic children failed this task, whereas over 80% of the younger language-impaired children (with somewhat *lower* verbal mental ages than the autistic children) passed the task. Normal young children master this task at around age 4, whereas the mean age of the autistic children in this study was around 15 (Perner et al., 1989).

More recent research has extended the number of paradigms on which the autistic deficit in understanding false belief is found, and has clarified which mental states autistics understand and do not understand (see Baron-Cohen, 1993, for a review). Briefly, autistics are unimpaired relative to developmental controls in their understanding of desire, perception, and simple emotions, but are impaired in understanding beliefs, knowledge, cognitive emotions, and the relation between seeing and knowing. Autistics appear to understand that situations and desires can cause emotions, but they do not understand that belief can cause emotions. Thus, a much more differentiated understanding of the early development of mental state concepts is emerging from studies of both autistic and normal children (Wellman, 1990). At this point, a deficit in theory of mind appears to be specific and primary in autism; in addition, this deficit fairly readily explains many other symptoms of the disorder.

However, there is still theoretical disagreement on several issues. Is this theory of mind deficit social or cognitive in nature? How does it relate to the other deficits in imitation, emotion perception, and symbolic play? Is the child's theory of mind really a theory? Could autistic failures on theory of mind tasks really be caused by executive function deficits? Three competing developmental theories of autism have been proposed: (a) a metarepresentation theory (Leslie, 1987), (b) an intersubjectivity theory (Rogers & Pennington, 1991), and (c) an affective theory (Hobson, 1989). Each addresses these issues somewhat differently.

Leslie's (1987) metarepresentation theory ties the development of both theory of mind and symbolic play to a hypothesized milestone in the second year of life, the development of metarepresentation. As described earlier, this is the ability to "decouple" primary, veridical representations from their objective referents so they can be used in pretense. This theory nicely accounts for the theory of mind and symbolic play deficits in autism, but it does not account for the imitation and emotion perception deficits, except by claiming that these are characteristics of minor subtypes of autism. Joint attention deficits in autism might also present some difficulty for this theory, because joint attention (a) emerges in normal development well before the appearance of metarepresentation or theory of other minds and (b) involves affect sharing (Mundy & Sigman, 1989, 1991). The affective component of the development of joint attention is problematic for the metarepresentational account because that account is assiduously cognitive. However, the metarepresentational theory can accommodate the joint attention deficits as early expressions of an innate deficit in a computational module, the "expression-raiser" (EXPRAIS) or decoupler (Uta Frith, personal communication, 1993).

The metarepresentational theory would be problematic if it posited a discontinuity in the development of intersubjectivity. Research indicates a fairly continuous development of intersubjectivity in the first year of life (Bruner, 1991; Stern, 1985); intersubjectivity is likely a precursor to theory of mind. As Bruner (1991) wrote, "You need to climb the ladder of praxis to get to the propositional attitudes"; he felt it is very unlikely that a theory of mind module suddenly turns on in the fourth year of life. Instead, he pointed to the various early social interactions (e.g., imitative episodes) that help infants "realize they are dealing with sentient beings" and shape the development of the child's theory of mind.

To address some of the possible problems in the metarepresentational account, we formulated an intersubjectivity theory (Rogers & Pennington, 1991). In this theory, the development of theory of mind is continuous, and its precursors are observable very early in the first year of life, in the infant's capacity for imitation. Our theory is based on Stern's (1985) theory of the development of intersubjectivity, which traces a continuous line of development from imitation, emotion perception, and joint attention in the first year of life to theory of mind and pragmatics in the second and later years of life. This theory can account for all of the social deficits in autism and their secondary consequences (e.g., deficits in symbolic play). In this theory, unlike the metarepresentational theory, the earliest behavioral deficit expected to occur in autism is in imitation, not in behaviors attributable to EXPRAIS, such as joint attention.

When we recently tested our theory by administering a variety of imitation tasks to high-functioning autistics and IQ-matched, clinical controls, we found clear imitation deficits in the autistic group (Pennington, Rogers, Bennetto, & Ozonoff, 1993). Meltzoff and Gopnik's (1993) recent account of the key role played by imitation in the development of intersubjectivity is similar to our theoretical position (Rogers & Pennington, 1991).

The third theory, that of Hobson (1989, 1991, 1993), regards the deficits in affective connectedness and emotion perception as primary. Hobson likewise argues for a continuous development of intersubjectivity from birth onward, and he focuses on the central role of affective engagement in this process. He argues that a normal infant's capacity for affective engagement is innate and biological, and that this capacity is deficient in autism; in this way, his theory is an elaboration of Kanner's (1943) original hypothesis. Hobson (1991) also argues against regarding the theory of mind as a theory, and feels that theory of mind researchers have focused too narrowly on the development of the propositional attitudes (i.e., belief, desire, and so on—the stuff of folk psychology), neglecting other, earlier psychological attitudes, such as bodily expression or affective attitudes. He argues that conceptual or propositional attitudes arise out of children's earlier experience of affective attitudes in themselves and others.

In summary, Hobson's affective theory and our theory are similar in positing a continuous development of intersubjectivity from birth onward and locating the primary deficit in autism in a very early-appearing behavioral capacity that is crucial for that development. The two theories differ on the nature of that capacity: Hobson focuses on early affective processes and our theory focuses on the cognitive or working memory requirements for these very early social behaviors. Both of these theories differ from the metarepresentational account because of their emphasis on the continuous development of intersubjectivity and on very early-appearing deficits.

The three theories can also be compared in terms of their reliance on philosophical analyses of social skills. The metarepresentational theory and Hobson's affective theory are similar in that they derive from philosophical analysis of social skills, although each relies on different philosophical traditions.

The metarepresentational account (Leslie, 1987) is rooted in the symbolic paradigm (Smolensky, 1988) and begins with an account of competence (in theory of mind) that is based on formal, symbolic accounts of competence. Russell (in press) provides a detailed critique of the philosophical basis of Leslie's theory and an explication of the problems these philosophical commitments entail. In his critique, Russell points out that Leslie's philosophy of mind is essentially Fodorian: nativistic, modular, mechanistic, and propositional. By propositional, he means that the correct description of mental processes is in terms of linguistic propositions similar to those found in the folk psychology of beliefs and desires or in classical, symbolic approaches to artificial intelligence. Russell argues that this is too high a level of description to be developmentally useful: "You will not only tend to ignore these mental processes which look more like action than language (e.g., attention), you will also be unable to dig beneath the level of discursive and explicit thought to find its well-springs in information processing and control" (p. 22).

As Russell also notes, this nativist and modular account says nothing about the mechanisms of developmental change; the theory of mind module just "turns on" at a certain point, either at birth or later. It is a generally recognized weakness of symbolic accounts of competence that they create developmental puzzles: it is difficult to imagine how the formal concepts posited by such accounts develop; for instance, how could a child have half a rule or concept (Bates, Thal, & Marchman, in press; Pennington, Wallach, & Wallach, 1980)?

Hobson's work is likewise rooted in philosophy, but the core philosophical concepts for him are the concepts of person and self. Again, given the formal account of these concepts, it is hard to imagine how they develop; Hobson deals with this problem by postulating that some aspects of personhood are innate. So we can see that theorizing about autism takes us into deep issues about normal early social development and into metatheoretical issues about the relation between formal, philosophical analyses and developmental theories.

Fortunately, these three competing theories can also be evaluated empirically, because they make specific predictions about the associations and dissociations that should occur among the relevant early social and cognitive skills (i.e., imitation, emotion perception, joint attention, theory of mind, nonsocial metarepresentation, symbolic play, and pragmatics) in both normal and autistic development. Longitudinal and cross-sectional studies of these early skills in both autistic and normal children could falsify the predictions of these competing theories.

We now turn from developmental to neuropsychological theories of autism. These are not exclusive categories; for instance, parts of the Rogers and Pennington (1991) theory are neuropsychological. Moreover, another constraint on these developmental theories is (or will be) neurospsychological: which can best be integrated with whatever the aberrant brain mechanisms in autism turn out to be? Let us say, for example, that Panksepp's (Panksepp & Sahley, 1987) neurobiological theory—that autism is an imbalance of endogenous opiates that prevents early social interaction from being reinforcing—turns out to be correct. This particular neurobiological account integrates very nicely with Hobson's affective theory; on this view, autistic infants would lack affective engagement because it provides no reinforcement to them—they would have a primary affective or *connative* deficit. In contrast, the primary, essentially cognitive deficits posited by the other two theories would really be secondary if this account were true.

What are other recent neuropsychological theories of autism? Essentially, there are three. One is that it is a frontal lobe disorder in which the primary deficit is in some aspect of executive functions. A second holds that the primary deficit is in attention/arousal modulation (Courchesne, 1991; Dawson, 1991), possibly due to subcortical dysfunction (e.g., cerebellar). The third maintains that it is a limbic disorder that causes a primary deficit in long-term, episodic memory (Bachevalier, 1991; Boucher & Lewis, 1989). Each of these theories provides a possible link between the developmental and brain results presented above. To be successful, one of the theories must not only provide a convincing account of these results, but also be supported by positive results from studies of both brain mechanisms and neuropsychological functions. We next consider each theory in turn, beginning with the frontal theory.

A frontal theory of autism was originally proposed by Damasio and Maurer (1978); they noted similarities between autistics and patients with acquired frontal lesions in terms of motor symptoms, communication defects, attentional deficits, and ritualistic and compulsive behaviors. They hypothesized that autism results from a neurochemical imbalance in mesolimbic cortex and related subcortical structures, all of which are the main target areas for dopaminergic neurons.

The main empirical support for a frontal theory of autism comes from neuropsychological studies that have documented fairly selective defects in high-functioning autistics on various executive function tasks (Prior & Hoffman, 1990; Rumsey, 1985; Rumsey & Hamberger, 1988; Steel, Gorman, & Flexman, 1984).

We conducted a study of executive functions and social cognition in high-functioning autistics who were compared to controls matched on VIQ, PIQ, age, sex, and race (Ozonoff, Pennington, & Rogers, 1991). As expected, the autistics were significantly worse on measures of social cognition, including measures of theory of mind and emotion perception. What was surprising was that the autistic group was even more consistently impaired on a cognitive measure of executive function, the Tower of Hanoi planning task, in that this task alone better discriminated autistics from controls than the other tasks. We also found the autistic sample to be impaired relative to controls on a second executive function task, the Wisconsin Card Sorting Task, which replicates the results of other studies of high-functioning autistics that have found deficits on this task. Together, these results suggest that: (a) there may be two primary deficits in autism, one in theory of mind and the other in executive function, or (b) the executive function deficits are primary, or (c) both deficits derive from some more basic deficiency in prefrontal functions, for which we currently lack a satisfactory formulation in terms of cognitive processes.

Half of this high-functioning autistic sample also met diagnostic criteria for Asperger's syndrome. When we compared the deficits in these two subgroups, we found that both had clear deficits in executive functions, but only the autistic group had deficits on theory of mind tasks. The Asperger's syndrome group, in contrast, performed like controls on theory of mind tasks, but were deficient on an emotion perception task (Ozonoff,

Rogers, & Pennington, 1991). These results provide evidence for the external validity of the distinction between high-functioning autism and Asperger's syndrome. Moreover, deficits in theory of mind do not appear to be primary in Asperger's syndrome, whereas executive function (EF) deficits do. Thus, across both autism and Asperger's syndrome, EF deficits are more central.

Because all the evidence for EF deficits in autism had come from older samples, we felt it was important to see whether such deficits were also present in younger autistic samples. Perhaps EF deficits were just a consequence of growing up autistic. We also thought it was important to examine a different aspect of social cognition and to use different EF tasks to test the robustness of the relation between EF and social cognition.

McEvoy (McEvoy, Rogers, & Pennington, 1993) studied preschool autistic children on both EF tasks and the Early Social Communication Scales (ESCS) developed by Seibert, Hogan, and Mundy (1987). These scales measure joint attention, social interaction, and behavior regulations. The 17 autistic children met DSM-III-R criteria for autism and scored above 30 on the Childhood Autism Rating Scale (CARS). They also had idiopathic autism; that is, they had been screened for Fragile X, encephalitis, and other medical conditions associated with autism. They were compared to two control groups: (a) a developmentally delayed group, similar in CA and nonverbal ability, and (b) a younger, normally developing group, matched on verbal ability.

The EF tasks in this study were a graded series of 4 object search and alternation tasks, based on nonhuman primate studies of frontal functions (Diamond & Goldman-Rakic, 1989) and piloted so as to cover the developmental range from about 1 to 6 years. The tasks were: the A-not-B task, delayed response, spatial reversal, and alternation. All the tasks involved searching for food rewards under two inverted caps and were designed to involve minimal language comprehension and no language production. In the spatial reversal task, the child does not see the reward being hidden; the reward is hidden on the same side until the child retrieves it successfully 4 times in a row. Then the hiding location is switched. Like the WCST, the spatial reversal task builds up a prepotent response set and then requires the subjects to shift set.

We found that all groups were essentially at ceiling on the two earlier tasks in this series and at floor on the hardest task. On a task of intermediate difficulty, the spatial reversal task, the young autistic children, who made many more perseverative responses, were significantly impaired relative to both control groups. The autistic subjects were also significantly lower than both control groups on the joint attention and social interaction scales of the ESCS, but not on the behavior regulation scale. Moreover, the perseveration score on the spatial reversal task correlated significantly (and negatively) with the joint attention and social interaction measures ($r = -.53$, $p < .001$ and $r = -.44$, $p < .01$, respectively). These relations remained significant after controlling for both verbal ability and group membership.

Ozonoff and colleagues (Ozonoff, Strayer, McMahon, & Filloux, 1994) have begun to dissect the EF deficit in autism using information processing paradigms. They compared nonretarded autistics to Tourette's syndrome children and normal controls on several simple inhibition tasks. The autistics were not impaired on a neutral inhibition condition, but were impaired at inhibiting a previously reinforced response. In contrast, Tourette's syndrome subjects performed similarly to normals on all tasks.

Loisa Bennetto, working with the first author (B.F.P.), has pursued the working memory aspect of the EF deficit in autism. She has used standard working memory (WM) tasks from cognitive psychology (Sentence Span and Counting Span) as well as a memory for temporal order task (Petrides & Milner, 1982), on which patients with prefrontal lesions are selectively impaired. She has found striking deficits on both the WM and temporal order memory tasks in high-functioning autistics, but no deficits in verbal short term memory or recognition memory. Moreover, performance on the WM tasks correlated with performance on EF tasks in the autistic group, as well as with imitation performance, suggesting that a deficit in WM may underlie both the executive and imitation deficits in autism (Pennington, Rogers et al., 1993).

Taken together, these studies indicate that both EF deficits and a relation between such deficits and social cognitive deficits appear to be reliable phenomena in autism.

Separate evidence for both conclusions has been provided by Russell and colleagues. Russell, Mauther, Sharpe, and Tidswell (1991) found a significantly higher rate of perseverative responding in an autistic group on the strategic deception task originally proposed by Premack and Woodruff (1978) to measure theory of mind in nonhuman primates. To evaluate whether the autistics' failure was caused by a theory of mind deficit or just by inability to shift cognitive set away from a present (and salient) stimulus, Russell and colleagues conducted several follow-up experiments (Hughes & Russell, 1993). In the first of these, they manipulated whether the task required deception and whether the subjects' response was manual or verbal, maintaining the key feature that success on the task required inhibiting a response to a salient, visible reward. They found that both autistics and normal three- (but not four-) year-olds continued to fail the task in a perseverative manner. In later experiments, they found a similar problem with mental disengagement on an object retrieval task that did not involve theory of mind or deception (Hughes & Russell, 1993). Thus, failure on theory of mind tasks can be caused by an EF deficit and not by a lack of understanding of others' minds. That is, most theory of mind tasks (like many Piagetian tasks) are conflict tasks in which failures caused by lack of a concept or just by executive or strategic problems in conflict resolution are inherently confounded.

In summary, there are two related but distinguishable ways in which the frontal hypothesis accounts for the intersubjectivity or theory of mind deficit in autism. One is that both executive functions and these aspects of early social cognition may rely on a frontally mediated working memory system, which is important for integrating contextual cues over time and selectively and strategically shifting attentional set in response to context (Pennington, in press).

We actually know very little about the neurological basis of intersubjectivity or theory of mind, although it is known that limbic and orbital-frontal structures play a special role in social behavior. Price et al. (1990) recently reported on two patients with bifrontal lesions acquired early in life. The lesions included paralimbic and heteromodal portions of the frontal lobes, as well as underlying white matter and possibly the basal ganglia. These patients had deficits on role-taking tasks that required theory of mind, as well as deficits in moral reasoning and formal operations. They were not autistic, however. These authors speculated that the frontal lobes may be uniquely important in these kinds of social and cognitive behaviors. If correct, this view would provide support for considering both theory of mind and EF deficits as manifestations of prefrontal dysfunction. Moreover, at a more abstract or deeper level of cognitive analysis, they may involve similar neural computations, which, as far as the brain is concerned, are not specifically cognitive or social.

The other possibility is that many theory of mind tasks may really be EF tasks; Russell's work demonstrates that when the theory of mind component is removed but the element of conflict is maintained, both autistics and young children still fail the task. Consistent with this view, Frye, Zelazo, and Palfai (1992) demonstrated that the normal developmental transition from age 3 to age 4 on theory of mind tasks is attributable to general cognitive changes in the ability to handle more complex rules; in a follow-up study, Zelazo, Frye, and Reznick (in review) demonstrated that the developmental change in rule complexity was mediated in part by a developmental change in executive functions. Taken together, the results of the studies from these two groups of researchers indicate that performance on theory of mind tasks is related to domain general cognitive processes, particularly the executive function of inhibitory control, rather than to a domain-specific cognitive process, such as EXPRAIS. Further work is needed to provide more specific tests of this frontal theory of autism (and theory of mind tasks).

One problem with a frontal hypothesis of autism in particular, and of psychopathology more generally, is that deficits in other neuronal systems may affect frontal functions, producing deficits that are similar to those produced by lesions actually within frontal cortex. Because the prefrontal cortices have broadly integrative functions, it is certainly reasonable that deficient inputs from other systems could disrupt their function, especially in the case of early or nonfocal brain lesions (Goldberg & Bilder, 1987).

This consideration is relevant for next evaluating the attention/arousal modulation theories proposed by Courchesne (1991) and Dawson (1991). In both these theories, processing of the complex, sequential, context-dependent information contained in social interactions is hypothesized to be disrupted in a "bottom-up" fashion by failures in the subcortical systems that are important for attention or arousal modulation. Courchesne (1991) advanced an intriguing neuropsychological theory of autism, and then conducted a behavioral test of this theory. Briefly, he argued that the neocerebellum plays an important coordinating role for the activities of the whole neocortex by synchronizing its arousal; the connectivity of the neocerebellum to the neocortex would permit such a role. The early absence of this neocerebellar coordination in autism would particularly disrupt the processing of sequential information whose significance unfolds over time. Social interaction sequences would be especially vulnerable to such disrupted processing because of their complexity and unpredictability.

Courchesne (1991) tested this theory by comparing the performance of autistics to individuals with late, acquired lesions of the neocerebellum on a vigilance task with superimposed attentional shifts. In this task, the requirement for a voluntary attentional shift between the auditory and visual channels was signaled by a distinctive cue. The critical experimental manipulation was the length of the time interval between the cue and a target in the new channel. The prediction was that neocerebellar lesions would impair attentional shifts only on trials with a brief warning period. Courchesne (1991) found that, unlike controls, both autistics and subjects with acquired neocerebellar lesions were impaired only on these brief trials.

In Dawson's (1991) theory, autistic children are seen as having a primary deficit in arousal regulation and response to novelty. Dawson reviewed evidence suggesting that autistic children have chronic autonomic overarousal and deficient orienting responses to novel stimuli, leaving them with a very narrow range for optimal stimulation. Because, as Dawson argued, social interactions are inherently unpredictable, novel, and arousing, autistic children are hypothesized to be overstimulated by social interactions and thus avoid them. This avoidance of early social interactions leads in turn to secondary deficits in imitation, emotion expression and perception, intersubjectivity, and theory of mind.

On reflection, we can see that Dawson's theory is the opposite of Panksepp's (Panksepp & Sahley, 1987). In Dawson's theory, the autistic child finds social relations too stimulating; in Panksepp's view, they are not stimulating enough. Dawson's theory, like Panksepp's, might be called connative, in that the basic deficit is in motivational rather than cognitive processes. Like Hobson, Dawson postulates that the other deficits found in autism are secondary to this early lack of engagement in social interactions. In terms of brain loci that are consistent with her neuropsychological theory, Dawson (1991) mentioned right hemisphere attention/arousal modulation mechanisms and subcortical centers.

In the third neuropsychological theory, that of Boucher and Lewis (1989) and Bachevalier (1991), autism is viewed as a developmental amnesia resulting from early damage to the limbic memory structures. Boucher (1981a, 1981b; Boucher & Lewis, 1989; Boucher & Warrington, 1976), who tested this theory with neuropsychological measures of memory function, found certain deficits in episodic memory in autistic samples. However, these results must be interpreted in light of the fact that frontal lesions can disrupt the encoding of complex material into memory (so-called frontal "amnesia"), whereas, in limbic amnesia, formation of new declarative memories is impaired regardless of their complexity. (See Shimamura, Janowsky, & Squire, 1991, for a comparison of the effects of frontal and limbic lesions on memory tasks.) Autistic children sometimes evidence extremely good memory for new declarative information (as in delayed echolalia), even though their retrieval of that information may not be appropriate to the situation at hand. Moreover, a recent direct test of this hypothesis using a well-validated memory test, the California Verbal Learning Test, on which limbic amnesics are clearly impaired, failed to find clear memory deficits in autistics (Minshew & Goldstein, 1993). Thus, our reading of the data on memory function in autism is that it is not consistent with the limbic amnesia hypothesis. However, the distinction between frontal and limbic memory deficits remains a lively issue in the cognitive psychology of memory, and a clear test of these competing explanations for autistic memory problems remains to be conducted.

Bachevalier (1991) tested the amnesia hypothesis of autism with an animal model. She found that amygdalohippocampal lesions in infant rhesus monkeys produced, on the delayed nonmatching to sample task, amnesic deficits similar to those produced in adult rhesus monkeys, establishing that it was possible to produce limbic amnesia early in life. Moreover, when the development of these amnesic infant monkeys was followed longitudinally, Bachevalier (1991) found they had abnormal social development, including motor sterotypies, social withdrawal, decreased eye contact, decreased facial expression, and catastrophic reactions, all similar to symptoms observed in autism. Although intriguing, this animal model study does not indicate whether the amnesia caused the autism or whether the limbic lesions also disrupted circuits important for functions other than memory, such as social functions. Kling and Steklis (1976) had found earlier that a combination of orbitofrontal, anterior temporal, and amygdala lesions produced in monkeys social withdrawal similar to that found by Bachevalier (1991), supporting the overall hypothesis that damage to limbic structures can produce autistic symptoms. But neither study tells us which brain structures are critical. For instance, would an early lesion that simply disconnects the limbic system from the prefrontal cortex, without specifically damaging the amygdala and hippocampus, also produce autistic symptoms?

In summary, these competing neuropsychological theories cannot be fully tested without better neuroanatomical and neuroimaging data than we currently possess. It may be that each theory is correct—for a subtype of autism. We still do not have enough constraining data at the developmental, neuropsychological, or neurological levels of analyses to sort out competing theories. However, given new data at each level of analysis, we could support or reject these specific theories.

It is also important to emphasize that recent work has narrowed considerably the set of behavioral phenomena that any adequate theory of autism must explain, so that current competing theories are less discrepant than they once were in terms of which behaviors they address. Moreover, this progress is impressive, given the complexity of the issues involved. As we have discussed, the phenomenon of autism takes us to the heart of metatheoretical and philosophical issues about what a person is, the relation between social and cognitive functions, the relative merits of symbolic versus subsymbolic theories in cognitive psychology, and how we conceptualize brain functions. All of these are key issues for both cognitive neuroscience and developmental psychopathology. As a result, autism research is both extremely exciting and, sometimes, overwhelmingly complex. Nonetheless, we think autism provides at least one case where the developmental psychopathology approach may yield further very impressive returns for basic developmental, cognitive, and neural science.

Dyslexia: A Disorder of Phonological Processes

Dyslexia was first described in 1896 by Kerr and Morgan, and its central research paradigm has been neuropsychological from the beginning. Early on, Hinshelwood (1907) theorized that it was the developmental equivalent of an acquired alexia and postulated that it resulted from a developmental anomaly of the left angular gyrus—a hypothesis that has possibly turned out to be much closer to the mark than early hypotheses for all the other disorders considered in this chapter. Although dyslexia researchers have disagreed about which cognitive processes are central to the disorder, the view that it is a cognitive disorder has remained central. Compared to the other disorders in this chapter, dyslexia research has been much less affected by paradigm shifts within mainstream psychopathology research, and has always had closer ties to behavioral neurology and neuropsychology, and more recently to cognitive psychology. In addition, the emergence of a mature cognitive psychology of reading has allowed recent dyslexia research to progress further than research on other disorders in cognitive domains that are not as well understood, such as the domains of attention and executive functions. Another reason for this greater progress is that the brain systems affected in dyslexia appear to be more modular and less central; we can recall Fodor's (1983) pessimism about the prospects for a neuropsychology of nonmodular, central cognitive processes. The other disorders considered in this chapter—schizophrenia, ADHD, and autism—are all arguably disruptions of such central processes, whereas dyslexia appears to be a circumscribed disruption of a posterior, modular system concerned with phonological processing. Indeed, it could be argued that dyslexia is not a psychopathology at all, because it does not disrupt the overall regulation of behavior. That issue aside, dyslexia does provide a useful contrast to the other disorders considered earlier.

Clinical Description. The key symptoms in dyslexia are difficulties in learning to read and spell, often with relatively better performance in arithmetic. These reading and spelling problems appear to be the consequence of a primary deficit in the phonological coding of written language. Parents and teachers may also report slow reading or writing speed, letter and number reversals, problems memorizing basic math facts, and unusual reading and spelling errors. Some of these impairments may be correlated with dyslexia but not necessarily directly related to the core phonological disorder. These correlated deficits involve impairments in language processes, such as articulation, naming, and verbal short- and long-term memory. Finally, dyslexic individuals may demonstrate problems in reading comprehension, math, and self-esteem, as well as letter reversals and abnormal eye movements during reading. These characteristics are generally considered to be secondary symptoms of the disorder.

Brain Mechanisms. We know less about the neurology of dyslexia than we know about either its genetics or its neuropsychology, but what we do know converges several broad conclusions: (a) electrophysiological and blood flow measures have documented left hemisphere functional differences in dyslexic individuals, particularly in posterior language areas; (b) there is structural evidence of an alteration in the usual posterior cortical asymmetry of the planum temporale; and (c) because this structural difference arises early in brain development, it may lead to more widespread differences in cortical connectivity and function. We also do not know the etiology of the structural differences, but, given the strong evidence that dyslexia is moderately heritable (Pennington, 1989), it is quite plausible that these structural differences are under genetic influence. We do not know whether the structural differences cause the physiologic differences, but this is a very likely inference. First, we will review the structural evidence and then the physiological evidence.

The most direct evidence of structural differences in dyslexic brains has been provided by neuropathological studies conducted by Galaburda and colleagues at Harvard Medical School (Galaburda & Kemper, 1979; Galaburda, Sherman, Rosen, Aboitiz, & Geschwind, 1985). Several autopsies on brains of dyslexic individuals have been conducted by this group. The most consistent finding is symmetry of the planum temporale in all cases. The planum temporale is the superior posterior surface of the temporal lobe. In the left hemisphere, it is part of Wernicke's area, which is involved in phonological processing. This neuropathological result is consistent with the extensive cognitive research on dyslexia, which has found that it is essentially a phonological processing problem.

Ectopias and architectonic dysplasias (i.e., malformations in the arrangement of neurons) were also found by Galaburda; their location has been less consistent across cases, but they are more frequent in left perisylvian regions. It is important to note that the size of these ectopias is smaller than the resolution of the MRI (or CT) scan, so the failure to find such anomalies in the MRI and CT scan studies is not a failure to replicate these autopsy findings. Neuropathological studies provide the most detailed neuroanatomical data, but extreme ascertainment biases are likely in an autopsy group, so confirmation of the planum temporale findings in a representative sample of dyslexic individuals is important.

In vivo structural studies have been conducted using both CT and MRI scans. The results of CT scan studies are less consistent than those of MRI studies. Some studies using CT scans have found alterations in the posterior cerebral asymmetry; others have not. In the majority of normal brains, the posterior left hemisphere is larger than its homologue on the right; in some studies of dyslexics, either symmetry or an opposite asymmetry (R > L) has been found.

Hier, Le May, Rosenberger, and Perlo (1978) found 10 of 24 dyslexic patients had a reversed occipital asymmetry on CT scan; these patients also had a lower mean verbal IQ (VIQ) than the 14 other dyslexic patients. Handedness was not a significant confound in this result. A similar high rate of reversed posterior asymmetry associated with low VIQ was found in a second dyslexic sample by these same investigators (Rosenberger & Hier, 1979). Because similar results were also obtained in an autistic sample (Hier, Le May, & Rosenberger, 1979), reversed occipital asymmetry is not specific to dyslexia. Moreover, a different set of investigators (Haslam, Dalby, Johns, & Rademaker, 1981) failed to find an increased frequency of this same reversed asymmetry or an association between asymmetry and either VIQ or dyslexia subtypes; they did find a higher than normal proportion of dyslexic subjects with symmetry of the occipital widths. In contrast, Roberts, Varney, Reinarz, and Parkens (1988) failed to replicate the finding of either reversed or symmetrical occipital width in a sample of 44 adult dyslexic males in which right- and left-handed dyslexics were examined separately. In sum, the CT scan data are inconsistent; recent MRI scan data are more consistent.

There have been three reported studies of neuroanatomical differences in dyslexia using MRI scans. Rumsey et al. (1986) studied 10 severely dyslexic adult men and failed to find developmental anomalies or pathologic changes, but did find apparent symmetry of temporal lobe volume in 9 of the 10 subjects. However, no measurements of the temporal lobes were reported. Two more recent MRI studies have measured the planum and both have essentially replicated the autopsy finding of altered planum asymmetry in dyslexia. The first study (Larsen, Hoien, Lundberg, & Odegaard, 1990) used MRI to compare left and right planum areas in 19 adolescent dyslexics and controls. They found significant group differences in the pattern of planum asymmetry: 70% of the dyslexics had symmetrical plana, whereas only 30% of the controls did. Moreover, planum symmetry was significantly associated with phonological coding deficits within the dyslexic group. The second study (Hynd, Semrud-Clikeman, Lorys, Novey, & Eliopulas, 1991) measured anterior and posterior width and area, as well as bilateral insular and planum length in 10 severely dyslexic, 10 ADHD, and 10 control children. They found that the dyslexics differed significantly from the other groups both in left planum length and in the pattern of planum asymmetry; the dyslexics had shorter left planum length and only one exhibited the typical L > R planum asymmetry, compared to 70% of each of the comparison groups. The dyslexics also had significantly shorter bilateral insular length than normal controls. Both the dyslexic and ADHD subjects had significantly smaller right anterior widths than normal controls, whereas measures of posterior width and area did not differentiate groups.

Hynd, Marshall, and Semrud-Clikeman (1991) tested relations between brain structures and brain functions, as measured by neuropsychological tests, in this same sample. These neurolinguistic relationships extend beyond the planum and other posterior language structures. Again, in this latter paper, there is an emphasis that a single localized alteration in brain morphology, such as planum symmetry, is unlikely to be sufficient to produce RD, and that, instead, we need to think of a pattern of alterations across several connected cortical zones.

In terms of brain physiology, several technologies have been employed. The results of electrophysiological studies (EEGs and EPs) are generally consistent in showing dyslexic differences in left hemisphere functioning on both reading and nonreading tasks (see Hughes, 1982, for a review). Wood, Flowers, Buchsbaum, and Tallal (1991) reviewed their work using three different physiologic measures of brain function dyslexia: (a) regional cerebral blood flow (rCBF), (b) positron emission tomography (PET), and (c) auditory evoked responses (AERs). Techniques such as these provide an important intervening level of analysis between studies of brain structure on the one hand and studies of behavior on the other. Structural differences do not necessarily lead to behavioral differences; even when they do, we are still uncertain about intervening mechanisms. What we would like to know is how a change in structure affects the neural computations that eventuate in complex behaviors; physiological studies such as these begin to address that issue.

These authors showed how converging results from different functional neuroimaging methods, all addressing multiple cortical regions, can begin to illuminate dyslexic alterations in the pattern of temporal lobe functioning during linguistic tasks. In contrast to normals, dyslexics exhibit effortful, nonautomatic processing in the superior left temporal lobe during a phonemic discrimination task; the pattern of correlations between blood flow task accuracy was negative in normals but positive in dyslexics. On an orthographic task, dyslexics exhibited a displacement of blood flow from superior temporal lobe to angular gyrus, consistent with a different functional organization of the language cortices in dyslexia. These authors also emphasized the methodological issues raised by their work. Finally, Rumsey et al., (1994) recently found similar altered blood flow patterns in posterior left hemisphere in dyslexia on a rhyming task studied with PET scans.

Related work on developmental language disorder (DLD) has also been done, and there are interesting similarities and differences, compared to the dyslexic work. Tallal, Sainburg, and Jernigan (1991) examined brain structure and functioning in DLD. Using MRI scans, they performed volumetric analyses of cortical and subcortical grey matter. They found bilateral volume reduction in DLD children (relative to controls) in the posterior perisylvian region (which includes the planum temporale), as well as subcortical volume reductions in the right diencephalon and caudate. Symmetry differences were found in the prefrontal and superior parietal/parietal-occipital regions. In the former, anterior region, DLDs exhibited a L < R asymmetry, whereas controls were symmetrical; in the latter, posterior region, DLDs had L > R asymmetry, whereas controls had a R > L pattern. These results are somewhat different from those found in dyslexia, but it is important to remember that DLD and dyslexia are distinct, if sometimes overlapping disorders. Moreover, the Tallal et al. (1991) study used different morphometric measures. These authors also reviewed their programmatic work indicating a basic temporal processing deficit in DLD, and offered two interesting theories for relating the structural and behavioral data.

In summary, both structural and physiological studies point to posterior left hemisphere structures, particularly the planum temporale, as being important in the brain mechanisms underlying dyslexia. Yet, structural and physiological differences have been found in other brain regions. For instance, Livingstone, Rosen, Drislane, and Galaburda (1991) recently reported decreased size of magnocellular (but not parvocellular) thalamic neurons in the same dyslexic brains in which the planum symmetry and neocortical ectopias were found.

Moreover, it is problematic theoretically to view planum symmetry per se as the causative neurological substrate in dyslexia (Steinmetz & Galaburda, 1991). Because planum symmetry is present in about 25% of neurologically normal individuals, as well as in left-handed persons (with only some of both groups being dyslexic), planum symmetry alone cannot be sufficient to produce dyslexia. Other possibilities discussed by these authors include planum symmetry's being a cofactor, nonpathological in itself, that limits the ability of the developing brain to compensate for pathological cortical anomalies, or planum symmetry's being a consequence or a correlate of other abnormalities in brain development in dyslexia. As these authors imply, twin studies employing both MRI scans and behavioral measures of dyslexia can help to resolve these issues, because such studies can not only determine the heritability of planum symmetry but also can estimate the extent of genetic covariation between dyslexia and a brain structure, such as the planum.

Neuropsychological Phenotype. The cognitive psychology of reading is a relatively mature field; consequently, our ability to ask and answer refined questions about the underlying deficit in dyslexia is greater than for the other developmental psychopathologies considered in this chapter. We now have a detailed understanding of which components of reading are impaired in dyslexia and of the underlying linguistic influences on that impairment.

In the vast majority of cases, the underlying deficit appears to be in phonological processing skills. That is, dyslexia is basically a subtle language processing disorder (Vellutino, 1979), not a disorder of visual or spatial processing, as has been commonly assumed. A variety of other cognitive explanations have been advanced for dyslexia, including faulty eye movements, vestibular system dysfunction, general problems in rule-learning or conceptual skills, differential sensitivity to certain light frequencies, failure of binocular convergence, problems in foveal vision, and so on. The important point is that none of these other, sometimes esoteric, explanations or treatments of dyslexia enjoys anything like the empirical support that the language processing explanation and corresponding treatments do.

The specificity and nature of the underlying neuropsychological deficit in dyslexia help us think about divisions within both the language and reading systems. Not all the components of the complex information processing system involved in reading are equally impaired in dyslexia. Reading involves: (a) visual perceptual processes to recognize letters, (b) word recognition, and (c) comprehension processes. Research has shown that the locus of difficulty in dyslexia is in word recognition, which Perfetti (1985) called the central recurrent component of reading. Dual process theorists have argued that word recognition can be accomplished either by "direct" access or through phonological coding. Of these two means of word recognition, developmental dyslexia appears to interfere mainly with phonological coding. Deficits in phonological coding (usually measured by nonword reading) are characteristic of the vast majority of developmental dyslexics (Olson, 1985; Stanovich, Nathan, & Vala-Rossi, 1986). These deficits are found when dyslexics are compared to younger normal readers matched for real word reading skill, and thus are unlikely to be just a consequence of dyslexia. Instead, a phonological coding deficit appears to be the proximal cause of dyslexia, at least in most cases.

A recent review (Van Orden, Pennington, & Stone, 1990) questioned the existence of a direct, nonphonological means of word recognition in normals or dyslexics, because there are no positive findings—rather, just inferences from null results—that support the direct access hypothesis. In an elegant series of experiments, Van Orden (1987; Van Orden, Johnston & Hale, 1988; Van Orden et al., 1990) has demonstrated that normal adult readers mistakenly accept homophonic "imposters" ("rows" or "roze" for *rose*) in semantic judgment tasks, and that this mistake is explained by their reliance on phonological coding, rather than by spelling similarity or some other alternative explanation. Van Orden et al. (1990) argued that a single process handles word recognition and that phonological coding is an inevitable aspect of that process. Phonological coding may be more central to both normal and abnormal reading development than previously supposed.

Further evidence for the centrality of phonological coding to word recognition has been provided by behavior genetic analyses of component word recognition processes. Because we now know that dyslexia has a substantial heritable component (DeFries, Fulker, & LaBuda, 1987), we can ask whether the contribution of a given phonological processing skill to dyslexia is likewise heritable. Olson, Wise, Conners, Rack, and Fulker (1989) analyzed the heritability (h^2g) of phonological versus orthographic coding deficits in single-word reading in the dyslexic twin sample studied by DeFries et al. (1987). Quite strikingly, they found significant heritability for phonological coding deficits measured by oral nonword reading speed and accuracy. In contrast, a measure of orthographic coding deficits skill in single-word reading was not found to be heritable. Moreover, the contribution of phonological coding deficits to the heritability of reading disability (RD) in these twins was substantial, whereas the contribution of orthographic coding was essentially zero. More recent analyses with a larger twin sample yielded h^2g estimates($\pm$ standard error) of .44($\pm$.11) for word recognition, .75($\pm$.15) for phonological coding, and .31($\pm$.20 n.s.) for orthographic coding. Again, there was a very substantial genetic overlap between the deficits in word recognition and phonological coding, indicating that the same genes are influencing deficits on both measures (Olson, Gillis, Rack, DeFries, & Fulker, 1991). Moreover, a similar pattern of large heritabilities for deficits in phonological coding and smaller heritabilities for deficits in exception word reading was found by Stevenson (1991) in a separate twin sample. As a further test of the robustness of this pattern of results, Olson et al. (1989), using confirmatory factor analysis, examined the heritability (h^2) of individual differences on phonological and orthographic coding within both the RD and control twin samples. Again, the h^2 estimates for phonological coding (.41 and .52, RD and normal samples, respectively) were significantly larger than those for orthographic coding (.05 and .20). Likewise, the genetic correlations between word recognition and phonological coding (.81 and .68) were significantly larger than those between word recognition and orthographic coding (.45 in both samples). In summary, there is now substantial evidence that dyslexics have heritable deficits in word recognition and phonological coding and that there is a strong genetic correlation between the two.

Thus, dyslexics' problem with word recognition is caused by a deficit in the use of phonological codes to recognize words. Over and over when we read, we must translate printed letter strings into word pronunciations. To do this, we must understand that the alphabet is a code for phonemes, the individual speech sounds in the language, and we must be able to use that code quickly and automatically so that we can concentrate on the meaning of what we read (Liberman, 1973; Liberman & Liberman, 1990; Liberman & Shankweiler, 1979; Liberman, Shankweiler, Fischer, & Carter, 1974). The difficulty that dyslexics have with "phonics," the ability to sound out words, makes reading much slower and less automatic, and detracts considerably from comprehension. Likewise, poor phonics ability makes spelling considerably less accurate and automatic. We do not simply memorize the spelling of words. If so, each new word would be completely novel, with no transfer of information from the words already known. Instead, what we already know about the regularities and exceptions of phonological codes in our language helps us learn and remember the spelling of a new word. Reading and spelling are very closely related; both use the same kind of codes, but in different directions. When we read, we go from letters to phonological representations; when we spell, we go from phonological representations to letters. These codes are probably not represented as explicit rules and exceptions, but, instead, as more implicit patterns of regularities. We know much more than we can say about phonological codes.

Behavior genetic (and other) evidence suggests there is a spoken language problem that leads to this phonological coding problem in written language. We can next ask: How specific is this spoken language problem? Research and clinical experience tell us that dyslexics have a higher rate of spoken language problems (Catts, 1989), including early articulation disorders, name-finding problems, and problems remembering verbal sequences (such as phone numbers, addresses, and the months of the year). Even adult dyslexics frequently mispronounce the name of their disorder, calling it "dylexia" or "dyslectia." It is important to emphasize that these symptoms occur in spontaneous speech and *not* in the context of dealing with the printed word. These spoken language symptoms of dyslexia are easily understood if dyslexia is conceptualized as a phonological processing disorder; they are harder to explain on a visual or other theory of dyslexia.

These various spoken language symptoms of dyslexia can be analyzed further: which are primary, secondary, correlated, and artifactual? One possibility is that all are primary and all are manifestations of a unitary, underlying phonological processing problem. This is an appealing, parsimonious hypothesis that several researchers are pursuing (e.g., Shankweiler & Crain, 1987). However, recent research indicates that even the seemingly narrow domain of phonological processing skills has a complex structure, and that different phonological processing skills have different relations to reading skill and disability. Problems in verbal short-term memory and name retrieval appear to be correlated and/or secondary symptoms, whereas problems in phoneme awareness appear to be primary (Bowey, Cain, & Ryan, 1992; Pennington, Van Orden, Kirson, & Haith, 1991), although the relation between reading and phoneme awareness appears to be one of reciprocal causation.

Consistent with this view, Olson et al. (1989) also found significant ($p < .05$) heritability estimates for the correlation between two different phoneme awareness measures, rhyming fluency (.99 $\pm$ .86) and Pig Latin (.81 $\pm$ .75), and the heritable nonword reading measure. This pattern of results is consistent with the overall argument we are developing here. We expect that the genetic influences on dyslexia do not affect reading directly; instead, they alter the development of spoken language skills that are important for later reading development. These behavior genetic analyses are consistent with the view that the heritable spoken language precursor to dyslexia is a deficit in phoneme awareness, which causes the heritable written language deficit in phonological coding. (The genes influencing dyslexia may also affect other components of early language development.)

We next consider longitudinal evidence bearing on whether phoneme awareness predicts later reading ability and disability, as well as evidence bearing on whether other closely related phonological processing skills, such as phoneme perception, verbal short-term memory, and lexical retrieval also make unique contributions to reading outcome.

In previous longitudinal studies, the strongest evidence for a predictive relation to reading outcome existed for phoneme awareness skills. A number of longitudinal studies (e.g., Liberman et al., 1974; Wallach & Wallach, 1976) found such a predictive relation, with at least 50% of the variance in reading outcome accounted for by phoneme awareness tasks in several studies (Calfee, Lindamood, & Lindamood, 1973; Lundberg, Olofsson, & Wall, 1980; Mann, 1984). However, Calfee et al. (1973) did not control for IQ, and the study by Lundberg et al. (1980) did not control for preexisting reading skill.

The study by Lundberg et al. (1980) tested the predictive relation between phoneme awareness skill and later reading skill using path analysis, and studied a variety of phoneme and syllable manipulation tasks, which involved both synthesis and analysis. The study found little predictive power for syllable or synthesis tasks, but impressive predictiveness for two phoneme analysis tasks: phoneme segmentation and phoneme reversal. This is an important study, but a reanalysis of the data by Wagner and Torgesen (1987) revealed that, when preexisting reading skill was partialled out, the predictiveness of the phoneme awareness tasks was considerably reduced.

Mann's (1984) study both controlled for IQ and screened early readers out of the sample, yet still found an impressive partial correlation of .75 between kindergarten phoneme reversal and first-grade reading achievement.

A study by Bradley and Bryant (1983) was unique in that it combined a longitudinal study with a training study, thus allowing a test of both the direction and specificity of the causal relation between phoneme awareness skills and reading outcome. The results supported a specific, causal relation between preschool phoneme awareness and later reading skill.

Two recent longitudinal studies have extended the predictive relation between phoneme awareness and later reading skill downward into the earlier preschool period. Maclean, Bryant, and Bradley (1987) found about a third of a broad sample of normal children showed evidence of some degree of phoneme awareness before age 4, and that early phoneme awareness skill was significantly related to later reading (but not arithmetic) skill, even when age, IQ, and maternal education were partialled out. In addition, early knowledge of nursery rhymes predicted later phoneme awareness skill. Similar results were obtained by Stuart and Coltheart (1988). Thus, it is possible that the behavioral precursor to dyslexia might be observable before age 4.

An early behavioral precursor to dyslexia was found in data from a longitudinal study of children at high familial risk for dyslexia. The study began when the children were 2½ years old (Scarborough, 1991). The future dyslexic subjects were significantly worse than both siblings and normal risk subjects on measures of natural language production (expressive syntax), but not on formal language measures. Nursery rhyme knowledge or other early measures of phoneme awareness were not evaluated in this study, so we do not know whether a deficit in phoneme awareness is detectable this early in dyslexic development. Scarborough's results argue for a wider range of early language deficits in dyslexia. However, these early deficits in syntax were no longer detectable at ages 4 and 5.

In contrast to the strong predictive relation between phoneme awareness and later reading skill, the unique predictiveness of other phonological processing skills is less strong, or absent, especially once the effect of phoneme awareness is accounted for. (See Pennington, Van Orden et al., 1991, for a review.) For instance, Mann and Ditunno (1989) included all four phonological processing skills discussed earlier (phoneme perception, phoneme awareness, verbal STM, and naming speed) in a longitudinal study with two cohorts. Phoneme perception was not predictive in either cohort, and verbal STM and naming speed were predictive in only one, but phoneme awareness was predictive in both. Moreover, phoneme awareness accounted for a very large portion of unique variance in reading outcome (e.g., 58% in one cohort), whereas the contributions of verbal STM and naming speed were much smaller.

In summary, previous longitudinal studies strongly suggest that phoneme awareness is a prerequisite or at least a facilitator of later reading skill. The training study by Bradley and Bryant (1983) helped to rule out the "third variable" or correlate relation, but a longitudinal study of all four phonological processing skills is still needed to completely address this possibility. In addition, it is not entirely clear from these studies whether phoneme awareness has the same predictive relation for developmental dyslexia that it does for later reading skill. Do the same processes underlie both dyslexic and normal reading? Are dyslexics at the low end of the same continuum as normal readers, or are different cognitive processes involved in reading success (Stanovich, 1986)? The existing research data do not permit a clear answer to these questions. We are currently conducting a longitudinal study comparing children at low and high family risk for dyslexia to help answer these questions.

It is also important to mention that there is evidence that naming speed may contribute to individual differences in component reading processes separate from those influenced by phoneme awareness. Both Bowers and Swanson (1991) and Lovett (1987) have found that naming speed is related to speed of word recognition and to reading comprehension; in phoneme awareness, accuracy is related to accuracy in both phonological coding and word recognition. Even though the largest contributor to individual differences in overall reading skill appears to be phoneme awareness, other phonological processes may influence particular component reading processes. Some of these, like naming speed, may be especially important for the development of automaticity in reading.

In summary, studies of cognitive and linguistic processes in dyslexia have clearly identified word recognition as the locus of difficulty, which is caused by a deficit in the phonological coding of written language (usually measured by nonword reading). Underlying this deficit in phonological coding is a spoken language deficit in the specific skill of phoneme segmentation. These results converge nicely with the behavior, genetic, and neuroanatomical results we have just reviewed. We can summarize all this information as suggesting that the genetic influences on dyslexia affect the development of the planum temporale, resulting in altered planum symmetry. Those alterations in planum structure (and connectivity) lead to phonological processing problems in both spoken and written language. Those phonological processing problems, which are primary in disrupting reading, lie in phoneme segmentation that causes problems in phonological coding. Undoubtedly, however, these genetic and neuroanatomical differences can also lead to correlated symptoms in other phonological and perhaps even nonphonological cognitive processes.

It is important to emphasize here that the development of phoneme segmentation can also be retarded by lack of sociocultural stimulation. Thus, subcultural variations in the early literacy skill experiences provided for preschoolers can produce a phenocopy of dyslexia in some children. Across languages and socioeconomic levels, poor readers have problems with phoneme segmentation skills. Some of these problems are caused by biological variation, some by deficient early stimulation, and some by simply not reading. In this regard, phoneme segmentation is a special language skill because it is not necessary for spoken language.

IMPLICATIONS FOR FUTURE RESEARCH

The overall thrust of this chapter has been to demonstrate the value of a neuropsychological approach to research on developmental psychopathology; less emphasized, but equally important, is a reciprocal relation—the relevance of developmental psychopathologies for key issues in neuroscience. Although the mainstay of traditional neuropsychology has been the study of the effects of acquired lesions in mature humans and nonhumans, such lesion studies are not particularly informative about how the nervous system is constructed, because acquired lesions frequently "cut across the grain" of developmental components. In contrast, a genetic lesion can be exquisitely precise, affecting a single developmental pathway that runs from gene to brain to behavior. However, there has been considerably less research on the neuropsychology of genetic disorders than on the effects of acquired lesions in adults, partly because of difficulties inherent to developmental neuropsychology and partly because well-characterized genetic disorders have become available for study only more recently. Thus, one strong implication for future research is that at least certain developmental psychopathologies will provide important insights for neuroscience.

Not all neurogenetic disorders will be equally informative about the mechanisms of brain and behavioral development; in some, the effect on development is both global and catastrophic. However, even in some severe retardation syndromes, such as Lesch-Nyan, Fragile X, and Down syndromes, there are specific lessons to be learned about the developmental pathways that run from genes to brain to behavior. For instance, the Fragile X gene, which was recently sequenced, includes repeated C-G-G sequences (Verkerk et al., 1991). Those with Fragile X have an abnormally large number of repeats, and that number varies among affected individuals. This genetic breakthrough potentially provides a clearer explanation for the wide range of phenotypic involvement among affected individuals, but, even more importantly, it is the beginning of a fundamental understanding of the mechanisms of both the disorder and aspects of normal intellectual development. As the above example illustrates, unlocking the lessons potentially available in developmental pathologies requires technical advances that have only recently become available. Three key technical advances—in molecular genetics, in brain imaging, and in neural network connectionist models—all have considerable significance for advancing our understanding of abnormal and normal brain-behavior development. By using these techniques in concert, a much more profound understanding of particular developmental psychopathologies is potentially within our grasp. We will sketch out an example of how such a concerted research program might look, using a disorder, dyslexia, in which parts of this research program are already in place.

As noted earlier, considerable progress in understanding the genetics of dyslexia has already been made. (See Pennington, 1989, for a review.) We know that dyslexia is familial, and heritable in part, and that the transmission in some families, if not a majority of families, follows a major gene pattern of transmission (Pennington, Gilger et al., 1991). Genetic linkage analyses have now identified a possible major locus influencing dyslexia on the shortarm chromosome 6 (Cardon, Smith et al., 1994). This result was found in two independent samples of sibling pairs, replicated across genetic markers, and was highly significant.

One of the samples studied for linkage was dizygotic (DZ) twin pairs (in which at least one twin is dyslexic) and their siblings. At the same time, these twins, as well as monozygotic (MZ) dyslexic twin pairs and MZ and DZ control pairs, are being studied with an extensive battery of neuropsychological measures, targeting both executive functions and linguistic processes important for reading. Thus, the study combines the techniques of molecular and behavior genetics with neuropsychology. We have now expanded this project to include a brain imaging component in which dyslexic twin pairs are being studied with MRI. By nesting a brain imaging study within a twin study of this kind, it will be possible to study the heritability and environmentality of particular brain-behavior relations. There is also the potential to identify specific genetic loci influencing brain-behavior relations, such as those influencing a hypothesized relation between alterations in planum temporale morphology and phonological processes in reading. If such loci were identified and sequenced, considerable insights into the neurobiology of normal and abnormal language development would be gained.

The last component of this concerted research effort would involve the use of neural network models to help us understand how alterations in brain structure could lead to the particular alterations observed in dyslexic reading. Two neural network simulations of normal and abnormal reading have recently been published (Hinton & Shallice, 1991; Seidenberg & McClelland, 1989). As our knowledge of brain structural differences in dyslexia becomes clearer, such knowledge could provide an additional constraint on a neural network model of developmental dyslexia.

Although we have highlighted the role that three new technical advances can play in further understanding dyslexia, it is very important to point out the foundation that had already been provided by basic cognitive and developmental research on normal and abnormal reading. This research provided a specific and well-characterized behavioral phenotype to which the techniques of molecular genetics and neuroscience can be applied. Behavioral scientists will continue to have a very important role to play in developing a comprehensive understanding of normal and abnormal behavior.

The general neuroscientific strategy sketched above could easily be applied to other developmental psychopathologies discussed in this and other chapters. One benefit of this strategy that should be highlighted is that it can potentially provide a much clearer understanding of environmental influences on normal and abnormal behavioral development. Longitudinal studies of subjects classified according to both genetic and environmental risk for a given disorder can be potentially illuminating about both the size of the genetic and environmental main effects and the particulars of their interaction. Ideally, genetic risk would be measured by the presence or absence of a genetic marker for the disorder; in the absence of a marker, family history could provide a cruder measure of genetic risk. Ottman (1990) nicely outlined five different testable models of genetic-environment relations in the etiology of disorder; her examples focus on diseases such as skin cancer and emphysema, but her conceptual framework is readily applicable to developmental psychopathologies. Only by controlling for genetic effects can we get clear answers about environmental effects on psychopathology.

Another broad implication of the work reviewed here is the value of considering various developmental psychopathologies to be *cognitive* disorders and pursuing which cognitive processes are deficient and what their brain bases are. For some disorders, this is clearly a paradigm shift away from previous conceptualizations. In this regard, we have tried to demonstrate how research on frontal lobe functions appears to be central to understanding several developmental psychopathologies. We have also emphasized the questions and issues raised by a frontal hypothesis: the discriminant validity problem (how can all these different disorders be frontal?) and the possibility of producing frontal symptoms by nonfrontal lesions. Nonetheless, further research on the normal and abnormal development of frontal functions appears to hold great promise for both developmental psychopathology and developmental psychology generally. For instance, the construct of working memory may provide a unified explanation of both developmental and individual differences in intelligence (see Pennington, in press).

This chapter has reviewed the use of neuropsychology in developmental psychopathology with two broad aims in mind: (a) to provide a current review of the use of neuropsychology in the analysis of several specific disorders and (b) to provide a general view of the relevance of neuroscience for research on developmental psychopathology and of the place of neuropsychology within neuroscience. In closing, it is interesting to note that both neuropsychology and developmental psychopathology are interdisciplines, lying at the intersection of several established, and traditionally separate, disciplines. They thus inherit whatever conceptual and methodological problems divide the separate disciplines, but they also hold out an exciting possibility for a new integration. In bringing together the two interdisciplines of neuropsychology and developmental psychopathology, we are generally more excited by the latter than daunted by the former.

REFERENCES

Aarkrog, D. (1968). Organic factors in infantile psychosis and borderline psychosis. *Danish Medical Bulletin, 11,* 283–287.

Abrams, R., & Taylor, M. (1981). Importance of schizophrenic symptoms in diagnosis of mania. *American Journal of Psychiatry, 138,* 658–661.

Adler, L., Pachtman, E., Franks, R., Pecevich, M., Waldo, M., & Freedman, R. (1982). Neurophysiological evidence for a defect in neuronal mechanisms involved in sensory gating in schizophrenia. *Biological Psychiatry, 17,* 639–654.

Adler, L., Rose, G., & Freedman, R. (1986). Neurophysiological studies of sensory gating in rats: Effects of amphetamine, phencyclidine, and haloperidol. *Biological Psychiatry, 21,* 787–798.

Aitken, K. J. (1991). Examining the evidence for a common structural basis to autism. *Developmental Medicine and Child Neurology, 33,* 930–938.

Allen, H. A. (1984). Positive and negative symptoms and the thematic organization of schizophrenic speech. *British Journal of Psychiatry, 144,* 611–617.

Andreasen, N. (1988). Brain imaging: Applications in psychiatry. *Science, 239,* 1381–1388.

Arbib, M. A. (1989). *The metaphorical brain 2.* New York: Wiley.

Asarnow, R., & MacCrimmon, D. (1978). Residual performance deficit in clinically remitted schizophrenics: A marker of schizophrenia? *Abnormal Psychology, 87,* 597–608.

Bachevalier, J. (1991). An animal model for childhood autism memory loss and socioemotional disturbances following neonatal damage to the limbic system in monkeys. In C. A. Tamminga & S. C. Schulz (Eds.), *Advances in neuropsychiatry and psychopharmacology: Vol. I. Schizophrenia research* (pp. 129–140). New York: Raven Press.

Baddeley, A. D. (1986). *Working memory.* Oxford, England: Clarendon Press.

Baker, N., Adler, L., Franks, R., Waldo, M., Berry, S., Nagamoto, H., Muckle, A., & Freedman, R. (1987). Neurophysiological assessment of sensory gating in psychiatric inpatients: Comparison between schizophrenia and other diagnoses. *Biological Psychiatry, 22,* 603–617.

Barkley, R. A. (1977). The effects of methylphenidate on various types of activity level and attention in hyperkinetic children. *Journal of Abnormal Child Psychology, 5,* 351–369.

Baron-Cohen, S. (1989). Are autistic children behaviorists? An examination of their mental-physical and appearance-reality distinctions. *Journal of Autism and Developmental Disorders, 19,* 579–600.

Baron-Cohen, S. (1993). From attention-goal psychology to belief-desire psychology: The development of a theory of mind and its dysfunction. In S. Baron-Cohen, M. Tager-Flusberg, & D. S. Cohen (Eds.), *Understanding other minds* (pp. 59–82). Oxford: Oxford University Press.

Baron-Cohen, S., Leslie, A. M., & Frith, U. (1985). Does the autistic child have a "theory of mind"? *Cognition, 21,* 37–46.

Baron-Cohen, S., Leslie, A. M., & Frith, U. (1986). Mechanical, behavioral and intentional understanding of picture stories in autistic children. *British Journal of Developmental Psychology, 4,* 113–125.

Bartsch, K., & Wellman, H. (1989). Young children's attribution of action to beliefs and desires. *Child Development, 60,* 946–964.

Bates, E., Thal, D., & Marchman, V. (in press). Symbols and syntax: A Darwinian approach to language development. In N. Krasnegor, D. Rumbaugh, R. Schiefelbusch, & M. Studdert-Kennedy (Eds.), *Behavioral foundation of language.* Hillsdale, NJ: Erlbaum.

Bauman, M., & Kemper, T. L. (1985). Histoanatomic observations of the brain in early infantile autism. *Neurology, 35,* 866–874.

Beitchman, J. H., Nair, R., Clegg, M., Ferguson, B., & Patel, P. G. (1986). Prevalence of psychiatric disorders in children with speech and language disorders. *Journal of the American Academy of Child Psychiatry, 25,* 528–535.

Benes, F., Davidson, J., & Bird, E. (1986). Quantitative cytoarchitectural studies of the cerebral cortex of schizophrenics. *Archives of General Psychiatry, 43,* 31–35.

Berman, K. F., Illowsky, B. P., & Weinberger, D. R. (1988). Physiologic dysfunction of dorsolateral prefrontal cortex in schizophrenia: IV. Further evidence for regional and behavioral specificity. *Archives of General Psychiatry, 45,* 616–622.

Berman, K. F., Zec, R. F., & Weinberger, D. R. (1986). Physiologic dysfunction of dorsolateral prefrontal cortex in schizophrenia: II. Role of neuroleptic treatment, attention, and mental effort. *Archives of General Psychiatry, 43,* 126–135.

Bogerts, B., Meertz, E., & Schonfeldt-Bausch, R. (1985). Basal ganglia and limbic system pathology in schizophrenia: A morphometric study of brain volume and shrinkage. *Archives of General Psychiatry, 42,* 784–791.

Bornstein, R. A., Nasrallah, H. A., Olson, S. C., Coffman, J. A., Torello, M., & Schwarzkopf, S. B. (1990). Neuropsychological deficit in schizophrenia subtypes: Paranoid, nonparanoid, and schizoaffective subgroups. *Psychiatric Research, 31,* 15–21.

Boucher, L. (1981a). Memory for recent events in autistic children. *Journal of Childhood Schizophrenia, 11,* 293–302.

Boucher, L. (1981b). Memory impairment in relatively high functioning autistics. *Journal of Child Psychology and Psychiatry, 30,* 99–122.

Boucher, L., & Lewis, J. (1989). Memory impairment in relatively high functioning autism. *Journal of Child Psychology and Psychiatry, 30,* 99–122.

Boucher, L., & Warrington, E. K. (1976). Memory deficits in infantile autism: Some similarities to the amnesic syndrome. *Journal of Psychology, 67,* 73–87.

Bowers, P. G., & Swanson, L. B. (1991). Naming speed deficits in reading disability: Multiple measures of a singular process. *Journal of Experimental Child Psychology, 51,* 195–219.

Bowey, J. A., Cain, M. T., & Ryan, S. M. (1992). A reading-level design study of phonological skills underlying fourth-grade children's word reading difficulties. *Child Development, 63,* 999–1011.

Bradley, L., & Bryant, P. E. (1983). Categorizing sounds and learning to read: A causal connection. *Nature, 301,* 419–421.

Braff, D., & Saccuzzo, D. (1982). Effect of antipsychotic medication: Speed of information processing in schizophrenic patients. *American Journal of Psychiatry, 139,* 1127–1130.

Bruner, J. (1991, April). *Discussion of Development of Theory of Mind Symposium.* Paper presented to the Society for Research in Child Development, Seattle, WA.

Bruton, C., Crow, T., Frith, C., Johnstone, E., Owens, D., & Roberts, G. (1990). Schizophrenia and the brain: A prospective clinico-neuropathological study. *Psychological Medicine, 20,* 285–304.

Bryant, P., & Bradley, L. (1985). *Children's reading problems.* Oxford, England: Blackwell.

Burg, C., Rapoport, J., Bartley, L., Quinn, P., & Timmins, P. (1980). Newborn minor physical anomalies and problem behavior at age 3. *American Journal of Psychiatry, 137,* 791–796.

Calfee, R. C., Lindamood, P., & Lindamood, C. (1973). Acoustic-phonetic skills and reading—Kindergarten through twelfth grade. *Journal of Educational Psychology, 64,* 293–298.

Campbell, M., Rosenbloom, S., Perry, R., George, A. E., Kircheff, I. I., Anderson, L., Small, A. M., & Jennings, S. L. (1982). Computerized axial tomography in young autistic children. *American Journal of Psychiatry, 139,* 507–512.

Cardon, L. R., Smith, S. D., Fulker, D. W., Kimberling, W. J., Pennington, B. F., & DeFries, J. C. (1994). Quantitative trait locus for reading disability on chromosome 6. *Science, 266,* 276–279.

Carpenter, P. A., & Just, M. A. (1989). The role of working memory in language comprehension. In D. Klahr & K. Kotovsky (Eds.), *Complex information processing: The impact of Herbert A. Simon* (pp. 31–68). Hillsdale, NJ: Erlbaum.

Carpenter, P. A., Just, M. A., & Shell, P. (1990). What one intelligence test measures: A theoretical account of the processing in the Raven Progressive Matrices Test. *Psychological Review, 97,* 404–431.

Case, R., Kurland, M., & Goldberg, J. (1982). Operational efficiency and the growth of short-term memory span. *Journal of Experimental Child Psychology, 33,* 386–404.

Catts, H. W. (1989). Phonological processing deficits and reading disabilities. In A. G. Kamhi & H. W. Catts (Eds.), *Reading disabilities: A developmental language perspective* (pp. 101–132). Boston: College-Hill.

Changeaux, J. P. (1985). *Neuronal man.* New York: Oxford University Press.

Chelune, G. J., & Baer, R. L. (1986). Developmental norms for the Wisconsin Card Sorting Test. *Journal of Clinical and Experimental Neuropsychology, 8,* 219–228.

Churchland, P. M. (1988). *Matter and consciousness.* Cambridge, MA: MIT Press.

Churchland, P. S. (1986). *Neurophilosophy.* Cambridge, MA: MIT Press.

Cicchetti, D. (1984). The emergence of developmental psychopathology. *Child Development, 55,* 1–7.

Clementz, B., & Sweeney, J. (1990). Is eye movement dysfunction a biological marker for schizophrenia? A methodological review. *Psychological Bulletin, 108,* 77–92.

Cohen, J. D., & Servan-Schreiber, D. (1992). Context, cortex, and dopamine: A connectionist approach to behavior and biology in schizophrenia. *Psychological Review, 99,* 45–77.

Colter, N., Bruton, C., Johnstone, E., Roberts, G., Brown, R., & Crow, T. (1987). Neuropathology of schizophrenia: II. Lateral ventricle. *Neuropathology in Applied Neurobiology, 13,* 499–500.

Conners, C. K. (1970). Symptom patterns in hyperkinetic, neurotic, and normal children. *Child Development, 41,* 667–682.

Conners, C. K. (1975). Minimal brain dysfunction and psychopathology in children. In A. Davids (Ed.), *Child personality and psychopathology: Current topics.* New York: Wiley.

Conners, C. K., & Wells, K. C. (1986). *Hyperkinetic children: A neuropsychosocial approach.* Beverly Hills, CA: Sage.

Conrad, A., & Scheibel, A. (1987). Schizophrenia and the hippocampus: The embryological hypothesis extended. *Schizophrenia Bulletin, 13,* 577–587.

Courchesne, E. (1991, April). *The theory of mind deficit in autism: Possible biological bases.* Paper presented to the Society for Research in Child Development, Seattle, WA.

Courchesne, E., Yeung-Courchesne, R., Press, G. A., Hesselink, J. R., & Jernigan, T. L. (1988). Hypoplasia of cerebellar vermal lobules VI and VII in autism. *The New England Journal of Medicine, 318,* 1349–1354.

Creasey, H., Rumsey, T. M., & Schwartz, M. (1986). Brain morphometry in autistic men as measured by volumetric computed tomography. *Archives of Neurology, 43,* 669–672.

Cromwell, R., Baumeister, A., & Hawkins, W. (1963). Research in activity level. In N. Ellis (Ed.), *Handbook of mental deficiency* (pp. 632–663). New York: McGraw-Hill.

Damasio, A. R., & Maurer, R. G. (1978). A neurological model for childhood autism. *Archives of Neurology, 35,* 777–786.

Damasio, A. R., Maurer, R. G., Damasio, A. R., & Chui, H. C. (1980). Computerized tomography scan findings in patients with autistic behavior. *Archives of Neurology, 37,* 504–510.

Dawson, G. (1991). A psychobiological perspective on the early socioemotional development of children with autism. In D. Cicchetti & S. L. Toth (Eds.), *Rochester Symposium on Developmental Psychopathology* (Vol. 3, pp. 207–234). Rochester, NY: University of Rochester Press.

DeFries, J. C., Fulker, D. W., & LaBuda, M. C. (1987). Reading disability in twins: Evidence for a genetic etiology. *Nature, 329,* 537–539.

Dennett, D. C. (1987). *The intentional stance.* Cambridge, MA: MIT Press.

DeVolder, A., Bol, A., Michel, C., Cogneau, M., & Goffinet, A. M. (1987). Brain glucose metabolism in children with the autistic syndrome: Positron tomography analysis. *Brain and Development, 9,* 581–587.

Diamond, A., & Goldman-Rakic, P. S. (1989). Comparison of human infants and rhesus monkeys on Piaget's AB task: Evidence for dependence on dorsolateral prefrontal cortex. *Experimental Brain Research, 74,* 24–40.

Douglas, V. I. (1972). Stop, look, and listen: The problem of sustained attention and impulse control in hyperactive and normal children. *Canadian Journal of Behavioral Science, 4,* 259–282.

Douglas, V. I. (1984). Attentional and cognitive problems. In M. Rutter (Ed.), *Developmental neuropsychiatry* (pp. 280–329). New York: Guilford.

Douglas, V. I. (1988). Cognitive deficits in children with attention deficit disorder with hyperactivity. In L. M. Bloomingdale & J. Sergeant (Eds.), *Attention deficit disorder: Criteria, cognition, intervention* (pp. 65–81). Oxford, England: Pergamon.

Douglas, V. I., & Peters, K. G. (1979). Toward a clearer definition of the attentional deficit of hyperactive children. In G. A. Hale & M. Lewis (Eds.), *Attention and cognitive development* (pp. 173–247). New York: Plenum.

Drewe, E. A. (1975). Go-no-go learning after frontal lobe lesions in humans. *Cortex, 11,* 8–16.

Eccles, J. (1969). *The inhibitory pathways of the central nervous system.* Liverpool, England: Liverpool University Press.

Edelman, G. M. (1987). *Neural Darwinism.* New York: Basic Books.

Eimas, P. (1974). Linguistic processing of speech by young infants. In R. Schiefelbusch & L. Lloyd (Eds.), *Language perspectives: Acquisition, retardation and intervention* (pp. 55–74). Baltimore: University Park Press.

Falkai, P., Bogerts, B., & Rozumek, M. (1988). Limbic pathology in schizophrenia: The entorhinal region—a morphometric study. *Biological Psychiatry, 24,* 515–521.

Fein, D., Pennington, B. F., Markowitz, P., Braverman, M., & Waterhouse, L. (1986). Towards a neuropsychological model of infantile autism: Are the social deficits primary? *Journal of the American Academy of Child Psychiatry, 25,* 198–212.

Ferguson, H. B., & Rapoport, J. L. (1983). Nosological issues and biological validation. In M. Rutter (Ed.), *Developmental neuropsychiatry* (pp. 369–384). New York: Guilford.

Fey, E. T. (1951). The performance of young schizophrenics and young normals on the Wisconsin Card Sorting Test. *Journal of Consulting Psychology, 15,* 311–319.

Filipek, P. A., Kennedy, D. N., & Caviness, V. S. (1992). Neuroimaging in child neuropsychology. In I. Rapin & S. J. Segalowitz (Eds.), *Handbook of neurology: Vol. 6. Child neuropsychology.* New York: Elsevier.

Fodor, J. A. (1983). *The modularity of mind.* Cambridge, MA: MIT Press.

Franks, R., Adler, L., Waldo, M., Alpert, J., & Freedman, R. (1983). Neurophysiological studies of sensory gating in mania: Comparison with schizophrenia. *Biological Psychiatry, 18,* 989–1005.

Freedman, R., Adler, L., Gerhardt, G., Waldo, M., Baker, J., Rose, G., Drebing, C., Nagamoto, H., Bickford-Wimmer, P., & Franks, R. (1987). Neurobiological studies of sensory gating in schizophrenia. *Schizophrenia Bulletin, 13,* 669–677.

Freedman, R., Adler, L., Waldo, M., Pachtman, E., & Franks, R. (1983). Neurophysiological evidence for a defect in inhibitory pathways in schizophrenia: Comparison of medicated and drug-free patients. *Biological Psychiatry, 18,* 537–551.

Frith, C. D., & Frith, U. (1991). Elective affinities in schizophrenia and autism. In P. E. Bebbington (Ed.), *Social psychiatry: Theory, methodology and practice* (pp. 65–68). New Brunswick, NJ: Transaction.

Frye, D., Zelazo, P. D., & Palfai, T. (1992). *The cognitive basis of theory of mind.* Manuscript under review.

Gaffney, G. R., Kuperman, S., Tsai, L. Y., & Minchin, S. (1989). Forebrain structure in autism. *Journal of the American Academy of Child and Adolescent Psychiatry, 28,* 534–537.

Galaburda, A. M., & Kemper, T. L. (1979). Cytoarchitectonic abnormalities in developmental dyslexia: A case study. *Annals of Neurology, 6,* 94–100.

Galaburda, A. M., Sherman, G. F., Rosen, G. D., Aboitiz, F., & Geschwind, N. (1985). Developmental dyslexia: Four consecutive patients with cortical anomalies. *Annals of Neurology, 18,* 222–232.

Goldberg, T. E., Berman, K. F., Mohr, E., & Weinberger, D. R. (1990). Regional cerebral blood flow and cognitive function in Huntington's disease and schizophrenia: A comparison of patients matched for performance on a prefrontal-type task. *Archives of Neurology, 47,* 418–422.

Goldberg, T. E., & Bilder, R. M. (1987). The frontal lobes and hierarchical organization of cognitive control. In E. Perecman (Ed.), *The frontal lobes revisited* (pp. 159–187). New York: IRBN Press.

Goldberg, T. E., & Weinberger, D. R. (1988). Probing prefrontal function in schizophrenia with neuropsychological paradigms. *Schizophrenia Bulletin, 14,* 179–183.

Goldberg, T. E., Weinberger, D. R., Berman, K. F., Pliskin, N. H., & Podd, M. H. (1987). Further evidence for dementia of the prefrontal type in schizophrenia? *Archives of General Psychiatry, 44,* 1008–1014.

Goldman-Rakic, P. (1987). Development of cortical circuitry and cognitive function. *Child Development, 58,* 601–622.

Goldman-Rakic, P. (1988). Topography of cognition: Parallel distributed networks in primate association cortex. *Annual Review of Psychology, 11,* 137–156.

Goldman-Rakic, P. S. (in press). Prefrontal cortical dysfunction in schizophrenia: The relevance of working memory. In B. Carroll (Ed.), *Psychopathology and the brain.* New York: Raven Press.

Goldman-Rakic, P. S., & Friedman, H. R. (1991). The circuitry of working memory revealed by anatomy and metabolic imaging. In H. Levin, H. M. Eisenberg, & A. L. Benton (Eds.), *Frontal lobe function and dysfunction* (pp. 72–91). New York: Oxford University Press.

Grant, D., & Berg, E. (1948). A behavioral analysis of degree of reinforcement and ease of shifting to new responses in a Weigle-type card-sorting problem. *Journal of Experimental Psychology, 38,* 404–411.

Greenough, W. T., Black, J. E., & Wallace, C. S. (1987). Experience and brain development. *Child Development, 58,* 439–459.

Gruzlier, J. (1975). The cardiac responses of schizophrenics to orienting, signal, and non-signal tones. *Biological Psychiatry, 3,* 143–155.

Gur, R. E., Gur, R. C., Skolnick, B. E., Caroff, S., Obrist, W. D., Resnick, S., & Reivich, M. (1985). Brain function in psychiatric disorders: III. Regional cerebral blood flow in unmedicated schizophrenics. *Archives of General Psychiatry, 42,* 329–334.

Harcherick, D. F., Cohen, D. J., Ort, S., Paul, R., Shaywitz, B. A., Volkmar, F. R., Rothman, S. L. G., & Leckman, T. F. (1985). Computed tomographic brain scanning in four neuropsychiatric disorders of childhood. *American Journal of Psychiatry, 142,* 731–737.

Haslam, R. H., Dalby, J. T., Johns, R. D., & Rademaker, A. W. (1981). Cerebral asymmetry in developmental dyslexia. *Archives of Neurology, 38,* 679–684.

Hauser, S., Delong, R., & Rosman, P. (1975). Pneumographic findings in the infantile autism syndrome. *Brain, 98,* 667–688.

Heath, A., & Martin, N. (1991). *Alcoholism: Clinical & Experimental Research, 15,* 122–128.

Heaton, R. (1981). *Wisconsin Card Sorting Test Manual.* Odessa, FL: Psychological Assessment Resources.

Herold, S., Frakowiak, R. S. J., LeCouteur, A., Rutter, M., & Howlin, P. (1988). Cerebral blood flow and metabolism of oxygen and glucose in young autistic adults. *Psychological Medicine, 18,* 823–831.

Hier, D. B., Le May, M., & Rosenberger, P. B. (1979). Autism and unfavorable left-right asymmetries of the brain. *Journal of Autism and Developmental Disorders, 9,* 153–159.

Hier, D. B., Le May, M., Rosenberger, P. B., & Perlo, V. B. (1978). Developmental dyslexia: Evidence of a subgroup with reversal of cerebral asymmetry. *Archives of Neurology, 35,* 90–92.

Hillyard, S. A., Pfefferbaum, S., Hink, R., Schment, V., & Pieton, T. (1973). Electrical signs of selective attention in the human brain. *Science, 182,* 177.

Hinshelwood, J. (1907). Four cases of cogenital word-blindness occurring in the same family. *British Medical Journal, 2,* 1229–1232.

Hinton, G. E., & Shallice, T. (1991). Lesioning an attractor network: Investigations of acquired dyslexia. *Psychological Review, 98,* 74–95.

Hobson, R. P. (1989). Beyond cognition: A theory of autism. In G. Dawson (Ed.), *Autism: New perspectives on diagnosis, nature and treatment* (pp. 22–48). New York: Guilford.

Hobson, R. P. (1991). Against the theory of 'Theory of Mind'. *British Journal of Developmental Psychology, 9,* 33–51.

Hobson, R. P. (1993). Understanding persons: The role of affect. In S. Baron-Cohen, H. Tager-Flusberg, & D. J. Cohen (Eds.), *Understanding other minds* (pp. 204–227). Oxford: Oxford University Press.

Holtzman, P., & Matthysse, S. (1990). The genetics of schizophrenia: A review. *Psychological Science, 1,* 279–286.

Horwitz, B., Rumsey, J. M., Grady, C. L., & Rapoport, S. I. (1988). The cerebral metabolic landscape in autism: Intercorrelations of regional glucose utilization. *Archives of Neurology, 45,* 749–755.

Hughes, C., & Russell, J. (1993). Autistic children's difficulty with mental disengagement from an object: Its implications for theories of autism. *Developmental Psychology, 29,* 498–510.

Hughes, J. R. (1982). The electroencephalogram and reading disorders. In R. N. Malatesha & P. G. Aaron (Eds.), *Reading disorders: Varieties and treatments* (pp. 233–253). New York: Academic Press.

Hynd, G. W., Marshall, R. M., & Semrud-Clikeman, M. (1991). Developmental dyslexia, neurolinguistic theory and deviations in brain morphology. *Reading and Writing, 3,* 345–362.

Hynd, G. W., Semrud-Clikeman, M., Lorys, A. R., Novey, E. S., & Eliopulas, D. (1991). Brain morphology in developmental dyslexia and attention deficit disorder/hyperactivity. *Archives of Neurology, 47,* 919–926.

Iacono, W., Smith, G., & Moreau, M. (1988). Ventricular and sulcal size at the onset of psychosis. *American Journal of Psychiatry, 145,* 820–824.

Jakob, H., & Beckmann. (1986). Prenatal development disturbances in the limbic allocortex in schizophrenics. *Journal of Neural Transmission, 65,* 303–326.

Kanner, L. (1943). Autistic disturbances of affective contact. *Nervous Child, 2,* 217–250.

Kelsoe, J., Jr., Cadet, J., Pickar, D., & Weinberger, D. (1988). Quantitative neuroanatomy in schizophrenia. *Archives of General Psychiatry, 45,* 533–541.

Kerr, J. (1896). School hygiene, in its mental, moral, and physical aspects. Howard Medical Prize Essay. *Journal of the Royal Statistical Society, 60,* 613–680.

Kerwin, R., Patel, S., Meldrum, B., Czudek, C., & Reynolds, G. (1988). Asymmetric loss of glutamate receptor subtype in left hippocampus in schizophrenia. *Lancet, 1,* 583–584.

Kling, A., & Steklis, H. D. (1976). A neural substrate for affiliative behaviors in non-human primates. *Brain, Behavior, and Evolution, 13,* 126–238.

Klonoff, H., Fibiger, C. H., & Hutton, G. H. (1970). Neuropsychological patterns in chronic schizophrenia. *Journal of Nervous and Mental Disease, 150,* 291–300.

Klove, H., & Hole, K. (1979). The hyperkinetic syndrome: Criteria for diagnosis. In R. L. Trites (Ed.), *Hyperactivity in children: Etiology, measurement and treatment implications.* Baltimore: University Park Press.

Kolb, B., & Wishaw, I. Q. (1983). *Fundamentals of human neuropsychology.* New York: Freeman.

Kornetsky, C., & Orzack, M. (1978). Physiologic and behavioral correlates of attention dysfunction in schizophrenic patients. In R. L. Cromwell, L. C. Wynne, & S. Matthysse (Ed.), *The nature of schizophrenia: New approaches to research and treatment* (pp. 196–204). New York: Wiley.

Kraepelin, E. (1919). *Dementia Praecox* (R. Barclay, Trans.). Edinburgh, Scotland: Livingstone.

Landau, S., Buchsbaum, M., Carpenter, W., Strauss, J., & Sacks, M. (1975). Schizophrenia and stimulus intensity control. *Archives of General Psychiatry, 32,* 1239–1245.

Largen, J., Jr., Calderon, M., & Smith, R. (1983). Asymmetries in the densities of white and gray matter in the brains of schizophrenic patients. *American Journal of Psychiatry, 140,* 1060–1062.

Larsen, J. P., Hoien, T., Lundberg, I., & Odegaard, H. (1990). MRI evaluation of the size and symmetry of the planum temporal in adolescents with developmental dyslexia. *Brain and Language, 39,* 289–301.

Leslie, A. (1987). Pretence and representation: The origins of "theory of mind." *Psychological Review, 94,* 412–426.

Leslie, A. (1991, April). *The theory of mind deficit in autism: The metarepresentation theory.* Paper presented to the Society for Research in Child Development, Seattle, WA.

Lewis, B. A., Ekelman, B. L., & Aram, D. M. (1990). A familial study of severe phonological disorders. *Journal of Speech and Hearing Research, 32,* 713–724.

Liberman, I. Y. (1973). Segmentation of the spoken word and reading acquisition. *Bulletin of the Orton Society, 23,* 65–77.

Liberman, I. Y. (1984). *Biology and evolution of language.* Cambridge, MA: Harvard University Press.

Liberman, I. Y., & Liberman, A. M. (1990). Whole language vs. code emphasis: Underlying assumptions and their implications for reading instruction. *Annals of Dyslexia, 40,* 51–76.

Liberman, I. Y., & Shankweiler, D. (1979). Speech, the alphabet, and teaching to read. In L. B. Resnick & P. A. Weaver (Eds.), *Theory and practice of early reading* (Vol. 2, pp. 109–132). Hillsdale, NJ: Erlbaum.

Liberman, I. Y., Shankweiler, D., Fischer, F. W., & Carter, B. (1974). Reading and the awareness of linguistic segments. *Journal of Experimental Child Psychology, 18,* 201–212.

Livingstone, M., Rosen, G., Drislane, F., & Galaburda, A. (1991). Physiological and anatomical evidence for a magnocellular deficit in developmental dyslexia. *Proceedings of the National Academy of Science, 88,* 1–5.

Losonczy, M. F., Song, I. S., Mohs, R. C., Small, N. A., Davidson, M., Johns, C. A., & Davis, K. L. (1986). Correlates of lateral ventricular size in chronic schizophrenia: I. Behavioral and treatment response measures. *American Journal of Psychiatry, 143,* 976–981.

Lou, H. C., Henriksen, L., & Bruhn, P. (1984). Focal cerebral hypoperfusion and/or attention deficit disorder. *Archives of Neurology, 41,* 825–829.

Lou, H. C., Henriksen, L., Bruhn, P., Borner, H., & Nielson, J. B. (1989). Striatal dysfunction in attention deficit and hyperkinetic disorder. *Archives of Neurology, 46,* 48–52.

Lovett, M. W. (1987). A developmental approach to reading disability: Accuracy and speed criteria of normal and deficient reading skill. *Child Development, 58,* 234–260.

Lundberg, I., Olofsson, A., & Wall, S. (1980). Reading and spelling skills in the first school years predicted from phonemic awareness skills in kindergarten. *Scandinavian Journal of Psychology, 21,* 159–173.

Luria, A. (1966). *Higher cortical functions in man.* New York: Basic Books.

Maclean, M., Bryant, P., & Bradley, L. (1987). Rhymes, nursery rhymes, and reading in early childhood. *Merrill-Palmer Quarterly, 33,* 255–282.

Mahler, M. (1952). On child psychosis and schizophrenia: Autistic and symbiotic infantile psychosis. *Psychoanalytic Study of the Child, 7,* 286–305.

Malmo, H. (1974). On frontal lobe functions: Psychiatric patient controls. *Cortex, 10,* 231–237.

Mann, V. A. (1984). Longitudinal predictions and prevention of early reading difficulty. *Annals of Dyslexia, 34,* 117–136.

Mann, V. A., & Ditunno, P. (1989). Phonological deficiencies: Effective predictors of future reading problems. In G. Paulides (Ed.), *Dyslexia: A neuropsychological & learning perspective.* New York: Wiley.

Mattes, J. A., & Gittelman, R. (1979). *A pilot trial of amantadine in hyperactive children.* Paper presented at the NCDEU meeting, Key Biscayne, FL.

McEvoy, R. E., Rogers, S. J., & Pennington, B. F. (1993). Executive function and social communication deficits in young autistic children. *Journal of Child Psychology and Psychiatry, 34,* 563–578.

McGhie, A., & Chapman, J. (1961). Disorders of attention and perception in early schizophrenia. *Journal of Medical Psychology, 34,* 103.

Meehl, P. E. (1989). *Psychodiagnosis—selected papers.* Minneapolis: University of Minnesota Press.

Meltzoff, A., & Gopnik, A. (1993). The role of imitation in understanding persons and developing a theory of mind. In S. Baron-Cohen, H. Tager-Flusberg, & D. J. Cohen (Eds.), *Understanding other minds* (pp. 335–366). Oxford: Oxford University Press.

Menyuk, P., & Menn, L. (1979). Early strategies for the perception and production of words and sounds. In P. Fletcher & M. Garman (Eds.), *Language acquisition* (pp. 49–70). Cambridge, England: Cambridge University Press.

Mesulam, M. (1988). Neural substrates of behavior: The effects of brain lesions upon mental state. In *The new Harvard guide to psychiatry* (pp. 91–128). Cambridge, MA: Harvard University Press.

Mesulam, M. (1990). Schizophrenia and the brain. *The New England Journal of Medicine, 322,* 842–845.

Milner, B. (1966). Effects of different brain lesions on card sorting. *Archives of Neurology, 9,* 90–100.

Minshew, N. J., & Goldstein, G. (1993). Is autism an amnesic disorder? Evidence from California Verbal Learning Test. *Neurology, 7,* 209–216.

Minshew, N. J., Dombrowski, S. M., Panchalingam, K., & Pettegrew, J. W. (1993). A preliminary ^{31}P MRS study of autism: Evidence for undersynthesis and increased degradation of brain membranes. *Society of Biological Psychiatry, 33,* 762–773.

Morgan, W. P. (1896). A case of congenital word-blindness. *British Medical Journal, 2,* 1543–1544.

Morice, R. D., & Ingram, J. C. L. (1983). Language complexity and age of onset in schizophrenia. *Psychiatry Research, 9,* 233–242.

Mundy, P., & Sigman, M. (1989). The theoretical implications of joint-attention deficits in autism. *Development and Psychopathology, 1,* 173–183.

Mundy, P., & Sigman, M. (1991, April). *The autistic person's theory of mind and early nonverbal joint attention deficits.* Paper presented to the Society for Research in Child Development, Seattle, WA.

Nelson, H., Pantelis, C., Carruthers, K., Speller, J., Baxendale, S., & Barnes, T. (1990). Cognitive functioning and symptomatology in chronic schizophrenia. *Psychological Medicine, 20,* 357–365.

Nittrouer, S., & Studdert-Kennedy, K. (1987). The role of coarticulatory effects in the perception of fricatives by children and adults. *Journal of Speech and Hearing Research, 30,* 319–329.

Nowakowski, R. S. (1987). Basic concepts of CNS development. *Child Development, 58,* 568–595.

Oades, R. D. (1987). Attention deficit disorder with hyperactivity: The contribution of catecholaminergic activity. *Progress in Neurobiology, 29,* 365–391.

Olson, R. (1985). Disabled reading processes and cognitive profiles. In D. B. Gray & J. K. Kavanaugh (Eds.), *Biobehavioral measures of dyslexia* (pp. 215–243). Parkton, MD: York Press.

Olson, R., Gillis, J. J., Rack, J. P., DeFries, J. C., & Fulker, D. W. (1991). Confirmatory factor analysis of word recognition and process measures in the Colorado Reading Project. *Reading and Writing: An Interdisciplinary Journal, 3,* 235–248.

Olson, R., Wise, B., Conners, F., Rack, J., & Fulker, D. (1989). Specific deficits in component reading and language skills: Genetic and environmental influences. *Journal of Learning Disabilities, 22,* 339–348.

Ottman, R. (1990). An epidemiologic approach to gene-environment interaction. *Genetic Epidemiology, 7,* 177–185.

Ozonoff, S., Pennington, B. F., & Rogers, S. (1990). Are there emotion perception deficits in young autistic children? *Journal of Child Psychology and Psychiatry, 31,* 343–361.

Ozonoff, S., Pennington, B. F., & Rogers, S. J. (1991). Executive function deficits in high-functioning autistic individuals: Relationship to theory of mind. *Journal of Child Psychology and Psychiatry, 32,* 1081–1105.

Ozonoff, S., Rogers, S. J., & Pennington, B. F. (1991). Aspergens syndrome: Evidence of an empirical distinction from high-functioning autism. *Journal of Child Psychology and Psychiatry, 32,* 1107–1122.

Ozonoff, S., Strayer, D. L., McMahon, W. M., & Filloux, F. (1994). Executive function abilities in autism and Tourette syndrome: An information processing approach. *Journal of Child Psychology and Psychiatry, 35,* 1015–1032.

Panksepp, J., & Sahley, T. L. (1987). Possible brain opiod involvement in disrupted social intent and language development of autism. In E. Schopler & G. B. Mesibov (Eds.), *Neurobiological issues in autism* (pp. 357–372). New York: Plenum.

Parry, P. (1973). *The effect of reward on the performance of hyperactive children.* Unpublished doctoral dissertation, McGill University, Montreal.

Pennington, B. F. (1989). Using genetics to understand dyslexia. *Annals of Dyslexia, 39,* 81–93.

Pennington, B. F. (1991). *Diagnosing learning disorders: A neuropsychological framework.* New York: Guilford.

Pennington, B. F. (in press). Working memory and cognitive differences: The frontal lobes and intelligence revisited. In M. M. Haith, J. Benson, R. Roberts, & B. F. Pennington (Eds.), *Future oriented processes in development.* Chicago: University of Chicago Press.

Pennington, B. F., Gilger, J., Pauls, D., Smith, S. A., Smith, S. D., & DeFries, J. C. (1991). Evidence for major gene transmission of developmental dyslexia. *Journal of the American Medical Association, 266*(11), 1527–1534.

Pennington, B. F., Groisser, D., & Welsh, M. C. (1993). Contrasting deficits in attention deficit hyperactivity disorder versus reading disability. *Developmental Psychology, 29,* 511–523.

Pennington, B. F., & Ozonoff, S. (1991). A neuroscientific perspective on continuity and discontinuity in developmental psychopathology. In D. Cicchetti (Ed.), *Rochester Symposium on Developmental Psychopathology* (Vol. III, pp. 117–159). Rochester, NY: University of Rochester Press.

Pennington, B. F., Rogers, S., Bennetto, L., & Ozonoff, S. (1993, April). *Executive functions and imitation skill in autistic children: Working memory study and theoretical integration.* Paper presented to the Society for Research in Child Development, New Orleans.

Pennington, B. F., Van Orden, G., Kirson, D., & Haith, M. M. (1991). What is the causal relation between verbal STM problems and dyslexia? In S. Brady & D. Shankweiler (Eds.), *Phonological processes in literacy* (pp. 173–186). Hillsdale, NJ: Erlbaum.

Pennington, B. F., Wallach, L. W., & Wallach, M. A. (1980). Nonconservers' understanding of invariance and arithmetic. *Genetic Psychology Monographs, 101,* 231–243.

Perfetti, C. A. (1985). *Reading ability.* New York: Oxford University Press.

Perner, J., Frith, U., Leslie, A. M., & Leekam, S. R. (1989). Exploration of the autistic child's theory of mind: Knowledge, belief and communication. *Child Development, 60,* 689–700.

Petrides, M., & Milner, B. (1982). Deficits on subject-ordered tasks after frontal- and temporal-lobe lesions in man. *Neuropsychologia, 20,* 249–262.

Pfefferbaum, A., Horvath, T., Roth, W., Tinklenberg, J., & Kopell, B. (1980). Auditory brain stem and cortical evoked potentials in schizophrenia. *Biological Psychiatry, 209,* 209–223.

Piven, J., Berthier, M. L., Starkstein, S. E., Nehme, E., Pearlson, G., & Folstein, S. (1990). Magnetic resonance imaging evidence for a deficit of cerebral cortical development in autism. In S. Chase & M. E. Hertzig (Eds.), *Annual progress in child psychiatry and child development* (pp. 455–465). New York: Brunner/Mazel.

Plomin, R. (1990). The role of inheritance in behavior. *Science, 248,* 183–188.

Porges, S. W., Walter, G. F., Korb, R. J., & Sprague, R. L. (1975). The influence of methylphenidate on heart rate and behavioral measures of attention in hyperactive children. *Child Development, 46,* 727–733.

Posner, M. I., & Petersen, S. E. (in press). The attention system of the human brain. *Annual Review of Neuroscience.*

Premack, D., & Woodruff, G. (1978). Does the chimpanzee have a theory of mind? *Behavioral and Brain Sciences, 1,* 515–526.

Price, B. H., Daffner, K. R., Stowe, R. M., & Mesulam, M. M. (1990). The comportmental learning disabilities of early frontal lobe damage. *Brain, 113,* 1383–1393.

Prior, M., & Hoffman, W. (1990). Neuropsychological testing of autistic children through an exploration with frontal lobe tests. *Journal of Autism and Developmental Disorders, 20,* 581–590.

Rapin, I. (1987). Searching for the cause of autism: A neurologic perspective. In D. J. Cohen & A. M. Donnellan (Eds.), *Handbook of autism and pervasive developmental disorders* (pp. 710–717). New York: Wiley.

Rapoport, J. L., & Quinn, P. O. (1975). Minor physical anomalies (stigmata) and early developmental deviation: A major biological subgroup of "hyperactive children." *International Journal of Mental Health, 4,* 29–44.

Reiss, D., Hetherington, M., & Plomin, R. (1994). The separate worlds of teenage siblings: An introduction to the study of the nonshared environment and adolescent development. In M. Hetherington, D. Reiss, & R. Plomin (Eds.), *The separate worlds of siblings: The impact of nonshared environment on development,* (pp. 63–109). Hillsdale, NJ: Erlbaum.

Reite, M., Teale, P., Zimmerman, J., Davis, K., Whalen, J., & Edrich, J. (1988). Source origin of a 50-msec latency auditory evoked field component in young schizophrenic men. *Biological Psychiatry, 24,* 495–506.

Reveley, M., Reveley, A., & Baldy, R. (1987). Left cerebral hemisphere hypodensity in discordant schizophrenic twins: A controlled study. *Archives of General Psychiatry, 44,* 625–632.

Reynolds, G. (1983). Increased concentrations and lateral asymmetry of amygdala dopamine in schizophrenia. *Nature, 305,* 527–529.

Reynolds, G., Czudek, C., & Andrews, H. (1990). Deficit and hemispheric asymmetry of GABA uptake sites in the hippocampus in schizophrenia. *Biological Psychiatry, 27,* 1038–1044.

Ritvo, E. R., Freeman, B. J., Scheibel, A. B., Doung, P. T., Robinson, H., & Guthrie, D. (1986). Decreased Purkinje cell density in four autistic patients: Initial findings of the UCLA-NSAC Autopsy Research Project. *American Journal of Psychiatry, 43,* 862–866.

Roberts, G., Colter, N., Lofthouse, R., Bogerts, B., Zech, M., & Crow, T. (1987). Implications of normal brain development for the pathogenesis of schizophrenia. *Archives of General Psychiatry, 44,* 660–669.

Roberts, R. J., Hager, L., & Heron, C. (in press). Prefrontal cognitive processes: Working memory and inhibition in the antisocial task. *Journal of Experimental Psychology: General.*

Roberts, R. J., Varney, N. R., Reinarz, S. J., & Parkens, R. A. (1988). CT asymmetries in developmentally dyslexic adults. *Developmental Neuropsychology, 43,* 231–237.

Rochester, S. R., & Martin, J. R. (1979). *Crazy talk: A study of the discourse of schizophrenic speakers.* New York: Plenum.

Rodnick, E., & Shakow, D. (1940). Set in the schizophrenic as measured by a complete reaction time index. *American Journal of Psychiatry, 97,* 214–225.

Roemer, R., Shagass, C., Straumanis, J., & Amadeo, M. (1979). Somatosensory and auditory evoked potential studies of functional differences between the cerebral hemispheres in psychosis. *Biological Psychiatry, 14,* 357–373.

Rogers, S. J., & Pennington, B. F. (1991). A theoretical approach to deficits in infantile autism. *Development and Psychopathology, 3,* 137–162.

Rosenberger, P. B., & Hier, D. B. (1979). Cerebral asymmetry and verbal intellectual deficits. *Annals of Neurology, 8,* 300–304.

Roth, W., & Cannon, E. (1972). Some features of the auditory evoked response in schizophrenics. *Archives of General Psychiatry, 27,* 466–471.

Rumsey, J. M. (1985). Conceptual problem-solving in highly verbal, nonretarded autistic men. *Journal of Autism and Developmental Disorders, 15,* 23–36.

Rumsey, J. M., Dorwort, R., Vermess, M., Denckla, M. B., Kruesi, M., & Rapoport, J. L. (1986). Magnetic resonance imaging of brain anatomy in severe developmental dyslexia. *Archives of Neurology, 43,* 1045–1046.

Rumsey, J. M., Duara, R., Grady, C., Rapoport, J. L., Margolin, R. A., Rapoport, S. I., & Cutler, N. R. (1985). Brain metabolism in autism: Resting cerebral glucose utilization rates as measured with positron emission tomography. *Archives of General Psychiatry, 42,* 448–455.

Rumsey, J. M., & Hamberger, S. D. (1988). Neuropsychological findings in high-functioning men with infantile autism, residual state. *Journal of Clinical and Experimental Neuropsychology, 10,* 201–221.

Rumsey, J. M., Zametkin, A., Andreason, P., Hanahan, A. P., Hamberger, S. D., Aguino, T., King, A. C., Pikus, A., & Cohen, R. M. (1994). Normal activation of frontotemporal language cortex in dyslexia as measured with oxygen in positron emission tomography. *Archives of Neurology, 51,* 21–38.

Rund, B. (1986). Verbal hallucinations and information processing. *Behavior and Brain Science, 9,* 531–532.

Russell, J. (in press). The theory theory: "So good they named it twice"? *Cognitive Development.*

Russell, J., Mauther, N., Sharpe, S., & Tidswell, T. (1991). The "windows task" as a measure of strategic deception in preschoolers and autistic subjects. *British Journal of Developmental Psychology, 9,* 331–349.

Rutter, M., Graham, P., & Yule, W. (1970). A neuropsychiatric study in childhood. In *Clinics in developmental medicine.* Philadelphia: Lippincott.

Saccuzzo, D., & Braff, D. (1981). Early information processing deficits in schizophrenia: New findings using schizophrenic subgroups and manic controls. *Archives of General Psychiatry, 38,* 175–179.

Sapolsky, R. M. (1990). Stress in the wild. *Scientific American, 262,* 116–122.

Sarason, I. G., & Sarason, B. R. (1989). *Abnormal psychology* (6th ed.). Englewood Cliffs, NJ: Prentice-Hall.

Scarborough, H. (1991). Very early language deficits in dyslexic children. *Child Development, 61,* 1728–1743.

Schopler, E. (1985). Convergence of learning disability, higher-level autism and Asperger's syndrome. *Journal of Autism and Developmental Disorders, 15,* 359–360.

Schlusinger, F., Parnas, J., Petersen, E., Schlusinger, H., Thomas, W., Mednick, S. A., Meller, L., & Silverton, L. (1984). Cerebral ventricular size in the offspring of schizophrenic mothers: A preliminary study. *Archives of General Psychiatry, 41,* 602–606.

Sejnowski, T. J., & Churchland, P. S. (1989). Brain and cognition. In M. Posner (Ed.), *Foundations of cognitive science* (pp. 301–356). Cambridge, MA: MIT Press.

Seibert, J. M., Hogan, A. E., & Mundy, P. C. (1987). Assessing social communication skills in infancy. *Topics in Early Childhood Special Education, 7,* 32–48.

Seidenberg, M., & McClelland, J. (1989). A distributed, developmental model of word recognition and naming. *Psychological Review, 96,* 523–568.

Shagass, C. (1977). Early evoked potentials. *Schizophrenia Bulletin, 3,* 80.

Shallice, T. (1982). Specific impairments in planning. *Philosophical Transactions of the Royal Society of London B, 298,* 199–209.

Shallice, T. (1988). *From neuropsychology to mental structure.* Cambridge, MA: Cambridge University Press.

Shankweiler, D., & Crain, S. (1987). Language mechanisms and reading disorder: A modular approach. In P. Bertelson (Ed.), *The onset of literacy* (pp. 139–168). Cambridge, MA: MIT Press.

Shaywitz, B. A., Cohen, D. J., & Bowers, M. B. (1977). CSF monoamine metabolites in children with minimal brain dysfunction: Evidence for alteration of brain dopamine. *Journal of Pediatrics, 90,* 67–71.

Shaywitz, S. E., & Shaywitz, B. A. (1988). Attention deficit disorder: Current perspectives. In J. F. Kavanaugh & T. J. Truss (Eds.), *Learning disabilities: Proceedings of the national conference.* Parkton, MD: York Press.

Shaywitz, S. E., Shaywitz, B. A., Cohen, D. J., & Young, J. G. (1983). Monoaminergic mechanisms in hyperactivity. In M. Rutter (Ed.), *Developmental neuropsychiatry* (pp. 330–347). New York: Guilford.

Shelton, R., & Weinberger, D. (1986). In H. Nasrallah & D. Weinberger (Eds.), *The neurology of schizophrenia.* Amsterdam: Elsevier/North-Holland.

Shimamura, A. P., Janowsky, J. S., & Squire, L. R. (1991). What is the role of frontal lobe damage in memory disorders? In H. S. Levin, H. M. Eisenberg, & A. L. Benton (Eds.), *Frontal lobe function and injury* (pp. 173–195). New York: Oxford University Press.

Siegel, C., Waldo, M., Miznor, G., Adler, L., & Freedman, R. (1984). Deficits in sensory gating in schizophrenic patients and their relatives. *Archives of General Psychiatry, 41,* 607–612.

Smolensky, P. (1988). On the proper treatment of connectionism. *Behavioral and Brain Sciences, 11,* 1–74.

Stanovich, K. E. (1986). Matthew effects in reading: Some consequences of individual differences in the acquisition of literacy. *Reading Research Quarterly, 21,* 360–406.

Stanovich, K. E., Nathan, R. G., & Vala-Rossi, M. (1986). Developmental changes in the cognitive correlates of reading ability and the developmental lag hypothesis. *Reading Research Quarterly, 21,* 267–283.

Steel, J. G., Gorman, R., & Flexman, J. E. (1984). Neuropsychiatric testing in an autistic mathematical idiot-savant: Evidence for nonverbal abstract capacity. *Journal of the American Academy of Child Psychiatry, 23,* 704–707.

Steinmetz, H., & Galaburda, A. M. (1991). Planum temporale asymmetry: In-vivo morphometry affords a new perspective for neuro-behavioral research. *Reading and Writing: An Interdisciplinary Journal, 3,* 331–343.

Stern, D. N. (1985). *The interpersonal world of the infant: A view from psychoanalysis and developmental psychology.* New York: Basic Books.

Stevenson, J. (1991). Which aspects of processing text mediate genetic effects? *Reading and Writing: An Interdisciplinary Journal, 3,* 249–269.

Stuart, M., & Coltheart, M. (1988). Does reading develop in a sequence of stages? *Cognition, 30,* 139–181.

Suddath, R., Casanova, M., Goldberg, T., Daniel, D., Kelsoe, J. J., & Weinberger, D. (1989). Temporal lobe pathology in schizophrenia: A quantitative magnetic resonance imaging study. *American Journal of Psychiatry, 146,* 464–472.

Suddath, R., Christison, G., Torrey, E., Casanova, M., & Weinberger, D. (1990). Anatomical abnormalities in the brains of monozygotic twins discordant for schizophrenia. *The New England Journal of Medicine, 322,* 789–794.

Sykes, D. H., Douglas, V. I., & Morgenstern, G. (1973). Sustained attention in hyperactive children. *Journal of Child Psychology and Psychiatry, 14,* 213–220.

Sykes, D. H., Douglas, V. I., Weiss, G., & Minde, K. K. (1971). Attention in hyperactive children and the effect of methylphenidate (Ritalin). *Journal of Child Psychology and Psychiatry, 12,* 129–139.

Tallal, P., Sainburg, R. L., & Jernigan, T. (1991). The neuropathology of developmental dysphasia: Behavioral, morphological, and physiological evidence for a pervasive temporal processing disorder. *Reading and Writing, 3,* 363–377.

Templin, M. (1957). *Certain language skills in children.* Minneapolis: University of Minnesota Press.

Tulving, E. (1983). *Elements of episodic memory.* Oxford, England: Clarendon Press.

Van Orden, G. C. (1987). A ROWS is a ROSE: Spelling sound and reading. *Memory & Cognition, 15,* 181–198.

Van Orden, G. C., Johnston, J. C., & Hale, B. L. (1988). Word identification in reading proceeds from spelling to sound to meaning. *Journal of Experimental Psychology: Learning, Memory, and Cognition, 14,* 371–385.

Van Orden, G. C., Pennington, B. F., & Stone, G. O. (1990). Word identification in reading and the promise of subsymbolic psycholinguistics. *Psychological Review, 97,* 488–522.

Vellutino, F. R. (1979). *Dyslexia: Theory and research.* Cambridge, MA: MIT Press.

Verkerk, A. J., Pieretti, M., Sutcliffe, J. S., Fu, Y. H., Kuhl, D. P., Pizzuti, A., Reiner, O., Richards, S., Victoria, M. F., Zhang, F. P., Eussen, B. E., VanOmmen, G. J. B., Blonden, L. A. J., Riggins, G. J., Chastain, J. L., Kunst, C. B., Galjaard, H., Caskey, T. C., Nelson, D. L., Oostra, B. A., & Warren, S. T. (1991). Identification of a gene (FMR-1) containing a CGG repeat coincident with a breakpoint cluster region exhibiting length variation in fragile X syndrome. *Cell, 65,* 904–914.

Volkmar, F. R., Paul, R., & Cohen, D. J. (1985). The use of "Asperger's syndrome." *Journal of Autism and Developmental Disorders, 15,* 437–439.

Wagner, R. K., & Torgesen, J. K. (1987). The nature of phonological processing and its causal role in the acquisition of reading skills. *Psychological Bulletin, 101,* 192–212.

Walker, E., Davis, D., & Gottlieb, L. (1991). Charting the developmental trajectories to schizophrenia. In D. Cicchetti & S. L. Toth (Eds.), *Rochester Symposium on Developmental Psychopathology.* Rochester, NY: University of Rochester Press.

Wallach, M. A., & Wallach, L. (1976). *Teaching all children to read.* Chicago: University of Chicago Press.

Weinberger, D., Berman, K. F., & Zec, R. F. (1986). Physiologic dysfunction of dorsolateral prefrontal cortex in schizophrenia. *Archives of General Psychiatry, 43,* 114–124.

Weinberger, D., DeLisi, L., Perman, G., Targum, S., & Wyatt, R. (1982). Computed tomography in schizophreniform disorder and other acute psychiatric disorders. *Archives of General Psychiatry, 39,* 778–783.

Weinberger, D., Torrey, E., Neophytides, A., & Wyatt, R. (1979). Lateral cerebral ventricular enlargement in chronic schizophrenia. *Archives of General Psychiatry, 36,* 735–739.

Wellman, H. M. (1990). *The child's theory of mind.* Cambridge, MA: MIT Press.

Welsh, M. C., & Pennington, B. F. (1988). Assessing frontal lobe functioning in children: Views from developmental psychology. *Developmental Neuropsychology, 4,* 199–230.

Welsh, M. C., Pennington, B. F., & Groisser, D. B. (1991). A normative-developmental study of executive function: A window on prefrontal function in children? *Developmental Neuropsychology, 7*(2), 131–149.

Welsh, M. C., Wall, B. M., & Towle, P. O. (1989, April). *Executive function in children with attention deficit: Implications for a prefrontal hypothesis.* Paper presented at the biennial meeting of the Society for Research in Child Development, Seattle, WA.

Werry, J. S., Minde, K., Guzman, D., Weiss, G., Dogan, K., & Hoy, R. (1972). Studies of the hyperactive child: VIII. Neurological status compared with neurotic and normal children. *American Psychologist, 42,* 441–450.

Wilkins, A. J., Shallice, T., & McCarthy, R. (1987). Frontal lesions and sustained attention. *Neuropsychologia, 25,* 359–365.

Williams, A., Reveley, M., Kolakowska, T., Arden, M., & Madelbrote, B. (1985). Computed tomography in schizophreniform disorder and other acute psychiatric disorders. *Archives of General Psychiatry, 146,* 239–246.

Wing, L. (1986). Clarification of Asperger's syndrome. *Journal of Autism and Developmental Disorders, 16,* 513–515.

Witelson, S. F. (1987). Neurobiological aspects of language in children. *Child Development, 58,* 653–688.

Wood, F., Flowers, L., Buchsbaum, M., & Tallal, P. (1991). Investigation of abnormal left temporal functioning in dyslexia through rCBF, auditory evoked potentials, and positron emission tomography. In B. F. Pennington (Ed.), *Reading disabilities: Genetic and neurological influences* (pp. 379–393). Dordrecht, The Netherlands: Kluwer.

Yates, A. (1966). Psychological deficit. In P. R. Farnsworth (Ed.), *Annual review of psychology* (pp. 111–144). Palo Alto, CA: Annual Reviews.

Zahn, T. (1976). On the bimodality of the distribution of electrodermal orienting responses in schizophrenic patients. *Journal of Nervous Mental Disorders, 162,* 195–199.

Zametkin, A., Nordahl, T., Gross, M., Semple, W., Rapoport, J. L., & Cohen, R. (1990). Cerebral glucose metabolism in adults with hyperactivity of childhood onset. *The New England Journal of Medicine, 323,* 1361–1415.

Zametkin, A. J., & Rapoport, J. L. (1987). Neurobiology of attention deficit disorder with hyperactivity: Where have we come in 50 years? *Journal of the American Academy of Child and Adolescent Psychiatry, 26,* 676–686.

Zelazo, P. D., Frye, D., & Reznick, J. S. (in review). Age-related changes in the execution of explicit rules: The roles of logical complexity and executive function.

CHAPTER 10

Nature, Nurture, and the Development of Psychopathology

RICHARD RENDE and ROBERT PLOMIN

In 1943, the child psychiatrist Leo Kanner introduced the term "autism" to characterize a severe syndrome of disturbed development (Kanner, 1943). In presenting the salient clinical features of this syndrome, Kanner's speculation and observation are especially fascinating through the hindsight of modern quantitative genetics. First, Kanner suggested that the core of this syndrome was a biological (and probably innate) inability to develop an attachment to other human beings. Second, Kanner noted that some of the parents of children with this syndrome had peculiar personality traits, such as aloofness and coldness.

In the years following Kanner's paper, an interesting trend emerged: Kanner's observations about parental characteristics were translated into environmental theories of autism in which "refrigerator mothers" made infants withdraw into a world of their own. As recently as 1967, a book was published that emphasized psychodynamic pathways by which infants became autistic (Bettelheim, 1967). In such environmental theories, Kanner's speculation that autism was due to biological and probably innate factors was dismissed, as evidenced by the following: ". . . stories about autistic children being unresponsive from birth on do not, in and by themselves, suggest an innate disturbance. Because it may be a very early reaction to their mothers that was triggered during the first days and weeks of life" (Bettelheim, 1967, p. 399).

Over time, psychodynamic theories of autism died out because empirical studies demonstrated that parents of autistic children did not show severe deficits in parenting. In addition, a number of studies suggested that the syndrome of autism had a biological basis, as reflected by findings such as increased rates of seizures in autistic individuals. Hence, by the 1970s, researchers had returned to Kanner's notion that the etiology of autism involved biological factors. However, as recently as the mid-1970s, it was believed that genetic factors did not play a significant role in the etiology of autism (Hanson & Gottesman, 1976). Little attention was given to Kanner's observation about the personality characteristics of some parents of autistic children.

Since the mid-1970s, research on autism has suggested that genetic influences play a major and perhaps primary role in the etiology of this syndrome (Rutter, Macdonald et al., 1990). Furthermore, Kanner's original observations about personality characteristics in the relatives of autistic individuals have been translated into *genetic* theories, in which a genetic predisposition to autism may be reflected in lesser variants of problems in first-degree relatives, including social abnormalities (e.g., impaired social reciprocity) and repetitive behaviors (e.g., circumscribed interests) (Bolton et al., 1991). We have come full circle in the 50 years since Kanner published his landmark paper. His observations have been united with modern quantitative genetic theory, and the result is an etiological theory that places primary emphasis on genetic factors.

This brief history of research on autism is symbolic of trends in current research on psychopathology. A very similar picture may be painted for research on schizophrenia, in which neo-Freudian theories placing blame on "schizophrenogenic mothers" (see Torrey, 1992) have been replaced by quantitative models of genetic diathesis to schizophrenia (Gottesman, 1991). In fact, very few forms of psychopathology are *not* believed to have a genetic component, and genetic strategies represent a primary component in research on psychopathology (e.g., Plomin, Rende, & Rutter, 1991; Rutter, Bolton et al., 1990).

The case may be made that the nature-nurture pendulum has in fact swung too far in the direction of genetic influence in recent theories. In the late 1980s, there was much enthusiasm regarding the purported discovery of single genes that caused schizophrenia (Sherrington et al., 1988) and bipolar disorder (Egeland, Gerhard, Pauls, Sussex, & Kidd, 1987). Suggestions were made about the possible implications of the genetic findings, such as revamping our classifications of psychopathology based on genetic findings. However, the excitement generated during this time period was soon replaced with a more somber tone as the discoveries of single genes for schizophrenia and bipolar disorder were not replicated and were, in some cases, retracted (see Plomin & Rende, 1991). Models of psychopathology that place total emphasis on genetic factors are going the way of models that focused exclusively on environmental theories.

Because neither genetic nor environmental theories have provided satisfactory explanations of the development of most forms of psychopathology (the only exceptions are rare genetic disorders such as Huntington's disease), developmental psychopathology

Dr. Rende acknowledges the support of an Aaron Diamond Postdoctoral Fellowship in the Biomedical and Social Sciences, and a NARSAD Young Investigator Award.

must recognize, as have other disciplines, the importance of studying nature AND nurture rather than nature VERSUS nurture (e.g., Plomin & McClearn, 1993). This middle ground, although probably theoretically correct, presents the possibility of misinterpretation for individuals not intimately acquainted with its methods: environmentalists may misconstrue what is meant by the phrase "genetic influence," and geneticists may disregard the importance of "environmental influence." In addition, there is an old argument that, because we need to study nature and nurture in order to understand both adaptive and maladaptive development, it makes no sense to try to disentangle one from the other.

Our goal in this chapter is to convey to readers the current thinking about the ways in which both nature AND nurture influence the development of psychopathology through the life span. We begin with an overview of quantitative genetics and normal developmental processes. We define "genetic" and "environmental" influences, discuss how they are studied, review our current knowledge about these influences on normal development through the life span, and address possible misconceptions about both nature and nurture. We then discuss our current knowledge about nature, nurture, and the development of psychopathology across the life span, illuminating some of the differences that emerge between the study of the normal and abnormal in terms of quantitative genetic theory and method. We examine what the study of genetic and environmental influences on the development of psychopathology can contribute to our understanding of normal development. The concluding section is a future perspective on what must be done in the next decade.

NATURE, NURTURE, AND NORMAL DEVELOPMENT

What Are Nature and Nurture?

The first issue to be addressed is definitional: what are nature and nurture? Many individuals may feel that they have an intuitive sense of these terms, but their definitions are specific and technical, and a complete understanding of the nuances involved is essential for an informed and critical discussion of how nature and nurture contribute to normal development.

Nature refers to what is typically thought of as inheritance—in this context, the DNA differences transmitted from generation to generation. However, the word nature is not synonymous with DNA. Many DNA events, such as changes in gene expression that occur in response to events in the intracellular and extracellular environment, are not inherited. Nature refers here to a specific biological process by which genetic events are coded in DNA at conception. Other genetic events that may have a large impact on development are not inherited. An example is Down syndrome. Although Down syndrome is due to a chromosomal abnormality, in most cases the abnormality is not inherited.

Because *nature* has a specific meaning, *nurture* also takes on a special, much broader definition than is usually considered. Nurture refers to all noninherited factors. These factors may include prenatal occurrences and effects of viruses as well as psychosocial factors. A crucial aspect of this definition is that genetic strategies are essential in understanding environmental effects because genetic approaches can help determine what events are truly environmental (Rutter, 1991). These definitions of nature and nurture are, like all definitions, arbitrary and debatable (Plomin, 1994). Because they are offered as a heuristic for guiding and interpreting research, it is most important that they be explicit.

Most strategies used to study the impact of nature on behavioral development rely on "indirect" strategies such as twin and adoption designs or similar natural experiments that help to disentangle inherited and noninherited influences. (These strategies are discussed in the following section.) However, the continuing explosion of molecular genetic techniques is making direct study of genetic influences (both inherited and noninherited) increasingly possible, even on complex phenotypes such as behavior (see Plomin, 1990; Plomin, Rende, & Rutter, 1991).

Basic ideas of *how* nature can impact development should be reviewed because there is often confusion about the ways in which genes influence behavior, especially with the increasing attention given to molecular genetic techniques in recent years. One mistaken notion is that genes encode behavior directly (see Plomin, 1990). There are no genes for behavior per se. Genes are chemical structures that can only code for amino acid sequences. All effects of genes on behavioral variability are indirect, representing the cumulative effects of stretches of amino acids that differ among individuals and that interact with the intracellular and extracellular environment. Introductory discussions of the pathways by which genetic processes affect development are found in Plomin (1990, 1994), and more advanced discussion is available in Plomin, DeFries, and McClearn (1990).

Another crucial point is that the word nature in this context does not refer to the nature of the human species (Plomin, 1994). Rather, it refers to genetically instigated differences among individuals within the species. Species-typical behavior—such as the use of language as a means of communication—is not examined. What is examined is *individual differences* in language use, e.g., why some children are slow in learning to use language, and others are fast. The goal is to understand the relative contributions of nature and nurture to individual differences in behavioral traits, not differences between species. The next section reviews the techniques currently used to understand how both nature and nurture influence development.

How Are Nature and Nurture Studied?

Human behavior genetics began over a century ago, with Darwin's cousin, Francis Galton. Reading Darwin's *On the Origin of Species,* Galton was inspired to devote the rest of his life to the investigation of the inheritance of human behavior. At the turn of the century, when Mendel's laws of inheritance were rediscovered, a bitter argument erupted between Mendelians and Galtonians. The Mendelians looked for discontinuous traits such as disorders and Mendelian segregation ratios that implicate the transmission of a single gene responsible for a disorder. The Galtonians, also called biometricians, at first argued that Mendel's laws were not applicable to complex traits because such traits are distributed continuously as dimensions. The resolution of the controversy, and the birth of quantitative genetics, came from the realization that a continuous distribution would emerge for a trait if several genes affect the trait.

Despite the resolution of the controversy, which was generally accepted before 1920, the two genetic approaches went their different ways. The Galtonians moved outward from the gene, toward the functioning of the whole organism; developed quantitative genetic strategies for animal and human research; and documented the important role of heritable genetic factors for complex traits, including behavioral dimensions and disorders. The Mendelians moved inward toward the gene at the cellular level, primarily using mutational analysis, and eventually developed the molecular genetic tools known as the new genetics.

This section begins with a brief overview of quantitative genetic theory and methods as applied to behavior, and then considers possibilities for harnessing the power of the new genetics to address quantitative genetic analyses of behavior. Details concerning behavioral genetic methods are available in texts (e.g., Plomin, DeFries, & McClearn, 1990) and in a recent discussion focused on child psychiatry (Rutter, Bolton et al., 1990).

Quantitative genetic methods assess genetic influence even when many genes and substantial environmental variation affect a disorder or dimension. Applied behavior genetics began thousands of years ago, when animals were bred for their behavior as much as for their morphology. The results of such artificial selection can be seen most dramatically in differences in behavior as well as physique among dog breeds—differences that testify to the great range of genetic variability within a species, and its effect on behavior. Selection studies in the laboratory still provide the most convincing demonstrations of genetic influence on behavior. For example, in one of the longest mammalian selection studies of behavior, replicated high and low lines of mice were selected for activity in a brightly lit open field, an aversive situation thought to assess emotional reactivity (DeFries, Gervais, & Thomas, 1978). After 30 generations of selection, a 30-fold difference exists between the activity of the high and low lines, with no overlap between them. It is noteworthy that such selection studies of behavior typically yield steady divergence of selected lines after many generations. These data provide the best available evidence that many genes affect behavior. If only one or two major genes were responsible for genetic effects on behavior, the relevant alleles would be sorted into the high and low lines in a few generations.

Other methods that have been used to demonstrate ubiquitous genetic influence on animal behavior include family studies and studies of inbred strains. Family studies assess the sine qua non of transmissible genetic influence, resemblance between genetically related individuals. More so than in human studies, the family method suggests genetic sources of resemblance among family members because individuals are reared in the same laboratory conditions. Inbred strains are created by mating brother to sister for at least 20 generations. This severe inbreeding eliminates heterozygosity and results in animals that are virtually identical genetically. Behavioral differences between inbred strains reared under the same laboratory conditions can be ascribed to genetic differences. An especially powerful inbred strain method involves recombinant inbred (RI) strains, which are multiple inbred strains derived from the same genetically segregating cross between two progenitor inbred strains (Bailey, 1971; Taylor, 1989). Although RI strains were developed to identify and map single-gene effects, they also are valuable for identifying associations between behavior and genes that account for relatively small amounts of variation in behavior (Plomin, McClearn, Gora-Maslak, & Neiderhiser, 1991).

For human behavior, no quantitative genetic methods as powerful as selection or inbred strain studies exist. Human behavioral genetic research relies on family, adoption, and twin designs. As in studies of nonhuman animals, family studies assess the extent of resemblance for genetically related individuals, although they cannot disentangle possible environmental sources of resemblance. That is the point of adoption studies. Genetically related individuals adopted apart provide evidence of the degree to which familial resemblance is attributable to hereditary resemblance. This is like a natural experiment in which family members share heredity but not environment. The other side of the adoption design tests the influence of nature by studying the resemblance of genetically unrelated individuals living together in adoptive families. The concern with this experiment is that nature and nurture are not neatly cleaved if selective placement occurs in which children are placed with adoptive parents who resemble the birth parents. However, the extent of selective placement can be assessed empirically.

Twin studies are also natural experiments in which the resemblance of identical twins, whose genetic identity can be expressed as genetic relatedness of 1.0, is compared to the resemblance of fraternal twins, first-degree relatives whose coefficient of genetic relatedness is 0.50. If heredity affects a behavioral trait, identical twins will resemble each other on the trait to a greater extent than will fraternal twins. The concern with the twin experiment is that identical twins may experience more similar environments than fraternal twins; thus, the greater similarity of identical twins as compared to fraternal twins may be mediated in part by environmental factors. This issue, referred to as the equal environments assumption of the twin method, is discussed in detail elsewhere (Plomin, DeFries, & McClearn, 1990).

Other genetic designs exist, in addition to the classical adoption and twin designs. For example, a variant of the adoption design is a cross-fostering design in which adopted children are reared by parents who have the disorder under study. Variations of the classical twin design include the families-of-identical-twins design, cotwin control studies in which members of identical twin pairs are treated differently, and studies of discordant identical twin pairs. Combinations of designs are particularly important to triangulate on estimates of quantitative genetic parameters. For example, family and adoption designs can be combined by including nonadoptive or control families in which family members (siblings as well as parents and offspring) share both heredity and family environment, in addition to adoptive families. Twin and adoption designs can be combined by studying twins reared apart as well as control twins reared together. Analysis of research employing such multiple groups is facilitated by model fitting, which is discussed below.

Behavioral genetic methods can assess the statistical significance and the magnitude of the genetic effect. Heritability is a descriptive statistic that assigns an effect size to genetic influence.

For example, the correlation for identical twins reared apart in uncorrelated environments directly estimates heritability. This correlation represents the proportion of variance that covaries for identical twins who share all their heredity but not their rearing environments. If hereditary influence were unimportant, their correlation would be low; their correlation would be high if heredity was primarily responsible for phenotypic variance. Although behavioral scientists reflexively square correlations to estimate variance—and this is appropriate to estimate the amount of variance in one trait that can be predicted by another trait—correlations for family members, such as the correlation for identical twins reared apart, represent components of variance and are not squared. Thus, a correlation of .40 for reared-apart identical twins implies that heritability is 40%. That is, genetic variance accounts for 40% of the observed variance in the population.

Model-fitting techniques are routinely used in behavioral genetic analyses to estimate heritability because they test a model, make assumptions explicit, analyze data from multiple groups simultaneously, provide standard errors of estimate, and make it possible to compare the fit of alternative models. Model fitting essentially involves solving a series of simultaneous equations. For example, the twin method consists of two equations that express the observed correlations for identical and fraternal twins in terms of two unknowns that represent expected components of variance (1.0 G + E for identical twins and 0.5 G + E for fraternal twins). The solution to these two equations with two unknowns merely involves doubling the difference between the identical and fraternal twin correlations to estimate G; E is estimated as the residual twin similarity not explained by G. As data for other family groups are added, more equations are available, making it possible to solve for more parameters and to compare alternative models. An excellent introduction to model fitting that includes behavioral genetic model fitting is available (Loehlin, 1987). Three recent behavior genetics books include introductions to model fitting in quantitative genetic analysis (Eaves, Eysenck, & Martin, 1989; Plomin, DeFries, & Fulker, 1988; Plomin, DeFries, & McClearn, 1990), and a special issue of *Behavior Genetics* is devoted to LISREL model-fitting analyses of twin data (Boomsma, Martin, & Neale, 1989).

As mentioned at the outset of this chapter, quantitative genetics is limited to describing observed variation between individuals in a population and ascribing these phenotypic differences to genetic and environmental sources of variability. This focus on variance leads to several limitations. First, universal genetic and environmental factors may be critical for development, but they cannot be detected by quantitative genetic methods unless these factors create observable differences between individuals. For example, genes are undoubtedly responsible for bipedalism and binocular vision, but because these are essentially nonvarying characteristics of the human species, quantitative genetics will not detect such universal genetic influences. Similarly, light, food, and oxygen are essential for development, but quantitative genetics can only assess the extent to which variation in such environmental factors creates variability among individuals. In terms of disease, if all individuals were exposed to a particular pathogen but only genetically susceptible individuals succumb to the disease, quantitative genetics would indicate the genetic variability responsible for expression of the disease but would not provide any clues that the ultimate cause of the disease is an environmental pathogen. Yet the disease would not occur if the pathogen were eradicated.

A second limitation of focusing on variance in a population is that variance describes average differences among individuals in the population. Moderate heritability in a population could mask total environmental etiology for some individuals and total genetic etiology for others. A related point is that genetic and environmental etiologies that completely explain a disorder for a few individuals account for a negligible amount of variance in the population as a whole and could thus remain undetected if quantitative genetic analyses are restricted to total variation in the population. These issues have been put in extreme form in order to emphasize that the proportion of population variance explained should not be misinterpreted as a measure of strength of effect as it applies to individuals.

Three complications of behavioral genetic analyses should also be mentioned. Although multiple genes can add up linearly in their effect on behavior, it is likely that some genetic effects involve interactions among genes, that is, nonadditive rather than additive effects. Identical twins are identical genetically and thus resemble each other for all genetic effects, including higher-order interactions among several genes. For this reason, genetic designs that involve identical twins assess all genetic variance, whether additive or nonadditive. In contrast, first-degree relatives share half of the additive genetic variance but very little nonadditive genetic variance. This distinction may be particularly important for psychiatric disorders, which often suggest evidence for nonadditive genetic variance in that identical twins are much more than twice as similar as first-degree relatives such as fraternal twins.

Other complications are assortative mating and genotype-environment interaction and correlation. The adage that opposites attract is not borne out by research—the maxim that birds of a feather flock together is closer to the truth for behavioral dimensions and disorders. For couples, this resemblance is known as positive assortative mating. It increases additive genetic variance in the population, and it has implications for estimating heritability. For example, in the twin method, unless taken into account, assortative mating will lead to underestimates of heritability. Assortative mating increases the genetic resemblance among first-degree relatives beyond 0.50; however, it cannot increase the genetic resemblance of identical twins because they are identical genetically. Thus, assortative mating has the effect of lowering the difference between identical and fraternal twin correlations, and decreasing heritability estimates for traits that show assortative mating. Genotype-environment correlation and interaction are effects at the interface of nature and nurture—they literally refer to the extent to which genetic and environmental effects correlate or interact. Although these concepts are important for conceptualizing transactions between genetic and environmental effects during development, their effect on quantitative genetic estimates is not easily assessed (Plomin, DeFries, & Loehlin, 1977).

Despite these complications, quantitative genetic methods provide a powerful approach to the etiological analysis of behavioral development. In the next two sections, we review important themes that have emerged from the application of these methods, and address possible misconceptions that surround behavioral genetic approaches to behavior and development.

Current Knowledge about Nature, Nurture, and Normal Development

Over the past 20 years, there has been an explosion of behavioral genetic research on prototypical dimensions of behavior such as personality traits and cognitive abilities. The impact of this work is reflected in a recent survey of behavioral scientists: most of the over 1,000 researchers surveyed believed that there is a heritable component to IQ (Snyderman & Rothman, 1988).

Recent overviews of the major empirical findings to date are available (Plomin, DeFries, & McClearn, 1990; Plomin & Rende, 1991). In this section, we highlight important themes that have emerged from this large body of research and that reflect current thinking on the ways in which nature and nurture impact normal development.

Genes Are Important

A first theme is that genes undoubtedly exert an important influence on the variance observed in the population—the ubiquitous individual differences that developmentalists study. Much attention has been given to the heritable nature of IQ and other cognitive abilities; more behavioral genetic data have been obtained for IQ than for any other trait. A number of studies, utilizing different paradigms (e.g., twin design, adoption designs, twin-adoption designs), have converged on the finding that individual differences in IQ are substantially influenced by genetic influences. A review of many studies involving over 100,000 individuals and essentially every behavioral genetic design concluded that the heritability of IQ is between .30 and .70 (Bouchard & McGue, 1981). More recent model-fitting analyses of the world's IQ literature continue to yield heritability estimates of about .50 (Chipuer, Rovine, & Plomin, 1990). Hence, although arguments may be made against the validity and value of IQ test scores, these traits, as typically measured, show evidence of substantial genetic influence.

A similar picture may be painted for temperament and personality traits, another domain of development that has received much attention from behavior geneticists (see Plomin, DeFries, & McClearn, 1990; Plomin & Rende, 1991). A review of research involving over 25,000 pairs of twins for the personality "superfactors"—extraversion and neuroticism—yielded average heritability estimates exceeding .50 for these two traits (Henderson, 1982), and the continuing behavior genetic evidence supports these findings (Eaves et al., 1989; Loehlin, 1992). Similarly, temperamental traits such as the EAS dimensions (emotionality, activity, and sociability) also show evidence for genetic influence (e.g., Plomin, 1986a). Although the actual estimate of heritability may fluctuate from study to study and across paradigms, there is substantial support for the notion that temperamental and personality traits are influenced in part by heritable factors.

Environment Is Important

A second theme that has emerged in behavioral genetic research over the past two decades is that the environment is an important influence on individual differences in behavior. The same data that point to significant genetic influence provide the best available evidence for the importance of nongenetic factors. As has been the case for cognitive abilities and personality traits, rarely do behavioral genetic data yield heritability estimates that exceed .50, which means that behavioral variability is due at least as much to environment as to heredity. A point made earlier bears repeating because of its importance: in quantitative genetics, the word *environment* includes any nonhereditary influence, such as biological factors (e.g., nutrition, viruses), in addition to the psychosocial environmental factors that are thought of as being prototypical indexes of environmental influences.

Environment Is of the Nonshared Type

One of the most important discoveries in human behavior genetics is that environmental factors important to development are experienced differently by children in the same family. In the past, the assumption was made that resemblance within families was caused by environmental factors shared by children growing up together in the same family. Nevertheless, behavioral genetic research indicates that sibling resemblance for most traits is due to shared genes, not shared environments. However, environmental factors are very important, although experiences shared by siblings are not. The significant environmental variation lies in experiences not shared by siblings. This implication is consistently supported by data from various designs, such as the direct test of shared environment provided by the resemblance of adoptive siblings, or pairs of genetically unrelated children adopted early in life into the same family. This category of environmental influence has been referred to by different labels over the years, including nonshared, within-family, unique, or specific. A main article in *Behavioral and Brain Science,* discussing the evidence for and the importance of nonshared environment, was followed by 32 commentaries and a response to the commentaries (Plomin & Daniels, 1987). Two recent books discuss late developments in this blossoming area of research (Dunn & Plomin, 1990; Hetherington, Reiss, & Plomin, 1994).

The evidence for the importance of nonshared environment in development is exemplified by recent research on IQ. IQ had been thought to be an exception to the rule that environmental influence is nonshared. For example, the average correlation for adoptive siblings is generally reported to be about .30, and data on twins are also consistent with an appreciable shared environment for IQ. However, studies of twins greatly overestimate shared environmental influence because the IQs of fraternal twins are nearly twice as similar as those of nontwin siblings (Plomin, 1988). The most compelling evidence comes from a 10-year longitudinal follow-up of the Texas Adoption Project, which has found that shared environment declines to negligible influence from childhood to early adulthood (Loehlin, Horn, & Willerman, 1989). Although shared environmental influences are important in childhood, their influence wanes to insignificant levels during adolescence.

Environmental Measures May Be Genetically Influenced

Another prominent finding in the behavioral genetic literature concerns the environment: measures once assumed to assess the environment have been shown to be influenced by heredity (Plomin & Bergeman, 1991). The first studies on this topic showed that adolescent identical twins are more similar to their perceptions of parental affection than are fraternal twins (Rowe, 1981, 1983). These findings were replicated in analyses of adult twins retrospectively rating their childhood rearing environment (Plomin, McClearn, Pedersen, Nesselroade, & Bergeman, 1988), and genetic influences were also found for adults' ratings of the family in which they are now the parent (Plomin, McClearn, Pedersen, Nesselroade, & Bergeman, 1989). A number of observational studies have also revealed genetic influence on directly observable interactions between family members such as mother-child and sibling dyads (e.g., Rende, Slomkowski, Stocker, Fulker, & Plomin, 1992). Other putative "environmental" measures that show evidence of genetic influence include perceptions of life events and social support as well as socioeconomic status (SES) (see Plomin & Bergeman, 1991). Two recent books (Plomin, 1994; Rowe, 1994) discuss the findings to date and the implications for future research.

Finding genetic influence on "environmental" measures should not be surprising; many of the indexes of psychosocial environment are partly products of heritable traits such as dimensions of personality. For example, it may be that a construct of family environment such as "parental affection" may reflect in part the genetically influenced trait neuroticism. This line of research has been especially important in refining the assumed distinction between nature and nurture, and has proved to be a catalyst for researchers to examine the interface of nature and nurture in development (Plomin, 1994).

Common Genes May Affect Multiple Domains

Another important advance in the study of genetic influences on development has been the refinement of methods to examine the covariation between traits rather than variance within a trait. Any quantitative genetic strategy that can be used to decompose the variance of a trait into genetic and environmental components can also be used to decompose the covariance between two traits. Rather than comparing MZ and DZ resemblance for single trait X, the basis for multivariate genetic analysis is "cross-twin" resemblance for one twin on trait X and the cotwin on trait Y. The phenotypic correlation between X and Y is assumed to be mediated genetically to the extent that MZ cross-twin resemblance exceeds DZ cross-twin resemblance. This genetic contribution to the phenotypic correlation can be shown to be the genetic correlation weighted by a function of the heritabilities of the two traits (Plomin & DeFries, 1979). Thus, even if the genetic correlation is high, the genetic contribution to the phenotypic correlation will be low if the heritability of one or both of the traits is low. A second type of question addressed by multivariate genetic analysis focuses on the genetic correlation itself. The genetic correlation indexes the extent to which genetic effects on one trait overlap with genetic effects on the other trait, independent of the heritabilities of the two traits.

Multivariate genetic strategies have been applied in recent years to the study of both cognition and personality. For example, in the cognitive domain, genetic correlations have been reported for reading and math performance (Gillis, DeFries, & Fulker, 1992) and for cognitive abilities and scholastic achievement (Thompson, Detterman, & Plomin, 1991). Evidence also exists, however, for independent genetic effects on a battery of specific cognitive abilities (Cardon, Fulker, DeFries, & Plomin, 1992). In the personality domain, a series of multivariate analyses of items of the Eysencks' personality questionnaire suggests that the genetic structure of the items can differ from the phenotypic structure, especially for the psychoticism dimension (Heath, Eaves, & Martin, 1989; Heath, Jardine, Eaves, & Martin, 1989; Heath & Martin, 1990). Hence, a general conclusion is that the genetic relationship among traits should be studied directly, because phenotypic covariation does not necessarily reflect genetic covariation.

Genetic Effects Can Change over Time

For many developmentalists, genetic influences are assumed to be static and unchanging, and these developmentalists are justifiably uneasy about such nondevelopmental phenomena. However, quantitative genetic research describes sources of variance for a particular population at a particular occasion of measurement and a particular age that will change as genetic and environmental factors change. The new subdiscipline of developmental behavior genetics focuses on genetic sources of change as well as continuity during behavioral development (Plomin, 1986a). Evidence to date, for example, suggests that, when heritability changes during development, it increases. This finding is counterintuitive for developmentalists, who make the reasonable but wrong assumption that only environmental influences, not genetic ones, accumulate during development.

In addition to investigating age changes in heritability, quantitative genetic techniques developed during the past decade can address the issue of the genetic contribution to age-to-age change (Plomin, 1986a). The simplest way to approach age-to-age genetic change is to analyze a change score, asking directly whether genetic factors contribute to change from age to age (Plomin & Nesselroade, 1990). More generally, the concepts and analysis of age-to-age change are similar to the multivariate genetic approach described in the previous section (Plomin, 1986b). Instead of analyzing the covariance between two traits, longitudinal analysis focuses on the covariance between the measurements of a trait at different ages. The genetic correlation in this longitudinal analysis indicates the extent to which genetic effects at one age are correlated with genetic effects at another age; the extent to which the genetic correlation is less than 1.0 indicates that genetic factors contribute to developmental change.

Age-to-age genetic change in this context refers to changes in the effects of genes on behavioral differences among individuals, not to changes in the transcription and translation of DNA. For example, a genetic correlation between two ages would be zero even though the same genes are transcribed at both ages, if their gene products have different effects at the two ages. Conversely, the same genes need not be transcribed at two ages even if the genetic correlation between the two ages is 1.0. That is, the relevant genes at the second age might no longer be actively transcribed, but their structural legacy (e.g., differences in neural networks) could produce a genetic correlation between the two ages.

As in the case of multivariate genetic analysis of genetic correlations, any behavioral genetic design that can estimate genetic and environmental components of the variance of a single trait can also be used to estimate genetic and environmental components of covariance across time, if longitudinal data are available. Also similar to multivariate genetic analysis, the basis for estimating age-to-age genetic correlations, for example, for twin data, is the twin "cross correlation" across ages rather than the usual twin correlation at each age. In the case of IQ, genetic correlations from childhood to adulthood are surprisingly high (DeFries, Plomin, & LaBuda, 1987; Fulker, DeFries, & Plomin, 1988). Personality data, however, suggest more genetic change than continuity, especially during childhood (Plomin & Nesselroade, 1990).

Misconceptions about Nature, Nurture, and Development

Thus far, we have reviewed the primary methods that have been used to examine the impact of nature and nurture on behavioral development, and the most important themes that have emerged from the large body of research using these methods over the past two decades. Although the major conclusions presented are generally accepted by developmentalists, there are still a number of misconceptions about the implications derived from behavioral genetic studies.

A basic misconception is that it is not possible to disentangle genetic and environmental influences on development. It is true, in a descriptive sense, that individual development reflects both genetic and environmental influences. However, as discussed earlier, behavior genetics involves the study of individual differences, not individual development. It is possible to attempt to determine, using the methods reviewed earlier, the extent to which genes and environment contribute to individual differences, which may be due primarily to genetic differences across individuals, environmental factors, or a combination of genetic and environmental influences. Behavior genetics sets out a theory of individual differences, applies methods that ascribe variation to different latent classes of effects, and interprets these findings based on the methods used and populations studied (as discussed earlier, in the section on behavioral genetic methods). In this sense, the prediction of individual differences using behavioral genetic techniques is as appropriate as the many other techniques used by developmentalists to understand behavioral variation (e.g., Goldsmith, 1993).

Another fundamental misconception surrounding behavioral genetic approaches is that genetic influences are deterministic. In the next section of this chapter, we discuss some disorders that are caused by single genes that have sledgehammer effects on development. However, there is no evidence that the domains of behavior studied by developmentalists are governed by such deterministic disease genes. Moreover, as the review of current tenets in behavior genetics has revealed, although genes are important in development, they by no means provide a complete understanding of individual differences. Hence, modern behavior genetics involves the study of *probabilistic* genes, many of small effect size, which contribute partially to individual differences on normative traits (e.g., Plomin, 1990), rather than *deterministic* genes that completely explain development.

The implication for genetic influences on development is that genes represent only a partial contribution to behavior, and their contribution is probabilistic rather than deterministic. For example, it is estimated that an individual with a schizophrenic genotype has only a 50% chance of eventually developing schizophrenia (Gottesman, 1991). It is also believed that, for most individuals at risk for schizophrenia, the pathway from genotype to phenotype is probabilistic and reflective of both genetic and nongenetic influences (e.g., Goldsmith & Gottesman, in press). This probabilistic influence of genes on behavioral development has been described as setting a "reaction range" or "reaction surface" (Turkheimer & Gottesman, 1991) of behavior rather than deterministically establishing a phenotype. Hence, the concept of a reaction surface by no means implies that potential in various domains is determined by genes in an absolute sense (e.g., Rutter, 1991).

A related point is that there may be a mistaken notion that genetic effects imply that environmental manipulations cannot exert a change. As outlined in a previous section, behavioral genetic methods that ascribe variation to genetic and environmental sources are limited to the populations studied at particular points in time—they do not imply "what should be" or "what will be" but rather "what is." As discussed by Rutter (1991), one example of this point is that environmental factors can effect levels of a trait even if individual differences on the trait are due primarily to heritable factors, as is the case with nutritional improvements leading to gains in average height in a population. Another example is IQ: adoption data demonstrate that rearing by a socially advantaged parent can lead to a significant increase in IQ as compared to rearing by a socially disadvantaged parent (Capron & Duyme, 1986).

Another misconception about genetic influences on development is that there are "good" and "bad" genes (Rutter, 1991). A general principle in genetics is pleiotropy (e.g., Plomin, DeFries, & McClearn, 1990), which refers to the fact that the effects of a single gene may be diffuse across various domains of behavior rather than specific to one domain. As discussed later, one example of pleitropy is the Fragile X anomaly, in which a localized genetic mutation may lead to a wide range of symptomatology, including social, cognitive, and behavioral dysfunction. Furthermore, the diffuse effects of genes may mean that disease genes may also confer benefits (Rutter, 1991), as is the case with the genetic locus for sickle cell, which may also lead to resistance to malaria (Childs, Moxon, & Winklestein, 1992). Hence, it is simplistic and incorrect to assume that "good" and "bad" genes will be found, and the study of genetic influences must incorporate the potential diffuse effects of genes.

A point made in a previous section of this chapter, but worth repeating, is that behavioral genetic approaches are useful for understanding and studying the environment. It is not the case that genetic strategies will only inform us on the genome (e.g., Rutter, 1991). For example, the often replicated finding of the importance of nonshared environment for development has led to major research projects devoted to the understanding of this type of environmental influence. In addition, there are theoretical models that attempt to understand the ways in which the influences of nature and nurture come together in development. Two fundamental ways in which genetic and environmental influences may be linked—genotype-environment (GE) interaction and genotype-environment (GE) correlation—were highlighted in the 1970s (Plomin et al., 1977). Genotype-environment interaction refers to an interaction in the statistical sense, as in an analysis of variance. In contrast, genotype-environment correlation refers to a correlation between the genetic and environmental influences that affect a particular trait. Three types of GE correlation—passive, reactive, and active—have been described (Plomin et al., 1977) and translated into a model of development (Scarr & McCartney, 1983). In the Scarr and McCartney model, the emphasis was on the extent to which "genes drive experience" (or active GE correlation) throughout the life span. More recently, interest in genetic influences on the environment has led to *environmental* theories about nature and nurture, such as a model in which behavioral propensities that are genetically influenced lead to the shaping of environments through selective patterns of interaction (Bronfenbrenner & Ceci, 1993; see also Horowitz, 1993, and Wachs, 1992, 1993). The overall point is that, rather than pitting nature versus nurture, modern quantitative genetic research not only examines both but is beginning to explore ". . . the hyphen in the phrase nature-nurture" (Plomin, 1994).

NATURE, NURTURE, AND ABNORMAL DEVELOPMENT

The major application of behavioral genetic methods has involved the examination of individual differences in the development of quantitative, continuous dimensions. Historically, however, research on abnormal development has focused on diagnosed conditions, and this has been the case for genetic approaches to psychopathology. This difference in orientation has led to the use of a number of strategies to understand the nature and nurture of abnormal development, other than the primary methods reviewed in the previous section of this chapter. Because the range of available strategies may not be appreciated by nongeneticists (e.g., Rutter, Macdonald et al., 1990), we begin this section of the chapter with a review of these approaches and a discussion of how the traditional methods of behavior genetics have been applied to the study of abnormal development.

How Are the Nature and Nurture of Abnormal Development Studied?

One strategy used to understand genetic influences on abnormal development is to examine the consequences of known genetic conditions. There are thousands of single-gene disorders, many of which display behavioral effects (McKusick, 1990). Many chromosomal abnormalities have documented behavioral consequences, such as Down syndrome (Cicchetti & Beeghly, 1990; Plomin, DeFries, & McClearn, 1990). An example of a genetic condition with notable behavioral symptomatology is the Fragile X syndrome. Fragile X refers to an observable break or fragile site in the structure of the X chromosome (as detected using specific culture conditions to examine the chromosomal structure of cells). Although Fragile X has been known to be strongly associated with mental retardation, in recent years the diverse clinical symptomatology associated with Fragile X has been appreciated. Additional forms of disturbance that may be displayed by some individuals with the Fragile X condition include hyperactivity, attentional deficits, and deficits typical of the syndrome of autism, such as stereotyped behavior and abnormal nonverbal communication (e.g., Bregman, Leckman, & Ort, 1988; Reiss & Freund, 1990). There is also an increasing understanding of the adaptive and behavioral functioning of individuals with the Fragile X syndrome (e.g., Dykens & Leckman, 1990).

Studying known genetic conditions is an important method for assessing genetic influences on behavior. However, because most types of psychopathology do not have a known etiology, the task is to take a behavioral condition of interest and determine whether genetics plays a role in the behavior. Over the past decade, molecular genetic techniques—sometimes referred to as the "new genetics"—have been used to isolate single-gene influences on a number of medical conditions. The most prominent technique used is linkage analysis, in which specific sites on the genome are shown to be linked to the presence of disease (see Rutter, Macdonald et al., 1990, for a brief description of linkage techniques). Generally, linkage analysis is performed after analyzing patterns of familial aggregation using statistical methods such as segregation analysis, which test how these patterns fit with genetic models. In addition, current attention has been given to molecular genetic strategies capable of identifying specific genes that have a small, rather than large, effect on behavior (Plomin, 1990).

Although there was much excitement about the promise of the "new genetics" for revealing the etiological basis of many forms of psychopathology, there also has been increasing interest in the classical methods of behavior genetics—for example, twin and adoption methods—reviewed in a previous section of this chapter (McGuffin & Murray, 1991). This interest has been spurred in part by the development of the many sophisticated model-fitting techniques that are available (e.g., Kendler, 1993). Most important is the recognition that behavioral genetic methods are most suited to assess the impact of *both* genes and environment on development (Rende & Plomin, 1994). Hence, behavioral genetic methods are still essential in sorting out the extent to which genetic and environmental factors play a role in the development of psychopathology, and should be included as part of the "new genetics" (McGuffin & Murray, 1991).

Although the basic design issues discussed earlier apply to studies of abnormal as well as normal development, there is one important difference: studies of normal development examine continuously distributed traits, whereas most studies of abnormal development focus on diagnosed conditions. Because of this, the quantitative methods used to study psychopathology differ from those used to study individual differences, and these merit discussion. One approach is to analyze rates of disorders across individuals who vary in genetic relatedness. For example, twin studies can compare concordance rates of MZ and DZ twins, with genetic influence being inferred if the MZ concordance exceeds the DZ concordance. A limitation of this approach, however, is that it does not partition the effect sizes of nature and nurture as do the model-fitting approaches of modern quantitative genetics.

A related approach has been to apply "liability" models to the study of psychopathology. Geneticists have long recognized that disorders that are defined categorically may be due to a continuum of genetic and environmental risk factors. It has been suggested that a hypothetical distribution of risk or "liability" to categorical disorders may be assumed (Falconer, 1965). The normal distribution of liability may then have a "threshold" that determines whether an individual is diagnosed as having the disorder. Estimates of genetic and environmental influences on the liability to disorders may be made from the calculation of concordance rates by modifying the model-fitting approaches used earlier.

Current Knowledge about Nature, Nurture, and Abnormal Development

All of the methods reviewed above have been used to contribute to our current knowledge about the impact of nature and nurture on abnormal development. In this section, we provide an overview of the most important themes to emerge in the quantitative genetic study of abnormal development through the life span.

Some Disorders May Be Due Entirely to Genes

The major success of the linkage approach in psychiatry has been the identification of the genomic location of the gene responsible for Huntington's disease (Gusella et al., 1983). Other major accomplishments have been the discovery of the genetic site of the Fragile X mutation (Oberle et al., 1991; Yu et al., 1991) and the localization of the genetic site for early-onset Alzheimer's disease (see Crawford & Goate, 1992). All of these disorders represent examples of genetic problems that lead to significant and substantial clinical symptomatology.

There are other disorders for which the hypothesis of a single or major gene effect has received much attention; among them is Tourette's syndrome (TS). Both twin studies and family studies using segregation analysis have consistently pointed to a genetic etiology for this syndrome (Pauls, 1992). Most studies point to the effects of a single or major gene (an autosomal dominant genetic locus) (e.g., Eapen, Pauls, & Robertson, 1993), although conclusive evidence is lacking (Rutter, Bolton et al., 1990), especially since the actual site or sites on the genome involved in the development of TS have not been isolated (e.g., Gelernter, Kennedy, Grandy, & Zhou, 1993). Another area of active genetic research focuses on developmental dyslexia or reading disability (RD). Twin studies have suggested that heritable factors are important for the emergence of RD (e.g., Pennington, Gilger, Olson, & DeFries, 1992). A number of studies have suggested that single or major gene models may provide an adequate fit to patterns of familial aggregation (Gilger, Borecki, DeFries, & Pennington, 1994). However, as is the case with TS, there is, to date, no evidence of an actual site on the genome which is associated with RD, and suggestions that there is a single or major gene must be regarded with caution.

Most Disorders Involve Effects of More Than One Gene

The promise of linkage strategies for finding single genes for other forms of psychopathology has diminished over the past few years, as demonstrated by the lack of replication of purported linkage findings for schizophrenia and bipolar disorder (e.g., Plomin & Rende, 1991). In part, this result is not surprising, because the patterns of familial aggregation for most forms of psychopathology do not conform to the expectations generated by Mendelian (i.e., single-gene) models (Rutter, Bolton et al., 1990).

What has become clear, however, is that almost all forms of psychopathology show evidence of genetic influence. In all cases, the evidence comes from behavioral genetic strategies rather than molecular genetic techniques. Complete reviews of the findings to date are available (see Rutter, Bolton et al., 1990); here, we present an overview to demonstrate the repeated finding of significant heritabilities for most disorders.

One way to organize the findings to date is to take a life-span perspective based on age of first onset. Most diagnosed disorders have a specified range for age of onset—for example, autism is usually diagnosed before age 3, whereas the onset of Alzheimer's disease is much later in the life span. Reviewing the evidence for genetic influence on psychopathology based on age of onset provides a starting point for understanding how genetic influences contribute to abnormal development through the life span.

As discussed in our Introduction, autism is now considered to be due substantially to genetic influences (Smalley, Asarnow, & Spence, 1988). Twin studies have provided the strongest evidence for genetic influence: the concordance rates for MZ twins greatly exceed the rates for DZ twins (Folstein & Rutter, 1977; Steffenburg et al., 1989). In addition, some cases of autism may be associated with the Fragile X anomaly, which, as already described, has a clear genetic basis (see Rutter, Bolton et al., 1990). Hence, the importance of genetic factors in autism is not questioned, although the genetic site involved has yet to be identified.

There is much interest in the possible role that genes play in the etiology of attention deficit/hyperactivity disorder (ADHD). Twin studies of both the dimension of attention problems (Goodman & Stevenson, 1989) and diagnosed ADHD (Gillis, Gilger, Pennington, & DeFries, 1992; Stevenson, 1992) have found evidence for genetic influence. A recent report suggested that ADHD might be due to mutations in the thyroid receptor-beta gene (Hauser, Zametkin, Martinez, & Vitiello, 1993). However, application of this finding to the vast majority of cases of ADHD is not warranted (Alessi, Hottois, & Coates, 1993), because it would be valid for no more than 3% of the cases of ADHD. The evidence to date is most consistent with moderate genetic effects rather than the impact of single or major disease genes.

More controversial findings have surrounded research on antisocial behavior, including oppositional and conduct disorders. The developmental trajectory of these behaviors is complex, because phenotypic characteristics can range from oppositional behavior in early childhood to delinquent behavior in adolescence to antisocial personality disorder in adulthood. Twin and adoptee studies have suggested a genetic component to antisocial personality disorder and criminality in adulthood (e.g., Cloninger & Gottesman, 1987; McGuffin & Gottesman, 1985). However, the impact of genetic influences on antisocial behavior—broadly conceptualized as including delinquency as well as problems of conduct—is less clear (see Rutter, Bolton et al., 1990). One potential problem is the high rate of delinquent behavior in adolescence: if delinquent behavior is part of a typical developmental phase, then it may be difficult to reveal genetic predispositions (DiLalla & Gottesman, 1989). One possibility is that genetic influences are more important in the development of antisocial behavior that persists throughout all life stages than in transient antisocial behavior that is largely confined to adolescence (Moffitt, 1993). Hence, the role of genetic influences on antisocial behavior in childhood and adolescence has yet to be clarified.

Because the developmental trajectory of antisocial behavior may often incorporate substance abuse, we next turn to evidence on genetic influences on alcohol and drug abuse. In recent years, much attention has been given to a purported association between gene markers in the dopaminergic system and both alcohol and substance abuse (e.g., Uhl, Blum, Noble, & Smith, 1993). Although some of the findings are suggestive, they are best interpreted as a possible genetic locus to vulnerability to alcohol and substance abuse rather than genes that cause alcoholism. Similarly, although twin and adoptee studies support the idea that genetic factors play a role in alcohol and substance abuse, the evidence suggests that genes have only a moderate effect (e.g., Dinwiddie & Cloninger, 1991). Most theoretical models emphasize that genetic influences on alcoholism and substance abuse are moderate at best and contribute to vulnerability or susceptibility to these syndromes, as opposed to functioning as "disease" genes that directly cause disorders involving substance abuse (e.g., Dinwiddie, 1992; George, 1993; Hill, 1992; Searles, 1991).

We have moved our focus from disorders with onsets in childhood to disorders with the usual age of first onset in adolescence or adulthood. We now turn to evidence surrounding genetic factors in affective disorders. Research on affective disorders may be divided into studies of bipolar disorder and unipolar or major depressive disorder. There is consensus that bipolar disorder has a substantial genetic basis, as evidenced by numerous twin and adoptee studies (see McGuffin & Katz, 1989; Tsuang & Faraone, 1990). The focus of most recent genetic studies of bipolar disorder has been to uncover the site or sites on the genome that are involved in the development of this disturbance. As mentioned earlier, the initial report of the discovery of a gene for bipolar disorder was retracted (Kelsoe, Ginns, Egeland, Gerhard, & Goldstein, 1989), and recent reports have continued to exclude rather than report linkage to various sites on the genome (e.g., Bredbacka, Pekkarinen, Peltonen, & Lonnqvist, 1993; Mitchell, Selbie, Waters, & Donald, 1992). Attempts to resolve the best-fitting genetic models have been inconclusive; both single-gene and polygenic models are compatible with patterns of familial aggregation (Sham, Morton, & Rice, 1992). Hence, although the importance of genetic factors in the etiology of bipolar disorder is unquestioned, the specific genetic loci involved, as well as the mode of inheritance (e.g., one vs. several vs. many genes), have yet to be determined.

More controversy has surrounded the role of genetic factors in the development of unipolar or major depression (MDD). Although many studies have documented that MDD aggregates in families, the resolution into genetic and environmental components of variance has been debated (e.g., McGuffin & Katz, 1993). However, recent twin studies, using state-of-the-art model-fitting techniques, have converged on the conclusion that MDD shows evidence of moderate to substantial genetic influence (Kendler, Neale, Kessler, Heath, & Eaves, 1992a; McGuffin & Katz, 1993). The emerging picture, then, is that genetic factors are important in the development of MDD.

Recent studies also point to the importance of genetic influences on the development of anxiety disorders. A number of papers by Kendler and colleagues provide the most recent evidence. They have demonstrated, using a population-based twin registry in Virginia, the importance of heritable factors for generalized anxiety disorder (Kendler, Neale, Kessler, Heath, & Eaves, 1992b); phobias, including agoraphobia, social phobia, situational phobia, and simple phobia (Kendler, Neale, Kessler, Heath, & Eaves, 1992c); and panic disorder (Kendler, Neale, Kessler, Heath, & Eaves, 1993a).

We complete our overview of genetic influences on psychopathology with a discussion of schizophrenia, a disorder that has been the target of a tremendous amount of genetic research. Twin and adoptee studies have supported and established the importance of heritable factors in the emergence of schizophrenia (Gottesman, 1991; Kendler & Diehl, 1993; Prescott & Gottesman, 1993). Consequently, there has been hope that the genetic basis of schizophrenia will be uncovered by molecular genetic techniques. However, as mentioned earlier, the reported discovery of genetic linkage was not replicated (Owen & Mullan, 1990), and, to date, the relevant sites on the genome involved in the etiology of schizophrenia remain unknown. Although some genetic models of schizophrenia still emphasize the possibility of effects of single or major genes (e.g., Holzman, 1992), other approaches have turned away from single-gene models, favoring instead theories that postulate the effects of several or many genes (e.g., Gottesman, 1991; McGue & Gottesman, 1991).

This brief and broad overview of current thinking on the genetic basis of the primary forms of psychopathology reveals that most disorders are believed to have a genetic basis. However, equally important is the increasingly accepted belief that these disorders, unlike Huntington's disease, are not the result of a single gene with "sledgehammerlike" effects on development. Even severe disruptions of development, such as schizophrenia, do not appear to be under such deterministic genetic control, and more common forms of dysfunction, such as MDD and ADHD, are clearly not inherited as straightforward genetic diseases. Hence, although evidence for genetic contributions to psychopathology continue to mount, current thinking is that heritable influences reflect the probabilistic impact of several or many genes rather than the control of single disease genes.

Environmental Effects Are Also Important

For almost every disorder reviewed above, the behavioral genetic evidence also points to the importance of the environment. To date, the one exception is autism; it has been suggested that autism is the most strongly genetic of all psychiatric disorders (with the exception of Huntington's disease). For all other disorders studied, heritability estimates are often less than 50%, suggesting that environmental and genetic factors are of similar magnitude. To make this point explicit, consider that the concordance rate for schizophrenia in MZ twins is usually less than 50%, meaning that more than half the time MZ twins are *discordant* for schizophrenia. If environmental factors—defined as all nongenetic sources of variance (see our Introduction)—were unimportant, then MZ twins should always be concordant for schizophrenia.

The MZ concordance for schizophrenia also serves as impressive testimony to the importance of nonshared environment in the development of psychopathology. Differences within pairs of MZ twins can only be caused by nonshared environment and error of measurement. That is, no genetic factors or genotype-environment interactions can explain differences within pairs of genetically identical individuals. Hence, concordance rates lower than 50% indicate that substantial differences related to nonshared environment are important for many MZ pairs at risk for schizophrenia. The reader is reminded that the term *environment* refers to nongenetic sources of variance, and research on schizophrenia considers both pre- and postnatal stressors, both biological and psychosocial (Gottesman, 1991; Prescott & Gottesman, 1993). The impact of these stressors, however, can clearly differ for MZ twins, and in this sense, the stressors are nonshared environmental factors.

Most other disorders also show evidence for nonshared environmental effects. For example, the behavioral genetic studies of MDD, anxiety disorders, panic disorder, and phobias, conducted by Kendler and colleagues and reviewed above, all indicate the statistical necessity of including nonshared environmental effects along with genetic effects in the best-fitting biometrical models. The only area of problem behavior in which shared environmental effects appear to be important is antisocial or delinquent behavior (see Rutter, Bolton et al., 1990, for a review). Hence, most common forms of psychopathology appear to be influenced by environmental as well as genetic factors, and, most often, environmental influences operate in a nonshared rather than shared manner.

Genetic Effects May "Turn on" at Different Points in the Life Span

Another prominent theme to emerge from a review of genetic influences on psychopathology is that genetic effects may "turn on" or become especially apparent at different points in the life span. The Fragile X syndrome and autism are two examples of genetic conditions in which the phenotypic expression occurs very early in development. In contrast, schizophrenia, which as reviewed above, has a genetic component, has a typical first age of onset of late adolescence (Weinberger, 1987), and it is not clear that there are obvious phenotypic markers prior to the first onset. Moreover, the clinical symptoms of Huntington's disease, which is known to be a single-gene disorder, do not emerge until adulthood. Genetic effects on psychopathology should not be automatically equated with having an effect early in development. The impact of genes on behavior is dynamic and may unfold at various points in the life span.

Phenotypically Defined Disorders May Be Etiologically Heterogeneous

An important issue in the study of psychopathology is the possibility that a "disorder" classified on the basis of phenotypic characteristics may actually reflect a set of conditions with different etiological bases (see Plomin & Rende, 1991). A recent review of research on autism concluded that this disorder shows evidence of genetic heterogeneity, because nearly 10% of the cases of autism may be associated with a known medical condition such as the Fragile X anomaly (Rutter, Bailey, Bolton, & Le Couteur, 1993). In addition, the authors make the point that the remaining 90% of cases of autism not due to medical conditions are not necessarily genetically homogenous. A similar speculation has been made about schizophrenia. Gottesman (1991) has made "guesstimates" of the proportional etiologies ranging from single rare genes to multifactorial models to primary environmental influences. In the cases of both autism and schizophrenia, there is current appreciation of the possibility that clinically defined syndromes may reflect a heterogeneous collection of disorders with differing etiologies. A review of current research examining heterogeneity of psychopathology is available (Plomin & Rende, 1991).

Phenotypically Distinct Disorders May Be Etiologically Homogenous

Although much genetic research on psychopathology has focused on heterogeneity within conditions, a complementary approach has been to examine whether there are genetic influences that spill over beyond a diagnosed disorder to other disorders or to a spectrum of less severe symptoms (Plomin & Rende, 1991). For example, a central question in research on Tourette's syndrome is the relation between cardinal features of the disorder, such as multiple motor and phonic tics, and other areas of dysfunction, including obsessive-compulsive behavior and attentional and learning difficulties (Cohen & Leckman, 1994; Robertson, 1989). Similarly, although the Fragile X anomaly is clearly related to mental retardation, a host of other symptoms has been identified, including hyperactivity, attention deficits, and anxiety in males (Bregman et al., 1988), and schizotypal and affective symptomatology in females (Reiss, Hagerman, Vinogradov, Abrams, & King, 1988). In a similar vein, it has been suggested that genetic influence on autism affects a range of social and cognitive abnormalities that extends beyond the typical phenotypic boundaries of this syndrome (Rutter et al., 1993).

Recent research on genetic covariation using biometrical model-fitting approaches has examined whether comorbid conditions may result from common genetic influences. The issue of comorbidity is of special interest because comorbid conditions may be the rule rather than the exception for many domains of psychopathology (Caron & Rutter, 1991). To date, common genetic influences have been found for the following comorbid conditions: alcoholism and major depression (Kendler, Heath, Neale, Kessler, & Eaves, 1993), major depression and phobias (Kendler, Neale, Kessler, Heath, & Eaves, 1993a), and major depression and generalized anxiety disorder (Kendler, Neale, Kessler, Heath, & Eaves, 1992d). Hence, the common impact of genes on comorbid conditions may be as prominent as the heterogeneous genetic influences within single diagnostic categories.

Genetic and Environmental Influences May Be Linked in "Surprising" Ways

A final theme of this section is that research on psychopathology has begun to demonstrate that nature and nurture may come together in ways that may be surprising to some individuals because of common misconceptions about genetic influences (Rutter, 1991). One way in which nature and nurture may be linked is that genetic conditions may have environmental effects (Plomin, Rende, & Rutter, 1991). A notable example of this is research on Huntington's disease (HD). HD families show an increased rate of conduct disorder. However, it appears that the occurrence of conduct disorder is a consequence of the family discord associated with parental psychopathology that accompanies the emergence of HD (Folstein, Franz, Jensen, Chase, & Folstein, 1983). Similarly, a recent adoption study found that antisocial behavior in adoptive parents is associated with a markedly increased risk for affective disturbance in the adopted offspring, and it appears that this risk may be caused by environmental stresses rather than direct genetic paths (Cadoret, Troughton, Moreno, & Whitters, 1990). Thus, genetic factors may lead to one form of psychopathology, which may, in turn, predispose to a second type of disorder through nongenetic mechanisms.

A second novel way in which genetic and environmental influences may be linked is through the effects of environmental interventions on genetic conditions. The best example to date is research on phenylketonuria (PKU). Although PKU is known to be a genetic disorder, the simple environmental intervention of providing low phenylalanine diets may prevent PKU children from becoming retarded. In this case, an environmental treatment program based on knowledge of the genetic deficit may be used to circumvent the deleterious effects of a genetic condition.

A third way in which nature and nurture may be linked is provided by research on psychosocial stressors as a risk factor for major depression. Historically, stressors such as recent life events have been regarded as a salient environmental risk factor for depression. However, current studies have begun to yield the conclusion that the relationship between stressors and depression is more complex: reports of life events, coping, and social support all show evidence of genetic influence (e.g., Kendler, Neale, Kessler, Heath, & Eaves, 1993c; Kessler, Kendler, Heath, Neale, & Eaves, 1992). It is postulated that a common genetic liability to experience both psychosocial stressors and depression may account for the link between the two (e.g., McGuffin & Katz, 1993). This example serves as a reminder that it may be misleading to classify risk factors for psychopathology as "environmental" on an a priori basis, because the possibility exists that such risk factors may involve, in part, the influence of genes. It must be appreciated that individuals may, to some extent, create their own risk environments (Scarr & McCartney, 1983), and genetically influenced traits may play a role in this process (Rutter, 1991).

HOW CAN QUANTITATIVE GENETIC RESEARCH ON DISORDERS INFORM THEORIES OF NORMAL DEVELOPMENT?

Thus far, we have reviewed current thinking in quantitative genetic research on normal and abnormal development, respectively. This division of research is reflective of the state of the field; the majority of quantitative genetic studies can be placed in one of the two categories fairly easily. However, it is becoming increasingly clear that quantitative genetic strategies hold much promise for integrating our knowledge about normal and abnormal development (e.g., Rende & Plomin, 1990). In this section, we consider a few prominent ways in which such an integration may take place.

Convergence between Findings on Normal and Abnormal Development

One way in which quantitative genetic research can help integrate the study of both normal and abnormal development is through the emergence of converging findings. There is considerable overlap between the general themes that have arisen from quantitative genetic research on the normal and abnormal. Both approaches have come to the following conclusions:

1. Genetic influences (a) are important, (b) primarily reflect the impact of many genes of small probabilistic effect rather than the sledgehammer effects of single deterministic genes, and (c) can change throughout the life span.
2. Environmental influences (a) are important, (b) are primarily nonshared rather than shared, and (c) can have an impact even for traits or disorders that are primarily caused by genetic factors.
3. Environmental variables may be partially influenced by genes.

In addition, there has been a carryover of methodologies across perspectives, as exemplified by the use of multivariate genetic methods to examine covariation between traits (or disorders). In many ways, then, although the behaviors of interest may differ, quantitative genetic research on both normal and abnormal development has led to an impressive overlap in the body of evidence on the role of nature and nurture in development.

This convergence of findings may allow quantitative genetic research on psychopathology to magnify the ways in which nature and nurture impact development because of its overt significance to society. For example, the dismissal of psychodynamic theories of autism and schizophrenia highlights the importance of determining empirically the extent to which familial aggregation for any trait is caused by genetic and environmental factors. Similarly, if a profound disturbance of development, such as schizophrenia, is believed to be caused by probabilistic genetic vulnerability as well as a host of nongenetic factors, it becomes less plausible to think of normative traits such as IQ and personality as being the result of deterministic genes. Similarly, the finding that MZ twins are, more often than not, discordant for schizophrenia may serve as a powerful example of how pronounced nonshared environmental factors may be in development. It is hoped that (a) these findings on the abnormal may help to highlight how nature and nurture impact behavioral development, and (b) the continuing clarification of the terms *genetic influences* and *environmental influences* on complex phenotypes may not only inform models of development, but also help to assuage concerns about genetic determinism.

Using Maladaptation to Highlight Normal Developmental Processes

An explicit way in which quantitative genetic research on abnormal development can inform us about normal development is by magnifying processes responsible for normal development through the study of maladaptation (see Rende & Plomin, 1990). This strategy has been used profitably in the field of genetics: examinations of inborn errors of metabolism have led to the "one gene, one enzyme" hypothesis that is the basic mechanism of normal gene action (Beadle & Tatum, 1941).

Currently, there is promise that investigations of known genetic conditions will lead to a body of knowledge about normal development. One discrete, although small, window on normal development is provided by research on PKU. Understanding the genetic basis of this disorder has revealed that sufficient amounts of tyrosine are necessary for normal cognitive development, although it must be stressed that this gene is not responsible for variation in normal cognitive development (Rende & Plomin, 1990).

A second example is how research on the Fragile X syndrome has provided the potential for understanding normal development (see Rende & Plomin, 1994). As reviewed earlier, because of the range of symptoms observed in individuals with the Fragile X anomaly, research on this syndrome demonstrates that a single genetic factor can influence a vast array of behavioral domains, including cognition and language, as well as psychopathological characteristics such as atypical personality and affective symptoms. The diversity of domains affected reveals an important principle, referred to as pleiotropy, in genetics: localized genetic sites (such as the Fragile site on the X chromosome) may affect multiple domains of functioning. Future study of the Fragile X syndrome holds out the promise of identifying the specific mechanisms by which genes have their diffuse effect on behavior. For Fragile X, the recent discovery of the genetic site of the mutation will intensify this search (Oberle et al., 1991; Yu et al., 1991). Knowing the molecular basis of the Fragile X syndrome may eventually reveal not only the specific gene product responsible for the mutation, but also the biological pathways that result in the behavioral symptoms associated with the Fragile X site (Reiss & Freund, 1990). The eventual combination of both molecular genetic techniques and other biological methods may reveal how this genetic condition affects neural development and may pinpoint specific areas in the brain that underlie the behavioral consequences of Fragile X. In turn, understanding the complex gene-brain-behavior pathways involved in this syndrome may highlight how these pathways work in normal development, as was the case when study of inborn errors of metabolism led to the "one gene, one enzyme" hypothesis of normal gene action.

Applying an Individual Differences Perspective to Research on Psychopathology

As discussed in an earlier section of this chapter, behavioral genetic research is based on an individual differences perspective rather than a normative or "species typical" framework. Although the utility of this approach has been well recognized for studying normative dimensions of behavior, such as cognitive abilities and personality traits, this approach can be used to study variation in the population in terms of psychopathology. This perspective is enticing because lesser variants of pathological conditions may be seen, and, rather than clearly stand out as disorders, these variants may blend more gradually into variations seen across individuals. It is important to note that such an individual differences perspective does not imply that the "disordered" behavior is not problematic; rather, it is seen as problematic against a background of variation instead of a background of a static norm. However, applying an individual differences perspective to psychopathology yields data on both normal and abnormal development, because the entire range of functioning is examined rather than focusing a priori on either a normative range or affected individuals (Rende, in press).

One example of the utility of an individual differences perspective is research on common behavior problems in childhood and adolescence (see Rende, in press). Common behavior problems offer an opportunity to apply behavioral genetic techniques aimed at individual differences because the defining symptoms—such as oppositional behavior, aggressive behavior, attentional problems, and depressed mood—are often present in varying degrees in individuals. The variance in problem behaviors, which is observed among children and adolescents, raises the question of the etiology of these differences. From a quantitative genetic perspective, individual differences in a continuum of symptoms (i.e., ranging from no problems to some problems to many problems) could be caused by genetic differences among individuals, environmental differences among individuals, or a combination of genetic and environmental effects. By focusing on the range of symptoms in the population (from none to many), quantitative genetic approaches provide information on the etiology of both adaptive and maladaptive behavior.

Recent behavioral genetic studies have begun to provide a database on the influences of genes and environment on common behavior problems in childhood and adolescence, and a few general trends have begun to appear. A number of studies have indicated that two forms of behavior problems in childhood and adolescence—aggressive behavior and attention problems—may be especially influenced by genetic differences across individuals (Edelbrock, Rende, Plomin, & Thompson, in press; Goodman & Stevenson, 1989). There is also emerging evidence that depressed mood in adolescence is caused partly by genetic influences (Edelbrock et al., in press; Rende, Plomin, Reiss, & Hetherington, 1993). In contrast to the general finding of genetic influence, twin studies of delinquent behavior have suggested that genetic influences are less prominent, whereas shared environmental factors seem to be especially important (Carey, 1992; Edelbrock et al., in press; Rowe, 1983, 1986).

The findings discussed above may be viewed as initial attempts to construct developmental models of genetic and environmental influences on diverse behavior problems through childhood and adolescence. What is notable about this approach is that the focus is not on normative development or pathological development per se, but rather on the range of individual differences that is seen when one considers dimensions of problem behaviors in childhood and adolescence. Focusing on the roots of this variation represents a prototypical way in which quantitative genetic research may contribute to understanding the etiology of adaptive and maladaptive behavior in an integrated fashion.

Empirical Investigation of the Etiology of Individual Differences and Extreme Cases

Perhaps the most explicit way of integrating quantitative genetic approaches with the study of developmental psychopathology is to generate empirical tests to determine the most appropriate models for specific forms of psychopathology. That is, an explicit focus on determining the continuity or discontinuity between adaptive and maladaptive development, which is a hallmark of developmental psychopathology (Cicchetti, 1984), may be accomplished through the application of new quantitative genetic methods (e.g., Plomin, Rende, & Rutter, 1991; Rende & Plomin, 1990).

In terms of quantitative genetics, the crucial question from this perspective is whether the genetic and environmental influences on disorders also contribute to normal variations in the general population; that is, are there discrete etiological factors specific to a disorder, or is there a continuum of risk factors that contributes to the etiology of the disorder? Depending on the finding, the implications for normal development may vary.

As reviewed earlier, geneticists have allowed for the possibility that disorders that are defined categorically may be caused by a continuum of genetic and environmental risk factors through the application of liability models. The concept of liability has been useful in research on some diseases. For example, convulsive threshold, a dimension that underlies the diagnostic category of epilepsy, can be detected only by special tests; it is not manifest in minor or infrequent seizures (see Plomin, Rende, & Rutter, 1991). However, a difficulty with the liability approach in research on psychopathology is that it assumes that a normal distribution of risk factors underlies a disorder, rather than assessing the risk factors empirically. It has been suggested that there can be no presuppositions that the extremes do or do not involve the same etiological mechanisms that operate in the normative range of functioning (Rutter, 1988); there must be empirical tests for similarities and dissimilarities between etiological mechanisms. The challenge is to translate the hypothesized liability into something measurable, such as a behavioral dimension representing degrees of a categorical disorder or processes related to a disorder.

Recently, DeFries and Fulker (1985, 1988) developed a quantitative genetic method that assesses the extent to which dimensions are etiologically related to disorders. This technique, which has been called "DF" analysis (Plomin & Rende, 1991), makes it possible to assess the extent to which the magnitude of genetic and environmental influences on extreme scores (on a quantitative measure) differs from the magnitude of etiological influences on the entire range of individual differences. As such, the method represents a way of determining, in terms of etiology, the extent to which extreme symptomatology (e.g., characteristic of a psychiatric disorder) reflects a qualitative or quantitative departure from the normal range of variation (see Plomin, 1991; Plomin, Rende, & Rutter, 1991; Rende, in press; Rende & Plomin, 1990).

The conceptual framework for DF analysis is presented most easily by using the more straightforward case of siblings (rather than twins or adoptees). DF analysis introduces a new concept of familial resemblance (group familiality), which it contrasts with the traditional concept of individual familiality. The traditional concept of individual familiality is indexed by sibling resemblance for a quantitative trait. Specifically, the correlation between siblings indicates the extent to which individual differences—or variability—on the trait of interest may be attributable to familial factors (i.e., genetic or environmental factors operating to produce similarities within families), and hence is termed "individual familiality."

A novel index of familial resemblance derived from DF analysis estimates familial factors involved in the expression of extreme scores on the trait (as in the case of clinical populations). This estimate, called "group familiality," represents in general terms the extent to which family members—in this case, siblings—deviate from normality on the trait of interest. For example, if extreme scores on a trait are caused by familial factors, then the siblings of "probands" (i.e., individuals diagnosed as cases because their scores exceed a cutoff on the scale of interest) would also be expected to have scores that deviate from normality and perhaps begin to approach the clinical range.

Technically, group familiality is indexed by the regression toward the mean of sibling scores on the quantitative measure in order to provide a quantitative estimate of the degree to which extreme scores are caused by familial factors. For a quantitative measure relevant to a particular disorder, the mean of diagnosed probands will fall toward the extreme of the distribution. The mean of the siblings of the probands will regress to the unselected population mean, to the extent that familial factors are unimportant in the etiology of the disorder. In contrast, if familial factors are important, the mean of the siblings of the probands will be greater than the population mean. The extent to which the mean difference between the siblings and the population approaches the mean difference between the probands and the population on a quantitative measure provides an estimate of the extent to which the mean difference between the probands and the population on the quantitative measure is caused by familial factors.

One example of the utility of this approach is provided by family studies on mental retardation (Nichols, 1984), which used IQ tests as a continuous measure of cognitive ability (see Plomin, Rende, & Rutter, 1991). Siblings of severely retarded children (IQs less than 50) had an average IQ of 103, and none was retarded. In contrast, the average IQ of siblings of mildly retarded children (IQs from 60 to 69) was 85, and one-fifth of the siblings were retarded. This research yielded two important findings: (a) severe retardation shows no familiality and is thus etiologically distinct from the rest of the IQ distribution; and (b) mild retardation is familial and is thus etiologically connected with the rest of the IQ distribution.

Twins or adoptees are needed to determine the extent to which familiality is caused by heredity rather than environment shared by siblings. Group heritability (h^2_g) indicates the proportion of the difference between the probands and the unselected population that is attributable to genetic differences. It is based, for example, on the differential regression toward the mean for cotwins of MZ and DZ probands. For instance, h^2_g is 0 if MZ and DZ cotwins regress to the population mean to the same extent. In contrast, h^2_g is 1.0 if MZ cotwins do not regress toward the mean and if DZ cotwins regress halfway back to the mean. Two important differences between the twin approach and the sibling approach should be emphasized. In the case of twins, note that two types of "siblings" are studied; hence, information is provided by comparing the difference between MZ and DZ cotwin means rather than using a single sibling mean. In addition, the sibling approach indicates the extent to which familiality is important, whereas the twin approach attempts to decompose familiality into genetic and environmental components.

Similar to individual familiality, individual heritability (h^2) is based on the traditional estimates of heritability reviewed earlier, such as doubling the difference in correlations for MZ and DZ twins. In addition, estimates of both individual and group shared environment (c^2 and c^2_g, respectively) may be determined in this approach. A multiple regression approach that estimates h^2, h^2_g, c^2, and c^2_g was presented by DeFries and Fulker (1985, 1988).

It should be emphasized that the reliance on quantitative measures in DF analysis does not preclude the use of clinically diagnosed individuals. Rather, the inclusion of diagnosed individuals as probands strengthens the approach. The key, however, is to utilize quantitative measures that are relevant to the symptomatology of interest, so that links between the normal and abnormal may be addressed empirically (see Rende & Plomin, 1990). Indeed, many behavioral disorders of interest—for example, unipolar depression, hyperactivity, anxiety, and conduct problems—clearly are present in varying degrees in the population, and the etiological links or breaks between normative ranges of functioning and the extremes in these cases may be investigated directly.

The DF analysis was first applied to reading disability. Probands and twins were assessed using a continuous discriminant function score of reading-related tests (DeFries, Fulker, & LaBuda, 1987). Group heritability was found to be only about half the magnitude of individual heritability, suggesting that reading disability is etiologically different from the continuous dimension of reading ability. A related study also suggested that group heritability for reading recognition may be of smaller magnitude than individual heritability (Olson, Wise, Conners, Rack, & Fulker, 1989). A multivariate extension of the DF analysis suggested that phonological coding ability (e.g., speed and accuracy in pronouncing nonwords such as "ter" and "tegwop") may be a key element in the genetics of reading disability (Olson et al., 1989).

Recently, DF analysis has been applied to the study of depressive symptomatology in adolescence (Rende et al., 1993). Individual differences in depressive symptomatology—as assessed by the Children's Depression Inventory (CDI; Kovacs, 1983)—were accounted for by moderate genetic influence and nonshared environmental influences. Moderate genetic influence was also observed when analyses focused on probands—adolescents who exceeded the suggested cutoff score of 13, which is used to index risk for clinical depression. (Higher cutoff scores could not be used because of the small number of subjects who had scores in this range.) In contrast to the findings on individual differences, however, shared environmental influences were pronounced for the extremes, and these were significantly greater than the shared environmental effects on individual differences. The results were interpreted using a diathesis-stress model, which speculated that there is a continuum of genetic risk (or diathesis) for depression, along with specific familial psychosocial stressors (such as family discord or major life events), and together they lead to the expression of extreme depressive symptomatology in some adolescents. It must be stressed that the adolescents in this study were not assessed clinically, and research with clinical samples is necessary before firm conclusions can be drawn. However, an implication of the study is that the mix of genetic and environmental influences on extreme scores may indeed differ from that of individual differences.

Two recent twin studies have applied the DF methodology to assess genetic influence on diagnosed Attention Deficit/Hyperactivity Disorder (ADHD). In both studies, group heritability was highly significant and substantial, providing strong evidence for genetic influence on this syndrome (Gillis et al., 1992; Stevenson, 1992). The findings in both studies are consistent with the results reported earlier for the dimension of attention problems (Edelbrock et al., in press; Goodman & Stevenson, 1989). In contrast to the findings on reading disability and depression presented above, the data from the studies of ADHD indicate that genetic factors play a similar role in the etiology of both the dimension of attention problems and symptoms characterizing diagnosed cases of the disorder, suggesting continuity between the etiology of individual differences and the extremes for this domain of psychopathology.

Although a minimal number of studies have used the DF approach, the results to date are exciting and promising. The most important contributions of this approach are its move away from arguments regarding the most appropriate etiological model, and its replacement of rhetoric with empirical tests about links between variation in the population and the extreme cases assessed as disorders. This new quantitative genetic approach carries many implications for studying links and breaks between the normal and abnormal (see Rende & Plomin, 1990), and the implications for investigation are as profound for normal development as they are for abnormal development. Most notable is the attempt to consider both the normal and abnormal in an integrated fashion. Such work is a defining characteristic of the field of developmental psychopathology and may help to determine whether the normal range of variability for different forms of symptomatology includes the extremes of the distribution.

The results of DF analysis are directly relevant to the study of normal development, if the etiology of the extremes does not differ from the etiology of individual differences in the population (Rende & Plomin, 1990). Such a finding would be consistent with the hypothesis that disorders are the extremes of the normal distribution. The payoff in terms of understanding normal development would be that the genetic and environmental contributions to affected cases may be the same as those contributing to normative or adaptive development. In this case, studying abnormal development may highlight the mechanisms that also contribute to positive outcomes. Such research may refine our study of the "normal" and "abnormal" and may lead to a more integrated approach that focuses on behaviors and processes along a continuum of adaptation/maladaptation as opposed to presence or absence of disorders.

If, on the other hand, the etiology of the extremes differs from the etiology of individual differences in the population, the range in symptomatology that may be considered normative may be specified, as well as the range that indexes an etiologically different phenomenon (Rende & Plomin, 1990). DF analysis may contribute to our definitions of both normal ranges of variability and the extremes that are considered as pathological. For example, one crucial piece of information would be the "breakpoint" in the distribution that best distinguishes the normal range of variability from extreme cases. In this way, DF analysis may be of great benefit in providing proper definitions of a clinical phenotype that may be etiologically distinct from normal variation and highly heritable, and hence perhaps more amenable to molecular genetic strategies that work best with rarer forms of dysfunction rather than normal variation (Rende, in press). In this case, however, an empirical demonstration of etiological discontinuity would be available, rather than merely an assumption that this is the case.

Another quantitative genetic approach that broaches the issue of continuity and discontinuity between the normal and abnormal is an application of latent class analysis recently developed by Eaves and colleagues. A mathematical discussion of this approach is provided in Eaves, Silberg, Hewitt, and Rutter (1993), and a more conceptual discussion may be found in Eaves, Silberg, Hewitt, Meyer et al. (1993). In brief, in this method, latent class analysis is used to determine empirically whether psychopathology represents a categorical break with normal variation on a trait, such as symptoms of conduct disorder. As outlined in Eaves, Silberg, Hewitt, Meyer et al. (1993), a first step is to determine the number of underlying categories of subjects or latent classes that is necessary to explain the pattern of associations between variables, such as the items on a symptom checklist. For example, in their analysis of data on ADHD, Eaves, Silberg, Hewitt, Meyer et al. (1993) reported that a three-class model was necessary to explain data on ADHD symptoms in a sample of male twins. This model supported a distinction between general symptoms of ADHD and a more severe pattern of symptoms that appeared to be of clinical relevance.

Most importantly, in terms of the theme of this section, the latent-class approach also is applied to examine the issue of continuity or discontinuity between normal variation and psychopathology from a quantitative genetic perspective. In essence, this approach determines the extent to which MZ and DZ twins are correlated for class membership, and then decomposes this correlation into genetic and environmental sources. The various models that may be postulated are outlined in Eaves, Silberg, Hewitt, Meyer et al. (1993), and they are conceptually similar to the basic model-fitting approach outlined earlier in this chapter. What is novel about this approach is that it moves away from models that *assume* a continuous liability to psychopathology in favor of empirical tests to determine whether there is a break between the normal and abnormal, both phenotypically and etiologically. In summary, this approach carries the same profound implications for studying the etiology of normal and abnormal development in an integrated manner as the DF analysis outlined above.

FUTURE DIRECTIONS FOR QUANTITATIVE GENETIC RESEARCH IN DEVELOPMENTAL PSYCHOPATHOLOGY

The review of research in this chapter is testimony to the enormous progress that has been made in studying how nature and nurture contribute to both normal and abnormal development. However, although a number of general principles have emerged from this vast area of research, many basic questions remain about the precise ways in which nature and nurture impact the course of development through the life span. In this section, we review some of the most fundamental themes that should be considered in the next decade of research.

Identifying Specific Genes That Affect Behavior

A first goal is to make progress in identifying, through the technology of the "new genetics" or molecular genetics, specific genes that contribute to behavioral development. As reviewed earlier, although there is a large body of data on single-gene disorders and their impact on development, such disorders are atypical and not representative of the way genes will influence behavior. Most important is the recognition that, for most complex forms of behavior, including most forms of psychopathology that emerge through the life span, genetic influence refers to the small, probabilistic effect of many genes rather than the deterministic sledgehammer effects of single disease genes (Plomin, 1990).

Applications of the new genetics to the study of developmental psychopathology have been presented elsewhere (Plomin, Rende, & Rutter, 1991; Rende & Plomin, 1994); here, we emphasize the most crucial concerns for the next decade of research. Quantitative genetic techniques assess genetic variation through indirect means such as comparing MZ and DZ twins. This has been and will continue to be a source of great strength, because quantitative genetics addresses the "bottom line" of genetic influences on variability. That is, these methods assess the total impact of genetic variability of any kind, regardless of the complexity of its molecular source of variation. However, the advent of the new genetics has yielded many genetic markers that can be screened for their contribution, independently and jointly, to the variance of quantitative traits, even in the case of traits for which perhaps scores of genes each contribute small portions of variances in the population and for which environmental factors are important. Such multiple loci that affect quantitative traits have been called quantitative trait loci (QTL; Gelderman, 1975), although the notion of multiple-gene influence is just as relevant to qualitative traits such as psychiatric diagnoses.

The use of molecular techniques to clarify the inheritance of complex traits is not new, but the idea gains tremendous power from the thousands of genetic markers that are now available. Such analyses were previously limited to about 80 genetic markers expressed peripherally in blood, saliva, or urine. Nearly 2,000 DNA markers are now available that assess variability in

DNA itself, not just DNA expressed as polypeptides in peripheral systems (Kidd et al., 1989). Moreover, this is just the beginning: About 1 in 1,000 nucleotide DNA bases differs for unrelated humans, which means that about 3 million of our 3 billion bases are variable.

Applications of molecular genetic techniques to the study of behavior are unlikely to succeed if they need to assume that a major gene is largely responsible for genetic variation. This is the problem with linkage analyses of large family pedigrees that have failed to uncover replicable major gene effects for psychiatric disorders, as reviewed earlier. The alternative hypothesis emphasized in this chapter is that major gene effects will not be found for behavior (both normative traits and diagnosed forms of psychopathology). Rather, for each individual, many genes may make small contributions toward variability and vulnerability. The genetic quest is not to find *the* gene for a psychiatric disorder or psychological trait, but to find the *many* genes that increase the likelihood of displaying the disorder or trait in a probabilistic rather than a predetermined manner.

One possibility is to employ allelic association strategies rather than linkage, because sample sizes can be increased to provide sufficient power to detect associations that account for small amounts of variance among individuals in a population (Plomin, Rende, & Rutter, 1991). Allelic association, usually called linkage disequilibrium, refers to covariation between allelic variation in a marker and phenotypic variation among individuals in a population (Edwards, 1991). Most importantly, instead of using random DNA markers to look painstakingly through the human genome for QTL, a more efficient initial strategy is to screen polymorphic candidate genes with known function, especially genes involved in neurological processes, for their individual and joint contributions to behavior. Two examples are: (a) research on the association between a dopamine receptor gene and susceptibility to substance abuse (Uhl et al., 1993), and (b) a recent study that has begun to explore DNA markers associated with high versus low IQ (Plomin et al., 1994).

What good is it if we find QTL associations with behavior? Success in the QTL quest will revolutionize behavior genetics. We can begin to replace our anonymous components of genetic variance, estimated in twin and adoptee studies, with specific DNA variation measured directly in individuals, which will provide indisputable evidence of genetic influence on behavior. We will be able to transform quantitative genetic analyses of a complex phenomenon, such as comorbidity, by revealing whether the same genes are involved in the development of different disorders. Knowledge about the specific genes that impact behavior will also allow a more precise understanding of the complex biological pathways by which genetic variation contributes to behavioral variation. In addition, the application of techniques such as the QTL approach will revolutionize the way in which we study how genes contribute to both normal and abnormal development by revealing whether the genetic loci involved in psychopathology are the same loci that contribute to normal variation. We will no longer need to rely on the indirect evidence provided by the statistical approaches reviewed earlier, such as DF analysis. In summary, quantitative genetic methods have provided evidence of genetic influence on a wide range of traits and disorders; the next step is to begin to isolate the genes that contribute to behavior and to understand how they have their effect on development.

Redefining the Phenotype and Genotype in Studies of Genetic Influence on Psychopathology

Another important issue in research on psychopathology is to consider that the dimensions of symptomatology influenced by genes do not necessarily coincide with the symptoms used to define disorders. We reviewed evidence that genetic influences can, for example, be common across different disorders (e.g., depression and anxiety) or extend to areas of functioning not considered as core symptomatology (e.g., as in autism). These examples serve as strong reminders that genetic strategies that are rigidly confined to clinically defined disorders are likely to be unsuccessful.

Future research should aggressively apply the multivariate techniques reviewed earlier to aid in the search for the genetically influenced phenotypes underlying different forms of psychopathology. The multivariate approach to comorbidity and heterogeneity has already begun to clarify, broadly speaking, the genetic architecture within and across different syndromes (as reviewed in this chapter), and this strategy is essential for future studies (e.g., Rende & Plomin, 1994; Rutter et al., 1993). Furthermore, an important developmental extension of this general multivariate model will be to utilize longitudinal designs to examine how the genetically influenced phenotype is expressed over time.

Another notable approach is to search for biological markers of psychopathology that may be more heritable than the diagnosed conditions they underlie. One example is the research on schizophrenia that examines eye movement abnormalities as a potential biological marker for schizophrenia that may be caused by a single or major gene (Holzman & Matthysse, 1990). There are, however, many other potential biological markers or indexes of biological liability to schizophrenia, in addition to eye movement abnormalities; the specific form of pathophysiology involved in the development of schizophrenia has yet to be resolved. Other potential markers that have received intensive study include structural brain abnormalities, biochemical markers, and attentional and cognitive disturbances (see Moldin & Erlenmeyer-Kimling, 1994). Such work is notable in that attempts are made to specify which biobehavioral pathways may be compromised in individuals at risk for schizophrenia in order to help identify the genetic liability to the complex phenotype of clinically defined schizophrenia (Moldin, 1994).

A second example of biological markers of liability to disorders is research on behavioral inhibition to the unfamiliar, which is a temperamental construct characterized by shy and fearful behavior and believed to have a substantial genetic basis (Kagan, Reznick, & Snidman, 1988). A number of recent studies have indicated that this temperamental construct may be an early risk factor for the development of anxiety disorders (see Rosenbaum et al., 1993, for a review). For example, children of parents with panic disorder with agoraphobia are at increased risk for behavioral inhibition (Rosenbaum et al., 1988), and children with behavioral inhibition have high rates of anxiety disorders with onsets in childhood (Biederman et al., 1990). Such work is suggestive that behavioral inhibition is a genetically influenced trait that may be a marker of risk for anxiety disorders and may be observed in early childhood or, perhaps, infancy. Hence, this work demonstrates the potential of identifying specific phenotypic profiles—in the form of temperamental constructs—that may also be biological markers for the development of specific forms of psychopathology.

Research on attentional dysfunction and schizophrenia, and behavioral inhibition and anxiety disorders, respectively, illustrate the potential utility of defining early emerging phenotypic markers of risk for psychopathology that have a familial basis. More work of this nature—especially studies using multivariate behavioral genetic approaches—may help tremendously in defining more precisely phenotypic characteristics that reflect genetic predispositions of psychopathology. Such work would undoubtedly inform research on the genetic contributions of psychiatric disorders (e.g., Rende & Plomin, 1994).

Identifying Specific Environmental Factors That Affect Behavior

Identifying environmental influences that contribute to behavioral development, both adaptive and maladaptive, is as important a goal in quantitative genetics as the identification of genes that affect behavior. As discussed throughout this chapter, quantitative genetics involves the study of both nature and nurture, and quantitative genetic methods provide the best evidence for environmental influences by controlling for genetic effects.

The conclusion that environmental factors operate primarily in a nonshared manner has important implications for research over the next decade. The overall point is that researchers need to think about the environment on an individual-by-individual rather than a family-by-family basis. The message is not that family experiences are unimportant but rather that environmental influences in behavioral development are specific to each child rather than general to an entire family.

Research on nonshared environment can be categorized into (a) analyses of the magnitude of the nonshared environment component of variance, (b) attempts to identify specific nonshared factors that are experienced differently by siblings in a family, and (c) explorations of associations between nonshared factors and behavior. Most is known about the first issue. Although research on the second issue has just begun, it seems clear that siblings growing up in the same family experience quite different family environments in terms of their parents' treatment, their interactions with their siblings, experiences beyond the family, and chance (Dunn & Plomin, 1990). Concerning the third direction for research, the few initial attempts to relate nonshared environmental factors to sibling differences in outcome are promising. As such associations are found, it becomes necessary to untangle their possible genetic sources. Because siblings differ genetically, associations between differences in their experience and behavioral outcomes may be caused by their genetic differences rather than their nonshared experiences. Identical twins provide a stringent test of differential experiences of siblings that cannot be caused by genetic differences within sibling pairs (Baker & Daniels, 1990).

It is ironic that, after decades of environmentalism, the limiting factor in this effort is the need for better measures of the environment. Especially scarce are environmental measures that are specific to a child rather than general to a family, measures of experience (the subjective, experienced environment) in contrast to measures of the objective environment, and measures that move beyond the passive model of the child as merely a receptacle for environmental influence to measures that can capture the child's active selection, modification, and creation of environments. These needs are great because researchers often apply measures designed to assess between-family effects to examine nonshared influences on children. Rather than assessing indirectly the way in which siblings may have different experiences within the family, we need to develop methods for capturing what each child experiences within the family as well as outside the family. Such advances in environmental assessment will contribute to our understanding of specific nonshared environmental influences, for example, by investigating observations of family interaction, differences in perceptions of the family environment, and ways in which children contribute to the creation of differential experiences. This research direction can also begin to elucidate the processes by which children in the same family experience different environments.

The relevance to the study of psychopathology may be illustrated by considering the effects of maternal depression on development (e.g., Rende & Plomin, 1993). Many known negative characteristics of parenting are displayed by depressed parents (see Rutter, 1990). However, to date, no studies have examined how a depressed parent interacts with multiple children within the family. Such a strategy is important because of the possibility that a depressed parent may show differential behavior within the family, perhaps based in part on differences among children in areas such as temperamental characteristics. A necessary step in research is to abandon assumptions that parents with specific forms of psychopathology present a homogeneous environment to multiple offspring. Empirical efforts examining the extent to which environmental risk is not shared by children in a family, as well as the association between nonshared experiences and outcome, are essential for understanding how high-risk environments contribute to the development psychopathology.

Understanding the Construction of Risk Environments

Another conclusion about the environment has emerged from behavioral genetic research: that the environment may be subject to genetic influence. This conclusion carries strong implications for research in developmental psychopathology, especially because it suggests that genetic factors may influence how certain individuals actively create risk environments. That is, genetic factors undoubtedly play a role in the wide range of individual differences seen in exposure to risk environments (Rutter, 1991), as was the case with the association between depression and life events. Because genetics may play a role in how individuals create their own environmental influences, such as risk factors for psychopathology, research in this area should attempt in the near future to sort out the environmental measures most and least influenced genetically. Research should also be aimed at identifying processes by which heredity affects measures of the environment. So far, the obvious candidates—for example, parental IQ and personality in the case of genetic influence on the family environment—do not seem to be the answer (Plomin & Bergeman, 1991). Continued research on the genetics of environmental measures is likely to enrich our understanding of the developmental interface between nature and nurture in the development of psychopathology.

Reconceptualizing Risk and Resilience from a Quantitative Genetic Perspective

An important concept in developmental psychopathology is the distinction between proximal and distal risk factors. Distal factors are variables that are grouped to subsume specific environmental influences; a notable example is social class, a labeled environmental factor that may reflect many specific environmental influences (Wachs & Gruen, 1981). Proximal factors are the actual environmental experiences nested within distal factors. With respect to psychopathology, family history of psychopathology has been classified as a distal variable in that it is not what is experienced by individuals at risk (Baldwin, Baldwin, & Cole, 1990; Luthar, 1993; Richters & Weintraub, 1990). It has been suggested that the risk posed by such distal variables is mediated by proximal variables such as ineffective parenting or family discord (Luthar, 1993; Richters & Weintraub, 1990).

Traditionally, proximal risk factors have been conceptualized as representing environmental risk factors for psychopathology. Quantitative genetics can make an important contribution to this area of research by clarifying the extent to which proximal risk factors are truly environmental (Rende & Plomin, 1993). First, genetic influences should also be considered as potential proximal risk factors because they may represent biological pathways by which some individuals are placed at risk for psychopathology. Second, because measures of the environment, such as stressors, may show genetic influence, proximal risk factors should not be considered as environmental a priori, and quantitative genetic studies can help determine what aspects of risk environments are nongenetic influences on development.

In addition to contributing to our understanding of risk for psychopathology, another application of quantitative genetic theory and methods is to clarify conceptions of resilience (Rende & Plomin, 1993). One consideration is that an understanding of the genetic contributions to psychopathology may help explain why some individuals at risk for psychopathology do not develop disorders and, in fact, may have positive outcomes. Although good outcomes in the face of known risk factors have been a prominent theme in research on resilience, genetic theory predicts that heritable dimensions and disorders will show differences as well as resemblances within families because, with the exception of identical twins, family members are not genetically identical. This point is important because some individuals in high-risk families may be considered as resilient, when in fact they may not be at risk genetically. For example, even in the case of single-gene disorders such as Huntington's disease, only 50% of the first-degree relatives at risk for the disorder will actually have the gene, and those individuals who do not develop the disorder are not resilient but, rather, not at risk, because they did not inherit the mutated form of the disease gene (see Rende & Plomin, 1993). In addition, because variation within families is the rule rather than the exception, the same general argument may be made for studying nonshared environment. For example, although one child in a family may be exposed to risk factors posed by particular parenting styles, another child may not be exposed to the same degree, and hence may not necessarily be resilient (Rende & Plomin, 1993).

A related point is that genetic influences may directly contribute to resilience as well as to liability to disorders. Genetic factors that affect resistance (resilience) as well as susceptibility (vulnerability) to infectious disease have been found, such as several genes that increase resistance to malaria (e.g., Childs et al., 1992). Although there are no comparable examples in the study of psychopathology to date, it has been argued that genetic effects on psychopathology may carry some benefits in terms of other areas of functioning, as may be the case with certain features of autism (Rutter, 1991). It is also possible that other traits, such as dimensions of personality, which are moderately heritable, may play a role in resilience (Rende & Plomin, 1993). This theme is important because genetic influences are often considered in psychopathology only as predisposing factors to maladaptation, whereas their potential protective functions are not considered (Rende, in press). Such is the case with diathesis-stress models in which genetic influences are usually conceptualized as conveying risk for psychopathology (Rende & Plomin, 1992). We emphasize that it is important to consider not only genetic risk but also heritable influences that may be protective.

An important direction for the next decade, then, is to merge the findings on genetic and environmental influences on the development of psychopathology with theories on risk and resilience. This approach is critical because it represents a prototypical way in which we can move away from deterministic etiological models to models that examine the probabilistic effects of genetic and environmental influences. Understanding the quantitative genetics of risk and resilience is, in some ways, a primary goal for the next decade, and data gathered from this perspective will clarify how both nature and nurture contribute to, rather than determine, both adaptive and maladaptive patterns of development.

Merging the Study of Normal and Abnormal Development

Another prominent theme for the next decade should be the integrated study of normal and abnormal development using quantitative genetic strategies. As discussed earlier, most quantitative genetic studies to date have been investigations of either normative traits or diagnosed conditions. However, cleaving development into normal or abnormal pathways is not consistent with the theoretical basis of developmental psychopathology (e.g., Cicchetti, 1984), and quantitative genetic studies should explore more intensively the potential links between adaptive and maladaptive developmental pathways (e.g., Rende, in press; Rende & Plomin, 1990).

This integrated approach to development is important. It is possible that dimensions of behavior—dimensions normally distributed in the population—reflect, in part, the genetically influenced contribution to disorders. Although, as reviewed earlier, geneticists have invoked and applied the concept of liability to disorders to account for this possibility, in most studies of psychopathology the liability has been inferred statistically rather than measured empirically. Hence, identifying the liability in behavioral terms may move us closer to understanding how genes contribute to the development of psychopathology, and may remove the artificial distinction between normal and abnormal development. A related point is that direct attempts to include measures of liability in quantitative genetic studies may help in removing the misinterpretation that we are looking for deterministic disease genes by reinforcing the notion that our search is for probabilistic genes that contribute partly to a vulnerability to psychopathology.

We discussed new quantitative genetic methods—DF analysis pioneered by DeFries and Fulker, and the latent class analysis developed by Eaves and colleagues—that have been developed to broach directly the links or breaks between the normal and abnormal in etiological terms. Applications of these new methods will undoubtedly advance our knowledge of how genetic and environmental influences contribute to both adaptive and maladaptive developmental pathways, and especially to the potential overlap between the normal and abnormal.

Merging the Study of Nature and Nurture

At the beginning of this chapter, we discussed how modern quantitative genetics involves the study of nature AND nurture rather than nature VERSUS nurture. As a concluding theme, we wish to emphasize how the merging of the study of nature and nurture reflects, in part, a new and exciting direction for quantitative genetic research (Plomin, 1994).

Theories of the intersection of nature and nurture have been available for a number of years. For example, two primary ways in which nature and nurture could be linked in normal development—(a) genotype-environment interaction and (b) genotype correlation—were outlined in the 1970s (Plomin, DeFries, & Loehlin, 1977) and translated into a theory of development in the 1980s (Scarr & McCartney, 1983). Similarly, the implications of GE correlation and interaction for the development of psychopathology have been recognized and integrated into diathesis-stress models of psychopathology (Rende & Plomin, 1992). The current impetus to examine the interplay between nature and nurture comes from the large body of studies, reviewed earlier, that have documented genetic influence on the environment, in terms of normative measures of the environment as well as risk environments. This database has inspired both environmentalists and geneticists to construct theories of development that emphasize the interplay of nature and nurture (see Plomin, 1994). Representative of this new spirit of collaboration is the suggestion that we need "to construct actual empirical bridges between nature and nurture" through the combined efforts of environmentalists and geneticists (Wachs, 1993, p. 388).

A fitting conclusion to this chapter, then, is to suggest that the nature-nurture link should be a prominent theme in quantitative genetic research on psychopathology in the next decade. Although a number of methodological difficulties are embedded in this task, concrete starting points are available in the form of testable hypotheses (see Plomin, 1994). Applications of this perspective to the study of psychopathology through the life span will provide firm empirical support of the importance of both nature and nurture for development.

REFERENCES

Alessi, N., Hottois, M., & Coates, J. (1993). The gene for ADHD? Not yet. *Journal of the American Academy of Child and Adolescent Psychiatry, 32,* 1073–1074.

Bailey, D. W. (1971). Recombinant-inbred strains: An aid to finding identity, linkage, and function of histocompatibility and other genes. *Transplantation,* 11, 325–327.

Baker, L., & Daniels, D. (1990). Nonshared environmental influences and personality differences in adult twins. *Journal of Personality and Social Psychology, 74,* 187–192.

Baldwin, A., Baldwin, C., & Cole, R. (1990). Stress-resistant families and stress-resistant children. In J. Rolf, A. Masten, D. Cicchetti, K. Nuechtelein, & S. Weintraub (Eds.), *Risk and protective factors in the development of psychopathology* (pp. 257–280). New York: Cambridge University Press.

Beadle, G. W., & Tatum, E. L. (1941). Experimental control of developmental reaction. *American Naturalist, 75,* 107–116.

Bettelheim, B. (1967). *The empty fortress: Infantile autism and the birth of the self.* New York: Free Press.

Biederman, J., Rosenbaum, J., Hirshfeld, D., Meminger, S., Herman, J., & Kagan, J. (1990). Psychiatric correlates of behavioral inhibition in young children of parents with and without psychiatric disorders. *Archives of General Psychiatry, 47,* 21–26.

Bolton, P., Macdonald, H., Murphy, M., Scott, S., Yuzda, E., Whitlock, B., Pickles, A., & Rutter, M. (1991). Genetic findings and heterogeneity in autism. *Psychiatric Genetics, 2,* 49.

Boomsma, D. I., Martin, N. G., & Neale, M. C. (1989). Structural modeling in the analysis of twin data. *Behavior Genetics, 19,* 5–8.

Bouchard, T., & McGue, M. (1981). Familial studies of intelligence: A review. *Science, 212,* 1055–1059.

Bredbacka, P., Pekkarinen, P., Peltonen, L., & Lonnqvist, J. (1993). Bipolar disorder in an extended pedigree with a segregation pattern compatible with X-linked transmission: Exclusion of the previously reported linkage to F9. *Psychiatric Genetics, 3,* 79–87.

Bregman, J. D., Leckman, J. F., & Ort, S. I. (1988). Fragile X syndrome: Genetic predisposition to psychopathology. *Journal of Autism and Developmental Disorders, 18,* 343–354.

Bronfenbrenner, U., & Ceci, S. (1993). Heredity, environment, and the question "how?" A first approximation. In R. Plomin & G. E. McClearn (Eds.), *Nature, nurture, and psychology* (pp. 313–324). Washington, DC: American Psychological Association.

Cadoret, R. J., Troughton, E., Moreno, L., & Whitters, A. (1990). Early life psychosocial events and adult affective symptoms. In L. N. Robins & M. Rutter (Eds.), *Straight and devious pathways from childhood to adulthood* (pp. 300–313). Cambridge, England: Cambridge University Press.

Capron, C., & Duyme, M. (1986). Assessment of the effects of socioeconomic status on IQ in a full cross-fostering study. *Nature, 340,* 552–554.

Cardon, L., Fulker, D., DeFries, J., & Plomin, R. (1992). Multivariate genetic analysis of specific cognitive abilities in the Colorado Adoption Project at age 7. *Intelligence, 16,* 383–400.

Carey, G. (1992). Twin imitation for antisocial behavior: Implications for genetic and family environment research. *Journal of Abnormal Psychology, 101,* 18–25.

Caron, C., & Rutter, M. (1991). Comorbidity in child psychopathology: Concepts, issues, and research strategies. *Journal of Child Psychology and Psychiatry, 32,* 1063–1080.

Childs, B., Moxon, E. R., & Winkelstein, J. A. (1992). Genetics and infectious diseases. In R. King, J. Rotter, & A. Motulsky (Eds.), *The genetic basis of common diseases* (pp. 71–91). New York: Oxford University Press.

Chipuer, H., Rovine, M., & Plomin, R. (1990). LISREL modelling: Genetic and environmental influences on IQ revisted. *Intelligence, 14,* 11–29.

Cicchetti, D. (1984). The emergence of developmental psychopathology. *Child Development, 55,* 1–7.

Cicchetti, D., & Beeghly, M. (Eds.). (1990). *Children with Down syndrome: A developmental perspective.* New York: Cambridge University Press.

Cloninger, C. R., & Gottesman, I. I. (1987). Genetic and environmental factors in antisocial behavior. In S. A. Mednick, T. E. Moffitt, & S. A. St ack (Eds.), *Causes of crime: New biological approaches* (pp. 92–109). Cambridge, England: Cambridge University Press.

Cohen, D. J., & Leckman, J. F. (1994). The developmental psychopathology and neurobiology of Tourette's syndrome. *Journal of the American Academy of Child and Adolescent Psychiatry, 33,* 2–15.

Crawford, F., & Goate, A. (1992). Alzheimer's disease untangled. *Bioessays, 14,* 727–734.

DeFries, J. C., & Fulker, D. W. (1985). Multiple regression analysis of twin data. *Behavior Genetics, 15,* 467–473.

DeFries, J. C., & Fulker, D. W. (1988). Multiple regression analysis of twin data: Etiology of deviant scores versus individual differences. *Acta Geneticae Medicae et Gemellologiae, 37,* 205–216.

DeFries, J. C., Fulker, D. W., & LaBuda, M. C. (1987). Evidence for a genetic aetiology in reading disability of twins. *Nature, 329,* 537–539.

DeFries, J. C., Gervais, M., & Thomas, E. A. (1978). Response to 30 generations of selection for open-field activity in laboratory mice. *Behavior Genetics, 8,* 3–13.

DeFries, J. C., Plomin, R., & LaBuda, M. C. (1987). Genetic stability of cognitive development from childhood to adulthood. *Developmental Psychology, 23,* 4–12.

DiLalla, L., & Gottesman, I. (1989). Heterogeneity of causes for delinquency and criminality: Lifespan perspectives. *Development and Psychopathology, 1,* 339–349.

Dinwiddie, S. H. (1992). Patterns of alcoholism inheritance. *Journal of Substance Abuse, 4,* 155–163.

Dinwiddie, S. H., & Cloninger, C. R. (1991). Family and adoption studies in alcoholism and drug addiction. *Psychiatric Annals, 21,* 206–214.

Dunn, J. F., & Plomin, R. (1990). *Separate lives: Why siblings are so different.* New York: Basic Books.

Dykens, E., & Leckman, J. F. (1990). Developmental issues in Fragile X syndrome. In R. Hodapp, J. Burack, & E. Zigler (Eds.), *Issues in the developmental approach to mental retardation* (pp. 226–245). New York: Cambridge University Press.

Eapen, V., Pauls, D., & Robertson, M. (1993). Evidence for autosomal dominant transmission in Tourette's syndrome: United Kingdom cohort study. *British Journal of Psychiatry, 162,* 593–596.

Eaves, L. J., Eysenck, H. J., & Martin, N. (1989). *Genes, culture and personality.* New York: Academic Press.

Eaves, L., Silberg, J., Hewitt, J., Meyer, J., Rutter, M., Simonoff, E., Neale, M., & Pickles, A. (1993). Genes, personality, and psychopathology: A latent class analysis of liability to symptoms of attention-deficit hyperactivity disorder in twins. In R. Plomin & G. E. McClearn (Eds.), *Nature, nurture, and psychology* (pp. 285–303). Washington, DC: American Psychological Association.

Eaves, L., Silberg, J., Hewitt, J., & Rutter, M. (1993). Analyzing twin resemblance in multisystem data: Genetic applications of a latent class model for symptoms of conduct disorder in juvenile boys. *Behavior Genetics, 23,* 5–19.

Edelbrock, C., Rende, R., Plomin, R., & Thompson, L. (in press). Twin study of behavioral problems and social competence in adolescence. *Journal of Child Psychology and Psychiatry.*

Edwards, J. H. (1991). The formal problems of linkage. In P. McGuffin & R. Murray (Eds.), *The new genetics of mental illness* (pp. 58–70). Oxford, England: Butterworth-Heinemann.

Egeland, J., Gerhard, D., Pauls, D., Sussex, J., & Kidd, K. (1987). Bipolar affective disorders linked to DNA markers on chromosome 11. *Nature, 325,* 783–787.

Falconer, D. S. (1965). The inheritance of liability to certain diseases, estimated from the incidence among relatives. *Annals of Human Genetics, 29,* 51–76.

Folstein, S. E., Franz, M., Jensen, B., Chase, G., & Folstein, M. F. (1983). Conduct disorder and affective disorder among the offspring of patients with Huntington's disease. *Psychological Medicine, 13,* 45–52.

Folstein, S. E., & Rutter, M. L. (1977). Infantile autism: A genetic study of 21 twin pairs. *Journal of Child Psychology and Psychiatry, 18,* 297–321.

Fulker, D. W., DeFries, J. C., & Plomin, R. (1988). Genetic influence on general mental ability increases between infancy and middle childhood. *Nature, 336,* 767–769.

Gelderman, H. (1975). Investigations on inheritance of quantitative characters in animals by gene markers: I. Methods. *Theoretical and Applied Genetics, 46,* 319–330.

Gelertner, J., Kennedy, J., Grandy, D., & Zhou, Q. (1993). Exclusion of close linkage of Tourette's syndrome to D-sub-1 dopamine receptor. *American Journal of Psychiatry, 150,* 449–453.

George, F. R. (1993). Genetic models in the study of alcoholism and substance abuse mechanisms. *Progress in Neuropsychopharmacology and Biological Psychiatry, 17,* 345–361.

Gilger, J., Borecki, I., DeFries, J. C., & Pennington, B. (1994). Commingling and segregation analysis of reading performance in families of normal reading probands. *Behavior Genetics, 24,* 345–356.

Gillis, J., DeFries, J., & Fulker, D. (1992). Confirmatory factor analysis of reading and mathematics performance: A twin study. *Acta Geneticae Medicae et Gemellologiae Twin Research, 41,* 287–300.

Gillis, J., Gilger, J., Pennington, B., & DeFries, J. C. (1992). Attention deficit disorder in reading-disabled twins: Evidence for a genetic etiology. *Journal of Abnormal Child Psychology, 20,* 303–315.

Goldsmith, H. H. (1993). Nature-nurture issues in the behavioral genetics context: Overcoming barriers to communication. In R. Plomin & G. E. McClearn (Eds.), *Nature, nurture, and psychology* (pp. 325–340). Washington, DC: American Psychological Association.

Goldsmith, H. H., & Gottesman, I. I. (in press). Heritable variability and variable heritability in developmental psychopathology. In M. Lenzenweger & J. Haugaard (Eds.), *Frontiers of developmental psychopathology.* New York: Oxford University Press.

Goodman, R., & Stevenson, J. (1989). A twin study of hyperactivity: II. The aetiological role of genes, family relationships and perinatal adversity. *Journal of Child Psychology and Psychiatry, 30,* 691–709.

Gottesman, I. I. (1991). *Schizophrenia genesis: The origins of madness.* New York: Freeman.

Gusella, J., Wexler, N., Conneally, P., Naylor, S., Anderson, M., & Tanzi, R. (1983). A polymorphic DNA marker genetically linked to Huntington's disease. *Nature, 306,* 234–238.

Hanson, D. R., & Gottesman, I. (1976). The genetics, if any, of infantile autism and childhood schizophrenia. *Journal of Autism and Schizophrenia, 6,* 209–233.

Hauser, P., Zametkin, A., Martinez, P., & Vitiello, B. (1993). Attention deficit-hyperactivity disorder in people with generalized resistance to thyroid hormone. *The New England Journal of Medicine, 328,* 997–1001.

Heath, A., Eaves, L., & Martin, N. (1989). The genetic structure of personality: III. Multivariate genetic item analysis of the EPQ scales. *Personality and Individual Differences, 10,* 877–888.

Heath, A., Jardine, R., Eaves, L. J., & Martin, N. (1989). The genetic structure of personality: II. Genetic item analysis of the EPQ. *Personality and Individual Differences, 10,* 615–624.

Heath, A., & Martin, N. (1990). Psychoticism as a dimension of personality: A multivariate genetic test of Eysenck and Eysenck's psychoticism construct. *Journal of Personality and Social Psychology, 58,* 111–121.

Henderson, N. D. (1982). Human behavior genetics. *Annual Review of Psychology, 33,* 403–440.

Hetherington, E. M., Reiss, D., & Plomin, R. (Eds.) (1994). *Separate social worlds of siblings: Impact of nonshared environment on development.* Hillsdale, NJ: Erlbaum.

Hill, S. Y. (1992). Is there a genetic basis of alcoholism? *Biological Psychiatry, 32,* 955–957.

Holzman, P. S. (1992). Behavioral markers of schizophrenia useful for genetic studies. *Journal of Psychiatric Research, 26,* 427–445.

Holzman, P. S., & Matthysse, S. (1990). The genetics of schizophrenia: A review. *Psychological Science, 1,* 279–286.

Horowitz, F. D. (1993). Bridging the gap between nature and nurture: A conceptually flawed issue and the need for a comprehensive new environmentalism. In R. Plomin & G. E. McClearn (Eds.), *Nature, nurture, and psychology* (pp. 341–353). Washington, DC: American Psychological Association.

Kagan, J., Reznick, S., & Snidman, N. (1988). Biological bases of childhood shyness. *Science, 240,* 167–171.

Kanner, L. (1943). Autistic disturbances of affective contact. *Nervous Child, 2,* 217–250.

Kelsoe, J., Ginns, E., Egeland, J., Gerhard, D., & Goldstein, A. (1989). Re-evaluation of the linkage relationship between chromosome 11p loci and the gene for bipolar affective disorder in the Old Order Amish. *Nature, 342,* 238–243.

Kendler, K. (1993). Twin studies of psychiatric illness. *Archieves of General Psychiatry, 50,* 905–915.

Kendler, K., & Diehl, S. (1993). The genetics of schizophrenia: A current, genetic-epidemiologic perspective. *Schizophrenia Bulletin, 19,* 261–285.

Kendler, K., Heath, A., Neale, M., Kessler, R., & Eaves, L. (1993). Alcoholism and major depression in women: A twin study of the causes of comorbidity. *Archives of General Psychiatry, 50,* 690–698.

Kendler, K., Neale, M., Kessler, R., Heath, A., & Eaves, L. (1992a). A population-based twin study of major depression in women: The impact of varying definitions of illness. *Archives of General Psychiatry, 49,* 257–266.

Kendler, K., Neale, M., Kessler, R., Heath, A., & Eaves, L. (1992b). Generalized anxiety disorder in women: A population-based twin study. *Archives of General Psychiatry, 49,* 267–272.

Kendler, K., Neale, M., Kessler, R., Heath, A., & Eaves, L. (1992c). The genetic epidemiology of phobias in women: The interrelationship of agoraphobia, social phobia, situational phobia, and simple phobia. *Archives of General Psychiatry, 49,* 273–281.

Kendler, K., Neale, M., Kessler, R., Heath, A., & Eaves, L. (1992d). Major depression and generalized anxiety disorder: Same genes, (partly) different environments? *Archives of General Psychiatry, 49,* 716–722.

Kendler, K., Neale, M., Kessler, R., Heath, A., & Eaves, L. (1993a). Major depression and phobias: The genetic and environmental sources of comorbidity. *Psychological Medicine, 23,* 361–371.

Kendler, K., Neale, M., Kessler, R., Heath, A., & Eaves, L. (1993b). Panic disorder in women: A population-based twin study. *Psychological Medicine, 23,* 397–406.

Kendler, K., Neale, M., Kessler, R., Heath, A., & Eaves, L. (1993c). A twin study of recent life events and difficulties. *Archives of General Psychiatry, 50,* 789–796.

Kessler, R., Kendler, K., Heath, A., Neale, M., & Eaves, L. (1992). Social support, depressed mood, and adjustment to stress: A genetic epidemiologic investigation. *Journal of Personality and Social Psychology, 62,* 257–262.

Kidd, K. K., Bowcock, A. M., Schmidtke, J., Track, R. K., Ricciuti, F., Hutchings, G., Bale, A., Pearson, P., & Willard, H. F. (1989). Report of the DNA committee and catalogs of cloned and mapped genes and DNA polymorphisms. *Cytogenetics and Cell Genetics, 51,* 622–647.

Kovacs, M. (1983). Children's Depression Inventory: A self-rated depression scale for school-aged youngsters. Unpublished manuscript, University of Pittsburgh.

Loehlin, J. C. (1987). *Latent variable models: An introduction to factor, path, and structural analysis.* Hillsdale, NJ: Erlbaum.

Loehlin, J. C. (1992). *Genes and environment in personality development.* Newbury Park, CA: Sage.

Loehlin, J. C., Horn, J. M., & Willerman, L. (1989). Modeling IQ change: Evidence from the Texas Adoption Project. *Child Development, 60,* 993–1004.

Luthar, S. S. (1993). Annotation: Methodological and conceptual issues in research on childhood resilience. *Journal of Child Psychology and Psychiatry, 34,* 441–453.

McGue, M., & Gottesman, I. I. (1991). The genetic epidemiology of schizophrenia and the design of linkage studies. *European Archives of Psychiatry and Clinical Neuroscience, 240,* 174–181.

McGuffin, P., & Gottesman, I. I. (1985). Genetic influences on normal and abnormal development. In M. Rutter & L. Hersov (Eds.), *Child and adolescent Psychiatry: Modern approaches* (2nd ed., pp. 17–33). Oxford, England: Blackwell.

McGuffin, P., & Katz, R. (1989). The genetics of depression and manic-depressive disorder. *British Journal of Psychiatry, 155,* 294–304.

McGuffin, P., & Katz, R. (1993). Genes, adversity, and depression. In R. Plomin & G. E. McClearn (Eds.), *Nature, nurture, and psychology* (pp. 217–230). Washington, DC: American Psychological Association.

McGuffin, P., & Murray, R. (Eds.). (1991). *The new genetics of mental illness.* Oxford, England: Butterworth-Heinemann.

McKusick, V. A. (1990). *Mendelian inheritance in man* (9th ed.). Baltimor Johns Hopkins University Press.

Mitchell, P., Selbie, L., Waters, B., & Donald, J. (1992). Exclusion of close linkage of bipolar disorder to dopamine D-sub-1 and D-sub-2 receptor gene markers. *Journal of Affective Disorders, 25,* 1–11.

Moffitt, T. E. (1993). Adolescence-limited and life-course-persistent antisocial behavior: A developmental taxonomy. *Psychological Review, 100,* 674–701.

Moldin, S. (1994). Indicators of liability to schizophrenia: Perspectives from genetic epidemiology. *Schizophrenia Bulletin, 20,* 169–184.

Moldin, S., & Erlenmeyer-Kimling, L. (1994). Measuring liability to schizophrenia: Progress report 1994. *Schizophrenia Bulletin, 20,* 25–29.

Nichols, P. (1984). Familial mental retardation. *Behavior Genetics, 14,* 161–170.

Oberle, I., Rousseau, F., Heitz, D., Kretz, C., Devys, D., Hanauer, A., Boue, J., Bertheas, M. F., & Mandel, J. L. (1991). Instability of a 550-base pair DNA segment and abnormal methylation in Fragile X syndrome. *Science, 252,* 1097–1102.

Olson, R., Wise, B., Conners, F., Rack, J., & Fulker, D. W. (1989). Specific deficits in component reading and language skills: Genetic and environmental influences. *Journal of Learning Disabilities, 22,* 339–348.

Owen, M., & Mullan, M. (1990). Molecular genetic studies of manic-depression and schizophrenia. *Trends in Neurosciences, 13,* 29–31.

Pauls, D. L. (1992). The genetics of obsessive compulsive disorder and Gilles de la Tourette's syndrome. *Psychiatric Clinics of North America, 15,* 759–766.

Pennington, B., Gilger, J., Olson, R., & DeFries, J. C. (1992). External validity of age versus IQ discrepant diagnoses in reading disability: Lessons from a twin study. *Journal of Learning Disabilities, 25,* 562–573.

Plomin, R. (1986a). *Development, genetics, and psychology.* Hillsdale, NJ: Erlbaum.

Plomin, R. (1986b). Multivariate analysis and developmental behavioral genetics: Developmental change as well as continuity. *Behavior Genetics,* 16, 25–43.

Plomin, R. (1988). The nature and nurture of cognitive abilities. In R. Sternberg (Ed.), *Advances in the psychology of human intelligence* (pp. 113–141). Hillsdale, NJ: Erlbaum.

Plomin, R. (1990). The role of inheritance in behavior. *Science, 248,* 183–188.

Plomin, R. (1991). Genetic risk and psychosocial disorders: Links between the normal and abnormal. In M. Rutter & P. Casaer (Eds.), *Biological risk factors for psychosocial disorders* (pp. 101–138). Cambridge, England: Cambridge University Press.

Plomin, R. (1994). *Genetics and experience: The interplay between nature and nurture.* Thousand Oaks, CA: Sage.

Plomin, R., & Bergeman, C. S. (1991). The nature of nurture: Genetic influence on "environmental" measures. *Behavioral and Brain Sciences,* 14, 373–386.

Plomin, R., & Daniels, D. (1987). Why are children in the same family so different from each other? *Behavioral and Brain Sciences, 10,* 1–16.

Plomin, R., & DeFries, J. C. (1979). Multivariate behavioral genetic analysis of twin data on scholastic abilities. *Behavior Genetics, 9,* 505–517.

Plomin, R., DeFries, J. C., & Fulker, D. W. (1988). *Nature and nurture in infancy and early childhood.* New York: Cambridge University Press.

Plomin, R., DeFries, J. C., & Loehlin, J. C. (1977). Genotype-environment interaction and correlation in the analysis of human behavior. *Psychological Bulletin, 84,* 309–322.

Plomin, R., DeFries, J. C., & McClearn, G. (1990). *Behavioral genetics: A primer* (2nd ed.). New York: Freeman.

Plomin, R., & McClearn, G. E. (Eds.) (1993). *Nature, nurture, and psychology.* Washington, DC: American Psychological Association.

Plomin, R., McClearn, G. E., Gora-Maslak, G., & Neiderhiser, J. M. (1991). Use of recombinant inbred strains to detect quantitative trait loci associated with behavior. *Behavior Genetics, 21,* 99–116.

Plomin, R., McClearn, G. E., Pedersen, N. L., Nesselroade, J. R., & Bergeman, C. S. (1988). Genetic influence on childhood family environment perceived retrospectively from the last half of the life span. *Developmental Psychology, 24,* 738–745.

Plomin, R., McClearn, G. E., Pedersen, N. L., Nesselroade, J. R., & Bergeman, C. S. (1989). Genetic influence on adults' ratings of their current family environment. *Journal of Marriage and the Family, 51,* 791–803.

Plomin, R., McClearn, G., Smith, D., Vignetti, S., Chorney, M., Chorney, K., Venditti, C., Kasarda, S., Thompson, L., Detterman, D., Daniels, J., Owen, M., & McGuffin, P. (1964). DNA markers associated with high versus low IQ: The IQ Quantitative Trait Loci (QTL) Project. *Behavior Genetics, 24,* 107–118.

Plomin, R., & Nesselroade, J. R. (1990). Behavioral genetics and personality change. *Journal of Personality, 58,* 191–220.

Plomin, R., & Rende, R. (1991). Human behavioral genetics. *Annual Review of Psychology, 42,* 161–190.

Plomin, R., Rende, R. D., & Rutter, M. (1991). Quantitative genetics and developmental psychopathology. In D. Cicchetti & S. L. Toth (Eds.), *Rochester Symposium on Developmental Psychopathology: Vol. 2. Internalizing and externalizing expressions of dysfunction* (pp. 155–202). Hillsdale, NJ: Erlbaum.

Prescott, C., & Gottesman, I. (1993). Genetically mediated vulnerability to schizophrenia. *Psychiatric Clinics of North America, 16,* 245–267.

Reiss, A. L., & Freund, L. (1990). Neuropsychiatric aspects of the Fragile X syndrome. *Brain Dysfunction, 3,* 9–22.

Reiss, A. L., Hagerman, R., Vinogradov, S., Abrams, M., & King, R. (1988). Psychiatric disability in female carriers of the Fragile X chromosome. *Archives of General Psychiatry, 45,* 25–30.

Rende, R. (in press). Adaptive and maladaptive pathways in development: A quantitative genetic perspective. In M. LaBuda, E. Grigorenko, I. Ravich-Scherbo, & S. Scarr (Eds.), *On the way to indivudality: Current methodological issues in behavioral genetics.*

Rende, R., & Plomin, R. (1990). Quantitative genetics and developmental psychopathology: Contributions to understanding normal development. *Development and Psychopathology, 2,* 393–407.

Rende, R., & Plomin, R. (1992). Diathesis-stress models of psychopathology: A quantitative genetic perspective. *Applied and Preventive Psychology, 1,* 177–182.

Rende, R., & Plomin, R. (1993). Families at risk for psychopathology: Who becomes affected and why? *Development and Psychopathology, 5,* 529–540.

Rende, R., & Plomin, R. (1994). Genetic influences on behavioral development. In M. Rutter & D. Hay (Eds.), *Developmental principles and clinical issues in psychology and psychiatry* (pp. 26–48). Oxford, England: Blackwell.

Rende, R., Plomin, R., Reiss, D., & Hetherington, E. (1993). Genetic and environmental influences on depressive symptomatology in adolescenc Individual differences and extreme scores. *Journal of Child Psychology and Psychiatry, 34,* 1387–1398.

Rende, R., Slomkowski, C., Stocker, C., Fulker, D., & Plomin, R. (1992). Genetic and environmental influences on maternal and sibling interaction in middle childhood: A sibling adoption study. *Developmental Psychology, 28,* 484–490.

Richters, J., & Weintraub, S. (1990). Beyond diathesis: Toward an understanding of high-risk environments. In J. Rolf, A. Masten, D. Cicchetti, K. Neuchterlein, & S. Weintraub (Eds.), *Risk and protective factors in the development of psychopathology* (pp. 67–96). New York: Cambridge University Press.

Robertson, M. M. (1989). The Gilles de la Tourette syndrome: The current status. *British Journal of Psychiatry, 154,* 147–169.

Rosenbaum, J., Biederman, J., Gersten, M., Hirshfeld, D., Meminger, S., Herman, J., & Kagan, J. (1988). Behavioral inhibition in children of parents with panic disorder and agoraphobia: A controlled study. *Archives of General Psychiatry, 45,* 463–470.

Rosenbaum, J. F., Biederman, J., Bolduc-Murphy, E., Faraone, S., Chaloff, J., Hirshfeld, D., & Kagan, J. (1993). Behavioral inhibition in childhood: A risk factor for anxiety disorders. *Harvard Review of Psychiatry, 1,* 2–16.

Rowe, D. C. (1981). Environmental and genetic influences on dimensions of perceived parenting: A twin study. *Developmental Psychology, 17,* 203–208.

Rowe, D. C. (1983). Biometric models of self-reported delinquent behavior: A twin study. *Behavior Genetics, 13,* 473–489.

Rowe, D. C. (1986). Genetic and environmental components of antisocial pairs: A study of 265 twin pairs. *Criminology, 24,* 513–532.

Rowe, D. C. (1994). *The limits of family influence.* New York: Guilford.

Rutter, M. (1988). Epidemiological approaches to developmental psychopathology. *Archives of General Psychiatry, 45,* 486–495.

Rutter, M. (1990). Commentary: Some focus and process considerations re the effects on children of parental depression. *Developmental Psychology, 26,* 60–63.

Rutter, M. (1991). Nature, nurture, and psychopathology: A new look at an old topic. *Development and Psychopathology, 3,* 125–136.

Rutter, M., Bailey, A., Bolton, P., & Le Couteur, A. (1993). Autism: Syndrome definition and possible genetic mechanisms. In R. Plomin & G. E. McClearn (Eds.), *Nature, nurture, and psychology* (pp. 269–284). Washington, DC: American Psychological Association.

Rutter, M., Bolton, P., Harrington, R., Le Couteur, A., Macdonald, H., & Simonoff, E. (1990). Genetic factors in child psychiatric disorders: I. A review of research strategies. *Journal of Child Psychology and Psychiatry, 31,* 3–37.

Rutter, M., Macdonald, H., Le Couteur, A., Harrington, R., Bolton, P., & Bailey, A. (1990). Genetic factors in child psychiatric disorders: II. Empirical findings. *Journal of Child Psychology and Psychiatry, 31,* 39–82.

Scarr, S., & McCartney, K. (1983). How people make their own environments: A theory of genotype-environment effects. *Child Development, 54,* 424–435.

Searles, J. S. (1991). The genetics of alcoholism: Impact on family and sociological models of addiction. *Family Dynamics of Addiction Quarterly, 1,* 8–21.

Sham, P., Morton, N., & Rice, J. (1992). Segregation analysis of the NIMH Collaborative Study: Family data on bipolar disorder. *Psychiatric Genetics, 2,* 175–184.

Sherrington, R., Brynjolfsson, J., Petursson, H., Potter, M., Dudleston, K., Barraclough, B., Wasmuth, J., Dodds, M., & Gurling, H. (1988). Localization of a susceptibility locus for schizophrenia on chromosome 5. *Nature, 336,* 164–167.

Smalley, S. L., Asarnow, R. F., & Spence, M. A. (1988). Autism and genetics: A decade of research. *Archives of General Psychiatry, 45,* 953–961.

Snyderman, M., & Rothman, S. (1988). *The IQ controversy, the media and public policy.* New Brunswick, NJ: Transaction Books.

Steffenburg, S., Gillberg, C., Hellgren, L., Anderson, L., Gillberg, I., Jakobsson, G., & Bohman, M. (1989). A twin study of autism in Denmark, Finland, Iceland, Norway, & Sweden. *Journal of Child Psychology and Psychiatry, 30,* 405–416.

Stevenson, J. (1992). Evidence for a genetic etiology in hyperactivity in children. *Behavior Genetics, 22,* 337–344.

Taylor, B. A. (1989). Recombinant inbred strains. In M. F. Lyon & A. G. Searle (Eds.), *Genetic variants and strains of the laboratory mouse* (2nd ed., pp. 773–789). Oxford, England: Oxford University Press.

Thompson, L. A., Detterman, D. K., & Plomin, R. (1991). Associations between cognitive abilities and scholastic achievement: Genetic overlap but environmental differences. *Psychological Science, 2,* 158–165.

Torrey, E. F. (1992). *Freudian fraud: The malignant effect of Freud's theory on American thought and culture.* New York: HarperCollins.

Tsuang, M. T., & Faraone, S. V. (1990). *The genetics of mood disorders.* Baltimore: Johns Hopkins University Press.

Turkheimer, E., & Gottesman, I. I. (1991). Individual differences and the canalization of behavior. *Developmental Psychology, 27,* 18–22.

Uhl, G., Blum, K., Noble, E., & Smith, S. (1993). Substance abuse vulnerability and D-sub-2 receptor genes. *Trends in Neuroscience, 16,* 83–88.

Wachs, T. D. (1992). *The nature of nurture.* Newbury Park, CA: Sage.

Wachs, T. D. (1993). The nature-nurture gap: What we have here is a failure to collaborate. In R. Plomin & G. E. McClearn (Eds.), *Nature, nurture, and psychology* (pp. 375–391). Washington, DC: American Psychological Association.

Wachs, T. D., & Gruen, G. E. (1981). *Early experience and human development.* New York: Plenum.

Weinberger, D. R. (1987). Implications of normal brain development for the pathogenesis of schizophrenia. *Archives of General Psychiatry, 44,* 660–669.

Yu, S., Pritchard, M., Kremer, E., Lynch, M., Nancarrow, J., Baker, E., Holman, K., Mulley, J. C., Warren, S. T., Schlessinger, D., Sutherland, G. R., & Richards, R. I. (1991). Fragile X genotype characterized by an unstable region of DNA. *Science, 252,* 1179–1181.

CHAPTER 11

Temperament, Attention, and Developmental Psychopathology

MARY K. ROTHBART, MICHAEL I. POSNER, and KAREN L. HERSHEY

In this chapter, we consider possible relationships between individual differences in temperament and attention and the development of psychopathology. We define temperament as constitutionally based individual differences in reactivity and self-regulation, as observed within the domains of emotionality, motor activity, and attention (Rothbart, 1989c; Rothbart & Derryberry, 1981). By reactivity we mean characteristics of the individual's responsivity to changes in the environment, as reflected in somatic, autonomic, and endocrine nervous systems. By self-regulation, we mean processes modulating this reactivity, including behavioral approach, avoidance, inhibition, and attentional self-regulation. In our view, individual differences in temperament constitute a subset of the broader domain of personality and the substrate from which personality develops.

The chapter has two major sections. First, we present some recent findings on temperament that have implications for the study of developmental psychopathology. We then discuss ideas and research relating temperament to the development of risk conditions for psychopathology. In our view, individual differences in the deployment of attention, seen as a major aspect of temperament, are critical to an understanding of these issues. In the second section, we describe an approach to the study of attention that we believe has important implications for our thinking about the development of psychopathology.

We begin the chapter with a brief historical introduction, followed by a discussion of dimensions of temperament that have emerged from both conceptual (Rothbart, 1989d) and factor-analytic studies of parent-reported temperament in early life (Bates, Freeland, & Lounsbury, 1979; Hagekull & Bohlin, 1981; Sanson, Prior, Garino, Oberklaid, & Sewell, 1987). These dimensions include fear (distress and behavioral inhibition to novelty), general distress proneness (irritability), positive affect and approach, activity level, and attentional persistence. We note similarities between these dimensions and the "Big Five" and "Big Three" personality factors identified in research on adults (Goldberg, 1990).

We are very grateful to Myron Rothbart, Scott Monroe, and Ann Sanson for their comments on an earlier version of this chapter, and to Scott Monroe for his contributions to Table 11.1.

We consider temperamental dimensions in connection with models for developmental psychopathology, and then review recent research on temperament and psychopathology in childhood. This research has been based chiefly on the work of Thomas and Chess and their colleagues in the New York Longitudinal Study (NYLS, Thomas & Chess, 1977; Thomas, Chess, Birch, Hertzig, & Korn, 1963). Finally, we discuss systems of attentional self-regulation and their underlying neural networks (Posner & Petersen, 1990), and the relation of attention to the development of several neurological and psychiatric pathologies.

TEMPERAMENT AND PSYCHOPATHOLOGY

The Greco-Roman Typology

The ancient Western typology of temperament was developed by early Greek and Greco-Roman physicians, including Theophrastus, Vindician, and Galen (Diamond, 1974). Like later approaches to temperament, this typology related individual differences in behavior and emotionality to variability in human physiology as it was understood at the time. The temperamental syndrome of *melancholia* (a tendency to quiet, and to negative and depressed mood) and its relation to a predominance of black bile was developed in the 4th century B.C. writings of Theophrastus, and the complete fourfold typology of temperament related to the Hippocratic bodily humors was present by the time of the writings of Vindician in the 4th century A.D. (Diamond, 1974).

In addition to the melancholic type as described above, the fourfold typology of temperament included descriptions of the *choleric* type (quick-tempered and touchy, easily aroused to anger, with a predominance of yellow bile), the *phlegmatic* type (apathetic and sluggish, not easily stirred to emotion, with a predominance of phlegm), and the *sanguine* type (characterized by warmth, optimism, and expressiveness, with a predominance of blood). The fourfold typology was endorsed throughout the Middle Ages and Renaissance (Cf. Burton, 1621/1921; Culpeper, 1657) and discussed by Kant (1798/1978). Most recently, Eysenck's (1970) work made use of the typology, and Merenda (1987) argued that it constitutes a four-factor model for our current understanding of temperament and personality. However, most current researchers and with the notable exception of Kagan (1989), conceptualize temperament in terms of dimensions of variability rather than categories of human beings.

If we look at woodcuts from the Middle Ages, representing the four temperament types, we may be surprised to see the depiction of behaviors that appear pathological. The choleric man is depicted beating a woman, the phlegmatic person is asleep in bed while others are working, the melancholic person is in an attitude of depression or portrayed as a distraught lover (e.g., Carlson, 1984, p. 613). The sanguine type is often depicted as apparently more adjusted than the other three, but even the sanguine individual may be seen engaging in overeating or overdrinking. These images suggest that, at the extreme, individual differences in temperament may in themselves constitute maladaptations. In the current literature, we see this idea expressed in the argument by Gorenstein and Newman (1980) that the extravert and psychopath have a good deal in common. One of the issues immediately raised by these historical treatments of temperament and psychopathology is the relation between a temperamental extreme and a psychopathological condition.

Several of the ways in which temperament may be conceptually linked to the development of risk conditions or psychopathology are proposed in Table 11.1. In some instances, a psychopathological condition may map relatively directly on a temperamental extreme, such as agoraphobia on fear of novelty (Table 11.1, items 1 and 2). In other instances, however, the condition may be constructed out of concerns closely related to temperament, but the condition itself may appear unrelated or even contradictory to the temperamental characteristics that contributed to its development (Table 11.1, item 6). Thus, extreme sensitivity to emotional stimuli may be found to contribute to an individual's tendency to dissociate feeling from consciousness, leading to self-reports of low negative affect in persons who are actually autonomically highly reactive (see descriptions of the repressive personality style in Weinberger, 1990). Some of these links will be explored and elaborated in this chapter; others are listed as possible directions for future work linking temperament and psychopathology. Throughout the chapter, we will refer to Table 11.1 to order the literature and point out possible research directions for the field.

The Approach of Carl Jung

In this century, the type construct has been conceptually modified, leading to dimensional and factor-analytically derived approaches to an understanding of individual differences. Even the psychological types put forward by Jung (1923) differ in important ways from the fourfold typology. To Jung, introverted and extraverted were predominant attitudes, and he described four kinds of information nested within these attitudes: (a) thinking, (b) feeling, (c) sensation, and (d) intuition. Unlike the ancients, or Kagan's (1989) view of inhibited and uninhibited types as qualitatively different classes of individuals, Jung (1923) did not view the psychological types as representing qualitative differences. Instead, he described types as "Galtonesque family-portraits, which sum up in a cumulative image the common and therefore typical characters, stressing these disproportionately, while the individual features are just as disproportionately effaced" (Jung, 1923, p. 513).

Jung's approach to the type is similar to the idea of the prototype in cognition (Posner & Keele, 1968; Rosch, 1973); it can also be seen to be related to the individual trait construct. In deriving a

TABLE 11.1 Ways in Which Temperament May Be Related to "High Risk" Conditions and Psychopathology

1. A temperamental extreme constitutes the psychopathology (extreme shyness, attention deficit disorder).
2. A temperamental extreme predisposes the person to a closely related disorder or risk condition (fear → general anxiety disorder or agoraphobia/panic disorder; low attentional control → conduct disorder; fear and irritability → shame and guilt).
3. The temperamental characteristic acts as a protective factor for some forms of psychopathology or risk factors (fear protecting against psychopathy, positive affect against peer/parental rejection).
4. The temperamental characteristic may heighten or buffer the individual's response to a given event (e.g., in stress-related depression).
5. The temperamental characteristic may lead to a set of experiences that structure the immediate social environment, influencing the development of psychopathology (high stimulation seeking → leaving home early, marrying "poorly," early pregnancy, etc.).
6. Self-regulation of a temperamental extreme may lead to quite different expressed characteristics from the original temperament (e.g., high negative emotionality → repressive personality).
7. Problems with attentional self-regulation may allow expression of reactive temperamental extremes that would otherwise have been controlled, but now constitute a disorder (e.g., hyperactivity).
8. Problems with attentional self-regulation may lead to chronic worrying and anxiety.
9. The temperamental characteristic may bias processing of information about self and others, predisposing an individual to a more cognitively based psychopathology (seeing others as hostile or dangerous, seeing the self as unworthy).
10. The temperamental characteristic may bias others to behave in ways that will provide a set of experiences leading to development of a risk factor (infant negative affect → maternal withdrawal → insecure attachment).
11. Different temperamental characteristics may predispose different developmental pathways to similar risk conditions (shyness, inappropriate social behavior, lack of social interest: all → later social isolation).
12. Temperamental characteristics may affect the particular symptomatology of a disorder, e.g., anxiety versus hopelessness in connection with depression.
13. Temperamental characteristics may influence the course of the disorder once initiated (chronicity). Subsequent temperament may also be influenced by the disorder.
14. Temperamental characteristics may influence response to psychotherapy and/or psychopharmacological treatment.

score for an individual on a trait, the individual's item scores on a scale are aggregated to describe a single score that represents similar responses across time and situations. This trait score can be seen as the *individual's* "common and therefore typical" characteristics, "stressing these disproportionately"; the influence of particular situations or other important factors is also "just as disproportionately effaced." The type can then be seen to refer to a set of traits that tend to occur together in groups of individuals. Factor-analytic approaches to temperament and personality identify clusters of characteristics that tend to covary; results of this work will be described in more detail below.

Jung suggested that introverted *and* extraverted tendencies are present in all persons, but, for a given person, one attitude tends to become more elaborated and conscious, while the other is less elaborated, more primitive, and, for the most part, unconscious. Differentiation between extraversion and introversion, he wrote, can be seen early in life:

> The earliest mark of extraversion in a child is his quick adaptation to the environment, and the extraordinary attention he gives to objects, especially to his effect upon them. Shyness in regard to objects is very slight; the child moves and lives among them with trust. He makes quick perceptions, but in a haphazard way. Apparently he develops more quickly than an introverted child, since he is less cautious, and as a rule, has no fear. Apparently, too, he feels no barrier between himself and objects, and hence he can play with them freely and learn through them. He gladly pushes his undertakings to an extreme, and risks himself in the attempt. Everything unknown seems alluring. (1928, p. 303)

By objects, psychoanalysts such as Jung include both physical and social entities, so that the more introverted child would be expected to show a tendency to dislike new social situations and to approach strangers with caution or fear, and the introverted adult to dislike new situations or social gatherings, and to demonstrate hesitation and reserve. Jung suggests the introvert would also be inclined toward pessimism about the outcome of future events. The extraverted person would be expected to show more ready approach and action toward social and physical objects (impulsivity), and more sociability and greater optimism about the future (Jung, 1923).

Jung also related extraversion-introversion to psychopathology. He took over a distinction between two types of neurosis originally made by Janet, and developed the idea that the extravert is predisposed to hysteria, "characterized by an exaggerated rapport with the members of his circle, and a frankly imitatory accommodation to surrounding conditions" (Jung, 1923, p. 421), combined with a tendency toward experiencing somatic disorders. The introvert was seen as prone to psychasthenia, "a malady which is characterized on the one hand by an extreme sensitiveness, on the other by a great liability to exhaustion and chronic fatigue" (Jung, 1923, p. 479).

Factor-Analytic Studies

Extraversion-introversion also emerged from factor-analytic studies of temperament in adults. Early factor-analytic studies were carried out in Great Britain by Webb and Burt. Webb (1915) analyzed items assessing emotionality, activity, qualities of the self, and intelligence, and identified two factors that preceded extraction of the factor of extraversion-introversion. One was a factor "w," defined as "consistency of action resulting from deliberate volition or will" (Webb, 1915, p. 34). This factor may be similar to the higher-order personality factor recently labeled control, constraint, or conscientiousness (Digman & Inouye, 1986). A second factor assessed individuals' tendency to negative emotionality, sometimes labeled emotional stability-instability; Eysenck would later call it neuroticism. By 1939, Burt had also identified the factor of extraversion-introversion. Later factor-analytic work has repeatedly identified three factors similar to these: (a) extraversion (the first factor that is usually extracted from a large data set of personality descriptors), (b) neuroticism, and (c) conscientiousness (Costa & McCrae, 1988; Goldberg, 1990; John, 1989). These three factors, with the additional factors of agreeableness and openness to experience, constitute what have been called the "Big Five" personality factors.

In Eysenck's (1944, 1947) early factor-analytic work on scores from a group of male neurotic subjects, factors of extraversion-introversion and neuroticism were extracted. In addition, he reported support for Jung's distinction between more extraverted (hysteric) symptoms and more introverted (dysthymic or psychasthenic) symptoms in neurosis. Eysenck (1947) also reviewed results of a factor analysis of Ackerson's (1942) data describing a large sample of children studied by the Illinois Institute for Juvenile Research. These data yielded a general neuroticism factor, along with a factor distinguishing among more introverted behavior problems "(sensitive, absent-minded, seclusive, depressed, daydreams, inefficient, queer, inferiority feelings, and nervous), and extraverted behavior problems (such as stealing, truancy from home and school, destructive, lying, swearing, disobedient, disturbing influence, violent, rude and egocentric)" (Eysenck & Eysenck, 1985, p. 53).

There has since been extensive replication of this factor structure of psychopathology in childhood, distinguishing between internalizing problems, including inhibition, shyness, and anxiety related to introversion, and externalizing problems, including aggressive and acting-out problems related to extraversion (Achenbach & Edelbrock, 1978; Cicchetti & Toth, 1991). Results of these analyses, combined with evidence for stability of extraversion-introversion across long periods (see reviews by Bronson, 1972; Kagan, 1989; and Rothbart, 1989a), suggest that individual differences on extraversion-introversion may be basic to both a description of temperament and, in their extremes, to an individual's likelihood of demonstrating particular kinds of behavior problems or psychopathology (Table 11.1, items 1 and 2).

Temperament Dimensions in Infancy and Childhood

Most of the research and thinking in the field of temperament in childhood has relied on Thomas and Chess's pioneering work on the subject in the New York Longitudinal Study (NYLS, Thomas et al., 1963; Thomas & Chess, 1977). Dimensions of temperament identified by the NYLS included activity level, threshold, mood, rhythmicity, approach/withdrawal, intensity, adaptability, distractibility, and attention span/persistence.

In the original, highly clinical use of the NYLS dimensions (Thomas, Chess, & Birch, 1968), no attempts were made to avoid conceptual overlap across these dimensions. Questionnaires and other instruments based on the NYLS dimensions have thus dealt with constructs that are sometimes highly overlapping in meaning. Findings of relatively high intercorrelations among scale scores designed to assess the dimensions have not been too surprising, given that a behavioral item might, in some cases, belong as easily to any one of three different NYLS-based scales (Rothbart & Mauro, 1990). Lack of internal homogeneity within individual scales based on some of the NYLS dimensions has also been found, which, when combined with lack of independence among scales, has led researchers in Sweden and Australia to attempt item-level factor analysis of NYLS-based parent report scales (Hagekull & Bohlin, 1981; Sanson et al., 1987).

Results of item-level factor-analytic work have in turn led to identification of a smaller number of factors that correspond well with dimensions of temperament developed from other developmentally based theoretical approaches to temperament (Buss & Plomin, 1975, 1984; Rothbart & Derryberry, 1981). These factors include distress to novelty (including behavioral inhibition), other distress proneness or irritability, positive affect and approach, activity level, and persistence (Rothbart & Mauro, 1990). We (Ahadi & Rothbart, 1994; Rothbart, 1989d; Rothbart & Ahadi, 1994) and Martin and Presley (1991) have indicated possible relationships between temperament factors identified for infants and children and personality factors identified for adults.

In the next section, we discuss possible links between several variables from this shorter list of temperamental dimensions and the development of risk conditions for psychopathology. Whenever possible, we refer to conceptual and neural models developed to enhance our understanding of these dimensions. The first two dimensions we discuss are positive affect and approach, and fear (distress and latency to approach novel or challenging stimuli). The third dimension, negative affectivity or irritability, is seen as a general susceptibility to negative affect. These dimensions are particularly interesting because of the degree to which they might map on the factor structures extracted from studies of personality in adults. The fourth dimension, attention, related to effortful control, will be discussed more thoroughly in the second section of the chapter. We begin our more specific discussion with a consideration of positive affect and fear.

Neural Models

Gray (1979, 1982), LeDoux (1987, 1989), and Panksepp (1982, 1986) have all made contributions to the development of neural models for temperament (Rothbart, Derryberry, & Posner, 1994). LeDoux's analysis gives a neural basis for emotions as broadly integrative systems ordering feeling, thought, and action. In his analysis, emotions are seen as the output of information processing networks that assess the meaning or affective significance of events for the individual (LeDoux, 1989). Whereas object recognition systems and spatial processing systems address, respectively, "What is it?" and "Where is it?", neural emotion processing systems give answers to "Is it good for me?" and "Is it bad for me?", in turn influencing the organism's behavioral answers to "What shall I do about it?" or, simply, "What shall I do?"

In the neural processing of emotion, thalamic connections route information about object qualities of a stimulus through sensory pathways while simultaneously routing information for evaluative analysis to the limbic system and the amygdala, where memories of the affective meaning of the stimulus further influence the process (LeDoux, 1989). Later stages of object processing update the emotional analysis based on early sensory information, but, in the meantime, back projections from the amygdala influence the subsequent sensory processing of the stimulus. Output of the amygdala to organized autonomic reactions via the hypothalamus and to motor activation via the corpus striatum constitutes the motivational aspect of the emotions.

In this view, emotional processing can be seen as data processing of a special sort. Attentional neural networks can then act on emotional information in a way that is similar to their action on other data processing systems, including those for object recognition, language, and motor control, each of which in turn has its own underlying neural networks (Posner & Petersen, 1990). We have speculated that connections between emotional processing networks and the anterior attention system, including the anterior cingulate, allow attentional influence on the selection of emotional information for conscious processing, so that we may or may not be aware of emotional evaluations (Posner & Rothbart, 1992). Recent positron emission tomography (PET) studies of pain, for example, indicate the importance of the anterior cingulate in the pain pathway (Talbot et al., 1991).

Attentional systems can thereby be seen to act on and influence the conscious aspects of emotional analyses, and emotion is also seen to influence the focusing and shifting of attention (Gray, 1982). An important aspect of social adaptation involves the individual's appropriate social interaction and acceptance by others (Parker & Asher, 1987). Information about the state of others is an important contributor to appropriate social action, and the access of this information to action and consciousness can be a critical element in the development of disordered functioning (Table 11.1, item 9). Affective states associated with an attentional focus either on threatening stimuli or on the self may make access to information about others less accessible.

Approach

We now briefly consider neural models developed to describe a physical substrate for approach and inhibition. Based on animal research, Gray (1979, 1982) described the Behavioral Activation System (BAS), involving sensitivity to rewards, and the Behavioral Inhibition System (BIS), involving sensitivity to punishment, nonreward, novelty, and innate fear stimuli. These two systems are seen as mutually inhibitory; their balance determines extraversion-introversion. Gray also posited a fight-flight system moderating unconditioned punishment (Gray, 1971, 1975). He traced the BAS through structures previously identified with self-stimulation (Olds & Olds, 1963), including the medial forebrain bundle and lateral hypothalamus, and with neurochemical influences of the transmitters dopamine (DA) and norepinephrine (NE) (Stein, 1980).

In an account of bipolar affective disorders, Depue and Iacono (1989) posited a Behavioral Facilitation System (BFS) that is quite similar to Gray's Behavioral Activation System (BAS). The BFS involves the individual's initiation of locomotor activity, incentive-reward motivation, exploration of environmental novelty (if the stimulus and its context do not induce opposing fear reactions), and irritative aggression. In Depue and Iacono's model, nucleus accumbens DA activity "appears to modulate the flow of motivational information from the limbic system to the motor system, and thereby contributes to the process of initiating locomotor activity, incentive, and goal-directed behavior" (1989, p. 470).

Panksepp (1982, 1986) also reviewed the literature on DA effects, concluding that "the general function of DA activity in appetitive behavior is to promote the expression of motivational excitement and anticipatory eagerness—the heightened energization of animals searching for and expecting rewards" (1986, p. 91). Cloninger (1986, 1987a, 1987b) also specified a novelty-seeking dimension related to DA functioning, as did Zuckerman (1984) in his dimension of sensation seeking (see review by Rothbart, 1989b). Tellegen's (1985) factor-analytic research on personality in adults identified positive emotionality, a broad factor that includes positive affect and anticipation. In research on infants (Rothbart, 1988; Rothbart, Hershey, & Derryberry, 1991), we have found expressions of positive affect (smiling and laughter) (a) to be positively related to infants' rapid latency to approach objects, and (b) to predict anticipatory eagerness about upcoming positive events when the same children were 7 years old.

Fear and Behavioral Inhibition

Factor analyses of infant temperament questionnaires have reliably yielded two distress factors: one involves distress to novelty, and the other, general distress proneness or irritability, including distress to limitations (Rothbart & Mauro, 1990). The distress to novelty factor is linked to an extended latency to approach new objects (Rothbart, 1988), and the combination of behavioral inhibition and distress proneness to novelty appears to correspond to the introverted pole of a broader extraversion-introversion dimension. As noted above, the amygdala has been identified as a critical structure in the processing of emotional information (LeDoux, 1987, 1989), and evidence has been found that emotional networks involving the amygdala respond more strongly to novel than to familiar stimuli (Nishijo, Ono, & Nishino, 1988).

The Behavioral Inhibition System (BIS) described by Gray includes the orbital frontal cortex, the medial septal area, and the hippocampus, involving the neurotransmitters NE and serotonin (Gray, 1977, 1979, 1982). Other investigators have also identified serotonin influences on behavioral inhibition in connection with cues indicating punishment (see review by Soubrie, 1986). Because stimulus conditions identified by Gray as leading to behavioral inhibition include novelty, innate fear stimuli, conditioned signals for punishment, and conditioned signals for reward (the fight-flight system is seen as moderating unconditioned punishment and nonreward), multiple networks are likely to be identified in the BIS.

Other models have postulated cerebral hemispheric differences in tendencies toward approach versus inhibition-withdrawal. Fox and Davidson (1984), developing a theory proposed by Kinsbourne and Bemporad (1984), proposed that the left hemisphere is predominantly associated with positive affect and approach, and the right, with negative affect and avoidance. Evidence from both electrophysiological (EEG) and lesion studies has found increases in anterior left hemisphere activation to be associated with increased positive affect and/or decreased negative affect. The reverse relationships—higher negative affect and/or decreased positive affect—are found for increased anterior right hemisphere activation (reviewed in Davidson & Tomarken, 1989). In addition, some studies have provided support for resting EEG asymmetries predicting positive and negative emotional reactivity (e.g., Davidson & Fox, 1989; Tomarken, Davidson, Wheeler, & Doss, 1992). Fox and Davidson (1984) suggested that, toward the end of the first year of life, development of commisural transfer allows left hemisphere inhibition of right hemisphere function, attenuating expression of negative affect and leading to behavioral alternation between approach and avoidance.

Inhibitory Control

As noted above, the existence of extraverted behavior problems, including overactivity, aggression, and general conduct problems, has been frequently documented in the literature. In exploring the relationship between extraversion and psychopathology, it is important to consider the influence of multiple inhibitory controls on extraverted behavior (Table 11.1, items 3 and 8). The first of these, represented directly in the extraversion-introversion dimension, is behavioral inhibition or fear control. If a disposition to behavioral inhibition is strong, both positive and negative expressive and approach behavior will be moderated under novel or challenging situations. We have found that measures of infants' fearfulness in the laboratory negatively predict mothers' reports of the same children's behaviors, at age 7, of impulsivity, activity, and aggression, and positively predict susceptibility to guilt and shame, two powerful socializing emotions (Rothbart et al., 1991; Rothbart, Ahadi, & Hershey, 1994). In research that combines temperamental assays with information about parent child-rearing techniques, Kochanska (1991) found that toddlers with low behavioral inhibition and high defiance to their mothers show low evidence of internalized conscience 6 years later.

A second inhibitory influence on impulsivity is the attentionally influenced capacity to withhold prohibited responses, that is, effortful inhibitory control. Inhibitory control in our 7-year-old sample was predicted by the infants' longer latency to approach toys (caution) at 11 and 13 months and by their lower activity level in the laboratory at 13 months (Rothbart et al., 1991). In mothers' reports on the 7-year-olds, inhibitory control was concurrently related positively to attentional control and empathy, and negatively to aggression. Inhibitory control was also moderately positively related to guilt/shame, although uncorrelated with concurrent behavioral inhibition as assessed in shyness.

Both the behavioral inhibition associated with fear and effortful inhibitory control demonstrate a developmental time course; the former develops earlier than the latter (see review by Rothbart, 1989d), and both may be seen as protective factors for the development of extraverted psychopathologies (Table 11.1, item

3). In keeping with a developmental view of control, externalizing problems have been associated with description of a child as immature, and a lack of control in expressing emotion and action would be seen as characteristic of the more reactive younger child. We believe that inhibitory control is established with development of the anterior attention system, as described later in this chapter.

Extraversion and Risk for Psychopathology

Individual extremes on extraversion (Table 11.1, item 1) have been associated with psychopathology in Gorenstein and Newman's (1980) model. Gorenstein and Newman (1980) extended Gray's ideas to psychopathology, proposing that the effects of septal lesions provide a model for disinhibiting psychopathologies exhibited in individuals with antisocial, psychopathic, alcoholic, hyperactive, and extraverted tendencies. They based their argument in part on observations of extraverts and psychopaths who emitted dominant responses in spite of punishment, extinction, or reversal of contingencies (McCleary, 1966).

The study of psychopathy from an information processing viewpoint is not very advanced, but Harpur and Hare (1990) reviewed evidence suggesting that psychopaths, like extreme extraverts (see below), find it difficult to inhibit responses (Newman, 1987). In studies of extraversion, Newman and his associates used a passive avoidance procedure, the "go-no go" situation, where the subject is required to withhold responses associated with punishment. In this paradigm, extraverts make more errors of commission to punished no-go responses (Newman, Widom, & Nathan, 1985). Nichols and Newman (1986) also asked subjects to view a visual pattern and match a subsequent pattern against it. Rewards and punishments were preprogrammed and noncontingent on subject response. On trials following punishment, introverts responded more slowly and extraverts responded more quickly. This response tendency is related to subjects' performance on a "go-no go" task: subjects who were more slowed by punishment performed better on the go-no go task (Patterson, Kosson, & Newman, 1987).

The energizing effect of punishment on extraverts' response in the Nichols and Newman (1986) study is interesting for students of developmental psychopathology. In a study with young children, Saltz, Campbell, and Skotko (1983) found, in support of Luria's (1961) observations, that increasing the loudness of a "no go" command increased 3- to 4-year-old children's likelihood of performing a prohibited act. They also found that increasing loudness decreased the likelihood of responding for children 5 to 6 years of age, indicating developmental change in the development of inhibitory control during the preschool years.

These findings may be important with respect to the development of conduct problems in children. Patterson (1980) reported that parents of nonaggressive problem children are effective in stopping their children's aversive behavior on three out of every four occasions of punishment. When parents of aggressive problem children employ punishment, however, the likelihood that the child will persist in the problem behavior increases rather than decreases (Patterson, 1977, 1980; Snyder, 1977). In our laboratory, we have found (Hershey, 1992) that more aggressive (by mothers' report) 7-year-old children show less caution (respond more quickly) after encountering catch trials punishment than less aggressive 7-year-olds. When children prone to negative affect and with low inhibitory control are brought up in a family where causing pain to others is the major strategy for gaining satisfaction, children might be expected to be particularly at risk for conduct problems.

Campbell (1991) recently reported results from two samples that speak to these issues. The first included 3-year-olds referred by parents; the second was a sample of 3-year-old boys, including a group rated by their teachers as inattentive, overactive, and impulsive, and a matched control group from the same classes. Data were collected in home visits, laboratory, and preschool classrooms, and children in both samples have been followed longitudinally. This research found consistency of ratings of externalizing behavior problems across parents and teachers of preschool, 1st-grade, and 4th-grade children. Relationships were found between early inattention, hyperactivity, and poor impulse control, and aggression and noncompliance. In addition, higher levels of externalizing problems in preschool children were found to be related to both higher levels of stress in the family and the mother's use of more negative control strategies.

Campbell's research thus identified both biological and environmental contributions to the development of behavior problems, "consistent with a transactional model of developmental change that emphasizes the complex and dynamic interactions among child characteristics and family factors in determining outcome (Cicchetti & Schneider-Rosen, 1986; Sameroff & Chandler, 1975)" (Campbell, 1991, p. 81). Results of prediction of childhood problems from the Australian Temperament Project are also consistent with this model (Sanson, Oberklaid, Pedlow, & Prior, 1991). Campbell's case history examples further suggest that, in some cases, individual temperament may make the larger contribution to the problem, but, in others, the treatment of the child by the caregivers is more significant. In the future, temperament research might contribute to such studies with development of more detailed assays of subjects' self-regulatory attentional and impulse control.

In addition to their relation to disinhibiting psychopathologies, positive, outgoing characteristics of the young child have been identified as a general *protective* factor for the development of risk factors and psychopathology (Table 11.1, item 3). More active and outgoing children are likely to show fewer negative effects of institutionalization, possibly because they are more likely to receive greater attention from adult caregivers (Schaffer, 1966). Werner's longitudinal studies in Hawaii indicate that more positive affective and expressive characteristics in the young child from an at-risk population are associated with fewer psychosocial problems later in life (Werner, 1986; Werner & Smith, 1982).

Chess and Thomas (1986; Thomas et al., 1968) developed the important idea of "goodness-of-fit" to describe situations in which there is a "match" between the temperamental characteristics of the child and the expectations of others and/or demands of the situation. In their model, a good fit would be predictive of a more favorable mental health outcome; a poor fit, or "incompatibility" would be predictive of impaired function and risk of development of behavior disorders (Table 11.1, item 10).

In their case studies of children who have survived an upbringing in multiproblem families with mental illness in one or more parents, Radke-Yarrow and Sherman (1990) identified two key protective factors. The first protective factor is very similar to Chess and Thomas's (1986) "goodness-of-fit" idea: "One key factor is a *match* between a psychological or physical *quality* in the child and a core *need* in one or both of the parents that the child fulfills . . . The second factor, an extension of the first, is the child's clear conception that there is something good and special about himself or herself. The child quality is then a source of positive self-regard for the child, as well as need-satisfying to the parent" (Radke-Yarrow & Sherman, 1990, p. 112). Child qualities providing a match or mismatch with parental need could be gender, appearance, intellectual or physical aptitude, or temperament. Within American society generally, a positive outgoing temperament may represent a particularly auspicious "match" between the child and many situational requirements; in the school, inhibitory and/or fear control may provide a better match (Lerner, Nitz, Talwar, & Lerner, 1989).

Introversion and Risk for Psychopathology

Considering now the relation of more introverted tendencies to the development of psychopathology, we might expect individual differences in behavioral inhibition to be relatively directly related to susceptibility to anxiety and a tendency toward social withdrawal. Wolfson, Fields, and Rose (1987) found that preschool children with anxiety disorders were reported by their mothers to be less adaptable, more negative in mood, and more "difficult" than a nonanxious control group. Overall, internalizing problems were also found to be related to high temperamental withdrawal. Rosenbaum et al. (1988) studied 2- to 7-year-old children of parents with agoraphobia or panic disorder. Compared with children of psychiatric controls, the rates of behavioral inhibition were close to 80% for the children of the agoraphobic or panic disorder parents, and approximately 15% for non-major-depression controls. In a study of adult subjects with major depression, the codiagnosis of agoraphobia or panic disorder has been found to be positively related to risk for psychiatric disorders in their children, especially risk for major depression and separation anxiety (Weissman, 1989). Weissman concluded that there may be a common underlying process that constitutes a vulnerability (diathesis) for both panic disorder and major depression (Table 11.1, item 2).

Although sex differences are rarely found in early assessments of temperament (Rothbart, 1986), behavior problems develop disproportionately in boys, girls are at greater risk than boys for depression (Zahn-Waxler, Cole, & Barrett, 1991), and antisocial behavior is generally found at higher rates for males than for females (Eagly & Steffen, 1986). Research results currently describe an interplay among temperament, social experience, and gender in the development of depressive mood; two recent studies suggest that antecedents for depressive mood may be somewhat gender-specific (Block, Gjerde, & Block, 1991; Patterson & Capaldi, 1990).

Measuring depressive mood at age 18, with self-reported anxiety partialled out, Block et al. (1991) found that girls' depressive mood was predicted from intropunitive, oversocialized, and overcontrolling behavior at age 7 and from higher preschool IQ. Boys' depressive mood was predicted from higher aggressive, self-aggrandizing, and undercontrolled behavior at age 7, and from lower preschool IQ. Variables assessing undercontrol for males and overcontrol for females were also found to be concurrently related to depressive mood at age 18 for this sample (Gjerde, Block, & Block, 1988). Block et al. (1991) noted that their findings were congruent with findings of a positive relationship between conduct disorder and depression for male but not for female clinically depressed preadolescents (Edelbrock & Achenbach, 1980; Puig-Antich, 1982).

Patterson and Capaldi (1990) provided further information on this point, in research with two samples of 4th-grade boys. Their research results supported a model in which peer rejection is a central mediating influence on depressed mood. In this model, for at least some boys, undercontrolled behavior is seen to lead to peer rejection, which in turn is related to development of depressive mood (Table 11.1, item 10). For girls, on the other hand, Zahn-Waxler et al. (1991) offered a developmental model for depression, highlighting vulnerability to depression in highly socialized girls. Once again, gender may be a moderating variable in the relation between temperament and the development of depressive mood (Table 11.1, item 12).

In a further analysis of gender and psychopathology, Maziade, Cote, Bernier, Boutin, and Thivierge (1989b) suggested that boys' "difficult" temperament is more stable than girls', and that girls are prone to become less difficult over time even when there is stress in the family. In addition, Earls and Jung (1987) reported that marital discord and maternal depression are related to behavior problems in boys but not in girls. They speculated that boys may be under different socialization pressures than girls, especially when the mother is under stress, although the direction of effects might also be reversed, with boys' more externalizing problems creating higher levels of stress for the mother and for her relationship with the father.

In this section, we have considered temperamental extraversion-introversion differences in connection with the development of internalizing and externalizing disorders. We would expect, however, that at most, early temperament would be only one of many influences on the development of behavior problems, mood problems, or disorders. Antisocial and aggressive behaviors appear to be particularly sensitive to reinforcing outcomes, whether positive (when the person achieves a desired goal or is directly rewarded for the aggressive act) or negative (where the aggressive act terminates the pain being inflicted by another) (Bandura & Walters, 1963; Patterson, 1977). Individual differences in fear and inhibitory control would be expected to influence the effects of punishment, and the effects of planning, on externalizing behavior. The individual's experiences in a coercive family would have an additional influence, and parental attitudes of rejection might contribute further to the antisocial behavior (Rohner, 1986).

Negative Affectivity and Development of Risk Conditions

Because distress proneness is a basic temperamental characteristic, and particularly because, unlike behavioral inhibition and inhibitory control, it can be measured developmentally very early (Rothbart, 1989c), it provides an excellent starting place for studies of the child's development of adaptations to a social world. In this section, we consider studies that have investigated how the interaction between negative emotionality and the social environment might place children at risk for behavior problems. Several studies have investigated the association between negative emotionality and other temperament dimensions and characteristics of the mother-child relationship (e.g., Bates, Maslin, & Franke, 1985; Hinde, Easton, Meller, & Tamplin, 1982; Lee & Bates, 1985; Stevenson-Hinde & Simpson, 1982; van den Boom, 1989). This kind of research allows one to address the question of whether children's temperament affects their relations with others in a way that might help to explain subsequent behavior problems (Table 11.1, item 10). An advantage of this research is that it frequently involves direct observation of the child's interactions with others (usually the mother), removing the potential bias of having all data based on the mother's perceptions.

Van den Boom (1989) carried out, in The Netherlands, an excellent quasi-experimental study that illuminates both the relation between early distress proneness and the development of avoidant patterns in the child, and presents a powerful model for studying temperament/child-rearing interactions. In the first phase of her research, van den Boom found that infants' attachment classification at 12 months was not predicted directly by maternal sensitive treatment of the infant during early infancy. Children who were temperamentally more distress prone at 15 days (as assessed in Brazelton examinations), however, were much more likely to be later classified as avoidant in the strange situation. She then examined her longitudinal home observation data in detail, to find how mothers of the distress-prone children tended to treat their infants. In these data, van den Boom found that mothers of distress-prone babies tended to increasingly ignore their infants over time, engaging in little positive play with them.

She therefore developed a study in which she identified a large group of distress-prone, low socioeconomic status (SES) infants. For a group of 6-month-old experimental subjects, a 3-month mother-training procedure taught mothers how to soothe their infants and how to play with them. In comparison with controls, this intervention resulted in more positive and less negative behavior of the infants in the home, and greater involvement of the mothers with their infants through interaction. The experimental infants were also much less likely than control subjects to be categorized as avoidant at 1 year. In an independent assessment, the children from the experimental group also demonstrated higher levels of exploratory play with toys than did children in the control groups. Van den Boom's (1989) research suggested that infant proneness to distress may, at least in The Netherlands, have led mothers to increasingly interact less with their infants, which, in turn, may have led the infants to develop avoidant strategies of interaction with their mothers because the mothers were less available (Table 11.1, item 10).

It is interesting to note that the attachment category predicted by infant distress proneness appears to differ, depending on the culture of child rearing (van Ijzendoorn & Kroonenberg, 1988). Thus, distress-prone infants from the United States or Japan are more likely than less distress-prone infants to be identified in the insecure-ambivalent category (Category C) by the end of the first year (Goldsmith & Alansky, 1987; Miyake, Chen, & Campos, 1985). Distress-prone infants from West Germany or The Netherlands are more likely than less distress-prone infants to be later found in the insecure-avoidant category (Category A) (Grossman, Grossman, Spangler, Suess, & Unzner, 1985; van den Boom, 1989). Japanese and U.S. parents may tend to employ somewhat different strategies with their distress-prone infants than parents in northern Europe, perhaps maintaining more closeness with the infants during the children's distress rather than pulling away from the infants. Closeness might lead to frustration and ambivalent and resistant behavior from the child and the insecure-ambivalent designation (van den Boom, 1989).

It is not appropriate to identify attachment classifications as psychopathology, but this series of studies does indicate that, for infants who are likely to develop less positive patterns of interaction with parents, parent training in easing the child's distress and providing positive experiences may prove useful for children's later adjustment to both persons and objects.

Such a model is also congruent with current ideas about effectance and mastery motivation. In Harter's (1978, 1983) model for the development of competence in children, she identified two approaches to objects and challenges, one mastery-related and one avoidant. Given temperamental individual differences in tendencies toward negative versus positive reactions to objects, a predisposition to distress, combined with a set of negative experiences, may make avoidance of challenges particularly likely and approach less likely. Similarly, a predisposition to positive reactions, combined with a set of positive experiences, may make approach toward challenges especially likely and avoidance or withdrawal less likely. Thus, small early temperamental differences with repeated experiences of positive (success) or negative (failure) results may lead to quite different self-regulatory strategies in dealing with the social and physical worlds. These effects could operate prior to the effects of any caregivers' verbal expressions of approval or disapproval of the child. As suggested by van den Boom's (1989) research, early temperamental differences may also influence caregivers' behavior toward the child, with the child then adapting to the caregivers' adaptations.

Two kinds of research would be helpful in tracing these developments; both are similar to the approach used by van den Boom (1989). One would trace the development of approach and avoidance strategies, especially those involving social objects, in light of early individual differences in temperament and developmental experience. The second would test the extent to which negative trajectories of interaction and children's outcomes may be altered through intervening to produce changes in adult caregivers' behavior and understanding. In this approach, observations like those of van den Boom, where the individual variability of children is observed in an interactional context, will be of utmost importance. Werner (1986) has argued: "What we need in the future are more sophisticated assessments of their (neonates and infants) environments (like those rendered by gifted anthropologists), *and* novel ways to change those environments, so that the impact of risk factors can be attenuated and children's competencies can be enhanced" (p. 19).

Other studies have investigated the relationship of temperament to observations of naturalistic mother-child interaction in preschool age children. Hinde et al. (1982) found that negative mood, intensity, high activity, irregularity, and shyness in preschoolers as reported by mothers was concurrently related to more tense or hostile interactions with mothers, especially for girls. Lee and Bates (1985), observing mothers' interaction with 2-year-olds at home, in situations where the mothers were attempting to control their toddlers' "trouble" behavior, found that more distress-prone ("difficult") children approached trouble more often, tended to resist the mothers' attempts to control them, and had mothers who were more likely both to use more aversive discipline and to give in to their children. Lee and Bates indicated that the pattern of these early interactions resembles the coercive cycle of behavior described in socially aggressive boys and their mothers (Patterson, 1977, 1980). Even at early ages, children who present their mothers with more troublesome, resistant behavior may encourage mothers to use aversive discipline tactics more frequently or to give in (Table 11.1, item 10), and these in turn may be the antecedents of a coercive cycle of parent-child interactions related to problems with aggression (Patterson, 1980).

There is also evidence that children's relationships with others are related to temperament. Stevenson-Hinde and Simpson (1982) found that mothers reported effects of difficult-to-manage behavior on all relationships in the family, including interactions with siblings and mother-father interactions. In comparison to mothers of more manageable children, these mothers also reported higher levels of anxiety and irritability in themselves, many commenting that they "did not used to be like this." Rutter and Quinton (1984) reported that children showing negative mood, low regularity, low malleability, and fastidiousness were more likely to be the focus of depressed parents' criticism, hostility, and irritability. In Rutter's (1990) terms, "the interactive process reflects a pattern in which the children's attributes make them a focus for the discord (thus increasing exposure to the risk variable) and increase the probability that exposure will set in motion a train of adverse interactions that will prolong the risk" (p. 191) (Table 11.1, item 10).

Rubin, LeMare, and Lollis (1990) put forward two scenarios for the development of behavior problems in children. Their model specified outcomes of both mother and child interaction and peer interaction, but we briefly describe only the latter here. In their first model, infants who demonstrated a low threshold for arousal, high wariness, and relative unsoothability were considered. These children were seen to adopt socially withdrawn positions in the peer group; peers' perception of such a child as an "easy mark" possibly increased the children's insecurity in group situations, leading to greater withdrawal (Table 11.1, items 2 and 10). The developmental outcome for this scenario is internalizing problems.

In the second model, infant temperamental conditions described as "difficult" (defined as fussy, overactive, and relatively unsoothable) are discussed. The difficult child is more actively rejected by the peer group because of the child's aggression and hostility toward other children; the outcome is seen as externalizing problems and possibly dropping out of school (Table 11.1, item 10). Rubin et al.'s (1990) characterization of their model for externalizing disorders is congruent with data reported above on the development of depressive mood in boys.

Rubin et al.'s (1990) scenarios are offered speculatively, and research will be needed to support or elaborate them, but they are important in that they distinguish between two kinds of temperamental negative affect identified in very young children, and they elaborate further instances of our Table 11.1, item 10. Eisenberg and Fabes (1992) have also developed a model for predicting prosocial behavior and behavior problems based on temperamental reactivity and self-regulation in the context of development and social experience. Their model is also very much in keeping with our analysis. These approaches are promising for further understanding the interaction between temperament and social experience in the development of disorders and more positive social adaptations, including the development of mastery motivation.

Adult Relationships between the "Big Five" and Psychopathology

In our earlier discussion, we indicated potential relationships between childhood temperament and the Big Five personality factors. Three of the Big Five factors map fairly readily on dimensions of approach (adult extraversion), negative affectivity (adult neuroticism), and inhibitory control (adult conscientiousness) found in infancy and childhood. The Big Five factors in adulthood are of particular interest because of work by Wiggins and his colleagues (Trapnell & Wiggins, 1990; Wiggins & Pincus, 1994; Wiggins, Trapnell, & Phillips, 1988), who related them to the structure of personality disorders. Wiggins and Pincus (1994) have factor-analyzed Minnesota Multiphasic Personality Inventory (MMPI) personality disorder measures and Personality Adjective Check List (PACL) measures for personality styles associated with Millon's (1981, 1986) theory of psychopathology. These measures were administered to a large sample of undergraduate psychology students. Students were also administered instruments to get at three measures of the five-factor personality model: (a) Costa and McCrae's (1985, 1989) Neuroticism Extraversion Openness Personality Inventory (NEO-PI); (b) Wiggins' (1979; Trapnell & Wiggins, 1990; Wiggins, Phillips, & Trapnell, 1989) Interpersonal Adjective Scales (IASR-B5); and (c) the Hogan Personality Inventory (HPI; Hogan, 1986).

The five factors extracted from the three personality scales were closely enough related to the four factors of the personality styles/disorders to justify a conjoint factor analysis including both sets of data. The first component extracted included neuroticism, with avoidant and MMPI dependent and borderline personality disorders loading positively, and narcissistic personality loading negatively on the factor. The second component included personality extraversion, with histrionic personality disorder loading positively and schizoid personality disorder loading negatively. The third component included personality agreeableness (vs. antagonistic hostility), with dependent (PACL) personality disorder loading positively and paranoid and antisocial (PACL) personality disorder loading negatively. Personality conscientiousness was related positively to compulsive and negatively to antisocial (MMPI) personality disorders. The openness factor was related only to schizotypal disorder.

Secondary loadings indicate that avoidant personality disorders are related to both neuroticism and introversion, and that schizoid disorders are chiefly related to introversion. They also indicate ways in which the MMPI and PACL scales differ from each other: the PACL antisocial disorder scale is related to hostility, extraversion, and lack of neuroticism; the MMPI antisocial disorder scale is mainly related to low conscientiousness.

These findings are important. To the extent that temperamental extraversion-introversion and neuroticism/distress proneness, anger/aggression, and effortful control are closely related to the Big Five, and the personality dimensions in adulthood can be seen as on a continuum with personality disorders/styles (Table 11.1, item 2), we may be able to detect temperamental variables that would be most appropriate in the longitudinal study of the development of personality disorder. As we will argue below, overlap of the constructs of personality disorders and personality/temperament may account to a large degree for these findings. However, to the degree that these constructs are meaningfully related to developmental analyses, the overlap may be useful to our understanding of these disorders.

In the next section, we review recent studies that have been designed to investigate more direct relationships between temperament and the development of behavior problems and psychopathology. In almost all cases, these studies have used Thomas and Chess's (1977) New York Longitudinal Study (NYLS) dimensions of temperament.

Research on Temperament and Psychopathology Using the NYLS Framework

As noted above, dimensions of childhood temperament identified by the New York Longitudinal Study (NYLS) include: activity level, persistence, threshold, mood, rhythmicity, approach/withdrawal, intensity, adaptability, distractibility, and/or categorizations of types of children: "easy," "difficult," "intermediate," "slow-to-warm-up" (Thomas et al., 1963). The dimensions are not defined in such a way as to make them independent of one another (see discussion above). In research on temperament and psychopathology using this framework, mothers' temperament ratings are in most cases collected in questionnaires based on the NYLS conceptualization. The incidence of children's behavior problems has also been frequently assessed by mothers' reports through questionnaires or interviews. Problems of bias of these ratings are discussed below.

In the studies to be described, there was extensive use of the construct of "difficultness," employed also in some of the studies we have already discussed. This construct stemmed from results of a factor analysis of data from the original NYLS, which identified a cluster of five temperament dimensions: (a) approach/withdrawal, (b) mood, (c) intensity, (d) adaptability, and (e) rhythmicity, as "difficult" (Thomas et al., 1963). In algorithms for assessing difficulty, developed by Carey and McDevitt (1978), Fullard, McDevitt, and Carey (1984), and others, "difficulty" is derived from extreme scores on all of these five dimensions.

There are several problems with the use of the difficulty construct in temperament research. (For a discussion of this issue, see Rothbart, 1982.) One problem is the wide variability of operationalizations of the construct. Because factor analyses of data collected on the NYLS dimensions have frequently failed to replicate the presence of rhythmicity in the "difficulty" factor (Bates, 1989), studies based on such analyses often delete rhythmicity measurements and use varying composites, depending on the outcome of the factor analysis; those based on the Carey & McDevitt (1978) or Fullard et al. (1984) algorithms always include it. Inconsistency in the use of difficulty as a construct then creates serious problems for knowing what is meant by difficulty in any given study. We attempt below to indicate some of the multiple operationalizations of this term, but feel that precision will result only when assessments of a given construct are both psychometrically sound and comparable across studies.

Bates (1980, 1989) argued that the core variable of measures of difficulty is the presence of negative emotionality, and his work utilized measures assessing this variable. Factor-analytic work by Bates and others also identified two kinds of negative emotionality in infancy: (a) negative affect related to children's responses to novelty and (b) more general distress proneness (Bates et al., 1979). Bates's research indicated that the two varieties of negative emotionality may be differentially related to specific behavior problems that develop later, and this important distinction is lost in the more general NYLS-based difficulty construct.

Two other cautions must be taken into account in reviewing this literature. Although studies reported below have found some links between temperament and behavior problems or psychopathology, a clear drawback lies in determining the direction of influence. Although the implication is usually that certain temperament extremes and/or the constellation of dimensions defined as difficult *predispose* one to behavior problems (Table 11.1, item 2), an alternative interpretation is that the child's psychological problems associated with the behavioral disorder lead to extremes in the behavior measured as temperament.

Another important issue, raised by a number of investigators (e.g., Barron & Earls, 1984; Prior, Sanson, Oberklaid, & Northam, 1987; Sanson, Prior, & Kyrios, 1990; Wertlieb, Wiegel, Springer, & Feldstein, 1987), is the possible confounding of the concepts of extreme or difficult temperament and behavior problems, especially when they are assessed by the same rater (usually, the mother). For example, items assessing temperamental dimensions such as activity, approach/withdrawal, and adaptability may bear considerable similarity to items assessing such behavior problems as hyperactivity, shyness, and oppositional behavior. Sanson et al. (1990) asked practicing child psychologists to rate items from temperament and behavior problem questionnaires for their fit to both constructs. Although they found temperament items to be generally regarded as better measures of temperament than of behavior problems, two scales (activity/intensity and irritability) showed considerable confounding across both areas. Behavior problem items also were not rated as significantly better at measuring behavior problems than were temperament items. Bates (1990), however, argued that if temperament is seen as contributing to the development of behavior problems, conceptual overlap across constructs might be theoretically expected.

Although their number is relatively small, most studies investigating concurrent links between parent-reported temperament and parent-reported behavior problems have found significant relationships (e.g., Barron & Earls, 1984; Earls, 1981; Maziade, Cote, Bernier, Boutin, & Thivierge, 1989a; Prior et al., 1987; Wertlieb et al., 1987). One exception, done with deaf children as subjects, did not find mothers' or fathers' perceptions of their children's temperament to be related to behavior problem scores, but did find a relationship for ratings by the children's teachers (Prior, Glazner, Sanson, & Debelle, 1988). Most studies—one important exception being Maziade et al. (1989a)—do not distinguish between statistically significant differences in behavior problems within the normal range and clinically significant differences in behavior problems. Consequently, it remains unclear whether the temperament dimensions and/or "difficulty" are associated with relatively greater frequency of mild behavior problems, or with more serious psychopathology.

The Martha's Vineyard Child Health Survey, a total population study of the prevalence and correlates of behavior problems in 3-year-old children on the rural island of Martha's Vineyard, Massachusetts (Barron & Earls, 1984; Earls, 1981), used a questionnaire adapted from that of Thomas and Chess (1977). They found children rated as less distractible, more intense, and less adaptable to be seen as having more problem behaviors. In particular, low distractibility (renamed by Barron & Earls, 1984, as "inflexibility" because relevant items appeared to reflect stubborn, resistant behavior more than attention-related behavior) was most strongly predictive of behavior problems, although the authors noted the possible overlap between "inflexible" and "problematic" behavior. Analyzing data from a different cohort of children and using Carey and McDevitt's (1978) and Fullard et al.'s (1984) temperament measures, Earls and Jung (1987) found that high activity, low adaptability, and negative mood contributed unique predictability to behavior problems in 3-year-olds. A zero-order relationship with intensity and behavior problems was also found, but the distractibility finding was not replicated.

Examining the link between temperament and behavior problems in older children (6- and 9-year-olds), Wertlieb et al. (1987) found high activity, withdrawal, distractibility, and intensity, and low adaptability, persistence, negative mood, and unpredictability to be significantly related to higher behavior problem scores. Internalizing behavior scores (reflecting anxiety, phobias, social withdrawal, and so on) and externalizing behavior scores (reflecting hyperactivity, aggression, and so on) were also found to be differentially related to temperament. Withdrawal was more associated with internalizing scores, and high activity, distractibility, and low threshold were more associated with externalizing scores.

In comparing the Baron and Earls (1984) and Wertlieb et al. (1987) results, the relationship between distractibility and behavior problems is in the opposite direction, possibly due to differences in ages of the children, differences in measures, or a failure of replication of the Barron and Earls (1984) results. Another possibility is lack of agreement on what distractibility is. When items assessing distractibility pertain to children's coming when called, ignoring parental bids to stop an activity, and so on, then *low* distractibility may be related to behavior problems (i.e., those assessing stubbornness, disobedience, manageability, and so on). Low distractibility also seems equated by some researchers (e.g., Maziade et al., 1990 following the item content of Carey & McDevitt's 1978 scale) with low *soothability,* for example, the parent's inability to distract the child from emotional upset, which lends itself to relationships with behavior problems. On the other hand, when distractibility items are more attention-related, *high* distractibility may be found to be related to behavior problems such as hyperactivity or ADHD-related items.

Concurrent relationships between temperament and behavior problems have been found in other geographical regions as well. As part of the large-scale prospective Australian Temperament Project (described by Prior, Sanson, & Oberklaid, 1989), Prior et al. (1987) found toddlers categorized as "difficult" and "slow-to-warm-up"—using Fullard et al.'s (1984) algorithm—to have more mother-reported behavior problems than "easy" and "intermediate" children. Similarly, Maziade et al. (1989a), using a representative French-speaking sample in Quebec, found preschool children scoring high on a factor assessing low adaptability, approach, negative mood, high intensity, and low distractibility (labeled "difficult") to be more likely to be rated by psychiatrists (based on a clinical interview with the parents) as having slight or definite behavioral disorders than "average" or "easy" subjects. This association remained significant even when controlling for the effects of other risk factors (e.g., SES, stressful life events, family functioning, and so on). However, the risk for behavior problems posed by "difficult" temperament was significantly increased when the family was also assessed as being more dysfunctional in terms of the parents' exerting less clear, firm, consistent behavioral control.

Relatively little research beyond Maziade et al.'s (1985) work has compared the temperament profiles of clinically disturbed children with normal children. Wolfson et al. (1987) compared preschool children diagnosed as having anxiety disorders with matched peers from normal preschools and found the anxious group to be significantly less adaptable, more negative in mood, and more likely to be classified as "difficult"—according to Carey and McDevitt's (1978) algorithm—than the control group. Maziade, Caron, Cote, Boutin, and Thivierge (1990) compared temperament assessments of 3- to 12-year-old children referred to a psychiatric clinic with norms obtained from their earlier work, which used random samples of the general population. They defined "difficult" as scoring above the 30th percentile for 4 of 5 measures: (a) low adaptability, (b) high withdrawal, (c) intensity, (d) negative mood, and (e) *low* distractibility. They, too, found a higher proportion of clinic children categorized as "difficult" than was found in the general population. Even with this overproportion, however, two-thirds of the clinic children had not been identified as having a difficult temperament.

Longitudinal research, particularly studies beginning with assessment of temperament in infancy, before parents generally identify their children's behaviors as problems, helps address a concern with the direction of influence between temperament and behavior problems. In this research, evidence for a predictive link between *infant* temperament and later behavior problems appears mixed. Cameron (1978), reanalyzing NYLS data, found first-year temperament "risk" scores (corresponding roughly to Thomas & Chess's "difficulty" with high persistence added) to predict only mild subsequent behavior problems. For boys, an unexpected finding in the reverse direction was reported: *lower* risk scores in the first year related to later, more severe problems. Bates et al. (1985) did not find home observations of infant temperament to predict mother-reported behavior problems at age 3, but found a modest relationship between mothers' early perceptions of "difficulty" (measured as more frequent and intense negative emotion rather than employing the more extensive NYLS construct) and behavior problems at age 3. Maziade et al. (1989a), using Carey & McDevitt's (1978) measure, found no relationship between mothers' ratings of infant temperament and behavior problems at 4 years of age.

Evidence of predictability of behavior problems in later years *has* been found in studies of children beyond the period of infancy, although, again, the danger exists that temperament and disorder measures may be assessing an overlap between constructs. Earls and Jung (1987), assessing children at age 2 and again at age 3 as part of the Martha's Vineyard project, found that low adaptability and high intensity at the earlier age uniquely predicted behavior problems later, and in fact were better predictors that any of the home environment variables (e.g., marital discord, maternal depression, and so on). Kyrios and Prior (1990), studying slightly older preschoolers, also found temperament to better predict behavior problems one year later than such environmental variables as marital adjustment, family stress, and child-rearing practices. Both groups of investigators, however, noted the similarity between their temperament and behavior problem constructs.

Maziade and colleagues (Maziade et al., 1985; Maziade, Caron, Cote, Merette et al., 1990) used clinical diagnoses of psychiatrists, based on interviews with the children and parents, as their main outcome variable. In comparing subgroups of children from the general population who, at 7 years, had been assessed as extremely "easy" or extremely "difficult," they found the extremely difficult children to be significantly more likely to have clinical diagnoses at age 12. By age 16, however, extremely difficult temperament predicted a poor clinical outcome only if the family had also been assessed earlier as dysfunctional in terms of parental behavioral control. Nevertheless, 16-year-olds who had been described as more "difficult" reported significantly more behavioral symptoms and lower self-image than their previously "easy" peers.

Although it is questionable, from these studies, whether infant temperament predicts later behavior problems, there is stronger evidence that temperament assessed later in childhood does so. One possible reason for this may be methodological: there may be greater similarity between the constructs of "difficult" childhood temperament and behavior problems. For the young infant, "difficulty" may be evidenced chiefly in terms of emotionality; for the older infant or young child, manageability becomes part of the construct (Hagekull, 1991). The characteristics of activity/intensity and irritability, found by Sanson et al. (1990) to be most confounded with behavior problems, also constitute a large part of the "difficulty" construct in most studies. It is possible that much longitudinal research is mainly documenting continuity among these characteristics rather than predicting behavior problems from temperament. In this light, Maziade et al.'s (1985; Maziade, Caron, Cote, Merette, et al., 1990) use of clinical diagnoses as the outcome variable is important.

There are other reasons why associations between infant temperament and later psychopathology might not be found. "Difficulty" shows some stability from infancy to childhood, but as many as half or more of difficult infants lose that categorization when they become older (e.g., Lee & Bates, 1985; Maziade et al., 1989b). Noting the instability of the "difficult" classification from infancy to later childhood and the lack of predictability of infant "difficult" temperament leading to later behavior problems, Maziade et al. (1989b) cautioned against large-scale, community prevention programs aimed at early identification of temperamentally difficult infants. We agree. Also, given that most parents of "difficult" infants describe their babies as no more difficult than average, or even in positive terms (Chess, 1982; Maziade, Boudreault, Thivierge, Caperaa, & Cote, 1984), one must consider whether, under most circumstances, more harm than good would be done by encouraging parents to label their infants as "difficult."

ATTENTION AND SELF-REGULATION

In the preceding sections of this chapter, we have described ways of thinking about the relation among temperament, risk factors, and the development of pathology, and some of the kinds of research designed to assess the relationship. One major approach to research in this area has been correlational analysis of relations between temperament and disorder or behavior problem assessments, of the sort we have described above. Another has been the "risk study" approach, in which multiple variables at different levels of analysis are assessed (some demographic, some assessing intelligence, characteristics of child rearing, and temperamental characteristics of the child, often as reported by the mother) and related to later outcomes (see Rutter & Garmezy, 1983). Outcomes of the risk studies may include children's problems with adaptation within the family or community, or "survival" of children who have grown up at risk but do not show serious problems at the time of later assessment.

Results of several large-scale risk studies of this sort are quite similar to those in studies of health risk: the more factors (up to an asymptote) identified as putting the child at risk, the more likely the child will be to develop difficulties in adjustment, with some risk factors interacting in their relationships with outcome (Rutter, 1979, 1983). As in the Truffaut film *The 400 Blows* each challenge to the adaptive capacity of the child—poverty, parental divorce, school failure, the physical threat of a dangerous neighborhood, and so on—can be seen as another injury inflicted on the child's functioning, further straining the child's ability to adjust. These risk factors represent immediate challenges to our society, because, in many cases, they may be remediable.

Outcomes may also be moderated to a degree by variables such as gender, and by positive protective factors such as (a) in Werner and Smith's (1982) study, the mothers' perception of the children as positive and outgoing in infancy, (b) the children's later ability to focus attention and control impulses, and (c) in Masten and her associates' work, IQ (Masten, 1990). Although variables such as attentional focusing, impulse control, and IQ may moderate the influences of risk factors, we may nevertheless ask how they might operate as psychological influences on development. This question was posed in an excellent review article by Masten (1990), without an altogether satisfactory answer. Risk research gives us an idea about the variables that are predictive of the development of disorder, but it does not get us very far in understanding the psychological *processes* involved in its development.

We have already suggested ways for including temperamental variables in smaller-scale studies of the development of problem behaviors and disorders. One of the most important of recent ideas that may address the question of process will now be discussed in more detail: the possibility that individual differences in attentional systems and their development play an important role in disordered versus positive outcomes (Rothbart & Ahadi, 1994). A framework now exists for looking at attentional self-regulatory processes in detail (Posner & Petersen, 1990), and we present this framework in the hope that it may be more widely applied to studies of individual differences. The framework is also appropriate for gaining insights, from studies of populations with psychiatric disorder, for our understanding of self-regulatory processes.

In the past five years, our understanding of three networks involved in selective attention—(a) the posterior, (b) the anterior, and (c) the vigilance attention networks—has tremendously increased (see Posner & Petersen, 1990; Posner, 1992; Posner & Raichle, 1994). Each is involved in the selective aspects of attention in somewhat different ways. As we have defined temperament (Rothbart & Derryberry, 1981; Rothbart & Posner, 1985), it involves individual differences in both emotional and motor reactivity and in mechanisms of self-regulation, including attention. Responses to stimuli in older children and adults always involve the extensive influence of both reactivity and self-regulation, but the study of infants allows some separation between reactivity and attentional self-regulation. In early infancy, the mechanisms of attention undergo considerable maturation, producing dramatic changes in the ability to exercise voluntary control during the first year of life (Johnson, Posner, & Rothbart, 1991; Rothbart & Posner, 1985). We also review briefly the early development of these self-regulatory mechanisms.

The Posterior Attention Network

Anatomically, the posterior attention network involves at least portions of the parietal cortex, associated thalamic areas of the pulvinar and reticular nucleus, and parts of the midbrain's superior colliculus. These areas cooperate in performing the operations needed to bring attention to a location in space. The posterior network also has close anatomical connections to anterior attention networks and to arousal or vigilance systems (Posner & Petersen, 1990; Posner & Raichle, 1994).

The posterior attention network is involved in the individual's orienting to sensory stimuli. Most is known about the orienting of visual attention, but similar systems are available for other sensory modalities as well (Posner, 1990). The posterior network directs attention to relevant locations, as in visual search or in selection of a relevant scale for examining visual input. The metaphor of a zoom lens has been useful in guiding research on this system. When one attends to a location in visual space, not only is information increased in processing efficiency at that location, but information at other locations is processed less efficiently (Posner & Presti, 1987). This basic selective property of attention has been demonstrated for the posterior network in cellular recordings, electrical recording from the scalp, detection of near threshold stimuli, and reaction time techniques. There is evidence that injury to the posterior attention system is closely related to specific deficits in the ability to make selections from information contralateral to the lesion (Posner, 1988).

The Anterior Attention Network

A second attention network involves areas of the midprefrontal cortex (including the anterior cingulate gyrus and closely related but more superior supplementary motor area) that together appear to be active in a wide variety of situations involving the detection of events (Posner & Petersen, 1990). Detection plays a special role in the production of attentional interference. People can monitor many input channels at once with little or no interference, but if a target on any one channel is detected, the probability of detection on other channels is greatly restricted (Duncan, 1980).

A source of evidence favoring an anterior attention network comes from studies of the activity of brain systems during target detection. The degree of activation of the anterior attention system during detection tasks appears to be related to the number of targets detected, not the number of events presented (Posner, Petersen, Fox, & Raichle, 1988). The anterior attention system is also much more active during conflict blocks of the Stroop task than during nonconflict blocks (Pardo, Pardo, Janer, & Raichle, 1990). Finally, the anterior attention system is active during all tasks requiring subjects to detect target visual stimuli, whether the targets involve color, form, motion, or word semantics (Corbetta, Meizin, Dobmeyer, Shulman, & Petersen, 1991; Petersen, Fox, Snyder, & Raichle, 1990).

There is a great deal of cognitive evidence on the functional role of attention in relation to word association. We have known for 15 years, for example, that words can have relatively automatic input to their semantic associations, at least under some conditions (Posner, 1978). However, attending to words can modify this effect. If one attends to one meaning of a word, activation of other meanings is suppressed (Burgess & Simpson, 1988; Nakagawa, 1991). Attending to a word meaning also reduces the ability to detect unrelated words; that is, attending to a semantic category retards the speed at which words in other categories are detected. These effects are similar to the enhancements, described previously, in posterior attention when a visual location is attended. We do not have conclusive evidence that these enhancements require activation of the anterior cingulate, but data indicating that shadowing abolishes differences between lateralized lexical decisions suggest that they are caused by anterior cingulate interaction with lateral frontal areas (Nakagawa, 1991).

There is also experimental evidence on the effects of lesions of the anterior cingulate on performance. Bilateral lesions in this area can cause akinetic mutism (Damasio & Van Hoesen, 1983). The presence of recovery of function from lesions in this area (Janer & Pardo, 1991) and the relatively benign effect of cingulotomy for psychiatric disorders suggest that this area may not be alone in mediating attentional effects. PET studies suggest that a whole band of areas are (as inferior as the anterior cingulate or as superior as the supplementary motor area) involved in attentional effects on language (Petersen, Fox, Posner, Mintun, & Raichle, 1989). The more closely the task is related to actual motor output, the more superior the location of the activation. The structure of the anterior cingulate in nonhuman primates is consistent with its role in relation to both semantics and control of the posterior attention network. Research involving labeling of cells in this area shows that alternate columns are connected to the lateral prefrontal cortex (semantic processing) and to the posterior parietal cortex (posterior attention network) (Goldman-Rakic, 1988).

Relation between Posterior and Anterior Networks

There are strong anatomical connections between the anterior cingulate and the posterior parietal lobe, at least in the monkey (Goldman-Rakic, 1988). The obvious fact that we can command orienting via high-level cognitive strategies requires that there be some connection between the two networks, and this is also suggested by the anatomy. Nonetheless, cognitive studies suggest that the networks also maintain considerable independence. It is important that there be a degree of independence in the development and function of the two systems, as we shall indicate below.

A number of recent studies have tried to examine the ability of peripheral and central cues to produce orienting (i.e., to activate the posterior attention system) when the subject is processing another task that would be likely to tie up the anterior attention system (Jonides, 1981; Pashler, 1993; Posner, 1988; Posner, Sanson, Dhawan, & Shulman, 1989). These studies have found some independence between the two systems; the actual degree of independence appears to depend on the amount of on-line mental activity required for the other task.

A number of pathological states appear to show specific deficit in using cues to orient attention covertly to visual stimuli. These include neglect, Balint's syndrome, Parkinson's disease, closed head injury, attention deficit hyperactivity disorder (ADHD), schizophrenia, and PKU. Some of these disorders involve posterior and some anterior brain injury. In addition, a number of them involve reduced DA or NE input. These findings suggest that there may be many different types of lesions that can affect the orienting system.

The Vigilance Network

A third attentional network influences our ability to maintain the alert state. This system involves the locus coeruleus norepinephrine (NE) input to the cortex (see Harley, 1987, for a review). When subjects are required to maintain the alert state in the foreperiod of a reaction time task, or when they attend to a source of signal while waiting for an infrequent target to occur (vigilance), there is strong activity in this system (see Posner & Petersen, 1990, for a review of this evidence). This activity shows up in PET scans in the right lateral frontal lobe. When lesioned, this area gives rise to deficits in the ability to develop and maintain the alert state. This network is likely to be important in disorders like ADHD (see below) that impair the maintenance of attention.

Lateralization of a network for alerting may seem puzzling. Both hemispheres need to maintain alertness, and the function seems so basic and simple that there would appear to be little reason for lateral asymmetries. We believe that lateralization of this system to the right hemisphere may reflect its close involvement with regulation of the heart (Rothbart, Posner, & Boylan, 1990). Heart rate, as well as other autonomic systems, intimately reflects attentional state. The heart is asymmetric, and there is evidence connecting heart rate changes to the left stellate ganglion, which in turn is controlled by the right cerebral cortex. There is much reason to believe that the right hemisphere develops earlier in infancy than does the left (Tucker, 1985), possibly reflecting the need to replace the rapid shifts between sleep and wakefulness in newborns with sustained periods of alertness as the infant develops. The ability to control the alert state is what is called "vigilance" in adults; it is indexed by marked slowing of the heart. We speculate that the asymmetric control of the heart produces the asymmetry found in the cortical control of vigilance.

Cohen and Servan-Schreiber (1992) found an area of the right lateral midfrontal cortex that appears to be the most active during an auditory vigilance task, with the higher metabolic activation accompanied by reduced activation of the anterior cingulate. If one views the anterior cingulate as related to target detection, this makes sense. In tasks where one needs to suspend activity while waiting for low probability signals, it is important not to interfere with detecting the external event. Subjectively, one feels empty-headed, trying to avoid any stray thoughts that might detract from detection of the signal. Objectively, this suspended state has been shown to be effective in reducing loss of information in short-term memory (Reitman, 1971) and in producing a widespread inhibitory effect that includes not only cortical activity but also sympathetically controlled autonomic activity (Kahneman, 1973).

In addition to its effect on the anterior attention system, vigilance has a clear effect on the posterior attention system. It appears to tune the posterior system so that its interaction with accumulating information in object recognition systems is faster (Posner, 1978). Anatomically, it is known that the locus coeruleus (lc) has its primary NE input to the areas of the posterior attention system, including the parietal, pulvinar, and collicular systems (Morrison & Foote, 1986). Within these systems, the receptive field sizes of cells can be altered by the simultaneous activity of lc cells. Cognitively, this means that attention can interact more efficiently with the ventral data collection system. Thus, in highly alert states, responses are faster, with more anticipatory reactions and higher error rates (Posner, 1978).

The operations of the brain's attentional system boost signals within various brain areas. This basic fact has been illustrated both in PET studies (Corbetta et al., 1991) and in studies of recording of the brain's electrical activity (Mangun & Hillyard, 1990). For example, these studies show that attention to a visual dimension increases blood flow and electrical activity in prestriate areas, and attention to semantic associations boosts activity in lateralized frontal areas.

Development of Attentional Networks

One of the important aspects of regarding attention as a neural system with its own anatomy is that one can ask quite specific questions about development of the brain areas involved (Clohessy, Posner, Rothbart, & Vecera, 1991; Johnson, 1990; Johnson et al., 1991; Rothbart et al., 1990). As we have pointed out previously, the development of these networks is likely to relate to the attentional pathologies we discuss later in this section.

As a model of the development of attention, we have been exploring the way in which the posterior (orienting) attention network develops over the first year of life in connection with the laminar development of the visual system. We have used the method of marker tasks—tasks that have been shown in adults to involve specific aspects of attention—to connect the maturation of brain systems to behavior. Thus, it has been shown that the superior colliculus carries out a computation that reduces the probability of reorienting attention to an already examined visual location (inhibition of return; Posner, 1988). We have studied this function in infants ages 3 to 12 months, and have shown that it is not fully mature at 3 months, but it appears by 6 months to be at about the same level as in adults (Clohessy et al., 1991).

Other forms of attention shifting that may well involve the posterior attention network include the ability to disengage from a stimulus and the ability to develop an expectation of the location of a stimulus from an arbitrary prior event (Haith, Hazan, & Goodman, 1988; Johnson et al., 1991). These aspects of attention also show development in the period from 3 to 6 months. At 4 months, the infant is capable of learning that an arbitrary stimulus means the next event is likely to occur to the left rather than to the right (Johnson et al., 1991), and recent observations in our laboratory suggest relatively little development of these expectations over the next year (Clohessy, Posner, & Rothbart, 1992). We suspect that much of the improvement in learning involves new mechanisms that depend on later maturation of frontal areas.

One of the most striking aspects of 4-month-olds in visual orienting tasks is the degree to which, once locked on to stimulus events, their attention can be moved to various events at the will of the experimenter. They appear almost to look compulsively until distress or fatigue overtakes them. This contrasts strongly with the laboratory behavior of 12-month-olds, who appear to have an agenda of their own. They look for a while, but appear to have other activities pressing on them and may quickly turn to those instead. Thus, at 4 to 6 months, there is clear evidence of selection in terms of orienting to stimuli, even orienting based on clearly learned expectations, but behavioral evidence suggests that further development is needed for operation of the anterior attentional network. Much of this development appears to occur late in the first year.

Recently, Lalonde & Werker (1990) studied three seemingly quite separate tasks said to involve mental coordination. Two of the tasks were: (a) the ability to search for a hidden object and (b) the ability to recognize the correlation between features of a visual object. These abilities become highly correlated at 9 months when infants tend to pass all or none of them. The period from 7 to 12 months also marks the infant's ability to dissociate reaching from the line of sight (Diamond, in press). To reach away from where they are looking, infants must inhibit the prepotent tendency to reach along the line of sight. In an abstract sense, this is like the well-known Stroop effect, where the word name must be inhibited in order to make a highly related vocal response based on ink-color name. In adults, the conflict condition in naming the ink color of colored words (Stroop effect) has been shown to activate the anterior attention network (Pardo et al., 1990). Thus, it seems reasonable to suppose that the anterior attention network is involved in these coordinative activities developing in the period around 9 months.

Nine months is also about the time when infants begin to use single words. PET data suggest that the semantic association among words involves a left lateral frontal area very close to the area thought to be related to reaching (Petersen et al., 1989). Indeed, the early use of words is very closely related to infants' gestures toward objects (Dore, Franklin, Miller, & Ramer, 1976). Gesturing is also frequently used to aid in the development of word use by language-delayed children (Pien & Klein, 1989).

McCall (1979) reviewed research indicating the presence of a shift, between 7 and 13 months, in infants' means-ends competencies, their coordination of action schemes on an object, motor and vocal imitation, and the beginnings of response uncertainty (wariness). McCall summarized the changes in this way: "At approximately 7 months of age, the child's cognitive development first permits the separation of means from ends and infant from environment. Whereas previously the infant's response and its consequences were unitary, now their separation introduces an element of response uncertainty—either, 'Will this response have a desired consequence?' and/or 'Which of several responses shall I make?'" (1979, p. 207).

Thus, age 9 months seems crucial for the development of coordination between cues and responses in a number of domains. Put in popular terms, infants are developing a mind of their own, in the sense of having an internal agenda that controls behavior. Self-regulative systems continue to mature well into the preschool years (Rothbart & Posner, 1985). This maturation is under the control of both genetic plans and the child's specific experiences of socialization (Luria, 1973), and both factors are important in understanding psychopathology. In our more recent work, we have identified a second major transition in executive control occurring at about 18 months (see review in Ruff & Rothbart, in press).

Attention and Pathology

Neurological

Many neurological and psychiatric disorders, such as neglect, depression, schizophrenia, and ADHD, have been said to involve pathologies of attention. However, without a real understanding of the neural substrates of attention, this has been a somewhat empty classification. This situation should be changed with the systematic application of our understanding of attentional networks to pathological issues (Posner & Raichle, 1994). On this topic, we review work mainly on neglect (Posner & Rafal, 1986), schizophrenia (Early, Posner, Reiman, & Raichle, 1989) and ADHD (Swanson et al., 1991).

In each of these pathologies, we have found it possible to document at least one deficit in attention that was specific and implied a particular anatomical basis for the disorder. Further, in each case, the disorder proved to involve not only portions of the cortex that compute attentional operations, but also abnormal regulation by transmitter systems that influence those computations. To illustrate the general principle involved in these two kinds of influences, we consider the way in which the norepinephrine (NE) system interacts with computations of the posterior visual-spatial attention network to influence neglect. Principles from this section will then be applied to the disorder of schizophrenia and ADHD.

We have noted that computations of the parietal lobe, pulvinar, and colliculus constitute the posterior visual-spatial attention system. From work in monkeys, it is known that each of these areas receives a very heavy input of NE from the locus coeruleus (Morrison & Foote, 1986). NE input to these areas is much greater than to the classical geniculo-striate pathway or to the areas along the ventral pathway from primary cortex to the inferior temporal lobe visual areas. This anatomy corresponds well to a view of visual pattern recognition put forward many years ago, based solely on cognitive experiments (Posner, 1978). That view suggested that arousal, such as is induced by task-relevant warning signals, influences the operation of attention but has relatively little direct influence on the pattern recognition system. The basis for this idea was that the time course of retrieval of information from internal codes appeared little changed by providing a warning signal. What changed were the probability and the speed with which the subject would become aware of these retrieved products and could thus note them, store them, and respond to them. In anatomical terms, the warning signal induces changes in the posterior attention network, allowing faster interaction with pattern recognition and thereby producing a more efficient routing of input information to the anterior attention network.

By far the most common lesion site to produce contralateral neglect of visual stimuli is the posterior parietal lobe. Damage to this area produces a specific abnormality in dealing with visual stimuli contralateral to the lesion. Shortly after the lesion, there is widespread dysregulation of metabolic activity that might extend over the whole hemisphere, but after about 6 months this usually has cleared (Duell & Collins, 1984). Neglect as a clinical syndrome has many features, but the lasting deficit appears to be primarily attentional. Subjects may appear to be normal, but their impairment is revealed in their inability to deal with a contralateral target when they are already attending to visual information, with a greatly magnified cost in reaction time.

These basic results have now been replicated with many patients with parietal lesions, and the time course of recovery has been thoroughly traced (Morrow & Ratcliff, 1988; Posner, Walker, Friedrich, & Rafal, 1984, 1987). The parietal damage need not result from trauma. Recently, Parasuraman, Greenwood, Haxby, and Grady (1992) studied a subset of Alzheimer's patients with reduced metabolism of the parietal lobe consequent to their degenerative process. These patients showed the same attentional deficit as stroke patients, and the degree of deficit was correlated with the amount of metabolism reduction in this area.

It has been known for many years that neglect as a clinical syndrome is more prevalent with right than with left hemisphere damage (Heilman, Watson, & Valenstein, 1985; Mesulam, 1980), leading some to suppose that the right hemisphere controls attention to both sides of space. Recent PET data strongly support this view (Corbetta, Meizin, Shulman, & Petersen, 1993). However, two other asymmetries could also contribute to the difference between right and left parietal lesions. Right parietal patients have difficulty in maintaining the alert state unless given a specific cue before the start of each trial; left parietal patients appear virtually normal in this respect (see Posner & Petersen, 1990, for a review). In addition, right posterior lesions appear to influence perception of more global aspects of external visual signals; left posterior lesions influence more detailed information (Robertson, Lamb, & Knight, 1988). These three influences apparently combine to produce the very noticeable attentional orienting deficits found in patients with right posterior lesions.

As noted above, the right cerebral hemisphere appears to be specialized for maintaining the alert state (Posner & Petersen, 1990). There is abundant evidence that patients with right-side lesions have reduced ability to stay alert during vigilance tasks. This corresponds to findings that lesions of the right but not the left hemisphere of rats can deplete NE input to the cortex. Heilman and colleagues (e.g., Heilman et al., 1985) have argued for many years that the right hemisphere has a special role in arousal. In this, he appears to be quite correct. However, they seem to think of arousal as being the same as the operation of attention; our view has been that arousal modifies specific orienting computations by the posterior attention system.

There appear to be two different influences on the efficiency of the posterior attentional systems. Lesions of the parietal lobe produce great difficulty in shifting from a focus of visual attention to deal with targets in the contralesional direction. This tends to produce an abnormal fixation on target events and difficulty in disengaging. However, if the normal modulation of this system by transmitter input (e.g., NE) is blocked, the opposite set of effects occurs. The person has difficulty in maintaining concentration on a source of signals and is easily distracted by events outside of that focus. In that sense, he or she is distractable. It seems likely that the idea of a cortical computation being modified by transmitters from subcortical areas might serve as a very general model for a number of pathological states. Below, we consider the relevance of these ideas for the study of schizophrenia and ADHD.

Attention and Psychopathology

From our perspective, the distinguishing factor in a number of neurological and psychiatric disorders is mainly what is known about the underlying pathophysiology. In a case of neglect from stroke or tumor, one can observe the lesions through neuroimaging. Confirmation of the lesion location can lead to the application of various cognitive tests and, through them, to an understanding of the deficit in terms of the underlying computations. Thus, when the same general cognitive deficits were found in some patients with Alzheimer's disease as for patients with parietal strokes, functional scanning in Alzheimer's patients showed a reduction of metabolism in the posterior parietal lobe that was correlated with the extent of the attentional deficit (Parasuraman et al., 1992). This finding supports the view that when a brain abnormality is unknown, as in many disorders labeled psychiatric, it may be possible to use the details of the attentional deficit to infer the nature of the underlying pathology.

In this section, we try to illustrate this logic by examining two well-known psychiatric disorders: schizophrenia (Early et al., 1989) and ADHD (Swanson et al., 1991). Both of these disorders have been said to involve attention; they clearly involve different aspects of self-regulation. However, these terms have been used only very generally. We are very far from understanding either disorder, but it is possible to report some evidence supporting rather specific attentional abnormalities that allow us to consider how a disorder may affect regulatory mechanisms and vice versa.

Schizophrenia

Several aspects of schizophrenia suggest an abnormality of the circuitry involving the anterior attention system, including the ventral tegmentum and pallidum, the anterior cingulate, and the dorsolateral prefrontal cortex (Early et al., 1989; Goldman-Rakic, 1988). Moreover, in most studies, the initial nature of the deficit supports mainly left hemisphere pathology. It has been known for many years that schizophrenic subjects are very slow in responding to input stimuli and that this slowing is somehow related to the predictability of the input signal (Zahn, Rosenthall, & Shakow, 1963). However, this general slowing provides very little localizing information, because it could result from motivational, attentional, or other processing difficulties.

In our studies, in addition to a general slowing, we found a specific difficulty in dealing with right visual field targets following cues to the left visual field (Posner, Early, Reiman, Pardo, & Dhawan, 1988). In this, the schizophrenic patients appeared to resemble neglect patients with left parietal damage. The specificity of this result is important because it means the deficit cannot be seen as caused by general factors such as motivational effects or a failure to understand the task. We also found the pattern of the disorder was not present in other psychiatric groups such as depressives (Pardo, Pardo, Humes, & Posner, in press).

However, from many cognitive and imaging studies, there was reason to suppose that the core of the schizophrenic deficit was *not* in posterior but rather in frontal areas (Early et al., 1989). In addition, our studies of attention shifting of normal subjects engaged in a simultaneous shadowing task showed that right visual field cues were ineffective, and this could explain the pattern of data found in our schizophrenics (Posner et al., 1989). Because shadowing is a task that involves the anterior attention network, it seemed reasonable to suppose patient deficits might be in this network. In addition, similar deficits in moving rightward have been found in schizophrenics' eye fixations (Potkin et al., 1990) and in their motor movements (Bracha, 1987). These findings also fit with a more general attention deficit, as would be true if the anterior attention network were involved.

Studies using the Stroop effect have also revealed a deficit in schizophrenic patients (Cohen & Servan-Schreiber, 1992). By itself, the increased difficulty schizophrenics had in naming the ink color in the presence of conflicting information did not indicate a very specific deficit. Often, brain damage of almost any kind will increase the relative difficulty of the task. However, when normal subjects were required to perform the Stroop color-naming task while undergoing PET scans, it was found that the anterior cingulate gyrus was the most activated area in the brain (Pardo et al., 1990). In addition, in our studies of a version of the Stroop task that is differentially affected by right and left lateralized strokes (Sandson et al., 1988), the never medicated schizophrenic patients resembled those with left- rather than right-sided damage. The Stroop effect in normals has now been shown to involve the anterior cingulate (a part of the anterior attention system), and the fact of a schizophrenic deficit in this task suggests a problem in the anterior attention system.

More recent studies using visual orienting tasks (Nestor et al., in press; Pardo, 1992; Potkin et al., 1990; Strauss, Alphs, & Boekamp, 1991; Wigal, Potkin, Richmond, Swanson, & LaBerge, 1991) have confirmed this position in part and have raised additional issues. In one study (Potkin et al., 1990), first break, never medicated schizophrenics showed the same pattern of deficit found in our patients and in normal subjects' shadowing, but this was not true in patients who had been on medication for a long period. Several other studies showed that chronic schizophrenic patients did not exhibit the same pattern of deficit that we had found (Nestor et al., in press; Strauss et al., 1991).

Additional support for the idea of a frontal deficit arises from findings that suggest deficit in both the Wisconsin Card Sorting Test and in pursuit eye movements in schizophrenic patients (Holtzman, 1985; Weinberger, Berman, & Zec, 1986). These findings have usually been thought to implicate dorsolateral prefrontal cortex and eye movement systems. It is well established that patients with chronic schizophrenia exhibit a number of signs of frontal lobe damage, including a reduction in frontal blood flow and metabolism. The eye movement abnormalities found in pursuit movements of schizophrenics could also relate to the inhibitory control that areas of the basal ganglia exercise over the superior colliculus. Deficits in dopamine could reduce this control and make it more difficult to suppress intrusive saccadic eye movements during tracing of visual objects.

Chronic schizophrenic patients tend to show withdrawal and poverty of expression; first break patients often exhibit auditory hallucinations and symptoms of thought disorder. In terms of their verbal behavior, the chronic patients use few words, and the first break patients seem to have poor control over a flood of vivid associations. Chronic patients' performance shows withdrawal and is said to exhibit the negative symptoms of the disorder; first break patients exhibit positive symptoms. We do not think that these differences between early and later stages of the disorder are absolute. Rather, both patterns may be present in all patients but may mix in differing degrees, depending on their current state.

These results suggest that deficits in schizophrenia relate to specific abnormalities of attention. The finding of a left globus pallidus deficit in PET studies of never medicated schizophrenics (Early et al., 1989), together with signs of neglect of the right side of space and the specific deficits in versions of the Stroop effect, all point to problems in the anterior attention system. The specific difficulty may occur as a result of dysregulation of dopamine (DA) input from the ventral tegmental area to the anterior cingulate. It is possible to relate problems in regulation by the anterior attention systems to symptoms of difficulties in concentration, alien thought insertion, and bizarre use of language, all seen as positive symptoms in first break schizophrenics (Early et al., 1989).

A recent study of phenylketonuria (PKU) patients who have been treated to avoid mental retardation provides a developmental perspective to the visual orienting results. Phenylketonuria is a deficiency of phenylalanine that results in severe retardation unless treated by a specific diet. Although treated patients do not show the mental retardation that would otherwise occur, they do have reduced aminergic production, particularly in dopamine (DA). These patients have a deficit in dopamine and other transmitter systems, but do not show other symptoms of mental retardation or schizophrenia. However, male patients in this group were found to be slower on shifting attention to right than to left visual field—exactly the deficit found in first break schizophrenic patients (Craft, Gourvitch, Dowton, Swanson, & Bonforte, 1992). The female PKU patients did not show this abnormality; they resembled the normal control subjects. There was no direct confirmation of transmitter deficits, but this study suggests important ties between depletion of transmitter input in childhood and a pattern of visual spatial orienting related to that found in at least one form of schizophrenia.

As schizophrenia progresses and/or as a result of the medication, a different and more pervasive pattern of deficit emerges. In chronic patients, as mentioned above, there is evidence of reductions of blood flow and metabolism in the frontal lobes and deficits in neuropsychological tasks associated with lateral as well as medial frontal lobe function (Weinberger et al., 1986). In these chronic patients, the deficit in attention appears to reflect difficulty in maintaining the alert state and a more pervasive attention problem than we have described for the initial state of the disorder.

It is also clear that schizophrenia has a strong genetic basis (Gottesman, 1991). However, the specific attentional deficits found in the cognitive tasks we have been describing appear to be caused by the particular form of the disorder that patients are exhibiting and not to its genetic precursor. This conclusion is most strongly supported by studies of monozygotic twins discordant for schizophrenia (Pardo, 1992). The twin with schizophrenia showed clear evidence of the right visual field abnormality in roughly the form found in the first break patients. The nonschizophrenic cotwin appeared to be entirely normal in both general speed and in the specific spatial attention associated with schizophrenia. This result confirms that the attention deficits are related to the disorder as manifested in schizophrenia, not to the genotype.

The findings of schizophrenic deficits in the Wisconsin Card Sorting Test and in pursuit eye movements have been shown to occur in monozygotic twins and in relations of schizophrenics who are not suffering from the disorder. These findings support the genetic basis of the disorder and suggest that at least some of the cognitive deficits may be related to the genetic precursors.

Judging from the sensitivity of the cognitive tasks to deficits present in stroke patients, it is possible that the presence of abnormalities in attention could serve as a warning sign of possible environmental influences that could convert a genetic predisposition into a schizophrenic break. If, for example, stress during adolescence affected DA levels in persons who had a genetic predisposition to the disorder, one might first expect to see subtle changes in attention and only later the other symptoms we associate with the disorder. This might suggest possibilities for early pharmacological intervention to prevent expression of the disorder. Basic research on the effect of transmitter systems on attentional operations could be useful in the development of such an intervention strategy. This kind of speculation turns our attention to the importance of developmental factors in the expression of attentional psychopathology. To explore this idea, we turn to some studies of attention deficit hyperactivity disorder.

Attention Deficit Disorder

Attention deficit hyperactivity disorder (ADHD) has been studied from many viewpoints, but, to date, work from a cognitive-neuroscience perspective has not been extensive. Earlier in this chapter, we reported that blocking NE in normal subjects can produce a pattern of reduced cost in shifting to an unexpected target. The term "reduced cost" may be a bit misleading because it sounds like improved performance. In fact, the reduction in cost can be seen as increased distractibility, because nonattended locations have an increased chance of influencing judgments. Because of the common descriptions of ADHD as involving increases in distractibility and because the symptoms of ADHD are often improved by drugs that affect DA and NE (Zametkin & Rapoport, 1987), it is reasonable to suppose that, for ADHD children, cognitive tasks would show reduced costs in shifting to unattended target locations.

Two studies have been guided by this hypothesis. The first study used manual responses and the second, eye movement responses to visual stimuli (Rothlind, Posner, & Schaughency, 1991; Swanson et al., 1991). The results of the first study showed a very specific abnormality in ADHD children. At longer delay intervals, they showed little difference between valid and invalid trials compared to normal age-matched controls, who demonstrated the expected cost in reaction time (RT) for invalid trials.

This evidence for greatly reduced cost was apparent only for left visual field stimuli. The result confirmed the expectation of a lack of cost as would be expected if there was reduced NE.

Rothlind et al. (1991) also found evidence of a difference between ADHD and normal children in eye movements toward visual events. Under conditions of low alertness, leftward eye movements controlled by the right cerebral hemisphere were faster than rightward eye movements in normal children, but not in ADHD children. These two findings taken together give some support to the idea of a specific deficit in ADHD children in maintaining the alert state. The deficit might operate through reduction in right hemisphere availability of NE and, through this mechanism, reduction in the ability to restrict information to a selected location. This view would be supported by evidence in neuroimaging studies of deficiency of right hemisphere activation during vigilance. The most thorough PET study of this hypothesis to date (Zametkin et al., 1990), however, conducted with adults who had ADHD when children, showed a large number of activated areas that were mainly left frontal and did not correspond to the arousal system in normal subjects.

Other Pathologies

A few studies of other pathological abnormalities have used cognitive methods similar to the ones described above. For example, as noted above, it has been possible to study children with treated phenylketonuria (PKU) who have a deficit in dopamine and other transmitter systems. Neuropsychological studies of children with this deficit support the idea that they show reduced performance in tasks having a relationship to executive function (Welsh, Pennington, Ozonoff, Rouse, & McCabe, 1990). These tasks would draw heavily on frontal lobe systems and their regulation by the anterior attention system. As mentioned earlier, attention shifting in male PKU children (Craft et al., 1992) showed a deficit very similar to that found in schizophrenics. Similar methods of study are being applied to work on psychopathy; the underlying hypothesis is that psychopaths have difficulty in inhibiting prepotent responses to stimuli (Harpur & Hare, 1990).

In this section, we have illustrated the range of deficits that might arise from pathologies of the brain's attentional system. It is impressive that disorders such as schizophrenia and ADHD show very specific abnormalities in orienting that cannot be credited to general effects. The presence of deficits to one visual field or to one type of trial suggests very specific disorders that can be related to the neural machinery underlying the brain's attention system. These disorders provide clues as to the pathophysiology that might be present in psychiatric disorders. What seems most firmly established, primarily from the work with ADHD and schizophrenia, is the presence of abnormalities indicating very specific attention deficits that can be linked to anatomically restricted hypotheses. It is important to keep in mind that these deficits appear to change with the developmental progression of the disorder. There is still much we do not know and considerable complexity and controversy in the current findings. However, at the very least, they illustrate that the full range of cognitive and neuroscience methods can be fruitfully applied to the analysis of these psychopathological disorders.

DIRECTIONS FOR FUTURE WORK

In the first section of this chapter, we stressed the importance of looking at the interaction between individual differences and experience in environmental contexts, with two goals in mind. One goal is theoretical: to understand some of the influences on the development of psychopathology or its risk factors. The second goal is applied: to identify times and places in the course of development when intervention might be particularly appropriate to enhance the life chances of the child. In pursuing these goals, we investigated relations between individual differences in temperament and the development of risk for psychopathology by putting forward a set of temperamental dimensions, considering their psychobiological substrate and changes with development of the disorder, and relating them to a set of environmental experiences that might further influence the development of disorder. In several sections of the chapter, we have also suggested possible directions for future research. Here, we suggest some further areas for future research based on findings from research on temperament and development. Such research requires implementation of psychometrically sound measures of individual differences, and sensitive measures of behaviors in an interactive setting.

Future research needs to explore an understanding of emotion and motivation in terms of information processing networks that can be linked to neural functioning. Marker tasks for components of emotional-motivational functioning might then also be developed to better understand mental disorders, and to allow investigation of the disorders themselves as a way of furthering our understanding of temperament. We expect, in addition, that an increased understanding of the development of attention and of individual differences in the ability to shift and focus attention related to the control of impulses and affective displays will enhance our understanding of the development of psychopathology. This work will require a concern with the environmental context and requirements for self-regulation, as well as the environmental supports or "other regulation" available (Rothbart, 1984, 1989d), which we have not developed in this chapter.

An important contribution that we have only touched on in our review is the way in which the study of disorders can illuminate our understanding of individual differences in temperament. Ganiban, Wagner, and Cicchetti (1990), for example, have investigated the development of Down syndrome in a way that advances our understanding of temperament. Studies of the comorbidity of disorders (the co-occurrence of two or more syndromes at the same point in time) also contribute to our understanding of temperament. Butler and Nemeroff (1990) suggested that corticotropin-releasing factor (CRF) may be a possible cause of comorbidity of anxiety and depression in its regulatory role within the hypothalamic-pituitary-adrenal (HPA) axis. Such a mechanism identified in the study of psychopathology might then be considered with respect to nonclinical individual differences in stress reactivity; indeed, Panksepp (1986) discussed this relationship. Panksepp noted that central administration of CRF can lead to intense arousal, and that the anatomy of the CRF system maps closely on the anatomy of distress vocalization systems. On this basis, he suggested that the CRF system can be seen to be a general modulator of distress reactivity.

In childhood, the comorbidity of aggression-related disorders and depression has already proved to be of great interest. Although chiefly explored to date through social learning (Patterson & Capaldi, 1990) and social cognitive processing (Garber, Quiggle, Panak, & Dodge, 1991) models, more constitutionally based analyses might further illuminate our understanding of this relationship and its general relevance to temperament.

Further studies are suggested by some items in Table 11.1 that we have not cited or developed in this chapter. These include considering the tendencies of individuals to put themselves in situations associated with risk. The example we give in Table 11.1, item 5, is that temperamental stimulation seeking (or lack of fear or effortful control as protective factors) may be related to a woman's choice of partner, place of residence, and/or pregnancy, which may then put her at risk for affective disorder (Brown & Harris, 1978). Temperamental characteristics would also be expected to be related to the psychological impact of negative or positive life events (Table 11.1, item 4).

Other research suggests that problems with attentional self-regulation may be related to chronic anxiety (Mathews & MacLeod, 1986) (Table 11.1, item 8). In addition, emotional biases may prime the information processing biases noted in the development of disorder (or vice versa) (Table 11.1, item 9), and temperamental characteristics may be related to the particular symptomatology of a clinical disorder, such as anxiety versus hopelessness in depression (Table 11.1, item 12).

We also suggest that temperamental characteristics may influence the chronicity of a disorder (Table 11.1, item 13) and may be related to the individual's response to psychopharmacological or psychotherapeutic therapy (Table 11.1, item 14). In general, these suggestions implicate temperamental variables not only in research with infants and children, where their importance has been already indicated (e.g., Werner, 1986), but in research on links between temperament and psychopathology in adults. The basic importance of individual differences in reactivity and self-regulation to the development of adaptation suggests that thinking and research in these directions across the life span will continue to be fruitful.

REFERENCES

Achenbach, T. M., & Edelbrock, C. S. (1978). The classification of child psychology: A review and analysis of empirical efforts. *Psychological Bulletin, 85,* 1275–1301.

Ackerson, L. (1942). *Children's behavior problems* (Vol. 2). Chicago: University of Chicago Press.

Ahadi, S. A., & Rothbart, M. K. (1994). Temperament, development and the Big Five. In C. Halverson, R. Martin, & G. Kohnstamm (Eds.), *The developing structure of temperament and personality from infancy to adulthood* (pp. 189–208) Hillsdale, NJ: Erlbaum.

Bandura, A., & Walters, R. H. (1963). *Social learning and personality development.* New York: Holt, Rinehart and Winston.

Barron, A. P., & Earls, F. (1984). The relation of temperament and social factors to behavior problems in three-year-old children. *Journal of Child Psychology and Psychiatry, 25,* 23–33.

Bates, J. E. (1980). The concept of difficult temperament. *Merrill-Palmer Quarterly, 26,* 299–319.

Bates, J. E. (1989). Applications of temperament concepts. In G. A. Kohnstamm, J. E. Bates, & M. K. Rothbart (Eds.), *Temperament in childhood* (pp. 321–355). New York: Wiley.

Bates, J. E. (1990). Conceptual and empirical linkages between temperament and behavior problems: A commentary on the Sanson, Prior, and Kyrios study. *Merrill-Palmer Quarterly, 36,* 193–197.

Bates, J. E., Freeland, C. A. B., & Lounsbury, M. L. (1979). Measurement of infant difficultness. *Child Development, 50,* 794–803.

Bates, J. E., Maslin, C. A., & Franke, K. A. (1985). Attachment security, mother-child interaction, and temperament as predictors of behavior-problem ratings at age three years. In I. Bretherton & E. Waters (Eds.), *Growing points in attachment theory and research* (pp. 167–193). Society for Research in Child Development Monographs, Serial No. 209.

Block, J. H., Gjerde, P. F., & Block, J. H. (1991). Personality antecedents of depressive tendencies in 18-year-olds: A prospective study. *Journal of Personality and Social Psychology, 60,* 726–738.

Bracha, H. S. (1987). Asymmetric rotational circling behavior, a dopamine-related asymmetry: Preliminary findings in unmedicated and never-medicated schizophrenic patients. *Biological Psychiatry, 22,* 995–1003.

Bronson, W. C. (1972). The role of enduring orientations to the environment in personality development. *Genetic Psychology Monographs, 86,* 3–80.

Brown, G. W., & Harris, T. (1978). *Social origins of depression.* New York: Free Press.

Burgess, C., & Simpson, G. B. (1988). Cerebral hemispheric mechanisms in the retrieval of ambiguous word meanings. *Brain and Language, 33,* 86–103.

Burton, R. (1921). *The anatomy of melancholy.* Oxford: Oxford University Press. (Original work published 1621)

Buss, A. H., & Plomin, R. (1975). *A temperament theory of personality development.* New York: Wiley.

Buss, A. H., & Plomin, R. (1984). *Temperament: Early developing personality traits.* Hillsdale, NJ: Erlbaum.

Butler, P. D., & Nemeroff, C. B. (1990). Corticotropin-releasing factor as a possible cause of comorbidity in anxiety and depressive disorders. In J. D. Maser & C. R. Cloninger (Eds.), *Comorbidity of mood and anxiety disorders* (pp. 413–607). Washington, DC: American Psychiatric Press.

Cameron, J. R. (1978). Parental treatment, children's treatment, and the risk of childhood behavioral problems: 2. Initial temperament, parental attitudes, and the incidence and form of behavioral problems. *American Journal of Orthopsychiatry, 48,* 140–147.

Campbell, S. B. (1991). Longitudinal studies of active and aggressive preschoolers: Individual differences in early behavior and in outcome. In D. Cicchetti & S. L. Toth (Eds.), *Rochester Symposium on Developmental Psychopathology: Vol. 2. Internalizing and externalizing expressions of dysfunction.* Hillsdale, NJ: Erlbaum.

Carey, W. B., & McDevitt, S. C. (1978). Revision of the infant temperament questionnaire. *Pediatrics, 61,* 735–739.

Carlson, N. R. (1984). *Psychology: The science of behavior.* Boston: Allyn & Bacon.

Chess, S. (1982). The "blame the mother" ideology. *International Journal of Mental Health, 11,* 95–107.

Chess, S., & Thomas, A. (1986). *Temperament in clinical practice.* New York: Guilford.

Cicchetti, D., & Schneider-Rosen, K. (1986). An organizational approach to childhood depression. In M. Rutter, P. Read, & C. E. Izard

(Eds.), *Depression in young people: Clinical and developmental perspectives.* New York: Guilford.

Cicchetti, D., & Toth, S. L. (1991). *Rochester Symposium on Developmental Psychopathology: Vol. 2. Internalizing and externalizing expressions of dysfunction.* Hillsdale, NJ: Erlbaum.

Clohessy, A. B., Posner, M. I., & Rothbart, M. K. (1992, May). *Anticipatory eye movement learning during the first year of life.* Paper presented at the annual meeting of the Western Psychological Association, Portland, Oregon.

Clohessy, A. B., Posner, M. I., Rothbart, M. K., & Vecera, S. (1991). The development of inhibition of return in early infancy. *Journal of Cognitive Neuroscience, 3,* 345–350.

Cloninger, C. R. (1986). A unified biosocial theory of personality and its role in the development of anxiety states. *Psychiatric Developments, 3,* 167–226.

Cloninger, C. R. (1987a). A systematic method for clinical description and classification of personality variants. *Archives of General Psychiatry, 44,* 573–588.

Cloninger, C. R. (1987b). Neurogenetic adaptive mechanisms in alcoholism. *Science, 236,* 410–416.

Cohen, J. D., & Servan-Schreiber, D. (1992). Contact, cortex, and dopamine: A connectionist approach to behavior and biology in schizophrenia. *Psychological Review, 99,* 45–77.

Corbetta, M., Meizin, F. M., Dobmeyer, S., Shulman, G. L., & Petersen, S. E. (1991). Selective and divided attention during visual discrimination of shape, color and speed: Functional anatomy by positron emission tomography. *Journal of Neuroscience, 11,* 2392–2402.

Corbetta, M., Meizin, F. M., Shulman, G. L., & Petersen, S. E. (1993). Shifts of visuo-spatial attention: A PET study. *Journal of Neuroscience, 13,* 1202–1226.

Costa, P. T., Jr., & McCrae, R. R. (1985). *The NEO Personality Inventory manual.* Odessa, FL: Psychological Assessment Resources.

Costa, P. T., Jr., & McCrae, R. R. (1988). From catalog to classification: Murray's needs and the five-factor model. *Journal of Personality and Social Psychology, 55,* 258–265.

Costa, P. T., Jr., & McCrae, R. R. (1989). *NEO PI/FFI manual supplement.* Odessa, FL: Psychological Assessment Resources.

Craft, S., Gourvitch, M. L., Dowton, S. B., Swanson, J. M., & Bonforte, S. (1992). Lateralized deficit in visual attention in males with developmental dopamine depletion. *Neuropsychologia, 30,* 341–351.

Culpeper, N. (1657). *Galen's art of physik, Translated with a gloss. by N. Culpeper.* London.

Damasio, A. R., & Van Hoesen, G. W. (1983). Emotional disturbance associated with focal lesions of the limbic frontal lobe. In K. M. Heilman & P. Satz (Eds.), *Neuropsychology of human emotion* (pp. 85–110). New York: Guilford.

Davidson, R. J., & Fox, N. A. (1989). Frontal brain asymmetry predicts infants' response to maternal separation. *Journal of Abnormal Psychology, 98,* 127–131.

Davidson, R. J., & Tomarken, A. J. (1989). Laterality and emotion: An electrophysiological approach. In F. Boller & J. Grafman (Eds.), *Handbook of neuropsychology* (pp. 419–441). Amsterdam, The Netherlands: Elsevier.

Depue, R. A., & Iacono, W. G. (1989). Neurobehavioral aspects of affective disorders. In M. R. Rosenzweig & L. Y. Porter (Eds.), *Annual review of psychology* (Vol. 40, pp. 457–492). Palo Alto, CA: Annual Reviews.

Diamond, A. (in press). Retrieval of an object from an open box: The development of visual-tactile control of reaching in the first year of life. *Child Development Monographs.*

Diamond, S. (1974). *The roots of psychology.* New York: Basic Books.

Digman, J. M., & Inouye, J. (1986). Further specification of the five robust factors of personality. *Journal of Personality and Social Psychology, 50,* 116–123.

Dore, J., Franklin, M. B., Miller, R. T., & Ramer, A. L. H. (1976). Transitional phenomena in early language acquisition. *Journal of Child Language, 3,* 13–27.

Duell, R. M., & Collins, R. C. (1984). The functional anatomy of frontal lobe neglect in the monkey: Behavioral and quantitative 2 DG studies. *Annals of Neurology, 15,* 521–529.

Duncan, J. (1980). The locus of interference in the perception of simultaneous stimuli. *Psychological Review, 87,* 272–300.

Eagly, A. H., & Steffen, V. J. (1986). Gender and aggressive behavior: A meta-analytic review of the social-psychological literature. *Psychological Bulletin, 100,* 309–330.

Earls, F. (1981). Temperament characteristics and behavior problems in three-year-old children. *Journal of Nervous and Mental Disease, 169,* 367–373.

Earls, F., & Jung, K. G. (1987). Temperament and home environment characteristics and causal factors in the early development of childhood psychopathology. *Journal of the American Academy of Child and Adolescent Psychiatry, 26,* 491–498.

Early, T. S., Posner, M. I., Reiman, E. M., & Raichle, M. E. (1989). Hyperactivity of the left striato-pallidal projection; Parts I & II. *Psychiatric Developments, 2,* 85–121.

Edelbrock, C., & Achenbach, T. M. (1980). A typology of Child Behavior Profile patterns: Distribution and correlates in disturbed children aged 6 to 16. *Journal of Abnormal Child Psychology, 8,* 441–470.

Eisenberg, N., & Fabes, R. A. (1992). Emotion, self-regulation, and social competence. In M. Clark (Ed.), *Emotion and social behavior: Vol. 14. Review of personality and social psychology* (pp. 119–150). Newbury Park, CA: Sage.

Eysenck, H. J. (1944). Types of personality: A factorial study of 700 neurotics. *Journal of Mental Science, 90,* 851–861.

Eysenck, H. J. (1947). *Dimensions of personality.* London: Routledge & Kegan Paul.

Eysenck, H. J. (1970). *The structure of human personality* (3rd ed.). London: Methuen.

Eysenck, H. J., & Eysenck, M. W. (1985). *Personality and individual differences.* New York: Plenum.

Fox, N. A., & Davidson, R. J. (1984). Hemispheric substrates of affect: A developmental model. In N. A. Fox & R. J. Davidson (Eds.), *The psychology of affective development* (pp. 353–382). Hillsdale, NJ: Erlbaum.

Fullard, W., McDevitt, S. C., & Carey, W. B. (1984). Assessing temperament in one- to three-year-old children. *Journal of Pediatric Psychology, 9,* 205–217.

Ganiban, J., Wagner, S., & Cicchetti, D. (1990). Temperament and Down syndrome. In D. Cicchetti & M. Beeghly (Eds.), *Children with Down syndrome: A developmental perspective* (pp. 63–100). New York: Cambridge University Press.

Garber, J., Quiggle, N. L., Panak, W., & Dodge, K. A. (1991). Aggression and depression in children: Comorbidity, specificity, and social cognitive processing. In D. Cicchetti & S. L. Toth (Eds.), *Rochester Symposium on Developmental Psychopathology: Vol. 2. Internalizing and externalizing expressions of dysfunction.* Hillsdale, NJ: Erlbaum.

Gjerde, P. F., Block, J., & Block, J. H. (1988). Depressive symptoms and personality during late adolescence: Gender differences in the externalization-internalization of symptom expression. *Journal of Abnormal Psychology, 97,* 475–486.

Goldberg, L. R. (1990). An alternative "Description of Personality": The Big-Five factor structure. *Journal of Personality and Social Psychology, 59,* 1216–1229.

Goldman-Rakic, P. S. (1988). Topography of cognition: Parallel distributed networks in primate association cortex. *Annual Review of Neuroscience, 11,* 137–156.

Goldsmith, H. H., & Alansky, J. A. (1987). Maternal and infant temperamental predictors of attachment: A meta-analytic review. *Journal of Consulting and Clinical Psychology, 55,* 805–816.

Gorenstein, E. E., & Newman, J. P. (1980). Disinhibitory psychopathology: A new perspective and a model for research. *Psychological Review, 87,* 301–315.

Gottesman, I. I. (1991). *Schizophrenia genesis.* New York: Freeman.

Gray, J. A. (1971). *The psychology of fear and stress.* New York: McGraw-Hill.

Gray, J. A. (1975). *Elements of a two-process theory of learning.* New York: Academic Press.

Gray, J. A. (1977). Drug effects on fear and frustration: Possible limbic site of action of minor tranquilizers. In L. L. Iverson, S. P. Iverson, & S. H. Snyder (Eds.), *Handbook of psychopharmacology: Vol. 8, Drugs, neurotransmitters and behavior.* New York: Plenum.

Gray, J. A. (1979). A neuropsychological theory of anxiety. In C. E. Izard (Ed.), *Emotions in personality and psychopathology.* New York: Oxford University Press.

Gray, J. A. (1982). *The neuropsychology of anxiety.* New York: Oxford University Press.

Grossman, K., Grossman, K. E., Spangler, G., Suess, G., & Unzner, L. (1985). Maternal sensitivity and newborn orientation responses as related to quality of attachment in Northern Germany. In I. Bretherton & E. Waters (Eds.), Growing points of attachment theory and research. *Monographs of the Society for Research in Child Development, 50,* 233–256.

Hagekull, B. (1991, April). *The search for meaning in factor analytically derived dimensions.* Paper presented at the biennial meeting of the Society for Research in Child Development, Seattle, WA.

Hagekull, B., & Bohlin, G. (1981). Individual stability in dimensions of infant behavior. *Infant Behavior and Development, 4,* 97–108.

Haith, M., Hazan, C., & Goodman, G. S. (1988). Expectation and anticipation of dynamic visual events by 3.5-month-old babies. *Child Development, 59,* 467–479.

Harley, C. W. (1987). A role for norepinephrine in arousal, emotion and learning? Limbic modulation by norepinephrine and the Kety hypothesis. *Progress in Neuropsychopharmacology and Biological Psychiatry, 11,* 418–458.

Harpur, T. J., & Hare, R. D. (1990). Psychopathy and attention. In J. T. Enns (Ed.), *The development of attention: Research and theory. Advances in psychology* (pp. 429–444). Amsterdam, The Netherlands. North Holland.

Harter, S. (1978). Effectance motivation reconsidered: Toward a developmental model. *Human Development, 21,* 34–64.

Harter, S. (1983). Developmental perspectives on the self-system. In P. H. Mussen (Ed.), *Handbook of child psychology: Vol. IV. Socialization, personality and social development* (E. M. Hetherington, Vol. Ed.) (pp. 275–386). New York: Wiley.

Heilman, K. F., Watson, R. T., & Valenstein, E. (1985). Neglect and related disorders. In K. F. Heilman & E. Valenstein (Eds.), *Clinical neuropsychology* (pp. 243–293). New York: Oxford University Press.

Hershey, K. (1992). *Concurrent and longitudinal relationships of temperament to children's laboratory performance and behavior problems.* Doctoral dissertation, University of Oregon, Eugene.

Hinde, R. A., Easton, D. F., Meller, R. E., & Tamplin, A. M. (1982). Temperamental characteristics of 3-4-year-olds and mother-child interaction. In *Temperamental differences in infants and young children* (pp. 66–86). Ciba Foundation Symposium 89. London: Pitman.

Hogan, R. (1986). *Hogan Personality Inventory manual.* Minneapolis, MN: National Computer Systems.

Holtzman, P. S. (1985). Eye movement dysfunction and psychosis. *Internal Review of Neurobiology, 27,* 179–205.

Janer, K. W., & Pardo, J. V. (1991). Deficits in selective attention following bilateral anterior cingulotomy. *Journal of Cognitive Neuroscience, 3*(3), 231–241.

John, O. P. (1989). Towards a taxonomy of personality descriptors. In D. M. Buss & N. Cantor (Eds.), *Personality psychology: Recent trends and emerging directions* (pp. 261–271). New York: Springer-Verlag.

Johnson, M. H. (1990). Cortical maturation and the development of visual attention in early infancy. *Journal of Cognitive Neuroscience, 2,* 81–95.

Johnson, M. H., Posner, M. I., & Rothbart, M. K. (1991). Components of visual orienting in early infancy: Contingency learning, anticipatory looking and disengaging. *Journal of Cognitive Neuroscience, 3,* 335–344.

Jonides, J. (1981). Voluntary versus reflexive control over the mind's eye movement. In J. B. Long & A. D. Baddeley (Eds.), *Attention and performance IX* (pp. 187–203). Hillsdale, NJ: Erlbaum.

Jung, C. G. (1923). *Psychological types or the psychology of individuation.* New York: Harcourt.

Jung, C. G. (1928). *Contributions to analytic psychology.* New York: Harcourt Brace. Cited in Fordham, F. (1953). *An introduction to Jung's psychology.* New York: Plenum.

Kagan, J. (1989). The concept of behavioral inhibition to the unfamiliar. In J. S. Resnick (Ed.), *Perspectives on behavioral inhibition* (pp. 1–24). Chicago: University of Chicago Press.

Kahneman, D. (1973). *Attention and effort.* Englewood Cliffs, NJ: Prentice-Hall.

Kant, I. (1978). *Anthropology from a pragmatic point of view.* Carbondale: Southern Illinois University Press. (Originally published in 1798.)

Kinsbourne, M., & Bemporad, B. (1984). Lateralization of emotion: A model and the evidence. In N. A. Fox & R. J. Davidson (Eds.), *The psychology of affective development* (pp. 259–292). Hillsdale, NJ: Erlbaum.

Kochanska, G. (1991). Socialization and temperament in the development of guilt and conscience. *Child Development, 62,* 1379–1392.

Kyrios, M., & Prior, M. (1990). Temperament, stress and family factors in behavioral adjustment of 3-5-year-old children. *International Journal of Behavioral Development, 13,* 67–93.

LaLonde, C. E., & Werker, J. F. (1990, April). *Cognitive-perceptual integration of three skills at 9 months.* Paper presented at the 7th International Conference on Infancy Studies, Montreal, Quebec, Canada.

LeDoux, J. E. (1987). Cognitive-emotional interactions in the brain. *Cognition and Emotion, 3*(4), 267–289.

LeDoux, J. E. (1989). Emotion. In F. Plum (Ed.), *Handbook of physiology: Vol. V. Higher functions of the brain. Section 1. The nervous system* (pp. 419–460). Bethesda, MD: American Physiological Society.

Lee, C. L., & Bates, J. E. (1985). Mother-child interaction at age two years and perceived difficult temperament. *Child Development, 56,* 1314–1325.

Lerner, J. V., Nitz, K., Talwar, R., & Lerner, R. M. (1989). On the functional significance of temperamental individuality: A developmental contextual view of the concept of goodness of fit. In G. A. Kohnstamm, J. E. Bates, & M. K. Rothbart (Eds.), *Temperament in childhood* (pp. 509–522). Chichester, England: Wiley.

Luria, A. R. (1961). *The role of speech in the regulation of normal and abnormal behavior.* New York: Liveright.

Luria, A. R. (1973). *The working brain: An introduction to neuropsychology.* New York: Basic Books.

Mangun, G. R., & Hillyard, S. A. (1990). Electrophysiological studies of visual selective attention in humans. In A. B. Scheibel & A. F. Wechsler (Eds.), *Neurobiology of higher cognitive function* (pp. 271–294). New York: Guilford.

Martin, R., & Presley, R. (1991, April). *Dimensions of temperament during the preschool years.* Paper presented at the biennial meeting of the Society for Research in Child Development, Seattle, WA.

Masten, A. S. (1990). Resilience in development: Implications of the study of successful adaptation for developmental psychopathology. In D. Cicchetti (Ed.), *Rochester Symposium on Developmental Psychopathology: Vol. 1. The emergence of a discipline.* Hillsdale, NJ: Erlbaum.

Mathews, A., & MacLeod, C. (1986). Discrimination of threat cues without awareness in anxiety states. *Journal of Abnormal Psychology, 93,* 131–138.

Maziade, M., Boudreault, M. Thivierge, J., Caperaa, P., & Cote, R. (1984). Infant temperament: SES and gender differences and reliability of measurement in a large Quebec sample. *Merrill-Palmer Quarterly, 30,* 213–226.

Maziade, M., Caperaa, P., Laplante, B., Boudreault, M., Thivierge, J., Cote, R., Boutin, P. (1985). Value of difficult temperament among 7-year-olds in the general population for predicting psychiatric diagnosis at age 12. *American Journal of Psychiatry, 142,* 943–946.

Maziade, M., Caron, C., Cote, R., Boutin, P., & Thivierge, J. (1990). Extreme temperament and diagnosis. A study in a psychiatric sample of consecutive children. *Archives of General Psychiatry, 47,* 477–484.

Maziade, M., Caron, C., Cote, R., Merette, C., Bernier, H., Laplante, B., Boutin, P., & Thivierge, J. (1990). Psychiatric status of adolescents who had extreme temperaments at age 7. *American Journal of Psychiatry, 147,* 1531–1536.

Maziade, M., Cote, R., Bernier, H., Boutin, P., & Thivierge, J. (1989a). Significance of extreme temperament in infancy for clinical status in preschool years. I: Value of extreme temperament at 4–8 months for predicting diagnosis at 4.7 years. *British Journal of Psychiatry, 154,* 535–543.

Maziade, M., Cote, R., Bernier, H., Boutin, P., & Thivierge, J. (1989b). Significance of extreme temperament in infancy for clinical status in preschool years. II: Patterns of temperament and implications for the appearance of disorders. *British Journal of Psychiatry, 154,* 544–551.

McCall, R. B. (1979). Qualitative transitions in behavioral development in the first two years of life. In M. H. Bornstein & W. Kessen (Eds.), *Psychological development from infancy: Image to intention* (pp. 183–224). Hillsdale, NJ: Erlbaum.

McCleary, R. A. (1966). Response-modulating function of the limbic system: Initiation and suppression. In E. Stellar & J. M. Sprague (Eds.), *Progress in physiological psychology* (Vol. 1, pp. 209–271). New York: Academic Press.

Merenda, P. F. (1987). Toward a four-factor theory of temperament and/or personality. *Journal of Personality Assessment, 51,* 367–374.

Mesulam, M. M. (1980). A cortical network for directed attention and unilateral neglect. *Annals of Neurology, 10,* 309–325.

Millon, T. (1981). *Disorders of personality.* New York: Wiley.

Millon, T. (1986). A theoretical derivation of pathological personalities. In T. Millon & G. L. Klerman (Eds.), *Contemporary directions in psychopathology: Towards the DSM-IV* (pp. 639–669). New York: Guilford.

Miyake, K., Chen, S., & Campos, J. J. (1985). Infant temperament, mother's mode of interaction, and attachment in Japan: An interim report. In I. Bretherson & E. Waters (Eds.), Growing points of attachment theory and research. *Monographs of the Society for Research in Child Development, 50,* 276–297.

Morrison, J. H., & Foote, S. L. (1986). Noradrenergic and seretoninergic innervation of cortical, thalamic and tectal visual structures in old and new world monkeys. *Journal of Comparative Neurology, 243,* 117–128.

Morrow, L. A., & Ratcliff, G. (1988). The disengagement of covert attention and the neglect syndrome. *Psychobiology, 16,* 261–269.

Nakagawa, A. (1991). Role of anterior and posterior attention networks in hemispheric asymmetries during lexical decisions. *Journal of Cognitive Neuroscience, 3,* 313–321.

Nestor, P. G., Faux, S. F., McCarley, R. W., Penhume, V., Shenton, M. E., Pollak, S., & Sands, S. F. (in press). Attentional cues and performance asymmetry in schizophrenia: Abnormal disengagement of attention. *Journal of Abnormal Psychology.*

Newman, J. P. (1987). Reaction to punishment in extraverts and psychopaths: Implications for the impulsive behavior of disinhibited individuals. *Journal of Research in Personality, 21,* 464–480.

Newman, J. P., Widom, C. S., & Nathan, S. (1985). Passive avoidance in syndromes of disinhibition: Psychopathy and extraversion. *Journal of Personality and Social Psychology, 48,* 1316–1327.

Nichols, S., & Newman, J. P. (1986). Effects of punishment on response latency in extraverts. *Journal of Personality and Social Psychology, 50,* 624–630.

Nishijo, H., Ono, T., & Nishino, H. (1988). Single neuron responses in amydgala of alert monkey during complex sensory stimulation with affective significance. *Journal of Neuroscience, 8,* 3570–3583.

Olds, M. E., & Olds, J. (1963). Approach-avoidance analysis of the rat diencephalon. *Journal of Comparative neurology, 120,* 259–295.

Panksepp, J. (1982). Toward a general psychobiological theory of emotions. *Behavioral and Brain Sciences, 5,* 407–468.

Panksepp, J. (1986). The neurochemistry of behavior. *Annual Review of Psychology, 37,* 77–107.

Parasuraman, R., Greenwood, P. M., Haxby, J. V., & Grady, C. L. (1992). Visuospatial attention in dementia of the Alzheimer type. *Brain, 115,* 711–733.

Pardo, P. J. (1992). *Twin studies of attentional dysfunction in schizophrenia.* Unpublished doctoral dissertation, Washington University, St. Louis, MO.

Pardo, J. V., Pardo, P. J., Humes, S. W., & Posner, M. I. (in press). Alerting and covert orienting of visuospatial attention in unipolar depression. *British Journal of Psychiatry.*

Pardo, J. V., Pardo, P. J., Janer, K. W., & Raichle, M. E. (1990). The anterior cingulate cortex mediates processing selection in the Stroop attentional conflict paradigm. *Proceedings of the National Academy of Science, 87,* 256–259.

Parker, J. G., & Asher, S. R. (1987). Peer relations and later personal adjustment: Are low-accepted children at risk? *Psychological Bulletin, 102,* 357–389.

Pashler, H. (1993). Dual task interference and elementary psychological mechanism. In D. Meyer & S. Kornblum (Eds.), *Attention and performance: XIV* (pp. 245–264). Hillsdale, NJ: Erlbaum.

Patterson, C. M., Kosson, D. S., & Newman, J. P. (1987). Reaction to punishment, reflectivity and passive avoidance learning in extraverts. *Journal of Personality and Social Psychology, 52,* 565–575.

Patterson, G. R. (1977). Accelerating stimuli for two classes of coercive behaviors. *Journal of Abnormal Child Psychology, 5,* 335–350.

Patterson, G. R. (1980). Mothers: The unacknowledged victims. *Monographs of the Society for Research in Child Development, 45*(5, Serial No. 186).

Patterson, G. R., & Capaldi, D. M. (1990). A mediational model for boys' depressed mood. In J. Rolf, A. S. Masten, D. Cicchetti, K. H. Neuchterlin, & S. Weintraub (Eds.), *Risk and protective factors in the development of psychopathology* (pp. 141–163). New York: Cambridge University Press.

Petersen, S. E., Fox, P. T., Posner, M. I., Mintun, M., & Raichle, M. E. (1989). Positron emission tomographic studies of the processing of single words. *Journal of Cognitive Neuroscience, 1,* 153–170.

Petersen, S. E., Fox, P. T., Snyder, A. Z., & Raichle, M. E. (1990). Activation of extrastriate and frontal cortical areas by visual words and word-like stimuli. *Science, 249,* 1041–1044.

Pien, D., & Klein, J. M. (1989). *Gestures: The missing link to language.* Seattle, WA: University of Washington Press.

Posner, M. I. (1978). *Chronometric explorations of mind.* Hillsdale, NJ: Erlbaum.

Posner, M. I. (1988). Structures and functions of selective attention. In T. Boll & B. Bryant (Eds.), *Master lectures in clinical neuropsychology and brain function: Research, measurement and practice.* Washington, DC: American Psychological Association.

Posner, M. I. (1990). Hierarchical distributed networks in the neuropsychology of selective attention. In A. Carramaza (Ed.), *Cognitive neuropsychology and neurolinguistics: Advances in models of cognitive function and impairment* (pp. 187–210). New York: Plenum.

Posner, M. I. (1992). Attention as a cognitive and neural system. *Directions in Psychology Science, 1*(1), 11–14.

Posner, M. I., Early, T. S., Reiman, E., Pardo, P. J., & Dhawan, M. (1988). Asymmetries in hemispherical control of attention in schizophrenia. *Archives of General Psychiatry, 45,* 814–821.

Posner, M. I., & Keele, S. W. (1968). On the genesis of abstract ideas. *Journal of Experimental Psychology, 77,* 353–363.

Posner, M. I., & Petersen, S. E. (1990). The attention system of the human brain. *Annual Review of Neuroscience, 13,* 25–42.

Posner, M. I., Petersen, S. E., Fox, P. T., & Raichle, M. E. (1988). Localization of cognitive functions in the human brain. *Science, 240,* 1627–1631.

Posner, M. I., & Presti, D. (1987). Selective attention and cognitive control. *Trends in Neuroscience, 10,* 12–17.

Posner, M. I., & Rafal, R. D. (1986). Cognitive theories of attention and the rehabilitation of attentional deficit. In R. J. Meir, L. Diller, & A. C. Benton (Eds.), *Neuropsychological rehabilitation.* London: Churchill-Livingston.

Posner, M. I., & Raichle, M. E. (1994). *Images of Mind.* New York: Scientific American Library.

Posner, M. I., & Rothbart, M. K. (1992). Attention and conscious experience. In A. D. Milner & M. D. Rugg (Eds.), *The neuropsychology of consciousness* (pp. 91–112). London: Academic Press.

Posner, M. I., Sanson, J., Dhawan, M., & Shulman, G. L. (1989). Is word recognition automatic? A cognitive-anatomical approach. *Journal of Cognitive Neuroscience, 1,* 50–60.

Posner, M. I., Walker, J. A., Friedrich, F. J., & Rafal, R. D. (1984). Effects of parietal lobe injury on covert orienting of visual attention. *Journal of Neuroscience, 4,* 1863–1874.

Posner, M. I., Walker, J. A., Friedrich, F. J., & Rafal, R. D. (1987). How do the parietal lobes direct covert attention? *Neuropsychologia, 25A,* 135–146.

Potkin, S. G., Swanson, J., LaBerge, D. L., Costa, J., Heh, C., & Wigal, S. B. (1990). Lateralized visual field abnormalities in schizophrenia. *Biological Psychiatry, 27,* 48A.

Prior, M. R., Glazner, J., Sanson, A., & Debelle, G. (1988). Temperament and behavioral adjustment in hearing impaired children. *Journal of Child Psychology and Psychiatry, 29,* 209–216.

Prior, M. R., Sanson, A. V., & Oberklaid, F. (1989). The Australian Temperament Project. In G. A. Kohnstamm, J. E. Bates, & M. K. Rothbart (Eds.), *Temperament in childhood* (pp. 537–554). New York: Wiley.

Prior, M. R., Sanson, A., Oberklaid, F., & Northam, E. (1987). Measurement of temperament in one- to three-year-old children. *International Journal of Behavioral Development, 10,* 131–132.

Puig-Antich, J. (1982). Major depression and conduct disorder in prepuberty. *Journal of the American Academy of Child Psychiatry, 21,* 118–128.

Radke-Yarrow, M., & Sherman, T. (1990). Hard growing: Children who survive. In J. E. Rolf, A. S. Masten, D. Cicchetti, K. H. Neuchterlein, & S. Weintraub (Eds.), *Risk and protective factors in the development of psychopathology* (pp. 97–119). New York: Cambridge University Press.

Reitman, J. (1971). Mechanisms of forgetting in short-term memory. *Cognitive Psychology, 2,* 131–157.

Robertson, L. C., Lamb, M. R., & Knight, R. T. (1988). Effects of lesions of the temporal parietal junction on perceptual and attentional processing in humans. *Journal of Neuroscience, 8,* 3757–3769.

Rohner, R. P. (1986). *The warmth dimension: Foundations of parental acceptance-rejection theory.* Beverly Hills, CA: Sage.

Rosch, E. (1973). On the internal structure of perceptual and semantic categories. In T. E. Moore (Ed.), *Cognitive development and the acquisition of language.* New York: Academic Press.

Rosenbaum, J. F., Bierderman, J., Gersten, M., Hirshfeld, D. R., Meminger, S. R., Herman, J. B., Kagan, J., Reznick, J. S., & Snidman, N. (1988). Behavioral inhibition in children of parents with panic disorder and agoraphobia: A controlled study. *Archives of General Psychiatry, 45,* 463–470.

Rothbart, M. K. (1982). The concept of difficult temperament: A critical analysis of Thomas, Chess & Korn. *Merrill-Palmer Quarterly, 28,* 35–40.

Rothbart, M. K. (1984). Social development. In M. J. Hanson (Ed.), *Atypical infant development* (pp. 207–236). Baltimore, MD: University Park Press.

Rothbart, M. K. (1986). Longitudinal observation of infant temperament. *Developmental Psychology, 22,* 356–365.

Rothbart, M. K. (1988). Temperament and the development of inhibited approach. *Child Development, 59,* 1241–1250.

Rothbart, M. K. (1989a). Behavioral approach and inhibition. S. Reznick (Ed.), *Perspectives on behavioral inhibition* (pp. 139–157). Chicago: University of Chicago Press.

Rothbart, M. K. (1989b). Biological processes of temperament. In G. Kohnstamm, J. Bates, & M. K. Rothbart (Eds.), *Temperament in childhood* (pp. 77–110). Chichester, England: Wiley.

Rothbart, M. K. (1989c). Temperament in childhood: A framework. In G. Kohnstamm, J. Bates, & M. K. Rothbart (Eds.), *Temperament in childhood* (pp. 59–73). Chichester, England: Wiley.

Rothbart, M. K. (1989d). Temperament and development. In G. Kohnstamm, J. Bates, & M. K. Rothbart (Eds.), *Temperament in childhood* (pp. 187–248). Chichester, England: Wiley.

Rothbart, M. K., & Ahadi, S. A. (1994). Temperament and the development of personality. *Journal of Abnormal Psychology, 103,* 55–66.

Rothbart, M. K., Ahadi, S. A., & Hershey, K. L. (1994). Temperament and social behavior in childhood. *Merrill-Palmer Quarterly, 40,* 21–39.

Rothbart, M. K., & Derryberry, D. (1981). Development of individual differences in temperament. In M. E. Lamb & A. L. Brown (Eds.), *Advances in developmental psychology* (Vol. I, pp. 37–86). Hillsdale, NJ: Erlbaum.

Rothbart, M. K., Derryberry, D., & Posner, M. I. (1994). A psychobiological approach to the development of temperament. In J. E. Bates & T. D. Wachs (Eds.), *Temperament: Individual differences at the interface of biology and behavior* (pp. 83–116). Washington, DC: American Psychological Association.

Rothbart, M. K., Hershey, K. L., & Derryberry, D. (1991, November). Poster, Stability of temperament in childhood: Laboratory observations in infancy to parent reports at seven years. "Lives Through Time" meeting in honor of Jack Block, Palm Springs, CA.

Rothbart, M. K., & Mauro, J. A. (1990). Questionnaire measures of infant temperament. In J. W. Fagen & J. Colombo (Eds.), *Individual differences in infancy: Reliability, stability and prediction* (pp. 411–429). Hillsdale, NJ: Erlbaum.

Rothbart, M. K., & Posner, M. I. (1985). Temperament and the development of self-regulation. In L. C. Hartlage & C. F. Telzrow (Eds.), *The neuropsychology of individual differences: A developmental perspective* (pp. 93–123). New York: Plenum.

Rothbart, M. K., Posner, M. I., & Boylan, A. (1990). Regulatory mechanisms in infant development. In J. T. Enns (Ed.), *The development of attention: Research and theory* (pp. 139–160). Amsterdam, The Netherlands: Elsevier.

Rothlind, J., Posner, M. I., & Schaughency, E. (1991). Lateralized control of eye movements in attention deficit hyperactivity disorder. *Journal of Cognitive Neuroscience, 3,* 377–381.

Rubin, K. H., LeMare, L. J., & Lollis, S. (1990). Social withdrawal in childhood: Developmental pathways to peer rejection. In S. R. Asher & J. D. Coie (Eds.), *Peer rejection in childhood* (pp. 217–249). New York: Cambridge University Press.

Ruff, H. A., & Rothbart, M. K. (in press). Attention in early development: Themes and variations. New York: Oxford University Press.

Rutter, M. (1979). Protective factors in children's responses to stress and disadvantage. In M. W. Kent & J. E. Rolf (Eds.), *Primary prevention of psychopathology: Vol. 3. Social competence in children* (pp. 49–74). Hanover, NH: University Press of New England.

Rutter, M. (1983). Stress, coping, and development: Some issues and some questions. In N. Garmezy & M. Rutter (Eds.), *Stress, coping, and development in children* (pp. 1–41). New York: McGraw-Hill.

Rutter, M. (1990). Psychosocial resilience and protective mechanisms. In J. Rolf, A. S. Masten, D. Cicchetti, K. H. Neuchterlein, & S. Weintraub (Eds.), *Risk and protective factors in development of psychopathology* (pp. 181–214). New York: Cambridge University Press.

Rutter, M., & Garmezy, N. (1983). Developmental psychopathology. In P. Mussen (Ed.), *Handbook of child psychology: Vol. IV. Socialization, personality, and social development* (E. M. Hetherington, Vol. Ed.) (pp. 776–911). New York: Wiley.

Rutter, M., & Quinton, D. (1984). Long-term follow-up of women institutionalized in childhood: Factors promoting good functioning in adult life. *British Journal of Developmental Psychology, 18,* 225–234.

Saltz, E., Campbell, S., & Skotko, D. (1983). Verbal control of behavior: The effects of shouting. *Developmental Psychology, 19,* 461–464.

Sameroff, A. J., & Chandler, M. J. (1975). Reproductive risk and the continuum of caretaking casualty. In F. D. Horowitz (Ed.), *Review of child development research* (Vol. 4). Chicago: University of Chicago Press.

Sandson, J., Crosson, B., Posner, M. I., Barco, P. P., Velozo, C. A., & Brobeck, T. C. (1988). Attentional imbalances following head injury. In J. M. Williams & C. J. Long (Eds.), *Cognitive approaches to neuropsychology.* New York: Plenum.

Sanson, A. V., Oberklaid, F., Pedlow, R., & Prior, M. (1991). Risk indicators: Assessment of infancy predictors of preschool behavioural maladjustment. *Journal of Child Psychology and Psychiatry, 32,* 609–626.

Sanson, A., Prior, M., Garino, E., Oberklaid, F., & Sewell, J. (1987). The structure of infant temperament: Factor analysis of the revised Infant Temperament Questionnaire. *Infant Behavior and Development, 10,* 97–104.

Sanson, A., Prior, M., & Kyrios, M. (1990). Contamination of measures in temperament research. *Merrill-Palmer Quarterly, 36,* 179–192.

Schaffer, H. R. (1966). Activity level as a constitutional determinant of infantile reaction to deprivation. *Child Development, 37,* 595.

Snyder, J. A. (1977). A reinforcement analysis of interaction in problem and nonproblem children. *Journal of Abnormal Psychology, 86,* 528–535.

Soubrie, P. (1986). Reconciling the role of central serotonin neurons in human and animal behavior. *Behavioral and Brain Sciences, 9,* 319–364.

Stein, L. (1980). The chemistry of reward. In A. Routtenberg (Ed.), *Biology of reinforcement* (pp. 109–130). New York: Academic Press.

Stevenson-Hinde, J., & Simpson, A. E. (1982). Temperament and relationships. In *Temperamental differences in infants and young children* (pp. 51–65). Ciba Foundation Symposium 89. London: Pitman.

Strauss, M. E., Alphs, L., & Boekamp, B. A. (1991). Disengagement of attention in chronic schizophrenia. *Psychiatry Research, 37,* 139–146.

Swanson, J. M., Posner, M. I., Potkin, S., Bonforte, S., Youpa, D., Fiore, C., Cantwell, D., & Crinella, F. (1991). Activating tasks for the study of visual-spatial attention in ADHD children: A cognitive anatomic approach. *Journal of Child Neurology, 6,* S119–S127.

Talbot, J. D., Marrett, A., Evans, A. C., Meyer, E., Bushnell, M. C., & Duncan, G. H. (1991). Multiple representation of pain in human cerebral cortex. *Science, 251,* 1355–1357.

Tellegen, A. (1985). Structures of mood and personality and their relevance to assessing anxiety, with an emphasis on self-report. In A. H. Tuma & J. D. Maser (Eds.), *Anxiety and the anxiety disorders* (pp. 681–706). Hillsdale, NJ: Erlbaum.

Thomas, A., & Chess, S. (1977). *Temperament and development.* New York: Brunner/Mazel.

Thomas, A., Chess, S., & Birch, H. G. (1968). *Temperament and behavior disorders in children.* New York: New York University Press.

Thomas, A., Chess, S., Birch, H. G., Hertzig, M. E., & Korn, S. (1963). *Behavioral individuality in early childhood.* New York: New York University Press.

Tomarken, A. J., Davidson, R. J., Wheeler, R. E., & Doss, R. C. (1992). Individual differences in anterior brain asymmetry and fundamental dimensions of emotion. *Journal of Personality and Social Psychology, 62,* 676–687.

Trapnell, P. D., & Wiggins, J. S. (1990). Extension of the Interpersonal Adjective Scales to include the Big Five dimensions of personality. *Journal of Personality and Social Psychology, 59,* 781–790.

Tucker, D. M. (1985). Neural control of emotional communication. In P. Blanck, R. Buck, & R. Rosenthal (Eds.), *Nonverbal communication in the clinical context* (pp. 258–308). New York: Oxford University Press.

van den Boom, D. (1989). Neonatal irritability and the development of attachment. In G. Kohnstamm, J. Bates, & M. K. Rothbart (Eds.), *Temperament in childhood.* Chichester, England: Wiley.

van Ijzendoorn, M. H., & Kroonenberg, P. M. (1988). Cross-cultural patterns of attachment: A meta-analysis of the strange situation. *Child Development, 59,* 147–156.

Webb, E. (1915). Character and intelligence. *British Journal of Psychology Monographs,* Nos. 1 & 3.

Weinberger, D. A. (1990). The construct validity of the repressive coping style. In J. L. Singer (Ed.), *Repression and dissociation* (pp. 337–386). Chicago: University of Chicago Press.

Weinberger, D. R., Berman, K. F., & Zec, R. F. (1986). Physiological dysfunction of dorsolateral prefrontal cortex in schizophrenia. *Archives of General Psychiatry, 43,* 114–124.

Weissman, M. M. (1989). Anxiety disorders in parents and children: A genetic-epidemiological perspective. In J. S. Reznick (Ed.), *Perspectives on behavioral inhibition* (pp. 241–254). Chicago: University of Chicago Press.

Werner, E. E. (1986). The concept of risk from a developmental perspective. In B. Keogh (Ed.), *Advances in special education: Developmental problems in infancy and the preschool years.* Greenwich, CT: JAI Press.

Werner, E. E., & Smith, R. S. (1982). *Vulnerable, but invincible: A longitudinal study of resilient children and youth.* New York: McGraw-Hill.

Wertlieb, D., Wiegel, C., Springer, T., & Feldstein, M. (1987). Temperament as a moderator of children's stressful experiences. *American Journal of Orthopsychiatry, 57,* 234–245.

Wigal, S. B., Potkin, S. G., Richmond, G., Swanson, J. M., & LaBerge, D. L. (1991). Asymmetries in attention filtering in left and right visual fields in schizophrenic patients. *Schizophrenia Research, 4,* 396.

Wiggins, J. S. (1979). A psychological taxonomy of trait-descriptive terms: The interpersonal domain. *Journal of Personality and Social Psychology, 37,* 395–412.

Wiggins, J. S., Phillips, N., & Trapnell, P. (1989). Circular reasoning about interpersonal behavior: Evidence concerning some untested assumptions underlying diagnostic classification. *Journal of Personality and Social Psychology, 56,* 296–305.

Wiggins, J. S., & Pincus, A. L. (1994). Personality structure and the structure of personality disorders. In P. T. Costa & T. A. Widiger (Eds.), *Personality disorders and the five-factor model of personality.* Washington, DC: American Psychological Association.

Wiggins, J. S., Trapnell, P., & Phillips, N. (1988). Psychometric and geometric characteristics of the revised Interpersonal Adjective Scales (IAS-R). *Multivariate Behavioral Research, 23,* 517–530.

Wolfson, J., Fields, J. H., & Rose, S. (1987). Symptoms, temperament, resiliency, and control in anxiety-disordered preschool children. *Journal of the American Academy of Child and Adolescent Psychiatry, 26,* 16–22.

Zahn, T. P., Rosenthall, D., & Shakow, D. (1963). Effects of irregular and regular preparatory periods on reaction time in schizophrenia. *Journal of Abnormal and Social Psychology, 72,* 44–52.

Zahn-Waxler, C., Cole, P. M., & Barrett, K. C. (1991). Guilt and empathy: Sex differences and implications for the development of depression. In J. Garber & K. A. Dodge (Eds.), *The development of emotion regulation and dysregulation* (pp. 243–272). New York: Cambridge University Press.

Zametkin, A. J., Nordahl, T. E., Gross, M., King, A. C., Semple, W. E., Rumsey, J., Hamburger, S., & Cohen, R. M. (1990). Cerebral glucose metabolism in adults with hyperactivity of childhood onset. *The New England Journal of Medicine, 323*(20), 1361–1415.

Zametkin, A. J., & Rapoport, J. L. (1987). Neurobiology of attention deficit disorder with hyperactivity: Where have we come in 50 years? *Journal of American Child Adolescent Psychiatry, 26,* 676–686.

Zuckerman, M. (1984). Sensation seeking: A comparative approach to a human trait. *Behavioral and Brain Sciences, 7,* 413–471.

PART FOUR

Cognitive and Social-Cognitive Processes

CHAPTER 12

Theory of Mind and Face-Processing: How Do They Interact in Development and Psychopathology?

SIMON BARON-COHEN

My intention in this chapter is to focus on just two topics: (a) the development, in the child, of an understanding of mental states (or "theory of mind"), and (b) the development of face-processing. Let me begin by addressing the question of why theory of mind and face-processing are of special interest.

WHY FOCUS ON THEORY OF MIND AND FACE-PROCESSING?

A number of reasons guided my selection of these two topics. First, these are two of the most exciting growth areas in the field of social cognition, probably because both are being studied at multiple levels—face-processing, in terms of computational theory (Bruce, 1988) and neurobiology (Perrett et al., 1985), and theory of mind, in developmental psychology (Astington, Harris, & Olson, 1988; Wellman, 1990), primatology, and artificial intelligence (Whiten, 1991). Second, both of these areas are vulnerable to impairment (Baron-Cohen, Tager-Flusberg, & Cohen, 1993; Ellis & Young, 1989). I shall explore what psychopathology can teach us about the normal processes underlying these two abilities, and vice versa, thus illustrating a key principle of developmental psychopathology (Cicchetti, 1984). The major relevant clinical syndromes are autism and prosopagnosia, although I discuss other disorders briefly along the way.

My third reason for selecting these two areas is that they have remained almost entirely unconnected. Although a sizable body of research has studied emotion-recognition in facial expressions (Ekman & Friesen, 1971; Hobson, 1986), no work has looked at whether the broader range of mental states that we attribute to others (thoughts, desires, goals, and so on) is influenced to some degree by information contained in their faces. My main aim here will be to suggest that there are important, but hitherto unacknowledged, connections between face-processing and theory of mind. I begin by reviewing the literature on theory of mind.

UNDERSTANDING MENTAL STATES

When we attribute mental states such as thoughts, beliefs, desires, and intentions to ourselves and others, we employ what Premack and Woodruff (1978) called a theory of mind. What is a theory of mind for? Might it have a biological basis? If so, why might it have evolved? We will consider, later, some evidence from autism that suggests a theory of mind may have a biological basis, but the function and evolutionary value of a theory of mind have recently been considered by Cheney and Seyfarth (1990), who invited us to imagine some possible scenarios in evolutionary history:

> (I)magine a group of baboons in which individuals are extremely skilled at judging behavioral contingencies . . . but unable to identify the motives or knowledge of others. . . . Imagine further that among these baboons . . . adult males solicit each other for support in alliances. . . . If male baboons are incapable of recognizing the motives of other animals . . . [they] will always be vulnerable to those who *cheat*. . . .
>
> Now imagine that into this group of nonintentional baboons comes a mutant male capable of attributing states of mind to others. . . . (H)e recognizes a distinction between an animal's behavior and the motives that underlie it. As a result, he recognizes that however much a solicitor *seems* likely to reciprocate, this may not actually be his intention. Such knowledge will not necessarily make the mutant male any less vulnerable to cheaters on his first interaction with them, but is certainly likely to make him more sceptical in subsequent interactions. . . . In short, the new male will have a competitive advantage over others in his group, because in being able to assess his companions' motives, he is better able to predict their behaviour. (pp. 249–251, italics added)

This chapter was written while the author was supported by grants from the Mental Health Foundation and the Medical Research Council. I am grateful to Ruth Campbell, Uta Frith, and Dante Cicchetti for comments on the first draft of this chapter. Correspondence should be addressed to the author.

Figures 12.3 and 12.4 originally appeared in the Fairburn System of Visual References (1978). Efforts at tracing this publisher have been unsuccessful, but their source is gratefully acknowledged.

This example underscores important adaptive advantages that possession of a theory of mind confers on an individual: the capacity to recognize deception, and the capacity to predict how a person will behave on the basis of his or her mental states. Having a concept of another persons' knowledge or belief also opens up the possibility of manipulating what they believe (practicing persuasion and deception). Cheney and Seyfarth (1990) suggested that the capacity to *teach* is a further adaptive advantage conferred by possession of theory of mind:

> Suppose there exists a group of macaques in which one animal . . . suddenly develops a new method for acquiring and preparing food. . . . (I)f the inventor can attribute ignorance to others . . . there is an immense amount to be gained. An inventor who possesses a theory of mind can selectively *transmit* her knowledge to kin. . . . She can also selectively *withhold* her knowledge from rivals. . . . (S)he need not depend on the relatively slow process of observational learning to transmit her skill but instead can engage in active pedagogy. Once again, an individual capable of attribution would seem to have a clear selective advantage over others. (p. 251, italics added)

These are just some of the major benefits that ensue from possession of a theory of mind. Others include the ability to: predict behavior on the basis of beliefs, judge intended meanings in language, and show empathy (Baron-Cohen, 1988; Dennett, 1978b; Happé, 1993).

Given the apparent importance of a theory of mind, a recent wave of research in developmental psychology has attempted to trace its development. One starting point has been to ask whether infants understand that actions are *caused* by mental states. Infants can distinguish animate movement from inanimate movement (Gelman & Spelke, 1981)—they are sensitive to the difference between internal and external causation of movement—but it is still unresolved whether they recognize the internal causes of animate movement as *mental* states (Premack, 1990; Wellman, 1990). By the time toddlers start to talk, however, it is clear that they talk about actions in terms of mental states. From as early as 18 to 24 months, normal children refer to a range of mental states: desires, beliefs, thoughts, dreams, pretense, and so on (Shatz, Wellman, & Silber, 1983; Wellman, 1990). This suggests that, at the very least, they have what Bretherton, McNew, and Beeghly-Smith (1981) called an *implicit* theory of mind. Studies with slightly older children have focused on obtaining evidence for an *explicit* theory of mind. These studies are reviewed next.

Developing a Theory of Mind: A Review

Research into the development of a theory of mind gathered considerable momentum following Premack and Woodruff's (1978) "Does the Chimpanzee Have a 'Theory of Mind'?", a provocative article that reviewed a series of fascinating experiments suggesting that chimpanzees can take into account an actor's mental states. For example, in one experiment, a chimpanzee watched a film of an actor struggling to obtain bananas that were inaccessible. The film was frozen at the point of the struggle, and the animal was given a choice of photographs indicating various outcomes. Typically, the chimpanzee chose the picture showing the solution to the actor's frustration (stepping onto a box in order to reach the bananas). This led Premack and Woodruff to conclude that "the chimpanzee solves problems such as the present one . . . by imputing states of mind to the human actor" (p. 518).

Understanding Belief

In the discussion that followed, several commentators raised the criticism that the solution of such tasks does not necessarily require any reasoning about mental states (Dennett, 1978a). Instead, they proposed that the "acid test" of when an organism is judging another's mental state arises in situations of *false belief,* in which the subject is exposed to current reality but another person is exposed to only partial (or wrong) information about reality. Under such conditions, it is possible to separate, unambiguously, judgments based on the subjects' *own* mental state (their true belief) from judgments based on the other persons' different mental state (their false belief). Thus, suppose a subject knows that (a) the key is in the hallway but (b) Dante *thinks* it's in the bedroom. If asked where Dante would look for the key, the subject should judge that Dante will look in the *wrong* place—the bedroom.

Within developmental psychology,[1] Wimmer and Perner (1983) employed such a test and showed that not until around 4 years of age do normal children pass such a test. An adaptation of their test (Baron-Cohen, Leslie, & Frith, 1985) is illustrated in Figure 12.1.

The test involves appreciating that, because Sally was absent when her marble was moved from its original location, she won't *know* it was moved, and therefore must still *believe* it is in its original location. On the belief question ("Where will Sally look for her marble?"), 85% of normal children answered correctly. All subjects passed a memory control question ("Where was the marble in the beginning?") and a reality control question ("Where is the marble really?"), as well as a naming question ("Which doll is Sally?"), thus ruling out the possibility that the normal 3-year-olds' failure on the belief question was caused by such factors as inattention, memory or language overload, or lack of motivation. The result replicated that of Wimmer and Perner (1983), and later studies essentially confirmed the finding that false beliefs are not well understood until 4 years of age (Perner, Leekam, & Wimmer, 1987).

In recent years, the finding that age 4 is a turning point in understanding false beliefs has been challenged by a number of investigators. Thus, whereas Wimmer and Perner (1983) argued that the false belief data indicated the presence of a *cognitive deficit* in younger normal children, newer studies (Freeman, Lewis, & Doherty, 1991; Wellman, 1990) suggested that, when simpler experimental methods are employed, normal children younger than 4 years of age do show some evidence of understanding false belief. The age at which there is a genuine cognitive limitation on young children's understanding of other people's beliefs remains controversial.

---

[1] Research into children's developing theory of mind has its roots both in Piaget's work and in the philosophy of mind and language. (See Perner & Wilde-Astington, 1991.)

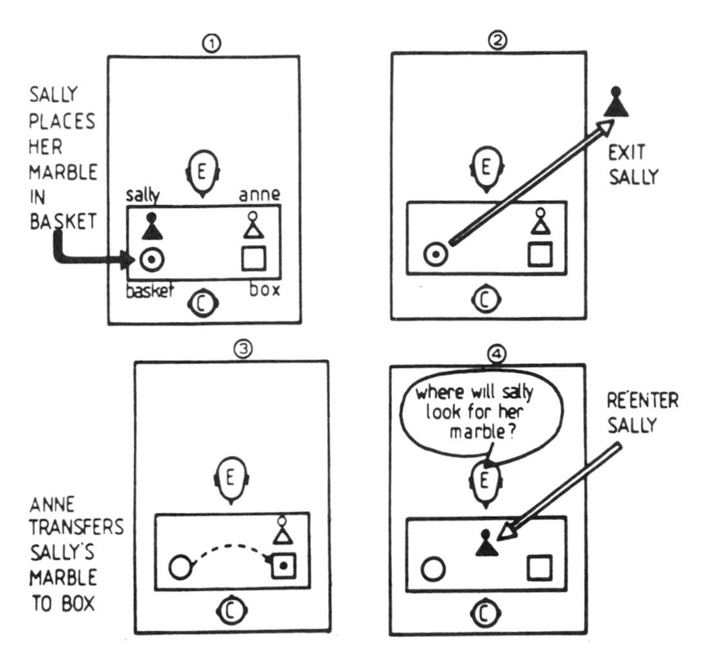

Figure 12.1 A simple test for children's understanding of false belief. From "Does the Autistic Child Have a 'Theory of Mind'?" by S. Baron-Cohen, A. M. Leslie, and U. Frith, 1985, *Cognition, 21,* pp. 37–46. Copyright 1985 by Elsevier Science Publishers BV. Reprinted by permission.

Understanding Desire and Intention

Desire is often thought to be *the* other key mental state, next to belief, in our folk psychology (Dennett, 1978b). With beliefs and desires, all kinds of behavior become interpretable. For example, when watching a movie and trying to understand why John Wayne suddenly dived under a table, we might refer to his *belief* that the loud noise he heard was a gunshot and his *desire* to stay alive. Several studies have shown that, for normal children, desire is understood earlier than belief—in fact, desire is clearly understood by normal 2-year-olds (Wellman, 1990). The "terrible twos" have been interpreted as evidence of this age group's growing awareness of the frustrating difference between their own and their parents' desires (Wellman, 1990).

A mental state closely related to desire is intention. The two states are distinguishable, as Astington and Lee (1991) and Phillips (1993) made clear: it is possible to desire something and yet to have no intention of fulfilling that desire. (One might desire to visit a friend in Australia, but have no intention of going there.) Intention is related to desire in that one way of fulfilling one's desires is to formulate an intention—a plan of action—to fulfill them. Desires are sometimes fulfilled fortuitously (your Australian friend might turn up on your doorstep unexpectedly), but the principal means for fulfilling desires is via intentional actions. When do young children grasp the concept of intention?

A large part of the literature on children's understanding of morality centers on their appreciation of the distinction between intentional and accidental acts and on their judgments of responsibility and blame. Understanding intention has also been studied separately from moral development. Some early studies in this area (Berndt & Berndt, 1975; King, 1971; Smith, 1978) found a significant change around 4 years of age in the ability to distinguish acts "done on purpose" from accidental acts. Children younger than this were reported to err on the side of assuming that *everything* was intentional—an echo of Piaget's (1929) findings.

More recent studies by Astington and Lee (1991) extended this work by investigating young children's ability to distinguish outcomes that appear the same but differ in the crucial respect of the actor's intention. Thus, in one story, a girl intends to feed her breadcrumbs to the birds, and then she does so; in another story, a girl accidentally drops some bread crumbs. The birds end up being fed just the same. In such a test, the child is asked, "Which girl *meant* to feed the birds?" These findings are broadly similar to the earlier studies: chance performance occurs before age 4.

Understanding Pretense

Children begin to produce pretend play from as early as 10 to 18 months of age (Bates, Benigni, Bretherton, Camaioni, & Volterra, 1979). Experiments with verbal children also show that, as soon as they can answer questions, they seem to understand that pretense is distinct from reality (Wellman, 1990). This is clearly a complex achievement. In terms of the acquisition of different mental state concepts, understanding pretense may even predate understanding desire (Baron-Cohen, 1991a; Gopnik & Slaughter, 1991), although longitudinal data on this are needed.

Pretense was, for a long time, studied as part of symbolic development (McCune-Nicholich, 1981; Piaget, 1962). In an important article rethinking the nature of pretense, Leslie (1987) put forward a theory that focused on children's understanding of pretense as a mental state. He argued that the logical properties of pretense resembled the logical properties of other mental states (such as belief), and, on these grounds, children's understanding of pretense might reflect an important stage in the origins of a theory of mind.

Part of Leslie's claim also centered on the sort of cognitive architecture that would be needed to support comprehension not only of pretense but of all mental states. His suggestion was that a capacity for *metarepresentation* would be minimally required. He defined metarepresentation as the ability to represent an agent's mental attitude toward a proposition. (For details of the component parts of this system, see Leslie, 1987; Leslie & Roth, 1993; for counter-arguments, see Perner, 1988, 1991, 1993.) The implication is that pretense might mark not only a developmental stage in the acquisition of a theory of mind, but a qualitative change in the sort of representational mechanisms available to cognition.

Understanding Perception

Piaget and Inhelder's (1956) "three-mountains task" broke new ground in suggesting that children between 4 and 6 years old were unable to select a picture that showed how a view would appear to different people at different locations. Such children, Piaget and Inhelder reported, tended to attribute their own spatial perspective to other people—an error that became the hallmark of Piaget's concept of "childhood egocentrism."[2]

Flavell, Shipstead, and Croft (1978) challenged this view by employing far simpler experimental techniques. They distinguished between two levels of visual perspective-taking. The first they called Level 1—the ability to infer *what* another person can see. This appears to be present by age 2 (Flavell, Everett, Croft, & Flavell, 1981; Flavell et al., 1978; Lempers, Flavell, & Flavell, 1977). Thus, 2-year-olds can put things out of or bring things into sight, when requested to do so. Level 2 of visual perspective-taking is the ability to infer *how* the object appears to another person. This ability seems to take longer to develop; in fact, not until 3 to 4 years of age do children reliably pass Level 2 tasks. For example, when shown a picture of a turtle that appears either right-side up or upside-down (depending on the location of the viewer), young 3-year-olds fail to identify correctly which of these two perspectives the experimenter would have (Flavell et al., 1981).

Before moving on to consider abnormalities in the development and use of a theory of mind, it is worth noting that relatively little work has looked at later normal development of this ability. Perner and Wimmer (1985) studied slightly older children for the ability to attribute beliefs about beliefs to others (so-called *second-order belief attribution*), and found this appears for the first time at around 6 years of age. Riviere (1993), using a simpler paradigm, found this ability appearing slightly earlier—in 5-year-olds. Leekam (1991) reported on related developments in the use and comprehension of figurative speech such as irony and sarcasm. Studies that tap adult levels of functioning in this domain are still needed. In the next section, I consider what happens when a theory of mind fails to develop normally.

ABNORMALITIES IN THE COMPREHENSION OF MENTAL STATES

Autism

Autism is a developmental disorder characterized by severe social and communication abnormalities (Baron-Cohen, 1988; Frith, 1989; Kanner, 1943; Rutter, 1983). A sizable body of work documents the deficits in understanding mental states in children with autism (Baron-Cohen, Tager-Flusberg, & Cohen, 1993). For example, on tests of false belief comprehension, children with autism make more errors than both normal and mentally handicapped children of a younger mental age (Baron-Cohen, 1989a, 1989b; Baron-Cohen, Leslie, & Frith, 1985, 1986; Leekam & Perner, 1991; Leslie & Frith, 1988; Perner, Frith, Leslie, & Leekam, 1989; Reed & Petersen, 1990). This deficit appears to relate to the symptoms these children show in social and communicative development (Baron-Cohen, 1988; Happé, 1993; Frith, Happé, & Siddons, 1994).

Most children with autism fail tests of belief understanding, but a minority of them, ranging from 20–35% in different samples, do pass. When these subjects are given a more taxing test of belief understanding (comprising understanding second-order, nested beliefs, or *beliefs about beliefs* ("Anne thinks Sally thinks x"))—these being well within the comprehension of normal 6- to 7-year-old children (Perner & Wimmer, 1985)—even most teenagers with autism fail outright (Baron-Cohen, 1989b; Ozonoff, Pennington, & Rogers, 1991). It appears, then, that although most children with autism do not understand beliefs even at the level of normal 3- to 4-year-old children, some do; but these show impaired understanding of beliefs at the level of normal 6- to 7-year-old children. Something is going wrong in the development of the concept of belief in children with autism. This has been discussed in terms of specific developmental deviance and delay in autism (Baron-Cohen, 1989b, 1991a, 1992a).

An inability to understand others' beliefs reveals itself most dramatically on tests of deception in autism (Sodian & Frith, 1992). As discussed earlier, because deception entails belief manipulation, performance is consistent with difficulties in belief comprehension. Thus, in the Penny Hiding Game (Gratch, 1964), a simple test of deception, children with autism fail to hide the clues that enable the guesser to infer the whereabouts of the penny (Baron-Cohen, 1992b; Oswald & Ollendick, 1989). For example, they leave the empty hand open, or they hide the penny in full view of the guesser, or they show the guesser where the penny is, before the guesser has guessed. Subjects with mental handicap and normal 3-year-old children make far fewer errors of this sort.

When children with autism are asked how a story character will feel when given something the children either *want* or do not want, no impairments are found, relative to a mental-age matched control group without autism (Baron-Cohen, 1991b). Understanding these simple aspects of desire thus seems to be within their ability, although more complex aspects of desire and intention pose problems for them (Phillips, 1993). On tests of understanding *perception,* children with autism have been tested at both levels of visual perspective-taking (Baron-Cohen, 1989d, 1991a; Hobson, 1984; Leslie & Frith, 1988; Reed & Petersen, 1990; Tan & Harris, 1991) and appear to show no deficits. However, in studies of *pretense* (Baron-Cohen, 1987; Ungerer & Sigman, 1981), children with autism seem to produce significantly less spontaneous pretend play than mentally handicapped control groups. Similarly, on tests of understanding *knowledge,* children with autism make more errors than control groups (Baron-Cohen & Goodhart, 1994; Leslie & Frith, 1988; Perner et al., 1989).

The indication from these studies is that not *all* mental states pose difficulties for children with autism: certain aspects of perception and desire do not; pretense, knowledge, intention, and belief do. Explaining this specific pattern of intact and impaired comprehension is currently the focus of debate (Baron-Cohen, Tager-Flusberg, & Cohen, 1993). However, the claim that these deficits are specific to autism appears less controversial, and relies on experimental evidence from other clinical groups. Other childhood clinical populations tend to pass false belief tests. These populations include children with Down syndrome (Baron-Cohen et al., 1985), mental handicap of unknown etiology (Baron-Cohen, 1989b), language impairment (Leslie & Frith, 1988), conduct disorder (Frith et al.,

[2] Light and Nix (1983) showed, however, that even the notion that children are biased to select their *own* view is not correct: rather, children are biased to select a "good" view.

1994), deafness (Sellars & Leslie, 1990), William's Syndrome (Karmiloff-Smith, 1992), and callosal agenesis (Temple & Vilarroya, 1990). Further clinical populations remain to be tested, but the deficit does seem to be autism-specific. That most disorders leave the development of a theory of mind relatively intact is some confirmation for Fodor's (1987, pp. 132–133) view that a theory of mind is so important that it has been innately *built in* to the human mind and is a universal. Avis and Harris (1991) provided some cross-cultural data in support of this view.

Abnormal Development of a Theory of Mind in Other Clinical Groups

Autism seems to reflect the most severe disruption to the normal acquisition of a theory of mind—these children often do not arrive at the fundamental stage of appreciating that mental states such as beliefs even *exist*—but there are other disorders in which children reach this basic level but show difficulties in the *accurate use* of a theory of mind. Thus, in schizophrenia, some have argued that symptoms of paranoia (Baron-Cohen, 1989e) are an expression of inaccurate attribution of beliefs to others (for example, the paranoid delusion: "The man on the television *knows* what I am thinking"). This comparison with autism may be of considerable theoretical value (Frith & Frith, 1991). Similarly, in conduct disorder (Dodge, 1980), aggressive behavior is often reported to be the outcome of inaccurate attribution of intentions to others ("You *deliberately* bumped into me").

A third disorder in which it has been hypothesized that abnormal theory of mind development may occur is narcissistic personality disorder (Fonagy, 1989). In these patients, it is argued—on the basis of clinical rather than experimental studies—that the striking lack of empathy such individuals show may reflect not a lack of awareness that other people have minds, but a psychological defense against confronting the contents of other people's minds.

Finally, patients with semantic-pragmatic disorder (Bishop, 1989) are thought to have particular difficulties in accurately identifying a speaker's communicative intent and taking into account a listener's informational needs—what the listener needs to know for an utterance to be understood. These subjects may well overlap considerably with autism (Baron-Cohen, 1988; Lister-Brook & Bowler, 1992), but it is possible that the two conditions are also distinguishable. Future work is needed to establish the extent to which they are indeed separable disorders, and to what extent deficits in theory of mind use differ between them.

In summary, the impressive ability of even very young normal children to use a theory of mind, apparently effortlessly, and the serious consequences of its impairment in autism, suggest the existence of a specialized cognitive mechanism for understanding mental states. The studies from autism have been enriched by and in turn have challenged models of the normal development of a theory of mind (Baron-Cohen, 1990, 1991c, 1995). A theory of mind is a strong candidate for a modular mechanism in the brain (Leslie, 1991)—a mechanism that is neurologically and informationally independent. It is assumed to be biological in origin (a) because autism has a biological basis (Rutter, 1983) and (b) because it appears to be universal (Avis & Harris, 1991). In the next section, I review the development of face-processing, before considering the interesting question as to whether face-processing may play a role in the functioning of our theory of mind.

FACE-PROCESSING

Normal Face-Processing in Childhood: A Brief Review

Any parent can relate how faces seem to hold a particular fascination for infants, almost from birth. In the scientific literature, it is 30 years since the simple but important experiments (Fantz, 1961, 1963) showing that newborn infants prefer a drawing of a human face over other kinds of drawings. Newborns also are more interested in tracking schematic face-patterns than either scrambled faces or blank head outlines (Goren, Sarty, & Wu, 1975; Johnson, Dziurwiec, Bartrip, & Morton, 1991; Maurer & Young, 1983). By 2 months, infants prefer looking at (and not just tracking) a real face rather than a drawing of a face (Lewis, 1969), and a regularly arranged schematic face rather than a scrambled face (Caron, Caron, Caldwell, & Weiss, 1973; Fantz, 1961, 1963).[3]

Why should infants show such a strong preference for faces? Morton and Johnson (1991) suggested that, for newborns and 1-month-old infants, a preference for faces appears to be driven by an innate mechanism that guides the infants' attention toward conspecifics' faces. They call this mechanism "Conspec," and they argue that it ensures that the neonate attends to faces—and, therefore, likely caregivers. To quote Morton and Johnson (1991): "The information contained within Conspec need only be sufficient to select the parents' face from the set of likely stimuli in the species-typical environment. It need not be species- or even class-specific" (p. 85). Conspec information, they argue, is available without the organism having to be exposed to specific stimuli.

Which aspects of the face do infants attend to? One aspect seems to be the *movement* properties. They prefer to look at moving rather than stationary heads (Carpenter, 1974; Sherrod, 1979), and movement such as nodding and changing facial expression causes them to smile and imitate (Meltzoff, 1990). In contrast, faces that remain entirely stationary have the effect of provoking distress in infants, even as young as 2 months of age (Field, 1979; Tronick, Als, Adamson, Wise, & Brazelton, 1978). Precisely which parts of the face are preferred seems to vary with age. Thus, 1-month-old infants appear to attend to the contour of the head, 2-month-olds focus more on the eyes, and 5-month-olds attend to the nose-mouth area of the face (Caron et al., 1973).

The importance of the *eyes* over other parts of the face is suggested by a range of studies. Parents report their subjective experience of obtaining eye contact after their babies are about 4 weeks of age (Berger & Cunningham, 1981). Two- to 3-month-olds look longer at a face when its eyes are open rather than closed, and they show strongest preference for a face with its eyes moving (Maurer, 1985), but show no comparable preference

[3] After this, a different response pattern can often be found (see Morton & Johnson, 1991).

for a face with an open rather than a closed mouth. Maurer and Barrera (1981, study 1) also found that 2-month-olds looked less than half as long at a face in which eyes and eyebrows were omitted than at a naturally drawn face or at a face in which mouth and nose were omitted. There was no significant difference between how long they looked at a drawing of a complete face versus one with the mouth and nose omitted. These results, shown in Figure 12.2, strongly suggest that the preference for faces is actually a preference for the eyes (or eye region), and is not influenced to the same degree by the nose and mouth. (In Maurer and Barrera's second study, they demonstrated that this preference for the eyes was not affected by the position of the eyes.)

Most studies assume that the main function underlying infants' fascination with the face is to ensure that they learn to recognize people's *identities*. Thus, Morton and Johnson (1991) emphasized that one key ability that becomes available after the maturation of a new mechanism (which they called "Conlern") at 2 months of age is the ability to distinguish between one face and another. "Conlern is a device that acquires and retains specific information about the visual characteristics of individual conspecifics" (Johnson & Morton, 1991, p. 90). These authors then discussed the possibility that this second mechanism is neurologically and informationally dissociable from the earlier (Conspec) mechanism. Conlern, then, is held responsible for children's rapid acquisition of expertise in identity recognition.

This emphasis on the identity-recognition function of face-processing in the early infancy period would in no way lead one to think of any connection between face-processing and theory of mind. However, in the next section, I explore some arguments suggesting that face-processing may play a role in the development and use of a theory of mind.

Could Face-Processing Play a Role in the Development of a Theory of Mind?

Evidence from Joint Attention

One function of face-processing that appears to entail some early use of a theory of mind is seen in *joint attention* (Bruner, 1983). The earliest of these behaviors appears to be *deictic gaze:* the infant spontaneously looks across in the direction of another person's gaze, in order to check what the person is looking at. Scaife and Bruner (1975) found that 30–40% of infants showed this skill by 2 to 7 months, 60–70% by 8 to 10 months, and 100% by 11 months (Scaife & Bruner, 1975). Presumably, the information being used by the infant to judge what another person is looking at is derived from the *direction of the eyes.* The infant appears to be reading this information from the eyes very much as it reads information from the index finger later, recognizing that it *points* (or refers) to things (Butterworth, 1991).

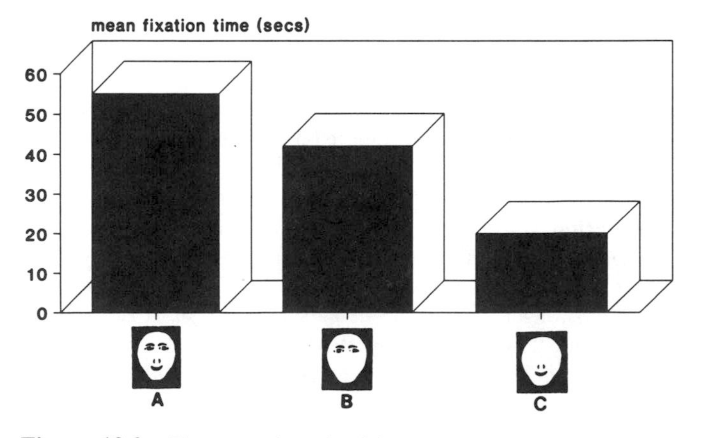

Figure 12.2 The mean length of fixation on facelike drawings by 2-month-olds. Adapted from data in Maurer (1985).

Other joint-attention behaviors include giving, showing, and pointing out objects to others; all of these behaviors appear by 10 to 14 months of age (Bates et al., 1979). The production of these three behaviors directs other people to *look at* objects. They all involve face-processing in that the child makes eye contact, then alternates the gaze with a look at the target of the other person's gaze, and then resumes eye contact. This sequence is known as *gaze alternation* (Gomez, 1991). Exactly the same pattern of gaze alternation is seen in children's comprehension of these gestures.

The link I wish to draw between joint attention and theory of mind requires one critical premise: what children are doing during joint attention is not simply computing what is in someone's visual field or calculating the geometry of objects in the environment; rather, they are computing what that person is *attending* to (Baron-Cohen, 1989c, 1989d, 1991c). Having computed this, they then either *monitor* the person's attention (during deictic gaze and in comprehension of another person's showing and pointing gestures) or *direct* it (in pointing things out with the index finger or the eyes, or showing objects to another person). Given that attention itself is a mental state, joint attention could be viewed as comprising an early stage in the development of a theory of mind.

There is some evidence in support of the premise that joint-attention behaviors entail the child's possessing a concept of attention. First, in producing pointing and showing behaviors, the child does not seem to be simply trying to get the person to move his or her head in the appropriate direction or to change his or her visual field. Rather, the child appears to clearly intend the person to look at a *particular* object: the child will repeat the gesture insistently if the person looks at the wrong thing (Baron-Cohen, 1989d). If we define attention as *selective perception,* the infant's attempt to direct the person's perception to a particular object justifies the use of the term *attention.* Second, the child appears to then check how the person reacts (smiles, looks alarmed, or gives other responses) to the pointing or showing gesture. As in social referencing (Sorce, Emde, Campos, & Klinnert, 1985), the other person's *appraisal* of the particular object being pointed out, shown, or reacted to, seems to be a critical part of the goal of the behavior (Baron-Cohen, 1991c; Hobson, 1990). The child is therefore not just directing the person to look in a given direction, but rather to *selectively attend* to a particular object of *interest* (concern, delight, and so on).

One possible function of eye-processing then, from about 8 months of age on, is to monitor and direct other people's attention. The important work by Perrett et al. (1985), showing that a specialized group of cells in the temporal cortex of macaque monkeys responds selectively to gaze, opens up lines of neuroscientific research that may specify the brain bases of such cognitive mechanisms and cognitive deficits. In a recent study, we found computation of eye direction to be easily within the ability of normal 3-year-olds (Baron-Cohen & Cross, 1992). Subjects were asked which of two children, in a photograph of children's faces, was looking at them. Each pair contained one child looking straight ahead and one looking slightly away (see Figure 12.3). Available cues were either eye direction or eye direction plus nose direction, but it was apparent that even 3-year-old normal children could make this distinction, and, from the work of Butterworth and his colleagues (Butterworth, 1991), it is likely that this skill is present in infancy.

Evidence from Goal Detection

A second possible function of eye contact (and thus, of face-processing) that relates to the use of a theory of mind is in *goal detection*—the ability to judge another person's goal. Goal detection is a fundamental part of our understanding of action: we recognize actions as being *goal-directed.* Because people always *look at* the object they act on, it follows that eye direction provides information not only about what a person is attending to, but also about the target (or goal) of the person's next action. It may be, then, that one reason for making eye contact is to facilitate goal detection. And because goals are mental states, face-processing again appears to interact with theory of mind.

At what age might such goal detection via face-processing begin? Phillips, Baron-Cohen, and Rutter (1992) investigated this with normal infants ranging from 9 to 18 months. The child was presented with either an ambiguous or an unambiguous action. One ambiguous action comprised blocking the child's hands during manual activity; an adult's hands were cupped over the child's. A second ambiguous action comprised offering an object to the child, but then, at the last minute, teasingly withdrawing it, just as the child began to reach for it. The unambiguous action simply comprised giving or presenting an object to the child. This study found that, on at least half of the trials, 100% of the infants responded to the ambiguous actions by instantly looking at the adult's eyes (within the first 5 seconds after the tease or the block); only 39% did so following the unambiguous action. This suggests that, under conditions in which the goal of an act is uncertain, the first place young children (and indeed, adults) look for information to disambiguate the goal is the eyes. In a further study, we demonstrated that children indeed use eye direction in the goal-detection function of face-processing (Baron-Cohen, Campbell, Karmiloff-Smith, Grant, & Walker, in press). Thus, when 3-year-olds are asked, "Which chocolate will Charlie take?", after being shown a display of 4 chocolates and Charlie's

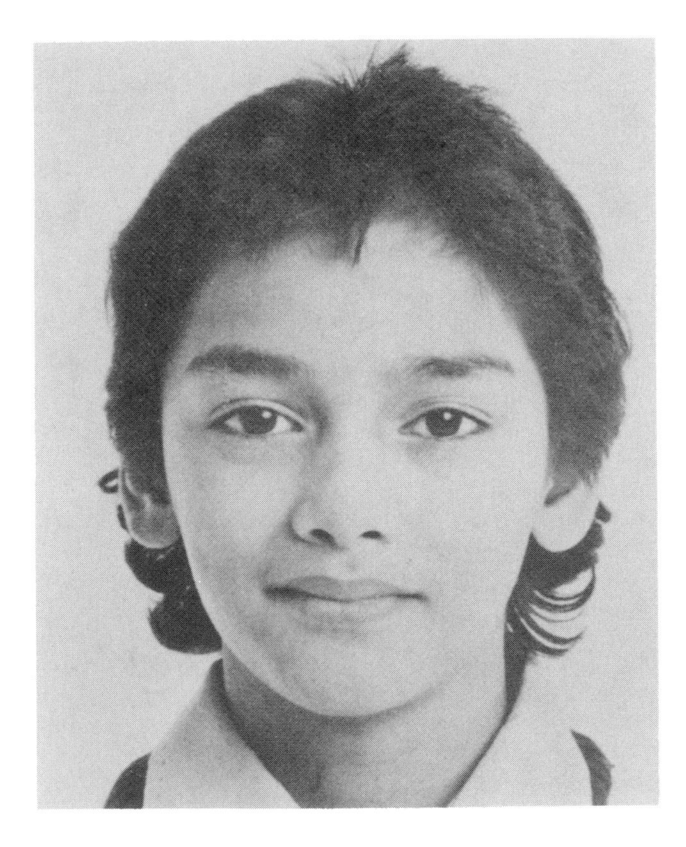

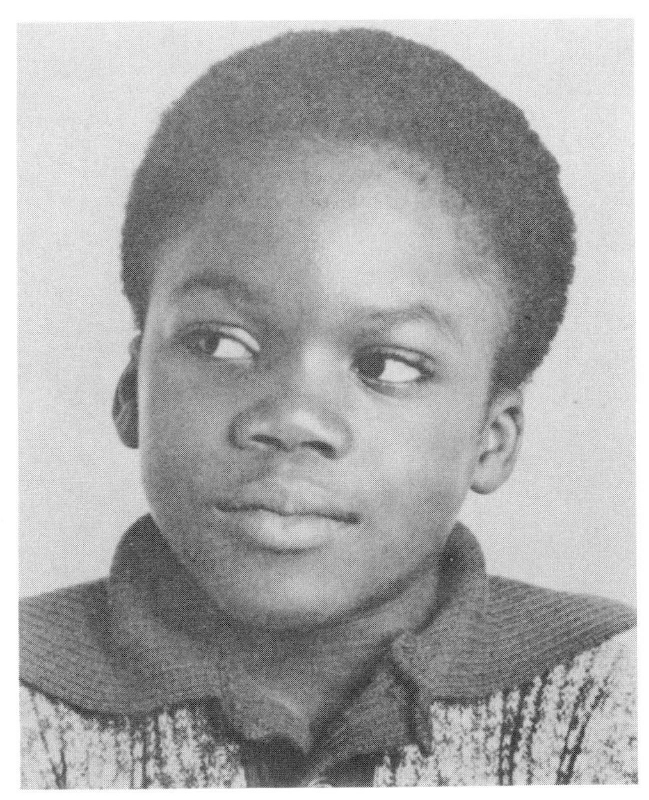

Figure 12.3 Test of "Which one is looking at you?" From "Reading the Eyes: Evidence for the Role of Perception in the Development of a Theory of Mind" by S. Baron-Cohen and P. Cross, 1992, *Mind and Language, 6,* pp. 172–186. Reproduced from Fairburn System of Visual References (1978).

face (a cartoon representation) looking at one of these, they tend to pick the one he is *looking at* as the goal of his next action.

Evidence from Thought Detection

Joint attention and goal detection are two face-processing phenomena that suggest a mentalistic function might drive them. A further phenomenon we have tested (Baron-Cohen, Campbell et al., in press; Baron-Cohen & Cross, 1992) is in *thought detection*—the ability to judge when another person is thinking. We do not mean being able to recognize the *content* of someone's thoughts, only that someone is thinking. In this experiment, normal 3- and 4-year-olds were shown a series of photographs of pairs of children's faces, in which one child was looking straight ahead and one was looking upward and sideways, with neutral emotional expression in the mouth (see Figure 12.4). The subject was asked, "Which one is thinking?". The vast majority of children chose the person in the photo who was looking upward and sideways as the one who was thinking. The only difference in the pictures was eye direction, so this again suggests that aspects of face-processing continue to have mentalistic functions, at 3 to 4 years of age and from then on.

Does Eye Direction Cue Recognition of Other Mental States?

In a further study, we considered whether face-processing might be used by normal children (and adults) in drawing inferences about *other* mental states too. When Baron-Cohen, Campbell et al. (in press) presented normal 3- and 4-year-olds with a display of 4 chocolates, and placed the cartoon face of Charlie in the center of the display, Charlie's eyes were depicted as pointing toward one of the 4 chocolates, randomly selected. In one condition, the subjects were asked, "Which one does Charlie *want?*"; in another, "Which one does Charlie *say* is the (x)?". Children of this age had no difficulty at all in inferring Charlie's desire, or intended referent, from his eye direction. This was particularly striking because, in a retest of this experiment, the display included a distractor cue—a large black arrow pointing at another of the 4 chocolates. Normal 3- and 4-year-olds appeared to ignore this "unnatural" cue, and predominantly used the "natural" cue of eye direction to infer this range of mental states.

In summary, we have presented some evidence that, from early childhood onward, one function of face-processing is to recognize not only emotional states (Ekman & Friesen, 1971), but also other mental states such as attention, desire, goal, and thought. This

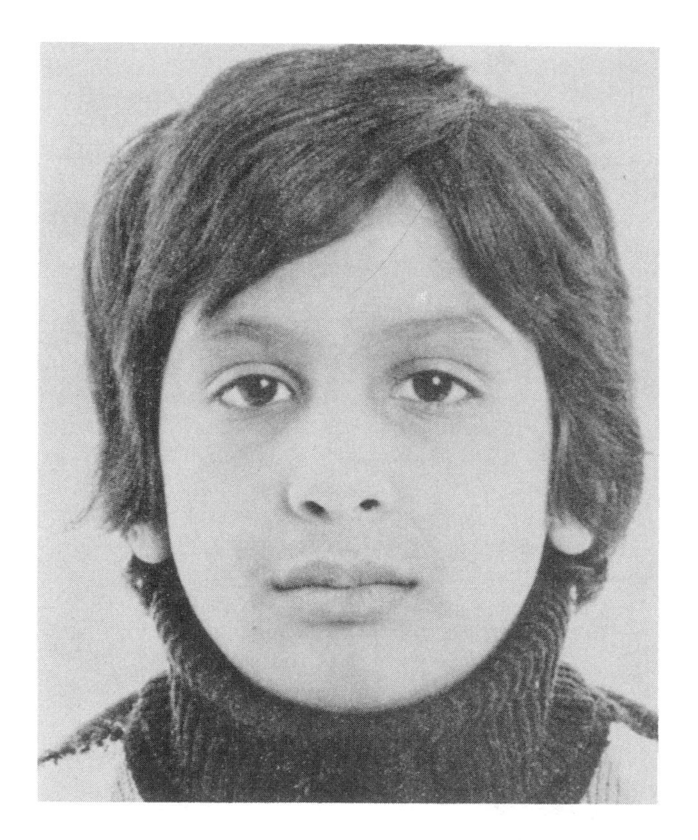

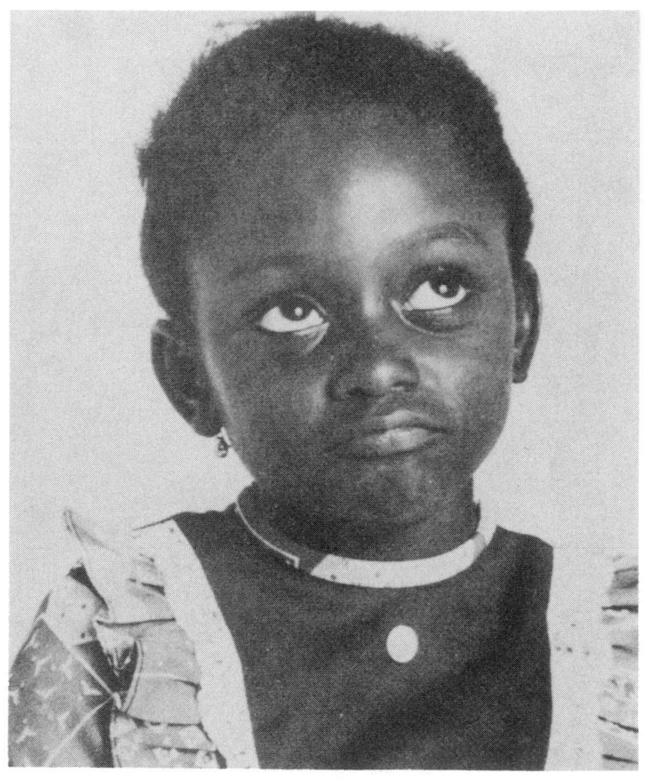

Figure 12.4 Test of "Which one is thinking?" From "Reading the Eyes: Evidence for the Role of Perception in the Development of a Theory of Mind" by S. Baron-Cohen and P. Cross, 1992, *Mind and Language, 6,* pp. 172–186. Reproduced from Fairburn System of Visual References (1978).

idea builds on Hobson's (1990) notion of "visual coorientation" being involved in the development of a theory of mind.

ABNORMALITIES IN THE USE OF FACE-PROCESSING FOR THEORY OF MIND

Autism

Face-processing appears to be impaired in children with autism. Although these children have no difficulties in recognizing a person's *identity* in faces (Campbell, Walker, & Baron-Cohen, 1993; Langdell, 1978; Volkmar, Sparrow, Rende, & Cohen, 1989) and can recognize age and gender in faces (Baron-Cohen, 1991d; Campbell et al., 1993), they nevertheless seem to use unusual face-processing strategies. For example, they do not appear to show the normal inversion effect in identity recognition (Hobson, Ouston, & Lee, 1988b; Langdell, 1978). From Diamond and Carey's (1986) study,[4] one might interpret this abnormality in terms of a relative lack of expertise with faces, because of the limited amount of social experience they have had; others have speculated that this abnormality might reflect featural rather than configural face-processing (Langdell, 1978).

Children with autism have been reported to show some difficulties in recognizing facial expressions of emotion (Hobson, 1986). However, such deficits are not found when control groups are matched for verbal mental age (Braverman, Fein, Lucci, & Waterhouse, 1989; Hobson, Ouston, & Lee, 1988a, 1988b, 1989; Ozonoff, Pennington, & Rogers, 1990; Prior, Dahlstrom, & Squires, 1990; Tantam, Monaghan, Nicholson, & Stirling, 1989).[5] There may, nevertheless, be autism-specific deficits in recognizing "complex" emotions such as surprise, rather than "simple" emotions such as happy and sad (Baron-Cohen, Spitz, & Cross, 1993). This deficit may relate to difficulties in developing a theory of mind; emotions such as surprise entail understanding that a person had held a false belief about what was going to happen.

Some evidence in support of the earlier argument that joint-attention behaviors entail the child's possessing the concept of attention can also be found in autism. Children with autism show little, if any, joint-attention behaviors (Leekam, Baron-Cohen, Perrett, Milders, & Brown, 1993; Sigman, Mundy, Ungerer, & Sherman, 1986), yet they pass Level 1 visual perspective-taking tasks (Baron-Cohen, 1989d; Hobson, 1984; Tan & Harris, 1991), as reviewed earlier. One way of accounting for this dissociation is to assume that Level 1 visual perspective-taking tasks can be solved using geometric, "line of sight" algorithms (Lempers et al., 1977), which do not necessarily require any understanding of the mental state of attention. In contrast, joint-attention behaviors, on the analysis given above, do require understanding the mental state of attention. Abnormalities in joint attention in autism may therefore reflect an inability to recognize eye direction information as indicating a person's attentional state. Such joint-attention deficits may be developmentally and conceptually related to the later theory of mind deficits found in autism.

Phillips et al. (1992), using the ambiguous and unambiguous actions described earlier, tested very young children with autism for their ability to use face-processing to detect goals. These children did not seem to use eye contact to disambiguate the ambiguous actions; in each test, in both conditions, less than 11% used looking. This result suggests that they may have lacked the concept of people's actions being caused by mental states such as goals. Again, it is plausible to assume that these face-processing deficits may be developmentally related to the deficits in their theory of mind, reviewed earlier.

Baron-Cohen, Campbell et al. (in press) tested children with autism (a) on the tests originally developed by Baron-Cohen and Cross (1992), to see whether these children could use eye direction to deduce a person's mental state of thinking, and (b) on the 4 chocolates task, to see whether they were able to use eye direction to infer the mental states of want, goal, and refer. They found significant impairments in the children's use of eye direction in inferring all of these. In addition, the children were significantly more likely to use the "unnatural" cue of the large black arrow than the "natural" cue of gaze, when responding to questions like "Which one does Charlie want?". The researchers concluded that these children may be blind to the mentalistic significance of the eyes, a deficit that may contribute to the observation of unusual use of eye contact by children with autism (Mirenda, Donnellan, & Yoder, 1983).

Blindness

A second condition in which abnormalities have been suggested in the use of face-processing in developing a theory of mind is congenital blindness (Hobson, 1990). Hobson noted the converging reports that autisticlike symptoms are sometimes reported in children who are congenitally blind, or partially blind and partially deaf (e.g., Fay, 1973; Fraiberg & Adelson, 1977; Wing, 1969). These symptoms include delayed onset of pretend play and referential communication (such as pointing), problems in pronoun usage, deixis, flexible thought, and the

---

[4] Configural processing in normal subjects is severely disrupted when inverted faces are presented (Sergent, 1984). The temptation is to interpret this inversion data as evidence for a purpose-built face-processing mechanism. Diamond and Carey (1986) show, however, that this assumption is probably mistaken. Similar orientation effects can be achieved with other objects, as long as subjects possess "expert" experience of the stimulus. Thus, they demonstrated that identification of (specific breeds of) *individual* champion dogs by experts is also vulnerable to the inversion effect.

[5] Emotion recognition deficits are found in a range of other clinical disorders, such as schizophrenia (Cutting, 1981; Novic, Luchins, & Perline, 1984), mental handicap (Gray, Frazer, & Leuder, 1983), abused children (Camras, Grow, & Ribordy, 1983), deaf children (Odom, Blanton, & Laukhuf, 1973), and prosopagnosia (De Kosky, Heilman, Bowers, & Valenstein, 1980; Kurucz, Feldmar, & Werner, 1979), but *not* children with visual impairment (Ellis, Young, & Markham, 1987). Future research in this area needs to untangle how emotion perception deficits in different clinical groups relate to each other. At present, it is not clear whether these deficits are the same (i.e., caused by the same underlying neuropathology), or constitute only superficially similar patterns of impairment (i.e., caused by different underlying patterns of neuropathology).

presence of echolalia. Given that these symptoms are also characteristic of autism, Hobson proposed that "there may be a common psychological deficit underlying the specific constellation of impairments common to autistic and congenitally blind children" (1990, pp. 118–119). He went on to outline what this common psychological deficit might be.

In essence, he argued that, in the normal case, "vision greatly facilitates the child's grasp of shared reference" (p. 119), as is clear in both joint attention and social referencing. Shared reference, he argued, is an important stage in the development of an understanding of other minds.

Prosopagnosia

Prosopagnosia is a neurological condition in which patients, following brain injury, no longer recognize famous faces, friends, relatives, or even their own face in a mirror (Benton, 1980). Prosopagnosic patients can say when they are looking at *a* face, but not whose it is, simply from the facial information alone. When they do recognize the person, it is on the basis of other information (voice, clothing, context, etc.).

Early cases of this disorder were discussed by Charcot (1883) and Wilbrand (1892), in the context of widespread cognitive impairment. Bodamer (1947) coined the term *prosopagnosia* to describe the specific deficit of face recognition. The term literally means "loss of knowledge of faces." Whether such cases are indeed cases of "pure" face recognition deficits (De Renzi, 1986) or always occur in the context of wider deficits in object recognition, remains controversial (see Morton & Johnson, 1991). Prosopagnosia can occur in both childhood and adulthood, although the differential effects of age of onset of the condition are not well understood (De Haan & Campbell, 1991).

It has long been recognized that there are different forms of prosopagnosia. The handicap does not always extend to all aspects of face perception, and the particular patterns of impairment have added important evidence to neuropsychological models of face-processing. For example, some patients with prosopagnosia can recognize facial expressions of emotion but still not recognize identity from faces (Shuttleworth, Syring, & Allen, 1982). Others have the exact opposite pattern of deficit: they can identify faces but have difficulty interpreting their facial expressions (Kurucz & Felmar, 1979; Kurucz et al., 1979). The latter pattern remains to be replicated, but such *double dissociations* are held to be strong evidence of the independence between the neurocognitive systems responsible for these two abilities.

Other dissociations in prosopagnosia have also been reported. For example, Campbell, Landis, and Regard (1986) reported a prosopagnosic woman who could neither recognize (nor even identify the sex of) faces nor interpret their expressions, but who could judge what phonemes were mouthed in photographs of faces and was susceptible to the McGurk illusion (McGurk & MacDonald, 1976). A second patient, they reported, had the exact opposite set of impairments. She could identify faces and categorize their expressions, but was not susceptible to the McGurk illusion. De Haan and Campbell (1991) reported a case (AB) who was unable to detect eye direction. Given the role of eye direction in computing the mental states of attention, goal, desire, and reference, suggested earlier, we might predict that cases with this subtype of prosopagnosia would, like the blind, show delay in the development of a theory of mind. At the time of writing, there is no evidence of what the development of a theory of mind is like in such patients' childhood.[6]

CONCLUSIONS AND FUTURE DIRECTIONS

Theory of mind and face-processing represent well-studied domains within developmental psychology. Both appear vulnerable to impairment, the clearest expression of such deficits being found in autism and prosopagnosia, respectively. Both disorders have shaped the development of models of normal functioning in these areas (Baron-Cohen, 1994, 1995). The development of face-processing and theory of mind may interact in important ways, from about the 8th month of infancy onward. Evidence for such interaction comes from the toddler's ability to judge a person's mental states of *attention, goal, desire, refer,* and *think* from the direction of the person's eyes. Perceiving eye direction may also give the child a first lesson in (at least some aspects of) intentionality, or aboutness, because gaze direction always points to (or is about) something.

In a volume of this nature, it is useful to speculate about future directions for research. What might we expect for theory of mind research? There has been enormous interest in this field over the past 10 years. Will this (like many other "fashions" in science) be shortlived?

On one view, a single topic cannot continue to sustain such a high level of interest. The alternative view (the one that I am drawn to support) is that theory of mind will continue as a major research area in the future. My reasons for this prediction are based on the kind of topic that theory of mind is. It is not a narrow topic, with limited implications. On the contrary, as a psychological process or capacity, it appears to be as basic as several other important processes, such as language or memory. Just as language or memory research will continue to be fundamental areas of cognitive science, so (in this view) will theory of mind.

Future lines of investigation that are opening up (I shall mention just a few) include the development of nonverbal theory of mind tests for potential use with nonhuman primates (Povinelli, Parks, & Novak, 1991), neonates (Premack, 1990), and language-impaired clinical populations (Whiten, 1993); the investigation of cross-cultural aspects of theory of mind (Avis & Harris, 1991); and the brain basis of theory of mind (Baron-Cohen, Ring et al., 1994; Brothers, 1992).

Similarly, the interface between theory of mind and face-processing, on which this chapter has focused, is likely to continue to raise many new questions. Although this interface (albeit under a different guise) was an important topic in the initial pioneering studies by Ekman and Friesen (1971) and by Scaife and Bruner (1975), face-processing and theory of mind subsequently

[6] The only relevant study is a single case study by Young and Ellis (1989). The subject (KD) passed a false belief test at 8 years of age. This is too late an age to investigate subtle delays.

became rather divorced from one another. The work in autism may serve to refocus research on this interface.

Examples of just a few of the important questions that will, it is hoped, be part of future investigations in this area include: the possible neural connections between face-processing and theory of mind "modules" in the brain (Brothers, 1992; Frith, 1992; Baron-Cohen & Ring, 1994); the differential pathology underlying emotion-recognition impairments in a large range of clinical populations (Cutting, 1981; De Kosky et al., 1980; see also note 5); and the relationship between inferences about one's own mental states and inferences (from facial expressions) about another person's mental states (Gopnik, 1993). I hope that this chapter will encourage further empirical work on the interface between face-processing and theory of mind, from the perspective of both the normal and the abnormal.

REFERENCES

Astington, J., Harris, P., & Olson, D. (1988). *Developing theories of mind.* New York: Cambridge University Press.

Astington, J., & Lee, E. (1991, April). *What do children know about intentional causation?* Paper presented at the Society for Research in Child Development Conference, Seattle, WA.

Avis, J., & Harris, P. (1991). Belief-desire reasoning among Baka children: Evidence for a universal conception of mind. *Child Development, 62,* 460–467.

Baron-Cohen, S. (1987). Autism and symbolic play. *British Journal of Developmental Psychology, 5,* 139–148.

Baron-Cohen, S. (1988). Social and pragmatic deficits in autism: Cognitive or affective? *Journal of Autism and Developmental Disorders, 18,* 379–402.

Baron-Cohen, S. (1989a). Are autistic children behaviourists? An examination of their mental-physical and appearance-reality distinctions. *Journal of Autism and Developmental Disorders, 19,* 579–600.

Baron-Cohen, S. (1989b). The autistic child's theory of mind: A case of specific developmental delay. *Journal of Child Psychology and Psychiatry, 30,* 285–298.

Baron-Cohen, S. (1989c). Joint attention deficits in autism: Towards a cognitive analysis. *Development and Psychopathology, 1,* 185–189.

Baron-Cohen, S. (1989d). Perceptual role-taking and protodeclarative pointing in autism. *British Journal of Developmental Psychology, 7,* 113–127.

Baron-Cohen, S. (1989e). Thinking about thinking: How does it develop? Critical notice. *Journal of Child Psychology and Psychiatry, 30,* 931–933.

Baron-Cohen, S. (1990). Autism: A specific cognitive disorder of "mind-blindness." *International Review of Psychiatry, 2,* 79–88.

Baron-Cohen, S. (1991a). The development of a theory of mind in autism: Deviance and delay? *Psychiatric Clinics of North America, 14,* 33–51.

Baron-Cohen, S. (1991b). Do people with autism understand what causes emotion? *Child Development, 62,* 385–395.

Baron-Cohen, S. (1991c). Precursors to a theory of mind: Understanding attention in others. In A. Whiten (Ed.), *Natural theories of mind* (pp. 223-254). Oxford, England: Basil Blackwell.

Baron-Cohen, S. (1991d). The theory of mind deficit in autism: How specific is it? *British Journal of Developmental Psychology, 9,* 301–314.

Baron-Cohen, S. (1992a). On modularity and development in autism: A reply to Burack. *Journal of Child Psychology and Psychiatry, 33,* 623–629.

Baron-Cohen, S. (1992b). Out of sight or out of mind? Another look at deception in autism. *Journal of Child Psychology and Psychiatry, 33,* 1141–1155.

Baron-Cohen, S. (1993). From attention-goal psychology to belief desire psychology: The development of a theory of mind, and its dysfunction. In S. Baron-Cohen, H. Tager-Flusberg, & D. J. Cohen (Eds.), *Understanding other minds: Perspectives from autism.* Oxford, England: Oxford University Press.

Baron-Cohen, S. (1994). How to build a baby that can read minds: Cognitive mechanisms in mind reading. *Cahiers de Psychologie Cognitive, 13*(5), 513–552.

Baron-Cohen, S. (1995). *Mindblindness.* Cambridge, MA: MIT Press/Bradford Books.

Baron-Cohen, S., Campbell, R., Karmiloff-Smith, A., Grant, J., & Walker, J. (in press). Are children with autism blind to the mentalistic significance of the eyes? *British Journal of Developmental Psychology.*

Baron-Cohen, S., & Cross, P. (1992). Reading the eyes: Evidence for the role of perception in the development of a theory of mind. *Mind and Language, 6,* 172–186.

Baron-Cohen, S., & Goodhart, F. (1994). The "seeing leads to knowing" principle: Deficit in autism. The Pratt and Bryant probe. *British Journal of Developmental Psychology, 12,* 397–402.

Baron-Cohen, S., Leslie, A. M., & Frith, U. (1985). Does the autistic child have a "theory of mind"? *Cognition, 21,* 37–46.

Baron-Cohen, S., Leslie, A. M., & Frith, U. (1986). Mechanical, behavioural and intentional understanding of picture stories in autistic children. *British Journal of Developmental Psychology, 4,* 113–125.

Baron-Cohen, S., & Ring, H. (1994). A model of the mindreading system: Neuropsychological and neurobiological perspectives. In P. Mitchell, & C. Lewis (Eds.), *Orgins of an understanding of mind.* Hove: Erlbann.

Baron-Cohen, S., Ring, H., Moriarty, J., Schmitz, P., Costa, D., & Ell, P. (1994). Recognition of mental state terms: A clinical study of autism, and a functional neuroimaging study of normal adults. *British Journal of Psychiatry, 165,* 640–649.

Baron-Cohen, S., Spitz, A., & Cross, P. (1993). Do children with autism recognize surprise? A research note. *Cognition and Emotion, 7,* 507–516.

Baron-Cohen, S., Tager-Flusberg, H., & Cohen, D. J. (Eds.). (1993). *Understanding other minds: Perspectives from autism.* Oxford, England: Oxford University Press.

Bates, E., Benigni, L., Bretherton, I., Camaioni, L., & Volterra, V. (1979). *The emergence of symbols: Cognition and communication in infancy.* New York: Academic Press.

Benton, A. (1980). The neuropsychology of facial recognition. *American Psychologist, 35,* 176–186.

Berger, J., & Cunningham, C. (1981). The development of eye-contact between mothers and normal versus Down's syndrome infants. *Developmental Psychology, 17,* 678–689.

Berndt, T., & Berndt, E. (1975). Children's use of motives and intentionality in person perception and moral judgement. *Child Development, 46,* 904–912.

Bishop, D. (1989). Autism, Asperger's syndrome, and Semantic-Pragmatic Disorder: Where are the boundaries? *British Journal of Disorders of Communication, 24,* 107–122.

Bodamer, J. (1947). Die Prosopagnosie. *Archiv für Psychiatrie und Zeitschrift für Neurologie, 179,* 6–54.

Braverman, M., Fein, D., Lucci, D., & Waterhouse, L. (1989). Affect comprehension in children with pervasive developmental disorders. *Journal of Autism and Developmental Disorders, 19,* 301–316.

Bretherton, I., McNew, S., & Beeghly-Smith, M. (1981). Early person knowledge as expressed in gestural and verbal communication: When do infants acquire a "theory of mind"? In M. Lamb & L. Sharrod (Eds.), *Infant social cognition* (pp. 333–374). Hillsdale, NJ: Erlbaum.

Brothers, L. (1992). Perception of social acts in primates: Cognition and neurobiology. *Seminars in the Neurosciences, 4.*

Bruce, V. (1988). *Recognizing faces.* E. Sussex, England: Erlbaum.

Bruner, J. (1983). *Child's talk: Learning to use language.* Oxford, England: Oxford University Press.

Butterworth, G. (1991). The ontogeny and phylogeny of joint visual attention. In A. Whiten (Ed.), *Natural theories of mind* (pp. 223–231). Oxford, England: Basil Blackwell.

Campbell, R., Landis, T., & Regard, M. (1986). Face recognition and lip-reading: A neurological dissociation. *Brain, 109,* 509–521.

Campbell, R., Walker, J., & Baron-Cohen, S. (1993). Face-processing in autism: An experimental investigation. Unpublished manuscript, Department of Psychology, Goldsmiths College, University of London.

Camras, L. A., Grow, G., & Ribordy, S. C. (1983). Recognition of emotional expression by abused children. *Journal of Child Psychology and Psychiatry, 12,* 325–328.

Caron, A., Caron, R., Caldwell, R., & Weiss, S. (1973). Infant perception of structural properties of the face. *Developmental Psychology, 9,* 385–399.

Carpenter, G. (1974). Mother's face and the newborn. *New Scientist, 61,* 742–744.

Charcot, J. (1883). Un cas de suppression brusque et isolée de la vision mentale des signes et des objets (formes et couleurs). *Le Progres Medicale, 88,* 568–571.

Cheney, D., & Seyfarth, R. (1990). *How monkeys see the world.* Chicago: University of Chicago Press.

Cicchetti, D. (1984). The emergence of developmental psychopathology. *Child Development, 55,* 1–7.

Cutting, J. (1981). Judgement of emotional expression in schizophrenics. *British Journal of Psychiatry, 139,* 1–6.

De Haan, E., & Campbell, R. (1991). A 15-year follow-up of a case of developmental prosopagnosia. *Cortex, 27,* 1–21.

De Kosky, S., Heilman, K., Bowers, M., & Valenstein, E. (1980). Recognition and discrimination of emotional faces and pictures. *Brain and Language, 9,* 206–214.

Dennett, D. (1978a). Beliefs about beliefs. *Behaviour and Brain Sciences, 4,* 568–570.

Dennett, D. (1978b). *Brainstorms: Philosophical essays on mind and psychology.* Brighton, England: Harvester Press.

De Renzi, E. (1986). Current issues on prosopagnosia. In H. Ellis, M. Jeeves, F. Newcombe, & A. Young. (Eds.) *Aspects of face processing.* Dordrecht, The Netherlands: Nijhoff.

Diamond, R., & Carey, S. (1986). Why faces are not special: An effect of expertise. *Journal of Experimental Psychology: General, 115,* 107–117.

Dodge, K. (1980). Social cognition and children's aggressive behaviour. *Child Development, 51,* 162–170.

Ekman, P., & Friesen, W. (1971). Constants across cultures in the face and emotion. *Journal of Personality and Social Psychology, 17,* 124–129.

Ellis, A., & Young, A. (1989). *Human cognitive neuropsychology.* Hillsdale, NJ: Erlbaum.

Ellis, H., Young, A., & Markham, R. (1987). The ability of visually impaired children to read expressions and recognize surprise. *Journal of Visual Impairment and Blindness, December,* 485–486.

Fantz, R. (1961). The origin of form perception. *Scientific American, 204,* 66–72.

Fantz, R. (1963). Pattern vision in newborn infants. *Science, 140,* 296–297.

Fay, W. (1973). On the echolalia of the blind and of the autistic child. *Journal of Speech and Hearing Disorders, 38,* 478–489.

Field, T. (1979). Visual and cardiac responses to animate and inanimate faces by term and preterm infants. *Child Development, 50,* 188–194.

Flavell, J., Everett, B., Croft, K., & Flavell, E. (1981). Young children's knowledge about visual perception: Further evidence for the level 1–level 2 distinction. *Developmental Psychology, 17,* 99–103.

Flavell, J., Shipstead, S., & Croft, K. (1978). Young children's knowledge about visual perception: Hiding objects from others. *Child Development, 49,* 1208–1211.

Fodor, J. A. (1987). *Psychosemantics: The problem of meaning in the philosophy of mind.* Cambridge, MA: MIT Press.

Fonagy, P. (1989). On tolerating mental states: Theory of mind in borderline personality. *Bulletin of the Anna Freud Centre, 12,* 91–115.

Fraiberg, S., & Adelson, E. (1977). Self-representation in language and play. In S. Fraiberg (Ed.), *Insights from the blind* (pp. 248–270). London: Souvenir Press.

Freeman, N., Lewis, C., & Doherty, M. (1991). Preschoolers' grasp of desire for knowledge in false-belief prediction: Practical intelligence and verbal report. *British Journal of Developmental Psychology, 9,* 139–158.

Frith, C. (1992). *The neuropsychology of schizophrenia.* Hillsdale, NJ: Erlbaum.

Frith, C., & Frith, U. (1991). Elective affinities in schizophrenia and childhood autism. In P. Bebbington (Ed.), *Social psychiatry: Theory, method, and practice.* New Brunswick, NJ: Rutgers University Press.

Frith, U. (1989). *Autism: Explaining the enigma.* Oxford, England: Basil Blackwell.

Frith, U., Happé, F., & Siddons, F. (1994). Autism and theory of mind in everyday life. *Social Development, 3,* 108–124.

Gelman, R., & Spelke, E. (1981). The development of thoughts about animate and inanimate objects: Implications for research on social cognition. In J. Flavell & L. Ross (Eds.), *Social cognitive development* (pp. 43–66). Cambridge, England: Cambridge University Press.

Gomez, J. C. (1991). Visual behaviour as a window for reading the mind of others in primates. In A. Whiten (Ed.), *Natural theories of mind.* Oxford, England: Basil Blackwell.

Gopnik, A. (1993). How we know our own minds: The illusion of first person knowledge of intentionality. *Behavioural and Brain Sciences, 16,* 1–14.

Gopnik, A., & Slaughter, V. (1991). Young children's understanding of changes in their mental states. *Child Development, 62,* 98–110.

Goren, C., Sarty, M., & Wu, R. (1975). Visual following and pattern discrimination of facelike stimuli by newborn infants. *Pediatrics, 56,* 544–549.

Gratch, G. (1964). Response alternation in children: A developmental study of orientations to uncertainty. *Vita Humana, 7,* 49–60.

Gray, J. M., Frazer, W. L., & Leudar, I. (1983). Recognition of emotion from facial expression in mental handicap. *British Journal of Psychiatry, 142,* 566–571.

Happé, F. (1993). Communicative competence and theory of mind in autism: A test of relevance theory. *Cognition, 48,* 101–119.

Hobson, R. P. (1984). Early childhood autism and the question of egocentrism. *Journal of Autism and Developmental Disorders, 14,* 85–104.

Hobson, R. P. (1986). The autistic child's appraisal of expressions of emotion. *Journal of Child Psychology and Psychiatry, 27,* 321–342.

Hobson, R. P. (1990). On acquiring knowledge about people and the capacity to pretend: Response to Leslie (1987). *Psychological Review, 97,* 114–121.

Hobson, R. P., Ouston, J., & Lee, A. (1988a). Emotion recognition in autism: Coordinating faces and voices. *Psychological Medicine, 18,* 911–923.

Hobson, R. P., Ouston, J., & Lee, A. (1988b). What's in a face? The case of autism. *British Journal of Developmental Psychology, 79,* 441–453.

Hobson, R. P., Ouston, J., & Lee, T. (1989). Naming emotion in faces and voices: Abilities and disabilities in autism and mental retardation. *British Journal of Developmental Psychology, 7,* 237–250.

Johnson, M., Dziurwiec, S., Bartrip, J., & Morton, J. (1991). Infants' preference for facelike stimuli: Effects of the movement of internal features. *Infant Behaviour and Development.*

Johnson, M., & Morton, J. (1991). *Biology and cognitive development.* Oxford, England: Basil Blackwell.

Kanner, L. (1943). Autistic disturbance of affective contact. *Nervous Child, 2,* 217–250. (Reprinted in Kanner, L. (1973). *Childhood psychosis: Initial studies and new insights.* New York: Wiley.

Karmiloff-Smith, A. (1992). *Beyond modelarity.* Cambridge, MA: MIT Press/Bradford Books.

King, M. (1971). The development of some intention concepts in children. *Child Development, 42,* 1145–1152.

Kurucz, J., & Feldmar, G. (1979). Prosopo-affective agnosia as a symptom of cerebral organic disease. *Journal of the American Geriatrics Society, 27,* 225–230.

Kurucz, J., Feldmar, G., & Werner, W. (1979). Prosopo-affective agnosia associated with chronic organic brain syndrome. *Journal of the American Geriatrics Society, 27,* 91–95.

Langdell, T. (1978). Recognition of faces: An approach to the study of autism. *Journal of Child Psychology and Psychiatry, 19,* 225–238.

Leekam, S. (1991). Jokes and lies: Children's understanding of intentional falsehood. In A. Whiten (Ed.), *Natural theories of mind* (pp. 159–174). Oxford, England: Basil Blackwell.

Leekam, S., Baron-Cohen, S., Perrett, D., Milders, M., & Brown, S. (1993). *Gaze-monitoring and perceptual role-taking: A dissociation in autism.* Unpublished manuscript, Department of Social and Applied Psychology, University of Kent, Canterbury.

Leekam, S., & Perner, J. (1991). Does the autistic child have a metarepresentational deficit? *Cognition, 40,* 203–218.

Lempers, J., Flavell, E., & Flavell, J. (1977). The development in very young children of tacit knowledge concerning visual perception. *Genetic Psychology Monographs, 95,* 3–53.

Leslie, A. M. (1987). Pretence and representation: The origins of "theory of mind." *Psychological Review, 94,* 412–426.

Leslie, A. (1991). The theory of mind impairment in autism: Evidence for a modular mechanism of development? In A. Whiten (Ed.), *Natural theories of mind* (pp. 63–78). Oxford, England: Basil Blackwell.

Leslie, A., & Roth, D. (1993). What can autism teach us about metarepresentation? In S. Baron-Cohen, H. Tager-Flusberg, & D. J. Cohen (Eds.), *Understanding other minds: Perspectives from autism.* Oxford, England: Oxford University Press.

Leslie, A. M., & Frith, U. (1988). Autistic children's understanding of seeing, knowing, and believing. *British Journal of Developmental Psychology, 6,* 315–324.

Lewis, M. (1969). Infants' responses to facial stimuli during the first year of life. *Developmental Psychology, 1,* 75–80.

Light, P., & Nix, C. (1983). Own view versus good view in a perspective-taking task. *Child Development, 54,* 480–483.

Lister-Brook, S., & Bowler, D. (1992). Autism by another name? Semantic and pragmatic impairments in children. *Journal of Autism and Developmental Disorders, 22,* 61–82.

McCune-Nicholich, L. (1981). Towards symbolic functioning: Structure of early use of pretend games and potential parallels with language. *Child Development, 52,* 785–797.

McGurk, H., & MacDonald, J. (1976). Hearing lips and seeing voices. *Nature, 264,* 746–748.

Maurer, D. (1985). Infants' perception of facedness. In T. Field & N. Fox (Eds.), *Social perception in infants* (pp. 73–100). Norwood, NJ: Ablex.

Maurer, D., & Barrera, M. (1981). Infants' perception of natural and distorted arrangements of a schematic face. *Child Development, 52,* 196–202.

Maurer, D., & Young, R. (1983). Newborns' following of natural and distorted arrangements of facial features. *Infant Behavior and Development, 6,* 127–131.

Meltzoff, A. (1990). Towards a developmental cognitive science: The implications of cross-modal matching and imitation for the development of representation and memory in infancy. *Annals of the New York Academy of Sciences, 608,* 1–37.

Mirenda, P., Donnellan, A., & Yoder, D. (1983). Gaze behavior: A new look at an old problem. *Journal of Autism and Developmental Disorders, 13,* 397–409.

Morton, J., & Johnson, M. (1991). Conspec and Conlern: A two-process theory of infant face-recognition. *Psychological Review, 98,* 164–181.

Novic, J., Luchins, D. J., & Perline, R. (1984). Facial affect recognition in schizophrenia: Is there a differential deficit? *British Journal of Psychiatry, 144,* 533–537.

Odom, P. B., Blanton, R. L., & Laukhuf, C. (1973). Facial expressions and interpretations of emotion-arousing situations in deaf and hearing children. *Journal of Abnormal Child Psychology, 1,* 139–151.

Oswald, D. P., & Ollendick, T. (1989). Role taking and social competence in autism and mental retardation. *Journal of Autism and Developmental Disorders, 19,* 119–128.

Ozonoff, S., Pennington, B., & Rogers, S. (1990). Are there emotion perception deficits in young autistic children? *Journal of Child Psychology and Psychiatry, 31,* 343–363.

Ozonoff, S., Pennington, B., & Rogers, S. (1991). Executive function deficits in high-functioning autistic children: Relationship to theory of mind. *Journal of Child Psychology and Psychiatry, 32,* 1081–1106.

Perner, J. (1988). Developing semantics for theories of mind: From propositional attitudes to mental representations. In J. Astington,

P. Harris, & D. Olson (Eds.), *Developing theories of mind* (pp. 141–172). Cambridge, England: Cambridge University Press.

Perner, J. (1991). *Understanding the representational mind.* Cambridge, MA: MIT Press.

Perner, J. (1993). The theory of mind deficit in autism: Rethinking the metarepresentation theory. In S. Baron-Cohen, H. Tager-Flusberg, & D. J. Cohen (Eds.), *Understanding other minds: Perspectives from autism* (pp. 112–137). Oxford, England: Oxford University Press.

Perner, J., Frith, U., Leslie, A. M., & Leekam, S. (1989). Exploration of the autistic child's theory of mind: Knowledge, belief, and communication. *Child Development, 60,* 689–700.

Perner, J., & Wilde-Astington, J. (1991, May). The child's understanding of mental representation. *Proceedings of the 20th Anniversary Symposium of the Jean Piaget Society,* Philadelphia.

Perner, J., & Wimmer, H. (1985). "John *thinks* that Mary *thinks* that . . .": Attribution of second-order beliefs by 5-10-year-old children. *Journal of Experimental Child Psychology, 39,* 437–471.

Perrett, D., Smith, P., Potter, D., Mistlin, A., Head, A., Milner, A., & Jeeves, M. (1985). Visual cells in the temporal cortex sensitive to face view and gaze direction. *Proceedings of the Royal Society of London, B223,* 293–317.

Phillips, W. (1993). *Comprehension of intention and desire by children with autism.* Unpublished doctoral dissertation, Institute of Psychiatry, University of London.

Phillips, W., Baron-Cohen, S., & Rutter, M. (1992). The role of eye-contact in goal detection: Evidence from normal infants, and children with mental handicap or autism. *Development and Psychopathology, 4,* 375–383.

Piaget, J. (1929). *The child's conception of the world.* New York: Harcourt Brace.

Piaget, J. (1962). *Dreams, play and imitation in childhood.* London: Routledge & Kegan Paul.

Piaget, J., & Inhelder, B. (1956). *The child's conception of space.* London: Routledge & Kegan Paul.

Povinelli, D., Parks, K., & Novak, M. (1991). Do rhesus monkeys (Macaca mulatta) attribute knowledge and ignorance to others? *Journal of Comparative Psychology, 105,* 318–325.

Premack, D. (1990). The infant's theory of self-propelled objects. *Cognition, 36,* 1–16.

Premack, D., & Woodruff, G. (1978). Does the chimpanzee have a "theory of mind"? *Behaviour and Brain Sciences, 4,* 515–526.

Prior, M., Dahlstrom, B., & Squires, T. (1990). Autistic children's knowledge of thinking and feeling states in other people. *Journal of Child Psychology and Psychiatry, 31,* 587–602.

Reed, T., & Petersen, C. (1990). A comparative study of autistic subjects' performance at two levels of visual and cognitive perspective-taking. *Journal of Autism and Developmental Disorders, 20,* 555–568.

Riviere, A. (1993). Second-order belief attribution in 5- and 6-year-old normal children. Unpublished manuscript, Universidad Autonoma de Madrid.

Rutter, M. (1983). Cognitive deficits in the pathogenesis of autism. *Journal of Child Psychology and Psychiatry, 24,* 513–531.

Scaife, M., & Bruner, J. (1975). The capacity for joint visual attention in the human infant. *Nature, 253,* 265.

Sellars, L., & Leslie, A. (1990). *The deaf child's theory of mind.* Unpublished manuscript, MRC Cognitive Development Unit, London.

Sergent, J. (1984). An investigation into component and configural processes underlying face recognition. *British Journal of Psychology, 75,* 221–242.

Shatz, M., Wellman, H., & Silber, S. (1983). The acquisition of mental verbs: A systematic investigation of the first reference to mental states. *Cognition, 14,* 301–321.

Sherrod, L. (1979). Social cognition in infants: Attention to the human face. *Infant Behaviour and Development, 2,* 279–294.

Shuttelworth, E., Syring, V., & Allen, N. (1982). Further observations on the nature of prosopagnosia. *Brain and Cognition, 1,* 307–322.

Sigman, M., Mundy, P., Ungerer, J., & Sherman, T. (1986). Social interactions of autistic, mentally retarded, and normal children and their caregivers. *Journal of Child Psychology and Psychiatry, 27,* 647–656.

Smith, M. (1978). Cognizing the behavioral stream: The recognition of intentional action. *Child Development, 49,* 736–748.

Sodian, B., & Frith, U. (1992). Deception and sabotage in autistic, retarded, and normal children. *Journal of Child Psychology and Psychiatry, 33,* 591–606.

Sorce, J., Emde, R., Campos, J., & Klinnert, M. (1985). Maternal emotional signaling: Its effect on the visual cliff behavior of 1-year-olds. *Developmental Psychology, 21,* 195–200.

Tan, J., & Harris, P. (1991). Autistic children understand seeing and wanting. *Development and Psychopathology, 3,* 163–174.

Tantam, D., Monaghan, L., Nicholson, H., & Stirling, J. (1989). Autistic children's ability to interpret faces: A research note. *Journal of Child Psychology and Psychiatry, 30,* 623–630.

Temple, C., & Vilarroya, O. (1990). Perceptual and cognitive perspective-taking in two siblings with callosal agenesis. *British Journal of Developmental Psychology, 8,* 3–8.

Tronick, E., Als, H., Adamson, L., Wise, S., & Brazelton, T. (1978). The infant's response to entrapment between contradictory messages in face-to-face interaction. *Journal of the American Academy of Child Psychiatry, 17,* 1–13.

Ungerer, J., & Sigman, M. (1981). Symbolic play and language comprehension in autistic children. *Journal of Abnormal Child Psychology, 9,* 149–165.

Volkmar, F. R., Sparrow, S., Rende, R. D., & Cohen, D. J. (1989). Facial perception in autism. *Journal of Child Psychology and Psychiatry, 30,* 591–598.

Wellman, H. (1990). *The child's theory of mind.* Cambridge, MA: MIT Press.

Whiten, A. (Ed.). (1991). *Natural theories of mind.* Oxford, England: Basil Blackwell.

Wilbrand, H. (1892). Ein Fall von Seelenblindheit und Heminaopie mit Sectionsbefund. *Deutscher Zeitschrift für Nervenkrantkheiten, 2,* 361–387.

Wimmer, H., & Perner, J. (1983). Beliefs about beliefs: Representation and constraining function of wrong beliefs in young children's understanding of deception. *Cognition, 13,* 103–128.

Wing, L. (1969). The handicaps of autistic children: A comparative study. *Journal of Child Psychology and Psychiatry, 10,* 1–40.

Young, A., & Ellis, H. (1989). Childhood prosopagnosia. *Brain and Cognition, 9,* 16–47.

CHAPTER 13

Causal Modeling: A Structural Approach to Developmental Psychopathology

JOHN MORTON and UTA FRITH

Nel mezzo del cammin di nostra vita mi ritrovai per una selva oscura che la diritta via era smarrita

DANTE: INFERNO, CANTO 1

Dante's poetic words very aptly express our position at the beginning of this chapter. We are lost in a dark wood in the middle of life where no straight paths exist. How can we find our way in the crisscrossing paths of developing abilities that forever seem to change direction? Like Dante, we have a vision of a distant hill. If we had a view *from* such a hill, we could discern the paths and draw a map.

In this chapter, we survey a few of the paths that others have already traced, and we show which directions might be fruitful, if followed. The problem we are addressing is the creation of a framework within which *different* views of developmental disorders can be modeled. We can clarify matters by introducing two major distinctions. First, we distinguish among various *levels of discourse*. Most commonly, when defining disorders or conditions, workers in developmental psychopathology have concerned themselves with the biological level and the behavioral level. People coming from a medical background have tended to stress the biological, and those coming from a psychological or psychodynamic background have tended to focus on the behavioral. The problem of relating these levels is great and, usually, there have been no more than gestures toward it. We have pointed out elsewhere (Frith, Morton, & Leslie, 1991) that an understanding of autism, at least, requires a third level between the biological and the behavioral. This third level we have called the cognitive level. We will rehearse the arguments and the scope of the terms in the next section.

The second general distinction we make is between *descriptive* models and *causal* models. Descriptive models are especially useful for the stable state, and description can be at any level—biological, cognitive, or behavioral, whichever is most appropriate for the current question. Indeed, it is sometimes argued that unless the current question is explicitly that of mapping between levels, descriptive models should always be at one level only (Mehler, Morton, & Jusczyk, 1984). When discussing development, descriptive models can sometimes be like snapshots of a moving scene. Causal models, on the other hand, have the principle of change over time built in, and will often require all levels to be represented. This is the case for autism, for example, where the very definition of the condition requires an intervening cognitive level between the biological and behavioral levels. The choice of levels here is an empirical issue rather than depending on what question is being asked. We would expect to find conditions where there is a direct link between the biological and behavioral levels without cognitive intervention. Tics in Tourette's syndrome are a possible example.

This chapter is concerned mainly with exploring and developing a framework within which *causal* models can be expressed. It is important to note that the framework of itself makes no empirical claims about any condition nor does it commit the user to any particular theory about anything. This feature makes the framework a neutral forum for the comparison of alternative or even contradictory theories. Our aim is that any coherent theory about developmental psychopathology—even one considered to be wrong—should be expressible within the framework. For example, the consequences of a claim about a single biological cause of a particular condition can be mapped out over different levels and compared against the consequences following from a claim about multiple biological causes of that condition. Empirical data can then be brought to bear on those points that emerge as critical, when the two competing theories are represented in a directly comparable fashion.

We are grateful to our colleagues at the MRC Cognitive Development Unit for extensive discussions on the topics of this chapter. Alison Gallagher, Francesca Happé, and Annette Karmiloff-Smith gave particular help and critical support. Erich Herrman prepared the figures. We wish to thank Martin Bellman, Dante Cicchetti, Chris Frith, Peter Hobson, Alan King, Brian Neville, Mike Rutter, Marion Sigman, Digby Tantam, and Guinevere Tufnell for their helpful comments on an earlier draft.

In almost all cases of developmental disorders, there is continuing controversy as to what constitutes the unique and universal features. These are usually contrasted with what are called associated features or secondary features. Diagnostic schemes generally strive toward defining disorders in terms of presumed primary features. Indeed, in some cases, the notion of primary features seems to have been constrained in terms of what could be defined within a particular diagnostic structure. We will see later that, when we want to explain rather than describe a condition, the so-called secondary features are as vital as the core features in constraining a theory.

In this chapter, we first review our approach to autism, the area for which the framework was first developed. While reviewing the development of our notation, we draw most of our examples from a particular causal theory for autism—a theory postulating a specific deficit at the cognitive level, with its origin at the biological level. It is important to note that we are not concerned with arguing the merits of one over other causal accounts of autism, although our preferences will certainly reveal themselves. Our own causal theory (Frith, Morton, & Leslie, 1991; Morton, 1989b) proposes a computational fault in a particular mechanism. We use the framework to show how it contrasts with others, but we do not review empirical work; such a review would only result in replicating information provided in other chapters of this volume.[1]

After establishing the framework, we explore its properties. In particular, we show how the notation reveals three distinct patterns of diagnostic practice. We work through a few examples of diagnostic categories of current interest and show how, in each case, a potentially useful definition of the category can be achieved. We then discuss some major problems in diagnosis, such as the variability of symptoms and the action of compensatory and protective factors. We present the concept of psychosocial pathways, along with the related technique of developmental contingency modeling. This is a modeling technique devised to enable us to represent the normal cognitive prerequisites of any particular behavior. Finally, we apply the framework to dyslexia in order to review the causal modeling approach.

A NOTE ON TERMINOLOGY

To start with, *levels* are not to be confused with *domains* (a term used to distinguish between, for example, cognitive and affective functions), which are placed at the same level in the present framework. The interactions among different domains, and especially the interactions of emotions and rational thinking, have been of concern to theorists in psychology from the time of Aristotle, in about 300 B.C., and these interactions would certainly be amenable to being represented inside the cognitive level.

We are also aware that our levels of discourse—*biological, cognitive,* and *behavioral*—could give rise to problems of definition. At any stage in development, the biological component includes extensive contributions from the environment. Any reference to the biological origins of a particular problem should, then, be taken to include the appropriate environmental and social factors. Johnson and Morton (1991) discussed this issue at some length.[2] Such considerations, as well as our need to refer to the genetic contributions to psychopathological disorders, rule out use of the term *neural* or *organic* in place of *biological.*

Cognitive has a variety of meanings. We will try to make clear the scope of the word as we intend it. On one hand, the term is contrastive with *biological* and *behavioral.* For example, when we use *cognitive,* we do not necessarily imply conscious constructions, although that is still the way the term is used in such environments as cognitive therapy, where "cognitions" are always conscious. The other problem for our use of the term comes from the contrast that has been made, since Kant, between *cognitive* and *affective.* We have already pointed out that this contrast involves domains, not levels.

In our framework, affects and cognitions occur at the same level, intervening between biology and behavior. Affects in other frameworks might well be defined simply at the biological level, as physiological responses. In this case, it would still be necessary to bring in a special process capable of interpreting these responses so that they could exert an influence over mental activities. This process would have to be placed within the cognitive level of discourse. In yet other frameworks, affects might be defined simply at the behavioral level, for instance, as facial expressions, voice modulations, body language, and so on. Again, these outward behavioral expressions of affect need to be related to internal processes that interpret feelings in the same way as in the former case. It seems that affects can be defined, described, and discussed at all three levels, but the cognitive level is the one that explains how affects can have meaning.

It should be clear from the above that we use the term *cognitive* in a general sense of referring to the functional description of the brain's activity. We know of no other term suitable for this purpose, except perhaps *psychological.* This term is confusing, however, because it is commonly used to refer to behavior as well as to cognitive activity. These two levels must be kept distinct from each other.

GROUND RULES OF CAUSAL MODELING

The rules of causal modeling of a developmental disorder are informally well established but rarely made explicit. We propose

[1] The preceding chapter by Baron-Cohen presents a detailed discussion of autism and of the particular cognitive deficit that we propose in order to account for this disorder. Here, we merely summarize the facts that are essential to the understanding of our general framework.

[2] While accepting that no clear partition can be made of the contribution of genetic factors, Johnson and Morton (1991) argued that it is still useful to make distinctions along a continuum. They proposed that the term *genetic* should be reserved for referring to the genome, and interactions of the genome with the internal environment should be termed *innate.* They then made a major distinction between the Species-Typical Environment and the Individual-Specific Environment. Where development is facilitated through interaction with nonspecific aspects of the Species-Typical Environment, they proposed the term *primal.*

here a short but expandable list of the most important maxims, which we shall illustrate later with examples. The maxims are:

1. *Start with biology.* Let the causal chain start with the biological origins.[3]
2. *Build causal chains.* The causal chain should be specified, or at least sketched, from the origin to behavior.
3. *Give full account.* All signs and symptoms of the disorder must be accounted for.[4]
4. *Specific over general.* A distinction between specific and general conditions must be made.[5] Features that can be accounted for as part of a general condition need not be accounted for within the causal theory for the specific condition.
5. *Correlation is not causation.* Do not confuse correlation with cause.

Violation of all these rules for causal modeling has been common in the history of autism.

Maxim 1: Start with Biology

The biological origin of autism has often been ignored. Some time ago, in the absence of evidence, this was understandable. Autism manifested itself most obviously in terms of social isolation, and it was easy for people to believe that social problems must have a social cause. Purely nonbiological psychosocial causes of autism can no longer be invoked. The evidence for a genetic origin, for example, is accumulating rapidly (Bolton & Rutter, 1990).

Unfortunately, belief in a psychosocial origin of autism still lingers on, much to the detriment of autistic people and their families. They suffer unnecessarily from self-blame and often follow punishing and entirely unproven regimes assumed to reverse or ameliorate supposedly disastrous interpersonal relationships.

Focus on the behavioral level alone has, for a while, been the hallmark of intervention programs. This has led to practical benefits in many cases, because behavior modification has been a successful tool for the management of "difficult" children in general. On the negative side, such programs have also allowed unrealistic hopes about restoration of normality.

It is not advised to start with the behavioral level and work backward. The same behavior can be shown for different reasons. Autistic children who are emotionally aloof may, on the surface, look like children who avoid social contact because of extreme shyness. Children who superficially show fluent reading may be severe dyslexics with excellent compensatory skills.[6] We would expect to reveal the compensation by use of suitable tests (such as dual tasks) and measures (such as reading time rather than errors).

Maxim 2: Build Causal Chains

A claim such as the following is unhelpful: Limbic system abnormality causes social impairment. Even if the statement were true, in that it pinpointed correctly a critical brain structure, we would still have an insufficient account of social impairment. A single causal statement is not the same as a causal model. We need plausible links in the causal chain from origin to signs and symptoms.

Maxim 3: Give Full Account

A number of early cognitive explanations of autism suffered from a problem that could be caricatured as ring-around-a-rosy. When the job is to explain all the symptoms, it is hazardous to choose one of them as the most important, suggest an underlying process fault for this single symptom, and ignore the other symptoms or assume that they derive from the same underlying psychological dysfunction. The remaining symptoms are in as much need of causal explanation as the supposed primary ones. It is tempting to relegate all problems not accounted for in the primary explanation to the position of secondary consequences. For example, in a social deficit account of autism, the social deficit would be assumed to result in poor learning of language; conversely, in a language-based account of the disorder, the language deficit would be assumed to result in poor social relations.

Maxim 4: Specific over General

Mental retardation is an example of a general deficit that, to varying degrees, is present in a large proportion (often estimated at around 75%) of autistic individuals. Fombonne and du Mazaubrun (1992), in a study of the prevalence of autism in four French regions, found that more than 66% of the autistic group were severely or profoundly retarded. Only 13% showed no intellectual retardation. Mental retardation affects almost all cognitive functions and is manifest in a very wide range of behavior. It implies brain abnormalities of the type that would affect the basic efficiency of biological and of cognitive information processing.

[3] The precise biological origins of developmental disorders are very rarely known. This does not mean, however, that we should ignore biology. This is true even where we might want to explicitly rule out any biological component explicitly.

[4] For our causal model, the quality of the information on these matters is of vital importance. We try to use the most up-to-date epidemiologically based evidence, as well as clinical practice as laid down in DSM-III, DSM-III-R, and DSM-IV (American Psychiatric Association, 1980, 1987, 1994) and ICD-10 (WHO, Geneva, 1992), but we must leave open the possibility that received wisdom as to the symptomatology will be overturned by new research.

[5] The developmental disorders we are concerned with here are all specific disorders; that is, there is a particular deficit (identifiable at some level—biological, cognitive, or behavioral) that has particular consequences for development and that may occur in a pure form (with all other psychological functions intact). The pure form may be rare; more often, there are associated problems of a variable kind. If the original damage was large, then many functions are affected and this may lead to general deficits. Specific deficits have to be demonstrated over and above general deficits.

[6] Different underlying representations can give rise to the same behavior by the same individual at different developmental stages (Karmiloff-Smith, 1984). This is to be distinguished from the observation of the same behavior shown by different individuals on different developmental paths.

The effect of such damage on development is grave. Delays and capacity limitations in many cognitive areas are common in autism. These have to be taken into account separately from specific deficits. After controlling for developmental level (MA), degree of mental retardation (IQ), and chronological age (CA), many supposedly typical symptoms were found to be neither unique nor universal to autism (Hermelin & O'Connor, 1970). They can be attributed to the general condition of mental retardation, and therefore should not be accounted for in the theory of the specific condition of autism.

Maxim 5: Correlation Is Not Causation!

We have included this maxim partly as a reminder to ourselves, because the temptation to interpret correlation as causation is ever present. Examples of using correlational evidence as causal proof abound in all areas of psychology. It would be a violation of the previous maxim to single out autism researchers for specific blame.

A CAUSAL ACCOUNT OF AUTISM

The Biological Origin of Autism

It has now been generally accepted that there must be a biological origin to autism (see chapters in Gillberg, 1989, and in Schopler & Mesibov, 1987). There are several reasons for this acceptance. First, it is known that people with autism have a greatly increased chance of having diverse medical conditions as background factors. Second, the majority of autistic individuals show direct signs of brain dysfunction. This shows through MRI scans, cerebral spinal fluid investigations, brain stem auditory potentials, presence of epilepsy, and many other factors (Gillberg, 1992; Steffenburg, 1991). Third, there are indirect indications of brain damage in that autism is strongly associated with mental retardation. As one includes progressively more retarded samples of children, the likelihood of autism increases (Smalley, Asarnow, & Spence, 1988; Wing & Gould, 1979). One simple model for this pattern is that a specific brain system is necessary for normal development, disturbance of which leads to autism. Brain damage that results in general intellectual retardation could be seen as caused by randomly distributed lesions. The more the damage, the higher the probability that the critical brain system will be affected.

Even in high-functioning autistic people, in whom we can assume that the general level of damage is low, MRI techniques have revealed abnormalities in the cerebellar vermis (Courchesne, Yeung-Courchesne, Press, Hesselink, & Jernigan, 1988). Autopsy studies have suggested neuronal disruption in a number of brain areas, particularly in the limbic system (Bauman & Kemper, 1985), and recent reviews of the literature conclude that there is cortical as well as subcortical involvement (Dawson & Lewy, 1989a). However, such studies have not yet separated causal and correlative relationships between these various kinds of brain damage and autism. Given the range of possible brain damage in autistics, we cannot be sure which particular kind of damage is actually responsible for the autism.

The damage that causes the autism also has a cause. The latter causal factor could give rise to other damage that is unrelated to the autism. In Figure 13.1, the flat, unfilled arrow is the symbol we have chosen to represent the causal relationship. A horizontal line is used to separate levels. A hypothesized single origin, O, could be a particular genetic condition, for example, that gives rise to two consequences in the brain during the course of development. We have called these br_1 and br_2. We have supposed that br_1 is solely responsible for the cluster of behavioral signs S_1 to S_3, which, in our special case, are the main diagnostic criteria for autism. However, in this not implausible scenario, the kind of damage we have termed br_2 will always be found, but will, by the terms of the scenario, have no causal role in the autism. This, then, illustrates the difference between correlation (br_2) and cause (br_1). It is possible, for example, that the cerebellar damage found in many autistic people has no causal effect on the defining symptoms of autism. The symbol S is used for signs and symptoms at the behavioral level. We have indicated subcategories S_1 to S_3 without specifying them. They would be easily formed, for instance, by using the distinction between positive and negative signs, or between signs and symptoms. Signs are the objectively observable behaviors. They are positive if they are abnormal by their presence and negative if they are abnormal by their absence. Symptoms we only know about through the patient's self-report or through indirect inference. For instance, if one saw a person talking and listening intently when no one is there, one might infer that the person hears "voices."

We have mentioned a variety of kinds of brain damage that have been associated with autism. These correspond to kinds of damage found at the end of an early occurring developmental process and are thought to persist throughout life. The adult autistic brain is just as good a source for data about these abnormalities as that of the child. However, the cause of the damage is located in the developmental history of the autistic individual. As to such biological origins of autism, genetic factors have recently received particularly strong confirmation (Rutter et al., 1990). The results from both twin and family studies suggest that the genetic causes account for more than 80% of the phenotypic variance and are themselves likely to be heterogeneous (Szatmari & Jones, 1991). Genetic factors may well be the major cause of the majority of

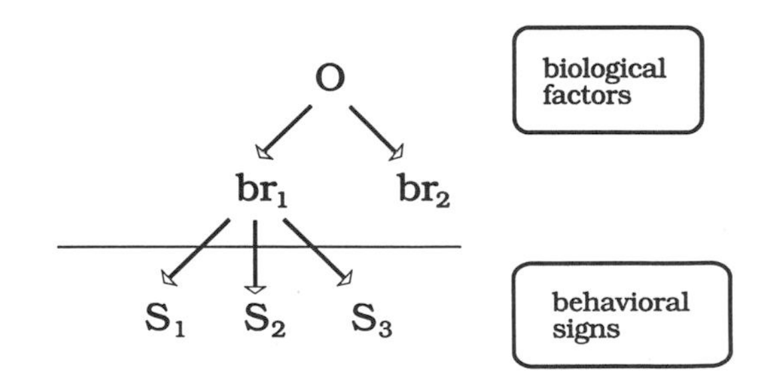

Figure 13.1 A hypothetical relationship between biological origin and autistic signs. S_n refers to signs and symptoms; br_n refers to conditions in the brain. The origin has two consequences in the brain, called br_1 and br_2. The former is responsible for the autism syndrome, and the latter gives rise to correlated disorders.

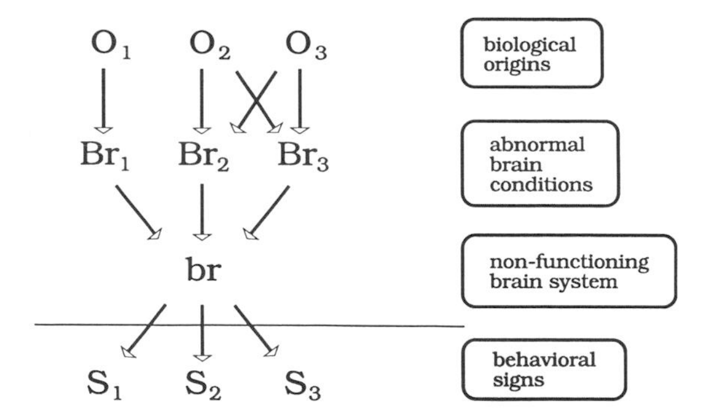

Figure 13.2 A hypothetical summary statement representing the theory that autism is always caused by a particular nonfunctioning brain system, which could be caused by any one of a number of possible origins.

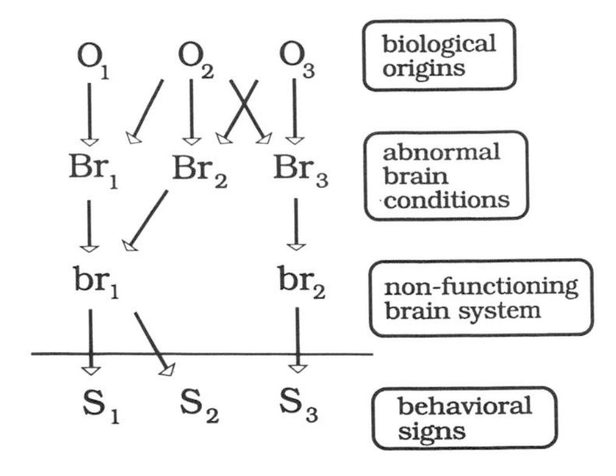

Figure 13.3 A representation of the hypothesis that two brain systems are involved in autism rather than the single one represented in Figure 13.2.

autistic disorders, but other causal factors, such as viral disease, are still being considered as additional, independent causes (Nunn, Lask, & Cohen, 1986; Tsai, 1989).

At the biological level, then, a variety of prime causes is possible. The effect of these is always autism, and, therefore, we suppose they will all eventually be shown to affect the same brain system in some way. By brain system we mean that part of the brain that performs a particular identifiable function. The possible causal effects include destruction of the system, disconnection, or malfunction. In the absence of more precise information, we can still discuss the available biological evidence in terms of a causal analysis.

In Figure 13.2, we represent the material we have just summarized. The items at the top level, O_1 to O_3, represent the postulated biological origins—genetic and other factors. This portion of the diagram represents a summary statement, ideally across the full range of the disorder; for any one child, only one of the biological origins will usually apply. From these origins come a variety of abnormal conditions over the course of development, in a way as yet to be established. Such nonspecific brain conditions we have symbolized as Br_n.[7] Having identified the place in the model for the autism-critical brain condition, we can go a step further. The kinds of general brain abnormality (Br_n) required for a causal account will be those that affect a common system, here called br. Damage to the specific system br or interruption of the functioning of system br causes autism. In Figure 13.2, then, we have added another link to the causal chain on the biological level. Note that we could do this even though very little is as yet known about the anatomical and physiological, let alone the molecular biological facts. Having added the link, we immediately see an interesting consequence: it may turn out that two or even more identifiable cortical systems are responsible for the autistic behavioral complex.

We have illustrated this possibility in Figure 13.3, where we propose two biological systems, br_1 and br_2, responsible for different aspects of the behavioral manifestations of autism. This exercise illustrates what it means to say that different symptoms, even though they co-occur, are not necessarily traceable to the same underlying fault.

How would we know when this was the case? We would see occasional dissociations between otherwise related behaviors. An example will be considered in Figure 13.5, in the next section.

We have claimed elsewhere that the causal chain between candidate biological factors and the resulting behavioral impairment requires an intervening *cognitive* level (Frith et al., 1991). The final form of our diagram, then, must include the cognitive level, and, within it, a number of further links in the causal chain. The general form of this causal model is shown in Figure 13.4. For purposes of simplified exposition, we show just a single link in the cognitive level and with the biological level. The hollow, struck-out C symbolizes a cognitive system that is found in normal development but is missing in autism, the abnormal developmental path being described.

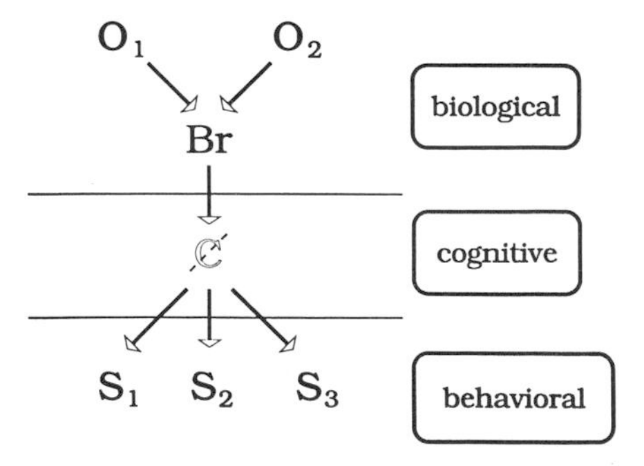

Figure 13.4 Introduction of a cognitive level between the biological and behavioral levels. The general hypothesis expressed is that autism can be seen as a cognitive deficit with a biological origin. The hollow, struck-out C indicates that a particular cognitive function, which is present in all normal children, is absent in autistics by virtue of the brain condition Br, which, in turn, could be caused by one of two different origins, genetic or nongenetic.

[7] We use Br to refer to general conditions and br to refer to specific conditions.

All the primary elements of the causal model are now in place. We may have given the impression, in the preceding paragraphs, that outcome in the causal model is determined. As a matter of empirical fact, all outcomes of developmental abnormalities appear to be probabilistic, and the causal diagrams for conditions as a whole should be interpreted in this way.

The Behavioral Picture

The history of autism has been fraught with problems of diagnosis. For any causal account of a condition, it is vital to be able to agree on what one wishes to account for. "Is there such a thing as autism?" is a question that continues to be asked when there is uncertainty about the behavioral as well as the biological level of description. "Every autistic child is different" is a frequent cry from bewildered caregivers. And yet, over the past 50 years, the consensus about autism as a clinical entity with special needs and a predictable course has grown steadily.

Where do we start? Despite continuing controversy about the precise diagnostic criteria,[8] there is agreement that there are different variants of autism. A matter for debate is whether the variants are to be described merely in terms of degree of severity (i.e., "spectrum") or in terms of qualitative differences. From the point of view of this chapter, the outcome of this debate would only result in variation in the detail of the causal model. For simplicity, let us take the concept of the *autistic spectrum.* Disorders of this spectrum have in common three core features (Wing, 1988):

1. *Impairment in socialization*—specific impairment in the quality of reciprocal interactions, ranging from aloof to passive to odd.
2. *Impairment in communication*—delay in language acquisition and poor use of verbal and nonverbal means of communication.
3. *Impairment in imagination*—lack of understanding make-believe.[9]

These three features were first found as a triad of impairments in the course of epidemiological research (Wing & Gould, 1979). They were discovered to form a syndrome, that is, to be closely associated in the same individual and to manifest themselves in a variety of behaviors according to age and ability. Although the triad was found in children with classic autism it was also present in children who had not been so diagnosed. Furthermore, it was found not only in children who suffered at the same time from general intellectual retardation but also, occasionally, in those of average intelligence.

Even if there were no argument about the definition of the core features of autism, there are usually many more problems to be considered in each individual autistic child, in addition to any core features. We frequently find specific language impairments, motor coordination problems, and general learning disability. Other features often seen in autism may include anxiety and bewilderment as well as slow learning and lack of generalization. Impairments in attention, memory, and perception have also been described in children within the spectrum of autistic disorders (Gillberg, 1992). The range of signs and symptoms is indeed great, and the problem of accounting for all of them is still wide open.

The Role of Cognition in Defining Autism

According to our maxims, a causal analysis of autism will have to account for all of the *core* features (maxim 3) and all of what have been called the *associated* features. Specific accounts, however, are only developed if general accounts do not suffice (maxim 4). Thus, we do not have to account for mental retardation and its consequences in the same way that we account for the triad of impairments and its consequences. That is to say, although any account of the biological origins of autism must also explain the accompanying mental retardation, it is not appropriate to attempt a single cognitive account of the two. We explore this concept in Figure 13.5, where we show two specific consequences, br_1 and br_2, of one and the same general damage, Br. They have different consequences at the cognitive level: C_1 leads to impaired intellectual function and C_2 leads to the criterial signs of autism. In any child who suffers from this general type of brain damage, we will always find autism in conjunction with severe mental retardation.

According to maxim 3, the analysis must also allow for the principled explanation of all the features, including secondary ones. It is often a matter of controversy as to what constitute primary and secondary features. As an example, let us take anxiety, a frequent symptom in autism. People who regard the anxiety as primary see it as springing directly from a malfunction of the arousal mechanism, which, in turn, is seen as directly caused by the biological conditions underlying the disorder. Others see the anxiety as a secondary and not a primary feature.

---

[8] DSM-III (American Psychiatric Association, 1980, pp. 87–90) gave the following criteria for Infantile Autism:

- Pervasive lack of responsiveness to other people;
- Gross deficits in language development;
- Peculiar speech patterns;
- Bizarre responses to various aspects of the environment, e.g., resistance to change, peculiar interest in or attachments to animate or inanimate objects.

DSM-III-R (American Psychiatric Association, 1987, pp. 38–39) specified the following criteria for Autistic Disorder:

- Qualitative impairment in social interaction;
- Qualitative impairment in verbal and nonverbal communication, and in imaginative activity;
- Markedly restricted repertoire of activities and interests.

DSM-IV (American Psychiatric Association, 1994, pp. 70–71) requires:

- Qualitative impairment in social interaction;
- Qualitative impairment in communication;
- Restricted repetitive and stereotyped patterns of behavior, interests, and activities.

[9] The phrasing of this particular impairment in Wing and Gould's (1979) epidemiological study was "repetitive activities in place of imaginative symbolic interests" (p. 26).

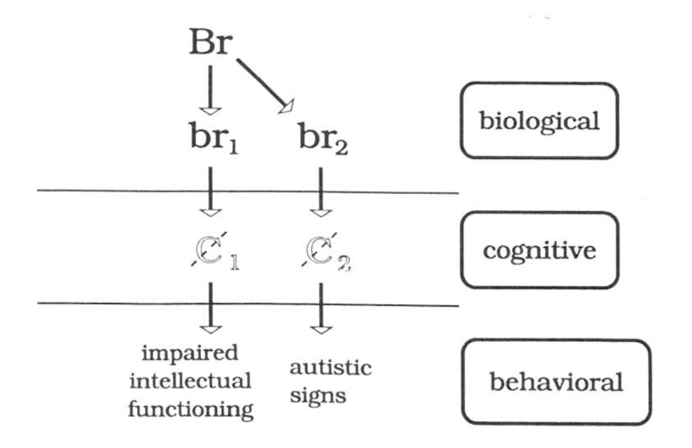

Figure 13.5 The frequent association of intellectual retardation with autism can be explained as resulting from a single brain condition, Br, with two separate consequences, br_1 and br_2.

Thus they would derive it as a result of the autistic child's incomprehension of features of the environment. In other words, they believe that autistic anxiety is a normal (and possibly functional) response.

One particular claim that we wish to make is that pathological features involving a component of the environment in their causal chain will always be secondary and not core features. (This is explored later, in the context of Figure 13.10.) Such subchains could be broken by appropriate manipulation of the environment at the appropriate time.

We also need to allow for the components that are identified with the large individual differences in the clinical picture of autistic people. These include, in particular, processes of *compensation,* and changes over time, attributable either to internal factors such as maturation or to external factors such as teaching.

From our brief review (above) of current work on the biology of autism, we concluded that autism has no single biological origin. Nevertheless, autism, or rather the developmental disorder underlying the spectrum of autistic features, continues to be seen as a single diagnostic category. If there is no single origin nor any single kind of damage that can be used as criterial, what, then, justifies the application of a single label?

The triad of impairments and the already envisaged spectrum that encompasses different degrees of autism seem, at first glance, to provide justification enough. However, the triad, or any similarly defined behavioral phenotype, is only a collection of symptoms that happen to co-occur with sufficient regularity to convince us that this co-occurrence is meaningful and has implications at other levels. Therefore, although the term *behavioral phenotype* has descriptive value, it has no explanatory value.

As we have already pointed out, the common constellation of signs and symptoms points to an underlying single cognitive deficit (Rutter, 1983). Clinical experience and the history of autism itself suggest that there is such a diagnostic entity and that it is much more than a chance constellation. Despite proven heterogeneity at the biological and behavioral levels, we assume that it is possible to justify a single label in a causal account and propose that what all autistic people have in common is a single *cognitive* deficit. This deficit gives rise to the core symptoms in the course of development.

To define the specific deficit that underlies the triad of impairments, we have to draw attention to a particular aspect of normal development that has been explored only recently (Astington, Harris, & Olson, 1988; Butterworth, Harris, Leslie, & Wellman, 1991; Whiten, 1991): the development of theory of mind (Premack & Woodruff, 1978), or "mentalizing"—our ability to predict and explain the behavior of other humans in terms of their mental states. Our ability to mentalize is revealed in our use and understanding of such words as *believe, know, wish, desire, intend,* and *pretend,* which are acquired remarkably early (Wellman, 1990). A central feature of our proposal is that autistic children lack this ability (Baron-Cohen, Leslie, & Frith, 1985; Leslie, 1987).

The term *theory* in the phrase *theory of mind* can lead to certain misunderstandings of our position. In particular, it can lead to a belief that we are talking about conscious constructions concerning not only other individuals, but also other minds in general. This is most certainly *not* what we—or, indeed, Premack and Woodruff (1978), who coined the term—intend to imply. Human beings do develop explicit theories concerning other minds, and autistic people are notably deficient in such development; however, this is not the difference we consider basic. The ability we are talking about, mentalizing, is primarily unconscious or implicit. It is a property of our cognitive apparatus that comes into action when triggered by particular stimuli, and it "makes sense" of other people's and our own behavior fully automatically.

What Is Mentalizing?

The hypothesis is that the ability to mentalize is dependent on a primal[10] mechanism and cannot be explained by learning. The ability manifests itself gradually in behavior over the first 5 years. By age 1, infants already internally represent many physical states of the world; that is, they can remember and manipulate in their heads what they perceive in the world. These are first-order representations.[11] From some time in their second year (or arguably, even earlier), children have at their disposal second-order representations and can represent mental states as well as physical states (Leslie, 1987).

What is the difference between first- and second-order[12] representations? We know that <*ducks are fowl*> and can represent that idea in memory as a first-order representation. At the same time, we can represent the idea <*ducks are fish*>, as long as we ascribe it to someone else, in a form such as "Some monks believed

[10] *Primal* is defined by Johnson and Morton (1991) as the interaction of the genotype with the internal environment and the nonspecific component of the Species-Typical Environment (see note 2).

[11] Note that when we talk about representations, we mean *mental* representations, not pictures.

[12] We use "first- and second-order representation" because these two terms make a clear and unambiguous contrast. In other places, Leslie has used "meta-representations" when referring to what we have called second-order. Unfortunately, there are other meanings of "meta-representation," and the theory of mind literature has become very confused through lack of distinction among the various senses of this term. In response to this confusion, Leslie (Leslie & Thaiss, 1992) has started to use "M-representation" in this context.

that <ducks are fish>." Second-order representations—in this case, the representation of someone's belief—can be used to predict people's behavior. For instance, monks could eat ducks on Fridays if they believed them to be fish. In this way, we can establish relationships between external states of affairs and internal states of mind.

We postulated that the cognitive cause of autism is damage to a particular part of the mentalizing mechanism, termed EXPRAIS.[13] This theory enabled us to explain difficulties with pretend and, more importantly, to predict special problems with other mental state computations. The first test of our theory was as follows: Will autistic children, taking into account CA and MA, have special problems with understanding a false belief about something, as opposed to understanding a real state of affairs? This was confirmed by the Sally-Anne experiment (Baron-Cohen et al., 1985).[14]

The Sally-Anne task tested whether the child would know that Sally will look for her toy in the place she hid it, in spite of the child's knowing that the toy has been moved elsewhere. If so, then the child can represent Sally's false belief as well as the true state of things. Normal children have no problems with this sort of task from about 4 years of age. Down syndrome children with a mental age of 5 or 6 can also answer correctly. However, of a group of 20 autistic children, with a mean mental age of 9 years, 16 failed the task in spite of being able to answer correctly a variety of questions of fact about what happened. They knew where Sally had put the toy, and they knew that Anne had moved it and that Sally had not seen the move. Their problem did not lie in perception, in memory, or in language. The autistic children just could not conceptualize the possibility that Sally believed something that was not true.

We believe that the mentalizing deficit goes some way toward explaining the three core features in the autistic spectrum. It does not explain certain other criterial features of autism, such as "restricted, repetitive, and stereotyped patterns of behavior, interests and activities" (DSM-IV, American Psychiatric Association, 1994; also in ICD-10, World Health Organization, 1992). It may well be that the autism spectrum demands explanation in terms of more than one cognitive deficit. Some symptoms whose precise status as part of the behavioral phenotype is as yet unclear, notably those associated with repetitive actions, special skills, and so-called frontal signs, may need additional explanation. These would also be mediated through the cognitive level but could require a second component at the biological level, as in Figure 13.3.

Changes over Time

In all studies reported so far, there is a minority of autistic children who perform mentalizing tasks correctly. We ourselves have now tested over 50 able autistic children on the false belief and related tasks. So far, we have found that, for autistic children to succeed on a mentalizing task, they have to have a much higher chronological and mental age than is the case in normal development. On the whole, those autistic subjects who pass theory of mind tasks are teenagers with a mental age in excess of 8 years (Frith et al., 1991). Could the successful autistic children have acquired some mentalizing ability after all? If so, how? We consider two possibilities under the headings of *compensation* and *residual deficits*.

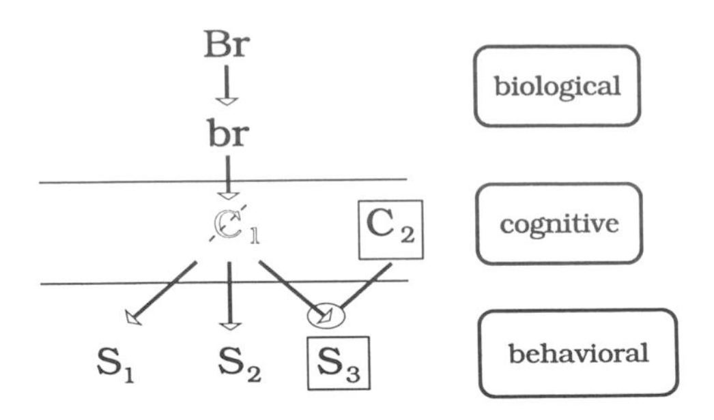

Figure 13.6 Compensation in a causal model. This diagram is intended to indicate that whereas S_3 is normally the consequence of the absence of C_1, this sign is attenuated in the presence of another cognitive factor, C_2. This outcome is more easily thought of in positive terms. If we think of S_3 as the absence of a particular piece of behavior which is normally mediated by C_1, this piece of behavior is now mediated by C_2 instead.

In Figure 13.6, we use a special symbol to represent compensation in the causal model. We have the usual range of behavioral signs, S_1–S_3, arising from the cognitive deficit, the hollow, struck-out C_1. The behavior S_3 would occur in a set of conditions that the autistic child cannot understand or respond to as a normal child would. The supposition is that the individual develops knowledge or skill in response to these environmental conditions in order to cope with the problem. We symbolize such knowledge or skill with C_2, and show a connection from C_2 to S_3 with an elliptical surround to the $C_1 \rightarrow S_3$ causal arrow. This indicates that C_2 provides a compensation for the missing or dysfunctional C_1 in respect of S_3.

Next, we will consider residual deficits. This possibility would assume that all individuals in the autistic spectrum initially share the same underlying deficit but that, for some, mentalizing ability eventually develops because the innate mechanism matured late. Normally, children structure their experience of others, from a very early age, taking into account mental states. A child who spends extra years without the benefit of this ability will have established habit patterns and interpretive frameworks whose influence will be difficult to eradicate.[15] Another example, from the area of vision, is that a squint uncorrected in a young child means that the individual lacks stereopsis. Correction of the squint in adulthood does not correct the residual deficit.

[13] EXPRAIS is short for "expression raiser." This, in Leslie's 1987 paper, is the single most crucial computational process in forming representations of other people's beliefs, desires, and intentions.

[14] A number of experimenters have now carried out similar studies worldwide, confirming that autistic children have a specific impairment with beliefs. (See Happé & Frith, in press, for a recent review.)

[15] The converse explanation would apply in schizophrenia, where the already established good habit patterns serve to sustain the patients' understanding of mental states, even though the critical mechanism has ceased to function (C. Frith, 1992).

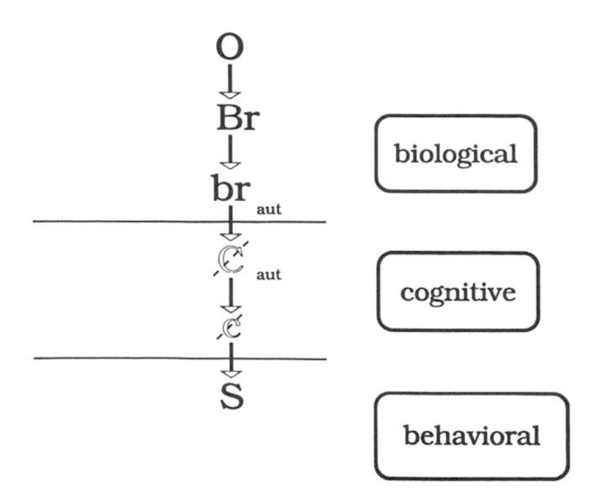

Figure 13.7 The essential components of a causal model for autism.

Competing Causal Accounts of Autism

We are concerned with providing a notation that enables alternative accounts of the cause of developmental disorders to be satisfactorily represented. As we have seen, such a notation requires, at least, that biological, cognitive, and behavioral levels be represented. Most of the current competing accounts have the same general structure as the ones already discussed. However, as we shall see, the formalism of the present framework helps to focus on the crucial differences between these accounts.[16]

Nearly all researchers now agree that a biological disorder is at the root of autism. Reducing the causal model down to its essence, we arrive at Figure 13.7, which indicates that there is some origin, O, of the condition with one of a set of possible biological consequences, Br. This has a specific effect, br_{aut}, affecting a particular brain system, which underlies the cognitive function C_{aut}.[17] Damage to C_{aut} affects the development of the set of cognitive functions, c, which, in turn, leads to a variety of signs and symptoms, S. The only theories that do not subscribe to this general account—the pure psychoanalytic account and the ethological account (Tinbergen & Tinbergen, 1983)—require the causal diagram to represent the role of agents outside the child. We have done this in Figure 13.8, where the dotted vertical line divides internal from external effects. The external circumstance—let us suppose for the moment that these are family circumstances, P—are seen as affecting the cognitive function, C_{aut}. The role of genetic factors in this case would need specification. The logic of the formalism allows one possibility: that both factors, damage to br_{aut} and external factor P, are required for autism to occur. To indicate this conjunction, we have used the symbol &. Whenever this symbol is used it is to be understood as saying that both causal factors have to be present for the effect to occur. If only one of the two factors is present, then the condition will not arise. The theory expressed in Figure 13.8 would next be

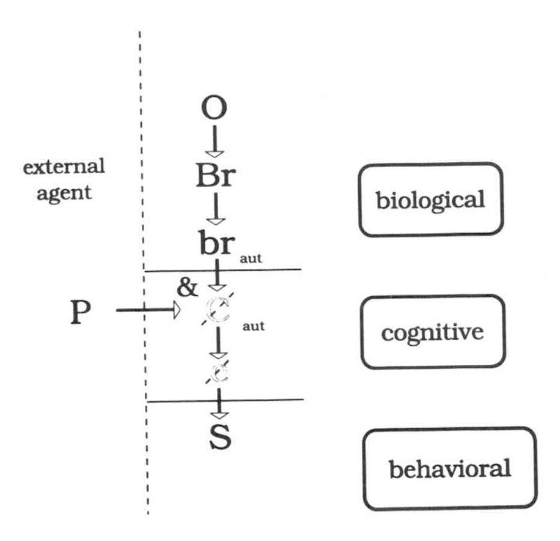

Figure 13.8 A theory of autism where family circumstances, P, interact with biological factors. The dotted vertical line divides internal from external effects.

obliged to specify, or at least to indicate, the nature of C_{aut} such that there is (or, at least, that it is plausible that there might be) a brain state that maps onto it. Such a constraint would, for example, rule out knowledge states (such as a belief or a feeling about mother) as candidates for C_{aut}.

A more plausible scenario, perhaps, is shown in Figure 13.9. This diagram represents a scenario where the autistic child behaves in some way so as to provoke a particular kind of response in the caregivers. This, in turn, changes the child's cognitive states to create the autistic spectrum of behavior. In the abstract, then, the biologically based cognitive condition, C_{aut}, leads to behavior that disrupts parental bonding. The behavior is not indicated in the diagram because it is not (ex hypothese) a part of the autistic spectrum. However, the parental response, in turn, feeds back into the child to create a change at the cognitive level. This leads to behavior which, by virtue of being part of the autistic spectrum, has to be represented in the diagram.

Psychodynamic accounts emphasize the role of interpersonal factors as both cause and effect of conditions such as autism.

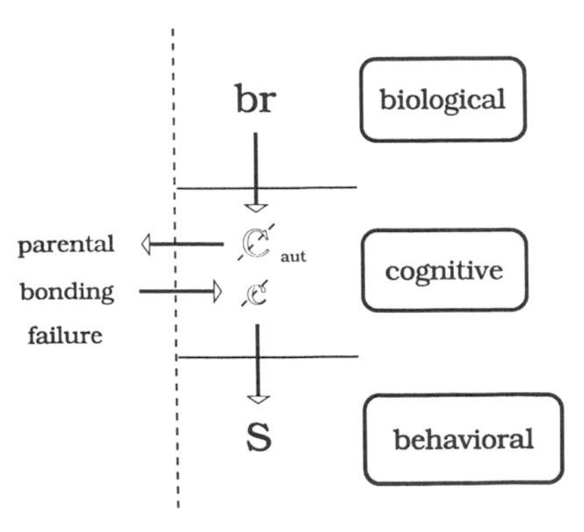

Figure 13.9 A hypothesis that autism is caused by a disruption of parental bonding.

---

[16] We will, in any case, only mention a few of the current accounts of autism. Furthermore, new versions are bound to be created in the future.

[17] We identify C_{aut} with the Expression Raiser—the function required to create second-order representations. Other theories will identify C_{aut} differently.

Interpersonal factors clearly exist, but their causal role is not clear. In our own account of autism, we would want to allow a place for secondary problems that were the reaction of the child to the parent's response to the manifestation of the child's basic disorder. In previous articles on this subject (Frith et al., 1991; Morton, 1989b), we have represented the social level as equivalent to the other three but causally related to the behavioral level only. This is not the only option. It is also possible to represent the social environment as interacting with the individual at any of the three levels. For instance, we can understand family variables, from psychiatric conditions to stress and deprivation, as affecting the cognitive level rather than the behavioral level; that is, behavioral change would take place by virtue of the cognitive change and not independently.

A different kind of possibility involving the environment would occur where one wished to postulate that some external event created a changed brain state. This is shown in Figure 13.10. The first parts of the biological chain represented in previous diagrams is missing from this figure because the claim in question would relate to a child without genetic or other developmental abnormality. An example would be the occasional report that a child developed normally until the age of 3 or so but then had a viral condition leading to brain damage, a rapid regression of language gains, and subsequent autistic symptoms.

Rogers and Pennington (1991) proposed that the root cognitive cause of autism is an inability to imitate. They pointed to "the potential power of an early deficit in imitation to disrupt other early developing interpersonal processes" (p. 137). While accepting that there is no evidence of any deficit in autistic children during the first year of life, Rogers and Pennington pointed to deficits in imitation skills in older autistic children. Note, however, that it is unlikely that early imitation skills are mediated by the same mechanisms as later skills (they differ in the intentional component, for example). In addition to deficits in imitation, Rogers and Pennington supposed that autistic infants also lack the ability of emotion sharing. These defects "would greatly affect the baby's ability to organise *social* information concerning other people by depriving the baby of primary sources of social data" (p. 147, original italics). These two deficient skills, together with the theory of mind deficit that emerges later, are viewed as "increasingly complex expressions of the ability to form and coordinate certain representations of self and of another and to use these representations to guide the planning and execution of one's own behavior" (p. 150). Such functions are, apparently, supposed to be mediated by biological circuits involving the prefrontal cortex and the limbic system.

The underlying deficit in this theory as currently expressed is "impaired formation/coordination of specific self-other representations." This is clearly a description of the outcome of a variety of information processing operations spread out over time. In this formulation, there is nothing corresponding to a deficit in any single function that could find its way into a cognitive model. The theory could not, then, be represented formally in the same way as our own theory, with a number of possible biological origins converging onto a single cognitive core, as in Figure 13.4. Rather, the core impairment seems to be at the biological level. Rogers and Pennington depicted their own model in the form shown in Figure 13.11. The triad of impairments, shown as part of a causal chain, are all being affected by the core impairment. We are inclined, then, to represent the Rogers and Pennington model inside our framework in the form shown in Figure 13.12.

This is a much more complex model than one in which deficit in imitation is the primary cognitive cause. The disadvantage of the latter formulation is that imitation in the older child is a complex cognitive skill and cannot be readily mapped onto a biological substrate. Thus, it would be necessary to specify the elements of this skill in such a way as to make the possibility of a biological mapping plausible. This is much the same kind of problem as would arise with our own model if the underlying deficit were seen simply as an inability to create a theory of mind. This complex, cognitive, conscious activity is clearly the result of a good deal of cognitive development and interaction with the environment, and not at all the kind of factor that one would want to introduce into a developmental theory. The mentalizing theory, however, reduces to a core computational ability—the ability needed to create second-order representations. This order of things could well correspond to a simple biological deficit that

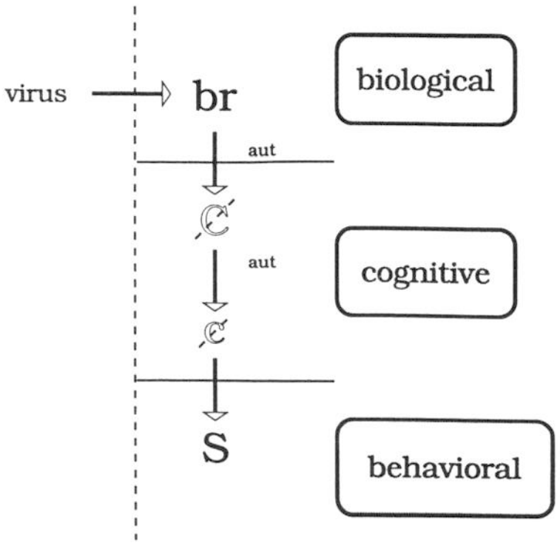

Figure 13.10 An example of an external influence operating at the biological level.

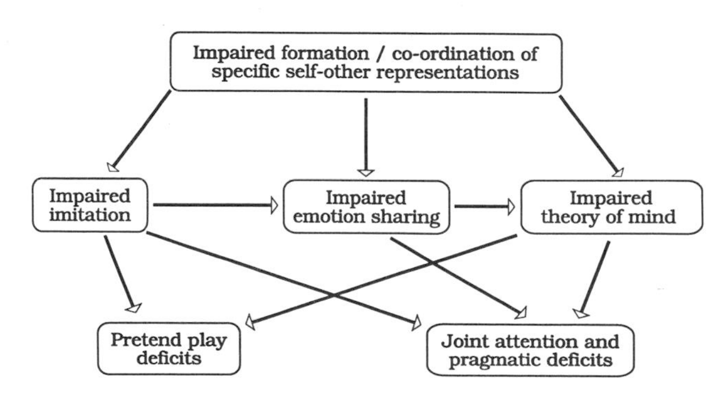

Figure 13.11 Adaptation of the Rogers and Pennington model. From "A Theoretical Approach to the Deficits in Infantile Autism" by S. J. Rogers and B. F. Pennington, 1991, *Developmental Psychopathology, 3,* p. 152. Copyright 1991 by Cambridge University Press. Adapted by permission.

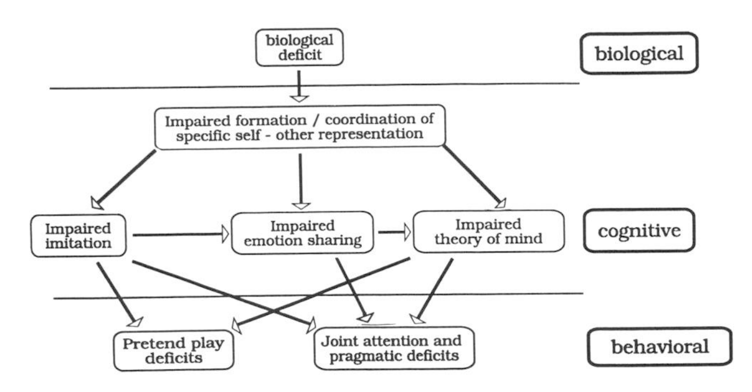

Figure 13.12 Our interpretation of the Rogers and Pennington model. Compare with the version in Figure 13.11.

might have no clearly visible signs over the first year of life (Johnson, Siddons, Frith, & Morton, 1992). If ability to imitate were to be fitted into a causal, developmental, multilevel representation, then it would require breaking down in a similar way.

A theoretical explanation that is close to our own and that postulates a cognitive deficit was proposed by Mundy, Sigman, and Kasari (1993). Predating Rogers and Pennington's approach, they postulated a seemingly simple and early appearing cognitive function as faulty, and focused on joint attention and the component of shared affect in this particular cognitive function. Now, it seems plausible to analyze deficits in joint attention as early manifestations of deficits of second-order representational skills (Mundy, Sigman, Ungerer, & Sherman, 1986). However, Mundy, Sigman, and Kasari (1993) rejected this "in the light of developmental data indicating that gestural joint attention skills emerge prior to meta-representational skills in normal development" (p. 126, n. 3). This represents a confusion between an underlying ability and the manifestation of that ability. Baron-Cohen et al. (1985) initially demonstrated the specific mentalizing deficit with a task that normal children could not do until they were around 4 years old. But that task also requires a number of other abilities, and it is those other abilities that are not developed until age 4. The underlying computational process, EXPRAIS, is supposed to be innate and will operate in other situations earlier. The Mundy and Sigman view (Mundy & Sigman, 1989; Mundy, Sigman, & Kasari, 1993) of our theory (e.g., Frith, 1989; Frith, Morton, & Leslie, 1991) is given in Figure 13.13, and the model

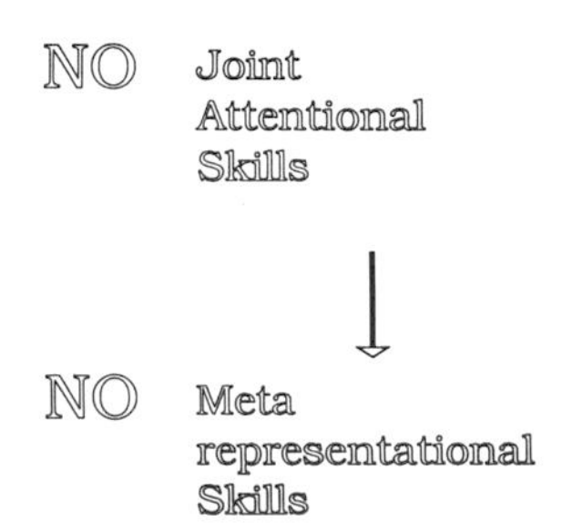

Figure 13.13 The Sigman and Mundy view of the Frith/Morton/Leslie theory of autism diagrammed using our notation.

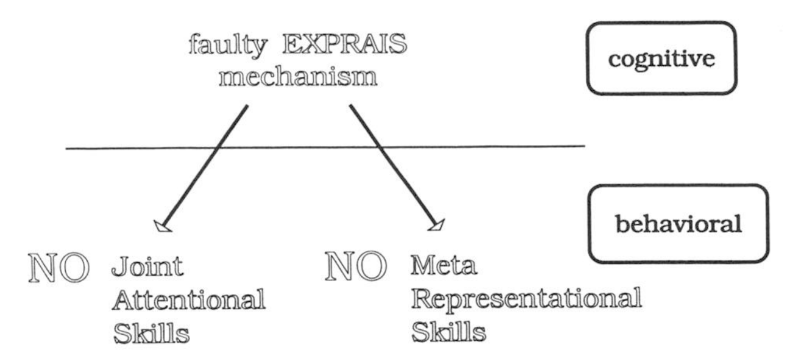

Figure 13.14 Our view of the Frith/Morton/Leslie theory of autism. Compare with Figure 13.13.

we actually support is shown in Figure 13.14. Let us reiterate that performance on tasks such as the Sally-Anne task is a manifestation of the core ability in interaction with a good deal of knowledge together with a variety of cognitive skills, including language. Within the theory we espouse, there is no early limit for the manifestation of mentalizing. We would, for example, be happy to include joint attention skills such as pointing (Baron-Cohen, 1991; Leslie & Happé, 1989), eye-gaze engagement, and teasing (Reddy, 1991), all of which occur within the first year.[18]

We turn now to the alternative proposed by Hobson (1989, 1990, 1993; Leslie & Frith, 1990). Hobson supposed that the primary deficit in autism is a disturbance of affective contact. He would accept that there is a biological origin to this problem—this much he has in common with us. He would also agree that it would be necessary to provide a causal chain from the affective disorder to the full range of autistic symptoms. The problem then arises as to how to represent the core affective disorder in the framework we have created.[19] The account by Dawson and Lewy (1989b) also emphasized the role of an impairment in very early socioemotional interaction.

At first glance, it might seem as though there is a clear contrast between Hobson's *affective* theory and our *cognitive* theory. But when we diagram Hobson's theory as a causal model, we can see that what Hobson calls the affective level has the same relationship to biological and behavioral levels as does what we call the cognitive level. That is, Hobson would not want to say that the affective problem he alludes to was either biological or behavioral. In terms of the contrast we have been using, Hobson's theory is of the same kind as all the other cognitive models.

This puts us into something of a representational dilemma. Hobson will also want to specify cognitive consequences of this affective, or, rather, interpersonal disorder, as well as its behavioral consequences. The affective and the cognitive are different domains but belong at the same level of description. The most convenient way to represent Hobson's theory, then, is as shown in Figure 13.15.

---

[18] See the previous chapter, by Baron-Cohen, for links between mentalizing and early eye-gaze detectors.

[19] Hobson suggests that there is "an interpersonal psychological system that is impaired as the final common pathway in autism" (personal communication, June 18, 1992).

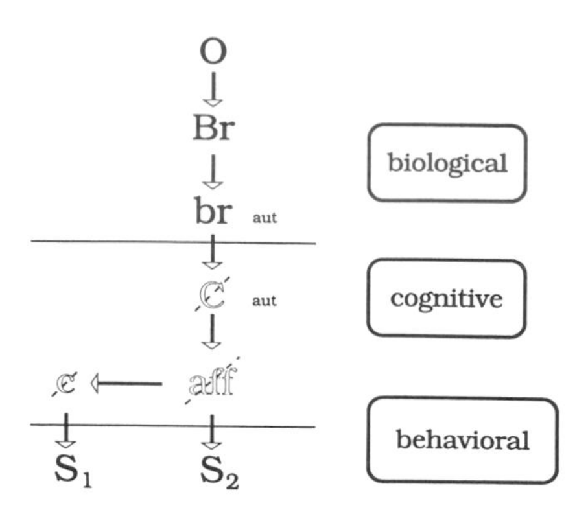

Figure 13.15 A simplified view of Hobson's theory of autism. The cognitive deficit, c, is seen as deriving from an affective disorder rather than being directly consequent on a biological deficit.

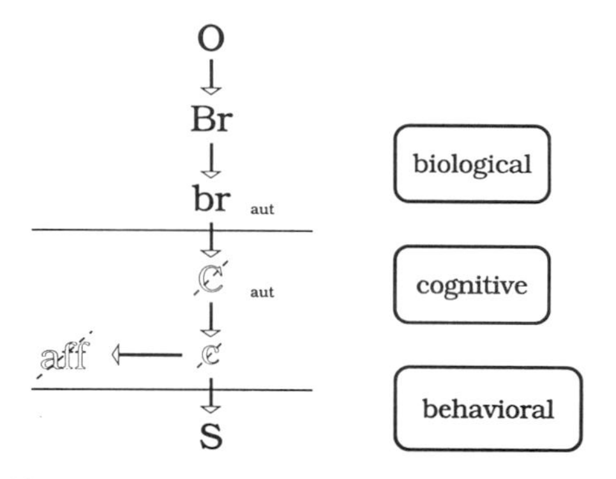

Figure 13.16 An affective disorder shown as a secondary consequence of a cognitive disorder.

In the expansion of our own theory, we would interpret the affective disorders as secondary consequences of the child's interaction with the environment. One way of doing this is shown in Figure 13.16, where the affective disorder, aff, is seen as a consequence of the cognitive disorder, c, at the same level.

PROBLEMS OF DIAGNOSTIC PRACTICE

Now that we have defined and explored the properties of the notation, we can begin to put it to use. First, we will consider the way pathological conditions are diagnosed. Conditions—that is, syndromes or disease entities—are, in practice, defined at all of the biological, cognitive, and behavioral levels. In many cases, the levels are mixed haphazardly and, in the case of the cognitive level, intuitive psychology often takes over from scientific concepts.

Basically, the definition of an entity can have a strong form or a weak form. The strong form corresponds to a singularity in the causal nexus. This would be revealed in our causal diagram by the existence of three types of causal model, resembling, respectively, the shapes of the letters A, X, and V (see Figure 13.17). Each of these letter shapes shows a convergence of paths at a single point: the top, the middle, and the bottom, respectively. These

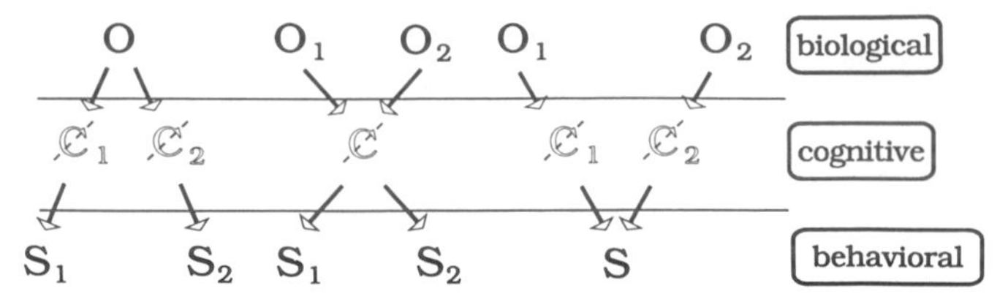

Figure 13.17 Idealized diagnostic types, resembling the letters A, X, and V.

three locations of "pinch-points" correspond to biological, cognitive, and behavioral levels. The convergence or pinching means that there is just one feature at that level or sublevel. In the weak forms of the three types, there would be two or more nodes at the pinch-point. In the illustrations that follow, we will restrict ourselves to the strong forms.

A typical example of a strong biologically defined syndrome would be a specific genetic defect, such as phenylketonuria (PKU). This would be an A-shape definition, a form of which is shown in Figure 13.18, where C_1 and C_2 represent the cognitive consequences of a single defect that is of genetic origin. In PKU, there appear to be global cognitive impairments as well as emotional disorder (Taylor, 1991). S, as usual, represents signs and symptoms, the behavioral manifestations.

Two aspects of Figure 13.18 need to be strongly marked. First, as we have already stressed, we do not intend the notation to imply that there is a deterministic relationship between origin at one end and signs and symptoms at the other. The notation is descriptive, not prescriptive, and causal theories of any degree of complexity can be represented to any required level of detail. Thus, one might want to represent the fact that the presence of the particular genetic defect characteristic of PKU is not sufficient for the full cognitive and behavioral expression of the disorder, but that certain other biological, environmental, or cognitive preconditions would be necessary as well. Thus, PKU children's difficulties depend strongly on how well the prescribed diet is kept to. To give a dramatic example of the amazing diversity following from a single major gene disorder, we could take neurofibromatosis. Manifestations in a single family may vary from a few skin blemishes, requiring an expert to note them, to grotesque multiple nerve tumors, causing gross deformity.

The second aspect is related to the first. The diagram could be seen either as the description of an individual or as the

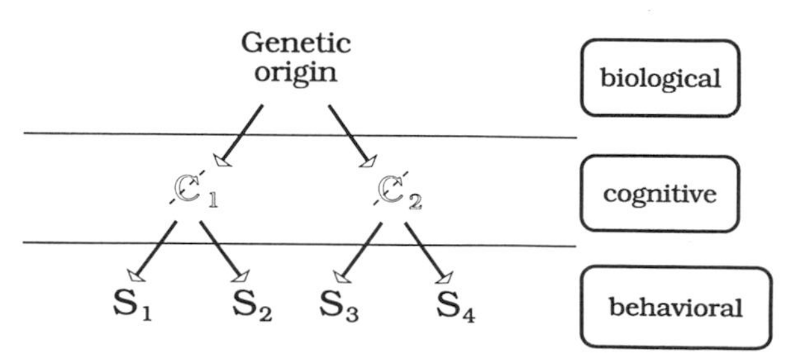

Figure 13.18 The archetypal A-type causal model.

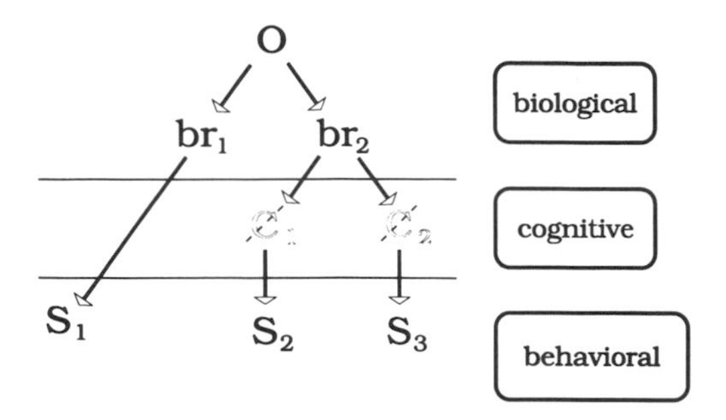

Figure 13.19 A variant on the A-type causal model.

description of a type. If we are describing an individual, then we enter only those elements that are germane for that individual, and we represent the specific determinants of the signs and symptoms for that individual. The causal links would then be seen as clinically real. On the other hand, we could use the diagram for the description of a type in order to answer the question: What is the range of clinical picture possible for PKU? For this kind of question, the causal connections should be seen as probabilistic rather than deterministic.

Note that a number of variations are possible in this general form of the diagram. One example is that the primary biological defect has a number of biologically defined consequences. This would be represented by a causal nexus entirely within the biological level. A second variant is that a biological defect may directly lead to behavioral consequences without cognitive mediation. Thus, dopamine deficiency in Parkinson's disease (in interaction with other factors) can lead to tremor. The way in which these two examples would be incorporated into our diagram is shown in Figure 13.19. In this case, br_1 and br_2 are biological consequences of the primary deficit; br_1 is shown as directly causing the behavioral consequences S_1; br_2 has consequences C_1 and C_2 which, together, have a variety of signs and symptoms, S_2 and S_3. All these variations would still roughly conform to the A-shape.

An example of a cognitively defined syndrome is that of autistic spectrum disorder, which we have already briefly outlined above. This would be represented as an X-shape, as shown in Figure 13.20. A variety of possible biological causes, O_1 to O_3, all lead to the same cognitive deficit. The single cognitive deficit then results in (some subset of) a large number of signs and symptoms. Again, variations at all three levels are possible, as we have already shown in our discussion of competing theories. All would maintain a relative convergence at the cognitive

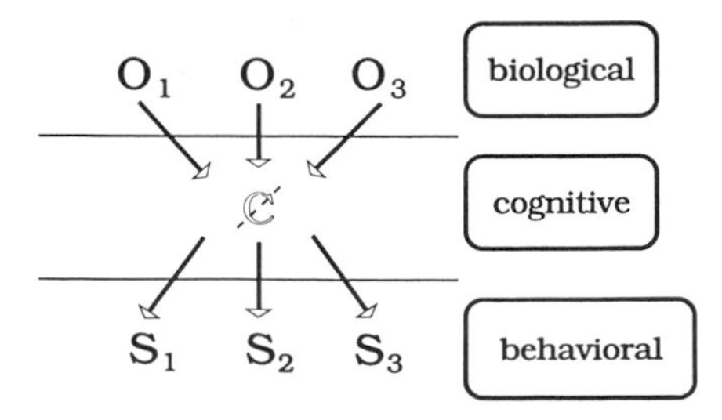

Figure 13.20 The archetypal X-type causal model.

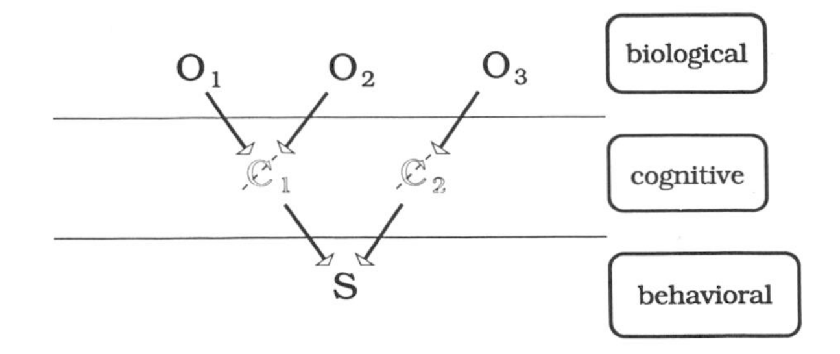

Figure 13.21 The archetypal V-type causal model.

level. Even if it were necessary to postulate two or three separate cognitive deficits for a full explanation of the condition, the causal analysis would still roughly conform to the X-shape.

Note that the links do not at the moment make a distinction between conjunctive and disjunctive causation; that is, the preceding diagram is to be interpreted as saying that C can be caused by O_1 or by O_2 or by O_3. It will be necessary in a full causal account to allow for restrictions such as that C is caused by the conjunction of O_2 and O_3. This is equivalent to the "additional preconditions" discussed in the context of Figure 13.18.

Finally, we can represent the behaviorally defined syndrome, which would have the general form of a V-shape, as shown in Figure 13.21. S represents the defining behavior or behavior pattern which, in the example, can be caused directly or through cognitive mediation. We use the example of hyperactivity, which is defined as a diagnostic entity at the behavioral level.

Hyperactivity: An Example of a V-Type Causal Model

The diagnosis of hyperactivity is contentious. Not only are there major differences between U.S. and European practice (as represented in DSM-IV and ICD-10; see Taylor, 1986, for other differences) but also there appear to be differences within each of the communities with respect to the status of the diagnosis. It is not our intention to attempt to legislate in these debates. We can, however, represent the position of at least some of the protagonists.

Hyperactivity is a "pattern of restless, inattentive, and impulsive behavior in childhood" (Schachar, 1991, p. 155); such a pattern is what is called a *diagnostic entity.* There is much concern with the face validity of diagnostic entities. Rutter (1978) suggested that, to be *valid,* a diagnostic entity must differ in etiology, course, characteristics, or treatment response from those of other child psychiatric entities as well as from normality. At the moment, there is concern over the validity of the distinction between hyperactivity and conduct disturbance (Hinshaw, 1987). We discuss the implications of such a concern below.

Essentially, hyperactivity and associated disorders have been defined behaviorally. This is confirmed by a glance at the DSM-III and the DSM-III-R (American Psychiatric Association, 1980, 1987) criteria. In DSM-III (1980), the diagnosis of attention deficit disorder with hyperactivity (ADDH) required inattentiveness, impulsiveness, and overactivity. These had to continue for more than 6 months, starting before the age of 7. If a child presented with inattentiveness and impulsiveness but without overactivity, the diagnosis of attention deficit disorder without hyperactivity (ADD/WO) was applied in the belief that this combination delineated a distinct syndrome (see Lahey, Schaughency, Hynd, Carlson, & Nieves, 1987). DSM-III-R introduced a further category of attention deficit hyperactivity disorder (ADHD). To qualify for this category, a child had to exhibit 8 symptoms from a menu of 14 symptoms of hyperactivity, inattention, and impulsiveness. Schachar (1991) pointed out that this created two new subcategories of hyperactivity, one characterized by overactivity and impulsiveness but without inattention, and the other by inattention and overactivity but without impulsiveness. These have now been introduced in DSM-IV.

The ICD-9 criteria differed in a number of ways, as described in some detail by Schachar (1991). One feature that he focused on was the treatment of comorbid psychopathology. He commented:

> The syndrome of hyperactivity is viewed, for the most part, as an epiphenomenon or non-specific correlate of various forms of psychopathology that carries no particular etiological significance. Consequently, when hyperactivity occurs as part of a mixed presentation, the clinician is encouraged to diagnose the underlying condition. (p. 158)

In this case, then, the focus of diagnosis was to be either at the cognitive or the biological level rather than at the behavioral level. Schachar commented that "a diagnosis of hyperkinetic syndrome is usually limited to a presentation uncomplicated by co-morbid psychopathology" (p. 158). There was clearly potential for enormous variability of symptoms that might or might not lead to distinct subgroups.

We have chosen the example of hyperactivity because it is specified at the behavioral level. What can we say about the rest of the causal tree? We can surmise that the intentions of the two diagnostic systems are different from each other in some respects. In particular, DSM-III (1980) permitted diagnosis of ADDH when the symptoms occurred at school but not at home, or vice versa. In contrast, the ICD-10 diagnosis of hyperkinetic syndrome requires that the behavior be reported consistently in several situations. One might surmise that ICD-10 regards it as being more of an endogenous problem. DSM-III-R (1987), on the other hand, with its explicit "some people . . . show signs of the disorder in only one setting, such as at home or at school" (p. 50) suggested a more temporary and exogenously caused problem. The statement clearly indicated that the behavior, rather than the precipitating circumstances, was important. In this classification, the notion of cause seemed to be submerged under the behavioral criterion.[20] In DSM-IV the behavioral emphasis is less marked.

Cantwell (1977), on the basis of studies of response to stimulant drugs, follow-ups, and neurological and neurophysiological studies, concluded that all of these techniques indicate that hyperactive children are a heterogeneous group. In an earlier paper examining the genetics of hyperactivity, Cantwell (1975) concluded that "if there is a genetic component to the syndrome, it is operating in one sub-group of these children; or there may be several genetically distinct sub-groups" (p. 264). We can see, then, that there are a number of causal possibilities in the definition of hyperactivity. All of these can be represented in the V-shape.

Taylor (1986) also considered pharmacological effects as a means of establishing diagnostic categories. The underlying principle is that patients who respond in the same way to drugs belong to the same biologically defined category. We can illustrate this principle using the causal notation. In Figure 13.22, we suppose two subgroups of children with the same sign, S. The groups differ in that they have different abnormal brain states, br_1 and br_2, which have the same cognitive consequence, C. Whether the operation of a drug may be useful in helping to define subgroups will depend on the level at which it interacts with the causal tree. If the drug is operating at the biological level in the causal tree and the response of two patients is the same, then we would be justified in classifying the two as being in the same group. On the other hand, if two patients have different responses to such drugs, then they would be classified as coming from different subgroups. Thus, $drug_1$ could operate selectively on br_1. Patients in this group would no longer suffer the cognitive dysfunction and would not, then, exhibit the characteristic signs. Patients with damage to br_2, on the other hand, would remain unchanged by the drug. In contrast, $drug_2$ could operate selectively on br_2, abolishing the signs in that group but not in the first one. Use of these two drugs, then, will serve to distinguish the two subgroups of children. However, another drug, $drug_3$, might operate by suppressing the behavior without otherwise interacting with the causal tree. In this case, the two groups of children would be responding in the same way to $drug_3$ in spite of their underlying biological differences. The existence of a common response to $drug_3$ would demonstrate nothing about the homogeneity of the groups but would be equivalent to suppressing the signs by behavior modification techniques or even simple physical restraint.

Taylor's (1986) review of childhood hyperactivity and, even more, his review (1991) of child neuropsychiatry in general allude to many of the problems that explanations of developmental

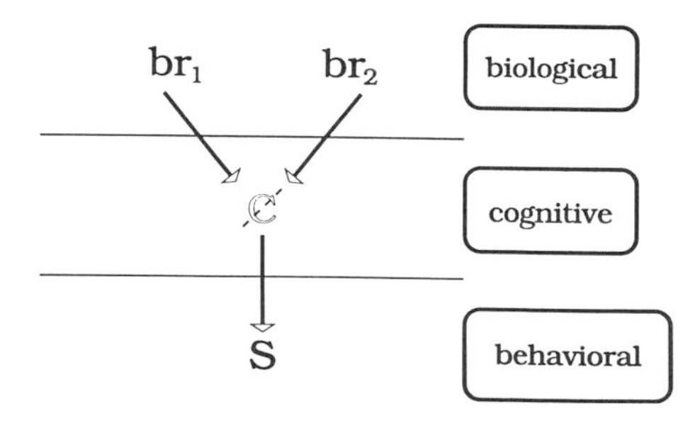

Figure 13.22 A simple causal model to help understand whether reaction to drugs can decide diagnostic categories (see text).

[20] It would be more correct to talk about *reported* behavior rather than *actual* behavior, because much of the research in this area has been done with teacher-based checklists rather than observation.

disorders encounter. It is precisely for these reasons that we are suggesting the present framework.

The approach followed by Sonuga-Barke, Taylor, and Heptinstall (1992) and Sonuga-Barke, Taylor, Sembi, and Smith (1992) suggests that it would be fruitful now to consider an X-shape of causal modeling with a hypothesized underlying cognitive deficit, such as *impulsiveness* or *inability to delay reward.* This approach is possible because of the convergence of clinical, epidemiological, and neuropsychological studies, which (just as in the case of autism) together strongly point to hyperactivity as a valid diagnostic entity, not in terms of behavior but in terms of underlying causes. Like autism, hyperactivity is likely to be defined as a cognitively based and biologically caused developmental disorder. If this happens, however, it is essential that a separate diagnostic category be created for children with the same behavior but different cognitive cause.

As yet, we cannot go further in the X-shape causal model of hyperactivity because we lack a psychological theory of hyperactivity that would relate the phenomena to normal control of movement, as well as to impulsivity and attention deficits. We can show in simplified causal diagrams how various causal theories can be represented (Figures 13.23–13.28). Taylor (1986) suggested two possibilities: (a) genetic or other biological factors may affect activity levels directly (Figure 13.23) or (b) the biological effects are mediated through cognitive factors (Figure 13.24). In either case, the condition could be exacerbated by psychosocial factors that, for example, increase levels of stress. In Figure 13.25, we have indicated the environmental factors as in-

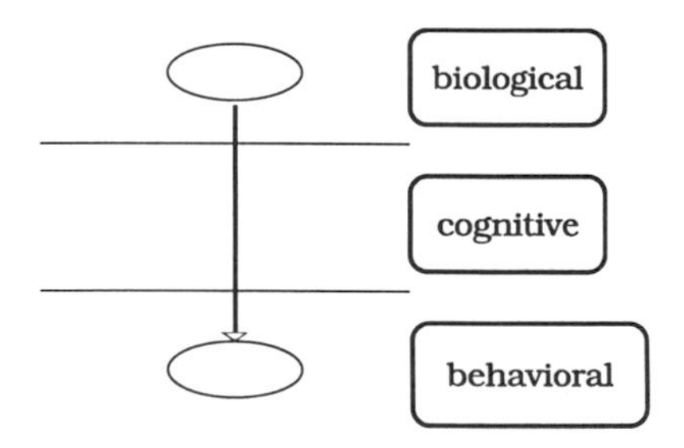

Figure 13.23 A schematic representation of direct causation of hyperactivity from biological factors.

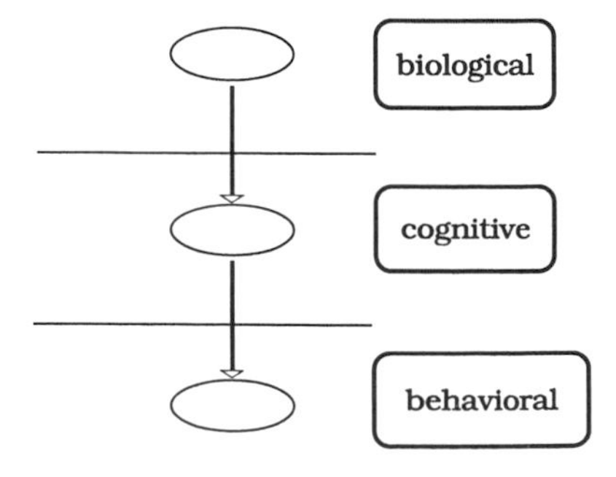

Figure 13.24 A schematic representation of biological cause of hyperactivity being mediated through cognitive factors.

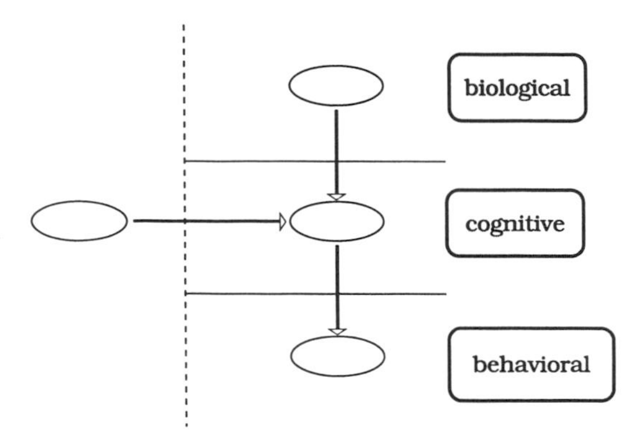

Figure 13.25 A schematic representation of environmental factors interacting with genetic factors to produce hyperactivity symptoms.

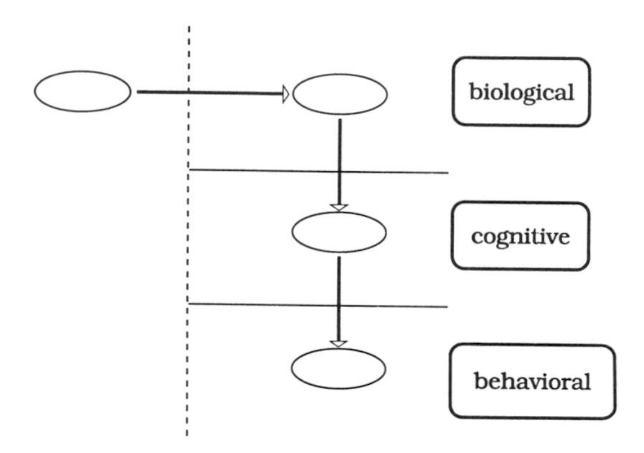

Figure 13.26 The effects of the environment operating at the biological level.

teracting with some genetic factor to precipitate a state not describable at the biological level. The theory that hyperactivity is caused by an environmental toxin of sorts (suggestions include lead intake and dietary additives) is illustrated in Figure 13.26, where we diagram the possibility of an external cause operating at the biological level. A factor originating in the environment need not operate at the biological level in the causal chain. It may affect general attitudes toward schooling, while interacting with other factors. This possibility is represented in Figure 13.27.

At the behavioral level, all of these diagrams refer to the same behavioral complex. Thus, we can put them all together into a single causal diagram, as in Figure 13.28. There is, in all cases, some degree of freedom left for specification of the involvement of alternative constructs at the cognitive level.

Variability

One of the irritating as well as fascinating problems in developmental psychopathology is the variability among individuals. If selection of a group of people is based on their identity by some definition, then it will inevitably be discovered that they are

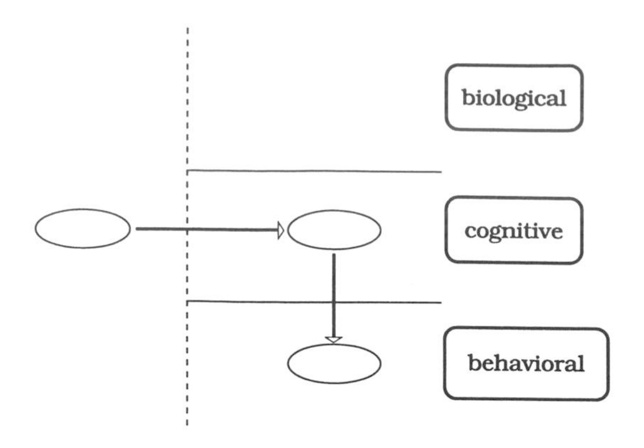

Figure 13.27 The effects of the environment operating directly at the cognitive level with no biological involvement.

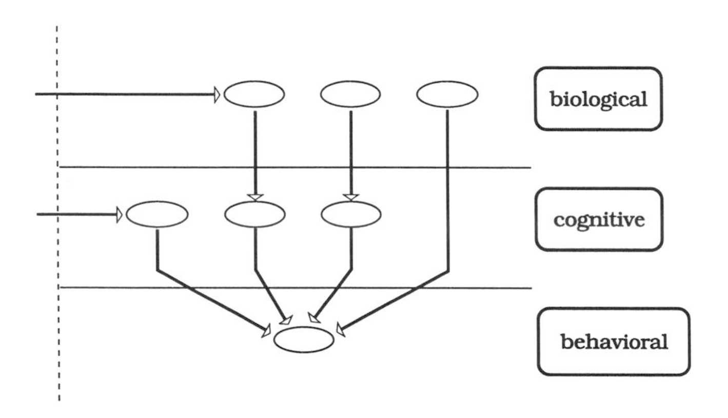

Figure 13.28 A compilation of Figures 13.23–13.27 showing, schematically, a variety of causal pathways for the hyperactivity behavioral phenotype. This is a classic V-shaped causal model.

different, sometimes wildly different, by some other definition, particularly if this definition is at another level. Thus, a group of Fragile X children will display a range of severity of symptom from the mildly hyperactive to full-blown autism. Such a phenomenon is not the same as convergence, which has already been alluded to. Convergence is what happens when a group of autistics, presenting as a single diagnostic entity, are discovered to manifest a variety of biological causes. This is not a problem when one considers any system that develops with multiple contingency and when there are no inconsistencies to unravel.

Variability can be handled in a number of ways. Sometimes, we have embarrassments such as the DSM II-R definition of hyperactivity, where having any 3 out of 8 symptoms qualifies a child. Such pragmatics—categories at all costs—have little scientific content and could even be thought of as antiscientific. In some accounts of hyperactivity, there are signs of uneasiness with this approach and indications that more consistency might be found through redefining the concept at a cognitive or biological level (see above). In other cases, symptoms might be ordered in terms of severity. The ideal patient will show all the signs from the mildest up to the most severe for that patient. What will not

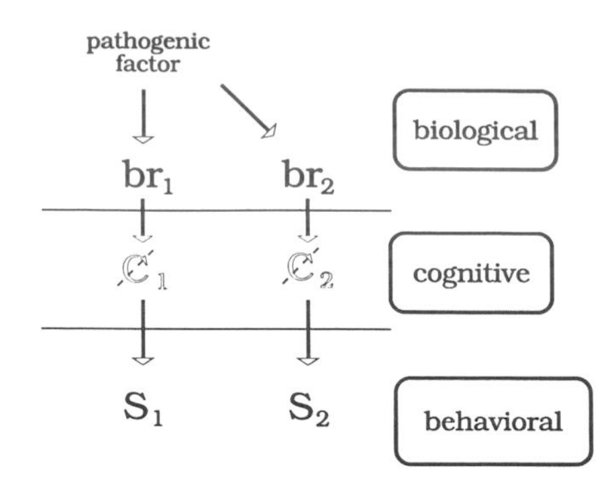

Figure 13.29 In this figure and in Figure 13.30, we illustrate one theory concerning the variability of the expression of a particular condition. Here, the condition has full expression.

be found is a scattering of symptoms of different severity, with some medium severity symptoms missing. The underlying model for the concept of variability would then be that of a quantitative disorder, either at the biological or cognitive level. At the biological level, one could imagine gauging the severity of the affliction in terms of the amount of tissue damaged or the level of a particular neurotransmitter. Another way of referring to this would be in terms of the genetically mediated penetrance of the disorder. At the cognitive level, the diagnostic tasks could be ordered in terms of their information processing demands. Patients would then be located on this continuum as a function of some cognitive measure—for example, the available working memory.

Let us look at one simpler example of variability, a genetic condition where in some cases we find signs S_1 and S_2, but in others we find only S_1. How can we conceptualize this condition? Of the possibilities available, let us illustrate a couple where we examine explanations in terms of a second biological factor that can be either protective (in which case, only S_1 results) or precipitating. In Figure 13.29, we model the assumption that the pathogenic condition would normally give rise to two brain abnormalities, br_1 and br_2. These cause the nondevelopment of the two cognitive systems, C_1 and C_2, which give rise to the symptom complex in its full-blown form. In Figure 13.30, we see how the

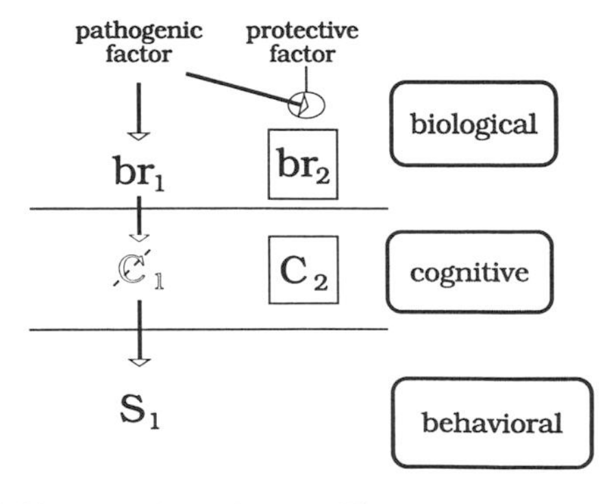

Figure 13.30 In this variant on Figure 13.29, a protective factor mitigates the condition so that only some signs and symptoms are found.

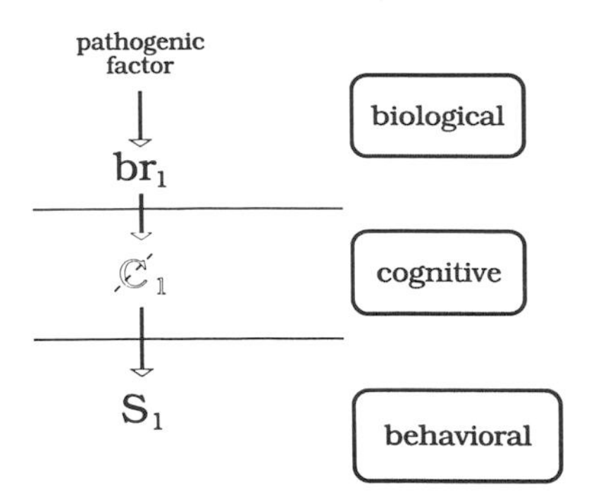

Figure 13.31 An alternative theory of variability of expression of a particular condition. C_2 is not shown because it is not affected by the pathogenic factor. Individuals will not show the group symptom S_2 found in Figure 13.32.

extra factor serves to counteract the effect of the condition on br_2, which will then develop normally. The cognitive structure, C_2, will then be intact (symbolized by the box around it). In this case, the extra factor can be seen as protective.

A second possibility is illustrated in Figures 13.31 and 13.32, where the assumption is that the extra factor works in a negative way. By itself, as shown in Figure 13.31, the pathogenic factor only gives rise to br_1. In such a case, br_2 is not found unless the extra, precipitating factor is present, as shown in Figure 13.32. The two factors are seen as acting in concert—symbolized by the & sign—in producing the br_2 condition. The extra factor here can be seen as making the individual vulnerable to the effects of the genetic condition.

In many cases, we suspect that the source of variation will be hidden at a level well below the one at which the causal model is operating. Johnson and Morton (1991) discussed the sense in which genetic and environmental effects could be equivalent. Thus, differences between individuals can be brought about by "normal" variations within the genotype. Such differences give rise to the range of color, the body type, and some characteristics of the central nervous system that lead to differences in speed of processing. This kind of variation is usually referred to

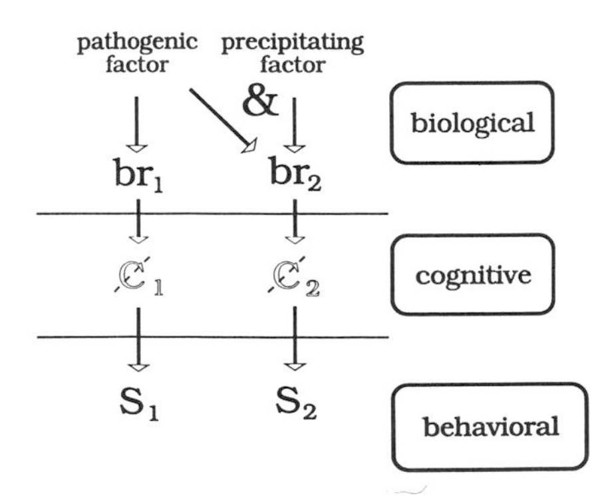

Figure 13.32 A variant on Figure 13.31, where an extra factor works in a negative way, for example, making the individual especially vulnerable. In this case, C_1 and C_2 are both defective.

as *individual differences.* "Normal" variations in lower-level environments (especially the in utero environment) would be functionally equivalent here. Thus, maternal variations in diet shift the average height without affecting the genotypic variation. Another source of variation discussed by Johnson and Morton is traceable to abnormalities within the genotype. Down syndrome would be one such variation. Another example is maternal rubella, which, in combination with genotypic factors, can lead to autism in the child (Chess, Korn, & Fernandez, 1971).

Finally, we can review cases where the condition has a known biological origin. For this, we move outside the developmental area and consider a case of a left middle cerebral artery infarct. The variability in symptoms following a hemorrhage will surprise no one and will call for no special principles of explanation. Lesions will differ in their extent as a function of both the exact location of the problem and the individual variation in distribution of the artery. In addition, the effects of two roughly equivalent lesions can be widely different because of the differences in the way that particular psychological functions have become implemented in a particular region of the cortex. All patients who have suffered from a left middle cerebral artery infarct will have symptoms that are related. All will have some form of aphasia and most, if not all, will have some form of dyslexia. At one time, such a description might have been thought sufficient to justify the single diagnostic category, but work in cognitive neuropsychology has established a number of clear categories of dyslexia with different patterns of symptoms and different possibilities of compensatory strategies. The variation, then, is accountable in terms of the cognitive models of the reading process (Patterson, 1981; Shallice, 1981).

PSYCHOSOCIAL PATHWAYS

The causal model, as we have developed it, has a similarity with the psychosocial pathway developed by Rutter (1989) and his colleagues. The main difference is that pathways represent, broadly, trends over time for groups of individuals. They show the contingent relationships among events in the lives of individuals. The pathways are variously termed "chains of adversity" or "chains of circumstance." Usually, these pathways are constructed from correlation or contingency tables. Causality is implied, not explicitly claimed. In these cases, as in our own model, the causal links are not determinate. Where two events are linked by an arrow:

$$x \rightarrow y$$

One is to understand that in those cases where x is found, there is an increasing likelihood of y occurring later. Note that y could occur for other reasons, and that pathway analysis seems to concentrate more on the forward implications. Figure 13.33, based on a study of Gray, Smith, and Rutter (1980), gives a simplified pathway from poor schooling to poor job success, controlling for other variables such as the individual's measured intelligence and social circumstance. It seems to focus more on a series of forward questions such as:

"What are the consequences of poor schooling?"

rather than backward ones such as:

"What are the causes of poor employment records?"

Figure 13.33 indicates comparative rates of traversing each subpath. We see that children with poor schooling are twice as likely to have poor school attendance (compared to children with good schooling). The next stage of the pathway, rather than being the continuation of the first part (that is, using only children with poor schooling) is actually recomputed from scratch, using all children with poor school attendance. Thus, the relationship of poor school attendance and early school leaving is a twofold increase over the group with good school attendance. Remember that this calculation ignores the quality of the schooling. In fact, we are also told that the poor schooling group is only twice as likely to leave school early. This means that we can infer that poor attendance with good schooling has a *worse* outcome than poor attendance with poor schooling. Poor schooling might then be seen as a mitigating circumstance for early school leaving in the poor attendance group!

In the rest of the pathway, we are not given the necessary data to see whether the same complex contingency is a factor. However, it is possible that, although a child with poor schooling was more likely to lack scholastic qualifications, a child who lacked scholastic qualifications because of poor schooling was less likely to end up in unskilled work than someone without qualifications who had good schooling.

Rutter (1989) described the figure from Gray et al. (1980) as "simplified," and in this form the figure may be less than helpful for thinking about some of the problems. Rutter also brought together a number of examples of how the psychosocial pathway was used to show different outcomes. One example, shown in Figure 13.34, comes from a study by Quinton and Rutter (1988) on the

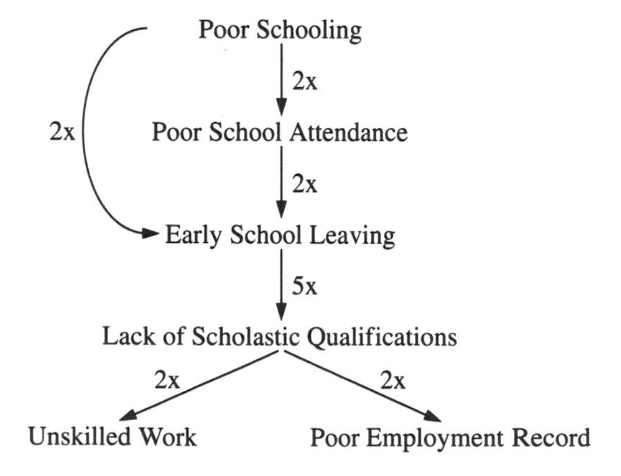

Figure 13.33 The psychosocial pathway from poor schooling to poor job success. From "Pathways from Childhood to Adult Life" by M. Rutter, 1989, *Journal of Child Psychology and Psychiatry, 30,* p. 31. Copyright 1989 by the Journal of Child Psychology and Psychiatry. Reprinted by permission.

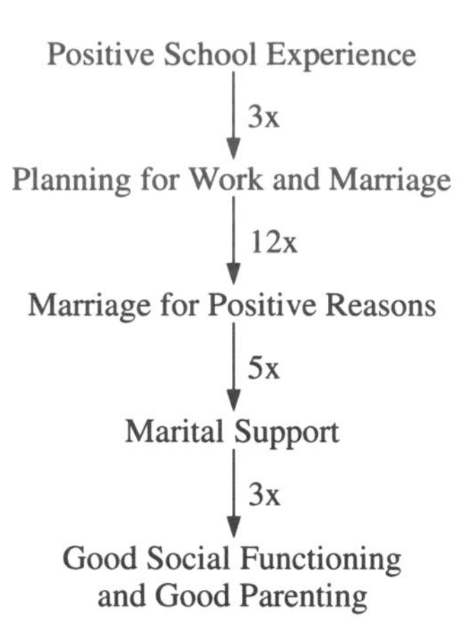

Figure 13.34 The psychosocial pathway: the outcome for institutionally reared girls. From "Pathways from Childhood to Adult Life" by M. Rutter, 1989, *Journal of Child Psychology and Psychiatry, 30,* p. 33. Copyright 1989 by the Journal of Child Psychology and Psychiatry. Reprinted by permission.

outcome of institutionally reared girls, a third of whom manifested parenting breakdown. More detailed analysis showed that this was not caused by the institutionalization per se, but rather by the quality of the family home. If, on leaving the institution, the child returns to a discordant family in adolescence, the likelihood of an early marriage with poor prospects is increased. This is associated with increased risk of poor social functioning which, in turn, is associated with an increase in breakdown of parenting. Girls who return from the institution to a harmonious home during adolescence are much more likely to end up as adequate parents. It is tempting to see such intergenerational transmission as inevitable, but there is at least one other major factor, the quality of the schooling. Children's homes tend to distribute the children in their care around the local schools. This leads to a variety of school experience which has a major impact on outcome, as indicated in Figure 13.34.[21]

We have analyzed these examples in some detail as a means of contrasting them with the causal model. One clear difference that emerges from the above analysis is that, although *cause* propagates down the causal model, it does not propagate down the psychosocial pathway as usually constructed. This is not accidental, we feel; rather, it expresses a view of life-span development that is gaining currency. By this view, adverse early life events are no longer seen as *determining* later outcomes (Clarke & Clarke, 1992). Instead, such events place the child in a disadvantaged situation from which it is more difficult to achieve a satisfactory outcome at the next stage. They cause more vulnerability to bad outcomes from later setbacks. The adverse early events certainly are a disadvantage, but this is not the same as life-span determination.[22] This analysis may all look dangerously close to a social

[21] Note, however, that there could well be contingencies between family background and the ability to profit from school, even when intelligence and other individual variables are taken into account.

[22] The fault ". . . is not in our stars but in ourselves . . ." (Shakespeare).

philosophy rather than a scientific analysis, but cause and responsibility are not to be equated.[23] In summary, it is possible to say that a particular behavioral sign is caused by a genetic abnormality at the beginning of the causal chain. However, we are not on so good a ground in saying, for example, that someone's poor employment record is caused by his or her poor schooling.

Another, related difference can be found between psychosocial pathways and causal models. In the causal models, we can represent the full causal path for the condition for any affected individual or, alternatively, for all individuals in a defined group with the full variety of possibilities. With respect to the time dimension, we can note that the psychosocial pathway is restricted to the historical events, whereas the causal model may or may not represent temporal sequence. A notation that has temporal sequence at its core is Developmental Contingency Modeling (Morton, 1986). This notation also is more natural when discussing the preconditions for normal development.

DEVELOPMENTAL CONTINGENCY MODELING

To give an example, let us start with the following question: "What is the cause of the development of pretend play?" A question of this form seems distinctly odd because it has to do with the relative uniqueness of A in a claim that *A caused B.* The uniqueness takes these forms:

1. There should not be many other examples of x for which it would be the case that *x caused B.*
2. Condition A should not be common in the population.
3. There should not be too many people for whom A is true but B is not.

Notice that this use of *cause,* which is the way it is used in ordinary language (including in medicine), is very much weaker than the notion of implication: if *A implies B,* then there would be no cases of A without B. *Cause,* in the developmental domain (and, indeed, in the human domain as a whole), is not nearly so strict, for reasons we will explore below.

The above constraints on *cause* mean that we cannot (that is to say, we normally do not) talk about the cause of a normal condition. In particular, too many things would count as causes to make the notion worthwhile. Instead, we might refer to the *preconditions* for a particular aspect of normal development. For such reasons, Morton (1986) developed the Developmental Contingency Model (DCM), which allows one to trace the normal developmental preconditions for a particular process or skill. We will illustrate DCMs in the area for which this theoretical device was developed: the emergence of mentalizing in normal development. This brings us back to the question on the cause of the development of pretend play, posed at the beginning of this section. Here, instead of asking about the *cause* of pretend play, we are asking about the *preconditions* of pretend play, and the related abilities. In fact, we will focus on only one of the many necessary preconditions.

[23] An extreme example of the separation is given in a guidebook to Bali. The traveler is warned of the consequences of being involved in a traffic accident. Irrespective of the cause of the accident, it is claimed, the tourist will be deemed responsible because if the tourist had not visited the island, the accident would not have taken place.

Figure 13.35 is a developmental contingency model, not a flow chart or an information processing model. The symbol on the lines in Figure 13.35 is to be read as "(normally) requires the (pre) existence of." Thus, pairs of connected elements are related developmentally, and each such pair effectively represents a hypothesis about developmental contingencies. We have choices regarding which elements to represent and their relationship.

The particular form of Figure 13.35 was driven as follows. We wanted to separate representations having to do with things from those having to do with people. We called these representations material (MAT) and individual (IND), respectively. IND constitutes those representations that have to do with individual people. MAT refers to all other representations. This division is based solely on content; we are *not* postulating the existence of two different memory stores. In Figure 13.35, then, MAT is to be understood as the *ability* to create representations with respect to objects. IND is to be understood as the *ability* to create representations with respect to individual people. We have separated IND from MAT because there will be prerequisites for IND that are not shared by MAT. These will relate to the differentiation of individuals from each other, an ability not necessarily tied to the differentiation of objects from each other. It may

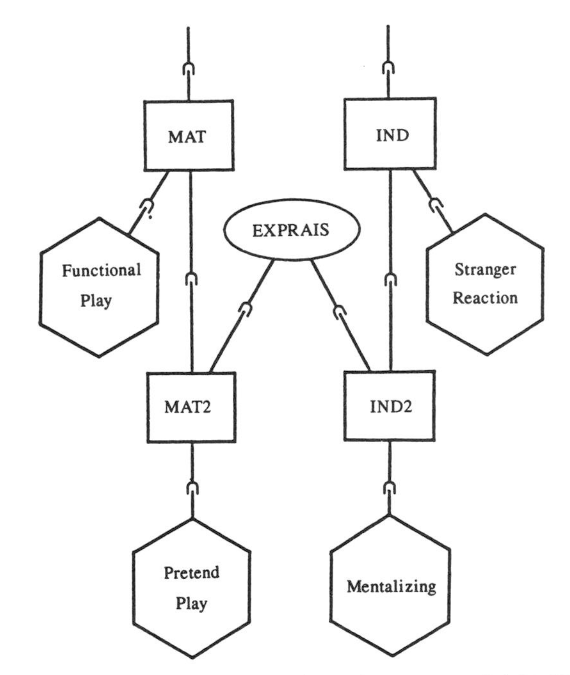

Figure 13.35 A developmental contingency model (DCM) relating to autism. From "Developmental Contingency Modelling: A Framework for Discussing the Processes of Change and the Consequence of Deficiency" by J. Morton, 1986, in P.L.C. van Geert (Ed.), *Theory Building in Developmental Psychology* (p. 148). Copyright 1986 by Elsevier Science Publishers. Reprinted by permission.

also be important to separate MAT and IND for the reason that the understanding of individuals as agents and the understanding of objects as physical causes seem to be separate developmental achievements (Carey, 1985; Gelman, 1990).

MAT and IND are first-order representations. The equivalent second-order representations are created by the action of a specific mechanism, first called expression raiser (EXPRAIS) by Leslie (1987). EXPRAIS operates on first-order representations. Thus, a first-order representation can be decoupled from its job of representing a real state of affairs ("It is raining.") and used inside a phrase (She thinks, "It is raining."). We call the resulting ability to create second-order representations MAT2 and IND2. A single knowledge fragment, or "thinks," could include all four kinds of representation. The following fragment is an example:

> Daddy is on his brown chair (which I am pretending is my space machine) and he pretends I'm an alien.

In this fragment, the four kinds of representation are as follows:

MAT: the chair is brown
MAT2: the chair is a space machine
IND: Daddy is on the chair
IND2: Daddy pretends I'm an alien.

We maintain the separation among these four classes of knowledge because we believe that some people cannot create some of them and because they do not appear to develop at the same time (Leslie, 1987). In Figure 13.35, the relationship between MAT and MAT2 should be understood as follows: the development of the ability to form MAT2 representations is contingent on having previously developed the ability to form MAT representations.

In Figure 13.35, we have represented a number of claims made with respect to mentalizing and other skills. Thus, the existence of pretend play presupposes the existence of MAT2 representations. In the same way, mentalizing (the ability to attribute mental states) requires the ability to create IND2 representations. The contrast is made, on the one hand, with so-called functional play, which only requires first-order MAT representations, and, on the other hand, with the stranger reaction, which only requires first-order IND representations. If someone cannot mentalize, it is because that person cannot form IND2 representations. The diagram makes it obvious that an inability to form IND2 representations could arise for two reasons. First, if the EXPRAIS was missing, there could be no IND2. This was our original supposition for autism. The resulting inability to mentalize would be accompanied by a lack of pretend play, which also relies on the existence of EXPRAIS. At the same time, the ability to represent objects and individual agency would be presumed intact.

Second, there may be an absence of IND representations, or the ability to create IND representations may be computationally insufficient to allow the creation of IND2 representations. Such an individual would fail the Sally-Anne experiment but would be able to pretend play—so long as EXPRAIS existed. This is the case in the normally developing 2- to 3-year-old child.

One important feature in developmental contingency modeling is that there are always unexpressed contingencies. We only consider here the developing abilities and the kinds of knowledge that are germane to the particular theory of development being represented.

The Properties of the Notation

In the DCM shown in Figure 13.35, there is the objective that contingencies should be traced back to the biological givens.[24] A second presupposition is that such biological givens will be buried deep with respect to behavior. Each one will be implicated in a wide range of activities, and the absence of any one will have far-ranging consequences. A third presupposition is that no special environmental conditions are required for the normal fruition of the givens. That is not to say that there is no learning, but only that the learning is effort-free. The child learns about language, objects, family, causality, number, and so on, in an effort-free way because what is happening in the course of such learning is that the givens are being used. There is almost a teleological element about this process. The processing machinery and the innate structures are constructed in the way they are in order that the goals shall always be reached. This is the achievement of evolution. The child has no choice in the matter; its "learning" is under the control of its processes. A child can choose not to speak but it cannot choose not to learn its native language. The biological givens that subsume language learning make sure of that.

In the DCM framework, the focus is on the prerequisites for the emergence of a particular process or structure. Such properties of the infant brain form "elements" in a DCM model. Although our direct evidence for the existence of such an element will be behavioral, our primary focus will be on the elements and not on the behavior. There are two main reasons for this. First, an element may be present without being visible in behavior. Thus, a profoundly deaf infant who has no experience of sign language still has the innate component of the language learning apparatus. The presence of this component becomes revealed as soon as signing starts. Before this point, the component is not able to exert any significant influence on behavior.

Second, a particular piece of behavior could be mediated by a variety of means. For example, autistic children may learn to have exchanges of utterances with adults. However, in the majority of cases, such exchanges would not, on close analysis, be confusable with the conversations that normal children have. Normally, conversations are driven by IND2 representations (among other things) and are intrinsically "reinforcing" for normal children. The autistic child would only slowly learn that they were appropriate modes of behavior.

In the preceding paragraphs, we indicated why the focus of the DCM method is on the elements of the child's cognitive apparatus rather than on behavior. We should now look at the elements more closely. Elements are either primitive or not. By "primitive" we mean innate and irreducible. Trivially, either a particular element E can only emerge if some specific element D has already emerged (to some level of specification), or E is a primitive. The development of nonprimitives depends on the prior functioning of particular primitives plus exposure to specific kinds of stimuli.

---

[24] This is, of course, the first of our maxims of causal modeling.

Primitives require, at most, a minimal environment. Primitives need not be present from birth; they can arise in the course of maturation.

In practice, there will be a variety of patterns of contingencies. Thus, one can imagine a skill whose emergence is a function of a late maturing structure but which also depends on the prior existence of other processes or knowledge. We would want to be able to represent all such contingencies. The general form of the contingency model is that of elements connected in a directed graph. The elements can be of a variety of kinds—processes, structures, knowledge, perceptual or other experiences, or biological elements. The symbols on the connecting lines have temporal/causal implications.

The Relation between DCMs and Causal Models

We noted in the previous section that it doesn't make much sense to talk about the *cause* of normal development. For this reason, we introduced the Developmental Contingency Model (DCM). The relation between the two is quite straightforward. Suppose we are interested in the development of an ability, A—say, speech. We establish that the normal development of A depends on the prior development of at least two features, X and Y, ears and mouth. The DCM for this development is shown in Figure 13.36.

From what we have already said, it should be clear that the normal development of A (speech) will be prevented or impeded if there is delay of development or malfunction of either X (ears) or Y (mouth). Thus, there will be two different causal models of malfunction of A, depending on whether hearing or producing speech sounds is affected. The two causal models are shown in Figure 13.37.

In case (i), it is possible that feature Y (producing sounds) is still intact; in case (ii), it is possible that feature X is still intact. Let us examine case (i). The first step in establishing that feature Y is functioning would be to test some other ability, B, which would normally also depend on the existence of feature Y. Thus, a more complete DCM would be as shown in Figure 13.38.

Children categorized under case (i) would show ability B; children under case (ii) would not. We would, however, expect case (ii) children to show other abilities that depend on feature

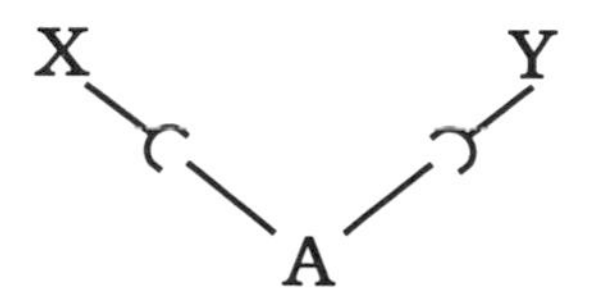

Figure 13.36 A simplified developmental contingency model.

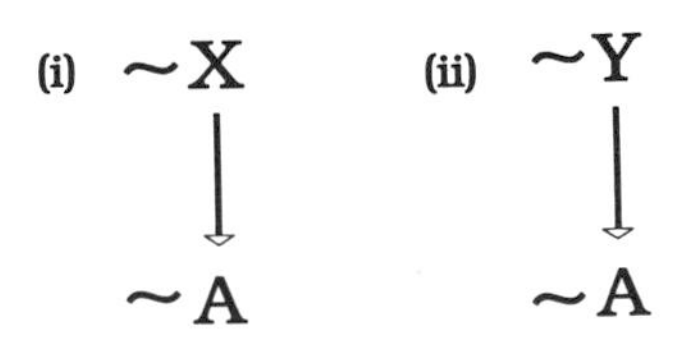

Figure 13.37 The causal implications of DCM in Figure 13.36: no X leads to no ability A; no Y also leads to no ability A.

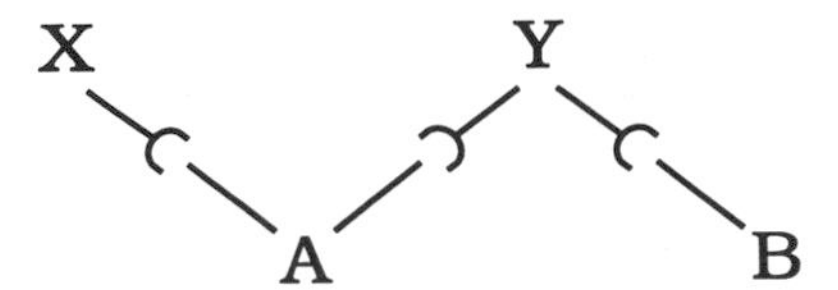

Figure 13.38 A DCM that slightly elaborates the one shown in Figure 13.36: two abilities, A and B, presuppose Y. Ability A also presupposes X.

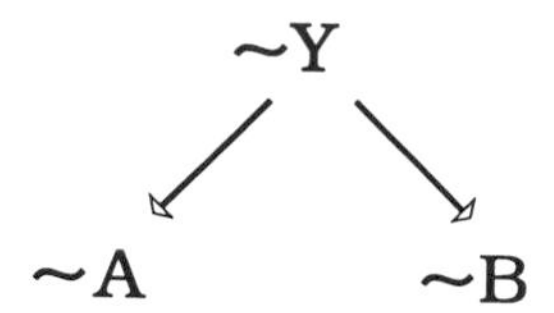

Figure 13.39 A causal model related to the DCM in Figure 13.38: no Y leads to double disability A and B.

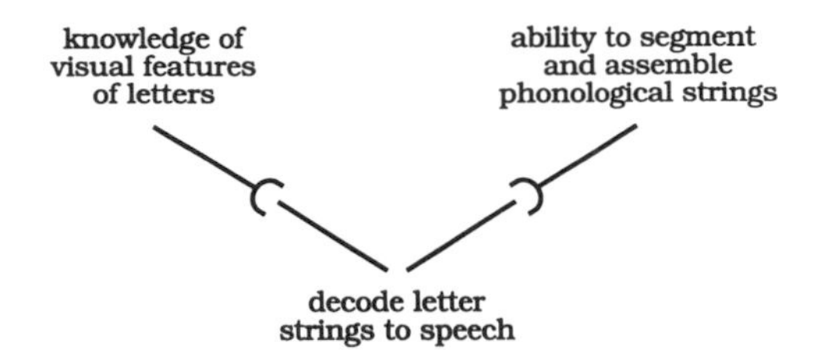

Figure 13.40 A fragment of a DCM for acquisition of reading.

X.[25] The more complete causal model for case (ii) would take into account both abilities A and B, as shown in Figure 13.39.

We can illustrate this principle with an example from the area of literacy development. One component of mature reading is the ability to decode letter strings into speech. Many factors are prerequisites for this skill. We will select two: (a) knowledge of the visual features of letters and (b) the ability to segment and assemble phonological strings. The relationships among these abilities are shown in the DCM fragment in Figure 13.40. If a child has failed to acquire either the letter knowledge or the phonological skills, then this child will not be able to acquire the decoding skill. These simple causal relationships are shown in Figure 13.41. If we only know that a particular child has no decoding skills, we cannot tell whether this is because the child lacks one or another of the prerequisites (not to mention other possibilities). However, the phonological abilities will reveal themselves in other simple tasks, such as an "I spy" game.[26] This dependency is represented in

[25] The prediction of the absence of an ability depends on the child's being unable to develop the ability through a compensatory strategy. As we shall see, this is not always the case; a case (ii) child might not demonstrate ability B because of the absence of Y, but may exhibit ability A through compensation. Thus, a deaf child can learn to speak via lip reading, even though the normal route for doing so is blocked.

[26] The "I spy" game involves one person saying, "I spy, with my little eye, something beginning with b" (or some other letter name). The other person has to guess the object in question.

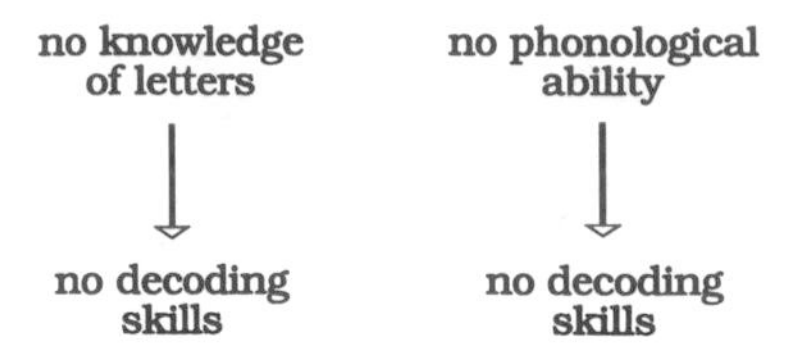

Figure 13.41 The causal implications of the DCM in Figure 13.40. Absence of either of the two abilities in Figure 13.40 will lead to an inability to decode letter strings into speech.

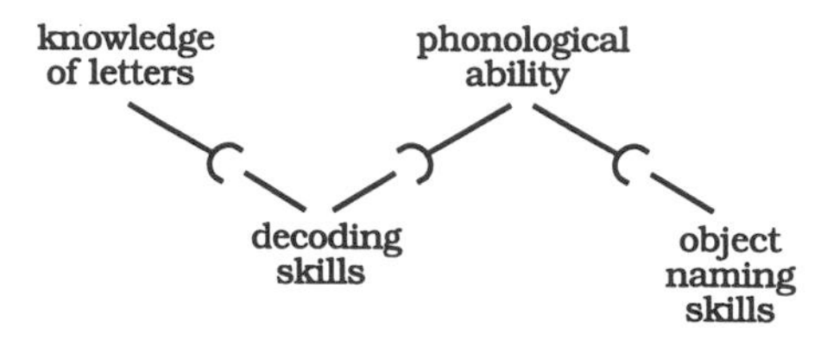

Figure 13.42 An example of the DCM in Figure 13.38. This indicates that phonological ability is necessary not just for decoding but also for object-naming skills.

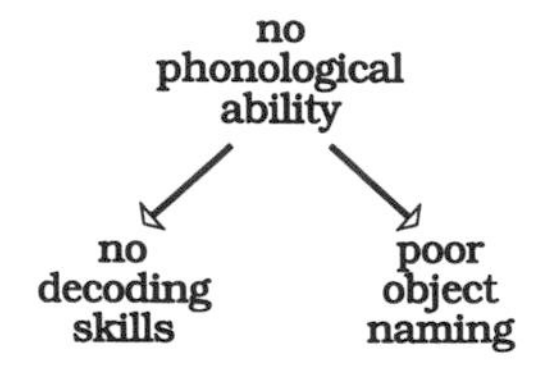

Figure 13.43 The causal model implications of the DCM in Figure 13.42.

Figure 13.42. The causal consequences of an absence of phonological skills can now be extended, as in Figure 13.43. Other things being equal, we can tell the difference between a child who cannot decode simply because letter knowledge is absent and a child who lacks the requisite phonological skills. In the next section, we look at performance on the "I spy" game and on a letter-naming game, using dyslexia as a way of illustrating the generality of the notation that we have been developing.

A CAUSAL ANALYSIS OF DYSLEXIA

The Dyslexia Debate: Is There Such a Thing as Dyslexia?

The first distinction we have to make is between *true dyslexia* and reading difficulty of the type that is sometimes called the garden variety (Gough & Tunmer, 1986). This is not as easy a task as might initially appear (Stanovich, 1988). What we are seeking to know is the difference between those children who are delayed for reasons stemming from the relationship between the child and the educational process, and those children who have some clear and specific cognitive deficit that gives rise to a reading problem. There appear to be major differences in the literature with respect to the delineation of these groups. On the one hand, we have the biological school, exemplified by Galaburda and his team. The advance publicity information for a conference cosponsored by the New York Academy of Sciences, in September 1992, and organized by Galaburda, contained the following (Tallal, 1988):

> Despite normal intelligence some 10% of our school children have great difficulties in learning to read and write. This severe handicap, which is often combined with developmental language impairment (dysphasia), seems to have a neurological etiology.

The implication is that all 10% are to be seen as neurologically impaired. The basis of the claim is work comparing the brains of dyslexics and of normals with respect to certain parameters (Galaburda, 1989; Galaburda, Rosen, & Sherman, 1989; see also Hynd & Semrud-Clikeman, 1989, for a review).

This position contrasts with that of educationalists such as Marie Clay, who see reading difficulties as educational problems from a variety of causes, all of which have educational solutions (Clay, 1979). Clay's work in New Zealand involved retesting children after a year's reading instruction. Those children in the bottom 10–20% in reading attainment, irrespective of the apparent cause, were given remedial teaching, individually designed and delivered by highly trained specialists, half an hour a day for 12–20 weeks. Clay reported that 70–90% of these children responded to this special teaching by attaining class-appropriate performance (Clay, 1987). The children who did not respond included some who arrived at satisfactory performance levels the following year, without further intervention, and some children who turned out to be significantly handicapped. The implication is that less than 1% of the original population had a permanent, specific handicap.

How is one to reconcile these two sets of ideas and facts? There are a number of possibilities:

1. Educationalists tend to use a behavioral definition of reading difficulties and are concerned only with children at primary school age. Neurologists tend to consider only cases that evidence a lifelong handicap in reading and reading-related skills, regardless of systematic improvement over time.
2. Educationalists might argue that the Galaburda team sampled a set of extreme dyslexics with brains not typical of the reading-impaired population (the sample were self-referred by willing their brains for scientific research). The vast majority of dyslexics, by this argument, would not be expected to show any brain abnormalities.
3. Neurologists might argue that all people with developmental reading difficulties have some kind of cortical abnormality but only in a minority of cases is the difficulty not remediable. This account also requires a particular assumption: that most cases of reading difficulty are remediable if caught in time, or are only remediable if they are treated by a method that includes a feature contained in the Clay method.

We will attempt to take these possibilities into account in the discussion that follows.

The Discrepancy Definition of Specific Reading Disability

It is well known that there are great difficulties in defining reading failure as opposed to generally low academic achievement. The pioneering work in studying the total population of a particular age group in the Isle of Wight (Rutter, Tizard, & Whitmore, 1970; Rutter, Tizard, Yule, Graham, & Whitmore, 1976) showed that it was hard to establish clear-cut differences on the behavioral level between children who were specifically reading disabled and those who were merely backward. Their reading patterns were equivalent. To identify the target subpopulation of dyslexics, intelligence had to be taken into account. Using a discrepancy definition based on the regression between reading test scores and intelligence test scores, a group of underachievers could be identified who had "specific" difficulties—they were unexpectedly failing to become literate at the pace of their peers (Rutter & Yule, 1975).

Ultimately, this method, which seemed very promising as a basis for identifying dyslexia, was defeated by its own strength: its behavioral descriptive basis. In the measures available, no consistent and meaningful neurological correlates could be found that would allow the delineation of a biologically based syndrome. On the contrary, the *backward* group exhibited neurological symptoms such as clumsiness, deafness, visual problems, and epilepsy. Particularly damaging was the later claim that the originally proposed "hump" in the normal distribution of discrepancy scores was the result of a statistical artifact (van der Wissel & Zegers, 1985). What was actually shown was that the hump *could have been* an artifact. In any case, it is very difficult to demonstrate the presence of two different distributions when one of them is a very small subsample.

The next step, which proved irresistible to critics, was to deny that there is such a thing as dyslexia (Bryant & Impey, 1986; Prior, 1989; Treiman & Hirsh-Pasek, 1985). However, this is a step too far (Miles & Haslum, 1986). There is good evidence that reading and spelling problems can be caused by genetic factors (Pennington, 1991). On the other hand, the discrepancy definition of dyslexia does not map on to such a concept, as is already apparent in the Isle of Wight studies. How could this state of affairs come about?

The behavioral definition of reading difficulties is not the same as a cognitive definition. A discrepancy definition is a definition at the behavioral level and can only distinguish between two broad categories:

1. There are children who show no discrepancies. Their poor scores on reading tests could be a consequence of general developmental delay, general learning disability, or adverse external circumstances, such as lack of reading experience.
2. There are children with poor reading test scores relative to IQ. This could be a sign of a specific cognitive deficit, but not necessarily.

Some children may be found to be reading-disabled relative to their IQ for rather tangential reasons: they may not speak the language, or they may have missed out on schooling because of illness, bullying, or poor teaching. Some children may appear to be specifically reading-disabled simply because they are growing up in a culture where schooling and literacy are not valued. All these children would be picked up in big sweeps of educational tests and would look worse off even than true dyslexics, in terms of their reading test scores. They may be shown to be dyslexic in terms of a discrepancy definition; however, they are only pseudo-dyslexic. The Clay sweep at the end of the first school year gathers up the bottom 15 + % of readers to place in a remedial program, and includes these types of children. One would expect particularly high success rates if these children were taught individually and might be given their first real chance at learning to read.

Current reading test scores do not identify particular types of specific disability. Therefore, the category of specific underachievement necessarily lumps together children whose deficit could also be caused by, say, visual impairment. Not all children with an unexpected reading failure suffer from a specific underlying cognitive deficit. Let us stress the causal asymmetry here. We agree that if there is an underlying cognitive problem, then there will be behavioral signs. However, the presence of such behavioral signs does not necessarily imply an underlying cognitive problem. There is another reason for dissatisfaction with a discrepancy definition of dyslexia.[27] Within the framework we have set up, we can readily make the required distinctions within the area of specific reading difficulties. The notation introduced in the previous section can help us solve the problem of representing true dyslexia as well as representing different causes for dyslexia, or subtypes of dyslexia. We can also separate out pseudodyslexia, the reading failure originating from external and often reversible causes.

Toward a Cognitive Definition

Beginning with the Isle of Wight studies, a large body of work on specific reading difficulty has succeeded in sharpening the distinction and in laying the foundations of genetic studies of a particular type of dyslexia that seems to run in families and to be more frequent in boys than in girls (Critchley, 1970; Pennington, 1989). The main outcome from the genetic studies (twin studies and family pedigree studies) is that the phenotype for the disorder is a phonological processing problem (Olson, Wise, Conners, & Rack, 1990; Olson, Wise, Conners, Rack, & Fulker, 1989; Stevenson, Graham, Fredman, & McLoughlin, 1987). This outcome was independently arrived at in a wide variety of psychological studies comparing dyslexic readers and reading-age-matched normal readers. We shall focus on this particular condition as a prototype of dyslexia and will model it in an X-type causal diagram. We make no theoretical claim other than those implicit in the position we are modeling.

Why is there continuing disagreement as to the existence of such a prototype? It has been suggested that a simple yet sensitive

[27] A further reason for not trusting the behavioral discrepancy definition is that it excludes dyslexics who are compensated sufficiently to be accurate readers but still read very slowly and with effort.

behavioral measure that will distinguish dyslexics with phonological problems is performance on nonword reading and spelling (Rack, Snowling, & Olson, 1992; Siegel, 1989; Snowling, 1987). Ordinary reading tests that consist of real word recognition and text comprehension are likely to camouflage the problem because, by sheer rote learning, a child may acquire a large sight vocabulary, and, by sheer intelligence, may be able to use sentence context to guess the gist of the message.[28] The question that fires the debate is: What is special about dyslexic readers that is not also shown by garden variety poor readers or indeed by young normal children before they have learned to read? In other words, are there differences among these groups at the cognitive level? Before we can address these questions, we need to look at the prerequisites for the normal development of literacy. We do this because what applies to deficits also applies to development.

Contingencies in Literacy Acquisition

In Figure 13.44, we diagram some of the main contingencies for learning to become literate in an alphabetic script. One important internal prerequisite is a minimum of general processing efficiency.[29] Furthermore, we need to assume that there is adequate vision and hearing—the normal input channels for the skill to be learned. (Children with impairments in these channels would have to be acknowledged separately.) In addition to these very basic prerequisites, which figure in a great many developmental contingencies, we require two cognitive capacities that are specifically relevant: (a) a normally developing phonological system, P, which many researchers have proposed is damaged in true dyslexics, and (b) a normally developing Supervisory Attentional System (SAS), as proposed by Shallice (1988). This general SAS needs to function efficiently if any formal learning is to take place, and we assume that, when this SAS is immature or damaged, the acquisition of any taught skills, including reading, would be difficult or impossible, even if all other prerequisites were available. This might be the case with certain types of attention disorder (see the section on Hyperactivity, above). External input—specifically, teaching—will be required for any progress in learning to read. If all of these internal and external conditions are fulfilled, then an automated system for handling grapheme-phoneme (GP) correspondence will be established, and, as a result, alphabetic skills will be evident.[30] Only after achieving a certain degree of proficiency with alphabetic skills will the child go on to become an orthographically skilled reader (Frith, 1985; Morton, 1989a).

[28] That the vocabulary score correlates very highly with all other reading measures, including those that stress comprehension at the most abstract level, is another problem. The correlation is valid only for the normal population. Where there is a cognitive deficit and the child has adopted a compensatory strategy, normal population statistics are no longer applicable.

[29] The concept of general processing efficiency is discussed extensively by Anderson (1992).

[30] The alphabetic skills will, of course, depend on more than GP. Thus, the ability to segment at the level of onset/rime enables children to use spelling patterns in familiar words (beak) when decoding unfamiliar words (peak) (Goswami, 1986, 1990).

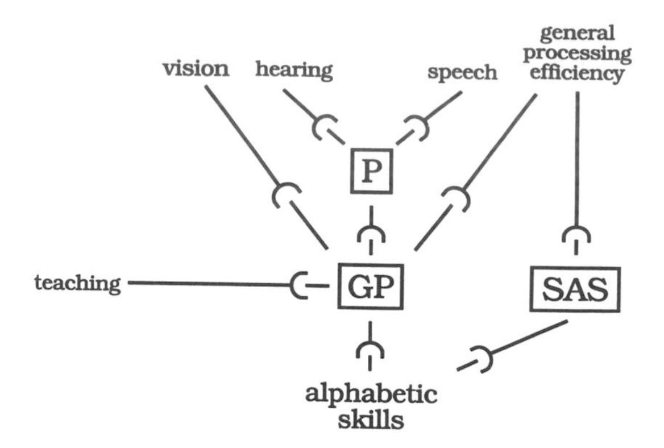

Figure 13.44 A minimal set of contingencies for learning to become literate in an alphabetic script.

An X-Type Causal Model of Dyslexia

As with autism, enough facts are available at both biological and behavioral levels of description to suggest that there is a diagnostic entity. This occurs even though (a) the biological origins of dyslexia are unknown and are likely to be multiple, and (b) the signs and symptoms are extremely variable and have not yet been sorted out into core symptoms, additional associated problems, and secondary consequences.

The causal model for dyslexia that seems to be well supported by the weight of the evidence is given in Figure 13.45. As with autism, the model includes alternative biological origins, a single, defining cognitive deficit, and a variety of core and other signs and symptoms. We would not be surprised, however, if, in the future, different or additional deficits were

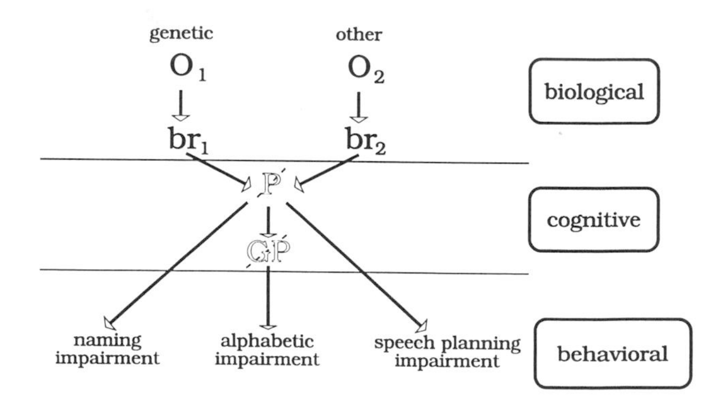

Figure 13.45 A schematic causal model for dyslexia, involving all three levels of description. The defining condition is a cognitive deficit, an absence of the cognitive structure P. This leads to absence of structure GP, involving automated routines that relate sounds and letters. The biological causes may be of different types, genetic and other. Behavioral consequences include problems other than lack of decoding skills.

considered necessary for a full explanation of the many varieties of reading problems.

Biological Factors

As yet, the biological basis of dyslexia is a matter of speculation. Galaburda (1989) reviewed the anatomical evidence from 8 brains analyzed up to that time. The brains all showed an absence of ordinary asymmetry in the planum temporale, a particular area of the temporal lobes that is thought to subserve speech and language. Exactly what this implies in terms of developing psychological functions is unknown.

More recently, Livingstone, Rosen, Drislane, and Galaburda (1991) reported further anatomical findings, this time concerning the visual cortex, in particular, V1. Here, too, abnormalities were found in dyslexic brains, specifically in the magnocellular system, which is responsible for low-contrast, high-speed visual processing. Experimental evidence for a deficit in this process has been provided by Lovegrove, Garzia, and Nicholson (1990). Although a visual cognitive deficit underlying reading failure is a perfectly reasonable option (see the models in Figures 13.49 and 13.50, below), we cannot jump to the conclusion that there is a deficit that is different from our previously assumed P structure. We shall have to await further evidence before we can talk about contrasting biological causes that may or may not be connected with contrasting cognitive deficits.

The genetic findings (Olson et al., 1989; Smith, Kimberling, Pennington, & Lubs, 1983; Stevenson et al., 1987) all agree that there is an identifiable, single component underlying dyslexia, namely, a deficit in phonological processing. Scarborough (1990) studied preschool children whose parents were dyslexic. Of these children, 65%, a remarkably high level, were later themselves diagnosed dyslexic. These children had tended to show deficits in certain speech processes by age 3. In a recent theory concerning brain lateralization, Annett (1992) went one step further, postulating a single gene for left hemisphere specialization, which enables efficient phonological processing. Thus, in the normal population there will be wide variation in the extent to which speech is supported by dedicated neural systems. Individuals at the extremes of the normal variation may be at risk for dyslexia (Annett & Kilshaw, 1984).

It is notable that scarcely any theories of the origins of dyslexia have implicated other than genetic factors. A possible exception is the somewhat speculative Geschwind-Galaburda hypothesis explaining abnormalities in brain asymmetry that might be relevant to dyslexia in terms of complex interactions of intrauterine environments and sex of fetus (Geschwind & Galaburda, 1985). The biological level in our causal model will have only one node, corresponding to genetic disorders, although it is anticipated that a number of different types of genetic disorder will be identified. Bishop (1990), who provided a critical evaluation of both Annett's and Geschwind's theories of cerebral lateralization and dyslexia, concluded:

> [T]here is little support for the theory that individual differences in the direction and degree of laterality of language representation are the basis for developmental dyslexia. (p. 129)

Cognitive Factors

The consensus of the best available research is that a proportion of poor readers—garden variety as well as true dyslexics—is deficient in the formation of the particular cognitive structure that is responsible for grapheme-phoneme correspondence (Frith, 1985; Johnston, 1982; Snowling, 1991; Snowling, Stackhouse, & Rack, 1986). This can have a number of different causes. In true dyslexia, as we have described it in our X-type model, the cause is a deficient P structure. This deficit results in not only a faulty GP structure and poor alphabetic skills but additional impairments as well. Some agreement has been reached as to the crucial impairments (Catts, 1989; Pennington, 1989). These all concern problems in the phonological processing of spoken language and are termed by Pennington: "name retrieval," "verbal short-term memory," and "speech production." It will be apparent from this description that the deficit proposed by such theorists to underlie dyslexia will reveal itself well before the normal onset of literacy.[31]

There is widespread agreement that the developmental deficit in system P, which we assume characterizes dyslexia (Olson et al., 1989; Shankweiler, Liberman, Mark, Fowler, & Fischer, 1979; Snowling, 1987; Stanovich, 1988), can be indexed by a variety of phonological tests. Such tests include alliteration and rhyming (Bradley & Bryant, 1983; Bryant, Maclean, Bradley, & Crossland, 1990), nonword reading (Rack, Snowling, & Olson, 1992), and rhyme matching (Lenel & Cantor, 1981), all of which involve the use of certain components of phonological skills.[32] Many studies have shown that the critical component P is also absent in normal children below school age (see Figure 13.46), presumably because of a relatively late process of maturation (Byrne & Fielding-Barnsley, 1989; Liberman, Liberman,

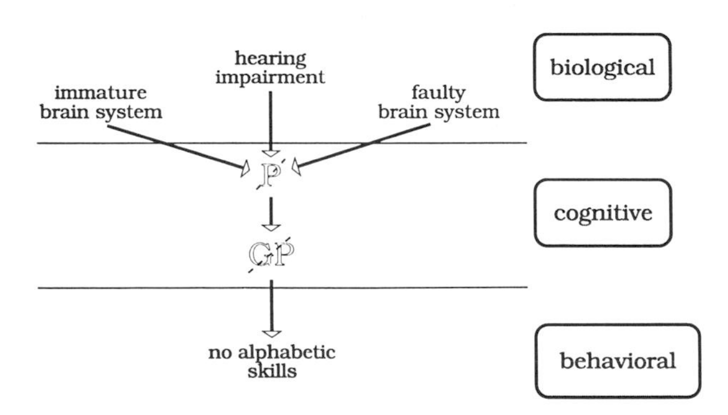

Figure 13.46 Failure of structure P can come about either through a fault at the biological level or, with young children, because of immature biological structures. In the latter case, the "dyslexia" is purely temporary.

[31] It also follows that the deficit underlying dyslexia in English-speaking children should be found in all cultures, including nonliterate cultures and nonalphabetic cultures.

[32] At the moment, it is unclear how this developing process might be characterized. Its identification at the cognitive level is a major goal for researchers in the field.

Mattingly, & Shankweiler, 1980; Lundberg, Frost, & Peterson, 1988).[33] A third reason for the lack of development of the critical component, P, could be hearing impairment, including intermittent impairments such as otitis media with effusion (OME).

Difficulties of the Beginning Reader

The reciprocal relationship between literacy acquisition and phonological skills (Cataldo & Ellis, 1990; Ehri, 1984; Perfetti, 1991; Stuart & Coltheart, 1988) means that clear causal pathways for reading failure are difficult to establish. For instance, subsyllabic segmentation and blending skills appear simultaneously with alphabetic reading skills. However, it seems likely that different components of phonological processes are evoked when typical phoneme awareness tasks are given to a person who is literate and when given to a preliterate child (Morais, 1991).

There is a clear correlation between the emergence of P-indexed skills in preschool children and their subsequent smooth and early entry into an alphabetic system, but there is also evidence from training studies (Lundberg et al., 1988) to strengthen the notion of a causal relationship. Wimmer, Landerl, Linortner, and Hummer (1991) showed that prereaders with poor P-indexed skills (e.g., "mis-repetition," not being able to substitute one particular vowel for another vowel in a single word) could be divided into two groups after the first school year: (a) those whose P component was simply delayed compared to their peers but who subsequently became competent readers, and (b) those who remained persistently poor readers, with the possible explanation that their P component was faulty.

In its simplest form, this hypothesis supposes that, at preschool age and on standard tasks, an immature P system is not distinguishable from a faulty P system. The implication of this theory is that the brain systems involved in Figure 13.46 should be the same in the case of fault and delay. The study by Scarborough (1990) of preschool children at risk for dyslexia suggested, however, that a careful analysis of speech processes may pick out a dysfunctional from a merely immature P system even at this early stage. On this view, one would expect the biological components in the causal chains of the two to be different from each other. We would also expect remediation in the case of delay to be much more straightforward than in the case of deficit.

Behavioral Signs and Symptoms

There are other reasons for not developing a GP system, and we have already alluded to several other prerequisites apart from the phonological system in Figure 13.44. In other words, specific evidence is needed in order to draw the conclusion that a child is truly dyslexic—which we equate here with a faulty P component. Figure 13.47 is a diagram of the possibility of different types of biological causes, one of which affects both the P component and the SAS component. This would be the case for an individual suffering from a severe learning difficulty affecting not only literacy, but also any other type of formal learning. Figure 13.48 illustrates a case where only the SAS component is directly affected by a biological malfunction. This could occur with attentional deficit disorder. When certain aspects of the SAS system are affected, absence of a GP system would result. The solid box around the P system indicates that it is intact.[34]

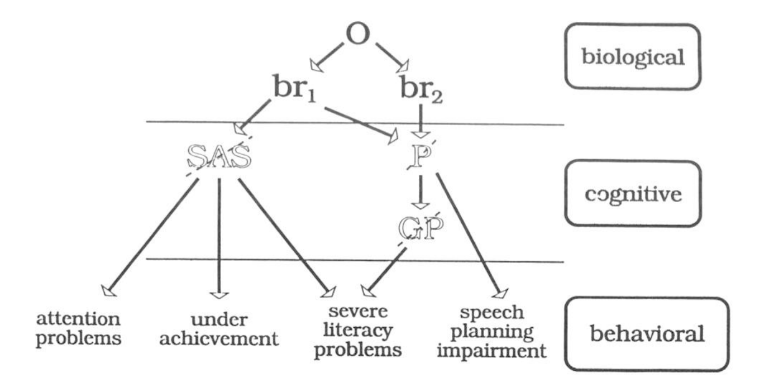

Figure 13.47 A hypothesis of aggravated dyslexia where a biological deficit can cause not only a lack of the P system but also a deficit in the supervisory attentional system (SAS).

As our maxim 4 of causal modeling demands, we must distinguish between general and specific deficit. If a deficit is explicable in terms of a general deficit, then we need have no recourse to specific accounts. Poor reading achievement can often be explained as part and parcel of general mental retardation or social disadvantage. We would not want to talk about specific reading problems in such circumstances.

Associated and Secondary Problems

A number of authors have reported that children with severe reading problems have more attentional deficits than would be expected by chance (Taylor, 1986). It remains to be seen whether these children would be classified as dyslexic by virtue of a faulty P component. If they are, then there would be two ways in which the association could come about, each of which would have a particular representation in a causal model. One possibility is that the attentional problem is secondary—that is, it is caused by the effects of being backward in reading on the child's attitude toward himself and toward the process of education (Stanovich, 1986). The other account of the attentional problem involves the SAS component, and the behavior would be classified as associated. Fergusson and Horwood (1992) claimed to have evidence for the latter account and not for the former. An association between reading problems and conduct disorder has also long been known

[33] There is reason to believe that another component of phonology is derivative on alphabetic skills and only develops in individuals who had a minimum of experience with alphabetic scripts. Thus, Morais, Cary, Alegria, and Bertelson (1979) showed that adult illiterates found it difficult to understand, for instance, what was meant by the request to say "Ted" without the "tuh." Because letters are visible manifestations of the artificial concept phoneme, it is not surprising that so-called phoneme awareness is dependent on knowing letters.

[34] We note here that there exist other children who are hyperlexic in the presence of potentially severe SAS problems, and, indeed, general intellectual impairments. In these cases, it has been shown that a GP system is fully operative, presumably in the presence of a normal P structure (Cossu & Marshall, 1990; Frith & Snowling, 1983; Seymour & Evans, 1992).

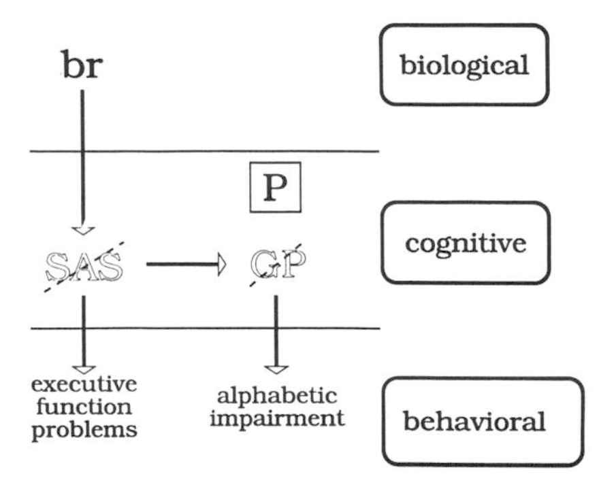

Figure 13.48 A hypothesis relating a deficit in SAS to subsequent dyslexic symptoms in the presence of an intact P system. The setting up of the GP structure is assumed to be dependent on an intact attentional structure. Hence, GP would be absent despite intact P.

(Sturge, 1982; Yule & Rutter, 1985) and might receive a similar explanation.

Competing Theories of Dyslexia

There are, of course, challenges to the particular causal model of dyslexia that we have adopted. Clay (1987), for instance, argued that children learn to become learning-disabled and that a biological basis may be an unsound assumption to start with. Another challenge is that we focused on a phonological deficit when there may be others (e.g., visual deficits) that underlie at least a subtype of dyslexia. Our notation enables us to represent competing theories of dyslexia, and, just as in the case of autism, the potential to compare theories on neutral ground can be demonstrated by some examples.

Figures 13.49 and 13.50 illustrate a specific visual impairment as a cause of dyslexia. Such a cause has been suggested by several researchers, notably Stein (1991) and Lovegrove, Martin, and

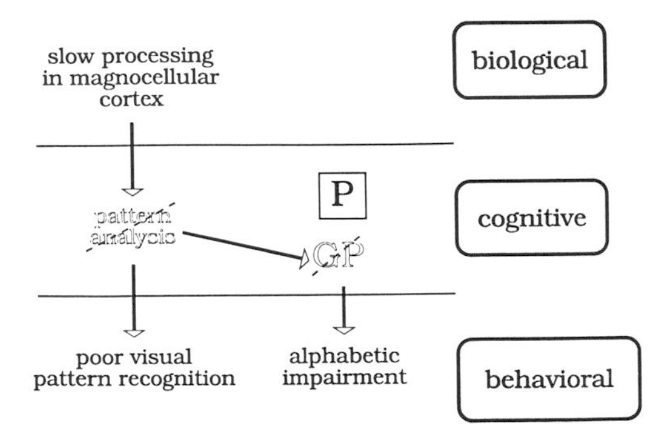

Figure 13.49 A representation of a hypothesis implicating a visual deficit caused by a biological problem which, in turn, leads to a dyslexic syndrome in the presence of an intact P system. GP is absent or diminished because the visual component of letter sound routines (letter analysis) is deficient.

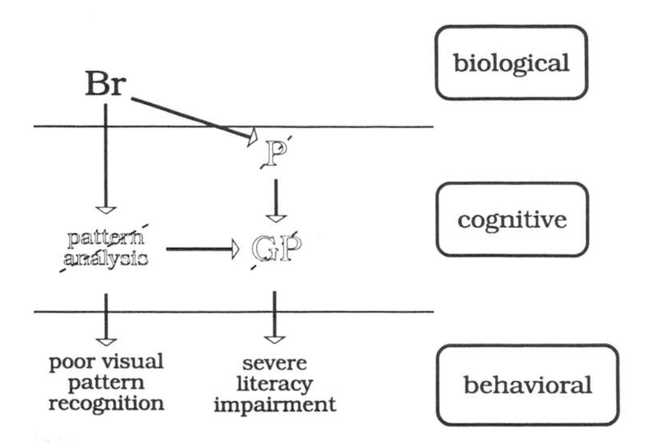

Figure 13.50 A representation of a hypothesis of a biological deficit that affects both visual and phonological systems. This illustrates a case that could be termed "can't read" rather than "won't read."

Slaghuis (1986). We expect that, in some cases at least, a cognitive component will be identified whose absence, quite separately from the P component, will inhibit the development of alphabetic skills. In Figure 13.49, we propose *pattern analysis* as such a component. The biological cause could be as Livingstone et al. (1991) suggested: a defect within the magnocellular system. Cases of dissociation between phonological and visual skills exist (Seymour, 1990) and strongly suggest the possibility of subgroups that can be defined at the cognitive level. Figure 13.50 illustrates the possibility of a more complex picture: a double deficit, at the cognitive level, both in phonological skills and in visual pattern analysis. This double deficit may nevertheless be caused by a single biological fault (Stein, 1991).

Nonbiological Causes

Figures 13.51, 13.52, and 13.53 show examples of externally generated causes of poor reading—lack of language knowledge, poor teaching/learning environment or severe emotional resistance to school, and test performance brought about by negative external influences. Sometimes, these causes directly affect the GP component (Figure 13.51). More often, the SAS component is affected

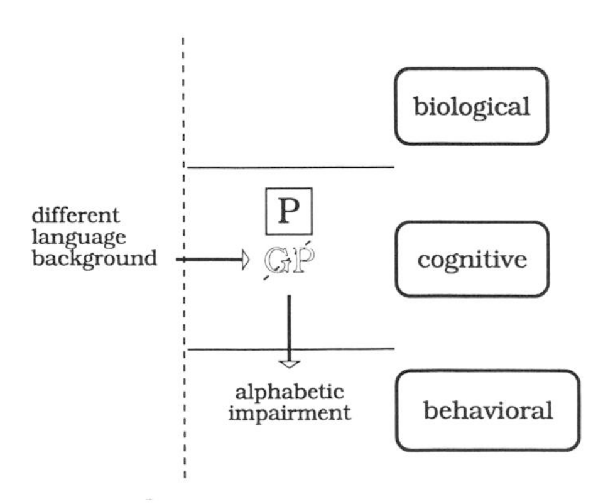

Figure 13.51 Reading problems caused by virtue of a different language background.

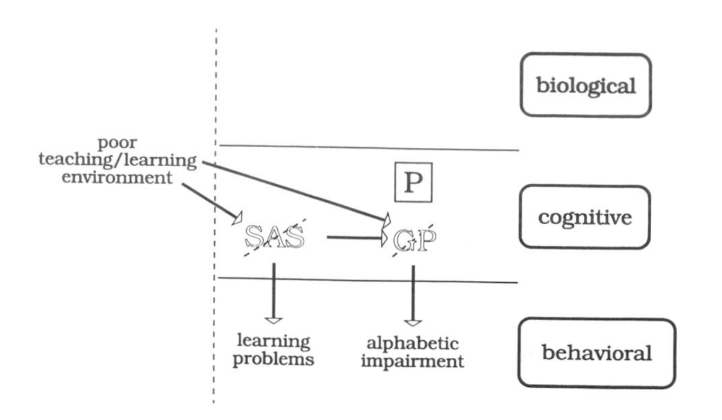

Figure 13.52 Reading problems caused by problems in an attentional component, which is, in turn, caused by external factors (poor teaching). Here, the external influences have impeded the establishment of the GP system. The P system is intact. The deficit in SAS will give rise to additional learning problems (and possibly conduct disorder).

(in the form of attentional problems), as illustrated in Figures 13.52 and 13.53.

A "normal" variant of externally motivated causes that accidentally impair reading acquisition is the effect of a child's being newly confronted by a different language and phonology, or simply not getting instruction because he or she is growing up in a nonliterate culture. In such cases, we would have no reason to suppose that process P is dysfunctional; rather, we could point to incomplete knowledge of the phonology of the particular language that the child is still in the process of acquiring. Figure 13.51 illustrates such a cultural factor.

Figures 13.52 and 13.53 show the effects of a different class of factors—a disturbed home life, a hostile relationship with a teacher, or, simply, misguided teaching (all of which have been claimed to inhibit reading acquisition). These external causes may primarily affect the SAS component; that is, they have potentially

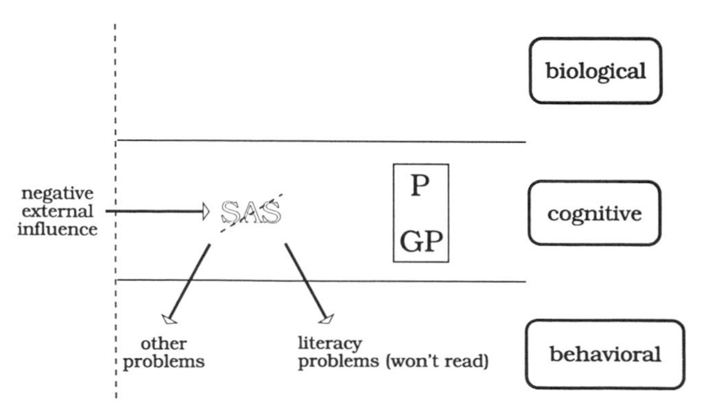

Figure 13.53 Reading problems caused via external influences acting on the attentional systems to create reading difficulties in the presence of an intact P system and an intact GP system. This might be termed "won't read," as opposed to "can't read."

more widespread effects than mere reading difficulties. We have indicated that behavioral disorders would be expected in this group, given the association of conduct disorder and reading difficulty, delinquency, and illiteracy. These externally caused reading problems (part of the large garden variety group) may be mediated either through an effect on the GP system (as in Figure 13.52, where we would expect poor performance specifically in reading and spelling nonwords) or only at the behavioral level (Figure 13.53).[35] Figure 13.53 presents the case of a poor reader who won't read rather than can't read. We are suggesting that the child's not wanting to read can and should be treated as a cognitive link in the causal chain. An external cause that is not mediated by the SAS system and yet has a specific and detrimental effect on setting up a GP system might be an impenetrable orthographic writing system. English, with its complex orthography, is a possible candidate (Wimmer, 1993).

In another version of the causal theories just discussed, the damage done has its effect solely at the behavioral level. For instance, counterproductive reading strategies may have been induced by incompetent or misguided teaching. Such patterns of behavior are established instead of the normal reading strategies, which generally function as self-teaching mechanisms. This is in contrast to the first version illustrated above, where the effect occurs at the level of cognitive structures and the acquisition of a well-functioning GP system is prevented.

Other Biological Causes of Reading Failure

We can imagine a case of reading failure attributable to a cognitive deficit and yet not of biological origin. We would claim that this condition, if it exists, is pseudo-dyslexia. True dyslexia, in contrast, is defined by a cognitive deficit (whether in a visual or in a phonological system) and has a biological origin. The question that we now need to ask is whether all biological causes of reading failure are connected with a specific cognitive deficit and therefore qualify as true dyslexia.

The case of a blind person (who has not learned Braille) illustrates the answer to this question (Figure 13.54). There would undoubtedly be a biological origin that we would want to call the cause of the person's being unable to read. We would not, however, want to link this through the cognitive factor P, in spite of the fact that the blind person (lacking the relevant teaching) has no grapheme-phoneme system. The immediate/local cause of absence of a GP system, then, is the absence of Braille stimuli and a teacher, not the absence of P. It would be more sensible to stick with the remote cause and to show the behavioral problem, lack of alphabetic skills, as being caused (remotely) by the blindness, but not by a specific cognitive problem. A similar case might be made for some types of hearing impairment. However,

[35] The effect of lead in the environment has repeatedly been shown in lower scores on reading tests (Fulton et al., 1987; Silva, Hughes, Williams, & Faed, 1988). We would suggest that this sort of external cause of reading impairment may act in the same way as certain psychosocial causes. Thus, there would be an effect on the behavioral level (alphabetic skills), which would be mediated through the attentional (SAS) component rather than the phonological (P) component.

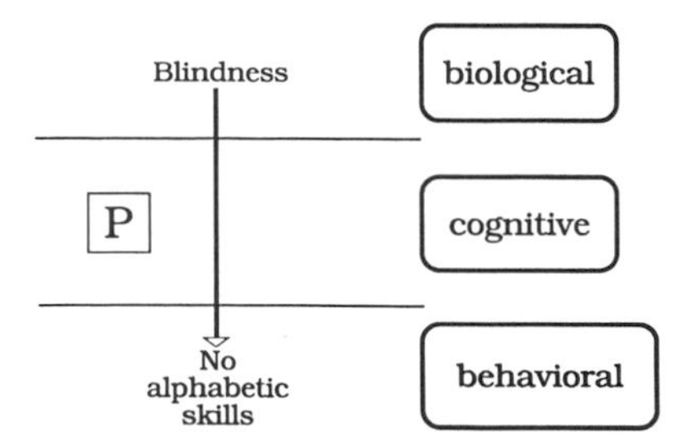

Figure 13.54 A scarcely necessary causal model of the relationship between blindness and inability to read. We do not show the absence of a GP system as being causal in the lack of decoding ability because it is preempted by the visual impairment.

in the absence of a clear theory of the normal development of the P system, we feel such a case would have to be heavily qualified.

CAUSE AND CONTINGENCY: FUTURE DEVELOPMENT

We have introduced a method of transcribing causal theories into a graphical notation. In doing so, we have made the case that, at least for higher cognitive functions, the route from biology to behavior must be through cognition. This is the only substantive theoretical claim we have made in this chapter. The justification for this position is that, without the cognitive level, we cannot account for patterns of breakdown within individuals, nor can we account for the nature of the variability of breakdown in the population. We have used existing work on autism as an example. The essential aspect of this work is the claim that the vast range of symptoms found in autistics, which include disorders of communication, socialization, and imagination, can be accounted for on the basis of a single cognitive deficit. Such a unification requires, of course, theories of cognitive development in the normal population as well as in autistics. The theories of cognitive development enable us to account for the variability in the population. Matters of intelligence, other individual sources of variability (including the extent of brain damage), and environmental considerations will interact in complex ways. This complexity is not manageable if one only looks at the behavior, because the invariant core of autism and most of the interactions between the variables that affect the behavioral manifestations can only be described at the cognitive level.

In addition to our account of autism, we have analyzed developmental dyslexia in the same terms. There are many other candidate pathologies. Laszlo's (1990) approach to the development of motor skills is similar to the one we have used in this chapter. Instead of talking about *cognition* and *behavior,* she referred to the "process-oriented approach" and the "task-oriented approach." She pointed out that, with the task-oriented methods:

> . . . assessment results in a list of tasks the child can perform at a certain age. However, confounding variables, such as motivation, opportunity and interest, will have a decisive influence on the types of skills the child has practised and can perform well. If, on the other hand, developmental progression in underlying processes, which contribute to learning and performance, can be established—performance-oriented approach—it should be possible to assess which tasks the child is ready to acquire and whether the child is functioning according to his ability level or below it.
>
> Secondly, for a child presenting motor difficulties, task-oriented assessment can only reconfirm the list of tasks the child cannot perform adequately. The process-oriented diagnosis can establish the reason or reasons why the child cannot master some of the skills expected of him. That is, process dysfunction can be diagnosed and, following causal diagnosis, focal therapy, aiming at improvement of the defective process can be given. (Laszlo, 1990, p. 281)

We do not claim that all invariance is at the cognitive level. There will be many cases where the invariance is at the biological level. An example is Lesch-Nyhan syndrome, where a diverse set of signs—mental retardation, self-injury involving the upper limbs and mouth, and gout—co-occur simply because there is a missing enzyme, hypoxanthine-guanine-phospho-ribosyl-transferase. The converse of this case is represented by the example of reading disability, where a variety of kinds of breakdown at the biological level may give rise to the same functional breakdown. This functional breakdown is properly described at the cognitive level. We reiterate that "cognition" is just the label that we give to the middle level of our model, and that, where affective factors enter into the causal chain, they will generally do so at the same level as cognitive factors. For example, we have shown that affective disturbance in autism, if postulated as the root cause, will lead to a causal model very similar to the one based on the cognitive causes discussed earlier in the chapter.

Much as we champion consideration of cognitive causes of developmental disorders, we would readily agree that interest in a pathological condition does not have to be focused on the cognitive level, nor indeed on the point of convergence, at whatever level this point may be. Much will depend on the type of question that is being asked. For example, questions of prevention will almost always involve consideration of the biological level. On the other hand, the practicalities of management and teaching devolve on the behavioral level. Thus, to someone whose job involves managing severely brain-damaged autistic individuals, the technical details of the relationship between high-ability autism and Asperger's syndrome will be irrelevant. On the other hand, for a variety of activities, including the design and evaluation of new tests or therapeutic methods, the cognitive approach is essential. Irrespective of the focus of the particular work, however, a multilevel causal model will provide a framework that allows the relationship between different approaches to emerge.

The method we have described in this chapter is not tied to any theory, although in our illustrations we have been partisan. Roughly speaking, if you can say it, then it can be represented in the causal notation. One major advantage of the notation is that it is explicit with respect to the causal chain from its biological, social, or other origin, to the signs and symptoms. The pathway itself will be explicit even if some of the intervening links lack detail. Once the causal chain is made explicit, two things follow:

1. What is missing will be more apparent. Thus, in our discussion of dyslexia, we are inevitably drawn to considering the precise nature of the process that, in the normal child, is a required factor in making the phonological system available in the construction of a grapheme-phoneme system.
2. The notation simplifies the task of distinguishing among core behaviors and those that are secondary or merely associated through correlated defects at the biological levels. This is illustrated in a general fashion in Figure 13.55.

Equipped with nothing more than the five maxims of causal modeling, it is possible to make sense of topics that are of current concern for developmental psychopathology. Looking at diagnostic practice in a variety of examples, we have identified three diagnostic types, which we have termed the A-type, the X-type, and the V-type. Each will likely be appropriate in particular circumstances, but it has seemed to us important to establish which type is being discussed at any time. Again, the notation is a powerful way of revealing the underlying structure of a diagnostic concept.

Some Future Prospects of Causal Modeling

The Problem of Variability

Some readers may suspect that the phenotypic causal model makes a deterministic claim. This would be a grave error. The model is neutral in that respect; the facts are overwhelmingly against. Just because the individuals in a group have a particular genetic abnormality, it does not follow that they manifest the same abnormal brain condition. The likelihood of their behaving in the same way is even more remote. The facts of variability are undeniable, and we have to be able to indicate in our notation, at least in principle, what the sources of variation might be. We have already mentioned protective factors and precipitating factors as being two such possibilities, acting at the biological level. Such factors might be seen as variables, with values that are within the normal range of variability; that is, by itself, such a value would be unremarkable—only in combination with something else do we find abnormal development.[36] We could take as an example a mild phonological difficulty, within the "normal" range, and undetectable preliterately or where the individual belongs to a community with a nonalphabetic script (such as Kannada). When faced with learning to read English, for example, this individual could be revealed to be dyslexic.

If we look at the relationship between the cognitive and the behavioral levels, there are numerous important sources of variability. Frith (1992) analyzed both autism and dyslexia in this respect. She pointed to motivation, compensation, experience, and maturation, each of which could have a positive or negative role. These factors all intervene between stable cognitive structures and behavior.

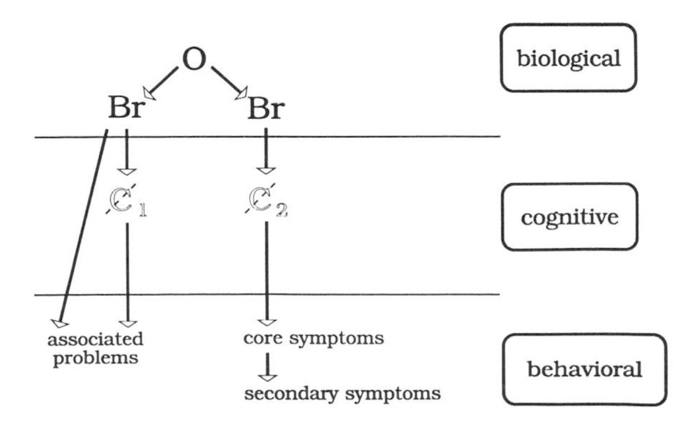

Figure 13.55 A generalized schematic causal model showing how the core signs and symptoms can be distinguished from secondary symptoms and from associated problems.

The Problem of Comorbidity

In clinical practice, it is often very difficult to know whether a particular constellation of features in a few individuals represents a diagnostic entity or a chance combination. Furthermore, we have to rule out the possibility that correlated symptoms represent the secondary consequences of a particular core symptom. The causal modeling approach offers a method and a solution to these difficulties. We propose that the definition of a diagnostic entity could be validated by the existence of a single causal chain.

We have occasionally touched on the problem of explaining overlapping or superimposed disorders, for example, when we considered the association of attention disorder and reading disability. Any rigorous account of comorbidity must avoid many pitfalls. As Caron and Rutter (1991) pointed out, fully representative epidemiological data are vital in order to assess comorbidity. In many cases, this information is not yet available. In this relatively new field of diagnostic refinement, there will certainly be a need for a tool to enable the comparison of alternative accounts.

Changing Patterns of Diagnosis

Often, the most obvious aspects of developmental abnormality, as with disease, are the outward manifestations. It is natural for a clinician, upon noticing a new pattern of signs and symptoms, to classify the individuals together as a group and to refer to the signs and symptoms as a syndrome. This behaviorally defined group would give rise to a V-shaped causal model. For some aspects of management and treatment, this might be sufficient, but, in most cases, there seems to be a process of search for the underlying cognitive or biological condition. This would lead to an X-shaped causal model or, if a single biological cause were identified, to an A-shaped causal model. The way of thinking about autism, for example, has changed, largely to keep pace with the advance of its scientific study. The current debate rests on the precise nature of the underlying cognitive deficit, rather than on behavioral description. It remains to be seen whether a

[36] It is, of course, possible to find two variables, either of which could take particular values without disturbing the developmental trajectory, but which, in combination, could lead to some developmental abnormality. Such conditions would, in any case, strain any attempt to precisely define "abnormal." Because of such limiting conditions, we would not want to abandon analysis of clear cases of pathology.

division of autism into subgroups as a function of their biological origin will be useful.

Latent Developmental Disorders

A further point arises in terms of the relationship between behavior and cognition. Let us take again the example of autism. From a behavior-based view, the search for early indicators reduces solely to a question of increasing refinement of the detection instruments. From a cognitive developmental viewpoint, which assigns the root of autism to the cognitive level, the pursuit of earliest signs has natural limitations. It therefore remains entirely possible that there will be no behavioral index of autism earlier than 18 months (Johnson et al., 1992; Lister-Brook, 1992). The particular cognitive deficit that we postulate in autism may have no visible manifestations in behavior for the first year of life. As a matter of fact, our particular theory leads us to suspect that autism can only be detected at the age when certain critical kinds of behavior would normally be expected to emerge. Delay between root and manifestation applies to almost all genetically based conditions. The first manifestation may occur as late as adulthood (e.g., Huntington's chorea and certain kinds of schizophrenia).

Finally, we would like to stress that the notation gives us a ready method of relating abnormal development, as expressed with a causal model, with normal development, as expressed with a contingency model. Only by keeping this relationship firmly in mind shall we be able to follow the straight as well as the crooked pathways.

REFERENCES

American Psychiatric Association. (1980, 1987, 1994). *Diagnostic and statistical manual of mental disorders* (3rd ed., 3rd ed. rev., 4th ed.). Washington, DC: Author.

Anderson, M. (1992). *Intelligence and development: A cognitive theory.* Oxford, England: Blackwell.

Annett, M. (1992). Phonological processing and right minus left hand skill. *Quarterly Journal of Experimental Psychology, 44A,* 33–46.

Annett, M., & Kilshaw, D. (1984). Lateral preference and skill in dyslexics: Implications of the right-shift theory. *Journal of Child Psychology and Psychiatry, 25,* 357–377.

Astington, J., Harris, P., & Olson, D. (Eds.). (1988). *Developing theories of mind.* Cambridge, England: Cambridge University Press.

Baron-Cohen, S. (1991). Precursors to a theory of mind: Understanding attention in others. In A. Whiten (Ed.), *Natural theories of mind: Evolution, development and simulation of everyday mindreading* (pp. 233–251). Oxford, England: Basil Blackwell.

Baron-Cohen, S., Leslie, A. M., & Frith, U. (1985). Does the autistic child have a "theory of mind"? *Cognition, 21,* 37–46.

Bauman, M., & Kemper, T. L. (1985). Histoanatomic observations of the brain in early infant autism. *Neurology, 35,* 866–874.

Bishop, D. V. M. (1990). *Handedness and developmental disorder.* London: MacKeith Press.

Bolton, P., & Rutter, M. (1990). Genetic influences in autism. *International Review of Psychiatry, 2,* 67–80.

Bradley, L. L., & Bryant, P. E. (1983). Categorizing sounds and learning to read: A causal connection. *Nature, 301,* 419.

Bryant, P. E., & Impey, L. (1986). The similarities between normal children and dyslexic adults and children. *Cognition, 24,* 121–137.

Bryant, P. E., Maclean, M., Bradley, L. L., & Crossland, J. (1990). Rhyme and alliteration, phoneme detection and learning to read. *Developmental Psychology, 26,* 429–438.

Butterworth, G., Harris, P., Leslie, A. M., & Wellman, H. (Eds.). (1991). *The child's theory of mind.* Oxford, England: Oxford University Press.

Byrne, B., & Fielding-Barnsley, R. (1989). Phonemic awareness and letter knowledge in the child's acquisition of the alphabetic principle. *Journal of Educational Psychology, 81,* 313–321.

Cantwell, D. P. (1975). Genetics of hyperactivity. *Journal of Child Psychology and Psychiatry, 16,* 261–264.

Cantwell, D. (1977). Hyperkinetic syndrome. In K. F. Rutter & L. Hersov (Eds.), *Child psychiatry: Modern approaches* (pp. 524–555). Oxford, England: Blackwell.

Carey, S. (1985). *Conceptual change in childhood.* Cambridge, MA: MIT Press.

Caron, C., & Rutter, M. (1991). Comorbidity in childhood psychopathology: Concepts, issues and research strategies. *Journal of Child Psychology and Psychiatry, 32,* 1063–1080.

Cataldo, S., & Ellis, N. (1990). Learning to spell, learning to read. In P. D. Pumfrey & C. D. Elliott (Eds.), *Children's difficulties in reading, spelling and writing* (pp. 101–125). London: Falmer Press.

Catts, H. W. (1989). Defining dyslexia as a developmental language disorder. *Annals of Dyslexia, 39,* 50–64.

Chess, S., Korn, S. J., & Fernandez, P. B. (1971). *Psychiatric disorders of children with congenital rubella.* New York: Brunner/Mazel.

Clarke, A. M., & Clarke, A. D. B. (1992). How modifiable is the human life path? In N. Bray (Ed.), *International review of research in mental retardation, 18,* 137–157. New York: Academic Press.

Clay, M. M. (1979). *The early detection of reading difficulties.* London: Heinemann.

Clay, M. M. (1987). Learning to be learning disabled. *New Zealand Journal of Educational Studies, 22,* 155–172.

Cossu, G., & Marshall, J. C. (1990). Are cognitive skills a pre-requisite for learning to read and write? *Cognitive Neuropsychology, 7,* 21–40.

Courchesne, E., Yeung-Courchesne, R., Press, G. A., Hesselink, J. R., & Jernigan, T. L. (1988). *The New England Journal of Medicine, 318,* 1349–1354.

Critchley, M. (1970). *The dyslexic child.* London: Heinemann.

Dawson, G., & Lewy, A. (1989a). Arousal, attention, and the socioemotional impairments of individuals with autism. In G. Dawson (Ed.), *Autism: Nature, diagnosis and treatment* (pp. 49–74). New York: Guilford.

Dawson, G., & Lewy, A. (1989b). In G. Dawson (Ed.), *Autism: Nature, diagnosis and treatment* (pp. 144–173). New York: Guilford.

Ehri, L. C. (1984). How orthography alters spoken language competencies in children learning to read and spell. In J. Downing & R. Valtin (Eds.), *Language awareness and learning to read* (pp. 119–147). New York: Springer-Verlag.

Fergusson, D. M., & Horwood, L. J. (1992). Attention deficit and reading achievement. *Journal of Child Psychology and Psychiatry, 33,* 375–385.

Fombonne, E., & du Mazaubrun, C. (1992). Prevalence of infantile autism in four French regions. *Social Psychiatry and Psychiatric Epidemiology, 27,* 203–210.

Frith, C. (1992). *The cognitive neuropsychology of schizophrenia.* Hove, Sussex, England: Erlbaum.

Frith, U. (1985). Beneath the surface of developmental dyslexia. In K. Patterson, M. Coltheart, & J. Marshall (Eds.), *Surface dyslexia* (pp. 301–330). London: Erlbaum.

Frith, U. (1989). *Autism: Explaining the enigma.* Oxford, England: Blackwell.

Frith, U. (1992). Cognitive development and cognitive deficit. *The Psychologist, 5,* 13–19.

Frith, U., Morton, J., & Leslie, A. M. (1991). The cognitive basis of a biological disorder: Autism. *Trends in Neurosciences, 14,* 433–438.

Frith, U., & Snowling, M. (1983). Reading for meaning and reading for sound in autistic and dyslexic children. *British Journal of Developmental Psychology, 1,* 329–342.

Fulton, M., Raab, G., Thomson, G., Laxen, D., Hunter, R., & Hepburn, W. (1987, May 30). Influence of blood lead on the ability and attainment of children in Edinburgh. *The Lancet,* 1221–1226.

Galaburda, A. M. (1989). Ordinary and extraordinary brain development: Anatomical variation in developmental dyslexia. *Annals of Dyslexia, 39,* 67–80.

Galaburda, A. M., Rosen, G. D., & Sherman, G. F. (1989). The neural origin of developmental dyslexia: Implications for medicine, neurology and cognition. In A. M. Galaburda (Ed.), *From reading to neurons.* Cambridge, MA: MIT Press.

Gelman, R. (1990). First principles organize attention to and learning about relevant data: Number and the animate-inanimate distinction as examples. *Cognitive Science, 14,* 79–106.

Geschwind, N., & Galaburda, A. (1985). Cerebral lateralization: Biological mechanisms, associations and pathology. Part I. A hypothesis and programme for research. *Archives of Neurology, 42,* 428–459.

Gillberg, C. (Ed.). (1989). *Diagnosis and treatment of autism.* New York: Plenum.

Gillberg, C. (1992). Autism and autistic-like conditions: Subclasses among disorders of empathy. *Journal of Child Psychology and Psychiatry, 33,* 813–842.

Goswami, U. (1986). Children's use of analogy in learning to read: A developmental study. *Journal of Experimental Child Psychology, 42,* 73–83.

Goswami, U. (1990). A special link between rhyming skills and the use of orthographic analogies by beginning readers. *Journal of Child Psychology and Psychiatry, 31,* 301–311.

Gough, P. B., & Tunmer, W. E. (1986). Decoding, reading and reading disability. *Remedial and Special Education, 7,* 6–10.

Gray, G., Smith, A., & Rutter, M. (1980). School attendance and the first year of employment. In L. Hersov & I. Berg (Eds.), *Out of school: Modern perspectives in truancy and school refusal* (pp. 343-370). Chichester, England: Wiley.

Happé, F., & Frith, U. (in press). Theory of mind in autism. In E. Schopler & G. B. Mesibov, *Learning and cognition in autism.* New York: Plenum.

Hermelin, B., & O'Connor, N. (1970). *Psychological experiments with autistic children.* Oxford, England: Pergamon.

Hinshaw, S. P. (1987). On the distinction between attention deficits/hyperactivity and conduct problems/aggression in child psychopathology. *Psychological Bulletin, 101,* 443–463.

Hobson, R. P. (1989). Beyond cognition: A theory of autism. In G. Dawson (Ed.), *Autism: Nature, diagnosis and treatment* (pp. 22–48). New York: Guilford.

Hobson, R. P. (1990). On acquiring knowledge about people, and the capacity to pretend: A response to Leslie (1987). *Psychological Review, 97,* 114–121.

Hobson, R. P. (1993). Understanding persons: The role of affect. In S. Baron-Cohen, H. Tager-Flusberg, & D. Cohen (Eds.), *Understanding other minds: Perspectives from autism.* Oxford, England: Oxford University Press.

Hynd, G. W., & Semrud-Clikeman, M. (1989). Dyslexia and brain morphology. *Psychological Bulletin, 106,* 447–482.

Johnson, M., & Morton, J. (1991). *Biology and cognitive development: The case of face recognition.* Oxford, England: Blackwell.

Johnson, M., Siddons, F., Frith, U., & Morton, J. (1992). Can autism be predicted on the basis of infant screening tests? *Developmental Medicine and Child Neurology, 34,* 314–320.

Johnston, R. S. (1982). Phonological coding in dyslexic readers. *British Journal of Psychology, 73,* 455–460.

Karmiloff-Smith, A. (1984). Children's problem solving. In M. E. Lamb, A. L. Brown, & B. Rogoff (Eds.), *Advances in developmental psychology* (Vol. III, pp. 39–90). Hillsdale, NJ: Erlbaum.

Lahey, B. B., Schaughency, E. A., Hynd, G. W., Carlson, C. L., & Nieves, N. (1987). Attention deficit disorder with and without hyperactivity: Comparison of behavioral characteristics of clinic-referred children. *Journal of the American Academy of Child and Adolescent Psychiatry, 26,* 718–723.

Laszlo, J. (1990). Child perceptuo-motor development: Normal and abnormal development of skilled behavior. In C.-A. Hauert (Ed.), *Developmental psychology: Cognitive, perceptuo-motor and neurological perspectives* (pp. 273–308). Amsterdam, The Netherlands: Elsevier.

Lenel, J. C., & Cantor, J. H. (1981). Rhyme recognition and phonemic perception in young children. *Journal of Psycholinguistic Research, 10,* 57–68.

Leslie, A. M. (1987). Pretense and representation: The origins of "theory of mind." *Psychological Review, 94,* 412–426.

Leslie, A. M., & Frith, U. (1990). Prospects for a cognitive neurospsychology of autism: Hobson's choice. *Psychological Review, 97,* 122–131.

Leslie, A. M., & Happé, F. G. E. (1989). Autism and ostensive communication: The relevance of metarepresentation. *Development and Psychopathology, 1,* 205–212.

Leslie, A. M., & Thaiss, L. (1992). Domain specificity in conceptual development: Neuropsychological evidence from autism. *Cognition, 43,* 225–251.

Liberman, I., Liberman, A. M., Mattingly, I., & Shankweiler, D. (1980). Orthography and the beginning reader. In J. F. Kavanagh & R. I. Venezky (Eds.), *Orthography, reading and dyslexia* (pp. 137–153). Baltimore: University Park Press.

Lister-Brook, S. (1992). *Early detection of social and communication impairment.* Unpublished doctoral dissertation, London University.

Livingstone, M. S., Rosen, G. D., Drislane, F. W., & Galaburda, A. M. (1991). Physiological and anatomical evidence for a magnocellular deficit in developmental dyslexia. *Proceedings of the National Academy of Science, 88,* 7943–7947.

Lovegrove, W., Garzia, R. P., & Nicholson, S. B. (1990). Experimental evidence for a transient system deficit in specific reading disability. *Journal of the American Optometric Association, 61,* 137–146.

Lovegrove, W., Martin, F., & Slaghuis, W. (1986). A theoretical and experimental case for a visual deficit in specific reading disability. *Cognitive Neuropsychology, 3,* 225–267.

Lundberg, I., Frost, J., & Peterson, O. (1988). Effects of an extensive program for stimulating phonological awareness in preschool children. *Reading Research Quarterly, 23,* 263–284.

Mehler, J., Morton, J., & Jusczyk, P. W. (1984). On reducing language to biology. *Cognitive Neuropsychology, 1,* 83–116.

Miles, T., & Haslum, M. (1986). Dyslexia: Anomaly or normal variation? *Annals of Dyslexia, 36,* 103–117.

Morais, J. (1991). Metaphonological abilities and literacy. In M. J. Snowling & M. Thompson (Eds.), *Dyslexia: Integrating theory and practice* (pp. 95–107). London: Whurr.

Morais, J., Cary, L., Alegria, J., & Bertelson, P. (1979). Does awareness of speech as a sequence of phones arise spontaneously? *Cognition, 7,* 323–331.

Morton, J. (1986). Developmental contingency modelling: A framework for discussing the processes of change and the consequence of deficiency. In P. L. C. van Geert (Ed.), *Theory building in developmental psychology* (pp. 141–165). Amsterdam, The Netherlands: North Holland-Elsevier.

Morton, J. (1989a). An information-processing account of reading acquisition. In A. M. Galaburda (Ed.), *From reading to neurons* (pp. 43–65). Cambridge, MA: MIT Press.

Morton, J. (1989b). The origins of autism. *New Scientist, 9,* 44–47.

Mundy, P., & Sigman, M. (1989). The theoretical implications of joint attention deficits in autism. *Development and Psychopathology, 1,* 173–183.

Mundy, P., Sigman, M., & Kasari, C. (1993). Theory of mind and joint attention deficits in autism. In S. Baron-Cohen, H. Tager-Flusberg, & D. Cohen (Eds.), *Understanding other minds: Perspectives from autism.* Oxford, England: Oxford University Press.

Mundy, P., Sigman, M., Ungerer, J., & Sherman, T. (1986). Defining the social deficit of autism: The contribution of non-verbal communication measures. *Journal of Child Psychology and Psychiatry, 27,* 657–669.

Nunn, K. P., Lask, B., & Cohen, M. (1986). Viruses, neurodevelopmental disorder and childhood psychosis. *Journal of Child Psychology and Psychiatry, 27,* 55–64.

Olson, R. K., Wise, B., Conners, F., & Rack, J. (1990). Organization, heritability and remediation of component word recognition and language skills in disabled readers. In T. H. Carr & B. A. Levy (Eds.), *Reading and its development: Component skills approaches* (pp. 261–322). New York: Academic Press.

Olson, R. K., Wise, B., Conners, F., Rack, J., & Fulker, D. (1989). Specific deficits in component reading and language skills: Genetic and environmental influences. *Journal of Learning Disabilities, 22,* 339–348.

Patterson, K. E. (1981). Neuropsychological approaches to the study of reading. *British Journal of Psychology, 72,* 151–174.

Pennington, B. F. (1989). Using genetics to understand dyslexia. *Annals of Dyslexia, 39,* 81–93.

Pennington, B. F. (1991). *Reading disabilities: Genetic and neurological influences.* Dordrecht, The Netherlands: Kluwer.

Perfetti, C. A. (1991). Representations and awareness. In L. Rieben & C. A. Perfetti (Eds.), *Learning to read: Basic research and its implications* (pp. 33–44). Hillsdale, NJ: Erlbaum.

Premack, D., & Woodruff, G. (1978). Does the chimpanzee have a theory of mind? *Behavioral and Brain Sciences, 4,* 515–526.

Prior, M. R. (1989). Reading disability: "Normative" or "pathological"? *Australian Journal of Psychology, 41,* 135–158.

Quinton, R., & Rutter, M. (1988). *Parental breakdown: The making and breaking of intergenerational links.* Aldershot, England: Gower.

Rack, J., Snowling, M., & Olson, R. K. (1992). The nonword reading deficit in developmental dyslexia: A review. *Reading Research Quarterly, 27,* 29–53.

Reddy, V. (1991). Playing with others' expectations: Teasing and mucking about in the first year. In A. Whiten (Ed.), *Natural theories of mind: Evolution, development and simulation of everyday mindreading* (pp. 143–158). Oxford, England: Basil Blackwell.

Rogers, S. J., & Pennington, B. F. (1991). A theoretical approach to the deficits in infantile autism. *Developmental Psychopathology, 3,* 137–162.

Rutter, M. (1978). Diagnostic validity in child psychiatry. *Advances in Biological Psychiatry, 2,* 2–22.

Rutter, M. (1983). Cognitive deficits in the pathogenesis of autism. *Journal of Child Psychology and Psychiatry, 24,* 513–531.

Rutter, M. (1989). Pathways from childhood to adult life. *Journal of Child Psychology and Psychiatry, 30,* 23–51.

Rutter, M., Macdonald, H., Le Couteur, A., Harrington, R., Bolton, P., & Bailey, A. (1990). Genetic factors in child psychiatric disorders: II. Empirical findings. *Journal of Child Psychology and Psychiatry, 31,* 39–83.

Rutter, M., Tizard, J., & Whitmore, K. (Eds.). (1970). *Education, health and behaviour.* London: Longmans.

Rutter, M., Tizard, J., Yule, W., Graham, P., & Whitmore, K. (1976). Research report, Isle of Wight studies (1964–1976). *Psychological Medicine, 6,* 313–332.

Rutter, M., & Yule, W. (1975). The concept of specific reading retardation. *Journal of Child Psychology and Psychiatry, 16,* 181–197.

Scarborough, H. S. (1990). Very early language deficits in dyslexic children. *Child Development, 61,* 1728–1743.

Schachar, R. (1991). Childhood hyperactivity. *Journal of Child Psychology and Psychiatry, 32,* 155–191.

Schopler, E., & Mesibov, G. B. (Eds.). (1987). *Neurobiological issues in autism.* New York: Plenum.

Seymour, P. H. K. (1990). Developmental dyslexia. In M. W. Eysenck (Ed.), *Cognitive psychology: An international review* (pp. 135–196). New York: Wiley.

Seymour, P. H. K., & Evans, H. M. (1992). Beginning reading without semantics: A cognitive study of hyperlexia. *Cognitive Neuropsychology, 9,* 89–122.

Shallice, T. (1981). Neurological impairment of cognitive processes. *British Medical Journal, 37,* 187–192.

Shallice, T. (1988). *From neuropsychology to mental structure.* Cambridge, England: Cambridge University Press.

Shankweiler, D., Liberman, I. Y., Mark, L. S., Fowler, C., & Fischer, F. W. (1979). The speech code and learning to read. *Journal of Experimental Psychology: Human Learning and Memory, 5,* 531–545.

Siegel, L. (1989). IQ is irrelevant to the definition of learning disabilities. *Journal of Learning Disabilities, 22,* 469–486.

Silva, P. A., Hughes, P., Williams, S., & Faed, J. M. (1988). Blood lead, intelligence, reading attainment and behaviour in eleven-year-old children in Dunedin, New Zealand. *Journal of Child Psychology and Psychiatry, 29,* 43–52.

Smalley, S. L., Asarnow, R. F., & Spence, A. (1988). Autism and genetics: A decade of research. *Archives of General Psychiatry, 45,* 953–961.

Smith, S. D., Kimberling, W. J., Pennington, B. F., & Lubs, H. A. (1983). Specific reading disability: Identification of an inherited form through linkage analysis. *Science, 219,* 1345–1347.

Snowling, M. (1987). *Dyslexia: A cognitive developmental perspective.* Oxford, England: Blackwell.

Snowling, M. (1991). Developmental reading disorders. *Journal of Child Psychology and Psychiatry, 32,* 49–77.

Snowling, M., Stackhouse, J., & Rack, J. (1986). Phonological dyslexia and dysgraphia—A developmental analysis. *Cognitive Neuropsychology, 34,* 309–339.

Sonuga-Barke, E. J. S., Taylor, E., & Heptinstall, E. (1992). Hyperactivity and delay aversion: II. The effect of self versus externally imposed stimulus presentation periods on memory. *Journal of Child Psychology and Psychiatry, 33,* 399–409.

Sonuga-Barke, E. J. S., Taylor, E., Sembi, S., & Smith, J. (1992). Hyperactivity and delay aversion: I. The effect of delay on choice. *Journal of Child Psychology and Psychiatry, 33,* 387–398.

Stanovich, K. E. (1986). Matthew effects in reading: Some consequences of individual differences in the acquisition of literacy. *Reading Research Quarterly, 21,* 360–407.

Stanovich, K. E. (1988). Explaining the differences between the dyslexic and the garden-variety poor reader: The phonological-core variable-difference model. *Journal of Learning Disabilities, 21,* 590–612.

Steffenburg, S. (1991). Neuropsychiatric assessment of children with autism: A population-based study. *Developmental Medicine and Child Neurology, 33,* 495–511.

Stein, J. F. (1991). Vision and language. In M. J. Snowling & M. Thomson (Eds.), *Dyslexia: Integrating theory and practice* (pp. 31–43). London: Whurr.

Stevenson, J., Graham, P., Fredman, G., & McLoughlin, V. (1987). A twin study of genetic influences on reading and spelling ability and disability. *Journal of Child Psychology and Psychiatry, 28,* 229–247.

Stuart, M., & Coltheart, M. (1988). Does reading develop in a sequence of stages? *Cognition, 30,* 139–181.

Sturge, C. (1982). Reading retardation and antisocial behaviour. *Journal of Child Psychology and Psychiatry, 23,* 21–31.

Szatmari, P., & Jones, M. B. (1991). IQ and the genetics of autism. *Journal of Child Psychology and Psychiatry, 32,* 897–908.

Tallal, P. (1988). Developmental language disorders. In J. Kavanagh & T. Truss (Eds.), *Learning disabilities: Proceedings from the National Conference* (pp. 181–272). Tarkington, MD: York Press.

Taylor, E. A. (1985). Syndromes of overactivity and attention deficit. In M. Rutter & L. Hersov (Eds.), *Child and adolescent psychiatry: Modern approaches* (2nd ed., pp. 424–443). Oxford, England: Blackwell.

Taylor, E. A. (1986a). Causes and development of hyperactive behaviour. In E. Taylor (Ed.), *The overactive child.* Clinics in Developmental Medicine No. 97. London: MacKeith Press.

Taylor, E. A. (1986b). Childhood hyperactivity. *British Journal of Psychiatry, 149,* 562–573.

Taylor, E. A. (1991). Developmental neuropsychiatry. *Journal of Child Psychology and Psychiatry, 32,* 3–47.

Tinbergen, N., & Tinbergen, E. A. (1983). *"Autistic" children: New hope for a cure.* London: Allen & Unwin.

Treiman, R., & Hirsh-Pasek, K. (1985). Are there qualitative differences in reading behaviour between dyslexics and normal readers? *Memory and Cognition, 13,* 357–364.

Tsai, L. Y. (1989). Recent neurobiological findings in autism. In C. Gillberg (Ed.), *Diagnosis and treatment of autism* (pp. 83–104). New York: Plenum.

van der Wissel, A., & Zegers, F. E. (1985). Reading retardation revisited. *British Journal of Developmental Psychology, 3,* 3–9.

Wellman, H. M. (1990). *The child's theory of mind.* Cambridge, MA: MIT Press.

Whiten, A. (ed.). (1991). *Natural theories of mind: Evolution, development and simulation of everyday mindreading.* Oxford, England: Blackwell.

Wimmer, H. (1993). Characteristics of developmental dyslexia in a regular writing system. *Applied Psycholinguistics, 14,* 1–33.

Wimmer, H., Landerl, K., Linortner, R., & Hummer, P. (1991). The relationship of phonemic awareness to reading acquisition: More consequence than precondition but still important. *Cognition, 40,* 219–249.

Wing, L. (1988). The autistic continuum. In L. Wing (Ed.), *Aspects of autism: Biological research* (pp. v–viii). London: Gaskell and Royal College of Psychiatrists.

Wing, L., & Gould, J. (1979). Severe impairments of social interaction and associated abnormalities in children: Epidemiology and classification. *Journal of Autism and Developmental Disorders, 9,* 11–30.

World Health Organization. (1992). *The ICD-10 classification of mental and behavioural disorders: Clinical descriptions and diagnostic guidelines.* Geneva, Switzerland: Author.

Yule, W., & Rutter, M. (1975). *Effects of lead on children's performance: A critical review.* In K. R. Mahaffey (Ed.), *Health implications of typical levels of lead exposure: Dietary and environmental sources.* Amsterdam, The Netherlands: Elsevier.

Yule, W., & Rutter, M. (1985). Reading and other learning difficulties. In M. Rutter & L. Hersov (Eds.), *Child and adolescent psychiatry: Modern approaches* (2nd ed., pp. 444–464). Oxford, England: Blackwell.

CHAPTER 14

Cognitive Processing, Academic Achievement, and Psychosocial Functioning: A Neurodevelopmental Perspective

BYRON P. ROURKE and DARREN R. FUERST

Following this brief introduction, there are three major sections in this chapter: (a) a consideration of three hypotheses linking learning disabilities (LD) and psychosocial functioning, including a description of the Windsor Taxonomic Research project; (b) a discussion of the syndrome and model of nonverbal learning disabilities (NLD); (c) future directions for research in the study of the interactions of cognitive processing, academic achievement, and psychosocial functioning. The emphasis in all of these sections is squarely on matters germane to the theoretical and applied aspects of developmental psychopathology in the domain of LD.

In our society, children are expected to go to school from roughly the age of 5 years until well into late adolescence. Indeed, attending and benefiting substantially from school constitute what most consider to be the principal developmental demands for children during these years. While in school, children are expected to acquire a large number of skills and to learn a large amount of material. They are expected to emerge from this experience as literate young adults who are capable of comporting themselves in an adaptive manner in the world of work and in the social pursuits that are common to our society. For many—as a result of the burgeoning academic requirements of our increasingly sophisticated technological society, or out of a love of learning, or because of parental expectations, or for any number of other reasons—"school" will continue well past this point. Indeed, for most young persons in our society, postsecondary education or formal training of some sort is now the norm rather than the exception, and we can expect this pattern to continue.

Whether one is in school or not, the capacity to benefit from experience and to fashion one's responses to meet the demands of such experience in an adaptive fashion (i.e., to learn) lies at the very core of what it is to be human. Hence, it should come as no surprise that significant difficulties in learning are thought to eventuate in much more than simple failure in school or failure to learn or hold a job. Indeed, it is a commonly held notion that persons who experience significant difficulties in learning—especially when these are thought to be LD—are most definitely prone to disorders in other areas of human existence, such as the "emotional" and "social" dimensions of life. It is in this sense that some characterize LD as "life" or "lifetime" disabilities.

In the first section of this chapter, we present a précis of our review of some of the more important psychological and neuropsychological literature that has addressed the issues surrounding the relationships among LD, academic achievement, and psychosocial functioning (Rourke & Fuerst, 1991). Most of this research was designed to answer the following questions: Are LD and socioemotional disturbance inextricably intertwined? Does psychosocial dysfunction cause LD? Are children with LD more at risk for socioemotional disturbance than are normal learners? Does psychosocial dysfunction become more prominent with advancing years in those who exhibit LD? Are the learning disabled more prone to delinquency, conduct disorder, and other forms of externalized psychopathology than are normal learners? Is there a distinct psychosocial profile of disabled learners? Are distinct subtypes of psychopathology evident in children with LD? Are children who exhibit different subtypes of LD more or less at risk for the development of socioemotional disturbance? Are problems in social judgment, social competence, and social learning more prevalent in children with LD?

Some of the conclusions that flow from our review may apply to children and adolescents who fail in school but who have the necessary cognitive attributes to learn at a normal rate and to a normal extent in ordinary academic instructional and social learning settings (i.e., who are not, in the usual sense of the term, disabled with respect to learning). However, in the present context, we have set as our task the explanation of the interrelationships of central processing assets/deficits, academic learning, and psychosocial functioning in those who exhibit LD. At this point, therefore, it would be well to define what we mean by LD. The following excerpt constitutes what we consider to be a "generic" definition (Rourke, 1989):

Pages 391–392, 395–400, 404–409, and 411–414 of this chapter contain some material previously published in *Learning Disabilities and Psychosocial Functioning* and *Nonverbal Learning Disabilities: The Syndrome and the Model.* Permission to cite this material has been granted by Guilford Press.

LD is a generic term that refers to a heterogeneous group of disorders manifested by significant difficulties in the mastery of one or more of the following: listening, speaking, reading, writing, reasoning, mathematical, and other skills and abilities that are traditionally referred to as "academic." The term LD is also appropriately applied in instances where persons exhibit significant difficulties in mastering social and other adaptive skills and abilities. In some cases, investigations of LD have yielded evidence that would be consistent with hypotheses relating central nervous system dysfunction to the disabilities in question. Even though learning disabilities may occur concomitantly with other handicapping conditions (e.g., sensory impairment, mental retardation, social and emotional disturbance) or environmental influences (e.g., cultural differences, insufficient/inappropriate instruction, psychogenic factors), they are not the direct result of those conditions or influences. However, it is possible that emotional disturbances and other adaptive deficiencies may arise from the same patterns of central processing assets and deficits that generate the manifestations of academic and social LD. LD may arise from genetic variations, biochemical factors, events in the pre- to perinatal period, or any other subsequent events resulting in neurological impairment.

It would take us too far afield to discuss the *specific* definitions of various subtypes of LD, although some statements regarding the issues surrounding subtypes and the specific definitions implied thereby will be discussed below. (For a fuller discussion of specific definitions of subtypes of LD, the interested reader is referred to Rourke, 1989, especially Chapter 8.)

As in our comprehensive review (Rourke & Fuerst, 1991), we have organized this presentation around three major hypotheses regarding the relationships between socioemotional functioning and LD that have held sway from time to time over the past 20 years. For each of these hypotheses, we present our characterization of the general and specific conclusions that can be arrived at on the basis of this review. Where appropriate, we highlight the results of studies from our own laboratory that we feel are appropriate to address the issues in question. We also present some clinical observations and generalizations that are felt to flow from the empirical evidence gathered to this point. The presentation closes with some suggestions for future investigations that are needed in order to fill in the gaps of our knowledge in this important area of neurodevelopmental investigation.

For the most part, we have confined our presentation to studies involving children and adolescents. Initially, we anticipated covering the entire age range in our review of this topic. However, we discovered quickly that relatively little of the research in this area has studied the relations between psychosocial functioning and LD in adults. This should not have come as a surprise: LD have been a subject of serious scientific scrutiny for only a very short period of time. Hence, there has been little opportunity to examine the long-term (adult) impact of childhood LD. Notable exceptions are the work of Bruck (1987) and Spreen (1988), the recent volume of research by Johnson and Blalock (1987), and the studies of McCue and Goldstein (1991) and Morris and Walter (1991). These sources are referred to in our review. However, the essentially exploratory nature of much of this research with adults and the unavailability of cross-validation attempts make it difficult to do much more than comment on what appear to be the very interesting hypotheses raised in research with adults.

HYPOTHESIS 1: SOCIOEMOTIONAL DISTURBANCE CAUSES LD

The notion that socioemotional disturbance causes LD is a widely held position. In this view, learning problems that children face in school and elsewhere are thought to constitute one reflection of systematic disturbances in socioemotional functioning (e.g., unresolved psychic conflicts). The evidence for this assertion comes from a variety of sources: some are empirical (e.g., Colbert, Newman, Ney, & Young, 1982), but most are "clinical" in nature (e.g., Brumback & Staton, 1983; Ehrlich, 1983). Many professionals whose work brings them into contact with youngsters who are experiencing problems in academic achievement have observed that a significant proportion of these children suffer from one or more socioemotional difficulties: personality conflicts with their teachers, which render learning in the classroom difficult, if not impossible; strain associated with difficulties in meeting the (exaggerated) perceived demands of their parents and teachers; extreme psychic conflicts that render them almost incapable of benefiting from ordinary scholastic instruction; "inappropriate" motivation for academic success and social expectancies at variance with those of the school; and major psychiatric disorders, such as depression, that remain undiagnosed and/or untreated (Rourke, Bakker, Fisk, & Strang, 1983; Rourke, Fisk, & Strang, 1986). These examples illustrate the following: that social conflict between teacher and student should be kept to a minimum if academic learning is to proceed apace; that unrealistic ego-ideals can, and usually do, have a profound negative impact on performance; that significant intrapsychic conflicts or psychiatric disorders, no matter how generated and maintained, can impact significantly on academic performance; and that the school is predominantly a middle-income institution that requires at least the temporary adoption of its standards (in North America, largely those of the Protestant Ethic) for success in its programs.

These few examples should illustrate the enormous number of complex sets of interactions that can limit significantly the academic progress of untold numbers of students. In all of these instances, even the personality conflict with teachers, the socioemotional "problem" antedates the difficulty in learning. Furthermore, it is assumed that, were the socioemotional problem to be resolved, satisfactory academic performance would ensue. Thus, solving the student-teacher personality conflict, bringing ego-ideals more closely in tune with reality, rectifying the intrapsychic conflict or psychiatric disorder, and leading the student to adopt a motivational posture and social-expectancy set that are more in line with those of the school would be expected to lead eventually to satisfactory academic progress.

This having been said, it is also necessary to point out that these matters involve academic and other learning difficulties that are not usually included under the rubric of LD. The latter designation is commonly reserved for persons whose significant problems in learning are *not* a result of primary emotional disturbance (or mental retardation, primary sensory handicap, inadequate instruction, inappropriate motivation, or cultural/linguistic deprivation—the "exclusionary" criteria embodied in most definitions of LD). Thus, although interesting in and of themselves, and of obvious importance for the total understanding and treatment of children's problems in learning, these factors are not properly considered within the context of socioemotional correlates of LD. Hence, this chapter is devoted to those considerations that fall quite precisely within the defined domain.

HYPOTHESIS 2: LD CAUSE SOCIOEMOTIONAL DISTURBANCE

This first *major* hypothesis of interest within the present context proposes a causal link between learning difficulties and socioemotional disturbance (Rourke & Fisk, 1981). The differences in this instance are: (a) LD, as commonly defined (Rourke, 1975, and above), are the focus of interest, and (b) the causal relationship is reversed: it is proposed that LD lead to disrupted or aberrant psychosocial functioning. This general proposition has a very compelling, tacit appeal for most clinicians; it concretizes a view that is widely held and that has become almost a cornerstone of clinical lore in this area. The reasons for the *prima facie* appeal of this view are numerous. For example, it appears to make good clinical sense to maintain that a youngster with LD who persists in his or her learning problems throughout the elementary school years will be the butt of criticism and negative evaluations by parents, teachers, and age-mates; that these criticisms will render the child with LD more anxious and less self-assured in learning situations; that a vicious circle will develop and will increasingly hamper academic success and encourage progressively more debilitating degrees of anxiety (i.e., learning failure results in increased anxiety, which results in feelings of inferiority, which result in additional learning failure, and so on); and that this sort of undesirable situation is virtually inevitable and can be expected to increase in severity as the child fails to make advances in learning.

Research in support of this position has focused on the emotional, social, and behavioral functioning of children with LD, with particular regard to their interpersonal environment. In our comprehensive review of this literature (Rourke & Fuerst, 1991), we examined current research relevant to, or advanced in support of, variants of this general hypothesis. Four specific areas of investigation were scrutinized: (a) patterns of general psychosocial functioning and pathology; (b) social status with respect to peers and teachers; (c) self-concept/self-esteem and attributions; and (d) social competence. Summaries and conclusions regarding the first three of these areas are presented next. Considerations regarding social competence are raised within the contexts of subsequent sections of the chapter.

Patterns of General Psychosocial Functioning and Pathology

The results of classroom observation, checklist/rating scale, personality inventory, and longitudinal studies are often contradictory, but it would appear that, as a group, children with LD are at somewhat greater than average risk for aberrant psychosocial development or psychopathology. However, it is also clear that not all children with LD fare poorly in these respects: the range of psychosocial outcomes is probably as great as that seen in any other group of children (i.e., some do very well, some do moderately well, and some do poorly). Although, on average, children with LD may fare worse relative to their normal peers, reliable estimates of the incidence of various degrees and types of disordered psychosocial adaptation have not emerged from the literature. Thus, a simple and clear causal link between LD and psychopathology has not been demonstrated.

Social Status with Respect to Peers and Teachers

The available evidence indicates that, as a group, children with LD may have somewhat lower social status relative to normally achieving peers. This should not be surprising; research with other groups of children has also shown that, in general, academic achievement and social status are positively (but weakly) correlated (Green, Forehand, Beck, & Vosk, 1980). However, it would appear that only some children with LD have truly low social status and are actively disliked/rejected by peers. On the other hand, some children with LD are quite popular, perhaps because they exhibit attributes that are important to their peers. In most respects, children with LD are heterogeneous with regard to social status. As yet, the nature and extent of relations between peer status and other aspects of psychosocial adaptation are poorly understood, as are other predictors and correlates of social status. Little is known of teacher perceptions and attitudes toward children with LD; however, the available evidence suggests that further investigation of these potentially important issues is warranted.

Self-Concept/Self-Esteem and Attributions

There is some evidence that some children with LD demonstrate reduced self-concept with respect to academic and, perhaps, intellectual domains. However, the evidence that children with LD have lower self-concept/self-esteem either globally or in other specific domains is not convincing. There is no evidence that children with LD demonstrate a particular pattern of attributions with respect to success or failure in academic and other settings (Bender, 1987). Thus, there is no convincing evidence that, in children with LD, reduced self-concept is related to attributions and locus of control. There is no compelling evidence that: (a) children with LD demonstrate a pattern of attributions and behaviors consistent with a condition of learned helplessness, (b) self-concept and attribution patterns of LD children are adversely affected by experience of failure, and (c) self-concept and attribution patterns are related to aberrant behavior in children with LD.

The conclusions of the research that appears to have established a causal link between LD and patterns of psychosocial dysfunction may seem fairly straightforward and unambiguous. However, there are a number of serious flaws in most of the investigations that have led to those conclusions. Some of the major shortcomings of this research are discussed in the following sections.

Methodological/Theoretical Considerations

The research that we reviewed, relating to the interpersonal environments of children with LD, has not been terribly contributory. The results of many studies are trivial, contradictory to one another, and not supported in replication attempts. There is little to suggest that the factors identified as "characteristic" of children with LD in these studies are related to one another in any meaningful fashion. In sum, the evidence that emerges from this research regarding socioemotional functioning is, at best, equivocal. A coherent and meaningful pattern of personality characteristics (including psychopathology, problems with self-concept/self-esteem, attributions and locus of control, social status, and so on) of children with LD does not emerge from this literature—perhaps because such a univocal pattern does not obtain. At this juncture, it would be well to point out some of the more obvious methodological inadequacies of this research.

Definition of LD

There was no consistent formulation of the criteria for LD in these studies. For example, some employed vague or undefined groups; others used the ratings of teachers and other school personnel who remain otherwise unspecified. This lack of clarity and consistency had a negative impact on the generalizability of such findings. Clear, consensually validatable definitions are vital in this area of investigation.

Measurement of Maladjustment

"Emotional disturbance," "socioemotional adjustment," "behavior disorder," "antisocial behavior," and other constructs of psychosocial functioning have been operationalized at least as inadequately as have LD, in many of these studies. The use of reliable and valid psychometric instruments would be preferable to the largely subjective nature of the judgments of these crucial dependent variables that has characterized much of this research.

Developmental Considerations

Several studies offer support for the notion that the nature of the skill and ability deficits of (some subtypes of) children with LD varies with age (e.g., McKinney, Short, & Feagans, 1985; Morris, Blashfield, & Satz, 1986; Ozols & Rourke, 1988; Rourke, Dietrich, & Young, 1973). It would seem reasonable to infer that the socioemotional functioning of (some subtypes of) children with LD would also vary as a function of age (considered as one index of developmental change). The aforementioned inconsistencies in research results, therefore, may reflect differences in the ages of the subjects employed. To investigate this possibility, cross-sectional or longitudinal studies, such as those carried out by Spreen (1988) and colleagues, are necessary.

Heterogeneity

Virtually all of the studies on which the conclusions stated above were based have employed a research design that involves comparisons of undifferentiated groups of children with LD to equally undifferentiated groups of normal achievers. This approach, which aims to identify the particular pattern of socioemotional disturbance characteristic of children with LD, tends to obscure within-group differences. As Applebee (1971) pointed out, employment of this "comparative-populations" approach can only be justified if one can safely assume that children and adolescents with LD are homogeneous in terms of their abilities and deficits.

Homogeneity of psychosocial functioning, or the lack thereof, has become an increasingly important topic of investigation in recent years. Although some investigators have previously noted that not all children with LD behave in a similar manner in the psychosocial domain, discussion of this issue has been largely confined to brief, post-hoc descriptions. These descriptions are often couched as explanations for unexpected or contradictory findings, rather than as proper subjects of investigation. However, research into the neuropsychological aspects of LD has suggested strongly that: (a) children with LD constitute a markedly heterogeneous population in terms of their skills and abilities, and (b) meaningful subtypes of children with LD can be identified in a reliable fashion, using a variety of methods (e.g., Fletcher, 1985; Morris, Blashfield, & Satz, 1981; Rourke & Finlayson, 1978; Rourke & Strang, 1978; Strang & Rourke, 1983).

Apart from our continuing work at the University of Windsor, presented in detail in the next section, relatively few systematic attempts to develop a psychosocial typology of children with LD have been reported in the literature. Notable exceptions are the work of Loveland, Fletcher, and Bailey (1990), McConaughy and Ritter (1986), and, to a lesser extent, Silver and Young (1985).

Lack of a Conceptual Model

In the vast majority of the studies that we reviewed, there was an obvious absence of a conceptual model to guide the research efforts in question. This was especially true in the area of social competence. A notable exception was the formulation of Wiener (1980). For example, at the very minimum, a componential analysis of social competence should sensitize the researcher to the possibility that, whereas some subtypes of children with LD may experience social competence problems because they lack certain perceptual, cognitive, or behavioral skills, others may manifest such problems as a more direct result of attitudinal/motivational difficulties. It should also be clear that different patterns of perceptual, cognitive, and behavioral skills and abilities may encourage different types or degrees of socially incompetent behavior.

Model Development: An Example. To evaluate the hypotheses that arise from such a view, the emphasis of our neuropsychological approach has been to attempt to integrate dimensions of social and emotional development on the one hand with relevant central processing features on the other, thereby fashioning a useful model by which to study crucial aspects of individual human development, including LD. Models and explanatory concepts developed with this aim in mind (e.g., Rourke, 1976, 1982, 1983, 1987, 1988b, 1989) contain explanations that are thought to apply to some types of children with frank brain injuries, to those with LD, and to some aspects of normal human development. This content should come as no surprise: maximum generalizability is one goal of any scientific model or theory. Specifically with respect to children with LD, the aspects of these concepts and models that are most relevant are those that propose linkages between patterns of central processing abilities and deficits that may predispose a youngster to predictably different patterns of social as well as academic LD. In addition, these models are designed to encompass developmental change and outcome in patterns of learning and behavioral responsivity. Hence, these models are of central concern for the theoretical and applied dimensions of developmental psychopathology, as well as for those of "normal" development.

Model Development: Group R-S and Group A. Since 1971, at the University of Windsor laboratory, two subtypes of children with LD have been the subject of intensive investigation. Children in one group (referred to as Group R-S) are those who exhibit many relatively poor psycholinguistic skills in conjunction with very well-developed abilities in visual-spatial-organizational, tactile-perceptual, psychomotor, and nonverbal problem-solving skills. They exhibit very poor reading and spelling skills and significantly better, though still impaired, mechanical arithmetic competence. The other group (Group A) exhibits outstanding problems in visual-spatial-organizational, tactile-perceptual, psychomotor, and nonverbal problem-solving skills, within a context of clear strengths in some psycholinguistic skills such as rote verbal learning, regular phoneme-grapheme matching, amount of verbal output, and verbal classification. Group A children experience their major academic learning difficulties in mechanical arithmetic, while exhibiting advanced levels of word recognition and spelling. Both of these subtypes of children with LD—especially the second subtype of child, characterized as having "nonverbal learning disabilities"—have been the subject of much scrutiny in our laboratory (for reviews, see Rourke, 1975, 1978, 1982, 1987, 1989; Rourke & Strang, 1983; Strang & Rourke, 1985a, 1985b).

The results of one of the studies in this series (Ozols & Rourke, 1985) can be used to illustrate our approach to the determination of the psychosocial ramifications of these two subtypes of LD. In this study, the performances of two groups of children with LD—one exhibiting a pattern of relatively poor auditory-perceptual and language-related skills within a context of well-developed visual-spatial-organizational skills (similar to Group R-S), and the second exhibiting the opposite pattern of abilities and deficits (similar to Group A)—were compared on four exploratory measures of social judgment and responsiveness. As predicted on the basis of the Rourke (1982) model, this study revealed that children in the language-disorder group performed more effectively than did those in the visual-spatial disorder group on tasks requiring nonverbal responses; in contrast, tasks requiring verbal responses yielded exactly the opposite results. These results suggest that social awareness and responsiveness vary markedly for these two subtypes of children with LD, probably as a result of an interaction between their particular patterns of central processing abilities and deficits and the specific task demands of the four measures employed. A recent study by Loveland et al. (1990) has replicated and extended these findings.

The results of the Ozols and Rourke (1985) study should be viewed within the context of a study by Ackerman and Howes (1986), which demonstrated that, although social competence deficits often occur in many children with LD, some children with LD do not exhibit such deficits and are seen as popular with their peers and active in after-school interests. These findings, taken together, would suggest that a study designed along the lines of the Porter and Rourke (1985) investigation (described below) may reveal an analogous set of "social competence" subtypes (i.e., some "normal" and others "disturbed" in terms of social competence). (The studies by Speece, McKinney, and Apelbaum (1985) and McKinney and Speece (1986) contain some data that could be used to address this question directly.) As in the investigation of emotional disturbance in youngsters with LD, the examination of their social competence should eschew the homogeneous, contrasting groups methodology that has heretofore characterized all but a few studies in the field in favor of one that does justice to the heterogeneity of subtypes evident in the LD population.

Furthermore, it would appear that efforts to relate patterns of abilities and deficits on the one hand and components of social competence on the other may generate much more interesting data and conclusions than do approaches that simply search for correlates of LD (considered as a univocal phenomenon) and either emotional disturbance or problems in social competence. The studies reviewed in connection with the examination of Hypothesis 3 constitute another step beyond the latter type of simplistic contrasting groups/unitary deficit methodologies.

The Windsor Taxonomic Research

Before turning our attention to the most recent formulations of the psychosocial functioning of children with LD (Hypothesis 3 approaches), we examine in detail one issue raised in the previous section: heterogeneity.

In our laboratory, we have undertaken a research program with the immediate aim of more precisely describing the psychosocial functioning of children with LD. We have applied multivariate statistical subtyping methods, such as *Q*-factor analysis and some of the many variants of cluster analysis, to selected scales of the Personality Inventory for Children (PIC; Wirt, Lachar, Klinedinst, & Seat, 1977, 1984), in an attempt to derive both reliable and valid psychosocial subtypes of children with LD. These studies are the initial steps in a comprehensive research program aimed at the development of a psychosocial typology of children with LD; for want of a better term, we refer to them here as the Windsor Taxonomic Research. Note that, in this section, we concentrate on describing the characteristics and reliability of the typology that has emerged from this research. Other aspects of these studies are more germane to issues raised in connection with Hypothesis 3 approaches (see below).

The results of five of our studies (Fuerst, Fisk, & Rourke, 1989, 1990; Fuerst & Rourke, 1993, in press; Porter & Rourke, 1985) are summarized schematically in Figure 14.1. Each box represents a subtype derived from the source noted at the left of the chart. Within each box, a descriptive label characterizes the mean PIC profile of the subtype and, in the lower right corner, the relative size of the subtype is expressed as a percentage of the subjects classified within the study. Correlations between corresponding subtypes across studies appear on the connecting lines. Although some of the subtypes are arranged hierarchically, this order is based on the temporal course of our research and is not meant to imply that such a hierarchical division does, in fact, exist. Whether certain broad categories of psychosocial functioning can be usefully and accurately divided into subcategories, as implied by Figure 14.1, can only be determined by further research.

The four top rows of the figure present chronologically the subtypes found in the first four studies—Porter and Rourke (1985), Fuerst et al. (1989, 1990), and Fuerst and Rourke (1993), respectively. In the fifth row ("Overall"), which summarizes the typology that emerged across studies 1–4, the relative size values represent the average percentage of subjects assigned to a subtype across the four studies. The bottom four rows present the results from Fuerst and Rourke (in press). The results of that study are broken down into young "cluster-analysis-derived" (CAD) subtypes, middle CAD subtypes, old CAD subtypes, and "profile-matching-derived" (PMD) subtypes based on the entire sample. In this portion of the figure, the correlations on connecting lines represent the correlation between the mean PIC profile of the subtype and the corresponding prototype developed from studies 1–4.

Internal Validity (Reliability) of the Typology

Ideally, subtyping methods of any type should produce reliable, homogeneous groups that can be replicated across different samples and classification techniques (Everitt, 1980). This issue is of

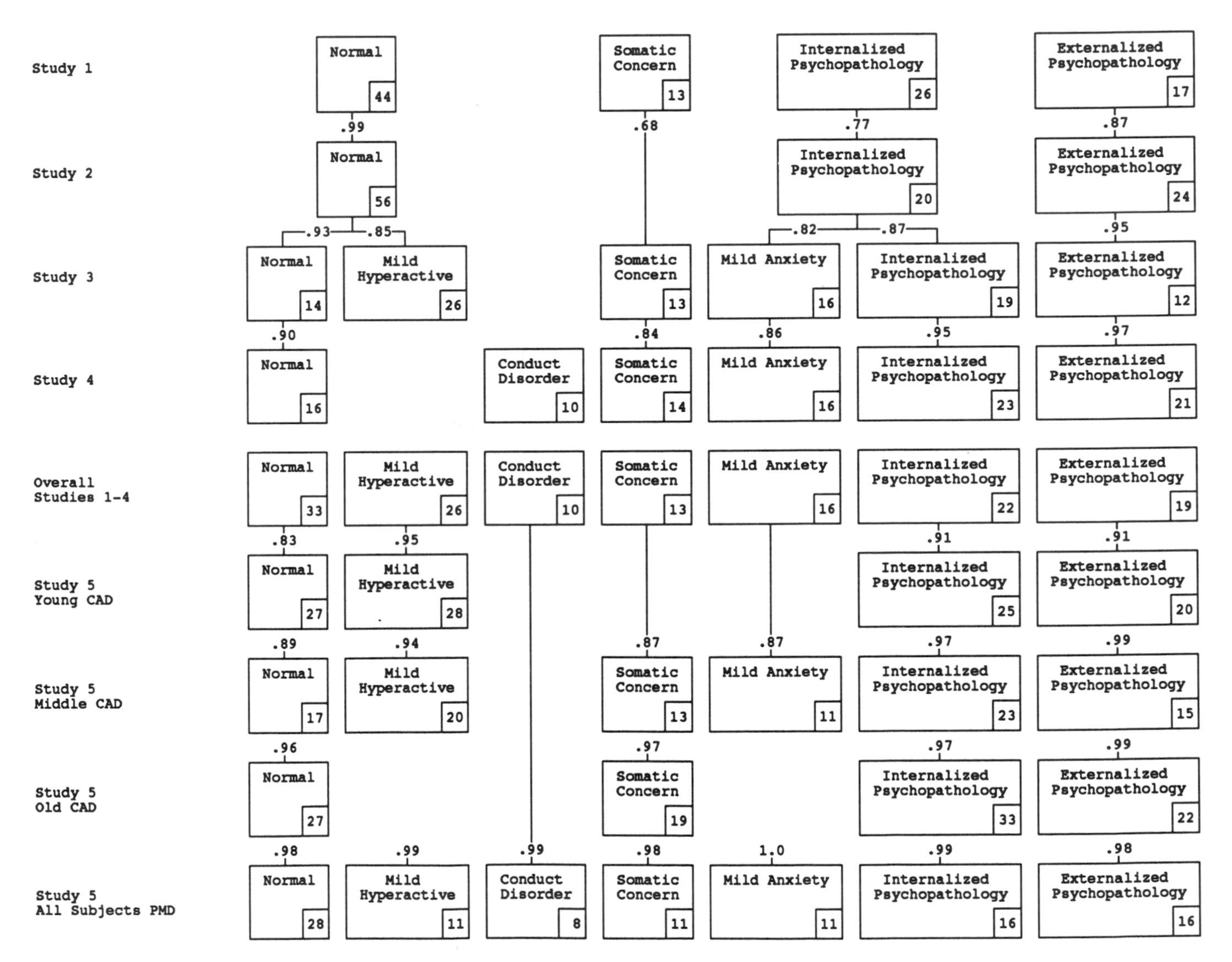

Figure 14.1 Summary of the psychosocial typology developed in the Windsor Taxonomic Research program. References for the studies are: study 1, Porter and Rourke (1985); study 2, Fuerst, Fisk, and Rourke (1989); study 3, Fuerst, Fisk, and Rourke (1990); study 4, Fuerst and Rourke (1993); study 5, Fuerst and Rourke (in press). CAD, cluster-analysis-derived; PMD, profile-matching-derived.

particular concern when multivariate subtyping techniques are applied in an exploratory fashion to data with relatively unknown statistical properties. Multivariate subtyping techniques, such as cluster analysis and *Q*-factor analysis, will always produce some grouping of cases, even if purely random data are used in the procedures, and different statistical subtyping techniques can, and often do, produce disparate solutions when applied to the same data. Replicability of solutions across different samples from the same population, and across different subtyping techniques, is a crucial step in determining the validity of the subtypes so derived (Fletcher, 1985). When the results of our five studies are considered, it is apparent that four of the subtypes—(a) Normal, including Mild Hyperactive; (b) Somatic Concern; (c) Internalized Psychopathology, including Mild Anxiety; and (d) Externalized Psychopathology—are readily replicable using different samples, statistical techniques, and sets of PIC scales. The reliability of the conduct disorder subtype is currently unknown.

Description of the Typology

Correlation coefficients (calculated between the mean PIC profiles of the subtypes) were used in Figure 14.1 to match up corresponding subtypes across the five studies. Overall, across studies 1–5, seven distinct subtypes were identified: (a) Normal; (b) Mild Hyperactive; (c) Mild Anxiety; (d) Somatic Concern; (e) Conduct Disorder; (f) Internalized Psychopathology; and (g) Externalized Psychopathology. By averaging the PIC scores of corresponding subtypes across studies (e.g., PIC scores of all of the Normal subtypes), it is possible to obtain "prototypical" mean PIC profiles for the seven subtypes. Prototypical profiles are presented in Figures 14.2 to 14.8.

Presentation of PIC profiles without interpretation does not describe behavior, because the scale labels are, in some respects, arbitrary. For example, elevation of the Psychosis scale above 70 *T* does not mark a child as psychotic. Similarly, the labels given to the subtypes, such as Normal or Mild Hyperactive, were used more as descriptions of the pattern of scores on the mean PIC profiles than as descriptions of behavior. For example, the PIC profile of the Normal subtype is, in fact, abnormal, with clinically meaningful elevations on some PIC scales. However, elevations on the Academic Achievement, Intellectual Screening, and Development scales, in the context of an otherwise roughly flat profile, are unremarkable, or *normal,* in samples of children with LD.

In this section, the subtypes are discussed in terms of psychosocial adaptation, or general patterns of behavioral function/dysfunction that would be expected, based on our current understanding of the PIC. Note that these characterizations are actually *expectations* or predictions that, in the process of establishing the external validity of the typology, must be tested in future research.

Two of the subtypes have mean PIC profiles that suggest relatively good psychosocial functioning. The profile of the Normal subtype (Figure 14.2) shows mean elevations above 70 *T* on the Achievement, Intellectual Screening, and Development scales (the so-called cognitive triad—a pattern found, to a greater or lesser extent, in all subtypes), and a very flat profile on all other clinical scales. The caretakers of these children are most concerned with cognitive development and academic performance.

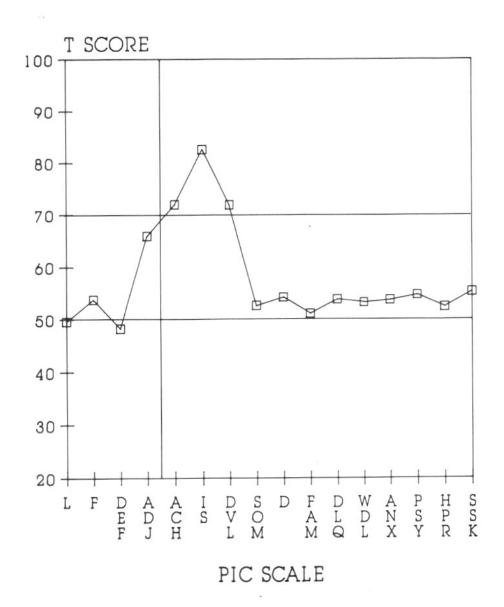

Figure 14.2 PIC profile for the Normal prototype. Abbreviations used in Figures 14.2 through 14.8 are: L, Lie; DEF, Defensiveness; ADJ, Adjustment; ACH, Achievement; IS, Intellectual Screening; DVL, Development; SOM, Somatic Concern; D, Depression; FAM, Family Relations; DLQ, Delinquency; WDL, Withdrawal; ANX, Anxiety; PSY, Psychosis; HPR, Hyperactivity; SSK, Social Skills.

The mean PIC profile of the Somatic Concern subtype (Figure 14.5) is similar to that of the Normal subtype, but it is marked by elevation of the Somatic Concern scale. The caretakers of these children are likely to express distress about their child's physical well-being and health. Physical complaints could span a wide range of difficulties, including visual problems, dizziness, headaches, syncope, fatigue, and gastrointestinal dysfunction. However, it should be noted that, as with other psychosocial measures tapping somatic domains, it is not possible to determine the degree to which such complaints might be "functional" rather than "organic" in nature, on the basis of the PIC profile. Elevation of this scale may be indicative of a need for medical assessment and intervention rather than reflective of psychosocial dysfunction.

Two of the subtypes evidence modest degrees of psychosocial dysfunction. Children in the Mild Hyperactive subtype (Figure 14.3) show a relatively unremarkable PIC profile that is distinguished by a single significant elevation above 70 *T* on the Intellectual Screening scale, and a somewhat higher than usual mean score on the Hyperactivity scale. This suggests fairly good psychosocial adaptation in most domains, as in the Normal subtype, with the possibility of rather mild acting-out behaviors. The profile of the Mild Anxiety subtype (Figure 14.4) suggests mild psychosocial disturbance, with notable, but relatively modest, peaks on the Intellectual Screening, Depression, and Anxiety scales. Overall, this profile suggests symptoms of mild anxiety and depression, and is somewhat reminiscent of the PIC profile of the Internalized Psychopathology subtype.

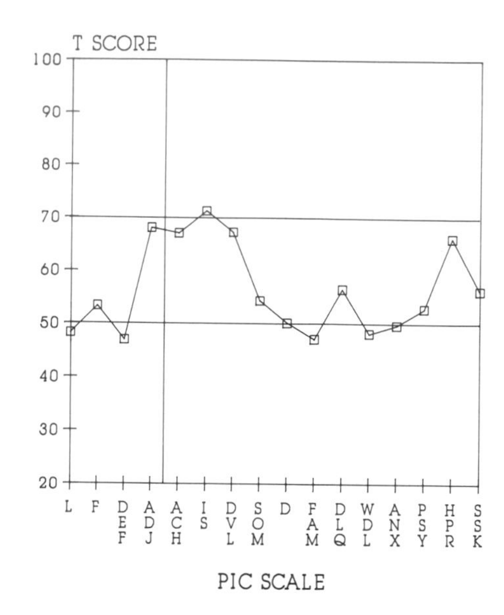

Figure 14.3 PIC profile for the Mild Hyperactive prototype.

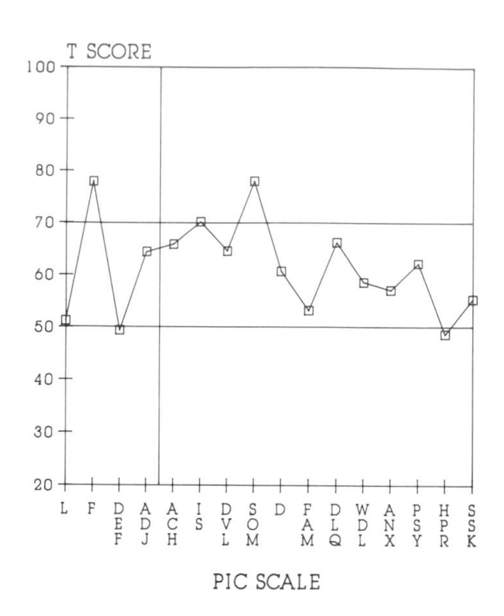

Figure 14.5 PIC profile for the Somatic Concern prototype.

In some respects, the PIC profile of the Conduct Disorder subtype (Figure 14.6) also suggests modest psychosocial dysfunction, with a single peak on the Delinquency scale. However, the behaviors that may be demonstrated by such children are likely to be more problematic for caretakers and peers than are those demonstrated by children in the Mild Hyperactive or Mild Anxiety subtypes. Children with this profile may show insensitivity toward others, a disregard for rules and limits, impulsivity, and hostility. Truly delinquent behavior, such as verbal and physical aggression, destructiveness, lying, and stealing, may be exhibited by some children.

The mean PIC profile of the Internalized Psychopathology subtype (Figure 14.7) displays prominent elevations on a number of subscales that suggest significant, internalized, socio-emotional difficulties. High scores appear on the Adjustment, Depression, Withdrawal, Anxiety, and Psychosis scales, with moderate, though clinically relevant, elevations on Achievement, Development, and Social Skills scales. Children in the

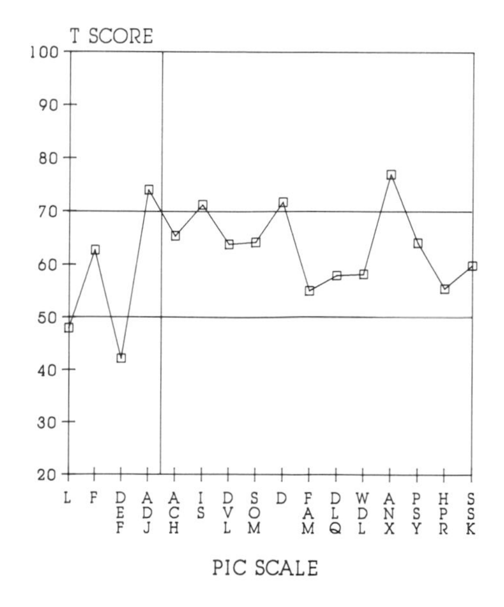

Figure 14.4 PIC profile for the Mild Anxiety prototype.

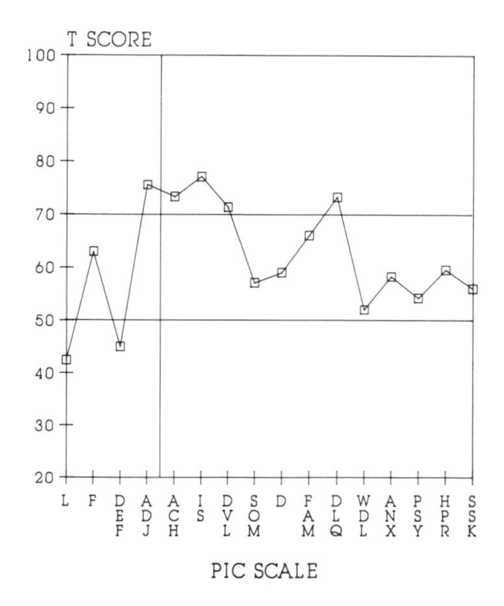

Figure 14.6 PIC profile for the Conduct Disorder prototype.

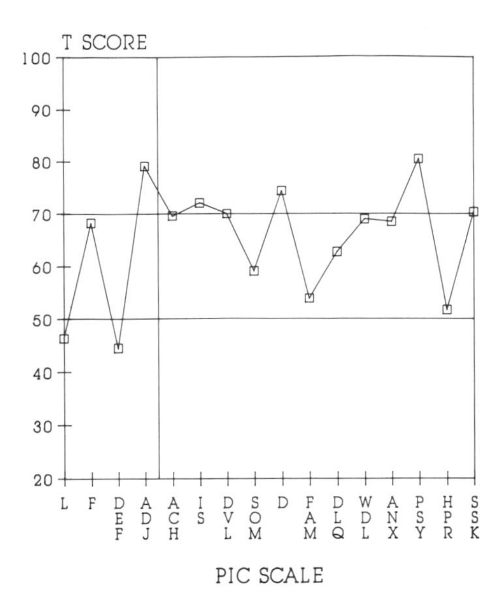

Figure 14.7 PIC profile for the Internalized Psychopathology prototype.

Internalized Psychopathology subtype are likely to be depressed, anxious, and emotionally labile. Inappropriate affect, difficulties with cognition and with orientation to reality, and social isolation have been associated with this profile. Social interaction and general interpersonal functioning may present serious problems for these children.

The mean PIC profile of the Externalized Psychopathology subtype (Figure 14.8) is also elevated on a number of scales. Children in this subtype have particularly high mean scores on the Adjustment, Delinquency, Hyperactivity, and Social Skills scales.

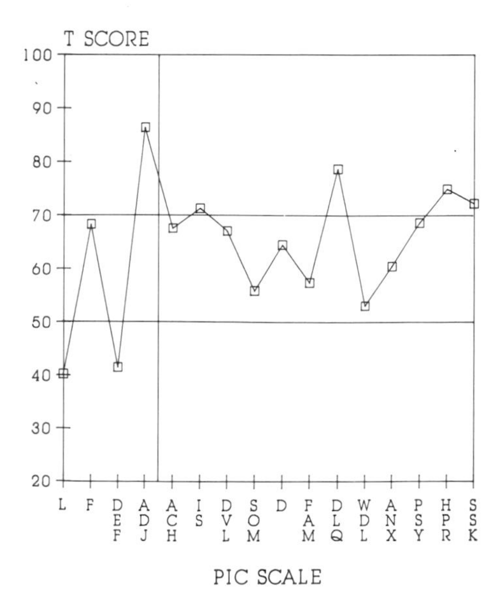

Figure 14.8 PIC profile for the Externalized Psychopathology prototype.

This profile also suggests significant behavioral disturbance; however, unlike the Internalized Psychopathology subtype, these children are apt to exhibit hyperkinetic, acting-out types of behavior. Such children may be hostile, impulsive, restless, and emotionally unstable, and have low frustration tolerance. Aggressive, violent, and destructive behavior may also be part of the clinical picture.

Relations between Age and Psychosocial Functioning

Of the five studies discussed above, the relations between age and patterns of psychosocial functioning were directly examined only in Fuerst and Rourke (in press). In this study, we examined the relations between age and patterns of psychosocial functioning in children with LD. To this end, we constructed a sample of 728 children with LD, between the ages of 7 and 13 years. For some analyses, the children were subdivided into three age levels: (a) young (7–8 years; 201 subjects), (b) middle (9–10 years; 258 subjects), and (c) old (11–13 years; 269 subjects). As in the first four studies, psychosocial functioning was defined by subtypes derived from PIC scores. Two methods were used to derive the subtypes.

The first method employed *k*-means cluster analysis, applied separately to each of the young, middle, and old samples. The resulting *k*-means partitions were validated by replication, using a variety of hierarchical-agglomerative clustering techniques. The subtypes—referred to as cluster-analysis-derived (CAD) subtypes—at each of the three age levels were very similar and were strongly related to clusters found in our previous studies. At each age level, roughly the same number of subtypes were found (4, 6, and 4 subtypes at young, middle, and old age levels, respectively), which suggests that, with increasing age, children with LD do not show greater diversity of psychosocial functioning. Also, at all three age levels, Normal, Internalized Psychopathology, and Externalized Psychopathology subtypes were found, which suggests that major *patterns* of psychosocial functioning are consistent across ages 7 through 13. Finally, the Internalized Psychopathology and Externalized Psychopathology CAD subtypes were very similar across the young, middle, and old samples. Thus, it appears that, with increased age, there is no change in the *level* of pathology evidenced by children in frankly maladjusted subtypes.

The second classification method used in this study involved assigning subjects to the subtypes of the typology derived in previous research, on the basis of similarity of PIC profile shape. As outlined earlier and summarized in Figure 14.1, previous research in our laboratory had produced a typology of seven psychosocial subtypes. Calculation of the mean PIC scores on all (16) scales for the seven previously derived subtypes resulted in the creation of "prototypical" PIC profiles for those subtypes. Correlations between each subject's PIC profile and the seven prototypical PIC profiles were calculated, and subjects were assigned ("matched") to the subtypes to which their PIC profiles correlated most strongly. When the profile-matching-derived (PMD) subtypes formed by this profile matching technique were further broken down at the young, middle, and old age levels, there were no differences between the resulting mean PIC profiles in terms of either profile shape or elevation within each subtype. Furthermore, the distribution of subjects across the subtypes was comparable at each of the three age levels. Again, these results demonstrated that children with LD show similar patterns of psychosocial functioning and similar forms and levels of psychopathology, from ages 7 through 13.

The results of the Fuerst and Rourke (in press) study show that there is remarkable stability in patterns of psychosocial adaptation of children with LD across the elementary school years. No evidence was found to support the notion that children with LD are likely to develop more serious types or degrees of psychopathology as they grow older. Similarly, these results indicate that, given a particular pattern of psychosocial adaptation, there is no substantial change in level of adaptation with increasing age. Thus, overall, as children with LD grow older, they show no increased risk for the development of pathological patterns of psychosocial adaptation, nor do they show any deterioration in level of psychosocial functioning.

These results are very much at variance with Hypothesis 2 formulations of the psychosocial functioning of children with LD. Recall that such formulations generally hold that the negative consequences of having a learning disability (such as frustration, anxiety, or peer rejection because of continued academic failure, or a discrete cognitive deficit that perpetually disrupts psychosocial functioning) in time produce maladjustment by grinding down the child's adaptive capacity in some fashion. Cumulative negative experiences may be deleterious to some children with LD, but the results of Fuerst and Rourke (in press) and others (e.g., Chapman, 1988; Chapman & Boersma, 1980; Jorm, Share, Matthews, & Maclean, 1986; Strang, 1981) suggest strongly that this is not generally the case. Some children with LD evidence significant maladjustment (e.g., the Internalized Psychopathology and Externalized Psychopathology subtypes); however, the development of pathological patterns of functioning is not more likely with increasing age, nor is deterioration in level of adaptation.

This conclusion must, of course, be tempered by the same consideration that motivated the studies reviewed in this section: heterogeneity. Just as some children with LD will not fall neatly within the typology presented above (to the chagrin of statistically oriented researchers, outliers *do* have the annoying habit of showing up in the clinic waiting room), experience dictates that some children with LD demonstrate abnormal psychosocial development. However, this series of studies suggests that, when such changes are observed in clinical settings, factors other than simple increased age and cumulative exposure to negative experiences must be considered. An example of a specific, well-delineated subpopulation of children with LD who *do* show abnormal psychosocial development with advancing age, and the factors that may cause or contribute to this process, will be presented in a subsequent section of this chapter.

General Conclusions

The results of the foregoing studies conducted in our laboratory constitute a formidable, perhaps irrefutable, challenge to the view that children with LD are relatively uniform in terms of their socioemotional functioning. Furthermore, these studies cast doubt on the notion that LD, broadly considered, constitute a sufficient condition for the production of emotional disturbance. The results of these studies suggest strongly that some children who meet commonly accepted definitions of LD show signs of significant socioemotional disturbance, whereas others do not; on balance, it appears that most do not. The important question at this juncture becomes: Is there a set of characteristics that differentiates: (a) children with LD who develop adaptive socioemotional functioning from those children who develop maladaptive socioemotional functioning (i.e., presence or absence of psychopathology, and/or level of psychopathology); and (b) children with LD who develop particular patterns of psychosocial functioning (i.e., type of pathology, such as internalized versus externalized)? This issue is discussed in greater detail in the following section wherein relations between neuropsychological skill/ability patterns and socioemotional disturbance are examined.

HYPOTHESIS 3: SPECIFIC PATTERNS OF CENTRAL PROCESSING ABILITIES AND DEFICITS CAUSE SPECIFIC MANIFESTATIONS (SUBTYPES) OF LD AND SPECIFIC FORMS OF SOCIOEMOTIONAL DISTURBANCE

This hypothesis proposes a causal connection between particular patterns of central processing assets and deficits on the one hand and particular subtypes of both LD and socioemotional functioning on the other (Rourke & Fisk, 1981). In other words, the academic and behavioral adaptation of children with LD is not seen as directly related (except in a correlational sense), as in Hypothesis 2 approaches, but, instead, as primarily determined by neurocognitive or neuropsychological strengths and deficiencies.

This formulation of the interrelations between LD and psychosocial functioning is relatively new. Unfortunately, some of the research in this area has been of less than stellar quality (see Weller & Strawser, 1987, for a brief review of relevant studies). A rather extreme example is found in a study by Stellern, Marlowe, Jacobs, and Cossairt (1985), in which they attempted to relate hemispheric cognitive modes (or styles) to academic performance, classroom behavior, and emotional disturbance in a sample of behaviorally disordered and normal control children. Cognitive style (i.e., left hemisphere preferred, right hemisphere preferred, or integrated) was assessed by means of a paper-and-pencil self-report scale. Briefly, Stellern et al. (1985) found that emotional disturbance was weakly associated with a right hemisphere cognitive mode. In addition to poor subject selection procedures, unsophisticated and questionable statistical methods, and the use of an unvalidated measurement instrument, the entire premise of left versus right hemisphere cognitive modes reveals a rather limited and largely erroneous view of brain-behavior relations.

A marginally better study is one by Glosser and Koppell (1987), who divided 67 children with learning problems (so identified by referral sources, with no other criteria used) into left hemisphere impaired, right hemisphere impaired, or nonlateralized impairment. Unfortunately, the classification scheme used was only vaguely described by the authors, and appeared to have been developed more to provide adequate coverage when the sample was partitioned than on a rational or empirical basis. The three groups were compared on scores derived from behavioral checklists created by the investigators. Overall, children showing left hemisphere impairment (as judged by the authors) tended to show more evidence of depression and anxiety, whereas children showing right hemisphere impairment tended to have more somatic complaints. Those children with nonlateralized impairment tended to show more distractibility, motor activity, and aggression. Roughly comparable results have been reported by Nussbaum and Bigler (1986), who found that children with putative left hemisphere impairment (judged on the basis of measures of psychometric intelligence and academic achievement) showed somewhat greater levels of personality and behavioral deviance.

More recently, Nussbaum et al. (1988) administered a battery of neuropsychological tests to 219 children, from 7 to 12 years old, referred for testing because of learning problems. The investigators developed composite "anterior" and "posterior" cortical impairment scores based on neuropsychological measures used in the assessment. On the basis of these composite scores, they classified 33 subjects into either anterior or posterior impairment groups. These two groups were then compared on the Child Behavior Checklist (CBCL; Achenbach & Edelbrock, 1983) and PIC (Wirt et al., 1984) measures completed by parents. The results showed that the anterior impairment group exhibited more evidence of social withdrawal, aggression, hyperactivity, and externalizing pathology, whereas the posterior impairment group showed somewhat greater levels of anxiety.

These and other studies fall within the framework of Hypothesis 3 investigations, but they clearly represent little or no improvement over many of the Hypothesis 2 investigations reviewed above, for much the same methodological reasons (poor or absent definitions of LD, poor operationalization of psychological constructs, questionable classification procedures, and so on). Disregard of developmental considerations is also of particular concern in these investigations.

In our view, the central importance of developmental considerations in this area cannot be overemphasized. Unfortunately, there is a tendency in some studies to assume that brain-behavior relations derived from research with adults can be extrapolated without modification to children with LD—for example, that a particular test that may have some value for localization of dysfunction in adults with demonstrated cerebral insult necessarily has similar significance across all age ranges and populations. As Rourke et al. (1983) pointed out, there are numerous reasons (e.g., rapid maturation of the nervous system, loss of existing ability versus failed acquisition of ability, abnormal or atypical development) why generalizations of adult models of cerebral functioning to children must be done with extreme caution and must be subject to careful empirical testing. Similarly, in some studies, there is a tendency to frame research problems within static models of limited scope (or, worse, to present entirely atheoretic investigations). Research undertaken within a limited or trivial theoretical framework tends to produce limited or trivial results. Recent reviews and theoretical papers by Spreen (1989) and Rourke (1988a) have emphasized the need to consider both the components and the dynamics of neurologic, cognitive, academic, and psychosocial development and adaptation when developing models to account for the socioemotional difficulties faced by children with LD. Although this is a monumental task, choosing to ignore complexity when formulating research questions does not make a phenomenon under investigation simpler.

A more sophisticated test of Hypothesis 3 involves an examination of the results of several LD subtype investigations aimed at the determination of patterns of central processing abilities and deficits that characterize such subtypes, and the patterns of socioemotional responsivity that appear to be related to them. Regarding the first issue, the results of studies by Rourke and Finlayson (1978), Rourke and Strang (1978), and Strang and Rourke (1983) demonstrated that 9- to 14-year-old children with LD who exhibit a pattern of impaired reading (word recognition) and spelling within a context of a significantly better, though still impaired, level of performance in mechanical arithmetic (Group R-S) differ markedly in their patterns of neuropsychological abilities and deficits from those who exhibit a pattern of above-average reading and spelling and an outstandingly deficient level of mechanical arithmetic performance (Group A).

As summarized in Strang and Rourke (1985b), the differences between these subtypes cover a wide range of skills and abilities. Specifically, Group A children exhibit below-normal performances on tasks requiring visual-spatial-organizational, psychomotor, tactile-perceptual, and conceptual skills and abilities, within a context of normal performances on verbal tasks that require rote, overlearned verbal skills; they also have difficulties on measures that involve novel task requirements, whether these are "verbal" or "nonverbal" in nature. Group R-S children exhibit the virtually opposite pattern of neuropsychological skills and abilities: mild to moderate difficulties in almost all areas of linguistic endeavor and marked problems in auditory-perceptual tasks that tax their capacities for exact hearing of speech-sounds; normal visual-spatial organizational, psychomotor, tactile-perceptual, and nonverbal concept-formation skills and abilities. In addition, complex problem solving, hypothesis testing, and concept formation in situations where verbal instructions and response requirements are kept to a minimum pose no difficulties for Group R-S children.

We turn now to a review of studies carried out in our laboratory that have focused on the psychosocial functioning of subtypes of children and adolescents with LD. These studies have their origins in the discovery of the neuropsychological dimensions of the Group R-S and Group A children, and they have followed a course best described as an attempt to develop a nomological net and the exploitation of a form of the multitrait-multimethod approach to validity (Cook & Campbell, 1979). Furthermore, they were designed specifically to capitalize on a framework squarely within the purview of developmental psychopathology.

Strang and Rourke (1985a)

When the average PIC profiles of children chosen to approximate the characteristics of these two subtypes of learning-disabled children were compared (Strang & Rourke, 1985a), it was clear that the profile for Group A was similar to that exhibited by the "emotionally disturbed" (internalized psychopathology) group in the Porter and Rourke (1985) and Fuerst et al. (1989)

studies, whereas the profile for Group R-S children was virtually identical to that exhibited by the "normal" group in those studies. Additional examination of three factor scores derived from the PIC revealed that Groups R-S and A did not differ significantly on the "concern over academic achievement factor" but differed sharply on the factors of "personality deviance" and "internalized psychopathology." In both of the latter cases, the Group A levels of deviation were significantly higher (i.e., more pathological) than were those for Group R-S.

These two sets of results, taken together, offer strong support for Hypothesis 3—that particular patterns of central processing abilities can eventuate in (a) markedly different subtypes of LD and academic functioning (Groups R-S and A) and (b) markedly different patterns of socioemotional functioning (one characterized by normalcy; the other, by an internalized form of psychopathology and personality deviance). Because such group results can be deceiving when applied to the individual case, we emphasize that very little variance was evident in the PIC protocols of the children classified into Groups R-S and A in these studies. Furthermore, the interested reader may wish to consult case studies of such youngsters in four recent works (Rourke, 1989; Rourke et al., 1983; Rourke & Fisk, 1992; Rourke, Fisk, & Strang, 1986) to find evidence of such consistent differences in socioemotional manifestations.

The Fuerst et al. (1990) and Fuerst and Rourke (1993) investigations (reviewed above) also attempted to address Hypothesis 3 considerations. However, in these studies, we took the opposite approach to that employed in the Strang and Rourke (1985a) investigation, in that we first attempted to develop a psychosocial typology (using the PIC and statistical methods), and then examined the manner in which these subtypes differed on cognitive and academic measures.

Fuerst et al. (1990)

In this study, the subjects were selected so as to comprise three (equal-sized) groups with distinctly different patterns of Wechsler Intelligence Scale for Children (WISC; Wechsler, 1949, 1974) Verbal IQ (VIQ) and Performance IQ (PIQ) scores. One group had VIQ greater than PIQ by at least 10 points (VIQ > PIQ), a second had VIQ less than PIQ by at least 10 points (VIQ < PIQ), and a third had VIQ-PIQ scores within 9 points of each other. As discussed in the earlier section on the Windsor Taxonomic Research, the application of several cluster analytic techniques yielded an apparently reliable solution that suggested the presence of six distinct personality subtypes. The frequencies of the three VIQ-PIQ groups within each of these psychosocial subtypes were calculated and compared.

Within the Normal subtype, we found children with VIQ > PIQ at a much lower frequency (roughly 6% of the subtype) than either children with the opposite pattern of VIQ-PIQ discrepancy or children with no significant difference between VIQ and PIQ. This was also the case in the Mild Anxiety subtype, in which subjects with VIQ > PIQ were found at a rate significantly below expectation (about 5% of the subtype). In the Mild Hyperactivity subtype, the frequencies of subjects from the three VIQ-PIQ groups were approximately equal. These results indicated that, overall, within normal and mildly disturbed subtypes of children with LD, there was a tendency for VIQ > PIQ children to be found at lower frequencies than VIQ = PIQ or VIQ < PIQ children. There were only about half as many VIQ > PIQ children in these three groups as there were VIQ = PIQ or VIQ < PIQ children.

In the Internalized Psychopathology subtype, subjects with VIQ = PIQ were found at significantly lower than expected frequencies (about 15% of the subtype). On the other hand, subjects with VIQ > PIQ were found at a higher frequency than would be expected (roughly 46% of the subtype), and at a higher frequency than VIQ < PIQ subjects (39%). Within the Externalized Psychopathology subtype, subjects with VIQ > PIQ were found at a much higher frequency (about 63% of the group) than were children with either VIQ = PIQ or VIQ < PIQ. Thus, unlike the normal and mildly disturbed groups, within subtypes showing severe psychosocial disturbance there was a strong tendency for VIQ > PIQ subjects to be found at higher frequencies than either the VIQ = PIQ or VIQ < PIQ subjects. There were about twice as many VIQ > PIQ children in these two "severe" groups as there were VIQ = PIQ or VIQ < PIQ children.

Fuerst and Rourke (1993)

In this investigation, six personality subtypes were also generated (see discussion of the Windsor Taxonomic Research, above). With one exception, these were the same subtypes as those found in the Fuerst et al. (1990) study. The differences among these six subtypes on WRAT Reading, Spelling, and Arithmetic standard scores were examined. Overall, the six subtypes were indiscriminable on WRAT Arithmetic. However, there were significant differences among some of the subtypes on WRAT Reading and Spelling. The Externalized and Internalized Psychopathology subtypes had mean WRAT Reading scores that were significantly higher than those of the Normal and Somatic Concern subtypes. Similarly, the Externalized and Internalized Psychopathology subtypes scored higher on WRAT Spelling than did the Conduct Disorder and Normal subtypes, and the Internalized Psychopathology group also scored higher than did the Somatic Concern subtype.

These findings were echoed when WRAT Reading, Spelling, and Arithmetic were considered simultaneously in a canonical discriminant analysis. The first canonical function was significant, providing better than chance discrimination among the groups. When the standardized scoring coefficients for this function were considered, it was apparent that scores on this variable were, in fact, essentially simple sums of WRAT Reading and Spelling scores, with Arithmetic playing a trivial role. Examination of group means on the canonical variables indicated that the Normal, Somatic Concern, and Conduct Disorder groups were indistinguishable on this variable. These three groups were, however, clearly separated from the higher-scoring Externalized and Internalized Psychopathology groups, which appeared to form a second "clump" on their own. The Mild Anxiety group fell about midway between these two sets of subtypes.

These results suggest that children referred for neuropsychological assessment (mostly because of suspected LD) with relatively well-developed reading and spelling skills (but with deficient mechanical arithmetic skills) are more likely to appear in PIC subtypes with profiles suggestive of severe psychopathology, be it of the internalizing or externalizing type. On the other hand, children with relatively mild somatization or conduct disorder problems are indistinguishable from normal children on the basis of these reading and spelling skills. Children with symptoms of mild anxiety and depression appear to fall between these two extremes, and cannot be distinguished from either on the basis of these skills.

Fuerst and Rourke (1993) compared the subtypes on WRAT Reading minus Arithmetic (RA) and Spelling minus Arithmetic (SA) scores. Overall, the Internalized Psychopathology group had not only the largest absolute difference on RA and SA, but also showed deficient Arithmetic relative to both Reading and Spelling (i.e., a pattern identical to that shown by the Group A subtype in previous studies). The other subtypes showed much smaller discrepancies on RA and SA, and, in some instances, discrepancies in the opposite direction (e.g., the Normal, Somatic Concern, and Conduct Disorder subtypes had Arithmetic scores that were *higher* than their Spelling scores). This contrast (Internalized Psychopathology versus all other subtypes) was statistically significant. None of the other subtypes could be differentiated from any other on the basis of these measures.

Related Developmental Studies

Two investigations that were designed to determine the developmental outcome for Group A children are also useful for evaluating Hypothesis 3. Rourke, Young, Strang, and Russell (1986) compared the performances of Group A children and a group of clinic-referred adults on a wide variety of neuropsychological variables. The adults presented with VIQ-PIQ discrepancies and WRAT patterns that were virtually identical to the analogous patterns in Group A children. It was demonstrated that the patterns of age-related performances of the adults and the children on the neuropsychological variables were remarkably similar. In addition, the adults were characterized by internalized forms of psychopathology that bore a striking resemblance to those exhibited by Group A youngsters. In a related study, Del Dotto, Rourke, McFadden, and Fisk (1987) confirmed the stability of the neuropsychological and personality characteristics of this subtype of LD over time.

Implications of Hypothesis 3 Studies

The results of these studies are quite straightforward, but the patterns of relations revealed by them, and their implications for the current discussion, are fairly complex and require the following detailed explanation.

1. Strang and Rourke (1985a) demonstrated that Group A subjects (good reading and spelling performance relative to arithmetic) evidence greater, clinically significant, psychopathology as compared to Group R-S subjects (poor reading and spelling relative to arithmetic). Fuerst and Rourke (1993) also demonstrated that children evidencing severe psychopathology tend to perform better in reading and spelling relative to children with normal psychosocial functioning or relatively benign psychosocial problems. Both the Strang and Rourke (1985a) and Fuerst and Rourke (1993) studies also revealed that children showing a Group A pattern of academic performance tend to evidence a particular *type* of psychopathology (internalized). Thus, there is a relationship between patterns of academic functioning and patterns of psychosocial functioning (both level and type of pathology) in at least one subtype of children with LD.

2. It is difficult to argue that patterns of academic performance (i.e., good reading and spelling relative to arithmetic, or vice versa) influence psychosocial functioning. That is, there is no obvious explanation for the observation that Group A children evidence greater psychopathology as compared to Group R-S children. Similarly, it is also difficult to argue that different patterns of psychosocial functioning can directly produce different patterns of academic achievement. (An exception to this assertion might be cases of primary psychopathology, such as major depressive disorder or attention deficit disorder. As explained in the discussion of Hypothesis 1, these cases lie outside the realm of LD.)

3. Considering point 2, it is logical to propose that a third factor accounts for the apparent relationship between patterns of academic functioning and psychosocial functioning. It is certainly possible that many different factors could be producing this apparent relationship, but a single factor would provide the most parsimonious explanation.

4. The most likely candidate for this intervening factor is cognitive functioning. Previous research has clearly indicated that patterns of academic functioning are strongly related to patterns of cognitive functioning, as measured by neuropsychological/psychometric instruments. These measures include—but are by no means limited to—WISC VIQ-PIQ discrepancies (Rourke et al., 1973; Rourke & Finlayson, 1978; Rourke & Telegdy, 1971; Rourke, Young, & Flewelling, 1971). The logical direction of causation in this relationship is that cognitive factors influence academic performance.

5. The results of Fuerst et al. (1990) have demonstrated that patterns of cognitive functioning, measured by WISC VIQ-PIQ discrepancy, are associated with psychosocial functioning. Specifically, children showing the pattern of WISC VIQ > PIQ tend to be found in subtypes demonstrating severe psychopathology, whereas children with VIQ = PIQ or VIQ < PIQ tend to be found in subtypes with normal or mildly disturbed psychosocial functioning. As before, it is difficult to conceive of patterns of psychosocial functioning as causative with respect to patterns of cognitive functioning (with the exceptions noted in point 2 above). It is more logical to propose that patterns of cognitive functioning influence psychosocial functioning.

6. Thus, cognitive/neuropsychological functioning may, at one and the same time, influence academic performance on the one hand and psychosocial functioning on the other. Patterns of cognitive/neuropsychological functioning may be the intervening factors accounting for the apparent relationship between academic performance and socioemotional adjustment. However, further investigation, using more direct and detailed measures of cognitive/neuropsychological functioning, is required in order to have greater confidence in this conclusion.

Psychosocial Dynamics in Groups R-S and A

It would appear that children who exhibit the Group A (Nonverbal Learning Disabilities, NLD) profile of neuropsychological abilities and deficits are likely to be described by parents as emotionally or behaviorally disturbed. In contrast, Group R-S children (with outstanding difficulties in many aspects of psycholinguistic functioning) are so described at much lower frequencies. More generally, it may be that the pattern of NLD described approximates a sufficient condition for the development of some sort of socioemotional disturbance (Rourke, 1987, 1989), whereas the pattern of central processing assets and deficits exhibited by the subtype of psycholinguistically impaired children examined in this series of studies may not constitute the same sufficient basis for such an outcome.

This is not meant to imply that children characterized by the Group R-S pattern—which we have come to characterize as the Basic Phonological Processing Disorder subtype (Rourke, 1989)—will never experience socioemotional disturbance. Indeed, clinical experience (e.g., Rourke et al., 1983; Rourke, Fisk, & Strang, 1986) suggests that many do. Rather, these results suggest that, for the Group R-S subtype, factors in addition to psycholinguistic deficiency may be necessary for disturbed socioemotional functioning to occur. Such "additional" factors may include some of those mentioned in connection with the emotional disturbance-learning problem relationship outlined in the Hypothesis 1 section of this review (e.g., teacher-pupil personality conflicts, unrealistic demands by parents and teachers, inappropriate motivation and social expectancies). Others would appear to include the presence of salient antisocial models, selective reinforcement of nonadaptive and socially inappropriate behaviors, and any number of other factors that have the potential for encouraging problems in the socioemotional functioning of even normally achieving youngsters.

Refinements of these findings and detailed theoretical explanations of their interrelations are contained in several recent publications (e.g., Rourke, 1982, 1987, 1989, 1990; Rourke & Fisk, 1988; Strang & Rourke, 1985a). It is relatively easy to demonstrate and outline this pattern of relations, as we have done in the previous section. The development and articulation of a model capable of accounting for those relations, however, is a far more complex undertaking.

NONVERBAL LEARNING DISABILITIES: THE SYNDROME AND THE MODEL

A detailed model that attempts to account for the propensity of Group A (NLD) children to develop a particular configuration of academic learning difficulties and a specific type of severe socioemotional disturbance (plus many other unusual features often noted by clinicians when dealing with children with NLD) is presented in Rourke (1989). Figure 14.9 is an illustration of the developmental dynamics that are thought to obtain in the NLD syndrome.

The principal clinical features of the NLD *syndrome* are thought to be deficiencies in visual-perceptual-organizational abilities, complex psychomotor skills, tactile perception, and nonverbal problem solving, with age-appropriate development of many rote verbal, simple motor, and psycholinguistic skills and abilities. In addition to describing the clinical features of the NLD syndrome, Rourke (1987, 1988b, 1989) has proposed a model to explain the syndrome's dynamics. The model involves an extension of the theoretical tenets of Goldberg and Costa (1981), some integration with Piagetian developmental theory, and some relationships to known age-related developmental changes in the neuropsychological test performance. Summaries of the syndrome and the model follow; in these, we accentuate the developmental dimensions of both the syndrome and the model.

Characteristics and Dynamics of the NLD Syndrome

The following summary of the assets and deficits of the NLD syndrome should be viewed in the specific context of cause-effect relationships; that is, the primary neuropsychological assets and deficits are thought to lead to the secondary neuropsychological assets and deficits, and so on; and the foregoing are seen as causative vis-à-vis the academic and socioemotional/adaptive aspects of the syndrome. In this sense, the latter dimensions are, essentially, *dependent* variables (i.e., effects rather than causes) in the NLD syndrome. Reference to Figure 14.9 should be of assistance in understanding the dynamics that are proposed to obtain in the NLD model.

Neuropsychological Assets

(a) Primary

Simple motor. Simple, repetitive motor skills are generally intact, especially at older age levels (middle childhood and beyond).

Auditory perception. After a very early developmental period when such skills appear to be lagging, auditory perceptual capacities become very well developed.

Rote material. Repetition and/or constancy of stimulus input—especially through the auditory modality, but not confined to it—is well appreciated. Repetitious motor acts, including some aspects of speech and well-practiced skills, such as handwriting, eventually develop to average or above-average levels.

(b) Secondary

Attention. Selective and sustained attention to simple, repetitive verbal material (especially that delivered through the auditory modality) becomes very well developed.

(c) Tertiary

Memory. Rote verbal memory and memory for material that is readily coded in a rote verbal fashion become extremely well developed.

(d) Verbal

Speech and language. Following an early developmental period when linguistic skills appear to be lagging, a number of such skills emerge and develop in a rapid fashion. Excellent phonemic hearing, segmentation, blending, and

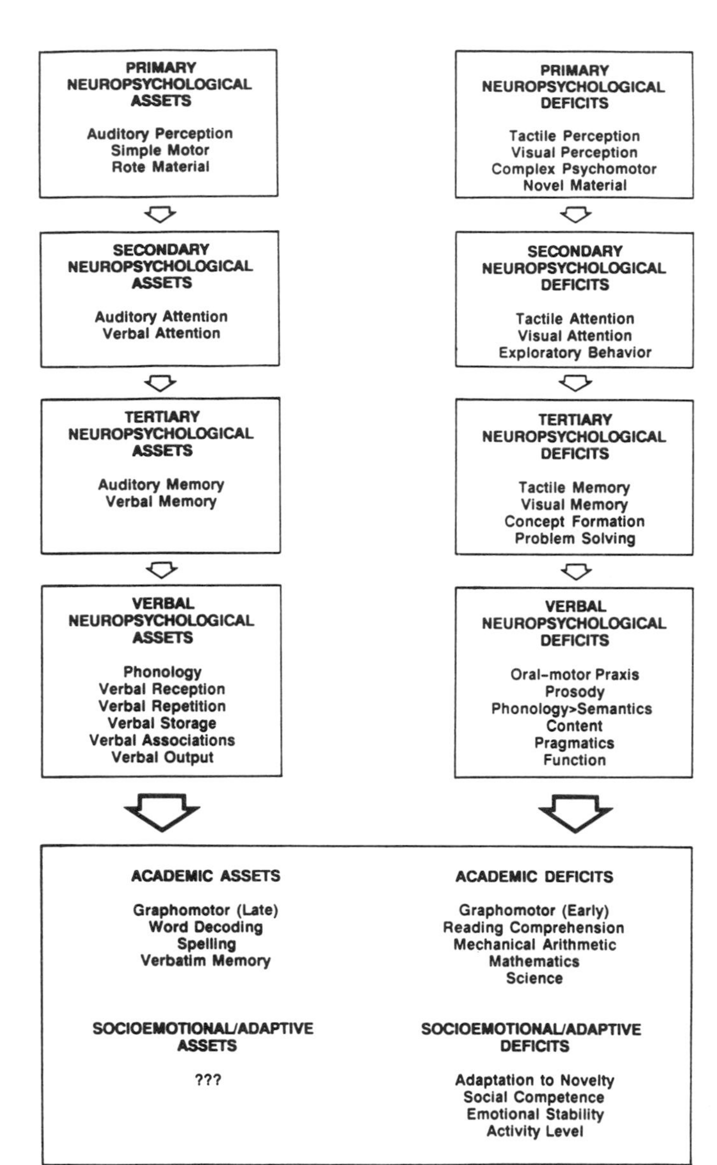

Figure 14.9 NLD syndrome and dynamics.

repetition and very well developed receptive language skills and rote verbal capacities are evident, as are a large store of rote verbal material and verbal associations, and a very high volume of speech output. All of these characteristics tend to become more prominent with advancing years.

Academic Assets

Following initial problems with the visual-motor aspects of writing and much practice with a writing instrument, graphomotor skills (for words) reach good to excellent levels. Following initial problems with the development of the visual-spatial feature-analysis skills that are necessary for reading, good to excellent single-word reading (decoding) skills become evident. Single-word spelling-to-dictation skills also develop to above-average levels. Misspellings are almost exclusively of the phonetically accurate variety. Verbatim memory for oral and written verbal material can be outstanding in the middle to late elementary school years and thereafter.

Neuropsychological Deficits

(a) Primary

Tactile perception. Bilateral tactile-perceptual deficits, usually more marked on the left side of the body, are apparent early in development. These deficits tend to become less prominent with advancing years.

Visual perception. Impaired discrimination and recognition of visual detail and visual relationships are evident, as are outstanding deficiencies in visual-spatial-organizational abilities. Deficits in these areas tend to increase with advancing years.

Complex psychomotor. Bilateral psychomotor coordination deficiencies are prominent; these are often more marked on the left side of the body. These deficits, except for well-practiced skills such as handwriting, tend to increase in severity with age.

Novel material. Stimulus configurations that are novel are dealt with very poorly and inappropriately. Difficulties in age-appropriate accommodation to novel events, and a marked tendency toward overassimilation of novel events, increase with advancing years.

(b) Secondary

Attention. Attention to tactile and visual input is poor. Deficiencies in these areas tend to increase over the course of development, except for material that is programmatic and overlearned (e.g., printed text). Deployment of selective and sustained attention is much better for simple, repetitive verbal material (especially that delivered through the auditory modality) than for complex, novel nonverbal material (especially that delivered through the visual or somatosensory modalities). The disparity between attentional deployment capacities for these two sets of materials tends to increase with age.

Exploratory behavior. There is little physical exploration of any kind. This is the case even for objects that are immediately within reach and that could be explored through visual or tactile means. A tendency toward sedentary and physically limited modes of functioning increases with age.

(c) Tertiary

Memory. Memory for tactile and visual input is poor. Deficiencies in these areas tend to increase over the course of development, except for material that is programmatic and overlearned (e.g., spoken natural language). Memory for nonverbal material, whether presented through the auditory, visual, or tactile modalities, is poor if such material is not readily coded in a verbal fashion. Relatively poor memory for complex, meaningful, and/or novel verbal and nonverbal material is typical. Differences between good to excellent memory for rote material and impaired memory for complex material and material that is not readily coded in a verbal fashion tend to increase with age.

Concept formation, problem solving, strategy generation, and hypothesis testing; Appreciation of informational feedback. Marked deficits in all of these areas are apparent, especially when the concept to be formed, the problem to be solved, and/or the problem-solving milieu are novel or complex. Also evident are significant difficulties in dealing with cause-effect relationships and marked deficiencies in the appreciation of incongruities (e.g., age-appropriate sensitivity to humor). Most noticeable as formal operational thought becomes a developmental demand (i.e., in late childhood and early adolescence), deficits in these areas tend to increase markedly with advancing years, as does the gap between performance on rote (overlearned) and novel tasks.

(d) Verbal

Speech and language. Mildly deficient oral-motor praxis, little or no speech prosody, and much verbosity of a repetitive, straightforward, rote nature are characteristic. When paraphasic errors are made, these are much more likely to be phonological than semantic. Also typical are content disorders of language, characterized by very poor psycholinguistic pragmatics (e.g., "cocktail party" speech) and reliance on language as a principal means for social relating, information gathering, and relief from anxiety. All of these characteristics, except for oral-motor praxis difficulties, tend to become more prominent with advancing years.

Academic Deficits

Graphomotor. In the early school years, much difficulty with printing and cursive script is evident; with much practice, handwriting most often becomes quite good.

Reading comprehension. Reading comprehension is much poorer than is single-word reading (decoding). Deficits in reading comprehension, especially for novel material, tend to increase with advancing years.

Mechanical arithmetic and mathematics. Outstanding relative deficiencies in mechanical arithmetic as compared to proficiencies in reading (word recognition) and spelling are apparent in the middle school years. With advancing years, the gap between good to excellent single-word reading and spelling and deficient mechanical arithmetic performance widens. The absolute level of mechanical arithmetic performance only rarely exceeds the grade 5 level; mathematical reasoning, as opposed to programmatic arithmetic calculation, remains poorly developed.

Science. Persistent difficulties in academic subjects involving problem solving and complex concept formation (e.g., physics) are prominent. The gap between deficiencies in these types of complex academic endeavors and other, more rote, programmatic academic pursuits widens with age.

Socioemotional/Adaptive Deficits

Adaptation in novel situations. Extreme difficulties in adapting to (i.e., countenancing, organizing, analyzing, and synthesizing) novel and otherwise complex situations are prominent. There is an overreliance on prosaic and rote (and, in consequence, inappropriate) behaviors in such situations. These characteristics tend to become more prominent with advancing years.

Social competence. Significant deficits in social perception, social judgment, and social interaction skills are prominent; these deficits become more apparent as age increases. A marked tendency toward social withdrawal and even social isolation is apparent with advancing years.

Emotional disturbance. Often characterized during early childhood as afflicted with some type of acting-out/conduct disorder, children with NLD are very much at risk for the development of "internalized" forms of psychopathology. Indications of excessive anxiety, depression, and associated internalized forms of socioemotional disturbance tend to increase with advancing years.

Activity level. Frequently, children with NLD are perceived as hyperactive during childhood. With advancing years, they tend to become normoactive and, eventually, hypoactive.

DETAILS OF THE CHARACTERISTICS AND DYNAMICS OF THE NLD SYNDROME

This section is designed to provide a fuller description of the characteristics of the NLD syndrome and to place these characteristics within the context of their developmental dynamics. In structuring the section, we have assumed that the reader will refer to Figure 14.9 whenever necessary to follow the discussion.

Throughout this section, we refer to the "developmental presentation" of the NLD syndrome, that is, the presentation that appears to have been evident at birth or shortly thereafter, and is not complicated by subsequent neurological disease, disorder, or dysfunction. Although the same general principles—and especially the dynamics of the syndrome—hold for other children and adolescents who have experienced a normal course of development before suffering an untoward event (e.g., significant traumatic brain injury) that eventuates in the NLD syndrome, there are important differences between the "developmental" and "other" (neurological disease superimposed on a normally developing brain) presentations of the syndrome. These differences are especially evident when we compare the neuropsychological presentations of children whose early months and years of cognitive development have been "normal" with those of children who have been affected adversely by the elements and dynamics of the NLD syndrome since a very early developmental stage.

Early Presentation: Basic Neuropsychological Skills and Abilities

The principal neuropsychological asset of the child who exhibits the NLD syndrome is his or her capacity to deal with information delivered through the auditory modality. Virtually all other assets of such a child appear to flow from this basic "strength." However, it should be pointed out that, in infancy, it is often suspected that a child who is eventually shown to have a "developmental" presentation of the NLD syndrome is "hard of hearing." This impression is reinforced by a discernible delay in the acquisition of speech. (Fortunately, advances in evoked audiometry now make it possible to discern the integrity of the auditory apparatus at very tender ages.) Adding to the seriousness of this situation during the first months and years of the child's life is the fact that developmental milestones, including speech, are clearly delayed. Indeed, it is fairly common for such a child to be scrutinized carefully during his or her early months of life with the differential diagnostic possibilities of mental retardation, deafness, and/or severe (pervasive) emotional disturbance in mind.

This being the case, it should come as no surprise that parents and other caretakers are overjoyed when such a child utters the first sounds of speech. This joy mounts thereafter as the child progresses through the various stages of speech and language development at what seems to be an above-normal rate of speed. This is usually accompanied by the parents' selective and effusive positive reinforcement of the child's linguistic output, with a correlative disregard for the fact that the child is still not making normal progress in the attainment of other developmental milestones, especially those having to do with locomotor and manipulative skills. The child remains essentially sedentary, exploring the world not through vision or locomotion, but rather through receiving verbal answers to questions posed about the immediate environment.

Even within this context, at relatively tender ages, we can see the beginnings of the complex interactions that tend to transpire between and among the neuropsychological abilities and deficits of a child with NLD. For example, it would appear quite probable that such a child will become progressively less likely to engage in physical exploration of his or her environment precisely because the patent auditory channel and its rapidly emerging receptive linguistic correlates provide information without the difficulties and large expenditures of energy attendant upon the engaging of (deficient) psychomotor skills for such purposes. Indeed, the more often and the more elaborate the parents' and other caretakers' verbal answers to the child's questions, the more likely it becomes that the child will engage in sedentary rather than exploratory behaviors. This, in turn, reduces the opportunities for encountering truly novel stimuli, with consequent negative repercussions for an already diminished capacity to deal with such stimuli. In all of this, the reinforcement history of the child would be expected to exacerbate or partially mollify some of these effects.

As a final consideration with respect to early presentations of basic neuropsychological skills and abilities, some note should be made regarding simple motor skills. It is a basic principle of the NLD syndrome and model that the reduction of novelty to familiarity and the invocation of the stereotypy that comes from sustained practice of simple motoric acts should lead to proficiency in them. Thus, unsurprisingly, throughout this developmental process, particular skills (e.g., graphomotor), although extremely difficult for the child initially, tend to be mastered to a considerable extent as a result of extensive practice. This mastery is a function of the repetitive nature of the task and the familiar nature of the surroundings within which it is to be executed.

Attention, Exploratory Behavior, and Memory

The patent auditory channel of the NLD child, in concert with difficulties in dealing with visual and tactile signals, would be expected to increase the likelihood of (a) good auditory attentional deployment, and (b) poor tactile and visual attentional deployment. In addition, it would be expected that, for the distance senses (audition and vision), the gap between "attention" within these modalities would tend to widen with advancing years.

Tactile perception is a special case. Little effort is required to engage this sensory modality: it can be developed within the proximate space of even a virtually immobile child, and it can be "practiced" extensively by a child who is prone to engage in repetitive, rote behavior. For all of these reasons, it is expected that the child who exhibits NLD will eventually show little or no marked (i.e., "hard") signs of deficiencies in the tactile modality, including the capacity to deploy attention within this modality. Hence, although visual attention (and other skills and abilities that are dependent on this rather basic processing level) would be expected to decline relative to age-appropriate norms, such would not be expected in the case of the "contact" sense of touch.

Exploratory behavior is expected to be quite deficient in terms of frequency and quality because of (a) the NLD child's penchant for rote material, (b) a correlative avoidance of novelty (because of an inability to "handle" its informational processing demands), (c) problems in deploying complex psychomotor skills (e.g., climbing), and (d) a tendency to prefer the auditory over the visual modality for the processing of information. All of these features should conspire early in the child's life to limit exploration of the environment: Thus, for example, it is expected that the child will come to prefer to *hear* about the environment rather than to *see* or to *touch* it.

It is a small step from the latter developmental point to expectations regarding relative proficiency in auditory (especially auditory-verbal) memory over visual memory. Several investigators have found that the auditory-verbal memory skills of Group A children are superior to their visual memory skills (see Fletcher, 1985). Similar results have been obtained recently in our own laboratory (Brandys & Rourke, 1991). The chain of events in the case of the child exhibiting NLD would seem to suggest very strongly that well-developed attention and memory for auditory stimuli and poorly developed attention and memory for visual stimuli follow a cause-effect sequence as follows: good or poor sensory-perceptual capacity → good or poor attentional deployment skills → good or poor memory. Furthermore, the interactions along this cause-effect sequence are important; that is, it would be expected that, just as all biological organisms have a strong tendency to practice what they do well and to avoid what they do poorly, the very existence of a "strength" (auditory analysis) would be expected to interfere with the practice of a "weakness." In other words, within the perception → attention → memory sequence, it would appear quite probable that the rich (i.e., patent perceptual processing channels) will get richer, and the poor, poorer. Only with a balance between and among these capacities would one expect that "normal" information processing development would occur.

Concept Formation, Problem Solving, Strategy Generation, Hypothesis Testing; Appreciation of Informational Feedback

The analysis, organization, and synthesis of information constitute the cognitive "building blocks" that are the foundation of the ability to form and modify concepts, generate reasonable solutions to complex problems, apply these solutions in a testable fashion, and deal systematically with feedback regarding the acceptability of solutions to the problems. Another important basis for such activity is the capacity to tolerate (even relish) novelty.

Such engagement in novel experiences would require (a) systematic, careful visual and (sometimes) tactile exploration of the evidence, (b) (perhaps) complex psychomotor manipulation of the elements of the problem, (c) a capacity for dealing with novel material, and (d) memory for what one has seen during the exploration of the problem. These capacities are deficient in the child with NLD and, in the developmental presentation of this syndrome, would be expected to have been deficient since the child's earliest days.

Previous references to Piaget's (1952, 1954) notions regarding the genesis of intelligent behavior are certainly relevant here. The necessity for the "contributions" of the sensorimotor phase of development for the eventual attainment of formal operational thought forms the basis for the series of events proposed above. The disabilities in concept formation and other forms of higher cognitive processes that are exhibited by the child with NLD are seen as a fairly direct consequence of a failure to acquire these cognitive building blocks.

Speech and Language

In this formulation of the NLD syndrome, it is hypothesized that the NLD child's speech and language assets are fairly direct reflections of his or her more basic neuropsychological assets, and that deficits in this area are a reflection of more basic neuropsychological deficits.

Well-developed capacities for auditory perception, attention, and memory would seem to be excellent (and virtually sufficient) for the development of natural language in nonretarded persons who attain rather elementary enunciatory and word-finding skills. Thus, good phonemic hearing, segmentation, and blending capacities should lead to good to excellent verbal reception, verbal repetition, verbal storage, and verbal associative skills. In the child with NLD, these characteristics tend to develop to above-average, even extreme, degrees; such developments are accompanied by increasingly larger volumes of verbal output.

In the child's early years, oral-motor praxis problems are in evidence; these are rarely severe or even moderate in degree. Mild difficulties in the enunciation of complex, multisyllabic words tend to persist throughout development. These are inferred to be one reflection of a more general problem in praxis that persists over time.

More telling deficits evident in the linguistic performance of children with NLD include their problems in appropriate prosody and, more important, the sometimes grossly deficient content and pragmatics of their linguistic productions. The deficiencies in content and pragmatics are viewed as direct results of difficulties in concept-formation and other higher-order cognitive skills that are, in turn, inferred to be reflections of more basic neuropsychological deficiencies. A marked tendency to favor the phonological aspects of oral communication over its semantic content is also seen as a reflection of these more basic deficiencies.

The end result of this pattern of linguistic deficits is poor "functional" language—a concept that is conveyed somewhat by the aforementioned deficiencies in linguistic pragmatics. It is included here because the means-end relationships that language promotes in normal persons are notably absent from the spoken and written language of persons with NLD. This shortcoming is usually evident as a general and pervasive deficit touching virtually every aspect of their communicative behavior. It almost always appears to reflect a much more basic problem in appreciating the functional role that language can play in achieving one's goals.

Academic Performance

After a rather slow start in kindergarten, grade 1, and perhaps into grade 2, the child with NLD exhibits remarkable gains in single-word reading (decoding). It is not uncommon for such children to be rated on word-decoding at the grade 6 level when they are in grade 3, at the grade 9 level when they are in grade 4, and at the grade 11 level when they are in grade 5. Indeed, beyond grade 3, their word-recognition skills are usually well in excess of their age-expected grade level.

Another important aspect that should be emphasized in this discussion of the dynamics of the NLD syndrome is that graphomotor script becomes smooth and effortless even though it involves the most basic neuropsychological deficits included within this syndrome. This would appear to attest to the capacity of the NLD child to routinize this activity to the point where it becomes a completely rote activity. As noted in connection with the Rourke (1982) model, the capacity for such routinization and stereotypic application is thought to be a process for which left hemispheral systems are particularly geared.

An important dimension of spelling for children with NLD is their fidelity to the phonetic composition of the words to be spelled. This is certainly a predictable attribute in view of their basic neuropsychological assets in phonemic hearing, segmentation, and blending. Misspellings are almost exclusively of the phonetically accurate variety (e.g., "nacher" for nature; "ocupie" for occupy). In fact, it is common to find that better than 95% of their misspelled syllables are rendered in a phonetically accurate manner (see Sweeney & Rourke, 1978, for an explanation of our syllable-by-syllable system for assessing phonetic accuracy).

This rather high percentage becomes more than an idle curiosity, in light of the fact that English is approximately 75% "regular" with respect to phoneme-grapheme correspondences. (This should be compared with virtually 100% phoneme-grapheme correspondences in Finnish.) Normal adolescent and adult misspellings tend to be approximately 75% phonetically accurate. Taking these facts together, it becomes clear that the English-speaking NLD child/adolescent is "hyperphonetic" in the analysis of words to be spelled.

Other aspects of this tendency to accentuate the phonetic aspects of words (often, to the detriment of their semantic content) can be seen in the NLD child's tendency to make far more phonological than semantic paraphasic errors during sentence repetition tasks. It is as though, when given the opportunity to "choose" between the way words sound and what they mean, the former triumphs over the latter.

Mechanical arithmetic poses considerable difficulty for the NLD child. As pointed out above, the problems in evidence appear to reflect basic neuropsychological deficits in visual-spatial-organizational and psychomotor skills, appreciation for novel data, and the interrelated dimensions of concept formation, strategy generation, and hypothesis testing. Limitations in judgment and reasoning tend to predominate in the productions of older NLD children; these would include their apparent failure to realize the inappropriateness of some answers to arithmetic problems. Perseveration and failure to shift set in serial arithmetic problem solving would appear to reflect such difficulties, as do the related penchants for stereotyped, routinized, programmatic unfolding of behavior in any number of situations.

Rarely does the mechanical arithmetic prowess of the NLD adolescent or adult exceed the grade 5 to grade 6 level. Until the grade 2, grade 3, or even grade 4 level, it is sometimes not possible to see the emerging discrepancy between word recognition and spelling (high) and arithmetic (low) because of the nature of the arithmetic problems that are considered to be within the ken of the 7- to 8-year-old child. However, after this point and beyond, this discrepancy is easily discernible.

One particular proclivity of the NLD child in mechanical arithmetic deserves further comment because it bears on subsequent discussions regarding frankly brain-damaged individuals. NLD children and adolescents have a marked tendency to "forget to remember." This phrase applies to individuals who have stored memories that would be applicable to a given situation but who fail to realize that a particular time and place call for the particular stored material in question. Thus, it can usually be shown that the 10-year-old NLD child "knows" how to "carry" and "borrow," but does not access these stored arithmetic rules when it would be appropriate to do so. This problem is easy to understand when we consider that a normal person does not ordinarily commit to memory the *occasions* when particular memories need to be employed, but rather trusts that his or her judgment at any particular time will produce a decision to scan memory for the appropriate rule. This trust is probably a long-term consequence of the assurances (reinforcements) that ensue from repeated efficacious problem-solving performances in novel situations.

This interaction between memory/remembering and (good and poor) higher-order reasoning skills is analogous to the difference between skilled and unskilled mathematicians. The skilled mathematician would never dream of committing to memory (say) the Pythagorean theorem, but would, instead, "reason it through" when required to do so. The person who must commit the theorem to memory so as to regurgitate it when asked to do so (on an exam) is to be applauded for his or her verbal memory and for the capacity to respond appropriately to the cue (exam question) that calls forth this remembered material. What such a person may very well lack is the capacity to engage in elementary mathematical thinking. In this connection, it is often found that adolescents with NLD perform much better in secondary school mathematics courses than they did in elementary school arithmetic, to the extent that the secondary school mathematics courses require verbatim memory, as opposed to adaptive problem solving, for theorems, corollaries, and the like. When the adolescent with NLD turns to subjects such as physics, his or her problems in concept formation, problem solving, and hypothesis testing become very apparent. These deficiencies are compounded by failure to benefit from informational feedback in such problem-solving situations.

Psychosocial Adaptation

As with the academic deficits described above, the psychosocial difficulties of the child with NLD appear to result from interactions among and between his or her neuropsychological assets and deficits. The following are some examples of such interactions:

1. The NLD child's deficits in social judgment would appear to result from more basic problems in reasoning, concept formation, and the like, which also lie at the root of difficulties in mechanical arithmetic and scientific reasoning.

2. Difficulties in visual-spatial-organizational skills are reflected in problems in identifying and recognizing faces, expressions of emotion, and other subtle nonverbal identifiers of important dimensions of human communication.

3. Lack of prosody, in conjunction with a high volume of verbal output, tends to encourage negative feedback from those who find themselves forced to listen to the seemingly endless recitation of dull, drab, colorless statements that the NLD child or adolescent seems impelled to deliver. In a word, the speech and language characteristics exhibited tend to alienate others, thus increasing the probability that the child will experience socio-emotional/adaptational difficulties.

4. The tactile-perceptual and psychomotor prowess required for smooth affectional encounters, in conjunction with the NLD child's typically inappropriate judgments regarding nonverbal cues, render intimate relationships all but impossible.

5. Adaptability to novel interpersonal situations is the hallmark of socially appropriate individuals. A combination of aversion for novelty, failure sometimes even to appreciate that an event *is* novel, poor problem-solving and hypothesis-testing skills—all of these conspire to render spontaneous, smooth adaptation to the constantly changing milieux of social groups and the interactions nascent therein all but impossible for the NLD individual.

The dynamics of the changes in activity level that are quite commonly seen in the developmental presentation of NLD are relevant within this context. Typically, such children are seen as "hyperactive" when they are 4 or 5 years of age: they are constantly getting in the way of others; they seem to be disinhibited; they bump into other persons and objects; and they persist in such behavior over protracted periods of time. These manifestations of the sensorimotor and other deficiencies of the NLD syndrome are often taken as indicators of the presence of hyperactivity and, presumably, an underlying attentional deficit disorder as well. For this reason, methylphenidate is often prescribed for such youngsters. After a time in school, their behavior tends to "normalize" in terms of activity level. This may occasion the cessation of the administration of the drug. Thereafter (usually during the middle of the elementary school years), it is noticed that they appear to be somewhat hypoactive.

This is, of course, another example of a situation wherein it would be easy to infer that the pharmacological agent and/or any other form of intervention employed (e.g., behavioral shaping) has been effective in the reduction of hyperactivity. The fact that the child reads and spells well after a course of such therapy also suggests that any underlying attentional deficit has also been "cured."

However, it must be pointed out that the "natural history" of the NLD child involves moving from apparent hyperactivity through normoactive behavior and then on to a hypoactive response style. This occurs largely, if not exclusively, as a result of the rebuffs and outright physical punishments that NLD children experience as a result of their failure to anticipate the consequences of their actions. Age-mates and adult caretakers tend to react very negatively to such shenanigans. And, because there is no reason to think that the NLD child is anhedonic, there is good reason to infer that the negative consequences of his or her behavior will eventuate in the reduction of activity level. A very unfortunate by-product of this reduction in activity level is an even further reduction in exploratory behavior, with the negative consequences that this can entail for the child's cognitive development (see above).

These few examples should suffice to illustrate the main point of this exercise: psychosocial and adaptation deficiencies are, essentially, dependent variables in the NLD matrix. As with academic deficits, they arise out of a common mix of neuropsychological abilities and deficits that all but ensures that they will occur and grow in intensity with the passing of years. Unfortunately, the eventual social and personal outcome for the NLD person is almost never pleasant. Withdrawal, isolation, and loneliness are common.

MANIFESTATIONS OF NLD IN NEUROPATHOLOGICAL CONDITIONS

Although the NLD syndrome was isolated in studies that were geared to the determination of the neuropsychological and psychosocial assets and deficits of children chosen solely on the basis of their presenting profile of academic learning skills (Group A), it became clear that children whom we had examined for other reasons also exhibited this syndrome. Some of the groups of children with various forms of neurological disease, disorder, and dysfunction who manifest this syndrome are as follows (citations of our own case studies and the research reports of some others appear in parentheses):

1. Many children with moderate to severe head injuries who are able to undergo a comprehensive neuropsychological investigation (Ewing-Cobbs, Fletcher, & Levin, 1985; Fletcher & Levin, 1988).

2. Most children with a hydrocephalic condition that was not treated promptly and/or with success (Rourke et al., 1983, pp. 290–297; Rourke, Fisk, & Strang, 1986, pp. 59–68); most children with shunted hydrocephalus beginning during the perinatal period (Fletcher et al., 1992).

3. Survivors of acute lymphocytic leukemia and other forms of childhood cancer who had received very large doses (treatments) of X-irradiation over a prolonged period of time (Copeland et al., 1985; Fletcher & Copeland, 1988; Rourke, Fisk, & Strang, 1986, pp. 108–116; Taylor, Albo, Phebus, Sachs, & Bierl, 1987).

4. Children who had congenital absence of the corpus callosum and who exhibited no other demonstrable neurological disease process (Casey, Del Dotto, & Rourke, 1990; see case study in Rourke, 1987).

5. Children with significant tissue removal from the right cerebral hemisphere (Rourke et al., 1983, pp. 230–238).

All of the above types of cerebral lesions involve significant destruction or disturbance of function of white matter (long myelinated fibers) in the brain, although the mechanisms of destruction and/or disturbance differ significantly (e.g., *shearing* in the case of the head-injured child, *absence* in the case of children with corpus callosum agenesis, and *removal of tissue* within the right hemisphere). With respect to lesions affecting large portions of the right cerebral hemisphere, much destruction of white matter is quite probable. In such instances, because the ratio of white matter to gray matter is much larger in the right cerebral hemisphere than in the left cerebral hemisphere (Goldberg & Costa, 1981)—that is, there is considerably less gray matter relative to white matter in the right, compared to the left, cerebral hemisphere.

Other conditions in which the NLD syndrome is manifest include: myelomeningocele (Wills, Holmbeck, Dillon, & McLone, 1990), metachromatic leukodystrophy (Shapiro, Lipton, & Krivit, 1992), Williams syndrome (Udwin & Yule, 1991), fetal alcohol syndrome (Streissguth & LaDue, 1987), congenital hypothyroidism (Rovet, 1990), Turner's syndrome (Rovet & Netley, 1982), velo-cardio-facial syndrome (Golding-Kushner, Weller, & Shprintzen, 1985), insulin-dependent diabetes mellitus (Rovet, Ehrlich, Czuchta, & Akler, 1993), adrenal hyperplasia (Nass, Speiser, Heier, Haimes, & New, 1990), Asperger's syndrome (Stevens & Moffitt, 1988), and autism (Szatmari, Tuff, Finlayson, & Bartolucci, 1990). Of crucial importance in this connection is that there are thought to be significant perturbations of white matter development and/or functioning in most of the aforementioned diseases and disabilities. Disordered myelinization and/or myelin functioning has been hypothesized to be the "final common pathway" that eventuates in the NLD syndrome (Rourke, 1987, 1988b, 1989); current and future research will indicate whether and to what extent this is the case (Rourke, 1995). (For an example of such efforts, see Fletcher et al., 1992.)

We turn now to an explication of the model that was designed to account for the dynamics underlying these neurodevelopmental processes. The model is presented in two stages: the first emphasizes its roots in a more general neuropsychological model; the second traces the etiology, course, and dynamics of NLD.

The NLD Model

The Goldberg and Costa and Rourke Models

The Goldberg and Costa (1981) model was based primarily on data gathered and speculations derived from investigations of human adults. Its principal developmental dimension is its emphasis on the progressive left hemispheral lateralization of functions throughout the life span. The Rourke (1982) model was an attempt to expand the elements of this model to encompass early developmental phenomena, especially as these relate to the etiology, course, and persistence of central processing deficiencies in children.

In the Rourke (1982) model, special emphasis was afforded formulations regarding children who exhibit outstandingly deficient mechanical arithmetic performance relative to word-recognition and spelling performances. Of particular importance in the present context is the fact that these Group A children exhibit virtually all of the characteristics of the NLD child. In the Rourke (1982) model, it was emphasized that Group A children exhibit deficiencies in intermodal integration and in problem solving and concept formation (especially in novel situations), and that they have profound difficulty in benefiting from experiences that do not fit or mesh well with their only existing well-developed, overlearned descriptive system (i.e., natural language). In terms of the formulations of the Goldberg and Costa model, it was hypothesized that these children exhibit deficient right hemispheral capacities within a context of well-developed, modality-specific, intramodal, routinized, and stereotyped left-hemispheral skills.

It was emphasized that the deficiencies exhibited by these children in tactile-perceptual, visual-spatial, visual-perceptual, and psychomotor capacities (deficits that are assumed to have been present from their earliest years), within a context of adequate auditory-perceptual and (eventually) verbal expressive capacities, would be expected to alter substantially the normal course of their development of sensorimotor skills. In turn, it was thought probable that this state of affairs would contribute to considerable developmental deviation in their acquisition of cognitive skills. Specifically, it was thought that their problems in establishing cause-and-effect relationships on a physical, concrete basis during infancy and early childhood would be expected to limit their capacity to develop more abstract levels of thought. Furthermore, this constellation of deficiencies was viewed as causative vis-à-vis the academic and social learning disabilities that these children eventually develop. (The dynamics of the NLD syndrome outlined previously constitute, essentially, a systematic expansion of the interplay of these features, first proposed in the 1982 model.)

As an explanation for this state of affairs, it was hypothesized that, in such children, one or both of two scenarios could obtain: (a) deficient right hemispheral systems, or (b) insufficient access to initially intact right hemispheral systems. This level of model development was felt to be sufficient to account for the differences that were evident in the neurodevelopmental course and neuropsychological profiles of the Group A youngster (i.e., one manifestation of the NLD syndrome) as compared to those who exhibited other patterns of central processing abilities and deficits.

The Rourke (1987, 1988b, 1989) model is an extension of the Goldberg and Costa (1981) and Rourke (1982) models to account for the specific aspects of early and subsequent neuropsychological development within those domains that are thought to characterize *all* children who exhibit the NLD syndrome.

Main Theoretical Principles

The main theoretical principles on which an explanation of the phenomena of NLD in children appears to rest are articulated in terms of three principal dimensions of the model:

1. *Amount of white matter destroyed/dysfunctional.* In general, the more white matter (relative to total brain mass) that is lesioned, removed, or dysfunctional, the more likely that the NLD syndrome will be in evidence. (This is reminiscent of the "mass action" hypothesis of Lashley, 1938.)

2. *Developmental stage of destruction/dysfunction.* Which white matter is lesioned, removed, or rendered dysfunctional, and at which stage of development this occurs has an important bearing on the manifestations of the NLD syndrome. (This formulation is in clear contradistinction to Lashley's notion of strict equipotentiality.)

3. *Development and maintenance of learned behavior.* Right hemisphere white matter is crucial for the *development* and *maintenance* of its specific proclivities (such as intermodal integration, especially when novel information processing situations are encountered). For example, significant destruction or permanent disruption of right hemisphere white matter would be expected to pose a permanent handicap to the acquisition of new descriptive systems at any developmental stage.

Left hemisphere white matter is essential for the *development,* but not necessarily for the *maintenance,* of its specific penchants. For example, isolable linguistic skills are often found to remain intact after significant damage to the left cerebral hemisphere in adults. In terms of the model under consideration, once natural language is acquired and automatized, specific functions presumably subserved by the prominent opercula of the left hemisphere would be expected to be relatively impervious to destruction or permanent disruption of white matter not immediately adjacent to and/or forming an integral part of the functioning of these opercula. However, it would be expected that significant disruption of white matter within the left hemisphere during early ontogenetic stages would hamper or even prevent the development of language in the child.

Main Deductions

These theoretical principles lead to the following deductions:

1. *Sufficiency.* A significant lesion confined to the right cerebral hemisphere may constitute a *sufficient* condition for the production of the NLD syndrome.

2. *Necessity.* The *necessary* (and "dose-sensitive") condition for the production of the NLD syndrome is the destruction or dysfunction of white matter that is necessary for intermodal integration. (For example, a significant reduction of callosal fibers or any other neuropathological state that interferes substantially with "access" to right hemispheral systems—and, thus, to those systems that are necessary for intermodal integration—would be expected to eventuate in the NLD syndrome.)

White Matter

At this point, it would be well to describe briefly the three principal types of white matter fibers that are in the brain. In the following, a designation regarding the three principal axes of neurodevelopment is employed for each type of white matter:

1. *Commissural fibers (right ↔ left).* These nerve fibers cross the midline and interconnect similar regions in the two cerebral hemispheres. There are three sets of such fibers: (a) the corpus callosum (made up of fibers that radiate to interconnect the left and right homologous regions of the frontal, parietal, temporal, and occipital lobes); (b) the anterior, posterior, and habenular commissures; and (c) the hippocampal commissural fibers (very few in humans). By far, the set of these fibers that constitutes the corpus callosum is the largest.

2. *Association fibers (back ↔ front).* These fibers interconnect cortical regions of the same cerebral hemisphere. They are classified as short association (or, arcuate) fibers (connecting adjacent convolutions within the hemisphere), and long association fibers (connecting cortical regions of the different lobes within the same hemisphere).

3. *Projection fibers (up ↔ down).* These fibers project from the diencephalon to the cerebral hemispheres and from the hemispheres to the diencephalon, the brain stem, and the spinal cord. The internal capsule, which handles the "input-output" of the hemispheres, contains projection fibers.

All of these fibers can be destroyed or rendered dysfunctional by various sorts of neurological disease. However, some observations should be made at this point regarding the *probability* of destruction/disorder within these various types of white matter:

1. It is clear that general white matter disease would be expected, by definition, to affect all three types of white matter, with consequent negative impact(s) on all three of the principal axes of neural development.

2. Conditions such as hydrocephalus would be expected to have their principal effects on commissural (right ↔ left) and projection (down ↔ up) fibers, leaving association (back ↔ front) fibers relatively intact.

3. A disease that affects the callosal fibers would be expected to interfere with right hemisphere ↔ left hemisphere "communication." Such a disease would be expected to have a more profound effect on the functioning of the right than that of the left cerebral hemisphere because of the right hemisphere's greater "dependence" on white matter functioning, especially with regard to its apparent "specialization" for the intermodal integration of novel stimuli. On the other hand, left hemispheral systems, many of which are relatively "encapsulated" within the three major opercula (gray matter and short association fibers), may maintain enough stimulation within and between each other so that some fairly sophisticated intramodal integrations can proceed without much (or any) input from the right cerebral hemisphere. The upshot of all of this is that left hemispheral systems are probably able to function reasonably well in the face of callosal and projection fiber damage, so long as association fibers are intact. However, even in the latter instance, intact associational fibers would appear to be necessary for the *development* but not for the *maintenance* of left hemispheral functioning.

From this state of affairs, one would expect to see the principal (primary, secondary, and tertiary) neuropsychological features of the NLD syndrome *plus* global linguistic deficiencies (as in autism) only if there is early associational fiber disease within the left cerebral hemisphere *plus* white matter disease that affects intermodal integration. Associational fiber destruction, disorder, or dysfunction in the left hemisphere *after* natural language has been acquired should lead to aphasia (of the conduction or similar varieties) but not to autism.

It is expected that close clinical neuropsychological monitoring of children and adolescents with the various types of neurological disease, disorder, and dysfunction referred to above will eventuate in profiles characterized as being typical of the NLD child. Investigation of children and adolescents with neuropsychiatric disorders, the published accounts of which bear a striking resemblance to the manifestations of the NLD syndrome (e.g., those who exhibit Asperger's syndrome, alexithymia, and/or inadequate-immature types of delinquency), would be expected to yield similar findings. In Asperger's syndrome, this certainly seems to obtain (Sparrow, 1993). In addition, it is our expectation that, in the future, studies employing sophisticated neural imaging techniques that are capable of assessing metabolic changes during central processing tasks will eventually demonstrate that the white matter versus gray matter relationships suggested in this model are causative with respect to the NLD syndrome. The latest evidence regarding the relationship between impaired corpus callosum functioning and deficient right hemispheral systems in children with very early shunted hydrocephalus (Fletcher et al., 1992, 1993) is entirely in accord with this prediction.

DEVELOPMENTAL EXAMPLE: SIGNIFICANCE OF EARLY SOMATOSENSORY IMPAIRMENT

In the developmental presentation of the NLD syndrome, basic and early emergent deficits in tactile-perceptual skills are thought to play a very significant role in the eventual manifestations of impaired problem-solving, concept-formation, and related cognitive abilities. One of the conceptual bases for this linkage is the position of Piaget (1952, 1954) regarding the importance of intact sensorimotor functioning as one of the early developmental pillars on which formal operational thought is based.

The world of the young child could, in the main, be characterized as searching, locating, encountering, and exploring objects in the physical world. For the most part, the manipulations of the elements of this world are through the contact senses of touch and taste, although one would not want to suggest a diminished role for vision in this process. Indeed, the processes of searching, locating, and exploring are greatly enhanced thereby. However, the young child's *encounters* with the physical world are largely haptic in nature. Smooth affectional encounters between persons, regardless of age or stage of development, are greatly enhanced by the presence of intact somatosensory capacities. Indeed, one would be inclined to think that intimate exchanges between persons would be all but impossible without such capacities. The early bonding between parent and child, thought to be so important for subsequent psychosocial development, is largely a function of exchanges through the somatosensory systems.

With growth and maturity, the child comes to depend more on the distance senses for knowledge of the world. Encounters with this world are largely representational in nature rather than characterized by immediate physical contact—haptic or otherwise. Nevertheless, the knowledge gained through immediate haptic contact, especially during the early phases of development, is thought by many to be essential for normal intellectual growth. (See Casey & Rourke, 1992, for a fuller account of this view.)

SUMMARY AND GENERAL DEVELOPMENTAL IMPLICATIONS OF THE MODEL

Integrity of white matter (long myelinated fiber) function would appear to be (a) necessary for the *development* of systems within both hemispheres, and (b) crucial for both the *development* and the *maintenance* of those functions subserved primarily by systems within the right hemispheral systems, but (c) not necessary for the *maintenance* of some functions subserved primarily by systems within the left hemisphere.

The NLD syndrome would be expected to develop under any set of circumstances that interferes significantly with (a) the functioning of right hemispheral systems (as in the case of any general deterioration of white matter or of substantial destruction of white matter within the right hemisphere) and/or (b) access to (neuronal intercommunication with) these systems (as in the case of callosal agenesis).

Furthermore, any neurological disease that has the effect of "isolating" (from each other and/or from right hemispheral systems) one or more of the three prominent opercula of the left hemisphere that play a crucial role in its essentially intramodal functions of routinization and stereotypic application of previously acquired descriptive systems (e.g., natural language) would be expected to increase the likelihood that the NLD syndrome will be manifest. Such a scenario would effectively handicap the individual in the acquisition of new descriptive systems, and would increase the likelihood that he or she would apply previously acquired descriptive systems in a rigid, stereotyped, perseverative fashion within situations where such application is not necessarily adaptive. The set of phenomena associated with normal aging may be one example of such a state of affairs; symptoms associated with advanced stages of any number of demyelenating diseases may be another. It should be noted that, for both of these examples, a *general* deterioration in white matter, rather than a *specific* deterioration of left hemisphere white matter, would be expected to be the rule rather than the exception.

In any case, the loss of the capacity to generate new descriptive systems helps to explain the essentially "downward" course over successive developmental epochs that is observed in individuals who manifest the NLD syndrome. Considering the entire developmental course of this syndrome, it would seem that it is less apparent at the age of 7 to 8 years (Ozols & Rourke, 1988, 1991) than at 10 to 14 years (Casey, Rourke, & Picard, 1991; Rourke & Finlayson, 1978; Rourke & Strang, 1978; Strang & Rourke, 1983), and that it becomes progressively more apparent (and more debilitating) as adulthood approaches (Rourke et al., 1983, pp. 247–253; Rourke, Young, Strang, & Russell, 1986).

In connection with this last observation, it should be noted that formal operational thought (a feature of higher-order cognitive functioning that is notably deficient in older children and adolescents who manifest the NLD syndrome) is not within the developmental capacities of the 7- to 8-year-old child. Because it becomes a developmental task/demand as the child approaches puberty—and, of course, increases in adaptive importance as the individual progresses through adolescence and into adulthood—it should come as no surprise that progressive deterioration in skills associated with such capacities (e.g., socioemotional adaptation) is the rule rather than the exception. Evidence of such deterioration is apparent in the cross-sectional and longitudinal studies of such individuals cited above.

THEORETICAL AND CLINICAL IMPLICATIONS OF THE NLD MODEL

The heuristic implications of this explanatory model may be seen best in specific instances of the presence or absence of the NLD syndrome in various forms of neurological disease, disorder, and dysfunction. Because of space limitations, only one of these will be examined.

Theoretical Implications: General or Diffuse Destruction of White Matter

The neurological diseases and disorders (mentioned above) that eventuate in the NLD syndrome do so to the extent that they involve destruction of white matter; the more white matter that is destroyed or permanently disordered, the more likely the syndrome will be manifest. This would be especially expected in conditions that involve general or diffuse destruction of white matter (e.g., as may result from intensive or extensive radiotherapy of the brain; extensive white matter shearing, as in significant craniocerebral trauma following acceleration-deceleration injuries;

or disordered development of white matter, as in congenital hypothyroidism). In this connection, Taylor et al. (1987) showed that, in elementary school children who survived acute lymphocytic leukemia (ALL), higher doses of brain radiation used to prevent or treat the disease were associated with lower IQ scores (WISC-R Full Scale and Performance IQs), poorer neuropsychological performances (tests of eye-hand coordination and visual-motor integration), and greater difficulties in school as judged by parent ratings and by special help received. Furthermore, the ALL group as a whole in this study exhibited a pattern of relatively high scores on the WRAT Reading and Spelling subtests as compared to their performances on the WRAT Arithmetic subtest. Similar conclusions have been arrived at by Fletcher and Copeland (1988) in their review of the ALL literature.

Clinical Implications

The ramifications of this particular pattern of abilities and deficits are far-reaching, usually affecting every aspect of vocational and social life. Hence, the therapeutic programs necessary to handle these difficulties are always complex and need to be comprehensive and integrated. The treatment program that we have found to be helpful for children and adolescents who present with this neuropsychological profile is outlined in Rourke (1989; 1995).

Although our clinical experiences suggest that there are some differences in the severity of the psychosocial manifestations of NLD, we have found a number of dimensions of these manifestations almost universally present in individuals who exhibit the syndrome. With this proviso in mind, the following generalizations are framed so as to relate to the expected prognosis in the area of psychosocial functioning for individuals who exhibit the NLD syndrome. In this discussion, we focus on the hypothesized etiologies of these psychosocial difficulties and the linkages that are thought to exist between the neuropsychological deficits exhibited by persons with NLD and their particular patterns of psychopathology. In our experience, this pattern gradually emerges in late childhood and is quite clearly manifest during adolescence. The crucial transition from "concrete" to "formal" operational thought at this time (Piaget, 1952), with the concomitant impact on developmental demands that this transition involves, is thought to be particularly troublesome for adolescents with NLD. Their difficulties with problem solving, hypothesis testing, concept formation, conceptual flexibility, and capacity to benefit from informational feedback become more obvious to those around them, and possibly to themselves. It may be for this reason that self-injurious behavior looms large in the histories of such individuals during late adolescence and early adulthood (Rourke, Young, & Leenaars, 1989).

ETIOLOGY OF SOCIOEMOTIONAL DIFFICULTIES

The socioemotional difficulties of persons with NLD appear to result from interactions among and between their neuropsychological assets and deficits. Some examples of such interactions are listed on page 409.

INTERRELATIONSHIPS THAT USUALLY TRANSPIRE IN THE NLD SYNDROME

Psychomotor Clumsiness and Problems in Tactile Sensitivity

The importance of psychomotor coordination and of basic sensory-perceptual competencies (such as tactile sensitivity) is characteristically undervalued in most psychosocial treatments of adult competencies, primarily because of the overwhelming emphasis accorded to linguistic proficiencies in connection with adult competency/adaptation. Not for a moment do we deny the importance of linguistic competence for mature adaptation, but we must also point out that adult interactions, especially intimacy, are largely functions of smooth, coordinated, integrated sensorimotor functioning and spontaneous adaptive alterations to meet sometimes rapidly changing social circumstances. These processes involve not only sensorimotor integrity but also a number of other "nonverbal" dimensions that have been discussed above in connection with the NLD syndrome. Persons who are incapable of deploying such behaviors are seldom, if ever, "popular" with their peers. Indeed, they are often viewed as social misfits. The serious clinical ramifications of this state of affairs would be expected to include an increase in the probability of social withdrawal, social isolation, and depression.

Visual-Spatial-Organizational Deficits

Standing too close or too far away from other persons while engaged in various forms of social interaction; failure to appreciate subtle—and, sometimes, even obvious—visual details in configurations, with consequent misinterpretation of them; extreme difficulties in appreciating others' nonverbal "body language"; poor appreciation of visual-spatial relationships when locomoting, driving a car, engaging in gestures of affection—all of these are examples of the predictable ramifications of deficits in visual-spatial-organizational skills. In addition to encouraging social ostracism for the person with NLD (with unfortunate consequences such as an increase in the likelihood of withdrawal, isolation, and depression), it should also be clear that these disabilities render such persons at risk for personal injury—at the hands of others or through their own misperception and mismanagement of physical dangers. Their tendency to "rush in where angels fear to tread" is not a reflection of their courage, but rather of their failure to appreciate the dangers inherent in any number of physical and social situations and the consequences of their actions within them.

Difficulties in Dealing with Novelty

The person with NLD is expected to have particular difficulty in adapting to situations that require systematic orientation to, and analysis of, novel stimulus material, especially when there exist no overlearned descriptive systems and/or patterns of adaptation for coping with them. Instead of orienting successfully to such novel situations, planning and executing adequate coping strategies, and dealing flexibly with changing patterns of interaction within them, the person with NLD will probably attempt to apply previously overlearned strategies to such situations in a stereotyped, rigid fashion. It goes without saying that such inflexible approaches are likely to meet with considerable resistance from others involved in the interaction. The predicament becomes even worse when, as is very likely, the person with NLD attempts to deal with such situations in a verbal fashion although some other mode of interaction (e.g., touching, psychomotor expression, appropriate gesturing) is demanded. As the inevitable social rebuffs that the person experiences are multiplied many times over, it is reasonable to expect that he or she will become prone to withdraw from such contacts. Indeed, he or she may eventually become seriously isolated and avoid social encounters almost entirely. Thus, we see another manifestation of the NLD syndrome that would be expected, under a wide variety of circumstances, to lead directly to marked isolation and withdrawal from social intercourse, with consequent increases in the likelihood of depression.

Problems in Intermodal Integration

Included among the difficulties that arise from limitations in the capacities of the person with NLD for intermodal integration are the following: problems in the assessment of another's emotional state through the integration of information gleaned from his or her facial expressions, tone of voice, posture, psychomotor patterns, and so on; limitations in the assessment of social cause-and-effect relationships because of a failure to integrate data from a number of sources, as is often necessary in order to generate reasonable hypotheses regarding the chain of events in social intercourse; failure to appreciate humor because of the complex intermodal judgments required for assessing the juxtaposition of the incongruous; imputing of unreasonable, trite, and/or oversimplified causes for the behavior of others, and imparting such assignations in situations that would lead to embarrassment for the person so described. These are but a few of the consequences that accrue for the person with NLD because of the difficulties that he or she experiences in integrating information from a variety of sources. Such unfortunate outcomes, of course, are much worse when he or she is anxious and confused (as becomes increasingly common) in novel or otherwise complex situations.

ADULT CONSEQUENCES OF THE NLD SYNDROME

The practical, concrete ramifications of the NLD syndrome in adults are straightforward and would include examples such as the following: (a) efforts to pursue their chosen "professions" (i.e., those for which they were "educated") are forsaken for "less demanding" jobs; (b) these "less demanding," second-choice jobs often require smooth psychomotor coordination, trouble shooting, and dealing adaptively with the demands of new or otherwise complex situations (abilities and skills that are notably deficient in such individuals); (c) they have a virtual inability to reflect on the nature and seriousness of their problems (anosognosia), and outstanding difficulties in generating adequate solutions for those problems that they do appreciate; (d) they have marked deficiencies in the appreciation of subtle and even fairly obvious nonverbal aspects of communication, inviting consequent social disdain and even rejection.

This state of affairs, developing over a period of years, would increase greatly the probability that those individuals so afflicted will feel that others do not wish to be with them; that their behavioral expressions are seen as silly and the object of ridicule; that they are impotent in the face of what are for them challenging circumstances (but with which others seemingly deal without difficulty). Depression and suicide attempts are greater than average in individuals who exhibit this syndrome (Rourke, Young, Strang, & Russell, 1986).

Despite the damaging effects of their early experiences, many of these individuals manage to complete secondary school and move on to obtain college and university degrees. It is likely that the structure inherent in the academic milieu increases the probability that they will be able to cope and even succeed within its confines (especially if courses in mathematics, science, and similar subjects can be avoided). The most serious crises seem to occur at the point when they leave school and attempt to enter the competitive work force. At this juncture, they begin to experience the most devastating effects of their deficits. Attempting to find work in line with their academic achievement, they seldom get past the interview stage, primarily because of their social ineptitude. Should they manage to obtain work, they typically fail because jobs that are seen as commensurate with their level of scholastic attainment are too complex for them. Lacking insight into this mismatch, they may continue to look for similar jobs. However, they eventually opt for less demanding work. Even then, failure is common.

The important point in the present context is that the academic and psychosocial deficits envisioned in the dynamics of the NLD syndrome and model are *dependent* variables; that is, the academic and psychosocial deficits are seen as *effects* of the deficits that are part-and-parcel of the neurodevelopmental dynamics of the syndrome.

Empirical evidence consistent with many dimensions of this model (e.g., Loveland et al., 1990; White, Moffitt, & Silva, 1992) has been growing very rapidly. In a recent study, Casey et al. (1991) contrasted the psychosocial functioning of samples of younger (about 8 years of age) and older (about 13 years) children who met criteria for NLD. Casey et al. (1991) found that the mean PIC profiles exhibited by both groups were very similar to the prototypical Internalized Psychopathology profile derived from the Windsor Taxonomic Research. However, the mean PIC profile of the older children was clearly more deviant than that of the younger children, with an extreme score on the Psychosis scale (greater than 90 *T*), and significant elevations on the Depression and Social Skills scales. Overall, the PIC profiles of the older children with NLD were more elevated (i.e., more disturbed), especially on scales related to internalized psychopathology. Children with LD may show no apparent predisposition for increased psychopathology with advancing age, but a specific subpopulation of children, those with NLD, are at risk for the development of significant psychopathology (of the internalizing kind) as they grow older.

The actual model presented by Rourke (1989) is much more complex than this brief synopsis. The dynamic interplay and development of the components within the model is further cast on a foundation of empirical and theoretical models of central nervous system development in children. Thus, the model is also capable of encompassing some of the complex manifestations of specific neuropathological conditions (such as head injury, extensive radiotherapy of the central nervous system, and neurotoxic conditions) that are likely to produce the NLD syndrome. At the same time, it is clear that the etiologies of NLD are by no means limited to frank cerebral insult. There is a good fit between the model and clinical experience, and rapidly mounting empirical evidence to support it, but further research is required to test many aspects of the model (Rourke, 1995).

GENERAL TREATMENT IMPLICATIONS

The preceding considerations would suggest strongly that the following principles of treatment for children and adolescents who manifest the NLD syndrome are viable (these would appear to apply, mutatis mutandis, to adults as well):

1. The earlier in development that white matter disease of significant dimensions occurs, the more propitious it would be to "attack the deficits" of the child in a direct fashion. The rationale for such a principle is fairly straightforward: it would seem reasonable to attempt to stimulate the functioning of the remaining white matter to the maximum in an effort to "encourage" the development of centers of gray matter that are dependent on input from white matter for their adequate development. (It is at this time that intensive physiotherapy and related interventions aimed at increasing sensorimotor integration would be expected to be most efficacious.) Failure to do so during these early years may lead to "secondary degeneration" of such gray matter (Rourke et al., 1983, p. 178). Perhaps most important, the stimulation of the principal clumps of ganglia (opercula) of the left cerebral hemisphere that are crucial for the development of natural language may be encouraged thereby. In any case, during these early stages of development it would seem to be particularly unpropitious to adopt a laissez-faire attitude toward child-rearing with such youngsters; this would essentially encourage them to languish in a neuropsychologically isolated and largely understimulated personal world.

2. The longer the NLD syndrome persists and the later it occurs in the development of the individual, the more probable it becomes that accentuation of compensatory techniques (e.g., the use of intact rote verbal memory skills) will prove to be efficacious for adaptational/therapeutic purposes. For example, it would appear to be particularly appropriate to encourage the adoption of compensatory strategies for older children who have acquired natural language to an advanced level prior to the onset of significant white matter disease or dysfunction. For such children, the use of compensatory strategies (largely of the verbal variety) for social and vocational adaptation would appear to be one of the very few feasible and efficacious therapeutic/rehabilitational tacks to pursue. A more specific therapeutic program for persons exhibiting NLD is described in Rourke (1989; 1995).

GENERAL CONCLUSIONS REGARDING THE NLD SYNDROME AND MODEL

In a first attempt at the formulation of a developmental neuropsychological model aimed at the explication of central processing abilities and deficiencies in children (Rourke, 1982), the salience of the right hemisphere → left hemisphere distinction and interactions was emphasized. It was noted at the time that it would eventually become necessary to incorporate the so-called "up-down" and "front-back" dimensions into this model if it were to constitute a reasonably complete theoretical formulation of developmental neuropsychological functioning. The NLD model, which constitutes an attempt to account for the behavioral consequences of destruction or permanent incapacity of various types of white versus gray matter at various stages of development, is a step in the direction of this more general developmental neuropsychological theory.

In this context, it would appear that Lashley's formulations regarding *mass action* (remember that he was dealing with lesions in rat brain, where the proportion of white to gray matter is considerably greater than is the case in the human brain) loom large in the explanation of the neurological diseases and developmental learning disabilities under consideration and in what appears to be their final common pathway, the NLD syndrome. That is, it is proposed in the NLD model that positive, "dose-sensitive" (although not necessarily linear) relationships obtain between amount (mass) of brain substance destroyed, disordered, or rendered dysfunctional and the degree of neuropsychological deficit that ensues therefrom. This relationship is inferred to obtain in the case of white, not gray, matter.

At the same time, Lashley's notion that neurons are *equipotential* vis-à-vis their capacity to mediate behavior stands in marked contrast to the formulations enunciated in the NLD model. Indeed, this model points to the necessity for particular, unique, hemispheric-specific (i.e., not substitutable) processes to be extant and functioning at particular stages of ontogeny if normal development is to proceed, and to the abnormal developmental consequences that are thought to ensue if such is not the case.

PRINCIPAL THEORETICAL CONCLUSIONS AND GENERALIZATIONS

Our understanding of the psychosocial development and functioning of children with LD is far from complete. However, our review of the available literature suggests that, although many studies have been less informative than might be hoped, research efforts in this area have not been wasted. The conclusions that flow from our review are as follows:

1. No single, unitary pattern of personality characteristics, psychosocial adaptation, social competence, self-concept, locus of control, or other facet of socioemotional functioning is characteristic of all children with LD.

2. Some children with LD experience mild to severe disturbance of socioemotional functioning. However, most children with LD appear to achieve adequate psychosocial adaptation.

3. Distinct types of socioemotional disturbance and behavior disorder may be displayed by children with LD. These various manifestations of emotional and behavioral disorder may occur more frequently among children with LD than among their normally achieving peers; however, the precise incidence of emotional and behavioral problems in children with LD is, as yet, not accurately known.

4. One pattern of central processing abilities and deficits (NLD) appears to lead to both a particular configuration of academic achievement (well-developed word recognition and spelling as compared to significantly poorer mechanical arithmetic), increased risk of psychopathology, and a tendency to develop an internalized form of socioemotional disturbance. Other patterns of central processing abilities and deficits (those marked by outstanding difficulties in psycholinguistic skills) appear to lead to particular patterns of academic achievement (striking problems in reading and spelling, and varying levels of performance in mechanical arithmetic), with some correlative effect on the incidence of psychopathology but no particular effect on its specific manifestations.

5. There is no conclusive evidence that children with LD are prone to developing problems with substance abuse, truly antisocial behavior, or delinquency. Carefully conducted longitudinal research suggests that, as a group, children with LD are no more likely to develop these problems than are children who do not exhibit LD.

6. There is no conclusive evidence that children with LD, as a group, tend to become more prone to socioemotional disturbance with advancing age, relative to normally achieving peers.

7. One exception to point 6 is the worsening in the manifestations of psychopathology and the increasing discrepancies between abilities and deficits that are exhibited by children and adolescents of the NLD subtype, in spite of the fact that the *pattern* of neuropsychological abilities and deficits and the specific manifestations of psychopathology in such individuals remain quite stable over time.

One additional conclusion, not raised as a question at the outset of this chapter, relates to whether the model developments are broad enough and articulated enough to address the complex interactions that take place between patterns of central processing abilities and deficits on the one hand and academic learning difficulties and socioemotional disturbances on the other. Our review of the literature to this point would lead to the conclusion that continuing to carry out essentially atheoretical, correlational studies of matched groups of normally achieving children and those with LD to address the important theoretical and clinical issues in this area is counterproductive. Model developments sufficient to deal with the latter (e.g., Fletcher & Taylor, 1984) must be complex and sophisticated.

CLINICAL GENERALIZATIONS AND CONCLUSIONS

General Observations and Guidelines

Some children, adolescents, and adults experience socioemotional problems that prevent progress in learning in school and elsewhere. It is important to direct treatment at the socioemotional disturbances exhibited by such individuals. The following general observations and guidelines may help to direct such efforts:

1. For persons whose learning problems are caused by socioemotional disturbance, one would expect that, once this disturbance is treated effectively (especially if treated at an early age), learning would proceed apace.

2. For those individuals whose psychosocial difficulties are (largely or in part) the direct result of, or strongly linked to, their LD, it is necessary to direct therapeutic attention in some systematic way to both of these sets of problems.

3. For persons whose LD and socioemotional difficulties result from a common cause (e.g., some form of central processing abilities and deficits), clinicians should attempt to ameliorate those basic central processing deficits that are amenable to change and provide compensatory coping strategies and techniques for those deficits that are not likely to change.

Clinical Conclusions

The following clinical conclusions, arising from our review, should be made quite explicit:

1. The social status of persons with LD would appear to be an important dimension relating to their feelings of well-being and their level of psychosocial functioning. It appears that some children and adolescents with LD have lower social status (in the judgment of others) than do their normally achieving peers. However, the variance in this dimension exhibited by children and adolescents with LD (i.e., ranging from well below average to well above average social status) would suggest strongly that the presence of LD is not an unambiguous marker for level of social status. Hence, if clinically justified, a specific determination of the social status of the person with LD should be carried out in conjunction with other assessment methods. Failure to measure such a dimension explicitly may limit the understanding of the clinician and, in turn, jeopardize the treatment of the person with LD.

2. The evidence relating self-esteem to LD is equivocal. Among other things, this would suggest that the person with LD who presents with significant deficits in self-esteem may not be suffering from such problems as a result of deficits in learning. Rather, it is much more probable that, in such a case, problems in self-esteem have a separate etiology quite apart from the learning disability. Hence, it is likely that a coordinated therapeutic program that takes into consideration the essentially unrelated nature of each of these sets of disorders would be most effective.

3. Learned helplessness may be exhibited by some children and adolescents with LD. However, in this instance as well, it is quite probable that such dimensions of "problem" behavior are the result of etiological factors that are not directly attributable to LD per se. Hence, treatment will, in all probability, be directed at changing "learned helplessness" without particular regard to the person's LD.

4. The absence of any apparent relationship between advancing years and degree of psychosocial disturbance in children and adolescents with LD should not be taken to imply that early intervention with such persons is not desirable. The apparent absence of age-related changes in these important dimensions of behavior may reflect the operation of compensatory behaviors that are, in the long run, undesirable. In any case, significant socioemotional disturbance should be treated without regard to data that suggest that such disturbance does not increase with age.

5. Every clinician aims to treat patients on an individualized basis. However, there is something to be gained from taking into consideration the notion of subtypes, both with respect to LD per se and with respect to the psychosocial problems and difficulties that may accompany them, be caused by them, or arise from a similar or identical source, as do the LD themselves. Several dimensions of the subtype issue should be mentioned within this context. These issues have been outlined before (Rourke, 1985) and are spread here as a general statement of this rather complex problem:

> The classification of children into "homogeneous" subtypes does *not* imply that the children so classified are identical. Indeed, it would appear quite likely that children classified (into subtypes) . . . would exhibit, together with their similarities, fairly substantial individual differences. That is, although they may be quite similar to one another with respect to their pattern of adaptive abilities and deficits (and, by implication, with respect to their central processing characteristics), any number of differences in early or current environmental circumstances, reinforcement patterns, and so on would be expected to have a differential impact on the psychosocial functioning of the children. It is for this reason that predictions (prognoses) and treatments must be framed and designed as individual amalgams reflecting common (subtypal) and unique (historical) characteristics.
>
> In this connection, it should be borne in mind that the common (subtypal) variance is itself a reflection of a certain level of uniqueness or individuality, insofar as it differentiates each child within a particular subtype from those in other subtypes and from those who are not classified. In addition, the idiographic formulation of the treatment plan should take into consideration the final level of individualization that is afforded by an examination and understanding of a child's unique socio-historical milieu and characteristics. It is in this (combined) sense that we view the identification of more general clusters of learning-disabled children who share common dimensions or factors as a complementary form of individualization that (we hope) contributes to the formulation and execution of appropriate individual education/therapeutic plans (Fisk & Rourke, 1983; Rourke et al., 1983). (p. 12)

IMPORTANCE OF THE STUDY OF ABNORMAL DEVELOPMENT FOR THE UNDERSTANDING OF NORMAL DEVELOPMENT

In the normally developing child, it would be very difficult to determine which skills are particularly crucial for the development of higher forms of cognitive and psychosocial functioning. What we have been able to demonstrate (by studying children whose development is nonnormal in significant ways) is the crucial importance of basic visual-spatial-organizational, tactile-perceptual, and psychomotor skills for the development of such functions. At the same time, we have demonstrated the relative unimportance of many linguistic skills for the development of such functions.

The mediating factor responsible for such differences would appear to be the impact of visual, tactile, and psychomotor competencies—in conjunction with attraction to novelty—on exploratory behavior, problem solving, hypothesis testing, and concept formation. Thus, the crucial importance of exploratory behavior and "sensorimotor intelligence" for the development of formal operational thought, as advocated and elaborated by Piaget (1954), would appear to receive strong support from our work.

Furthermore, the attraction to novelty and the exploration of the environment can be characterized as crucial dimensions of a "pure desire to know"—a notion that has been central to theories of intellectual development since the time of Aristotle. The effects of the absence or paucity of curiosity and exploration, as seen in children with NLD, would appear to lead to serious limitations of this type of motivation and to devastating consequences with respect to intellectual and psychosocial development.

Although it is abundantly clear that language is important for the enhancement and elaboration of the intellectual and psychosocial dimensions of human experience, the results of our studies suggest strongly that many language functions per se are of relatively little importance for the fundamental dimensions of either intellectual or psychosocial growth. Indeed, we have demonstrated that the presence of many linguistic skills is certainly no guarantee of sound development in these areas. So too, the relative absence of such skills appears to pose no particular impediment to adaptive psychosocial development.

It is difficult to imagine how these conclusions could have been arrived at firmly and with confidence except through the study of children whose course of development is altered substantially as a result of a relative absence of many important psycholinguistic skills (Group R-S) and those who exhibit such skills within a context of markedly deficient visual-spatial-organizational, tactile-perceptual, and psychomotor skills (children with NLD).

As Piaget suggested (1952, 1954), language and thought are distinct, and "sensorimotor intelligence" is a sine qua non for adequate development of formal operational thought—and, we would add, adequate psychosocial functioning.

FUTURE DIRECTIONS

Several dimensions of the complex interactions discussed in this chapter require much more investigative effort in order to expand and refine the conclusions spread above. We view the following as particularly important:

1. Continued specification of the reliability and validity of subtypes of LD and subtypes of psychosocial functioning within the population of children with LD.
2. Continued specification of the relationships between neuropsychological assets and deficits, as manifested in various subtypes of LD in children, and the interaction between these and patterns of normal and disordered psychosocial functioning.

3. Continued investigation of the developmental dimensions of the interactions mentioned in points 2 and 3 above.
4. Attempts to frame these complex interrelationships within theoretical frameworks that are capable of encompassing their complexity. We feel that a good start has been made with the models presented herein, but much is left to do in the area of creative theory and model development.

We feel that these developments will be enhanced by trends that are anticipated in neuropsychology more generally (Rourke, 1991):

1. There will be more accent on what brain structures and systems do, rather than what they do not do when they are damaged or absent. In this connection, the study of the development of normal brain-behavior relationships will be especially relevant.

2. There will be intensive investigations involving simultaneous measurement of brain activity and important neuropsychological dimensions. Many neuroscientists are very much involved in investigations that exploit the latest in brain-imaging technology. They are especially interested in the type envisioned here—simultaneous brain and behavior measurement. Important new information will, undoubtedly, be learned when we can, essentially, watch the human brain engage in learning.

3. Sophisticated statistical methods and mathematical models will be employed on an ever-increasing basis. Methods for applying cluster analysis, confirmatory factor analysis, structural equations, and a host of other sophisticated mathematical and statistical techniques and procedures are now readily available in software form. Although the use of these programs is anything but routine, we can expect to see the exploitation of these techniques expand considerably during the foreseeable future.

4. There will be intense interest in the investigation of the socioemotional and personality correlates of brain disease. In a sense, this prediction suggests that neuropsychologists will *return* to an emphasis on psychosocial functioning that was alive and well in the middle part of this century but has been set aside considerably in favor of the investigation of perception, memory, learning, and cognition during the past two to three decades. Neuropsychologists, especially those with a life-span developmental orientation, can be expected to participate in the thrust of much investigative effort along these lines.

5. The "natural history" or developmental course of brain-behavior relationships in children with disordered brain functions will move to the forefront of research interest. Although we know a great deal about "normal" development, we know relatively little about the course of development of important perceptual, mnestic, cognitive, linguistic, and psychosocial dimensions in children with various types of disordered brain functions. There is no doubt that the accumulation of such knowledge will pose some interesting challenges to our understanding of both normal and abnormal development.

6. Neuropsychological taxonomies will increase in number and sophistication. The Windsor Taxonomic Research outlined in this chapter is an example of a rigorous effort to fashion a reliable and valid taxonomy of some important dimensions of the behavior of children with LD. The development and refinement of other taxonomies would be expected to enhance considerably our understanding of the developmental dimensions of normal and disordered behavior in children.

7. New paradigms, models, and theories will be abundant. Developments in this area are always difficult to predict with any amount of confidence. However, sophisticated data-gathering techniques and technologies, when seen in conjunction with new ways of analyzing large amounts of data in a delicate and precise manner, usually serve as the harbingers for such activity. We are seeing such investigative proceeding today (e.g., Fletcher et al., 1992; Rovet, 1990). This type of solid longitudinal research would be expected to eventuate in much more model building and theorizing.

8. There will be much more truly comparative neuropsychology. Sophisticated developmental and phylogenetic comparisons should be of considerable benefit to those who are interested in human developmental neuropsychology. Indeed, we would anticipate that much of the theorizing and model building that we expect to see flower in the 1990s will have reference to data and theory within a developing comparative psychology that is attuned to developments in comparative neuroscience.

9. Investigation of the neurochemical dimensions of human brain-behavior relationships will expand exponentially. Although they have languished in the shadow of "structural" investigations for the past few decades, the explosive dimensions of nervous system biochemistry will revolutionize the manner in which we structure our views of brain-behavior relationships. This may be especially important for the science of developmental psychopathology because much of the unexplained variance in our prognostications vis-à-vis various forms of developmental abnormalities (e.g., very low birth weight, juvenile onset diabetes, congenital hypothyroidism, traumatic brain injury) may very well relate to neurochemical anomalies that have yet to be determined with any degree of accuracy.

10. Investigations of various medical diseases with neurological impact will intensify. Research dealing with the impact, on the brain, of vascular disease, hormonal disturbances, lung and kidney disease, and the like will continue to develop. The potential for positive impact on developmental psychopathology should be considerable.

11. The neuropsychological investigation of psychiatric syndromes will intensify. The zeitgeist of psychiatry is clearly focused on biological concerns, and a significant number of neuropsychologists, nicely situated in psychiatric settings, can provide their expertise in the investigation of psychiatric syndromes in both children and adults. This should contribute much to the mix of relevant research referred to above.

12. Clinical neuropsychology will be increasingly turned to for solutions to pressing social problems. Lead ingestion, teratogens, toxins in the home and workplace, head injury—all of these are problems with which the practicing clinical neuropsychologist comes into contact. And they are problems that cry out increasingly for data that will convince social policy makers to adopt measures that will deal effectively with their nefarious impact on the brain. In the process, we expect to learn a great deal about the psychosocial impact of these neurotoxins, especially with respect to any transient and permanent developmental alterations that they may cause.

REFERENCES

Achenbach, T. M., & Edelbrock, C. S. (1983). *Manual for the Child Behavior Checklist and Revised Child Behavior Profile.* Burlington: Department of Psychiatry, University of Vermont.

Ackerman, D., & Howes, C. (1986). Sociometric status and after-school activity of children with learning disabilities. *Journal of Learning Disabilities, 19,* 416–419.

Applebee, A. N. (1971). Research in reading retardation: Two critical problems. *Journal of Child Psychology and Psychiatry, 12,* 91–113.

Bender, W. N. (1987). Correlates of classroom behavior problems among learning disabled and nondisabled children in mainstream classes. *Learning Disabilities Quarterly, 10,* 317–324.

Brandys, C. F., & Rourke, B. P. (1991). Differential memory capacities in reading- and arithmetic-disabled children. In B. P. Rourke (Ed.), *Neuropsychological validation of learning disability subtypes* (pp. 73–96). New York: Guilford.

Bruck, M. (1987). Social and emotional adjustments of learning-disabled children: A review of the issues. In S. J. Ceci (Ed.), *Handbook of cognitive, social, and neuropsychological aspects of LD* (Vol. 1, pp. 361–380). Hillsdale, NJ: Erlbaum.

Brumback, R. A., & Staton, R. D. (1983). LD and childhood depression. *American Journal of Orthopsychiatry, 53,* 269–281.

Casey, J. E., Del Dotto, J. E., & Rourke, B. P. (1990). An empirical investigation of the NLD syndrome in a case of agenesis of the corpus callosum. *Journal of Clinical and Experimental Neuropsychology, 12,* 29.

Casey, J. E., & Rourke, B. P. (1992). Disorders of somatosensory perception in children. In I. Rapin & S. J. Segalowitz (Eds.), *Handbook of neuropsychology: Vol. 6. Child neuropsychology* (pp. 477–494). Amsterdam, The Netherlands: Elsevier.

Casey, J. E., Rourke, B. P., & Picard, E. (1991). Syndrome of nonverbal learning disabilities: Age differences in neuropsychological, academic, and socioemotional functioning. *Development and Psychopathology, 3,* 329–345.

Chapman, J. W. (1988). Cognitive-motivational characteristics and academic achievement of learning disabled children: A longitudinal study. *Journal of Educational Psychology, 80,* 357–365.

Chapman, J. W., & Boersma, F. J. (1980). *Affective correlates of LD.* Lisse, The Netherlands: Swets & Zeitlinger.

Colbert, P., Newman, B., Ney, P., & Young, J. (1982). LD as a symptom of depression in children. *Journal of Learning Disabilities, 15,* 333–336.

Cook, T. D., & Campbell, D. T. (1979). *Quasi-experimentation: Design and analysis issues for field settings.* Boston: Houghton Mifflin.

Copeland, D. R., Fletcher, J. M., Pfefferbaum-Levine, B., Jaffe, M., Reid, H., & Maor, M. (1985). Neuropsychological sequelae of childhood cancer in long-term survivors. *Pediatrics, 75,* 745–753.

Del Dotto, J. E., Rourke, B. P., McFadden, G. T., & Fisk, J. L. (1987). Developmental analysis of arithmetic-disabled children: Impact on personality adjustment and patterns of adaptive functioning. *Journal of Clinical and Experimental Neuropsychology, 9,* 44.

Ehrlich, M. I. (1983). Psychofamilial correlates of school disorders. *Journal of School Psychology, 21,* 191–199.

Everitt, B. (1980). *Cluster analysis.* New York: Halsted Press.

Ewing-Cobbs, L., Fletcher, J. M., & Levin, H. S. (1985). Neuropsychological sequelae following pediatric head injury. In M. Ylvisaker (Ed.), *Closed head injury rehabilitation: Children and adolescents* (pp. 71–89). San Diego: College Hill.

Fisk, J. L., & Rourke, B. P. (1983). Neuropsychological subtyping of learning disabled children: History, methods, implications. *Journal of Learning Disabilities, 16,* 529–531.

Fletcher, J. M. (1985). External validation of learning disability typologies. In B. P. Rourke (Ed.), *Neuropsychology of learning disabilities: Essentials of subtype analysis* (pp. 187–211). New York: Guilford.

Fletcher, J. M., Bohan, T. P., Brandt, M., Beaver, S. R., Thorstad, K., Brookshire, B. L., Francis, D. J., Davidson, K. C., & Thompson, N. M. (1993). Relationships of cognitive skills and cerebral white matter in hydrocephalic children. *Journal of Clinical and Experimental Neuropsychology, 15,* 40–41.

Fletcher, J. M., Bohan, T. P., Brandt, M. E., Brookshire, B. L., Beaver, S. R., Francis, D. J., Davidson, K. C., Thompson, N. M., & Miner, M. E. (1992). Cerebral white matter and cognition in hydrocephalic children. *Archives of Neurology, 49,* 818–825.

Fletcher, J. M., & Copeland, D. R. (1988). Neurobehavioral effects of central nervous system prophylactic treatment of cancer in children. *Journal of Clinical and Experimental Neuropsychology, 10,* 495–537.

Fletcher, J. M., & Levin, H. (1988). Neurobehavioral effects of brain injury in children. In D. K. Routh (Ed.), *Handbook of pediatric psychology* (pp. 258–295). New York: Guilford.

Fletcher, J. M., & Taylor, H. G. (1984). Neuropsychological approaches to children: Towards a developmental neuropsychology. *Journal of Clinical Neuropsychology, 6,* 39–56.

Fuerst, D. R., Fisk, J. L., & Rourke, B. P. (1989). Psychosocial functioning of learning-disabled children: Replicability of statistically derived subtypes. *Journal of Consulting and Clinical Psychology, 57*(2), 275–280.

Fuerst, D. R., Fisk, J. L., & Rourke, B. P. (1990). Psychosocial functioning of learning-disabled children: Relations between WISC Verbal IQ–Performance IQ discrepancies and personality subtypes. *Journal of Consulting and Clinical Psychology, 58*(5), 657–660.

Fuerst, D. R., & Rourke, B. P. (1993). Psychosocial functioning of learning-disabled children: Relationships between personality subtypes and achievement test scores. *Journal of Abnormal Child Psychology, 21,* 597–607.

Fuerst, D. R., & Rourke, B. P. (in press). Psychosocial functioning of children with learning disabilities: Relations with age and cognitive functioning. *Child Neuropsychology, 1.*

Glosser, G., & Koppell, S. (1987). Emotional-behavioral patterns in children with LD: Lateralized hemispheric differences. *Journal of Learning Disabilities, 20,* 365–368.

Goldberg, E., & Costa, L. (1981). Hemispheric differences in the acquisition and use of descriptive systems. *Brain and Language, 14,* 144–173.

Golding-Kushner, K. J., Weller, G., & Shprintzen, R. J. (1985). Velocardio-facial syndrome: Language and psychological profiles. *Journal of Craniofacial Genetics and Developmental Biology, 5,* 259–266.

Green, K. D., Forehand, R., Beck, S. J., & Vosk, B. (1980). An assessment of the relationship among measures of children's social competence, and children's academic achievement. *Child Development, 51,* 1149–1156.

Johnson, D. J., & Blalock, J. W. (Eds.). (1987). *Adults with learning disabilities: Clinical studies.* Orlando, FL: Grune & Stratton.

Jorm, A. F., Share, D. L., Matthews, R., & Maclean, R. (1986). Behavior problems in specific reading retarded and general reading backward children: A longitudinal study. *Journal of Child Psychology and Psychiatry, 27,* 33–43.

Lashley, K. S. (1938). Factors limiting recovery after central nervous system lesions. *Journal of Nervous and Mental Diseases, 88,* 733–755.

Loveland, K. A., Fletcher, J. M., & Bailey, V. (1990). Verbal and nonverbal communication of events in learning-disability subtypes. *Journal of Clinical and Experimental Neuropsychology, 12,* 433–447.

McConaughy, S. H., & Ritter, D. R. (1986). Social competence and behavioral problems of learning disabled boys aged 6–11. *Journal of Learning Disabilities, 19,* 39–45.

McCue, M., & Goldstein, G. (1991). Neuropsychological aspects of learning disability in adults. In B. P. Rourke (Ed.), *Neuropsychological validation of learning disability subtypes* (pp. 311–329). New York: Guilford.

McKinney, J. D., Short, E. J., & Feagans, L. (1985). Academic consequences of perceptual-linguistic subtypes of learning disabled children. *Learning Disabilities Research, 1,* 6–17.

McKinney, J. D., & Speece, D. L. (1986). Academic consequences and longitudinal stability of behavioral subtypes of learning disabled children. *Journal of Educational Psychology, 78,* 365–372.

Morris, R., Blashfield, R., & Satz, P. (1981). Neuropsychology and cluster analysis: Potentials and problems. *Journal of Clinical Neuropsychology, 3,* 79–99.

Morris, R., Blashfield, R., & Satz, P. (1986). Developmental classification of reading-disabled children. *Journal of Clinical and Experimental Neuropsychology, 8,* 371–392.

Morris, R. D., & Walter, L. W. (1991). Subtypes of arithmetic-disabled adults: Validating childhood findings. In B. P. Rourke (Ed.), *Neuropsychological validation of learning disability subtypes* (pp. 330–346). New York: Guilford.

Nass, R., Speiser, P., Heier, L., Haimes, A., & New, M. (1990). White matter abnormalities in congenital adrenal hyperplasia. *Annals of Neurology, 28,* 470.

Nussbaum, N. L., & Bigler, E. D. (1986). Neuropsychological and behavioral profiles of empirically derived subgroups of learning disabled children. *International Journal of Clinical Neuropsychology, 8,* 82–89.

Nussbaum, N. L., Bigler, E. D., Koch, W. R., Ingram, W., Rosa, L., & Massman, P. (1988). Personality/behavioral characteristics in children: Differential effects of putative anterior versus posterior cerebral asymmetry. *Archives of Clinical Neuropsychology, 3,* 127–135.

Ozols, E. J., & Rourke, B. P. (1985). Dimensions of social sensitivity in two types of learning-disabled children. In B. P. Rourke (Ed.), *Neuropsychology of learning disabilities: Essentials of subtype analysis* (pp. 281–301). New York: Guilford.

Ozols, E. J., & Rourke, B. P. (1988). Characteristics of young learning-disabled children classified according to patterns of academic achievement: Auditory-perceptual and visual-perceptual abilities. *Journal of Clinical Child Psychology, 17,* 44–52.

Ozols, E. J., & Rourke, B. P. (1991). Classification of young learning-disabled children according to patterns of academic achievement: Validity studies. In B. P. Rourke (Ed.), *Neuropsychological validation of learning disability subtypes* (pp. 97–123). New York: Guilford.

Piaget, J. (1952). *The origins of intelligence in children.* New York: International Universities Press.

Piaget, J. (1954). *Construction of reality in the child.* New York: Basic Books.

Porter, J., & Rourke, B. P. (1985). Socioemotional functioning of learning-disabled children: A subtypal analysis of personality patterns. In B. P. Rourke (Ed.), *Neuropsychology of learning disabilities: Essentials of subtype analysis* (pp. 257–279). New York: Guilford.

Rourke, B. P. (1975). Brain-behavior relationships in children with learning disabilities. *American Psychologist, 30,* 911–920.

Rourke, B. P. (1976). Reading retardation in children: Developmental lag or deficit? In R. M. Knights & D. J. Bakker (Eds.), *Neuropsychology of learning disorders: Theoretical approaches* (pp. 125–137). Baltimore, MD: University Park Press.

Rourke, B. P. (1978). Reading, spelling, arithmetic disabilities: A neuropsychologic perspective. In H. R. Myklebust (Ed.), *Progress in learning disabilities* (Vol. 4, pp. 97–120). New York: Grune & Stratton.

Rourke, B. P. (1982). Central processing deficiencies in children: Toward a developmental neuropsychological model. *Journal of Clinical Neuropsychology, 4,* 1–18.

Rourke, B. P. (1983). Reading and spelling disabilities: A developmental neuropsychological perspective. In U. Kirk (Ed.), *Neuropsychology of language, reading, and spelling* (pp. 209–234). New York: Academic Press.

Rourke, B. P. (Ed.). (1985). *Neuropsychology of learning disabilities: Essentials of subtype analysis.* New York: Guilford.

Rourke, B. P. (1987). Syndrome of nonverbal learning disabilities: The final common pathway of white-matter disease/dysfunction? *The Clinical Neuropsychologist, 1,* 209–234.

Rourke, B. P. (1988a). Socioemotional disturbances of learning disabled children. *Journal of Consulting and Clinical Psychology, 56,* 801–810.

Rourke, B. P. (1988b). The syndrome of nonverbal learning disabilities: Developmental manifestations in neurological disease, disorder, and dysfunction. *The Clinical Neuropsychologist, 2,* 293–330.

Rourke, B. P. (1989). *Nonverbal learning disabilities: The syndrome and the model.* New York: Guilford.

Rourke, B. P. (1990). Human neuropsychology in the 1990s. In P. J. D. Drenth, J. A. Sergeant, & R. J. Takens (Eds.), *European perspectives in psychology* (Vol. 2, pp. 305–320). New York: Wiley.

Rourke, B. P. (Ed.). (1991). *Neuropsychological validation of learning disability subtypes.* New York: Guilford.

Rourke, B. P. (Ed.). (1995). *Syndrome of nonverbal learning disabilities: Manifestations in neurological disease, disorder, and dysfunction.* New York: Guilford.

Rourke, B. P., Bakker, D. J., Fisk, J. L., & Strang, J. D. (1983). *Child neuropsychology: An introduction to theory, research, and clinical practice.* New York: Guilford.

Rourke, B. P., Dietrich, D. M., & Young, G. C. (1973). Significance of WISC verbal-performance discrepancies for younger children with LD. *Perceptual and Motor Skills, 36,* 275–282.

Rourke, B. P., & Finlayson, M. A. J. (1978). Neuropsychological significance of variations in patterns of academic performance: Verbal and visual-spatial abilities. *Journal of Abnormal Child Psychology, 6,* 121–133.

Rourke, B. P., & Fisk, J. L. (1981). Socioemotional disturbances of learning disabled children: The role of central processing deficits. *Bulletin of the Orton Society, 31,* 77–88.

Rourke, B. P., & Fisk, J. L. (1988). Subtypes of learning-disabled children: Implications for a neurodevelopmental model of differential hemispheric processing. In D. L. Molfese & S. J. Segalowitz (Eds.),

Developmental implications of brain lateralization (pp. 547–565). New York: Guilford.

Rourke, B. P., & Fisk, J. L. (1992). Adult presentations of learning disabilities. In R. F. White (Ed.), *Clinical syndromes in adult neuropsychology: The practitioner's handbook* (pp. 451–473). Amsterdam, The Netherlands: Elsevier.

Rourke, B. P., Fisk, J. L., & Strang, J. D. (1986). *Neuropsychological assessment of children: A treatment-oriented approach.* New York: Guilford.

Rourke, B. P., & Fuerst, D. R. (1991). *Learning disabilities and psychosocial functioning: A neuropsychological perspective.* New York: Guilford.

Rourke, B. P., & Strang, J. D. (1978). Neuropsychological significance of variations in patterns of academic performance: Motor, psychomotor, and tactile-perceptual abilities. *Journal of Pediatric Psychology, 3,* 62–66.

Rourke, B. P., & Strang, J. D. (1983). Subtypes of reading and arithmetical disabilities: A neuropsychological analysis. In M. Rutter (Ed.), *Developmental neuropsychiatry* (pp. 473–488). New York: Guilford.

Rourke, B. P., & Telegdy, G. A. (1971). Lateralizaing significance of WISC verbal-performance discrepancies for older children with learning disabilities. *Perceptual and Motor Skills, 33,* 875–883.

Rourke, B. P., Young, G. C., & Flewelling, R. W. (1971). The relationships between WISC verbal-performance discrepancies and selected verbal, auditory-perceptual, visual-perceptual, and problem-solving abilities in children with LD. *Journal of Clinical Psychology, 27,* 475–479.

Rourke, B. P., Young, G. C., & Leenaars, A. (1989). A childhood learning disability that predisposes those afflicted to adolescent and adult depression and suicide risk. *Journal of Learning Disabilities, 21,* 169–175.

Rourke, B. P., Young, G. C., Strang, J. D., & Russell, D. L. (1986). Adult outcomes of central processing deficiencies in childhood. In I. Grant & K. M. Adams (Eds.), *Neuropsychological assessment in neuropsychiatric disorders: Clinical methods and empirical findings* (pp. 244–267). New York: Oxford University Press.

Rovet, J. F. (1990). Congenital hypothyroidism: Intellectual and neuropsychological functioning. In C. S. Holmes (Ed.), *Psychoneuroendocrinology: Brain, behavior, and hormonal interactions* (pp. 273–322). New York: Springer-Verlag.

Rovet, J. F., Ehrlich, R. M., Czuchta, D., & Akler, M. (1993). Psychoeducational characteristics of children and adolescents with insulin-dependent diabetes mellitus. *Journal of Learning Disabilities, 26,* 7–22.

Rovet, J., & Netley, C. (1982). Processing deficits in Turner's syndrome. *Developmental Psychology, 18,* 77–94.

Shapiro, E. G., Lipton, M. E., & Krivit, W. (1992). White matter dysfunction and its neuropsychological correlates: A longitudinal study of a case of metachromatic leukodystrophy. *Journal of Clinical and Experimental Neuropsychology, 14,* 610–624.

Silver, D. S., & Young, R. D. (1985). Interpersonal problem-solving abilities, peer status, and behavioral adjustment in learning disabled and non-learning disabled adolescents. *Advances in Learning and Behavioral Disabilities, 4,* 201–223.

Sparrow, S. S. (1993). Asperger's syndrome and nonverbal learning disabilities syndrome: Developmental and clinical aspects. (1993). *Journal of Clinical and Experimental Neuropsychology, 15,* 41.

Speece, D. L., McKinney, J. D., & Apelbaum, M. I. (1985). Classification and validation of behavioral subtypes of learning-disabled children. *Journal of Educational Psychology, 77,* 67–77.

Spreen, O. (1988). *Learning disabled children growing up: A follow-up into adulthood.* New York: Oxford University Press.

Spreen, O. (1989). The relationship between LD, emotional disorders, and neuropsychology: Some results and observations. *Journal of Clinical and Experimental Neuropsychology, 11,* 117–140.

Stellern, J., Marlowe, M., Jacobs, J., & Cossairt, A. (1985). Neuropsychological significance of right hemisphere cognitive mode in behavior disorders. *Behavioral Disorders, 2,* 113–124.

Stevens, D. E., & Moffitt, T. E. (1988). Neuropsychological profile of an Asperger's syndrome case with exceptional calculating ability. *The Clinical Neuropsychologist, 2,* 228–238.

Strang, J. D. (1981). *Personality dimensions of learning disabled children: Age and subtype differences.* Unpublished doctoral dissertation, University of Windsor, Windsor, Canada.

Strang, J. D., & Rourke, B. P. (1983). Concept-formation/non-verbal reasoning abilities of children who exhibit specific academic problems with arithmetic. *Journal of Clinical Child Psychology, 12,* 33–39.

Strang, J. D., & Rourke, B. P. (1985a). Adaptive behavior of children with specific arithmetic disabilities and associated neuropsychological abilities and deficits. In B. P. Rourke (Ed.), *Neuropsychology of learning disabilities: Essentials of subtype analysis* (pp. 302–328). New York: Guilford.

Strang, J. D., & Rourke, B. P. (1985b). Arithmetic disability subtypes: The neuropsychological significance of specific arithmetical impairment in childhood. In B. P. Rourke (Ed.), *Neuropsychology of learning disabilities: Essentials of subtype analysis* (pp. 167–183). New York: Guilford.

Streissguth, A. P., & LaDue, R. A. (1987). Fetal alcohol syndrome: Teratogenic causes of developmental disabilities. In S. R. Schroeder (Ed.), *Toxic substances and mental retardation: Neurobehavioral toxicology and teratology* (pp. 1–32). Washington, DC: American Association on Mental Deficiency.

Sweeney, J. E., & Rourke, B. P. (1978). Neuropsychological significance of phonetically accurate and phonetically inaccurate spelling errors in younger and older retarded spellers. *Brain and Language, 6,* 212–225.

Szatmari, P., Tuff, L., Finlayson, M. A. J., & Bartolucci, G. (1990). Asperger's syndrome and autism: Neurocognitive aspects. *Journal of the American Academy of Child and Adolescent Psychiatry, 29,* 130–136.

Taylor, H. G., Albo, V. C., Phebus, C. K., Sachs, B. R., & Bierl, P. G. (1987). Postirradiation treatment outcomes for children with acute lymphocytic leukemia: Clarification of risks. *Journal of Pediatric Psychology, 12,* 395–411.

Udwin, O., & Yule, W. (1991). A cognitive and behavioural phenotype in Williams syndrome. *Journal of Clinical and Experimental Neuropsychology, 13,* 232–244.

Wechsler, D. (1949). *Wechsler Intelligence Scale for Children.* New York: Guilford.

Wechsler, D. (1974). *Wechsler Intelligence Scale for Children—Revised.* New York: Psychological Corp.

Weller, C., & Strawser, S. (1987). Adaptive behavior of subtypes of learning disabled individuals. *Journal of Special Education, 21,* 101–115.

White, J. L., Moffitt, T. E., & Silva, P. A. (1992). Neuropsychological and socioemotional correlates of specific-arithmetic disability. *Archives of Clinical Neuropsychology, 7,* 1–16.

Wiener, J. (1980). A theoretical model of the acquisition of peer relationships of learning disabled children. *Journal of Learning Disabilities, 13,* 42–47.

Wills, K. E., Holmbeck, G. N., Dillon, K., & McLone, D. G. (1990). Intelligence and achievement in children with myelomeningocele. *Journal of Pediatric Psychology, 15,* 161–176.

Wirt, R. D., Lachar, D., Klinedinst, J. K., & Seat, P. D. (1977). *Multidimensional description of child personality: A manual for the Personality Inventory for Children.* Los Angeles: Western Psychological Services.

Wirt, R. D., Lachar, D., Klinedinst, J. K., & Seat, P. D. (1984). *Multidimensional description of child personality: A manual for the Personality Inventory for Children Revised 1984.* Los Angeles: Western Psychological Services.

CHAPTER 15

Clinical-Developmental Psychology: Constructivism and Social Cognition in the Study of Psychological Dysfunctions

GIL G. NOAM, MICHAEL CHANDLER, and CHRIS LALONDE

This chapter relates the normative course of social-cognitive development to psychopathology. In it we use a broad perspective on social cognition, referring to the construction and development of meanings about the self and other social world. This social world includes not only the self and personal biography, but also interpersonal and small group relationships and conceptions about the wider society, including the development of social norms and morality. While the theoretical roots of social cognition can be traced to the cognitive theory traditions of Piaget (1960), Vygotsky (1962), Werner (1948), and others, the relationship to affectivity, individual differences, and personal meaning has become increasingly important. In this shift from abstract and general cognitive-developmental theory to conceptions of the experiencing person with a personal history, real relationships, and typical motivations and feelings, the possibility for understanding psychopathology in new ways has increased as well.

In fact, constructivist theories have made their greatest mark in research and practice, where general patterns cutting across large groups of people were at the fore. These theories have been less useful in exploring individual differences and the interplay between life history and present cognitive functioning. Typically, abstractions in developmental descriptions have been favored, forgetting that the so-called "epistemic subject" has a real and often painful socioemotional history and complex motivations. This shift in focus has been accepted through the social-cognitive study of psychopathology since psychological problems are usually related not only to general cognitive functions, but also entail individual thought and feeling patterns (e.g., Noam, 1988b, 1990). It is this increasing focus of social cognition on clinical issues and personal biographical pathways and the resultant new theories and applications that are the focus of this chapter.

Social-cognition, which has a solid base in the constructivist traditions of cognitive theory, always addresses the person as a meaning-maker of self and social reality. The constructivist perspective posits that the same events and social conditions are given very diverse subjective interpretations. That these forms of diverse interpretation are not entirely idiosyncratic has made it possible to generate developmental typologies of meaning-making that have come to be known as "stages." Every person continuously attempts to bring some organization to varied and often fragmented social experiences. Today we are less convinced, however, that the acquisition of social cognition entails a stepwise and unitary progression, from stage to stage than were the contributors to the field even a decade ago. We are also less convinced that the constructions about the many social and self domains progress in neatly parallel fashion. Instead, the constructivist approach to making-meaning of varied social experiences as we use it here should be viewed as a fundamentally interactive and dysynchronous process. From early on, the child has interaction with different partners and settings that require very different responses. Even in the most intimate relations to the parents, the interaction requirements can be quite contradictory and require flexible and differentiated responses from the child. Much as we have the model parents in mind when we develop theories—parents who "work out" their differences and are consistent in their goals and values—the reality is usually quite different. Most parents cannot afford the time to achieve consensus on every issue and live with a great deal of unresolved conflict and differing views about child rearing. The child is left to make sense of these differences and to develop strategies to deal with these incongruities. These differences in interaction experiences and demands become greater with development as the child is exposed to increasingly differentiated institutional settings and an exposure to separated peer and adult worlds.

We would like to thank Bracha Molad and Andrew Rhein for their continuous work on this chapter and Philip Hodkins for his help in creating the bibliography. Without their intelligent and creative input, this chapter would not have been nearly as strong. The Institute for Advanced Studies in Berlin provided excellent support, to Gil Noam, in the writing phase of this chapter. The American Suicide Foundation, the Alden Trust, and the Simches Family Trust all supported the Laboratory of Developmental Psychology and Developmental Psychopathology where the clinical-developmental research presented in this chapter was conducted. As always, our friend and colleague, Dante Cicchetti provided us with excellent comments and supported us throughout.

The complex and often contradictory set of relationships and institutions leads to a great deal of uneven development of differing meanings about the self and the social world. It is thus not surprising that the social interactions represented in the self do not follow neat and organized forms. Instead, they are typically contradictory and conflictual, leading to very different abilities and complexity levels in different domains, even within a single relationship. We should begin to view this unevenness in development not as a pathological exception, but as a dynamic and creative aspect in the evolution of personality.

Such a perspective in personality formation makes the study of social cognition exceedingly interesting and challenging by promoting a more dynamic view of development (e.g., Case, 1988; Fischer & Ayoub, 1994; Noam, 1990) and demanding far more complex theories and empirical strategies than have been applied in the past. As a consequence, the study of psychological dysfunctions can work to uncover strengths and weaknesses in social-cognitive theories in both normality and pathology.

Thus, our goal in this chapter is not to "apply" a cognitive frame about self and relationships to the phenomenon of psychological dysfunctions, but to allow for transformations of theories and underlying paradigms that may provide insights into relationships among meaning-making, social interaction, and the development of psychopathological symptoms. In the process, it is the transformation, and not the application of theory, that is essential. Too often have theories been exported to more and more areas of application (e.g., Stimulus and Response theories, or cognitive models to education) without reflecting on the ways in which the new domain also requires a change in the underlying paradigm (e.g., Noam 1988a). This form of dogmatism also existed in Piagetian circles, where the excitement about the cognitive and social-cognitive principles led to a mushrooming of stage theories and applications in distant domains (e.g., animal love, vegetarianism). Instead, we need to pursue the question of how the study of psychological dysfunction has changed, or needs to change, our basic views of human development.

Using a series of examples, we argue that some, but by no means all, psychological disorders can be viewed as instances of normative social-cognitive development "gone wrong." Along with Rutter (1988) and others, we take the view that certain constellations of symptoms and syndromes (e.g., mania in bipolar affective disorders) may contain few elements of normal development. These symptoms might represent entirely different mechanisms than can be observed in the course of normative development. But most psychological symptoms, such as anxiety, behavioral problems, and mood disorders are not as clearly separable from states also found in the course of a person's growing-up.

Following this initial effort to outline distinctive ways in which theories of normal development can explain psychological dysfunctions, we begin by laying out a number of prototypical ways in which social cognition and psychological dysfunctions relate. We also review how notions of fixation and delay have customarily been invoked as a way of accounting for such phenomena as moral immaturity or social role-taking deficits. Next, we describe how early processes of development can be vertically or horizontally "encapsulated" (Noam, 1988a, 1988c, 1988d) in such ways as to yield still other clinically recognizable forms of psychological dysfunction. We conclude by putting forward developmental typologies of a number of disorders, focusing on borderline psychopathology and suicidality.

The research literature we build on for a discussion of the ways social cognition and psychopathology relate is the study of moral judgment, ego development, and role-taking. These developmental domains are chosen for review because most research efforts in social cognition and psychopathology have used these theory and measurement traditions. Our goal is not to provide an exhaustive overview of all the studies conducted, but to outline a broader path along which the studies of social-cognition and psychopathology might join to produce a full-fledged field, clinical-developmental psychology.

HISTORICAL REFLECTIONS

Disagreement about the relationship between theories of normal and deviant development has focused on how far this supposed "union" has already progressed. Nannis and Cowan (1988), for example, describe the arranged "marriage between the two fields" as an established fact, with "developmental psychopathology as its latest offspring." Santostefano (1990), seeing these matters as having advanced further, comments upon developmental psychopathology's recent "baptism," as do Nannis and Cowan (1988) who—perhaps losing sight of their initial metaphor—point to its "adolescent awkwardness." While there is disagreement about the exact nature of the union between theories of normal and deviant functioning, clinical and developmental theories are already very much intertwined. Keating & Rosen (1990) acknowledge this common perspective by commenting that "It is by now commonplace to assert that the study of normal development informs our understanding of atypicality and pathology and that the study of differences in development informs our understanding of normal development" (p. 4).

The notion that normative developmental theories can be put to work to explain psychopathology is far from new. In fact, among many developmental psychology's progenitors, the majority have emphasized the value of normative research and theory to a better understanding of psychopathology (e.g., Elkind, 1979; Kagan, 1989). Piaget and Inhelder (e.g., Inhelder, 1976), Kohlberg (Kohlberg, Scharf, & Hickey 1972), and their associates applied their theoretical models to specific forms of psychopathology. In so doing, they chose those pathologies that had the greatest potential to exemplify their developmental sequences. Thus, it is not surprising that "the Genevans" (e.g., Inhelder, 1966) studied mental retardation as a natural ceiling effect for the development of cognition. Similarly, the work on psychotic children (e.g., Ajuriaquerra, Inhelder, Jaeggi, Roth, & Sterlin, 1970; Schmid-Kitsikis, 1990) represented an attempt to understand the irrational as an instance of delayed logic, such as magical thinking still operant in the adolescent and adult.

Kohlberg's moral development theory (e.g., 1969, 1984) lent itself neatly to the study of delinquency. For centuries, antisocial activities have been viewed as problems in moral thought and behavior. In a variety of studies with prison populations, Kohlberg and associates found that the delinquent adolescents and adult law-violators often functioned at delayed, preconventional positions (for a review, see Jennings, Kilkenny, & Kohlberg, 1983, Noam & Young, 1990). These findings represented important real-life validations of the developmental model (e.g., finding links between judgment and action) and pointed to ways of intervention (i.e., to support development to the conventional developmental stages). But neither Piaget nor Kohlberg and their associates could explain with these studies and interpretations why so many individuals who are developmentally delayed are delinquent, nor why so many highly developed individuals can show antisocial and psychotic behaviors and other pathological symptoms.

These issues suggest that some problems in psychopathology could be quite independent of the developmental station. It is not hard to imagine, for example, circumstances under which persons of varying ages or developmental positions might fall victim to the same reign of terror, abuse, or adversity (e.g., Rutter, 1988). Under such circumstances, specific knowledge regarding the developmental stage or history of such individuals may count for very little. That is, there undoubtedly exists a number of deviant psychological reactions that naturally arise in response to general stressors, for which it ultimately does not matter that one happens to be old or young, or functioning at different developmental stages. Under such adverse circumstances, persons of greater or lesser developmental maturity may react in slightly different ways, but ultimately neither these problems, nor their solutions, are determined by matters central to the developmental process itself.

It is also quite possible that the causal explanation for later-arriving forms of psychopathology is to be found in certain traumatic and stressful events of early childhood. Such "early insult models" have been firmly in place in clinical circles throughout the greater part of this century, and were central to psychoanalytic fixation theory (e.g., Abraham, 1968; Freud, 1910). When Piagetian thinking became a dominant force in academic developmental psychology, some investigators steeped in both traditions (e.g., Anthony, 1976; Feffer, 1982; Wolff, 1960) became very interested in comparing and contrasting Freud's psychoanalysis and Piaget's genetic epistemology. These comparisons were driven by a recognition that both systems had significant strengths and weaknesses and that especially for the understanding of clinical issues, a new synthesis would need to produce a more comprehensive model.

Even Piaget, who is otherwise not credited for his interest in psychoanalytic theory and practice, claimed to have spent time, as we do now, "looking forward with great expectation to the emergence of developmental psychopathology as a product of the union between these two disciplines" (Piaget, 1975). In fact, Piaget was well acquainted with psychoanalytic thinking, heard Freud present, and underwent a personal analysis. But with few exceptions, especially his Sorbonne manuscript on the relationship between cognition and affectivity, Piaget's commitment was firmly focused on the development of thought. As we introduce a new clinical-developmental synthesis, the attempts to bridge cognitive and dynamic thinking can serve as both historical stepping stones and as a useful foundation to build on. However, clinical-developmental psychology draws on a wider set of tradition than introduced by Freud and Piaget.

Psychodynamic and Cognitive Theories

Many links between psychoanalysis and cognitive theory in Piaget's tradition have been found over the past three decades. These varied explorations have been especially important as they connect a sophisticated model of psychopathology with a significant developmental model of normal cognition. While these interparadigm comparisons and integrations posed many problems (e.g., different theoretical assumptions, different empirical methods), similarities in outlook promised important innovations (e.g., Feffer, 1982). These similarities included a focus on underlying, rather than manifest meanings about self and relationships, an emphasis on the developing nature of these meanings, and the centrality of logic and self-reflection in human growth and mental health. Because the link between social cognition and psychological dysfunctions can be enhanced by psychodynamic principles, we turn to the attempts that integrate psychoanalysis and cognitive theory to provide the literature for further in-depth explanations.

Conceptual Contributions

Odier's seminal work (1956) on the relationship between anxiety and magical thinking represents one of the first scholarly integrations between psychoanalytic thinking and Piaget's evolving paradigm. Odier believed that the psychoanalysts had neglected the study of the development of thoughts, while the genetic psychologists had overlooked affectivity, including its origins and impact on personality. He proposed that instead of treating these two schools of thought like two rivers that are condemned "never to meet," there is a need and a possibility for an integration. These two schools of thought complement and enrich each other in that they share the view that emotion and thought are neither different nor distinct from one another. On the contrary, "emotions pervade every aspect of life, and it is up to logical thinking to use them in a productive and healthy way. Every psychology that wishes to be clinical must be also genetic. Both methods must be used and then combined into what may be termed the genetic-analytic method" (pp. 32–33).

Thus, Odier suggested that some bridges are needed "across the river joining the intellectual and affective banks," in every major stage of development. In this spirit, he attempted to apply principles of genetic theory to the analysis of certain neurotic symptoms, such as anxiety. Accordingly, anxiety produces regression to the prelogical stage of infantile thinking, which is governed by "realistic tendencies" (infantile realism, in Piagetian terms, is the tendency to attribute one's own psychic structures to others, and to accept these attributes as real and absolute). Odier created a connection between child-like thinking and psychoneurosis in adults. Where the child realism originates from the inability to differentiate self and other, the parallel mode of thinking in the adult is externalism; that is, the adult is unaware of the projected elements of the self rather than unable to differentiate the self. This tendency for "reification" of ideas, perceptions, or sensations (e.g., making absolute reality of them) is common to children's thinking and to adults with neurotic symptoms such as nightmares or phobias. Hence, the phobia is a product of primary realism following both the laws of prelogical thinking and affectivity. Odier's suggestions to treatment, in light of these connections, is that "before attacking the adult beliefs, all the elements of the infantile structure which produced them must be analyzed" (p. 76). Thus, the therapist should attend first to the underlying pathological thinking structure by exploring the process of the regression itself rather than the consequences. By this call for therapeutic intervention utilizing both Freudian and Piagetian theories, Odier was showing one direction for a future clinical-developmental approach.

In a similar tradition, Wolff (1960) systematically compared Freud's psychosexual stages with Piaget's theory of six sensorimotor stages. He concluded that the two theories are essentially compatible, especially through the modification of psychoanalytic ego psychology. Along with Wolff, earlier psychoanalytic theorists (e.g., Hartmann, Kris, & Loewenstein, 1953), were especially concerned with the "conflict-free" sphere of the ego, which encompasses learning, perception, coping, as well as cognitive and emotional synthesis. By focusing on these ego capacities, rather than on sexual drive, psychoanalysis had come closer to Piagetian concerns.

Identifying compatibilities, James Anthony (1976) described both Freud and Piaget as epistemologists, developmentalists, and moralists. He cited four common theoretical commitments:

1. Moral sense is not innate, but acquired;
2. Acquisition of moral values takes place in the course of childhood;
3. Moral acquisition begins with external sources (parental injunctions) and is subsequently internalized; and
4. This shift leads generally from an external to an internal locus of control.

Basch (1980) has presented a model through which he modified the psychoanalytic notions of regression and repression in the analytic process from a cognitive and developmental perspective. Instead of using only one idea about repression, Basch suggested that there are a number of different ways in which experiences become repressed and available to consciousness. He believed that new cognitive abilities are related to what and how experiences, thoughts and feelings become part of the unconscious.

Greenspan (1979) and Greenspan and Lourie (1981) also integrated the Piagetian and psychoanalytic models applying their synthesis to clinical work with infants and young children. They showed that to a large extent the Piagetian stages that represent cognitive development are highly interactive with those psychodynamic stages that represent social and emotional development. By linking these cognitive and emotional processes, they described principles regulating ego boundaries—concepts that have proven highly relevant to clinicians.

Noam and Kegan (1982, 1989) have taken the psychoanalytic ideas of boundaries of the ego and the self and showed that, depending on the cognitive-developmental level, the shape of the boundary of what is taken as self and as other differs fundamentally. They suggested that clinicians use terms like boundaries, regression, and so on, in ways that take account of qualitative developmental differences emerging throughout the lifespan.

Malerstein and Ahern (1979) took the psychoanalytic idea of character fixation and introduced three character structures based on characteristics of the thought pattern described by Piaget. These three structures—the operational, the intuitive, and the symbolic—each represent the individual's most basic concerns and systems of processing interpersonal relations. Similarly, Santostefano's (1978) biodevelopmental perspective is a synthesis of ego psychology concerning cognitive controls (e.g., controls against aggression and depression) and Piaget's stages of intellectual development.

Recently, Furth (1987) has also related Piagetian and Psychoanalytic work. He, too, believes that there is a need to overcome the split between intellectual development and emotional development. Furth accepts the primary themes of Freudian theory and interprets them using Piagetian developmental framework. He stresses that behind any symbol or knowledge formation there is a necessary individual motivational base: "The new object of knowledge would have never been grasped unless its creator has a passionate personal relation to it that provides the drive and the commitment to risk the unknown and turn possibility into new ability" (p. 160). In light of this synthesis, Piaget's theory of knowledge acquisition appears to be social and emotional (unlike what it is traditionally assumed to be), while Freud's notions of the id, the unconscious, repression, and life and death drives lose their mystical quality and become part of a personal development of knowledge. Furth maintains that knowledge and emotion are closely related and both stem from the "biological evolution of human sociability" (p. 172).

Integrating Psychoanalytic and Piagetian Principles in Empirical Research: The Examples of Object Permanence, Defense, and Attachment

While conceptual discussions of psychoanalysis and Piagetian developmental psychology have yielded a slow, yet consistent, set of conceptual comparisons and creative integrations, systematic research has been less successful. An important exception is the systematic work of Decarie (1978), who studied the relationship between the Piagetian construct of object constancy and the psychoanalytic notion of object relations. She specifically considered how the timing of the development of internal representations (object permanence) parallels the development of the affective tie between the child and the mother.

More recently, Westen and Cohen (1993) have attempted to integrate a social-cognitive perspective with a psychodynamic one in their empirical analyses of the self in borderline personality disorder. They suggested that typical forms of object representations seen in psychoanalysis as occurring early (e.g., some forms of splitting) are, in fact, social-cognitive capacities of middle childhood and adolescence.

In Bowlby's ethological reinterpretation of psychoanalysis, we also find many cognitive elements. Most importantly, the idea of a "working model" of relationships which is both conservative, yet undergoes important updating in development has essential constructivist and cognitive elements. Many of the significant contributors to the longitudinal study of attachment (e.g., Main, Kaplan, & Cassidy, 1985; Sroufe, 1979) have written about the significance of cognition and self in the continued evolution of the working model of relationships (see also Noam, in press b).

One research group which has built heavily on a social cognitive perspective (Edelstein, Grundmann, Hoffmann, & Schellhas, 1992; Edelstein, Keller, & Schröder, 1990) explored the relationship between attachment patterns (e.g., secure or insecure) and cognitive development. They describe the cognitive consequences of insecure attachment (ambivalent or avoidant), chronic anxiety, and childhood depression. They hypothesized that these constraints "operate by limiting the exploratory or assimilatory activity of the individual" (p. 25). Furthermore, if the individual is chronically suffering from these conditions, he will be likely to experience a negative cumulative effect on cognitive development. Jacobsen, Edelstein, and Hoffmann (1992) differentiated insecure attachment from chronic anxiety and depression. While insecure attachment is conceptualized as a risk factor for producing an enduring maladaptive "working model" for interpretation of relationships and events, anxiety and depression are viewed as elements of such a working model. Edelstein argues that insecurely attached children who lack consistent parental support are often inhibited from exploration of their environment. Their fear of dealing with novel situations lead to withdrawal from external "epistemic objects" which, in turn results in deficiency in cognitive development. Edelstein writes, "Insecure children may have added difficulties confronting the novelty and stress implied in a venture entirely within the abstract realm of the mind: their model of novelty may be based on painful childhood experience with a deficient holding environment, causing panic in the face of the challenge, failure to engage in the cognitive task, or perhaps defensive reinterpretation of the facts that constitute it" (p. 29). Both depression and anxiety limit the individual attempts and strategies of exploration. Excessive anxiety often generate defenses that "paralyze" the individual's self-assured response to new situations. Depression, is even more destructive since it not only generates inadequate responses, but often involve a lack of will, a sense of hopelessness, and passivity.

In a longitudinal study following 95 subjects from age 7 to 17, Edelstein and associates found that the secure group was significantly more cognitively advanced, with formal operational thought often arising as early as age 12. In contrast, subjects who had avoidant attachment patterns were dramatically less cognitively developed, with most subjects barely having entered formal operation at age 17. Subjects characterized by disorganized attachment patterns seemed to exhibit the most problematic path of cognitive development as they rarely proceed beyond concrete operation. Edelstein concludes that "The age-equivalent developmental discrepancy increases steadily and cumulatively between groups as a function of the attachment pattern measured at age 7" (p. 28). Interestingly, it seems that at age 7 there is not much differentiation in cognitive level between different attachment patterns. However, with age the gap in cognitive development among the different groups increases.

The most active research relating cognitive and dynamic thinking has been in the area of defenses. Haan (1977) introduced a way of understanding adaptational processes from the perspective of Piaget's and Kohlberg's developmental theories of structure and cognitive transformation. Haan's view of the ego is one of a process of assimilation and accommodation to environmental demands restructuring thinking, feeling, and action. These ego processes are not themselves organized structurally but are expressions of a person's changeable forms of adaptation. Haan's taxonomy includes a hierarchy of ten generic processes (such as detachment, delayed response, and selective awareness), which are subdivided into defense coping and fragmentation.

Chandler and colleagues (Chandler, Paget, & Koch, 1978; Koch, Harder, Chandler, & Paget, 1982) studied the effect of parents' defense style on children's mental health. Their principal hypothesis was that when the child is forced to grapple with socioemotional circumstances that are structurally more complex than their own capacity, negative developmental consequences follow. A clear example of such structural mismatch is provided by typical outcomes of children who are obliged to first learn about the world of thoughts and feelings from adults who use maladaptive psychological defense styles. One of the adaptational problems that faces growing children is that of acquiring a set of conceptual tools for discussing affective experience. That is, children need to gradually grasp tacit rules of behavior such as "she acted that way because she was angry," or "he was afraid that he was unable to act," or more generally, "he showed otherwise unexpected behavior 'X' because of emotion or affect state 'Y'." Because it is generally believed that children are born into the world without such a tacit "belief-desire psychology" (Bartsch & Wellman, 1989) it is assumed that children learn about such matters from their parents.

In an effort to ground such intuitions, and set them in relation to what is already known about the maturing skills with which children gradually learn to decode the complexities of emotional experience, a systematic research effort was made to classify and order the different psychological defenses into groups of structurally similar transformations (distortions) of "truth" (Chandler, Paget, & Koch, 1978). Some defenses (e.g., denial and repression) appear to consist of only simple negations according to which an emotion (e.g., anger or fear) is merely replaced by its inverse (i.e., not angry or not afraid). In other defenses, such as reaction formation or displacement, feelings that actually unfold in one direction (e.g., I feel anger toward you) are transformed into their reciprocals (i.e., you are angry at me). Still other defenses (secondary projection, for instance) negate propositions such as "I feel attracted to you" by the double negation "you are attracted to me." The aim of the research was to understand these defense mechanisms as examples of different logical levels and try to understand their intergenerational transfer.

The research showed (e.g., Koch, Harder, Chandler, & Paget, 1982) that in the majority of the cases, the children whose parents regularly relied upon psychological defenses that were difficult to decode by the children (based on their cognitive capacity) would be more likely to fall victim to psychological disorders. The researchers concluded that such efforts to identify the interrelations between the various socioemotional hazards to which children are subject and their maturing abilities to come to grips with such experiences emphasize the importance of looking at, not only the developmental station of children at risk, but the variable complexities inherent in the social world.

In a study exploring the relationship between ego and moral development, and defense style, Noam (1984) used Vaillant's (1977) hierarchy of defenses which include immature defenses (e.g., projection, acting out), neurotic defenses (e.g., intellectualization, denial, reaction formation, repression, displacement), and mature defense (e.g., altruism, suppression). The goal in this study was to find whether the psychoanalytic developmental hierarchy which Vaillant posits and has shown to be an important tool in understanding adult development would (a) be observable in a group of adolescents and (b) be related to the social cognitive developmental hierarchy captured by ego and moral development. As hypothesized, Noam found significant negative associations between ego development and the immature and neurotic defenses and substantial positive associations with mature defenses. Similar correlations were observed between these defense groups and moral development.

In more recent studies, Noam and colleagues have used the Defense Mechanisms Inventory (DMI) (Gleser & Ihilevich, 1969; Ihilevich & Gleser, 1971), one of the most widely used measures of defenses. The DMI is a paper-and-pencil test in which subjects are asked to describe their reactions of ten hypothetical dilemmas. The responses involve a forced choice method, where each of the alternative responses represents one of five defense clusters entitled: Turning-Against-the-Object (TAO), Principalization (PRN), Turning-Against-the-Self (TAS), Reversal (REV), and Projection (PRO).

Several studies using the DMI and Loevinger's measure in normal populations have found a relationship between ego development and defenses. In a study of normal adolescents, Levit (1989) reported that Turning-Against-the-Object (TAO) was inversely related to ego development. In a study of normals (aged 10–77), Labouvie-Vief, Hakim-Larson, & Hobart, (1987) demonstrated that ego development is related to defenses even when the variance due to age is partialed out. Specifically, they found that TAO and PRO were negatively associated with ego development while TAS, REV, and PRN were positively associated with ego development. Although these investigators support the theoretical claims of relationship between defenses and development, a clear consensus has yet to emerge. This is especially so since not all studies have shown such a relationship between ego development and defenses (i.e., Vaillant & McCullough, 1987).

In a longitudinal study analyzing the development in a group of adolescents in a residential treatment facility, it was found that ego progressors differed significantly from nonprogressors in defense use (Noam, Recklitis, & Paget, 1991). Progressors not only demonstrated a significant decrease in psychiatric symptoms over the course of nine months, but also had a significant change in their use of coping and defense processes compared with the nonprogressors. The progressors showed a significantly greater increase in the use of five coping strategies than did nonprogressors. These five strategies were: investing in close friends, solving family problems, engaging in a demanding activity, seeking diversions, and self-reliance. The group of progressors also showed a significant decrease in Projection (PRO) and showed an increase in the use of Reversal (REV) a more internalizing defense. Taken together these findings suggest an important link between social cognition and defenses, a link that can provide a bridging construct between thought and feeling, adaptive and maladaptive cognition, as well as mature and immature meaning-making.

The attempts to integrate psychoanalytic and cognitive theories have generated considerable interest but have not led to true integrations of the two traditions. The paradigmatic differences have proven too great between unconscious motivations, affective development, and regression from a normal development model primarily concerned with cognitive organization and transformation.

In contrast to Piaget's work which was mainly dedicated to the uncovering of the development of intelligence and cognition (as it encompassed the changing meaning and understanding of physical properties), the social-cognitive perspective more strongly emphasizes those developmental dimensions that are important to psychodynamic and clinical focus, including an interest in self and self representations, the changing patterns of relationships, the interaction between cognition and emotion, the tension between impulsivity and self-reflection, and so on (e.g., Noam, Kohlberg, & Sharey, 1983). Because of this conceptual and empirical thrust, social-cognition is proving itself to be a powerful model in the evolution of a clinical-developmental psychology which we will sketch in the next section.

Social Cognition and the Emergence of Developmental Psychopathology

With the emergence of developmental psychopathology as a central theoretical concern and research focus, many new resources were brought to its study (e.g., Cicchetti, 1990). For example, psychoanalytic concerns and object-relation issues were now studied with rigorous methodologies characteristic of longitudinal attachment research (Ainsworth, 1982; Sroufe, 1979). Delinquency, psychosis, and mental retardation became far more researchable than in Piaget and Kohlberg's time through reliable interview schedules that helped in differentiating these disorders (e.g., Costello, Edelbrock, Dulcan, Kalas, & Klarie, 1984). Large-scale epidemiological studies with nonclinical samples have helped to provide baselines of symptom occurrence by age in the general population. And the strengthening of a risk and protective factor approach has helped to move the field away from a simple distinction between normality and pathology. This approach, which posits that most people are exposed to psychosocial risks whose effects on personality and health are better understood in terms of profiles of strengths and dysfunctions, (Garmezy, 1983; Noam, 1993; Rolf et al., 1990), is supported by the many creative studies of resilience in at-risk children and adolescents (Werner, 1990, for an overview). Finally, the biological and neuroscience revolution in psychiatry has created an immense potential for understanding the neural and physiological mechanisms underlying various forms of disorders.

This progress has also yielded sophisticated research perspectives regarding the continuities and discontinuities of disorders. Such a perspective not only addresses the occurrence of symptoms and syndromes, but also emphasizes the meaning the symptom choice has for the person. As contributors to this new perspective have made clear, it is not sufficient to address some characteristic list of adversity and risk factors in order to fully predict or understand a set of consequences. Instead, much has been shown to hinge upon the cognitive interpretations of such adverse events and the affective and attitudinal outlooks of those who suffer from them (e.g., Cicchetti, 1991; Gilligan, Rogers, & Tolman, 1991; Noam, 1988c; Perry, 1970; Rutter, 1990).

Fundamental elements of the constructivist approach could be found in the conclusions which Garmezy (1981) drew from his own pioneering work in stress research. Garmezy looked beyond simple behavioral responses to stress in children, instead viewing coping as an interaction between stressors and the individual who cognitively evaluates or imposes meaning upon potentially stressful events. Garmezy's new insight had critical implications to pathology and recovery. The focus shifted from the "objective" account of stress to a "subjective" construction of the meaning of the stressful event.

What remains surprising is that the call to take into consideration the interpretive mode with which life events, stressors, and risks are being faced, strengthens constructivist principals without taking into account developmental dimensions of these constructions. Only if we explore specific age-graded ways in which experiences are ordinarily processed can we truly understand their typical stressful dimensions. Are there typical ways in which children and adolescents interpret reality that leave them at risk for potential stressors? For example, the preschooler who has fluid boundaries between reality and fantasy is particularly anxious about the monsters that appear in his or her dreams. For most children, monsters and other fantasy figures become less threatening over time as they more clearly distinguish between "reality" and the products of their imagination. The firming up of boundaries between reality and fantasy in the school-aged child represents a loss of the "magical era" of early development. This loss of magical thinking simultaneously produces a significant gain in predictability and control over self and environment, and a significant decrease in stress about threatening objects thought to be real before (see Noam, in press a; Odier, 1956).

In the past decade, a number of investigators in the social-cognitive tradition (e.g., Noam, 1988a, 1988c, 1988d, 1992; Perry, 1970; Selman & Schultz, 1990) have begun to relate cognitive-conceptual *development* of self and self-other relationships to risk factors in the etiology of psychological disorder. This work has created the basis of an emerging clinical-developmental psychology, incorporating some of Werner's (1948) ideas while building on a variety of other theoretical, clinical, and research traditions. Werner's paradigm of differentiation and integration in development and psychopathology has proven very useful in a variety of domains, such as schizophrenia, as well as general health, and illness conception (e.g., Bibace & Walsh, 1981). In addition, our clinical-developmental orientation combines concepts from cognitive-developmental theory with Erikson's (1968) work on the meaning of life tasks, as well as developmental models of interpersonal relationships that have their origins in Sullivan's (1953) ideas. Although researchers in clinical-developmental psychology generally pursue different developmental strands (e.g., Basseches, 1984; Parks, 1986), explore a variety of disorders, and view the relationship between dysfunction and growth quite differently (e.g., Rogers & Kegan, 1990), assumptions that are shared and create important commonalties will be discussed next.

KEY PRINCIPLES IN CLINICAL DEVELOPMENTAL PSYCHOLOGY

In this section, we outline several key principles underlying approaches to clinical-developmental psychology. These ideas are used to organize the following sections of the chapter, which deal with the intersection of social cognition and psychological dysfunctions.

Mental Representations and Meaning Frames

For clinical-developmental psychologists, mental representations, especially the ways people represent themselves, their relationships, and their social world are essential in understanding the individual's psychological world. These representations are not fixed, but are continuously updated based on maturation and social interaction (e.g., Belenky, Clinchy, Goldberger, & Tarule, 1986), providing an important key to a developmental understanding of health and dysfunction. Many cross-sectional and longitudinal studies have shown that children, adolescents, and even adults shape and reshape their understanding of the social world. Piaget's early work on the moral judgment of the child (Piaget, 1932, 1965) was a milestone in uncovering developmental differences in how children construct and perceive social rules. Since then many cognitive perspectives of the social world have been introduced (e.g., Basseches, 1984; Broughton, 1978; Damon, 1977; Kegan, 1982; Noam, 1988a; Oser, 1991; Piaget, 1970; Selman, 1980). All of these studies have shared the view that developmental levels are best understood in terms of the complexity of the representation of social reality. What the new clinical-developmental focus brings to this body of knowledge is an interest in: (a) the tension between the constructive nature of these representations and their transformational potential; (b) the fluctuations between progress and regress in development; (c) the domain-specific achievements and lags which create complex profiles of individual functioning instead of overall capacities.

Normative Development

In order to understand the developmental dimensions in cognition and social cognition implied in psychopathology, we need prospective studies of what occurs in "normality." We are fortunate to have a variety of solid developmental studies that give us indications of what to expect with different populations. These normative studies have provided us with maps that are useful when we begin to explore clinical populations. These maps allow us to meaningfully apply the concepts of delay and deterioration that have proven important in the study of mental retardation, delinquency, psychosis, and other psychological and psychiatric disorders.

Clinical-developmental psychology is not, however, simply the application of normal cognitive development in the realm of psychological dysfunction. Instead, it reformulates a number of traditionally held assumptions of normative theory. Key among these reformulations is the view that various symptomatic expressions may take different forms as a function of the individual's level of development (e.g., Shirk, 1988b). Accordingly, the idea that higher stages of development are necessarily more adaptive, as implied by the theories of Piaget and Kohlberg, requires serious reconsideration. The same developing capacity that ordinarily produces more self-knowledge and adaptation can also be used for more complex forms of self-deception, and self-destruction. Similarly, the idea that overall psychological development necessarily occurs in neat and stepwise progressions must also be called into question, as some capacities in disordered populations seem to be able to progress, or indeed regress, while others do not (e.g., Noam, 1993). This issue will be addressed in fuller detail later on.

Age Chronology

From these assumptions about development come significant questions about the usefulness of chronological age in the study of development and psychopathology. There are evident and interesting age trends in the emergence of certain forms of psychopathology. For example, certain phobias and anxieties, such as separation anxiety and nightmares, are especially prevalent in early childhood and tend to decrease in middle childhood (e.g., Rutter & Garmezy, 1983). Suicide rates rise dramatically in adolescence, as well as a number of other disorders such as obsessive-compulsive disorders, depression, and conduct problems. Evidently, age can serve as a simple organizer of a range of underlying pathogenic processes. But the simplicity of any such age-graded approach is deceptive (see also Rutter, 1988; Wohlwill, 1973). As in the case of progressive development, we may quickly find that chronological age is by no means a guarantor that basic cognitive and social cognitive processes have actually occurred. For example, despite claims to the contrary, many adolescents and adults never achieve formal-operational thought. The notion that chronological age indicates certain cognitive development level is a common misapplication of cognitive-developmental theory. For example, while many adolescents function at the formal operational level, the existence of certain maturational capacities in and of themselves do not necessarily precipitate a transformation in cognitive development. Many adolescents continue to function at concrete operational levels and may remain at such levels for the rest of their lives (e.g., Noam, Powers, Kilkenny, & Beedy, 1990).

Consequently, if we use chronological age as a primary marker in the study of developmental psychopathology, those important variations evident among every group of normally developing individuals are missing. For that reason, clinical-developmental psychologists study the complexity of meaning systems along cognitive, social, and emotional lines and in relation to symptoms, syndromes, or types of maladaptations without primary reference to chronological age. Paradoxically, from such a perspective, chronological age gains even greater importance than it does it we use it as a simple developmental marker. Any focus on mental representation has to deal with the question of when developmental capacities have 'fallen behind' and should be called "delayed."

In addition, one has to assume that different cognitive and social cognitive capacities, even when they have the same formal structure, will have a very different function at different ages in the life span. For instance, it is quite typical for a person to reach a third-person perspective-taking position in early adolescence and to continue throughout adulthood using the same basic structure of thought. It is unlikely, though, that the basic ways in which the seventy-year-old adult reflects on self and other, and interprets present, past, and future events will be similar to the ways in which the fifteen-year-old goes about solving these same problems.

Lifelong Development

A very important aspect of clinical-developmental psychology is its ability to address issues of adult as well as child and adolescent development. There is a great deal of evidence that representations of self and others are transformed throughout the life span (e.g., Commons, Richards, & Armon, 1984; Parks, 1986; Valliant 1977). Many clinical perspectives, especially psychoanalysis, have attempted to build theoretical bridges between child and adult development and link them to psychopathology. For example, a child's ambivalent relationships to his or her parents are thought to be connected to later self-destructive behavior. Adult psychopathology in these traditions is therefore derivative of primitive internalizations of relationships and is viewed as signifying uneven or even primitive development in early "object relations" (e.g., Fairbairn, 1952; Klein, 1930, 1932).

The clinical-developmental perspective, by contrast, tends to be more focused on the continued transformations of the self and relationships. Throughout life, human beings have the capacity to create new forms of relationships to themselves and to others. While undoubtedly there are examples of "fixated" patterns of object relations, it is perhaps more representative that individuals regularly create new and restructure old concepts of themselves and others. That is, old relationships to one's self, one's parents and siblings, and meaningful others change throughout life, not only as a function of new interactions with these primary figures, but also because of transformation of one's cognitive structures, which can lead to different perceptions of the past. Important developmental changes can and regularly do occur far beyond childhood and adolescence and can serve as essential forces toward recovery as well as dysfunction (e.g., Baltes & Schaie, 1973; Noam, 1988d). This capacity for reframing relationships from birth to death, however, does not exclude the possibility that certain representations about past relationships remain unresolved and pathological.

Interpersonal Relationships

Quite apart from any consideration about how the past might be conceptualized in the present, clinical-developmental psychology is committed to an interactionist perspective which places a great deal of emphasis on relationships. Gilligan's (1982) theorizing and research on adolescent development has given this focus an enormous impetus and new direction as have certain lines of clinical work emerging from contemporary feminist theory (e.g., Rogers, 1991; Jordan, in press). While in traditional cognitive theories "relationships" tend to be viewed in rather abstract ways (e.g., interactions with the "environment"), the new clinical focus represented here has brought an interest in relationships for their own sake, especially relationships with significant others. This new emphasis on people and relationships came about at a time when the field of social-cognition began to put forward many important distinctions about how people represent other people and relationships (see also Smetana, 1989, 1991). While the focus on relationships is then shared with psychoanalyists and attachment theorists, the clinical-developmental perspective outlined here contributes to these approaches by tracing the transformations of how others and relationships are described and experienced across time (e.g., Bretherton, in press; Cicchetti, 1991; Cicchetti, Cummings, Greenberg, & Marvin, 1990; Noam, in press b). The fact that the level of representation of relationships is associated with types of symptoms and syndromes has created an important focus in clinical-developmental research.

A necessary first step in expanding a constructivist model of developmental psychopathology requires making a distinction between change and development in all the above categories and mental representations, dysfunctions, and adaptational capacities. Do symptoms change or develop? Do the interpretive tools of a person simply change, or do they undergo qualitative transformations? These are central questions for any developmental psychopathologist, which we will explore in the next section.

CHANGE AND DEVELOPMENT IN CLINICAL-DEVELOPMENTAL PSYCHOLOGY

The clinical-developmental framework we present here builds on the observation that the usual course of social-cognitive development regularly unfolds as a potential set of progressive, discontinuous, qualitative transformations that differ from simple, reversible, and directionless changes (Overton, in press). Development in this special sense is not aimless in its course, but ordinarily provides an increasingly better "fit" to a reality (von Glasersfeld, 1984). That is, while we are aware that talk of developmental "progress" can often mask poorly disguised convictions about spiritual or personal outlooks (Chandler, 1993), we are, nevertheless, committed to the views that: (a) both normal and deviant development are marked by novel and fundamental change; (b) our understanding is deepened by distinguishing those structures and processes that promote behaviors and actions from thought; and (c) even though the ideal path of human development may be unavoidably hidden from view, it is still possible to explore ways of being that are "better" or "healthier" than others.

From these shared constructivistic positions, we see children's maturing understanding of themselves and their social world to be subsumptive and increasingly consistent, which in turn provides them with a better fit to reality in general, and their own experiences in particular. However, it is incorrect to assume that any simple linear relationship exists between increasing sociocognitive complexity and adaptation or mental health. As later parts of this chapter will bring out, many psychological dysfunctions are associated with complex sociocognitive structures. This seeming contradiction—that higher developmental positions represent better adaptations and that they can be related to specific maladaptations as well—provides both challenges and opportunities to the sociocognitive approach to the study of developmental psychology.

This set of understandings about sociocognition development helps us to bracket our own perspective on psychological dysfunctions by: (a) setting important limits on what would qualify as disorders of development; (b) helping to understand the different ways in which developmental processes might take psychopathological turns; and (c) allowing for a revision of traditional cognitive-developmental principles based on the findings of developmental psychopathology research.

Trying to work out the important distinction between development and change is not, however, the same thing as clarifying what makes certain psychological disorders developmental and others not. In fact, the idea that maladaptive developments of some description "are the cause of subsequent psychopathology is so widely held," according to Lewis (1990), "that to argue its necessity seems redundant" (p. xiii). One part of moving beyond all such endorsements of the automatic importance of human development is to work toward some greater precision in sorting developmental from nondevelopmental change. We are quick to assume that, in contrast to ordinary, substitutive, either/or conceptions of contingent change, "true" developmental changes are somehow internal, quasi-permanent, structural or systemic, and directional. Central are distinctions such as that voiced by Watzlawick, Weakland, and Fisch (1974), between *first-order* and *second-order* changes, which also allow for the fact that certain simple, quantitative (first-order) additions or subtractions can be made to systems without such alterations leading to other qualitative (second-order) changes in that system itself. The benefit of such intentionally restrictive criteria is clear: It allows us to give up the hollow, if fashionable, position that everything about psychopathology is seen more clearly when viewed in its developmental aspect, while still insisting that not every way of becoming psychopathological need qualify as some second- or higher order form of truly "developmental" change.

In support of such exclusionary criteria, Overton and Horowitz (1991) makes a strong case that the language of "central states" adopted by at least some contemporary cognitive-behavioral approaches actually works to promote a confusion between more fully fledged developmental accounts of directional change and their own more contingent views. As Overton argues, such views are best seen as direct outgrowths of a still earlier version of "social learning" theories—according to which antecedent conditions and instrumental behaviors have traditionally been understood to be linked through associative chains assumed to have the same theoretical status as the overt matters to which they refer. Despite the fact that such heady rhetoric concerning so-called cognitive changes was invented in an effort to span the gap between observable inputs and outputs, such cognitive behavioral accounts never really escaped the antecedent-consequent conditions that have historically dominated traditional learning theories, and so need to be understood as all about first- rather than second-order developmental change.

The commentaries on psychopathology arising from this cognitive-behavioral tradition tend to explain psychological disorder in terms of the same deficiencies in the linear sequence of contingent relations that are assumed to account for the linkages thought to mark more progressive age-graded changes. Pointing out that cognitive-behavioral approaches to the study of developmental psychopathology are more about simple or first-order change is intended as a reminder that the changes to which they refer are meant to be about first-order mediational, as opposed to second-order structural-qualitative, or systemic change, and that the putting together of words like "cognitive" and "development" and "psychopathology" can be accomplished in ways that are quite different and altogether distinct from what is being attempted here.

Over and above the foregoing matter of what is and is not legitimately "developmental," even among those who work out of a common "constructivist" or "interpretive" tradition, there exists the related problem that there seems to be no common understanding of how such *directional* changes might somehow reverse their field to produce recognizable instances of psychopathology. Is pathology outside of this development? In other words, is it just orthogonal, or also causative—a risk factor in itself?

In particular, there are good reasons, more fully detailed below, to suppose that those directional and subsumptive forms of change that many developmentalists see as constitutive of real ontogenetic development can in no way be seen to operate in reverse—not for any empirical reason but because the explanatory mechanisms relied upon in development only make sense when operating in a "forward gear." This issue will be addressed later, but for the moment, we point out that among the natural limitations on the formation of a cognitive, or structural-developmental psychopathology is that regressive forms of certain developmental changes are simply inconceivable. This issue represents an important starting point for much needed theory transformation of the social-cognitive frame, which we will return to.

Development and Dysfunctions: Is Psychopathology Viewed as Primitive in Clinical-Developmental Psychology?

Having just addressed the incorrect notion that each and every sort of change, for better or worse, is necessarily a developmental change, we need to lay out the ways in which progressive qualitative development could conceivably take a wrong turn. We will address this issue by means of a typology of underlying mechanisms that give rise to different developmental disorders. The first and simplest is a broad class of psychological disorders that are said to arise when development *slows* or *stops*. The second broad class of developmental disorders are related to social-cognitive *complexity*. The third concerns those vertical and horizontal "encapsulations" that Noam (1988c) has shown to operate whenever developmentally earlier structures coexist with their more mature counterparts or give rise to entirely separate developmental lines within the self. Detailing how such developmental asynchronies of this more elaborate sort are the same as or different from delays in social role taking, ego development, or moral reasoning is one important theme to follow.

Some cautionary remarks are needed here. What has seemingly first come to mind, whenever matters of normal development and psychopathology are discussed together, is the possibility that symptoms that differentiate persons with and without psychological disorders may be directly traceable to some delay in the normal ontogenetic course. From Erikson (1950), Freud (1910), Werner (1948), and backward in time to a whole history of commentators upon the human condition, almost every developmentally oriented thinker has suggested that to be psychologically disturbed is to be somehow developmentally delayed. The fact that a similar idea has co-occurred in all of these seminal minds is not by itself a condemnation. It should alert us, however, to the prospect that the association between psychopathology and developmental delay may be less an empirical fact than a shared limitation of theoretical options. The psychopathological was viewed as the primitive or fixated, the healthy as the mature and complex. Accusations of this sort were leveled against Heinz Werner (1948), whose facile, and likely misunderstood, comments about possible similarities between the minds of children, the insane, and those living in certain preliterate societies are partially responsible for why many have tended to shy away from attempts to draw related parallels.

Still, it is critical to point out that accepting the view that serious developmental delays are equivalent to being pathological, in no way compels one to accept the opposite case. As a part of their general campaign against what they refer to as "developmental reductionism," (i.e., the tendency to reduce all psychopathology to developmental delay), Noam (1988d) and Borst and Noam (1993) have shown that continued development can produce new and more complex forms of dysfunction. Rogers and Kegan (1990) conclude that there is "no support for Werner's hypotheses that there is a reciprocal relationship between mental growth (developmental level) and mental health (the degree of psychiatric disturbance)" (p. 124). While perhaps an overstatement of the case, such a strong warning is useful if it leaves us less likely to simply reduce all psychopathology to developmental delay. Most theories of normal development are not up to explaining much of what is considered psychopathological because such theories often detail the linear course of supposed monolithic, universally trodden pathways (Van Den Daele, 1969), thereby considering failure in one aspect of life to be an indication for overall pathology. That is, except perhaps in the special case of mental retardation, many disorders held out as examples of development "gone wrong" are not actually intended to be illustrative of some across-the-board problem in developmental rate, but rather are examples of developmental asymmetries, where one dimension of development slows or stops while others go on progressing.

The ego development, role-taking, or moral reasoning difficulties often said to characterize delinquent or antisocial behavior are cases in point. Individuals acting in morally immature ways, or lagging behind normal developmental norms in social role-taking are generally held out to be of interest theoretically, precisely because they are not equally bad at everything. Such saw-toothed patterns of uneven developmental accomplishment are not a problem for more modern theories that see the ontogenetic course as being made up of potentially distinct developmental pathways (e.g., Case, 1984, 1985; Fischer, 1980). Piaget, for example, has been commonly read as such a champion of monolithic development. Some of his interpreters (e.g., Chapman, 1988) are quick to disagree and claim that developmental rate is a partial function of the materials idiosyncratically put at each individual's disposal, making for just those spotty kinds of developmental histories common to persons marked by some form of psychopathology. This leaves us in some confusion over whether fixations or delays in areas such as moral maturation, role-taking competence, or ego development should be regarded as problems in overall developmental rate or problems of developmental asynchrony.

THE INTERSECTION OF SOCIAL COGNITION AND PSYCHOLOGICAL DYSFUNCTIONS

Developmental Delay

Historically, the area of study most often viewed as the object of special attention while considering developmental delay is the course of moral maturation. Trading, perhaps, on the Judeo-Christian notion of original sin, or its still more ancient analogs, early childhood is often read as a kind of savagery over which the cloak of civilization, with its civilizing moral constraints, very badly needs to be drawn. Once headed down this interpretive pathway it begins to seem inevitable that all acts of barbarism are expressions of moral immaturity. Therefore, if patient X or inmate Y acts barbarously, then they must of necessity be morally delayed. On the strength of such reasoning those whom we now diagnose as psychopaths were once labeled "moral imbeciles," and remedies for the breaking of civil as well as religious law were thought to be the proper province of the church. Nor have such ideas particularly fallen out of fashion for the simple reason that many social scientists with more secular, but still presumably universal, accounts of moral maturation have replaced earlier ideas of divine law and divine guidance.

Beginning with the classical studies of Hartshorne and May (1928–1932) and of Kohlberg (1958), numerous social scientists, broadly concerned with possible relations between moral thoughts and morally relevant actions, have both searched for and commonly found close connections between varying sorts of antisocial behavior and evidence of developmental delays in the ordinary course of moral maturation. While a small corner of this research enterprise has been devoted to studying the role of developing moral knowledge in shaping everyday behaviors (e.g., Harré, 1983; Turiel, 1978; Smetana, 1989, 1991), the lion's share of such studies has sought to demonstrate some correspondence between criminal or delinquent behaviors, on the one hand, and immature forms of moral reasoning on the other (for reviews of this literature see Hayes & Walker, 1986; Jurkovic, 1980; Kohlberg & Candee, 1984; Noam & Young, 1990). The regular finding to emerge from the studies listed by these several reviewers is that, at least in the case of adolescents, adjudicated or institutionalized delinquents do demonstrate, almost without exception, serious delays in their ability to reason about moral matters in an age-appropriate fashion (see Chandler & Moran, 1990; Gibbs, Arnold, Ahlborn, & Cheesman, 1984; Haines & Ryan, 1983; and Jurkovic & Prentice, 1977 for discussions of the occasional exception of this standard finding). Beyond such attempts to link criminality and delinquency with any sort of fixation or delay in moral maturation, others have attempted to further narrow their sights by showing some relation between the seriousness of various criminal behaviors and the degree of accompanying moral immaturity (i.e., Kohlberg, 1976; Petronio, 1980; Thornton & Reid, 1982). Still others (i.e., Campagna & Harter, 1975; Chandler & Moran, 1990; Fodor, 1973; Jurkovic & Prentice, 1977; Trevethan & Walker, 1989) have extended such refocusing efforts by demonstrating a particular link between moral immaturity and the diagnosis of psychopathy.

Although generally correlational in character, the credence of this data, and the occasional finding (e.g., Kohlberg & Candee, 1984) linking advanced maturity of moral reasoning to reductions in criminality, is augmented by the fact that they are all consistent with a large body of well-received theory (e.g., Cleckley, 1976; Kohlberg, 1958, 1976) that predicts just those results obtained. All of this follows for the reason that the constructivistic paradigm common to Piaget and Kohlberg is not only intrapsychic in its focus, but also claims to be "interactive" or predicated on a constant exchange between actions in the world and internalizations. For this reason, thought and action, or cognition and adaptation, need to be seen as two sides of the same coin, and the split sometimes imagined to exist between them ought to be regarded as illusory. Higher stages, by these lights, are simply better adaptations—more mature forms of thought, as well as more adequate responses to the world.

Age-Stage Dysynchrony in Ego Development

As mentioned, Loevinger (1976), a theorist strongly influenced by a social cognitive perspective in personality theory, posits that each person has a customary orientation to self and world and that there are stages and transitions, independent of age, along which these "frames of reference" can be conceptualized. Cross-sectional and longitudinal studies provide evidence for individual differences and individual change patterns in adolescent and adult ego development along the sequence outlined by Loevinger (e.g., Hauser, 1976; Loevinger & Wessler, 1970; Redmore & Loevinger, 1979). There is a growing body of research investigating the relationship between ego development and maladaptive behavior. Although developmental approaches to psychopathology have often focused on the description of age-based chronologies of symptoms and disorders (e.g., Rutter & Garmezy, 1983), there is increasing interest in approaches that go beyond age as the central developmental variable (Achenbach, 1982; Kazdin, 1989).

Noam and associates at the Harvard-McLean Hospital (e.g., 1984, 1988, 1990, 1992) have conducted research demonstrating different forms and expressions of pathology at different levels of ego development. For example, a large group of hospitalized adolescents were studied and 90% were found to be delayed (Noam et al., 1984; Noam & Valliant, 1993). Similar results were found comparing moral development in this sample of adolescents where the great majority of hospitalized adolescents were reasoning on preconventional levels and the majority of high school students on conventional levels. These findings supported the theoretical and clinical view that developmental analyses might prove a useful framework to address psychopathology as, at least in part, an instance of "age-stage dysynchrony."

Tasks of a given life phase can be approached in very different ways, depending on the frame of reference or meaning applied at a given ego stage. Important adolescent phasic requirements, such as reworking the relationships with parents and other authority figures and the inevitable anxieties and frustrations associated with integrating into the peer group, are especially difficult at lower stages of ego development. The self-protectiveness of the earlier developmental positions, or the lack of impulse control, while developmentally adequate at earlier phases in the life cycle, become inadequate for coping with adolescent issues. The conformist level brings with it important developmental gains: the establishment of mutuality, the ability to curb impulses, and the delay of some need gratification. These gains bring out new and more complex abilities to deal with adolescent tasks and conflict situations. Thus, a lag in ego development can create severe problems in the resolution of phasic life tasks (Noam et al., 1984). Furthermore, delay in one phase of development can carry over and increase ego vulnerability, which in turn exacerbates the delay in subsequent phases of development.

Aggressive behaviors are among the most widespread and rapidly increasing problems of today's adolescents and are especially present in the delayed developmental positions (e.g., Kazdin, 1987). In clinical populations, the most common psychiatric diagnosis among adolescents is conduct disorder (Rutter & Giller, 1984), which often includes physical aggression as a primary symptom. In a study of normal adolescents, 35% reported having committed an assaultive act (Feldman, Caplinger, & Wodarski, 1983).

While many studies have examined the relationship of neurological and diagnostic variables to adolescent aggression, few studies have attempted to show the role of personality development in the expression of such behaviors. If conduct disorders or other aggressive behavioral problems are the result of a failure to develop in accordance with "major age-appropriate societal norms" (American Psychiatric Association, 1987, p. 53), it is essential to look at aggressive behavior in light of what is known about children's normal development. In studies of adolescents, a significant delay in ego development has been found with both delinquent (Frank & Quinlan, 1976) and psychiatric groups (Noam, 1984; Noam et al., 1984, Noam & Houlihan, 1990). Building on these earlier findings, Recklitis and Noam (1990) conducted a study to examine how ego development was related to specific aggressive behaviors in a group of adolescent psychiatric patients. Ego development was negatively associated with aggression, even when age and gender were accounted for. Subjects who were assaultive during hospitalization had lower levels of ego development than those who were not. These various studies demonstrate that early forms of ego development, also known as "preconformist," significantly raise the risk for aggression, delinquency, and other behavioral and externalizing disorders. The findings point to an important link between the frame of meaning a person uses to understand self and relationships and typical, often destructive, behavior patterns. By uncovering this link between thought and action, we are one step closer to creating interventions that are geared both to supporting social-cognitive development and new adaptational styles.

Early Developmental Forms of Role-Taking

Moral and ego development are not the only areas of social-cognitive functioning within which problems of developmental delay can occur, or about which psychopathologists have maintained a serious and long-standing interest. Perhaps because of the emphasis that Baldwin (1925), Mead (1934), and Piaget in his earlier work (1926) placed on egocentrism as a matter in the course of cognitive development, the study of developing social role-taking competence began to emerge in the 1960s and 1970s (e.g., Enright & Lapsley, 1980; Hudsen, 1978; Rubin, 1978) as a common meeting ground for child clinical and developmental scholars, who had begun to take seriously the prospect that theories of normal development (such as those of Baldwin, Piaget, and Werner) were critical to any deep understanding of psychopathology. As mentioned, some took as their point of entry the possible connections that might obtain between the "undifferentiated," "pre-operational," or "magical" thoughts of preschoolers and the thought disorders of the psychoses (e.g., Anthony, 1958, 1970; Cohen, 1974, 1958; Feffer, 1967; Odier, 1956; Rapaport, 1960). Others began programs of research meant to bring out the ways that varying forms of lesser psychopathology (e.g., delinquencies, impulse disorders, psychopathy) might be traced to delays in the rate at which young persons are scheduled to abandon their earlier egocentric ways in favor of other more mature and "sociocentric" displays of role- or perspective-taking competence (Rubin, 1973; Selman, 1980).

Early works by Feffer and Gourevitch (1960), Elkind (1967), and Flavell, Botkin, Fry, Wright, & Jarvis (1968) were quickly joined by many related contributors (Chandler, 1972, 1973a, 1973b; Chandler, Greenspan, & Barenboim, 1974; Coie & Pennington, 1976; Higgins, 1981; Kurdek, 1978; Selman, 1971, 1975, 1980; Selman & Byrne, 1974). Although differing in small details, the common finding of these investigators, was that, when compared to their undiagnosed, better "adjusted" age-mates, middle school children and adolescents who had been earmarked as somehow pathological were also characterized by marked delays in coming to a mature capacity to take other people's roles and perspectives. Further confirming this close association between persistent egocentrism and a broad spectrum of acting out problems, such as impulsivity, delinquency, and so on, is the fact that several intervention studies (e.g., Chalmers & Townsend, 1990; Chandler, Greenspan, & Barenboim, 1974; Gaffney, 1984; Iannotti, 1978; Kennedy, 1984; Rosen, 1974) demonstrated that therapeutic steps taken to upgrade the substandard role-taking skills of persons with manifest socioemotional difficulties were uniquely associated with notable improvements in the social competence of these troubled youths.

Selman and colleagues made the link between social cognition and behavior in a number of studies of children's level of interpersonal understanding, or social perspective taking, and interpersonal negotiation strategies in real-life interactions (e.g., Selman, 1980; Selman & Schultz, 1990). The studies demonstrated that there is a positive relationship between level of reflective understanding and the level of behavioral negotiation strategies used with other children. Children who were at developmentally early levels of reflective interpersonal understanding were more likely to use developmentally less advanced negotiation strategies. They also appear to be more withdrawn or aggressive when their needs were not met. Children at higher levels were more likely to use age-appropriate negotiation strategies such as working collaboratively with peers which, in turn, facilitated positive responses and increased capacities to share experiences. A clinical intervention called "pair therapy," in which the therapist treats two children who are considered developmentally lagging behind their peers, simultaneously by helping them to establish a cooperative relationship and learn new negotiation strategies (Selman & Schultz, 1990), was introduced. We will return to this form of therapy in the intervention section.

Complexity versus Maturity in Development: Social-Cognitive Complexity in Psychopathology

As we have seen, Kohlberg (1984) called the sequence and measurement of moral development "moral maturity," a term that implies a combination of cognitive complexity and adaptive abilities. Like in Piaget's work, every stage is defined by a new and more complex logic, in the sense of incorporating earlier structures into a more encompassing unity. Kohlberg considered this new gestalt function not only as a more complex form of understanding the moral world but simultaneously as a more adaptive way of referring to and interacting with the social world. Thus, in Piaget's and Kohlberg's models, higher stages are better stages. But better in what way? What is a better moral judgment? Is it logically more coherent and complex, or better in adaptive terms? The paradigm of Piaget-Kohlberg and many social-cognitive theories is not only intrapsychic; it claims to be interactive, consisting of a constant exchange between internalizations and actions in the world. For that reason, the split between thought and action, cognition and adaptation cannot be firm; they are two sides of the same coin. Higher stages are defined also as better adaptations, more mature forms of thought as well as more adaptive responses to the world.

Piagetian principles of structural wholeness, sequentiality, and hierarchical integration have been applied to social cognition as if they were dealing with the development of cognitive operations. Building on Piaget's and Kohlberg's foundation, a group of theorists we have called "maximalist self theorists" (Noam, 1990, 1992) (e.g., Fowler, 1981; Kegan, 1982; Loevinger, 1976), constructed abundant distinctions about cognitive categories for understanding the self, such as interpersonal relationships, faith, and many other developmental domains. Because the area of study had become so much broader than in the original moral judgment work, firmer distinctions about psychological functions should have been drawn when venturing out in such breadth (see also Broughton & Zahaykevich, 1977). Instead, the same basic stage categories had to hold many more adaptive processes and cognitive functions.

Among the maximalist theorists, it was quite literally assumed that each stage transformation was reorganizing broad categories of self and personality into a new and structured whole (e.g., Loevinger, 1976). But since more and more contents have been included in the models, it was incorrect to assume that a stage change would reorganize and transform *all* of these aspects of self and personality as these theorists claim. And even within one more closely defined developmental arena it is quite possible that important discrepancies in developmental perspective exist. Hence, since the self is viewed as more complex and developed, there seems to be a need to change the traditional model of a unified stage to a more flexible model that allows for uneven transformation from one developmental point to another. Evidence for this skepticism exists even in the narrow cognitive realm where studies show that some cognitive capacities can transform while others do not (e.g., Fischer, 1980).

Psychopathology consists in part of serious disequilibrations and maladaptions (e.g., fragmentation under stress, inability to act willfully, difficulty tolerating ambiguity, projecting inner conflict onto others) associated not only with the lower levels of ego and self-development but also with complex ones. We have argued that the developmental point of view can help overcome the widely held position that psychopathology should be equated to developmentally primitive cognitions, emotions, and behaviors (e.g., Noam, 1984, 1988d, 1990). It has also proven empirically untenable, to view psychopathology as a phenomenon of developmental transitions (posited for example by Kegan, 1982). A great deal of psychopathology can be observed in individuals who function solidly within a given developmental position. Many people organize their reality from within one rigidly organized form of knowing that their problems relate to the inability to flexibly understand and experience themselves and others.

Thus, complex developmental forms of understanding reality do not necessarily indicate better mental health. Were we to speak of a more complex self, without any interest in mental health issues, we could understand high stages as better (more complex) stages. However, definitions of complexity go hand-in-hand with implicit descriptions of better mental health even if the theorists view development and mental health as unrelated (e.g., Rogers & Kegan, 1990). One has only to read a variety of cognitive-developmental stage descriptions (e.g., Loevinger & Wessler, 1983; Kohlberg, 1984) to see that earlier positions are viewed as weaker (e.g., impulsive, deceptive, projective, grandiose) and more mature stages are labeled in terms of strengths (e.g., capable of intimacy with boundaries, tolerant, empathic, accepting).

Each new developmental position of the self was considered simultaneously a cognitively more complex form of perspective-taking and a more adaptive form of "being in the world." The more complex self was viewed as the more mature, integrated, adapted self. This idea was in part rejected (Loevinger, 1968), but moral judgment theory created the basic architecture for these self theories, at first elegant and convincing, yet upon closer scrutiny, problematic and confusing. For one could not truly account for the fact that so-called mature levels of development could be levels of entrapment of the self, procedures of hating the self more elaborately, and contexts for rejecting others on increasingly sophisticated grounds (see, e.g., Dobert & Nunner-Winkler, 1994; Noam, 1988a). Additional lines of research that speak out especially strongly against traditional views of the usual growth process are Berkowitz (1992), Boyes (1987), Chandler (1975), Chandler, Boyes, and Ball (1990) and King, Kitchner, Wood, and Davidson (1989). These investigators point out ways in which the ordinary developmental course not only moves young persons away from the hazards of egocentric and absolute thought, but also routinely carries them dangerously close to excessive self-doubts and risk of "epistemological loneliness" that have been shown to trigger problems in identity formation and to serve as breeding ground for various self-destructive impulses.

How is it, then, that one can move up in a developmental sequence which also addresses positive mental health and, in fact, end up more seriously disturbed, disorganized, symptomatic, or maladapted than in earlier developmental positions?

Addressing this question, Borst, Noam, and Bartok (1991) conducted a study investigating the connection between ego development and suicidal behavior in a group of hospitalized adolescents. One important finding was that increased ego development did not, in most cases, protect these adolescents from suicide. On the contrary, the data showed that with developmental complexity, psychopathology became more internalized and less action oriented. Internalization led to greater self-blame and depression which in turn led to increase in suicidal behavior. In contrast, subjects who functioned on lower developmental level, showed more externalizing behavior, namely, greater acting out as well as a tendency to blame others for their own problems. Another approach to studying the developmental impact of ego complexity was pursued through studying the differences between depression (affective disorders) and delinquency/aggression (conduct disorders) and mixed conduct-affective problems using adolescent psychiatric nosology and measurement. Analyses revealed that patients diagnosed with affective disorder were more likely to be functioning at the conformist stages of ego development than those with conduct or mixed, conduct-affective diagnoses (Noam, Paget, Bartok, & Borst, 1994).

These results suggest that there is a need to view developmental delay not only as risk, but also as a protective factor. For many adolescents who have been abused, hurt and seriously disillusioned, the self-protective capacities at the preconformist level provide an important shield. The developmental move to the conformist level entails becoming more vulnerable to others as the self defines itself more deeply in relation to expectations of and identifications with others. Clinically, this is more often experienced by adolescents as regressive and as putting them again at the mercy of potentially abusing others.

These studies challenge the idea that higher stages are, in fact, more adaptive, a position supported by Loevinger when she states that psychopathology is possible at any stage (Loevinger, 1968). For example, a person may use more advanced intellectual and social capacities to develop a consistent theory of self, but one that is based on self-hate and self-rejection. This position should lead to viewing ego development, not as a sequence moving toward more *maturity* and integration, but toward more *complexity.* That is, development can lead to more complex reasoning but not necessarily to more adaptive judgments and behaviors.

Fischer and Ayoub (1994) and Calverley, Fischer and Ayoub (in press) conducted a set of studies in collaboration with Noam, which support the observation that pathology can be very complex (as opposed to primitive). These researchers explored the patterns of splitting and dissociation in normal and maltreated children and how these patterns are indicative of developmental pathways for the self in relationships. Specifically, Calverley, Fischer, and Ayoub (1994), compared sexually abused adolescent girls to nonsexually abused girls in the way they perceive themselves and the world. They found that sexually abused girls attributed significantly more negative characteristics (such as badness) to their core selves, were significantly more depressed, and showed a greater "polarized affective splitting" (e.g., described the real self as "happy," "sad," "lonely," "good" without apparent conflict) than nonabused girls. However, although the sexually abused group clearly showed more emotional disturbance, they showed no evidence of developmental delay—"To the contrary [the sexually abused girls] produced developmental levels that were the same as nonabused and better" (p. 207). Fischer et al. concluded that sexual abuse, or any kind of traumatic experience for that matter, does not necessarily cause delay in development. Rather, it leads to *different paths* of adaptation. The abused girls seem to adapt to their reality in ways that are as complex as the nonabused girls. But because they have experienced different and extreme objective conditions in many aspects of their lives, their unique paths of adaptations may look "pathological" or "strange" to an outside observer. Fischer et al. concluded that, "contradictory to traditional theories of psychopathology as developmental delay . . . sexual trauma apparently does not delay overall cognitive development but, instead shifts processing to create alternative developmental pathway. Instead of not growing up, sexually abused girls grow up differently" (p. 209). Thus Calverley et al. conclude that traumatic experiences are not fixated but transformed throughout development, producing ever more complex splitting at what the authors call "level of abstractions and identity constructions."

In regards to patients with multiple personality disorder, Fischer and Ayoub (1994) further suggest the presence of advanced skills in pathology. Fischer et al. suggest that the mind consists of "many distinct control systems that are strongly connected with each other, but not coordinated or integrated" (Fischer & Ayoub, 1994, p. 6). Accordingly, he posits, as we do, that in a "fragmented mind" coordination and integration are considered steps toward development. In multiple personality disorder, there is an apparent disintegration that may be mistakenly diagnosed as a lower developmental level. However, according to Fischer's ideas about the "naturally fractionated mind," the person has first to learn to coordinate experience and meaning before he or she can separate and dissociate it. In this light, the dissociative symptoms observed in people with multiple personality disorder are not regressive; rather they can be viewed as indication of complex skills. The multiple "personalities" are not independent, but connected in ways that utilize sophisticated skills. Fischer lists three of these skills: the ability to actively separate the personalities, the ability to switch from one personality to another and relate the two, and the ability to influence/affect each other (e.g., in action, memory, experience). Hence, these two studies further demonstrate that in many cases pathological symptoms are not manifestations of regression or delay, but actually suggest developmentally complex and advanced skills.

Similarly, Schorin and Hart (1988) discuss the ways in which self-understanding influences anorexic girls. Building on a model of self development (Damon & Hart, 1982), they observed that anorexic girls deviated from nonanorexic girls in their subjective sense of volition and individuality. Their understanding of individuality and volition seemed to be less mature (i.e., qualitatively different) than that of the control group. For example, they defined individuality in terms of others not doing or not wearing the same things as they did. Thus, they tended to use lower level reasoning about individuality based on actions and material possessions, excluding psychological dimensions. But relevant to our discussions about complexity in psychopathology, the anorexic girls also differed from normal girls in their self-understanding regarding their relationships with their mothers. When asked "What are you like when you are with your mother?" (Schorin & Hart, 1988, p. 181), they tended to describe how they *felt* in the presence of their mothers unlike the girls in the control group, who tended to describe the way they communicated. This pattern may indicate that the anorexic girl perceives herself as an ineffective communicator; she does not use unevolved forms of thought. When anorexic and nonanorexic girls were asked how they thought their mother would describe them, the anorexic girls believed that their mother would describe qualities related to competence (e.g., successful, intelligent) whereas the nonanorexic believed that their mothers would describe them in terms of autonomy and maturity (e.g., independent, reliable, patient). These results show that anorexic girls differ from controls in several dimensions of self-concept (e.g., volition, individuality, effectiveness) in relation to peers and mothers. Consequently, Schorin & Hart argue that, ". . . anorexic girls' cognitive understanding of themselves may be as important to . . . [the] interpretation of their difficulties as their early history, intrapsychic conflicts, affective experiences, or environmental reinforcements" (p. 182).

This line of work is very promising in its combination of theoretical exploration and empirical fact-finding. Fischer, Calverley, and Ayoub and Schorin and Hart take a strong position against the traditionally held view in psychoanalysis and most other clinical circles that psychopathology is primitive and related to early developmental fixations. (Even in cognitive behavior therapy, where one finds less of a commitment to early development, self-attributions underlying depression, such as global thinking, are viewed as "child-like.") Our own ego development work, has also stressed the importance of viewing psychological dysfunctions as evolving to more complex developmental levels.

However, the differentiation from models that stress delay and fixation, should not lead to a dichotomous view on these matters (either primitive or developmentally sophisticated). There are complex symptom expressions that have their roots in childhood. There is also in some symptoms and psychopathology an experience of "time frozen," of traumatic experiences creating a constriction and rigidity that defends against further growth. There is also, as noted above, a strong indication from many cognitive-developmental studies that delay and psychopathology often go hand-in-hand. Thus, we should work towards models that allow us to move freely between a concept of delay and regression, and one of complexity and differentiation in psychopathology.

Most interestingly, many forms of psychopathology, including trauma, multiple personality disorders, and anorexia, are simultaneously expression of delayed functioning and sophisticated expressions of developmental capacities. We will return to this important issue in the section of vertical and horizontal encapsulations. It is impossible to answer these difficult questions without a detailed and sophisticated theory of biography, a life history that evolves with development.

In summary, this recent line of research suggests high levels of self complexity in some forms of psychopathology, necessitates distinctions which has traditionally been overlooked in developmental theories. Noam (1992) has called for distinguishing between *complexity* and *maturity* in development. Maturity is viewed as the relationship between the *complexity of judgments and the capacity to transform judgments into positive adaptations.* Complexity without this ability to react flexibly to different situations and to think productively serves as segway toward more self-alienation and negation of a basic vitality in development. This insight might be one of the most important contribution clinical-developmental psychology is making for future work into the atypical and normal course of development.

Beyond the Delay-Complexity Distinction: Life History and Fluctuations in Development

The problem is that growth models, of the sort articulated by Piaget or Kohlberg, are widely assumed to be progressive in character disallowing the occurrence of "structurally regressive forms of behavior" and thought (Bearison, 1974, p. 22). It is widely known that individuals regularly behave in ways that are of a quality well beneath their best ability. Short of jettisoning any theory that threatens to render such seemingly regressive steps impossible, one can choose, as Bearison did, to interpret such instances of apparent regression as merely symptomatic of a widening gap between competence and performance, or in ways that we document below, one can seek new theoretical ways of allowing for the possibility of regression within otherwise progressive models of development.

This suggests that certain forms of psychological dysfunction might qualify as instances of what classic Piagetian theory would have described as horizontal decalage. The present section shows how attention to developmental asynchronies of a different sort can help us to better understand other ways in which one's mental health can become divided or disintegrated. In particular, we will turn our attention to certain asynchronous processes that Noam (1986a, 1986b) has referred to as "*encapsulations.*" But in order to address these asynchronies of development in detail, we will have to pursue issues of life history and biography in greater theoretical depth.

The Lost Dimension in Social Cognition: Biography

Is there a living biography of earlier self-other relationships that continues to shape the person's choices, experiences, and self-understandings? If so, how does this biographical dimension of self relate to the development of role-taking and new internalizations throughout life? To try to answer these questions, we must trace simultaneously the developmental line of self-other complexity (schemata), which has been the topic of this chapter to this point, and a biographical structure (themata), which we will now deal with. (See Noam, 1990 for a detailed discussion of the schemata/themata distinction.)

Cognitively based theorists have overlooked the central structuring activities of the self by defining the epistemic self as the sole representative of structure. In the process, the cart was placed before the horse, life history became content to the structure of the epistemic self. The five or six generalized perspectives that define moral, ego, or role-taking development were viewed as the organizing principles of that which "makes meaning" in a person's life. Epistemology replaced life history. But as cognitive ideas become applied to research on the life course and to clinical questions, we observe the power of another narrative—a biographical one. We cannot consider it a cognitive structure in any strict way, but it reveals a pattern, produces meanings, and provides typical motivations. Biography is not necessarily organized by the most mature social-cognitive structure of ego, self, or personality, but it must be viewed as other than content in a Piagetian sense. To call it content is misleading since it is coherent, systematic; it *organizes* action, cognition, and emotion.

Others have also expressed their doubts about the adequacy of cognitive-structural interpretations in the study of the self. Bruner (1986), for example, states that while we know a great deal about a paradigmatic mode of thinking (organized by cognitive, logical, mathematical, and scientific principles) we still know little about "narrative structure." This structure, he states, follows the logic of a story line about "the vicissitudes of human intentions."

A central theoretical impetus for this broadened constructivist perspective has also come from Habermas' philosophical work (1979). He states that (a) a theory of self requires dimensions of biography since the unique experiences of one life symbolize the generalized patterns that span across lives and (b) a focus on biography necessitates an understanding of ways in which earlier selves become incorporated and integrated into the present self organization.

Habermas' starting point in discussing the self is the notion of ego-identity. For Habermas, identity is the sociological equivalent of the ego or the self. It refers to the symbolic structures that create continuity and consistency across different social contexts and social interactions in accordance with the biographical nature of the person. He defines ego-identity as proving itself

> in the ability of the adult to construct new identities in conflicting situations and to bring these into harmony with older superseded identities so as to organize himself and his interactions—under the guidance of general principles and modes of procedure—into a unique life history. (1979, pp. 90–91)

Identity and self include the tension between universal stages and the uniqueness of the one life. In addition, for Habermas, self and identity include typical patterns of adaptation, coping, and an array of defenses. They also involve ways to communicate competently within an evermore complex radius of social interactions.

Habermas sees psychoanalysis as possessing a powerful method of producing enlightenment through self-reflection: Actions and nonverbal behavior of a person belie what is expressively stated even though they are the expressions of the subject. Habermas states that "their symbolic character, which identifies them as split-off parts of a symbolic structure, cannot be permanently denied. They are the scars of a corrupt text that confronts the author as incomprehensible" (p. 127). He describes rules through which the private communication becomes "public" (communicated). Through therapy systematic distortions are traced back to two developmentally separate stages of symbol organization. In other words, a previously inappropriately symbolized text becomes resymbolized; in the process, it becomes reappropriated as a formerly lost part of the self.

In contrast, cognitive-developmental ideas imply only one symbolic structure: the symbolic and rational one. In the process, Kohlberg and the self-theorists in his tradition lost the other, "developmentally separate stage of symbol organization." That Habermas keeps this second dimension of self alive ends up providing him with a significantly larger radius of exploration than does the social-cognitive stage conception.

The analysis of the self, for Habermas, can occur in a systematic way not only because we have theories of the "epistemic self" traced by Piaget, Kohlberg, and Loevinger but also because the self follows what he calls a "causality of fate." In the tradition of Hegel, he distinguishes "causality of fate" from "causality of nature." Causality of fate is biographical in the sense that motives, meanings, and actions are laid down in a life history and are filtered through the symbolic organization of the mind. This inner world of self does not follow laws of nature, but is an invariance of life history that can be dissolved by the power of reflection.

The belief in man's ability to overcome this "causality of fate" places ego identity in the dominant position in Habermas' overall theoretical considerations about autonomy and emancipation. In relationship to the moral domain, Habermas repeatedly states that principled moral judgment is an insufficient condition for freedom from conventions. He states:

> as long as the ego is cut off from its internal nature and disavows the dependency on needs that still await suitable interpretations, freedom, no matter how much it is guided by principles, remains in truth unfree in relation to existing systems of norms. (Habermas, 1979)

This passage raises the question of how one can evolve a social-cognitive theory of self and morality where both phenomena are not disembodied from their own history and part of their internal nature. This is indeed, a central task when moral judgment and action are addressed in terms of the development of self and should be important to our discussions. Habermas states that the earlier resolutions of developmental crises are critical for whatever present-day solutions the self has available. However, a specific proposal for a theory that details the relationships between transformational and biographical dimensions of self remains outstanding. Even Erikson, who combines an interest in early development with a commitment to the developing ego's changing psychosocial tasks, neither systematically describes nor adequately explains their influence upon each other (Erikson, 1968). We now explore the issue of biographical dimensions of self in greater depth as they have been introduced in a number of papers (e.g., Noam, 1990, 1993, in press).

Themata: Biography Dimensions of the Self

Despite situational variability and powerful developmental discontinuities, each person has core existential issues that help organize the many events, relationships, and contexts encountered in a life. Because of the basic organizing nature of these themes, one can view them as biographical structures and call them *themata.* Gerald Holton has used the term with a different connotation to describe themes in the history of scientific discoveries. In the present context, themata refer to life themes that create a frame of knowing, experiencing, and relating in the ongoing relationship between person and environment. They further convey four points:

1. Multiple life experiences are organized into key interpersonal and intrapsychic patterns of adaptation;
2. These patterns can be described and defined in terms of some basic existential themes;
3. Life themes have a certain enduring quality, spanning across time and space;
4. Life themes contribute to the organizing of behavior, cognition, and affect.

This last point especially calls attention to the incomplete position of social-cognitive developmental perspective and theories in which only the most complex self-organization is viewed as having structuring power. Themata provide structuring frames on our basic ways of knowing the world.

Themata are subjective constructions of meanings about the self's evolution, not objective accounts of life history. Every new clinician or researcher makes the discovery that it is impossible to predict the qualitative or quantitative effect of certain events on patients or research subjects. They learn that it is the *meanings* people attribute to these events that make them formative, powerful or traumatic. And only those meanings that have an enduring quality should be labeled biographical. For that reason, we use the term *living biography* in contrast to lived life history. "Living" conveys the sense that these constructions still shape a person's way of being. Once they have become *history* they have been reflected upon, worked through, and have lost their organizing power. This leads us to a second issue, that of internalization.

Biography continues to shape experience long after original events have occurred and social environments have ceased to exist because experiences and actions become internalized. Interestingly, this is the same process through which schemata get established. Schemata, however, are defined by a generalizable logic of knowing, understanding, and role-taking. Thematic structures are concerned with internalization of specific relationships and relationship patterns. These relationships are specific, their affective valences and cognitive understandings are tied to meanings transmitted through the generations, to family constellation, and life circumstances.

For this reason, it is natural to assume that themata refer to one life rather than to many. Since internalization and social construction always occur from one self's perspective to the important others in friendship, family, and community, themes emerge individually. They are the stamp of identity as important as one's name, making the one life different from all others. Living biography is a personal expression of the meanings of one life lived and unfolding. Nonetheless, there are generalizable patterns. From each life, we can generalize to the many lives that solidly embed the individual in his or her cohort, the historic moment. From each life, we can also generalize to the epistemic structures.

Uncovering the relationship between the specific and the general, the biographical self, and the epistemic self makes this work particularly challenging. The theory of biography and transformation posits that early life history does not just get replayed. Thus, we cannot find a life history that is not also filtered through the most mature developmental self position. There is also no expression of the self that exists in a vacuum, abstracted from its genesis. Each level of organization requires its own descriptions and explanations. The two structures have their own shape and properties, yet each structure affects the other. The experiences in one structure will reframe experience of the other. Each frame is incomplete and thus we are required to focus on both for an encompassing view of the self. With this expose about the relevance of biography in clinical-developmental psychology, we can now return to the concept of encapsulation and problem pathway.

Encapsulations

Encapsulations refer to certain sequestered schema or biographical structures that, while related to the past, live on in the present. Two types of encapsulations, vertical and horizontal, have been distinguished, which will be outlined in the following sections.

As is widely known, a schema is a cognitive or mental structure by which individuals intellectually adapt to and organize the environment. By means of these structures, events are organized into groups according to common characteristics. Perhaps Piaget's greatest contribution was to describe the developmental nature of schemas from birth to maturity. Each new life situation creates the opportunity for a developmental spurt, a reorganization of a cognitive (and affective) schema. This change is what Piaget refers to as accommodation—that is, the organism's ability to adapt to the world by changing its internal structure or schema. Important events in a person's life hold the potential for such critical, qualitative changes. It is, however, possible even for dramatic experiences to be integrated into the existing developmental schemes. Piaget describes this integration as assimilation—the incorporation of an object into the existing structure.

The nature of the relationship between assimilation and accommodation, what Piaget terms equilibration, represents the process of development. Equilibrium is the state of balance between assimilation and accommodation; disequilibrium is the state of imbalance between these two processes. Piaget stressed that equilibrium is a condition toward which the organism strives. When disequilibrium occurs, the individual is motivated to further assimilate and accommodate in order to achieve equilibrium. These processes are based on the idea that the organism finds new equilibrium after a state of disequilibrium or transition in which all earlier self-structures are synthesized into a new structure considered a stage. Piaget's theoretical perspective on development has influenced many of the more recent social-developmental theories discussed above.

Noam (1986a, 1986b, 1990) extended Piaget's work by conceptualizing those aspects of development that remain unaccommodated even when overall transformation occurs. Such an analysis can account for what Piaget referred to as the "multiple, divided, and contradictory" nature of self and personality and is central dimension of theory of biography and transformation discussed above. This theory emphasizes how particular experiences resist integration into a higher order system—a process we termed *overassimilation.* This process refers to incorporating experiences into an earlier structure when a more developed structure exists. The consequences or products of these overassimilations are *encapsulations.* Vertical encapsulations begin as developmentally appropriate modes of meaning-making, but become a strong unresolved, living part in an otherwise developing self-system. This process creates pockets of old meaning systems that are guided by the cognitive and affective logic that governed at an earlier time. But encapsulations do not refer to unchanged internal "time capsules." Instead overassimilative activity is a process that does not return to us a replica of the past but rather to a constructed living biography. This living biography implies, however, that even with a great deal of continued interaction with the environment and reconstructions of the past, old meaning systems—those that are less differentiated and less integrated—continue to be used.

Overassimilation and encapsulations are concepts less concerned with momentary regressions but convey systematic ways of viewing self and world. Used in this context, earlier meaning systems are not truly tested against an external reality. Only those aspects of the internal and interpersonal world become transformed that are challenged through interactions. Some ways of thinking and feeling are so much related to trauma or require such radical separations from people, ideas, or basic stances in life, that they are kept away from self reflection and interpersonal dialogue. Often shame and the danger implied in new knowledge keep these ways of organizing meaning sequestered from the general thrust of development. At other times loyalty to family and friends makes a reexamination too threatening. Too much knowledge can lead to unwanted separations, conflicts and resultant isolation. Whatever the specific reasons, the result is an encapsulated form of thinking and feeling that can exert a tremendous power on the life of a person.

Depending on the developmental level the beliefs are associated with, they can be more physical (based on magical thinking or focused on the body and bodily images), concrete-action oriented (based on a view of the self as an agent that acts on the world or needs to manipulate the world deceptively to achieve need gratification), or psychological (a state where needs are expressed in symbolic form and around identification with others). Continued development and the present-day experiences will influence these basic beliefs, yet a great deal of the energy to maintain these less-differentiated thought and feeling states emerges from this living biography and cannot be subsumed under the most mature aspect of the self. The fact that many people have certain earlier meaning systems co-existing with later ones, and often in ways that are quite disorganizing, indicate that we might have to change Piaget's notion that psychological adaptation is in large part about "equilibration." Instead, we might have to view disequilibration, if defined as the fluctuations between different complexity levels of meaning-making, as more the norm than the exception.

Examples of an old meaning systems still organizing present-day world views of a person are plenty. The five-year-old child whose parents divorce will often carry the sense of being at fault well into adolescence and adulthood. The undercutting voices in the adult who simultaneously knows about the many competence and success, represents another typical example. Often such self-criticism can be traced to undermining interactions in the family and the peer world.

This model of development provides an alternative to traditional views of psychopathology as remaining somehow primitive, due to developmental fixation or arrest. In the model presented here, the less-evolved side of the self is always in relationship with the more-evolved one. This new model of development stands in contrast to a cognitive-developmental view in that not all aspects of the self have to be viewed as functioning at one level of development. When we introduce clinical cases in the borderline psychopathology section, the concept of encapsulations will become further elaborated.

Horizontal Encapsulation (Problem Pathway)

There are a number of different patterns that emerge, when we focus on different levels of meaning-making operating simultaneously in a person. As we have seen, vertical encapsulations relate to hierarchical discrepancies between different complexity levels of meaning construction. Another type of encapsulation can be called horizontal encapsulation or problem pathway. Here, camouflaged discrepancies appear under the governance of the most advanced developmental position. In reality, the earlier systems of thinking and feeling are very much involved but have led not so much to an arrest as to a specific derailment with a continued developmental pathways (for that reason we chose the term problem pathway, Noam, 1990). The early experience continues to shape an aspect of the person's world view but reappears, at higher levels of complexity, often transforming at each point in development. It is this continued transformation, that gives the term "developmental psychopathology" a literal meaning. By adulthood, the person has usually attained a complex system that can observe the self and develop an ideology and theory of relationships. It will appear, therefore, that the most complex developmental position dominates. In fact, however, the earlier derailment has caused a separate developmental line in the self that has transformed an early state along the lines of the complex self. For that reason we use the term "horizontal," suggesting that there is no discrepancy of complexity level as is the case in vertical encapsulations. We have provided some empirical evidence for this phenomenon in an earlier section, entitled complexity vs. maturity in development.

Although the integration of horizontal encapsulations into the overall self-system might seem simpler because there has been continued development, the dissolution of a problem pathway is clinically often extremely difficult. Narcissistic patients can serve as an example. Their rage and grandiosity is often referred to as extremely primitive and part of an unevolved self. But while there is often truth to such interpretation, problems of perfectionism, the feelings of alienation and psychological imprisonment which underlay the great sense of despair and anger are directly related to the complex nature of self development. The person has made the self part of a totalizing system, which derives its essence not from positive experiences and feelings, but from a theoretical ideal. To reduce such idealizations of the adult self to the child's relationship with the parents, misses the point that there is a complicated subsuming of the self under the governance of rigid theoretical principles about issues such as achievement, respect, authority at work. An earlier paper has dealt with this phenomenon through an analysis of Franz Kafka's letter to his father (Noam, 1988b).

Of course, the biographical origins of the self-alienation and the sense of feeling insignificant are often found in childhood. But the developmental organization and the framing of the experience is directly tied to the level of the complex forms of meaning-making. In fact, the person often experiences the meanings and behaviors as a matter solely of the present, which makes the critical return to the earlier, yet living source of the derailment a matter of particular difficulty. The "totalitarian rule" of the alienated formal-operational self can only be overcome by returning to some moments in biography which gave hope, if only fleetingly so, to the experience of a vital and exploring self. These moments, often tied to the immediacy of childhood experiences, serve as a point of reference from where the imprisonment can be recognized and transformed.

The fact that problems can develop along problem pathways, give rise to different manifestations of the same disorder at different developmental levels. Most problems, symptoms, or disorders can exist at different complexity levels. We will now exemplify this phenomenon by developmentally subtyping different disorders.

Social Cognition and the Subtyping of Disorders

A final issue is the use of social cognition for differentiating existing disorders. We are at present in an exciting phase where sufficient research has been conducted of psychiatric disorders that subtypes of symptoms, syndromes, etiology, or course have become increasingly well researched. As a consequence of the detailed and empirically derived descriptions of different disorders in DSM III, III-R, and IV, the heterogeneity of many disorders, such as affective disorders, conduct disorders, and so on has been recognized. An example is the difference between unipolar and bipolar depression, which have different symptom patterns, etiologies, course, sequel, and responses to treatment. These observations have made the subclassification of depression essential.

Establishing subtypes for other disorders is equally important because they can point the way toward differential treatment and provide information relating to etiology and natural history. These subtypes are usually introduced around different symptom clusters or different clinical manifestations. But few attempts have been made to include a developmental dimension to the study of subtypes. The findings described earlier, showing connections between social-cognitive level and disorders such as conduct disorders, anorexia, and so on suggest that important distinctions could be made not only between, but also within disorders. It is likely that at different levels of development treatment requests and treatment course will differ as patients make use of the treatments offered based on their understanding of themselves and the relationship with their therapist/treatment staff.

We have very important and encouraging results that show differences in clinical manifestations with different disorders by finding different combinations of thoughts, feelings, and symptoms within certain disorders such as borderline psychopathology (Noam, 1988d), depression (Kegan, Noam, & Rogers, 1984) and suicidality (Borst & Noam, 1993; Chandler, 1994). This is a welcome development that needs to be expanded to other disorders. We will provide two examples, first, adolescent suicide, where a number of developmental typologies have been introduced (see Noam & Borst, 1994 for a compilation of approaches) and researched. We will then turn to borderline psychopathology, where psychoanalytic typologies of early disorders have been used to distinguish between different disorder types. We will show what a clinical-developmental perspective built on constructivist and social cognitive theories can further contribute. When we turn to the borderline disorders, we will briefly introduce three patients and treatment implications in order to explore the meaningfulness of a developmental typology for treatment.

Suicide

Numerous authors have shown that there are multiple subtypes of suicidal adolescents, such as an aggressive type and a depressive type who demonstrate little, if any, aggressive behavior (Brent, 1987; Pfeffer, Newcorn, Kaplan, Mizruchi, & Plutnick, 1989). The aggressive type makes impulsive attempts of variable intent, whereas the depressive type is hopeless, and makes planned attempts of high suicidal intent. Pfeffer and her colleagues (1989) demonstrated important differences between adolescents with both suicidal and assaultive behavior and adolescents who were suicidal but not assaultive. Thus far, these subtypes have been classified predominantly on the basis of symptomatology, and the internalizing and externalizing distinctions have never been explored in terms of developmental differences. Social-cognitive development should play an important role in understanding the differences between the various suicidal profiles that have been delineated and account for some of the differences between these subtypes.

The Borst-Noam Model. Borst and Noam (1993) and Noam and Borst (1994) hypothesized that there would be two subtypes of adolescent suicide attempters: the first subtype are those who are developmentally delayed, functioning at the preconformist level of ego development and as a result have great difficulty taking the perspective of other people. This subtype was expected to present as impulsive and aggressive, prone to using externalizing defenses and viewing conflict as outside of the self. Adolescent attempters of the second subtype, functioning at developmentally age-appropriate levels (conformist levels) were expected to be more self-blaming and depressed and to use more internalizing defense mechanisms. To investigate these hypotheses, suicide attempters functioning at preconformist developmental levels were compared with attempters who had reached conformist developmental levels in psychopathology, defensive styles, hopelessness, and frequency of attempt.

The studies discerned two distinct developmental profiles of suicidal girls that corresponded to the nondevelopmental typologies based on symptomatology introduced by prior researchers (Brent, 1987; Pfeffer et al., 1989). Female attempters who have reached more advanced social-cognitive development were found to differ significantly on diagnosis, symptomatology, and defense mechanisms from female attempters who still function on preconformist levels. The preconformist attempters are angry and action-oriented, have a limited capacity for self-reflection, and have a tendency to direct their aggression toward others as well as themselves. They present with both externalizing and internalizing symptoms and seem at risk for impulsive suicide attempts. This group was referred to as "the angry-defiant suicidal type."

The conformist attempters, in contrast, present as depressed and do not blame others for their despair. It is likely that their strong identification with other people's opinion leaves them vulnerable to criticism and feelings of guilt. They tend to use more complex defenses such as intellectualization and reaction formation, and present with few aggressive and delinquent symptoms. This group we call "the self-blaming suicidal type." Borst and Noam (1993) concluded that social-cognitive development has an important impact on the expression of suicidal behavior in adolescent girls.

Age by itself is not strongly associated with the risk and preconditions of suicide. Dimensions of personality, such as the degree of impulsivity and the capacity for delay of gratification, are also closely linked to psychopathology and suicidality. In the clinical-developmental tradition, it is assumed that people systematically organize meanings about themselves and their lives, and that these perspectives on self and significant others develop across the life span. In addition, these meaning systems are seen as related to expressions and outcomes of psychopathology. Given this orientation, it was hypothesized that Loevinger's theory of ego development (Loevinger, 1976), with its emphasis on impulse control, complexity of self-reflection, and emotional experience, would lend itself well to the study of suicidality. Loevinger's model encompasses major ego functions of concern in the study of adolescent suicidality.

Although evidence has accumulated that ego development and psychopathology are significantly related, no studies had examined this construct in relation to suicidal behavior (Borst, Noam, & Bartok, 1991). As shown in an earlier section of this chapter, findings from earlier studies indicate that there are important relationships between ego development, symptomatology, defenses, and treatment requests and an important clinical use for developmental information (Browning, 1986; Dill & Noam, 1990; Noam & Dill, 1991; Noam & Houlihan, 1990). For example, studies reviewed above on the relationship between ego development and psychopathology have shown that delinquency, conduct disorders, and externalizing behaviors are associated with preconformist levels of ego development (Frank & Quinlan, 1976; Noam et al., 1984; Paget, Noam, Borst, & Bartok, 1990). Two studies have also suggested a greater degree of maladjustment and psychiatric impairment among adolescents at the preconformist stages, as compared to adolescents at conformist stages (Browning, 1986; Frank & Quinlan, 1976). As we have mentioned before, research investigating a link between higher levels of ego development and internalizing symptomatology has been less conclusive. However, some findings indicate an association between ego maturity and emotional disorders (Gold, 1980; Paget et al., 1990), supporting the hypothesis that with increasing developmental complexity, psychopathology becomes more internalized, more experienced in psychological than in physical terms, and less action oriented. Because suicidality is, in part, a turning against the self (e.g., Recklitis, Noam, & Borst, 1990) the authors pursued the hypothesis that maturation of developmental capacities does not necessarily lead to better adjustment but may in fact lead to a greater vulnerability for suicidality. Although suicidal behavior was not hypothesized to be exclusively a phenomenon of conformist stages, the authors expected to find a higher percentage of suicide attempters within the conformist group than within the group of preconformist adolescents. It was hypothesized that adolescents at conformist levels of ego development are more prone to self-rejection, feelings of depression, guilt, and despair, and more likely to see causes of intrapsychic and interpersonal problems within themselves than preconformist adolescents, who are more likely to externalize and to blame others for their problems.

This study demonstrates the relevance of a clinical-developmental approach to the study of adolescent suicide attempts. In addition to the established risk factors of gender and diagnosis, it was found that with increasing ego development, adolescents diagnosed with a conduct and/or affective disorder became more vulnerable to suicidal behaviors. The study further supports the importance of going beyond age as the key developmental variable, as the authors did not find any association between age and suicidal attempts in this adolescent sample. Instead, the adolescent's "frame of reference" proved to be a useful concept for understanding the developmental dimensions of suicidality.

In line with the ego development construct, it was hypothesized that with the social-cognitive reorganization that generally occurs in puberty, the unhappiness that was formerly attributed to external sources and dealt with behaviorally becomes increasingly part of inner evaluations of the self. Such transformations are likely to lead to more self-blame and overtly self-destructive symptomatology as typical reactions to interpersonal disappointments (e.g., Noam, 1988d). This idea has been influential among clinical theorists (e.g., Blos, 1962; Erikson, 1968) but has not been systematically studied from a developmental perspective.

The Chandler Model. Chandler (1994) takes a social-cognitive approach in a developmental account of protective factors against the risk of suicide in adolescence. By first reviewing how individuals come to understand personal stability and self-continuity when faced with personal change, he forges a link to adolescent suicidality. Chandler proposes that a loss of self-continuity makes the individual vulnerable to self-destructive impulses. Without the ability to find a continuous thread in one's own identity, the individual may be prone to respond to difficulties or disappointments with attempts on their own lives. Adolescents who get temporarily derailed perceive themselves as lacking resources and as poorly prepared to deal effectively with those standard threats to identity development easily brushed aside by individuals who possess a stronger sense of personal continuity. In particular, Chandler (1994) found that those young individuals who dismiss as immature their earlier strategies for reasoning about self-continuity without, at the same time, being able to articulate some more effective means of warranting personal sameness in the face of change are especially likely to be characterized by recent attempts to end their own lives. Specifically, of the more than 100 suicidal and nonsuicidal control subjects Chandler and his colleagues have so far tested, no adolescent who sustained a sense of continuous personal identity is known to have ever made a serious attempt at suicide. By contrast, more than 80% of the suicidal adolescents so far tested have proven themselves to be caught in some transitional moment that has left them bereft of any working method of effectively counting themselves as continuous in time. In light of this accumulating database, Chandler and colleagues are increasingly confidant that an important reason many more adolescents attempt suicide than do individuals in other age groups is the fact that the usual course of identity development repeatedly leads adolescents to the brink of a hazard-filled moment during which all connections between the present and some owned future are momentarily suspended.

Developmental Typology of Borderline Personality Disorders

Developmental typologies of borderline psychopathology have been proposed repeatedly in the psychiatric and psychoanalytic literature. Masterson and Rinsley (1975), for example, have suggested that different borderline vulnerabilities (i.e., more engulfment fears or more abandonment fears) correspond to different points of arrest in the separation-individuation phase of development. Kernberg's developmental differentiation (1975) is based on a model of object relations along dimensions of object differentiation and integration. According to Kernberg, these developments or arrests occur early in life. The developmental typology presented here differs from previous ones which all share an emphasis on the earliest years. In contrast, a social cognitive perspective traces the continued development of the self to the most advanced position and relates the most mature self-other organization to present and earlier problems. This approach has produced a new typology of borderline psychopathology. Table 15.1 briefly describes the three types of borderline patients.

The typology is applicable to adolescent and adult patients. Predictably, there are phasic differences which are relevant to a developmental description of borderline patients. In order to demonstrate the developmental aspects more clearly, adolescent patients were chosen as examples who all share the same age, yet are functioning on very different social-cognitive levels. There are also many examples of borderline patients in adulthood that fit the typology. Among the adult patients, different life tasks will be at the fore (i.e., marriage, work, children), but the differential logic of the disorder will remain quite similar.

This section, building on earlier accounts (Noam, 1986b), will depict three borderline groups by focusing on three patients and a short description of the hospitalization phase of their treatment. The patients share a number of features. All have been hospitalized and were seen in intensive evaluation or psychotherapy. The borderline diagnosis, all based on DSM criteria, were established by means of Gunderson's diagnostic interview schedule (Retrospective) (Gunderson, 1984) using psychiatric history and medical chart information.

The Subjective-Physical Borderline Patient: The Case of Daniel. Daniel was hospitalized at a major psychiatric hospital in the Northeast. Fifteen years old, the youngest of five children, Daniel was a chubby, preadolescent-looking boy who had been in intensive, individual psychotherapy for treatment of severe depression, school phobia, and psychosomatic milk allergy. The referral to the intensive family treatment center was made by his treating psychiatrist who felt Daniel's condition was deteriorating. He was particularly concerned about Daniel's "lack of self," his severe separation anxiety, and the increasing frequency of rage outbursts and tantrums, which were followed by long crying spells. He reported that Daniel became encopretic when

TABLE 15.1 Developmental Typology of Borderline Personality Disorder

1. *The Subjective-Physical Borderline Disorder*
   Most important aspect is lack of self-control; consequent characteristics—impulsivity, hyperactivity and attention-deficit. Tendency toward magical thinking, but can distinguish between fantasy and reality. Prone to short psychotic episodes and overwhelming anxiety. No observational capacity to view action as symbolic; to understand interpretation; concomitant sense of being at the mercy of the impulses. Concrete perspective on self and others with accompanying split view of "good" or "bad." Others viewed as powerful and punitive perceived relation to others limited to submitting or physically hiding.*

2. *The Reciprocal-Instrumental Borderline Personality*
   Major aspect seemingly "overdifferentiated." Little magical thinking. Emphasis on concrete, here and now. Cognitive distinction between "public self" and "inner hidden self." Thus possibility of planned deception, as a means for self to affirm itself. Psychotic episodes and acknowledged anxiety rare. More prone to feelings of rage, entrapment, and antisocial features. Can endanger self *and* others when depressed (e.g., drug and alcohol related accidents). Instrumental perspective on self and other; relationships often exploitative. Conflicts around self-protective assertion of control. Earlier, encapsulated abandonment of primary relationships emerging in a distancing posture or the "lone ranger syndrome" (i.e., others perceived unhelpful in goal-attainment, pleasure pursued alone or with rapidly changing partners).

3. *The Mutual-Overinclusive Borderline Disorder*
   More complex psychological system with greater observing potential. Capable of insight into action and seeing things in a symbolic way. Can coordinate different points of view and take perspective of others. Major aspect—overidentification with the views of the other. Typical feelings—"loss of self" in close relationships, low self-esteem, depression and anxiety. Concomitant defining of self through important relationships and complaints of exclusion, guilt, abandonment, and identity confusion. Suicidal gestures typically seek attention from loved others.

*Note: These attributes can also exist in borderline patients at more advanced developmental positions but they represent regression points. For the subjective-physical borderline patient, they are part of the most advanced organization.

he entered school, and would leave school frequently for home where his mother awaited him to watch morning soap operas.

In the first phase of psychotherapy, Daniel felt very threatened by the closeness of the setting; illustratively, he wore a green T-shirt that he would stretch to cover his body from nose to toes, as if to give him a limited sense of protection. He often would hide behind a big chair, pointing its four legs at the therapist like guns. He seemed threatened by what he perceived as the clinician's wish to control him and to guide his mind. He was frequently preoccupied with fears about homosexuality and death and could only sustain very short therapy. Similarly, in family therapy Daniel felt overwhelmed by the group's disorganization. The sessions were mainly concerned with the anger and anxiety of the family over the separation induced by the hospitalization.

Daniel, dreading separation from his parents, began a weekly routine of visiting his family without permission. A part of this routine was the implicit understanding that his mother, joined by the father, took him to dinner in elegant restaurants. They presented themselves as the "good" and giving parents in contrast to the withholding and "bad" staff. Although relieved that they had found a safe place for their son, the family suffered greatly from the separation. After each dinner ceremony they decided anew that Daniel could not be kept at home, brought him back to the hospital, and criticized the night staff for "having allowed their son to leave." Any attempt by Daniel to settle into the center led to signals of parental disapproval.

Daniel escalated his behavior after the early months of treatment and fluctuated in individual therapy. Moments of appreciation for the attention and help he was receiving were interspersed with long spans of furious, bored, covertly sadistic, and incoherent behaviors. He needed very structured interview sessions, which by now lasted almost the full hour; he was able to respond only very concretely, but in an organized manner. He gradually began to worry about my absences between sessions, especially during weekends. He described the images of explosions after visits from his parents or sessions with his therapist. After such experiences, he was convinced that there would not be a reunion. Whenever treatment brought him closer to the feelings of desperation (usually experienced as unbearable boredom), his fears became so great that he had to remove himself physically from the place that "caused" his problems. Psychological well-being was attached to the physical space; when painful feelings occurred at the treatment center, he thought a change of settings would make the problems disappear.

After seven months of treatment, Daniel had begun to display more manipulative and overtly aggressive behavior. The staff began to complain that one could not trust his intentions. He became a leader of a somewhat dangerous "hall riot," throwing furniture at staff and setting a small fire. This phase of treatment ended with another crisis: Daniel had not received the privileges required to leave the hospital, but his family and he had made plans to go on an important out-of-town trip. A confrontation with the staff was inevitable. That same afternoon, after the parents had told him about their decision that he was to stay in the hospital, he cried bitterly about the first real acknowledgment of a process of separation occurring in the family. Daniel came to his therapy appointment feeling sad, but at the same time relieved. It was the first time that he linked two ideas in one sentence. He said that he hated to stay in the hospital, but that his parents had finally made a decision for him to be in the hospital. Now, he said, he could concentrate on his work, while still voicing fears that he might never be allowed to leave.

Daniel began to translate a new sense of responsibility into other areas of his life. He became a good student at the hospital-affiliated school, was better able to concentrate on the task of learning, and slowly moved into the group of adolescents whom he had earlier detested with such passion. Daniel focused in therapy on work and competency. He wanted a job at a local restaurant and decided on future career as a restaurant owner and chef. After a year of hospitalization, the staff agreed that he had worked out important aspects of his borderline disorder. He had given up much of the self-destructive behavior and had built a better inner structure that protected him from unmanageable impulses and affect. Daniel was subsequently discharged.

Interpretation and Implications for Treatment. At the subjective-physical stage, inner and outer reality is experienced in physical terms. Thus, Daniel did not realize that outer actions could reveal inner feelings. When he lost his privileges—always shortly before the weekend—members of the treatment staff suggested to him that he might be leaving the hospital without a pass in order to lose his privileges, so that he would not have to go home for the weekend. He denied this interpretation.

At this level, motives are taken at face value, unconscious thoughts and feelings have not as yet been discovered, and the concept of self-deception is not part of a personal lexicon. In addition, as part of the physical perspective, the person lacks the capacity to control and distance himself from many of the impulses that guide behavior. Daniel was at the mercy of intense feelings of annihilation. His fears and thoughts about accidents and explosions were experienced as if they had in fact taken place, leading the staff to wonder at times about an underlying psychotic process (a hypothesis which was rejected in the end). Daniel experienced thoughts as open to the world and readable by therapist and parents alike. Thus, protection from overwhelming adults was found only through physical hiding or running away.

Given Daniel's age, the delay seen in his level of self-organization is quite remarkable since his organization is more typical for children between the ages of five and seven. Despite this delay, it is important to note that a Piagetian account would place his most mature self-system beyond the early separation-individuation period at 12 to 16 months, typically described as the borderline fixation point. It is also important that Daniel progressed during one year of hospitalization to the reciprocal-instrumental state.

By comparing Daniel both with children at the age of around six and with older patients who function at this stage but present a different clinical picture, the clinicians became convinced that other developmental processes were at work. Daniel's intense fantasies of death and explosion whenever his parents (and later his therapist) left him cannot be solely explained from within his, self-other perspective. Rather, these fears point to the replay of encapsulated materials of separation-individuation fears from an earlier era. Not every person at the subjective-physical stage who moves into the reciprocal-instrumental stage experiences separations as final or avoids self-asserting behavior because of the danger of annihilation. The former experiences are, however, quite typical of the young child who has not achieved object permanence. Thus, one can see Daniel's behavior as both a biographical recapitulation of earlier developmental positions and an attempt at resolving these problems within his most advanced position.

Regressive phenomena like Daniel's need to be viewed as attempts to resolve conflict. The context in which this happens is the transforming self. The impulsive expression of desires and anxieties without understanding their symbolic value (e.g., running between hospital and home) point to a concrete-physical attempt at dealing with the more primitive separation-individuation fears. During later developmental positions, patients can be subject to the same history of separation fears, but express them and resolve them in the context of a different psychological system. The fears then become expressed around the ups and downs of relationships, and the self observes the fluctuation in psychological terms (e.g., feeling hurt, abandoned) rather than in physical terms (e.g., running home because "my feet tell me to").

This physical/psychological distinction is usually not made in the treatment of borderline patients. Moreover, the guiding treatment notion concerning early separation individuation problems failed to provide sufficient specificity and explanation to Daniel's disorder. Such a notion was also in variance with the interpretation that his movement between hospital and home was an expression of an unconscious wish. Although this observation may well have been accurate, making it explicit to the patient was geared toward a system of self-observation far beyond Daniel's level. To place Daniel's acting-out behavior into an appropriate context for him, it was necessary to understand the organization of his developmental "cutting edge" and speak from that level. Focusing on his early childhood separation fears made him feel infantilized, and interpretations oriented toward understanding unconscious motivation made him feel stupid.

Daniel's impulsive behavior became worse, if viewed from the danger posed to himself and others. It can, however, also be viewed as an attempt to gain control by moving from unreflective impulsivity to preplanned manipulation. That the transition did not lead to more complex pathology at a new developmental level (a frequent clinical occurrence where symptoms transform from an external action-orientation to a more internal, affective position without getting better) can be attributed to the skill of the treatment staff and the ultimate cooperation of patient and family. In developing a more complex developmental world, Daniel found more adaptive ways of dealing with his old issues of work, relationships and school. For example, as a five-year-old, Daniel was terrified of separation from his mother. His encopresis became a way to reunite with her and to convince himself she was still alive. Daniel recreated this scene as an adolescent by a pattern of returning home from the hospital. A central biographical pattern had re-emerged. In the process of becoming more manipulative (which also meant both coordinated and setting a boundary between inner plans and outer appearance), his past fears had become more workable. In transition to a new psychological organization he, along with his parents, was able to break this form of recapitulation and to integrate the encapsulationed part of the self, intricately linked to his fusion with his mother, into a higher order system.

An adolescent (or adult) patient diagnosed as borderline who fits the first level of this developmental typology requires a great deal of clinical input. The lack of capacity for psychological interpretation of what happens inside and outside the self does not make a traditional "insight-oriented" form of therapy a viable alternative. The person has to learn how to set concrete boundaries both internally and externally. The internal boundaries relate to impulse control: that is, to an ability to delay wish-fulfillment and turn away from fantasies in order to be and to work. The difficulty with these issues makes this patient especially prone to short psychotic intrusions and overwhelming anxiety.

The patient's external boundaries are attached to a severe dependency on others who have the role of maintaining internal functions. The arrest is usually part of an overinvolved family environment that does not provide the patient with a sufficient combination of support and limits necessary for building these self-regulatory functions. The research literature that reports difficult peer relations as an important factor in psychopathology and its long-term prediction (Kohlberg, LaCrosse, & Ricks, 1972) is relevant here. We hypothesize that the child has never learned the basic functions that make an adaptation to the peer group possible. Simultaneous therapeutic work with the person and the context, therefore, become crucial. At first the boundary conditions have to be set in the treatment. Slowly, and through behavior-oriented support systems, these conditions become internal. This work often requires a residential treatment center to provide an adequate holding environment.

The Instrumental-Borderline Patient: The Case of Richard. Richard, a 16-year-old adolescent, was referred to a psychiatric hospital by a juvenile court. Before deciding his case, the court asked for a recommendation from the hospital. The parents had originally asked the court to intervene, because they could not control Richard's "acting-out behavior" at home. He was frequently truant from school, ran away from home on several occasions, was involved in drug and alcohol abuse, and had threatened his parents on numerous occasions. One disagreement with the father had led to a dangerous, physical fight.

Richard was the second of two sons of a lawyer father and a mother who was a teacher. Richard described a long history of problems. He felt his parents never understood him, were belligerent toward him, and tried to enforce inappropriate rules at home. He described his father as a weak man and his mother as cold, manipulative, and aggressive. He remembered with pride his physical fight with his father. The major problems began when his brother was found to have an incurable (but not life-threatening) illness and when his grandmother died. Richard, 11 at the time, was very depressed and scratched his wrist and hurt himself with a knife repeatedly. Over the next two years, he became harder to manage and frequently exploded at his parents, who were frightened of his intense outbursts of anger. Richard fluctuated between aggressive behaviors and self-destructive acts.

During the course of hospitalization, Richard wanted to return home on his parents' terms, if they would retract the court petition. To the treatment staff, the proposal seemed like a way to negotiate himself out of the hospital, rather than a genuine change of direction. Richard refused to talk about himself and his parents in detail, so that most of the information came from observation in family therapy, which he had begun to attend with some interest. Indeed, he was confronted with much distance from both his parents, who showed only superficial concern for him. Richard felt close only to the family dog. He became very sad when he described his relationship with his dog, whom he missed greatly. "She is the only one who really is happy when I come home." He often shared his room with her and took her on long walks.

Richard had many friends and found it easy to make new ones. But they found pleasure mainly in the shared distribution and consumption of drugs and alcohol, "We go out, have fun and get high." He liked to talk about one friend, who was different, "He is someone who is really there when you need him, and I am there for him." The friend left the area and Richard missed him. Because his mother disapproved of this friend, however, Richard could only make occasional secret phone calls to him. Although he did well academically, Richard never liked school very much and began to stay away frequently. He rarely cooperated with the teachers, got into power struggles, and did not develop any goals for the future.

Richard's preoccupation with his own self-interest and his "manipulation" of the staff (by setting different people up against each other) earned him the title "staff-splitter." While for Daniel, the problem was a mind which was too open and in need of structure, Richard was too self-contained. He gave the staff an unsettling sense of a master plan behind all his actions. He became part of the adolescent patient group and sadistically planned trouble, especially for the more vulnerable and dependent patients.

With regard to treatment, Richard could see no purpose in psychotherapy meetings and came only because it was required. As a result, he tried to find ways to avoid coming, while not losing "privileges." For example, he would become ill just before our therapy hour, but recover soon thereafter. The initial period of therapy, however, was quite positive. He described in greater detail (with much focus on the concrete actions) what he most liked to do and why he hated the hospital, parents, and all other authorities. Although he could not understand what talking would do to help him, he began to see the therapist as an ally against other authority. He did not consider the meetings therapeutic, since he did not feel that he should be in the hospital in the first place. His definition of his problem was that he was getting in trouble with the law and his parents, and it was their inflexibility that led to this "punishment." Richard frequently said that he would plan an escape, if there was nothing in the hospitalization for him. However, he wanted the staff to protect him from the judges. Given the choice between a psychiatric institution and a setting for juvenile delinquency, he preferred the hospital. As he saw it, the meetings with staff were negotiations with an implicit deal in which the clinicians were to help him in the legal actions. The brief work ended with the court decision of a transfer to a residential school where Richard remained for over a year and succeeded in mastering a number of his problems.

Interpretation and Implications for Treatment. Richard was already functioning at a more complex social-cognitive level when he was hospitalized than Daniel. Richard shares with Daniel the "external" and rather concrete interpretation of self and social reality. The physical orientation was organized on a higher order level than Daniel's. The instrumental borderline patient can usually curb and control immediate impulses and act in a more planned fashion (although there can be many impulsive breakthroughs, as observable in Richard's case). Associated with this increased control over the concrete physical needs is the ability to mentally leave the self and view thoughts and actions through an outside perspective. This capacity to self-reflect provides individuals with a more constant sense of themselves over time than was evident in the subjective-physical orientation. Nevertheless, this kind of patient is unable to integrate his needs with those of others, resulting in a self-protective or nonmutual stance. Kohlberg's description of the "I scratch your back, you scratch my back" type of moral thinking captures this social perspective, which often leads to antisocial features in the borderline disorders. It is in the transition to the next developmental position that the self can fully take the perspective of the other in relationships.

The ways in which Richard's early separation-individuation concerns re-emerge are dramatically different when compared with Daniel. Richard's conscious feelings were expressed as rage against his parents ("I am going to kill them") and a sense of frustration that "they don't understand, anyway." His fear of abandonment was expressed in his belief that people did not care. He interpreted the parents' appeal to the court as a renewed sign of uncaring parents. Only in the relationships with his brother and his friend was he able to express the wish to be close and be taken care of. But here his experience was that they, too, would become ill or leave him. In Richard's case, as is common at the instrumental stage, the fear of engulfment was much more visible, as seen in his need to distance himself, to be isolated and removed, and distrust any adult. Specifically, he feared that adults would take over, and he would be forced to submit. He was not aware that this fear could have also contained an element of wish. He struggled for independence from the family, but in ways that would recreate the child's experiences of running away and being brought home. On many occasions, beginning at age four, Richard ran away from home and was brought home by the police. The parents were incapable of providing the safety net he needed. He increasingly experienced them as distant and overly involved in their careers and their marital relationship.

Similarly, later on, the treatment staff observed a painful formality and distance in their relationship with Richard: it was as if they talked with him over a telephone a continent apart. This stance of separateness makes Richard less prone to psychotic intrusions. It is rare that anxiety and depression are reported as subjective experiences. Instead, one can observe an immediate transformation of these feelings (usually experienced as a feeling of being caged, or victimized) into action. Drugs, promiscuous sexuality, and exploitative relationships serve as buffers against dysphoria and are in the service of need-gratification.

Early on, in most of the therapies with borderline patients at the instrumental level, therapy breaks down in the initial contract. The relationship is defined by the patient as "helping me out." If such a construction does not fit all the time and is replaced by limit-setting and exploration, power struggles—the hallmark of the acting-out adolescent—soon follow. The patient begins to feel victimized and his conviction that no one can be trusted is reinforced. If the patient has a choice, he or she stops coming; if the therapist has a choice, he stops performing the services. Usually the break-up of the relationship occurs when the adolescent storms out of the therapy session. The calmer, yet equally angry, therapist labels the patient as primitive. If a total breakdown of the therapy does not occur, it is often because the adolescents and the therapist force themselves to continue and a new compromise is found. The therapist and patient are seen walking together to the cafeteria or interact around sports or other activities; ideally they share in an activity which is of interest to both. A relationship is built around the mutual need satisfaction which helps trust to emerge slowly.

By this point in the therapy, the therapist builds a relationship around helping the patient pursue goals more adaptively. Actively developing trust is for the instrumental borderline patient as crucial as boundary establishment is for the patient within the physical level. The early abandoning interactions in the family have led to a profound belief that the world is unsafe and that one cannot rely on anyone. Coming close means getting hurt. It is not surprising that the instrumental patient often comes from an overly distant and critical family, in contrast to the enmeshed family of the physical borderline patient. The developmental thrust to the interpersonal role-taking stage, with its opening of boundaries and strong group identification, is experienced in part as a regression. Evoked for the patient are memories of a time when the self was little protected, often abandoned, and within the cycle of running away and being brought home.

Meanwhile, the patient follows an "oath": never to allow the self to be hurt again, never to care that much again. This early attitude contributes to an arrest at the preconventional and preconformist stages, observed so consistently in the research literature. Since the recapitulations stand in contradiction to the continued developmental thrust. The repetitive theme is to avoid closeness while feeling abandoned and victimized. The resultant self-protective stance stands in the way of those experiences that support the move to the mutual-inclusive stage. Often group environments and group therapy provide the patient with peer experiences that support change by sidestepping biographical recapitulations with adult authority figures. In place of the latter, the patient experiences shared values and emotional ties with his peers, and a tentative intimacy is established.

As Richard moved beyond the self-protective stance, he was able to overcome the cycle of disappointment, resentment, and running away. In the process, he was able to open up toward friends, but not without consequences like becoming more depressed. As with Daniel, Richard's transition involved more symptomatology, making him look like as though he was getting worse. Such a view is misleading. As the self opens, all earlier intimate relationships along with their great disappointments become the focus of treatment. Experiences of loneliness, emptiness and sadness come to the fore, and lead, at first, to more symptoms like dangerous acting out. But ultimately, this hard sequence is the road to recovery. The move to the next developmental position makes the reworking of the past possible, and the reworking of the past creates the opportunity for real maturation of the self.

The Mutual-Inclusive Borderline Patient: The Case of Denise. Denise, 15 years old, was admitted to a psychiatric treatment center after she tried to commit suicide. Six months prior to the suicide attempt, Denise's parents separated. Before the separation, Denise's mother and father argued often, and Denise assumed the role of mediator. Following the separation, Denise isolated herself by withdrawing from friends and attending school sporadically. Denise first experienced anxiety attacks and felt she was "losing herself" after her father left the household. Her sense of self deteriorated rapidly, and soon she began drinking while alone. She described herselfin this period of being "miserable all the time." She reported short episodes of derealization and wrist scratching, the latter in order to "feel myself." She also described two very short psychotic episodes.

Her situation worsened and she tried to end her life by taking a large quantity of painkillers with alcohol. Denise was quite sure that her mother would return from work in time to discover her, but was willing to "take the risk" in case her mother was delayed. Denise's reaction to her parents' separation was exacerbated by a long history of separation anxiety. In treatment she remembered how her parents had to drive behind the bus bringing her to kindergarten, so that she would not panic. As a child, she was excessively shy around other children and secure only around her parents. Her mother reported that her later school experience was colored by much anxiety, a submissive attitude toward teachers, and frequent psychosomatic illnesses. Whenever an important separation occurred, she became insecure, retreated into herself, and cried. Both parents were concerned about her strong attachment to them, yet brought her into their marital drama from early on in her life.

After an initial period of "homesickness," Denise settled into the milieu of the hospital. She was well-liked by the patients and was always trying to help others. Similar to behavior at home, she became a mediator on the unit and was never seen by the staff as a significant "management problem." Of most concern to staff were a chameleon-like quality and romanticized relationships with male nursing staff. The latter inevitably led to feelings of pain and rejection when her romantic feelings were not reciprocated. Throughout, she rarely showed anger; when she did, it was out of control with an explosive quality that caused her considerable anxiety.

Consistent with this history, Denise became strongly involved in therapy. The appointments with her therapist were an important part of her hospital life. She talked readily about her disappointments and the many rejections she experienced. She frequently wanted to know what her therapist thought about her situation and the decisions she had to make (e.g., whether to live with her father or her mother). Her helplessness, paired with her hypervigilance around rejection, made it necessary to spend much time discussing the reasons why her therapist would not make the decision for her. She often interpreted her clinician's refusal as a sign of lack of interest. She would then withdraw, become silent, and be convinced her therapist would not meet with her again. She also was preoccupied with what her therapist might think and how she could "help him." After some of the sessions, she became enraged and threatened suicide. A great deal of patience and empathy were required so that she could experience closeness and explore separateness within the treatment. Each rupture of the relationship needed to be discussed in great detail. Over time, Denise was able to give up her interest in living through her therapist or her parents. She learned strategies for being concerned without giving up all sense of self.

Interpretation and Implications for Treatment. Denise viewed herself through the eyes of others, especially her parents and close friends. She removed herself from others because she could not tolerate the disappointment and confusion that came with two sets of contradicting expectations and self-views: that of her mother who hurt her father and that of her father who felt abandoned by her mother. She could understand both positions and identified with both. Her mother's wish to free herself from an unhappy marriage was as convincing to Denise as her father's attempt to avoid a painful separation and to keep the family together. At stake in this situation, however, was her self-definition, at the core of the mutual-inclusive stage. The loss of each parent led to feelings of self-loss, self-doubts, and self-hate. Anger and other assertive feelings could not be tolerated. When she did experience anger, it revolved around feeling abandoned and unloved and led to extreme anxiety. It could not be expressed toward the loved one and so turned against the self.

Denise's suicidal reaction to the break-up of her parents cannot be understood solely from the perspective of her most mature developmental position. She has a history of separation anxieties, exaggerated needs for affirmation, and overattachment to parents. Her early separation anxieties (e.g., her parents driving behind the school bus), and her sense that she could not physically survive without powerful adults, were related to unquestioned childhood beliefs. She had always tried to give adults what she thought they wanted and struggled generally with shyness. The result of these earlier problems was that she experienced an imminent dissolution of self in a most basic and existential way (e.g., derealizations). From a Piagetian perspective, Denise's problems with self-integration could easily be misinterpreted as one aspect of the interpersonal, mutual perspective-taking capacity. This would ignore, however, the recapitulation of earlier themes found within her otherwise relatively mature self-system. For Denise, the reopening of ego boundaries through identification, typical for the mutual-inclusive stage combined with earlier forms of the self's openness (e.g., loss of body integrity, loss of a sense of survival during separations).

From such a perspective it is not surprising that Denise's rarely displayed anger frequently turned into the earlier developmental forms of tantrum and rage. The latter often resulted in fragmentation, short episodes of derealizations, but also guilt about the loss of control. (This is in contrast to Daniel and Richard who never reported feeling guilty.) The recapitulation of these earlier forms of thinking and feeling contributed to her difficulties of moving beyond the mutual-inclusive stage. Her need for others to define herself inhibited her ability to differentiate from her parents' conflict.

In therapy, premature attempts at self-observation and reflection are often experienced as cold and analytic. The mature self emerges only in the transition from the mutual-inclusive to the systemic-organizational self. In Denise's case, this began gradually and after many months of treatment. The mixture of supportive therapy and insight orientation (i.e., where the fluctuation of the feelings and thoughts is observed in the important relationships of the patient) requires a further understanding of the self's transformational capacities in adolescence and adulthood. Many therapists either underestimate or overestimate the capacities of the patient to do "insight-oriented" therapy. This leads to misunderstandings in treatment where the patient feels criticized for not being "smart enough" or patronized.

Denise's development was visible over time. The transition involved systematic reflection both about the ways in which she felt bound into the needs and wishes of others and how this pattern precluded her ability to protect herself. In this transition, which parallels Erikson's description of the identity crisis, she began to examine her future and her ideological commitments. As Denise began to want more autonomy, she noticed that her belief that she could not survive without others was based on a longstanding misconception. In the process of uncovering this biographic reality, she began to experiment with distancing herself from her therapist. These experiences, in turn, allowed her to use her most mature insights to examine her past beliefs: for example, that separation equals physical death and that movement toward autonomy would be met with revenge and punishment.

In summary, Denise's recurring themes of separation, abandonment, and depression created a life narrative in which the earlier fears resurfaced within the context of the later self. The focus on recapitulation permitted experimentation with new forms of relating. The developmental transition of the most mature part of herself provided Denise with those tools that made it possible to gain a new perspective—and therefore overcome—the recapitulations of the past. The role of the clinician was to ensure that the development of the self was brought into unity with the strengthening of that self.

This section has served as an introduction to social-cognitive typologies of suicidal and borderline patients. We have also addressed the clinical usefulness of one such developmental typology. We will now turn to a more general discussion of clinical-developmental approaches to intervention.

CLINICAL-DEVELOPMENTAL PSYCHOLOGY AND INTERVENTION

Constructivist psychology has provided educators with great inspiration and many creative school interventions. These programs have built on diverse sources, such as Piaget's (1926) and Vygotsky's (1978) theories. Since learning can readily be viewed as part of an intellectual process, this bond between cognitive development and education is not surprising. Kohlberg and Mayer (1972) radicalized the relationship between education and cognition asserting, along with John Dewey, that *the* aim of education *is* development—understood predominantly as cognitive development.

In contrast to this long and distinguished line of educational interventions, there have been few social cognitive applications in clinical settings. This is especially surprising because psychoanalysis, and especially dynamic child and adolescent psychotherapy, have a strong, if not always acknowledged, cognitive base (e.g., making the unconscious conscious; fostering the observing ego, focusing on identity issues). In another tradition, the extension of behavioral psychology to cognitive behavior therapy has produced many effective applications. But the different cognitive theories established in academic developmental psychology, which have proven so useful, complex, and elegant, have had only a small influence on clinical practice.

Of the scholars and clinicians who have created bridges between cognitive ideas and practical clinical techniques are, among others, Ivey, Ivey, and Simek-Morgan (1993), Guidano and Liotti (1983), Noam (1988c), Rosen (1985), Selman and Schultz (1990), and Shirk (1988b). All of these theorists provide a unique view of developmental therapy, in this section we will outline only central common themes of an emerging clinical-developmental therapy.

First, the constructivist lens focuses on the ways therapists and patients develop meaning and how symptoms are related to underlying beliefs and theories about the self. Second, developmental contributors point to the important distinction between competence and performance. Instead of assuming that children, adolescents, and adults resist insights offered them, the research indicates that the tools are often not available to understand the insight offered by therapists, frequently rendering the concept of resistance useless. Third, the constructivist clinicians often stress the importance of multiple level functioning, instead of applying a single-stage model traditionally put forward by their academic peers. Such a perspective is in line with what we have addressed in earlier parts of this chapter: therapy and development are not only about continued creation of self reflection, but also about accessing and integrating earlier forms of knowing and experiencing.

Gaining Perspective

As to the first point, central to all the constructivist principles is the idea of "multiple seeing" (Ivey, Ivey, & Simek-Morgan, 1993); that is, the therapist's and the client's ability to hold several perspectives at once. The underlying assumption for a mature level of functioning is that by acquiring a more holistic word view, the client can be mobilized toward gaining greater flexibility and fluidity in her perspectives. Acknowledgment of multiple realities helps the client explore the tacit structure and beliefs about herself and the world. It is hoped that in the process, the client's beliefs and casual theories regarding her problems will shift from being perceived as *the* truth to *a* truth (one among many possibilities). This shift from a dualistic to a relativistic perspective is also at the center of Perry's clinical and educational work (1970), and has proven especially useful (see also Henderson, 1989). Guidano and Liotti (1983) refer to this "process of relativity" when they write, "[the therapists'] job is to make the patient well aware that his or her declarations concern nothing but *theories*, and not absolute truths" (p. 139). This new awareness enables the patient to see more clearly the ways in which her tacit set of beliefs prevent psychological growth and/or maintain disturbing emotion or self-defeating behaviors (Guidano & Liotti, 1983).

Guidano and Liotti show that a cognitive-constructionist approach to therapy helps the client explore the tacit structure and beliefs about herself and the world. When the ways of making meaning and casual theories about the self move from the abstract and the impersonal to being the object of examination, the client usually is able to see more clearly how her tacit set of beliefs direct, maintain, and prevent from growing and changing self-defeating behavior or disturbing emotion. For the Italian team, this perspective builds on cognitive-behavioral therapy while introducing developmental and attachment principles.

In this model, the therapist should be more concerned about the patient's formulation of internal consistency of the patient's "subjective" past life events (e.g., the way the events influenced her life theme and her present reconstruction of casual theories) than to "objective" facts. Interestingly, such a constructivist perspective has also been developed in psychoanalysis through the creative work of Spence (1984). These authors argue that the narration of a cohesive life story is more significant and healing than the historical facts. Guidano and Liotti show that only after the "subjective" account of the patients inner reality is established, she would be able to see how the present irrational beliefs developed. The patient's problematic behavior is understood as a rigid cognitive organization (e.g., overassimilation; see Noam, 1986a, 1986b) that resist development in the face of ever-changing environmental demands. This avoidance of change relates to the idea of equilibration, which is at the center of Rosen's work (1985) on clinical applications.

Rosen argues that equilibration is the essential factor in Piaget's theory of development. With each new equilibrated stage, a wider perspective is achieved, consisting of the ability to coordinate more perspectives. He states, "A way of looking at patients in therapy from a Piagetian prospective is that they are stuck in a state of disequilibrium. The problem they are facing cannot be adequately assimilated and resolved at their present level of knowledge organization, but neither are they inventing new and more adaptive ways to handle the situation successfully. That is precisely why they have come into therapy" (pp. 185–186). Piagetian theory stresses the importance of peer interaction in producing "confrontation" and "conflict" that facilitate decentration from the person's egocentric beliefs and promote growth (p. 230). For example, it was found that two pre-operational children paired in order to solve problems were able to reach concrete operational levels of reasoning and judgments (Doise & Mugny, 1984). Rosen describes this phenomena as ". . . the impetus to development came from the dialogue and conflict predicted upon a confrontation of contradictory *incorrect* centrations" (p. 231).

For many children, the creation of a perspective on their behavior is key to clinical work. Selman and his group have explored strategies of treatment with a method they call "pair therapy." This social-cognitive developmental training focuses on improving the individual's ability to take a third-person prospective. That is, to have the ". . . ability to take the view of another person, when that view differs from one's own" (Selman & Schultz, 1988, p. 232).

Selman and Schultz believe that, for children, a therapeutic intervention that focuses solely on introspection and insight is unlikely to facilitate behavioral change. Children can intellectually grasp the concepts of collaboration and reciprocity, but experience difficulty in translating "interpersonal thought" to "interpersonal action." They suggest shifting the focus of intervention from interview/discussion to real-life interactions with peers. By doing so, children will achieve "felt understanding"—they will learn to connect affect to action through immediate reflection on feeling within an ongoing interaction. Selman and Schultz write, "the pair therapy context raises action to the level of thought by solving the puzzle of high-level understanding—low, level behavior through felt understanding in a 'real-life' peer relationship" (1988, p. 243).

Using this method, the therapist treats two children who are considered developmentally lagging behind their peers, simultaneously helping them to establish a cooperative relationship and learn new negotiation strategies. By pairing children at the same developmental level, the therapy enables them to work on assimilating more adaptive behaviors. It was found that the most effective match is of two children who are on the same level of social functioning, but who have predominantly different orientations (e.g., one accommodative the other assimilative styles). This allows the children to learn from the other's opposite mode and to feel safe to experiment with different orientations.

This approach is illustrative of taking social-cognitive development into account to work toward improved health. Especially creative in this model is the combination of individual development (e.g., more flexibility in orientations and prosocial thinking and behavior) and interpersonal communication patterns. Psychological reality is not viewed solely as an "intrapsychic" phenomenon, but as a shared activity of interacting people who "co-construct" their world. The focus on two converging and diverging communication partners can be very effective as shown in adult couples' therapy. But this technique has rarely been applied to children and their friendships, despite the fact that many issues of creating intimacy while establishing differentiation and autonomy have some resemblance with adult couples.

Many publicly funded institutions and agencies throughout the United States and beyond initiated intervention programs relying on one or another type of role- or perspective-taking training. One example of these diverse efforts is provided by the work of Chalmers and Townsend (1990), who successfully overcame the delayed role-taking skills of a group of institutionalized delinquent girls in New Zealand. A related technique was developed by Chandler, Greenspan, and Barenboim (1974). This is a group training, in which each member of the group plays a role in a sketch and continues to switch roles until he or she acts all the different roles in the play. After the role-taking exercise, the participants are encouraged to reflect on the thoughts, motivations, and feelings of the different personalities and on the insights they gained by assuming multiple perspectives.

In these studies of Chandler, Selman, and others, role-taking training not only resulted in a broad improvement in the performance of such troubled youth on standard measures of social perspective-taking, but also on various "hard" measures of real-world social competence, such as recidivism or behavioral ratings by institutional staff. Most therapeutic perspectives build on the notions of insight, perspective, and understanding. But it is the clinical-developmental therapist who uses models of progressive growth to promote these capacities. Instead of producing the insight, the therapist can ally herself with an inherent developmental potential and can concentrate on creating conditions for social interaction that support such development.

Limits of Understanding Instead of Resistance

A number of developmental child clinicians and researchers address the second point—the view of children not having developed certain skills that previously were interpreted as being present but resisted. *Cognitive Development and Child Psychotherapy* edited by Shirk (1988b) represents an important volume dealing with cognitive, self, and interpersonal aspects of child therapy from a constructivist perspective. Shirk believes that the interaction of the child's psychological and behavioral problems with his developmental stage presents a complex and challenging task for the child therapist since children's cognitive-developmental level mediates their involvement in and response to therapy. Shirk stresses that the therapist needs to assess the child's developmental level accurately and communicate on the child's level, otherwise the child is unlikely to benefit from the interaction (e.g., the child either ignores the communication or will assimilate it to his developmental level and thereby distort its content).

According to Shirk (1988a) as well as Noam (1986a, 1986b), an especially difficult concept for children is unconscious motivation. The paradoxical nature of unconscious motivations—their causes are purposeful but at the same time they are not done on purpose—reaches beyond the capacities of the child's mind as does the fact that there are usually multiple causes. Shirk (1988a) gives the example of a troubled child who was put in a foster home. The child began to "act out" against a substitute teacher in school. In a discussion with the school principle, the child attributed his disruptive behavior to the fact that the teacher gave too much classwork. The child's therapist, however, suspected that the amount of classwork presents only a partial answer for the child's intense reaction. He believed that this behavior was also a result of an "unconscious transference reaction . . . [in which] feelings intended for the 'substitute' parent have been transferred to the substitute teacher" (p. 80). When the therapist presented him with this interpretation, the child dismissed it, called it "stupid," and continued in blaming the teacher for having excessive demands. Shirk argues that this response should be understood in its whole complexity, not merely as "resistance." It is likely that the child's cognitive level prevented him from acknowledging the multiple causes for his behavior as well as recognizing his internal psychological processes (as also indicated in the case of Daniel presented in an earlier section of this chapter).

Similarly, Nannis (1988) argues that children's conceptions of emotions are related to their cognitive level. Therefore children's denial of conflicted feelings are not necessarily manifestations of their pathology, rather they may not posses the cognitive capacities to experience and express them. One important implication is that child therapists should be especially careful in their assessment. They must not have "intuitive" assumptions concerning the child's understanding of feeling, rather they need to examine it directly. For example, a child who is highly verbal is often perceived as having a higher level of reasoning. This impression seems to work, giving the therapist "a false sense of progress" (p. 112). Later in therapy, when the child demonstrates an age-appropriate cognitive level, therapists tend to interpret it as "regression" (p. 112). Nannis describes this unfortunate misunderstanding well when she writes ". . . It is more likely that the child had never truly functioned at a higher level. Rather, the child sounded as if he or she had. It is part of the therapist's responsibility to assess how information is internalized and processed, not just how it is verbalized" (p. 112).

Harter (1988) makes a similar point regarding an adequate evaluation of competence. She believes that the degree of similarity between the child's developmental level and the therapist's communication will determine whether the insight offered by the therapist would be ignored or facilitate change. She points out that the therapist's interest in self-reflection, thoughts, and emotions often stands in sharp contrast to children's interest in concrete activities in the outside world. As a result, overly "psychological" interventions that consist of introspection and self-reflection are likely to fail since they do not match the child's interests. Thus, for school-age children, action-oriented methods such as direct modeling are likely to be more effective than insight-oriented ones.

Bierman (1988) argues that preschoolers and younger school-age children are unable to integrate inconsistent information about other people. For example, if they learn that a movie star committed a crime, most young children will deny that he can still be a star or even act in a show. Similarly, a child's abrupt change in feelings towards a friend or a significant other may not reflect psychopathology (e.g. lack of object permanence), but rather a normative reaction typical for his level of cognitive development.

All of these approaches are extremely important in creating a map of children's capacities that can support empathic responses. Accepting the limits of the client's meaning-making system depathologizes and avoids a sense of not living up to the expectations of the therapist. Paradoxically, accepting the existing limitations produces better chances for development than demanding responses that are beyond the patient's capacities. Vygotsky's (1978) idea of the zone of proximal development can serve as an important, and underutilized, construct for the clinical-developmentalist. This notion of a developmental space simultaneously addresses the acceptance of the present organization while challenging the limitations.

Multiple Functioning

As we have seen earlier in this chapter, according to Noam (1988a, 1988d) and Noam and Borst (1994b), advances in social cognition may transform symptoms to a higher developmental level (e.g., a similar underlying conflict will be expressed through a different or "higher level" symptom), but not necessarily guarantee their reduction. In fact, in many cases greater complexity in self-conception can lead to more sophisticated ways of self-deception, alienation, and internalized problems. In addition, social-cognitive development is not uniform across all aspects of personality, rather there are areas of "encapsulations" of old meaning systems. These old meaning systems, usually in the area of emotional and interpersonal functioning, are governed by a lower cognitive level and resist integration to the higher level system. Noam argues that within child therapy too much emphasis on advancing structural development may not be helpful since it neglects encapsulated areas that are problematic in social interactions. Instead, the therapist must attend to the interrelation between the different developmental levels. That is, the therapist should engage in careful analysis of (a) the broader gestalt of the client's "core life themes" in their relationship to (b) encapsulations and (c) the most complex psychological organization of the self. Stages of development, be they cognitive, moral, or self, have not captured the interrelationships between the different organizational levels. Noam (1988d) provides an example that illustrates this point. Jay, a 10-year-old who showed an excessive need to control situations (e.g., requested strict structure in sessions, asked for rule-bound games) while exhibiting an inability to control a great many psychological and physical functions (e.g., encopresis, excessive-eating, and temper tantrums). In this case, if the therapist would have attended only to treating the most mature level trying to mobilize his ego, moral, or perspective-taking capacities to the next stage, it would have proven quite destructive. The full shift to the age-appropriate reciprocal, self-protective level brings with it a strong focus on control. But it proved very important to focus on meanings of the insufficient control that were strongly tied to a long history of struggles with his extremely demanding and strict parents. Helping Jay to control his behavior without addressing the fact that the symptoms were related to a search, albeit self-destructive, for a freer expression of his wishes and will, might have led to further rigidities of character. These forms of more complex coping, can indeed lead to symptom reduction and support for higher cognitive functions, but they do not necessarily produce more flexibility and vitality and solutions that are "truer" to the self.

In support of Noam, Leahy (1988) writes that individuals' maladaptive notions regarding themselves or their relationships might be a product of the earlier developmental stage in which they were formed (like encapsulation). These early self-schemas often do not change despite cognitive development in other areas. Furthermore, Leahy suggests that progression in social-cognitive development may have negative implications. For example, a growing ability to take a third-person perspective can lead to excess self-reflection which, in turn, may cause self-reproach. Similarly, more complex moral development can produce excessive guilt feelings. These new abilities may make the person more vulnerable for "self-critical depression" (p. 196). Thus, higher stages are not necessarily better; they can bring positive changes as well as new vulnerabilities.

Russell and van den Broek (1988) hold that children's difficulties with therapeutic tasks are not a result of their general cognitive level, but of excessive demands on a certain domain such as attention or memory. They suggest that therapists will complement less-developed aspects of children cognitive functions in order to counterbalance demands that are beyond their cognitive abilities. Russell and Broek view child psychotherapy as "a process of collaborative problem solving in which the therapist's cognitive abilities support the child's active attempts at problem mastery" (p. 325).

From a cognitive point of view, Schmid-Kitsikis (1990) offers an integrative approach to understanding mental functioning and stresses the vital connection between cognition and emotion. She believes that the intersection between the various mental factions (e.g., cognition, emotion) and their modes of construction (e.g., unconscious, preconscious, and conscious), constitutes our symbolic representations both in rational and imaginative thinking. In other words, creative thought requires openness to primary thought processes even when the individual is predominantly using secondary processes. Accordingly, pathology occurs when the different spheres of mental functioning, such as emotion and cognition, are not linked, are unavailable to the client, or are immobilized in some way.

In therapy, the clinician presents the client with novel challenges (e.g., tasks, play, questions) which often touch on or trigger unconscious processes related to the client's motivations and behaviors. By so doing, the therapist activates relational conflicts that allow her to assess the significance of certain behaviors as well as their degree of variety and mobility. Hence, a goal of the therapeutic intervention is to explore and "mobilize" the "mental potentialities" of the client. The various tasks during a session call the client to explore new and creative ways of "being together" with the therapist. It is hoped that learning alternative ways of "being together" improve the quality and nature of object relations and experience a greater sense of continuity (psychic as well as sociohistorical). Schmid-Kitsikis writes, ". . . the central issue in therapy is, in our view, that the connections between developments in different spheres, i.e., of object relations and of cognitive energies, as well as the quality of the mental constructions and acquisitions that are already present" (p. 74). Finally, she maintains that her therapeutic method is not directed toward quantitative changes such as improvement of intellectual performance. Rather, it focuses on *integration* of mental functions (e.g., qualitative change) which, in turn, build a stronger foundation and enhance the individual's capacity for further developments.

From a moral development point of view, Blakeney and Blakeney (1990) introduced a creative conceptual and clinical synthesis. They classified three common types of "moral misbehavior" in a population of emotionally and behaviorally disturbed girls in a residential treatment facility by combining symptoms, behaviors, and thought. The group of girls who fell under the first category was usually diagnosed as having a conduct disorder. They defied authority (e.g., parents, teachers, police officers) and often claimed (in a derogatory manner) that they did not know how to do their work. They tended to skip school and were often suspected in instances of substance abuse, including stealing and selling of drugs. The girls tended to justify their behavior as the "practical solution to the problem of unfair distribution" (p. 101).

The girls in the second category of moral misbehavior tended to run away from their homes or schools. They often engaged in self-abusive behavior, ranging from drug and alcohol abuse to self-mutilation with knives or razor blades to sexual activity with strangers. Their behavior vacillated from being disobedient and having temper tantrums to inviting protective attention. They often described "feelings" as the motivation for their behavior, particularly feelings of sadness, abandonment, and rage.

The girls in the third category often showed extreme behaviors, both alone and in public. Such behaviors included hiding in closets, setting fires, masturbating in public, and disrupting classroom activities. They often justified their behavior by claiming that they were "just playing."

Blakeney and Blakeney's position is that "by understanding the relationship between the pattern of moral misbehavior and the structure of moral thought and feeling in the social context, we are able to understand the *function* of the child's misbehavior" (p. 102). Only when the function the deviant behavior serves in maintaining the child's psychic equilibrium is understood can a child be treated by bringing latent moral claims to awareness and trying to construct new ways of feeling, thinking, behaving and interacting with adults and peers. Blakeney and Blakeney argue that an assessment of type of moral misbehavior and the meaning that a particular behavior holds for the child is essential for deciding on a treatment strategy. Such treatment, they say, should be focused on reconstructing the child's underlying moral beliefs. Relevant to the issue of multiple-level functioning, the Blakeney's found that the girls had a preponderance of split-responses at different stages of complexity on the moral judgment interview (Kohlberg, 1984).

Blakeney and Blakeney proposed three treatment plans corresponding with each of the three categories of moral misbehavior. In treating the child in the first category, they stress that any attempts to modify a subject's way of thinking are likely to fail because the subject inevitably "already knows better." Rather, they suggest that the therapist focus on the subject's underlying feelings, which are often split from the behavior. For example, when a child complains about unfairness and favoritism (i.e., "the counselor wasn't doing her job. She was sleeping when she should have been checking chores," p. 111), the therapist should attend not only the actual incident, but also to the child's need for nurturing. Another important issue for these girls is their unwillingness to take the perspective of authority figures. According to Blackeney and Blackeney, this unwillingness can be treated through role playing with peers or "role reversal" with a staff member.

While affect and behavior are split in the first category, they are parallel in the second category, although do not inform each other. That is, behavior is often "impulsive, and not subject to cognitive evaluation or transformation" (p. 112). The treatment of this second group therefore focuses on the logical relationship between feelings and behavior (a subject may be asked to make lists and charts indicating the logical linkage between his or her feelings and behavior, for example). Unlike the first group, the girls have little trouble role-reversing, although the subjects need training to be able to do it with some consistency.

Finally, for the third group, neither feeling nor steady cognitive structure influence moral judgment or behavior. Since the subject frequently is not able to tell whether his or her own actions are playful, imaginary, or real, other people's reactions to that behavior do little to modify it. Accordingly, a behavioral approach that helps the child acknowledge the differences between social contexts proves to be the most beneficial. For example, if a child is "lost" in a movie theater, he or she may be hiding while shouting loudly for help. The therapist must begin by joining the child in the fantasy, and then move on to focus on the delusional parts of that fantasy. Next, the therapist should focus on the logical context of the misbehavior (e.g., play or reality) rather than the specific misbehavior. In other words, the therapist has to join the child's fantasy so that the child feels safe enough to enter the larger social world.

In a theoretical discussion entitled "Toward a Constructive-Developmental Understanding of the Dialectics of Individuality and Irrationality," Basseches (1979) addressed the issue of multiple levels of functioning. He argues that two of the limitations of the constructive-developmental tradition can be transcended without excluding its dialectical assumptions. The first limitation is the insensitivity to individual differences. The constructive-developmental theories support the structural approach that assumes stage unity, thus failing to recognize diversity and richness of individual meaning-making. These theoretical notions often stand in sharp contradiction to what clinicians experience in the context of therapy (e.g., that people's differences in the ways they understand themselves and their environment are as notable as their similarities). To overcome this limitation, Basseches proposes that the stages should be understood as *philosophical,* and not as psychological concepts, where each individual possesses a unique psychological origination. The second limitation he points out is that constructive-developmental theory assumes a complete transformation of all psychological domains to a more sophisticated structure. Assuming such high level of mental integration, it is difficult to explain incidents where individuals feel and behave in ways that contradict their rational meaning making. Basseches suggests that instead of viewing structural transformation in a "totalistic" fashion, we should view developmental reorganization as processes in which "differentiation and integration is always imperfect and incomplete" (p. 190).

These diverse clinical approaches are all freeing social-cognition and constructivist thinking from an exclusive focus on thought and a simple stage-wise notion of development. The clinical explorations are messy, supporting the theory while deconstructing it. But they lead to a richer understanding of human adaptation and growth. They have led to a rediscovery of emotions and the symbolic, unconscious life and a multitude of responses at different levels in the same person. The modern constructivist accounts can build on many of the insights of psychoanalysis mentioned in an early section of this chapter. Within that tradition, psychological life is seen as conflicted, fluctuating between insight and unknown parts of the self, prone to getting pulled to unresolved interpersonal relationships. The essential contribution of the clinical-developmental perspective is to free these constructs from their fixations on early childhood. This new perspective on humans, fully incorporating our knowledge about the ways meaning about self and relationships develop across time, is enriching not only our understanding of at-risk populations but also our theories of normative growth as well.

Differential Treatment

While most theorists in the earlier sections explore issues in child psychotherapy, Ivey (1986) and Ivey, Ivey, and Simek-Morgan (1993) focus on adults. These authors describe two major theoretical foundations used in developmental counseling and therapy to facilitate a multiple-perspective/holistic world view in the client: (a) co-construction of knowledge and the relationship between therapist and client and (b) adaptation of Piagetian four cognitive stages as useful ways in understanding clients cognitive and emotional states.

Developmental therapy with adults is built on Piagetian cognitive stages who, like children, exhibit different levels of cognitive development (e.g., sensory motor, pre-operational, concrete-operational, formal-operational, and dialectic/systemic). Each level is characterized by "different complexity of language and meaning" (Ivey, Ivey, & Simek-Morgan, 1993, p. 132). In therapy, the clinician evaluates the predominant developmental level in which the patient operates and works towards fostering development. In order to promote cognitive development, the counselor matches the intervention with the client's cognitive style. In so doing, she helps the client explore issues in his developmental level. Only after the client feels grounded and understood within his predominant developmental stage can the therapist begin to expand the inquiries to integrate different levels of development. The goal is that the client will expand the experience and functioning to engage all levels. All of the categories are important and necessary for full and healthy functioning, where one is not superior to the other. By "traveling" through the different developmental levels the client gains a broad perspective on his issues The problem is understood and felt differently when viewed from different levels (Ivey, Ivey, & Simek-Morgan, 1993). The combination of both forms of development is useful to address a range of cognitive and emotional aspects in the client.

Ivey posits that different therapy schools seem more useful in working with different cognitive levels. For example, Gestalt exercises, body work, and relaxation techniques are most effective in dealing with clients who present difficulties around sensory motor issues. These techniques help the client connect with her emotional world directly, be more spontaneous, and reduce denial and splitting. Behavioral techniques seem to fit concrete thinkers since they focus on facts and on "if/then thinking." Psychodynamic and Rogerian therapies appear to work best with formal operational clients, because of their focus on reflection, introspection, and analysis of recurrent patterns.

This last point is especially important as a clinical-developmental approach should not only be viewed as creating new forms of assessment, prevention, and intervention, but also as a way to deal with the important issue of differential treatment. For too long, the therapy schools have defined how a patient gets treated. Instead, the person struggling with difficulties and symptoms should be evaluated to receive those treatments that have proven to produce the best results. Recently, eclectic and integrating treatment approaches are receiving deserved attention. However, most approaches focus on diagnostic issues. A clinical approach that is tied to development, where the person's capacities for insight and perspective and typical meaning systems and symptom patterns are combined has a far greater likelihood for success. The distinctions about what the client can understand, will view as salient issues and themes, and will apply to new adaptational capacities should be directly related to the way the therapist can expect to support recovery.

Noam (1992) has introduced a differential treatment model for adolescents that is summarized in Table 15.2. Introducing a constructivist grid of meanings about the self and relationships, different treatment foci are suggested. These treatment methods cannot be neatly attributed to one or another therapy tradition,

TABLE 15.2 Clinical-Developmental Interventions with Adolescents

The Subjective-Physical Position	The Reciprocal-Instrumental Position	The Mutual-Overinclusive Position
Treatment focus		
• Interventions that focus on cognitive and emotional disorganization, impulsivity, attention problems, the constant need for physical presence of attachment figures, and the lack of body control (e.g., supportive and behavioral treatments in a structured environment, helping in creating a firmer family structure, if possible).	• Treatment with focus on issues of fairness and support for behavior that takes other people into consideration. • Central role for peer learning, as struggles with authority figures are typical (e.g., AA). • Activities with adult role models who work on skills and competencies (e.g., coaches).	• "Interpersonal therapy" with focus on depression and low self-esteem emerging in close relationships.
Setting		
• Sometimes residential setting needed to contain serious impulsivity, depression, and potential for short psychotic episodes. But any regular school or community setting has to provide strong limits and rules that foster the learning of consequences of self's actions. • Predictable staff must be readily available.	• Containment in residential or special school classroom settings, sometimes needed for a long period of time, especially when antisocial and violent trends are strong. • But despite seeming disinterest in individual therapy, one-to-one relationships are important to create trust, but need to entail mutually satisfying activities (e.g., eating, sports, walks).	• Individual treatment (often in conjunction with family treatment) to help adolescents express internalized feelings and, when necessary, short hospitalization (long, regressive hospitalizations to be avoided).
Support		
• Strong boundaries and limits with goal of internalizing external rules. Support with often enmeshed family system.	• Support in experience of unfairness of rules and situations and with the world that confronts externalizing stance. • Experience of nurturant relationship is critical as many have experienced trauma and neglect. • Confrontations to address manipulations.	• Strong commitment in every aspect of adolescents' experiences even when it seems more like friends talking. • Support for assertiveness needed. • Encouraging the expression of anger and frustration.
Insight		
• Work with emerging ability to review behaviors, feelings, and thoughts. • Begin to recognize that multiple feelings can coexist about the same person or situation. • Learn about the fact that strategies are being used that are self-destructive.	• Emerging recognition that world can be influenced in productive ways and that rejections by others do not have to be addressed in terms of revenge and hostility. • Close relationships provide a possibility to begin to view the world through a sense of mutuality and community.	• Beginning reflection of what is occurring in the relationship as a pattern (e.g., "Everytime I am silent, I feel ashamed"). • Framing regression and low self-esteem in terms of a lack of inner agency. • Explore the problems of anger.
Typical therapeutic binds		
• Attempt by the therapist to interpret behavior in terms of symbolic meanings, when they are only understood in concrete and behavioral terms. • Feeding into split between "good family, bad treatment staff" (or vice versa) often leads to a breakdown of the work.	• Adolescent confuses the therapist "being on my side" with jointly breaking rules (e.g., smoking in office before age). • Fear of consequences can lead to a style of nondisclosure. • Difficulty in talking about problems emerging in the relationship and past hurts because a biographical and transference focus has not yet developed.	• Silences in the treatment and feeling rejected by therapist require impossible proofs of acceptance (e.g., midnight phone calls). • Danger that therapist demand when this ability is not fully present too much insight and self-observation and underestimating the capacity to observe relationship patterns and feeling states.

Source: Adapted from Noam, 1992.

but are instead organized around what adolescents typically view as motivating and alliance building, what insights they can make use of, and what the typical therapeutic binds are that one encounters in development.

A great deal of further work is necessary to specify differential treatments from a developmental point of view. These attempts are beginning to bear fruit, as a central healing dimension in therapy is related to the potential for development each person brings to the process.

Even without being able to describe the entire evidence that has come from the social-cognitive studies, it is possible to generalize the findings reviewed and to discuss the implications of theory. We will briefly outline the implications of the clinical-developmental approach for present discussions in developmental psychology, psychiatry, developmental psychopathology, and psychoanalysis.

Conclusion and Outlook for Developmental Psychology and Developmental Psychopathology

A parsimonious conclusion from the work presented is that self theory inspired by social-cognitive ideas (in the case of this chapter: moral and ego development as well as social-role taking) can help organize something as seemingly disorganized as psychopathology. This line of work further shows that self theory can be "validated" in relationship to behavioral problems and emotional states. The broad personality dimensions included in Loevinger's model are associated to psychopathology, as are the more circumscribed and cognitive levels of Piaget and Kohlberg.

But the research presented here raises almost as many questions as it answers. For example, is it the stage of psychological self-organization that "produces" the psychopathology? Or, are problems that have existed for some time been structured in new ways with development? Furthermore, why is it that many people function at these same developmental positions and do not manifest any psychological dysfunction? In the adolescent research reviewed in this chapter, one could argue that delay produces a discrepancy between life tasks and developmental abilities ("age-stage dysynchrony"). Still, theorists often have difficulty dealing with the many adolescents who are developmentally delayed and yet asymptomatic. Furthermore, in most adult samples, the subjects function at age appropriate, normative developmental levels, and at the same time their symptoms are also associated significantly to developmental stage (e.g., Dill & Noam, 1990). These questions all require more than empirical studies, they demand new and encompassing models.

Existing cognitive self-theories can help a great deal, because the self and interpersonal relationships are usually centrally involved in psychological dysfunction. But clinical-developmental studies also point to the limitations and over-simplifications of normative developmental theory.

As discussed in this chapter, two theoretical issues can serve as examples of how clinical-developmental psychology can point to changes necessary in normative developmental theory. The first deals with the "higher-is-better" hypothesis, the second with the underlying architecture of constructivism. In contrast to those investigators of normal development who have stated that higher stages are more adaptive than lower stages, the findings reviewed in this chapter suggest that more mature ego levels can be associated with very destructive and personally injurious behaviors. Similar findings have been reported in the literature on moral development (e.g., Noam & Young, 1990). We have found that developmental delay can serve as a protective factor for certain serious internalizing disorders, such as suicidality and depression. Thus it will be important to begin to carefully distinguish psychological maturity from psychological complexity, with both normal and pathological samples.

In the past ten years, a great deal of progress has been made in establishing a bridge between the developmental and mental health disciplines. Developmental psychopathology research has advanced with new journals, special issues of developmental and clinical journals and books appearing at a rapid pace. However, as funding has become available in the United States for this line of work, the output of research is far outpacing the careful conceptual delineation of what constitutes development; what models should be used to classify and observe maladaptation; and what bridging constructs are needed to discover essential interplays between development and psychopathology.

Large-scale longitudinal-epidemiological studies (e.g., Rutter's Isle of Wright Study) establish prevalence and incidence of psychiatric disorder at different age points. Similarly, a great many developmental studies of disordered populations (e.g., Robbins classic study of delinquent children) follow children into adulthood to establish prediction rates and risk factors in development. Because of the scope and theoretical orientations of these sets of studies, age is generally used as the critical developmental marker. But as we noted in the beginning of this chapter, developmental research has shown chronological age to be a very crude indicator, and most developmental processes are better understood in psychological terms defined independently of age.

But even within this research camp, dissatisfaction about crude age-developmental measurement is voiced. Achenbach (1982), for example, ends the first textbook of developmental psychopathology, which is largely dedicated to an age-graded, psychometric approach by stating:

> Many approaches to psychopathology neglect children's capacity for constructive cognitive adaptation and reorganization. The child's mental representations are end products of many organic and experiential factors, but these mental representations may yield a better prediction of behavior than all the separate determinants would. Modification of the mental representations may therefore be an important step in promoting more adaptive development. (pp. 654–655)

The clinical-developmental research focuses on mental representations, defined as cognitive, social-cognitive dimensions in the development of the self. In fact, in most social-cognitive studies of adolescents age is not significantly associated with psychopathology and symptomatology, whereas developmental level is.

This clinical-developmental approach is also relevant to the more theoretical developmental psychopathology approach provided by the attachment paradigm. Bowlby and the researchers using his theory (e.g., Ainsworth, Bretherton, Cicchetti, Grossman, Main, Sroufe) have had to address the issue of how early dyadic attachment patterns continue to shape adaptation despite a great many developmental transformations that occur in a child's life. Many investigators have used Bowlby's theory of the working model to describe the process whereby primary attachments become part of the self over time. In this tradition, it is assumed that with development—as social interaction and cognitive and emotional development become more differentiated—internal working models must be increased in complexity and revised to fit new relationship experiences.

If the working model is also defined in cognitive and representational terms, one has to assume that changes of cognitive and social cognitive capacity can significantly influence attachment configurations (and vice versa). Future work will be necessary to shed light on the important relationship between normative social cognitive development and the growth of the working model. In this conceptual and empirical marriage lies the potential for very important new findings about how people outgrow their problems and symptoms, or how they create resilience in development and recover. (For an overview, see Noam and Fischer, in press.)

Implications for Psychiatry

The field of psychiatry has moved with great vigor over the past decade toward establishing a research base from which to diagnose mental disorders. Two descriptive-nosological approaches have emerged as the standards in the field of clinical and research psychiatry: the *Diagnostic and Statistical Manual* (now in its 4th edition) and the World Health Organization's modified classification system, the ICD 10. Both manuals pay a great deal more attention to issues of reliability and validity than did diagnostic systems in the past and both have contributed to the routine use of a number of diagnostic instruments for epidemiological and clinical studies. Earlier versions of the DSM system were far less focused on research issues and had a strong psychoanalytic developmental orientation (i.e., neurotic disorders which have been eliminated since DSM III). But the attention to precision provided by the descriptive-phenomenological approach has led to the elimination of practically all developmental thinking in clinical diagnosis.

Interestingly, this has occurred at a time when there is growing recognition of the importance of cognitive and longitudinal-developmental properties (see for example, Yates, 1991). The studies described above are, thus, not only relevant to the study of the self, but show that it is possible both to use a research perspective in psychiatry *and* to reintroduce a developmental perspective to psychiatric diagnosis, as well as the related study of the etiology, antecedents and course of psychiatric disorders and their biological roots.

Implications for Psychoanalysis

While psychoanalysis has been an important, if indirect, contributor to cognitive self-psychology, especially in the transformed models introduced by Erikson and Sullivan, we continue to be confronted with a central problem in most of psychodynamic thinking. Conceptualizations about the etiology of psychopathology as well as clinical theory (e.g., transference) all relate to the early periods in life. While it used to be the Oedipal struggle of the young child that provided the essential lens for psychoanalytic thinking and treatment, the changes in patient populations and types of psychopathology (e.g., narcissism and borderline states) have changed the focus: These more serious disorders were developmentally tied to *earlier* stages of life, especially the "separation-individuation phase" of 12 to 24 months. This overemphasis on early childhood is found even in the brilliant reworkings of psychoanalysis in object relations theory (e.g., Fairbairn, Guntrip, Winnicott) and self-psychology (e.g., Kohut, Wolff). Both of these theoretical traditions have remained too closely tied to classical analysis in their attempt to understand the adult by reconstructing the child. In the process, both of these creative movements are lacking an adequate theory of adolescence and adulthood.

The clinical-developmental approach adds credence to the importance of understanding the architecture of the continuously developing and organizing self. The adolescent and adult construct meanings about self and other and produce symptoms in systematically new ways. It is an essential discovery of cognitive self-theory that these transformations follow a logical and empirical sequence that occurs, or at least has the potential to occur, throughout the lifespan.

IMPLICATIONS FOR A DEVELOPMENTAL DEFINITION OF MENTAL HEALTH

In summary, theoretical preparations for a new synthesis have occurred over the years; we have described a variety of psychoanalytic-cognitive integrations have been proposed (e.g., Wolf, 1960; Greenspan, 1979; Noam, 1985) and, more recently, papers relating Vygotsky to clinical issues have appeared. But, in contrast to educational interventions, the tools of most therapists are not guided by these theories. Child and adolescent clinicians are rightly weary of cognition built on pure logic, "upwardly mobile" stage sequences of intellectual development, and of moral judgment and perspective-taking. Fluctuations of competencies and regressions in the face of seemingly insurmountable conflicts are the daily bread of every clinician. Furthermore, what looks to the cognitive researcher like a complex and serious explanation or rationale, reveals itself to the clinician as a manipulation and rationalization. High scores on cognitive and social-cognitive tests are often accompanied by limited coping styles and fragile self integration. In addition, few clinicians, child or adult, can work without a strong focus on attachment history, present-day interpersonal processes and emotional capacities. Fortunately, developmental researchers have begun to take seriously the clinician's focus and experience—while not abandoning their orientation on normative development and health.

Despite the limitations of a cognitive perspective, we need to explore the inherent power of this tradition for understanding clinical phenomena, especially when we embed cognition in relationships, life history, and affective development. Human beings are essential cognitivists and epistemologists in their capacity to reflect on themselves and their actions, to symbolize inner and outer experiences, and to create complex interpretive systems about relationships, culture, and faith. Any videotape of a clinical encounter or a transcript of a therapist-client interaction reveals how many epistemological assumptions and meanings are being introduced and negotiated by both parties. For example, we have consistently observed that the antisocial adolescent who usually complains about parents and other authority figures will argue in terms of fairness introducing a wide set of assumptions about disappointed obligations, revenge for afflicted injuries, and so on. The fact that many of these assumptions have a present-day developmental core and are organized by observable principles is an essential, yet mostly unappreciated insight that has its roots mostly in academic developmental psychology.

However, "exporting" these insights into the therapy world may result in little more than dogmatic misapplication. The excitement captured by the field of developmental psychopathology (e.g., Cicchetti, 1984; Sroufe & Rutter, 1984) is that new problems and issues—in our case clinical in nature—produce innovative insights and tools. The psychologist's fallacy (Kohlberg, 1984) in education is to treat the educator as an applied psychologist who can readily use the laboratory findings in schools. We would like to suggest that the "developmentalist's fallacy" is that normative principles and findings can be directly assimilated by the clinician in a one-way relationship. The lack of mutually enhancing theoretical debate, research, and clinical exploration has contributed to the paucity of innovation, now being addressed by scholars and clinicians.

Slowly a fit has emerged and continues to evolve requiring reinterpretation of a new definition of mental health. Love and work as markers of health do not suffice once we take a constructivist and developmental perspective, because they are adaptational outcomes that potentially diagnose as healthy those who produce and procreate without ever experiencing the basic creativity and vitality inherent in lifelong development. For that reason, we must find new, developmentally focused definitions.

Social cognitive work will need to shed light on how continued development creates new opportunities for recovery. This is the most important applied question for the developmental psychopathologist: What developmental processes, if any, are at work when people move from dysfunction to adaptation? Most studies have been more interested in continuities of psychopathology and tracing the evolution of disorders. But we know from most clinical approaches, such as cognitive behavior therapy, client-centered psychotherapy, and psychoanalysis, that recovery is connected to relationships, self observation and the reframing of experiences and attributions. Clinical-developmental psychology is concerned with tracing those cognitive, social and emotional capacities that are at work when people reflect on themselves and important relationships. Much research is needed to relate the developing capacities about the construction of the self and relationships to recovery.

Interpreting the evolution of cognitive functioning as a progression to adaptation and health represents an overly simple extrapolation of cognitive principles to the study of psychopathology. As we have seen in this chapter, many people use their newly developing cognitive and social cognitive skills to create more complex forms of alienation, self-hate, and psychopathology. It is an important aspect of clinical-developmental psychology to differentiate productive and destructive developmental pathways, and to learn to understand under what conditions the same capacities can be used for very different purposes.

In a recent paper, we dealt with the related question whether one should define development as the aim of many clinical interventions (Noam, 1992). If development can be related to more complex forms of pathology in addition to expanded mental health, one would be inclined to dismiss the claim. If we broaden our view on development, however, we do not have to abandon this important idea prematurely. Up to recently all cognitive-developmental models, even when applied to morality, role-taking, ego, and self, have had difficulty addressing central clinical dimensions because maturity and complexity have been used interchangeably. As we have shown in this chapter, from the emerging clinical-developmental perspective maturity and complexity should be viewed as very different constructs. Maturity implies insight and perspective with an adaptational quality. Complexity refers to the shape and form of the self's organization, not its adaptational value.

This distinction of self-complexity and self-maturity is an important aspect of our developmental framework. In this model, both self-complexity and the different forms in which biographical themes, such as attachment history and traumatic experiences, are *integrated* into the overall self are defined in developmental terms. The interrelationships between self-complexity and self-integration are viewed to determine—at least in part—how well the person is adapted. A well-integrated person has more freedom to pursue new experiences in work and love and to explore and experiment in ways that produce enhanced self-complexity. This, in turn, produces new windows of opportunity to bring into focus earlier vulnerabilities and to finally overcome them. Addressing these issues then produces new freedom for exploration and emboldens the self to create deeper forms of intimacy and greater autonomy. It is this continuous cycle we should call development, rather than the stepwise progression from stage to stage, which marks cognitive-developmental models to this day; and it is this developmental courage, vitality, and flexibility that we should call mental health, rather than the ability to function smoothly and to produce appropriately.

REFERENCES

Abraham, K. (1968). A short study of the development of the libido, viewed in the light of mental disorders. In K. Abraham (Ed.), *Developmental Psychology* (pp. 418–501). London: Hogarth Press.

Achenbach, T. M. (1982). *Developmental Psychopathology* (2nd ed.). New York: Wiley.

Ainsworth, M. (1982). Attachment: retrospect and prospect. In C. Parkes & J. Stevenson-Hinde (Eds.), *The place of attachment in human behavior.* London: Tavistock.

American Psychiatric Association. (1987). *Diagnostic and statistical manual of mental disorders* (3rd ed.). Washington DC: Author.

Anthony, E. J. (1976). Freud, Piaget and human knowledge: Some comparisons and contrasts. *Annual of Psychoanalysis, 4,* 253–277.

Anthony, F. J. (1958). An experimental approach to the psychopathology of childhood autism. *British Journal of Medical Psychology, 32,* 19–37.

Anthony, F. J. (1970). Behavior disorders. In P. Mussen (Ed.), *Carmichael's manual of child psychology* (pp. 667–764). New York: Wiley.

Baldwin, J. M. (1925). *Mental development in the child and the race.* London: Macmillan.

Baltes, P. B., & Schaie, K. W. (1973). On life-span developmental research paradigms: Retrospects and prospects. In P. B. Baltes & K. W. Shaie (Eds.), *Life-span developmental psychology: Personality and socialization* (pp. 366–395). New York: Academic Press.

Bartsch, K., & Wellman, H. (1989). Young children's attribution of action to beliefs and desires, *Child Development, 60*(4), 946–964.

Basch, M. (1980). *Psychoanalytic interpretation and cognitive transformation.* Unpublished manuscript, Center for Psychosocial Studies, Chicago, IL.

Basseches, M. (1979). Towards a constructive-developmental understanding of the dialectics of individuality and rationality. In D. A. Kramer & M. Bopp (Eds.), *Transformation in clinical and developmental psychology.*

Basseches, M. (1984). *Dialectical thinking and adult development.* Norwood, NJ: Ablex.

Bearison, D. J. (1974). A Piagetian approach. *Merrill-Palmer Quarterly, 20*(1), 21–31.

Belenky, M. F., Clinchy, B. M., Goldberger, N. R., & Tarule, J. M. (1986). *Women's ways of knowing.* New York: Basic Books.

Berkowitz, M. W. (1992, April). *Adolescent moral thinking and drug use.* Paper presented at the annual meeting of the American Educational Research Association, San Francisco, CA.

Bibace, R., & Walsh, M. E. (1981). *Children's conceptions of health, illness, and bodily functions.* San Francisco: Jossey-Bass.

Bierman, K. L. (1988). The clinical implications of children's conceptions of social relationships. In S. R. Shirk (Ed.), *Cognitive development and child psychotherapy* (pp. 247–272). New York: Plenum.

Blakeney, C., & Blakeney, R. (1990). Reforming moral misbehaviour. *Journal of Moral Education, 19*(2), 101–113.

Blos, P. (1962). *On adolescence.* New York: Free Press.

Borst, S. R., & Noam, G. G. (1993). Developmental psychopathology in suicidal and non-suicidal adolescent girls. *Journal of the American Academy of Child and Adolescent Psychiatry, 32,* 501–508.

Borst, S. R., Noam, G. G., & Bartok, J. A. (1991). Adolescent suicidality: A clinical-developmental approach. *Journal of the American Academy of Child and Adolescent Psychiatry, 30,* 796–803.

Boyes, M. (1987). *Epistemic development and identity formation in adolescence.* Unpublished doctoral dissertation, University of British Columbia, Vancouver, British Columbia.

Brent, D. (1987). Correlates of medical lethality of suicide attempts in children and adolescents. *Journal of the American Academy of Child and Adolescent Psychiatry, 26,* 87–89.

Bretherton, I. (in press). Internal working models of attachment relationships as related to coping. In G. G. Noam & K. W. Fischer (Eds.), *Development and vulnerabilities in close relationships.* Hillsdale, NJ: Erlbaum.

Broughton, J. (1978). *The development of concepts of self, mind, reality, and knowledge. New direction in child development: Social cognition.* San Francisco: Jossey-Bass.

Broughton, J., & Zahaykevich, M. (1977). Review of J. Loevinger's "Ego Development." *Telos, 32,* 246–253.

Browning, D. L. (1986). Psychiatric ward behavior and length of stay in adolescent and young adult inpatients: A developmental approach to prediction. *Journal of Consulting and Clinical Psychology, 54,* 227–230.

Bruner, J. (1986). *Actual minds, possible worlds.* Cambridge, MA: Harvard University Press.

Calverley, R. M., Fischer, K. W., & Ayoub, C. (1994). Complex affective splitting in sexually abused adolescent girls. *Development and psychopathology,* 195–213.

Campagna, H. F., & Harter, S. (1975). Moral judgement in sociopathic and normal children. *Journal of Personality and Social Psychology, 31,* 199–205.

Case, R. (1984). The process of stage transition: A neo-Piagetian view. In R. J. Sternberg (Ed.), *Mechanisms of cognitive development* (pp. 20–44). New York: Freeman.

Case, R. (1985). *Intellectual development: Birth to adulthood.* New York: Academic Press.

Case, R. (1988). The whole child: Toward an integrated view of young children's cognitive, social, and emotional development. In A. D. Pellegrini (Ed.), *Psychological bases for early education.* New York: Wiley.

Chalmers, J. B., & Townsend, M. (1990). The effects of training in social perspective taking on socially maladjusted girls. *Child Development, 61,* 178–190.

Chandler, M. J. (1972). Egocentrism in normal and pathological childhood development. In W. H. F. Monks & J. DeWitt (Eds.), *Determinants of behavioral development* (pp. 569–576). New York: Academic Press.

Chandler, M. J. (1973a). Egocentrism and anti-social behavior: The assessment and training of social perspective taking skills. *Developmental Psychology, 9,* 326–332.

Chandler, M. J. (1973b). The picture arrangement subtest of the WAIS as an index of social egocentrism: A comparative study of normal and emotionally disturbed children. *Journal of Abnormal Child Psychology, 1,* 340–349.

Chandler, M. J. (1975). Relativism and the problem of epistemological loneliness. *Human Development, 18*(3), 171–180.

Chandler, M. J. (1993). Contextualism and the postmodern condition: Learning from Las Vegas. In L. J. H. S. C. Hayes, H. W. Reese, & T. R. Sarbin (Eds.), *Varieties of scientific contextualism* (pp. 227–247). Reno, NV: Context Press.

Chandler, M. J. (1994a). Adolescent suicide and the loss of personal continuity. In D. Cicchetti & S. L. Toth (Ed.), *Rochester symposium on developmental psychopathology: Disorders and dysfunctions of the self* (pp. 371–390). Rochester, NY: University of Rochester Press.

Chandler, M. J. (1994b). Self-continuity in suicidal and non-suicidal adolescents. In G. Noam & S. Borst (Eds.), *Child and adolescent suicide: Clinical-developmental perspectives.* San Francisco: Jossey-Bass.

Chandler, M. J., Boyes, M., & Ball, L. (1990). Relativism and stations of epistemic doubt. *Journal of Experimental Child Psychology, 50*(3), 370–395.

Chandler, M. J., Greenspan, S., & Barenboim, C. (1974). Assessment and training of role taking and referential communication skills in institutionalized emotionally disturbed children. *Developmental Psychology, 10,* 546–553.

Chandler, M. J., & Moran, T. (1990). Psychopathology and moral development: A comparative study of delinquent and non-delinquent youth. *Development and Psychopathology, 2,* 227–246.

Chandler, M. J., Paget, K. J., & Koch, D. (1978). The child's demystification of psychological defense mechanisms: A structural and developmental analysis. *Developmental Psychology, 14*(3), 197–205.

Chapman, M. (1988). *Constructive evolution: Origins and development of Piaget's thought.* Cambridge: Cambridge University Press.

Cicchetti, D. (1984a). *Developmental psychopathology.* Chicago: University of Chicago Press.

Cicchetti, D. (1984b). The emergence of developmental psychopathology. *Child Development, 55,* 1–7.

Cicchetti, D. (1990). A historical perspective of developmental psychopathology. In A. M. J. Rolf, D. Cicchetti, K. Neuchterlein, & S. Weintraub (Eds.), *Risk and protective factors in the development of psychopathology* (pp. 2–28). New York: Cambridge University Press.

Cicchetti, D. (1991). Fractures in the crystal: Developmental psychopathology and the emergence of self. *Developmental Review, 11,* 271–287.

Cicchetti, D., Cummings, E. M., Greenberg, M. T., & Marvin, R. S. (1990). An organizational perspective on attachment beyond infancy. In M. Greenberg, D. Cicchetti, & E. M. Cummings (Eds.), *Attachment in the pre-school years: Theory, research, and intervention* (pp. 87–137). Chicago: University of Chicago Press.

Ciompi, S. L. (1982). *Affektlogik [Affective Logic].* Stuttgart: Klett-Cotra.

Cleckley, H. (1976). *The mask of sanity* (5th ed.). St. Louis: Mosby.

Cohen, B. D. (1974). Referant Communication disturbances in acute schizophrenia. *Journal of Abnormal Psychology, 83,* 1–13.

Coie, J. D., & Pennington, B. F. (1976). Children's perceptions of deviance and disorder. *Child Development, 47,* 407–413.

Commons, M. L., Richards, F. A., & Armon, C. (1984). *Beyond formal operations: Late adolescent and adult cognitive development.* New York: Praeger.

Costello, A., Edelbrock, C., Dulcan, M., Kalas, R., & Klarie, S. (1984). *Development and testing of the NIMH diagnostic interview schedule for children on a clinical population: Final report (Contract RFP-DB-81-0027).* Center for Epidemiologic Studies, National Institute for Mental Health.

Damon, W. (1977). *The social world of the child.* San Francisco: Jossey-Bass.

Damon, W., & Hart, D. (1982). The development of self-understanding from infancy through adolescence. *Child Development, 53,* 841–864.

Decarie, T. (1978). Affect development and cognition in a Piagetian context. In T. Decarie, M. Lewis, & L. Rosenblum (Eds.), *The development of affect* (pp. 183–204). New York: Plenum.

Dill, D. L., & Noam, G. G. (1990). Ego development and treatment request. *Psychiatry, 53,* 85–91.

Dobert, R., Habermas, J., & Nunner-Winkler, G. (1977). Zur Einfuhrung [Toward Understanding]. In J. H. R. Dobert & G. N. Winkler (Eds.), *Entwicklung des Ichs [Development of Self]* (pp. 9–30). Cologne: Kiepenheuer and Witsch.

Dobert, R., & Nunner-Winkler, G. (in press). Commonsense understandings about suicide as a resource for coping with suicidal impulses. In G. Noam & S. Borst (Eds.), *Children, youth, and suicide: New directions in child development.* San Francisco: Jossey-Bass.

Doise, W., & Mugny, G. (1984). *The social development of the intellect* (A. St. James-Emler & N. Emler, Trans.). New York: Pergamon.

Edelstein, W. (in press). Social development. In G. Noam & K. Fischer (Eds.), *Development and vulnerabilities in close relationships.* Hillsdale, NJ: Erlbaum.

Edelstein, W., Grundmann, M., Hoffmann, V., & Schellhas, B. (1992, September). *Family determinants and cognitive consequences of the development of anxiety and depression.* Poster presented at the fifth European Conference on Developmental Psychology, Seville, Spain.

Edelstein, W., Keller, M., & Schröder, E. (1990). Child development and social structure: A longitudinal study of individual differences. In P. B. Baltes, D. L. Featherman, & R. M. Lerner (Eds.), *Life-span development and behavior* (Vol. 10, pp. 152–185). Hillsdale, NJ: Erlbaum.

Elkind, D. (1967). Egocentrism in adolescence. *Child Development, 38,* 1025–1034.

Elkind, D. (1979). Cognitive development and psychopathology: Observations on ego-centrism and ego defense. In D. Elkind (Ed.), *The child and society.* New York: Oxford University Press.

Enright, R., & Lapsley, D. (1980). Social role-taking: A review of the construct, measures, and measurement properties. *Review of Educational Research, 28,* 647–674.

Erikson, E. (1968). *Identity, youth, and crisis.* New York: Norton.

Erikson, E. H. (1950). Growth and crisis of the healthy personality. *Psychological Issues, 1,* 50–100.

Fairbairn, W. (1952). *Psychoanalytic studies of the personality.* London: Routledge and Kegan Paul.

Feffer, M. (1967). Symptom expression as a form of primitive decentering. *Psychological Review, 7774,* 16–28.

Feffer, M. (1982). *The structure of Freudian thought.* New York: International Universities Press.

Feffer, M., & Gourevitch, V. (1960). Cognitive aspects of interpersonal behavior. *Psychological Review, 77,* 197–214.

Feldman, R. A., Caplinger, T. E., & Wodarski, J. S. (1983). *The St. Louis conundrum: The effective treatment of antisocial youths.* Englewood Cliffs, NJ: Prentice-Hall.

Fischer, K. W. (1980). A theory of cognitive development: The control and construction of hierarchies of skills. *Psychological Review, 87,* 477–531.

Fischer, K. W., & Ayoub, C. (1994). Affective splitting and dissociation in normal and maltreated children: Developmental pathways for self in relationships. In D. Cicchetti & S. Toth (Eds.), *Rochester symposium on developmental psychopathology: Disorders and dysfunctions of the self.* (pp. 1–73). New York: University of Rochester Press.

Flavell, J. H., Botkin, P. T., Fry, C. L., Wright, J. W., & Jarvis, P. E. (1968). *The development of role-taking and communication skills in children.* New York: Wiley.

Fodor, E. M. (1973). Moral development and parent behavior antecedents in adolescent psychopaths. *Journal of Genetic Psychology, 122,* 37–43.

Fowler, J. W. (1981). *Stages of faith: The psychology of human development and the quest for meaning.* New York: Harper & Row.

Frank, S., & Quinlan, D. (1976). Ego development and adjustment patterns in adolescence. *Journal of Abnormal Psychology, 85,* 505–510.

Freud, S. (1910). Five lectures on psycho-analysis. *SE, 11,* 7–55.

Furth, H. G. (1987). *Knowledge as desire: An essay on Freud and Piaget.* New York: Columbia University Press.

Gaffney, L. R. (1984). A multiple-choice test to measure social skills in delinquent and non-delinquent adolescent girls. *Journal of Consulting and Clinical Psychology, 52,* 911–912.

Garmezy, N. (1981). Children under stress: Perspectives on antecedents and correlates of vulnerability and resistance to psychopathology. In A. I. Rabin, J. Aronoff, A. M. Barclay, & R. A. Zuckers (Eds.), *Further explorations in personality* (pp. 196–270). New York: Wiley.

Garmezy, N. (1983). Stressors of childhood. In N. Garmezy & M. Rutter (Eds.), *Stress, coping, and development in children.* New York: McGraw-Hill.

Gibbs, J. C., Arnold, K. D., Ahlborn, H. H., & Cheesman, F. L. (1984). Facilitation of sociomoral reasoning in delinquents, *Journal of Consulting and Clinical Psychology, 52,* 37–45.

Gilligan, C. (1982). *In a different voice.* Cambridge, MA: Harvard University Press.

Gilligan, C., Rogers, A. G., & Tolman, D. L. (1991). *Women, girls and psychotherapy: Reframing resistance.* New York: Harrington Park Press.

Gleser, G. C., & Ihilevich, D. (1969). An objective instrument for measuring defense mechanisms. *Journal for Consulting and Clinical Psychology, 33,* 51–60.

Gold, S. N. (1980). Relations between level and ego development and adjustment patterns in adolescence. *Journal of Personality Assessment, 44,* 630–638.

Greenspan, S. I. (1979). *Intelligence and adaptation: An integration of psychoanalytic and Piagetian developmental psychology.* New York: International Universities Press.

Greenspan, S. I., & Lourie, R. S. (1981). Developmental structuralists approach to the classification of adaptive and pathologic personality organizations: Infancy and early childhood. *American Journal of Psychiatry, 138,* 725–735.

Guidano, V. F., & Liotti, G. (1983). *Cognitive processes and emotional disorders: A structural approach to psychotherapy.* New York: Guilford.

Gunderson, J. G. (1984). *Borderline personality disorder.* Washington, DC: American Psychiatric Press.

Haan, N. (1977). *Coping and defending.* New York: Academic Press.

Habermas, J. (1971). *Knowledge and human interests.* Boston: Beacon Press.

Habermas, J. (1979). Moral development and ego identity. In J. Habermas (Ed.), *Communication and the evolution of society* (pp. 69–94). Boston: Beacon Press.

Haines, A. A., & Ryan, E. B. (1983). The development of social cognitive processes among juvenile delinquents and nondelinquent peers. *Child Development, 54,* 1536–1544.

Harré, R. (1983). *Personal being: A theory for individual psychology.* Oxford: Blackwell.

Harter, S. (1988). Development and dynamic changes in the nature of the self-concept: Implications for child psychotherapy. In S. R. Shirk (Ed.), *Cognitive development and child psychotherapy* (pp. 119–160). New York: Plenum.

Hartmann, H., Kris, E., & Loewenstein, R. (1953). The function of theory in psychoanalysis. *PPP,* 117–143.

Hartshorne, H., & May, M. A. (1928–1932). *Studies in the nature of character: Vol. 1. Studies in deceit; Vol. 2. Studies in self-control; Vol.3. Studies in organization of character.* New York: Macmillan.

Hauser, S. T. (1976). Loevinger's model and measure of ego development: A critical review. *Psychological Bulletin, 83*(5), 928–955.

Hauser, S., Powers, S. I., & Noam, G. G. (1991). *Adolescents and their families: Paths of ego development.* New York: Macmillan.

Hayes, S. C., & Walker, W. L. (1986). Intellectual and moral development in offenders: A review. *Australian and New Zealand Journals of Criminology, 19,* 53–64.

Henderson, A. F. (1989). Perry's developmental scheme: Implications for counseling. Paper presented at the Perry Network Conference, Washington, DC.

Higgins, E. T. (1981). Role-taking and social judgement: Alternative developmental perspectives and processes. In J. H. Flavell & L. Ross (Eds.), *Social cognitive development: Frontiers and possible futures* (pp. 119–153). New York: Cambridge University Press.

Hudson, L. (1978). On the coherence of role-taking abilities: An alternative to correlation analysis. *Child Development, 49,* 223–227.

Iannotti, R. J. (1978). The effects of role-taking experiences on role-taking, altruism, empathy, and aggression. *Developmental Psychology, 14,* 119–124.

Ihilevich, D., & Gleser, G. C. (1971). Relationship of defense mechanisms to field dependence-independence. *Journal of Abnormal Psychology, 77,* 296–302.

Inhelder, B. (1966). Cognitive development and its contribution to the diagnosis of some phenomena of mental deficiency. *Merrill-Palmer Quarterly, 12,* 299–321.

Inhelder, B. (1976). Some pathologic phenoma analyzed in the perspective of developmental psychology. In B. Inhelder & H. Chipman (Eds.), *Piaget and his school.* New York: Springer-Verlag.

Ivey, A. E., Ivey, M. B., & Simek-Morgan, L. (Eds.). (1993). *Counseling and psychotherapy.* Boston, MA: Allyn and Bacon.

Ivey, A. F. (1986). *Developmental Therapy.* San Francisco: Jossey-Bass.

Jacobsen, T., Edelstein, W., & Hoffmann, V. (1992). *Security of attachment and cognitive development: A longitudinal study of the relation between attachment in childhood and cognitive development in later childhood and adolescence.* Unpublished manuscript, University of Illinois at Chicago and Max Planck Institute for Human Development and Education, Berlin.

Jennings, W., Kilkenny, R., & Kohlberg, L. (1983). Moral developmental theory and practice for youthful and adult offenders. In W. W. Laufer & J. M. Day (Eds.), *Personality theory, moral development and criminal behavior.* Lexington, MA: Lexington Books.

Jordan, J. (in press). *Clarity in connection: Empathic knowing, desire, and sexuality.* Stone Center.

Jurkovic, G. J. (1980). The juvenile delinquent as moral philosopher: A structural-developmental perspective. *Psychological Bulletin, 88,* 709–727.

Jurkovic, G. J., & Prentice, N. M. (1977). Relation of moral and cognitive development to dimensions of juvenile delinquency. *Journal of Abnormal Psychology, 86,* 414–420.

Kagan, J. (1989). *Unstable ideas: Temperament, cognition, and self.* Cambridge, MA: Harvard University Press.

Kazdin, A. E. (1987). *Conduct disorder in childhood and adolescence.* Newbury Park, CA: Sage.

Kazdin, A. E. (1989). Developmental psychopathology. *American Psychologist, 44,* 180–187.

Keating, D. P., & Rosen, H. (1990). *Constructivist perspectives on developmental psychopathology and atypical development.* Hillsdale, NJ: Erlbaum.

Kegan, R. (1982). *The evolving self.* Cambridge, MA: Harvard University Press.

Kegan, R., Noam, G. G., & Rogers, L. (1982). The psychology of emotion: A neo-Piagetian view. In D. Cicchetti & P. Hesse (Eds.), *New direction for child development, No. 16.* San Francisco: Jossey-Bass.

Kennedy, R. (1984). Cognitive-behavior interventions with delinquents. In A. W. Meyers, & W. Craighead (Eds.), *Cognitive behavior therapy with children* (pp. 350–376). New York: Plenum.

Kernberg, O. (1975). *Borderline conditions and pathological narcissism.* New York: Aronson.

King, P., Kitchner, K., Wood, P., & Davidson, M. (1989). Relations across developmental domains: A longitudinal study of intellectual, moral, and ego development. In M. Commons, J. Sinnot, F. Richards, & C. Armon (Eds.), *Adult development* (pp. 57–72). New York: Praeger.

Klein, M. (1930). *Die bedeutung der symbolbildung für die ichentwicklung.* London: Hogarth Press.

Klein, M. (1932). *The psychoanalysis of children.* London: Hogarth Press.

Koch, D. A., Harder, D. W., Chandler, M. J., & Paget, K. F. (1982). Parental defense style and child competence: A match-mismatched hypothesis. *Journal of Applied Developmental Psychology, 3*(1), 11–21.

Kohlberg, L. (1958). *The development of modes of moral thinking and choice in years 10 to 16.* Unpublished doctoral dissertation, University of Chicago, Chicago, IL.

Kohlberg, L. (1969). Stage and sequence: The cognitive-developmental approach to socialization. In D. Gloslin (Ed.), *Handbook of socialization, theory and research* (pp. 347–480). New York: Rand McNally.

Kohlberg, L. (1976). Moral stages and moralization: The cognitive-developmental approach. In T. Lickona (Ed.), *Moral development and behavior: Theory, research, and social issues* (pp. 31–53). New York: Holt, Rinehart & Winston.

Kohlberg, L. (1984). *Essays on moral development: Vol. 2. The psychology of moral development.* San Francisco: Harper & Row.

Kohlberg, L., & Candee, D. (1984). The relation of moral judgement to moral action. In W. Kurtines & J. Gerwitz (Eds.), *Morality, moral behavior and moral development.* New York: Wiley.

Kohlberg, L., LaCrosse, J., & Ricks, D. (1972). The predictability of adult mental health from childhood behavior. In B. Wolman (Ed.), *Manual of child psychopathology* (pp. 1217–1284). New York: McGraw-Hill.

Kohlberg, L., & Mayer, R. (1972). Development as the aim of education. *Harvard Educational Review, 42,* 449–496.

Kohlberg, L., Scharf, P., & Hickey, J. (1972). The justice of the prison: A theory and intervention. *Prison Journal, 51,* 3–14.

Kramer, D. A., & Bopp, M. (Eds.). (1989). *Transformation in clinical and developmental psychology.*

Kurdek, L. (1978). Perspective taking as the cognitive basis of children's moral development: A review of the literature. *Merrill-Palmer Quarterly, 24,* 3–28.

Labouvie-Vief, G., Hakim-Larson, J., & Hobart, C. J. (1987). Age, ego, and the life-span development of coping and defense processes. *Psychology and Aging, 2*(3), 286–293.

Leahy, R. L. (1988). Cognitive therapy of childhood depression: Developmental Considerations. In S. R. Shirk (Ed.), *Cognitive development and child psychotherapy* (pp. 187–206). New York: Plenum.

Levit, D. B. (1989). *A developmental study of ego defenses in adolescence.* Unpublished doctoral dissertation, Boston University, Boston, MA.

Lewis, M. (1990). Models of developmental psychopathology. In M. Lewis & S. Miller (Eds.), *Handbook of developmental psychopathology.* New York: Plenum.

Loevinger, J. (1968). The relation of adjustment to ego development. In S. Sales (Ed.), *The definition and measurement of mental health.* Washington, DC: Government Printing Office.

Loevinger, J. (1976). *Ego development.* San Francisco: Jossey-Bass.

Loevinger, J., & Wessler, R. (1970). *Measuring ego development* Vol. 1. San Francisco: Jossey-Bass.

Loevinger, J. L., & Wessler, R. (1983). *Measuring ego development.* London: Jossey-Bass.

Main, M., Kaplan, N., & Cassidy, J. (1985). Security in infancy, childhood, and adulthood: A move to the level of representation. *Monographs of the Society of Research in Child Development, 51,* 66–104.

Malerstein, A. J., & Ahern, M. J. (1979). Piaget's stages of cognitive development and adult character structure. *American Journal of Psychotherapy, 23,* 197–218.

Masterson, J., & Rinsley, D. (1975). The borderline syndrome: The role of the mother in the genesis and psychic structure of the borderline personality. *International Journal of Psychoanalysis, 56,* 163–177.

Mead, G. H. (1934). *Mind, self, and society.* Chicago: University of Chicago Press.

Nannis, E. D. (1988). A cognitive-developmental view of emotional understanding and its implications for child psychotherapy. In S. R. Shirk (Ed.), *Cognitive development and child psychotherapy* (pp. 91–118). New York: Plenum.

Nannis, E. D., & Cowan, P. A. (1988). Developmental psychopathology and its treatment. *New Directions for Child Development, 39.*

Noam, G. G. (1984). *Self, morality and biography: Studies in clinical-developmental psychology.* Unpublished doctoral dissertation, Harvard University, Cambridge, MA.

Noam, G. G. (1985). Stage, phase, and style: The developmental dynamics of the self. In M. Berkowitz & F. Oser (Eds.), *Moral education: Theory and application* (pp. 322–346). Hillsdale, NJ: Erlbaum.

Noam, G. G. (1986a). Borderline personality disorders and the theory of biography and transformation (part 1). *McLean Hospital Journal, 11*(1), 19–43.

Noam, G. G. (1986b). The theory of biography and transformation and the borderline personality disorders: A developmental typology. *McLean Hospital Journal, 11,* 79–105.

Noam, G. G. (1988a). A constructivist approach to developmental psychology. In E. Nannis & P. Cowan (Eds.), *Developmental psychopathology and its treatment* (pp. 91–122). San Francisco: Jossey-Bass.

Noam, G. G. (1988b). The self, adult development and the theory of biography and transformation. In D. R. Lapsky & P. F. Clark (Eds.), *Self, ego and identity-integrative approaches.* New York: Springer-Verlag.

Noam, G. G. (1988c). Self-complexity and self-integration: Theory and therapy in clinical-developmental psychology. *Journal of Moral Education, 17,* 230–245.

Noam, G. G. (1988d). The theory of biography and transformation: Foundation for clinical-developmental therapy. In S. R. Shirk (Ed.), *Cognitive development and child psychotherapy* (pp. 273–317). New York: Plenum.

Noam, G. G. (1990). Beyond Freud and Piaget: Biographical worlds—interpersonal self. In T. E. Wren (Ed.), *The moral domain* (pp. 360–399). Cambridge, MA: MIT Press.

Noam, G. G. (1992). Development as the aim of clinical intervention. *Development and Psychopathology, 4,* 679–696.

Noam, G. G. (1993a). Ego development: True or false? *Psychological Inquiry, 4*(1), 43–48.

Noam, G. G. (1993b). "Normative Vulnerabilities" of self and their transformations in moral actions. In G. G. Noam & T. E. Wren (Eds.), *The moral self* (pp. 209–238). Cambridge, MA: MIT Press.

Noam, G. G. (in press a). High risk children and youth: Transforming our understanding of human development. *Human Development.*

Noam, G. G. (in press b). Reconceptualizing maturity: Beyond the myth of integration. In G. G. Noam & K. W. Fischer (Eds.), *Development and vulnerabilities in close relationships.* Cambridge, MA: Harvard University Press.

Noam, G. G., & Borst, S. (Eds.). (1994a). *Children, youth, and suicide: Developmental perspectives.* San Francisco: Jossey-Bass.

Noam, G. G., & Borst, S. (1994b). Developing meaning, losing meaning, understanding suicidal behavior in the young. In W. Damon (Ed.), *New directions for child development, No. 64.* San Francisco: Jossey-Bass.

Noam, G. G., & Dill, D. L. (1991). Adult development and symptomatology. *Psychiatry, 54,* 208–216.

Noam, G. G., & Fischer, K. W. (in press). *Development and vulnerabilities in close relationships.* Hillsdale, NJ: Erlbaum.

Noam, G. G., Hauser, S., Santostefano, S., Garrison, W., Jacobson, A., Powers, S., & Mead, M. (1984). Ego development and psychopathology: A study of hospitalized adolescents. *Child Development, 55,* 184–194.

Noam, G. G., & Houlihan, J. (1990). Ego development and DSM-III diagnoses in adolescent psychiatric patients. *American Journal of Orthopsychiatry, 60,* 371–378.

Noam, G. G., & Kegan, R. (1982). Social cognition and psychodynamics. In W. Edelstein & M. Keller (Eds.), *Perspektivitat und interpretation* (pp. 397–426). Frankfurt: Suhrkamp.

Noam, G. G., & Kegan, R. G. (1989). On boundaries and externalization: Clinical-Developmental perspectives. *Psychoanalytic Inquiry, 9*(3), 397–426.

Noam, G. G., Kohlberg, L., & Snarey, J. (1983). Steps towards a model of the self. In B. Lee & G. Noam (Eds.), *Developmental approaches to the self* (pp. 59–142). New York: Plenum.

Noam, G. G., Paget, K., Borst, S., & Bartok, J. (1994). Conduct and affective disorders in developmental perspective: A systematic study of adolescent developmental psychology. In *Development and Psychopathology, 6,* 519–532.

Noam, G. G., Powers, S. I., Kilkenny, R., & Beedy, J. (1990). The interpersonal self in life-span developmental perspective: Theory, measurement, and longitudinal case analyses. In P. B. Baltes & D. L. Lerner (Eds.), *Life-span development and behavior* (pp. 60–104). Hillsdale, NJ: Erlbaum.

Noam, G. G., & Recklitis, C. (1990). The relationship between defenses and symptoms in adolescent psychiatric patients. *Journal of Personality Assessment, 54*(11), 311–327.

Noam, G. G., Recklitis, C., & Paget, K. (1991). Pathways of ego development: Contributions to maladaptation and adjustment. *Development and Psychopathology, 3,* 311–321.

Noam, G. G., & Young (1990). *Ego development and moral development in psychopathology: A critical review.* Unpublished manuscript, Harvard University, Cambridge, MA.

Odier, C. (1956). *Anxiety and magical thinking.* New York: International Universities Press.

Oser, F. K. (1991). The development of religious judgement, *New Directions for Child Development, 52,* 5–26.

Overton, W. F. (in press). The arrow of time and cycles of time: Concepts of change, cognition and embodiment. *Psychological Inquiry.*

Overton, W. F., & Horowitz, H. (1991). Developmental psychopathology: Differentiations and integrations. In D. Cicchetti & S. Toth (Eds.), *Rochester Symposium on Developmental Psychopathology* (Vol. 3, pp. 1–41). Rochester, NY: University of Rochester Press.

Parks, S. (1986). *The critical years: The young adult search for a faith to live.* San Francisco: Harper & Row.

Perry, W. S. (1970). *Forms of intellectual and ethical development in the college years.* New York: Holt Rinehart.

Petronio, R. J. (1980). The moral maturity of repeater delinquents. *Youth and Society, 12,* 51–59.

Pfeffer, C. R., Newcorn, J., Kaplan, G., Mizruchi, M. S., & Plutnick, R. (1989). Subtypes of suicidal and assaultive behaviors in adolescent psychiatric patients: A research note. *Journal of Child Psychology and Psychiatry, 30,* 151–163.

Piaget, J. (1926). *The language and thought of the child.* New York: Harcourt.

Piaget, J. (1932). *The moral judgement of the child.* New York: Harcourt.

Piaget, J. (1960). *The child's conception of the world.* (J. Tomilson & A. Tomilson, Trans.) Totowa, NJ: Littlefield Adams. (Originally published 1926)

Piaget, J. (1965). *The moral judgment of the child.* New York: Free Press.

Piaget, J. (1970). *Structuralism.* New York: Basic Books.

Piaget, J. (1975). Foreward. In E. J. Anthony (Ed.), *Explorations in child psychiatry.* New York: Plenum.

Rapaport, D. (1960). Psychoanalysis as a developmental psychology. In D. Kaplan & S. Wapner (Eds.), *Perspectives in psychological theory.* New York: International University Press.

Recklitis, C. J., & Noam, G. G. (1990, August). *Aggression in adolescent psychopathology: Developmental and personality dimensions.* Poster presented at the American Psychological Association meeting, Boston, MA.

Recklitis, C. J., Noam, G. G., & Borst, S. R. (1990, March). *Adolescent suicide and defense mechanisms: Differentiating attempters from ideators and non-attempters.* Paper presented at the Society for Research in Adolescence biannual meeting, Atlanta, Georgia.

Redmore, C., & Loevinger, J. (1979). Ego development in adolescence: Longitudinal studies. *Journal of Youth and Adolescence, 8,* 1–20.

Rogers, A. G. (1991). A feminist poetics of psychotherapy. In C. Gilligan, A. G. Rogers, & D. L. Tolman (Eds.), *Women, girls, and psychotherapy: Reframing resistance.* New York: Harrington Park Press.

Rogers, L., & Kegan, R. (1990). Mental growth and mental health as distinct concepts in the study of developmental psychopathology: Theory, research, and clinical implications. In D. Keating & H. Rosen (Eds.), *Constructivist perspectives on developmental psychopathology and atypical development* (pp. 103–148). Hillsdale, NJ: Erlbaum.

Rolf, J., Masten, A. S., Cicchetti, D., Nuechterlein, K. H., & Weintraub, S. (Eds.). (1990). *Risk and protective factors in the development of psychopathology.* Cambridge: Cambridge University Press.

Rosen, C. E. (1974). The effects of socio-dramatic play on problem solving behavior among culturally disadvantaged preschool children. *Child Development, 45,* 920–927.

Rosen, H. (1985). *Piagetian dimensions of clinical relevance.* New York: Columbia University Press.

Rubin, K. H. (1978). Role-taking in childhood: Some methodological considerations. *Child Development, 49,* 428–433.

Russell, R. L., & van den Broek, P. (1988). A cognitive-developmental account of storytelling in child psychotherapy. In S. R. Shirk (Ed.),

Cognitive development and child psychotherapy (pp. 19–52). New York: Plenum.

Rutter, M. (1988). Functions and consequences of relationships: Some psychopathological considerations. In R. A. Hinde & J. Stevenson-Hinde (Eds.), *Relationships within families: Mutual influences.* Oxford: Oxford University Press.

Rutter, M. (1990). Psychosocial resilience and protective mechanisms. In Rolf & Jon et al. (Eds.), *Risk and protective factors in the development of psychopathology* (pp. 181–214).

Rutter, M., & Garmezy, N. (1983). Developmental psychopathology. In E. M. Hetherington (Ed.), *Mussen's handbook of child psychology. Socialization, personality, and social development* (pp. 775–911). New York: Wiley.

Rutter, M., & Giller, H. (1984). *Juvenile delinquency: Trends and perspectives.* New York: Penguin.

Santostefano, S. (1978). *A biodevelopmental approach to clinical child psychology: Cognitive controls and cognitive control therapy.* New York: Basic Books.

Santostefano, S. (1990). Coordinating outer space with inner self: Reflections on developmental psychopathology. In D. Keating & H. Rosen (Eds.), *Constructivist perspectives on developmental psychopathology and atypical development* (pp. 11–40). Hillsdale, NJ: Erlbaum.

Schmid-Kitsikis, E. (1990). *An interpersonal approach to mental functioning: Assessment and treatment.* Switzerland: Thür AG Offsetdruck.

Schorin, M. Z., & Hart, D. (1988). Psychotherapeutic implications of the development of self-understanding. In S. R. Shirk (Ed.), *Cognitive development and child psychotherapy* (pp. 161–186). New York: Plenum.

Selman, R. L. (1971). The relation of role-taking to the development of moral judgements in children. *Child Development, 42,* 79–91.

Selman, R. L. (1975). Level of social perspective taking and the development of empathy in children: Speculations from a social cognitive viewpoint. *Journal of Moral Education, 5*(1), 35–43.

Selman, R. L. (1980). An analysis of "pure" perspective taking: Games and the delights of deception. In R. L. Selman (Ed.), *The growth of interpersonal understanding* (pp. 49–68). New York: Academic Press.

Selman, R. L., & Byrne, D. F. (1974). A structural developmental analysis of levels of role-taking in middle childhood. *Child Development, 45,* 803–806.

Selman, R. L., & Schultz, L. H. (1990). *Making a friend in youth: Developmental theory and pair therapy.* Chicago: University of Chicago Press.

Shirk, S. R. (1988a). Causal reasoning and children's comprehension of therapeutic interpretations. In S. R. Shirk (Ed.), *Cognitive development and child psychotherapy* (pp. 53–90). New York: Plenum.

Shirk, S. R. (1988b). *Cognitive development and child psychotherapy.* New York: Plenum.

Shirk, S. R. (1988c). Introduction: A cognitive-developmental perspective on child psychotherapy. In S. R. Shirk (Ed.), *Cognitive development and child psychotherapy* (pp. 319–331). New York: Plenum.

Smetana, J. G. (1989). Adolescents' and parents' reasoning about actual family conflict. *Child Development, 60*(5), 1052–1067.

Smetana, J. G. (1991). Adolescent-parent conflict in married and divorced families. *Developmental Psychology, 27*(6), 1000–1010.

Spence, D. P. (1984). *Narrative truth and historical truth: Meaning and interpretation in psychoanalysis.* New York: Norton.

Sroufe, L. A. (1979). The coherence of individual development: Early care, attachment and subsequent developmental issues. *American Psychologist, 34,* 834–841.

Sroufe, L. A., & Rutter, M. (1984). The domain of developmental psychopathology. *Child Development, 55,* 17–29.

Strauss, J. S., Harder, D. W., Chandler, M. J., & Paget, K. (1979). Egocentrism in children of parents with a history of psychotic disorders. *Archives of General Psychiatry, 36,* 191–202.

Sullivan, H. S. (1953). *The interpersonal theory of psychiatry.* New York: Norton.

Thorton, D., & Reid, R. L. (1982). Moral reasoning and type of criminal offense. *British Journal of Social Psychology, 21,* 231–238.

Trevethan, S. D., & Walker, L. J. (1989). Hypothetical versus real-life moral reasoning among psychopathic and delinquent. *Developmental and Psychopathology, 1,* 91–103.

Turiel, E. (1978). The development of concepts of social structure: Social convention. In J. Glick & A. C. Stewart (Eds.), *The development of social understanding.* New York: Gardner Press.

Vaillant, G. E. (1977). *Adaptation to life.* Boston: Little Brown.

Vaillant, G. E., & McCullough, L. (1987). The Washington University Sentence Completion Test compared with other measures of adult ego development. *American Journal of Psychiatry, 144*(9), 1189–1194.

Van Den Daele, L. (1969). Quantitative models in developmental analysis. *Developmental Psychology, 1,* 303–310.

Von Glasersfeld, E. (1984). An introduction to radical constructivism. In P. Watzlawick (Ed.), *The invented reality* (pp. 17–40). New York: Norton.

Vygotsky, L. (1962). *Thought and language.* E. Haufmann & G. Vakar (Trans.), Cambridge, MA: MIT Press.

Vygotsky, L. (1978). *Mind and society: The development of the higher psychological processes.* Cambridge, MA: Harvard University Press.

Watzlawick, P., Weakland, J., & Fisch, R. (1974). *Change: Principles of problem formation and resolution.* New York: Norton.

Wenar, C. (1984). Commentary: Progress and problems in the cognitive approach to clinical child psychology. *Journal of Consulting and Clinical Psychology, 52*(1), 57–62.

Werner, E. (1990). Protective factors and individual resilience. In S. Meisels & J. Shonkoff (Ed.), *Handbook of early childhood intervention.* Cambridge, MA: Cambridge University Press.

Werner, H. (1948). *Comparative psychology of mental development.* New York: International Universities Press.

Westen, D., & Cohen, R. P. (1993). The self in borderline personality disorder: A psychodynamic perspective. In Z. V. Segal & S. J. Blatt (Eds.), *The self in emotional distress: Cognitive and psychodynamic perspectives.* New York: Guilford.

Wicks, R. J., Parsons, R. D., & Capps, D. (Eds.). (1985). *Clinical handbook of pastoral counseling.* New York: Paulist Press.

Wohlwill, J. F. (1973). The concept of human development: S or R? *Human Development, 16,* 90–107.

Wolff, P. (1960). *The developmental psychologies of Jean Piaget and psychoanalysis.* New York: International Universities Press.

Yates, T. (1991). Theories of cognitive development. In M. Lewis (Ed.), *Child and adolescent psychiatry* (pp. 109–128). Baltimore, MD: Williams & Wilkins.

PART FIVE

Socioemotional Processes

CHAPTER 16

Emotional Development and Developmental Psychopathology

CARROLL E. IZARD and PAUL HARRIS

There are several reasons why any discussion of developmental psychopathology would be incomplete without considering the role of emotions. First, as Cicchetti (1990) iterated, numerous astute observers of human behavior have noted that the etiology, symptoms, and course of psychological disorders cannot be fully explained without recourse to emotion concepts.

Second, converging evidence from normal and abnormal populations suggests that the emotions constitute a separate, albeit interdependent, developmental system (e.g., Hesse & Cicchetti, 1982; Izard & Malatesta, 1987). This underscores the need for research concerned specifically with the emotions system. Studies focused only on cognitive variables cannot fulfill this need. Analyses of the mechanisms, processes, and effects of interaction among the emotions system and the cognitive and action systems are essential to understanding normal and psychopathological development (Harris, 1989; cf. Zigler, 1971).

Third, a substantial body of evidence supports the hypothesis that emotions are motivational and hence must be involved in explaining the causes of normal and abnormal behavior. The current trend toward studying the functions of emotions (Barrett & Campos, 1987) gained impetus from theories that considered emotions as the primary motivational system for human beings and, perhaps, all mammalian species (Izard, 1971; Plutchik, 1980; Tomkins, 1962, 1963).

The final reason for involving emotion constructs in theory and research on developmental psychopathology may seem a bit paradoxical. Whereas there is ample evidence to indicate that emotions figure in the explanation of psychological disorders, there is also theory and evidence to support the idea that in evolutionary-developmental perspective each of the basic emotions is inherently adaptive. Thus, the fear of an agoraphobic patient may be incapacitating, but an infant's cautious exploration of a novel environment accompanied by frequent return to a secure base (Bowlby, 1973) is adaptive. Similarly, the guilt and self-recrimination of a depressive patient can lead to suicide, but guilt in healthy individuals can serve a useful reparative function within a social group.

This leads to two possibilities that must be considered in the analysis of relations among emotions and psychological disorders. One, although emotions typically have adaptive functions, they can also be determinants of psychopathological development. Two, emotions remain essentially functional, adaptive systems; if development goes awry, it is not because of malfunctioning within the emotions system but because the emotions are not appropriately integrated with other systems at each stage of development. It is possible to make a case for each of these two positions, and this chapter will reflect theory and research related to both. It is important to note that neither of these positions represents the outdated notions that emotions are mainly reactive in nature, primarily transient and situational, and essentially disruptive and disorganizing (Pribram, 1967). The relatively recently accumulated body of evidence on the adaptive functions of emotion in development has thoroughly vitiated these ideas.

In this chapter, we are concerned with the normal and abnormal development of the mechanisms and processes involved in emotion activation, emotion expressions and emotion-related behavior, the feeling/experiential component of emotions, and emotion-cognition relations. In discussing these developmental processes, we address, wherever possible, the issues described above. When is the influence of emotion adaptive and when maladaptive, and under what circumstances is it one or the other? What sorts of emotion-related biological, sociocultural, and cognitive processes lead to developmental psychopathology? Can phenomena as seemingly disparate as genetic anomalies and inappropriate belief systems be implicated? Although we would say yes in answer to the latter question, no quick answer is available for the others, and our tentative affirmation will require elaboration.

THE NEURAL SUBSTRATES OF EMOTION

In this section, we present a few general remarks on the neural basis of emotions and then focus on those aspects that have clear implications for developmental psychopathology. More extensive treatments of the neural substrates of emotion can be found elsewhere (Gray, 1982; Izard & Saxton, 1988; LeDoux, 1987; Panksepp, 1986; Rolls, 1986).

The neuroanatomical and neurochemical substrates of emotions constitute a highly complex and intricately interrelated set of structures, pathways, and neurotransmitters. Added to this physiological and biochemical complexity is the factor of differential rates of development for various brain structures and hormone-releasing mechanisms. In the simplest terms, the brain consists of (a) incoming sensory pathways, both specific and lemniscal systems, and diffuse arousal systems; (b) outgoing motor pathways to the smooth muscles of vital organs and the striated muscles that perform voluntary actions, and (c) central—cortical and subcortical—integrative structures. All of these neural systems may be involved in emotion and emotion-related activity.

In addition to these structures and pathways of the central nervous system, the peripheral nervous system is intrinsic to emotion. Somatic branches of the peripheral nervous system control the mimetic muscles used in the facial expressions of emotions as well as such emotion-related activities as heart rate and blood pressure. Although current evidence indicates that central mechanisms are responsible for evaluation of the emotional significance of sensory information (the initial stage of emotion activation), it also shows that peripheral structures (muscles and end organs) involved in emotion expression provide critical information for the processes that lead to emotion experience (LeDoux, 1987).

Some theorists (e.g., Barrett & Campos, 1987; Emde, 1983; Izard, 1977) hold that the core of emotion experience is a feeling state and that this feeling becomes further defined psychologically by virtue of the information it provides to the cognitive system. Emotion feeling influences perceptual and interpretive processes, memory, and anticipation, and these cognitive activities, in turn, influence emotion feeling. In general terms, this is the basis for the development of emotion-cognition relations, which, over time, come to define an individual's emotional life—emotion experiences and emotion-based traits of personality.

The great complexity of the interplay between central neural processes and peripheral neural and neuromuscular processes involved in activating emotion-feeling and the virtually limitless array of feeling-cognition interactions alerts us to potential problems that might lead to maladaptive behavior in developmental psychopathology. For example, a genetic anomaly or environmental condition that delayed either motor or cognitive development could have adverse effects on emotional development. Motor system delay could alter observable emotion expressions and social communication, and cognitive delay could create deficits in feeling-thought interactions that contribute to the appropriateness of emotion responses and the development of sociality and empathy—phenomena that ultimately depend on higher-order representational processes. In a later section, we shall discuss the data showing that clinical populations with delayed and deviant cognitive or motor development can result in abnormal emotion responses that create problems for atypical individuals and their families.

Three concepts relating to the neural substrates of normal emotion processes and emotional development have implications for developmental psychopathology: (a) dual pathways for emotion activation, (b) noncognitive activators of emotions, and (c) differential rates of development of brain mechanisms involved in emotions and emotion-cognition interactions. To place the dual-pathways hypothesis of emotion activation in perspective, we now present a summary of the evidence on neural processes in emotion expression and emotion experience.

The Evaluation of Emotion Information and Emotion Activation

The global concept of emotion activation ignores the evidence that pathways serving emotion expression and emotional behavior are not necessarily the same as those serving emotion feeling/experience. It is often assumed that spontaneous emotion expression and emotional behaviors are accompanied by emotion feelings. However, in humans, some forms of emotion expression can be encoded voluntarily without activating emotion feelings. The activation of involuntary emotion expression may indeed involve the same pathways that generate emotion experience, but this is a point of view not yet supported by empirical data. There is substantial neuroanatomical and neurophysiological evidence relating to emotional behavior at both the level of observable phenomena and the level of hormonal changes and activity in the autonomic nervous system and the organs it innervates. On the other hand, little is known about the neurophysiological circuitry of emotion feelings or about the processes whereby neural activity is transformed into conscious experiences of any kind.

Although necessarily incomplete, our discussion of the biological basis of emotions includes separate consideration of the neural substrates underlying (a) the evaluation of sensory information for emotional significance, (b) emotion expression, and (c) emotion experience. It is readily conceivable that one circuit (or different components of the same circuit) activates all three components of emotion, but there are few data to support this idea. The hard evidence at the neural level comes from animal research, where evaluation of stimuli for emotional significance is indexed by emotion expression (somatic and autonomic activity) and emotion-related instrumental behavior. Thus, the neurophysiological evidence relating to the pathways for the evaluation of the emotional significance of sensory information is at the same time evidence relating to the substrates of expressive behavior.

Because the hard data on the neural substrates of emotion are largely from nonhuman animals, expression-feeling correlation can only be inferred. Although the bulk of the evidence from neuroscience does not speak directly to the issue of emotion feeling/experience, it does, we believe, have some bearing on the notion of separate systems for emotion and cognitive processes and some implications for clinical phenomena such as repression and unconscious motivation.

The Role of the Limbic System

It has long been thought that the evaluation of stimuli for emotional significance (as well as subsequent emotion experience) was a function of a network of structures and pathways in the limbic lobe (see Durant, 1973). Its functional borders, no longer anatomically defined, have expanded over time. Papez (1937) proposed that limbic system functioning involved the relay of sensory information to the hypothalamus and then to the anterior thalamus, cingulate cortex, hippocampus, and back to the hypothalamus. MacLean (1952, 1975) added to Papez's circuit the neuronal pathway known as the forebrain bundle, which connects the ventral forebrain, hypothalamus, and mesencephalic brain stem. MacLean maintained that this enlarged limbic system mediated all aspects of emotion.

Neuroscientists have now questioned the integrity of the concept of a limbic system and have concluded that the idea of a unified network of limbic area structures mediating emotion processes has little empirical support (Durant, 1973; LeDoux, 1987). This does not mean, however, that the search for specific brain structures that mediate the different aspects of emotion has ended.

A Revised Emotion Circuit

Current evidence indicates that emotion circuits involve the thalamus, amygdala, neocortex, and, possibly, the hippocampus, with the amygdala being considered the sensory gateway to the emotions. Efferent (outputs) from the amygdala project to the basal forebrain and several deep subcortical structures, including the hypothalamus, midbrain, medulla, substantia nigra, central gray, locus coerulus, parabrachial nuclei, dorsal motor nucleus of the vagus, and the nucleus of the solitary tract (Aggleton & Mishkin, 1986). The great complexity and extent of the emotion circuitry and its roots in phylogenetically old structures are consistent with the notion that emotions are a fundamental part of our evolutionary heritage and have inherently adaptive functions. The complex nature of the emotion circuitry also reminds us that damage in any of a number of structures and pathways, and deficits in the numerous neurotransmitters that serve them, can affect emotion responses adversely.

The Amygdala as Sensory Gateway in Two Pathways to the Emotions

There is consensus among neuroscientists that the amygdala is the key structure in evaluating sensory information for emotional significance. Over 100 years ago, it was discovered that bilateral damage to the temporal lobes (which contain the amygdala) rendered animals unnaturally tame and fearless. Since that time, the amygdala has been identified as the crucial structure in this syndrome, and many investigators have contributed to our knowledge of its role in emotion activation (see Aggleton & Mishkin, 1986, and Kling, 1986, for review).

Recent neurobehavioral studies of the role of the amygdala in emotion activation, conditioned fear, and emotional memory have clear implications for normal and abnormal emotion development. In a series of carefully controlled experiments with rats, LeDoux (1987) and his colleagues showed that classical conditioning of fear reactions to acoustic stimuli could be mediated by a thalamo-amygdala pathway. Because the circuit bypasses the auditory cortex, it constitutes a subcortical mechanism that can mediate emotional learning. This suggests that theories that describe emotion activation exclusively in terms of higher-order cognitive processes (e.g., complex appraisals), language, and reasoning (e.g., causal attribution) need to be extended or complemented in order to account for classically conditioned, and possibly other, emotion responses mediated subcortically.

The work on auditory fear conditioning through subcortical pathways has been extended to visual fear conditioning (LeDoux, Romanski, & Xagoraris, 1989). Animals without visual cortex were still able to acquire conditioned fear responses to a flashing light, indicating the efficacy of a subcortical (thalamo-amygdala) sensory pathway in mediating emotional behavior.

LeDoux (1987) proposed, for emotion activation, a second pathway that involves cognitive processes such as appraisal, attribution, and belief. This pathway involves transmission of sensory information from the thalamus to the neocortex, and thence to the hippocampus and amygdala. In this pathway, too, the amygdala is the final gateway to hormonal release, autonomic changes, and emotional behavior.

Having demonstrated that fear expression and behavior can be activated by acoustic or visual stimuli in the absence of auditory or visual cortex, LeDoux (1989) concluded that his data supported the hypothesis of separate systems for processing emotional and nonemotional information (Izard, 1984; Zajonc, 1984). This condition is also consistent with Cicchetti's (1990) observation, derived from comparative developmental studies of normal and atypical children, that the emotions constitute a separate developmental system.

The concepts of dual activation pathways and a separate developmental system for emotions have implications for developmental psychopathology. First, deviant or delayed development may affect the emotions system or the cognitive system or both. For example, the genetic anomaly of Down syndrome may have independent effects on emotion responses as well as on cognitive development. Evidence suggesting that this is the case will be reviewed in a later section.

LeDoux's research also showed that subcortically mediated emotion responses tend to be locked in memory with high resistance to extinction (LeDoux, Romanski, & Xagoraris, 1989). The conditioned stimulus (CS) was readministered to lesioned and sham (control) animals in 5 test sessions over a 30-day period. The sham animals showed gradual and ultimately complete extinction of fear behavior. In contrast, the animals without visual cortex failed to extinguish the fear responses. The authors suggested that subcortically mediated emotion responses and memories may continue for an indefinite period.

The foregoing evidence suggests that any psychological disorder involving subcortically mediated conditioned emotion responses may be very difficult to treat with methods based on extinction procedures. There are two reasons for this:

1. Because the memory is stored subcortically, it will not have the usual links to language and cognition that enable the person to articulate the emotion experience.
2. Because the emotion in question is subcortically mediated, cortical inhibitory processes, including cognition relevant to the emotion, cannot operate.

The Neural Substrates of Emotion Expression

Evidence for the key role of the amygdala in the evaluation of emotion information continues to mount, but evidence identifying the structures and pathways of emotion expression is less clear. Several areas have been strongly implicated.

Hypothalamus and Central Gray

A substantial body of evidence has shown that stimulation of the hypothalamus elicits aggressive attack behavior in animals (e.g., Flynn, 1967). A fascinating aspect of the studies of Flynn and his colleagues showed that physical aggression (cat attacking rat) was dependent on three sensory systems: (a) vision, (b) olfaction, and (c) touch. When feedback from the perioral region (sense of touch) was interrupted by cutting sensory branches of the trigeminal nerve, aggression fell from 100% to 0% in over half the cats. In a second phase of the experiment, the cats that continued to show aggression were blindfolded. With both tactile and visual feedback interrupted, aggressive attack was entirely eliminated. These studies were among the first in a line of research demonstrating the role of the peripheral nervous system, and particularly sensory feedback, in the neural processing of emotional behavior. Numerous other studies have implicated the hypothalamus in emotion expression and emotional behavior. However, increasingly sophisticated neuroscience methods have cast doubt on the centrality of the role of the hypothalamus. Although it is clear that, for example, stimulation of the ventromedial nucleus of the hypothalamus elicits displays of emotional behavior (hissing, baring of teeth) and autonomic activity (piloerection, changes in blood pressure), it now appears that the stimulated neurons are fibers of passage with cell bodies lying elsewhere. Thus, the hypothalamus may be an important relay station but not the effective structure for neural processing of emotional behavior (Bandler, 1982b).

Research using microinjection and defensive conditioning techniques suggests that the central gray region of the midbrain may be an important area for mediating emotion responses (Bandler, 1982b). Evidence shows that it is a target of efferent outputs from emotion responses originating in the limbic forebrain (LeDoux, 1987).

Autonomic Nervous System

Another important component of emotional behavior is activity of the autonomic nervous system (ANS) and the organs it innervates. In the early part of this century, Cannon (1927, 1929) demonstrated that threatening emotional stimuli resulted in activation of the sympathetic branch of the ANS and the mobilization of the animal's resources for "fight or flight." It should be noted that Cannon worked with a limited range of emotion activators—intense aversive stimuli that typically elicited emergency responses. Partly as a result of his method, Cannon's model of ANS involvement in emotion proved to be overly simplistic. In some emotion-eliciting situations, the parasympathetic branch of the ANS is activated (LeDoux, 1987), and many situations elicit a far wider range of emotion responses than anger/fight and fear/flight (Izard, 1972). Among other weaknesses, this model cannot explain the role of positive emotion expression in adaptation, nor can it account for the effects of negative emotions such as sadness, shame, and guilt.

Cannon was quite correct about one very important aspect of emotions: they do indeed mobilize the resources of the individual for emotional activity. This idea is broadened and elaborated in a number of contemporary theories that view emotions as the primary motivational system and each emotion as having the capacity to organize and motivate adaptive behavior.

Peripheral Nervous System and Sensory Feedback

Two aspects of the research on the neural substrates of emotion expression have implications for developmental psychopathology. First, the evidence shows that both the central and peripheral nervous systems are involved. More specifically, feedback through one or more sensory systems may be critical. Some of Flynn's (1967) attack cats showed no aggressive behavior when facial feedback was interrupted, and none attacked when their trigeminal sensory fibers were sectioned and their eyes covered. The attack behavior of these cats was dependent on tactile and visual information and possibly on feedback from facial muscle activity. This suggests that abnormal emotional development may occur as a result of defect or deficiency in either the central or peripheral nervous systems. Sensory deficits are not uncommon in atypical children, but the role of these sensory deficits in emotional development has been neglected.

A second implication of the research on the neural substrates of emotion expression is that interruption of sensory feedback and subsequent emotion expression may lead to inappropriate or uncontrolled emotional behavior. When brain lesions inhibit fear responses in monkeys, they show interest in and exploratory behavior toward potentially dangerous stimuli (Kluver & Bucy, 1939). Many factors could contribute to these abnormal emotion responses, but, in social interactions with higher-status animals, the lack of appropriate expressive signals could be a major contributor to victimization. The role of expressive behavior in the regulation of emotion is discussed in a later section.

Neural Processes in Emotion Experience

Damage to either the frontal or temporal lobes of the brain dramatically alters emotion expression and emotional behavior. The effects of experimentally induced brain lesions in nonhuman animals suggest that defects in the neural substrates of emotion alter the feeling state or conscious experience of emotion, as well as observable behavior. The limited data from surgical procedures and clinical investigations with human subjects indicate that emotion experience is affected as much as emotion expression and emotional behavior. Research and clinical evidence also show that abnormal levels of hormones and neurotransmitters specific to the neural pathways of emotion expression/emotional behavior can contribute to anxiety and depression (Post & Ballenger, 1984).

Two Approaches to Explaining Emotion Experience

In emotion theory, there are two approaches to the problem of explaining how emotion experiences are generated. The first, which is addressed in this section, is that emotion feeling is a direct product of the central neural processes involved in the evaluation of the emotional significance of information and the peripheral (sensory) feedback from expressive behavior. The relative contribution of the central and peripheral nervous systems in emotion experience is a matter that has been debated since William James (1884) argued the extreme position that peripheral structures are essential and that emotion experience is the perception of changes in the striated muscles of emotional behavior, the smooth muscles of visceral organs, and the endocrine system.

Despite Cannon's (1927) rather successful experimental assault on aspects of James's hypothesis of emotion-feeling activation (see also the work of Bard and his associates, e.g., Bard, 1928), contemporary neuroscience has done little to resolve the controversy over the role of the peripheral nervous system and sensory feedback. However, despite the lack of evidence at the neural level, a substantial body of evidence at the behavioral level supports aspects of James's position, particularly with respect to the role of facial behavior in contributing to emotion experience directly through sensory feedback or indirectly through changes in cerebral blood temperature or self-perception (Izard, 1990; Laird & Bresler, 1990; Zajonc, Murphy, & Inglehart, 1989). Patients with facial muscle paralysis still experience emotions, but this can be explained in terms of developmental changes in expression-feeling relations (Izard & Malatesta, 1987). We shall return to the importance of these data for developmental psychopathology when we consider the development of emotion regulation.

In a later section, we discuss the generation of emotion experience by cognitive appraisal processes that can involve beliefs, desires, and expectations. Because they are concerned with explanation at different levels of conceptualization (neural and cognitive), there may be little fundamental conflict between the two approaches. This is especially so if we view the neurochemically produced feeling state as subject to the influence of cognition. Thus, emotion experience, in a broader sense, consists of feelings plus cognition (appraisals, attributions, beliefs, desires) or affective-cognitive processes.

There is one potentially important consequence for maintaining the view that feeling states, with their complex and powerful motivational properties, can be generated directly by neurochemical processes, independently of cognition. The point is that some feelings may arise without antecedent cognitive causes and may not be immediately related to or integrated with subsequent cognition, a topic that is addressed in the following section. With this framework for thinking about emotion feeling/experience, we return to the data from neuroscience and neurosurgery.

Socioemotional Deficits from Brain Lesions

The evidence from research with nonhuman animals clearly demonstrates that damage to particular neural substrates radically reduces the animals' ability to respond appropriately to emotion-eliciting events. Lesions or chemical blocking of activity in these brain structures create drastic deficits and defects in emotion expression and social behavior. The social affiliative behaviors so crucial to attachment, sociality, and social support are lost or ineffective. If we are willing to infer concomitant changes in consciousness, we would assume the presence of affective states associated with anxiety, depression, or other psychopathology, depending on the nature of the damage.

The sparse and methodologically weak data from human patients support the foregoing assumption. However, as Kling (1986) noted, discussion of brain-emotion relations in humans is complicated by a number of factors. First, trauma to emotion substrates is rarely specific to emotion structures/pathways, and damage to the amygdala, for example, is almost never bilateral. These factors, especially the latter, tend to hold even in some surgical procedures. Second, surgical procedures in the deep structures of the emotions system are applied only to patients with serious psychopathology that does not yield to drugs and psychotherapy. Because such procedures have been documented only on adult patients, their effect on emotional development is unknown. Third, in humans, emotion expression and emotional behavior are closely linked to language, and language is the only direct means of assessing emotion feelings. People's verbalizations about their feelings are imprecise; often, they have difficulty finding any suitable words at all, especially if they are psychologically disturbed. Finally, socioemotional behavior, including emotion-related verbal behavior, is regulated by environmental (particularly sociocultural) factors. Despite these limitations and the incompleteness of the data, clinical evidence from psychosurgery and brain trauma in humans is generally consistent with the data from nonhuman animals.

Proposed Pathways for Mediating Emotion Experience

Panksepp's (1986) review of the evidence from human psychosurgery and basic research on animals led him to suggest that the "higher representations" for four "primal emotions" were as follows: (a) positive expectancy: basal ganglia, orbito-frontal-basal-forebrain mechanisms; (b) anger and rage: corticomedial amygdala and surrounding temporal lobe; (c) fear: basolateral and central amygdala and surrounding temporal-pyriform cortex; (d) social emotions: bed-nucleus of the stria terminalis and cingulate gyrus. The role of these mechanisms in emotional behavior is better understood than their role in emotion experience.

There is wide agreement that the amygdala is involved in mediating emotion experience. Amygdalectomy to relieve epilepsy produces greatly reduced emotionality (Kling, 1986). The most common emotion feeling elicited by stimulation of the amygdala is fear. Anger was reported much less frequently, but the relation of activity in the amygdala and anger experience is suggested by effects of stereotaxic lesions in the amygdala on violent, hyperactive patients (see Aggleton & Mishkin, 1986). Data on the role of the amygdala and other structures in mediating positive emotion experiences are particularly scarce.

LeDoux (1987) suggested that emotion experience may be a function of neural connections among deep structures and the neocortical areas subserving language functions. He based his argument, in part, on the assumption that "conscious experiences in humans are predicated on the cognitive processes underlying natural language" (1987, p. 449). Although attractive, this view could not explain emotion experiences in animals (including human infants) that have no language. Another limitation, as pointed out by LeDoux (1987), is that the language areas of the neocortex have extensive connections to other cortical areas but limited connections with the limbic forebrain that subserves emotion expression and emotional behavior.

It is known that subcortical structures such as the hippocampus are critically involved in cognitive processes, and that the amygdala, so important in emotion processes, can also affect perception and memory (Aggleton & Mishkin, 1986). Perhaps emotion experience can be mediated by subcortical as well as corticolimbic pathways, and the former may be relatively more important in early development, in noncognitively activated emotions, and in emotion experiences linked to repression, dissociation, and developmental psychopathology. The view, based in part on cortical stimulation studies of Penfield (1958), that emotion experiences in humans are mediated by the neocortex has been challenged. Later research has shown that emotion feelings from stimulation of neocortex were reported only if there were discharges in subcortical structures such as the amygdala (Gloor, Oliver, & Quesney, 1981).

Much remains to be done before we can understand precisely how emotion feeling/experience is generated through neural processes. Yet, neuroscientists and behavioral scientists agree that this is a highly desirable goal. The importance of emotion experience was eloquently articulated a long time ago: "Individuality is founded in feeling; and the recesses of feeling, the darker, blinder strata of character, are the only place in the world in which we catch real fact in the making, and directly perceive how events happen, and how work is actually done" (James, 1910/1985, p. 395).

Maturational and Environmental Influences on Neural Processes in Emotion

As indicated earlier, differential maturational rates of brain structures may influence the course of emotional development and increase vulnerability in certain periods of development. For example, according to Jacobs and Nadel (1985), the relatively late maturation of the hippocampus may be a factor in the development of fears and phobias.

Jacobs and Nadel (1985) began their argument with several assumptions about characteristics of phobias that they thought could not be explained in terms of current laws of learning. For example, they noted that phobic patients are often unable to report when and where the feared object was paired with the noxious experience of fear. Phobias sometimes simply appear following stressful but noncontingent events. They seem to generalize very broadly, and they often persist after many years of traditional extinction procedures—exposure to the presumed feared stimulus in the absence of aversive consequences.

Jacobs and Nadel suggested a model based on differential rates of maturation of brain mechanisms, with consequent differential effects on two types of learning, and the effects of stress on neural processes. The gist of their model is that some infantile learning experiences have lasting influences because they occur before the hippocampus, which mediates context learning, has matured sufficiently to become functional. Evidence indicates that the hippocampus does not become functional until some time after the first year of life, perhaps as late as 2.5 or 3 years. Thus, although the young infants are capable of forming associations between noxious conditions and fear feelings (taxon or procedural learning), they are incapable of autobiographical or context learning—learning the where and when of the event and the specificity of the stimulus. Because young infants are capable of learning associations (with the taxon learning system) but not capable of learning the details of time and space (for lack of a functional context learning system), they are unable to recall early experiences. According to Jacobs and Nadel, "infantile amnesia" is lack of contextual information, the information that makes it possible to access memories and put them in temporal and spatial perspective.

Jacobs and Nadel reviewed research that suggested that hormonally induced stress renders the hippocampally based context-learning system dysfunctional, and potentiates the taxon learning system. This would mean that circuits for learning context-free fears are prepared for the formation of strong associations, and the likelihood of establishing a phobia is thus increased.

The foregoing analysis of fears and phobias suggests that children subjected to stress through maltreatment, handicap, illness, accident, or other negative life events may be more likely to acquire irrational fears and phobias. Evidence consistent with this hypothesis is reviewed in a later section.

Although Jacobs and Nadel's model offers a needed explanation for facts about phobias, McNally's (1989) critique of their position raises some questions about its validity. McNally maintained that some of Jacobs and Nadel's assumptions about phobic people were unfounded. The validity of McNally's criticism seems to hinge, at least in part, on definitions of terms. For example, it is true, as Jacobs and Nadel assumed, that phobic people are unable to report when and where the feared object was initially paired with the noxious event, if the noxious event is defined as the unconditioned stimulus (analogous to electric shock, in the case of laboratory conditioning). This assumption is not true for agoraphobic people, however, if the noxious event is defined as a panic attack. According to McNally, most agoraphobic people trace their phobias to panic attacks that occurred in places they currently avoid. Defining the noxious event as a panic attack, however, would still leave the noxious event or cause of the panic attack unexplained. McNally acknowledged that people with animal phobias do often fail to describe an initial frightening experience.

McNally also maintained that the extinction of phobic responses may not be as difficult as Jacobs and Nadel had claimed. Because most phobics are skilled avoiders, they do not give extinction many opportunities. Finally, McNally argued that it was the disposition to respond fearfully, not the specific phobic response, that is difficult to treat. However, it seems possible that McNally's idea of a phobic disposition may not really differ from Jacobs and Nadel's notion of neural circuits prepared for strong fear associations.

AFFECTIVE AND BEHAVIORAL PROCESSES IN EMOTION ACTIVATION

In the foregoing section, we reviewed the evidence for dual pathways for emotion activation. The data supported the hypothesis that both subcortical and corticolimbic pathways can effectively mediate emotion responses. In this section, we review research on affective and behavioral processes in emotion activation.

The behavioral data relating to the activation of emotions seem to fall into two classes: (a) cognitive and (b) noncognitive. We propose that noncognitive processes that generate emotions are subserved largely by subcortical pathways such as the thalamo-amygdala circuit that LeDoux found to be effective in auditory and fear conditioning.

We hypothesize that cognitive processes (e.g., appraisal, attribution, belief) that activate emotions are subserved by pathways involving the neocortex. A number of researchers have proposed such pathways (e.g., Aggleton & Mishkin, 1986; Kling, 1986; LeDoux, 1987; Panksepp, 1986). The role of cognitive processes in emotion activation is discussed later in the chapter. Research at the behavioral level has identified several types of emotion activators that might be subserved primarily by subcortical pathways. These include emotions themselves (one emotion activating another), pain, changes in cerebral blood temperature, and facial expressions.

One Emotion Activating Other Emotions

A number of studies of self-reported emotion experiences have indicated that emotion-eliciting events rarely produce a single emotion. Instead, an effective stimulus situation typically produces a pattern of emotions (Izard, 1972). Indeed, the evidence from different laboratories indicates that these are reliably identifiable patterns (Hansen & Hansen, 1988; Izard, 1972). Thus, a situation that elicits joy typically elicits interest and surprise as well, and, on the average, conditions that evoke anger also elicit disgust and contempt.

In the foregoing studies, emotions were elicited by having the subject imagine/visualize a scene from memory that had elicited the target emotion at an intense level. The elicited pattern of emotions in these studies could also be explained by the complexity of the situation or the array of elicitors and appraisals. However, similar emotion-emotion sequences have been found to occur regularly in certain psychopathological conditions and as a result of experimentally induced feelings.

Evidence that is reviewed in a later section indicates that there are patterns of emotions specific to anxiety and depression in children (Blumberg & Izard, 1985, 1986) and in adults (Izard, 1972). For example, sadness, which is generally recognized as the dominant emotion in depression, is almost always reported to co-occur with anger. Clinicians frequently describe the affective symptomatology of depression in children and adults as a sad-mad pattern, and they often observe acting-out and aggressive behavior by depressive patients. This sad-mad emotion profile has been empirically identified through self-report inventories. In the data from depressed people, as with the data from normals, there is no direct evidence that it is the target emotion—say, sadness—rather than some cognitive antecedent that elicited the other emotion (say, anger). However, some clinical opinion and some empirical data suggest that one emotion causes the other. Finman and Berkowitz (1989) have shown that experimentally induced depression elicited anger. Berkowitz's research led him to conclude that the "depressed mood in itself produces angry feelings and hostile intention" (1990, p. 496). Berkowitz recognized that even in affect-induced emotion, cognition can play a role in modifying (intensifying, prolonging) the emotion.

That the neural pathways for sadness and anger might be biologically prepared for interaction is suggested by the fact that, in some circumstances, it is adaptive for sadness to recruit anger. Sadness has a slowing effect on mental and motor processes which, up to a point, may serve to focus the individual on the troubling situation. Left unabated, however, intense sadness may lead to maladaptive inaction and withdrawal. Anger has an opposite effect. It mobilizes energy for action against frustrating, goal-blocking barriers and exploitations (Izard, 1977; Nesse, 1990; Plutchik, 1980). Although there may be both noncognitive and cognitive activators of patterns of emotions that co-occur with regularity, there is much less likelihood that cognitive processes are necessary antecedents in the cases described below.

Pain as an Activator of Anger

Several types of data suggest a causal relation between pain and anger. Most people can remember a time when they reacted to unanticipated pain with an angry expletive and, perhaps, a blow to the offending object. Empirical research has shown that animals often respond to pain with physical aggression, and human infants respond with facial expressions of anger.

Berkowitz (1983) reviewed the research on pain-elicited aggression in animals and concluded that aversive stimulation was an effective elicitor of aggressive actions in a wide variety of species. Although the literature shows that a number of environmental factors determine whether aversive stimulation will elicit "fight" or "flight," aggressive responses to pain occur under many circumstances. Even though learning can modify behavioral responses to aversive stimulation, pain-elicited aggressive behavior appears to be unlearned. The aim of the aggressive action is to eliminate or reduce the noxious stimulation.

In a later review, Berkowitz (1990) reinforced his earlier conclusion regarding the effectiveness of aversive stimulation in eliciting anger and aggression. In this account, he also argued that the instigator of anger was the stimulus-induced negative affect (pain, physical distress). He concluded that the elicitation of anger by painful stimulation did not require cognitive mediation.

A longitudinal study of infants' emotion responses to the acute pain of diphtheria-pertussis-tetanus (DPT) inoculation reported evidence of noncognitive activation of emotion expression (Izard, Hembree, & Huebner, 1987). Infants' faces were videotaped with a close-up camera when they received the DPT injection at 2, 4, 7, and 19 months of age. Their facial behavior was objectively coded with an anatomically based coding system (Izard, 1979). Immediately following needle penetration and serum injection, all the 2- to 7-month-old infants regularly encoded a facial movement pattern identified as a pain expression. Immediately following the pain pattern, the infants expressed anger.

Several tests were made of the infants' knowledge of the nurse and syringe as agents of aversive stimulation. Even at 19 months of age, infants failed to show negative emotion expressions or avoidance behavior to the nurse or syringe. In the early months of life, this can be explained in terms of limited memory capacity, and, at the oldest age, by forgetting or memory inaccessibility. When the infants were inoculated at 19 months, they had not been to the clinic for several months—enough time to account for forgetting. There is a possibility that the infants had a memory of the previous pain experience, but, because of an immature context-learning system, were unable to access it (Jacobs & Nadel, 1985).

In any case, during the inoculation procedure they showed no signs of pain anticipation.

Several factors support the notion that, in the study of DPT inoculations, emotion expressions of anger resulted from pain or aversive feelings (cf. Berkowitz, 1990). Because there was no evidence that the infants had any knowledge of or hypothesis about the agent of harm, it is reasonable to assume that cognitive processes (appraisals, attributions) did not play a role in mediating the anger expression.

Expression-Mediated Changes in Cerebral Blood Flow and Emotion Activation

At the beginning of this century, a French physician, Israel Waynbaum, proposed that facial muscles acted as ligatures on blood vessels supplying the brain and that changes in cerebral blood flow produced changes in emotion experiences (see Zajonc, 1985). Zajonc (Zajonc et al., 1989) modified Waynbaum's theory and hypothesized that facial-muscle contractions affect venous blood flow to the cavernous sinus of the brain, an important structure in thermoregulation. It is thought that temperature changes in cerebral blood affect neurochemical processes like those that mediate emotion.

Zajonc reasoned that facial movements that facilitate venous flow to the cavernous sinus and the cooling of the brain would result in a hedonically pleasant subjective state. Once venal blood is in the veins of the cavernous sinus, it is cooled by the air of normal breathing. Cooling the blood in the cavernous sinus may also cool the hypothalamus, an important structure in thermoregulatory and emotion responses. It was hypothesized that facial movements that restrict blood flow to the cavernous sinus would impede cooling, increase cerebral blood temperature, and result in unpleasant subjective feelings.

Although the changes in brain blood temperature are thought to occur as a function of facial expressions of emotion, Zajonc and his colleagues decided to test their vascular theory of emotional efference (VTEE) by instigating nonemotional facial actions. This choice was determined by Zajonc's conviction that, in experiments that manipulate emotion-expressive behavior, it is difficult to eliminate the possibility that subjects infer the subjective feelings they "should experience" with the facial expression that is being manipulated.

Zajonc et al. (1989) conducted a series of five experiments to test hypotheses of VTEE. For example, they had subjects pronounce phonemes that involved facial muscle contractions that either facilitated or inhibited venal flow from facial veins to the cavernous sinus. They indexed changes in brain blood temperature with thermographic images of two points on the left and right sides of the forehead, points near the place where a branch of the anterior cerebral artery issues from the carotid sinus as it enters the brain. As predicted, facial muscle contractions (from phoneme pronunciation) that facilitated or inhibited venal flow and the cooling of cerebral blood resulted in an increase in pleasant and unpleasant feelings, respectively. Correspondingly, forehead temperature was significantly lower when cerebral blood flow was facilitated than when it was inhibited.

In addition to the experiments using facial movements to alter cerebral blood temperature, Zajonc et al. (1989) had subjects breathe slightly cooled or slightly warmed air. To conceal the purpose of the study and eliminate any possible connection to emotion, subjects were told that the experiment was evaluating reactions to olfactory stimulations. This direct physical manipulation of cerebral blood temperature by breathing cool or warm air produced results comparable to those obtained with facial muscle contractions. Breathing cool air resulted in pleasant feelings and lower forehead temperature, and breathing warm air produced negative feelings and higher forehead temperature.

Zajonc's VTEE and empirical data complement the facial feedback theory of emotion activation, to be reviewed in the next section. The data of Zajonc and his colleagues add two potentially significant factors. First, they suggest a mechanism for explaining how manipulation of emotion expressions produces emotion feeling states. Second, they offer convincing support for the notions of noncognitive activation of emotions and separate systems for emotions and cognition. Zajonc's studies seem to have eliminated the possibility of explaining the observed feeling states in terms of cognitive antecedents. Zajonc recognized that cognitive processes frequently activate emotions, but he argued that they are not necessary antecedents for all feeling states.

Three questions can be raised about Zajonc's data: (a) Are the observed subjective states truly emotional or simply changes on a pain-comfort dimension? (b) Are changes in cerebral blood temperature and subsequent brain neurochemistry fast enough to account for the rapidity of emotion reactions? As Zajonc (1980) and others have noted, rapidity of response is a characteristic of the emotions system generally accepted as important in evolution and adaptation. (c) If thermoregulation of cerebral blood and brain neurochemistry produces only changes in the positivity and negativity of hedonic states, how do we account for discrete emotion experiences? The literature on the facial feedback hypotheses describes data relevant to these questions.

Facial Expressions and Emotion Experience

In this section, we summarize the evidence for emotion activation by facial expression. In a later section, we shall examine the role of expressive behavior in emotion regulation. If facial expressions contribute to either the activation or the regulation of emotions, then any genetic or environmental condition that adversely affects expressive behavior development, a topic to be dealt with later, might be a factor in developmental psychopathology.

In the first controlled experiment on the effects of facial expression on emotion experience, Laird (1974) instructed subjects to pull the corners of their mouth back and up or to pull the browheads downward. These movements result in a simple smile or anger frown. Following the expression manipulation, subjects rated cartoons portrayed on slides. Subjects in the smile condition rated the cartoons significantly more pleasant than did the subjects in the frown condition. Laird concluded that his results were basically consistent with James's (1884) position that information from peripheral systems activated emotion experience. Thus, facial movements simulating a smile made subjects happier and caused them to rate cartoons more positively. The movements of the frown had the opposite effect.

Since Laird's original study, about 28 experiments that tested the facial feedback hypothesis have been published. The published accounts supported the hypothesis, with varying degrees of strength. Some of these experiments used well-disguised manipulations. For example, Strack, Martin, and Stepper (1988) had subjects hold a pencil with their teeth (which produced movements simulating a smile) or with their pursed lips (an action contrary to smiling). Subjects reported being significantly happier after the first (smile) manipulation than after the second.

Winton's (1986) review of the facial feedback literature indicated that expression manipulation only affected positive and negative emotionality, not discrete emotion experiences such as joy and sadness. In attempting to answer this criticism, Duclos et al. (1989) manipulated expressions of fear, anger, sadness, and disgust. They reported that each of these expressions produced significantly greater increases in the appropriate feeling than in other negative feelings. Others have challenged the strength of the facial feedback effect. Matsumoto's (1987) meta-analysis of the facial feedback experiments showed the average effect size for manipulated facial expressions was statistically significant although relatively small.

Despite the number of supporting publications, there remain criticisms and doubt regarding the methodology of the facial feedback experiments. Perhaps the most difficult criticism to assess is that subjects consciously or unconsciously infer the subjective feelings they "should" be having under the experimental conditions (Zajonc et al., 1989). Postexperimental inquiry could not be expected to identify subjects who make unconscious inferences or those who make conscious inferences but want to please the experimenter.

The criticisms notwithstanding, the weight of evidence and opinion indicates that expressive behavior can activate emotion feelings and that, in some cases, the feelings are elicited without causal cognitive antecedents. Two areas require future research: (a) more evidence is needed regarding the specificity of the expression effect (does an anger expression lead to the feeling of anger or simply to negative feelings?); (b) further work is needed to identify and elucidate the mechanism by which facial expression influences feelings. Three mechanisms have been proposed: (a) self-perception of the expressive behavior (Laird, 1974); (b) sensory feedback from expressive behavior (Gellhorn, 1964; Izard, 1977; Tomkins, 1962); (c) changes in cerebral blood temperature and brain neurochemistry resulting from the effects of facial muscle actions on blood flow to the cavernous sinus (Zajonc et al., 1989).

Summary

In this section, we have presented evidence for four types of noncognitive activators of emotions: (a) emotion, (b) pain, (c) change in cerebral blood temperature and brain neurochemistry, and (d) facial expression. It is not possible to say precisely how often emotion feelings occur as a result of noncognitive activators. They probably occur more frequently in people subject to chronic pain and less frequently in people with biologically or socially determined restrictions of expressive behavior. If we accept the evidence that one emotion feeling can elicit another, then noncognitive activation of feelings may be commonplace. In any case, there is clear evidence that various cognitive processes activate emotion; these are considered in a later section.

NORMAL AND ABNORMAL EXPRESSIVE BEHAVIOR DEVELOPMENT

Charles Darwin greatly influenced emotion theory and research by relating emotions to evolution and adaptation, social communication, and emotion regulation. He made his greatest impact on the field with his astute observations of the expressions of emotions, the only objectively measurable aspect of emotions readily available to 19th-century scientists. It was no accident that the resurgence of scientific interest in the emotions in the late 20th century was initially focused on expressive behavior.

Since Darwin's (1872/1965) seminal volume on emotions, ethologists and psychologists have done extensive investigations of expressive behavior (e.g., Charlesworth & Kreutzer, 1973; Eibl-Eibesfeldt, 1972; Ekman, Friesen, & Ellsworth, 1972; Izard, 1971). This widespread research activity was owed in part to Darwin's views on the relations among emotion expressions, socialization, and self-regulation, and his data indicating the phylogenetic continuity of expressions and their origins and functions in evolution and adaptation. Although Darwin's explanation of the evolution of expressions as dependent on inherited traits rather than natural selection was faulty, he was clear and correct in describing their significance as the first means of communication between infant and mother and a primary vehicle for socialization in human development. Later scientists have argued that the communicative function of expressions accounted for their selection in evolution (Andrew, 1963). In any case, expressive behavior has been shown to have important effects in mother-infant interactions and social relationships.

Darwin may have been the first scientist to note the causal role of expressive behavior in regulating emotion experiences. He wrote: "The free expression . . . of an emotion intensifies it . . . the repression . . . of all outward signs softens our emotions" (Darwin, 1872/1965, p. 365).

The Functions of Emotion Expressions

We have already discussed one potential function of expression—its role in the activation of emotion feelings. Although some theorists question the importance of this function, others believe that it is of great importance and that the evidence of its validity is substantial.

A second function of emotion expression is communication. Precisely what is communicated to whom and for what purpose is still a matter of debate and research. There is controversy in developmental psychology as to whether expression and feeling are biologically connected or become associated through social learning (Izard & Malatesta, 1987; Lewis & Michalson, 1983). Although there is evidence that young infants' discrete expressions are interpreted as signaling specific feelings (Izard, Huebner, Risser, McGinnes, & Dougherty, 1980), there are few data to show that young infants' specific expressions are related in a logical way to subsequent behavior.

The third function of emotion expressions is clear and unequivocal. Expressions motivate others to respond and affect the quality of their behavior. Mothers reported different feelings and behavioral tendencies in response to infants' expressions of sadness, anger, and pain (Huebner & Izard, 1988). Apparently, these expressions provided mothers with expression-specific cues for the amelioration of negative affect and the prevention of trauma. Several studies have shown that children modify their behavior in response to others' expressions (Izard & Malatesta, 1987).

Any breakdown in the parent-child communication system based on emotion expressions could have adverse effects on parents and children. For example, the dampened expressions of infants with Down syndrome can create serious problems, even reactive depression, in their parents (Emde, Katz, & Thorpe, 1978).

The Emergence of Discrete Emotion Expressions

We have already discussed the central neural substrates of emotion expressions. The efferent pathway that controls the facial movements of expressions is the VII (facial) cranial nerve. The sensory nerve that provides feedback from facial expression to the brain is the V (trigeminal) nerve. These pathways and the facial muscles they innervate are functional by the end of the 28th week of gestation (Oster, 1978), and the newborn is quite capable of expressive behavior. The facial expressions of interest, neonatal smiling, and disgust, and the affect expression of pain are present at birth. At least one of these expressions (disgust) has been elicited in anencephalic infants, confirming that its substrates lie in phylogenetically old parts of the brain (Steiner, 1973). The expressions of sadness and anger are observable as early as 2 to 3 months. The emergence of these basic emotion expressions has a predictable time course that is apparently independent of cognitive development (Izard & Malatesta, 1987).

Most of the relevant evidence indicates that the fear expression and avoidant behavior emerge at about 6 or 7 months. Whether some particular cognitive attainment is a prerequisite to fear expression is debatable. For example, it was once thought that the emergence of depth perception was a trigger for the expression of fear on the visual cliff, but clear signs of avoidant behavior and correlated physiological responses only occur on the visual cliff months after the first indications of depth perception and even a few weeks after the commencement of self-locomotion (Campos, Hiatt, Ramsay, Henderson, & Svejda, 1978).

It is generally thought that the emergence of behavioral signs of contempt, shame, shyness, and guilt are dependent on cognitive development. The idea is that these emotions are triggered by social comparison (contempt), self-reference (shame, shyness), or reference to an internalized standard (guilt). Social comparison, self-reference, and the learning and remembering of moral standards are functions of cognitive processes that do not occur in the early months of life. Empirical studies of these emotions usually involve subjects in the second year of life (e.g., Kagan, Reznick, & Snidman, 1988; Lewis, Sullivan, Stanger, & Weiss, 1989).

Theory and evidence relating to contempt, shame, shyness, and guilt suggest that they emerge well after the first year of life, but this does not mean that they are not part of a separate developmental system. Conceivably, the neural substrates of these emotions mature more slowly, and their behavioral and experiential manifestations are very likely influenced by learning. That neither biological or environmental influences guarantee these emotions is evidenced by the apparent lack of guilt in the psychopath.

Emotion Expressions in Normal Development

Given the foregoing picture of emotion expression ontogeny, it is possible to sketch an outline of early emotional development. Expressive behaviors and the capacity to respond to them are available from birth. From the beginning of life, the emotional and social experiences of the infant are influenced by expressive behavior. The young infant learns about the caregiver through the affective exchange mediated by vocal and facial expressions. Concepts of the traits of significant others begin to form on the basis of these emotion communications, and these affective-cognitive structures become part of the child's working model of the attachment figure. When this model is that of a sensitive and emotionally available caregiver, the child experiences a secure attachment relationship (Cicchetti, Cummings, Greenberg, & Marvin, 1990; Main, Kaplan, & Cassidy, 1985). Secure attachment has proven to be a predictor of socioemotional competence (Cicchetti et al., 1990; Erickson, Sroufe, & Egeland, 1985; Sroufe, 1988).

The young infant shares the emotional life of the caregiver through direct imitation of emotion signals and vicariously through social referencing and observational learning (Termine & Izard, 1988; Walden, 1991). Mother influences the emotional life of the infant through conscious and unconscious selective reinforcement of the infant's expressions. For example, mothers respond differentially to the facial expressions of 3- to 6-month-old male and female infants (Malatesta & Haviland, 1982), and there are grounds for believing that they also respond differentially to individual differences in emotion/temperament characteristics (Izard, Haynes, Chisholm, & Baak, 1991). A child who is prone to negative emotionality will expose caregivers to a different array of expressive signals and demands for attention than will a child who has a high threshold for negative emotions.

By the end of the first year of life, the role of expressive behavior has broadened considerably. At 10 to 12 months, it is possible to demonstrate the functional significance of emotion expressions through studies of social referencing. In social referencing, an infant or child looks to the face of the mother or another adult in order to facilitate interpretation of an object or situation. If the mother's face provides unambiguous information about her feelings toward the object, the infant can easily make an appraisal. As a result of this appraisal or interpretation, the infant may modify its emotion expression and experience and its actions. (For a discussion of the relative importance of the infant's modification of its emotion responses and actions, see Campos, 1983, and Feinman, 1982.) Because social referencing requires the infant to look at the mother's face, it also provides the infant an opportunity to display its initial emotion feeling about the object.

The power of mothers' emotion expressions to modify the actions of their children has been amply demonstrated. (For reviews, see Feinman, 1985, and Klinnert, Campos, Sorce, Emde, & Svejda, 1983.) A study of social referencing on the visual cliff provides an example with clear implications for emotional development (Sorce, Emde, Campos, & Klinnert, 1985). The stimulus, a visual cliff modified to show an apparent drop-off of about 12 inches, provided a situation of uncertainty and possible danger to the infants. The mother stood by the deep side of the visual cliff (which shows the apparent drop-off while the infant is placed on the shallow side). When mothers smiled, 74% of their infants crossed over the deep side; when mothers expressed fear, none of the infants crossed. The results suggest that infants used the emotional information in their mothers' faces to interpret the visual cues afforded by the apparent drop-off. A variation in this experiment indicated that emotional information obtained through social referencing is less likely to modify the infants' behavior in the face of clear and strong cues of danger. When the experimenters used the regular visual cliff with an apparent 42-inch drop-off, infants would not cross to a smiling mother. One explanation of this behavior is that infants are biologically prepared to respond with fear to certain conditions (Seligman & Hager, 1972). Thus, a 42-inch drop-off (height) activated sufficiently intense fear to nullify or preclude the influence of the mother's smiling face. The cliff-induced fear feeling provided the information that organized and motivated the infant's avoidance behavior.

Developmental changes occur in various aspects of social referencing (Walden & Ogan, 1988). When confronted with a new and ambiguous stimulus, infants become more selective in their looking behavior as age increases from 6 to 22 months. Looks to the parent increased markedly during this period, when the child was exposed to a fearful stimulus (robot). Also, with increasing age, children looked more directly at their parents' faces. Not until 14 months of age would infants refuse to touch "fearful" toys until they had looked at their parents' faces. In later free-play sessions, infants' behavior showed that they had learned (e.g., avoidance behavior) from their parents' emotional reactions. Thus, social referencing studies show the potential for parental expressive behavior to affect socialization.

The combined effects of (a) biological preparedness to learn and (b) emotional information in mothers' expressive behavior seem evident in a study of observational conditioning of snake fear in rhesus monkeys (Mineka, Davidson, Cook, & Keiri, 1984). Six laboratory-reared adolescent/young adult monkeys showed no fear of a snake and freely reached over the snake to obtain a food reward. Wild-reared adult monkeys in the same colony displayed strong signs of fear upon seeing the snake, even though they had not been exposed to one during their many (up to 15) years in the laboratory. Five of 6 of the young monkeys quickly acquired an intense and persistent fear of the snake after observing a wild-reared monkey's reaction to one. The strength of the learned fear was greatest when the model was the young monkey's mother. Mineka et al.'s findings suggest that observational learning is involved in the origins of many fears and phobias.

We can now consider aspects of emotional development beyond the first few months of life, a period characterized by sharing the emotional life of the caregiver through initiation and imitation of emotion expressions. Beginning in the latter part of the first year, infants learn about the emotional significance of objects and situations through social referencing and observational learning—processes that depend on the integration of information in expressive behavior with information afforded by the environment. These processes may affect changes in emotional behavior throughout the life span.

Casual observation of the expressive behavior of infants and that of preschool children reveals remarkable changes. Preschool children show a much greater capacity to regulate expression. They can delay expression (signaling) and be selective in choosing a receiver. Differential rates of development of expression regulation undoubtedly reflect emerging differences in socioemotional competence and personality. The patterns and directions of expression regulation that begin to take shape in toddlerhood probably continue through the life span. However, there are few empirical data on the mechanisms and processes whereby the developmental changes in expressive behavior occur.

The Stability of Expressive Behavior in Early Development

There is evidence of stability in emotion expression characteristics over the first 2 years of life. In a longitudinal study of emotion responses to acute pain, early-infancy indexes of sadness and anger expressions were significantly correlated with sadness and anger expression at 19 months. Thus, for example, young infants (2 to 7 months) who expressed a relatively great amount of anger in response to pain of inoculation tended to express a relatively great amount of anger to the same stimulus at 19 months (Izard et al., 1987). Studies of the strange situation and similar separation-reunion procedures have also found evidence for stability of expressive behavior (Hyson & Izard, 1985; Malatesta, Culver, Tesman, & Shepard, 1989). A study of behavioral and psychophysiological indexes of emotion and temperament in a variety of stimulus situations showed stability from 2 months to 2 years (Izard, Simons, & Porges, 1991). The stability coefficients, including those for two indexes of resting-state heart-rate variability, were highly significant.

The foregoing evidence of stability of emotion characteristics in early development, when some indexes of cognitive development are unstable, suggests that emotion characteristics and the personality traits they organize and motivate emerge very early in the life of the individual. Further research is greatly needed on the continuity of expressive and other emotion characteristics through the preschool years and beyond.

Development of Expressive Behavior in Atypical Populations

In assessing and understanding abnormal expressive behavior, it is essential to consider the kinds of processes that can contribute to the deviant behavior. Because there are always at least two people involved in emotion communication, both individuals can play a part in breakdowns or failures.

Consider a mother and young infant in face-to-face interaction. Either the mother or the infant can encode ambiguous or difficult-to-interpret expressions. The mother, more than the infant, might be thought responsible for noncontingency or asynchrony in sending emotion signals. However, an intellectually delayed or abused child might fail to respond expressively to a mother in time for the exchange to be smooth and synchronous. The delayed infant might need more time to decode the mother's expression and respond appropriately. The abused child might delay a response because of wariness or ambivalence about the consequences. These discrepancies in timing might become even more disturbing to the parent or participant observer as the child grows older and more is expected.

Emotion Expressions in Children with Down Syndrome

A series of studies comparing normal infants and infants with Down syndrome showed that a serious developmental disorder can have dramatic effects on emotion expression (Cicchetti & Sroufe, 1978). The investigators studied the emotional reactions of infants with Down syndrome to the visual loom (apparent colliding object), visual cliff (height or apparent drop-off), and a variety of items designed to elicit smiling and laughing. As expected, they found great differences in the emotional behavior of normal infants and infants with Down syndrome. For example, in response to an apparent impending collision (of object with infant), no 4- or 8-month-old infants with Down syndrome cried, and at 12 months only 6% cried. The corresponding figures for normal infants at these ages were 3%, 33%, and 57%. When placed on the visual cliff, far fewer infants with Down syndrome cried or experienced heart-rate acceleration than did normal infants. Similarly, positive stimuli elicited significantly less smiling and laughing in infants with Down syndrome than in normal infants.

Cicchetti and Sroufe also compared the emotional reactions of infants with Down syndrome and normal infants matched in terms of cognitive development. Their data suggested that the differences in emotional reactions of infants with Down syndrome and normal infants could not be explained by cognitive factors alone. Even when the two groups were equivalent in developmental age, infants with Down syndrome showed a marked diminution in both positive and negative emotion expressions and emotional behavior toward the stimuli. Data like these led Cicchetti (1990) to conclude that the emotions constitute a separate developmental system.

It is reasonable to expect that different genetic conditions (e.g., Down syndrome) or environmental processes (e.g., child abuse) affect the development of the emotions system differently. Cicchetti and Sroufe summarized a number of ways in which Down syndrome might affect the emotions system. These included low levels of an enzyme necessary to the synthesis of norepinephrine, abnormal catecholamine metabolism, and deficiencies in the functioning of the sympathetic nervous system. There is also evidence of deficiencies in the cholinergic and serotonergic systems that could affect the parasympathetic and reticular activating systems, which are important to the individual's arousal levels (see Cicchetti, 1990).

Overall, the evidence from neurochemical studies suggests that persons with Down syndrome may have dampened reactive systems. This condition could result in attenuated emotion-expressive behavior and a deficiency in emotion communication. The behavioral studies of Cicchetti and his colleagues (see Cicchetti, 1990; Ganiban, Wagner, & Cicchetti, 1990) and Emde and his associates (Emde, Katz, & Thorpe, 1978) indicate that this is the case. Children with Down syndrome show delay in age-appropriate emotion responses, even in comparison with normal children of the same mental age, and the expressions they do encode are dampened.

Emotion Communication in Mentally Retarded Children

Research by Walden (1991) and her associates showed how deviations in different developmental processes resulted in substantial deficiencies in social referencing and infant-mother communication. A preliminary study showed that, when confronted with ambiguous stimuli, intellectually delayed children engaged in about as much referential looking to their mothers as normal children. The delayed children, however, did not show the expected changes in playing with toys that had been referents of positive and fearful parental expressions. Walden did a follow-up experiment to determine why intellectually delayed children looked to their parent but failed to use information from parental expressions to regulate their behavior.

The subjects were 11- and 21-month-old normal children and an intellectually delayed group of equal mental age. The mean chronological ages for the younger and older delayed children were 28 and 43 months, respectively. Again, they presented children with ambiguous toys. They not only measured the child's looks to mother, but they determined whether the mother saw the look and how well the mother's expression and the child's look were coordinated.

They found that mothers of intellectually delayed children often "jumped the gun" or otherwise mistimed their emotion expression so that it was noncontingent with the child's look. By making the expression noncontingent, the emotion information was unavailable or less available to the child. Delayed children whose parents timed their expressions effectively showed appropriate behavior regulation. Normal children were not affected by the contingency of the parental expression. The normal children were apparently better able than the intellectually delayed to integrate the uncoordinated (noncontingent) information.

Walden found two types of parental miscommunication: (a) noncontingent response (mother's expression not within 3 seconds of infant's look) and (b) false alarms (unsolicited expressions). Delayed and normal children also differed in their responses to the two types of miscommunication. Delayed children were adversely affected by both noncontingent expressions and false alarms. Normals were affected only by the latter.

The foregoing findings exemplify the need for a multifactor approach to understanding deficits in developmental processes. On the average, delayed children were less competent in integrating appraisals of the ambiguous toy with emotion information from parental expressions. Therefore, they were less effective in regulating their behavior in relation to the toy. The work of Walden and her colleagues clearly showed that the mothers of the delayed children, as well as the children themselves, contributed to the children's deficiency in self-regulation. As compared to mothers of normal children, mothers of the delayed children more often mistimed their expressions and gave false alarms.

Expressive Behavior of Premature Infants

Premature infants, especially in the first year of life, show atypical expressive behaviors (Malatesta et al., 1989). They express more negative emotion and less positive emotion than normals. Although prematures typically catch up with normals in cognitive development during the first year of life, this may not be so in the domain of emotions. In the study by Malatesta et al., the prematures continued to lag behind normals in emotional development well into the second year.

Other studies have shown that, compared to normals, the cry of the premature infant is more strident (Lester, 1985). The premature's more frequent negative emotion expressions and more strident cry may create problems in parent-infant interactions and the development of attachment. The likelihood of the development of parent-infant problems in families with prematures is very likely to be increased when parents are psychologically unprepared for the deficiencies in the expressive component of the emotions system—deficiencies that are probably caused by a neurophysiological immaturity.

Emotion Expression and Emotional Behavior in Maltreated Children

Several studies have shown that abused children have marked defects in emotion expression and emotional behavior. The extensive investigations of maltreated children by Cicchetti and his colleagues (see Cicchetti, 1990) have increased our understanding of abnormal and normal emotional development.

For a long time, clinical reports have suggested that abused children often become abusing parents, thus creating a kind of deviant cultural evolution of abnormal emotionality. Many factors contribute to the maltreated child's defective emotional development. Studies of normal emotional development (Izard et al., 1980) have shown the enormous potential of expressive behavior for influencing infant-parent relations: it is the primary basis for infant-parent communication, particularly in the preverbal months of life.

Gaensbauer and his colleagues (Gaensbauer, Mrazek, & Harmon, 1981; Gaensbauer & Sands, 1979) have shown that parental maltreatment destroys or seriously disrupts the normal patterns of affective communication. The expressive behavior is deficient in positive emotion expression and high in negative emotion expression. Expressive behavior in parent-child dyads that involve an abusive parent is also characterized by ambivalence/ambiguity, inconsistency/unpredictability, and withdrawal. That such withdrawal might be a sign of infants' inability to make sense of ambiguous parental expressions is suggested by the work of Tronick and his colleagues (Tronick, 1989). Even when presented with the apparently benign stimulus of about 180 seconds of mother's still and silent face, the infant displays abnormal expressive behavior that sometimes ends in withdrawal.

The work of Gaensbauer and his colleagues revealed one quite remarkable deviation in the expressive behavior of the abused child: infants as young as 3 or 4 months might display fear expressions on being approached by a strange adult of the same sex as the maltreating parent. Emotion theorists (Izard, 1977; Tomkins, 1963) have hypothesized that the neural substrates of fear do not normally mature until the infant is 6 or 7 months of age. The late-maturing fear system protects the very young child from the toxic and potentially lethal effects of extreme fear or terror. Consistent with these theoretical notions, normal infants under 7 months did not display fear even to separation (Malatesta et al., 1989) or the acute pain of inoculation (Izard et al., 1987). The observations of Gaensbauer et al. (1981) suggest that chronic maltreatment of children can even hasten the development of the fear system. These researchers identified four groups of maltreated children characterized by different types of deviant expressive behavior: (a) developmentally and affectively retarded, characterized by lack of social and environmental responsiveness and emotional blunting; (b) depressed, showing excessive sadness, inhibition, and withdrawal; (c) ambivalent/affectively labile, exhibiting sudden shift from positive to negative emotion expression; and (d) angry, characterized by angry outbursts and disorganized play. Although cause-effect relations for these emotional behaviors is not yet validated, Cicchetti and his colleagues have confirmed the existence of early aberrations in emotion communication in mother-infant dyads characterized by maltreatment (e.g., Aber & Cicchetti, 1984). Given the power of a simple stimulus like a still, silent face to disrupt communicative and relational behavior, it is reasonable that the kinds of deviant parental expression identified by Gaensbauer and Cicchetti and their colleagues, combined with the emotional turmoil resulting from parental abuse, are quite sufficient to contribute substantially to the abnormal emotional behavior of maltreated children. For example, because fear of the caregiver is thought to be a determinant of disorganized (type D) attachment, it is conceivable that maltreatment-induced acceleration in the development of fear (as suggested by the work of Gaensbauer and Cicchetti and their colleagues) is one of the factors that mediates the development of type D attachment (cf. Carlson, Cicchetti, Barnett, & Braunwald, 1989).

It seems a long road from being an abused infant to becoming a maltreating parent, but there is evidence that the processes that underlie the transition from being a recipient of abuse to being a perpetrator do not lie dormant until adulthood. Apparent relations have been found between parental maltreatment of a child and the aggressive behavior of that child toward peers in 1- to 3-year-old children in a day-care setting (Main & George, 1985). When the investigators classified the responses of economically disadvantaged children and disadvantaged abused children to distress in a peer, only 5.6% of the disadvantaged children responded unusually to a peer's distress, whereas 55.4% of the abused children responded with fear, nonphysical aggression, diffuse anger, or a physical attack on the distressed toddler.

Abused children's emotional behavior toward a distressed peer is clearly different from that of nonabused children's reactions to distress exhibited by others (Zahn-Waxler, Radke-Yarrow, & King, 1979). The modal response of 1.5- to 2.5-year-old normal children was to attempt to make reparation. This was especially so of children whose mothers were rated high on empathic caregiving and frequently used emotionally toned explanations of the need for empathic and altruistic behavior (Zahn-Waxler et al., 1979).

Adverse Effects of Others' Emotion Expressions

Normal children are adversely affected, at least temporarily, by exposure to genuine anger expression in others' quarrels. In this circumstance, 24% of 1.5- to 2.5-year-old normal children express anger, including hitting, pushing, or scolding one of the antagonists (Cummings, Zahn-Waxler, & Radke-Yarrow, 1981). Several subsequent studies have verified that very young children are capable of detecting the anger expressions of others. Their own anger responses while observing agonistic encounters clearly show that they are influenced by others' anger expressions.

The expressive behavior of depressed parents can be a factor in abnormal emotional development of their children. Zahn-Waxler, Kochanska, Krupnick, and McKnew (1990) found that 5- to 9-year-old children of depressed mothers experienced about the same amount of guilt as children of nondepressed mothers, but the children of depressed mothers had significantly more atypical reactions to guilt. Normal guilt has adaptive functions; it helps facilitate empathic concern and motivates reconciliation and reparative behavior (Hoffman, 1982; Izard, 1977). Abnormal or distorted guilt, however, can contribute to depression in children and adults (Blumberg & Izard, 1985; Seligman et al., 1984).

In the study of Zahn-Waxler et al. (1990), interview-based guilt scores of children with depressed mothers correlated significantly with hostility scores derived from a semiprojective technique. Their responses on the latter test showed that they tended to become overly aroused and involved in the distress of another person. The investigators speculated that children who become overinvolved in a parent's depression-related problems may develop tendencies to distance or protect themselves from the distress of others. They would show less empathy and prosocial behavior to others' distress because the normal adaptive functions of guilt would be rendered dysfunctional.

As Zahn-Waxler et al. (1990) noted, some of the characteristics of depressed mothers probably contribute to the processes by which their children develop distorted reactions to guilt. Feelings of despair and helplessness may make the depressed mothers more sensitive to issues of blame and responsibility. Depressed mothers are more likely than normal mothers to make negative attributions about their children and to use more guilt- and anxiety-induction techniques in their child-rearing practices (Zahn-Waxler et al., 1979, 1990; Zahn-Waxler & Kochanska, 1990). Two processes that are probably involved in the intergenerational transmission of emotional maldevelopment are emotion contagion and modeling. Emotion expression is involved in both of these processes. Emotion contagion is expression-induced emotion feeling, and modeling consists, in part, of emotion expression and emotional behavior in the presence of the child.

Early-Infancy Emotion Expressions as Predictions of Developmental Outcomes

In a longitudinal project on normal emotional development (Izard et al., 1991), facial expressions of emotion were measured in a variety of pleasant and mildly stressful mother-infant interactions at 2.3, 3, 4.5, 6, and 9 months. Recordings of cardiac activity provided two measures of resting-state heart-rate variability. When the infants were 13 months old, a continuous index of attachment was derived from data obtained in the strange-situation procedure. Both the facial expression and heart-rate variability indexes contributed to the prediction of level-of-attachment security. The greater the infants' negative emotion expression and the higher their heart-rate variability, the higher were their attachment insecurity scores. Because insecure attachment can be a causal factor in the development of psychopathology in later childhood (see Cicchetti, 1990, for a review), the data of Izard et al. suggest that emotion expressive behavior can provide an early window on dysadaptive development. Consistent with this notion was the finding from the same project that early-infancy indexes of emotion expression predicted temperament problems at the end of the second year of life.

There are several reasons why expressive behavior might function as an index of normal and abnormal emotional development. Emotion expressions are a valid index of emotion feelings, especially in infants and young children, and the stability of expressive behaviors indicates that patterns of emotion experiences remain stable (Izard & Malatesta, 1987). These recurring patterns of emotion experiences tend to manifest themselves as traits of the emerging self or personality.

In adults, there is substantial evidence of strong relations among emotion experiences and specific traits and dimensions of personality (Izard, Libero, Putnam, & Haynes, 1993; Lyons-Ruth, Zoll, Connell, & Grunebaum, 1989; Malatesta, 1990; Watson & Clark, 1992). Positive emotion experiences are correlated with specific traits like affiliation and broad dimensions like sociability. Negative emotion experiences are correlated with specific traits like aggressiveness and broad dimensions like neuroticism and psychoticism. Lyons-Ruth et al. showed that mothers whose childhood relationships were characterized by excessive negative emotion were much more likely than mothers with more sanguine childhood relationships to exhibit hostile-intrusive reactions to their own infants. Their finding is quite consistent with the notion that emotion characteristics—in this case, hostility-aggressiveness—show a great deal of stability from early childhood to adulthood. In the case of child maltreatment, as in other forms of emotion-related behavior, both biological and social factors probably play a role.

Differential emotions theory (Izard, 1977, 1989; Malatesta, 1990) explains the relations among emotion experiences and personality characteristics on the basis of the organizational and motivational properties of emotions. Each emotion organizes and motivates a particular range or type of responses, not a random set of responses. For example, interest motivates approach, exploration, engagement in the environment, and learning. The feeling of interest also provides cues for cognition and facilitates creativity (cf. Isen, Daubman, & Nowicki, 1987). In contrast, sadness typically causes a slowing of both motor and mental activity. Sadness experience and expression appropriate to the occasion and in moderation can be adaptive. The slowing down can provide a new perspective, and the sadness experience can motivate remedial thoughts and actions. However, frequent and intense sadness can contribute to inaction, withdrawal, and depression. Similarly, frequent exposure to a threatening environment and frequent fear experiences can contribute to anxiety disorders (Barlow, 1989).

In addition to the contribution of patterns of emotions to anxiety and depressive disorders, some specific emotions have traitlike characteristics. For example, behaviors indicative of extreme shyness have been shown to be stable over the first 7 years of life (Kagan, Reznick, & Snidman, 1987). Overt Type A behaviors, which are probably organized and motivated by anger, have shown stability from 2 to 5 years and from 6 to 12 years. The stability of Type A behaviors is comparable to that for other cardiovascular risk factors in children (Visintainer & Matthews, 1987).

Persistent, open, and uncontrolled expression of anger (aggressive actions, fighting) from kindergarten through early school years is associated with an increase in nonaggressive behavior problems such as lying, stealing, and cheating (Loeber, Tremblay, Gagnon, & Charlebois, 1989). Perhaps persistent uncontrolled expression of anger through aggression, which is easily observed, should serve as a warning that other emotions such as guilt may be developing abnormally.

Differential emotions theory holds that any emotion may show traitlike characteristics as a function of biologically based individual differences in emotion thresholds, environmental conditions, and personal experience. Each of these broad sources of influences helps determine whether an emotion will be so regulated that it emerges as a trait within the normal range. As shown in the foregoing review, genetic defects, maltreatment, parental mental health, and other adverse conditions can contribute to the development of psychopathological emotionality.

We said at the outset that each emotion has inherently adaptive functions—joy inspires affiliation; fear, protection; and so on. When an emotion becomes pathological, it has become associated with maladaptive thought and actions, often derived from adverse circumstances. As a result, one may experience anger unjustifiably or fear without real threat. The development of this sort of overgeneralized emotion responding is more likely to occur when early experiences such as those created by maltreating or depressive parents are fraught with sadness, anger, or fear.

Several rather vague constructs that are related to the development or prevention of psychopathology probably could be described more precisely in terms of discrete emotion expressions and emotional behavior. For example, a "positive relationship" with one parent can help protect a child from the risks of growing up in a severely discordant home (Rutter, 1979). Such a positive relationship is undoubtedly characterized by positive emotion expressions and emotional behavior. Similarly, "maternal warmth" has been shown to be a protective factor against adjustment problems associated with peer rejection (Patterson, Cohn, & Kao, 1989). These investigators demonstrated that nonverbal and verbal expressions of positive feelings were substantial components of maternal warmth. Further, "differential affection" on the part of a mother toward her children is associated with behavior problems in middle childhood (Dunn, Stocker, & Plomin, 1990). Such differential affection is probably manifested through both positive and negative emotion expressions.

Another significant factor in determining the pathogenicity of an emotion is the development of emotion regulation. We turn next to the rule of expressive behavior in regulating emotion feelings.

Expressive Behavior and Emotion Regulation

In an earlier section, we reviewed the substantial evidence supporting the hypothesis that facial expressions contribute to the activation of emotion feelings. This evidence also supports a corollary of that hypothesis: emotion-expressive behavior is a mechanism for the regulation of emotion experiences. Like the emotion activation hypothesis, the emotion-regulation corollary can be traced to Darwin (1872/1965) and James (1890/1950). Darwin believed that there was a direct relation between voluntarily produced expressive behavior and the subjective experience of emotion. Similarly, James wrote: "Refuse to express a passion and it dies . . ." and if you wish to experience an emotion, ". . . go through the outward movements . . ." (p. 463).

Contemporary research has shown that Darwin and James were essentially correct; for example, exaggeration or suppression of facial expressions increases and decreases, respectively, both the subjective experience of emotion and the accompanying physiological arousal (see Izard, 1990, for a review).

Compared to the evidence for the role of emotion expression in emotion activation, the evidence for the effect of voluntarily controlled expressive behavior on altering ongoing emotion experiences is substantially stronger. A meta-analysis of 16 facial feedback studies showed that the effect size (in Pearson r) for the expression manipulation was .343, accounting for only 11.8% of the total variance in emotion feelings (Matsumoto, 1987). An examination of the methodology of these 16 studies (Izard, 1990) showed that 10 of them used Laird's subject-blind experimenter-manipulation to activate emotion experience, and 6 of them requested subjects to exaggerate or attenuate event-elicited expression to attain some goal (e.g., concealing their feelings from an observer). The effect size for the 10 studies of experimenter-manipulated expression was .275; for the studies of subject-controlled expression, it was .457. The data indicate that individuals who can effectively regulate expressive behavior can exercise considerable control over their emotion experiences.

The substantial effect size for subject-controlled expression has direct implications for the socialization of emotions (Izard, 1990). The evidence suggests that when the infant or child imitates or otherwise learns expressive behavior from parents with psychological disorders, the child may be placed at risk for similar mental health problems.

Thus, if a child assumes the expression of a depressed parent, the expression may induce depressive affect. If a maltreating parent models angry expressions and behavior and the child learns to encode the same expressive behaviors under similar circumstances, the child may experience and express anger and engage in aggressive behavior. This could be one of the mechanisms for the intergenerational transmission of child abuse. The data of Main and George (1985) are consistent with this model. Many of the abused children in their sample expressed anger and acted aggressively on witnessing a peer experience distress. Similarly, when depressed mothers express depressive affect—sadness, anger, guilt—and their children incorporate these expressive behaviors as part of their coping strategy, the children are more likely to experience depressive affect. The data of Zahn-Waxler et al. (1990) are relevant here. Their data suggested that depressed mothers' maladaptive responses to their own feelings of guilt led to distorted guilt and guilt-related behavior in their children.

The experimental data on the effect of manipulated or self-regulated expression on emotion experience and the congruent data from clinical investigations strongly suggest that the socialization of expressive behavior contributes to the socialization or regulation of emotion feelings. As children learn the adaptive and maladaptive techniques modeled by parents for expression and emotional behavior control, they are learning adaptive or maladaptive techniques for the regulation of emotion feelings.

Once the child has acquired language and verbal representational skills, facial and bodily expression of emotion is complemented by verbal expression. Language development and memory enable the child to learn about the causes and consequences of emotion and to deal with emotions conceptually. Language and thought provide the resources for the development of a different set of techniques for emotion regulation. These will be discussed in a later section.

Cicchetti, Ganiban, and Barnett's (1991) review of the research on children with Down syndrome and maltreated children shows that this work has contributed to our understanding of emotion regulation in normal children. For example, the importance of the timely development of neural inhibitory systems is underscored by the fact that delayed maturation of neuroregulatory systems in children with Down syndrome apparently limits their ability to inhibit emotion-elicited arousal in response to a caregiver's effort to ameliorate and soothe. As already noted, maltreatment may lead to the early emergence of the fear system, a phenomenon that highlights the adaptiveness of the normal timetable for the development of discrete emotions (Izard & Malatesta, 1987).

The salubrious effects of normal socialization on the development of emotion regulation are better appreciated in the light of Rieder and Cicchetti's (1989) finding that, compared to normal children, maltreated children have greater difficulty in processing and managing aggressive stimuli. Aggressive maltreatment apparently lowers children's threshold for perception of and attention to aggressive stimuli. Thus, aggressively abused children have greater difficulty in focusing attention on tasks when aggressive stimuli are part of the context. Such a context is probably uncommon in the life of maltreated children, given their tendency to perceive or interpret stimuli as aggressive.

EMOTION EXPERIENCES IN ANXIETY AND DEPRESSION

Although there is a large body of literature on anxiety and depression, relatively little of it relates these phenomena to emotion concepts and variables. Even less of it has examined anxiety and depression in both children and adults with the same or conceptually similar instruments.

This section focuses on the discrete emotions approach to understanding anxiety and depression. It is brief because of the relative scarcity of studies in this tradition and because reviews of this work are readily available (Izard & Blumberg, 1985; Izard & Schwartz, 1986).

The research reviewed here was guided by differential emotions theory (Izard, 1977; Izard & Malatesta, 1987). This theory shares a number of tenets with various discrete emotion approaches that underlie much of the research reviewed in the foregoing sections. Two of these propositions are especially relevant here.

1. Each of the discrete emotions of human experience has unique organizational and motivational properties. This premise suggests that all psychodiagnostic and therapeutic endeavors should include an attempt to discern the complete profile of emotions that characterize the patient. As we shall see, the profiles are very different in anxiety and depression.

2. Anxiety and depression, like other psychological disorders, occur in two ways. (a) Genetic factors can establish proneness to depression or anxiety by altering or creating deficiencies in the underlying neural substrates. Such factors may increase sensitivities to stressful stimulation, which amounts to changing emotion thresholds. (b) Environmental stress, for example, from insensitive caregiving, maltreatment, separation, or loss, can change emotion thresholds so as to render the individual more susceptible to anxiety or depression.

Earlier sections of this chapter have shown how it is possible to determine children's understanding of a few of their own and others' basic emotion experiences through experimental manipulations and direct queries. By the time children are 9 or 10 years of age, they can give a reliable account of their emotion experiences across the range of emotions (Kotsch, Gerbing, & Schwartz, 1982). They can even demonstrate their understanding of multiple emotions toward the same person or event, suggesting that they have some appreciation of ambivalence (Harter, 1983).

Two studies illustrated the usefulness of the discrete emotions approach to measuring the affective symptomatology of anxiety and depression. These studies drew on earlier evidence of the existence of differential patterns of emotions in anxiety and depressive disorders in adults (Izard, 1972). The first study examined the affective characteristics of depression in 10- and 11-year-old children. The Differential Emotions Scale IV (DES IV), the self-report measure of emotions, is essentially the same as the DES III described by Kotsch et al. (1982), with the addition of separate scales for shame and inner-directed hostility. The latter scales were considered necessary for a complete assessment of the emotion expressions in depression. The results showed that childhood depression is characterized by essentially the same pattern of emotions as in adults, when the children's version of Beck's Depression Inventory (CDI) is the index of depression. The discrete emotion scales of sadness, inner-directed hostility, shame, and anger were highly correlated with the CDI scores. To help control for method variance, a separate nonaffect depression index was derived by eliminating CDI items that contained emotion words. The correlations between the relevant

DES scales and the nonaffect items of the CDI remained highly significant and approximately of the same magnitude as the correlations between DES scales and the total CDI (Blumberg & Izard, 1985).

The second study compared the profiles of emotions in anxiety and depression in another sample of 10- and 11-year-old children (Blumberg & Izard, 1986). As predicted, the profiles of emotions in these two conditions were substantially different. Whereas sadness was the key, or most prominent, emotion in depression, fear was the key emotion in anxiety. The anxiety measure was the State Trait Anxiety Inventory for Children (STAIC; Spielberger, Edwards, Lushene, Montuori, & Platzek, 1973). Other aspects of the two patterns were distinctly different. Inner-directed hostility was the second most prominent feature of the affective symptomatology of depression, but it did not figure in anxiety at all. Similar results obtained when the nonaffect items of the STAIC constituted the anxiety index.

In the first of the foregoing studies, the children's teachers rated them on depression. The correlations between DES scales and teacher ratings were similar to those for the self-report index of depression. Although they were not as great in magnitude, they were statistically significant.

On the assumption that each discrete emotion always retains unique organizational and motivational properties, the foregoing data confirm the notion that a careful assessment of the complete pattern of emotions should facilitate both understanding and intervention. The literature summarized here reported average profiles of emotions for large groups. Individual profiles for anxious or depressed individuals show variation while retaining the key features found in group averages (Izard, 1972). These individual differences can be an important guide for psychodiagnosis and therapy.

In this chapter and elsewhere (e.g., Izard, 1989), we have presented evidence supporting the hypothesis that each emotion has a unique capacity to organize and motivate cognition and action. This capacity makes an emotion adaptive—a particular emotion tends to organize and motivate behavior appropriate to the emotion-eliciting situation.

We hypothesize that, even in anxiety or depression, the specific emotions retain adaptive features. For example, the sadness in depression causes a slowing of mental and motor functions. This change in the rate of information processing may enable the individual to see new relations, gain a better grasp of the problem, and initiate corrective actions. The anger in depression tends to have an effect opposite to that of sadness. Anger mobilizes energy for action and fosters feelings of strength and confidence in one's powers. This amounts to an antidote to sadness and the helplessness one feels in depression. In this way, anger can attenuate sadness and keep the depressive mood from becoming overwhelming.

When adequate regulatory mechanisms and techniques are deficient or absent, the sadness in depression can become so intense that it overwhelms the patient. The anger, in the form of inner-directed hostility, can lead to self-destructive behavior and, in the extreme, suicide. These deficient control processes call for a search for genetically and experientially induced defects within the emotions system (e.g., altered emotion thresholds) and for inappropriate or ineffective links among the emotions, cognition, and action systems.

APPRAISAL PROCESSES IN EMOTION ACTIVATION

Earlier, we considered several noncognitive activators of emotion. In this section, we look more closely at cognitive processes that lead to emotion. Because this is a complex topic, it is important to be clear about just what will be discussed. The main focus is on the appraisal processes that can give rise to an emotional state and its accompanying action tendencies. The emotions selected for special study are fear and guilt. This gloomy pair has been chosen for several reasons. First, each emotion illustrates the role that appraisal can play, albeit in different ways. Second, these two emotions are central to discussions of abnormal development, particularly the development of phobias and depression. Third, the two emotions provide an intriguing contrast with one another. Fear is usually regarded, quite uncontroversially, as a basic and universal emotion. By contrast, the status of guilt is more controversial: some see it as a secondary rather than a basic emotion, and some judge it to fall short of universality. By considering both emotions, therefore, we can weigh the contributions of both biology and culture to emotional development.

Appraisal Processes and Fear

In his overview of the emotions, Frijda (1986) claimed that emotions give rise to action tendencies. The way in which a person construes a situation, especially in relation to his or her ongoing concerns and values, will engender an impulse or willingness to maintain or change the situation in specific ways. The nature of this action tendency will vary sharply from emotion to emotion. In the case of fear, for example, there will be an impulse to reduce the threat of harm, usually by means of escape or avoidance. In the case of guilt, there will be an impulse to invite or express criticism of the self, or to undo the wrong that has been done.

For these action tendencies to be generated, the situation in which the person finds himself or herself must be evaluated in a specific way. Emotion theorists have wavered in their thinking about how best to specify the link between situation and emotion. Life—or at least, research—would be easier if a particular emotion could be neatly linked back to a coherent and unified set of external stimuli. Even a modest survey shows, however, that such alleged links soon amount to an unwieldy and heterogenous list. Consider the stimuli that are often considered to be biologically prepared or natural elicitors of fear in young children: strangers, animals, heights, and loud noises. These stimuli have no common physical parameter; what, for example, does an animal have in common with a high place? One solution is to abandon the search for such a parameter, and to assume instead that here is a heterogeneous set of triggers that all result in the same discrete emotion—namely, fear. Figure 16.1 illustrates this simple model.

Note that this model also permits the acquisition of new fears. These are elicited by otherwise neutral stimuli that happen to be associated with a natural elicitor. Consistent with this model, a good deal of research on the acquisition of fear has emphasized

Figure 16.1 A system that responds directly to fearful stimuli with no common appraisal.

the role of conditioning. One disadvantage of such an approach from a developmental point of view is that it ignores the possibility that new fears are acquired, not via conditioning, but via a cognitive appraisal that assesses seemingly innocent situations for the harm that they can engender. In this second model, illustrated in Figure 16.2, some stimuli trigger fear directly whereas others require cognitive appraisal before activating fear.

This dualistic approach offers room for the acquisition of fear based on new information. As children become more sophisticated, they can assess the likelihood of harm in situations that they have been told about but have not actually encountered. Situations such as being approached by a well-known bully or by a police officer would be processed by the same harm-appraisal system and would produce a similar emotional reaction. Such assessments might be inaccurate, but they would allow the child to increase his or her repertoire of fears.

Note that, according to this account, the fear response itself is the same whether it is triggered directly or via the appraisal system. Only the mode of activation varies. Thus, some fears are more directly and quickly evoked than others. In particular, this analysis suggests that certain fears will persist unchanged throughout the life span.

However, it is possible to extend the role of appraisal still further. It may not simply lead to the anticipation of harm in a situation that has no natural significance. It may also lead to the reassessment of stimuli that have natural significance. Thus, we may postulate a grand appraisal system that assesses both neutral and natural stimuli. Whether the same mode of appraisal will occur remains an open question. For example, repeated exposure and habituation may be especially effective in attentuating fear with respect to natural stimuli, whereas instruction and information may dispel fear of nonnatural stimuli, such as police officers or monsters. With this possibility in mind, Figure 16.3 depicts such a grand appraisal system tentatively divided into two parts, one directed at natural clues and the other at seemingly neutral situations.

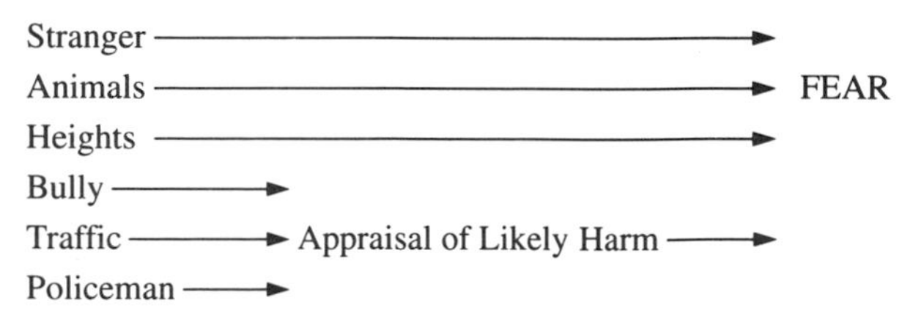

Figure 16.2 Illustration of system that responds directly to selected stimuli, and cognitively to others.

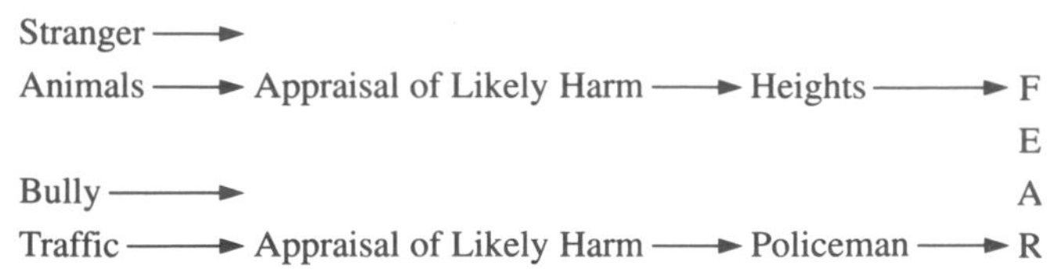

Figure 16.3 A system that responds indirectly to fearful stimuli via an appraisal system.

Next, we turn to a more detailed examination of the developmental evidence in order to compare the validity of these three models (Figures 16.1–16.3). In making an assessment, we examine three sources of evidence: (a) the existence of prepared or natural fears, (b) the way new fears are acquired, and (c) the coherence and stability of the alleged appraisal system.

Natural Elicitors of Fear

There is considerable evidence that some situations or stimuli are prevalent causes of fear. From this evidence, some authors have concluded that such stimuli are "natural clues" to danger: fear of the harm that they signal is unlearned. For example, Bowlby (1973, p. 85) argued that unfamiliarity, a sudden noise, an object that rapidly approaches, darkness, and isolation constitute such clues, and that there is a genetic bias to take avoiding action or run away. He pointed out that these clues to danger make evolutionary sense. Although each of them in isolation may not constitute a danger, they may well presage danger when they co-occur: an approaching predator, for example, is strange, approaches rapidly and perhaps noisily, and may strike at night when the victim is alone.

Seligman's (1971) concept of prepared stimuli was quite similar to Bowlby's. Reviewing research on phobias, Seligman claimed that human phobias are usually directed at objects that have threatened survival, for example, potential predators and darkness. His claim was not that such stimuli elicit fear with no learning whatsoever, but that, at the very least, fear of them is easily learned.

Both of these theories imply that children's fears might be directed at a small set of elicitors, as depicted in Figure 16.1. In addition, both imply that there should be considerable continuity, throughout development, in the stimuli that elicit fear. Is this the case? Some of the best evidence on children's fears was gathered nearly 50 years ago by Arthur Jersild (1947). In one study, parents were asked to keep detailed records, over a 3-week period, of any occasion when their children showed fear; these detailed records were combined with occasional records from a further sample. The children ranged up to 6 years of age. The following situations proved to be prevalent sources of fear, especially in infancy: noise, strange entities (including objects, situations, and persons), pain, falling, or loss of support. The following situations were common sources of fear, especially beyond infancy: animals, the threat of injury (e.g., from traffic, drowning, fire, jail, and so on), and imaginary creatures (especially when the child was alone in the dark).

This list of fears is remarkably congruent with the fears that adults report. For example, in a survey of the normal population, Agras, Sylvester, and Oliveau (1969) found that fear of animals (particularly snakes), heights, injury or illness, and public places and transport (agoraphobia) was common. Combining these two surveys, there is considerable continuity in the situations that elicit fear. The notion that certain situations serve as natural or prepared triggers of fear throughout the life span is strengthened, lending some support to the alleged links depicted in Figure 16.1.

A scrutiny of Jersild's findings (cf., Jersild, 1947, fig. 1) also reveals an important developmental trend—an increasing fear of hypothetical or imaginary outcomes that the child has not actually encountered: being hurt by a car, being put in jail, and imaginary creatures. The obvious implication is that the cognitive system increasingly leads the child to imagine or anticipate possible harm in otherwise neutral situations. The child fears what *might* happen as much as what he or she actually encounters. The emergence of this anticipatory system does not transform the child's fears beyond recognition: the child continues to fear pain and injury but is now able to conjure up such threats in his or her imagination. These findings suggest that the simple model depicted in Figure 16.1 will not do. As implied by Figure 16.2, situations that the child has been told about can be appraised and judged potentially harmful even if they have never been directly experienced.

Other findings supplied by Jersild make the further point that the set of primordial and persistent fears is not just supplemented by new, cognitively based fears. Some fears that are widespread in infancy (fear of noise or of strangers) undergo a sharp decline in later childhood. The implication is that early fears can also come under the sway of the appraisal system (the possibility allowed for in Figure 16.3). Whether we should construe such reassessments as operating by the same appraisal process remains unclear: hence, Figure 16.3 is tentatively divided between the reassessment of natural or prepared stimuli and the anticipation of harm in nonnatural contexts.

We may now consider the acquisition of new fears in more detail. Earlier, two possible mechanisms for acquisition were discussed: (a) learning by association and (b) a more cognitive, information-based appraisal. After each of these mechanisms is considered in turn, a third mechanism, the vicarious transmission of information, will be explored.

Learning by Association

Traditional approaches to fear, especially those concerned with the treatment of phobias, have frequently adopted an associative model. Indeed, developmental research on the conditioned acquisition of fear (Watson & Rayner, 1920) and its amelioration (Jones, 1924) offered a source of inspiration for such clinical endeavors. Referring to Figure 16.1, it is easy to imagine that neutral situations that are presented along with natural clues (e.g., a loud noise or a painful injection) might gain fear-inducing properties through conditioning. This approach to fear acquisition, advocated by authors such as Wolpe and Rachman (1960), dominated research during the 1960s.

As Rachman (1990) observed, however, the conditioning theory ran into difficulties, for several reasons. First, conditioning in the laboratory, and naturalistic analogues such as air-raid sirens, do not systematically lead to conditioned fear reactions. Indeed, the original experimental procedure of Watson and Rayner (1920) had proved difficult to replicate (Bregman, 1934). Second, the uneven distribution of fears appears to reflect the stability and persistence of natural or prepared stimuli for fear, rather than their extension through conditioning to arbitrary stimuli. Third, it has gradually become clear that the conditioning model ignores other potent modes of acquisition, notably the acquisition of new information and vicarious transmission, which are discussed below.

Despite these problems, the conditioning model continues to exert its grip on developmental research. Hence, it is worth examining its validity in some detail. Consider, for example, the interesting study, by Yule, Udwin, and Murdoch (1990), of the reactions of adolescents who had survived the sinking of a cruise ship. The ship had collided with a tanker, rapidly took water, and listed as it did so. The children were forced to get into tugs alongside the cruise ship, which meant that they had to negotiate the ship's tilted decks. As the ship sank, many had to jump into the water, even though they were nonswimmers. Darkness had fallen by the time of the rescue. One schoolgirl, one teacher, and two seamen died in the disaster.

Five months later, the survivors were questioned about their fears of situations that were and were not related to the original traumatic experience. Consistent with the conditioning model, the survivors reported more fear of related situations (e.g., deep water, traveling by boat, swimming) than unrelated situations (e.g., lizards, meeting someone for the first time). This difference was not found among a control group of adolescents with no ship-sinking experience, nor among a "near-miss" group who had wanted to go on the cruise but did not do so. At first glance, these results provide support for the traditional conditioning model, but closer scrutiny reveals several problems. First, certain stimuli that the authors judged to be closely related to the original experience (e.g., loud sirens; dark places; being in a crowd) showed no increment in fear. Second, several stimuli that the authors judged to be unrelated to the cruise (e.g., riding on a train; having to talk to the class) did show an increment. Third, the authors concentrated on increments with respect to situations already known to elicit some fear (they administered a previously developed fear questionnaire; Ollendick, 1983). Yet, the traditional conditioning model predicts that fear should generalize to any stimuli contiguous with the disaster (e.g., naval uniforms; sloping surfaces) and not simply to those that already elicit fear. In short, the results of Yule et al. (1990) provide only loose support for the conditioning model.

An alternative explanation may be formulated in terms of the likelihood of flashbacks or intrusive thoughts about the disaster. The children had undergone a memorable, indeed a traumatic experience; mental rehearsal of that experience would be likely to reawaken the fear they had originally felt, and situations that reminded them of the disaster would prompt such mental rehearsal and re-evoke fear. These straightforward assumptions may be conjoined with a more speculative possibility: the repeated rehearsal of the original disaster, along with the accompanying fear, would lead to a subjective reassessment of those cues that served as reminders.

When we ask what cues might serve as potent reminders, three different factors may be considered: (a) some cues will have a conceptual rather than a physical similarity to the disaster—for example, a train journey might be a reminder of a boat journey;

Conditioning Model

TIME OF DISASTER	AFTER DISASTER
Sinking Ship → Fear	
+	
Loud Noise	Loud Noise
+	+
Water → Conditioned Fear	Water → Fear
+	+
Boat Travel	Boat Travel

Flashback Model

TIME OF DISASTER	AFTER DISASTER
	Travel
	+
Sinking Ship → Fear	Swimming → Rehearsal → Fear
	+
	Going to School

Figure 16.4 Conditioning model and flashback model of fear-increment.

(b) certain venues—for example, going to school and seeing other survivors—may trigger memories of the disaster; (c) situations that arouse the same affective state (i.e., fear) would serve as reminders (Bower, 1981).

As a result of the flashback process, which may last several months, survivors reassess the fear that they experience in relation to reminders. The difference between these two models is illustrated in Figure 16.4. According to the conditioning model, the basic transfer process is set in motion at the time of the traumatic event. This original learning is subsequently displayed in the context of later encounters via stimulus generalization. By contrast, in the flashback model, the reassessment does not begin until after the original event. Thus, contexts that have no obvious contiguity with the original incident (e.g., going to school) but serve as potent contexts for being reminded of the incident will be subsequently reevaluated as fearful.[1] Similarly, situations that have a purely cognitive relationship to the original incident (e.g., other modes of transport, such as a train journey) but thereby serve as reminders should also be reevaluated as fearful. Both of these predictions are supported by the findings of Yule et al. (1990).

The above account relies heavily on the notion of flashback memories. Despite earlier doubts (Garmezy & Rutter, 1985), recent evidence on children exposed to traumatic events (e.g., shootings; transport disasters) shows that there are important similarities between the reactions of children and adults (Terr, 1991). Like adults, children often report intrusive thoughts and imagery in the first weeks following a trauma. Such reports are much more frequent among those who witnessed or participated in the traumatic event than among those who were in the vicinity but learned about the event second-hand (Pynoos, Frederick, & Nader, 1987). One year later, intrusive imagery and thoughts—coupled with the desire to avoid such thoughts—remain widespread among those directly exposed but are rare among those not directly exposed (Nader, Pynoos, Fairbanks, & Frederick, 1990). Thus, children display a mental conflict between their wish to cease being reminded of such emotionally charged material and their involuntary recollections or flashbacks of that same material. Research with adults has uncovered a similar conflict between avoidance and intrusion. Victims report an intensification of both processes after a traumatic disaster or loss (Zilberg, Weiss, & Horowitz, 1982).

Consistent with the speculations set out earlier, children exposed to a traumatic event also report that they experience fear or distress when thinking of the event both in the immediate aftermath of the event and months later (Nader et al., 1990). Thus, traumatized children would be likely to avoid or fear stimuli that did not co-occur with the traumatic event but subsequently trigger intrusive thoughts and images. Indeed, the most frequently reported reaction among children who had witnessed a shooting one year earlier was an avoidance of reminders (Nader et al., 1990).

A study of a ferry disaster in Zeebrugge, The Netherlands, illustrates in more detail how such fears might arise in relation to stimuli that trigger intrusive thoughts or images. Yule and Williams (1990) interviewed children who had survived the ferry disaster, in which many passengers, including relatives or traveling companions of the children, had lost their lives when the ferry capsized. They found that adults familiar with the children, particularly teachers, were inclined to underestimate the impact of the disaster. Accordingly, some of the most revealing evidence came from assessments of the children themselves. The high level of intrusive thoughts, measured using the Horowitz Impact of Events Scale, was comparable to that seen among adults being treated for trauma (Horowitz, Wilner, & Alvarez, 1979). One child explained how, when standing over his desk, he would think that it was going to topple over. He had dreamed that the world itself was going over on its side, flinging people up into the sky. On one occasion, when traveling in a bus that swayed as it negotiated a roundabout (a circular intersection), he shouted to his father that the bus was going over, and he had to be taken off the bus because he was so terrified. Although the researchers provided no information on the matter, it would not be surprising if this child subsequently became nervous about traveling by bus, as the flashback model would predict.

[1] The claim that contexts for being reminded of a disaster will themselves become fearful is supported by the findings of Dollinger, O'Donnell, and Staley (1984), who studied adolescents who had been struck by lightning. The authors interpreted the subsequent elevation of fear to other stimuli (e.g., the disaster victims expressed more fear of bodily penetration than did a control group) in terms of conditioned stimulus generalization. However, this concept cannot easily explain the finding that the most noticeable increment in fear surrounded sleep (although Dollinger et al. do provide post hoc suggestions; cf. p. 1035, note 5). By contrast, if we assume that going to sleep is a potent context for thinking back to such a disaster, the increment in fear concerning sleep is readily explained. Similarly, the ensuing sleep problems shown by the disaster victims can be easily explained.

The flashback model leads to several untested predictions. First, there is good evidence that the process of reminding is state-dependent. As Bower (1981) has shown, a reminder is likely to be especially effective if it is accompanied by the affective state surrounding the original learning. Thus, after a sea disaster, survivors who take an elevator and are afraid of elevators are more likely to have a flashback of the sinking ship than are survivors who have no fear of elevators. From this analysis, it follows that situations that have a cognitive relationship to the traumatic incident and also serve as triggers of the same affective state will be especially likely to act as effective reminders and hence to undergo reassessment.

Completely novel situations that start to become contexts for recollection of the trauma (e.g., meeting a psychiatrist or lawyer who asks for a detailed account of the disaster) and thereby reactivate the earlier feelings will also be subject to reassessment. This prediction, if correct, is particularly important from a therapeutic point of view. It means that efforts to help traumatized victims will be unsuccessful if they simply increase the likelihood of flashback memories and the fear that ensues. The victim will be tempted to avoid the source of such reminders—the therapist.[2]

Information Acquisition

Traditional approaches to the acquisition of fear have, as Rachman (1990) noted, downplayed the role of information. Yet its impact on adults appears undeniable. Consider, for example, the precipitous drop in the use of public transport, particularly airlines, during the Gulf War. Such avoidance is not caused in any obvious sense by the greater salience or prevalence of natural clues to danger; it cannot be explained by any known conditioning model. If imitation or modeling played a role, it seems exceedingly indirect: prospective passengers are not likely to observe other people avoiding airplanes. They are much more likely to hear or read about the threat of terrorist attacks.

Fear can be suppressed or increased in the context of new information. For example, most adults have occasionally experienced an electric shock, and they try to avoid any repetition by not tinkering with electric plugs, switches, and fuses. If, however, they have switched off the main power supply and are sure that the current has been thereby interrupted, they will calmly approach stimuli that they would typically avoid: they will replace a fuse and handle formerly live wires.

What role does information transmission play among children? Studies of adult phobics who are asked about the origin of their fear suggest that at least some phobias are acquired during childhood via information of instruction (Ost, 1987). Adults suppose that instruction is effective and they rely on it to caution children against a variety of hazards. Yet there is very little research with children that directly assesses the impact of instruction or information. However, as noted earlier, children beyond infancy report a variety of fears regarding objects or situations that they have presumably never encountered, including supernatural creatures such as monsters, witches, and ghosts, and improbable events such as being put in jail or meeting a burglar. It seems absurd to insist that all these fears are based on stimulus generalization; it is much more likely that children acquire information about these hypothetical entities or situations, and the information alone induces fear.

Can children's fears be extinguished or attenuated via instruction or information? Early investigations suggested that verbal reassurance (Jones, 1924) or explanation (Hagman, 1932) is rarely effective in reducing fear. Reviewing several intervention studies, Jersild (1947) recommended methods that helped the child "by degrees to have active experience with, or successful direct participation, in the feared situation." He observed that this procedure was probably effective "because it helped the child to acquire a changed conception of his ability to cope with his weakness and this might entail a changed attitude toward himself." These astute remarks anticipated the notion of self-efficacy (Bandura, 1977) by about 30 years. The implication is that it is important to convince children that they are not afraid, and that is best done through direct exposure. Verbal efforts to convince children that there is nothing to be afraid of will rarely work. It is important to emphasize, however, that the focus on direct exposure rather than on information or verbal reassurance derives chiefly from attempts to reduce persistent and intense fear, or fear of natural clues to danger (e.g., heights; dark passages). Where a fear has been induced through information or instruction, it may be much easier to secure extinction through the same means, provided a genuine reappraisal is achieved.

Vicarious Transmission

The vicarious transmission of fear was first highlighted in World War II. Studies were made of the reactions of children and adults in the course of air raids and blackouts (John, 1941; Solomon, 1942). A fairly close relationship was noted between the amount of fear displayed by the mother and the child. The authors concluded that learning took place vicariously: when children saw the adults around them expressing fear, they began to feel afraid themselves. It may be no coincidence, of course, that such emotional contagion was found in the presence of stimuli that we have referred to as natural clues to danger: darkness and sudden loud noises.

A more recent set of studies has provided experimental (rather than correlational) evidence for emotional contagion and has shown that it occurs during the first year of life. One of the most convincing is the visual-cliff study of Sorce et al. (1985). As already noted, the majority of infants crossed the cliff if the mother smiled, but none did so if she looked fearful. Again, it is interesting to note that this contagious reaction was not directed toward a totally neutral or innocent stimulus: fear of heights is, as we have seen, a common fear. The implication is that vicarious learning

---

[2] It is interesting to note that children who had been the victims of the ferry disaster voiced their reluctance to see the psychologist who had previously interviewed them (Yule & Williams, 1990). On the other hand, they were quite keen to meet one another for a group discussion. It is also noteworthy that the victims were selective about the family members or friends with whom they discussed the disaster: the same child might rarely or never discuss it with one person while talking about it obsessively with another. The exact conditions that lead victims to seek rather than avoid reminding and rehearsal are obviously of important therapeutic significance, but they have not been systematically investigated.

can readily bias the appraisal of natural clues to danger. Whether it can bring about such changes for a completely "innocent" stimulus is an open question. Research with monkeys showed that vicarious transmission is much more effective for some stimuli than others. Although they became fearful of snakes after watching a videotape of monkey models displaying fear in the presence of a snake, they failed to show a parallel reaction to flowers when the videotapes were altered so as to show monkeys displaying fear of flowers (Mineka, 1988). As Rachman (1990) pointed out, there are important constraints on vicarious transmission. For example, the children of agoraphobic patients rarely acquire their parents' fears themselves, perhaps because they are immunized by the availability of a wide range of adults who display no such fear (Ost & Hugdahl, 1983).

Research has shown that vicarious transmission can be a powerful technique for the extinction as well as the acquisition of fear. Much of this work has been carried out with adults (Bandura, 1977). Given the phenomenon of emotional contagion in infancy, however, there is every reason to expect that the technique will work with children. Indeed, in one of the earliest successful intervention studies with a child, Jones (1924) made systematic use of the technique: the rabbit that Peter feared was introduced while Peter played with three other children chosen because of their "entirely fearless attitude toward the rabbit."

General Shifts in Appraisal

We can now take a closer look at the unity of the appraisal system. One strong argument for that unity would be the following pattern: under certain circumstances, the infant or child shows a generalized shift in his or her appraisal of a whole variety of disparate stimuli that would normally elicit fear. These shifts might be in an "upward" direction: disparate stimuli elicit greater fear; or in a "downward" direction: disparate stimuli are approached with more confidence.

Evidence for such pervasive shifts is provided by studies on the presence of a familiar caretaker. A long experimental tradition has shown that a child's fear of a stranger's approach is less marked in the presence of the caretaker. Jersild and Holmes (1935) carried out an experimental study in which they examined children's reactions to a wide variety of potentially frightening situations. Entering a dark passage, approaching a large dog, and reaching into a box containing a snake proved to be frightening to roughly half of the children, who ranged from 24 to 59 months: they either refused to perform alone or they refused to perform at all. Across these situations, the authors found that children who refused to perform alone would do so when accompanied by an adult who was familiar to them. The implication of these findings is that the presence of a familiar adult brings about a wholesale shift in the appraisal process: a variety of different situations that would typically elicit fear are approached with less hesitation. Such shifts extend to what are usually regarded as prepared stimuli (snakes and darkness). Thus, Figure 16.3 provides a more adequate model than Figure 16.2.

A generalized shift in the appraisal system may eventually become a relatively stable part of the personality rather than a temporary shift that depends on local conditions. For example, there is evidence that securely attached infants exhibit curiosity and confidence in exploring a novel environment (Arend, Gove, & Sroufe, 1979) whereas abused children who develop an insecure attachment are apprehensive (Egeland & Sroufe, 1981).

Further support for the notion of a unified and unifying appraisal system comes from observations on so-called "compound" stimuli. Bowlby (1973) pointed up the observations made by Jersild and Holmes (1935) on parental observation of fear: the situations described often contained more than one element, for example, a strange dog that barks, an unexpected noise heard in the dark. The implication is that the different elements summate with one another within the same appraisal system. Again, the evidence points to Figure 16.3, in which such summation is feasible, rather than to Figure 16.1 or 16.2, in which prepared or natural clues to danger serve as discrete and autonomous triggers.

Summary

There is considerable stability from childhood to adulthood in the stimuli that elicit fear. Nevertheless, new fears are acquired and old fears are extinguished. Three mechanisms for change have been discussed: (a) learned association, (b) information transmission, and (c) vicarious transmission. The simple model depicted in Figure 16.1 would be adequate if most new fears were acquired simply by learned association. However, even in contexts where learning by association seems to have occurred, close inspection of the data suggests that the standard notions of conditioning and stimulus generalization are problematic. An alternative based on intrusive flashbacks was proposed instead.

Learning by conditioning is unlikely to explain all the fears that children exhibit. New fears can be acquired through information or vicarious transmission; moreover, there is evidence that vicarious transmission can lead to the extinction of preexisting fears. These findings suggest that some type of appraisal process supplements the existence of prepared fears or their extension by conditioning.

Finally, there is evidence for the overall unity of the appraisal system. Certain circumstances—for example, the immediate availability of a familiar caretaker—can lead to a shift in the appraisal of a wide variety of situations. Such shifts may eventually become part of the individual's characteristic mode of appraisal, and may constitute a relatively stable personality trait rather than a temporary shift.

Appraisal Processes and Guilt

In discussing fear, it was plausible to invoke an action tendency that can be observed in the latter part of the first year; there is also considerable evidence that certain activators serve as natural or prepared stimuli. To the extent that appraisal occurs, it supplements or modifies that early-emerging fear system. Can we make the same claims with respect to guilt?

Some authors (e.g., Izard, 1977) have suggested that guilt should be seen as a discrete emotion, on a par with fear. There are several reasons for caution, however. The expressive component of guilt is less clear than the expressive component for fear. The action tendency linked with guilt (reparation and/or self-criticism) is considerably more complex than the action tendency associated with fear (i.e., avoidance). Finally, the claim that there are natural or prepared activators for guilt is not well-established. We examine this last claim more closely in the next section.

Natural Elicitors of Guilt

There have been few systematic efforts to describe "natural" elicitors for guilt. However, Hoffman (1982) suggested that the observation of another's distress might be such a natural elicitor. He proposed that guilt in such contexts is due to the conjunction of an empathic response to another person's distress and the awareness of being the cause of that distress. According to Hoffman, self and other are increasingly differentiated during infancy so that the distinct and separate nature of distress in the other person is eventually recognized. In addition, there is a growing appreciation of what the self as agent can accomplish. Thus, the stage is set (around 2 years of age) for the child to recognize that he or she has hurt another person, and to feel guilty about it. Unfortunately, the empirical base for these claims is slender, even though Hoffman has worked and reworked his theory over many years.

It is true that, in the course of the second and third years, children make increasingly active and planful efforts to comfort a person in distress (Zahn-Waxler & Radke-Yarrow, 1982). Between 10 and 12 months, children rarely do anything beyond watching the other person or becoming upset themselves. But in the months that follow, they intervene more often: they touch or pat the person who is upset, bring objects that might be comforting, or put their sympathy into words.

Are such concerned interventions prompted by guilt in any way? If Hoffman's analysis is correct, we should expect children to be especially likely to intervene and make reparation if they are the cause of the distress rather than simply witnesses to it. However, in a study of toddlers ranging from 38 to 134 weeks, no such differentiation was observed (Zahn-Waxler & Kochanska, 1990). There was the same increase in the proportion of interventions (especially during the second year), whether toddlers had caused the distress themselves or simply witnessed distress caused in other ways. The obvious implication of this nonspecific developmental change is that children are becoming increasingly sensitive to the needs of others in distress. Their intervention is not prompted by guilt even when they are the cause of the distress; it is prompted simply by concern for the others' plight, irrespective of whether they were the ultimate cause.[3]

Zahn-Waxler and Kochanska (1990, p. 219) do not accept this straightforward interpretation. In line with the proposals made by Hoffman (1982), they claim that: "Since young children sometimes have difficulty distinguishing between harm they cause and harm they observe, early forms of altruism and conscience overlap." On this account, children's sympathetic interventions are provoked by guilt not only when they have caused the distress, but even when they have not caused it! This theoretical excess of guilt seems unwarranted on two counts. First, children's sympathetic interventions can be explained in terms of their concern for the other person; the appeal to guilt as a trigger is unparsimonious. Second, if guilt were the trigger, one would expect older toddlers to respond more selectively than younger toddlers because they should be better able to identify when they themselves are the cause of the distress. Yet, Zahn-Waxler and Kochanska report no developmental trend toward increasing selectivity.

Three-Pronged Appraisal

Accepting the conclusion that guilt cannot be inferred from toddlers' sympathetic interventions, when can it be inferred? To answer this question, we need a working definition of what will count as guilt. Frijda's conceptual analysis provides a helpful starting point. He defined guilt as: "painful self-evaluation due to some action evaluated negatively and for which action the person holds himself responsible" (Frijda, 1986, p. 201). This definition implies that guilt calls for a complex three-pronged appraisal process: (a) an evaluation of the act as bad, (b) an evaluation of responsibility for the act, and (c) a consequent negative evaluation of the self. Let us consider these components one-by-one, to assess when children might be capable of feeling guilt.

First, there is plenty of evidence that toddlers know that various acts cause distress and that distress is bad. As we have just seen, by comforting people in distress, toddlers show that they understand something about the nature of distress. A parallel age-change in strategies for hurting and teasing other people shows that toddlers know what acts cause distress: they show many signs of well-planned aggression (Harris, 1989, chapter 2). In addition, children of 3 to 4 years know that actions such as hitting other persons or taking others' possessions are bad; they evaluate them as bad, and they realize they would be bad even in the absence of any specific rule prohibiting them (Smetana, 1981). In short, there are a variety of indications that preschoolers judge certain acts and their consequences negatively.

Second, can young children appreciate when they themselves have caused such undesirable consequences? There is a good deal of experimental evidence showing that preschoolers are quite capable of assessing whether an act has been deliberately caused. They distinguish deliberate acts from mistakes, reflexes, and passive movements (Poulin-Dubois & Shultz, 1988). The implication is that, when 3-year-olds hit another child or appropriate a toy, they know that their action is deliberate. We cannot assume from these results that 3-year-olds will always make an accurate diagnosis of their responsibility for another child's distress. If they deliberately throw a ball and accidentally hit another child, they may not always distinguish between their responsibility for the act itself and their responsibility for its consequences (Yuill, 1984). Nonetheless, in simple cases where the intention to hurt coincides with the outcome, preschoolers can assess responsibility.

We turn now to the final and perhaps the most critical component: the consequent negative evaluation of the self. Recent

[3] Zahn-Waxler and Kochanska (1990, appendix A) presented individual records as well as a statistical overview. Yet, virtually all of these records were quite ambiguous about whether children had guilt feelings. For example, children engaged in self-injurious behavior (e.g., one child, aged 75 weeks, having attacked another child and been reprimanded, directed a similar attack against the self, i.e., pulling own hair; hitting self in face). This type of attack might have been provoked by frustration or curiosity as much as by guilt. One child (aged 106 weeks) told his mother that his playmate bit him because he had pushed her. This can be construed as a "confession" or "an acknowledgment of responsibility" or as a (naive) bid for sympathy. When children say they are sorry, it is not obvious that they are feeling sorry. Often, they have been instructed to say the word, or they have learned to say it to forestall being reprimanded.

research has shown that toddlers express self-conscious emotions such as embarrassment when they are made the focus of public attention (Lewis et al., 1989). Guilt is more complex than embarrassment, however, because it is triggered by an evaluation of the self relative to some moral standard. It is not obvious that young children are capable of this type of self-appraisal. For example, when 3-year-olds hit another child, who then bursts into tears, they know that they have caused the victim's distress, but do they feel bad about themselves as a result? It is not enough for children to say that they have been bad or to say that it is bad to hit other children. Such remarks may be simply an evaluation that they have repeatedly heard and may not signify that a child feels bad about the self. We need clear evidence of an emotionally charged judgment of the self, as opposed to mere parroting.

A possible way to answer this question is to tell children stories about moral transgressions—for example, to narrate how a protagonist hits another child or takes someone's possessions, and then ask children how the protagonist will feel as a result. This method is indirect: the children must imagine how the *protagonist* will feel; we are not observing children's own emotional reactions to such transgressions. We shall return to this caveat shortly.

Several experiments have shown that a clear age-change takes place. Young children of 4 to 5 years rarely anticipate that the protagonist will feel bad (although they sometimes mention fear in connection with possible punishment). By contrast, older children (8 to 9 years) do anticipate such bad feelings (Barden, Zelko, Duncan, & Masters, 1980; Harter & Whitesell, 1989; Nunner-Winkler & Sodian, 1988; Thompson & Hoffman, 1980). The results obtained by Nunner-Winkler and Sodian were especially clear. The older children explained their expectations in moral terms by referring to the protagonist's misdeed and to the fact that he or she would feel bad about doing something that violated a moral rule. Harter and Whitesell (1989) also found that older children had a well-articulated grasp of confession. Most of them expected the protagonist to tell an adult about the misdeed, because this would relieve feelings of guilt. As one child put it: "If you tell, then you wouldn't have a guilty conscience and that feeling would go away."

Thus, the story judgment method suggests a fairly slow timetable for the emergence of guilt. The implication is that preschool children know what counts as a misdeed but do not view misdeeds as triggers of emotion. If one child hits another child, preschoolers know that the victim's distress is bad and they can work out that the hitting was deliberate, but they draw no conclusions for the affective life of the perpetrator. They do not expect him or her to feel bad about the misdeed. By contrast, children of 8 years and older do.

Can we conclude from these findings that preschool children do not feel guilt? Because they appraise the implications of a situation differently from older children, does that mean that they are effectively guilt-free? Such a conclusion would be premature because of difficulties in interpreting the story judgment method. This method has been widely used since the 1960s, when there was a great deal of work (inspired both by learning theory and psychoanalytic theory) on the question of what type of parental discipline fostered moral development. Stories about transgression were used to assess children's willingness to attribute guilt feelings to the perpetrator (see Hoffman, 1970, for a review). The standard assumption was that the technique tapped the child's own guilt feelings. It was acknowledged that the method was indirect, but insofar as it was assumed that children might feel guilty without being consciously aware of what they felt, the tacit nature of the measure was deemed an advantage.

However, as will be argued in a subsequent section on children's understanding of emotion, it is dangerous to assume any direct link between the capacity to experience a feeling and the capacity to recognize and attribute that feeling. Children may have certain feelings long before they can recognize and attribute them appropriately. Yet the story judgment effectively assumes that the two are closely connected. In our view, it is necessary to recognize two distinct cognitive systems: (a) the appraisal system that enables a child to experience a feeling, and (b) what we shall refer to as the attributional system by which children recognize and understand emotions.[4] Thus, children's capacity to appraise their own transgressions and to experience guilt as a result should be distinguished from their capacity to recognize and attribute guilt to someone else. Children need to imagine themselves in the shoes of a story character who has transgressed, reconstruct that person's appraisal process, and work out the emotional reaction that will ensue.

Recent results with the story judgment method provide convincing evidence that children of approximately 8 years of age can attribute guilt to a story character. This sophisticated capacity almost certainly means that they also possess the capacity to experience guilt themselves. More generally, if children can attribute an emotion appropriately, it seems reasonable to use story projection methods to tap their own likely feelings in an equivalent situation. Yet, story judgment methods may be misleading indexes of children's emotional experience, if they are used with children who make inappropriate attributions. Hence, it remains an open question whether young children of, say, 3 or 4 years experience guilt themselves when they transgress. Their inability to attribute guilt appropriately to a story character cannot be used as evidence that they themselves do not experience guilt. In the absence of any firmly established criteria for the facial expression of guilt, it will not be easy to decide when they do start to experience guilt. What is needed is a developmental study of children's action tendencies in relation to guilt, notably reparation, self-criticism, and confession. A start has been made using these techniques (Zahn-Waxler & Kochanska, 1990), but the developmental pattern is not yet clearly established.

THE DEVELOPMENT OF EMOTION UNDERSTANDING

Turning now to the development of the attributional system introduced above, we look at the ways in which children begin to

[4] We use the term *attributional system* without wishing to confine ourselves to the particular tenets of attribution theory. For example, we discuss the crucial role of mental states, especially beliefs and desires, in making appropriate attributions. Their role has usually been ignored by attribution theorists, who focus instead on attributions to "internal" factors that need not be mental (e.g., effort or ability).

identify, predict, and explain the emotions felt by others and by themselves. We review some of the main developmental changes in that understanding, beginning with infants' recognition of emotion. Later, we consider how research on children's attributional system for emotion is relevant to clinical practice and to psychopathology.

Emotion Recognition

Infancy

In his classic work on the facial expression of emotion, Darwin (1872/1965) not only insisted that there was an innate repertoire for the production of facial expressions, but also claimed that there is an innate capacity to comprehend emotional expressions in others. He pointed out, for example, that his 6-month-old son appeared to understand the meaning of his nurse's facial expression when she leaned over him and pretended to cry. He looked at her and then became distressed himself. Darwin noted that his son had never seen an adult crying. The implication, therefore, was that an innate recognition device signaled the meaning of the facial expression and led to an appropriate emotional reaction.

A great deal of work on emotion during infancy has reexamined Darwin's claims about the early production of facial expression. However, a smaller body of work is now available on comprehension. In reviewing this work, we need to make an important conceptual distinction. An infant might see a difference between two facial expressions, in the sense that he or she sees them as different facial configurations. Darwin had something more in mind. His idea was that the baby not only picked out a given facial expression as a distinct visual configuration, but also realized the emotional significance of the expression. Thus, not only could the baby see a difference between a downturned and an upturned mouth, but the baby could also grasp that the former conveys sadness and the latter, happiness. Given this important distinction, we need to look for evidence that the baby not only reacts differently to two distinct facial expressions but also reacts appropriately, i.e., in accordance with the emotional meaning of the facial expressions. In the review below, we shall focus on appropriate reactions rather than mere discrimination.

Recent evidence for early appropriate reactions lends support to Darwin's claims. Haviland and Lelwica (1987) showed that when 10-week-old babies watched their mothers expressing happiness, sadness, or anger, they subsequently reacted appropriately. In the case of happiness, they looked happy; in response to the mother's anger, they looked angry or remained still; and in response to sadness, they did not look sad, but they often engaged in mouthing, chewing, or sucking. Parallel results were obtained by Termine and Izard (1988) with older babies. They found that 9-month-olds responded differentially and appropriately to mother's happiness or sadness, and this carried over to a subsequent play session with toys.

These two experiments suggest that caretaker and infant can engage in an emotional dialogue: the emotional state of the caretaker can be communicated to the baby, who then responds appropriately. However, it is important to stress that, in themselves, these experiments do not show that Darwin was correct to stress an innate emotion comprehension device. We can scarcely assert (even if Darwin was prepared to do so with respect to his son) that the babies have never seen such emotional expressions before. Considerable opportunity for learning exists; nevertheless, in sympathy with Darwin, it is difficult to spell out a plausible learning device. Consider the following possibilities. First, we might argue that the baby comes to treat an adult's emotional expression as a signal that precedes certain pleasant or unpleasant consequences. For example, the baby learns that a caretaker who smiles is about to do something pleasant: offer an interesting spectacle, or an embrace, or an enjoyable feed. Conversely, the baby learns that a caretaker who looks angry is about to do something unpleasant: for example, terminate an embrace, insert a nasty-tasting substance into the baby's mouth, and so forth. The problem with this argument is that the infant's comprehension must necessarily remain egocentric: the other's expression is narrowly understood in terms of what it signals for the self rather than what it expresses for the other.

A second possibility is that the baby learns by mimesis. For example, suppose that the mother's smile leads the baby to copy that facial expression. Suppose further that the production of a smile by the baby makes the baby feel happy (in line with the experimental evidence reviewed earlier). Finally, suppose that this felt mood is used as a gloss with which to interpret the meaning of the facial expression of the mother. So far so good, but the argument is difficult to press home. Infants do not invariably respond to a caretaker's facial expression with the same expression. In response to an angry face, for example, they can become subdued rather than express anger.

In short, with respect to the comprehension of emotion, we are in a position that is roughly similar to the acquisition of language. We are driven back toward nativist claims, precisely because it is very difficult to advance a convincing learning account. In future research, the study of atypical populations (e.g., children who are handicapped in facial movement or imitation) may prove revealing.

How does the child's comprehension of emotion progress? So far, we have emphasized the emotional dialogue that can occur between caretaker and infant as they face one another. Toward the end of the first year, an important new competence emerges. The baby starts to understand that the caretaker is not only in a particular emotional state but also that the emotional state is targeted at a particular object or event in the environment. The caretaker is understood to be afraid of object X, or angry at person Y, or happy with outcome Z. Such targeting reflects what has been called the "intentionality" of emotion (Brentano, 1874/1973).

Evidence for an understanding of intentionality has been gathered by researchers interested in the phenomenon of social referencing. Essentially, at around 9 months, babies regulate their behavior in a given situation by attending to the facial expression of their caretaker. For example, suppose the baby approaches a ledge or step and is uncertain whether to crawl over it; the baby will frequently look up at its mother, and having checked whether she is looking on with a positive or a negative expression on her face, the baby will either attempt to traverse the obstacle or will avoid it (Sorce et al., 1985).

Evidence that the baby appreciates that the mother's emotional state is being targeted at a particular object or event has been provided by Hornik, Risenhoover, and Gunnar (1987). They observed that when the mother expressed positive emotion (delight) or negative emotion (disgust) toward a particular toy, babies of 12 months subsequently approached or avoided it appropriately. Their behavior toward other toys was unaffected. A comparable type of selectivity was observed by Walden and Ogan (1988) among 1-year-old infants. If mothers expressed delight toward one toy and fear toward another, the infants spent more time touching the "delightful" toy than the "fearful" one, when later given a choice between them. How did the babies know which toy was associated with which emotion? The most plausible interpretation is that the mother's line of regard had earlier provided a critical cue. We know from work on joint attention that babies of 12 months will turn to gaze in the direction that a caretaker is looking (Butterworth & Cochran, 1980), and the mothers in these experiments presumably looked at a particular toy as they expressed their emotion toward it. Infants noticed their mothers' direction of gaze and took the concurrent emotional expression as a reaction to the target of that gaze.

Beyond Infancy

In the second year of life, the child's understanding of other people's emotions progresses still further. In social referencing, the baby merely reacts to the emotional signals that the mother sends; he or she does not seek to activate or terminate those emotional states. However, this is precisely what we see emerging in the second year of life. We can divide the toddler's interventions into roughly two sorts. On the one hand, the toddler seeks to offer comfort or solace to another person, in order to reduce or stop an expression of distress. On the other hand, the toddler seeks to hurt, thwart, or tease another person, in an effort to provoke distress.

As described earlier, efforts at comforting become increasingly complex and planful in the course of the second year (Zahn-Waxler & Radke-Yarrow, 1982). Teasing also becomes increasingly complex. At around 9 months, the baby is capable of proffering an object and withdrawing it as the other person reaches out to take it (Reddy, 1990). In the course of the second and third years, such teasing becomes both more strategic and farsighted: the toddler will retrieve a sibling's comfort object and then make off with it in a deliberate effort to upset the sibling (Dunn & Kendrick, 1979); alternatively, the toddler will retrieve an object that is known to cause fear—for example, a toy spider—and thrust it at the sibling (Dunn & Munn, 1985).

Talking about Emotion

Toward the end of the second year and increasingly in the third year, the toddler starts to label and talk about emotion states. A variety of studies suggest that toddlers start by concentrating on the basic set of discrete emotions: they employ terms such as happy, sad, mad, and scared (Bretherton & Beeghly, 1982; Izard, 1971; Smiley & Huttenlocher, 1989). It is tempting to speculate that these terms are used because infants' comprehension of the facial expression of these emotions provides a set of anchors or focal points. In much the same way, it has been argued that the child's early color lexicon is guided by the perception of focal colors (Heider, 1971). Still, it is important to emphasize that other explanations are available. For example, because these emotion terms are the ones that caretakers commonly use, guidance may be supplied by the socializing environment as much as by internal perceptual constraints (Smiley & Huttenlocher, 1989).

Whatever the exact explanation, it is clear that toddlers rapidly move beyond the mere identification of facial expression. First, they begin to talk about past and future emotional states (Bretherton & Beeghly, 1982). Second, they begin to describe the emotional states of various nonhuman entities such as animals and dolls used in pretend play (Wolf, Rygh, & Altshuler, 1984). Third, and in line with what we might have expected from the earlier discussion of emotional targeting, they start to talk about the situations that provoke emotion (Bretherton & Beeghly, 1982).

Toddlers also go beyond talking about emotion in a descriptive mode. In a longitudinal study of children's spontaneous utterances, we have found that they use talk about emotion to regulate and control emotional states. For example, toddlers try to ward off a particular emotional experience by telling an adult that a given object or event will make them scared or mad. They seek to terminate an emotion experience by asking an adult to stop doing something that upsets them (Sinclair & Harris, 1991). Three-year-olds also make remarks that are aimed at influencing other people's feelings: they make provocative and teasing remarks as well as comforting remarks (Dunn, Brown, & Beardsall, 1991). Thus, language is much more than a descriptive tool for young children. They make use of it in seeking to alter the course of their own emotions and those of other people.

Children differ in their acquisition of this tool. For example, research with maltreated toddlers (aged 30 months) shows that these children are broadly comparable to nonmaltreated children in terms of the type of mental states that they talk about (e.g., both groups talk about perception and volition). Nevertheless, the maltreated children produce fewer utterances about negative affect. One plausible interpretation of this finding is that caretakers who maltreat their children are less likely to comment on or question their children about their emotions, especially their feelings of sadness or anger (Cicchetti, 1990).

In summary, children's early talk about emotion picks up some of the themes that we saw in discussing their behavioral reactions to the expression of emotion. They identify particular emotional states; they articulate their grasp of the way in which emotions are targeted at particular objects and situations; and, finally, they start to talk about those targets in such a way as to exert control over emotion: they ask for frightening or distressing targets to be withdrawn or withheld. Moreover, just as children vary in their tendency to tease or comfort, so too they vary in the language that they use to describe and regulate emotion.

Understanding the Role of Beliefs and Desires

Hitherto, we have implied that the child's understanding of emotion might be reduced to an appreciation of the way that particular emotional states, as indexed by discrete facial expressions, are targeted at particular objects or situations in the environment. From the age of 3 years and upward, such a description definitely underestimates the child's comprehension. Starting at around 3 years, and possibly earlier, children begin to integrate what they know about emotion with their developing appreciation of the central role of desires and beliefs in motivating and guiding conduct.

This important development means that children start to understand that particular situations do not automatically provoke the same emotion in everyone; rather, the same situation can arouse different emotions in different people, depending on how it fits in with the desires and beliefs that an individual brings to the situation.

A variety of studies suggest that 3-year-olds have a clear appreciation of the subjective nature of desires or preferences. For example, they realize that a given food may be something that A likes but that B dislikes. Accordingly, if A and B are both given that food, their emotional reactions will differ. A will be happy and B will not (Flavell, Flavell, Green, & Moses, 1990; Harris, Johnson, Hutton, Andrews, & Cooke, 1989).

By the age of 4 to 5 years, children also grasp the role of beliefs. Consider the following experiment (Avis & Harris, 1991). Children watched while an adult cooked some tasty fruit kernels and then, having placed them in a covered bowl, announced that he would leave but would return shortly to eat them. After he had left, a second adult encouraged children to play a trick on the absent cook by removing the kernels from the bowl and hiding them in a different container. Once this had been accomplished, children were asked how the cook would feel on his return, before he had lifted the cover of the bowl and found the contents missing. Almost all the older group of children (ranging from 4 to 6 years) realized that the cook would feel pleased. Effectively, they could put themselves in the shoes of the returning cook and realize that the objective situation would not provoke his emotion because he did not yet know what the objective situation was. Rather, his mistaken assumption (that the kernels were ready and waiting for him) would determine his emotion. By contrast, the younger children (aged 2 to 3 years) were more likely to assume that the returning cook would be upset. They ignored his mistaken assumption and based their prediction on the actual situation that confronted him.

These results were obtained with children of the Baka pygmies, a community of traditional hunter-gatherers who live in the tropical rain forests of Southeast Cameroons. The age-change parallels that which has been observed in a variety of other studies carried out with children living in industrialized countries. The implication is that children's understanding of the mind in general and emotion in particular undergoes a universal elaboration in the course of normal development. When we turn to a discussion of autistic children, we shall see what happens when this elaboration goes awry.

In summary, from around the age of 3 years, children begin to acknowledge that emotional reactions are subjective. They cannot be predicted by simply scrutinizing the objective situation that faces a person. Instead, one must take into account how the person appraises the situation. Essentially, children begin to develop what we might call a cognitive theory of emotion: they appreciate that a person's emotion is determined not by the inherent features of the situation but by the way in which the person appraises it. Critical for an understanding of appraisal processes are the twin contributions of desires and beliefs. Children appreciate the subjective nature of desires—and their impact on emotion—before they take account of beliefs. The exact reason for this decalage is not yet known. Insofar as 4- to 5-year-old children appreciate the joint contribution of desires and beliefs, they have a more complete understanding of the cognitive antecedents of emotion.

The Acknowledgment and Denial of Emotional Experience

The use of the word *denial* may lead readers with a psychoanalytic background to anticipate, at this juncture, a discussion of the mechanisms of defense. Our aim, however, is different. In the preceding section, it was argued that children develop an increasingly sophisticated and articulate understanding of their own emotions and those of other people. Not only can they individuate emotions, but they also understand what provokes emotion, and they put that knowledge into words in seeking to regulate their own emotions and those of other people. Finally, as was discussed in the previous section, they increasingly understand the role of appraisal processes.

This analysis may have given the impression that children are highly insightful creatures who are constantly "in touch" with their emotions and what causes them. We now try to correct that possible impression. Our goal in this section is not to reiterate the traditional claim that children are motivated to use defense mechanisms that distort their capacity to engage in clear-eyed introspective analysis. Rather, we argue that the developmental process of understanding emotion is slow and painstaking: it imposes important conceptual constraints on the child's capacity for reflexive self-awareness. Admittedly, children may sometimes attempt to avoid thoughts or reminders of an emotionally charged experience—as discussed earlier in connection with posttraumatic stress reactions. They may even altogether deny that they experience a particular emotion, because it is too painful to bring that emotion into conscious awareness—as implied by psychoanalytic theory. There is, however, the additional possibility that they cannot conceptualize the conditions for having such an emotion. This limitation is likely to apply to positive as well as negative emotion. Two examples of this phenomenon are discussed here.

Understanding Surprise

To introduce the first illustration, it is necessary to make a brief digression. In the previous section, it was argued that 3-year-olds often have difficulty in understanding the impact that false beliefs will have on emotion. This is part of a much wider difficulty in appreciating the impact of false beliefs. Three-year-olds often ignore the fact that what a person will say or do depends on what the person believes to be the case and not on what actually is the case. For example, if someone wrongly believes that a box contains candy (when it really contains a pencil), 3-year-olds do not grasp that the person will say that candy (rather than a pencil) is in the box and will search for candy (rather than a pencil) in the box. By contrast, 4- to 5-year-olds appreciate that the person will be mistaken in what he or she says and does (Perner, Leekam, & Wimmer, 1987).

Other studies have shown that this age-change occurs when children are asked to assess their own mistakes as well as those of other persons. For example, if 3-year-olds discover that what they thought was a candy box with candy inside it actually contains a pencil, they frequently deny that they ever thought there was candy in the box (Gopnik & Astington, 1988; Wimmer & Hartl, 1991). So, whether it is a question of assessing someone else's beliefs or their own, 3-year-olds have difficulty in appreciating that beliefs and reality may be out of line with one another. Consider, now, the conditions under which surprise occurs. A person approaches a situation with an expectation about what will happen (the expectation may be more or less conscious); the situation does not match this expectation; the perceived mismatch between expectation and reality provokes surprise. Whenever we diagnose the reason for a person's surprise, we acknowledge, more or less explicitly, that an assumption that the person brought to a situation has turned out to be mistaken.

We have already seen that 3-year-olds have difficulty in acknowledging that someone might hold a belief that is out of line with reality. Yet this is the essential precondition for surprise. Hence, we can make two straightforward predictions: 3-year-olds will have difficulty in correctly predicting surprise in another person, and (even more surprising!) they should have difficulty in understanding their own surprise. Recent findings lend support to both of these predictions. Hadwin and Perner (1991) reported studies in which 3- to 5-year-olds listened to stories about a protagonist whose expectations were violated. They found that 5-year-olds, but not 3-year-olds, understand that if someone is given a box and thinks it contains a favorite candy, that person will be surprised if, when the box is opened, it does not contain the favorite candy after all. In a similar study, Wellman and Banerjee (1991) found that 3- and 4-year-olds did somewhat better if they were told that a story character was surprised and were asked to explain why. Yet, even with this explanation task (as opposed to the prediction task used by Hadwin and Perner, 1991), there was still an age-change in the children's citation of the critical precondition for surprise: the mistaken expectation of the story character.

What about children's insight into the reasons for their own surprise? Here too, recent data suggest that there is an age-change. Consider the following experiment: children were shown a familiar container (e.g., a matchbox) and either they were asked to guess what was inside it or they were shown that there were matches inside and the box was closed again. A few seconds later, the box was opened. All the children now discovered an unexpected switch: the box contained candy (the experimenter used a matchbox with two compartments to bring about this apparently magical switch). Children were presumably surprised by these contents, especially if they had seen matches inside the box. Nonetheless, whether they had guessed or seen the contents of the box, 3-year-olds tended to deny the reason for their surprise. They often claimed that they had thought the box contained candy from the start. Five-year-olds, by contrast, were more accurate in reporting this mistaken belief (Catchpole & Harris, 1991).

This line of experimentation shows, then, that it is important to distinguish between two systems for achieving cognition-emotion linkages (Harris, 1989). On the one hand, there is a basic appraisal system that allows a person to assess a situation in terms of his or her beliefs and desires, and generates emotions depending on the outcome of that appraisal; on the other hand, there is an attributional system that enables that appraisal sequence and its emotional output to be conceptualized. A child may appraise a situation, find that it contains something unexpected, and express surprise in terms of facial expression and, perhaps, exclamation. That reaction does not mean that the child's attributional system can make sense of what has happened. The child may be unable to conceptualize the reasons for his or her surprise, even when that emotion has been triggered by the appraisal system and expressed overtly. Such an acknowledgment requires an ability to realize the conditions under which an emotion is felt. When surprised, the child must be able to grasp how surprise is triggered by the mismatch between a false expectation and reality. If the child has no insight into his or her false expectations, an understanding of the emotion of surprise is blocked. Finally, it is worth underlining the fact that surprise is mostly (although not always) a positive emotion. Young children tend to associate it with positive outcomes such as gifts and treats (Wellman & Banerjee, 1991). Hence, young children's difficulties in acknowledging the reasons for their surprise cannot be construed as a defensive strategy.

Understanding Mixed Emotions

We may now turn to another example of the gap between the appraisal system and the attributional system: the expression and acknowledgment of mixed feelings. Attachment theorists have shown that a minority of infants display an ambivalent reaction when they are reunited with their mother after a brief separation. The child approaches the mother as if to seek comfort, but then tends to resist being picked up or cuddled (Ainsworth, Blehar, Waters, & Wall, 1978). Preschool children often show a similar vacillation in their emotional reaction to siblings: they can oscillate between a kindly caress and overt hostility within the space of a few seconds (Dunn, 1984). Despite these early expressions of ambivalence, there is now ample evidence that young children find it difficult to conceptualize ambivalent feelings, especially if (as in the cases described above) these feelings are aroused by the same target. For example, if children are told a story that contains an episode likely to arouse mixed feelings (the return of a lost dog with a cut ear) and asked how the main character will feel, 6-year-olds typically focus on one aspect of the outcome: they claim that the child in the story would feel happy (because the dog had come home) or sad (because the dog had cut its ear); rarely do they acknowledge that the child might feel both happy and sad. By contrast, the recognition of this mixed reaction is much more frequent among 10-year-olds (Harris, 1983).

Similar results emerge if children are asked to invent or remember situations in which mixed feelings are possible (Harter & Buddin, 1987). Six-year-olds often describe a situation likely to elicit two distinct and successive feelings rather than a blend; for example, "If you were in a haunted house, you'd be scared but then you'd be happy after you got out of it." At about 10 years of age, children successfully describe two concurrent situations that elicit feelings of the opposite valence; for example, "I was sitting in school feeling worried about all the responsibilities of a new pet, but I was happy that I got straight As on my report card." Roughly a year later, they describe a single situation with two interlinked components; for example, "I was happy that I got a present but mad that it wasn't what I wanted."

Why is there this considerable lag between the expression of mixed or ambivalent feelings and the ability to acknowledge them? As Harter (1977) has pointed out, children's difficulties in recognizing ambivalent feelings are especially evident in clinical settings because the acknowledgment of conflicting emotional reactions is often a therapeutic goal. Within that setting, there is a temptation to interpret the child's difficulties in psychodynamic terms. However, cognitive-developmental constraints may operate for disturbed as well as normal children. To conceptualize those constraints, we may refer once again to the distinction introduced earlier between the appraisal system and the attributional system. The developmental data show that the appraisal system can operate quite rapidly and exhaustively, concurrently scanning more than one aspect of a situation. For example, reunited with his or her mother, the infant anticipates being comforted, and expresses this positive expectation by approaching the mother. At the same time, the infant is also reminded of previous occasions when such expectations have not been met, and this produces resistance or withdrawal.

By contrast, the attributional system appears to operate in a nonexhaustive fashion: the child focuses on one aspect of the situation and recognizes the emotion that would be triggered by it; having done so, the child neglects other aspects of the situation. Recent studies in this domain have begun to ask how the child might be brought to acknowledge the mixed feelings that he or she expresses. It follows from the above analysis that the child needs to be prompted to engage in a more thorough and exhaustive analysis of the situation, using the attributional system. Suppose children are told a story with two conflicting components. They are asked to think first about one of those components, and to say what emotion it would elicit. Next, their attention is directed at the other component, and they are again asked to say what emotion it would elicit. Finally, children are asked to say how the story character would feel at the end of the story. Note that this kind of step-by-step analysis and integration resembles in certain respects the type of emotional reworking that children are guided through in a therapeutic session. Such a procedure should encourage children to engage in a more exhaustive analysis of the situation, and might also prompt them to examine other dual-faceted situations with equal systematicity. In a training study of this type (Peng, Johnson, Pollock, Glasspool, & Harris, 1992), we obtained this effect with 6- to 7-year-olds who denied the possibility of experiencing mixed emotion when they were questioned before the intervention.

In conclusion, these findings suggest that children who face complex, emotionally charged situations (e.g., starting at a new school; meeting a parent who has left the family home) will have difficulty in conceptualizing the mixed feelings that such situations are likely to provoke. A variety of studies using different techniques suggest that an acknowledgment of mixed feelings is quite difficult for children younger than 10 years. Nevertheless, training studies suggest that increased insight might be attained where it is deemed appropriate. Theoretically, and empirically, the recommended strategy is to encourage the child to focus on the different aspects of the situation one-by-one, and eventually to lead the child toward a more integrated overview. To the extent that emotionally disturbed children suffer from the same cognitive constraints as normal children, that strategy may also be effective in therapeutic contexts.

Emotions and Autism

In earlier sections, we have described the way in which the normal child's understanding of emotion proceeds. We can now use that description as a blueprint with which to study emotion comprehension in autism. We shall see that, in some respects, the autistic child's perception and understanding of emotion is fairly normal, particularly when due allowance is made for the intellectual retardation that often accompanies autism. Nevertheless, some aspects of the autistic child's understanding are markedly deficient, even when due allowance is made for intellectual retardation. Plotting both the competence and the deficits that accompany the autistic syndrome is critically important for constraining causal explanations.

In his initial case study of 11 autistic children, Kanner (1943) emphasized their inability "to form the usual, biologically provided affective contact with people." Recent research has begun to probe the nature of this alleged deficit more carefully. One possibility is that autistic children do not express or experience basic emotions such as joy, anger, and fear. Indeed, clinical observers have described several aberrations in the emotion expressions of autistic children. Some observers have noted a deficiency of emotion expressions and others have suggested that emotion expressions are exaggerated, but there is no consensus regarding the exact nature of the problem.

Yirmiya, Kasari, Sigman, and Mundy (1989) examined the facial expressions of 4- to 5-year-old autistic children in a social situation in which they had already demonstrated social responsiveness. Comparison groups consisted of mentally retarded and normal children matched for mental age and maternal educational level. The investigators predicted that the autistic children's facial expressions of emotions would be fewer in number and more ambiguous. The social interactions were with the experimenter who presented toys and games to the children. Expressions were reliably coded with an objective, anatomically based system (Izard, 1979).

The results revealed that autistic children displayed about the same amount of emotions as normal children but significantly less than the mentally retarded group. Contrary to prediction, the autistic children encoded a significantly greater variety of expressions than either normal or retarded children. However, the autistic children displayed a significantly greater number of negative and incongruous blends (simultaneous signals of two or more emotions) than either of the other groups. They encoded eight negative blends and five incongruous blends (e.g., anger-joy, fear-anger) not displayed by any of the normal or mentally retarded children.

This innovative study suggests that there may be a critical malfunction within the emotion system. Nonetheless, there is evidence that some aspects of the emotion system are intact. For example, when autistic children are briefly separated from their mother or caretaker, they seek her out on reunion in the same way that normal children do (Sigman, Mundy, Ungerer, & Sherman, 1987). Reading Kanner's account from a Darwinian perspective, it is tempting to speculate that autistic children may be deficient in the interpretation of emotion, over and above any potential deficit they may have in the expression of emotion. Recall that normal children rapidly interpret the emotional signals of their caretakers. As we saw in an earlier section, they respond appropriately to displays of emotion by their caretaker during the first few months of life, and, by the end of the first year, they are capable of "social referencing"—they can use their caretaker's emotional "comment" about an object or situation to regulate their own emotional stance toward that same object. What if this interpretive device were damaged or deficient among autistic children? They would fail to enter (with any comprehension) into the emotional face-to-face dialogue that is common in the early months, and they would not exhibit normal social referencing. The stage would be set for the marked disruption of human social relationships that is typical of autistic children, and also for the atypical emotional expressions reported by Yirmiya et al. (1989).

Peter Hobson has examined this line of interpretation in a variety of experiments. Autistic children have been shown a variety of emotional signals (facial expressions of emotion, gestures associated with particular emotions, and so forth) and asked to identify the emotion displayed. When the performance of the autistic children was then compared with that produced by normal and retarded children of the same mental age, the results have been mixed. Although Hobson himself has usually found that autistic children perform less accurately than retarded children matched for mental age (Hobson, 1986a, 1986b), these results have not always been replicated, especially when a stringent matching procedure is used by comparing the autistic children with controls of equivalent verbal rather than nonverbal ability (Ozonoff, Pennington, & Rogers, 1990).

In any case, there are other difficulties facing the hypothesis that the primary deficit in autism is a difficulty in interpreting and identifying expressions of emotion. First, autism is rarely diagnosed until well into the second year of life. Yet, if autistic children were deviant in the emotional dialogue and social referencing that can be observed during the first year of life, one would expect the syndrome to be more rapidly identified. Second, a longitudinal study of language acquisition by autistic and Down syndrome children (Tager-Flusberg, 1992) shows that the two groups acquire and use simple emotion terms (e.g., happy, fun, hate, sad) at the same rate. Third, experimental studies of autistic children show that they understand how particular situations typically provoke emotions such as happiness and sadness (Baron-Cohen, 1991; Tan & Harris, 1991). Finally, the hypothesis does not offer a satisfying explanation for other well-known symptoms of autism, especially the deficits in pretend play.

Nevertheless, the notion that autistic children have difficulty in understanding certain mental states has begun to receive widespread attention. There is convincing experimental evidence that autistic children have difficulty in understanding beliefs (Baron-Cohen, Leslie, & Frith, 1985; Leslie & Frith, 1990), belief-based emotions (Baron-Cohen, 1991), and attentional states (Baron-Cohen, 1990). In line with these findings, their linguistic reference to cognitive and attentional states is also markedly reduced relative to that of children with Down syndrome (Tager-Flusberg, 1992).

Overall, research with autistic children has produced an unexpected and interesting conclusion. Kanner's initial description led many investigators to focus on the autistic child's alleged lack of affective contact with other people, and some investigators have maintained that emphasis (Hobson, 1990). Yet recent research suggests that they particularly lack what we might call cognitive contact with others. Although autistic children show some limited appreciation of what others feel, they have great difficulty in appreciating what others think or heed. The implications are that there are distinct subsystems for these two types of contact with other people and that autistic children show a more severe disturbance in one than the other. These findings illustrate a major contribution that the study of developmental psychopathology can make to our understanding of normal development. Abilities that appear to be inextricably intertwined in the course of normal development may cleave into distinct capacities when we turn to pathological development.

NORMAL AND ABNORMAL DEVELOPMENT OF EMOTIONS: SOME CONCLUDING PROPOSITIONS

We have provided a number of sectional summaries throughout the text. Rather than attempt an overall synopsis, we conclude with some general propositions, based on the conceptual framework and the findings that we have described.

1. The capacity for expressing and experiencing many of the basic emotions is in place in early infancy. The motivational properties of these emotions are also functional, preceding and helping to organize various aspects of cognitive and motor development. Different types of input activate different emotions. The infant is biologically prepared to respond with positive or negative emotions to a limited set of stimuli (e.g., with joy to the human face; with fear to sudden or loud noises). Nevertheless, an infant must learn how to appraise many of the situations that elicit emotion-behavior sequences. Indeed, for some emotions (e.g., guilt), the case for natural or prepared elicitors remains unproven. The emergence of some emotions, therefore, may depend entirely on developmental changes in the appraisal system.

2. Socialization, particularly parenting practices during early development, creates an emotional climate that can have long-term effects on emotional development. It can determine whether the child perceives a given context as threatening or rewarding and whether the child expresses negative or positive emotions. Parenting practices can also bring about a wide-ranging recalibration of the appraisal system. Following such alterations, the infant can be more disposed to appraise a variety of contexts as fearful or distressing. Such early developing affective-cognitive structures become the personality dispositions or traits of adulthood. In normal development, within the context of sensitive, affectionate, and empathic caregiving, the emotions become connected to age-appropriate antecedents (activators) and consequents (cognitions, actions). In a more disturbed emotional climate of repeated anger or persistent depression, maladaptive emotional patterns will emerge. For example, children of physically abusive parents are hypervigilant toward potentially threatening stimuli as a result of their frequent threat-fear experiences. In addition, there is evidence for the cross-generational continuity of these abusive parenting practices. Distortions in the development of the emotions system and the self concept are also evident in the children of depressed mothers. Such children have more difficulty responding constructively to guilt.

3. Noncognitive activators of emotion, such as pain, are present from birth. Others, such as normal hormonal changes, peak in adolescence. Little is known about the role and developmental course of noncognitive activators. However, it is reasonable to assume that they too develop differently in response to normal as compared with abnormal parenting and socialization. Consider, for example, the socialization of emotion responses to pain in physically maltreated children. There is substantial evidence to show that pain, particularly unanticipated pain, is an innate activator of anger, requiring no cognitive mediation. Anger can be an adaptive response to pain because it mobilizes energy for defensive actions. In the case of physically abused children, however, the anger response to pain is apparently thwarted. Abused children learn to anticipate pain on seeing an anger expression or other telling signs of impending punishment in the abusive parent. Anticipation of pain is a compelling stimulus for fear. Thus, the stage is set for physically abused children to develop abnormal emotional reactions to signals of pain in themselves and others, and to pain anticipation. The normal anger response to pain may be thwarted in the presence of the abusive parent, only to emerge later in an exaggerated form that triggers aggression.

4. The processes that activate emotions—be they cognitive or noncognitive—need to be conceptually distinguished from the processes that enable children to identify, understand, and attribute emotions. For example, the ability to experience and express fear or guilt should be distinguished from the ability to attribute such feelings to other people. The attributional process also gets under way in the first year of life: infants begin to identify and react appropriately to another person's emotion and the objects to which a given emotion is directed. Toddlers show some understanding of the causes of emotion. They understand which situations typically provoke a given emotion, and they use that knowledge to regulate other people's emotions. Preschoolers begin to understand the role of the appraisal system. They grasp that two people may differ in their appraisal of the same situation. Specifically, they realize that people bring their own desires and beliefs to a given situation so that the emotion that is activated will vary from person to person.

5. In the course of normal development, children also become more insightful about their own emotional lives. For example, faced with multifaceted situations—divorce or separation—older children are better able to identify and understand the reasons for their own multiple or ambivalent emotional reactions. This cognitive process of identification and interpretation allows the child to think through complex emotional experiences. Nevertheless, full assimilation of an emotional experience may not always occur. There are at least two different sources of assimilation difficulty: (a) motivation and (b) cognition. First, irrespective of age, children can encounter unexpected, traumatic events (e.g., the sudden death of a friend; a transport disaster) that are not assimilated into the attribution system. The child experiences involuntary flashbacks, but because these memories arouse fear or distress, the child is motivated to avoid such thoughts and any external reminders that trigger them. Second, depending on their age, children may lack the cognitive ability to make sense of their own emotional reactions. Thus, toddlers and preschool children exhibit mixed or ambivalent emotional reactions to a parent, but think of positive and negative emotions as mutually exclusive.

FUTURE DIRECTIONS

There are promising areas of research on emotions and the development of psychopathology. We list the topics in the order used in the text.

The neurosciences are making significant progress in identifying the neural substrates of emotion, but more neurophysiological research is needed on discrete emotions. There has been an even greater neglect of a discrete emotions approach in neurophysiological studies of psychopathology. For example, any depressive disorder is likely to involve multiple negative emotions, each of which may have unique biochemical properties.

For the most part, emotion theorists and researchers concerned with the activation of emotions have concentrated their efforts on cognitive processes. There is now ample evidence from neural and behavioral sciences to show that several noncognitive processes—sensorimotor activity, pain, cyclical motivational/drive states—lead directly to emotion without cognitive mediation. We need research on the relative contribution of cognitive and noncognitive processes to the activation of emotions in both normal and abnormal populations. Noncognitive activators may be relatively more important in the preverbal infant and remain a significant source of emotions in developmentally delayed children and in children whose socialization has led to distorted appraisal processes.

Our knowledge of the development of expressive behavior development in normal children exceeds that for children with psychological disorders. Careful studies of expressive behavior have been conducted with only a few clinical populations. Expressive behavior is particularly important in early (preverbal) phases of development, but it remains an important means of communication throughout the preschool years and beyond. Long after language acquisition, children continue to look to parents for emotion expressions that provide guidance and reassurance.

Research on the relationship between cognition and emotion can be divided into two important themes. First, there are the appraisal processes that give rise to a particular emotional reaction such as fear, guilt, surprise, or ambivalence. Second, there are the conceptual processes by which children recognize, understand, and attribute mental states, including emotion, either to the self or to another person. With respect to a given emotion, these distinct processes may or may not emerge at different points in development. For example, children express fear in the first year of life; they also show some ability to recognize and respond appropriately to other people's fear expressions. On the other hand, children express surprise and ambivalence early in life, but the appropriate attribution of these emotional experiences comes much later. Traditionally, these distinct processes have often been collapsed together. For example, children's guilt reactions have been measured by their tendency to attribute guilt using story projection techniques. Future research will benefit by studying both aspects of emotional development while recognizing the important conceptual distinction between them. The study of autism provides an illustrative example. On the one hand, we can ask about autistic children's emotional reactions, including their facial expressions. On the other hand, we can ask about their ability to recognize and attribute mental states, including emotional states, both to themselves and to others.

Research on the attributional system is quite recent and has been chiefly directed at describing the course of normal development. In future research, it will be important to examine individual differences in the emergence of that system, and the background factors that facilitate or impede its emergence. For example, parents differ dramatically in the way that they seek to regulate emotions in their children and in their willingness to broach emotionally charged topics. We need to study the impact of these sharp variations on children's developing insight into emotion.

REFERENCES

Aber, J., & Cicchetti, D. (1984). Socioemotional development in maltreated children: An empirical and theoretical analysis. In H. Fitzgerald, B. Lester, & M. Yogman (Eds.), *Theory and research in behavioral paediatrics* (Vol. 2, pp. 147–205). New York: Plenum.

Aggleton, J. P., & Mishkin, M. (1986). The amygdala in emotion. In R. Plutchik & H. Kellerman (Eds.), *Emotion: Theory, research, and experience: Vol. 3. Biological foundations of emotion* (pp. 281–299). New York: Academic Press.

Agras, C., Sylvester, D., & Oliveau, D. (1969). The epidemiology of common fears and phobias. *Comprehensive Psychiatry, 10,* 151–156.

Ainsworth, M. D., Blehar, M. P., Waters, E., & Wall, S. (1978). *Patterns of attachment: A psychological study of the strange situation.* Hillsdale, NJ: Erlbaum.

Andrew, R. J. (1963). Evolution of facial expression. *Science, 142,* 1034–1041.

Arend, R., Gove, F., & Sroufe, L. A. (1979). Continuity of individual adaptation from infancy to kindergarten: A predictive study of ego resiliency and curiosity in preschoolers. *Child Development, 50,* 950–959.

Avis, J., & Harris, P. L. (1991). Belief-desire reasoning among Baka children: Evidence for a universal conception of mind. *Child Development, 62,* 460–467.

Bandler, R. (1982a). Induction of "rage" following microinjections of glutamate into midbrain but not hypothalamus of cats. *Neuroscience Letters, 30,* 183–188.

Bandler, R. (1982b). Neural control of aggressive behavior. *Trends in Neurosciences, 5*(11), 390–394.

Bandura, A. (1977). Self-efficacy: Toward a unifying theory of behavioral change. *Psychological Review, 84,* 191–215.

Bard, P. A. (1928). A diencephalic mechanism for the expression of rage with special reference to the sympathetic nervous system. *American Journal of Physiology, 84,* 490–515.

Barden, R. C., Zelko, F. A., Duncan, S. W., & Masters, J. C. (1980). Children's consensual knowledge about the experiential determinants of emotion. *Journal of Personality and Social Psychology, 39,* 968–976.

Barlow, D. H. (1989). *Anxiety and its disorders.* New York: Guilford.

Baron-Cohen, S. (1990). Precursors to a theory of mind: Understanding attention in others. In A. Whiten (Ed.), *Natural theories of mind* (pp. 233–251). Oxford, England: Blackwell.

Baron-Cohen, S. (1991). Do people with autism understand what causes emotion? *Child Development, 62,* 385–395.

Baron-Cohen, S., Leslie, A. M., & Frith, U. (1985). Does the autistic child have a theory of mind? *Cognition, 21,* 37–46.

Barrett, K. C., & Campos, J. J. (1987). Perspectives on emotional development II: A functionalist approach to emotions. In J. D. Osofsky (Ed.), *Handbook of infant development* (2nd ed., pp. 555–578). New York: Wiley.

Berkowitz, L. (1983). Aversively stimulated aggression: Some parallels and differences in research with animals and humans. *American Psychologist, 38,* 1135–1144.

Berkowitz, L. (1990). On the formation and regulation of anger and aggression: A cognitive-neoassociationistic analysis. *American Psychologist, 45*(4), 494–503.

Blumberg, S. H., & Izard, C. E. (1985). Affective and cognitive characteristics of depression in 10- and 11-year-old children. *Journal of Personality and Social Psychology, 49*(1), 194–202.

Blumberg, S. H., & Izard, C. E. (1986). Discriminating patterns of emotions in 10- and 11-year-old children's anxiety and depression. *Journal of Personality and Social Psychology, 51*(4), 852–857.

Bower, G. H. (1981). Mood and memory. *American Psychologist, 36,* 129–148.

Bowlby, J. (1973). *Attachment and loss: Vol. 2. Separation.* London: Pelican.

Bregman, E. (1934). An attempt to modify the emotional reactions of infants by the conditioned response technique. *Journal of Genetic Psychology, 45,* 169–196.

Brentano, F. (1973). *Psychology from an empirical standpoint.* London: Routledge & Kegan Paul. (Original work published 1874)

Bretherton, I., & Beeghly, M. (1982). Talking about internal states: The acquisition of an explicit theory of mind. *Developmental Psychology, 18,* 906–921.

Butterworth, G. E., & Cochran, E. (1980). Towards a mechanism of joint visual attention in human infancy. *International Journal of Behavioral Development, 3,* 253–270.

Campos, J. J. (1983). The importance of affective communication in social referencing. *Merrill Palmer Quarterly, 29,* 83–87.

Campos, J. J., Hiatt, S., Ramsay, D., Henderson, C., & Svejda, M. (1978). The emergence of fear on the visual cliff. In M. Lewis & L. A. Rosenblum (Eds.), *The development of affect: Vol. 1. Genesis of behavior* (pp. 149–182). New York: Plenum.

Cannon, W. B. (1927). The James-Lange theory of emotions: A critical examination and an alternative theory. *American Journal of Psychology, 39,* 106–124.

Cannon, W. B. (1929). *Bodily changes in pain, hunger, fear and rage: An account of recent researches into the function of emotional excitement* (2nd ed.). New York: Appleton-Century-Crofts.

Carlson, V., Cicchetti, D., Barnett, D., & Braunwald, K. (1989). Finding order in disorganization: Lessons from research on maltreated infants' attachments to their caregivers. In D. Cicchetti & V. Carlson (Eds.), *Child maltreatment: Theory and research on the causes and consequences of maltreatment* (pp. 55–67). New York: Cambridge University Press.

Catchpole, A., & Harris, P. L. (1991). *Children's reactions to "magical" substitutions.* Unpublished manuscript, Department of Experimental Psychology, University of Oxford.

Charlesworth, W. R., & Kreutzer, M. A. (1973). Facial expressions of infants and children. In P. Ekman (Ed.), *Darwin and facial expression: A century of research in review* (pp. 91–168). New York: Academic Press.

Cicchetti, D. (1990). The organization and coherence of socioemotional, cognitive, and representational development: Illustrations through a developmental psychopathology perspective on Down syndrome and child maltreatment. In R. Thompson (Ed.), *Nebraska Symposium on Motivation: Vol. 36. Socioemotional development* (pp. 259–366). Lincoln: University of Nebraska Press.

Cicchetti, D., Cummings, E. M., Greenberg, M. T., & Marvin, R. S. (1990). An organizational perspective on attachment beyond infancy. In M. T. Greenberg, D. Cicchetti, & E. M. Cummings (Eds.), *Attachment in the preschool years* (pp. 3–49). Chicago: University of Chicago Press.

Cicchetti, D., Ganiban, J., & Barnett, D. (1991). Contributions from the study of high risk populations to understanding the development of emotion regulation. In K. Dodge & J. Garber (Eds.), *The development of emotion regulation* (pp. 15–48). New York: Cambridge University Press.

Cicchetti, D., & Sroufe, L. A. (1978). An organizational view of affect: Illustration from the study of Down syndrome infants. In M. Lewis & L. A. Rosenblum (Eds.), *The development of affect* (pp. 309–350). New York: Plenum.

Cummings, E. M., Zahn-Waxler, C., & Radke-Yarrow, M. (1981). Young children's responses to expressions of anger and affection by others in the family. *Child Development, 52,* 1274–1281.

Darwin, C. (1965). *The expression of the emotions in man and animals.* London: Murray; Chicago: University of Chicago Press. (Original work published 1872)

Dollinger, S. J., O'Donnell, J. P., & Staley, A. A. (1984). Lightning-strike disaster: Effects on children's fears and worries. *Journal of Consulting and Clinical Psychology, 52,* 1028–1038.

Duclos, S. E., Laird, J. D., Schneider, E., Sexter, M., Stern, L., & Van Lighten, O. (1989). Emotion-specific effects of facial expressions and postures on emotional experience. *Journal of Personality and Social Psychology, 57*(1), 100–108.

Dunn, J. (1984). *Sisters and brothers.* London: Fontana.

Dunn, J., Brown, J., & Beardsall, L. (1991). Family talk about feeling states and children's later understanding of others' emotions. *Developmental Psychology, 27,* 448–455.

Dunn, J., & Kendrick, C. (1979). Interaction between young siblings in the context of family relationships. In M. Lewis & L. A. Rosenblum (Eds.), *The child and its family* (pp. 143–168). New York: Plenum.

Dunn, J., & Munn, J. (1985). Becoming a family member: Family conflict and the development of social understanding in the first year. *Child Development, 50,* 306–318.

Dunn, J., Stocker, C., & Plomin, R. (1990). Nonshared experience within the family: Correlates of behavioral problems in middle childhood. *Development and Psychopathology, 2,* 113–126.

Durant, J. R. (1973). The science of sentiment: The problem of cerebral localization of emotion. In P. P. G. Bateson & P. H. Klopfer (Eds.), *Perspectives in ethology: Vol. 6. Mechanisms* (pp. 1–30). New York: Plenum.

Egeland, B., & Sroufe, L. A. (1981). Developmental sequelae of maltreatment in infancy. *New Directions for Child Development, 11,* 77–92.

Eibl-Eibesfeldt, I. (1972). Similarities and differences between cultures in expressive movements. In R. A. Hinde (Ed.), *Nonverbal communication* (pp. 297–311). New York: Cambridge University Press.

Ekman, P., Friesen, W. V., & Ellsworth, P. C. (1972). *Emotion in the human face: Guidelines for research and in integration of findings.* New York: Pergamon.

Emde, R. (1983). The pre-representational self and its affective core. *Psychoanalytic Study of the Child, 38,* 165–192.

Emde, R., Katz, E. L., & Thorpe, J. K. (1978). Emotional expression in infancy: II. Early deviations in Down syndrome. In M. Lewis & L. A. Rosenblum (Eds.), *The development of affect* (pp. 351–360). New York: Plenum.

Erickson, M. F., Sroufe, L. A., & Egeland, B. (1985). The relationship between quality of attachment and behavior problems in preschool in a high risk sample. In I. Bretherton & E. Waters (Eds.), Growing points in attachment theory and research (pp. 147–156). *Monographs of the Society for Research in Child Development, 50* (1–2, Serial No. 209).

Feinman, S. (1982). Social referencing in infancy. *Merrill Palmer Quarterly, 28,* 445–470.

Feinman, S. (1985). Emotional expression, social referencing, and preparedness for learning in infancy: Mother knows best, but sometimes I know better. In G. Zivin (Ed.), *The development of expressive interactions* (pp. 291–318). Orlando, FL: Academic Press.

Finman, R., & Berkowitz, L. (1989). Some factors influencing the effect of depressed mood on anger and overt hostility toward another. *Journal of Research in Personality, 23,* 70–84.

Flavell, J. H., Flavell, E. R., Green, F. L., & Moses, L. J. (1990). Young children's understanding of fact beliefs versus value beliefs. *Child Development, 61,* 915–928.

Flynn, J. P. (1967). The neural basis of aggression in cats. In D. C. Glass (Ed.), *Neurophysiology and emotion* (pp. 40–60). New York: Rockefeller University Press and Russell Sage Foundation.

Frijda, N. (1986). *The emotions.* London: Cambridge University Press.

Gaensbauer, T. J., Mrazek, D., & Harmon, R. (1981). Emotional expression in abused and/or neglected infants. In N. Frude (Ed.), *Psychological approaches to child abuse* (pp. 120–135). Totowa, NJ: Rowman & Littlefield.

Gaensbauer, T. J., & Sands, K. (1979). Distorted affective communications in abused/neglected infants and their potential impact on caretakers. *American Journal of Child Psychiatry, 18,* 236–250.

Ganiban, J., Wagner, S., & Cicchetti, D. (1990). Temperament and Down syndrome. In D. Cicchetti & M. Beeghly (Eds.), *Children with Down syndrome* (pp. 63–100). New York: Cambridge University Press.

Garmezy, N., & Rutter, M. (1985). Acute reactions to stress. In M. Rutter & L. Hersov (Eds.), *Child and adolescent psychiatry: Modern approaches* (2nd ed., pp. 152–176). Oxford, England: Blackwell.

Gellhorn, E. (1964). Motion and emotion: The role of proprioception in the physiology and pathology of the emotions. *Psychological Review, 71*(6), 457–472.

Gloor, P., Oliver, A., & Quesney, L. F. (1981). The role of the amygdala in the expression of psychic phenomena in temporal lobe seizures.

In Y. Ben-Ari (Ed.), *The amygdaloid complex* (pp. 395–408). Amsterdam, The Netherlands: Elsevier/North-Holland.

Gopnik, A., & Astington, J. W. (1988). Children's understanding of representational change and its relation to the understanding of the appearance-reality distinction. *Child Development, 59,* 26–37.

Gray, J. A. (1982). Précis of: The neuropsychology of anxiety: An enquiry into the functions of the septo-hippocampal system. *Behavioral and Brain Sciences, 5,* 469–534.

Hadwin, J., & Perner, J. (1991). Pleased and surprised: Children's cognitive theory of emotion. *British Journal of Developmental Psychology, 9,* 215–234.

Hagman, C. (1932). A study of fear in pre-school children. *Journal of Experimental Psychology, 1,* 110–130.

Hansen, C. H., & Hansen, R. D. (1988). Finding the face in the crowd: An anger superiority effect. *Journal of Personality and Social Psychology, 54*(6), 917–924.

Harris, P. L. (1983). Children's understanding of the link between situation and emotion. *Journal of Experimental Child Psychology, 36,* 490–509.

Harris, P. L. (1989). *Children and emotion: The development of psychological understanding.* Oxford, England: Blackwell.

Harris, P. L., Johnson, C. N., Hutton, D., Andrews, G., & Cooke, T. (1989). Young children's theory of mind and emotion. *Cognition and Emotion, 3,* 379–400.

Harter, S. (1977). A cognitive developmental approach to children's expression of conflicting feelings and a technique to facilitate such expressions in the conduct of play therapy. *Journal of Consulting and Clinical Psychology, 45,* 417–432.

Harter, S. (1983). Developmental perspectives on the self-system. In P. H. Mussen (Ed.), *Handbook of child psychology* (Vol. 4, pp. 275–385). New York: Wiley.

Harter, S., & Buddin, B. (1987). Children's understanding of the simultaneity of two emotions: A five-page developmental acquisition sequence. *Developmental Psychology, 23,* 388–399.

Harter, S., & Whitesell, N. (1989). Developmental changes in children's emotion concepts. In C. Saarni & P. L. Harris (Eds.), *Children's understanding of emotion* (pp. 81–116). New York: Cambridge University Press.

Haviland, J. M., & Lelwica, M. (1987). The induced affect response: 10-week-old infants' responses to three emotional expressions. *Developmental Psychology, 23,* 97–104.

Heider, E. R. (1971). "Focal" color areas and the development of color names. *Developmental Psychology, 4,* 447–455.

Hesse, P., & Cicchetti, D. (1982). Perspectives on an integrated theory of emotional development. *New Directions for Child Development, 16,* 3–48.

Hobson, R. P. (1986a). The autistic child's appraisal of expressions of emotion. *Journal of Child Psychology and Psychiatry, 27,* 321–342.

Hobson, R. P. (1986b). The autistic child's appraisal of expressions of emotion: A further study. *Journal of Child Psychology and Psychiatry, 27,* 671–680.

Hobson, R. P. (1990). On the origins of self and the case of autism. *Development and Psychopathology, 2,* 163–181.

Hoffman, M. L. (1970). Moral development. In P. H. Mussen (Ed.), *Carmichael's manual of child psychology* (Vol. 2, pp. 261–359). New York: Wiley.

Hoffman, M. L. (1982). Development of prosocial motivation: Empathy and guilt. In N. Eisenberg (Ed.), *The development of prosocial behavior* (pp. 281–313). New York: Academic Press.

Hornik, R., Risenhoover, N., & Gunnar, M. (1987). The effects of maternal positive, neutral, and negative affective communications on infant responses to new toys. *Child Development, 58,* 937–944.

Horowitz, M. J., Wilner, N., & Alvarez, W. (1979). Impact of event scale: A measure of subjective stress. *Psychosomatic Medicine, 41,* 209–218.

Huebner, R. R., & Izard, C. E. (1988). Mothers' responses to infants' facial expressions of sadness, anger, and physical distress. *Motivation and Emotion, 12,* 185–196.

Hyson, M. C., & Izard, C. E. (1985). Continuities and changes in emotion expressions during brief separation at 13 and 18 months. *Developmental Psychology, 21,* 1165–1170.

Isen, M., Daubman, K. A., & Nowicki, G. G. (1987). Positive affect facilitates creative problem solving. *Journal of Experimental Psychology, 52,* 1122–1132.

Izard, C. E. (1971). *The face of emotion.* New York: Appleton-Century-Crofts.

Izard, C. E. (1972). *Patterns of emotions: A new analysis of anxiety and depression.* New York: Academic Press.

Izard, C. E. (1977). *Human emotions.* New York: Plenum.

Izard, C. E. (1979). The maximally discriminative facial movement coding system (MAX). Newark: Office of Academic Computing and Technology, University of Delaware.

Izard, C. E. (1984). Emotion-cognition relationships and human development. In C. E. Izard, J. Kagan, & R. B. Zajonc (Eds.), *Emotions, cognition, and behavior* (pp. 17–37). New York: Cambridge University Press.

Izard, C. E. (1989). The structure and functions of emotions: Implications for cognition, motivation, and personality. In I. S. Cohen (Ed.), *The G. Stanley Hall lecture series* (pp. 35–73). Washington, DC: American Psychological Association.

Izard, C. E. (1990). Facial expressions and the regulation of emotions. *Journal of Personality and Social Psychology, 58*(3), 487–498.

Izard, C. E., & Blumberg, S. H. (1985). Emotion theory and the role of emotions in anxiety in children and adults. In A. H. Tuma & J. D. Maser (Eds.), *Anxiety and the anxiety disorders* (pp. 109–129). Hillsdale, NJ: Erlbaum.

Izard, C. E., Haynes, O. M., Chisholm, G., & Baak, K. (1991). Emotional determinants of infant-mother attachment. *Child Development, 62*(5), 905–917.

Izard, C. E., Hembree, E. A., & Huebner, R. R. (1987). Infants' emotion expressions to acute pain: Developmental change and stability of individual differences. *Developmental Psychology, 23*(1), 105–113.

Izard, C. E., Huebner, R. R., Risser, D., McGinnes, G., & Dougherty, L. (1980). The young infant's ability to produce discrete emotion expressions. *Developmental Psychology, 16,* 132–140.

Izard, C. E., Libero, D., Putnam, P., & Haynes, O. M. (1993). *Stability of emotion experiences and their relations to traits of personality. Journal of Personality and Social Psychology, 64,* 847–860.

Izard, C. E., & Malatesta, C. Z. (1987). Perspectives on emotional development I: Differential emotions theory of early emotional development. In J. D. Osofsky (Ed.), *Handbook of infant development* (2nd ed., pp. 494–554). New York: Wiley.

Izard, C. E., & Saxton, P. M. (1988). Emotions. In R. C. Atkinson, R. J. Herrnstein, G. Lindzey, & D. Luce (Eds.), *Stevens' handbook of experimental psychology* (2nd ed., pp. 627–676). New York: Wiley.

Izard, C. E., & Schwartz, G. M. (1986). Patterns of emotion in depression. In M. Rutter, C. E. Izard, & P. B. Read (Eds.), *Depression in young people: Developmental and clinical perspectives* (pp. 33–70). New York: Guilford.

Izard, C. E., Simons, R. F., & Porges, S. W. (1991, August). Stability of emotion-temperament variables during the first two years of life. Paper presented at the meeting of The American Psychological Association, San Francisco.

Jacobs, W. J., & Nadel, L. (1985). Stress-induced recovery of fears and phobias. *Psychological Review, 92*(4), 512–531.

James, W. (1884). What is emotion? *Mind, 4,* 188–204.

James, W. (1950). *The principles of psychology* (Vol. 2). New York: Dover. (Original work published 1890)

James, W. (1985). *The varieties of religious experience.* Cambridge, MA: Harvard University Press. (Original work published 1910)

Jersild, A. T. (1947). Emotional development. In L. Carmichael (Ed.), *Manual of child psychology* (2nd ed., pp. 833–917). New York: Wiley.

Jersild, A. T., & Holmes, F. B. (1935). Children's fears. *Child Development Monograph, No. 20.* New York: Teachers College, Columbia University.

John, E. (1941). A study of the effects of evacuation and air raids on pre-school children. *British Journal of Educational Psychology, 11,* 173–179.

Jones, M. C. (1924). A laboratory study of fear. *Pedagogical Seminars, 31,* 308–315.

Kagan, J., Reznick, J. S., & Snidman, N. (1987). The physiology and psychology of behavioral inhibition in children. *Child Development, 58,* 1459–1473.

Kagan, J., Reznick, J. S., & Snidman, N. (1988). Biological bases of childhood shyness. *Science, 240,* 167–171.

Kanner, L. (1943). Autistic disturbances of affective contact. *Nervous Child, 2,* 217–250.

Kling, A. S. (1986). The anatomy of aggression and affiliation. In R. Plutchik & H. Kellerman (Eds.), *Emotion: Theory, research, and experience: Vol. 3. Biological foundations of emotion* (pp. 237–264). New York: Academic Press.

Klinnert, M., Campos, J., Sorce, J. F., Emde, R. N., & Svejda, M. (1983). Emotions as behavior regulators: Social referencing in infancy. In R. Plutchik & H. Kellerman (Eds.), *Emotion: Theory, research, and experience* (pp. 57–86). New York: Academic Press.

Kluver, H., & Bucy, P. (1939). Preliminary analysis of functions of the temporal lobes in monkeys. *Archives of Neurology and Psychiatry, 42,* 979–1000.

Kotsch, W. E., Gerbing, D. W., & Schwartz, L. E. (1982). The construct validity of the differential emotions scale as adapted for children and adolescents. In C. E. Izard (Ed.), *Measuring emotions in infants and children* (pp. 251–278). Cambridge, England: Cambridge University Press.

Laird, J. D. (1974). Self-attribution of emotion: The effects of expressive behavior on the quality of emotional experience. *Journal of Personality and Social Psychology, 29,* 475–486.

Laird, J. D., & Bresler, C. (1990). William James and the mechanisms of emotional experience. *Personality and Social Psychology Bulletin, 16*(4), 636–651.

LeDoux, J. E. (1987). In F. Plum (Ed.), *Handbook of physiology. Section 1. The nervous system: Vol. V. Higher functions of the brain* (pp. 419–460). Bethesda, MD: American Physiological Society.

LeDoux, J. E. (1989). Cognitive-emotional interactions in the brain. In C. E. Izard (Ed.), *Development of emotion-cognition relations* (pp. 267–289). Hillsdale, NJ: Erlbaum.

LeDoux, J. E., Romanski, L., & Xagoraris, A. (1989). Indelibility of subcortical emotional memories. *Journal of Cognitive Neuroscience, 1*(3), 238–243.

Leslie, A. M., & Frith, U. (1990). Prospects for a cognitive neuropsychology of autism. *Psychological Review, 97,* 122–131.

Lester, B. M. (1985). There's more to crying than meets the ear. In B. M. Lester & C. F. Z. Boukydis (Eds.), *Infant crying: Research and theoretical perspectives* (pp. 1–26). New York: Plenum.

Lewis, M., & Michalson, L. (1983). *Children's emotions and moods: Developmental theory and measurement.* New York: Plenum.

Lewis, M., Sullivan, M. W., Stanger, C., & Weiss, M. (1989). Self development and self-conscious emotions. *Child Development, 60,* 146–156.

Loeber, R., Tremblay, R. E., Gagnon, E., & Charlebois, P. (1989). Continuity and desistance in disruptive boys: Early fighting at school. *Development and Psychopathology, 1,* 39–50.

Lyons-Ruth, K., Zoll, D., Connell, D., & Grunebaum, H. U. (1989). Family deviance and family disruption in childhood: Associations with maternal behavior and infant maltreatment during the first two years of life. *Development and Psychopathology, 1,* 219–236.

MacLean, P. D. (1952). Some psychiatric implications of physiological studies on frontotemporal portion of the limbic system (visceral brain). *Electroencephalography and Clinical Neurophysiology, 4,* 407–418.

MacLean, P. D. (1975). Evolution of three mentalities. *Man–Environment Systems, 15,* 213–224.

Main, M., & George, C. (1985). Responses of abused and disadvantaged toddlers to distress in agemates: A study in the day-care setting. *Developmental Psychology, 21*(3), 407–412.

Main, M., Kaplan, N., & Cassidy, J. (1985). Security in infancy, childhood, and adulthood: A move to the level of representation. In I. Bretherton & E. Waters (Eds.), Growing points in attachment theory and research (pp. 66–104). *Monographs of the Society for Research in Child Development, 50* (1–2, Serial No. 209).

Malatesta, C. Z. (1990). The role of emotions in the development and organization of personality. In R. Thompson (Ed.), *Nebraska Symposium on Motivation: Vol. 36. Socioemotional development* (pp. 1–56). Lincoln: University of Nebraska Press.

Malatesta, C. Z., Culver, C., Tesman, J. R., & Shepard, B. (1989). The development of emotion expression during the first two years of life: Normative trends and patterns of individual differences. (A commentary by A. Fogel, M. Reimers, & G. Zivin). In I. Bretherton & E. Waters (Eds.), Growing points in attachment theory and research (pp. 42–54). *Monographs of the Society for Research in Child Development, 54* (1–2, Serial No. 219).

Malatesta, C. Z., & Haviland, J. M. (1982). Learning display rules: The socialization of emotion expression in infancy. *Child Development, 53,* 1001–1003.

Matsumoto, D. (1987). The role of facial response in the experience of emotion: More methodological problems and a meta-analysis. *Journal of Personality and Social Psychology, 52*(4), 769–774.

McNally, R. J. (1989). On "stress-induced recovery of fears and phobias." *Psychological Review, 96*(1), 180–181.

Mineka, S. (1988). A primate model of phobic fears. In H. Eysenck & I. Martin (Eds.), *Theoretical foundations of behavior therapy* (pp. 81–111). New York: Plenum.

Mineka, S., Davidson, M., Cook, M., & Keiri, R. (1984). Observational conditioning of snake fear in rhesus monkeys. *Journal of Abnormal Psychology, 93*(4), 355–372.

Nader, K., Pynoos, R., Fairbanks, L., & Frederick, C. (1990). Children's PTSD reactions one year after a sniper attack at their school. *American Journal of Psychiatry, 147,* 1526–1530.

Nesse, R. M. (1990). Evolutionary explanations of emotions. *Human Nature, 1*(3), 261–289.

Nunner-Winkler, G., & Sodian, B. (1988). Children's understanding of moral emotions. *Child Development, 59,* 1323–1338.

Ollendick, T. H. (1983). Reliability and validity of the revised Fear Survey Schedule for Children (FSSC-R). *Behavior Research and Therapy, 21,* 685–692.

Ost, L. G. (1987). Age of onset in different phobias. *Journal of Abnormal Psychology, 96,* 223–229.

Ost, L. G., & Hugdahl, K. (1983). Acquisition of agoraphobia, mode of onset and anxiety response patterns. *Behavior Research and Therapy, 21,* 623–631.

Oster, H. (1978). Facial expression and affect development. In L. Lewis & L. Rosenblum (Eds.), *The development of affect* (pp. 43–75). New York: Plenum.

Ozonoff, S., Pennington, B. F., & Rogers, S. J. (1990). Are there emotion perception deficits in young autistic children? *Journal of Child Psychology and Psychiatry, 31,* 343–361.

Panksepp, J. (1986). The anatomy of emotions. In R. Plutchik & H. Kellerman (Eds.), *Emotion: Theory, research, and experience: Vol. 3. Biological foundations of emotions* (pp. 91–124). New York: Academic Press.

Papez, J. W. (1937). A proposed mechanism of emotion. *Archives of Neurology and Psychiatry, 38,* 725–743.

Patterson, C. J., Cohn, D. A., & Kao, B. T. (1989). Maternal warmth as a protective factor against risks associated with peer rejection among children. *Development and Psychopathology, 1,* 21–39.

Penfield, W. (1958). *The excitable cortex in conscious man (Sherrington Lectures, V).* Springfield, IL: Thomas.

Peng, C., Johnson, C. N., Pollock, J., Glasspool, R., & Harris, P. L. (1992). Training young children to acknowledge mixed emotions. *Cognition and Emotion, 6,* 387–401.

Perner, J., Leekam, S., & Wimmer, H. (1987). Three-year-olds' difficulty in understanding false belief: Cognitive limitation, lack of knowledge, or pragmatic misunderstanding? *British Journal of Developmental Psychology, 5,* 125–137.

Plutchik, R. (1980). *Emotion: A psychoevolutionary synthesis.* New York: Harper & Row.

Post, R., & Ballenger, J. (Eds.). (1984). *Neurobiology of mood disorders.* Baltimore: Williams & Wilkins.

Poulin-Dubois, D., & Shultz, T. R. (1988). The development of the understanding of human behavior: From agency to intentionality. In J. W. Astington, P. L. Harris, & D. R. Olson (Eds.), *Developing theories of mind* (pp. 109–125). Cambridge, England: Cambridge University Press.

Pribram, K. (1967). Emotion: Steps toward a neuropsychological theory. In D. C. Glass (Ed.), *Neurophysiology and emotion* (pp. 3–40). New York: Rockefeller University Press and Russell Sage Foundation.

Pynoos, R. S., Frederick, C., & Nader, K. (1987). Life threat and posttraumatic stress in school age children. *Archives of General Psychiatry, 44,* 1057–1063.

Rachman, S. (1990). *Fear and courage* (2nd ed.). New York: Freeman.

Reddy, V. (1990). Playing with others' expectations: Teasing and mucking about in the first year. In A. Whiten (Ed.), *Natural theories of mind* (pp. 143–158). Oxford, England: Blackwell.

Rieder, C., & Cicchetti, D. (1989). An organizational perspective on cognitive control functioning and cognitive-affective balance in maltreated children. *Developmental Psychology, 25,* 382–393.

Rolls, E. T. (1986). Neural systems involved in emotion in primates. In R. Plutchik & H. Kellerman (Eds.), *Emotion: Theory, research, and experience: Vol. 3. Biological foundations of emotion* (pp. 125–143). New York: Academic Press.

Rutter, M. (1979). Protective factors in children's responses to stress and disadvantage. In M. W. Kent & J. E. Rolf (Eds.), *Primary prevention of psychopathology: Vol. 3. Social competence in children* (pp. 207–223). Hanover, NH: University Press of New England.

Seligman, M. E. P. (1971). Phobias and preparedness. *Behavior Therapy, 77,* 406–418.

Seligman, M. E. P., & Hager, J. L. (1972). *Biological boundaries of learning.* New York: Appleton-Century-Crofts.

Seligman, M. E. P., Peterson, C., Kaslow, N., Tanenbaum, R., Alloy, L., & Abramson, L. (1984). Attributional style and depressive symptoms among children. *Journal of Abnormal Psychology, 93,* 235–238.

Sigman, M., Mundy, P., Ungerer, J. A., & Sherman, T. (1987, April). *The development of social attachments in autistic children.* Paper presented at the Society for Research in Child Development Biennial Meeting, Baltimore.

Sinclair, A., & Harris, P. L. (1991). *A longitudinal study of children's talk about emotion.* Unpublished manuscript, Department of Experimental Psychology, University of Oxford.

Smetana, J. G. (1981). Preschool children's conception of moral and social rules. *Child Development, 52,* 1333–1336.

Smiley, P., & Huttenlocher, J. (1989). Young children's acquisition of emotion concepts. In C. Saarni & P. L. Harris (Eds.), *Children's understanding of emotion* (pp. 27–49). New York: Cambridge University Press.

Solomon, J. (1942). Reactions of children to black-outs. *American Journal of Orthopsychiatry, 12,* 361–364.

Sorce, J. F., Emde, R. N., Campos, J. J., & Klinnert, M. D. (1985). Maternal emotional signalling: Its effects on the visual cliff behavior of 1-year-olds. *Developmental Psychology, 21,* 195–200.

Spielberger, C. D., Edwards, C. D., Lushene, R. F., Montuori, J., & Platzek, D. (1973). *STAIC: Preliminary Manual.* Palo Alto, CA: Consulting Psychologists Press.

Sroufe, L. A. (1988). The role of infant-caregiver attachment in development. In J. Belsky & T. Nezworski (Eds.), *Clinical implications of attachment* (pp. 18–30). Hillsdale, NJ: Erlbaum.

Steiner, J. E. (1973). The human gustofacial response. In J. F. Bosma (Ed.), *Fourth Symposium on Oral Sensation and Perception.* Rockville, MD: U.S. Dept. of Health, Education & Welfare.

Strack, F., Martin, L. L., & Stepper, S. (1988). Inhibiting and facilitating conditions of the human smile: A nonobtrusive test of the facial feedback hypothesis. *Journal of Personality and Social Psychology, 54*(5), 768–777.

Tager-Flusberg, H. (1992). Autistic children's talk about psychological states: Deficits in the early acquisition of a theory of mind. *Child Development, 63,* 161–172.

Tan, J., & Harris, P. L. (1991). Autistic children understand seeing and wanting. *Development and Psychopathology, 3,* 163–174.

Termine, N. T., & Izard, C. E. (1988). Infants' responses to their mothers' expressions of joy and sadness. *Developmental Psychology, 24,* 223–229.

Terr, L. C. (1991). Childhood traumas: An outline and overview. *American Journal of Psychiatry, 148,* 10–20.

Thompson, R. A., & Hoffman, M. L. (1980). Empathy and the arousal of guilt in children. *Developmental Psychology, 15,* 155–156.

Tomkins, S. S. (1962). *Affect, imagery, consciousness: Vol. 1. The positive affects.* New York: Springer.

Tomkins, S. S. (1963). *Affect, imagery, consciousness: Vol. 2. The negative affects.* New York: Springer.

Tronick, E. Z. (1989). Emotions and emotional communication in infants. *American Psychologist, 44*(2), 112–119.

Visintainer, P. F., & Matthews, K. A. (1987). Stability of overt Type A behaviors in children: Results from a two- and five-year longitudinal study. *Child Development, 58,* 1586–1591.

Walden, T. A. (1991). Infant social referencing. In J. Garber & K. A. Dodge (Eds.), *The development of emotion regulation and dysregulation* (pp. 69–88). New York: Cambridge University Press.

Walden, T. A., & Ogan, T. A. (1988). The development of social referencing. *Child Development, 59,* 1230–1240.

Watson, D., & Clark, L. A. (1992). On traits and temperament: General and specific factors of emotional experience and their relation to the five-factor model. *Journal of Personality, 60,* 441–476.

Watson, J., & Rayner, R. (1920). Conditioned emotional reactions. *Journal of Experimental Psychology, 3,* 1–22.

Wellman, H. M., & Banerjee, M. (1991). Mind and emotion: Children's understanding of the emotional consequences of beliefs and desires. *British Journal of Developmental Psychology, 9,* 191–214.

Wimmer, H., & Hartl, M. (1991). The child's understanding of own false beliefs. *British Journal of Developmental Psychology, 9,* 125–138.

Winton, W. M. (1986). The role of facial response in self-reports of emotion: A critique of Laird. *Journal of Personality and Social Psychology, 50,* 808–812.

Wolf, D. P., Rygh, J., & Altshuler, J. (1984). Agency and experience: Actions and states in play narratives. In I. Bretherton (Ed.), *Symbolic play* (pp. 195–217). Orlando, FL: Academic Press.

Wolpe, J., & Rachman, S. (1960). Psychoanalytic evidence: A critique based on Freud's case of Little Hans. *Journal of Nervous and Mental Diseases, 131,* 135–145.

Yirmiya, N., Kasari, C., Sigman, M., & Mundy, P. (1989). Facial expressions of affect in autistic, mentally retarded and normal children. *Journal of Child Psychology and Psychiatry, 30,* 725–735.

Yuill, N. (1984). Young children's coordination of motive and outcome in judgements of satisfaction and morality. *British Journal of Developmental Psychology, 2,* 73–81.

Yule, W., Udwin, O., & Murdoch, K. (1990). The "Jupiter" sinking: Effects on children's fears, depression and anxiety. *Journal of Child Psychology and Psychiatry, 31,* 1051–1061.

Yule, W., & Williams, R. A. (1990). Post-traumatic stress reactions in children. *Journal of Traumatic Stress, 3,* 279–295.

Zahn-Waxler, C., & Kochanska, G. (1990). The origin of guilt. In R. A. Thompson (Ed.), *Nebraska Symposium on Motivation: Vol. 36. Socioemotional development.* Lincoln: University of Nebraska Press.

Zahn-Waxler, C., Kochanska, G., Krupnick, J., & McKnew, D. (1990). Patterns of guilt in children of depressed and well mothers. *Developmental Psychology, 26,* 51–59.

Zahn-Waxler, C., & Radke-Yarrow, M. (1982). The development of altruism: Alternative research strategies. In N. Eisenberg (Ed.), *The development of prosocial behavior* (pp. 109–137). New York: Academic Press.

Zahn-Waxler, C., Radke-Yarrow, M., & King, R. A. (1979). Child rearing and children's prosocial initiations towards victims of distress. *Child Development, 50,* 319–330.

Zajonc, R. B. (1980). Feeling and thinking: Preferences need no inferences. *American Psychologist, 35*(2), 151–175.

Zajonc, R. B. (1984). On the primacy of affect. *American Psychologist, 39,* 117–123.

Zajonc, R. B. (1985). Emotion and facial efference: A theory reclaimed. *Science, 228,* 15–21.

Zajonc, R. B., Murphy, S. T., & Inglehart, M. (1989). Feeling and facial efference: Implications of the vascular theory of emotion. *Psychological Review, 96*(3), 395–416.

Zigler, E. (1971). The retarded child as a whole person. In H. E. Adams & W. K. Boardman III (Eds.), *Advances in experimental clinical psychology* (Vol. 1, pp. 116–141). New York: Pergamon.

Zilberg, N. J., Weiss, D. S., & Horowitz, M. J. (1982). Impact of event scale: A cross-validation study and some empirical evidence supporting a conceptual model of stress response syndromes. *Journal of Consulting and Clinical Psychology, 50,* 407–414.

CHAPTER 17

Psychoanalytic Perspectives on Developmental Psychopathology

PETER FONAGY, MARY TARGET, MIRIAM STEELE, and ANDREW GERBER

PSYCHOANALYTIC THEORIES OF DEVELOPMENT: AN OVERVIEW

The emerging field of developmental psychopathology (Cicchetti, 1990a) has brought psychoanalysis and developmental psychology into close contact. The developmental approach to psychopathology is the traditional framework of psychoanalysis (see Tyson & Tyson, 1990); it aims to uncover the course of different disorders of childhood and adulthood, their developmental stages and sequelae, and factors that may influence developmental patterns in a potentially therapeutic way (Sroufe, 1990; Sroufe, Egeland, & Kreutzer, 1990). This chapter provides a review of psychoanalytic theories, including classical and contemporary structural theories, developments of ego psychological models, and British and U.S. object relational approaches. The discussion of each of these psychoanalytical schools is organized to illustrate the contributions each may be seen to provide to developmental psychopathology. It is argued that the bringing together of psychoanalysis and developmental psychopathology is a matter of making explicit what has been at the core of psychoanalytic theorizing and treatment from Freud's day onward, while acknowledging that major problems in psychoanalytic theory remain.

The psychology that Freud both discovered and invented has enjoyed considerable success as an explanatory framework for linking development and psychopathology because its few basic assumptions and propositions are open to endless elaboration, revision, and refinement, and, arguably, because the clinical procedure that provides its evidential base offers a unique perspective on the developing human mind. Most specific propositions to be reviewed in this chapter are data-dependent; that is, they may be revised or even omitted without any damage to the integrity of the psychoanalytic theoretical structure. The core assumptions of the basic psychoanalytic model (Sandler, 1962; Sandler & Joffe, 1969) include: (a) *psychic determinism*—cognitive, emotional, and behavioral aspects of pathology may be most conveniently studied in terms of psychological causes (rather than physical causality or random biological events); (b) *the pleasure-unpleasure principle*—behavior may be seen as an adaptive effort at minimizing psychic pain and maximizing psychic pleasure and a sense of intrapsychic safety; (c) *the biological nature of the organism,* which drives its psychological adaptation; (d) *the dynamic unconscious*—mental forces contend for control over access to actions and determination of which ideas and feelings may have access to consciousness; and (e) *the genetic-developmental proposition*—all behaviors are understandable as sequences of actions developing out of earlier (or even earliest infantile) events. Thus, the developmental framework lies at the very heart of all psychoanalytic formulations.

An essential idea that runs through all phases of Freud's thinking is the notion that pathology recapitulates ontogeny (see, e.g., Freud, 1905/1991b). In connection with neurosis and psychosexual development, this implies that personality types and neurotic symptoms could be linked with specific developmental stages and symptoms understood in terms of fixations at and regressions to earlier periods of normal development. For example, Freud's theory of narcissism or self-development during infancy has been regularly invoked to explain adult psychotic conditions; conversely, his view of psychic life during infancy was constructed, at least in part, on the basis of observations of adult psychopathology. His notion of infantile grandiosity was derived from the grandiosity observed in many instances of psychosis, and the presumed confusion, presumed hallucinatory experiences, and lack of reality testing of Freud's infant seem to link to the psychotic phenomena of schizophrenic and other psychotic patients. For Freud, and almost all psychoanalysts who have followed him, there is a tacit assumption of an isomorphism between pathology and development, which permits bidirectional causal inference from childhood to pathology and vice versa. The assumption is of sufficient power to cover all types of pathology and all stages of development. For example, psychosis in the first instance should be seen as a regression to infantile functioning. Neurotic pathology was developmentally dated by Freudian analysts as representing a residue of oedipal concerns, appearing mainly from the third to fifth years of life, and character disorder was placed somewhere in between the infantile and the oedipal stages, mostly from the second year of life.

Despite these apparently fixed assumptions, psychoanalytic theory is not a static body of knowledge; rather, it is in a state of constant evolution. Historically, it has evolved from an early concentration on identifying the roles of instinct in development and psychopathology (drive theory) to a focus on the development and functions of the ego (ego psychology), to a current interest in the early mother-infant dyad and its long-term effect on interpersonal relationships and their internal representation (object relations). Concurrently, a psychology of the self has evolved as part of most psychoanalytic theories. With its integration into mainstream theories, there is a better conceptual basis for a comprehensive and phenomenological clinical theory. There has been movement away from metapsychological constructs couched in a natural science framework and toward an experience-near clinical theory that has the representational world as its core focus (see particularly Jacobson, 1964; Sandler, 1962). Contemporary theories attempt to trace the elusive link between formative interpersonal relationships and the complex interactions that underpin them, and the formation of mental structures throughout development.

This theoretical move was made possible by two factors: (a) observation-based psychoanalytic developmental theories (Mahler, Pine, & Bergman, 1975) and (b) the development of object relations theory, which, within a developmental framework, explores the evolution of a differentiated, cohesive, and integrated representational world within the context of a mother-infant matrix that Winnicott (1960) termed "the holding environment." At its broadest, object relations theory concerns the development of schemata from a diffuse set of sensorimotor experiences in the infant, into a differentiated, consistent, and relatively realistic representation of the self and object in interaction. This evolution is toward increasingly symbolic levels of representation, but with the general assumption that earlier levels of representations of interactions are retained in the mind and continue to exert influence.

Freud's (1905/1991b) psychosexual theory of development was revolutionary in presenting a predominantly developmental view of adult psychopathology; he began to construct an understanding of adult disturbances in terms of infantile and early childhood experience. The details of the model were etched in by Abraham (1927/1979), who identified specific links between character formation, neurosis, and psychosis on the one hand, and instinctual development on the other. Contemporary followers of Freud proposed alternative foci for clinical study, but all were based on developmental formulations. Adler's (1916) focus was on the child's feelings of inferiority as the roots of the adult's striving for power and maturity; Ferenczi (1913/1980) outlined the vicissitudes of the child's development of a sense of reality and the simultaneous sacrifice of fantasized omnipotence; Rank's (1924/1929) focus was on an even earlier time—that of the birth trauma—which, in his view, underpinned all subsequent human conflicts, defenses, and strivings; and even Jung's (1913/1949) model may be considered a developmental one, if in a somewhat negative sense, for he proposed that true maturity and mental health lie in the giving up of the "child-self."

More recent psychoanalytic theories continue to follow a strictly developmental motif. Anna Freud (1936/1946) provided a developmental model of ego defenses and, later (1965), a comprehensive model of psychopathology based on the dimensions of normal and abnormal personality development. Melanie Klein (1935/1975a), influenced by Ferenczi and Abraham, was a pioneer in linking interpersonal relationships to instinctual developmental factors to provide a radically different perspective both on severe mental disorders and on child development. Meanwhile, in the United States, Heinz Hartmann, with Ernst Kris and Rudolph Loewenstein (1946), provided an alternative, developmentally oriented framework that focused on the evolution of mental structures necessary for adaptation, and elaborated on the common developmental conflicts between mental structures in early childhood. Margaret Mahler and her colleagues (1975) provided psychoanalysts in the American tradition with a dynamic map of the first three years of life, and ample opportunities for tracing the developmental origins of disorders. Fairbairn (1952a) traced the development of object seeking from immature to mature dependence; Jacobson (1964) explored the development of representations of self and other. Kernberg (1975) drew on previous work by Klein, Hartmann, and Jacobson to furnish a developmental model of borderline and narcissistic disturbances; Kohut (1977) constructed a model of narcissistic disturbances based on presumed deficits of early parenting.

Unfortunately, early theories have not been supplanted in the minds of analysts by later formulations, and most psychoanalytic writers assume that a number of explanatory frameworks are necessary to account for the relationship of development and psychopathology (see Sandler, 1983). So-called neurotic psychopathology is presumed to originate in later childhood, at a time when there is self-other differentiation and when the various agencies of the mind (id, ego, superego) have been firmly established. The structural frame of reference (Arlow & Brenner, 1964) is most commonly used in developmental accounts of these disorders. Personality or character disorders, as well as most nonneurotic psychiatric disorders, are most commonly looked at in frameworks developed subsequent to structural theory (e.g., borderline personality disorder, narcissistic and schizoid personality disorders). Here, a variety of theoretical frameworks are available, including the structural, most of which point to developmental pathology arising when psychic structures are still in formation (see for example, Kohut, 1971; Modell, 1985).

CONTROVERSIAL ISSUES

Psychoanalytic theories of development are plagued by a number of long-standing debates. It may be helpful to mention them, because they provide the dimensions along which models may be evaluated.

1. Are psychoanalytic accounts biased toward abnormality because, in most cases, developmental propositions are retrospective extrapolations from clinical observations based either exclusively on adult patients, particularly those with severe disturbances, or on children who have not progressed in developmentally expectable ways?
2. Do clinically based developmental accounts merely mirror the specific meta-psychological commitment of the author (Klein, 1976b) and the population of patients that has preoccupied particular theoreticians (Holzman, 1985)?
3. What is the relative importance of early childhood (infantile) experiences in contrast to later oedipal and middle-childhood events (see Cooper, 1983)?

4. Is the self an individual (intrapsychic) construction as conceived by Freud, or is it an intersubjective (interpersonal) unit derived from the interaction of mother and infant (Winnicott, 1956) or infant and self-objects (Kohut, 1971)?
5. Is the basic constitution of human nature in conflict with its environment, which must tame and inhibit it as Freud (1930/1991) and Klein (1957/1975b) conceived, or is it potentially consonant with the external world, provided that the latter does not thwart its desire for self-actualization through malevolence and unresponsiveness (Kohut, 1977; Sullivan, 1953; Winnicott, 1965c)?
6. Can stage theory used to describe child development be extended to the adult, as, for example, Erikson (1950) suggested (see also Benedek, 1959; Bibring, Dwyer, Huntington, & Vallenstein, 1961), or is development better seen as the repetition of characteristic positions throughout an individual's life course (Klein, 1946/1975e)?
7. If development continues throughout life, is such development merely a shift of concerns (e.g., Colarusso & Nemiroff, 1981; Pollock, 1981; Tyson & Tyson, 1990), or does the structure of the mind remain flexible, and open to drastic alteration and the generation of new structures (Emde, 1985; Settlage, Curtis, Lozoff, Silberschatz, & Simburg, 1988)?

We will return to many of these issues at the end of the chapter.

MAJOR SHIFTS IN FREUD'S MODEL OF DEVELOPMENT

Freud (1895/1991) initially believed that he had discovered the etiology of neurosis in the actual event of childhood seduction. In this conception, the interpersonal event of the early trauma was represented in a distorted form in the neurotic symptom. For example, an 8-year-old child with hysterical blindness may have achieved relative internal safety by "shutting his eyes" to the memory of having witnessed his mother's rape. This model posited no mental apparatus and reflected only the physical conversion of energy.

When Freud turned away from his seduction hypothesis in favor of his second model, emphasizing fantasy organized by a biological drive state, psychoanalytic theory moved away from a social theory of development. Freud (1905/1991b) attempted to explain all actions in terms of the failure of the child's mental apparatus to deal adequately with the pressures of a predetermined sequence of drive states. Adult psychopathologies, as well as dreaming, jokes, and parapraxes, were seen as the revisiting of unresolved childhood conflicts over sexuality (Freud, 1900/1991, 1901/1991, 1905/1991a). For example, he saw anxiety as arising from the failure of repression of unacceptable sexual wishes (Freud, 1905/1991b).

The influence of the social environment again found a preeminent place with the second major shift in Freud's thinking (Freud, 1920/1991, 1923/1991, 1926/1991). A new structural theory, which grew and prospered long after Freud, arose because of its compelling fit with clinical experience in the dual-instinct theory (sexuality and aggression) (Freud, 1920/1991). For example, the significance for psychopathology of the child's struggle with innate destructive and self-destructive forces was finally fully recognized. Freud (1926/1991) also revised his view of anxiety: formerly seen as a biologically determined epiphenomenal experience associated with inhibited drives, anxiety was now a psychological state linked to the perception of internal (instinctual or moral) or external danger. The danger situation was specified as the fear of helplessness resulting from loss (loss of the mother or of her esteem; loss of a body part; loss of self-regard). This revision restored adaptation to the external world as an essential part of the psychoanalytic account, and recast the theory into more cognitive terms (Schafer, 1983). Freud nevertheless retained the concept of a more primitive form of anxiety that arises in an involuntary automatic way and is warded off with the help of *signal anxiety,* which functions to limit the threat of a basic danger situation (see Yorke, Kennedy, & Wiseberg, 1981).

This final revision in Freud's thinking provided a developmental framework based around the tripartite structural schema of id, ego, and superego (Freud, 1923/1961, 1933/1991, 1940/1991). The hypothesis that conflicts within the mind are chiefly organized around three themes—(a) wish versus moral injunction, (b) wish versus reality, and (c) internal reality versus external reality—has had extraordinary explanatory power. In particular, the ego's capacity to create defenses that organize characterological and symptomatic constructions as part of the developmental process became the cornerstone of psychoanalytic theorization and clinical work in the United States and the United Kingdom.

Perhaps the most important post-Freudian contributions have been in the domains of the cultural and social context of development: the significance of early childhood experiences; the developmental significance of the real behavior of the real parents; the role of dependency, attachment, and safety in development, alongside the role of instinctual drives; the synthesizing function of the self; and the importance of the nonconflictual aspects of development. Many of these shortcomings were pointed out by Freud's contemporaries but were not recognized at the time because of Freud's efforts to exclude them from the psychoanalytic mainstream. For example, Jung's rejection of libido theory drew attention away from the undoubted advances he made in the understanding of narcissism and from his development of a theory of the self throughout the life cycle (Jung, 1916).

THE STRUCTURAL APPROACH TO DEVELOPMENT

Hartmann's Ego Psychology Model

Freud (1923/1961) introduced the tripartite or structural model of the mind as composed of instinctual derivatives (id), an internalization of parental authority (the superego), and a structure independent of both these pressures and oriented toward internal and external adaptation (the ego). In *Inhibitions, Symptoms, and Anxiety* (1926/1991), he added that innate features and the social environment both play important roles in the evolution of these structures and in the conflictual interactions among them. Freud's proposed sequence for the development of the libidinal drive in relation to different erotogenic zones remained the cornerstone of developmental theory until the advent of ego psychology (Hartmann et al., 1946).

Freud's model was refined and advanced in the ego psychology of Heinz Hartmann and his colleagues. Hartmann (1939/1958) demonstrated how psychoanalysts frequently used the developmental point of view in an oversimplified and reductionist way. His concept of the "change of function" (Hartmann, 1939/1958) highlighted how behavior originating at one point in development may serve an entirely different function later on. For example, the internalization of parental injunction may, through the mechanism of reaction formation, lead the child to repudiate the anal wish to mess and soil and become excessively clean and orderly. The same behavior in the adult may serve quite different functions and is likely to be independent—that is, to have achieved *secondary autonomy* (Hartmann, 1950/1964)—from the original wish. The failure to recognize this discontinuity has been termed the *genetic fallacy* (Hartmann, 1955/1964). Similarly, the persistence of dependent behavior in adulthood cannot be treated as if it were a simple repetition of the individual's early relationship with the mother. Sandler and Dare (1970) pointed out that, whereas the infant's first year of life may be considered as characterized by oral dependency, such longings are likely to occur at any phase, during times of stress, when the child wishes to have what he or she fantasizes. Adult behaviors are invariably seen as having multiple functions (Brenner, 1959; Waelder, 1930/1976).

Hartmann's admonition continues to be relevant. The identification of what are presumed to be primitive modes of mental functioning in individuals with severe personality disorders (e.g., Kernberg, 1975; Kohut, 1977) is often regarded as evidence for the persistence or regressive recurrence of early pathogenic developmental experiences. Yet, even if splitting or identity diffusion were representative of early modes of thought (an issue that is, in any case, highly controversial; see Westen, 1990b), their reemergence in adult mental functioning may be linked to later or persistent trauma. The structural view of development, perhaps more than any other psychoanalytic developmental framework, attempts to take a holistic view of the developmental process, resisting the temptation to identify particular, especially early, critical periods (Tyson & Tyson, 1990).

Hartmann et al. (1946) postulated an initial undifferentiated matrix, which contains the individual's endowment and from which both the id and the ego originate. They also introduced the concept of an *average expectable environment,* affirming the importance of the parental contribution to development, and outlined a scheme for the phase-specific maturation of autonomous, conflict-free ego functions, accommodating both environmental and maturational influences. They described the gradual differentiation of the self from the world during the first half of the first year, and the evolution of the child's relationship to his or her own body and objects in the second half, as the influence of the reality principle is increasingly felt. In the second year, an ego-id differentiation phase emerges, marked by ambivalence, as the reality principle begins to assert its influence over the pleasure principle. The final phase is that of superego differentiation as a consequence of social influences, identification with parental values, and the resolution of the oedipal conflict. Rapaport (1950) suggested a stage theory of the development of thinking: the individual proceeds from hallucinatory wish fulfillment through the drive organization of memories, to primitive modes of ideation and the conceptual organization of memories, and finally attains the capacity for abstract thought.

Structural theorists see development as driven by a maturational pull whereby independently emerging components and functions come to be linked, forming a coherently functioning organization (the ego) that is more complex than the sum of its parts (Hartmann, 1939/1958). Stages of ego development represent nodal points at which *fixation* may occur and to which, under the pressure of intense internal conflict, the individual may return. For example, obsessive-compulsive disorder is seen by structural theorists (Arlow & Brenner, 1964) as a regression to the phase of ego functioning characteristic of the 2-year-old (magical phenomenalism; repetitive, ritualistic behaviors). Kris (1952), however, emphasized that ego regressions should be considered part of normal development and may serve adaptive functions in, for example, artistic or scientific creativity. (See Blos, 1962, for an exposition of adaptive ego regression in adolescent development.) Abrams (1977) pointed out that the forward spurts of internal reorganization are frequently accompanied by "backward slides," and the recapitulation or reemergence of earlier structures in later developmental phases is a ubiquitous observation of psychoanalytic theoreticians (Brody & Axelrad, 1970; Neubauer, 1984). J. Sandler and A. -M. Sandler (1992) went so far as to suggest that active inhibition of a natural regressive tendency is essential in order for the position of the individual to be maintained at a particular developmental phase.

Partly in response to the growth of object relations theory (see below), there has been a revival of the structural theory in psychoanalysis. Modern structural theory (see, e.g., Boesky, 1989) retains Freud's tripartite model of id, ego, and superego, but dispenses with concepts of psychic energy and other problematic notions. The theory takes as its central premise the ubiquitous nature of internal psychic conflict; Brenner (1982) suggested that all mental contents (thoughts, symptoms, etc.) are compromises among an intense wish, an unpleasant affect in relation to the wish, a defense against the wish, and guilt or atonement. From a developmental standpoint, the interrelationship of these psychic agencies is studied, rather than either chronological age or libidinal phase.

Developmental Work within the Structural Model

An important developmental schema was proposed by Erikson (1950), whose primary concern was the interaction of social norms and biological drives in generating self and identity. His well-known description of eight developmental stages was based on biologically determined life events that disturb the equilibrium between drives and social adjustment. Personality would be arrested if the developmental challenge was not mastered through the evolution of new skills and attitudes, and later developmental stages would be compromised. Erikson was remarkable among psychoanalysts for his attention to cultural and family factors and his extension of the developmental model to the entire life cycle. His theory introduced plasticity to the psychoanalytical developmental model, as well as attributing critical importance to the need for a coherent concept of self fulfilled in a supportive social milieu (see Stechler & Kaplan, 1980).

René Spitz (1959), one of the first empiricists of the psychoanalytic tradition, formulated a general understanding of the developmental process in structural terms as early as 1936. He drew on Kurt Lewin's (1952) field theory as well as embryology (Spemann, 1938) and proposed that major shifts in psychological organization, marked by the emergence of new behaviors and new forms of affective expression (e.g., social smiling), occur when functions are brought into new relation with one another and are linked into a coherent unit. He drew attention to the meaning of new forms of emotional expression such as initial differentiation of self and object, 8-month anxiety indicating differentiation among objects, and the assertion of self in the "no" gesture between 10 and 18 months. The way in which these *psychic organizers* herald dramatic changes in interpersonal interactions was elaborated in a highly influential series of papers by Robert Emde (1980a, 1980b, 1980c). Spitz saw self-regulation as an important function of the ego. Psychoanalytic observational studies repeatedly showed the ways in which constitutional, early environmental, and interactional factors contribute to the self-regulatory process, leading to adaptation or maladaptation (Greenacre, 1952; Spitz, 1959; Weil, 1978). In particular, psychoanalysts have highlighted the role of affect; the mother's emotional expression at first serves a "soothing" or "containing" function, which facilitates the restoration of emotional equilibrium. Later, the infant uses the mother's emotional response as a signaling device to indicate safety. Later still, the infant internalizes the affective response and uses his or her own emotional reaction as a signal of safety or danger (Call, 1984; Emde, 1980c).

Edith Jacobson (1964) reconstructed a wide variety of sequences over the life span on the basis of her experience of adult patients. She included in her theory the emergence of self and object representations, and advanced the idea that the infant acquires self and object images with good or bad valences, depending on experiences of gratification or frustration with the caretaker. She used the term *self-representation* to stress the notion of the self and object as they were experienced, as distinguished from external objects. She stated that the ego was a structure—in contrast to the self, which is the totality of the bodily and psychic person. She assumed that early drive states shifted continuously from object to self with very weak boundaries between them. Distributional (good versus bad) and directional (self versus other) considerations were thought to shape all future growth as more stable self and object representations emerge. She assumed that, through introjections and identifications, traits and actions of objects became internalized parts of self-images. She was particularly concerned with superego formation, which she saw as initially polarized between pleasure and unpleasure, then by issues of strength and weakness, and finally as the internalization of ethical considerations that regulate self-esteem as well as behavior. Jacobson applied her developmental perspective to a wide variety of disorders, most particularly to depression. She was the first psychoanalyst to suggest that depression was associated with the gap at an unconscious level, between self-representation and ego ideal.

Settlage et al. (1988) proposed a novel structural view of development across the life span. They considered the stimulus for development to be a disturbance of the previously adequate self-regulatory functioning, which creates a disequilibrium with varying degrees of emotional stress. Such *developmental challenges* may be caused by biological maturation, environmental demand, traumatic experiences, or, simply, the perception of superior possibilities for adaptation. The motivating tension can lead to regression, which may involve pathological solutions, or to progression through conflict, resolved by adaptive structure formation or reorganization—in Piagetian (1958/1977) terms, accommodation or assimilation self-regulated by means of equilibration. For example, pregnancy (Bibring et al., 1961) or parenthood (Benedek, 1959) may serve as the stimulus for psychic reorganization.

There are serious doubts about the viability of such a Piagetian/constructivist model of the process of internalization. Developmentalists and cognitive scientists have demonstrated that Piaget's *conflict-equilibration model* of cognitive development provides only a partial account of the internalization process leading to the establishment of more and more complex levels of structural representation (see Piattelli-Palmarini, 1980). More recent developmental writings appear to favor a constitutional hypothesis of language acquisition, concept formation, object and event perception, thinking and reasoning, and causal perception (Bower, 1989; Chomsky, 1968; Fodor, 1981; Gelman & Baillargeon, 1983; Leslie, 1986; Meltzoff, 1990). These have more in common with Kleinian than with structural developmental theory (see below). Both approaches assume a rich, domain-specific, constitutionally given structural basis for the acquisition of higher-order knowledge structures.

Criticism was raised in the 1960s against the associationist learning theory account of development, on the grounds that it could not explain the internalization of highly complex and abstract structures that must be posited to account for human cognitive capacities, such as language (e.g., Chomsky, 1968). This objection is equally applicable to some aspects of the structural theory of development (Gergely, 1991). The originators of the theory were increasingly forced to move away from the notion that ego capacities could be seen as evolving out of the "taming of instinctual desires," and were forced to resort to a nativistic account (see, e.g., Rapaport, 1958).

A STRUCTURAL MODEL OF DEVELOPMENTAL PSYCHOPATHOLOGY

The classical developmental model of the neurosis is well known, and we will not elaborate it in detail here. Childhood sexual wishes arouse conscious repugnance when experienced in adulthood, and therefore can reach awareness only when disguised. The neurotic compromise involves a disguised id derivative of childhood sexuality, the ego's defense, and signal anxiety marking the ego's experience of internal danger. It unifies the wish and the reaction against it in a part of the personality that is experienced as separate (ego dystonic). This compromise is characterized by a subjective experience of punishment, suffering, and irritation, which originates from, and is designed to placate, the superego.

Within the structural model, psychosis as well as neurosis is seen as arising when an individual's urge for drive gratification reverts from an age-appropriate mode of satisfaction to a formerly outgrown infantile mode. Such regressions are brought about by psychic conflict that the ego is incapable of resolving. The id's regression and the associated revival of infantile urges intensify the clash with parts of the personality that have maintained a mature level of functioning, and intense internal conflict is the outcome. The ego's failure to manage such conflict, manifested in the intensification of guilt and drive demands, and the greater inappropriateness of these demands as a consequence of the regression lead to the formation of symptoms. Symptoms are compromises, reflecting the ego's attempts to restore inner equilibrium. In other cases, the ego regression itself, owing to psychological and organic causes, results in pathology. In psychosis, the ego is seen as threatened by complete dissolution. Essential ego functions come to be dominated by irrational, magical thought and a failure to control impulses. Thus, although mental health is seen as harmonious interaction between psychic agencies that function at age-appropriate levels, mental ill health is seen as the result of the ego's attempt to reconcile impulses and aims that may become contradictory when seen across the different stages of development. The pathogenic sequence is then as follows: (a) frustration, (b) regression, (c) internal incompatibility, (d) signal anxiety, (e) defense by regression, (f) return of the repressed, and (g) compromise formation and symptomatic disorders.

Symptomatic disorders are not the invariable developmental consequences of childhood fixations. Within the classical structural model, inhibition is seen as a powerful way of reducing conflict between the psychic agencies, and extreme levels can lead to personality disorders (Freud, 1926/1991). An individual who avoids any kind of human contact that might stimulate drives and their associated affects, may be seen as schizoid in personality type; sexual inadequacy (erectile dysfunction) may be seen as the inhibition of the expression of the sexual drive. An ego function that has become psychically painful may be abandoned (A. Freud, 1936/1946). Restriction of affect may occur in individuals who experience emotion as highly threatening.

The Structural Theory of Personality Disorder

Whereas notions of neurotic pathology have, on the whole, evolved little since the structural theory of Freud, models of personality disorder have become paradigmatic of various psychoanalytic models. As subsequent sections will illustrate, extremes of personality types are formulated radically differently in diverse theoretical models. Classical psychoanalysis, embodied in the structural model, also offers a view of personality disorders, often sharply contrasting with more recent models, as if to demonstrate that a revision of psychoanalytic theory is unnecessary. Some have examined post-Freudian contributions to the field of character neurosis, pointing to many ambiguities. Others have opposed distinctions between severe personality disorders when these do not correspond to theoretical differences in terms of the structural frame of reference. Rangell (1982), for example, said that the differentiation between borderline states and narcissistic disorders is a false one, and that these groups should be brought together under the rubric of "disturbed cases."

Structural theory distinguishes those character disorders that resemble neurosis in terms of dynamic considerations and those that reflect a nonneurotic pattern based on structural deficit (see Waelder, 1960). The so-called character neurosis (a concept introduced by Alexander, 1930) of the former category is assumed to be dynamically similar to neurosis except that symptoms are not experienced as alien or ego-dystonic. Yorke, Wiseberg, and Freeman (1989) referred to microstructures of character neurosis, which, like the microstructures of id, ego, and superego, become synthesized and achieve permanence within the personality. The obsessional character neurosis reflects the same compromise among id derivatives, ego, and superego; the critical difference is that the drive derivatives are better tolerated.

The notion of character neurosis is a problematic one. It suggests some kind of continuum between disorder and character type, the difference being chiefly in quantity rather than quality. There is good evidence that certain typical neurotic reactions may be found in nonclinical subjects, in character types, as well as in disorders. For example, Rachman and de Silva (1978) found that transient obsessions and compulsions occur within a fairly large proportion of the population, whereas the prevalence of the disorder is relatively low. There is some evidence to suggest that frank obsessions or compulsions correlate with obsessional traits (Flament & Rapaport, 1984); however, only 15% to 20% of obsessive-compulsive disordered children have what may be termed obsessive character neurosis (Swedo, Rapoport, Leonard, & Lenane, 1989). These findings suggest that the continuum model of character neurosis is inappropriate, and that character pathology and neurotic symptomatology imply different underlying processes (King & Noshpitz, 1990).

More severe personality disorders, such as narcissistic personality disorder, are regarded as consequences of a developmental arrest or deviation. The structural view of such cases tends to be in terms of faulty ego development (Frank, 1956; Gitelson, 1955; Rangell, 1955). Important ego functions such as reality testing, anxiety tolerance, and stable defenses are impaired, but others appear to retain their integrity, thus giving the patient a semblance of normality.

A Model of Borderline Personality Disorder

Individuals with borderline personality disorder were initially described in the psychoanalytic literature as unlikely to do well in classical psychoanalysis (Deutsch, 1942; Stern, 1938). The issue of modification of classical technique was raised at an early stage (Schmideberg, 1947). Knight (1953) was the first to propose a comprehensive developmental model of the disorder in terms of ego functions impaired by traumatic development. Among the ego functions he considered were "integration, concept formation, judgment, realistic planning, and defending against eruption into conscious thinking of id impulses and their fantasy elaborations" (p. 6). Erikson (1959), in his epigenetic sequence of identity formation, described the syndrome of identity diffusion as reflecting deficiencies in continuity of self-experience, and a feeling of affiliation with a social group of reference. Jacobson (1964) drew attention to how these individuals, at times, experience their mental functions and bodily organs not as belonging to them, but as objects that they wish to expel. She saw these individuals as retaining an "adolescent fluidity of moods" (p. 159). Abend, Porder, and Willick (1983), however, questioned the usefulness of the term *borderline*. They maintained that profound ego weakness and identification with disturbed parents were the only characteristics that separated these patients from those with neurotic disorders. Otherwise, their disturbance could be understood as reflecting a regressive defense against deeply disturbing oedipal issues.

The Structural Theory of Antisocial Personality Disorder

Aichhorn (1925/1935) was the first psychoanalyst to work seriously with delinquent individuals. He posited a failure of progression from the pleasure principle to the reality principle, with a corresponding malformation of the superego. He stressed deprivation as impeding the renunciation of the pleasure principle, and the internalization of poor parental norms as an explanation of superego dysfunction. Reich (1933) suggested that the ego kept the superego at a distance, causing it to be isolated and therefore unable to prevent the individual from yielding to an impulse. Fenichel (1946) emphasized that the superego was not absent in these individuals, but pathological; not just isolated by the ego, but also "bribed." Johnson and Szurek (1952) suggested that superego lacunae (lack of superego in certain circumscribed areas) form, because of the parents' unconscious wish to act out forbidden impulses; the child is unconsciously encouraged by the parents to act in amoral ways, but consciously discouraged from doing so. Lampl-de-Groot (1949) suggested that the relative strengths of the superego and ego ideal explained why certain individuals became neurotically depressed and others became antisocial. The former corresponds to a severe superego and strong ego ideal, and the latter is a consequence of a menacing superego and a weak ego ideal. Singer (1975) proposed a tripartite model of antisocial personality: (a) drive disturbances (e.g., stealing as acquiring an aggrandized penis to undo hidden feelings of being small, impotent); (b) disturbances of ego functions (e.g., disturbed reality testing, inability to delay action by fantasy); and (c) superego, which is corruptible (Alexander, 1930), isolated (Greenacre, 1945), and riddled with lacunae (Johnson & Szurek, 1952).

Critique and Evaluation

The notion of the id has changed in current structural theory (Arlow & Brenner, 1964; Hayman, 1969; Schur, 1966). Instincts are no longer seen as firmly anchored to developmental stages (Greenacre, 1952), and the simplistic drive-reduction model has been abandoned by most theoreticians (Sandler, 1985). The quasi-physiological character of the original model has been the subject of intense criticism (Compton, 1981; Klein, 1976a; Rosenblatt & Thickstun, 1977b). Schafer (1974) criticized the classical model on the grounds that it forces us to consider all forms of sexual pleasure, other than heterosexual genital sexuality, as abnormal (arrested or deviant). Others saw the primacy of sexuality in explanations of psychopathology as a misconception (Klein, 1981; Peterfreund, 1978). Fonagy and Target (in press b) suggest that the apparent centrality of conflicts related to bodily functions in many forms of psychological disturbance is misleading; frequently, the failure to resolve psychological conflicts in the domain of ideas and wishes causes them to be experienced somatically (rather than vice versa). Because the body is not an appropriate arena for the resolution of psychological conflict, the conflict can become intensified at the level of drives or instincts—for example, through aggression.

MODIFICATIONS AND DEVELOPMENTS OF THE STRUCTURAL MODEL

Anna Freud's Developmental Model

Developmental Lines and Other Developmental Concepts

That development is both cumulative and epigenetic (i.e., each developmental phase is constructed on the previous one) is a fundamental tenet of all psychoanalytic developmental models. Anna Freud (1965) was one of the first to adopt a coherent developmental perspective on psychopathology. She provided a comprehensive developmental theory using the metaphor of developmental lines and stressing the interactions and interdependencies between maturational and environmental determinants in developmental steps. For example, aspects of the child's relationship to the mother may be described as a line moving from "dependency to emotional self-reliance to adult object relationships," "from sucking to rational eating," "from wetting and soiling to bladder and bowel control," and "from irresponsibility to responsibility in body management." Other lines, such as the movement from egocentrism to social partnership, are concerned with the mastery of the environment. Pathology is assessed (Yorke, 1980) in terms of large discrepancies between positions along the lines and notable lags along each line.

The notion of developmental lines is important for two reasons. First, it evaluates the child's emotional maturity or immaturity apart from psychiatric symptoms. It could also be integrated with the second axis of diagnosis (American Psychiatric Association, 1987, 1994) with prognostic implications. The developmental lines focus the clinician on (a) the phase-appropriate developmental issues, (b) the meaning of the behavior in the context of the phase, and (c) the profile of adaptation shown by the child's cutting across aspects of development. Second, unevenness of development may be regarded as a risk factor for psychiatric disturbance; a child's problem may be understood in terms of arrest or regression on a particular line of development. The clinical implication is that the psychoanalytic clinician should focus not only on the determinants of symptomatic aspects of the disorder, but also on offering "developmental help" to the child and restoring him or her to the "path of normal development" (Fonagy & Target, in press a; A. Freud, 1976/1981; Kennedy & Moran, 1991).

Anna Freud's Views of Developmental Psychopathology

General Model of Pathology. Anna Freud (1955/1968) regarded the child as enormously resilient, with a self-righting capacity to return to the course of normal development after trauma. Her views foreshadowed recent questioning of the inevitability of pathogenic effects of early deprivation (e.g., Anthony & Cohler, 1987).

Structural theorists (Boesky, 1989; Brenner, 1982), following Hartmann, have repeatedly stressed that the child is continually challenged by incompatibility, and is constitutionally capable of resolving conflict by environmental manipulation and the internalization of conflict, leading to internal compromises and the modification of psychic structure. Nagera (1966), strongly influenced by the work of Anna Freud, termed these conflicts "developmental" in order to stress the expectable and usually transitory nature of the tensions and, sometimes, the symptoms that accompany progress. The mother's phase-appropriate demands for bowel control may lead to temper tantrums, which subside as the conflict is internalized and an equilibrium is reestablished. Developmental conflicts may be potentially resolvable (convergent) or inherently insoluble (divergent) (see Kris, 1984). In the latter case, the child faces incompatible but equally desirable courses of action, such as masculinity and femininity or dependence and autonomy. Divergent conflicts remain part of the ego and may create subsequent difficulties for the individual in specific situations—for example, in initiating sexual relationships.

An "Anna Freudian" Model of Anxiety. Yorke and his coworkers (Yorke et al., 1989) put forward a developmental model of anxiety that illustrates well the "Anna Freudian" psychoanalytic approach. They proposed that anxiety matures from a diffuse somatic excitation to signal anxiety as conceived by Freud (1926/1991). At a stage when the infant is seen as part of an undifferentiated mother-baby unit, the pathways between psyche and soma are assumed to remain open so that psychic tension will be discharged somatically. As mentalization is established (but the ego's capacity to regulate affect is still limited), such somatic experiences give way to experiences of psychic panic, as seen in temper tantrums. The preverbal child is easily plunged into complete helplessness by automatic anxiety, which can be alleviated only by outside intervention from an auxiliary ego.

With the development of thought and language ("trial action"; Freud, 1933/1991), the ego acquires the capacity to use "trial affect" where anxiety is restricted to a signal level. This capacity allows for the restriction of anxiety by crude defensive measures such as denial or projection. During the phallic and oedipal phases (3–5 years old), there is a fear of helplessness; but the anxiety is not automatic, although it remains pervasive. With latency, anxiety becomes a signal for the use of increasingly mature defenses, such as rationalization, intellectualization, and humor. The support of parents, teachers, and peers, as well as social institutions, is essential to maintain the child's developmental progress at this stage. Biological maturation at puberty can lead to a reemergence of the basic anxiety and a shift back to pervasive or even automatic forms.

The assumption that pervasive panic and helplessness are the predominant modes of emotional expression during infancy and early childhood is not well supported by empirical evidence. As we will detail below, such a view may underestimate the constitutional capacities of infants and young children. Harris (1989), who martialed a substantial body of observational and experimental data that illustrate the surprisingly rapid development of emotional processing in infants, found little evidence to support the notion of primitive affects at early stages of development (see also Emde, 1980b; Stern, 1985).

The Notion of Developmental Disharmonies. Anna Freud proposed that discrepancies between the relative strengths of the psychic agencies result from constitutional and environmental factors and may be critical for a predisposition to psychopathology. Normal development is threatened, for example, if parental support is withdrawn too early, leaving the child confronted with archaic fears of being alone or in the dark, and requiring the adult's participation as an auxiliary ego. If the ego matures too late or if the parents are neglecting, the child may tend to regress to earlier, more intense forms of anxiety. The child's capacity to develop an independent identity may also be jeopardized by an inability to move away from the mother (e.g., as a consequence of physical handicap) or to ascertain the mother's distal presence, for example, as a result of blindness (see Wills, 1965). Developmental pathology is seen as separate and to some degree independent of the symptomatic pathology of Hartmann's structural model; a simple insight-oriented treatment method is unlikely to be able to tackle the psychological difficulties faced by such a child (A. Freud, 1974; Kennedy & Yorke, 1980). Treatment directed toward developmental assistance may, however, help to correct developmental discrepancies (Fonagy & Target, in press a). Minor degrees of disharmony are ubiquitous (Yorke et al., 1989), but gross disharmony may in itself constitute pathology as well as being the focus of later neurotic development. In general terms, disharmony is seen as a "fertile breeding ground" (A. Freud, 1981) for later neurosis and more severe psychopathology and as the major constituent of nonneurotic developmental disturbances of the personality (personality disorders).

The Anna Freudian Model of Severe Personality Disorders. Anna Freud agreed with structural theorists that severe personality disorders reflect structural deficits, for example, in reality testing, capacity for anxiety tolerance, and superego development. She explained these as developmental deviations or disharmonies. For example, Yorke et al. (1989) suggested that inadequate response by the mother to an infant's instinctual needs creates conflict, most intensely felt when structuralization is not ready to sustain the pressures caused by the internal and external stresses. Ego development will suffer because the internalizing and identificatory processes will be specifically threatened. Object constancy, for example, may not develop if the early relationship with the mother is disrupted by trauma. Narcissistic character disorder is seen as rooted in early emotional deprivation, which compromises the process by which representations of people are invested with instinctual energy. The individual attempts to identify with the frustrating and disappointing object, providing a focus for attachment that heightens narcissism and egocentrism.

Evaluation

Developmental conflict should be differentiated from *developmental interference* (Nagera, 1966), where environmental demands are so grossly out of keeping with the child's needs that the consequent frustration and distress interfere with the child's forward movement. Conflict may lead to neurotic compromises where, for example, keeping the mother's affection is at odds with the desire for unrestricted gratification and leads to neurotic inhibition of aggressive or libidinal wishes. *Infantile neurosis* implies that internalized conflict was not tackled successfully by the developing ego, and the conflict of drive-related wishes and internalized standards (superego) threatens the ego's sense of safety. Such infantile neurosis may be crippling and may significantly interfere with the child's development; yet the underlying conflict falls into the expectable range, is resolved by further maturational development of the mental structures, and motivates further adaptive efforts and independent psychological functioning. Developmental interference will disrupt the process of development itself and may result in the inhibition of entire psychological functions such as abstract thinking (Weil, 1978), body integrity (Greenacre, 1952), or the capacity for mentalization (Fonagy & Moran, 1991).

The model suggested by Anna Freud, who may be considered to be a modern structural theorist, is fundamentally developmental, at least in that the individual is seen as capable of moving back along developmental lines to deal with some current, potentially overwhelming challenge, and then moving forward again. Also, within this framework, a given behavior may reflect a temporary or circumstantial perturbation rather than a true symptom. These ideas (mobility of function and the meaning of behavior) are key assumptions of developmental approaches to psychopathology (Cicchetti, 1984, 1989; Sroufe, 1989; Sroufe & Rutter, 1984). Anna Freud's model is limited by its literal use of the structural model of drives (the balance among id, ego, and superego, drive fixation, and so on). She was unwilling to abandon what she perceived as the most scientific aspect of her father's contribution. Her use of metaphors as part of causal accounts naturally risks reification, which some of her followers avoided through the development of less reductionist theoretical frameworks. Interestingly, her observational work during World War II, in the Hampstead Nurseries (A. Freud, 1941–1945/1974), yielded many findings consistent with those of contemporary developmental research (e.g., the development of attachment relationships during the first 6 months of life, the rise in ambivalence to the caregiver at 6–12 months, the parent's use of withdrawal of affection to socialize the child, the early sociability of the infant). Unfortunately, her work was buried in the annual report of the Nurseries, and her later work was driven by theory and clinical observation of later developmental phases and draws little on her early findings (Tyson & Tyson, 1990).

Margaret Mahler's Developmental Model

Margaret Mahler (Mahler & Furer, 1968; Mahler, Pine, & Bergman, 1975) offered a developmental model within which object relations and the self are seen as outgrowths of instinctual vicissitudes. She asserted that the "biological birth of the human infant and the psychological birth of the individual are not coincident in time" (Mahler et al., 1975, p. 3). Separation refers to the child's emergence from a symbiotic fusion with the mother whereas "individuation consists of those achievements making the child's assumption of his own individual characteristics" (Mahler et al., 1975, p. 4). Mahler's model assumes that the child develops from *normal autism* through a *symbiotic period* to the four sequentially unfolding subphases of the separation-individuation process. Each step is strongly influenced by the nature of the mother-infant interaction, in particular by such factors as early symbiotic gratification and the emotional availability of the mother.

The first few weeks of life are labeled as normal autism. Mahler assumed that experiences are limited to "deposits of memory traces of the two primordial qualities (pleasure-good versus painful-bad)" (Mahler & Furer, 1968, p. 8). The infant is thought to be surrounded by a "quasi-solid stimulus barrier," that is, an "autistic shell which [keeps] external stimuli out." From the second month, the infant enters the symbiotic phase, marked by dim awareness of the need-satisfying object. This is a state of undifferentiated fusion with the mother. For Mahler, this phase is "an inferred intrapsychic state rather than an observable behavioral condition . . . [which refers] to the character of the infant's primitive, cognitive affective life at a time when differentiation between self and mother has barely begun to take place" (Mahler & McDevitt, 1980, p. 397). Thus, during the first half of the first year, Mahler's infant lives "in a state of primitive hallucinatory disorientation" (Mahler et al., 1975, p. 42). This is not unequivocally so. Mahler and Furer (1968) alluded to "mutual cuing" as circular interaction in which the infant adaptively alters its behavior in response to the mother's selective reactions to her infant's cues. For each mother, this results in the creation of "her child."

A satisfactory symbiotic phase development was seen by Mahler as the source of benevolent feelings about the self and toward the object. If the mother's preoccupation with her infant is anxiety-ridden, inconsistent, or hostile, the individuating child will not have a reliable frame of reference for checking back perceptually and emotionally to the symbiotic mother. Mahler (1963) recognized the resilience of children and their capacity to extract benevolence from their mothers even against considerable odds. A severely compromised symbiotic phase is, however, thought to leave permanent characterological scars in the form of fragmented identity, mindless hedonism, cognitive delay, more than average amounts of destructive aggression, and overall lack of affection (see Burland, 1986).

The separation-individuation process is thought to begin at 4 to 5 months, in the subphase of *differentiation* identified as hatching, when the infant's pleasure in sensory perception can begin if his or her symbiotic gratification has been optimal. The infant begins to differentiate the self from mother. Playing peek-a-boo games may indicate a nascent reaction to, as well as adaptation to, the anxiety associated with the mother's occasional disappearance. From 9 months to about 15–18 months is the second subphase of *practicing*. The child practicing locomotion has a sense of sharing the mother's magical powers. There is a "love affair with the world," although the child returns to the mother for "emotional refueling." Physical prowess is important "for the establishment of body boundaries and a greater awareness of body parts and body self" (Mahler & McDevitt, 1980, p. 403). The toddler is elated with "the escape from the tendency toward fusion with, or engulfment by, the mother" (pp. 403–405). Parens (1979), using Mahler's framework, pointed out that aggression begins to emerge in this subphase in the service of both separation and individuation, implying a departure from Freud's assumptions concerning innate aggression.

The *rapprochement* subphase is dated from 15–18 to 24 months. The infant is more aware of separateness and, consequently, of separation anxiety. Mahler described the child's shadowing of the mother at the same time as it darts away, and the child's clinging while pushing the mother away, and terms these activities *ambitendency.* The handling of this subphase is thought to be critical for future development. The mother must combine emotional availability with "the gentle push" toward independence; otherwise, the infant may become desperately dependent, investing the environment with little interest, and his own functioning with little pleasure.

Settlage (1977) identified the developmental tasks of the rapprochement subphase as: (a) mastery of intensified separation anxiety, (b) affirmation of basic trust, (c) gradual deflation of the sense of omnipotence of symbiotic unity, (d) compensation for this deflation by increased autonomy, (e) firming up of the core sense of self, (f) establishment of affect and drive regulation, (g) healing of the tendency to split the representation of the object into good and bad parts, and (h) replacing of splitting with repression.

The fourth subphase, *the consolidation of individuality and the beginnings of emotional object constancy,* begins with the third year of life. The main task is the achievement of individuality and affective object constancy, which assumes that the cognitive symbolic inner representation of the object has been established. Other tasks underscore the lifelong importance of this phase: the internalization of parental demands, unifying good and bad representations into an integrated whole, gender identity, and so on.

Separation-Individuation and Psychopathology

Mahler (1974) hoped to enable clinicians treating adults to make more accurate reconstructions of the preverbal period, thereby making patients more accessible to analytic interventions. Like Spitz, Mahler implicitly proposed an alternative model of psychopathology based on developmental imbalances in childhood. Several psychoanalytic workers have built on this, addressing developmental deficits relatively directly through the relationship with the therapist (see Blanck & Blanck, 1979; Pine, 1985; Settlage, 1977).

The rapprochement subphase is seen by Mahlerians as the critical period of character formation. Its crucial conflict between separateness and closeness, and between autonomy and dependency, is repeated throughout development, particularly in illness and drug-induced states (Kramer & Akhtar, 1988). This part of her theory has been put to extensive use by those working with borderline personality disorder. Mahler et al. (1975) observed that some mothers responded to their returning infants in the rapprochement subphase with either aggression or withdrawal, and that the behavior of their infants was similar to that of borderline patients. Residues of rapprochement subphase conflicts are seen in this group in the form of persistent longings for, and dread of, fusion with the mother, and in continued splitting of self- and object representations, which cumulatively prevent the establishment of object constancy and identity (Mahler & Kaplan, 1977; see also Kramer, 1979).

Masterson (1976) elaborated Mahler's views of borderline pathology, enriching them with Bowlby's (1973) and Kernberg's (1976b) perspectives. He suggested that the mother of the borderline individual was likely to have been borderline herself and thus encouraged symbiotic clinging and withdrew her love when the child strived toward independence. The father did not, or could not, perform his role of focusing the child's awareness toward reality. Masterson believed that borderline patients experience a deep conflict between the wish for independence and the threat of loss of love, and thus search for a clinging tie with a mother substitute. Such a tie will temporarily ensure a feeling of safety, but any wish for self-assertiveness will present the terror of abandonment. A lifelong and vicious cycle of brief blissful unions, ruptures, emptiness, and depression will ensue.

Rinsley (1982) further elaborated on Masterson's model, based on the introjection of borderline interpersonal relationship patterns from a pathological primary object. Masterson and Rinsley (1975) suggested that a dual image of such objects exists in the borderline individual's mind: (a) the *withdrawing object relations unit,* which represents the critical withdrawing maternal image, associated anger and frustration, and a self-representation as helpless and bad, and (b) the *rewarding object relations unit,* which is made up of an image of the mother as approving, associated good feelings, and an image of the self as compliant and passive.

From retrospective studies, there is evidence that is consistent with Masterson and Rinsley's formulation. Loranger, Oldham, and Tullis (1982) showed that mentally ill relatives of borderline personalities are, usually, themselves borderline (see also Baron, Gruen, & Asnis, 1985; Links, Steiner, & Huxley, 1988). Borderline patients appear to be more likely to have parents who have had mental illness, personality disorder, drug abuse, or severe marital discord (Ogata, Silk, & Goodrich, 1990). Borderline patients have experienced more early separations, family breakdown, family violence, foster placements, and physical and sexual abuse than those with depressive pathology (Ogata, Silk, Goodrich, Lohr et al., 1990), schizophrenia (Byrne, Velamoor, & Cernovsky, 1990), antisocial personality disorder (Zanarini, Gunderson, & Frankenburg, 1990b), or those with borderline traits (Links et al., 1988). Empirical research supports the psychoanalytic view of the distrusting, dark quality of depression in borderlines as compared to nonborderline depressed patients, with the former being far more preoccupied with concerns about loss, abandonment, alienation, and desperation with respect to attachment figures (see Westen et al., 1992).

Burland (1986), using Mahler's framework, described an *autistic character disorder* that resembles schizoid personality. He suggested that early, sustained, and severe deprivation results in the incomplete psychological birth of the infant from the normal autistic phase, and subsequent subphases of separation-individuation are compromised. This developmental arrest manifests in affectionlessness, fragmented identity, cognitive impotence, and mindless hedonism. Burland's description was based on severely deprived ghetto children and has greater ecological validity than many other psychoanalytic descriptions.

Evaluation of Mahler's Framework

Mahler's theory has been generally accepted by psychoanalysts because it dovetails with classical oedipal theory as well as being compatible with the theory of pregenital drives (see Parens, 1980). Chief among its virtues is the way it has strengthened the tendency to reconstrue the psychoanalytic situation as a developmental one (see Fleming, 1975; Loewald, 1960; Settlage, 1980). There is a shift of emphasis from classical theory, in that it is thought that the psychoanalytic situation resolves separation-individuation conflicts through the analyst's coming to be heard and experienced as "a real person" in the interactions.

As we have seen, according to Mahler, during the first half of the first year, the infant is in a state of primary narcissism, its psychic functioning dominated by the pleasure principle; the structuralizations of the mind to id and ego, self and other, and inner versus outer have not yet taken place. Evidence from infant research casts considerable doubt on this formulation. The newborn is sensitive to specific kinds of external stimuli, such as the human face (Fantz, 1963), the human voice (Friedlander, 1970), and any stimulus over which the infant experiences *mastery* (Bower, 1977; Watson, 1979). Bahrick and Watson (1985) demonstrated a capacity to differentiate degrees of action-event contingencies and cross-modal stimulus defenses in 3-month-old infants. There is also innate coordination of perception and action, evidenced by imitation of facial gestures of adults based on a short-term memory system available at birth (Meltzoff & Moore, 1989). There is even evidence for long-term memory capacity in motor recognition at 3 to 5 months (Rovee-Collier & Fagan, 1981). This and other evidence casts serious doubt on Mahler's notion of normal autism and self-object merger (see also Lichtenberg, 1987; Peterfreund, 1978; Soref, 1992; Stern, 1985).

Similarly, the notion of the lack of object permanence during the first year of life has been seriously questioned. Early evidence on the relative lateness of object permanence was based on the Piagetian manual search task (see Piaget, 1954; Werner & Kaplan, 1963). More recent studies using occlusion tasks and surprise as a dependent variable have shown that infants are able to represent the continuous existence of a hidden object, and to reason about expectable "behavior" (e.g., to reappear after a period of occlusion) as early as 3 months of age (Baillargeon, 1987; Spelke, 1985). Gergely (1991) and Stern (1994) both argue that the key feature of these early capacities is the infant's sensitivity to abstract, amodal properties and cross-modal invariances, rather than to modality-specific, physical features. Thus, the infant seems not to be a concrete experiencer of the physical world, as Mahler and classical psychoanalytical theory (see also Klein, 1935/1975a) had assumed.

Mahler's developmental framework, however, may well be appropriate to the truly psychological world of the human infant. Fonagy, Moran, and Target (1993) argued that whereas the infant is well aware of the self and the object in the physical domain, he or she might well assume that psychological states extend beyond the physical boundaries. Full comprehension of mental states seems not to be acquired until the third or fourth year (see Baron-Cohen, 1993a; Leslie, 1987; Perner, 1991; Wellman, 1990). Thus, a symbiotic intersubjective unity may indeed characterize infancy and even early childhood, but solely at the level of mental representations of mental states.

Sandler's Representational Model

The structural hypothesis can encompass extensions at various levels of abstraction. One such important development was Joseph Sandler's restatement of the model in terms of the child's representational world (Sandler & Rosenblatt, 1962). With the collapse of associationist stimulus-response psychology and the emergence of cognitive science, a real possibility for the integration of cognitive psychology and psychoanalysis presented itself (see Bucci, 1985; Erdelyi, 1985; Foulkes, 1978; Stern, 1985; Westen, 1991b, for some significant attempts at achieving this). Sandler described how complex self- and object representations are shaped by everyday affectively laden experiences, fantasies, and memories, and attributed a central role to them in the causation of behavior (Sandler, 1960/1987a).

Sandler's contributions to psychoanalysis are firmly rooted in this developmental perspective. Sandler (1987b) elaborated a model of the two-person interaction where one has influence on the other by the evocation of particular roles in the mind of the other. The behavior or role of the influencing person is crucial in eliciting a complementary response from the participant. Sandler suggested that, in this way, infantile and childhood patterns of relationships may be actualized or enacted in adult relationships, even suggesting that all relationships are guided by individuals' needs to explore the *role-responsiveness* of the other.

J. Sandler and A. -M. Sandler (1978) saw mother-infant interactions as the context for the earliest self- and object representations, providing the basic unit of self-representation. Emde (1988a), who should perhaps be credited with bringing the notion of mental representation to the forefront of the controversy concerning developmental continuity, also saw the sense of self and other as arising from the reciprocal exchanges with the mother, which at the same time form the basis of a sense of "we" (see also Winnicott, 1965c). Most psychoanalytic workers who adopt the developmental framework now assume that the cognitive-affective structures of self- and other representation regulate children's behavior with the caregiver and, in due course, behavior in all significant relationships—including, eventually, their relationships with their own children. Sandler provided the psychoanalytic theoretical framework linking this view with classical conceptualization.

Mental representations of the self and other in interaction, as elaborated by developmentalists, particularly attachment theorists, correspond closely to Sandler's psychoanalytic formulations (Sandler, 1990; Sandler & Sandler, 1978). His ego psychological model of the representational world and the suggestions of developmentalists concerning *internal working models* of attachment relationships may differ in terms of the respective roles given to fantasy and drives, but, even here, they agree in many fundamentals. Sandler (1985) placed an inborn wish to maintain safety at the center of the infant's motivational field, in a manner analogous to Bowlby's (1969/1982) emphasis on the innate propensity for attachment.

A focus of the convergence between psychoanalysts and developmentalists is research on representational structures underlying interpersonal (in particular, attachment) behavior (Bretherton, 1985; Crittenden, 1990; Main, Kaplan, & Cassidy, 1985; Zeanah & Barton, 1989). Using Bowlby's (1973) notion of internal working models, research on the development and influence of attachment patterns has now moved quite close to object relations theory, particularly as formulated by British theorists (see, for example, Bretherton, 1992). The cognitive notion of mental representation is congenial to developmental and social psychologists working from a sociocognitive perspective (see Fonagy & Higgitt, 1984; Sherman, Judd, & Park, 1989; Westen, 1991b) and may be extended to encompass numerous psychoanalytic ideas (see, e.g., Blatt & Behrends, 1987; Fonagy, Moran, Edgcumbe, Kennedy, & Target, 1993; Jacobson, 1964; Sandler, 1990).

General Systems Theory Implementations

General systems theory, as explicated by Bertalanffy (1968), successfully removed the study of biological systems from the epistemological world of physics and created a frame of reference more appropriate for the study of human behavior. The mind is an open system, available to influence and modification from outside. Systems theory has been extensively applied to structural psychoanalytic formulations of development (Basch, 1977; Boesky, 1988; Noy, 1977; Peterfreund, 1980; Rogers, 1980; Rosenblatt & Thickstun, 1977a; Sander, 1983; Stechler & Halton, 1987; Tyson & Tyson, 1990) as well as outside this framework (see, e.g., Bowlby, 1980). The motivation for adopting this model is primarily rooted in the reification and anthropomorphism of psychoanalytic metapsychological formulations (Fonagy, 1982), with their inevitable contradictions. Systems theory formulation of the structural hypothesis of development enables theoreticians to address multiple components of developmental processes at several levels of abstraction simultaneously. Comprehensive general systems theory accounts are to be found in the work of psychoanalysts most influenced by British object relations theory (Bowlby, 1980; Horowitz, 1987; Stern, 1985).

INTRODUCTION TO OBJECT RELATIONS THEORY

Object relations theory includes various sets of ideas of greater and lesser coherence and specificity. As object relations theories have come to dominate psychoanalytic thinking, most theorists have appeared to aspire to this category, making a definition of the term even more problematic. Greenberg and Mitchell (1983), in their definitive review, used the term to include all theories "concerned with exploring the relationship between real, external people and the internal images and residues of relations with them and the significance of these residues for psychic functioning" (p. 14). A strict application of this definition would not exclude structural theories, which was, in fact, Greenberg and Mitchell's implicit aim. Lussier (1988) reminded us that psychoanalysts such as Edith Jacobson (1964, 1971), in writing about depression, used object relations concepts but remain rooted in a structural framework. Jacobson noted, for example, that the child will prefer a bad mother to no mother at all, and may choose to destroy him or herself rather than kill that bad internal object. She also wrote that the child was frequently ready to sacrifice pleasure for the sake of security.

Kernberg (1976a) identified three ways in which the term object relations theory is used: (a) an understanding of present interpersonal relations in terms of past ones, which would include the study of intrapsychic structures as deriving from fixation on modifying and reactivating earlier internalizations; (b) a specialized approach within psychoanalytic meta-psychology, one that stresses the building-up of mental representations of dyadic self and object relationships, which are rooted in the original relation of the infant and the primary caregiver, and its later development into dyadic, triadic, and multiple internal and external interpersonal relationships in general; and (c) the specific approaches of the Kleinian school, the British school of independent psychoanalysts, and those theoreticians who attempted to integrate the ideas of these schools into their own developmental theory. Kernberg's (1976b) own theory best fits the second of these definitions. In the present context, we will use his third pragmatic definition, because object relationships are as much the concern of structural theorists as they are of the Kleinian and British (independent) schools and their followers. As Spruiell (1988) pointed out, Freud saw objects in terms of drives, and it is almost impossible to imagine drives without objects.

A genuine shift of interest toward developmental issues is associated with the rise of object relations theories. There is an implicit or explicit move away from the study of intrapsychic conflict, particularly conflict relating to the sexual and aggressive drives, the central organization of oedipal compromises, and the complementary influences of biological and experiential forces in development (see Lussier, 1988; Rangell, 1985; Spruiell, 1988). Psychoanalysis seems to have moved increasingly toward a perspective that emphasizes the individual's experience of being with others and with the analyst during analytic work (see, for example, Loewald, 1986; Schwaber, 1983). This approach inevitably emphasizes phenomenological constructs such as individuals' experiences of themselves (see Stolorow, Brandchaft, & Atwood, 1987) and their experiences of psychic as opposed to actual reality (see McLaughlin, 1981; Michels, 1985). The clinical emphasis on experience inevitably drives theory away from a structural mechanistic model and toward what Mitchell (1988) broadly termed *relational theory.*

Object relations theories share several assumptions (see Akhtar, 1992; Kernberg, 1988): (a) that severe pathology has origins in the first three years of life, (b) that the pattern of relationships with objects becomes increasingly complex with development, (c) that this development follows a maturational sequence that exists across cultures but may be distorted by pathological personal experiences, (d) that early patterns of object relations are repeated, (e) that the developmental continuum of these relationships is isomorphic with the continuum of pathology (see Westen, 1989), and (f) that patients' clinical reactions to their therapists provide a window for examining healthy and pathological aspects of early relationship patterns.

There exist, however, considerable differences among psychoanalytic theories in terms of the rigor with which the problem of object relationships is tackled. Friedman (1988) differentiated between hard and soft object relations theories. Hard theories, in which he included those of Melanie Klein, Fairbairn, and Kernberg, see much hate, anger, and destruction, and dwell on obstacles, illness, and confrontation; soft object relations theories (those of Balint, Winnicott, and Kohut) deal with love, innocence, fulfillment, and progressive unfolding.

Akhtar (1992) offered an extremely helpful overview of two contrasting approaches to object relations theory. In the classic view, humans are seen as inherently limited but able in part, to overcome their tragic flaws and become "fairly decent." The romantic view sees humans as intrinsically good and capable, but vulnerable to restriction and injury by circumstance. The classic view corresponds to the tradition represented by Anna Freud, Melanie Klein, American ego psychologists, Kernberg, Horowitz, and some exponents of the British object relations tradition. The romantic approach perhaps originated with the work of Ferenczi and is well represented in the work of Balint, Winnicott, and Guntrip in the United Kingdom, and that of Kohut, Modell, and Adler in the United States. The first approach views psychopathology largely in terms of conflict; the other, in terms of deficit. For example, acting out might be seen as an inevitable consequence of deep-rooted pathology in the classic view; the other view sees it as a manifestation of hope that the environment might reverse the damage done. In the classic view, conflict and destructiveness are encountered only in cases of environmental failure. In this latter view, there is no escape from conflict and destructiveness. In the romantic view, there is primary love; in the classic view, love is a developmental achievement that can never be totally free of early transferences. Naturally, there are approaches that combine the classic and the romantic, such as those of Kohut and Kernberg, who proposed models of development that are pure representatives of neither tradition.

THE KLEIN-BION MODEL OF DEVELOPMENT

General Characteristics of the Model

Melanie Klein's (1935/1975a) model of development combines the structural model with an interpersonal, object relations model of development. Until 1935, Klein was basically working within the theoretical framework of Freud and Abraham. Her papers on the *depressive position* (1935/1975a, 1940/1975c), her paper on the *paranoid-schizoid position* (1946/1975e), and her book *Envy and Gratitude* (1957/1975b) established her as the leader of an original psychoanalytic tradition. There are several excellent introductions to the work of Klein, including those of Segal (1974), Meltzer (1978), Caper (1988), and Hinshelwood (1989).

Klein, who began her work in the 1920s, noticed that the internal images of objects were much more ferocious than the actual parents appeared to be. She assumed that these internal figures were distorted by sadistic fantasies. She developed the conception of internal objects and an inner world that was far from a replica of the external world, built up through the mechanisms of introjection and projection from the beginning of life. This led to a reformulation of the developmental stages of the ego and the superego—for instance, the enrichment of the ego by introjections and its impoverishment by projection into the superego.

Klein (1932/1975h) saw mental structures arising out of a variety of internal objects, which changed in unconscious fantasy (Isaacs, 1943/1952) as the child developed from infancy. The model is interpersonal in that it relates the development of the ego and the internal objects to personal relationships (Klein, 1931/1964a). At every stage, the infant's fantasies are modified by actual experience of interaction with the environment, and the individual is seen as continuing to use the external object world in the service of an internal, primarily defensive, system of relationships (Klein, 1935/1975a). Klein's view of development included a rather uncritical acceptance of Freud's (1920/1991) speculation about a death instinct, which Klein saw as a real psychological phenomenon present from birth (if not before) and powerfully altering the positions the psyche assumes in relation to the external world.

The Two Basic Positions

In the Kleinian model, the human psyche has two basic positions: (a) the paranoid-schizoid and (b) the depressive (Klein, 1935/1975a, 1946/1975e). In the paranoid-schizoid position, the relationship to the object (the caregiver) is as to a part object; the relationship, as well as the ego (self), is split into persecutory and idealized components. In the depressive position, the relation is to integrated parents, both loved and hated, and the ego is more integrated. The paranoid-schizoid superego is split between an idealized omnipotent ego ideal and the extremely persecutory superego of paranoid states. In the depressive position, the superego is a hurt love object with human features.

The term *position* is appropriate because it implies a particular constellation of external and internal object relationships, fantasies, anxieties, and defenses to which the individual is likely to return throughout life. They arise out of developmental stages; the paranoid-schizoid precedes the depressive, and maturity implies the predominant presence of the depressive position. Klein implicitly discarded Freud's (1905/1991b) view of developmental stages and saw anal and phallic phantasies occurring alongside oral ones (Spillius, 1994). Klein and her followers unequivocally asserted that development is never complete, and fluctuation between these positions never ceases (Klein, 1945/1975f).

The paranoid-schizoid position is the infant's earliest relationship with the external world and is dominated by innate internal representations (Klein, 1959/1975g). The infant's initial attempt at organizing internal and external perceptions is dominated by splitting. All goodness, love, and pleasure are attributed to an ideal object; and all pain, distress, and badness, to a persecutory one. The model of this persectuory experience is the hungry infant who, without the ability to represent the breast as absent, experiences in its place a gnawing sensation of being, as it were, attacked from within by a bad internal breast. All good feelings of affection and desire are aimed at the idealized good object, which the infant wishes to possess, take inside (introject), and experience as self (identify with). Negative affect (hatred, disgust, and so on) is directed to the persecutory object and projected (externalized) onto it because the infant wishes to be rid of everything bad. The infant's mental life is envisaged as extremely labile; good rapidly turns into bad, the bad gets worse, and the good gets increasingly idealized. Each external object has at least one good and one bad representation, but both are just parts rather than the whole object.

The depressive position is marked by the infant's capacity to perceive the mother as a whole object who provides both good and bad experiences, and was seen by Klein as the central achievement in the child's development. The infant becomes aware of his or her own capacity to love and hate the parent. This ambivalence, along with a growing capacity to recognize absence and potential loss of the attacked object, opens the child to the experience of guilt over hostility. This is what Klein called *depressive anxiety,* as distinct from the *persecutory anxieties* of the earlier paranoid-schizoid position. Working through the characteristic experiences of the depressive position brings with it reparative feelings (Klein, 1935/1975a; Riviere, 1936). The psychic pain associated with the integration is so great that it can lead to defenses characteristic of this position, including manic or obsessional reparation, total denial of damage, or contempt. Segal (1957) linked the capacities for symbolization and sublimation to depressive reparation. As projections diminish in the depressive position, the individual begins to gain an understanding of the nature of his or her own impulses and fantasies. Spillius (1994) suggested that the depressive position may be initiated by the child's perception of the caregiving figure as thinking and feeling (having a theory of mind; see Fonagy, 1991). Mentalizing is closely related to Bion's (1962, 1962/1967) notion of *K*—getting to know oneself or the other person—and the evasion of the process, which he called *minus K.*

Modern Kleinian writers (e.g., Quinodox, 1991; Steiner, 1992) see the critical aspect of the depressive position in terms of the child's achievement of separateness. This brings Kleinian formulations closer to the Mahlerian model. The emphasis on the object's separateness also links the concept of the depressive position to classical ideas about oedipal conflict. Once the object is perceived as a mentally independent entity, it is seen as having desires and attachments of its own, and concerns about the "third" may arise (Britton, 1989, 1992; O'Shaughnessy, 1989).

Projective Identification and Other Developmental Concepts

The concept of *projective identification* is central to the Kleinian model of development (Klein, 1946/1975e). Whereas in classical theory projected impulses and wishes are seen as part of the object rather than the self, and identification implies attributing to the self qualities of the object, projective identification involves the externalization of attempts to control these via manipulative behavior toward the object. Consequently, projective identification is a more interactive concept than either projection or identification. There is a much closer relation to the object, which now "stands for" the projected aspects of the self (Greenberg & Mitchell, 1983).

For Klein (1957/1975b), projective identification was an unconscious infantile phantasy by which the infant is able to relocate persecutory experiences by separating (splitting) them from the self-representation and making them part of the image of a particular object. Disowned unconscious feelings of rage or hostility are firmly believed by the infant to exist within the mother. By acting in subtle ways, the infant may achieve a confirming reaction of criticism or even persecution. Projective identification has explanatory power far beyond that of a mechanism of defense. Projective identification is not just an internal process; it involves the object, who may experience it as manipulation, seduction, or a myriad of other forms of psychic influence. Bion's (1962) work suggested a distinction between normal projective identification, where less pathological aspects of the self are externalized and may underpin normal empathy and understanding, and more pathological projective identification, which is linked to an absence of empathy and understanding.

Bion (1959) pointed to the necessity for projective identification in infancy, a time when the individual is ill-equipped to absorb his or her impressions of the world. By projecting these elements into another human mind (a container) that has the ability to absorb and transform them into meanings, mental survival is ensured. The absence of a suitable container makes projective identification a pathogenic process of evacuation. Bion (1962) discussed the significance of the mother's capacity to contain both the affective state and the cause of the distress. This significance goes beyond *mirroring* (Meltzoff & Gopnik, 1993) as the caregiver conveys her capacity not to be overwhelmed by, but to deal with, the distress; this, we believe, is the central, and potentially measurable, aspect of Bion's containment concept.

Freud's assumption of an *aggressive drive* is extensively used by Kleinian theorists. Klein was impressed that the children she analyzed had extremely sadistic fantasies about which they felt guilty and anxious (Spillius, 1994). Klein (1935/1975a) assumed that the infant's self is, from the beginning, threatened by destruction from within by an aggressive drive. Klein (1948/1975i) posited an unconscious fear of annihilation, called *primary anxiety.* The mother's breast, her body, and parental intercourse are the main targets for the projection in phantasy of the child's destructive impulses. Combined with fantasies deriving from frustration and the wish to take possession of these sources of "good" things, anxiety about attacks on the other's body means that the other's body comes to feel dangerous and a persecutor. The death instinct was seen by Klein (1946/1975e) as only partly projected onto the bad object; some of it is retained and continues to exist, throughout life, as a threat to the individual of being annihilated from within.

Klein (1957/1975b) suggested that early, primitive *envy* represents a particularly malignant form of innate aggression. Unlike other forms, which are turned against objects already seen as persecutory, envy is hatred directed to the good object and arouses premature depressive anxiety about damage to the good object. The child resents the inevitable limitations of maternal care, cannot tolerate the mother's control over it, and would prefer to destroy it rather then experience the frustration. This may interfere with the primal differentiation of "good" and "bad," and may ultimately be the developmental precursor of some confusional states (Rosenfeld, 1950).

The Place of Experience in Klein's Model

Klein (1960/1975d) saw parents as mitigating influences who may modify the child's anxieties arising from constitutional tendencies. In favorable circumstances, good experiences predominate over bad ones; the idea of a good object is firmly established, as is the child's belief in his or her capacity to love. Klein's belief in the innateness of the earliest objects and their independence of actual experience (Klein, 1936/1964b, 1959/1975g; see Sutherland, 1980, for a critical account) may appear to belie this statement, but post-Kleinian psychoanalysts have successfully integrated environmental accounts into her ideas (see Bion, 1957, 1962; Meltzer, 1974; Rosenfeld, 1965; Segal, 1981).

Balint (1968) took Kleinian psychoanalysts to task for concentrating exclusively on what happens inside one person rather than essentially between two people. The actual state of the object while the child is in the depressive position is, however, thought to be extremely important. If the mother appears to be damaged, the child's depressive anxiety and guilt are increased; if she appears well and can empathize with her child about his or her state, fear of his own destructiveness is decreased.

KLEINIAN MODELS OF PSYCHOPATHOLOGY

General Models of Pathology

Psychological illness reflects the predominance of the paranoid-schizoid position, whereas health implies the stabilization of the depressive framework. Klein considered the intense anxiety aroused by sadistic infantile phantasies to be at the root of mental illness either as direct cause (childhood psychosis) or as defense. For example, Klein (1932/1975h) developed a new conception of obsessional neurosis as a defense against early psychotic anxiety, instead of regarding it as a regression to a fixation point in the anal phase of libidinal development. Bion (1962) outlined the processes that can lead to pathology in the paranoid-schizoid position. He named two factors: (a) deficiencies in the mother's capacity for *reverie* (see also Winnicott's, 1962, formulation of primary maternal preoccupation) and (b) overwhelming envy in the infant.

Persecutory anxiety arises as a result of the perceived threat of the bad object for the ego. Excessive anxiety leads to fragmentation, giving rise to typical schizoid fears of annihilation and disintegration. Although this idea is implicitly present in Klein's early work, its adoption follows Fairbairn's work on ego splitting in the early 1940s (Fairbairn, 1940/1952c). Another feature of primitive anxiety is pathological projective identification, where part of the ego is fragmented and projected into the representation of the object, which, in turn, becomes fragmented. This gives rise to terrifying perceptions of what Bion called "bizarre objects" containing projected fragments of the self and imbued with hostility and anxiety. Segal (1985) cited the example of a patient who experienced the onset of a psychotic episode as his mind being invaded by millions of little computers that would destroy it. The experience was linked to an omnipotent fantasy that, through his work, he would supply all British universities with computers and this would enable him to dominate the whole of British university life. The computers represented fragments of his own personality invading the world, which would dominate and disintegrate it, then reinvade him in the form of tiny bizarre ideas.

In neurotic states, the transition between schizoparanoid and depressive positions is perceived as partial; the superego contains both paranoid and depressive features, manifesting as persecutory guilt. The most common anxiety is the fear of guilt and the possibility of the loss of the loved object. If the depressive position is not approached, the anxiety will be about fragmentation, annihilation, and persecution, and the reality sense will be grossly distorted by projections. This picture is more fitting for patients with severe personality disorders, such as borderline or narcissistic personalities.

In treatment, Kleinians prefer to work exclusively with interpretations—that is, primary transference interpretations—aimed at the patient's current anxieties. They work analytically with very severe disorders, and stress early interpretation of negative transferences derived from the paranoid-schizoid position. Kleinians have contributed enormously to our understanding and use of projective and introjective aspects of the countertransference (Ogden, 1986; Racker, 1968; Spillius, 1988b). A pioneer in this respect was Bion (1962), for whom transference and countertransference are about the transfer of intolerable mental pain by projective identification, originally from infant to mother, and, in the treatment situation, from patient to therapist.

Rosenfeld's Developmental Model of Narcissism

Rosenfeld (1964) viewed narcissistic states as characterized by omnipotent object relations and defenses that deny the separateness and identity of the object. He stressed the destructiveness of the relationship with others, the ruthless use of people, and denial of their value. By introjective identification, narcissistic individuals lay claim to the good part of the object and, in fantasy, own it. Projective identificatory processes help them to deposit their own perceived inadequacies in others, whom they can then denigrate. Grandiosity, contempt, and profound dependency are explained in terms of the manic defense (Klein, 1940/1975c). To deal with envy, these individuals devalue their objects (therapist, spouse); denigration avoids the recognition of goodness in others, which these persons find threatening to their delusional state of self idealization. If the destructive (aggressive, envious) parts of the self are idealized, these individuals will be tempted to destroy any love or goodness that is offered, to maintain the state of infantile omnipotence. To achieve an identification with the omnipotent destructive self, they will attack the sane and loving part of the mind and will, at times, feel completely barren and empty.

Models of Borderline Personality

Klein's (1964) formulations were vital to the psychoanalytic understanding of borderline conditions. The paranoid-schizoid position is the template for borderline personality functioning:

1. In object relationships, splitting predominates over repression, others are either idealized or denigrated, and the inner world is populated by parts (or caricatures) of the object.
2. Because the depressive position is avoided and all badness is pushed into the object, there can be no genuine sadness, mourning, or guilt.
3. Projective identification predominates; communication cannot be meaningful, and the object is manipulated by being forced to experience unacceptable aspects of the borderline individual's personality.

Recent Kleinian thinking (see Spillius, 1988a) has examined the defensive arrangements that many conditions linked to borderline pathology appear to have in common. The term *organization* (Rosenfeld, 1971; Steiner, 1987) refers to a relatively stable construction of impulses, anxieties, and defenses that creates a very precious internal state. An individual in that state is protected from the chaos of earlier developmental stages but "voluntarily" deprives himself or herself of more advanced modes of psychic functioning, which would lead to intolerable depressive anxiety. This rigid, precarious system makes change or therapeutic progress difficult, and rarely is it entirely successful. It is as if the organization becomes the embodiment of the destructive impulses that called it into existence. Bion (1962) provided one explanation of this puzzling state of affairs. He described the ego's identification with an object that is felt to be full of envy and hate. The result is an early disabling of certain psychic processes involved with understanding cognitive and affective aspects of interpersonal relationships. Thus, in this model, intrapsychic conflicts are resolved through adopting a state of quasi-deficit.

Evidence Consistent with Kleinian Formulations

Klein (1935/1975a) assumed that infants' experiences are classified on the basis of affective states (see Bower, 1981; Zajonc, 1984) as either good or bad objects. Early affect-based categorization is consistent with modern semantic models based on "family resemblance" (Rosch, 1978) and is seen in the incapacity of infants to use natural categories during much of the first year of life (Younger & Cohen, 1986). Gergely (1991) suggested, on the basis of similar evidence, that the baby may start out with multiple representations of the mother defined by the infant's current affective state (see also Stern, 1994).

Klein's early critics focused on her assumption of the early development of higher-order cognitive and perceptual capacities (see King and Steiner's, 1991, remarkable account of the scientific discussions that took place in the British Psycho-Analytical Society in 1944). For example, projection in the paranoid-schizoid position assumes a differentiated sense of self and other, and a causal component: the infant fantasizes that his or her unpleasurable state is caused by the object, an external agent. There is now detailed documentation of remarkably abstract and complex cognitive capacities of the human infant (Bower, 1989; Osofsky, 1987; Spelke, 1990; Watson, 1984)—in particular, compelling evidence that the infant differentiates between the self and other (Field, 1979; Papousek & Papousek, 1974; Watson, 1991). For example, at 5 months, an infant differentiates a video image of his or her own legs moving from images of another baby's legs (Bahrick & Watson, 1985). Studies of the perception of causality (Bower, 1989; Leslie & Keeble, 1987) and causal reasoning (Golinkoff, Hardig, Carlson, & Sexton, 1984; Shultz, 1982) in infancy suggest that the human mind is innately predisposed to impose a causal structure on perceptual experience. Klein may therefore have been correct that the infant blames the mother for an experience of frustration. However, there is no evidence for Klein's implicit contention that the infant relates to the object as a mental entity. Fonagy, Moran, and Target (1993) suggested that the infant's vulnerability in fact arises from an inability to conceive of the other as a psychological as opposed to a physical being, and that Kleinian descriptions of *concrete* or *nonsymbolic* functioning in severely personality-disordered patients may be understood in these terms (see Premack, 1990, and Trevarthen, 1979, 1980, for opposing nativist views).

Criticisms and Evaluation

The concept of projective identification has been extensively criticized (see, e.g., Meissner, 1980) but continues to be used because of its clinical relevance (see Sandler, 1987). Searles (1986), Giovacchini (1987), and many other North American analysts working with borderline patients make use of the construct of projective identification in its broader sense of unconscious communication. The concept is appealing because it conveys the undoubted ability of these patients to "get under the skin" of all those with whom they develop close relations. Whether a psychologically implausible concept such as projective identification is essential, or whether a more parsimonious concept such as Sandler's (1976) role responsiveness or King's (1978) reverse transference may suffice, is a controversial issue.

The notion of the death instinct is also controversial within current psychoanalytic theory; many find it both problematic and unnecessary (see Parens, 1979, for a comprehensive treatment). Envy may not be rooted in a biological predisposition but, instead, triggered by frustration, inconsistent mothering, or the child's as yet inadequate capacity to appreciate time and space (see Greenberg & Mitchell, 1983). The clinical value of the concept, however, remains in relation to patients who regard potential helpers with powerful malice and are totally unable to tolerate the limitations of any therapeutic relationship.

Current criticisms address the "fuzziness" (Greenberg & Mitchell, 1983) of Klein's descriptions of the development of mental structure. (For more rigorous formulations, see Fairbairn, 1952a; Kernberg, 1980; Modell, 1968.) The emphasis on *phantasy* as the building block of mental structure confounds the experiential and nonexperiential aspects of mental functioning (see Sandler & Joffe, 1969). Klein and post-Kleinians have moved mental structuralization into the experiential realm, which has the advantage of experience-nearness for clinicians and rids theory of much reified pseudo-scientific terminology. However, it bypasses essential questions concerning the nature of the mechanisms underpinning the organization of mental functions.

The attainment of the depressive position provides a good illustration of some of the ambiguities of Kleinian nomenclature.

This change clearly implies a qualitative shift in the perception of the object from part to whole. What is not clear, however, is whether the attainment of this phase would be indicated by: (a) consciousness of conflicting feelings about the same person (e.g., love and hate), (b) unconscious integration of various images with no necessary conscious correlate, (c) the ability to recognize that one can have diverse feelings about a person, but that these do not necessarily pertain to the reality of that individual, (d) the ability to be aware of mixed feelings toward an individual (e.g., knowing that one simultaneously, or in quick succession, feels love and hate), and (e) the ability to be aware of loving feelings at the moment of feeling anger and hate. The problem in having such diverse interpretations of a single developmental construct is that these capacities develop at very different times in the child's life. For example, children younger than age 5 have great difficulty understanding mixed emotions (see Harris, 1989; Harter, 1986), but would be expected to be able to represent the same person as sometimes angry and sometimes loving from the first year of life, without difficulties in object constancy (Stern, 1985). An understanding of their own feelings about that person is likely to be very partial until the awareness of some degree of reflective capacity toward the end of the second and the beginning of the third year of life (Harris, 1989, 1994).

The work of Kleinian writers represents a major advance in clarifying the relationship of emotional development and the psychological functioning of the individual. Many of their ideas remain to be operationalized, but many models, such as Bion's (1962) model of the container and contained, have lessened the divide between cognitive development and emotional disorder, a process that, in our view, is essential to further advances in the field of developmental psychopathology.

THE DEVELOPMENTAL MODEL OF THE INDEPENDENT SCHOOL OF BRITISH PSYCHOANALYSIS

Overview of the British School

The "Independent" tradition is not a misnomer; unlike other psychoanalytic schools, it is the work of a number of individual analysts, has no single leader or reference point, and therefore lacks the internal coherence of a more unified approach. Fairbairn and Guntrip were the systematic theory builders, but major contributions came from Winnicott, Balint, Klauber, and Khan. (There are some excellent overviews of their work, e.g., Hughes, 1989; Kohon, 1986; Rayner, 1991; Sutherland, 1980.) This group has made a major contribution to the exploration of earliest child development and the fateful effects of the environment in facilitating or disrupting the child's moves from total early dependence to mature independence. This focus led them away from a libidinally driven structural model to develop a self-object theory. Although the theory remains dynamic in its emphasis on repudiated desires and wishes, now different aspects of the ego, or parts of the self, are seen as dynamically interacting with each other and with complementary internal and external objects.

Fairbairn changed psychoanalytic views of internalization processes that he saw as consisting of a part of the self representation in a specific relation to an object representation. Fairbairn (1954) envisaged the self as a crucial agent of motivation: there is no emotion without the self and no self without emotion. Winnicott (1958b) described the powerful desire to develop a sense of self and, conversely, how powerfully it may be hidden or falsified (see also Bollas's, 1989, contributions on destiny and fate). The impact of these ideas cannot be underestimated. They gradually permeated the entire psychoanalytic literature and radically altered dynamic developmental models of psychopathology.

Developmental Contributions of the Independent Group

Balint (1937/1965a) influenced by the Budapest group of Ferenczi and Herman, took issue with Freud's (1914/1991) concept of primary narcissism (that the infant's love of self, associated with autoerotism, precedes object love). Balint proposed that a desire to be loved was a primary form of love. This is conceived of as a lack of differentiatedness felt toward benign early objects (Balint, 1968). The infant assumes that they are present for the self and have no independent interest; the ego's attitude toward them is one of *omnipotence.* Serious trauma prior to the stable differentiation of self and objects creates a *basic fault* in the structure of the psyche, which Balint (1968) envisaged not as a fracture, but as a misordering (equivalent to mismatched genetic coding on chromosomes). Persons manifesting a basic fault have an underlying feeling that something is not right about them; they are not resentful about this, but invariably seek a solution in the environment. The basic fault is seen as the developmental root of personality disorder. With object differentiation, Balint (1959) identified two characteristic defenses in the child's management of anxiety: one is to love, even to be intensely dependent on, the newly emerging objects (*the ochnophilic attitude*), and the other is to dislike attachment to objects, but to love the spaces between them (*the philobatic attitude*). Instead of investing in objects, the philobat invests in his or her own ego skills.

Fairbairn (1952a) was the most forthright of the object relations theorists: "The libido is primarily object-seeking (rather than pleasure-seeking as in classical theory)" (p. 82). Pleasure is gained and anxiety reduced by the quality of ego-object relations (internal or external), rather than in discharge of energy. Thus, the baby stops crying when the image of the good breast is evoked by its sight or smell, not when it starts sucking. Fairbairn's implicit psychological model was far closer to general systems theory than to classical psychoanalytic formulations (see Basch, 1976; Boesky, 1988; Peterfreund, 1975, 1980; Sander, 1983; Tyson & Tyson, 1990). The most important shift is from a psychoanalytic model, primarily concerned with the unconscious and repression, to one focused around the notion of incompatible ideas. The loss of optimal intimacy with the primary object is seen as giving rise to splitting in the self (the ego). Conflicting ego-object systems are seen as the developmental roots of psychopathology.

Winnicott's (1965c) psychoanalytic model was rooted in his work with infants and mothers as well as with severely personality-disordered patients. He saw the child as evolving from an infant-mother unity in which three functions facilitate healthy development: (a) holding-integration, (b) handling-personalization, and (c) object-relating (Winnicott, 1960, 1962). The mother holds the infant, both actually and figuratively, and so gives cohesion to its sensorimotor elements. Her *primary maternal preoccupation* (a partial withdrawal from activities other than care of the baby and a heightened sensitivity to her own self, her body, and the baby) helps the mother achieve a state whereby the baby is provided with the illusion that the mother responds accurately to its gesture because she is a part of the baby.

Winnicott (1953) also introduced the idea of *transitional phenomena.* A favorite blanket may help to soothe the infant because it is grasped as the infant fantasizes about breast feeding, and is associated with calling the mother (and the breast) to mind in her absence. The physical object is both the infant and the mother; it facilitates the transition from omnipotent relating to a subjectively created object, to relating to the mother, who is seen as part of external reality. Because the physical object is under the infant's control and helps to bridge the gap between "me and not-me" as the infant becomes aware of separation, the infant and the transitional object may become inseparable. Transitional objects are in the space between the self and external reality, a space in which sharing-yet-separate companionship and love take place, where play symbolization and illusion are maintained in the spontaneous, creative activities of healthy individuals (Winnicott, 1971).

The concept of the transitional object has been controversial, with some writers suggesting that Winnicott overstated his case (e.g., Bowlby, 1969/1982; Brody, 1980; Elmhirst, 1980; Olinick, 1982; Sperling, 1963; Tolpin, 1972). Others have pointed out that transitional objects may be peculiar to Anglo-Saxon culture (see Gaddini & Gaddini, 1970; Hong & Townes, 1976; Litt, 1981), where prolonged physical contact with the mother is less likely to be available. The concept has been enthusiastically embraced by a large number of analysts who have linked transitional objects and relatedness to a wide variety of psychological disorders such as borderline personality disorder (Gunderson, Morris, & Zanarini, 1985; Modell, 1963, 1968; Perry & Cooper, 1985), schizophrenia (Searles, 1960), hospitalism (Provence & Ritvo, 1961), psychosomatic disorders (McDougall, 1974), fetishism (Greenacre, 1970; Sperling, 1959), autism (Tustin, 1981), obsessional disorder (Solomon, 1962), learning difficulties, and pervasive developmental disorders (Sherman & Hertzig, 1983).

Winnicott (1951/1958e) saw object relations as beginning with the experience of magical omnipotence. At this stage, when self-object differentiation is incomplete, object representations are best designated self-objects. The infant's muscular "attacks" on the mother, and her survival of them, facilitate the development of the self and the infant's perception of the mother as a separate person who can be used properly and not just omnipotently. Holding is based on comprehension—that is holding in mind—of the infant's mental state. Winnicott (1967) suggested that optimal development of self-esteem depends on the mother's capacity for affective mirroring. Unlike Balint (1965b), Winnicott did not assume that even early infancy is an idyllic era; the mother has to be *good enough,* but failure is inevitable and is the motivator of growth.

Winnicott (1956/1958d) stressed that the baby must not be challenged too soon about the mother's independent existence, and asked to negotiate the "me and the not-me." The baby's omnipotence gives rise to the ego nuclei, which will in time, become integrated in the *real* experience of the *I* (the true self). Winnicott (1962/1965b) differentiated frustration of wishes from frustration of ego needs, where the child's knowing is impinged on or confused. This, he believed, leads to disorientation, withdrawal, and a sense of annihilation: experience is traumatic if it is incomprehensible. Individuals who, as adults, live in fear of breakdown may have unconscious memories of such infantile experiences (Winnicott, 1973). If trauma occurs at the stage of absolute dependency, a *caretaker self* may develop (Winnicott, 1971). The mother's gestures do not "give meaning" to the infant's reactions, and symbolic communication cannot be said to develop between them. The infant, and then the child, will have the capacity to "go through the motions" of interpersonal relationships, but these encounters will be with the *false self,* which will serve to hide the true self (Winnicott, 1965c).

Khan's (1963, 1974, 1978/1983b) work is helpful in elaborating the concept of trauma in the mother-infant relationship. He pointed out that single experiences are less traumatic than repeated breaches in the protective shield provided by the mother from childhood to adolescence. These have the quality of strains that do not so much distort the development of the ego but cumulatively create a vulnerability to later stresses. This is the converse of the attainment of resilience through a secure and understanding infant-mother relationship (Fonagy, Steele, Steele, Higgitt, & Target, 1994).

The Independent Group's Contributions to Developmental Psychopathology

General Views of Psychopathology

The key contribution of the Independents (Fairbairn, 1944/1952b) has been the proposition that early trauma is stored in memories that are "frozen" or dissociated from a person's severe functional self. This conception steps beyond the classical psychoanalytic notion of repression. The classical model of pathogenesis (conflict → repression → reactivation of conflict → neurotic compromise) is still seen to apply to conflicts that reach the oedipal (3–4 years) level. The Independent Group's model applies to disorders of the self, thought to arise out of traumatic events before that age. Although their clinical formulations apply particularly to narcissistic and borderline personality disorders, the notion of multiple self-representations is of profound importance in all domains of psychoanalysis. For example, the Independent approach to dream interpretation differs from the classical position in seeing dreams as communication patterns between different parts of the self (see Bollas, 1987; Rycroft, 1966, 1979).

All pathological states are rooted in the conflicts over infantile dependence. The regressive wish to be dependent carries with it the threat of loss of identity. The progressive goal of separation generates anxiety over feeling isolated and unsupported.

Personality Disorder

A schizoid personality (Fairbairn, 1940/1952c, 1952a) arises out of the infantile experience that love is destructive for the mother and therefore has to be inhibited along with all intimacy. In schizoid states, the ego is so split that the individual may be mystified about the self and sometimes about reality (finding the familiar in the unfamiliar, and vice versa). He or she resists perceiving others as whole persons, and substitutes bodily for emotional contacts. Often, because the enjoyment of love relationships is forbidden, the individual may give him or herself over to the pleasure of hating and destruction. Fairbairn (1952a) differentiated depressive disorder from schizoid conditions in that it derives from later in infancy.

Winnicott (1956/1958a, 1963/1965d) used his formulation of the false self to elaborate a theory of antisocial behavior, particularly in children. He saw antisocial behavior as starting in the environment's failure to adjust to the child, but its continuation is an expression of hope, an attempt by the child to restore the pretraumatic situation. With development, the original symbolic meaning of the antisocial act is lost, and it is replaced by secondary gain (economic gain from stolen goods replaces the symbolic possession of love). In the case of destructive behavior, "the child is seeking that amount of environmental stability which will stand the strain resulting from impulsive behavior" (p. 310).

Winnicott (1960/1965a, 1965c) viewed the schizoid personality as a variety of false-self organization. Beyond the overly compliant self lie deep anxieties about the cohesiveness of the self, and a loss of relationship to the body. Winnicott (1965c) did not see the false self as invariably pathological; in fact, it may be an essential aspect of social adaptation, particularly in certain cultures. At the extreme, it is (like Fairbairn's picture of schizoid personality) only functional outside of intimate relationships; within such relationships (for example, psychoanalysis), it may break down and leave unprotected a poorly developed sense of true self. The false self provides a screen behind which the true self can secretly search for actualization. If the false self is undermined, suicide may be the only means left for the false self to protect the true self from annihilation.

Balint's (1968) notion of "the basic fault" is also important to understanding borderline and other serious personality pathology—for instance, differences in the experience of oedipal feelings, the absence of conflict, and the idiosyncratic use of language. Khan (1963, 1974, 1983a) put forward a developmental model based on the notions of cumulative trauma from a mother who repeatedly fails in her protective function, and *symbiotic omnipotence,* whereby the mother, through collusion, maintains an exclusive closeness to the child, which actively discourages involvement with other objects. Khan also contributed to integrating Fairbairn's and Winnicott's views of schizoid personality. His description was very similar to Kernberg's structural-theory-based description in stressing poor affect tolerance, impulse control, and integration of aggression. Khan (1966) went further in identifying schizoid aspects of disorders classically regarded as neurotic. For example, he considered that the safety aspect of phobias, not the danger, is critical (there is a desire to cling to primary internal object representations)—an approach very like certain behavioral formulations of agoraphobia (Rachman, 1984).

Evidence Consistent with the Independent Group's Developmental Model

Balint's Theory of Two Forms of Defense

There is a remarkable correspondence between Balint's model of ochnophilic and philobatic defenses and more recent empirical work on internal working models of adult relationship patterns. Mary Main's and Eric Hesse's work, which emerged out of attachment theory, used the Adult Attachment Interview (George, Kaplan, & Main, 1985; Main & Hesse, 1991) as an indicator of these models. The interview elicits the individual's account of his or her childhood attachment and separation experiences, and evaluates the effects of those experiences on present functioning. Ratings of emotional and cognitive features of the individual's representational world constitute the basis of a four-way classification scheme (Bakerman-Kranenburg & van IJzendoorn, 1993; Main & Goldwyn, 1991). Secure individuals are able to describe both pleasant and painful aspects of their lives in a coherent and realistic manner. The *insecure-preoccupied* group manifests an ochnophilic attitude: they appear entangled in their past experiences with attachment figures. By contrast, the *insecure-dismissing* group may be described as philobats: they show limited recall, a highly restricted range of affective responses, denigration of past relationships, and idealization of independence.

Evidence Consistent with Winnicott's Image of the Infant

Research provides consistent support for Winnicott's (1960, 1962) view that a major feature of the infant's experience of the social world is a sense of control over the caregiver's contingent responses (Trevarthen, 1977, 1990; Watson, 1972). The infant tries to ensure that the mother maintains her interaction, decreases the frequency of nonresponsive or aversive gestures, and increases instances where she imitates the infant's actions (Beebe & Lachman, 1988; Brazelton, Kowslowski, & Main, 1974; Schaffer, 1977; Stern, 1974; Trevarthen, 1977). Gianino and Tronick (1988) referred to the reciprocal pursuit of social aims as "a mutual regulation model" (p. 47). There has been considerable empirical research on transitional objects. The pervasiveness of comforting objects is well demonstrated, but there is no convincing evidence that their presence or absence implies either mental health or illness (Ekecrantz & Rudhe, 1972; Horton & Gewirtz, 1988; Newson, Newson, & Mahalski, 1982; Schaffer & Emerson, 1964; Sherman, Hertzig, Austrian, & Shapiro, 1981). Free (1988) demonstrated, however, that adolescents who recalled having a transitional object in childhood and those who currently used one were more likely to engage in creative activities such as dancing, and writing poetry.

Evidence Consistent with Winnicott's Model of the Caregiver

More controversy surrounds Winnicott's view of sensitive maternal care and mirroring. As we have seen, Winnicott stated that the mother has to be good enough, but some failure is inevitable and is the motivator of growth. Gianino and Tronick (1988) found that the ratio of "miscoordinated" states to coordinated or matched interchanges between infant and mother is 70 to 30. Research supports Winnicott's view that a moderate level of acceptance (Murphy & Moriarity, 1975) and maternal involvement (Belsky, Rovine, & Taylor, 1984; Grolnick, Frodi, & Bridges, 1984) is more beneficial to growth than perfect matching. Evidence suggests that the infant is more active in the process of repair than was perhaps assumed by Winnicott. Demos (1989) described sequences of infant-mother interactions in which relations are at first good, then disrupted, then infant and caregiver jointly restore good relations.

Winnicott's assumptions concerning the traumatic effects of early maternal failure, particularly maternal depression, are also supported by research. Children of depressed parents are at increased risk for the development of psychopathology (e.g., Orvaschel, 1983), particularly behavioral problems (Fendrich, Warner, & Weissman, 1990; Welsh-Allis & Ye, 1988). Abnormalities appear early as difficult temperaments—for example, social unresponsiveness and hypersensitivity (Field, 1992; Garrison & Earls, 1986)—although it is possible that elevated risk for psychopathology and infant behavioral abnormalities are caused by genetic, prenatal, or perinatal correlates of maternal depression. There is ample evidence to suggest that impairment of parent-child relations associated with maternal depression is an important pathogen.

Maternal depression may interfere with the development of secure mother-child attachments (see Cummings & Cicchetti, 1990, for an extended discussion). Parental emotional unavailability and psychological insensitivity have been shown to be strongly linked to maternal depression (Burbach & Borduin, 1986; Webster-Stratton & Hammond, 1988). Laboratory studies of face-to-face interactions involving simulated depressive behavior (negativity, intrusiveness, and withdrawal) have been shown to elicit infant responses of anger, reduced activity, dysphoria, and social withdrawal (Cohn & Campbell, 1992; Cohn & Tronick, 1983; Field, Healy, Goldstein, & Guthertz, 1990; Zekoski, O'Hara, & Wils, 1987). Prolonged exposure to this pattern of interaction leads to depressive behavioral styles in other social contexts (Cohn, Campbell, Matias, & Hopkins, 1990; Field et al., 1988).

Insensitive parental behavior induces distress and physiological arousal (Field, 1987) and may interfere with the child's emerging capacities to regulate these reactions (Tronick, 1989). Field (1989) demonstrated a relationship among maternal depression, aversive mother-child interactions, and the infant's sympathetic arousal, a finding suggesting that the infant's arousal system may become sensitized to all potentially stressful or challenging social contacts (see Cummings & Cicchetti, 1990; Cummings & Zahn-Waxler, 1992). Tronick and Gianino (1986) suggested that children of depressed parents may resort to social withdrawal to avoid the aversive state of disregulation. This is consistent with Winnicott's picture of the incomprehensible caregiver who impinges on the child, causing later disturbance (Winnicott, 1960, 1962).

Research does not support the exclusive concern of Winnicott with the infant-mother relationship. Yogman (1982) showed that, from birth, father and infant are available for meaningful social interaction, although there appear to be qualitative differences between mother-infant and father-infant interactions. H. Steele, M. Steele, and Fonagy (in press) demonstrated that the internal representation of object relationships of both mothers and fathers are independently transmitted to their children during the first 18 months of life. The correlation in the patterns of relationship between infants and mothers and infants and fathers appears totally accounted for by the overlap in the internal working models of the two caregivers. Studies by Grossmann and his colleagues (Grossmann et al., 1993) also illustrated that the security of the child's early relationship to the father has an important and developmentally independent impact on the child's development. There is little in Winnicott's model that speaks to the nature of the paternal element in the child's development, or even an implied account of how a person might develop the capacity for fathering.

Critique and Evaluation

The major weakness of the British object relations school is what may be called naive reconstruction of infancy in the adult mind. Although infant research confirms speculation and informal observation, it cannot sustain the developmental argument of a linear evolution from infancy to adulthood. To the extent that such research is available, longitudinal studies from infancy suggest that personality organization is subject to reorganization throughout development, based on significant positive and negative influences (Emde, 1988a, 1988b). The infantile experiences described by Winnicott and others are thus metaphorical and partial, as were the ego psychological formulations they aimed to replace.

NORTH AMERICAN OBJECT RELATIONS THEORISTS

Modell's Two-Instinct Theory

Modell's View of Development

Modell (1975) attempted to integrate the challenges from British object relations theory with traditional structural theory. He suggested that two classes of instincts should be considered: (a) id instincts (libidinal and aggressive) and (b) the newly recognized object relations instincts, which may be considered the instincts of the ego. Modell suggested that "affects are essentially object seeking." Object relations provide a context in which the developing ego can gain mastery over id instincts mainly by identification with good objects. The failure in the taming of the id, particularly the failure to develop a coherent sense of self, is Modell's (1975) major route to pathology. Unlike British theorists, Modell (1985) saw object relations theory to be relevant only for a restricted group of patients, especially those with narcissistic personality disorders.

Modell's View of Personality Disorders

Modell (1975, 1984) used both Kernberg's formulations (see below) and Winnicott's concept of mirroring, suggesting that narcissistic individuals have been traumatized by parents who fail in mirroring. He assumed that such children perceived that their parents had inadequate capacities for reality testing, and fell back on a compensatory self-structure. Their "self-sufficiency" is illusory and their autonomy unreal.

Modell (1963, 1968) was the first to describe the *transitional relatedness* of borderline patients. Borderline individuals frequently make use of inanimate objects in their adult lives as babies obtain comfort in mother's absence in the same way. Even more striking is their use, usually in primitive and demanding ways, of other people as if they were inanimate (much as a toddler uses a teddy bear). Searles (1986) and Giovacchini (1987) saw this as an indication that borderline patients may have been treated as transitional objects by their parents. Modell (1968) saw the borderline individual's self-image as divided into a helpless infant and someone who is omnipotently giving or destructive. The lack of stability of the self and of object representations leaves the person with a "harrowing dilemma" (p. 286) of extreme dependence and a terror of closeness.

Evaluation of Modell's Approach

Modell differed from object relations theorists (Winnicott, 1965c) in conceptualizing object relations as an instinct of the ego. Many theoreticians feel that this is inconsistent with structural formulations of the ego (Eagle, 1984; Greenberg & Mitchell, 1983). Indeed, it may seem more logical to expand the concept of the id to include object relations—along the lines Bowlby (1969/1982) proposed and Loewald (1955/1980) attempted.

Kohut's Self-Psychology

Developmental Theory

In brief, Kohut's (1971, 1977; Kohut & Wolf, 1978) formulation is that narcissistic development proceeds along a path of its own and that caregiving individuals serve within this line of development as *self-objects.* A self-object performs particular functions for the self; these functions evoke the experience of selfhood (Wolf, 1988). To begin with, a mirroring self-object (assumed to be the mother) allows the unfolding of exhibitionism and grandiosity. Frustration, when manageable and phase-appropriate, permits a gradual modulation of infantile omnipotence through a *transmuting internalization* of this mirroring function. Transmuting internalization of the self-object leads gradually to consolidation of the *nuclear self* (Kohut, 1971; Kohut & Wolf, 1978). The idealization of self-objects, also through internalization, leads to the development of ideals. The internalizing of the mirroring function and idealized self-object leads to the emergence of a "bipolar self," with ambitions, ideals, and the natural talents available to it. Although the mirroring and idealized self-objects come to be internalized, the self continues to require self-objects to varying degrees throughout life, to help in the maintenance of self-cohesion (Kohut, 1984).

Kohut did not provide a clear timetable for his model of development, although he implied that grandiosity changes into ambition, with the help of the mother's mirroring, between the second and fourth years. In this, he seems in line with a Mahlerian rather than a Winnicottian timetable of development. Idealized goals appear from the fourth to sixth years as they do according to classical Freudian superego development.

In Kohut's early work (1971), the self was conceptualized as part of the ego structure; in his later writings (1977, 1984), the self was regarded as a superordinate structure including drives and defenses. Kohut proposed that the main developmental achievement for any individual is a cohesive self. He suggested (1977) that it is the "enfeebled self" that turns defensively toward pleasure aims (drives) and then secondarily involves the ego in managing these aims. Drives are breakdown products of disappointments to the self, usually involving failures in emotional attunement of self-objects. Self-cohesion is the primary human motivation and is derived from inevitable disappointments of grandiosity and exhibitionistic needs (Kohut, 1971).

Kohut attempted to take a number of phenomena of structural psychoanalytic theory and redefine them in terms of self-cohesion. For example, he differentiated between anxiety related to danger situations, such as the fear of instinctual gratification leading to self-reproach or object loss, and anxiety related to the fear of disintegration of the self. Anxiety was primarily the self's experience of defect and a lack of cohesiveness and continuity. Kohut reexamined the Freudian concept of the Oedipus complex and identified a group of individuals for whom oedipal preoccupation is a defense against a fragmentary or enfeebled self. He saw the Oedipus complex, as classically described, as the child's reaction to the parent's failure to enjoy and participate empathically in the child's growth. Unempathic parents are likely to react to their oedipal child with counterhostility or counterseduction, stimulating destructive aggression and isolated sexual fixation. This is a reversal of Freud's model, in that Kohut identified castration anxiety and penis envy as imposed from outside, rather than the consequence of a constitutional predisposition to oedipal experiences.

Working from a Kohutian framework, Stolorow et al. (1987) attempted to redefine the experiential nature of the self-concept. Stolorow and Atwood (1984) distinguished the self as an initiator of action from the self as an organizer of experience. They saw their experiential orientation as an empathic introspective perspective that focuses on the structuralization of experience, rather than on the acquisition of observable skills. Stolorow et al. (1987) criticized Kohut for confounding self as structure with the person as agent. Kohut's view of the self as a superordinate structure with a mental apparatus, in their view, ran into the same problems of mechanistic thinking and reification that, as has been noted, hindered ego psychology. Kohut's motivational metaphor of an attention arc between idealizing and mirroring functions was just as remote from experience as the interagency conflict of the structural model. It moved psychoanalysis back to meta-psychology and away from an experiential focus on the self.

A Model of Developmental Psychopathology

Kohut's General Model of Pathology. Kohut suggested that when parents consistently fail to provide for the child's narcissistic needs, the archaic grandiose self and the idealized parental imago may become hardened and may fail to be integrated into later structures. They then cause various forms of disturbance in the individual's view of the self and his or her relationship with others.

Narcissistic Personality Disorder. Kohut (1971) refused to offer a behavioral description of narcissistic personality disorder, claiming that diagnosis is only possible in terms of the evolving transference relationship. Akhtar and Thompson, however (1982), summarized some of the behavioral features noted in Kohut's writing (see Kohut, 1966, 1968, 1971) and included rage and need for revenge to deal with narcissistic injury, a lack of capacity to form and maintain relationships, perverse sexuality or a lack of sexual interest, lack of empathy, pathological lying, humorlessness toward the self, hypomanic states, and overconcern with the body.

Kohut and Wolf (1978) described five narcissistic personality types: (a) mirror-hungry personalities who compulsively need to evoke others' admiration to deal with a sense of worthlessness, (b) ideal-hungry personalities who search for others whom they can idealize to draw emotional sustenance, (c) alter-ego personalities who need a relationship that will conform to and confirm their own value system, (d) merger-hungry personalities who need to control others to actualize their feeble inner structure in the outside world, and (e) contact-shunning personalities who avoid others to control their desperate need for objects. The last two categories seem to have much in common with borderline and schizoid personality disorders, respectively.

Kohut's conception of narcissistic personality was as a form of developmental arrest. An individual's disappointment in his or her caregivers impinges on primary infantile narcissism and is fended off by the *normal grandiose self,* a quasi-megalomaniac self-image, which helps the child to regain narcissistic equilibrium. The grandiose self is gradually neutralized by age-specific mirroring by the parental figures. Similarly, the ideal parental images with which the young child wishes to merge are eventually modified as the child gradually perceives their limitations and integrates these into the child's own system of values and ideals.

In narcissistic personality disorder, the normal sequence is disrupted in the following ways: (a) the grandiose self persists in an unneutralized way because the child is not met with appropriate mirroring responses, and (b) if the parent is unable to help the child appreciate his or her real limitations, or if the child is disappointed in a traumatic rather than a gradual way, the idealized parental imago will remain and the child will be left with an unattainable, unrealistic, or partial system of values and ideas. The patient in Kohutian treatment is allowed to express both an idealization of the therapist and his or her own grandiosity without being confronted or met by interpretation. The empathic stance taken by the therapist will reactivate the developmental process and, through the inevitable and gradual disappointment of the patient, neutralization of the grandiose self and a decline in the idealization of the caregiving figures will be resumed.

Kohut assumed that, in Freud's time, children were largely overstimulated and that, in the late 20th century, children are reared in an understimulating and lonely psychological environment. He argued on this basis that self-pathology is the dominant psychological illness of modern times.

Other Disorders. Kohut linked perversions and other isolated manifestations of a sexual drive to prolonged empathic failures in the self-object environment. The breakdown of self-assertiveness by way of the mirroring self-object is manifested in exhibitionism. Similarly, the breakdown of a healthy admiration for the idealized self-object is manifested in voyeuristic preoccupation with the breast or the penis. In Kohut's (1971) view, the schizoid personality is a defensive organization motivated by the individual's preconscious awareness of the possibility of a narcissistic injury, which could initiate an "uncontrollable regression" (p. 12). Consequently, the individual channels energy into nonhuman interests.

A number of Kohutians consider the *borderline concept* to be iatrogenic, an indication of the failure of therapist empathy. Kohut (1977, 1984) put forward a trauma arrest model that has been expanded and elaborated in the context of borderline pathology by a number of American authors, including Buie and Adler (1982) and Brandchaft and Stolorow (1987). Buie and Adler (1982) saw the self-pathology of borderline patients in terms of a disjointedness of thinking, feelings of loss of integration of body parts, and a subjective sense of losing control of the self.

Adler (1985), influenced by self-psychology, suggested that the fundamental developmental pathology of narcissistic patients is a failure to achieve an evocative memory of objects, resulting in an inability to hold onto self-objects that might sustain the self. The consequent inner emptiness is primary, and, without internal objects, the self cannot be adequately organized. Borderline patients retain recognition memory, which draws them into intense and deep relationships. When such relationships are threatened by separation or other causes, the patient faces an "annihilatory panic," which, in turn, evokes intense rage to protect the self. The loss of contact with soothing and supporting others leads to a collapse of the self and to identity confusion because, as Kohut (1977) suggested, the self is built up and nourished through the "transmuting internalization" of soothing and mirroring functions provided by early caregivers. Adler's emphasis on memory deficit may help explain why such patients, when in panic and rage, may fail to emotionally recognize their therapists even when physically present. This theory, like all Kohutian developmental models of psychopathology, is thus essentially a deficiency theory: deficiency of necessary facilitating experiences leads to a primary psychic deficit, an inadequately developed sense of self. The clear therapeutic implication is that meaningful intervention must focus on the nature of the individual's deficit and aim at the provision of a therapeutic environment, which may be expected to lead to personal growth to make good the early deprivation—in Kohutian terms, the provision of a soothing and mirroring function that leads to the restoration of the self through the mastery of omnipotence.

Evidence Consistent with the Concept of Mastery

There is little evidence that grandiosity is a normal stage of development. Kohut's evidence, such as it was, came from his analysis of adult patients. Infancy research has identified mastery as a significant feature of the infant's early interaction. DeCasper and Carstens (1981) demonstrated that infants a few days old were able to elongate customary pauses between bursts of sucking in order to activate a recording of female singing. When, in the next phase of the experiment, their "omnipotence" was lost and the singing was produced randomly, not contingent on their sucking pauses, the infants' reactions were negative ("grimacing and vigorous crying," p. 32). The notion of infantile omnipotence is, however, challenged by recent findings, which indicate that, on the majority of occasions, the infant is not able to elicit synchronous behavior from the mother (Gianino & Tronick, 1988). This is not disastrous for Kohut's view: he stressed that the inevitable shortcomings of maternal care, rather than absolute perfection, lead to the development of healthy narcissism. The infant's subjective response beyond observable emotional indicators cannot be tested using presently available techniques.

The evidence concerning children's need for unconditional admiration from their caretakers is questionable (Gedo, 1980). There is certainly a relationship between inconsistent, power-assertive, and lax parental monitoring and antisocial behaviors in children (e.g., Patterson & Stouthamer-Loeber, 1984). Miller, Eisenberg, Fabes, Shell, and Gular (1989) reported on an interesting study of 4- to 5-year-old children and their mothers. Children who showed more sympathy in social situations had mothers who independently indicated that, should their child hurt a peer, they would use reasoning techniques with their children; by contrast, mothers whose children tended to show less sympathy felt equally strongly about such incidents, but indicated they would use negative control practices to encourage the child to have sympathy. Thus, the mother's capacity to try to understand the child's motivation at such times of intense affect appears to have been conveyed to the child, whereas an unempathic attempt to induce concern appears to be counterproductive.

Developmental research does not, by and large, confirm the existence of a narcissistic period in the first 2 to 3 years of life, which is superseded by the oedipal period, as Kohut (1977) suggested. (Kohut, 1984, was less specific about the developmental phase associated with normal narcissism and narcissistic pathology.) There is plenty of evidence to suggest that egocentrism and excessive investment of the self do not normally come to an end in the oedipal period (see Ford, 1979; Westen, 1990a). Rather, they persist throughout childhood and adolescence, with new forms of egocentrism simply replacing old ones. For example, concern about the impact of one's emotions on the mental state of another may not be fully established until the fourth and fifth years of life (see Wellman, 1993).

Furthermore, as we shall detail below, the abandonment of egocentrism and the development of understanding of another's mental state are not all-or-nothing phenomena; they form a process of piecemeal development. The process may indeed start in early infancy in a biological preparedness to attend to people as entities (e.g., Nelson, 1987) and to see interpersonal causation as different from mechanical causation (see Bertenthal, Proffit, Spetner, & Thomas, 1985; Poulin-Dubois & Shultz, 1988). An understanding of others as having intentional subjective experiences is evident early in the second year, from studies of joint perception (e.g., Butterworth, 1991), attention to emotional reactions (Adamson & Bakeman, 1985), and social referencing (Sorce, Emde, Campos, & Klinnert, 1985). Three-year-olds appear to understand how desires are involved in emotions such as happiness (Wellman & Banerjee, 1991), and consider desires imputed to characters as potential explanations of their behavior (Bartsch & Wellman, 1989; Moses & Flavell, 1990). Only 4-year-olds consistently evidence the capacity to consider the beliefs of others (Perner, Leekam, & Wimmer, 1987; Wellman & Bartsch, 1988). Understanding the point of view of another by no means implies a willingness to act on this understanding under most circumstances. Research on childhood social interaction tends to highlight the pragmatic self-interest of children, in terms of both their friendship behavior (Shantz, 1983) and their morality (Rest, 1983). This kind of complex developmental path implies the need to consider the development of normal narcissism in a far more differentiated way than was done by Kohut and self psychologists in general.

Critical Appraisal of Kohut's Model

There are numerous critical reviews of Kohut's theory from within structural psychoanalytic models (see, e.g., Blum, 1982; Loewald, 1973). Schwartz (1978) found Kohut's descriptions overinclusive: fragmentations of the self include depressions, depersonalizations, and disorganizing anxieties, as well as temporary or encapsulated psychotic states. Rothstein (1980) criticized Kohut's failure to acknowledge the link between his ideas and those of others—for example, the link between Kohut's concept of fragmentation and Reich's (1960/1973) construct of catastrophic feelings of annihilation; and between his emphasis on the therapist as a real person and the work of Alexander and French (1946), Stone (1954), Loewald (1960), and Klein (1976b). To these criticisms can be added the scant references to the work of Winnicott.

Many have criticized Kohut's relative deemphasis of aspects of optimal functioning other than the individual's relation to his or her own grandiosity and exhibitionism, such as the capacity for intimacy, mutuality, and reciprocity in interpersonal relationships. P. Tyson and R. L. Tyson (1990) took issue with the prominence Kohut gave to the pathogenic role of the parents at the expense of the infant's innate potential and capacity to modify his or her own environment.

A major problem in Kohut's more recent formulation was the implicit confusion between self and self-representation. The self was presented by Kohut in representational terms, yet Kohut ascribed to it motivational properties and tendencies such as goals, plans, and self-esteem motivation (see Kohut, 1971). In this way, the self came to denote most, if not all, of the personality and therefore became a superfluous term, much as the concept of ego was overextended by ego psychologists (see, e.g., Schafer, 1976). By contrast, Sandler's use of the term *self* (see Sandler, 1962,

1987b) was logically coherent because it was restricted to mental models or representations that persons form of themselves, analogous to representations that others might form of them.

Kernberg's Integration of the Object Relations and Structural Schools

Kernberg's Developmental Theory

Kernberg, an analyst with a Kleinian training, who wrote and practiced in the environment of ego psychology, achieved a remarkable level of integration between these quite possibly epistemologically inconsistent (Greenberg & Mitchell, 1983) developmental frameworks (see Kernberg, 1975, 1976b, 1980, 1984, 1987b). In Kernberg's theory of development, affects serve as the primary motivational system (Kernberg, 1982). He suggested that the *combinations* of a self-representation, an object representation, and an affect state linking them are the essential units of psychic structure. He saw affects as organized into libidinal and aggressive drives, always by way of interactions with a human object. To put this differently, he treated drives as hypothetical constructs manifested in mental representations and affects; these representations are of the self and object, linked by some dominant affect state. The object is not just a vehicle for drive gratification. The major psychic structures (id, ego, superego) are seen as internalizations of object representations and self-object relationships under the influence of various emotional states. The characteristics of internalization depend on the affects active at the time. A superego may be harsh because of a prevailing affect of anger and criticism. Kernberg (1976b) described three functions of internalization—(a) the concept of self-image, (b) the forming of object representations, and (c) the forming of dispositions to affective states—and three processes of internalization—(a) introjection, (b) identification, and (c) ego identity.

Introjection exists at the most basic level of the internalization process. It involves the reproduction of an interaction with the environment by means of the clustering of memory traces attached to the self-image or object-image and the interactions of the two in their affective context. This notion is based on the propositions of Spitz (1965) and Jacobson (1964), that self- and object-images are not yet distinguishable during the earliest stages of interaction. We have already looked at the untenability of this assumption in the light of current infant research, and at the need for the proposition to be reformulated, perhaps in terms of awareness of the boundedness of mental functioning rather than self-object distinction. The second internalization process is identification, which presumes the child's cognitive ability to recognize the variety of role dimensions that exist in interactions with others. Identification, for Kernberg (1976b), involved the capacity of the self to model itself after the object. Kernberg saw such identifications as strongly influenced by fantasy and affect. The individual's experiences of gratification and frustration influence affective states and determine the degree to which self-representation is flexible, true, and complex. Finally, ego identity is borrowed from Erikson (1956/1959) as the overall organization of introjections and identification under the synthesizing influence of the ego.

Kernberg's model of early development was based on reconstructions, strongly influenced by Kleinian theory, from the treatment of severely disturbed adults. It was focused on the force of introjects and fantasies and was less concerned with the child's real experience. Kernberg was also strongly influenced by the work of Jacobson (1964) and proposed a three-stage developmental theory associated with a theory of character pathology based on developmental failure.

Kernberg's Model of Developmental Psychopathology

Kernberg's Framework of Pathology. Kernberg differed from other proponents of object relations theory, such as Klein, Fairbairn, and Mahler, in that he focused less on any particular time at which the dominant pathogenic conflicts and structural organization of the personality may have originated, and more on the current state of the patient's ideation. He accepted that subsequent development makes any one-to-one link between current state and the past risky. He sidestepped a distinction between oedipal or preoedipal problems, which characterizes much of structural psychoanalytic writing. He believed that all levels of disturbance are more complex in severe personality disturbance but all exist, to a greater or lesser extent, across the entire spectrum of psychopathology.

Kernberg (1984) saw neurotic pathology as regression to a relatively integrated, although repressed, infantile self, connected to relatively integrated although also unconscious representations of the parental object. Patients with a neurotic rather than a borderline level of personality organization are able to integrate positive and negative representations of self and others because they have passed through infantile and early childhood phases of development where good and bad representations of self and others are combined across affective valences and a complex, integrated representation of these, containing both loving and hostile elements, has evolved. These unconscious representations come to govern future object relationships in the therapeutic situation and elsewhere. Even such relatively integrated internal representations, however, contain dyadic units that reflect either a defensive or an impulsive aspect of psychic conflict.

An individual is highly susceptible to anxiety when configurations of self and object representations are highly charged affectively and are poorly differentiated. For example, a representation of the self as being weak and vulnerable may be coupled with an object representation of ruthless domination with a violent affective tone. When this configuration is activated in therapy or elsewhere, the individual may become highly anxious. The defensive side may emerge separately, triggered by activation of the impulse-based relationship pattern. Thus, for example, in a masochistic character structure, the experience of a good relationship may trigger an unconscious fantasy of sexual intimacy between the child and the parent and propel into consciousness a critical, nagging relationship pattern where the self is seen as criticized by an unsympathetic and misunderstanding other (the therapist or another figure) (Kernberg, 1987a, p. 487). The results are: lack of superego integration, severe mood swings, contradictory feelings and behavior, a mixture of repression and other defenses, and mixed pregenital and genital aims in relationships at this intermediate level of personality functioning. This level includes passive-aggressive personalities, sadomasochistic personalities, and some infantile and narcissistic personalities.

In more severe psychopathology, there is a much greater likelihood of rapid reversal. In the example cited above, although an individual may feel criticized, the criticism can very quickly shift from the self onto the other; the critic is then seen as the self who is hurt and mistreated, and the individual identifies with the critical stance. This oscillation of self and other accounts for many instances where impulses appear to change into their opposite (active into passive, good into bad).

At very severe levels of character pathology, Kernberg (1984) identified a defensive primitive dissociation or splitting of internalized object relations. This level of character pathology is marked by a lack of integration of self and object representations, projections of primitive superego nuclei, splitting, impulsivity, lack of empathy, and the unmodulated expression of libido and aggression. Kernberg saw such splitting as occurring in borderline personality organization, antisocial personalities, patients with multiple sexual deviations in narcissistic personalities, addictions, and analytically approachable psychosis.

Here, the tolerance of ambivalence characteristic of higher-level neurotic object relationships is replaced by a defensive disintegration of the representation of self and objects into libidinally and aggressively invested part-object relations. Instead of the more realistic and readily comprehensible relationship patterns of neurotic personalities, Kernberg found highly unrealistic, idealized, or persecutory self and object representations. These cannot be traced back to actual or fantasized relationships in the past; Kernberg believed they do not correspond to any real relationship. Because the object relations are very poorly integrated, the reversals of the enactment of self and other representations may be very rapid. This can make relationships with such individuals confusing and even chaotic. For example, love and hate may exist in a dissociated way side by side; several object relations may be condensed into single images, and so on. He identified the central problems of borderline patients as the activation of primitive, overwhelming part-object relations that continuously alternate.

In contrast, the problem in the case of psychosis is the blurring of boundaries between self and object representations. Here, the protective quality of the defensive object relation fails because the confusion between self and object blurs the origin of the intolerable impulse. The impulse is therefore reactivated without the protection of the defensive relationship pattern into which it was cast. Such patients will be frequently overwhelmed in any kind of intimate relationship.

Kernberg's Model of Narcissistic Personality Disorder. Kernberg (1970) described "a narcissistic personality structure" in individuals who display an overreliance on acclaim, grandiose fantasies, intense ambition, and extreme self-absorption. He described their behavior as superficially adaptive; they lack empathy, tend to exploit others, feel empty and unable to love, and have no enjoyment in life other than from admiration. He noted that such individuals have a capacity for consistent work and success, but their activities are focused around opportunities for exhibitionism, lacking in genuine commitment, and corruptible in the search for praise. Less well socially adjusted individuals may seek treatment because of a failure to establish long-term relationships and a general sense of aimlessness. Some narcissistic individuals function at the borderline level and display major deficiencies in anxiety tolerance, impulse control, and sublimation. For all these individuals, Kernberg (1975) noted that feelings of inferiority coexist with notions of grandiosity, and this he saw as rooted in the "chronic intense envy and defenses against such envy, particularly devaluation, omnipotent control and narcissistic withdrawal" (p. 264). The envious attacks sooner or later encompass their own achievements, and, with the approach of middle age, their destructive self-devaluations may lead to a "gradual deterioration of the patient's internal past" (Kernberg, 1980, p. 138). Their omnipotent approach to reality may lead them to deny natural aging, feel rivalrous with youth (in their children and colleagues), and develop full-blown midlife crises, with major vocational shifts and inappropriate love relationships.

Kernberg saw narcissistic pathology as rooted in experiences of a rejecting primary caregiver who was cold but who was the only available source of comfort. The child falls back on the grandiose self. The child's rage reaction to protect the grandiose self is projected onto the parents, who are then perceived as even less likely to meet the child's needs, and the child is increasingly restricted to the grandiose self for soothing and comfort. The term *grandiose self* was also used by Kohut (1968), but in a different way. In Kernberg's model, this aspect of the self contains the admired aspects of the child, the compensatory fantasies about the self as all-powerful, and a fantasized image of a loving and understanding caregiver. The needy parts of the individual remain out of awareness. The grandiose self differentiates narcissistic personality from borderline disorder; whereas both manifest a predominance of splitting over repression, narcissistic personalities have a more cohesive, albeit highly pathological self. In psychotherapeutic treatment, the grandiose self increasingly emerges in the therapeutic relationship. Interpretive exploration of this will give insight about the role of these distortions in maintaining self-esteem and self-continuity, in the context of helplessness and rage.

Kernberg's Model of Borderline Personality Disorder. For Kernberg, borderline was a level of psychic organization rather than a nosological entity. His criteria for the disorder included: (a) nonspecific manifestations of ego weakness (poor affect tolerance, impulse control, and sublimatory capacity), (b) primitive defenses, (c) identity diffusion, and (d) intact reality testing but a propensity to shift toward dreamlike thinking. There is some empirical evidence in support of Kernberg's criteria (see Kernberg, 1981).

For Kernberg (1967, 1977), the root cause of borderline states was the intensity of destructive and aggressive impulses and the relative weakness of ego structures available to handle them. The good introjects are repeatedly threatened with destruction by the predominance of negative, hostile images and impulses, which are necessary to achieve stability. Kernberg saw the borderline individual as using developmentally early defenses in an attempt to separate contradictory images of self and others. This separation is necessary to protect positive images from being overwhelmed by negative and hostile ones. The wish to protect the object from destruction with only the most rudimentary psychic mechanisms available leads to the defensive fragmentation of self and object representations. Manifestations of the borderline condition therefore represent a continuation of an unresolved infantile conflict state.

The defenses of borderline individuals center on the splitting (defensive separating) of contradictory self and object representations in order to forestall the terror associated with ambivalence. Primitive idealization, also a consequence of splitting, protects the individual from the "all bad" objects through creation, in fantasy, of an omnipotent object that is the container of grandiose identifications. Projective identification was seen by Kernberg as a by-product of the absence of self-object differentiation; the individual using this defense is left with a sense of empathy for the object of projection as well as a need to control it. The use of primitive denial ensures that the individual can totally disregard an experience of "good" feelings toward the object when "bad" feelings dominate his or her consciousness. Splitting also results in a diffuse sense of identity, which is characterized by a confused internal representation of the "real" object, and an unintegrated primitive superego, which sets unattainable ideals and internalized persecutory images. Because representations of the self are organized in a parallel fashion with those of others, splitting also leads to "extreme and repetitive oscillation between contradictory self concepts . . . the patient, lacking in a stable sense of self or other, continually experiences the self in shifting positions with potentially sharp discontinuities—as victim or victimizer, as dominant or submissive, and so on" (Kernberg, Selzer, Koenigsberg, Carr, & Appelbaum, 1989, p. 28).

Kernberg (1987a) illustrated how self-destructiveness, self-mutilating behavior, and suicidal gestures tend to coincide with intense attacks of rage toward the object. They can serve to reestablish control over the environment by evoking guilt feelings or expressing unconscious guilt over the success of a deepening relationship. In some patients, self-destructiveness occurs because their self-image becomes "infiltrated" with aggression; they experience increased self-esteem and a confirmation of their grandiosity in self-mutilation or masochistic sexual perversions. The caring professions can respond only with despair to these patients' obvious sense of triumph in their victory over pain and death. Remedial efforts seem futile to the patient, who at an unconscious level experiences a sense of being in control over death. Self-mutilation, such as cutting, may also protect against identity diffusion (de-realization), which is a constant threat to the fragmented internal world of the borderline individual.

Kernberg (1970) grouped together borderline and schizoid personality disorders, viewing both of these as lower-level character organizations (see also Kernberg, 1967). The overlap is substantiated by empirical investigations demonstrating comorbidity between the two conditions (Plakum, Burkhardt, & Muller, 1985) as well as overlaps in pathological psychic mechanisms (Grinker, Werble, & Drye, 1968; Gunderson, 1985).

Kernberg's Model of Antisocial Personality Disorder. Kernberg (1975, 1976c, 1984, 1989) believed that patients with antisocial personality disorder usually have underlying borderline personality organizations. Because superego integration is minimal at this level and its sadistic forerunners are easily projected outward, there is deficient guilt, lack of goals, inauthenticity, and erratic potential for sublimation. Antisocial behavior occurs in most severe personality disorders because of the common underlying personality organization. Superego pathology is particularly evident in an absence of loyalty, guilt, and anticipatory anxiety, and in an incapacity to learn from prior experience. Kernberg (1989) also mentioned the importance of an absence of self-reflection in these individuals.

Evidence Consistent with Kernberg's Formulations

Some empirical work, using projective techniques, draws on Kernberg's theoretical model. Krohn's object representation scales for dreams (see Hatcher & Krohn, 1980; Krohn & Mayman, 1974) were constructed to assess levels of capacity for interpersonal relatedness. The aim of the measures is to examine the degree to which people are experienced as whole, consistent, alive, and complex, as opposed to absent, desolate, fragmented, and malignant. They are used primarily with Rorschach responses but can also be applied to early memories and dreams. There is a relationship between scores on these measures and general mental health (Grey & Davies, 1981) and the capacity to engage in psychotherapy (Hatcher & Krohn, 1980) as well as its outcome (Frieswyk & Colson, 1980).

A similar measure, also based on Rorschach protocols, was developed by Urist (1977; Urist & Schill, 1982). It draws on the work of Mahler and Kohut, as well as Kernberg, and identifies a 7-point continuum in which a rating of 1 indicates reciprocity of mutuality, and a rating of 7 indicates envelopment-incorporation. In between are points indicating collaboration, cooperation, simple interaction, analytic dependency, reflection-mirroring, and magical control-coercion. The measure is correlated with outcome of psychotherapy (Kavanagh, 1985) and hospital treatment (Blatt, Ford, Berman, Cook, & Meyer, 1988), as well as the differential diagnosis of borderline personality disorder and schizophrenia (Spear & Sugarman, 1984).

Ryan's object relations scale (Ryan & Bell, 1984; Ryan & Cicchetti, 1985) also identified borderline disorders and differentiated them from (a) depressed or pathologically narcissistic states and (b) neurotic disturbances in relatedness. Using the scale, Ryan and Cicchetti (1985) demonstrated an association between object relations and therapeutic alliance, and Ryan and Bell were able to predict the length of remission from hospital treatment for psychotic patients. Westen and his associates (Westen, Ludolph, Block, Wixom, & Wiss, 1990; Westen, Ludolph, Lerner, Ruffins, & Wiss, 1990) developed a four-scale model for scoring object relations: (a) complexity and differentiation of the representation of people, (b) affective tone of relationships, (c) capacity for emotional investment in relationships and morals, and (d) understanding of social causality. The scale discriminates the borderline group of patients from psychotic and normal controls, demonstrating more malevolent representations, less emotional investment in relationships and values, and less accurate and logical attributions of causality. The complexity of the borderline representation was apparently greater than those of the other two groups.

The latter finding is, however, confounded by the issue of accuracy. Blatt, Brenneis, Schimek, & Glick (1976; see also Ritzler, Wyatt, Harder, & Kaskey, 1980), using a different scoring system, also reported borderline patients showing higher developmental levels (levels of complexity) than normal, but questioned the accuracy and reality of their perceptions.

Perhaps the strongest support for Kernberg's model has come from the work of Drew Westen (Westen & Cohen, 1993). Westen and his coworkers designed a structured interview to elicit general characterization and specific memories of relationships with important others, and to provide self-descriptions at increasing levels of abstraction. These workers gave empirical backing to Kernberg's view of the transitory, split, and poorly integrated quality of borderline self-representation. Such individuals show egocentrism, an apparent lack of concern for the listener's perspective, poor differentiation between self and others, little awareness of contradictions, and extremely negative self-representations. In line with previous work (e.g., Bell, Billington, & Cicchetti, 1988; Nigg, Lohr, Westen, Gold, & Silk, 1992; Westen, Lohr, Silk, Gold, & Kerber, 1990), borderline individuals described relationship schemata with others that were generally malevolent in character; most commonly, the self and others fell into the roles of victim and victimizer. Westen's group also found evidence of the interchangeability of self and other in these schemata (see Kernberg, 1984), and the descriptions of roles would reverse rapidly. The relationship schemata appear transitory, with the subject showing limited awareness of contradictions. Evaluative representations of borderline patients reflect an all-or-nothing character; for example, wishes or ideals are either totally achieved or not achieved at all. They are also unrealistic and confused about both feared and ideal self-representations. Their self-esteem is subject to extreme fluctuation, particularly in a negative direction. Their sense of self is usually disrupted by dissociative experiences (see Zanarini, Gunderson, & Frankenburg, 1990a). More generally, there is much support for the diffusion of identity concept proposed by Kernberg (1975), manifest in the lack of consistent investment in goals, values, ideals, and relationships over time.

Memory and identity are intrinsically linked (Klein, 1970); an individual is, by and large, a memory of himself or herself. Westen and Cohen (1993) demonstrated that the historical memory of borderline patients tends to be filled with large gaps or discontinuities, and the self is represented as totally different during different time periods. It is suggested that the social construction of identity may be disrupted in these patients by their failure to sustain long-term intimate relationships.

Evaluation of Kernberg's Model

Otto Kernberg's work has been extremely influential in the United States, Europe, and Latin America. He succeeded in systematizing psychoanalytic object relations theory into a unitary framework that is consistent with both classical and structural theory and the work of British object relations theorists. The integration is not perfect; for example, Kernberg leaped between drive theory and object relations approaches by using common terminology in the two frameworks (e.g., "good" and "bad" constellations of relations with objects). He made extensive use of affects as explanatory constructs, but his view of these ill fit classical (drive theory) formulations. Kernberg's bias was toward abandoning drive theory in favor of a relational approach (Greenberg & Mitchell, 1983). Kernberg achieved integration by radically altering the meaning of terms that have been part of the classical model, such as id, drives, and objects.

Even if Kernberg's attempt at providing an integrated psychoanalytic model may not be regarded as an unqualified success, he has advanced the field dramatically in terms of providing operational definitions for many of the constructs that he uses. Kernberg's commitment to research has spanned his career (Kernberg, 1974, 1989). His technical recommendations are unambiguous and open to scientific scrutiny (Kernberg & Clarkin, 1993). His descriptions of psychopathology, particularly his contribution to the diagnosis of personality disorder, may be appropriately contrasted with the operational criteria provided by the DSM (Miller, 1993). His etiological hypotheses remain largely untested and suffer from many of the historical weaknesses of psychoanalytic formulations (see below). His contribution is a landmark, not simply in terms of the advancement of psychoanalytic developmental formulations of severe personality disorders, but also bringing about a major shift in the epistemic stance taken by psychoanalysts, from a clinical/hermeneutic toward an empirical perspective.

Stern's Approach to Infant Development

Stern's Developmental Schema

Stern's (1985) work has been distinguished by being normative rather than pathomorphic, and prospective rather than retrospective. His focus is the reorganization of subjective perspectives on self and other as these occur with the emergence of new maturational capacities.

His model uses four different senses of self, each with an associated domain of relatedness:

1. The sense of *emergent self* involves the process of the self coming into being and forming connections (from birth to 2 months of age);
2. The sense of *core self* (from between 2 and 6 months of age) and the domain of *core relatedness* are based on a single organizing subjective perspective and a coherent *physical self;*
3. The sense of *subjective self* and the domain of *intersubjective relatedness* (between 7 and 15 months) emerge with the discovery of subjective mental states beyond physical events;
4. The sense of *verbal self* forms after 15 months.

The capacities underlying the sense of subjective self include a number that are clinically relevant. The earliest manifestation may be an understanding of the mental state of attention, which appears in normal infants from about 9 months of age in a monitoring of the gaze of the mother (Butterworth, 1991; Scaife & Bruner, 1975) and in gestures such as protodeclarative pointing (Bates, Benigni, Bretherton, Camaioni, & Volterra, 1979). It is evident from gaze monitoring that infants apprehend the intentions and motives of others and seem to check not only where someone is looking but also how the person is evaluating what he or she sees (social referencing; Sorce et al., 1985). Such emotional communication can be conveyed through the face or the voice by a parent or familiar caretaker, and it can regulate behavior toward an object, a location, or a person (Boccia & Campos, 1989; Camras & Sachs, 1991). In protodeclarative pointing, children appear to use the pointing gesture as a comment on a topic of interest, concern, or fun (Baron-Cohen, 1991; Tomasello, 1988). Phillips, Baron-Cohen, and Rutter (1992) found that normal 9- to 18-month-old toddlers respond to an ambiguous action of an adult by instantly looking at the adult's eyes; they do so on only a minority of occasions, when the adult's action is not ambiguous. Thus, infants from this stage appear to sense the congruence or lack of congruence between their own state and that of another person.

The sense of verbal self and the domain of verbal relatedness represent a move to a stage where the subject and other people can be represented as storehouses of knowledge and experience. This experience may be shared, involving abilities to objectify the self, reflect on mental contents, and use language to communicate. Baron-Cohen (1993b) identified six different classes of mental states that the developing child comes to appreciate at different moments: (a) *understanding beliefs,* particularly that a belief may be false; (b) *desire*; (c) *understanding knowledge*; (d) *understanding pretense,* that is, understanding that an identity is inappropriate; (e) *understanding perception*; and (f) *understanding emotion.*

Infants of depressed mothers "expect" less emotional responsiveness and therefore gaze less at their mothers (see, e.g., Cohn, Matias, Tronick, Connell, & Lyons-Ruth, 1986). Infants generalize this expectation toward a stranger (Field et al., 1988). There is evidence that the effect is cumulative and shapes the behavior of strangers interacting with the infant, who behaves less positively toward them (Cohn et al., 1990; Field et al., 1988).

Infants also understand anger in the caregiver and respond to it by crying, looking angry, or just watching in expressionless fashion (Haviland & Lelwica, 1987). Toddlers understand affect between others, such as covert tension between the parents or overt conflict (Cummings, Zahn-Waxler, & Radke-Yarrow, 1981, 1984). Laboratory observations indicate that a simulated quarrel is most likely to be associated with a freezing response and subsequent aggression, and sensitizes children to further similar experiences (Cummings, Iannotti, & Zahn-Waxler, 1985). Children appear to understand a quarrel differently: for some, it serves as a license to engage in hostile behavior; for others, it is a stimulus that arouses solicitous concern. Children assimilate such exchanges into larger causal schemata encoding general assumptions about how quarrels arise, who is to blame, and how one may avoid and ameliorate these experiences (Harris, 1994).

Two- to 3-year-olds can appropriately distinguish and name various emotional states, and appear to understand the equivalence between their own states and those of other people (Bretherton, Fritz, Zahn-Waxler, & Ridgeway, 1986; Brown & Dunn, 1991; Dunn, Bretherton, & Munn, 1987). Wellman, Harris, Banerjee, and Sinclair (in press) report that children up to 4 years of age almost invariably explain emotion in terms of an intentional target, that is, a person or a physical object at which the emotion is aimed.

Stern (1994) concurs with Sandler in focusing on the consciously or unconsciously experienced aspects of the representational world, as opposed to the nature of the nonexperiential mental structures (or mental processes; see Fonagy & Moran, 1991), which underpin and create mental representations. Stern's starting point is the *emergent moment,* the subjective integration of all aspects of lived experience, which takes its input from emotions, behaviors, sensations, and all other aspects of the internal and external world. The emergent moment is seen as deriving from schematic representations of various types: event representations or scripts; semantic representations or conceptual schemata; perceptual schemata; and sensorimotor representations. To these, Stern has added two clinically relevant modes of representation: (a) *feeling shapes* and (b) *protonarrative envelopes.* These schemata form a network that he terms the *schema of a-way-of-being-with* (see also Horowitz, 1991; Kernberg, 1976b).

The schema of a-way-of-being-with is conceptualized by Stern from the assumed subjective point of view of the infant who is in interaction with the caregiver. The infant's experiences across a number of domains are organized around a motive and a goal, and in this sense echo Freud's (1905/1991b) original formulation of drives and object relationships in the *Three Essays.* The goals that organize these moments are not only biological but also include object relatedness, affect states, and states of self-esteem and safety, as well as physical need gratification, be it hunger, thirst, sexuality, or aggression. The representation will contain a protoplot, with an agent, an action, an instrumentality, and a context—all necessary elements for the comprehension of human behavior (see Bruner, 1990).

Stern (1994) offers a compelling example of a-way-of-being-with a depressed mother and describes the infant's reaction to a nonresponsive object by trying repeatedly to recapture and reanimate her. He describes how depressed mothers, monitoring their own failure to stimulate, may make huge efforts to enliven their infant in a forced and unspontaneous way, to which infants respond with what is probably an equally false response of enlivened interaction. This model maps very closely onto Sandler's model of projection and projective identification, and the two need to be combined to achieve a fully coherent account. The child identifies with the representation of the mother's distorted representation of him or her, which is communicated by a process of projective identification and eventually evolves into an expectation of "a false way-of-being-with" the other.

The schemata of ways-of-being-with come closest to providing a neuropsychologically valid model of the representation of interpersonal experience. Certain features of the model are critical in this regard. First, these schemata are emergent properties of the nervous system and the mind. Second, they make use of multiple simultaneous representations of the lived experience. This is consistent with the clinical observation that even in pervasive brain injury, aspects of experience are retained. Third, they are based on prototypes, are less affected by single experiences, and naturally aggregate common patterns of lived experience. Emergent moments are represented in the simultaneous activation of a set of nodes within a network and the strengthening of the connections between these nodes, with each activation automatically constituting a *learning process.* By conceptualizing schemata of way-of-being-with as networks, Stern links his model to that of the dominant model of cognitive science, parallel distributed processing (see Rumelhart & McClelland, 1986). Fourth, the model allows room for modification from inside as well as outside. In postulating refiguration as a process whereby attention can scan representation, Stern offers a way in which internally generated activation (fantasy) may strengthen or alter and potentially distort objective experience. Fifth, in adopting Edelman's (1987) concept of neural Darwinism, Stern opens an important avenue for further work on the fate of representations that lost out in the process of natural selection (see below).

Stern's schema of a-way-of-being-with concept seems to have much in common with other important, relatively recent, developments in cognitive science. His formulation is perhaps most closely linked to Barasalou's (1991) work on the concept of *frame,* which is an overlapping construct with that of *schema* but is less vague and unspecified than Bartlett's (1932) overused concept (for reviews, see Alba & Hasher, 1983; Brewer & Nakamura, 1984). The notion of frames was originally proposed by Fillmore (1968). In his model of syntactic knowledge, syntactic structures were represented by frames that had several attributes associated with them (e.g., an agent, a theme, a source, or an instrument), and each of these attributes was assumed to acquire a value in a specific sentence. Thus, for Fillmore, the frame for the verb "buy" specified an agent who buys, a theme of what is bought, a source of where it is bought, and an instrument with which it is bought. Stern's formulation of object relations in terms of a schema of a way-of-being-with also provides a frame with attributes such as an agent, an action, an instrumentality, and a context.

Numerous similar models in the field of cognitive science (e.g., Minsky, 1977, 1985; Schanck, 1975, 1982) have been a subject of psychoanalytic commentary in the past. Our reason for highlighting the work of Barasalou as particularly relevant to Stern's ideas is motivated by Barasalou's contributions on the representation and organization of autobiographical memories (1988), and on the contextual variability of contextual representation (Barasalou, 1987, 1989; Barasalou & Billman, 1989), as well as his ambitious work on providing a model for the representation of all knowledge in human cognition (Barasalou, 1991). Unlike some other schema theories, Barasalou's implementation of the frames concept has, in common with Stern's schema of a-way-of-being-with, a certain flexibility in the configuration of these mental structures. In most schema theories, such structures are envisaged as relatively rigid configurations of independent attributes. In frames theory, attributes vary in systematicity with relevant attributes varying across contexts.

Closer scrutiny, from a psychoanalytic standpoint, may teach us much more of great explanatory value. For example, the notion of "constraint" on values—the assumption that the values of attributes in a frame are not independent of one another—provides a framework for understanding the pervasive influence of prototypical experiences between infant and caregiver. Past experience will constrain the possible values that the mother's affective emotional response attribute may take on, given a particular value of the child's motivational state. Constraints, as Barasalou pointed out, are self-perpetuating and thus resilient to change.

Stern's formulation also touches on mental model theory (see Johnson-Laird, 1983). Mental model theory assumes that higher-order cognitive processes are based on an individual's understanding of a situation, where the starting point is a set of models—typically, a single model for a single situation—constructed from perceiving the world, from understanding discourse, or from both. To understand is to construct mental models from knowledge and from perceptual or verbal evidence. To formulate a conclusion is to describe what is represented in the models. To test validity is to search for alternative models that refute the putative conclusion. Mental models, just as Stern's schema of a-way-of-being-with, may or may not be accessible to consciousness. What matter for both Stern's and Johnson-Laird's proposed mechanisms are the structures created, which are isomorphic with the structures of the states of affairs to which they pertain, whether perceived or conceived, and which they are thus able to represent. It is a highly attractive aspect of Johnson-Laird's formulation, from a psychoanalytic standpoint, that irrationality in the sense of invalid deductions is an emergent property of the model.

Taken together, the psychoanalytic propositions of Sandler and Stern have created a number of new bridges between clinically grounded psychoanalytic observations and progress in modern neuroscience. They offer the potential for dramatic revisions of psychoanalytic metapsychology. For example, what was previously thought of as a qualitatively different structure of cognition, primary process thought, may simply be the activation of neural networks or representations selected out in the process of neural evolution. Prelinguistic children are likely to organize their physical world in nonconceptual ways in some instances, according to the physical appearance of objects. Studies of language development show that the early use of language is frequently dominated by the physical appearance of objects (e.g., children frequently refer to all round objects with the same word). Such neural networks are selected out as the child understands more complex and conceptual relationships between these elements. In states of reverie, dreaming, or intense emotional arousal, these old "vestigial" structures may become reactivated. Schemata may also lose out in the process of neural natural selection, through deliberate separation of frames or parts of a network that interfere with efficient adaptive neural functioning. Ideas that give rise to conflict and anxiety may thus be eliminated from neural nets. When schemata of ways-of-being-with have been eliminated in this way, they may re-emerge or persist (Sandler & Joffe, 1967), if other constraints on the system are temporarily lifted by dream sleep, by reverie, or by free association.

A Model of Developmental Pathology in Stern's Framework

Although Stern (1985, 1994) has implied many links to pathological states, he has not proposed a comprehensive model of psychopathology. Some proposed models, loosely based on Stern's developmental approach, integrate findings from developmental research with clinical goals (Fonagy & Moran, 1991; Fonagy, Moran, Edgcumbe, Kennedy, & Target, 1993). Work with case records at the Anna Freud Centre (Fonagy & Target, 1994; Target & Fonagy, 1994), in conjunction with research on the determinants of early relationships (Fonagy, Steele, Moran, Steele, & Higgitt, 1991; Fonagy, Steele, & Steele, 1991; Steele et al., in press) has led to an extension of certain psychoanalytic assumptions concerning the nature of psychic change in child analysis (Fonagy & Moran, 1991). In these papers, two psychoanalytic models of mental disturbance are delineated. The first (the *synthetic model*) describes the mechanism by which the patient is helped to recover threatening ideas and feelings that had been repudiated or distorted in the course of development, as a result of conflict and defense. The second model (the *mental process model*) draws attention to the therapeutic effects of engaging previously inhibited mental processes within the psychoanalytic encounter. This engagement tends to occur primarily when the patient and analyst focus on the thoughts and feelings of each person and on how the child understands these. The two models entail two types of pathology, requiring two types of analytic work, with different predicted rates of change.

The notion of unutilized mental processes offers a conceptual bridge between psychoanalytic work with children and advances in cognitive science; it also stresses the therapeutic value of a mentalizing or reflective capacity, which independently emerges as a predictor of secure parent-child attachment relationship (Fonagy, Steele, Moran et al., 1991). Furthermore, it offers a theoretical explanation of a long-established clinical finding: children with marked developmental or personality disturbances require longer treatment, with modifications of classical psychodynamic technique (e.g., A. Freud, 1965). This theoretical basis leads us to predict that there will be clear differences in technique, levels of change, and rates of change, depending on the depth of personality disturbance in a child.

This approach is exemplified in an understanding of the role of inhibition of mental functioning in borderline personality disorder (Fonagy, 1991; Fonagy et al., in press; Fonagy & Higgitt, 1989). The hypothesis is that an early and sustained history of trauma and abuse in these individuals would be associated with inhibition of their capacity to envisage mental states (reflective self-function). This has been supported by both cross-sectional and longitudinal investigations. Patients who met Gunderson's criteria for borderline personality disorder were rated as having lower reflective self function than control groups of patients with nonpsychotic psychiatric disorders of equal severity. The inpatient psychotherapeutic treatment of borderline patients was associated with an improvement in reflective self-function in all those who showed substantial symptom reductions in response to the treatment. These findings offer preliminary support for the hypotheses that (a) part of the disturbance of borderline patients may be understood in terms of a deficit of mentalizing functions, and (b) these functions are inaccessible to such patients, but may be recovered in the course of psychotherapeutic treatment.

Considerable evidence supports the possibility of conflict-induced deficits in the functioning of mental processes that normally evolve through constitution-determined developmental pathways—or, to use Waddington's (1966) term are "canalised." For example, in one study, 9-year-old boys attending ordinary schools were compared with boys of the same age attending schools for the emotionally disturbed (Adlam-Hill & Harris, 1988). The latter group frequently failed to distinguish real from apparent emotion, implying that the disturbed family environment that characterized most of these children impeded, in some way, the normal development of the capacity to understand how and in what situation feelings could be hidden. They were particularly unlikely to see any need for concealing feelings if the other person's feelings were at stake. Mary Main (1991), from an attachment theory perspective, found evidence that ambivalently attached children, who are most likely to have had experiences of emotional entanglement with their primary caregiver, are also most likely to deny the inherent privacy of mental state. Main argued that such children continue to assume that their caregivers have access to their innermost selves, and that they themselves can read the thoughts of an attachment figure. From a broader psychoanalytic perspective, we would claim that the child defensively inhibits his or her capacity to accept the mental separateness of the mother because to do so would entail the pain of experiencing her incomprehension of the child's feelings, beliefs, and desires (Fonagy et al., in press).

Accumulating evidence also suggests that these fundamental cognitive processes underlying the understanding of mental states are far more vulnerable to the vicissitudes of environmental experiences than had previously been thought. There is evidence to suggest that the development of the capacities underlying the false belief task may be enhanced by the proximity of a sibling (see Jenkins & Astington, 1993; Perner, Ruffman, & Leekam, in press). Close interaction with a sibling who is close in age enhances the child's understanding of mental states. Preliminary data from our own prospective study, as well as data reported by Main (1991), are consistent with the view that a secure attachment to a caregiver enhances the child's capacity to explore the mind of that person and facilitates the evolution of emotional self-awareness and a theory of mind.

Following the philosopher Davidson (1983), and psychoanalytic exponents of his work (see Cavell, 1988a, 1988b, 1991), it is suggested that getting to know one's own mind is a process of familiarizing oneself with the mind of another. Children perceive and eventually come to recognize themselves in their caregivers' perceptions of them. We believe that the development of the self entails the internalization not of the object, good or bad, as classical object relations theory posits, but of the caregiver's image of the intentional infant which, when internalized, comes to constitute the core of the child's mentalizing self. Incoherent perception of the child's mental state therefore places the child's self-development at risk. Accurate perception of the child as a psychological being is particularly critical when the caregiver's own adverse history places her at risk of recapitulating, with her child, her own adverse early relationship experiences (Fonagy et al., 1994).

UNDERSTANDING NORMAL DEVELOPMENT: CONTRIBUTIONS FROM THE STUDY OF PSYCHOPATHOLOGY

Psychoanalytic Theory at the Interface of Development and Pathology

Psychoanalytic models have evolved as diverse attempts to explain why and how a particular individual in psychoanalytic treatment has deviated from the normal path of development and has come to experience major intrapsychic and interpersonal difficulties. All of the models reviewed in this chapter focus on particular developmental phases and outline a model of normal development derived almost exclusively from the analyst's interpersonal experience with patients.

Freud was the first to give meaning to mental disorder by linking it to childhood experiences (Freud & Breuer, 1895/1991), and to the vicissitudes of the developmental process (Freud, 1900/1991). Freud's greatest contribution was undoubtedly the recognition of childhood sexuality (Freud, 1905/1991). Few would now doubt that children experience sexual feelings from the earliest days (Green, 1985). Freud's discoveries radically altered our perception of the child from one of idealized naïveté and innocence to a human being struggling to adapt his or her biological and constitutional characteristics to constraining social circumstances. Freud's image of the child is of a person in turmoil (Freud, 1933/1991), struggling to achieve control over biological needs and to make them acceptable to society at large through the microcosm of the family (Freud, 1930/1991).

Ego psychologists balanced this view by focusing on the evolution of adaptive capacities (Hartmann, 1939/1958), which the child brings to bear on the struggle with biological needs. Hartmann's model attempted to take a wider view of the developmental process, linking drives and ego functions and showing how negative interpersonal experiences beyond the expectable range can jeopardize the evolution of the psychic structures essential to adaptation. He also showed that the reactivation of earlier structures (regression) is the most important component of psychopathology. Epidemiological research confirms that disadvantaged children in modern society appear to be protected by superior constitutional endowment (Garmezy & Masten, 1991; Kandel et al., 1988; Rutter & Quinton, 1984). Children with good adaptive capacities have the opportunity to acquire protective and nonaggressive problem-solving skills (Huesmann, Eron, & Yarmel, 1987). Social and cognitive abilities and effective problem-solving skills appear to commonly mark resilient children (Cowen, Wyman, Work, & Parker, 1990; Masten, 1989; Werner, 1990).

Child analysts working with children in distress (e.g., Fraiberg, 1969, 1980; A. Freud, 1965) have taught us that symptomatology is not a fixed formation, but rather a dynamic entity superimposed on and intertwined with an underlying developmental process. Anna Freud's study of symptomatic and asymptomatic children under great social stress led her to formulate a relatively comprehensive developmental theory, in which the child's emotional maturity can be identified independently of diagnosable pathology. Particularly in her early work in the war nurseries (A. Freud, 1941–1945/1974), she identified many of the characteristics that later research linked to the so-called *resilient* child (Rutter, 1990). For example, her observations spoke of the importance of the social support that children can give one another in situations of extreme stress (concentration camps), helping to ensure their physical and psychological survival. More recent research on youngsters experiencing trauma has confirmed her assertion of the protective power of sound social support (Garmezy, 1983; McFarlane, 1987; O'Grady & Metz, 1987; Werner, 1989).

Anna Freud was also a pioneer in identifying the importance of an equilibrium among developmental processes (A. Freud, 1965). Her work is particularly relevant in explaining why children who are deprived of certain capacities, by environment or constitution, appear to be at greater risk of psychological disturbance. Epidemiological studies substantiate that children with specific developmental disorders, such as reading retardation or chronic physical illness (Taylor, 1985; Yule & Rutter, 1985), are at greater risk of psychiatric disturbance. Harmonious development is threatened by constitutionally acquired weaknesses.

Margaret Mahler drew attention to the paradox of self-development, in that a separate identity implied the giving up of a highly gratifying closeness with the caregiver. Her observations of the ambitendency of children in their second year of life were helpful in understanding individuals with chronic problems of consolidating their individuality. Mahler's framework highlights the importance of the caregiver in facilitating separation, and helps explain the difficulties experienced by children whose parents fail to perform a social referencing function for the child, evaluating for them the realistic danger associated with unfamiliar environments (Feinman, 1991; Hornik & Gunnar, 1988). A panicked and traumatized parent may hinder rather than help a child's adaptation (Terr, 1983). An abusive parent may altogether inhibit the process of social referencing (Cicchetti, 1990b; Hesse & Cicchetti, 1982). The pathogenic potential of the withdrawing object, when confronted with the child's wish for separateness, was further elaborated by Masterson (1972) and Rinsley (1980), and is helpful in accounting for the transgenerational aspects of psychological disturbance (see Baron et al., 1985; Links et al., 1988; Loranger et al., 1982).

Melanie Klein and her followers constructed a developmental model which, at the time, met with great opposition because of the extravagant assumptions these workers were ready to make about the cognitive capacities of infants. Surprisingly, developmental research appears to be consistent with many of Klein's claims concerning perception of causality (e.g., Bower, 1989) and causal reasoning (Golinkoff et al., 1984). Modern Kleinian psychoanalysts (Bion, 1962, 1963; Rosenfeld, 1971b) were particularly helpful in underscoring the potential impact of emotional conflict on the development of cognitive capacities.

The early relationship with the caregiver emerged as a critical aspect of development from psychoanalytic studies of severe character disorders by psychoanalysts in Britain. Winnicott's (1965c) notions of the holding environment, and the mirroring function of the caregiver, provided a clear research focus for developmentalists interested in individual differences in the development of self-structure. The significance of the parent-child relationship is consistently borne out by developmental studies of psychopathology. Research in many respects supports Winnicott's assertions concerning the traumatic effects of early maternal failure, particularly maternal depression (see Cummings & Davies, 1994), and the importance of maternal sensitivity for the establishment of a secure relationship (Ainsworth et al., 1978; Belsky et al., 1984; Bus & van IJzendoorn, 1992; Grossmann, Grossmann, Spangler, Suess, & Unzner, 1985).

A unique longitudinal study showed that youngsters who remained "invincible" despite chronic poverty, low maternal education, family conflict, and moderate to severe perinatal stress, were temperamentally better positioned to develop good relationships with their primary caregivers (they appeared to elicit greater attention, were more active and socially responsive) and were viewed as better natured (boys) and more cuddly (girls) by their mothers when compared with children in the high-risk sample who had developed problems (Werner, 1989, 1990; Werner & Smith, 1982). Other investigations have found that easy temperament is a feature of resilience (Cowen et al., 1990), and that difficult temperament may be associated with a greater likelihood of maltreatment in families where child abuse occurs (Berger, 1985; Carey, 1982; Huttuen & Nyman, 1982). Although these data are consistent with an account phrased in terms of the superior endowment of this group, it has been argued that superior temperament and fewer congenital defects reduced the likelihood of the adverse affect of an unresponsive, withdrawn, disinterested parental object whose presence may be essential for the normal development of autonomy and competence. This latter version is supported by the well-known findings of De Vries (1984), who showed that in the Masai culture, where assertiveness is a highly valued trait and where many caregivers are involved with a single child, temperamentally difficult infants are more likely to survive than easy babies. The child's temperament is given meaning by the caregivers' culturally rooted value system, and the impact on the child-caregiver relationship will determine the child's fate.

The central developmental idea of Kohut's formulation was the need for an understanding caretaker to counteract the infant's sense of helplessness in facing the biological striving for mastery. Kohut emphasized the need for understanding and empathetic objects throughout life, consistent with accumulating evidence for the powerful protective influence of social support identified across a wide range of epidemiological investigations (Brown & Harris, 1978; Brown, Harris, & Bifulco, 1986). Kohut's hypotheses concerning the profound and long-term consequences of a self "enfeebled" by the failure of emotional attunement of the self-object are supported by the literature on risk factors in psychopathology. The work of Cicchetti (1990a, 1990b; Cicchetti & Carlson, 1989) has identified a clear link between early trauma and disorganization and delay in self-development. Researchers working with maltreated infants and toddlers have noted striking attachment behaviors in spontaneous play and in laboratory observations (Carlson, Cicchetti, Barnett, & Braunwald, 1989; Crittenden & Ainsworth, 1989; Fraiberg, 1982). In the Strange Situation procedure, the behavior of such children is often marked by disorganization or inconsistency (Carlson et al., 1989). Main and Solomon (1986) described such children's reaction to reunion as lacking in coherent strategy. Maltreatment appears to jeopardize the organization and development of the attachment relationship and the self, and the regulation of all mental processes underlying social behavior (Masten & Braswell, 1991). Crittenden (1992) found support for the hypothesis that abused and neglected children lack coherent and distinct internal representational models of relationships with their mothers and siblings.

The effectiveness of actions undertaken by the child is at the center of Kohut's concept of self-esteem and is also the core of Bandura's notion of self-efficacy (Bandura, 1982). Kohut's formulations were probably helpful in the operationalization of the concept of self-confidence (Garmezy, 1985; Rutter, 1990; Werner, 1990), although, in some recent studies, problem-solving skills and self-esteem appear to be independent indicators of resilience (Cowen et al., 1990). Although the linking of personal mastery, self-efficacy, and self-esteem may be criticized for reflecting a predominantly Western bourgeois view of individual attainment (see Anthony & Cohler, 1987), it is also inherently a social developmental concept. The response of others within the child's social network creates the experience of mastery by acknowledging the child's success and sometimes verbally persuading the child of his or her own effectiveness (Amato & Ochiltree, 1986).

Limitations of Psychoanalytic Theory

As we have seen, the assumption of an isomorphic relationship between development and psychopathology is present in all psychoanalytic formulations. There may be divergences in terms of the exact period of development involved in particular disorders, or the aspect of the developmental process most pertinent to a particular pathology, but the assumption that the study of development and the study of pathology concern the same psychic processes is universally accepted. Here, we would like to tackle two aspects of this assumption.

First, although there is no doubt that critical analogies exist between aspects of mental functioning in psychosis and style of thinking characteristic of early development (e.g., metonomic aspects of language use, loss of reflective capacity, idiosyncratic use of words, and so on), it is fallacious to argue from the presence of *some* characteristics that the best and only description is in terms of the reactivation of infantile modes of functioning, for the following reasons: (a) there exist important and striking differences between infantile mode of thought and the adult mind "in regression" (there is no evidence for hallucinatory processes, persecutory experiences, delusions of grandeur, and so on; see above); (b) even in the case of shared characteristics, the assumption of identity is unwarranted because later development must be assumed to substantively alter both the mechanism and function of the early structures assumed to be reactivated in severe psychopathology. It is an oversimplification of a very complex developmental process to explicitly or implicitly ignore the manner in which a deficit present from a developmentally early stage might affect subsequent development. Logically, we should assume that so-called primitive aspects of severe psychopathologies have quite different functions in the context of an adult mind from the ones they served in childhood.

Second, throughout the object relations theories review, perhaps with the exception of the ideas of Anna Freud, there has been a consistent emphasis on the relationship between severe personality pathology and intrapsychic or external experiences in the first 2 or 3 years of life. Both structural and object relations accounts depend for their explanatory power on developmental descriptions of the evolution of the ego, the self-structure, and self-other differentiation in the context of primary object relationships (see Kernberg, 1975, 1980; Kohut, 1971; Masterson, 1976). Mechanisms that are seen as explaining the phenomenology of these disorders are all assumed to be rooted in early stages of development. However, as we have seen, many of these developmental models have little empirical support, and some actually conflict with the empirical evidence that is available. Further, even if the pathology observed is analogous to an early mode of mental functioning, it is illogical to link the etiology of the disorder to this phase of development (see Gunderson, 1985). It is equally likely that later or cumulative trauma exerts pressure on the individual to abandon more mature forms of functioning (which had, in fact, developed quite adequately) and return to developmentally earlier forms of interaction.

For psychoanalysis to become a proper developmental theory, it will have to broaden its scope and evolve a new set of concepts that pertain to later childhood, adolescent, and adult development. It is important to identify a few developmental ideas that generalize to the developmental process itself (for example, Klein's idea of the schizo-paranoid and depressive position, or Bowlby's construct of attachment). Beyond these generalizations, developmental concepts pertaining to later developmental phases will be necessary in order to encompass the impact of environmental events and intrapsychic circumstances that continue to profoundly influence the trajectory of a person's development beyond the first 4 years of life.

CONCLUSIONS AND FUTURE PERSPECTIVES

In this section, we consider the most important limitations highlighted by our review of current psychoanalytic ideas, and indicate some possible directions for their development. We also consider certain strengths of the psychoanalytic approach, which, by contrast, indicate aspects of this body of knowledge and thought that should be retained and, if possible, protected from change.

Limitations of the Psychoanalytic Models: A Review

The Evidential Basis of Theories

Most psychoanalytic theorizing has been done by clinicians who have not tested their conjectures empirically. Not surprisingly, therefore, the evidence for these theories is often unclear. For example, Melanie Klein, without any direct evidence (see Spillius, 1994), asserted that the infant forms representations of the mother's breast and the father's penis. In asking for this evidence, we are not returning to operationalism, verificationism, or other discredited residues of logical positivism (see, e.g., Leahey, 1980; Meehl, 1986). By placing explanation outside controlled observations and testable hypotheses, psychoanalysis deprives itself of the *interplay* between data and theory which has contributed so much to the growth of 20th-century science. In the absence of data, psychoanalysts are frequently forced to fall back on either the indirect evidence of clinical observation or an appeal to authority. The validation of variables implicated by psychodynamic theories poses a formidable challenge to the researcher. Most of the variables are private, complex, remote, and difficult to operationalize or test; concepts such as splitting of the ego, masochism, and omnipotence are rarely defined with the necessary exactitude.

There is a further logical problem with the reconstructionist clinical stance. At the simplest level, clinical theories of development are based on accounts of distressed individuals who attempt to recall events that occurred during early, particularly preverbal, childhood. Psychoanalysis has contributed significantly to our understanding of the sources of bias in memories of early experience (see Brewin, Andrews, & Gotlib, 1993). The danger is of the fallacy in assuming that something must have gone amiss during childhood, otherwise these individuals would not be in such difficulties. Thus, most developmental theories assume various errors by the mother, many of which would be difficult to verify. The converse is also true: the presence of healthy responses in an otherwise severely disturbed individual may lead clinicians to postulate moderating factors such as the presence of a "good object" in an otherwise devastated interpersonal environment. This confirmatory bias is inherent to enumerative inductivism. Clinical illustrations have value in summarizing recurrent themes in a particular patient group, and in generating hypotheses; however, they are unlikely to be helpful in resolving arguments over early events considered to place an individual at risk for a disorder. We hope this chapter has illustrated that the observations of perceptive and experienced clinicians do not always lead to the same interpretations.

It should not, however, be assumed that optimally controlling variables, minimizing threats to validity, and maximizing the possibility of causal influence are also most helpful in the *construction* of psychological theory. Westen (1990a) pointed to few rich theories within current psychiatry and psychology that derive from controlled studies. Indeed, many psychological theories of psychopathology explicitly acknowledge that psychoanalytic ideas have inspired specific lines of empirical investigation—for example, Seligman's (1975) work on learned helplessness and depression; Ainsworth et al. (1978), on attachment; Beck's (1967, 1976) schema theory of depression; and Slade's (1982) functional analysis of eating disorders. Clinical data offer a fertile ground for theory building but not for distinguishing good theories from bad or better ones. Future psychoanalytic work should develop closer links with data-gathering methods available in modern social science. To do this without violating the phenomena that we aim to scrutinize is an important challenge to the current generation of analysts.

The Assumption of Uniformity

Psychoanalytic developmental models aim at a level of abstraction where there is a one-to-one relationship between a pattern of abnormality and a developmental course. Thus, within any theory, there is a single model for borderline personality disorder, narcissistic pathology, and so on. Empirical studies, on the whole, are at odds with these accounts, showing diversity within domains essential to psychoanalytic formulations. For example, in eating disorders, where most psychoanalytic accounts presume a severe pathology of early family relationships, empirical studies testify to the variations in parent-child interactions (see Kog & Vandereycken, 1985) and family dynamics (Grigg, Friesen, & Sheppy, 1989), and none of these has specific links to eating disorders (Stern et al., 1989; Strober & Humphrey, 1987; Yager, 1982).

There is a further sense in which uniformity is often inappropriately assumed by psychoanalytic theories, perhaps accounting for the point just made. Object relationships tend to be treated as a singular phenomenon encompassing a number of functions—for example, empathy, the ability to maintain relationships, and self and object representations (see Kernberg, 1984). Current research is at odds with this kind of hierarchical model and suggests the existence of a number of linked but independent mental functions that sustain social behavior (see Fonagy, Moran, Edgcumbe et al., 1993). Westen (1991a), for example, discussed four aspects of object relations and offered data to show patterns of deficit in different pathologies. For example, borderline individuals show no deficit in the complexity of their representations of people, but considerable pathology on the other dimensions. Too little is known about the common object relations abnormalities in specific disorders and the heterogeneity within major groupings.

Alternative Accounts

Psychoanalytic theoreticians tend not to contemplate explanations of clinical observations, other than those generated within psychoanalysis. Even within it, the tradition is not for comparative studies where alternative frameworks are compared; rather, each is expanded to incorporate new data, making the studies unwieldy and difficult to contrast. These considerations apply to the ubiquitous concept of splitting. Following Fairbairn (1952a), most psychoanalysts assume that splitting occurs to protect representations of the object as good. When it is operationalized (see, e.g., Kernberg, 1989), it is usually considered as extreme "black and white" thinking. It may be appropriate to consider splitting as a behavior that can normally occur in response to extreme psychosocial stress (see, e.g., Linehan & Heard, 1993); borderline individuals may engage in it more frequently because of greater exposure to stressful experiences.

The hostility of borderline patients in analysis is a well-established fact (Kernberg et al., 1989), but explanations beyond psychoanalytic accounts—for example, constitutional aggression (Kernberg, 1977) or experiences of unempathic caregiving (Adler, 1985)—are rarely considered. Many aspects of contact with the therapist may elicit hostility from such an individual; examples include the subtle hostility of an anxious or highly frustrated therapist (Brandchaft & Stolorow, 1987) and a patient's inability to understand what the therapist means (Fonagy, 1991). The challenge is to explore alternative ideas as potentially complementing and, in some cases, to replace traditional psychoanalytic accounts.

The Stance toward the Environment

Although psychoanalytic accounts vary in terms of the emphasis placed on the environment, they share a certain lack of sophistication in this area. We have already touched on the exclusive focus on events within the earliest mother-infant relationship. Winnicott (1948/1958c) may well have been right to correct the Kleinian tendency to pathologize the infant and to attribute this pathology, more or less exclusively, to the baby's own drives. However, when Winnicott said that "ordinary babies are not mad" (i.e., they are neither paranoid nor depressive), he left open only one alternative to account for pathology: the mother. This "mother-baiting," present in the work of Kohut, Adler, Modell, Masterson, Rinsley, and even Bowlby and Stern, is tantamount to the imposition of a burden of responsibility on mothers, whose deficiencies are seen as the cause of all psychopathology. As noted earlier, constitutional and parental factors interact in the generation of risk (see, e.g., Rutter, 1989, 1994). A transactional approach suggests a poorness-of-fit model in which the individual's temperament and the family's behavior combine to generate risk, but neither is sufficient by itself. Such an approach shows more respect for both child and parent and may advance our understanding of prevention and treatment.

There is a further respect in which psychoanalytic views of environmental influences fall short. The wider social context within which object relationships develop is, by and large, ignored by psychoanalytic theorists. This may be a residue of the biological origin of psychoanalytic formulations (Pine, 1985), and is not true of all dynamic models (see, e.g., Lasch, 1978; Sullivan, 1953). Some developmental phenomena may be so deeply biologically rooted that they are invariant cross-culturally (Bowlby, 1969/1982). However, evidence is accumulating that even basic psychological processes are accelerated or inhibited by cultural factors. Sissons Joshi and MacLean (in press) found that, in India, 4-year-olds were fairly accurate when they were asked about a child's concealing emotions from an adult in an appearance-reality task, whereas, in England, children consistently failed. The authors attributed these differences to the greater deference toward adults demanded of Indian children, particularly girls. In view of the central role cultural factors play in the development of the self (Mead, 1934), psychoanalysts may, at their own peril, be ignoring their rootedness in Western culture. The individuated self, at the center of most psychoanalytic formulations, is a particularly Western aspiration and contrasts with the relational self more valued by non-Western cultures (see Sampson, 1988). The latter is characterized by more fluid self-other boundaries and by an emphasis on social control that reaches far beyond the person; its unit of identity is the family or community, not an internal representation of the other, or its abstraction or elaboration as an ego ideal.

The psychoanalytic bias toward parental behavior in the etiology of childhood disorder precludes consideration of the broader social context. Belsky (1993), in a useful review of the ecological factors at play in bringing about childhood maltreatment, linked social isolation and limited social ties with risk of child abuse and neglect. For example, Garbarino and Sherman (1990) documented that two neighborhoods matched for social class varied significantly in maltreatment rates as a function of the quality of social networks in the local community. Although such findings might reflect negative social attitudes toward maltreating families, cross-cultural evidence also supports the importance of a broader social context. Cultures that value community and social relationships use physical punishment of children less frequently and have fewer instances of severe abuse and neglect (Zigler & Hall, 1989).

Lack of Specificity

Most psychodynamic models are nonspecific in their explanations of different forms of pathology. All too often, when this is raised, theoreticians invoke constitutional factors (see, e.g., Freud, 1908/1991). Etiological models do not identify specific remote and proximal variables to account for specific symptoms, or define the interaction among contributing factors. As a result, there is poor correspondence between demographic and descriptive characteristics of specific disorders and psychoanalytic formulations. Few psychoanalytic theories would predict the relative decline in one form of pathology (e.g., conversion reaction), and the increase in others (e.g., eating disorders). There is also little understanding of the prevalence of disorders across the life span—for instance, the spontaneous improvement of borderline personality disorder over time (McGlashan, 1986). Many theories fail to distinguish between subprocesses and developmental lines; many concepts referred to (e.g., narcissism) have multiple referents, some pertaining to developmental course (e.g., inadequate experience of mirroring and soothing), some to covert mental states (e.g., a fragile sense of self), and some to manifest presentation (e.g., grandiosity).

The Weakness of the Developmental Perspective

Most of the theories reviewed suffer from a surprisingly narrow view of the developmental process, evident in propositions concerning the self (for critical appraisal, see Eagle, 1984; Stern, 1985; Westen, 1990a, 1992) and object relations (Peterfreund, 1978; Robbins, 1989; Westen, 1990b). Two closely related issues have been raised by critics. The first pertains to unjustified confidence in mapping particular forms of psychopathology to specific developmental epochs (e.g., borderline disorder and the rapprochement subphase of separation and individuation). The second concerns the overemphasis on early experience, which is frequently at odds with developmental data. Westen (1990a, 1990b) presented clear evidence that pathological processes of self-representation and object relationships actually characterize developmental phases far later than those that have traditionally concerned psychoanalysts. The emphasis on preverbal periods is a particular problem for psychoanalytic theory because it places so many hypotheses beyond a realistic empirical test.

Major challenges of psychoanalytic work will have to be a proper expansion of the notion of "the past and the present" and a more comprehensive tracing of developmental continuities between infancy and old age. The metaphorical "baby" of psychoanalytic theory, which stands for the past, will probably have to be abandoned and replaced by notions consistent with what we now understand about the development of the central nervous system.

The Strengths of Psychoanalytic Models

The Distinction between Overt and Covert Characteristics

Psychoanalytic theories emphasize the importance of understanding and therapeutically addressing the structure of unconscious representations. These theories assume qualitative differences between the way in which an individual presents and underlying characteristics. For example, in narcissistic personality disorders, the individual may present as grandiose, preoccupied with fantasies of success, totally self-sufficient, and claiming to be unique; yet, clinical exploration may uncover a sense of inferiority, constant self-doubt, shame, and fragility. Such individuals may present as socially charming, successful, and hardworking, yet feel aimless, superficial, and bored. A dynamic model shows how, for example, unconscious self-representation may be defensively transformed to avoid unpleasant affects, particularly guilt, anxiety, or shame. The distinction between manifest and latent dysfunction, which permeates psychoanalytic theory, is essential because of the limitations of self-report data. Westen and Cohen (1993) reviewed self-report measures with severely personality-disordered individuals. Whereas such individuals can describe disruption in their sense of self (see William James, 1890, on "the self as subject"), dissociative episodes, or periods of amnesia (Silk, Lohr, Westen, & Goodrich, 1989), it is unlikely that they can accurately assess their self-representation. Many borderline patients endorse a large number of pathological items in any inventory (Evans, Ruff, Breff, & Ainsworth, 1984); others underreport pathology, yet show it on indirect measures such as physiological functioning (Shedler, Mayman, & Manis, 1993; Weinberger, 1990). Nisbett and Wilson (1977) showed that the individual may not be in a privileged position for understanding his or her own experiences; the information processing that underpins psychological disorders is by now usually seen as nonconscious (see Dixon, 1981; Marcel, 1983a, 1983b, 1988a, 1988b). Thus, claims that individuals make about habitual behavior or motivation could be distorted by self-serving bias. Observation, as in the clinical setting, is far more likely to give an accurate picture of an individual's characteristic ways of behaving, thinking, and feeling.

Implicit in these models is a search for developmental explanation. Why are narcissistic individuals often forgetful of names, prejudiced, inconsiderate of others' time, and unable to remain in love? Psychoanalytic accounts, whether self-psychological or based on other object relations views, attempt to find a single explanation for such diverse phenomena. The development of a strategy for protecting a fragile self-structure, by seeking ways of enhancing its importance relative to others, does provide a good unified account of most features of narcissistic disorders, even if it does not explain others, such as why there appear to be more male narcissistically disordered individuals (Akhtar & Thomson, 1982).

Development as Compromise Formation

A major and, to our knowledge, unique feature of the psychoanalytic model is that it allows us to see development as a series of compromise formations (see particularly Brenner, 1982). For example, both unconscious and conscious representations of the self are helpfully viewed as the product of competing environmental pressures and intrapsychic processes in an effort to regulate positive and negative affect. These compromises may have involved the defensive distortion of mental representations; where the competing pressures have occurred particularly early or intensely, there may also have been a wholesale distortion or disabling of some of the mental processes that generate representations. This leads to far more pervasive and extensive abnormalities of development (Fonagy, 1991; Westen, 1985).

The Clinical Focus of Psychoanalytic Formulation

The efficacy of therapeutic interventions with children and adults following classically defined psychoanalytic procedures has always been controversial and is currently particularly in doubt (Bachrach, Galatzer-Levy, Skolnikoff, & Waldron, 1991; Waldron, in press). Sandler (1983), among others (Wallerstein, 1989; Hamilton, 1990), drew attention to the loosely coupled relationship between theory and practice in psychoanalysis. Practice has not advanced at the same rate as theory. It is questionable whether practice, even if it were shown to be effective, could ever validate any particular theoretical formulation, when all formulations seem more or less equally compatible with practice. Nevertheless, the practical orientation of psychoanalytic theorization makes it extremely valuable as a device for enabling the therapist to make a link with an individual whose thoughts, feelings, and behavior are beyond the normal range of conscious experience and common-sense psychology. Notwithstanding the inadequacy and partial nature of psychoanalytic explanations, they facilitate human interaction with individuals whose general stance toward others places them at the edge of society. Well-trained psychoanalytic clinicians have the potential to offer vital understanding to these individuals by virtue of their theoretical framework. Other so-called omnibus theories of human behavior—behavioral, humanistic, and systemic approaches—offer something similar, but perhaps psychoanalytic theory equips clinicians to handle and make sense of particularly intense and disturbing human encounters. This, we believe, is the inherent appeal of psychoanalytic developmental ideas for clinicians and is the central reason for the continued and, in some respects, increasing popularity of an approach flawed by so many epistemic, logical, and empirical problems.

REFERENCES

Abend, S. M., Porder, M. S., & Willick, M. S. (1983). *Borderline patients: Psychoanalytic perspectives.* New York: International Universities Press.

Abraham, K. (1979). *Selected papers of Karl Abraham.* New York: Brunner/Mazel. (Original work published 1927)

Abrams, S. (1977). The genetic point of view: Historical antecedents and developmental transformations. *Journal of the American Psychoanalytic Association, 25,* 417–426.

Adamson, L B., & Bakeman, R. (1985). Affect and attention: Infants observed with mothers and peers. *Child Development, 56,* 582–593.

Adlam-Hill, S., & Harris, P. L. (1988). *Understanding of display rules for emotion by normal and maladjusted children.* Unpublished manuscript, Department of Experimental Psychology, University of Oxford.

Adler, A. (1916). *The neurotic constitution.* New York: Moffat Yard.

Adler, G. (1985). *Borderline psychopathology and its treatment.* New York: Aronson.

Aichhorn, A. (1935). *Wayward youth.* New York: Viking. (Original work published 1925)

Ainsworth, M. D. S., Blehar, M. C., Waters, E., & Wall, S. (1978). *Patterns of attachment: A psychological study of the Strange Situation.* Hillsdale, NJ: Erlbaum.

Akhtar, S. (1992). *Broken structures: Severe personality disorders and their treatment.* Northvale, NJ: Aronson.

Akhtar, S., & Thomson, J. (1982). Overview: Narcissistic personality disorder. *American Journal of Psychiatry, 139,* 12–21.

Alba, J. W., & Hasher, L. (1983). Is memory schematic? *Psychological Bulletin, 93,* 203–231.

Alexander, F. (1930). The neurotic character. *International Journal of Psycho-Analysis, 11,* 292–311.

Alexander, F., & French, T. (1946). The principle of corrective emotional experience: The case of Jean Valjean. In *Psychoanalytic theory, principles and application* (pp. 66–70). New York: Ronald Press.

Amato, P. R., & Ochiltree, G. (1986). Family resources and the development of child competence. *Journal of Marriage and the Family, 48,* 47–56.

American Psychiatric Association (1987, 1994). *Diagnostic and statistical manual of mental disorders* (3rd ed. rev., 4th ed.). Washington, DC: Author.

Anthony, E. J., & Cohler, B. J. (1987). *The invulnerable child.* New York: Guilford.

Arlow, J. A., & Brenner, C. (1964). *Psychoanalytic concepts and the structural theory.* New York: International Universities Press.

Bachrach, H. M., Galatzer-Levy, R., Skolnikoff, A., & Waldron, S. (1991). On the efficacy of psychoanalysis. *Journal of the American Psychoanalytic Association, 39,* 871–916.

Bahrick, L. R., & Watson, J. S. (1985). Detection of intermodal proprioceptive-visual contingency as a potential basis of self-perception in infancy. *Developmental Psychology, 21,* 963–973.

Baillargeon, R. (1987). Object permanence in 3.5- and 4.5-month-old infants. *Developmental Psychology, 23,* 655–664.

Bakerman-Kranenburg, M. J., & van IJzendoorn, M. H. (1993). A psychometric study of the Adult Attachment Interview: Reliability and discriminant validity. *Developmental Psychology, 29,* 870–879.

Balint, M. (1959). *Thrills and regressions.* London: Hogarth Press.

Balint, M. (1965a). Early developmental states of the ego, primary object of love. In *Primary love and psycho-analytic technique.* London: Tavistock. (Original work published 1937)

Balint, M. (1965b). *Primary love and psycho-analytic technique* (enlarged ed.). London: Tavistock.

Balint, M. (1968). *The basic fault.* London: Tavistock.

Bandura, A. (1982). Self-efficacy mechanism in human agency. *American Psychologist, 37,* 122–147.

Barasalou, L. W. (1987). The instability of graded structure in concepts. In U. Neisser (Ed.), *Concepts and conceptual development: Ecological and intellectual factors in categorization* (pp. 101–140). New York: Cambridge University Press.

Barasalou, L. W. (1988). The content and organization of autobiographical memories. In U. Neisser (Ed.), *Remembering reconsidered: Ecological and traditional approaches to the study of memory* (pp. 193–243). New York: Cambridge University Press.

Barasalou, L. W. (1989). Intra-concept similarity and its implications for inter-concept similarity. In S. Vosniadou & A. Ortony (Eds.), *Similarity and analogical reasoning* (pp. 76–121). New York: Cambridge University Press.

Barasalou, L. W. (1991). *Cognitive psychology: An overview for cognitive scientists.* Hillsdale, NJ: Erlbaum.

Barasalou, L. W., & Billman, D. (1989). Systematicity and semantic ambiguity. In D. Gorfein (Ed.), *Resolving semantic ambiguity* (pp. 146–203). New York: Springer-Verlag.

Baron, J., Gruen, R., & Asnis, L. (1985). Familial transmission of schizotypal and borderline personality disorders. *American Journal of Psychiatry, 142,* 927–934.

Baron-Cohen, S. (1991). Precursors to a theory of mind: Understanding attention in others. In A. Whiten (Ed.), *Natural theories of mind.* Oxford, England: Blackwell.

Baron-Cohen, S. (1993a). The development of a theory of mind: Where would we be without the intentional stance? In M. Rutter & D. Hay (Eds.), *Developmental principles and clinical issues in psychology and psychiatry.* Oxford, England: Blackwell.

Baron-Cohen, S. (1993b). From attention-goal psychology to belief-desire psychology: The development of a theory of mind, and its dysfunction. In S. Baron-Cohen, H. Tager-Flusberg, & D. J. Cohen (Eds.), *Understanding other minds: Perspectives from autism* (pp. 59–82). New York: Oxford University Press.

Bartlett, F. C. (1932). *Remembering: A study in experimental and social psychology.* Cambridge: Cambridge University Press.

Bartsch, K., & Wellman, H. M. (1989). Young children's attribution of action to beliefs and desires. *Child Development, 60,* 946–964.

Basch, M. F. (1976). Psychoanalysis and communication science. *Annals of Psychoanalysis, 4,* 385–421.

Basch, M. F. (1977). Development psychology and explanatory theory in psychoanalysis. *Annals of Psychoanalysis, 5,* 229–263.

Bates, E., Benigni, L., Bretherton, I., Camaioni, L., & Volterra, V. (1979). Cognition and communication from 9–13 months: Correlational findings. In E. Bates (Ed.), *The emergence of symbols: Cognition and communication in infancy.* New York: Academic Press.

Beck, A. T. (1967). *Depression: Causes and treatment.* Philadelphia: Universitiy of Pennsylvania Press.

Beck, A. T. (1976). *Cognitive therapy and the emotional disorders.* New York: International Universities Press.

Beebe, B., & Lachman, F. M. (1988). The contribution of mother-infant mutual influence to the origins of self and object representations. *Psychoanalytic Psychology, 5(4),* 305–337.

Bell, M. B., Billington, R., & Cicchetti, D. (1988). Do object relations deficits distinguish BPD from other diagnostic groups? *Journal of Clinical Psychology, 44,* 511–516.

Belsky, J. (1993). Etiology of child maltreatment: A developmental-ecological analysis. *Psychological Bulletin, 114,* 413–434.

Belsky, J., Rovine, M., & Taylor, D. G. (1984). The Pennsylvania Infant and Family Development Project: III. The origins of individual differences in infant-mother attachment: Maternal and infant contributions. *Child Development, 55,* 718–728.

Benedek, T. (1959). Parenthood as a developmental phase. *Journal of the American Psychoanalytic Association, 7,* 389–417.

Berger, M. (1985). Temperament and individual differences. In M. Rutter & L. Hersov (Eds.), *Child and adolescent psychiatry: Modern approaches.* Oxford, England: Blackwell.

Bertalanffy, L. von (1968). *General system theory: Foundations, development, applications.* New York: Braziller.

Bertenthal, B. I., Proffit, D. R., Spetner, N. B., & Thomas, M. A. (1985). The development of infant sensitivity to biomechanical motions. *Child Development, 56,* 531–543.

Bibring, G. L., Dwyer, T. F., Huntington, D. S., & Vallenstein, A. F. (1961). A study of the psychological processes in the pregnancy and earliest mother-child relationship. *The Psychoanalytic Study of the Child, 16,* 9–72.

Bion, W. R. (1957). Differentiation of the psychotic from the non-psychotic personalities. *International Journal of Psycho-Analysis, 38,* 266–275.

Bion, W. R. (1959). Attacks on linking. *International Journal of Psycho-Analysis, 40,* 308–315.

Bion, W. R. (1962). *Learning from experience.* London: Heinemann.

Bion, W. R. (1967). A theory of thinking. In *Second thoughts* (pp. 110–119). London: Heinemann. (Original work published 1962)

Bion, W. R. (1963). *Elements of psycho-analysis.* London: Heinemann.

Blanck, G., & Blanck, R. (1979). *Ego psychology: Vol. 2. Psychoanalytic developmental psychology.* New York: Columbia University Press.

Blatt, S. J., & Behrends, R. S. (1987). Internalization, separation-individuation, and the nature of therapeutic action. *International Journal of Psycho-Analysis, 68,* 279–297.

Blatt, S. J., Brenneis, C. B., Schimek, J. G., & Glick, M. (1976). Normal development and psychopathological impairment of the concept of the object on the Rorschach. *Journal of Abnormal Psychology, 85,* 364–373.

Blatt, S. J., Ford, R. Q., Berman, W., Cook, B., & Meyer, R. (1988). The assessment of change during the intensive treatment of borderline and schizophrenic young adults. *Psychoanalytic Psychology, 5,* 127–158.

Blos, P. (1962). *On adolescence: A psychoanalytic interpretation.* New York: Free Press.

Blum, H. P. (1982). Theories of the self and psychoanalytic concepts: Discussion. *Journal of the American Psychoanalytic Association, 30,* 959–978.

Boccia, M., & Campos, J. J. (1989). Maternal emotional signals, social referencing, and infants' reactions to strangers. *New Directions for Child Development, 44,* 24–29.

Boesky, D. (1988). The concept of psychic structure. *Journal of the American Psychoanalytic Association, 36* (Suppl.), 113–135.

Boesky, D. (1989). A discussion of evidential criteria for therapeutic change. In A. Rothstein (Ed.), *How does treatment help? Models of therapeutic action of psychoanalytic therapy* (pp. 171–180). Madison, CT: International Universities Press.

Bollas, C. (1987). *The shadow of the object.* London: Free Association Books.

Bollas, C. (1989). *Forces of destiny.* London: Free Association Books.

Bower, T. R. (1977). *A primer of infant development.* San Francisco: Freeman.

Bower, T. R. (1981). Mood and memory. *American Psychologist, 36,* 129–148.

Bower, T. R. (1989). *The rational infant: Learning in infancy.* San Francisco: Freeman.

Bowlby, J. (1982). *Attachment and loss: Vol. 1. Attachment.* New York: Basic Books. (Original work published 1969)

Bowlby, J. (1973). *Attachment and loss: Vol. 2. Separation, anxiety and anger.* New York: Basic Books.

Bowlby, J. (1980). *Attachment and loss: Vol. 3. Loss: Sadness and depression.* London: Hogarth Press and Institute of Psycho-Analysis.

Brandchaft, B., & Stolorow, R. D. (1987). The borderline concept: An intersubjective view. In J. S. Grotstein, M. F. Solomon, & J. A. Lang (Eds.), *The borderline patient: Emerging concepts in diagnosis, psychodynamics, and treatment* (pp. 103–126). Hillsdale, NJ: Analytic Press.

Brazelton, T., Kowslowski, B., & Main, M. (1974). The origins of reciprocity: The early mother-infant interaction. In M. Lewis & L. Rosenblum (Eds.), *The effect of the infant on its caregiver* (pp. 49–76). New York: Wiley.

Brenner, C. (1959). The masochistic character: Genesis and treatment. *Journal of the American Psychoanalytic Association, 7,* 197–226.

Brenner, C. (1982). *The mind in conflict.* New York: International Universities Press.

Bretherton, I. (1985). Attachment theory: Retrospect and prospect. In I. Bretherton & E. Waters (Eds.), *Growing points of attachment theory and research* (pp. 3–35). *Monographs of the Society for Research in Child Development, 50,* (1–2, Serial No. 209).

Bretherton, I. (1992). *Internal working models: Cognitive and affective aspects of attachment representations.* Paper presented at the 4th Rochester Symposium on Developmental Psychopathology, Rochester, NY.

Bretherton, I., Fritz, J., Zahn-Waxler, C., & Ridgeway, D. (1986). Learning to talk about emotions: A functionalist perspective. *Child Development, 57,* 529–548.

Brewer, W. F., & Nakamura, G. V. (1984). The nature and function of schemes. In R. S. Wyer & T. K. Srull (Eds.), *Handbook of social cognition* (Vol I., pp. 119–160). Hillsdale, NJ: Erlbaum.

Brewin, C. R., Andrews, B., & Gotlib, I. H. (1993). Psychopathology and early experience: A reappraisal of retrospective reports. *Psychological Bulletin, 113,* 82–98.

Britton, R. (1989). The missing link: Parental sexuality in the Oedipus complex. In J. Steiner (Ed.), *The Oedipus complex today* (pp. 83–102). London: Karnac Books.

Britton, R. (1992). The Oedipus situation and the depressive position. In R. Anderson (Ed.), *Clinical lectures on Klein and Bion* (pp. 34–45). London: Routledge.

Brody, S. (1980). Transitional objects: Idealization of a phenomenon. *Psychoanalytic Quarterly, 49,* 561–605.

Brody, S., & Axelrad, S. (1970). *Anxiety and ego formation in infancy.* New York: International Universities Press.

Brown, G. W., & Harris, T. O. (1978). *Social origins of depression: A study of psychiatric disorders in women.* London: Tavistock.

Brown, G. W., Harris, T. O., & Bifulco, A. (1986). Long-term effects of early loss of parent. In M. Rutter, C. E. Izard, & P. B. Read (Eds.), *Depression in young people: Developmental and clinical perspectives* (pp. 251–296). New York: Guilford.

Brown, J. R., & Dunn, J. (1991). "You can cry, mum": The social and developmental implications of talk about internal states. *British Journal of Developmental Psychology, 9,* 237–257.

Bruner, J. (1990). *Acts of meaning.* Cambridge: Harvard University Press.

Bucci, W. (1985). Dual coding: A cognitive model for psychoanalytic research. *Journal of the American Psychoanalytic Association, 33,* 571–608.

Buie, D. H., & Adler, G. (1982). Definitive treatment of the borderline personality. *International Journal of Psychoanalytic Psychotherapy, 9,* 51–87.

Burbach, D. J., & Borduin, C. M. (1986). Parent-child relations and the etiology of depression: A review of methods and findings. *Clinical Psychology Review, 6,* 133–153.

Burland, J. A. (1986). The vicissitudes of maternal deprivation. In R. F. Lax, S. Bach, & J. A. Burland (Eds.), *Self and object constancy: Clinical and theoretical perspectives* (pp. 324–347). New York: Guilford.

Bus, A. G., & van IJzendoorn, M. H. (1992). Patterns of attachment in frequently and infrequently reading mother-child dyads. *Journal of Genetic Psychology, 153,* 395–403.

Butterworth, G. E. (1991). The ontogeny and phylogeny of joint visual attention. In A. Whiten (Ed.), *Natural theories of mind.* Oxford, England: Blackwell.

Byrne, C. P., Velamoor, V. R., & Cernovsky, Z. Z. (1990). A comparison of borderline and schizophrenic patients for childhood live events and parent-child relationships. *Canadian Journal of Psychiatry, 35,* 590–595.

Call, J. D. (1984). From early patterns of communication to the grammar of experience and syntax in infancy. In J. D. Call, E. Galenson, & R. L. Tyson (Eds.), *Frontiers of infant psychiatry* (pp. 15–29). New York: Basic Books.

Camras, L. A., & Sachs, V. B. (1991). Social referencing and caretaker expressive behavior in a day care setting. *Infant Behavior and Development, 14,* 27–36.

Caper, R. (1988). *Immaterial facts.* Northvale, NJ: Aronson.

Carey, W. B. (1982). Clinical use of temperament data in pediatrics. In R. Porter & G. M. Collings (Eds.), *Temperamental differences in infants and young children.* London: Pitman.

Carlson, J., Cicchetti, D., Barnett, D., & Braunwald, K. G. (1989). Finding order in disorganization: Lessons from research on maltreated infants' attachments to their caregivers. In D. Cicchetti & V. Carlson (Eds.), *Child maltreatment: Theory and research on the causes and consequences of child abuse and neglect.* Cambridge, England: Cambridge University Press.

Cavell, M. (1988a). Interpretation, psychoanalysis and the philosophy of mind. *Journal of the American Psychoanalytic Association, 36,* 859–879.

Cavell, M. (1988b). Solipsism and community: Two concepts of mind in psychoanalysis. *Psychoanalysis and Contemporary Thought, 11,* 587–613.

Cavell, M. (1991). The subject of mind. *International Journal of Psycho-Analysis, 72,* 141–154.

Chomsky, N. (1968). *Language and mind.* New York: Harcourt, Brace & World.

Cicchetti, D. (1984). The emergence of developmental psychopathology. *Child Development, 55,* 1–7.

Cicchetti, D. (1989). Developmental psychopathology: Some thoughts on its evolution. *Development and Psychopathology, 1,* 1–4.

Cicchetti, D. (1990a). An historical perspective on the discipline of developmental psychopathology. In J. Rolf, A. Masten, D. Cicchetti, K. Nuechterlein, & S. Weintraub (Eds.), *Risk protective factors in the development of psychopathology* (pp. 2–28). New York: Cambridge University Press.

Cicchetti, D. (1990b). The organization and coherence of socioemotional, cognitive, and representational development: Illustrations through a developmental psychopathology perspective on Down syndrome and child maltreatment. In R. Thompson (Ed.), *Nebraska Symposium on Motivation: Socioemotional development.* Lincoln: University of Nebraska Press.

Cicchetti, D., & Carlson, V. (1989). *Child maltreatment: Theory and research on the causes and consequences of child abuse and neglect.* New York: Cambridge University Press.

Cohn, J. F., & Campbell, S. B. (1992). Influence of maternal depression on infant affect regulation. In D. Cicchetti & S. Toth (Eds.), *Rochester Symposium on Developmental Psychopathology: Vol. 4. A developmental approach to affective disorders* (pp. 103–130). Rochester, NY: University of Rochester Press.

Cohn, J. F., Campbell, S. B., Matias, R., & Hopkins, J. (1990). Face-to-face interactions of postpartum depressed and nondepressed mother-infant pairs at 2 months. *Developmental Psychology, 26,* 15–23.

Cohn, J. F., Matias, R., Tronick, E. Z., Connell, D., & Lyons-Ruth, K. (1986). Face-to-face interactions of depressed mothers and their infants. In E. Z. Tronick & T. Field (Eds.), *Maternal depression and infant disturbance* (pp. 31–45). San Francisco: Jossey-Bass.

Cohn, J. F., & Tronick, E. (1983). Three-month-old infants' reaction to simulated maternal depression. *Child Development, 54,* 185–190.

Colarusso, C. A., & Nemiroff, R. A. (1981). *Adult development: A new dimension in psychodynamic theory and practice.* New York: Plenum.

Compton, A. (1981). On the psychoanalytic theory of instinctual drives: Part IV. Instinctual drives and the ego-id-superego model. *Psychoanalytic Quarterly, 50,* 363–392.

Cooper, A. M. (1983). Psychoanalytic inquiry and new knowledge. In J. D. Lichtenberg & S. Kaplan (Eds.), *Reflections of self psychology* (pp. 19–34). Hillsdale, NJ: Analytic Press.

Cowen, E. L., Wyman, P. A., Work, W. C., & Parker, G. R. (1990). The Rochester Child Resilience Project: Overview and summary of first year findings. *Development and Psychopathology, 2,* 193–212.

Crittenden, P. A. (1992). Children's strategies for coping with adverse home environments: An interpretation using attachment theory. *Abuse and Neglect, 16,* 329–343.

Crittenden, P. M. (1990). Internal representational models of attachment relationships. *Journal of Infant Mental Health, 11,* 259–277.

Crittenden, P. M., & Ainsworth, M. D. S. (1989). Child maltreatment and attachment theory. In D. Cicchetti & V. Carlson (Eds.), *Child maltreatment: Theory and research on the causes and consequences of child abuse and neglect.* Cambridge, England: Cambridge University Press.

Cummings, E. M., & Cicchetti, D. (1990). Towards a transactional model of relations between attachment and depression. In M. Greenberg, D. Cicchetti, & E. M. Cummings (Eds.), *Attachment in the preschool years: Theory, research, and intervention* (pp. 339–372). Chicago: The University of Chicago Press.

Cummings, E. M., & Davies, P. T. (1994). Maternal depression and child development. *Journal of Child Psychology and Psychiatry, 35,* 73–112.

Cummings, E. M., Iannotti, R. J., & Zahn-Waxler, C. (1985). Influence of conflict between adults on the emotions and aggression of young children. *Developmental Psychology, 21,* 495–507.

Cummings, E. M., & Zahn-Waxler, C. (1992). Emotions and the socialization of aggression: Adults' angry behavior and children's arousal and aggression. In A. Fraczek & H. Zumkley (Eds.), *Socialization and aggression* (pp. 61–84). New York: Springer.

Cummings, E. M., Zahn-Waxler, C., & Radke-Yarrow, M. (1981). Young children's response to expressions of anger and affection by others in the family. *Child Development, 52,* 1275–1282.

Cummings, E. M., Zahn-Waxler, C., & Radke-Yarrow, M. (1984). Developmental changes in children's reactions to anger in the home. *Journal of Child Psychology and Psychiatry, 25,* 63–74.

Davidson, D. (1983). *Inquiries into truth and interpretation.* Oxford, England: Oxford University Press.

DeCasper, A. J., & Carstens, A. A. (1981). Contingencies of stimulation: Effects on learning and emotion in neonates. *Infant Behavior and Development, 4,* 19–35.

Demos, E. V. (1989). Resiliency in infancy. In T. F. Dugan & R. Coles (Eds.), *The child in our times* (pp. 3–22). New York: Brunner/Mazel.

Deutsch, H. (1942). Some forms of emotional disturbance and their relationship to schizophrenia. *Psychoanalytic Quarterly, 11,* 301–321.

De Vries, M. W. (1984). Temperament and infant mortality among the Masai of East Africa. *American Journal of Psychiatry, 141,* 1189–1194.

Dixon, N. F. (1981). *Preconscious processing.* Chichester, England: Wiley.

Dunn, J., Bretherton, I., & Munn, P. (1987). Conversations about feeling states between mothers and their young children. *Developmental Psychology, 23,* 132–139.

Eagle, M. N. (1984). *Recent developments in psychoanalysis: A critical evaluation.* Cambridge, MA: Harvard University Press.

Edelman, G. M. (1987). *Neural Darwinism.* New York: Basic Books.

Ekecrantz, L., & Rudhe, L. (1972). Transitional phenomena: Frequency, forms and functions of specially loved objects. *Acta Psychiatrica Scandinavica, 48,* 261–273.

Elmhirst, S. (1980). Transitional objects in transition. *International Journal of Psycho-Analysis, 61,* 367–373.

Emde, R. N. (1980a). Emotional availability: A reciprocal reward system for infants and parents with implications for prevention of psychosocial disorders. In P. M. Taylor & F. Orlando (Eds.), *Parent-infant relationships* (pp. 87–115). New York: Grune & Stratton.

Emde, R. N. (1980b). Toward a psychoanalytic theory of affect: Part I. The organizational model and its propositions. In S. I. Greenspan & G. H. Pollock (Eds.), *The course of life: Infancy and early childhood* (pp. 63–83). Washington, DC: U.S. Department of Health and Human Services.

Emde, R. N. (1980c). Toward a psychoanalytic theory of affect: Part II. Emerging models of emotional development in infancy. In S. I. Greenspan & G. H. Pollock (Eds.), *The course of life: Infancy and early childhood* (pp. 85–112). Washington, DC: U.S. Department of Health and Human Services.

Emde, R. N. (1985). From adolescence to midlife: Remodeling the structure of adult development. *Journal of the American Psychoanalytic Association, 33,* 165–192.

Emde, R. N. (1988a). Development terminable and interminable: I. Innate and motivational factors from infancy. *International Journal of Psycho-analysis, 69,* 23–42.

Emde, R. N. (1988b). Development terminable and interminable: II. Recent psychoanalytic theory and therapeutic considerations. *International Journal of Psycho-analysis, 69,* 283–286.

Erdelyi, M. H. (1985). *Psychoanalysis: Freud's cognitive psychology.* New York: Freeman.

Erikson, E. H. (1950). *Childhood and society.* New York: Norton.

Erikson, E. H. (1959). The problem of ego identity. In *Identity and the Life Cycle* (pp. 104–164). New York: International Universities Press, 1959. (Original work published 1956)

Erikson, E. H. (1959). *Identity and the life cycle.* New York: International Universities Press.

Evans, R., Ruff, R., Breff, D., & Ainsworth, T. (1984). MMPI characteristics of borderline personality inpatients. *Journal of Nervous and Mental Disease, 172,* 742–748.

Fairbairn, W. R. D. (1952a). *An object-relations theory of the personality.* New York: Basic Books.

Fairbairn, W. R. D. (1952b). Endopsychic structure considered in terms of object-relationships. In *An object-relations theory of the personality.* New York: Basic Books. (Original work published 1944)

Fairbairn, W. R. D. (1952c). Schizoid factors in the personality. In *An object-relations theory of the personality.* New York: Basic Books. (Original work published 1940)

Fairbairn, W. R. D. (1954). Observations on the nature of hysterical states. *British Journal of Medical Psychology, 29,* 112–127.

Fantz, R. (1963). Pattern vision in newborn infants. *Science, 140,* 296–297.

Feinman, S. (1991). *Social referencing and the social construction of reality in infancy.* New York: Plenum.

Fendrich, M., Warner, V., & Weissman, M. M. (1990). Family risk factors, parental depression, and psychopathology in offspring. *Developmental Psychology, 26,* 40–50.

Fenichel, O. (1946). *The psychoanalytic theory of neurosis.* London: Routledge.

Ferenczi, S. (1980). Stages in the development of the sense of reality. In *First contributions to psycho-analysis.* London: Karnac, 1980. (Original work published 1913)

Field, T. (1979). Differential behavioral and cardiac responses of 3-month-old infants to a mirror and peer. *Infant Behaviour and Development, 2,* 179–184.

Field, T. (1987). Interaction and attachment in normal and atypical infants. *Journal of Consulting and Clinical Psychology, 55,* 853–859.

Field, T. (1989). Maternal depression effects on infant interaction and attachment behavior. In D. Cicchetti (Ed.), *Rochester Symposium on Developmental Psychopathology: Vol.1. The emergence of a discipline* (pp. 139–163). Hillsdale, NJ: Erlbaum.

Field, T. (1992). Infants of depressed mothers. *Development and Psychopathology, 4,* 49–66.

Field, T., Healy, B., Goldstein, S., & Guthertz, M. (1990). Behavior-state matching and synchrony in mother-infant interactions of non-depressed vs. depressed dyads. *Developmental Psychology, 26,* 7–14.

Field, T., Healy, B., Goldstein, S., Perry, S., Bendell, D., Schanberg, S., Zimmerman, E., & Kuhn, C. (1988). Infants of depressed mothers show "depressed" behavior even with nondepressed adults. *Child Development, 59,* 1569–1579.

Fillmore, C. J. (1968). The case for case. In E. Bach & R. Harms (Eds.), *Universals in linguistic theory* (pp. 1–88). New York: Holt, Rinehart, & Winston.

Flament, M., & Rapaport, J. L. (1984). Childhood obsessive-compulsive disorders. In T. R. Insel (Ed.), *New findings in obsessive-compulsive disorder* (pp. 24–43). Washington, DC: American Psychiatric Press.

Fleming, J. (1975). Some observations on object constancy in the psychoanalysis of adults. *Journal of the American Psychoanalytic Association, 23,* 743–759.

Fodor, J. A. (1981). *Representations: Philosophical essays on the foundations of cognitive science.* Cambridge, MA: MIT Press.

Fonagy, P. (1982). Psychoanalysis and empirical science. *International Review of Psychoanalysis, 9,* 125–145.

Fonagy, P. (1991). Thinking about thinking: Some clinical and theoretical considerations concerning the treatment of a borderline patient. *International Journal of Psycho-Analysis, 72,* 639–656.

Fonagy, P., & Higgitt, A. (1984). *Personality theory and clinical practice.* London: Methuen.

Fonagy, P., & Higgitt, A. (1989). A developmental perspective on borderline personality disorder. *Révue Internationale de Psychopathologie, 1,* 125–159.

Fonagy, P., & Moran, G. S. (1991). Understanding psychic change in child analysis. *International Journal of Psycho-Analysis, 72,* 15–22.

Fonagy, P., Moran, G. S., Edgcumbe, R., Kennedy, H., & Target, M. (1993). The roles of mental representation and mental processes in therapeutic action. *Psychoanalytic Study of the Child, 48,* 9–48.

Fonagy, P., Moran, G. S., & Target, M. (1993). Aggression and the psychological self. *International Journal of Psycho-Analysis, 74,* 471–485.

Fonagy, P., Steele, M., Moran, G., Steele, M., & Higgitt, A. C. (1991). The capacity for understanding mental states: The reflective self in parent and child and its significance for security of attachment. *Infant Mental Health Journal, 13,* 200–216.

Fonagy, P., Steele, H., & Steele, M. (1991). Maternal representations of attachment during pregnancy predict the organization of infant-mother attachment at one year of age. *Child Development, 62,* 891–905.

Fonagy, P., Steele, M., Steele, H., Higgitt, A., & Target, M. (1994). Theory and practice of resilience . *Journal of Child Psychology and Psychiatry, 35,* 231–257.

Fonagy, P., Steele, M., Steele, H., Leigh, T., Kennedy, R., Mattoon, G., & Target, M. (in press). The predictive validity of Mary Main's Adult Attachment Interview: A psychoanalytic and developmental perspective on the transgenerational transmission of attachment and borderline states. In S. Goldberg & J. Kerr (Eds.), *Attachment research: The state of the art.* New York: Analytic Press.

Fonagy, P., & Target, M. (1994). The efficacy of psycho-analysis for children with disruptive disorders. *Journal of the American Academy of Child and Adolescent Psychiatry, 33,* 43–45.

Fonagy, P., & Target, M. (in press a). Psychodynamic developmental therapy for children: A contemporary application of child psychoanalysis. In E. D. Hibbs & P. S. Jensen (Eds.), *Psychosocial treatment research with children and adolescents.* Washington, DC: National Institutes of Health/American Psychological Association.

Fonagy, P., & Target, M. (in press b). Understanding the violent patient: The use of the body and the role of the father. *International Journal of Psycho-Analysis.*

Ford, M. E. (1979). The construct validity of egocentrism. *Psychological Bulletin, 86,* 1169–1189.

Foulkes, D. (1978). *A grammar of dreams.* New York: Basic Books.

Fraiberg, S. (1969). Libidinal object constancy and mental representation. *The Psychoanalytic Study of the Child, 24,* 9–47.

Fraiberg, S. (1980). *Clinical studies in infant mental health.* New York: Basic Books.

Fraiberg, S. (1982). Pathological defenses in infancy. *Psychoanalytic Quarterly, 51,* 612–635.

Frank, J. (1956). Contribution to scientific proceedings, reported by L. L. Robbins. *Journal of the American Psychoanalytic Association, 4,* 561–562.

Free, K. (1988). Transitional object attachment and creative activity in adolescence. In P. C. Horton, H. Gewitz, & K. J. Kreutter (Eds.), *The solace paradigm: An eclectic search for psychological immunity* (pp. 145–158). Madison, CT: International Universities Press.

Freud, A. (1946). *The ego and the mechanisms of defence.* New York: International Universities Press. (Original work published 1936)

Freud, A. (1974). Reports on the Hampstead Nurseries. In *The writings of Anna Freud.* New York: International Universities Press. (Original work published 1941–1945)

Freud, A. (1968). The concept of the rejecting mother. In *The writings of Anna Freud* (pp. 586–602). New York: International Universities Press. (Original work published 1955)

Freud, A. (1965). *Normality and pathology in childhood.* Harmondsworth, England: Penguin Books.

Freud, A. (1971). Child analysis as a subspeciality of psychoanalysis. In *The writings of Anna Freud* (pp. 204–219). New York: International Universities Press. (Original work published 1970)

Freud, A. (1974). A psychoanalytic view of developmental psychopathology. In *The writings of Anna Freud* (pp. 119–136). New York: International Universities Press.

Freud, A. (1981). *Changes in psychoanalytic practice and experience.* New York: International Universities Press. (Original work published 1976)

Freud, A. (1981). *The writings of Anna Freud: Vol. 8. Psychoanalytic psychology of normal development 1970–1980.* London: Hogarth Press/Institute of Psychoanalysis.

Freud, A. (1983). Problems of pathogenesis. *The Psychoanalytic Study of the Child, 36,* 129–136.

Freud, S. (1991). The interpretation of dreams. In J. Strachey (Ed. and Trans.), *The standard edition of the complete psychological works of Sigmund Freud* (Vol. 4 & 5, pp. 1–715). London: Hogarth Press. (Original work published 1900)

Freud, S. (1991). The psychopathology of everyday life. In J. Strachey (Ed. and Trans.), *The standard edition of the complete psychological works of Sigmund Freud* (Vol. 6, pp. 1–190). London: Hogarth Press. (Original work published 1901)

Freud, S. (1991a). Jokes and their relation to the unconscious. In J. Strachey (Ed. and Trans.). *The standard edition of the complete psychological works of Sigmund Freud* (Vol. 8, pp. 1–236). London: Hogarth Press. (Original work published 1905)

Freud, S. (1991b). Three essays on the theory of sexuality. In J. Strachey (Ed. and Trans.). *The standard edition of the complete psychological works of Sigmund Freud* (Vol. 7, pp. 123–230). London: Hogarth Press. (Original work published 1905)

Freud, S. (1991). "Civilized" sexual morality and modern nervous illness. In J. Strachey (Ed. and Trans.). *The standard edition of the complete psychological works of Sigmund Freud* (Vol. 9, pp. 177–204). London: Hogarth Press. (Original work published 1908)

Freud, S. (1991). On narcissism: An introduction. In J. Strachey (Ed. and Trans.). *The standard edition of the complete psychological works of Sigmund Freud* (Vol. 14, pp. 67–104). London: Hogarth Press. (Original work published 1914)

Freud, S. (1991). Beyond the pleasure principle. In J. Strachey (Ed. and Trans.). *The standard edition of the complete psychological works of Sigmund Freud* (Vol. 18, pp. 1–64). London: Hogarth Press. (Original work published 1920)

Freud, S. (1991). The ego and the id. In J. Strachey (Ed. and Trans.). *The standard edition of the complete psychological works of Sigmund Freud* (Vol. 19, pp. 1–59). London: Hogarth Press. (Original work published 1923)

Freud, S. (1991). Inhibitions, symptoms, and anxiety. In J. Strachey (Ed. and Trans.). *The standard edition of the complete psychological works of Sigmund Freud* (Vol. 20, pp. 77–172). London: Hogarth Press. (Original work published 1926)

Freud, S. (1991). Civilization and its discontents. In J. Strachey (Ed. and Trans.). *The standard edition of the complete psychological works of Sigmund Freud* (Vol. 21, pp. 57–146). London: Hogarth Press. (Original work published 1930)

Freud, S. (1991). New introductory lectures on psychoanalysis. In J. Strachey (Ed. and Trans.). *The standard edition of the complete psychological works of Sigmund Freud* (Vol. 22, pp. 1–182). London: Hogarth Press. (Original work published 1933)

Freud, S. (1991). An outline of psychoanalysis. In J. Strachey (Ed. and Trans.). *The standard edition of the complete psychological works of Sigmund Freud* (Vol. 23, pp. 141–207). London: Hogarth Press. (Original work published 1940)

Freud, S., & Breuer, J. (1991). Studies on hysteria. In J. Strachey (Ed. and Trans.). *The standard edition of the complete psychological works of Sigmund Freud* (Vol. 2, pp. 1–305). London: Hogarth Press. (Original work published 1895)

Friedlander, B. Z. (1970). Receptive language development in infancy. *Merrill-Palmer Quarterly, 16,* 7–51.

Friedman, L. (1988). The clinical polarity of object relations concepts. *Psychoanalytic Quarterly, 57,* 667–691.

Frieswyk, S., & Colson, D. (1980). Prognostic considerations in the hospital treatment of borderline states: The perspective of object relations theory and the Rorschach. In J. Kwawer, H. Lerner, P. Lerner, & A. Sugarman (Eds.), *Borderline phenomena and the Rorschach test* (pp. 229–256). New York: International Universities Press.

Gaddini, R., & Gaddini, E. (1970). Transitional objects and the process of individuation: A study in three different social groups. *Journal of the American Academy of Child Psychiatry, 9,* 347–365.

Garbarino, J., & Sherman, D. (1990). High-risk neighborhoods and high-risk families: The human ecology of child maltreatment. *Child Development, 51,* 188–198.

Garmezy, N. (1983). Stressors of childhood. In N. Garmezy & M. Rutter (Eds.), *Stress, coping, and development in children.* New York: McGraw-Hill.

Garmezy, N. (1985). Stress-resistant children: The search for protective factors. In J. E. Stevenson (Ed.), *Recent research in developmental psychopathology* (Journal of Child Psychology and Psychiatry Book). Oxford, England: Pergamon.

Garmezy, N., & Masten, A. (1991). The protective role of competence indicators in children at risk. In E. M. Cummings, A. L. Greene, & K. K. Karraker (Eds.), *Life-span developmental psychology: Perspectives on stress and coping.* Hillsdale, NJ: Erlbaum.

Garrison, W. T., & Earls, F. J. (1986). Epidemiologic perspectives on maternal depression and the young child. In T. Field & Z. Tronick (Eds.), *Maternal depression and infant disturbance* (pp. 13–30). San Francisco: Jossey-Bass.

Gedo, J. E. (1980). Reflections on some current controversies in psychoanalysis. *Journal of the American Psychoanalytic Association, 28,* 363–383.

Gelman, R., & Baillargeon, R. (1983). A review of some Piagetian concepts. In P. Mussen (Ed.), *Handbook of child psychology* (pp. 157–199). New York: Wiley.

George, C., Kaplan, N., & Main, M. (1985). The Adult Attachment Interview. In *Privileged communication.* Berkeley: Department of Psychology, University of California.

Gergely, G. (1991). Developmental reconstructions: Infancy from the point of view of psychoanalysis and developmental psychology. *Psychoanalysis and Contemporary Thought, 14,* 3–55.

Gianino, A. F., & Tronick, E. Z. (1988). The mutual regulation model: The infant's self and interactive regulation and coping and defensive capacities. In T. Field, P. McCabe, & N. Schneiderman (Eds.), *Stress and coping.* Hillsdale, NJ: Erlbaum.

Giovacchini, P. (1987). The "unreasonable" patient and the psychotic transference. In J. S. Grotstein, M. F. Solomon, & J. A. Lang (Eds.), *The borderline patient: Emerging concepts in diagnosis, psychodynamics and treatment* (pp. 59–68). Hillsdale, NJ: Analytic Press.

Gitelson, M. (1955). Contribution to scientific proceedings, reported by L. Rangell. *Journal of the American Psychoanalytic Association, 3,* 294–295.

Golinkoff, R. M., Hardig, C. B., Carlson, V., & Sexton, M. E. (1984). The infant's perception of causal events: The distinction between animate and inanimate objects. In L. P. Lipsitt & C. Rovee-Collier (Eds.), *Advances in infancy research.* Norwood, NJ: Ablex.

Green, R. (1985). Atypical psychosexual development. In M. Rutter & L. Hersov (Eds.), *Child and adolescent psychiatry: Modern approaches* (pp. 638–649). Oxford, England: Blackwell.

Greenacre, P. (1945). Conscience in the psychopath. *American Journal of Orthopsychiatry, 15,* 495–509.

Greenacre, P. (1952). Pregenital patterning. *International Journal of Psycho-Analysis, 33,* 410–415.

Greenacre, P. (1970). The transitional object and the fetish with special reference to the role of illusion. *International Journal of Psycho-Analysis, 51,* 447–456.

Greenberg, J. R., & Mitchell, S. A. (1983). *Object relations in psychoanalytic theory.* Cambridge, MA: Harvard University Press.

Grey, A., & Davies, M. (1981). Mental health as level of interpersonal maturity. *Journal of the American Academy of Psychoanalysis, 9,* 601–614.

Grigg, D. N., Friesen, J. D., & Sheppy, M. I. (1989). Family patterns associated with anorexia nervosa. *Journal of Marital and Family Therapy, 15,* 29–42.

Grinker, R., Werble, B., & Drye, R. C. (1968). *The borderline syndrome: A behavioral study of ego functions.* New York: Basic Books.

Grolnick, W., Frodi, A., & Bridges, L. (1984). Maternal control style and the mastery motivation of one-year-olds. *Infant Mental Health Journal, 5*(2), 72–78.

Grossmann, K., Grossmann, K. E., Spangler, G., Suess, G., & Unzner, L. (1985). Maternal sensitivity and newborns' orientation responses as related to quality of attachment in Northern Germany. In I. Bretherton & E. Waters (Eds.), *Growing points of attachment theory and research* (pp. 233–256). Minnesota: SRCD Monograph.

Grossmann, K. E., Loher, I., Grossmann, K., Scheuerer-Englisch, H., Schildbach, B., Spangler, G., Wensauer, M., & Zimmermann, P. (1993, March). *The development of inner working models of attachment and adaptation.* Paper presented at 60th anniversary meeting of the Society for Research in Child Development, New Orleans.

Gunderson, J. G. (1985). *Borderline personality disorder.* Washington, DC: American Psychiatric Press.

Gunderson, J. G., Morris, H., & Zanarini, M. (1985). Transitional objects and borderline patients. In T. McGlashan (Ed.), *The borderline: Current empirical research.* Washington, DC: American Psychiatric Press.

Hamilton, V. (1990). Interpretation of transference in North American and British psychoanalysis: An empirical study. Unpublished doctoral thesis, University of London.

Harris, P. L. (1989). *Children and emotion: The development of psychological understanding.* Oxford, England: Basil Blackwell.

Harris, P. L. (1994). The child's understanding of emotion: Developmental change and the family environment. *Journal of Child Psychology and Psychiatry, 35,* 3–28.

Harter, S. (1986). Cognitive-developmental processes in the integration of concepts about emotions and the self. *Social Cognition, 4,* 119–151.

Hartmann, H. (1958). *Ego psychology and the problem of adaptation.* New York: International Universities Press. (Original work published 1939)

Hartmann, H. (1964). *Comments on the psychoanalytic theory of the ego.* New York: International Universities Press. (Original work published 1950)

Hartmann, H. (1964). Notes on the theory of sublimation. In *Essays on ego psychology* (pp. 215–240). New York: International Universities Press. (Original work published 1955)

Hartmann, H., Kris, E., & Loewenstein, R. (1946). Comments on the formation of psychic structure. *The Psychoanalytic Study of the Child, 20,* 11–38.

Hatcher, R., & Krohn, A. (1980). Level of object representation and capacity for intense psychotherapy in neurotics and borderlines. In J. Kwawer, H. Lerner, P. Lerner, & A. Sugarman (Eds.), *Borderline phenomena and the Rorschach test.* New York: International Universities Press.

Haviland, J. M., & Lelwica, M. (1987). The induced affect response: 10-week-old infants' responses to three emotional expressions. *Developmental Psychology, 23,* 97–104.

Hayman, A. (1969). What do we mean by "id"? *Journal of the American Psychoanalytic Association, 17,* 353–380.

Hesse, P., & Cicchetti, D. (1982). Perspectives on an integrated theory of emotional development. *New Directions for Child Development, 16,* 3–48.

Hinshelwood, R. (1989). *A dictionary of Kleinian thought.* London: Free Associations Press.

Holzman, P. S. (1985). Psychoanalysis: Is the therapy destroying the science? *Journal of the American Psychoanalytic Association, 33*(4), 725–770.

Hong, M. K., & Townes, B. (1976). Infant's attachment to inanimate objects: A cross-cultural study. *Journal of the American Academy of Child Psychiatry, 15,* 49–61.

Hornik, R., & Gunnar, M. R. (1988). A descriptive analysis of infant social referencing. *Child Development, 59,* 626–634.

Horowitz, M. J. (1987). *States of mind: Configurational analysis of individual psychology.* New York: Plenum.

Horowitz, M. J. (1991). Person schemas. In M. J. Horowitz (Ed.), *Person schemas and maladaptive interpersonal patterns* (pp. 13–31). Chicago: University of Chicago Press.

Horton, P. C., & Gewirtz, H. (1988). Acquisition and termination of first solacing objects in males, females, and in a clinic and nonclinic population: Implications for psychological immunity. In P. C. Horton, H. Gewirtz, & K. J. Kreutter (Eds.), *The solace paradigm: An eclectic search for psychological immunity* (pp. 159–184). Madison, CT: International Universities Press.

Huesmann, L. R., Eron, L. D., & Yarmel, P. W. (1987). Intellectual functioning and aggression. *Journal of Personality and Social Psychology, 52,* 232–240.

Hughes, J. (1989). *Reshaping the psychoanalytic domain.* Berkeley: University of California Press.

Huttuen, M. O., & Nyman, G. (1982). On the continuity, change and clinical value of infant temperament in a prospective epidemiological study. In R. Porter & G. M. Collings (Eds.), *Temperamental differences in infants and young children.* London: Pitman.

Isaacs, S. (1952). The nature and function of phantasy. In M. Klein, P. Heimann, S. Isaacs, & J. Riviere (Eds.), *Developments in psychoanalysis.* London: Hogarth Press. (Original work published 1943)

Jacobson, E. (1964). *The self and the object world.* New York: International Universities Press.

Jacobson, E. (1971). *Depression: Comparative studies of normal, neurotic, and psychotic conditions.* New York: International Universities Press.

James, W. (1890). *Principles of psychology.* New York: Holt.

Jenkins, J. M., & Astington, J. W. (1993, March). *Cognitive, linguistic, and social factors associated with theory of mind development in young children.* Paper presented at the meeting of the Society for Research in Child Development, New Orleans.

Johnson, A. M., & Szurek, S. A. (1952). The genesis of antisocial acting out in children and adults. *Psychoanalytic Quarterly, 21,* 323–343.

Johnson-Laird, P. N. (1983). *Mental models.* Cambridge, MA: Harvard University Press.

Jung, C. G. (1949). *Psychology of the unconscious.* New York: Dodd, Mead. (Original work published 1913)

Jung, C. G. (1916). *Psychology of the unconscious.* London: Routledge & Kegan Paul.

Kandel, E., Mednick, S. A., Kirkegaard-Sorensen, L., Hutchings, B., Knop, J., Rosenberg, R., & Schulsinger, F. (1988). IQ as a protective factor for subjects at high risk for antisocial behavior. *Journal of Consulting and Clinical Psychology, 56,* 224–226.

Kavanagh, G. (1985). Changes in patients' object representations during psychoanalysis and psychoanalytic psychotherapy. *Bulletin of the Menninger Clinic, 49,* 546–564.

Kennedy, H., & Moran, G. (1991). Reflections on the aims of child psychoanalysis. *The Psychoanalytic Study of the Child, 46,* 181–198.

Kennedy, H., & Yorke, C. (1980). Childhood neurosis v. developmental deviations: Two clinical case histories. *Dialogue: A Journal of Psychoanalytic Perspectives, 4,* 20–33.

Kernberg, O. F. (1967). Borderline personality organisation. *Journal of the American Psychoanalytic Association, 15,* 641–685.

Kernberg, O. F. (1970). A psychoanalytic classification of character pathology. *Journal of the American Psychoanalytic Association, 18,* 800–822.

Kernberg, O. F. (1974). Barriers to falling and remaining in love. *Journal of the American Psychoanalytic Association, 22,* 486–511.

Kernberg, O. F. (1975). *Borderline conditions and pathological narcissism.* New York: Aronson.

Kernberg, O. F. (1976a). *Object relations theory and clinical psychoanalysis.* New York: Aronson.

Kernberg, O. F. (1976b). Technical considerations in the treatment of borderline personality organisation. *Journal of the American Psychoanalytic Association, 24,* 795–829.

Kernberg, O. F. (1977). The structural diagnosis of borderline personality organization. In P. Hartocollis (Ed.), *Borderline personality disorders: The concept, the syndrome, the patient* (pp. 87–121). New York: International Universities Press.

Kernberg, O. F. (1980). *Internal world and external reality: Object relations theory applied.* New York: Aronson.

Kernberg, O. F. (1981). Structural interviewing. *Psychiatric Clinics of North America, 4,* 169–195.

Kernberg, O. F. (1982). Self, ego, affects and drives. *Journal of the American Psychoanalytic Association, 30,* 893–917.

Kernberg, O. F. (1984). *Severe personality disorders: Psychotherapeutic strategies.* New Haven, CT: Yale University Press.

Kernberg, O. F. (1987a). Borderline personality disorder: A psychodynamic approach. *Journal of Personality Disorders, 1,* 344–346.

Kernberg, O. F. (1987b). An ego psychology-object relations theory approach to the transference. *Psychoanalytic Quarterly, 51,* 197–221.

Kernberg, O. F. (1988). Object relations theory in clinical practice. *Psychoanalytic Quarterly, 57,* 481–504.

Kernberg, O. F. (1989). The narcissistic personality disorder and the differential diagnosis of antisocial behavior. *The Psychiatric Clinics of North America, 12,* 553–570.

Kernberg, O. F., & Clarkin, J. F. (1993). Developing a disorder-specific manual: The treatment of borderline character disorder. In N. E. Miller, L. Luborsky, J. P. Barber, & J. P. Docherty (Eds.), *Psychodynamic treatment research: A handbook for clinical practice* (pp. 227–246). New York: Basic Books.

Kernberg, O. F., Selzer, M. A., Koenigsberg, H. W., Carr, A. C., & Appelbaum, A. H. (1989). *Psychodynamic psychotherapy of borderline patients.* New York: Basic Books.

Khan, M. (1963). The concept of cumulative trauma. *The Psychoanalytic Study of the Child, 18,* 283–306.

Khan, M. (1966). The role of phobic and counter-phobic mechanisms and a separation anxiety in the schizoid character formation. *International Journal of Psycho-Analysis, 47,* 306–313.

Khan, M. (1974). *The privacy of the self.* London: Hogarth Press.

Khan, M. (1979). *Alienation in perversions.* London: Hogarth Press.

Khan, M. (1983a). *Hidden selves.* London: Hogarth Press.

Khan, M. (1983b). Secret and potential space. In *Hidden selves.* London: Hogarth Press. (Original work published 1978)

King, P. (1978). Affective response of the analyst to the patient's communications. *International Journal of Psycho-Analysis, 59,* 329–334.

King, P., & Steiner, R. (1991). *The Freud-Klein controversies.* London: Routledge.

King, R., & Noshpitz, J. D. (1990). *Pathways of growth: Essentials of child psychiatry: Vol. 2. Psychopathology.* New York: Wiley.

Klein, G. S. (1970). *Perception, motives and personality.* New York: Knopf.

Klein, G. S. (1976a). Freud's two theories of sexuality. *Psychological Issues, 36,* 14–70.

Klein, G. S. (1976b). *Psychoanalytic theory: An exploration of essentials.* New York: International Universities Press.

Klein, M. (1964a). A contribution to the theory of intellectual inhibitions. In *Contributions to psychoanalysis, 1921–1945.* New York: McGraw-Hill. (Original work published 1931)

Klein, M. (1964b). The psychotherapy of the psychoses. In *Contributions to psychoanalysis, 1921–1945.* New York: McGraw-Hill. (Original work published 1936)

Klein, M. (1975a). A contribution to the psychogenesis of manic-depressive states. In *The writings of Melanie Klein* (pp. 236–289). London: Hogarth Press. (Original work published 1935)

Klein, M. (1975b). Envy and gratitude. In *The writings of Melanie Klein* (pp. 176–235). London: Hogarth Press. (Original work published 1957)

Klein, M. (1975c). Mourning and its relation to manic-depressive states. In *The writings of Melanie Klein* (pp. 344–369). London: Hogarth Press. (Original work published 1940)

Klein, M. (1975d). The narrative of a child analysis. In *The writings of Melanie Klein* (pp. 15–30). London: Hogarth Press. (Original work published 1960)

Klein, M. (1975e). Notes on some schizoid mechanisms. In *The writings of Melanie Klein* (pp. 1–24). London: Hogarth Press. (Original work published 1946)

Klein, M. (1975f). The Oedipus complex in the light of early anxieties. In *The writings of Melanie Klein* (pp. 370–419). London: Hogarth Press. (Original work published 1945)

Klein, M. (1975g). Our adult world and its roots in infancy. In *The writings of Melanie Klein* (pp. 247–263). London: Hogarth Press. (Original work published 1959)

Klein, M. (1975h). The psycho-analysis of children. In *The writings of Melanie Klein.* London: Hogarth Press. (Original work published 1932)

Klein, M. (1975i). On the theory of anxiety and guilt. In *The writings of Melanie Klein* (pp. 25–42). London: Hogarth Press. (Original work published 1948)

Klein, M. (1981). On Mahler's autistic and symbiotic phases: An exposition and evaluation. *Psychoanalysis and Contemporary Thought, 4,* 69–105.

Knight, R. (1953). Borderline states. *Bulletin of the Menninger Clinic, 17,* 1–12.

Kog, E., & Vandereycken, W. (1985). Family characteristics of anorexia nervosa and bulimia: A review of the research literature. *Clinical Psychology Review, 5,* 159–180.

Kohon, G. (Ed.). (1986). *The British school of psycho-analysis: The independent tradition.* London: Free Association Books.

Kohut, H. (1966). Forms and transformations of narcissism. *Journal of the American Psychoanalytic Association, 14,* 243–272.

Kohut, H. (1968). The psychoanalytic treatment of narcissistic personality disorders. *The Psychoanalytic Study of the Child, 23,* 86–113.

Kohut, H. (1971). *The analysis of the self.* New York: International Universities Press.

Kohut, H. (1977). *The restoration of the self.* New York: International Universities Press.

Kohut, H. (1978). *The search for the self. Selected writings 1950–78.* P. H. Ornstein (Ed.). New York: International Universities Press.

Kohut, H. (1984). *How does analysis cure?* Chicago: University of Chicago Press.

Kohut, H., & Wolf, E. S. (1978). The disorders of the self and their treatment: An outline. *International Journal of Psycho-Analysis, 59,* 413–425.

Kramer, S. (1979). The technical significance and application of Mahler's separation-individuation theory. *Journal of the American Psychoanalytic Association, 27,* 241–262.

Kramer, S., & Akhtar, S. (1988). The developmental context of internalized pre-oedipal object relations: Clinical applications of Mahler's theory of symbiosis and separation-individuation. *Psychoanalytic Quarterly, 57,* 547–576.

Kris, A. O. (1984). The conflicts of ambivalence. *Psychoanalytic Study of the Child, 39,* 213–234.

Kris, E. (1952). *Psychoanalytic explorations in art.* New York: International Universities Press.

Krohn, A., & Mayman, M. (1974). Object representations in dreams and projective tests. *Bulletin of the Menninger Clinic, 38,* 445–466.

Lampl-de-Groot, J. (1949). Neurotics, delinquents and ideal formation. In K. R. Eissler (Ed.), *Searchlights on delinquency* (pp. 225–245). New York: International Universities Press.

Lasch, C. (1978). *The culture of narcissism: American life in an age of diminishing expectations.* New York: Norton.

Leahey, T. H. (1980). The myth of operationism. *Journal of Mind and Behavior, 1,* 127–143.

Leslie, A. M. (1986). Getting development off the ground: Modularity and the infant's perception of causality. In P. L. C. van Geert (Ed.), *Theory building in developmental psychology.* Amsterdam: Elsevier/North Holland.

Leslie, A. M. (1987). Pretense and representation: The origins of "theory of mind." *Psychological Review, 94,* 412–426.

Leslie, A. M., & Keeble, S. (1987). Do six-month-olds perceive causality? *Cognition, 25,* 265–288.

Lewin, K. (1952). *Field theory and social science.* London: Tavistock.

Lichtenberg, J. D. (1987). Infant studies and clinical work with adults. *Psycho-Analytic Inquiry, 7,* 311–330.

Linehan, M. M., & Heard, H. L. (1993). Commentary. In Z. V. Segal & S. J. Blatt (Eds.), *The self in emotional distress: Cognitive and psychodynamic perspectives* (pp. 161–370). New York: Guilford.

Links, P. S., Steiner, M., & Huxley, G. (1988). The occurrence of borderline personality disorder in the families of borderline patients. *Journal of the Personality Disorders, 2,* 14–20.

Litt, C. (1981). Children's attachment to transitional objects: A study of two pediatric populations. *American Journal of Orthopsychiatry, 51,* 131–139.

Loewald, H. W. (1980). Hypnoid state, repression, abreaction, and recollection. In *Papers on psychoanalysis* (pp. 33–42). New Haven, CT: Yale University Press. (Original work published 1955)

Loewald, H. W. (1960). On the therapeutic action of psycho-analysis. *International Journal of Psycho-Analysis, 41,* 16–33.

Loewald, H. W. (1973). The analysis of the self. *Psychoanalytic Quarterly, 42,* 441–451.

Loewald, H. W. (1986). Transference-countertransference. *Journal of the American Psychoanalytic Association, 34,* 275–288.

Loranger, A., Oldham, J., & Tullis, E. (1982). Familial transmission of DSM-III borderline personality disorder. *Archives of General Psychiatry, 39,* 795–799.

Lussier, A. (1988). The limitations of the object relations model. *Psychoanalytic Quarterly, 57,* 528–546.

Mahler, M. S. (1963). Thoughts about development and individuation. *The Psychoanalytic Study of the Child, 18,* 307–324.

Mahler, M. S. (1974). Symbiosis and individuation: The psychological birth of the human infant. In *The selected papers of Margaret S. Mahler.* New York: Aronson.

Mahler, M. S., & Furer, M. (1968). *On human symbiosis and the vicissitudes of individuation.* New York: International Universities Press.

Mahler, M. S., & Kaplan, L. (1977). Developmental aspects in the assessment of narcissistic and so-called borderline personalities. In P. Hartocollis (Ed.), *Borderline personality disorders: The concept, the syndrome, the patient* (pp. 71–86). New York: International Universities Press.

Mahler, M. S., & McDevitt, J. F. (1980). The separation-individuation process and identity formation. In S. I. Greenspan & G. H. Pollock (Eds.), *Infancy and early childhood: The Course of Life. Psychoanalytic contributions toward understanding personality development* (Vol. 1, pp. 395–406). Washington, DC: National Institute for Mental Health, Publication No. (ADM) 80-786.

Mahler, M. S., Pine, F., & Bergman, A. (1975). *The psychological birth of the human infant: Symbiosis and individuation.* New York: Basic Books.

Main, M. (1991). Metacognitive knowledge, metacognitive monitoring, and singular (coherent) vs. (incoherent) models of attachment: Findings and directions for future research. In P. Harris, J. Stevenson-Hinde, & C. Parkes (Eds.), *Attachment across the life cycle.* New York: Routledge.

Main, M., & Goldwyn, R. (1991). *Adult Attachment Classification System. Version 5.* Unpublished manuscript, University of California, Berkeley.

Main, M., & Hesse, E. (1990). Parents' unresolved traumatic experiences are related to infant disorganized attachment status: Is frightened and/or frightening parental behavior the linking mechanism? In M. Greenberg, D. Cicchetti, & E. M. Cummings (Eds.), *Attachment in the preschool years: Theory, research and intervention* (pp. 161–182). Chicago: University of Chicago Press.

Main, M., & Hesse, E. (1991). The insecure disorganized/disoriented attachment pattern in infancy: Precursors and sequelae. In M. Greenberg, P. Cicchetti, & E. M. Cummings (Eds.), *Attachment in the preschool years: Theory, research and intervention.* Chicago: University of Chicago Press.

Main, M., Kaplan, N., & Cassidy, J. (1985). Security in infancy, childhood and adulthood: A move to the level of representation. In I. Bretherton & E. Waters (Eds.), *Growing points of attachment theory research* (pp. 66–104). *Monographs of the Society for Research in Child Development, 50,* (1–2, Serial No. 209).

Main, M., & Solomon, J. (1986). Discovery of an insecure-disorganized/disoriented attachment pattern. In T. B. Brazelton & M. W. Yogman (Eds.), *Affective development in infancy.* Norwood, NJ: Ablex.

Marcel, A. J. (1983a). Conscious and unconscious perception: An approach to the relations between phenomenal experience and perceptual processes. *Cognitive Psychology, 15,* 238–300.

Marcel, A. J. (1983b). Conscious and unconscious perception: Experiments on visual masking and word recognition. *Cognitive Psychology, 15,* 197–237.

Marcel, A. J. (1988a). Electrophysiology and meaning in cognitive science and dynamic psychology: Comments on "Unconscious conflict: A convergent psychodynamic and electrophysiological approach." In M. J. Horowitz (Ed.), *Psychodynamics and cognition* (pp. 169–190). Chicago: University of Chicago Press.

Marcel, A. J. (1988b). Phenomenal experience and functionalism. In A. J. Marcel & E. Bisiach (Eds.), *Consciousness in contemporary science* (pp. 121–158). Oxford, England: Clarendon Press.

Masten, A. S. (1989). Resilience in development: Implications of the study of successful adaptation for developmental psychopathology. In D. Cicchetti (Ed.), *Rochester Symposium on Developmental Psychopathology: The emergence of a discipline.* Hillsdale, NJ: Erlbaum.

Masten, A. S., & Braswell, L. (1991). Developmental psychopathology: An integrative framework for understanding behaviour problems in children and adolescents. In P. R. Martin (Ed.), *Handbook of behaviour therapy and psychological science: An integrative approach.* New York: Pergamon.

Masterson, J. F. (1972). *Treatment of the borderline adolescent: A developmental approach.* New York: Wiley.

Masterson, J. F. (1976). *Psychotherapy of the borderline adult: A developmental approach.* New York: Brunner/Mazel.

Masterson, J. F., & Rinsley, D. (1975). The borderline syndrome: The role of the mother in the genesis and psychic structure of the borderline personality. *International Journal of Psycho-Analysis, 56,* 163–177.

McDougall, J. (1974). The psycho-soma and the psychoanalytic process. *International Review of Psycho-Analysis, 1,* 437–460.

McFarlane, A. C. (1987). Post-traumatic phenomena in a longitudinal study of children following a natural disaster. *Journal of the American Academy of Child and Adolescent Psychiatry, 28,* 764–769.

McGlashan, T. (1986). Long-term outcome of borderline patients. *Archives of General Psychiatry, 40,* 20–30.

McLaughlin, J. T. (1981). Transference, psychic reality and countertransference. *Psychoanalytic Quarterly, 50,* 639–664.

Mead, G. H. (1934). In C. Morris (Ed.), *Mind and society.* Chicago: University of Chicago Press.

Meehl, P. E. (1986). Diagnostic taxa as open concepts: Metatheoretical and statistical questions about reliability and construct validity in the grand strategy of nosological revision. In T. Millon & G. L. Klerman (Eds.), *Contemporary directions in psychopathology: Toward DSM IV* (pp. 215–231). New York: Guilford.

Meissner, W. W. (1980). A note on projective identification. *Journal of the American Psychoanalytic Association, 28,* 43–67.

Meltzer, D. (1974). Mutism in infantile autism, schizophrenia and manic-depressive states. *International Journal of Psycho-Analysis, 55,* 397–404.

Meltzer, D. (1978). *The Kleinian development.* Strathtay, England: Clunie Press.

Meltzoff, A. N. (1990). Foundations for developing a concept of self: The role of imitation in relating self to other and the value of social mirroring, social modeling and self practice in infancy. In D. Cicchetti & M. Beeghly (Eds.), *The self in transition: Infancy to childhood* (pp. 240–263). Chicago: University of Chicago Press.

Meltzoff, A. N., & Gopnik, A. (1993). A role of imitation in understanding persons and developing a theory of mind. In S. Baron-Cohen, H. Tager-Flusberg, & D. Cohen (Eds.), *Understanding other minds: Perspectives from autism* (pp. 335–366). New York: Oxford University Press.

Meltzoff, A. N., & Moore, M. K. (1989). Imitation in newborn infants: Exploring the range of gestures imitated and the underlying mechanisms. *Developmental Psychology, 25,* 954–962.

Michels, R. (1985). Perspectives on the nature of psychic reality: Panel introduction. *Journal of the American Psychoanalytic Association, 33,* 515–525.

Miller, N. E. (1993). Diagnosis of personality disorder: Psychodynamic and empirical issues. In N. E. Miller, L. Luborsky, J. P. Barber, & J. P. Docherty (Eds.), *Psychodynamic treatment research* (pp. 127–151). New York: Basic Books.

Miller, P. A., Eisenberg, N., Fabes, R. A., Shell, R., & Gular, S. (1989). *Mothers' emotional arousal as a moderator in the socialization of children's empathy.* New York: Wiley.

Minsky, M. L. (1977). A framework for representing knowledge. In P. H. Winston (Ed.), *The psychology of computer vision* (pp. 211–277). New York: Wiley.

Minsky, M. L. (1985). *The society of mind.* New York: Simon & Schuster.

Mitchell, S. A. (1988). *Relational concepts in psychoanalysis: An integration.* Cambridge, MA: Harvard University Press.

Modell, A. H. (1963). Primitive object relationships and the predisposition to schizophrenia. *International Journal of Psycho-Analysis, 44,* 282–292.

Modell, A. H. (1968). *Object love and reality.* New York: International Universities Press.

Modell, A. H. (1975). A narcissistic defense against affects and the illusion of self-sufficiency. *International Journal of Psycho-Analysis, 56,* 275–282.

Modell, A. H. (1984). *Psychoanalysis in a new context.* New York: International Universities Press.

Modell, A. H. (1985). Object relations theory. In A. Rothstein (Ed.), *Models of the mind: Their relationships to clinical work* (pp. 85–100). New York: International Universities Press.

Moses, L. J., & Flavell, J. H. (1990). Inferring false beliefs from actions and reactions. *Child Development, 61,* 929–945.

Murphy, L. G., & Moriarity, A. E. (1975). *Vulnerability, coping and growth.* New Haven, CT: Yale University Press.

Nagera, H. (1966). *Early childhood disturbances, the infantile neurosis, and the adulthood disturbances.* New York: International Universities Press.

Nelson, L. A. (1987). The recognition of facial expressions in the first two years of life: Mechanisms of development. *Child Development, 58,* 889–909.

Neubauer, P. B. (1984). Anna Freud's concept of developmental lines. *The Psychoanalytic Study of the Child, 39,* 15–27.

Newson, J., Newson, E., & Mahalski, P. (1982). Persistent infant comfort habits and their sequelae at 11 and 16 years. *Journal of Child Psychology and Psychiatry, 23,* 421–436.

Nigg, J., Lohr, N. E., Westen, D., Gold, L., & Silk, K. R. (1992). Malevolent object representations in borderline personality disorder and major depression. *Journal of Abnormal Psychology, 101,* 61–67.

Nisbett, R. E., & Wilson, T. D. (1977). Telling more than we can know: Verbal reports on mental processes. *Psychological Review, 84,* 231–259.

Noy, P. (1977). Metapsychology as a multimodel system. *International Review of Psychoanalysis, 4,* 1–12.

O'Grady, D., & Metz, J. R. (1987). Resilience in children at high risk for psychological disorder. *Journal of Pediatric Psychology, 12,* 3–23.

O'Shaughnessy, E. (1989). The invisible Oedipus complex. In J. Steiner (Ed.), *The Oedipus complex today* (pp. 129–150). London: Karnac Books.

Ogata, S. N., Silk, K. R., & Goodrich, S. (1990). The childhood experience of the borderline patient. In P. Links (Ed.), *Family environment and borderline personality disorder.* Washington, DC: American Psychiatric Press.

Ogata, S. N., Silk, K. R., Goodrich, S., Lohr, N. E., Westen, D., & Hill, E. (1990). Childhood abuse and clinical symptoms in borderline patients. *American Journal of Psychiatry, 147,* 1008–1013.

Ogden, T. (1986). *The matrix of the mind: Object relations and the psychoanalytic dialogue.* New York: Aronson.

Olinick, S. (1982). Meanings beyond words: Psychoanalytic perceptions of silence and communication, happiness, sexual love and death. *International Review of Psycho-Analysis, 9,* 461–472.

Orvaschel, H. (1983). Maternal depression and child dysfunction. In B. Lahey & A. Kazdin (Eds.), *Advances in clinical child psychology* (pp. 169–197). New York: Plenum.

Osofsky, J. D. (1987). *Handbook of infant development.* New York: Wiley.

Papousek, H., & Papousek, M. (1974). Mirror-image and self recognition in young human infants: A new method of experimental analysis. *Developmental Psychobiology, 7,* 149–157.

Parens, H. (1979). *The development of aggression in early childhood.* New York: Aronson.

Parens, H. (1980). An exploration of the relations of instinctual drives and the symbiosis/separation-individuation process. *Journal of the American Psychoanalytic Association, 28,* 89–114.

Patterson, G. R., & Stouthamer-Loeber, M. (1984). The correlation of family management practices and delinquency. *Child Development, 55,* 1299–1307.

Perner, J. (1991). *Understanding the representational mind.* Cambridge, MA: MIT Press.

Perner, J., Leekam, S. R., & Wimmer, H. (1987). Three-year-olds' difficulty with false belief. *British Journal of Developmental Psychology, 5,* 125–37.

Perner, J., Ruffman, T., & Leekam, S. R. (in press). Theory of mind is contagious: You catch it from your sibs (if you are close to them). *Child Development.*

Perry, J., & Cooper, S. (1985). Psychodynamics, symptoms, and outcome in borderline and antisocial personality disorders and bipolar type II affective disorder. In T. McGlashan (Ed.), *The borderline: Current empirical research.* Washington, DC: American Psychiatric Press.

Peterfreund, E. (1975). The need for a new general theoretical frame of reference for psychoanalysis. *Psychoanalytical Quarterly, 44,* 534–549.

Peterfreund, E. (1978). Some critical comments on psychoanalytic conceptualizations of infancy. *International Journal of Psycho-Analysis, 59,* 427–441.

Peterfreund, E. (1980). On information and systems models for psychoanalysis. *International Review of Psycho-analysis, 7,* 327–345.

Phillips, W., Baron-Cohen, S., & Rutter, M. (1992). The role of eye-contact in goal-detection: Evidence from normal toddlers and children with autism or mental handicap. *Development and Psychopathology, 4,* 375–384.

Piaget, J. (1954). *The construction of reality in the child.* New York: Basic Books.

Piaget, J. (1977). Equilibration processes in the psychobiological development of the child. In H. E. Gruber & J. J. Voneche (Eds.), *The essential Piaget* (pp. 832–841). New York: Basic Books. (Original work published 1958)

Piattelli-Palmarini, M. (1980). *Language and learning: The debate between Jean Piaget and Noam Chomsky.* Cambridge, MA: Harvard University Press.

Pine, F. (1985). *Developmental theory and clinical process.* New Haven, CT: Yale University Press.

Plakum, E. M., Burkhardt, P. E., & Muller, J. P. (1985). Fourteen-year follow-up of borderline and schizotypal personality disorders. *Comprehensive Psychiatry, 26,* 448–455.

Pollock, G. H. (1981). Aging and aged: Development on pathology. In S. I. Greenspan & G. H. Pollock (Eds.), *The course of life* (pp. 549–581). Washington, DC: U.S. Department of Health and Human Services.

Poulin-Dubois, D., & Shultz, T. R. (1988). The development of the understanding of human behavior: From agency to intentionality. In J. Astington, P. Harris, & D. Olson (Eds.), *Developing theories of mind.* New York: Cambridge University Press.

Premack, D. (1990). The infant's theory of self-propelled objects. *Cognition, 36,* 1–16.

Provence, S., & Ritvo, S. (1961). Effects of deprivation on institutionalized infants: Disturbances in development of relationships to inanimate objects. *The Psychoanalytic Study of the Child, 16,* 189–204.

Quinodox, J. M. (1991). Accepting fusion to get over it. *Review Francais de Psychoanalyse, 55,* 1697–1700.

Rachman, S. (1984). Agoraphobia: A safety-signal perspective. *Behavioral Research and Therapy, 22,* 59–70.

Rachman, S., & de Silva, P. (1978). Abnormal and normal obsessions. *Behaviour Research and Therapy, 16,* 233–248.

Racker, H. (1968). *Transference and countertransference.* New York: International Universities Press.

Rangell, L. (1955). The borderline case. *Journal of the American Psychoanalytic Association, 3,* 285–298.

Rangell, L. (1982). The self in psychoanalytic theory. *Journal of the American Psychoanalytic Association, 30,* 863–891.

Rangell, L. (1985). On the theory of theory in psychoanalysis and the relation of theory to psychoanalytic therapy. *Journal of the American Psychoanalytic Association, 33,* 59–92.

Rank, O. (1929). *The trauma of birth.* New York: Harcourt. (Original work published 1924)

Rapaport, D. (1950). On the psychoanalytic theory of thinking. *International Journal of Psycho-Analysis, 31,* 161–170.

Rapaport, D. (1958). The theory of ego autonomy: A generalization. *Bulletin of the Menninger Clinic, 22,* 13–35.

Rayner, E. (1991). *The independent mind in British psychoanalysis.* London: Free Association Books.

Reich, A. (1973). Empathy and countertransference. In *Psychoanalytic Contributions* (pp. 344–360). New York: International Universities Press. (Original work published 1960)

Reich, W. (1933). *Character analysis* (3rd ed.). (V.R. Carfagno, Trans.). New York: Farrar, Straus & Giroux.

Rest, J. R. (1983). Morality. In J. H. Flavell & E. M. Markman (Eds.), *Handbook of child psychology: Vol. 3. Cognitive development* (pp. 556–629). New York: Wiley.

Rinsley, D. (1980). The developmental etiology of borderline and narcissistic disorders. *Bulletin of the Menninger Clinic, 44,* 127–134.

Rinsley, D. B. (1982). *Borderline and other self disorders: A developmental and object relations perspective.* New York: Aronson.

Ritzler, B., Wyatt, D., Harder, D., & Kaskey, M. (1980). Psychotic patterns of the concept of the object on the Rorschach. *Journal of Abnormal Psychology, 89,* 46–55.

Riviere, J. (1936). On the genesis of psychical conflict in early infancy. *International Journal of Psycho-Analysis, 55,* 397–404.

Robbins, M. (1989). Primitive personality organization as an interpersonally adaptive modification of cognition and affect. *International Journal of Psycho-Analysis, 70* , 443–459.

Rogers, R. (1980). Psychoanalytic and cybernetic models of mentation. *Psychoanalysis and Contemporary Thought, 3,* 21–54.

Rosch, E. (1978). Principles of categorization. In E. Rosch & B. B. Floyd (Eds.), *Cognition and categorization.* Hillsdale, NJ: Erlbaum.

Rosenblatt, A. D., & Thickstun, J. T. (1977a). Modern psychoanalytic concepts in a general psychology. In *Psychological issues* (pp. 229–264). New York: International Universities Press.

Rosenblatt, A. D., & Thickstun, J. T. (1977b). Modern psychoanalytic concepts in a general psychology: Part 2: Motivation. In *Psychological issues* (pp. 217–230). New York: International Universities Press.

Rosenfeld, H. (1964). On the psychopathology of narcissism: A clinical approach. *International Journal of Psycho-Analysis, 45,* 332–337.

Rosenfeld, H. (1965). *Psychotic states: A psychoanalytic approach.* New York: International Universities Press.

Rosenfeld, H. (1971). A clinical approach to the psychoanalytic theory of the life and death instincts: An investigation into the aggressive aspects of narcissism. In E. B. Spillius (Ed.), *Melanie Klein today* (pp. 239–255). London: Routledge.

Rosenfeld, H. (1988). Contribution to the psychopathology of psychotic states: The importance of projective identification in the ego structure and object relations of the psychotic patient. In E. B. Spillius (Ed.), *Melanie Klein Today* (pp. 117–137). London: Routledge. (Original work published 1971)

Rosenfeld, J. (1950). Notes on the psychopathology of confusional states in chronic schizophrenia. *International Journal of Psycho-Analysis, 31,* 132–137.

Rothstein, A. (1980). Toward a critique of the psychology of the self. *Psychoanalytic Quarterly, 49,* 423–455.

Rovee-Collier, C. K., & Fagan, J. W. (1981). The retrieval of memory in early infancy. In L. P. Lipsitt (Ed.), *Advances in infant research.* Norwood, NJ: Ablex.

Rumelhart, D. E., & McClelland, J. L. (1986). *Parallel distributed processing.* Cambridge, MA: MIT Press.

Rutter, M. (1989). Epidemiological approaches to developmental psychopathology. *Archives of General Psychiatry, 45,* 486–500.

Rutter, M. (1990). Psychosocial resilience and protective mechanisms. In J. Rolf, A. S. Masten, D. Cicchetti, K. H. Neuchterlein, & S. Weintraub (Eds.), *Risk and protective factors in the development of psychopathology.* New York: Cambridge University Press.

Rutter, M. (1994). Developmental psychopathology as a research perspective. In D. Magnusson & P. Casaer (Eds.), *Longitudinal research on individual development: Present status and future perspectives.* New York: Cambridge University Press.

Rutter, M., & Quinton, D. (1984). Long-term follow-up of women institutionalized in childhood: Factors promoting good functioning in adult life. *British Journal of Developmental Psychology, 18,* 225–234.

Ryan, E. R., & Bell, M. D. (1984). Changes in object relations from psychosis to recovery. *Journal of Abnormal Psychology, 93,* 209–215.

Ryan, E. R., & Cicchetti, D. V. (1985). Predicting the quality of alliance in the initial psychotherapy interview. *Journal of Nervous and Mental Disease, 12,* 717–725.

Rycroft, C. (1966). *Psycho-analysis observed.* London: Constable.

Rycroft, C. (1979). *The innocence of dreams.* London: Hogarth Press.

Sampson, E. E. (1988). The debate on individualism: Indigenous psychologies of the individual and their role in personal and societal functioning. *American Psychologist, 43,* 15–22.

Sander, L. W. (1983). Polarity, paradox, and the organizing process. In E. Galenson, J. D. Call, & R. L. Tyson (Eds.), *Frontiers of infant psychiatry* (pp. 333–346). New York: Basic Books.

Sandler, J. (1962). The Hampstead Index as an instrument of psychoanalytic research. *International Journal of Psycho-Analysis, 43,* 287–291.

Sandler, J. (1976). Countertransference and role-responsiveness. *International Review of Psycho-Analysis, 3,* 43–47.

Sandler, J. (1983). Reflections on some relations between psychoanalytic concepts and psychoanalytic practice. *International Journal of Psycho-Analysis, 64,* 35–45.

Sandler, J. (1985). Towards a reconsideration of the psychoanalytic theory of motivation. *Bulletin of the Anna Freud Centre, 8,* 223–243.

Sandler, J. (1987a). The background of safety. In *From safety to superego: Selected papers of Joseph Sandler* (pp. 1–8). London: Karnac. (Original work published 1960)

Sandler, J. (1987b). *From safety to the superego: Selected papers of Joseph Sandler.* New York: Guilford.

Sandler, J. (1990). Internal objects and internal object relationships. *Psychoanalytic Inquiry, 10,* 163–181.

Sandler, J., & Dare, C. (1970). The psychoanalytic concept of orality. *Journal of Psychosomatic Research, 14,* 211–222.

Sandler, J., & Joffe, W. G. (1967). The tendency to persistence in psychological function and development, with special reference to fixation and regression. *Bulletin of the Menninger Clinic, 31,* 257–271.

Sandler, J., & Joffe, W. G. (1969). Towards a basic psychoanalytic model. *International Journal of Psycho-Analysis, 50,* 79–90.

Sandler, J., & Rosenblatt, B. (1962). The concept of the representational world. *The Psychoanalytic Study of the Child, 17,* 128–145.

Sandler, J., & Sandler, A.-M. (1978). On the development of object relationships and affects. *International Journal of Psycho-Analysis, 59,* 285–296.

Sandler, J., & Sandler, A.-M. (1992). Psychoanalytic technique and theory of psychic change. *Bulletin of the Anna Freud Centre, 15,* 35–51.

Scaife, M., & Bruner, J. (1975). The capacity for joint visual attention in the infant. *Nature, 253,* 265–266.

Schafer, R. (1974). Problems in Freud's psychology of women. *Journal of the American Psychoanalytic Association, 22* , 459–485.

Schafer, R. (1976). *A new language for psychoanalysis.* New Haven, CT: Yale University Press.

Schafer, R. (1983). *The analytic attitude.* New York: Basic Books.

Schaffer, H. R. (1977). *Studies in mother-infant interaction.* London: Academic Press.

Schaffer, H. R., & Emerson, P. E. (1964). Patterns of response to physical contact in early human development. *Journal of Child Psychology and Psychiatry, 5,* 1–13.

Schanck, R. C. (1975). *Conceptual information processing.* Amsterdam: North Holland.

Schanck, R. C. (1982). *Dynamic memory: A theory of reminding and learning in computers and people.* New York: Cambridge University Press.

Schmideberg, M. (1947). The treatment of psychopathic and borderline patients. *American Journal of Psychotherapy, 1,* 45–71.

Schur, M. (1966). *The id and the regulatory principles of mental functioning.* New York: International Universities Press.

Schwaber, E. (1983). Psychoanalytic listening and psychic reality. *International Review of Psycho-Analysis, 10,* 379–392.

Schwartz, L. (1978). Review of "The restoration of the self" by Heinz Kohut. *Psychoanalytic Quarterly, 47,* 436–443.

Searles, H. (1960). *The nonhuman environment.* New York: International Universities Press.

Searles, H. F. (1986). *My work with borderline patients.* New York: Aronson.

Segal, H. (1957). Notes on symbol formation. *International Journal of Psycho-Analysis, 38,* 391–397.

Segal, H. (1974). *An introduction to the work of Melanie Klein.* London: Hogarth Press.

Segal, H. (1981). *The work of Hanna Segal.* New York: Aronson.

Segal, H. (1985). The Klein-Bion model. In A. Rothstein (Ed.), *Models of the mind: Their relationships to clinical work* (pp. 35–48). New York: International Universities Press.

Seligman, M. E. P. (1975). *Helplessness.* San Francisco: Freeman.

Settlage, C. F. (1977). The psychoanalytic understanding of narcissistic and borderline personality disorders: Advances in developmental theory. *Journal of the American Psychoanalytic Association, 25,* 805–833.

Settlage, C. F. (1980). Excerpt from the Report of the Preparatory Commission on Child Analysis. *Psychoanalysis and Contemporary Thought, 3,* 131–138.

Settlage, C. F., Curtis, Z., Lozoff, M., Silberschatz, G., & Simburg, E. (1988). Conceptualizing adult development. *Journal of the American Psychoanalytic Association, 60,* 347–370.

Shantz, C. U. (1983). Social cognition. In J. H. Flavell & E. M. Markman (Eds.), *Handbook of child psychology: Vol. 3. Cognitive developments.* New York: Wiley.

Shedler, J., Mayman, M., & Manis, M. (1993). The illusion of mental health. *American Psychologist, 48,* 1117–1131.

Sherman, M., & Hertzig, M. (1983). Treasured object use: A cognitive and developmental marker. *Journal of the American Academy of Child Psychiatry, 22,* 541–544.

Sherman, M., Hertzig, M., Austrian, R., & Shapiro, T. (1981). Treasured objects in school-aged children. *Pediatrics, 68,* 379–386.

Sherman, S., Judd, C. M., & Park, B. (1989). Social cognition. *Annual Review of Psychology, 40,* 281–326.

Shultz, T. (1982). Rules of causal attribution. *Monographs of the Society for Research in Child Development, 47*(1, Serial No 194).

Silk, K. R., Lohr, N. E., Westen, D., & Goodrich, S. (1989). Psychosis in borderline patients with depression. *Journal of Personality Disorders, 3,* 92–100.

Singer, M. (1975). The borderline delinquent: The interlocking of intrapsychic and interactional determinants. *International Review of Psycho-Analysis, 2,* 429–440.

Sissons Joshi, M., & MacLean, M. (in press). Indian and English children's understanding of the distinction between real and apparent emotion. *Child Development.*

Slade, P. (1982). Towards a functional analysis of anorexia nervosa and bulimia nervosa. *British Journal of Clinical Psychology, 21,* 167–179.

Solomon, J. D. (1962). The fixed idea as an internalized transitional object. *American Journal of Psychotherapy, 16,* 632–644.

Sorce, J., Emde, R., Campos, J., & Klinnert, M. (1985). Maternal emotional signalling: Its effect on the visual cliff behavior of 1-year-olds. *Developmental Psychology, 21,* 195–200.

Soref, A. R. (1992). The self in and out of relatedness. *The Annual of Psychoanalysis, 20,* 25–48.

Spear, W., & Sugarman, A. (1984). Dimensions of internalized object relations in borderline and schizophrenic patients. *Psychoanalytic Psychology, 1,* 113–129.

Spelke, E. S. (1985). Preferential looking methods as tools for the study of cognition in infancy. In G. Gottlieb & N. Krasnegor (Eds.), *Measurement of audition and vision in the first year of postnatal life.* Hillsdale, NJ: Erlbaum.

Spelke, E. S. (1990). Principles of object perception. *Cognitive Science, 14,* 29–56.

Spemann, H. (1938). *Embryonic development and induction.* New Haven, CT: Yale University Press.

Sperling, M. (1959). A study of deviate sexual behavior in children by the method of simultaneous analysis of mother and child. In L. Jessnor & E. Davenstad (Eds.), *Dynamic psychopathology in childhood.* New York: Grune & Stratton.

Sperling, M. (1963). Fetishism in children. *Psychoanalytic Quarterly, 32,* 374–392.

Spillius, E. B. (1988a). General introduction. In E. B. Spillius (Ed.), *Melanie Klein today: Developments in theory and practice: Vol. 1. Mainly theory.* London: Routledge.

Spillius, E. B. (1988b). *Melanie Klein today: Developments in theory and practice: Vol. 1. Mainly theory; Vol. 2. Mainly practice.* London: Routledge.

Spillius, E. B. (1994). Developments in Kleinian thought: Overview and personal view. *Psychoanalytic Inquiry, 14,* 324–364.

Spitz, R. A. (1959). *A genetic field theory of ego formation: Its implications for pathology.* New York: International Universities Press.

Spitz, R. A. (1965). *The first year of life.* New York: International Universities Press.

Spruiell, V. (1988). The indivisibility of Freudian object relations and drive theories. *Psychoanalytic Quarterly, 57,* 597–625.

Sroufe, L. A. (1989). Pathways to adaptation and maladaptation: Psychopathology as a developmental deviation. In D. Cicchetti (Ed.),

Rochester Symposium on Developmental Psychopathology: The emergence of a discipline (pp. 13–40). Hillsdale, NJ: Erlbaum.

Sroufe, L. A. (1990). An organizational perspective on the self. In D. Cicchetti & M. Beeghly (Eds.), *The self in transition: Infancy to childhood* (pp. 281–307). Chicago: University of Chicago Press.

Sroufe, L. A., Egeland, B., & Kreutzer, T. (1990). The fate of early experience following developmental change: Longitudinal approaches to individual adaptation in childhood. *Child Development, 61,* 1363–1373.

Sroufe, L. A., & Rutter, M. (1984). The domain of developmental psychopathology. *Child Development, 83,* 173–189.

Stechler, G., & Halton, A. (1987). The emergence of assertion and aggression during infancy: A psychoanalytic systems approach. *Journal of the American Psychoanalytic Association, 35,* 821–838.

Stechler, G., & Kaplan, S. (1980). The development of the sense of self: A psychoanalytic perspective. *The Psychoanalytic Study of the Child, 35,* 85–105.

Steele, H., Steele, M., & Fonagy, P. (in press). Associations among attachment classifications of mothers, fathers and their infants: Evidence for a relationship-specific perspective. *Child Development.*

Steiner, J. (1987). The interplay between pathological organisations and the paranoid-schizoid and depressive positions. *International Journal of Psycho-Analysis, 68,* 69–80.

Steiner, J. (1992). The equilibrium between the paranoid-schizoid and the depressive positions. In R. Anderson (Ed.), *Clinical lectures on Klein and Bion* (pp. 46–58). London: Routledge.

Stern, A. (1938). Psychoanalytic investigation and therapy in borderline group of neuroses. *Psychoanalytic Quarterly, 7,* 467–489.

Stern, D. N. (1974). The goal and structure of mother-infant play. *Journal of Academy of Child Psychiatry, 13,* 402–421.

Stern, D. N. (1985). *The interpersonal world of the infant: A view from psychoanalysis and developmental psychology.* New York: Basic Books.

Stern, D. N. (1994). One way to build a clinically relevant baby. *Infant Mental Health Journal, 15,* 36–54.

Stern, S. L., Dixon, K. N., Jones, D., Lake, M., Nemzer, E., & Sansone, R. (1989). Family environment in anorexia nervosa and bulimia. *International Journal of the Eating Disorders, 8,* 25–31.

Stolorow, R., & Atwood, G. (1984). Psychoanalytic phenomenology: Toward science of human experience. *Psychoanalytic Inquiry, 4,* 87–104.

Stolorow, R., Brandchaft, B., & Atwood, G. (1987). *Psychoanalytic treatment: An intersubjective approach.* Hillsdale, NJ: Analytic Press.

Stone, L. (1954). The widening scope of indications for psychoanalysis. *Journal of the American Psychoanalytical Association, 2,* 567–594.

Strober, M., & Humphrey, L. L. (1987). Familial contributions to the etiology and course of anorexia nervosa and bulimia. *Journal of Consulting and Clinical Psychology, 55,* 654–659.

Sullivan, H. S. (1953). *The interpersonal theory of psychiatry.* New York: Norton.

Sutherland, J. D. (1980). The British object-relations theorists: Balint, Fairbairn, Guntrip. *Journal of the American Psychoanalytic Association, 28,* 829–860.

Swedo, S. C., Rapoport, J. L., Leonard, H. I., & Lenane, M. (1989). Obsessive-compulsive disorders in children and adolescents: Clinical phenomenology of 70 consecutive cases. *Archives of General Psychiatry, 46,* 335–341.

Target, M., & Fonagy, P. (1994). The efficacy of psychoanalysis for children: Prediction of outcome in a developmental context. *Journal of the American Academy of Child and Adolescent Psychiatry, 33,* 1134–1144.

Taylor, D. C. (1985). Psychological aspects of chronic sickness. In M. Rutter & L. Hersov (Eds.), *Child and adolescent psychiatry: Modern approaches* (pp. 614–624). Oxford: Blackwell.

Terr, L. C. (1983). Chowchilla revisited: The effects of psychic trauma four years after a school-bus kidnapping. *American Journal of Psychiatry, 140,* 1543–1550.

Tolpin, M. (1972). On the beginnings of a cohesive self. *The Psychoanalytic Study of the Child, 26,* 316–352.

Tomasello, M. (1988). The role of joint-attentional processes in early language acquisition. *Language Sciences, 10,* 69–88.

Trevarthen, C. (1977). Descriptive analyses of infant communicative behavior. In H. Schaffer (Ed.), *Studies in mother-infant interaction* (pp. 227–270). New York: Academic Press.

Trevarthen, C. (1979). Communication and cooperation in early infancy: A description of primary intersubjectivity. In M. M. Bullowa (Ed.), *Before speech: The beginning of interpersonal communication.* New York: Cambridge University Press.

Trevarthen, C. (1980). The foundations of intersubjectivity: Development of interpersonal and cooperative understanding in infants. In D. R. Olson (Ed.), *The social foundations of language and thought: Essays in honor of Jerome Bruner.* New York: Norton.

Trevarthen, C. (1990). Intuitive emotions: Their changing role in communication between mother and infant. In M. Ammaniti & N. Dazzi (Eds.), *Affetti: Natura e Sviluppo delle Relazione Interpersonali [Affects: Nature and Development of Interpersonal Relationships]* (pp. 97–139). Roma-Bari: Laterza.

Tronick, E. Z. (1989). Emotions and emotional communication in infants. *American Psychologist, 44,* 112–119.

Tronick, E. Z., & Gianino, A. F. (1986). The transmission of maternal disturbance to the infant. In E. Z. Tronick & T. Field (Eds.), *Maternal depression and infant disturbance* (pp. 5–11). San Francisco: Jossey-Bass.

Tustin, F. (1981). *Autistic states in children.* London: Routledge & Kegan Paul.

Tyson, P., & Tyson, R. L. (1990). *Psychoanalytic theories of development: An integration.* New Haven, CT: Yale University Press.

Urist, J. (1977). The Rorschach test and the assessment of object relations. *Journal of Personality Assessment, 41,* 3–9.

Urist, J., & Schill, M. (1982). Validity of the Rorschach mutuality of autonomy scale: A replication using excerpted responses. *Journal of Personality Assessment, 46,* 450–454.

Waddington, C. H. (1966). *Principles of development and differentiation.* New York: Macmillan.

Waelder, R. (1976). The principle of multiple function: Observations on overdetermination. In S. A. Guttman (Ed.), *Psychoanalysis: Observation, theory, application* (pp. 68–83). New York: International Universities Press. (Original work published 1930)

Waelder, R. (1960). *Basic theory of psychoanalysis.* New York: International Universities Press.

Waldron, S. (in press). Review of efficacy studies of psychoanalysis. *Journal of the American Psychoanalytic Association.*

Wallerstein, R. S. (1989). Psychoanalysis and psychotherapy: A historical perspective. *International Journal of Psycho-Analysis, 70,* 563–591.

Watson, J. S. (1972). Smiling, cooing, and "the game." *Merrill-Palmer Quarterly, 18,* 323–339.

Watson, J. S. (1979). Perception of contingency as a determinant of social responsiveness. In E. B. Thoman (Ed.), *The origins of social responsiveness* (pp. 33–64). Hillsdale, NJ: Erlbaum.

Watson, J. S. (1984). Bases of causal inference in infancy: Time, space, and sensory relations. In L. P. Lipsitt & C. Rovee-Collier (Eds.), *Advances in infancy research.* Norwood, NJ: Ablex.

Watson, J. S. (1991). Detection of self: The perfect algorithm. In *Self-recognition.* Sonoma, CA: Sonoma State University Press.

Webster-Stratton, C., & Hammond, M. (1988). Maternal depression and its relationship to life stress, perceptions of child behavior problems, parenting behaviors, and child conduct problems. *Journal of Abnormal Child Psychology, 16,* 299–315.

Weil, A. P. (1978). Maturational variations and genetic-dynamic issues. *Journal of the American Psychoanalytic Association, 26,* 461–491.

Weinberger, D. A. (1990). The construct validity of the repressive coping style. In J. L. Singer (Ed.), *Repression and dissociation.* Chicago: University of Chicago Press.

Wellman, H. (1990). *The child's theory of mind.* Cambridge, MA: MIT Press.

Wellman, H. M. (1993). Early understanding of mind: The normal case. In S. Baron-Cohen, H. Tager-Flusberg, & D. J. Cohen (Eds.), *Understanding other minds: Perspectives from autism* (pp. 10–39). New York: Oxford University Press.

Wellman, H. M., & Banerjee, M. (1991). Mind and emotion: Children's understanding of the emotional consequences of beliefs and desires. *British Journal of Developmental Psychology, 9,* 191–214.

Wellman, H. M., & Bartsch, K. (1988). Young children's reasoning about beliefs. *Cognition, 30,* 239–277.

Wellman, H. M., Harris, P. L., Banerjee, M., & Sinclair, A. (in press). Early understandings or emotion: Evidence from natural language. *Cognition and Emotion.*

Welsh-Allis, G., & Ye, W. (1988). Psychopathology in children of parents with recurrent depression. *Journal of Abnormal Child Psychology, 16,* 17–28.

Werner, E. E. (1989, April). Children of the garden island. *Scientific American,* 106–111.

Werner, E. E. (1990). Protective factors and individual resilience. In S. J. Meisels & M. Shonkoff (Eds.), *Handbook of early intervention.* New York: Cambridge University Press.

Werner, E. E., & Smith, R. S. (1982). *Vulnerable, but invincible: A longitudinal study of resilient children and youth.* New York: McGraw-Hill.

Werner, H., & Kaplan, B. (1963). *Symbol formation.* New York: Wiley.

Westen, D. (1985). *Self and society: Narcissism, collectivism, and the development of morals.* New York: Cambridge University Press.

Westen, D. (1989). Are "primitive" object relations really pre-oedipal? *American Journal of Orthopsychiatry, 59,* 331–345.

Westen, D. (1990a). The relations among narcissism, egocentrism, self-concept, and self-esteem. *Psycho-analysis and Contemporary Thought, 13,* 185–241.

Westen, D. (1990b). Towards a revised theory of borderline object relations: Contributions of empirical research. *International Journal of Psycho-Analysis, 71,* 661–694.

Westen, D. (1991a). Cognitive-behavioural interventions in the psychoanalytic psychotherapy of borderline personality disorders. *Clinical Psychology Review, 11,* 211–230.

Westen, D. (1991b). Social cognition and object relations. *Psychological Bulletin, 109,* 429–455.

Westen, D. (1992). The cognitive self and the psychoanalytic self: Can we put our selves together? *Psychological Inquiry, 3,* 1–13.

Westen, D., & Cohen, R. P. (1993). The self in borderline personality disorder: A psychodynamic perspective. In Z. V. Segal & S. J. Blatt (Eds.), *The self in emotional distress: Cognitive and psychodynamic perspectives* (pp. 334–360). New York: Guilford.

Westen, D., Lohr, N., Silk, K., Gold, L., & Kerber, K. (1990). Object relations and social cognition in borderlines, major depressives, and normals: A TAT analysis. *Psychological Assessment: A Journal of Consulting and Clinical Psychology, 2,* 355–364.

Westen, D., Ludolph, P., Block, M. J., Wixom, J., & Wiss, C. (1990). Developmental history and object relations in psychiatrically disturbed adolescent girls. *American Journal of Psychiatry, 147,* 1061–1068.

Westen, D., Ludolph, P., Lerner, H., Ruffins, S., & Wiss, F. C. (1990). Object relations in borderline adolescents. *Journal of the American Academy of Child and Adolescent Psychiatry, 29,* 338–348.

Westen, D., Moses, M. J., Silk, K. R., Lohr, N. E., Cohen, R., & Segal, H. (1992). Quality of depressive experience in borderline personality disorder and major depression: When depression is not just depression. *Journal of Personality Disorders, 6,* 383–392.

Wills, D. M. (1965). Some observations on blind nursery school children's understanding of their world. *Psychoanalytic Study of the Child, 20,* 344–364.

Winnicott, D. W. (1953). Transitional objects and transitional phenomena. *International Journal of Psycho-Analysis, 34,* 1–9.

Winnicott, D. W. (1956). The mirror role of mother and family in child development. In *Playing and reality.* New York: Basic Books.

Winnicott, D. W. (1958a). The antisocial tendency. In D. W. Winnicott (Ed.), *Collected papers: Through paediatrics to psycho-analysis.* London: Tavistock. (Original work published 1956)

Winnicott, D. W. (1958b). *Collected papers: Through paediatrics to psycho-analysis.* London: Tavistock.

Winnicott, D. W. (1958c). Paediatrics and psychiatry. In D. W. Winnicott (Ed.), *Collected papers* (pp. 157–173). New York: Basic Books. (Original work published 1948)

Winnicott, D. W. (1958d). Primary maternal preoccupation. In D. W. Winnicott (Ed.), *Collected papers: Through paediatrics to psycho-analysis* (pp. 300–315). London: Tavistock. (Original work published 1956)

Winnicott, D. W. (1958e). Transitional objects and transitional phenomena. In D. W. Winnicott (Ed.), *Collected papers: Through paediatrics to psycho-analysis.* London: Tavistock. (Original work published 1951)

Winnicott, D. W. (1960). The theory of the parent-infant relationship. *International Journal of Psycho-Analysis, 41,* 585–595.

Winnicott, D. W. (1962). The theory of the parent-infant relationship: Further remarks. *International Journal of Psycho-Analysis, 43,* 238–288.

Winnicott, D. W. (1965a). Ego distortion in terms of true and false. In *The maturational process and the facilitating environment* (pp. 140–152). New York: International Universities Press. (Original work published 1960)

Winnicott, D. W. (1965b). Ego integration in child development. In E. W. Winnicott (Ed.), *The maturational processes and the facilitating environment.* London: Hogarth Press. (Original work published 1962)

Winnicott, D. W. (1965c). *The maturational processes and the facilitating environment.* London: Hogarth Press.

Winnicott, D. W. (1965d). Psychotherapy of character disorders. In D. W. Winnicott (Ed.), *The maturational processes and the facilitating environment.* London: Hogarth Press. (Original work published 1963)

Winnicott, D. W. (1967). Mirror role of mother and family in child development. In P. Lomas (Ed.), *The predicament of the family.* London: Hogarth Press.

Winnicott, D. W. (1971). *Playing and reality.* London: Tavistock.

Winnicott, D. W. (1973). Fear of breakdown. *International Review of Psycho-Analysis, 1,* 103–107.

Wolf, E. S. (1988). Case discussion and position statement. *Psychoanalytic Inquiry, 8,* 546–551.

Yager, J. (1982). Family issues in the pathogenesis of anorexia nervosa. *Psychosomatic Medicine, 44,* 43–60.

Yogman, M. (1982). Observations on the father-infant relationship. In S. Cath, A. Gurwitt, & J. Ross (Eds.), *Father and child: Developmental and clinical perspectives* (pp. 101–122). Boston: Little Brown.

Yorke, C. (1980). The contributions of the diagnostic profile and the assessment of developmental lines to child psychiatry. *Psychiatric Clinics of North America, 3,* 593–603.

Yorke, C., Kennedy, H., & Wiseberg, S. (1981). Some clinical and theoretical aspects of two developmental lines. In *The course of life* (pp. 619–637). Adelphi, MD: U.S. Department of Health.

Yorke, C., Wiseberg, S., & Freeman, T. (1989). *Development and psychopathology: Studies in psychoanalytic psychiatry.* New Haven, CT: Yale University Press.

Younger, B. A., & Cohen, L. B. (1986). Developmental change in infants' perception of correlations among attributes. *Child Development, 57,* 803–815.

Yule, W., & Rutter, M. (1985). Reading and other learning difficulties. In M. Rutter & L. Hersov (Eds.), *Child and adolescent psychiatry: Modern approaches* (pp. 444–464). Oxford, England: Blackwell.

Zajonc, R. B. (1984). On the primacy of affect. *American Psychologist, 39,* 117–123.

Zanarini, M. C., Gunderson, J. G., & Frankenburg, F. R. (1990a). Cognitive features of borderline personality disorder. *American Journal of Psychiatry, 147,* 57–63.

Zanarini, M. C., Gunderson, J. G., & Frankenburg, F. R. (1990b). Discriminating borderline personality disorder from other Axis II disorders. *American Journal Psychiatry, 147,* 161–167.

Zeanah, C., & Barton, M. (1989). Internal representations and parent-infant relationships [Special issue]. *Infant Mental Health Journal, 10*(3).

Zekoski, E. M., O'Hara, M. W., & Wils, K. E. (1987). The effects of maternal mood on mother-infant interaction. *Journal of Abnormal Child Psychology, 15,* 361–378.

Zigler, E., & Hall, N. (1989). Physical child abuse in America. In D. Cicchetti & V. Carlson (Eds.), *Child maltreatment* (pp. 38–75). Cambridge, MA: Cambridge University Press.

CHAPTER 18

The Contributions of Ego Psychology to Developmental Psychopathology

STUART T. HAUSER and ANDREW W. SAFYER

Ego psychology represents one perspective within psychoanalytic theory. It builds on and extends drive theory by combining a biological and psychological view of individuals with an appreciation of the influence of sociocultural dimensions. In doing so, it broadens the scope of psychoanalysis from the study of unconscious phenomena and psychopathology to include the exploration of adaptive processes within a matrix of interpersonal, familial, societal, and cultural influences. More specifically, ego psychology deals with the development of those processes (referred to as ego functions or ego processes) by which individuals adapt to the demands of intrapsychic life (drives, conscience prohibitions, inner ideals) *and* to the external environment.

HISTORICAL OVERVIEW

We begin our elaboration of the meaning of ego psychology and its relevance to developmental psychopathology through considering the history of ego psychology, tracing key paths in its evolution.[1] From its inception, ego psychology provided new understandings about human growth and adaptation. Contributions from this perspective continue to have implications for psychoanalytic theory and for the practice of psychoanalysis and psychoanalytic psychotherapy; therapists are urged to move beyond viewing human beings as impulse driven toward identifying and clarifying purposeful, adaptive processes (Waelder, 1969).

Ego psychology represents an optimistic view of development and the possibilities of adaptation. Four major assumptions underlie many of the constructs and theoretical models within ego psychology: (a) individuals are born with an innate capacity to adapt to their environment, a capacity that evolves as a consequence of both maturation and learning (Hartmann, 1939a, 1939b); (b) societal influences on psychological functioning and psychopathology are significant (e.g., cultural practices and values) and are transmitted primarily through the family (Erikson, 1963); (c) besides sex and aggression, there are important motivations, such as competence and mastery (White, 1959); and, (d) individual psychopathology can be found at early stages of development (i.e., outside the realm of conflict) and is significantly influenced by the child's environment (Blanck & Blanck, 1974).

We consider two broad groupings of ego psychologists: (a) Freud and those closely associated with his early writings; and (b) theorists who subsequently departed from these conceptualizations, laying out new vistas and thereby opening up directions not previously imagined for developmental and clinical research.

First Soundings: Discoveries and Refinements

Sigmund Freud

Freud's definition of "the ego" can be understood in terms of the three phases through which his definition evolved (Rapaport, 1959). During the first phase, the ego was defined with the least precision: the term was used interchangeably with one's own person or the self. Despite this vagueness, one aspect of ego processes was already apparent: the defensive functions of the ego. The ego was here conceptualized as preventing painful memories from entering awareness. Because of this censoring, important emotions (associated with the repressed or censored traumas) are not directly expressed. Instead, these emotions are expressed through neurotic symptoms (Rapaport, 1959).

During the second phase, Freud's interest in ego functions temporarily receded as he now more fully addressed drives, their vicissitudes and their derivatives (Freud, 1915a, 1915b). This diminished interest in the individual's experiences with traumatic events, and in his or her attempts at coping with their effects—through censoring awareness of them—is argued by some as being associated with Freud's discovery that his patients' reports of

Preparation of this chapter was supported by an NIMH Research Scientist Award (#K05-70178-09), and by a grant from the John D. and Catherine T. MacArthur Foundation for partial support to Stuart Hauser while a Fellow at the Center for Advanced Study in the Behavioral Sciences, Stanford, California; and by an NIMH Faculty Scholar Award (#MH-19144) to Andrew Safyer.

[1] For related reviews see: Blanck & Blanck, 1974; Goldstein, 1984; Greenberg & Mitchell, 1983; Hauser & Daffner, 1980; Klein, 1970; and Rapaport, 1959.

childhood seductions were derived from their fantasies, not from real experiences (Rapaport, 1959). Nonetheless, Freud distinguished central aspects of ego functioning: secondary process, the reality principle, and repression. Of interest is the fact that these important distinctions, still used in discussions of ego development and clinical phenomena, may have arisen because of Freud's intensified interest in unconscious processes and the strength and impact of drives (Rapaport, 1959).

The final phase begins with Freud's introduction of the structural model, characterizing the ego as a coherent organization which, together with id and superego functions, is included in a tripartite personality structure. In this newest and most comprehensive formulation, ego functioning refers to far more than compromises among opposing ideas and feelings. The work of the ego is now more clearly specified as involving active maintenance of harmonious relations between ego functions and the two other major psychic structures. In other words, ego processes resolve conflicts among drives, cognitions, and prohibitions.

This third phase culminated with Freud's construction of a new anxiety paradigm: he posited that ego processes had adaptive biological functions that extended beyond those of defense (Freud, 1932). From this perspective, anxiety was seen as a byproduct of conflict to which the ego could respond by invoking a defense (Rapaport, 1959). Defenses were no longer deployed simply to censor awareness of traumatic experiences, as in Freud's earlier (first phase) view. In this newest model, which delineated the ego as a central structure devoted to coping with anxiety, Freud laid the groundwork for recognizing the ego as an *active agent* with its own independent interests, not simply passively responding to other psychic structures and impulses (Blanck & Blanck, 1974; Rapaport, 1959).

Anna Freud

Anna Freud (1936) both served as "guardian of the psychoanalytic tradition of her father's legacy and she pressed relentlessly toward new frontiers" (Neubauer, 1983, p. 507). With respect to ego processes, she identified a broad array of defenses and pointed out the diversity of events connected with the use of defenses by children and adults. Defenses can be evoked by threatening impulses, conflicts over these impulses, and external events. In her classic monograph, *The Ego and the Mechanisms of Defense,* Anna Freud (1936) described many defense mechanisms including: intellectualization, identification with the aggressor, altruism, asceticism, denial, avoidance, acting out, and displacement. These constructs continue to be recognized in contemporary psychoanalytic discourse as well as relevant clinical and empirical research (e.g., Blos, 1962; Vaillant, 1992, 1993). Moreover, launching a still unresolved theoretical and empirical debate, she explicitly speculated about the chronological emergence of defenses, a theme most evident in Vaillant's "developmental hierarchy" of defenses (Vaillant, 1971).

In this clearly abbreviated recognition of her role in the evolution of ego psychology, it is important to note Anna Freud's consistent tying of ego processes to an understanding of the development of theory (Freud, 1952), of young children (Freud, 1965), and of adolescents (Freud, 1958). Recurrent in her many contributions is her emphasis on the significance of child observations as sources of data for theoretical and clinical knowledge of development and ego functioning. For example, she argued that a variety of disturbances were not the result of intrapsychic "oedipal" conflicts, but instead began at earlier developmental stages and were significantly influenced by the child's environment. Finally, there are many indications of her prescience, as she anticipated connections between ego psychology and developmental psychopathology (Freud, 1952, 1966, 1968, 1974).

Other Early Contributions

In this early period, several other psychoanalytic writers also studied ego development and ego processes, continuing to conceptualize adaptive aspects of the ego. Foremost among these contributors were Herbert Nunberg (1931), Robert Waelder (1936), and Wilhelm Reich (1949). Each considered ego processes beyond defenses.

Nunberg (1931, 1948), conceptualizing the synthetic capacity of the ego, foreshadowed the writings of Hartmann (1939a, 1939b). The synthetic capacity, representing a force inherent within the ego that both "unites and binds" and "simplifies and generalizes," is responsible for integrating various aspects of psychic life into a coherent form (Nunberg, 1948, p. 125). Moreover, the synthetic function is intermediary between intrapsychic life and external reality, and thereby is involved in the individual's assimilations of these two realms of experience. Nunberg, like Waelder (below), saw the ego as an active agent synthesizing cognitions and affects, rather than being driven by competing and converging internal and external forces. Nunberg's synthetic principle was a central component in Loevinger's view and measure of ego development (Hauser, 1976; Loevinger, 1976; Loevinger & Wessler, 1970).

Waelder (1936) delineated a more powerful executive role served by the ego in relation to drives. His "principle of multiple function" posited that every psychic action should be understood from the side of the ego and from the side of the id, in that psychic events represent both libidinal (impulse) expression and purposeful (ego) activities. In his writings, Waelder pointed to the kinds of problems for which the ego seeks solutions: meeting the demands of impulse expression, conscience prohibitions, and external events, and dealing with a presumed biological compulsion to repeat. He conceived of personality as being largely determined by psychologically specific solutions that are unique to each individual, and as remaining constant throughout the life span.

Reich (1949) wrote in a more explicitly developmental direction. Focusing on how individuals form character traits in early childhood, he argued that these traits emerge as reactions against libidinal drives. With respect to how ego defenses evolve, Reich theorized that, during early childhood, individuals develop habitual patterns of behavior that serve as an "armor," or defense, against stimuli they experience as threatening. There are several characteristic patterns of such armor, including compulsive character disorder and the hysterical personality. Reich concluded that it is through these and other enduring patterns of defensive armor (e.g., hysteria) that ego processes become so distorted that psychopathology, rather than adaptive functioning, results.

New Paradigms of Ego Processes and Ego Development: Movements toward Empirical Research

Heinz Hartmann

Heinz Hartmann revised and refined Freud's structural theory, giving strong consideration to the ego's relation to external events. First independently (Hartmann, 1939a, 1939b), and then in several major collaborations with Ernst Kris and Rudolph Loewenstein (Hartmann, Kris, & Loewenstein, 1946, 1949, 1953), Hartmann's writings set the stage for exploring connections between development and the "non-conflictual sphere" of mental functioning, a theoretical direction seen as necessary in order for psychoanalysis to become a psychology of both normal and abnormal human behavior.

Hartmann assumed that the ego and the id develop simultaneously from the same common matrix, a formulation in striking contrast with earlier psychoanalytic views characterizing ego structures as resulting from the *conflict* between impulses and reality. In so demarcating ego development and ego processes, he drew attention to the importance of thorough systematic investigations of ego functioning, from theoretical, empirical, and clinical perspectives. For instance, Hartmann stressed that motives and other psychological forces are uniquely associated with ego activities. In other words, ego processes are not simply the by-products of acute and chronic clashes among wishes, dangers, and prohibitions. Pursuing this line of thought, ego processes influence, and are influenced by, all aspects of behavior, rather than only by impulses and moral precepts. A major concern for Hartmann was the ego's role in adaptation, in line with his view that individuals are born with a biologically guaranteed coordination with an "average expectable environment" (Hartmann, 1939a). From this perspective, the ego is seen as endowed with a range of innate capacities, encompassing perception, memory, and motility. These capacities—representing primary autonomy—develop outside conflicts over impulses or drives and are pleasurable "in their mere exercise," enabling individuals both to change themselves (autoplastic activities) and to effect responses from the environment (alloplastic activities) (Blanck & Blanck, 1974; Hartmann, 1939a).

In addition, behaviors originally resulting from coping with conflict, may be transformed, becoming "autonomous" from the original conflicts, and may then be drawn into other adaptive activities. For example, although the initial defensive function of intellectualization in adolescence may be evoked by conflicts over sexual or aggressive impulses, possibly involving superego prohibitions (e.g., against masturbation), this ego process may subsequently be reflected as intellectuality (Haan, 1977), the productive use of intelligence in solving problems (Benjamin, 1966). Regression may also be adaptive, as exemplified by the harnessing of feelings and fantasies associated with earlier development for new goals of creative writing and visual products ("regression in the service of the ego") (Haan, 1977; Kris, 1952). Hartmann referred to such transformations as "secondary autonomy." Psychological adaptation, then, arose from two sources: (a) innate adaptive capacities (in the "conflict-free" realm) and (b) transformed psychic functions, previously associated with the resolution of psychic conflict (Hartmann, 1939a). An extensive appreciation of the many implications of Hartmann's ego psychology contributions can be found in the volume edited by Loewenstein, Newman, Schur, and Solnit (1966).

Leopold Bellak

A new line of theoretical and empirical studies was stimulated by the conceptualizations of Hartmann and his colleagues (cf. Loewenstein et al., 1966). In the decades following Hartmann's major theoretical monograph (1939a), a series of sophisticated contributions appeared, investigating a broad and differentiated range of ego functions, their development, and their role in adaptation (Bellak, Hurvich, & Gediman, 1973; Beres, 1965; Grinker, Werble, & Drye, 1968; Haan, 1977; Prelinger & Zimet, 1964; Semrad, Grinspoon, & Feinberg, 1973; Vaillant, 1977; see also the review in Hauser & Daffner, 1980).

Especially noteworthy is that these studies represented the first attempts to draw ego psychology constructs into the design of empirical research; innovative, theoretically relevant investigations were begun, shaped by the new ego psychology constructs. These research programs involved clinical and nonclinical samples, and applied assessment approaches developed with a clear eye to measuring the very processes conceptualized by Anna Freud, Hartmann, Nunberg, and their collaborators (Bellak et al., 1973; Haan, 1977; Hauser, 1986; Loevinger & Wessler, 1970; Prelinger & Zimet, 1964). We review these programs of research in the next section, where we consider significant empirical research about ego processes and ego development. Among the first empirical contributors in this literature were Bellak and colleagues (Bellak et al., 1973; Bellak & Sheehy, 1976), who identified and assessed an array of ego functions, including defenses, impulse control, and reality testing. Applying these instruments to psychological test protocols, interviews, and experimental observations, Bellak compared patient samples (schizophrenic and neurotic) and nonpatients. As predicted, the schizophrenic patients showed the lowest overall levels of adaptation, in marked contrast to the nonpatient subjects.

Erik Erikson

Drawing on such predecessors from the ego psychology as Hartmann and Anna Freud, as well as other relevant theorists from psychiatry (Sullivan, 1953) and anthropology (Kroeber, 1963), the rich corpus of Erikson's books and papers has persistently focused on understanding the complex interplay of individual development, social history, and contemporary sociocultural forces. Working with classical psychoanalytic concepts, such as unconscious motivations and drives, Erikson dramatically broadened the scope of traditional psychoanalytic theory to incorporate considerations of "macro" dimensions—institutions, rituals, shared symbols systems—and considerations of lifespan development from infancy through old age. Through all of these contributions is the theme that personality development follows an epigenetic sequence. As the individual matures, he or she passes through various stages, at the center of which are specific psychosocial crises.

> [Crisis is used] . . . in a developmental sense to connote not a threat or catastrophe but a turning point, a crucial point of increased vulnerability and heightened potential, and therefore the ontogenetic source of generational strength and maladjustment. (Erikson, 1963, p. 294)

"Erikson's definition of crisis is reminiscent of the ancient conception of crisis as both a danger and a challenge: Each successive crisis contains potentials for maladjustment as well as for growth" (Hauser & Follansbee, 1984, p. 210). In resolving each crisis, the individual progresses to the next stage and its corresponding crisis. These resolutions require interactions by the individual with significant others and with societal institutions. Erikson's writings, influenced by Hartmann's conceptualization of autonomous ego functions, proposed a detailed timetable for ego development, a timetable closely coordinated with social structures and cultural values (Erikson, 1959, 1963). For instance, there is the adolescent crisis of "identity versus role confusion" The danger is in remaining in role diffusion, not holding a clear sense of self or place in the world. Successful resolution of the challenge of this crisis results in the formation of ego identity, reflecting

> . . . more than the sum of childhood identifications. It is the accrued experience of the ego's ability to integrate these identifications with the vicissitudes of the libido, with the aptitudes developed out of endowment, and with the opportunities afforded in social roles. The sense of ego identity, then, is the accrued confidence that the inner sameness and continuity are matched by the sameness and continuity of one's meaning for others. (Erikson, 1950, p. 228)

In a series of widely read and cited publications, Erikson conceptualized dynamic linkages among social institutions, interpersonal relationships, and individual development. This interplay is illustrated in the epigenetic life cycle, the sequence of eight incremental stages shaped by psychosexual drives, ego functions, and moral understandings (Erikson, 1959, 1963). These inner influences set the stage for significant specific interactions between the developing individual and an increasingly wider social world. While arguing that this progression of stages is universal, Erikson allowed that individual developmental patterns are culturally defined. He distinguished eight "psychosocial stages," reaching from infancy through the late adult years:

1. Trust vs. mistrust;
2. Autonomy vs. shame and doubt;
3. Initiative vs. guilt;
4. Industry vs. inferiority;
5. Identity vs. role confusion;
6. Intimacy vs. isolation;
7. Generativity vs. stagnation; and
8. Integrity vs. despair.

Signs of these stages can be seen throughout development. Yet, the crisis associated with a given stage is most pronounced during the specific chronological age associated with its unfolding (e.g., identity vs. role confusion in adolescence). At each stage, there is a phase-specific "psychosocial crisis" that becomes dominant in the form of a dilemma, a pattern of conflicts surrounding a core theme or issue that the individual is struggling to resolve. Among the core themes are basic trust vs. mistrust (infancy), autonomy vs. shame (toddler years), and, as already noted, identity conflicts in the adolescent years. Crisis resolution depends on mastery of psychosocial challenges inherent at each stage (e.g., in toddlerhood, the acquisition of autonomy and self-control). In other words, stage-specific conflicts are pervasive for the developing individual and critical at particular times in his or her life cycle. But these conflicts can be traced throughout life; they do not simply exist at one point in life and then move off-stage as the individual ages. The issue of autonomy, for instance, is especially important to toddlers, but any observer of adolescents is surely aware of the often poignant autonomy conflicts and the sometimes highly original solutions that individuals bring to them during this transition between childhood and the adult years (Blos, 1962; Erikson, 1963; Hauser & Levine, 1994; Steinberg, 1990).

Erikson (1963) conceptualized individual development and identity as more than simply childhood identifications. The resolutions achieved during each of the eight successive phases contribute to the important synthesis of ego processes, identifications, and values, which Erikson conceptualized as "ego identity." This important task of ego integration is most apparent during adolescence. From a broader perspective, the adolescent identity crisis is an important point in lifelong identity formation, and adolescence is neither the beginning nor the end of this extended process. The sense of identity that can evolve prepares the rapidly developing youth—fast approaching adulthood—for new tasks and associated obstacles involving commitments to work, career, and intimacy (For more detailed description and discussion of these years from Erikson's perspective, see Hauser & Follansbee, 1984.)

Robert White

Related and similar to Erikson, with respect to the impressive scope of his interests and his inclusion of additional personality characteristics in conceptualizing individual development, is Robert White (1959, 1963). White characterized individuals as beginning life with motivations besides sex and aggression, and considered these motivations as inherently involved with adaptation. His writings are at odds with the psychoanalytic theories of normal functioning and adaptation proposed by Hartmann and his colleagues, who invoked such concepts as "neutralization of libidinal energies" for basic ego functions and aspects of ego development (Hartmann, 1939a, 1939b). Like Erikson, White drew from several related domains of inquiry—ethology, child development, and ego psychology—in constructing his theory of how the child and adult cope effectively with their surroundings. Hartmann's psychoanalytic ego psychology certainly covers a striking range of functioning (ego strengths as well as defenses). Yet, from White's perspective, there are adaptive behaviors, including grasping, crawling, language, and perception, that are handled poorly by psychoanalytic ego psychology explanations based exclusively on drive motivations, whether transformed by neutralization or not.

White proposed that these kinds of exploratory behaviors have biological significance and can be categorized under the general heading of *competence.* He applied the term "effectance" to describe the motivational aspects of competence. Effectance is reflected in feelings of pleasure (efficacy) gained from successful, repetitive interactions with one's environment (White, 1959, 1963).

Theorists from the Child Observation Tradition

These theorists, not ordinarily included in discussions of ego psychology, are relevant with respect to their focus on early interpersonal "conditions," optimal and dysfunctional, for ego development. Within this group are René Spitz and Margaret Mahler, who blended systematic infant observations with psychoanalytic theory to specify the "average expectable environment," primarily from the point of view of the mother-infant relationship. Each portrayed the infant's future relationships as being shaped by those established in the very first maternal relationship.[2] Their writings set the stage for object relations and attachment theory contributions to our understanding of early contexts of ego development.

René Spitz

Spitz's writings (1945, 1946a, 1946b, 1959, 1961, 1965, 1983) are an outgrowth of his clinical observations of harmful effects on babies awaiting adoption in institutions for extended periods of time. "Anaclitic depression" and "hospitalism" refer to the developmental disturbances seen in infants separated early from their mothers. Spitz became interested in discerning the essential aspects of early development that were absent in these deprived infants. His studies led to an increasing appreciation of the importance of the emotional availability from the mother for an infant's development. For Spitz, key element in the parent-infant relationship was the *emotional dialogue* that occurs between the participants. He systematically described ways in which emotional exchanges provide adaptive information for both the parent and the infant. His use of the term *dialogue* emphasized ". . . that a basic communication process exists in infancy, even before speech" (Emde, 1992, p. 355). "Although [these] communications are not verbal, they are complex, emotional, and two-way, providing adaptive information for both parent and infant" (p. 355)

Spitz also addressed the significance of those critical periods when the infant is separated from his or her mother. The optimal outcome of these separations is a reorganizing of the psychic system on a higher level of complexity. Three behavioral markers—(a) the smiling response, (b) separation and stranger anxiety, and (c) the expression of "no"—indicate that developmental organization is proceeding satisfactorily. Spitz (1961) also described biological precursors that serve as prototypes for the formation of specific defenses (e.g., vomiting as a form of projection). His assumption was that, in the course of development, physiological functions are ". . . psychologically processed and give rise to adaptive mechanisms of defense" (p. 627). In addition, Spitz focused on when these transformations occur. "We would thus acquire what might be called an inventory of the age-adequate appearance of defense mechanisms. This knowledge would make a more systematic approach to the question of the influence of mother-child relations on the formation of defenses possible" (Spitz, 1961, p. 629).

Margaret Mahler

Mahler's contributions were first sparked by her studies of different childhood psychoses, which she conceptualized as outcomes of profound disturbances in the mother-infant relationship (Mahler, Pine, & Bergman, 1975). In this and subsequent work, she underscored the psychological significance of the infant's initial attachment to his or her mother. Her clinical studies of disturbed infants eventually broadened to encompass normal mother-child interactions during various phases of the child's early development, and to closely examine "psychological birth"—how infants achieve an integrated self-identity separate from their mothers (Mahler et al., 1975).

Mahler's widely cited theory of separation-individuation charts the infant's development as a series of stages from normal autism to object constancy. In Mahler's perspective, the overall sequence of this early maturation begins with the infant's progression from nonrelatedness ("normal autism") to merged self-object relatedness ("symbiosis"), and then moves to the separation-individuation phase, which ends with the realization of a stable autonomous identity. Mahler maintained that it is during the separation-individuation phase that a central conflict, the desire for autonomy versus the wish to stay merged with the mother occurs (Greenberg & Mitchell, 1983). The way in which children resolve this central conflict determines the extent to which they will develop without psychological disturbances.

INVESTIGATIONS OF EGO PSYCHOLOGY CONSTRUCTS

Several of the earlier theorists—including Hartmann, Bellak, Mahler, and Spitz—ventured beyond the "consulting room." However, only in recent years have a growing cadre of investigators been willing to tackle the daunting problems inherent in designing and carrying out rigorous research programs based on ego psychology theory. The domain of ego psychology is too vast to be systematically investigated through any single program of empirical studies, regardless of their rigor and thoughtfulness. Nonetheless, several key constructs that are highly relevant for general developmental theory and developmental psychopathology have been the object of continuing empirical research; among them are defenses and ego processes.

Defense Mechanisms

Defense mechanisms have long been regarded by psychoanalytic theorists and psychoanalytically oriented clinicians as providing an important window on intrapsychic conflicts and on how these

[2] These two theorists are only briefly covered here, for the purpose of offering some specific examples of this genre of work; their mention by no means exhausts other scholars in this domain. Absent, but hardly irrelevant, are attachment theorists such as John Bowlby (1969, 1973, 1979, 1980), and object relations theorists such as Michael Balint (1965) and D. W. Winnicott (1958). A more extended discussion of these theorists can be found in Greenberg and Mitchell (1983).

conflicts are handled. Defenses have multifaceted connections with development. There is still the unresolved question of the chronological development of defenses, raised many years ago by Anna Freud (1936) and, more recently, by theorists such as Vaillant (1992). Other questions touch on the role of biological and environmental forces. Are constitutional dimensions (e.g., temperament) and other individual differences associated with varied profiles and/or sequences of defenses? Do specific environmental conditions—parenting, other family and peer context experiences—influence defense development and defense repertoires? With respect to empirical study, there are several outstanding dilemmas. What degree of standardization in data collection is required so that measuring instruments can be "calibrated" to permit meaningful comparisons across studies? This is not a simple problem; more highly structured data collections (e.g., a structured clinical interview) run the risk of interfering with expression of the more spontaneous thoughts, feelings, and fantasies in the very sequences that might be most revealing of inner conflicts and the individuals's defensive handling of them. A second problem concerns the selection of defenses. Can an agreed-on inventory be constructed that will be used by investigators in this area? Such a list needs to be neither so narrow that it excludes clinically and theoretically important processes, nor so broad that it becomes diffuse and unmanageable for both investigators and raters. Related to the preceding problems, and perhaps most pressing, is the need for investigators to be using the same battery of reliable and valid approaches for assessing these processes. Fortunately, we are furthest along in solving this third problem (Hauser, 1986; Perry & Cooper, 1986; Vaillant, 1986, 1992).

Conceptual Dilemmas

It is generally agreed that defenses are *inferred mental processes* mediating between individuals' impulses, cognitions, and affects on the one hand, and internalized prohibitions or external reality on the other (Hauser, 1986, p. 91). There remain, however, major questions regarding the systematic classification of these inferred processes. What is the universe of defense mechanisms? What is the most theoretically meaningful way to classify these processes? Researchers generate different lists of defenses, and then use contrasting classification principles to order them (e.g., Bellak et al., 1973; Bibring, Dwyer, Huntington, & Valenstein, 1963; Perry & Cooper, 1986; Vaillant, 1992). Not surprisingly, each of these taxonomies views defenses differently in terms of their role in aspects of development and in psychopathology (Hauser, 1986). These differences can almost always be traced to varied underlying assumptions, based on differing theoretical perspectives and sometimes different research populations (Vaillant, 1986, 1992).

Such basic conceptual issues, lurking in the most general theoretical frameworks and implicit in specific definitions, lead to a second set of problems, which interfere with the task of deriving crisp empirical operational definitions. For example, empirical definitions of defenses frequently differ among investigators, even when the defense is one that is commonly discussed, such as denial (e.g., Jacobson, Beardslee, Hauser, Noam, & Powers, 1986; Vaillant, 1986). Although Vaillant (1986) argued that this lack of perfect convergence among researchers must be viewed in light of the "elusiveness" of studying intrapsychic variables, our more optimistic stance is to see these nonalignments as understandable consequences of diverse but resolvable conceptualizations.

Measurement Dilemmas

Two basic approaches have been used in assessing defenses: (a) self-report questionnaires and (b) clinical observer ratings. Each approach comes with its assets and liabilities (see Hauser, 1986; Jacobson et al., 1986). Self-report measures depend on the subject's conscious recognition and subsequent inference about his or her own behaviors. This approach has the virtue of minimizing problems of interrater reliability, assessment time, and professional participation in the assessment process. Its cost is that the obtained data about defenses are derived from a limited number of standardized statements that the subject can evaluate and consciously choose among (Jacobson et al., 1986). Turning to observational data (specifically, clinical interviews), the major benefit is the richness of the data, providing the opportunity to detect subtler influences that may be present but are not recognized by the subject because they are outside of his or her conscious awareness. Limitations of this approach include difficulty in developing reliable ratings, the need to often obtain professional input through clinician judges, and variability in the database, caused by interview style and methods of observation (Hauser, 1986; Jacobson et al., 1986).

Realms of Inquiry

Empirical and clinical study of defense mechanisms is highly relevant for three related domains of inquiry: (a) the diagnosis and course of psychopathology, (b) stress and coping, and (c) developmental studies (Hauser, 1986).

Psychopathology. Clinically meaningful questions can be conceptualized, and empirically studied, in terms of defense mechanisms and psychopathology. Moreover, many of these questions have developmental implications. For example, do certain patterns of defenses or changes in primary defenses precede, and thereby presage, the expression of specific forms of psychopathology, such as major depressive episodes? With respect to psychiatric diagnoses, are specific profiles of defenses consistently associated with certain syndromes or symptom patterns? These questions also highlight an important methodological point: assessments of psychiatric symptoms and defenses must be based on *independent measurement approaches,* using different instruments and coders. In other words, here, as in other questions involving links between defenses and psychopathology, we must carefully consider issues of discriminant validity: are the same phenomena being measured, although labeled with different terms (Hauser, 1986)?

Another direction in studies of psychopathology and defenses addresses consistency or constancy across time. Are some diagnoses or developmental deviations characterized by dramatic shifts in individual defense profiles following successful interventions, or over the natural course of the specific pathology? On the other hand, are there some individuals, such as those with personality disorders, whose defenses remain stubbornly the same over time? Similar questions can be raised about age and psychopathology. Do younger patients have defenses that are more likely to change following treatment? Or does the likelihood of such fluidity depend on other variables, such as diagnosis and severity?

Stress and Coping. Several research programs focus on how individuals and families cope with, or adapt to, stressful life circumstances (e.g., Anthony & Cohler, 1987; Garmezy & Rutter, 1983; Lazarus & Folkman, 1984; Reiss & Oliveri, 1991). This area of work is vast, and thorough coverage of relevant contributions would take us far beyond the scope of this chapter. Nonetheless, a brief review of some of the major issues can convey how studies of defenses are pertinent to important questions in this active and complex literature. Adaptation, from an individual perspective, depends on a spectrum of processes ranging from enduring affective and behavioral responses to more situationally driven responses (Hauser & Bowlds, 1990; Hauser, Borman, Bowlds et al., 1991).

Investigators considering coping processes usually attend with great rigor to environmental characteristics, such as the nature of the stressors and social support networks. Many are also concerned with individual dimensions—how the person manages major acute stresses and chronic strains. Much of this work examines conscious strategies, including information seeking, support seeking, and modes of appraisal (Lazarus & Folkman, 1984). But within the range of ways that children and adults deal with specific difficulties there are also discrete, often less conscious strategies (or strengths), such as diversity of thought, persistence, and viewing oneself as an active agent (Beardslee et al., 1986; Jacobson et al., 1986). In our recent longitudinal studies of adolescents, we examined how these adaptive strengths combine with specific defenses, like denial, suppression, and anticipation (Hauser, 1986; Jacobson et al., 1986). Findings from these and similar fine-grained analyses of individuals facing acute and chronic stresses are likely to offer a fuller picture of the determinants of competence under varied conditions, including those of great adversity.

An example of one such study was reported by Snarey and Vaillant (1985), who considered how working-class youths become middle-class adults—how they defy the odds that children's social class will stubbornly predict their adult social class. Through a series of systematic defense ratings of interview materials and multivariate analyses, Snarey and Vaillant found that three defense mechanisms, scored from adult interviews, strongly predicted upward social mobility. Intellectualization, altruism, and anticipation were highly correlated with upward mobility, even after accounting for intelligence, childhood ego strengths, and parent education. This unusual investigation is an outstanding illustration of how investigating defenses—and other adaptive strengths—can contribute to the understanding of resilient as well as pathological developmental pathways.

Developmental Studies. Investigations of the interplay between defenses and child, adolescent, and adult development are most directly relevant to developmental psychopathology. One of the first empirical investigations of defenses from a developmental perspective was *Adaptation to Life* (Vaillant, 1977), a study of changing defenses between early adulthood and middle age. From a more theoretical and speculative vantage point, Anna Freud (1936, 1965) considered the thesis that defenses may follow a developmental course, in terms of their emergence and relations with other ego functions (see Cramer, 1991a). Despite recent empirical and theoretical contributions, major questions remain unanswered. How do defense mechanisms contribute (and respond) to developmental variation over time—both qualitative (stage) and more gradual cumulative change? How are defenses embedded in psychosexual, ego, and cognitive development? For instance, does the use of certain defenses in adolescence require specific levels of cognitive and ego development? To what extent are developmental advances in a particular domain (e.g., psychosexual) contingent on the availability of particular defense mechanisms and other personal resources?

Some argue that defenses can be hierarchically ordered in terms of their association with psychosocial maturity (Vaillant, 1977). The most "primitive" defenses (e.g., projection) appear earliest in the life of an individual; the more complex defenses (e.g., altruism) do not appear until later years (Vaillant, 1977). This pattern of emergence is believed to be similar to other ego processes, such as cognitive ones, which originate in specific developmental phases and typify different developmental periods (Cramer, 1987). Although there have been numerous contributions to the empirical literature regarding defenses, there are relatively few studies of the development of defenses (Cramer, 1991a). Moreover, programs focusing on defense development are usually based on observations of adults, and must thus infer developmental sequences (e.g., Vaillant, 1977). We review investigations addressing defense and development below. Significant characteristics of these studies include their samples (children and adolescents), longitudinal designs, and analyses specifying relations between defenses and other developmental constructs (e.g., moral and ego development).

Norma Haan: Coping and Defending. Haan's (1977) model of coping led to one of the earliest empirical attempts to measure defenses (which she referred to as ego processes) from a developmental perspective. She conceptualized 30 ego processes, with conceptual and empirical definitions of each process (Haan, 1977). Her investigations examined connections between these ego processes and conceptually relevant individual difference variables (e.g., intelligence, ego development) (Haan, 1963, 1974, 1977, 1978; Haan, Aerts, & Cooper, 1985; Haan, Stroud, & Holstein, 1973).

The longitudinal program and several cross-sectional research programs linked with this perspective are based on a conceptualization of defenses and coping mechanisms that clearly differs from many psychoanalytically driven studies.[3] Haan did not assume that a major function of defenses involves warding off anxiety associated with the expression of drives. Defenses are also creative efforts to deal with external stresses in every day life. Ego processes (including defenses) are "strategically evoked" and mark the person's need to preserve a coherent self-organization (Haan, 1977).

[3] The theoretical model used in these studies, and its links with other psychoanalytic writings, was also discussed by Kroeber (1963).

Haan's taxonomy begins with ten generic dimensions, each having three modes of expression: (a) coping, (b) defending, and (c) fragmenting. These modes can be distinguished from one another by specific formal properties. *Coping* allows choice, is reality-oriented, and enables the individual to experience a wider range of affective and cognitive expression. *Defending* is rigid and compelled; it distorts or misdirects an individual's experiences and reactions. Fragmenting is automated, ritualistic, and irrationally expressed (Haan, 1977). The generic dimension of sensitivity includes the processes of empathy (coping mode), projection (defending mode), and ideas of reference (fragmenting mode). These processes can be further classified in terms of general functions: cognitive, self-reflective (whereby people interact with their own feelings and thoughts), attention focusing, and emotion regulating.

Haan distinguished between coping and defending responses to stressors, and posited coping as the normative mode: "When all other matters are equal, the person will cope" (Haan, 1977, p. 49). During those times when a stressful situation surpasses an individual's capacities, defensive processes ". . . are brought into play . . . which entail some negation or distortion" (p. 49). Fragmentation is an indicator of more serious pathology, and occurs when ". . . the required accommodations are not only beyond the person's capability, but also irrefutably contradict and confuse his self-constructions and make intersubjective reality preferable" (p. 49).

Ego processes do not develop through an invariable sequence of stages. Moreover, contextual influences must be assessed. Although cognitive capabilities precede, or at least coincide with, the emergence of the mature form of each broad dimension (e.g., the coping process of objectivity requires capacity for abstract thinking), individuals do not always utilize those ego processes reflecting their highest level of cognitive functioning. There are other influences (e.g., social, moral, and affective) that shape their response in particular situations (Haan, 1977).

Haan's research program was primarily based on a longitudinal, normative sample (the Oakland Growth study) using extensive clinical interviews (each lasting about 12 hours). Ego processes were measured through a Q-sort, applied to the interviews. Trained coders sorted cards with defining characteristics of specific ego processes in a forced distribution, assigning specific ratings from "most uncharacteristic" to "most characteristic."

Ego processes have been found to be related to intelligence and its developmental pattern of change (Haan, 1964) to gender (Haan, 1977), and to socioeconomic status (Haan, 1964) in expected ways. In terms of other ego functions, Haan et al. (1973) examined relations between defenses and levels of moral (Kohlberg, 1964) and ego development (Loevinger, 1976) in a sample of 58 late adolescent "hippies." Defenses were not significantly related to moral development. For ego development, two defenses (projection and intellectualizing) were used more frequently by individuals at higher levels of ego development. These findings may be related to the specialized nature of the sample. A number of methodological concerns have been raised regarding these studies of defending and coping (see Morrissey, 1977, for an extensive review). They include the use of nonrepresentative samples, the "idiosyncratic nature" of some of the definitions, and a liberal (.10) significance criterion.

George Vaillant: A Defense Hierarchy. In his ongoing longitudinal research program, Vaillant conceptualizes and assesses defenses along the lines of maturity and psychopathology. Clearly influenced by earlier psychoanalytic writers who also addressed aspects of defenses and related ego psychology phenomena (e.g., Bibring et al., 1963; Semrad, 1967), Vaillant delineates 18 defenses, and, in a series of methodological and substantive contributions, illustrates their meaning and significance (Snarey & Vaillant, 1985; Vaillant, 1971, 1975, 1976, 1977, 1978, 1983, 1986, 1992, 1993; Vaillant & Drake, 1985; Vaillant & McCullough, 1987; Vaillant & Vaillant, 1990).

Vaillant orders the chronological appearance of the 18 defenses into four "maturity" levels. He suggests that primitive defenses (e.g., delusional projection, distortion) are common in individuals before the age of 5, and, in adult life, appear in dreams and fantasy. In contrast, mature defenses (e.g., altruism, anticipation, and humor) are common in healthy individuals from adolescence onward (Vaillant, 1971, 1977).

Included in Vaillant's hierarchy are the following levels of defenses:

1. Immature defenses (e.g., projection and acting out behaviors), believed to be common in youngsters as well as those individuals with personality and mood disorders and often in adults in psychotherapy;
2. Intermediate defenses (e.g., repression, displacement, reaction-formation), observed in normal adults and in those with neurotic disorders;
3. Mature defenses (e.g., altruism, humor), generally characterize healthy, mature adults (Snarey & Vaillant, 1985; Vaillant, 1976, 1977).

This hierarchy of defenses was first examined through the Harvard Study of Adult Development, a longitudinal program of research on college men (Heath, 1945). This project, popularly called "the Grant study," was an investigation of college sophomores, selected on the basis of psychological and physical "health." The men, nominated by their college deans as promising adults, have continued to respond to questionnaires, psychological tests, and interviews for over four decades. Defenses are assessed from excerpts, systematically gathered from their files, that are illustrated instances of the men's responses to crises and conflicts in their lives.

To replicate findings from the Grant study, Vaillant explored defense use among economically disadvantaged inner-city boys, using a mixture of ethnic groups from either lower- or working-class families, who had initially served as the control group in an investigation of juvenile delinquency (Glueck & Glueck, 1968). Similar to the Grant study, these subjects have been followed for over 40 years. At age 47, they participated in a two-hour interview, and subsequently completed biennial questionnaires. More recently, the original subjects' adult children were assessed at age 25, thus extending the investigation to the next generation (Snarey & Vaillant, 1985).

Vaillant's prolific theoretical and empirical writings support the clinical validity of his hierarchy of defenses, showing that defense maturity relates in expectable ways with theoretically relevant variables (e.g., marital success, career choice, psychopathology, and physical health) (Vaillant, 1971, 1975, 1976, 1977, 1978, 1983, 1986, 1992, 1993; Vaillant & Drake, 1985; Vaillant & McCullough, 1987; Vaillant & Vaillant, 1990).

In terms of developmental dimensions, Vaillant (1977) described defense usage over many years. In an examination of vignettes from late adolescence through midlife, he found that use of mature defenses (sublimation, anticipation) increased with age, while use of immature defenses (projection) decreased. He also reported predictions from emotional health in childhood to more mature defense use in adulthood (Vaillant & Vaillant, 1990).

Late adjustment among the Grant sample was recently examined (Vaillant & Vaillant, 1990). A total of 173 men (85% of the original sample) were still active members of the study. The major cause of attrition was death: 23 men died before age 60. Five overarching variables were important to late life adjustment: "They were long-lived ancestors (for physical health only), sustained familial relationships (prior closeness to parents was important in young adulthood, prior closeness to siblings loomed more important in late midlife), maturity of defenses, and absence of alcoholism and depressive disorder" (Vaillant & Vaillant, 1990, p. 36). "Paradoxically, a warm childhood environment made an important independent contribution to predicting physical not mental health" (p. 31).

Phebe Cramer: The Emergence of Defenses. Shaping Cramer's investigations (Cramer, 1979, 1983, 1987, 1988, 1991a, 1991b; Cramer & Blatt, 1990; Cramer, Blatt, & Ford, 1988; Cramer & Carter, 1978; Cramer & Gaul, 1988) is the idea that defenses emerge during childhood and adolescence along a continuum, and that certain defenses are salient for particular time periods (Cramer, 1987, 1991a). The use of a given defense is determined by *both* the developmental level of the child and the cognitive complexity of the particular defense (Cramer, 1987). In addition, there are gender-related differences in the frequency of defense use (Cramer, 1979).

Cramer's conceptualizations have strong intellectual roots in Piaget's (1932) cognitive theory and in Anna Freud's (1936, 1965) child observations. Piaget (1932) described qualitatively different forms of reasoning emerging in a predictable developmental sequence (e.g., abstract thinking during adolescence). In her writings, Anna Freud described more mature children as less likely to use defenses that deny the anxiety-provoking circumstance. Such defense mechanisms are replaced by more cognitively sophisticated operations to distort reality. Also contributing to Cramer's program were several studies exploring children's understanding of defenses (Chandler, Paget, & Koch, 1978; Dollinger & McGuire, 1981; Whiteman, 1967). Chandler and colleagues (1978), for example, demonstrated that repression and denial were easiest for concrete operational children to decode; next in order were rationalization, displacement, and reaction formation. Cramer (1991a) has argued that children's ability to explain the reasoning behind the defense strategies used by fictitious story characters predicts when the defense is no longer effective. Thus, "there should be a close correspondence between the chronology of defense understanding and the chronology of defense use with the use of each defense characteristically preceding its understanding" (Cramer, 1991a, p. 31).

Prior empirical support for a developmental approach toward understanding children's defense preference had come from studies of young children (e.g., Ames, Learned, Metraux, & Walker, 1974; Brody, Rozek, & Muten, 1985). These investigations indicated that defenses are observed as early as age 2 and increases during the preschool years. Younger children tend to use more denial than older children, who use more projection and intellectualization (Cramer, 1987).

Cramer has extended the developmental sequencing of defenses beyond early childhood. Her investigations focus on three defenses—(a) denial, (b) projection, and (c) identification—as representative of different points on the developmental continuum. She conceives of denial as the most primitive defense, because it protects the individual by withdrawing attention from noxious stimuli. On the other hand, Cramer postulates that projection is more mature than denial, because it entails the ability to differentiate between internal and external stimuli, together with the capacity to make judgments about what is acceptable or unacceptable (Cramer, 1987, 1991a). From her perspective, the most mature defense is identification, requiring "the capacity to differentiate self from other, to differentiate among many others, and to form enduring internal mental representations of those others" (Cramer, 1987, p. 599). To chart the developmental sequencing of these three defenses, Cramer uses children's responses to the Children's Apperception Test (CAT) and Thematic Apperception Test (TAT). These measures were chosen to provide relatively extensive verbal narratives, in which "no stereotyped response [would be] readily available"; the CAT and TAT ask subjects to tell stories in response to ambiguous situations (Cramer, 1991a, p. 215). A basic and important assumption is that responses to these cards accurately reflect the subject's characteristic responses to actual anxiety-arousing situations (Cramer, 1991a).

Cramer's coding procedure, The Defense Mechanism Manual, is used to determine which defenses are expressed in these narratives. Findings from a study of children and adolescents indicate expected age differences. Denial was the most salient defense for preschool children. Projection was most frequent during adolescence (Cramer, 1987). Identification was employed most by late adolescents. To explore the frequency of these defenses beyond the high school years, Cramer (1991b) assessed first-year college students' use of denial, projection, and identification in response to two TAT cards. Once again, results were consistent with Cramer's developmental prediction: projection and identification were used more than denial.

Several investigations have examined gender differences in defenses (Cramer, 1979, 1991a; Cramer & Carter, 1978). In one study, Cramer (1979) used a self-report measure, the Defense Mechanism Inventory (Gleser & Ihilevich, 1969), to assess the relative strength of five clusters of defenses—(a) turning against the self, (b) turning against the object, (c) projection, (d) reversal, and (e) principalization—among adolescents. Findings were consistent both with gender role theory (e.g., Maccoby & Jacklin,

1974) and psychoanalytic formulations (Deutsch, 1944), which theorize that boys will utilize more externalizing defenses (e.g., projection), whereas girls will use more internalizing defenses (e.g., turning against the self). Gender-related choices of defense mechanisms may become strong during the adolescent period. Prior to early adolescence, males begin to externalize conflict (via projection and/or overaggression). In contrast, females employ defenses that internalize the conflict, primarily through turning the aggression inward.

Hauser and Colleagues: Adolescent Ego Processes and Ego Development. Hauser and his collaborators (Beardslee et al., 1986; Hauser, Powers, Noam, 1991; Hauser, Borman, Bowlds et al., 1991; Hauser, Borman, Jacobson, Powers, & Noam, 1991; Jacobson, Hauser, Powers, & Noam, 1991; Jacobson et al., 1986) have approached the developmental nature of defenses by viewing these mechanisms within the spectrum of ego processes, and examining their relationship to ego development during adolescence. Guiding this longitudinal research program are two themes: (a) defenses represent one type of ego process; and (b) individuals can use defenses in adaptive *and* maladaptive ways. In other words, defenses do not simply represent the pathological end of the spectrum for individual coping. Identifying a defense and its intensity does not sufficiently characterize the outcome of its use. This position argues against characterizing defenses as "pathological" or "rigid," and differs from Haan's dichotomous distinction between coping and defense processes (Haan, 1977; Hauser, Borman, Bowlds et al., 1991; Hauser, Borman, Jacobson, Powers, & Noam, 1991).

These studies represent one facet of a long-term project considering the interplay of adolescent and young adult development with family processes. To identify a wide range of adolescent developmental trajectories ("paths"), Hauser and colleagues follow both clinically defined samples of adolescent subjects, who are likely to be developmentally impaired or at risk for future impairment, and same-age nonpatient high school students, not at apparent risk for developmental impairment. The clinically defined sample includes adolescents who are psychiatrically hospitalized for nonpsychotic disorders (e.g., conduct disorders, depression).

In one series of studies (Hauser, Borman, Bowlds et al., 1991; Hauser et al., 1991), Haan's (1977) Q-sort assessment of coping and defending was applied to clinical research interviews. However, the dichotomous categories of coping versus defending were recast as representing poles of a theoretical continuum ranging from differentiated/engaged to undifferentiated/detached coping strategies. In other words, coping and defending *can* be adaptive, depending on the context and individual (developmental, personality) variables. At one pole of this theoretical coping strategies continuum are those ways that an adolescent narrows his or her affective and cognitive responses to conflict, and rigidly detaches from confronting difficulties at hand. At the other pole are differentiated and flexibly engaging ways that an adolescent may handle specific problems, involving such matters as developmental conflicts (bodily changes) or situational difficulties (family conflicts over emergent independence strivings). In contrast to Haan, no assumptions are made about immediate or long-term consequences associated with the individual's use of these strategies. Outcomes depend on many additional factors besides individual coping processes (e.g., school, family, interpersonal strengths). Questions about which strategies are adaptive or maladaptive must be examined empirically, not settled through a priori definitions of each strategy. Individual functioning or adaptation is contingent on many factors besides coping strategies; among them are: school and family dimensions, peer relationships, and work settings (for extended discussion of this point, see Hauser, Powers, & Noam, 1991).

These new explorations of ego development and coping strategies describe consistent differences between high school and patient samples in terms of types of coping strategies used. The patient sample had higher mean scores on undifferentiated/detached coping strategies and lower mean scores on differentiated/engaged coping strategies, when compared with the nonpatients. In addition, findings point to theoretically meaningful ties between ego development stages and all but one coping strategy (reaction-formation) expressed by all the adolescents. Yet another set of observations addresses relations between parental ego development and adolescent coping strategies, highlighting links between parenting characteristics (ego development) and developmentally relevant aspects of adolescent functioning (e.g., coping strategies).

In another set of related studies, an interview-based measure of adolescent ego processes were constructed (Beardslee et al., 1986; Jacobson et al., 1985, 1986). Twelve defenses and 15 other ego processes were conceptualized, drawn from several psychoanalytically derived rating scales (e.g., Bellak et al., 1973; Grinker & Werble, 1977; Prelinger & Zimet, 1964). These ego processes, theoretically and clinically relevant to adolescent development, were empirically defined and scored on 5-point scales. Analyses of adolescents' expression of defenses and their ego development revealed the alignment of variables that was theoretically predicted: projection, acting out, denial, repression, displacement and avoidance were inversely associated with ego development; altruism, intellectualization, and suppression varied directly with the adolescent's ego development (Jacobson et al., 1986).

Ego Development

The Measurement of Ego Development: Two Models

Ego development is a central construct for many psychotherapists and most psychoanalysts. Arrests and lags in ego development often signal psychopathology; the difficulties are then treated in differing ways by the various available psychotherapies. Although ego processes (reviewed in the preceding section) and ego development are related, the complex components of this relationship are only beginning to be disentangled (Hauser, 1993; Hauser & Daffner, 1980). A clear illustration of the complex relationship between these two realms is in two prevailing models of ego development. One model focuses on the collection of ego mechanisms, defining ego development in terms of how these processes unfold and are used by the growing individual; the other model strongly emphasizes the centrality of one ego process, the synthetic function, in its definition of ego development (Hauser, 1976). Thus, from these perspectives, ego development is defined in terms of change in ego processes, or, conversely, ego processes are defined with respect to developmental change. The choice of emphasis is closely linked with the concept of the ego underlying each model.

Research programs directed by Bellak and colleagues (Bellak et al., 1973; Bellak & Sheehy, 1976; Sharp & Bellak, 1978), and by Grinker and colleagues (Grinker et al., 1968; Grinker & Werble, 1977) exemplify the ego processes tradition, conceiving of the ego as a patterning of related processes whose overall function is "task solving" or "attempted solution," in contrast with impulse expression. Viewed in this way, ego development refers to the development of multiple functions: adaptive strengths, cognitive processes, defenses, and aspects of object relations (Hauser & Daffner, 1980). Empirical investigations assess arrays or profiles of ego processes through instruments that are applied to interviews, behavioral observations, and data drawn from clinical psychological tests, such as Rorschach and Thematic Apperception tests. Complex inventories are used to rate the individual's ego processes with respect to such dimensions as their degree of adaptiveness (Bellak et al., 1973) or their level of intensity (Prelinger & Zimet, 1964). The ego process approach to conceptualizing ego development has met with limited success when used in systematic empirical studies; it requires further research in terms of demonstrating distinctions within and between levels of adaptive ego functioning (Hauser & Daffner, 1980).

A second conceptualization of ego development emphasizes the individual's integrative processes and overall frame of reference. This perspective has major intellectual roots in cognitive-developmental theory (Kohlberg, 1964; Piaget, 1932), theories of self-system development (Sullivan, 1953), and contemporary psychoanalytic emphases on the relationship of internalizations and their transformations to ego development (Loewald, 1980). Using this second conceptualization, Loevinger and her associates have elaborated a model of ego development and closely linked assessment technique (Loevinger, 1976; Loevinger & Wessler, 1970; Loevinger, Wessler, & Redmore, 1970). In the past 20 years, numerous studies have used this approach and instrument to study ego development from psychological and sociocultural perspectives (Cohn, 1991; Hauser, 1976, 1993; Loevinger, 1979a, 1979b). Running through much of this research is a focus on clarifying relations between the individual's level of ego development and other dimensions of his or her psychological functioning. This broad theme is clearly relevant for research in developmental aspects of psychopathology. More precise knowledge of relations among individual behavior, individual experience, and ego development can clearly contribute in important ways to diagnostic and longitudinal studies of various psychopathologies and developmental arrests (Hauser, Powers, & Noam, 1991).

Loevinger's model of ego development assumes that each person has a customary orientation to the self and to the world, and that there is a continuum (ego development) along which these frames of reference can be arrayed. "In general, development is marked by a more differentiated perception of one's self, of the social world, and the relations of one's feelings and thoughts to those of others" (Candee, 1974, p. 621). Specific ego processes (e.g., cognition, impulse control) cannot be distinguished from one another, they are aspects of one integrated structure of the developing ego (Loevinger, 1979b). Ego development is one of four lines of human development, the other three being physical, psychosexual, and intellectual. These four are viewed as being conceptually distinct, although probably empirically related (Hauser, 1978).

Loevinger conceived of the ego as a relatively stable structure, which maintains its coherence by initially screening out information that would disrupt its homeostasis. However, this definition does not postulate that the ego does not experience periods of disequilibrium. Qualitative changes occur gradually as the ego continues to confront phenomena that is incompatible with its current framework of meaning. Thus, inconsistencies in experience can trigger periods of disequilibrum, facilitating changes to a higher ego level (Loevinger, 1976; Loevinger et al., 1970).

Stages of Ego Development

Each of the ego development stages differs from the others along the dimensions of impulse control, conscious concerns, and interpersonal and cognitive style. These variations are described by Loevinger in detail in two monographs (Loevinger, 1976; Loevinger et al., 1970). Seven stages and three transition phases are distinguished. In brief, individuals at the earliest stages are impulsive and fearful, and they tend to use stereotypes and dependent and/or exploitative interpersonal styles. Immediate gratification and avoidance of punishment are salient conscious themes held by individuals at these stages (Hauser, 1976). The two stages (impulsive and self-protective) and the transition phase (transition to conformist) that share these characteristics comprise the *preconformist* level.

A second set of stages comprise the *conformist* level. Individuals at these stages are concerned with social acceptance and approval. The "right" way is dictated by social norms, which are perceived as universal. Inner states are verbally expressed, for the most part, as clichés, stereotypes, and generalizations. Nonetheless, there is a gradual increase of self-awareness and an appreciation of multiple possibilities in different situations. Individuals who reach the most advanced stages—the conscientious, autonomous, and integrated stages—are characterized by their self-awareness and capacity for introspection. Social norms are no longer regarded as immutable: they are followed because they are understood as just, not because their violation leads to punishment and social disapproval. Interpersonal relationships are guided by principles of mutuality and empathy, alongside a growing appreciation of and interest in individual differences. This final *postconformist* set of stages is less commonly found in any given population and usually emerges in late adolescence and adulthood. All of the stages and transitions are summarized and discussed in greater detail in several reviews of this framework and measure (Hauser, 1976, 1993; Loevinger, 1976, 1979a, 1979b), and in Table 18.1.

Over the past two decades, Loevinger has been mapping the conceptual terrain covered by her complex measure—tracing, often in some detail, convergences between her approach and neighboring theoretical perspectives (e.g., Loevinger, 1976, 1979b, 1984). This line of inquiry continued in a contribution

TABLE 18.1 Loevinger's Stages of Ego Development

Stage	Impulse Control "Moral" Style	Interpersonal Style	Conscious Preoccupations	Cognitive Style
Preconformist				
Presocial (I-1)	. . .	Autistic	Self vs. nonself	. . .
Symbiotic (I-1)	. . .	Symbiotic	Self vs. nonself	. . .
Impulsive (I-2)	Impulsive, fear	Receiving dependent, exploitive	Bodily feelings, especially sexual and aggressive	Stereotype, conceptual confusion
Self-protective Δ	Fear of being caught, externalizing blame, opportunistic	Wary, manipulative, exploitive	Self-protection, wishes, things, advantages, control	. . .
Transition from self-protective to conformist (Δ/3)	Obedience and conformity to social norms are simple and absolute rules	Manipulative, obedient	Concrete aspects of traditional sex roles, physical causation as opposed to psychological causation	Conceptual simplicity, stereotypes
Conformist				
Conformist (I-3)	Conformity to external rules, shame, guilt for breaking rules	Belonging, helping, superficial niceness	Appearance, social acceptability, banal feelings, behavior	Conceptual simplicity, stereotypes, clichés
Transition from conformist to conscientious; self-consciousness (I-3/4)	Dawning realization of standards, contingencies, self-criticism	Being helpful, deepened interest in interpersonal relations	Consciousness of the self as separate from the group, recognition of psychological causation	Awareness of individual differences in attitudes, interests and abilities; mentioned in global and broad terms
Postconformist				
Conscientious (I-4)	Self-evaluated standards, self-criticism	Intensive, responsible, mutual, concern for communication	Differentiated feelings, motives for behavior, self-respect, achievements, traits, expression	Conceptual complexity, idea of patterning
Transition from conscientious to autonomous	Individuality, coping with inner conflict	Cherishing of interpersonal relations	Communicating, expressing ideas and feelings, process and change	Toleration for paradox and contradiction
Autonomous (I-5)	Add: Coping with conflicting inner needs[a]	Add: Respect for autonomy	Vividly conveyed feelings, integration of physiological and psychological causation of behavior, development, role conception, self-fulfillment, self in social context	Increased conceptual complexity; complex patterns, toleration for ambiguity, broad scope, objectivity
Integrated (I-6)	Add: Reconciling inner conflicts, renunciation of unattainable	Add: Cherishing of individuality	Add: Identity	. . .

Source: From Loevinger and Wessler, 1970 and Hauser et al., 1993.
[a]"Add" means in addition to description applying to previous level.

where Loevinger suggested that her model can best be viewed within the camp of what she calls "self-theory," referring to ". . . a kind of filter, template, or frame of reference for one's perceptions and conceptions of the interpersonal world" (Loevinger, 1984, p. 49). This template is not simply a reified theoretical entity derived from abstruse theoretical premises or psychoanalytic metapsychology:

> I am convinced that the self, ego, I, or me is in some sense real, not created by our definition. My purpose is to comprehend the way the person navigates through life, not to create artificially demarcated entities [self, ego, I, me]. . . . What I have called ego development is, I believe, the closest we can come at present to tracing the developmental sequences of the self, or major aspects of it. (Loevinger, 1984, p. 50)

When we consider the domains referred to by ego development, together with previous theoretical arguments about the sequence of stages and their assessment, three important implications become apparent. First, the notion of a template, or frame of reference, is surely too vast to be equivalent to a trait or even a collection of traits. Patterns, clusters of perceptions, cognitions, feelings, and other intrapsychic forces represent points along the continuum of ego development. Repeatedly, Loevinger refers to milestones, sequences, and cohesive organizations of perceptions and cognitions held by the individual. In light of this view that such patterns and configurations represent stages—or, as Loevinger now suggests, "gradual transitions" along a continuum (Loevinger, 1993)—of ego development, it is inconceivable that any simple tests of attitudes (conformism, authoritarianism) or traits could measure ego development. Moreover, the sentence completion test used to assess ego development is, without doubt, measuring more than "reasoning," a limited goal sometimes attributed to this instrument. Reasoning, perceiving, and ways of conceptualizing feelings and relationships are all included within the domain of ego development.

A second implication is that assessment of adolescent and young adult ego development taps the template, the "filter," through which the individual is currently experiencing his or her interpersonal world. The assessed development may be at a stage generally associated with an earlier chronological age—self-protective or impulsive, for instance. Certain individuals, for yet unknown reasons, delay or arrest at these early stages. A consequence of this nonadvance is the salience, in the person's perceptions and understandings, of the framework associated with the specific level at which he or she has delayed or arrested. The final implication is a generalization of the preceding idea about ego development arrests. In the adult years, individual personality differences can be found with respect to the imprint of the ego development stage that the individual has reached.

These implications, emphasizing complexity, coherence, and individual differences, are surely meaningful to clinical investigators, who tend to veer away from overly simple reductionistic concepts and their accompanying measures. In addition to these conceptual and methods points, are there aspects of the definition of ego development that are of special importance? We can begin by describing Loevinger's conceptualization as pointing to the *framework of meaning* that the individual imposes on his or her experience (Hauser, 1976). But so abstract a definition certainly does not capture important intricacies within this conceptualization—perhaps those very intricacies that attract diverse investigators to think about and measure ego development. Through its very abstractness, this first definition does not reveal what are theorized as the key components of ego development, and the complex patterning of these components that represents "the way the person navigates through life." In other words, after granting that Loevinger is talking about constructions, or individual meaning-making, our next pressing questions become: What is being constructed? What is the developmental nature of these constructions?

Perceptions and conceptions of the interpersonal world are certainly salient aspects of ego development, but more is included in the model. Cognitive style, cognitive complexity, impulse control, and conscious preoccupations are repeatedly cited as components of ego development (Hauser, 1976, 1993; Loevinger, 1976, 1984; Loevinger & Wessler, 1970). The components are not simply isolated lists of properties. They are dynamically connected in specific ways along a continuum of increasing self-integration, differentiation, and complexity of thought. The relatively distinct patterns of components can be demarcated as "milestones" of advancing development, and are referred to as "stages" or levels of ego development by Loevinger and her colleagues. Whether these stages "exist" as separate logical entities has been a topic of lively debate over the years, together with the associated question of what is meant by "transitions." For instance, do these transitions represent points of conflict or instability in development? Or might they reflect increasing refinement of our observational powers to recognize intervals between previously distinguished stagelike patterns?

We think that the question of the existence of stages misses a fundamental point of this perspective: the stages themselves are constructions of the individual's constructions, the best model that we can articulate of the special ways that he or she constructs his or her inner and interpersonal world. So too, the topic of transitions represents too concrete a view of stages. Moreover, when so many individuals are found to express such a "transition" as the self-aware, then it is even less persuasive to view this pattern as a transitional one (Loevinger, 1993).

Ego Development Motifs

Turning to specific motifs embedded within this ego development perspective, we can discern three central themes (Hauser, 1993): (a) psychological mindedness; (b) integration, synthesis, coherence of perceptions and cognitions; (c) agency, active mastery. They are strongly implied as one reads "up" the sequence of advancing levels of development (see Table 18.1).

Psychological Mindedness. Within the component of conscious concerns is a multifaceted strength described by Loevinger and other investigators of personality development (e.g., Loewald, 1980; Vaillant & McCullough, 1987). This strength includes certain kinds of awareness: recognition that one's internal states are separate from those of others; knowledge that inner feelings and standards can stand apart, and yet are not totally isolated from those of others; and awareness of the psychological impacts of one's actions, emotional expressions, and verbal expressions on another person. These related forms of self-awareness constitute an important set of dimensions noted by many clinical observers and systematically studied in terms of coping and defending (Beardslee et al., 1986; Haan, 1977; Vaillant, 1977, 1986).

Integration, Synthesis, Coherence of Perceptions and Cognitions. Such an integration is not achieved by sacrificing complexity or truncating ideas and perceptions so that they artificially "fit" together. Rather, the coherence comes about through an implicit or overt connectedness of thoughts revealing relevance to the subject at hand—for instance, a given sentence completion stem. The idea of coherence also appears in investigations of adult attachment representations (Main, Kaplan, & Cassidy, 1985). As predicted, analyses of young adults have found significant correlations between their coherence of attachment representations and ego development (Hauser, Powers, & Noam, 1991).

Agency, Active Mastery. This theme can be seen as included under the rubric of psychological mindedness, but it is different enough to deserve separate emphasis. The basic idea is that one can and does influence his or her environment—immediate settings and even larger institutional contexts. The individual believes that he or she is able, within limits, to shape ongoing relationships, has affected previous ones, and can anticipate affecting future events. This belief contrasts with being at the mercy of the environment (Hauser, 1993; Swensen, 1980).

These themes do not exhaust all the important meanings within Loevinger's perspective. Our purpose has been to discern those themes that are at the heart of this model and measure. The breadth and richness of the themes is one reason that Loevinger's approach has been recognized and applied by an increasing number of investigators studying theoretically and clinically meaningful issues across the life span.

The Measurement of Ego Development: The Sentence Completion Test

Ego development is assessed with the Washington University Sentence Completion Test. The projective nature of this test enables identification of underlying developmental structures in an individual's responses. The test instructions request subjects to complete 36 sentences; slightly different versions are used for males and females. Examples of the stems include: "When people are helpless," "When they talked about sex, I," "At times she worried about."

A complex scoring system, provided by Loevinger and colleagues, is elaborated with a specific rationale for scoring decisions in their empirically derived, exemplar-based manual (Loevinger et al., 1970). Each of the subject's responses, separated from his or her other completions, is assigned to one of nine levels (including three transitional phases). After all responses are scored and reassembled, the profile of scores then generates a composite stage score, using a distribution (ogive) algorithm (Hauser, 1976). A second scoring technique is based on the assignment of weighted scores to each successive stage or transition. The sum of these values represents the item sum score (ISS), a summary score used most frequently in research designs that treat ego development as a continuous variable (Hauser, 1976).

Psychometric properties of this assessment approach have been extensively reviewed over the past 16 years (Hauser, 1976, 1993; Holt, 1965; Loevinger, 1979a, 1979b, 1984). The internal consistency and interrater agreement are consistently reported as high. Favorable evidence for validity has been presented with respect to discriminant, construct, and predictive construct validity (Hauser, 1976, 1993; Loevinger, 1976, 1979a, 1984). Among important unsolved validity problems are those involving structural characteristics (coherence of the stages) and finding evidence for the hypothesized invariant stage sequence (Hauser, 1976; Loevinger, 1979a, 1979b).

Empirical Studies of Ego Development

Loevinger's conceptualization and measure of ego development have been incorporated in over 280 published and unpublished empirical studies, translated into 6 languages, and administered to subjects of diverse ages and social backgrounds (Cohn, 1991). In addition, this measure of ego development is clearly of interest to individuals working in clinical settings (e.g., evaluating progress in psychotherapy, assessing developmental impairments, and so on) (Hauser, 1993).

Hauser (1993) distinguished four related conceptual domains covered by these numerous studies: (a) personality and development; (b) adjustment and psychopathology; (c) interpersonal relationships; and (d) social contexts. The domains of personality and development, and of adjustment and psychopathology, and interpersonal relationships are most relevant to the field of developmental psychopathology.

Personality and Development. There is much evidence for theoretically expected relations between ego development and personality, including openness to different facets of experience (McCrae & Costa, 1980), psychological mindedness (Vaillant & McCullough, 1987), use of flexible coping mechanisms (Hauser, Borman, Bowlds et al., 1991; Labouvie-Vief, Hakim-Larson, & Hobart, 1987), empathy (Carlozzi, Gaa, & Liberman, 1983), and expression of positive emotions (Safyer & Hauser, 1994). Because the studies leading to these findings are all cross-sectional, conclusions regarding direction of influence (e.g., advances in ego development leading to higher levels of empathy) cannot be drawn. It is also important to note that the reported correlations are modest and thus do not raise discriminant validity concerns.

Longitudinal analyses examining ego development address questions about direction of influence and developmental trajectories. Of interest here is the question of when people reach their upper limit of ego development (Loevinger, Cohn, Redmore et al., 1985). Several contributors report that during college years there are significant gains over high school ego development levels (Hauser, 1993). For example, Redmore (1983) found slight gains in ego level over a 5-year period in a community college group. Loevinger and colleagues (1985) also found that the majority of college students showed modest increases in ego development during their college years, although some women in the sample showed small but consistent decreases in ego level. Adams and Fitch (1982), on the other hand, did not find such clear indications of progressive change among their sample of college students over a 2-year period. Two studies, currently in progress, consider ego development change beyond high school years in longitudinal samples (Block, 1993; Hauser & Allen, 1991). Preliminary findings from one of these studies (Hauser & Allen, 1991) reveal significant advances in ego development stages and strong correlations between ego development levels over a 10-year period (e.g., $r = .66$).

Adjustment and Psychopathology. Many investigators now include ego development in their studies and discussions of clinical populations. Loevinger's model and ego development measure were not originally developed with clinical research in mind, but this application of the measure is likely to prove valuable by providing more evidence for its validity as well as advancing systematic study of psychopathology through incorporating developmental considerations. Extensions of studies from healthy populations to those with psychiatric and medical impairments are hardly surprising, in light of the fact that ego development refers to such clinically relevant dimensions as impulse control, anticipation, responsibility taking, and social judgment. Such dimensions are among the most important features considered in analyses of impaired individual functioning. The findings of recent clinical research indicate meaningful relations between ego development and:

1. Adolescent delinquency (Frank & Quinlan, 1976) and substance abuse (Wilbur, Rounsaville, Sugarman, Casey, & Kleber, 1982);
2. Adolescent externalizing symptoms (Noam et al., 1984);
3. Adolescent psychiatric ward behavior and length of hospital stay (Browning, 1986);
4. Adolescent coping processes (Beardslee et al., 1986; Hauser, Borman, Bowlds et al., 1991; Jacobson et al., 1986);

5. Adult women's adaptation to divorce (Bursik, 1991);
6. Adolescent adaptation to a chronic physical illness (Hauser et al., 1993).

These studies, and several previously cited, strongly support Loevinger's often expressed belief that there is no simple relation between ego development and adjustment. Many factors influence connections between ego development and adaptation, including sample characteristics, adjustment and diagnostic criteria, psychopathology assessments, and the social setting in which the psychopathology or medical pathology is being expressed. It is encouraging that recent studies in this area (e.g., Noam, Recklitus, & Paget, 1989) recognize this complexity, while using ego development as one of their major probes for asking important clinically relevant questions about antecedent conditions, mediating processes (coping), social setting determinants, and outcome status in unusually stressed samples.

These primarily cross-sectional studies of ego development and psychopathology have stimulated and informed new longitudinal projects that are tracing changes in ego development and symptom patterns (Noam et al., 1989), and are investigating hypothesized predictions from adolescent ego development to early adult adjustment, close relationships, and adult attachment representations (Hauser & Allen, 1991).

Interpersonal Relationships. In earlier reviews of ego development research (Hauser, 1976; Loevinger, 1979a), several studies referring to social functioning were cited. Since then, a series of papers has added even stronger support to the idea that there are theoretically meaningful connections between ego development and interpersonal relations (e.g., Browning, 1987; Hauser, 1978; Helson & Wink, 1987; McCrae & Costa, 1980; Rosznafsky, 1981; Vaillant & McCullough, 1987; White, 1985). The most persuasive data supporting such links are based on actual behavioral ratings or naturalistic data, thereby circumventing the bias inherent in data drawn from multiple self-reports. Several studies used this important design (Frank & Quinlan, 1976; Hauser, 1978; Helson & Wink, 1987; Rosznafsky, 1981; Vaillant & McCullough, 1987). In general, findings indicated that higher levels of ego development are associated with greater nurturance, trust, interpersonal sensitivity, valuing of individuality, psychological mindedness, responsibility, and inner control. This direction of work provides yet another impetus for mounting longitudinal designs, as discussed in the preceding section, to identify possible contributions of ego development to interpersonal dimensions such as close relationships and attachment representations (Main, Kaplan, & Cassidy, 1985).

Ego Control and Ego Resiliency

Another important set of ego psychology contributions has come from Jeanne and Jack Block, personality and clinical psychologists. The Blocks consider whether there are recurrent personality patterns that influence the ways that individuals perceive and act in the world. Their explorations began during an era when there was little interest in the concept of personality. Psychology was heavily influenced by the writings of social learning theorists (e.g., Mischel, 1968) who believed that human beings were controlled by aspects of the environments they confronted, and developmentalists (e.g., Kagan, 1975) who argued against continuities in development (Block, 1993).

Although recognizing the importance of environmental forces, the Blocks conceptualized coherency in personality functioning and personality development. Human beings, they argued, are not "simply linear response systems effectively at the mercy of the situations they encounter" (Block, 1993, p. 15). The limited empirical evidence for personality constructs, in their view, can be attributed to poor conceptualizations or inadequate methodologies.

Beginning with their dissertations, the Blocks have focused on two broad personality constructs: (a) ego control and (b) ego resiliency. From their perspective, these conceptualizations are of central theoretical relevance for understanding individual functioning. Much of their theoretical and empirical work examines the implications of ego control and ego resiliency with respect to individual behavior over time, and varying styles of adaptation.

In considering the question of personality consistency, the Blocks argued against viewing all individuals as developing in essentially the same way, with any variations attributable to the rate or timing of development (Block, 1971). In other words, individuals differ "in kind and in direction, rather than simply" in terms of "rate of transversal" (Block, 1971, p. 11). Thus, their writings introduced and underlined the notion of different developmental paths (e.g., Block, 1971), an idea clearly influential in the subsequent work of D. Offer and J. Offer (1975) and Hauser, Powers, and Noam (1991).

The Blocks' interest in the constructs of ego control and ego resiliency can be traced to psychoanalytic theory—in particular, ego psychology. As discussed in several preceding sections of this chapter, through the lens of ego psychology, personality is viewed in terms of "motivations operating through ego structures which respect and react to both the drives energizing the person and the environmental context in which that individual necessarily must function" (Block, 1971, p. 9). To study these two fundamental aspects of ego functioning—motivational control and adaptation—more precise terms were required. Psychoanalytic theory, rich with respect to conceptualizations of dynamic processes underlying manifest personality functioning, was, for the Blocks' purposes, "inaccessible scientifically" (Block & Block, 1980, p. 42). These overarching investigative goals, together with their strong interest in psychoanalytic theory, led to the Blocks' formulations of ego-control and ego-resiliency constructs. In addition to this general psychoanalytic background, two psychologists were especially influential in the development of these constructs. Consistent with the Blocks' broad reach, one of these figures was Kurt Lewin (1946), who addressed personality functioning and social contexts through his field theory. The second was Otto Fenichel (1945), one of the first psychoanalysts to consider in detail interfaces between drives and ego controls.

Ego Control

Fenichel (1945) posited that drives must be modulated and tolerated. The development of this ability is the product of maturation and of various structures within the ego that are experientially derived over time. Functions of these ego structures include delay of gratification, inhibition of aggression, and caution in unstructured situations. Shared by these varied ego processes involved in tolerating drives is the capacity for impulse control (Block & Block, 1980).

In Lewin's perspective, behavior is a function of the psychological field existing at the time a behavior transpired (Lewin, 1946). This psychological field can be identified through its various elements (individual needs and environmental contexts), separated by a boundary system. The characteristics of boundary systems are highly relevant to the concepts of ego control and ego resiliency. In terms of ego control, permeability is of the most interest. Permeable boundaries allow for neighboring systems to mutually interact with each other; impermeable boundaries tend to impede interaction with other systems (Block & Block, 1980).

Together, the concepts of impulse control (Fenichel, 1945) and boundary permeability (Lewin, 1946) represent key intellectual roots for the Blocks' conceptualization of ego control. Ego control is ". . . the threshold or operating characteristics of an individual with regard to the expression or containment of impulses, feelings, and desires" (Block & Block, 1980, p. 43). Ego control is similar to, yet different from seemingly related personality constructs (e.g., extroversion-introversion, externalizing-internalizing). For example, the construct of extroversion and introversion is a "blend" of impulsivity and sociability. Consequently, it is more "concerned with whether need tensions are discharged" as opposed to the controls placed on motivated responses (Block & Block, 1980, p. 45).

The Blocks suggested that genetic and constitutional factors are major antecedents of ego control. In terms of environmental influences, overcontrolled adults in their mid-30s were found to come from highly structured and ordered families (Block, 1980). On the other hand, the families of undercontrolled adults were described as conflict-ridden and showing poor impulse control. In an earlier study (1971), Block also considered the early family environments of his subjects and speculated about continuities, in his longitudinal findings, between "constructive family situations" and more optimal individual adjustment in later life (Block, 1971, p. 258). Consistent gender roles and family cohesion are major family components that may be the source of later "healthy" personality functioning.

Ego Resiliency

Lewin's second property of boundary systems—elasticity—leads to the construct of ego resiliency. Elasticity refers to the ability of a "boundary to change its characteristic level of permeability-impermeability," [in relation to] "impinging psychological forces" (Block & Block, p. 47). Elasticity also enables a boundary to return to its original form when environmental stressors are no longer pressing. A permeable boundary is flexible and pliant; a rigid boundary resists change (Block & Block, 1980).

Ego resiliency, then, refers to ". . . the dynamic capacity of an individual to modify his/her modal level of ego control, in either direction, as a function of the demand characteristics of the environmental context" (Block & Block, 1980, p. 48). Ego resiliency can be dimensionalized along a continuum. The "ego resilient" pole of this continuum refers to "resourceful adaptation to changing environmental circumstances" (Block & Block, 1980, p. 48). In contrast, the opposite pole describes "ego brittleness," a limited adaptive flexibility accompanied by a tendency to become disorganized when encountering new challenges, especially those that are traumatic (Block & Block, 1980).

Like ego control, ego resiliency differs from other seemingly similar personality constructs, such as competence, ego strengths, and coping. With respect to competence, for example, the Blocks argued that the term has become too widely used and so generalized that it requires a modifier (e.g., social competence vs. intellectual competence). Such specifications limit the construct to the domain in which the behavior occurs. In contrast, the term ego resiliency is "applicable across domains and across cultures" (Block & Block, 1980, p. 50).

Determinants of ego resiliency include both genetic and constitutional factors. In terms of experiential factors, findings suggest that resilient individuals came from warm, caring, and competent families. On the other hand, family settings of ego-brittle individuals were "observed to be conflictful, discordant, with neurotic and anxious mothers ambivalent about their maternal role, and without intellectual or philosophical emphasis, among other qualities" (Block & Block, 1980, p. 51).

Conceptualizing Ego Control and Ego Resiliency

To explore the development of ego control and ego resiliency, the Blocks began a longitudinal study that has come to serve as a model for other programmatic efforts exploring personality development and personality change (e.g., Hauser, Powers, & Noam, 1991; Offer & Offer, 1975). The goals of their project were to: (a) examine the relations of these two constructs, and their interaction, to other aspects of personality functioning (e.g., cognitive functioning, affective differentiation, moral development, and interpersonal behaviors); (b) discern key environmental dimensions associated with differences in ego control and ego resiliency; and (c) assess the predictive utility of these constructs to behaviors and adaptations in the preadolescent and adolescent years (Block & Block, 1980). To meet these ends, it was necessary to ". . . seek out or create assessment procedures and concept-representing measures that were new, age-appropriate, theoretically interesting, technically sound, and perhaps even elegant" (Block, 1993, p. 21).

Their initial sample included 128 children from two nursery schools in the Berkeley, California, area. Together, these two schools attracted children from heterogeneous backgrounds with regard to education, socioeconomic level, racial and ethnic origin (Block & Block, 1980). To date, extensive individual assessments of these children have been conducted at ages 3, 4, 5, 7, 11, 14, 18, and 23. At age 23, a total of 104 subjects were seen.

Within each assessment period, multiple variables, conceptually related to ego control and ego resiliency, were studied. Two core questions were examined. First, how are ego control and ego resiliency associated with a wide variety of social behaviors and cognitive behaviors? Second, what other aspects of personality functioning are conceptually relevant to ego control and ego resilience? Both questions led to rigorous and repeated assessments of cognitive functioning and affective differentiation. Block and Block (1980) detailed the measures used at each assessment period.

The constructs of ego control and ego resiliency are operationalized in terms of experimentally based and naturalistic (observer-based) indexes. The experimentally based ego-control assessment, for example, includes such measures as a "curiosity box" and a motor inhibition tasks situation. Examiners, independently of each other, rated every child on a 7-point set of behavioral dimensions (e.g., talkative, involved in tasks, gives up easily). The results of the assessments were subsequently composited: the summarized scores for measures administered "within any given year were standardized to give equal weighting to each procedure" (Block & Block, 1980, p. 63). They were then further composited to provide an experimentally derived index of ego control at each assessment period (Block & Block, 1980).

Observer-based assessments were drawn from teachers trained to use the California Child Q-set (CCQ); adapted from the adult form of the California Q-set (Block, 1978). Using the CCQ, judges rated each child along the lines of salient psychological characteristics (for example, at ages 3 and 4: considerate of other children, is physically cautious, is able to concentrate). The ratings were carried out by arranging 100 such Q-set items in a forced, choice 9-step, rectangular distribution.

Within each of the assessment periods, multiple independent Q-sort formulations were obtained (e.g., CCQ descriptions were completed by 11 nursery school teachers when the children were 3 years old, and by 9 entirely different teachers when the children were 4 years old). Internal consistency reliability, based on correlations among observers, averaged .65 at ages 3 and 4. At age 7, the average item reliability was .47. During early adolescence, the average item reliability was .72 (Block & Block, 1980; Block, Block, & Gjerde, 1986).

These independently generated Q-sort descriptions were averaged to form composite descriptions of each child. An important application of the Q-sort ratings involved referencing these composite scores against criterion *prototype* sorts already generated for individuals exemplifying ego control and ego resiliency. To generate such criterion Q-sorts, three clinical psychologists used the CCQ to describe a hypothetical ego-undercontrolling child, and, separately, a hypothetical ego-resilient child. The criterion raters showed high levels of agreement (.90).

These criterion definitions were then compared with the actual composite Q-descriptions of each child through correlational analyses. In other words, the array of ratings for a given child was correlated against the prototype sort for undercontrol and, separately, against the prototype sort for ego resiliency. A high correlation indicated that the child was similar or close to the prototypical definition (i.e., resilient); a low or negative correlation signified that the child was dissimilar or far from the prototypical definition (i.e., brittle).

In summary, the constructs of ego control and ego resiliency were operationalized in several ways, using a variety of data (e.g., task performance, self-reports, observer ratings). The Blocks then demonstrated favorable convergent and discriminant validity across these domains of measurement and with regard to other investigations (Block & Block, 1980).

Empirical Findings

To what extent are these constructs relevant for understanding aspects of individual functioning? Overall, ego control and ego resiliency have been shown to be related to a variety of indexes both in the personality (e.g., delay of gratification) and cognitive (e.g., egocentrism) realms (see Block, 1993; Block & Block, 1980; Block, Block, & Gjerde, 1986; Block, Block, & Keyes, 1988; Block, Gjerde, & Block, 1991; Funder & Block, 1989; Funder, Block, & Block, 1983; Gjerde, Block, & Block, 1986). Interestingly, gender differences are seen as early as age 7 in several of these analyses. These differences are apparent with respect to the correlational patterns that characterized males as compared to females, rather than as absolute differences (main effects) on particular variables (Block, 1993).

Are these two constructs related? Ego control and ego resiliency are virtually uncorrelated with each other during childhood, but their relative position within the child has been shown to have much consequence for his or her behavior and adaptive functioning (Block & Block, 1980). In the undercontrolled child, the presence of ego resiliency tends to temper impulsive expression without suppressing spontaneity and enthusiasm. Where resiliency is absent, the impulsivity of the undercontrolled child is unmodulated. The child behaves impulsively when stressed, is easily distractible, and may be described by others as hyperactive. In the overcontrolled child, the presence of resiliency contributes to a high degree of socialized and anxiety-free exploratory behavior. Where resiliency is minimal or absent, the overcontrolled child is often overwhelmed with anxiety, views the world as unpredictable, and becomes immobilized when confronted by stress (Block & Block, 1980, p. 88).

Is there a consistency to these two personality constructs over time? "Are children who are relatively ego-resilient or relatively ego-controlled at an early age relatively ego-resilient or relatively ego-controlled at later stages (i.e., in middle childhood, in preadolescence, adolescence, and young adulthood?" (Block, 1993, p. 32). Block (1993) pointed out that this question is not about "stability." People at age 23 are certainly more resilient and controlled than at age 3. The more important question is whether individuals "maintain their relative positions" with respect to these two constructs (Block, 1993, p. 32).

Considering ego control, the correlations are consistently positive for both sexes throughout the years. Regarding ego resiliency, the correlations for the boys are also consistently positive. For girls, the correlations for ego resiliency present a different picture. During childhood, the correlations are reasonably consistent. From adolescence onward, they are also consistent. There is no relation, however, between childhood and adolescent periods for girls. This finding of discontinuity suggests that, for girls, to be resilient (or brittle) during childhood has no implications for "being resilient (or brittle) in adolescence or beyond" (Block, 1993, p. 33).

"What happened to the girls as they left childhood and moved into puberty?" (Block, 1993, p. 34). To understand the meaning of this observation, Block (1993) cited another interesting finding: around puberty, the relation between overcontrol and ego resiliency becomes substantially *negatively* correlated after being uncorrelated during childhood. This relationship appears to diminish during the adolescent years, but, at age 23, the relation becomes low again. Thus, during the preadolescent and adolescent years, the presence of ego resiliency is accompanied by a decrease in over-control for girls. Block (1993) speculated that the above connection may be caused by differences in the girls' socialization. Literature in this area (e.g., J. H. Block, 1983) suggests that, during childhood, girls' environments are more structured and predictable. These gender differences ". . . can be expected to have cumulative, powerful and general effects on the adaptive strategies invoked when the world in which one has been living changes in a fundamental way" (Block, 1993, p. 35).

Although the advent of puberty may present "a larger and more abrupt adaptational problem for girls than for boys," it may also afford them the opportunity to restructure their prior adaptational modes (Block, 1993, p. 35). The ability to do so is "encompassed" by the construct of ego resiliency. Block also believes the restructuring is dependent on their ability to emerge "from the cocoons of security and restriction in which they have grown up" (Block, 1993, p. 35).

CONTRIBUTIONS OF PSYCHOPATHOLOGY

Ego psychology and psychopathology have shared an intimate relationship from the very beginning. Thus, commenting on the interplay of psychopathology study and ego psychology may at first blush seem superfluous, or even silly. In contrast to other areas of developmental psychology, where recognition and immersion in psychopathology can possibly add new insights and research directions (Cicchetti, 1990, 1993), ego psychology first emerged from the crucible of psychoanalysis and its detailed observations of neurotic symptoms. As detailed in the preceding sections, Hartmann and colleagues later suggested that this realm be expanded into a general psychology. Since then, writers hailing from developmental psychology and psychopathology quarters have been close neighbors, intermingling in many ways. Often, the interplay between a clinical and a developmental mind is within the same thinker (e.g., Bellak, Emde, Erikson, A. Freud, Haan, Hartmann, Hauser, Holt, Vaillant). What has this long marriage produced? Are there, nonetheless, problems that might profitably be addressed by this couple in the future? In this section, we briefly review what has been gained by the tradition of close collaboration between investigators from developmental and psychopathology disciplines.

The insight that defenses cannot simply be thought of as "pathological" or "normal" has been present since the earliest discussions and observations of how defenses must be understood within the context of the patient's overall psychopathology and functioning. Thus, thinking about the pathological functions of a given defense apart from the actual ways it is used by the given patient makes no sense in psychoanalytic theories of defenses. Nor does the notion of healthy coping and pathological defenses ring true to the practicing clinical observer. A related understanding from psychopathology concerns how what appear to be ego strengths may sometimes be drawn into pathological patterns, and how aspects of pathology (e.g., intense intellectualization) may have adaptive value in certain contexts. In other words, there are dynamic relationships between environment and ego functioning, and between large patterns of psychopathology and more molecular ego processes.

No one has more clearly celebrated these associations among context, history, development, and the workings of the mind than Erik Erikson. Through rich and coherent psychohistory portraits (e.g., Erikson, 1958, 1968) and a broad rendering of life-span developmental psychology (Erikson, 1950, 1959, 1968), Erikson returned again and again to the central importance of recognizing the normal and abnormal within each of us, our leaders, and social institutions. Remarkably, in these creative efforts, neither social complexities nor intrapsychic complexities are reduced to oversimple terms or to the other's framework.

A large area that is clearly affected by observations and treatment of psychopathology is ego development itself. As we discussed earlier, there have been at least two prominent conceptions of ego development, one from psychoanalysis (e.g., Bellak et al., 1973) and the other from structural developmental theory (e.g., Loevinger, 1976). The importance of constructing a coherent theoretical framework is emphasized in Loevinger's work. The complexity of functioning—the multiple aspects of ego development and its unevenness—is a theme highlighted more clearly by clinical observations and theory. As clinically experienced investigators have turned to Loevinger's measure and framework, issues involving unexpected regression, affect development, advances, and regressions (moratoria) in the same individual have come to the fore (Hauser, 1976, 1993). Although no clear resolutions for these new complexities are in sight, a richer ego development theory and measure (or measures) may result from this fruitful exchange by clinical and basic developmental investigators.

FUTURE PERSPECTIVES

Two overarching principles guide our vision of how the interplay between ego psychology and developmental psychopathology can be most fully realized. First, the concepts inspired by psychoanalytic data and theory must be more explicitly integrated with the insights, theories, and empirical approaches of neighboring disciplines (Holzman & Aronson, 1992). Adjoining fields that systematically study stress, coping, and individual development have certainly been influenced by work on defenses, adaptive transformations, and levels of awareness, but explicit *integrations* between ego psychology constructs and underlying models to these other fields are indeed rare. The second principle builds on a theme of the chapter: in order to more precisely understand connections between ego psychology and developmental psychopathology, more systematic theoretically driven empirical analyses must be launched. We have already reviewed several major programs of relevant research; we outline below our recommendations for the next stages of this work.

Recommendations

In detailing the following 10 programmatic directions that we advocate, we consider *ego processes* and *ego development,* which are key aspects of ego psychology. Although these areas are intermingled in theoretical and empirical studies, there are crucial differences, and these differences influence our recommendations for future directions.

1. *Definition of ego processes.* To broaden analyses of individual adaptation so that they will include multiple significant contexts—family, school, work, other institutions—continued advances are required in precise conceptual and empirical definitions of ego processes. This greater exactness should then more smoothly lead to specific instruments that can be used by investigators in varied settings. In the ideal case, an interview-based approach and self-report questionnaire instrument would operationalize a standard set of defined ego processes involving defenses and other ego strengths. Others have already presented both definitions and/or linked measures (Bellak et al., 1973; Bibring et al., 1963; Jacobson et al., 1986; Perry & Cooper, 1986; Prelinger & Zimet, 1964; Vaillant, 1986, 1992). What is now needed is a synthesized, theoretically derived list of ego processes, with one or more linked instruments that can be used to assess their presence, patterning, and strength in individuals over varied developmental periods, social settings, and contrasting cultural contexts. Only through such ambitious efforts can we meaningfully consider some pressing, yet unanswered, questions about family contributions to individual adaptation, and cross-cultural variations in individual adaptation to culturally salient stressors.

2. *Resilient development.* Observers continue to be puzzled by how certain individuals grow and perform remarkably well in the face of major adversities. Although studies dealing with this intriguing question are available (Garmezy & Rutter, 1983; Masten & Garmezy, 1985; Masten, Morison, Pellegrini, & Telegen, 1990; Rutter, 1985, 1990; Vaillant, 1977, 1993; Werner & Smith, 1982, 1992), and many more are ongoing, we are still only dimly aware of specific psychological *mechanisms* underlying these optimal outcomes. For instance, much of the work on resiliency has addressed behaviors, competences, and risk factors. Not considered as intensively is a connection of these observable actions with cognitive, perceptual, and affective dimensions. Exceptions include J. Block (1971, 1993), Beardslee and colleagues (1986), and related work exploring how cognitive processes may mediate specific protective mechanisms (Rutter, 1990).

3. *Development and ego processes.* Using Loevinger's framework and instrument (Loevinger, 1976), several investigators have focused on the interplay of ego development and: (a) ego processes (Hauser, Borman, Bowlds et al., 1991; Jacobson et al., 1986); (b) psychopathology (Noam et al., 1984); (c) moral development (Lee & Snarey, 1988); and (d) family processes (Hauser, Powers, & Noam, 1991; Hauser et al., 1984; Hauser, Houlihan et al., 1991). Ego development is highly relevant to understanding ego processes, but other lines of development also need to be considered in terms of how they interface with ego processes. Vicissitudes in physical development, psychosexual development, and cognitive development can pose specific challenges to daily and long-term adaptation. How do the individual's ego strengths and defenses foster his or her adaptation in these circumstances? For example, during the early adolescent years, unexpected spurts in body growth, and changes in body parts, can be stressful for many boys and girls and are sometimes associated with psychopathology (Brooks-Gunn & Petersen, 1991; Brooks-Gunn & Reiter, 1990; Susman et al., 1987). Do specific ego processes, or arrays of ego processes, underlie successful coping during these transitions? Which defenses are connected with unfavorable outcomes or with specific vulnerabilities?

A second way to ask about development points to the development of ego processes. Are there specific sequences in which ego defenses and strengths evolve? To what extent are such unfoldings influenced by age, gender, or cultural dimensions? Or, more likely, are there *trajectories* of ego process development, varying in terms of gender, social class, and cultural influences? Theoretical questions about the development of ego processes have been considered by Anna Freud (1936) and Vaillant (1977, 1993). However, other than in the work of Cramer (1979, 1991a), these questions have not been investigated through nonclinical approaches.

4. *Cognition and ego processes.* In light of current understandings of cognitive development and information processes (Seigler, 1989), what can we say about the interplay between cognitive processes and ego processes, as well as the even more interesting questions regarding transformations in ego processes? For instance, do certain ego processes require specific individual cognitive resources for their appearance and use?

5. *Emotions and ego processes.* Ego psychology has, at times, been characterized as affect-free—unconcerned with conflict or impulse life. From this view, one might legitimately wonder why we are writing so extensively about ego psychology in a book about developmental psychopathology. Recent challenges to this overly narrow understanding of ego psychology conceptualize how ego development and ego processes intersect with expression, tolerance, and awareness of emotions (Busch, 1993; Hauser & Smith, 1992). So far, these contributions are theoretical; they provide an important starting point for new empirical efforts. Next steps for this direction of work involve building bridges between ego psychology and two groups: (a) those conceptualizing emotions from relational and differential perspectives (Campos, Campos, & Barrett, 1989; Izard, 1991; Izard & Malatesta, 1987), and (b) those addressing empirical assessments of emotion, using verbal discourse (Gottman, 1988; Hauser & Safyer, 1994; Safyer & Hauser, 1994; Shaver, Schwartz, Kirkson, & O'Connor, 1987) and nonverbal (e.g., Scherer, 1986) approaches.

Many fascinating questions are connected with this topic. Does affect awareness and tolerance depend on specific levels of ego development? Which ego processes promote greater tolerance of intense affect states? Which processes are associated with labile mood, with impulse expression, and with aggressive and sexual emotions?

6. *Relationship development and ego psychology.* How individuals' relationships evolve over time, how close relationships begin and are sustained—or are rejected and avoided—represent fundamental questions being pursued by scholars from many perspectives (Blumstein & Kollock, 1988; Brown & Gilligan, 1992; Gilligan, 1987; Hazan & Shaver, 1990; Maccoby, 1990). In the literature, sharp debate continues over whether there are gender differences in this development and in ongoing relationship experience (Gilligan, 1987; Hauser &

Levine, 1994; Maccoby, 1990). In the midst of this debate, questions have not been posed about how an individual's relationships are shaped by his or her ego defenses and ego strengths, and about reciprocal influences between ego development and relationship development (Hauser & Levine, 1994; Hauser & Smith, 1992).

Clinical writings, especially from psychoanalytic perspectives, consistently and intensively examine ties between intrapsychic processes and relationships, both normal and pathological (Greenberg & Mitchell, 1983; Hauser & Smith, 1992; Kernberg, 1991; Mitchell, 1988; Modell, 1990). A second group of clinical contributions, briefly reviewed above, addresses relationship precursors in future ego development (Mahler et al., 1975; Spitz, 1983). Now needed are empirical studies that can identify points of connection among ego development, ego processes, and relationship development. There are strong reasons to look more closely at these domains, given the mounting evidence for links between social support (built on relationships) and health (Cohen & Syme, 1985; House, Landis, & Umberson, 1988). In the newest phase of our longitudinal research program, we explore predictive links from adolescents' ego development and ego processes to both close relationships and attachment representations (Allen & Hauser, 1992). Findings from these analyses, and others exploring attachments and psychopathology, should begin to illuminate important issues regarding ego psychology and relationship dimensions.

7. *Family processes and ego psychology.* Thinking about close relationships and attachment leads us to families, the settings of the earliest and often most influential relationships. Psychoanalytically oriented writings, long attentive to implications of early parent-child experience, conceptualize probable links between the early family environment and individual development (e.g., Lidz, 1968; Shapiro, 1968; Stierlin, 1981; Wynne, Ryckoff, Day, & Hirsch, 1958). Contemporary psychoanalytic writing also focuses on family influences as unidirectional, from family to child. More recent views of child development within the family emphasize *reciprocal* influences—how children and adolescents may shape their families (Bell, 1968; Bell & Harper, 1977; Maccoby, 1990; Maccoby & Martin, 1983). Explicit recognition of two-way relationships between a child and other family members characterizes contemporary conceptualizations and empirical analyses of the family's interplay with ego process and ego development. Haan (1977), in examining parent and child coping and defending processes, was one of the first to directly study ego processes with respect to the family. An overarching goal of all of our study, begun in 1976, was to identify family dimensions that promote and retard adolescent ego development (Hauser, Powers, & Noam, 1991; Hauser et al., 1984; Hauser, Houlihan et al., 1991). These ongoing studies, by assessing and enabling the constraining and discourse change processes from direct family observations, have delineated (a) some of the ways that parental and adolescent ego development contributes to family interactions, and (b) how family interactions may shape adolescent ego development. Besides analyses of the frequency of specific interactions, a second direction is application of sequential analyses to determine how specific sequences (e.g., mother-son mutual enabling) are associated with the ego development of both members of given dyads (Hauser, Houlihan et al., 1991).

These approaches, until now focused primarily on ego development, now need to extend to ego processes, considering questions like the contributions of family interaction and sequence to members' ego strengths and vulnerabilities. Yet another extension is forward in time, as we now examine how family processes, observed in the adolescent era, predict young adult ego development, attachment representation, and psychopathology (Allen & Hauser, 1992; Hauser & Allen, in press). The range of questions associated with family relationships is indeed vast, and the issues are of much import. How families may foster and respond to individual adaptation—ego processes and ego development—thus represents a key direction for future work.

8. *Intergenerational transmission of ego development and ego processes.* A central unsolved question is how patterns of adaptive functioning are passed between generations. To what extent are these functions determined by genetic processes? How may the family environment independently— or, more likely, in concert with—these biological forces shape such transmission? This large, multifaceted question leads to detailed considerations of parenting, parent temperament, marital interactions, and child temperament. Also likely involved as component dimensions are such basic processes as child attachment to the parents and parent attachment representations. Although intergenerational transmission is a lively topic in attachment research (e.g., Bowlby, 1988; Ricks, 1985), researchers from the ego psychology perspective have not systematically pursued these important issues. In the newest phase of our longitudinal program, we assess subjects' ego development and, for the first time, examine attachment dimensions: the attachment representations of young adult subjects who were originally studied, together with their families, in their adolescent years, and the attachment relationships formed by the children of these subjects (Allen & Hauser, 1992; Hauser & Allen, 1991). Through these new data, we will be in a position of looking at how family processes are linked with continuity and discontinuity in ego development, as well as how ego development and attachment variables may be interconnected.

9. *Ego processes, ego development, and psychopathology.* Although often discussed in psychoanalytically oriented theoretical and clinical writings (e.g., A. Freud, 1936; S. Freud, 1915a, 1915b; Sandler, 1985; Semrad, 1967; Shapiro, 1965; Wallerstein, 1983), few systematic empirical studies have addressed questions regarding intrapsychic forces and psychopathology. Important exceptions, discussed above, are Bellak and colleagues (1973), J. Block (1971), and Vaillant (1986, 1992). Yet, although interesting and relevant, these research programs have not built on one another's efforts and are rarely considered in more "contemporary" analyses of child, adolescent, or adult psychopathology. Indeed, current studies of psychopathology are characterized by their dual attention to neuroscience and pharmacology perspectives and epidemiological/diagnostic questions. These perspectives are important for unraveling the rich and varied questions about etiologies, treatment, and mental health service delivery. However, what is eclipsed in these often highly sophisticated discussions is attention to details of *mediating processes*—those intrapsychic and interpersonal processes found in the causal chains linking biological events, the onset of psychopathology, and the expression and continuation of psychopathology (Allen & Hauser, 1992; Bowlby, 1973, 1980; Hauser & Bowlds, 1990).

10. *Ego psychology from cross-cultural perspectives.* How do variations in social structures and cultural settings influence individual adaptation? There is a strong tradition within anthropology, and in collaboration with psychology, to examine questions about "mind and society" (Laboratory of Comparative Human Cognition, 1983, p. 296). Investigators have considered links between values (and other facets of culture) and cognition, affective experience, personality, and psychopathology (e.g., Cole, 1975; Laboratory of Comparative Human Cognition, 1983; LeVine, 1973, 1982; Mead, 1930; Whiting, 1963; Whiting & Whiting, 1975). From a purely psychological direction, Hartmann (1939a) envisioned a universal understanding (across cultures) as an overarching goal of ego psychology. More recently, through his cross-cultural and psychohistorical studies, Erikson (1958, 1963) continued this important line of work. However, like systematic studies in the ego process-psychopathology domain, cross-cultural investigations show limited cumulative thrust, often appearing to be relatively isolated from one another. Were it possible to develop crisp conceptual and empirical definitions of key dimensions, such as ego processes and ego development, such progress would facilitate the design and implementation of empirical research programs addressing questions in a variety of cross-cultural domains: family contributions to ego development, evolution of particular ego functions, varied adaptive profiles, and connections between ego processes and central values and rituals. In our own heterogeneous country, there are scientifically and socially pressing questions involving adaptation of minority individuals to oppressive social conditions, poverty, and racism; and links between family process and adaptation that are not apparent in the more typical Caucasian middle-income samples that are usually studied (see Hauser, Powers, & Noam, 1991, for a fuller discussion). Related to this point are problems regarding vastly differing cultural assumptions about the nature of health, progressive development, and attachment (Dasen, Berry, & Sartorius, in press; LeVine, 1989; Miyake, Chen, & Campos, 1985).

REFERENCES

Adams, G. R., & Fitch, S. A. (1982). Ego stage and identity status development: A cross-sequential analysis. *Journal of Personality and Social Psychology, 43,* 574–583.

Allen, J. P., & Hauser, S. T. (1991, April). *Predictions of adult attachment representations, psychological distress, and competence from family interactions in adolescence.* Paper presented at the biennial meeting of the Society for Research on Child Development, Seattle, WA.

Allen, J. P., & Hauser, S. T. (1992, March). *Longitudinal prediction of young adult attachment representations at age 25 from family structure and observed interactions with parents at age 14.* Paper presented at biennial meeting of Society for Research on Adolescence, Washington, DC.

Ames, L., Learned, J., Metraux, R., & Walker, R. (1974). *Child Rorschach responses: Developmental trends from 2 to 10 years.* New York: Hoeber.

Anthony, E. J., & Cohler, B. J. (Eds.). (1987). *The invulnerable child.* New York: Guilford.

Balint, M. (1965). *Primary love and psycho-analytic technique.* New York: Liveright.

Beardslee, W. R., Jacobson, A. M., Hauser, S. T., Noam, G. G., Powers, S., Houlihan, J., & Rider, E. (1986). An approach to evaluating adolescent adaptive processes: Validity of an interview-based measure. *Journal of Youth and Adolescence, 15,* 355–376.

Bell, R. (1968). A reinterpretation of the directions of effects in studies of socialization. *Psychological Review, 75,* 81–95.

Bell, R., & Harper, L. (1977). *Child effects on adults.* Hillsdale, NJ: Erlbaum.

Bellak, L., Hurvich, M., & Gediman, H. K. (1973). *Ego functions in schizophrenics, neurotics and normals: A systematic study of the conceptual, diagnostic, and therapeutic aspects.* New York: Wiley.

Bellak, L., & Sheehy, M. (1976). The broad role of ego function assessment. *American Journal of Psychiatry, 133,* 1259–1264.

Benjamin, J. (1966). Discussion of Hartmann's ego psychology and the problem of adaptation. In R. Loewenstein (Ed.), *A general psychology: Essays in honor of Heinz Hartmann.* New York: International Universities Press.

Beres, D. (1965). Structure and functions in psychoanalysis. *International Journal of Psychoanalysis, 46,* 53–65.

Bibring, G. L., Dwyer, T. F., Huntington, D. S., & Valenstein, A. F. (1963). A study of the psychological process in pregnancy and the earliest mother-child relationship: II. Methodological considerations. *Psychoanalytic Study of the Child, 16,* 25–72.

Blanck, G., & Blanck, R. (1974). *Ego psychology in theory and practice.* New York: Columbia University Press.

Block, J. (1971). *Lives through time.* Berkeley, CA: Bancroft Books.

Block, J. (1978). *The Q-sort method in personality assessment and psychiatric research.* Palo Alto, CA: Consulting Psychologists Press. (Original work published in 1961)

Block, J. (1993). Studying personality the long way. In D. Funder, R. Parke, C. Tomlinson-Keasey, & K. Widaman (Eds.), *Studying lives through time* (pp. 9–41). Washington, DC: American Psychological Association.

Block, J. H. (1983). Differential premises arising from differential socialization of the sexes: Some conjectures. *Child Development, 54,* 1335–1354.

Block, J. H., & Block, J. (1980). The role of ego control and ego resiliency in the organization of behavior. In W. A. Collins (Ed.), *Minnesota Symposia on Child Psychology* (Vol. 13, pp. 39–101). Hillsdale, NJ: Erlbaum.

Block, J. H., Block, J., & Gjerde, P. F. (1986). The personality of children prior to divorce: A prospective study. *Child Development, 57,* 827–840.

Block, J., Block, J. H., & Keyes, S. (1988). Longitudinally foretelling drug usage in adolescence: Early childhood personality and environmental precursors. *Child Development, 59,* 336–355.

Block, J., Gjerde, P., & Block, J. H. (1991). Personality antecedents of depressive tendencies in 18-year-olds: A prospective study. *Journal of Personality and Social Psychology, 60,* 726–738.

Blos, P. (1962). *On adolescence.* New York: Free Press.

Blumstein, P., & Kollock, P. (1988). Personal relationships. *Annual Review of Sociology, 14,* 467–490.

Bowlby, J. (1969). *Attachment and loss: Vol. 1. Attachment.* New York: Basic Books.

Bowlby, J. (1973). *Attachment and loss: Vol. 2. Separation: Anxiety and anger.* New York: Basic Books.

Bowlby, J. (1979). *The making and breaking of affectional bonds.* London: Tavistock/Routledge.

Bowlby, J. (1980). *Attachment and loss: Vol. 3. Loss: Sadness and depression.* New York: Basic Books.

Bowlby, J. (1988). *A secure base: parent-child attachment and healthy human development.* New York: Basic Books.

Brody, L. R., Rozek, M. K., & Muten, E. O. (1985). Age, sex, and individual differences in children's defensive styles. *Journal of Clinical Child Psychology, 14,* 132–138.

Brooks-Gunn, J., & Petersen, A. C. (1991). Studying the emergence of depression and depressive symptoms during adolescence. *Journal of Youth and Adolescence, 20,* 115–119.

Brooks-Gunn, J., & Reiter, E. O. (1990). The role of pubertal processes and the early adolescent transition. In S. Feldman & G. Elliot (Eds.), *At the threshold: The developing adolescent* (pp. 16–53). Cambridge, MA: Harvard University Press.

Brown, L. M., & Gilligan, C. (1992). *Meeting at the crossroads: Women's psychology and girls' development.* Cambridge, MA: Harvard University Press.

Browning, D. L. (1986). Psychiatric ward behavior and length of stay in adolescent and young adult inpatients: A developmental approach to prediction. *Journal of Consulting and Clinical Psychology, 54,* 227–230.

Browning, D. L. (1987). Ego development, authoritarianism, and social status: An investigation of the incremental validity of Loevinger's Sentence Completion Test (short form). *Journal of Personality and Social Psychology, 53,* 113–118.

Bursik, K. (1991). Adaptation to divorce and ego development in adult women. *Journal of Personality and Social Psychology, 60,* 300–306.

Busch, F. (1993). "In the neighborhood": Aspects of a good interpretation and a "developmental lag" in ego psychology. *Journal of the American Psychoanalytic Association, 41,* 151–177.

Campos, J. J., Campos, R. G., & Barrett, K. C. (1989). Emergent themes in the study of emotional development and emotional regulation. *Developmental Psychology, 25,* 394–402.

Candee, D. (1974). Ego development aspects of new left ideology. *Journal of Personality and Social Psychology, 30,* 620–630.

Carlozzi, A. F., Gaa, J. P., & Liberman, D. B. (1983). Empathy and ego development. *Journal of Counseling Psychology, 30,* 113–125.

Chandler, M. J., Paget, K. F., & Koch, D. A. (1978). The child's demystification of psychological defense mechanisms: A structural developmental analysis. *Developmental Psychology, 14,* 197–205.

Cicchetti, D. (1990). Perspectives on the interface between normal and a typical development. *Development and Psychopathology, 2,* 329–333.

Cicchetti, D. (1993). Developmental psychopathology: Reactions, reflections, projections. *Developmental Review, 13,* 471–502.

Cohen, S., & Syme, S. L. (Eds.). (1985). *Social support and health.* New York: Academic Press.

Cohn, L. (1991). Sex differences in the course of personality development: A meta-analysis. *Psychological Bulletin, 109,* 252–266.

Cole, M. (1975). An ethnographic psychology of cognition. In R. W. Brislin, S. Bochner, & W. J. Lonner (Eds.), *Cross-cultural perspectives on learning.* New York: Halstead Press.

Cramer, P. (1979). Defense mechanisms in adolescence. *Developmental Psychology, 15,* 476–477.

Cramer, P. (1983). Children's use of defense mechanisms in reaction to displeasure caused by others. *Journal of Personality, 51,* 78–94.

Cramer, P. (1987). The development of defense mechanisms. *Journal of Personality, 55,* 597–614.

Cramer, P. (1988). The Defense Mechanism Inventory: A review of research and discussion of the scales. *Journal of Personality Assessment, 52,* 142–164.

Cramer, P. (1991a). The development of defense mechanisms. *Journal of Personality, 59,* 39–55.

Cramer, P. (1991b). Anger and the use of defense mechanisms in college students. *Journal of Personality, 59,* 39–55.

Cramer, P., & Blatt, S. J. (1990). Use of the TAT to measure change in defense mechanisms following intensive psychotherapy. *Journal of Personality Assessment, 54,* 236–251.

Cramer, P., Blatt, S. J., & Ford, R. Q. (1988). Defense mechanisms in the anaclitic and introjective personality configuration. *Journal of Consulting and Clinical Psychology, 56,* 610–616.

Cramer, P., & Carter, T. (1978). The relationship between sexual identification and the use of defense mechanisms. *Journal of Personality Assessment, 42,* 63–73.

Cramer, P., & Gaul, R. (1988). The effects of success and failure on children's use of defense mechanisms. *Journal of Personality, 56,* 729–742.

Dasen, P. R., Berry, J. W. & Sartorius, N. (Eds.). (in press). *Health and cross-cultural psychology: Toward applications.* Beverly Hills, CA: Sage.

Deutsch, H. (1944). *The psychology of women.* New York: Grune & Stratton.

Dollinger, S. J., & McGuire, B. (1981). The development of psychological-mindedness: Children's understanding of defense mechanisms. *Journal of Clinical Child Psychology, 10,* 117–121.

Emde, R. (1992). Individual meaning and increasing complexity: Contributions of Sigmund Freud and René Spitz to developmental psychology. *Developmental Psychology, 28,* 347–359.

Erikson, E. H. (1950). Growth and crises of the "healthy and personality." In M. J. E. Senn (Ed.), *Symposium on the healthy personality.* New York: Josiah Macy Jr. Foundation.

Erikson, E. H. (1958). *Young man Luther.* New York: Norton.

Erikson, E. H. (1959). Identity and the life cycle. *Psychological Issues: Vol. 1.* New York: International Universities Press.

Erikson, E. H. (1963). *Childhood and society.* New York: Norton.

Erikson, E. (1968). *Identity: Youth and crisis.* New York: Norton.

Fenichel, O. (1945). *The psychoanalytic theory of neurosis.* New York: Norton.

Frank, S. J., & Quinlan, D. M. (1976). Ego development and female delinquency: A cognitive-developmental approach. *Journal of Abnormal Psychology, 85,* 505–510.

Freud, A. (1936). *The ego and the mechanisms of defense.* New York: International Universities Press.

Freud, A. (1952). The mutual influences in the development of the ego and the id: Introduction to the discussion. *Psychoanalytic Study of the Child, 7,* 42–50.

Freud, A. (1958). Adolescence. *Psychoanalytic Study of the Child, 13,* 255–278.

Freud, A. (1965). *Normality and pathology in childhood.* New York: International Universities Press.

Freud, A. (1966). Links between Hartmann's ego psychology and the child analyst's thinking. In R. Loewenstein, L. M. Newman,

M. Schur, & A. J. Solnit (Eds.), *Psychoanalysis—A general psychology: Essays in honor of Heinz Hartmann.* New York: International Universities Press.

Freud, A. (1968). Acting out. In *The writings of Anna Freud* (Vol. 7, pp. 94–109). New York: International Universities Press.

Freud, A. (1974). A psychoanalytic view of developmental psychopathology. *Journal of the Philadelphia Association for Psychoanalysis, 1,* 7–17.

Freud, S. (1915a). Instincts and their vicissitudes. In J. Strachey (Ed. and Trans.). *The standard edition of the complete psychological works of Sigmund Freud* (Vol. 14, pp. 117–140). London: Hogarth Press.

Freud, S. (1915b). Repression. In J. Strachey (Ed. and Trans.). *The standard edition of the complete psychological works of Sigmund Freud* (Vol. 14, pp. 146–158). London: Hogarth Press.

Freud, S. (1932). New introductory lectures on psychoanalysis. In J. Strachey (Ed. and Trans.). *The standard edition of the complete psychological works of Sigmund Freud* (Vol. 22, pp. 5–32). London: Hogarth Press.

Funder, D. C., & Block, J. (1989). The role of ego-control, ego-resiliency, and IQ in delay of gratification in adolescence. *Journal of Personality and Social Psychology, 57,* 1041–1050.

Funder, D. C., Block, J. H., & Block, J. (1983). Delay of gratification: Some longitudinal personality correlates. *Journal of Personality and Social Psychology, 44,* 1198–1213.

Garmezy, N., & Rutter, M. (Eds.). (1983). *Stress, coping and development in children.* New York: McGraw-Hill.

Gilligan, C. (1987). Adolescence mental health reconsidered. In C. Irwin (Ed.), *Adolescent social behavior and health* (pp. 63–92). San Francisco: Jossey-Bass.

Gjerde, P. F., Block, J., & Block, J. H. (1986). Egocentrism and ego-resiliency: Personality characteristics associated with perspective-taking from early childhood to adolescence. *Journal of Personality and Social Psychology, 51,* 423–434.

Gleser, G. C., & Ihilevich, D. (1969). An objective instrument for measuring defense mechanisms. *Journal of Consulting and Clinical Psychology, 33,* 51–60.

Glueck, S., & Glueck, G. (1968). *Delinquents and nondelinquents in perspective.* Cambridge, MA: Harvard University Press.

Goldstein, E. (1984). *Ego Psychology and Social Work Practice.* New York: The Press.

Gottman, J. M. (1988). *Specific affect coding system manual.* Unpublished. Seattle: University of Washington.

Greenberg, J., & Mitchell, S. (1983). *Object relations in psychoanalytic theory.* Cambridge, MA: Harvard University Press.

Grinker, R., & Werble, B. (1977). *The borderline patient.* New York: Basic Books.

Grinker, R., Werble, B., & Drye, R. (1968). *The borderline syndrome.* New York: Basic Books.

Haan, N. (1963). Proposed model of ego functioning: Coping and defense mechanisms in relationship to IQ change. *Psychological Monographs, 77*(8), 1–23.

Haan, N. (1964). The relationship of ego functioning and intelligence to social status and social mobility. *Journal of Abnormal and Social Psychology, 6,* 594–605.

Haan, N. (1974). The adolescent antecedents of an ego model of coping and defense and comparisons with Q-sorted ideal personalities. *Genetic Psychology Monographs, 89,* 273–306.

Haan, N. (1977). *Coping and defending.* New York: Academic Press.

Haan, N. (1978). Two moralities in social contexts. *Journal of Personality and Social Psychology, 36,* 286–305.

Haan, N., Aerts, E., & Cooper, B. A. B. (1985). *On moral grounds: The search for practical morality.* New York: New York University Press.

Haan, N., Stroud, J., & Holstein, C. (1973). Moral and ego stages in relationship to ego processes: A study of "hippies." *Journal of Personality, 41,* 569–612.

Hartmann, H. (1939a). *Ego psychology and the problem of adaptation.* New York: International Universities Press.

Hartmann, H. (1939b). Psychoanalysis and the concept of health. *International Journal of Psychoanalysis, 20,* 308–321.

Hartmann, H., Kris, E., & Loewenstein, R. (1946). Comments on the formation of psychic structure. *Psychoanalytic Study of the Child, 2,* 11–38.

Hartmann, H., Kris, E., & Loewenstein, R. (1949). Notes on the theory of aggression. *Psychoanalytic Study of the Child,* 3/4, 9–36.

Hartmann, H., Kris, E., & Loewenstein, R. (1953). The function of theory in psychoanalysis. In R. M. Loewenstein (Ed.), *Drives, affects, and behavior* (Vol. 1, pp. 13–37). New York: International Universities Press.

Hauser, S. T. (1976). Loevinger's model and measure of ego development: A critical review. *Psychological Bulletin, 83,* 928–955.

Hauser, S. T. (1978). Ego development and interpersonal style in adolescence. *Journal of Youth and Adolescence, 7,* 333–352.

Hauser, S. T. (1986). Conceptual and empirical dilemmas in the assessment of defenses. In G. E. Vaillant (Ed.), *Empirical studies of ego mechanisms of defense* (pp. 89–99). Washington, DC: American Psychiatric Press.

Hauser, S. T. (1993). Loevinger's model and measure of ego development: A critical review II. *Psychological Inquiry, 4,* 23–29.

Hauser, S. T., & Allen, J. (1991, April). *Antecedents of young adult ego development: The contributions of adolescent and parent ego development.* Paper presented at the biennial meeting of the Society for Research in Child Development, Seattle, Washington.

Hauser, S. T., & Allen, J. P. (in press). *Outstanding outcomes: Portraits of adolescent recovery and resilience.* Cambridge, MA: Harvard University Press.

Hauser, S. T., Borman, E. H., Bowlds, M. K., Powers, S., Jacobson, A., Noam, G., & Knoebber, K. (1991). Understanding coping within adolescence: Ego development trajectories and coping styles. In A. L. Greene, E. M. Cummings, & K. Karraker (Eds.), *Life-span developmental psychology: Perspectives on stress and coping.* Hillsdale, NJ: Erlbaum.

Hauser, S. T., Borman, E. H., Jacobson, A. M., Powers, S. I., & Noam, G. G. (1991). Understanding family contexts of adolescent coping: A study of parental ego development and adolescent coping strategies. *Journal of Early Adolescence, 11,* 96–124.

Hauser, S. T., & Bowlds, M. K. (1990). Stress, coping, and adaptation within adolescence: Diversity and resilience. In S. Feldman & G. Elliot (Eds.), *At the threshold: The developing adolescent* (pp. 388–413). Cambridge, MA: Harvard University Press.

Hauser, S. T., & Daffner, K. (1980). Ego functions and development: Empirical research and clinical relevance. *McClean Hospital Journal, 5* 87–109.

Hauser, S. T., DiPlacido, J., Jacobson, A., Paul, E., Bliss, R., Milley, J., Lavori, P., Vieyra, M., Wolfsdorf, J., Herskowitz, R., Willett, J., & Cole, C. (1993). The family and the onset of their youngster's insulin-dependent diabetes: Ways of coping. In R. Cole & D. Reiss (Eds.), *Family processes and chronic illness.* Hillsdale, NJ: Erlbaum.

Hauser, S. T., & Follansbee, D. (1984). Developing identity: Ego growth and change during adolescence. In H. Fitzgerald, B. Lester, & M. Yogman (Eds.), *Theory and research in behavioral pediatrics* (Vol. 2, pp. 207–268). New York: Plenum.

Hauser, S. T., Houlihan, J., Powers, S. I., Jacobson, A. M., Noam, G. G., Weiss-Perry, B., Follansbee, D., & Book, B. (1991). Adolescent ego development within the family: Family styles and sequences. *International Journal of Behavioral Development, 14,* 165–193.

Hauser, S. T., & Levine, H. A. (1994). Relatedness and autonomy in adolescence: Links with ego development and family interactions. In *Adolescent psychiatry.* Chicago: University of Chicago Press.

Hauser, S. T., Powers, S. I., & Noam, G. G. (1991). *Adolescents and their families: Paths of ego development.* New York: Free Press.

Hauser, S. T., Powers, S. I., Noam, G. G., Jacobson, A. M., Weiss, B., & Follansbee, D. J. (1984). Familial contexts of adolescent ego development. *Child Development, 55,* 195–213.

Hauser, S. T., & Safyer, A. (1994). Ego Development and Adolescent Emotions. *Journal of Research on Adolescence, 4,* 487–501.

Hauser, S. T., & Smith, H. F. (1992). The development and experience of affect in adolescence. *Journal of the American Psychoanalytic Association, 39,* 131–165.

Hazan, C., & Shaver, P. (1990). Love and work: An attachment-theoretical perspective. *Journal of Personality and Social Psychology, 59,* 270–280.

Heath, C. (1945). *What people are.* Cambridge, MA: Harvard University Press.

Helson, R., & Wink, P. (1987). Two conceptions of maturity examined in the findings of a longitudinal study. *Journal of Personality and Social Psychology, 53,* 531–541.

Holt, R. (1965). Ego autonomy revisited. *International Journal of Psychoanalysis, 46,* 151–167.

Holzman, P. S., & Aronson, G. (1992). Psychoanalysis and its neighboring sciences. *Journal of the American Psychoanalytic Association, 40,* 63–88.

House, J. S., Landis, K. R., & Umberson, D. (1988). Social relationships and health. *Science, 241,* 540–545.

Izard, C. F. (1991). *The psychology of emotions.* New York: Plenum.

Izard, C. F., & Malatesta, C. W. (1987). Perspectives on emotional development: I. Differential emotions theory of early emotional development. In J. Osofsky (Ed.), *Handbook of infant development* (2nd ed.). New York: Wiley.

Jacobson, A. M., Beardslee, W. R., Hauser, S. T., Noam, G. G., & Powers, S. (1986). An approach to evaluating ego defense mechanisms using clinical interviews. In G. Vaillant (Ed.), *Empirical studies of ego mechanisms of defense* (pp. 47–59). Washington, DC: American Psychiatric Press.

Jacobson, A. M., Hauser, S. T., Powers, S., & Noam, G. (1985). The influence of chronic illness and ego development on self-esteem in diabetic and psychiatric adolescent patients. *Journal of Youth and Adolescence, 13,* 489–507.

Kagan, J. (1975). Emergent themes in human development. *American Scientist, 64,* 186–196.

Kernberg, O. F. (1991). Aggression and love in the relationship of the couple. *Journal of the American Psychoanalytic Association, 39,* 45–70.

Klein, G. (1970). The ego in psychoanalysis-A concept in search of identity. *The Psychoanalytic Review, 54,* 511–525.

Kohlberg, L. (1964). Development of moral character and moral ideology. In M. Hoffman & L. Hoffman (Eds.), *Review of children development research.* New York: Russell Sage Foundation.

Kris, E. (1952). *Psychoanalytic explorations in art.* New York: International Universities Press.

Kroeber, T. C. (1963). The coping functions of the ego mechanisms. In R. W. White (Ed.), *The study of lives.* New York: Atherton.

Laboratory of Comparative Human Cognition. (1983). Culture and cognitive development. In W. Kessen (Ed.), *Handbook of child development* (Vol. 1, pp. 240–296). New York: Wiley.

Labouvie-Vief, G., Hakim-Larson, J., & Hobart, C. (1989). Age, ego level, and the life-span development of coping and defense processes. *Psychology and Aging, 2,* 286–293.

Lazarus, R. S., & Folkman, S. (1984). *Stress, appraisal, and coping.* New York: Springer.

Lee, L., & Snarey, J. (1988). The relationship between ego and moral development: A theoretical review and empirical analysis. In D. K. Lapsley & F. C. Power (Eds.), *Self, ego and identity: Integrative approaches* (pp. 151–178). New York: Springer-Verlag.

LeVine, R. (1973). *Culture, behavior, and personality.* Chicago, Illinois: Aldine.

LeVine, R., (1982). *Culture, behavior, and personality: An introduction to the comparative study of psychosocial adaptation.* New York: Aldine.

LeVine, R. (1989). Cultural environments in child development. In W. Damon (Ed.), *Child development today and tomorrow* (pp. 52–68). Cambridge, MA: Jossey-Bass.

Lewin, K. (1946). Behavior and development as a function of the total situation. In L. Carmichael (Ed.), *Manual of child psychology* (pp. 918–970). New York: Wiley.

Lidz, T. (1968). *The person: His development throughout the life cycle.* New York: Basic Books.

Loevinger, J. (1976). *Ego development: Conceptions and theories.* San Francisco: Jossey-Bass.

Loevinger, J. (1979a). Construct validity of the sentence completion test of ego development. *Applied Psychological Measurement, 3*(3), 281–311.

Loevinger, J. (1979b). *Scientific ways in the study of ego development.* Worcester, MA: Clark University Press.

Loevinger, J. (1984). On the self and predicting behavior. In R. A. Zucker, J. Aronoff, & A. I. Rabin (Eds.), *Personality and the prediction of behavior* (pp. 43–68). Orlando, FL: Academic Press.

Loevinger, J. (1993). Measurement of personality: True or false. *Psychological Inquiry, 4,* 1–16.

Loevinger, J., Cohn, L., Redmore, C., Bonneville, L., Streich, D., & Sargent, M. (1985). Ego development in college. *Journal of Personality and Social Psychology, 48,* 947–962.

Loevinger, J., & Wessler, R. (1970). *Measuring ego development* (Vol. 1). San Francisco: Jossey-Bass.

Loevinger, J., Wessler, R., & Redmore, C. (1970). *Measuring ego development: Vol. 2. Scoring manual for women and girls.* San Francisco: Jossey-Bass.

Loewald, H. (1980). *Papers on psychoanalysis.* New Haven, CT: Yale University Press.

Loewenstein, R., Newman, L. M., Schur, M., & Solnit, A. J. (Eds.). (1966). *Psychoanalysis—a general psychology: Essays in honor of Heinz Hartmann.* New York: International Universities Press.

Maccoby, E. E. (1990). Gender and relationships: A developmental account. *American Psychologist, 45,* 513–520.

Maccoby, E. E., & Jacklin, C. (1974). *Psychology of sex differences.* Stanford, CA: Stanford University Press.

Maccoby, E. E., & Martin, J. A. (1983). Socialization in the context of the family: Parent-child interactions. In M. Hetheringon (Ed.), *Handbook of child psychology* (Vol. 4). New York: Wiley.

Mahler, M. S., Pine, F., & Bergman, A. (1975). *The psychological birth of the human infant.* New York: Basic Books.

Main, M., Kaplan, N., & Cassidy, J. (1985). Security in infancy, childhood, and adulthood: A move to the level of representation. In I. Bretherton & E. Waters (Eds.), Growing points in attachment theory and research (pp. 66–104). *Monographs of the Society for Research in Child Development, 50* (Serial No. 209).

Masten, A. S., & Garmezy, N. (1985). Risk, vulnerability and protective factors in developmental psychology. In B. B. Lahey & A. E. Kazdin (Eds.), *Advances in clinical child psychology* (Vol. 8, pp. 1–52). New York: Plenum.

Masten, A. S., Morison, P., Pellegrini, D., & Telegen, A. (1990). Competence under stress: Risk and protective factors. In J. Rolf, A. S. Masten, D. Cicchetti, K. H. Neuchterlein, & S. Weintraub (Eds.), *Risk and protective factors in the development of psychopathology* (pp. 236–256). Cambridge, England: Cambridge University Press.

McCrae, R., & Costa, P. (1980). Openness to experience and ego level in Loevinger's sentence completion test: Dispositional contributions to models of personality. *Journal of Personality and Social Psychology, 39,* 1179–1190.

Mead, M. (1930). *Growing up in New Guinea.* New York: Morrow.

Mischel, W. (1968). *Personality and assessment.* New York: Wiley.

Mitchell, S. A. (1988). *Relational concepts in psychoanalysis.* Cambridge, MA: Harvard University Press.

Miyake, K., Chen, S., & Campos, J. (1985). Infant temperament, mother's mode of interaction, and attachment in Japan: An interim report. In I. Bretherton & E. Waters (Eds.), Growing points in attachment theory and research (pp. 276–297). *Monographs of the Society for Research in Child Development, 50* (Serial No. 209).

Modell, A. H. (1990). *Other times, other realities.* Cambridge, MA: Harvard University Press.

Morrissey, R. F. (1977). The Haan model of ego functioning: An assessment of empirical research. In N. Haan, *Coping and defending* (pp. 250–279). New York: Academic Press.

Neubauer, P. (1983). Anna Freud's legacy. *The Psychoanalytic Quarterly, 53,* 507–513.

Noam, G. G., Hauser, S. T., Santostefano, S., Garrison, W., Jacobson, A. M., Powers, S. I., & Mead, M. (1984). Ego development and psychopathology: A study of hospitalized adolescents. *Child Development, 55,* 184–194.

Noam, G. G., Recklitis, C., & Paget, K. (1989). Ego development, psychopathology and adaptation: A longitudinal study. *Acta Paedopsychiatrica, 52,* 254–265.

Nunberg, H. (1931). The synthetic function of the ego. In *Practice and theory of psychoanalysis* (pp. 120–136). New York: International Universities Press.

Nunberg, H. (1948). *Practice and theory of psychoanalysis.* New York: International Universities Press.

Offer, D., & Offer, J. (1975). *From teenage to young manhood: A psychological study.* New York: Basic Books.

Perry, J. C., & Cooper, S. H. (1986). Preliminary report on defenses and conflict associated with borderline personality. *Journal of the American Psychoanalytic Association, 34,* 863–893.

Piaget, J. (1932). *The moral judgment of the child.* London: Kegan Paul.

Prelinger, E., & Zimet, C. (1964). *An ego psychological approach to character assessment.* New York: Free Press.

Rapaport, D. (1959). An historical survey of psychoanalytic ego psychology. *Introduction to Psychological Issues, 1,* 5–17.

Redmore, C. (1983). Ego development in the college years: Two longitudinal studies. *Journal of Youth and Adolescence, 12,* 301–306.

Reich, W. (1949). *Character analysis.* New York: Orgone Institute.

Reiss, D., & Oliveri, M. E. (1991). The family's conceptualization of accountability and competence: A new approach to the conceptualization and assessment of family stress. *Family Process, 30,* 193–214.

Ricks, M. (1985). The social transmission of parental behavior: Attachment across generations. In I. Bretherton & E. Waters (Eds.), Growing points in attachment theory and research (pp. 211–227). *Monographs of the Society for Research in Child Development, 50* (Serial No. 209).

Rosznafsky, J. (1981). The relationship of level of ego development to Q-sort personality ratings. *Journal of Personality and Social Psychology, 41,* 99–120.

Rutter, M. (1985). Resilience in the face of adversity: Protective factors and resistance to psychiatric disorder. *British Journal of Psychiatry, 147,* 598–611.

Rutter, M. (1990). Psychosocial resilience and protective mechanisms. In J. Rolf, A. S. Masten, D. Cicchetti, K. H. Nuechterlein, & S. Weintraub (Eds.), *Risk and protective factors in the development of psychopathology* (pp. 181–214). Cambridge, England: Cambridge University Press.

Safyer, A., & Hauser, S. T. (1994). A microanalytic method for exploring adolescent emotional expression. *Journal of Adolescent Research, 9*(1), 50–66.

Sandler, J. (1985). *The analysis of defense.* New York: International Universities Press.

Scherer, K. (1986). Vocal affect expression: A review and a model for future research. *Psychological Bulletin, 99*(2), 143–144.

Semrad, E. (1967). The organization of ego defenses and object loss. In D. M. Moriarity (Ed.), *The loss of loved ones.* Springfield, IL: Thomas.

Semrad, E., Grinspoon, L., & Feinberg, S. E. (1973). Development of an ego profile scale. *Archives of General Psychiatry, 28,* 70–77.

Shapiro, D. (1965). *Neurotic styles.* New York: Basic Books.

Shapiro, D. (1968). *Aspects of internalization.* New York: International Universities Press.

Sharp, V., & Bellak, L. (1978). Ego function assessment of the psychoanalytic process. *Psychoanalytic Quarterly, 47,* 52–72.

Shaver, P., Schwartz, J., Kirkson, D., & O'Connor, C. (1987). Emotion knowledge: Further exploration of a prototype approach. *Journal of Personality and Social Psychology, 52* 1061–1086.

Siegler, R. S. (1989). Mechanisms of cognitive development. *Annual Review of Psychology, 40,* 353–379.

Snarey, J., & Vaillant, G. E. (1985). How lower and working class youth become middle class adults: The association between ego mechanisms of defense and upward social mobility. *Child Development, 56,* 899–910.

Spitz, R. (1945). Hospitalization: An inquiry into the genesis of psychiatric conditions in early childhood. *Psychoanalytic Study of the Child, 1,* 53–74.

Spitz, R. (1946a). Anaclitic depression: An inquiry into the genesis of psychiatric conditions in childhood. *Psychoanalytic Study of the Child, 2,* 313–342.

Spitz, R. (1946b). Hospitalism: A follow-up report. *Psychoanalytic Study of the Child, 2,* 113–117.

Spitz, R. (1959). *A genetic field theory of ego formation: Its implications for pathology.* New York: International Universities Press.

Spitz, R. (1961). Some early prototypes of ego defenses. *Journal of the American Psychoanalytic Association, 9,* 626–651.

Spitz, R. (1965). *The first year of life: A psychoanalytic study of normal and deviant development of object relations.* New York: International Universities Press.

Spitz, R. (1983). The evolution of dialogue. In R. Emde (Ed.), *René A. Spitz: Dialogues from infancy* (pp. 179–195). New York: International Universities Press.

Steinberg, L. (1990). Autonomy, conflict, and harmony in the family relationship. In S. S. Feldman & G. Elliott (Eds.), *At the threshold: The developing adolescent.* Cambridge, MA: Harvard University Press.

Stierlin, H. (1981). *Separating parents and adolescents: Individuation in the family.* New York: Aronson.

Sullivan, H. S. (1953). *Interpersonal theory of psychiatry.* New York: Norton.

Susman, E., Inoff-Germain, G., Nottelman, E. D., Loriaux, D. L., Cutler, G. B., & Chrousos, G. P. (1987). Hormones, emotional dispositions, and aggressive attributes in young adolescents. *Child Development, 58,* 1114–1134.

Swensen, C. H. (1980). Ego development as general model for counseling and psychotherapy. *Personality and Guidance Journal, 6,* 382–388.

Vaillant, G. E. (1971). Theoretical hierarchy of adaptive ego mechanisms. *Archives of General Psychiatry, 24,* 107–118.

Vaillant, G. E. (1975). Natural history of male psychological health: III. Empirical dimensions of mental health. *Archives of General Psychiatry, 32,* 420–426.

Vaillant, G. E. (1976). Natural history of male psychological health: V. The relation of choice of ego mechanisms of defense to adult adjustment. *Archives of General Psychiatry, 33,* 535–545.

Vaillant, G. E. (1977). *Adaptation to life.* Boston: Little Brown.

Vaillant, G. E. (1978). Natural history of male psychological health: VI. Correlates of successful marriage and fatherhood. *American Journal of Psychiatry, 135,* 653–569.

Vaillant, G. E. (1983). Childhood environment and maturity of defense mechanisms. In D. Magnusson & V. L. Allen (Eds.), *Human development: An interactional perspective* (pp. 343–352). New York: Academic Press.

Vaillant, G. E. (Ed.). (1986). *Empirical assessment of ego mechanisms of defense.* Washington, DC: American Psychiatric Press.

Vaillant, G. E. (Ed.). (1992). *Ego mechanisms of defense.* Washington, DC: American Psychiatric Press.

Vaillant, G. E. (1993). *The wisdom of the ego.* Cambridge, MA: Harvard University Press.

Vaillant, G. E., & Drake, R. E. (1985). Maturity of ego defenses in relation to DSM-III Axis II personality disorder. *Archives of General Psychiatry, 42,* 597–601.

Vaillant, G. E., & McCullough, L. (1987). The Washington University sentence completion test compared with other measures of adult ego development. *American Journal of Psychiatry, 144,* 1189–1194.

Vaillant, G. E., & Vaillant, C. (1990). Natural history of male psychological health: XII. A 45-year study of predictors of successful aging at age 65. *American Journal of Psychiatry, 147,* 31–37.

Wallerstein, R. (1983). Defense mechanisms and the structure of the mind. *Journal of the American Psychoanalytic Association, 31,* 201–225.

Waelder, R. (1936). The principle of multiple function: Observations on overdetermination. *Psychoanalytic Quarterly, 5,* 45–62.

Werner, E., & Smith, R. (1982). *Vulnerable, but invisible: A longitudinal study of resilient children and youth.* New York: McGraw-Hill.

Werner, E., & Smith, R. (1992). *Overcoming the odds: High risk children from birth to adulthood.* Ithaca, New York: Cornell University Press.

White, M. S. (1985). Ego development in adulthood. *Journal of Personality, 53,* 561–574.

White, R. F. (1959). Motivation reconsidered: The concept of competence. *Psychological Review, 66,* 297–333.

White, R. F. (1963). *The study of lives: Essay on personality in honor of Henry A. Murray.* New York: Atherton.

Whiteman, M. (1967). Children's conception of psychological causality. *Child Development, 38,* 143–156.

Whiting, B. (1963). *Six cultures, studies of child rearing.* New York: Wiley.

Whiting, B. & Whiting, J. (1975). *Child of six cultures: A psycho-cultural analysis.* Cambridge, MA: Harvard University Press.

Wilbur, C. H., Rounsaville, B., Sugarman, A., Casey, J., & Kleber, H. (1982). Ego development in opiate addicts: An application of Loevinger's stage model. *Journal of Nervous and Mental Disease, 170,* 202–208.

Winnicott, D. W. (1958). *Through pediatrics to psycho-analysis.* London: Hogarth Press.

Wynne, L., Ryckoff, I., Day, J., & Hirsch, S. (1958). Psuedomutuality in the family relations of schizophrenics. *Psychiatry, 21,* 205–220.

CHAPTER 19

Contribution of Attachment Theory to Developmental Psychopathology

ELIZABETH A. CARLSON and L. ALAN SROUFE

Developmental psychopathology is a domain replete with promise. A central task of this field is to describe the origins, nature, and course of disordered behavior. The accomplishment of such a goal would have profound implications for both prevention and intervention. First, much would be learned about the early origins of patterns of maladaptation. Precursors of pathology might be recognized long before the emergence of frank pathology, enhancing prevention and early intervention. Second, descriptive developmental study of individual patterns of adaptation over time would promote understanding of developmental transformations. Recognizing varying manifestations of the same pattern is critical for demonstrating continuity and for longitudinally evaluating intervention efforts. Third, the study may reveal critical junctures in development where change is more or less likely, providing further keys for intervention. Finally, developmental study of patterns of adaptation and maladaptation over time can reveal processes associated with change in the trajectory of development—for example, why some individuals on a course often leading to pathology do not develop disorder, or why some individuals show late-emerging deviations from normalcy. This information will help further to define risk and protective mechanisms and to provide guidance for intervention.

Although conceptually straightforward, fulfilling the promise of this field is incredibly challenging in practice. Human psychological functioning is complex, and the course of behavior is unique to each individual. The study of developmental psychopathology becomes the study of individual development, and the challenge of the domain becomes distinguishing meaningful order among the infinite variety of individual patterns of adaptation and maladaptation (Sroufe, 1990a; Sroufe & Rutter, 1984). Patterns of positive adaptation and maladaptation, however, are not predefined or obvious to casual observers. They must be discerned, and the search poses difficult questions. Without theoretical guidance, the task of discerning and documenting useful patterns could take decades or generations to accomplish.

Preparation of this work was supported by a grant from the National Institute of Mental Health (MH 40864) to the second author and a National Institute of Mental Health postdoctoral training grant (MH 09744) to the first author.

Herein lies the importance of Bowlby's attachment theory and the research it has inspired in the field of developmental psychopathology. First, Bowlby defined and documented the fundamental importance of infant-caregiver attachment for development. Second, he carefully described normative aspects of the phenomenon, including its origins in dyadic interaction. Third, he pointed toward the conceptualization and assessment of deviations in attachment relationships. Fourth, he outlined a theory and reviewed preliminary research suggesting mechanisms by which early patterns of regulation in the attachment relationship provide continuity in later functioning, linking attachment deviations with psychopathology. His work represents an exemplary interweaving of the normative and the clinical (Sroufe, 1990a). In all, he provided one starting point for a truly developmental perspective of psychopathology.

In this chapter, we first review assumptions guiding an organizational developmental perspective and Bowlby's theory of attachment. Next, we provide an overview of attachment theory. We then review the evidence with respect to the major claims of attachment theory: (a) that individual differences in attachment are rooted in patterns of early interaction (the quality of care), (b) that patterns of dyadic regulation provide the basis for individual differences in the emerging self, and (c) that such early differences have implications for evolving patterns of adaptation in later development. Following this discussion, we review theory and research on processes and mechanisms of continuity in development within attachment theory. Finally, we present recent work on implications of attachment differences for psychopathology. In conclusion, we point to future directions for research.

A DEVELOPMENTAL PERSPECTIVE

Integral to the domain of developmental psychopathology and to the theory of attachment is the concept of development. The term suggests a perspective on psychopathology that extends beyond the description or differentiation of disordered behavior and the examination of early pathology and etiological factors (Sroufe & Rutter, 1984). From a developmental perspective, the study of psychopathology focuses on patterns of adaptation as constructed or evolved over time from the interaction of biological and psychological factors within an environmental context. This study attends to the process by which individuals develop ways of regulating emotion, coping, relating to others, and organizing attitudes and expectations concerning the self, others, and relationships. By understanding the nature of these processes, including the progressive transformation of structures and mechanisms, it may be possible to understand the complex links between early adaptation and later disorder (Sroufe, 1989b; Sroufe & Rutter, 1984) and to define families of developmental profiles, some associated with psychopathology with high likelihood and others with low likelihood (Sroufe, 1990a).

There is no single theory of development, however a developmental perspective includes a set of models and regulative principles that guide research and theory about human behavior (Bowlby, 1973; Cicchetti & Schneider-Rosen, 1986; Santostefano, 1978; Sroufe, 1990a; Sroufe & Rutter, 1984; Werner, 1957). Derived from the study of embryology and evolution, these organizational guidelines reflect unifying characteristics of biological and psychological development (Sameroff, 1983). The principles serve as heuristic tools in the search for order among the range of research findings from studies of human development and psychopathology (Cicchetti & Schneider-Rosen, 1986).

From an organizational view, development is conceived as a dynamic multidetermined process (Magnusson, 1992; Sameroff, 1983). Variables and processes at many levels of analysis (genetic, physiological, behavioral, psychological, and environmental) operate in transaction with one another to contribute to individual functioning (Cicchetti & Schneider-Rosen, 1986; Sameroff & Chandler, 1975). The interactive process is central at all levels of functioning, from physiological organization (Edelman, 1987, 1992) to individual functioning in relation to the environment (Cairns, 1979; Kuo, 1967; Magnusson, 1992; Sameroff, 1983; Werner, 1948, 1957).

Development is viewed as a unified process: the individual develops and functions as an integrated whole (Block, 1971; Cairns, 1979; Sameroff, 1983; Santostefano, 1978; Sroufe, 1979a; Sroufe & Rutter, 1984; Werner, 1948, 1957). Aspects of interactive structures and processes derive meaning from the role each plays in the total functioning of the individual (Sroufe, 1979a). Within the totality, as well as within organized subsystems, processes of development are governed by lawful relations (Sroufe & Waters, 1977). Adaptive patterns and competencies emerge in a lawful manner from that which has gone before (Sroufe, 1979a). Through processes of differentiation and integration, increasingly complex modes of functioning and organization (whether adaptive or maladaptive) evolve from relatively diffuse and globally undifferentiated states (Cicchetti & Schneider-Rosen, 1986; Sroufe, 1979a; Sroufe & Rutter, 1984; Werner, 1957).

Within this process, the individual organism is viewed as an active participant, shaping and creating experience through preprogrammed physiological and psychological biases and with the development of more complex interrelated capacities (Sroufe & Rutter, 1984). What characterizes the individual and distinguishes one individual from another is the patterning of various aspects that comprise the totality (Magnusson, 1988). Variations in patterning reflect variations in the ongoing regulation of biological and psychological processes within an environmental context.

The potential for variation in individual functioning or patterns of organization is vast; however, evolutionary theory suggests that neither individual choices nor environments are limitless (Breger, 1974; Kuo, 1967). Adaptational styles evolve within and are constrained by what already exists (for both the organism and the environment).

Drawing from Waddington (1957), Bowlby (1973) incorporated these and other evolutionary principles into a model of development. Bowlby described variations in development in terms of individual pathways that diverge from a central path. Within this model, interactions between genetic potentialities and environmental influences determine the particular pathway followed. In infancy, developing processes are highly sensitive to environmental change and a wide range of behavioral potentials is available. With development, sensitivity to environmental influence is reduced, and internal mechanisms increasingly constrain flexibility in the pathway. At branchings or points of developmental transition (choice points), current organization (the cumulation of all prior adaptations) interacts with environmental conditions to further consolidate or alter the developmental direction (Sroufe & Egeland, 1991). Within such a framework, pathology involves a series of deviations (branchings or "choices") over time (Sroufe, 1990a).

Adapted to the study of patterns of adaptation, maladaptation, and pathology, the developmental model suggests six guiding principles (Sroufe, 1990a):

1. Even prior to the onset of psychopathology, certain developmental pathways represent adaptational failures that probabilistically forecast later pathology.
2. Not all outcomes of a given pathway need be pathological (or nonpathological).
3. Diverse, but conceptually related, patterns of pathological outcomes may emerge from a given early pathway.
4. Alternative early pathways may lead to the same outcome (principle of equifinality).
5. Change is possible at each phase of development; however, change is constrained by prior adaptation, and alterations in some forms of adaptation may be more likely for certain individuals.
6. Following change, prior adaptations may still be reactivated in certain circumstances (Sroufe, Egeland, & Kreutzer, 1990).

Within this framework, the study of psychopathology, or developmental deviation, requires the study of normal and pathological development in tandem (Sroufe, 1990a). Disordered behavior is defined with respect to normative developmental tasks, and basic developmental phenomena are brought into relief by development that goes awry (Cicchetti, 1984; Freud, 1974, 1976; Sroufe, 1990a; Sroufe & Rutter, 1984; Werner, 1948, 1957). Both patterns of functioning are defined with respect to critical developmental issues (Sroufe & Rutter, 1984) that, in turn, are determined through examination of consequences of adaptation and adaptational failure (Sroufe, 1990a).

For each child, adaptive negotiations of stage-salient developmental issues are unique, based on characteristics of the child and the environment with which the child interacts. Adaptation in one developmental period lays the groundwork for, though is not thought of as determining, later development (Sander, 1975; Sroufe & Rutter, 1984). With the "resolution" of issues at each phase, alternative resolutions become more difficult or less likely, and variation in individual functioning is increasingly restricted. In this way, adaptation may be serviceable at one point in development but may compromise the child's ability to draw upon the environment to flexibly negotiate later issues (Sroufe & Rutter, 1984).

From this organizational perspective, psychopathology is defined in terms of process: it is a pattern of adaptation coconstructed by the individual and the environment. The search for lawfulness among variations in individual functioning is focused on shared developmental trajectories or pathways, and emphasis is placed on understanding processes that maintain or deflect individuals from these pathways. Bowlby's formulation of the phenomenon of attachment makes a critical contribution to this investigation. Defined in terms of behavioral and affective regulation, attachment represents a fundamental normative process in early development. Dyadic regulatory patterns reflect the history of early caregiver-infant interaction and provide a significant link to later individual functioning. Variations in these patterns may represent the emergence of diverging trajectories, nascent developmental pathways that may forecast adaptation as well as pathology.

OVERVIEW OF ATTACHMENT THEORY

Attachment theory as a formulation of personality development based on early relationships has its origins in Bowlby's (1944) observations and inquiries into the lives of 44 juvenile thieves who had experienced early emotional deprivation. These clinical investigations of deviant parent-child relationships marked a beginning of convergent studies of normal and pathological processes from which emerged an ethological approach to the study of socioemotional development. The recent application of these ideas to the study of developmental psychopathology begins to fulfill Bowlby's original desire to contribute to the understanding and treatment of emotional difficulties in children and adults (Bowlby, 1988).

Bowlby described attachment as "a special type of social relationship" between infant and caregiver, which evolves over the first year of life (Bowlby, 1969/1982, p. 376). The relationship involves "an affective bond" between infant and caregiver (Bowlby, 1988) that may be characterized in terms of regulation of infant emotion (Sroufe, 1990b). Attachment, the emerging pattern of dyadic regulation of emotion, represents the culmination of all infant development in the first year and the basis from which self-regulation evolves.

Evolution of Attachment Theory

Bowlby (1969/1982) transformed and integrated ideas from a variety of theories of human development and psychopathology to formulate his theory of attachment; however, his work falls primarily within the psychoanalytic tradition begun by Freud (Sroufe, 1986). Bowlby retained and built on Freud's core clinical and developmental insights, incorporating concepts from evolutionary biology, control systems theory, and cognitive psychology to explain the attachment phenomenon.

Drawing on Freud, Bowlby emphasized the importance of early experience and especially early relationships as the foundation for later functioning (Sroufe, 1986). Bowlby incorporated Freud's idea of an internal world of mental processes as the key to the ongoing power of early history. Bowlby also retained Freud's emphasis on development as a series of stages or sequences, with relevant issues expanded at each stage, and traditional psychoanalytic ideas of fixation and regression in development replaced with the concept of "prototype." From Bowlby's view, regardless of the nature of care, development proceeds, but it proceeds within the framework established by previous patterns of functioning (Sroufe, 1986).

Bowlby departed from psychoanalytic tradition in his emphasis on the quality of care as the central issue of infancy and his view of the individual as active, adapting, coping, and shaping his or her own experience in the developmental process. Bowlby abandoned the psychoanalytic notion of attachment as a secondary drive derived from the mother's gratification or frustration of instinctual needs as well as Freud's mechanistic view of the individual (motivated by a desire to keep tension at the lowest level).

Bowlby found evidence for his view of attachment as independent of need gratification in the ethological work of Lorenz (1965) on the following response of ducklings, and of Harlow (1958) on infant-mother relationships of macaque monkeys. Lorenz (1965) demonstrated that attachment behavior can develop in ducklings and goslings without the young animals' receiving food or any other reward. In studies by Harlow (1958) and his colleagues, infant macaques showed clear preference for cloth surrogate mothers over wire mesh mothers under stressful conditions, even though the wire mothers were sources of food. When frightened, these primate infants scurried to the mother they could clutch rather than the one who fed them. From Bowlby's (1969/1982) view, the cloth surrogate monkeys supported the inborn capacity for clinging, the focus of monkey attachment.

More recent studies support ideas of the critical importance of reciprocity in early relationships as well as the independence of attachment from feeding and sexuality. Cloth surrogate mothers proved adequate as attachment figures for infant macaques, but the attachments were not fully adequate for the development of adult parenting behavior (Harlow & Harlow, 1966). More normal development in macaques resulted when alternate relationships provided a sufficient level of reciprocity (Mason & Kenney, 1974; Ruppenthal, Arling, Harlow, Sackett, & Suomi, 1976).

Attachment as Behavior

Incorporating aspects of evolutionary biology, Bowlby (1969/1982) conceptualized attachment as a repertoire of preadapted behaviors that promote interaction. The behaviors (e.g., orienting, smiling, crying, clinging, signaling, and, with locomotion, proximity seeking) are thought to have evolved in social species (including primates) because of the role they play in promoting survival. The initial repertoire of infant behavior, however, does not provide for the capacity to adapt alone. In order to survive, the infant must become attached to a specific other, one who is available and responsive in emergencies.

Built-in infant behaviors emerge and are organized around an available and interactive (generally adult) figure. From an evolutionary perspective, adults are thought to be equipped with complementary attachment behaviors (e.g., smiling, touching, holding, rocking) that promote a response to infant signals (Bowlby, 1958, 1969/1982). In most environments, infants organize behaviors around one caregiving figure (a primary caregiver) and one or more secondary figures (Ainsworth, 1982; Rutter, 1981). The infant may demonstrate attachment behaviors or derive security from secondary adult or peer figures when more appropriate figures are not available (Harlow, 1963) or in response to less stressful environmental stimuli. In times of extreme stress, however, the infant shows preference for the principal figure.

Bowlby distinguished the attachment relationship or affectional bond from the behaviors that mediate the relationship (Bowlby, 1969/1982, 1973). Various behaviors may serve the attachment relationship, but no behavior is exclusively an attachment behavior. Smiling, vocalizing, and proximity seeking may serve attachment as well as exploration and affiliation. Attachment is defined, not by the presence, intensity, or frequency of particular behaviors (e.g., proximity seeking), but by their organization with other behaviors in a particular context. Biologically based variation in infant behavior is transformed in the context of the caregiver relationship. Behavior becomes organized and directed toward the caregiver under conditions of stress, fatigue, illness, or threat, thus promoting survival of the infant (Bowlby, 1969/1982; Tracy, Lamb, & Ainsworth, 1976). This emerging organization or regulation of infant behavior with respect to the caregiver is attachment.

From an attachment theory perspective, by the end of the first year, virtually all normal infants, however treated, become attached (Bowlby, 1969/1982). Attachment organization develops even in the face of maltreatment and severe punishment (Ainsworth, 1969; Belsky & Nezworski, 1988; Crittenden, 1981; Egeland & Sroufe, 1981; Harlow & Harlow, 1965). Individual variation in attachment is found in the quality of attachment organization, which, in turn, depends on the responsivity of the caregiver and the degree of reciprocity between the infant and the caregiver.

Attachment as an Organizational Construct

Bowlby (1969/1982) conceptualized the organization of attachment behavior in terms of control systems theory. He proposed the concept of a behavioral control system to account for the way a child maintains his or her relation to an attachment figure between certain limits of distance or accessibility. Bowlby described the attachment behavioral system as one of several systems encoded at a biological level, each with its own activations, functions, and outcomes that emerge at different times in early development (Bischof, 1975; Bowlby, 1969/1982). The attachment system is thought to have evolved to "insure the preservation of the individual and continuation of the species within its own environment of evolutionary adaptedness" (Bowlby, 1969/1982, p. 38). Thus, in control system terminology, protection from predators is seen as the biological "function" of the system, and proximity to caregivers, the "set goal." Within this "goal-corrected system," innate action patterns or behaviors are automatically activated when a distance threshold between infant and caregiver is exceeded. When the set goal, or proximity, is achieved, behaviors are terminated through the operation of a feedback loop.

Within an evolutionary framework, the attachment system supports a second function critical for human adaptation: infant exploration and mastery of the environment. As a secure base (Ainsworth, 1963, 1967), the attachment figure supports both the infant's engagement of novelty—or the unknown, until it becomes familiar—and the infant's adaptive use of social and nonsocial opportunities.

Attachment as an Emotional Relationship

Fixed action patterns and imprinting models (Bowlby, 1969/1982) adequately explain duckling behavior and infant caregiver relationships of primates who cling where the set goal is contact (Harlow, 1963). Human functioning, however, is more flexible, and interrelated components of emotion (and later, language) make possible more complex forms of subjective experience and social interaction (Breger, 1974). Although Bowlby (1958, 1988) emphasized affective components of attachment relationships in many of his writings, these observations were not well integrated in his original control systems model (Bowlby, 1969/1982). Affect, however, may be viewed as the core of human psychological experience, the central feature of infant activity and regulation (Emde, 1989). From an evolutionary perspective, emotions give special value to events and make particular actions likely to occur. Emotions inform the organism about what to pay attention to and what to ignore, what to approach and what to avoid (Breger, 1974). The specific meaning of perceptions and actions is shaped through affective as well as cognitive experience with specific others (Sroufe, 1979b, 1990b).

Within an expanded view of attachment—incorporating subjective experience as a core feature—infant proximity seeking is no longer conceived as automatically activated. Instead, attachment behavior depends on the infant's evaluation of a range of external and internal cues, resulting in a subjective experience of security-insecurity (Bishof, 1975; Bowlby, 1969/1982; Sroufe, 1979b). Immediate context, history of care, and infant developmental level all influence the initiation of bids for contact or closeness through their impact on the infant's emotional experience. Within this conceptualization, the attachment system is defined in terms of regulation of emotion. Felt security is viewed as the set goal, and affect is seen as mediating adaptive behavior (Ainsworth, 1973; Sroufe & Waters, 1977).

The special emotional quality of the attachment relationship is reflected in the infant's preference for the caregiver when threatened or distressed, and the infant's use of the caregiver as a secure base for exploration (Ainsworth, Blehar, Waters, & Wall,

1978; Tracy Lamb, & Ainsworth, 1976; Vaughn, 1977). The affective quality of the infant-caregiver relationship is thought to underlie stability in attachment organization over time. Thus, although the developing child may evolve varied means of communicating information about emotional states and ways of actively pursuing proximity and maintaining contact with the caregiver, the patterning of behaviors remains stable in most environments. Stability lies in the quality of the affective bond that is the core around which attachment behaviors are organized.

Bowlby's formulations of infant experiences of separation from and loss of the caregiver highlight the emotional quality of the attachment relationship and its survival advantage. From an evolutionary perspective, emotional reactions to separation (e.g., anxiety, fear) are viewed as important aspects of normal adaptation (Breger, 1974). Physical separations represent a threat to the ongoing availability of a protective caregiver for the infant. In an evolutionary environment, such separations would leave the infant defenseless and vulnerable to predation. Being separated and being alone are "natural clues" to danger (Bowlby, 1973). Emotional reactions to brief separations motivate the infant to seek proximity and to signal distress so that the caregiver also will seek reunion. Infant reactions to prolonged separations include periods of protest, despair, and detachment (thought to be related to conservation-withdrawal in an ethological view). Reunions are characterized by avoidance, anger, and ambivalence, followed by rapprochement (Bowlby, 1973; Breger, 1974; Heinicke & Westheimer, 1966; Robertson & Robertson, 1971). Anxiety, from an ethological perspective, is pathological only when it is pervasive, when it occurs in the absence of a real threat, or when it does not lead to the activation of attachment behavior (Sroufe, 1986).

Bowlby's view of the experience of loss and mourning also follows logically from the significance of early affective relationships in an environment of evolutionary adaptedness (Bowlby, 1980; Sroufe, 1986). From an evolutionary perspective, loss of an attachment figure places the primate infant at extreme risk. The associated experience of vulnerability is thought to be profound. Lost figures must be sought and, if not recovered, intense and prolonged emotional reactions and behavioral disorganization follow. Such reactions reflect the emotional investment of individuals in the relationship and the critical importance of the relationship for survival and well-being. Thus, despite intense psychic pain and curtailed functioning, mourning is not pathological. Rather, from an ethological perspective, the absence of mourning or failure to recover from mourning may be pathological. Through the expression of feelings of vulnerability and distress, the survivor recovers, forming new relationships or deepening already existing alternative ones.

Development of the Attachment Relationship

The evolutionary theory of attachment is founded on the idea that the infant enters the world with biologically based propensities for interaction and self-regulation (Bowlby, 1969/1982). From birth, the infant has "capacities for initiating, maintaining, and terminating social interactions" (Emde, 1989, p. 38), including attending to human facial features and being soothed by human touch (Ainsworth, Bell, & Slayton, 1974; Emde, 1989). Infant capabilities alone, however, are insufficient to ensure survival and self-regulation; caregiver interaction is required (Breger, 1974; Emde, 1989; Kopp, 1982). Environment makes possible the steady progress of maturational processes. In particular, during early months of rapid growth and maturation, caregiver assistance in infant regulation may have long-term effects on infant biological organization (Cicchetti, Ganiban, & Barnett, 1991; Collins & Depue, 1992; Greenough & Black, 1992; Greenough, Black, & Wallace, 1987; Kraemer, 1992).

From the perspective of neurobehavioral systems, experience with the caregiver during an early sensitive period may confer a survival advantage to the infant through the "fine tuning" of neural system development (Collins & Depue, 1992, p. 71). The evolution of infant-caregiver attachment is formulated in terms of "experience expectant" development. Experience expectant processes are associated with the "highly predictable occurrence of an environmental context for young members of the species" (Collins & Depue, 1992, p. 68). Development is characterized by the overproduction of synapses, which are strengthened or eliminated through regulatory experiences with the caregiver. Through the competition of neurobiological systems, enduring regulatory patterns (including patterns of emotion regulation) are established. Within this model, "experience dependent" synaptic modifications continue to occur with new emotional experiences throughout the life span.

Central to the infant's biologically based activity and development of regulatory patterns is the infant's affective experience in the relationship with the caregiver (Emde, 1989). Affective monitoring (of what is pleasurable and not pleasurable) guides infant behavior, and infant affective expression guides caregiving actions.

During the first phase of development, from birth to 3 months, a synchrony related to physiological needs is established between infant and caregiver through the built-in regulatory capacities of the infant and a responsive caregiving environment (Sroufe, 1989a, 1990b). Through trial and error, the caregiver learns to discriminate among the child's reflexive signals (e.g., cries) and affective communications. The caregiver's response to infant behaviors is guided by his or her interpretations of these early cues (meaning assigned to behavior). This early pattern of physiological regulation in the caregiving relationship serves as a prototype for later psychological regulation characterized by the coordinated sequence of behavioral interactions (Sroufe, 1990b).

During the next 3 months of life, the caregiver and the child develop chained interaction sequences (Sander, 1975). Through these coordinated, apparently give-and-take sequences, the caregiver helps the infant to remain engaged or to maintain organized behavior in the face of increasing levels of arousal (Brazelton, Koslowski, & Main, 1974; Stern, 1974). Dyadic regulation at this stage, however, is characterized by caregiver responsiveness: the caregiver organizes behavioral sequences around the infant (Sroufe, 1989a, 1990b, in press). The infant has action schemes and can participate in sequences, but, as yet, the child cannot achieve the organization intentionally or independently.

This level of organization lays the groundwork for later phases in two ways: (a) the repetition of organized behavioral sequences provides the infant with a resource of action schemes from which to draw, and (b) affective exchanges (most often of pleasure and delight) become established as a standard for matching subsequent interpersonal interactions (Sander, 1975; Waters, Wippman, & Sroufe, 1979). Shared affective experience serves as a reservoir of positive feelings that underlies the infant-caregiver bond and is coordinated with the infant's developing schema of relationship interactions (Sroufe, 1989a).

Facilitated by infant sensorimotor and cognitive developmental accomplishments, a new level of dyadic organization is achieved in the second half-year. With the emergence of locomotion, directed reaching, and grasping, the child develops the ability to distinguish means and ends (Piaget, 1952). Behavior becomes intentional, and alternate response patterns are adapted to changing situations. With increasing intentionality, the child assumes a more active and creative role in initiating, maintaining, and continuing coordinated exchanges orchestrated by the caregiver in earlier phases. The infant can follow and embellish on the caregiver's lead, and there is movement toward genuine reciprocity (Sroufe, 1989a). Separate attachment behaviors (e.g., crying, smiling, following, and clinging) become organized into patterns in relation to the attachment figure and are extended to include goal-corrected schemes (e.g., attempting to follow the primary caregiver on departure, and greeting on return) (Bowlby, 1969/1982). An increase in specific affective expressions (e.g., aversive response to strangers, anger, surprise, and fear) marks the coordination of affect and cognition, the beginning of inner organization of experience (Sroufe, 1979b, in press). From early organized dyadic interaction, a particular attachment relationship emerges.

In the final months of the first year, behavioral organization reflects the increased mobility and increasingly active role of the infant in the dyadic system. The caregiver assumes the role of "home base" (Mahler, Pine, & Bergman, 1975) or secure base (Ainsworth, 1973) around which the infant centers expanding exploratory activities. The child moves away to explore the world, retreating when fatigued, frustrated, or threatened, and approaching to share positive affect; "affect, cognition, and social behavior of the infant are smoothly coordinated and organized with respect to the caregiver" (Sroufe, 1989a, p. 78). During this period, infant behavior becomes more purposeful, and goals and expectations are more specific. The infant intentionally directs communications to a specific caregiver, and flexibly selects and alters behaviors from an expanded repertoire of signals to achieve contact or to restore emotional stability when distressed. The child persists toward these goals when initial attempts fail.

This new level of behavioral organization suggests a new level of inner organization (Sroufe, 1990b). By the end of the first year, the infant has developed clear expectations about the availability and responsiveness of the caregiver. The infant responds to new situations in light of past experience, selecting behavior that is expected to elicit known responses from the caregiver. Bowlby (1973) referred to this organization of expectations of the caregiver and self in the relationship as an "internal working model." Derived from the history of interactions over the course of the first year, the model is thought to represent "tolerably accurate reflections" of the infant's actual experience. In most circumstances, the model is reflected in the quality and organization of infant attachment behavior shown in relation to the caregiver.

In summary, development over the first year proceeds from an organizational caregiving matrix constructed around the infant to patterns of dyadic regulation that make room for increasing participation of the infant (Sander, 1975; Sroufe, 1990b). Caregiver responses to an infant's fluctuating states and primitive signals give the infant behaviors meaning, incorporating them into a dyadic regulatory system (Sroufe, 1990b). Central to the dyadic system, or attachment relationship, is the regulation of infant emotion. Through repeated interactions in the relationship over the first half-year, most infants experience that arousal in the context of the caregiver does not lead to disorganization and that, when arousal is disorganizing or beyond the infant's coping capabilities, the caregiver will re-establish equilibrium. Increasingly, the infant develops expectations about the caregiver in regulating emotion and maintaining organization and his or her own role in eliciting caregiver assistance. When emotional regulation is consistently achieved through active signaling and proximity seeking, the infant gains confidence in the relationship and in his or her ability to tolerate increased internal arousal as well as external novelty and challenge in the environment.

Two hypotheses derive from Bowlby's organizational developmental view of attachment: (a) that differences in quality of care (caregiver regulation) will lead to coherent differences in the quality of attachment (dyadic regulation) and (b) that such differences in patterns of attachment will significantly influence later self-regulation of emotion.

Individual Differences in Quality of Attachment

Testing the propositions that history of caregiver-infant interaction leads to the organization of infant behavior with respect to a particular caregiver, or that dyadic patterns provide the basis for self-regulation, requires a valid assessment of patterns of early attachment. Drawing on cross-cultural field research (Ainsworth, 1967) and on hundreds of hours of home observation (Ainsworth et al., 1978), Ainsworth developed an assessment procedure to examine individual differences in the quality of the attachment relationship. The procedure takes into account the organization of individual behavior with respect to the caregiving relationship, with a focus on the effectiveness of the relationship in serving infant regulation of emotion and exploration.

Assessment of Attachment

The laboratory procedure, the Strange Situation, consists of eight episodes (Ainsworth et al., 1978): (a) the caregiver and infant are introduced to an unfamiliar, sparsely furnished room containing a variety of attractive, age-appropriate toys, (b) the infant is allowed to explore with the caregiver present, seated in a chair, (c) a stranger enters, sits quietly, converses with the caregiver, then initiates interaction with the infant, taking cues from the baby, (d) the caregiver leaves, (e) the caregiver returns and the stranger leaves unobtrusively, (f) the caregiver leaves the infant alone, (g) the stranger enters, attempts to comfort the infant if needed, and (h) the caregiver returns.

The procedure represents a series of increasingly stressful infant-caregiver separations and reunions. It was designed to approximate situations that most 12- to 18-month-old infants in Western societies encounter in everyday life. Increments in stress for the infant include exposure to a novel environment, stranger presence, the caregiver's departure, a second departure, and the infant's being left alone.

Individual differences in the quality of the attachment relationship are coded with respect to the infant's gaining comfort in the mother's presence and the child's use of the mother as a secure base from which to explore. In an effective attachment relationship, the infant readily separates from the caregiver to explore and derives comfort from the caregiver when distressed. The relationship is judged to be ineffective when infants cannot separate to explore or do not seek or derive comfort from the relationship when distressed. Emphasis in classification is placed on behavioral organization during reunion episodes. Reunions are thought to elicit individual differences in the capacity to manage the threat to the emotional bond posed by separations. Four categorical rating scales used to examine reunion behavior (proximity seeking, contact maintaining, contact resistance, and avoidance) take into account the degree of infant activity, the initiative and promptness of infant behavior, and the frequency and duration of behavior (Ainsworth et al., 1978).

Patterns of Behavior in the Strange Situation

Based on ratings of reunion behavior and patterns of infant behavior throughout the procedure, infant-mother dyads are classified into one of three major categories: (a) secure attachment, (b) anxious, avoidant attachment, (c) anxious, resistant attachment (Ainsworth et al., 1978).

Secure Attachment. Typically, secure infants readily separate from the caregiver and become easily absorbed in exploration. When wary of a stranger, threatened, or distressed by separation, these infants actively seek contact or proximity and maintain it until settled. They often cling, sink in, or mold to caregivers, demonstrating their desire for contact and its effectiveness in providing comfort. Their recovery from an overly aroused, disorganized state is smooth and carried to completion (the infant returns to exploration/play). If not threatened or distressed, they may not seek physical contact, but actively seek interaction. Securely attached infants show a clear preference for the caregiver when distressed. Upon reunion, they show no reluctance to re-engage the caregiver and no mixture of anger, petulance, or rejection with contact seeking in relation to the caregiver.

When the caregiver's presence does not reduce distress or support exploration, the infant exhibits a nonoptimal pattern of behavior and is said to be anxiously attached.

Anxious, Avoidant Attachment. Anxious, avoidant infants often become engaged in exploration, but with little affective interaction with caregivers (Ainsworth et al., 1978). They show little or no wariness of a stranger and generally are upset only if left alone. Avoidant infants do not show preference for the caregiver over the stranger. Most notably, when the caregiver returns following a separation, these infants fail to actively initiate interaction, are not responsive to caregiver attempts at interaction, and may pointedly look away or turn away from the caregiver. Such avoidance tends to be greater in the second reunion; thus, as stress increases, avoidance increases. Exploration is compromised in reunions despite the lack of overt distress.

Anxious, Resistant Attachment. Anxious, resistant infants show impoverished exploration and play and are wary of a stranger and novel situations (Ainsworth et al., 1978). They may seek contact with the caregiver, or cry, even before being separated from the caregiver. Upon reunion with the caregiver, they have great difficulty settling and may mix active contact-seeking with struggling, stiffness, batting away toys, and continued crying; or, they may cry or fuss in a passive way. These infants are not reassured by the mother's presence or comforting, in part because their anxiety and explicit anger interfere with effective attempts to derive comfort through proximity (Sroufe, 1990b). They lack flexibility in behavioral organization and cannot use the caregiver to regulate arousal; as a result, they do not return to active exploration.

For resistant infants, the anxious, insecure quality of attachment is revealed in their obvious ambivalence and failure to explore. The anxious quality of avoidant attachment is inferred from the lack of expectable organization of attachment behavior in stressful conditions. Both resistant and avoidant infants are thought to be uncertain about caregiver availability. For avoidant infants, however, the presumed desire for contact and feelings of anger are not expressed. The infant copes with arousal and ambivalence through precocious overcontrol of affect, or through ignoring or displacement behavior (Main, 1981; Sroufe, 1990b). It is presumed that avoidance mitigates further alienation of the parent and thus serves proximity.

The three major patterns are thought to represent organized strategies for coping with the arousal of attachment-related feelings (Main & Hesse, 1990; Sroufe & Waters, 1977). Avoidant and resistant strategies reflect coherent means of maintaining proximity (in case of extreme threat) in the context of rejection or unpredictable caregiving.

Disorganized/Disoriented Attachment. For some infants, however, no coherent strategy may evolve from the caregiver relationship. These infants may exhibit an array of disorganized/disoriented and seemingly undirected behavioral responses in the Strange Situation (Main & Solomon, 1990). These include inconsistencies in usual sequences of behavior and unusual behaviors such as freezing, stilling, hand flapping, and other stereotypies. Such cases are referred to as anxiously attached, disorganized/disoriented. It is believed that, for these infants, incomprehensible or frightening caregiver behavior has interfered with the formation of a coherent strategy with respect to attachment (Main & Hesse, 1990). In contrast to moderate levels of anger or anxiety that may serve to maintain closeness in avoidant and resistant attachment relationships, the concurrent activation of fear and attachment behavioral systems produces strong conflicting motivations for the disorganized child. For this infant, the caregiver has served as both a source of fear and a biologically based, expectable source of reassurance. Such extreme conflict is thought to interfere in a dramatic way with the development and stability of effective strategies of emotional communication and the ability to maintain internal organization.

Patterns of Emotion Regulation

Secure Attachment. For securely attached infants, emotions are thought to operate in an integrated, smoothly regulated fashion to serve the inner organization and felt security of the child (Sroufe, 1990b). Through repeated well-coordinated positive interactions with the caregiver, the secure infant has experienced that: the caregiver is available and responsive when the infant is overaroused; stimulation in the context of the caregiver is rarely overarousing; and, should arousal be disorganizing in the presence of the caregiver, restabilization is readily achieved. As a result, children with histories of secure attachment are likely to explore confidently in the caregiver's presence, use the caregiver as a source of reassurance when threatened or distressed, express emotions directly, and respond quickly to caregiver interventions. With increased stress, communication becomes increasingly direct (Grossmann, Grossmann, & Schwan, 1986). Later, these children are expected to remain relatively organized in stressful situations and to seek help directly from others when their own efforts fail. Emotions, particularly negative emotions, are not experienced as threatening but are expected to serve a communicative function (Bowlby, 1969/1982; Sroufe, 1979b). Having experienced such signals as successful in eliciting a response and restoring emotional stability (felt security), these infants are confident in the availability of the other and in their own abilities to elicit care (Sroufe, in press).

In situations when responsive care is unavailable or inconsistently available, a disjunction exists between inner emotional experience and outward expression of feelings. The expression of emotion has not led to responsive care, and heightened arousal often has been experienced as disorganizing.

Anxious, Avoidant Attachment. It is hypothesized that avoidant children have experienced an overly rigid style of emotion regulation (Bowlby, 1980; Sroufe, 1990b). The caregiver may repeatedly ignore the infant or actively reject the child's expression of distress and attempts to gain reassurance, presumedly based on the caregiver's own relationship experiences. At times, the child's demands for attention and support may result in overt resentment by the caregiver. Heightened arousal is experienced as disorganizing; the expression of such emotion, particularly negative signals, however, is not experienced as effective in eliciting care or even as "acceptable." These children are likely to build expectations of the caregiver as unavailable and unresponsive, especially to clear signals of distress. As a result, avoidant children may fail to seek contact or to initiate interaction in response to perceived threats; instead, they may redirect distress or anger to the environment and withhold the desire for closeness. In time, with development, attentional processes also may be modified. Avoidant children may come to exclude the perception of threat, steering away from situations that are likely to be emotionally arousing.

Anxious, Resistant Attachment. Resistant children are thought to have experienced intermittent caregiver responsiveness to signals of distress, supporting a constant state of arousal in the children (Bowlby, 1980; Sroufe, 1990b). These infants openly express distress and anger, but their expressions have not led to restabilization or to felt security. Affect is not effectively modulated, and the children remain chronically vigilant and may heighten expressions of distress in an effort to elicit caregiver response. Children with histories of resistant attachment are thought to form expectations that the caregiver will not be consistently available or responsive to help manage high levels of tension or arousal. In time, these children may come to view a range of situations as threatening, and exaggerated emotional displays may preempt more subtle forms of communication (Bell & Ainsworth, 1972). These children may develop low thresholds for threat, be preoccupied with having contact with the caregiver, and show signs of frustration regarding contact when distressed.

From all three relationship patterns, internalized regulatory patterns or expectations derived from a history of parent-child interactions form the basis for rules that govern the child's interpretation and expression of emotions and behavior. Well-functioning regulatory styles or distortions in early dyadic regulation serve as prototypes for later mediating processes for maintaining organization or felt security under stress (Kobak & Shaver, 1987; Main & Hesse, 1990; Sroufe & Waters, 1977).

RESEARCH ON EMPIRICAL CLAIMS OF ATTACHMENT THEORY

Bowlby hypothesized that differences in quality of care will lead to differences in quality of attachment and to dyadic regulation of emotion. From an interactive history with the caregiver, the child forms "internal working models"—expectations regarding caregiver responsiveness and, in a complementary manner, expectations of the self in eliciting care. Through coordinated exchanges orchestrated by the caregiver, the infant learns whether the caregiver is likely to be available and how emotional regulation may be maintained or reachieved if lost. These expectations are thought to be revealed in the organization of attachment behavior.

Central to Bowlby's second hypothesis is the idea that the experience of dyadic regulation provides a basis for self-regulation. To the degree that the caregiver is responsive, the child acquires confidence in his or her own ability to influence the environment as well as internal states. The development of self-regulation proceeds through a series of phases as the child develops the capacity to make more distal and flexible use of the caregiver as an aid in regulation. Confidence in the caregiver becomes confidence in the self in relationship with the caregiver and, in time, confidence in the self.

Attachment Relationships as a Product of Quality of Care

History of Care and Patterns of Attachment

The idea that effectively organized attachment behavior emerges from a history of responsive care has been documented empirically. Observations of caregiver responsivity at various points in the first year have been found to predict later quality of attachment behavior in both home and laboratory. Ainsworth and her colleagues (Ainsworth et al., 1978) found that infants of mothers who had characteristically responded to signals promptly and effectively cried less at home, responded more positively when held, explored more actively, and showed fewer undesirable behaviors than infants with histories of insensitive care. In the Strange Situation, these infants were assessed as securely attached. Ainsworth and her colleagues (Ainsworth et al., 1978; Ainsworth, Bell, & Stayton, 1971) have emphasized that mothers of secure infants also express negative feelings about the demands of mothering; however, these feelings are "integrated" or balanced with more positive feelings.

Mothers of insecurely attached infants responded less sensitively to infant signals across contexts at home, beginning early in the first year (Ainsworth et al., 1978; Blehar, Lieberman, & Ainsworth, 1977). They delayed more often in responding to crying and demonstrated a lack of affectionate behavior toward the child. By the end of the first year, insecurely attached infants, both avoidant and resistant, cried more frequently at home. They responded less positively to being held, were less responsive in face-to-face interactions, and were less compliant with commands.

Avoidant infants were observed to be more angry at home, unlikely to "sink in" (i.e., mold to their mothers), and less affectively positive. Mothers of these infants were described as rejecting (Ainsworth, Bell, & Stayton, 1971; Ainsworth, Blehar, Waters, & Wall, 1978). They specifically rebuffed their infants when the infants initiated contact, despite holding their infants as much as other mothers (Main, 1981), and they expressed affection through kissing rather than hugging or cuddling. In free-play settings, mothers of avoidant infants were observed to withdraw from their infants when the infants expressed depressed affect (Grossmann & Grossmann, 1991). Withdrawal during times of negative affect reinforces for the infant that such affect is unacceptable (Stern, 1985). In contrast, mothers of securely attached infants were more likely to join in play in a supportive way when infants expressed negative affect.

Mothers of infants assessed as anxious resistant were described as a diverse group who exhibited interfering, ignoring, and inconsistent behavior (Ainsworth et al., 1978; Cassidy & Berlin, 1994; Grossmann & Grossmann, 1991). These mothers seemed to enjoy holding their infants, but they failed to respond reliably to the infants' bids for contact and to support the infants' initiatives (e.g., attempts to feed themselves).

The relationship that Ainsworth and her colleagues found between quality of attachment in the laboratory assessment and sensitivity of care and synchrony of dyadic interaction at home has been replicated by numerous researchers (Bates, Maslin, & Frankel, 1985; Belsky & Isabella, 1988; Egeland & Farber, 1984; Grossmann, Grossmann, Spangler, Suess, & Unzer, 1985; Isabella, 1993; Isabella & Belsky, 1991; Kiser, Bates, Maslin, & Bayles, 1986). Dyads developing secure attachments have been observed to interact in a well-timed reciprocal manner; dyads developing insecure relationships have been characterized by interactions in which mothers were minimally involved, unresponsive to infant signals, or intrusive. In each case, Ainsworth's sensitivity scale ratings in early infancy (3 to 6 months) were related to independently derived attachment classifications at 12 months. The relationship between caregiver rejection and avoidance also has been replicated (Isabella, 1993).

Assessments of infant behavioral capacities and dispositions in the first year, either from behavioral observation or parental report, do not predict attachment security (Bates et al., 1985; Blehar et al., 1977; Bohlin, Hagekull, Germer, Andersson, & Lindberg, 1990; Egeland & Farber, 1984; Vaughn, Lefever, Seifer, & Barglow, 1989). Parental report of temperament and cortisol reactivity to stress predict amount of crying during separation episodes of the Strange Situation procedure (i.e., proneness to distress in general), but these assessments do not predict amount of crying during reunion or ratings of avoidance or resistance (Gunnar, Mangelsdorf, Larson, & Herstgaard, 1989; Spangler & Grossmann, 1993; Vaughn et al., 1989).

From an organizational perspective, variations in infant temperament and in attachment quality based on history of caregiving are viewed as independent. Through a transactional process, variations in infant behavior are mediated by caregiver sensitivity to become part of dyadic organization. An initially difficult infant may become an easier infant through dyadic experience with a sensitive mother, or an infant may become more difficult in the context of insensitive care (Susman, Kalkoske, & Egeland, in press). In caregiving environments characterized by adequate support and only ordinary stress, irritable newborns may become securely attached with usual probability (Belsky & Isabella, 1988; Crockenberg, 1981). Irritable infants reared by caregivers with low social support, however, are likely to show anxious attachment patterns.

Maltreatment Studies

Maltreatment studies also provide support for the relationship between quality of care and quality of attachment relationship. Unpredictable, chaotic home environments provide the context for parent-child maltreatment (Cicchetti, Toth, & Bush, 1988; Egeland, Breitenbucher, & Rosenberg, 1980; Garbarino & Gillian, 1980; Gil, 1970). Enduring problematic characteristics include emotional or physical rejection, aggression, hostile child management, threatening affective or verbal assaults, and lack of appropriate responsivity (Crittenden, 1981). In addition, there is a strong likelihood that parents in these families have had insecure attachment relationships with their own parents (DeLozier, 1982; Main & Goldwyn, 1984).

The effects of maltreatment experience on the development of attachment relationships have been well-documented. Maltreated infants and toddlers are significantly more likely to form insecure attachment relationships with primary caregivers than infants drawn from matched lower socioeconomic status (SES) comparison groups (Carlson, Cicchetti, Barnett, & Braunwald, 1989; Crittenden, 1988; Egeland & Sroufe, 1981; Schneider-Rosen, Braunwald, Carlson, & Cicchetti, 1985). Estimates of insecurity range from approximately 50% to 100% across studies. In accord with Main's theoretical predictions, nearly 80% of one sample of 12-month-old infants from maltreating families were assessed as anxiously attached, disorganized/disoriented, compared to 19% of SES matched control groups (Carlson et al., 1989).

History of Care and Disorganization

Disorganization/disorientation of attachment organization in infancy has been related to parental experience of unresolved mourning (Main & Hesse, 1990) as well as to infant histories of maltreatment (Carlson et al., 1989), maternal depression (Radke-Yarrow, Cummings, Kuczynski, & Chapman, 1985), and prenatal alcohol (O'Connor, Sigman, & Brill, 1987) and drug (Rodning, Beckwith, & Howard, 1991) exposure. In addition, Lyons-Ruth and her colleagues (Lyons-Ruth, Repacholi, McLeod, & Silva, 1991) have found disorganized attachment to be related to maternal history of loss due to divorce or separation (foster care) as well as death. In this study, disorganizing effects of maternal history of parental death were evident at 12 months, and disorganizing effects associated with parental divorce or out-of-home care were evident at 18 months. Disorganization also was significantly associated with maternal psychosocial problems (e.g., depression, maltreatment) and hostile-intrusive behavior toward the infant in the home.

Attachment Variation and the Emergent Self

The quality of dyadic regulation of emotion in infancy has consequences for emerging expectations concerning emotional arousal and the expression, modulation, and flexible control of emotions by the child. Through participation in dyadic regulation during the first year, the infant has repeatedly experienced particular patterns of coping with arousal in the context of the caregiver, at first orchestrated by the caregiver but with increasing participation by the child. From these experiences, in particular caregiver responses to infant initiatives, individual patterns of organizing attachment behavior in the face of arousal evolve. Along with behavioral organization, the child develops expectations about the caregiver and the self in the regulation of emotion. As regulation orchestrated by the caregiver provided the basis for dyadic regulation in infancy, self-regulation supported and guided by the caregiver precedes regulation by the child outside of the caregiving matrix.

During the second and third years, major developmental changes include the emergence of symbolic representation and language, self-awareness, and the beginnings of self-control. With cognitive and social advances and increased motor skills, the toddler actively pursues his or her own goals and plans, initiating separations both physically and psychologically from the caregiver (Sroufe, 1989a). Psychological contact maintained through distance interaction (e.g., visual contact, vocalizations) increasingly replaces the need for physical contact (Feldman & Ingham, 1975; Sorce & Emde, 1981; Sroufe & Waters, 1977), and inner aims, even those contrary to those of the caregiver, take precedence over coordinating interactions with the caregiver (Sander, 1975). Conflict resolved within the context of relationship security and emotional closeness deepens the child's trust in the relationship, the foundation of autonomous functioning (Erikson, 1963).

Cognitive, social, and motoric developmental advances provide the child with new experiences and capacities for regulating emotion. The child is challenged to cope with arousal and frustration and to control impulses on his or her own, relying on the caregiver when needed. Increased control allows the child to move toward ownership of inner experience and come to recognize the self as competent to elicit regulatory assistance, to upset and then to reachieve inner regulation. Through independent action and the pursuit of inner plans, the child develops an understanding of self and other as autonomous agents (Sroufe, 1990b). These developmental advances are paralleled by the emergence of self-assertions (Breger, 1974), self-recognition (Lewis & Brooks, 1978; Mans, Cicchetti, & Sroufe, 1978), and differentiated emotional experiences (e.g., shame, new expressions of anger and joy) that, in turn, influence capacities for regulating emotion (Sroufe, in press).

From an organizational/process view, the emerging inner organization, or core of self, concerns regularities in experience. From early patterns of caregiver-infant interaction, an abstracted history of behavioral and affective regulation is carried forward. The internal organization of attitudes and expectations includes recognition of others as part of regulation; recognition of oneself as effective or ineffective in eliciting care and regulation; and recognition of the self as author of experience (Sroufe, 1989a, 1990b). Patterns of behavior and affective regulation and associated expectations of self and other provide continuity in experience, despite transformations in development and changes in context.

Qualitative Differences in Attachment Organization

Secure Attachment. For the secure child, a history of effective dyadic regulation of arousal is expected to support a smooth transition to effective autonomous functioning. Through experiences of well-regulated caregiver-infant interactions, these children have evolved positive expectations concerning their exploratory competence, the capacity to modulate arousal and communicate affectively within the relationship, and confidence in the ongoing availability of the caregiver (Sroufe, in press). Direct expression of emotion is based on early experiences of flexible access to feelings and freedom to express emotion. Based on these experiences, secure children are likely to actively engage in opportunities and challenges in the environment to the limit of their abilities and to flexibly draw on caregiver resources when needed. A sense of self as autonomous agent emerges from and in connection to a supportive caregiving relationship (Emde & Buchsbaum, 1990; Lieberman & Pawl, 1990).

The demands of toddlerhood and the separation individuation process, including challenges to control and modulate emotion and to express emotion openly, may pose difficulties for infants with histories of avoidant and resistant attachment.

Anxious, Avoidant Attachment. For children with histories of avoidant attachment, overly rigid patterns of dyadic regulation may provide the basis for patterns of self-regulation characterized by restrictions or distortions in affective experience and expression. These children may be expected to have difficulty maintaining emotional closeness as a basis for the separation individuation process (Sroufe, in press). The avoidant child may show limited engagement in emotionally arousing situations (withholding affective involvement in play), indirect expression of emotions (e.g., distress, anger), and an inability to draw on caregiver resources when guidance or comfort is needed. Experiences of caregiver rejection of infant signals and restrictions of affect support a precocious independence in toddlerhood, compromising the child's development of a genuine sense of competence and autonomy.

Anxious, Resistant Attachment. For children with resistant histories, a lack of positive experiences in effective regulation of emotion, insecurity about separating from the caregiver, and poverty of exploration may contribute to difficulties in the negotiation of separation individuation issues in toddlerhood (Sroufe, in press). Early experiences of chronic dysregulation may support a self-regulatory style characterized by heightened arousal and exaggerated emotional expression. Continued preoccupation with the caregiver (including frustration behavior with the goal of involving the caregiver) may prevent these children from engaging in environmental opportunities and making use of caregiver support. Such experiences are likely to support a view of self as unworthy and/or incompetent.

Empirical Findings

Empirical findings support the relationship between early attachment experience and patterns of adaptation based on stage-salient issues of the toddler period: self-regulation under caregiver guidance (Sroufe, 1989a, 1990b). Assessments in infancy predict key aspects of toddler functioning: inner security; feelings of self-worth, self-reliance, and personal power of the emerging self; and the development of autonomy (Bates et al., 1985; Gove, 1983; Londerville & Main, 1981; Matas, Arend, & Sroufe, 1978).

In an early longitudinal study of middle-income families in Minnesota (Matas et al., 1978), toddlers were assessed in a tool-using/problem-solving situation designed to challenge the children's cognitive and motivational capacity and their ability to draw on personal and environmental resources. Assessment focused on the ability to become engaged in and persist with tasks, to maintain organization in the face of arousal, and to directly signal and make use of adult support. Compared with toddlers who had been insecurely attached as infants, toddlers who had been secure in their early attachments were found to be more enthusiastic, persistent, flexible, and affectively positive in the tool/problem situation. Secure children were more smoothly cooperative with their mothers, informing the mothers when a problem was beyond their own resources, attending to the mothers' verbal and postural cues, and complying with their requests. As predicted by numerous theorists (Bowlby, 1969/1982; Erikson, 1963; Kohut, 1977; Mahler et al., 1975), infants with histories of well-regulated relationships with caregivers (i.e., infants who sought out caregivers when needed, actively achieved physical contact when distressed, and used contact to support encounters with novelty) had moved toward more autonomous functioning by age 2 than those with less well-coordinated relationships.

Toddlers who had been avoidant as infants sought little assistance from their mothers even with the most difficult problem in the tool-using situation (Matas et al., 1978). They showed little physical contact or affective investment. Anger was expressed indirectly through noncompliance and object-directed aggression. Infants assessed as anxious, resistant were easily frustrated in the problem situation. They were negativistic, fussy, and angry, and engaged with their mothers in power struggles that took precedence over problem solving.

The findings from the problem-solving task in the Minnesota study have been replicated in middle-income (Bates et al., 1985) and high-risk poverty (Gove, 1983) samples. In addition, Bates and his colleagues extended the generalizability of results by relating problem-solving factors to home observations. Toddler functioning in the tool task was predicted by 6-, 13-, and 24-month home observation factors describing both verbal and behavioral interaction (Frankel & Bates, 1984).

Attachment Variation and Patterns of Adaptation in Childhood

Self-reliance, flexible self-management, and positive self-evaluations continue to be salient issues in early childhood. In contrast to the guided regulation of toddlerhood, however, the preschool child is expected to follow rules and prohibitions and protect himself or herself from overwhelming stimulation and disorganizing feelings even without adult supervision.

The preschool child assumes a greater role in self-regulation through processes of identification (Breger, 1974). Caregiver standards for behavioral control and patterns of regulating emotion and maintaining organization are internalized. As a result, emotional reactions are based less on the affective response of parents and more on the child's own standards for performance. Emotions such as guilt and pride (based on self-evaluations) are distinguished from more global feelings of anxiety and joy (Kochanska, 1993; Lewis, Alessandri, & Sullivan, 1992; Sroufe, 1979b). Internalized standards lead to an improved capacity to direct, monitor, and inhibit behavior (Arend, 1983; Kopp, Krakow, & Vaughn, 1983). The child develops new ways of coping with frustration and modulating emotional expression (e.g., aggression).

The developing internalization of caregiver standards is also reflected in children's concern for others, shown in early childhood. The preschool child responds to and seeks to make reparations for accidents or injury to others (Cole, Barrett, & Zahn-Waxler, 1992). Rudiments of perspective-taking ability and empathy (Flavell, 1977; Radke-Yarrow, Zahn-Waxler, & Chapman, 1983) enable the child to establish a truly goal-corrected partnership (Bowlby, 1969/1982; Sroufe, 1989a, 1990b).

Protective processes (defenses) evolve as part of the internalization of regulatory schemes, promoting the child's move toward self-reliance or emotional independence (Sroufe, 1979b). For preschoolers, self-reliance involves the ability to operate in the environment without constant attention from adults, but to rely on adults when injured or to share experiences (Sroufe, Fox, & Pancake, 1983). Emotional dependence is seen in children who hover or cling to adult figures at the expense of exploration and in those who act out in order to receive attention.

The development of emotional self-sufficiency is facilitated through cognitive and linguistic advances and through imaginative play. With the rise of symbolic capacity, the child develops the ability to understand that actions may have positive as well as negative outcomes and that outcomes may be delayed. The child develops a shared awareness of experience, recognizing that the caregiver is aware of and may even oppose his or her plans. By intentionally disrupting the dyadic synchrony and purposefully acting to reinstate the cooperative relationship with the parent, the child acquires increased confidence in the constancy of the relationship (trust) and the ability of the self to maintain organization (Sander, 1975; Sroufe, 1990b).

Through fantasy play and the use of imagination, the child imitates caregiver behavior, expresses vital feelings, and works through conflicts in a controlled or safe environment (Breger, 1974). Through play, the child experiments with relationships, trying out and experiencing feedback from his or her own actions, all of which contribute to the child's sense of ownership of acts and intentions. Individual differences in fantasy play may be an important indicator of emotional regulation during this period.

A developing sense of self and capacities for self-regulation provide the basis for establishing relationships with peers, a central issue of early childhood. Adequate peer involvement requires the abilities to understand rules of reciprocity, to be emotionally engaged, to understand and respond to feelings of others, and to regulate tension in social interactions (Sroufe, Schork, Motti, Lawroski, & LaFreniere, 1984). These capacities continue to provide the basis for peer relations in middle childhood, when challenges include effective functioning in group settings, mastering peer group norms, and forming loyal friendships (Cicchetti et al., 1988; Elicker, Englund, & Sroufe, 1992; Park, 1991; Sullivan, 1953). Because peer involvement draws on the child's capacities for emotion regulation, these relationships represent good indicators of individual functioning during the preschool and middle childhood periods, predicting later adaptive and maladaptive functioning. Defective peer relationships have been found to be a powerful, broad-band predictor of later pathology (Cowen, Pederson, Babijian, Izzo, & Trost, 1973; Kohlberg, Ricks, & Snarey, 1984; Robins, 1978; Roff, Sells, & Golden, 1972), and the ability to garner social support has been shown to be a prominent buffer or protective factor (Rutter, 1988).

Individual styles of adaptation with respect to self-control, emotional regulation, fantasy play, empathy, and peer relationships become more distinct during the early childhood period. Features of this more stable organization of self, or personality, include characteristic patterns of regulating emotion and arousal, expectations of self and other in the regulatory process, and variations in openness to emotional experience.

Qualitative Differences in Attachment Organization

Attachment theory makes clear predictions with regard to individual differences in negotiating these developmental issues and the emergence of patterns of adaptation. Bowlby (1973) theorized that children with histories of secure attachment or experiences of early "effective dependence" (directly expressing dependence on the caregiver) would be more self-reliant or emotionally independent later than children with histories of anxious attachment. In contrast, infants with avoidant histories who remain aloof or fail to seek contact when distressed may be viewed as being precociously independent. In the Bowlby/Ainsworth theory, such behavior is viewed rather as an indicator of an ineffective attachment relationship, which would impede the growth of self-reliance.

Secure Attachment. Children who have participated in responsive and smoothly regulated attachment relationships are expected to carry forward a capacity for self-regulation, a core sense of security and effectance, and a fundamental confidence in others as caring and in the self as worthy. Children with secure histories have experienced a range of emotions and inner aims as acceptable and the self as competent in maintaining some degree of emotional regulation. Based on such experience, these children have developed positive expectations of self and others in relationships, and the capacity to flexibly regulate emotion, including abilities to contain impulses when necessary, to express feelings when appropriate, and to become emotionally invested in activity (Elicker et al., 1992). For secure children, an understanding of relationships (including peer relationships) includes features of emotional openness, reciprocity, and responsiveness (Sroufe, 1983; Sroufe & Fleeson, 1986).

For children with avoidant and resistant histories, distortions in early dyadic regulatory processes serve as prototypes for individual patterns of overly rigid self-regulation or dysregulation. Children who are not able to flexibly regulate emotion and lack experiences of effectance in relationships may be expected to be vulnerable to feelings of low self-esteem, a sense of incompetence, and distortions in interactive patterns with peers (Sroufe, in press).

Anxious, Avoidant Attachment. Children with histories of avoidant attachment who have been forced toward precocious independence by harsh or emotionally unavailable caregiving have experienced and internalized a restricted range of emotions as acceptable and rigid patterns of regulating emotion. Based on these experiences, children are expected to exhibit patterns of functioning characterized by underlying anger or negativism that children have learned not to express at its source. Avoidant children may develop individual styles—characterized by hostility and aggression, emotional isolation, or profound disconnection from experience—that distance feelings and people (Sroufe, 1983).

Anxious, Resistant Attachment. From histories of inconsistent care, resistant children lack experience in well-coordinated dyadic regulation as a guide to self-management and lack confidence in the caregiving relationship (self and other) as a source of regulation. As a result, these children may demonstrate individual styles that tend to postpone autonomous functioning (Main, in press). Anxious resistant histories may leave children easily frustrated, overstimulated, impulsive, and overtly anxious, or, alternately, dependent, passive, and helpless (Sroufe, 1983).

Empirical Findings

Early Childhood. In accord with Bowlby's theory, prospective longitudinal research has found children with histories of secure attachment, compared to anxiously attached groups, to be higher on measures of self-esteem, agency, self-confidence, self-reliance, and ego resiliency, all based on ratings of judges blind to history (Sroufe, 1983; Waters et al., 1979). For example, in a sample of low SES preschoolers, all 16 secure cases had positive correlations with the Q-sort-based ego-resiliency criterion of J. H. Block and J. Block (1980), and 13 of 15 children with avoidant histories had negative correlations. Thus, as predicted by attachment theory, children with secure attachment relationships had internalized the capacity for flexible, well-modulated expression of impulses, desires, and feelings. Likewise, differences in dependency, as rated by teachers and bolstered by ample detailed behavioral observation, showed marked, almost nonoverlapping differences between secure and anxious groups in preschool (Sroufe et al., 1983), a powerful confirmation of Bowlby's theory.

Given these differences in personal competence, it is not surprising that children with secure histories also have been found to be competent with peers (LaFreniere & Sroufe, 1985; Sroufe, 1983; Sroufe et al., 1990; Waters et al., 1979). As assessed through sociometrics, direct observation, and teacher reports, children with secure attachment histories were more effective in peer groups and formed deeper relationships with individual partners (Pancake, 1985; Sroufe, 1983). They approached and responded to others with more positive and less negative affect (Sroufe et al., 1984). They more often had friends, were more capable of reciprocity, and with more socially oriented, frequently imitated, popular, and empathic (Kestenbaum, Farber, & Sroufe, 1989). The empathy finding marks another strong confirmation of the Bowlby relational perspective. Having been part of a responsive dyadic system, the child is later responsive to others.

Three additional studies (Lieberman, 1977; Park & Waters, 1989; Seuss, Grossmann, & Sroufe, 1992) have supported the prediction of continuity between infant-parent relationship and early peer competence. Attachment security has been related to peer reciprocity and the absence of negative behavior in play sessions at home (Lieberman, 1977) and to social competence ratings concerning quality of play, conflict resolution, and occurrence of problem behaviors in preschool (Seuss et al., 1992). Using contemporaneous Q-sort assessments of attachment, Park and Waters (1989) found that secure-secure friendship pairs were more harmonious, less controlling, more responsive, and happier than secure-insecure pairs in preschool.

In studies of peer competence, well-functioning children demonstrated a variety of patterns of healthy adaptation. Some children were reserved and quiet, others boisterous and energetic, and physical dominance influenced popularity among boys' and girls' groups differently. What the children had in common were the abilities to manage themselves, to adjust their behavior in keeping with requirements and opportunities of the circumstances, to utilize resources in the environment effectively, and to remain emotionally engaged with peers.

Although children with avoidant and resistant attachment histories received similar ratings of overall poor functioning on molar measures in these studies, the two groups were distinguished by some differences in patterns of behavior (Sroufe et al., 1983). For example, although both groups were rated high on dependency, avoidant children were found to be slow to show their dependency needs. They often approached teachers indirectly or in restricted or safe conditions in times of low stress, and frequently failed to seek out teachers when injured, disappointed, or stressed. Avoidant children appeared to elicit punitive reactions from teachers, reproducing familiar relationship patterns and expectations of rejection (Sroufe & Fleeson, 1988). Teachers demonstrated more discipline and control, lower expectations of compliance, less warmth, and, at times, anger toward avoidant children. When observing distress in other children, those with avoidant histories were more likely to respond in an antiempathic manner, showing inappropriate affect and behavior (Kestenbaum et al., 1989); for example, some ridiculed a crying child or poked an injured one. Peer interactions with avoidant children were characterized by frequent hostility and aggression, or, alternately, by emotional distance (Cicchetti, Lynch, Shonk, & Todd Manly, 1992; LaFreniere & Sroufe, 1985; Sroufe, 1983). Paired with play partners, avoidant children were identified as victimizers, systematically exploiting the other by hitting or physically punishing or through derogation and hostility (Troy & Sroufe, 1987). The negativity and hostility that characterize peer relationships of avoidant children often perpetuate a cycle of rejection and social isolation.

Children with resistant attachment histories demonstrated dependency needs in a chronic low-level style, constantly staying physically near or oriented to teachers. These children waited for teachers to take the initiative to invite them to participate. Preschool teachers seemed to perceive the emotional immaturity of resistant children (Sroufe & Fleeson, 1988), showing them more nurturance and tolerance, making allowances for them, and accepting their minor infractions of classroom rules. Because peer relations of resistant children also were characterized by immaturity and social ineptitude, these children had difficulty sustaining close relationships. Although capable of showing empathy toward other distressed children, resistant children demonstrated difficulty establishing appropriate personal boundaries (for example, going for comfort themselves when another child was injured). In peer interactions with bullies or oppressors, resistant children were vulnerable to exploitation and victimization. With socially adept play partners, resistant children were nurtured and led. Both patterns of interaction supported and perpetuated models of the self as immature and incompetent.

Middle Childhood. In the Minnesota study, attachment history has been related to measures of social competence in a camp setting in middle childhood (Elicker et al., 1992). Ten-year-old children classified as securely attached as infants differed from anxious groups on molar measures of adaptation, including social competence and ego resilience on Q-sort descriptions of overall personality (Urban, Carlson, Egeland, & Sroufe, 1991). Securely attached children were consistently ranked higher than children with anxious histories, on broad-band measures of social competence, emotional health/self-esteem, and self-confidence. Children with secure histories spent a greater portion of time with peers and less time with adults or in isolation, and were rated as more socially adept with peers. These children were more likely to display positive biases in evaluating the performance of their own peer group and to form camp friendships. They were attracted to others with secure histories, and the quality of their friendships was more often characterized by openness, trust, coordination, and complexity of activity.

Children with anxious attachment histories were rated by counselors as more dependent on adults, and were observed to spend dramatically more time interacting with them (Elicker et al., 1992; Urban et al., 1991). In particular, children with resistant histories were found more often to be recipients of adult-initiated contact—specifically, support and nurturance—than were children with avoidant histories. Compared to children with secure and resistant histories, children with anxious avoidant histories showed undifferentiated levels of interpersonal sensitivity in their inferences about thoughts and feelings of others in their peer group, and children with anxious resistant histories displayed negative biases in evaluating the performance of peers. Thus, resistant children were not deficient in level of understanding of others' internal states, but had some negative biases (e.g., anxieties or anger) with regard to peer relations. Avoidant children exhibited both impaired interpersonal understanding and more negative social-evaluative biases.

In a German longitudinal study (Grossmann & Grossmann, 1991), early attachment history was related to children's reported behaviors in stressful situations. Children with secure histories more readily reported negative feelings and more often reported relationship-oriented strategies (e.g., seeking help or comfort from another individual). In contrast, children with avoidant histories reported attempting to work out problems alone. Children's peer relationships, as reported by the children themselves as well as their parents, were also related to early caregiving histories. Children with early secure histories reportedly had one or a few good friends who were considered trustworthy and reliable. Children with avoidant or resistant histories reported having either no friends or "many" friends without being able to specify their names. They more often reported being exploited, ridiculed, or excluded from group activities by peers.

Many of the findings reviewed here also hold up into adolescence. Thus, 15-year-old children with histories of secure attachment were observed to be more competent with peers and less dependent on counselors in a camp setting (Sroufe, Carlson, & Shulman, 1993).

It is expected that strong continuity across this long period hinges, at least in part, on continuity in environment. If there is notable change in caregiving circumstances, notable changes in the child will follow. In fact, research has shown that change in the fundamental quality of adaptation is related to changing stability and social support in the caregiving environment, both in the preschool years (Erickson, Egeland, & Sroufe, 1985) and the early elementary school years (Egeland, Kalkoske, Gottesman, & Erickson, 1990).

PROCESSES AND MECHANISMS OF CONTINUITY IN ATTACHMENT THEORY

Theoretical Ideas

Self-Regulatory Processes in Developmental Continuity

From an organizational/adaptational perspective, several mechanisms are believed to underlie continuity in adaptation (Sroufe, 1988). As stated above, continuity in both environmental influences (e.g., quality of care) and individual traits supports stability in individual functioning over time. A third factor is prior history of adaptation (Sroufe & Egeland, 1991). Continuity is viewed as a transactional process involving an active self-regulating organism and the environment. From this perspective, the child actively participates in constructing his or her experience. First, individuals behave in ways that elicit from the environment responses that support prior adaptation. For example, the aggressive child behaves in antisocial ways that elicit punishment and rejection from teachers and peers, deepening feelings of alienation. Second, individuals make choices, selectively engaging aspects of the environment that support a particular adaptive style; for example, a child doubting the availability of others may isolate himself or herself and fail to experience supportive peer experiences. Third, individuals interpret new and ambiguous situations in ways that are consistent with earlier experience. For example, some children interpret ambiguous social gestures as implying hostile intent (Dodge, Pettit, McClaskey, & Brown, 1986; Suess et al., 1992) and respond in ways that alienate others. These processes presume some internal self-regulatory mechanisms as integral in guiding the transactional process.

From a developmental perspective, these self-regulatory structures and mechanisms are viewed as characteristic modes of affect regulation and associated expectations, attitudes, and beliefs internalized from patterns of dyadic regulation (Sander, 1975; Stern, 1985). These processes, or internalized "models" (Bowlby, 1980), serve not as static traits, but as guides to ongoing social interaction, supporting the maintenance of existing patterns of adaptation. What is incorporated from the caregiving experience are not specific behavioral features, but the quality and patterning of relationships, mediated by affect (Sroufe, 1990b).

Processes of internalization or incorporation of experience are critical at all levels of functioning, in biological as well as psychological domains (Edelman, 1987; Kuo, 1967; Magnusson, 1992). Such processes are of great theoretical and practical importance, not only because they may explain continuity in individual development but also because they may lead to an understanding of pathogenesis itself. From an organizational view of normal and deviant socioemotional development, the development of the attachment relationship and its internalized mechanisms represents the emergence of a fundamental coordination of developmental processes. Developing attentional, sensory, motoric, cognitive, and affective processes become organized, with respect to the regulation of emotion, around the primary caregiver. Emerging patterns of dyadic regulation guide behavioral organization and the sharing of intimate experience; in time, these patterns become characteristic modes of individual regulation.

Representational Organization and Strategies of Communication

From the perspective of developmental attachment theory, internalized regulatory processes evolve from biologically predisposed behaviors and expressions that have become organized and have been assigned meaning through repeated early experiences with the caregiver. These survival-enhancing regulatory patterns emerge from relatively undifferentiated abilities in early infancy. With development, increasingly differentiated capacities of perception, cognition, language, and behavior are coordinated with existing patterns of regulating and expressing emotion and maintaining organization. In well-functioning organisms, individually developing processes are integrated into flexible patterns that vary with function and context. Whether the organization of regulatory patterns follows a flexible and integrative course depends on the history of dyadic experience, individual capacities that have evolved from such experiences, and opportunities in the environment (Breger, 1974).

In early infancy, regulatory patterns consist of sensorimotor (Piaget & Inhelder, 1969; Rovee-Collier, 1993) or procedural (Mandler, 1983; Tulving, 1985) memory processes. Sensorimotor schemata are thought to be preconscious in nature, continuing to influence behavior in the face of contradictory information and the development of more sophisticated and conscious memory processes. These early schemata, or "ways of being with the other" (Stern, 1994), integrate diverse simultaneous aspects of experience: affects, movements, and visual and tactile stimuli. All are organized around basic functions and, in the case of attachment, around the regulation of emotion.

Early sensorimotor schemata give rise to the capacity to symbolize, which, in turn, provides the basis for language (Piaget & Inhelder, 1969). With the development of language, information may be acquired not only through perceptions or observations but also through what others say about behavior, the self, and relationships (Bowlby, 1980; Stern, 1985; Sullivan, 1953). Experiences may be compared over time and with those of others, and elaborated patterns of emotional expression become possible (Nelson, 1992). Interpretations from others may fulfill a clarifying and correcting function or, if they diverge from the child's direct experience with the world, may miscommunicate and create distortions and confusions (Bretherton, 1987, 1990; Crittenden & Ainsworth, 1989).

Language allows information extracted from experience to be recategorized into differentiated memory processes. These include mechanisms such as semantic memory processes related to the formation of generalizations (e.g., nature of relationships), and episodic or autobiographical memory processes related to anecdotal or basic information coordinated with memories of the self as participant (Tulving, 1989). The developing child responds to internal cues and outer stimuli in terms of this increasingly complex organization of regulatory and representational patterns (Bretherton, 1987). Individual differences in response relate in part to differences in the flexible coordination and employment of these interrelated processes.

With the gradual transfer of regulatory functions from the caregiving relationship to the child, developing motoric, cognitive, and linguistic patterns are engaged in ways that maintain existing regulatory styles. In particular, cognitive mechanisms (e.g., expectations, attitudes, beliefs) that determine ways in which the individual organizes, interprets, and makes use of information are viewed as central to the process of self-regulation (Reider & Cicchetti, 1989).

Qualitative Differences in Attachment Organization

Secure Attachment. In well-regulated dyadic relationships, infants experience a range of affective signals (e.g., expressions of joy and pleasure as well as signals of distress and anger) as acceptable (to be shared within social relationships) (Stern, 1985). No single emotion dominates. The caregiver assists the infant in coping constructively with negative emotions by remaining engaged with the child during times of anger and sadness, thereby transforming the infant's feelings into a tolerable form (Bion, 1962). The caregiver aids the child in distinguishing what is external and what is internal, and in acquiring a sense of mastery or manageability and of the availability of others to assist in arousal. Thus, the experience of security is based not on the denial of negative affect or arousal, but on the regulation of affect and the ability to temporarily tolerate negative affects in order to achieve mastery over threatening or frustrating situations (Kobak, 1985). Well-integrated regulatory patterns derived from early experience provide the basis for an integrated sense of self—the experience of self as a coherent whole.

Critical to this process are infant experiences of effectance in the caregiving relationship, experiences in which the caregiver responds to the infant's needs or communications in understandable ways. From such experiences, the infant develops confidence in the ability to influence what happens in his or her world in a meaningful way. Through attempts to act on problems and engagement with others, the child develops capacities for emotional and cognitive coordination, integrating aspects of experience and coordinating compensatory skills across naturally occurring fractionations/separations (Breger, 1974).

Through experiences of well-coordinated regulation, or "affective attunement" (Stern, 1985), developing cognitive processes and linguistic patterns are integrated with early regulatory patterns. Emerging representational processes reflect the positive experiences of self and other in managing emotion or arousal. Flexibility in coordination of regulatory processes and a reservoir of positive regulatory experiences provide the basis for short- and long-term adaptation to the environment. Environmental cues are flexibly perceived and interpreted, behavior varies with context, and experience is integrated with existing patterns of functioning. Internalized mechanisms that include experience of the self as competent promote engagement and purposeful action in the social world and in response to challenges of maturation and social demands.

From a history of responsive caregiving, the secure infant has developed a strategy of openly expressing attachment behavior and feeling. The secure child expects that such expression (communications of distress or desire for closeness) will reduce distress and increase a sense of emotional security. For this child, the awareness and expression of particularly negative emotion has a positive effect on organization. As a result, emotional information is readily accepted and communication of feelings of distress, fear, and anger to the caregiver is open and direct. Defensive mechanisms are flexibly employed to maintain organization temporarily until more effective means of coping can be utilized. From experience in open interactions, the child builds beliefs about the self as worthy of love and effective in gaining it from others (Bowlby, 1973, 1980; Kobak & Shaver, 1987). The concordant sense of confidence encourages the child to explore the external world of real events as well as the internal world of thoughts and feelings.

In less well-regulated dyadic relationships, a disjunction exists between inner experience and outward expression. If the caregiver is rejecting of needs for comfort or only intermittently supportive, the child's expression of distress and his or her attempts to gain reassurance fail to elicit care and lead only to heightened anxiety. A sense of organization or security is not maintained through the expression of attachment feeling or behavior, and the two levels function separately.

Anxious, Avoidant Attachment. In a relationship characterized by rejection or overly rigid regulatory patterns, the child may experience particular thoughts, impulses, feelings, and actions (e.g., proximity seeking, signals of distress) as unacceptable or confusing. Such thoughts, feelings, and actions are not integrated with experience, and their arousal leads to internal conflict. To minimize conflict, the expression and, in time, the experience and perception of cues that arouse such feelings are defensively restricted or cut off and not consciously perceived as part of the self. Ideas, wishes, actions, and emotions experienced as unacceptable by external or internal standards are disowned or split off from awareness and from one's sense of conscious self.

When early regulation of emotional experience has been overly restrictive, vital emotions (e.g., fears, joys, rages, pleasures) that have been experienced as unacceptable, in time, are more likely to be experienced as arising outside of the existing organization of self—externally imposed or just happening to the self. The self is likely to be viewed as "one to whom things happen" rather than as a competent active agent, the legacy of a well-regulated relationship. Defensive patterns are perpetuated in part by such a passive view of self in relation to others. Aspects of functioning are no longer part of conscious social interchange and no longer subject to social influence or revision.

With development (without intervention or alternate experiences of caregiving), more complex cognitive, linguistic, and behavioral patterns become organized around the separation of aspects of thought and feeling. Attempts to regulate underlying affect may result in further distortions of behavior, language, and thought. The child may become increasingly socially compliant, expressing vital thoughts and feelings (the "inner self") only in fantasy play or activity. Hostility, aggression, and desire for closeness may be expressed indirectly or may be directed away from the original source (Kobak & Sceery, 1988; Main, 1973; Pastor, 1981).

For the avoidant child with a history of overly rigid regulatory experience, negative expectations are associated with the processing of emotional information, particularly the awareness and communication of distress and anger (Kobak & Shaver, 1987). To reduce anxiety, incoming information leading to distress is increasingly excluded, and the expression of emotion that may heighten conflict and alienation is minimized or cut off (Cassidy & Kobak, 1988). Based on fundamental expectations of caregiving that include the rejection of signals of distress and desire for closeness, the avoidant child comes to experience the self as unworthy of love and comfort (Bowlby, 1973, 1980). These fundamental expectations and feelings are modified by a defensive strategy. Painful feelings associated with rejection are minimized, and views of the self as independent and invulnerable to disappointment are supported. In a similar manner, resentment toward the parent is mastered through the reconstruction of belief systems whereby the caregiver is viewed as strong and above reproach.

Anxious, Resistant Attachment. When dyadic interaction has been chaotic or inconsistent and arousal has not been well regulated, intermittent responses from the caregiver support a constant state of arousal in the child. Anxiety regarding the caregiving relationship may be evident in the child's exaggerated displays of attachment feeling and behavior and/or extreme passivity. From a history of chronic dysregulation, the resistant child develops uncertain or negative expectations regarding the processing and expression of emotions (Kobak & Shaver, 1987). The child may lack both the necessary confidence in self and others and positive experience in regulation (effective means of reading affective cues and of modulating and communicating emotions; Bell & Ainsworth, 1972) to guide individual efforts or flexible experimentation with regulation. Based on such experience, the resistant child builds expectations about the self as unworthy and lacking in personal resources to cope with distress (Bowlby, 1973, 1980). Experiences of chronic dysregulation and corresponding expectations of the self as helpless or incompetent leave individuals vulnerable to continued dysregulation and passivity in the face of challenge, without an awareness of the source of frustration. Heightened awareness of the self and attentiveness to the attachment figure foster beliefs that exaggerate personal difficulties and prevent perspective-taking and the accurate formulation of beliefs about others in relationships.

Patterns of restricted regulation or chronic dysregulation evolve as protective mechanisms against continued disorganization or extreme arousal. The patterns represent strategies for maintaining organization in the context of selective caregiving insensitivities or restrictions on emotional communication (e.g., caregiver failure to aid infant regulation of overwhelming feelings by perceiving, recognizing, or responding to infant communications). For example, children with histories of early dysregulation may employ perceptive skills primarily to monitor and anticipate actions and emotions of others in relationships, and, as a result, may be less aware of their own internal states. Such protective or defensive strategies may compromise the ability of these children to use emotions to communicate and reflect on experience and to gain comfort or closeness from others.

Distortions of the early dyadic regulatory process serve as prototypes for later dysregulation. Emerging developmental capacities (cognitive, linguistic, behavioral) become organized with respect to restricted regulation or emotional dysfunction. Organization exists, but only in distorted or poorly integrated forms. With development, individuals construct more complex and elaborated types of defensive coordination, separating multiple components of complex relations.

Defensive Processes

Defensive mechanisms refer to processes that maintain aspects of experience compartmentalized from or unintegrated with other organizational aspects of the self. Defensive processes operate in such a way that current modes of perceiving and interpreting situations, feelings, and actions are determined or strongly influenced by earlier responses to emotionally significant events (daily interactions as well as traumatic experiences). To minimize conflict or pain associated with such experiences, aspects of individual functioning are modified, and portions of experience are cut off from conscious processing (Bowlby, 1973). As a result, individual behavioral and affective responses are inflexibly applied and may be maladapted to new situations and opportunities (Bowlby, 1988).

Drawing on work from neurophysiology and cognitive psychology, Bowlby (1980) described defensive mechanisms in terms of normal human processes. Bowlby noted, for example, that humans and other organisms do not process all incoming information at the same level. Information is monitored and processed, and inferences may be drawn from input that does not reach usual levels of awareness (Clyman, 1991; Kihlstrom, 1987). Bowlby employed the term *defensive exclusion* to suggest that individuals rely on similar mechanisms to exclude information that has previously led to disorganization or conflict, and to maintain control over anger and distress too intense for behavioral organization (Heinicke & Westheimer, 1966). Bowlby distinguished the adaptive function of selective exclusion from the varying adaptive value of defensive processes motivated by painful affect.

Defensive processes are thought to evolve from the natural separation of processes, states, and skills that occur routinely in early development. For example, Harter (1986) found that the development of emotion recognition starts with the ability to recognize single emotions and proceeds to capacities to group similar emotions, understand different emotions occurring sequentially, and recognize simultaneously different emotions about the same situation or person. As Bowlby noted, the natural separation of processes is distinguished from controlled separation in defense mechanisms motivated by internal conflict. Early forms of normal functioning, however, may provide patterns for defensive processes when ongoing conflict or trauma interferes with the normal integration of skills and processes or disrupts established modes of functioning.

The flexible employment of defensive mechanisms is thought to allow the individual to become aware of and adjust to experience, and to put aside wishes and feelings until he or she is capable of coping with or working through such feelings (Breger, 1974; Epstein, 1973, 1991). Disturbances in development occur when the moratorium is not reopened and defensive solutions become rigid, pervasive, and not integrated with development, or when inadequate defenses allow the individual to be overwhelmed (Epstein, 1973). For example, it is not avoidance per se (that can be identified in all infants), but the marked or pervasive tendency to avoid that is thought to be an early indicator of disturbance in infant-mother relationships (Escalona, 1968).

With increasing control over the environment, the child maintains defensive organization in more complex and elaborated ways. These involve modifications of encoding and retrieval functions, and alterations in the coordination of memory processes—in addition to the control and manipulation of attention (Tulving, 1989).

Bowlby (1980) noted that, to be effective, defense mechanisms must control both information that activates particular behavior and feelings and the display of such behavior and feelings. The more information that is controlled, the less crucial it becomes to control behavior. Distortions in encoding may be seen in perceptual exclusion, whereby aspects of events or experience are excluded as a result of active deletion or distortion. Distortions in retrieval processes may result in an inability to recall information or make connections among memory processes. Such modifications may result in more complex distortions in memory and a lack of information available for interpretation (Cassidy & Kobak, 1988). Cognitive representations of an event or events may be separated from normally accompanying affect (i.e., "isolation of affect," according to A. Freud, 1946), affective elements may be separated along a positive/negative dimension (splitting), or experiences may be disconnected from the self. All such mechanisms are thought to be motivated by anxiety, representing attempts to deal with internal conflict through a process of disowning or dissociating parts of the self, relegating them to the category that Sullivan (1953) calls the "not me."

Bowlby (1988a) suggested that experiences that tend to be excluded or distorted include those that parents wish children not to know, those in which parents treated children in ways unbearable to think about, and those in which children have done or thought things about which they feel unbearably guilty or ashamed. The exclusion of thoughts, feelings, and impulses to action that are natural responses to extreme events results in distorted representational patterns and difficulties in personality functioning. The child may develop expectations about relationships or the self that dismiss the importance of giving and receiving care and minimize negative components of the self or other that are experienced as distressing.

The defensive distortion of representational processes may result in the formation of multiple incompatible belief systems (Bowlby, 1980). In a simple form, one system of beliefs (of which a person may be more consciously aware) may distort a second set of beliefs (more closely based on experience), which continues to influence thoughts and behavior (Bowlby, 1980). One explanation for individual continuity may be that such unconscious, underlying processes are no longer a part of conscious social interchange and, as a result, no longer subject to environmental feedback and revision. This was the essence of Freud's idea of the "dynamic unconscious" (Loevinger, 1976).

Dissociation. The general category of defensive mechanisms includes the more specific compartmentalization of experiences referred to as dissociation (e.g., Kihlstrom, 1987; Putnam, 1989). The phenomenon of dissociation is characterized by the coexistence or the simultaneous activity of two or more organizational aspects of personality within one individual (Putnam, 1989). These systems are viewed as relatively coherent patterns of behavior with sufficient complexity to represent some degree of internal organization (Hilgard, 1977). If repeated, these symptoms or alternative identities may develop identifying characteristics and be capable of independent life and development (Putnam, 1989). In ordinary experience, a sense of wholeness in organization is maintained through continuity of memories (Hilgard, 1977), and one is aware of variations in behavior and roles. Within the phenomenon of dissociation, however, subordinate systems appropriate to varying roles are disconnected from one other. Whereas in the normal defensive process, unavailable ideas are largely bound up with affect and impulse and enter consciousness only indirectly, in dissociative phenomena, an amnesic barrier exists among usually available memories (Hilgard, 1977). Unavailable memories need have no special affective or impulsive significance.

As with general defensive mechanisms, dissociative phenomena are thought to originate in traumatic, potentially disorganizing early experiences (Putnam, 1989). In harsh or particularly chaotic caregiving contexts, the process of regulation—the consolidation of self across behavioral states and acquisition of control over modulation of states—is disrupted. Recurring trauma in the context of inadequate or overly restrictive caregiving increases the level of arousal and the need to separate or compartmentalize overwhelming affects and memories. Dissociative mechanisms serve survival functions by providing for automatization of behaviors (minimum expenditure of conscious control over behavior), escape from reality constraints, containment of overwhelming memories or feelings, and, in extreme form, assignment of painful feelings to alternate personalities (Ludwig, 1983). Variations in outward manifestations result from differences in individual psychological capacities, caregiving experience, and social and cultural factors (Ludwig, 1983).

The psychobiological mechanisms of dissociation are thought to underlie a wide variety of altered forms of consciousness, including minor disturbances of everyday functioning determined by the modification of controls (daydreaming) and more serious dissociative disorders (e.g., conversion hysteria, multiple personality disorder, fugue states) (Hilgard, 1977; Ludwig, 1983).

Summary

Attachment organization is viewed as a system of internal structures and related interactive processes that emerge with development and provide the basis of personality functioning. The organization regulates the processing of emotional information and provides direction in interpersonal relationships. Developing cognitive and linguistic capabilities increase the complexity of processing of emotional information and the meaning assigned to experience. More complex representations and beliefs concerning relationships with caregivers, the self, and the world develop. In optimal functioning, communication remains open, and meaning and affect are related directly and flexibly to experience. In less than optimal functioning, defensive mechanisms distort or dissociate meaning and affective aspects of experience as a means of maintaining felt security.

According to attachment theory, conscious processing of early emotional attachment-related experience plays a crucial role in the continued reappraisal and modification of unrealistic or maladaptive beliefs and representational models (Bowlby, 1969/1982). Bowlby defined conscious processing as the inspection or examination of overlearned and automated action systems and representational models linked to them. Such conscious processing depends in part on the nature of representations or memory processes: some types of representations are more accessible to awareness; other, more biologically preprogrammed or routinized schemata may be more difficult to access (Kihlstrom, 1987). This examination is itself thought to be a product of attachment strategies.

Conscious processing, and the modification of representations and belief systems based on experience, involves the ability to link representations, affective experience, and the self as agent or experiencer (James, 1980). Such links are forged in early relationships where emotion is openly communicated and the self is experienced as actor, as competent in maintaining or reestablishing internal organization and influencing relationships with others. In contrast, for individuals with insecure attachment histories, defensive strategies evolved from early dysregulation are likely to maintain distortions in patterns of emotion regulation and associated patterns of expectations, attitudes, and beliefs. The capacity for conscious processing and metacognitive control has been limited. Individuals may have difficulty viewing objectively feelings and thoughts of self and others, observing inconsistencies in beliefs, and separating the actions of others from beliefs about the self. In turn, inaccurate impressions of thoughts and feelings of others may provide the basis for continued vulnerability and distortions in relationships.

Empirical Support of Processes and Mechanisms of Continuity

Research on Self-Regulation and Affective Expression in Childhood

Claims regarding continuity from patterns of early attachment relationships (dyadic regulation of emotion) to individual styles of self-regulation in early childhood have been supported empirically. In the Minnesota longitudinal study (Sroufe et al., 1984), assessments of infant attachment at 12 and 18 months predicted affective expression and control on observer checklists and Q-sort measures in preschool. Children who were securely attached in infancy were rated significantly higher on measures of composite positive affect and lower on negative affect than children who had been classified as anxiously attached. Those with secure histories also were observed to be more affectively expressive and more affectively responsive to others. Attachment assessments and measures of affect in toddlerhood were also related to measures of social competence in preschool.

In a study of children in middle-income families, those who had been securely attached as infants scored higher on measures of ego resiliency in kindergarten (Arend, Gove, & Sroufe, 1979). Ego resiliency is defined as the ability to respond flexibly and resourcefully to challenge, in contrast to ego brittleness or inability to respond to changing requirements of the situation and a tendency to become disorganized in the face of novelty or stress (Block & Block, 1980). Ego resiliency implies the ability to modulate emotion in appropriate ways. Children were also assessed with respect to ego control, the disposition of the individual regarding the expression or containment of feelings and impulses. Ego undercontrollers are spontaneous and impulsive; ego overcontrollers are constrained. In kindergarten, children with resistant histories were rated significantly higher on a measure of ego undercontrol than were children with avoidant histories. Securely attached children received moderate ratings on ego control measures, falling in between the two anxious groups.

An association between infant attachment and ego resiliency was also found in the Minnesota longitudinal study of a high-risk sample (LaFreniere & Sroufe, 1985; Sroufe, 1983). Teacher

Q-sorts for ego resiliency for children with secure attachment histories were consistently correlated with the ego resiliency criterion sort, compared with small or negative correlations for children with anxious histories. Children with secure attachment histories were ranked or rated higher on measures of emotional health, self-esteem, social competence, and positive affect, and lower on measures of dependency and negative affect. Impressionistic findings also relate patterns of ego resiliency to functioning in peer relationships. Secure children were able to modulate affect in service of social relationships, but relationships of avoidant children were characterized by rigidity and exclusivity. Avoidant children were unable to negotiate individual relationships with group participation. On the other hand, relationships of children with resistant histories were transient and not sustainable in group settings.

Lutkenhaus, Grossmann, and Grossmann (1985) found evidence for attachment-related defensive mechanisms in affective displays of 3-year-olds. Infant attachment status was related to children's affective reactions to winning and losing in social and problem-solving contexts with an unfamiliar adult. Secure and avoidant children did not differ in frequency of negative affective displays, but the groups did differ in the contexts in which reactions occurred. Secure children showed sadness related to games when adult figures were available for social interaction, whereas children with avoidant histories tended to replace negative affect expressed during procedures with smiling when adults were available for communication. The findings support the notion that effective dyadic regulation of emotion in infancy may allow for direct and flexible communication of emotion and problem solving in relationships in early childhood. Attachment insecurity may promote distorted or restricted individual styles of communication.

The relationship between early caregiving experience and later affect regulation (or foreclosure) has also been demonstrated by Lay, Waters, and Posada (in press). In this study, attachment security of 3.5-year-old children, as measured through a home observation Q-sort (Waters & Deane, 1985), was related to children's affective responses to mood induction vignettes. The vignettes were designed to induce positive or negative mood with and without the mother as cause of the mood. No significant differences between securely and insecurely attached children were found with respect to positive vignettes. Negative vignettes, however, elicited a variety of "paradoxical" or defensive responses (positive responses or mixed responses to negative mood induction vignettes). A strong interaction was found between attachment status and mother versus not-mother involvement. Securely attached children gave more paradoxical responses than insecurely attached children in the not-mother condition and fewer paradoxical responses than insecurely attached children in the mother-involved condition. The findings suggest differences, between securely and insecurely attached children, in the employment of cognitive transformation to regulate affect. For securely attached children, defensive processes may be employed to modulate affect in the absence of adult caregivers (secure base from which to derive support); for insecurely attached children, based on a history of unavailable caregiving, defensive processes may be employed in place of engaging the attachment behavioral system.

Consistent with attachment theory, patterns of early dyadic regulation of emotion have been found to be related to individual styles of self-regulation. In early childhood, securely attached children with histories of well-coordinated dyadic regulation of emotion have been found to be more affectively expressive and responsive to others and to express more positive affect than children with histories of anxious attachment. In addition, attachment history and early affective style have been found to be related to social competence. Securely attached children have been found to respond flexibly and resourcefully to challenge, to adapt to environmental demands, and to modulate emotion in appropriate ways (ego resiliency). Secure attachment has been associated with later emotional health, self-esteem, social competence, and emotional independence. Anxious attachment has been associated with increased negative affect and with difficulties in the modulation of emotion, expression of affect, and flexible negotiation and maintenance of peer relationships.

Research on Representational Organization in Childhood

Continuity in the representational organization of attachment has been demonstrated through empirical studies of projective storytelling, fantasy play, and interview coordination of language and thought. Early expectations and rules regarding the regulation and expression of emotion in relationships have been found to be related to patterns of attention, memory, and cognition associated with attachment in childhood, adolescence, and adulthood (Main, Kaplan, & Cassidy, 1985).

In early childhood (3-year-olds), representational organization of attachment relationships has been assessed using a story completion task (Bretherton, Ridgeway, & Cassidy, 1990). In this study, children's story presentations of attachment-related issues were classified with respect to structure and content, taking into account the child's total performance. Children classified as secure in infancy were found to acknowledge negative emotions (i.e., pain, fear, anger) and provide positive solutions to stressful dilemmas (e.g., the child's physical injury or fear was addressed by the parent, the child was reassured or hugged by the parent) or positive coping behavior (e.g., the child portrayed an adaptive solution to the parent's absence). Responses of children with anxious attachment histories were characterized by avoidance of story issues (e.g., not responding to questions and probes; labeling figures rather than completing the story) or incoherent or odd responses (e.g., violent solutions or intrusions in the story; bizarre or unrelated responses to probes).

Variations in quality of early mother-child attachment have predicted differences in elaboration, investment, and quality of fantasy play of 4.5-year old children in the Minnesota longitudinal study (Rosenberg, 1984). Children who were securely attached in infancy became strongly engaged in fantasy play, incorporated work on social relationship skills in their play, balanced positive and negative themes in fantasy, worked with persistence (without fear) on frightening experiences, and routinely brought conflictual themes to successful resolutions. Based on experiences of sensitive caregiving and open communication of affective experience, the child with a secure history is thought to have internalized a positive view of self in relationships and an ability to flexibly regulate affective experience. These expectations and attitudes are reflected in the child's enthusiastic engagement in social relationships in fantasy play, employment of a range of emotions, and tolerance of feelings of fear or conflict in the course of working through experiences.

Anxious groups differed in the adeptness with which negotiations and cooperative fantasy play were promoted (Rosenberg, 1984). Avoidant children showed impoverished themes and low-level engagement in fantasy play. People and social relationships were notably absent, and aggression was a prevalent theme. These qualities are consistent with the defensive strategy of cutting off or restricting the expression of emotion, difficulties in social interactions, and indirect expression of underlying anger. In particular, the paucity of themes and elaboration may limit the adaptive use of play for social feedback by these children. For resistant children, early experiences of overarousal and difficulties in regulating arousal were reflected in fantasy play characterized by conflicted relationships, fear, aggression, and danger in the environment.

Extensive study of attachment at the representational level has been undertaken by Main and her colleagues (Main et al., 1985). This longitudinal study of children in middle-income families began in infancy with Strange Situation procedures at 12 and 18 months. At 6 years, children's representational organization was assessed through the following measures: (a) separation pictures adapted from the Klagsbrun and Bowlby (1976) version of the Hansburg (1972) Separation Anxiety Test, (b) responses to family photo during separation from parent, (c) child drawings of the family, (d) parent-child conversations upon reunion after a one-hour separation.

In response to a series of separation pictures, 6-year-old children classified as secure with mother in infancy gave coherent elaborated responses, sometimes volunteering information regarding their own separation experiences (Kaplan, 1987). These children were described as emotionally open and able to maintain an easy balance between self-exposure and self-containment. They described the child in the picture as lonely, sad, fearful, or angry during many separations, but were able to offer reasons for these emotions. Children assessed as avoidant with mother in infancy described children in more severe separation pictures as sad, but provided no coping solution to the separation. Children classified as resistant showed no clear pattern of response. Children classified as disorganized/disoriented were either completely silent or gave irrational or bizarre responses.

In response to a family photograph, 6-year-olds classified as secure with mother readily accepted the photograph, smiled, showed some interest, and released the picture casually after inspection (Main, 1985). Children classified as avoidant refused to accept, turned away from, or dropped the photograph. Children classified as disorganized showed a depressed affect or became disorganized while viewing the picture. No clear pattern was reported for children classified as resistant.

In family drawings, 6-year-olds classified as secure depicted family members as close, but also individuated and animated (Kaplan & Main, 1989). In contrast, drawings of children classified as avoidant were described as having an "aura of falseness," with all family members bearing similar smiles, and with greater distance among family members. Bodies appeared tense and rigid, and figures tended to be armless. Such signs are associated with emotional unavailability, with a withholding affective communication style. An overall impression of vulnerability characterized drawings of children classified as resistant in infancy. Figures were either very tiny or very large with exaggerated facial features, or body parts were depicted in extreme proximity or separated by barriers and were drawn randomly on the page (not in the center or grounded). Drawings by children judged to have disorganized/disoriented attachment showed a mixture of elements observed in the drawings of secure and avoidant children, but were bizarre in a number of ways. Strange marks were added, unfinished objects or figures were present. Parts of the work were sometimes scratched out, and overbright and cheery elements such as hearts and rainbows were added without being integrated into the overall design (Kaplan & Main, 1989). Many of these findings have been replicated in a high-risk poverty sample (Fury, 1993).

Discourse patterns during mother-child reunions at the 6-year assessment also were related to early attachment classifications (Strage & Main, 1984). Dyads classified as secure in infancy were fluent and discussed a wide range of topics. Dyads classified as avoidant in infancy were restricted in discourse, emphasized impersonal topics (e.g., activities or objects), showed little topic elaboration, and asked questions that were rhetorical or suggested yes/no responses. Dyads classified as disorganized were dysfluent, with much stumbling and false starts. For some, the focus of the conversation was on relationship topics with the child steering the conversation.

In summary, for 6-year-old children with secure reunion behavior, communication with parents appeared fluid and warm, and communication about attachment issues (e.g., separation) suggested that these children had relatively free access internally to affect, memory, and planning. Negative affect (anger, sadness) did not obstruct resourceful planning or access to caregiving help.

Children rated as avoidant exhibited communication patterns characterized by attempts to direct attention away from caregivers and to avoid attachment-related issues, suggesting that these children may use patterns of restriction organized to avoid affective exchanges. In projective drawings, avoidant children tended to idealize family relationships. When distress or sadness was acknowledged, children were unable to provide reasons or strategies for coping with negative affect.

Expressions of negativity or hostility on projective tasks were most frequent among children classified as anxious, resistant, or controlling, even though both open and idealized responses were also characteristic of these groups. Consistent with experience characterized by dysregulation and hypervigilance, children classified as resistant combined incompatible strategies to solve attachment-related problems and became preoccupied with bodily characteristics in drawings, perhaps because of anxiety concerning relationships. Children classified as disorganized demonstrated mixed communication and representational patterns, combining those associated with secure and avoidant groups with controlling strategies, dissociative reactions, and bizarre elements.

Using a puppet interview and story completion task, Cassidy (1988) has shown children with secure histories to be open and flexible in dealing with emotions; these children convey a sense of self-worth and acceptance. Children with avoidant histories exhibited defensive communication styles (insisting on perfection and dismissing the importance of relationships) in interview tasks while endorsing items associated with low esteem on a self-report measure of perceived competence. Extreme negativity (hostility), overt statements about lack of worth, and/or bizarre behavior characterized responses of children classified as anxiously attached, nonavoidant (resistant or controlling) in infancy.

In the Minnesota longitudinal study, differences in children's representational organization of relationships were assessed in a day camp experience and through projective measures. As part of a 4-week summer camp, 10- to 11-year-old children were interviewed about friendships made while at the camp and about thoughts and feelings involving themselves, their peers, and the group processes during a camp activity (Elicker, 1991). Videotapes and transcripts of interviews were coded for: (a) interpersonal sensitivity, a composite measure of self-other differentiation in inferences about thoughts and feelings of group members and the psychological depth of the inferences; (b) peer group evaluation bias, a measure of the tendency to rate one's own group's performance either positively or negatively; and (c) balance in group/self presentations, a measure of distinction between perspectives of self and other. Children with histories of secure and resistant attachment displayed higher levels of interpersonal sensitivity than children with avoidant histories. Children with secure and resistant histories differed in ratings of peer competence, despite similarities in interpersonal sensitivity. The findings suggested that anxieties or ambivalence about peer relationships, rather than deficiencies in level of understanding of others, may interfere with competent functioning for children with resistant histories. As expected, children with secure histories tended to evaluate their own groups positively, avoidant children tended to exhibit a negative bias, and resistant children showed intermediate levels of positive-negative bias. Depth of inference distinguished secure and avoidant children. No significant group differences emerged for balancing group/self presentations.

In the Minnesota study, children were assessed at age 12, using sentence completion stems and projective stories (McCrone, Carlson, & Engler, 1993; Ramirez, Carlson, Gest, & Egeland, 1991). Significant relationships were found between security of attachment and positive expectations concerning primary caregivers on the sentence completion stems (e.g., "My mother never . . .") (Ramirez et al., 1991). On projective stories, children with avoidant histories incorporated significantly more negativity, ambivalence, and victimization/aggression than did children with secure histories (McCrone et al., 1993). Children with secure histories described more positive peer relations and more competently resolved problems. Projective measures of positive relationship models were found to be related to contemporary measures of observed competence with peers (Sroufe et al., 1993).

Research on Adults and Adolescents

Differences in the ability to consciously process attachment-related experiences have provided a basis for inferences regarding attachment organization in adolescence and adulthood (Main et al., 1985). Three patterns of adult attachment organization have been revealed from the analysis of transcripts of the Adult Attachment Interview (George, Kaplan, & Main, 1984): (a) secure/autonomous, (b) dismissing of attachment, and (c) preoccupied with attachment (Main & Goldwyn, 1989).

Adults classified as secure/autonomous present either a believable picture of one or both parents serving as a secure base in early childhood or are relatively reflective and objective about relationships with unsupportive parents (Main & Goldwyn, 1989). These individuals value attachment relationships and regard attachments and experiences related to attachment as influential on personality. The valuing of attachment and the ability to freely discuss difficult early experiences reflect a strategy characterized by open communication of attachment feelings and behavior, and consciousness in the reappraisal of expectations and attitudes.

In contrast, interviews with adults rated as dismissing and preoccupied are characterized by a lack of consciousness and of integration of attachment-related information, and by incoherencies in the form of contradictions between stated beliefs and specifically described memories (Main & Goldwyn, 1989). Adults classified as dismissing of attachment have difficulty recalling events and feelings and/or tend to minimize attachment as being of little value. Idealized beliefs about parents, alongside episodic descriptions of rejecting and unsupportive caregiving, characterize the defensive strategy. Individuals classified as preoccupied are able to recall attachment-related experiences easily; however, they lack effective strategies to organize experience and resolve attachment-related issues. Unable to identify the source of conflicts, they remain perpetually concerned with past or current parental relationships.

In addition to the classification of three principal patterns, some adults were classified as unresolved with respect to experiences of loss or trauma. These individuals were judged to have not completed a process of mourning a significant caregiver lost in childhood or of resolving an early experience of trauma. The interviews were characterized by irrational or disorganized thinking regarding the lost attachment figure or traumatic experience.

Stability in secure/autonomous, dismissing, and preoccupied categories has been found to range from 78% to 90% over 2 to 3 months in the United Kingdom, the Netherlands, Israel, and the United States, and over a 15-month period in Canada (Main, in press). Stability including the unresolved category is lower. Average interjudge agreement across studies is about 85%. In four studies, adult state of mind with respect to attachment has been found to be unrelated to measures of general intelligence, memory, or verbal fluency (Van IJzendoorn, in press). In addition, state of mind assessed in the adult classification system has been found to be unrelated to general style of discourse (Waters et al., 1993).

Caregiving Relationships. Variations in adult organization of attachment-related experience are thought to account for individual differences in caregiving sensitivity to infant signals and communication (Main et al., 1985). The similarity between parent and infant strategies may be a product of the style of emotional communication related to the adult's attachment strategy (Kobak & Shaver, 1987). A parent who is able to acknowledge and easily integrate attachment-related experiences, particularly painful experiences, is likely to be free to respond to a child's attachment signals in a sensitive manner. A parent who adopts a defensive strategy of dismissing and avoiding attachment-related memories and feelings may not be able to respond to the child's attachment needs in a contingent and sensitive manner. Similarly, the parent who is preoccupied with his or her own attachment needs is likely to be inconsistently responsive in caregiving.

Three retrospective studies of child-rearing history and subsequent infant-caregiver attachment (Main et al., 1985; Morris, 1980; Ricks, 1985) support this view. Each of these investigators found that mothers' reports of their early experiences of nurturance were strongly associated with secure or anxious patterns of attachment in the subsequent infant-caregiver relationship.

In a middle-income sample, individual differences in attachment organization assessed with the adult attachment interview corresponded to differences in their infants' attachment strategies as assessed in the Strange Situation (Main et al., 1985). Parents who were coherent in discussing early experiences during adult attachment interviews, and who were rated as secure, tended to be parents of secure infants; whereas incoherent parents tended to have insecure infants. Main et al.'s findings have been replicated in two middle-income samples (Ainsworth & Eichberg, 1991; Eichberg, 1987; Grossmann, Fremmer-Bombik, Rudolph, & Grossmann, 1988) and with high-risk adolescent mothers (Carlson, 1990). In addition, mothers' prenatal attachment status has been found to predict infant attachment classification for both adult and adolescent mothers (Fonagy, Steele, & Steele, 1991; Ward & Carlson, in press).

Main's findings suggest a particular relationship between experiences of early rejection and lack of nurturance, and anxious avoidant patterns of attachment in the next generation. Morris (1980) found similar relationships between maternal history and infant-caregiver attachment in a poverty sample from the Minnesota longitudinal study. Anxious patterns of attachment were predicted by lack of a stable family relationship structure and the caregiver's perception of his or her own mother as not nurturant and not competent in the maternal role. For some subjects, however, there were discordances between mother self-reports of their own childhood experiences and their attachments to their infants. Recent research on defensive self-reporting may explain notable "misses" in Morris's study (e.g., dyads including mothers who reported harmonious families of origin, little or no crises, and plentiful support but who, nonetheless, had anxiously attached infants).

Ricks (1985) conducted two studies relating mothers' retrospective views of relationships and self-esteem to their children's attachment and preschool outcomes. In the first study, history of mother acceptance and current high self-esteem in adult mothers were related to infant attachment security. In a follow-up study, maternal defensiveness and idealization of parents were related to insecurity in infant attachment. Controlling for maternal defensiveness and idealization, mothers' self-esteem and recollections of childhood related to emotional functioning of their preschoolers.

Recently, individual differences in caregiver organization have also been related to quality of parent-child relationship in preschool (Cohn, Cowan, Cowan, & Pearson, 1992; Crowell & Feldman, 1988; Crowell, O'Conner, Wollmers, Sprakin, & Rao, 1991). In a middle-income sample (Cohn et al., 1992), mothers and fathers classified as autonomous in the Adult Attachment Interview received higher ratings of overall warmth (high warmth and responsiveness; low anger, displeasure, and coldness) and structure (limit-setting, maturity, demands, providing adequate structure and clear communication) in a series of structured and unstructured laboratory tasks than did parents classified as insecure (dismissing or preoccupied). In high-risk samples, compared with mothers classified as insecure, mothers classified as secure/autonomous were rated as more helpful and supportive in a series of teaching tasks with preschool (Crowell & Feldman, 1988) as well as school-age children (Crowell et al., 1991).

Noncaregiving Relationships. Longitudinal data are not yet available to support the notion of continuity in behavioral and representational strategies from childhood to adolescence; however, the relationship between styles of emotion regulation and coordination of attachment-related thought and language have been investigated in a series of empirical studies (Dozier & Kobak, 1992; Kobak, Cole, Ferenz-Gillies, Fleming, & Gamble, 1993; Kobak & Sceery, 1988). Adolescent attachment organization has been related to peer ratings of individual functioning, adolescents' beliefs about others and self (Kobak & Sceery, 1988), and adolescents' patterns of regulating emotion during mother-teen problem-solving tasks (Kobak et al., 1993). In addition, Dozier and Kobak (1992) examined the psychophysiology of defensive attachment strategies in adolescents.

In a study of adolescents from middle-income families during their transition to college, individuals classified as secure/autonomous in the Adult Attachment Interview were rated by peers as higher on social relatedness, insight, and ego resiliency (able to modulate negative feelings constructively) in problem-solving and social contexts than dismissing or preoccupied groups (Kobak & Sceery, 1988). Insecure adolescents were found to be less ego-resilient. Adolescents classified as dismissing were rated as more hostile and condescending with peers. Preoccupied individuals were judged by peers to be more anxious and reported more symptoms of distress.

Attachment-related strategies also were associated with adolescents' beliefs about self and others (Kobak & Sceery, 1988). Individuals classified as secure/autonomous demonstrated high levels of perceived self-competence as well as high levels of perceived support from others. In contrast, adolescents adopting a dismissing strategy reported positive beliefs about the self in terms of high levels of perceived competence, but negative beliefs about others as suggested by low levels of perceived support from family and a sense of loneliness. Adolescents classified as preoccupied demonstrated low levels of perceived competence and high levels of perceived support.

These patterns of correlates may be explained in terms of differences in affect regulation (Kobak & Sceery, 1988). Adolescents classified as secure/autonomous may organize their experiences in ways that leave them free to evaluate attachments, to acknowledge vulnerability and distress, and to seek support from others when needed. Based on negative expectations of others, individuals classified as dismissing tend to bolster a self-reliant image. Anger is dissociated and displaced onto peer relationships, perpetuating beliefs that others are not trustworthy as well as a personal sense of isolation. Individuals classified as preoccupied may initially seek friends, but their hypervigilant attention to distress or suffering as well as to relationship figures may inhibit the development of a sense of competence and of the autonomy necessary for enduring personal relationships.

In a two-part study, Kobak and his colleagues (Kobak et al., 1993) examined the relationship between adolescent attachment organization and emotion regulation during a mother-teen problem-solving assessment. First, Q-sort prototypes for "primary" strategies of secure/insecure and "secondary" strategies of deactivating/hyperactiving (dismissing/preoccupied) were found to differentiate Main and Goldwyn's (1989) Adult Attachment classifications. Q-sort-based attachment classifications then were related to four aspects of dyadic problem-solving: (a) support validation, (b) dysfunctional anger, (c) avoidance of problem solving, and (d) maternal dominance. Adolescents with secure strategies were found to demonstrate more functional patterns of emotion regulation during problem solving with their mothers than adolescents with insecure strategies. Problem-solving interactions were characterized by less dysfunctional anger and more engagement in problem-solving discussion. These adolescents demonstrated "balanced assertiveness": the expression of negative emotion served to restore rather than disrupt the mother-adolescent relationship. Secondary strategies were also linked to problem-solving behavior. Adolescents described as employing a deactivating strategy engaged in problem-solving interactions characterized by high levels of maternal dominance and dysfunctional anger. Allowing mothers to dominate conflictual discussion and expressing anger (as a distancing strategy) are consistent with a strategy of minimizing negative exchanges.

Dozier and Kobak (1992) examined the relationship between interview demands to coordinate attachment-related thought and language and physiological status, in a sample of 50 adolescents. In this study, skin conductance scores of individuals who scored high on a repression scale (characteristic of those classified as dismissing; Kobak et al., 1993) did not differ from those of remaining subjects when all subjects responded to low-stress background questions about parents and childhood. When asked more stressful questions about feelings during times of separation, rejection, or threat, individuals with high repression scores showed significantly greater conflict than other individuals, as evidenced by higher skin conductance scores, even as they verbally denied having difficulties in early attachment relationships. The findings are consistent with the notion that a disjunction may exist between emotional experience and expression for individuals adopting an avoidant/dismissing strategy. The defensive strategy of shifting attention away from attachment information may not be fully effective in regulating feelings aroused during the attachment interview.

In summary, Bowlby's assumptions regarding the internalization of qualities of early primary relationships have been supported by modest empirical findings. Individual variations in affect regulation have been related to representations of the self and other in the social world. Stability in such internal processes is thought to be supported by transaction with the social environment. In turn, these internal mechanisms may provide the key to understanding links between attachment experience and later pathology. For some individuals, early experiences of responsive caregiving may facilitate the development of styles of emotional communication and social involvement that serve to protect or buffer the individual in times of stress. For others, distorted early caregiving may lead to the development of maladaptive patterns of affect regulation and inflexible defensive processes that restrict social relationships and promote feelings of low self-worth. These conditions may be exacerbated in times of stress, or, alternately, may lead to recognized forms of pathology.

ATTACHMENT AND PSYCHOPATHOLOGY

The link between attachment and psychopathology may be viewed in two principal ways. One is to directly consider deviations in attachment that are so extreme as to be considered disturbances meriting intervention even in the infancy or preschool period. A beginning conceptualization (not restricted to the early years) is reflected in DSM-IV (American Psychiatric Association, 1994) and ICD-9 (World Health Organization, 1992). Two types of attachment disorder of childhood are described. Both refer to marked disturbances in the child's social relatedness, which begins before age 5, extends across social contexts, and is distinguished from pervasive developmental disorders. One type of disorder is characterized by excessively inhibited, hypervigilant, or highly ambivalent responses to adult caregivers. A second is characterized by indiscriminant sociability (excessive sociability with strangers) and a relative failure to show appropriate selective attachments. In addition, DSM-IV requires evidence of grossly pathogenic care, including persistent disregard of the child's emotional and physical needs or repeated changes in primary caregiver.

Zeanah, Mammen, and Lieberman (1994) have elaborated on this scheme, defining the following disorders: nonattachment, indiscriminate attachment, inhibited attachment, aggressive attachment, and role-reversed attachment. The disorders may be diagnosed in children ages 1 to 4 years, based on behavior of the child alone; with few exceptions, behaviors need only be shown in the presence of one attachment figure. Nonattachment disorder represents a failure to develop a preferred attachment figure. Indiscriminate attachment disorder is characterized by indiscriminate and promiscuous use of others for comfort or support. The child fails to use the caregiver as a secure base in unfamiliar settings or a source of comfort when frightened or threatened. In inhibited attachment disorder, the child fails to venture away from the caregiver to engage in age-appropriate exploration. This disorder is characterized by excessive clinging and affective constriction or, alternately, hypervigilance and compulsive compliance. Children with aggressive attachment disorder show pervasive anger and aggression toward the attachment figure and/or the self that exceeds transitory expressions of frustration. The role-reversed disorder or controlling pattern includes children who are overly nurturant and solicitous toward the caregiver and children who are overly punitive toward the caregiver. While these relationship disturbances are supported by clinical evidence, the phenomena have not been validated as disorders.

A second approach to the attachment-psychopathology link is to consider disturbed attachment relationships not as disorders of the infant, but as markers of a beginning pathological process or as risk factors for later pathology (Sameroff & Emde, 1989). A principal aim of the domain of developmental psychopathology is to identify differences in patterns of socioemotional functioning, including experiences that leave individuals vulnerable or buffered with respect to stressful life circumstances and differences in capacity of individuals to draw strength from available social support (Cicchetti, 1984; Sroufe, 1988). Bowlby's work emphasizing vital human relationships, the quality of early adaptation, and continuity in experience provides a framework for looking at individual adaptation in such a developmental manner (Sroufe, 1986).

The organization of expectations, attitudes, and feelings related to attachment promotes continuity in socioemotional functioning across periods of discontinuous growth and despite fundamental transformations in manifest behavior (Sroufe & Rutter, 1984). Affective regulatory processes influence new relationships and social adaptation by determining what information is perceived or ignored, what persons or situations to pursue or avoid, and how new experience is interpreted (Bowlby, 1973). Internal organization and the environment interact in mutually reinforcing or validating ways to maintain an established developmental path.

Disordered behavior typically does not spring forth without connections to a previous quality of adaptation or without changing environmental supports (Sroufe, 1990a). Previous modes of functioning are currently available and are part of individual ongoing adaptation—at times, promoting an improved fit to the environment and, at other times, compromising growth. More recently integrated patterns of behavior are thought to be most susceptible to disruption (during periods of stress or transition), giving way to earlier, less differentiated forms (Sroufe & Rutter, 1984). Pathology is associated not with the presence or employment of these less differentiated patterns, but with the inflexible use of behavior in relation to ongoing adaptational tasks. In this section, we examine recent work on the implication of differences in early attachment organization and patterns of emotion regulation for developing psychopathology.

Early Care as Risk or Protective Factor

From an organizational attachment perspective, variations in responses to stressful life conditions and the development of specific disorders may be related to early experiences of caregiving. For individuals for whom the caregiver has been a source of effective emotional regulation and comfort, the other is valued and relationships are viewed as worthwhile. From the earliest relationship, the individual has experienced the rudiments of reciprocity, including how to receive care and how to respond empathically to others (Sroufe & Fleeson, 1986). This child has developed a sense that he or she is worthy of care and efficacious in attaining it. The child's expectations and complementary behavior about self and others elicit feedback from others that supports an adaptive style. As a result, under conditions of minimal stress, the relationship pattern serves to enhance the child's ongoing positive emotional involvement in challenges and opportunities. In the face of extreme stress or challenge, the child is likely to take the initiative to seek comfort and support with the expectation that others will be available and willing to provide aid.

In contrast, individuals who have adopted insecure strategies may be particularly vulnerable to normative stresses (Cicchetti et al., 1988; Kobak & Shaver, 1987; Sroufe & Fleeson, 1986). Based on experiences with caregivers who were unavailable or inconsistently responsive, these individuals may be prone to forming relationships that are not supportive and that may be easily disrupted. For the avoidant child, early experiences support a view of self as isolated, unable to achieve emotional closeness, and unworthy of care. The social world is viewed as alien and may be treated with anger and hostility. As stress is elevated, the child may fail to seek comfort from others and remain isolated with his or her problems. Care may be sought only in times of low stress. From unpredictable or inconsistent caregiver experiences, the resistant child develops patterns of relating to others based on heightened displays of emotion or extreme passivity. This anxious style, in which negative emotions function to disrupt rather than restore relationships, inhibits the development of stable close relationships.

For both avoidant and resistant children, the critical factor in the quality of relationships is the way negative emotions are communicated and utilized. Emotions that optimally would facilitate affective communication and exchange are defensively modified. As a result, when experiencing distress, the avoidant child may fail to signal directly a need for support from others, and the resistant child may become excessively caught up in negative emotion and unable to stay engaged constructively in social relationships. These children may sacrifice supportive relationships that form an important buffer against stress and psychopathology. What has begun as personal distress may be compounded by isolation, lack of support, and relationship dysfunction (Kobak & Shaver, 1987).

For individuals with insecure attachment histories, strategies for maintaining felt security may themselves be vulnerable to breaking down under stress (Kobak & Shaver, 1987). The brittleness of insecure strategies is evident in low ratings of ego resiliency, an inability to cope with frustration, and the pervasive presence of negative affect, documented earlier in this chapter. Insecure children have difficulty being flexible in problem solving. They either give up or fall apart when faced with challenging or stressful situations, or they may tend to perseverate on tasks (Block & Block, 1980). In the context of stressful life events or personal challenges, these children must cope with the activation of attachment feeling and behavior and the re-experiencing of emotional conflict that their defensive strategy was originally designed to control. Distorted or symptomatic forms of attachment behavior may result. For example, hypochondriacal reactions may serve unfulfilled attachment needs (desire for closeness/care), or suicidal behavior may represent a desire to reunite with a lost attachment figure (Bowlby, 1980).

In the context of a history of distorted communications of attachment feeling and behavior, a child's symptomatic behavior may be misinterpreted and the symptom may be disconnected from the context in which it originated (Kobak & Shaver, 1987).

Early miscommunications and misinterpretations by others may be reemployed, reinforced, and elaborated. For example, a child's emerging resentment may be interpreted as negative attention seeking or willful behavior, or fears and anxiety may be attributed to immaturity. The child's attempts to further control such emotional expression may exacerbate the original problem.

Insecure attachment organizational styles are thought to represent working defensive strategies, not symptoms or disorders (Main, in press). Although these characteristic strategies may pose difficulties for children in the face of added stress, attachment theory emphasizes that a child is neither made invulnerable nor doomed to psychopathology by early relationship patterns. For example, not all insecurely attached infants develop behavioral problems or fail to resolve successfully stage-salient issues (Bates et al., 1985; Erickson et al., 1985; Lewis, Feiring, McGuffog, & Jaskir, 1984; Sroufe, 1990b).

Insecure attachment may be considered a risk factor for the development of psychopathology in the context of a complex model that includes interactive biological and environmental factors (Cicchetti et al., 1988), rendering individuals more likely to respond adversely to stress and more vulnerable to pathological problems (Sroufe, 1990b). Adaptation at one point in development may compromise the child's long-term development by limiting his or her ability to draw on the environment in a flexible manner.

Attachment and Disorder

Theoretical Claims

Particular styles of personality functioning or strategies of maintaining organization under stress may predispose individuals to certain types of symptomatic behavior (Bowlby, 1973, 1977, 1980). Individual patterns of emotion regulation, beliefs about the self and others, abilities to revise and reflect on experience, and biases in interpreting and responding to stress provide a coherent basis for specific disorders.

Secure/autonomous attachment strategies may be expected to provide a protective function against major and repeated difficulties or disorders—in particular, those most closely related to attachment (e.g., caregiving and close relationships in adulthood). Individuals with secure histories, however, may nevertheless experience psychological suffering. In response to such experiences, from a history of effective regulation of emotion and experience of self as competent in eliciting care, these individuals may be expected to seek out and make effective use of supportive relationships or services. A history that includes trust in relationships, the direct communication of emotion, flexibility and openness in interpreting information, and the ability to reflect on mental states of self and others may provide the basis for the successful reworking of ineffective adaptational patterns and the resolution of experiences of trauma or loss.

For individuals employing an avoidant/dismissing strategy, symptomatic behavior is likely to be consistent with attempts to minimize attachment behavior and feeling. Symptoms may reflect a tendency to mask emotional expression and to maintain beliefs about the self as invulnerable or impervious to hurt, beliefs about others as untrustworthy, and idealized beliefs about attachment relationships (Kobak & Shaver, 1987). Attachment feelings are likely to emerge in the form of anger or resentment. Conduct disorders or antisocial personality styles are congruent with this pattern of emotional regulation. Bowlby (1944) observed this association of misconduct and lack of expressive affect in his investigation of juvenile thieves. Because of extreme emotional isolation and low self-worth, individuals maintaining an avoidant/dismissing strategy may also be prone to depressive symptoms when attempts to maintain an independent self-reliant image repeatedly fail (Guidano & Liotti, 1983).

For the resistant/preoccupied individual, anxiety in relationships is likely to reduce exploration and increase attachment behavior. Consistent with this strategy are difficulties in managing anxiety, manifested in phobias and conversion reactions, including preoccupation with personal suffering (Bowlby, 1973, 1977). The resistant/preoccupied individual's tendency to exaggerate emotion, to maintain negative beliefs about the self, and to experience anxiety and confusion when reflecting on the nature of attachment difficulties supports these forms of symptomatic behaviors (Kobak & Shaver, 1987). As Bowlby (1973) noted, school refusal or phobias are often associated with family patterns in which the child is anxious about the availability or well-being of the attachment figure. The anxiety manifests itself in personal fears about leaving home, accompanied by related fears (e.g., of the dark; of animals) and psychosomatic symptoms.

For individuals adopting avoidant/dismissing and resistant/preoccupied strategies (particularly children), death or major separation may confirm the individual's worst expectations about the psychological availability of the attachment figure and may lead to despair as well as anxiety (Bowlby, 1980). For these individuals, without supportive social relationships, reactions to loss and separation are likely to take an atypical course. Supportive relationships serve affective and behavioral reorganization processes by allowing for the expression of feelings of distress and vulnerability. For those with histories of avoidant attachment, mourning may be delayed for months or years; nevertheless, strain and irritability may be present and depression may occur long after the connection with loss or separation is readily apparent. The response of individuals with a history of resistant attachment is likely to be characterized by unusually intense anger and/or self-reproach with depression that may persist for much longer than normal.

Empirical Findings: Direct Research

From an organizational view of the developing personality, disorders of the early years of life may be characterized best as relational problems that have occurred as a result of dysfunction in the parent-child transactional system (Cicchetti et al., 1988; Sameroff & Emde, 1989; Sroufe & Fleeson, 1986). With development, these dysfunctional relationship patterns become part of the individual organization and emerge through a variety of developmental pathways (Bowlby, 1988b). Empirical findings lend direct support to the idea that trends in symptom formation develop in a coherent way from early relationship patterns and styles of personality functioning.

Autism. The study of childhood autism from an organizational perspective has contributed to an understanding of both normative and distorted processes of early attachment and development (Sigman, 1989). The autistic child has been shown to develop some core self and attachment to others; however, social understanding and the development of intersubjectivity is limited. Social-cognitive and symbolic systems are compromised. The developmental pattern highlights the critical nature of the integration of cognitive, social, and sensorimotor experiences in infancy. Emotional regulatory patterns may be viewed as a central feature of this early organization or coordination of developing processes; such patterns provide the basis for later adaptation through the development of the capacity for intersubjectivity and relatedness.

Behavior Problems/Aggression. The relationship between the quality of the early attachment relationship and later psychopathology has been examined by a number of investigators (Lewis et al., 1984; Lyons-Ruth, Alpern, & Repacholi, 1993; Marvinney, 1985; Renken, Egeland, Marvinney, Sroufe, & Mangelsdorf, 1989). Lewis and his colleagues (1984) found different outcomes for male and female 6-year-old children, using Achenbach's (1978) Child Behavior Profile (CBP) as an outcome measure. For boys, attachment classification at one year was significantly related to later psychopathology. Insecurely attached boys showed more psychopathology than securely attached boys. Attachment classification alone, however, did not predict later behavior problems. The development of psychopathology was influenced by factors including stressful life events (i.e., death, divorce, family moves) and family demographic variables (i.e., planning, birth order). The findings support a transactional multidetermined model of development and psychopathology wherein organismic and environmental influences interact to determine adaptation. Thus, although secure early attachment experiences may serve a protective function in a high-risk environment, insecure attachment need not lead to psychopathology; rather, difficult early attachment experiences may predispose boys to psychopathology in the context of environmental stressors. Boys with insecure attachment histories may be more vulnerable to the effects of environmental stress.

Consistent with a probabilistic view of the development of psychopathology, Lyons-Ruth and her colleagues (Lyons-Ruth et al., 1993) found child behavior problems (characterized by aggression) to be related to disorganized/disoriented attachment in infancy, although only a minority of children classified as disorganized in infancy were highly aggressive in preschool. In this study, maternal psychosocial problems contributed to the outcome for one subgroup of children who were classified as disorganized in infancy and later developed behavior problems. The effects of attachment status and maternal psychosocial problems were independent and additive rather than interactive; however, the authors noted that previous analyses had indicated that mothers with psychosocial problems were more likely to develop insecure attachment relationships. The findings support the view that individual functioning may be influenced by environmental risk factors through multiple direct and indirect pathways.

In the Minnesota longitudinal study (Egeland & Sroufe, 1981; Erickson et al., 1985; Sroufe, 1983), attachment history and early social adaptation were significantly related to teacher ratings of aggression and passive withdrawal in middle childhood (Renken et al., 1989). Attachment history predicted aggressive outcomes for boys, and the factors of harsh parental treatment and stressful life circumstances were related to aggression in both boys and girls. As the authors emphasized, the attachment relationship predicts aggression in boys before aggression is even part of the child's behavioral repertoire. Findings from the Minnesota project support claims that avoidant and resistant patterns of anxious attachment have different sequelae. For boys in this study, aggressive antisocial behavior was related to avoidant attachment in infancy, and passive/withdrawn behavior was associated with resistant attachment history (Renken et al., 1989). The two sets of predictors failed to discriminate between aggression and passive withdrawal in girls to the same degree. The authors suggested that a restricted degree of variability among girls in the direction of nonpathological signs produced a weaker overall relationship, and cultural factors may influence girls in the direction of internalizing behaviors. In earlier investigations, however, passivity in girls in kindergarten was predicted by anger ratings in a tool use/problem-solving assessment in toddlerhood (Marvinney, 1985).

Findings from the Minnesota study are consistent with previous evidence that parental emotional unavailability is highly predictive of aggression (Egeland & Sroufe, 1981; Sroufe, 1983; Troy & Sroufe, 1987). From an attachment perspective, the avoidant child may approach the world with underlying resentment derived from unmet emotional needs and with relationship experiences that include exploitation and victimization. This child enters the world of peers with a tendency to be hostile and deliberately hurtful toward others and, as a result, is actively rejected by peers (LaFreniere & Sroufe, 1985; Sroufe & Fleeson, 1986). Through processes of internalization, patterns of maladaptation (regulation of emotion, expectations, and attitudes) that begin in the caregiver-infant relationship are carried forward to the child's relationship with peers (Cicchetti et al., 1992).

The links between the child's internal world of representations and expectations and external aggressive behavior have been explored in the work of Dodge and his colleagues (Dodge, Bates, & Pettit, 1990; Dodge & Frame, 1982) and Suess (1987). Dodge and Frame (1982) demonstrated that aggressive children more frequently interpret ambiguous social situations as entailing hostile intent. More recently, Dodge, Bates, and Pettit (1990) demonstrated social cognitive style to be a significant mediator of the relationship between harsh punishment and behavior problems. In a prospective longitudinal study in West Germany, Suess (1987) found that children with avoidant attachment who experienced rejection in early life showed this same attributional style. Although congruent with Dodge's cognitive style interpretation, Suess's data suggest that the roots of these differences lie in the child's actual experience.

Depressive Symptomatology. Using a developmental pathway model, Kobak, Sudler, and Gambler (1991) investigated the relationship of attachment, as measured by the Adult Attachment Interview (George et al., 1984), and depressive symptoms, as measured by the Dimensions of Depression Profile for Adolescents (Harter, Marold, & Nowakowski, 1987). The findings from this study suggest that deviations from secure pathways increase the likelihood of adolescents' reporting depressive symptomatology. Insecure (dismissing and preoccupied) attachment strategies were associated with adolescents' reports of depressive symptoms.

Life stress (maternal ratings of stress) and gender (females at higher risk) also contributed to the model. The authors suggested that the ability to flexibly process information about the self and others related to secure/autonomous classification may reduce the risk of developing dysfunctional expectations, thoughts, and feelings associated with depressive symptoms.

Empirical Findings: Collateral Research

Beyond research based on an attachment organizational perspective designed to assess directly links between relationship experience and later psychopathology, numerous studies corroborate the idea that early experience, including stressful events, influences the child's ability to use external and internal resources and, ultimately, the development of psychopathology.

Depression. Several researchers have demonstrated that early environmental factors can lay the groundwork for affective symptoms later in life. Early experiences of major separation, loss of a parent, or disruption of the parent-child relationship have been consistently linked to greater risk for depressive symptomatology and suicide in adolescents and adults (Bilfulco, Harris, & Brown, 1992; Bowlby, 1980; Brown & Harris, 1978; Brown, Harris, & Bilfulco, 1986; Cadoret, Troughton, Merchant, & Whitters, 1990).

Using an adoption model and data, Cadoret and his colleagues (Cadoret et al., 1990) found an association between environmental factors occurring in the first and second years of life and the report of lifetime depressive and manic symptoms in adult males. The most relevant environmental factor was social disruption or change in home placement from a foster family to an adoptive family. Analysis of data of females from the same adoption studies indicated an association between major depression in adulthood and earlier loss (by death) of adoptive parents.

Similarly, Brown and Harris (1978) found that the loss of mother (by death or separation) alone may not pose a risk for later depressive symptomatology. The risk, however, increases if loss is accompanied by threatening life events, long-term problems, and problematic personal relationships. In two studies (Bilfulco, Brown, & Harris, 1987; Harris, Brown, & Bilfulco, 1986), the increased risk was largely explained in terms of lack of adequate care, which predicted later depression even in the absence of maternal loss (Brown et al., 1986). In both studies, childhood and adulthood helplessness were related to adult depressive symptoms, and substantial continuity was found between the two forms of helplessness (Harris, Brown, & Bilfulco, 1990). Through more recent analyses of these data (Bilfulco et al., 1992), inadequate caregiving prior to loss (rather than care following loss) was found to be related to childhood helplessness and to adult disorder. The series of findings supports (a) the importance of adequate caregiving from natural and surrogate caregivers for socioemotional development and (b) a developmental pathways perspective on the evolution of depressive symptoms in adulthood. Quality of care—in particular, early care—rather than trauma alone may be critical to later psychological functioning.

In the Minnesota longitudinal study (Egeland & Sroufe, 1981; Sroufe, 1983), the association of antecedents and early risk factors with depressive outcomes in middle childhood has been investigated prospectively (Bacon, 1988; Erickson, Bacon, & Egeland, 1987). Children who manifested chronic and severe depressive symptoms, as measured by mother and teacher ratings in middle childhood, began to show depressed-like adaptation as early as 24 months. In a problem-solving situation, depressed children demonstrated a lack of enthusiasm and low positive affect. They were noncompliant and dependent, and they expressed negative affect toward mother. By 42 months, in laboratory and preschool evaluations, a lack of enthusiasm and sad affect were identified across situations of being with mother, being alone, and being in a preschool setting (Erickson et al., 1985).

Early risk factors in the mother-child relationship of later depressed children included insecure attachment and abuse or neglect. In addition, children exhibiting depressive symptoms in middle childhood had experienced a higher incidence of loss or death in their families before the age of 42 months than children in comparison groups. Fifty percent of depressed children had experienced a significant early separation from the caregiver through foster placement.

Borderline. Poor quality early infant-mother interactions are often viewed as the primary cause of childhood borderline disorders, even though little empirical evidence is available to support this position. The majority of theories suggest that the presence of developmental deviation or arrest during early interaction, most likely during the stage of separation-individuation, underlies the disorder (Bemporad, Smith, Hanson, & Cicchetti, 1982; Kohut, 1977; Mahler et al., 1975). Bemporad et al. cited family disturbances—abuse, chaotic family life, history of neglect with bizarre behavior, and inconsistent care—as causal. In this study, mothers were seen as unstable, easily frustrated, and unable to maintain many aspects of interpersonal relationships. Families were characterized by a sense of turmoil and impending violence combined with a lack of consistency in parental behavior. Bemporad and his colleagues speculated that this type of environment impairs the child's development of a "secure self" and his or her ability to manage anxiety. The impaired development and experiences of trauma underlie difficulties in reality testing and preoccupations with destruction and self-annihilation. Consistent with an adaptational view, these researchers suggested that borderline disorders are a heterogeneous group of disorders with no unitary etiology. Multiple divergent pathways that may result from multifactorial etiologies include organicity, deprivation of early socialization, and constant exposure to chaotic traumatic environments.

Dissociative Disorders. Disorganized/disoriented infants may be particularly vulnerable to the development of dissociative disorders (e.g., fugue states, multiple personality disorder), should traumatic circumstances intervene in later life (Liotti, 1992). The disorganized/disoriented attachment style is characterized by lapses or slippages in control, orientation, or organization—characteristics that do not represent organized defensive structures or strategies and are associated with dissociative disorders (Putnam, 1989). Liotti suggested that it is likely that paradoxical frightened/frightening behavior on the part of the attachment figure may represent a form of trance induction and lead to the onset of hypnotic states. Such trancelike states and behavior patterns are observed in some disorganized/disoriented infants.

Maltreatment Sequelae. Studies of maltreating families also support an association between early relational experiences and later difficulties in adaptation. Prospective longitudinal studies demonstrate the continued difficulties in the regulation of affect and negotiation of stage-salient issues of maltreated children (Cicchetti, 1990; Cicchetti & Beeghly, 1987; Egeland & Sroufe, 1981; George & Main, 1979; Kaufman & Cicchetti, 1989).

In the Minnesota study, toddlers with experiences of physical abuse were described as more angry, noncompliant, and frustrated with mother, and less enthusiastic than controls in a problem-solving task (Egeland & Sroufe, 1981). Physically abused maltreated children exhibited a higher frequency of aggression, frustration, and noncompliant behaviors, and a lower frequency of positive affect. Neglected children expressed less positive and more negative affect, and obtained higher noncompliance, frustration, and anger scores than controls did.

Maltreatment histories place children at risk for communication problems in early childhood (Coster, Gersten, Beeghly, & Cicchetti, 1989). Compared with nonmaltreated toddlers, children with experiences of maltreatment demonstrated less well-developed expressive language and showed deficits in discourse abilities, in a study by Coster and his colleagues (1989). Maltreated toddlers differed from normal toddlers on internal state language variables as well. In this study, maltreated children used fewer internal state words, showed less differentiation in attribution, and were more context-bound in their use of internal state language. Maltreating mothers also reported that their children produced fewer internal state words about the self and others (Cicchetti & Beeghly, 1987).

Continued interpersonal difficulties of maltreated children have been demonstrated in studies of peer relations of preschool and school-age children in a variety of settings. George and Main (1979) found that preschool children with histories of physical abuse were rated higher on measures of avoidance and aggression toward peers than matched comparison groups. Most noteworthy in this study was the finding that negative behaviors often occurred in response to friendly overtures from others. Physically abused children also were more likely to respond negatively or aggressively to the naturally occurring distress of peers than were nonabused children (Main & Goldwyn, 1984).

Notable similarities were found among the maltreatment groups when children in the Minnesota longitudinal study were assessed at age 4 to 6 years (Erickson, Egeland, & Pianta, 1989). All children exhibited notable anxiety and anger, were unpopular with peers, and had difficulty functioning independently to meet the kindergarten demands. The authors related these common problems to the lack of nurturance central to all patterns of maltreatment. Children who were identified as physically abused were found to be aggressive and noncompliant, and to exhibit externalizing behavior in kindergarten (Erickson et al., 1989). In a laboratory situation, these children were impulsive, expressed considerable negative affect, and were quick to seek examiner attention or assistance. Children whose mothers were judged to be psychologically unavailable functioned more poorly both on academic tasks and in social situations than children in the control group in kindergarten. Their aggression and disruptive behavior resembled that of physically abused children. Children of psychologically unavailable mothers were described as uninvolved on the laboratory task. The neglected group presented the most severe and varied problems in this study (Erickson et al., 1989). In social situations, neglected children exhibited both aggressive and withdrawn behavior, little positive affect, and unpopularity with their peers. In the classroom, they performed poorly on cognitive tasks, were anxious and inattentive, lacked initiative, and relied heavily on the teacher for help, approval, and encouragement. Similarly, children who had been sexually abused exhibited a range of social behavior and were unpopular with peers and highly dependent on adults for approval and closeness.

Lynch and Cicchetti (1991) examined differences in maltreated and nonmaltreated children's reports of relationships with others (i.e., mother, teacher, and best friend) in middle childhood. Relational dimensions of emotional quality (positive affect and a sense of security) and psychological proximity seeking (desire to feel closer) were investigated. In this study, nonmaltreated children were more likely to show optimal patterns of relatedness (high positive emotional quality and low need for increased psychological closeness). Maltreated children were more likely than nonmaltreated children to show confused patterns (high emotional quality and high need for increased psychological closeness). For all children, substantial concordance was found among patterns of relationships with mother, teacher, and best friend. For all relationships, maltreated children reported greater need for psychological proximity. Consistent with previous maltreatment findings (Cicchetti & Beeghley, 1987), Lynch and Cicchetti suggested that maltreated children have a predominantly negative self-organization, which may impair the functioning of cognitive controls and direct social information processing. Discordant emotional patterns of relationships, reflected in the defensive idealization of relationships, may contribute to the difficulties maltreated children experience in peer relationships—in particular, in children's approaches to new relationships with peers. The authors hypothesized that such approach/avoidance qualities may relate to histories of disorganized/disoriented attachment.

Adult Pathology and Attachment. For children of parents with affective or severe personality disorders, psychological unavailability or the recurrent loss of function during difficult periods (i.e., depressive episodes) may be equivalent to the impact of major separation or loss on the child's self-concept (Cummings & Cicchetti, 1988). In addition, parents may be unable to respond to differences in affect and may be perceived as inconsistent or unavailable (Cicchetti et al., 1988). Maternal affective illness may interfere with parents' capacity to relate in ways that promote the development of reliable patterns of physiological regulation and emotional communication.

Differences in regulation and differentiation of affect emerge very early in the lives of infants exposed to a depressed parent (Cicchetti et al., 1988). In a Rochester longitudinal study (Sameroff, Seifer, & Zax, 1982), infants of depressed parents had greater difficulty with self-quieting than infants of nonaffectively ill parents. At 4 months, infants of depressed parents were less responsive to others, and their mothers were less spontaneous, less happy, less vocal, and less proximal to infants.

Numerous studies demonstrate a greater likelihood of insecure attachment relationships in children of depressed parents (Gaensbauer, Harmon, Cytryn, & McKnew, 1984; Radke-Yarrow, 1991; Radke-Yarrow et al., 1985; Spieker & Booth, 1988; Zahn-Waxler, Cummings, McKnew, Davenport, & Radke-Yarrow, 1984). In the study by Radke-Yarrow and colleagues, insecure attachment was found to be infrequent in children of normal parents or parents with minor depression. Attachment disturbances (avoidant and mixed avoidant/resistant) were found in children of affectively ill parents, and children of bipolar parents showed the highest percentage of insecure attachments.

Studies of toddlers of affectively ill parents provide evidence of the continued effect of depression on the development of an autonomous self and the regulation of emotion. In collaborative NIMH/Colorado studies (Gaensbauer et al., 1984; Radke-Yarrow et al., 1985; Zahn-Waxler et al., 1984), children of parents with bipolar disorder demonstrated increased socioemotional difficulties and were less competent in interpersonal relationships than control groups of children at age 2. Similar difficulties in modulation of affect were seen in toddlers of mothers with unipolar depression (Zahn-Waxler et al., 1984). In this study, nondepressed mothers and mothers with unipolar depression expressed comparable content and quantity of attributions to their children; however, the affective tone of child attributions of depressed mothers was found to be significantly more negative in tone. The investigation of process variables such as these is important for the evaluation of genetic and experiential explanations of these data.

Direct and collateral research on attachment or early care and pathology supports a transactional multidetermined view of the development of psychopathology. The studies highlight the importance, in early care, of sensitivity, responsiveness, and perhaps continuity, for later psychological functioning. Based on empirical findings, the relationship between attachment and stressful life experiences is less clear, in part due to variations in design and methodology employed by relevant studies. Four models are suggested by the data presented here: (a) attachment and stress may be viewed as multiplicative interactive risk factors; (b) attachment may be viewed as mediating the effects of stressful life events; (c) the consequences of attachment may depend on level of stress; or (d) the relationship between attachment and life stress may be viewed in terms of a diathesis/stress model. Within a diathesis/stress model, experiences of anxious attachment (difficulties in dyadic regulation of emotion, and distortions in related expectations and attitudes) may leave individuals vulnerable to the effects of stressful life events. For individuals with avoidant, resistant, or disorganized attachment histories, moderate levels of stress may have adverse effects on socioemotional functioning; individuals with histories of secure attachment may be vulnerable to psychopathology only under conditions of severe stress. Within the context of high stress and anxious attachment, a variety of pathways (based on variations in risk configurations) may nevertheless determine common outcomes of pathology.

FUTURE DIRECTIONS OF ATTACHMENT RESEARCH

Models linking early regulatory experiences, or attachment, and later psychopathology suggest directions for continued investigation. A principal focus of study remains: tracing the origins and course of individual variations in personality functioning. Thus, it is important to build on current research, to follow the pathways of children in high-risk caregiver-child relationships (e.g., abusive or affectively ill caregivers) and of children who presently show specific patterns of socioemotional difficulties in childhood (e.g., aggressive or withdrawn behavior). Disorganized/disoriented attachment patterns as precursors of maladaptation warrant particular study. Questions concern etiologies and correlates of disorganization, the stability and transformations of disorganization over time, and the relationship between disorganization and change (reworking) of coherent organizational strategies.

The careful study of deviant early relationships and interactional precursors of individual malfunctioning will provide a basis for investigating mechanisms that link developmental processes (e.g., cognition and affect) and provide continuity in development. Research is needed on normal and atypical patterns of affect regulation and representational organization across different phases of development. How do individual styles of affect regulation evolve from their beginnings in early attachment relationships? How do affective regulatory styles and representational processes mediate behavior? How do defensive processes develop? A particularly fruitful area of research may be the study of processes of change. What factors facilitate change in organization of behavior and feeling, and how do previous patterns of adaptation continue to influence behavior following significant change?

To fully conceptualize the evolution of developmental pathways, a multidisciplinary investigative approach may be useful. Collaborative efforts involving ideas from relational and family systems theory, research on risk and resilience, and biobehavioral mechanisms may enhance the assessment and interpretation findings related to attachment and development. For example, family systems and relational theoretical perspectives may guide the study of influences of children's experiences of multiple concurrent or sequential caregivers and of the formation and integration of multiple models of experience. The coordination of neurophysiological research with social behavioral investigations of attachment may lead to an understanding of the physiological underpinnings of the development of attachment and the application of principles and findings from neurobiology to the study of human emotional behavior.

Within an organizational/developmental perspective, such research efforts are guided by a view of psychopathology as process, a pattern of adaptation co-constructed by the individual and environment. Pathology is viewed as a complex product of strengths and vulnerabilities, risk and protective processes, with even resilience defined as developmental process. Within this framework, a central role is reserved for relationship history. From early relationships emerges the inner organization of attitudes, feelings, expectations, meanings, and behavior that is the self

(Block & Block, 1980; Breger, 1974; Loevinger, 1976; Sroufe, 1979a). Just as regularities in early dyadic interaction become regularities in individual organization, early relationship difficulties may result in distortions in individual functioning.

Although many childhood problems reflect such troubled relationship histories, most early attachment difficulties are not well thought of as disorders. From an organizational perspective, attachment may best be conceived as a marker of emerging differences in developmental trajectories, dyadic regulatory patterns that represent the history of the infant caregiver relationship over the first year, and the foundation for individual functioning. Such an organizational approach to the study of pathology, with emphasis on mechanisms that influence the early direction of development and that maintain or deflect individuals from developmental pathways, may significantly contribute to our understanding of normal development and provide a truly developmental perspective on psychopathology.

REFERENCES

Achenbach, T. (1978). The child behavior profile, I: Boys aged 6–11. *Journal of Consulting and Clinical Psychology, 46*(3), 478–488.

Ainsworth, M. D. S. (1963). The development of infant-mother interaction among the Ganda. In B. M. Foss (Ed.), *Determinants of infant behavior II.* New York: Wiley.

Ainsworth, M. D. S. (1967). *Infancy in Uganda.* Baltimore: Johns Hopkins University Press.

Ainsworth, M. D. S. (1969). Object relations, dependency and attachment: A theoretical view of the infant-mother relationship. *Child Development, 40,* 969–1025.

Ainsworth, M. D. S. (1973). The development of infant-mother attachment. In B. Caldwell & H. Ricciati (Eds.), *Review of child development research* (Vol. 3, pp. 1–94). Chicago: University of Chicago Press.

Ainsworth, M. D. S. (1982). Attachment: Retrospect and prospect. In C. M. Parkes & J. Stevenson-Hinde (Eds.), *The place of attachment in human behavior* (pp. 3–30). New York: Basic Books.

Ainsworth, M. D. S., Bell, S., & Stayton, D. (1971). Individual differences in Strange Situation behavior of one-year-olds. In H. R. Schaffer (Ed.), *The origins of human social relations* (pp. 17–57). New York: Wiley.

Ainsworth, M. D. S., Bell, S., & Stayton, D. (1974). Infant-mother attachment and social development: Socialization as a product of reciprocal responsiveness to signals. In M. Richards (Ed.), *The integration of the child into the social world* (pp. 99–135). Cambridge, England: Cambridge University Press.

Ainsworth, M. D. S., Blehar, M., Waters, E., & Wall, S. (1978). *Patterns of attachment.* Hillsdale, NJ: Erlbaum.

Ainsworth, M. D. S., & Eichberg, C. G. (1991). Effects on infant-mother attachment of mother's unresolved loss of an attachment figure or other traumatic experience. In P. Marris, J. Stevenson-Hinde, & C. Parkes (Eds.), *Attachment across the life cycle* (pp. 160–183). New York: Routledge.

American Psychiatric Association. (1994). *Diagnostic and statistical manual of mental disorders* (4th ed.). Washington, DC: Author.

Arend, R. (1983). *Infant attachment and patterns of adaptation in a barrier situation at age $3^1/_2$ years.* Unpublished doctoral dissertation, University of Minnesota, Minneapolis.

Arend, R. A., Gove, F. L., & Sroufe, L. A. (1979). Continuity of individual adaptation from infancy to kindergarten: A predictive study of ego-resiliency and curiosity in preschoolers. *Child Development, 50,* 950–959.

Bacon, M. S. (1988). *Antecedents and correlates of depressive symptoms in middle childhood: A longitudinal perspective.* Unpublished doctoral dissertation, University of Minnesota, Minneapolis.

Bates, J., Maslin, C., & Frankel, K. (1985). Attachment security, mother-child interactions, and temperament as predictors of behavior problem ratings at age three years. In I. Bretherton & E. Waters (Eds.), Growing points in attachment theory and research (pp. 167–193). *Monographs of the Society for Research in Child Development, 50* (1-2, Serial No. 209).

Bell, S., & Ainsworth, M. (1972). Infant crying and maternal responsiveness. *Child Development, 43,* 1171–1190.

Belsky, J., & Isabella, R. A. (1988). Maternal, infant, and social-contextual determinants of attachment security. In J. Belsky & T. Nezworski (Eds.), *Clinical implications of attachment* (pp. 41–94). Hillsdale, NJ: Erlbaum.

Belsky, J., & Nezworski, T. (1988). *Clinical implications of attachment.* Hillsdale, NJ: Erlbaum.

Bemporad, J. R., Smith, H. F., Hanson, G., & Cicchetti, D. (1982). Borderline syndromes in childhood: Criteria for diagnosis. *American Journal of Psychiatry, 139,* 596–602.

Bilfulco, A., Brown, G., & Harris, T. (1987). Childhood loss of parent, lack of adequate parental care and adult depression: A replication. *Journal of Affective Disorders, 12,* 115–128.

Bilfulco, A., Harris, T., & Brown, G. (1992). Mourning or early inadequate care? Reexamining the relationship of maternal loss in childhood with adult depression and anxiety. *Development and Psychopathology, 4,* 433–449.

Bion, W. R. (1962). A theory of thinking. In *Second thoughts* (pp. 110–119). London: Heinemann.

Bischof, N. (1975). A systems approach toward the functional connections of attachment and fear. *Child Development, 46,* 801–817.

Blehar, M. C., Lieberman, A. F., & Ainsworth, M. D. S. (1977). Early face-to-face interaction and its relation to later infant-mother attachment. *Child Development, 48,* 182–194.

Block, J. (1971). *Lives through time.* Berkeley, CA: Bancroft Books.

Block, J. H., & Block, J. (1980). The role of ego-control and ego-resiliency in the organization of behavior. In W. A. Collins (Ed.), *Minnesota Symposia on Child Psychology* (Vol. 13, pp. 39–101). Hillsdale, NJ: Erlbaum.

Bohlin, G., Hagekull, B., Germer, M., Andersson, K., & Lindberg, L. (1990, April). *Early antecedents of attachment: Avoidant and resistant reunion behaviors as predicted by maternal interactive behavior and infant temperament.* Paper presented at the International Conference on Infant Studies, Toronto.

Bowlby, J. (1944). Forty-four juvenile thieves: Their characters and home life. *International Journal of Psychoanalysis, 25,* 19–52, 107–127.

Bowlby, J. (1958). The nature of child's tie to his mother. *International Journal of Psychoanalysis, 39,* 350–373.

Bowlby, J. (1973). *Attachment and loss: Vol. 2. Separation.* New York: Basic Books.

Bowlby, J. (1977). The making and breaking of affectional bonds. *British Journal of Psychiatry, 130,* 201–210.

Bowlby, J. (1980). *Attachment and loss: Vol. 3. Loss.* New York: Basic Books.

Bowlby, J. (1982). *Attachment and loss: Vol. 1. Attachment* (2nd ed.). New York: Basic Books. (Original work published 1969.)

Bowlby, J. (1988a). *A secure base: Parent-child attachment and healthy human development.* New York: Basic Books.

Bowlby, J. (1988b). Developmental psychiatry comes of age. *American Journal of Psychiatry, 145*(1), 1–10.

Brazelton, T. B., Koslowski, B., & Main, M. (1974). The origins of reciprocity: The early mother-infant interaction. In M. Lewis & L. Rosenblum (Eds.), *The effect of the infant on its caregiver* (pp. 49–76). New York: Wiley.

Breger, L. (1974). *From instinct to identity: The development of personality.* Englewood Cliffs, NJ: Prentice-Hall.

Bretherton, I. (1987). New perspectives on attachment relations: Security, communication and internal working models. In J. Osofsky (Ed.), *Handbook of infant development* (2nd ed., pp. 1061–1100). New York: Wiley.

Bretherton, I. (1990). Open communication and internal working models: Their role in the development of attachment relationships. In R. A. Thompson (Ed.), *Socioemotional development: Nebraska Symposium on Motivation, 1988* (pp. 57–113). Lincoln: University of Nebraska Press.

Bretherton, I., Ridgeway, D., & Cassidy, J. (1990). Assessing internal working models of the attachment relationship: An attachment story completion task for 3-year-olds. In M. T. Greenberg, D. Cicchetti, & E. M. Cummings (Eds.), *Attachment in the preschool years* (pp. 273–308). Chicago: University of Chicago Press.

Brown, G., & Harris, T. (1978). *Social origins of depression.* London: Tavistock.

Brown, G., Harris, T., & Bifulco, A. (1986). Long-term effects of early loss of parent. In M. Rutter, C. Izard, & P. Read (Eds.), *Depression in young people* (pp. 251–296). New York: Guilford Press.

Cadoret, R. J., Troughton, E., Merchant, L. M., & Whitters, A. (1990). Early life psychosocial events and adult affective symptoms. In L. Robins & M. Rutter (Eds.), *Straight and devious pathways from childhood to adulthood* (pp. 300–313). Cambridge, England: Cambridge University Press.

Cairns, R. B. (1979). *Social development: The origins and plasticity of interchanges.* San Francisco: Freeman.

Carlson, E. (1990). *Individual differences in quality of attachment organization of high-risk adolescent mothers.* Unpublished doctoral dissertation, Columbia University, New York.

Carlson, V., Cicchetti, D., Barnett, D., & Braunwald, K. (1989). Disorganized/disoriented attachment relationships in maltreated infants. *Developmental Psychology, 25,* 525–531.

Cassidy, J. (1988). Child-mother attachment and the self in six-year-olds. *Child Development, 59,* 121–134.

Cassidy, J. (1994). Emotion regulation: Influences of attachment relationships. In N. Fox (Ed.), Biological and behavioral foundations of emotion regulation (pp. 228–249). *Monographs of the Society for Research in Child Development, 59*(2–3, Serial No. 240).

Cassidy, J., & Berlin, L. J. (1994). The insecure/ambivalent pattern of attachment: Theory and research. *Child Development, 65,* 971–991.

Cassidy, J., & Kobak, R. (1988). Avoidance and its relation to other defensive processes. In J. Belsky & T. Nezworski (Eds.), *Clinical implications of attachment theory* (pp. 300–323). Hillsdale, NJ: Erlbaum.

Cicchetti, D. (1984). The emergence of developmental psychopathology. *Child Development, 55,* 1–7.

Cicchetti, D. (1990). The organization and coherence of socioemotional, cognitive, and representational development: Illustrations through a developmental psychopathology perspective on Down syndrome and child maltreatment. In R. Thompson (Ed.), *Nebraska Symposium on Motivation: Vol. 36. Socioemotional development* (pp. 266–375). Lincoln: University of Nebraska Press.

Cicchetti, D., & Beeghly, M. (1987). Symbolic development in maltreated youngsters: An organizational perspective. In D. Cicchetti & M. Beeghly (Eds.), *Symbolic development in atypical children* (pp. 47–68). San Francisco: Jossey-Bass.

Cicchetti, D., Ganiban, J., & Barnett, D. (1991). Contributions from the study of high-risk populations to understanding the development of emotion regulation. In K. Dodge & J. Garber (Eds.), *The development of emotion regulation and dysregulation* (pp. 15–48). New York: Cambridge University Press.

Cicchetti, D., Lynch, M., Shonk, S., & Todd Manly, J. (1992). An organization perspective on peer relations in maltreated children. In R. D. Parke & G. W. Ladd (Eds.), *Family-peer relationships: Modes of linkage.* Hillsdale, NJ: Erlbaum.

Cicchetti, D., & Schneider-Rosen, K. (1986). An organizational approach to childhood depression. In M. Rutter, C. Izard, & P. Read (Eds.), *Depression in young people: Clinical and developmental perspectives* (pp. 71–134). New York: Guilford Press.

Cicchetti, D., Toth, S., & Bush, M. (1988). Developmental psychopathology and incompetence in childhood: Suggestions for intervention. In B. Lahey & A. Kazdin (Eds.), *Advances in clinical child psychology* (Vol. 11, pp. 1–71). New York: Plenum Press.

Clyman, R. B. (1991). The procedural organization of emotions: A contribution from cognitive science to the psychoanalytic theory of therapeutic action. *Journal of the American Psychoanalytic Association, 39,* 349–382 (Supplement).

Cohn, D. A., Cowan, P. A., Cowan, C. P., & Pearson, J. (1992). Mothers' and fathers' working models of childhood attachment relationships, parenting styles, and child behavior. *Development and Psychopathology, 4,* 417–431.

Cole, P., Barrett, K., & Zahn-Waxler, C. (1992). Emotion displays in two-year-olds during mishaps. *Child Development, 63,* 314–324.

Collins, P., & Depue, R. (1992). A neurobehavioral systems approach to development psychopathology: Implications for disorders of affect. In D. Cicchetti & S. Toth (Eds.), *Rochester Symposium on Developmental Psychopathology: Vol. 4. Developmental perspectives on depression* (pp. 29–101). Hillsdale, NJ: Erlbaum.

Coster, W., Gersten, M., Beeghly, M., & Cicchetti, D. (1989). Communicative functioning in maltreated toddlers. *Developmental Psychology, 25,* 1010–1029.

Cowen, E., Pederson, A., Babijian, H., Izzo, L., & Trost, M. (1973). Long-term follow-up of early detected vulnerable children. *Journal of Consulting and Clinical Psychology, 41,* 438–446.

Crittenden, P. M. (1981). Abusing, neglecting, problematic, and adequate dyads: Differentiating by patterns of interaction. *Merrill-Palmer Quarterly, 27,* 201–208.

Crittenden, P. M. (1988). Relationships at risk. In J. Belsky & T. Nezworski (Eds.), *Clinical implications of attachment theory* (pp. 136–174). Hillsdale, NJ: Erlbaum.

Crittenden, P. M. (1990). Internal representational models of attachment relationships. *Infant Mental Health Journal, 11,* 259–277.

Crittenden, P. M., & Ainsworth, M. D. S. (1989). Child maltreatment and attachment theory. In D. Cicchetti & V. Carlson (Eds.), *Child maltreatment: Theory and research on the causes and consequences of child abuse and neglect* (pp. 432–463). New York: Cambridge University Press.

Crockenberg, S. (1981). Infant irritability, mother responsiveness and social support influences on the security of infant-mother attachment. *Child Development, 52,* 857–865.

Crowell, J. A., & Feldman, S. S. (1988). Mothers' internal models of relationships and children's behavioral and developmental status: A study of mother-child interaction. *Child Development, 59,* 1273–1285.

Crowell, J. A., O'Connor, E., Wollmers, G., Sprakin, J., & Rao, U. (1991). Mothers' conceptualizations of parent-child relationships: Relation to mother-child interaction and child behavior problems. *Development and Psychopathology, 3,* 431–444.

Cummings, E. M., & Cicchetti, D. (1988). Toward a transactional model of relations between attachment and depression. In M. T. Greenberg, D. Cicchetti, & E. M. Cummings (Eds.), *Attachment in the preschool years* (pp. 339–372). Chicago: University of Chicago Press.

DeLozier, M. (1982). Attachment theory and child abuse. In C. M. Parkes & J. S. Stevenson-Hinde (Eds.), *The place of attachment in human behavior* (pp. 95–117). London: Tavistock.

Dodge, K., Bates, J., & Pettit, G. (1990). Mechanisms in the cycle of violence. *Science, 250,* 1678–1683.

Dodge, K. A., & Frame, C. L. (1982). Social cognitive biases and deficits in aggressive boys. *Child Development, 53,* 620–635.

Dodge, K. A., Pettit, G. S., McClaskey, C. L., & Brown, M. M. (1986). Social competence in children. *Monographs of the Society for Research in Child Development, 51* (2, Serial No. 213).

Dozier, M., & Kobak, R. R. (1992). Psychophysiology in attachment interviews: Converging evidence for deactivating strategies. *Child Development, 63,* 1473–1480.

Edelman, G. (1987). *Neurodarwinism.* New York: Basic Books.

Edelman, G. (1992). *Bright air, brilliant fire.* New York: Basic Books.

Egeland, B. (1991). From data to definition. *Development and Psychopathology, 3,* 37–43.

Egeland, B., Breitenbucher, M., & Rosenberg, D. (1980). A prospective study of the significance of life stress in the etiology of child abuse. *Journal of Clinical and Consulting Psychology, 48,* 195–205.

Egeland, B., & Farber, E. (1984). Infant-mother attachment: Factors related to its development and changes over time. *Child Development, 55*(3), 753–771.

Egeland, B., Kalkoske, M., Gottesman, N., & Erickson, M. F. (1990). Preschool behavior problems: Stability and factors accounting for change. *Journal of Child Psychology and Psychiatry, 31*(6), 891–910.

Egeland, B., & Sroufe, L. A. (1981). Developmental sequelae of maltreatment in infancy. In D. Cicchetti & R. Rizley (Eds.), *Developmental approaches to child maltreatment: New directions in child development* (Vol. 11, pp. 77–92). San Francisco: Jossey-Bass.

Eichberg, C. G. (1987, April). *Quality of infant-parent attachment: Related to mother's representation of her own relationship history.* Paper presented at the biennial meeting of the Society for Research in Child Development, Baltimore, MD.

Elicker, J. (1991, April). *Attachment history, interpersonal sensitivity peer competence and preadolescence.* Poster presented at the biennial meeting of the Society for Research in Child Development, Seattle, WA.

Elicker, J., Englund, M., & Sroufe, L. A. (1992). Predicting peer competence and peer relationships in childhood from early parent-child relationships. In R. Parke & G. Ladd (Eds.), *Family-peer relationships: Modes of linkage* (pp. 77–106). Hillsdale, NJ: Erlbaum.

Emde, R. (1989). The infant's relationship experience: Developmental and affective aspects. In A. Sameroff & R. Emde (Eds.), *Relationship disturbances in early childhood* (pp. 33–51). New York: Basic Books.

Emde, R., & Buchsbaum, H. (1990). "Didn't you hear my mommy?" Autonomy with connectedness in moral self-emergence. In D. Cicchetti & M. Beeghly (Eds.), *The self in transition* (pp. 35–60). Chicago: University of Chicago Press.

Epstein, S. (1973). The self-concept revisited: Or a theory of a theory. *American Psychologist, 28,* 404–416.

Epstein, S. (1991). Cognitive-experiential self theory: Implications for developmental psychology. In M. Gunnar & L. A. Sroufe (Eds.), *Minnesota Symposia on Child Psychology* (Vol. 23, pp. 79–123). Hillsdale, NJ: Erlbaum.

Erickson, M. F., Bacon, M., & Egeland, B. (1987, April). *Developmental antecedents and concomitants of depressive symptoms in preschool children.* Paper presented at the biennial meeting of the Society for Research in Child Development, Baltimore, MD.

Erickson, M. F., Egeland, B., & Pianta, R. (1989). The effects of maltreatment on the development of young children. In D. Cicchetti & V. Carlson (Eds.), *Child maltreatment: Theory and research on the causes and consequences of child abuse and neglect* (pp. 647–684). New York: Cambridge University Press.

Erickson, M., Egeland, B., & Sroufe, L. A. (1985). The relationship between quality of attachment and behavior problems in preschool in a high-risk sample. In I. Bretherton & E. Waters (Eds.), Growing points in attachment theory and research (pp. 147–186). *Monographs of the Society for Research in Child Development, 50* (1-2, Serial No. 209).

Erikson, E. H. (1963). *Childhood and society* (2nd ed.). New York: Norton.

Escalona, S. (1968). *The roots of individuality.* Chicago: Aldine.

Feldman, S. S., & Ingham, M. E. (1975). Attachment behavior: A validation study in two age groups. *Child Development, 46,* 319–330.

Flavell, J. H. (1977). *Cognitive development.* Englewood Cliffs, NJ: Prentice-Hall.

Fonagy, P., Steele, H., & Steele, M. (1991). Maternal representations of attachment during pregnancy predict the organization of infant-mother attachment at one year of age. *Child Development, 62,* 891–905.

Frankel, K. F., & Bates, J. E. (1984). *Mother-toddler interactions while solving problems: Correlations with attachment security and interaction at home.* Unpublished manuscript, Indiana University, Bloomington.

Freud, A. (1946). *The ego and mechanisms of defense.* New York: International Universities Press.

Freud, A. (1974). A psychoanalytic view of developmental psychopathology. *Journal of the Philadelphia Association for Psychoanalysis, 1,* 7–17.

Freud, A. (1976). Psychopathology seen against the background of normal development. *British Journal of Psychiatry, 129,* 401–406.

Fury, G. (1993, March). *The relationship between infant attachment history and representations of relationships in school-aged family drawings.* Poster presented at the biennial meeting of the Society for Research in Child Development, New Orleans.

Gaensbauer, T., Harmon, R., Cytryn, L., & McKnew, D. (1984). Social and affective development in infants with a manic-depressive parent. *American Journal of Psychiatry, 141,* 223–229.

Garbarino, J., & Gillian, G. (1980). *Understanding abusive families.* Lexington, MA: Lexington Books.

George, C., Kaplan, N., & Main, M. (1984). *Attachment interview for adults.* Unpublished manuscript, University of California, Berkeley.

George, C., & Main, M. (1979). Social interactions of young abused children: Approach, avoidance, and aggression. *Child Development, 50,* 306–318.

Gil, D. B. (1970). *Violence against children: Physical child abuse in the United States.* Cambridge, MA: Harvard University Press.

Gottlieb, G. (1991). Experiential canalization of behavioral development: Theory. *Developmental Psychology, 27,* 4–13.

Gove, F. (1983). *Patterns and organizations of behavior and affective expression during the second year of life.* Unpublished doctoral dissertation, University of Minnesota, Minneapolis.

Greenough, W., & Black, J. (1992). Induction of brain structure by experience: Substrates for cognitive development. In M. R. Gunnar & C. A. Nelson (Eds.), *Minnesota Symposia on Child Psychology* (Vol. 24, pp. 155–200). Hillsdale, NJ: Erlbaum.

Greenough, W., Black, J., & Wallace, C. (1987). Experience and brain development. *Child Development, 58,* 535–559.

Grossmann, K., Fremmer-Bombik, E., Rudolph, J., & Grossmann, K. E. (1988). Maternal attachment representations is related to patterns of child-mother attachment patterns and maternal sensitivity and acceptance of her infant. In R. A. Hinde & J. Stevenson-Hinde (Eds.), *Relationships within families* (pp. 241–260). Oxford, England: Oxford University Press.

Grossmann, K. E., & Grossmann, K. (1991). Attachment quality as an organizer of emotional and behavioral responses in a longitudinal perspective. In C. M. Parkes, J. Stevenson-Hinde, & P. Marris (Eds.), *Attachment across the life cycle.* London: Tavistock/Routledge.

Grossmann, K. E., Grossmann, K., & Schwan, A. (1986). Capturing the wider view of attachment: A reanalysis of Ainsworth's Strange Situation. In C. E. Izard & P. B. Read (Eds.), *Measuring emotions in infants and children* (Vol. 2, pp. 124–171). New York: Cambridge University Press.

Grossmann, K., Grossmann, K. E., Spangler, G., Suess, G., & Unzer, L. (1985). Maternal sensitivity and newborn orienting responses as related to quality of attachment in Northern Germany. In I. Bretherton & E. Waters (Eds.), Growing points of attachment theory and research (pp. 233–256). *Monographs of the Society for Research in Child Development, 50* (1-2, Serial No. 209).

Guidano, V. F., & Liotti, G. (1983). *Cognitive processes and emotional disorders: A structural approach to psychotherapy.* New York: Guilford Press.

Gunnar, M., Mangelsdorf, S., Larson, M., & Hertsgaard, L. (1989). Attachment, temperament, and adrenocortical activity in infancy: A study of psychoendocrine regulation. *Developmental Psychology, 25,* 355–363.

Harlow, H. F. (1958). The nature of love. *American Psychologist, 13,* 673–685.

Harlow, H. F. (1963). The maternal affectional system. In B. M. Foss (Ed.), *Determinants of infant behavior* (pp. 3–29). New York: Wiley.

Harlow, H. F., & Harlow, M. K. (1965). The affectional systems. In A. M. Schrier, H. F. Harlow, & F. Stollnitz (Eds.), *Behavior of nonhuman primates* (Vol. 2, pp. 1–28). New York: Academic Press.

Harlow, H. F., & Harlow, M. K. (1966). Learning to love. *American Scientist, 54,* 244–272.

Harris, T., Brown, G. W., & Bifulco, A. (1986). Loss of parent and adult psychiatric disorder: The rule of lack of adequate parental care. *Psychological Medicine, 16,* 641–659.

Harris, T., Brown, G. W., & Bifulco, A. (1990). Loss of parent and adult psychiatric disorder: A tentative overall model. *Development and Psychopathology, 2,* 311–328.

Harter, S. (1986). Cognitive-developmental processes in the integration of concepts about emotions and self. *Social Cognition, 4,* 119–151.

Harter, S., Marold, D., & Nowakowski, M. (1987). *Manual for the Dimensions of Depression Profile for Children and Adolescents.* Department of Psychology, University of Delaware, Newark, DE.

Heinicke, C., & Westheimer, I. (1966). *Brief separations.* New York: International Universities Press.

Hilgard, E. R. (1977). *Divided consciousness: Multiple controls in human thought and action.* New York: Wiley.

Isabella, R. A. (1993). Origins of attachment: Maternal interactive behavior across the first year. *Child Development, 64,* 605–621.

Isabella, R. A., & Belsky, J. (1991). Interactional syncrony and the origins of infant-mother attachment: A replication study. *Child Development, 62,* 373–384.

James, W. (1980). *Principles of psychology.* New York: Holt.

Kaplan, N. (1987). *Individual differences in 6-year-olds' thoughts about separation: Predicted from attachment to mother at age 1.* Unpublished doctoral dissertation. Department of Psychology, University of California, Berkeley.

Kaplan, N., & Main, M. (1989). *A system for the analysis of family drawings.* Unpublished manuscript, Department of Psychology, University of California, Berkeley.

Kaufman, J., & Cicchetti, D. (1989). Effects of maltreatment on school-age children's socioemotional development: Assessments in a day-camp setting. *Developmental Psychology, 25,* 516–524.

Kestenbaum, R., Farber, E., & Sroufe, L. A. (1989). Individual differences in empathy among preschoolers' concurrent and predictive validity. In N. Eisenberg (Ed.), *Empathy and related emotional responses: New directions for child development* (pp. 51–56). San Francisco: Jossey-Bass.

Kihlstrom, J. F. (1987). The cognitive unconscious. *Science, 237,* 1445–1452.

Kiser, L., Bates, J., Maslin, C., & Bayles, K. (1986). Mother-infant play at six months as a predictor of attachment security at thirteen months. *Journal of the American Academy of Child Psychiatry, 25,* 68–75.

Klagsbrun, M., & Bowlby, J. (1976). Responses to separation from parents: A clinical test for young children. *British Journal of Projective Psychology, 21,* 7–21.

Kobak, R. R. (1985). *Attitudes towards attachment relations and social competence among first year college students.* Unpublished doctoral dissertation, University of Virginia, Charlottesville.

Kobak, R. R., Cole, H. E., Ferenz-Gillies, R., Fleming, W., & Gamble, W. (1993). Attachment and emotion regulation during mother-teen problem solving: A control theory analysis. *Child Development, 64,* 231–245.

Kobak, R. R., & Sceery, A. (1988). Attachment in later adolescence: Working models, affect regulation, and perceptions of self and others. *Child Development, 59,* 135–146.

Kobak, R. R., & Shaver, P. (1987, June). *Strategies for maintaining felt security: A theoretical analysis of continuity and change in styles of social adaptation.* Paper presented at the Conference in Honor of John Bowlby's 80th Birthday, London.

Kobak, R. R., Sudler, N., & Gambler, W. (1991). Attachment and depressive symptoms during adolescence: A developmental pathways analysis. *Development and Psychopathology, 3,* 461–474.

Kochanska, G. (1993). Toward a synthesis of parental socialization and child temperament in early development of conscience. *Child Development, 64,* 325–347.

Kohlberg, L., Ricks, D., & Snarey, J. (1984). Childhood development as a predictor of adaptation in childhood. *Genetic Psychology Monographs, 110,* 91–172.

Kohut, H. (1977). *The restoration of the self.* New York: International Universities Press.

Kopp, C. (1982). Antecedents of self-regulation: A developmental perspective. *Developmental Psychology, 18*(2), 199–214.

Kopp, C., Krakow, J., & Vaughn, B. (1983). The antecedents of self-regulation in young handicapped children. In M. Perlmutter (Ed.), *Minnesota Symposia on Child Psychology* (Vol. 17). Hillsdale, NJ: Erlbaum.

Kraemer, G. W. (1992). A psychobiological theory of attachment. *Behavioral and Brain Sciences, 15,* 493–541.

Kuo, Z.-Y. (1967). *The dynamics of behavior development: An epigenetic view.* New York: Random House.

LaFreniere, P. J., & Sroufe, L. A. (1985). Profiles of peer competence in the preschool: Interrelations among measures, influence of social ecology, and relation to attachment history. *Developmental Psychology, 21,* 56–66.

Lay, K., Waters, E., & Posada, G. (in press). Security of attachment and preschoolers' mood induceability. *Monographs of the Society for Research in Child Development.*

Lewis, M., Alessandri, S., & Sullivan, M. (1992). Differences in shame and pride as a function of children's gender and task difficulty. *Child Development, 63,* 630–638.

Lewis, M., & Brooks. J. (1978). Self-knowledge and emotional development. In M. Lewis & L. Rosenblum (Eds.), *The development of affect.* New York: Plenum Press.

Lewis, M., Feiring, C., McGuffog, C., & Jaskir, J. (1984). Predicting psychopathology in six-year-olds from early social relations. *Child Development, 55,* 123–136.

Lieberman, A. F. (1977). Preschooler's competence with a peer: Relations of attachment and peer expenses. *Child Development, 55,* 123–126.

Lieberman, A. F., & Pawl, J. H. (1990). Disorders of attachment and secure base behavior in the second year of life: Conceptual issues and clinical intervention. In M. T. Greenberg, D. Cicchetti, & E. M. Cummings (Eds.), *Attachment in the preschool years* (pp. 375–398). Chicago: University of Chicago Press.

Liotti, G. (1992). Disorganized/disoriented attachment in the etiology of the dissociative disorders. *Dissociation, 4,* 196–204.

Loevinger, J. (1976). *Ego development.* San Francisco: Jossey-Bass.

Londerville, S., & Main, M. (1981). Security of attachment, compliance, and maternal training methods in the second year of life. *Developmental Psychology, 17,* 238–299.

Lorenz, K. (1965). *The evolution and modification of behavior.* Chicago: University of Chicago Press.

Ludwig, A. M. (1983). The psychobiological functions of dissociation. *American Journal of Clinical Hypnosis, 26,* 93–99.

Lutkenhaus, P., Grossmann, K. E., & Grossmann, K. (1985). Infant-mother attachment at twelve months and style of interaction with a stranger at the age of three years. *Child Development, 56,* 1538–1542.

Lynch, M., & Cicchetti, D. (1991). Patterns of relatedness in maltreated and nonmaltreated children: Connections among multiple representational models. *Development and Psychopathology, 3,* 207–226.

Lyons-Ruth, K., Alpern, L., & Repacholi, B. (1993). Disorganized infant attachment classification and maternal psychosocial problems as predictors of hostile-aggressive behavior in the preschool classroom. *Child Development, 64,* 572–585.

Lyons-Ruth, K., Repacholi, B., McLeod, S., & Silva, E. (1991). Disorganized attachment behavior in infancy: Short-term stability, maternal and infant correlates and risk-related subtypes. *Development and Psychopathology, 3,* 377–396.

Magnusson, D. (1988). *Individual development from an international perspective: A longitudinal study.* Hillsdale, NJ: Erlbaum.

Magnusson, D. (1992). Back to the phenomena: Theory, methods, and statistics in psychological research. *European Journal of Personality, 6,* 1–14.

Mahler, M., Pine, R., & Bergman, A. (1975). *The psychological birth of human infants.* New York: Basic Books.

Main, M. (1973). *Play, exploration and competence as related to child-adult attachment.* Unpublished doctoral dissertation, Johns Hopkins University, Baltimore, MD.

Main, M. (1981). Avoidance in the service of attachment: A working paper. In K. Immelmann, G. Barlow, L. Petrinovich, & M. Main (Eds.), *Behavioral development: The Bielefeld interdisciplinary project* (pp. 651–693). New York: Cambridge University Press.

Main, M. (1985, April). *Adult mental organization with respect to attachment: Related to infant Strange Situation attachment status.* Paper presented at the biennial meeting of the Society for Research in Child Development, Toronto.

Main, M. (in press). Discourse, prediction, and studies in attachment: Implications for psychoanalysis. In T. Shapiro & R. Emde (Eds.), *Some empirical issues in psychoanalysis. Journal of the American Psychoanalytic Association* (Supplement).

Main, M., & Goldwyn, R. (1984). Predicting rejection of her infant from mother's representation of her own experiences: A preliminary report. *International Journal of Child Abuse and Neglect, 8,* 203–217.

Main, M., & Goldwyn, R. (1989). *Adult attachment rating and classification system.* Unpublished scoring manual, Department of Psychology, University of California, Berkeley.

Main, M., & Hesse, E. (1990). Parents' unresolved traumatic experiences are related to infant disorganized attachment status: Is frightened and/or frightening parental behavior the linking mechanism? In M. T. Greenberg, D. Cicchetti, & E. M. Cummings (Eds.), *Attachment in the preschool years* (pp. 161–182). Chicago: University of Chicago Press.

Main, M., Kaplan, N., & Cassidy, J. (1985). Security in infancy, childhood, and adulthood: A move to the level of representation. In I. Bretherton & E. Waters (Eds.), Growing points in attachment theory and research (pp. 66–104). *Monographs of the Society for Research in Child Development, 50* (1-2, Serial No. 209).

Main, M., & Solomon, J. (1990). Procedures for identifying infants as disorganized/disoriented during the Ainsworth strange situation.

In M. T. Greenberg, D. Cicchetti, & E. M. Cummings (Eds.), *Attachment in the preschool years* (pp. 121–160). Chicago: University of Chicago Press.

Mandler, J. M. (1983). Representation. In P.H. Mussen (Ed.), *Handbook of child psychology: Vol. III. Cognitive development* (pp. 420–494); J. H. Flavell & E. M. Markman (Eds.). New York: Wiley.

Mans, L., Cicchetti, D., & Sroufe, L. A. (1978). Mirror reactions of Down's syndrome infants and toddlers: Cognitive underpinnings of self-recognition. *Child Development, 49,* 1247–1250.

Marvinney, D. (1985). *Sibling relationships in middle childhood: Implications for social-emotional development.* Unpublished doctoral dissertation, University of Minnesota, Minneapolis.

Mason, W., & Kenney, M. (1974). Redirection of filial attachments in rhesus monkeys: Dogs as mother surrogates. *Science, 183,* 1209–1211.

Matas, L., Arend, R. A., & Sroufe, L. A. (1978). Continuity of adaptation in the second year: The relationship between quality of attachment and later competence. *Child Development, 49,* 547–556.

McCrone, E., Carlson, E., & Engler, J. (1993, March). *Relations of attachment to defensive organization in middle childhood.* Poster presented at the biennial meeting of the Society for Research in Child Development, New Orleans, LA.

Morris, D. (1980). *Infant attachment and problem solving in the toddler: Relations to mother's family history.* Unpublished doctoral dissertation, University of Minnesota, Minneapolis.

Nelson, K. (1992). Emergence of autobiographical memory at age 4. *Human Development, 35,* 172–177.

Nelson, K., & Gruendel, J. (1981). Generalized event representations: Basic building blocks of cognitive development. In M. Lamb & A. Brown (Eds.), *Advances in developmental psychology* (pp. 131–158). Hillsdale, NJ: Erlbaum.

O'Connor, M. J., Sigman, M., & Brill, N. (1987). Disorganization of attachment in relation to maternal alcohol consumption. *Journal of Consulting and Clinical Psychology, 55,* 831–836.

Pancake, V. (1985, April). *Continuity between mother-infant attachment and ongoing dyadic peer relationships in preschool.* Paper presented at the biennial meeting of the Society for Research in Child Development, Toronto.

Park, K. A. (1991). *A developmental model of the relations between mother-child attachment and friendship.* Unpublished manuscript, Kent State University, Kent, OH.

Park, K. A., & Waters, E. (1989). Security of attachment and preschool friendships. *Child Development, 60,* 1076–1081.

Pastor, D. L. (1981). The quality of mother-infant attachment and its relationship to toddlers' initial sociability with peers. *Developmental Psychology, 17,* 323–335.

Piaget, J. (1952). *The origins of intelligence in children.* New York: Norton.

Piaget, J., & Inhelder, B. (1969). The psychology of the child. New York: Basic Books.

Putnam, F. W. (1989). *Diagnosis and treatment of multiple personality disorder.* New York: Guilford Press.

Radke-Yarrow, M. (1991). Attachment patterns in children of depressed mothers. In P. Harris, J. Stevenson-Hinde, & C. Parkes (Eds.), *Attachment across the life cycle* (pp. 115–126). London: Routledge.

Radke-Yarrow, M., Cummings, E. M., Kuczynski, L., & Chapman, M. (1985). Patterns of attachment in two- and three-year-olds in normal families and families with parental depression. *Child Development, 56,* 884–893.

Radke-Yarrow, M., Zahn-Waxler, C., & Chapman, M. (1983). Children's prosocial dispositions and behavior. In P. Mussen (Ed.), *Carmichael's manual of child psychology: Vol. 4* (4th ed.). New York: Wiley.

Ramirez, M., Carlson, E., Gest, S., & Egeland, B. (1991, July). *The relationship between children's behavior at school and internal representations of their relationships as measured by the sentence completion method.* Paper presented at the biennial meeting of the International Society for the Study of Behavioral Development, Minneapolis.

Reider, C., & Cicchetti, D. (1989). Organizational perspective on cognitive control functioning and cognitive-affective balance in maltreated children. *Developmental Psychology, 25*(3), 382–393.

Renken, B., Egeland, B., Marvinney, D., Sroufe, L. A., & Mangelsdorf, S. (1989). Early childhood antecedents of aggression and passive-withdrawal in early elementary school. *Journal of Personality, 57*(2), 257–281.

Ricks, M. (1985). The social transmission of parental behavior: Attachment across generations. In I. Bretherton & E. Waters (Eds.), Growing points in attachment theory and research (pp. 211–227). *Monographs of the Society for Research in Child Development, 50* (1-2, Serial No. 209).

Robertson, J., & Robertson, J. (1971). Young children in brief separation: A fresh look. *Psychoanalytic Study of the Child, 26,* 264–315.

Robins, L. (1978). Sturdy childhood predictors of adult antisocial behavior: Replications from longitudinal studies. *Psychological Medicine, 8,* 611–622.

Rodning, C., Beckwith, L., & Howard, J. (1991). Quality of attachment and home environments in children prenatally exposed to PCP and cocaine. *Development and Psychopathology, 3,* 351–366.

Roff, M., Sells, S., & Golden, M. (1972). *Social adjustment and personality development in children.* Minneapolis: University of Minnesota Press.

Rosenberg, D. M. (1984). *The quality and content of preschool fantasy play: Correlates in concurrent social-personality function and early mother-child attachment relationships.* Unpublished doctoral dissertation, University of Minnesota, Minneapolis.

Rovee-Collier, C. (1993). The capacity for long-term memory in infancy. *Current Directions in Psychological Science, 2*(4), 130–135.

Ruppenthal, G. C., Arling, G. L., Harlow, H. F., Sackett, G. P., & Suomi, S. J. (1976). A 10-year perspective of motherless-mother monkey behavior. *Journal of Abnormal Psychology, 85*(4), 341–349.

Rutter, M. (1981). Epidemiological-longitudinal approaches to the study of development. In W. A. Collins (Ed.), *Minnesota Symposia on Child Psychology* (Vol. 15, pp. 105–144). Hillsdale, NJ: Erlbaum.

Rutter, M. (1988). Functions and consequences of relationships: Some psychopathological considerations. In R. A. Hinde & J. Stevenson-Hinde (Eds.), *Relationships within families: Mutual influences* (pp. 332–353). New York: Oxford University Press.

Sameroff, A. (1983). Developmental systems: Contexts and evolution. In P. H. Mussen (Ed.); *Handbook of child psychology* (4th ed.) (pp. 237–294). New York: Wiley.

Sameroff, A., & Chandler, M. (1975). Reproductive risk and the continuum of caretaking casualty. In F. D. Horowitz (Ed.), *Child development research* (Vol. 4, pp. 187–244). Chicago: University of Chicago Press.

Sameroff, A., & Emde, R. (1989). *Relationship disturbances in early childhood.* New York: Basic Books.

Sameroff, A., Seifer, R., & Zax, M. (1982). Early development of children at risk for emotional disorder. *Monographs of the Society for Research in Child Development, 47* (Serial No. 199).

Sander, L. W. (1975). Infant and caretaking environment. In E. J. Anthony (Ed.), *Explorations in child psychiatry.* New York: Plenum Press.

Santostefano, S. (1978). *A biodevelopmental approach to clinical child psychology.* New York: Wiley.

Schneider-Rosen, K., Braunwald, K. G., Carlson, V., & Cicchetti, D. (1985). Current perspectives in attachment theory: Illustration from the study of maltreated infants. In I. Bretherton & E. Waters (Eds.), Growing points in attachment theory and research (pp. 194–210). *Monographs of the Society for Research in Child Development, 50* (1-2, Serial No. 209).

Sigman, M. (1989). The application of developmental knowledge to a clinical problem: The study of childhood autism. In D. Cicchetti (Ed.), *Rochester Symposium on Developmental Psychopathology: Vol. 1. The emergence of a discipline* (pp. 165–187). Hillsdale, NJ: Erlbaum.

Sorce, J., & Emde, R. (1981). Mother's presence is not enough: The effect of emotional availability on infant exploration and play. *Developmental Psychology, 17,* 737–745.

Spangler, G., & Grossmann, K. E. (1993). Biobehavioral organization in securely and insecurely attached infants. *Child Development, 64,* 1439–1450.

Spieker, S., & Booth, C. (1988). Maternal antecedents of attachment quality. In J. Belsky & T. Nezworski (Eds.), *Clinical implications of attachment* (pp. 95–135). Hillsdale, NJ: Erlbaum.

Sroufe, L. A. (1979a). The coherence of individual development. *American Psychologist, 34*(10), 834–841.

Sroufe, L. A. (1979b). Socioemotional development. In J. Osofsky (Ed.), *Handbook of infant development* (pp. 462–516). New York: Wiley.

Sroufe, L. A. (1983). Infant-caregiver attachment and patterns of adaptation in preschool: The roots of maladaptation and competence. In M. Perlmutter (Ed.), *Minnesota Symposia in Child Psychology* (Vol. 16, pp. 41–83). Hillsdale, NJ: Erlbaum.

Sroufe, L. A. (1986). Bowlby's contribution to psychoanalytic theory and developmental psychopathology. *Journal of Child Psychology and Psychiatry, 27,* 841–849.

Sroufe, L. A. (1988). The role of infant-caregiver attachment in development. In J. Belsky & T. Nezworski (Eds.), *Clinical implications of attachment* (pp. 18–38). Hillsdale, NJ: Erlbaum.

Sroufe, L. A. (1989a). Relationships, self, and individual adaptation. In A. J. Sameroff & R. N. Emde (Eds.), *Relationship disturbances in early childhood: A developmental approach* (pp. 70–94). New York: Basic Books.

Sroufe, L. A. (1989b). Pathways to adaptation and maladaptation: Psychopathology as developmental deviation. In D. Cicchetti (Ed.), *Rochester Symposium on Developmental Psychopathology: Vol. 1. The emergence of a discipline* (pp. 13–40). Hillsdale, NJ: Erlbaum.

Sroufe, L. A. (1990a). Considering normal and abnormal together: The essence of developmental psychopathology. *Development and Psychopathology, 2,* 335–347.

Sroufe, L. A. (1990b). An organizational perspective on the self. In D. Cicchetti & M. Beeghly (Eds.), *The self in transition: Infancy to childhood* (pp. 281–307). Chicago: University of Chicago Press.

Sroufe, L. A. (in press). *Emotional development.* New York: Cambridge University Press.

Sroufe, L. A., Carlson, E., & Shulman, S. (1993). The development of individuals in relationships: From infancy through adolescence. In D. C. Funder, R. Parke, C. Tomlinson-Keesey, & K. Widaman (Eds.), *Studying lives through time: Approaches to personality and development* (pp. 315–342). Washington, DC: American Psychological Association.

Sroufe, L. A., & Egeland, B. (1991). Illustrations of person and environment interaction from a longitudinal study. In T. Wachs & R. Plomin (Eds.), *Conceptualization and measurement of organism-environment interaction* (pp. 68–84). Washington, DC: American Psychological Association.

Sroufe, L. A., Egeland, B., & Kreutzer, T. (1990). The fate of early experience following developmental change: Longitudinal approaches to individual adaptation in childhood. *Child Development, 61,* 1363–1373.

Sroufe, L. A., & Fleeson, J. (1986). Attachment and the construction of relationships. In W. Hartup & Z. Rubin (Eds.), *Relationships and development.* Hillsdale, NJ: Erlbaum.

Sroufe, L. A., & Fleeson, J. (1988). The coherence of family relationships. In R. A. Hinde & J. Stevenson-Hinde (Eds.), *Relationships within families: Mutual influences* (pp. 27–47). Oxford: Oxford University Press.

Sroufe, L. A., Fox, N., & Pancake, V. (1983). Attachment and dependency in developmental perspective. *Child Development, 54*(6), 1615–1627.

Sroufe, L. A., & Rutter, M. (1984). The domain of developmental psychopathology. *Child Development, 55,* 17–29.

Sroufe, L. A., Schork, E., Motti, E., Lawroski, N., & LaFreniere, P. (1984). The role of affect in social competence. In C. Izard, J. Kagan, & R. Zajonc (Eds.), *Emotion, cognition and behavior* (pp. 289–319). New York: Plenum Press.

Sroufe, L. A., & Waters, E. (1977). Attachment as an organizational construct. *Child Development, 48,* 1184–1199.

Stern, D. N. (1974). The goal of structure of mother and infant play. *Journal of the American Academy of Child Psychiatry, 13,* 402–421.

Stern, D. N. (1985). *The interpersonal world of the infant.* New York: Basic Books.

Stern, D. N. (1994). One way to build a clinically relevant baby. *Infant Mental Health Journal, 15*(1), 9–25.

Strage, A., & Main, M. (1984). *Attachment and parent-child discourse patterns.* Unpublished manuscript, University of California, Berkeley.

Suess, G. (1987). *Auswirkungen fruhkindlicher bindungserfahrungen auf die kompetenz in kindergarten* (Consequences of early attachment experiences on competence in preschool). Doctoral dissertation, University of Regensburg.

Suess, G. J., Grossmann, K. E., & Sroufe, L. A. (1992). Effects of infant attachment to mother and father on quality of adaptation in preschool: From dyadic to individual organization of self. *International Journal of Behavioral Development, 15*(1), 43–66.

Sullivan, H. S. (1953). *The interpersonal theory of psychiatry.* New York: Norton.

Susman, A., Kalkoske, M., & Egeland, B. (in press). Infant temperament and maternal sensitivity as predictors of attachment security. *Infant Behavior and Development.*

Tracy, R., Lamb, M., & Ainsworth, M. D. S. (1976). Infant approach behavior as related to attachment. *Child Development, 47,* 571–578.

Troy, M., & Sroufe, L. A. (1987). Victimization among preschoolers: The role of attachment relationship history. *Journal of the American Academy of Child and Adolescent Psychiatry, 26*(2), 166–172.

Tulving, E. (1985). How many memory systems are there? *American Psychologist, 40,* 385–398.

Tulving, E. (1989). Remembering and knowing the past. *American Scientist, 77,* 361–367.

Urban, J., Carlson, E., Egeland, B., & Sroufe, L. A. (1991). Patterns of individual adaptation across childhood. *Development and Psychopathology, 3,* 445–460.

Van IJzendoorn, M. H. (in press). Attachment representations in mothers, fathers, adolescents, and clinical groups: A meta-analytic search for normative data. *Journal of Clinical and Consulting Psychology.*

Vaughn, B. (1977). *The development of greeting behavior in infants from 6 to 12 months of age.* Unpublished doctoral dissertation, University of Minnesota, Minneapolis.

Vaughn, B., Lefever, G., Seifer, R., & Barglow, P. (1989). Attachment behavior, attachment security, and temperament during infancy. *Child Development, 60,* 728–737.

Waddington, C. H. (1957). *The strategy of the genes.* London: Allen & Unwin.

Ward, M. J., & Carlson, E. (in press). The validity of the adult attachment interview for adolescent mothers. *Child Development.*

Waters, E., Crowell, J., Treboux, D., O'Connor, E., Posada, G., & Golby, B. (1993, March). *Discriminant validity of the Adult Attachment Interview.* Poster presented at the biennial meeting of the Society for Research in Child Development, New Orleans.

Waters, E., & Deane, K. (1985). Defining and assessing individual differences in attachment relationships: Q-methodology and the organization of behavior in infancy and early childhood. In I. Bretherton & E. Waters (Eds.), Growing points of attachment theory and research (pp. 41–65). *Monographs of the Society for Research in Child Development, 50* (1-2, Serial No. 209).

Waters, E., & Sroufe, L. A. (1983). Social competence as a developmental construct. *Developmental Review, 3,* 79–97.

Waters, E., Wippman, J., & Sroufe, L. A. (1979). Attachment, positive affect, and competence in the peer group: Two studies in construct validation. *Child Development, 50,* 821–829.

Werner, H. (1948). *Comparative psychology of mental development.* New York: International Universities Press.

Werner, H. (1957). The concept of development from a comparative and organismic point of view. In D. Harris (Ed.), *The concept of development.* Minneapolis: University of Minnesota Press.

World Health Organization (WHO). (1992). *International classification of diseases: Clinical descriptions and diagnostic guidelines* (9th ed.). Geneva: Author.

Zahn-Waxler, C., Cummings, E. M., McKnew, D. H., Davenport, Y. B., & Radke-Yarrow, M. (1984). Altruism, aggression and social interaction in young children with a manic depressive parent. *Child Development, 48,* 555–562.

Zeanah, C. H., Mammen, O. K., & Lieberman, A. T. (1994). Disorders of attachment. *Handbook of infant mental health* (pp. 332–349). New York: Guilford Press.

CHAPTER 20

Autonomy, Relatedness, and the Self: Their Relation to Development and Psychopathology

RICHARD M. RYAN, EDWARD L. DECI, and WENDY S. GROLNICK

Concepts related to autonomy figure prominently in organismic and dynamic theories of development and psychopathology. Developmental theorists, for example, consider the movement toward greater autonomy and self-initiation to be a hallmark of healthy development (e.g., Hartmann, 1947/1964; Jahoda, 1958; Loevinger, 1976; Piaget, 1981; Werner, 1948), and the promotion of autonomy is an important focus of research on parenting (e.g., Baumrind, 1971; Grolnick & Ryan, 1989). In a similar vein, the literature on psychopathology includes frequent mention of autonomy disturbances (e.g., Bruch, 1973; Shapiro, 1965), and the obstruction of children's autonomy has been implicated in the onset of many psychopathologies (e.g., Miller, 1981).

Although the concept of autonomy is implicit or explicit in many theories, relatively few writers have addressed the issue directly, explicating its developmental, experiential, and motivational facets, its role in psychopathology and mental health, and its relation to aspects of the social context. Furthermore, most of the seminal discussions of autonomy that do exist (e.g., Angyal, 1965; Shapiro, 1981) were based on clinical observations and considerations, and thus have neither been stimulated nor constrained by relevant empirical investigations.

In this chapter, we critically examine the concept of human autonomy as it relates to both normal and psychopathological development. We set forth a definition of autonomy that is informed by philosophical and clinical analyses, and that differentiates it from closely related constructs such as independence and detachment. We then explore how autonomy is intertwined with the developmental processes of intrinsic motivation, internalization, and emotional integration, paying particular attention to how conditions in the social context either support the motivational and emotional bases of normal development or, alternatively, undermine these bases and contribute to psychopathology. Further, we examine how the development of individual autonomy is intertwined with issues in attachment and the development of interpersonal relatedness, and how both autonomy and relatedness represent critical aspects of the development of self. Finally, we discuss the dynamics of autonomy and relatedness with regard to varied clinical disorders of a psychological nature, which we view as outcomes of nonoptimal developmental antecedents.

Preparation of this chapter was facilitated by a research grant from the National Institute of Child Health and Human Development (HD 19914) to the Human Motivation Research Program, Department of Psychology, University of Rochester.

AUTONOMY IN DEVELOPMENT

The term *development* refers to an essential feature of animate objects. Whereas many entities can be changed, altered, or transformed, living things, through continuous activity, grow in the direction of increased complexity, differentiation, and refinement, on the one hand, and increased coordination of parts, cohesion, and integration on the other (Blasi, 1976; Ryan, 1993). As a number of theoretical biologists (e.g., Mayr, 1982; Rosenberg, 1985) have pointed out, development is thus an aspect of an overarching negentropic characteristic of *organization,* which refers to the tendency of systems to extend themselves, while at the same time preserving their overall integrity.

The concept of organization applies not only to biological systems per se, but also to the cognitive and epistemic systems that are both aspects and extensions of the biological ones (Piaget, 1971; Werner, 1948). In Piaget's view, for example, cognitive development in particular entails the progressive differentiation of elements and their assimilation and integration into organized regulatory structures. He thus conceptualized the growth of knowledge structures as merely an extension of the overall, organizational tendency of living things.

In addition to issues of the elaboration and refinement of cognitive structures, however, the organizational principle has often been applied to an understanding of the development of personality and self. Indeed, the overall process of psychological development entails individuals' working to elaborate or expand themselves while at the same time striving to maintain or enhance integration and cohesion among all aspects of themselves. Angyal (1965), for example, spoke of development as a continual process of self-expansion in which people enhance and consolidate their self-regulatory capacities (autonomy) as well as their relations to the social world (homonomy). In other words, Angyal proposed, the integrative tendency functions in both the intrapersonal and interpersonal realms. As Dewey (1934) similarly argued, the self seeks ever to extend itself.

The view that personality development is a process governed by the principle of organization can also be found in other theoretical traditions. Freud (1923/1962), for example, spoke of the ego as an organization of mental processes that aims for both greater complexity and greater unity. He conceptualized these interrelated organizational tendencies as the ego's "synthetic function" (Nunberg 1931). More recently, Loevinger (1976), extending Freud's model, saw this synthetic process as the essence of ego development.

The integrative tendency is central in many humanistic theories as well. Rogers (1963) and Maslow (1943), like Goldstein (1939), postulated that the primary thrust of life is toward actualization of one's potentials. In these and related theories, actualization describes the healthy growth of personality, which involves nurturing differentiated potentials and bringing them into harmony with other aspects of personality. Accordingly, many theories within this tradition portray the therapeutic process as stimulating the healing forces within the individual (Frank, 1961), and the inherent organizational tendency is understood as the core of those healing forces (Deci & Ryan, 1985b; Rogers, 1951).

Motivation and Development

Implicit in the organismic, ego-analytic, and humanistic descriptions of life change is the view that psychological development emanates from within and results from the *activity* of the organism. Stated differently, organisms are assumed by these approaches to be inherently active and to operate on (as well as be operated on by) their inner and outer environments. Flavell (1977), in discussing Piagetian theory, stated that the human is an "active kind of knower" who selects and interprets information to construct knowledge, rather than a passive copier of the information presented by the environment. Elkind (1971), in discussing cognitive development, suggested that humans seek out stimuli that provide the nutriments for their growth, both motoric and mental. From the time of birth, they exercise their physical capacities, exploring and manipulating their environments to expand their capacities and assimilate those environments. The concept of seeking, of course, presumes proactivity.

Theories for which *organismic integration* is posited as the central process of development assume that organisms are inherently proactive, yet most of them give little or no attention to the energization of that developmental process. These theories have instead portrayed the movement toward greater organization as occurring naturally or automatically. Piaget (1952), for example, suggested that it is simply the nature of structures, once existing, to function and to elaborate themselves as they function. In this, he made the processes underlying development so integral to the definition of life itself that a differentiated analysis of their motivation was considered unnecessary (Flavell, 1963; Piaget, 1971).

Conceiving of an organizational tendency operating simply or automatically because that is the nature of life can have the unfortunate consequence of masking the *human agency* that is essential for development. Many developmental processes, particularly those involved in psychological development, do not just happen; they occur through the motivated exercise of structures, and through behavior that is often organized purposively (Blasi, 1976; Kaplan, 1983; Ryan, 1993). For cognitive schemata to "elaborate themselves," for personality structures to "differentiate," or for the self to "actualize," an individual must act on his or her world. A full understanding of development thus requires attending to people's aims and purposes, to their ongoing struggles to do and to grow, to their decisions to engage challenges or avoid them. It requires attending to the motivational considerations that facilitate—or, alternatively, that impede—the movement toward organization.

One type of motivation inextricably involved in the unfolding of human development is what we and other theorists have labeled *intrinsic motivation.* Within empirical psychology during the 1940s and 1950s, a wide range of studies and observations had indicated that organisms freely engage in certain types of activities in the absence of demands or reinforcement contingencies (e.g., Harlow, 1953). Such activities as exploration and manipulation were thus said to be intrinsically motivating. Simultaneously, within the psychoanalytic tradition, the compatible idea of an independent ego energy evolved to explain various phenomena of normal development (e.g., Hartmann, 1939/1958; White, 1960). Said to be primary and innate (rather than derivative of the libido), this energy is theorized to initiate and sustain the types of activity that promote psychological organization and ego development. Thus, in widely differing schools of thought, it was increasingly acknowledged that individuals try new activities, persist at challenging tasks, and strive to master their surroundings simply because of the experience that accompanies such behaviors. In the words of Bruner (1962), the process of discovery is itself rewarding.

Intrinsically motivated behaviors are not merely random behaviors; rather, they are clearly purposive, performed for the satisfaction and interest they yield. And, as it turns out, the types of activities that are intrinsically satisfying are those that promote expansion of one's capacities and thus foster development (Elkind, 1971). Accordingly, we have proposed that intrinsic motivation energizes organismic integration (Deci & Ryan, 1985b, 1991; Ryan, 1993).

The postulate that intrinsically motivated activities promote development is quite different from the postulate that development occurs naturally as structures function. The critical difference is that the former explanation is organized with respect to people's desires and strivings for the experience that we term intrinsic satisfaction. As such, the concept of intrinsic motivation provides a starting point for exploring aspects of human development that would not otherwise be adequately addressed. For example, studies have outlined the dynamic forces that both facilitate and forestall intrinsic motivation, and thus, in turn, bespeak the factors that shape developmental and organizational processes more generally.

A number of theorists have critically examined the meaning and nature of intrinsic motivational phenomena. In an early landmark paper, White (1959) proposed gathering together, under the rubric of *competence,* all those behaviors that seem to be rewarding in their own right (behaviors such as grasping, exploring, attending, and playing). He argued that competence should be treated as a motivational concept, suggesting that people have an innate *psychological need* to feel effective or competent in dealing with their environment. This psychological need, which may have adaptive value and yet is unrelated to biological drives, underlies a variety of directed, selective, and persistent behaviors. The experience of competence can thus be understood as one type of intrinsic satisfaction that people freely pursue and that promotes development. As Bruner (1962) put it, people's exercise of the competence motive has the effect of strengthening their control over behavior.

deCharms (1968), agreeing that some behaviors appear to be done for their own sake, suggested that preferred among such behaviors are ones that result in "maximum evidence of the effectiveness of the actor" (p. 328). More specifically, he argued that those competent actions that *emanate from oneself,* and of which one is an *origin,* are intrinsically motivating. Behaviors initiated by external controls or pressures, even when competently done, do not supply the inherent satisfactions associated with being an origin. This viewpoint, although close to White's, placed less emphasis on competence per se than on being an origin—that is, on personally causing one's actions.

Recognizing the similarity, as well as the subtle but important difference, in the positions expressed by White and deCharms, Deci (1975) proposed that *competence* and *self-determination* (i.e., autonomy) are the primary psychological needs that underlie intrinsically motivated activity. Deci argued that people, when intrinsically motivated, engage in activities that *interest* them. These activities typically involve seeking and conquering optimal challenges, and thus they promote development. Infants explore their surrounds, ever distinguishing novel objects and attempting complex uses for their motoric capacities; adults struggle to improve their tennis game or create more refined paintings. Such activities require no prompts or prods; they are what people do freely, "between episodes of homeostatic crisis" (White, 1959, p. 321). However, as Deci and Ryan (1980) later argued, the conquering of challenges must be autonomous to be intrinsically motivated. Even the successful or efficacious pursuit of goals and challenges under conditions where one is compelled or coerced to do so is not likely to be experienced as intrinsically satisfying.

The psychological needs for competence and autonomy do not tell the full story of the inherent energy underlying healthy development, however, for they are concerned primarily with *intra*personal growth and integration, thus underplaying the importance of *inter*personal integration. In the words of Angyal (1965), they relate more to the developmental trend for autonomy than to the complementary trend for homonomy.

Research and theorizing by a wide range of psychologists make it clear that the desire for relatedness or connectedness to others is not only a crucial ingredient for optimal development (Bowlby, 1988; Harlow, 1958; Winnicott, 1965c), but also appears to be an intrinsic motivator. That is, relationships seem to offer satisfactions that are independent of the drive-based satisfactions and securities they often provide. Thus, an inherent psychological need for *relatedness* provides yet a third intrinsic motivational trajectory of tremendous significance for those interested in the energization of human development (Connell & Wellborn, 1990; Deci & Ryan, 1991; Ryan, 1991).

Not only does the need for relatedness energize interpersonal explorations and interactions, it also interacts with needs for autonomy and competence. For young children to explore and experiment—that is, to seek novelty—they must feel a sense of security in their relations to primary caregivers (Ainsworth, 1989; Ainsworth, Blehar, Waters, & Wall, 1978). In fact, the importance of security of attachment for a wide range of developmental outcomes suggests that the need for relatedness represents a primary psychological need throughout the life span (Ryan, 1991, 1993).

As we and others (e.g., Deci & Ryan, 1991; White 1959) have pointed out, the recognition of *psychological needs* as a basis for motivation is essential to account for both the trajectory and sustenance of human development. The specific postulation of psychologically based needs for autonomy, competence, and relatedness helps the explication and empirical study of intrinsically motivated action, because it provides an account of why various contextual conditions support (versus impair) such action. Conditions that allow satisfaction of these needs support intrinsic motivation; those that thwart their satisfaction undermine intrinsic motivation.

These psychological needs also bear importantly on developmentally relevant classes of behavior that are not directly intrinsically motivated. For example, in adapting to the demands of the social world, individuals must at times engage in activities that are not interesting to them but are socially valued or mandated. A central motive that helps to initiate and maintain much of this nonintrinsically motivated action is the need for relatedness. Put differently, people often engage in activities that do not interest them, in order to maintain or strengthen their connections with others.

This process of social learning would be simply a study of conformity, were there not also a tendency to psychologically transform these outer mandates into inner regulations, a process we and others refer to as *internalization* (Ryan & Connell, 1989; Ryan, Connell, & Deci, 1985). When internalized, initially external contingencies have become part of the psyche. Relevant behaviors no longer require external prompts, and the person experiences a sense of both competence and relatedness with respect to such actions. However, one further distinction must be made to clarify the picture of the development of self-regulation. For full internalization, or *integration,* to occur, the person must not only have "taken in" regulatory processes, but must have made them his or her own. These regulations must indeed have been transformed: they must have been integrated with other aspects of one's self. The need for autonomy is essential for explaining this developmental thrust toward transformation of regulations from external to self-determined. Accordingly, successful internalization and integration can be understood as being energized by and allowing satisfaction of the needs for autonomy, competence, and relatedness. A thorough consideration of these three basic needs is thus critical for the study of social development.

To summarize, we have proposed that the needs for competence, autonomy, and relatedness are primary psychological needs, and that opportunities to satisfy these needs promote agentic activity and organization. As people engage the world in an attempt to feel competent, autonomous, and related, they develop through the operation of the organismic integration process. Development is thus an interplay of the unfolding or actualizing of intrinsic potentials and interests and the incorporation of knowledge, values, and regulatory processes that are brought into coherence with these intrinsic tendencies.

Development and Social Contexts

Attention to the motivational underpinnings of development has the advantage of clarifying the important role played by the social context in promoting development. It is obvious that exposure to some environments promotes development, and exposure to others slows or sidetracks it. A focus on motivation helps to explicate the processes through which this facilitation or inhibition occurs. Because psychological development results largely from motivated activity—particularly activity energized by the innate needs for competence, autonomy, and relatedness—the rate and trajectory of development can be understood, in part, as a function of the social-contextual conditions that allow (versus thwart) the satisfaction of these basic human needs.

In our own work (e.g., Grolnick & Ryan, 1989; Grolnick, Ryan, & Deci, 1991; Ryan, 1991), we have specified three dimensions to characterize the nutriments necessary for the child's optimal development. They are: (a) *autonomy support,* which refers to caregivers' encouraging self-initiation, providing choice, allowing independent problem solving, and minimizing control and power assertion—in short, acting with attunement to the child's perspective; (b) *structure,* which refers to caregivers' organizing of the environment so as to guide and provide for a coherent field of operations for their offspring—that is, clarifying contingencies, providing a rationale for requested activities, and administering meaningful feedback or guidance concerning the child's agentic activity; and (c) *involvement,* which refers to the caregivers' devoting time, attention, and resources to the child as he or she takes on challenges, explores new territory, and expresses himself or herself.

A considerable amount of research, to be reviewed later in the chapter, has substantiated that these contextual nutriments are important for sustaining intrinsic motivation, promoting internalization, and supporting emotional integration—and, accordingly, for the associated outcomes of self-regulation and autonomy. By contrast, caregiving environments deficient with regard to the provision of autonomy, involvement, and structure forestall the processes of intrinsic motivation and internalization, and thus result in varied delays and disruptions of development.

Autonomy and Self

In self-determination theory, the process of *organismic integration* is the defining feature of *self.* It is theorized to be the means through which one assimilates ongoing experience into an organized coherence. We thus use the term *self* to refer both to the agentic activity that promotes integration and to the structures resulting from this integrative activity. The phenomenological correspondent of the integrative function is referred to as one's core *sense of self,* and the primary motivational underpinnings of self are the three psychological needs that energize agentic activity.

This definition of self can thus be seen to have organizational, motivational, and phenomenological components (Ryan, 1993). The organizational component concerns the degree of "reciprocal assimilation" and structural integrity underlying personality functioning; the motivational component is the set of psychological needs underlying agentic activity, which both emanates from and further elaborates one's organizational core; and the phenomenological component is the experience of self that accompanies acting from that core—it is the experience of autonomy.

To the extent that one is operating agentically, from one's core sense of self, one is said to be autonomous. To be autonomous thus means to be *self*-initiating and *self*-regulating. In contrast, to the extent that one feels coerced or seduced into behaving—with one's actions not emanating from one's core sense of self—one would not be described as autonomous. The reader might therefore anticipate, with regard to developmental psychopathology, that many of the derailed developmental processes that come to be viewed as pathological will be characterized by both structural and experiential manifestations of disturbed autonomy. Put differently, under nonoptimal conditions, people tend to develop contradictory motives, experience incompetence and inconsistencies in the regulation of behavior, and feel that much of what they do is caused by forces outside themselves. These, of course, are central characteristics in various forms of psychopathology.

Our use of the term self differs significantly from its use in current social cognitive theories (e.g., Bandura, 1977; Markus & Sentis, 1982). In these theories, self is a set of internalized schemata, rather than a synthetic process. Although we agree that people do internalize aspects of the social context to form parts of their self-concepts, we also argue (a) that there are intrinsic aspects of the self that precede consciousness and symbolization, and (b) that, using the synthetic, assimilative process, people actively construct their self-concepts from these intrinsic elements and social nutriments. The development of self is thus not a passive process in which the environment implants various selves into the person; but rather, it is an active, constructive process in which the person makes use of information from the environment.

Autonomy, Organization, and Developmental Psychopathology

Organismic integration is the process through which personality develops and people become more autonomous or self-regulated. When the integrative process functions optimally and people act agentically from the self, personality integration proceeds and healthy development results. In contrast to integration, which signifies healthy development and autonomous activity, fractionation and/or stagnation are considered the principal markers of psychopathology. To the extent that the integrative process is impaired—whether by organic, intrapsychic, or interpersonal processes—fractionation, psychopathology, and nonautonomous actions would be expected to result. In this model, the concepts of autonomy and organization are intimately linked. To the extent that behavior emanates from one's core self-organization, one feels autonomous. Indeed, as we shall later see, the phenomenological sense of autonomy and the wholeness reflected in integrated psychological functioning are two aspects of the same phenomenon.

The emerging field of developmental psychopathology also uses the term *organization* as a central concept (Cicchetti,

Beeghly, Carlson, & Toth, 1990). Psychopathology is understood as a developmental sequela of interruptions to a natural organismic propensity, manifest as nonsynchronous relations among the biological, emotional, and cognitive systems.

It is, however, important to distinguish between organization as we employ the term (the integration of processes and structures in personality to the self) and the view of organization as defined by *synchrony,* in which there is a high correlation or consistency among cognitive, affective, physiological, and behavioral indexes (e.g., Shields, Cicchetti, & Ryan, 1994; Sroufe & Waters, 1977). For us, integration within personality is the basis of autonomy and the hallmark of mental health, and its absence signifies a disturbance of autonomy and is an indicator of psychopathology. In this perspective, with organization will often come synchrony, but synchrony does not ensure organization. Theoretically at least, a person could have a high degree of synchrony among systems without being well integrated with respect to the self. For example, an angry, aggressive, acting-out child, operating with an externalizing cognitive set, may be showing synchrony but not integration.

Our interest in organization is focused primarily on the processes through which the self ongoingly seeks to expand and grow, to assimilate experience, and to initiate and sustain action in concert with systemic needs. This subtle difference in emphasis is highlighted when one considers that the growth of the self would not be explainable if mere synchrony were the goal of development, for activity would stop once systems acted in concert, regardless of the degree of personality coherence.

Much of our research has explored optimal (i.e., autonomous) and nonoptimal (i.e., nonautonomous) functioning in relatively normal populations, across the life span. In applying that work to the field of developmental psychopathology, we make several important assumptions. First, like many other authors (e.g., Cameron & Rychlak, 1985; Cicchetti, 1991), we assume that psychopathology is a dysfunctional condition involving extreme and chronic instances of nonoptimal processes (termed controlling and amotivational in our theory) that, in weaker and more transitory forms, are evident in nonpathological individuals. Thus, we argue, research on the antecedents and consequences of nonoptimal processes in normal populations has direct relevance for understanding developmental psychopathology, as well as development. Second, we assume that the organismic integration process operates across the life span and that the interpersonal and intrapsychic forces that interrupt organizational processes at one age are theoretically related to those that impair such processes at other ages. Finally, although psychopathological outcomes are considered maladaptive, we also understand that they are the most adaptive developmental outcomes a person could achieve under the circumstances in which his or her integrative tendency was impaired.

THEORETICAL ASPECTS OF AUTONOMY

Etymologically, the term autonomy refers to "self-rule," and indeed we apply the term to actions that are initiated and regulated by the self. Thus, autonomy describes behaviors that one volitionally initiates and endorses, whereas nonautonomous behaviors are those that are compelled and thus not initiated by the self. It would be a mistake, however, to assume that all authors who use the term are referring to the same thing (Dworkin, 1988; Ryan 1991). In this section, we discuss various interpretations of the concept of autonomy that are compatible with our current usage. We then turn to a discussion of interpretations that are not compatible with our meaning.

Autonomy as True Self

Autonomous actions emanate from the phenomenal core we label self. Self is the metaphorical "agent" that acts autonomously and integrates experience, and it is the ever-expanding set of coherent structures and processes that result from the ongoing assimilation of new values, propensities, and regulatory functions. When used in this way, the term self does *not* refer to all internal regulatory processes and structures; rather, it refers only to those that either are intrinsic to one's agentic core or have been fully assimilated with it. As will become increasingly clear throughout this chapter, our concept of self is thus akin to what some writers have referred to as one's "real" or "true" self (Horney, 1950; Winnicott, 1960a).

The idea of true self conveys that individuals sometimes behave in ways that reveal their core spirit and communicate a sense of integrity and personal endorsement; yet, at other times, they behave in ways that do not express that inner core but instead are more superficial and less integrated. Unintegrated regulatory processes typically develop as an adaptation to being contingently valued and/or controlled, and thus serve both to manipulate others and to defend or preserve oneself.

Winnicott (1960a) distinguished between "true self" and "false self" by suggesting that, when acting from the true self, people feel real and "in touch" with their core needs and emotions. True self embodies their creative nature, their ability to freely initiate, to be vital, to enjoy existence. True self begins as inherited potentials. Through organismic integration, it acquires, at its own speed and in its own way, a personal psychic reality. True self is the product and expression of the experience of aliveness and vitality. In contrast, when acting from false self, people display "as-if" personalities that formed while they were attempting to gain approval in a nonaccepting social context. False self involves taking in aspects of the social context without accepting them as one's own. It thus conveys a splitting between one's nature and what one has become.

The experience of acting from true self is the phenomenological essence of autonomy, and individuals can be described as more (versus less) autonomous to the extent that they live in accord with the true self rather than the false self. This perspective was apparent in Winnicott's (1986) description of autonomy as living one's own life and taking responsibility for one's own actions and inactions.

Whereas true self is the source of spontaneous perceptions, needs, and behaviors, false self reflects habitual perceiving and responding that a child adopts instrumentally, in accord with narcissistic needs. According to Winnicott (1949/1958), false self employs cognitive functions to know what is required of it—that is, what the situation demands—and, in so doing, cognitive processes can gradually become separated from their affective and somatic grounding. We see here how the idea of autonomy as activity regulated by one's true self also has implications for the idea of psychological integration as coordination or synchrony among aspects of one's personality. To the extent that one acts from other than the true self, fractionization and splitting of functioning often results.

Other writers in the psychoanalytic tradition have also discussed the concept of true or real self. Horney defined the real self in terms of an intrinsic potentiality, a tendency toward personal growth and fulfillment. She tied neurosis to alienation from the real self, which results in the loss of the vital energy that is available to the real self. Jung (1951/1959) described the self as an organismic endowment representing the "center" of personality and possessing the tendency toward integration. Although, in Jung's theory, the self is largely unconscious and is manifest through dreams and symbols, the concept still conveys the sense of one's having a vital core that is related to integration in personality.

In self-determination theory (Deci & Ryan, 1991), an individual's internal processes, structures, and urges can also be described in terms of the extent to which they represent "true" versus "false" self. More precisely, we speak of self, or *integrated self,* as that set of coherently organized processes, structures, and energies that are the developmental outcome of organismic integration. All aspects of one's psychological makeup can thus be understood in terms of the degree to which they are integrated with the self. Those that are more integrated are akin to what Winnicott and others have called true self.

Autonomy as Authenticity

The term *authentic* typically applies to something that actually proceeds from its reputed "author." Authentic actions are those with which the person identifies and for which he or she accepts responsibility. Accordingly, authenticity can be represented as a continuum describing the extent to which an action is a true expression of oneself (and thus autonomous) versus an expression of pressures or causes external to the self (and thus controlled or amotivated) (Ryan, 1991, 1993).

The concept of authenticity has appeared primarily in the writings of existentially oriented philosophers (e.g., Kierkegaard 1849/1968). Still, the concept is highly apt for describing the phenomenological experience of acting from one's sense of self. When an action is fully endorsed by its author, the experience is one of integrity or authenticity. As Laing (1969) put it, "To be authentic is to be true to oneself" (p. 127). Authenticity is thus acting from the self; it is self-determination. When viewed in this way, authenticity becomes a quality of behavior rather than just an abstract philosophical concept.

Although literatures emphasizing authenticity tend to focus on the behaviors and experiences of adults, the term authenticity can be applied even to very young children. Observation of toddlers in the context of controlling or maltreating families will reveal the sense of surface compliance, as-if affects, and false consciousness as early as the second year of life (e.g., Crittenden, 1988).

Autonomy as Will

Autonomy has also been equated with will by some authors (e.g., Deci, 1980; Easterbrook, 1978), although the concept of will has not been readily accepted within the psychological literature. In part, this stems from confusion between the concepts of will and free will, and the crux of the issue has to do with whether behaviors that are willed are free from causation. The philosophical debate between free will and determinism concerned whether all behaviors are lawful and thus predictable: free will was interpreted as meaning freedom from causation, and determinism was interpreted as meaning that behavior is lawfully caused.

As Sperry (1976) pointed out, however, the concept of will does not mean freedom from causation; rather, it refers to the capacity to determine one's own actions on the basis of one's motivational, affective, and cognitive processes. Sperry's view suggests that behaviors that are "willed" can be said to be caused or determined so long as one does not equate cause with "bottom-up" efficient causes. Willed behaviors are "caused" in the sense that higher-order organizational processes can entrain and make use of lower-order ones in the service of purposive actions. Understood in this way, it is entirely possible for a person to experience a sense of freedom while engaging in actions that can also be described in terms of their material and efficient causal underpinnings.

Pfander (1908/1967) used a phenomenological approach in discussing will, distinguishing actions that reflect one's will from other forms of motivated behaving. Acts are said to be willed if they are experienced as being caused by oneself as agent—if they emanate from one's "ego-center." In contrast, other forms of action are experienced as caused by a different agent—by a force "outside one's ego-center." When interpreted in this way, only willed acts would be considered autonomous, for only they emanate from what we term the self.

Parenthetically, it is worth noting that the term *willpower* is sometimes used to describe the process of countering one's urges or organismic nature through force (e.g., Deci, 1980). As we will discuss later, May (1969) suggested that willpower involves self-deceit, and Shapiro (1965) stated that the use of willpower is central to rigid character disorders. Behavior that is regulated through "will *power,*" when the term is used in that sense, would not typically be considered autonomous, because it frequently refers to one part of personality dominating another.

Autonomy as Agency

To be autonomous means to act agentically and to experience a sense of choice and willingness in one's actions. Agency thus connotes something different from merely deciding to act, for one can "decide" to do what one feels compelled or coerced to do. To convey fully the meaning of autonomy as agency thus requires that we distinguish between the concepts of intentionality and autonomy.

Intentionality refers to purposefulness, to pursuing a desired outcome. Autonomy, however, is a more restrictive term; it necessitates the experience of feeling free, of feeling that intended actions are an expression of oneself. An action would thus be considered intentional, but not autonomous, when one feels one "has to" do it, or when one feels pressured by one's craving for the praise it is expected to yield. When one acts compulsively—for example, in aligning the magazines on a coffee table or washing one's hands yet again—the behavior is intentional, but it is surely not autonomous: it lacks the sense of freedom and flexibility that are the phenomenological accompaniments of autonomy.

Precisely because humans have the capacity to act other than from their core—that is, to be self-deceiving and act from fractionated regulatory processes or divided consciousness (Hilgard, 1977)—the concept of human agency takes on its import. To be agentic requires more than being intentional; it requires being autonomous. As Williams (1992) put it, agency means engaging the world truthfully, free from self-deceit.

When one recognizes that true agency requires autonomy, as we define that term, it is easy to see the problem with Bandura's (1989) formulation of human agency. In Bandura's self-efficacy theory, the term agency is ascribed to all intentional behaviors, without distinguishing those behaviors that are freely chosen and authentic from those that are pressured and not well-anchored within the self. Only the former are truly agentic. A person who is a pawn (deCharms, 1968) to forces external to the self, no matter how "self-efficacious," is neither autonomous nor agentic.

Autonomy and the Attribution of Causality: Toward an Empirically Accessible Construct of Autonomy

As we have seen, several psychological theories, largely within the psychoanalytic and humanistic traditions, have considered the concept of autonomy to be highly important, whether treated in terms of freedom, authenticity, will, or true self. Different theories have used different terminologies and have addressed different problems; yet a shared idea, which we term autonomy, is woven through these various conceptions. Because these theories have been based primarily on clinical practice and experiential discoveries, however, the concept of autonomy has been slow in making inroads into empirical psychology.

Fortunately, the "common sense language" of attributions proposed by Heider (1958) and extended by deCharms (1968) set the stage for empirical investigations of autonomy that have begun to shed new light on the issues that so many theorists have judged important—issues like freedom, volition, and the true self. Based on an extensive program of research on autonomy, we have been able to sketch out the self-determination framework and relate it to normal versus psychopathological development.

Heider (1958) began by distinguishing between personal and impersonal causality in terms of intentionality. Actions and their effects are said to be *personally caused* to the extent that they were intended. In contrast, those not intended, resulting from forces beyond one's control, are said to be *impersonally caused*.

deCharms (1968) suggested, however, that some intentional behaviors may not embody a true sense of personal causation. He pointed out that, although intrinsically motivated behaviors are clear instances of personal causation, extrinsically motivated behaviors represent a complex case with respect to the personal/impersonal distinction. Extrinsic behaviors, as deCharms portrayed them, are performed intentionally because of a reward contingency, so, in a sense, that contingency can be viewed as the locus of initiation or causation. To handle this issue, deCharms introduced the concept of an *internal* versus an *external perceived locus of causality*. Both internal and external causality fall within the category of personally caused (or intended) behaviors, but only internal causality conveys the prototypic sense of personal causation.

deCharms argued that an intentional action has an internal perceived locus of causality to the extent that it is intrinsically motivated, and an external perceived locus of causality to the extent that it is extrinsically motivated. Thus in deCharms's work, both the internal/external causality distinction and the intrinsic/extrinsic motivation distinction referred to whether the locus of initiation of an intentional action appeared to be inside the actor (and thus, according to deCharms, intrinsically motivated) or outside the actor (and thus extrinsically motivated).

Deci and Ryan (1985b) agreed with deCharms that intrinsically motivated behaviors invariantly have an internal perceived locus of causality. Such actions are experienced as a spontaneous self-expression and are wholly volitional. However, Deci and Ryan disagreed that all extrinsically motivated behaviors necessarily have an external perceived locus of causality. Instead, these authors proposed that extrinsically motivated (i.e., instrumental) behaviors can vary considerably in their relative autonomy. Some extrinsically motivated actions are clearly pressured or compelled by outside forces, and thus have an external perceived locus of causality. Other actions that are extrinsically motivated can be endorsed by the self if the values underlying them are well integrated. Thus, these behaviors would have an internal perceived locus of causality. Indeed, the relative autonomy of extrinsically motivated action directly corresponds to the degree to which the regulation of such action has been internalized and integrated.

Ryan and Connell (1989) pointed out that this conceptualization of perceived locus of causality shifts the boundary between internal and external from the person to the self. One's phenomenal core, here referred to as self, is the most appropriate referent for distinguishing between an internal and external perceived locus of causality. In other words, a behavior would be said to have an internal perceived locus of causality to the extent that one experiences it as expressive of one's true self—one feels both authentic in and responsible for one's actions.

There is an important implication to the use of the self as the boundary referent: the proximal cause of an action could be a force within the person that is not integral to the self and thus would have an external perceived locus of causality. This is the case in introjection, for example, in which one part of the personality is heteronomous with respect to the self (e.g., Meissner, 1981; Schafer, 1968). More specifically, we suggest that some extrinsically motivated behaviors are initiated by processes *external* to the person (e.g., another person says that one must do something to avoid a punishment), some are initiated by *introjects* within the person but external to the self (e.g., one feels one must do something to avoid guilt), and some are initiated by processes that have been *identified* with and/or *integrated* into the self (e.g., one does something because of a personally endorsed value). Although these varied types of extrinsic regulation all involve intentionality and instrumentality, they differ substantially in the degree to which they involve autonomy; each falls at a different place along a gradient of perceived causality. Sources of extrinsic motivation that are external to the person represent the extreme of an external perceived locus of causality; sources of extrinsic motivation that are internal to the person but external to the self represent a less external perceived locus of causality; and sources of extrinsic motivation that have been integrated with the self have an internal perceived locus of causality and are considered autonomous. Later in this chapter, we look more closely at the developmental antecedents and dynamic character of these varied regulatory processes.

Because intrinsically motivated behaviors are the prototype of an internal perceived locus of causality, their experiential qualities represent a kind of template against which extrinsically motivated behaviors can be compared to determine the degree of autonomous regulation of the latter behaviors. Using a person's experience of an internal versus external locus of causality as a marker of the relative autonomy of an action provides an empirical means for describing the extent to which an action emanates from the true (or integrated) self—that is, the extent to which it is authentic.

Whether children are intrinsically or extrinsically motivated, they are engaged in intentional behavior. By contrast, the absence of intentionality represents an amotivational state. Thus, a person is motivated (and actions are personally caused) only to the extent that the person intends an action and follows the intention with an expenditure of effort. *Amotivation,* in contrast, most often refers to a relative lack of action—for example, when one feels hopeless and gives up behaving. The term amotivation also describes actions if the person does them without intending to. A spasm, for example—although an action emanating from one's body—is not mediated by intention and thus is amotivated and has an impersonal locus of causality. More interesting, however, from both phenomenological and clinical viewpoints, are behaviors such as a reflexive emotional "outburst" in which regulatory processes are overpowered by a sudden surge of energy. In Heiderian terminology, these behaviors have an impersonal perceived locus of causality. A person might, for example, say, "I don't know what came over me," conveying the sense of an impersonal cause. Such behaviors are, of course, motivated in the sense of being energized and explicable. Nonetheless, we refer to them as amotivated to convey the extent to which they are experienced as nonintentional and outside of personal control.

Most empirically based theories of motivation and self-regulation contrast motivation with amotivation, but treat the former as a unitary concept (e.g., Bandura, 1977; Seligman, 1991). Yet, a consideration of autonomy requires differentiating the concept of motivation. Specifically, we focus on the extent to which one's motivated actions are autonomous (i.e., have an internal perceived locus of causality and emanate from the self) versus controlled (i.e., have an external perceived locus of causality and are coerced by some interpersonal or intrapsychic force external to the self).

It is important to recognize that an internal versus external perceived locus of *causality* is quite different from an internal versus external locus of *control* (Rotter, 1966). An internal locus of *control* and the closely related concepts of perceived control (E. Skinner, 1985) and self-efficacy (Bandura, 1977) refer to the belief that one can attain desired outcomes—in other words, that one understands how to achieve the outcomes and possesses the requisite competence to carry out that understanding. An external locus of control refers to believing that one cannot control outcomes, instead believing that they are controlled by some unpredictable external source. Accordingly, one would expect to find intentional (i.e., motivated) behavior in cases of an internal locus of control, and a lack of intentionality (i.e., amotivation) in cases of an external locus of control.

The concept of an internal versus external locus of control parallels the distinction between personal versus impersonal causation (Heider, 1958). An internal locus of control does *not,* however, imply autonomy or an internal perceived locus of causality. For instance, a girl who learns to successfully hide her feelings and to outwardly comply with demands in order to avoid arousing her father's aggression or abuse would have both an internal locus of control (Rotter, 1966) and self-efficacy (Bandura, 1989). However, even though she has internal control over the outcome, she would undoubtedly experience an external perceived locus of causality. Indeed, someone with an internal locus of control who is high in self-efficacy can as easily be a pawn as an origin (deCharms, 1981). One can thus have an internal locus of control accompanied by either an internal *or* an external perceived locus of causality.

Because of the extent to which these various motivational terminologies overlap in both substance and source, we present Table 20.1 for clarity. As can be seen from this classification table, self-determination theory differentiates not only between motivated and amotivated acts, but also between motivated acts characterized by autonomy and those characterized by being controlled (i.e., by being a pawn to forces outside the self).

As stated earlier, the importance of this phenomenological and attributional approach to autonomy rests primarily on the fact that, by using the perceived locus of causality construct, we have been able to address issues concerning the development and experience of autonomy versus heteronomy with empirical strategies. Factors that affect the perceived locus of causality are, in fact, those that affect autonomy and self-regulation, and thus bear importantly on issues of self-development.

Human Autonomy: A Reprise

Autonomy pertains to both processes and outcomes in development. Organismic integration represents the developmental process of autonomy; integration of self and the self-determination of behavior represent the developmental outcomes of autonomy. In turn, these outcomes promote further development: as people behave more autonomously, they more fully assimilate their experiences, resulting in still greater elaboration and coherence of the self.

Phenomenologically, autonomy relates to the experience of freedom and authenticity, that is, to the experience of an internal perceived locus of causality. In the case of intrinsically motivated activities, the experience is one of spontaneous interest and vitality; in the domain of extrinsic actions, autonomy more typically appears through enactment of fully integrated values and intentions.

Table 20.1 Various Theoretical Concepts as They Relate to Autonomous Regulation, Controlling Regulation, and Non-Regulation

Types of Regulation	Locus of Control (Rotter, 1966)	Efficacy Theory (Bandura, 1977)	Helplessness Theory (Seligman, 1975)	Attribution Theory (Heider, 1958)	Personal Causation (deCharms, 1968)	Self-Determination (Deci-Ryan, 1985b)
Autonomous regulation	a	a	a	Personal causation	Intrinsic motivation; "origin"	Intrinsic motivation; Integrated extrinsic motivation; Internal PLOC[b]
Controlling regulation	Internal locus of control	Self-efficacy	Perceived controllability	Personal causation	Extrinsic motivation; "pawn"	Introjected extrinsic motivation; External control; External PLOC[b]
Non-regulation	External locus of control	Ineffectance	Helplessness	Impersonal causation	Impersonal causality	Amotivation; Impersonal PLOC[b]

[a]The autonomy control differentiation (or a comparable one) is not made within these theories. All intentional actions would nonetheless be said to involve an internal locus of control, self-efficacy, and perceived controllability.
[b]PLOC refers to Perceived Locus of Causality.

Starting with the concept of autonomy as a phenomenological issue has been important in empirical pursuits, insofar as perceived autonomy—that is, an internal perceived locus of causality—can be employed to help differentiate between different types of motivational processes. As will be seen in the subsequent review of our empirical work, this approach has been validated in two important ways: first, people's perceptions of autonomy have been greater in social contexts that support autonomy rather than control behavior (Deci & Ryan, 1987); and, second, people's having greater perceived autonomy has been found to have important and expectable accompaniments such as flexibility, creativity, integration, and both psychological and physical health (e.g., Amabile, 1983; Grow & Ryan, 1994; Koestner, Bernieri, & Zuckerman, 1992; McGraw & McCullers, 1979; Rodin & Langer, 1977; Sheldon & Kasser, in press).

The concept of human autonomy applies directly to developmental psychopathology in that failures of organismic integration, manifest as controlling or amotivational processes, represent impairments in the development of self. Although all people display some nonautonomous regulation, excessive and chronic instances of being controlled and/or amotivated are quite broadly implicated in developmental psychopathology.

WHAT AUTONOMY IS NOT

Having provided a theoretical overview of autonomy as being based in the organizational tendencies at the heart of development and the corresponding experience of freedom and volition, we turn to the question of what autonomy is not. We have mentioned already that autonomy (or will) does not mean freedom from causation, and it is also clear that autonomy does not mean freedom from environmental influence, as Bandura (1989) portrayed it. Quite to the contrary, we will see that social contexts play a crucial role in supporting or thwarting autonomy. We now briefly discuss some of the other ways in which autonomy has been interpreted—ways that are *not* consistent with our conceptualization.

Autonomy as Independence?

A common usage of the word autonomy equates it with "independence." Although autonomy and independence overlap in their secondary dictionary definitions, they can refer to quite distinct attributes. Independence typically refers to not relying on others. Its opposite, dependence, correspondingly means being provided or cared for by others (Memmi, 1984). In contrast, autonomy as we use it describes being self-initiating, and feeling a sense of freedom or volition. Its opposite, heteronomy or control, conveys that one's actions stem from forces external to the self, as when one is pressured or coerced.

Once these distinct definitions are clarified, it is easy to see how it is possible for various configurations to arise: one could feel heteronomously independent, heteronomously dependent, autonomously dependent, or both autonomous and independent. The first category applies when one feels forced to give up reliance on another; the second would pertain to one's feeling compelled to rely on another; the third is possible when one volitionally and willingly enters into or accepts dependence or interdependence; and the fourth is conceivable when one desires and initiates self-reliance.

When dependence (versus independence) is viewed in terms of relying on (versus not relying on) others, dependencies of varied sorts can be construed as both natural and healthy at all stages of development. Newborns are highly dependent, and as they grow older they become gradually less dependent in many respects, but there are significant areas of dependence that remain and are appropriate.

The important issue, therefore, is whether a person's dependence, whatever its level and at whatever stage of development, is autonomous or controlled. It is possible for someone to be provided for—that is, to be dependent—with a full sense of willingness and volition, just as it is possible to feel pressured or coerced in one's dependence. Often, the issues of dependence and autonomy become dynamically fused, insofar as caregivers use their resources as instruments of control.

Similarly, independence can be accompanied by either autonomy or control. One can be quite volitional in one's independence from another, genuinely choosing not to be provided for by that other. But being independent does not ensure autonomy, for one can be pressured into independence, as, for example, when a child is forced to "do for oneself" by parents with immoderately high expectations.

The conceptual demarcation between independence and autonomy is crucial not only for developmental thinking, but also for theories of gender and cultural differences. Numerous writers have derogated the importance of autonomy, suggesting that too much self-reliance is unnatural and unhealthy. For example, the Western (Markus & Sentis, 1982), market-economy-based (Broughton, 1987), masculine (Gilligan, 1982) cast toward non-interdependence has often been criticized under the rubric of autonomy. As critiques of extreme independence, these arguments have considerable merit, but they are not meaningful critiques of autonomy. To construe autonomy as an exclusively male and/or Western cultural value and preoccupation is to inappropriately equate autonomy with self-reliance rather than to appropriately equate it with volition. Unfortunately, this confusion then runs the risk of denying the importance of volition and authenticity in women and Eastern individuals, which, of course, constitutes a regressive and potentially disempowering theoretical and clinical stance (see, for example, Lerner, 1988; Ryan, 1991). It also precludes an ideal of many relational theories that recognize mutuality of autonomy and volitional interdependencies as optimal forms of interpersonal engagement.

Autonomy as Detachment?

Human beings, out of their innate need for relatedness, are oriented toward attachments with caregivers (Ainsworth et al., 1978) just as they begin immediately to express and strive for greater autonomy. Still, some theorists have cast the development of autonomy in terms of a relinquishing of familial attachments, especially during adolescence (e.g., Blos, 1962; A. Freud, 1958; Steinberg & Silverberg, 1986). In doing this, they are construing autonomy in terms of detachment rather than volition. In addition to the conceptual confusion this creates, there is the empirical fact that detachment (especially from parents) is typically counterproductive with regard to the development of autonomy and self-regulation.

Ryan and Lynch (1989) applied this formulation in their reconsideration of research by Steinberg and Silverberg (1986) on what the latter authors had termed *emotional autonomy* in adolescence. Steinberg and Silverberg (1986) drew on Blos's theory of adolescence, defining emotional autonomy as the relinquishing of dependence on parents, and they developed a measure to assess this construct. Ryan and Lynch, while acknowledging the significance of reliance issues in adolescent development, criticized the labeling of such nonreliance as autonomy. They regarded the so-called "emotionally autonomous" youths as those who, for a variety of reasons, indicated less willingness to turn to their parents for support, guidance, or help. Rather than indicating volition and agency, such nondependence could be better understood in most cases as reflecting emotional *detachment*.

Ryan and Lynch suggested that, under most circumstances, teenagers who detach from their parents, and thus do not utilize or rely on them for emotional support, should tend to show more negative developmental consequences, whereas autonomy (i.e., volition) should have positive consequences. To support this view, Ryan and Lynch showed, within varied adolescent samples, that a high degree of what was labeled "emotional autonomy" by Steinberg and Silverberg was negatively correlated with indexes of adjustment such as self-esteem, perceived competence, and lovability. Autonomy, in contrast, has frequently been found to be positively correlated with those same indexes of adjustment (e.g., Deci & Ryan, 1987). Furthermore, Ryan and Lynch (1989) provided evidence that the typical familial context associated with high degrees of adolescent emotional autonomy is lacking in cohesion and support and is characterized by insecure attachments. Such evidence points toward (a) the positive confluence of attachment and autonomy and (b) the need to differentiate the idea of autonomy from that of detachment and independence. Specifically, a good deal of emotional attachment to caregivers is, according to Ryan and Lynch, conducive rather than antithetical to autonomy and healthy development.

Autonomy as Just a Stage?

The development of autonomy, when viewed as an increasing sense of volition and choice resulting from the integration of regulatory processes, is ongoing throughout life. The form and content of the dialectical struggle for autonomy varies at different developmental stages, but the general striving is the same. Specifically, people engage challenges that are optimal for their current capacities, and through such activity they assimilate and elaborate the structures and processes of self.

Various writers, however, have portrayed the struggle for autonomy as being primarily evident at particular developmental stages. Perhaps the best known of these theories is Erikson's (1950) reformulation of Freud's (1908/1959, 1913/1959) theory of psychosexual development. Erikson identified the second and third years of children's lives as the crucial ones for the development of autonomy. At this time, having achieved a primitive sense of self as a separate entity, children begin to assert themselves, generally in accord with their biological urges, but, at times, as all parents know, apparently just to be oppositional toward the word or will of others.

Erikson argued that, if allowed to respond to their urges and inner cues, children will develop a sense of autonomy and pride.

By contrast, if they face rigid dominance and are thus not allowed to act on their drives and desires, children will instead develop a sense of shame and doubt. Such children may find it necessary to block awareness of their own inner cues and develop a more passive stance toward the initiation of behavior.

This period in children's lives, when their sense of self is still quite rudimentary, is crucial for their long-term sense of autonomy, and the responsiveness of the social context is critically important for that development. However, the struggle for autonomy is ongoing across the life span, and although Erikson's theory acknowledges the importance of integration throughout one's life, his relegating the concept of autonomy development to this brief stage diminishes greatly the meaning of autonomy. The dynamic in which people attempt to be self-regulating—to assert their autonomy—and are responded to in either an autonomy-supportive or a controlling manner is played out at all stages of life with regard to varied issues and in varied domains. Our research has consistently shown that the social context's being autonomy-supportive versus controlling of people at various ages affects not only their immediate motivation but also their ongoing tendencies to be autonomous.

Piaget (1967) suggested that will (which is closely related to autonomy) is a regulatory capacity that comes into existence during middle childhood (7 to 12 years of age) in relation to moral issues. For a child of that age, morality is gradually shifting from being based wholly on authority to being determined more by mutuality and consent. The shift away from exclusive reliance on authority necessitates the development of internal regulatory processes that will, as Piaget conceived it, allow a morally superior principle to win out over a morally inferior drive. In our view, this process of developing internal regulatory processes to manage one's drives and emotions is merely an example of the development of one's more general sense of will or autonomy. This process begins before and continues long after middle childhood.

Adolescence has often been said to be the important period for the development of autonomy (e.g., A. Freud, 1958). As noted, adolescence is a period of individuation in which teenagers develop both greater independence and greater autonomy. However, the rebellion of a child struggling to free himself or herself from parental control is often said to reflect autonomous regulation. Rebellion, which typically means insistently doing the opposite of what was demanded of one, does not, however, constitute autonomy. Instead, rebellion is merely the defiant rather than compliant form of being controlled and is not accompanied by the experience of choice, volition, and coherence. The period of adolescence is surely important for the development of autonomy, for as teenagers gradually individuate from parental authority, they are faced with the challenge of developing the type of internal regulatory processes that constitute autonomous rather than controlled regulation. However, as with the struggles in early and middle childhood, this represents one aspect and form of the striving for autonomy that is central to development across the life span.

Loevinger (1976) used the term autonomy to describe a stage of adulthood that most individuals never attain. This stage is characterized by the ability to accept responsibility for one's actions and emotions, and to respect the needs of others. Loevinger's description of autonomy thus bespeaks the concepts of integration and awareness that are the hallmarks of self-determination. Still, these characteristics can be found, to varying degrees, in behavior at all ages, not only in some people during adulthood.

These various theories all emphasize the importance of people's striving for autonomy, but they localize the struggle to specific, but different, developmental epochs, ranging from infancy to adulthood. When taken together, however, the theories highlight how significant the dynamics of autonomy are across all stages of development. In infancy, autonomy concerns the consolidation of self and the development of initiative. Progressively, as the child gets older, autonomy relates (a) to assimilating socially important behaviors and ideals while preserving one's initiative, (b) to individuating and forming new attachments while preserving the old, and (c) to fully accepting and integrating aspects of oneself. In all cases, the issues concern reaching an accommodation to the social world in a way that allows an internal perceived locus of causality and the experience of agency and volition.

AUTONOMY IN DEVELOPMENT

Having conveyed what is (and is not) meant by autonomy, we turn now to an elaboration of the role of autonomy in development. We focus on three developmental processes in which autonomy figures heavily: (a) intrinsic motivation, (b) internalization, and (c) emotional integration. We then turn to the dynamic interactions of autonomy and relatedness, which further forge and temper these three central developmental processes.

Intrinsic Motivation

The natural tendencies of exploration, manipulation, and curiosity are present from the time of birth, are manifest as an initial sense of volitional self by the end of 6 months (Stern, 1985), are expressed as a clear preference for novelty by the 9th month (Hunt, 1965), lead to persistent mastery attempts by the time of the child's first birthday (Ainsworth et al., 1978), and differentiate into more specific interests as the child grows older (Deci, 1975). These tendencies are intrinsically motivated (Deci & Ryan, 1985b); they require no incentives or pressures, but instead occur spontaneously when the social context does not forestall them. These intrinsically motivated activities provide their own rewards in the form of the excitement, interest, and enjoyment that accompany them. They are autotelic (Csikszentmihalyi, 1975) rather than being instrumental for some separable consequence.

The concept of intrinsic motivation emerged from the experimental literature during the 1950s and 1960s, in opposition to the two dominant behavioral, associationist theories of that period (operant theory and drive theory). Operant theory (Skinner, 1953) had proposed that all operant behavior is under the control of contingencies of reinforcement in one's environment—in other words, all nonreflexive behaviors are maintained by extrinsic consequences. Proponents of intrinsic motivation, in contrast, held that many behaviors, such as play and exploration, are "rewarding in their own right"; they are done out of interest and do not require extrinsic rewards or reinforcements (Deci, 1975). This conceptualization of an innate and natural source of activity oriented toward exercise and growth has been an important coordinate for the study of developmental and learning processes (Elkind, 1971; Flavell, 1977).

In our research on intrinsic motivation, we work with the general thesis that intrinsic motivation represents an autonomous organismic striving and is accompanied by people's experiencing their actions as emanating from themselves and as having an internal perceived locus of causality. We also reason that maintaining intrinsic motivation, and thus promoting optimal development and positive well-being, depends on social conditions that support and preserve one's autonomy. Thus, intrinsic motivation—and the curiosity, assimilative tendency, and joy that attend it—have been predicted to be undermined in conditions that are overly controlling or inconsistent, leading to nonoptimal development and the onset of psychopathology.

Numerous studies, using widely varied methods, have linked intrinsic motivation to the effective negotiation of one's surrounds. For example, children's intrinsic motivation has been positively related to their creativity on artistic endeavors (e.g., Amabile, 1983; Koestner, Ryan, Bernieri, & Holt, 1984), and both elementary school and college students' intrinsic motivation has been positively associated with fuller processing of information and greater conceptual understanding (Benware & Deci, 1984; Grolnick & Ryan, 1987). These studies thus indicate that undermined intrinsic motivation has negative consequences for normal functioning across a person's first two decades.

Even more importantly, perhaps, individuals' intrinsic motivation has been positively related to mental health. For example, children's intrinsic motivation in a classroom setting has been positively associated with their feelings of self-worth (e.g., Deci, Schwartz, Sheinman, & Ryan, 1981; Ryan & Grolnick, 1986), and lower levels of intrinsic motivation have been linked to more aggressive projections (Ryan & Grolnick, 1986), more maladaptive coping (Ryan & Connell, 1989), more tension and anxiety (Ryan, Mims, & Koestner, 1983), and a more negative emotional tone (Garbarino, 1975). Thus, these and related studies strongly suggest that, to the extent that intrinsic motivation is undermined, negative developmental consequences will follow.

Studies with later adolescents have made the point even more definitively. For example, Kasser and Ryan (1993, in press) found that college students' and adults' aspiring for the intrinsic goals of personal growth, meaningful relationships, and making community contributions was positively associated with markers of good mental health, including self-actualization, vitality, global social functioning, and social productivity. In the Kasser and Ryan research, these three aspirations were considered akin to intrinsic motivation because achieving them tends to be a reward in its own right and because they are theoretically congruent with concepts such as growth tendencies and a secure sense of self. Greater relative importance (to individuals) of these intrinsic (versus extrinsic) aspirations was negatively associated with indicators of poor mental health, including anxiety, depression, physical symptoms, and conduct disorders.

Taken together, the various studies just reviewed provide good evidence that a high level of intrinsic motivation has a clear positive relation to strong mental health, whereas a low level points toward psychopathology. It thus seems important to explicate the social-contextual conditions that have been found to enhance versus undermine intrinsic motivation.

The Social Context

A substantial amount of research has explored the effects of various social contexts on intrinsic motivation. These studies have been done with subjects ranging from toddlers to adults, and it is particularly striking that the effects are parallel across ages. This fact lends credence to our assertion that the striving for autonomy is operative throughout the life span, and it allows us to draw at least tentative inferences about fundamental aspects of human development.

The experimental paradigm most often used involves groups of subjects working on the same activity under different conditions (usually varied in terms of factors affecting perceived autonomy, perceived competence, or both). Subsequently, intrinsic motivation is assessed by placing subjects in a free-choice situation where the target activity is available along with alternative activities. The amount of time subjects spend spontaneously engaging the target activity is recorded and used as the "free choice" or "free play" measure of intrinsic motivation. Subjects' ratings of how interesting and enjoyable they found the task are used as a secondary measure of intrinsic motivation. When these two measures are significantly correlated, we are most confident that the free-choice behavior is a true reflection of intrinsic motivation (Ryan, Koestner, & Deci, 1991).

In the earliest studies, Deci (1971, 1972) found that subjects who received monetary rewards for solving intrinsically interesting puzzles subsequently displayed significantly less intrinsic motivation than those who had solved the puzzles for no rewards. Deci (1971) postulated that rewarded subjects were more likely to see the impetus or "cause" of their activity as stemming from external, as opposed to internal, sources, thus prompting a shift in the perceived locus of causality (deCharms, 1968). This proposal was provocative precisely because so many psychologists had emphasized that rewards are the primary impetus behind individual behavior. Here, not only was that not the case, but rewards were shown to have a detrimental effect on spontaneous challenge-seeking behaviors.

A study by Lepper, Greene, and Nisbett (1973), in which preschool children were given good-player awards for drawing with magic markers, found results complementary to those of Deci (1971, 1972). The Lepper et al. study not only showed the generalizability of the undermining of intrinsic motivation by rewards to young children, but also indicated that the negative effects persisted across a considerable delay period. A plethora of studies soon converged on this point (see, Harackiewicz, 1979; Ross, 1975, for examples with elementary and high school children), documenting that the allure of attractive extrinsic rewards can have a negative effect on people's autonomy. People gradually become pawns to the rewards (deCharms, 1968), and their intrinsic motivation is undermined.

Not only can controlling rewards undermine intrinsic motivation, but so can coercive motivational tactics, such as threatened punishment (Deci & Cascio, 1972). Further, surveillance (Lepper & Greene, 1975; Pittman, Davey, Alafat, Wetherill, & Kramer, 1980; Plant & Ryan, 1985), evaluations (Smith, 1974), and controlling language (Ryan, 1982) have also been found to decrease intrinsic motivation. In these studies, the external events employed (e.g., reward, surveillance, threat, controlling language) are those that are frequently used as methods of controlling behavior. Such events tend to acquire a psychological meaning or *functional significance* of being controlling, which, in turn, tends to negatively affect people's sense of autonomy.

Although material rewards are not widely used during the early years of a child's development, the use of controlling interpersonal rewards is very prevalent. Parents, for example, often use controlling, directive language and "withdrawal of love" to shape their children's attitudes and behavior. The general point of this literature is that, to the extent that adults use these salient prods, prompts, or pressures to induce performance at an interesting activity, they are likely to disrupt intrinsic motivation and autonomous functioning, which may result in the emergence of psychopathological outcomes.

The significance of this idea for development cannot be overstated. Children's exploration, challenge seeking, and curiosity with respect to the physical and social worlds, from which specific competencies derive, appear to be curtailed in an impinging, surveilling, contingency-managed environment. The intrinsically motivated basic tendencies supporting growth can, accordingly, be stifled by well-meaning caretakers who attempt to elicit development through reinforcement or control. Thus, even though, as Piaget (1952) emphasized, the tendency toward assimilation is a basic fact of psychic life, such findings suggest that even this natural process requires circumstances supportive of autonomy to remain vital and active.

A classic study illustrating this principle was performed by Danner and Lonky (1981). Using Piagetian tasks, they preclassified children with regard to their current level of cognitive development. They then allowed the children to choose activities freely. Children left free to choose activities at any level of complexity gravitated to tasks that were optimally challenging—to those just exceeding their cognitive capacities. However, children who were extrinsically rewarded for problem solving tended to avoid challenge during subsequent free-choice play. Such results illustrate how attempts to "enhance" development through rewards can clearly backfire (see also Kruglanski, Stein, & Riter, 1977; Pittman, Emery, & Boggiano, 1982).

These studies underscored the idea that developmentally relevant activity has its own fuel and requires conditions supportive of autonomy and challenge, rather than external controls, to be sustained.

It is particularly troubling that the use of controlling strategies is so pervasive; it seems to bring about a general shift away from people's active, autonomous engagement with their surroundings and toward a more passive and rigid orientation. Thus, in experiments exploring the effects of rewards and controls on variables such as cognitive flexibility, investigators have found that controlling external events also have negative effects on these outcomes (McGraw & McCullers, 1979). Rigidity, of course, has regularly been implicated in various forms of psychopathology, as we will see later in this chapter.

A few studies have considered whether any external events will enhance rather than undermine the sense of autonomy essential to intrinsic motivation and related psychological processes. Zuckerman, Porac, Lathin, Smith, and Deci (1978) had college student subjects work on interesting puzzles. Half were allowed to make task choices, and, using a yoking procedure, the other half were assigned the tasks selected by the choice subjects. Results indicated that subjects who had been given choices were significantly more intrinsically motivated than subjects who had not. Swann and Pittman (1977) found similar results with children.

A second external event that has had positive effects on intrinsic motivation is acknowledging the individual's feelings. For example, Koestner et al. (1984) found that, when setting limits for early elementary school children, their intrinsic motivation remained high for an activity if their feelings of not wanting to observe the limits were acknowledged, whereas their intrinsic motivation was significantly lowered when their feelings were not acknowledged. A study by Deci, Eghrari, Patrick, and Leone (1994) found that acknowledging college-age subjects' conflicting feelings also led to more autonomy and a more positive emotional tone than not acknowledging their feelings.

Taken together, these studies indicate that providing choices and acknowledging feelings enhance intrinsic motivation and positive affect because these events leave subjects feeling less pressured and more autonomous. In summation, then, numerous laboratory experiments suggest that contextual conditions that are experienced as controlling (i.e., conveying pressure to think, feel, or behave in specific ways) undermine autonomy, resulting in less self-initiation and greater psychological rigidity, whereas contextual conditions that are autonomy-supportive (i.e., taking the target individual's frame of reference, providing choice, and encouraging self-initiation) have comparably positive effects on psychological functioning. Extrapolating from this suggestion, it is easy to predict that contexts that are overly controlling rather than optimally autonomy-supportive represent one identifiable input to the development of various psychopathologies.

Although it is not the central focus of this chapter, it is worth noting that numerous studies have shown that persistent feedback indicating one's incompetence at a task or within an activity domain undermines not only intrinsic motivation but also extrinsic motivation (e.g., Deci, Cascio, & Krusell, 1973; Hiroto & Seligman, 1975; Koestner & McClelland, 1990). We refer to contexts that continually signify incompetence, potentially resulting in helplessness and depression, as *amotivating*.

Field Studies

In addition to the laboratory exploration of the effects of controlling versus autonomy-supportive social structures, numerous field studies of parents and teachers have investigated factors that influence intrinsic motivation and development.

Grolnick, Bridges, and Frodi (1984), in a study of infants, found that those whose mothers were more controlling evidenced less mastery motivation and persistence in independent problem solving than did those whose mothers tended to support and encourage their initiations and autonomous play. Deci, Driver, Hotchkiss, Robbins, and Wilson (1993) found similar results in a sample of 5-to 7-year-old children. They reported that mothers who, during an interactive play period, were rated as being relatively controlling had children whose subsequent intrinsic motivation was lower than those whose vocalizations were rated as more autonomy-supportive.

A study by Deci, Schwartz, Sheinman, and Ryan (1981) found comparable results for late elementary school teachers and their students. When teachers were oriented toward supporting autonomy, the students displayed higher levels of intrinsic motivation, perceived cognitive competence, and self-esteem than when the teachers were oriented toward controlling behavior. Ryan and Grolnick (1986) reported comparable results, and Flink, Boggiano, and Barrett (1990) also found that when teachers were more controlling students performed less well.

The results of such field studies cohere on several points. When people in positions of responsibility or authority—for example, parents and teachers—support the autonomy of those with whom they interact, the latter individuals tend to display enhanced autonomy, intrinsic motivation, and self-regard. Overcontrol, conversely, is typically associated with diminished motivation and self-esteem. It is particularly noteworthy that the results of these field studies parallel the results of laboratory experiments in which autonomy-supportive versus controlling interpersonal climates were created.

Internally Controlling Regulation

In the research thus far discussed, intrinsic motivation has been the only form of internal motivation identified, and the only controlling elements discussed have been aspects of the social context. Another line of experimental research has highlighted another form of internal motivation—referred to as *internally controlling regulation*—that is quite different from intrinsic motivation. Ryan (1982) showed that when individuals become *ego involved* in outcomes, they tend to be internally controlling in their regulation; that is, they tend to pressure themselves and display the qualities of being controlled. In turn, Ryan found that these ego-involved subjects displayed significantly less intrinsic motivation than task-involved subjects, thus confirming that internally controlling regulation does not represent autonomous functioning. Ryan et al. (1991) replicated this result.

Plant and Ryan (1985) took a complementary approach to exploring this issue, based on Sartre's (1956) discussion of the "look phenomenon." This refers to a form of "inauthentic" or nonautonomous being in which people's awareness of themselves is "as if through the eyes of another." Plant and Ryan found that when subjects were induced to become "objectively self-aware" (Duval & Wicklund, 1972), a state analogous to the look phenomenon, their intrinsic motivation was undermined, thus indicating that evaluating oneself "as if" through the eyes of another entails internally controlling regulation and impairs autonomy.

Studies on internally controlling regulation (see Ryan & Stiller, 1991, for a fuller review) demonstrate how a motivational force that is "internal" to the person can, like external forces, be heteronomous with respect to the self, thus disturbing one's autonomy. They highlight the critical importance of employing a more differentiated conception of internal forms of motivation, which is all the more critical in the discussion of internalization to which we now turn.

Internalization

When intrinsically motivated, children do what interests them, whether it be exploring a novel space, building a model, or playing with a doll. Although a source of delight for caretakers, it is also a challenge. Often, caregivers think it important to redirect the children's attention and energy away from what interests them to other activities that promote family harmony, improve school performance, or are socially sanctioned. There are many activities, in fact, that children may not find intrinsically interesting but that parents, school systems, and society believe are "in the children's best interest." It is thus the task of parents and teachers, as primary socializing agents, to encourage children not only to perform such nonintrinsically motivated activities, but also to aid them in developing an internal motivation and willingness to do so.

The shift from an external impetus and sustenance of behaviors to an internal one is characterized herein as the process of *internalization* (Ryan, Connell, & Deci, 1985). Internalization is the means through which someone can become more autonomous in performing an activity that was initially externally prompted. It is an active process of taking in information or regulatory processes and transforming them into personal values or motivational propensities (Meissner, 1988; Ryan, Connell, & Grolnick, 1992; Schafer, 1968).

Internalization is an instance of organismic integration. It is the means through which people, by integrating experiences and the regulatory processes implicit in them, can become, simultaneously, more autonomous and more homonomous. Through internalization, people acquire values and behaviors that allow them to be effective, to relate to others, and to experience a true sense of willingness in doing so. In other words, internalization functions primarily in the service of people's needs for competence, autonomy, and relatedness; through effective internalization, people become both more homonomous and more autonomous. Conversely, failures of internalization typically imply less effective functioning and a vulnerability to psychopathology.

Because internalization operates in the service of the three basic psychological needs, we can readily predict that aspects of the social context that support autonomy, are adequately structured, and provide interpersonal involvement, will facilitate it. When the context allows satisfaction of these needs, and particularly when they are not in any way pitted against each other, there will be optimal socializing circumstances for children to naturally acquire social values subserving nonintrinsically motivated activity.

Conceptualized in this way, one can see that both intrinsic motivation and internalization are related to the construct of autonomy. Intrinsic motivation is the prototype of autonomous regulation, and internalization and integration represent the means by which activities that are not intrinsically interesting can become more autonomous. By integrating values and regulatory processes into one's self, those values and processes become the basis for self-determination of extrinsically motivated (i.e., instrumental) activities. And, although behaviors for which the regulatory processes have been fully integrated do not necessarily become intrinsically motivated (because they usually retain an "instrumental" rather than autotelic quality), the more closely the qualities of one's extrinsically motivated behaviors match those of intrinsically motivated behavior, the more likely the extrinsic regulation has been integrated.

In developmental terms, infants express their autonomy through intrinsically motivated engagement and mastery. Gradually, as they develop into toddlerhood, childhood, and adulthood, their autonomous activity is expanded by the integration of regulatory processes that originally had an external impetus or source. It may well be that adults express less intrinsically motivated behavior than children, and, instead, display their autonomy in the form of integrated regulation.

When functioning optimally, the internalization process results in values and regulations that are fully integrated with the self, and we hypothesize that supports for autonomy and relatedness are necessary for such optimal internalization. Unfortunately, such ideal contextual conditions are not widely prevalent, and full integration of regulations is often not attained. Instead, when socializing agents are controlling or uninvolved, the internalization process operates nonoptimally, resulting in values and regulations that are only introjected and never fully assimilated (Ryan, 1993; Schafer, 1968).

Introjection is only partial assimilation in which the internal regulatory process retains essentially the same form it had when it was still external. Perls (1973), for example, described introjection as a process in which some aspect of the environment is "swallowed whole" and never "digested." Metaphorically, it is as if the regulator and regulatee were still separate even though they are the same person; the regulatory process has *not* been integrated with the self and is thus a source of tension and inner conflict. When a regulation has been introjected (rather than integrated), it tends to be rigid and controlling. Indeed, introjection supplies the developmental basis for *internally controlling* regulation, such as that evidenced in ego-involvement. Several studies have now demonstrated that introjection is related to anxiety, self-derogation, and other maladaptive patterns, whereas fuller integration is associated with more positive adaptation (e.g., Ryan & Connell, 1989; Ryan, Rigby, & King, 1993). This suggests that, to the extent that values and regulatory processes are stuck in the form of introjects and thus not integrated with the self, a child is at risk for psychopathology.

The importance of distinguishing between types of internalization is crucial for developmental theories concerned with the nature and quality of behavioral and psychological functioning. Even in early life, it is clear that infants and young children can be either self-regulating or merely compliant. As Crockenberg and Litman (1990) argued, there is an important difference between a toddler's doing something compliantly, out of fear or force, and doing it autonomously, with a full sense of willingness. The autonomous (rather than merely compliant) performance of uninteresting, though important, activities is a significant goal of socialization.

To provide a framework for making distinctions between various types of internalization, we have specified four regulatory styles that are pertinent to extrinsically motivated behavior (Deci & Ryan, 1985b): (a) external, (b) introjected, (c) identified, and (d) integrated. *External* regulation describes extrinsically motivated behavior that is initiated and maintained by external rewards and structures; a girl who does her chores to avoid parental wrath would be externally regulated. When an external regulation has been internalized but not accepted as one's own, it is said to be *introjected;* a boy who picks up his room because he thinks he should—because that is what "good boys" do—would have introjected the regulation. Gradually, as a child identifies with a value or regulatory process, the child begins to accept it as his or her own. In such a case, the behavior is governed by what we call *identified* regulation, which can be viewed as transitional between introjected and integrated regulation. A girl who studies arithmetic because she believes it is important for her self-selected goal of becoming an architect would be considered identified in terms of this regulation. *Integrated* regulation, the most advanced form of internalized regulation, indicates that a value and its accompanying regulatory process have been reciprocally assimilated with all other aspects of one's self. The internalization process will have been completed, representing further development of oneself. A young man who identifies with working hard at his studies and also identifies with being a good soccer player, and who has organized these differing values within a relatively harmonious regulatory network, can be said to have integrated these regulations.

These varied forms of behavioral regulation are schematically depicted in Figure 20.1. The four styles of extrinsic regulation are placed along a continuum of relative autonomy; external regulation is the least autonomous form of extrinsically motivated behavior, and integrated regulation is the most autonomous form.

Ryan and Connell (1989) assessed children's external, introjected, and identified regulatory styles for doing schoolwork, as well as their intrinsic motivation. Data confirmed that the external, introjected, identified, and intrinsic subscales formed a simplexlike pattern, indicating that these four regulatory styles can be ordered along a single dimension of autonomy. The more autonomous styles (identified and intrinsic) were positively correlated with positive affect and proactive coping, whereas the less autonomous styles (i.e., external and introjected) were correlated with negative affect and maladaptive coping. Introjection, in particular, was highly correlated with anxiety and with anxiety amplification following failure, thus highlighting the inner stress and vulnerability caused by these controlling prescriptions.

Ryan and Connell (1989) also found that more autonomous regulation in the prosocial domain was associated with greater empathy, more mature moral reasoning, and more positive relatedness to others, thus signifying the importance of autonomous self-regulation for healthy adaptation in the prosocial as well as the academic domain.

Ryan, Rigby, and King (1993) examined the degree of internalization of religious values in late adolescents and adults. Results indicated that introjected regulation of religious behaviors predicted greater susceptibility to depression, anxiety, and low self-esteem, whereas identified regulation was negatively associated with these indicators of ill-being.

Blais, Sabourin, Boucher, and Vallerand (1990) assessed adults' reasons for maintaining their primary relationship. Six types of reasons that vary in their degree of autonomy were used:

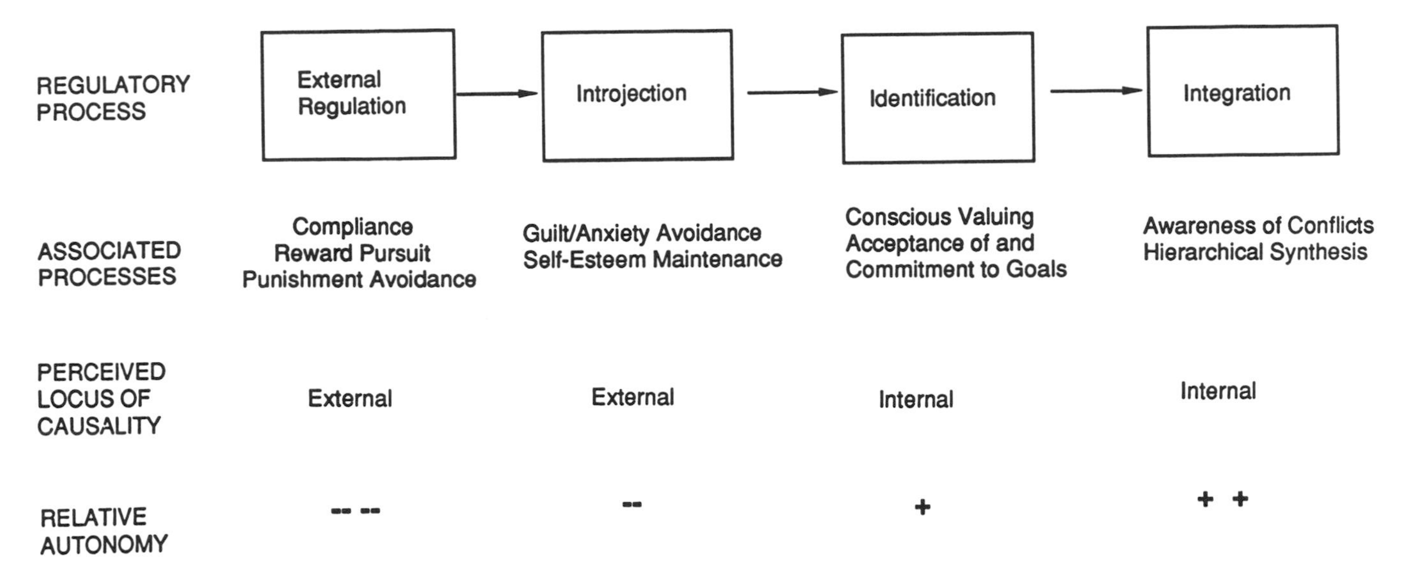

Figure 20.1 Schematic of regulatory styles associated with internalization.

(a) amotivation, (b) external, (c) introjected, (d) identified, (e) integrated, and (f) intrinsic. From a sample of 63 heterosexual couples, the three regulatory styles constituting non-self-determination (i.e., amotivation, external, and introjected) all correlated significantly negatively with dyadic adjustment and general marital satisfaction; the three regulatory styles constituting greater self-determination (i.e., identification, integration, and intrinsic) all correlated significantly positively with those variables.

Work on self-regulation using the questionnaire method and the construct outlined above is continuing in the domains of religion (O'Connor & Vallerand, 1990), health care (Ryan, Plant, & O'Malley, in press; Williams, Grow, Ryan, Friedman, & Deci, 1994), aging (Grow & Ryan, 1994; Vallerand & O'Connor, 1989), and education (Grolnick et al., 1991; Vallerand & Bissonnette, 1992; Vallerand et al., 1993), and has indicated consistently that the less integral and autonomous one's motivations, the less positive one's adjustment and well-being.

Introjection results in internally controlling regulation, which, if it persists beyond the point of developmental appropriateness, is not considered part of one's true or integrated self, but instead can be thought of as akin to false self. If the organismic integration process continues to function with respect to an introjected value or process (as, for example, it would in psychotherapy), that value or regulatory process may, in time, be integrated, but insofar as the integrative process is stalled, introjected aspects of the person remain alien to the self.

Internalization and the Social Context

Although internalization and integration are natural processes, they, like all such processes in the organismic dialectic, require nutriments and supports from the social context. The critical contextual nutriments in our analysis are involvement, structure, and autonomy support.

Parents' being involved with their children—relating to them and providing a moderate amount of consistent, clear structure—facilitates internalization of values and regulatory processes, but for those internalized processes to be integrated, the parents must also provide autonomy support. If, instead, parents are excessively controlling, it is likely that any internalized processes will merely be introjected, not integrated.

Being autonomy-supportive for a child implies that one attempts to grasp and acknowledge the child's perspective, uses minimal controls to foster behavior, and provides choice when possible. When that occurs, the child will understand the reasons for self-regulating and will feel understood. Further, the behaviors that are encouraged will be performed with a relatively more internal perceived locus of causality. In contrast, being controlling involves parents' pressuring the child to do what *they* want, emphasizing obedience and compliance.

Most theories of parenting employ a variable that is anchored on one end by a concept essentially equivalent to being controlling. For example, Becker (1964) spoke of restrictive parenting, Schaefer (1959) described controlling parenting, and Baldwin (1955) discussed an autocratic style of parenting. These terms apply to parents who place paramount value on compliance. Children of parents high on these attributes have been found to be hostile (Hoffman, 1960), dysphoric and disaffiliated (Baumrind, 1967), and obedient, low in social interaction, and dominated by peers (Baldwin, 1955).

Although there is general agreement about the controlling end of a parent dimension, there is less agreement about the other end. Some researchers have contrasted control with permissiveness (e.g., Becker, 1964); others have contrasted it with democracy (Baldwin, 1949). We emphasize that autonomy support does not imply permissiveness, neglect, or the absence of action on the part of the parent; instead, it conveys an active support of the child's capacity to be self-initiating and autonomous. Of the various concepts that have previously been used in contrast to control, Baldwin's (1949) concept of democratic parenting comes closest to autonomy support.

Baumrind (1967, 1971), who empirically examined the effects of parental styles on internalization, contrasted authoritative and authoritarian parental styles. The *authoritative* parent communicates openly with the child and encourages independence and individuality, while at the same time holding expectations and standards for mature behavior. The *authoritarian* parent, in contrast, values obedience and compliance and attempts to shape the child according to an absolute standard.

Baumrind (1977) found that, among nursery school children from authoritarian homes, girls were withdrawn and dependent and boys were aggressive. From our perspective, these two seemingly contrasting behavior patterns are two sides of a coin: they are both manifestations of being controlled by authoritarian parents. In one the child relies excessively on others to control behavior and in the other the child rebels against the controls and aggresses with little provocation. In contrast, children from authoritative homes were more adaptive in their behavior, displaying assertive, independent, and friendly actions.

Grolnick and Ryan (1989) extended the work of Baumrind and others by proposing a set of independent parenting dimensions from which the important parenting styles could be derived. The dimensions are: autonomy-supportive (versus controlling); structured (versus unstructured), and involved (versus uninvolved). Their dimensionalization recognizes that parenting behaviors can be either structured (i.e., consistent and clear with respect to expectations and rules) and autonomy-supportive, or unstructured and autonomy-supportive. The first configuration captures Baumrind's "authoritative" construct, and the second represents permissiveness. Furthermore, any of these parenting styles can be embedded in relationships characterized by various levels of involvement.

Using this three-dimensional model, Grolnick and Ryan (1989) interviewed separately, in their homes, the mothers and fathers of late elementary school students, to determine how they deal with their children concerning doing homework and chores. In addition, the children, in their classrooms, completed a self-regulation questionnaire developed by Ryan and Connell (1989), as well as a measure of their understanding of control over outcomes (Connell, 1985). Teachers rated the children's classroom adjustment and motivation, and school records were accessed to examine objective competence outcomes. Results indicated that parental controllingness predicted children's failure to internalize regulations, as well as poor adjustment and low achievement. Lack of involvement predicted children's not understanding how to control outcomes and contributed to poor adjustment and achievement. Parental inconsistency predicted children's not understanding what controls outcomes. Thus, the data indicated that parents' autonomy support, structure, and involvement contribute to their children's mastering the social context and developing the capacities to function effectively within it. Parents' failure to provide these necessary nutriments leads to poor adjustment and achievement and may set the stage for more profound disturbances.

Grolnick, Ryan, and Deci (1991) tested a model proposing that the effects of the parental environment on children's outcomes is mediated by the children's self-relevant motivations and perceptions. Children rated the degree to which their parents were involved with them and supported their autonomy. Results indicated that children who perceived their mothers and fathers as less involved and autonomy-supportive also reported poorer self-regulation, perceived competence, and control understanding relative to those who perceived more involvement and autonomy support. These self-relevant motivation variables, in turn, predicted the children's school performance, thus serving as mediators between the home context and children's performance. Elmen, Mounts, and Steinberg (1989) found comparable results using Baumrind's conceptualization.

Deci et al. (1994) performed a laboratory experiment to explore social contextual influences on internalization and integration. They manipulated three contextual factors that were thought to constitute autonomy support and involvement: (a) a meaningful *rationale* so the individual would understand the personal importance of the requested activity; (b) an *acknowledgment* of the individual's feelings so he or she would feel understood; and (c) an interpersonal style that emphasizes *choice* and minimizes control. Results revealed that the absence of these three facilitating factors impaired internalization, thus complementing the findings from the Grolnick and Ryan (1989) field study. Further, Deci et al. showed that the internalization that occurred in the conditions not supportive of self-determination (those with, at most, one of the facilitating factors) was introjected, as reflected by negative relations between subsequent behavior and subjects' self-reports of perceived choice, perceived importance of the activity, and enjoyment. In contrast, the internalization that occurred in the self-determination supporting conditions (those with two or more facilitating factors) was more integrated, as reflected by coherence between subsequent behavior and the same three affective self-report variables.

It appears, then, that if the context fails to support self-initiation and choice—that is, if significant others are controlling and uninvolved—people are less likely to internalize values, attitudes, and behaviors than if the significant others are autonomy-supportive and involved. Furthermore, when the context fails to provide the necessary nutriments, internalization that does occur is likely to have the quality of introjection, thus being rigid, conflicted, and marked by negative emotionality.

Weiss and Grolnick (1991) studied the relation of parental involvement and autonomy support to adolescents' internalizing and externalizing symptomatology (Achenbach & Edelbrock, 1987). Adolescents rated their mothers and fathers on dimensions of involvement and autonomy support, and they completed the self-report profile of symptoms. Analyses indicated that parents who were perceived to be *both* highly involved and autonomy-supportive had children who reported very low levels of either internalizing or externalizing symptoms. However, there were significant interactions between perceived parental involvement and autonomy support on both types of symptoms, indicating that the combination of high involvement and low autonomy support yielded a high level of symptoms. It thus appears that feeling close to very controlling parents can be detrimental to a developing child's well-being. Having to give up one's autonomy to satisfy the need for relatedness to parents can be quite costly indeed.

From these and related studies, we conclude that parental involvement, structure, and autonomy support are necessary for optimal internalization of social values and regulations and, in turn, for adjustment. It is particularly important to note that parental involvement and structure are not enough, for without autonomy support whatever internalization occurs is likely to be introjected rather than integrated, and the accompanying tension and inner conflict are likely to be associated with greater symptomatology.

Emotional Regulation and Integration

The third function of organismic integration (in addition to maintaining intrinsic motivation and fostering integrated internalization) is to develop capacities for integrated emotional regulation. *Emotional regulation* refers to the capacity to modulate or manage one's emotions and impulses; *emotional integration* refers to the most mature and autonomous form of emotional regulation. Specifically, emotional integration involves a differentiated awareness of one's emotional states and the capacity to use this sensitivity and awareness in the choiceful regulation of action.

From our perspective, integration is essential for optimal emotional regulation because it allows the experience, rather than the control or stifling, of emotion. In contrast to integrated regulation, internally controlling regulation, which involves blocking or suppressing one's emotions, not only is not optimal but, as we will see later, is implicated in various forms of psychopathology. Successful self-regulation of emotions is a flexible process in which the person experiences autonomy while using emotions as a guide to adaptive behavior. Emotional integration presupposes regulatory capacity in that being able to choicefully use emotional experience requires that an individual not be overwhelmed by inner experiences, which would result in dysregulation and impulsivity.

Within the developmental and child-clinical literatures, a great deal has been written under the broad rubric of emotion regulation referring to the management or control of affect (e.g., Garber & Dodge, 1991). This important area of work has, however, not often considered the problem of the relative autonomy of such management or control. This latter problem of emotional integration (rather than regulation or management per se) is more pertinent to empirical studies on the topic of coherence among aspects of the self. Because the literatures addressing these two aspects of developing autonomy in the emotional realm are separate, we discuss them in successive, though interrelated, sections.

Emotional Regulation

Many theorists view the development of self-regulation of inner impulses and affects as beginning from the time of birth and involving homeostasis as a neurologically based function. Greenspan (1979), for example, described infants during the early weeks of life as being centrally concerned with inner equilibrium. The signals a child sends when experiencing disequilibrium alert caregivers to respond in ways intended to allow the child's return to equilibrium. Emde (1983) suggested that this initial regulation through caregiver mediation is the basis on which the child gradually learns to monitor and manage his or her own equilibrium.

As children move beyond the first year, they must increasingly acquire the capacity to voluntarily control impulses and emotional expressions. Indeed, Vaughn, Kopp, and Krakow (1984), elaborating the work of Mischel on delay of gratification (e.g., Mischel, Ebbesen, & Zeiss, 1972; Mischel & Underwood, 1974), found a linear increase in children's ability to control their urges and delay gratification over the period from 18 to 30 months. The failure to develop this and related regulatory capacities, of course, is likely to result in maladaptive behaviors and thoughts, such as aggressive acting out (Dodge, 1991) and having depressive ideation and self-deprecating expectancies (Garber, Broafladt, & Zeman, 1991).

We argue, however, that the regulation of emotions and impulses is not just a matter of controlling oneself. Some children in a negatively arousing situation, such as being asked to delay gratification, will exert great effort, "forcing" themselves to push emotions out of their minds. But controlling themselves in this way requires attention and energy and diminishes the children's capacity for adaptive engagement with the environment. When used as a chronic way to deal with distress, it leads the children to experience being controlled by their own harsh thoughts and to display nonadaptive engagement. In contrast, other children in the same stressful settings may be more flexible (i.e., less rigid and pressured) in dealing with the situation—for example, by doing alternative activities or talking about their disappointment, signifying that they have developed more adaptive capacities for self-regulation of emotion.

Adaptive modes of self-regulating emotions thus entail gradual movement from reliance on mediation by others for modulation of one's inner forces to reliance on one's own inner resources (Cicchetti, Ganiban, & Barnett, 1991). But increasing self-reliance in coping with emotions does not ensure true emotional self-regulation; the latter requires being able to flexibly use inner experiences to adaptively interact with the environment.

Block and Block (1980) characterized ego resiliency in terms of a balance between overcontrol and undercontrol, thus conveying that neither dysregulation nor being rigidly regulated is an optimal outcome in developing self-regulation of emotions. Kopp (1982) made a similar distinction between self-control, which is the ability to inhibit behavior in the face of external demands, and self-regulation, which involves a greater capacity for adapting to new situations. From Kopp's viewpoint, self-control and self-regulation are sequential stages of early childhood development, whereas for us the rigid versus flexible forms of regulation represent markers on a developmental continuum of autonomous regulation that is relevant throughout life. This movement toward autonomous regulation of emotions and impulses, as noted, is considered a natural aspect of the development of self (Deci & Ryan, 1991; Ryan, 1993).

Greenspan (1979) referred to the development of regulatory processes for autonomously managing one's emotions and impulses as integration at "the internal boundary" (i.e., the boundary between the self and other aspects of the person), whereas he referred to the development of regulatory processes for engaging in activities deemed important by the social world as integration at "the external boundary" (i.e., the boundary between the self and the world). Although these two developmental functions (which we have called the development of emotional regulation and the internalization of regulatory capacities) are somewhat different, they are similar in many respects. Both involve gaining the capacities to regulate oneself with respect to behavior that is not intrinsically motivated, and both entail a developmental progression in which the child gradually relies less on cues and structures from the social context and more on internal cues and structures.

The movement toward greater self-regulation of emotion in young children can be understood as involving both emotional responsiveness and strategies for initiating, maintaining, and modulating this emotionality (Grolnick & Bridges, 1992). Identifying these two processes sets the stage for an empirical examination of how children develop autonomous regulation of, rather than the stifling of, emotions.

Emotional self-regulatory strategies involve behaviors used by the individual to regulate emotional experience. They can be more or less autonomously initiated and more or less active with respect to maintaining engagement with the environment. Rudimentary self-regulatory strategies are apparent from birth in such behaviors as head turning and sucking (Gianino & Tronick, 1988), and they develop into more autonomous, flexible strategies over time. In studies of 24-month-old children, a team of investigators (Bridges & Grolnick, 1995; Grolnick, Bridges, & Connell, 1993) developed a continuum of emotion-regulation strategies ranging from least to most autonomous for toddler-age children. Children were observed in two sets of mildly stressful situations—a delay in which they had to wait to play with an attractive toy (or eat a food), and a brief separation from mother. The child's emotionality (i.e., level of upset) and strategies to regulate this upset were then coded. Results supported an autonomy continuum in that the more autonomous (i.e., proactive) strategies were associated with the least upset whereas the least autonomous (i.e., the more controlled or passive) strategies were associated with the most upset. Further, there was some consistency across situations in that some children tended to use more autonomous and effective strategies in each situation whereas others used less autonomous and effective strategies. The results suggest that, within the first two years, individual differences in the self-regulation of affect have developed.

This raises the question of what aspects of the social environment facilitate the capacity to regulate affects, motives, and impulses. Before addressing that, however, it is important to emphasize that emotional responsiveness and the creation of effective regulatory strategies is not solely a function of the caretaking environment: temperamental qualities may intensify particular emotional states and influence the sequential flow of those states (Lewis & Michalson, 1983). Temperamental factors, which are relatively stable tendencies with biological underpinnings (Goldsmith et al., 1987), may include soothability and irritability (Brazelton, 1973); sociability, adaptability, and difficulty (Thomas, Chess, & Birch, 1968); and reactivity and self-regulation (Rothbart & Derryberry, 1981). Such factors play a significant role in the development of emotional self-regulation, although we view these individual differences in temperament as aspects of the child's "starting point" that interact with the caretaking environment as he or she develops emotional self-regulation. Temperament thus influences how formidable a task the development of emotional self-regulation will be for a child, and, as with all developmental processes, the magnitude of the challenge faced by different children can be quite different.

The challenge faced by children with difficult temperaments can also be exacerbated because their temperament and emotional expressiveness affect the socializing environment, which, in turn, further affects them. Children who are irritable and not very soothable may affect the caretakers in ways that make them less nurturing and supportive. As Dix (1991) pointed out, children's behavior can stimulate emotions in parents that undermine their effectiveness and responsiveness, thus making it even more difficult for the children to develop personal autonomy and interpersonal relatedness.

Emotion Regulation and the Social Context

There has been less research about contextual influences on emotional regulation than on intrinsic motivation and integrated internalization. Nonetheless, there is some work, both theoretical and empirical, that falls directly in line with the emerging picture of the importance of parental involvement and autonomy support for the development of self.

Winnicott (1960b) described the "holding environment" as one in which the infant's impulses, affects, and frustrations are satisfied by the parent before they become overwhelming, and in which the parent is sensitive to the cues and initiations of the infant. For Winnicott, a responsive holding environment facilitates the infant's developing sense of agency and vitality, although the dynamics of such responsiveness are complex and subtle. For example, when impulses and affects are experienced in the presence of a caregiver who is sensitive to what the child can tolerate, the caregiver will hold and soothe the child when that limit has been reached, and the borders of the child's self-experience will be broadened. The child will learn more about his or her own inner world and its relation to the social context; the child will experience both the force of the urges and the nature of gratification. In contrast, to the extent that the child is left alone with strong, unsatisfied urges, the child may either suppress them because they are so threatening or be overwhelmed by them, ending up disoriented. The experience of being responded to and thus, in a sense, regulated by an empathic other is thus crucial for the child's developing the capacities for regulating himself or herself.

Brazelton, Koslowski, and Main (1974) similarly emphasized the importance of the parents' ability to attend to infants' cues and to appreciate their need to withdraw from stimulation following periods of intense interaction. Sensitive parents recognize their infants' attempts to elicit interaction, but, equally importantly, they respect the infants' need to be without stimulation. Such parents adjust their own rhythm and behavior to that of their infants.

Greenspan's (1981) notion of a growth-promoting early environment emphasizes the capacity of the environment to balance the infant's need to engage the world and to experience self-regulation or homeostasis with respect to inner states. In a growth-promoting environment, the parent is available, providing soothing and comfort to supplement the child's emerging capacities to modulate inner states. The parent also provides stimulation and opportunities to engage the environment at times when the child is alert and ready. In the growth-inhibiting environment, the parent may be unavailable to provide comfort and regulatory help and the child does not then experience comfort and harmony. Without self-regulatory help, the child will need to shut out external stimulation, and engagement of the environment will be undermined.

In a study of normal mother-infant interactions, Field (1987) found that the mother adjusts her behavior to her infant's to provide adequate stimulation and arousal modulation. In an optimal interaction, the mother's and infant's attention and affective behavior are synchronized. If, however, the mother is emotionally unavailable or unresponsive, as in the case of depressed mothers (Tronick & Gianino, 1986), the relationship is asynchronous and the child would be likely to experience disorganization and to manifest disturbed state regulation. Field, Healy, Goldstein, and Guthertz (1990), in fact, found more negative affect and greater asynchrony between mood states in depressed mother-child dyads than in normals. The experiences of regulation and dysregulation within the mother-child dyad thus affect the child's developing the capacity for self-regulation.

In a recent study of emotional self-regulation (Shields et al., 1994), maltreated children and comparison children were observed on a playground, interacting with other children. Behaviors were coded for appropriate and inappropriate instances of positive and negative affect, and maltreated children displayed poorer emotional regulation than matched controls. Presumably, experiences within the family rendered the maltreated children deficient in the processes necessary to deal adaptively with stressful experiences. These children, who were less effective at emotion regulation, also displayed less social competence, emphasizing the adaptive importance of self-regulatory capacities.

In our view, as noted, three aspects of the optimal caretaking environment facilitate the young child's gradually becoming more able to self-regulate emotion. First, parental *involvement* helps a child maintain a tolerable level of distress so he or she is not overwhelmed and can learn to manage the inner forces of emotion. Second, parents' being *autonomy-supportive*—that is, taking the child's perspective and allowing the child the maximum amount of *self*-regulation he or she can tolerate—helps the child build confidence in his or her abilities to autonomously initiate and maintain regulatory strategies. This may, for example, mean supporting a child who is struggling in a distressing situation rather than removing the child from the situation. Third, providing *structure*—that is, offering optimal challenges (e.g., not expecting the child to behave in ways that are far beyond what is developmentally appropriate), being consistent, and setting limits that can be internalized—allows the child to trust and take interest in the environment and his or her affective relation to it.

Emotional Integration

Whereas emotional regulation is concerned with the modulation of emotional experience and expression, emotional integration is concerned specifically with the degree of flexibility and choice one feels in the regulation of emotions and emotion-related actions. To the extent that one's emotions and regulatory capacities are integrated aspects of the self, one is able to take interest in them and experience them as inputs to autonomous actions. In contrast, if regulatory capacities are merely introjected and thus in conflict with the emotions, a person is likely to suppress the feelings and ignore their personal meaning. The process of increasingly integrating one's emotions and regulatory capacities is merely a continuation of the work a child does in gaining regulatory capacities with respect to emotions, but it represents a mature version of that process.

The goal of emotional integration is not merely to have an individual comply with social norms by suppressing strong inner urges or acting in opposition to them; rather, it is to have the individual use inner experiences flexibly in acting autonomously. At times, a person may choose to act in a way that is counter to an urge or feeling, but suppression is not the integrated means through which this would occur. Instead, the person would allow the experience, take interest in its significance, and still act in a way that is counter to the urge but is in accord with a self-selected goal. When viewed in this way, the degree of integration of emotions cannot be judged on the basis of whether a person's behavior is socially appropriate. Failure to act in a socially sanctioned way could be quite choiceful and autonomous whereas acting in accord with social expectations could be achieved by rigid control of emotions.

How does the socializing environment impact the developing child so he or she can become more able to integrate emotional experiences with other aspects of the self? First, by accepting and nurturing the child, involved parents convey to the child a sense of personal worth. Acceptance by significant adults sets the stage for self-acceptance, particularly with regard to emotions. Parents' failure to respond or their negative reactions to certain feelings, in contrast, may be internalized as the nonacceptance of such feelings by oneself. Second, responsiveness of adults to the child's emotional initiations—as with any other type of initiation—supports and strengthens the child's sense of agency and autonomy and the child's definition of self as an initiating being. Third, parents' setting appropriate limits on behavior while allowing adequate expression of feelings (see Koestner et al., 1984) facilitates children's attunement to the social world and their acceptance of self in the process of adapting to it. Children can thus learn to be respectful of others—or, as Angyal (1965) put it, "to assume a homonomous attitude"—while seeking their own gratification and expression. Developing the capacities for respecting others and for delaying gratification represents a central agenda for the person from toddlerhood through adulthood; it involves learning when and how it is reasonable and appropriate to express one's feelings and being able to use that information in a choiceful way. Thus, emotional regulation entails internalizing values and regulatory structures provided by caregivers, a process that functions much like the internalization of any other behavioral regulation.

Emotional integration as herein viewed concerns the degree to which emotions can be assimilated and utilized by the self. It is important, once again, to contrast this view of integration with the conception of integration as the synchrony among affective, behavioral, and cognitive systems (Greenberg, Kusche, & Speltz, 1991). In part, synchrony has been equated with integration based on the fact that, quite often, synchrony represents the congruence among action, feelings, and consciousness. Thus, synchrony can be a *sign* that emotions have been fully acknowledged and freely expressed, and that the behaviors associated with them are integrated and endorsed. But, in our view, coordination among behaviors, affects, and cognitions (i.e., the fact of synchrony) does not guarantee integration of these processes into the self. Emotional expression and actions related to it can often be characterized by highly correlated systems, yet still can have an external perceived locus of causality. Conversely, one can have affects that one is fully aware of but meaningfully chooses not to express behaviorally in a certain context. Such apparent desynchrony can represent a high degree of integration in our current use of that term. Integration to the self and synchrony are thus not the same thing, the crucial issue being the degree to which emotions and regulatory processes have come into harmonious relations with other aspects of the integrated self.

Koestner et al. (1992) explored the relation of autonomy to the integration and synchrony of emotions, cognitions, and behavior. They separated subjects into an autonomy-oriented group and a control-oriented group based on a measure developed by Deci and Ryan (1985a), and then explored the consistency of behavior, attitudes, and traits among these two groups. Their general hypothesis was that autonomous subjects, because they are more integrated, would evidence greater consistency across these aspects of personality than would controlled subjects, who are theorized to be more rigid and fractionated. In the first two experiments presented, the researchers found very high correlations between the behavioral and self-report measures of intrinsic motivation within the autonomous groups, but no correlations within the controlled groups. The autonomy-oriented subjects displayed greater congruence between behaviors and feelings than did controlled subjects. In another experiment, Koestner et al. had subjects complete a trait measure of conscientiousness and then gave them an opportunity to behave conscientiously in the succeeding days. Subjects' conscientiousness scores and their conscientious behavior were significantly more highly correlated within the autonomous group than within the controlled group. Finally, a friend of each subject rated him or her on various traits, including conscientiousness, and the self-ratings and peer ratings were also more highly correlated for the autonomy-oriented subjects than for the control-oriented subjects. Taken together, this set of studies provides support for the theoretical proposition that autonomy is associated with greater congruence among traits, behaviors, and feelings, which we interpret as a reflection of greater integration in personality.

AUTONOMY AND RELATEDNESS AS INEXTRICABLY CONNECTED NEEDS

Thus far, we have emphasized the importance of autonomy by relating it to three vital developmental processes: (a) intrinsic motivation, (b) internalization, and (c) emotional integration. However, the construct of autonomy also figures heavily in the analysis of human relatedness and attachment, and the quality of relatedness, in turn, is a crucial factor in the development of mental health versus psychopathology.

The connection between autonomy and relatedness has been a hotly debated topic among psychological theorists over the past two decades. Some authors (e.g., Gilligan, 1982) see autonomy and relatedness as largely independent if not antithetical, and others (e.g., Bakan, 1966) see them as dialectically related to one another (again implying an original opposition that precedes synthesis). Our view differs from these because we do not view autonomy and relatedness as being in opposition. Indeed, we see them as integral to one another.

When we first began to explore the dynamics of autonomy and relatedness, we assumed that the strength and quality of one's connection to others in a given context could be examined separately from one's sense of autonomy. Accordingly, we attempted in several studies, using varied age samples and contexts, to do independent assessments of subjects' feeling related to others and feeling like their autonomy was supported by them. For example, we asked children to rate their parents with regard to both a sense of warmth and connectedness (indexes of relatedness) and a sense of their parents' taking their perspective, offering choices, and using minimal controls (indexes of autonomy support). Separable factors did not emerge; instead, warmth and connectedness ratings invariantly loaded with those representing autonomy support. Similar difficulties in obtaining independent factors for affection/warmth and autonomy support have occurred for other dyads such as teacher-child and physician-patient. Thus, for example, in studies of classroom climate, we typically cannot empirically separate perceived teachers' warmth and caring from their autonomy support. This series of psychometric "mishaps" strongly conveyed how closely connected one's feelings of attachment and relatedness are to the sense that the other acknowledges and supports one's self. This has led us to more deeply explore these seeming inextricable constructs.

With more clarity about the meaning of relatedness, we realized that, phenomenologically, one typically feels authentically related to another person only to the extent that one feels free to be oneself with him or her (Ryan, 1989, 1991). In other words, one feels warmly related to and secure in one's connection with others only to the extent that there is receptivity to and acceptance of one's real self. Conversely, insofar as there is a felt absence of autonomy support, the quality of relatedness suffers—one's connection is more superficial, insecure, and contingent.

How deep does this connection between autonomy and relatedness run? We suggest that, from the very beginning of life, the strength and security of attachment is in part a function of the autonomy support afforded by caregivers. We therefore begin our analysis of these intertwined needs during infancy, before further elaborating the analytic argument.

Autonomy and Relatedness in Infancy

It is particularly difficult to separate the development of autonomy and relatedness in the child's first year of life. During this period, according to Stern (1985), establishing a core self is a primary agenda for the infant. Although the self that is consolidated within the first 6 months does not take the form of a conscious representation, it is manifest as coherence and volition. Because infants are highly dependent on caregivers not only for biological necessities such as food and temperature regulation but also for interpersonal necessities such as love, contact, and comfort, these earliest experiences of the self as "initiator" of action occur within the context of very close parent-child relationships in which responsiveness to rising needs and to signals of them strengthens the sense of agency and its connections with action.

The interrelated development of autonomy and relatedness is described, albeit using different terms, in attachment theory. According to Bowlby (1969) and later theorists who have elaborated his framework (e.g., Bretherton, 1987), infants are innately prepared to engage in social relations from birth. The nature of these early social relations with primary caregivers shapes the security of attachment and the corresponding working models of self and others that function to organize future social relations.

Perhaps the most emphasized feature within attachment theory that contributes to security of attachment is the caregiver's responsiveness or *sensitivity* (Ainsworth et al., 1978; Brody & Axelrad, 1978). Sensitivity is defined as the provision of contingent, appropriate, and consistent responses to the child's signals and needs (Lamb & Easterbrooks, 1981). Sensitivity is thus a broad concept conveying that caregivers will respond to the child's initiations in ways that are empathic and appropriate to the child's needs.

To a large degree, the concept of sensitivity overlaps with what we have described as autonomy support, because what one is being "sensitive to" are the child's initiations, strivings, needs, and developing self. Indeed, Bretherton's (1987) description of sensitivity in terms of "maternal respect for the child's autonomy" (p. 1075) captures the essence of such contingent responsiveness. The sensitive caretaker responds to the initiations, cues, concerns, and needs that emerge from the child, and this contingent responsiveness gradually strengthens the child's inner sense of agency and coherence, and thus the meaningfulness of the child's self-initiated action and expression. When responded to, the child experiences a sense of safety and interconnection that is lacking for one whose biddings and expressions have fallen on deaf ears.

Autonomy support is thus a critical component of early relationships bcause it facilitates not only the solidity of attachment but also self-development more generally. Numerous studies have supported this perspective by linking sensitivity and/or autonomy support to more curiosity, effectance, and ego resiliency (Arend, Gove, & Sroufe, 1979; Grolnick et al., 1984; Waters, Wippman, & Sroufe, 1979), greater self-initiation (Stevenson & Lamb, 1981; Watson, 1966), improved learning (Lewis & Coates, 1980; Yarrow, Rubenstein, & Pederson, 1975), and, in general, more resourcefulness and better adjustment (Brody, 1956).

This interrelation among autonomy support, attachment, and self-development is also considered in Bowlby's (1969) speculations concerning infant exploration and mastery motivation. He postulated the existence of two innate systems that guide the child's behavior and development. The *attachment system* has as its goal the attainment and maintenance of close proximity to and contact with the caregiver, while the goal of the *exploratory system* is to discover and master the world around. These two systems are mutually dependent, however, and the satisfactory attainment of one will occur only in concert with the other. According to Bowlby, to the extent that a child experiences security (i.e., a sense that the caregiver will be accessible and responsive in times of need), the child will feel enabled to venture forth to explore with interest. However, to the extent that attachment is insecure, the child will stay close and monitor the parent's status and thus will not display healthy attempts at mastery and autonomous initiation.

This brief analysis of the role of autonomy and relatedness in infancy suggests the following: autonomy support (a) is a critical component of caregiving in infancy and (b) shapes both the experienced quality of relatedness (as reflected in the security of attachment) and the consolidation and vitality of the self (as reflected in both well-being and mastery motivation). Relatedness that is low in autonomy support, by contrast, will set the stage for attachment disturbances and impoverished agency.

Although we have emphasized the centrality of autonomy support to the formation of secure attachments, it is not the only component variable contributing to it. The sense of security in early relationships is also facilitated by caregiver involvement and structure. The involved parent dedicates resources to the child in the form of availability, effort, attention, and concrete nurturance. A caregiver also contributes to security by providing structure in the form of an optimal environment that modulates stimulation in accord with the infant's capacities and state. These contributions to well-being help to provide a sense of safety and comfort that is the backdrop of secure relations and the development of competencies. However, to facilitate the emerging self, the patterning of additional contributions must grow out of a reading of the child's actual needs and emotional states. That is, the optimal environment is one that provides resources and introduces structure in a context of autonomy support.

Autonomy and Relatedness beyond Infancy

As a result of their experiences with early caretakers, children develop models and expectancies regarding interpersonal interaction that are often referred to as object representations (Behrends & Blatt, 1985) or working models (Bretherton, 1991). These internal representations and models are *hypothetical* rather than inductively derived variables. They are used to explain how experiences in relationships with caregivers foster the characteristic patterns of interpersonal perceptions and behaviors that an individual exhibits. Because of their hypothetical status, such representations have been assessed and described in many different ways. Indeed, the methodological and content focus of representational assessments is as varied as the theoretical models that have been brought to bear on early childhood relatedness.

Given the emphasis in self-determination theory on the connections between relatedness and autonomy throughout development, one particularly intriguing conceptualization of object representations is that based on the *mutuality of autonomy* construct. Derived from object relational (Winnicott, 1965) and self-psychological (Kohut, 1971) theories, this construct assesses one's internalized schemata of relationships along a dimension ranging from those characterized by reciprocal dialogue and autonomy to those characterized by unifocal power and overwhelming control. Thus, the construct inherently assumes that the quality of one's relatedness is, to a great degree, a function of the autonomy supportiveness that characterizes it.

In a study of urban preadolescents, Ryan, Avery, and Grolnick (1985) employed a projective measure of mutuality of autonomy developed by Urist (1977). Based on the idea that experiences of relatedness that lack autonomy would be associated with less integrated functioning, these investigators hypothesized and found that poorer mutuality of autonomy predicted lower perceived control, poorer school grades, and, most importantly, worse interpersonal and classroom adjustment as rated by teachers. Tuber (1992) recently reviewed a number of studies with clinical samples that further document how various forms of psychopathology in childhood and adolescence are typically accompanied by lower levels of mutuality of autonomy.

Avery and Ryan (1988), also working with urban children in middle childhood, utilized a different projective assessment of object representations, developed by Blatt, Chevron, Quinlan, and Wein (1981), to examine the parental antecedents of the quality of children's object representations. Avery and Ryan found that perceived parental autonomy support and involvement—variables derived from self-determination theory—predicted the overall nurturant quality of parental representations. Furthermore, a wide array of functional outcomes, including peer sociometric ratings, general adjustment ratings, and perceived social and cognitive competence, were facilitated by parental autonomy support and involvement. As in infant attachment, these results bespeak the critical components of autonomy support and involvement underlying secure relatedness.

Ryan, Stiller, and Lynch (1994) recently investigated the relative and independent contributions of relatedness to parents, teachers, and friends to the prediction of motivation, adjustment, and self-esteem of early adolescents. They found that the quality of relatedness to parents and teachers, assessed in terms of felt security, as well as utilization and emulation of these target figures, predicted adjustment, again attesting to the facilitating effect of relatedness on one's integration and well-being. Furthermore, they found evidence that the quality of relatedness to parents predicted the quality of relatedness to both teachers and peers, and appeared to have priority among working models.

Ryan and Kuczkowski (1994) examined the effects of felt security on the development of autonomy in adolescence. In a cross-sectional design, they assessed adolescents' experience of private audiences (Elkind, 1967), arguing that the private-audience phenomenon, a precipitate of cognitive development in early adolescence, typically represents a heteronomous influence on adolescent behavior (Elkind, 1967; Piaget, 1965). This phenomenon is essentially akin to public self-consciousness and can be the basis of internally controlling regulation, particularly if it persists past early adolescence. Ryan and Kuczkowski supported this reasoning by showing that the salience of private audiences to adolescents was negatively related to public individuation.

Furthermore, based on theorizing by Lapsley and Rice (1988), Ryan and Kuczkowski predicted and found that whereas security of relatedness to parents was unrelated to the strength of private audiences in early adolescence (when it is an emerging and normative aspect of ego development), it was more strongly related in later adolescents. Those adolescents experiencing emotional insecurity with parents tended to remain more preoccupied with private audiences and were less capable of public individuation, in opposition to normative trends. This shows one specific way in which the growth of autonomy is dependent on one's embeddedness in secure relationships.

Ryan and Lynch (1989), in a study reviewed earlier in this chapter, examined both theoretically and empirically the issues of autonomy and attachment in early, middle, and late adolescent samples. They cited several theorists and researchers who have viewed adolescents' development of autonomy in terms of an increasing independence and nonreliance on parents. Ryan and Lynch argued, in contrast, that autonomy is more typically *facilitated* by attachment and dependence on parents than by detachment. Indeed, they suggested that, among the primary reasons that adolescents detach from and refuse to rely on parents is that parents have been overly controlling and/or underinvolved. According to Ryan and Lynch, adolescents whose parents provide a more optimal caretaking environment in which there is both involvement and autonomy support do not need to relinquish their attachment in order to become more autonomous and self-regulated. Rather than having to trade off relatedness for autonomy, such adolescents can maintain both, precisely because, in an autonomy-supportive context, the parent-adolescent relationship itself changes in accord with developing adolescent capacities and needs. In support of their perspective, Ryan and Lynch showed that adolescents with stronger positive ties to parents were, in fact, better adjusted and self-regulated than those whose connectedness with parents was poorer. This fits with a number of other extant perspectives and findings (e.g., Behrends & Blatt, 1985; Hill & Holmbeck, 1986; Kandel & Lesser, 1969).

In still another study, Dresner and Grolnick (1992) examined how the autonomy and interpersonal relatedness of college women was influenced by their parental object representations. The women's current relationships were classified as being caring, respectful, and intimate, or, alternatively, as being either superficial or enmeshed (Levitz-Jones & Orlofsky, 1985; Orlofsky, Marcia, & Lesser, 1973). Results indicated that whereas women whose relationships were caring and intimate had parental representations that were accepting and autonomy-supportive, the women with more superficial relationships had object representations that were nonaccepting and overcontrolling, and the women with enmeshed relationships had representations that were nonaccepting but idealized. Furthermore, the women who were high in autonomy orientation (Deci & Ryan, 1985a) had parental representations that were autonomy-supportive, and those not displaying high autonomy had representations that were overly controlling.

The most general point to be derived from these studies, which span from middle childhood to early adulthood, is that relatedness and autonomy, rather than being opposing or antithetical variables, function in a complementary, synergistic manner with respect to personality integration. Children who are provided with optimal care, characterized by an atmosphere of autonomy support and involvement (dedication of resources), are likely to experience both greater security of attachment and a greater sense of personal autonomy. In the context of autonomy-supportive relationships, one has the circumstances that conduce toward agency and mental health.

We have focused on three contextual dimensions—(a) autonomy support, (b) structure, and (c) involvement—in our research on social-contextual influences on development (e.g., Grolnick & Ryan, 1989). Our dimensional characterization of the social context can be understood as a differentiation of the general concept of "good parenting," at least during childhood and adolescence. However, this model has considerable relevance for the understanding of intimate relationships across the life span (Reis & Shaver, 1988). In particular, intimate relationships in adulthood not only depend on strong ties but also entail an acceptance and encouragement of the true self of one's partner. This affordance of autonomy support breeds a sense of trust and confidence, as well as facilitating self-expression and actualization.

AUTONOMY DISTURBANCES

When the development of self proceeds optimally, in social contexts where children experience ongoing supports for their autonomy, competence, and relatedness, they display increasing amounts of self-determination, appropriate to their developmental stage. Behaviors are undertaken with a sense of choice, for they emanate from the self in a harmonious fashion.

When development does not proceed optimally, however, because the social context does not provide autonomy support, competence, and involvement, the organismic integration process will be impaired, resulting in psychopathology characterized by disturbances of autonomy. This may involve blocking awareness of urges and developing rigid regulatory processes, or, alternatively, displaying inadequate regulatory capacities and being governed by one's urges. Stated differently, when organismic integration is impaired, people become either over- or undercontrolled, neither of which is adaptive, for both lack the experience of autonomy. In the case of overcontrol, self exploration and understanding can be constrained by the continuous regulation of action through introjected values and controls. In the case of undercontrol, internalization is forestalled, preventing the development of a well-anchored value system to organize and guide behavior.

In cases of either over- or undercontrol, the perceived locus of causality for behavior lies outside the self, and there are compromised or distorted volitional processes (Shapiro, 1981) and reduced personal freedom (Fromm, 1941). Such circumstances predominate when caregivers have not provided the interpersonal involvement and consistent responsiveness necessary for forming attachments that support the development of self-regulation in all its forms, including intrinsic motivation, internalization, and emotional integration.

Given the generality of this description, it is perhaps more clear why we stated at the outset of this chapter that, although varied in its form and etiology, psychopathology typically entails *impairments of autonomy* (Angyal, 1965) representing failures in organismic integration and the development of self. From the perspective of self-determination theory, explicating the autonomy disturbances that result from failed integration involves a consideration of the dialectical interplay between the psychological needs for autonomy, competence, and relatedness that subserve organismic integration and the social contexts that either nurture or thwart the individual with respect to these psychological needs.

The workings of this dialectical relationship were discussed in the review of research on intrinsic motivation, internalization, and emotional integration—or, more to the point, on the impairments of those processes. Although much of that research was conducted with nonclinical subject populations, we argue that the processes that hinder intrinsic motivation, internalization, and emotional integration are the same processes that underlie the disturbed autonomy evident in various forms of psychopathology.

Focusing on these processes, we discuss three general types of autonomy disturbances. First, we consider those in which rigidly introjected controls dominate one's psychic reality. Although there are a variety of "internalizing" disorders in which introjects play a critical role, we discuss a select few for illustrative purposes. To do that, we begin with a review of Shapiro's (1965, 1981) conception of rigid character as a dimension in psychopathology and then turn to specific diagnostic categories, including obsessive-compulsive disorders, in which internalized but unintegrated pressures and mandates exert periodic regulatory influence over behavior and thought, and both self-critical depression and eating disorders (i.e., anorexia and bulimia), in which unreasonable and unattainable introjected standards dominate one's experience and lead invariably to harsh self-evaluations and self-disparagement.

Second, to illustrate autonomy disturbances based in failures to internalize significant values and regulatory processes, we focus on selected externalizing disorders. In these cases, the structures and processes to manage one's urges or to regulate intentional actions are often transient, and there is an emphasis within personality on substitute goals intended to support an impoverished core sense of self. To illustrate these types of autonomy disturbance, we discuss problems of impulsivity, and then focus specifically on motivational dynamics in conduct and antisocial personality disorders.

Third, we address autonomy disturbance in the context of personality disorders by considering borderline syndromes. Here, our focus is on the integrative difficulties posed by controlling and inconsistent environments that produce the self-pathology associated with these personality styles.

In discussing each of these types of autonomy disturbance, our approach is twofold: (a) we illustrate how autonomy issues are integral to the disorders, in the sense that phenomenological and regulatory issues related to autonomy and perceived locus of causality are characteristically skewed; (b) we discuss factors relating to the social context of development that contribute to the etiology of these disorders. Although any factor that disrupts the organizational tendency, whether biological, interpersonal, or cultural in nature, can potentiate disturbances of autonomy, the sources of disrupted autonomy can, in many cases, be directly traced to deficiencies in the caregiving environment—that is, to its failure to provide appropriate autonomy support, structure, or involvement.

Internalizing Disorders and Autonomy

The process of introjection is central to a substantial amount of psychopathology. When values, regulations, and standards are taken in but not integrated, they exist as forces dissonant with one's true self and they pressure one to act. Thus, many instances of maladjustment involve introjection, particularly those often described as internalizing disorders.

Rigid Character

One class of psychopathology for which introjection is a defining feature is what Shapiro (1981) labeled *rigid character disorders.* Rigid character involves an ongoing struggle with authority that begins as a conflict between the strict demands of a socializing agent and the person's own organismic urges and desires. Over time, the person moves the conflict "inside" by introjecting the demands in the form of rigid, internally controlling structures that hold the urges in check.

Rigid introjects, although products of socialization, regulate action in part through blocking awareness of the person's organismic needs and urges (Rogers, 1951). This victory of the introjects is a peculiarly distorted one, for the person will align with the internalized authority by relinquishing aspects of his or her own organismic nature. Indeed, the process of introjecting rigid structures often results in the type of self-deception in which the person thinks he or she "wants" what the authority originally prescribed. This is an instance of what Winnicott (1960a) referred to as false self, in which cognitive functions gradually lose their grounding in organismic processes. Resolution of the authority conflict by introjecting the authority is therefore accomplished at the expense of a person's need for autonomy.

Intentionality in rigid character disorders is characterized by its heteronomy and inflexibility. Heteronomy is manifest in the pressured experience, backed by threat of anxiety, that drives much of the person's action, and inflexibility is evident in the absence of openness to novel ways of doing things or consideration of alternative values. Rigid character, with its internally controlling regulation, has a clear parallel with what we have observed in research on ego involvement, where self-esteem is hinged on particular outcomes so the person is pressured to perform (Ryan, 1982).

The internally controlling regulation of rigid character can, in some instances, be highly stable and self-sustaining, in part because it can yield ongoing external approval and derivative internal gratifications. Among these gratifications are what Deci (1980) referred to as *substitute needs.* In a case of rigid character, for example, the person will have developed a strong need to be in control as a substitute for the innate, though unsatisfied need for autonomy. The substitute need for control is reflected in the exercise of *willpower* (Shapiro, 1965), which Deci described as internally controlling regulations countering one's drives and emotions. Similarly, Lewin (1951) suggested that willpower involves concealing the motives that run counter to the controls, and May (1969) asserted that willpower involves rationalization and self-deceit. These various views converge to emphasize that rigid internal controls function to block conflicting aspects of the person from awareness, thus allowing the person to "disown" them. This self-deception is both a result of and a contributor to forestalled organismic integration, and thus represents impaired autonomy even though it involves clear intentionality and mental determination. In this vein, Shapiro (1981) described such displays of willpower as "pseudo-autonomy."

As an example of rigid character, we turn to a discussion of obsessive-compulsive disturbances.

The Obsessive-Compulsive Disorders

Two separable diagnoses carry the rubric of obsession compulsion: (a) Obsessive Compulsive Disorder (OCD) and (b) Obsessive Compulsive Personality (OCP) (APA, 1994). These two distinct entities share some common features in the dynamics of behavior regulation, but they also differ in meaningful ways. OCD is characterized by the experience of intrusive thoughts and demands that typically can be alleviated only by engaging in some ritualistic, rigid behavior. The thoughts are often ego-dystonic: they are unwelcome and anxiety-provoking and thus are experienced as having an origin outside the self. Indeed, these thoughts often are inconsistent with the person's conscious values and ideals. An example is a woman who was diagnosed with OCD and who reported continuing intrusive thoughts concerning hurting her baby whenever she was near certain objects. These intrusive thoughts raised considerable anxiety, precisely because they ran against her seemingly strongly held desire to keep her child safe. To alleviate this anxiety, she was compelled to check continuously for dangerous objects in her vicinity.

Important features of the dissonant thoughts often found in OCD are that they are persistent, unwanted, and difficult to control. From the perspective of the individual, the unwanted thoughts have an impersonal locus of causality—they "befall" him or her. The person then feels "coerced" into ritualistic behaviors; he or she must do them or face dreadful anxiety. The ritualistic actions that alleviate obsessional thoughts therefore have an external perceived locus of causality. As an aspect of this external causality, compulsive behavior patterns typically are performed under strict constraints—there is an inner demand to engage in actions in rigidly prescribed ways. These orders are experienced as heteronomous forces, albeit ones within the person. The costs of failure are guilt, anxiety, and self-disparagement, and, in more extreme cases, a sense of panic and fragmentation of the self. The regulatory process of compulsive acts is thus accompanied by a sense of inner pressure that we would describe as internally controlling.

OCP, in contrast to OCD, is more a life-style than a symptom, and many features of this controlled life-style are ego-syntonic rather than disturbing. For example, a patient with OCP might exhibit a stereotyped and rigid manner of organizing his or her possessions, and become distraught whenever things appear to have been moved or misplaced. Such a person might come to treatment not because he or she views the orderliness as problematic, but because his or her pattern of living is causing interpersonal or vocational difficulties. Nonetheless, the drivenness, compulsiveness, and inflexibility associated with OCP life-style practices bear similarities to the ritualistic behaviors often accompanying OCD.

It is particularly clear with OCP that the pathology of obsessive-compulsive actions is not defined by the behavior itself, for the behavior can be productive and beneficial. Rather, it is the rigid regulatory processes underlying compulsive behavior that are pathological. Still, the more severe the disorder, the more one's behaviors become separated from adaptive consequences, and the resulting ritualistic behaviors, which serve to bind anxiety, themselves become dysfunctional.

Persons with OCP, although not typically afflicted with intrusive or bizarre thoughts, are often inordinately concerned with carrying out the actual or presumed demands of authority. For example, a person with this personality style can be quite industrious and fastidious in complying with the introjected demands, and this may yield high productivity. This industriousness is quite different from the vitality of an autonomous individual, however. Miller (1981) described vitality as the freedom to be spontaneous and to experience one's inner feelings, and Ryan and Frederick (1994) argued that vitality concerns the free energy a person has at his or her disposal. The determination of the internally controlled individual (e.g., someone with OCD or OCP) involves neither freedom nor spontaneity and is often experienced as energy-draining. Resistance to inner dictates, when possible, may feel like a gargantuan effort. For instance, as Swedo and Rapoport (1990) reported, children with OCD often hide their symptoms in public and report feeling that it takes tremendous energy to stave off compulsive enactments. They then feel compelled to release the pressure of resistance at home, leading parents to attribute willfulness and control to a child who feels little of either with respect to these symptoms.

An interesting point about the obsessive-compulsive personality highlights an important aspect of disturbed autonomy. Although obsessive-compulsive individuals often act with haste and determination in carrying out their introjected dictates, they sometimes display confusion and indecision. The problem arises when there is no dictate, no established course to follow. At such times, these persons may be rocked with indecisiveness and ambivalence, and decisions that appear trivial can be the source of painful ruminations. This phenomenon illustrates clearly how dependence on nonintegrated controls leaves one without self-direction, without a sense of what one wants for oneself. Once a person has blocked access to his or her affective underpinnings and organismic needs, there is no basis for making decisions when a control or rule is not evident. The anxiety of indecision highlights how the determination of the obsessive-compulsive is not autonomous.

Although the obsessive-compulsive disorders represent clear instances of psychopathology with disturbed autonomy, it is not clear, nor theoretically necessary, that they are exclusively *outcomes* of parental control. Evidence has, in fact, been quite compelling for a biologic contribution to OCD. To date, research on social factors contributing to obsessive-compulsive behavioral patterns has been sparse, compared to studies attempting to document the biologic and genetic contributors. There is some evidence, however, that OCD can be related to rigidity and controllingness in one's family of origin. For example, Rasmussen and Tsuang (1986) examined the backgrounds of adult OCD patients and found evidence of strict, orderly, and inflexible religious styles. Hoover and Insel (1984) reported family entrapment as common among adolescents with OCD, but also emphasized the reciprocal nature of adult-child interactions that might produce such patterns.

Case literatures concerning OCP have typically pointed toward controlling, often intrusive parenting. However, here too, systematic investigation of the social context of development of OCP individuals is lacking. Thus, whether the controlling regulatory underpinnings of either OCD or OCP can be linked to excessive controllingness or other social-contextual factors in early caregiving awaits further study.

Introjection and Self-Disparagement

At the core of many rigid character pathologies are introjected demands that organize intentional behavior. Although this type of autonomy disturbance involves conflict and tension, individuals with rigid character are often able to behave intentionally and satisfy their introjects. There are other types of introjected demands, however, that individuals cannot easily attain, and they invariably result in experienced failure and self-disparagement. These forms of disturbed autonomy, like those of rigid character, begin with individuals' introjecting the demands of authorities and basing their self-worth on living up to those demands. But here, the pathology and experience are quite different because the individual's predominant experiences are failure and worthlessness. Among the many specific pathologies of introjection are self-critical depression and eating disorders.

Self-Critical Depression

Recent research on depression and its etiology has increasingly pointed toward two distinct pathways to the disorder, one primarily involving loss of relatedness, love, or attachment, and a second primarily involving internalization of excessive demands for achievement and characterized by harsh self-criticism and guilt (Blatt & Homann, 1992; Nietzel & Harris, 1990). Although both of these vulnerabilities involve self-esteem dynamics, and issues of autonomy and relatedness are intertwined in both, the latter, self-critical form of depression is particularly relevant to our discussion of internalizing disturbances of autonomy. We thus focus on the self-critical depression syndrome, which has been labeled variously as a disorder of achievement-autonomy (Neitzel & Harris, 1990), introjection (Blatt, 1974), self-worth (Swallow & Kuiper, 1988), and autonomy (Beck, 1983). By whatever label, this syndrome involves a type of disturbed autonomy in which one experiences dysphoric affect and lethargy resulting from the belief that one is a failure. In this disorder, rigid standards or ideals have been introjected, along with the belief that failure to attain them means one is unlovable and unworthy. Because little that the person does is good enough, self-derogation becomes ubiquitous.

The punitive introjects, with their ties to contingent self-worth, ultimately leave the person ongoingly vulnerable to feelings of both self-scrutiny and worthlessness. Individuals with such introjects are harsher in their self-judgments than in their judgments of others, and these self-judgments often form the precursors to depressive episodes (Beck, 1983).

The phenomenological set underlying self-critical depression is particularly relevant to the understanding of depression as involving disturbed autonomy. With respect to significant self-goals, the individual sees the self as responsible and yet incapable. Thus, the absence of felt competence to attain internalized goals results in a sense of amotivation (Deci & Ryan, 1985b) or personal helplessness (Abramson, Seligman, & Teasdale, 1978). At the same time, many of the specific demands on the self to achieve or succeed have the character of "have to" and "must," revealing their phenomenological character as having an external perceived locus of causality (i.e., as being heteronomous with respect to self). This, of course, is the case with all introjects: they are both internal to the person and external to the self.

Although the etiology and course of depression are complex, involving both biologic and social/environmental factors, the evidence that parental style can contribute to depressive problems is relatively clear. Factors such as loss of parents (and thus of attachment supports), depression in parents (and thus low involvement and/or autonomy support), and parental controllingness have all been implicated in the development of childhood depression (see Miller, Birnbaum, & Durbin, 1990) and are implicated in adult depression as well.

Studies of the parenting environments of self-critical depressives have been increasingly frequent. In one illustrative investigation, McCranie and Bass (1984) found that women high in self-critical depression had parents who maintained strict control, demanded high achievement, and were inconsistent and contingent in their conveyance of love. Similar results with respect to self-critical depression in males and females, were reported by Whiffen and Sassville (1991). The findings from these studies are consistent with our speculations more generally concerning the social context leading to introjection and internally controlling states. In this sense, one can view self-critical depression as a chronic and pervasive state of ego involvement in which one ongoingly fails to live up to the demands and is thus punished.

Anorexia and Bulimia

Bruch (1973), in her classic work on the topic, described eating disorders as "pathologies of autonomy." She argued that these eating pathologies typically involve a struggle for control that takes the form of obsession with eating and body image, dynamically staving off a pervasive sense of ineffectiveness. They thus illustrate how bodily states and desires can be manipulated by introjects to preserve the illusion of self-sufficiency and to feel a sense of control with respect to oneself and others. In restrictive anorexia, the introjects around eating and weight are more stable and effective in keeping one's eating behavior in abeyance; in bulimia, there is a more open conflict between rigid controls and akratic eating. Bulimics engage in binge eating—expressive, uncontrolled consumption—only to be overcome by guilt and self-derogation, which in turn lead to induced vomiting or abuse of diarrhetics.

The psychodynamics highlighted by Bruch were empirically described in a study by Strauss and Ryan (1987). Using Benjamin's (1980) circumplex measure of self-regulation, Strauss and Ryan found greater self-oppression and self-rejection in both anorexic and bulimic subjects than in a matched control group, who displayed more flexible self-management and self-acceptance. Furthermore, Strauss and Ryan documented the particularly heightened impersonal causality orientation (Deci & Ryan, 1985a) of restrictive anorexics, which is indicative of an impoverished sense of personal effectiveness.

Internally controlling forms of regulation are readily apparent in the dynamics of eating disorders. Whether anorexic or bulimic, these patients display inordinate concern with how others view them, and hypertrophied public self-consciousness. As Plant and Ryan (1985) argued, such consciousness potentiates an external perceived locus of causality in which one has to conform to the projected views of others. Although a focus on weight is often paramount, eating-disordered patients are typically self-conscious, demanding, and self-critical with regard to many aspects of appearance and behavior, which is experienced as a straitjacket to the self. And, although restrictive anorexics in particular appear to display a high degree of personal control, the regulatory basis of this control is dictatorial and built on a tenuous foundation of ineffectance.

Whereas the restrictive anorexic can display a high degree of control with respect to eating, bulimic patients often find their control overwhelmed by an impulse to binge eat. Binges typically occur at times of high stress or anxiety, thus showing how their introjected regulatory structures are not sufficiently stable to keep the impulse in check. The binge impulse often represents a reaction to the rise of unacceptable feelings or to being controlled or criticized, and thus is an attempt to escape from the painful sense of self that carries the burdensome, introjected standards (Baumeister, 1991). It is interesting to note that, as the psychic threat gets greater for someone with the bulimic –disorder, the person's regulatory capacity becomes weakened, whereas, in someone with obsessive-compulsive personality, the regulatory capacity often becomes even more rigid and dominant. The lack of stability of the regulatory introjects in the bulimic thus allows for the akratic action, but the self-evaluative introjects invariably result in self-disparagement and feelings of depression for having lost control. It is interesting to note, in this regard, that the long-term course for many restrictive anorexics is a shift to bulimic patterns of coping.

Again, there are multiple contributors to the development of bulimia and related eating disorders, but the role of familial factors in setting up the dynamics of introjection and internal control is quite salient. Bruch (1973, 1979) vividly depicted the role of parents in catalyzing anorexia by depriving their daughter of autonomy and the "right to live her own life" (1979, p. 38). Minuchin, Rosman, and Baker (1978) similarly reported high levels of enmeshment and intrusive control in the families of their eating-disordered patients. Convergent empirical findings are also extant. Strober and Humphrey (1987) reported that, compared to normals, both anorexics and bulimics experience their parents as blaming, rejecting, and critical. Strauss and Ryan (1988) found evidence for less mutuality of autonomy in the object representations of both bulimic and anorexic subjects compared with normals, and lower reported expressiveness within their families.

Each of the disorders we have considered thus far begins with rigid, demanding, critical introjects that are pervasive in one's psychic makeup. These rigid structures take varied forms and are more or less stable and effective in controlling the person's actions. In some cases, most notably the obsessive-compulsive personality and anorexia nervosa, the disordered individuals can feel a strong sense of personal control and self-efficacy—the OCP can keep his or her personal affairs quite orderly, for example, and the anorexic can keep her body image under control. But these, like the other disorders involving salient introjects, constitute disturbed autonomy and can terrorize the person with contingent self-esteem. They thus emphasize the important difference between personal control and autonomy.

We turn now to disorders characterized by the absence rather than the prevalence of introjects. These forms of psychopathology involve a lack of adequate regulatory structures that link one effectively to the socializing context.

Failures of Internalization and the Externalizing Disorders

As we argued earlier, the internalization process is dependent on certain affordances in the caregiving environment—autonomy support, structure, and involvement—which together facilitate both attachment to the caregivers and a readiness to assimilate the values they model. Some caretaking environments, particularly those characterized either by coldness and hostility or by neglect, foster a more impoverished quality of attachments and lessened internalization.

Disorders Related to Impulse Control

The distinction between motivated and amotivated behavior is based on whether the acts are mediated by intentionality. Accordingly, actions resulting from failures of internalization represent an interesting mix of motivation and amotivation. The actions are motivated, for they are both energized by an organismic condition and directed in a way that is implicit in that condition. However, these actions involve *amotivational regulation* in the sense that the person is incapable of modulating and regulating urges in accord with social values, because of a weakness or instability of internalized structures.

Often, the behavior of impulsive persons appears responsive to immediate impulses or stimulation rather than being deliberate or intentional (Wishnie, 1977). There is no sustained desire or decision, and impulsive individuals are not able to tolerate the frustration of delayed gratification. Further, they rarely accept responsibility for their actions, instead attributing them to external influences or overwhelming internal pressures. Externalization of responsibility (as in "He made me do it," or "I couldn't help it") illustrate the elements of external and impersonal perceived loci of causality that the impulsive person experiences regarding behavior. However, the external causality for the impulsive is quite different from that of the person with rigid character. In the latter case, the locus of causality for actions is the person's introjects; with the impulsive individual, the locus of causality is either his or her inner urges or the external temptations hooking them.

For a person with an impulsive disorder, nonregulated acts are characteristic aspects of ongoing experience. Most people display some impulsive actions when their regulatory capacities break down in times of undue stress, but this is different from the impulsive disorders because the impulsivity is not an ongoing aspect of their character.

An interesting example of a disorder involving discrete episodes of impulsivity is the *intermittent explosive disorder.* This pathology entails occasional acute loss of control of aggressive impulses. The strength of these responses, which involve assault to others or to property, is extreme and out of proportion to the apparent stimulus. People with this disorder typically report not knowing what came over them at the time of an incident, and they may even evidence amnesia with respect to it. In this disorder, one sees clearly the sense of amotivation with respect to regulating explosive actions, and the experience of impersonal causality in the reports that "something just came over me." With the intermittent explosive disorder, the person is typically not impulsive or aggressive between episodes, but the condition differs from the normal person's occasional loss of temper because of its intensity and complete lack of control. It also differs from the antisocial personality disorder because the latter involves ongoing impulsivity and aggressiveness between what may be more frequent but less intense outbursts than those of the intermittent explosive disorder.

Conduct Disorders and Antisocial Personality

The diagnosis of *antisocial personality disorder* (APD) applies to persons who lie, steal, manifest an impoverished sense of responsibility, are aggressive and manipulative toward others, and show evidence that these patterns are continuations of behavior disorders earlier in life. Children diagnosed with *conduct disorders,* the typical antecedent of APD, display control problems, lability, a lack of ability to give and receive affection, and delayed or impaired development of conscience. Often, they show an unusual interest in violence and sensational phenomena such as fire or gore (Magid & McKelvey, 1987). Furthermore, self-aggrandizement and egocentrism often characterize their behavior, and their lying about accomplishments highlights their excessive need to be shored up or esteemed by other people in an immediate way.

Etiologic theories of APD have been varied and include both biologic or genetic factors (such as poor autonomic reactivity) and familial or cultural inputs (see Richters & Cicchetti, 1993). Our contention is that, to the extent that APD is a psychopathology of *failed internalization,* it can be robustly linked to deficits during one's early development in the social contextual factors that we have argued are essential for internalization to occur.

Individuals with APD and its antecedents indeed display a lack of conscience. There is no deep concern with what is good or right, no stable sense of "I should." Societal norms and moral principles have not been internalized, whether in the form of introjected prescriptions or integrated values.

In an internalization conceptualization, we would thus look toward the family environment for the sources of internalized values of a prosocial nature that seem to be lacking in APD. Although there has been little research or theory directly connecting issues of autonomy support, involvement, or structure to the failure of internalization that characterizes APD, considerable evidence points to their importance. The general literature on prosocial value development locates the sources of such positive values in socialization patterns within the family (Kilby, 1993). Most of the theorists in this area have taken as their point of departure the idea that value transmission is accomplished through a process of *identification,* in which children emulate or model the values and attitudes of their caretakers. Such theoretical models, of course, implicitly assume that prosocial values must be "put in" to the psyche rather than nurtured. One might alternatively assume that human nature is already prosocial and simply requires conditions of nurturance to express that tendency. In any case, the empirical evidence supports either view insofar as prosocial values are most likely to be acquired (or expressed) when caregiving is characterized by warmth (Maccoby, 1980), low power-assertive discipline (Hoffman, 1960), and autonomy support (Ryan, 1993; Ryan et al., 1992).

The experience of growing up in a nurturant, caring, responsive familial environment undoubtedly facilitates prosocial values. As Kohn (1990) argued, a person who grows up in such an environment has many needs met and is freed from being self-preoccupied, so perhaps he or she is more able to turn toward homonomous strivings and to focus on others. Furthermore, the person will have been exposed to models of caring and concern about others, from figures whom he or she is likely to emulate. Support for this comes from many quarters. For example, Ryan and Connell (1989) reported that children who experience a high quality of relatedness to parents were more autonomously motivated in the prosocial domain. Similarly, Waters, Wippman, and Sroufe (1979) demonstrated a connection between security of attachment as measured with the Strange Situation paradigm and prosocial orientations.

Conversely, a variety of clinical and empirical perspectives have suggested that antisocial personality, oriented toward self-serving, manipulative, and hedonically gratifying acts, has its roots, in part, in a cold, inconsistent, and controlling family environment (e.g., Buss, 1966; Greenberg, Speltz, & DeKlyen, 1993; McCord & McCord, 1964). A plethora of studies has also shown that the common backdrop to APD and conduct disorders of childhood includes such factors as maternal depression, loss, high family conflict, other parental pathology, and impoverished conditions of life that fragment the family (Loeber & Stouthammer-Loeber, 1986). All of these factors potentiate a situation ultimately lacking in the basic nutriments on which internalization depends—autonomy support, adequate structure and guidance, and concerted involvement.

One limitation of these models of value acquisition, and their implications with regard to the development of externalizing disorders such as APD, is that they do not focus on how or why children might develop values of a nonprosocial or nonmoral nature, except as a converse or absence of moral internalization. For example, there are probably very few parents who strive to teach their children to be manipulative, materialistic, or machiavellian, but there are many children who develop such an orientation. Absence of identification does not explain why one proactively seeks to act in these ways. Thus, a full model of psychopathy requires explaining both why internalization fails, and why hedonic, aggressive, self-gratifying values predominate instead.

In recent theorizing (Kasser & Ryan, in press; Ryan, Sheldon, Kasser, & Deci, in press), we have argued that, to the extent that individuals lack the necessary nutriments of autonomy support and involvement (and therefore are deficient in the development of self), they often turn toward extrinsic, narcissistically oriented values to gain and sustain some minimal sense of power, importance, and worth. Thus, people place more value on issues of material wealth and other exteriorized qualities, to the extent that they have not consolidated a secure sense of an inner self. Put differently, to the extent that one is not anchored in a true self, behavior becomes increasingly organized by narcissistically oriented, "false self" values. In line with this theorizing, Kasser and Ryan (1993, in press) found, in late adolescent samples, that excessive emphasis on materialistic values was associated with greater maladjustment, including narcissism and conduct disorders.

Kasser, Ryan, Zax, and Sameroff (in press) examined the developmental antecedents of this greater emphasis on materialism relative to prosocial values and found that adolescents who were more materialistic came from homes where both they and their mothers reported less autonomy support, warmth, and security. They also found that more impoverished, high-crime neighborhoods, in confluence with these more controlling and hostile parenting styles, were likely to promote children's development of attachment to these extrinsic values. Finally, analysis of clinical interviews with subjects in an at-risk population (defined in terms of maternal psychopathology and low socioeconomic status) revealed that those with greater centrality of materialistic values were more likely to be clinically diagnosed as conduct-disordered. In a conceptual replication with a "not at risk" college population, subjects who perceived their parents to be controlling (versus autonomy-supportive) and cold (versus warm) were found to evidence a relatively higher centrality of materialism in their value orientation.

One important aspect of this work is its clarification that environments nonsupportive of development of the true self promote an emphasis on alienated or substitute rather than authentic needs and on the visible trappings of worth. This emphasis may be particularly salient within the so-called antisocial personality. This research also highlights the continuity of motivational dynamics between nonclinical and clinical populations.

From the perspective of self-determination theory, conduct disorders, and, more seriously, asocial, self-focused goal orientations, stem largely from inadequate attachments and failed internalization, which result from an externally controlling and affection-impoverished social contexts. To the extent that social values (and the economic conditions that structure them) disable, distract, or fragment the caretaking environment, children will be more oriented to narcissistic goals in order to gain a temporary sense of worth and importance. Not only is this model applicable to conduct-disordered children, but, increasingly, it represents American culture more generally. Put succinctly, the more we create conditions that disrupt the quality and stability of familial relationships, the more narcissistically oriented (Lasch, 1978) and antisocial our culture as a whole may become.

Borderline Disorders: Lack of a Stable Self

Personality disorders have become a predominant concern in clinical settings because of their increasing incidence and, thus, the personal resources demanded in their treatment. Borderline disorders highlight many issues in character pathology generally, and they represent a prototypic example of structural damage to the self that has been associated with failures in autonomy support and involvement of early caregivers.

The core of borderline disorders is a lack of a cohesive and stable sense of self. Among the central features that are associated with this lack of a consistent and organized self are emotional, interpersonal, and self-esteem lability. Borderline individuals show the externalizing attributes of impulsivity, along with some of the features of internalizing disorders such as susceptibility to depression, anxiety, and fragmentation in the face of self-esteem-related losses. A cardinal dynamic of borderline lability concerns anger, both self- and other-directed, which can result in destructive actions and magnify relationship instability and internal feelings of being overwhelmed and disintegrated. More generally, patients with borderline disorders have difficulty differentiating internal needs from external reality, and they are tremendously dependent on concrete supplies from others to maintain a sense of self. They lack the internal controls to modulate anxiety, which can escalate to panic proportions, particularly when no one is available to contain and comfort them.

Another central feature of borderline disorder is the lack of a stable sense of identity and commitment, either to a line of action such as a career choice or to a relationship (Meissner, 1988). Patients with this disorder may latch on to something or someone in an effort to derive a temporary feeling of cohesion, but these choices are often inappropriate or destructive. Commitments are difficult because the borderline individual lacks the stable cohesive self that might form the basis for sharing in committed relationships or endeavors.

Phenomenologically, patients with borderline disorders report being both controlled and helpless with respect to their behavior. They often feel like a victim of circumstances without a sense of personal initiative or responsibility for the direction of their own fate. One patient, for example, reported that, prior to self-mutilation, he entered into a "lost" state where the overwhelming impulse to cut "came upon" him (conveying an impersonal perceived locus of causality); at the same time, he felt he could only obtain relief and release from dysphoric self-hateful feelings by engaging in such acts (suggesting external causality). In no sense did he feel autonomous and volitional, rather than driven, desperate, and helpless, in these acts.

Connected with the lack of feeling of autonomy and identity, patients with borderline disorder may feel empty and isolated (Westen, 1991). There is a diminution of the true self whereby the individual loses connection to his or her interests and feelings. Patients with this disorder often report feelings of boredom and may engage in impulsive acts, such as substance abuse, careless spending, and binge eating, to counteract such feelings.

There is some evidence of genetic contributions to borderline disorder, in that there is a higher prevalence of borderline and other affective disorders in the relatives of individuals diagnosed with the disorder (Loranger, Oldham, & Tulis, 1982), but much of the work focuses on the early environment of the child. The formation of a stable and cohesive sense of self depends on the integration of positive identifications; thus, it is not surprising that theories and research point to the importance of early family relations. Two sets of characteristics have emerged from these literatures: (a) severely impoverished caregiving during the early years, and (b) the parents' (particularly the mothers') difficulty allowing the child to move toward self-sufficiency and autonomy during the separation-individuation phase. In both cases, the parents are thought to fail to bolster the child's autonomous self, which is needed for self functions such as identity and affect modulation.

Early caregivers of individuals with borderline disorder have been described as unavailable, inconsistent, and neglectful (Gunderson, 1984), with some reports of sexual, emotional, and physical abuse (Herman, Perry, & van der Kolk, 1989; Westen, Lodolph, Misle, Ruffins, & Block, 1990). In one study, 80% of borderline patients were reported to have been physically or sexually abused or to have witnessed serious domestic violence (Herman et al., 1989). Explicating more specifically the affect and behavior regulation difficulties of these patients, Linehan (1987) suggested that patients with borderline disorder come from families that invalidate the affective experience of their children, expecting them to be constantly cheerful. There is no tolerance for fears or anxieties in the children, and they do not experience soothing or comforting from the parent. Without such care, these children do not internalize the capacity to soothe themselves; as a result, they have difficulty regulating emotions and tolerating feelings of distress and grief that could help to guide their actions.

According to object relations theorists (Kernberg, 1967; Masterson, 1981), the disorder has its roots in the mother-child relationship, particularly during the phase of separation-individuation, when the child is striving to experience himself or herself as separate from the mother. Part of the phase involves a pushing away from the mother. In families of borderline individuals, the mother is not able to tolerate movement toward self-sufficiency because it brings up her own fears of abandonment. Consequently, the mother threatens to withdraw nurturance from the child if he or she moves to act as a separate autonomous individual. The child must therefore decide between autonomy and relatedness to the mother and, because of his or her helpless position in relation to the mother, the child gives up autonomy and the trajectory of true self. The connection to the mother, however, is not experienced as true relatedness because it is conflicted and fraught with hostility. Given this level of conflict, there is no "good" object that can be integrated into the child's representational world to form the basis for a sense of self.

The problems of the borderline patient thus illustrate how a lack of empathy, of consistent involvement, and of autonomy support undermines intrinsic interests and tendencies, as well as self-regulatory functions—all aspects of the autonomous self.

THE STUDY OF NORMAL AND ABNORMAL POPULATIONS

Unlike the research of most of the authors in this volume, ours has focused primarily, though not exclusively, on normal populations across the life span from infancy to old age. Although one of our aims in that work has been to explicate the social-contextual conditions that promote optimal development of self, we have focused considerable attention on specifying the conditions that undermine optimal development—those that are controlling, rejecting, cold, and chaotic. In studying normal populations, we have observed the undermining of intrinsic motivation, the introjection of rigid demands and punitive contingencies, and the failures of internalization, resulting in poor modulation of urges and emotions and inadequate self-regulation.

It is our contention that many of the processes integral to nonoptimal functioning in normal populations are also central to various psychopathologies. We do not discount the role of biologic influences but rather consider them interactive with interpersonal, familial influences. Thus, someone with biologic factors contributing toward psychopathology will influence the caretaking environment, which, in turn, will influence his or her further development. This interaction will be negatively synergistic to the extent that caretakers respond by restricting their provision of the critical nutriments for optimal development—autonomy support, structure, and involvement.

In the studies we have done with abnormal populations, we have found support for our view that disturbed autonomy exists within various pathologies. Further, the work of numerous investigators has confirmed that the caregiving environments of individuals with various disorders were lacking in critical nutriments. We thus see the study of normal and abnormal populations as wholly complementary for explicating the psychological factors involved in psychopathology and for detailing the social-contextual factors that contribute to diminished development and the onset of psychopathology.

CONCLUSION

The developmental antecedents of disturbed autonomy are surely multiple, with genetic, biologic, interpersonal, and sociocultural factors all being relevant. Genetic and biologic factors enter transactionally into interpersonal relationships, facilitating or forestalling the quality of these social contextual inputs; and cultural factors both shape and are emergent from patterns of social and familial functioning. Our focus has been on the social and familial factors, although our aim has not been to provide a complete account of the development of autonomy disturbances. Rather, we have attempted to describe the phenomenological significance of autonomy in normal and pathological development and to show empirically and theoretically how interpersonal factors contribute to the etiology of pathologically disturbed autonomy.

Within this approach, we have viewed the development of autonomy as proceeding most effectively in familial and social contexts that provide autonomy support, optimal structure, and interpersonal involvement. In the absence of these necessary social nutriments—in contexts that thwart satisfaction of the needs for autonomy, competence, and relatedness—disturbed self-development is expected, resulting in the emergence of psychopathology. Psychopathology is thus the result of disorganizing influences, that is, contexts that thwart or forestall personality integration.

We have reviewed a large number of studies indicating that the development of autonomy—the maintenance of intrinsic motivation, the internalization of values and regulatory processes, and the integration of emotions—is facilitated by the contextual nutriments of caregiver attention and interest, and of encouragement for exploration and self-initiation. Contexts where interpersonal involvement and autonomy support are absent have been found reliably to diminish autonomous regulation and impair the development of self. The contextual elements that have consistently been found, in our studies, to impair autonomy and development—controllingness and lack of interpersonal involvement—have also been emphasized in the clinical literature on the antecedents of disorders that involve either heteronomous introjects or failures of internalization. Thus, there appear to be clear parallels between the results of the empirical explorations of autonomy dynamics in normative development and the conclusions from clinical studies of psychopathology.

DIRECTIONS FOR FUTURE RESEARCH

Although the concept of autonomy—or closely related concepts such as integration, authenticity, and true self—appears in many theoretical writings related to the development of psychopathology, it has received relatively little empirical attention from investigators outside our group (Ryan, in press). And, as noted, our work has been skewed in the direction of normal rather than pathological development. The exciting thing about the convergence between our research results and the theorizing of many writers focused more on clinical populations is that it sets the stage for empirical investigations in which autonomy concepts—for example, perceived autonomy, autonomy orientation, and relative autonomy—can be employed to further test some of the general hypotheses contained in clinically oriented theories.

Needed research could begin by comparing diagnostic groups to matched control groups, much like Strauss and Ryan (1988) and Grolnick and Ryan (1990) have done with eating-disordered patients and learning-disabled students, respectively. Such strategies help establish that autonomy disturbances do exist within various clinical problems. Such research would specify the nature of the disturbed autonomy. For example, in disorders involving rigid introjects, it would be important to clarify the strength and centrality of introjects, whether the disordered individuals generally live up to or fall short of the introjected demands, and the nature of the intrapsychic punishment that follows inadequate performance. Additionally, in disorders involving inadequate internalization, research should clarify the nature of the impulses that prevail, the conditions within which regulation is more (versus less) effective, and so on.

More detailed work on the antecedents of specific autonomy disturbances within the various disorders will also be important. It is clear, for example, that a lack of autonomy support and of genuine relatedness by caregivers is antecedent to the development of a wide range of pathologies. Why an individual develops anorexia nervosa rather than pervasive self-punitive depression in familial contexts that are demanding and critical is an example of the kinds of questions that are important to tackle empirically. That autonomy disturbances are involved in a wide range of disorders and that familial and other interpersonal contexts play a role in their development seems certain, but the more specific whats, hows, and whys of this general conclusion remain to be clarified. The challenge this provides is at once formidable and intrinsically interesting.

More generally, we have pointed in this chapter to the connections between the development and integration of personality and the phenomenological experience of autonomy in the regulation of behavior. In our view, the issue of autonomy is a critical one for organizational perspectives on developmental psychopathology, because it supplies a deeper meaning to the concepts of organization and integration than mere synchrony or coordination between systems. That is, the experience of autonomy in action is a defining feature of organization, whereas disturbances of autonomy correspond to fragmentation and disorganization in psychological development. We have further pointed to environmental conditions that either thwart or nurture needs for self-determination, competence, and relatedness as central factors in development away from or toward greater organization and integrity, respectively. The differentiated study of how these psychological needs, in interaction with the biologic and social conditions of development, result in relative integration and, thus, experiences of integrity in action, supplies a broad and important agenda for future clinical research.

REFERENCES

Abramson, L. Y., Seligman, M. E. P., & Teasdale, J. D. (1978). Learned helplessness in humans: Critique and reformulation. *Journal of Abnormal Psychology, 87,* 49–74.

Achenbach, T., & Edelbrock, C. (1987). *Manual for the Youth Self Report.* Unpublished manuscript, University of Vermont.

Ainsworth, M. D. S. (1989). Attachments beyond infancy. *American Psychologist, 44,* 709–716.

Ainsworth, M. D. S., Blehar, M. C., Waters, E., & Wall, S. (1978). *Patterns of attachment.* Hillsdale, NJ: Erlbaum.

Amabile, T. M. (1983). *The social psychology of creativity.* New York: Springer-Verlag.

American Psychiatric Association. (1994). *Diagnostic and statistical manual of mental disorders* (4th ed.). Washington, DC: Author.

Angyal, A. (1965). *Neurosis and treatment: A holistic theory.* New York: Wiley.

Arend, R., Gove, F., & Sroufe, L. A. (1979). Continuity of adaptation from infancy to kindergarten: A predictive study of ego-resiliency and curiosity in preschoolers. *Child Development, 50,* 950–959.

Avery, R. R., & Ryan, R. M. (1988). Object relations and ego development: Comparison and correlates in middle childhood. *Journal of Personality, 56,* 547–569.

Bakan, D. (1966). *The duality of human existence.* Boston: Beacon Press.

Baldwin, A. L. (1949). The effect of home environment on nursery school behavior. *Child Development, 20,* 49–62.

Baldwin, A. L. (1955). *Behavior and development in childhood.* New York: Dreyden.

Bandura, A. (1977). Self-efficacy: Toward a unifying theory of behavioral change. *Psychological Review, 84,* 191–215.

Bandura, A. (1989). Human agency in social cognitive theory. *American Psychologist, 44,* 1175–1184.

Baumeister, R. (1991). *Escaping the self.* New York: Basic Books.

Baumrind, D. (1967). Child care practices anteceding three patterns of preschool behavior. *Genetic Psychology Monographs, 75,* 43–88.

Baumrind, D. (1971). Current patterns of parental authority. *Developmental Psychology Monographs, 4,* 1–102.

Baumrind, D. (1977). *Socialization determinants of personal agency.* Paper presented at the biennial meeting of the Society for Research in Child Development, New Orleans.

Beck, A. T. (1983). Cognitive treatment of depression: New perspectives. In P. J. Clayton & J. E. Barrett (Eds.), *Treatment of depression: Old controversies and new approaches* (pp. 265–290). New York: Raven Press.

Becker, W. C. (1964). Consequences of different kinds of parental discipline. In M. L. Hoffman & L. W. Hoffman (Eds.), *Review of child development research* (Vol. 1, pp. 169–208). New York: Russell Sage Foundation.

Behrends, R. S., & Blatt, J. S. (1985). Internalization and psychological development through the life cycle. *Psychoanalytic Study of the Child, 40,* 11–39.

Benjamin, L. (1980). *Validation of structural analysis of social behavior.* Unpublished manuscript.

Benware, C., & Deci, E. L. (1984). Quality of learning with an active versus passive motivational set. *American Educational Research Journal, 21,* 755–765.

Blais, M. R., Sabourin S., Boucher, C., & Vallerand, R. J. (1990). Toward a motivational model of couple happiness. *Journal of Personality and Social Psychology, 59,* 1021–1031.

Blasi, A. (1976). Concept of development in personality theory. In J. Loevinger, *Ego development* (pp. 29–53). San Francisco: Jossey-Bass.

Blatt, S. J. (1974). Levels of object representation in anaclitic and introjective depression. *Psychoanalytic Study of the Child, 29,* 107–157.

Blatt, S. J., Chevron, E. S., Quinlan, D. M., & Wein, S. (1981). *The assessment of qualitative and structural dimensions of object representation.* Unpublished manuscript, Yale University.

Blatt, S. J., & Homann, E. (1992). Parent-child interaction in the etiology of dependent and self-critical depression. *Clinical Psychology Review, 12,* 47–91.

Block, J. H., & Block, J. (1980). The role of ego-control and ego-resiliency in the organization of behavior. In W. A. Collins (Ed.), *Minnesota Symposium on Child Psychology: Vol. 13. Development of cognitive affect and social relations* (pp. 39–101). Hillsdale, NJ: Erlbaum.

Blos, P. (1962). *On adolescence: A psychoanalytic interpretation.* Glencoe, IL: Free Press.

Bowlby, J. (1969). *Attachment.* New York: Basic Books.

Bowlby, J. (1988). Developmental psychiatry comes of age. *The American Journal of Psychiatry, 145,* 1–10.

Brazelton, T. (1973). *Neonatal Behavioral Assessment Scale.* Philadelphia: Lippincott.

Brazelton, T. B., Koslowski, B., & Main, M. (1974). The origins of mother-infant interaction. In M. Lewis & L. A. Rosenblum (Eds.), *The effect of the infant on its caregiver.* (pp. 49–76). New York: Wiley.

Bretherton, I. (1987). New perspectives on attachment relations: Security, communication and internal working models. In J. Osofsky (Ed.), *Handbook of infant development* (pp. 1061–1100). New York: Wiley.

Bretherton, I. (1991). Pouring new wine into old bottles: The social self as internal working model. In M. R. Gunnar & L. A. Sroufe (Eds.), *Minnesota Symposia on Child Development: Vol. 23. Self processes and development* (pp. 1–41). Hillsdale, NJ: Erlbaum.

Bridges, L. J., & Grolnick, W. S. (1995). The development of emotional self-regulation in infancy and early childhood. In N. Eisenberg (Ed.), *Review of personality and social psychology: Vol. 15. Social development* (pp. 185–211). New York: Russell-Sage Foundation.

Brody, D. S. (1956). *Patterns of mothering.* New York: International Universities Press.

Brody, D. S., & Axelrad, S. (1978). *Mothers, fathers and children.* New York: International Universities Press.

Broughton, J. M. (1987). *Critical theories of psychological development.* New York: Plenum.

Bruch, H. (1973). *Eating disorders.* New York: Basic Books.

Bruch, H. (1979). *The golden cage: The enigma of anorexia nervosa.* New York: Vintage Books.

Bruner, J. S. (1962). *On knowing: Essays for the left hand.* Cambridge, MA: Harvard University Press.

Buss, A. H. (1966). *Psychopathology.* New York: Wiley.

Cameron, N., & Rychlak, J. F. (1985). *Personality, development, and psychopathology: A dynamic approach.* Boston: Houghton Mifflin.

Carver, C. S., & Scheier, M. F. (1981). *Attention and self-regulation: A control theory approach to human behavior.* New York: Springer-Verlag.

Cicchetti, D. (1991). Fractures in the crystal: Developmental psychopathology and the emergence of self. *Developmental Review, 11,* 271–287.

Cicchetti, D., Beeghly, M., Carlson, V., & Toth, S. (1990). The emergence of self in atypical populations. In D. Cicchetti & M. Beeghly (Eds.), *The self in transition: Infancy to childhood* (pp. 309–344). Chicago: University of Chicago Press.

Cicchetti, D., Ganiban, J., & Barnett, D. (1991). Contributions from the study of high-risk populations to understanding the development of emotion regulation. In J. Garber & K. A. Dodge (Eds.), *The development of emotion regulation and dysregulation* (pp. 15–48). New York: Cambridge University Press.

Connell, J. P. (1985). A new multidimensional measure of children's perceptions of control. *Child Development, 56,* 1018–1041.

Connell, J. P., & Wellborn, J. G. (1990). Competence, autonomy and relatedness: A motivational analysis of self-system processes. In M. R. Gunnar & L. A. Sroufe (Eds.), *The Minnesota Symposium on Child Psychology: Vol. 22. Self-processes in development* (pp. 43–77). Hillsdale, NJ: Erlbaum.

Crittenden, P. (1988). Relationships at risk. In J. Belsky & T. Nezworski (Eds.), *Clinical implications of attachment theory* (pp. 136–174). Hillsdale, NJ: Erlbaum.

Crockenberg, S., & Litman, C. (1990). Autonomy as competence in 2-year-olds: Maternal correlates of child defiance, compliance, and self-assertion. *Developmental Psychology, 26,* 961–971.

Csikszentmihalyi, M. (1975). *Beyond boredom and anxiety.* San Francisco: Jossey-Bass.

Danner, F. W., & Lonky, E. (1981). A cognitive-developmental approach to the effects of rewards on intrinsic motivation. *Child Development, 52,* 1043–1052.

deCharms, R. (1968). *Personal causation: The internal affective determinants of behavior.* New York: Academic Press.

deCharms, R. (1981). Personal causation and locus of control: Two different traditions and two uncorrelated measures. In H. M. Lefcourt (Ed.), *Research with the locus of control construct: Vol. I. Assessment methods.* New York: Academic Press.

Deci, E. L. (1971). Effects of externally mediated rewards on intrinsic motivation. *Journal of Personality and Social Psychology, 18,* 105–115.

Deci, E. L. (1972). Intrinsic motivation, extrinsic reinforcement, and inequity. *Journal of Personality and Social Psychology, 22,* 113–120.

Deci, E. L. (1975). *Intrinsic motivation.* New York: Plenum.

Deci, E. L. (1980). *The psychology of self-determination.* Lexington, MA: Lexington Books.

Deci, E. L., & Cascio, W. F. (1972, April). *Changes in intrinsic motivation as a function of negative feedback and threats.* Paper presented at the meeting of the Eastern Psychological Association, Boston.

Deci, E. L., Cascio, W. F., & Krusell, J. (1973, May). *Sex differences, verbal reinforcement, and intrinsic motivation.* Paper presented at the meeting of the Eastern Psychological Association, Washington, DC.

Deci, E. L., Driver, R. E., Hotchkiss, L., Robbins, R. J., & Wilson, I. M. (1993). The relation of mothers' controlling vocalizations to children's intrinsic motivation. *Journal of Experimental Child Psychology, 55,* 151–162.

Deci, E. L., Eghrari, H., Patrick, B. C., & Leone, D. R. (1994). Facilitating internalization: The self-determination theory perspective. *Journal of Personality., 62,* 119–142.

Deci, E. L., & Ryan, R. M. (1980). The empirical exploration of intrinsic motivational processes. In L. Berkowitz (Ed.), *Advances in experimental social psychology* (Vol. 13, pp. 39–80). New York: Academic Press.

Deci, E. L., & Ryan, R. M. (1985a). The general causality orientations scale: Self-determination in personality. *Journal of Research in Personality, 19,* 109–134.

Deci, E. L., & Ryan, R. M. (1985b). *Intrinsic motivation and self-determination in human behavior.* New York: Plenum.

Deci, E. L., & Ryan, R. M. (1987). The support of autonomy and the control of behavior. *Journal of Personality and Social Psychology, 53,* 1024–1037.

Deci, E. L., & Ryan, R. M. (1991). A motivational approach to self: Integration in personality. In R. Dienstbier (Ed.), *Nebraska Symposium on Motivation: Vol. 38. Perspectives on motivation* (pp. 237–288). Lincoln: University of Nebraska Press.

Deci, E. L., Schwartz, A. J., Sheinman, L., & Ryan, R. M. (1981). An instrument to assess adults' orientations toward control versus autonomy with children: Reflections on intrinsic motivation and perceived competence. *Journal of Educational Psychology, 73,* 642–650.

Dewey, J. (1934). *A common faith.* New Haven, CT: Yale University Press.

Dix, T. (1991). The affective organization of parenting: Adaptive and maladaptive processes. *Psychological Bulletin, 110,* 3–25.

Dodge, K. A. (1991). Emotion and social information processing. In J. Garber & K. A. Dodge (Eds.), *The development of emotion regulation and dysregulation* (pp. 159–181). New York: Cambridge University Press.

Dresner, R., & Grolnick, W. S. (1992). *Constructions of early parenting, intimacy, and autonomy in young women.* Unpublished manuscript, Clark University.

Duval, S., & Wicklund, R. A. (1972). *A theory of objective self-awareness.* New York: Academic Press.

Dworkin, G. (1988). *The theory and practice of autonomy.* New York: Cambridge University Press.

Easterbrook, J. A. (1978). *The determinants of free will.* New York: Academic Press.

Elkind, D. (1967). Egocentrism in adolescence. *Child Development, 38,* 1025–1034.

Elkind, D. (1971). Cognitive growth cycles in mental development. In J. K. Cole (Ed.), *Nebraska Symposium on Motivation* (Vol. 19, pp. 1–31). Lincoln: University of Nebraska Press.

Elmen, J., Mounts, N., & Steinberg, L. (1989). Authoritative parenting, psychosocial maturity and academic success among adolescents. *Child Development, 60,* 1424–1436.

Emde, R. (1983). The prerepresentational self and its affective core. *Psychoanalytic Study of the Child, 38,* 165–192.

Erikson, E. H. (1950). *Childhood and society.* New York: Norton.

Field, T. (1987). Interaction and attachment in normal and atypical infants. *Journal of Consulting and Clinical Psychology, 55,* 853–859.

Field, T., Healy, B., Goldstein, S., & Guthertz, M. (1990). Behavior-state matching and synchrony in mother-infant interactions of nondepressed versus depressed dyads. *Developmental Psychology, 26,* 7–14.

Flavell, J. (1963). *The developmental psychology of Jean Piaget.* New York: Van Nostrand.

Flavell, J. (1977). *Cognitive development.* Englewood Cliffs, NJ: Prentice-Hall.

Flink, C., Boggiano, A. K., & Barrett, M. (1990). Controlling teaching strategies: Undermining children's self-determination and performance. *Journal of Personality and Social Psychology, 59,* 916–924.

Frank, J. D. (1961). *Persuasion and healing: A comparative study of psychotherapy.* Baltimore: Johns Hopkins Press.

Freud, A. (1958). Adolescence. In R. S. Eissler, A. Freud, H. Hartmann, & M. Kris (Eds.), *Psychoanalytic study of the child* (Vol. 13, pp. 255–278). New York: International Universities Press.

Freud, S. (1959). Character and anal eroticism. In *Collected papers* (Vol. 2, pp. 45–50). New York: Basic Books. (Original work published 1908)

Freud, S. (1959). The predisposition to obsessional neurosis. In *Collected papers* (Vol. 2, pp. 122–131). New York: Basic Books. (Original work published 1913)

Freud, S. (1962). *The ego and the id.* New York: Norton. (Original work published 1923)

Fromm, E. (1941). *Escape from freedom.* New York: Holt, Rinehart & Winston.

Garbarino, J. (1975). The impact of anticipated reward upon cross-aged tutoring. *Journal of Personality and Social Psychology, 32,* 421–428.

Garber, J., Broafladt, N., & Zeman, J. (1991). The regulation of sad affect: An information processing perspective. In J. Garber & K. A. Dodge (Eds.), *The development of emotion regulation and dysregulation* (pp. 208–242). New York: Cambridge University Press.

Garber, J., & Dodge, K. A. (Eds.). (1991). *The development of emotion regulation and dysregulation.* New York: Cambridge University Press.

Gianino, A., & Tronick, E. Z. (1988). The mutual regulation model: The infant's self and interactive regulation and coping and defensive capacities. In T. M. Fields, P. M. McCabe, & N. Schneiderman (Eds.), *Stress and coping across development* (pp. 47–68). Hillsdale, NJ: Erlbaum.

Gilligan, C. (1982). *In a different voice.* Cambridge, MA: Harvard University Press.

Goldsmith, H. H., Buss, A. H., Plomin, R., Rothbart, M. K., Thomas, A., Chess, S., Hirde, R. A., & McCall, R. B. (1987). Roundtable: What is temperament? Four approaches. *Child Development, 58,* 505–529.

Goldstein, K. (1939). *The organism.* New York: American Book.

Greenberg, M. T., Kusche, C. A., & Speltz, M. (1991). Emotional regulation, self-control, and psychopathology: The role of relationships in early childhood. In D. Cicchetti & S. L. Toth (Eds.), *Internalizing and externalizing expressions of dysfunction* (pp. 21–56). Hillsdale, NJ: Erlbaum.

Greenberg, M. T., Speltz, M. L., & DeKlyen, M. (1993). The role of attachment in the early development of disruptive behavior problems. *Development and Psychopathology, 5,* 191–213.

Greenspan, S. I. (1979). *Intelligence and adaptation.* New York: International Universities Press.

Greenspan, S. I. (1981). *Psychopathology and adaptation in infancy and early childhood: Principles of clinical diagnosis and early intervention.* New York: International Universities Press.

Grolnick, W. S., & Bridges, L. (1992, May). *Emotional self-regulatory strategies, emotionality, and parent-infant interaction in the second year of life.* Paper presented at the International Conference on Infant Studies, Miami, FL.

Grolnick, W. S., Bridges, L. J., & Connell, J. P. (1993). *Emotional self-regulation in two-year-olds: Strategies and emotionality in four contexts.* Unpublished manuscript, Clark University.

Grolnick, W. S., Bridges, L., & Frodi, A. (1984). Maternal control style and the mastery motivation of one-year-olds. *Infant Mental Health Journal, 5,* 72–82.

Grolnick, W. S., & Ryan, R. M. (1987). Autonomy in children's learning: An experimental and individual difference investigation. *Journal of Personality and Social Psychology, 52,* 890–898.

Grolnick, W. S., & Ryan, R. M. (1989). Parent styles associated with children's self-regulation and competence in school. *Journal of Educational Psychology, 81,* 143–154.

Grolnick, W. S., & Ryan, R. M. (1990). Self-perceptions, motivation, and adjustment in children with learning disabilities: A multiple group comparison study. *Journal of Learning Disabilities, 23,* 177–184.

Grolnick, W. S., Ryan, R. M., & Deci, E. L. (1991). The inner resources for school achievement: Motivational mediators of children's perceptions of their parents. *Journal of Educational Psychology, 83,* 508–517.

Grow, V., & Ryan, R. M. (1994). *Autonomy and relatedness in the institutionalized elderly: Effects on health, vitality and well-being.* Unpublished manuscript, University of Rochester.

Gunderson, J. G. (1984). *Borderline personality disorders.* Washington, DC: American Psychiatric Press.

Harackiewicz, J. (1979). The effects of reward contingency and performance feedback on intrinsic motivation. *Journal of Personality and Social Psychology, 37,* 1352–1363.

Harlow, H. F. (1953). Motivation as a factor in the acquisition of new responses. In *Current theory and research on motivation* (pp. 24–49). Lincoln: University of Nebraska Press.

Harlow, H. F. (1958). The nature of love. *American Psychologist, 13,* 673–685.

Hartmann, H. (1958). *Ego psychology and the problem of adaptation.* New York: International Universities Press. (Originally work published 1939)

Hartmann, H. (1964). On rational and irrational action. In *Essays on ego psychology.* New York: International Universities Press. (Original work published 1947)

Heider, F. (1958). *The psychology of interpersonal relations.* New York: Wiley.

Herman, J., Perry, J. C., & van der Kolk, B. A. (1989). Childhood trauma in borderline personality disorder. *American Journal of Psychiatry, 146,* 490–495.

Hilgard, E. R. (1977). *Divided consciousness.* New York: Wiley.

Hill, J. P., & Holmbeck, G. (1986). Attachment and autonomy during adolescence. In G. Whitehurst (Ed.), *Annals of Child Development* (Vol. 3, pp. 145–189). Greenwich, CT: JAI Press.

Hiroto, D. S., & Seligman, M. E. P. (1975). Generality of learned helplessness in man. *Journal of Personality and Social Psychology, 31,* 311–327.

Hoffman, M. L. (1960). Power assertion by the parent and its impact on the child. *Child Development, 31,* 129–143.

Hoover, C. F., & Insel, T. R. (1984). Families of origin in obsessive-compulsive disorder. *Journal of Nervous and Mental Disorders, 172,* 207–215.

Horney, K. (1950). *Neurosis and human growth.* New York: Norton.

Hunt, J. McV. (1965). Intrinsic motivation and its role in psychological development. In D. Levine (Ed.), *Nebraska Symposium on Motivation* (Vol. 13, pp. 189–282). Lincoln: University of Nebraska Press.

Jahoda, M. (1958). *Current concepts of positive mental health.* New York: Basic Books.

Jung, C. G. (1959). Aion. In *Collected works* (Vol. 9). New York: Pantheon Books. (Original work published 1951)

Kandel, D., & Lesser, G. S. (1969). Parent-adolescent relationships and adolescent independence in the United States and Denmark. *Journal of Marriage and the Family, 31,* 348–359.

Kaplan, B. (1983). Genetic-dramatism: Old wine in new bottles. In S. Wapner & B. Kaplan (Eds.), *Toward a holistic developmental psychology.* Hillsdale, NJ: Erlbaum.

Kasser, T., & Ryan, R. M. (1993). A dark side of the American dream: Correlates of financial success as a central life aspiration. *Journal of Personality and Social Psychology, 65,* 410–422.

Kasser, T., & Ryan, R. M. (in press). Further examining the American dream: The differential effects of intrinsic and extrinsic goal structures. *Personality and Social Psychology Bulletin.*

Kasser, T., Ryan, R. M., Zax, M., & Sameroff, A. J. (in press). The relations of maternal and social environments to late adolescents' materialistic and prosocial values. *Developmental Psychology.*

Kernberg, O. F. (1967). Borderline personality organization. *Journal of the American Psychoanalytic Association, 15,* 641–685.

Kierkegaard, S. (1968). *The sickness unto death.* Princeton, NJ: Princeton University Press. (Original work published 1849)

Kilby, R. W. (1993). *The study of human values.* Lanham, MD: University Press of America.

Koestner, R., Bernieri, F., & Zuckerman, M. (1992). Self-regulation and consistency between attitudes, traits, and behaviors. *Personality and Social Psychology Bulletin, 18,* 52–59.

Koestner, R., & McClelland, D. C. (1990). Perspectives on competence motivation. In L. A. Pervin (Ed.), *Handbook of personality: Theory and research* (pp. 527–548). New York: Guilford.

Koestner, R., Ryan, R. M., Bernieri, F., & Holt, K. (1984). Setting limits on children's behavior: The differential effects of controlling versus informational styles on intrinsic motivation and creativity. *Journal of Personality, 52,* 233–248.

Kohn, A. (1990). *The brighter side of human nature: Altruism and empathy in everyday life.* New York: Basic Books.

Kohut, H. (1971). *The analysis of self.* New York: International Universities Press.

Kopp, C. B. (1982). Antecedents of self-regulation: A developmental perspective. *Developmental Psychology, 18,* 199–214.

Kruglanski, A. W., Stein, C., & Riter, A. (1977). Contingencies of exogenous reward and task performance: On the "minimax" strategy in instrumental behavior. *Journal of Applied Social Psychology, 7,* 141–148.

Laing, R. D. (1969). *Self and others* (2nd ed.). London: Tavistock.

Lamb, M. E., & Easterbrooks, M. A. (1981). Individual differences in parental sensitivity: Origins, components, and consequences. In M. E. Lamb & L. R. Sherrod (Eds.), *Infant social cognition: Empirical and theoretical considerations* (pp. 127–154). Hillsdale, NJ: Erlbaum.

Lapsley, D. K., & Rice, K. (1988). The "new look" at the imaginary audience and personal fable: Toward a general model of adolescent ego development. In D. K. Lapsley & F. C. Power (Eds.), *Self, ego and identity: Integrative approaches* (pp. 109–129). New York: Springer-Verlag.

Lasch, C. (1978). *The culture of narcissism: American life in an age of diminishing expectations.* New York: Norton.

Lepper, M. R., & Greene, D. (1975). Turning play into work: Effects of adult surveillance and extrinsic rewards on children's intrinsic motivation. *Journal of Personality and Social Psychology, 31,* 479–486.

Lepper, M. R., Greene, D., & Nisbett, R. E. (1973). Undermining children's intrinsic interest with extrinsic rewards: A test of the "overjustification" hypothesis. *Journal of Personality and Social Psychology, 28,* 129–137.

Lerner, H. G. (1988). *Women in therapy.* New York: Harper & Row.

Levitz-Jones, E. M., & Orlofsky, J. C. (1985). Separation-individuation and intimacy capacity in college women. *Journal of Personality and Social Psychology, 49,* 156–169.

Lewin, K. (1951). Intention, will, and need. In D. Rapaport (Ed.), *Organization and pathology of thought* (pp. 95–153). New York: Columbia University Press.

Lewis, M., & Coates, D. (1980). Mother-infant interaction and infant cognitive performance. *Infant Behavior and Development, 3,* 95–105.

Lewis, M., & Michalson, L. (1983). *Children's emotions and moods.* New York: Plenum.

Linehan, M. (1987). Dialectical behavior therapy for borderline personality disorder: Theory and method. *Bulletin of the Menninger Clinic, 51,* 261–276.

Loeber, R., & Stouthammer-Loeber, M. (1986). Family factors as correlates and predictors of juvenile conduct disorders. In M. Tonry & N. Morris (Eds.), *Crime and justice* (Vol. 7, pp. 29–149). Chicago: University of Chicago Press.

Loevinger, J. (1976). *Ego development.* San Francisco: Jossey-Bass.

Loranger, A. W., Oldham, J. M., & Tulis, E. H. (1982). Familial transmission of DSM-III borderline personality disorder. *Archives of General Psychiatry, 39,* 795–799.

Maccoby, E. E. (1980). *Social development: Psychological growth and the parent-child relationship.* New York: Harcourt Brace Jovanovich.

Magid, K., & McKelvey, C. A. (1987). *High risk: Children without a conscience.* New York: Bantam Books.

Markus, H. J., & Sentis, K. (1982). The self in social information processing. In J. Suls (Ed.), *Psychological perspectives on the self* (Vol. 1, pp. 41–70). Hillsdale, NJ: Erlbaum.

Maslow, A. H. (1943). A theory of human motivation. *Psychological Review, 50,* 370–396.

Masterson, J. F. (1981). *The narcissistic and borderline disorders.* New York: Brunner/Mazel.

May, R. (1969). *Love and will.* New York: Norton.

Mayr, E. (1982). *The growth of biological thought: Diversity, evolution, and inheritance.* Cambridge, MA: Harvard University Press.

McCord, W., & McCord, J. (1964). *The psychopath: An essay on the criminal mind.* Princeton, NJ: Van Nostrand.

McCranie, E. W., & Bass, J. D. (1984). Childhood family antecedents of dependency and self-criticism: Implications for depression. *Journal of Abnormal Psychology, 93,* 3–8.

McGraw, K. O., & McCullers, J. C. (1979). Evidence of a detrimental effect of extrinsic incentives on breaking a mental set. *Journal of Experimental Social Psychology, 15,* 285–294.

Meissner, W. W. (1981). *Internalization in psychoanalysis.* New York: International Universities Press.

Meissner, W. W. (1988). *Treatment of patients in the borderline spectrum.* Northvale, NJ: Aronson.

Memmi, A. (1984). *Dependence.* Boston: Beacon Press.

Miller, A. (1981). *The drama of the gifted child: The search for the true self* (R. Ward, Trans.). New York: Basic Books.

Miller, S. M., Birnbaum, A., & Durbin, D. (1990). Etiologic perspectives on depression in childhood. In M. Lewis & S. Miller (Eds.), *Handbook of developmental psychopathology* (pp. 311–325). New York: Plenum.

Minuchin, S., Rosman, B., & Baker, L. (1978). *Psychosomatic families.* Cambridge, MA: Harvard University Press.

Mischel, W., Ebbesen, E., & Zeiss, A. R. (1972). Cognitive and attentional mechanisms in delay of gratification. *Journal of Personality and Social Psychology, 21,* 204–218.

Mischel, W., & Underwood, B. (1974). Instrumental ideation in delay of gratification. *Child Development, 45,* 1083–1088.

Nietzel, M. T., & Harris, M. J. (1990). Relationship of dependency and achievement/autonomy to depression. *Clinical Psychology Review, 10,* 279–298.

Nunberg, H. (1931). The synthetic function of the ego. *International Journal of Psychoanalysis, 12,* 123–140.

O'Connor, B. P., & Vallerand, R. J. (1990). Religious motivation in the elderly: A French-Canadian replication and an extension. *Journal of Social Psychology, 130*(1), 53–59.

Orlofsky, J. L., Marcia, J. E., & Lesser, I. (1973). Ego identity status and the intimacy versus isolation crisis of young adulthood. *Journal of Personality and Social Psychology, 27,* 211–219.

Perls, F. S. (1973). *The Gestalt approach and eyewitness to therapy.* Ben Lomond, CA: Science and Behavior Books.

Pfander, A. (1967). *Phenomenology of willing and motivation* (H. Spiegelberg, Trans.). Evanston, IL: Northwestern University Press. (Original work published 1908)

Piaget, J. (1952). *The origins of intelligence in children.* New York: International Universities Press.

Piaget, J. (1965). *Moral judgment of the child.* Glencoe, IL: Free Press.

Piaget, J. (1967). *Six psychological studies* (D. Elkind, Ed.). New York: Vintage.

Piaget, J. (1971). *Biology and knowledge.* Chicago: University of Chicago Press.

Piaget, J. (1981). *Intelligence and affectivity: Their relationship during child development.* Palo Alto, CA: Annual Reviews.

Pittman, T. S., Davey, M. E., Alafat, K. A., Wetherill, K. V., & Kramer, N. A. (1980). Informational versus controlling verbal rewards. *Personality and Social Psychology Bulletin, 6,* 228–233.

Pittman, T. S., Emery, J., & Boggiano, A. K. (1982). Intrinsic and extrinsic motivational orientations: Reward-induced changes in preference for complexity. *Journal of Personality and Social Psychology, 42,* 789–797.

Plant, R., & Ryan, R. M. (1985). Intrinsic motivation and the effects of self-consciousness, self-awareness, and ego-involvement: An investigation of internally controlling styles. *Journal of Personality, 53,* 435–449.

Rasmussen, S., & Tsuang, M. (1986). Clinical characteristics and family history in DSM-III obsessive-compulsive disorder. *American Journal of Psychiatry, 143,* 317–322.

Reis, H. T., & Shaver, P. (1988). Intimacy as an interpersonal process. In S. Duck (Ed.), *Handbook of personal relationships* (pp. 367–389). Chichester, England: Wiley.

Richters, J. E., & Cicchetti, E. (Eds.). (1993). Toward a developmental perspective on conduct disorders [Special issue]. *Development and Psychopathology, 5,* 1–344.

Rodin, J., & Langer, E. J. (1977). Long-term effects of a control-relevant intervention with the institutionalized aged. *Journal of Personality and Social Psychology, 35,* 897–902.

Rogers, C. (1951). *Client centered therapy.* Boston: Houghton-Mifflin.

Rogers, C. (1963). The actualizing tendency in relation to "motives" and to consciousness. In M. R. Jones (Ed.), *Nebraska Symposium on Motivation* (Vol. 11, pp. 1–24). Lincoln: University of Nebraska Press.

Rosenberg, A. (1985). *The structure of biological science.* Cambridge, England: Cambridge University Press.

Ross, M. (1975). Salience of reward and intrinsic motivation. *Journal of Personality and Social Psychology, 32,* 245–254.

Rothbart, M. K., & Derryberry, D. (1981). Development of individual differences in temperament. In M. E. Lamb & A. L. Brown (Eds.), *Advances in developmental psychology* (Vol. 1, pp. 37–86). Hillsdale, NJ: Erlbaum.

Rotter, J. B. (1966). Generalized expectancies for internal versus external control of reinforcement, (pp. 1–28). *Psychological Monographs, 80*(1, Whole No. 609).

Ryan, R. M. (1982). Control and information in the intrapersonal sphere: An extension of cognitive evaluation theory. *Journal of Personality and Social Psychology, 43,* 450–461.

Ryan, R. M. (1989). The relevance of social ontology to psychological theory. *New Ideas in Psychology, 7,* 115–124.

Ryan, R. M. (1991). The nature of the self in autonomy and relatedness. In J. Strauss & G. R. Goethals (Eds.), *The self: Interdisciplinary approaches* (pp. 208–238). New York: Springer-Verlag.

Ryan, R. M. (1993). Agency and organization: Intrinsic motivation, autonomy and the self in psychological development. In J. Jacobs (Ed.), *Nebraska Symposium on Motivation: Vol. 40. Developmental perspectives on motivation* (pp. 1–56). Lincoln: University of Nebraska Press.

Ryan, R. M. (in press). Psychological needs and the facilitation of integrative processes. *Journal of Personality* [Special issue, "Levels and Domains in Personality," 1995].

Ryan, R. M., Avery, R. R., & Grolnick, W. S. (1985). A Rorschach assessment of children's mutuality of autonomy. *Journal of Personality Assessment, 49*(1), 6–12.

Ryan, R. M., & Connell, J. P. (1989). Perceived locus of causality and internalization: Examining reasons for acting in two domains. *Journal of Personality and Social Psychology, 57,* 749–761.

Ryan, R. M., Connell, J. P., & Deci, E. L. (1985). A motivational analysis of self-determination and self-regulation in education. In C. Ames & R. E. Ames (Eds.), *Research on motivation in education: The classroom milieu* (pp. 13–51). New York: Academic Press.

Ryan, R. M., Connell, J. P., & Grolnick, W. S. (1992). When achievement is *not* intrinsically motivated: A theory of self-regulation in school (pp. 167–188). In A. K. Boggiano & T. S. Pittman (Eds.), *Achievement and motivation: A social-developmental perspective.* New York: Cambridge University Press.

Ryan, R. M., & Frederick, C. M. (1994). *A theory and measure of vitality.* Unpublished manuscript, University of Rochester.

Ryan, R. M., & Grolnick, W. S. (1986). Origins and pawns in the classroom: Self-report and projective assessments of individual differences in children's perceptions. *Journal of Personality and Social Psychology, 50,* 550–558.

Ryan, R. M., Sheldon, K. M., Kasser, T., & Deci, E. L. (in press). All goals were not created equal: The relation of goal content and regulatory styles to mental health. In P. M. Gollwitzer & J. A. Bargh (Eds.), *The psychology of action: Linking motivation and cognition to behavior.* New York: Guilford.

Ryan, R. M., Koestner, R., & Deci, E. L. (1991). Varied forms of persistence: When free-choice behavior is not intrinsically motivated. *Motivation and Emotion, 15,* 185–205.

Ryan, R. M., & Kuczkowski, R. (1994). Egocentrism and heteronomy: A study of imaginary audience, self-consciousness, and public individuation in adolescence. *Journal of Personality, 62,* 219–238.

Ryan, R. M., & Lynch, J. (1989). Emotional autonomy versus detachment: Revisiting the vicissitudes of adolescence and young adulthood. *Child Development, 60,* 340–356.

Ryan, R. M., Mims, V., & Koestner, R. (1983). Relation of reward contingency and interpersonal context to intrinsic motivation: A review and test using cognitive evaluation theory. *Journal of Personality and Social Psychology, 45,* 736–750.

Ryan, R. M., Plant, R. W., & O'Malley, S. (in press). Initial motivations for alcohol treatment: Relations with patient characteristics, treatment involvement and dropout. *Addictive Behaviors.*

Ryan, R. M., Rigby, S., & King, K. (1993). Two types of religious internalization and their relations to religious orientations and mental health. *Journal of Personality and Social Psychology, 65,* 586–596.

Ryan, R. M., & Stiller, J. (1991). The social contexts of internalization: Parent and teacher influences on autonomy, motivation and learning. In P. R. Pintrich & M. L. Maehr (Eds.), *Advances in motivation and achievement: Vol. 7. Goals and self-regulatory processes* (pp. 115–149). Greenwich, CT: JAI Press.

Ryan, R. M., Stiller, J., & Lynch, J. H. (1994). Representations of relationships to teachers, parents, and friends as predictors of academic motivation and self-esteem. *Journal of Early Adolescence, 14,* 226–249.

Sartre, J. P. (1956). *Being and nothingness.* New York: Philosophical Library.

Schaefer, E. S. (1959). A circumplex model for maternal behavior. *Journal of Abnormal and Social Psychology, 59,* 226–235.

Schafer, R. (1968). *Aspects of internalization.* New York: International Universities Press.

Seligman, M. E. P. (1991). *Learned optimism.* New York: Knopf.

Shapiro, D. (1965). *Neurotic styles.* New York: Basic Books.

Shapiro, D. (1981). *Autonomy and rigid character.* New York: Basic Books.

Sheldon, K. M., & Kasser, T. (in press). When organism meets system: Exploring two views of personality integration. *Journal of Personality and Social Psychology.*

Shields, A., Cicchetti, D., & Ryan, R. M. (1994). The development of emotional and behavioral self-regulation and social competence among maltreated school-age children. *Development and Psychopathology, 6,* 57–75.

Skinner, B. F. (1953). *Science and human behavior.* New York: Macmillan.

Skinner, E. A. (1985). Action, control judgments, and the structure of control experience. *Psychological Review, 92,* 39–58.

Smith, W. E. (1974). *The effects of social and monetary rewards on intrinsic motivation.* Unpublished doctoral dissertation, Cornell University, Ithaca, NY.

Sperry, R. W. (1976). Changing conceptions of consciousness and free will. *Perspectives in Biology and Medicine, 20,* 9–19.

Sroufe, L. A., & Waters, E. (1977). Attachment as an organizational construct. *Child Development, 48,* 1184–1199.

Steinberg, L., & Silverberg, S. (1986). The vicissitudes of autonomy in adolescence. *Child Development, 57,* 841–851.

Stern, D. N. (1985). *The interpersonal world of the infant.* New York: Basic Books.

Stevenson, M. B., & Lamb, M. E. (1981). The effects of social experience and social style on cognitive competence and performance. In M. E. Lamb & L. R. Sherrod (Eds.), *Infant social cognition: Empirical and theoretical considerations* (pp. 375–394). Hillsdale, NJ: Erlbaum.

Strauss, J., & Ryan, R. M. (1987). Autonomy disturbances in subtypes of anorexia nervosa. *Journal of Abnormal Psychology, 96,* 254–258.

Strauss, J., & Ryan, R. M. (1988). Cognitive dysfunction in anorexia nervosa. *International Journal of Eating Disorders, 7,* 19–27.

Strober, M., & Humphrey, L. L. (1987). Familial contributions to the etiology and course of anorexia nervosa and bulimia. *Journal of Consulting and Clinical Psychology, 55,* 654–659.

Swallow, S. R., & Kuiper, N. A. (1988). Social comparison and negative self-evaluations: An application to depression. *Clinical Psychology Review, 8,* 55–76.

Swann, W. B., & Pittman, T. S. (1977). Initiating play activity of children: The moderating influence of verbal cues on intrinsic motivation. *Child Development, 48,* 1128–1132.

Swedo, S. E., & Rapoport, J. L. (1990). Obsessive-compulsive disorder in childhood. In M. Hersen & C. G. Last, *Handbook of child and adult psychopathology* (pp. 211–219). New York: Pergamon.

Thomas, A., Chess, S., & Birch, H. G. (1968). *Temperament and behavioral disorders in children.* New York: New York University Press.

Tronick, E. Z., & Gianino, A. F. (1986). The transmission of maternal disturbance to the infant. In E. Z. Tronick & T. Field (Eds.), *Maternal depression and infant disturbance* (pp. 5–12). San Francisco: Jossey-Bass.

Tuber, S. (1992). Empirical and clinical assessments of children's object relations and object representations. *Journal of Personality Assessment, 58,* 179–197.

Urist, J. (1977). The Rorschach test and the assessment of object relations. *Journal of Personality Assessment, 41*(1), 3–9.

Vallerand, R. J., & Bissonnette, R. (1992). Intrinsic, extrinsic, and amotivational styles as predictors of behavior: A prospective study. *Journal of Personality, 60,* 599–620.

Vallerand, R. J., & O'Conner, B. P. (1989). Motivation in the elderly: A theoretical framework and some promising findings. *Canadian Psychology, 30,* 538–550.

Vallerand, R. J., Pelletier, L. G., Blais, M. R., Briere, N. M., Senecal, C., & Vallieres, E. F. (1993). On the assessment of intrinsic, extrinsic, and amotivation in education: Evidence on the concurrent and construct validity of the Academic Motivation Scale. *Educational and Psychological Measurement, 53,* 159–172.

Vaughn, B. E., Kopp, C. B., & Krakow, J. B. (1984). The emergence and consolidation of self-control from eighteen to thirty months of age:

Normative trends and individual differences. *Child Development, 55,* 990–1004.

Waters, E., Wippman, J., & Sroufe, L. A. (1979). Attachment, positive affect, and competence in the peer group: Two studies in construct validation. *Child Development, 50,* 821–829.

Watson, J. S. (1966). The development and generalization of contingency awareness in early infancy: Some hypotheses. *Merrill-Palmer Quarterly, 12,* 123–135.

Weiss, L. A., & Grolnick, W. S. (1991, April). *The roles of parental involvement and support for autonomy in adolescent symptomatology.* Paper presented at the biennial meeting of the Society for Research in Child Development, Seattle, WA.

Werner, H. (1948). *Comparative psychology of mental development.* New York: International Universities Press.

Westen, D. (1991). Cognitive-behavioral interventions in the psychoanalytic psychotherapy of borderline personality disorders. *Clinical Psychology Review, 11,* 211–230.

Westen, D., Lodolph, P., Misle, B., Ruffins, S., & Block, J. (1990). Physical and sexual abuse of adolescent girls with borderline personality disorder. *American Journal of Orthopsychiatry, 60,* 55–66.

Whiffin, V. E., & Sassville, T. M. (1991). Dependency, self-criticism, and recollections of parenting: Sex differences and the role of depressive affect. *Journal of Social and Clinical Psychology, 10,* 121–133.

White, R. W. (1959). Motivation reconsidered: The concept of competence. *Psychological Review, 66,* 297–333.

White, R. W. (1960). Competence and the psychosexual stages of development. In M. R. Jones (Ed.), *Nebraska Symposium on Motivation* (Vol. 8, pp. 97–141). Lincoln: University of Nebraska Press.

Williams, G. C., Grow, V. M., Ryan, R. M., Friedman, Z., & Deci, E. L. (1994). *The role of perceived autonomy in maintained weight loss.* Unpublished manuscript, University of Rochester.

Williams, R. N. (1992). The human context of agency. *American Psychologist, 47,* 752–760.

Winnicott, D. W. (1958). Birth memories, birth trauma, and anxiety. In *Through pediatrics to psychoanalysis.* London: Hogarth Press. (Original work published 1949)

Winnicott, D. W. (1965a). Ego distortions in terms of true and false self. In *The maturational process and the facilitating environment.* New York: International Universities Press. (Original work published 1960)

Winnicott, D. W. (1965b). The theory of the parent-infant relationship. In *The maturational processes and the facilitating environment.* New York: International Universities Press. (Original work published 1960)

Winnicott, D. W. (1965c). *Maturational processes and the facilitating environment: Studies in the theory of emotional development.* New York: International Universities Press.

Winnicott, D. W. (1986). *Human nature.* New York: Schocken.

Wishnie, H. (1977). *The impulsive personality.* New York: Plenum.

Yarrow, L. J., Rubenstein, J. L., & Pederson, F. A. (1975). *Infant and environment: Early cognitive and motivational development.* New York: Halsted Press.

Zuckerman, M., Porac, J., Lathin, D., Smith, R., & Deci, E. L. (1978). On the importance of self-determination for intrinsically motivated behavior. *Personality and Social Psychology Bulletin, 4,* 443–446.

PART SIX

Systems Approaches

CHAPTER 21

General Systems Theories and Developmental Psychopathology

ARNOLD J. SAMEROFF

The discipline of developmental psychopathology has been promoted as the foundation for major advances in our ability to understand, treat, and prevent mental disorders (Cicchetti, 1989). One assumption underlying this expectation is that the perspectives of developmentalists and psychopathologists offer different conceptualizations of the same phenomena and that their unification would produce a clarification of the appearance and etiology of psychological disturbances. In this vein, Rutter and Garmezy (1983) characterize this difference as the developmentalist's concern with continuity in functioning such that severe symptoms are placed on the same dimension with more normal behaviors in contrast to the pathologist's concern with discontinuity, where the abnormal is differentiated from the normal. The division of the field into those who approach the problem from a developmental perspective and those who approach it from a clinical perspective has masked the fact that there are many different kinds of developmentalists and many different kinds of psychopathologists. These differences arise in contrasting interpretations of behavioral development and ultimately in contrasting views of the sources of behavioral deviation.

Recent progress in the technology of molecular genetics has led to a hope that the etiology of mental disorders will soon be revealed and that their treatment and prevention will follow. The editorial policies of major interdisciplinary scientific journals provide clear examples of such beliefs. Koshland (1993) presents an optimistic picture in which the future will be better than the past because of expected "insights into the effect on complex processes such as IQ, bad behavior, and alcoholism by single genes or chemical reactions" (p. 1861). What seems to be a technological statement of fact can alternatively be interpreted as the expression of a particular belief system about the nature of the child and especially the nature of pathology. The basis for such hopes is a view of humans as determined by their biology and of development as an unfolding of predetermined lines of growth. Among these lines of development are those that produce the emotionally disturbed, such as schizophrenics and depressives, the cognitively disturbed, such as the learning disabled and the retarded, and the undisturbed (normal) individuals. But would this model fit those individuals who do not stay on their predicted trajectories? There have been many full-term healthy infants who were predicted to have a happy course but instead ended up with a variety of mental disorders later in life. In these cases, researchers could argue that we have not yet developed the sophisticated diagnostic tools to identify their inherent deviancy at birth. However, how would investigators explain those infants who presented with major disabilities that somehow did not progress to adult forms of disturbance (Sameroff & Chandler, 1975).

The case of Helen Keller is probably the most telling counterpoint to the maturational view of development (Keller, 1904). The story of this deaf-blind woman required a model of development that went beyond the maturational blueprint to incorporate the powerful effect of environment on human potential. There are documented biographies of many individuals who were certain candidates for a life of institutionalization but whose fate was altered to a happier end (cf. Clarke & Clarke, 1976, Garmezy, 1985).

Because the fulfillment of the molecular biologist's promises are still in the future, there is time to examine the gap between our current scientific knowledge and the elimination of mental disease. On the one hand, we can view this gap as a technical one that will be closed by the accomplishments of federal empirical initiatives such as the "decade of the brain." On the other hand, we can view this gap as a conceptual one that will continue to exist despite major advances in the biological understanding of developmental processes. Notwithstanding vast scientific and technological advances over the past century, the solution to problems at both the individual and social level seem no closer. At the same time that there are major advances in our understanding of the biological underpinnings of such disorders as cancer, the rate of cancer has increased. At the same time that major advances are made in the understanding of ecological systems, the rate of environmental devastation is increasing. And at the same time that major advances are made in our understanding of economic processes, the rate of poverty is increasing. How can we explain such contradictions? At one level, the explanation may be that achievements in the laboratory are not readily translated into achievements in society at large and that eventually scientific reason will prevail. At another level, it may be that scientific reason itself is at fault. A belief that scientific knowledge directly changes social action may be akin to a reductionistic belief that the actions of atoms, molecules, and genes directly change human action. If such is the case, a model of human and social action that respects the complexity of both may be necessary as an alternative view.

In recent years, a number of respected developmental psychologists have argued that research efforts to understand the basic nature of the child have been rooted in the wrong scientific model of behavior. Reinstating a reductionist perspective, Scarr (1985) argues that constructions giving context a major role in human development underestimate the power of genetic influences on the characteristics of not only the child but also the child's environment. In contrast, Kessen (1979, 1993), supporting an expanded contextualist view, proposes that the technological shifts in society are altering our scientific view of the child from an isolate who develops independent of experience to an image of the child as a continuous creation of social and biological contexts.

This chapter will first discuss such alternative models for understanding living systems. From this analysis, it will be argued that the appropriate model for understanding developmental psychopathology is one that matches the complexity of human behavior. Such a view is in accord with the beliefs of most of the founding voices of developmental psychopathology. Sroufe and Rutter (1984) argued that a primary concern is the complexity of the adaptational process, with developmental transformation being the norm. This focus on complexity is amplified by Cicchetti (1989) who lists differentiation, organization, and hierarchic integration as principles at the cornerstone of developmental psychopathology. These ingredients will be included in a conception based on general systems theory that attempts to integrate individual and contextual processes in a model for understanding developmental psychopathology.

WORLD HYPOTHESES AND ROOT METAPHORS

The rationalist tradition that accompanied the rise of natural science diminished the role of speculation and philosophy in science in favor of obtaining a "true" view of the operation of the universe through the careful collection of facts. This view could be supported as long as the facts and their interrelationships are considered to exist independently of the scientific lens through which they are viewed.

More recently, a contrasting position developed within the history of science: Theory acts to select certain facts as more relevant than others and to impose an organization on observations rather than to have the organization determined by observations. Even Einstein drew back from a determining view of data: "It may be heuristically useful to keep in mind what one has observed. But on principle, it is quite wrong to try founding a theory on observable magnitudes alone. In reality the very opposite happens. It is the theory which decided what we can observe" (Einstein, cited in Heisenberg, 1971, p. 63). It is not implied here that scientists make up theories that have nothing to do with the facts but rather that there is a reciprocal relationship between theory and facts involving inseparable roles. This transactional position—in which what the scientist observes is strongly influenced by what theory is held and at the same time what theory is held is strongly influenced by what facts are observed—is analogous to what has come to be called the "constructivist" position in developmental psychology (Piaget, 1970).

Constructivism when applied to understanding psychological development focuses on the active role of children in creating their cognitive and social worlds. In their widely separate domains, developmental biologists (e.g., Waddington, 1962) and historians of science (e.g., Kuhn, 1962) have arrived at similar positions in which the organism in the former case and the scientist in the latter engage in constructive efforts imposing order on their environments.

Although the importance of theory may be discouraging to researchers who see scientific progress in the gathering of experimental facts, the historical fact is that attention to theory has produced scientific progress, albeit theory focused on empirical data. This chapter will consider data but only in the service of better understanding the kind of theory that will be necessary to explain the findings of developmental psychology. By starting at a very general level, a context will be described in which specific developmental theories and sets of empirical observations can be embedded. The most general level is that of world hypotheses. At this level, similarities can be explored into many other communalities of principle between psychology and biology, and at the same time these communalities can be extended into other scientific disciplines.

A basic difference between psychology and biology is in the possibility of observing developmental processes. Although behavioral changes are the central concern of the developmental psychologist, the organization of behavioral change is relatively hidden compared with the biological changes during individual human growth from zygote to maturity. The early Greeks were concerned with explaining such changes. Aristotle was able to differentiate between two alternative processes that moved life along on its path to maturity, preformationism and epigenesis. Preformationism is the idea that within the fertilized egg there are parts corresponding with each of the parts of the adult. Growth is a simple process of enlargement from the small seed to the adult form. The homunculus, the little man, that early microscopists claimed to have seen in the sperm cell was thought to be the final evidence for the preformationist position. In modern times, such homunculi have been regarded more abstractly in the hereditary material, each gene a preformed aspect of the adult organ. Epigenesis is the view that the organism initially contains only a few basic elements. All later complex structures are the result of the interactions of these original units. Local interactions have more to do with developmental outcomes than either divine or genetic plans. The epigenetic approach has consistently been the more complex, for its focus has always been on the interaction of parts in the developing system, and especially in its modern manifestation on the interaction of the parts with their environments.

What follows will be an effort to understand how perspectives such as preformationism and epigenesis have been translated within different scientific contexts. Although there is agreement that each discipline deals with different empirical phenomena, there is less agreement that there is a difference in theoretical principles. The views range from those who see each level of human functioning reflected in different disciplines obeying different principles, to those who recognize the separateness of scientific arenas but also see analogies among their principles, to those who perceive a unity in which all fields of science share the same principles.

A major source of unity between the empirical and theoretical world is to model one after the other. From this perspective, philosophies are fashioned in correspondence to theories of how the material world functions. Scientific understanding becomes a model for philosophical understanding. The debate between philosophical positions then becomes a debate between how well the metaphor fits the functioning of the material world. In an analysis of such root metaphors, Pepper (1942) proposed four "world hypotheses" that he claimed have been the basis for most modern scientific theories: formism, mechanism, contextualism, and organicism. At various times during this century, one or another of these hypotheses has been emphasized in the dominant developmental theories, although traces of each can be found at any one time.

Formism

Formism is based on Plato's philosophy of ideal forms. Concrete manifestations are viewed as the expression of abstract universals. Formism has not been a popular metaphor among developmentalists because it denies development. However, it is gaining in popularity as an explanation for developmental phenomena among nondevelopmentalists. The preformist view of growth is reflected in theories that explain social organization on the basis of genetic determinants (Wilson, 1975) or language on the basis of universal innate grammars (Chomsky, 1975).

Behavioral genetics (Plomin, DeFries, & McClearn, 1990) is one of the current homes of formist thinking. Efforts to partial out the components of phenotypic variance reflect a belief that heredity and environment have an existence prior to their interaction. Heredity brings one set of determinants and environment brings another set to the developmental equation (Scarr, 1993). The task of science is to untangle these factors so that the unique contribution of each can be understood. This formist belief system has interesting implications for the interpretation of probability and the usefulness of components of variance designs. Probability is associated with how close the investigator's empirical work can come to revealing the true mean, the true underlying genetic contribution. This view is in contrast to definitions of probability within an organicist root metaphor. As will be seen in the following section, the organismic view is that the underlying reality is itself probabilistic. Each living phenomenon is based on multiple interactions of multiple causal systems. From this perspective, the search for such things as heritability estimates is fundamentally misguided. At best, it is an abstraction of a moving target. When relatively stable heritability estimates are found, it is only because there is a relative stability in the interactions of these multiple systems rather than an underlying stable cause.

Mechanism and Organicism

Mechanism and organicism have been the most popular metaphors for theories of developmental psychology. A number of papers have been explicitly devoted to contrasting the models derived from these two world views (Ford & Lerner, 1992; Kuhn, 1978; Langer, 1969; Overton & Reese, 1973). Reese and Overton (1970) analyzed organismic and mechanistic models as applied to developmental phenomena in detail because they felt that these radically different models have had a pervasive effect generally on the nature of psychology and specifically on that of developmental psychology. Because each model has served as a lens through which scientists view their subject matter, Reese and Overton described a number of issues on which the two models differ with respect to the categories they impose on developmental research.

A central issue on which the models differ is the root metaphor, the machine versus the organism. When the universe is regarded as a machine, it is seen as being composed of discrete pieces. The pieces and their relationships form the basic reality to which all other complex phenomena can be reduced. Such a reality is capable of quantification, so that functional equations can be constructed mapping the relationships between the pieces in operation. The model is derived from the Newtonian version of the cosmos: The same laws that apply to irreducible fundamental elements and their interactions also apply to all more complex interactions. The early learning theorists proposed equations that would typify the behavior of all animals independently of their phyletic level (Hull, 1943). For example, the monotonically negatively accelerating relationship between strength of response and hours of food deprivation applies equally well to a sponge, a blowfly, a rat, or a human being: Only the exponent differs in the equation. The facts that no central nervous system mediates the response in the sponge, a single nerve mediates it in the blowfly, a combination of peripheral and central systems mediates it in the rat, to which the human adds a reflective consciousness, are irrelevant because the same curve can be used for all.

In contrast, when the universe is regarded as a living organized system, the parts gain some of their meaning from the whole in which they are embedded. From this perspective, research is directed toward discovering principles of organization, toward the explanation of the relations of parts and wholes rather than toward the derivation of the whole from some set of elementary processes. For example, "vision," a property of the visual system, is not reducible to the sum of its parts—the cornea, retina, optic nerve, and brain. The interpretation of an observable bit of behavior like the human smile will have different meaning depending on the developmental stage and situational context of the behavior. For the newborn, it is an endogenous concomitant of a particular state of sleep (Emde, Gaensbauer, & Harmon, 1976); for the older infant, it is the reflection of contingency awareness (Watson, 1972); for the adult, it may be a sign of manipulation, or of anxiety, or perhaps even of genuine happiness.

The source of motivation is another key issue on which the models differ. Reese and Overton describe the mechanistic position as the "reactive, passive, robot, or empty organism model or man." The individual is inherently at rest, only becoming active under the influence of outside forces. This Newtonian machine must have a source of power external to the central function. Human beings must have extrinsic drives that motivate thought, perception, and activity. Freudian theories of psychodynamics and behaviorist learning theories are based on such a need for underlying causes of behavior separate from the behavior. In contrast, from the organismic perspective, the essence of substance is not its parts but its activity. Based on the model of the living cell, it follows that the organism is in a continuous transition from one state to another in unceasing succession. No outside source of motivation is necessary because activity is a given in the definition of life. Herein is the basis for the active organism model of humans.

The several differences between the two models make for differences in the way investigators would study developmental change. The organicist would emphasize the study of processes over products and qualitative change over quantitative change (Reese & Overton, 1970). As applied to research, the method of the organicist would be to describe structures at each identifiable period, to discover the rules of transition from one period to another, and to determine the experiences that would enhance or retard these transitions. The mechanist, on the other hand, would focus on the basic parts and their principles of relationship to which complexities or organization can be reduced. Because a universal set of principles is presumed to explain the operation of parts at all levels of functioning, the only differences between the levels for the mechanist would be quantitative ones. Thus, development becomes analogous to simple growth: Just as the body enlarges, knowledge enlarges.

Contextualism

Where formism has not been found useful as a metaphor for development because of its simplicity, contextualism has been inadequate because of its complexity. Pepper (1942) sees the historical event as the metaphor of contextualism with the implication that the universe is a network of many causes interacting to produce uniquely determined events. Because each context has a different set of determinants, each development is nonreproducible as well as nonpredictable. Despite its complexity, contextualism has been popular in the theories associated with life-span developmental psychology (Baltes, 1979). The need to explain developmental changes in adulthood, where intrinsic biological factors are thought to play a minor role, has moved theorists to a greater consideration of the organization of the environment, that is, the context of development (Lerner & Busch-Rossnagel, 1981).

The original need for life-span developmentalists to emphasize the contextualist metaphor was the result of a misunderstanding about the distinction between the organismic metaphor and how it was presented as a theory of development. Baltes (1979) rejected organismic views because he believed they interpreted development as the unfolding of an intrinsic biological program. Few, if any, organismically inclined developmentalists share this view. Like biological development, behavioral development is viewed as being intimately connected with the environment. Lerner, one of the early proponents of the contextualist view, has reintegrated environmental concerns with an organismically based perspective in positing an unified developmental systems theory (Ford & Lerner, 1992).

In summary, the mechanistic and organismic world views have different categories for organizing searches for and ascribing meaning to empirical data. These interpretative schemes differ from one another in their units of investigation, sources of motivation, bases of knowing, concepts of developmental change, and possibilities for predicting such changes. To test the adequacy of such generalizations, it would be useful to examine the characteristics of these metaphors to determine the source of the abstracted properties of the model. In the process, additional properties of the organismic model that can enrich the analogies between biological development and behavioral development may be unearthed.

From the perspective of developmental psychopathology, a major question would be the identification of the sources of maladaptation. Abnormalities have been posited by various investigators as being situated wholly within the individual, the environment, or some combination of the two. Although these perspectives have equal status today, there have been historical shifts in the zeitgeist emphasizing one or the other model. A consideration of the history of research models in development may help illuminate the usefulness of attention to root metaphors.

MODELS OF DEVELOPMENT

The classic definition of development was that of a gradual unfolding as an image on a photographic plate (Neilson, 1942). The unfolding model (see Figure 21.1) fit embryological conceptions of a developmental plan that was either materially inherent in the original state of the organism as in early views of the operations of heredity or inherent in the organization of development as in vitalistic theories of developmental regulation (Jacob, 1976). Dominant gene theories of schizophrenia would fit in this mold. The effects of these genes would unfold leading to markers such as eye-movement abnormalities, attentional dysfunction, and ultimately a diagnosis of schizophrenia (Iacono & Grove, 1993).

The constitutional continuity model was countered by an environmental model of discontinuity in which each stage of development was determined by the contingencies in the contemporary context. Such a radical behaviorist approach tied all behavior to the current reinforcement schedules for the child (Bijou & Baer, 1961). If the context remained the same, the child remained the same. If the context changed, the child changed (see Figure 21.2). In explaining the etiology of schizophrenia, environmentalists saw the disorder as a consequence of family conflict or boundary problems (Lidz, 1973). To change the outcome for children in such disturbed families, family patterns of interaction needed to be changed.

An interactionist position combined these two as in Figure 21.3. Here continuities within child are moderated by possible discontinuities in experience. Current dominant views of the causes of intellectual and emotional problems are based on the interactionist model. For intellectual functioning, the standard

$$C_1 \longrightarrow C_2 \longrightarrow C_3 \longrightarrow C_4$$

Figure 21.1 Deterministic constitutional model of development. (C1 to C4 represent state of the child at successive points in time.)

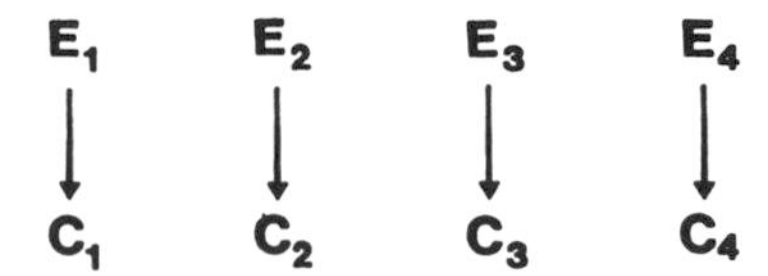

Figure 21.2 Deterministic environmental model of development. (El to E4 represent experiential influences at successive points in time.)

explanatory model is based on the combination of a genetic range of reaction and an environmental range of experience. Maximum intelligence is the result of excellent genes and enriching experience; middling performance can result from poor genes in a good environment or good genes in an impoverished one; and mental retardation is the result of poor genes in a poor environment (cf. Scarr, 1993). In this scenario, however, the constitutional endowment doesn't change. There are individuals with genes for higher IQs and individuals with genes for lower IQs.

The interactionist position as captured in analysis-of-variance models is an important advance over single-factor models that overemphasized either constitutional or environmental influences. However, the emphasis remains on separating influences into discrete categories rather than an appreciation of their interpenetration. Anastasi (1957) is credited with the important interactionist conceptual breakthrough in pointing out the inextricable connectedness between individual and context. There is no logical possibility of considering development of an individual independent of the environment. Anastasi argued that the core question was not whether nature and nurture worked together, but how—the issue was to identify the processes of development.

More recent conceptualizations of the developmental model added a dynamic component to the interactional model in which organism and context are viewed as interdependent. The behavior of the child actually changes the environment (Bell, 1968; Rheingold, 1966). These dynamic interactionists (Thomas, Chess, & Birch, 1968) or transactional models (Sameroff & Chandler, 1975) state that the environment cannot be identified or assessed apart from the child because different children will elicit different reactions from the same environment. Similarly, the state of the child cannot be taken out of context because different environments will elicit different reactions from the same child (see Figure 21.4). Continuity could not be explained as a characteristic of the child because each new achievement was an amalgam of characteristics of the child and his or her experience. Neither alone would predict later levels of functioning. If continuities were found, it was because there was a continuity in the relation between the child and the environment, not because of continuities in either taken alone.

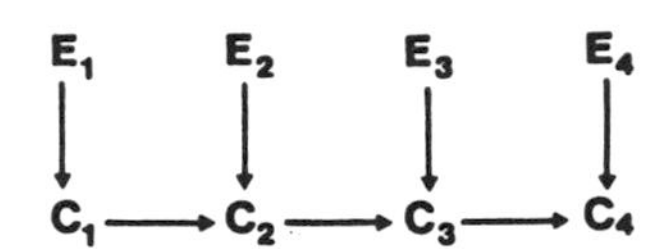

Figure 21.3 Interactionist model of development.

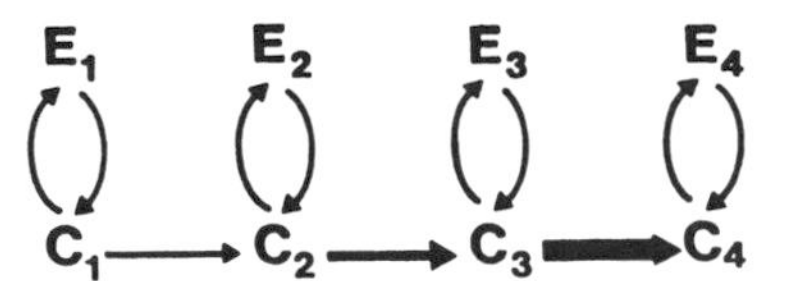

Figure 21.4 Transactional model of development.

THE TRANSACTIONAL MODEL

In the transactional model the development of the child is seen as a product of a continuous dynamic interaction of the child and the experience provided by his or her family and social context (Sameroff & Chandler, 1975). What is innovative in the transactional model is the emphasis placed on the effect of the child on the environment, so that experiences provided by the environment are not independent of the child.

Figure 21.5 shows a concrete example of such a transactional outcome. In this figure, the child's outcome at any point in time is neither a function of the initial state of the child nor the initial state of the environment, but a complex function of the interplay of child and environment over time. For example, complicated childbirth may have made an otherwise calm mother somewhat anxious. The mother's anxiety during the first months of the child's life may have caused her to be uncertain and inappropriate in her interactions with the child. In response to such inconsistency, the infant may have developed some irregularities in feeding and sleeping patterns that give the appearance of a difficult temperament. This difficult temperament decreases the pleasure that the mother obtains from the child and so she tends to spend less time with her child. If caregivers do not actively interact with the child, and especially, do not speak to the child, the youngster may not meet the norms for language development when entering preschool or kindergarten resulting in a diagnosis of language delay.

What determined the poor outcome in this example? Was the poor linguistic performance caused by the complicated childbirth, the mother's anxiety, the child's difficult temperament, or the mother's avoidance of verbal and social interaction? If we were to design an intervention program for this family, where would we direct it? If we were to select the most proximal cause, it would be the mother's avoidance of the child, yet such a view would oversimplify a complex developmental sequence. Should intervention

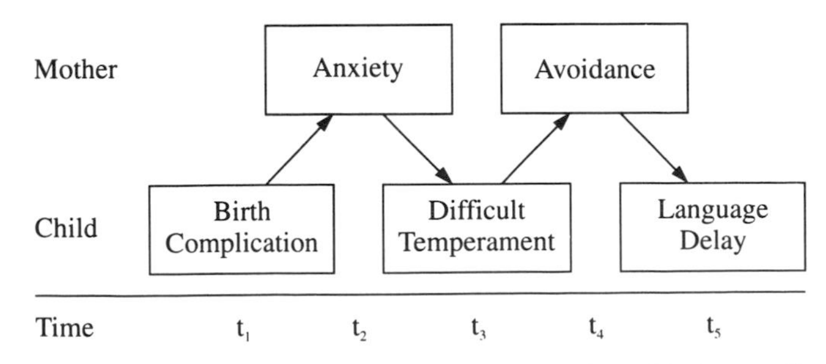

Figure 21.5 Transactional process leading from birth complications to language delays.

be directed at eliminating the child's difficult temperament or at changing the mother's reaction, or at providing alternative sources of verbal stimulation for the child? Each of these would eliminate a potential dysfunction at some contemporary point in the developmental system. But would any of these efforts ensure the verbal competence of the child or, perhaps more important, ensure the continued progress of the child after the intervention was completed?

For some children, there is indeed a linear connection between biological abnormalities and later language or learning disabilities. The continuum of reproductive causality (Pasamanick & Knobloch, 1961) has at one end a group of children who are so physically deviant that they are impervious to the normal range of caregiving experience. For the rest, however, experience is a major mediator of developmental outcome. A fascinating natural experiment helped to elucidate some of these developmental processes. During the late 1950s, a number of pregnant women who were taking a drug called thalidomide for nausea gave birth to physically abnormal infants. Because the teratogenic effects of thalidomide had not yet been discovered, it was left to the clinicians to make an uninformed diagnosis. In an investigation of the fate of a sample of these children in Canada, Roskies (1972) reported that about half the clinicians told the mothers that the infants would be hopelessly retarded and it would be better to have the children institutionalized. The other half of the clinicians told the mothers that the infants had a physical deformity but that there was no reason to expect retardation or to expect that they could not care for their infants at home. In longitudinal studies of these children, it was found that, indeed, there were no intellectual consequences of the thalidomide. Irrespective of the degree of physical deviance, the language performance of the children was related to whether they had been institutionalized or not. The infants of those mothers who followed the medical advice of institutionalization were retarded in their language skills. The infants who were reared at home showed no such effects. The transaction here was the clinician's redefinition of the child, which set one group of infants on a developmental trajectory of institutional isolation and educational deprivation and permitted another identical group to be reared at home as mentally normal infants.

Transactions can be caused by atypical behavior of the child for which the parent has no understanding or by normative behavior of the child that the parent understands from a distorted perspective. An example of parental misinformation is described by Parmelee (1989). A baby regurgitates some of each feeding, a not abnormal infant behavior, but one that is upsetting to some parents who believe the baby is not getting enough food. The parental response may be to overfeed the infant, which increases the regurgitation, which leads the parent to believe that the baby has a disorder. A visit to the physician by the worried parent may result in a diagnosis of a reflux disorder, the prescription of medication, and in some cases surgery. The transaction that occurred here was to convert a parent with a normal view of her infant into one with a disordered view and to convert a child who spits up into a medical case.

An example of a transaction arising from parental distortion is the case of Lisa described by Brazelton and Cramer (1990). A mother brought a 14-week-old infant for therapy because the infant cried too much. The mother interpreted the cries as anger rather than the discomfort or need for discharge that they actually were. The mother's fear was that her angry response to what she saw as the infant's angry cries would lead her to abuse the child. In this case, therapeutic intervention allowed a reinterpretation of the infant's cries as normal, interrupting the negative transaction. In many disordered families, however, the parent's inappropriate view of a young infant as angry or oppositional does lead to battering. The transaction in Lisa's case was that the parent changed her view of her baby from normalcy to deviancy, requiring angry retaliation instead of loving care.

When attempts are made to operationalize complex transactional processes within a specific research design, causal sequences are rarely simple. Crockenberg and Smith (1982) were able to separate transactional from linear influences when they examined the relation of infant and mother characteristics to the development of infant temperament and mother-infant interaction during the first 3 months of life. Mothers' responsive attitudes and infant irritability were measured during the newborn period. Three months later, the mothers who had responsive and flexible attitudes at birth responded more quickly when their infants cried, and their infants spent less time fussing and crying. On the other hand, the baby's irritability at birth was not related to the amount of crying at 3 months, but it was related to the amount of time required to calm down. In other words, some aspects of infant crying at 3 months are the result of transactional processes whereas other aspects can be explained more directly. Although time to calm down was not, amount of crying was a function of the subsequent caregiving experiences. From the infant's side, a transaction had occurred; the state of the child was changed as a function of the mother's behavior.

There was also evidence in the Crockenberg and Smith study that the behavior of the mother was changed by the specific characteristics of the child. Alert infants had mothers who spent more time in contact with them, and mothers of irritable females responded more quickly to fussing and crying than mothers of irritable males. Mothers' behavior was sensitive to both the behavioral and physical characteristics of the child. The evidence for transactional processes in this study is an example of the multidimensional nature of both maternal and child behavior. Depending on the antecedent and outcome measures and the ages of assessment, different relations will be found, some giving strong evidence for transactions and others not.

For a genuine transaction to occur, the parents must be influenced by the infant's behavior to do something they would not have done if the child behaved otherwise. In many cases, parents respond with love and affection to anything the child does; and in a few cases, parents respond with anger and abuse to anything the child does. These are not examples of transactions because the parent was not changed by the behavior of the child. It is difficult to separate transactional effects from these parental effects when only one child is involved. The study of twins, however, offers a clear opportunity for observing transactional processes. A transaction will have occurred if the same parent relates differently to the two infants.

It is a common clinical observation that parents generally prefer one twin over the other. Minde, Carter, Goldberg, and

Jeffers (1990) found that the majority of mothers maintained these preferences at least through the 4 years of their study. The preference was based on the infants' behavior usually during the first 2 weeks of life although some mothers took up to a year to establish a long-term choice. The preferred infant was not necessarily the one with the easiest temperament. Some mothers liked strong-willed, independent, active babies, others calm, easygoing infants, and others healthier ones. The consequences of these early choices were that at 4 years the preferred twins had fewer behavior problems and higher IQ scores. In a case study, Stern (1981) reported a mother's preference for the more active twin already during pregnancy. The mother explained her bias as her identification with the more active twin in contrast to the calmer baby, whom she identified with her more passive husband. Minde and colleagues described their mothers as making similar associations between the characteristics of the preferred twin and beloved relatives or idealized developmental outcomes such as becoming a future professor or deep thinker. In these twin studies, the same parent reacts differently to the different behaviors of her offspring. Transactions are occurring in which the behavior of the preferred twin is interpreted in a different system from that of the non-preferred twin, and consequently, it sets off a different course of development.

Observations of families in natural settings provide insights into possible causal sequences in development, but definitive evidence can only be produced by attempts to manipulate developmental variables (Bronfenbrenner, 1977). Experimental manipulations to illuminate transactional processes have been infrequent as yet. Bugental and Shennum (1984) assessed beliefs about causes of caregiving outcomes for a group of mothers who were then placed in interaction situations with children who had been trained to be more or less responsive and assertive. Short-term transactions were identified in some conditions where mothers responded differently as a function of the combination of their attributions and the actual behavior of the child. Other research projects have been directed at long-term transactions resulting from massive intervention programs.

Zeskind and Ramey (1978, 1981) examined the effects of an intensive early intervention program on the development of a group of growth-retarded infants with low socioeconomic status (SES). Intervention began at 3 months and included social work, medical, nutritional, and educational components. A control group received similar social work, medical, and nutritional services but did not participate in the educational program. As a group, the infants without educational intervention declined in developmental quotients from 3 to 18 months of age and continued to score lower on tests at 36 months of age. Within that group, however, the growth-retarded babies showed a much greater decline in developmental status. In contrast, in the group that received educational intervention, the malnourished infants who had scored significantly lower than the rest of the group at 3 months were doing as well as the others by 18 months. Zeskind and Ramey (1981) concluded that the educational program had interrupted the negative transaction found in the control group. The treated mothers were showing much higher levels of involvement in caregiving. Where low SES mothers would usually be put off by the characteristics of a fetally malnourished infant, contributing to a worsening developmental outcome as in the control group, intervention fostered the relationship between mother and child, thereby leading to an above-average outcome within this sample.

TRANSACTIONS AND PSYCHOPATHOLOGY

The study of severe forms of psychopathology is an arena in which, notwithstanding the continuing nature-nurture battles, a transactional perspective is beginning to appear. Areas in which little is known lend themselves to contrasting hypotheses. In an overview of research on the etiology of schizophrenia, Iacono and Grove (1993) concluded that despite the promise of new technology, the past 100 years have done little to explain the disorder. On the one side have been those who posited dominant genes as causal agents (Matthysse, Holzman, & Lange, 1986). On the other side are those who see family interaction patterns as the causal agents (Lidz, 1973). These single-factor models have been augmented by interactional models where schizophrenia has been interpreted as an outcome of combined biological vulnerabilities and environmental adversity (Rosenthal, 1970). The individual is born with an inherited diathesis but will not become schizophrenic unless the stress in the environment is above a certain threshold, thus an interactive model. The difference between an interactional model and a transactional one is that during interaction the vulnerability will not change: Only the variability in the context will result in the expression of the illness; the organismic and environmental factors are seen as independent. In a transactional system, organism and environment are interdependent as in the etiologic model for schizophrenia proposed by Asarnow, Asarnow, and Strandburg (1989). Children with the greatest psychobiological vulnerability were exposed to families with poor communication patterns that taxed, and perhaps worsened, the childrens' fragile attentional processes. There were different risks for exposure to stressful family interactions for children with and without attentional impairments, and it may be that these two groups of children responded differently to the same deviant family communication patterns. Additionally, family interaction patterns may be worsened in the presence of a child with attentional problems.

There are other empirically validated examples of transactional processes in development (cf. Sameroff, 1993) that are directly pertinent to psychopathology. One of the most compelling data sets emerges from the work of Patterson and his colleagues in a series of studies on the origins of antisocial behavior in childhood (Patterson, 1986). In the Patterson model, children normally engage in some proportion of noncompliance activities. If parents are inept in disciplining their children, they create a context where the child is reinforced for learning a set of coercive behaviors. Parental ineptitude is characterized by lack of monitoring, harsh discipline, lack of positive reinforcement, and lack of involvement with the child. The child develops noncompliant behaviors characterized by whining, teasing, yelling, and disapproval. These behaviors escalate parental negative coercive responses that promote further child noncompliance eventuating in increased aggressive behaviors, including physical attack. The high use of noncompliance with inept parents does not permit the child to learn a set of social strategies that will be necessary for coping with peers and in a school environment. When these aggressive noncompliant children enter the school setting, they elicit poor peer acceptance that maintains poor self-esteem and poor academic performance. This constellation of antisocial behavior, poor peer relations, and poor school achievement has been demonstrated by Patterson to unfold in the previously described developmental sequence of negative transactions (see Figure 21.6). The child's initial noncompliance does not lead directly to antisocial behavior, rather it is the inept parenting response that converts age-appropriate expressions of autonomy into a coercive interactive style.

The research on the transactional effects of child antisocial behavior gives further impetus to the need to appreciate the attributional framework of the transacting individuals. Olson (1992) observed the unfolding of transactions in the classroom where an antisocial child converted his classmates from benign playmates into hostile combatants. What was especially interesting in this study was that after the playmates retaliated, the antisocial child stopped his aggressive behaviors, but this change in interactive contingencies did not stop the newly formed aggressive behavior of the classmates. The child had now become labeled as different and served as a continuing target for other children.

Although the parents in the Patterson model are more blameworthy than in the temperament example, they too are embedded in transactional contexts with their own parents. In other research (Elder, Caspi, & Downey, 1985; Huesmann, Eron, Lefkowitz, & Walder, 1984), cross-generational effects have been found associated with antisocial child behavior. In two longitudinal studies, the poor disciplinary practices of the grandparents were related to antisocial behavior of the parents and the grandchild. Moreover, the child, parents, and grandparents were embedded in a social context that supported these child-rearing strategies as a means of successfully adapting to a particular level of socioeconomic existence (Kohn, 1969, 1973).

The etiology of depression is another area where transactional processes have been implicated. Cummings and Cicchetti (1990) examined the paths by which insecure attachments during early childhood can be connected to later depression. A direct relation has not been supported by the data because variations in early attachments did not predict depression (Bowlby, 1988). Cummings and Cicchetti propose a model where low internalized feelings of felt security mediate between early insecure attachment and the later development of depressed cognitions and affect.

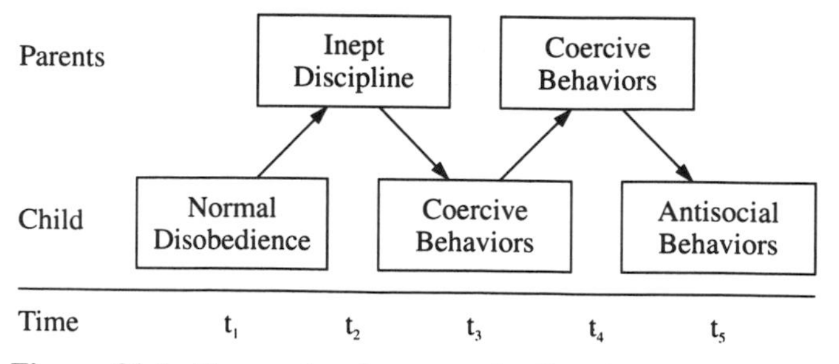

Figure 21.6 Transactional process leading from early child disobedience to later antisocial behavior.

This interpretation is given a life-span perspective in the work of Brown and his collaborators (Brown, Harris, & Bifulco, 1986; Harris, Brown, & Bifulco, 1987). They found that maternal loss led to depression only if mediated by lack of affectionate care. In the presence of an affectionate relationship, there was no connection between maternal loss and depression.

A more complex picture of transactions at many levels is found in the work of Hammen and her colleagues studying the school-age children of depressed mothers. Her basic conclusion, as reflected in the title of the book describing the study, is that depression runs in families (Hammen, 1991). She found support for an intergenerational hypothesis in which psychopathology in the family of origin limits the mother's psychosocial skills such that her children are also symptomatic. Stressful life events were related to the child's outcomes, but depressed mothers seemed to elicit more stress from the environment than other mothers. In this short-term longitudinal study, a number of bidirectional effects were found: The mother contributed to the child's depression, but the child's behavior also contributed to the mother's depression. Hammen (1992) emphasized the effect of the person on the environment as well as the environment on the person. Mother and child were part of each other's environments. The depressed mother and child engaged in a reciprocal process in which they directly impacted each other affecting their availability as a resource to each other for buffering the effects of stress.

The sets of transactions described here are examples of how developmental achievements are rarely sole consequences of immediate antecedents and even more rarely sole consequences of distal antecedents. The causal chain not only is extended over time, and even generations but is also embedded in an interpretive framework. In the birth complication example, the mother's anxiety is based on an interpretation of the meaning of a complicated childbirth, and her avoidance is based on an interpretation of the meaning of the child's irregular feeding and sleeping patterns. To understand why parents behave differently to their infants in the twin examples, it is necessary to understand their interpretive frameworks. In the antisocial behavior example, the extension across time was also across contexts. The relationship expectations the child developed in the home were carried forward into self-fulfilling prophecies as the child moved into the school. The parents in these examples had to rely on their own interpretive schemes for understanding and perhaps distorting the characteristics of their children. In the thalidomide example, another level of influence came into play when the professional community made its contribution to the transactional system. The clinical interpretations of an ambiguous situation placed some children in developmental jeopardy. In a later section, I will describe how more beneficial clinical interventions might be produced (Sameroff & Fiese, 1990).

The transactional model in Figure 21.4 is an improvement over the interactional model in Figure 21.3 by including reciprocal influences between child and environment. However, another step is required to complete the picture of the regulatory forces in development. The continuity implied in the organization of the child's behavior by the series of arrows from C_1 through C_2 and C_3 to C_4 in Figure 21.7 requires a parallel set of arrows indicating continuity in the organization of the environment. Experiences offered to

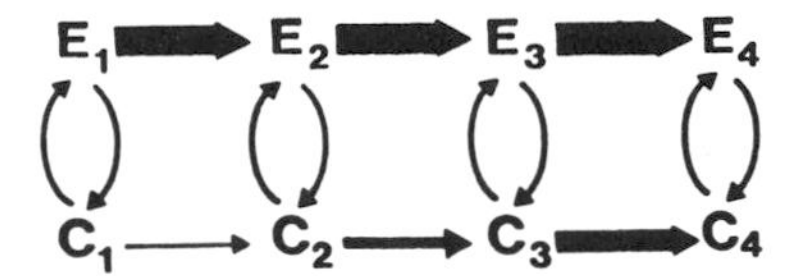

Figure 21.7 Social regulatory model of development.

the child are not random nor are they completely dependent on the eliciting characteristics of the child. There is a continuity in experience that may be highly organized as in some traditional cultures or highly disorganized as in some overburdened families in economically deprived subcultures. The degree of coherence in what has been called the developmental agenda (Sameroff, 1987) is indicated by a series of arrows from E_1 to E_2 to E_3 to E_4 and is a major component of the environtype.

THE ENVIRONTYPE

Just as there is a biological organization, the genotype, that regulates the physical outcome of each individual, there is a social organization that regulates the way human beings fit into their society. This organization operates through family and cultural socialization patterns and has been postulated to compose an "environtype" analogous to the biological genotype (Sameroff, 1985). The importance of identifying the sources of regulation of human development is obvious to investigators interested in developmental psychopathology. There will be different implications if the problem is situated in the child than if it is situated in the family or some interaction between the two. From the transactional perspective, a problem is never located completely in the child or the context, but always in their relationship.

The child's behavior at any point in time is a product of the transactions between the phenotype (the child), the environtype (the source of external experience), and the genotype (the source of biological organization [see Figure 21.8]). This regulatory system is reciprocally determined at each point in development. On the biological side, the genotype in each cell is identical but the particular set of genes that is active at any point is regulated by the state of the phenotype. Depending on the current chemical environment, certain genes are activated that alter the phenotype. The altered phenotype may then act reciprocally to deactivate the original genes and activate another set that will produce further developmental changes in the phenotype. On the environmental side, the environtype contains a range of possible reactions to the child, but the particular regulating experiences that are active at any point are in response to the behavioral status of the child's phenotype. Once the child changes as a consequence of one set of experiences, that set of experiences may be inhibited and another set activated in response to the child's changed status.

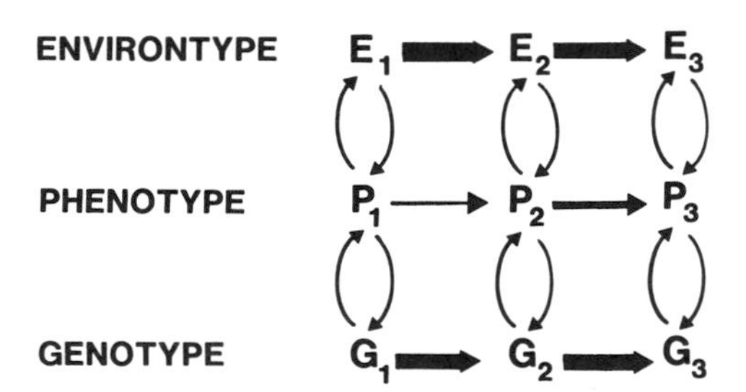

Figure 21.8 Transactional developmental model integrating environmental, genetic, and individual regulating systems.

Traditional research on child development has emphasized the child's utilization of biological capacities to gain experience and the role of experience in shaping child competencies, but there has been far less attention to how that experience is organized. Indeed, the organization of experience is explicit in the great amount of attention given to curriculum development in educational programs, but far less attention is given to the implicit organization of experience found in the family and social context that compose the environtype.

The environtype is composed of subsystems that not only transact with the child but also transact with each other. Bronfenbrenner (1977) has provided the most detailed descriptions of environmental organizations that influence developmental processes within categories of microsystems, mesosystems, exosystems, and macrosystems. The microsystem is the immediate setting of a child in an environment with particular features, activities, and roles (e.g., the home or the school). The mesosystem comprises the relationships between the major settings at a particular point in an individual's development (e.g., between home and school). The exosystem is an extension of the mesosystem and includes settings that the child may not be a part of but that affect the settings in which the child does participate, for example, the parent's world of work. Finally, the macrosystem includes the overarching institutional patterns of the culture including the economic, social, and political systems of which the microsystems, mesosystems, and exosystems are concrete expressions.

Bronfenbrenner (1986) went on to review the research paradigms that studied the influence of the environment on development. These paradigms varied in the detail in which they examined dimensions of external systems. The simplest is the social address model in which family process is not considered at all. Here the focus is on such variables as ethnicity or social status with no attention to the activities within these addresses that could affect the child. More complex are process-context models in which there is an examination of the impact of external environment on particular family processes. Here the more complex focus is on the interaction between context and family variables. As an example, Bronfenbrenner cites studies by Tulkin and his colleagues (Tulkin & Cohler, 1973; Tulkin & Covitz, 1975) in which the pattern of correlations between parenting behavior and child behavior in one social address, middle-class families, were different than in another social address, lower-class families.

At the most complex level were person-process-context models, which add a third term to the predictive equation. Interactions between process and context were studied in interaction with the specific characteristics of the individuals in the family. Crockenberg's (1981) study of the relations among mother's social support, child attachment, and child temperament serves as an example. She found that when the infant had a difficult temperament, there was a stronger relation between social support and secure attachment than when the infant had an easy temperament. Such interactions among variables in the person-process-context model show great similarity to what would be expected from transactional processes.

Bronfenbrenner's (1977) original ecological model provided a perceptive organization for an analysis of syncronic processes, a slice of life that incorporated the multiple contexts that could influence development. He stressed the importance of moving beyond the mother-child relationship to concerns with the effects of other relationships that the child participates in without the parent and that the parent participates in without the child. The mesosystem level of analysis integrated the multiple child contexts of family, school, and peer group. The exosystem analysis integrated the multiple parental contexts of the workplace, social networks, and community influences. To this synchronic approach, Bronfenbrenner (1986) added a diachronic dimension in a chronosystem level of analysis for examining over time the effects of environmental changes on individual development. The necessity for examining the lifelong coherence of environmental influences has become a more common theme in developmentalist thinking. The environtype was proposed as an organizational framework for capturing the quality of this coherence.

Although an endless range of environmental factors is involved in any given developmental ecology, this discussion, for clarity of presentation, will be restricted to levels of environmental factors within the culture, the family, and the individual parent. Developmental regulations at each of these levels can be conceptualized as being carried within codes: a cultural code, a family code, and an individual code for each parent. The developmental consequence of these codes is to produce an adult member of society who can play a role in reproducing society. Regulation during childhood is aimed at cognitive behavior and social-emotional adaptation so that the child ultimately will be able to occupy a role in society. The codes are hierarchically related in their evolution and in their current influence on the child. The experience of the developing child is partially determined by the beliefs, values, and personality of the parents, partially by the family's interaction patterns and transgenerational history, and partially by the socialization beliefs, controls, and supports of the culture.

A distinction must be recognized between codes and behaviors. The environtype is no more a description of the experiential environment than the genotype is a description of the child, but it may be no less. In each case, the code must be actualized through active processes at either the behavioral or biological level. The codes have an organizational and regulatory influence on parental behavior, but the behavior is not the same as the codes. Moreover, developmental goals are not necessarily recognized by all members of society, nor perhaps by any member of a particular society. They are the result of ultimate causes in the evolution of human cultures. If a culture was not successful in producing new adults to carry on roles, it would no longer exist. The proximate causes of why any particular set of parents is engaged in child rearing will have a wide range of variability as well as a wide range of coherence. Some parents have a clear philosophy of child rearing and clear desired goals for their children. For other parents, there is far less reflection on these issues. Reiss (1989) implicitly focused on this contrast in conceptualizing family behavior in terms of representation and practice. The representational level is where the family conceptualizes its behavior, whereas the practicing level is where the behavior actually takes place. This distinction will become clearer in the following discussion of the family code.

The environtype can be conceptualized independently of the child; school systems can describe their curricula, and some parents can describe their child-rearing systems. Expected increases in the abilities of the developing child are major triggers for these regulatory changes, and in most likelihood were major contributors to the evolution of the developmental agenda. In an analysis of developmental transitions, a distinction is generally made between normative transitions (the milestones), and non-normative transitions (accidents, societal changes, and historical events). This distinction is important when examining any individual life course, but for a general exposition the focus will be on normative events.

Although developmental milestones have always been thought to be a property of the child, their significance is much reduced unless there is a triggered regulation from the environtype. Different parents, different families, and different cultures may be sensitive to different behavior of the child as a regulatory trigger (deVries & Sameroff, 1984). For example, in the United States it was not until the major changes in the educational system, stimulated by evidence of advanced Soviet technology (i.e., the first Russian satellite, Sputnik), that newborn intellectual competence (the ability to perceive and learn), became an important milestone. Different cultures define adolescence independently of the pubertal status of the child (Worthman, 1993). In some, adolescence is closely tied to biological changes, in others it precedes or follows these changes, and in some it is independent of these changes.

Most behavioral research on the effects of the environment has been limited to the study of mother-child interaction patterns, which is only one component of the environtype. Parke and Tinsley (1987), in an extensive review of family interaction research, pointed to the important new trend of not only adding father-child interaction to mother-child interaction studies but combining these into studies of triadic interactions and behavioral patterns for the entire family. The behavioral research is slowly overcoming the technological difficulties embodied in analyses of multiple interacting individuals (Gottman, 1979; Sackett, 1978). Another growing empirical base comes from the direction of beliefs rather than behavior (Sigel, McGillicudy-DeLisi, & Goodnow, 1992). Parental belief systems include their child-rearing values as well as understanding of child behavior and the sources of developmental change (Sameroff & Feil, 1983; Kohn, 1969). Investigators have become increasingly articulate at defining the dimensions of parental belief systems (Baumrind, 1971; Darling & Steinberg, 1993) with the ultimate goal of describing the effects of these belief systems on parental behavior and ultimately, on the behavior of the child (Baumrind, 1991).

Cultural Code

The ingredients of the cultural code are the complex of characteristics that organize a society's child-rearing system and that incorporate elements of socialization and education. These processes are embedded in sets of social controls and social supports. They are based on beliefs that differ in the amount of community consensus ranging from mores and norms to fads and fashions. The content of such a cultural code is a core concern of both sociology and anthropology. Human societies vary greatly in the experiences they provide their children (Worthman, 1993). Infancy is a time period when these differences are first apparent in birthing practices (Lozoff, 1983), feeding and sleeping arrangements (Whiting, 1981), and the size of the family unit (Draper, 1976).

Cultural codes have not evolved independently of developmental capacities of the child but they have not been determined by these capacities. Many common biological characteristics of the human species have acted to produce similar developmental agendas in most societies. For example, in most cultures, formal education begins between the ages of 6 and 8 when children generally have acquired the cognitive ability to learn from such structured experiences (Rogoff, 1981). However, there are historical and cross-cultural differences where changes in child behavior are emphasized or ignored. Informal education can begin at many different ages depending on the culture's attributions to the child. Some middle-class parents have been convinced that prenatal experiences will enhance the cognitive development of their children and consequently begin stimulation programs during pregnancy, whereas others believe it best to wait until the first grade before beginning formal learning experiences. Such examples demonstrate the variability of human developmental contexts, and the openness of the regulatory system to modification.

A major contemporary risk condition for children in the United States is having an unmarried adolescent mother. Although for certain young mothers, pregnancy is the outcome of individual factors, for a large proportion it is the result of a cultural code that defines maturity, family relationships, and socialization patterns with adolescent motherhood as a normative ingredient. Teenage childbearing has never been uncommon in the United States (Wattenberg, 1976). In the 1950s, close to half of all women wed in their teens and well over a quarter had their first child before age 20 (Cherlin, 1981). The current concern results from two new trends. The first is that the number of families having children is declining in all age groups except adolescence; and the second is that the number of children born out of wedlock is increasing dramatically in this age group (Furstenberg, Brooks-Gunn, & Morgan, 1987). The reduced rate of marriage overall adds further to the numbers of single adolescent mothers. During the 1950s, there were estimates that 50% of women who married before the age of 20 were pregnant at the time (Cutright, 1972), but these premarital pregnancies were hidden by the consequent marriage. Furstenberg et al. (1987) point out that the current life-course perspective on families attributes the timing of marriage and childbearing to the interplay between personal, social, economic, and cultural beliefs about age-appropriate behavior. In such instances, to focus on the problem as residing wholly at the level of the pregnant individual would seriously undermine attempts to understand such behavior and ultimately to change it.

Adolescence is a developmental stage that is a clear example of how cultural codes produce a variety of meanings and behaviors as different developmental agendas are played out. Although biologists can define adolescence in terms of the maturation of the reproductive system and its hormonal changes, few cultures are so medically minded. Among these are the Kikuyu for whom the adolescent transition, marked by circumcision for boys and clitoridectomy for girls, was closely tied to the maturational appearance of the children as evidenced by the status of their sexual characteristics. Worthman (1993) describes the variability in cultural definitions that ranges from the nonexistent to the highly elaborated and prolonged. In the latter category are the Maasai who transitioned a cohort of children into adolescence every seven years. Thus the range of ages was from 7 to 14 at the start and 14 to 21 at the end. In Western culture, adolescence as a stage was not recognized until the 1800s (Aries, 1962) and continued to evolve through the middle of the 20th century. There has been a dramatic change in the social responsibilities of the 14- to 18-year age cohort over the past century in the United States (Elder, 1980). Where a century ago, nearly all these children were working, now nearly all these children are in school.

Family Code

Just as cultural codes regulate the fit between individuals and the social system, family codes organize individuals within the family system. Family codes provide a source of regulation allowing a group of individuals to form a collective unit in relation to society as a whole. As the cultural code regulates development so that an individual may fill a role in society, family codes regulate development to produce members that fulfill a role within the family and ultimately are able to introduce new members into the shared system. Traditionally, new members are incorporated through birth and marriage, although more recently, remarriage has taken on a more frequent role in providing new family members.

Over the past 20 years, a great deal of effort has been directed toward identifying patterns of parent-child interaction that may contribute to child outcome. Although issues of cause and effect have been addressed through sophisticated mathematical methodologies such as sequential analyses (e.g., Bakeman & Gottman, 1986; Sackett,1979) and structural equation modeling (e.g., Bentler, 1987; Patterson, 1986), direct influences rarely account for a large proportion of the variance related to child outcome. A consistent finding has been that global aspects of the environment such as socioeconomic status regularly account for some of the variance (e.g., Sameroff, Seifer, Barocas, Zax, & Greenspan, 1987) and microanalytic factors such as interaction patterns also account for some of the variance (e.g., Field, 1987). Intermediary between the cultural influences and individual interaction patterns are a series of factors that make up the family code.

The family regulates the child's development through a variety of processes that vary in their degree of explicit representation and conduct. Families have rituals that prescribe roles and dictate conduct within family settings, stories that transmit orientations and accounts to each family member as well as to whoever will listen, shared myths that influence individual interactions and exaggerate aspects of family stories, and paradigms that change individual behavior when in the presence of other family members. Reiss (1989) has contrasted the degree to which these processes are articulated and readily recounted by individual members with the degree to which each family member's behavior is regulated by a common practice evident only when the family members are together. Whereas family rituals may be recounted by each family member, family paradigms are constructed through group processes. The most represented regulations are exemplified by family rituals and the least by family paradigms. Stories and myths provide regulatory functions intermediate to rituals and paradigms. Issues that will have importance for developmental psychopathology are how these forms are transmitted behaviorally among family members and how they are represented in cognition.

Rituals

Family rituals are the most self-aware aspects of the family code (Bossard & Boll, 1950). Family rituals may range from highly stylized religious observances such as first communion or bar mitzvahs to less articulated daily interaction patterns such as the type of greeting made when someone returns home. Rituals mark the beginning and end of life within a family but also regulate behavior on a daily basis. Families can easily identify ritual practices they hold as well as describe the routines they perform on a daily, weekly, or annual basis (Fiese & Kline, 1993; Wolin, Bennett, & Jacobs, 1988). Rituals are practiced by the whole family and are frequently documented. They may be times for taking photographs, exchanging gifts, or preserving mementos. Family rituals include symbolic information as well as important preparatory phases, schedules, and plans. Rituals serve a regulatory function by assigning roles and providing meaning to family interactions.

Rituals of early childhood can be extrapolated from research on children's stories. Hudson and Nelson (1983) have demonstrated that preschool and first-grade children recall stories about birthday parties prior to recalling stories about routine events such as baking cookies. There is a high degree of saliency to rituals that facilitate participation by children, and encoding of family structure. The child's participation in family rituals may be facilitated by the child's own creation of rituals that regulate other family members. Bedtime and mealtime rituals frequently occur during early childhood. As families develop, their use of ritual also may develop. Fiese, Hooker, Kotary, and Schwager (1993) found that as the age of children advanced out of infancy, the number of family centered rituals increased. The age changes in the use of family rituals directly reflects the developmental aspects of the family code.

The role of family rituals in regulating dysfunctional behavior has been most clearly demonstrated in families of alcoholics. In a study of married children of alcoholic parents, certain aspects of family rituals were identified as protective factors that guarded against the children becoming alcoholics (Wolin, Bennett, & Jacobs, 1988). Children who came from families that were able to preserve family rituals, such as distinctive dinner and holiday routines, were less likely to become alcoholics themselves. Wolin and his colleagues speculate that rituals provide stability for dysfunctional families.

Fiese and Kline (1993) found that the level of ritualization in the family was related to the child's feelings of security and belongingness. More specifically, the symbolic and affective qualities associated with family rituals were positively related to adolescent attachment to the family. Fiese (1992) identified two distinct dimensions of family rituals: a meaning factor and a routine factor. The meaning factor included dimensions of regular occurrence, required attendance, symbolic significance, affective involvement, and deliberateness. The routine factor included dimensions of specific roles and detailed routines. The two factors were differentially related to measures of child outcome. The meaning factor was negatively related to a measure of anxiety and positively related to self-esteem, but the routine factor was not significantly related to either.

The distinction between meaning and routine was given further importance in a follow-up study of the intergenerational transmission of alcoholism. In accord with the findings of Wolin and Bennett (Bennett, Wolin, Reiss, & Teitelbaum, 1987; Wolin et al., 1988) who had sampled self-identified children of alcoholics, children of alcoholics who reported low levels of family ritual meaning had significantly higher anxiety scores than children of alcoholics who reported high meaning levels or children of nonalcoholic families regardless of family ritual meaning level (Fiese, 1992).

Family rituals may contribute to the family code by providing significance to patterned interactions. Although it is probable that a certain amount of routine and regularity would have to exist for rituals to have a powerful influence, it is apparently the meaning associated with family rituals that is significantly related to child outcome. Sociologists have pointed out that when cultures create rituals, the symbolic quality of patterned interactions transforms a routine into a ritual (Moore & Myerhoff, 1977). For the family, it may be the meaning associated with routine interactions that transforms momentary interactions into central features of family process and organization.

Stories

Stories provide a second form for family regulations. Reiss (1989) notes that although stories have long been of interest to developmental and cognitive scientists as a tool for understanding cognitive development, there is little systematic work on the importance of stories that families tell about themselves.

In a study of family folklore, Zeitlin, Kotkin, and Baker (1982) collected large numbers of family stories. From their analysis they proposed three broad functions for such stories: (a) to highlight conspicuous heroes or rogues in the family's history, (b) to dramatize and conserve significant family transitions and stressful events, and (c) to enshrine and preserve certain family customs. Thus stories are seen as having a stabilizing effect by preserving important events and passing on a value system to the next generation (Reiss, 1989).

There is a strong developmental component to family stories. As a source of regulation, the practice of telling stories is a major feature of early relationships between young children and other family members. Ratner and Bruner (1977) proposed that this early storytelling provides a framework for the learning of conversational turn-taking and facilitates language development. During these early years, the child engages in storytelling by being a story-listener and will often encourage others to tell or read a story.

If family stories provide a format for imparting lessons and values, then it would be reasonable to predict that different themes would predominate according to social and developmental context. Fiese (1990) found that mothers of 8- to 12-year-old boys told stories of their childhood that included themes of overcoming obstacles and facing adversity. These themes were not evident in the stories told to toddlers. From this dynamic perspective, family stories are adjusted to meet the agenda of the family. Although family stories may provide a link across generations, the connection is paired with the demands of the contemporary family.

Children are increasingly able to recall specific aspects of stories. Nelson and her colleagues found a developmental progression in the recall of stories. Preschool children readily talk about their experiential knowledge in scriptlike form, and these scripts affect the way in which children interpret and remember stories and everyday events (Nelson, 1981; Nelson & Gruendel, 1981). Children are receptive to hearing stories and organizing experiences along story lines, which provides parents with the opportunity to pass down values through their storytelling.

Myths

A third source of regulation within the family code is family myths. Family myths are beliefs that go unchallenged in spite of reality. Myths may have a traumatic origin and frequently have a strong affective component (Kramer, 1985). Family myths are not open for discussion, nor are they readily recognized as distortions (Ferreira, 1963).

Some family myths help to regulate role definitions. For example, a traditional family may consider women as unable to handle professional responsibilities of the work world even though they balance the family checkbook and organize a busy household. Subtle aspects of a particular role may become inflated and incorporated into the myth. For example, parents of a physically disabled child may believe that the child also is cognitively disabled despite examples of the child's intelligent behavior. A myth develops that casts the child in a "handicapped" role encompassing behaviors outside of physical limitations. In the same context, another family may create a myth that their mentally retarded child is unimpaired because of a bright-eyed look (Pollner & McDonald-Wikler, 1985; Roskies, 1972).

Family myths frequently provide a sense of continuity across generations. Individual family members carry with them their own beliefs and interpretations of their family of origin experiences and family heritage. Wamboldt and his colleagues (Wamboldt & Reiss, 1989; Wamboldt & Wolin, 1989) have proposed that family myths influence mate selection and marital satisfaction and may even be changed through the marriage. They found that when new couples are faced with the task of defining for themselves what their newly created family will be like, they include beliefs about their parent's marital relationship. However, it is possible for an individual to be "rescued" from a family of origin myth by pairing with another individual with a healthier background and deliberately changing that myth (Bennett et al., 1987).

Developmental problems can arise when the child must accept a distorted family myth to be congruent with the family or when the family imposes an inflated role on the child by creating a new myth. In the first instance, sexually abused children or witnesses to parental abuse may adapt their behavior to fit within the family structure (Belsky, 1980). In the second instance, a handicapped child may be treated as the youngest sibling despite birth order or chronological age (Sigel, 1985).

Paradigms

Family paradigms are a fourth form of family regulations. Reiss and his colleagues (Reiss, 1981; Reiss, Oliveri, & Curd, 1983) have described how families develop paradigms including a set of core assumptions, convictions, or beliefs that each family holds about its environment. The evidence that paradigms operate at the family level is that in the same problem-solving situations members will engage in different problem-solving strategies if they are with other members of their family than when they are alone. Reiss et al. (1983) argue that these paradigms generally persist for years, and even generations, and are manifested "in the fleeting fantasies and expectations by all members of the family and, even more important, in the routine action patterns of daily life" (p. 20). Based on empirically derived dimensions of configuration, coordination, and closure, these investigators have identified a four-category typology of paradigms including environment-sensitive, consensus-sensitive, achievement-sensitive, and distance-sensitive families. Environment-sensitive and consensus-sensitive families both are highly cohesive and cooperative internally, but they differ in how they understand and respond to stress. Environment-sensitive families believe the world is understandable and problems are solvable, whereas the consensus-sensitive ones believe the world operates by unknowable random laws and they become self-protective in response to stress. In achievement-sensitive and distance-sensitive families, the members are in competition with each other. Where they differ is that the achievement-sensitive family members seek alliances outside the family to support their roles, whereas distance-sensitive family members cannot relate to anyone, in or out of the family group.

Paradigms appear to be the form of family regulation that is the least articulated in awareness although they can be expressed in family stories and myths. The importance of family paradigms for prevention efforts is that, although they have been identified only in the course of family problem-solving tasks, they are manifested in the relationships that family members, including children, form with other individuals and groups. Thus, the normal or disturbed behavior of children must to some degree be interpreted as an outgrowth of the family paradigm (Reiss et al., 1983).

Current research on the effects of family factors on child development has emphasized observed interactions among family members—whether there are conflicted or harmonious relationships among family members. The family code is a domain of family functioning that organizes such behaviors and is only now being explored. A recognized risk condition for children is the effect of marital discord and divorce that produces behavioral problems in response to the family conflict or the absence of a parent (Wallerstein & Kelly, 1980). Studying the family code is important for understanding these problems because divorce involves a process of code disorganization and reorganization (Hetherington & Camara, 1984). As old members are less influential and new members are introduced through remarriage, existing family codes are altered. Hetherington (1991) found major differences in roles given to and assumed by stepfathers as compared with fathers, and to stepmothers as compared with mothers. To focus entirely on the individual child's reaction to the absence of a parent would ignore broader changes in the family context. To focus entirely on a parent's reaction to the child ignores the constraints that have been placed on the behavior of both by the family rituals, stories, myths, and paradigms.

Individual Code of the Parent

There is clear evidence that parental behavior is influenced by the family and social context. When operating as part of a family, the behavior of each member is altered (Parke & Tinsley, 1987), frequently without awareness of the behavioral change (Reiss, 1981). However, individuals undoubtedly bring their own contribution to family interactions. Because multiple levels compose parents' behavior, their contribution is determined much more complexly than that of young children.

In the Rochester Longitudinal Study, a cluster of variables labeled parental perspectives was examined across a 9-year span (Sameroff, Siefer, Baldwin, & Baldwin, 1993). Mothers completed a cluster of three scales, the Sameroff & Feil (1985) Concepts of Development Questionnaire, the Kohn (1969) parental values scale, and the Schaefer and Bell (1958) Parent Attitude Research Instrument when the children in the study were 4 years old and again when they were 13 years old. It might seem there would be a great deal of plasticity in parent attitudes, beliefs and values across the 9-year intervening period. In fact, there was not. When the 4- and 13-year measures were intercorrelated, the coefficients were in the 60s, all highly significant.

The stability of risk factors like low occupational and educational level, the things people do with their lives, is not terribly surprising. However, the stability of beliefs and values, the things people think about, is surprising. Both kinds of stability emphasize the importance of assessments of context as major regulators of how parents deal with children. It is important to recognize the parent as a major regulating agency, but it is equally important to recognize that parental behavior is itself embedded in social and family regulatory contexts (Goodnow, 1988). The richness of both health and pathology embodied in these parental responses is well described in the clinical literature. In terms of early development, Fraiberg and her colleagues (Fraiberg, Adelson, & Shapiro, 1980) have provided many descriptions of the attributions that parents bring to their parenting. These "ghosts" of unresolved childhood conflicts have been shown to have significant influences on current parental behavior.

The individualized interpretations that parenting figures impose on social and family practice are to a large extent conditioned by each parent's past participation in his or her own family's coded interactions, but they are captured uniquely by each member of the family. These individual influences further condition each parent's responses to his or her own child. Main and Goldwyn (1984) identified adult attachment categories that reflect parents' encoding of their interpretation of their attachment to their own parents. The resulting three major categories—secure/autonomous, insecure/dismissing, and insecure/preoccupied—were analogous to attachment categories that are used to characterize infant relationship behavior. What is compelling about these adult attachment categories is that they operate across generations and are predictive of the attachment categories of the infants of these parents (van IJnezdoorn, 1992). In fact, the maternal verbal descriptions of their attachment models have been better predictors of infant behavior than their actual interactive behavior with the child (Seifer, Schiller, Sameroff, Resnick, & Riordan, 1993).

Environtype as a System

The description of the environtype has emphasized a hierarchy of levels in the context of the child that has important regulatory functions on developmental outcomes. The manner in which the environtype operates is analogous to the operation of the genotype in its regulation of the biological development of the child. An organismic metaphor has been described that embodies many properties of developing systems. A further level of abstraction to describe the operation of living systems is embodied in General Systems Theory. Within the general systems framework can be found specific principles that may help to organize both the understanding and treatment of childhood behavioral disorders.

GENERAL SYSTEMS THEORY

Systems thinking, in general, is different from general systems thinking, in specific. Systems thinking alone is vaguely restricted to the proverbial idea that everything is connected to everything else. General systems theory refers to a specific category of formulations about *how* everything is connected to everything else. The general version seeks properties that can be described independently of the concrete data of individual disciplines. It has been described as lying midway between "the specific that has no meaning and the general that has no content (Boulding, 1956)." The goal of developmental theorists is to produce a systems theory that would be useful in interpreting past products of developmental research and organizing fruitful future efforts.

A discussion of general systems approaches to behavioral development can be viewed from two perspectives attributable to Boulding (1956). The first approach is to seek processes in development that are analogous to those in other disciplines. For example, in almost all disciplines there are populations of elements to which new ones are added or born and old ones are subtracted or die. Moreover, these elements exchange information or energy with each other and with an environment. The second approach is to include the development of behavior in a hierarchy of complexity with the developmental concerns of all other scientific disciplines. For example, psychological processes are composed of biological processes and compose social processes. One could combine these two perspectives by creating a general systems theory of development that is hierarchically organized and has each level operating on the same set of general principles. Such efforts have been elaborated by Werner (1957) and Piaget (1971).

Although there are a large number of general systems theories incorporating a multitude of levels and processes (Miller, 1978), five principles can capture the core issues in such perspectives

(Laszlo, 1972; Sameroff, 1983): wholeness and order, self-stabilization, self-reorganization, hierarchic interaction, and dialectical contradiction. In turn each of these general systems principles will have specific analogues in theories of development and psychopathology (see Table 21.1). Wholeness and order provide the basis for continuity and identity; self-stabilization for development; self-organization for evolution; hierarchical interaction for discontinuity; and dialectical contradiction for motivation.

Wholeness and Order

The reason that wholes are more than the sum of their parts is that relationships are added that can never be assigned to single elements. This antireductionistic principle is characterized by a favorite example of the Gestaltists, the melody. A melody can be composed of different sets of tones yet still retain its identity if a certain relationship among the parts is unchanged. More complex examples can be found in arbitrary systems that have been organized through evolution at the biological level, such as the genetic code, or at the psychosocial level, such as language. All living proteins result from combinations of 20 permutations of 4 biochemical bases. There is no intrinsic explanation why each one of the orderings of chemical bases on the DNA molecule encodes a specific amino acid. The origin of the genetic code was a probabilistic outcome of evolutionary processes which with other probabilities could have produced other codes for the same amino acids or other codes for other amino acids. Similarly, there is no intrinsic explanation why a specific ordering of sounds encodes a specific meaning in a language. The existence of a wide array of languages that can express the same meanings with very different words demonstrates both the arbitrariness of the origins of part-whole relationships, and the specificity of their contemporary interactions. Wholes and their parts create a system with dual constraints, neither will have continuity and identity without the other. Language would not exist without sound or other units to which meaning can be attached, and units of sound would not cohere without a semantic system that relates those meanings.

The contrary position has been that of the reductionists, who see no problem in attempting to explain the complexity of functioning found at higher levels by using principles derived from lower levels. In other words, there are no properties of collections of individuals that cannot be explained by the properties of the individuals analyzed apart from the collection. In an attempt to clarify the relationships between fundamental laws and the various fields of knowledge, P. M. Anderson (1972), a physicist, has subdivided reductionism into legitimate and illegitimate reductionism. He argues that the ability to reduce everything to simple fundamental laws does not imply the ability to start from those laws and reconstruct the universe. He sees reductionism as legitimate if it is restricted to the hypothesis that the functioning of higher levels of complexity is based on and cannot violate the laws of functioning of lower levels of complexity. Biological functioning cannot violate the laws of chemistry and physics that constrain the activity of an organism's constituent atoms and molecules. On the other hand, Anderson regards as illegitimate the "constructionist" use of reductionism, which attempts to argue that higher levels of complexity can be explained by the principles of the lower levels. The laws of chemistry and physics do not explain biological functioning even though such functioning cannot violate these laws. Similarly, the laws of biology do not explain psychological and social functioning even though these laws cannot be violated.

There is a certain irony in current debate on reductionism. The physicists, who have traditionally held the role of fundamentalists through their study of the basic units of the universe, have begun to turn more and more to metaphysical speculations (Gal-Or, 1972; Soodak, & Iberall, 1978). Physicists are facing an uncomfortable fact: Whenever someone seems to discover the ultimate building blocks of nature, be they molecular, nuclear, or subnuclear, someone else discovers a more fundamental unit (Perkins, 1987). Even more interesting are the names, such as truth and beauty, chosen to designate the latest ultimate particles—quarks. These labels reflect abstract process or system properties rather than any concrete characteristic of the particles. Moreover, quarks cannot exist in isolation, there must be at least two together. In other words at the most fundamental level of the universe there are no ultimate units, only ultimate relationships.

The traditional view of the relationship among the sciences has been that they represent a pyramid with physics providing the material base and the social sciences nebulously surmounting the summit. A more recent view is still of a pyramid, but one hanging in space, where the emergence of softer areas of science at the tip is matched by the dissolution of the harder areas at the bottom as each purported ultimate particle gives way to the next newly discovered ultimate particle. But most important, physicists have come to see that what appears as material, in reality, represents an organization in time and space of some underlying dynamic process. Nothing that can be defined as a thing-in-itself has been found to exist. In each case, dynamic processes give rise to the unit's appearance and continued existence.

Trefil (1980) after reviewing the history of the search for simplicity in physics feels that "the dream of explaining the entire physical world in terms of a few basic building blocks does not look realizable" (p. 208). Instead, the explanation may involve something that sounds similar to a general systems theory:

> The road that led us to quarks started with the assumption that nature was simple in the sense that it could be understood in terms of a few simple constituents. We could call this a search for structural simplicity. We can imagine another kind of simplicity, however. We can imagine a world in which we understand processes in terms of a few general principles. The simplicity here would be of an abstract

TABLE 21.1 Theoretical Principles of Development

General Systems	*Developmental Systems*
Wholeness and order	Continuity and identity
Self-stabilization	Development
Self-organization	Evolution
Hierarchical interaction	Discontinuity
Dialectical contradiction	Motivation

> and purely intellectual nature. . . . In practice, the search for intellectual simplicity has been concerned not so much with the structure of particles as with their interactions. Thus, instead of concentrating on the search for quarks, the theorist would concern himself with studying the fundamental interactions between elementary particles. (p. 208)

The emphasis of the new physics is on interactions rather than objects. The ultimates will not be found in products, but rather in processes. In short, scientists at every level of complexity now have difficulty clearly defining the essential parts of their science. At the atomic level, physicists no longer consider the solar system view of the atom with its electrons spinning around a nucleus core. Instead, there is the connection of a series of fields within which are embedded particlelike concentrations of energy and spin. The atom is currently conceived as functionally interacting nuclear and electronic fields rather than as mechanically interacting parts, the older notion (Anderson, 1972). At the biological level, wholeness and order are found to characterize all systems. Modern definitions of any biological element or structure interpret these as only visible indexes of regularities of the underlying dynamics operating in their domains (Weiss, 1969). In other words, static entities are illusions: At the core, everything is process.

The developmental analogue of wholeness and order is continuity and identity. As in the organismic metaphor of the cell, continuity is in the relationship of the parts rather than in their specificity. The parts of the body are in constant transformation as nutrients flow in and excretions flow out. At the psychological level, the organizational view of attachment is an example where the specific behaviors may change while the representation may remain the same (Sroufe & Waters, 1977). A family is defined independently of the specific actors, although this definition is itself in flux with the evolution of serial parenting in multimarriage families.

Self-Stabilization

Dynamic systems respond to contextual perturbations either by homeostatic or homeorhetic feedback processes. Systems have a set point (e.g., the setting of a thermostat) that they maintain by altering internal conditions to compensate for changes in external conditions. Human thermoregulation is an example of a homeostatic process that is organized biologically but can be facilitated by behavioral processes (e.g., putting on a coat or turning on the air conditioner). Egocentrism, perceptual constancy, and the use of attributions are examples of psychological homeostatic processes used to reinterpret environmental perturbations as congruent with existing mental organization.

For developmental systems, homeorhesis (Waddington, 1962) is a more important self-stabilizing process than the better known process of homeostasis. In homeorhesis, the system stabilizes around a trajectory rather than a set point. Physical growth is such a trajectory. There is an organized time course over which growth accelerates and decelerates until adulthood. If there is a deviation, the system does not return to the state at the point of deviation but to the point on the trajectory where the system would be if the deviation had not occurred. Underweight preterm infants are not permanently stunted because for these infants the time course is accelerated to provide a catch-up opportunity so that the child achieves normal physical development by the end of the second year. Swaddled infants who show motor lags when initially unwrapped, soon show normal age-appropriate locomotion skills no different from unswaddled infants. These examples of homeorhetic processes appear as self-righting tendencies.

What we observe as development is a product of self-stabilization. An active organism, subject to an ordered series of perturbations, will respond with an ordered series of adaptations. Most attention has been devoted to internal sources of perturbations, usually labeled as maturation. As the genotype regulates biological changes in the body, there is a continuous process of adaptation while each change is assimilated into the system's functioning. The genetic timetable of activity is stimulated in a transactional process by resulting changes in the body's physiology and anatomy.

Far less attention has been paid to the ordered series of external perturbations in the environtype that also serve to organize and regulate development. As described earlier, the environtype includes a developmental agenda for raising children in which graded changes in the child trigger changes in the environment and graded changes in the environment change the child. Some of these triggers are age graded and tied to specific points in time. At 3 years of age, for example, many children are placed in new physical environments: nursery schools, with new socializing agents (i.e., teachers) and a new peer group. Other graded changes are tied by different cultures to different developmental milestones (e.g., walking, talking, or puberty). The individual's adaptation to these sets of previously organized internal and external perturbations is what we label as development. The previous organization is the product of prior evolutionary processes at both the biological and social level. In contrast, evolution itself is a response to stable but less organized perturbations.

Self-Organization

Self-stabilization occurs within a range of environmental variation but new processes are required when the experience moves outside that range. Adaptive self-organization occurs when the system encounters new constants in the environment that cannot be balanced by existing system mechanisms. Adaptation is defined as a change that permits the system to maintain its set points best in new circumstances. Biological evolution is the best example of adaptive self-organization. The new adaptation is reflected in the stabilization of changed biological functioning, often in the form of a new species. Adaptation as in evolution frequently has the connotation of progress, but such teleology is foreign to general systems thinking. A misreading of the theory of evolution gave rise to the idea that psychological development is toward some better state of existence (Kessen, 1987) rather than to a state of better adaptation. The modern synthesis in the theory of evolution (Mayr, 1970) defines it as a probabilistic process rather than a deterministic one. Evolution results from changes in distributions of genetic material in a population produced by changes in individual reproductive success as a consequence of changed environmental conditions. If the environment turns cold from a period of glaciation, a newly stabilized contextual perturbation, individuals within a species or species within the ecosystem that are better able to stay warm will have greater reproductive success. Their increased reproductive success will change the distribution of individuals in the next generation, the modern synthesis in action.

The course of evolution is frequently represented as a tree diagram with a trunk of single-cell organisms subdividing to produce many branches that represent the currently existing species on earth. What is too often forgotten is that there is a similar tree diagram of environments in which the trunk of primordial magma cools to branch into water and land masses that further branch into areas of forest and plain containing continuously changing varieties of flora and fauna. This evolution of environments is part and parcel of the evolution of species; each species is in a continuous adaptive relation to the development of the other (Foerster, 1966). Fish could not leave the water until there was land to go to, primates could not climb into the trees until there were trees to live in.

Piaget's (1971) concept of adaptation is a psychological example of this process expressed through assimilation and accommodation. To the extent that the system cannot assimilate the new environmental conditions with existing regulatory subsystems, accommodation must occur in the form of new subsystems derived either from new relations between existing subsystems or by the establishment of a higher order subsystem with new functions. The Piagetian example is better suited to homeorhetic self stabilization than to evolutionary reorganization because human cognitive development is well buffered by both biological and educational constraints. On the other hand, there was a period in human evolution when environmental change provided the opportunities for the advances in cognition that led to modern human abstract thinking abilities. Such processes may still be active as indicated by data that abstract intelligence scores have risen dramatically in the last generation in a wide variety of countries around the world (Flynn, 1984, 1987).

To understand the future of human evolution we must consider social factors, not biological factors, as the major motivating force. The evolution of the environtype, the familial and social external regulator of development, has progressed at a much faster rate than the evolution of the genotype, the internal biological developmental regulator. E. O. Wilson (1975) described human society as autocatalytic. Fueled by positive feedback from its own social products, the evolution of the human species began to operate independently of the typical environmental constraints that influenced the evolutionary progressions of all other species. Such changes can be still found in recent times in socially determined modifications of women's roles and in the changing organization of the family.

Hierarchical Interactions

From the perspective of general systems theory, a system that has the first three principles—wholeness and order, self-stabilization, and self-reorganization—will change in the direction of hierarchical structuration (Laszlo, 1972). Simon (1973) put it more succinctly: "Nature loves hierarchies." He hypothesized that systems based on hierarchies are much more stable in evolution because a failure in organization will not destroy the whole system but only decompose it down to the next level of stable subsystems. Material hierarchies run from subatomic particles through people and nations to the universe. Cognitive hierarchies run from sensorimotor schemata through logical systems to social institutions.

An important aspect of hierarchical organization in natural systems is that systems at each level do not have unidirectional control functions over those of lower levels. There is a dual control (Polanyi, 1968) that is constrained by both the nature of the parts and the nature of the whole. The higher levels set boundary conditions for the subsystems, but they do not determine the activity of the subsystems. Polanyi sees these boundary conditions as extraneous to the processes they delimit. Boundary conditions set by higher-order systems harness the properties of the lower systems but cannot violate these properties.

A behavioral example of such hierarchical organization is language. Polanyi analyzes five levels of a hierarchy necessary to produce a spoken literary composition in terms of dual control. Each of the five levels—voice production, word utterance, sentence construction, style organization, and text composition—must conform to the laws that apply to the elements themselves as well as the laws of the higher level entity formed by the elements. Words are based on the rules of sound production, but the rules of sound production do not determine what words will be formed. Sentences are composed of words, but the meanings of words do not determine which sentences will be constructed. A vocabulary cannot be derived from phonetics nor can grammar be derived from a vocabulary. The correct use of grammar does not necessarily produce a good style nor does style produce content, except perhaps in certain rhetorical contexts like politics.

Within principles of hierarchical interaction, I have been able to find the most satisfying account of developmental discontinuities. The empirical judgment that a discontinuity has occurred in development is typically based on a lack of correlation between assessments at two points in time. The usual interpretation is that the individual got better or worse. Wohlwill (1973) pointed out that most such low correlations were explained by assessments that measured different kinds of functioning at the two points in time. Just because tests given to a 3-year-old and a 12-year-old are both DSM or ICD diagnostic schemes or well-normed intelligence tests does not mean that psychopathology or intelligence at the two ages consist of the same dimensions or functions. Although both children may have attained an IQ score of 100, the items they passed are very different. Moreover, a 12-year-old with an IQ of 80 knows a lot more than a 3-year-old with an IQ of 120.

A genuine discontinuity occurs when a new level of functioning is involved, or when a previously excluded element now is able to participate in a system. Children who are dyslexic and fail exams because they cannot write may show a radical discontinuity after learning to type, overcoming their expressive problems. Paraplegics who are given wheelchairs and the hearing impaired who are given hearing aids can participate in activities that were previously unavailable.

Although it may be true that any living system is an interconnected network with many components contributing to any observed activity, the relationship between a whole and its parts is one of abstraction. Tests are designed to filter an individual's behavior and produce a score. The score is then considered a description of the individual. The whole abstracts some aspect of its parts as a criterion for system membership. These aspects are what Pattee (1973) labeled alternative descriptions. Such abstracting properties of hierarchies are a common characteristic of perceptual and cognitive systems. The categorization of color is such an example. In spite of the continuous distribution of light wave frequencies, cultures cut the spectrum into color categories with different names.

In a hierarchy, superordinate levels, the whole, only utilize some properties (i.e., alternative descriptions) of the subordinate level, the part. A physiological example can be found in the hierarchical relationships of the body. The circulatory system includes the heart, which is composed of tissues that are composed of cells. A complete description of the heart would require a description of each tissue and cell part. From the perspective of the circulatory system, however, the significant alternative description of the heart includes only its pumping property. Many tissue and cell properties contribute to this functioning but these are irrelevant from the circulatory system's perspective. In fact, the heart can be replaced in the system by someone else's, or even a machine without any tissues or cells, as long as the pumping function is carried out. Alternative descriptions of the machine might include its rust resistance or hardness, but the significant feature for the circulatory system is solely its pumping ability.

The Piagetian theory of cognitive development is a sequence of such abstractions in which the content of experience is depreciated relative to some abstracted formal properties as the individual goes further and further in intellectual development. To demonstrate that liquid quantity can be conserved, the child must ignore the different appearances of the liquid in two glasses and infer an underlying logical reality that makes them the same. Yet, at the perceptually based peroperational level, the liquids *are* different.

All reality is organic in that it varies with the constant activity of its components, but in the realm of contemplation, mechanical categorization must intrude. This philosophical point about cognition is equally true for biology, chemistry, and physics. The genetic code is interpreted categorically even though the electrical potentials that characterized the atoms in the DNA molecules are in constant flux. Bonner (1973) describes the relationships among hierarchical levels in embryology as a series of developmental tests. Levels of the hierarchy act in an all-or-none fashion (an abstraction), to certain chemical regulators, even though the regulators are always present in some quantity. These biological systems have triggerlike mechanisms that go to a second state if the amount of regulator is above a threshold and remain in the current state if the amount is below the threshold.

Psychiatric diagnosis falls into the same category of hierarchical abstraction. Symptom dimensions have some continuous distribution in the patient but if they cross a threshold designated in the nosological scheme, the patient is judged to have the disorder where below the threshold he or she is not. Depression that lasts one week is not diagnostic but if it lasts two weeks, it is (American Psychiatric Association, 1994). Similarly, three additional symptoms of the disorder are not diagnostic but four may be. Patients may have many other personality characteristics that are relevant for the course of their disorder but for the purpose of psychiatic diagnosis only one set of alternative descriptions are relevant.

Discontinuity is found when alternative descriptions are important in different social contexts or different developmental periods. Much is made of the lack of correlation between developmental assessments during the first year of life and later intelligence scores. The ability to walk is an important developmental marker in the first 2 years of life, but has little relevance to later intellectual functioning unless it prevents a child from going to school. There may be continuity at the subsystem level (a motorically handicapped infant may still be a motorically impaired adult) but not necessarily at the superordinate level (the motorically handicapped adult can become a lawyer or a parent). In a similar vein, an individual who is effective intellectually may be incompetent socially, the proverbial nerd, because these different capabilities are alternative descriptions of the same individual from the perspective of different social groupings.

Developmental agendas provide alternative descriptions of children as they grow and exhibit new capacities for behavior. Physical development may produce a new description moving from infant to child to adult. The transactional changes in parents' attributions described earlier all fall into this category of alternative descriptions within a hierarchical organization.

Dialectical Contradiction

The last principle to be discussed is the motivational force in behavioral change. Self-stabilization and self-organization are reactions to environmental changes. Many of these perturbations, especially in development, are not random events. They are the result of the system's own activity. The basic premise of all constructivist theories of development is that individuals come to know the world through their own activity. It is through action that knowledge and development emerge. The contradiction is that by acting on the world, the individual is constantly changing it, so that the act of knowing is already changing what the person is trying to know. This transactional principle has had many names over the years, but its most general formulation has been in theories of the dialectic.

The dialectic was conceived by the Greeks as the process by which truth emerges through the intellectual conflict of several protagonists. Hegel (1807/1910) formulated a more psychological version of dialectics in which truth emerges through the interaction of subject and object. Prior to Hegel, these two had been separated by Kant, who described the knowing subject as having innate categories of mind and the object as having unknowable real properties. In contrast, Hegel believed that the categories of mind emerged from the experience with objects, and the properties of objects emerged through the application of mind. Subject and object endow existence on each other. Without objects that differ on a conceptual dimension, the mind does not develop categories. Without a subject to separate the objects on the basis of those categories, the objects do not exist. Development for Hegel is a unified system in which subject and object cannot be separated.

Compare Hegel's philosophical understanding of the developmental relationship between subject and object and the biological relationships between organism and environment discussed earlier. An organism cannot exist separated from its environment, and an environment cannot exist separated from the perspective of an organism. Further, the developmental differentiation and integration of both organism and environment are the result of their exchanges, the organism changing the environment through its activity and the environment changing the organism through its selective opportunities.

Levins and Lewontin (1985) push the dialectic to the ontological position that everything is in a state of contradiction. Every fundamental element that the physical sciences have discovered is eventually found to be composed of heterogeneous opposing forces, from the negative and positive subparticles that characterize the seemingly unitary atom to the combinations of quarks that characterize each hadron. Biological processes are more complex through the involvement of multiple molecules, cells, tissues, and organs in multiple interactions. In each of these, the appearance of persistence or stability is not a natural state. Continuity is the consequence of a more or less temporary balancing act of opposing forces, of negative and positive feedback processes.

In an attempt to apply this approach to developmental psychology, Sameroff and Harris (1979) explored the importance of the concept of dialectical contradiction as the major force motivating cognitive reorganizations. Hegelian dialectics considers development to be motivated by internal contradictions inherent in all things. The notion of inherent internal contradiction makes no sense in a psychology based on stable entities. It makes sense only when the focus turns to process. One of the internal contradictions in systems is that all entities are involved in hierarchies; they are, at one and the same time, parts and wholes. They are at once part of someone else's hierarchy while containing their own. Whether the entity be human beings or molecules, the issue is the same. Koestler (1967) has referred to this as the Janus principle. Like Janus, all elements are two-faced, one aimed outward at the wholes of which they are a part and one aimed inward at the parts that make them whole. The various social systems in which we participate place constraints on activity. At the same time, we are constrained by our physical, chemical, and biological constituents.

The contradiction arises out of the previously cited possibility for alternative descriptions. If each system participated in only one hierarchy, the dialectic would not operate, what we are part of would completely overlap our parts. However, this is rarely the case for complex systems. Coleman (1971) contrasts "whole-person" organizations with institutionalized bureaucracies. In the whole-person society characteristic of the Middle Ages in Western society, or any social system based on blood lines, each individual is within a group and has no social existence outside the group. Any activity with people outside the group must be carried out through group-relation channels. Bureaucracies, on the other extreme, are composed of abstracted roles in a set of organized relationships that can be filled by anyone who will carry out the required activities. For Coleman, the individual is a member of the whole-person group but only a participant in the bureaucracy. But the person can participate in a number of bureaucracies, each of which represents an alternative description of that person. These alternative roles could be salesman, student, father, or little-league coach, each requiring different activities and different interpersonal relationships. A child fills alternative descriptions in the family, the school, or the peer group.

As long as the values of the various roles that the individual fills are similar, there is no source of conflict, nor is there a need for adaptive change. However, when the values in one role are different from those in another, conflict arises. The recent rise of feminism is an example of such a dialectical contradiction reaching resolution. As long as the roles that men and women filled were nonoverlapping, there was no conflict with the value of equal opportunity. Each sex had the equal opportunity to fill its own roles (i.e., breadwinner vs. homemaker). When women attempted to fill roles traditionally held by men, it became clear that equal opportunity did not exist. The social system had to adapt by either changing the legal code to legitimize unequal treatment or to eliminate sex as a relevant dimension for filling institutional roles. In molecular genetics, repressors produced by regulatory genes can participate in two different systems as a function of the biochemical environment. In one circumstance, they can combine with certain genes to prevent their functioning; in another circumstance—the presence of certain regulatory metabolites—they are coopted into a different structure, and the gene is free to function.

At a psychological level, cognitive development presents many comparable instances; for example, as the child grows, older elements are redefined by being included in new systems. The shift from preoperational to operational thinking in the Piagetian system is characterized by a shift from incorporating information into perceptual systems to incorporating it into conceptual systems. Siegler's (1981) studies give examples of how children progress through a series of alternative understandings. The developmental sequences found in children are the result of such shifts. At an early stage, only one interpretation is placed on information; next, there is a period of instability in which the information is coded into two different systems; and, finally, a new period of stability emerges in which the information is now coded only into the new system.

Dialectical contradiction is most evident in evolutionary history. When bacteria first evolved, they did not use oxygen but began producing it as a by-product. This by-product changed the atmosphere to permit the evolution of new species of bacteria that used oxygen for energy. At the same time, the new oxygen killed off the species of bacteria that originally produced the atmospheric changes. The action of a species produced consequences that eventually destroyed it, the ultimate contradiction.

Our activity in the world changes it so that it can never be the way it was before. Technological advances such as the discovery of fire, the invention of electricity, or microchips all have nonreversible effects on evolution. Unintended developmental by-products such as pollution are further examples of the contradictory effects of human activity. Technological evolution spills over into social evolution. The rise of factories removed the father from the house reorganizing family life. The need for the mother to become the primary caregiver may have been a major basis for the institutionalization of sex-role differentiation in modern society. The contradictions between changed context and the system's current state of organization are what push for new levels of stabilization. Environmental protection laws and equal rights amendments are ways in which society reorganizes itself to adapt to these new circumstances.

Psychologically, dialectical contradiction has been most explicitly treated in Piaget's (1971) theory of cognitive development. Equilibration is the result of an individual's efforts to overcome contradictions between the subject's cognitive organization and the object. Each assimilation requires some accommodation to occur because no two experiences are ever identical, and each new accommodation means that the next experience will be assimilated somewhat differently because the subject will have been changed. Riegel (1976) enlarged the number of domains among which contradictions occurred to include the biological, the psychological, the social, and the physical setting. In his view, developmental changes that are thought to represent stages, such as adolescence, are the resolution of a cascade of dialectical contradictions between physical status, cognitive development, and social roles.

CHAOS THEORY AND DYNAMIC SYSTEMS PERSPECTIVES

References to the current literature in the sciences will find few references to general systems theory. Happily, this has a positive interpretation in that many of the previously described principles have been incorporated into the everyday empirical work of most biological and many behavioral scientists. Cognitive science, neuroscience, and their newer combination into cognitive neuroscience focus on the processes by which brain organization and consequent mental functioning occur. An overriding metatheoretical perspective is of little interest to those who are involved in the here-and-now investigation of dynamic processes. It only arises when problems do not lend themselves to easy experimental observation, as characterizes the understanding of abnormal patterns of behavioral organization.

At the metatheoretical level, chaos theory provides a contemporary view of complex processes. Chaos theory arose in the context of trying to explain what appeared to be probabilistic phenomena with deterministic models (e.g., predicting the weather). The popular view of chaos theory (Gleick, 1987) is associated with the "butterfly effect": A butterfly flapping its wings in Beijing will influence storms the following month in New York City. What was new was the idea that small changes can produce major longitudinal effects (i.e., there is a sensitive dependence on initial conditions). Chaos is not to be confused with randomness or stochastic processes because seemingly erratic behavior is the result of deterministic nonlinear equations. What was exciting for social scientists was the idea that sudden shifts in social organization could be modeled on equations that produced chaotic behavior in physics and biology (Gregersen & Sailer, 1993).

For the study of development, it is unlikely that we will discover simple equations to describe complex processes because of the dialectical contradictions described earlier. However, several other aspects of the theory have been incorporated into interesting models of human motor and communicative behavior (Fogel & Thelen, 1987). In contrast to hierarchical models like the environtype, in which the focus is on the dual regulation between superordinate and subordinate levels, chaos theory is more concerned with coregulation by processes at the same level. Thelen (1989) points out that pattern and order can emerge from the interaction of components of a system without the need for hierarchical instructions. Adult nervous system functions can be seen as dynamic, self-organizing processes that emerge from the assembly of more elemental processes. She invokes the field of synergetics, the physics of complex systems, to explain patterns of motor development.

What appear to be discontinuities in behavior can be explained by the shift from one attractor, a determinant of the system, to another. Using motor development as her prime example, Thelen explained the disappearance of newborn walking behavior and its reappearance later in the first year. What had previously been explained neurologically as the suppression of newborn reflexes by developing inhibitory brain processes and the subsequent reappearance of walking through a higher-order integration of excitatory and inhibitory processes, was now seen to be the correlate of the balance between fatty and muscle tissue in the leg. Thelen showed that the neurological mechanism that controlled assymetrical movement in the legs was continuous from birth. What changed was that after a few weeks the infant was too heavy for the legs to support the body, and it was not until the muscles were strong enough that walking reemerged. The "attractor" in this case was muscle development in the legs. Thelen describes additional systems in which shifts in attractors that characterize dynamic systems perspectives have been used to explain developmental transitions. These include shifts in arousal states in the infant (Wolff 1987), the transition in performance on Piagetian conservation tasks that occurs between 5 and 8 years of age (Church & Goldin-Meadow, 1986), and the timing of weaning in rat pups.

Of more specific interest to the field of developmental psychopathology has been Gottman's (1993) studies of marital distress. In searching for predictors of marital dissolution, Gottman and Levenson (1992) found that a cascade of precursor events led to dissolution: a period of unhappy marriage, a consideration of separation, actual separation, and then divorce. Whether this cascade would progress from one stage to another was predicted best by the balance between positive and negative interactive behavior, not the amount of either behavior considered separately. The shift between the positive and negative attractors was the determinant of whether the couple would move to the next state of dissolution.

The description of the process of marital dissolution is akin to the descriptions necessary to characterize the developmental progression of adaptive patterns of behavior. For most psychopathology, a dynamic balance exists between the individual's ability to maintain an adaptive self-integration and the stresses and strains of everyday life. It is in the dynamic characteristics of this process that investigators might hope to explain what leads certain individuals and not others to disorder.

The principles that have been described for a general systems theory of development can be seen to incorporate the properties of the dominant metaphors in developmental thinking. For each, we can ask the same questions: What is the network of relationships? What are the parts and what are the wholes? What are the regulations and what are the constraints, both contextual and hierarchical? And of most importance to our concerns in developmental psychopathology, where did specific patterns of adaptation arise and in what direction are they progressing?

The general systems theory approach will lead to common organizational parameters in every explanation of mental health—a theory of context and a theory of development. The theory of context must indicate the relation of parts to wholes and the mutual constraints imposed by hierarchical dual control. The theory of development must reveal the processes of self-stabilization and the sources of perturbations that lead to reorganization. Each future step is constrained by prior organization but not determined by the past. Predicting the future will require knowing the systems, their environments, and their transactions in dialectical terms. Because of its scope, this task may seem difficult; on the other hand, to return to the simplicity of seeing the world through linear eyes would make any understanding of the future an impossibility.

The difference between a study based on general systems theory principles and one that is not may not be in any empirical detail, but it will be in the conceptual frame. When a general systems researcher examines infants or school-age children, the design is based on an active decision not to study other ages because of the scope of the work or the questions asked. When nonsystems researchers use the same design, it is usually because they do not consider developmental status to be a relevant dimension. Similarly, researchers who ignore family structure, social class, or ethnic background usually do so by default rather than by choice. The data are increasingly clear that the default option can rarely be justified. In almost every domain of child functioning, contextual factors make significant contributions (Sameroff, 1987). To ignore these factors is no longer the reflection of a different point of view, it is just bad science.

GENERAL SYSTEMS THEORY AND MENTAL HEALTH

There are few explicit applications of general systems theory to developmental research although it has been emphasized in the family therapy literature (Hoffman, 1981). A number of approximations of a general systems model may help to indicate the usefulness of such an approach. Patterson and Bank (1989) describe the etiology of child antisocial behavior as a system unfolding over time through a series of social interactions that amplify trivial disobedience into serious deviance. A main point of their formulation is that the behavior or personality of the child cannot be explained without major attention to the family context. Wholeness and order were found in family interaction patterns. Self-stabilization was evident in the recurring negative interactions among family members in coercive families whenever the child's noncompliance occurred. Self-organization was seen in the development of the coercive family style itself. The initial perturbing effects of normal noncompliance produced a coercive parenting style that increased rather than decreased the noncompliant behavior. These reorganizations could be seen in a series of stages as the family moved toward the production of an antisocial child.

Although positive and negative feedback processes, as captured in the principles of self-stabilization and self-organization, are strongly exemplified in the Patterson and Bank analysis, hierarchical relationships are not. Although the family is clearly a part of the analysis, it is only considered as a collection of interacting individuals, either in terms of parent-child or child-child behavioral changes. What is not considered is the family as a unit, whether as a symbol system or a behavioral system in which individual family members are embedded. The discussion of the represented and practicing family (Reiss, 1989) as described in the family code would be relevant here. A general problem in the field of social development is that the family systems literature provides little bridging where there is an opposite problem. Much attention is paid to family level characteristics but little attention to individual characteristics. On the other hand, Patterson and Bank use their data to throw some interesting light on the issue of alternative descriptions.

In principle, each system in which the individual participates can incorporate a different aspect of the person. The school can relate to the child's academic performance, whereas the family can relate to the child's social performance. However, the opportunity of a setting to choose an alternative description might reflect an active process on the part of the child. Individuals can emphasize one or another of their characteristics in different situations. In the case of the antisocial child, the description given importance and exaggerated by the family interactions comes to dominate the child's behavior in other contexts. Instead of emphasizing their academic prowess in the school setting, children from coercive families emphasize their disruptive antisocial behavior, which alienates them from both teachers and schoolmates.

Dialectical contradictions permeate the Patterson and Bank data. In two major cases, the efforts of both parents and child produce opposite effects. The inept, coercive child rearing that parents believe will produce compliance in the child produces instead the contradictory behavior of noncompliance. This contradiction in outcome is produced by a discrepancy between the parent's good intentions and poor child-rearing knowledge. A similar contradiction occurs between the child's later attempts to engage peers in social relationships at school and the resulting rejection. The family has provided the child with only one aggressive model of social interaction, and that model does not serve to attract friends at school. The dialectical problems in these instances can be resolved only through therapeutic interventions where both the parents and child experience consciousness raising. The Patterson intervention strategies that help parents and children to change their interactive behavior and outcomes are good demonstrations of how the environtype can reorganize to alter family experience through action of the social context, in this case therapists in the social service system.

Another study with direct reference to systems interactions is the Belsky, Rovine, and Fish (1989) investigation of family development surrounding the birth of a first child. These researchers are explicit about the use of general systems principles especially around hierarchical relationships. Individuals are seen as participating in dyads that are organized into families.

The family subsystems are based on alternative descriptions of the members. The marital dyad emphasizes different aspects than the parenting dyads (i.e., mother-father vs. mother-child or father-child).

Self-stabilization is explicitly analyzed by observing the marital dyad before and after the perturbation of childbirth. The effect of this normative event can be assessed as a developmental change for the population as whole, or individual differences can be studied among couples who are better or worse at restabilizing. The normative event presents a major opportunity for self-organization as the new constant perturbation, the baby, becomes a permanent part of the system.

Hierarchical interactions are the exciting core of the analysis by Belsky and colleagues. These researchers are able to ask questions about the effects of parts on systems and subsystems, of wholes on parts and of subsystems on parts. Specifically, they examine the role of each individual in his or her different dyadic relationships and then the role of the dyadic relationships in the family. Moreover, they can then examine the effect of perturbations or changes in each family member on their behavior in dyads and the dyads' behavior in the family group. Such imaginative analyses show the power of general systems perspectives for illuminating the dynamic processes that mediate observed behavioral outcomes. Without some explicit realization of the importance of context for understanding individual behavior, these researchers (Belsky et al., 1989) never would have collected the interaction data that made systems analyses possible.

FROM THEORY TO PRACTICE

The principles of a general systems theory of development are at a level of abstraction that may seem far from clinical concerns to understand and treat the behavioral problems that are at the core of developmental psychopathology. The discussion of the environtype was a move closer to operationalizing systems principles and is more directly connected with human social and emotional life. In the next section, we will move even closer to behavioral problems by detailing some of the processes that may characterize the regulatory activity of the environtype. Finally, a therapeutic model will be presented that incorporates both prevention and intervention activities based on the systems principles that have been described.

DEVELOPMENTAL REGULATIONS

The description of the contexts of development is a necessary prologue to the understanding of developmental problems and to the eventual design of intervention programs. Once an overview of the complexity of systems is obtained, we can turn to the search for nodal points at which intervention strategies can be directed. These points will be found in the interfaces among the child, the family, and the social system, especially where regulations are occurring. To complete the picture of developmental processes we must elaborate on the complexity of regulatory processes reflected in their stability, time span, purposiveness, level of representation, and the nature of the child's contribution. Developmental regulations have been divided into three categories based on these considerations—macroregulations, miniregulations, and microregulations (Sameroff, 1987, Sameroff & Fiese, 1989, 1990). Macroregulations are predominantly purposive major changes in environmental action that demarcate enduring phases of child behavior. Examples would be transformations in feeding behavior marked by weaning or transformations in teaching behavior marked by the entry into the school system. Miniregulations are predominantly caregiving activities that punctuate daily experience, such as the activities of dressing, feeding, or disciplining the child. Microregulations are almost automatic patterns of momentary interactions, such as attunement (Stern, 1977) on the positive side, in which the parent and the child lock into a rhythmic pattern of vocalization or smiling; or coercion (Patterson, 1986) on the negative side, where the parent and child lock into a reciprocal pattern of hostile social interactions. Because of differences in the duration of the regulations, microregulations are embedded within miniregulations and miniregulations are embedded within macroregulatons.

Macroregulations

The most extensive cycle of regulations are macroregulations, which generally are part of a developmental agenda. This agenda is a series of points in time when the environment is restructured to provide different experiences to the child. Age of weaning, toilet training, and schooling may be initiated at different times in the child's course of development based on different cultural codes. The Digo and Kikuyu are two distinct cultures in East Africa that provide different experiences to infants according to cultural beliefs (deVries & Sameroff, 1984). The Digo view the infant as capable of learning within a few months after birth and begin socialization early on. The Kikuyu do not hold such beliefs and wait until the second year of life before educating their children. Cultural agendas are subject to change and are tolerant of variation found in contemporary Western culture described earlier.

Macroregulatory codes provide the basis for socialization in each culture. They are responses to major changes in the child that are easily identifiable as distinct events and are expected of all members of a culture. Temporally, macroregulations are epochal in nature, reflecting changes that mark major milestones and a restructuring of the child's activities. The validity of a cultural developmental agenda is not in its particular details, but in that culture's successful reproduction of generation after generation of offspring. Macroregulations are the most highly articulated of the regulatory functions and are known to socialized members of each culture and may be openly discussed or written down in the form of laws (e.g., all children aged 6 years and older must be registered for school). In Western culture, the recording of developmental milestones is an institutionalized practice of health personnel and family members. The stability of macroregulations is a correlate of the stability of society. In traditional societies, the same developmental agendas have been played out for hundreds of generations. In modern society, especially among developed countries, each generation has been faced with major changes in these agendas. This has been true for cohorts at both the beginning (infants) and end (adolescents) of childhood. Over the past hundred years, the period of adolescence has undergone a major cultural restructuring (Elder, 1980). In 1890, over 90% of children over age 14 in the United States had entered the workforce and for all intents and purposes were fulfilling adult roles in society. In contrast, by 1970 over 90% of 14- to 17-year-olds were still in school. Society had produced a new age cohort for which it had different social expectations than from both adults and younger children. In addition, the percentage of children aged 18 to 21 in school educational programs has risen from about 10% before 1930 to over 60% in 1990 creating another age cohort at a different social stage than adulthood. The major change at the beginning of the life span is that the age at which infants are introduced to group care is undergoing a normative modification as the proportion of children with mothers in the labor force increased from 10% in 1940 to 59% in 1990 (Hernandez, 1993).

Miniregulations

The second level is characterized by miniregulations that operate within a shorter time span. They include the daily caretaking activities of a family. Temporally, they operate on a daily basis reflecting repeated demands within the family. Such activities include feeding children when they are hungry, changing their diapers when they are wet, and disciplining them when they misbehave. Bell (1971) described such subsets of actions as repertoires that were used to regulate interactions to constrain the intensity, frequency, or situational appropriateness of behavior. Upper limit control reactions are directed at reducing excessive or inappropriate behavior (e.g., crying or impulsiveness in children). Lower limit control reactions are directed at stimulating or increasing insufficient behavior (e.g. lethargy or shyness in children).

Miniregulations are susceptible to a wide range of individual variability while still conforming to cultural codes. The family provides the arena for most of the early developmental miniregulations and throughout much of the child's growth and development. Families may develop their own codes, which are then transmitted to other members of the family (Sameroff & Fiese, 1990). Families may carry out caregiving practices such as disciplining in a variety of ways while still conforming to the cultural code. Deviances such as coercive parenting can have a detrimental effect on the child's behavior but be maintained as a form of regulation within the family (Patterson, 1986). Most family members can agree on the miniregulations although they may not be able to articulate them spontaneously (Reiss, 1989).

The child's contribution to miniregulations may be seen in instances where the caretaking behaviors of the family are restructured to meet the unique demands of the child. A child with cerebral palsy, for example, may present difficulties in established routine caretaking. However, adjustments are made to incorporate the child into daily routines through alterations in miniregulations.

Microregulations

The third level of regulation consists of microregulations that operate on the shortest time base. Microregulations are momentary interactions between child and caregiver that others have referred to as "behavioral synchrony" or attunement (Field, 1979; Stern, 1977). Microregulations are a blend of social and biological codes because, although they may be brought to awareness, many of these activities appear naturally and with seeming automaticity. Toward the biological end are the caregiver's smile in response to an infant's smile, and toward the socialized end are "microsocial" patterns of interaction that increase or decrease antisocial behavior in the child (Patterson, 1986). The child's contribution to microregulations may be seen in the effects of the level of infant activity on maternal responsivity. Premature infants or infants who have experienced multiple prenatal complications may exhibit a lower activity level overall and require less active stimulation from their mother than that required by a healthy, full-term newborn (Field, 1977; Goldberg, Brachfeld, & DeVitto, 1980). Thus, adjustment in maternal microregulations can be stimulated in part by the child's behavior (Brazelton, Koslowski, & Main, 1974).

The three sources of regulation that have been outlined are organized at different levels of the environtype. Macroregulations are the modal form of regulation within the cultural code. Many cultural codes are written down or memorized and may be passed on to individual members of society through customs, beliefs, and mythologies, in addition to actual laws that are aimed at regulating child health and education. Miniregulations are modal within the family code where less formal interactions condition the caregiving behavior of family members. Microregulations come into play at the individual level where differences in personality and temperament balance with commonalities in human species-specific behavior in regulating reactions to the child.

Although these levels of regulation have been described independently, they are in constant interaction and even transaction. The family develops its caretaking routines influenced by the transactions between the cultural and family codes (i.e., between social norms and family traditions). As children develop within the family, they participate increasingly in these transactions that serve as a foundation for social interaction. Families highlight the role defined for each child through rituals and develop myths that further regulate the child's development. The style of each family member contributes to the way in which the regulations will be carried out in relation to the individuality of each child.

The operation of the family code is characterized by a series of regulated transactions. The parents may hold particular concepts of development that influence their caretaking practices. As children are exposed to different role expectations and listen to the family stories, they make their own contribution by their particular styles. The child's acting out of roles within the family is incorporated into family stories, rituals, and myths. By becoming an active transactor in the family code, the child ultimately may affect the child-rearing practices of the parents and thereby influence the code to be passed down to the next generation.

TRANSACTIONAL MODEL OF INTERVENTION

Among the goals of the scientific enterprise are the prediction and control of behavior. Even though the principles of general systems theory have indicated that prediction and control are probabilistic rather than deterministic, influencing the sources of regulation in the developmental process can make it possible to gain greater control of the range of child outcomes. Consideration of developmental processes has important implications for understanding the success or lack of success of attempts to change development. Cicchetti & Toth (1992) note the complexity of conceptualization required to address issues of hierarchical interrelations, processes of differentiation and integration, disequilibriums, and reorganizations that characterize applied programs within developmental psychopathology. Program success will be limited unless attention is paid to the changing meaning of problems and symptoms at different developmental levels and to discontinuities where protective factors in the context or the child alter patterns of maladaptation.

The lack of a developmental perspective may be the source of psychotherapeutic failures with depressed children. Weisz, Rudolph, Granger, and Sweeney (1992) found that where posttreatment and follow-up benefits were large for adolescents, for children there were smaller posttreatment effects and no lasting improvement at follow-up. This dismaying circumstance is attributed to an inadequate developmental rationale for most therapy regimens. Even in cognitive approaches, there is little attention to the changing quality of thinking during childhood nor to the changing relation between cognition and depression.

Where a developmental perspective is used, much more successful interventions are possible. The Conduct Problems Prevention Research Group (1992) based their FAST Track (Families and Schools Together) intervention on a developmental analysis of the course of conduct disorder where nodal points for optimal effects were identified. Following on the Patterson (1986) studies demonstrating that children from coercive families carried their antisocial behavior into new contexts as they grew, these clinicians determined that the transition into school was a developmentally appropriate time in which to intervene: The children are then at most risk and the families are most receptive. Moreover, the intervention was based on a comprehensive model that has components directed at the child, the family, the school, and the peer group. Finally, the program takes into account reciprocal processes that will extend over time.

It is beyond the scope of this chapter to describe these processes throughout development so the discussion will be restricted to early childhood with a focus on a three-level system consisting of the child, the family, and the service-providing community. With older children, additional levels of process analysis need to be added to include the effects of additional contexts such as the school and peer group as in the FAST Track Program.

A sensitivity to the complexities of the regulatory systems for child development has encouraged the implementation of intervention strategies to include multiple members of the child's family (Dunst & Trivette, 1988; Turnbull, Summers, & Brotherson, 1983) as well as multiple disciplines concerned with early childhood (Bagnato & Neisworth, 1985; Bricker, 1986; Bricker & Dow, 1980; Golin & Ducanis, 1981). Increasingly, early intervention programs are being designed with a team approach that addresses the many facets of childhood problems (Greenspan, 1990). As it becomes less acceptable to focus on isolated aspects of developmental disorders, programs are considering the total environmental context of the child (Sameroff, 1982). Once multiple determinants have been recognized as being associated with childhood problems, a more targeted approach to implementing intervention is in order, based on the specific determinants identified in a specific situation.

A frequent problem in planning intervention strategies is deciding where to concentrate therapeutic efforts. As previously outlined, developmental regulatory systems may include individual, family, and cultural codes. Not only do economic and personnel limitations preclude global interventions across systems, all these regulatory codes incorporate different aspects of the child's development and imply different intervention strategies. A careful analysis of the regulatory systems is necessary to define what may be the most effective avenue and form of intervention. The cultural, familial, and individual codes are embedded in temporal and behavioral contexts that vary in magnitude of time and scope of behavior. A basic point that emerges from this analysis, in keeping with a systems analysis, is that there will never be a single intervention strategy that can solve all developmental problems. Cost-effectiveness will not be found in the universality of a treatment but in the individuation of programs that are targeted at the relevant nodal points for a specific child in a specific family in a specific social context.

In consideration of the temporal dimensions of regulation, what are the implications for intervention? Frequently, models of intervention attempt to cover a wide range of contexts for a single identified problem. Some early intervention programs for disabled infants are designed to intervene on the level of the child, family, and occasionally the larger context of social support systems (Dunst & Trivette, 1990; Dunst, Trivette, & Cross, 1986). Although well intentioned, a great deal of effort may be expended with minimal results. A more precise understanding of regulatory systems may provide more effective forms of intervention.

The transactional model (Sameroff & Chandler, 1975) has implications for early intervention, particularly for identifying targets and strategies of intervention. The nonlinear premise that continuity in individual behavior is a systems property rather than a characteristic of individuals provides a rationale for an expanded focus of intervention efforts (Garbarino, 1990). According to the model, changes in behavior are the result of a series of interchanges between individuals within a shared system following specifiable regulatory principles. There is an emphasis on the multidirectionality of change while pinpointing regulatory sources that mediate change. By examining the strengths and weaknesses of the regulatory system, targets can be identified that minimize the necessary scope of the intervention while maximizing cost-efficiency. In some cases, small alterations in child behavior may be all that is necessary to reestablish a well-regulated developmental system. In other cases, changes in the parents' perception of the child may be the most strategic intervention. In a third category are cases that require improvements in the parents' ability to take care of the child. These categories of intervention strategies have been labeled remediation, redefinition, and reeducation, respectively (Sameroff, 1987; Sameroff & Fiese, 1990).

Figure 21.9 contains an abstraction of the regulatory model of development during early childhood that incorporates all biologically regulated changes into the child line of development

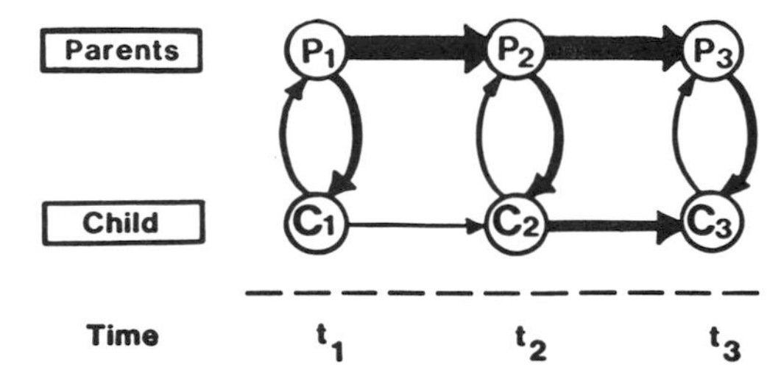

Figure 21.9 Transactional regulatory model.

and all environmentally regulated changes into the parent line of development.

A set of arrows leads from the child's initial state (C_1) to the child's state at succeeding points in time. This dimension refers to the child's development of self-regulatory capacities. Early in infancy these are primarily biological regulations of autonomic and state variables, to which are added an increasingly rich behavioral repertoire (Brazelton, 1973). As children increase in age, the line gets thicker because they learn more skills for taking care of themselves and buffering themselves from stressful experiences. Another set of arrows leads from the parents' initial state (P_1) to the parents' state at succeeding points in time. This dimension refers to the continuity in the parents' understanding of the cultural code and their competence in regulating their child's development. The discussion of intervention strategies will focus on the vertical arrows between parent and child and on the change in parents from time (1) to time (2). The arrows from child to parent represent changes in the child that transact with the parent and ultimately change the parents' behavior or attitudes. The downward arrows reflect changes in the parent that are directed toward eventual changes in the child. Horizontal arrows between P_1 and P_2 reflect changes initiated with the parent at time (1), which then influence the parents' behavior at time (2), which may then affect the child's behavior at time (2). Each direction of effect implies a different point and form of intervention.

A further abstraction of the regulatory model that focuses only on strategies of early intervention can be seen in Figure 21.10. Remediation changes the way the child behaves toward the parent. For example, in cases where children present with known organic disorders, intervention may be directed primarily toward remediating biological dysregulations. By improving the child's physical status, the child will be better able to elicit caregiving from the

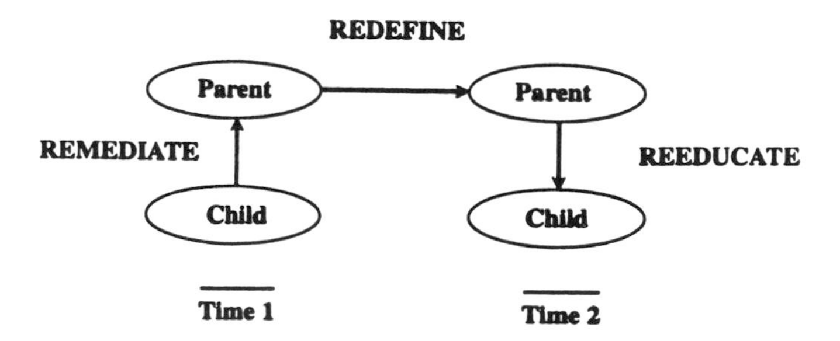

Figure 21.10 Transactional model for diagnosing intervention needs.

parents. Redefinition changes the way the parent interprets the child's behavior. Viewing the child as colicky or willful may deter a parent from positive interactions. By refocusing the parent on other, more acceptable, attributes of the child, positive engagement may be facilitated. Reeducation changes the way the parent behaves toward the child. Providing training in soothing a crying child or bringing a disengaged infant to an alert state are examples of this form of intervention. Each category of intervention will be described further, with examples of early intervention techniques used for each regulatory code.

Feeding disturbances are a common problem during infancy (Sameroff & Emde, 1989). The treatment of such problems will be used as the primary illustration of each aspect of the transactional approach. During the first year of life, children's development is regulated in part by their nutritional status. Failure to maintain growth may result from a variety of conditions, each requiring a different form of intervention. Severe primary malnutrition is a problem not only in economically deprived countries, but also in the United States and other Western countries (Listernick, Christoffel, Pace, & Chicaramonte, 1985). The following discussion will serve to highlight how a basic condition such as nutritional status may be regulated by a variety of systems requiring different forms of intervention.

Remediation

As represented in Figure 21.10, the strategy of remediation is the class of intervention techniques designed to change the child leading to changes in the parent (upward arrow). Remediation is not directed at changing the family or cultural codes. The intervention goal is to fit the child to preexisting caregiving competencies that could operate adequately given appropriate infant triggering responses. Remediation is typically implemented outside the family system by a professional whose goal is to change an identifiable condition in the child. Once the child's condition has been altered, intervention is completed.

The use of medication to control a school-age child's hyperactivity is an example of such an intervention. The request for treatment comes from parents or teachers who feel that the child cannot fit into their caregiving or classroom situation because of disruptive behavior (Sroufe, 1975). After the activity level of the child is reduced, the parents and teachers believe they can use their normative child-rearing and teaching strategies more effectively.

During infancy, the most clear-cut examples of remediation are those in which there are possibilities for structural repair of a biological condition, for example, the surgical correction of a mechanical blockage in the intestines. The child is presented to the parents as cured and they proceed to engage in the normative child-rearing appropriate to a healthy infant. Such direct solutions are excellent interventions for a number of early problems, but they occasionally involve controversial applications. The surgical alteration of the appearance of children with Down syndrome would be such a questionable procedure (Pueschel, 1984). In this example, the transactional hypothesis is the basis for the surgeon's belief that if the child looked more like a nonhandicapped child, he or she would be treated more like a nonhandicapped child and consequently would have a developmental outcome more like that of a nonhandicapped child. Controversy also surrounds the efficacy of medication for attentional and activity problems. Despite the lack of evidence for long-term effects on behavior (Jacobvitz, Sroufe, Stewart, & Leffert, 1990), in many communities over 10% of boys are treated with stimulants (Safer & Krager, 1984).

Less dramatic but more behaviorally oriented remediations may be appropriate for preterm infants with feeding difficulties due to immaturity of sucking and poor coordination in swallowing. In such cases, feedings may be regulated initially through tubes inserted into the stomach while the infant is in the neonatal intensive care unit (NICU). Poor nutrition may complicate the care of such an infant, and delayed development of the sucking reflex may prolong hospitalization, leading to a parental perception of a sick child with the possibility of associated dysfunctions in child-rearing behavior. Bernbaum, Peneira, Watkins, and Peckham (1983) demonstrated through conditioning procedures that premature infants who received an individualized remediation treatment in the special care nursery were able to normalize their feeding behavior earlier and be discharged from the hospital sooner. The transactional consequence was fewer discrepant effects on their parents' behavior (Anderson, Burroughs, & Measel, 1983; Field et al., 1982).

Als and her colleagues (Als et al., 1986) have demonstrated that individualized treatment of the premature infant was associated with higher degrees of social turn-taking, interactional synchrony, and overall quality of the interaction with their mothers during a free play session at 9 months of age. The remediation of the child as a neonate may have facilitated the parents' sensitivity in interacting with their child at a later age. The infants who did not receive the individualized intervention as neonates showed decreased levels of social interaction at 9 months of age.

The current emphasis on incorporating immediate members of the child's family and support group into intervention programs (Dunst & Trivette,1988) has been a result, in part, of the disappointing results obtained in using solely child-centered approaches to intervention. However, according to the principles of the transactional model and the regulatory system being presented here, there are circumstances where interventions directed toward the child alone may result in changes in the parent. In cases where the child's dysfunction is easily identified and successful intervention techniques are available, remediation of the child may lead to adaptive changes in the parent.

The case of treating malnutrition in infancy highlights how remediation of another child biological condition may influence the parents' behavior. Lower intelligence scores in infants who have been malnourished were originally believed to be the result of decreased cell growth in the brain (Stein & Susser, 1985). However, in cases where nutritional status could be improved, it has been demonstrated that poor intellectual performance in malnourished infants is the result of poor environments rather than poor biology (Cravioto & Arrieta, 1983; Read, 1982; Riccuti, 1993). Cravioto and DeLicardie (1979) found that the behavioral effects of malnutrition were most prevalent in families where mothers were more traditionally passive in their child care and provided little stimulation to their children. To examine how familial interactions may be influenced by nutritional status, Barrett, Radke-Yarrow, and Klein (1982) compared a group of children who had received caloric supplementation with a group that did not. The infants who received the nutritional supplements demonstrated greater social responsiveness, more expression of affect, greater interest in the environment, and higher activity at school age. Nutritional supplements increased the infants' energy level, but this did not directly affect their school-age social, emotional, and intellectual competence. Rather, their higher energy level, enabled the nourished infants to participate more fully in the socialization process, by increasing their ability to elicit optimal caregiving behaviors from their parents (Rutter, 1987). Healthy, well-nourished children were better able to give cues about their condition and elicit a wide range of behaviors, including more feeding. Their parents were prompted to provide more socially responsive stimulation, thereby further encouraging their children's interpersonal behavior.

Remedial interventions are regulators of child development in much the same way that the family and cultural code are regulators of development. Remediation strategies can be further analyzed in terms of the level of regulation addressed (Sameroff & Fiese, 1990). Microregulations were predominantly involved in the nutritional supplementation interventions. The child's ability to stimulate interactive sequences was enhanced, permitting parents to respond to the child's triggering cues. Alterations in miniregulations were more apparent in interventions that changed the child's overall behavioral repertoire, as in the sucking enhancement efforts. Here the change was not in the threshold or response to existing cues, but in the child's ability to produce a new organized behavioral episode. Finally, macroregulations changed major domains of experience. Remediations that fit in this latter category are the one-time structural changes wrought by surgical interventions that alter the child's functioning for long periods. The agent of remediation is a part of an expanded concept of the cultural code that includes all social agencies responsible for fostering child development. Because of the vagaries of government support, a large proportion of early intervention programs are experimental or demonstration efforts that have not been incorporated into the cultural code. In contrast, there are times when legislative efforts convert such experimental programs into a component of the environtype as was the case with the Headstart program.

The preceding examples of remediation are directed toward changing the child, with the expectation that changes in child behavior will result in a more optimal caregiving environment. Remediation is indicated where there is a reasonable expectation that the child's condition can be altered and the family and cultural codes do not prevent implementation of the intervention effort. There are instances, however, in which the cultural or familial code cannot operate successfully and a second strategy needs to be implemented—the strategy of redefinition.

Redefinition

Redefinition as an intervention strategy is indicated when existing family codes do not fit with the child's behavior. This intervention is represented by the horizontal arrow between

Parent(1) and Parent(2) in Figure 21.10. Redefinition strategies are warranted when parents have defined their child as abnormal and are unable or unwilling to provide normal caregiving. Such difficulties in providing caretaking may arise from two sources: failure of parents to adapt to physical or behavioral differences in the child, or failure of parents to distinguish between their emotional reactions to the child and the child's actual behavior (Sameroff & Fiese, 1990). Examples of the first kind of problem are parents who disqualify themselves as adequate caregivers by automatically translating a child's physical or mental condition into something that can only be treated by professionals (Roskies, 1972). Examples of the second kind are parents who become disenchanted with child rearing because they find a poor fit between their expectations of child behavior and the child's actual performance.

In the case of an atypical condition in the child, redefinition interventions are directed toward normalizing the parents' reactions to their child. An infant born with Down syndrome, for example, may be defined as abnormal because of differences in appearance or developmental pace or merely the label itself, leading the parents to believe that they are incapable of rearing such a child. Redefinition would be directed toward emphasizing the normal aspects of the child's behavior to facilitate caregiving behaviors that are in the parents' repertoire. Such normal child behaviors would include communication efforts (e.g., eye contact) and emotional responsivity (e.g., smiling, laughing). Redefinition interventions directed toward parents when a deviant condition in the child is not identified focus on the parent's misperceptions of the child. Redefinition is directed toward changing interactions in the context of immediate experience rather than past events. The case of an infant with a diagnosis of nonorganic failure to thrive (FTT) illustrates this process.

Failure to thrive is a condition diagnosed in the first 2 years of life when a child's weight drops below the third percentile of growth with no known organic etiology (Barbero & McKay, 1969). Nonorganic FTT, in contrast to organic FTT, is a diagnosis often made by the combined criteria of the exclusion of organicity and a weight gain in the hospital produced by nutritional supplements (Rosen, Loeb, & Jura, 1980). Children diagnosed with FTT are thought to be at risk for behavior problems, child abuse, and delays in development (Haynes, Cutler, Gray, & Kempe, 1984; Oates, Peacock, & Forrest, 1985; Singer, Drotar, Fagan, Devost, & Lake, 1983). A striking feature of nonorganic FTT is that, on removal from the home environment, hospitalized infants achieve significant weight gain with implementation of a standard nutritional program. In-hospital weight gain contrasted with in-home weight loss has led some to speculate that failure to thrive represents a failure in parenting (Haynes et al., 1984). However, there is increasing evidence that FTT may not represent a single syndrome but is a concomitant of a variety of disturbances in infancy (Gordon & Vazquez, 1985).

For redefinition to be the intervention of choice, a crucial aspect of the failure-to-thrive case must be in the parental perception of the child. It has been reported that many parents of FTT infants describe their children as oppositional or "bad" (Ayoub & Milner, 1985), and have difficulty in accepting them (Casey, Bradley, & Wortham, 1984). Redefinition efforts in this case would be directed toward relabeling the child's emotional expressions for the parent. In the case of a mother who refuses to feed a crying infant because the infant is perceived as being stubborn, the infant's cry may be redefined as a signal for hunger rather than anger. Simple relabeling may be sufficient to alter the parent-child relationship so that effective feeding interactions can take place. However, some cases of failure to thrive may not be responsive to altered labels of child behavior and may indicate a more intensive effort directed toward the parents' past history.

Fraiberg and her colleagues have described how past experiences of being parented influence current caretaking behaviors (Fraiberg, Adelson, & Shapiro, 1980). Parents engaging in routine caretaking activities with their children remember past experiences of their own childhoods. Individuals who experienced nurturant parenting recall these positive experiences as they parent their own children. However, individuals who have experienced inadequate parenting often repeat the same nonoptimal interactions. These "ghosts in the nursery" may influence how parents engage in routine caretaking activities. Returning to the case of FTT, mothers of FTT infants often recount their own upbringing as deficient in nurturance (Haynes et al., 1985; Altemeir, O'Connor, Sherrod, & Vietze, 1985). In this case, redefinition interventions may be directed at the parents' memories of past experiences. Chatoor and her colleagues report that redefining the baby as the mother's own, rather than as a symbol of past parenting experiences, has been effective in the treatment of infants failing to thrive (Chatoor, Dickson, Schaeffer, & Egan, 1985).

The mother, the father, or the entire family may be the source of inappropriate attributions concerning the infant. In fact, recognizing how a family may contribute to dysfunctions in the child is central to adapting the family code to fit the child's behavior. The family context may be particularly crucial in treating FTT infants (Drotar et al., 1985). Redefinition interventions may be directed at how the family, as a whole, views the child, and what roles the family code permits the infant to play. Minimizing the current influence of past parenting experiences can have a positive effect on caregiving in families with an FTT child (Drotar & Malone, 1982).

Redefinition may be directed toward parent-child interactions and a relabeling of the child's behavior. If a relabeling of behavioral interactions proves effective in facilitating weight gain, then no further intervention may be necessary. When relabeling is insufficient to facilitate change, however, redefinition efforts may be also directed toward examining the parents' past experiences of being parented.

Most of the discussion of redefinition has been directed at the family code but occasionally redefinition may be directed at the cultural code. For example, during the 1950s, a healthy infant was typified by the "Gerber baby"—full, round cheeks and a pudgy torso. This cultural image may have led to overfeeding and perhaps to weight problems later in childhood. As more emphasis has been placed on balanced nutrition, the image of the healthy baby in American culture has been redefined to emphasize a less rotund child. Cultural redefinitions are rarely in the purview of intervention programs. However, public education programs such as those directed toward defining the expectations of adequate parenting for teenage parents attempt to redefine behavior at the level of the cultural code.

Redefinitions at different levels of regulation move from a focus on specific child behaviors to a focus on general attributions to a specific child to a focus on attributions to children in general (Sameroff & Fiese, 1990). Interventions at the level of microregulation help parents to reinterpret their child's cues (e.g., as a cry of hunger instead of a cry of oppositionalism). Miniregulation interventions help parents redefine who their child is (e.g., "it is my baby and not myself as a baby, not my mother, not my father, and not my spouse,") so that the object of their caregiving becomes clarified. Interventions at the macroregulation level are directed at redefining cultural stereotypes to alter major segments of that culture's developmental agenda (e.g., redefining the ideal baby as mean and lean instead of fat and happy).

Whereas redefinition interventions attempt to alter parenting patterns caused by maladaptive perceptions or inadequate past parenting experiences, sometimes the parents do not have the requisite skills for effective parenting. In such cases, re-education is indicated.

Reeducation

Reeducation refers to teaching parents how to raise their children. Reeducation is represented by the downward arrow from Parent to Child in Figure 21.10. It is directed toward parents who do not have the knowledge base to use a cultural code to regulate their child's development.

Reeducation, like redefinition, has rarely involved intervention in the cultural code. However, public health initiatives have increasingly been utilized in such efforts. Teaching teenage fathers basic parenting skills is an example of reeducation at a cultural level that alters the expected roles for males. Providing information about the nutritional qualities of food types has been directed toward improving child-raising behaviors in impoverished societies (Messer, 1984). General cultural attitudes may also be altered to provide parents with enriched experiences as well. One such example is the recent value that parents of healthy children should be educated about the newborn's interactive capabilities (Worobey & Belsky, 1982).

Most reeducation efforts are directed at the family or individual parent level. Such efforts typically supply parents with information about specific caregiving skills. The care and feeding of premature infants illustrates reeducation interventions. Premature infants present parents with particular challenges in routine caretaking since the infant's immaturity may be characterized by irregularities in maintaining homeostasis (Gorski, 1983), irregular sleep patterns (Parmelee & Sigman, 1984), and inconsistencies in social interaction (Field, 1980; Goldberg et al., 1980). An intervention program developed to address the caregiving concerns of parents of premature infants is reported by Minde and his colleagues (Minde et al., 1980). A series of discussion groups was offered to parents while the infants were still in the nursery. The discussion groups included a "veteran mother" who had had a similar premature infant. The later course of the intervention included discussions led by hospital personnel to review medical procedures and the developmental needs of premature babies. Three months following discharge from the hospital, the infants whose parents participated in the intervention groups fed significantly longer than did the control group. These changes were mediated by changes in the parents' behavior. Mothers who had participated in the intervention engaged their infants more through talking and looking than did the control group.

An even more highly structured and educational approach is reported by Nurcombe and his colleagues (Nurcombe et al., 1984). Parents of premature infants were assigned either to a control condition or were enrolled in an intervention program that consisted of 11 sessions with a trained pediatric nurse. The nurse trained the parents in developmental aspects of prematurity including state regulation, motor system development, and recognition of cues and patterns of temperament. Mothers in the intervention and control groups were assessed 6 months following discharge from the hospital and 3 months following the end of the program. Those who participated in the intervention program were more confident in, more satisfied with, and more favorable toward child rearing than those in a low-birthweight control group. Intervention mothers perceived their infants as more adaptable, happy, and approachable, and less easily distressed. Reeducation efforts influenced their caretaking abilities and confidence in parenting premature infants with special needs. This form of intervention may have led the parents to perceive their infants as less difficult to raise and in turn made them more willing to interact with them in a social context.

In contrast with classroom programs for groups of parents are the individualized interactions in programs devoted to modifications of parent-child interactions through various forms of coaching (Field, 1983; McDonough, 1993). After being videotaped in dyadic interaction sessions, mothers, typically, are shown how changes in their interaction behavior produced changes in the infant's responsivity. Highlighting the relatively subtle cues produced by high-risk infants allows parents to participate in more optimal caregiving behaviors and facilitates the child's communication and interaction behaviors (Seifer, Clark, & Sameroff, 1991).

These programs show the contrast between interventions at the level of macroregulations, miniregulations, and microregulations (Sameroff & Fiese, 1990). Macroregulations are involved when parents are taught in didactic programs about developmental milestones and about what changes should be made when the child is weaned, begins to walk, and to talk. Miniregulations are involved when parents are given more hands-on training in changing diapers or positioning the infant for feeding. Microregulations are involved when parents receive interaction coaching to improve their interpretation of subtle interactional cues.

These studies have not been designed to separately manipulate regulation levels. When intervention programs are targeted at one level of regulation, it is not clear whether there are diffusion effects into other levels. It may be that teaching parents in a classroom will change the way they interact in face-to-face situations with their infant. On the one hand, the classroom situation is much less expensive and will ensure that infants will at least get the right feeding formula. On the other hand, it may be in the face-to-face situation, or perhaps the lack of it, that many feeding difficulties arise. Alternatively, there may be spillover from programs that focus on microregulations to broader areas of parenting. For example, parents who feel better about their minute-to-minute interactions with their infant may alter their developmental goals for the child.

Reeducation interventions are directed toward families that are deficient in certain skills that are necessary for optimal parenting. Remediation and redefinition are less salient for such families because even if the parent makes appropriate attributions to a child who is making appropriate elicitations, the parent does not know how to respond appropriately. Recent advances in our knowledge about teaching parenting skills allows professionals to impart this knowledge to parents in need of information and skill training. Reeducation is the intervention of choice when parents are expected to make use of this information, thus producing beneficial changes in the child's developmental course.

The transactional model of intervention is a working model at this point. It has been proposed to provide a framework for identifying more effective means of intervention while recognizing the complexities of human development. Several aspects of this model have not been addressed that may be salient for future research directives. Considering the systemic properties of change, for example, intervention focused in one area may lead to the need for intervention in another area. As a teenage mother becomes reeducated about child development, subsequent interventions may be directed toward a redefinition of her relationship with her infant if there are continued difficulties in the child's development. A better understanding of how the regulatory codes relate to each other and are involved in different processes of change may lead to more specific forms of intervention. An attempt to clarify the transactional model of intervention highlights again the complexities of human development.

LESSONS FROM THE STUDY OF DEVELOPMENTAL PSYCHOPATHOLOGY

The primary lesson we have learned from research in developmental psychopathology is that there is no line of demarcation between the processes that lead to adaptive or maladaptive outcomes for children. We must examine all behavior in context even to place evaluative labels. It is the developmental and situational context of behavior that determines whether it is normative or symptomatic. Normative behaviors include irritability and overdependence during infancy, defiance and poor impulse control during toddlerhood, aggression during early childhood, and even delinquency during adolescence. Hyperactivity is normative on the playground but not in the classroom. It is when these behaviors are not normative for the context that they become symptomatic; it is not their quality but their lack of organization within an adaptive relationship between child and context that is a sign of disorder.

The burgeoning field of infant mental health is a case in point. A major concern in this area is whether its title is a misnomer. A better one might be "relationship" mental health because, except for major biological anomalies, most infant behavioral problems are interactional ones (Sameroff & Emde, 1989). Diagnoses may be better applied to relationships than to the infant alone (Anders, 1989), although further developmental research is required to determine when such relationship disorders become part of the child so that they are recreated in multiple contexts with multiple partners. Even where relationship issues, such as attachment disorders, have been included in current diagnostic schemes, they have not been fully based on developmental research on the concept of attachment (Zeanah, Mammen, & Lieberman, 1993). Research in infant mental health has been a growing point for the entire area of developmental psychopathology because of the rapid transformation of the child from a primarily biological to a biopsychosocial existence. From its inception, the area has been multidisciplinary and multigenerational, with a developmental orientation toward the dynamic interchanges between organism and environment (Emde, Bingham, & Harmon, 1993).

We have learned a great deal from major advances in biological research. Although there is much to be appreciated in the practical achievements of identifying biochemical processes at the cellular level and perhaps even the genes that may play a role in some manifestations of psychopathology, we have learned even more from the discovery that biological activity operates according to complex models in which each developmental achievement is the outcome of multiple interacting processes in a regulated dynamic balance.

In the area of behavioral development, we have made the same discoveries. Each child behavior is the result of multiple interacting systems in a regulated dynamic balance. When we turn to the examination of child psychopathology, the questions we need to ask are (a) "What are the multiple systems involved in any particular child?" and (b) "What are the processes that regulate the expression of the atypical behavior?"

At Rochester, when my colleagues and I (Sameroff, Seifer, Zax, & Barocas, 1987) joined the Consortium on High Risk Studies of Schizophrenia in 1970, we became part of a cohort of some 14 longitudinal studies trying to discover how schizophrenic parents transmitted their disorder to their offspring (Garmezy, 1974). After following these children for 20 years in the Rochester Longitudinal Study, we have found only one child with a diagnosis of schizophrenia. Unfortunately for our original hypothesis, the parents of this child were not schizophrenic. Fortunately for us, we had abandoned this linear prediction when the children in our sample were 4 years of age. At that point in our study we had discovered, on the one hand, if the only developmental risk for a child was a schizophrenic mother, that child was doing fine. On the other hand, if the child had a schizophrenic mother, who was also poor, uneducated, without social supports, and with many stressful life events, that child was doing poorly. But, we also found that children whose mothers were poor, uneducated, without social supports, and with many stressful life events had bad outcomes, even if the mother did not have a psychiatric diagnosis.

Our findings in Rochester were not different from those found in the other high-risk studies of schizophrenia (Watt, Anthony, Wynne, & Rolf, 1984). Parental diagnosis alone was not predictive of child pathology unless there were additional behavioral stressors in the family or social context. Whatever the organic vulnerability that is transmitted in families with a schizophrenic parent, it needs fertile soil if it is to be expressed in child psychopathology.

In longitudinal studies of the continuity of depression from parent to child, the pathways by which children show deviations in emotional behavior have been examined (Hammen, 1992). The thrust of the findings from these studies is that having a mother with a lifetime diagnosis of major affective disorder is not alone predictive of child behavioral problems. In contrast, mothers with current symptoms of depression, married to a spouse with a current diagnosis, engaged in marital conflict, and with poor family functioning do have children who show signs of behavioral deviance (Sameroff, Seifer, Dickstein, Schiller, & Hayden, 1993).

What then is the risk that these children will begin or continue to show developmental psychopathology? Prevention scientists (Coie et al., 1993) have found that a number of environmental risks are common to the etiology of child psychopathology. These risks are at many levels of the child's ecology, from the most proximal in the form of abusive or unemotional parent-child interactions, through more removed levels of family conflict and distorted communication patterns, lack of social support, and stressful life events, to distal factors such as poverty, disorganized neighborhoods and inadequate school systems. In our longitudinal research, we have found that the continuity of such risk factors in the context of a child is much stronger than the continuity of any behavioral domain within the child. Whereas the correlations between adaptive behavior scores at 4 and 18 years of age was .40, the correlation for environmental risk across the same 14-year period was .80. For most families, the risk factors that children faced during the preschool years are the same risks they continue to face through adolescence (Sameroff, Seifer, Baldwin, & Baldwin, 1993).

Any major effort to understand patterns of adaptation during childhood must take careful note of the advances in biological research, but equal attention must be paid to the conceptual contributions as to the empirical. Every developmental achievement is multiply regulated through reciprocal transactions between the child and his or her context. Thus the identification of health and disorder must focus on the relationship between child and context.

CONCLUSION

A classic imperative of academic research is the application of Ockham's razor, the principle that it is vain to use more explanations for a phenomenon that can be explained by fewer (Boehner, 1962). The application of general systems approaches to the study of behavior moves us in the opposite direction, toward a principle that whatever seems to be explained by a simple cause is really the result of multiple causes and their interactions. In this chapter, we explored, on the one hand, the factors that would lead us to seek complexity instead of simplicity as an explanation for behavior and, on the other hand, the occasions when we can accept linear models that relate singular causes to singular effects.

The need for a complex understanding of behavior is rooted in the complex organization of the real world. The concern of clinicians has been with individuals in distress. General laws of behavior that are abstracted from the behavior of large populations have only a probabilistic relation to the specific responses of an individual in a specific set of circumstances. In fact, it has been suggested that the major scientific achievements of the 20th century have not been the obvious choices, the subnuclear organization of the atom or the structure of the gene, but rather advancements in the understanding of probability. Probability is everywhere and is always less than unity. Each individual is embedded in a multiplicity of contexts that contribute something to each behavioral act and to which each behavioral act will make a contribution. Beginning with Lewin's (1935) field theories and extending through Bronfenbrenner's (1979) ecological models to Elder's (1979) concern with historical events and the life course, there has been an expanding recognition of the number of social structures that impinge on individual psychological functioning. The growth of biopsychology and cognitive neuroscience has brought into juxtaposition the comparable complexity of the biological world and the behavioral one. The theoretical formulations of von Bertalanffy (1968) had already described the complexities to be expected in the biological world and begun the theoretical abstraction that produced general systems theory. But few took seriously, the extension of such complex models to the realm of human behavior.

For some reason, it was very difficult for most, and is still very difficult for some, to appreciate that discoveries about the complexity of the physical and biological world have important implications for the behavioral world. It was the purpose of this chapter to foster this appreciation. The model of biobehavioral simplicity was based on biological examples of unique structural genes that seemed to act linearly to produce unique phenotypic characteristics, such as blue eyes or brown hair. The model of biobehavioral complexity is based on intricate physical phenomena such as the functioning of the cardiovascular system where a multiplicity of genetic factors interact with a multiplicity of developmental factors, which interact with a multiplicity of psychological and social factors to produce either a better or worse functioning heart. In a quest for a stronger foundation for understanding developmental psychopathology, an analogous model of complexity is necessary for understanding the growth of better or worse behavioral adaptations.

The preceding discussion has been aimed at providing a model for interpreting the interplay between child and environment during development. The presentation has been sketchy in that there is little depth of research in most of the domains that have been touched on. Through an ecological analysis, some aspects of an environtype were highlighted as providing the regulatory framework for healthy child development. These factors included the cultural, familial, and parental codes. Although a case was made that the environment is an active force in shaping outcomes constrained by the state and potentialities of the individual, there is still much to be studied and understood in the dynamics of these systems.

How do we move from the generalities of risk factors to the specificities of child adaptation? The presentation on general systems theory focused on the commonalities between principles of biological and psychological functioning. The biological model that has been most salient for understanding developmental psychopathology is a transactional one in which gene expression requires a responsive cytoplasmic environment for either the activation or inhibition of inherited potentials. Although each cell contains exactly the same genotype, that genotype will be expressed differently in different kinds of cells and at different stages in the development of each cell. There is no expression of biological capacities for good or bad without a supportive transacting environment.

Using a formist or mechanistic metaphor, psychopathologists have searched for antecedent markers of many mental disorders.

In this book, you will find reference to precursors such as attentional problems, poor emotional regulation, atypical temperaments, and poor impulse control. But the predictive utility of these markers has been generally weak. For some, the weakness is in the empirical research, for others the weakness is in the metaphor. To use child characteristics alone to predict outcomes when complex systems are at play is inherently problematic. For most children in most families, biological variation is regulated through the economic, social, and individual constraints of the environtype to fit social norms. For example, despite the strong evidence of inherited factors in schizophrenia, 90% of the offspring of schizophrenics do not become schizophrenic nor do 55% of their identical twins (Masten, Best, & Garmezy, 1990). For these children who do not evidence the disorder, the social regulation implicit in organized family life and coherent, benign communities assists them to overcome poor emotional regulation, attentional deficits, shy reactive temperaments, or disobedient behavior. Thus, these behavioral variations will not be perpetuated into later diagnosable depression, anxiety, schizophrenia, or conduct disorder. On the other hand, for children with these same behavioral variations reared in disorganized family and community contexts, not only are there no social supports for the normalizing regulation of these behaviors, but there are risk conditions that will exacerbate these tendencies.

The conceptual framework for prevention research presented by Coie and his colleagues (Coie et al., 1993) is equally salient for the understanding of continuities and discontinuities in symptomatology and disorder during development. They concluded that (a) risk factors have complex relations to clinical disorders, (b) the salience of risk factors may fluctuate developmentally, (c) exposure to many risk factors has cumulative effects, and (d) diverse disorders share fundamental risk factors in common. Although the focus on risk factors is an abstraction from the dynamic interplay of developmental systems at many levels, the findings of risk research force investigators into more complex models of research design and analysis.

In an attempt to incorporate both the child and the context in a coherent model of development, the utility of the transactional model for designing programs to prevent cognitive and social-emotional problems was explored. The development of these behavioral problems was interpreted as deviations in a child-rearing regulatory system. The prevention of these problems has been defined as the adjustment of the child to better fit the regulatory system or the adjustment of the regulatory system to better fit the child.

Within this regulatory framework, transactions are ubiquitous. Wherever parents change their way of thinking about or behaving toward the child as a result of something the child does, a transaction has occurred. Most of these transactions are normative within the existing cultural code and facilitate development. Intervention only becomes necessary where these transactions are nonnormative. In our progress toward effective therapeutic programs, we have reached a key theoretical breakthrough. The source of children's behavioral problems is no longer seen as restricted to the children themselves (Sameroff & Emde, 1989). Social experience is now recognized as a critical component of all behavioral developments, both normal and abnormal. Unfortunately, we have not yet reached the level of sophistication in theory and research that would connect every childhood problem with the appropriate regulatory problem. There are many possible regulations to solve the same problem and, therefore, many possible interventions.

The complex model that characterizes our modern understanding of the regulation of development seems an appropriate one for analyzing the etiology of developmental disorders. It permits the understanding of intervention at a level necessary to identify targets of intervention. It helps us to comprehend why initial conditions do not determine outcomes, either positively or negatively. The model also helps us to grasp why early intervention efforts may not determine later outcomes. There are many points in development where regulations can facilitate or retard the child's progress. The hopeful part of this model is that these many points in time represent opportunities for changing the course of development.

In sum, theories that focus on singular causal factors are inadequate for either the study or manipulation of developmental outcomes. The evolution of living systems has provided a regulatory model that incorporates feedback mechanisms between the individual and regulatory codes. These cultural and genetic codes are the context of development. By appreciating the workings of this regulatory system, we can understand the process of development, for good or ill, and the possibilities for changing it.

REFERENCES

Als, H., Lawhon, G., Brown, E., Gibes, R., Duffy, F. H., McAnulty, G., & Blickman, J. G. (1986). Individualized behavioral and environmental care for the very low birth weight preterm infant at high risk for bronchopulmonary dysplasia: Neonatal intensive care unit and developmental outcome. *Pediatrics, 78,* 1123–1132.

Altemeir, W. A., O'Connor, S. M., Sherrod, K. B., & Vietze, P. M. (1985). Prospective study of antecedents for nonorganic failure to thrive. *Journal of Pediatrics, 106,* 360–365.

American Psychiatric Association. (1994). *Diagnostic and statistical manual of mental disorders* (4th ed.). Washington, DC: Author.

Anastasi, A. (1957). Heredity, environment, and the question, "How?" *Psychological Review, 75,* 81–95.

Anders, T. F. (1989). Clinical syndromes, relationship disturbances, and their assessment. In A. J. Sameroff & R. N. Emde (Eds.), *Relationship disturbances in early childhood: A developmental approach* (pp. 125–144). New York: Basic Books.

Anderson, G. E., Burroughs, A. K., & Measel, C. P. (1983). Nonnutritive sucking opportunities: A safe and effective treatment for preterm neonates. In T. Field & A. Sostek (Eds.), *Infants born at risk: Physiological, perceptual, and cognitive processes* (pp. 129–146). New York: Grune & Stratton.

Anderson, P. M. (1972). More is different. *Science, 177,* 393–396.

Aries, P. (1962). *Centuries of childhood.* New York: Vintage.

Asarnow, R. F., Asarnow, J. R., & Strandburg, R. (1989). Schizophrenia: A developmental perspective. In D. Cicchetti (Ed.), *Rochester Symposium on Developmental Psychopathology: Vol. 1. The emergence of a discipline* (pp. 189–220). Hillsdale, NJ: Erlbaum.

Ayoub, C. C., & Milner, J. S. (1985). Failure to thrive: Parental indicators, types and outcomes. *Child Abuse and Neglect, 9,* 491–499.

Bagnato, J. J., & Neisworth, J. T. (1985). Efficacy of interdisciplinary assessment and treatment for infants and preschoolers with congenital and acquired brain injury. *Analysis and Intervention in Developmental Disabilities, 1,* 107–128.

Bakeman, R., & Gottman, J. M. (1986). *Observing interaction: An introduction to sequential analysis.* New York: Cambridge University Press.

Baltes, P. B. (1979). Life-span developmental psychology: Some converging observations on history and theory. In P. B. Baltes & O. G. Brim, Jr. (Eds.), *Life-span development and behavior* (Vol. 2). New York: Academic Press.

Barbero, G., & McKay, N. (1969). Failure to thrive. In W. E. Nelson (Ed.), *Textbook of pediatrics* (pp. 1653–1654). Philadelphia: Saunders.

Barrett, D. E., Radke-Yarrow, M., & Klein, R. E. (1982). Chronic malnutrition and child behavior: Effects of early caloric supplementation on social and emotional functioning at school age. *Child Development, 18,* 541–556.

Baumrind, D. (1971). Harmonious parents and their preschool children. *Developmental Psychology, 4,* 99–102.

Baumrind, D. (1991). The influence of parenting style on adolescent competence and substance use [Special issue]. The work of John P. Hill: I. Theoretical, instructional, and policy contributions. *Journal of Early Adolescence, 11,* 56–95.

Bell, R. Q. (1968). A reinterpretation of the direction of effects in studies of socialization. *Psychological Review, 75,* 81–95.

Bell, R. Q. (1971). Stimulus control of parent or caretaker behavior by offspring. *Developmental Psychology, 4,* 63–72.

Belsky, J. (1980). Child maltreatment: An ecological integration. *American Psychologist, 35,* 430–435.

Belsky, J., Rovine, M., & Fish, M. (1989). The developing family system. In M. R. Gunnar & E. Thelen (Eds.), *The Minnesota Symposia on Child Psychology: Vol. 22. Systems and development* (pp.119–166). Hillsdale, NJ: Erlbaum.

Bennett, L. A., Wolin, S., Reiss, D., & Teitelbaum, M. A. (1987). Couples at risk for the transmission of alcoholism: Protective influences. *Family Process, 26,* 111–129.

Bentler, P. M. (1987). Drug use and personality in adolescence and young adulthood: Structural models with nonnormal variables. *Child Development, 58,* 65–79.

Bernbaum, J. C., Peneira, G. R., Watkins, J. B., & Peckham, G. J. (1983). Nonnutritive sucking during gavage feeding enhances growth and maturation in premature infants. *Pediatrics, 71,* 41–45.

Bijou, S. W., & Baer, D. M. (1961). *Child development.* New York: Appleton-Century-Crofts.

Boehner, P. (1962). *Ockham.* Edinburg: T. Nelson & Sons.

Bonner, J. (1973). Hierarchical control programs in biological development. In H. H. Pattee (Ed.), *Hierarchy theory: The challenge of complex systems.* New York: Braziller.

Bossard, J. H. S., & Boll, E. S. (1950). *Ritual of family living.* Philadelphia: University of Pennsylvania Press.

Boulding, K. (1956). General systems theory—The skeleton of science. *Management Science, 2,* 197–208.

Bowlby, J. (1988). Developmental psychiatry comes of age. *American Journal of Psychiatry, 145,* 1–10.

Brazelton, T. B. (1973). Neonatal behavioral assessment scale. *Clinics in Developmental Medicine, 50.* Philadelphia: Lippincott.

Brazelton, T. B., & Cramer, B. G. (Eds.). (1990). *The earliest relationship.* Reading, MA: Addison-Wesley.

Brazelton, T. B., Koslowski, B., & Main, M. (1974). The origins of reciprocity: The early mother-infant interaction. In M. Lewis & L. Rosenblum (Eds.), *The effect of the infant on its caregiver* (pp. 49–76). New York: Wiley.

Bricker, D. D. (1986). *Early education of at-risk and handicapped infants, toddlers, and preschool children.* Glenview, IL: Scott, Foresman.

Bricker, D. D., & Dow, M. (1980). Early intervention with the young severely handicapped child. *Journal of the Association for the Severely Handicapped, 5,* 130–138.

Bronfenbrenner, U. (1977). Toward an experimental ecology of human development. *American Psychologist, 32,* 513–531.

Brofenbrenner, U. (1979). *The ecology of human development.* Cambridge, MA: Harvard University Press.

Bronfenbrenner, U. (1986). Ecology of the family as a context for human development: Research perspectives. *Developmental Psychology, 22,* 723–742.

Brown, G., Harris, T., & Bifulco, A. (1986). Long-term effects of early loss of parent. In M. Rutter, C. Izard, & P. Read (Eds.), *Depression in young people: Developmental and clinical perspectives* (pp. 251–296). New York: Guilford.

Bugental, D. P., & Shennum, W. A. (1984). "Difficult" children as elicitors and targets of adult communication patterns: An attributional-behavioral transactional analysis. *Monographs of the Society for Research in Child Development, 49.*

Casey, P. H., Bradley, R., & Wortham, B. (1984). Social and nonsocial home environments of infants with nonorganic failure to thrive. *Pediatrics, 73,* 348–353.

Chatoor, I., Dickson, S., Schaeffer, S., & Egan, J. (1985). A developmental classification of feeding disorders associated with failure to thrive: Diagnosis and treatment. In D. Drotar (Ed.), *New directions in failure to thrive: Implications for research and practice* (pp. 235–258). New York: Plenum.

Cherlin, A. J. (1981). *Marriage, divorce, remarriage.* Cambridge, MA: Harvard University Press.

Chomsky, N. (1975). *Reflections on language.* New York: Pantheon.

Church, R. B., & Goldin-Meadow, S. (1986). The mismatch between gesture and speech as an index of transitional knowledge. *Cognition, 23,* 43–71.

Cicchetti, D. (1989). Developmental psychopathology: Some thoughts on its evolution. *Development and Psychopathology, 1*(1), 1–4.

Cicchetti, D., & Toth, S. L. (1992). The role of developmental theory in prevention and intervention. *Development and Psychology, 4,* 489–493.

Clarke, A. M., & Clarke, A. D. B. (1976). *Early experience: Myth and evidence.* London: Open Books; New York: Free Press.

Coie, J. D., Watt, N. F., West, S. G., Hawkins, J. D., Asarnow, J. R., Markman, H. J., Ramey, S. L., Shure, M. B., & Long, B. (1993). The science of prevention: A conceptual framework and some directions for a national research program. *American Psychologist, 48,* 1013–1022.

Coleman, J. S. (1971). Social systems. In P. A. Weiss (Ed.), *Hierarchically organized systems in theory and practice.* New York: Harcourt.

Conduct Problems Prevention Research Group. (1992). A developmental and clinical model for the prevention of conduct disorder: The FAST Track Program. *Development and Psychopathology, 4,* 509–528.

Cravioto, J., & Arrieta, R. (1983). Malnutrition in childhood. In M. Rutter (Ed.), *Developmental neuropsychiatry* (pp. 32–51). New York: Guilford.

Cravioto, J., & DeLicardie, E. R. (1979). Nutrition, mental development, and learning. In F. Falkner & J. M. Turner (Eds.), *Human growth (Vol. 3).* New York: Plenum.

Crockenberg, S. B. (1981) Infant irritability, mother responsiveness, and social support influences on the security of infant-mother attachment. *Child Development, 52,* 857–865.

Crockenberg, S. B., & Smith, P. (1982). Antecedents of mother-infant interaction and infant irritability in the first three months of life. *Infant Behavior and Development, 5,* 105–119.

Cummings, E. M., & Cicchetti, D. (1990). Toward a transactional model of relations between attachment and depression. In M. Greenberg, D. Cicchetti, & M. Cummings (Eds.), *Attachment in the preschool years* (pp. 339–372). Chicago: University of Chicago Press.

Cutright, P. (1972). Illegitimacy in the United States, 1920–1960. In C. W. Woestoff & R. Parke (Eds.), *Demographic and social aspects of population growth.* Washington, DC: U.S. Government Printing Office.

Darling, N., & Steinberg, L. (1993). Parenting style as context: An integrative model. *Psychological Bulletin, 113,* 487–496.

deVries, M. W., & Sameroff, A. J. (1984). Culture and temperament: Influences on temperament in three East African societies. *American Journal of Orthopsychiatry,* 54, 83–96.

Draper, P. (1976). Social and economic constraints on child life among the !Kung. In R. B. Lee & E. DeVore (Eds.), *Kalahari hunter gatherers* (pp. 199–217). Cambridge, MA: Harvard University Press.

Drotar, D., & Malone, C. A. (1982). Family-oriented intervention in failure to thrive. In M. Klaus & M. O. Robertson (Eds.), *Birth interaction and attachment: Johnson & Johnson pediatric round table* (Vol. 6, pp. 104–112). Skillman, NJ: Johnson & Johnson.

Drotar, D., Woychik, J., Mantz-Clumpner, C., Brickell, C., Negray, J., Wallace, M., & Malone, C. (1985). The family context of failure to thrive. In D. Drotar (Ed.), *New directions in failure to thrive: Implications for research and practice* (pp. 295–310). New York: Plenum.

Dunst, C. J., & Trivette, C. M. (1988). A family systems model of early intervention. In D. P. Powell (Ed.), *Parent education and support programs: Consequences for children and families.* Norwood, NJ: Ablex.

Dunst, C. J., & Trivette, C. M. (1990). Assessment of social support in early intervention programs. In S. J. Meisels & J. P. Shonkoff (Eds.), *Handbook of early childhood intervention* (pp. 326–349). New York: Cambridge University Press.

Dunst, C. J., Trivette, C. M., & Cross, A. H. (1986). Mediating influences of social support: Personal, family and child outcomes. *American Journal of Mental Deficiency, 90,* 403–417.

Elder, G. H., Jr. (1979). Historical change in life patterns and personality. In P. Baltes & O. Brim, Jr. (Eds.), *Life-span development and behavior* (pp. 117–159). New York: Academic Press.

Elder, G. H., Jr. (1980). Adolescence in historical perspective. In J. Adelson (Ed.), *Handbook of adolescent psychology.* New York: Wiley.

Elder, G. H., Jr., Caspi, A., & Downey, G. (1985). Problem behavior and family relationships: Life course and intergenerational themes. In A. Sørensen, F. Weinert, & L. Sherrod (Eds.), *Life course research on human development.* Hillsdale, NJ: Erlbaum.

Emde, R. N., Bingham, R. D., & Harmon, R. J. (1993). Classification and the diagnostic process in infancy. In C. H. Zeanah, Jr. (Ed.), *Handbook of infant mental health* (pp. 225–235). New York: Guilford.

Emde, R. N., Gaensbauer, T., & Harmon, R. (1976). Emotional expression in infancy: A biobehavioral study. *Psychological Issues Monographs Series, 10.* New York: International Universities Press.

Ferreira, A. (1963). Family myth and homeostasis. *Archives of General Psychiatry, 9,* 457–463.

Field, T. (1977). Effects of early separation, interactive deficits, and experimental manipulation in infant-mother face-to-face interaction. *Child Development, 48,* 763–771.

Field, T. M. (1979). Interaction patterns of preterm and term infants. In T. M. Field, A. M. Sostek, & H. H. Schuman (Eds.), *Infants born at risk: Behavior and development.* New York: SP Medical and Scientific Books.

Field, T. M. (1980). Interactions of preterm and term infants with their lower- and middle-class teenage and adult mothers. In T. Field, S. Goldberg, D. Stern, & A. M. Sostek (Eds.), *High-risk infants and children: Adult and peer interactions* (pp. 113–132). New York: Academic Press.

Field, T. M. (1983). Early interaction and intervention: Coaching of high-risk infants and parents. In M. Perlmutter (Ed.), *Development and policy concerns: Children with special needs. Symposium on Child Psychology.* Hillsdale, NJ: Erlbaum.

Field, T. M. (1987). Affective and interactive disturbances in infants. In J. Osofsky (Ed.), *Handbook of infant development* (2nd ed.) (pp. 972–1005). New York: Wiley.

Field, T. M., Ignatoff, E., Stringer, S., Brennan, J., Greenberg, S., Widmayer, S., & Anderson, G. C. (1982). Nonnutritive sucking during tube feedings: Effects on preterm neonates in an intensive care unit. *Pediatrics, 70,* 381–384.

Fiese, B. H. (1990, April). *Family stories: Mothers' stories of their childhood and relation to mother-toddler interaction in a free-play setting.* Paper presented at the International Conference on Infant Studies, Montreal.

Fiese, B. H. (1992). Dimension of family rituals across two generations: Relation to adolescent identity. *Family Process, 31,* 151–162.

Fiese, B. H., Hooker, K. A., Kotary, L., & Schwager, J. (1993). Family rituals in the early stages of parenthood. *Journal of Marriage and the Family, 55,* 633–642.

Fiese, B. H., & Kline, C. A. (1993). Development of the Family Ritual Questionnaire: Initial reliability and validation studies. *Journal of Family Psychology, 6,* 290–299.

Flynn, J. R. (1984). The mean IQ of Americans: Massive gains 1932–1978. *Psychological Bulletin, 95,* 29–51.

Flynn, J. R. (1987). Massive IQ gains in 14 nations: What IQ tests really measure. *Psychological Bulletin, 101,* 171–191.

Foerster, H. von. (1966). From stimulus to symbol: The economy of biological computation. In G. Kepes (Ed.), *Sign, image, symbol* (pp. 170–181). New York: Braziller.

Fogel, A., & Thelen, E. (1987). The development of expressive and communicative action in the first year: Reinterpreting the evidence from a dynamic systems perspective. *Developmental Psychology, 23,* 747–761.

Ford, D. H., & Lerner, R. M. (1992). *Developmental systems theory: An integrative approach.* Newberry Park: Sage.

Fraiberg, S., Adelson, E., & Shapiro, V. (1980). Ghosts in the nursery: A psychoanalytic approach to the problems of impaired mother-infant relationships. In S. Fraiberg (Ed.), *Clinical studies in infant mental health: The first year of life* (pp. 164–196). New York: Basic Books.

Furstenberg, F. F., Brooks-Gunn, J., & Morgan, S. P. (1987). *Adolescent mothers.* Cambridge, England: Cambridge University Press.

Gal-Or, B. (1972). The crisis about the origin of irreversibility and time anisotropy. *Science, 176,* 11–17.

Garbarino, J. (1990). The human ecology of early risk. In S. J. Meisels & J. P. Shonkoff (Eds.), *Handbook of early childhood intervention* (pp. 78–96). New York: Cambridge University Press.

Garmezy, N. (1974). Children at risk: The search for the antecedents of schizophrenia. *Schizophrenia Bulletin, 8,* 14–90.

Garmezy, N. (1985). Stress-resistant children: The search for protective factors. In J. E. Stevenson (Ed.), *Recent research in developmental psychopathology* (pp. 213–233). Oxford, England: Pergamon.

Gleick, J. (1987). *Chaos: Making a new science.* New York: Viking.

Goldberg, S., Brachfeld, S., & DiVitto, B. (1980). Feeding, fussing and playing parent-infant interaction in the first year as a function of prematurity and perinatal problems. In T. Field, S. Goldberg, D. Stern, & A. Sostek (Eds.), *High-risk infants and children: Adult and peer interactions* (pp. 133–153). New York: Academic Press.

Golin, A. J., & Ducanis, A. J. (1981). *The interdisciplinary team: A handbook for the education of exceptional children.* Rockville, MD: Aspen Systems.

Goodnow, J. J. (1988). Parents' ideas, actions, and feelings: Models and methods from developmental and social psychology. *Child Development, 59,* 286–330.

Gordon, E. F., & Vazquez, D. M. (1985). Failure to thrive: An expanded conceptual model. In D. Drotar (Ed.), *New directions in failure to thrive: Implications for research and practice* (pp. 69–76). New York: Plenum.

Gorski, P. (1983). Premature infant behavioral and physiological responses to caregiving interventions in intensive care nursery. In J. D. Call, E. Galenson, & R. L. Tyson (Eds.), *Frontiers of infant psychiatry* (pp. 265–263). New York: Basic Books.

Gottman, J. M. (1979). Detecting cyclicity in social interaction. *Psychological Bulletin, 86,* 338–348.

Gottman, J. M. (1993). A theory of marital dissolution and stability. *Journal of Family Psychology, 7,* 57–75.

Gottman, J. M., & Levenson, R. W. (1992). Marital processes predictive of later dissolution: Behavior, physiology, and health. *Journal of Personality and Social Psychology, 63,* 221–233.

Greenspan, S. I. (1990). Comprehensive clinical approaches to infants and their families: Psychodynamic and developmental perspectives. In S. J. Meisels & J. P. Shonkoff (Eds.), *Handbook of early childhood intervention* (pp. 150–172). New York: Cambridge University Press.

Gregersen, H., & Sailer, L. (1993). Chaos theory and its implications for social science research. *Human Relations, 46,* 777–802.

Hammen, C. (1991). *Depression runs in families: The social context of risk and resilience in children of depressed mothers.* New York: Springer-Verlag.

Hammen, C. (1992). The family-environmental context of depression: A perspective on children's risk. In D. Cicchetti & S. L. Toth (Eds.), *Rochester symposium on developmental psychopathology: Vol. 4. Developmental perspectives on depression* (pp. 251–281). Rochester, New York: University of Rochester Press.

Harris, T., Brown, G., & Bifulco, A. (1987). Loss of parent in childhood and adult psychiatric disorder: The role of social class position and premarital pregnancy. *Psychological Medicine, 17,* 163–183.

Haynes, C. F., Cutler, C., Gray, J., & Kempe, R. S. (1984). Hospitalized cases of nonorganic failure to thrive: The scope of the problem and short-term lay health visitor intervention. *Child Abuse and Neglect, 8,* 229–242.

Hegel, G. W. F. (1910). *The phenomenology of mind* (J. B. Baillie, Ed. and Trans.). London: Allen & Unwin. (Original work published 1807)

Heisenberg, W. (1971). *Physics and beyond.* New York: Harper & Row.

Hernandez, D. J. (1993). *America's children, resources from family, government, and the economy.* New York: Russell Sage Foundation.

Hetherington, E. M. (1991). The role of individual differences and family relationships in children's coping with divorce and remarriage. In P. A. Cowan & M. Hetherington (Eds.), *Family transitions* (pp. 165–194). Hillsdale, NJ: Erlbaum.

Hetherington, E. M., & Camara, K. A. (1984). Families in transition: The process of dissolution and reconstitution. In R. Parke (Ed.), *The family* (pp. 398–439). Chicago: University of Chicago Press.

Hoffman, L. (1981). *Foundations of family therapy: A conceptual framework for systems change.* New York : Basic Books.

Hudson, J., & Nelson, K. (1983). Effects of script structure on children's recall. *Developmental Psychology, 19,* 625–635.

Huesmann, L. R., Eron, L. D., Lefkowitz, M. M., & Walder, L. O. (1984). The stability of aggression over time and generations. *Developmental Psychology, 20,* 1120–1134.

Hull, C. L. (1943). *Principles of behavior.* New York: Appleton.

Iacono, W. G., & Grove, W. M. (1993). Schizophrenia reviewed: Toward an integrative genetic model. *Psychological Science, 4,* 273–276.

Jacob, F. (1976). *The logic of life: A history of heredity.* New York: Vintage.

Jacobvitz, D., Sroufe, L. A., Stewart, M., & Leffert, N. (1990). Treatment of attentional and hyperactivity problems in children with sympathomimetic drugs: A comprehensive review. *Journal of the American Academy of Child and Adolescent Psychiatry, 29,* 677–688.

Keller, H. (1904). *The story of my life.* New York: Doubleday, Page.

Kessen, W. (1979). The American child and other cultural inventions. *American Psychologist, 34,* 815–820.

Kessen, W. (1987, April). *Developmental psychology: Present and future.* Paper presented at a meeting of the American Psychological Association, New York.

Kessen, W. (1993). The child and other cultural inventions. In F. S. Kessel & A. W. Siegel (Eds.), *The child and other cultural inventions* (pp. 26–47). New York: Praeger.

Koestler, A. (1967). *The ghost in the machine.* New York: Macmillan.

Kohn, M. L. (1969). *Class and conformity: A study in values.* Homewood, IL: Dorsey Press.

Kohn, M. L. (1973). Social class and schizophrenia: A critical review and reformulation. *Schizophrenia Bulletin, 7,* 60–79.

Koshland, D. E., Jr. (1993). The molecule of the year. *Science, 258,* 1861.

Kramer, J. (1985). Family myth and homeostasis. *Archives of General Psychiatry, 9,* 457–463.

Kuhn, T. S. (1962). *The structure of scientific revolutions.* Chicago: University of Chicago Press.

Kuhn, T. S. (1978). Mechanisms of cognitive and social development: One psychology or two? *Human Development, 21,* 92–118.

Langer, J. (1969). *Theories of development.* New York: Holt, Rinehart & Winston.

Laszlo, E. (1972). *Introduction to systems philosophy: Toward a new paradigm of contemporary thought.* New York: Harper & Row.

Lerner, R. M., & Busch-Rossnagel, N. (1981). Individuals as producers of their development: Conceptual and empirical basis. In R. M. Lerner & N. A. Busch-Rossnagel (Eds.), *Individuals as producers of their development: A life-span perspective* (pp. 1–36). New York: Academic Press.

Levins, R., & Lewontin, R. C. (1985). *The dialectical biologist.* Cambridge, MA: Harvard University Press.

Lewin, K. (1935). *A dynamic theory of personality.* New York: McGraw-Hill.

Lidz, T. (1973). *The origin and treatment of schizophrenic disorders.* New York: Basic Books.

Listernick, R., Christoffel, K., Pace, J., & Chicaramonte, J. (1985). Severe primary malnutrition in U.S. children. *American Journal of Diseases in Childhood, 139,* 1157–1160.

Lozoff, B. (1983). Birth and "bonding" in non-industrial societies. *Developmental Medicine and Child Neurology, 25,* 595–600.

Main, M., & Goldwyn, R. (1984). Predicting rejection of their infant from mother's representation of her own experience: Implications for the abused and abusing intergenerational cycle. *Child Abuse and Neglect, 8,* 203–217.

Masten, A. S., Best, K. M., & Garmezy, N. (1990). Resilience and development: Contributions from the study of children who overcome adversity. *Development and Psychopathology, 2,* 425–444.

Matthysse, S., Holzman, P. S., & Lange, K. (1986). The genetic transmission of schizophrenia: Application of Mendelian latent structure analysis to eye tracking dysfunctions in schizophrenia and affective disorder. *Journal of Psychiatric Research, 20,* 57–76.

Mayr, E. (1970). *Populations, species, and evolution.* Cambridge, MA: Belknap Press.

McDonough, S. C. (1993). Interaction guidance: Understanding and treating early infant-caregiver relationship disturbances. In C. H. Zeanah, Jr. (Ed.), *Handbook of infant mental health* (pp. 414–426). New York: Guilford.

Messer, E. (1984). Sociocultural aspects of nutrient intake and behavioral responses to nutrition. In J. Galler (Ed.), *Nutrition and behavior* (pp. 417–471). New York: Plenum.

Miller, J. G. (1978). *Living systems.* New York: McGraw-Hill.

Minde, K., Corter, C., Goldberg, S., & Jeffers, D. (1990). Maternal preferences between premature twins up to age four. *Journal of the American Academy of Child and Adolescent Psychiatry, 29,* 367–374.

Minde, K., Shosenberg, N., Marton, P., Thompson, J., Ripley, J., & Burns, S. (1980). Self-help groups in a premature nursery—a controlled evaluation. *Journal of Pediatrics, 96,* 933–940.

Moore, S. F., & Myeroff, B. G. (1977). *Secular ritual.* Amsterdam, The Netherlands: Van Gorcum.

Neilson, W. A. (Ed.). (1942). *Webster's New International Dictionary of the English Language* (2nd ed., unabridged). Springfield, MA: Merriam.

Nelson, K. (1981). Social cognition in a script framework. In J. Flavell & R. Ross (Eds.), *Social cognitive development.* Cambridge, England: Cambridge University Press.

Nelson, K., & Gruendel, J. (1981). Generalized event representations: Basic building blocks of cognitive development. In A. Brown & M. Lamb (Eds.), *Advances in developmental psychology* (Vol. 1, pp. 131–158). Hillsdale, NJ: Erlbaum.

Nurcombe, B., Howell, D. C., Rauh, V. A., Teti, D. M., Ruoff, P., & Brennan, J. (1984). An intervention program for mothers of low-birthweight infants: Preliminary results. *Journal of the American Academy of Child Psychiatry, 23,* 319–325.

Oates, R. K., Peacock, A., & Forrest, D. (1985). Long-term effects of nonorganic failure to thrive. *Pediatrics, 75,* 36–40.

Olson, S. (1992). Development of conduct problems and peer rejection in preschool children: A social systems analysis. *Journal of Abnormal Child Psychology, 20,* 327–350.

Overton, W., & Reese, H. (1973). Models of development: Methodological implications. In J. Nesselroade & H. Reese (Eds.), *Life-span developmental psychology: Methodological issues* (pp. 65–86). New York: Academic Press.

Parke, R. D., & Tinsley, B. J. (1987). Family interaction in infancy. In J. Osofsky (Ed.), *Handbook of infancy* (2nd ed.) (pp. 579–641). New York: Wiley.

Parmelee, A. H. (1989). The child's physical health and the development of relationships. In A. J. Sameroff & R. N. Emde (Eds.), *Relationship disturbances in early childhood* (pp. 145–162). New York: Basic Books.

Parmelee, A. H., & Sigman, M. (1984). Perinatal brain development and behavior. In J. J. Campos & M. M. Haith (Eds.), P. H. Mussen (Series Ed.) *Handbook of child psychology: Vol. II. Infancy and developmental psychobiology* (pp. 95–155). New York: Wiley.

Pasamanick, B., & Knobloch, H. (1961). Epidemiologic studies on the complications of pregnancy and the birth process. In G. Caplan (Ed.), *Prevention of mental disorders in children.* New York: Basic Books.

Pattee, H. H. (1973). The physical basis and origins of hierarchical control. In H. H. Pattee (Ed.), *Hierarchy theory: The challenge of complex systems* (pp. 71–108). New York: Braziller.

Patterson, G. R. (1986). Performance models for antisocial boys. *American Psychologist, 41,* 432–444.

Patterson, G. R., & Bank, L. (1989). Some amplifying mechanisms for pathologic processes in families. In M. Gunnar & E. Thelene (Eds.), *The Minnesota Symposia on Child Psychology* (Vol. 22, pp. 167–210). Hillsdale, NJ: Erlbaum.

Pepper, S. C. (1942). *World hypotheses.* Berkeley: University of California.

Perkins, D. H. (1987). *Introduction to high-energy physics.* Reading, MA: Addison-Wesley.

Piaget, J. (1970). *Structuralism.* New York: Harper & Row.

Piaget, J. (1971). *Biology and knowledge.* Chicago: University of Chicago Press.

Plomin, R., DeFries, J., & McClearn, G. (1990). *Behavioral genetics, a primer* (2nd ed.). New York: Freeman.

Pollner, M., & McDonald-Wikler, L. (1985). The social construction of unreality: A case study of a family's attribution of competence to a severely retarded child. *Family Process, 24,* 241–254.

Polanyi, M. (1968). Life's irreducible structure. *Science, 160,* 1308–1312.

Pueschel, S. M. (1984). *The young child with Down syndrome.* New York: Human Sciences Press.

Ratner, N., & Bruner, J. (1977). Games, social exchange and the acquisition of language. *Journal of Child Language, 5,* 391–401.

Read, M. S. (1982). Malnutrition and behavior. *Applied Research in Mental Retardation, 3,* 279–291.

Reese H., & Overton, W. (1970). Models of development and theory of development. In L. Goulet & P. Baltes (Eds.), *Life span developmental psychology: Methodological issues* (pp. 115–145). New York: Academic Press.

Reiss, D. (1981). *The family's construction of reality.* Cambridge, MA: Harvard University Press.

Reiss, D. (1989). The represented and practicing family: Contrasting visions of family continuity. In A. J. Sameroff & R. N. Emde (Eds.), *Relationship disturbances in early childhood: A developmental approach* (pp. 191–220). New York: Basic Books.

Reiss, D., Oliveri, M. E., & Curd, K. (1983). Family paradigm and adolescent social behavior. In H. D. Grotevant & C. R. Cooper (Eds.), *Adolescent development in the family: New directions for child development* (Vol. 22, pp. 77–91). San Francisco: Jossey-Bass.

Rheingold, H. L. (1966). The development of social behavior in the human infant. In H. W. Stevenson (Ed.), *Concept of development. Monographs of the Society for Research in Child Development, 31.*

Riccuti, H. N. (1993). Nutrition and mental development. *Current Directions in Psychological Science, 2,* 43–46.

Riegel, K. F. (1976). The dialectics of human development. *American Psychologist, 31,* 689–700.

Rogoff, B. (1981). Schooling and the development of cognitive skills. In H. C. Triandis & A. Heron (Eds.), *Handbook of cross-cultural psychology: Developmental psychology* (Vol. 4). Boston: Allyn & Bacon.

Rosen, D., Loeb, J. S., & Jura, M. B. (1980). Differentiation of organic from nonorganic failure to thrive syndrome in infancy. *Pediatrics, 66,* 698–704.

Rosenthal, D. (1970). *Genetic theory and abnormal behavior.* New York: McGraw-Hill.

Roskies, E. (1972). *Abnormality and normality: The mothering of thalidomide children.* Ithaca, NY: Cornell University Press.

Rutter, M. (1987). Continuities and discontinuities from infancy. In J. Osofsky (Ed.), *Handbook of infant development* (2nd ed.) (pp. 1256–1296). New York: Wiley.

Rutter, M., & Garmezy, N. (1983). Development psychopathology. In E. M. Hetherington (Ed.), *Carmichael's manual of child psychology: Vol. 4. Social and personality development* (pp. 775–911). New York: Wiley.

Sackett, G. P. (1978). *Observing behavior: Data collection and analysis method* (Vol. 2). Baltimore: University Park Press.

Safer, D. J., & Krager, J. M. (1984). Trends in medication therapy for hyperactivity: National and international perspectives. *Advances in Learning Behavior Disorders, 3,* 125–149.

Sameroff, A. J. (1982). The environmental context of developmental disabilities. In D. Bricker (Ed.), *Intervention with at-risk and handicapped infants: From research to application* (pp. 141–152). Baltimore: University Park Press.

Sameroff, A. J. (1983). Developmental systems: Contexts and evolution. In W. Kessen (Ed.), P. H. Mussen (Series Ed.), *Handbook of child psychology: Vol. 1. History, theories, and methods* (pp. 237–294). New York: Wiley.

Sameroff, A. J. (1985, August). *Can development be continuous?* Paper presented at Annual Meeting of American Psychological Association, Los Angeles.

Sameroff, A. J. (1987). The social context of development. In N. Eisenberg (Ed.), *Contemporary topics in developmental psychology* (pp. 273–291). New York: Wiley.

Sameroff, A. J. (1993). Models of development and developmental risk. In C. Zeanah (Ed.), *Handbook of infant mental health* (pp. 3–13). New York: Guilford.

Sameroff, A. J., & Chandler, M. J. (1975). Reproductive risk and the continuum of caretaking casualty. In F. D. Horowitz, M. Hetherington, S. Scarr-Salapatek, & G. Siegel (Eds.), *Review of child development research* (Vol. 4, pp. 187–244). Chicago: University of Chicago Press.

Sameroff, A. J., & Emde, R. N. (Eds.). (1989). *Relationship disturbances in early childhood: A developmental approach.* New York: Basic Books.

Sameroff, A. J., & Feil, L. (1985). Parental concepts of development. In I. Sigel (Ed.), *Parent belief systems: The psychological consequences for children* (pp. 83–104). Hillsdale, NJ: Erlbaum.

Sameroff, A. J., & Fiese, B. H. (1989). Conceptual issues in prevention. In D. Shaffer, I. Philips, & N. Enzer (Eds.), *Prevention of mental disorders, alcohol and other drug use in children and adolescents* (OSAP Prevention Monograph 2, pp. 23–53). Washington, DC: U.S. Department of Health and Human Services.

Sameroff, A. J., & Fiese, B. H. (1990). Transactional regulations and early intervention. In S. J. Meisels & J. P. Shonkoff (Eds.), *Handbook of early childhood intervention* (pp. 119–149). New York: Cambridge University Press.

Sameroff, A. J., & Harris, A. (1979). Dialectic approaches to early thought and language. In M. H. Bornstein & W. Kessen (Eds.), *Psychological development from infancy: Image to intention* (pp. 339–372). Hillsdale, NJ: Erlbaum.

Sameroff, A. J., Seifer, R., Baldwin, A., & Baldwin, C. (1993). Stability of intelligence from preschool to adolescence: The influence of social and family risk factors. *Child Development, 64,* 80–97.

Sameroff, A. J., Seifer, R., Barocas, B., Zax, M., & Greenspan, S. (1987). IQ scores of 4-year-old children: Social-environmental risk factors. *Pediatrics, 79,* 343–350.

Sameroff, A. J., Seifer, R., Dickstein, Schiller, M., & Hayden, L. (1993, March). *Effects of family process and parental depression on children.* Paper presented at the meeting of the Society for Research in Child Development, New Orleans.

Sameroff, A. J., Seifer, R., Zax, M., & Barocas, R. B. (1987). Early indices of developmental risk: The Rochester Longitudinal Study. *Schizophrenia Bulletin, 13,* 383–394.

Scarr, S. (1985). Constructing psychology: Making facts and fables for our times. *American Psychologist, 40,* 499–512.

Scarr, S. (1993). Biological and cultural diversity: The legacy of Darwin for development. *Child Development, 64,* 1333–1353.

Schaefer, E., & Bell, R. (1958). Development of a parental attitude research instrument. *Child Development, 29,* 339–361.

Seifer, R., Clark, G. N., & Sameroff, A. J. (1991). Positive effects of interaction coaching on infants with developmental disabilities and their mothers. *American Journal on Mental Retardation, 96,* 1–11.

Seifer, R., Schiller, M., Sameroff, A. J., Resnick, S., & Riordan, K. (1993, April). *Attachment, maternal sensitivity, and temperament during the first year of life.* Paper presented at the annual meeting of the American Psychological Society, Chicago.

Siegler, R. S. (1981). Development sequences within and between concepts. *Monographs of the Society for Research in Child Development, 46* (2, Serial No. 189).

Sigel, I. E. (1985). Parental belief systems: *The psychological consequences for children.* Hillsdale, NJ: Erlbaum.

Sigel, I. E., McGillicuddy-DeLisi, A. V., & Goodnow, J. J. (1992). *Parental belief systems: The psychological consequences for children* (2nd ed.). Hillsdale, NJ: Erlbaum.

Simon, H. A. (1973). The organization of complex systems. In H. H. Pattee (Ed.), *Hierarchy theory: The challenge of complex systems.* New York: Braziller.

Singer, L. T., Drotar, D., Fagan, J. F., Devost, L., & Lake, R. (1983). The cognitive development of failure to thrive infants: Methodological issues and new approaches. In T. Field & A. Sostek (Eds.), *Infants born at risk* (pp. 211–242). New York: Grune & Stratton.

Soodak, H., & Iberall, A. (1978). Homeokinetics: A physical science for complex systems. *Science, 201,* 579–582.

Sroufe, L. A. (1975). Drug treatment of children with behavior problems. In F. Horowitz (Ed.), *Review of child development research* (Vol. 4, pp. 347–407). Chicago: University of Chicago Press.

Sroufe, L. A., & Rutter, M. (1984). The domain of developmental psychopathology. *Child Development, 55,* 17–29.

Sroufe, L. A., & Waters, E. (1977). Attachment as an organizational construct. *Child Development, 48,* 1184–1199.

Stein, Z., & Susser, M. (1985). Effects of early nutrition on neurological and mental competence in human beings. *Psychological Medicine, 15,* 717–726.

Stern, D. (1977). *The first relationship: Infant and mother.* Cambridge, MA: Harvard University Press.

Stern, D. (1981). A micro-analysis of mother-infant interaction: Behaviors regulating social contact between a mother and her three-and-a-half-month-old twins. *Journal of the American Academy of Child Psychiatry, 10,* 501–517.

Thelen, E. (1989). Self-organization in developmental processes: Can systems approaches work? In M. R. Gunnar & E. Thelen (Eds.), *The Minnesota Symposia on Child Psychology: Vol. 22. Systems and development* (pp. 77–117). Hillsdale, NJ: Erlbaum.

Thomas, A., Chess, S., & Birch, H. (1968). *Temperament and behavior disorders in children.* New York: New York University Press.

Trefil, J. S. (1980). *From atoms to quarks: An introduction to the strange world of particle physics.* New York: Scribner's.

Tulkin, S. R., & Cohler, B. J. (1973). Childrearing attitudes and mother-child interaction in the first year of life. *Merrill-Palmer Quarterly, 19,* 95–106.

Tulkin, S. R., & Covitz, F. E. (1975, April). *Mother-infant interaction and intellectual functioning at age six.* Paper presented at the meeting of the Society for Research in Child Development, Denver.

Turnbull, A., Summers, J., & Brotherson, M. (1983). *Working with families with disabled members: A family systems approach.* Lawrence: University of Kansas Research and Training Center.

van IJzendoorn, M. H. (1992). Intergenerational transmission of parenting: A review of studies in nonclinical populations. *Developmental Review, 12,* 76–99.

von Bertalanffy, L. (1968). *General system theory* (rev. ed.). New York: Braziller.

Waddington, C. H. (1962). *New patterns in genetics and development.* New York: Columbia University Press.

Wallerstein, J. S., & Kelly, J. B. (1980). *Surviving the break-up: How parents and children cope with divorce.* New York: Basic Books.

Wamboldt, F. S., & Reiss, D. (1989). Defining a family heritage and a new relationship identity: Two central tasks in the making of a marriage. *Family Process, 28,* 317–335.

Wamboldt, F. S., & Wolin, S. J. (1989). Reality and myth in family life: Changes across generations. In S. A. Anderson & D. A. Bagarozzi (Eds.), *Family myths: Psychotherapy implications* (pp. 141–166). New York: Haworth Press.

Watson, J. S. (1972). Smiling, cooing and "the game." *Merrill-Palmer Quarterly, 18,* 323–339.

Watt, N., Anthony, J., Wynne, L., & Rolf, J. (Eds.). (1984). *Children at risk for schizophrenia: A longitudinal perspective.* New York: Cambridge University Press.

Wattenberg, B. J. (Ed.). (1976). *The statistical history of the United States: From colonial times to the present.* New York: Basic Books.

Weiss, P. A. (1969). The living system: Determinism stratified. In A. Koestler & J. R. Smythies (Eds.), *Beyond reductionism: New perspective in the life sciences.* Boston: Beacon Press.

Weisz, J. R., Rudolph, K. D., Granger, D. A., & Sweeney, L. (1992). Cognition, competence, and coping in child and adolescent depression: Research findings, developmental concerns, therapeutic implications. *Development and Psychopathology, 4,* 627–653.

Werner, H. (1957). The concept of development from a comparative and organismic point of view. In D. B. Harris (Ed.), *The concept of development.* Minneapolis: University of Minnesota Press.

Whiting, J. W. M. (1981). Environmental constraints on infant care practices. In R. H. Munroe, R. L. Munroe, & B. B. Whiting (Eds.), *Handbook of cross-cultural human development* (pp. 155–179). New York: Garland.

Wohlwill, J. (1973). *The study of behavioral development.* New York: Academic Press.

Wilson, E. O. (1975). *Sociobiology: The new synthesis.* Cambridge, MA: Belknap Press.

Wolff, P. H.(1987). *The development of behavioral states and the expression of emotions in early infancy: New proposals for investigation.* Chicago: University of Chicago Press.

Wolin, S., Bennett, L., & Jacobs, S. (1988). Assessing family rituals. In E. Imber-Black, J. Roberts, & R. Whiting (Eds.), *Rituals and family therapy.* New York: Norton Press.

Worobey, J., & Belsky, J. (1982). Employing the Brazelton scale to influence mothering: An experimental comparison of three strategies. *Developmental Psychology, 18,* 736–743.

Worthman, C. M. (1993). Bio-cultural interactions in human development. In M. E. Pereira & L. A. Fairbanks (Eds.), *Juvenile primates: Life history, development and behavior.* Oxford, England: Oxford University Press.

Zeanah, C. H., Mammen, O. K., & Lieberman, A. F. (1993). Disorders of attachment. In C. H. Zeanah, Jr. (Ed.), *Handbook of infant mental health* (pp. 332–349). New York: Guilford.

Zeitlin, S. J., Kotkin, A. J., & Baker, H. C. (1982). *A celebration of American family folklore.* New York: Pantheon Press.

Zeskind, P. S., & Ramey, C. T. (1978). Fetal malnutrition: An experimental study of its consequences for infant development in two caregiving environments. *Child Development, 49,* 1155–1162.

Zeskind, P. S., & Ramey, C. T. (1981). Preventing intellectual and interactional sequelae of fetal malnutrition: A longitudinal, transactional, and synergistic approach to development. *Child Development, 52,* 213–218.

CHAPTER 22

Family Systems and Developmental Psychopathology: Courtship, Marriage, or Divorce?

BARRY M. WAGNER and DAVID REISS

Family systems theories of psychopathology were, in the main, created by the pioneers of the family therapy movement (e.g., Bateson, 1972; Bowen, 1978; Haley, 1964; Minuchin, 1974). By and large, the models were derived and supported through observations of families with severe psychopathology, in particular schizophrenia. The models of family processes are often complex and theoretically rich, and they have given birth to a large movement in family therapy using techniques that draw heavily on them. Concepts such as "family homeostasis" and "triangulation" are an integral part of the everyday practice of many family clinicians. Many of the founders of these clinical models, however, were not adherents of empirical research methodology, and most of the models and concepts of family systems theory have not been put to careful, rigorous empirical test. In fact, it has often been assumed by theoreticians and clinicians that the models are too complex to be adequately tested with empirical methods.

Nevertheless, in the past 15 years, a growing number of empirically based researchers have turned to family systems models to guide new research paradigms. This movement has been aided by the development of new research methods, including microanalytic observation of behavior (e.g., Bakeman & Gottman, 1986) and statistical analysis of sequences of behavior, transitions, and reciprocity (Falk & Miller, 1991; Gottman, 1987) that allow for more adequate testing of complex models. Research incorporating family systems concepts has been applied to the study of psychopathology (e.g., Patterson & Reid, 1984), and to stressful turning points in normal families (e.g., Cowan, Cowan, Heming, & Miller, 1991; Dunn & Munn, 1985). It is important now to take stock of the degree to which this work has yielded answers to the important questions regarding the utility and veracity of family systems concepts. What evidence exists to support the family systems models as frameworks for building an understanding of the development of symptoms and processes of psychopathology?

To review all work that has utilized notions of family systems would be beyond the range of a single chapter. Rather, our focus will be on several lines of research that have yielded promising data with regard to important and interesting family systems questions. Specifically, the plan is to (a) describe these promising areas in depth; (b) critique these bodies of research methodologically; (c) discuss the implications of the work in the context of the family systems models they seek to support; and (d) discuss prospects for future research in each of these areas.

The title of the chapter reflects our observation that the relationship between empirical research and family systems theories is still relatively new. As in any relationship, it takes some time before a clearheaded judgment can be made as to its true quality and endurance. In these early years of the field, a rush of excitement has been generated about the potential of this relationship. In this chapter, we will review some of the yield of the research efforts, to sort out whether the relationship will be an enduring and productive one, as in a good marriage, or, like many adolescent romances, will fizzle after a relatively brief emission of heat and light.

MAJOR FEATURES OF FAMILY SYSTEMS THEORIES

In clarifying the parameters of family systems theories, it is necessary to recognize that there is no single, definitive family systems theory. Instead, we must identify common threads among the various theories that purport to explain family processes. In the following section, we list and describe these common threads. It is important to note that not all of the family systems theories embrace all of these assumptions and conceptions.

Family as an Integral Whole

The most fundamental assumption is that researchers and clinicians achieve an important gain in understanding and prediction by considering the family as a system. The relationships in the family place constraints on the behavior of all family members, such that we cannot understand or predict the behavior of a particular family member by knowledge of his or her individual characteristics in isolation from other family members. For example, the behavior of a boy with the diagnosis of conduct disorder cannot be understood or predicted solely through knowledge of the child's individual symptoms or personality characteristics, but must be considered in the context of the patterns of organization (i.e., the regularities of behavior) that characterize the interactions of the child with other family members and of these members with each other.

Because of the importance of these mutual influences, many systems writers have maintained that the most important unit of observation and intervention should be *relationships,* and not the individual family members. This represents a radical departure from the thinking of mainstream psychiatric and psychological thought. Indeed, only recently have major research investigators begun to take seriously the study of relationships, and to refine theories and tools for examining relationships (e.g., Hinde & Stevenson-Hinde, 1988). Curiously, the clinical literature has begun to turn back to the importance of studying the individual within the relationship. A number of family systems theorists now maintain that family therapies that attempt to manipulate behaviors within relationships have become insensitive to the motivational and phenomenological worlds of individual family members. This movement in the clinical literature is occurring contemporaneously with an increasing awareness in the research literature that individual differences, including personality, history, temperament, genetic, and other biological factors, play an important role in determining the transactions of particular family members with each other. Thus both clinical and research worlds are moving toward an integrative stance in which the study of individual factors and the study of families are seen as mutually compatible.

Circularity

Circularity is an important dimension of all family systems theories. These theories eschew unidirectional notions of family functioning, instead emphasizing mutual patterns of reciprocity. This is probably the least controversial of the family systems concepts. Many family theorists argue that assigning the cause of a problem to a particular person at a particular point is often an arbitrary matter of "punctuation" in a process, and that it is always possible to find alternative causes at alternative points. Reciprocal patterns of interaction between family members have now been demonstrated in marital couples as well as in parent-child relationships (e.g., Gottman, 1979; Patterson, 1982). These findings stem from recent developments in the sequential analysis of data that have allowed for the analysis of patterns of interaction that follow each other at varying time lags.

Family Homeostasis

This term was first applied to families by Don Jackson (1965), and has formed an important backbone of the work of many schools of family therapy, including those developed by Haley (1976) and Watzlawick and colleagues at the Mental Research Institute in Palo Alto, California (e.g., Watzlawick, Weakland, & Fisch, 1974). The principle of family homeostasis holds that families act to maintain stability. Threats to family stability, in the organizational, power, or affective realm, tend to be counteracted by family members in a manner that will retain or restore their balance. In an important elaboration of the homeostatic model, Bateson (1972), borrowing from Wiener (1961), applied the theory of cybernetics to an understanding of how families regulate their internal environment. The cybernetic model involves the concept of a *servomechanism,* in which sensors detect fluctuations in the internal environment, and act through feedback loops to restore the internal environment to a set level. A simple example of a servomechanism is a thermostat, in which fluctuations in the temperature of a room above or below a preset level cause an electronic circuit to activate heating or cooling that brings about a return to a comfortable temperature. In family systems theory, symptoms are often thought to serve a homeostatic purpose in regulating the internal environment of the family. For example, in a couple with marital strife, an argument may trigger aggressive behavior in a child which in turn diverts attention from the couple onto the child, thus stopping short the argument before the family "overheats." Vogel and Bell (1960), in their classic article on the scapegoated child, asserted that emotionally disturbed children are *always* involved in tensions between parents, in which the parents' projection of their conflict onto the child allows the marital relationship to appear more harmonious than it is.

Because of the extensive literature on the homeostatic functions of symptoms among clinical populations, homeostasis sometimes has a negative connotation, (i.e., it is a mechanism through which families resist change). Thus, clinicians look for ways to counteract this force. Homeostatic patterns can be dysfunctional, for two reasons. First, they may be inadequate to meet the demands of stressors, and, the usual homeostatic routines may be ineffective or even destructive. This situation occurs when symptoms are a regular way of maintaining stability. Second, the patterns may be overly rigid, with the set point for triggering homeostatic mechanisms at such a low level that only a slight change in the environment triggers responses to maintain stability. Such families may not have clinical problems, but they are probably not open to exploring new environmental possibilities or allowing new information into the family. These families may be at risk for developing symptoms if sufficient stress impinges on the family. However, homeostasis can also be understood to be a way in which normal families maintain constancy and predictability in the face of constantly changing environmental demands. Without homeostatic mechanisms, it would be difficult for family members to maintain a sense of regularity in the presence of everyday stresses and changes. In this way, it is a healthy force that frees the family to be less vigilant about the environment.

Family systems theorists have been interested in identifying and understanding the mechanisms through which families maintain homeostasis. The following two concepts represent the mechanisms that are thought to be most important in providing families with the potential for maintaining stability.

Triangles

Most theories of family functioning stress the importance of triangles, although the particular conception of how the triangle functions varies somewhat from one theory to the next. The most influential formulation of the importance of triangles for family functioning is that of Murray Bowen (1978; Kerr & Bowen, 1988). According to Bowen, two-person systems are inherently less stable than three-person systems. Whenever anxiety increases among two people, either because of communication difficulties within the dyad or because of external stresses impinging on the dyad, a third person becomes involved to create a triangle. The triangle is thought to be more stable than the dyad because of the increased number of relationships among which anxiety can be shifted.

Triangles in Bowen's theory are fluid systems, so that the closeness and distance among the various relationships in the triangle can alter over time. For example, when anxiety is low, the relationship among two of the individuals tends to be close and the third person tends to be the outsider. This outsider typically makes efforts to try to become more of an insider with one or the other person. However, when anxiety increases between the two insiders (e.g., persons A and B), one of the two (e.g., B) seeks closeness with the previous outsider, C, often by confiding in or complaining to C. Sometimes, according to Bowen, the situation evolves so that C, now sympathetic with B's plight, becomes entangled in conflicts with A. This allows B to be more comfortable with A, so that in effect the tension between A and B is acted out in the conflict between B and C (Kerr & Bowen, 1988). Bowen also points out that, although in low anxiety the outside position is the most isolated, during high anxiety the outside position may be the most comfortable, and family members may jockey for this position. For example, a mother may seek the outside position by trying to get the father to discipline a teenage son.

Although Bowen (1978) does not use the word "homeostasis," it is clear from his descriptions that the triangles are thought to serve the function of relieving stress in the family and thus maintaining the system's stability. In Bowen's theory, triangles are also an important construct in understanding the development of symptoms in a family. In the preceding example, if person A becomes an outsider while B and C become closer, then person A may develop symptoms in attempting to reduce the new distance. Thus, person A may feel increasingly lonely, and may turn to drinking to relieve this feeling. Haley (1977) also invoked the concepts of triangles in explaining the development of symptoms in families. He observed that in families with a symptomatic member there generally is a "coalition"—a close relationship or alliance between two members of a family that excludes a third member—and this arrangement is not openly communicated in the family. Haley further noted that the most pathological form of coalition is one in which generational boundaries are crossed. He termed this type of coalition the "perverse triangle," and believed that it coincided with violence, symptoms, or even the breakup of the system.

Minuchin, Rosman, and Baker (1978) elaborated a number of different forms of triangles in the family. One of these they termed "triangulation," in which two parents, embroiled in conflict with one another, compete for the attention and sympathy of the child. In a second form termed the "parent-child coalition," one parent sides with the child against the other parent. A third type of triangle, the "detouring-attacking" triangle, occurs when both parents detour their conflict onto the child, as in the case of the scapegoated child. These second and third types of triangles are similar to those of Bowen, described earlier. Finally, in the "detouring-supportive" triangle, both parents avoid conflict with each other through overconcern and overinvolvement with their child's problem behavior. Minuchin et al. (1978) observed this last type of triangle frequently in families of psychosomatic teenagers. From Minuchin and colleagues' perspective, a rigid adherence to a certain pattern of triangulation is one of the markers of family disturbance.

Most published clinical descriptions of triangles concern the interface of the marital relationship with a parent-child relationship. As complex as these triangles may be, they still probably oversimplify many families' patterns of interactions. In particular, family theorists and clinicians have become increasingly interested in describing sibling relationships, and understanding the various enduring roles that these relationships play in the course of development (Bank & Kahn, 1982; Dunn & Kendrick, 1982). This work has begun to yield observations that may have important implications for our understanding of the workings of some family triangles. For example, it appears that, from an early age, children are keenly aware of differences in the ways in which they are treated by a parent versus the ways a brother or sister is treated. This raises the intriguing possibility that the negative effects of scapegoating may lie in part not in the actual negative treatment the child receives, but in the child's perception that his or her treatment by a parent compares unfavorably with the treatment of a sibling.

Boundaries

Whether explicitly an integral part of the theory or not, most family systems theories incorporate the notion of boundaries. Boundaries are invisible enclosures around subsystems (e.g., individuals, parent-child subsystem, marital subsystem, sibling subsystem) in the family, and around the family as a whole. Boundaries around subsystems differ in their *permeability,* the degree to which they allow for contact with other systems. In Minuchin's (1974) terms, rigid boundaries denote a subsystem that is *disengaged* from other systems, and diffuse boundaries imply an *enmeshed* subsystem. Disengaged systems promote autonomy and mastery, but at the expense of closeness. Enmeshed systems allow members to experience support and closeness, but at the expense of the autonomy of family members. Thus, in a family with permeable boundaries around the marital subsystem, children may receive a great deal of attention from the parents, but parents may have no time or privacy to promote the growth of their marital relationship. Minuchin's structural theory emphasizes the importance for healthy family functioning of a natural hierarchy in the family, in which parents have more power in decision making and rule setting than do children. Boundaries that are neither overly permeable nor overly rigid help to preserve these functional hierarchical arrangements.

Certain family subsystems have received considerably richer theoretical treatment in the literature than others. For example, far more has been written about the marital and parent-child subsystems than about the sibling subsystem, although increasing attention is being paid to the important impact that sibling relationships may have on development across the life span, from clinical, theoretical, and empirical perspectives (e.g., Bank & Kahn, 1982; Brody, Stoneman, & McCoy, 1992; Marvin & Stewart, 1990).

As noted, a number of family systems theorists discuss the importance of the nature of boundaries not only between subsystems of the family but also around the family as a whole (Constantine, 1986; Kantor & Lehr, 1975; Minuchin, 1974; Reiss, 1981). Some families are more or less open to the flow of information from the external world and from the family to the external world. Families who are overly closed to information may be more brittle in times of stress, because they are not open to information and support that can help them to manage a crisis. On the other hand, overly permeable boundaries with the world may leave a family in a state of chaos in which family members have little sense of family membership and family identity. This characterization presupposes that there indeed exists a shared sense of family boundaries among the various family members and subsystems, a supposition that has yet to be firmly empirically established.

Another aspect of boundaries that has been of theoretical and clinical interest is the intergenerational boundaries between the nuclear family and both the family of origin as well as preceding generations. The central question of interest in this area is whether and how certain psychopathology or family difficulties are transmitted from one generation to the next. Some theorists, particularly Bowen (1978) and Boszormenyi-Nagy (Boszormenyi-Nagy & Spark, 1973), have emphasized that any problem behavior of family members can only be understood in the context of distortions in family functioning across prior generations. Bowen describes a rather complex process of intergenerational transmission of psychopathology (explained in greater detail in a later section of the chapter) in which the mother projects anxiety onto her child, and the child learns to respond with the expected anxiety because this provides relief to the relationship to some extent. Boszormenyi-Nagy and Spark (1973) hold that the tie that connects generations is loyalty, in particular the child's commitment to repay benefits received—or denied—from his or her parents. Boszormenyi-Nagy and Spark maintain that each of us is a sort of bookkeeper of a mental ledger, in which we tally up the fairness with which we have been treated and with which we treat our parents and child, and there is a desire to achieve balanced books through repaying others in the present for debts incurred in the past. Other theorists invoke the importance of attachment processes (Sroufe & Fleeson, 1988; Sroufe & Ward, 1980) or family rituals (Bennett, Wolin, & Reiss, 1988) as mechanisms that transmit patterns of behavior across generations.

Morphogenesis

The counterpoint to family homeostasis is morphogenesis—growth and change in family systems. Homeostasis provides a model of how stability is maintained, but it does not explain the process of change in families. How do families evolve and grow, and how do they achieve greater levels of complexity? Clinical family systems models have been strongly influenced by two broad models of change.

Two Definitions

Before introducing these models, it is necessary to define two terms that are often utilized in discussing change in families, and represent mechanisms by which change is achieved in both of the broad models. The first of these is a two-part term, *first- and second-order change* (Watzlawick, Weakland, & Fisch, 1974). First-order change refers to fluctuations within a set of family rules or structures. Such changes represent minor corrections that keep a family maintaining a certain course. Second-order change represents an alteration of the structure itself, in which new rules and patterns or new ways of understanding are created.

A second, closely related term is *negentropy.* General systems theories (e.g., Miller, 1965) introduced the notion that a closed or self-contained system tends to progress over time from a relatively more ordered arrangement into a less ordered arrangement. This disorder is known as *entropy.* All living systems, however, are open systems that affect and are affected by their environment. Curiously, a number of theorists from differing scientific disciplines have noted that living systems tend toward the opposite of randomness over time: They tend toward increasing complexity and organization (e.g., von Bertalanffy, 1968; Weiss, 1969; Werner, 1948); that is, development can be characterized as a progression towards levels of increasing complexity. The term negentropy has been used to denote this tendency toward increased patterning.

An equivalent way of expressing lack of order or patterning is in terms of the degree of information that is available. Patterning means that we have information that allows us to bring order to a phenomenon, whereas lack of information is equivalent to lack of order. The point of contact between this line of thinking and clinical models of the family lies in communication theories (e.g., Watzlawick, Beavin, & Jackson, 1974). Communication theorists hold that clear and effective communication of high-quality information is essential for the growth and development of the family system. Similarly, in family therapy, a family might be presented with new information that allows it to make sense of its situation in a new way, thus allowing for systemic reorganization at a higher level. In other words, increased patterning or organization is one way to bring about second-order change.

Models of Family Change

The first dominant model of change in families holds that *stress and crisis are necessary precursors to change.* Second-order change, with the possibility of new patterned behavior and new meaning, is thought to occur when homeostatic mechanisms are tipped off balance by the occurrence of stress of sufficient intensity (e.g., Bowen, 1978; Minuchin, 1974). The stress might arise as a function of normal family transitions, such as change in family membership due to the birth of a child or death or divorce, entrance to school, or career change. Or, external stresses, such as crime, job loss, or accidents, may impinge on the family. These stresses may increase family conflict or tension beyond the family's capacity to compensate through its usual homeostatic patterns (i.e., first-order solutions). In such a state, the family needs to reorganize its regular patterns of operating so that new homeostatic patterns are instituted that are appropriate to the changing environment. This generally involves finding new patterns of response and interaction. If the family cannot successfully achieve such a reorganization, then the changing environmental circumstances may precipitate a severe crisis in the family, in which the anxiety becomes intolerable. This crisis may enable the family to find new solutions that do not follow logically from their old patterns of operation. Or, it may lead to the rupture of relationships in the family.

Because of the presumed importance of crisis as a precursor to change, family therapists have devised methods for inducing a crisis in families. One prime example is the use of paradoxical techniques, which, as Hoffman (1981) observed, place the family in a therapeutic sweat box to instigate change. Another example of this approach is the work of Minuchin and colleagues (1978) with families of teenage anorectics. In the hospital setting, a lunch is served to the teenager, and the parents are told to get the child to eat. Needless to say, with most anorectic teenagers this is not an easy feat. According to Minuchin and associates, it is even more difficult than might be imagined because these families have developed "structures," or preferred behavioral patterns, that serve to minimize conflict or that overprotect the teen. The therapist intervenes so as to prevent the parents from engaging in these typical patterns. If the family has difficulty finding alternative ways of responding to the teenager (i.e., if they are relatively nonadaptive), then they will find themselves in a crisis in which they are at a loss as to how to respond.

A second model of change is the *family development model.* The earliest conceptualization of family development was the theory of the family life cycle (Carter & McGoldrick, 1980; Duvall & Miller, 1985; Hill, 1970). In the initial formulation of this model, sociologists Duvall and Hill drew on Erikson's (1950) model of psychosocial stages of development in delineating a sequence of stages of family development. These stages were seen as invariate, with each stage containing specific developmental tasks that family members must master before moving successfully to the following stage. For example, in Stage 1, "married couple," the tasks include establishing a mutually satisfying marriage, adjusting to pregnancy and the promise of parenthood, and fitting into a kin network. Stage 2, "childbearing," includes having, adjusting to, and encouraging the development of infants, and establishing a satisfying home for parents and infant. Although this model describes the necessary steps for mastery within each stage, it does not describe the process by which families move from one stage to the next (i.e., the transition process or mechanism of change).

Carter and McGoldrick (1980), in contrast, developed a model that explicitly states the emotional process and the nature of the second-order changes that are necessary for the transition to proceed at each stage. For example, in the stage at which new couples are formed, the transition process consists of "commitment to the new system," and second-order changes that are necessary at this stage include formation of the marital relationship and realignment of each partner's relationship with his or her own extended family and friends to include the spouse.

An obvious difficulty with the life-cycle models is that they describe only certain family forms. The original models were based on two-parent families with only parents and children in the home. With the multiplicity of family forms that predominate today, these models are of limited usefulness. Although Carter and McGoldrick (1980) extended their model to single-parent and stepfamilies, it is questionable whether a framework that requires extensive revision for each family form is sufficiently parsimonious to be useful.

Partially in response to the inadequacy of the life-cycle models, Steinglass and colleagues (Steinglass, Bennett, Wolin, & Reiss, 1987) developed the Family Life History model of family development, which focuses on three developmental tasks that they believe are common to all families, whatever their form or structure. The universality of these tasks is thought to be possible because they are tied to change in the family as a system, not to individual family members whose roles may differ from one family to the next. Each of the three tasks is thought to reach ascendancy as the predominant task in sequence, at particular points in family development (i.e., it is an epigenetic model).

In the early phase of development, the most important requirement is for the family to develop an identity as an independent and distinct system. In particular, this involves determining the extent to which the characteristics of each member's family of origin are continued in the new family; this process may go smoothly for some families, or may be a source of struggles for others. Often, the struggles at this point involve issues of determining the *boundaries* within the new family, as well as the boundaries between the family and the families of origin.

Steinglass and associates argue that in a middle stage of development, the most important developmental task involves choosing and *committing* to a limited number of organizing themes around which family life will revolve. Unlike the early phase, in which families may find themselves in great flux with regard to such areas of family living as rituals, values, and the importance of work and child rearing, the middle phase in normal families is marked by a relative stability and commitment around these issues (although minor fluctuations are not uncommon).

Steinglass and colleagues also identify a late phase of family life, in which the family's focus is on *the future,* particularly the preservation of its identity in future generations. To this end, the family clarifies those aspects of family life that it perceives to be at its core, and verbalizes these aspects so that they can be accurately carried on by family members in the future. Steinglass and collaborators emphasize that the greatest difficulties in family development arise when the demands of individual family members—demands that perhaps emerge as a function of adding or losing members from a family, changes in individual member's developmental level, and so on—are not compatible with the ascendent developmental level of the family as a system, as described here. The authors have demonstrated the usefulness of this model in understanding the development of alcoholic families (Steinglass et al., 1987).

Another developmental alternative to the life-cycle models is the epigenetic relationship development model of Wynne (1984). This model describes processes, or relationship dimensions, that characterize increasingly complex and mature levels of relationship systems. These dimensions represent developmental issues that must be mastered for development to proceed properly to the succeeding level. The processes are, in order of emergence: (a) attachment/caregiving; (b) communication (sharing attention and meanings); (c) joint problem solving; (d) mutuality (the capacity for systems to renew themselves or change themselves in adaptive response to changing demands); and (e) intimacy (sharing with a partner the experiences and meanings associated with all levels of this developmental scheme).

The models of both Steinglass et al. (1987) and Wynne (1984) represent intriguing alternatives to the traditional family life-cycle theories. The two schemes appear to deal with differing notions of family development, and thus may prove to be complementary. Both schemes, however, involve some complex conceptions, and some of these concepts do not yet have adequate measurement devices. Not surprisingly, then, little data exist at this point to substantiate the reliability or validity of either scheme.

PSYCHOPATHOLOGY FROM A FAMILY SYSTEMS PERSPECTIVE

Although still subject to extensive debate, there is a growing international consensus on a multiaxial taxonomy of mental disorders. Working from within this frame, it would be possible to review the relationship of family process to psychopathology under rubrics that match those in the *Diagnostic and Statistical Manual of Mental Disorders* (4th ed., *DSM-IV,* American Psychiatric Association, 1994). Thus we might review family factors in mood disorders, schizophrenia, anxiety disorders, and so on. In the past few years, a number of family systems researchers have embraced these taxonomies and selected subjects for study using standardized psychiatric diagnostic interviews capable of assigning any troubled individual in the family to at least one diagnostic category.

Although this work plays an important role in the emerging field of family systems and psychopathology, we have not organized this chapter to parallel these current taxonomies of mental disorder such as that represented by the DSM-IV or the *International Classification of Diseases and Related Health Problems* (ICD-10; World Health Organization, 1990). Family systems approaches to psychopathology offer the prospect of reconceptualizing psychopathology and perhaps, in future years, helping to shape taxonomies of disorders that look quite different from those in current use. With this prospect in mind, our chapter is organized by the previously summarized principles of family process and change to which we will return in the next section. We review the relationship of family process to psychopathology by starting with the family and its special features, as understood by current systems perspectives, and then review data linking these processes to a range of psychopathology in childhood and adulthood. The contrast between some of the assumptions of DSM-IV and a perspective consistent with family systems helps to illuminate the potential contribution of the latter to psychiatric nosology and also clarifies the approach we take in this chapter.

DSM-IV versus Family Systems Perspectives

Along Axis I in DSM-IV are arrayed the major child and adult syndromes of psychiatric disorder. These are the aggregates of emotional, cognitive, and behavioral abnormalities that cause severe distress to the individual or to those in his or her immediate environment; often, they prompt the search for treatment. There are two fundamental criteria for delineating the syndromes of Axis I. A syndrome must have symptoms or abnormalities that regularly co-occur, and its critical components must be assessed by clear, reliable indicators. The validity of these syndromes is usually examined by data on their prodromes or early clinical development, subsequent clinical course, and response to treatment. These syndromes are often the launching pads for major programmatic research into etiology.

The family systems perspective does not center on this approach to psychopathology, for three reasons. First, the systems perspective is as sensitive to interpersonal dynamics between a mental health professional and a family as it is to the dynamics of relationships within the family. The act of diagnosis, systems theorists argue, is not just a cognitive event inside the head of the clinical researcher but a transaction between the professional and the family. On the negative side, it may label the designated patient as somehow defective and victimized by the illness. This labeling might derail a process by which clinician and family perceive transactional patterns in which the psychopathology is embedded. Some family therapists, particularly those who use psychoeducational approaches, see a positive side to the diagnostic transaction: A clear, medicalized diagnosis—applied to the patient—helps reduce the family's sense of blameworthiness for the illness and opens them and the identified patient to instruction on facts about the syndrome. Although it is doubtful that families retain many of these facts over the long haul, the reduction in guilt—secondary to this explicit and strategic diagnostic process—may open them to more positive therapeutic relationships.

The second objection, closely related to the first, is the family system theorist's concern about the prevailing perspective that locates psychopathology within the skin of the patient rather than in the transactions of which the patient is a major part.

The third objection concerns notions of etiology implied by DSM-IV. DSM-IV tried to use theoretically neutral terminology to elaborate a nosology that would be equally useful to clinicians of many theoretical perspectives. However, Axis I has many syndromes that are the object of intense and programmatic research on etiology.

In earlier editions of the diagnostic manual, a conspicuous and explicit example on Axis I of the linkage between etiology and diagnosis were the Organic Mental Disorders; here the etiologic base for a syndrome was part of the name of the disorder. This general label has been dropped in DSM-IV to avoid the implication that the Organic Mental Disorders are the only disorders with a biological cause. However, most of the specific diagnoses in this section continue to attach an etiology to the symptoms (e.g., Dementia due to Huntington's Disease, Vascular Dementia, Dementia due to Other General Medical Conditions, Substance-Induced Dementia, etc.). Family system thinkers are cautious about traditional concepts of etiology that imply a single, direct cause of a clinical phenomenon. For family systems thinkers, the concept of circularity described earlier is meant to indicate the importance of patterns and richly joined networks of relationships among events and circumstances in the family. It is only in primitive, closed systems that simple concepts of cause are possible. The notion of etiology does not, necessarily, imply simple causality but its association with biomedical conceptions of pathogenesis, and in turn with DSM-IV and ICD-10, make it suspect.

Organization of the Chapter

To convey the special perspective of family systems theory on psychopathology, we have organized this chapter along themes of family regulation and development. In each of the following sections, we emphasize social process that is central to the moment-to-moment regulation of family life or to its development across time. Within each of these sections, we review research that attempts to link psychopathology with these family processes. The conceptual links vary. In some sections, we examine data to show how pathological symptoms function as part of an aberrant, self-perpetuating control mechanism in family life. In other sections, we explore data investigating psychopathology as part of a breakdown in regulation in the family system as a whole.

Research methods to explore these subtle, multifaceted links between psychopathology and family systems are just being developed. In a paradoxical sense, methods of clinical observation of families are not a primitive, first step in this branch of science. Rather, the capacity of the perceptive clinician to appraise complex family process sets a standard for quantitative methods to reach. These clinicians recognize complex patterns in family process to track how they change over time, integrate historical with contemporaneous data, and note the effects of their own entry into the family system and the impact of the family on them. Three great strides in research methods have permitted research data to make a faltering approximation to clinical observation: techniques of direct observation of family process, techniques of analyzing sequences of interaction across time, and techniques of integrating biological and social process data.

The following sections present a number of important research efforts that have sought to test the validity of the family systems concepts we have been discussing. Some of these lines of investigation were originally undertaken a number of years ago. Thus, they could not have benefited from the substantial advances made in methods in family research in recent years, and some are lacking in several important ways. In particular, minimization of shared method variance by using multiple methods and informants to measure the various constructs in a model (e.g., observation, self-report, other-report), and reduction of error variance in constructs by using structural equation modeling have become mainstays of this field. Despite their limitations, however, each of the studies included here has made an important contribution to furthering our understanding of important areas of family research.

MAJOR FAMILY SYSTEMS RESEARCH EFFORTS

As already noted, systems theory has drawn heavily for its major concepts on family therapy and on the kinds of patterning of social processes that can be grasped by sophisticated clinical perception. Thus, in its present formulations, systems theory is neither a summary of nor an agenda for empirical research. Rather, it has been an important intellectual orientation for shaping specific research hypotheses, and it often has been illuminated by research that was not originally designed as an explicit test of systems theory. Thus, in reviewing the empirical literature, we cannot summarize research by using the central categories or ideas of systems theory: circularity, homeostasis, triangularity, systems development, and so on. Rather, we have sought to define major lines of research that draw on these ideas, that subject them to empirical scrutiny, and that have modified or extended systems ideas. To do so, we have identified five themes. Three themes relate to systems concepts on the organization and patterning of process in the immediate family and how these processes connect to psychological functioning and development and to psychopathology of its individual members. These three themes are (a) how psychopathology functions to regulate intimacy in family process, (b) how family interaction process relates to biological functioning of its members, and (c) how family systems differentiate into subsystems. We have selected two additional themes that examine the transactions between the immediate family and the social world in which that family lives. The first of these two themes concerns the extended family context—more specifically, intergenerational relationships among families. The second of these two themes concerns the family's relationship to other aspects of its social community.

1. *Psychopathology as a regulator of expression of intimacy and conflict in interpersonal relationships.* Research that investigates this question serves to test a number of the issues previously outlined. First, by its nature, this question reflects a systems concept, in that there is an assumption that the behavior of each person in family relationships, and the symptoms of the identified patient, can be understood only in the context of larger systems. Second, it assumes that the symptom serves a homeostatic function: It keeps the relationship from becoming a "runaway"—Jackson's (1967) term connoting a positive feedback loop that escalates rapidly to a breakdown or blowup—by regulating the intensity of affect in the relationship. Third, it is circular: The behavior of two or more persons is assumed to mutually influence one another. Fourth, it may involve triangles in the family, although a considerable degree of research in this area has focused only on marital or parent-child dyads. In Bowen's concepts of triangles, a third person would always be involved in any attempt to modulate intense stress, but to our knowledge, this proposition has never been empirically tested.

2. *Biological factors and family systems.* A body of research illustrates the compatibility between biological models and family systems models of functioning. This work indicates that pharmacological interventions (e.g., Ritalin, antidepressants) can dramatically reorder family structure, and that physiological parameters can enhance our understanding of moment-by-moment transactions on the affective and behavioral levels in dyads.

3. *Psychopathology and the differentiation of sibling subsystems.* Efforts that stem from a behavioral genetics perspective, particularly studies of the nonshared family environment, have reinvigorated an interest in sibling subsystems. These studies have important implications for understanding the development and functioning of triangles and family alliances and provide a fresh conceptual framework for understanding old concepts such as scapegoating.

4. *Psychopathology as a regulator of the healthy differentiation of succeeding generations within families.* In addition to studies of the conventional two-generational family unit, there has been a growing interest in the transmission of pathology or protective factors across multiple generations. The most programmatic research that has been brought to bear on this question is investigation of alcoholic families (Bennett & Wolin, 1990). This work serves as a test of the issue of whether and how multigenerational transmission of psychopathology takes place.

5. *Psychopathology, the family, and the social systems in which it is embedded.* Research focusing on the interface of the family system with the peer system (e.g., Dishion, 1990), with the medical system (Reiss, Gonzalez, & Kramer, 1986), and with the outside world generally (e.g., Boss & Greenberg, 1984) provides a test of the utility of conceptions of family boundaries.

PSYCHOPATHOLOGY AS A REGULATOR OF INTIMACY AND CONFLICT IN FAMILY RELATIONSHIPS

In this section, two bodies of research will be investigated that shed light on the issue of how psychopathology can regulate closeness in family relationships. The first involves research on depression as a regulator of emotional expression in dyadic or family relationships; the second investigates how a third family member entering into a conflict situation between two other members influences that conflict.

Depressive Symptoms as Regulators of Negative Emotions in Relationships

Traditionally, depression has been studied as a phenomenon of the individual, and psychodynamic, biological, or behavioral theories have been applied to explain its development and its course. Coyne (1976a) developed an interactional conception of depression, in which the reciprocity of behaviors between two persons serves as the context for the development, maintenance, and amplification of depressive symptoms. Coyne postulated that the behavior of depressed persons arises because the available sources of security, validation, and meaning are not sufficient or have been disrupted. The distressed behavior of the depressed person engages others, and elicits a sense of responsibility for the depressed person. However, the distress of the depressed person and the concomitant responsibility to pay attention and alleviate the distress tends to be perceived by the other as burdensome and aversive, while inducing feelings of guilt and inhibiting the direct expression of hostility or annoyance. Thus, others may act supportive and sympathetic on the surface, but subtly they will be impatient and will reject the depressed person. This is gradually sensed by the depressed person, who thus exhibits increased symptoms of distress, and so the reciprocal pattern is strengthened.

In the years since the development of these ideas, a number of research efforts have provided data that are consistent with this view of depression. Initial support for the model was provided by laboratory studies of an analogue nature, in which depressed persons interacted with strangers. These studies provided evidence that depressive behavior appears to be aversive to interactional partners, although they did not directly test whether depression elicits a sense of responsibility on the part of the interactional partner. Coyne (1976b) found that subjects who conversed with depressed outpatients on the telephone, compared with those who spoke with nondepressed outpatients or control subjects, showed more negative mood changes and were more rejecting, and Strack and Coyne (1983) found similar results with face-to-face contacts. Both Hammen and Peters (1977) and Howes and Hokanson (1979) utilized confederates to test the impact of conversing with depressed versus nondepressed persons, and in both studies subjects interacting with depressed confederates exhibited more rejecting comments and showed less interest in the confederate compared with subjects interacting with nondepressed confederates. These data, taken together, suggest that depressed persons have a negative impact on others, even when the other person has no prior knowledge of them.

Although the results of these studies are consistent with Coyne's model, it is quite possible that the interactions of depressed persons with strangers might be very different from the interactions of depressed persons with family members. Studies of marital interaction involving a depressed spouse provide a more pointed test of the validity of the interactional model. Hinchliffe, Hooper, and Roberts (1978) compared the interactions of 20 depressed inpatients with their spouses versus with a stranger, and utilized a comparison group of 20 surgical patients. Interaction was generated using Strodbeck's (1951) Revealed Difference technique and was videotaped. Two of their findings are most germane to the present discussion. First, interactions between patients and their spouses were more negative than were interactions between the patients and strangers. Thus, it appears that, if anything, the studies of strangers interacting with depressed patients may underestimate the degree of negative influence that depressed persons have on family members. Second, compared with the interactions of surgical patients and their spouses, the interactions of depressed couples were characterized by more tension, negative emotion, and lack of congruity between verbal content and nonverbal behavior (this latter finding is consistent with Coyne's view that subtle negative messages are sent by others to depressed persons).

It is still possible that the negative interactions of depressed couples reflect difficulties investigators would find in any distressed couple, and are not unique to depression. To address this possibility, Hautzinger, Linden, and Hoffman (1982) compared depressed couples seeking marital treatment with a group of nondepressed couples also seeking marital treatment, who were matched on level of marital distress. For each of the couples, eight 40-minute conversations were recorded over a period spanning 3 to 4 weeks, and the conversations were coded into 28 categories covering both nonverbal affect and verbalizations directed at self and at the partner. The findings indicated that the depressed couples expressed more negative and uncomfortable feelings than did nondepressed couples. Additionally, within the depressed couples, the depressed spouse spoke negatively about him- or herself and positively about their spouse, whereas the nondepressed spouse only rarely evaluated him- or herself but spoke negatively about the depressed spouse. The study illustrates that the interaction of depressed spouses is even more negative than for other distressed couples, and that the negative self-evaluations of the depressed spouse are reflected in negative evaluations of the patient by his or her spouse.

Coyne et al. (1987) provided further evidence that the experience of living with a depressed person can be burdensome and aversive. They examined the experience of 42 persons living with depressed inpatients and outpatients who were in a current depressive episode, and compared their experiences with those of 23 persons living with patients who had a history of depression but were not currently in a depressive episode. In this study, most but not all of the respondents were spouses of the patient (78.5% were spouses; others were lovers, friends, adult children, parent, or sibling). Based on their scores on an abbreviated version of the Hopkins Symptom Checklist (Derogatis, Lipman, Rickels, Uhlenhuth, & Covi, 1974), 40% of the respondents of currently depressed persons were sufficiently distressed so as to meet the criterion for needing psychological treatment themselves. Significantly fewer of those living with a person not in a current episode—only 17.4%—met this distress criterion. This suggests that the high percentage of distress among those living with depressed persons is not simply a function of the fact that distressed people marry distressed people (i.e., assortative mating), but rather is a function of the depressive episode itself; longitudinal tracking of symptoms of spouses of depressed patients would be necessary to more firmly demonstrate this point. The strongest predictor of distress among those living with a depressed person is their emotional reactions to the patient's symptoms (e.g., upset by patient's fatigue, burdened by patient's lack of interest in things; burdened by patient's indecisiveness; discouraged by patient's hopelessness). These results indicate that those living with a depressed person find the experience difficult and experience distress in association with this.

Krantz and Moos (1987) also compared spouses of depressed versus remitted subjects, and included a nonpatient control group as well. They found that spouses of remitted subjects were functioning better than those of depressed patients, but not as well as spouses of nonpatients, both at assessments at the time of intake and one year later.

Biglan, Rothlind, Hops, and Sherman (1989) used analogue methods and a sample of normal volunteer couples to study the reactions of spouses to distress in their partners. In one study, members of the couple were presented with written statements with self-denigrating, complaining, aggressive, or neutral content, and were asked to rate how they would respond both emotionally and behaviorally. In a second study, spouses were shown videotapes in which similar content was displayed by an actor, and were asked how they would respond emotionally and behaviorally if the person involved were their spouse. In both studies, spouses said they would respond to distressed statements/behavior with less happiness, more anxiety, and more sadness compared with how they would respond to neutral behavior; but they also said they would feel more sympathetic, caring, and supportive than they would toward spouses with neutral content, and would make comforting and supportive reactions to their spouse. In the first study, spouses reported they would be more likely to say something supportive and try to comfort their spouses if they exhibited self-denigrating or complaining behavior than if they displayed aggressive behavior. These findings are consistent with the interactional model of depression—that although distress of one spouse elicits negative emotions in the other spouse, it also invokes supportive and comforting behavior.

The Biglan et al. (1989), Coyne et al. (1987), and Krantz and Moos (1987) studies all provide further evidence of the effect of depression on spouse's functioning. However, they still tell us little about the process by which depressed spouses affect each other, and although the findings are consistent with Coyne's (1976a) interactional hypothesis, they do not provide a picture of how the symptoms reduce hostility and conflict in the spouse. Recent work by Biglan Hops, and colleagues at the Oregon Research Institute (Biglan et al., 1985; Hops et al., 1987) and by Nelson and Beach (1990) provide more detailed analysis of the interactions of couples with a depressed spouse.

Biglan, Hops, and Sherman (1988) applied Patterson's (1982) theory of coercive processes in families of aggressive children to families with a depressed mother. Patterson's theory was developed initially to account for the negative parent-child interactions in families with an aggressive child. Coercive behavior consists of aversive behavior that is utilized by family members to control one another. Patterson and colleagues have shown that in families of aggressive children, all family members exhibit higher rates of coercive behavior than in normal families. Further, the theory posits that a child's aggressive behavior is maintained by negative reinforcement in which, after a cycle of reciprocated negative exchanges between mother and child, mothers eventually yield to the child. This is reinforcing to these children, because they learn that if they persist in negative behavior they will ultimately win. It is also reinforcing to the parent because his or her behavior results in the cessation of the child's negative behavior.

In applying this theory to depression in mothers, Biglan et al. (1988) assert that (a) family environments of depressed spouses will be characterized by higher rates of aversive behavior than that of normal families; (b) depressed wives will emit more aversive behavior and less positive behavior than control subjects; and (c) the dysphoric behavior of depressed mothers may decrease other family member's aversive behavior, as well as elicit positive support and sympathy. In their first study aimed at testing the process of coercive exchange in depressed women, Biglan et al. (1985) observed 27 married couples in which the wife was clinically depressed, and 25 normal control married couples, recruited so as to be both nondepressed and maritally satisfied. Approximately 50% of the couples with a clinically depressed mother reported that they were dissatisfied with their relationship ("depressed/distressed couples") and 50% were nondistressed ("depressed couples"). Couples were observed in the laboratory discussing two disagreements in their relationship in two 10-minute sessions. The sessions were videotaped and coded using the LIFE (Living in Familial Environments) coding system that was devised from this study. This system is an adaptation of the Marital Interaction Coding System (Hops, Wills, Patterson, & Weiss, 1972) and the Family Interaction Coding System (Reid, 1978).

The between-group results on the frequencies of behaviors are important in that they again indicate the high levels of aversive behaviors present in couples with a depressed spouse. Both distressed and nondistressed couples with a depressed wife showed less self-disclosure than did normal couples. The depressed/distressed couples showed less facilitative behavior (e.g., empathy, acceptance of responsibility, humor/happiness) than either the depressed couples or normal couples. There was a near significant finding that normal couples showed less aggressive behavior (e.g., disapproval, threats, argument) than did the two depressed groups. Depressed wives emitted higher rates of depressive behavior (e.g., complaining, ignoring, self-derogation) than did their husbands or members of normal couples.

Most important with regard to coercion theory, sequential analyses indicated that in the depressed/distressed couples, wives' depressive behavior was more likely to reduce the odds of the husband responding immediately with aggressive behavior than in the other two groups. In addition, there was a statistical trend in the direction of a lower probability of an immediate depressive response among wives following husband's aggressive behavior in the depressed/distressed couples versus other couples. These findings suggest that, among distressed couples with a depressed wife, women can at least briefly control their husband's aggression by emitting depressive behavior, and husbands can at least momentarily control their wive's depressive behavior by emitting aggressive behavior.

In a second project (Hops et al., 1987), the same couples were observed interacting with their families, including children, at home. Families were observed in 10 one-hour sessions at home, and interaction was coded live by trained observers on the LIFE coding system. As in the Biglan et al. (1985) study, the dysphoric affect displayed by depressed mothers lowered the conditional probability that husbands or children would immediately emit aggressive affect. Further, there was a statistical trend in which the mother's dysphoria was suppressed by family members' aggressive behavior. These findings, together with the Biglan et al. (1985) results, suggest that a family member's aggression and the mother's dysphoria may be part of a negative cycle in which family members attempt to avoid the aversive behavior of each other. Interestingly, caring affect displayed by family members also effectively reduced immediately subsequent mother dysphoria, suggesting that family members may learn to develop a less aversive alternative for reducing mother's depressive behavior.

Nelson and Beach (1990) replicated and extended the work of Biglan, Hops, and colleagues, comparing couples' communication among samples of depressed/discordant couples, nondepressed/discordant couples, and normal couples. They utilized a slight modification of the Kategoriensystem fur Partnerschaftliche Interaktion (KPI; Hahlweg, Reisner et al., 1984) to code interaction obtained from discussions of a problem area. In the between-group analyses of frequency of behavior, they found that normal couples showed more facilitative behavior (e.g., positive self-disclosure, acceptance, agreement) and less aggressive behavior than either of the discordant groups. Further, depressed/discordant wives emitted more depressive behavior than did nondepressed or normal wives. As in the Biglan et al. (1985) study, sequential analysis of behavior revealed that the occurrence of wife depressive behavior reduced the likelihood of husband aggressive responses. Between-group analyses of the sequences indicated that this effect was more likely in the nondepressed/discordant group than in the normal controls, with the depressed/discordant group not differing significantly from the other groups in frequency of this sequence. They found that this sequence of depressive affect and suppressed aggression is less likely in couples with longer duration of discord.

Comments and Integration

Research on interactions of discordant couples has been accumulating that provides evidence of a tendency for spouses to become increasingly reactive to negative behaviors from each other, resulting in chains of reciprocated negativity (Gottman, 1979; Hahlweg, Revenstorf, & Schindler, 1984; Levenson & Gottman, 1983; Margolin & Wampold, 1981). The research reviewed here suggests that depressive behaviors of one spouse can halt this chain of negativity, effectively putting the brakes on what might otherwise be a runaway of hostility. Further, the Hops et al. (1987) data indicated that the mother's depressive affect could also stop aggressive behavior of her children. Thus, the evidence reviewed here suggests that depressive affect may serve a homeostatic function in some families, keeping the family from overheating with aggression. The cost for the family of maintaining this pattern, however, is that although chains of aggression are broken, a new sequence involving aversive depressive behaviors is substituted.

We still have much to learn in this line of investigation. Thus far, the evidence has only investigated sequences involving those behaviors that immediately follow depressive behaviors. Presumably, this immediate impact is reinforcing for the depressed person and increases the likelihood of repeating the depressed behavior. However, it is likely that depressive behavior would be even more strongly reinforced if aggression of family members were preempted for even longer sequences of behavior. The likelihood of family members to respond with aggressive behavior in these more distant sequences has not been reported.

The processes involved in research to clarify the interpersonal effects of depression are quite complex. In part, this is because the range of negative risk factors for family functioning is correlated with parental depression, and these factors in turn, may influence the patterning of the depressed parent's interpersonal relationships. First, in families of depressed mothers, both the spouse and children may well show behavioral and affective disturbances that have an impact on their interpersonal transactions. For example, Downey and Coyne (1990), in a review of the effects of parental depression on children, pointed out that depressed mothers tend to exhibit similar behavior with their children as they do with adults: Compared with nondepressed mothers, they tend to show constricted and flat affect, they respond less positively and less promptly to children's efforts to elicit their attention, and they tend to exhibit more hostility and irritability. However, these maternal behaviors may in part be a function of the interactional style of the child; it is apparent that even young children of depressed mothers tend to display more negative and hostile interactions, and tend to elicit discomfort in and rejection by others, in much the same manner as adult depressives (Coyne, Downey, & Boergers, 1992). Further, the characteristics of the depressed parent's relationship with the spouse as well as with other adults may mediate any association between parenting and child adjustment. For example, the availability to the depressed parent of social support appears to decrease the risk of child adjustment problems in these families (Billings & Moos, 1983), whereas marital distress seems to increase the risk of child behavior problems (Emery, Weintraub, & Neale, 1982).

Chronic stress represents another risk factor that may complicate the behavior of depressed parents. Hammen (1992) reported that whereas higher levels of depressive symptoms among parents are associated with less involvement and more withdrawal from their children, higher levels of chronic stress are associated with greater criticism and negative affect in interactions with children. Hammen points out that depressed parents typically report greater levels of stress, particularly interpersonal stresses, than do other parents; therefore, it may be important to take stresses into account when analyzing the influence of depression on parenting. In addition, because the level of depressive symptoms typically fluctuates to some degree over time depressed parents' interactional style with their children may not be stable, but rather may fluctuate with changes in mood state and depressive symptoms. Further work exploring the links between parental psychopathology, stresses, marital distress and interaction, parent-child interactions, and child psychopathology is necessary to clarify the processes in these families.

Third-Party Intervention in Family Dyadic Conflict

An important observational study of triangles and alliances was conducted by Vuchinich, Emery, and Cassidy (1988). Vuchinich and associates were interested in the frequency with which third parties enter family conflicts involving two others, and, if so, what impact this has. They videotaped the dinnertime conversations of 52 volunteer families, 75% of which were two-parent families. Children ranged in age from 2 to 22 years. The tapes were scanned for episodes of verbal conflict (i.e., episodes in which at least two parties made at least two consecutive verbal oppositions). Conflict episodes were considered to be finished when three consecutive conversational turns occurred without continued verbal conflict.

The conflict episodes were coded using a system devised for this project, the Third Party Intervention Coding System (TPICS). Using this system, each conversational "turn" (i.e., unit from the point a person starts speaking to the point the person stops and either silence or another person's talk follows) was coded for who spoke, who they sided against and/or with, whether the speaker was a fighter (one of the two persons involved in the conflict) or a third-party intervener, and the type of strategic move each speaker made. These moves included (a) continuation of conflict (by opposing what another does, says, or is), (b) giving in or compromising, (c) withdrawal (refusing to talk or leaving the room), or (d) making statements that are unconnected to the conflict. The third-party intervention was coded into five categories: (a) conflict continuation, (b) authority (use of power to stop the conflict), (c) mediation or provision of information, (d) distraction, or (e) nonintervention (making a statement unrelated to the conflict). The outcomes of the conflict were coded as either a compromise, submission (one fighter gives in), standoff, or withdrawal (one fighter refuses to talk or leaves).

Vuchinich and colleagues found that, of the 176 conflict episodes that they identified (i.e., more than 3 per dinner), a third party intervened in approximately 38%. Remarkably, in almost two-thirds of conflicts, no third party intervened. Thus, Bowen's statement that third parties always are brought into a conflict did not receive support. It is possible that triangulation could have occurred at other times than at dinner for arguments that origniated at dinner. That is, perhaps in some cases, a fighter spoke with a third party at a later time. Thus, the system could underestimate triangulation. On the other hand, it may be that the third parties are likely to intervene only after the conflict becomes meaningful, and perhaps many of the conflicts at the dinner table were not meaningful ones. Unfortunately, Vuchinich et al. did not code the affect that accompanied the conflicts. It may be that all high-intensity conflicts are likely to lead to third-party intervention.

Vuchinich and collaborators coded an alliance when one family member took sides with another family member. When third parties intervened, they formed an alliance with one or the other fighter in about half (54.3%) of the cases, generally by making a conflict continuation move. In the remaining cases, the third party did not form an alliance with a fighter; in these cases, the third party generally performed a distraction behavior, a mediation behavior, or a nonintervention. Third parties were very likely to intervene in conflicts between children (they intervened in 78.0% of such conflicts) and in father-child conflicts (80.0%), and were moderately likely to intervene in mother-child conflicts (55.2%). However, third parties intervened in only 34.9% of mother-father conflicts. Overall, daughters were significantly more likely to intervene in conflicts than any other family member, and sons were the least likely to intervene. Daughters however, were no more likely than sons to intervene in conflicts between their parents. Mothers were almost three times as likely to intervene in conflicts between children as were fathers.

Regarding the formation of alliances, the frequencies of family members taking sides with each other were approximately equal across the different dyads. More interesting were the data regarding taking sides against another family member (i.e., coalitions). The likelihood of a parent siding against the other parent (i.e., the number of such interventions divided by the number of opportunities the person had to intervene) was only .04, whereas the likelihood of a parent siding against a child was .28; the difference between these two likelihood ratios was significant. Thus, in these normal families, parents were very unlikely to side against each other, at least in the presence of their children.

Comments and Integration

Vuchinich et al.'s work represents an important step forward in our understanding of third-party interventions in conflict. It illustrates that family members do indeed become involved at high rates in family conflicts involving two others, although perhaps not as high as some family systems thinkers might have speculated. Further, it provides important information regarding the rates of intervention by various family members, and the frequencies with which various family members side with or against each other. The study is the only one of its kind to utilize observational methods to investigate third-party intervention in conflict. Further, it is one of only a few studies that have investigated alliances through using coded interactions.

There are several limitations to the work of Vuchinich and colleagues (1988). One already mentioned was the failure to code the affect involved in the conflict episode, thus restricting the degree to which conclusions could be drawn about the impact of different intensities of conflict episodes on third-party intervention. In addition, only incomplete information is presented on the relative frequency of use of conflict continuation versus noncontinuation moves by parents and children. This makes it more difficult to interpret some findings. For example, Vuchinich and colleagues report that daughters are the most likely to intervene in conflicts. However, we do not know if they are more or less likely than other family members to intervene with conflict continuation or in ways intended to stop the conflict.

Alternative Conceptualization and Measurement of Triadic Interaction

Two other research programs have used observational methods to document the presence and patterning of alliances in distressed families; because of the rarity of such work and the importance of these constructs in family theory, these will be discussed in some detail. One of these efforts is the work of Margolin, Christensen, and colleagues (Christensen & Margolin, 1988; Gilbert, Christensen, & Margolin, 1984). In one project, Gilbert et al. (1984) coded videotaped observations of 12 distressed families (with both marital distress and a child with behavior problems) and 12 nondistressed families, each containing mother, father, and at least one child. Families were observed performing a problem-solving task and a menu-planning task. This interaction was coded with the Family Alliances Coding System (Gilbert et al., 1981). The system contains positive alliance content codes (e.g., expression of affection, defending or protecting another) and negative alliance codes (e.g., attacking, disaffiliating). It also contains codes for positive and negative affect.

Two important findings emerged with regard to the patterns of alliances. First, Gilbert and colleagues (1984) found that in distressed families, compared with nondistressed families, the strength of the marital alliance was low relative to the strength of other family alliances (i.e., parent-child, sibling). This result was obtained only on the problem-solving task, not on the dinner negotiation task. This result is important because it suggests that in distressed families, relationships other than the marital relationship have more positive alliances and may nurture the parents.

A second set of analyses was performed to determine if there were imbalances in the mother-child versus father-child relationship in distressed families, in which one of the parent-child relationships is more positive than the other. In particular, a "perverse triangle" arrangement in which the distress of the marital relationship is offset with a positive parent-child relationship was hypothesized. For these analyses, a target child (i.e., the child with the poorest behavior problem rating) was selected in both distressed and nondistressed families. The results indicated that, only on the problem-solving task were there greater discrepancies between the alliances of mother-target child versus father-target child in the distressed families than in the nondistressed families; generally, the mother-target child relationship was more negative than the father-target child relationship. It is unclear from the data why this imbalance exists, however. Because families were defined as distressed on the basis of both marital and child difficulties, this imbalance may reflect that mothers in the distressed families have a more negative interaction with their children than do fathers, perhaps by virtue of being the primary caregiver of a behavior-problem child. Alternatively, it is possible that difficulties in the marital relationship are being transferred to the child in a scapegoating pattern. In either case, there is no evidence for the perverse triangle model, in which difficulties in the marital relationship are offset with a close relationship with a child. The design of this study may have precluded obtaining that finding, however, since the analyses always focused on a child who displayed negative behavior problems. This child is more likely to be a target of scapegoating than of an intergenerational positive alliance. The study was further hampered by the small cell sizes that were available (the low statistical power).

A second line of research that has incorporated observational assessment of triadic interaction is the work of Heatherington, Friedlander, and colleagues on relational control, utilizing the Family Relational Communication Control Coding System (FRCCCS; e.g., Friedlander & Heatherington, 1988; Gaul, Simon, Friedlander, Cutler, & Heatherington, 1991). Relational control involves the ways in which individuals utilize verbal messages to influence one another and is not concerned with the content of the messages. The work on relational control is an outgrowth of earlier writings of the family communication theorists (e.g., Watzlawick, Beavin, & Jackson, 1974) on the *pragmatics* of communication, the messages about power and control in the relationship that are implicit in the communication. The FRCCCS assigns each message that is sent from one speaker to another a "format code," which refers to the grammatical format of the message (e.g., assertion, question, talkover, interception of another's message) as well at least one "response mode" code, that indicates the pragmatic function of the message in relation to the other speaker's previous message (e.g., support, answer to a question, disconfirmation, topic shift, etc.). The "relational control code"—which is either "one-up" (asserting control), "one-down" (giving up control), or "noncontrol defining"—is derived from these two codes according to a set of rules. For example, a closed-ended question involving support is defined as "one-down," whereas a close-ended question involving an instruction is "one-up." This system has more in common with the codes utilized by Vuchinich et al. (1988), who also examined the function rather than the content of the communication, than it does with the work of Gilbert et al. (1984), who emphasized positive versus negative affect in the communication.

The FRCCCS has the potential to be of particular interest to family researchers because, as noted, it can be utilized to code triadic interactions. One way in which the system captures triadic interaction is by assigning two response codes to a single message, one for the direct target of the message (the person who is addressed) and one for the indirect target (a person mentioned by the speaker but not directly addressed). Reciprocal influences can then be examined between the speaker and persons who are both directly and indirectly addressed. A coalition is evident when a speaker utilizes opposite control codes for two persons simultaneously, going "one-up" to one and "one-down" to another (e.g., one parent addressing the other with regard to a child: "Why don't you leave him alone, for goodness sake!") (Raymond, Friedlander, Heatherington, Ellis, & Sargent, 1993). A second way in which the system represents triadic interaction is through use of "intercept" response codes, in which a dyadic exchange is interrupted by a third person; these interceptions are necessarily assigned a "one-up" control code.

Heatherington, Friedlander, and colleagues have found the reliability of the FRCCCS codes to be quite good (e.g., Friedlander, Wildman, & Heatherington, 1991), and they have provided evidence for the validity of sets of codes for both dyadic (Heatherington, 1988) and triadic interactions (Gaul et al., 1991). The FRCCCS has also been used to test assumptions about schools of family therapy. In one study, Raymond et al. (1993) examined videotapes of 15 sessions of a single structural family therapy case in which the therapy was successful in treating an anorexic teenager and her family. The therapy was conducted by two experienced structural therapists. The purpose of the study was to examine a number of hypotheses regarding the process by which structural therapy is purported to work; for example, rigidity of transactions (measured in relational control terms) is expected to decrease over the course of therapy, it is expected that there will be fewer intergenerational coalitionary moves as therapy progresses, and interpersonal distance between generations is expected to increase over time (providing evidence of decreased enmeshment). The results indicated mixed support for the structural model, in that rigidity did decrease over time but interpersonal distance did not shift as predicted. Further, the hypotheses concerning triadic moves could not be tested because there were very few instances of intergenerational coalitionary moves or intercepts during the family sessions (the authors speculated that this was because the therapists were very active and did not allow time for within-family interactions). In general, this system shows great promise, and further work needs to be conducted to test the extent of its utility, particularly as a system for capturing triadic interactions in a variety of contexts.

Summary: Psychopathology as a Regulator of Intimacy

The literature on interaction in depressed families, and, to a lesser extent, on third-party intervention in conflict, both point to ways in which families maintain homeostasis. The work on depression (e.g., Biglan et al., 1988; Coyne et al., 1987), although still in initial stages, is perhaps the most compelling because of the replication of findings in multiple laboratories and the rigor of the studies. This literature illustrates the power of understanding psychopathology in the family context, and points clearly to patterns of reciprocity within the family. The work of Vuchinich et al. (1988) and Margolin and colleagues (Gilbert et al., 1984) supports the family systems notions of the importance of triangles and alliances for sustaining homeostatic functioning. The Vuchinich et al. (1988) study also underlined the importance of family boundaries, in that parents were unlikely to side against their partner, and children were relatively unlikely to intervene in parental conflicts. The coding system of Friedlander, Heatherington, and colleagues (e.g., Friedlander & Heatherington, 1988) shows promise as a method of efficiently capturing the control dimension in triadic interactions. Thus far, the validity of the triadic codes has been tested primarily with family therapy transcripts and a videotape of clinical treatment of one family. It will be of interest to determine the extent to which the triadic dimensions it measures are present in families in naturalistic settings, and to investigate correlates of triadic dimensions in both clinical and nonclinical settings.

BIOLOGICAL FACTORS AND FAMILY SYSTEMS

Until recently, most work that sought to unravel the workings of family systems was entirely psychosocial in nature. A few lines of investigations, however, have sought to join biological parameters with psychosocial parameters. In a prime example, pharmacological advances in the treatment of hyperactive youth have been shown to have important ramifications for the family interactions of these youth. A second example involves innovative work pursued by Robert Levenson and John Gottman (Levenson & Gottman, 1983, 1985), showing that physiological indexes of responses of couples to verbal interactions are predictive not only of substantial proportions of variance in concurrent measures of marital satisfaction, but also of changes in marital satisfaction across a period of 3 years. In the following section, we detail the work involving hyperactive children, as exemplary of the ways in which measurement of biological phenomena can inform our understanding of family systems.

Pharmacology and Family Systems: The Example of Attention-Deficit/Hyperactivity Disorder

It is probably the case that few researchers would presently hold the position that attention deficit/hyperactivity disorder (ADHD) is a product of disturbances in the family system. However, it is also probably the case that few would deny the potential importance of family interactions in exacerbating or mollifying the disorder, and in providing the child with a basis for establishing a positive sense of self in the face of academic difficulties. In this latter context, it becomes important to understand the nature of family interactions and how they might or might not be modified by pharmacological treatments. But there is a further interest in this line of work. If pharmacological treatments, which have an effect on the behavior of the child, are able to effect change on the parent as well, then there is some evidence that the parent's behavior in these interactions was at least in part responsive to the behavior of the child. That is, it provides support for the idea that the interactions in these families are not entirely "parent-driven," but are either "child-driven," or perhaps transactional; a sequence of interactions between parent and child, perhaps originating in new behavior exhibited by the child, may cumulatively be responsible for new patterns of behavior in the parent (Sameroff, 1975).

Research investigating the pharmacological effects on family interaction has as its starting point the work that first documented interactions in these families. In an early study, Battle and Lacey (1972) found mothers of hyperactive boys to exhibit more negative behavior—critical, unaffectionate, harsh—than mothers of nonhyperactive boys. Compared with the nonhyperactive boys the hyperactive children were less compliant, required more supervision, and sought attention more frequently. These boys were not diagnosed as hyperactive, but were rather described as excessively impulsive, uninhibited, and uncontrolled by parents. In two studies utilizing boys diagnosed as hyperactive, Campbell (1973, 1975) observed hyperactive boys to be more attention seeking, to require more assistance, and to be less compliant than either normal or learning-disabled boys, and observed mothers of these boys to be more likely to offer help, encouragement, and structure to the boys, presumably because they appeared to require it. Cunningham and Barkley (1979) observed 20 hyperactive and 20 normal children interacting with mothers in a playroom setting, both in free play as well as on a series of tasks in which mothers were asked to have their child comply with several commands (pick up toys, complete math problems, etc.). In general, their results were similar to the earlier findings, with mothers of hyperactive children providing more directions and structure during the tasks, and being less likely than other mothers to respond positively to their child, or, in free play, to respond at all to their child. The hyperactive children were less compliant than normal children on the tasks, and remained at the tasks for shorter periods. However, these studies were unable to determine whether in fact the child's behavior elicited the behavior of the parent, or whether parent's structuring or critical behavior was responsible for the behavior of the child.

In an attempt to determine if changes in child behavior would have an impact on mother-child interaction, Humphries, Kinsbourne, and Swanson (1978) provided either a dose of methylphenidate (Ritalin) or placebo to 26 children diagnosed as hyperactive. A double-blind, crossover design was used. One hour after drug administration, mother and child were given mazes to complete together using an Etch-A-Sketch. Time to complete the task, errors, verbal directions (e.g., "Stop," "Turn"), and praise/criticism were recorded. Results indicated that in the drug condition, compared with the placebo condition, the number of errors was lower, there was a lower frequency of mother directions, and there was a lower frequency in the amount of criticism and a higher frequency of praise given by mothers and by children to each other.

Barkley and Cunningham (1979) extended these findings by replicating the methods while using their task situation that requires the mother to get the child to comply with a series of instructions, and by utilizing a free-play situation as well. Twenty hyperactive boys participated in a double-blind, crossover design. Half the children received Ritalin 45 minutes prior to the observation and half received a placebo, then one week later the boys crossed to the opposite condition. The results indicated differences between drug and placebo groups for both boys and their mothers. In the free-play situation, the children in the drug condition showed less initiation of social interactions and more solitary play. In turn, mothers responded more often to their child's initiations in the drug condition and encouraged the play of these children. On the structured tasks, children on Ritalin complied more often than those not on Ritalin, and the sustained duration of their compliance was considerably longer. Mothers, in turn, used fewer commands in the drug condition, and made more positive responses to the compliance of their child.

In a later study, Barkley, Karlsson, Pollard, and Murphy (1985) studied 60 hyperactive boys ranging in age from 5 to 9 years old, and their mothers, in a double blind, drug-placebo crossover design. The purpose was to investigate whether the patterns observed earlier differed depending on the age of the boy or the dosage of Ritalin. The boys were observed at baseline on no medication, and at three subsequent occasions spaced approximately 1 week apart. Two dosages of Ritalin were employed (0.3mg/kg twice daily, and 0.7mg/kg twice daily). Placebo or Ritalin was taken within 1 hour of the observation periods. As in prior studies, Barkley and associates (1985) began with free play of 20 minutes, followed by five tasks in which the mother requires the compliance of the child: picking up the toys, copying geometric shapes, completing math problems, using the Etch-A-Sketch to solve a maze (with mother), and playing quietly on one side of the room. There were no significant effects of group, age, or drug condition on behavior during free play. On the tasks, however, boys on Ritalin were more compliant, and for longer periods of time, than non-Ritalin boys, and the compliance was greatest at the higher dosage. Mothers of boys on the higher dosage of Ritalin showed fewer commands, and less disapproval and negative reactions to their child's compliance, compared with mothers of non-Ritalin boys. Further, even when boys were off-task, mothers of boys on Ritalin were more attentive and less negative than were non-Ritalin mothers. Numerous nonsignificant interaction terms indicated that the effects of the drug on behavior of child and mother were not age-specific within this sample. Very similar results were also reported by Barkley and colleagues with a different sample of hyperactive boys in which ages were partitioned somewhat less discretely (Barkley, Karlsson, Strzelecki, & Murphy, 1984).

More recently, Barkley (1989) examined gender differences in the response to medication among 20 boys and 20 girls, ages 3 to 10, and their mothers. As in prior studies, a blind, crossover design was utilized, including a placebo condition and two dose levels of Ritalin. The methods directly paralleled the prior study, including the use of free play and task periods. The results indicated that mothers of hyperactive boys are more controlling and directive during the free play compared with mothers of girls, but that boys are less compliant than girls during the task sessions. As in the prior study, Ritalin resulted in increased child compliance to commands, and for greater duration, and mothers became less directive after their child received Ritalin. These effects were similar for both boys and girls, and mothers of boys and girls.

Comments and Integration

These studies illustrate the complementarity of research on biological factors and family systems. The findings impressively demonstrate that Ritalin not only markedly improves the compliance behavior of both boys and girls, but also dramatically changes the behavior of the mothers with their child. They thus provide rather convincing evidence that parent behaviors may be, at least in part, driven by the behavior of the child. Although directives and negativity on the part of the parent decrease, however, the degree of praise provided by parents is not observed to increase during some of these studies. Thus, the negative behaviors but not positive behaviors of these parents seem dependent on that of the child. In the absence of negative behaviors, it appears that the parents may be inclined to make no response to the behavior of their child (Barkley, 1989). Medication is not sufficient to produce the sorts of parent behaviors that can be expected to sustain positive interactions in the family. To help these families, it appears that it is necessary to teach parents to respond positively to their children with praise and reinforcement.

Family Subsystems Specific for Siblings in the Same Family: Integrating Genetic and Family Process Data

In the preceding two sections, we have reviewed data showing the insights provided by considering the family as a system. In the first section, we examined data suggesting that psychopathology may serve as part of a family process that regulates intimacy and distance among members. In the second section, we reviewed data suggesting that the impact of pharmacological agents on psychopathology may be mediated, in part, by the effects of these agents on the family system. In this second section, much of the data concerned a *subsystem* of the family: the mother-child dyad. Recently, genetic data has been reviewed to point to the importance of another family subsystem. In particular, there is now a lively interest in how the family may be different for each sibling in a family. Fathers and mothers may each have different relationships with their different children, and the sibling relationships may be asymmetrical so that each sibling experiences a special or unique relationship with his or her other siblings. Although the primary impetus for examining these sibling-specific subsystems comes from behavioral genetics, it is the family systems perspective that is helping to map an interesting line of current research linking family process to developmental psychopathology.

The genetic data that have stimulated interest in this area have been exhaustively reviewed (Plomin, Chipeur, & Neiderhiser, 1994; Plomin & Daniels, 1987). These data are drawn primarily from twin and adoption studies and focus on the broad classes of influences on individual differences in the development of psychopathology as well as differences in areas of social and cognitive competence. For many of these differences, heritability, or genetic influence, plays an important role, often accounting for as much as 40% of the total variance. In almost all cases, however, environmental factors unrelated to genes account for even more variance. Recent data emphasize that these environmental factors are of a very particular kind: Factors that are specific for siblings in the same family. This has been termed the *nonshared environment,* and can be compared with the *shared environment,* which, by measurement or definition, must be the same for siblings in the same family.

Examples of environmental factors that are typically measures of shared environment include social class, neighborhood decay, and maternal depression. When measures of these factors do not take into account any differences between siblings in the same family, and this is traditionally the case, then they are all defined as measures of the shared environment. However, when sibling differences are taken into account, these factors are then measures of the nonshared environment. For example, a measure of a sibling-specific aspect of social class, the financial or training resources allocated to each sibling in contrast to other siblings, is a nonshared measure. Likewise, a measure of the exposure of one specific sibling to delinquent gangs in a decayed neighborhood is also a nonshared measure. If we focus on the differential withdrawal of depressed mothers for one child, in comparison to others, we again measure the nonshared environment.

Genetic data suggest that sibling-specific environments account for most of the nongenetic environmental component of the causes of individual differences both in psychopathology and the development of competence. However, the genetic data is mute on just what these differences might be: They could be toxological, geographic, climatological, intrauterine, family, peer, occupational, or other influences across the life span. Despite their lack of specificity, the genetic data coincide with observations and ideas of those family systems theorists, clinicians, and researchers who have also argued for the importance of sibling-specific subsystems within the family (Bank & Kahn, 1982; Dunn & Munn, 1987; Dunn, Plomin, & Daniels, 1986; Gilbert et al., 1984).

The genetic data are of two kinds. First are a series of studies of families of siblings who are genetically unrelated but have been reared together from birth or nearly so. Typically, these are children who have been adopted from different families or families with one biological and one adopted child. These siblings are compared with ordinary siblings who share 50% of their genes. For a broad range of measures, the unrelated siblings show little or no correlation or concordance, whereas modest correlations or concordances are the rule for biologically related siblings. These data argue that the modest similarities between siblings are likely to be due to their genes, not the environment they share. If they were exposed to the same environments and those environments were functionally equivalent, then we would expect, at least, some positive correlation between genetically unrelated siblings.

More direct evidence of the importance of the nonshared environment comes from studies of monozygotic twins; these twins are genetic carbon copies of one another. For most traits studied, concordance rates or correlations suggest considerable differences between these genetic carbon copies. For example, recent reviews (Gottesman & Shields, 1982) suggest that concordance rates for schizophrenia may be less than 50%. This means that in any sample of identical twins, one of whom has schizophrenia, at least half the cotwins will not have schizophrenia at any point in their late adolescent or adult life. Some nonshared protective factor must have shielded these cotwins or some nonshared pathological factor must have led to the illness in the affected cotwin.

As reviews have pointed out (Plomin & Daniels, 1987; Plomin et al., 1994), error in measurement may account both for near-zero correlations in unrelated sibs and low correlations in monozygotic twins. Thus, estimates of the nonshared environment may be exaggerated when measures of low reliability are used. However, even in those studies where the reliability of measurement is very high, the nonshared effects are very strong in comparison with the effects of the shared environment.

In recent years, both family systems research and genetic research have begun to make direct measures of the environment to locate differences between sibling exposure and experience and the impact of these differences on development. It is now recognized that there are four logical steps in the inquiry (Reiss, Plomin, & Hetherington, 1991; Reiss et al., 1994).

1. *We need to know along which parameters siblings differ in their exposure to and experience of the environment.* Developmental studies have not typically asked this question.

2. *We want to know which differences are associated with differences among individuals in important developmental outcomes.* For example, are differences between siblings in harsh and abusive treatment by their parents associated with differences in antisocial behavior? This question can be asked in two ways. First, are differences within a family between the siblings in exposure to parental violence associated with differences—again within the family—between the siblings in antisocial behavior? A second question is whether the amount of increased abuse suffered by one child, in comparison with a sibling, is correlated with the level of his or her antisocial behavior in comparison with all other children in the same sample. The former is a *within-family* analysis and has interesting practical and theoretical ramifications. The latter question, a *between-families* analysis, addresses questions that are more typically considered by developmentalists: What factors account for individual differences among persons from different families.

3. *To what extent can an association between nonshared environmental variables and any outcome variable be attributed to genetic rather than environmental mechanisms?* Recent data has suggested, for example, that some time-honored findings in developmental studies—linking environmental variables to developmental outcomes—may be due in part to genetic influences. There are two ways for this to occur. First, heritable traits in the child may elicit certain forms of response from parents or children. There is now substantial evidence that this may be the case, for example, for parental affection (Plomin & Bergeman, 1991; Plomin, Reiss, Hetherington, & Howe, 1994). A second mechanism for this genetic effect is attributable to genes shared in common by parents and children. The same genes, for example, that lead a parent to behave in ways that are intellectually stimulating to children also influence the child's linguistic and cognitive competence. Indeed, an effect of this kind, comparing adopting and biological parents, has been demonstrated for the association between Caldwell and Bradley's Home Observation for Measurement of the Environment (HOME; Caldwell & Bradley, 1978), and Bayley's Mental Development Test (Braungart, Fulker, & Plomin, 1992).

4. *Can a nonshared variable be shown as causal of the developmental outcome?* Once a variable has been shown to be different for siblings in the same family, that it is associated with a developmental outcome, and that this association is not primarily attributable to genes, then longitudinal designs must be employed to determine whether the nonshared variable is antecedent or consequent to the developmental outcome.

To date, most preliminary research in this field has focused on answers to the first two of these four questions. However, at least one major study, the Nonshared Environment in Adolescent Development study, is examining all four (Reiss et al., 1994). This is a study of over 700 families divided into six groups: those with monozygotic twins (100% genetically similar), dizygotic twins, ordinary siblings in nondivorced families, and full sibs in stepfamilies (all 50% related), half sibs in stepfamilies (25% genetically related), and unrelated sibs in stepfamilies (0% related).

What is known about nonshared effects? The preliminary data in this field have been reviewed elsewhere (Hetherington & Clingempeel, 1992; Plomin & Daniels, 1987; Reiss et al., 1994), and only the briefest summary will be given here. The importance of these early data is that they reduce one very distinct possibility raised by the genetic data. These data, it must be remembered, do not indicate any specific environmental influences. They indicate only that whatever these variables might be, they are those not shared by siblings in the same family. Thus, nonshared variables could be any social, biological, or physical factors that affect psychological development. Moreover, they could be random from family to family. In one family, differences in maternal affection may lead to depression, whereas in another the nonshared influence on depression may be differential exposure to toxins in utero.

The emerging data suggest, however, that at least certain nonshared variables have systematic influences on developmental outcomes. For example, some data point to the importance of differential parenting between siblings. Dunn, Stocker, and Plomin (1990) studied variation in internalizing and externalizing symptoms in 7-year-olds who had younger siblings of the same gender. Children who received more affection and less control from their mothers, as determined by interview and direct observation, were less likely to show signs of internalizing as rated by mothers. Two studies of adolescents also suggest that differential parenting by both their mothers and fathers is important (Daniels, 1986; Daniels & Plomin, 1985). For example, the sibling who received more paternal affection than the other was the sibling most likely to develop more ambitious educational and occupational objectives. Recent data have suggested that the influence of these differential parental experiences may extend well into adulthood (Baker, 1990).

Preliminary findings indicate that differential experiences in the family are not restricted to parenting. The previously cited Daniels and Baker studies (Baker & Daniels, 1990; Daniels, 1986; Daniels & Plomin, 1985) also show that differences in the siblings' experiences with one another constitute a significant part of the nonshared environment. For example, if one sibling in a pair is caregiving and the other sibling is care receiving, the sibling environment for each is quite different. Data suggest that the more caretaking of the two siblings is least likely to show patterns of fearfulness during adolescence and early adulthood (Daniels, 1986). In addition to sibling differences in their experiences with the same parent and with each other, two of the four studies suggested the importance of differential experiences in peer groups (Baker, 1990; Daniels, 1986).

These studies report on differences between siblings on simple variables. However, siblings may accumulate differences between them across time. They will have, in effect, different life careers. Initial data are beginning to map these compounded or combined differences. For example, data reported by Bennett and her colleagues (Bennett et al., 1988) suggest a compounded sequence of nonshared experiences that may serve to protect some siblings in a family, but not others, from becoming alcoholic when one or both parents are alcoholics. Early in life, the sibling who will grow up free of alcohol is protected by the family group from alcohol; the family keeps those of its practices most cherished by the child free from intrusion by the alcoholic behavior. For example, a family may keep the child from experiencing the parental alcoholism during the child's treasured family Christmas celebration. Later, when these protected children are capable of more self-directed action, they protect themselves from the influences of the alcoholic parent by distancing themselves from the family altogether. Still later in life, the protected and distancing child is likely to marry a spouse who has no alcohol problem and who does not have a parent who drinks heavily. The sequence of these experiences, unfolding over time, may have a strong, cumulative protective effect and clearly marks off that sibling from one who ultimately succumbs to alcoholism. Further findings by Bennett and colleagues regarding family influences on transmission of alcoholism are described in the following section of this chapter.

Comments and Integration

The study of nonshared environments in families offers a fresh and clear method of conceptualizing, assessing, and analyzing environmental influences in families. The method offers an empirical approach to studying subsystems in the family, which is in harmony with many of the traditions of clinical family models outlined earlier in the chapter. Such writers as Haley (1977) and Minuchin (1974) have long argued for the importance of interactions that are unique to specific dyads in the family (e.g., alliances, coalitions), and the data from behavioral genetics studies strengthens the case for the potential importance of such environmental effects.

Up to this point, however, much of the empirical support for the importance of the nonshared environment comes from work in behavioral genetics in which the environment is not measured directly, but rather is inferred on the basis of mathematical models. In the typical behavioral genetics models, the environment, partitioned into shared and nonshared components, is the proportion of variance that remains after subtracting the variance accounted for by genetic effects and error. Major research efforts are underway in which the genetic component of variance is estimated and the environmental components are carefully measured, using multiple informants and multiple assessment methods (Reiss et al., 1994). These efforts should help to clarify the nature and extent of the influence of the nonshared environment in the development of psychopathology.

PSYCHOPATHOLOGY REGULATES THE HEALTHY DIFFERENTIATION OF SUCCEEDING GENERATIONS WITHIN FAMILIES

There is no longer any question whether families influence the psychological well-being of future generations. Patterns of intergenerational transmission of psychological phenomena have been observed by researchers in areas as diverse as divorce (Catton, 1988), child abuse (Simons, Whitbeck, Conger, & Chyi-In, 1991), suicide attempts (Sorenson & Rutter, 1991), and attachment status (Fonagy, Steele, & Steele, 1991). However, much remains to be understood about the process governing intergenerational transmission. We have already discussed that cross-generational patterns may in part be genetically determined. Of the environmental component, to what extent are family factors important, and, specifically, what type of family factors are most important? In this section, we review the theoretical building blocks of family systems conceptions of multigenerational transmission, and then trace the work that has provided empirical documentation of family systems mechanisms involved in the transmission of alcoholism.

Family Systems Notions of Multigenerational Transmission

The two dominant theories of multigenerational transmission have been introduced in an earlier section: the theory constructed by Bowen (1978; Kerr & Bowen, 1988), and that of Boszormenyi-Nagy (Boszormenyi-Nagy & Spark, 1973). Each of these will be briefly described here.

Central to Bowen's theory is the notion of "differentiation of self." In this model, a fusing of intellect and emotion constitutes a low level of differentiation; a person in this situation is dominated by emotions and is therefore nonflexible. Such a person is ruled by trying to ease his or her anxieties concerning whether love and approval will be forthcoming. More highly differentiated individuals are not governed by emotions and anxieties and are therefore more free to problem-solve even under higher degrees of stress. Undifferentiation in this sense is an individual construct.

However, it is also a family system construct. Bowen theorizes that in each family there is a certain amount of chronic anxiety; the more undifferentiated the family members, the more chronic anxiety there is. The supposition is that in many families, the sources of anxiety will not be directly acknowledged or addressed. Instead, the family will find ways to tie this anxiety up in certain loci, so that other loci are relatively anxiety free. In Bowen's (1978) view, this is effective because there is only a finite amount of anxiety that a family must manage. If anxiety is effectively tied up or bound in certain people or in certain arenas of functioning, this leaves less anxiety to cause disturbance in other areas of family functioning.

The main ways in which families indirectly manage anxiety are (a) by withdrawing from each other; (b) in marital conflict; (c) by having one spouse become ill; (d) through the family projection process. In this latter process, which is the key to multigenerational transmission, mother and child are the primary players. Bowen states that mother and not father is generally the central figure because she typically feels the most responsibility for the child's well-being.

The process begins with her anxiety. Typically, mothers who perpetuate disorder in multiple generations have deep feelings of inadequacy, in part with regard to the parenting role. This is manifested in an extreme concern for the health and functioning of the child. She may look for defects or problems in the child, and exaggerate these in her mind. She begins to treat the child in accordance with her image of the child, as if the child really is the way she projects him or her to be. Mother's concerns may be a reaction to something the child actually did, to something she imagines the child did, or to something she is afraid the child will do. In any case, she attaches significance to her perception that there is a problem with the child, because of her high degree of anxious emotion. This causes the child to respond anxiously to her. The child learns that if he or she responds in accord with mother's image, then mother is calmer; if mother is calm, the child can be calm. Mother is calmer when the child responds in ways that fit her image because the cause for anxiety is now external. Finally, the child internalizes the mother's image of him or her. In this way, the mother can make the child fit her own image. This is perceived by the mother as further validation of her perception of problems in the child and leads to further overprotection, which in turn causes more dependent yet demanding behavior by the child, and so on.

This may proceed without the development of symptoms in the child until he or she is subjected to major stressful events. Bowen (1978) observed that symptoms often do not emerge in these families until adolescence, when there is a stressful renegotiation in the direction of increased autonomy on the part of the teenager. The family projection process continues through multiple generations, and in each generation there is one child who is less differentiated than the parents; thus, across generations, there is always one offspring who functions at lower and lower levels of differentiation. Bowen claims that individuals marry others at their same level of differentiation, which further explains how the generational process continues to head in a singular direction.

In the multigenerational model of Boszormenyi-Nagy and Spark (1973), loyalty to family members, and an unspoken commitment to repay debts that are accumulated primarily within the parent-child relationship, are the major threads that connect generations. Boszormenyi-Nagy and Spark hold that children generally feel a debt toward their parents for all the care that they received when they were little, and it is difficult to find direct ways to repay this debt. Further—and they consider this point the key to why individuals remain fixed by feelings of guilt regarding parents—most individuals do not acknowledge this debt. There are three main ways that the child can repay the debt. First, on becoming a parent, an individual can attempt to repay it through the care and responsibility directed at his or her own child. Second, emotional separation from the parent can be avoided (e.g., the child never leaves home, or remains overly close even as an adult) as repayment to the parent. Third, and most optimally, a balance can be achieved so that on becoming a parent, there is give-and-take in the relationship with the new child, and also some level of repayment to the parent in the first generation.

According to this theory, the child who perceives that he or she received very little positive care from the parent is placed in a difficult situation, since there is likely to be a desire to retaliate against the parent but to do so is to be disloyal. Any number of possible solutions may be attempted to achieve a balance. For example, the child may deny any desire for revenge and may instead be overly attentive and caring to their own child to avoid repeating the mistake. Alternatively, the parent may find a scapegoat to turn against—a marriage partner, a child—and thus remain loyal to the "bad" parent.

We present Bowen's (1978) model and Boszormenyi-Nagy and Spark's (1973) model in some detail here because these are the most influential clinical models of the multigenerational transmission process. It should be apparent that there is some overlap between the two models; the undifferentiated family of Bowen resembles Boszormenyi-Nagy and Spark's child who, because of a loyalty debt, will not separate from the parent. Further, in both models, psychopathology is transmitted through parent-child relationships in which parents interact with the child to meet their own emotional needs, rather than the needs of the child. Thus, there is a violation of intergenerational boundaries, similar to those described in the triangulation models proposed by Minuchin et al. (1978) and by Haley (1977).

Disturbed Parent-Child Boundaries and Transmission of Psychopathology

Both Bowen's (1978) and Boszornmenyi-Nagy and Spark's (1973) models are rather complex, incorporating higher order, abstract constructs that would need to be simplified before being put to empirical test. This has not yet been attempted in a systematic fashion. However, there is some empirical evidence that cross-generational alliances may be pathogenic. Engfer (1988) found support for the idea that cross-generational alliances between mothers and infants may be a function of distress in the marital relationship—that the mother-infant relationship can be used to try to compensate for closeness that cannot be achieved in the marriage. She found that mother's role-reversal in her relationship with her 4-month-old infant (i.e., the degree to which mother expects that she should receive love and comfort from her child, while also experiencing anxious overprotective feelings toward the baby) were positively related to the degree of concurrent conflict in her marital relationship. Marital conflict continued to predict overprotectiveness but not role reversal prospectively from 4 months to 18 months.

Other researchers have provided similar evidence that the quality of the marital relationship affects parental attitudes and parental behavior with a child, although without suggesting that cross-generational boundaries are involved (e.g., Meyer, 1988; Olweus, 1980). Parents who are involved in a difficult marriage may be less emotionally available to their children, they may be less consistent in their discipline with their children, and they may agree less with their spouse with regard to how to parent their children (Block, Block, & Morrison, 1981); each of these problems may in turn lead to more maladaptation in their children (Block et al., 1981; Patterson & Capaldi, 1991). Within any one generation, this model suggests a unidirectional direction of influence from parent to child.

Researchers working within the attachment paradigm (e.g., Bowlby, 1980) have developed a framework for understanding cross-generational replication of relationships that incorporates notions of boundary violations. Specifically, internal working models of the whole parent-child relationship are thought to be carried forward from infancy, so that when the child grows up to become a parent, the relationship may be reenacted with the new infant, either directly or with a reversal of roles (the mother playing the role of her own mother) (Sroufe & Fleeson, 1988). When the early relationship of caregiver and child involves violation of boundaries as in the case of maternal overprotection or incest, a template of this distorted relationship is carried forward and may be recreated in the next generation.

In partial support of this notion, Sroufe & Ward (1980) empirically identified a pattern of "boundary dissolution" in which mothers are overly seductive with their infants (i.e., they exhibited intimate physical contact in ways that were not responsive to the child, such as squeezing buttocks, stroking the stomach, or grabbing the genitals) and in which mothers take on a nonmaternal role—such as acting charmed by the child or like a peer—so that their own needs are apparently gratified by the child. In a follow-up paper (Sroufe, Jacobvitz, Mangelsdorf, DeAngelo, & Ward, 1985), this pattern was found to be relatively stable across an 18-month span (child ages 24 to 42 months), and, in cases where two siblings were available in a family, the pattern was apparently unique to one mother-child dyad (generally mother-son). Importantly, 42% of mothers exhibiting this seductive pattern reported a history of incest, versus 8% of the nonseductive mothers. This suggests that these mothers were, at least in part, replicating the treatment they received as a child.

Jacobvitz, Morgan, Kretchmar, and Morgan (1991) found that mothers who recalled having been overprotected by their own mothers were more likely to be overly intrusive in observed interactions with their infants. Also, mothers who, in observed interactions with their own mother, showed weaker generational boundaries (e.g., role reversal in which mothers act as parents of the grandmother) and less positive affect were more likely to show greater intrusiveness with their infants, compared with other mothers. Again, this suggests that mothers who carry a model of disturbed parent-child relationships from their own history are more likely to cross generational boundaries to gratify their own emotional needs, and interact with their small children in inappropriate ways. Howes and Cicchetti (1993) have suggested that a similar process takes place in many maltreating families. Specifically, they argue that maltreating mothers' insecure internal representation of the parent-child relationship underlies their failure in relationships with romantic partners, and leads them to seek nurturance and care from their infants (i.e., to engage in role reversal); this, in turn, inevitably results in disappointment as the child seeks autonomy from the mother during the toddler period.

Family Rituals as the Mechanism for Replication or Differentiation of Generations

An alternate approach maintains that family rituals are a key mechanism for replicating or rejecting patterns of behavior across multiple generations. This model has been empirically investigated in a series of studies over a 15-year period by Wolin, Bennett, and colleagues (Bennett & Wolin, 1990; Bennett, Wolin, Reiss, & Teitelbaum, 1987; Steinglass et al., 1987; Wolin & Bennett, 1984; Wolin, Bennett, Noonan, & Teitelbaum, 1980). The model has been developed specifically with regard to the role of transmission in alcoholic families in an effort to explain why certain offspring, in certain families, are insulated from the negative effects of alcoholism in the home, whereas others are severely affected by having one or more alcoholic parents.

The theory developed by Bennett and Wolin (1990) states that parents and offspring from certain alcoholic families practice disengagement behaviors that may protect the offspring from repeating the substance abuse of their parents. Recent research on adolescents has documented that separation and increasing autonomy during adolescence is necessary for healthy differentiation from the family, such that an adolescent can evolve from a position of dependence on parents to one of mutuality (Grotevant & Cooper, 1985; Smetana, 1988). However, the sort of disengagement discussed by Wolin and colleagues is qualitatively different from that which is found in the normal differentiation and autonomy process. Based on their initial studies, Wolin and colleagues have formulated the notion that, to survive the negative experience of growing up in an alcoholic family, a youth must develop a pervasive sense of "differentness" from the illness in his or her family of origin, and must deliberately establish a healthy, nonabusing social network. This sense of differentness is thought to provide the youth with the stance that their life does not have to inevitably turn out to be as painful and disrupted as the family life in which they grew up.

How do youth create such a possibility when they have grown up in disturbance? Seemingly, they would be compelled to re-create that which they have known. Wolin and colleagues argue that the presence of deliberately practiced family rituals provides an important influence in leading to this ability to disengage. That is, the parent's ability to deliberately carry out rituals that are distinct from the alcoholic disruption in the family provides a model for disengaging from alcoholic behavior. Before discussing how family rituals might have the power to affect transmission of alcoholism, it is important to clarify how these researchers understand rituals.

Rituals are a symbolic form of communication that are performed systematically and repetitively, because they bring satisfaction to the family. Through their execution, they contribute to a family's collective sense of itself. They do this by clarifying expected roles of family members, by delineating the boundary of the family (i.e., who is in vs. out of the family), and by defining rules about the way that the family is (Wolin & Bennett, 1984). In devising their model, these researchers drew on earlier conceptions of rituals and their importance for family life. Probably the earliest investigation of rituals using contemporary empirical methods was performed by Bossard and Boll (1950). They documented the ritual practices among 196 nonclinical families, and noted a relationship between these shared, repeated symbolic family activities and the family's level of "integration" (i.e., values, attitudes, and goals). Reiss (1981) has written extensively about the importance of family rituals in serving to perpetuate and maintain the family paradigm, or core of shared beliefs about the world. However, only the work of Wolin and colleagues has documented the place of family ritual in the clinical functioning of the family.

Wolin and Bennett (1984) identified three types of rituals. The first of these is *family celebrations*. These include occasions that are widely practiced in the culture, with symbols that are recognized by all in a culture or subculture. Examples in our culture include both religious holidays (e.g., Christmas, Passover, and Easter), secular holidays such as Thanksgiving, and rites of passage such as weddings, funerals, and bar mitzvahs. The way in which these celebrations are typically observed for a given family contributes to the family's sense of identity, and repetition of the rituals connected with these occasions contributes to the sense of stability of the family. They are also an expression of the family's sense of connectedness with a wider cultural or religious community.

A second type of ritual is the *family tradition.* These are regular observances that, although they are common to the culture, are typically observed in ways that are quite idiosyncratic to the family. These include birthdays, anniversaries, family vacations, family reunions, and so on. Like holidays, these events often contribute importantly to the family's shared sense of itself, and family members often attach exceptional meaning to the way in which these are marked in a given family.

The third type of ritual identified by Wolin and Bennett (1984) is the *patterned routine* (e.g., bedtime routines, dinnertime routines, regular leisure activities). These regular patterns, although more variable than traditions and celebrations both across families and across time, serve to organize daily life and to define the roles of each family member. They, too, are often an expression of shared beliefs and identity in the family.

Empirical Research on Family Rituals

In their first study, Wolin and colleagues hypothesized that families who maintained the form and content of their rituals even in the face of severe drinking by one or more parents would be likely to have a strong sense of family identity apart from the alcoholism and would thus be protected with regard to transmission of drinking to the children (Wolin et al., 1980). Families in which rituals were subsumed by the alcoholic behavior—families in which the rituals were altered to meet the demands of the alcoholic parent—would be more likely to transmit alcoholism to the next generation. Interviews were conducted with 25 families in which at least one parent had an alcohol problem. In 12 of the families, there were no children with drinking problems ("nontransmitter families"); in 7 families, at least one child was classified as a "heavy" drinker with potential for becoming an alcoholic ("intermediate" families); and in 6 families, there was at least 1 alcoholic or problem-drinking child ("transmitter" families). The interview gathered information on family behavior regarding dinnertime, holidays, evening, weekends, vacations, and visitors in the home. Activities that were both patterned and meaningful to family members were identified as ritual areas.

The interviews were coded with regard to whether the rituals changed during times of heavy parental drinking. In 8 of the families, rituals remained essentially unaltered (i.e., these were "distinctive" families). In 10 families, approximately half the rituals were changed ("intermediate" families), and in 7 families all rituals were altered ("subsumptive" families). The most important question concerned whether these changes in ritual life were related to differences in transmission of alcoholism. That is, was there a relationship between transmitter category (transmitter, intermediate, nontransmitter) and whether the family was subsumptive, intermediate, or distinctive with regard to rituals? The findings indicated that there was a pattern of association between these two variables, although the results were significant only if the intermediate families on both variables are dropped. The greater the change in family rituals during the period of heaviest parental drinking, the more likely the alcohol would be transmitted to the children's generation. After deleting the intermediate families, of the 5 subsumptive families, 4 were transmitter families and 1 was nontransmitter. Of the 5 distinctive families, 0 were transmitter and 5 were nontransmitter.

Anecdotically, Wolin and colleagues (Bennett & Wolin, 1990; Steinglass et al., 1987; Wolin et al., 1980) found that, during the period of heaviest drinking, the alcoholic parent in the transmitter families was usually home, drinking and intoxicated. The parent's level of participation in family rituals generally diminished during periods of heavy drinking, and this person's behavior was accepted and tolerated by other family members. In nontransmitter families, the family members tended to directly confront the alcoholic parent whose behavior altered during the ritual, or at least to discuss the behavior in a negative manner among themselves. In fact, holiday rituals were generally kept relatively intact among nontransmitter families, but during periods of heavy drinking, they were altered for transmitter families. Thus, this first study provided evidence that the distinctiveness of family rituals was indeed associated with lower risk for transmission of alcoholism across generations.

In a second study, Wolin and colleagues (Bennett et al., 1987; Steinglass et al., 1987) sought to understand more about how one child in the family could become alcoholic while the other did not, despite having been exposed to the same environment. They hypothesized that the adult child's decisions regarding choice of spouse might be an important variable in explaining differences in transmission. The work of Cloninger, Reich, and colleagues at Washington University School of Medicine (e.g., Reich, Cloninger, Lewis, & Rice, 1981) had suggested that direct phenotypic assortative mating seemed to be occurring in couples who became alcoholic; there is evidence that two individuals are attracted to each other and become a couple because they both have a strong tendency to become alcoholic. Their work suggests that choice of marital partners can have an important impact on transmission rates. However, we still understand little about how offspring of alcoholic parents make decisions with regard to couple choices.

Bennett and colleagues (1987) attempted to explore closely certain aspects of the process by which offspring of alcoholic parents make the decision with regard to marriage partners, and how these decisions affect transmission rates. They reasoned that an offspring of an alcoholic parent has four options: (a) the person could maintain his or her ritual heritage; (b) he or she could reject that past and adopt the new spouse's ritual legacy; (c) both new spouses could bring elements from their families of origin; or (d) they could together create an entirely new set of rituals. A factor other than this ritual selection process was also presumed to affect whether alcoholism was transmitted: the quality of the ritualization of their family of origin. Thus, if the rituals in the family of origin were subsumed, and if the new family adopted these subsumed rituals, they would be at highest risk for transmission of alcoholism; if in this case, however, the rituals of the nonalcoholic spouse were adopted, these would reduce the risk of transmission. The notion that the time period around the time of the formation of the new family is an important point for making decisions regarding the extent to which the traditions of the family of origin will be carried on is consistent with the Family Life History model of Steinglass and colleagues (1987), discussed earlier.

In this project, Bennett et al. (1987) interviewed 68 married offspring and their spouses from 30 families with at least one alcoholic parent. At least two married siblings from each family were interviewed. The offspring couples were assessed with a rituals interview that was similar to the one used in the initial project; in this case, however, emphasis was placed on holiday and dinnertime rituals in the family of origin and, in a conjoint interview with spouse, rituals in the current family. Changes in the rituals in the family of origin at points when the parent was drinking the heaviest were again assessed.

The results of the study indicated that those offspring from families with distinctive dinnertimes showed less transmission than those in which the dinnertime rituals became subsumed at times of heavy drinking. Further, when the spouse comes from a family in which the degree of ritualization at dinner is high, this reduces the likelihood of transmission. A strong predictor of transmission was the degree of deliberateness, or planfulness, with which the new couple made a final heritage selection. Interestingly, there was a statistical trend ($p = .11$) indicating that a high degree of contact with the alcoholic family of origin was related to transmission of alcoholism. These results add to the pattern that disengagement is an important theme for protection against alcoholism, although it isn't necessary to break from the alcoholic family altogether. Further, they indicate that there is a choice for offspring as they form their own families. It seems to matter less whether or not the couple emulates the family-of-origin rituals than it does whether they make a deliberate choice about their rituals. These results thus provide some support for the validity of the first phase of Steinglass et al.'s (1987) Family Life History model, in that they underline the importance of creation of boundaries with the family of origin during the formation of the new family.

In a third study, Bennett et al. (1988) investigated adjustment in 144 children aged 6 to 18 years, from alcoholic families. The investigators were interested in determining whether characteristics of the family rituals, including level of ritualization, deliberateness in choosing a ritual heritage, and level of ritual disruption in the face of drinking, would be related to measures of cognitive, behavioral, emotional, and social functioning in the children. The families included 37 alcoholic families and 45 matched, nonalcoholic control families. Not surprisingly, the results indicated that children growing up in nonalcoholic families had better scores on a number of indexes of behavioral and emotional functioning. More unique to this project, however, it was found that, although the level of deliberateness in establishing family rituals was lower in alcoholic families than in control families, there were fewer behavioral problems among children in alcoholic families that deliberately executed cohesive rituals.

Generally, then, the capacity on the part of families with alcoholic members to establish and maintain family rituals protects against transmission of alcoholism as well as behavior disorders in offspring. This may be because the ritual offers a way to deliberately disengage from the alcoholism. Carrying out a meaningful ritual despite the drinking sends a message that successful separation from the alcoholism is possible. Disengagement from the alcoholism is also evident when newly forming couples can deliberately set out to establish a ritual pattern that departs from their family of origins.

The vast majority of work on family rituals has been conducted by the single research group cited here, and with alcoholic families. However, Fiese (1992) recently developed a family ritual questionnaire, based on the interview utilized by Wolin, Bennett, and colleagues (e.g., Bennett et al., 1988). Fiese asked 241 undergraduate students to complete the questionnaire along with measures of self-esteem and identity integration, and to send copies of the ritual questionnaire home to parents for them to complete. In initial psychometric work, Fiese and Klein (1993) found that the instrument showed good internal consistency as well as test-retest reliability. Fiese (1992) hypothesized that the degree to which families are highly ritualized should be related to the strength and clarity of adolescents' identities, because if rituals contribute to families' collective sense of shared identity, then they should also contribute to a strong individual identity in each family member. The data yielded significant although modest correlations between the frequency, deliberateness, and significance of ritual life, averaged across family members, and adolescent identity integration. The findings also indicated that both mothers and fathers had higher scores on frequency, significance, strong feelings, and deliberateness of rituals, compared with adolescents; thus, parents are apparently more invested in family rituals than are teenagers. Differences between mother and adolescent (in either direction) on their perceptions of a ritualization summary score comprising frequency, strong feelings associated with rituals, and deliberateness of the rituals, were negatively related to adolescents' perceptions of themselves as lovable and identity integrated. The data suggests that, in nonclinical populations, shared perceptions of rituals may indeed be related to the degree to which offspring obtain a positive and strong sense of themselves, and lack of congruence in these perceptions may result in a less positive and less coherent sense of oneself.

Comments and Integration

The findings reviewed here provide evidence for alternate models of multigenerational transmission of psychopathology. Some of the empirical work supports the importance of maintaining boundaries between parent and child, and illustrates that boundaries may partially dissolve in cases of marital problems or when the caregivers have a history of overly permeable boundaries in their early relationships (e.g., Engfer, 1988; Jacobvitz et al., 1991). Engfer's (1988) findings that maternal role reversal with the infant is related to marital distress is also supportive of models of family triangles presented by Haley (1977) and by Minuchin et al. (1978), in which compensation for a lack of closeness in the marital relationship is obtained through a cross-generational alliance of parent and child.

Both the attachment models (Sroufe & Fleeson, 1988) and the family ritual approach (Bennett & Wolin, 1990) offer a mechanism for intergenerational transmission. In the attachment model, the "internal working model" of the early caregiver relationship is carried forward in the mind of the caregiver, to be replicated in other close relationships. In the family ritual model, it is the remembrance (or "working model") of important family rituals that is carried forward—or not—to re-create the family of origin in the new family. In the attachment model, a recollection of "us," the caregiver-infant dyad, is stored in memory. In the family ritual, it is a recollection of "us" as a family that is preserved.

Thus, in contrast to other empirically tested approaches to multigenerational transmission, Bennett and Wolin's (1990) theory of family rituals is a family-level construct. The cultural relativity of the construct also serves to increase its attractiveness as a research and clinical tool. Every culture has its family rituals, and thus the construct can be translated to investigate the model in virtually any culture without undue concern that the construct is irrelevant. Although the power of family rituals as a protective mechanism has mainly been investigated with regard to alcoholism, it may also serve to reduce the risk of transmission of other disorders.

Further work must be done before we move toward utilization of family rituals as a clinical tool. The data available until this point are suggestive at best. The results have not been particularly powerful, in part because of the modest sample sizes that have been used. Also, if family rituals do indeed serve to protect succeeding generations from negative influences of alcoholism, the way in which this mechanism operates is still relatively unclear. Although the rituals may allow young persons and nonalcoholic spouses to distance themselves from the drinking, there is little evidence on this point. It is feasible that certain preexisting personality characteristics of spouses act as a "third variable," facilitating the development and maintenance of family rituals while simultaneously allowing them to withstand the effects of alcoholism in the family and providing their offspring with the care and involvement they need to successfully differentiate. Similarly, personality characteristics of the youth may facilitate their participation in ritual behavior. The point here is that personality variables might be a more parsimonious protective factor, and the higher-order family construct of rituals might be an unnecessary addition to the array of protective factors already identified by Garmezy (1987), Rutter (1987), and others. Prospective research would be helpful in untangling whether rituals are a cause or an effect of healthy adaptation of family members.

THE INTERFACE BETWEEN MULTIPLE SYSTEMS

As the field of family interaction research has matured, there has been a growing recognition of the need to take into account the broader social systems in which families are embedded: peer groups (Parke, McDonald, Beitel, & Bhavnagri, 1988), work settings (Crockenberg & Litman, 1991; Crouter, Perry-Jenkins, Huston, & McHale, 1987), community networks (Belsky, 1984), and social institutions of various kinds. Moreover, it has become increasingly clear that the pattern of influences between social institutions and the family is bidirectional. The ways in which broader social structures and institutions have an impact on the family is probably more immediately apparent than the ways in which families influence outside institutions and groups. The most immediate example in most family's lives is the impact of the media, especially television, on the development of children and the values and attitudes of the family as a whole. But it is also true that families influence social institutions. The peer network, community institutions, and schools are all strongly influenced by the family members who make up these bodies. Moreover, families manage the extent to which their members interact with outside institutions and create their own relationships with these outside structures (Reiss, 1981). In this section, we explore recent research on three important aspects of the relationship of the family with outside systems: (a) work on the nature and permeability of boundaries between the family and outside systems; (b) research on the interface between the family and the peer context among children; and (c) investigations of the interface between families coping with chronic illness and the hospital setting.

Family Boundaries: Who Is In and Who Is Out of the Family?

In our discussion on structural therapy earlier in the chapter, we noted the importance in that approach of family boundaries, highlighting almost exclusively the importance of boundaries between subsystems in a family. Thus, families in which the boundaries between parental subsystems and child subsystems are overly permeable are thought to be less healthy for family members, and some empirical findings support this contention (e.g., Minuchin et al., 1978; Sroufe et al., 1985). It is also important to consider the boundaries between the family and the larger community. Boundaries can regulate the amount of contact that the family has with the outside world. Some families are relatively closed to others and protect themselves from contact with outsiders. Other families have more permeable boundaries, and in some cases family membership can change from week to week, with relatives and friends coming and going with regularity.

Pauline Boss observed that family boundaries may be a particularly important concept in understanding how families adapt to loss (Boss & Greenberg, 1984; Boss, Greenberg, & Pearce-McCall, 1990; Boss, Pearce-McCall, & Greenberg, 1987). She posited that in situations involving loss of a family member, the most stressful component is the ambiguity—the uncertainty about whether the person is still a member of the family and about who is performing what roles and tasks in the family. This ambiguity impedes the ability of the family to reorganize to meet the demands of the loss, leaving it in a state of relative limbo (Boss & Greenberg, 1984). Boss asserts that boundary ambiguity can be a function of an objective situation in which a person cannot get accurate facts (e.g., in the case of some chronic illnesses, or in the case of soldiers missing in action) or, alternatively, a situation in which the person can get the facts but chooses to ignore, distort, or deny them (Boss, 1987). That is, the boundary ambiguity may arise as a function of the actual situation or of the individual's appraisal of the situation; however, either way, the family's perception and ascribed meaning of the situation form the crux of boundary ambiguity. Boss and colleagues have conducted a series of studies examining the utility of the boundary ambiguity concept, and have devised a series of six boundary ambiguity scales (Boss, Greenberg, & Pearce-McCall, 1990) for use with different populations. These research efforts will be reviewed here.

In her first study, Boss (1977) obtained a sample of 47 families in which the father was missing in action (MIA) in the conflict in southeast Asia (i.e., the father's location and whether he was dead or alive were unknown). In this work, Boss conceptualized boundary ambiguity as the degree of psychological presence in the face of physical absence. Cross-sectional data obtained through self-report and interviewer ratings with the family members of MIAs indicated better psychological adjustment of family members if the family experienced a low degree of psychological father presence. However, only 19 of 165 possible correlation coefficients reached significance in the data analysis. The work from this initial project led to the development of the first Boundary Ambiguity Scale, for wives of MIAs (Boss, 1980). The scale consists of 18 items loading on a single factor (e.g., "I find myself still wondering if my husband is alive"; "My children still believe that their father is alive"). In a follow-up of 37 of the wives from the original sample who had not yet remarried, low boundary ambiguity on this scale was associated with higher psychological well-being among the wives and lower family conflict as measured by wife reports on the Family Environment Scale (Moos & Moos, 1981).

Boss (1987) believes that the process of adjustment involved in families of MIAs is not discontinuous with the adjustment processes that all families must undergo at certain points in their life cycle. Deaths, leaving home for school, getting married and moving away, having an elderly parent grow frail, and so on are loss events that touch virtually all families and require clarification of boundaries. For some families, these normative events can thrust members into a crisis, whereas others achieve adjustment with minimal stress. Boss speculated that family boundary ambiguity may be one construct that is pivotal in determining whether normative family transitions are smoothly achieved. To test this, she undertook a series of studies with families experiencing different normative life crises—an adolescent leaving home, death of a spouse, and caring for spouses with Alzheimer's disease.

In the adolescent study (Boss et al., 1987), 70 married couples who reported having had an adolescent leave home completed questionnaires on stress and mental and physical health, and an 11-item Boundary Ambiguity form that was created for this study (examples of items: "I feel that it will be difficult for me now that ______ has left home"; "I think about ______ a lot"). The sample was predominantly rural (70%). Adolescents had been gone from the home an average 2.3 years. Yet, there was a broad range of responses on both mothers and fathers Boundary Ambiguity scales.

To test the major hypotheses that Boundary Ambiguity would be related to parent's physical and psychological well-being, correlations were performed of mothers' and fathers' Boundary Ambiguity scores with the indexes of stress, general affect on a semantic differential questionnaire, and somatic symptoms. Boundary ambiguity was not related to level of life stress for mothers or fathers; thus, their perception of the adolescent's physical presence was not a function of how stressful their lives had been recently. Looking at the somatic and affective dependent variables, four of the eight correlations were significant; these included associations of mother's boundary ambiguity both with father's somatic symptoms and with mother's and father's general affect, and father's boundary ambiguity with his own somatic symptoms. The magnitudes of the associations were small, however, with 4% to 9% of the variance accounted for. Although the study relied solely on self-report methods, mother's boundary ambiguity was correlated as strongly with father's dependent measures as with her own, suggesting the results are not solely a function of informer bias. It is also noteworthy that there is no information regarding the actual state of the adolescents' home leaving; for example, no information is provided about whether adolescent are in college or have moved out to their own apartment, whether they live next door or visit nightly, and so on, and whether this affects the way they are perceived by parents. Thus, it is difficult to interpret the meaning of the findings. Nevertheless, the study does provide evidence that parents vary in the degree to which they perceive their adolescent offspring have left home, and that these perceptions are systematically related to father's somatic symptoms and mother and father's affective tone.

Further construct validation of the adolescent form of the scale was performed (reported in Boss, Greenberg, & Pearce-McCall, 1990), in which the scale was included in a larger eight-state project in the North Central states. The sample was randomly selected from a commercial market panel list, and was chosen to include families in which both parents were in the home, where wives were between 35 and 54 years, and where there was at least one child in the home. The response rate was 30% to 35%. Of the approximately 1,600 families identified in this way, a second-stage sampling was done to select families in which a child had left home in the past year. This reduced the sample to 355 families. Factor analysis of the adolescent form of the Boundary Ambiguity scale revealed two factors in this sample: an "Affective Preoccupation" factor concerning how it feels to let the child go ("It will be difficult for me . . ."; "I am bothered because I miss him/her"), and a "Cognitive Preoccupation" factor ("I think about ______ a lot"; "Our family talks about ______ quite often"). Factors for both husbands and wives were similar.

In the widowhood study, Boss and colleagues (Blackburn, Greenberg, & Boss, 1987), interviewed women in Montana using a slight modification of the original Boundary Ambiguity Scale at 6 months and 1 year after the death of their spouse. The findings indicated that approximately 25% of widows agreed with items representing high psychological presence of their dead husbands, and approximately 75% agreed with items representing low psychological presence. Thus, at 6 months after the death, most women have made the psychological shift toward accommodating the loss of the husband (given this finding, it would be interesting to examine the course of the progression in boundary ambiguity over the first 6 months). At 1 year, only 18% agreed with items indicative of high phychological presence of the husband; this indicates a decrease in boundary ambiguity over the span from 6 months to 1 year. Boundary ambiguity was significantly negatively related to self-esteem at 6 months, but not at 1 year. Thus, by the end of the first year, most women had "let go" of their husbands as family members. This contrasts with the wives of MIAs, who showed relations between boundary ambiguity and indexes of individual and family functioning at the follow-up time point, 3 to 5 years after the loss of their husband.

Boss and colleagues (Boss, Caron, Horbal, & Mortimer, 1990) are currently engaged in a 5-year longitudinal study on the caregiving burden on families of Alzheimer's patients. They hypothesized that the strain will be primarily due to the perception of boundary ambiguity associated with the physical presence but increasing psychological absence from the family. They speculated that the ambiguity of whether or not they have lost the family member will hinder the development of mastery-oriented behaviors and active coping, resulting in depressive symptoms. Seventy patients and their primary caregivers have been recruited into the study. In the first year of the study, caregivers, predominantly women in their 60s and 70s, participated in a semistructured interview, including indexes of the patient's current behavior problems and functional level, a modified version of the Boundary Ambiguity Scale, the Pearlin Mastery Scale (Pearlin, Lieberman, Menaghan, & Mullan, 1981), a 7-item scale that assesses the patients' sense of mastery versus helplessness over occurrences in their life, and the Zung Depression Scale (Zung, 1965).

The modified version of the Boundary Ambiguity scale includes items such as "I feel guilty when I get out of the house to do something enjoyable while ______ remains at home"; "I put ______'s needs before my own"; "I feel like I have no time to myself." These items appear to differ in some respects from items on other Boundary Ambiguity scales, in that they focus specifically on the caregiving burden and not on the degree to which the subject has or has not let another person go. Some items do seem specifically geared toward that earlier focus (e.g., "Family members tend to ignore ______"; "______ no longer feels like my spouse/parent/sibling"). Preliminary analyses have been performed on concurrent data from the first year of the study. Results indicate significant correlations between boundary ambiguity and caregiver functioning, including depression and mastery, as well as patient functioning, including mental state, activities of daily living, and behavior problems (e.g., aggressive or affective disturbance, phobia, delusions, etc.). The strongest association for boundary ambiguity was with patient behavior problems, $r = .48$. However, the strongest correlations with caregiver depression were boundary ambiguity, $r = .39$, and mastery, $r = -.39$. Thus, this work indicates that boundary ambiguity, as measured in this study, is moderately related to the well-being of caregivers.

Comments and Integration

Boundary ambiguity represents an important bridge between structural theories of families (e.g., Minuchin, 1974), and family stress theories (e.g., Hill, 1949; Reiss, 1981) in emphasizing the importance of the family's conception of boundaries as an important determinant of well-being. The model has emphasized the individual's perceptions of the family, and measurement has been restricted to the individual's perceptions of the family boundaries. Thus, although the theory is at the family level, the measurement is at the individual level. This is in accord with Boss's contention that the important component of boundary ambiguity is the individual's perception and what that means to him or her. It remains to be demonstrated however, whether there is significant concordance between various family members' conceptions of the boundaries. Is boundary ambiguity a shared construction in the family, and if this varies from family to family, is level of concordance meaningfully related to other variables? Further validation work is needed on the various boundary ambiguity scales. In particular, as was observed, the caregiver scale contains many items that seem more related to burden than to the perception of whether the patient is in or out of the family. In addition, much of Boss's work relies on a single informant for both independent and dependent variables, and a single method of measurement (self-report). As noted earlier, recent advances in measurement theory in family research dictate the use of multiple informants and methods. In general, though, Boss and colleagues' intriguing series of studies show promising results and offer a rich picture of one important dimension of how families adapt to loss.

The Interface of the Family and the Medical System

Another interface between the family and a broader social system has been recognized recently, involving the family with a member with a chronic medical illness (Reiss et al., 1986). Willy nilly, sustained illness binds the family to the medical care system. This link is enforced in many ways. For example, the complex regimen that is ordered and monitored by the medical care team for many chronic illnesses is a constant source of disruption of important family routines. Further, extended medical care, including frequent hospitalizations, requires the family to accompany the patient for care or brings medical staff into the family's home. Further, the doctor or other members of the team are continuing sources of information, advice, and prediction for the family facing the uncertainties of severe illness. Financial issues also are binding; the costs of medical care, and the special financial practices of any medical care team in particular, may play a huge role in the life of a family. Finally, the medical care team plays a decisive role in the decision about institutionalizing some patients with chronic, debilitating illness.

Data on this interface are just beginning to accumulate. One illustrative study focused on patients with chronic renal disease (Reiss et al., 1986). Severe renal disease is a useful model for studying this process of connection between the family and the medical system. First, the most prevalent treatment is dialysis: the use of a machine to substitute for ordinary kidney function. Thus the patient, and indirectly the family, is absolutely dependent on medical technology to preserve life; a patient in chronic renal failure cannot sustain life for more than a few days without dialysis. Second, the treatment is very demanding and potentially disruptive. Dialysis sessions are thrice weekly and last from 2 to 4 hours a session. There is a demanding medical regimen beyond that, and fluid and dietary restrictions are exacting. Further, patients may often feel mildly ill and are subject to many sudden, severe, and disabling complications. Finally death, often sudden, is always imminent with a mortality rate that equals many cancers.

Reiss and colleagues set out to study the impact of three family strengths they thought would predict positive adjustment of the family to the severe and sustained stresses of this illness: the level of coordination or cooperation in a standard problem-solving task, the level of the family's economic and educational accomplishments, and the number of family members, outside the household, available for support.

There were two surprising findings. First, these three family strengths turned out to be important predictors not just of adjustment but of survival in the reverse direction from what intuition would have expected: problem-solving coordination, achievement, and support all predicted *early death.* Second, most of this effect was mediated, as expected, by the level of patient compliance, but the direction of this mediation was the opposite of intuitive expectations. *High levels of compliance* mediated the effects of the three "strengths" on survival. That is, the strengths predicted high compliance but high compliance predicted *early* death. There were no noncompliant patients in the sample because these always die early. The contrast was between fastidious compliers, who died early, and occasional noncompliers who survived much longer.

Reiss and colleagues (1986) explained their findings with reference to the interaction of the medical team and family in chronic illness. There were three steps in their explanations. First, the three family strengths are probably very effective in acute situations but may be liabilities in chronic stress. For example, highly coordinated families might have members who too readily feel their relative's illness as their own or who feel a special responsibility to provide support. This heavy involvement with the ill member may, over the long haul, lead to stress and burnout. Accomplished families may be most vulnerable to having their successful and tightly scheduled routines disrupted by chronic illness. Finally, extended family can be a useful support in the short term, but the price for having a large network may increase over time as the family with illness feels an increasing obligation to repay the help given.

The second step in the interpretation of these data is that the paradoxically strong but vulnerable families begin, earlier than others, to experience severe stress. After all other coping methods fail, the family has one left: realignment of its major relationships. The family and patient collude in this process with the patient withdrawing from the family and the family beginning to fashion a future for itself that may not include the patient.

As a consequence of this process, the patient seeks refuge in the dialysis center staff-patient community; this serves as a substitute family. The best route into such a community is fastidious compliance with its medical rules, particularly its stipulations about the medical regimen. Thus, compliance is understood as a transaction among family, patient, and staff.

This research team is currently replicating the study and more directly testing its hypotheses about family-patient-medical team relationships. The study is an 8-year longitudinal effort in which direct measurements are made of family process, the course of illness and the interactions among patient, family, and medical staff on the dialysis units.

Comments and Integration

These data have important implications for our understanding of the family's adaptation to stressful circumstances. Earlier, we discussed the crisis theory of change, in which stress is thought to be necessary for family growth and change. The data on families of dialysis patients suggests that stress may indeed result in change, specifically a realignment of boundaries within these families and between families and other systems. Boundaries that may have been relatively stable since the earliest days of the formation of these families (cf. Steinglass et al., 1987) may gradually undergo a reorganization in the process of adapting to chronic stress. Specifically, in the case of these families, boundaries may become firmer around the family members other than the patient, and the patient, finding him- or herself on the "outside," may become aligned with a new "family" of medical staff. As noted, the patterns of reorganization in dialysis families are still speculative until confirmatory evidence is available from the current replication study. However, studies from other research groups have noted similar challenges to long-standing boundaries in times of stress. For example, in families characterized by child maltreatment, the birth of the first child is often an important stressor, since an emotionally needy mother may turn away from father and toward the infant for emotional caretaking (Howes & Cicchetti, 1993). Father may find himself "on the outside" of this new, close relationship, effectively on the losing end of competition with the child for mother's attention and affection.

The Interface of the Family System and Peer System

A number of investigators have begun to examine the ways in which processes within the family influence the development of peer relationships (see Parke & Ladd, 1992). These efforts have to a large extent focused on family processes within samples of normal youth, including the role of parenting techniques; parental coaching, education, and management of peer play; family affective processes; and attachments. The findings from this research suggest that the quality of the parenting and of the parent-child relationship are directly associated with levels of competence in the peer realm. For example, investigators have established linkages between security of infant attachment to the caregiver and the quality of peer relationships (Easterbrooks & Lamb, 1979; Sroufe, Egeland, & Kreutzer, 1990). Associations have also been demonstrated between children's competence with peers and a variety of indexes of parent-child relationships, including positive parent behaviors, mothers' and fathers' emotional expressiveness, and the length of time of parent-child sustained play (i.e., "play bouts") during observed play sessions (Cassidy, Parke, Butkovsky, & Braungart, 1992; MacDonald & Parke, 1984; Parke, Cassidy, Burks, Carson, & Boyum, 1992; Putallaz, 1987).

In addition to work with samples of normal children, research has been conducted on samples of at-risk children. As an example, Zahn-Waxler and colleagues (Zahn-Waxler, Denham, Iannotti, & Cummings, 1992) investigated peer relations among children of depressed versus nondepressed mothers. They found that, among depressed mothers of 2-year-olds, positive child-rearing behaviors (e.g., showing warmth, encouragement of prosocial behavior) during peer interactions were associated with lower levels of child aggression both in the toddler period and at follow up at ages 5 to 6. Among other results reported with this sample was a finding that depressed mothers with fewer close friends were likely to have children reporting greater numbers of problems with friends.

A second example of research on the interface of family and peer worlds with at-risk populations is Cicchetti and colleagues' work with physically maltreated children (Cicchetti, Lynch, Shonk, & Manly, 1992). Child maltreatment represents an extreme of parenting dysfunction. One important question is whether maltreatment may render a child unable to form healthy relationships outside the home, or whether children may be able to form healthy peer relationships, despite the lack of secure, predictable, and nurturing relationships with a caregiver. Cicchetti and colleagues report that, by and large, the evidence from a variety of different informants—including peers, teachers, and camp counselors—suggests that maltreated youth form less satisfactory relationships with peers. For example, peers rate the behavior of maltreated youth as more disruptive and aggressive, and as showing fewer leadership qualities, relative to other youth. Teachers indicate that maltreated youth find a range of interpersonal conflict situations to be more problematic than do other youth, and that maltreated youth show poorer prosocial skills compared with others. Cicchetti et al. (1992) report that those maltreated youth who report the poorest relationships with their mothers (i.e., deprived, disengaged, confused) are most likely to desire closeness with peers; thus, these youth may turn to their peers in an effort to find the acceptance and intimacy of which they were deprived with their parents.

The remainder of this section focuses on the work that has attempted to describe and explain the linkages between the family and the peer system in the worlds of conduct-disordered children. In particular, we examine the evidence that factors in the family are related to the child's tendency to form an antisocial peer network, which in turn influences the establishment of an antisocial career. What are the points of contact between the world of peers and the family system that guide the trajectory toward antisocial behavior?

The principal work in this area has been conducted by Dishion, Patterson, and colleagues (e.g., Dishion, 1990; Dishion, Patterson, Stoolmiller, & Skinner, 1991, Patterson, 1986). Their framework emphasizes the origins of antisocial behavior in poor parenting practices in the home. They further believe that poor parenting translates into poor academic skills, and that children with both antisocial behaviors and poor academic skills tend to be rejected by most peers, and thus to gravitate toward an antisocial peer group where they can find acceptance. The links between parental child rearing and antisocial behavior have been well established (Loeber & Dishion, 1983; Patterson, 1982). So, too, have links between antisocial behavior and peer rejection (Coie & Kupersmidt, 1983; Dodge, 1983). Ladd (1983) found that rejected children tended to play with other rejected children. Dishion and colleagues have sought to test an integrative model incorporating these various elements.

Dishion (1990), in two cohorts each consisting of approximately 100 antisocial boys, demonstrated associations of peer acceptance with parental discipline, academic performance, and antisocial behavior. Using structural equation modeling with both cohorts combined, he then showed that the relationship between parenting practices and peer acceptance was mediated by both antisocial behavior and academic achievement. Thus, parent's skill level as a disciplinarian was positively associated concurrently with better academic performance and less antisocial behavior; these in turn were associated with more peer acceptance. Once the associations with peer relationships of academic performance and antisocial behavior were taken into account, there was virtually zero relationship between parent discipline and peer acceptance. These data were all obtained concurrently and thus do not provide evidence that parent discipline is a causal influence on child behavior. They also do not provide a picture of the process by which antisocial boys may drift into a negative peer group.

In a later study (Dishion et al., 1991), the same two cohorts of boys were examined using data from two time points, when boys were ages 10 and 12. A focus of this report was whether school adjustment and antisocial behavior would predict changes in the youths' association with antisocial peers. A number of variables relevant to the model were examined at age 10, including child antisocial behavior (parent, teacher, and youth reports), peer relations (sociometric ratings based on classroom nominations), parental monitoring practices, home observations of parent discipline behaviors, child's academic performance, and antisocial behavior of peers (parent, teacher, youth reports). At age 12, antisocial behavior of peers was again examined. Correlational analyses, replicated with both cohorts, indicated that the following age 10 variables were associated with peer antisocial behavior at age 12: being less liked by peers, low academic skills, antisocial behavior of the youth, poor parent discipline practices and parental monitoring, parent occupation, and parent education (the magnitude of the coefficients for the demographic variables was somewhat lower than those of other coefficients).

Regression analyses were performed on the two cohorts combined, to test the unique predictive power of each variable. In the first step, peer acceptance, academic performance, and parental monitoring and discipline were all significant predictors of age 12 peer deviance. In the second step, child antisocial behavior at age 10 predicted an additional 10% of the variation. With this variable in the equation, parent discipline practices no longer predicted deviant peers at age 12. In the third step, age 10 peer antisocial behavior was included as a predictor, accounting for an additional 3% of variance in age 12 peer antisocial behavior. In this third step, parent discipline and monitoring were no longer significant predictors of age 12 peer antisocial behavior. However, peer acceptance, academic performance, and antisocial behavior at age 10 remained predictors of age 12 antisocial peers, indicating that they accounted for increases in peer antisocial behavior.

Comments and Integration

These data have several implications for the interface of the family and peer contexts. The fact that parent discipline practices were predictive of involvement with deviant peers in bivariate analyses but not after controlling for the youth's antisocial behavior is consistent with the mediational hypothesis (Dishion, 1990; Patterson, 1986) that parenting practices give rise to antisocial behavior, which then is predictive of difficulties in the peer world. However, the causal direction of parent discipline to child antisocial behavior is still open to debate (see Lytton, 1990). The data also suggest that failure in the academic and peer realms can be influential in leading to association with a deviant peer group, two years later. Dishion and collaborators (1991) discuss the possibility that these associations may be an outgrowth of tracking in schools, where antisocial children may find themselves in the same classroom with one another, thus strengthening the odds of developing antisocial friendships. At this point, we note that each of the variables in this study (parent monitoring, parent discipline, peer antisocial behavior, etc.) were amalgams of various indicators that were constructed through inspecting the results of principal components analyses. Although combining data from multiple informants and multiple methods can reduce shared method variance, difficulties often arise in this process. Some constructs included combinations of variables that were correlated very modestly but apparently loaded together on the first principle component. For example, $r = .15$ between parent and child reports of parental monitoring, and the correlations among the various informants of antisocial behavior were not reported, but are often quite low in the research literature (e.g., Phares, Compas, & Howell, 1989). It is important to determine whether the results of the study would have differed if investigators had analyzed the reports of various informants separately, and whether it muddles matters to combine data from informants in this manner.

Summary: The Interface of Multiple Systems

A unifying theme in this section has been the usefulness of the concept of boundaries, both within families and between families and other systems. The crisis theory of change, discussed early in the chapter, postulates that the impingement of stress on the family may bring about growth and reorganization of the family. Boss's work (e.g., Boss et al., 1987), presents evidence that lack of clarity with regard to this reorganization—conceptualized as ambiguous boundaries—may perpetuate the presence of stress and associated symptoms. It appears that, until clear boundaries are re-established following the loss of a family member, it is not possible for families to redefine their family identity and move forward. Similarly, reorganization of family boundaries is seen by Reiss and colleagues (Reiss et al., 1986) as a developmental process of adapting to stress among dialysis patients and their families.

In a similar manner, one could interpret the work of Dishion and colleagues (e.g., Dishion et al., 1991) regarding the process of development of antisocial behavior in boys as another case of realignment of boundaries. Antisocial youth frequently have experienced parenting that is harsh, rejecting, and lacking in positive involvement (Loeber & Dishion, 1983), and they are also frequently rejected by the majority of their peers (Coie & Kupersmidt, 1983). Thus, they apparently tend to drift away from attempting to maintain active membership in these groups, and drift toward a new "family" of antisocial peers, among whom they may feel a sense of belonging that they cannot obtain elsewhere. The findings of Cicchetti et al. (1992), noted earlier, that those maltreated youth who have experienced the most negative relationships with mother are most likely to desire closeness with peers, is consistent with this suggestion. That is, some youth who have received extremely negative treatment in the home may seek to establish a substitute family to attain the sense of positive connection that was not forthcoming in their homes.

CONTRIBUTIONS THAT THE STUDY OF PSYCHOPATHOLOGY HAS MADE TO THE STUDY OF NORMAL FAMILY PROCESSES

An important principle of developmental psychopathology is that knowledge and research regarding abnormal and normal processes can and should inform one another. Thus, principles of normal development should be applied to theory, research design, measurement, and interpretation of work in the area of psychopathology, *plus* the study of abnormal processes should be used to inform and expand knowledge about normal developmental processes (e.g., Cicchetti, 1993). It is often more obvious how the study of normal developmental processes can be applied to the study of disorder than it is how study of the atypical can be applied to the study of normal development. Thus, it may prove useful to explore the ways in which study of abnormal family processes has contributed to thinking about normal family development processes.

Work in the area of family systems contains a number of examples of ways in which the study of disordered families has yielded information and insights that have been (and could continue to be) applied to thinking about normal families. The basic tenets of family systems models were developed through observation of families with major psychopathology, primarily schizophrenia. For example, systematic observations by Bateson (1972), Bowen (1978), and Haley (1959) led to formulation of family communication theories, as well as constructs such as coalitions, triangles, and family differentiation. In current family systems thought, these constructs are all considered to be applicable to normal families. For example, family differentiation is thought to lie on a continuum, so that in a healthy, well-differentiated family, family members are able to voice their opinions and feelings, make some decisions autonomously, and so on. Triangles are presumed to be a family coping mechanism in all families (Kerr & Bowen, 1988); however, it is expected that they are used more flexibly in normal families than in pathological families.

Minuchin and colleagues' work with anorexic families as well as with low-income clinic families led to the development and refinement of conceptions of boundaries (Minuchin et al., 1978; Minuchin, Montalvo, Guerney, Rosman, & Schumer, 1967). Minuchin and associates' permeability dimension of enmeshed-disengaged boundaries, in theory, is applicable to all family systems and subsystems; hierarchical arrangements among subsystems and a balance along the permeability dimension are seen as signs of healthy family functioning.

Several of the models of multigenerational transmission that were reviewed here were developed with disturbed families, including research by Sroufe and Fleeson (1988) invoking attachment processes, Bowen's (1978) theoretical analysis of transmission of anxiety, and the empirical work on family rituals as a transmission mechanism (Bennett et al., 1987, 1988). Each of these models has implications for normal family development. Regarding attachment processes, internal representations of the parent-child relationship are thought to occur in all individuals and to have implications for how a person parents his or her own child. Bowen's model, although still lacking empirical support, also provides a model for relatively more healthy versus less healthy management of anxiety. Healthier families are ones in which anxiety is directly acknowledged and addressed; thus, anxiety is less likely to be "bound" in pathological ways (e.g., withdrawal, marital conflict, psychosomatic illness, family projection), and less likely to be transmitted across generations. Family rituals, too, are thought to be an important component of the functioning of all families because they provide a sense of shared meaning and family identity; the role of family rituals in normal family development has been empirically explored by Fiese (1992).

In this chapter we also have described work on observation of family interaction in disturbed families that has implications for normal family processes. For example, the work of Patterson and colleagues (e.g., Patterson, 1982) has documented that coercive reciprocal processes between parent and child characterizes families of antisocial boys. An indirect outgrowth of this work on disturbed families has been the refinement of constructs and methodologies for studying normal families. For example, chains of reciprocated negative behavior involving two family members that resemble those found in antisocial families may occur in nondisturbed families, but they are likely to have a shorter duration because there is less "continuance," in which a family member continues to respond negatively no matter how a second family member behaves.

Thus, there are a number of lines of work in which research and theorizing regarding disturbed family systems have important applications for normal family processes. In some cases, these applications have already been explored; in other cases, the implications for future work are ripe. The following section offers more specific suggestions for future work, some of which build on themes of normal development mentioned in this section.

CONCLUSION

Some specific suggestions for future directions have already been included with each section of this chapter. At this point, we return to some of the broad questions that were raised at the outset, as a way of integrating the needs for future research. To what extent has the material presented in this chapter provided answers to our initial questions? Where answers are still needed, we present some suggestions for future efforts that might prove useful.

The Importance of Studying the Family as a Whole

In the first pages of this chapter, we presented the family systems assumption that it is necessary to study the family as an integrated whole to fully understand the behavior of individual family members. However, much of the current family research literature focuses on dyads, with relatively less focus either on triadic interaction or entire families. Thus, the extent to which significant knowledge is to be gained by moving to more complex levels of analysis remains somewhat unclear. Researchers probably shy away from triadic methods because they are very complex both to measure and to analyze. Methods of assessing and analyzing triadic interaction need to be further developed, refined, and possibly simplified before they are popularly adopted.

Although it is not possible to state that knowledge of the entire family is necessary to understand each individual family member, a considerable body of data now attests that family influences—marital adjustment, parental psychopathology, parent-child relationships, sibling relationships—have an important impact on psychological symptoms of individual family members. The work cited earlier both on ADHD youth by Barkley and colleagues (e.g., Barkley, 1989) and on behavioral genetics and families (e.g., Reiss et al., 1991) points to the idea that the converse is also true: It may be necessary to study individual biological or temperamental differences in individuals to understand the workings of the family, or at least of dyadic relationships within the family.

Circularity

A number of the research programs that were considered here emphasized reciprocal, mutual influences between family members. Typically, reciprocal relationships are studied in one of two ways. First, they are studied at the microanalytic level (e.g., Biglan et al., 1988). Sequential analysis is performed of videotaped or audiotaped interactions, generally of a dyad, and the probability of a particular behavior of person B, following a particular behavior of person A at a given time lag, is calculated to determine if it exceeds chance levels. Most commonly, probabilities are calculated for behaviors occurring at succeeding intervals, although the probability of chains of behavior at greater time lags is sometimes studied.

The second way in which reciprocity in families is commonly studied incorporates causal models of groups of family members (e.g., mothers and children, mothers and fathers), using either linear regression or structural equation models. In this type of analysis, the degree to which a variable of one group at an initial time point (e.g., Time 1, maternal harsh discipline) is predictive of a variable of a second group at the second time point (e.g., Time 2, child aggression) can be calculated, and the degree to which this second variable is then predictive of the behavior of the initial group at a later time point (e.g., Time 3, maternal harsh discipline) can be computed, as an index of mutual reciprocity. Here, the time intervals can be of any length, although succeeding intervals typically span at least a few months.

In practice, the information about reciprocity that is yielded by these two differing methods is quite distinct, one being informative about moment-by-moment transactions, the other typically informative about processes unfolding over considerable time lags. However, too little attention has been paid to considering and carefully specifying the length of time that is necessary for the unfolding of various family constructs, and to developing methods for studying unfolding processes of varying lengths. For example, when discussing the Vuchinich et al. (1988) findings, we noted that the response of some family members to a disagreement may not be apparent during dinnertime itself;

rather, an earlier disagreement may be brought up later in the evening. Similarly, other family processes, such as coping with interpersonal stresses or shifts in family alliances, may unfold over a span of minutes, hours, or even days. Researchers need to be attentive to the appropriate time elements involved in the research questions of interest, and need to be creative in developing methods for capturing these unfolding processes.

Triangles

In general, little work has investigated the validity of the models of triangles that were presented (e.g., Bowen, 1978; Minuchin et al., 1978). Research has yet to systematically test the applicability of various forms of triangles that have appeared in theoretical writings (e.g., "triangulation," "detour-attacking,"). These constructs typically describe patterns that are thought to occur in two-parent families, and involve triangles that theoretically defuse tension between two parents and maintain family stability. Empirical work on triangles has been restricted to families with two parents (Friedlander et al., 1991; Gilbert et al., 1984; Raymond et al., 1993; Vuchinich et al., 1988); thus, we need to learn more about the types of triangles that appear in single-parent families (e.g., between a mother and two children). The existing evidence from Vuchinich et al. (1988) suggests that triangles are less likely to occur concerning disagreements in the marital relationship than in parent-child or sibling disputes.

Future studies are needed that build on the work of Friedlander et al. (1991), Gilbert et al. (1984), and Vuchinich et al. (1988). This initial work has yielded varying operational definitions and measurement systems for assessing alliances and coalitions, focusing either on affective or control dimensions. The findings that have emerged thus far are provocative, though tentative. An important extension of this work could document the degree to which triangles naturally appear in various settings as an automatic family coping mechanism, and whether they do in fact defuse tension and maintain family stability.

Boundaries

Boundaries are a feature of some of the programs of research that were discussed (e.g., Boss, Greenberg, & Pearce-McCall, 1990; Jacobvitz et al., 1991). However, much remains to be accomplished in terms of measurement of boundaries, and validation of boundary-related constructs. Boss and colleagues have operationalized boundary ambiguity with a set of pencil-and-paper, self-report measures; however, the development of alternative methods of assessing the clarity of boundaries (e.g., observation, reports of informants) would be desirable to advance construct validation. As discussed earlier, some progress has been made on measurement of dysfunctional boundaries among parent-child dyads. For example, Jacobvitz, Sroufe, and colleagues (e.g., Sroufe et al., 1985) discovered a pattern of seductive behavior mothers exhibited with their infants that they considered to be a violation of healthy mother-child boundaries. However, we lack systematic operational definitions of healthy and unhealthy boundaries for the various family subsystems as well as the family as a whole; we also lack a set of validated measures of healthy and unhealthy boundaries for the system and subsystems (although Wood [1985] has made some important steps in this direction). Widely used pencil and paper measures of whole family functioning (e.g., Moos & Moos, 1981; Olson, 1986) tap some aspects of boundaries, especially perceived family closeness, but they are limited by the self-report methodology and they tap only a limited aspect of the construct of boundaries. Thus, further measurement development work is needed, utilizing multiple methods including reports of various informants, observational methods, as well as self-report.

Regarding cross-generational boundaries, a promising avenue of research that was reviewed is the work on family rituals as a protective factor for transmission of psychopathology. As noted earlier, the conceptualization and measurement of family rituals has been largely restricted to work with alcoholic families (Bennett et al., 1987, 1988). Fiese (1992) has demonstrated that the work can be effectively translated to normal families. Further research is necessary to test whether the protective role of family rituals has applicability for other forms of psychopathology (e.g., families in which a parent is depressed or schizophrenic). In addition, cross-cultural studies of family rituals within a diagnostic category are necessary to test the universality of the construct: Are family rituals protective across different cultures, or are there cultures in which rituals do not seem to be as effective in mitigating the negative influence of psychopathology on succeeding generations? Further work is needed to devise and test ritual-strengthening interventions with alcoholic families; such interventions will provide a strong test of the power of rituals to protect against cross-generational transmission.

As noted earlier, the way in which family rituals provide a protective mechanism remains unclear and should be carefully tested in future work. Prospective studies in which potential third variables, such as personality features of parents and youth, are systematically controlled would be helpful in clarifying the precise role of family rituals as well as in strengthening the case that rituals are a precursor, and not an effect, of healthy adaptation of family members.

Family Growth and Development

Research evidence clearly indicates that stresses can bring about change, growth, and reorganization of families (e.g., Cowan et al., 1991; Reiss et al., 1986). It appears that a range of adaptational outcomes are possible for family members in the aftermath of stresses, depending in part on the nature and severity of the stress, the level of family functioning prior to the stress, and the family coping skills and resources. However, evidence for the validity of family development models is still tentative. The family development model of Steinglass et al. (1987), developed with alcoholic families, appears to be promising; importantly, unlike prior family development models, it is not tied to any particular type of family form. Still, further empirical work is needed to test the model with various family forms and various types of psychopathology, in examining the extent to which it is capable of predicting and explaining family growth.

Similarly, Wynne's (1984) epigenetic model of relationships is an important theoretical contribution. Each level of this model, with the exception of intimacy (the highest level), has received considerable validation, but the overall model requires stringent empirical testing to determine if the sequence of stages is invariant, and whether mastery of each stage is necessary for further advancement (e.g., Does secure infant attachment constitute a necessary prerequisite for communication skills and problem solving across the life span? Is problem-solving necessary for intimacy?). Some empirical work has yielded results that are consistent with this developmental framework. In particular, work by a number of attachment theorists suggests that secure infant attachments may be a prerequisite for later problem-solving skills during childhood (Arend, Gove, & Sroufe, 1979; Sroufe et al., 1990) and greater social competence during adolescence (Kobak & Sceery, 1988). In addition, research documenting associations between attachment processes and the development of healthy romantic relationships during adult years (Feeney & Noller, 1990; Hazan & Shaver, 1987) is also consistent with this framework.

Families and Diagnostic Systems

Earlier, we detailed the distinctions between a family systems approach and the typical classification approaches used in psychiatry. Most importantly, whereas the DSM-IV (American Psychiatric Association, 1994) locates disorders within an individual, the family systems approach focuses on disturbances within relationships in the family. Thus, an important direction for the future is to develop ways of incorporating evaluations of various dimensions of family systems into existing classification systems. There are several important reasons for developing a standardized means of classifying family disturbances. Like classification of individuals, such a standardized system would provide a common language for researchers and practitioners who treat and study families, and a standard yardstick for the measurement of change in families. Equally important, it would add legitimacy to the practice of family treatment. Currently, because there is no accepted system for "diagnosing" a family, insurers will not reimburse family treatment. Instead, it is necessary to diagnose one or more family members, with the implicit message that these individuals are the "real" problem.

A number of proposals have been provided for supplementing the current diagnostic system with family evaluation constructs. For example, some have proposed including a family systems axis (e.g., Axis VI) that might consist of either a global assessment of family functioning, evaluation of any of various family constructs (e.g., boundaries, coalitions, power, etc.), or common family typologies that may match the systemic problems observed in a range of families (e.g., Fleck, 1983; Frances, Clarkin, & Perry, 1984). The DSM-IV (American Psychiatric Association, 1994) provides a Global Assessment of Relational Functioning (GARF) scale in the appendix that includes criteria and axes in need of further study. Like the DSM's Global Assessment of Functioning Scale, the GARF scale would require clinicians to assign to the family a number from 1 to 100 that represents the overall level of functioning of the relationship unit. The instructions ask the clinician to consider the degree to which the relationship meets the affective and instrumental needs in each of three areas: problem solving, organization and emotional climate. We do not yet know the extent to which such a judgment can be made reliably and meaningfully. Anders (1989) has proposed a classification system of relationship dysfunction, in which the pathology is defined as residing within the relationship, and not in an individual. He terms the most severe type of dysfunctions "relationship disorders"; these are characterized by rigid patterns of interaction, and problems in regulatory functions (i.e., either over- or underregulated, or inappropriate, irregular, or chaotic regulation of the relationship). Further development of systems of classifying relationships is important for advancement of both the science and practical issues involved in treating, evaluating, and understanding families.

FAMILY SYSTEMS AND DEVELOPMENTAL PSYCHOPATHOLOGY: A RICH AND ENDURING RELATIONSHIP

Throughout this chapter, we have attempted to summarize the extent to which each line of empirical research provides support for the various family constructs that were introduced at the outset. As we stated at the start, we have not attempted to summarize all the research that might be relevant to determining the validity of these constructs, but the research we have summarized represents the current state of the field. Although the lines of research reviewed here provide encouraging evidence for the importance of family systems concepts, the work of providing support for these concepts has only begun. Nevertheless, the evidence suggests that the research efforts in this area provide a firm foundation for a harmonious and productive future of the union of family systems and developmental psychopathology.

REFERENCES

American Psychiatric Association. (1994). *Diagnostic and statistical manual of mental disorders* (4th ed.) Washington, DC: Author.

Anders, T. F. (1989). Clinical syndromes, relationship disturbances, and their assessment. In A. J. Sameroff & R. N. Emde (Eds.), *Relationship disturbances in early childhood* (pp. 125–144). New York: Basic Books.

Arend, R., Gove, F. L., & Sroufe, L. A. (1979). Continuity of individual adaptation from infancy to kindergarten: A predictive study of ego-resilience and curiosity in preschoolers. *Child Development, 50,* 950–959.

Bakeman, R., & Gottman, J. M. (1986). *Observing behavior sequences.* New York: Cambridge University Press.

Baker, L. A., & Daniels, D. (1990). Nonshared environmental influences and personality differences in adult twins. *Journal of Personality and Social Psychology, 58,* 103–110.

Bank, S. P., & Kahn, M. D. (1982). *The sibling bond.* New York: Basic Books.

Barkley, R. A. (1989). Hyperactive girls and boys: Stimulant drug effects on mother-child interactions. *Journal of Child Psychology and Psychiatry, 30,* 379–390.

Barkley, R. A., & Cunningham, C. E. (1979). The effects of Ritalin on the mother-child interactions of hyperactive children. *Archives of General Psychiatry, 36,* 201–208.

Barkley, R. A., Karlsson, J., Pollard, S., & Murphy, J. V. (1985). Developmental changes in the mother-child interactions of hyperactive boys: Effects of two dose levels of Ritalin. *Journal of Child Psychology and Psychiatry, 26,* 705–715.

Barkley, R. A., Karlsson, J., Strzelecki, E., & Murphy, J. V. (1984). Effects of age and Ritalin dosage on the mother-child interactions of hyperactive children. *Journal of Consulting and Clinical Psychology, 52,* 750–758.

Bateson, G. (1972). *Steps to an ecology of mind.* New York: Ballantine Books.

Battle, E. S., & Lacey, B. (1972). A context for hyperactivity in children over time. *Child Development, 43,* 757–773.

Belsky, J. (1984). Determinants of parenting: A process model. *Child Development, 55,* 83–96.

Bennett, L. A., & Wolin, S. J. (1990). Family culture and alcoholism transmission. In R. L. Collins & K. E. Leonard (Eds.), *Alcohol and the family* (pp. 194–219). New York: Guilford.

Bennett, L. A., Wolin, S. J., & Reiss, D. (1988). Deliberate family process: A strategy for protecting children of alcoholics. *British Journal of Addiction, 83,* 821–829.

Bennett, L. A., Wolin, S. J., Reiss, D., & Teitelbaum, M. A. (1987). Couples at risk for transmission of alcoholism: Protective influences. *Family Process, 26,* 111–129.

Biglan, A., Hops, H., & Sherman, L. (1988). Coercive family processes and maternal depression. In R. D. Peters & R. J. McMahon (Eds.), *Marriages and families: Behavioral systems approaches* (pp. 72–103). New York: Brunner/Mazel.

Biglan, A., Hops, H., Sherman, L., Friedman, L., Arthur, J., & Osteen, V. (1985). Problem solving interactions of depressed women and their husbands. *Behavior Therapy, 16,* 431–451.

Biglan, A., Rothlind, J., Hops, H., & Sherman, L. (1989). Impact of distressed and aggressive behavior. *Journal of Abnormal Psychology, 98,* 218–228.

Billings, A. G., & Moos, R. H. (1983). Comparison of children of depressed and nondepressed parents: A social environmental perspective. *Journal of Abnormal Child Psychology, 14,* 149–166.

Blackburn, J., Greenberg, J., & Boss, P. (1987). Coping with normative stress from loss and change: A longitudinal study of ranch and non-ranch widows. *Journal of Gerontological Social Work, 11,* 59–70.

Block, J. H., Block, J., & Morrison, A. (1981). Parental agreement-disagreement on child-rearing orientations and gender-related personality correlates in children. *Child Development, 52,* 965–974.

Boss, P. (1977). A clarification of the concept of psychological father presence in families experiencing ambiguity of boundary. *Journal of Marriage and the Family, 39,* 141–151.

Boss, P. (1980). The relationship of wife's sex role perceptions, psychological father presence, and functioning in the ambiguous father-absent MIA family. *Journal of Marriage and the Family, 42,* 541–549.

Boss, P. (1987). Family stress. In M. B. Sussman & S. K. Steinmetz (Eds.), *Handbook of marriage and the family* (pp. 695–723). New York: Plenum.

Boss, P., Caron, W., Horbal, J., & Mortimer, J. (1990). Predictors of depression in caregivers of dementia patients: Boundary ambiguity and mastery. *Family Process, 23,* 245–254.

Boss, P., & Greenberg, J. (1984). Family boundary ambiguity: A new variable in family stress theory. *Family Process, 23,* 535–546.

Boss, P., Greenberg, J. R., & Pearce-McCall, D. (1990). *Measurement of boundary ambiguity in families.* Station Bulletin 593-1990, Minnesota Agricultural Experiment Station, University of Minnesota, St. Paul, MN, 55108.

Boss, P., Pearce-McCall, D., & Greenberg, J. (1987). Normative loss in mid-life families: Rural, urban, and gender differences. *Family Relations, 36,* 437–443.

Bossard, J., & Boll, E. (1950). *Ritual in family living.* Philadelphia: University of Pennsylvania Press.

Boszormenyi-Nagy, I., & Spark, G. M. (1973). *Invisible loyalties.* New York: Harper & Row.

Bowen, M. (1978). *Family therapy in clinical practice.* New York: Jason Aronson.

Bowlby, J. (1980). *Attachment and loss, Vol. 3: Loss, sadness, and depression.* New York: Basic Books.

Braungart, J. M., Fulker, D. W., & Plomin, R. (1992). Genetic mediation of the home environment during infancy: A sibling adoption study of the HOME. *Developmental Psychology, 28,* 1048–1055.

Brody, G. H., Stoneman, Z., & McCoy, J. K. (1992). Associations of maternal and paternal direct and differential behavior with sibling relationships: Contemporaneous and longitudinal analyses. *Child Development, 63,* 83–92.

Caldwell, B. M., & Bradley, R. H. (1978). *Home observation for measurement of the environment.* Little Rock: University of Arkansas.

Campbell, S. B. (1973). Mother-child interaction in reflective, impulsive, and hyperactive children. *Developmental Psychology, 8,* 341–349.

Campbell, S. B. (1975). Mother-child interaction: A comparison of hyperactive, learning disabled, and normal boys. *American Journal of Orthopsychiatry, 45,* 51–57.

Carter, E. A., & McGoldrick, M. (1980). *The family life cycle: A framework for family therapy.* New York: Gardner Press.

Cassidy, J., Parke, R. D., Butkovsky, L., & Braungart, J. M. (1992). Family-peer connections: The roles of emotional expressiveness within the family and children's understanding of emotions. *Child Development, 63,* 603–618.

Catton, W. R. (1988). Family "divorce heritage" and its intergenerational transmission: Toward a system-level perspective. *Sociological Perspectives, 31,* 398–419.

Christensen, A., & Margolin, G. (1988). Conflict and alliance in distressed and non-distressed families. In R. A. Hinde & J. Stevenson-Hinde (Eds.), *Relationships within families: Mutual influences* (pp. 263–282). New York: Oxford University Press.

Cicchetti, D. (1993). What developmental psychopathology is about: Reactions, reflections, projections. *Developmental Review, 13,* 471–502.

Cicchetti, D., Lynch, M., Shonk, S., & Manly, J. T. (1992). An organizational perspective on peer relations in maltreated children. In R. D. Parke & G. W. Ladd (Eds.), *Family-peer relationships: Modes of linkage* (pp. 345–383). Hillsdale, NJ: Erlbaum.

Coie, J. D., & Kupersmidt, J. B. (1983). A behavioral analysis of emerging social status: A cross-age perspective. *Child Development, 54,* 1400–1416.

Constantine, L. L. (1986). *Family paradigms: The practice of theory in family therapy.* New York: Guilford.

Cowan, C. P., Cowan, P. A., Heming, G., & Miller, N. B. (1991). Becoming a family: Marriage, parenting, and child development. In P. A. Cowan & M. Hetherington (Eds.), *Family transitions* (pp. 79–109). Hillsdale, NJ: Erlbaum.

Coyne, J. C. (1976a). Toward an interactional description of depression. *Psychiatry, 39,* 28–40.

Coyne, J. C. (1976b). Depression and the response of others. *Journal of Abnormal Psychology, 85,* 186–193.

Coyne, J. C., Downey, G., & Boergers, J. (1992). Depression in families: A systems perspective. In D. Cicchetti & S. L. Toth (Eds.), *Rochester Symposium on Developmental Psychopathology, Vol. 4: Developmental perspectives on depression* (pp. 211–245). Rochester, NY: University of Rochester Press.

Coyne, J. C., Kessler, R. C., Tal, M., Turnbull, J., Wortman, C. B., & Greden, J. F. (1987). Living with a depressed person. *Journal of Consulting and Clinical Psychology, 55,* 347–352.

Crockenberg, S., & Litman, C. (1991). Effects of maternal employment on maternal and two-year-old child behavior. *Child Development, 62,* 930–953.

Crouter, A. C., Perry-Jenkins, M., Huston, T. L., & McHale, S. M. (1987). Processes underlying father involvement in dual-earner and single-earner families. *Developmental Psychology, 23,* 431–440.

Cunningham, C. E., & Barkley, R. A. (1979). The interactions of hyperactive and normal children with their mothers in free play and structured tasks. *Child Development, 50,* 217–224.

Daniels, D. (1986). Differential experiences of siblings in the same family as predictors of adolescent sibling personality differences. *Journal of Personality and Social Psychology, 51,* 239–346.

Daniels, D., & Plomin, R. (1985). Differential experience of siblings in the same family. *Developmental Psychology, 21,* 747–760.

Derogatis, L. R., Lipman, R. S., Rickels, K., Uhlenhuth, E. H., & Covi, L. (1974). The Hopkins Symptom Checklist (HSCL): A self-report symptom inventory. *Behavioral Science, 19,* 1–15.

Dishion, T. J. (1990). The family ecology of boys' peer relations in middle childhood. *Child Development, 61,* 874–892.

Dishion, T. J., Patterson, G. R., Stoolmiller, M., & Skinner, M. L. (1991). Family, school, and behavioral antecedents to early adolescent involvement with antisocial peers. *Developmental Psychology, 27,* 172–180.

Dodge, K. A. (1983). Behavioral antecedents of peer social status. *Child Development, 54,* 1386–1399.

Downey, G., & Coyne, J. C. (1990). Children of depressed parents: An integrative review. *Psychological Bulletin, 108,* 50–76.

Dunn, J., & Kendrick, C. (1982). *Siblings: Love, envy, and understanding.* Cambridge, MA: Harvard University Press.

Dunn, J., & Munn, P. (1985). Becoming a family member: Family conflict and the development of social understanding in the second year. *Child Development, 56,* 480–492.

Dunn, J., & Munn, P. (1987). Development of justification in disputes with mother and sibling. *Developmental Psychology, 23,* 791–798.

Dunn, J., Plomin, R., & Daniels, D. (1986). Consistency and change in mothers' behavior towards young siblings. *Child Development, 57,* 348–356.

Dunn, J., Stocker, C., & Plomin, R. (1990). Nonshared experiences within the family: Correlates of behavioral problems in middle childhood. *Development and Psychopathology, 2,* 113–126.

Duvall, E. M., & Miller, B. C. (1985). *Marriage and family development* (6th ed). New York: Harper & Row.

Easterbrooks, M. A., & Lamb, M. E. (1979). The relationship between the quality of mother-infant attachment and infant competence in initial encounters with peers. *Child Development, 50,* 380–387.

Emery, R., Weintraub, S., & Neale, J. (1982). Effects of marital discord on the school behavior of children of schizophrenic, affective disordered, and normal parents. *Journal of Abnormal Child Psychology, 16,* 215–225.

Engfer, A. (1988). The interrelatedness of marriage and the mother-child relationship. In R. A. Hinde & J. Stevenson-Hinde (Eds.), *Relationships within families: Mutual influences* (pp. 104–118). New York: Oxford University Press.

Erikson, E. H. (1950). *Childhood and society.* New York: Norton.

Falk, R. F., & Miller, N. B. (1991). *A soft models approach to family transitions.* In P. A. Cowen & E. M. Hetherington (Eds.), *Family transitions* (pp. 273–301). Hillsdale, NJ: Erlbaum.

Feeney, J. A., & Noller, P. (1990). Attachment style as a predictor of adult romantic relationships. *Journal of Personality and Social Psychology, 58,* 281–291.

Fiese, B. H. (1992). Dimensions of family rituals across two generations: Relation to adolescent identity. *Family Process, 31,* 151–162.

Fiese, B. H., & Klein, C. A. (1993). Development of the Family Ritual Questionnaire: Initial reliability and validation studies. *Journal of Family Psychology, 6,* 290–299.

Fleck, S. (1983). A holistic approach to family typology and the axes of DSM-III. *Archives of General Psychiatry, 40,* 901–906.

Fonagy, P., Steele, H., & Steele, M. (1991). Maternal representations of attachment during pregnancy predict the organization of infant-mother attachment at one year of age. *Child Development, 62,* 891–905.

Frances, A., Clarkin, J. F., & Perry, S. (1984). DSM-III and family therapy. *American Journal of Psychiatry, 141,* 406–409.

Friedlander, M. L., & Heatherington, L. (1988). Analyzing relational control in family therapy interviews. *Journal of Counseling Psychology, 36,* 139–148.

Friedlander, M. L., Wildman, J., & Heatherington, L. (1991). Interpersonal control in structural and Milan systemic family therapy. *Journal of Marital and Family Therapy, 17,* 395–408.

Garmezy, N. (1987). Stress, competence, and development: Continuities in the study of schizophrenic adults, children vulnerable to psychopathology, and the search for stress-resistant children. *American Journal of Orthopsychiatry, 57,* 159–174.

Gaul, R., Simon, L., Friedlander, L., Cutler, C., & Heatherington, L. (1991). Correspondence of family therapists' perceptions with FRCCCS coding rules for triadic interactions. *Journal of Marital and Family Therapy, 17,* 379–393.

Gilbert, R., Christensen, A., & Margolin, G. (1984). Patterns of alliances in nondistressed and multiproblem families. *Family Process, 23,* 75–87.

Gilbert, R., Saltar, K., Deskin, J., Karagozian, A., Severance, G., & Christensen, A. (1981). *The family alliances coding system (FACS) manual.* Unpublished manuscript, University of California, Los Angeles.

Gottesman, I. I., & Shields, J. (1982). *Schizophrenia: The epigenetic puzzle.* Cambridge, England: Cambridge University Press.

Gottman, J. M. (1979). *Marital interaction: Experimental investigations.* New York: Academic Press.

Gottman, J. M. (1987). The sequential analysis of family interaction. In T. Jacob (Ed.), *Family interaction and psychopathology* (pp. 453–478). New York: Plenum.

Grotevant, H., & Cooper, C. (1985). Patterns of interaction in family relationships and the development of identity exploration in adolescence. *Child Development, 56,* 415–428.

Hahlweg, K., Reisner, L., Kohli, G., Vollmer, M., Schindler, L., & Revenstorf, D. (1984). Kategoriensystem fur Partnerschaftliche Interaktion. [Development and validity of a new system to analyze interpersonal communication]. In K. Hahlweg & N. Jacobson (Eds.), *Marital interaction: Analysis and modification.* New York: Guilford.

Hahlweg, K., Revenstorf, D., & Schindler, L. (1984). Effects of behavioral marital therapy on couples' communication and problem-solving skills. *Journal of Consulting and Clinical Psychology, 52,* 553–566.

Haley, J. (1959). The family of the schizophrenic: A model system. *Journal of Nervous and Mental Diseases, 129,* 357–374.

Haley, J. (1964). *Strategies of psychotherapy.* New York: Grune & Stratton.

Haley, J. (1976). Problem-solving therapy: New strategies for effective family therapy. San Francisco: Jossey-Bass, 1976.

Haley, J. (1977). Toward a theory of pathological systems. In P. Watzlawick & J. Weakland (Eds.), *The interactional view.* New York: Norton.

Hammen, C. L. (1992). The family-environmental context of depression: A perspective on children's risk. In D. Cicchetti & S. L. Toth (Eds.), *Rochester Symposium on Developmental Psychopathology, Vol. 4: Developmental perspectives on depression* (pp. 251–281). Rochester, NY: University of Rochester Press.

Hammen, C. L., & Peters, S. D. (1977). Differential responses to male and female depressive reactions. *Journal of Consulting and Clinical Psychology, 15,* 994–1001.

Hautzinger, M., Linden, M., & Hoffman, N. (1982). Distressed couples with and without a depressed partner: An analysis of their verbal interaction. *Journal of Behavior Therapy and Experimental Psychiatry, 13,* 307–314.

Hazan, C., & Shaver, P. (1987). Romantic love conceptualized as an attachment process. *Journal of Personality and Social Psychology, 52,* 511–524.

Heatherington, L. (1988). Coding relational control in counseling: Criterion validity. *Journal of Counseling Psychology, 35,* 41–46.

Hetherington, E. M., & Clingempeel, W. G. (1992). Coping with marital transitions: A family systems perspective. *Monographs of the Society for Research in Child Development, 57* (Serial No. 227).

Hill, R. (1949). *Families under stress.* New York: Harper & Row.

Hill, R. (1970). *Family development in three generations.* Cambridge, MA: Schenkman.

Hinchliffe, M., Hooper, D., & Roberts, F. J. (1978). *The melancholy marriage.* New York: Wiley.

Hinde, R. A., & Stevenson-Hinde, J. (Eds.) (1988). *Relationships within families: Mutual influences.* New York: Oxford University Press.

Hoffman, L. (1981). *Foundations of family therapy: A conceptual framework for systems change.* New York: Basic Books.

Hops, H., Biglan, A., Sherman, L., Arthur, J., Friedman, L., & Osteen, V. (1987). Home observations of family interactions of depressed women. *Journal of Consulting and Clinical Psychology, 55,* 341–346.

Hops, H., Wills, T., Patterson, G.R., & Weiss, R.L. (1972). *Marital interaction coding system (MICS).* Unpublished manuscript, Oregon Social Learning Institute, Eugene.

Howes, M. J., & Hokanson, J. E. (1979). Conversational and social responses to depressive interpersonal behavior. *Journal of Abnormal Psychology, 88,* 625–634.

Howes, P. W., & Cicchetti, D. (1993). A family/relational perspective on maltreating families: Parallel processes across systems and social policy implications. In D. Cicchetti & S. L. Toth (Eds.), *Child abuse, child development, and social policy* (pp. 249–299). Norwood, NJ: Ablex.

Humphries, T., Kinsbourne, M., & Swanson, J. (1978). Stimulant effects on cooperation and social interaction between hyperactive children and their mothers. *Journal of Child Psychology and Psychiatry, 19,* 13–22.

Jackson, D. D. (1965). The study of the family. *Family Process, 4,* 1–20.

Jackson, D. D. (1967). *Therapy, communication, and change.* Palo Alto, CA: Science and Behavior Books.

Jacobvitz, D. B., Morgan, E., Kretchmar, M. D., & Morgan, Y. (1991). The transmission of mother-child boundary disturbances across three generations. *Development and Psychopathology, 3,* 513–527.

Kantor, D., & Lehr, W. (1975). *Inside the family: Toward a theory of family process.* San Francisco: Jossey-Bass.

Kerr, M. E., & Bowen, M. (1988). *Family evaluation.* New York: Norton.

Kobak, R. R., & Sceery, A. (1988). Attachment in late adolescence: Working models, affect regulation, and representations of self and others. *Child Development, 59,* 135–146.

Krantz, S. E., & Moos, R. H. (1987). Functioning and life context among spouses of remitted and nonremitted depressed patients. *Journal of Counsulting and Clinical Psychology, 55,* 353–360.

Ladd, G. W. (1983). Social networks of popular, average, and rejected children in school settings. *Merrill-Palmer Quarterly, 29,* 283–307.

Levenson, R. W., & Gottman, J. M. (1983). Marital interaction: Physiological linkage and affective exchange. *Journal of Personality and Social Psychology, 45,* 587–597.

Levenson, R. W., & Gottman, J. M. (1985). Physiological and affective predictors of change in relationship satisfaction. *Journal of Personality and Social Psychology, 49,* 85–94.

Loeber, R., & Dishion, T. J. (1983). Early predictors of male delinquency: A review. *Psychological Bulletin, 94,* 68–98.

Lytton, H. (1990). Child and parent effects in boys' conduct disorder: A reinterpretation. *Developmental Psychology, 26,* 683–697.

MacDonald, K., & Parke, R. D. (1984). Bridging the gap: Parent-child play interaction and peer interactive competence. *Child Development, 55,* 1265–1277.

Margolin, G., & Wampold, B. E. (1981). Sequential analysis of conflict and accord in distressed and nondistressed marital partners. *Journal of Consulting and Clinical Psychology, 49,* 554–567.

Marvin, R. S., & Stewart, R. B. (1990). A family systems framework for the study of attachment. In M. T. Greenberg, D. Cicchetti, & E. M. Cummings (Eds.), *Attachment in the preschool years: Theory, research, and intervention.* Chicago: University of Chicago Press.

Meyer, H. J. (1988). Marital and mother-child relationships: Developmental history, parent personality, and child difficultness. In R. A. Hinde & J. Stevenson-Hinde (Eds.), *Relationships within families: Mutual influences* (pp. 119–139). New York: Oxford University Press.

Miller, J. G. (1965). Living systems: Basic concepts. *Behavioral Sciences, 10,* 193–237.

Minuchin, S. (1974). *Families and family therapy.* Cambridge, MA: Harvard University Press.

Minuchin, S., Montalvo, B. G., Guerney, B. L., Rosman, B. L., & Schumer, F. (1967). *Families of the slums.* New York: Basic Books.

Minuchin, S., Rosman, B. L., & Baker, L. (1978). *Psychosomatic families: Anorexia nervosa in context.* Cambridge, MA: Harvard University Press.

Moos, R., & Moos, B. (1981). *Family environment scale.* Palo Alto, CA: Consulting Psychologists Press.

Nelson, G. M., & Beach, S. R. H. (1990). Sequential interaction in depression: Effects of depressive behavior on spousal aggression. *Behavior Therapy, 21,* 167–182.

Olson, D. H. (1986). Circumplex Model VII: Validation studies and Faces III. *Family Process, 25,* 337–351.

Olweus, D. (1980). Familial and temperamental determinants of aggressive behavior in adolescent boys: A causal analysis. *Developmental Psychology, 16,* 644–660.

Parke, R. D., Cassidy, J., Burks, V. M., Carson, J. L., & Boyum, L. (1992). Familial contribution to peer competence among young children: The role of interactive and affective processes. In R. D. Parke & G. W. Ladd (Eds.), *Family-peer relationships: Modes of linkage* (pp. 107–134). Hillsdale, NJ: Erlbaum.

Parke, R. D., & Ladd, G. W. (Eds.). (1992). *Family-peer relationships: Models of linkages.* Hillsdale, NJ: Erlbaum.

Parke, R. D., McDonald, K. B., Beitel, A., & Bhavnagri, N. (1988). The role of the family in the development of peer relationships. In R. D. V. Peters & R. J. McMahon (Eds.), *Social learning and systems approaches to marriage and the family* (pp. 17–44). New York: Brunner/Mazel.

Patterson, G. R. (1982). *Coercive family process.* Eugene, OR: Castalia.

Patterson, G. R. (1986). Performance models for antisocial boys. *American Psychologist, 41,* 432–444.

Patterson, G. R., & Capaldi, D. M. (1991). Antisocial parents: Unskilled and vulnerable. In P. A. Cowan & E. M. Hetherington (Eds.), *Family transitions* (pp. 195–218). Hillsdale, NJ: Erlbaum.

Patterson, G. R., & Reid, J. B. (1984). Social interactional processes within the family: The study of the moment-by-moment family transactions in which human social development is imbedded. *Journal of Applied Developmental Psychology, 5,* 237–262.

Pearlin, L. T., Lieberman, M. A., Menaghan, E. G., & Mullan, J. T. (1981). The stress process. *Journal of Health and Social Behavior, 22,* 337–356.

Phares, V., Compas, B. E., & Howell, D. C. (1989). Perspectives on child behavior problems: Comparisons of children's self-reports with parent and teacher reports. *Psychological Assessment: A Journal of Consulting and Clinical Psychology, 1,* 68–71.

Plomin, R., & Bergeman, C. S. (1991). The nature of nurture: Genetic influences on "environmental" measures. *Behavioral and Brain Sciences, 14,* 373–427.

Plomin, R., Chipeur, H. H., & Neiderhiser, J. (1994). Behavioral genetic evidence for the importance of the nonshared environment. In E. M. Hetherington, D. Reiss, & R. Plomin (Eds.), *Separate social worlds of siblings: Impact of the nonshared environment on development* (pp. 1–31). Hillsdale, NJ: Erlbaum.

Plomin, R., & Daniels, D. (1987). Why are children in the same family so different from one another? *Behavioral and Brain Sciences, 10,* 1–16.

Plomin, R., Reiss, D., Hetherington, E. M., & Howe, G. (1994). Nature and nurture: Genetic influence on measures of family environment. *Developmental Psychology, 30,* 32–43.

Putallaz, M. (1987). Maternal behavior and children's sociometric status. *Child Development, 58,* 324–340.

Raymond, L., Friedlander, M. L., Heatherington, L., Ellis, M. V., & Sargent, J. (1993). Communication processes in structural family therapy: Case study of an anorexic family. *Journal of Family Psychology, 6,* 308–326.

Reich, T., Cloninger, C. R., Lewis, C., & Rice, J. (1981). Some recent findings in the study of genotype-environment interaction in alcoholism. *National Institute on Alcohol Abuse and Alcoholism Research Monograph* (No. 5).

Reid, J. B. (Ed.)(1978). *A social learning approach to family intervention, Vol. 2: Observation in home settings.* Eugene, OR: Castalia.

Reiss, D. (1981). *The family's construction of reality.* Cambridge, MA: Harvard University Press.

Reiss, D., Gonzalez, S., & Kramer, N. (1986). Family process, chronic illness, and death. *Archives of General Psychiatry, 43,* 795–804.

Reiss, D., Plomin, R., & Hetherington, E. M. (1991). Genetics and psychiatry: An unheralded window on the environment. *American Journal of Psychiatry, 148,* 283–291.

Reiss, D., Plomin, R., Hetherington, E. M., Howe, G., Rovine, M., Tryon, A., & Hagan, M. S. (1994). The separate social worlds of teenage siblings. In E. M. Hetherington, D. Reiss, & R. Plomin (Eds.), *Separate social worlds of siblings: Impact of the nonshared environment on development* (pp. 63–109). Hillsdale, NJ: Erlbaum.

Rutter, M. (1987). Psychosocial resilience and protective mechanisms. *American Journal of Orthopsychiatry, 57,* 316–331.

Sameroff, A. (1975). Early influences on development: Fact or fancy? *Merrill-Palmer Quarterly, 21,* 263–294.

Simons, R. L., Whitbeck, L. B., Conger, R. D., & Chyi-In, W. (1991). Intergenerational transmission of harsh parenting. *Developmental Psychology, 27,* 159–171.

Smetana, J. (1988). Adolescents' and parents' conceptions of parental authority. *Child Development, 59,* 321–335.

Sorenson, S. B., & Rutter, C. M. (1991). Transgenerational patterns of suicide attempts. *Journal of Consulting and Clinical Psychology, 59,* 861–866.

Sroufe, L. A., Egeland, B., & Kreutzer, T. (1990). The fate of early experience following developmental change: Longitudinal approaches to individual adaptation in childhood. *Child Development, 61,* 1363–1373.

Sroufe, L. A., & Fleeson, J. (1988). The coherence of family relationships. In R. A. Hinde & J. Stevenson-Hinde (Eds.), *Relationships within families: Mutual influences* (pp. 27–47). New York: Oxford University Press.

Sroufe, L. A., Jacobvitz, D., Mangelsdorf, S., DeAngelo, E., & Ward, M. J. (1985). Generational boundary dissolution between mothers and their preschool children: A relationship systems approach. *Child Development, 56,* 317–332.

Sroufe, L. A., & Ward, M. J. (1980). Seductive behavior of mothers of toddlers: Occurrence, correlates, and family origins. *Child Development, 51,* 1222–1229.

Steinglass, P., Bennett, L. A., Wolin, S. J., & Reiss, D. (1987). *The alcoholic family.* New York: Basic Books.

Strack, S., & Coyne, J. C. (1983). Social confirmation of dysphoria: Shared and private reactions to depression. *Journal of Personality and Social Psychology, 44,* 806–814.

Strodbeck, F. L. (1951). Husband-wife interaction over revealed differences. *American Sociological Review, 16,* 468–473.

Vogel, E. F., & Bell, N. W. (1960). The emotionally disturbed child as the family scapegoat. In N. W. Bell & E. F. Vogel (Eds.), *The family* (pp. 382–397). Glencoe, IL: Free Press.

von Bertalanffy, L. (1968). *General system theory: Foundations, development, applications.* New York: Braziller.

Vuchinich, S., Emery, R. E., & Cassidy, J. (1988). Family members as third parties in dyadic family conflict: Strategies, alliances, and outcomes. *Child Development, 59,* 1293–1302.

Watzlawick, P., Beavin, J. H., & Jackson, D. (1974). *Pragmatics of human communication.* New York: Norton.

Watzlawick, P., Weakland, J., & Fisch, R. (1974). *Change: Principles of problem formation and problem resolution.* New York: Norton.

Weiss, P. (1969). *Principles of development.* New York: Hafner.

Werner, H. (1948). *Comparative psychology of mental development.* New York: International Universities Press.

Wiener, N. (1961). *Cybernetics, or control and communication in the animal and the machine.* Cambridge, MA: MIT Press.

Wolin, S. J., & Bennett, L. A. (1984). Family rituals. *Family Process, 23,* 401–420.

Wolin, S. J., Bennett, L. A., Noonan, D. L., & Teitelbaum, M. A. (1980). Disrupted family rituals: A factor in the intergenerational transmission of alcoholism. *Journal of Studies on Alcohol, 41,* 199–214.

Wood, B. (1985). Proximity and hierarchy: Orthogonal dimensions of family interconnectedness. *Family Process, 24,* 487–507.

World Health Organization (1990). *International classification of diseases and related health problems (ICD-10; 10th ed.).* Geneva: Author.

Wynne, L. C. (1984). The epigenesis of relational systems: A model for understanding family development. *Family Process, 23,* 297–318.

Zahn-Waxler, C., Denham, S., Iannotti, R. J., & Cummings, E. M. (1992). Peer relations in children with a depressed caregiver. In R. D. Parke & G. W. Ladd (Eds.), *Family-peer relationships: Modes of linkage* (pp. 317–344). Hillsdale, NJ: Erlbaum.

Zung, W. (1965). A self-rating depression scale. *Archives of General Psychiatry, 12,* 63–70.

Author Index

Subject Index